TWENTY-SEVENTH EDITION

KOVELS'

Antiques &
Collectibles
PRICE LIST

For the 1995 Market

ILLUSTRATED

CROWN TRADE PAPERBACKS   NEW YORK

BOOKS BY RALPH AND TERRY KOVEL

American Country Furniture 1780–1875

Dictionary of Marks—Pottery & Porcelain

A Directory of American Silver, Pewter and Silver Plate

Kovels' Advertising Collectibles Price List

Kovels' American Silver Marks

Kovels' Antiques & Collectibles Price List

Kovels' Book of Antique Labels

Kovels' Bottles Price List

Kovels' American Art Pottery: The Collector's Guide to Makers,
Marks, and Factory Histories

Kovels' Collector's Guide to American Art Pottery

Kovels' Collector's Source Book

Kovels' Depression Glass & American Dinnerware Price List

Kovels' Guide to Selling, Buying, and Fixing Your Antiques and Collectibles

Kovels' Guide to Selling Your Antiques & Collectibles

Kovels' Illustrated Price Guide to Royal Doulton

Kovels' Know Your Antiques

Kovels' Know Your Collectibles

Kovels' New Dictionary of Marks—Pottery & Porcelain

Kovels' Organizer for Collectors

Kovels' Price Guide for Collector Plates, Figurines,
Paperweights, and Other Limited Editions

TWENTY-SEVENTH EDITION

KOVELS'
Antiques &
Collectibles
PRICE LIST

Dear Reader,

This is a book for the average collector. We check prices all year, visit shops and shows, read our mail, and decide what antiques and collectibles are of most interest. We do not list the top of the market but concentrate on the average pieces in any category. We will often add one or two high-priced pieces in a category so you will be aware that some rarities are quite valuable. For example, Ohr pottery can sell for $300 to $22,000. Most pieces we list are under $10,000. Although pieces of furniture, silver, Tiffany, or art pottery may sell for over $50,000, we list few of those examples here. The highest price in this book is $38,500 for a Girl Skipping Rope mechanical bank. The lowest price is 10¢ for a bottle cap. We even list the weird and wonderful, so in this edition you can find prices for a flyswatter, casket, poultry punch, appleseed necklace, and cow kickers. The smallest object is a railroad collar pin; the largest, a seven-foot-high phone booth.

The book is changed slightly each year. Categories are added or omitted to make it easier for you to find your antiques. The book is kept at about 800 pages because it is written to go with you to sales. We try to have a balanced format—not too much glass, pottery, or collectibles, not too many items that sell for over $5,000. The prices are *from* the American market *for* the American market. Few European sales are reported. We take the editorial privilege of not including any prices that seem to result from "auction fever."

The computer-generated index is so complete it amazes us. Use it often. An internal alphabetical index is also included. For example, there is a category for "Celluloid." Most celluloid items will be found here, but if a toy is made of celluloid, it will be listed under "Toy" and also indexed under "Celluloid." All pictures and prices are new every year, except pictures that are pattern examples shown in "Depression Glass" and "Pressed Glass." Pictured antiques are not museum pieces but items offered for sale. The hints are set in easy-to-notice special type. Leaf through the book and learn how to wash porcelains, store textiles, guard against theft, and much more. Old Kovels' price books should be saved for future reference, tax, and appraisal information.

RECORD PRICES

Million-dollar tables, $24,000 Coca-Cola signs, and $2,624,635 English desks impress the media and get publicity in daily papers and TV news broadcasts. But these are not the prices found in the general market at the sales and flea markets where most of us buy our antiques and collectibles. Of course, each of us hopes that one of the family heirlooms will turn out to be worth a fortune, and each year one or two stories tell of these lucky finds. In May this year, an album of photographs of Central America and Mexico taken by Eadweard Muybridge sold for $57,500. It had been purchased by a man at a midwestern flea market because it was "an interesting old book" with nice pictures. He studied and learned that the photographs were originals, not reproductions, and very valuable. This year, an Oscar given in 1940 to Vivien Leigh for her role as Scarlett O'Hara in *Gone With the Wind* auctioned for an unexpectedly high $563,500. A Parker "Snake" model fountain pen sold for $21,800, and the original art from the March 1944 *Amazing Stories* brought $25,300. Toys set the most records: a 1932 cast-iron Arcade Checker cab was $68,200, a Hubley Beach Patrol surfer boy advertising Jantzen swimwear sold for $15,400, and a Mickey Mouse slate dancer set the top price for a comic toy at $29,150. The Tom Mix marble that sold for $2,510 was one of several previously unknown marbles that brought high prices. Dolls continue to rise in price. A Madame Alexander doll that represented Kathryn Grayson, the movie star, was $10,400. An Emile Jumeau Creole lady doll made in 1884 set a record of $231,000. The Kammer & Reinhardt blue-eyed, strawberry-blond schoolgirl set a record as the most expensive doll at $282,750. And the 1908 Steiff blue teddy bear "Elliot" was $74,000.

Several important bottle collections were sold at auction this year. A olive yellow Medallions and Diamonds Jared Spencer flask sold for $52,800, the record for a decorative flask. An olive yellow Jared Spencer flask, made about 1815 by the Pitkin Glass Works, brought $66,000, the record for a historical flask. The General Washington/Eagle Portrait flask of grayish amethyst glass brought $27,500, and the William H. Harrison cabin flask in aquamarine brought $26,400. The crossed keys Masonic flask also set a record when the olive yellow half-pint bottle auctioned for $33,000.

Furniture records were set only for European pieces. A Mackintosh tall chair went for $464,250 and an ebonized mahogany writing cabinet for $1,166,445, so expensive that it also set a record for any twentieth-century furnishing. The top price was $2,624,635 for an 1809 mahogany desk made in London.

Flow Blue sold well at many auctions. A 20-inch long Scinde pattern well and tree platter was $7,000 and a matching ladle was $3,200. A 1750–1760 figurine of a tea party made of creamware in Staffordshire auctioned for a record $453,500. A twentieth-century figurine of "The Duchess," a Beatrix Potter design, went for $2,590.

Many other types of collectibles set records. A Victor Glodo duck call went for $16,500 the same day a Perry Hooker call brought $11,550 and a Charles Perdew call $6,600. A glass globe shaped like a Texaco Firechief hat, made for the top of a 1932 gasoline pump, delighted a collector for

$16,500, and another gas globe made for Aerio Gas in the 1940s was $9,350. The pause that refreshes included a bid of $24,200 for a 6 1/2-by-10 1/2-inch 1896 tin Coca-Cola sign showing a woman holding a glass.

Other records include $14,000 for a blue Grape Arbor pattern carnival glass pitcher, $64,900 for a Wheeler black duck decoy; and $270 for a Hudepohl 1933 Cincinnati, Ohio, beer label.

The prices in this book are reports of the general antiques market, not the record-setting examples. Each year, every price in the book is new. We do not estimate or "update" prices. Prices are actual asking prices, although a buyer may have negotiated a price to a lower figure. No price is an estimate. We do not ask dealers and writers to estimate prices. Experience has shown that a collector of one type of antique is prejudiced in favor of that item, and prices are usually high or low, but rarely a true report. If a price range is given, it is because at least two identical items were offered for sale at different times. The computer records prices and prints the high and low figures. Price ranges are found only in categories like "Pressed Glass," where identical items can be identified. Some prices in *Kovels' Antiques & Collectibles Price List* may seem high and some may seem low because of regional variations. But each price is one you could have paid for the object. If you are selling your collection, do not expect to get retail value unless you are a dealer. Wholesale prices for antiques are from 20 to 50 percent less than retail. Remember, the antiques dealer must make a profit or go out of business.

ACKNOWLEDGMENTS

Special thanks should go to those who helped us with pictures and deeds: Alderfer Auction Company, Frank H. Boos Gallery, Butterfield & Butterfield Auctioneers & Appraisers, Christie's, The Cockpit, DuMouchelle's, Robert Edward Auctions, Robert C. Eldred Co., Inc., Garth's Auctions, Inc., Morton M. Goldberg, Leslie Hindman Auctioneers, Michael Ivankovich Antiques, Inc., Leland's, McGrath's Sporting Antiquities, Gary Metz Auctions, Minya International, Neal Auction Company, Northeast Auctions, Old Barn Annex Antiques, Richard Opfer Auctioneering, Inc., Pennyfield's, Alan R. Pereske Antiques, Phillip's, Postcards International, Skinner, Inc., Sotheby's, Sports Section, Strike Zone, Superior Galleries, Swann Galleries, Weschler's, Williston, Witherel's, Richard Wolffers Auctions, Inc. Special help was given by Lee Markley.

To the others in the antiques trade who knowingly or unknowingly contributed prices to this book, we say "thank you!" We could not do it without you. Some of you are: A Moment in Time Antiques, A Touch of Glass, Ltd., A Work of Art, Jo Abrams, Bob Alexander, Loretta Anderson, As We Were Antiques, Barbara's Dolls, William Beck, Joyce Bee, Cyril Bish,

Bluegrass, Stuart & Karen Brody, Martin Brown, Samantha Burdick, Alex Caiola, Harold Call, CDK Collectibles, Cedars-Antiques, Walrath M. Colella, Dials Antiques, Darcia Antiques, Dale I. Deckert, Dee's Antiques, Dennis & George Collectibles, Greg Dulla, Eden West Antiques, Martin Elfant, Encinas Antiques, Fenner's Antiques, Lois J. Finnerty, Helen Garneau, Tim Gaudet, Anne L. Gessler, Leigh Giarde, B. Gilchrist, Muriel Giodano, Grandma's Attic, Grantiques, Ron & Donna Haring, Vicki Harman Antiques, Frederic Hartl, Johnny J. Henard, Hi-De-Ho Collectibles, Hourglass Antiques, Arlene Jaffee, Jon Jenkins, Margaret Jennings, David Jones, Betty Kennedy, Krainik Gallery, Sue Langley, Susan Levine, Greg Little, The Magnificent Doll, Mango Tree, Matrix Quality Antique Dolls, Berniece Matthews, Mary McAnich, Melton's Antiques, Shelby Messinger, Larry Meyer, Mouse Man Ink, Nickel Enterprises, Inc., Pam & Dick Oestreicher, Old Timers' Antiques, Ted Osborn, Pen Fancier's Club, Plantation Galleries, Don Raitzer, Remember When Mail Auction, Mable Richardson, Rosalie J. Robinson, Roggow House Antiques, Meredith Saltzman, Mary Sathoff, Alice J. Schnabel, Dick Schwind, The Sign Sez, Skylark Antiques, Bill Smith, Brent Smith, Somewhere in Time, Spirit of 76 Antiques, Bob Stowe, Team Antiques, Trinity Collection, Turn of the Century Antiques, Jenny Tarrant, Theriault's, Billie Nelson Tyrrell, David Uzarowski, Norm Vigue, Yesterdays South, Inc., Roger W. Yost, Stephen R. Yost, Wolf's Gallery.

MORE ANTIQUE PRICE NEWS

Have you kept up with prices? They change! In recent months a Kammer & Reinhardt doll sold for $282,750, a Stanley Tool veneer scraper was $825, a Tom Mix marble with a mysterious past brought $2,510, a 1932 iron toy Checker cab auctioned for $68,200, Charles Rennie Mackintosh's 1904 desk brought an astounding $1,166,445, and a Jared Spencer olive yellow flask sold for $66,000. How did the owners know these collectibles had such a special value? Prices change with discoveries, auction records, even historic events. Every entry and every picture in this book is new and current thanks to modern computer technology, making this book a handy overall price guide. But you also need current news about collecting. Books on your shelf get older each month, and prices do change. Important sales produce new record prices. Rarities are discovered. Fakes appear. You will want to keep up with developments from month to month rather than from year to year. *Kovels on Antiques and Collectibles,* a nationally distributed, illustrated newsletter, includes up-to-date information on the world of collectors. This monthly newsletter reports current prices, collecting trends, landmark auction results for all types of antiques and collectibles, and tax, estate, security, and other pertinent news for collectors. Additional information and a free sample newsletter are available from the authors at P.O. Box 420420, Palm Coast, FL 32142.

If sports are your interest, write for a sample of our other newsletter, *Kovels Sports Collectibles*. It has news about old and new sports items including baseball cards, hockey shirts, golf clubs, and stadium seats. A special monthly feature is a "Freebies" list of the collectibles being offered with products from the grocery store.

HOW TO USE THIS BOOK

There are a few rules for using this book. Each listing is arranged in the following manner: CATEGORY (such as Pressed Glass or Furniture), OBJECT (such as vase), DESCRIPTION (as much information as possible about size, age, color, and pattern). Some types of glass are exceptions to this rule, so these are listed by CATEGORY, PATTERN, OBJECT, DESCRIPTION. All items listed are presumed to be in good condition and undamaged, unless otherwise noted.

Several special categories were formed to make the most sensible listing possible. For instance, the category "Tool" includes special equipment because the casual collector might not know the proper name for an "adze." Two years ago we reorganized the glass entries into these categories: "Glass-Art," "Glass-Contemporary," "Glass-Midcentury," and "Glass-Venetian." Major glass factories are still listed under the factory names, and well-known types of glass such as cut, pressed, carnival, etc., can be found in their own sections. New categories include "Erickson," "Hedi Schoop," "Susie Cooper," "typewriter ribbon tins," and "Westmoreland." The index can help you locate items.

Several idiosyncrasies of style appear because the book is printed by computer. Everything is listed according to the computer alphabetizing system. This means words such as "Mt." are alphabetized as "M-T," not as "M-O-U-N-T." All numerals appear before all letters; thus 2 comes before A. A quick glance will make this clear, as the system is consistent throughout the book.

We made several editorial decisions. A bowl is a "bowl" and not a dish unless it is a special dish, such as a pickle dish. A butter dish is a "butter." A salt dish is called "salt" to differentiate it from a saltshaker. It is always "sugar and creamer," never "creamer and sugar." Political collectors often refer to pinbacks, the round celluloid or tin pins that are decorated with candidates' names and faces. The word "button" is sometimes used in this book instead of the word "pinback." Of course, "button" is also used when listing the closings used on clothing. For measurements, where one dimension is given, it is the height; or if the object is round, the dimension is the diameter. Height of a picture is listed before width. Glass is clear unless a color is indicated.

Every entry is listed alphabetically, but the problem of language remains. Some antiques terms, like "Sheffield" or "snow baby," have two meanings. Be sure to read the paragraph headings to know the meaning used. All category headings are based on the language of the average person at an average show, and we use terms like "mud figures" even if not technically correct.

This book does not include price listings of fine art paintings, stamps, coins, most types of books (although *Big Little Books* are included), comic books (although original comic art is listed), and a few other special categories. All pictures in *Kovels' Antiques & Collectibles Price List* are listed with the prices asked by the seller. "Illus" (illustrated nearby) is part of the description if a picture is shown.

Misinformed comments have been made about how this book is written. We do use the computer. It alphabetizes, ranges prices, sets type, and does other time-consuming jobs. Because of the computer, the book can be produced quickly. The last entries are added in June; the book is available in October. This is six months faster than would be possible any other way. But it is human help that finds prices and checks accuracy. We read everything at least twice, sometimes more. We edit 100,000 entries to arrive at the 50,000 entries found here. We correct spelling, remove incorrect data, write category headings, and decide on new categories. We sometimes make errors. Information in the paragraphs is reviewed and updated each year. This year more than fifty corrections and additions were made in the category headings. Prices are reports from all parts of the United States and Canada (translated to U.S. dollars at the rate of $1.30 U.S. to $1 Canadian) between June 1993 and June 1994. A few prices are from auctions; most are from shops and shows. Every price is checked for accuracy, but we are not responsible for errors.

It is unprofessional for an appraiser to set a value for an unseen item. Because of this, we cannot answer your letters asking for specific price information. But please write if you have any requests for categories to be included in future editions or any corrections to information in the paragraphs.

When you see us at the shows, stop and say hello. Since our television show has been on in all parts of the country, we find we can no longer be anonymous buyers. It may mean the dealers know us before we ask a price, but it has been wonderful to meet all of you. Don't be surprised if we ask for your suggestions for the next edition of *Kovels' Antiques & Collectibles Price List*. Or you can write us at P.O. Box 22200-K, Beachwood, Ohio 44122.

Ralph & Terry Kovel,
Accredited Senior Appraisers,
American Society of Appraisers
July 1994

A. WALTER made pate-de-verre glass under contract at the Daum glassworks from 1908 to 1914. He started his own firm in Nancy, France, in 1919. Pieces made before 1914 are signed *Daum, Nancy* with a cross. After 1919 the signature is *A. Walter Nancy.*

Ashtray, Shell Shape, Conch Shell Under Seaweed, 7 In.	1380.00
Dish, Mouse Nibbling Wheat At Top, Signed, 6 5/8 In.	2300.00
Paperweight, Bluebird, Blue, Dark Blue Base, 4 x 3 In.	1500.00
Paperweight, Green Frog, Brown & Green Base, 1925, 2 In.	3450.00
Tray, Green Moths, Scroll-Shaped Ends, 9 x 4 In.	4000.00
Vase, Linear Stylized Leaves & Flowers, Oviform, Signed, 4 1/2 In.	3520.00

ABC plates, or children's alphabet plates, were most popular from 1780 to 1860, but are still being made. The letters on the plate were meant as teaching aids for children learning to read. The plates were made of pottery, porcelain, metal, or glass. Mugs and other items were also made with alphabet decorations.

Dish, Feeding, Cats & Turtle, 1920	45.00 to 65.00
Ice Cream Set, Pressed Glass, 7 Piece	450.00
Mug, Alphabet, Nursery Rhymes, Figural, 1950s, 8 In.	40.00
Mug, Orange Letters, A Through K, Animals In-Between, Germany, 3 3/4 In.	55.00
Plate, Alphabet, Months, Days, 3-Row Border, 7 In.	40.00
Plate, Bear With Cubs, 7 1/2 In.	90.00
Plate, Blind Girl, Children In Victorian Dress, 5 3/4 In.	150.00
Plate, Cat & Fan Center, Alphabet Around Rim, Flow Blue, Adams, 7 In.	165.00
Plate, Cat, Sign Language	150.00
Plate, Cereal, Peter Rabbit, England	35.00
Plate, Chairs To Mend, Black Transfer, Blue Rim, 7 In.	165.00
Plate, Child's Activities, Staffordshire	85.00
Plate, Chinonca Watching Departure Of Cavalcade	120.00
Plate, Clock Center, Black Transfer, Green Border, Ironstone, 8 1/2 In.	82.00
Plate, Clock Face, Alphabet, 7 1/8 In.	32.00
Plate, Clock Face, White & Blue Numbers, Graniteware, 4 1/3 In.	65.00
Plate, Cow In Center, Tin, 1 1/2 In.	85.00
Plate, Ducks, Rolled Edge, 8 In.	50.00
Plate, Elephant, Howdah On Back, 6 In.	125.00
Plate, Elephant, Tin	110.00
Plate, Federal Generals, 6 In.	175.00
Plate, Franklin's Proverbs, 5 In.	150.00
Plate, Gathering Cotton, Raised Alphabet Rim, England, 19th Century, 6 In.	550.00
Plate, George Washington, 13 Stars, Tin, 5 5/8 In.	125.00 to 170.00
Plate, Girl On A Swing, Tin Lithograph, 3 1/2 In.	55.00
Plate, Girl, 2 Dachshunds, Frightened By Bearskin Rug, Dresden	65.00
Plate, Hey, Diddle Diddle, Alphabet Rim, Bavaria, 7 1/2 In.	75.00
Plate, Hey, Diddle Diddle, Tin, 8 3/4 In.	203.00
Plate, Jack & Jill, Alphabet Rim	28.00
Plate, Jumbo, Tin, 6 1/8 In.	115.00
Plate, Kite Flying	165.00
Plate, Little Red Riding Hood, Wolf Center, Red, Blue Trim	165.00
Plate, Mary Had A Little Lamb, Tin, 8 In.	93.00 to 110.00
Plate, Organ Grinder & Children, Green Transfer, Ironstone, 6 3/4 In.	105.00
Plate, Oriental Donkey	145.00
Plate, Rip Van Winkle, Catskill Mountains, 8 In.	40.00
Plate, Sancho Panza	58.00
Plate, Tiger & Hunter	145.00
Plate, Village Blacksmith, 7 In.	135.00
Plate, Who Killed Cock Robin, Tin, 7 7/8 In.	80.00 to 150.00
Plate, Y Is A Youth, Staffordshire, 6 In.	67.00

ABINGDON POTTERY was established in 1934 by Raymond E. Bidwell as the Abingdon Sanitary Manufacturing Company. The company made art pottery and other wares. Sixteen varieties of cookie jars are known. The factory ceased production of art pottery in 1950.

Compote, White, 17 In.	18.00

◆◆◆◆◆◆◆◆◆◆◆◆◆◆◆◆◆◆◆◆◆◆◆◆

Keep art, paintings, prints, and textiles away from sunny windows.

◆◆◆◆◆◆◆◆◆◆◆◆◆◆◆◆◆◆◆◆◆◆◆

◆◆◆◆◆◆◆◆◆◆◆◆◆◆◆◆◆◆◆◆◆◆◆

For a pollution-free glass cleaner use a mixture of white vinegar and water.

◆◆◆◆◆◆◆◆◆◆◆◆◆◆◆◆◆◆◆◆◆◆◆

Abingdon, Cookie Jar, Jack-O'-Lantern

Console, Gray-Green, 14 x 9 In.	18.00
Console, Leaf Pattern, 17 In.	18.00
Console Set, Scalloped Bowl & Candlesticks, Floral	75.00
Cookie Jar, Elsie In Barrel	395.00
Cookie Jar, Fat Boy	450.00
Cookie Jar, Guardhouse Soldier	85.00
Cookie Jar, Hippo, Flowers	260.00 to 285.00
Cookie Jar, Hobby Horse	250.00
Cookie Jar, Humpty-Dumpty	165.00 to 300.00
Cookie Jar, Jack-In-The-Box	275.00
Cookie Jar, Jack-O'-Lantern	*Illus* 275.00 to 350.00
Cookie Jar, Little Bopeep	300.00 to 400.00
Cookie Jar, Little Miss Muffet	375.00
Cookie Jar, Little Old Lady, Burgundy	65.00
Cookie Jar, Little Old Lady, Green	135.00
Cookie Jar, Little Old Lady, Turquoise	150.00
Cookie Jar, Money Sack	100.00
Cookie Jar, Mother Goose	150.00 to 575.00
Cookie Jar, Owl	40.00
Cookie Jar, Pineapple	125.00
Cookie Jar, Pumpkin	325.00 to 385.00
Cookie Jar, Train	155.00 to 225.00
Cookie Jar, Wigwam	100.00
Cookie Jar, Windmill	225.00
Creamer, Sunflower Handle, White	6.00
Planter, Cornucopia, Green	15.00
Salt & Pepper, Little Bopeep	40.00
Tile, Geisha Girl	65.00
Urn, Leaf Wreath, Rose, Side Handles, Vertical Ribbed, Square Footed	9.50
Vase, 2 Handles, Green, 9 1/2 In.	12.50
Vase, Fan, Flower Holder, Horizontal Rib Base, 5 x 5 x 7 In.	22.00
Wall Pocket, Apron	75.00
Wall Pocket, Art Deco, Blue	45.00
Wall Pocket, Cherub, Wings, Yellow, 7 3/4 x 4 1/4 x 4 1/2 In.	30.00

ADAMS china was made by William Adams and Sons of Staffordshire, England. The firm was founded in 1769 and is still working. All types of tablewares and useful wares have been made through the years. Other pieces of Adams will be found listed under Flow Blue.

Biscuit Jar, Jasperware, Dark Blue & White, Curved Sides, Marked	175.00
Bowl, Vegetable, Columbus, Indian Scene, Pink, 9 3/4 In.	295.00
Bowl, Vegetable, Schenectady On The Mohawk River, Pink, 9 3/4 In.	325.00

Creamer, Blue Jasperware, White Classical Figures, 3 1/4 In. 44.00
Cup & Saucer, Weehawk, New York, Pink 225.00
Cup Plate, Columbus, Brown 85.00
Dish, Soup, Cows & Floral, Dark Blue, 10 In. 165.00
Ladle, Soup Tureen, Andalusia, Pink, Large 250.00
Plate, Blue Transfer, Hawthornden, Edinburghshire, 8 3/4 In. 115.00
Plate, Columbus, Brown, 10 1/2 In. 85.00
Plate, Mitchell & Freeman's China & Glass Warehouse, Dark Blue, 10 1/2 In. 850.00
Plate, Moorland Castle, Dark Blue, Staffordshire, 6 1/4 In. 140.00
Plate, Shakespeare Scene, 10 In. 80.00
Plate, Shannondale Springs, Virginia, Pink, 7 7/8 In. 85.00
Plate, Villa In Regents Park, Dark Blue, Pebbled Glaze, 9 In. 110.00
Platter, Bothwell Castle, Clydesdale, Dark Blue, 11 1/2 In. 195.00
Platter, Falls Of Niagara, U.S.Views Series, Black, 19 1/2 In. 1200.00
Platter, Kyber, Flow Blue, 10 In. 140.00
Platter, Kyber, Flow Blue, 14 1/2 x 11 In. 275.00
Platter, Part Of Regents Street, Dark Blue, 14 In. 375.00
Platter, Rose, Gaudy, Staffordshire, 19 1/2 In. 302.00
Platter, St. George Chapel, Blue & White, Staffordshire, 15 In. 467.00
Saucer, Black Transfer, Outdoor Tea Party 214.00
Soup, Dish, Kyber, Flow Blue, 10 In. 120.00

ADVERTISING containers and products sold in the old country store are now all collectibles. These stores, with the crackers in a barrel and a potbellied stove, are a symbol of an earlier, less hectic time. Listed here are many of the advertising items. Other similar pieces may be found under the product name, such as Planters Peanuts. We have tried to list items in the logical places, so large store fixtures will be found under the Architectural category, enameled tin dishes under Graniteware, paper items in the Paper category, etc. Store fixtures, cases, and other items that have no advertising as part of the decoration are listed in the Store category.

3-D Viewer, Nabisco Shredded Wheat Magic 25.00
Album, Cigarette, Premium, Allen & Ginter, Our Navy 149.95
Ashtray, Air France, Blue China, Embossed Winged Horse Logo, 4 Piece 20.00
Ashtray, Benson & Hedges, Ceramic 10.00
Ashtray, Big Mack Bulldog 15.00
Ashtray, Breyers Ice Cream, 95th Anniversary, Logo, Harker, 1961, 5 3/8 In. 6.50
Ashtray, Breyers Ice Cream, White Ceramic, Orange Over Green Leaf, Round 7.50
Ashtray, Carnation Ice Cream 5.00
Ashtray, Darigold At Your Door At Your Store, Metal, Bronze Color, Rectangular 6.00
Ashtray, Dodge, 50 Years Of Dependability, 1914-1964 .... 65.00
Ashtray, Firestone, Tire, Amber Glass Insert, 600 x 20 .... 35.00
Ashtray, Goodyear, Tire 25.00
Ashtray, Grinnell Fire Sprinkler, Brass 43.00
Ashtray, Horniman's Pure Tea, Woman, Tin 125.00
Ashtray, Indian, You Don't Have To Be Jewish To Love Levy's Rye, Ceramic 1320.00
Ashtray, Iron Fireman, Cast Iron, Nickel Plated, 7 In. 50.00
Ashtray, Kessler Whiskey 35.00
Ashtray, Kool Cigarettes, 1950s 8.00
Ashtray, Match Holder, Green River Whiskey, Copper 45.00
Ashtray, Michelin Man, Figural, Bakelite, 1950s, 4 1/2 In. 95.00
Ashtray, Mobil, Flying Horse 247.00
Ashtray, Mokaine Liqueur, Metal, Parrot Picture 100.00
Ashtray, O'Keefe's Old Vienna Beer, Porcelain 15.00
Ashtray, Pabbies & Peaches, Bull, Figural, Brass 50.00
Ashtray, Pontiac Fleet Sales, Figural Indian, Ceramic, 1950s, 5 1/2 In. .... 125.00 to 175.00
Ashtray, Reddy Kilowatt, Safety Award, Sept. 14, 1960, 7 In. 35.00
Ashtray, Reddy Kilowatt, Square, White 45.00
Ashtray, Security National Bank, Paperweight, Octagonal, 1927 .... 15.00
Ashtray, Shoney's Big Boy 45.00
Ashtray, Texaco, Glass, Sterling Silver Rim, 1902-1952, 6 In. 135.00
Ashtray, Yeungling's Quality Check Ice Cream, Clear, Red & Yellow, Square 5.00
Awning, Dr Pepper, Porcelainized Steel, 2 Poles, Lime Ground, 46 In. 4400.00

Bag, Massasoit Coffee, Indian In Headdress, 1 Lb. 3.00
Banner, Hires Root Beer, Canvas, 1940s, 35 x 55 In. 85.00
Banner, Jose & Juan, Carnival Side Show, Hand Painted Canvas, 8 x 9 Ft. 750.00
Banner, Kellogg's Krumbles, 8 Pieces Spell Out Kelloggs, Paper, 1938 .... 500.00
Banner, Lee Authentic Western Ware, Brown Lettering, 2 x 3 Ft. 250.00
Banner, Sinclair Gasoline, Dino, Plastic, 42 x 59 In. 75.00
Banner, Society Brand Clothes, Felt, For Window, 3 x 5 Ft. 47.00
Banner, Star Tobacco, Leyendecker Style Litho, 36 x 89 In. 95.00
Banner, Wild Money, Ladies Home Journal, Cloth, 34 x 46 1/2 In. 121.00
Belt Buckle, Marlboro 45.00
Bench, Red Goose Shoes 450.00
Bill Hook, Ask For Walker Products, 2 3/4 In. 16.50
Bill Hook, Blue Eagle Laundry Co., Celluloid, 3 1/4 In. 45.00
Bill Hook, Vogel's Star Brand Meats, Paperboard, 5 1/2 In. 11.00
Bill Hook, Walker's Mexene Chili 25.00
Bin, Jersey Coffee, J.A. Palmer, Montpelier, Worn Red Paint, 100 Lb. 300.00
Bin, Tea Bin, Revolving, Kiosk Form, 8 Lids, Center Funnel, Norton Bros., 26 In. 143.00
Blotter, Aetna Insurance, Fire Cracker Scene, 1936 .... 28.00
Blotter, Amoco, Child Aviator & Plane, 1943 .... 15.00
Blotter, Bauman Florist, Christmas Flowers, Die Cut, 1930 .... 12.00
Blotter, Bond Bread, Portable TV, Baseball Scene, 1939 .... 15.00
Blotter, Borden's Elsie, Christmas Scene 24.00
Blotter, Eagle Draughting Pencils, Draftsman 450.00
Blotter, Fleer's Double Bubble, How Uncle Sam Was Named, 1930s 25.00
Blotter, Handfords Balsam Of Myrrh Medicine, Picture, Unused 2.00
Blotter, Kellogg's Cereal, Boy In Wagon, 1916 .... 18.00
Blotter, Philadelphia Transit Safety, Children At Play, Calendar, 1920 .... 20.00
Blotter, Rice Krispies, 1940 .... 22.00
Blotter, Snap! Crackle! Pop! Kellogg's Rice Krispies, 1950, 3 1/2 x 5 1/4 In. .... 5.00 to 6.50
Blotter, The 50 Ford, 50 Ways Finer For '50 .... 5.00
Blotter, Underwood Portable Typewriter, Boston Store, 1935, Unused, 5 x 3 In. 7.00
Books may be included in the Paper category
Booklet, Coloring, Cap'n Crunch, 1968, Colored, 8 x 10 In. 30.00
Booklet, Jackson's Best Chewing Tobacco, Black, Lithograph 50.00
Booklet, Metropolitan Life, Mother Goose, 1930s 25.00
Booklet, Metropolitan Life, Records For Baby's First Year 20.00
Booklet, Red Goose Shoes, Reddy Goose In What Price Fame, 1961, 16 Pages 15.00
Booklet, Story Of Kellogg Cereals, c.1935 .... 8.00
Booklet, What Mrs. Dewey Did With New Jell-O, Recipes, 1933, 20 Pages 33.00
Boot, Figural, Pewter, 19th Century, Large 2500.00
Bottles are listed in their own category
Bottle Carrier, Hoody Says Hoods For Flavor Carry Me Home, 12 Bottle 28.00
Bottle Openers are listed in their own category
Bottle Topper, Heinz Ketchup, Figural Dinosaur 10.00
Bowl, Child's, Elsie, Borden's, Universal 28.00
Box, 40% Bran Flakes, Twist-Teezer Puzzle, 1956 .... 75.00
Box, see also Box category
Box, All Bran, 1940 .... 45.00
Box, Armour's Cloverbloom Cheese, Wooden, 2 Lb. 4.50
Box, Baker's Chocolate, Wooden, 12 Lb. 18.00
Box, Bear Brand Hosiery 30.00
Box, Black & White Scotch, Wooden 20.00
Box, Bluebird Drug Co., San Mateo, Cardboard Cylinder, 3 x 2 In. 16.00
Box, Captain Action, Aurora, 1966 .... 285.00
Box, Cheerios, Donald Duck, 1946 .... 395.00
Box, Chicklets, 1950s 50.00
Box, Choco Crunch, Quaker, 1982, 12 Oz. 85.00
Box, Cigar, Hunter & Bird Dog, Wooden 125.00
Box, Cigar, Old Virginia Cheroots 45.00
Box, Cretor's Popcorn, Blue & Orange, Cardboard, 1929, 2 x 5 In. 12.00
Box, Diamond A Cheese, Chillicothe, Mo., Wooden, 5 Lb. 5.00
Box, Diamond Dyes, Wooden, 17 x 20 x 9 1/2 In. 467.00
Box, Dubuque Biscuit Co., Cardboard, Red Label, Framed Glass Top 30.00

Box, Edgeworth Tobacco 20.00
Box, English Ovals Cigarettes, Cardboard, Holds 10 Cigarettes, 1940s 2.50
Box, Florfina Cigar, Indian, Gentlemen, Wooden, With Cigars, 7 1/2 In. 110.00
Box, Frankenstein, Aurora, Square, 1972, 8 x 8 In. 95.00
Box, Fun To Wash Soap, Black Mammy Design, 1910, 3 x 5 x 7 In. 34.00
Box, G.I. Joe Cereal, Ralston, 1980s 25.00
Box, Gold Dust Twins Washing Soap, Unopened 95.00
Box, Gold Dust Washing Powder, 9 x 6 In. 48.00
Box, Golden Tax Tea, Orange & Black, 1910 .... 6.88
Box, Hershey Soap Flakes, Unopened 70.00
Box, Hershey's Candy Bar, 5 Cents, 1940s 3.50
Box, Kate Litter's Candy Shop, Pralines, Mammy Picture 50.00
Box, Kellogg's Cereal, Display, 1935 .... 75.00
Box, Kellogg's Corn Flakes, Detroit Tigers Sun Visor, 1945 .... 66.00
Box, Kellogg's Corn Flakes, Jack Webb Dragnet 395.00
Box, Kellogg's Corn Flakes, Woody Woodpecker, Walter Lantz Characters, 1958 ...... 175.00
Box, Kellogg's Rice Krispies, Jumbo, 1935 .... 210.00
Box, Kellogg's Sugar Corn Pops, Andy Devine, 5 Oz. 225.00
Box, Kellogg's Sugar Pops, Wild Bill Hickok, Single Serving 135.00
Box, Kellogg's Sugar Smacks, 1961 .... 20.00
Box, Kellogg's Sugar Smacks, Huckleberry Hound 135.00
Box, Lux Soap, Store Display, 1930s To 1940s 8.00
Box, Maison Blanche Creole Pralines 20.00
Box, Mandeville's Triple Tested Flower Seeds 68.00
Box, Mitchell's Belladonna Plasters, Wooden, Labels, Original Pull 20.00
Box, Mother's Oats, Mother & Boy, Round, 1940s, 2 Lb., 10 Oz. 28.00
Box, Moxie, Wooden, Dovetailed, 15 x 11 In. 40.00
Box, Mr. Dee-Lish Popcorn, 1950s, 8 In. 3.00
Box, Nabisco Rice Honeys, Frontier Hero Medal, 1957 .... 75.00
Box, Nabisco Shredded Wheat, Rin Tin Tin Cavalry Rifle Pen Offer, 6 0z. 110.00
Box, Nabisco, 28 Palmer Cox Brownies Characters, 4 x 8 In. 100.00
Box, New Era Potato Chips, 1960s 20.00
Box, New York Biscuit Co., Wooden, Paper Labels 66.00
Box, Nufashod Shoe Laces, Cardboard 2.00
Box, Old Reliable, Dayton, Ohio, Wooden 115.00
Box, Pall Mall Cigarettes, Red & Gold Cardboard 2.25
Box, Post Crispy Critters, Baseball Cards, 1962 .... 150.00
Box, Post Grape Nuts Flakes, Mickey Mantle Baseball Cards, 1961 .... 400.00
Box, Post Sugar Crisp, Mickey Mouse, Canada, 1934 .... 495.00
Box, Post Toasties, 1920s 295.00
Box, Post Toasties, Pinocchio, 1939 .... 295.00
Box, Post Toasties, Snow White, 1938 .... 395.00
Box, Pure Olive Oil Candy, Square, 6 1/4 x 3 1/4 x 1 1/2 In. 300.00
Box, Queen Bee Cigar 25.00
Box, Raisin Bran, Woody Woodpecker, 1963 .... 195.00
Box, Ralston Shredded Wheat, Little Women, Peter Lawford, June Allyson, MGM 395.00
Box, Ralston's Matchless Stove Polish, Lithographs 150.00
Box, Remington Ammunition, Wooden 20.00
Box, Remington Sheath Knife 10.00
Box, Rub No More Cleanser, Elephant Scrubbing Baby, Unopened 95.00
Box, Scripto Pencil Lead, Cardboard, Wooden 1.50
Box, Seed, Dovetailed Wood, Picture Inside Lid, 9 x 6 1/2 x 3 1/4 In. 55.00
Box, Seed, Ferry New Seeds 98.00
Box, Seed, Ferry Seeds, Oak 200.00
Box, Seed, Label, Choice Vegetable Seeds, Hiram Sibley & Co, Packages 600.00
Box, Seltzer Bottle, Wooden, Metal Bands, Holds 10 Bottles 15.00
Box, Shoeshine, Griffin Shinemaster, Oak, Footrest Top, 10 3/4 x 8 x 5 In. 35.00
Box, Skeezix Handkerchiefs 90.00
Box, Smith Brothers Cough Drops, Sample 20.00
Box, Sperm Sewing Machine Oil, 12 3-Oz Bottles, Wooden 3000.00
Box, Staley's Laundry Starch Cubes, Girl Ironing Shirt, Unopened 10.00
Box, Stickley Brothers Cigars, Brass & Copper Drew, 10 x 6 In. 1980.00
Box, Superia Insect Spray, Wooden 50.00

Box, Sweet Moments Cigar 50.00
Box, Trix, Arabic Writing, Saudi Arabia 20.00
Box, Western Cartridge, Wooden 25.00
Box, Wheaties, Johnny Bench 65.00
Box, Winchester 12 Gauge Shells 35.00
Box, X-Cello Red Bird, Paper & Cardboard 10.00
Bucket, Big Top Coffee, Cover, 5 Lb. 37.50
Buckle, Belt, Carnation, Advertising 15.00
Bust, Dr. Warner's Health Corset, Ceramic, White, Pat. Feb. 13, 1877, 28 1/2 In. 231.00
Bust, Old Grand Dad, Bottled In Bond, Composition, Painted, 11 1/2 In. 22.00
Bust, Scholar, Teacher's Scotch Whiskey, Papier-Mache, Painted, 12 In. 28.00
Butter Pat, Viking Skibe, Blue Ceramic, Royal Copenhagen 13.00
Button Hook, Spencer Shoe Store, Iron 2.25
Cabinet, Adams Pepsin Tutti-Frutti, Mirrored Back, Oak, 17 1/2 x 12 1/2 In. 700.00
Cabinet, Belding's Silk, Mahogany, Revolving, Gold Stencil, 32 1/2 In. 880.00
Cabinet, Best Quality Sewing Needles, Wooden, 3 Drawers, Tin Front, 17 1/2 In. 66.00
Cabinet, Clark Thread, Paneled Sides, 6 Drawers 375.00
Cabinet, Diamond Dyes, Children With Balloons, Tin, Wooden, Refinished, 30 In. 825.00
Cabinet, Diamond Dyes, Fairy, Tin Front, Wooden 1200.00
Cabinet, Diamond Dyes, Mansion, Wooden, Sliding Rear Doors, 29 1/2 In. 743.00
Cabinet, Display, Jos. Knittel Show Case Co., Stained Wood, 30 In. 275.00
Cabinet, Dr. Daniels Dog & Cat Remedies, Tin, 13 x 20 In. 3300.00
Cabinet, Dr. Daniels, Stained Oak, Tin Lithograph, 28 1/2 In. 825.00
Cabinet, Eagle Brand Musical Accessories, Glass Fall Front, 20 Boxes, 17 In. 220.00
Cabinet, Electric Cutlery Co., Oak, Geometric Designs, 29 In. 660.00
Cabinet, Freihofer's Quality Cakes, Display, Hinged Rear Door 325.00
Cabinet, Hohner Harmonicas, 3 Drawers, Logo 200.00
Cabinet, J.P. Privley's Gum, California Fruit & Pepsin, Wooden, 18 1/2 In. 385.00
Cabinet, Jacques' Flavoring Extracts, Glass, Stenciled, Wooden, 35 In. 660.00
Cabinet, Linkman's Quality Pipe House, Wooden Door, Reverse Painted, 13 In. 275.00
Cabinet, Lorillard Tobacco, Glass Doors, Carved 1750-1883, Cherry, 32 In. 3000.00
Cabinet, Milwares Needles, 2 Small Drawers, Wooden 150.00
Cabinet, Norvell-Shapleigh Hardware, Oak, Revolving Rack, Hexagonal, 55 In. 550.00
Cabinet, Our Best Snuffs, George W. Helme Co., Wooden, 20 Filled Tins, 19 In. 237.00
Cabinet, Pratt's Veterinary Remedies, Tin Lithograph, Oak, 32 1/2 In. 523.00
Cabinet, Putnam Fadeless Dyes, Tin, 14 1/2 x 18 3/4 In. 165.00
Cabinet, Sheaffer Pen & Pencil 395.00
Cabinet, Shumate Razors & Strops, Wooden, Glass, Decal, 23 In. 880.00
Cabinet, Spool, A.N. Russell & Sons, Oak, 6 Glass Doors Each Side, 38 In. 770.00
Cabinet, Spool, Belding Bros. & Co., Oak, 4 Drawers 425.00
Cabinet, Spool, Brainerd & Armstrong Co., Mirrors, 14 Drawers .... 500.00 to 990.00
Cabinet, Spool, Clark's ONT, Roll Top 575.00
Cabinet, Spool, Corticelli Silk, 12 Glass Front Drawers, Mirrored Sides, 33 In. 745.00
Cabinet, Spool, Corticelli, 3 Drawers 285.00
Cabinet, Spool, Corticelli, Oak, 3 Drawers, Glass Fronts, 39 x 23 In. 300.00
Cabinet, Spool, Goffs Braid, 2 Drawers 325.00
Cabinet, Spool, J. & P. Coats, Figural Spool, 4 Drawers, 19 1/2 x 15 In. 600.00
Cabinet, Spool, J. & P. Coats, Oak, 2 Drawers, 1920s 255.00
Cabinet, Spool, J. & P. Coats' Cotton, Oak, Revolving, Ornate, 22 3/4 In. 1375.00
Cabinet, Spool, Merrick's, Walnut, Victorian, Contents 275.00
Cabinet, Sunoco Oil, Mercury-Made, Floor Standing 825.00
Calculator, Hershey's, Looks, Feels & Smells Like Chocolate, In Display 25.00
Calendars are listed in their own category
Can, Ace Highmotor Oil, Graphics, 1 Qt. 355.00
Can, Conoco Oil, 1 Gal. 300.00
Can, Dyer's Cough Drops, Indian 350.00
Can, En-Ar-Co C1 Oil, Metal, 1 Qt. 6.00
Can, Gunpowder, American Powder Mills, Label, Red Paint, 9 x 7 7/8 In. 140.00
Can, Imperial Motor Oil, 1920s, 5 Gal. 95.00
Can, Modell Anti-Freeze, Graphics, 1/2 Gal. 175.00
Can, Oil, Sinclair, 1930s 22.00
Can, Rokeach Scouring Powder, Hebrew Word Kosher, 1912, 4 7/8 In. 205.00
Can, Rubon Cleaner, Women Mopping & Dusting, 1950s, 1 Pt. 15.00

Can, Shoreline Motor Oil, Script Shorelube, Tin 200.00
Can, Veedal, Tide Water Oil Co., Square, 1 Gal. 50.00
Can Opener, Pet Milk, Blue Plastic, Covers Entire Can Top 6.00
Candy Box, Valentine, Red Velvet Heart, 1920s 25.00
Candy Wrapper, Marshfield's Homemade Peanut Bar, 1930s 2.00
Canisters, see introductory paragraph to Tins in this category
Car, Roi-Tan Cigars, Steel, Rubber Wheels, Sophie Tucker Sign, 1939 .... 125.00 to 225.00
Cards are listed in their own category
Card, Bell Telephone, Santa Claus Talking On Phone, 1911, 3 x 6 In. 55.00
Cart, Oibermeyer & Leibmann's Bottled Beers, Wooden, 43 In. 1650.00
Carton, Cigarettes, Eagle, White Eagle, Bright Red Ground, 8 Full Packs 35.00
Case, Beer, Anheuser Busch, Wooden, With 24 Bottles, 1916 .... 275.00
Case, Biscuit, Christie's, Ash, 1900, 54 x 47 x 12 1/2 In. 1210.00
Case, Eagle On Globe, Revolving Cast Iron Base, Display, 66 In. 2750.00
Case, Grieshaber Fountain Pens, 1900s 600.00
Case, Keen Kutter Kutlery, 2 Drawers, Velvet Insert, Oak, 54 In. 80.00
Case, Lion Brand Shirts, Collars & Cuffs, Wood, Pedestal, Display, 66 In. 825.00
Case, Milk Bottle, Jones Dairy, Corydon, Iowa, Wire 12.00
Case, Milk Bottle, Sealtest Dairy, St. Louis, Wire 12.50
Case, Sheaffer Fountain Pens, Early 1900s 600.00
Case, William Root Beer Extract, Metal 45.00
Case, Wilson Goggles 165.00
Casket, Wooden, Window To View, Salesman's Sample, Bavarian Style, 5 x 3 In. 225.00
Chalkboard, Budweiser The King Of Beers 45.00
Change Receiver, see Tip Tray in this category
Cigar Box, Golden Brown Panatelas, Cedar, Hinged, 6 1/2 x 6 x 3 In. 15.00
Cigar Cutter, Brunhoff Mfg. Co., Cast Iron, Dual Arms, 7 1/4 In. 220.00
Cigar Cutter, Cubanola, Turn Ships Wheel, Iron, 6 3/4 In. 303.00
Cigar Cutter, Hatchet, Gillen & Boney, 7 In. 67.00
Cigar Cutter & Knife, Wolf's Whiskey, Engraved Wolf 45.00
Cigarette Flag, Belgium, Early 1900s, Felt, 8 x 5 1/2 In. 3.00
Cigarette Flag, Japan, Early 1900s, Felt, 8 x 5 1/2 In. 3.00
Cigarette Flag, Mexico, Early 1900s, Felt, 8 x 5 1/2 In. 3.00
Cigarette Silk, Gibson Girl Type, 5 1/2 x 3 1/2 In. 20.00
Clicker, Poll Parrot Shoes 10.00
Clocks are listed in their own category
Coaster, Genesee Beer, 2 Colors, Mug With Beer, 3 1/2 In. 1.00
Coaster, Simon Pure Beer, Red & Green, 3 1/2 In. 1.00
Coaster Set, Wurlitzer, Wooden, 1940s, 6 Piece 24.00
Coffee Grinders are listed in their own category
Comic Book, Poll Parrot Shoes, Bandit Buster, 1959 .... 25.00
Crate, Shipping, Smith Bros., Wooden 225.00
Creamer, Borden's, Elsie The Cow, 1940s, 5 x 4 1/2 In. 45.00
Creamer, Progressive Dairy 10.00
Cuff Links, Chevy Truck Sales, 1960s 20.00
Cup, Anheuser-Busch, Cases In Wagon, Decal, Incised Letters 75.00
Cup, Coffee, The Nut Tree Diner, Tree Logo, China 20.00
Cup, Collapsible, Alka Seltzer, Speedy 30.00
Cup, Kool-Aid, Pitcher Form With Face, Frosted, Clear Plastic, 1960s, Set Of 4 .... 15.00
Cup, Mavix Chocolates, 4 In. 39.00
Cup, Quaker Oats, Figural, Plastic, 1950s, 3 1/2 In. 12.00
Cup, Walgreen, China 20.00
Cup & Saucer, Nestle's, Sterling China 7.50
Cutter Set, Calumet Baking Powder, Nested 15.00
Desk Set, Fisk Tires, Boy Holding Tire, Brass & Metal, Ohio, 1940s, 7 In. 326.00
Dish, Fleischmann & Co., Ohio Pottery, 4 1/2 x 6 In. 72.00
Dish, Haagen-Dazs Ice Cream, Ceramic, Tub Looks Like Carton, 1980 .... 5.00
Dispenser, Bromo-Seltzer, Purple Glass Bottle, Nickel Plated Bracket, 16 In. 198.00
Dispenser, Cherry Julep Syrup, White Lettering On Red, No Pump, 11 In 440.00
Dispenser, Cherry Smash Syrup, 5 Cents, Glass On Front, 14 x 8 1/2 In. 500.00
Dispenser, Concord Punch, Frosted Glass Reservoir, Cordley & Hayes, 19 In. 165.00
Dispenser, Cone, Metal Lid & Nickel Plated Base, Clear Glass, 13 1/2 In. 358.00
Dispenser, Drink Hires, It Is Pure, Corset Barrel Form, 14 1/2 In. 660.00

Dispenser, Feen-A-Mint, Tin, Oval Mirror, 16 In. 357.00
Dispenser, Hires Syrup, Maroon Letters On White, 11 1/2 In. .... 253.00 to 550.00
Dispenser, Jersey-Creme, Green & Red Lettering, 11 3/4 In. 468.00
Dispenser, Jersey-Creme, Green & Red Lettering, 15 In. 605.00
Dispenser, Lemon Crush, Ceramic 550.00
Dispenser, Monarch Pickle, Sheet Metal, Glass Lids, Painted Lions, 43 In. 825.00
Dispenser, Morton's Salt, Tin, Wall Mount 100.00
Dispenser, Orange Crush, Mission, Black & Pink, Brass Top, c.1900 .... 1200.00
Dispenser, Orange Julep Syrup, White Letters On Orange, 13 1/2 In. 413.00
Dispenser, Ward's Lime Crush 1350.00
Dispenser, Ward's Orange Crush Syrup, Orange Shape, Pump, 9 x 12 x 8 In. 632.00
Dispenser, Ward's Orange Crush Syrup, Porcelain Knob Pump, 14 1/2 In. 715.00
Dispenser, Ward's Orange Crush, 1905-1910, 12 1/4 In. 990.00
Dispenser, Ward's Orange Crush, No Pump, 10 In. 413.00
Display, 7-Up Bottle Resting On Large Ice Cube, Glass, 9 In. 523.00
Display, 7-Up, Exactly What It Is, A Fresh Up, 2 Sides, Hanging, 1944, 5 x 7 In. 34.00
Display, Beech-Nut Gum, Box Holder, Spring-Loaded, Picture, 7 x 11 In. 660.00
Display, Black Boy, Clockwork, Animated, Open-Close Mouth, 7 In. 1430.00
Display, Blue Jay Corn Plasters, Grandma & Grandpa, Tin Die Cut, Pair 1000.00
Display, Blue-Jay, Keep Your Feet Gay, Comical Rocking Display, Tin, 11 In. 325.00
Display, Box, 29 Children's Rings, 1920s 145.00
Display, Box, Story Book Knobs, Individual Packages, 1950s, 12 1/2 In. 75.00
Display, Budweiser, Ceramic Wagon, 2 Clydesdales 80.00
Display, Case, Oak, 1875, 97 x 42 x 27 In. 750.00
Display, Chandler's Chewing Laxative, 24 Original Packages, Card, 1930s 18.00
Display, Clairol, 23 Real Hair Samples, Card, 1950s 48.00
Display, Converse Shoes, Man, Woman, Tennis Rackets, Cardboard, 30 x 26 In. 330.00
Display, Crayola Crayons, 1950s, 16 x 18 x 11 .... 45.00
Display, Creaters Popcorn Popper, Clown & Glass Drum 275.00
Display, Dills Pipe Cleaners, 24 Packages, Card, 1920s 18.00
Display, Dixieland Sewing Needles, 20 Packages, Card, 1930s, 6 x 8 In. 38.00
Display, Dutch Boy Paint, Figural, Papier-Mache & Composition, 29 In. 300.00
Display, Edison Mazda, Tin Lithograph, Wooden Base, Light Bulbs 525.00
Display, Esterbrook Pens, Rotary, Tin, 14 x 10 1/2 In. 195.00
Display, Eveready Flashlight Batteries, Tester, 1950s 35.00
Display, Ferry's Seed, Empty Seed Packs 125.00
Display, Ferry's Seed, With Vegetable & Flower Packets 120.00
Display, Ford, 1947 Ford On Cardboard, Framed In Neon, 16 x 19 x 6 In. 247.00
Display, General Electric Co., Radio Bandmaster, Punch Out, Paper, 6 x 10 In. 44.00
Display, Heinz Ketchup, Stand-Up, Folds Out To Hold Bottle, 1940s, 12 x 15 In. 65.00
Display, Houbigant Perfume, Art Deco, Chrome 350.00
Display, Iron Horse Train, People, Boston Sunday Globe, Cardboard, 1896 .... 85.00
Display, Jitterbug Suspenders, Child's Size, Card, 1940s 15.00
Display, Kool Cigarettes, 7 x 8 In. 35.00
Display, Lanvin Perfume, Bottle, Reverse Painted, 7 1/4 In. 88.00
Display, Lemp Beer, Die Cut Tin, Teddy Roosevelt, 13 1/2 In. 3750.00
Display, Lowenbrau Beer, Embossed Figure, Holding Mug, 3-D, 1940s, 19 In. 15.00
Display, Lulu Holding Box Of Kleenex, 10 x 10 In. 38.00
Display, Mail Pouch Tobacco, Paper, Panama Pacific Expo, 1915, 36 x 45 In. 1100.00
Display, McDonald's, Mack Tonight, Cutout 25.00
Display, McGregor Happy Foot, Rubber Figure, Rubber Guild Of Montreal, 17 In. 684.00
Display, Mirror, Bob' Link Cigars, Easel Frame, 17 1/2 x 10 1/2 In. 115.00
Display, Nodding Goose, Red Goose School Shoes, Papier-Mache, 24 In. 1100.00
Display, Old Crow, Figural, Plastic, Electric Light, 29 In. 50.00
Display, Red Goose Shoes, Cardboard, Stand-Up, 6 1/2 x 10 1/2 In. 25.00
Display, Smile Soda, Bottle, Orange & Black Paint, 18 1/2 In. 245.00
Display, Snap, Crackle & Pop, Figural, Wooden, 1940s, 4 1/2 Ft., 3 Piece 1300.00
Display, Soldier, Sweet Corporal Cigarettes, Soldier, Cardboard, Stand-Up, 13 In. 75.00
Display, Stag Beer, Bottle, Teal Glass, Label, 1930s, 27 In. 178.00
Display, Straight Razor, Figural, Case Bros., Nickel Plated, 14 In. 413.00
Display, Supp-Hose Stockings, Woman, Cloth Dress, Seated, Hard Rubber, 18 In. 468.00
Display, U.S. Marshal Flashlights, Western, 12 Piece 95.00
Display, Uncle John's Syrup, Figural, 3-D, Cardboard, 12 x 14 In. 15.00

Advertising, Figure, Bobbin' Head, KFC Colonel, 1960s, 3 In.	Advertising, Figure, Budweiser, Bud Man, Rubber, 17 x 5 x 8 1/2 In.	Advertising, Figure, RCA, Radiotrons, Composition, Wood, Maxfield Parrish, 15 In.	Advertising, Figure, Alka-Seltzer, Speedy, Vinyl, 8 x 4 x 3 1/2 In.

Display, Urn, Richard Hudnut Perfumer, Lamp, Urn, Woman Scene, Metal, 20 In. 385.00
Display, Windmill, Heineken's Lager, Light-Up 110.00
Display Case, Boston Garters, Etched Glass, Interior Shelves, 14 1/4 x 14 In. 250.00
Display Case, Boye, Counter Top, Sewing Items, c.1919, 11 x 11 x 9 In. 225.00
Display Case, Double-K Nuts 225.00
Display Case, Pine, Glass Front, 2 Shelves, Rear Door, 19 x 8 3/4 x 25 1/2 In. 160.00
Display Rack, Life Savers 225.00
Display Rack, Pall Mall Cigarettes 125.00
Display Rack, PEZ, c.1960 .... 250.00
Dolls are listed in their own category
Door Pull, Dr Pepper, Figural Bottle, Embossed Aluminum, 9 3/4 In. 231.00
Door Pull, White Rock, Screen Door, Embossed Metal, 4 x 14 1/2 In. 85.00
Door Push, Bankers Merchants Secret Service Bureau, Porcelain 100.00
Door Push, Burtonb'w'g Co. Beer, Reverse On Glass, Pre-1914, 3 1/2 x 10 In. 105.00
Door Push, Delicious Salada Tea, Porcelain, Red Letters, Yellow 140.00
Door Push, Dr. Caldwell's, Porcelainized Steel, Yellow & Black, 6 1/2 x 3 3/4 In. 105.00
Door Push, Fresh Up With 7-Up, Porcelain 90.00
Door Push, Grapette, Thirsty Or Not 110.00
Door Push, Junges Bread, Porcelain 85.00
Door Push, Old Gold, Dancing Cigarette Pack, Metal 55.00
Door Push, Plate, Ex-Lax, Porcelainized Steel, Red, White & Blue, 8 x 4 In. 105.00
Door Push, Royal Crown Cola, Best By Taste Test 125.00
Door Push, Salada Tea 110.00
Door Push, Sun Drop Cola, Tin 55.00
Door Push, White Rock 115.00
Dress, Child's, McDonald's, Size 8 .... 10.00
Earrings, Reddy Kilowatt, On Card, 1955 .... 45.00
Fans are listed in their own category
Figure, Alka-Seltzer, Speedy, Vinyl, 8 x 4 x 3 1/2 In. .... *Illus* 600.00
Figure, American Brakeblok, Dog, Name Stopper On Collar, 1930s 45.00
Figure, Anheuser-Busch, Composition, Part Of Larger Display 60.00
Figure, Bobbin' Head, KFC Colonel, 1960s, 3 In. .... *Illus* 119.00
Figure, Budweiser, Bud Man, Rubber, 17 x 5 x 8 1/2 In. .... *Illus* 236.00
Figure, Budweiser, Spud McKenzie, Big 135.00
Figure, California Raisins, Drummer, Vinyl 25.00
Figure, Clayton Veterinarian Remedies, Bulldog, Papier-Mache, 28 x 15 In. 1400.00
Figure, Clicquot Club Soda, Eskimo, Papier-Mache, 33 In. 375.00
Figure, Colonel Sanders, Nodder, 1967 .... 145.00
Figure, Dairyland Chocolate Coated Ice Cream, Insulated Polar Bear, 5 Cents 1400.00
Figure, Deckers Iowana Ham, Pig, Papier-Mache, 16 x 19 In. 65.00

Figure, Doggone Good Beer & Ale, Frankenmuth Dog, Plaster 40.00
Figure, Dutch Boy Paints, Boy Kneeling With Paint Brush, 12 In. 300.00
Figure, First Aid Soda, Lady, Bottle Cover, Paper & Crepe, Art Deco, 7 x 13 In. 18.00
Figure, I Croak For Webster Wagon, Frog, Cast Iron, 5 In. 93.50
Figure, Kellogg's Frosted Flakes, Tony The Tiger, Inflatable, 5 Ft. 125.00
Figure, Kellogg's Rice Krispies, Pop & Snap, Paperboard, 12 & 15 1/2 In., Pair 458.00
Figure, Kellogg's Rice Krispies, Snap, Crackle & Pop, Hollow Rubber, 3 Piece 75.00
Figure, Mohawk Carpet Co., Tommy The Indian, Bisque 425.00
Figure, Monsieur De Coco, Wood, Tin & Cloth, French Cafe, 1850s 4900.00
Figure, RCA Radiotrons, Composition, Wood, Maxfield Parrish, 15 In. .... *Illus* 800.00
Figure, Reddy Kilowatt, 1960s 175.00
Figure, Robin Hood Shoes, Composition, 18 In. 145.00
Figure, Sony, Boy, 4 In. 500.00
Figure, Swift & Co., Mayrose Maid, 1973, 7 3/4 In. 50.00
Figure, Wm. Penn Cigar, Man, Standing, Papier-Mache, 3 Ft. 75.00
Flashlight, Little Green Sprout, Carton, 9 In. .... 25.00 to 30.00
Fly Swatter, Davis Hardware, Unionville, Mo., Small 1.00
Folder, School, Ronald McDonald, 1974 .... 10.00
Game, Dominoes, Budweiser, Dovetailed Box 65.00
Game, Put The Tail On Tony 40.00
Gas Can, Keen Kutter, 2 1/2 Gal. 55.00
Glass, Albany Brewery, Albany, Oreg. 112.00
Glass, Atlas All-American Beer, Chicago, Enameled 55.00
Glass, Bedrock City, Various Scenes, 5 1/2 In. 21.00
Glass, Buffalo Brewing Co., Sacramento, Calif., Etched Running Buffalo, 1900s 165.00
Glass, Burger Chef, Chef & Jeff 12.00
Glass, Burger King, Endangered Species, 1978, Set Of 4 .... 25.00
Glass, Burger King, Luke Skywalker 7.00
Glass, Chilly Willy & Smedly, Walter Lantz, Tall 18.00
Glass, Commander Milwaukee Beer, Enameled, 1940s 72.00
Glass, Coon Chicken Inn 27.00
Glass, Dennis The Menace 44.00
Glass, Dr Pepper, Star Trek, Enterprise, 1976 .... 22.00
Glass, Dr Pepper, Star Trek, Kirk, 1976 .... 18.00
Glass, E.T., Pizza Hut, 1982 .... 5.00
Glass, Fauerbach, Madison, Wis., Etched, 1900s 356.00
Glass, Hamm's Excelsior, St. Paul 72.00
Glass, Hardee's, Flintstones, 4 Piece 20.00
Glass, Heidel Brau, Sioux City Brewing Co., Enameled 47.00
Glass, Heinz Aristocratic Tomato Juice, Set Of 4 .... 60.00
Glass, Koppitz-Melcher's Brewing Co., Beer 95.00
Glass, Little Lulu & Tubby Tom 66.00
Glass, McDonald's, Checkerboard, Early Cat Gets The Hotcake 2.00
Glass, McDonald's, Steelers Hall Of Fame, 4 Piece 20.00
Glass, Mission, With Syrup Line 27.00
Glass, Rising Sun Brewery, Elizabeth, N.J. 165.00
Glass, Salute To Olympic Games, Multilanguage, 1976 .... 3.00
Glass, Sunoco, Wildlife, 4 Piece 20.00
Glass, Tab Soda 5.00
Glass, Upper Peninsula Brewery, Marquette, Mich. 159.00
Glass, Walters Bros. Factory Scene, Etched, Beer 50.00
Glass, Welch's Jelly, Flintstones 6.50
Glass, Western Springs Distributing Co., Chicago, Etched, 3 In. 60.00
Goblet, Moeliens National Lager Beer, Embossed 50.00
Gum Wrapper, Pink Yucatan 20.00
Gum Wrapper, Wrigley's Doublemint, 1920s 6.00
Hat, Adam Hats, Red Felt, Box, Sample 38.00
Hat, Dr Pepper, Soda Jerk, 1950s 15.00
Hat, Fire Chief, Texaco 70.00
Hat, Long's Hats For Men, Salesman's Sample, Felt, Box 38.00
Hat, Stetson, Felt, Box, 3 In. 35.00
Hat, Top, Dobb's, Composition, Salesman's Sample, 1880s 175.00
Heater, Dr Pepper Hot, 1950-1960 .... 40.00

Humidor, Cremo Cigar, Tin Litho, Simulated Wood Grain, 14 In. 28.00
Humidor, Polar Bear Tobacco, Tin, Slant Lift Lid, 18 x 14 In. 413.00
Ice Cooler, Dr Pepper, Portable 85.00
Ice Pick, Brookville 9.00
Ice Scraper, Firestone, Cobalt Blue, 1930s 20.00
Jar, American Oyster Co., Providence, R.I., Glass, 1 Pt. 104.50
Jar, Chicos Peanuts, Metal Holder 175.00
Jar, Curtis Chicos Spanish Peanuts, 5 Cents, Enameled Lid & Base 245.00
Jar, Fin-De-Sicle Epsin Gum 595.00
Jar, Globe Tobacco Co., Detroit Pat. Oct. 10, 1882, Amber, Barrel Shape, Handle 70.00
Jar, Heinz's Pickling Vinegar, 6 Sides, Labels, Stopper, 5 x 12 In. 247.00
Jar, Heyser's Oysters, Glass, 1 Pt. 110.00
Jar, Horlick's Malt, 3 1/2 Qt. 70.00
Jar, Koenig 5 Cents, Coffee, Clear, 3 Pt. 5.00
Jar, Lance Cracker, Glass, Lid 20.00
Jar, Pyramid Salted Nuts, Octagonal, Label 150.00
Jar, Smucker's Apple Butter, Bristol Glaze, Wire Bail 75.00
Jug, Cullamore Irish Whiskey, 8 In. 25.00
Key Holder, 7-Up, Moxie 10.00
Label, Ace Beer, Sioux City Brewing Co., Sioux City, Iowa, 1948 .... 14.00
Label, Bigger Bang Firecracker, Canada 20.00
Label, Black Cat Firecracker 8.00
Label, Bob White, Apple, Bobwhite Bird, 4 x 14 In. 1.00
Label, Bomb-Buster Pop Corn, Ray's Farm Foods, Mattoon, Ill. 1.00
Label, Chautauqua Maid, Grape Juice, Pretty Girl, 1940s, 3 1/4 x 4 1/4 In. 1.00
Label, China Beauty Firecracker 50.00
Label, Cigar Box, 1492 Havana, Smoke Exposition Cigars, 1892, 6 x 10 In. 35.00
Label, Cigar Box, Franklin D. Roosevelt 15.00
Label, Corn Belt Beer, Pointer Brewing Co., Clinton, Iowa, 1934-1939 .... 26.00
Label, Defender, Vegetable, 2 Sailing Ships & Tomato, 3 1/2 x 9 In. 2.00
Label, Don't Cry, Sweet Potatoes, Black Man Shooting Dice, 1940s, 9 x 9 In. 5.00
Label, Donald Duck Juice, Florida Citrus Canners, Lake Wales, Fla., 1942 .... 20.00
Label, Dr. Rowell's Celebrated Invigorating Tonic, 7 x 7 In. 15.00
Label, Dubuque Star Beer, Dubuque Star Brewing Co., Dubuque, Iowa, 1950s 13.00
Label, El West Delite, Citrus, Couple Dancing, 9 x 9 In. 2.00
Label, Elkay Mayo Salad Dressing, Bottle, L. Klein, Chicago .... .50
Label, Eureka, Citrus Fruit, Indian At River, 1940s, 9 x 9 In. 4.00
Label, Flying Fairy Brand Firecracker, 2 In. 22.00
Label, Glamour Girl Artichokes, Pretty Girl, 1950s, 6 3/4 x 11 In. 2.50
Label, Grizzly Brand Apples, Hotchkiss, Colo., 9 x 11 In. 15.00
Label, Hitts Devil Dog Firecracker, 1930s, 2 In. 35.00
Label, Jaguar Sweet Potatoes, Jaguar In Field, 9 x 9 In. 5.00
Label, Jet Bomber Firecracker 35.00
Label, Ken Kat, Sweet Potato, Black Cat Sitting, 9 x 9 In. 3.00
Label, Leader Citrus Fruit, Horse & Lemons, 1940s, 9 x 12 In. 3.00
Label, Luxburger Beer, Bavarian Luxburger Brewing Co., 1934-1935, 12 Oz. 23.00
Label, Mighty Atom Brick Firecracker, Canada 15.00
Label, Mista Joe, Black Porter Serving White Couple, Vegetable Crate, 1948 .... 12.50
Label, Noi-Zee Boy Firecracker 8.00
Label, Old Reliable Beer, Old Reliable Brewing Co., 1941, 12 Oz. 18.00
Label, Peacock, 1 1/2 In. 25.00
Label, Pointer, Pointer Brewing Co., Clinton, Iowa, 1937-1939 .... 29.00
Label, Red Tips Cigars, 6 x 10 In. 10.00
Label, Red Wagon Grapes, Boy Pushing Wagon, 1950s, 13 x 4 In. .... .50
Label, Ritz Beer, Pointer Brewing Co., Clinton, Iowa, 1934-1939 .... 27.00
Label, Safe Hit, Texas Vegetables, Baseball Player Hitting Homer, 5 x 7 In. 1.25
Label, School Boy Brand Apples, Paonia, Colo., 9 x 11 In. 18.00
Label, Shamrock Oranges, Shamrock Over Groves, 1940s, 11 x 10 In. 1.00
Label, Smoke Sardines, Mermaid, 1930s, 3 x 4 In. 1.00
Label, Sunkist Lemons, Santa Carrying Sack, 1928, 9 x 12 In. 3.00
Label, Sweet Lue, Sweet Potato, Little Girl, Rural Scene, 9 x 9 In. 1.50
Label, Texas Moon, Citrus Fruit, Cowboy Riding Horse, 9 x 9 In. 6.00
Label, Valley Royal, Valley Brewing Co., 1960, 12 Oz. 25.00

Label, Victoria, Citrus Fruit, Queen & Oranges, 1930s, 11 x 10 In. 2.00
Label, Welcome Brand Firecracker 62.00
Label, Western Brew, Sioux City Brewing Co., Sioux City, Iowa, 1934 .... 19.00
Lamp, Kilster Radio, Dancing Nudes 250.00
Lamp, Miller Highlife, Motion 20.00
Lamp, Parker Pens, Metal Shade, Reticulated Letter Over Wood Base, 18 1/4 In. 143.00
Laundry Kit, Carter's Ink, 1900s, Box 55.00
Letter Opener, Fuller Brush Man, Plastic, Red, 1950s, 10 In. .... 7.50 to 12.00
Letter Opener, MacGregor's Ice Cream, Celluloid Handle 22.00
Lunch Boxes are listed in their own category
Magnet, Pillsbury, Poppin' Fresh & Poppie, Plastic, 1970s, 2 x 4 In., Pair 20.00
Mannequin, Woman, 3-D, Fruit Of The Loom Girdle, Rubber, 29 In. 253.00
Marbles, Red Goose, Box, 5 In. 45.00
Menu, 7-Up, Masonite, 12 x 12 In. 70.00

Advertising pocket mirrors range in size from 1 1/2 to 5 inches in diameter.
Most of these mirrors were given away as advertising promotions.

Mirror, American Fashion Hats, As Good As The Name, Gold, Black, 24 x 12 In. 165.00
Mirror, Andes Stoves, Red, White & Blue, Pocket 22.00
Mirror, Bell Roasted Coffee, Pocket 40.00
Mirror, Campbell's Soup, 10 Cents A Can, Pocket 200.00
Mirror, Cresota Flour, Pocket 45.00
Mirror, Duffy Malt Whiskey, Celluloid, Pocket 95.00
Mirror, Garrett's Baker Rye, Nude At Water, Celluloid, Pocket, 2 3/4 In. 300.00
Mirror, Gillette Safety Razor, Black, Red, White & Yellow, Pocket 25.00
Mirror, H.S.B. & Co., Cutlery & Tools, Pocket 44.00
Mirror, Horlicks, Girl & Cow, Pocket 75.00
Mirror, Hubbard Fertilizer Company, Woman, Long Hair Picture, 1905, Pocket 279.00
Mirror, I Use Kleinert's Dress Shields, Round, Lithograph, Celluloid, Pocket, 2 In. 55.00
Mirror, International Tailoring Co., With Game, N.Y., London, Berlin, Pocket 150.00
Mirror, Johnny Walker Red, Framed, 1950s, Pocket 75.00
Mirror, Lava Chemical Resolvent Soap, Yellow Ground, 1910, Pocket 40.00
Mirror, Lava Soap, Multicolor, Graphic, Celluloid, Pocket 80.00
Mirror, Mascot Crushed Cut Tobacco, Celluloid, Pocket 50.00
Mirror, Mr. Liver Tablets, Pocket 30.00
Mirror, Ohio Silage Cutters, Pocket 68.00
Mirror, Ohio Silo Filler, Silver Mfg.Co., Celluloid, Oval, 1908, Pocket 179.00
Mirror, Oliver Chilled Plow Works, Ind., Celluloid, 1 3/4 x 2 3/4 In. 139.00
Mirror, Schaefer Beer Restaurant, World's Fair, 1939, Pocket 27.50
Mirror, Skeezix Shoes, Pocket 27.00
Mirror, Socony Motor Gasoline, Box, Pocket 85.00
Mirror, Southern Electrical Co., Pocket 45.00
Mirror, Star Egg Carriers & Trays, Rochester, N.Y., Celluloid, 1910, Pocket 179.00
Mirror, Starrett Tools, Pocket 37.00
Mirror, State Farm Life Insurance, Grieving Wife & Boy, Pocket 42.50
Mirror, Toberman-Mackey & Co., Pocket 48.00
Mirror, Warren Tanner Dry Goods, Building, Pocket 32.00
Mirror, Wilson's Corn King Bacon, Pocket 35.00
Mixer, Horlick's Milk Shake, Porcelainized Steel, Blue & Gold Letters, 14 In. 231.00
Money Bag, Federal Reserve Bank, Chicago, Ill., Cloth 2.25
Money Clip, Chesterfield Cigarettes, Enamel 20.00
Money Clip, Philip Morris, Celluloid 25.00
Money Clip, Singer Sewing Machine, Anniversary 25.00
Mug, Anheuser-Busch, 40 Million Barrels, 1978 .... 40.00
Mug, Anheuser-Busch, CS-11, Green Ceramarte Mark 347.00
Mug, Armour's Veribest Root Beer, Stoneware, 5 7/8 In. 22.00
Mug, Borden's, Beulah, TV Series 45.00
Mug, Budweiser Bud Man, Solid Head, Knot In Bowtie 305.00
Mug, Budweiser, Red Wagon, St. Louis, Mo., Black Decal 200.00
Mug, Carnation Hot Cocoa Mix, Red, White, Brown & Yellow 5.00
Mug, Chelmsford Spring Ginger Beer, Stoneware, 4 3/4 In 39.00
Mug, Cherokee Brewery, St. Louis 235.00
Mug, City Squire Motor Inn 20.00

Mug, Coburger Bier, Hoboken, N.J., Pre-Prohibition 33.00
Mug, Colonel Sanders, Figural 25.00
Mug, Coricidin, Schering, Medical, Brown Pottery 15.00
Mug, Dick's Beer, Pottery, Musical Note, High Note In Brewing, 11 In. 70.00
Mug, Fabachers, New Orleans, Pre-Prohibition 140.00
Mug, Foremost, Frostie Root Beer, Plastic, Beer Type 3.00
Mug, Hires Root Beer, Join Health & Cheer, Boy Holding Mug, 4 x 5 x 3 In. 247.00
Mug, Kuebler-Stang, Sandusky, Ohio, Pre-Prohibition 248.00
Mug, Leisey Beer, Desert Scene 6.00
Mug, McHenry Brewery, McHenry, Ill., Pre-Prohibition 145.00
Mug, Michelob Dry, Pewter, Box 45.00
Mug, Ovaltine, Uncle Wiggly, 1920s .... 45.00 to 55.00
Mug, Pabst, Brigham Young, 1897 .... 91.00
Mug, Pillsbury Doughboy 10.00
Mug, Pioneer Dairy, Great Falls, Mont., Milk Glass, Red Pyro, Indian, Cowboy 10.00
Mug, Quaker Oats Man .:... .... 14.00
Mug, Radeke Brewing Co., Kankakee, Ill. 194.00
Mug, Rheingold, Stoneware, Germany, 4 1/2 In. 20.00
Mug, Royal Beer, Transfer Motto, Stoneware, 3 3/4 In. 28.00
Mug, Sehring Brewing Co., Joliet, Ill., 1907 .... 85.00
Mug, Standard Cardinal, Beer, Monk, Smelling Flowers 75.00
Mug, Thewalt, Deutschland, Beer 100.00
Mug, Trader Vic, Painted Ribald Hawaiian Scenes, 1966, 4 Piece 160.00
Night-Light, Big Boy 95.00
Olive Pick, Heinz Pickle, 1950s, Pair 4.00
Opener, Cigar Box, Elverso 12.00
Opener, Cigar Box, R.G. Dunn 12.00
Pack, Home Run Cigarette, Liggett & Myers, Catcher, Batter, Unopened, 2 3/4 In. ... 143.00
Paper Clip, Merchants Motor Freight Co., Spring Loaded, Hinged Iron, Large 5.00
Paperweight, Jersey Creme Soda 125.00
Paperweight, John Frick Jewelry Co., New York, Rock Of Gibraltar, Lead 28.00
Paperweight, Largest Makers Of Quinine & Cocaine, Drug Co. 60.00
Paperweight, Pile Of Coins, Jewelry Store, Metal, 1942 .... 20.00
Paperweight, Rat, Queen City Pattern Works, Metal, 1 1/2 x 4 1/2 In. 95.00
Paperweight, Richfield Gasoline, Figural, Airplane Engine, Inset Clock, 6 In. 300.00
Paperweight, School Of Nursing, McKeesport, Pa. 25.00
Paperweight, Thomas Drills, Rooster, Cast Iron, 3 1/4 In. 137.00
Patch, Meadow Gold Products, Shield 75.00
Patch, Steere's Milk 75.00
Pen Holder, Cat, Standing Up, Dr. Alan Pickard, Katz Drug Co., 7 1/4 x 4 3/8 In. 715.00
Pencil Holder, Oxydol, Mammy, Sho Makes Clothes White 45.00
Pillowcase, Murad Cigarette Silks, 2 Sides, 32 Pieces, 26 x 28 In. 385.00
Pin, Canada Dry, Mary Hartline Picture, 1950s 25.00
Pin, Kellogg's, Little Joe, Comic Character, Pinback, 1947 .... 8.00
Pin, Made In America, Red, White & Blue, Center Star, Pinback 5.00
Pin, Squirt, Picture, Squirt Boy, A.B.C.B. Expo Atlantic City, 1948 .... 12.00
Pin, Sweet Caporal Cigarettes, Celluloid, 1930s 20.00
Pitcher, Ambassador Deluxe Scotch, Brown Keg, Chrome Luster, 5 In. 9.50
Pitcher, Nestle's Quik Bunny, Mixer 10.00
Pitcher, Usher's Whiskey, Clear, Reverse Painted Letters Base, 5 1/4 In. 50.00
Pitcher, Welch's, Handle, 7 3/4 In. 25.00
Pitcher, Windsor Supreme Canadian, Beefeater, Ice Lip, Triangular 7.00
Pitcher Set, Kool-Aid, With Cups, 1951 .... 25.00
Place Mats, Skippy, 12 x 12 In., 4 Piece 15.00
Plate, A Steady Customer, Given To Kellogg's Stockholders, 1985 .... 550.00
Plate, Anheuser-Busch, 1st Holiday, Box, 1989 .... 45.00
Plate, Arizona Biltmore, Indian, Shenango 225.00
Plate, Chicken Of The Sea Tuna, Fish Shape, Ivory, Calif. 55.00
Plate, Child's, Union Pacific Tea Co., 1907 .... 45.00
Plate, Coon Chicken Inn, Face 295.00
Plate, Crosley Dishwasher 20.00
Plate, Davis Ice Cream, 1910s 50.00
Plate, Falstaff Beer, Tin, Large 120.00

Plate, Georgia Diner, Stylized Peach Tree, Dark Brown Border, China, 7 In. 12.50
Plate, Michelob Light, Tennis League Aware, USTA, 9 1/2 In. 40.00
Plate, Ronald McDonald & Hamburglar, Share A Big Grin, Plastic, 1977 .... 15.00
Platter, Steak 'n Shake, Restaurant, Buffalo China, 1940s, Oval 10.00
Pocket Safe, American Bank & Trust, New Orleans, La., Metal, Mirror, Box 100.00
Popcorn Machine, Holkum & Hoke 4500.00
Pot, Heinz Baked Beans, Brown Glaze, Aluminum Lid, 12 1/2 In. 121.00
Potholder, Phillips 66, Pair 30.00
Punch Bowl, Hires Rootbeer, Villeroy & Boch .... *Illus* 22000.00
Puppet, Big Boy, Plastic 10.00
Puppet, Colonel Sanders, Finger, Soft Vinyl, Late 1960s, 1 x 2 1/4 In. 28.00
Puppet, Dolly Madison Bakery Products, Charlie Brown Character, Hand 5.00
Puppet, Dutch Boy Paint, Vinyl Head, Cloth Body, Hand, 1960s, 8 1/2 x 12 In. 25.00
Puppet, Sealtest, Mr. Cool 85.00
Push Bar, Fresh Up With 7-Up, Porcelain, 1950s 50.00
Push Bar, Triple XXX Root Beer, Porcelainized Steel, 29 1/2 In. 132.00
Push Bar, Uptown Soda, Porcelain 40.00
Puzzle, Black Jack Gum, 1933 .... 40.00
Puzzle, Burger King, 1973, 8 1/2 x 10 In., Pair 60.00
Puzzle, Campbell Soup, Soup Can, American Publishing Corp., 1968, 12 In. 55.00
Puzzle, Folger's Coffee, In Can 50.00
Puzzle, Kellogg's, Jigsaw, 1933 .... 125.00
Puzzle, Nabisco Shredded Wheat, 3 Piece 40.00
Rack, Bottle, Suncrest, On Wheels 90.00
Rack, Mobil Oil, Diamond Bottle Style, Full Pruf 150.00
Rack, Tire, Amoco Gasoline 200.00
Rack, Zeno Guns, Oak, 1880s 725.00
Radio, Fada, 4 Set In Cardboard Display, 1946 .... 8000.00
Record, Kellogg's Aerobics The Special K Way, Featuring Mary Decker 3.00
Ring, Ripley's Circus, Jack Earle 8 Ft. Giant Emblem, Pewter, 1 1/4 In. Diam. 25.00
Ruler, Breyer Ice Cream Co., Wooden, Red & Green Both Sides 6.00
Ruler, Christopher Milk, San Francisco, Wooden 5.00
Ruler, Kentucky Fried Chicken, Montgomery Blair Football Schedule, 1963, 12 In. ... 12.00
Ruler, McGraw Coal Co., Wooden, 1920s 2.00
Ruler, Owl Cement, Chicago, Railroad Bridge On Back, Celluloid, 6 In. 98.00
Ruler, Reddy Kilowatt, Plastic 6.00
Ruler, Watkins Products, Wooden, 6 In. 7.50
Ruler, Wonder Bread, Wooden, 1950, 12 In. 1.50
Sack, Potato, Farmer's Union, Butte, Mont., 25 Lb. 12.00
Sack, Potato, Mammy, 50 Lb., 20 x 30 In. 18.88
Sack, Salt, Jack Sprat, 10 Lb. 5.00
Sack, Washington Cut Plug, Cloth, Picture 20.00
Saddle, Leather, Salesman Sample, 9 In. 110.00
Salt & Pepper Shakers are listed in their own category
Scales are listed in their own category

Advertising, Punch Bowl, Hires Rootbeer,
Villeroy & Boch

♦♦♦♦♦♦♦♦♦♦♦♦♦♦♦♦♦♦♦♦♦♦♦
If you receive a package of glass
antiques during cold weather, let it
sit inside for a few hours before
you unpack it. The glass must return to room temperature slowly
or it may crack.
♦♦♦♦♦♦♦♦♦♦♦♦♦♦♦♦♦♦♦♦♦♦♦

Scraper, Sharples Cream Separators, Tin Lithograph, 1909 .... 275.00
Shaker, Malted Milk, Nestle's Quik Ice Cream, Lid 2.00
Sharpener, Knife, Time Labor Saver, Oak, Cast Iron 110.00
Shaving Brush, Ever-Ready, Cream & Black Handle 2.50
Shoe, Woman's, Brown Leather, Salesman's Sample, Early 1900s 75.00
Shoehorn, Crosby Square Shoes, Iron 1.00
Shoehorn, Elgin Clothing Store, Centerville, Iowa, Iron 1.00
Shoehorn, Freemans Shoes, Iron 1.00
Shoehorn, Peters Shoes, Fayetteville, Ark., Iron 1.25
Shot Glass, Coon Chicken Inn 65.00
Shovel, Treasure Line Stoves & Ranges, Tin Lithograph 150.00
Sign, 7-Up, 2 Sides, Hanging, 12 x 19 In. 90.00
Sign, 7-Up, As You Like It, And It Likes You, Mountains, 1940s, 8 x 10 In. 35.00
Sign, 7-Up, For A Real Treat, 1940s, 9 1/2 x 13 1/2 In. 35.00
Sign, 7-Up, Fresh Up, Porcelain, 20 x 28 In. 450.00
Sign, Alka-Seltzer, Cartoon Vignettes, People Praising Product, 28 x 24 In. 285.00
Sign, Altes Lager, Tivoli Brewing Co., Detroit, Mich., Wooden, 10 x 7 In. 60.00
Sign, American Express, Flange, 1903, 17 x 17 In. 550.00
Sign, American Express, Paper On Board, 2 Sides, 1916, 15 x 12 In. 32.00
Sign, American Oil, 6 x 4 Ft. 195.00
Sign, Anheuser-Busch, Custer's Last Fight, Frame, 37 x 46 In. 550.00
Sign, Anheuser-Busch, Malt Nutrine, Cardboard, Summer Flowers, 12 In. 85.00
Sign, Anheuser-Busch, Malt Nutrine, Spring Breezes, 1903, 12 In. 85.00
Sign, Austin's Dog Bread, Woman Feeding Dogs, Tin, Self-Framed, 26 x 38 In. 935.00
Sign, Ayer's Hair Vigor, Woman With Long Hair, Tin, 19 3/4 x 13 3/4 In. 350.00
Sign, Baker's Chocolate Woman, Chas.W. Shonk, Ornate Frame, 39 x 27 In. 1265.00
Sign, Baker's Cocoa, Woman Serving Cocoa, On Tray, Framed, 15 x 19 In. 475.00
Sign, Beech-Nut Tobacco, Porcelain, 11 x 21 In. 150.00
Sign, Big Al's, From Happy Days, Neon, 10 Ft. 2000.00
Sign, Bireley's, Round Cap, 3 Ft. Diam. 145.00
Sign, Bismarck Beer, Canvas, 1930s, 18 x 60 In. 100.00
Sign, Bixby's AA Brown Shoe Coloring, Fashionable Woman, Frame, 33 x 10 In. 275.00
Sign, Blackstone Cigars, Porcelain, 12 x 36 In. 65.00
Sign, Blatz Brewing Company, People, Park-Type Scene, Chalk, Frame, 42 x 25 In. .. 750.00
Sign, Blue Lick, Ky., Health Waters, Canvas, 12 x 48 In. 125.00
Sign, Bond Bread, Porcelain On Steel, 14 x 19 In. .... 68.00 to 105.00
Sign, Borden's, Chocolate Milkshake, Elsie Picture, 1950s, 17 x 19 In 24.00
Sign, Bowman Diary Co., Red, White & Gold, Celluloid, Stand-Up, 8 x 11 In. 110.00
Sign, Brewers' Best, New Name In Beer, Wooden, Cutout Letters, 1950s, 14 In. 45.00
Sign, Broadside, Willard The Wizard, Black & White, 9 x 24 In. 150.00
Sign, Brown's Jumbo Bread, Figural, Elephant, Orange & White Blanket, 12 In. 605.00
Sign, Buckskin Breeches, Etched Stag & Wolves, Metal, 10 x 15 In. 412.00
Sign, Budweiser Girl, Bottle, Anheuser-Busch, Frame, 26 x 13 In. 605.00
Sign, Buffalo Brewing Co., Indian Riding Buffalo, Frame, 5 x 7 In. 225.00
Sign, Bull Durham, A Royal Victor, Paperboard, Wooden Frame, 26 x 44 In. 550.00
Sign, Bulova, Pocket Watch Shape, Ring Top, 2 Sides, Gold, White & Black, 28 In. .. 192.00
Sign, Burgon-Peel Dry Goods Co., Woman, P. Boileau, Frame, 19 x 14 In. 275.00
Sign, Buster Brown Shoes, Blue Ribbon Shows, Cardboard, 1904, 10 1/2 x 5 In. 95.00
Sign, Buster Brown Shoes, Buster Brown & Tige, Tin, Round, 10 In. 1900.00
Sign, Campbell's Soup, Porcelain, Curved, 22 x 14 In. 3000.00
Sign, Campbell's Tomato Soup Can, Figural, Painted Sheet Metal, 22 x 14 In. 94.00
Sign, Canada Dry, Tin, 36 x 12 In. 65.00
Sign, Caps Polar Ice Cream, Polar Bear, Tin, 16 x 20 In. 525.00
Sign, Carnation Hair Tonic, J. Sarubi Co., Flange, 2 Sides, 7 x 18 In. 75.00
Sign, Carter's Overalls, Curved, Speeding Train, Porcelain, 3 x 11 In. 75.00
Sign, Cavalier Cigarettes, Tin, 11 x 9 In. 30.00
Sign, Champlin Hi-V-I Motor Oil, On Ground & In Sky, Porcelain, 20 x 32 In. 265.00
Sign, Chesterfield Cigarettes, Die Cut, Cardboard, 1930s, 40 In. 200.00
Sign, Chesterfield Cigarettes, Milder, They Satisfy, Tin, 24 x 29 In. 135.00
Sign, Chesterfield Cigarettes, Wood Frame, 33 x 15 In. 400.00
Sign, Chesterfield King Cigarettes, Metal, 20 x 24 In. 20.00
Sign, Cole's Peruvian Bark & Bitters, Steel, Blue, White, 6 x 16 1/4 In. 495.00
Sign, Conoco Gas Pump, Porcelain, Die Cut, 7 1/2 In. 65.00

Advertising, Sign, Crack-A-Jack Clothes,
Tin, 18 x 13 1/2 In.

Tin signs and cans will fade from the ultraviolet rays coming in a window or from a fluorescent light. Plexiglass UF-1 or UF-3 will cover the window and keep the rays away from your collection. There are also plastic sleeves to cover fluorescent tubes.

Sign, Conoco Gasoline, Colonial Soldier Trademark, Porcelain, 25 In. 850.00
Sign, Copenhagen, Best Chew Ever Made, Porcelain, 6 x 23 In. 145.00
Sign, Cortez Cigars, Girl Holding Box Of Cigars, Die Cut, Tin, 1915, 12 x 16 In. 550.00
Sign, Cosmopolitan, Sen. Joe McCarthy, Cardboard, 1950s, 20 x 14 In. 15.00
Sign, Crack-A-Jack Clothes, Tin, 18 x 13 1/2 In. .... *Illus* 2360.00
Sign, Crisco, Can-Shaped, Better Than Butter, Porcelain, 14 x 20 In. 1375.00
Sign, Cunninghham Radio Tubes, Tin, 5 x 5 In. 120.00
Sign, Dad's Root Beer, Tin, 12 x 32 In. 125.00
Sign, DeLaval Cream Separator, Frame, 31 x 41 In. 1540.00
Sign, DeLaval, Porcelain, 16 x 12 In. 210.00
Sign, Downie Bros. Circus, Clown, Figures Around, Metal Frame, 41 x 28 In. 440.00
Sign, Dr Pepper, Take Home A Carton, Embossed Tin Lithograph, 27 x 19 In. 385.00
Sign, Dr. Daniels Medicine, A.M. Bowen, General Merchandise, 20 x 14 In. 660.00
Sign, Dr. Drake's Remedy, Cough & Croup Remedy, Couple, Child, 14 x 11 In. 220.00
Sign, Dr. Harter's Iron Tonic, Brown Shades, Wooden Frame, 12 x 7 1/2 In. 83.00
Sign, Dr. Willis A. Myers Veterinary Medicines, Paperboard, 6 3/4 x 20 In. 88.00
Sign, Drink Dr Pepper, Embossed Metal, 12 x 32 In. 45.00
Sign, Duke's Mixture, Roll Of Fame, Porcelainized Steel, 8 x 5 1/4 In. 121.00
Sign, Dupont Gun Powder, Dogs In Field, Tin, Self-Framed, 22 1/4 x 28 1/4 In. 750.00
Sign, DX Gasoline, 2 Sides, Tin, 61 x 47 In. 95.00
Sign, Eat Here, Painted, Wood, Gray, Black, Green, White, 5 1/2 x 46 In. 200.00
Sign, Ebbert Wagon, Farmer & Wife, Tin, Self-Framed, 37 1/2 x 25 1/2 In. 1700.00
Sign, Eberhardt & Ober Brewing, Paperboard, Aerial View, Frame, 26 x 41 In. 385.00
Sign, Eisemann's Klondike Head Rub, Cardboard, Hanging, Bottle, 8 1/2 x 11 In. 66.00
Sign, Erickson's Pure Rye Whiskey, Tin, Wood Frame, 22 x 32 In. 660.00
Sign, Eskimo Pie, Bear & Boy, Red & Blue, Foil Ground, 1922, 9 1/2 x 19 1/2 In. 176.00
Sign, F.W. Woolworth Co., Reverse On Glass, 1900, 20 x 36 In. 585.00
Sign, Fatima Cigarettes, Turkish Girl, Tin, Self-Framed, 37 1/2 x 25 1/2 In. 550.00
Sign, Federal Tires, Authorized Sales Agency, Porcelain, 18 x 36 In. 400.00
Sign, Federal Tires, Blue Felt, 1915, 11 x 29 In. 50.00
Sign, Ferguson System, This Farm Uses, Tin, 11 x 22 In. 37.50
Sign, Fire Pumper Form, Sheet Metal, 36 In. 550.00
Sign, Fisk Tire, Cream, Maroon, Black, Tin, 38 x 32 In. 475.00
Sign, Ford, Genuine Parts, Porcelain, 16 x 24 In. 595.00
Sign, Ford, Used Cars, 2 Sides, Folding Floor Frame, Pat. 1933, 36 In. 467.00
Sign, Foremost Dairy, Brown, White, Orange Ground, Tin, Round, 2 Ft. 30.00
Sign, Francisco Auto Heater, Summer All Year, Tin, Self Framed, 18 x 40 In. 413.00
Sign, Fred Ives Famous Pork Sausage, Wood, English, 33 1/2 In. 165.00
Sign, Freeport Anchor Society, 2 Sides, 34 x 22 In. 2250.00
Sign, Frictionless Bearing Metal Co., Child, Tin, 1903, 22 x 16 In. 2200.00
Sign, General Electric, Mr. Magoo, Battery Operated, Cardboard, 1959, 2 Sides 275.00
Sign, Glendora Coffee, Blue & Gold Can Shape, Tin, 8 1/2 x 14 In. 138.00
Sign, Gold Dust Washing Powder, Wood & Gesso Frame, 16 1/2 x 14 In. 275.00
Sign, Gold Seal Special Dy Champagne, Tin, Framed, 14 x 20 In. 395.00
Sign, Golden Bridge Root Beer, Bottle With Mug, Metal, 12 x 3 3/4 In. 35.00

Sign, Goodrich Tires, Porcelainized Steel, White Letters On Blue, 60 In. 231.00
Sign, Goodyear Tires, Porcelain Enameled Steel, 1930s, 9 1/4 x 16 In. 20.00
Sign, Grain Belt Beer, Cardboard, 22 x 48 In. 75.00
Sign, Granger Tobacco, Sam Snead Picture, Paperboard, Frame, 19 x 14 In. 165.00
Sign, Grape-Nuts, To School Well Fed On Grape-Nuts, 1910, 30 x 20 In. .. 1100.00 to 2200.00
Sign, Griesedieck Bros., Reverse On Glass, Bottle, 11 1/2 In. 45.00
Sign, Guaranteed Occident-Russell Miller Milling Co., Metal, 9 1/2 x 14 In. 75.00
Sign, Gulf Gasoline, That Good Gulf, Porcelain, Round, 12 In. 80.00
Sign, Hall's Distemper, Porcelain, British, 48 x 18 In. 700.00
Sign, Hampden Beer, Grinning Guy, Handsome Waiter, 11 In. 70.00
Sign, Hanline Paints, Neon, Red Letters, Reverse Glass Logo, 20 In. 220.00
Sign, Hardware Shoe, Wears Like An Anvil, Red & Black Lettering, 7 x 19 In. 165.00
Sign, Hardy's Cutlery, Pocket Knife Shape, Wood, 1900s, 72 In. 2450.00
Sign, Harvard Cigars, Image Of Man, Red Sweater, Tin, 36 x 24 In. 200.00
Sign, Heddon's Dowagiac, Tin, 7 1/2 x 14 In. 4500.00
Sign, Helmbold's, Jelly Of Glycerin & Roses, Tin, 16 x 12 In. 175.00
Sign, Hereford Brothers, Cutout Man In Red Tuxedo, Tin, Wood Panel, 36 In. 242.00
Sign, Hires Root Beer, Woman Holding Glass, Caskell Coffin, 21 x 15 In. 660.00
Sign, Hires, Ask For Hires In Bottles, Embossed Tin, 9 3/4 x 27 3/4 In. 310.00
Sign, Hires, Enjoy, It's Always Pure, Tin Lithograph, Wooden Frame, 9 1/2 x 27 In. . 660.00
Sign, Hohner Harmonica, Hanging, Plastic, Marine Band, 24 In. 35.00
Sign, Honor Brand, Girl With Flowers, Oval, Tin, 1909, 17 1/2 x 14 In. 350.00
Sign, Hood Tire, Man, Die Cut Porcelain, 1940, 35 In. 1320.00
Sign, Hoosier Beer, Tin Over Cardboard, American Art Works, 1930s, 12 x 15 In. 556.00
Sign, Hudson, Authorized Service, Triangle Across Front, Porcelain, 42 In. 750.00
Sign, I.W. Harper, Oriental Design, Steel, 12 x 15 In. 60.00
Sign, Illinois Watches, Lincoln Portrait, 1913, 6 x 9 1/2 In. 595.00
Sign, Indian Gas, Curved, Porcelain, 18 x 12 In. 295.00
Sign, Jacob Ruppert, Colonial Man, Cardboard, Frame, Pat. 1918, 14 x 30 In. 65.00
Sign, Joe Cumming, Hunting Dog, Antonio Picciola, 1899, 16 x 22 In. 187.00
Sign, Keep Feet Off Seat, Wooden, 22 x 12 In. 20.00
Sign, Kelly Tires, Woman In Upholstered Car, Porcelain, Round, 42 In. 9350.00
Sign, Kendall Motor Oil, 2 Sides, Tin, Round, 23 3/4 In. 55.00
Sign, Kodak, Die Cut, Triangular, 17 x 16 In. 750.00
Sign, La Belle Chocolatiere, Walter Baker Co., Woman With Tray, 44 x 32 In. 495.00
Sign, Lion's Head, Copper, Late 19th Century, Round, 25 In. 495.00
Sign, Little Bobbie Cigar, 5 Cents, Hanging, Cardboard, 9 x 11 In. 75.00
Sign, Longhorn Soda Water, Paper, Blue Ground, Wooden Frame, 13 x 19 In. 467.00
Sign, Mabson Hotel, Montgomery, Ala., 1901 .... 350.00
Sign, Made Right Feeds, Wooden, 1935, 96 In. 110.00
Sign, Meadow Gold Ice Cream, Masonite, 16 x 11 In. 135.00
Sign, Michelin, Bib Laughs, Smokes Cigar, Tire, 1905, 28 x 23 3/4 In. 418.00
Sign, Miller High Life Beer, Tin Lithograph, Round, 1907, 24 In. .... 1350.00 to 1500.00
Sign, Miller High Life Brew, Tin Over Cardboard, 11 x 17 In. 410.00
Sign, Milwaukee Brewery, San Francisco, Aluminum, Red & Blue, Round, 10 In. 193.00
Sign, Milwaukee Waukesha Health Beers, Reverse Painted Glass, Frame, 11 In. 225.00
Sign, Mobil, Pegasus, Porcelain, Red & White, 1930-1940, 24 In. 1500.00
Sign, Model Smoking Tobacco, Gentleman With Pipe, 13 x 34 In. 275.00
Sign, Model Tobacco, Porcelain, 12 x 36 In. 140.00
Sign, Model Tobacco, Tin, Die Cut, 5 Colors, 15 x 18 In. 135.00
Sign, Mona Motor Oil, Tune In K-O-I-L, Tin, Self-Framed, 11 x 35 In. 176.00
Sign, Money Orders, United States Substation, 2 Sides, 10 1/2 x 13 In. 165.00
Sign, Monongahela Valley Rye, Reverse Glass, 12 x 24 In. 175.00
Sign, Monumental Brand Baltimore Oysters, Wm. Taylor, Frame, 22 1/2 x 19 In. 495.00
Sign, Mother's Oats, Naughty Boy Smoking Pipe, Dated 1902, Frame, 19 x 26 In. 115.00
Sign, Mountain Dew, Hillbilly, Tin, 35 In. 245.00
Sign, Moxie, 2 Sides, Screen Door, Square 139.00
Sign, Mr. Cola, Bottle Cap, Tin, 30 In. 165.00
Sign, Mr. Zip, Wooden, 4 Ft. 550.00
Sign, Murad Cigarettes, Gypsy Woman With Tray, Tin, 28 x 20 In. 90.00
Sign, Nabisco, Slicker Boy, Cornucopia Of Nabisco Products, Paper, 24 x 20 In. 35.00
Sign, National Brewery Co., White Seal, Crystaloid, Hanging, Frame, 14 x 10 In. 880.00
Sign, Nesbitt, Bottle Cap, Tin, 18 In. 145.00

*Advertising, Sign, OshKosh, Uncle Josh,
Cardboard, 1936, Life Size*

*Advertising, Sign, Union Leader, Paper Board,
Frame, 25 x 17 In.*

Sign, New American Weekly, Rita Hayworth, Cardboard, 1942, 24 x 17 In. 22.00
Sign, New Grape Soda, Tin, 15 x 43 In. 295.00
Sign, Noonan's Hair Petrole, Reverse Says Zepp's Hair Dressing, Steel, 12 x 16 In. .. 413.00
Sign, Nu-Grape, Bottle Shape, Die Cut, 17 In. 50.00
Sign, Old Gold Paint, Pocket Watch Shape, Wooden, Round, 24 In. 330.00
Sign, Oliver Farm Implements, Tin Lithograph, 14 x 48 In. 125.00
Sign, Omar Cigarettes, Joy Of Life, Men, Paperboard, Wooden Frame, 21 x 15 In. 110.00
Sign, Orange Crush, Bottle Picture, 1960s, 18 x 54 In. 225.00
Sign, Orange Crush, Enjoy, Celluloid Cover, Cardboard, Orange Ground, 9 In. 75.00
Sign, Orange Crush, Enjoy, Plastic, Embossed, Painted, 9 x 11 In. 33.00
Sign, Orcherade, 2 Women, Bottle, Paperboard, 14 1/2 x 11 1/2 In. 210.00
Sign, Oriental Ethyl Gasoline, Convex Glass, Blue, Frosted White, 13 1/2 In. 45.00
Sign, OshKosh, Uncle Josh, Cardboard, 1936, Life Size .... *Illus* 685.00
Sign, Overland, Service, Genuine Parts, Oval, Porcelain, 30 x 40 In. 695.00
Sign, Pabst Blue Ribbon, Reverse On Glass, Wooden Base, 9 x 4 1/2 In. 50.00
Sign, Pabst Blue Ribbon, Rip Van Winkle, 11 3/4 x 17 1/2 In. 176.00
Sign, Parke-Davis, Glass, 25 x 13 In. 60.00
Sign, Paul Jones Whiskey, Dead Game, Guns, Tin, 1914, 25 x 36 In. 300.00
Sign, Paul Jones Whiskey, Temptation Of St. Anthony, 13 1/2 x 19 1/2 In. 190.00
Sign, Penn Drake Motor Oil, 20 x 26 In. 1600.00
Sign, Philip Morris Cigarettes, Embossed Johnny & Pack, 12 x 14 In. 147.00
Sign, Phillips 66, 2 Sides, Orange & Black, Porcelain, 29 In. 145.00
Sign, Phillips 66, Logo, World's Finest Oil For Your Motor, 22 x 11 In. 655.00
Sign, Phillips 66, Porcelain Enameled Steel, 1932, 11 x 12 In. 15.00
Sign, Pike Fish, Winchester Lures Sold Here, Die Cut Cardboard, 20 In. 110.00
Sign, Polar Bear Tobacco, Porcelain, 8 1/2 x 5 In. 275.00
Sign, Poll Parrot Shoes, Neon, 38 x 22 In. 1265.00
Sign, Prince Albert Tobacco, Feathered Fighter, Tin, 25 1/2 x 19 In. 600.00
Sign, Prince Albert, National Joy Smoke, 12 x 24 In. 65.00
Sign, R.C. Cola, The Fresher Refresher, 29 x 12 In. 65.00
Sign, RCA Victor Records, Double Sided, Hanging, Weathered, 20 In. 385.00
Sign, Red Crown Gasoline, Porcelain Enameled Steel, c.1928, 11 1/4 In. 15.00
Sign, Red Goose Shoes, Porcelainized Steel, Yellow Ground, 17 x 12 In. 187.00
Sign, Red Seal Dry Battery, Figural, Porcelainized Steel, Flange, 24 x 13 In. 330.00
Sign, Richlube Motor Oil, Space Object, Porcelain, 1915-1925, 24 In. 2000.00
Sign, Rock Island Railroad, Reverse On Glass, Colorado Rockies, 1901, 100 In. 9000.00
Sign, Rollerback Roller Razor, Cardboard, 1920, 10 3/4 x 14 In. 60.00
Sign, Rooms, Hanging, Sheet Metal, Cardboard Insert, 14 1/2 x 28 1/2 In. 11.00
Sign, Route U.S. 66, 62 Glass Reflectors, Porcelain 1500.00
Sign, Royal Baking Powder, Royal Saves Eggs In Baking, 22 x 12 In. 77.00
Sign, Royal Crown Cola, Barbara Stanwyck, Cardboard, 11 x 28 In. 65.00

◆ ◆ ◆ ◆ ◆ ◆ ◆ ◆ ◆ ◆ ◆ ◆ ◆ ◆ ◆ ◆ ◆ ◆ ◆ ◆

To remove trade cards from album pages, first try soaking the pages in a mixture of 2 gallons of warm water and one cup of white vinegar. If this fails, put the album in the freezer overnight, then drop into the vinegar water in the morning. If the glue is made of flour paste, the cards come off or can be loosened in 20 minutes. Rinse the cards in clear warm water and rub off the remains of glue with a soft, wet towel. Sounds like a good system, but check the album to be sure there are no inked names or other wanted information that might wash off.

◆ ◆

Advertising, Sign, Whitman's Sampler, 1945, 18 1/2 x 6 1/2 x 7 1/2 In.

Sign, Royal Crown Cola, Die Cut Bottle, Tin, 5 Ft.		325.00
Sign, Royal Crown Cola, Lucille Ball, 2 1/2 x 1 Ft.		250.00
Sign, Royal Crown Cola, Sheet Metal, Flange, Stenciled, 10 1/2 x 17 1/2 In.		132.00
Sign, Sailor's Hat Shape, Canvas Covered Wood, Round, 62 In.		550.00
Sign, Sam Clay Whiskey, Monogrammed Center, Tin, 26 1/2 x 18 1/2 In.		200.00
Sign, San Felice Cigars, For Gentlemen Of Good Taste, Metal, 12 x 36 In.		135.00
Sign, Santa Fe Trail System, Porcelainized Steel, Bracket, 23 x 26 In.		3630.00
Sign, Schmidt's Beer, White Tail Deer, Cardboard, Color, 1940s, 24 x 16 In.		32.00
Sign, Service, Oakland Pontiac, Porcelain, 24 x 36 In.		550.00
Sign, Sharples Tubular Cream Separator, Metal, 10 x 14 In.		150.00
Sign, Sinclair Aircraft, 2 Sides, Airplane, Round, 48 In.		2970.00
Sign, Sinclair Gasoline, Dino, Porcelain, Enameled, 12 x 13 In.		95.00
Sign, Sinclair, For Fords, 1920s, 20 x 46 In.		650.00
Sign, Ski, Soda, Humanized Bottle On Water Skis, Tin, 1 x 3 Ft.		75.00
Sign, Southwest Utility Ice, Save With Ice, Steel, Blue, White, 14 x 44 In.		132.00
Sign, Spalding, Athletic Goods For Sale, Porcelain, 20 x 18 3/4 In.		1200.00
Sign, Spratt's Bait, Silvercloud, Porcelain, 12 x 12 In.		385.00
Sign, Sprinklin' Sambo Lawn Sprinkler, Tin Lithograph		275.00
Sign, Squirt, Golfing Girl, Cardboard, Die Cut, 1950, 16 In.		45.00
Sign, Stanley Hardware, 2 Sides, Script Logo, c.1910, 9 1/4 x 18 3/8 In.		695.00
Sign, Star Brand Shoes Are Better, R.J. & R. Girl, Frame, 1908, 42 x 20 In.		275.00
Sign, Stromberg, Carlson, Fiber, 6 x 13 Ft.		35.00
Sign, Studebaker, White Cloud, Cardboard, 8 x 24 In.		295.00
Sign, Sun-Rise Beverages, Old Man Sol, Straw In Sliced Orange, 2 x 3 Ft.		135.00
Sign, Sunlife Insurance, Porcelain, 12 x 18 In.		125.00
Sign, Sunray Mid-Continent Oil Co., Porcelain, 10 x 18 In.		250.00
Sign, Sunrise Beverages, Sun Drinking From Orange, 20 x 28 In.		100.00
Sign, Sweet, Orr & Co., Porcelain, 8 x 30 In.		575.00
Sign, Sweet, Orr & Co., Union Made Overalls, 14 x 21 In.		990.00
Sign, Swift's Premium Oleomargarine, Little Cook, Frame, 19 x 14 In.		523.00
Sign, Texaco, Made By The Texas Co., Porcelain, Round, 42 In.		50.00
Sign, Texaco, Porcelain, Round, 1938, 6 In.		195.00
Sign, Texas & South Western Cattle Raisers Assoc., Porcelain, 20 x 10 In.		65.00
Sign, Trade, Mortar & Pestle, Gilded Zinc, 19th Century, 28 In.		520.50
Sign, Trade, Rifle Form, Wooden, Painted Metal Barrel, 63 In.		1610.00

Sign, Tru Ade, Sheet Metal, Flange, Stencil, 14 x 20 In. 110.00
Sign, Tru Blu Beer, Northampton, Pa., Tin Over Cardboard, 9 x 13 In. 143.00
Sign, Tucketts Marguerite Cigars, Tin, Self-Framed, 28 x 22 In. 2100.00
Sign, Union Leader, Paper Board, Frame, 25 x 17 In. .... *Illus* 2090.00
Sign, Valvoline/Pennsylvania Motor Oils, Round, 30 In. 1760.00
Sign, Van Houten's Cocoa, Dutch Couple, Plaque, Wooden Frame, 27 x 16 In. 247.00
Sign, Van Houten's Cocoa, Fruit & Cans Of Cocoa, Cardboard, 16 1/2 x 23 In. 60.00
Sign, Veedol Motor Oils, 2 Sides, Porcelain, White, Orange & Black, 22 x 28 In. 650.00
Sign, Velvet Tobacco, Porcelain, 12 x 42 In. 550.00
Sign, Victor Collar Button, Mr.Pullhard & Mr.Slipeasy, 1914, 16 x 20 In. 25.00
Sign, W. Harry Jones, Importer, Wines & Liquors, Wooden, 8 x 34 In. 750.00
Sign, Watchmaker, Pocket Watch, Wooden, 19th Century, 29 In. 1540.00
Sign, Western Ammunition, Elk Fight, V.K. Murray, Wooden Frame, 23 x 14 In. 275.00
Sign, Whitman's Sampler, 1945, 18 1/2 x 6 1/2 x 7 1/2 In. .... *Illus* 1830.00
Sign, Winchester Ammunition Sold Here, Mallard Ducks, Die Cut 25.00
Sign, Winchester Arms Co., Man With Rifle, Bear, c.1900, 23 x 39 In. 320.00
Sign, Winchester Carpenter's Tools, 2 Sides, Color, 39 x 18 In. 110.00
Sign, Winchester Cartridges & Guns, We Recommend, Tin, 36 x 29 3/4 In. 550.00
Sign, Winchester Tie, Metal, 18 x 55 In. 350.00
Sign, Wm. M. Herrmann Jeweler, Hanging, Metal, 2 Sides, 40 In. 385.00
Sign, Yankees Cigars, Sweet Smoke, Reverse Glass, Uncle Sam, 11 x 9 In. 330.00
Sign, Yukon's Self-Rising Flour, Queen Of The West, Sheet Metal, 22 x 13 In. 198.00
Sleeping Bag, Kellogg's Cereal Characters 55.00
Spice Kit, Stickney & Poor, 39 Full Vials, Salesman's Sample, 14 x 13 1/2 In. 265.00
Spoon, Doe-Wah-Jack Oak Stoves, Indian Handle 65.00
Spoon, Hershey, Enameled Name 20.00
Spoon, Kellogg's, Tony The Tiger, 1965 .... 18.00
Stand, Old Hickory Shoelace, 8 Drawer, Tin Lithograph Top 55.00
Stand, Poll Parrot Shoes 100.00
Stickpin, Old Dutch Cleanser, Enameled Cleaning Lady, Blue 85.00
Stickpin, Reddy Kilowatt, Original Card, 1952 .... 30.00
Stickpin, Reddy Kilowatt, Original Card, 1955 .... 6.00
Stickpin, Victor Talking Machine Co., Nipper, Celluloid 85.00
Straw Holder, Clear Glass, Metal Top & Base, Bloomfield Industries, 13 In. 77.00
Straw Holder, Clear Glass, Notched Ridges, Brass Top, 11 5/8 In. 242.00
Straw Holder, Flower & Stem Pattern, Metal Top, Octagonal, 12 In. 413.00
Straw Holder, Raised Geometric, Glass Lid, Clear, 12 1/2 In. 220.00
Striker, Arizona Biltmore, Grand Opening, Hull 250.00
String Holder, Heinz 57 Varieties, Pickle, Tin .... *Illus* 8250.00
String Holder, Heinz Pickle, Die Cut Tin Pickles, Spool, Tin, 17 In. 7500.00
String Holder, Red Goose Shoes, Cast Iron, Painted, Puzzle Tag 9350.00
String Holder, Red Goose Shoes, Cast Iron, Repainted, 14 1/2 In. 523.00
String Holder, Red Goose Shoes, Die Cut Goose, Tin, 28 In. 2600.00
Sugar & Creamer, Ken-L-Ration 30.00
Sunglasses, McDonald's, Figural, Package 15.00
Swizzle Stick, Grace Line Oars 1.00

Advertising, String Holder, Heinz 57 Varieties,
Pickle, Tin

◆ ◆ ◆ ◆ ◆ ◆ ◆ ◆ ◆ ◆ ◆ ◆ ◆ ◆ ◆ ◆ ◆ ◆ ◆ ◆

To hang an old Coca-Cola tray,
use a wire plate holder. The bent
parts that touch the tray should
be covered with plastic tubing.
Thin tubing is sold for use in fish
aquariums.

◆ ◆ ◆ ◆ ◆ ◆ ◆ ◆ ◆ ◆ ◆ ◆ ◆ ◆ ◆ ◆ ◆ ◆ ◆ ◆

Swizzle Stick, Hutton's New Pound Over Room, Black Steer Head, 8 Piece .... .75
Swizzle Stick, Lamppost Corner, Hotel New Yorker, Red Lamppost, 4 Piece 1.00
Swizzle Stick, Ruby Foo's Sundial, New York World's Fair, 1939, 6 In. 12.00
Syrup, Log Cabin, Wigwam, Glass Pourer 25.00
Tap Knob, Blatz Pilsener, Chrome, White & Blue On Red Enameled Insert 40.00
Tap Knob, Duke's Ale, Black, Gold On Red Metal Insert 45.00
Tap Knob, Iron City Baseball, Baseball Shape, Beat Em Bucs! 40.00
Tap Knob, Silver Dime Premium, Chrome, Ball, Blue Enameled Insert 149.00
Tap Knob, Sunshine Porter, Ball, Chrome, Black On White Enameled Insert.............. 150.00
Thermometers are listed in their own category
Tie Bar, Reddy Kilowatt, On Card, 1953 .... 25.00
Tie Clasp, Elsie The Cow, Medallion, 1930s 40.00
Tie Clasp, Ford 20.00
Tie Clasp & Cuff Links, RCA Movie Projector, Box 25.00

Advertising tin cans or canisters were first used commercially in the United
States in 1819 and were called *tins*. The English language is sometimes
confusing. Today the word *tin* is used by most collectors to describe many
types of containers, including food tins, biscuit boxes, roly poly tobacco
containers, gunpowder cans, talcum powder sprinkle-top cans, cigarette flat-
fifty tins, and more. Beer cans are listed in their own category. Things made
of undecorated tin are listed under Tinware.

Tin, Abbey Tobacco, Pocket 295.00
Tin, Adams Chicklets, 3 Glass Sides, Held 200 1-Cent Packages 40.00
Tin, Americana Breakfast Coffee 65.00
Tin, Apple Blossom Talc, Lithograph 29.00
Tin, Arbuckles Coffee, 6 x 4 x 2 In. 175.00
Tin, Arnstein's Bicycle Enamel, Round, 2 3/4 x 2 1/8 In. 275.00
Tin, Bagdad Tobacco, Man, Fez, Flag, Blue, Pocket 145.00
Tin, Baker's Cocoa, Round, Sample, 1 3/4 x 1 1/4 In. 200.00
Tin, Bambino Tobacco, Ballplayer, Red, c.1927, Pocket 2350.00
Tin, Big Ben Smoking Tobacco, Clock, Red To Yellow, Pocket, 4 1/2 In. 425.00
Tin, Big Horn Coffee, 1 Lb. 325.00
Tin, Big John Plug Cut Tobacco, 5 x 4 3/4 In. 25.00
Tin, Blue Bird Toffee 65.00
Tin, Bonita Coffee, 3 Lb. 85.00
Tin, Bonnette Coffee, Dutch Kids At Table, 1 Lb., 4 x 6 In. 220.00
Tin, Bowl Of Roses Tobacco, Man, Fireplace, Roses, Pocket 165.00
Tin, Bridal Brand Coffee, Man With Donkeys, Harbor Scene, Oval, 8 In. 275.00
Tin, Briggs Pipe Mixture, Pocket 8.00
Tin, British Crawford Double-Decker Bus, Biscuit, c.1920 .... 5060.00
Tin, Buckingham Tobacco, Pocket 75.00
Tin, Burley Boy Tobacco, White Man's Hope, Pocket, 4 1/4 In. .... 300.00 to 750.00
Tin, Bury's Saltines, Coach & Horsemen Silhouette, 1 Lb. 5.00
Tin, California Nugget Tobacco, Nugget Shape 95.00
Tin, Calumet Baking Powder, Indian Head 3.50
Tin, Caravan Condoms .... 125.00 to 350.00
Tin, Carnation, Oconomowoc, Wis., Square, 5 Lb. 35.00
Tin, Carter's Typewriter Reel, Midnight, Pictures Heavens .... 10.00 to 20.00
Tin, Cascara Quinine Cold Tablets, Red & White 7.00
Tin, Chas. Neubert & Co. Oysters, Baltimore, Md., 1 Gal. 154.00
Tin, Checkers Tobacco, Red & Black, Pocket, 4 1/2 x 3 In. 225.00
Tin, Christy's Oysters, George Christy & Son, Crisfield, Md., 1 Gal. 99.00
Tin, City Club Tobacco, Pocket, 4 x 2 In. .... 295.00 to 375.00
Tin, Crispes Soda Crackers 27.00
Tin, Culture Tobacco, Black & Yellow, Pocket .... 75.00 to 115.00
Tin, Dan Patch Coffee, Horse & Driver, 10 1/2 In. 880.00
Tin, Darby's Swan Tolu, 3 3/4 x 3 1/2 x 1 1/2 In. 200.00
Tin, Del-Monte Ortho Cut Coffee, 1 Lb. 3.00
Tin, DeLaval Oil, T-Style Spout Attached, Paper Label, 8 Oz. 8.00
Tin, DeWitt's Witch Hazel Salve, Great Pile Cure, Embossed 15.00
Tin, Dill's Best Tobacco, Yellow, Pocket .... 12.00 to 15.00
Tin, Diplomat Mixture, Oval, Cardboard, Metal Top, 3 x 2 1/2 In. 275.00

Tin, Dixie Kid Cut Plug, Hinged Lid, Handle, Black Boy On Cotton, 7 3/4 In. 165.00
Tin, Dixie Kid Tobacco, Short 425.00
Tin, Dixie Queen Plug Cut Tobacco, Canister, 6 In. 175.00
Tin, Doctor Daniels Wonder Worker Lotion 10.00
Tin, Dr. Hobson's Witch Hazel & Glycerin Salve, 2 3/4 In. 18.00
Tin, Dr. Morse's Indian Root Pills 13.00
Tin, Dr. Whetzel's Powder For Paroxysms Of Asthma, 4 In. 12.00
Tin, Dunnsboro Tobacco, Hunters, Dogs, Vertical Pocket 800.00
Tin, Dupont Gunpowder, Red, Paper Label 72.00
Tin, Eureka Typewriter Ribbon, Metal 20.00
Tin, Fairmont Tobacco, Gold Lid, Pocket 245.00
Tin, Fixaco Cough Drops, Running Man In Zoot Suit 35.00
Tin, Foley's Banner Salve, Embossed, Partial Box 18.00
Tin, Forest & Stream Tobacco, Fishermen, Pocket 125.00
Tin, Fort Western Coffee, Round, 12 x 6 In. 175.00
Tin, Freeman's Face Powder, Sample Size, Box, 1910 .... 12.50
Tin, Fresh Oyster, Sterling & Son, Crisfield, Md., 1 Pt. 27.50
Tin, Fruit & Flowers Mixture Tobacco 250.00
Tin, Garth Cigars 42.00
Tin, George Washington Pipe Tobacco, Christmas Box 70.00
Tin, Giant Salted Peanuts, 11 In. 275.00
Tin, Gold Coin Chewing Tobacco, Pocket 600.00
Tin, Granulated Cut Plug, Pocket 1100.00
Tin, Gre-Solvent Hand Cleaner, Black & Silver 10.00
Tin, Gum, Colgans, With Baseball Card 165.00
Tin, Gum, Colgans, With Cherubs 575.00
Tin, Hand Made Tobacco, Pocket .... 165.00 to 425.00
Tin, Harrison Fisher, Heart Shape, His Pledge, 3 1/2 x 4 1/2 In. 85.00
Tin, Haywood's Poison Oak Salve 14.50
Tin, Hercules Blasting Caps, Strongman Picture 35.00
Tin, Hercules Gun Powder 100.00
Tin, Heyser's Oysters, Wm. Heyser Co., Baltimore, Md., 1 Gal. 577.00
Tin, Hi-Plane Tobacco, 1 Engine, Pocket 75.00
Tin, Hi-Plane Tobacco, 2 Engines, Pocket 90.00
Tin, Home Run Asparagus Tips, Paper Label, Round, 3 1/4 x 2 1/2 In. 325.00
Tin, Honey Moon Tobacco, Man Alone On Moon, Pocket 150.00
Tin, Horlick's Malted Milk, 10 Lb. 45.00
Tin, Howeth Oysters 65.00
Tin, Hudson Bay Co. Tobacco, Red, Lithograph 65.00
Tin, Humpty Dumpty, Potato Chips, 5 Lb. 15.00
Tin, Huntley & Palmers Biscuits, Elves Bank, Lithograph 253.00
Tin, Huntley & Palmers, Pansies 12.00
Tin, Huntley & Palmers, Street Scene, Biscuit 85.00
Tin, Ice Cream, Embossed, Lid, 10 Qt. 7.00
Tin, Jackson Square Coffee, Round, 10 1/4 x 5 1/2 In. 750.00
Tin, Jam-Boy Coffee, Full Face, 1 Lb. 430.00
Tin, Jan Logan Candy, Auto, DeSoto, 1950s 12.00
Tin, Jewel Tea Cocoa, 1 Lb. 37.50
Tin, Just Suits Cut Plug 65.00
Tin, King Cole Coffee, King Cole Being Served, Canadian, 4 1/4 In. 150.00
Tin, Kleenal, Cleanses Everything & Everybody, Cardboard, 1926, 4 In. 15.00
Tin, Kreamer Coffee, Measuring Top 84.00
Tin, Lime Kiln Tobacco, Gold, 4 x 6 In. 100.00
Tin, Little Red Riding Hood English Toffee, Oblong, 1950s, 4 x 6 In. 55.00
Tin, Log Cabin Syrup, Man At Pump, 936 Grams 75.00
Tin, London Dock Tobacco 7.00
Tin, Luzianne Coffee, Mammy, 3 Lb. 98.00
Tin, Mammoth Salted Peanuts, 11 In. 275.00
Tin, Maryland Club Tobacco, Pocket .... 245.00 to 275.00
Tin, Mason's Shoe Polish 55.00
Tin, Maxwell House Coffee, Paper Label, 6 x 5 In.. .... 55.00
Tin, McCormick Banquet Tea, Lithograph 50.00
Tin, Melachrino & Company Egyptian Cigarettes, 5 1/2 x 4 x 5/8 In. 8.00

Tin, Mentholatum, Gift Sample, Envelope & Brochure, 1920s 25.00
Tin, Merck's Pyro-Gallic Acid 12.50
Tin, Miss Princine Baking Powder, In 8-Oz. Measuring Cup 75.00
Tin, Mohican Coffee, 1 Lb. 225.00
Tin, Nabisco Biscuit Co., Country Scene Lid, Large 10.00
Tin, Noah's Ark, Biscuit 285.00
Tin, O-So-Good Coffee, Red, White & Blue, 10 In. 143.00
Tin, Ogden's Snuffs, Snuffbox 35.00
Tin, Old King Cole, Crayon, 1930s 25.00
Tin, Olympian Coffee, 1 Lb. 550.00
Tin, Orinoco Coffee, Ohio Coffee Co., 1 Lb. 150.00
Tin, Paragon Tobacco, Canada, Pocket 295.00
Tin, Parrot & Monkey Baking Powder, Label, Unopened 35.00
Tin, Peachy Tobacco, Pocket .... 125.00 to 160.00
Tin, Peacock, Condom 45.00
Tin, Pearl Brand Oysters, McNasby Oyster Co., Bail Handle, 1 Gal. 55.00
Tin, Pedro Tobacco, Playing Cards, Hinged Lid, 7 1/2 In. 187.00
Tin, Penny Post Tobacco 225.00
Tin, Pipe Major Tobacco, Butler, Pocket 32.50
Tin, Piper Heidsieck Chewing Tobacco, Pocket 20.00
Tin, Ponce De Leon Coffee, 1 Lb. 250.00
Tin, Pride Of Virginia Tobacco, Gold, Blue, Pocket 40.00
Tin, Prince Albert Tobacco, Pocket 3.50
Tin, Puritan Tobacco, Dark Gray, Letters, Pocket .... 155.00 to 175.00
Tin, Queed Tobacco, Pocket 165.00
Tin, R.J. Reynolds Co., Cigarette Tobacco 30.00
Tin, Rawleigh's Headache Tablets 4.50
Tin, Red Cow Coffee, Paper Label 675.00
Tin, Red Star Carriage Lubricant 50.00
Tin, Red Wing Linseed Oil, Lid, 5 Gal. 8.00
Tin, Reddings' Russia Salve, Embossed 20.00
Tin, Reese 100% Pure Hawaiian Kona Coffee, Lid 20.00
Tin, Revere Coffee, Paul Revere Riding, 4 x 2 x 1 In. 200.00
Tin, Richmond Mixture Tobacco, 4 1/2 x 3 1/4 x 2 1/4 In. 125.00
Tin, Roebke & Pieper Baking Powder, Round, 8 x 5 1/4 In. 400.00
Tin, Roi Tan Little Cigars, Lid, Pocket 2.50
Tin, Roly Poly, Cowboy, Tobacco, Chein, 1980s 30.00
Tin, Roly Poly, Mammy, Dixie Queen 325.00
Tin, Roly Poly, Man From Scotland Yard, Dixie Queen 1000.00
Tin, Roly Poly, Satisfied Customer, Mayo 400.00
Tin, Roly Poly, Singer, Tobacco, Chein, 1980s 30.00
Tin, Rough Rider Baking Powder, Unopened 45.00
Tin, Schraft's, Brass Chased Woman, Carried In Chair, Oval, 1 Lb., 7 1/2 In. 24.00
Tin, Schraft's, Hinged Lid, Rectangular 3.50
Tin, Shamrock Oil, Metal, 1 Qt. 22.00
Tin, Sheaffer's Pencil Lead, Sliding Lid 2.00
Tin, Snake Charmer Tobacco, England, Pocket 175.00
Tin, Standard Oil Co., With Handle, 5 Gal. 10.00
Tin, Starlight Marshmallows, 5 Lb. 100.00
Tin, Stein Club Cigars, Playing Stud, Black Butler, 20 x 28 In. ... 1300.00
Tin, Sun Brand Oysters, Leib Packing Co., Baltimore, Md., 1 Pt. ... 49.50
Tin, Sunset Peanut Butter, 25 Lb. 13.00
Tin, Sunset Trail Tobacco, White, Pocket 120.00
Tin, Sunshine Biscuit, Battleship, USS Iowa 60.00
Tin, Sure Shot Tobacco, 4 x 10 In. 478.00
Tin, Sweet Georgia Brown Hair Dressing, Sample 12.00
Tin, Taxi Tobacco, Upright, Pocket 3000.00
Tin, Three Flowers Powder, Art Deco, 1 1/2 In. 5.00
Tin, Tiger Tobacco, Blue, 4 x 6 In. 75.00
Tin, Tilghman Oysters, Tin, 1 Gal. 18.00
Tin, Tobacco Girl Cigars 2275.00
Tin, Totem Tobacco, Pocket 295.00
Tin, Turkey Brand Coffee, c.1910, 3 Lb. 400.00

Tin, Udder Salve, Green & Cream, Cow, 1930s 17.00
Tin, Uncle Daniel Tobacco, Yellow, 2 x 8 In. 175.00
Tin, Uniform Cut Plug Tobacco, 4 x 6 In. 345.00
Tin, Vantine's, Rose Incense, Original Contents, Art Deco Design, 1920s 9.00
Tin, Veach Brand Oysters, J.M. Clayton Co., Cambridge, Md., 1 Pt. 258.50
Tin, Venizelos Coffee, 1 Lb. 650.00
Tin, Victor Phonograph, Nipper Insert 45.00
Tin, Virginia Dare Tobacco, Pocket 125.00
Tin, Ward's Oysters, B. Ward & Son, Crisfield, Md., 1 Pt. 236.50
Tin, White Rose Grease, 1940s, 1 Lb. 35.00
Tin, Whitman's Marshmallows, 3 1/2 Oz. 45.00
Tin, Wild Fruit Tobacco 245.00
Tin, Wiles Biscuit Co., George Washington On Lid, Scenes, 9 1/2 In. 17500.00
Tin, Williams Baby Talc, Blue, Yellow, Red, 5 In. 88.00
Tin, Woodbury Talc, Nude Woman, 1920s 10.00
Tin, Woodfield's Oysters, Woodfield Fish & Oyster Co., Maryland, 1 Gal. 275.00
Tin, Yankee Boy Tobacco, Red & White, Upright Pocket, 3 1/2 x 4 In. .... 575.00 to 605.00

Advertising tip trays are decorated metal trays less than 5 inches in diameter. They were placed on the table or counter to hold either the bill or the coins that were left as a tip. Change receivers could be made of glass, plastic, or metal. They were kept on the counter near the cash register and held the money passed back and forth by the cashier. Related items may be listed in the Advertising category under Change Receivers.

Tip Tray, Allouez Mineral Water & Beverages Co. 80.00
Tip Tray, American Line, Ship 115.00
Tip Tray, Appollanaris Water, Pollyanna 70.00
Tip Tray, Berliner Gram-O-Phone 175.00
Tip Tray, Camel Cigarettes 15.00
Tip Tray, Cottolene Shortening, Blacks Picking Cotton .... 85.00 to 98.00
Tip Tray, DeLaval Cream Separators, 5 In. 120.00
Tip Tray, Fairy Soap, Child's Picture .... 35.00 to 65.00
Tip Tray, Garland Stoves 75.00
Tip Tray, Globe Wernicke, Book Cases 65.00
Tip Tray, Heptol Splits Laxative, 1904 .... 195.00
Tip Tray, Junket, Blond Girl Eating Dessert, 4 1/2 In. 125.00
Tip Tray, King's Pure Malt, Panama Pacific Exposition 95.00
Tip Tray, Kraft Foods Company, Chicago, Golden Anniversary, 1903-1953, 4 In. 6.00
Tip Tray, Monticello 125.00
Tip Tray, Moxie, Green Ground .... 250.00 to 275.00
Tip Tray, Moxie, I Just Love Moxie Don't You, Tin, 1910, 6 In. 425.00
Tip Tray, National Cigar 125.00
Tip Tray, Old Angus, Scotch Whiskey 20.00
Tip Tray, Prudential Insurance, Rock Of Gibraltar, Tin 100.00
Tip Tray, Red Raven, Rectangular 145.00
Tip Tray, Robert Burns Cigars, Burns Picture In Center, 1930s 150.00
Tip Tray, Ruhstaller, Woman & Dove 120.00
Tip Tray, Slades Spices, Game Around Edge 45.00
Tip Tray, Smith Bros. Typewriter, Horses .... 135.00 to 200.00
Tip Tray, Stegmaier, Factory Scene, Oval, 6 In. 95.00
Tip Tray, Stroh's Beer, Lion Trademark, Gold Rim, 3 1/2 In. 40.00
Tip Tray, Urbana Wine, St. Louis Exposition .... 95.00 to 140.00
Tip Tray, White Rock Beer, Girl Kneeling On Rock, Looking Into Pond 155.00
Tobacco Cutter, Brighton Store, Cast Iron, Counter Top 15.00
Tobacco Cutter, Cast Iron, Advertising Counter, Embossed Floral 45.00
Tobacco Cutter, May Brothers Grocery, Counter 100.00
Tobacco Cutter, Red Devil, 14 In. 65.00
Tobacco Cutter, Waples Platter Grocery Co., Counter 125.00
Toilet, White Porcelain, Saleman's Sample, 10 In. 550.00
Toothpick, Coon Chicken Inn 100.00
Toy, Airplane, Nesbitt Orange Soda, Wooden, Package 10.00
Toy, Cow, Lea & Perrins, Moos When Turned Over 22.00
Toy, Energizer Bunny, Plush 45.00

Toy, Periscope, Jiffy Peanut Butter, Jiffaroo 15.00
Toy, Puppet, Hand, Dutch Boy Paint, 1956, 11 In. .... 25.00 to 35.00
Toy, Puppet, Snap, Rice Krispies 45.00
Toy, Truck, Chevy, Curtiss Candy, Marx, 9 In., Box 125.00
Toy, Truck, Friendly's Ice Cream, Battery Operated, Box 75.00
Toy, Truck, Kellogg's, With Snap, Crackle & Pop 300.00
Toy, Truck, Tractor Trailer, Howard Johnson, Winross, Box 75.00
Tray, A. Walkowick Whiskey, Buffalo, Pre-Prohibition 80.00
Tray, A.F. Talt Duck Hunting Scene, 24 1/2 In. 825.00
Tray, Anheuser-Busch Brewing Co., Factory Scene, St. Louis, Mo., 18 x 15 In. 2310.00
Tray, Anheuser-Busch, Woman, Cherubs, 15 In. 750.00
Tray, Arctic Ice Cream, Polar Bear, Larhe 140.00
Tray, Aurora Beer, Evangeline Picture, 1910, 13 x 10 1/2 In. 176.00
Tray, Bartels Beer, Orange, Black Ground, Plastic, 12 In. 20.00
Tray, Benham's Ice Cream, Palmer Cox Brownies, 10 1/2 x 13 1/4 In. 150.00
Tray, Budweiser, 1870s St. Louis Levee, Multicolored, 1914, Rectangular 329.00
Tray, Canandaigua Beer & Ale, Red & Brown, Yellow Ground, Oval, 16 In. 50.00
Tray, Capudine Liquid, Cures Headaches, Neuralgia, Angels, Round, 1900 .... 170.00
Tray, Castle's Ice Cream, 1920s 35.00
Tray, Christian Fergenspan Brewing Co., Newark, N.J., 13 In. 85.00
Tray, Crescent Brewing Co., Nampa, Idaho, Factory 525.00
Tray, Fidelio Brewery, 12 In. 65.00
Tray, Frank's Pale Dry Ginger Ale, Lithograph, 1930s 50.00
Tray, Fro-Joy Ice Cream, Sealtest Emblem, Beige Ground, Blue Rim 25.00
Tray, Greatest Show On Earth, Entire Casting Movie 65.00
Tray, Hardings The Cream Of All Ice Cream, Art Deco Type, Rectangular 45.00
Tray, Hornung's Beer, Philadelphia 45.00
Tray, Imperial Ice Cream, For Health, Crown, Wood Type Ground, Rectangular 50.00
Tray, Knudsen's Velvet Cottage Cheese, Blue Enameled 40.00
Tray, Leinenkugell, Indian Maiden, 12 In. 90.00
Tray, Leisy Beer, Factory Scene, c.1902 .... 425.00
Tray, Maltosia German-American Brewery, Buffalo, Pre-Prohibition 85.00
Tray, McAvoy's Malt Marrow, Boy & Dog 475.00
Tray, National Brewing Co., San Francisco, Jockey 275.00
Tray, Orange Crush, Allover Floral, Black, 13 In. 45.00
Tray, Orange Julep, Beach Girl, 1920s, 10 1/2 x 13 In. 175.00
Tray, Pabst Blue Ribbon, Bartender, Bottle Of Beer 12.00
Tray, Phoenix Brewery, Buffalo, Pre-Prohibition 160.00
Tray, Prince Albert, Indian Chief, 1983 .... 55.00
Tray, Quaker State Motor Oil, 9 In. 28.00
Tray, Red Raven, Beverages Beside Bird, Ask Man For Raven, 12 In. 600.00
Tray, Rupert, Clinking Steins, 14 1/2 x 10 1/2 In. 48.00
Tray, Schlitz Beer, 1957 .... 5.00
Tray, Seipp Brewing Company, 2 Couples In Touring Car, Tin, 14 x 10 In. 467.00
Tray, Sheffer's Ice Cream, Red & Yellow, Round, 14 In. 45.00
Tray, Sidney Dillon Cigars, Sire Of Trotters, Horse Center 450.00
Tray, Soulas' Rathskeller, Betz Building, Tin, 12 In. 200.00
Tray, Standard Brewing, Mankato, Minn., 12 In. 550.00
Tray, Stegmaier Brewing Co., Hand Holding Bottles 35.00
Tray, Terre Haute Brewing Co., Cherubs Pouring Beer, Oval, 15 In. 226.00
Tray, Tip, see Tip Trays in this category
Tray, Utica Club West End Brewing Co., Factory Scene, Round, 12 In. 45.00
Tray, Van Merritt Burlington Brewing Co., Silver Letters, Green, 5 x 10 In. 30.00
Tumbler, Anheuser-Busch, Founders, Etched, Stemmed, 5 1/2 In. 226.00
Tumbler, Coon Chicken Inn 45.00
Tumbler, Forest City Brewing Co., Cleveland, Ohio, 3 1/2 In. 50.00
Tumbler, GE Oven, Measuring, Red Decal 4.00
Tumbler, Genesee, To Toddy, Red, 1947 .... 30.00
Tumbler, Grain Belt, Red, Sample, 4 1/4 In. 20.00
Tumbler, Hillcrest Casper Beer, Wyoming, Red, 4 1/2 In. 100.00
Tumbler, Leisy, Pilsener, Blue & Yellow, 8 1/2 In. 75.00
Tumbler, McDonald's Peanut Camp 2.00
Tumbler, McDonald's, McVote, "86" 8.00

Tumbler, Pizza Hut, Flintstone Kids, 1986, 4 Piece Set 45.00
Tumbler, Put A Tiger In Your Tank, Decal 4.00
Tumbler, Schlitz, Etched Shell, Gold Rim, 3 1/2 In. 65.00
Umbrella, Morton Salt 35.00
Waste Basket, Rayovac Battery, Tin.. 45.00
Wave Setting Cap, Beautiwave, Illustrations, Box, 1930s 45.00
Waving Kit, Marcel, Curling Iron, Salesman's Sample 20.00
Whistle, Oscar Mayer Weiner Mobile, 3 1/2 In. 4.00
Whistle, Weatherbird Shoe, 1930s 20.00
Wings, PSA Airlines, Plastic 10.00
Yardstick, Tupperware, Folding, Wooden 7.00

AGATA glass was made by Joseph Locke of the New England Glass
Company of Cambridge, Massachusetts, after 1885. A metallic stain was
applied to New England Peachblow and the mottled design characteristic of
agata appeared.

Bowl, Peachblow, Ruffled, Oil Spots, 5 In. 770.00
Tumbler, Pink, Rose, 3 3/4 In. 500.00
Tumbler, Purple Hue, 3 3/4 In. 1140.00
Vase, Lily, Mottled, 8 In. 700.00

AKRO AGATE glass was made in Clarksburg, West Virginia, from 1932 to
1951. Before that time, the firm made children's glass marbles. Most of the
glass is marked with a crow flying through the letter *A*.

Ashtray, Blue Marble, Ellipsoid 10.00
Ashtray, Leaf, Carmel, Orange & White, 4 x 3 In. 4.00
Ashtray, Scalloped Shell, Green & White, 4 x 3 3/4 In. 5.00
Bowl, Cereal, Child's, Concentric Ring, Blue, 3 1/8 In. 22.50
Cornucopia, Blue, 3 1/8 In. 4.50
Creamer, Stippled Band, Amber 30.00
Cup, Chiquita, Green, 1 1/2 In. 7.00
Cup, Concentric Ring, Green, 2 In. 4.50
Cup & Saucer, Green & White, After Dinner 13.00
Cup & Saucer, Orange & White, After Dinner 13.00
Flowerpot, Blue, 2 1/4 In. 3.50
Flowerpot, Chevrons, Flared, Gray, Brown & Blue, 3 3/4 In. 8.50
Flowerpot, Stacked Discs, 3-Footed, Blue & White, 2 3/4 In. 4.50
Flowerpot, Vertical Rib Top, Green, 3 In. 7.00
Jar, Mexicalli, Hat 45.00
Lamp, Stacked Discs, Beige, 6 1/2 x 6 In. 45.00
Plate, Child's, Blue Opaque, 3 1/4 In. 6.00
Plate, Concentric Ring, Green, 3 1/4 In. 4.50
Plate, Stippled Band, Topaz, 4 1/4 In. 6.50
Powder Box, Scotty 50.00
Powder Box, Woman 50.00
Powder Jar, Cover, Southern Belle, Blue 65.00
Sugar, Green Cover, Interior Panel, Yellow 40.00
Sugar, Interior Panel, Blue Opaque 22.50
Tea Set, Child's, Amber, 15 Piece 100.00
Teapot, White Cover, Octagonal, Blue 20.00
Tumbler, Interior Panel, Green 10.00
Tumbler, Stippled Band, Green 11.00
Vase, Oval, Flared, Handles, Orange & White, 4 3/8 x 4 3/4 In. 9.00
Window Box, 4-Footed, Blue & Green, 5 1/2 x 3 x 2 1/4 In. 9.00
Window Box, Vertical Rib, Orange & White, 6 x 3 3/4 x 2 3/4 In. 10.00

ALABASTER is a very soft form of gypsum, a stone that resembles marble. It
was often carved into vases or statues in Victorian times. There are alabaster
carvings being made even today. Because the alabaster is very porous, it will
dissolve if kept in water, so do not use alabaster vases for flowers.

Box, Dresser, Metal Mount, Harlequin's Head Finial, Rectangle, 5 x 3 1/2 x 6 In. 77.00
Box, Jewelry, Green, England 25.00
Bust, Apollo & Athena, Late 19th Century, P. Bazzanti, Florence, 18 In., Pair 1430.00

♦ ♦ ♦ ♦ ♦ ♦ ♦ ♦ ♦ ♦ ♦ ♦ ♦ ♦ ♦ ♦ ♦ ♦ ♦
Never allow water to evaporate
in a glass vase. It will leave a
white residue that may be impossible to remove.
♦ ♦ ♦ ♦ ♦ ♦ ♦ ♦ ♦ ♦ ♦ ♦ ♦ ♦ ♦ ♦ ♦ ♦ ♦

Alexandrite, Vase, Trumpet, 8 1/4 In.

Bust, George Washington, 19th Century, 11 In. 770.00
Bust, Woman With Poppies, Antonia Ugo, Marble & Wooden Base, 24 In. 3335.00
Bust, Woman, Lacy Hat & Collar, Marble Column, 62 In. 275.00
Bust, Young Woman, High Lace Collar, Removable Plinth, 17 In. 93.00
Bust, Young Woman, Lacy Coat & Hat, 11 In. 92.50
Bust, Young Woman, Renaissance Costume, 14 In. 275.00
Bust, Young Woman, Shoulder Length Hair, Marble, 6 In. 175.00
Compote, Carved Base, 3 Opposing Hawks, 14 x 11 1/2 In. 375.00
Ewer, Baroque Style, Mask Spout, Swirled Body, 18 In., Pair 330.00
Figurine, Nude Woman, Reclining On Recliner, 7 3/4 In. 137.50
Figurine, Woman, Kneeling, Holding Snake, Italy, c.1900, 14 1/4 In. 715.00
Figurine, Woman, Tiara, Short Dress, Cylindrical Column, 22 1/2 In. 1265.00
Lamp, Seminude Maiden, Urn At Feet, Art Deco, 1925, 31 3/4 In. 2875.00
Lamp, Urn, Square Pedestal Base, Floral Relief, Scrolled Leafy Borders, 19 In. 137.00
Night-Light, Urn Shape, Classical Maidens, Empire Style Bronze 550.00
Urn, Pierced Scrolled Handles, Ribbon Twist Border, 20 In., Pair 1840.00

ALEXANDRITE is a name with many meanings. It is a form of the mineral
chrysoberyl that changes from green to red under artificial light. A man-made
version of this mineral is sold in Mexico today. It changes from deep purple
to aquamarine blue under artificial light. The Alexandrite listed here is glass
made in the late nineteenth and twentieth centuries. Thomas Webb & Sons
sold their transparent glass shaded from yellow to rose to blue under the name
Alexandrite. Stevens and Williams had a cased Alexandrite of yellow, rose,
and blue. A. Douglas Nash Corporation made an amethyst-colored
Alexandrite. Several American glass companies of the 1920s made a glass
that changed color under electric lights and this was also called Alexandrite.

Goblet, Wine, Pedestal, 4 1/2 In. 1100.00
Nut Bowl, Art Glass, 4 1/2 x 2 In. 1200.00
Vase, Bulbous Base, Hexagonal Rim, 3 In. 450.00
Vase, Honeycomb, 4 1/4 In. 765.00
Vase, Trumpet, 8 1/4 In. ....*Illus* 2800.00

ALUMINUM was more expensive than gold or silver until the 1850s.
Chemists learned how to refine bauxite to get aluminum. Jewelry and other
small objects were made of the valuable metal until 1914, when an
inexpensive smelting process was invented. The aluminum collected today
dates from the 1930s through 1950s. Hand-hammered pieces are the most
popular.

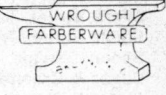

Basket, Acorn Design, Scalloped, Continental, 11 3/4 x 6 In. 12.00
Basket, Wheat, Double Twisted Handle, Milcraft, 14 In. 18.00
Bowl, 3 Masted Ship, Crimped, Handle, Hand Forged, 14 1/2 In. 10.00
Bowl, Bittersweet, Wendell August Forge, 7 1/2 In. 22.00
Bowl, Candy, 3 Sections, Farberware 18.00
Bowl, Centerpiece, Spun, Russel Wright 125.00
Bowl, Console, Lucite, Art Deco, Kensington, 12 In. 48.00
Bowl, Cover, Orange Ceramic Knob & Leaves, Shup Laird, 7 1/4 In. 15.00
Bowl, Cover, Wild Rose, Continental 18.50

Bowl, Iris Pattern, World Hand Forged, 11 In. 14.50
Bowl, Leaf Shape, Coiled Stem Handle, Triangular, Buenilum, 10 1/2 In. 6.00
Bowl, Pines & Mountains, Arthur Armour, 8 In. 35.00
Bowl, Stylized Flower Ring, Canterbury Arts, 7 1/ 2 In. 12.00
Bowl, Wheat Stems, Bar Handles, Milcraft, 15 1/2 In. 20.00
Box, Porch, Meadow Gold Milk, Insulated 45.00
Bread Tray, Fruits Pattern, Cromwell 22.50
Breakfast Set, Wild Rose, 4 Glass Dishes, Cover, Toast Holder, Tray, Continental ... 70.00
Butter, Deep Glass, Rodney Kent, 3 Piece 20.00
Candy Dish, Cover, Ring Holder, Glass, Rodney Kent, 3 Sections 27.00
Candy Dish, Rosette Knob, 3 Sections, Mums, Continental, 7 In. 7.00
Casserole, Cover, Buenilum 12.00
Coaster, Flying Geese, Reeds, Water, Set Of 6 .... 3.50
Coaster, Wine, Wilton 18.50
Coaster Set, Gadroon Rim, Polished, 3 1/4, 4 Piece 10.00
Cocktail Shaker Set, Norman Bel Geddes, Stamped Revere Rome, 8 Piece 2300.00
Comb Case, Wall, Embossed, Star & Shield 15.00
Compote, Applied Leaves At Base, Continental 14.50
Compote Set, Glass Ball, Candlesticks, Kensington, 3 Piece .... 195.00 to 250.00
Cooler, Wine, Bacchus, Chase, 9 1/4 In. 675.00
Crumber, Wild Rose, Pierced Handles, Continental, 2 Piece 25.00
Dish, Chrysanthemums, 2 Sections, Basket Handle, Continental, 11 x 7 1/2 In. 8.00
Dish, Grapes, Ruffled, Handle, Hammerkraft, 7 1/2 In. 4.00
Dish, Siesta Scene, Everlast, 5 1/4 In. 2.50
Holder, Casserole, Cover, Pyrex, Handled Tray, Rodney Kent 12.50
Ice Bucket, Basket Handle, Cromwell, 5 In. 9.00
Ice Bucket, Beaded Cover, Flattened & Grooved Handles, Buenilum 35.00
Ice Bucket, Light Blue Enameled Inset On Knobbed Lid, Buenilum 30.00
Ice Bucket, Open, Looped Handle, Cromwell 20.00
Lazy Susan, Applied Rosettes, Leaf & Acorn, Continental, 18 In. 27.00
Lazy Susan, Chrysanthemums, Continental, 18 In. 12.00
Lazy Susan, Chrysanthemums, NASCO, 16 In. 19.50
Lazy Susan, Tulip, 4-Part Insert, Rodney Kent, 18 In. .... 14.00 to 20.00
Lazy Susan, Tulips, Rodney Kent, 17 1/2 In. 14.00
Lazy Susan, Wild Rose, Continental 22.50
Napkin Holder, Flower & Ribbon Design, Footed, Rodney Kent 25.00
Pitcher, Ice Guard, Gailstyn, 8 In. 12.50
Pitcher, Wild Rose, Continental 27.00
Plate, Curvilinear Design, Canterbury Arts 19.50
Plate, Fern Circle, Turned Up Fluted Rim, Canterbury Arts, 11 1/2 In. 25.00
Platter, Metal, Griswold 95.00
Punch Set, Spun 1250.00
Relish, Glass Dish, Fruits & Flowers, Cromwell, 3 Sections 27.00
Salad Set, Flowers, Twisted Handles, Flower Shape, Servers, Buenilum, 12 1/4 In. .. 65.00
Scraper, Boot, Duck Form 57.00
Server, 2 Tiers, Bamboo, Round, Everlast, 7 3/4 x 6 In. 8.50
Server, Buffet, Rodney Kent 28.00
Server, Flower & Leaf Pattern, 3 Tiers, Gailstyn, 10 In. 29.00
Serving Cart, Everlast 300.00
Silent Butler, Tulip, Rodney Kent 7.00
Silent Butler, Wheat, Kraftware 18.00
Spoon, Serving, Wagner Ware 20.00
Sugar & Creamer, Cromwell, 3 Piece 35.00
Sugar & Creamer, Grape, Everlast, 3 Piece 20.00
Tidbit, Looped Center Handle, Finial, 2 Sections, Buenilum, 5 In. 14.00
Tray, Cattails, Gold Anodized, Arthur Armour, Square, 11 1/2 In. 35.00
Tray, Curvilinear Pattern, 3 Shaped Handles, Fluted, Canterbury Arts, 9 x 14 In. 20.00
Tray, Dahlias, Loop Handles, Openwork, Farber & Shlevin, 15 1/2 In. 10.00
Tray, Farberware, Round, 22 In. 50.00
Tray, Floral, Leaf, Crimped, Fluted, Farber & Shlevin, 7 In. 8.00
Tray, Flying Geese, 4 x 6 In., Set Of 8 .... 16.50
Tray, Gnarled Tree, Blossoms, Shup Laird, 8 1/4 x 11 1/4 In. 14.00
Tray, Grape Cluster, Looped Handle, Buenilum, 17 In. Diam. 20.00

Tray, Leaf & Bud Handles, Plain, Continental, 15 1/2 In. 12.00
Tray, Mum, Chopped Corners, Continental, 12 1/4 x 18 1/2 In. 45.00
Tray, Ribbon, Flower Handles, Rodney Kent, 12 x 15 In. 27.00
Tray, Ruffled, Fruits Pattern Center, Cromwell, 9 1/2 x 16 In. 22.50
Tray, Vegetables, Keystone, 13 x 10 In. 7.00
Tray, Zodiac, Handles, Arthur Armour, 20 In. 175.00
Tumbler, Turquoise 1.50
Tumbler Set, All Colors, 12 Piece 38.00
Vase, Cobalt Glass Top, Kensington 195.00

AMBER, see Jewelry category

AMBER GLASS is the name of any glassware with the proper yellow-brown
shading. It was a popular color just after the Civil War and many pressed
glass pieces were made of amber glass. Depression glass of the 1930s–1950s
was also made in shades of amber glass. All types are being reproduced.

Bottle, Liqueur, Pewter Overlay, Pewter Pedestal Foot, Amber, France, 8 3/4 In. 165.00
Bowl, Blue Salamanders & Trim, Sapphire Blue Feet, 4 1/2 In. 195.00
Bowl, Chameleons On Sides, Dolphin Feet, Sapphire Blue, 5 1/4 In. 245.00
Bowl, Underplate, Lotus, Frosted, 13 3/4 In. 55.00
Bowl, Wheel Cut Lines & Flowers, Rolled Rim, 10 1/2 x 3 In. 18.00
Box, Hinged Cover, Snowdrop Flowers, Leaves, Brass Feet, 4 1/2 x 3 1/2 In. 145.00
Candlestick, Lotus, Frosted, Double Twisted Stem, 9 In. 16.00
Creamer, Clear Handle, Gray & Green Enameled Bird, Flowers, 5 1/2 In. 85.00
Cruet, Pewter Stopper & Pedestal Foot, France, 8 3/8 In. 135.00
Rose Bowl, Jewel, 12-Crimp Top, Air Trap Zipper Pattern, 2 1/4 In. 118.00
Syrup, Robin's Nest, Worn Pewter Cap, Dated 1884 .... 125.00
Vase, 4 Entwined Thorny Tree Trunks, 16 3/8 In. 235.00
Wine, Pink Flowers & Gold Leaves 10.00

AMBERINA is a two-toned glassware made from 1883 to about 1900. It was
patented by Joseph Locke of the New England Glass Company, but was also
made by other companies. The glass shades from red to amber. Similar pieces
of glass may be found in the Baccarat and Plated Amberina categories. Glass
shaded from blue to amber is called *Blue Amberina* or *Bluerina*.

Berry Bowl, Daisy & Button, Hobbs & Brockunier, Square 90.00
Berry Set, Daisy & Button, 5 Piece 275.00
Biscuit Jar, Coralene Fruit, Branches & Leaves, Metal Rim, Handle & Lid 500.00
Bottle, Bar, Swirled Rib, Amber Stopper, 8 In. 350.00
Bowl, Diamond Optic, Blue, Gold Iridescent 150.00
Bowl, Finger, Diamond-Quilted, Tri-Folded-Over Rim, Fuchsia, New England 340.00
Butter, Cover, Baby Thumbprint 275.00
Celery Vase, Daisy & Button, Gold Color, 6 In. 165.00
Champagne, Flute, Wide Fuchsia Rim Band 265.00
Console, Heart Shape, Crenelated, Handle, Mt. Washington 375.00
Creamer, Square Neck & Shoulder, Reeded Handle, 4 1/4 In. 435.00

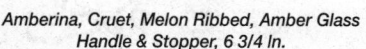

*Amberina, Cruet, Melon Ribbed, Amber Glass
Handle & Stopper, 6 3/4 In.*

*Amberina, Pitcher, Inverted Thumbprint, Ruby to
Deep Amber, 10 1/2 In.*

Cruet, Baby Thumbprint	225.00
Cruet, Blown, Applied Handle	215.00
Cruet, Melon Ribbed, Amber Glass Handle & Stopper, 6 3/4 In. .... *Illus*	200.00
Cruet, 8 Optic Panels, Amber Handle & Stopper, 6 1/2 In.	400.00
Cruet, Reverse Baby Thumbprint, Mt. Washington	365.00
Cruet, Swirl, Amber Faceted Stopper, 6 In.	535.00
Decanter, Inverted Thumbprint, Amber Stopper, 10 1/2 In.	395.00
Decanter, Stopper, Bulbous, 8 In.	45.00
Dish, Cover, Diagonal Block	235.00
Eggnog Cup, Allover White & Yellow Flowers	230.00
Pitcher, Cider, Inverted Thumbprint, 8 In.	225.00
Pitcher, Coin Dot, Amber Reeded Handle, 8 In.	295.00
Pitcher, Inverted Thumbprint, Ruby to Deep Amber, 10 1/2 In. .... *Illus*	385.00
Pitcher, Melon Ribbed & Inverted Thumbprint, 8 In.	350.00
Pitcher, Milk, Fuchsia, Applied Amber Reeded Handle, 6 In.	450.00
Pitcher, Pleated Top, Clear Reeded Handle, Amber To Fuchsia, 8 In.	225.00
Pitcher, Ruffled Top, Clear Handle, 8 In.	355.00
Pitcher, Thumbprint, 8 In. .... 230.00 to	250.00
Pitcher, Water, Thumbprint, Large	300.00
Plate, 12 Ribs New England Glass Co., c.1884, 8 1/2 In.	300.00
Punch Cup, Polished Rim	170.00
Punch Cup, Venetian Diamond-Quilted, Fuchsia, Amber Glass Handle, 3 x 2 5/8 In. .	200.00
Rose Bowl, Melon Ribbed, Threaded, 3 1/2 In.	70.00
Salt & Pepper, Blossom Time, Cattails, Wilcox Holder, Swan Feet	595.00
Saucer, Ice Cream, Daisy & Button	90.00
Spooner, Thumbprint, 4 3/4 In.	95.00
Sugar Sifter, Inverted Thumbprint	395.00
Syrup, Inverted Thumbprint, Sterling Silver Hinged Lid	450.00
Tankard, 10 Panels, Amber Reeded Handle, 6 3/4 In.	745.00
Toothpick, Daisy & Button, c.1886 .... 165.00 to	325.00
Toothpick, Tricorner	375.00
Tumbler, Baby Thumbprint	70.00
Tumbler, Diamond-Quilted, New England, 3 3/4 x 2 1/2 In.	150.00
Tumbler, Expanded Diamond-Quilted, Mt. Washington	120.00
Tumbler, Juice, Diamond-Quilted, 2 5/8 In.	125.00
Tumbler, Lemonade, 12 Optic Ribs, Curlicue Handle, 4 7/8 In.	185.00
Tumbler, Optic Ribs, 4 7/8 In.	185.00
Tumbler, Reverse Thumbprint	50.00
Tumbler, Silver Plated	425.00
Tumbler, Thumbprint, 4 In.	96.00
Vase, Ball, Hobnail Ivy, Beaded Stem, 5 3/4 In.	32.00
Vase, Celery, Fuchsia, Diamond Design, 6 1/4 In.	400.00
Vase, Lily, 6 In.	210.00
Vase, Red Platinum & Gold, Iridescent	165.00
Vase, Rigaree Trim, Blown, Squatty, Pinch Sides	225.00
Vase, Scalloped, 9 In.	215.00
Vase, Wheeling Drape, 10 In.	325.00
Whiskey, Yellow & White Floras, Green Leaves, Dotted Rim, 3 x 2 In.	425.00

AMERICAN ART CLAY Company of Indianapolis, Indiana, made a variety of art pottery wares, especially vases, from about 1930 to after World War II. The company used the mark AMACO, as well as the company name. Do not confuse this company with an earlier art pottery firm from Edgerton, Wisconsin, called the American Art Clay Works.

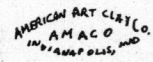

Figurine, Woman's Bust, Art Deco, White Glaze, 7 In.	110.00
Head, No. 158 & No. 159, Bright Blue Glaze, AMACO, 8 In., Pair	300.00

AMERICAN DINNERWARE is the name used by collectors for ceramic dinnerware made in the United States from the 1930s through the 1950s. Most was made in potteries in southern Ohio, West Virginia, and California. Dishes were sold in gift shops and department stores, or were given away as premiums. Many of these patterns are listed in this book in their own categories, such as Autumn Leaf, Coors, Fiesta, Franciscan, Hall, Harker, Harlequin, Red Wing, Riviera, Russel Wright, Vernon Kilns, and Watt. For

more information, see *Kovels' Depression Glass & American Dinnerware Price List.*

Ashtray, Green, Shenango China 25.00
Berry Bowl, Cavalier, Margaret Rose Pattern, Homer Laughlin, 6 In. 5.00
Biscuit Jar, Ivy, Purinton 75.00
Bowl, Century, Ivory, Homer Laughlin, 5 In. 7.00
Bowl, Cereal, Currier & Ives, Blue, Tab Handle, Royal .... 8.00 to 20.00
Bowl, Crab Apple, Red Rim, Blue Ridge, 9 1/4 In. 12.00
Bowl, Currier & Ives, Royal, 9 In. 18.00
Bowl, El Rancho, Wallace, 4 3/4 In. 25.00
Bowl, Little Brown Daisy, Marcrest, 5 In. 20.00
Bowl, Serving, Organdie, Vernonware 17.00
Bowl, Spaghetti, Apple, 14 1/2 In., Purinton 65.00
Bowl, Vegetable, Handle, Sculptured Daisy, 8 In. 28.00
Bowl, Vegetable, Pioneer Trails, Wallace, Oval 90.00
Box, Candy, Rose Marie, Blue Ridge 128.00
Butter, Cover, Della Robia, Metlox 23.00
Butter, Gold S On Lid, Gold Wedding Band, Knowles 8.50
Butter Chip, Ship, Blue Ridge 50.00
Cake Server, Kitchen Kraft, Homer Laughlin 25.00
Casserole, Cover, Colonial, Enoch Woods 55.00
Casserole, Mexican Village 16.00
Casserole, Red Rooster, Metlox 95.00
Celery Dish, Leaf, French Peasant 85.00
Chop Plate, California Ivy, Metlox, 13 In. 25.00
Chop Plate, Camellia, Metlox, 13 In. 25.00
Chop Plate, Currier & Ives, Royal, 12 In. .... 25.00 to 30.00
Cookie Jar, Humpty Dumpty, Purinton 80.00
Creamer, Ballerina, Universal 8.00
Creamer, Cattail, Universal 5.00
Creamer, Currier & Ives, Pink 15.00
Creamer, Currier & Ives, Royal 5.00
Creamer, Lu-Ray, Blue, Demitasse 35.00
Creamer, Rodeo, Wallace 55.00
Creamer, Tulip In Basket, Homer Laughlin 10.00
Cruet Set, Poppy Trail, California Provincial 25.00
Cup, Lu-Ray, Pink, Demitasse 10.00
Cup, Priscilla, Homer Laughlin 6.00
Cup, Tea, Rhythm Rose, Homer Laughlin 4.00
Cup & Saucer, Ballerina, Universal, Demitasse 20.00
Cup & Saucer, Bolero, George 6.00
Cup & Saucer, Cashmere, Georgian, Eggshell, 10 1/4 In. 8.50
Cup & Saucer, Colonial, Enoch Woods 15.00
Cup & Saucer, Country Life 40.00
Cup & Saucer, Currier & Ives, Pink 18.00
Cup & Saucer, Della Robia, Metlox 8.00
Cup & Saucer, Georgian, Eggshell, Gold Trim, Demitasse 9.00
Cup & Saucer, Lu-Ray, Blue, Demitasse 25.00
Cup & Saucer, Poppy Trail, California Provincial 12.00
Cup & Saucer, Priscilla, Homer Laughlin 10.00
Cup & Saucer, Provincial 12.00
Cup & Saucer, Sunnyvale, Castleton 20.00
Dinner Set, 30 Piece 190.00
Eggcup, Ballerina, Universal 12.00
Eggcup, Lu-Ray, Gray, Taylor-Smith-Taylor 15.00
Eggcup, Lu-Ray, Green 16.00
Flower Bowl, Peach, White, Low, Metlox 20.00
Gravy Boat, Attached Underplate, Rhythm Rose, Homer Laughlin 22.00
Gravy Boat, Ladle, Figural Chicken, Cleminson 30.00
Gravy Boat, Lu-Ray, Blue 20.00
Gravy Boat, Poppy Trail, Metlox 25.00
Gravy Bowl, Underplate, Currier & Ives, Royal 12.00
Jug, Purinton, Large 40.00

Mug, Muggsey, Pfhaltzgraff 38.00
Mug, Muscles Moe, Pfhaltzgraff 125.00
Pepper Mill, Rooster, Green 65.00
Pitcher, Apple, Green Trim, Purinton, 6 In. 16.00
Pitcher, Cover, Poppy Trail, Green 30.00
Pitcher, Lu-Ray, Blue, Flat 55.00
Pitcher, Rose Spiral, Blue Ridge 40.00
Pitcher, Sculptured Fruit, Blue Ridge 55.00
Plate, Autumn Apple, 10 1/2 In. 14.00
Plate, Avon, Blue Ridge, 8 3/4 In. 15.00
Plate, Ballerina, Universal 5.00
Plate, Blue Bell Bouquet, Blue Ridge, 10 In. 15.00
Plate, California Ivy, Metlox, 10 In. .... 9.00 to 30.00
Plate, Camellia, Metlox, 7 1/4 In. 8.50
Plate, Camellia, Metlox, 10 In. 12.50
Plate, Century, Ivory, Homer Laughlin, 6 1/4 In. 4.50
Plate, Century, Ivory, Homer Laughlin, 7 3/4 In. 6.50
Plate, Chicken, Blue Ridge, 6 1/4 In. 20.00
Plate, Chintz, Summertime, 9 In. 95.00
Plate, Christmas Tree, Blue Ridge, 10 1/2 In. 60.00
Plate, Colonial, Blue Ridge, 11 1/2 In. 28.00
Plate, Country Life, Stangl, 10 In. 25.00
Plate, Crab Orchard, Green Rim, Blue Ridge, 6 In. 2.50
Plate, Currier & Ives, Pink, 10 In. 12.00
Plate, Della Robia, Metlox, 9 1/2 In. 10.00
Plate, Intaglio, 10 In. 18.00
Plate, Lyonnaise, Blue Ridge, 6 In. 40.00
Plate, Priscilla, Homer Laughlin, 10 In. 6.00
Plate, Red Flowers & Bud Wreath, Piecrust Rim, Blue Ridge, 10 In. 8.00
Plate, Rhythm Rose, Homer Laughlin, 7 In. 6.00
Plate, Rhythm Rose, Homer Laughlin, 9 In. 8.00
Plate, Rooster, Poppy Trail, California Provincial, 10 In. 10.00
Plate, St. Augustine, Florida, Blue & White, Jonroth, 7 In. 26.00
Plate, Turkey & Acorns, Blue Ridge 50.00
Plate, Vistosa, Yellow, Taylor & Smith, 14 1/4 In. 17.50
Platter, Bolero, George, 11 In. 10.00
Platter, Cashmere, Georgian, Eggshell, Gold Rim, 12 In. 10.00
Platter, Cavalier, Margaret Rose Pattern, Eggshell, Homer Laughlin, 12 In. 10.00
Platter, Currier & Ives, Blue, Royal, 13 In. 25.00
Platter, Empress, Laughlin, 16 In. 15.00
Platter, Green Briar, Blue Ridge, 14 In. 14.00
Platter, Lifetime Mark, Homer Laughlin, 11 In. 12.00
Platter, Lu-Ray, Gray, 13 In. 25.00
Platter, Sculptured Daisy, Metlox, 14 1/2 In. 33.00
Platter, Turkey & Acorns, Blue Ridge, 16 In. 240.00
Relish, Intaglio, Ceramic Handle, 3 Sections, Purinton 60.00
Relish, Leaf Shape, French Peasant, Blue Ridge 50.00
Rolling Pin, Silhouette 85.00
Salad Plate, Homestead, Metlox 35.00
Salt & Paper, Chickens, Blue Ridge 95.00
Salt & Pepper, Ducks, Blue Ridge 250.00
Salt & Pepper, Fruit, Purinton 25.00
Saucer, Priscilla, Homer Laughlin 5.00
Server, Homestead Provincial, Tiered 30.00
Server, Pancake, Big Top Circus, Cleminson 45.00
Soup, Dish, Homestead Provincial, Metlox 8.00
Soup, Dish, Tam O'Shanter, Homer Laughlin 8.00
Stein, Bowling Scene, Metlox 500.00
Sugar, Apple, Purinton 18.00
Sugar, Ballerina 10.00
Sugar, Cover, Rhythm Rose, Homer Laughlin 14.00
Sugar, Currier & Ives, Royal 12.99
Sugar, Ivy, Purinton 12.00

Sugar, Tulip In Basket, Homer Laughlin 10.00
Sugar & Creamer, Bolero, George 20.00
Sugar & Creamer, Cover, Intaglio, Purinton 80.00
Sugar & Creamer, Cover, Pioneer Trails, Wallace 100.00
Sugar & Creamer, Cover, Rooster, Poppy Trail, California Provincial 20.00
Sugar & Creamer, Priscilla, Homer Laughlin 20.00
Tea & Toaster Set, Woodfield, Gray, Steubenville 15.00
Tea & Toaster Set, Woodfield, Seaform, Steubenville 15.00
Teapot, Apple & Pear, Purinton 65.00
Teapot, Apple, Individual, Purinton 38.00
Teapot, Jubilee, Homer Laughlin 24.00
Teapot, Purinton, 3 Cup 25.00
Teapot, Purinton, Fruit, 2 Cup 40.00
Tidbit, Apple Jack, 3 Tiers, Blue Ridge 20.00
Tray, Chocolate, Palace, Blue Ridge 400.00
Water Set, Apple, Purinton, 5 Piece 125.00
Water Set, Purinton, 9 Piece 135.00

AMERICAN ENCAUSTIC TILING COMPANY was founded in Zanesville, Ohio, in 1875. The company planned to make a variety of tiles to compete with the English tiles that were selling in the United States for use in fireplaces and other architectural designs. The first glazed tiles were made in 1880, embossed tiles in 1881, faience tiles in the 1920s. The firm closed in 1935 and reopened in 1937 as the Shawnee Pottery.

Soap Dish, Art Deco Nude, 8 In. 100.00
Tile, Elegantly Dressed Woman, Wooden Frame, 6 x 18 In., 3 Piece 143.00
Tile, Man In Formal Attire, Wooden Frame, 6 x 18 In., 3 Piece 121.00
Tile, Medusa, Gold Snake .... 300.00 to 450.00

AMETHYST GLASS is any of the many glasswares made in the dark purple color of the gemstone called amethyst. Included in this category are many pieces made in the nineteenth and twentieth centuries. Very dark pieces are called *black amethyst* and are listed under that heading.

Candlestick, Grape Design, Etched, 11 1/8 In., Pair 125.00
Decanter, Thumbprint Decoration, Cut To Clear, 17 In. 154.00
Jigger, 6 Panels, Flint, 1 7/8 In. 16.50
Jigger, Panels & Flattened Diamonds, 2 1/2 In. 22.00
Pitcher, Pittsburgh Glass, Large 8800.00
Toothpick, Silver Overlay, Bulbous To Flaring Top, 2 1/4 In. 75.00
Tumbler, 8 Panels, Flint, 3 1/2 In. 258.00
Vase, Applique 295.00
Vase, Flared, Crimped, 8 1/2 x 9 In. 45.00

ANIMAL TROPHIES, such as stuffed animals or fish, rugs made of animal skins, and other similar collectibles, are listed in this category. Collectors should be aware of the endangered species laws that make it illegal to buy and sell some of these items. Any eagle feathers, many types of cats (such as leopards), and many forms of tortoiseshell can be confiscated if discovered by the government.

2 Squirrels, Stuffed, Case, 14 1/2 In. 115.00
Black Bear, Upright, 6 Ft. 950.00
Brahma Bull, Bucking, Steel Ribcage To Support Rider, 2000 Lb. 7500.00
Bull Buffalo Head, Mounted 2000.00
Deer Antlers, Tombstone Plaque Mounted, Maine Camp 145.00
Owl, Fully Feathered, Mounted On Tree Branch, c.1930 .... 350.00
Rug, Zebra Skin, 1950s 350.00
Zebra, Mounted, Full Size 1800.00

ANIMATION ART collectibles include cels that are painted drawings on celluloid needed to make an animated cartoon. Hundreds of cels are made, then photographed in sequence to make a cartoon showing moving figures. Early examples made by the Walt Disney Studios are popular with collectors today. Original sketches used by the artists are also listed here.

Cel, 101 Dalmatians, Anita Walks Perdita In Park, Disney 1000.00
Cel, 101 Dalmatians, Anita Looks Out A Window, 1961, 8 x 10 In. 299.00
Cel, Adventures Of Ichabod & Mr. Toad, Walt Disney, 1949, 8 x 8 In. 633.00
Cel, Alice In Wonderland, King Of Hearts With Mallet, 1952, 6 x 6 In. 1100.00
Cel, Alice In Wonderland, The Flying Caterpillar, 1951, 4 1/2 x 9 1/2 In. 920.00
Cel, Alice In Wonderland, White Rabbit, Watch, Framed, 8 x 6 In. 1935.00
Cel, Ariel, The Little Mermaid, 13 x 8 In. 1320.00
Cel, Aristocats, Toulouse, 1970, 9 x 11 In. 299.00
Cel, Bambi & Thumper, 1942, 7 x 7 1/4 In. 3220.00
Cel, Bambi, Adult Bambi & Faline, 1942, 7 x 8 In. 3450.00
Cel, Bambi, Meets Flower, 1942, 8 1/2 x 11 1/4 In. 4025.00
Cel, Bambi, Skunk, Full Figure, Framed, 3 x 3 1/2 In. 905.00
Cel, Bambi, Thumper With Bluebird, Signed Mat, Inscribed, 7 x 7 1/2 In. 4025.00
Cel, Bambi, Thumper, 1942, 6 x 5 In. 1265.00
Cel, Batman, Be A Clown, Batman Jostles Joker, Warner Brothers 325.00
Cel, Beany & Cecil, And Friends, Bob Clampett Studio, Matted 860.00
Cel, Beatles, Yellow Submarine, John, Bulldogs & Blue Meanies, Framed 1200.00
Cel, Bugs & Marvin Martian, Tries To Blow Out Match, Framed, Warners 1100.00
Cel, Bugs Bunny, Bugs Zooms Away Of Flying Carpet, Fritz Freleng 900.00
Cel, California Raisins, 4 Raisins & Miss Rutabaga, Signed 175.00
Cel, Cinderella, 2 Seamstress Mice & A Bird Sew, 1950, 10 x 10 1/2 In. 805.00
Cel, Cinderella, Godmother, Framed, 9 x 9 In. 1028.00
Cel, Cinderella, Jaq, 1950, 5 1/4 x 9 1/2 In. 1265.00
Cel, Clarabelle Cow, Disney, 1930 .... 550.00
Cel, Daffy Duck, Joined By Speedy Gonzales, Freleng, Framed 750.00
Cel, Daffy Duck, Multiple Daffys Fly Up To Cloud In Sky, Warner Brothers 700.00
Cel, Dewey Duck, Disney, Matted 275.00
Cel, Donald Duck Gets Drafted, Marching, 1942, 7 x 9 In. 1035.00
Cel, Ducktales, Scrooge Stands In Money Bin, 1980s, 8 x 10 In. 403.00
Cel, Dumbo, 2 Clowns Ride Around Center Ring, 1941, 9 x 11 1/2 In. 805.00
Cel, Dumbo, With Timothy Mouse, Framed, 1941, 7 3/4 x 8 3/4 In. 3163.00
Cel, Fantasia, 2 Dewdrop Fairies, 1940, 8 x 6 1/2 In. 2760.00
Cel, Fantasia, Orchid Dancer, Framed, 6 x 5 In. 785.00
Cel, Ferdinand The Bull, Smiles Through Floral Reef, 1938, 17 x 16 In. 1840.00
Cel, Flintstones, Fred, Wilma, Pebbles & Dino, 8 1/2 x 10 1/2 In. 690.00
Cel, Foghorn Leghorn, Foggy's Wheeled By Miss Priss, Freleng 750.00
Cel, Gulliver's Travels, Princess Glory & Prince David, Framed, 10 x 13 In. 1495.00
Cel, How The Grinch Stole Christmas, Becoming A Reindeer, Max With Antlers 950.00
Cel, How The Grinch Stole Christmas, Grinch With Bag, 1966, 10 x 12 In. 1610.00
Cel, Huey Duck, Donald's Golf Game, Disney, Framed, Large 2400.00
Cel, Jetson Joyride, Hanna-Barbera, Framed 750.00
Cel, Jungle Book, Baloo With A Cactus On His Hand, 1967, 8 x 10 In. 863.00
Cel, Lady & The Tramp, Guests, Lady & Tramp, 5 x 5 In. 905.00
Cel, Lady & The Tramp, Smiling Lady, Framed, 12 1/2 x 16 1/2 In. 1935.00
Cel, Lady & The Tramp, Tony, 1955, 10 x 12 In. 1035.00
Cel, Little Mermaid, Ariel, Scuttle & Sebastian, Disney 1700.00
Cel, Little Mermaid, Prince Eric & Ariel, Framed, 5 x 7 1/2 In. 3870.00
Cel, Little Mermaid, Sebastian The Crab, Covers Head, Disney, Framed 1950.00
Cel, Little Mermaid, Swimming Dolphin, Framed, 1989, 11 1/2 x 34 In. 4600.00
Cel, Lord Of The Rings, Gandalf Gives Advice To Frodo, Matted 250.00
Cel, Make Mine Music, Songs, Framed, 8 x 9 1/2 In. 365.00
Cel, Mickey Mouse, Prince And The Pauper, 16 x 18 In. 1100.00
Cel, Peter Pan, Captain Hook, 1953, 11 x 15 In. 1955.00
Cel, Peter Pan, Captain Hook, Full Figure, Framed, 9 x 8 1/2 In. 1150.00
Cel, Peter Pan, John Darling Grasping Umbrella, Disney 700.00
Cel, Peter Pan, Peter & Pals Fly Over London At Night, Disney 1000.00
Cel, Pinocchio, Drowsy Pinocchio, 1940, 7 x 6 1/2 In. 3220.00
Cel, Pinocchio, Jiminy Stands In Front Of A Wheel, 1940, 9 x 10 In. 2300.00
Cel, Pinocchio, Stromboli, Disney 950.00
Cel, Popeye, Bluto Carries Flowers, 1930s, 6 x 7 1/2 In. 2760.00
Cel, Quick Draw McGraw, In Front Of Train Tracks, 7 x 9 In. 253.00
Cel, Robin Hood, Prince John On His Throne, 1973, 9 x 16 In. 2300.00
Cel, Rocky & Bullwinkle, Jay Ward Studio, Matted, 2 1/2 x 6 In. 248.00

Cel, Rocky & Bullwinkle, Wave To Their Fans, Jay Ward 375.00
Cel, Rocky, Bullwinkle, Boris & Natasha, Play Cowboys & Indians, Jay Ward 425.00
Cel, Saludos Amigos, Little Pedro & His Purse, 1943, 10 x 9 1/2 In. 575.00
Cel, Simpsons, Bart Ready For School, Krusty With Lunch Box 500.00
Cel, Sleeping Beauty, Princess Aurora, Framed, 12 1/2 x 16 1/2 In. 1025.00
Cel, Snow White, Sings To Birds, 1937, 9 x 9 1/2 In. 4600.00
Cel, Sword & The Stone, Archimedes Sits On A Bureau, 1963, 11 x 16 In. 2530.00
Cel, Sylvester, Sits Eating Ice Cream Cone, Framed, Warner Brothers 900.00
Cel, Tom & Jerry, Movie, Do Soft Shoe, Warner Brothers 525.00
Cel, Truth About Mother Goose, A Noble & Maiden Dance, 1957, 8 x 11 In. 403.00
Cel, Winnie The Pooh & Blustery Day, 8 x 10 In. 1450.00
Cel, Winnie The Pooh & Friends, Framed, 13 x 15 In. 3450.00
Cel, Winnie The Pooh, Piglet Brings Pool Tools, 1980s, 9 x 12 In. 633.00
Cel, Winnie The Pooh, Pooh Dreams Of Honey, 1970s, 10 x 14 In. 575.00
Cel, Winnie The Pooh, Pooh, Owl & Gopher Talk, 1970s, 10 x 13 In. 633.00
Cel, Yosemite Sam, Rabbitson Crusoe, Sam, Swinger, Warner Brothers 1250.00
Drawing, Barney Rubble, Swinging On Trapeze, 3 x 4 In. 40.00
Drawing, Figaro & Jiminy, Cleo, Monstro, 1940, 3 Sets 1495.00
Drawing, Fred Flintstone, Holding Thermos, Eyes Shut, 5 x 4 1/2 In. 20.00
Drawing, Mickey Mouse, Pencil, Signed, 10 1/2 x 8 In. 4600.00
Drawing, Mother Goose Goes To Hollywood, 1938, McCarthy, Fields, Pair 375.00
Drawing, Pinocchio Becomes A Boy, Brown Pencil, 1940, 5 x 6 In. 1265.00
Drawing, Pinocchio, Figaro Walks On Banister, 1940, 5 x 7 In. 483.00
Drawing, Scooby Doo, Zooming Along, 2 3/4 x 1 3/4 In. 25.00
Drawing, Tazmanian Devil, Running Wild, 6 1/2 x 4 1/2 In. 250.00
Drawing, Tom & Jerry, Pen & Ink, Inscribed, 9 1/2 x 7 1/2 In. 230.00
Drawing, Yosemite Sam, Dragon, Black Knight Riding Dragon, 7 1/2 x 12 In. 525.00

ARC-EN-CIEL is the French word for rainbow. A pottery factory named Arc-
en-ciel was founded in Zanesville, Ohio, in 1903. The company made art
pottery for a short time, then became the Brighton Pottery in 1905.

Vase, Applied Gold Luster, Swirling Rib, 7 1/2 In. 400.00
Vase, Oak Leaf Band Rim, Trailing Stems, Pale Blue-Green Glaze, 1904, 6 1/2 In. ... 247.00

ARCHITECTURAL antiques include a variety of collectibles, usually very
large, that have been removed from buildings. Hardware, backbars, doors,
paneling, and even old bathtubs are now wanted by collectors. Pieces of the
Victorian, Art Nouveau, and Art Deco styles are in greatest demand.

Backbar, Barber Shop, 9 x 21 Ft. 1800.00
Backbar, Cabinets Under Mirrored Back, Oak, 9 x 8 Ft. 3800.00
Backbar, English Pub, Stained Glass Canopy, Beveled Mirror, 8 Ft. 2900.00
Backbar, Marble Pillars, Mahogany, Stained Glass, 2 Doors, 1880s, 80 Ft. 10000.00
Backbar, Stained Glass Panels, Lit Side, Mirror, Marble Top, Oak, 9 x 8 Ft. 4200.00
Bathtub, Cast Iron, Claw Foot, Refinished, 5 Ft. 650.00
Bathtub, Copper Lined, Oak Panel Cabinet, Eastlake 2200.00
Bathtub, Copper, Cast Iron, Victorian, Scrolling Feet, 19th Century, 70 In. 1380.00
Bathtub, Copper, In Dovetailed Pine Shell, 1880 .... 900.00
Bathtub, Elliptical Form, Strapwork Braces, Brass, 37 x 63 In. 1495.00
Bathtub, Footed, 4 Ft. 50.00
Bathtub, Galvanized, Oak Trim, 5 Ft. 325.00
Bathtub, Zinc, c.1870 .... 650.00
Booth, Telephone, Laminate Interior, Rotary Dial, American, Maple, c.1950, 7 Ft. 275.00
Booth, Telephone, Metal Interior, Exhaust Fan, Maple, 6 Ft. 10 In. 385.00
Box, Post Office, Oak, With Slots 90.00
Box, Toilet, Child's, Pine, Varnished, Primitive, Porcelain Mug 45.00
Carving, Oak, Cherub, 18th Century, 54 x 36 x 18 In. 9850.00
Cupboard, Corner, Colonial, Shell Carved, Pine, 20th Century, 78 In. 3860.00
Door, Inset Leaded Glass Panel, Oak, 7 Ft. 10 In. x 42 In. 1600.00
Door, Leaded Glass, Stylized Lozenge Design, F.L. Wright, 1900, 79 5/8 In. 8050.00
Door, Louvered, Saloon, Pair 495.00
Door, Oak, Hammered Iron Hardware, Woven Iron Grating, 80 1/2 x 42 In. 220.00
Door, Saloon, Apple Green, Pair 60.00
Door, Screen, Cedar, 1907, 6 Ft. x 26 In., Pair 430.00

Door, Screen, Robin's-Egg Blue, 72 x 36 In. 95.00
Door, Swinging, Carved, Pair 300.00
Door Knocker, Woodpecker, Hubley, No. 251, 2 x 3 5/8 In. 77.00
Doorknob, Yellow Brass, Key Plate, Set 3.50
Doorknob & Escutcheons, Florals & Scrolls, Bronze, 9 1/2 In. 3220.00
Fence, Gate Posts, Art Nouveau, Cast Iron, Pair 375.00
Fence, With Gate, Wrought Iron, 34 x 70 In. 500.00
Fence Post, Octagonal Base, 49 1/2 In., Single 137.50
Figure, Lion's Head, Cast Iron 975.00
Figure, Lion's Head, Copper, Small 195.00
Floor Plate, Foliate Design, Copper Plated, 11 3/4 x 12 3/4 In. 3220.00
Frieze, Berry & Acanthus Leaf Design, Cast Iron, 87 In. 3220.00
Frieze, Stylized Geometric Pattern, Frank Lloyd Wright, 38 x 9 1/2 In. 1495.00
Gate, Bar Scene, Iron, 1920s, Each Panel 35 x 18 In., Pair 3250.00
Gate, Center Basket Issuing Flowers, Iron, 5 Ft. 3 In., Pair 6900.00
Gate, Gilt Rose Branches Upper Section, Iron, 5 Ft. 11 In. x 4 Ft. 6 In., Pair 2450.00
Gate, Scrolls & Panels, Iron, 6 x 10 Ft., 4 Sections 1840.00
Gate, Wooden, Turned Spindles, Worn Black Paint, 34 x 67 In. 104.00
Globe, Apothecary, Griffin Form Bracket, c.1900 .... 1980.00
Grille, Ceiling, Oak, Geometric Design, Frank Lloyd Wright, 36 1/2 x 7 In. 2760.00
Lamp, Street, Copper Post, Iron Wall Bracket, Trafalgar Sq., London, 36 In. 330.00
Mailbox, U.S., 1939, Restored 495.00
Mantel, Cast Iron, Reverse Painted, Inlaid Mother-Of-Pearl, Center Grate 400.00
Mantel, Dentil Carved Cornice, Garlands Of Flowers, Pine, 6 Ft. 6 In. 8050.00
Mantel, Fireplace, Side Pillars, Mirrored Top Doors, Oak, 60 x 86 In. 1500.00
Mantel, Grain-Painted, 1830 .... 550.00
Mantel, Oak, Beveled Mirror, Fruit & Flower Applied Carving 425.00
Mantel, Oak, Pillared Sides, Mirrored Doors On Top, Victorian, 60 x 86 In. 2000.00
Mantel, Painted Like White Marble, 73 x 63 In. 2400.00
Mantel, Revival, Pine, Painted, 62 1/4 x 44 1/2 In. 192.00
Mantel, White Marble, Inlaid Red Marble 5225.00
Model, Architect's, Victorian House, Turreted Roof, 1900 .... 110.00
Model, Palladian Manor House, 1844 .... 7200.00
Molding, Blocks Of Scrolling Foliage, Terra-Cotta, 10 1/2 x 22 In. 3220.00
Newel Post, Figural, Oak, 6 1/2 Ft. 3300.00
Newel Post, Mythological Face, Dark Red Finish 895.00
Newel Post, Walnut, Crystal, Mounted On Stand 165.00
Ornament, Angular Geometric Pattern, Terra-Cotta, 12 x 11 7/8 In. 1380.00
Ornament, Fence Post, Eagle, Outstretched Wings, Gilt Metal, 7 x 36 In. 935.00
Panel, Berry & Acanthus Leaf Design, Cast Iron, c.1896, 87 In. 9775.00
Panel, Martyrdom Of A Saint, Polychrome & Gilt, 39 1/2 In. 2640.00
Panel, Pantheon, Micro Mosaic, Italy, 9 x 14 1/2 In. 4730.00
Panel, St. Angelo Castle, St. Peter's In Distance, Micro Mosaic, Italy, 5 x 7 In. 2090.00
Panel, Trellis Work, Shell Designs, Riverscape Center, Italy, 5 Ft. 9 In., Pair. 4888.00
Partition, Door, Tavern Bar, Slatted Top, Paneled Base, 18th Century 3080.00
Radiator Cover, Iron, Marble, Paul Kiss, 1925, 40 x 34 x 15 In. 2300.00
Railing, Iron, Bronze, Fan-Like, Floral, Geometric, 1925, 29 In. x 7 Ft. 7763.00
Street Light, Globe, 10 Ft. 800.00
Surround, Carved, Gilt Bronze Berries, Majorelle, Walnut, 1900, 4 Ft. 11 In. 4600.00
Surround, Southern Virginia, c.1750 .... 3600.00
Toilet Seat, Oak, Varnished, Brass Hardware 14.00
Torchere Post, Iron, New York City 523.00
Valance Set, Green, Painted Scenes, 6 Piece 715.00

AREQUIPA POTTERY was produced from 1911 to 1918 by the patients of
the Arequipa Sanitarium in Marin County Hills, California.

Bowl, Closed-In Rim, 3 Panels, Stylized Leaves, Pink Glaze, Marked, 11 3/4 In. 385.00
Vase, Berries & Leaves, Mottled Green Ground, Signed, 8 1/2 In. 1900.00
Vase, Flowering Branch, Natural Ground, Ovoid, Cylindrical Neck, 1914, 8 In. 690.00
Vase, Gray Matte Glaze, Leaf Design, 6 1/2 In. 495.00
Vase, Plum Matte Glaze, Double Ribbed, Inverted Baluster, 1914, 6 In. 287.00
Vase, Raised Stylized Leaves & Vines, 6 1/4 In. 1500.00
Vase, Tan Glaze Ground, Marked, 3 1/2 In. 192.00

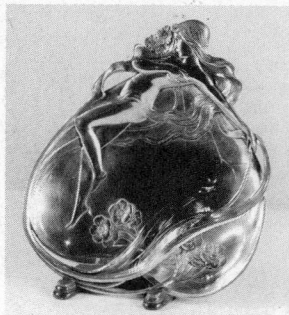

Art Nouveau, Card Tray, Nude, Flowers, Silvery Metal, WMF, 10 In.

Art Nouveau, Vase, Cupid, Nymph, Silvery Metal, WMF, 22 In.

Art Nouveau, Wine Set, Cooler, 14 In. Pitchers, Silvery Metal, WMF, 3 Piece

ARGY-ROUSSEAU, see G. Argy-Rousseau category

ARITA is a port in Japan. Porcelain was made there from about 1616. Many types of decorations were used, including the popular Imari designs, which are listed under Imari in this book.

Plate, Center Landscape, Green & Iron Red Border, Late 19th Century, 8 In.	65.00
Umbrella Stand, Blue & White, Flowers, Molded Dragon, 24 In.	385.00

ART DECO, or Art Moderne, a style started at the Paris Exposition of 1925, is characterized by linear, geometric designs. All types of furniture and decorative arts, jewelry, book bindings, and even games were designed in this style. Additional items may be found in the Furniture category or in various glass categories, etc.

Airplane, Sarsaparilla, Chrome, Cobalt Blue	150.00
Ashtray, Ball, Red & Yellow Glass	20.00
Box, Cigarette, Green Pot Metal & Glass, 1920s, 4 x 7 3/4 x 3 In.	225.00
Cigarette Case, Silver, 4 1/4 x 3 In.	80.00
Crumber Set, Brass, Blue-Green Patina, 2 Piece	25.00
Dresser Set, Perfume Atomizer, Box, Tray, Cut Glass, Ruby, 4 Piece	250.00
Mirror, Hand, Wooden Carved, From Hat Shop, Silver, Red, Black, 1920s, 16 In.	75.00
Newspaper Holder, Newsboy, Copper	60.00
Rug, Roses & Leaves, Oval Field, Fringe, Rectangular, Wool, 1930, 10 x 6 Ft.	4675.00
Sculpture, Clown Holding Roses, Bronze & Ivory, Gilt, Marble Base, 7 In.	1210.00
Traveling Set, Manicure Items, 1920s	53.00
Wall Pocket, Head, Porcelain, Pair	75.00

ART GLASS, see Glass-Art

ART NOUVEAU is a style of design that was at its most popular from 1895 to 1905. Famous designers, including Rene Lalique and Emile Galle, produced furniture, glass, silver, metalwork, and buildings in the new style. Ladies with long flowing hair and elongated bodies were among the more easily recognized design elements. Copies of this style are being made today. Many modern pieces of jewelry can be found. Additional Art Nouveau pieces may be found in Furniture or in various glass categories.

Brush & Mirror Set, Open Metal, Gold Brushed Leaves, Flowers, 13 In.	130.00
Card Tray, Nude, Flowers, Silvery Metal, WMF, 10 In. *Illus*	1200.00
Scissors, Brass & Steel, Brass Sheath, 11 In.	66.00
Vase, Cupid, Nymph, Silvery Metal, WMF, 22 In. *Illus*	6050.00
Vase, Enameled Peacock, Hammered Metal, 1900, 20 1/2 In.	3450.00
Vase, Maidens & Infants, Porcelain, Germany, Pair	900.00
Vase, Opalescent Glass, Reticulated Bronze Mistletoe, France, 1897, 17 In.	2587.00
Vase, Pottery, Buff, Bottle Shape, Dragonfly Handles, MB, 1900, 6 5/8 In.	2875.00
Wine Set, Cooler, 14 In. Pitchers, Silvery Metal, WMF, 3 Piece *Illus*	1750.00

ART POTTERY was first made in America in Cincinnati, Ohio, during the 1870s. The pieces were hand thrown and hand decorated. The art pottery tradition continued until the 1920s when studio potters began making the more artistic wares. American and English art pottery by less well-known makers is listed here. Other makers, such as Arequipa, Ohr, Rookwood, Roseville, and Weller, are listed in their own categories. More recent pottery is listed under the name of the maker or in the Pottery category.

Bowl, Fruit Basket, On Ivory Ground, Blue Rim, Byrdcliffe, 6 1/2 In.	190.00
Bowl, Raised Yellow Designs, Orange Glaze, Pine Ridge, S.D., 1937, 4 In.	120.00
Figurine, Gargoyles, On Casket, Crystalline Glaze, Pierrefonds, 5 In.	750.00
Group, Hillside, Young Couple, Boy With Birds, Flutist, Wiener Werkstatte, 11 In.	575.00
Jardiniere, Etruscan, Roman Figures, Redware, Black Matted Glaze, Signed	70.00
Lamp Base, Iridescent Blue Scene, Lessell, 8 In.	93.00
Pitcher, Exaggerated Spout, Head & Body Shaped Handle, W. Crane, 12 1/2 In.	2300.00
Planter, Molded Woman's Face, Flowers, Birds, Vance Avon, 5 x 10 In.	82.00
Powder Box, Scenic, Applied Bug, Valleris	65.00
Vase, Bison Band Borders, Geometric, Glazed, Charles Catteau, 15 3/4 In.	4025.00
Vase, Blue, Auguste Delaherche, 5 1/2 In.	950.00
Vase, Brown, Auguste Delaherche, 6 1/2 In.	950.00
Vase, Crystalline Glaze, Buff Ground, Pierrefonds, Early 1900s, 14 In.	1575.00
Vase, Glaze & Design In French Manner, France, 9 1/2 In.	160.00
Vase, Islamic Style Flowers & Foliage, Sanded Surface, 11 In., Pair	1250.00
Vase, Luster Ware, John Lessell, 1912, 9 1/2 In.	975.00
Vase, Peacock, Pine Cones, Brown, Green, 3 Handles, B. Barum, 17 In.	345.00
Vase, Purple, Auguste Delaherche, 8 In.	950.00
Vase, Sterling, Gloss Brown Over Blue-Green Drip Glaze, Walley, 3 3/8 In.	220.00
Vase, Swastika, Keramos, Luster, 10 1/2 In.	650.00

ARTS & CRAFTS was a design style popular in American decorative arts from 1894 to 1923. In the 1970s collectors began to rediscover Mission furniture, art pottery, metalwork, linens, and light fixtures from this period. The interest has continued. Today everything from this era is collectible, including jewelry, graphics, and silverware. Additional items may be found in the Furniture category, various glass categories, etc.

Bowl, Closed-In Rim, Embossed Lines, Speckled Glaze, Ted Randall, 7 1/4 In.	950.00
Bowl, Silver & Copper, Gebelein Silversmiths, Boston, 4 x 8 1/4 In.	192.00
Box, Carved & Painted Village Landscape On Lid, Oak, 3 x 5 In.	100.00
Candlestick, Hammered Copper, 2 Angular Handles, 9 x 4 3/4 In.	88.00
Chandelier, Hanging, 4 Suspending Lanterns, Slag, Iron, 22 1/2 In.	375.00
Charger, Iris, Hand-Painted Blossoms, Dragonfly, Theodore Deck, 12 In.	700.00
Desk Set, Etched & Verdigris Flying Cranes, Frost Co., 5 Piece	375.00
Frame, Egyptian, Benedict	35.00
Lamp, Electric, Copper, Abalone Leaf-Form Shade, E. Eaton Burton, 1912, 11 In.	690.00
Pitcher, Chrome Plated, Normandie, Muller-Monk, 1936, 12 In.	2530.00

Purse, Painted Flowers, Silver Clasp, Black Leather, 6 x 8 In. 77.00
Table Mat, Tooled Suede, Red Velvet Poppies, E. Eaton Burton, 28 x 19 In. 402.00
Tablecloth, Yellow Border, Tulip Designs On White, 6 Napkins, 38 x 38 In. 95.00
Tankard, Copper & Brass, Marked GBN, 12 In. 285.00
Tray, Hammered, Dragon, Pierced Handles, Oval, Fred Brosi, 32 x 19 In. 1035.00
Tray, Hammered Copper, Bone Handles, Albert Berry, 14 1/4 x 9 1/4 In. 245.00
Tray, Marsh Scene, Enamel On Copper, Round, 11 1/2 In. 75.00
Vase, Dead-Matte Brown & Terra-Cotta Glaze, Daniel Rhodes, 11 1/2 In. 1200.00
Vase, Double Bulbous Top, Textured Glaze, Daniel Rhodes, 22 In. 1500.00
Vase, Porcelain, Circles, Copper Overlay, Cylindrical, Continental, 4 3/8 In. 460.00
Wallet, Red Flowers On Swirling Stems, Leather, Paragon, 4 x 4 1/2 In. 65.00
Wood Block, Japanese Infant & Dog, Helen Hyde, Frame, 4 1/4 x 7 In. 350.00

AURENE glass was made by Frederick Carder of New York about 1904. It is
an iridescent gold or blue glass, usually marked *Aurene* or *Steuben*.

AURENE

Basket, Iridescent, Signed, 8 x 8 In. 600.00
Bowl, Blue, Signed, Steuben, 10 In. 695.00
Bowl, Calcite, Gold Interior, Steuben, 8 1/4 In. 150.00
Bowl, Flattened Circular Form, 3 Legs, Signed, Steuben, 14 In. 747.00
Bowl, Scalloped Rim, Gold, Signed, Steuben, 6 In. 322.00
Candleholder, Twisted Stem, Blue Signed, Steuben, 8 In. 325.00
Compote, Gold, No. 2642, Steuben, 5 3/4 In., Pair 825.00
Finger Bowl, Underplate, Calcite, Steuben, 2 Piece 650.00
Perfume Bottle, Blue, Steuben 750.00
Perfume Bottle, Golden Amber, Stopper, Steuben Signed, c.1920, 8 In. 345.00
Perfume Bottle, Stopper, Gold Iridescent, Steuben 450.00
Vase, Amber Iridescent, Steuben, 16 1/2 In. 5175.00
Vase, Blue Waisted Neck, Everted Rim, Ovoid, 1930, Steuben, 11 7/8 In. 1093.00
Vase, Blue, Steuben, 1920s, 6 1/2 In. 1100.00
Vase, Floriform, Ruffled Lip, Amber, Leaves, Millefiori Blossoms, No. 576, 11 In. ... 3450.00
Vase, Green Pulled Loops, Gold Iridescence, No. 209, Steuben, 4 3/4 In. 1210.00
Vase, Millefiori Design, Heart-Shaped Flowers, 1925, Steuben, 6 1/2 In. 2185.00
Vase, Red, Art Glass, Steuben, 7 x 5 1/2 In. 1100.00
Vase, Tapered Body, Flared, Blue, Signed No. 723, Steuben, 6 1/4 In. 550.00

AUTO parts and accessories are collectors' items today. Gas pump globes and
license plates are part of this specialty. Prices are determined by age, rarity,
and condition. Signs and packaging related to automobiles may also be found
in the Advertising category. Lalique hood ornaments will be listed in the
Lalique category.

Air Pump, Clock Face 1595.00
Book, Gas Ration Coupon, Issued For 1931 Model A Ford, Book-B, 1945 .... 35.00
Booklet, Ford V-8 For 1935 Through A Woman's Eyes, 16 Pages, 5 1/2 x 7 In. 35.00
Bumper Plate, U.S. Army, Brass Eagle Emblem, Enameled, Large 9.50
Car Jack, Pratt, Embossed Cast Iron 3.50
Catalog, Carb. Equipment, With Hot Spot For Chevrolet 490 .... 22.00
Catalog, General Motors Corp., Pontiac, 1941, 37 Pages 11.00
Catalog, Gofkauf's Automotive, New England, 1936, 63 Pages 8.00
Catalog, Lark, Studebaker, 1961 .... 20.00
Chart, Lube, Hupmobile 9.00
Clock, Attached To Dashboard, Chevrolet, 1950s 75.00
Clock, Built Into Mirror, Chevrolet, 1920s & 1930s 150.00
Door Sill, Mark III, Aluminum, Right & Left, Pair 70.00
Figure, Cleopatra, Watch Her Shimmy, Rear Car Window, 1950s, Box 75.00
Gas Measure, Butler, Service Station, Pour Spout, 5 Gal. 9.50
Gas Pump, Good Gulf Gasoline, Clock Face 1430.00
Gas Pump, Mobil, Bennet Electric, Upright 1950.00
Gas Pump Globe, AllFire, Security Oil Co., Red Anchor, Blue Sky 1870.00
Gas Pump Globe, American Express, Selling Agents For, Milk Glass, 16 In. 275.00
Gas Pump Globe, American Liberty Regular, Statue Of Liberty 2090.00
Gas Pump Globe, American, Statue Of Liberty, Wide Body 400.00
Gas Pump Globe, Atlantic Premium Gasoline, Milk Glass, 17 x 15 In. 200.00
Gas Pump Globe, Bell Regular, Blue Bell 1430.00

Gas Pump Globe, Ben Franklin, Premium, Regular, Picture Of Franklin 2090.00
Gas Pump Globe, Blue Sonoco Gasoline, Metal Body, 18 x 16 In. 175.00
Gas Pump Globe, Champlin Gas, Red, White & Blue, 17 In. 187.00
Gas Pump Globe, Chief Gasoline, Indian Chief, Feather In Headdress 1750.00
Gas Pump Globe, Crown, Milk Glass, 1 Piece, 15 1/2 In. 121.00
Gas Pump Globe, D-X Boron 175.00
Gas Pump Globe, Derby's Flexgas Gas, Red, Yellow & Black, 16 In. 176.00
Gas Pump Globe, Dixie Gasoline, Oils, Power To Pass 2310.00
Gas Pump Globe, Dixokine, Yellow 275.00
Gas Pump Globe, Enarco, White/Rose, Green Stripes, Little Boy In Center 375.00
Gas Pump Globe, Esalene 195.00
Gas Pump Globe, Ethyl Gasoline, Olympic Runner, Milk Glass Body, 16 1/2 In. 300.00
Gas Pump Globe, Hudson Oil Co., Transport Gasoline, White Tanker Truck 1210.00
Gas Pump Globe, Indian 525.00
Gas Pump Globe, Lion Gasoline, Lion Inserts, Milk Glass Frame, 17 x 15 In. 425.00
Gas Pump Globe, Mobil, Marine 750.00
Gas Pump Globe, Mobil, Pegasus, Gas Special 425.00
Gas Pump Globe, Mobilgas, Red Pegasus, Black Letters 300.00
Gas Pump Globe, Mutual Gasoline, Running Rabbit, Plastic Body, 17 x 15 In. 100.00
Gas Pump Globe, Petroleum Products Co., Dog-On-Good, c.1978 .... 2530.00
Gas Pump Globe, Phillips 66 Gas, Red & Black, Plastic, 16 In. 176.00
Gas Pump Globe, Phillips 66, Shield, Red, 1933 .... 300.00
Gas Pump Globe, Polly Gas 1100.00
Gas Pump Globe, Pure Oil Company, Blue & White, Metal, 19 In. 154.00
Gas Pump Globe, Red Crown Ethyl, Etched, White Glass, 1914-1931 .... 1800.00
Gas Pump Globe, Roxanna Hell, 1917, Pair 8100.00
Gas Pump Globe, Shell, Clamshell Shape 340.00
Gas Pump Globe, Sinclair, Vertical Stripe 600.00
Gas Pump Globe, Skelly, Powermax, Red & Blue On White 275.00
Gas Pump Globe, Sky Trak 125.00
Gas Pump Globe, Soline 145.00
Gas Pump Globe, Super Shell-Ethyl, Red Lettering 1045.00
Gas Pump Globe, Texaco Ethyl, Raised Lettering 1350.00
Gas Pump Globe, Texaco Ethyl, Threaded Base, Texaco Star 1980.00
Gas Pump Globe, Texaco, Clock Face 1840.00
Gas Pump Globe, Texaco, Star Embossed 450.00
Gas Pump Globe, Tioga Gasoline, Indian In Headdress 3575.00
Gas Pump Globe, Tydol, Flying A 400.00
Gas Pump Globe, Union Oil 76 .... 350.00
Gas Pump Globe, Wayne No. 60, Clock Face 1500.00
Gas Pump Globe, White Eagle, Gasoline & Oils, Hexagonal Design 375.00
Gauge, Air Pressure 130.00
Gauge, Tire Pressure, Schrader's, Brass 15.00
Hood Ornament, Donkey, Chrome, 8 In. 35.00
Hood Ornament, Fish, Glass, France, c.1920 .... 235.00
Hood Ornament, Flying Lady, Chrome, Rolls-Royce, c.1930, 5 3/4 In. 500.00
Hood Ornament, Helmeted Archer, Pierce Arrow, Bronze & Brass, 5 1/2 In. 800.00
Hood Ornament, Indian, Pontiac, Bronzed, 2 3/4 In. 500.00
Hood Ornament, Kangaroo, Babies In Pouch, Nickel 933.00
Hood Ornament, Knight's Head, Enameled Brass 3.50
Hood Ornament, Man Throwing Outsize Arrows, French 400.00
Hood Ornament, Nude Woman, Long Hair, Lying Down 12.00
Hood Ornament, Ram's Head, Art Deco, 1930s 15.00
Hood Ornament, Rocket Shape 20.00
Hood Ornament, Roman Boy, Holding Wheel & Hammer 800.00
Hood Ornament, Tiger, Ivory 800.00
Horn, Lovell, Klaxon, Hand Operated, 1908 .... 50.00
Hubcap, Auburn 30.00
Hubcap, Mercury Monterey, 1956 .... 30.00
Jack, Yellow Cab, 1920s 100.00
Key Ring, Texaco, Plastic Mileage Dial For Gallons Used, Miles Driven 12.00
Knob, Gear Shift, Triumph 10.00
License Plate, Florida, 1966 .... 3.50

License Plate, Georgia, 1938 .... 10.00 to 11.00
License Plate, Georgia, 1977 .... 3.75
License Plate, Illinois, 1940, Official State, Soybean Made Product 14.00
License Plate, John Deere 5.00
License Plate, Massachusetts, Porcelain, 1915 .... 250.00
License Plate, Mississippi, 1932, Original Wrapper 12.00
License Plate, Mississippi, 1977 .... 3.75
License Plate, Missouri, 1967 .... 3.50
License Plate, Missouri, 1969 .... 3.50
License Plate, Wisconsin, 1973, Red On White 5.00
License Plate, Wisconsin, America's Dairyland, 1963 .... 5.00
License Tag, IV Olympische Winterspiele, Enamel On Steel, 1936, 3 1/2 In. 229.00
Manual, Chevrolet, 1931 .... 25.00
Manual, Chevrolet, 1959 .... 35.00
Manual, Chevrolet, Corvette, Workshop Manual, 1968-1982, Haynes, 368 Pages 20.00
Manual, Chevrolet, Passenger Car, Owner's Manual, 1939 .... 30.00
Manual, DeSoto, 1951 .... 50.00
Manual, Dodge, 1954 .... 45.00
Manual, Olds, 1980 .... 20.00
Manual, Plymouth, 1937 .... 50.00
Manual, Volkswagen, Service Repair Handbook, 1961-1972, Clymer, 267 Pages 25.00
Mirror, Cobra, Box, 1950s 20.00
Mirror, Rear View, Pontiac, Box 18.00
Odometer, Studebaker, 1926 .... 35.00
Radiator Emblem, Dodge Bros. 30.00
Radio, Tucker, Factory Box 475.00
Registration, Michigan, 1919 .... 20.00
Sign, Gulf Oil, Touring Car, Porcelain, 2 x 5 Ft. 750.00
Sign, Pump, Blue Sunoco, Porcelain 200.00
Sign, Pump, Dynafuel, Porcelain 85.00
Sign, Pump, Flying A Service, Porcelain, Round 880.00
Sign, Pump, Flying A, Porcelain, Square 150.00
Sign, Pump, Gulf No Nox, Porcelain, Round 75.00
Sign, Pump, Mobil Premium, Porcelain, Small 75.00
Sign, Pump, Pacer 200 Hi-Test, Porcelain 250.00
Sign, Pump, Pure Pep, Porcelain 70.00
Sign, Pump, Texaco Fire Chief, Porcelain, Curved 150.00
Sign, Pump, Texaco, Truck, Porcelain, Dated 1937 .... 275.00
Sign, Pump, Tokheim Pump Service Station, Porcelain 450.00
Sign, Sinclair Gas, With Pole, 12 Ft. 650.00
Sign, Texaco, Truck, Round, 15 In. 295.00
Sign, Veedol Flying A, Flange 85.00
Steering Wheel, Model T Ford 17.50
Tag Reflector, Owl Shape, Red Eyes, Box 36.00
Tester, Battery, Cardboard Cylinder, Marked Boss, 1918 .... 25.00
Tin, Oilzum, 5 Qt. 130.00
Tire Gauge, Balloon, Goodyear Tire, 1909 .... 5.00
Tire Gauge, Brass, Leather Case 16.00
Tire Gauge, Schnader Universal, Firestone, Case, 1899 .... 25.00
Tire Gauge, Schraders, Service Station, Brass, Large 5.00
Tool Kit, Ignition, Chevrolet, Key Shape 50.00
Vase, Model T, Bracket, Marigold Glass, Pair 125.00
Wrench, Hand Brace & Connecting Rod, Model T Ford 7.00
Wrench, Head Bolt & Spark Plug, Ford Model T 3.00

AUTUMN LEAF pattern china was made for the Jewel Tea Company
beginning in 1933. Hall China Company of East Liverpool, Ohio,
Crooksville China Company of Crooksville, Ohio, Harker Potteries of
Chester, West Virginia, and Paden City Pottery, Paden City, West Virginia,
made dishes with this design. Autumn Leaf has remained popular and was
made by Hall China Company until 1978. Some other pieces in the Autumn
Leaf pattern are still being made. For more information, see *Kovels'
Depression Glass & American Dinnerware Price List.*

Baker, Fluted.	30.00
Basket, Wastepaper, Jewel Tea.	900.00
Bowl, Radiance, 9 In.	15.00
Butter, 1/4 Lb.	115.00
Butter, Cover, Winged	650.00
Candy Dish, Pedestal	495.00
Casserole, Cover	25.00
Casserole, Gold Trim, Hall	50.00
Cookie Jar, Zeisel	120.00 to 195.00
Cup, Custard, Hall	4.00
Cup & Saucer, St. Dennis, Hall	18.00
French Baker, Hall	15.00
Jug, Hall	35.00
Pitcher, Ball, Ice Lip, Hall	65.00
Pitcher, Lip, Hall, 8 In.	55.00
Salt & Pepper, Ruffled	16.00
Sugar, Jewel Tea	60.00
Teapot, Aladdin, Infuser	40.00
Tray, Hall	120.00
Tumbler, Frosted, 5 1/2 In., 6 Piece	90.00
Tumbler, Frosted, Jewel Tea	12.00

BACCARAT glass was made in France by La Compagnie des Cristalleries de Baccarat, located 150 miles from Paris. The factory was started in 1765. The firm went bankrupt and began operating again about 1822. Cane and millefiori paperweights were made during the 1860 to 1880 period. The firm is still working near Paris making paperweights and glasswares.

Bottle, Dresser, Swirl Pattern, Amberina	105.00
Box, Textured Wall, Pink Flowers, Scrolls & Lattice, Signed, Round, 5 1/4 In.	400.00
Candelabra, Spire Finials, 2 Arms Hung With Prisms, 24 1/2 In., Pair	550.00
Candlestick, Snake Entwined Base, Bamboo, Opalescent, Enameled, 8 In., Pair	2300.00
Candlestick, Vestal, c.1872, Pair	1500.00
Chandelier, 10 Scrolled Arms, Etched Hurricane Shades, Prisms, 36 In.	5290.00
Chandelier, 12-Light, Scrolled Arms, Draped With Faceted Prism Swags, 43 In.	3680.00
Cologne, Panel Cut, Stopper, 5 7/8 In.	71.00
Decanter, Cognac, Louis XIII, Protruding Scallops, Signed	275.00
Decanter, Liquor, Piccadilly	425.00
Decanter, Paneled Body, Mushroom Stopper, 11 1/2 In.	185.00
Decanter, Rose Fades To Clear, Fluted Bottle Shape, 10 1/2 In., Pair	412.00
Dresser Jar, Brass Lid, Amberina, Oval, 5 In.	55.00
Figurine, Cat, Crystal, Etched, Signed, 3 5/8 In.	120.00
Figurine, Frog, Crystal, Signed, 2 1/2 In.	75.00
Figurine, Owl, No. 764455	285.00
Figurine, Pelican, Crystal, Signed, 6 1/2 In.	110.00
Figurine, Raven, 7 In.	115.00
Figurine, Turtle, Crystal, Signed, 4 In.	65.00
Garland, Multicolored Star Cane In Circles	950.00
Inkwell, Swirl, Enameled Flower Bands	125.00
Lamp, Fairy, Pinwheel Pattern, Rose Teinte, 4 1/4 x 5 1/4 In.	265.00
Paperweight, Anemone, White Petals, Clear Ground, Star Cut Base, 2 3/4 In.	775.00
Paperweight, Black & Yellow Pansy, Pink & White Muslin Ground, 1971	350.00
Paperweight, Black Bear	95.00
Paperweight, Clematis, Pale Blue & White Buds, Clear, 2 13/16 In.	1035.00
Paperweight, Diamond & Oval Design, 2 1/2 In.	370.00
Paperweight, Different Multicolored Canes, Muslin Ground, 1968	285.00
Paperweight, Faceted Pompon, Clear, Star Cut Base, 3 1/8 In.	1725.00
Paperweight, Garland Pansy, Purple & Pale Yellow, Clear, 3 1/8 In.	1725.00
Paperweight, Millefiori, Mushroom, Clear, Star Cut Base, 3 3/16 In.	1265.00
Paperweight, Millefiori, Star & Animal Canes, 3 In.	1980.00
Paperweight, Pansy, Purple & Amber Petals, Clear, Star Cut Base, 3 1/16 In.	690.00
Paperweight, Red, White & Blue Circles, Green Canes & Ground, 2 In.	1045.00
Paperweight, Scenes Around Circle, Clear Ground, Dupont, 1920-1930	150.00
Paperweight, Stylized Flower, Clear, Canes, Upset Muslin Ground, 2 7/16 In.	2990.00

Paperweight, Sulphide, A. Stevenson, Ruby Ground 65.00
Paperweight, Sulphide, Herbert Hoover, Dark Blue 60.00
Paperweight, Sulphide, Joan Of Arc .... 70.00 to 195.00
Paperweight, Sulphide, Pope John XXIII, Amber Ground 95.00
Paperweight, Sulphide, Simon Bolivar, Amber 65.00
Paperweight, Sulphide, Woodrow Wilson 90.00
Perfume Bottle, Diorama, White, 6 3/4 In. 325.00
Perfume Bottle, Guerlain, Shalimar 150.00
Perfume Bottle, Laura, Swirl, Signed, Label 128.00
Perfume Bottle, Mal Maison 275.00
Perfume Bottle, Marcel, France, 2 3/4 x 1 1/2 In. 110.00
Perfume Bottle, Stopper Resembles Gears, Gray, Frosted, 1950s, 6 3/8 In. 633.00
Tray, Vermeil, Gold-Washed Silver Insert, Footed, 1860, Pair 4500.00
Urn, Louis XVI, Cut Glass, Gilt Bronze Mounted & Handles 4600.00
Vase, Cockatoo, Foliage, Opaline, Paper Label, 8 In., Pair 330.00
Vase, Coiled Gold Snake, Leaves, Signed, 8 In. 1500.00
Vase, Green Clover In Base, Paneled, 4 1/4 In. 50.00
Vase, Ruffled Rim, Etched Blooming Cyclamen Plants, Signed, 5 In. 325.00
Vase, Standard Headed By Bronze Leaf Tips, Scalloped, 16 In., Pair 4025.00

BADGES have been used since before the Civil War. Collectors search for examples of all types, including law enforcement and company identification badges. Well-known prison or law enforcement badges are most desirable. Most are made of nickel or brass. Many recent reproductions have been made.

Air Force Security 45.00
Chauffeur, California, 1931 .... 65.00
Chauffeur, City Of Toledo, No. 23, 1942 .... 7.00
Chauffeur, Illinois, Arrowhead, 1926 .... 35.00
Chauffeur, Indiana, Celluloid, 1925 .... 25.00
Chauffeur, Kansas, Sunflower Design, 1945 .... 20.00
Chauffeur, Michigan, 1916 .... 115.00
Chauffeur, Michigan, 1924 .... 30.00
Chauffeur, Michigan, 1937 .... 20.00
Chauffeur, New York, 1924 .... 22.50
Chauffeur, Ohio, 1947 .... 15.00
Chauffeur, Pennsylvania Special Licensed Driver, 1910 .... 200.00
Chauffeur, Quebec, 1922 .... 60.00
Chauffeur, Quebec, 1929 .... 30.00
Chauffeur, Utah, Beehive Shape, 1930 .... 110.00
Chauffeur, Vermont, 1919 .... 30.00
City Police, Plankton, S.D. 55.00
Deputy Sheriff, Escambia County, Fla. 25.00
Deputy Sheriff, Gold Plated 60.00
Driver, Teamster, 1958 .... 12.50
Fireman, Rockville Center 30.00
Gunner's Medal, Ft. McKinley, 1935 .... 24.00
Hat, 7th Cavalry, Crossed Swords, Brass 3.50
Hat, Letter Carrier, U.S. Post Office, No. 1117, Type 30.00
Highway Patrol, Florida 75.00
Hunting, New York, 1930 .... 20.00
National Air Races, 1928 .... 100.00
National Lock Co., No. 320, Shield 50.00
Pabst Breweries, No. 466 .... 50.00
Pilot, Winged Propeller, Brass, Large 4.00
Police, Miami 72.00
Post Office, U.S.A., Man Riding Horse, Red, White & Blue, No. 13452 .... 6.00
Sheriff, Florida 60.00
Sheriff, Scotland County, Mo. 65.00
Smokey The Bear, Tin 15.00
Star Of David, Israeli Military, Enameled Silver, Large 15.00
State Police, Connecticut 75.00
Texaco, Port Arthur, Tex., 1952 .... 35.00

U.S. Navy, Anchor, Gold 3.75
W.W. & Co., Iron, Padlock Shape, Brass Key Door 9.50

BANKS of metal have been made since 1868. There are still banks, mechanical banks, and registering banks (those which show the total money deposited on the face of the bank). Many old iron or tin banks have been reproduced since the 1950s in iron or plastic. Pottery, glass, and plastic banks are also listed here.

3 Coin, Tin Lithograph, Dime Register 40.00
Administration Building, World's Fair, 1933 .... 125.00
Antlered Deer, Cast Iron, Large 200.00
Auto, 1905 Ford First Delivery, Ertle Yuengling, Box 45.00
Auto, Guarantee Savings Bank, Brass 9.50
Auto, Sterling Martin, Raybestos, Ford Thunderbird #8 .... 23.00
Bank Of Thrift, 1920 .... 26.00
Battleship Iowa, Stevens 1870.00
Battleship Maine, Cast Iron 20.00
Battleship Oregon, Brown Japanning & Gold, Cast Iron, 5 In. 275.00
Bear, Domino Sugar 20.00
Bear, Snow Crest, Fiesta 15.00
Bear, With Honey & Bees, Cast Iron 150.00
Big Boy, 9 In. .... 16.00 to 35.00
Billiken, Gold & Red, Cast Iron, 4 1/8 In. 33.00
Black Boy, 2-Faced, Cast Iron, 3 In. 55.00
Black Boy, Nodder, Gold Earrings, Fruit, Pink Hat 25.00
Black Chef, Cast Iron, 8 In. 14.00
Black Man, High Hat, Nodder, Carved Wood, Dark Paint, 8 1/2 In. 44.00
Black Man, With Top Hat, Cast Iron, 4 1/2 In. 513.00
Black Woman, Painted Cast Iron, 5 3/4 In. 120.00
Bomb, Composition, 1942 .... 40.00
Book, Dated 1923, Miniature 40.00
Book, Greenpoint Savings Bank, Brooklyn, N.Y., Key, Ivory, 3 1/2 x 3 1/8 In. 8.00
Book, Rock Of Gibraltar, Prudential Insurance Company, 4 5/8 x 3 1/2 In. 15.00
Bottle, Galaxy Syrup, Interplanetary Commander, Spaceman Shape, 1950s, 3 x 8 In. 45.00
Boxer, Gold, Cast Iron, 4 3/8 In. 71.50
Boy On Trapeze, Blue Pants, Red Shirt, Barton & Smith Co., c.1891, Square, 5 In. .. 3505.00
Boy Scout, Cast Iron, 5 7/8 In. 32.50
Buffalo, Cast Iron, 4 3/8 In. 70.00
Building, City Bank, Chimney, Cast Iron, Thomas Swan, Pat. 1873, 6 5/8 In. 1650.00
Bullwinkle, Vinyl 55.00
Bust, Duke Of Wellington, Ceramic, 7 In. 45.00
Buster Brown & Tige, Cast Iron .... 165.00 to 190.00
Cadet Officer, Cast Iron 210.00
Calemeter, Bakelite & Chrome, Key 75.00
Calumet, Edward Barnes, Pat. Sept. 16, 1924 .... 330.00
Camel, Gray, Red Trim, Cast Iron, Small 140.00
Camel, Resting On Ground, Cast Iron 425.00
Campbell Kids, Cast Iron 325.00
Cap'n Crunch, Niagara Plastics, Late 1960s, 4 x 7 In. 30.00
Captain Kidd, Cast Iron, 5 In. 450.00
Case Eagle, Cast Iron 350.00
Caspar The Friendly Ghost, Hard Plastic, 1967, 12 In. 175.00
Cat, Seated, Cast Iron, c.1900 .... 250.00
Charlie The Tuna 35.00
Cleveland Indian, Stanford Pottery 145.00
Cliquot Club Ginger Ale, Eskimo, Bottle, Plaster, 1930s, 4 x 5 In. .... *Illus* 345.00
Clown, Cast Iron .... 50.00 to 60.00
Clown, Chein, Tin 75.00
Clown, Silver & Red, Cast Iron, 6 1/4 In. 72.00
Colonel Sanders, Plastic, Margardt Corp., Late 1960s, 4 1/2 x 9 1/2 In. .... 35.00 to 38.00
Conoco Man, Plastic, 5 In. 85.00
Cop, Williams, Mulligan, Cast Iron, 6 In. 325.00
Corky Pig, H.P. Co., China, 1958 .... 20.00

Bank, Clicquot Club Ginger Ale, Eskimo, Bottle, Plaster, 1930s, 4 x 5 In.

We once pulled some of the silver plating from a Sheffield candlestick when we removed the cellophane tape that held a Christmas decoration to the candlestick. A friend pulled some of the glaze from a plate when she pulled masking tape off the plate. Don't use anything with a strong glue on an antique surface.

Covered Wagon, Copper Finish, Banthrico, 4 x 3 In.	150.00
Deer, Original Paint, Label, Arcade	165.00
Delivery Truck, Meadow Gold	26.00
Dime, Prince Valient	65.00
Dinah, Yellow Dress, John Harper & Co., c.1911, 4 9/16 In.	905.00
Dog, Boston Bull, Black & White, Cast Iron, 4 3/8 In.	110.00
Dog, Bulldog, 19th Century, 4 In.	77.00
Dog, Bulldog, Mack Truck, Hard Plastic, 8 In.	25.00
Dog, Hound, Ford Motor Co. Credit Union, Union Tag Around Neck	32.00
Dog, Hushpuppies, Vinyl	35.00
Dog, Retriever, Gold Paint, Cast Iron, 5 1/4 In.	50.00
Dog, Spaniel, Stoneware, Albany Brown Glaze, c.1830, 8 1/2 In.	450.00
Dog, St. Bernard, I Hear A Call Motto On Side, Cast Iron	130.00
Dog, St. Bernard, With Pack, Large	265.00
Dog, With Backpack, Large	48.00
Dog's Head, Staffordshire, 1840s	275.00
Doghouse, Snoopy, Silver Plate	20.00
Donkey, Gillette Razor	20.00
Doughboy, Pillsbury	85.00
Doughboy, World War I, Cast Iron	350.00
Duck, Save For A Rainy Day, Cast Iron	95.00
Duck On Tub, Cast Iron	225.00
Dutch Boy Seated On Barrel, Cast Iron, 10 In.	195.00
Dutch Girl With Flower, Cast Iron	135.00
Eagle, Pottery, White	15.00
Eight O'Clock Coffee Tin, Red	6.00
Elmer Fudd, 1950s, Iron	65.00 to 110.00
Emigrant, Eagle, Ceramic, Box	55.00
Esso Gasoline, Red Plastic, 7 In.	55.00
Esso Tiger, Bust	250.00
Faith, Hope, Charity	4025.00
Fidelity Trust Vault, Iron	975.00
Fidelity Trust/Counting House, Cast Iron, J. Barton Smith Co., 1890, 6 In.	495.00
Fido On Pillow, 6 In.	550.00
Fred Flintstone, Vinyl Products, 13 In.	38.00 to 55.00
Galloping Cowboy, Battery Operated, Box	775.00
Gasoline Truck, Hess, 1984	35.00
Globe, Tin, Chein, Key	15.00
Globe Universal Stoves, Tin Lithograph, 1930s	275.00
Goat, Chalkware	150.00

Golliwog, Cast Iron 350.00
Good Luck Horse Shoe, Cast Iron 295.00
Graf Zeppelin, Silver Color, Cast Iron, 6 3/4 In. 138.00
Grinning Face, Green Glaze, White Clay, 3 In. 115.00
Gulfpride HD Select, Oil Can, 1950-1960, 2 13/16 In. 5.00
Happy Days, Barrel, Tin, Chein 20.00
Head, Phrenology, Numbered Skull Markings, Papier-Mache 155.00
Hershey Bar Vending Machine, 1950s, Box 150.00
High Score, Bowing Pin & Ball, Score Card, 300 Game, Ceramic ... 25.00
Hippopotamus, Bennington 150.00
Hockey Stick & Puck, New York Rangers, Hand Painted, Box, 1960s .... 25.00 to 28.00
Hole In One, Battery Operated, Box .... 165.00 to 200.00
Hoop-La, Clown, Dog & Barrel, Cast Iron, Harper, Willenhall, England, 1897, 8 In. .. 522.00
Horse, Front Legs Up On Drum, Cast Iron 195.00
Horse, Rearing, Crab Orchard Whiskey, Cast Iron 185.00
Horse On Tub, Cast Iron, 5 In. .... 95.00 to 365.00
Humble Oil, Tiger 30.00
Humpty Dumpty, Cast Iron 1000.00
Humpty Dumpty, Plastic, Colors 35.00
I Hear A Call, Black & Silver, Cast Iron, 5 1/2 In. 38.00
Indian, Cast Iron 33.00
Indian Scout, Cast Iron 275.00
Jack & Beanstalk, Tin 55.00
John Deere, Mailbox, Metal 80.00
Johnny Griffin, Black 95.00
King Kong, Relic Art, 1977, 13 In. 35.00
Laurel & Hardy, Plastic, 1974, 13 1/2 In. 80.00
Leap-Frog, Shepard Hardware Co., Patent 9/15/1891, 7 1/2 In. 968.00
Liberty Bell, Dark Bronze Finish, Arcade 125.00
Lion, Brown Glaze, White Clay, 3 3/4 In. 16.50
Lion, On Tub, Blue, Gold & Red, Cast Iron, 5 1/2 In. 120.00
Little Audrey, American Bisque 395.00
Little Joe, England, c.1910, 4 In. 575.00
Little Lulu, Rubber 65.00
Little Lulu, Vinyl 25.00
Little Nigger Boy, Iron 175.00
Little Red Riding Hood, Standing 325.00
Lord Fauntleroy, Fidelity Trust Vault 975.00
Magic, Yellow Building, Red Roof, J. & E. Stevens, Iron, Patent 1876, 4 3/4 In. 1695.00
Magic Mouse, Yone, Box 35.00
Majestic Radio, Cast Iron, 3 x 5 In. 95.00
Mammy, 19th Century, 5 In. 110.00
Mammy, Apron, Cast Iron, 5 In. 150.00

Mechanical banks were first made about 1870. Any bank with moving parts is considered mechanical. The metal banks made before World War I are the most desirable. Copies and new designs of mechanical banks have been made in metal or plastic since the 1920s. This year we are including some record-setting prices for groups of banks in excellent condition that were sold at auction. The high prices show how much condition determines value.

Mechanical, Always Did Spise A Mule, Cast Iron, Stevens, 1897, 10 In. .... 690.00 to 1050.00
Mechanical, Artillery, Blue Coat, J. & E. Stevens, c.1905, 6 In. 3220.00
Mechanical, Artillery, Shepard Hardware Co. 1430.00
Mechanical, Bank Of Education & Economy, Proctor-Raymond Co., Original Paper 2300.00
Mechanical, Barney Flintstone, Plastic 30.00
Mechanical, Bear & Tree Stump, Cast Iron, Judd Mfg. Co., 5 In. 690.00
Mechanical, Bear, Tin Lithograph, Saalheimer & Strauss, Germany 2300.00
Mechanical, Billy Goat, J. & E. Stevens Co. 770.00
Mechanical, Bird In House, Tin, c.1950, Germany 125.00
Mechanical, Bird On Roof, J. & E. Stevens Co. 550.00
Mechanical, Bismark Pig, J. & E. Stevens Co., 1883 .... 1485.00
Mechanical, Black Boy Dancer, Tin Plate, American, 20th Century, 7 In. 748.00
Mechanical, Boy & Bulldog, Cast Iron, Judd Mfg. Co., 1870s, 4 3/4 In. 1093.00

Bank, Mechanical, Girl Skipping Rope,
J. & E. Stevens

♦♦♦♦♦♦♦♦♦♦♦♦♦♦♦♦♦♦♦♦♦♦♦

Be sure copies of lists of valu-
ables, photographs, and other
information can be found in case
of an insurance loss. Give copies to a trusted friend. Do not
keep them in the house. If you
keep them in your safe deposit
box, be sure you have a key off
site. The key could be lost in a
house fire.

♦♦♦♦♦♦♦♦♦♦♦♦♦♦♦♦♦♦♦♦♦♦♦

Mechanical, Boy Scout 8800.00
Mechanical, Bucking Mule, Cast Iron, Judd Mfg. Co., 1870s, 4 3/4 In. 748.00
Mechanical, Bulldog, Cast Iron, J. & E. Stevens, 7 3/4 In. .... 625.00 to 800.00
Mechanical, Bulldog, Glass Eye, J. & E. Stevens, Cast Iron, c.1880, 5 5/8 In. 1100.00
Mechanical, Cabin, Cast Iron, J. & E. Stevens, 4 1/4 In. 489.00
Mechanical, Cabin, Man Kicks Coin In Cabin, J. & E. Stevens, 1883, 6 3/4 In. 2420.00
Mechanical, Cabin, Polychrome, 4 1/4 In. 632.00
Mechanical, Calamity, J. & E. Stevens Co., Repaired Foot 9350.00
Mechanical, Candy Vender, Strollwercks Victoria, No. 548, Tin, 10 1/2 In. 950.00
Mechanical, Candy Vender, Strollwercks, Penny Lane, No. 543, Tin, 6 1/2 In. 625.00
Mechanical, Cat & Mouse, Cast Iron, J. & E. Stevens, 11 3/8 In. 1840.00
Mechanical, Chief Big Moon, J. & E. Stevens, c.1905, 10 In. 1725.00
Mechanical, Chief Big Moon, Worn Paint, 10 1/8 In. 1925.00
Mechanical, Clown On Globe, Cast Iron, 1880s .... 1980.00 to 3300.00
Mechanical, Columbian Magic Savings Bank 450.00
Mechanical, Creedmore, Cast Iron, J. & E. Stevens & Co., c.1877, 10 1/8 In. 950.00
Mechanical, Creedmore, Red Aluminum Variant, J. & E. Stevens Co., Pat.1877 .... 660.00
Mechanical, Cupola, Diedrich Diekmann, J. & E. Stevens, Jan. 27, 1874, Cast Iron .. 4950.00
Mechanical, Dancing Clown, Clockwork, Tin Plate, American, 20th Century, 7 In. ... 748.00
Mechanical, Dandy Jim, Dancing Clown, Tin Plate, Unique Art, 1922, 10 In. 575.00
Mechanical, Darktown Battery, Cast Iron, J. & E. Stevens, 1888, 9 7/8 In. 4485.00
Mechanical, Dentist Pulling Black Boy's Tooth, Book Of Knowledge .... 135.00 to 265.00
Mechanical, Dinah 600.00
Mechanical, Dog On Turntable, Cast Iron, Judd Mfg. Co., 1870s, 5 In. ...... 374.00 to 1100.00
Mechanical, Eagle & Eaglets, Cast Iron, J. & E. Stevens, 1883, 6 3/4 In. ... 863.00 to 1675.00
Mechanical, Elephant & 3 Clowns 3190.00
Mechanical, Elephant & Howdah, Hubley 1934 .... 475.00 to 605.00
Mechanical, Elephant, Ru-Garnet 200.00
Mechanical, Ferris Wheel, Wheel Mounted Top Of Base, Hubley 8800.00
Mechanical, Football Player .... 500.00 to 2900.00
Mechanical, Frankenstein's Hand, Tin, Box 65.00
Mechanical, Frog, On Rock 550.00
Mechanical, Frog, Round Base, J. & E. Stevens Co., Pat. 8/20, 1872, Cast Iron, 4 In. . 357.00
Mechanical, Giant In Tower, John Harper 8250.00
Mechanical, Girl Skipping Rope, J. & E. Stevens .... *Illus* 38500.00
Mechanical, Great Garloo, Chair Medallion, Box 295.00
Mechanical, Guessing, Seated Man, McLoughlin Bros., Pat, 5/22/1877 .... 3190.00
Mechanical, Hall's Lilliput Bank, Cast Iron, 4 1/2 In. 49.50
Mechanical, Hall's, Excelsior, Yellow, Green & Red Roof, Teller, 1869, 5 In. 275.00
Mechanical, Harold Lloyd, Saalhelmer & Strauss, Germany, 1910-1920 .... 2860.00
Mechanical, Hawaii Pineapple, Cast Iron 175.00

Mechanical, Hen & Chick, Cast Iron 2310.00
Mechanical, Home Bank, Teller In Doorway 302.50
Mechanical, Humpty Dumpty, Shepard Hardware, 1884, 7 1/2 In. .... 600.00 to 4300.00
Mechanical, Independence Hall Tower, Cast Iron, 1875, 9 1/2 In. 518.00
Mechanical, Indian & Bear, Cast Iron, J. & E. Stevens, 10 1/2 In. .... 460.00 to 1320.00
Mechanical, Indian Shooting Bear, J. & E. Stevens, c.1900, 10 1/4 In. 900.00
Mechanical, Jolly Nigger, Cast Iron, c.1880 .... 475.00
Mechanical, Jolly Nigger, Stevens 9350.00
Mechanical, Jonah & The Whale, Cast Iron, Shepard Hardware, 1890, 10 1/4 In. 1610.00
Mechanical, Jonah & Whale, Shepard Hardware Co., Iron, 1890, 10 In. ..... 1600.00 to 1815.00
Mechanical, Jumbo, Black, Gold Accents, c.1884, 7 3/4 In. 845.00
Mechanical, Jumbo, Cast Iron 325.00
Mechanical, Leap Frog, Shepard Hardware, c.1890, 7 1/2 In. 3000.00
Mechanical, Lion & 2 Monkeys, Cast Iron, Kyser & Rex, 1883, 9 In. ...... 1495.00 to 3200.00
Mechanical, Lion Hunter, J. & E. Stevens Co., Pat. 8/22/1911 .... 5720.00
Mechanical, Little Jocko Musical Bank 6200.00
Mechanical, Lost Dog, Cast Iron, Judd Mfg.Co., 5 1/2 In. 690.00
Mechanical, Magic Mouse, Come Out Of Shoe, Metal 45.00
Mechanical, Magician, J. & E. Stevens Co., Pat. 1901, 7 In. 2530.00
Mechanical, Mammy Katzenjammer, Kenton Mfg. Co. 8800.00
Mechanical, Minstrel, With Verse, Germany, Pat. 6/4/1909 .... 440.00
Mechanical, Money Hungry, Tongue Comes From Teeth, Hard Plastic, Box 65.00
Mechanical, Monkey & Coconut, Cast Iron, Stevens, 1886, 8 1/2 In. .... 2185.00 to 7150.00
Mechanical, Mule Entering Barn, Cast Iron, Stevens, 1880, 8 1/2 In. .... 1610.00 to 1815.00
Mechanical, Multiplying, J. & E. Stevens Co., 1883 .... 4620.00
Mechanical, Novelty, Yellow Building, J. & E. Stevens, 1873, 4 1/4 In. 1028.00
Mechanical, Opium, Wood Carving, 1850 .... 522.00
Mechanical, Organ, Monkey Doffs Hat, Bell Noise, Kyser & Rex, Cast Iron, c.1881 1100.00
Mechanical, Organ, Monkey Tipping Hat, 2 Rotating Dancers 195.00
Mechanical, Owl Turns Head, 1880 .... 425.00 to 1250.00
Mechanical, Owl, Gray-Brown, White Highlights, Glass Eyes, No Tap, 7 1/4 In. 495.00
Mechanical, Paddy & The Pig, Cast Iron, J. & E. Stevens, 1877, 8 In. 3200.00
Mechanical, Parrot & Monkey, Tin 600.00
Mechanical, Pay Phone, J. & E. Stevens Co., Pat. 6/19/1928 .... 1320.00
Mechanical, Piano, E.M. Roche Novelty Co., Newark, N.J., 1900 .... 4070.00
Mechanical, Play Golf, Ferdinand Strauss, 1925, Box, 12 In. 460.00
Mechanical, Poverty Pup 45.00
Mechanical, Preacher, Ives, Box 7150.00
Mechanical, Professor Pug Frog's Great Bicycle Feat 9900.00
Mechanical, Punch & Judy, Cast Iron, Shepard Hardware, 1884, 7 3/8 In. 1100.00 to 5500.00
Mechanical, Rabbit, In Cabbage, 4 1/4 In. .... 360.00 to 1075.00
Mechanical, Rabbit, Standing, Japanning Traces, 5 3/4 In. 467.00
Mechanical, Robot, Starkie's Burnley, Lancaster, England, 1900 .... 3520.00
Mechanical, Rocket Ship, Silver Metal, Red Accents, Astro Co., 1950s, 13 In. 42.00
Mechanical, Rocket Ship, Spring Loaded, Fires Coin Into Nose Cone, Astro, 1950s . 32.00
Mechanical, Santa Claus, Polychrome, 6 In. 522.00

Bank, Reddy Kilowatt, Clouds, 1960s,
Plastic, 5 x 3 1/2 x 6 1/2 In.

◆◆◆◆◆◆◆◆◆◆◆◆◆◆◆◆◆◆◆◆◆◆◆

Plastic should be cleaned gently.
Wipe with a damp cloth, then
dry. Do not use an abrasive
cleaner. Soapy water can be
used.

◆◆◆◆◆◆◆◆◆◆◆◆◆◆◆◆◆◆◆◆◆◆◆

Mechanical, Smyth X-Ray, Henry C. Hart Mfg. Co., Pat. 5/31/1898 .... 4070.00
Mechanical, Snapping Bulldog, Clockwork Mechanism 4400.00
Mechanical, Spic & Span 1350.00
Mechanical, Springing Cat, Mouse, Pull String, Lead & Wood, Charles Bailey, 9 In. 6900.00
Mechanical, Stump Speaker, Brown Face, 10 In. .... 1800.00 to 2700.00
Mechanical, Tabby, Cast Iron 1675.00
Mechanical, Tammany Bank, Polychrome, J. & E. Stevens, 1873, 5 5/8 In. . 250.00 to 675.00
Mechanical, Teddy & Bear, Polychrome Paint, 9 1/4 In. .... 1210.00 to 2350.00
Mechanical, Treasure Chest 85.00
Mechanical, Trick Dog, Cast Iron, Hubley, 1920s, 8 5/8 In. 431.00
Mechanical, Trick Dog, Hubley, Pat. July 31, 1888, 8 In. 2200.00
Mechanical, Trick Dog, Shepard Hardware, c.1890, 8 1/2 In. .... 633.00 to 1495.00
Mechanical, Trick Pony .... 900.00 to 1100.00
Mechanical, Tricky Pig 797.00
Mechanical, Two Frogs, J. & E. Stevens, c.1890, 8 In. .... 1495.00 to 7150.00
Mechanical, Two Owls, Turn Heads, Cast Iron 650.00
Mechanical, Uncle Sam, Polychrome Paint, Cast Iron, 11 1/4 In. 495.00
Mechanical, Uncle Sam, Shepard Hardware, c.1890, 11 1/2 In. .... 1760.00 to 2530.00
Mechanical, Uncle Sam, With Umbrella 1200.00
Mechanical, Vender, Pascal Ambrosia Milk Chocolate, Penny Lane, No. 534, 5 In. ... 275.00
Mechanical, Whale, 1930s 605.00
Mechanical, William Tell, Cast Iron, J. & E. Stevens, 1896, 10 1/2 In. .... 345.00 to 1100.00
Mechanical, World, Tinplate, c.1900 .... 75.00
Mechanical, Zoo 1870.00
Merry-Go-Round, Cast Iron, 1930s, 4 In. 180.00
Middy, Original Paint, Cast Iron 65.00
Milk Bottle, Glass, Lock, Key Label, 1/2 Pt. 15.00
Model T Ford, Bronze Color Metal, 5 1/2 In. 90.00
Monk, Figural, Thou Shall Not Steal, Ceramic 32.00
Mutt & Jeff, Cast Iron, Gold & Silver Traces, 5 1/4 In. .... 190.00 to 285.00
My Pet, Slot In Belly Of Horse 275.00
Nestle, Bunny Money 15.00
New York Life, Calendar, Velour & Hard Plastic, 1950s, Box 50.00
OK Tire Man 65.00
Old Black Joe Beans, 1940s, 5 1/2 In. 18.00
Old South Church, Gray Building, Dark Roof, Cast Iron, 9 1/2 In. 3600.00
Orange Shape, Pottery, 3 1/8 In. 30.50
Organ Grinder, Battery Operated, Box 1050.00
Pabst, 100 Million Barrels, Tin.. 30.00
Palace, Ives 2645.00
Papoose, China, C.D. Kenny Co., Austria, 4 In. 400.00
Pass Around The Hat, Lincoln High Hat 165.00
Peanut, Jimmy Carter 35.00
Phineas T. Bluster... 40.00
Pig, Green & Orange Sponged, Pottery, 5 3/4 In. 93.50
Pig, Harley Davidson 70.00
Pig, Old Red Paint With Gold, 4 5/8 In. 50.00
Pig, R.B. Rice Sausage, Plastic 75.00
Pig, Running Tan & Brown Glaze, Pottery, 6 1/4 In. 104.00
Piggy, Dark Blue Glass 3.50
Piggy, Head Nods, Plastic, Large 38.00
Pineapple, Hawaiian Statehood Commemorative, 9 In. 193.00
Pittsburgh Glass, Block 25.00
Planter's Peanuts, Figural, Cast Iron, 11 1/2 x 5 In. 25.00
Pocket Safe, American Bank & Trust, Brass Name Plate, Mirror, Metal 100.00
Polar Bear, Pale Green Repaint, Cast Iron, 5 1/4 In. 65.00
Policeman, Die Cast Nickel Plated, 1950s 125.00
Popeye, American Bisque .... 295.00 to 350.00
Popeye, Octagonal, Dime Register, 1930s 110.00
Popeye, Tin Lithograph, Dime Register, 1956 .... 75.00
Porky Pig, Hubley 350.00
Possum, Sitting Upright, Green-Glazed, Hollow Ware Form, 5 3/4 In. 575.00
Post Office, Metal, Lithographed, Box, 3 1/2 x 5 In. 15.00

Poverty Pup, Battery Operated, Plastic, 1950s 75.00
Premium Metz Beer, Barrel Shape, Pottery 75.00
President Goldwater's Head 5.00
Puppy, Black & Red, Cast Iron, 3 7/8 In. 45.00
Quarter Register, Honest Abe 47.50
R.C.A. Serviceman, 1950s 65.00
Rabbit, Lying Down, Cast Iron, 2 In. 350.00
Rabbit, Sitting, Cast Iron, Paint Traces, 3 1/2 In. 80.00
Raggedy Ann & Andy, Plastic, 8 1/2 In. 60.00
Red Goose Shoes, Cast Iron, 4 3/8 In. 79.95
Red Goose Shoes, Gold Colored Hollow Plastic, Egg Shape, 1950s, 2 x 3 In. 40.00
Reddy Kilowatt, Clouds, 1960s, Plastic, 5 x 3 1/2 x 6 1/2 In. .... *Illus* 1605.00
Refrigerator, Electrolux, c.1950 .... 28.00
Rival Dog Food, Tin Can Shape, Lithographed 45.00
Rooster, Gold & Red, Cast Iron, 4 3/4 In. 73.50
Roy Rogers On Trigger, Rearing, Porcelain 245.00
Santa Claus, Animated, Tin Lithograph, Plush, Battery Operated, Box 60.00
Santa Claus, Battery Operated, Animated, Box 35.00
Santa Claus, Green, Pottery, 1918 .... 250.00
Santa Trimming Tree, Battery Operated, Box 150.00
Save With Pittsburgh, Corning Glass Blocks 35.00
Scooby Doo, Vinyl 40.00
Seaman's Saving Sailor, Ceramic .... 50.00 to 95.00
Sharecropper, Cast Iron, 5 1/2 In. 88.00
Shows Amount, Day Of Week, Blue, Gold, Dime Register 10.00
Sinclair, Dinosaur, Metal 135.00
Sinclair Oil Can, 1950s 18.00
Skyscraper, Black Paint, Cast Iron, 6 1/2 In. 126.50
Snoopy, Silver Plate, Box, 1958 .... 35.00
Soldier, Bobbing Head, Wooden, 10 1/2 In. 50.00
Speedy, Alka-Seltzer, Die Cut Coin Slot On Head, Vinyl, 1960s, 3 x 5 1/2 In. 240.00
Spider Man, Cookie Promotion, 6 In. 5.00
Spuds MacKenzie, Sitting, Cast Iron 8.50
Squirrel, Goebel 25.00
Stag, Cast Iron, 6 3/8 In. 71.50
Star War Set, Darth Vader, R2-D2, C-3PO, 24k Gold Plated, Box, 3 Piece 250.00
Streetcar, Cast Iron 250.00
Suitcase, Tin, Marx 75.00
Sun Maid Raisins, Top Coin Slot, Raisin Box Shape, Hard Vinyl, 1987, 6 1/2 In. 50.00
Sunoco Gas, Tin Litho 35.00
Sweet Pea, American Bisque Co. 1200.00
Sweet Thrift, Tin Lithograph, Beverly Novelty Co. 110.00
Tammany, Black Coat, Gray Trousers, J. & E. Stevens, 1873, 5 3/4 In. 270.00
Tank, A.C. Williams, Cast Iron 100.00
Tank, Cast Iron, 5 3/4 In. 170.00
Telephone, Structo, 1920s, 10 In., Box 135.00
Television Shape, ABC, Plastic, 1950s, 3 x 3 1/2 In. 50.00
Texaco Gasoline, Fat Man, Green 140.00
Thing, Addams Family, 1960s, Box .... 75.00 to 85.00
Three Little Pigs, Chein 95.00
Three Wise Monkeys, Cast Iron 335.00
Tiger, Humble Oil, Vinyl 35.00
Tootsie Roll, Hasbro, Early 1960s 35.00
Traders Bank Of Canada, A.E. Jarvis, 1891, Cast Iron, 5 x 10 x 8 3/8 In. 180.00
Treasure Chest, Pirates, Metal, Skull & Crossbones, Latch, 1950s, 4 x 3 x 3 In. 18.00
Truck, Carlisle Flea Market, Ertl 25.00
Truck, Hawkeye Motor, Ertl Heinekin, 1931, Box 25.00
Truck, Texaco 50.00
Trunk, Pioneer Life Insurance Co. 30.00
Turkey, Cast Iron, Large 375.00
U.S. Tank, Gold, Cast Iron, 4 In. 65.00
U-Haul, Truck 10.00
Uncle Mose, Cast Iron 75.00

Uncle Sam, Dime Register	25.00 to 35.00
Van, 1913 Ford Model T, Ertl Yuengling, Box	75.00
Victorian Gothic Cottage, Painted, Tin, George Brown, 1870s, 5 3/4 In.	425.00
W.C. Fields, Vinyl	25.00
Wiener Mobile, Oscar Mayer, Pull Toy Type, 1970s, 10 In.	30.00 to 45.00
William Tell, Cast Iron, J. & E. Stevens, June 23, 1896, 10 1/2 In.	770.00
Windup, Coffin, Yone, Box	100.00
World Globe, Columbian Exposition, Lithographed, 1893	325.00
World's Fair, 1939, Figural Typewriter	50.00
Yellow Cab, Arcade, c.1921, 7 3/4 In.	655.00
Zoo, Kyser & Rex Co., Cast Iron, c.1894, 4 1/4 In.	2050.00

BANKO, Korean ware, and Sumida are terms that are often confusing. We use the names in the way most often used by antiques dealers and collectors. Korean ware is now called *Sumida Gawa* or *Sumida* and is listed in this book in the Sumida category. Banko is a group of rustic Japanese wares made in the nineteenth and twentieth centuries. Some pieces are made of mosaics of colored clay, some are fanciful teapots. Redware and other materials were also used.

Group, Monkeys, 4 In.	385.00
Vase, Carved Terra-Cotta Teahouse Landscape, Brown Glaze, 2 3/4 x 4 1/2 In.	42.00
Vase, Contorted Face, Grayware, c.1920, 2 1/2 In.	115.00

BARBED WIRE was first patented in 1867. Collectors want eighteen-inch samples.

Concave Tail, 1885	200.00
Dent, Barbed Strip, 1897	200.00
Diamond Pin Wire, Underwood, 1884	200.00
Giant Three Strand, Wermley, 1875	200.00
Serpent Wire, Carpenter, 1882	300.00
Serrated Triangle Fence Rod, Beresford, 1891	100.00
Split Diamond, Crowell, 1879	200.00
Spread With Barb, Ellwood, 1882	200.00
Wheel Barb, Bacon, 1884	200.00
Wooden Rail, Carpenter, 1873, Per Inch	20.00

BARBER collectibles range from the popular red and white striped pole that used to be found in front of every shop to the small scissors and tools of the trade. Barber chairs are wanted, especially the older models with elaborate iron trim.

Brush, Neck, Long Handle, Hanging Clip, 13 1/2 In.	8.00
Brush, Neck, Varnished Wooden Handle, Marked Sterilized U.S.A.	8.00
Can, Shaving Soap, Colgate, Contents	8.00
Chair, Child's, Horse Head, Green Porcelain	1895.00
Chair, Child's, Horse's Head To Hold Onto, 19th Century	2850.00
Chair, Emil Padiar	350.00
Chair, Green Leather Seat, Oak	1800.00
Chair, Hercules, Cast Iron, Oak, 1901	300.00
Chair, Koch, Porcelain & Leather, Maroon & Tan, 24 x 46 x 40 In.	880.00
Chair, Koken, Leather, Porcelain Trim	750.00
Chair, Koken, White Porcelain, Chrome Trim, Hydraulic Pump, 1940s	650.00
Chair, Koken, White Porcelain, Leather Cushions, 24 x 52 x 36 In.	209.00
Chair, Lion's Head, Walnut	950.00
Chair, Oak, Dated 1873	500.00
Chair, Oak, Victorian, 1890	2000.00
Chair, Pleated Seat, Oak, 46 x 27 x 44 In.	1450.00
Chair, Swan Arms, Spread Eagle Underneath, c.1860	950.00
Clipper, Hand, Pranafa, Small	5.00
Globe, Red, White & Blue Stripes, 4 In.	40.00
Hair Net, Bestyette Real Human Hair, 1930	2.50
Hair Net, Duro Belle Bob Human, 1920s	3.00
Pole, Gilt & Paint, 19th Century, 23 1/2 In.	1980.00
Pole, Glass & Porcelain, Steel, Electrified, 16 x 96 In.	935.00

Pole, Koch, Revolving, Yellow & Green 475.00
Pole, Koken, Leaded Glass, 48 In. .... 975.00 to 1100.00
Pole, Koken, Red, White & Blue, 1909, 108 In. 2995.00
Pole, Marvey, Top Light, 1950s 600.00
Pole, Milk Glass, Painted, Ball, Cast Iron, Lighted, 25 In. 303.00
Pole, O.A. Kochs Co., Milk Glass, Red Stripes, Electrified, 20 3/4 In. 193.00
Pole, Plaster Gold Ball, Red & White Stripes, c.1940, 45 In. 450.00
Pole, Red & White Stripes, Green Iron Wall Mounts, 4 Ft. 415.00
Pole, Stained Glass, Wall Mount 1275.00
Pole, Striped, Porcelain, 52 In. 90.00
Pole, Wooden, Painted, 48 In. 295.00
Rack, Razor Blades, Gillette, Clamped To Top Of Cash Register 60.00
Scissors, Carl Monkhouse, Hammered Finish Shanks, Germany 5.00
Scissors, Pebbled Handle, Sheffield 8.00
Shaving Brush, Badger, Marbleized Catalin Handle 15.00
Shaving Brush, Ershine, Ivory 15.00
Shears, Thinning, Soligen, West Germany 6.50
Sign, Cast Iron, Screws To Wall, 4 3/8 x 13 1/2 In. 145.00
Soap, Colgate, 8 Unused Cakes, 1920 .... 30.00
Sterilizer, Glass, Metal Lid 45.00

BAROMETERS are used to forecast the weather. Antique barometers with elaborate wooden cases and brass trim are the most desirable. Mercury column barometers are also popular with collectors. It is difficult to find someone to repair a broken one, so be sure your barometer is in working condition.

Abatte, England, Inlaid Mahogany, 1830s, 40 1/2 In. 660.00
Banjo, George III Style, Inlaid Mahogany, Floral & Shell Medallion, 37 In. 165.00
Banjo, Rosewood Veneer, England, B. Riva Langefin, 19th Century 412.00
Black Forest, Thermometer Top, Dated 1933 .... 165.00
Broken Swan's-Neck Pediment, Inlaid Baluster, J. & N. Lettey, 38 1/2 In. 1495.00
Center Clock, Thermometer In Neck, Gilt Bronze, Mahogany, 44 1/4 In. 9200.00
D. Stampa, Edinburgh, Mahogany, 19th Century, 39 In. 1430.00
E.C. Spooner, Boston, 1850s, 42 In. 220.00
Eagle Crest, Carved Wood & Plaster, French, 36 In. 605.00
English, Inlaid Wood, Dated 1820s 850.00
George III, Thermometer, Lione & Somalvico, Mahogany, 1770s, 36 In. 2875.00
H. Abraham Optician, Liverpool, Walnut & Walnut Veneer, 29 1/4 In. 935.00
Inlaid Satinwood, Mahogany, James Gally, c.1830, 36 In. 2200.00
Joseph Solcha, Engraved Steel Dial, England, 39 In. 520.00
Louis XVI, Painted & Parcel Gilt, Urn Finial, Ronquelle Of Paris, 40 In. 1650.00
Neoclassical, Thermometer Above, Acorn Terminal, Giltwood, 40 1/4 In. 1380.00
Stick, George III, Bowed Glass Panel, Cary, 1830s, 40 In. 2530.00
Stick, George III, Provincial, Mahogany, John Ballard, Nuneaton, c.1800, 36 In. 2530.00
Thermometer-Hydrometer, Chart Recording 75.00
Victorian, Gold, Wishbone Shaped Holder, 30 In. 25.00
Walnut, Rope Carved, England, 5 1/2 In. 80.00
Wheel, George III Style, J. Schalfino, Taunton, 19th Century 412.50
Wheel, George III, Mahogany, 38 In. 357.50
Wheel, Victorian, Carved Leaves, 7 1/2 In. 302.50

BASKETS of all types are popular with collectors. Indian, Japanese, African, Shaker, and many other kinds of baskets can be found. Of course, baskets are still being made, so the collector must learn to tell the age and style of the basket to determine the value.

Bushel, Wooden, Bail Handle, Quarter Size 3.50
Buttocks, Albra Lord, Handles, 11 1/2 In., Pair 880.00
Buttocks, Splint, Bentwood Handle, 10 1/2 x 11 1/2 In. 71.00
Buttocks, Splint, Bentwood Handle, 13 x 17 1/2 In. 126.00
Buttocks, Splint, Bentwood Handle, Square, Weathered, 13 x 14 In. 71.50
Buttocks, Splint, Rectangular Rim 60.00
Buttocks, Splint, Worn Black Paint, 15 x 17 x 9 In. 137.00
Cheese, Splint, 15 In. 126.00

Cheese, Splint, White Repaint, 16 In. 27.50
Corn Drier, Rye, Round, Large 110.00
Egg, Wicker, Notched Handles, Round, 11 1/2 In. 135.00
Gathering, Oak, Round 225.00
Gathering, Splint, 2 Bentwood Handles, Ovoid 90.00
Gathering, Splint, Bentwood Handle, 17 x 27 In. 71.00
Goose Feather, Domed Lid, Woven Splint, Bentwood Rim Handles, 25 In. 77.00
Herb Drying, Splint, Open Weave Base, Bentwood Rim Handles, 16 x 7 In. 236.00
Laundry, Splint, 22 x 40 x 12 In. 60.50
Laundry, Splint, Dark Blue Paint, Bentwood Rim Handles, 18 1/2 x 29 x 14 In. 385.00
Laundry, Splint, Rectangular, 21 x 31 x 10 In. 71.00
Laundry, Splint, Ribbed, Open Rim Handles, 20 x 24 x 11 In. 93.50
Melon, Splint, Handle, 12 x 10 In. 99.00
Nantucket, c.1900, 7 1/2 In. 605.00
Nantucket, Carved Swing Handle, Oval, 15 1/2 In. 605.00
Nantucket, Cover, Handle, Paul Whitten, 1968 .... 440.00
Nantucket, Oval, c.1900, 12 In. 880.00
Nantucket, Paper Label, Sands Bury On South Shoal Lighthouse, 11 x 7 1/8 In. 825.00
Nantucket, Swing Handle, 3 1/2 x 5 In. 770.00
Nantucket, Swing Handle, Incised Base, Massachusetts., 9 In. Diam. 550.00
Pack, Splint, Web Harness 55.00
Pie, Ash Splint 60.00
Potato Stamp, Cover, Blue Painted, 19th Century, 30 In. 2250.00
Potato Stamp, Cover, Indian, Rectangular, Large 88.00
Round Painted Panels, Boy With Kite, Japanese, 6 x 14 1/2 In. 125.00
Rye, Straw, Nested, Pennsylvania, 19th Century, 12, 11 & 9 In., 3 Pieces 275.00
Rye Straw, Bentwood Handle 145.00
Rye Straw, Rim Handles, Partially Restored, Side Handles, 18 x 9 In. 104.00
Splint, Double Wrapped Rim, 2 Carved Handles, 12 x 18 In. 121.00
Splint, Early 19th Century, 16 x 10 In. 88.00
Splint, Natural Patina, Faded Blue, Square, 12 x 12 x 4 1/2 In. 198.00
Splint, Natural, Wooden Base, H.S.B. In Red Paint, 15 x 11 1/2 In. 60.50
Splint, Old Green Paint, Polychrome Fruit, 4 3/4 x 9 1/4 In. 105.00
Splint, Single Wrapped Rim, Hand Carved Handles, Pencil Signed, 12 x 15 1/2 In. ... 220.00
Splint, Swing Handle, Round 70.00
Splint, Wooden Base, Bentwood Rim Handles, Weathered, 11 x 10 1/2 In. 38.50
Swing Handle, 19th Century, 11 1/4 x 8 In. 22.00
Wall, Half Round, Green 550.00
Wicker, Marked Charles & Company Grocers & Fruiter, New York, Handle 45.00

BATCHELDER products are made from California clay. Ernest Batchelder
established a tile studio in Pasadena, California, in 1909 and expanded until
in 1916 he built a larger factory with a new partner. The Batchelder-Wilson
Company made all types of architectural tiles, garden pots, and bookends.
The plant closed in 1932. In 1936 Batchelder opened Batchelder Ceramics,
also in Pasadena, and made bowls, vases, and earthenware pots. He retired in
1951 and died in 1957. Pieces are marked *Batchelder Pasadena* or
Batchelder Los Angeles.

BATCHELDER
LOS ANGELES

Ashtray, Hexagonal Bowl, Light Blue Glaze, 1926, 4 1/2 In. 165.00
Bowl, Advertising, 2 x 4 In. 420.00
Tile, Blue & Purple, Square, 2 3/4 In. 28.00
Tile, Geometric Design, Black & Orange, Square, 4 In. 38.00
Tile, Geometric Design, Black & Tan, Square, 4 In. 38.00
Tile, Tree By A Brook, Blue & Green, Matte Glaze, 8 x 8 In. 357.00
Vase, Mottled Chinese Red & Green Glaze, Marked, 11 In. 1000.00
Vase, White Dripping Glaze, Blue-To-Green Body, 5 x 4 In. 440.00

BATMAN and Robin are characters from a comic strip by Bob Kane that
started in 1939. In 1966, the characters became part of a popular television
series. There have been radio and movie serials that featured the pair. The
first full-length movie was made in 1989.

Bank, Figural, 1974 .... 35.00
Bank, Figural, Robin, Box, 1966 .... 75.00

Batboat, Plastic, Replica From T.V. Series, Corgi, 1966, 5 In. 39.00
Batchute, Plastic, 27-In. Parachute, 1966 .... 58.00
Batcraft, Battery Operated, Marx, 1966, Box 225.00
Batmobile, Battery Operated, Batman & Robin, Alps, 11 1/2 In. 400.00
Batmobile, No. 267, Corgi, 1973, 5 In., Box 95.00
Batmobile, With Batman & Robin Figures, Mego, 1979 .... 200.00
Book, Coloring, Whitman, 1967 .... 15.00 to 30.00
Bowl, Cereal, Joker, Plastic, Sun Valley, 1966, 5 In. 29.00
Car-Boat, Corgi, Box 295.00
Clock, Alarm, Talking .... 40.00 to 75.00
Comic Book, No. 9 .... 895.00
Compass, Wrist, On Card, 1966 .... 25.00
Container, Batman Orange Drink 12.50
Container, Slam Bang Vanilla Ice Creamer 17.50
Costume, Box 20.00
Figure, Joker, Mego, 1979, 3 3/4 In. 40.00
Figure, Lex Luthor, Mego, 1979, 3 3/4 In. 15.00
Flashlight, On Card, 1980s 12.00
Frisbee, Bat Logo 20.00
Game, Batman, Board, Milton Bradley, Adam West Autograph, 1966 .... 165.00
Game, Batman, Hasbro, 1978 .... 32.00
Lunch Box, Prototype Kit, 1985 .... 863.00
Mask, Batman-Robin, Reversible, Cardboard, 1966 .... 15.00
Model, Batmobile, Aurora, Box, 1966 .... 275.00
Mug, Red Robin & Black Batman, 1966, Pair 35.00
Night-Light, Figural, Marked DC Comics 4.25
Night-Light, Yellow Plastic, Logo, 1966 .... 22.00
Pennant, Batman & Robin, Felt, 1966, 29 In. 18.00
Pix-A-Go-Go, Full Of Fun, c.1966 .... 50.00
Planter, Batman Super Plants, 1976 .... 20.00
Puppet, Hand, 1966, 11 In. 30.00
Puppet, Hand, Ideal, 1966, 12 In. .... 60.00 to 79.00
Puppet, Hand, Vinyl Body, 1966 .... 45.00
Puzzle, Jigsaw, 1966 .... 40.00
Puzzle, Jigsaw, Action Scene, England 75.00
Radio, Wrist, Box 70.00
Record, 33 1/3 RPM, 1975 .... 10.00
Slippers, 1966 .... 35.00
Thermos, Batman & Robin, Scene, Lithograph, Steel, Aladdin, 1966, 7 In. 49.00
Troll, Wishnik, 1960s 95.00
Utility Belt, Gun, Handcuffs, Ideal, 1966 .... 1500.00
Walkie-Talkie, Unopened Package 45.00
Wristwatch, Robin, Timex, 1978 .... 150.00

BATTERSEA enamels, which are enamels painted on copper, were made in
the Battersea district of London from about 1750 to 1756. Many similar
enamels are mistakenly called *Battersea*.

Box, Blue, Wreath, Absent, Not Forgotten On Top, Mirror Cover, 1 1/8 x 1 5/8 In. 190.00
Box, Patch, Floral, Inscription 195.00
Box, Pink, Roses, Late 1800s, 1 3/4 x 2 3/4 In. 80.00
Tieback, Enamel Mirror, Portrait, General Washington, 1830s, 2 In. 1325.00

BAUER pottery is a California-made ware. J.A. Bauer moved his Kentucky
pottery to Los Angeles, California, in 1909. The company made art pottery
after 1912 and dinnerwares marked *Bauer* after 1929. The factory went out of
business in 1962.

Bowl, Ring, Green, 9 In. 30.00
Bowl, Ring, Orange, 4 In. 15.00
Butter, Cover, Monterey, Yellow 65.00
Carafe, Coffee, Blue, 1930s, 9 In. 130.00
Casserole, Cover, La Linda, Green, Copper Holder 75.00
Chop Plate, Orange 12.00
Chop Plate, Ring, Yellow, 13 In. 45.00

Coffee Server, Orange, Red, Plain	50.00
Coffeepot, Yellow Ring	60.00
Cookie Jar, Dutch Boy & Girl	50.00
Cornucopia, Double, Light Blue, White Interior, 6 1/4 x 11 1/4 In.	40.00
Creamer, La Linda, Maroon	25.00
Cup, La Linda, 6 Piece	45.00
Cup, Tea, Green, 1930s	40.00
Flowerpot, Attached Saucer	15.00
Mixing Bowl, Yellow, 9 1/2 In.	20.00
Pie Plate, La Linda, Copper Holder, 10 1/2 In.	35.00
Pitcher, Barrel, Iced Tea, Burgundy	85.00
Pitcher, Ice Lip, La Linda, Signed, 1940s, 6 In.	120.00
Planter, Orange, Matt Carlton, 1930s, 3 x 8 In.	35.00
Planter, Swan	25.00
Plate, Jade, 15 In.	30.00
Punch Bowl, Burgundy	200.00
Relish, 5 Sections, Orange, Signed, 1930s, 10 In.	125.00
Salt & Pepper, Green, 1930s, 2 In.	40.00
Sauceboat, Black, 1930s, 3 In.	250.00
Sugar, Cover, Light Green	30.00
Teapot, Rings, Yellow, Large	37.50
Tray, Monterey, Burgundy, Rectangular	55.00
Tumbler, Burgundy, 12 Oz.	25.00
Vase, Fan, Leaf Shape, Art Deco, Turquoise Glaze, Footed, 13 3/4 x 10 1/4 In., Pair	95.00
Vase, Handles Near Shoulder, Green, Carlton, 1930s, 8 In.	600.00
Vase, Orange, 1930s, 12 In.	350.00
Vase, Pillow, White	495.00
Vase, Red-Orange, Fred Johnson, 1940s, 14 In.	650.00
Vase, Ruffled Rim, White, 1930s, 8 In.	450.00

BAVARIA is a region in Europe where many types of porcelain were made. In the nineteenth century, the mark often included the word *Bavaria*. After 1871, the words *Bavaria, Germany* , were used. Listed here are pieces that include the name *Bavaria* in some form, but major porcelain makers, such as Rosenthal, are listed in their own categories.

Basket, Hand Painted Roses, Scrolls, Scalloped, Z & Co., 5 1/4 x 4 In.	36.00
Bowl, Panels, Flower Spray, Scalloped, Marked, 9 1/4 In.	22.00
Bowl, Prospect Point, Niagara Falls, Reticulated, Schwarzenburg, 5 1/4 In.	4.00
Cake Plate, Swans, Water Lilies, Raspberry, Gold Tracery, 12 1/2 In.	125.00
Coffee Set, Gold & Lavender Leaves, Royal Heidelberg, 12 Piece	42.00
Coffee Set, Multicolor Floral, Melon Ribbed, Creidlitz, 3 Piece	125.00
Compote, Underplate, Reticulated, Multicolored Flowers, Schumann	220.00
Dish, Oak Leaf, Pink Blossoms, Gold Stem, Old Nuremberg, 4 1/2 x 11 In.	20.00
Plate, Arts & Crafts Fashion, Repeating Design, 12 In.	95.00
Plate, Fruit, Gold Tracery Border, Millerteich, Set Of 12	150.00
Plate, Red Poppies, Gold Beading & Trim, Leaves, Pastel Ground, 6 1/2 In.	15.00
Tea Set, Allover Flowers, Scalloped, 3 Piece	115.00
Vase, Dome Cover, Urn Shape, Floral Spray, Gold Trim, Waldershof, 12 x 7 In.	55.00
Vase, Large Floral Spray, Gold Trim, Waldershof, 12 x 6 In., Pair	115.00

BEATLES collectors search for any items picturing the four members of the famous music group or any of their recordings. Because these items are so new, the condition is very important and top prices are paid only for items in mint condition. The Beatles first appeared on American network television in 1964. The group disbanded in 1971. Ringo Starr, George Harrison, and Paul McCartney are still performing. John Lennon died in 1981.

Alarm Clock, Yellow Submarine, Sheffield	480.00
Album Cover, Meet The Beatles, Signed On Back, 12 1/2 In.	1760.00
Award, Single Album, I Want To Hold Your Hand, Framed, 17 x 13 In.	2990.00
Award, Single Album, You're Sixteen, Ringo Starr, Framed, 17 In.	748.00
Bag, Booty, Pictures All 4, Vinyl, 1964, 10 1/2 x 15 In.	100.00
Bank, Drum	15.00
Bank, Make A Deal With The Beatles, Plastic	65.00

Beatles, Glass,   Beatles, Glass,   Beatles, Glass,   Beatles, Glass,
John, Bust   George, Bust   Paul, Bust   Ringo, Bust

Bank, Ringo, Composition 400.00
Book, All About The Beatles, No. 1, 1964, 74 Pages 20.00
Book, Authorized Biography, Hunter Davies, McGraw-Hill, 1968, 372 Pages 25.00
Book, Punch-Outs, Yellow Submarine 115.00
Bottle, Soap Bubbles, NEMS Enterprises, Unused, 1964 .... 35.00
Carrying Case, White Handle, Black & White Group Photo, Airflite, 1960s 650.00
Case, Disk Go, Yellow, 1960s 125.00
Clock, Alarm, Yellow Submarine, Clapper Bells, Sheffield, 1960s, 4 In. ...... 850.00 to 1230.00
Coloring Book, Saalfield, 1960s 65.00
Comic, Official Beatles Comic Book, 8 Pin-Up Pictures, Dell, 1964 .... 180.00
Doll, Bobbin' Head, Gray Suits, Carmascot Inc., 1964, Box, 8 In., 4 Piece 1725.00
Doll, Paul, No Guitar, 1964, 4 1/2 In. 40.00
Doll, Set Of 4 Stuffed Cloth 175.00
Drum, Ringo 675.00
Figurine, Set Of 4 Ceramic, Blue Suits, Brown Guitars, 1960s, 6 1/2 In. 175.00
Figurine, Vinyl, Remco, 4 Piece 335.00
Game, Flip Your Wig, Milton Bradley, 1964, 9 1/2 x 19 In. .... 75.00 to 145.00
Glass, George, Bust .... *Illus*   88.00
Glass, John, Bust .... *Illus*   91.00
Glass, Paul, Bust .... *Illus*   88.00
Glass, Ringo, Bust .... *Illus*   91.00
Glass Set, Beatle On Each, Musical Notes & Record, NEMS, Set Of 4 .... 425.00
Hair Spray 600.00
Halloween Costume, Body Suit, Beatles Yellow Submarine, 1968 .... 125.00
Jigsaw Puzzle, England, 17 x 11 In. 185.00
Kit, Fan Club, Photos, Stickers, Bulletin, 1964 .... 30.00
Lunch Box, Blue, 1966 .... 250.00 to 575.00
Lunch Box, Metal, Thermos, Aladdin, 1965 .... 275.00 to 350.00
Lunch Box, Yellow Submarine, Metal, King Seeley, 1969 .... 300.00 to 375.00
Magazine, Young Miss, February 1967 .... 15.00
Mirror, Celluloid, Group Picture, 1964, Pocket 3.50
Model, Kit, Paul McCartney, The Great McCartney, Revell, 1964, 6 x 9 1/2 In. 250.00
Model, Kit, Ringo, Revell, 1964 .... 225.00
Model, Kit, Yellow Submarine, 1966, Box 195.00
Nodder, Bobbin' Head Beatles, Plastic, Carmascot Inc., 1964, 14 In. Figures 3000.00
Nodder, Ringo, Carmascot Inc., Early 1960s 175.00
Nodder Set, Plastic, Package, 4 Piece 15.00
Photograph, Autographed, All Members, Framed, 16 x 18 In. 1870.00

Photograph, Autographed, All Members, Holding Teacups, Framed, 8 1/4 In. 1955.00
Pillow, Red, White, Blue, Black Picture, Signatures, Saltzman Corp., 12 In. 150.00
Pin, Guitar & Drum, Medallion Of Beatles Picture Hanging On Card, 1964 .... 25.00
Pin, I'm An Official Beatles Fan 10.00
Pin, Ringo Starr 15.00
Pin, Yellow Submarine 50.00
Pin, Yellow Submarine, Dated 1968, 3 1/2 In. Diam., 4 Piece 28.00
Postcard Set, 1964, 8 Piece 25.00
Poster, A Hard Day's Night 165.00
Poster, Candlestick Park, Here Come The Beatles, Aug. 29, 1966, 24 x 17 1/4 In. 1495.00
Poster, Movie, Yellow Submarine 625.00
Puzzle, Sergeant Pepper Band, Jaymar, 650 Pieces 150.00
Record, Album, Let It Be, Apple Records 20.00
Record, Album, Meet The Beatles, Capitol Records, First Pressing 35.00
Record, Album, Something New, Capitol Records 25.00
Ring, Blue Flasher, Set Of 4 .... 30.00
Rug, 22 x 34 In. 326.00
Ruler, 1964 .... 12.00
School Bag, Plastic, Paper Insert 25.00
Sheet Music, Day Tripper, 1964 .... 50.00
Sheet Music, Michelle, McCartney, 1965 .... 10.00
Sheet Music, Please, Please Me, Photo Cover, 1964 .... 18.00
Skateboard, Wood, Surf Skater Co., 1965, 19 x 6 In. 145.00
Sketch, John Lennon, Pen & Ink On Paper, Framed, c.1976, 20 x 23 In. 935.00
Soaky, Paul & Ringo, NEMS, Colgate Palmolive, 1965, Box, Pair 450.00
Soaky, Ringo, 1965 .... 75.00 to 85.00
Stationery, Yellow Submarine, 32 Piece 100.00
Stockings, Original Package 75.00
Sweatshirt, White, NEMS, 1963 .... 150.00
Tie Tack, 4 Raised Faces, On Card, 1964 .... 20.00
Tie Tack, Ringo, On Card, 1964 .... 25.00
Toy, Bongos, Red, Black & White Drawing Of Group, Mastro, 1960s 3000.00
Toy, Colorforms, Cartoon Kit 470.00
Toy, Guitar, Electric, Red Jet, Red & Cream, Amp Plug, Selcol, 31 In. 1400.00
Toy, Guitar, Pink, 6 Strings, Mastro, 30 In. 650.00
Toy, Swingers Music Set, Plastic Figures, With Instruments, Microphones, Box 175.00
Toy, Yellow Submarine, Pop-Up Figures, Corgi, 1969, 5 1/4 In. .... 175.00 to 375.00
Tray, 4 Photographs, Fab 4, Tin, England, 1964, Square, Unused 20.00
Tray, Pictures, Tin, 1960s 95.00
Wig, Red Card, Plastic Bag, Lowell Toys, 1964 .... 68.00 to 100.00
Wrapper, Krunch Coated Ice Cream Bar, c.1960 .... 40.00
Wristwatch, John Lennon 40.00

BEEHIVE, Austria, or Beehive, Vienna, are terms used in English-speaking
countries to refer to the many types of decorated porcelain bearing a mark
that looks like a beehive. The mark is actually a shield, viewed upside down.
It was first used in 1744 by the Royal Porcelain Manufactory of Vienna. The
firm made porcelains, called *Royal Vienna* by collectors, until it closed in
1864. Many other German, Austrian, and Japanese factories have reproduced
Royal Vienna wares, complete with the original shield or *beehive* mark. This
listing includes the expensive, original Royal Vienna porcelains and many
other types of beehive porcelain. The Royal Vienna pieces include that name
in the description.

Compote, Cupid In Wagon Pulled By Maidens, Gold Border, Marked, 9 1/4 In. 245.00
Plaque, Biblical Subject Frame, 22 x 19 In. 2970.00
Plaque, White Water Lilies, Shaded Ground, Gold Rim, Marked, 9 1/2 In. 45.00
Plate, 3 Women, Cherub, Gold, Austria, 9 1/2 In. 50.00
Plate, Diana Et Endymeon, Marked, 10 In. 160.00
Plate, Portrait, Woman, Gold Shell & Scroll Rim, Square, 9 1/2 In. 450.00
Plate, Portrait, Woman, Marked, 11 In. 155.00
Platter, Boar Hunting Scene 2200.00

Beehive, Vase, Throne Room, Classical Women, Cobalt Ground, 24 In.

Several types of glue are needed to repair broken pottery and porcelain. Commercial glues found in a local hardware store are often satisfactory. Read the labels. Some types work only with pieces that are porous, others only with pieces that are not porous. Instant glue is difficult to use if the break is complicated.

Tray, Handles, Kauffmann, 16 1/2 In. 135.00
Urn, Cover, Painted, Cherubs, Putti, Gilt Handles, Late 19th Century, 19 In. 2530.00
Vase, Meditation, 3 1/2 In. 395.00
Vase, Portrait, Woman, Blue Gown, Center Reserve, Marked, 8 1/2 In. 595.00
Vase, Throne Room, Classical Women, Cobalt Ground, 24 In. .... *Illus* 11000.00
Vase, Woman, Flowing Hair, Gilt Flowers, Beading, Maroon Luster, 9 3/4 In. 1095.00

BEER CANS are a twentieth-century idea. Beer was sold in kegs or returnable bottles until 1934. The first patent for a can was issued to the American Can Company in September of that year; and Gotfried Kruger Brewing Company, Newark, New Jersey, was the first to use the can. The cone-top can was first made in 1935, the aluminum pop-top in 1962. Collectors should look for cans in good condition, with no dents or rust. Serious collectors prefer cans that have been opened from the bottom.

Aristocrat 30.00
Billy Beer .... 2.00 to 4.00
Blitz Weinhard, Blue 45.00
Burgermeister, Picture Label, 1 Qt. 90.00
Cooke's, Cherokee 173.00
Duquesne Keg-A-Beer, Concave Bottom 156.00
Edelweiss, Cone, 1 Qt. 65.00
Fox DeLuxe Bock 100.00
Ilser's, Cone, 1 Qt. 65.00
Krueger Ale 80.00
Mr. Lager 185.00
Maverick, Buckner, Mo., Unopened 2.00
Milwaukee Club 60.00
O'Keefe's Old Vienna Style 193.00
Oerteis 92, Cone Top 25.00
Red Top, Cone 75.00
Robin Hood 35.00
Schlitz, Cone, 6 Pack 160.00
Schmidt's Ale, Cone, 1 Qt. 25.00
Stag's Head Ale 45.00
World's Fair, Set, Empty Bottom, 1982 .... 100.00

BELL collectors collect all types of bells. Favorites include glass bells, figural bells, school bells, and cowbells. Bells have been made of porcelain, china, or metal through the centuries. Be careful not to buy a bell made from an old glass goblet.

Bronze, Animal, Plant Frieze, Johnnes, Mateus, Marcus, Lucas, 3 x 2 5/8 In. 28.00

Christmas, Red & Silver, Honeycomb, 9 1/2 x 12 In. 34.00
Church, Cast Iron, Yoke, 1870, 27 x 32 In. 1500.00
Church, Iron Funeral Hammer, With Bracket 25.00
Colonial Woman, Long Hair, Full Skirt, Brass, 5 3/4 In. 88.00
Cow, Full-Bodied, Cast Iron Bracket, Painted, 1880s, 29 In. 3220.00
Dinner, Halloween Cat, Chrome, 5 In. 60.00
Door, Chain Operated, Brass, 16 In. 45.00
Locomotive, Boston Revere Beach & Lynn Railroad, 1870 .... 4100.00
Locomotive, Brass, Iron, 1930, 24 x 18 In. 1900.00
Muffin, Kennebunk, Maine, Fire Department, Turned Handle, 10 In. 220.00
Pewter, Hand Type, Clapper 3.00
School, Brass, Red Paint, Wooden Handle, 7 3/4 In. 50.00
School, Brass, Ringed Pattern, 4 1/2 In. 35.00
Silver, Dinner, Water Lilies, Hammered Ground, Dominick & Haff 550.00
Silver, Molded Border, Baluster Handle, Peter & Ann Bateman, 1791, 4 1/4 In. 1265.00
Sleigh, Brass Plated, Leather Strap, 7 Ft. 30.00
Sleigh, Leather Strap, 29 Bells, 1870s, 90 In. 345.00
Sleigh, Nickel, Leather Mounted, 7 In. 26.00
Sleigh, Strap, Bevin's, 1882, 24 Piece 265.00
Table, Metal, Cast, Scroll Handle, Metal Clapper 5.00
U.S.N., Cast Iron, 9 1/2 Diam. 125.00
Woman, Curtsying, Bow In Hair, Brass, 5 In. 75.00
Woman, Fancy Dress, Hat & Fan, Brass, 5 3/4 In. 85.00

BELLE WARE glass was made in 1903 by Carl V. Helmschmied. In 1904 he started a corporation known as the Helmschmied Manufacturing Company. His factory closed in 1908 and he worked on his own until his death in 1934.

Vase, Allover Glass Beads, Pink Orchid, Buds, Surrounded By Leaves, Signed, 6 In.   385.00
Vase, Orchid Blossom, Textured Tapestry Surface, Red Mark, 6 In. 302.50

BELLEEK china was made in Ireland, other European countries, and the United States. The glaze is creamy yellow and appears wet. The first Belleek was made in 1857. All pieces listed here are Irish Belleek. The mark changed through the years. The first mark, black, dates from 1863 to 1890. The second mark, black, dates from 1891 to 1926 and includes the words *Co. Fermanagh, Ireland.* The third mark, black, dates from 1926 to 1946 and has the words *Deanta in Eirinn.* The fourth mark, same as the third mark but green, dates from 1946 to 1955. The fifth mark, green, dates from 1955 to 1965 and has an R in a circle added in the upper right. The sixth mark, green, dates after 1965 and the words *Co. Fermanagh* have been omitted. The seventh mark, gold, was used from 1980 to 1993 and omits the words *Deanta in Eirinn.* The eighth mark, introduced in 1993, is similar to the second mark but is printed in blue. The word *Belleek* is now used only on the pieces made in Ireland even though earlier pieces from other countries were sometimes marked *Belleek.* These early pieces are listed by manufacturer, such as Ceramic Art Co., Haviland, Lenox, Ott & Brewer, and Willets.

Basket, Floral Lattice, Contrasting Parian, Floralware, 5th Mark, Green, 9 In. 475.00
Bowl, Shell, Oval, 4th Mark, Green 85.00
Cake Plate, Basket Weave & Shamrock, 2nd Mark, Black 80.00
Cake Plate, Twig Handled, 4 Strand, 2nd Mark, Black, 1921, 10 In. 665.00
Candelabrum, Cherub, 2nd Mark, Black, 14 In. 3500.00
Centerpiece, Raised Flowers, 4th Mark, Green 495.00
Cheese Dish, Cottage Shape, Luster Trim, 6th Mark, Green 80.00
Coffee Set, 3rd Mark, Black, 13 Piece 850.00
Coffee Set, Limpet, 3rd Mark, Black, Demitasse, 15 Piece 950.00
Coffeepot, Limpet, 3rd Mark, Black 210.00
Compote, Fish Bottom, Shell Top, 1st Mark, Black, 5 x 4 In. 550.00
Creamer, Girl Kneeling, 5th Mark, Green 89.00
Creamer, Lily, Green Trim, 2nd Mark, Black, 3 1/2 In. 50.00
Creamer, Scale, 1st Mark, Black 165.00
Cup, Neptune, Green Trim, 2nd Mark, Black 85.00

Cup & Saucer, Neptune, Demitasse, 2nd Mark, Black, 8 Sets 240.00
Cup & Saucer, Tridacna, 2nd Mark, Black 60.00
Dish, Heart Shape, Shell, 4th Mark, Green, 6 In. 25.00
Figurine, Pig, 2nd Mark, Black, 3 In. 230.00
Figurine, Round Tower, 6th Mark, Green 345.00
Jar, Honey, Limpet, 6th Mark, Green 80.00
Mug, Shamrock, 6th Mark, Green 38.00
Pitcher, Basket Weave & Shamrock, 3rd Mark, Black, 6 In. 198.00
Pitcher, Shamrock, 3rd Mark, Black, 4 In. 75.00
Plate, Basket Weave & Shamrock, 3rd Mark, Black, 7 In., Pair 85.00
Plate, Limpet, 3rd Mark, Black, 7 1/4 In. 30.00
Plate, Shell Pattern, Pink Trim, Gold Edge, 4th Mark, Green, 7 1/8 In. 60.00
Plate, Shell, 5th Mark, Green, 8 In., 8 Piece 160.00
Sugar & Creamer, Lotus, 3rd Mark, Black .... 130.00 to 135.00
Sugar & Creamer, Neptune, 4th Mark, Green .... 90.00 to 165.00
Sugar & Creamer, Shamrock On Basket Weave, 3rd Mark, Black 95.00
Sugar & Creamer, Shamrock, 3rd Mark, Black 135.00
Sugar & Creamer, Tulip, 6th Mark, Green 55.00
Teapot, Harp, 6th Mark, Green 210.00
Teapot, Neptune, 6th Mark, Green, 5 1/4 In. 120.00
Teapot, Neptune, 6th Mark, Green, 6 1/2 In. 160.00
Teapot, Shamrock, 2nd Mark, Black 250.00
Toothpick, Pleat & Panel, Shamrocks, Square, 2nd Mark, Black, 1 5/8 In. 295.00
Vase, Bird & Tree Stump, 1st Mark, Black 425.00
Vase, Bud, Shamrock Tree, 6th Mark, Green 70.00
Vase, Lily, 3rd Mark, Black, 13 1/2 In. 1200.00
Water Font, 5th Mark, Green 135.00

BENNINGTON ware was the product of two factories working in Bennington, Vermont. Both the Norton Company and the Lyman Fenton Company were out of business by 1896. The wares include brown and yellow mottled pottery, Parian, scroddled ware, stoneware, graniteware, yellowware, and Staffordshire-type vases. The name is also a generic term for mottled brownware of the type made in Bennington.

Bar Counter, Swiss Woman Cover, Rockingham Glaze, 6 5/8 In. 2530.00
Bottle, Coachman, Rockingham Glaze, 1849, 10 3/8 In. 220.00
Bottle, Toby Barrel, Old Tom, Rockingham Glaze, 8 1/2 In. 330.00
Bottle, Toby, Mustache, Tassels, Rockingham Glaze, L. Fenton & Co., 1849, 11 In. .. 1540.00
Bowl, Flared Rim, Rockingham Glaze, 4 3/8 x 12 5/8 In. 220.00
Bowl, Wash, Flint Enamel, Alternate Rib Pattern, c.1855, 14 1/2 In. 522.00
Candlestick, Turned, Domed Feet, Mottled Brown & Yellow Glaze, 7 7/8 In., Pair ... 330.00
Creamer, Cow, Marked F, 7 In. 385.00
Cuspidor, Brown Glaze 27.50
Cuspidor, Rockingham Glaze, 1849 Mark, 9 3/4 In. 38.50
Cuspidor, Shell Pattern 100.00
Dish, Vegetable, Oval, 1860-1870 .... 65.00
Figurine, Lion, Coleslaw Mane, Tongue Up, Flint Enamel, 1849-1858, 10 3/4 In. 4400.00
Figurine, Poodle, Standing, Basket In Mouth, Olive Green, Flint, 8 3/8 In. 3850.00
Flask, Book Shape, Bennington Battle On Spine, Flint Enamel, 1849-1858, 7 3/4 In. .. 825.00
Flask, Book Shape, Flint Enamel, 1849-1858, 7 5/8 In. 467.50
Flask, Book Shape, Hermits, Suffering & Death, Fenton's Works Mark, 5 5/8 In. 1100.00
Flask, Figural, Daniel Webster, 7 5/8 In. 360.00
Flowerpot, Molded Cattails, Attached Saucer, 10 1/4 In. 148.50
Frame, Scalloped Edge, Flint, 1850s, 6 1/2 x 6 In. 825.00
Frame, Scalloped Edge, Paper Label, Flint, 1850s, 11 1/4 In. 990.00
Jar, Snuff, Olive Green, Flint, 1849, 4 3/8 In. 385.00
Lamp Base, Stepped Base, Olive Green Pedestal, Flint, 1849, 8 7/8 In. 1760.00
Mold, Pineapple 55.00
Paperweight, Dog, Spaniel, Reclining, Rockingham Glaze, 1849, 3 In. 550.00
Paperweight, Dog, Spaniel, Recumbent, Rockingham, 1849-1858, 3 x 4 1/2 In. 192.50
Pitcher, Anchor & Chain 95.00

Pitcher, Embossed Scenes, Brown, Green Drizzle Glaze, Horsehead Handle 125.00
Pitcher, Flint Enamel, c.1850, 7 1/4 In. 253.00
Pitcher, Ice, Cover, Stag & Eagle, Hound Handle, 11 In. 176.00
Pitcher, Molded Grape Design, Rockingham Glaze, 7 In. 165.00
Pitcher, Monastery, Blue & White, 8 In. 175.00
Pitcher, Paneled, Mask Spout, 7 3/4 In. 110.00
Pitcher, Paul & Virginia, Blue & White, USP Ribbon Mark, 9 1/2 In. 220.00
Pitcher, Pond Lily, Blue & White, Ribbon Mark, 8 1/2 In. 137.50
Pitcher, Presentation, To My Wife, Gold & Blue, Vintage Pattern, 7 5/8 In. 885.00
Pitcher, Toby, Ben Franklin, Sitting, Pipe & Wine Goblet, Rockingham, 6 3/8 In. 550.00
Toby, Barrel, All For James Crow, 9 In. 395.00
Vase, Applied Grapes On Handles, 19th Century, 9 In. 44.00
Washbasin, Floral Relief Base, Scroll Rim, Flint Enamel, 1849, 13 3/8 In. 110.00

BERLIN, a German porcelain factory, was started in 1751 by Wilhelm Kaspar
Wegely. In 1763, the factory was taken over by Frederick the Great and
became the Royal Berlin Porcelain Manufactory. It is still in operation today.
Pieces have been marked in a variety of ways.

Cup & Saucer, Boy With Basket Of Flowers, Seated Shepherd, Marked, 1764 .... 1150.00
Dish, Sweet Meat, Central Putti Figure, 12 Oval Bowls, Acanthus Leaf Base 258.00
Figurine, Figures Around Stove, Marked, 7 In. 132.00
Figurine, Venus & Paris, Pearls In Tresses, Paris On Crutch, Marked, 9 5/8 In., Pr. 1725.00
Jug, Milk, Cover, Pink & Gold Floral Sprig Knob, Bowknots, Marked, c.1770 .... 1495.00
Plaque, Woman, Sitting, Late 19th Century, Frame, Pair 9200.00
Platter, Gilt Banding, Enameled Floral Border, Marked, 14 In. 880.00
Vase, Enameled Floral Panels, Pink Ground, Arled, 17 1/2 In. 495.00
Vase, German Successionist Design, 1920s, 12 In. 2200.00
Vase, Triple Gourd Form, Chinoiserie Design, Birds & Flowers, 21 1/4 In., Pair 5750.00

BESWICK started making earthenware in Staffordshire, England, in 1936.
The company is now part of Royal Doulton Tableware, Ltd. Figurines of
animals, especially dogs and horses, Beatrix Potter animals, and other wares
are still being made.

Figurine, A Double Act, Kitty Macbride 75.00
Figurine, Alsatian, Running 50.00
Figurine, Bulldog 38.00
Figurine, Camel 65.00
Figurine, Cat, Label 55.00
Figurine, Cedar Waxwing 85.00
Figurine, Donkey, 5 3/4 In. 85.00
Figurine, Eagle, 6 In. 30.00
Figurine, Fisherman Otter, 6 In. 35.75
Figurine, Gardener Rabbit, 6 In. 35.75
Figurine, Guilty Sweethearts, Kitty Macbride 70.00
Figurine, Horse, Head Down, Brown .... 42.00 to 45.00
Figurine, Lazy Bones, Kitty Macbride 70.00
Figurine, Mrs. Tittlemouse, Label 55.00
Figurine, Owl, No. 2026, 4 1/2 In. .... 32.00 to 38.00
Figurine, Queen Elizabeth II, 9 1/2 x 10 1/2 In. 120.00
Figurine, Race Course, Kitty Macbride 65.00
Figurine, Spaniel, 8 In. 45.00
Figurine, Tommy Brock, Label 55.00
Mug, Christmas, 1971 .... 60.00
Mug, Christmas, 1981 .... 80.00
Mug, Christmas, 1982, Box 80.00
Plate, Christmas In Bulgaria 30.00
Plate, Christmas In England 20.00
Salt & Pepper, Laurel & Hardy, Heads, Ceramic 225.00
Tankard, Christmas, 1974 .... 66.00
Teapot, Peggotty 45.00
Teapot, Sairey Gamp 70.00

BETTY BOOP, the cartoon figure, first appeared on the screen in 1931. Her face was modeled after the famous singer Helen Kane and her body after Mae West. In 1935, a comic strip was started. Her dog was named Bimbo. Although the Betty Boop cartoons ended by 1938, there was a revival of interest in the Betty Boop image in the 1980s and new pieces are being made.

Ashtray, Betty & Bimbo, Luster Ware, Fleisher Studios, 1930s	475.00
Ashtray, Figural, Glazed Bisque	275.00
Bank, Betty Boop On National Boop & Trust Co.	45.00
Bank, Betty Boop, Winks When Coin Deposited, Sorts Coins	12.50
Bank, Betty's Face	20.00
Bank, Jukebox	25.00
Blanket, Baby, 1930s	200.00
Bookends	70.00
Box, Candy, 1931	150.00
Card, Playing, 1950s	40.00
Clock, Alarm	100.00
Clock, Key Wind	17.50
Cookie Jar, Head, Vandor	100.00 to 125.00
Cookie Jar, King Features	625.00 to 750.00
Cookie Jar, Standing, Vandor	750.00
Cookie Jar, Top Hat	195.00
Doll, Composition, Wooden, Jointed, Needs Restringing, 12 In.	425.00
Doll, Wooden, Jointed, Heart, Fleischer Studios, Graphic Cotton Shirt, 1930s	475.00
Figurine, Sitting, Chalk, 6 1/4 In.	30.00
Jewelry, Pin, Card	55.00
Lunch Box, Plastic, Thermos	25.00
Perfume Bottle	25.00 to 45.00
Salt & Pepper, 1930s	29.00
Salt & Pepper, Betty In Boat	18.00
Tray, Soda, Mexico, Round, 6 1/2 In.	50.00
Wall Pocket, Blue, Betty & Bimbo, Japan, 1930s	235.00
Wall Pocket, Luster	125.00

BICYCLES were invented in 1839. The first manufactured bicycle was made in 1861. Special ladies' bicycles were made after 1874. The modern safety bicycle was not produced until 1885. Collectors search for all types of bicycles and tricycles. Bicycle-related items are also listed here.

Columbia, 5 Star, 1948	650.00
Columbia, Chainless, Maple Rims, c.1897	1500.00
Columbia, High Wheel, c.1886	5200.00
Columbia, Red & White, Built-In Generator	550.00
Double Eagle, Woman's, Built-In Horn, 26 In.	150.00
Fleet Wing, Boy's, Maroon & White, c.1950	110.00
Gendron Wheel Co., Man's, Red Frame, Fenders, Toledo, Ohio, 1910	55.00
Good Humor Ice Cream, Wagon	3200.00
Hopalong Cassidy, Hand Tooled Leather Saddle Bags, 24 In.	4800.00
J.C. Higgins, Boy's, Repainted, 1940s	275.00
J.C. Higgins, Girl's	1100.00
Monarch, Man's, Deluxe	700.00
Murray, Boy's, Tank Carriage	60.00
Raleigh, Girl's, 3-Speed, England	90.00
Roadmaster, Boy's, Lights, Tank	100.00
Roadmaster, Stingray	450.00
Rollfast, Girl's, 1936	2250.00
Schwinn, Boy's, 1960s	700.00
Shelby, Donald Duck, Quacking Horn, Lighted Eyes, Walt Disney, 20 In.	2650.00
Tricycle, Child's, Iron, Small	20.00
Tricycle, Minute Man	300.00
Tricycle, Olson, 1930s	345.00
Tricycle, Rear Wheel Steering	300.00
Tricycle, Sky King, Red & Black, Restored, 1935, 38 In.	1725.00
Tricycle, Yellow, Our Gang Pedal Car Company, Restored, 1935	1850.00

Velocipede, 1880s 1200.00
Velocipede, 38-In. Front Wheel, 32-In. Rear Wheel, Wooden Wheels, c.1865 .... 3000.00
Velocipede, Child's 425.00

BING & GRONDAHL is a famous Danish factory making fine porcelains from 1853 to the present. Underglaze blue decoration was started in 1886. The annual Christmas plate series was introduced in 1895. Dinnerwares, stoneware, and figurines are still being made today. The firm has used the initials B & G and a stylized castle as part of the mark since 1898.

B&G
JØGENHAVN
MADE IN
DENMARK

Cup, Stork Nest, Handleless 20.00
Dish, Eskimo Boy Sitting On Snow Bank, Signed, 6 1/2 In. 375.00
Figurine, Boy & Girl Embracing, Reading Book, No. 1567 .... 165.00
Figurine, Boy, With Bear, No. 2231 .... 70.00
Figurine, Boy, With Flowers, No. 2390 .... 120.00
Figurine, Bulldog, Standing, 4 In. 75.00
Figurine, Bullfinch, No. 1909 .... 90.00
Figurine, Cellist, No. 2032 .... 330.00 to 475.00
Figurine, Child, Bellyache, White, No. 2208, 4 1/2 In. 25.00
Figurine, Children Reading, No. 1567 .... 135.00
Figurine, Fisherman, Seated, No. 2370, Signed 150.00
Figurine, Fisherwoman, No. 2233, Signed .... 800.00 to 900.00
Figurine, Girl, Cat In Basket, No. 2249 .... 105.00
Figurine, Girl, Feeding Cat, No. 1746 .... 125.00
Figurine, Girl, With Ball, No. 2391 .... 120.00
Figurine, Girl, With Doll, No. 1721 .... 175.00
Figurine, Owl, No. 2424, 10 In. 155.00
Figurine, Penguin, No. 1822, 9 3/4 In. 650.00
Figurine, Penguin, No. 3003 .... 65.00
Figurine, Peter, No. 1696 .... 145.00
Figurine, Polar Bear, No. 1785, 12 1/2 In. 130.00
Plate, Christmas, 1895, Behind The Frozen Window .... 3400.00 to 5500.00
Plate, Christmas, 1930, Yule Tree In Town Hall Square Of Copenhagen 75.00
Plate, Christmas, 1932, Lifeboat At Work 70.00
Plate, Christmas, 1933, Korsor-Nyborg Ferry 80.00
Plate, Christmas, 1943, Ribe Cathedral 40.00
Plate, Christmas, 1968, Christmas In Church 12.00
Plate, Christmas, 1971, Christmas At Home 15.00
Plate, Christmas, 1972, Christmas In Greenland 15.00
Plate, Christmas, 1974, Christmas Eve At Rockefeller Center 45.00
Plate, Christmas, 1974, Christmas In The Village .... 14.00 to 15.00
Plate, Christmas, 1976, Christmas Welcome 7.00
Plate, Christmas, 1982, Christmas Tree 35.00
Plate, Christmas, 1987, Snowman's Christmas Eve 29.00
Plate, Mother's Day, 1972 .... 75.00
Plate, Mother's Day, Swan Family 20.00

BINOCULARS of all types are wanted by collectors. Those made in the eighteenth and nineteenth centuries are favored by serious collectors. The small, attractive binoculars called *opera glasses* are listed in their own category.

Bausch & Lomb, Cased, World War II, 6 x 20 .... 175.00
Built-In Compass, Chavalier Opticina Paris 35.00
Colmont, Black Enameled Brass, Worn Leather Trim, Paris 11.00
Folding, Pocket, Adjustable, Case, c.1890 .... 80.00
German Military, 10 x 80, World War II, Head Rests, Tripod 375.00
Gilt Brass & Mother-Of-Pearl, Le Fils, Black Leather Case 77.00
Hensoldt, Dialyt, 10 x 15, Wide Angle Eyepieces, Military, 1930s 120.00
Jockey Club Sportiere, Paris, Case 35.00
Kalimar, 7 x 50, Fully Coated, Case 60.00
La Fayette, 6 x 15, Miniature Prism 40.00
Leather Case, Paris 15.00
LeMaire, Mother-Of-Pearl, Needlepoint Case 65.00
Nighthawk, 7 x 50, Center Focus, Case 32.50

Ofuna, 7 x 50, Case	32.50
Sard, 6 x 42, Case	900.00
Tripod Adapter, Celestron, 11 x 80, Case	160.00
Verex, 7 x 50, Center Focus, Japanese Glass	40.00
Wide Angle, Commodore Mark II, Case	120.00

BIRDCAGES are collected for use as homes for pet birds and as decorative objects of folk art. Elaborate wooden cages of the past centuries can still be found. The brass or wicker cages of the 1930s are popular with bird owners.

Brass, Victorian, Patent 1870	145.00
Carved Wood, Domed Top, China, 17 1/2 In.	82.50
Cathedral Form, Bell Tower, Turrets, Mexico, Wire & Parcel Gilt, 26 1/4 In.	920.00
Folk Art, Domed Wire Top, Old Red Paint	108.00
French Chateau Form, Wire, Bamboo & Painted Wood, Evans & Co.	2800.00
Hendryx, Wooden Finial, Rectangular, Blue	135.00
Iron Figures Holding Base, Victorian	225.00
Parrot, Brass, English, 39 In.	770.00
Red, Black Trim, Accessories, Stand, 52 In.	155.00
Tin & Wire, Tin Handle, 7 x 4 x 5 1/4 In.	55.00
Tin & Wire, Wooden Finial, Orange & Blue Paint, 16 In.	60.00
Turned Wooden Finial, Bell Shape	75.00
Twisted Wire, Wooden Base, Victorian	150.00
Wicker, Crescent Moon Floor Stand	795.00
Wire, Wooden, Primitive, Rectangular, Ring Handle	65.00
Wire Lattice, Brass Pulls, Tin Tray, Pine Frame, Tabletop, 24 x 11 x 15 In.	200.00
Wooden, Chinese Trade, Hand Made, 1840s, 15 In.	335.00
Wooden, Paktong & Ivory, Porcelain Feeders, China, c.1860, 36 In.	1200.00
Wooden, Robin's-Egg Blue	145.00
Wooden & Scrolled Wire, Victorian, 36 In.	200.00
Wooden Shingled Roof, Mustard Paint, Brass & Copper, 1892, 50 x 48 In.	7200.00

BISQUE is an unglazed baked porcelain. Finished bisque has a slightly sandy texture with a dull finish. Some of it may be decorated with various colors. Bisque gained favor during the late Victorian era when thousands of bisque figurines were made. It is still being made. Additional bisque items may be listed under the factory name.

Bust, Girl & Boy, Victorian, Pair	95.00
Dish, Chicken & Egg, Basket Weave Base, 4 x 5 1/2 In.	500.00
Figurine, Blond Girl, Pastel, Ruffled Pink Hat, Pair	48.00
Figurine, Choir Boy, Germany, Box, 3 In., 6 Piece	25.00
Figurine, Dog, Bulldog Face, Amber Glass Eyes, Seated, Roselane, 5 1/2 In.	10.00
Figurine, Early Bird Catches Worm	40.00
Figurine, Hen & Chick In Egg, Nest, Small	500.00
Figurine, Man & Woman, With Monkey's Heads, Country Clothes	325.00
Figurine, Man, With Lyre, L & M, 14 In.	60.00
Group, Putti, With Ram, Italy, Crowned N, 12 x 15 In.	330.00
Night-Light, Owl Head, Gray Bead, Amber Glass Eyes, 4 1/2 In.	245.00
Vase, Girl, Man, Pastel, Gilt, 6 1/4 In.	93.00

BLACK memorabilia has become an important area of collecting since the 1970s. The best material dates from past centuries, but many recent items are also of interest. Objects that picture a black person may also be listed in this book under Advertising, Tins; Banks; Bottle Openers; Cookie Jars; Salt & Pepper; Sheet Music; etc.

Apron, Aunt Jemima, Yellow, Pancake Jamboree	50.00
Ashtray, Coon Chicken Inn, Glass, With Cartoon Head, 3 1/2 In.	20.00 to 25.00
Ashtray, Full Head, Cartoon Like Mammy, Smoke Through Nostrils, 5 x 4 In.	100.00
Ashtray, Nodder, Boy, With Cigar In Mouth, Brass, 5 In.	140.00 to 145.00
Ashtray, Outhouse, Children, Japan	20.00
Ashtray, Union Station, Black Man's Face	145.00
Badge, Hire, Porter, 1836	2100.00

Badge, Hire, Porter, 1853 .... 3600.00
Badge, Hire, Porter, 1858 .... 2750.00
Badge, Hire, Servant, 1811 .... 7500.00
Badge, Hire, Servant, 1840 .... 4000.00
Badge, Hire, Servant, 1862 .... 5500.00
Bell, Aunt Jemima, Figural, Box, Dated 1941 .... 145.00
Bill Of Sale, Slaves Hardany & 2 Children, November 14, 1864 .... 330.00
Black Face, Pull String To Roll The Eyes, Tin, 1910 .... 55.00
Book, Little Black Sambo, 1959 .... 32.00
Book, Little Black Sambo, Platt & Munk, 1955 .... 55.00
Book, Most Popular Plantation Songs, Copyright 1911 .... 25.00
Booklet, Amos 'n' Andy, Radio Broadcast, Amos's Wedding, c.1935 .... 22.50
Box, Gold Dust Washing Powder 45.00
Brush, Aunt Jemima, Doll Type, Wooden, Mother & Child, Box, 1930-1940 .... 65.00
Brush, Butler 30.00
Candy Container, Amos 'n' Andy, New Paint 525.00
Candy Container, Papier-Mache Watermelon, Boy Holding Slice, Celluloid, Japan ... 150.00
Card, Story, 10 Little Niggers, Die Cut 185.00
Cookbook, Dixie Cookbook, c.1935 .... 65.00
Cookie Jar, Black Chef, Red Bowtie, Small 65.00
Cookie Jar, Black Wash Woman 30.00
Cookie Jar, Mammy, Wicker Handle, Yellow Rose Finial Cover, Japan 1350.00
Cruet, Oil & Vinegar, Mammy & Chef 60.00
Decanter, Whiskey, Black Man 75.00
Doll, Aunt Jemima, Red & White Checkered Dress, Oilcloth 80.00
Doll, Aunt Jemima, Uncle Mose, Children, Oilcloth, Stuffed, Set Of 4 .... 185.00
Doll, Baby, Terra-Cotta On Cloth, Happy Features, Thumb Fits Into Mouth, 26 In. 895.00
Doll, Boy, Celluloid Head, Flocked Hair, Jointed, Pants, Checkered Shirt, 20 In. 275.00
Doll, Composition, Ethnic, Painted Eyes, 9 In. 60.00
Doll, Mammy, Black Face, Plaid Body & Arms, Original Clothing, 12 In. 85.00
Doll, Mammy, Cloth, Red & White Gingham, 19 In. 330.00
Doll, Mammy, Ise Your Honey Girl Front, Stuffed, 5 In. 395.00
Doll, Mammy, Wooden Carved, Dressed 475.00
Doll, Plastic, Sleep Eyes, Original Red Cherries On White Dress, 19 In. 95.00
Doll, Rag, Painted Features, Wool Hair, Colorful Dress, 9 In. 35.00
Doll, Rag, Red & White Dress, White Apron, Red Bandanna, 1930s, 14 1/2 In. ... 125.00
Doll, Topsy Turvy, Black & White, Molded Hair, Composition, Painted Eyes 95.00
Figurine, Black Man, Eating Watermelon, Staffordshire, 3 In. 35.00
Figurine, Girl & Boy, Bisque, Painted, 2 3/4 In., Pair 110.00
Figurine, Man With Articulated Arms, Green Jacket & Trousers, Carved, 4 1/2 In. 195.00
Figurine, Man With Pipe, Yellow, Blue & Red Clothing, Metal, 4 In. 375.00
Figurine, Outhouse, Children On Potty, Bisque, England 50.00
Frame, Picture, Golliwog 45.00
Glass, Water, Coon Chicken Inn, 1940s, 4 In. 28.00
Hat, Aunt Jemima 45.00
Humidor, Congo Tobacco, Boy Sitting On Bale Of Cotton Scene 150.00
License, Marriage, Freed Man & Freed Woman, Handwritten, 1866, 8 x 12 1/4 In. ... 52.00
Match Holder/Ashtray, Amos 'n' Andy, Chalkware, I'se Regested 155.00
Match Holder/Cigarette, Yellowware, Old Woman 325.00
Mirror, Puzzle Picture Back, Place Teeth In Black Woman's Smile, 1915, 2 1/2 In. 298.00
Mold, Pancake, Aunt Jemima 165.00
Peg Board, Grocery, Mammy, Reckon Ah Needs, Wooden 65.00
Pen Holder, Boy, With Hat, White Metal, Middletown 95.00
Pie Bird, Chef, Yellow 125.00
Pie Bird, Mammy 150.00
Pin, Aunt Jemima Pancake Club 12.50
Pin, Aunt Jemima, Campaign Chairman, Pinback 20.00
Pin Dish, Booker T. Washington's Home Transfer, Porcelain, Dresden 32.50
Pincushion, Face, 1 1/4 In. 25.00
Planter, Black Boy & Pineapple, Japan 28.00
Planter, Figural Man, Gold, Brayton Laguna 70.00
Planter, Plaid Mammy 95.00

Plaque, Woman's Face, 2 x 6 In. 55.00
Potholder, Mammy, Folk Art, Wooden 65.00
Print, Wake Up Dar, Harry Roseland, Frame, 12 x 10 In. 135.00
Rack, Potholder, Watermelon Boy, Girl, Chalkware 38.00
Recipe Card, Aunt Jemima, 15 Piece 140.00
Shelf Sitter, Fishing Couple, Bisque 52.00
Slave Collar, Iron, Brass Covered, Engraved Tom Hier, W. Newbury Mass. 3300.00
Sparkler, Amos 'n' Andy, 2 Piece 2100.00
Spice Rack, Aunt Jemima, Yellow Plastic 150.00
Sprinkler, Water, Sambo 250.00
String Holder, Mammy, Lattice & Dot Cream Dress, Red Bandanna, 7 x 4 1/4 In. 120.00
String Holder, Mammy, Pottery 115.00
String Holder, Mammy, Signed Fred Hirode 185.00
String Holder, Mammy, Standing 45.00
String Holder, Man's Head, Chalkware 75.00
String Holder, Woman's Head, Chalkware 75.00
Sugar & Creamer, Aunt Jemima, F & F 135.00
Sugar Shaker, Mammy 80.00
Syrup, Aunt Jemima, F & F 45.00
Syrup, Little Black Sambo, Glass, Plastic Lid 275.00
Syrup, Mammy, F & F 36.00
Teapot, Mammy, Gone With The Wind 150.00
Toaster Cover, Mammy, 1950s .... 16.00 to 48.00
Toothbrush Holder, Tray, Black Baker 400.00
Watch Holder, Boy, Sitting, Basket, Chalkware, By Jino, 6 In. 135.00

BLACK AMETHYST glass appears black until it is held to the light, then a
dark purple can be seen. It has been made in many factories from 1860 to the
present.

Ashtray, Round, 5 In. 8.00
Bottle, Victorian, Crane In Rushes, White Enamel 45.00
Bowl, Flowers & Scroll, 11 1/2 In. 100.00
Bowl, Rolled Edge, Gold Rim, 9 x 3 1/4 In. 30.00
Bowl, Silver Deposit, Flowers, Scrolls, 3 Footed, 12 1/4 x 3 1/8 In. 65.00
Box, Lift-Off Lid, Enameled Leaves & Strawberries, 3 3/8 In. 75.00
Candy Dish, Cover, Cloverleaf Shape, Pierced Finial, Monogram, 7 In. 22.00
Coaster, 5 In. 4.00
Jar, Polychrome Floral Enameling, 15 1/2 In. 82.50
Plate, 8 In. 4.50
Tumbler, Diamond Point, 10 Oz. 8.00
Vase, Bud, Multicolor Floral Decal, Bulbous Base, Crimped, 8 In. 15.00
Vase, Ecru Flower, Leaves, Flared, Ruffled, 8 3/4 In. 25.00
Vase, Enameled Vines Bound By Gold Tassel, 8 1/4 In. 385.00
Vase, Tulip, Butterfly & Berry, Gold Design 250.00
Vase, Vines Bound Together At Top With Gold Tassel, 8 1/4 In. 385.00

BLOWN GLASS was formed by forcing air through a rod into molten glass.
Early glass and some forms of art glass were hand blown. Other types of
glass were molded or pressed.

Basket, Cobalt Blue 20.00
Basket, Tortoiseshell Spatter Pattern 200.00
Bottle, 3 Mold, Grass Green, 8 1/4 In. 2750.00
Bottle, 24 Swirl Ribs, Amber, Zanesville, 7 7/8 In. 330.00
Bottle, Pitkin, Light Green, 31 Broken Swirl Ribs, 1/2 Post Neck, 6 In. 220.00
Bottle, Pitkin, Light Olive, 36 Broken Swirl Ribs, 6 1/8 In. 385.00
Bottle, Stiegel Type Floral Enameling, Pewter, 1/2 Pt., 5 1/4 In. 115.00
Bottle, Vinegar, 3 Mold, Sapphire Blue, Flint 250.00
Bowl, Aqua, Applied Foot, Flared, 7 1/4 x 2 1/2 In. 82.50
Bowl, Cover, Pewter Dragon Finial, Enamel Swirls, 14 1/2 In. 579.50
Bowl, Cut Stars, Strawberry Diamonds & Panels, Flint, 3 3/4 x 5 In. 159.50
Bowl, Flared Rim, Folded Edge, 5 1/2 x 6 1/2 In. 27.50
Compote, Cut Strawberry Diamonds, Knop Stem, Pittsburgh, 9 1/2 x 7 1/2 In. 495.00

Compote, Ivory, 6 1/4 x 4 3/4 In. 121.00
Creamer, Applied Rings & Handle, 4 1/4 In. 5.50
Creamer, Cobalt Blue, 12 Diamond, Applied Foot & Handle, 3 1/2 In. 456.00
Creamer, Cobalt Blue, 12 Ribs, Pittsburgh, 5 3/8 In. 1045.00
Creamer, Opaque White Looping, Clear Handle, 3 In. 55.00
Cruet, 12 Ribs, Folded Lip, 6 5/8 In. 38.50
Cruet, 14 Ribs, Applied Hollow Handle, 6 1/2 In. 50.00
Decanter, 2 Applied Rings, Ribbed, Mushroom Stopper, 9 1/4 .... 82.50
Decanter, 3 Applied Rings, 3 Mold, Stopper, 8 In. 148.00
Decanter, 3 Applied Rings, Amber, 8 1/2 In. 71.50
Decanter, 3 Applied Rings, Engraved Leaves & Acorns, Lacy Stopper, 7 In. 27.50
Decanter, Applied Rings, Folded Lip, Lacy Flower Stopper, 8 1/ 2 In. 27.50
Decanter, Copper Wheel Engraved Ships, Windmills, Stopper, 9 1/4 In. 60.50
Decanter, Cut Wheat Design, 12 In. 49.50
Decanter, 3-Mold, Blown-Ribbed Stopper, 1 Qt. 250.00
Decanter, 3-Mold, Hollow Stopper, Rayed Base, 1 Pt. 110.00
Decanter, 3-Mold, Ringed Base, Clear Stopper, 1 Qt. 275.00
Decanter, Strawberry Diamonds, Roundels, Fans, Stopper, Pittsburgh, 8 In. 264.00
Decanter, Thick Tooled Top, Amethyst, 9 1/2 In., Pair 1200.00
Fish Bowl, Clear, Applied Base, 13 1/2 x 10 1/4 In. 203.00
Flask, Chestnut, Broken Swirl, 18 Ribs, Pale Green, Midwestern, 6 3/8 In. 165.00
Funnel, Wine, Applied Rim, 17 1/4 In. 27.50
Funnel, Wine, Applied Rim, 21 In. 154.00
Jar, Applied Rings, Hollow Finial, 14 In. 165.00
Jug, Swirled Ribs At Base, Copper Wheel Engraved Wreath, 4 3/4 In. 1540.00
Lamp, Lacemaker's, Cobalt Blue, Flared Base, Clear Font, Knop Stem, 7 In. 4070.00
Pitcher, 3 Mold, Applied Handle, 5 1/2 In. 577.00
Pitcher, Applied Handle, 2 1/8 In. 27.50
Pitcher, Double Chain Design 945.00
Pitcher, Engraved Design, 19th Century, 9 In. 132.00
Pitcher, Lily Pad, Aqua, Applied Handle, Threaded Neck, 7 1/4 In. 5200.00
Pitcher, Lily Pad, Deep Amber, Applied Handle, 7 1/4 In. 55.00
Salt, 11 Diamond, 3 1/8 In. 71.50
Salt, Peacock Green, 2 3/8 In. 440.00
Salt, Ribbed Bowl, Amethyst, 3 In. 14.00
Salt, Ribs & Diamonds, 2 3/4 In. 49.50
Sugar, Cover, Blue Finial, White Looping, Electric Blue, Folded Rim, 7 In. 1925.00
Sugar, Cover, Cobalt Blue, 12 Ribs, Pittsburgh, 6 1/2 In. 2860.00
Sugar, Galleried Rim, Thick Base, Domed Cover, Folded Rim, 9 3/8 In. 330.00
Sugar, Honeycomb Cut Design, 6 7/8 In. 82.50
Sugar, Knob Finial On Lid, Flint, 7 3/4 In. 1182.50
Syrup, Pillar Mold, Amber, 12 Ribs, Pewter Lid, Pittsburgh, 7 In. 2640.00
Tumbler, Amber, 24 Vertical Ribs 2640.00
Tumbler, Copper Wheel, Engraved Floral Wreath, Initials C.A.R., 3 1/2 In. 82.50
Tumbler, Pale Green, 18 Rib Broken Swirl 3905.00
Vase, Bubbles, Flared, Amber Threading, 7 1/4 In. 115.00
Vase, Cornucopia Shape, Sterling Silver Base, 11 In., Pair 297.00
Vase, Pillar Mold & Drape, Hollow Baluster Stem, Pittsburgh, 10 1/4 In. 495.00
Vase, Thorn Stem, Clear, 5 1/2 In. 60.00
Wine, Applied Foot, Panel Cut Stem, 4 3/4 In. 14.00
Wine, Cut Panels, Strawberry Diamonds, Fans, Star Foot, Pittsburgh, 4 3/8 In. 137.50
Wine, Emerald, 5 In. 82.00
Wine, Peacock Green, 4 1/2 In. 93.50
Wine, Ribbed Bowl, Polychrome Enamel Floral Band, 3 3/4 In. 22.00
Witch's Ball, Pink Loopings, White Ground 907.50
Witch's Ball, Red Loopings, White Ground 990.00
Witch's Ball, Salmon, Green & Blue, Milk Glass 1650.00
Witch's Ball, Stand, Teal Green 742.50
Witch's Ball, White Loopings, Cobalt Blue Ground 880.00

BLUE GLASS, see Cobalt Blue category

BLUE ONION, see Onion category

BLUE WILLOW pattern has been made in England since 1780. The pattern has been copied by factories in many countries, including Germany, Japan, and the United States. It is still being made. Willow was named for a pattern that pictures a bridge, birds, willow trees, and a Chinese landscape.

Bowl, 2 Spouts, Straight Sides, 5 x 3 In.	4.50
Bowl, Cereal, Japan, 5 3/4 In.	6.40
Bowl, Handles, Burslem, 6 1/2 x 8 In.	5.50
Bowl, Royal, Sebring, Ohio, 9 In.	13.00
Bowl, Salad, Royal, Sebring, Ohio, 5 1/2 In.	3.50
Bowl, Square, Johnson, Large	135.00
Bowl, Vegetable, Allerton, Rectangular, 8 1/4 In.	70.00
Cake Plate, Child's	45.00
Cake Plate, Square, Handles, Taylor & Kent	25.00
Cheese Dish, Cover	135.00
Chop Plate, Royal, 12 1/4 In.	16.00
Coffeepot, Johnson Bros.	95.00
Coffeepot, Transfer Design, Pearlware, 18th Century	110.00
Condiment Set	135.00
Creamer, Child's	15.00
Creamer, Cow, England	445.00
Cruet, Vinegar, Handle, Stopper, Japan, 5 1/2 In.	24.00
Cup, Occupied Japan	5.00
Cup & Saucer, Floral Sprays, Gold Trim, SGK China, Demitasse	8.50
Cup & Saucer, Japan	7.60
Cup & Saucer, Japan, Demitasse	9.60
Cup & Saucer, Mush	95.00
Cup & Saucer, Royal	6.80
Dinner Set, Child's, Staffordshire, 54 Piece	1800.00
Gravy, 2 Spouts, Royal	8.00
Grill Plate, Japan, 11 1/4 In.	7.60
Lamp, Kerosene	90.00
Pitcher, Cover, Mariyama, Paneled	125.00
Pitcher, High Handle & Spout, Burslem, 9 In.	150.00
Pitcher, Octagonal, Mason, 11 In.	425.00
Pitcher, Royal Corona, 10 In.	225.00
Plate, Japan, 6 In.	2.80
Plate, Japan, 9 1/2 In.	7.00
Plate, Logo, Occupied Japan, 9 In.	13.00
Plate, Maddock & Son, England, 8 In.	7.00
Plate, Occupied Japan, 6 3/8 In.	3.50
Plate, Rolled Edge, 7 7/8 In.	3.75
Plate, Royal, 6 1/4 In.	2.00
Plate, Royal, 7 1/4 In.	4.00
Plate, Royal, 9 In.	5.50
Plate, Royal, 10 In.	5.00
Plate, Royal, Sebring Ohio, 12 In.	15.00
Platter, Blue, Meakin, 16 In.	50.00
Platter, Ironstone, 14 1/2 In.	66.00
Platter, Maastricht, Oval, 16 In.	120.00
Platter, Mandarin, Copeland	145.00
Platter, U.S.A., 13 In.	16.00
Platter, Well & Tree, 17 x 13 3/4 In.	360.00
Salt & Pepper, Bulbous, Japan, 3 1/8 In.	32.00
Salt Box, Hanging	90.00
Saucer, Kakusa	2.00
Soup, Dish, Royal, 8 3/8 In.	7.50
Soup, Dish, Royal, 8 1/2 In.	8.50
Sugar & Creamer, Cover, Ridgway	70.00
Sugar & Creamer, Homer Laughlin	15.00
Sugar Shaker	75.00
Teapot, 6 Cup	125.00
Teapot, Child's	35.00

Teapot, McCormick Tea, Box, Unused 40.00

BOCH FRERES factory was founded in 1841 in La Louviere in eastern Belgium. The wares resemble the work of Villeroy & Boch. The factory is still in business.

Jardiniere, Black-Outlined Flowers, Cream, Cobalt, Brown Glaze, c.1890, 9 3/8 In. .. 825.00
Vase, 5 Panels, Polar Bear, Various Poses, Signed, 16 In. 6900.00
Vase, Flower Frog, Art Deco, Signed, 9 x 6 1/2 In. 495.00
Vase, Overall Floral Design, 5 In. 190.00
Vase, Stylized Leaves & Berries, Blue & Green Ground, Marked, 12 5/8 In. 1035.00
Vase, Stylized Leaves, Black Ground, c.1925, 9 1/2 In. 467.00
Vase, Yellow & Rust Blossoms, Cream Crackle Ground, c.1925, 12 In. 357.00

BOEHM is the collector's name for the porcelains of Edward Marshall Boehm. In 1953 the Osso China Company was reorganized as Edward Marshall Boehm, Inc. The company is still working in England and New Jersey. In the early days of the factory, dishes were made, but the elaborate and lifelike bird figurines are the best-known ware. Edward Marshall Boehm, the founder, died in 1961, but the firm has continued to design and produce porcelain. Today, the firm makes both limited and unlimited editions of figurines and plates.

Bowl, Bird, With Berries, Small 20.00
Figurine, Baby Bald Eagle, Inauguration Day, 1973 .... 4000.00
Figurine, Baby Blue Jay 60.00
Figurine, Baby Chickadee, 3 1/4 In. 60.00
Figurine, Baby Goldfinch 40.00
Figurine, Baby Wood Thrush, 4 1/4 In. 90.00
Figurine, Ballet Dancer 139.00
Figurine, Brindle Boxer .... 195.00 to 400.00
Figurine, Brown Pelican, 14 In. 880.00
Figurine, Canada Geese, No. 308, Pair 598.00
Figurine, Catbird With Hyacinth 1800.00
Figurine, Cygnet 175.00
Figurine, Fledgling Canada Warbler, No. 491 .... 2000.00
Figurine, Fledgling Red Poll .... 80.00 to 185.00
Figurine, Kestral, Pair 1850.00
Figurine, Magnolia Grandiflora, 11 1/2 x 13 In. 1540.00
Figurine, Moses, 13 1/2 In. 275.00
Figurine, Nativity Set, 16 Piece 1800.00
Figurine, Panda, On His Back, Playful, With Bamboo, 6 x 8 In. 275.00
Figurine, Pontiff Iris, 16 In. 935.00
Figurine, Poodle, White Bisque, Signed 225.00
Figurine, Waxwing 150.00
Figurine, Yellow Throated Warbler, No. 431 .... 265.00 to 400.00
Group, Prothonotary Warbler, No. 445, 5 1/2 In. 250.00
Plate, Mockingbirds 95.00
Plate, Mountain Bluebird 95.00

BOHEMIAN GLASS is an ornate overlay or flashed glass made during the Victorian era. It has been reproduced in Bohemia, which is now a part of the Czech Republic. Glass made from 1875 to 1900 is preferred by collectors.

Beaker, Ruby Cut To Clear, Flared, C-Scroll, Etched Fawn & Duck, 5 In. 220.00
Candlestick, Ruby Glass, Panel Shaft, Crystal Prism Drops, 9 1/2 In. 330.00
Candy Dish, Cover, Ruby Cut To Clear, 3 Footed, Grapes, Large 88.00
Compote, Cover, Ruby Overlay, Cut Glass, Buck & Doe, 19 In. 4400.00
Compote Set, Cranberry Glass, 19th Century, Graduated, 3 Piece 1705.00
Cordial, Scrolls & Birds, Stemmed 18.00
Cordial Set, Decanter, Tray & 3 Wines, 5 Piece 160.00
Decanter, Deer & Castle, Red 150.00
Decanter, Engraved Animals & Cattle, 1870s, 15 In. 120.00
Decanter, Wine, Ruby Cut, 1910, 14 1/2 In., Pair 110.00
Jar, Cover, Cranberry Cut To Clear, Scrolling Grape & Leaf Design, 7 In. 90.00
Jar, Cover, Deer & Castle, Ruby, 10 In. 160.00

Vase, Deer & Castle, Flared, 5 In. 42.00
Vase, Gold Cut To Clear, Engraved Grapes, Star Base, 6 x 5 In. 90.00
Vase, Pedestal, Ruby Overlay, 12 In. 250.00
Vase, Red, Cut Back With Deer 80.00
Vase, Stag & Lodge Reserves, Ruby, Cut, 8 1/2 In., Pair 247.00

BONE DISHES were considered a necessary part of a table setting for the Victorian table. The crescent-shaped dish was kept at the edge of the dinner plate so the bones removed from the fish could be stored away from the uneaten food. Some bone dishes were made in more fanciful shapes and many resemble fish.

    Argyle, Flow Blue 80.00
    Astoria 55.00
    Bluebird 20.00
    Bolingbroke, Ridgway 50.00
    Molland, Flow Blue, Alfred Meakin 45.00
    Touraine 65.00

BOOKENDS have probably been used since books became inexpensive. Early libraries kept books in cupboards, not on open shelves. By the 1870s bookends appeared, especially homemade fret-carved wooden examples. Most bookends listed in this book date from the twentieth century.

    Alfred Neuman, Mad Magazine, Metal 30.00
    Ancestral Home Of George Washington, Bronze Finish 40.00
    Apple, Pear, Glass, Gold Interior, Encased Bubbles, Italy 150.00
    Art Deco Maidens, 1 Seated & 1 On Knee, Gilt Ground, Metal, 7 1/2 & 6 3/4 In. ... 488.00
    Blacksmith, Iron, Bronze Plated, Gilt Traces 28.00
    Centaurs Playing, Seated In Scrolled Column, Bronze, 7 In. 440.00
    Church, Metal 16.00
    Clipper Ship, 5 7/8 x 3 3/4 In. 77.00
    Cocker Spaniels, Standing, Gilt Metal, Onyx Base 65.00
    Dante & Beatrice Busts, Polychrome, Bronze Armor 62.00
    Dante's Bust, Copper, Red & Bronze Paint 35.00
    Deer, Resting, Frosted Clear 8.00
    Dog, Pointer, Worn Bronze Finish, Cast Iron, 8 In. 70.00
    Dutch Children Kissing, Hubley, 4 7/8 x 4 3/8 In. 245.00
    Eucalyptus Pods & Leaves, Copper Craft, Mission, 5 x 6 In. 500.00
    Farmer & Wife, Praying In Fields, Wheelbarrow, Pitchfork, Bronze Finish 45.00
    Fitted Column Form, Lignum Vitae, 6 1/2 In. 920.00
    Foo Dogs, Brass, China, c.1900 .... 150.00
    Fox & Grapes, Art Nouveau, Signed, Bronze, 6 5/8 In. 185.00
    Gazelle, Metal, 1930 .... 200.00
    George Washington, Cast Iron, c.1870 .... 215.00
    German Shepherd, Cast Iron 25.00
    German Shepherds, Seated, Iron, Bronzed, 4 5/8 In. 18.00
    Hammered Copper, Pillow Backs, Gustav Stickley, 5 1/2 x 5 1/2 In. 660.00
    Hobo, Full Figure, Iron, 7 x 2 3/4 In. 357.00
    Horsehead, Clear, Federal 18.00
    Indian Chief, Cast Iron, Painted 45.00
    Jardiniere, Ming Tree Design, Carved Soapstone, China 52.50
    Kittens In Basket, 5 x 5 5/8 In. 385.00
    Kneeling Dancers, Painted Metal & Onyx, 7 In. 65.00
    Mallard Duck, Wildfowler 170.00
    Old Salt, FF, Painted Iron, 5 7/8 x 2 1/2 In. 120.00
    Owl, Art Deco, Bronze, Foundry Mark, M. Carr, 5 In. 700.00
    Owl, Metal, Telescoping 15.00
    Owl On Book, Bronze Finish, 5 1/8 x 3 1/2 In. 77.00
    Parakeet, Green, No. 401, 7 In. 1262.00
    Parrots, Copper, 5 1/2 x 6 1/4 In. 54.00
    Penguins, Glass, Crystal To Amber, 7 In. 175.00
    Pine, Carved, Folding Ends, Rustic Openwork Pickets 14.00
    Poppies, Cutout, Copper, Dirk Van Erp, 1912, 5 x 6 In. 775.00

Sailing Ship, Repousse, Copper, Harry Dixon, Signed, 6 x 7 3/4 In. 495.00
Scotty, Standing, Iron, 5 1/8 x 5 1/4 In. 198.00
Setters, Seated, Heads Up, Iron, Gilt Paint 25.00
Sunbonnet Girl, Iron, 6 1/4 x 4 In. 247.00

BOOKMARKS were originally made of parchment, cloth, or leather. Soon
woven silk ribbon, thin cardboard, celluloid, wood, silver, tortoiseshell, and
metals were used. Examples made before 1850 are scarce, but there are many
to be found dating before 1920.

Andes Stoves, Lithographed 10.00
Anne Of Green Gables, Anne Shirley RKO Radio Picture, Black & White 6.00
Centennial, George Washington, B.B. Tilt & Son, Silk 137.50
Civil War Centennial, Cannon & Flags, Silk 3.00
Eastman's Wild Rose, Lithographed 10.00
Hoskins Stationery, Picture Of Father Time, Celluloid, c.1910 .... 35.00
Trojans Football Team, Silk 2.00

BOSSONS character wall masks, plaques, figurines, and other decorative
pieces are made by W.H. Bossons, Limited of Congleton, England. The
company was founded in 1946 and is still working.

Figurine, Cheyenne Warrior, Shield, Label, 1965 .... 65.00
Head, Arab Sheik 55.00
Head, Basset Hound 60.00
Head, Beefeater 75.00
Head, Bretonne 65.00
Head, Bush Baby, In Tree 50.00
Head, Horse, Palomino 90.00
Head, Sea Captain 60.00
Head, Welsh Lady 60.00
Plaque, Afridi, Embossed Full Figure, 1959 .... 110.00
Plaque, Berber, Embossed Full Figure, 1959 .... 110.00
Plaque, Owl 78.00
Plaque, Ralmora, Artist Initials 100.00
Plaque, Westward Ho, Artist Initials 100.00
Plaque, Zulu Chief, Embossed Full Figure, 1959 .... 125.00

BOTTLE collecting has become a major American hobby. There are several
general categories of bottles, such as historic flasks, bitters, household, and
figural. For more bottle prices, see the book *Kovels' Bottles Price List* by
Ralph and Terry Kovel.

Apothecary, Black, Pontil, England, 13 In. 425.00
Apothecary, Eglomise Label, 11 1/4 In. 11.00

Avon started in 1886 as the California Perfume Company. It was not until
1929 that the name *Avon* was used. In 1939, it became Avon Products, Inc.
Avon has made many figural bottles filled with cosmetic products. Ceramic,
plastic, and glass bottles were made in limited editions.

Avon, Captain's Lantern, 1964-1976 .... 5.00
Avon, Car, Electric Charger, 1970-1972, 5 Oz. .... 4.00 to 6.00
Avon, Car, Packard Roadster, 1970-1972 .... 6.00
Avon, Car, Sterling Six, Brown, 1968-1970, 7 Oz. 4.00
Avon, Car, Stutz Bearcat, 1914 Model, 1974-1977 .... 6.00
Avon, Casey's Lantern, Red, 1966-1967 .... 20.00
Avon, Coleman Lantern, 1977-1979 .... 6.00
Avon, Dog, Seated, Dark Amber 8.00
Avon, Electric Charger, Black, Red Trim, 5 Oz. 4.00
Avon, Golf Cart, Wild Country After Shave, Olive, 5 Oz. 4.00
Avon, Jaguar, Wild Country After Shave, Emerald Green, 1973-1976, 5 Oz. 4.00
Avon, Piano, Amber, 1972 .... 3.00
Avon, Spirit Of St. Louis, 1970-1972, Box 55.00
Bar, Pillar Mold, 8 Flattened Ribs, Amethyst, c.1850, 10 In., Pair 6870.00
Barber, Bay Rum, Milk Glass, E.W. Co. 110.00
Barber, Fern Pattern, Melon Ribbed, Blue Opalescent 245.00

Barber, Flower & Vine Pattern, Lace Art Cameo, Orange Opalescent, Stopper, 8 In. .. 121.00
Barber, Hair Oil, Heckle Bros., Painted Flowers, Milk Glass, Metal Stopper, 7 1/2 In. 165.00
Barber, Hair Oil, Ruby Glass, Frosted, Gold Letters, 11 1/4 In. 55.00
Barber, Kokens Quinine Tonic, For The Hair, Clear, Label, 7 1/2 In. 215.00
Barber, Nelbro's Dandruff Herbicide, Embossed 8.00
Barber, Pressed Glass, Cork & Metal Applicator, 8 1/2 In. 20.00
Barber, Red, Blue & Green Swirled Stripes, Porcelain Stopper, 9 3/4 In. 210.00
Barber, Swirled & Raised White Stripes, Clear, 10 3/4 In. 220.00
Barber, White & Blue Flower & Dot Pattern, Cranberry, Orange, Pontil, 8 In. 44.00
Barber, White & Orange Flowers, Cobalt Blue, Gold Trim, Stopper, 11 In. 286.00

Beam bottles were made to hold Kentucky Straight Bourbon, made by the
James B. Beam Distilling Company. The Beam series of ceramic bottles
began in 1953.

Beam, Buffalo Hunter, Box 8.00
Beam, Cathedral Radio, 1979 .... 25.00
Beam, Civil War Centennial, Blue 50.00
Beam, Clydesdale Figural Lid, Decanter, St.Louis Arch 45.00
Beam, Decanter, Fire Wagon 30.00
Beam, Indian Maiden, Box 8.00
Beam, Pickwick 70.00
Beam, Racing Car, Unser Olsonite Eagle 48 .... 32.50
Beam, Town Crier 70.00
Beam, Whistler's Mother, Box 8.00
Beer, A. Laforme, Ale & Lager, Nashua, N.H., Porcelain Stopper, 1 Pt. 15.00
Beer, Anheuser-Busch Bottling Co., Brooklyn, N.Y., A With Eagle Applied Top 75.00
Beer, Bevo, A/B Brewing Assn., Front & Back Label 100.00
Beer, Blob Top, Amber, 1870s 7.00
Beer, Buffalo Brewing Co., Running Buffalo, Logo On Porcelain Bail, Dug 25.00
Beer, Bunker Hill Lager, Amber, Blob Top, 1 Pt. 22.00
Beer, C.D. Postel, San Francisco Sheaf Of Wheat 150.00
Beer, Clawons Birch, Paper Label 50.00
Beer, D. Lagrange, Moravia, N.Y., Honey Amber, 1 Pt. 20.00
Beer, E.L. Kerns, Embossed Elk Head, Green-Aqua, 1 Pt. 35.00
Beer, El Dorado Brewing Co., Stockton, Calif., Porcelain Bail Top 35.00
Beer, Fredricksburg Bottling Co., Monogram, Olive Green, 1 Qt. 70.00
Beer, Grain Belt, Logo 75.00
Beer, Grand Rapids Brewing Co., Embossed, Amber Glass, 1 Quart 5.00
Beer, Hoyt Bros., Lynn & Salem, Mass., Smoky Gold, 1 Pt. 35.00
Beer, Huelner, Embossed, Pure & Without Drugs Or Poison, Amber 7.00
Beer, J.Q. Doyle, Springfield, Mass., Aqua, 1 Pt. 25.00
Beer, J.W. Beck, Stoneware 15.00
Beer, Jacob Wirth, Boston, Mass., Honey Amber, 1 Pt. 22.00
Beer, John Weiland's Export, Amber & Whittled Applied Top, Amber, 1/2 Pt. 100.00
Beer, Joseph Demer, Pawtucket, R.I., Amethyst, Blob Top 10.00
Beer, Liquid Bread, Adolphus Busch, St. Louis, Blue, Blob Top, Label 215.00
Beer, Madison Original Ale, John Fennell, Louisville, Ky., Cylinder, 1/2 Pt. 125.00
Beer, Patrick Gillan, Milford, Mass., Round Slug, Lightning Stopper 15.00
Beer, Rock Island Brewing Co., Amber, 1/2 Gal. 40.00
Beer, Schlitz, Ruby, Label 20.00
Beer, Stoddard Ale, 3 Mold, Olive Green, Cylindrical, 9 1/2 In. 8.00
Beer, Terre Haute Brewing, Terre Haute, Ind., Amber, Blob Top, 1 Qt. 15.00
Beer, Twin City Bottling Co., Clasped Hands, Amber, Blob Top 17.00
Beer, U.S. Bottling, John Fauser, Amber, 1 Qt. 30.00
Beer, Wagner & Mathes, Lawrence, Mass., Amber, Ceramic Stopper 25.00
Bitters, Ad-La-Wa, Lenoxville, Mass., Indian On Label 75.00
Bitters, American Life Bitters, Tiffin, Ohio, Log Cabin, Amber, 1870s, 9 In. 4950.00
Bitters, Boeset 125.00
Bitters, Carter's Liver 125.00
Bitters, Clarks Sherry Wine, 25 Cents, 7 3/4 In. 140.00
Bitters, Colombo Peptic 45.00
Bitters, Damiana, Light Blue 75.00
Bitters, Dexter Lovegrove Wahoo 7150.00

Bottle, Creamer,	Bottle, Creamer,	Bottle, Creamer,	Bottle, Creamer,
Blanding's,	Country Club	Mac Donald's	Suncrest Farms,
Greenville, Mich.	Dairy	White House Dairy	Mowrer's

Bitters, Dr. George Pierce's Indian Restorative, Aqua, Open Pontil 135.00
Bitters, Dr. Harter's Wild Cherry, Light Amber, 4 In. 45.00
Bitters, Dr. Henley's Wild Grape Root, Medium To Deep Root Beer, 1868-1872 .... 4730.00
Bitters, Dr. J. Hostetter's Stomach, Deep Olive Amber 110.00
Bitters, Dr. J. Hostetter's Stomach, Yellow Amber 60.00
Bitters, Dr. Loew's, Apple Green 250.00
Bitters, Dr. M. McHenry Stomach, Exchange, Penna. 185.00
Bitters, Dr. Stephen Jewett's Celebrated Health Restoring, Aqua, Open Pontil 95.00
Bitters, Drake's Plantation, 4 Log, Amber, Whittled 65.00
Bitters, Drake's Plantation, 4 Log, Yellow 150.00
Bitters, Drake's Plantation, 6 Log, Chocolate Amber 150.00
Bitters, Drake's Plantation, 6 Log, Dark Strawberry 225.00
Bitters, Drake's Plantation, 6 Log, Strawberry Puce 200.00
Bitters, Drake's Plantation, Cabin, Green, Yellow, 1870s, 10 In. 5825.00
Bitters, Fenner's Capitol 75.00
Bitters, Greeley's Bourbon, Barrel Shape, Grayish Amber, 1860-1880, 9 In. 495.00
Bitters, Hall's, Barrel Shape, Yellow Amber 225.00
Bitters, Harzer Krauter 150.00
Bitters, Hertrich's Gesundheits, Globular Shape, Olive Green 2860.00
Bitters, Hooflands, Pontil 85.00
Bitters, J.T. Higby Tonic, Yellow Amber, Square Applied Top 55.00
Bitters, Old Homestead Wild Cherry, Yellow-Green 9020.00
Bitters, Old Man's Stomach 3080.00
Bitters, Old Sachem, Chocolate 395.00
Bitters, Pepsin Calisaya, Light Grass Green, 4 In. 200.00
Bitters, Prickley Ash, Blown In Mold 45.00
Bitters, Rex, Orange & Yellow, Blown In Mold 60.00
Bitters, Sazerac, Milk Glass 290.00
Bitters, Steven Jewett's Restorative 90.00
Bitters, Wm. Allen's Congress, Aqua 195.00
Blown, Club, Broken Swirl, Midwestern, Aqua, 8 3/8 In. 157.00
Clear Pressed Glass, Metal & Cork Stopper, 6 1/2 In. 60.00
Coca-Cola bottles are listed in the Coca-Cola category
Cordial, Booth & Sedgewicke, Green, Square 110.00
Cosmetic, Ayer's Hair Vigor, Midnight Blue, Stopper 50.00
Cosmetic, Barry's Tricopherous, Skin & Hair, Aqua, Pontil 20.00
Cosmetic, Benton's Hair Grower Co., Clear, Round 25.00
Cosmetic, Boswell & Warners, Colorific, Cobalt Blue, 5 1/2 In. 100.00
Cosmetic, Clock's Excelsior Hair Restorer, Aqua, 7 1/4 In. 15.00
Cosmetic, Colgate's Handkerchief Extract, Label, Box, 3 1/4 In. 22.50
Cosmetic, Evening In Paris Talcum, Dark Blue, Chrome Lid, Contents 18.00

Cosmetic, H.C. Hunter's Palm Lotion, Marlboro, Mass., Amber, 5 1/4 In. 38.00
Cosmetic, H.H. Sterling's Ambrosia For The Hair, New York, Aqua, 6 1/8 In. 28.00
Cosmetic, Mrs. Allen's World Hair Restorer, Golden Amber 18.00
Cosmetic, Mrs. H.E. Wilson's Hair Regenerator, Long Neck, Aqua 140.00
Cosmetic, Mrs. S.A. Allen's World Hair Balsam, Aqua 10.00
Cosmetic, Ostol Hair Colour Restorer, Edwards Hairlene Co., Amber, 7 In. 15.00
Cosmetic, Parker's Hair Balsam, Bimal, Label, Contents 25.00
Cosmetic, Star Hair Remedies, Golden Amber, 8 5/8 In. 35.00
Cosmetic, White Clover Cream, L.A. Gould, Portland, Me., Clear, 4 1/2 In. 16.00
Creamer, Blanding's, Greenville, Mich. .... *Illus* 21.00
Creamer, Blue Jay Cafe, Blue 20.00
Creamer, Country Club Dairy .... *Illus* 24.00
Creamer, Creamland, Albuquerque, Green 20.00
Creamer, Golden State Real Cream, Roberts Brothers 20.00
Creamer, Gray's Red Star Dairy, Red Star 60.00
Creamer, Mac Donald's White House Dairy .... *Illus* 21.00
Creamer, Plains Creamery, Red 20.00
Creamer, Quality Dairy, None Better, Red 12.50
Creamer, Suncrest Farms, Mowrer's .... *Illus* 26.00
Creamer, Sunshine Quality, Check Mark, Red 20.00
Cure, Alepizone A Certain Cure For Fits & Epilepsy, Aqua, Small 80.00
Cure, Alexander's Sure Cure For Malaria, Akron, Oh., Amber, 8 In. 65.00
Cure, Chase's Dyspepsia, Newburgh, N.Y., Label, Contents, Box 55.00
Cure, Clavert's Derby, Influenza & Colds, Dark Aqua, 5 1/4 In. 30.00
Cure, Craigs Kidney & Liver Cure, Amber 160.00
Cure, Craigs Kidney, Amber, 1 Pt. 100.00
Cure, D.L.C.S. & Co. Dysentery, Avon, N.Y., 4 1/2 In. 25.00
Cure, Dr. Sykes Sure Cure For Catarrh, Aqua, 4-Piece Mold, 7 In. 75.00
Cure, Gold Dandruff Cure, Clear, 7 1/2 In. 40.00
Cure, Hall's Catarrh 7.00
Cure, Himalya, Kola Compound Natures Cure For Asthma, Amber, 7 1/2 In. 65.00
Cure, K & L Remedy, Clear, Blob Top, 16 Oz. 60.00
Cure, Log Cabin Liver Pills 10.00
Cure, Polar Star Cough Cure, Aqua, 4 In. 35.00
Cure, S.B. Catarrh Cure, Smith Bros., Fresno, Calif., Aqua, 7 3/4 In. 65.00
Cure, Safe Cure, Rochester, Amber, 1/2 Pt. 25.00
Cure, Warner's Safe Cure, Embossed Shoulder, 1 Pt. 85.00
Cure, Warner's Safe Cure, Rochester, Amber, 1 Pt. 180.00
Cure, Warner's Safe Nervine, Pin, Slug Plated 65.00
Cure, Wm. Radam's Microbe Killer Cures, All Diseases, Amber, 10 1/4 In. 50.00
Decanter, Keene, Dark Green 2310.00
Decanter, Pillar Molded, Swirled Ribs, Green, Pewter Stopper, 10 1/2 In., Pair 660.00
Demijohn, Dark Green, Blown, 16 In. 66.00
Drug, Allen Hanburns Castor Oil, Cobalt Blue, 3 1/2 In. 35.00
Drug, Ayers Cherry Pectoral, Lowell, Mass., Aqua, 7 In. 14.00
Drug, Bromo Seltzer, Cobalt Blue, Measuring Cap, 5 In. 8.50
Drug, California Fig Syrup, Wheeling, W.V. 10.00
Drug, Ely McGill Nevada Clarks Drug Store, 4 1/2 In. 150.00
Drug, Evanston Drug, Evanston, Wyo., Clear, 3 5/8 In. 85.00
Drug, Flemings Pharmacy, Denver, Colo., Amber, 5 1/4 In. 75.00
Drug, Fuller, Anaconda, Mont., Amethyst, 5 3/4 In. 35.00
Drug, Leslie E. Keeley Co., Druggist, Ill., Keeley's Variant, Clear, 6 In. 65.00
Drug, Milk Of Magnesia Tablets, Blue Glass, Embossed 5.00
Drug, Red Cross Drug, Fairbanks, Alaska, Clear, 4 In. 85.00
Drug, Reed & Cutlass Druggist, Boston, Flared Lip, 7 3/4 In. 90.00
Drug, Sanborn's Kidney & Liver Vegetable Laxative, Amber 150.00
Drug, Sanitarium, Vicksburg, Miss., Embossed 7.00
Drug, Sweet Springs, Saline County, Mo., Aqua, Cork 18.00
Drug, Vick's VapoRub, Cobalt Blue, Screw Top, 3 In. 5.00
Figural, Cat 40.00
Figural, Derringer, Ceramic 25.00
Figural, Dolls, Milk Glass, Box 8.00
Figural, Ear Of Corn, National, Medium To Dark 275.00

Figural, Fish, Green, Tooled Lip, 10 In. 12.00
Figural, Gun, Ceramic 25.00
Figural, Indian, Peruvian Inca Chief, Black Painted, 12 In. 10.00
Figural, Lady, Upside Down, Clear & Frosted, 19th Century, France, 14 In. 150.00
Figural, Lion, Standing, Gilt, Cream Plinth, Rear Cork, Barsottini, 1970, 8 1/2 In. 24.00
Figural, Mammy, Soda, Large 45.00
Figural, Napoleon, Black Hat Stopper, Robj, 1930 .... 350.00
Figural, Robot, Brown, Clanky Chocolate Syrup 50.00
Figural, Schoolmarm, Stopper, Craquel, 3 In. 50.00
Figural, Violin, Amethyst, Molded F-Holes & Strings, 9 1/2 In. 16.00
Flask, A Little More Grape, Gen. Taylor, Aqua, 1 Pt., 7 1/4 In. 302.00
Flask, A Little More Grape, Monument, Reddish Puce, 1/2 Pt. 2475.00
Flask, Blown, Cornucopia & Urn, 3 Mold, Olive, 1 Pt.7 1/4 In. 495.00
Flask, Chestnut, 10 Diamonds, Amber, Blown, Zanesville, Ohio, 4 5/8 In. 3410.00
Flask, Chestnut, 16 Ribs, Swirled, Aqua, Mantua, Ohio, 6 In. 165.00
Flask, Chestnut, 18 Ribs, Swirled, Pale Green, Midwestern, 6 1/2 In. 192.00
Flask, Chestnut, 24 Ribs, Amber, Zanesville, Ohio, 4 7/8 In. 220.00
Flask, Chestnut, 24 Ribs, Vertical, Zanesville, Ohio, Amber, 4 5/8 In. 330.00
Flask, Coming Through The Rye, Blue Pottery, 3 5/8 x 4 7/8 x 1 5/8 In. 220.00
Flask, Corn For World, Aqua, Rough & Ready, Taylor, 7 1/4 In. 330.00
Flask, Corn For World, Washington Monument, Baltimore, Amber 400.00
Flask, Cornucopia, Olive Green, 5 1/2 In. 121.00
Flask, Custom House Wine Store, Boston, Mass., Aqua, Label, 1 Qt. 50.00
Flask, Double Eagle, Concentric Rings, Medium Green, 7 In. 4730.00
Flask, Double Eagle, Concentric Rings, Green, 1 Pt. 4300.00
Flask, Double Franklin, Deep Aqua, 8 In. 1075.00
Flask, Eagle Sunburst, Yellow Tint 2035.00
Flask, Eagle With Shield, Grapes, Deep Aqua, 1/2 Pt. 300.00
Flask, Eagle, Cornucopia, Light Green, Pontil, 5 1/2 In. 2310.00
Flask, Eagle, Flag, Aqua, Open Pontil 200.00
Flask, Eagle, Grapes, Aqua, Open Pontil 145.00
Flask, Eagle, Masonic, Light Green, 5 3/4 In. 440.00
Flask, Eagle, Prospector, Deep Aqua 120.00
Flask, Eagle, Willington Glass Co., Olive Amber, Double Collared Lip, 1 Pt. 110.00
Flask, Embossed Roses, Aqua Green, Frosted Handle, Hand Blown, 1840-1850 .... 65.00
Flask, Engraved Deer, Blue Overlay 495.00
Flask, Flattened Chestnut, Swirled 24 Rib Design, 6 7/8 In. 110.00
Flask, Flute, For Illicit On-Duty Nips Of Whiskey, Amber, c.1895 .... 165.00
Flask, For Pikes Peak, Hunter, Olive, 1 Pt., 7 5/8 In. 550.00
Flask, Franklin, Dyott, Portrait 1732.00
Flask, General Jackson, Flowers, Aqua, 1 Pt., 6 1/2 In. 907.00
Flask, General Washington & Eagle, Aqua, 1 Pt., 6 3/4 In. 226.00
Flask, George Washington Bust, Strawberry Amethyst, New Jersey, 1850s, 1 Qt. 3300.00
Flask, Jenny Lind, Calabash, Sapphire Blue 4840.00
Flask, Masonic, Eagle, Keene, Olive, Bubble, 7 5/8 In. 137.00
Flask, Masonic, Eagle, Light Green, Open Pontil 325.00
Flask, Monument, Baltimore, Liberty & Union, Aqua, 1 Pt. 220.00
Flask, Picnic, Chocolate Amber, No Design, 5 1/2 In. 20.00
Flask, Pumpkinseed, Amber, Screw Lid, 4 1/2 In. 20.00
Flask, Pumpkinseed, Clear, Sloping Collar With Ring, 4 1/2 In. 10.00
Flask, Pumpkinseed, Crisscross Design, Aqua, Small 35.00
Flask, Pumpkinseed, South Carolina Dispensary, 8 1/2 In. 65.00
Flask, Pumpkinseed, Union Pacific Tea Co., 2 Men On Elephant, Clear, 1873, 1/2 Pt. 135.00
Flask, Shepards & Co., Masonic, Aqua, 6 3/4 In. 220.00
Flask, Striped Red, White & Blue, White Casing, Nicholas Lutz, c.1870, 8 In. 525.00
Flask, Success To The Railroad, Olive Amber, 7 In. 242.00
Flask, Sunburst, Greenish Aqua, 1820s, 1 Pt. 137.50
Flask, Sunburst, Open Pontil, Light Green 375.00
Flask, Tam O'Shanter, Green, Kingsware Pottery 1490.00
Flask, Traveler's Companion, Bluish Aqua, Ravenna Glass Co. 110.00
Flask, Union Clasped Hands, Aqua, 1/2 Pt. 55.00
Flask, Urn & Cornucopia, Olive Amber, 5 1/4 In. 50.00
Flask, Washington & Jackson, Emerald Green, Open Pontil, 1 Pt. 200.00

Flask, Washington, Taylor, Aqua, 1 Qt. 98.00
Flask, Washington, Taylor, Cobalt Blue 3740.00
Flask, Washington, Taylor, Dark Green, 8 In. 412.50
Flask, Washington, Taylor, Yellow Green, 1 Qt. 290.00
Flask, Whiskey, Hard Cider, Harrison & Tyler, 2 In. 231.00
Food, Baker's Pride Maple Extract, Sedalia, Mo. 2.00
Food, Chestnuts, Metal Overlay, Monkey 1 Side, Woman In Corset Other, 5 1/4 In. ... 83.00
Food, J. Fan-Prunes Dente-Bordeaux, Aqua, 1840-1860, 10 In. 82.50
Food, Johnny Walker Orange Extract 3.00
Food, Juice, Lenker Brook Farms Milk, Refrigerator 11.00
Food, Meharry's Best 100% Pure Honey, San Francisco, Square, 1/2 Pt. 50.00
Food, Pepper Sauce, Ribbed, Aqua, 8 1/2 In. 20.00
Food, Pickle, Barrel, Emerald Green 50.00
Food, Pickle, Cathedral, 6 Sides, Aqua, 13 1/4 In. 82.50
Food, Pickle, Cathedral, Aqua, Crosshatch Design, 7 1/2 In. 125.00
Food, Pickle, Cathedral, Green, 1800s 350.00
Food, Smith's Bile Beans, Watch Type 7.00
Food, Towles Log Cabin Syrup, Embossed, Cork Top, 1900s 25.00
Food, White House, Vinegar, Embossed 7.00
Fruit Jar, Amazon, Swift Seal, Ball Blue, 1 Pt. 10.00
Fruit Jar, Ambler Globe, Pat. 1886, 1/2 Gal., 1 Qt., & 1 Pt., 3 Piece 350.00
Fruit Jar, Atlas E-Z Seal, Aqua, Glass Top, 1 Qt. 10.00
Fruit Jar, Atlas, E-Z Seal, Cornflower Blue, 1 Qt. 25.00
Fruit Jar, Atlas, Mason's Patent, Apple Green, 1 Pt. 10.00
Fruit Jar, Ball Ideal, Aqua, Glass Top, 1 Qt. 5.00
Fruit Jar, Ball Ideal, Aqua, Wire Bail, 1908, 1 Qt. 3.50
Fruit Jar, Ball Mason, Script Writing, Patent 1858, Aqua, 1 Qt. 5.00
Fruit Jar, Ball Perfect Mason, Dropped A, 1 Pt. 45.00
Fruit Jar, Ball Perfect Mason, Olive Green, 1 Qt. 25.00
Fruit Jar, Ball, Zinc Cap, Blue, 1/2 Pt. 48.00
Fruit Jar, Beaver, Clear, Heavy Embossing, 1 Canadian Qt. 35.00
Fruit Jar, Calcuts Patent, 1 Pt. 25.00
Fruit Jar, Cohansey, Barrel Shape, Aqua, 7 3/8 In. 110.00
Fruit Jar, Columbia, Clear, Lid Patent Dec. 29th 1896, 1 Qt. 20.00
Fruit Jar, Drey, Square Mason, Clear, 1 Pt. 5.00
Fruit Jar, Gem, Reverse H.G.W., Heavy Embossed Lid, Aqua, 1/2 Gal. 15.00
Fruit Jar, Globe, Amber, 1/2 Gal. 110.00
Fruit Jar, H.W. Pettit, Westerville, N.J., Lid, Steel Clamp, Aqua, 6 In. 6.60
Fruit Jar, Hazel Preserve, 1/2 Pt. 30.00
Fruit Jar, Improved Corona, Clear, Made In Canada, 1/2 Gal. 3.00
Fruit Jar, Improved Gem, Clear, Canada, 1/2 Gal. 3.00
Fruit Jar, Knox Mason, Zinc Top, Clear, 2 Qt. 3.50
Fruit Jar, L.G. Co., Improved Jam Reverse, Clear Lid, Aqua, 1 Pt. 125.00
Fruit Jar, Lafayette, Aqua, Clear Lid 115.00
Fruit Jar, Lightning, Amber, 1/2 Gal. 110.00
Fruit Jar, Lightning, Aqua, Wire Bail Handle, Glass Top, 1 Qt. 5.00
Fruit Jar, Mason's Patent Nov. 30th, 1858, Green, Zinc Cap, The Marion Jar, 1 Pt. 25.00
Fruit Jar, Mason's, G.C. Co., Patent Nov. 30th, 1858, Aqua, 1 Pt. 3.00
Fruit Jar, Mason's, Improved, Butter Jar, C.F.J. Co., Aqua, 2 Qt. 100.00
Fruit Jar, Mason, Black Lettering, 1/2 Gal. 180.00
Fruit Jar, Millville Atmospheric, Whitall's Pat. June 18th 1861, Aqua, 1/2 Gal. 45.00
Fruit Jar, Pottery, Macomb, Zinc Lid, 1898, 2 Qt. 85.00
Fruit Jar, Quick Seal, Wire Bail, Glass Lid, 1 Pt. 4.00
Fruit Jar, Salt Glaze, Wax Seal, 1 Qt. 17.50
Fruit Jar, Stevens Tin Top, Lewis & Neblett, Cincinnati, Ohio, 1 Pt. 275.00
Fruit Jar, Stoddard, Orange Amber, Octofoil Body, 1856-1871, 1 Gal. 457.00
Gin, Charles London Cordial, Emerald Green, Square, Beveled Edge, 1870s, 9 1/2 In. ... 93.50
Household, Buckingham Whisker Dye, Amber, 5 In. 7.00
Household, Hart's Delight Stove Polish, Troy, N.Y., Embossed Hearts, Crude 30.00
Ink, Blown, 3 Mold, Olive Amber, 2 5/8 In. 137.00
Ink, Carter's, Cathedral, Cobalt Blue, 1 Qt. 95.00
Ink, Carter's, Triangular Shape, Turtle, Label 15.00
Ink, Free-Blown, Handmade Link Chain Cork Stopper, Olive Green, c.1740, 2 In. 1155.00

Ink, Geometric, Sunburst Motif, 3 Mold, Cylindrical, c.1820, 2 x 2 In. 3850.00
Ink, Green-Aqua, Ribbed 32.00
Ink, Peacock Blue Ink, Tin 30.00
Ink, Phrenology-Type, F. Bridges, Phrenologist, Graniteware, 1850s, 5 7/16 In. 1870.00
Ink, Pitkin, 36 Ribs, Swirled To Right, Medium Green, 1 1/2 x 2 1/4 In. 500.00
Ink, Plantation, Cone 6.00
Ink, Ross's Excelsior Ink, Emerald Green 7475.00
Ink, Stafford's Jet Black, Cobalt Blue, Label, 6 In. 60.00
Ink, Teakettle, Barrel, Brass Cap, Sandwich Glass 1265.00
Ink, Teakettle, Free-Blown, Green 300.00
Ink, Warren's Congress Ink American, Olive-Green, c.1860, 7 1/4 x 2 1/2 In. 3850.00
Jar, Borden's Malted Milk, Clear, Stenciled Milk Glass Label, Tin Lid, 8 1/2 In. 633.00
Jar, Cream, Alden Bros. Co., Mass., Gray Cast, Clouded, 1/2 Pt. 20.00
Jar, Cream, Rhodes Bros. Co., Amethyst, Round, 1/2 Pt. 20.00
Jar, Crushed Fruit, Clear, 10 Sides, Heisey Mark, 10 In. 77.00
Jar, Dilling's Candies, Clear, Raised Letters, 11 In. 110.00
Jar, Eat Heos' Peanut Butter Sandwiches, Clear, Stenciled Letters, 14 In. 77.00
Jar, Fenway Candy Co., Boston, Aqua, 15 In. 85.00
Jar, Gibford's Pure Honey Apiaries, Riverside, Calif., Red, Straight Sides, 8 Oz. 30.00
Jar, Kis-Me-Gum, Raised Letters, 11 In. 66.00
Jar, Morrell Meat, Tin Lid, Square 2.00
Jar, Paste, Sanford Mfg. Co., Chicago & New York, Pat. July 10, 1900, Lid, Clear 8.00
Jar, Peerless Hard Water Soap, Clear Glass, Metal Lid, 10 In. 132.00
Jar, Preserving, Blue Stenciled Label, A.P. Donaghho, 8 1/4 In. 137.50
Jar, Pure Food Cigar, Tin Lid, Brown, 6 1/2 In. 33.00
Jar, Squirrel Brand Peanuts, Clear Glass, Tin Lid, Square, 9 1/2 In. 72.00
Jar, Uneeda Bakers Biscuit, Raised Letters, Metal Lid, Clear, 9 In. 143.00
Jar, Victoria's Yogurt Bulgarian Culture Made, San Bernardino, Calif., 1 Pt. 6.50
Jar, Walla Walla Gum, Indian, Headdress, Clear, 12 3/4 In. 275.00
Jar, Zatek Chocolate Billets, Pennsylvania, Gold Painted Letters, Clear, 17 In. 352.00
Jug, E. Demers & Co., Spencer, Mass., Wine & Liquors, Ironstone, 1/2 Gal. 65.00
Jug, St. Thomas, W.I., Rum, Label, 1 Gal. 75.00
Jug, Welch & Sullivan, Concord, N.H., Ironstone, Cream, Tan Top 150.00
Jug, West End Wine & Spirits Boston, Mass., Ironstone 75.00
Medicine, D. Wistars Balsam Of Wild Cherry 37.00
Medicine, Davis Vegetable Pain Killer, Aqua, 6 In. 12.50
Medicine, Dr. Caldwell's Syrup Pepsin, Sample 6.00
Medicine, Dr. Fahrney & Son Teething Syrup, For Babies, Aqua 7.50
Medicine, Dr. J. Gesteria, Regulador Gesteira, Amber, 5 In. 20.00
Medicine, Dr. J.W. Poland, Olive Amber, 1850-1870, 7 3/4 In. 302.50
Medicine, Dr. James' Cherry Tar Syrup, Pittsburgh, Pa., Aqua, 6 In. 12.50
Medicine, Dr. Jones' Liniment, Embossed Beaver, Aqua, 6 1/2 In. 15.00
Medicine, Dr. Kennedy's Rheumatic Liniment, Roxbury, Mass., Aqua, 7 In. 20.00
Medicine, Dr. Kilmer's Swamp Root Remedy, Cork, 1800s 6.00
Medicine, Dr. King's New Discovery, Cork, 1800s 6.00
Medicine, Dr. McClean's Strengthening Cordial & Blood Purifier, Aqua, 9 In. 45.00
Medicine, Dr. Miles' Medical Co., Restorative Nervine, Aqua, 8 In. 15.00
Medicine, Dr. Pierce Extract Of Smart Weed, Aqua, 5 1/4 In. 15.00
Medicine, Dr. Pierce's Golden Medical Discovery, Lime Green, 8 1/4 In. 45.00
Medicine, Dr. Porter, New York, Aqua, Rolled Lip, Open Pontil, 5 In. 25.00
Medicine, Dr. Simmon's Squaw Fine Wine, Aqua, 9 In. 25.00
Medicine, Dr. Thatcher's Liver & Blood Syrup, Chattanooga, Tenn., Amber, 3 3/8 In. . 28.00
Medicine, Dr. Thatcher's Liver & Blood Syrup, Chattanooga, Tenn., 8 1/2 In. .. 35.00 to 45.00
Medicine, Dr. V.N.H. Down's Vegetable Balsamic Elixir, Aqua, 12 Sides, 4 1/4 In. ... 35.00
Medicine, Dutton's Angleworm Liniment, Aqua, Bimal, 6 In. 16.00
Medicine, Father John, Amber 8.00
Medicine, Fiad Richer's Pain Expeller, Aqua, 4 3/4 In. 12.50
Medicine, Holman's Natures Grand Restorative, Olive Amber, 1850, 7 In. 3190.00
Medicine, L.M. Green Prop., Woodbury, N.J., Cork Top 6.00
Medicine, Lightning Hot Drops, No Relief, No Pay, Springfield, Oh., Aqua, 5 In. 10.00
Medicine, Liquozone, Amber, Embossed Cork, Chicago 1.50
Medicine, Prof. Lorman's Indian Oil, Philadelphia, Pa., Aqua, 5 1/8 In. 20.00
Medicine, Pure Cod Liver Oil, N.E. Atwood, Provincetown, Mass., Tombstone 60.00

Medicine, Rowler's Rheumatism Medicine, Apple Green 4235.00
Medicine, Scotts Emulsion Cod Liver Oil, Aqua Haze, 9 In. 8.50
Medicine, Shaker Syrup No.1, Canterbury, N.H., Aqua, Sloping Collar, 1800s, 7 In. . 165.00
Medicine, Sloan's Liniment, Clear, Languages, Box, 1929 .... 9.00
Medicine, Tom's Russian Liniment, Aqua 120.00
Medicine, Ubert's Tar, Boneset & Honey, Brooklyn, N.Y., Aqua, 6 1/2 In. 17.00
Medicine, Vapo Cresolene, Cornflower Blue, 5 1/2 In. 85.00
Medicine, Veterinary, Humphrey's Homopathic 265.00
Milk, Alpenrose Dairy Golden Crest Milk, Portland, Ore., Cream Top, 1 Qt. 65.00
Milk, Borden's, Elsie's Head, Red, Square, 1/2 Pt. 20.00
Milk, Brighton Place, Rochester, N.Y., Green 475.00
Milk, Burroughs Brothers Walnut Grove Farm, Knightsen, Calif., Cream Top, 1 Qt. ... 13.00
Milk, Cambridge Dairy, Black & Orange Pyro, Round, 1 Qt. 35.00
Milk, Carnation Fresh, Red, Square, 1/2 Pt. 25.00
Milk, Cedar Grove Dairy, Memphis, Tenn., Embossed, 1 Qt. 12.50
Milk, Charles W. Shuler, 1 Qt. 15.00
Milk, City Dairy, Bay City, Mi., Square, Orange 6.00
Milk, Clover Brand, 3-Leaf Clover, Round, 1 Pt. 9.00
Milk, Cloverleaf Blue Ribbon Farms, Stockton, Calif., Round Top, 1 Qt. 19.00
Milk, Cloverleaf Creamery Co., Boulder, Colo., Cream Top, 1 Qt. 80.00
Milk, College View Dairy, Jumping Horse, Rider, Maroon, Square, 1 Pt. 10.00
Milk, Collegian Dairy, Laramie, Wyo., Neck Ring, 1 Qt. 25.00
Milk, Dairy Mart, San Diego Farms, Hand With Test Tube, Amber, 1/2 Pt. 50.00
Milk, Dodds Alderney Dairy, Round, 1 Qt. 15.00
Milk, Eblings Golden Jersey Milk, Embossed, Round 10.00
Milk, Enjoy Reed's Homogenized Good Guernsey Milk, Amber, Square, 1 Qt. 12.50
Milk, Equity Top Of Ohio, Mountains, Sunrise, Paper Label, 1 Gal. 70.00
Milk, Eureka Dairy, Amethyst, Churn Shape, 1 Pt. 20.00
Milk, Family Dairy, Salem, Ohio, Cream Top, 1/2 Pt. 25.00
Milk, Golden Arrow, California, 1/2 Cup Measures, Amber, Square, 1 Qt. 12.00
Milk, Golden Royal, Amber, 1/2 Gal. 8.50
Milk, Grade A Cloverleaf, Cream Top, Maroon, 1 Pt. 75.00
Milk, Greenleaf Dairy, Petersburg, Va., Green, Square, 1 Qt. 45.00
Milk, Hagerstown Dairy Company, Shield Design, 1/2 Pt. 8.00
Milk, Hill's Dairy, This Side Up, Cream Separator, Amber, 1 Qt. 80.00
Milk, Hilo Dairymen's Center Gr. A., Black Pyro, Round, 1/2 Pt. 75.00
Milk, Hoppy's Favorite, Hoppy's Picture, Maroon, Square, 1 Qt. 40.00
Milk, J.H. Rich Dairy, Banner Over Neck, 16 Neck Panels, 1 Pt. 13.00
Milk, Jo-Mar Farm Guernsey Milk, Round, Emblem, Jug Style, 1/3 Qt. 25.00
Milk, Jones Dairy, Corydon, Iowa, 15 Cent Deposit, 1/2 Gal. 3.00
Milk, Kline's, Cream Top, 1 Pt. 22.50
Milk, Liberty Dairy, Pink, 1 Pt. 5.50
Milk, Loma Linda Sanitarium Dairy, Orange, Square, 1 Qt. 27.00
Milk, Mayflower Milk, Pilgrim, Red, Round Top, 1 Qt. 50.00
Milk, Middlesex Farm Dairy, New Brunswick, N.J., Cream Top, Red, 1 Qt. 10.00
Milk, Mission Milk Creameries Inc., Building, Orange Pyro, Round, 1 Qt. 11.00
Milk, Ohio Farmers, Script Over Map Of Ohio, 1 Pt. 35.00
Milk, Pacific Union Angwin College, 1 Pt. 30.00
Milk, Peplau's, New Britton, Conn., Embossed, Pink Tint, 10 Oz. 8.50
Milk, Portland Damascus Milk Co., Ribbon Overlay, Amethyst, 1/2 Pt. 15.00
Milk, Reno Model Dairy Inc., 14 Neck Ribs, 1/4 Pt. 40.00
Milk, Rosedale Dairy Dial Real Milk, Laramie, Wyo., Cream Top, 1 Qt. 95.00
Milk, Shamrock Dairy, Emblem, 1 Qt. 40.00
Milk, Shy-Der's 100% Pure Undiluted Health, Green Pyro, Round, 1 Pt. 15.00
Milk, Sunland Dairy, Yuma, Ariz., Square, Amber, 1 Qt. 25.00
Milk, Sunset Dairy, Inc., Hand With Glass Of Milk, Square, Amber, 1 Qt, ... 25.00
Milk, Terrace Farm Dairy Co., Round, 1 Qt. 18.00
Milk, Tri-State Milk Bottle Supply Co., Ashland, Ky., Round, 1 Qt. 30.00
Milk, Universal Store Bottle, 5 Cents, 4 Oz. 9.00
Milk, Universal Store Bottle, Embossed, Round, 1 Qt. 15.00
Milk, Vale Edge Dairy, A Bottle Of Health, Brown Pyro, Round, 1 Qt. 35.00
Milk, Weiland, Clear, 1 Qt. 8.00
Milk, Wm. Weckerle & Sons Inc., Buffalo, N.Y., Round, Amber, 1 Qt. 30.00

Milk, Wm. Weckerle & Sons, Buffalo, N.Y., Amber, 1/2 Pt. 39.00
Mineral Water, Akesion Spring, Owned By Sweet Springs Co., Amber 140.00
Mineral Water, Blue Lick Water Co., Ky., Emerald Green, c.1860, 8 1/8 In. 3520.00
Mineral Water, Clark & White, Golden Olive, Backwards N In N.Y., 1 Qt. 235.00
Mineral Water, Clark & White, New York, Olive Green, 1 Qt. 50.00
Mineral Water, Clark & White, Saratoga, N.Y., 1 Qt. 58.00
Mineral Water, Clarke & Co., New York, Olive Green, 1 Pt. 75.00
Mineral Water, D.A. Knowlton, Saratoga, N.Y., Olive Green, 1 Qt. 185.00
Mineral Water, Empire Spring Co., Emerald Green, 1880s, 1 Qt. 55.00
Mineral Water, Geyser Springs, Saratoga Springs, N.Y., 1 Pt. 50.00
Mineral Water, J. Schwepps, Torpedo, Blue, Aerated 175.00
Mineral Water, John Clarke, New York, Light Olive, 3 Mold, 1 Qt. 170.00
Mineral Water, Middletown Healing Springs, Grays & Clark, Middletown, Vt., 1 Qt. 80.00
Mineral Water, Oak Orchard Acid Springs, Lockport, N.Y., Green, 1 Qt. 160.00
Mineral Water, Star Springs Co., Saratoga, N.Y., Red Amber, 1 Pt. 85.00
Mineral Water, Vermont Springs Sax & Co., Sheldon, Vt., Emerald, 1 Qt. 75.00
Mineral Water, Vichy Water Hanbury Smith, Yellow Olive, 1/2 Pt. 85.00
Mineral Water, Wm. Otto, Philadelphia, Pa., Deep Blue-Green, Slug Plate, Blob Top 55.00
Nurser, Armstrong, Lays Flat 15.00
Nurser, Avondale Milk, Emblem Of Quality, Screw Top, Oz. & Cc. Marks 15.00
Nurser, Echo Farm Milk, Blue, Pullover Finish 12.00
Nurser, Embossed Rings Prevent Rolling, Oval, 8 Oz. 4.50
Nurser, Evenflo, Salesman's Sample, 1950s, 3 In. 14.00
Nurser, Golden Arrow, Double Homogenized, Oz. & Ml. Graduations, 6 Sides 30.00
Nurser, Guilford Feeder, Banana Shape, 1/2 Size 25.00
Nurser, Hygenic Feeder, Embossed, 1/2 Size 25.00
Nurser, National Baby's Formula Service, Chicago, Graduations, Square, Orange 40.00
Nurser, Pyrex, Hexagonal 12.00
Nurser, Rexall, Stork 15.00
Nurser, Ross Chemist, Turtle, Small 30.00
Nurser, San Diego State University, Evenflo Emblem, Graduations, 6 Sides 35.00
Nurser, Taxston Dairy, Good Health For Baby, Red, Round 15.00
Oil, Kickapoo Indian, Embossed 10.00
Oil, Shell, Raised Logo, Ribbed, 1 Qt., 14 In. 85.00
Oil, Sonoco Motor Oil, Raised Letters, Spout, 1 Qt., 17 In. 85.00
Oil, Tyolene, Embossed 40.00
Oil, Wm. Penn Valve-Ease 20.00
Perfume bottles are listed in their own category
Poison, Acme, Paris, Scover, Green 2.00
Poison, C.L.G. Co., Cobalt Blue, Ribbed Hexagon, 4 1/2 In. 55.00
Poison, Casket Shape, Cobalt Blue, 4 3/4 In. 4785.00
Poison, Champion Embalming Fluid 6.45
Poison, Diamond Antiseptic, Triangular, Label, 4 3/4 In. 20.00
Poison, Dick's Ant Destroyer, New Orleans 95.00
Poison, Dr. Perry's Dead Shot 9.00
Poison, Euvalerol Elixer B. Poison, Amber, Cylinder, Label, 20 Oz. 48.00
Poison, Green, 6 Sides 24.00
Poison, Light Cobalt Blue, Poison On Shoulder, Cylinder, 7 In. 35.00
Poison, Lin Bellad, Metho, Chocolate Brown, Label, 3 Mold, Stopper, 7 1/2 In. 48.00
Poison, McCormick & Co., Embossed Bee, Cobalt Blue, Triangular, 3 In. 150.00
Poison, Not To Be Taken, Embossed, Octagonal, 6 In. 38.00
Poison, P.R.R. Disinfectant, Amber, Embossed, Round, 6 In. 50.00
Poison, Permal Solution, Cobalt Blue, Oval, 6 1/2 In. 120.00
Poison, Pinched Spout, Cork Stopper, Mercury Finish 85.00
Poison, Poisonous, Not To Be Taken Front, Ribbed, Stopper, 9 1/2 In. 220.00
Poison, Skull Shape, Cobalt Blue, Pat. June 26, 1894, 3 1/2 In. 1000.00
Poison, Skull, 2 7/8 In. 3080.00
Poison, Skull, 3 1/2 In. 3135.00
Poison, Star, Light Apple Green, 6 In. 280.00
Poison, Wide Mouth, Light Blue, Cork, Label, 5 1/2 In. 40.00
Poison, Wrights Lysol, Amber, 4 In. 50.00
Sarsaparilla, Dr. Belding's Wild Cherry, Script 40.00
Sarsaparilla, Dr. Marshall's Extract Of Sarsaparilla & Dandelion, Aqua 25.00

Sarsaparilla, Dr. Townsend's, Albany, N.Y., Aqua, Tooled Top, 4 1/2 In. 85.00
Sarsaparilla, Dr. Townsend's, Albany, N.Y., Olive, Pontil 125.00
Sarsaparilla, Dr Townsend's, Emerald Green, Iron Pontil 50.00
Sarsaparilla, Dr. Wood's Wild Cherry Bitters, Open Pontil 300.00
Sarsaparilla, Skoda's Concentrated Extract Of Sarsaparilla, Amber, 8 1/2 In. 145.00
Seal, David Provost 1723, Olive Green 1925.00
Seltzer, Good Health, Harrison Bottle Co., Brooklyn, N.Y., Emerald Green 20.00
Seltzer, Good Health, Jos. Steckler, Brooklyn, N.Y., Aqua 20.00
Seltzer, Grand Seltzer Works, Weitzman & Sons, N.Y., Green, 10 Sides 22.00
Seltzer, Jay-EFF, Sparkling Beverages, Brooklyn, N.Y., Bright Blue 22.00
Seltzer, Petaluma Soda & Seltzer Works, Acid Etched, Shield Mark, c.1930s 22.00
Seltzer, Sara Ford, Frank Vesc Co., Orient Heights, 10 Sides 10.00
Snuff, Agate, Carved, Oriental, 2 1/4 In. 247.50
Snuff, Black Opalescent, Carved 330.00
Snuff, China, Jade Stopper, With Wooden Spoon 48.00
Snuff, Continuous Picture Of Travelers On Road, Porcelain, China 110.00
Snuff, Enameled Copper, Oriental Scenes, 2 1/2 In. 126.00
Snuff, Glass, Mold Blown, Olive Amber, 4 1/2 In. 137.00
Snuff, Glass, Painted Interior, Village In Valley, Flattened Form, China, 3 In. 145.00
Snuff, Green Stone, Star Design, Smoky Interior, Enameled Silver Lid, 2 1/2 In. 82.50
Snuff, Ivory, Men, Trees, Mountains, Paneled, Spoon 175.00
Snuff, Ivory, Shishis & Blossoms, Korea 1125.00
Snuff, Jadite, Carved Horsemen, In Battle, China, 19th Century 5500.00
Snuff, Lapis, Ornately Carved 285.00
Snuff, Malachite, Carved Trees, Oriental Figures, 2 1/2 In. 214.00
Snuff, Porcelain, Confronting Figures On Country Road, 2 3/4 In. 180.00
Snuff, Rock Crystal, Interior Painted, 2 Frolicking Pups, 1900 .... 2587.00
Snuff, Rock Crystal, Interior Painted, Ye Zhongsan, 1930 .... 862.00
Snuff, Rock Crystal, Painted, Zhou Leyuan, 1886 .... 1610.00
Snuff, Rose Quartz, Branches Of Flowers, Silver Mounted, Silver Hinged Top 245.00
Snuff, Soapstone, Brown Shaded To White, Carved, 3 In. 60.50
Soaky, Casper 30.00
Soaky, Felix The Cat, Colgate-Palmolive, 1960s 40.00
Soaky, Felix The Cat, Red 75.00
Soaky, Mighty Mouse 20.00
Soaky, Mummy 75.00
Soaky, Wolfman, Blue 75.00
Soda, Albert Pick & Co., Root Beer, Clear, Painted Black & White Label, 11 3/4 In. ... 60.00
Soda, C.D. Dows Ginger Ale, Boston, Mass., Aqua, Round, 5 Fancy Panels 25.00
Soda, Canada Dry, Marigold, 9 3/4 In. 55.00
Soda, Canada Dry, White, Signed, 12 In. 55.00
Soda, Chicquot Club, Eskimo Logo, Green, Original Label 5.00
Soda, Cottle Post & Co., Embossed Eagle, Emerald Teal, 1/2 Gal. 400.00
Soda, Diamond, Albin, Iowa, 7 Oz. 2.00
Soda, Dillon, Cowboy On Bronco, Orange & White, 12 Oz. 5.00
Soda, Donald Duck, 1950s, 7 1/2 In. 48.00
Soda, Double Cola Junior, 7 1/2 Oz. 1.50
Soda, Dr. J. Townsend's, Albany, N.Y., No. 1, Open Pontil, Bubbles, Olive Green 175.00
Soda, Dr. J. Townsend's, New York, Iron Pontil, Medium Blue Green 250.00
Soda, Green Spot Orange, 1/2 Pt. Milk Bottle Shape 2.50
Soda, Highland Park Mineral Co., Mi., Embossed, Slug Plate, Crown Top, Qt. 6.00
Soda, Hires Root Beer, Extract, Contents 8.00
Soda, Jones Sibley & Co., St. Louis, Mo., 6 Mold, Aqua, Round Base 225.00
Soda, Maumee Valley, Red & White, Indian Rowing Canoe 9.00
Soda, Moxie, With Carrying Case, Stopper, 2 Bottles 149.00
Soda, Pokagon, Angola, Ind., Indian Head, Red 8.00
Soda, Red Rock Cola, Unopened 5.00
Soda, Rudman & Son, Bangor, Maine, Hutchinson, Aqua 8.00
Soda, Silfvast & Kangas, Diamondville, Wyo., Hutchinson, Aqua 95.00
Soda, Sprite Boy, Springtime In Atlanta, 1984 .... 35.00
Soda, Wm. Lappeus Premium Soda, Albany, Cobalt, 10 Sides, Iron Pontil, 1/2 Gal. ... 575.00
Stopper, Bust Of Black Man, Painted Bisque, 2 3/4 In. 88.00
Tonic, Dr. Groves Chill, Cork, 1800 .... 6.00

Tonic, Elixir Of Cod Liver Oil, Amber, 7 5/8 In. 25.00
Tonic, Indian Liver & Kidney, Label, Cork Top, Contents 18.00
Tonic, Jones & Primley Co., Elkhart, Ind., Label, Contents 250.00
Wheaton, Billy Graham, Christmas, 1974 .... 6.00
Wheaton, MacArthur, Commemorative 6.00
Wheaton, Nixon-Agnew, 1972, Commemorative 6.00
Wheaton, President Washington Through Nixon, Box, Miniature, 36 Piece 180.00
Whiskey, A.M. Bininger & Co., Barrel Shape, Amber, Double Collar, 1860s, 8 In. 93.50
Whiskey, A.M. Bininger Old Kentucky Bourbon, Barrel Shape, Small 140.00
Whiskey, Champion Monogram Kessler & Co., New York, Honey Amber 50.00
Whiskey, Chopin & Gore, Sour Mash, Barrel Shape, Amber, Stopper, 1870s, 9 In. 110.00
Whiskey, Cyrus Eaton, Denver, Says 1 Qt. You Bet, Glob Top 750.00
Whiskey, Decanter, Fire Engine, Mooseheart, 1976, Original Tag 90.00
Whiskey, Devils Island, Embossed 15.00
Whiskey, E.C. Booz Old Cabin, Brown 27.50
Whiskey, Flask, Old Crow Bourbon, Rawlins, Wyo., Freedman Dandy, 1 Pt. 300.00
Whiskey, H. Melzer, Eagle On Barrel 2200.00
Whiskey, Haig & Haig, Pinched, Sterling Silver Floral Cage 150.00
Whiskey, Hiram Walker, Amber, Embossed, 1 Pt. 2.50
Whiskey, Mist Of The Morning, Barrel Shape, Amber, 1860-1880, 10 1/4 In. 192.50
Whiskey, Old Spring, Clear, Red Painted Raised Letters, 10 In. 22.00
Whiskey, Potts & Potts, Atlanta, Ga., Amber, Squatty Mold 325.00
Whiskey, Pullman Pure Rye, Stoneware, Brown & White, Missing Handle, 9 In. 154.00
Whiskey, Spears Old Pioneer, Golden Amber 2805.00
Wine, French Bordeaux, Unopened, 1908 .... 90.00
Wine, Green, Design, Long Neck, Europe, 1950-1960, 31 In. 695.00
Wine, J.T. Hartnett & Co. Wines & Liquors, Charlestown, Mass., Clear, 1/2 Pt. 45.00

BOTTLE CAP collectors search for the printed cardboard caps used during
the past 80 years.

Aunt Mary's Root Beer, Country Home, Cork Lined, 1940s .... .50
Broguiere's Homogenized Milk, Clamp Over, 1 1/2 In. .... .10
Brownie Root Beer, Picture Of Brownie, Cork Lined, 1950s 1.00
Crush Lemon-Lime, Caricature Holding Lemon, Cork Lined 2.00
Dandy Cola, Cork Lined, 1950s 1.00
Darigold Watcom Co., Dairymen's Assn., Metal, 2 1/4 In. 1.00
Foremost Milk, Orange Plastic, Clamp Over, 1 3/4 In. .... .10
Frost King, Soda, Snowman, Trees, Cork Lined, 1940s 1.50
Monebello Sanitary Dairy Low Fat Milk, Clamp Over, 1 1/2 In. .... .10
Moxie, Cork Lined, 1950s 1.00
MSC, Michigan State Pasteurized Cream, Plug Type, 2 1/4 In. .... .50
Old Fashioned Buttermilk, Plug Type, 2 1/4 In. .... .10
Shadow Lawn Dairy Pasteurized Milk, Plug Type, 2 1/4 In. .... .20
Walla Walla College Dairy Milk, Paper, 2 1/4 In. 25.00
Wink, Cork 2.00

BOTTLE OPENERS are needed to open many bottles. As soon as the commercial bottle was invented, the opener to be used with the new types of closures
became a necessity. Many types of bottle openers can be found, most dating
from the twentieth century. Collectors prize advertising and comic openers.

4-Eyed Man, Wall Mount, J.W. Co., 3 15/16 x 4 1/16 In. 11.00
4-Eyed Woman 65.00
Alligator, Brass 35.00
Alligator, Bronze 70.00
Bear, Wall Mount, Cast Iron 65.00
Bear Face, Brown 75.00
Bear On Fence 50.00
Bicycle 50.00
Black Face, Iron 75.00
Budweiser Beer, Iron .... .25
Bull Moose, Brass 65.00
Canada Goose, Brass 55.00
Canada Goose, Cast Iron 65.00

Clown, Head, Brass	75.00
Cockatiel	250.00
Cowboy, Cast Iron	125.00
Cowboy, With Guitar, Aluminum, Painted	35.00
Cowboy & Cactus, Cast Iron	125.00
Crab, Brass	6.00
Crab, John Wright Co., Iron, 1 x 3 3/4 In.	33.00
Dog, Pointer, Cast Iron	40.00
Dolphin, Chrome	20.00
Donkey, Iron	25.00
Donkey, Iron, Polychrome, 3 In.	38.50
Dr Pepper, Wall Mount, Box	27.00
Drunk, Lamppost	25.00
Drunk On Signpost, With Ashtray	50.00
Duck's Head, 3 1/4 x 5 1/4 In.	110.00
Elephant, Iron, Polychrome, 3 5/8 In.	27.50
Elephant, Iron, Red	40.00
Fish, Trout, 5 x 4 1/4 In.	100.00
Grain Belt, Chopper Shape, Royalton Beverage Co., Box	75.00
Gretz Beer, Man On Unicycle, Carrying Cheese, Mouse	9.00
Indian Boy, Iroquois Beverages	65.00
Jimmy Carter	25.00
Lobster, Brass, 2 3/4 In.	65.00
Lobster, Iron, 1/4 x 5 1/8 In.	66.00
Man, Saluting, Pith Helmet, Nickel On Brass, England	23.00
Nifty, Iron, Folding Corkscrew	2.25
Nude Woman, On Pedestal, Brass, 1930s	38.00
Palm Tree, Brass	45.00
Parrot, Brass, Small	45.00
Parrot, Chrome, With Corkscrew	55.00
Peacock, Bronze	95.00
Pelican, Wilton Products, 3 3/8 x 3 3/4 In.	93.00
Pumpkin Head	50.00
Putnam Bros., Milk & Cream, Peabody, Mass.	5.00
Sailor, John Wright Co., Iron, 3 3/4 x 2 1/4 In.	60.00
Seahorse, John Wright Co., 4 1/4 x 2 1/4 In.	106.00 to 140.00
Skeleton	50.00
Squawking Parrot, Corkscrew, Art Deco, Chrome, Negbauer, 5 In.	25.00
Sterling Silver Handle, 5 1/2 In.	25.00
Teeth, Full Set, Wall Mount	69.00
White Rock Ginger Ale, Wall Mount	10.00

BOXES of all kinds are collected. They were made of thin strips of inlaid wood, metal, tortoiseshell, embroidery, or other material. Additional boxes may be listed in other sections, such as Advertising, Battersea, Ivory, Shaker, Tinware, and various Porcelain categories. Tea Caddies are listed in their own category.

Apple, Poplar, Green Paint, 9 3/4 x 10 1/4 x 3 1/2 In.	236.00
Apple, Square Nail Construction, Pine, 9 1/2 In.	88.00
Ballot, Election, Wooden, Side Handle, Locking Lid	25.00
Ballot, Mahogany, Civil War, 16 In.	140.00
Band, Wallpaper Covered, 1845	225.00
Beetle Nut, Brass, Polynesian	60.00
Bentwood, Cutout Lid, Polychrome Floral Design, Original Paint, 8 1/2 In.	385.00
Bentwood, Poplar, Worn Salmon Red Paint, White & Blue Design, Oval, 4 1/2 In.	302.00
Bentwood, Round, Cover, Poplar & Chestnut, Red Finish, 20 x 12 In.	82.00
Bentwood, Round, Cover, Swivel Handle, Poplar & Chestnut, 14 1/4 x 9 1/2 In.	176.00
Bentwood, Swivel Handle, Cover, 9 3/4 In.	71.50
Bible, Carved Panel, Iron Lock & Hasp, Oak, England, 10 x 28 x 18 In.	700.00
Bible, Lift Top, Bracket Feet, Dovetailed Joinings, Walnut	1375.00
Bible, On Frame, Oak, Carved On Top IH:1690, 18th Century, England, 38 x 32 In.	825.00
Bible, Slant Front, On Stand, 18th Century, 28 In.	275.00
Book, Lock, Brass Escutcheon, Oak, 1843 Newspaper Lined, 9 1/2 x 15 1/4 In.	192.50

◆◆◆◆◆◆◆◆◆◆◆◆◆◆◆◆◆◆◆◆◆◆◆

When restoring antiques
or houses, take color pictures before and after for
records of colors used,
exact placement of deco-
rative details, and insurance claims.

◆◆◆◆◆◆◆◆◆◆◆◆◆◆◆◆◆◆◆◆◆◆◆

Box, Document, Wooden, Floral Wallpaper Lining, 1820

Book Shape, Marquetry, Horsehead 1 Side, Bird On Other, 7 1/2 x 8 1/4 In. 100.00
Bride's, Chromolithograph Of Children On Cover, German Inscription, 17 3/4 In. 550.00
Bride's, Cover, Vinegar & Sponge Design, 14 1/2 x 22 x 18 In. 3000.00
Bride's, Geometric Punch-Work Design, Norway, 20 In. 165.00
Bride's, Oval, Bentwood, Pine, Floral Design, German Inscription, 19 In. 770.00
Bride's, Pine, Floral, Black Ground, Soldier On Lid, 17 3/4 In. 1045.00
Bride's, Polychrome Design, Flowers On Sides, Chicken On Lid, Bentwood, 1872, 15 In. 220.00
Bride's, Spring-Clip Lid, Oval, Bentwood, 18 In. 82.50
Burled Walnut, Cover, Mahogany Interior, Divided, 6 x 3 1/2 In. 20.00
Button, Sliding Door, Shelves, Amish, Signed 350.00
Cake, Wooden, Pennyslvania German, Gold Stenciling, Rosewood Graining, Round .. 325.00
Candle, Beveled-Edge Sliding Lid, Chip Carved, Poplar, 10 3/4 In. 127.00
Candle, Cover, Canted Sides, Old Red Paint, 15 In. 330.00
Candle, Hanging, Dovetailed, Handcut Nails, Initials I.I.B., 12 In. 185.00
Candle, Hanging, Green Painted Stripes, Shaped Crest, Butternut, 18 In. 1100.00
Candle, Hanging, Pine, 12 1/2 In. 137.50
Candle, Hinged Lid, Strap Hanging Supports, Painted Tin, 1820s, 16 1/4 In. 495.00
Candle, Natural Finish, Sliding Top, Thumb Groove, 4 1/4 x 9 x 3 In. 105.00
Candle, Pine, Handcut, Paint Design, No Lid, Victorian, 12 x 24 In. 190.00
Candle, Slide Top, Grained, 19th Century, 7 x 4 x 3 In. 95.00
Candle, Sliding Lid, Dovetailed Drawer, Sectioned, Walnut 250.00
Candle, Tin, Hanging, Black Paint, 10 1/2 In. 132.00
Candle, Walnut, 1 Drawer, 19 In. 412.00
Candle, Walnut, No Lid, Wall, Carved Resin Plugs, 11 x 5 x 18 3/4 In. 485.00
Candle, Wooden, Sliding Top, Natural Finish, 4 1/4 x 9 x 3 In. 96.00
Candy, Nude Picture 30.00
Cash, Country Store, Walnut, Key, Bell, Instruction Label, 6 3/4 x 17 3/4 x 6 In. 265.00
Cedar, Cedar Chest Shape, Side Handles, English Thatched House Lid, 11 x 6 x 4 In. 22.00
Cedar, Hinged Dome Lid, Coney Island, Engraved Ann 1958, 6 1/2 x 3 1/2 In. 12.00
Checkerboard Parquetry, Whalebone Trim, 19th Century, 6 x 10 1/2 x 7 1/4 In. 1540.00
Cherry, Dovetailed, Original Lock, 17 1/2 x 10 x 7 3/4 In. 220.00
Cherry Geometric Designs, Shields & Stars, Inlaid, Poplar, 12 In. 38.50
Cigarette, Inlaid Checkerboard Sides, Tambour Top, Brass Handle, 4 x 3 1/2 x 2 In. 15.00
Cigarette, Shagreen, Hinged Cover, Ivory Inset & Handles, France, c.1930, 7 1/2 In. 460.00
Collar & Cuff, Celluloid, Embossed Cherubs 70.00
Collar & Cuff, Octagonal, 6 Cuffs, 14 Collars, Silk Lined, 5 3/4 x 7 3/4 In. 225.00
Copper, Hammered, Enameled Floral Medallion, Boston School, c.1910, 3 x 5 In. 385.00
Crate, Shipping, Sent To Philadelphia From China, March 31, 1812 .... 775.00
Cubed Oval Body, 2 Figures On Lid, Metal Chains, Bronze & Silver, 12 In. 3450.00
Curly Maple, Dovetailed, Beveled Edge Lid, Worn Refinishing, 10 5/8 In. 286.00
Cutlery, Scouring, Slide Cover, 13 x 7 x 3 1/2 In. 190.00
Document, Chinese, Pigskin, Lacquered, Gilt Design, 17 In. 275.00
Document, Chippendale, Massachusetts, c.1790, 10 1/2 x 20 x 11 In. 3575.00
Document, Georgian, Brass Studded, Bail Handle, Leather, 8 x 4 1/2 In. 110.00
Document, Lacquered Pigskin & Parcel Gilt, 19th Century, China, 17 1/4 In. 165.00
Document, Multicolored Floral & Swag Design, Wooden, Painted, 9 x 6 x 6 In. 225.00
Document, Wooden, Floral Design, Painted, Hinged Top, 11 x 7 x 6 In. 300.00
Document, Wooden, Floral Wallpaper Lining, 1820 .... *Illus* 4950.00

Dome Top, Black & Red Paint, Yellow Striping, Side Handles, Small 995.00
Dome Top, Blue, Red & White Compass Design, Lancaster City, Pa., 19 In 15400.00
Dome Top, Child's, Pine, Grain Painted, Ditty Box, Bracket Footed, 12 x 18 x 11 In. 935.00
Dome Top, Engraved Tortoiseshell On Pine, Metal Fittings, Miniature 325.00
Dome Top, Overall Floral & Paisley Design, 19th Century 6270.00
Dome Top, Pine, Brown Vinegar Grained, 1822, Dovetailed, 12 3/4 In. 357.00
Dome Top, Pine, Red Brown Grained, Rose Panel, 15 1/4 In. 467.00
Dome Top, Pine, Red Traces, Fitted, 2 Tills, Missing Lock, 12 3/4 In. 93.00
Dome Top, Salmon Paint, Freehand Design, Pennsylvania, 22 x 12 In. 3000.00
Dome Top, Wallpaper Covered, New England, 19th Century, 9 x 20 x 10 In. 192.00
Dome Top, Wooden, Black Design, Dovetailed Corners 522.00
Dome Top, Wooden, Cigar Paper Covered, Red, Green, 9 x 4 1/2 x 3 In. 125.00
Dough, Molded Sides, Handles, Painted Red, Pine, 19th Century, 32 1/2 In. 515.00
Dough, Pine, Old Red Stain, 15 1/2 x 34 In. 121.00
Dough, Poplar Base, Walnut Lid, Dark Brown Repaint 1540.00
Dough, Poplar, Red Paint, 19 3/4 x 42 x 27 3/4 In. 836.00
Dough, Tabletop, Dark Green Paint 100.00
Dough, Walnut, Breadboard Ends, Dovetailed, Pinned Construction 900.00
Dovetailed, Pine, Yellow Striping Over Red, Iron Strap Hinges, 12 In. 93.00
Dovetailed, Poplar, 24 3/4 In. 60.00
Embossed, Chromolithographic Design, Books In Tiered Case, Tin., 6 1/4 In. 247.00
Enameled, Frosted Glass Elephant Finial, Silver Gilt, Basse Taille, 4 1/2 In. 1100.00
Epaulet, c.1860, 10 3/4 x 4 1/2 x 7 In. 290.00
Federal, Grain Painted, 13 x 26 1/2 In. 632.00
Figural, Carved & Gessoed Bas Relief, Animal Footed, Europe, 5 x 6 1/2 In. 1430.00
Finger, Design, Pennsylvania Dutch, 1790-1810, Oval 825.00
Frisian, Carved Poplar, Worn Dark Finish, 3 1/2 x 9 1/4 x 9 1/4 In. 72.00
Glove, Pyrography, Woman's Portrait Under Lid 10.00
Gold Stenciled, Blue Paint, Black Frame Border, 1840s 350.00
Gum, Spruce, Carved, Painted, Inlaid, Contents, Rectangular 130.00
Gum, Spruce, Inlaid, Rectangular, Contents, Small 115.00
Hanging, Walnut, Cutout Crest, Dovetailed, 12 1/2 x 13 In. 935.00
Hat, Flowers & Leaves, Wooden, New England, c.1830 .... 2400.00
Hat, Hannah Davis Label, 10 1/2 In. 950.00
Hat, Schiaparelli, Pink 65.00
Hat, Tin, Brown Grain Painted, Green Interior, 9 3/4 x 11 3/4 x 9 3/4 In. 115.00
Hat, Wallpaper Covered, Bird & Flower Pattern, 19th Century, 19 In. 110.00
Hat, Wallpaper Covered, Drapery Swag With Three Roses & Vase, 10 1/2 In. 495.00
Hat, Wallpaper Covered, The Three Days, c.1830, 17 In. 110.00
Hat, Wallpaper Covered, Walking Beam Side-Wheeler, 19th Century, 17 1/2 In. 137.00
Hat, Wallpaper, Swag & Tassel, Lined, Patriot Marine Journal, 1833, 12 x 19 In. 600.00
Hat, Wooden, Wallpaper Covered, Hannah Davis, East Jaffrey, N.H., 7 1/4 In. 440.00
Inlaid Ivory Top, Bottom As Chess Board, Interior As Backgammon 880.00
Inlaid Rosewood, Victorian, Velvet-Lined Interior, 15 In. 165.00
Inro, Abalone Shell Design, Branch With Fruit, 4 Compartments, Black Lacquer 440.00
Inro, Gold Lacquer Ground, Inlaid Mother-Of-Pearl, Birds Amid Flowers 550.00
Inro, Mountainous Landscape, Waterfall, Ivory Dragon Netsuke, 5 Compartments 1650.00
Jewelry, Capitol Building Shape, 1920s 35.00
Jewelry, Chest Shape, Inlaid Checkerboard, 5 1/2 x 3 x 6 In. 25.00
Jewelry, Floral Petit Point Lid, Beveled Edge, Oval, 4 1/2 In. 82.00
Jewelry, Glass Top, Filigree, Glass Paneled Sides, Hexagonal, Red Velvet Interior 15.00
Jewelry, Harlequin, Black, Red Velvet Interior, Lloyderson, 1980s, 6 x 5 In. 10.00
Jewelry, Hinged Glass Floral Lid, Pierced Floral Sides 35.00
Jewelry, Marquetry, 19th Century, Dutch, 9 x 7 In. 66.00
Jewelry, Marquetry, Late 19th Century, 12 1/2 x 7 In. 302.00
Jewelry, Oriental Enameled, Black, Hand Painted, Mirror, 7 x 5 In. 18.00
Jewelry, Regency, Rosewood, 13 In. 83.00
Knife, Dovetailed, Pine, Heart Cutout Handle, 12 x 9 In. 137.00
Knife, Figural Mahogany Veneer, Inlaid 550.00
Knife, George III, Fruitwood, 15 3/4 In., Pair 2090.00
Knife, George III, Inlaid Mahogany, Late 18th Century, 14 1/2 In., Pair 2310.00
Knife, George III, Mahogany Veneer, 14 In. 440.00
Knife, Georgian, Pierced Central Handle, Walnut, 17 1/2 In. 175.00

Knife, Hepplewhite, Inlaid Mahogany, Pair 5750.00
Knife, Hepplewhite, Interior Star With Grid Design, Flame Veneer, Mahogany, 15 In.   412.00
Knife, Light Grayish Paint, Poplar, 15 1/2 x 34 1/2 In. 335.00
Knife, Mahogany, Inlaid Veneer, Interior Inlaid Stars, England, 14 1/4 In., Pair 600.00
Knife, Scouring, Pine, 1850 .... 200.00
Knife, Walnut, Dovetailed, Cutout Handle Of Bird In Flight, 12 x 16 In. 192.50
Lacquered Leather, Chinoiserie, Oriental, Cylindrical, 15 x 17 In. 99.00
Leather Covered, Brass Stud Trim, Brass Bale & Lock, Key, 8 1/8 In. 137.50
Lift Top, Grain Painted, Concealed End Opening Panel, 7 7/8 x 6 x 12 In. 250.00
Lift Top, Pine, Green Paint, Strap Hinges, 16 x 36 x 16 In. 132.00
Lift Top, Pine, Old Red Stain, Snipe Hinges, 18 x 40 x 17 In. 143.00
Lift Top, Pine, Sponge Painted, C.A.D. 1865, 35 x 18 In. 110.00
Lift Top, Rosewood Nails, Salmon & Black Paint 1017.00
Lift Top, Tulipwood, Grain Painted Design, Original Hardware, 10 1/2 x 28 x 14 In. .   143.00
Linen Over Cardboard, Embroidered Penn. Dutch Style Florals, 5 1/4 x 2 1/2 In. 8.50
Mahogany, Exotic Wood Fan Design, Whale Bone Escutcheon, 7 x 12 In. 412.00
Napoleon III, Nest With 3 Eggs, Gilt Metal, Opaline Glass, 9 In., Pair 1725.00
Nautical Scene, Hand Painted, Hinged Top, Lacquered, 5 In. 150.00
Painted, Tack Design, New York Newspaper Interior, Dovetailed, 1836 ....   308.00
Pantry, Natural, Varnish, Dated 1857, 6 In. 98.00
Pantry, Oak, Natural Finish, Bail Handle, 11 1/2 x 6 1/2 In. 195.00
Pantry, Red Paint, 19th Century, 6 In. 120.00
Paper Cover, Glass Top, Papier-Mache Bird, Mid-19th Century, 5 x 3 x 2 1/2 In. 220.00
Pine, Lift Top, Red Stain, 2 Base Drawers, 13 x 14 x 10 In. 467.00
Pine, Rosewood Graining, Girl On Horseback Decoupage Scene 137.00
Pine, Spring Closure, Tooled & Burned Design, Oval, 20 1/4 In. 110.00
Pine & Poplar, 2 Applied Panels On Lid, Interior Tray, 13 1/2 In. 192.00
Pine & Poplar, Painted Buildings, Green Ground, 12 3/4 In. 357.00
Pipe, Drawer, Pine, Painted, 18th Century 935.00
Pipe, Hanging, Recessed Heart Above Box, Stained Pine, 18 1/2 In. 2585.00
Pipe, William & Mary, Painted Red, Pine, 1750, 24 1/8 In. 1760.00
Polychrome Foliage, Dome Top, Interior Tray, Marked Sater, 10 3/8 In. 165.00
Poor, Mahogany, Dovetailed, Kingston, Kings County 190.00
Poplar, Wire Hinges, Red Paint, Stenciled & Floral Design, 10 1/4 In. 522.00
Puzzle, Ivory & Tortoiseshell, Rectangular, 19th Century 1210.00
Puzzle, Ivory & Wood, Hinged Top, 19th Century, 2 1/4 In. 385.00
Salt, Hanging, Mahogany 577.00
Shagreen Cover, White Metal & Wrought Iron Mount, J.P. Cooper, 4 3/4 In. 3000.00
Shoeshine, Wooden, Red Paint, Hand Made, Iron Footrest 35.00
Silverware, Gold & Red Birds, Squirrels, Fence, Scalloped, Green Paint 675.00
Single Finger Construction, Iron Tacks, Bentwood, 7 3/4 In. 110.00
Sliding Lid, Painted, Bright Blue Paint, Dovetailed, Machine Cut, 11 In. 104.00
Straw, Tunbridge Ware, Round, 2 1/4 In. 20.00
Success To Fleet, 3-Masted Ship, Floral Border, English, 19th Century, 2 3/4 In. 522.00
Tiger Maple, Till, 14 In. 825.00
Tiger Maple, Wavy Birch Burl Veneer, 3 Drawers, 9 3/4 x 13 1/2 In. 3575.00
Tobacco, 2 Interior Covers, Engraved Biblical Scenes, Dutch, 1730s 862.00
Tobacco, Return Of Prodigal Son, Brass, Holland, 6 In. 1100.00
Tobacco, Silver Medallion, Engraved Musical Instruments, Wooden, 6 In. 27.00
Toilet, Papier-Mache, Mother-Of-Pearl, 1865 ....   795.00
Trinket, Figural, Girl Kissing Chicken, Porcelain, 4 In. 60.00
Trinket, Orange Design, Tile & Mahogany, Glass Top, 10 1/2 x 4 1/2 In. 40.00
Trinket, Rosewood, 9 In. 77.00
Vanity, Crocodile, Silk Lined, Mirror, England, 13 x 9 In. 355.00
Vanity, Rosewood, Secret Drawers, T. Dalton, London 264.00
Vanity, Traveling, Inset Mother-Of-Pearl Shield, Compartment For Bottles, 12 x 9 In.   465.00
Wall, Hourglass & Heart Design, Wooden 110.00
Wall, Scrolled Crest, Sectioned Drawer, Floral, Painted Red, 14 1/2 In. 880.00
Walnut, Painted Paper Panel, 19th Century, Continental, 3 3/4 x 11 x 9 In. 690.00
Watch, Federal, Bird & Foliage, Inlaid Mahogany & Satinwood, 12 1/2 In. 1840.00
Watch, Keyhole Shape, Floral Bouquet, Wooden Carved, Latvia 95.00
Watch, Sliding Top, Wooden Carved, Lucerne, Square 95.00
Wooden, Beech, Floral Design, Natural Ground, Threaded Lid, 4 In. 275.00

Writing, Nacre & Ivory Marquetry Inlay On Lid, Fitted Interior, Bird's-Eye Veneer ... 110.00
Writing, Rosewood Veneer, Silver Line Inlaid, Fitted, Nacre Inlaid Lid, 16 In. 77.00
Writing, Victorian, Brass Swing Handles, Leather Surface, Mahogany, 21 In. 460.00

BOY SCOUT collectibles include any material related to scouting, including patches, manuals, and uniforms. The Boy Scout movement in the United States started in 1910. The first Jamboree was held in 1937. Girl Scout items are listed under their own heading.

Arrowhead Flint Chip Kit, 1950s 75.00
Ax-Knife, Kit Carson, Box 120.00
Bandanna, Cub Scouts, 1950s 12.00
Book, 1957 4th National Jamboree, Valley Forge, Pa. 40.00
Book, Boy Scout Encyclopedia, Rand McNally, 1958 .... 18.00
Book, Boy Scouts Requirements, 1966 .... 4.00
Book, Den Mother's Handbook For 1969 .... 5.00
Book, Scout Jamboree, James E. West, Yellow Cover, 1933 .... 42.50
Book, Scouting & The Jewish Boy, 1944, Orange Cover 18.00
Book, Scouting For Boys, R. Baden-Powell, Jan.1908 .... 265.00
Book, Scouting For Rural Boys, 1938 .... 38.00
Book, Scouting In The U.S.A., Steamer Cover, Scout Blowing Bugle 7.00
Book, The Boy Scout, Richard Harding Davis, 1914 .... 26.00
Book, Yarns For Boy Scouts, R. Baden-Powell, 1909 .... 75.00
Booklet, How To Organize A Boy Scout Troop, 1938 .... 16.00
Booklet, Merit Badge, Firemanship, 1961 .... 2.00
Bugle, Brass, Inscribed 60.00
Calendar Top, Boy Scouts Of America, The Right Way, Rockwell, 16 x 21 In. 22.00
Car, Ford, Promotion, 1950 .... 185.00
Card, Membership, National Council, Boy Scouts Of America, Trifold, 1939 .... 12.00
Catalog, Scout Executive Equipment, 1932 .... 25.00
Drum, Troop 399, Oakley, Sponsored By Cincinnati Milling Machine Co. 85.00
Handbook, 1929-1930 .... 23.00
Handbook, Cub Scout Den Chiefs, 1942 .... 7.00
Handbook, Norman Rockwell Cover, 1946 .... 12.50
Hat, 1930s 12.50
Hatchet, Red Wooden Handle 15.00
Holder, Neckerchief, Bronze, Eagle Emblem, Domed, 1 1/2 x 1 1/4 In. 8.00
Kit, First Aid, Tin 55.00
Match Holder, Camping, Metal Tube, Screw Cap 20.00
Match Safe, Boy Scout Insignia, Metal, Belt Loop On Lid, 1925-1930, 3 In. 8.00
Medal, Boy On Horse, Shoe Co. On Back, Bronze, 1910 .... 6.00
Pencil Case, Tin, Pictures Encampment, c.1917 .... 95.00
Signaler, Morse Code, 1920s 95.00
Stone, Sharpening, Official Carborundum, Round, Leather Belt Case, 2 1/4 In. 10.00
Token, Good Deed Lucky, Yellow Brass, Dollar Size 5.00
Watch Fob, Boy Scouts Of America, Emblem, Enameled Brass 8.50
Wristwatch, Boy Scouts Of America, National Council, N.Y., 1930s 175.00
Wristwatch, Cub Scouts, 1950s 75.00

BRADLEY & HUBBARD is a name found on many metal objects. Walter Hubbard and his brother-in-law, Nathaniel Lyman Bradley, started making cast iron clocks, tables, frames, andirons, lamps, chandeliers, sconces, and sewing birds in 1854 in Meriden, Connecticut. The company became Bradley & Hubbard Manufacturing Company in 1875. Charles Parker Company bought the firm in 1940. Their lamps are especially prized by collectors.

Bookends, Acropolis, Signed 40.00
Bookends, Moonlit Owl Figures, Green Patina, Copper, 6 x 4 In. 150.00
Bookends, Scottie Dog, Brass, Paper Label 75.00
Bookends, Women's Heads On Pillar, Marked 42.00
Candlestick, Jarvie-Style, 12 In., Pair 425.00
Clock, John Bull, Blinking Eye, Signed, 1857 .... 2200.00
Desk Set, Art Deco, 3 Piece 165.00
Inkwell, Jumping Deer 110.00

Lamp, Art Nouveau, Red Jewel Inset, Scrolled Handle, 13 In., Pair 431.00
Lamp, Blue, Red Shade, Brass Trim & Foot 825.00
Lamp, Brass, Spread Wing Eagle On Standard, Star Finial 55.00
Lamp, Kerosene, Painted Flower Bud Shade, Signed 75.00
Lamp, Oil, Embossed Filigree Base, Nickel 165.00
Lamp, Oil, Sugar Bowl Style, Silver Finish, Pair 265.00
Lamp, Palm Trees, 24 In. 3275.00
Lamp, Prairie School, No. 216, Green Slag Glass Shade, 1908, 20 x 16 In. 1320.00
Lamp, Rayo, White Shade, Miniature 185.00
Letter Opener, Cherubs, Brass, Art Nouveau, Signed 155.00
Letter Stand, Bronze, Figural, Dogs Chasing Stag, c.1900 .... 110.00
Vase, Urn Shape, Dolphins, Sea Lion Handles, Footed, 19 1/2 In. 425.00

BRASS has been used for decorative pieces and useful tablewares since
ancient times. It is an alloy of copper, zinc, and other metals. Additional brass
items may be found under Bell, Candlestick, Tool, or Trivet.

Ashtray, Enameled Slipper, Hinged Cigarette Rest, Dragon, 3 3/4 x 2 In. 18.00
Ashtray, Owl, Deep Feathers, England, 5 1/2 x 3 1/2 In. 24.00
Ashtray, Scalloped Shell, Anodized Blue Top, Israel, 3 3/4 In. 3.50
Bed Warmer, Engraved Lid, Turned Maple Handle, 41 In. 275.00
Bed Warmer, Floral Tooled Lid, Turned Wooden Handle, 36 In. 192.50
Bed Warmer, Peafowl Decoration, 45 In. 325.00
Bed Warmer, Pierced & Floral Lid, Rope Twist Wooden Handle, 43 In. 495.00
Bed Warmer, Tooled Design On Copper Lid, 44 1/2 In. 192.50
Bed Warmer, Tooled Floral Design Lid, Hardwood Handle, 42 In. .... 330.00 to 385.00
Bed Warmer, Turned Handle, Floral Engraved Lid, 44 In. .... 248.00 to 302.00
Biscuit Barrel, Form Of Fort, Soldier Finial, France, 8 In. 10.00
Book Stand, Adjustable Tilt & Height, Mahogany Rest, c.1840, 14 To 18 1/2 In. 165.00
Bucket, Hand Hammered, Wrought Iron Rim & Bail Handle, 13 x 20 In. 176.00
Bucket, Iron Bail Handle, 19th Century, 23 In. 335.00
Bucket, Iron Bail Handle, 21 In. 145.00
Candle Sconce, Wall Bracket, Stylized Deer, 3 Branch Socket, 9 1/2 In. 100.00
Cauldron, Iron Bail Handle, 12 In. 27.50
Center Bowl, Hammered, Shallow Dished Form, Van Erp, 3 x 17 5/8 In. 345.00
Chamber Stick, Angular Handle, Ovoid Top, Jarvie, 6 In. 500.00
Chamber Stick, Cast Foliage Design Base, 6 1/4 x 3 1/2 In. 115.00
Cigar Cutter, Chrome, Black & Green Enameled, Plunger, Germany, 6 In. 30.00
Coffee Urn, Brass Trim, 13 1/2 In. 33.00
Cup & Saucer, Abalone Shell Inlay, Demitasse 22.00
Cuspidor, 9 1/2 x 4 1/2 In. 45.00
Cuspidor, Embossed Locomotive, Union Pacific R. R., 10 1/2 In. 82.50
Cuspidor, Funnel Top, Round 25.00
Dog Tag, New York City, 1935 .... 6.50
Door Knocker, Engraved, J. Frey, 1805, 7 3/4 In. 82.00
Door Knocker, Figural, Whale, Iron Bolts, c.1800, 12 In. 985.00
Door Knocker, Kissing Couple, Roses In Background, 5 1/2 In. 74.00
Door Knocker, Lion Head, 8 1/2 In. 77.00
Easel, Scrolled Base & Crest, 21 In. 71.00
Figurine, Arnaud, Female Torso, Plexiglas Base, 1930, 33 In. 1495.00
Figurine, Drunk, Holding Signpost, Canterbury Coat Of Arms, England, 4 1/2 In. 15.00
Figurine, Woman, Top Hat & Opera Glasses, Worn Black & White Paint, 5 3/4 In. 148.00
Flask, Gunpowder, American Flask Co., Large 52.00
Flask, Shot, Embossing, G. & J.W. Hawksley, 8 1/2 In. 82.50
Frame, Open Work Scrolled Foliage, 12 3/4 x 10 In. 50.00
Frame, Tooled, Virginia Creeper Design, 3-In. Molding, 17 x 20 1/2 In. 93.00
Holder, Wig, 2 Arms, Porcelain Knobs, Wooden Handle, With Hook, 14 1/2 In. 82.00
Incense Burner, Incised Dragon, Footed, Handle, Chinese Characters, China 12.00
Jardiniere, Boat Form, Pierced Sides & Bracket Handles, France, 22 In. 35.00
Jardiniere, Floral Basket Frieze Rim, Ring Handles, Footed, 10 1/2 In. 28.00
Kettle, Side Handles, Waterbury, Conn., 1863, 26 In. 675.00
Mirror, Petticoat, 8 In. 24.00
Monteith, Scalloped, 1720, 13 x 8 x 4 In. 585.00

Mortar & Pestle, Zigzag, Square Handles, 3 7/8 x 4 3/8 In. 64.00
Pail, Spun, Wrought Iron Bale Handle, American Brass Label, 22 1/2 x 15 In. 137.00
Paper Cutter, Victorian, Dragons & Foliage, England 275.00
Planter, Lion's Head Design, Saber Legs, Paw Footed 121.00
Plaque, Fruit, Leaves, Beetle, Ring, England, 14 1/2 In. 8.00
Plate, Pierced Band, Griffin Heads, 10 1/4 In. 45.00
Pot, Side Spout, Turned Wooden Handle, Hand Engraved Foliage, 6 1/2 In. 313.00
Powder Box, Hand Painted Garden Scene On Lid, Glass Lined 60.00
Roaster, Chestnut, Hunter & Hounds Handle, England, 18 3/8 In. 50.00
Scissors, Wick Trimmer, Tray, 9 1/4 In. .... 71.50 to 82.50
Scoop, Joseph Coe Inscribed On Handle, 1793 .... 325.00
Shoehorn, Brown Patina, English, c.1770, 8 In. 110.00
Skimmer, Pierced Handle, England, 23 1/2 In. 93.50
Spigot Handle, Swan Head, 7 1/2 In. 50.00
Stand, 2 Tiers, Inset Onyx Top, Scroll Border, 14 x 14 x 30 In. 90.00
Stand, Kettle, Paw Footed, Cutout Squirrel Design Top, 6 x 10 3/4 In. 115.00
Teapot, Gooseneck, Tin Lined, Bail Handle, 8 1/4 In. 28.00
Teapot, Melon Rib, Oriental, 8 In. 230.00
Teapot, Rekin & Loverridge, 1881 .... 55.00
Tieback, Gilded, Minerva Head, 12 x 9 In., Pair 181.00
Tray, Card, Girl's Face, Bonnet, Victorian, 4 1/4 x 4 1/2 In. 84.00
Tray, Card, Landing Of Columbus, 3 3/4 x 5 1/4 In. 92.00
Tray, Ebonized Wooden Handle, Peter Behrens, 1908, 8 In. 880.00
Tray, Engraved Flowers, Double Bamboo Bail Handle, China, 10 In. 40.00
Vase, Bud, Engraved Floral, Scalloped, China, 5 In. 7.00
Watering Can, Basket Handle & Spout, Chase, 7 In. 22.00

BRASTOFF, see Sascha Brastoff category

BREAD PLATE, see various silver categories, porcelain factories, and pressed glass patterns

BRIDE'S BASKETS OR BRIDE'S BOWLS were usually one-of-a-kind novelties made in American and European glass factories. They were especially popular about 1880 when the decorated basket was often given as a wedding gift. Cut glass baskets were popular after 1890. All bride's baskets lost favor about 1905.

BRIDE'S BASKET, Bird, Fruit & Putti, C-Scroll Handle, Silver Plate, 18 1/4 In. 625.00
    Hand Painted Florals Inside, Apricot Overlay, Silver Plated Frame 225.00
BRIDE'S BOWL, Blown-Out Swags & Tassels, 8 Pointed Scallops, Toronto Frame 395.00
    Cranberry, Ruffled Edge & Handle, Clear, 4 x 9 1/2 In. 225.00
    Embossed Tassel Edging, Enamel Floral, Cranberry To Pink, 11 1/2 In. 350.00
    Hobnail, Barbour Frame, Parrots On Handles, Mt. Washington 875.00
    Ruffled, Tomato Color, Square, 4 x 9 In. 295.00
    Vaseline, White Opalescent Rim, Enameled Flowers 125.00

BRISTOL glass was made in Bristol, England, after the 1700s. The Bristol glass most often seen today is a Victorian, lightweight opaque glass that is often blue. Some of the glass was decorated with enamels.

Biscuit Jar, Herons, Trees & Foliage, Silver Top, Rim & Handle, 7 1/4 In. 245.00
Box, Lift-Off Lid, Gold Scrolls Top & Sides, Turquoise Blue, 2 1/4 x 3 In. 45.00
Decanter, Green, Stopper, 13 In. 121.00
Jar, Sweetmeat, Black & Yellow Bird, Flowers, Brass Top, Rim & Handle, Blue 70.00
Lamp, Peg, Brass Burners, Blue, 13 In., Pair 120.00
Lamp, Pink, Hand Painted Floral Beaded Design, Fabric Shade, 21 In., Pair 275.00
Mug, Traces Of Enameling, Opaque White, 3 7/8 In. 5.50
Patch Box, Enameled Bird On Lid, Pink Ground, 1 1/4 x 2 In. 135.00
Patch Box, Gold Bands, Yellow Enameled Flowers, Turquoise Blue, 1 1/4 x 2 In. 185.00
Plate, Tulip, Delft Type, 1730-1740, 13 In. 863.00
Urn, Enameled Roses, Flowers & Butterfly, Pink, 20 1/2 In. 110.00
Vase, Aqua, Bluebells & Bittersweet, 11 1/4 x 4 1/2 In. 35.00
Vase, Bird On Branch, Flowers, Gold Trim, 10 1/8 In. 145.00
Vase, Coach & Horses, White, Hand Painted Foliage, Gold Trim, Footed, 14 In. 140.00

Bronze, Figurine, Ferville-Suan, Man of Renaissance, Late 19th Century

Bronze, Figurine, Fredericks, Boy, On Bear, 1908, 11 1/2 In.

Bronze, Figurine, Kaesbach, Archer, Kneeling, Marble Plinth, 15 1/2 In.

Bronze, Bust, Ezekiel, Robert E. Lee, Signed

Vase, Floral, Pink Cased, 13 In.	100.00
Vase, Gold Bands & Garlands, Enameled Outlining, 7 In., Pair	145.00
Vase, Gold Leaves, Gold Band With Flowers, Handles, 6 3/4 In.	95.00
Vase, Gold Leaves, Pink Roses, Leaves, Turquoise Blue, 4 3/4 In., Pair	135.00
Wine, Green, 1830, 5 In., Pair	250.00

BRITANNIA, see Pewter category

BRONZE is an alloy of copper, tin, and other metals. It is used to make figurines, lamps, and other decorative objects.

Ashtray, Bull's Head	42.00
Ashtray, Bulldog, Flint Striker On Head, 6 x 4 In.	98.00
Ashtray, Deer, Standing Over Fallen Hunter, England	42.00
Ashtray, Mounted With Figural Pheasants, 8 1/4 x 6 1/2 In.	82.00
Ashtray, Oakleaf, Oval, Noroia, 4 3/8 x 1 7/8 In.	4.00
Bottle Vase, Crabs Appearing From Surface Holes, Japan, 19th Century, 9 In.	412.50
Box, Hinged Lid, Drop Handle, 1876-1891, Espanol	60.00
Bust, A.K. Nelson, Woman, Orchids & Roses In Hair, 12 1/4 In.	862.00
Bust, Benjamin Franklin, Circular Base, Marked, 1810-1892, 21 1/2 In.	1980.00

Bust, Colombo, Napoleon, 1885, 23 In. 2310.00
Bust, Csaky, Woman, Geometric Haircut, Silvered Bronze, 13 1/4 In. 4025.00
Bust, E. Grego, Fundicion Victoria Barcelona & Fundicion Bichini, Pair 605.00
Bust, E. Villanis, Nude, Celia 450.00
Bust, E. Villanis, Woman, Tanagra, c.1900, 24 1/2 In. 2875.00
Bust, Ezekiel, Robert E. Lee, Signed .... *Illus* 2860.00
Bust, Fix-Masseau, Maiden, Alexandria, c.1910, 15 1/2 In. 2875.00
Bust, Gaudez, Oriental Maiden, Marble Base, Signed 3850.00
Bust, Gemito, Laughing Boy, 18 In. 2970.00
Bust, Gruber, Maiden, Art Nouveau, 1900, 5 1/8 In. 1320.00
Bust, J. Causse, Maiden, Violette, c.1900, 22 1/2 In. 2760.00
Bust, J. Ofner, Maiden, Poppy, Oval Wooden Base, c.1900, 13 1/2 In. 2580.00
Bust, M. Bouval, Maiden, Poppy, c.1900, 13 3/4 In. 8625.00
Bust, Marin, Jeune Fille, F. Barbedienne Mark, Late 19th Century, 9 In. 137.00
Bust, Raoul Larche, Jesus, 14 1/2 In. 1610.00
Bust, Schwarz, Mozart, Marble Base, 12 1/2 In. 550.00
Bust, Van Der Straeten, Jan Van Beers, 18 1/2 In. 1430.00
Cigarette Box, Rockwell Kent, Goatherd On Lid, Cedar Lined, Chase, 1930 .... 230.00
Desk Set, Jennings Brothers, 4 Piece 325.00
Desk Set, Quercy, Early 20th Century, Letter Opener 11 3/8 In., 5 Piece 1840.00
Desk Set, Ramband, Louis XV Style, Mask Heads, Acanthus Scrolls, 3 Piece 1045.00
Desk Tray, Scottie Dog, Onyx Base 70.00
Dish, Cover, Scrolled Grapes, Leaves, Portrait Medallion, High Handles 125.00
Dish, Nude Mermaid Figural On Edge, Art Deco 35.00
Door Knocker, Green Patina, 6 1/4 In. 105.00
Door Knocker, Scrolls, Brass On Bronze, Keyhole Plate, 6 In. 10.00
Ewer, Napoleon III, Rouge Marble Base, Late 19th Century, 14 In., Pair 1045.00
Figurine, A. Gruber, Young Woman, Long Hair, Lily Corsage, Germany, c.1900, 7 In. 575.00
Figurine, A. Renzetti, Mother & Child, 1915 .... 2750.00
Figurine, A.J. LeVee, Warrior On Horse, Signed 2970.00
Figurine, Ageladas, Greek Maiden, Marble Base, 19 In. 412.00
Figurine, Albert-Ernest Carrier De Belleuse, Cavalier, Standing 2200.00
Figurine, Albin Polasek, Cupid With Turtle, Resting On Sphere, 26 In. 1650.00
Figurine, Azch, Ballet Dancer En Pointe, Stepped Red Marble Base, 19 3/8 In. 1150.00
Figurine, B. Putnam, Child At Pond, 20 In. 5750.00
Figurine, Berke, Old Woman Gathering Wood, Dated 1966, 12 1/2 In. 920.00
Figurine, Boucher, Nymph, Granite Rockery Base, 1900, 27 1/2 In. 7475.00
Figurine, Bruno Zach, Dancer, Green Marble Base, c.1925, 24 In. 1380.00
Figurine, C. Kauba, Indian On Horse, 1917, 27 1/4 In. 8800.00
Figurine, Carlier, Bear Hunter, With Dog, Signed 1650.00
Figurine, Carrier-Belleuse, Classical Woman, Pair, Large 3850.00
Figurine, Cartier, Lion In Fury, 1870s, 26 In. 1045.00
Figurine, Celine Lepage, Moroccan Woman, 20 1/4 In. 5750.00
Figurine, Ch. Korschann, Maiden, Gown, Standing On Hydrangea Blossoms, 13 In. .. 920.00
Figurine, China, Venerable Scholar, Mid-1800s 1200.00
Figurine, Chiparus, Dourga, Ivory, Marble Pedestal, 13 1/2 In. 6325.00
Figurine, Chiparus, Newspaper Boy, Knickers, Ivory Face & Hands, 9 In. 2588.00
Figurine, Chiparus, Scarf Dancer, Art Deco, Marble Plinth, 26 3/4 In. 4600.00
Figurine, Cordonnier, Monk, Reading & Writing, c.1900, 14 In. 825.00
Figurine, Cornik, Horse-Drawn Sleigh & Driver, 1910 .... 2750.00
Figurine, Cross-Country Skier, Art Deco, Silvered 255.00
Figurine, Duchoiselle, Indian Maiden In Canoe, Walnut Pedestal 9775.00
Figurine, E. Dame, Fairy, Pedestal 935.00
Figurine, E. Villanis, Maiden, Orient, c.1900, 19 7/8 In. 2530.00
Figurine, Emil Fuchs, Nude Woman, Butterfly On Foot, 1866-1929, 14 In. 1140.00
Figurine, F. Preiss, Cabaret Girl, Parcel Silvered, Ivory Limbs & Face, 14 1/2 In. 7150.00
Figurine, F. Preiss, Skier, Ivory Head, Cold Painted, 1925, 8 7/8 In. 7475.00
Figurine, Farnsworth, Resting Man, 21 In. 600.00
Figurine, Ferdinand Pautrot, Grouse, 13 1/2 In. 1430.00
Figurine, Ferville-Suan, Man Of Renaissance, Late 19th Century .... *Illus* 5175.00
Figurine, Fix-Masseau, Le Secret, Reddish Brown Patina, 1895, 24 1/4 In. 5750.00
Figurine, Fredericks, Boy, On Bear, 1908, 11 1/2 In. ....*Illus* 11000.00
Figurine, Frismuth, Nude, With Vine 7200.00

Figurine, G.H. Laurent, Pelican, Parcel Silvered & Gilt, 15 1/4 In. 2640.00
Figurine, Gamboge, Archer, Antique Costume, 20 In. 690.00
Figurine, Gaudez, Blacksmith, Working On Anvil, 20th Century, 11 1/2 In. 330.00
Figurine, Georg Roch, Seal, Balancing Striped Ball, c.1925, 14 1/2 In. 1035.00
Figurine, George Washington, Standing, Holding Scroll, Inscribed, 26 In. 935.00
Figurine, Gilbert, Harlequin With Rose, Ivory Head & Hands, 1925, 17 1/4 In. 4600.00
Figurine, Gilbert, Nude Woman, Kneeling, Holding Grapes, 1925, 31 1/4 In. 6613.00
Figurine, Gomer, Rin Tin Tin, Ivory Face, Black Marble Sockle, c.1925, 6 1/4 In. 1035.00
Figurine, Gregoire, Leda & Swan, 19 3/4 In. 3450.00
Figurine, H.M. Shrady, Robert E. Lee, On Horse, c.1900, 18 1/2 x 15 In. 4675.00
Figurine, Hagenauer, Child's Head, c.1940, 6 3/8 In. 920.00
Figurine, Hagenauer, Dancing Nude, Signed, 12 In. 750.00
Figurine, I. Bonheur, Bull, 13 1/2 In. 3960.00
Figurine, I. Bonheur, Horse & Jockey, 24 In. 770.00
Figurine, J. Guillot, Woman With Cherub, Signed, 19th Century, 16 1/2 In. 770.00
Figurine, J. Licaritz, Humpback Whale Pushing Baby To Surface, 30 In. 975.00
Figurine, Jacques Gauthier, Mephistopheles, c.1900, 34 1/ 2 In. 3450.00
Figurine, Japan, Crab, Movable Claws, 8 In., Pair 1092.00
Figurine, Japan, Crane, 19th Century, 58 In. 550.00
Figurine, Jean Louis Gregoire, Mozart, 30 1/2 In. 4888.00
Figurine, Jean-Jules Cambos, Maiden, Metal Label, 30 In. 4313.00
Figurine, John Good, Horse & Jockey, Silvered, Marble Base, 10 1/2 x 12 In. 1400.00
Figurine, Kaesbach, Archer, Kneeling, Marble Plinth, 15 1/2 In. .... *Illus* 1210.00
Figurine, Keck, Lacrosse Player, 30 In. 9900.00
Figurine, Kelety, Affection, Silvered & Gilt, Hungary, c.1925, 14 1/4 In. 3738.00
Figurine, Kelety, Seagull, Belgian Marble Base, 24 1/4 In. 575.00
Figurine, Ken Kendall, Mare & Foal, 1/5 Scale, 12 In. 1200.00
Figurine, L. Thompson, Civil War Soldier, With Flag, 38 In. 1540.00
Figurine, Lady In The Moon, 24 x 16 In. 1800.00
Figurine, Le Faguays, Ballerina, Ivory, Tooled Headband, 1925, 8 1/2 In. 3450.00
Figurine, Le Faguays, Dancer, Marble Base, 1925, 21 3/4 In. 3163.00
Figurine, Le Faguays, Diana The Huntress, 1930, 26 In. 2250.00
Figurine, Le Faguays, Girl With Puppets, Black Marble Base, 19 In. 1760.00
Figurine, Le Faguays, Wheel Man, 19 3/4 In. 1840.00
Figurine, Le Faguays, Woman, Marble Plinth, 1920, 23 1/2 In. 7475.00
Figurine, Liberty, Allegorical, Silvered, Late 19th Century, France, 14 In. 467.00
Figurine, Lorenzl, Dancer, Bolero Jacket, Cold Painted, Ivory Head, c.1925, 9 5/8 In. 800.00
Figurine, Louis Vidal, Stalking Lion, 20 1/8 In. 1980.00
Figurine, Luca Madrassi, La Danse Apres La Moisson, 35 In. 4840.00
Figurine, M. Guiraud-Riviere, Cloaked Woman, c.1925, 12 In. 3738.00
Figurine, M. Guiraud-Riviere, Nude Maiden, Stepped Black Marble, 1925, 19 In. 8050.00
Figurine, Marcellini, Medusa, Square Marble Base 795.00
Figurine, Marguerite Kirmse, Playful Scottie, 2 x 3 3/4 In. 650.00
Figurine, Mars Vallett, Sarah Bernhardt, 23 3/4 In. 9775.00
Figurine, Masson, Dog, Pointer 357.00
Figurine, McKenzie, Benjamin Franklin, Holding Bag & Cane, 3 Ft. 8800.00
Figurine, Mene, Pointer, Late 19th Century, Signed, 4 3/4 x 49 In. 330.00
Figurine, Moigniez, 2 Bulls, 13 In. 2860.00
Figurine, Moigniez, Bird, Golden Patina, 1880s, 12 1/4 In. 825.00
Figurine, Moigniez, Pointer, 7 1/2 x 13 1/2 In. 1200.00
Figurine, Moreau, Chamois, Goat, Standing On Rock, 11 3/8 x 8 3/4 In. 412.00
Figurine, Moreau, Grecian Huntress, Classical Maiden, 21 In., Pair .... *Illus* 5500.00
Figurine, Moreau, Song Of The Sea 3300.00
Figurine, Moreau, Water Nymph, 1900, 38 In. 5750.00
Figurine, Moreau, Woman Clam Digger, Revolving Stand, Marble Base, 28 In. 2200.00
Figurine, Mythological Ram, Cubist, Marble Base, c.1938, 6 In. 200.00
Figurine, Neoclassical Woman, Hammer & Raised Torch, Late 19th Century, 15 In. .. 275.00
Figurine, Omerth, Dutch Girl, Seated, Duck, Wings Open, 6 1/2 x 6 1/4 In. 1385.00
Figurine, Orpheus, Seated, Tortoise, Lyre & Fur Cloak, Gilt, 10 1/2 x 9 x 4 1/2 In. ... 285.00
Figurine, Peleschka, Woman, Partially Nude, Fringed Skirt, Marble Plinth, 13 In. 495.00
Figurine, Philippe, Seated Girl, Ivory Head & Arms, 12 1/4 In. 4600.00
Figurine, Picault, Fisherman, Revolving Stand, 19th Century, 31 In. 3300.00
Figurine, Picault, Rabbit, Standing 950.00

Bronze, Group, Amy, Barrel, 2 Cupids, Signed, 1876

Bronze, Group, Amy, Cupids, Playing, 19th Century

Bronze, Figurine, Moreau, Grecian Huntress, Classical Maiden, 21 In. , Pair

Figurine, Poertzel, Golfer, Ivory Head & Hands, Cold Painted, 1925, 9 1/4 In. 6613.00
Figurine, Pope, Gorham, Horse, c.1900, 15 In. 5060.00
Figurine, Raoul Larche, 21 Year Old, Young Man, Siot Paris, 35 In. 1100.00
Figurine, Rissner, Cat, Hollow Cast, 1900, 5 1/4 x 6 In. 275.00
Figurine, Roman Soldier, Penseur, Marble Pedestal, 19th Century, 12 3/8 In. 220.00
Figurine, Rousseau, Allegorical Figure, Floral Spray Aloft, 32 In. 2875.00
Figurine, Samurai, Full Armor, Wooden Base, Meiji Period, 25 In. 2200.00
Figurine, Sana Takachika, Geisha With Cat, Meiji Period, Late 19th Century, 31 In. .. 1320.00
Figurine, Seifert, Nude Woman, Marble Base, 18 In. 715.00
Figurine, Seifert, Nude, Standing, Drinking From Bowl, Marble Plinth, 14 5/8 In. 720.00
Figurine, Siefert, Seminude Woman, Red Marble Base, Art Nouveau, 14 1/2 In. 500.00
Figurine, Sorensen-Ringi, Sarah Bernhardt, 1899, 25 1/2 In. 6900.00
Figurine, Stanier, Sleeping Shepherdess, 18 In. 805.00
Figurine, Tereszczuk, Little Boy, Hands In Pockets, 3 In. 325.00
Figurine, Thila's Girl With Flowers & Vase 525.00
Figurine, Thila's Lovers, Late 1920s 565.00
Figurine, Two Lions, Attacking Arabs, Late 19th Century, 19 x 18 1/2 In. 1980.00
Figurine, Victor Demanet, Archer, 24 In. 2185.00

Figurine, Vienna, Arab Praying, Standing On Carpet, Foundry Mark, 1900, 9 In. 880.00
Figurine, Vienna, Cockatoo, Worn Paint, Austria, 4 x 3 1/2 In. 195.00
Figurine, Vienna, Dancing Woman, 11 In. 825.00
Figurine, Vienna, Man, Praying, Cold Painted, 19th Century, 4 3/8 In. 330.00
Figurine, Vienna, Mandolin Player, Marble Base, 3 1/2 In. 330.00
Figurine, Vienna, Pheasant, 1920 .... 350.00
Figurine, Vienna, Treasure Seeker On Hill, Lift Robe Reveals Nude, Erotic, 1880 ..... 3600.00
Figurine, W.S. Resch, Dancer, c.1920, 21 1/4 In. 1495.00
Figurine, Winged Victory, 19th Century, 30 In. 385.00
Figurine, Woman, Gilt Bronze, Marble Base, 19 In. 275.00
Garniture, Clock, Louis XV Style, 3 Scrolled Arms Candelabra 1320.00
Group, Amy, Barrel, 2 Cupids, Signed, 1876 .... *Illus* 4312.00
Group, Amy, Cupids, Playing, 19th Century .... *Illus* 2300.00
Group, Ary Bitter, Faun, Sleeping, Young Deer Other Side, Stepped Plinth, 33 In. 1340.00
Group, Bequerel, Woman & Borzoi, Venetian, 1920, Ivory, 13 3/4 In. 3450.00
Group, Bouraine, 2 Nude Women Dancing, Marble Base, 20 5/8 In. 1092.00
Group, Bousquet, Horse Pulling A Stone, Green Marble Base, 20 1/2 In. 935.00
Group, Chodet, Babies In Cradle, Basket Weave, Rockers, 11 1/2 In. 1840.00
Group, Cossack On Horse, Girl In Front, Wolf, 12 In. 1725.00
Group, Coustou, Marly's Horse, 9 In. 165.00
Group, Dubucand, Two Hunting Dogs, Wooden Base, 13 In. 715.00
Group, Elischer, Woman Dancing With Satyr, 11 1/2 In. 1150.00
Group, Eugene Lanceray, 3 Mounted Steeplechase Jockeys, 17 In. 7475.00
Group, Eugene Lanceray, Boy Riding Donkey, Pack Mules, 1870s, 8 1/2 In. 1610.00
Group, Eugene Lanceray, Equestrian, Czar's Falconer, 19 In. 3450.00
Group, Eugene Lanceray, Peasant Man On Sleigh, Horses, 1872, 12 In. 2185.00
Group, G. Lavroff, Polar Bears, White Marble Base, 1925, 11 1/2 In. 3450.00
Group, Grath, Europa & Bull, Stepped Black Marble Base, 24 In. 9200.00
Group, Mene, Ewe & Lamb, 5 1/2 x 9 In. 440.00
Group, Pozene, Cart Pulled By Oxen, Peasant Man, 30 In. 4025.00
Group, Pozene, Peasants By Wagon, Cow, Horse, 1880s, 31 1/2 In. 6613.00
Group, Roland Paris, 2 Costumed People, Ivory, Painted, 1925, 15 3/4 In. 8625.00
Group, Theodore Riviere, Sarah Bernhardt, In Play Carthage, 1895, 16 In. 5750.00
Group, U. Gemignani, 2 Satyrs, Cymbals, 1930, 23 1/2 In. 5175.00
Group, Zach, Man & Woman, Ballet Clothes, Oval Onyx Base, 14 7/8 In. 1092.00
Jardiniere, Art Nouveau Maiden, Diaphanous Drapery, 1900, 19 3/4 In. 4888.00
Jardiniere, Charles Korschann, Medium Relief, 1900, 5 1/2 In. 3450.00
Jardiniere, G. Flamand, Maiden, Butterfly In Her Hair, Handles, 1900, 15 In. 1438.00
Jardiniere, Writhing Dragons, Wan Li, China, 19th Century, 7 In. 330.00
Plaque, Dancing Girls, 19th Century, 4 1/2 x 9 5/8 In. 145.00
Plaque, Newman, Pres. Theodore Roosevelt, 100% American, 20 x 13 In. 550.00
Sconce, Albert Cheuret, Stork In Flight, Stylized Wings, Copper Painted, 36 In. 7475.00
Tazza, Charles, Neptune & Court Design, Triton Support, 6 3/8 x 6 3/4 In. 385.00
Vase, Cylindrical, Stylized Bird & Tree, Japan, 20th Century, 8 3/8 In. 302.00
Vase, Figural, J.H. Moraud, 1900s, 16 1/4 In. 4600.00
Vase, Figural, Tortoise Among Waves, 1775, 15 In. 715.00
Vase, Flaring Rim, Animal Head Handles, Japan, Meiji Period, 13 In. 440.00
Vase, Georges Recipon, Nude Attached At Rim, Liner, c.1900, 10 In. 1380.00
Vase, Hugo Elmquist, Trailing Ivy Vines, Grasshopper, c.1900, 12 In. 2875.00
Vase, J. Ofner, Art Nouveau Figure On Side, 1900, 14 In. 2300.00
Vase, J. Sorram, Frogs At Base, Extended Arms, 14 7/8 In. 1380.00
Vase, Joseph Cheret, Angels With Wings, Silvered, c.1898, 22 1/2 In. 6900.00
Vase, Mausch, Art Nouveau, Figural, c.1900, 17 3/4 In. 3450.00
Vase, Poinsettia, Japan, 19th Century, 15 In. 395.00
Vase, Robsjohn-Gibbings, Ivy Leaf, Copper Liner, 1936, 17 In. 5175.00

BROWNIES were first drawn in 1883 by Palmer Cox. They are characterized by large round eyes, downturned mouths, and skinny legs. Toys, books, dinnerware, and other objects were made with the Brownies as part of the design.

Booklet, Palmer Cox, 1897 .... 25.00
Candlestick, Figural, Uncle Sam, Pairpoint, 9 In. 300.00
Game, Target Ball, With Box 85.00

Pin, Brownie Club, Celluloid 35.00
Pitcher, Playing Golf, Tan, Pairpoint, 6 In. 300.00
Skittle Set, Palmer Cox 1050.00

BRUSH Pottery was started in 1925. George Brush first worked in 1901 in Zanesville, Ohio. He started his own pottery in 1907, but it burned to the ground and he joined McCoy in 1909. After a series of name changes, the company became The Brush Pottery. It closed in 1982. Collectors favor the figural cookie jars made by this company.

Bank, Little Audrey	495.00
Cookie Jar, Angel	750.00
Cookie Jar, Balloon Boy	650.00 to 1395.00
Cookie Jar, Bear, Green Apron	100.00
Cookie Jar, Chick & Nest	600.00 to 650.00
Cookie Jar, Cinderella, Pumpkin	190.00 to 295.00
Cookie Jar, Circus Horse, Brown	465.00
Cookie Jar, Clown Bust	495.00
Cookie Jar, Clown, Standing	325.00
Cookie Jar, Covered Wagon	750.00
Cookie Jar, Cow, Purple	1200.00
Cookie Jar, Cow, With Cat Finial	145.00
Cookie Jar, Crock, Cat Finial	50.00
Cookie Jar, Crock, Duck Finial	50.00
Cookie Jar, Crock, Little Girl Praying	75.00
Cookie Jar, Davy Crockett, Gold	895.00
Cookie Jar, Elephant, Wearing Baby Hat	325.00 to 400.00
Cookie Jar, Elephant, With Ice Cream Cone, Blue	130.00
Cookie Jar, Fish, Blue & White	550.00
Cookie Jar, Formal Pig, Black Jacket, Pink Shirt	350.00
Cookie Jar, Formal Pig, Green	325.00
Cookie Jar, Granny, Green Dress	450.00
Cookie Jar, Happy Bunny	195.00
Cookie Jar, Hen, On Basket	190.00
Cookie Jar, Hippo, Sitting, Green	450.00 to 550.00
Cookie Jar, Humpty Dumpty, Beanie & Bowtie	300.00
Cookie Jar, Lantern	65.00
Cookie Jar, Little Boy Blue, Large	800.00
Cookie Jar, Little Red Riding Hood	650.00 to 795.00
Cookie Jar, Old Shoe	150.00
Cookie Jar, Owl, Stylized, Salesman's Sample Label	750.00
Cookie Jar, Panda, Black & White	395.00
Cookie Jar, Peter Pan, Large	1000.00
Cookie Jar, Peter Pan, Small	450.00
Cookie Jar, Peter Pumpkin	300.00 to 400.00
Cookie Jar, Pig, Sitting	425.00
Cookie Jar, Pumpkin With Lock On Door	400.00
Cookie Jar, Rabbit, Gray	150.00
Cookie Jar, Rabbit, White	195.00
Cookie Jar, Smiling Bear	375.00
Cookie Jar, Squirrel, On Log	85.00 to 120.00
Cookie Jar, Squirrel, With Top Hat	300.00 to 495.00
Cookie Jar, Teddy Bear, Feet Together	200.00
Cookie Jar, Treasure Chest	170.00
Flower Frog, Bird Series	90.00
Jardiniere Base, Blue & Gold Glazes, 1920s, 16 In.	150.00
Planter, Beaver On Log, Gold Trim	28.00
Planter, Green, Flared, Scalloped, 4 Footed, 11 1/4 x 5 1/4 In.	12.00
Planter, Humpty Dumpty	34.00
Planter, Little Red Riding Hood	95.00
Vase, Flecked Tan Glaze, 9 In.	50.00
Vase, Mottled Rust & Gray, Akimbo Handles, Horizontal Ribbed Waist, 8 x 5 In.	16.00
Vase, Swan Handles, Green Onyx, 5 In.	30.00

BRUSH MCCOY, see McCoy category

BUCK ROGERS was the first American science fiction comic strip. It started in 1929 and continued until 1965. Buck has also appeared in comic books, movies, and, in the 1980s, a television series. Any memorabilia connected with the character Buck Rogers is collectible.

Badge, Solar Scouts, Brass	175.00
Book, Big Little Book, Buck Rogers Vs. The Fiend Of Space, Whitman, 1940	167.00
Book, Big Little Book, Depth Men	80.00
Book, Kellogg's Premium, 1930s	100.00
Book, Paint, 1935	85.00
Box, Pencil, Rogers In 25th Century, American Lead Pencil Co., 1936, 4 x 6 In.	80.00
Car, Twinpack, Die Cast, Corgi, Box	85.00
Card, Rocket Rangers, 1940s	92.00
Colorforms, Adventure Set, 1979, Box	16.00
Comics, Sunday, Full Page, 1938	25.00
Doll, Buck Rogers, Mego, 1979, Box	45.00
Doll, Twiki, Mego, 1979, Box	50.00
Figure, Ardella, Action, Mego, 1979, 3 3/4 In.	13.00
Game, 25th Century, Transogram, 1965	75.00
Glasses, Sun, Plastic, Red, 1930s	402.00
Gun, Pop, Break Handle	195.00
Holster Set, Leather, Pressed Steel Pop Gun, Daisy, c.1935	425.00
Matchbook Cover, 1940	25.00
Pistol, Atomic, 10 In.	70.00 to 100.00
Pistol, Rocket, Daisy, 1934	200.00 to 275.00
Ring, Of Saturn, Booklet	950.00
Rocket Ship, Box	1800.00
Rocket Ship, Windup	475.00
Skates, Futuristic Style, Louis Marx & Co.	1500.00
Sonic Ray Gun, c.1950, Box	150.00
Spaceship, Battle Cruiser, Toosietoy, 1930s, Box	350.00
Spaceship, Lithographed Metal, Windup, Marx, 12 In.	455.00
Spaceship, Marx	350.00
Spaceship, Wyandotte	455.00
Walkie Talkies, Complete Set, Remco, Box	350.00
Whistling Rocket Ship	145.00

BUFFALO POTTERY was made in Buffalo, New York, after 1902. The company was established by the Larkin Company, famous manufacturers of soap. The wares are marked with a picture of a buffalo and the date of manufacture. Deldare ware is the most famous pottery made at the factory. It has khaki-colored or green background with hand painted transfer designs.

BUFFALO POTTERY DELDARE, Bowl, Fruit, Ye Village Tavern	450.00
Bowl, Ye Village Street, 1908, 9 In.	500.00
Candlestick, Shield Back, Village Scenes, 7 In.	950.00
Chop Plate, Dr. Syntax Sells Grizzle, 1911, 13 1/2 In.	1500.00
Chop Plate, Fallowfield Hunt, The Start, 14 In.	625.00
Mug, Fallowfield Hunt, 4 1/4 In.	250.00
Mug, Sailboats, 1912, 4 1/4 In.	495.00
Mug, Ye Lion Inn, c.1908, 4 1/2 In.	375.00
Pitcher, All You Have To Do To Teach The Dutch English	850.00
Pitcher, Emerald, Art Deco, 1910, 7 In.	595.00
Pitcher, Fallowfield Hunt, 6 3/4 In.	425.00
Pitcher, Their Manner Of Telling Stories, 1909, 6 In.	475.00
Pitcher, To Demand My Annual Rent, 8 In.	595.00
Plaque, Ye Lion Inn, 12 In.	500.00
Plate, Dr. Syntax Making A Discovery, 1911, 10 In.	1000.00
Plate, Dr. Syntax Reading His Tour, 10 1/2 In.	165.00
Plate, Fallowfield Hunt, Breaking Cover, c.1909, 10 In.	450.00
Plate, Misfortune At Tulip Hall, 1911, 8 1/4 In.	595.00
Plate, Ye Olden Times, Signed, 1909, 9 1/4 In.	155.00 to 275.00

Buffalo Pottery, Plate, Modern Woodman of America, Buffalo, c.1911, 7 1/2 In.   *Buffalo Pottery, Plate, Hunter, Deep Blue-Green, c.1907, 9 In.*

Plate, Ye Village Gossips, 1909, 10 In.	165.00
Sugar, Village Life, Open Handles, 1909	125.00
Tankard, Vicar Of Wakefield Scene, 12 In.	800.00
Tea Set, Village Life In Ye Olden Days, 3 Piece	1000.00
Teapot, Village Life In Ye Olden Days, Hexagonal, 7 In.	285.00
Tile, Traveling In Ye Olden Days, 1908	245.00
Tray, Calling Card, Fallowfield Hunt, 1909, 7 3/4 In.	395.00
Tray, Calling Card, Ye Lion Inn	225.00
BUFFALO POTTERY, Charger, Sheep In Fog, Floral Border, Ralph Stuart, 13 In.	1870.00
Pitcher, Blue Willow, 1909	165.00
Pitcher, Cinderella	500.00
Pitcher, George Washington	495.00
Pitcher, Gloriana, Blue & White	395.00
Pitcher, Landing Of Roger Williams	345.00
Pitcher, Marine, Brown	625.00
Plate, Gunner, 9 1/4 In.	125.00
Plate, Hunter, Deep Blue-Green, c.1970, 9 In. *Illus*	385.00
Plate, Landing Of Lafayette, 9 In.	145.00
Plate, Modern Woodman of America, Buffalo, c.1911, 7 1/2 In. *Illus*	83.00
Plate, Mt. Vernon, 10 In.	36.00
Plate, Sailboat, Abino, 10 In.	500.00
Platter, Cairo, Lune Ware, Blue, 12 In.	55.00
Tray, Windmill, Boat Scene, Abino, 1911, 13 5/8 x 10 3/8 In.	975.00
Tumbler, Blue Scrolls & Flowers, White Ground, Flared Rim, 4 1/2 In., 6 Pc.	295.00

BURMESE GLASS was developed by Frederick Shirley at the Mt. Washington Glass Works in New Bedford, Massachusetts, in 1885. It is a two-toned glass, shading from peach to yellow. Some pieces have a pattern mold design. A few Burmese pieces were decorated with pictures or applied glass flowers of colored Burmese glass. Other factories made similar glass also called *Burmese*. Related items may be listed in the Fenton category, the Gunderson category, and under Webb Burmese.

Basket, Hat, Crimped, 5 In.	58.00
Bell, Yellow To Pink, Blue Tip & Rim, Clear Handle, 11 1/2 In.	450.00
Bowl, 3-Footed, 2 1/4 x 4 In.	80.00
Bowl, Berries & Leaves, 2 1/2 x 2 3/4 In.	275.00
Bowl, Enameled 5-Petal Flowers, Blue Butterfly, 2 1/2 x 4 1/4 In.	395.00
Bowl, Pinched Sides, Mt. Washington, 2 1/2 x 6 1/2 In.	750.00
Bowl, Rigaree Rim, Squeezed-In Sides, Mt. Washington, 6 In.	750.00
Bowl, Ruffled Rim, Applied Molded Leaf, 2 3/4 x 4 In.	700.00

Burmese, Epergne, 3 Fairy Lamps,
4 Flower Holders, 8 In.

◆◆◆◆◆◆◆◆◆◆◆◆◆◆◆◆◆◆◆◆◆

To clean dirt and corrosion from lamps and lanterns, use brass polish and steel wool. Or, to avoid rubbing off the nickel plating, first clean the surface with Fantastik or Formula 409. Then apply naval jelly with a brush. Rub for several minutes with the brush. Let stand for 30 minutes and wash the piece off. Let it dry. Polish gently with steel wool.

◆◆◆◆◆◆◆◆◆◆◆◆◆◆◆◆◆◆◆◆◆

Condiment Set, Pairpoint Holder, Mt. Washington, 4 Piece	1495.00
Cruet, Melon-Ribbed Body, Mushroom Stopper, Mt. Washington, 6 1/2 In.	1085.00
Cruet Set, Holder, Mt. Washington, 4 Piece	1275.00
Cup & Saucer, Demitasse, Mt. Washington	465.00
Epergne, 3 Fairy Lamps, 4 Flower Holders, 8 In. *Illus*	3100.00
Fairy Lamp, 3 Flower Holders, Triangular Base, 4 3/4 x 5 1/2 In.	650.00
Fairy Lamp, Clarke Base, Mt. Washington, 7 3/4-In. Saucer	220.00
Fairy Lamp, Flowers, Ruffled Base	1400.00
Fairy Lamp, Gilded & Decorated With Flowers, Clarke, 6 1/2 x 8 1/4 In.	750.00
Fairy Lamp, Matching Base, Ruffled Rim, Clarke Candleholder, 4 x 5 In.	800.00
Goblet, Flared Mouth, 6 1/2 In., Pair	2500.00
Inkwell, Hinged Lid, Swirl, Large	525.00
Lamp, Oil, Burmese, Clarke, 10 1/2 In.	250.00
Perfume Bottle, Lay Down, Gorham Sterling Silver Top	800.00
Pitcher, Acid Finish, Yellow Handle, Pink To Cream, Mt. Washington, 6 1/2 In.	1050.00
Pitcher, Hobnail, Pink To Yellow, Applied Handle, Mt. Washington, 5 1/2 In.	605.00
Pitcher, Tea Roses, Applied Handle, Mt. Washington, J. Hood, 7 1/2 In.	330.00
Rose Bowl, Applied Molded Leaf	700.00
Rose Bowl, Chrysanthemum Blossoms, Bronze & Gold, 3 3/8 x 3 3/8 In.	650.00
Rose Bowl, Flowers & Leaves, 2 1/2 In.	275.00
Salt & Pepper, Melon Ribbed	250.00
Tazza, Matte Finish, 4 1/2 x 7 In.	650.00
Toothpick, Diamond-Quilted, Square Top	345.00
Toothpick, Fig Mold, Unfired	350.00
Toothpick, Florals & Berries, Scalloped Crimped Rim, 2 1/2 In.	385.00
Tumbler, 1-In. Yellow Band Base, Mt. Washington	375.00
Tumbler, Mt. Washington	750.00
Vase, Acorns & Oak Leaves, Flared Petal Rim & Pedestal Base, 5 1/2 In.	500.00
Vase, Berries & Leaves, 3 3/4 In., Pair	500.00
Vase, Flowers & Leaves, Hexagon Rim, 2 1/2 x 3 1/2 In.	225.00
Vase, Gourd Shape, Forget-Me-Nots, Pink To Yellow, Mt. Washington, 8 In.	495.00
Vase, Ivy Leaves & Vines, Applied Ribbed Feet, Signed, 7 In.	950.00
Vase, Jack-In-The-Pulpit, Mt. Washington, 12 1/2 In.	250.00
Vase, Lily, Forget-Me-Nots, Mt. Washington, 8 In.	975.00
Vase, Oak Leaves & Acorns, Ruffled Rim, 3 1/4 x 3 1/2 In.	325.00
Vase, Pinched Sides, 3 1/4 x 3 1/4 In.	150.00
Vase, Prunus Blossom, Classic Shape, Mt. Washington, 8 3/4 In.	1500.00
Vase, Queen's Design, 60 White Enameled Dots, Mt. Washington, 8 3/4 In.	150.00
Vase, Raised Gold Florals, Prunts On Shoulders, Mt. Washington, 10 In.	1250.00

Vase, Ruffled Top, Mt. Washington, 5 In. 1150.00
Vase, Trumpet, Lily Form, Yellow Rim, Mt. Washington, 7 In. 335.00
Vase, Tulip, 6 In. 50.00
Vase, Tulip, 10 In. 85.00
Vase, Yellow Enamel Daisy With Leaves, Bulbous Bottom, 3 x 3 1/2 In. 850.00

BUSTER BROWN, the comic strip, first appeared in color in 1902. Buster
and his dog, Tige, remained a popular comic and soon became even more
famous as the emblem for a shoe company, a textile firm, and others. The
strip was discontinued in 1920, but some of the advertising is still in use.

Bank, Buster Brown & Tige, Shaped As Heads, Advertising 185.00
Bank, Buster Brown & Tige, Good Luck Horseshoe, Cast Iron, Arcade, Pre-1932 ...... 82.00
Banner, Cloth, Red, Black & Yellow, Red Border, 35 x 58 In. 33.00
Box, Socks, Children On Bicycles 25.00
Camera, Box 350.00
Card, Birthday, Buster Brown & Tige, 1960s, 4 1/4 x 5 1/2 In 15.00
Card, Ferndell Coffee, Color, 1903, 2 x 4 3/4 In. 25.00
Cigar, With Band 12.00
Cigar Cutter, Christmas Giveaway, 1920s 10.00
Compact, Buster Brown Shoes, Brass, 1930, 2 In. 70.00
Creamer, Buster Brown & Tige, 4 In. 45.00
Cup, China 75.00
Dish, Feeding, Buster Brown & Tige Picture, Porcelain 125.00
Doll, Composition & Cloth, Marked Brownie September 3, 1916, 11 x 32 In. 330.00
Figure, Tige, Hand Painted, Bisque, 1920s, 3 1/2 x 4 In. 65.00
Knife & Fork 27.50
Mannequin, Boy, 32 In. 275.00
Mannequin, Girl, 32 In. 275.00
Mask, Die Cut Paper, 1905, 7 1/2 x 10 In. 75.00
Mask, Froggy The Gremlin, Die Cut Paper, 1946, 8 1/2 x 10 1/4 In. 29.00
Mirror, Buster Brown Shoes Decals, Wood Frame, Hand Held, 16 1/2 x 24 In. 110.00
Paint Box, 1900 .... 75.00
Paper Doll, Original Envelope 175.00
Pattern, Cloth Doll, With Tige, Uncut, 1974 .... 35.00
Pattern, Cloth Doll, With Tige, Uncut, 18 x 42 In. 150.00
Periscope .... 15.00 to 26.00
Pin, Buster Brown Bread 25.00
Shoe Stretcher, Figural, 1950s 40.00
Shoe Tree, Package 38.50
Sign, Buster Brown Shoes, 11 x 14 In. 20.00
Socks 12.00
Thermometer, Buster Brown Shoes, Paper Dial, Brown & White, 9 In. 187.00
Toy, Bell Ringer, Windup, Painted Tin, Muller & Kadeder, 8 In. 1330.00
Toy, Buster Brown In 3-Wheel Wagon, Windup, Germany, 4 1/2 In. 875.00

BUTTER CHIPS, or butter pats, were small individual dishes for butter. They
were the height of fashion from 1880 to 1910. Earlier as well as later
examples are known.

Fan Shape, Majolica 110.00
Insect & Fan, Majolica 98.00
Leaves, Majolica 25.00
Wicker & Begonia Leaf, Majolica 120.00
Young Boy & Girl, 18th Century Costumes, Heubach, 2 3/4 In., Pair 95.00

BUTTONS have been known throughout the centuries, and there are millions
of styles. Gold, silver, or precious stones were used for the best buttons, but
most were made of natural materials, like bone or shell, or from inexpensive
metals. Only a few types are listed for comparison.

A Sentinel At Cracow, Large 6.00
Animal & Bird, Bronze, Framed, 30 Piece 450.00
George Washington, Relief Bust, Brass, 1850s, 1/2 In. 185.00

George Washington Inaugural, Eagle Surmounted By Star, Copper, 1789 .... 440.00
George Washington Inaugural, Linked States Border, Brass 935.00
Miniature Painting On Ivory, Maidens, Framed, 6 Piece 375.00
Napoleon, Gilt Brass, Cuff, Presented By Mrs. White, May 17, 1849, Display Card .. 550.00
Pearl, On Hand Painted Shirt Card, 1920s 8.00
Pearl, Rainbow Ocean, Sears, Roebuck, On Card, Early 1900s 1.00
Pierrot & Pierrette, Large 6.00
Police, Hartford, Macon Providence, Brass, 23 Piece 55.00
Uniform, Great Northern Railway, 8 Piece 25.00

BUTTONHOOKS have been a popular collectible in England for many years
but only recently have gained the attention of American collectors. The
buttonhooks were made to help fasten the many buttons of the old-fashioned
high-button shoes and other items of apparel.

Helena, Montana, L. Smithers Co. 15.00
Pearl Handle 18.00
Physical Culture Shoes, & Shoehorn, Folding, Pat.1917 .... 16.00
Shoaf Bros., Folding, Metal 18.00
Sterling Silver, Raised Flowers & Scrolls, Pat.1891 .... 35.00

CALENDARS made to hang on the wall or to be displayed on a desk top have
been popular since the last quarter of the nineteenth century. Many were
printed with advertising as part of the artwork and were given away as
premiums. Calendars with guns, gunpowder, or Coca-Cola advertising are
most prized.

1888, Hoods Sarsaparilla, Girl With Blue Bonnet, Paperboard, 9 3/4 In. 198.00
1890, Hoods Sarsaparilla, Girl's Profile, Paperboard, 9 3/4 In. 165.00
1893, Buckeye, Farm Picture, April Through September Only, 7 1/4 In. 33.00
1893, J. Miles, Gallipolis, Marble & Granite Works 85.00
1893, Prudential Insurance, Cherubic Child Center, Round 85.00
1894, John Hancock Ins. Co., Horse-Drawn Carriage, 15 x 12 In. 55.00
1897, Hood's Sarsaparilla, Child, Lilac Hat, Oct. Through Dec., 7 x 4 In. 37.50
1899, Colgate & Co., Patriots, Miniature 20.00
1899, Youth's Companion, Victorian Girls 35.00
1899, Singer Sewing Machine, Trifold, Songbird Lithographs 45.00
1901, Capewel Horse Nail Co., 10 1/2 x 14 In. 350.00
1901, Union Cartridge, Boy With Shotgun, 1/2 Pad, 13 x 26 In. 1265.00
1902, Lipton Tea, Girl Drinking Tea, 12 x 10 In. 55.00
1902, Marlin, Desk 275.00
1903, Malt-Nutrine, Spread Winged Eagle 240.00
1904, Fowler Nail Co., Vulcan Horse Nails, 14 x 18 In. 100.00
1906, Compliments Of W.P. Parker, Dealer In Carriages, 11 x 14 In. 100.00
1906, John Hancock Insurance, Colonial Shipboard Scene 20.00
1906, R.R. Himmelberger Carriage & Wagon Builders, 15 x 22 In. 575.00
1907, Nelson & Patrick Monuments, Bust Of Woman, Roses, 15 x 11 In. 45.00
1908, The Poppy, Die Cut 45.00
1909, Chattanooga Medicine Co., Weather Chart, 12 Pages, 13 x 20 In. 16.00
1909, Gibson Girl 45.00
1909, McCormick Line, 13 1/2 x 21 In. 70.00
1913, Colgate & Co., Perfumes, 1 3/4 x 2 1/4 In. 12.00
1913, Pretty Woman, Johnson's Market 12.00
1913, The Nature, Wild Flowers, Green Leather Covers 22.00
1914, Lowell Fertilizer, Girl With Roses, 21 1/2 x 14 1/2 In. 95.00
1916, The Nest, Twin City Coal Co., Moline, Ill. 40.00
1917, Grocery, Sheep Grazing 27.00
1917, Know College, Photographs Of Buildings 15.00
1918, June Caprice, 5 x 9 In. 275.00
1920, De Laval, Miss Liberty, Haskell Coffin 50.00
1923, Blue Star Line 225.00
1925, Parrish, Contentment 150.00
1925, Woman, Haskell-Coffin, Frame 45.00
1926, J.C. Penney Dept. Store, Pocket Notebook, Unused 2.25

1928, Chiropractor	22.00
1928, Flapper	25.00
1928, In Valley Of Enchantment, R.A. Fox	100.00
1929, Dog Print, Steady, F.M. Spiegle	77.00
1929, J.H. Strait Milling Co., 14 1/2 x 27 In.	100.00
1930, Shawnut Bank Of Boston, Shawnut Indian, 15 x 20 In.	60.00
1931, G.N. Bartemus Co., Millers Of Grain, 10 1/2 x 28 In.	20.00
1932, Cash Market, Oriental Design, 10 x 17 In.	20.00
1933, Goodyear, Leicht Tire Shop, Green Bay, Woodland Scene, 16 x 10 In.	10.00
1935, Chase & Sanborn	15.00
1937, McCord Groceries, Sailing Ship, 8 x 16 In.	2.50
1937, Mobil Gas, Full Color	150.00
1940, Alka-Seltzer, Miles Laboratory, 10 x 12 In.	13.50
1940, Goodyear, Industrial Rubber Goods, L. Bah Call, Inc., 37 x 20 In.	45.00
1943, De Laval	45.00
1943, Esquire, Vargas Girls, 9 x 12 In.	105.00
1944, John Morrell, Wyeth Illustrations, 17 3/4 x 8 1/4 In.	50.00
1944, Shoe Repair Shop, Pretty Woman With Horse	30.00
1944, There'll Always Be An England, Raphael Tuck & Sons, 11 1/2 x 12 In.	25.00
1944, Vargas, Original Glassine Envelope	75.00
1946, It's A Date, Seattle Jewelers Date Book, Armstrong, 5 1/2 x 7 In.	25.00
1947, Esquire, Vargas Girls	138.00
1948, Petty Girl, Original Envelope	85.00
1949, Nu-Grape	75.00
1949, Squirt	75.00
1950, Royal Crown Cola, Wanda Hendrix, 11 x 24 In.	125.00
1952, Schlitz, 6 Scenes, Shrink Wrapped, 12 x 25 In.	20.00
1953, Judd & Payne Funeral Home & Ambulance Service, Newton, Mo.	3.00
1953, Mobil Service Station, Girl In Nightie, Dog, Titled Playmates	8.00
1953, Nesbitt's	85.00
1955, Marilyn Monroe	39.00 to 48.00
1956, Union Pacific, Photographs, 8 Pages, 12 x 23 In.	20.00
1957, Nu-Grape	75.00
1958, New Moon, T.J. Lanphier Co., 24 x 17 In.	465.00
1958, Standard Oil Of Michigan, Santa Claus Cover	30.00
1960, Winchester	20.00
1963, Chessie System	18.00
1967, Walnut Hall Horse Farm, 75th Anniversary	25.00
1970, Hummel, Full Pad	6.00
1972, Evans Dairy, Portland, Ind., Desk, Mirror Back	8.00
1981, Fantasies Of Women, Icart	195.00
1984, Hochschild, Kohn	12.00

CALENDAR PLATES were very popular in the United States from 1906 to 1929. Since then, plates have been made every year. A calendar and the name of a store, a picture of flowers, a girl, or a scene were featured on the plate.

1909, Appleton, Wisconsin	25.00
1909, Freeport, Illinois	45.00
1909, Portrait, Woman, 9 1/4 In.	55.00
1910, Holly, Hitchcock Hardware, Woodbury, Connecticut.	37.00
1910, Old Rose Distilling Co.	55.00
1911, John W. Caldwell, Fitchburg Remnant Store, Poppies, 8 1/2 In.	16.50
1911, Victorian Woman & Cherubs, Carnation On Back	40.00
1912, Owl, J.R. Hess, Leesburg, Virginia.	35.00
1913, Ragged Boy	45.00
1914, Floral	35.00
1915, Panama Canal, American Flags	40.00
1923, Hunting Scene, Quail	35.00
1984, Star Spangled Banner, 9 In.	9.00

CAMARK POTTERY started in 1924 in Camden, Arkansas. Jack Carnes founded the firm and made many types of glazes and wares. The company was bought by Mary Daniel. Production was halted in 1983.

Bank, Monkey, 6 In.	38.00
Basket, Yellow, 5 x 3 In.	6.00
Bowl, Cabbage Leaf, Blue, Signed, 12 In.	35.00
Bowl, Green, Melon Ribbed, Scalloped, Label, 9 1/2 x 4 In.	10.00
Console, Pink, Butterfly, Frog	32.00
Cornucopia, Cream, Horizontal Rib, 8 x 9 In.	8.00
Cornucopia, Orange, 10 In	55.00
Cup & Saucer, Pink	10.00
Pitcher, Bead, Scroll, Green, 3 1/4 In.	4.00
Pitcher, Blue	25.00
Pitcher, Maroon, Yellow Interior, Scrolled Handle, 10 x 6 In.	25.00
Planter, 2 Swans, Figural, White, 7 x 7 In.	14.00
Planter, Rooster, Maroon	35.00
Vase, Cherokee, Bulbous, Green, 6 1/2 In.	80.00
Vase, Loving Cup, Black, Melon Rib, High Handles, 5 3/4 x 7 In.	6.00
Vase, Nautilus, Black, Footed, 4 1/4 In.	8.00
Vase, Yellow & Blue Drip, 17 1/2 In.	60.00
Wall Pocket, Fan, Paper Label	18.00

CAMBRIDGE GLASS Company was founded in 1901 in Cambridge, Ohio. The company closed in 1954, reopened briefly, and closed again in 1958. The firm made all types of glass. Their early wares included heavy pressed glass with the mark *Near Cut*. Later wares included Crown Tuscan, etched stemware, and clear and colored glass. The firm used a C in a triangle mark after 1920. Some Cambridge patterns may be included in the Depression Glass category.

Alpine Caprice, Lamp, 3-Light, Pair	195.00
Apple Blossom, Bowl, Footed, Amber, 12 In.	70.00
Apple Blossom, Bowl, Yellow, 12 1/2 In.	48.00
Apple Blossom, Cocktail, Oyster, Gold Krystol, 4 1/2 Oz., 4 Piece	50.00
Apple Blossom, Goblet, Water, Yellow	32.50
Apple Blossom, Mayonnaise Set, Yellow, 3 Piece	95.00
Apple Blossom, Pitcher, Yellow	395.00
Apple Blossom, Plate, Dessert	15.00
Apple Blossom, Plate, Gold Krystol, Metal Center Handle, 8 In.	15.00
Apple Blossom, Plate, Yellow, 6 In.	8.50
Apple Blossom, Plate, Yellow, 7 1/2 In.	13.50
Apple Blossom, Plate, Yellow, 10 1/2 In.	95.00
Apple Blossom, Platter, Yellow, 11 1/2 In.	85.00
Apple Blossom, Relish, 5 Sections	65.00
Apple Blossom, Salt & Pepper, Tilt Handle, Farberware Base, Green	30.00
Apple Blossom, Server, Amber, Center Handle, Gold Trim, 11 In.	40.00
Apple Blossom, Soup, Cream, Liner, Yellow	45.00
Apple Blossom, Sugar & Creamer, Yellow	47.50
Apple Blossom, Tumbler, Gold Krystol, Footed, 12 Oz.	45.00
Apple Blossom, Wine, Yellow	40.00
Arcadia, Candlestick, 2-Light, Pair	70.00
Bashful Charlotte, Flower Frog, Light Green	60.00
Bashful Charlotte, Flower Frog, Square Candleholder Base, 13 In.	275.00
Blue Jay, Flower Frog, 5 1/2 In.	100.00
Bookends, Eagle	115.00
Bookends, Scotty	100.00
Buzz-Saw, Creamer	25.00
Calla Lily, Candlestick, Amber, 6 In., Pair	75.00
Caprice, Ashtray, Footed, Blue	12.50
Caprice, Ashtray, Shell, 3-Footed, Blue	10.00
Caprice, Bonbon, Footed, Blue, Square, 6 In.	35.00
Caprice, Bonbon, Upright Handles, Square, 5 In.	12.00
Caprice, Bowl, Salad, Blue, 10 In.	165.00
Caprice, Candlestick, Prism, 7 In., Pair	75.00
Caprice, Candy Dish, 3-Footed, Blue	125.00
Caprice, Candy Dish, Cover, Blue, 6 In.	125.00
Caprice, Cigarette Set, Box & 4 Ashtrays, Dolphin Footed	70.00

Caprice, Cigarette Set, Box & 4 Ashtrays 32.00
Caprice, Cocktail Shaker, 32 Oz. 22.00
Caprice, Creamer, Blue 24.00
Caprice, Cruet Set, 3 Piece .... 55.00 to 60.00
Caprice, Cup & Saucer, Blue 45.00
Caprice, Dish, Nut, Shell, 3-Footed, Blue, 3 In. 10.00
Caprice, Goblet, Blue, 9 Oz. .... 27.50 to 48.00
Caprice, Ivy Ball, Crystal, 5 In. 40.00
Caprice, Jelly, 2 Handles. 15.00
Caprice, Plate, Blue, 6 1/2 In. 25.00
Caprice, Plate, Liner, Blue, 5 3/4 In. 9.00
Caprice, Relish, 3 Sections, Blue, 8 1/2 In. 45.00
Caprice, Salt & Pepper, Glass Lids 30.00
Caprice, Sherbet, Low, Blue 32.50
Caprice, Sherbet, Tall 12.50
Caprice, Sugar & Creamer, Blue 45.00
Caprice, Sugar & Creamer, Individual 40.00
Caprice, Sugar, Blue 30.00
Caprice, Tray, Center Handle, Blue 75.00
Caprice, Tumbler, Amethyst 20.00
Caprice, Tumbler, Blue, 12 Oz. 45.00
Caprice, Vase, Amber, 4 1/4 In. 50.00
Caprice, Vase, Amber, 8 1/2 In. 115.00
Caprice, Vase, Amethyst, 4 In. 40.00
Caprice, Vase, Blue, 4 1/2 In. 225.00
Caprice, Vase, Blue, Crimped, 5 1/2 In. 170.00
Caprice, Vase, Royal Blue, 4 1/2 In. 65.00
Caprice, Vase, Ruffled Top, Crystal, 9 1/2 In. 130.00
Caprice, Wine, Blue 65.00
Carmen, Jug, Ball, Crystal Handle, 80 Oz. 150.00
Cascade, Goblet 7.50
Cascade, Vase, Mandarin Gold, 9 1/2 In. 70.00
Chantilly, Cake Plate, Handle, 10 1/2 In. 50.00
Chantilly, Celery, Martha Etch, 3 Sections, 8 1/2 In. 30.00
Chantilly, Cocktail 9.00
Chantilly, Cocktail, Silver Overlay, 32 Oz. 125.00
Chantilly, Decanter, Cordial, Sterling Silver Base, 12 Oz. 70.00
Chantilly, Goblet, Water 30.00
Chantilly, Ice Bucket 58.00
Chantilly, Jam Jar, Sterling Silver Foot & Lid 80.00
Chantilly, Relish, 2 Sections, 6 In. 38.00
Chantilly, Salt & Pepper, Flat 25.00
Chantilly, Sugar & Creamer 40.00
Chantilly, Sugar & Creamer, Sterling Silver Bases .... 55.00 to 60.00
Chantilly, Vase, Peg 120.00
Chintz, Creamer, Individual 16.00
Cleo, Champagne, Green 32.50
Cleo, Cup & Saucer, Blue 30.00
Cleo, Cup, Blue 20.00
Cleo, Goblet 30.00
Cleo, Ice Bucket, Blue 135.00
Cleo, Ice Bucket, Pink 80.00
Cleo, Plate, Blue, 7 3/4 In. 20.00
Cleo, Plate, Green, 9 In. 50.00
Cleo, Sandwich, Tray 90.00
Cleo, Service For 6, Luncheon Set, Green, 22 Piece 340.00
Cleo, Sherbet 22.00
Cleo, Sugar, Footed, Emerald 25.00
Cleo, Tumbler, Pink, Gold Rim, 5 1/2 In. 45.00
Colonial, Creamer, Child's 25.00
Colonial, Punch Cup, Near Cut 5.50
Colonial, Spooner, Green 30.00
Corinth, Tumbler, Iced Tea, 9 Piece 85.00

Crown Tuscan, Ashtray, 3-Footed, 4 In. 20.00
Crown Tuscan, Bowl, Footed, 11 1/4 In. 55.00
Crown Tuscan, Bowl, Oval, 11 In. 50.00
Crown Tuscan, Bowl, Pedestal, 10 1/2 x 4 1/2 In. 42.00
Crown Tuscan, Candlestick, Double, 6 In. 63.00
Crown Tuscan, Candy Dish, Cover, 3 Sections 45.00
Crown Tuscan, Candy Dish, Cover, Divided 37.50
Crown Tuscan, Candy Dish, Cover, Shell Finial 50.00
Crown Tuscan, Cocktail, Mandarin Gold Bowl, Nude 140.00
Crown Tuscan, Compote, Shell 40.00
Crown Tuscan, Compote, Shell, With Nymph 225.00
Crown Tuscan, Cornucopia, Curled Tail, 9 In. 75.00
Crown Tuscan, Cornucopia, Miniature 20.00
Crown Tuscan, Decanter, Cordial, Tilt, Amber 28.00
Crown Tuscan, Plate, Shell, 6 In. 28.00
Crown Tuscan, Plate, Shell, Roses, 7 In. 35.00
Crown Tuscan, Swan, 3 In. .... 28.00 to 35.00
Crown Tuscan, Urn, Cover, 10 In. 240.00
Daisy Design, Decanter, Stopper, Handle, 24 Oz. 40.00
Decagon, Bowl, Pink, 12 In. 47.50
Decagon, Ice Bucket, Black Amethyst, Silver Overlay 40.00
Decagon, Ice Pail, Metal Bail, Handle & Tongs, Amethyst 30.00
Decagon, Ladle, Mayonnaise, Green 18.00
Decagon, Plate, Green, 8 3/4 In. 12.50
Decagon, Plate, Handles, Blue, 6 3/4 In. 10.00
Decagon, Platter, Green, 10 1/2 In. 35.00
Decagon, Sugar & Creamer, Tray, Green 65.00
Diane, Ice Bucket .... 30.00 to 85.00
Diane, Ice Bucket, Bail Handle 70.00
Dianthus, Bowl, Dolphin Head Handles, 12 In. 120.00
Draped Lady, Compote, Green, 8 1/2 In. 120.00
Draped Lady, Compote, Rose, 8 1/2 In. 200.00
Draped Lady, Flower Frog, 4 Candle Centerpiece, Peach-Blo, 8 1/2 In. 300.00
Draped Lady, Flower Frog, Amber, 8 1/2 In. .... 155.00 to 195.00
Draped Lady, Flower Frog, Amber, Frosted 230.00
Draped Lady, Flower Frog, Blue, 8 1/2 In. 295.00
Draped Lady, Flower Frog, Green, 13 1/2 In. 230.00
Draped Lady, Flower Frog, Peach-Blo, 8 1/2 In. 62.00
Draped Lady, Flower Frog, Pink, 13 1/2 In. 230.00
Elaine, Cruet, Oil, Ball Stopper, 2 Oz. 30.00
Elaine, Plate, 8 In. 150.00
Elaine, Relish, 2 Sections 24.00
Everglade, Candlestick, 4 In., Pair 35.00
Everglade, Vase, Blue 250.00
Everglade, Vase, Cinnamon, 5 In. 35.00
Everglade, Vase, Amber Flower Frog 225.00
Feather, Jar, Cover, Side Handles, Near Cut, 6 1/2 In. 60.00
Feather, Pitcher, Near Cut, 5 1/ 2 In. 30.00
Fernland, Rose Bowl, Near Cut, 6 In. 35.00
Fernland, Toothpick 15.00
Gadroon, Basket, 6 In. 15.00
Gadroon, Relish, 3 Sections, 10 In. 25.00
Gadroon, Relish, 4 Sections, Lily-Of-The-Valley Cut, 11 In. 35.00
Georgian, Sherbet, Amber 10.00
Georgian, Sherbet, Gold Krystol 8.00
Georgian, Tumbler, 5 Oz. 22.50
Georgian, Tumbler, Amber, 5 Oz. 7.60
Georgian, Tumbler, Blue, 5 Oz. 10.00
Georgian, Tumbler, Gold Krystol, 2 1/2 Oz. 7.50
Georgian, Tumbler, Peach-Blo, 9 Oz., Pair 20.00
Georgian, Tumbler, Pink, 9 Oz. 10.00
Gloria, Baker, Green, 10 In. 70.00
Gloria, Sherbet, Peach-Blo, Pedestal, 6 Oz. 130.00

Gloria, Tumbler, Amber, 12 Oz., Pair 45.00
Gloria, Tumbler, Gold Krystol, 12 Oz., 4 Piece 124.00
Guernsey, Semi-Colonial, Cake Stand, Child's 40.00
Helio, Bonbon, Cover, 5 In. 70.00
Helio, Bowl, Gold Daisy Band, Opaque, 12 In. 58.00
Helio, Bowl, Gold Laurel Band, Opaque, 8 3/4 In. 50.00
Helio, Bowl, Gold Rim, 11 In. 17.50
Helio, Candlestick, 7 1/2 In., Pair 60.00
Helio, Compote, 5 1/2 In. 25.00
Helio, Plate, 8 In. 25.00
Heron, Flower Frog, 9 In. .... 50.00 to 65.00
Heron, Flower Frog, 12 In. .... 50.00 to 100.00
Holder, Dog, Amber, 1 7/8 In. 28.00
Hunt Scene, Tumbler Set, Impressed, 6 Piece 175.00
Japonica, Candlestick, Royal Blue, 3 1/2 In., Pair 85.00
Jefferson, Sherbet, Stem, Green, 6 Oz. 30.00
Keyhole, Candlestick, 2-Light, Pair 25.00
Lily Of The Valley, Sugar & Creamer, Etched .... 70.00 to 80.00
Mandolin Lady, Flower Frog, Green, 9 In. .... 360.00 to 400.00
Marjorie, Tumbler, Near Cut 12.00
Marjorie, Vase, Bulbous, Near Cut, 7 1/2 In. 70.00
Martha, Compote, Blossom Time Etch, 6 In. 20.00
Martha, Hurricane Lamp, No Shade, Pair 25.00
Martha, Mug 22.00
Martha Washington, Finger Bowl, Cobalt Blue 18.00
Martha Washington, Sherbet, Forest Green, Footed, 7 Oz., 7 Piece 49.00
Martha Washington, Sugar & Creamer 15.00
Martha Washington, Tumbler, Carmen, 5 Oz. 16.00
Martha Washington, Vase, Fan, Milk Glass, 2 In. 45.00
Mt. Vernon, Butter Tub, Cover, Amethyst 80.00
Mt. Vernon, Celery, 5 Sections, 12 In. 25.00
Mt. Vernon, Cocktail, 3 1/2 Oz. 40.00
Mt. Vernon, Compote, Handles, Carmen, 6 In. 85.00
Mt. Vernon, Cordial, Milk Glass, 1 Oz., 4 Piece 40.00
Mt. Vernon, Decanter, Amber, 12 In. 40.00
Mt. Vernon, Decanter, Stopper 65.00
Mt. Vernon, Goblet, 12 Oz. 14.00
Mt. Vernon, Ice Bucket, Chrome Bail 25.00
Mt. Vernon, Pitcher, Water, 80 Oz. 55.00
Mt. Vernon, Sherbet 3.00
Muddler, Rooster Head, 5 In., 3 Piece 60.00
Nautilus, Salt & Pepper, Cobalt Blue 28.00
Nude Stem, Champagne, Saucer, Green 120.00
Nude Stem, Claret, Carmen 125.00
Nude Stem, Compote, Green 125.00
Oakwood, Ewer, Mottled Brown, 7 x 6 In. 65.00
Portia, Cabaret Plate, Gold Trim, 14 In. 105.00
Portia, Champagne .... 26.00 to 27.50
Portia, Goblet, 9 Oz. 18.00
Portia, Ice Tub 9.50
Portia, Jug, Ball, Amber 75.00
Portia, Jug, Ball, Carmen 165.00
Portia, Plate, 8 In. 10.00
Portia, Sherbet, 7 Oz. 14.00
Portia, Syrup, Chrome Top, 9 Oz. 140.00
Portia, Tray, Sandwich, Gold Krystol, Center Handle, 11 In. 65.00
Portia, Vase, 10 In. 110.00
Primrose, Cigarette Box, Ashtray Cover, 3 x 6 In. 55.00
Primrose, Compote, 5 1/2 In. 25.00
Primrose, Compote, Black Trim, 6 3/4 In. 35.00
Primrose, Vase, Bulbous, 12 In. 75.00
Pristine, Celery, 5 Sections, 10 In. 20.00
Pristine, Cocktail Shaker, 32 Oz. 28.00

Pristine, Relish, 3 Sections, Handle, 12 In. 24.00
Ram's Head, Console Set, Jade, Column Candlestick, 3 Piece 325.00
Ribbon Candy, Cracker Jar, Cover, Near Cut 30.00
Rose Point, Candlestick, Pair 150.00
Rose Point, Candy Box, Cover 130.00
Rose Point, Cheese & Cracker 95.00
Rose Point, Dish, Gold Etched Design, Open Handles, 6 1/2 In. 35.00
Rose Point, Goblet, Amber 45.00
Rose Point, Ice Bucket, Scalloped, Chrome Handle, Tongs 150.00
Rose Point, Relish, 3 Sections 65.00
Rose Point, Relish, Footed, 7 In. 27.50
Rose Point, Sherbet, 6 Oz. 16.00
Rose Point, Sugar & Creamer 38.00
Rose Point, Vase, Gold Etch Design, 8 In. 60.00
Round, Creamer, Amber 5.00
Round, Saucer, Amber 1.00
Round, Soup, Cream, Loop Handles, Amber 8.00
Round, Sugar & Creamer, Amber 11.00
Sea Gull, Flower Frog, 8 1/2 In. 55.00
Sea Gull, Flower Frog, 9 1/2 In. 50.00
Strawberry, Bowl, 9 In. 22.50
Strawberry, Plate, 7 1/2 In. 7.50
Swan, Ebony, 8 1/2 In. 95.00
Swan, Punch Bowl, 16 In. 450.00
Swan, Style II, Signed, 3 In. 15.00
Swan, Twisted Neck, Crystal, Gold, 3 In. 40.00
Tally-Ho, Bowl, Chrome Rim, Amber, 6 3/4 In. 8.00
Tally-Ho, Cocktail, Gold Flashed 55.00
Tally-Ho, Compote, Amber, 6 1/2 In. 30.00
Tally-Ho, Ice Pail, Yukon Etch, Chrome Handle 35.00
Tally-Ho, Sherbet, Carmen, Sterling Silver Overlay 55.00
Tally-Ho, Stein, Carmen, 12 Oz., Pair 80.00
Tally-Ho, Tumbler, Handle, Amber, 2 1/2 Oz. 8.00
Thistle, Cake Stand, 4 1/2 x 9 In. 45.00
Valencia, Candy Box, Cover, Ram's Head Handles, 6 In. 105.00
Vintage, Candy Dish, 3 Sections, 3-Footed, 2 1/2 x 7 In. 20.00
Wheat, Punch Bowl, Child's 20.00
Wheat, Punch Set, Child's, 5 Piece 80.00
Wheat, Whiskey, 2 1/2 Oz. 7.50
Wildflower, Bowl, 3 Sections, 10 1/2 In. 80.00
Wildflower, Cake Plate, Handles, 13 1/2 In .... 34.00 to 42.00
Wildflower, Celery Tray, Gold Trim, 11 In. 45.00
Wildflower, Champagne, 6 Oz. 24.50
Wildflower, Pitcher, Ball, 80 Oz. 130.00
Wildflower, Sherbet, Crystal, Low, 6 Oz. 15.00
Wildflower, Tumbler, Gold Krystol, Footed, 10 Oz. 30.00
Ye Olde Ivy, Compote, Low Foot, 8 In. 35.00

CAMBRIDGE POTTERY was made in Cambridge, Ohio, from about 1895 until World War I. The factory made brown-glazed decorated art wares with a variety of marks, including an acorn, the name *Cambridge*, the name *Oakwood*, or the name *Terrhea*.

Vase, 2 Fish, Sea Vegetation, Yellow, Brown, Aqua, 15 In. 385.00
Vase, Terrhea, c.1909, 12 In. 300.00

CAMEO GLASS was made in much the same manner as a cameo in jewelry. Parts of the top layer of glass were cut away to reveal a different colored glass beneath. The most famous cameo glass was made during the nineteenth century. Signed cameo glass pieces are listed under the glasswork's name, such as Daum or Galle.

Jam Jar, Notched Lid, White Floral & Leaves, Blue, England, 5 1/4 In. 1630.00
Perfume Bottle, White Flower & Leaves, Silver Lid, England, 3 In. 1925.00
Perfume Bottle, White Flowers & Leaves, Silver Lid, England, 2 In. 2150.00

*Campbell Kids, Thermometer, Figural,
Plaster, 1940s, 7 In.*

◆◆◆◆◆◆◆◆◆◆◆◆◆◆◆◆◆◆◆◆◆◆

Don't store old paint rags. They
may ignite spontaneously.

◆◆◆◆◆◆◆◆◆◆◆◆◆◆◆◆◆◆◆◆◆◆

◆◆◆◆◆◆◆◆◆◆◆◆◆◆◆◆◆◆◆◆◆◆

Never bid at an auction if you
have not previewed the items.

◆◆◆◆◆◆◆◆◆◆◆◆◆◆◆◆◆◆◆◆◆◆

Rose Bowl, White Flower & Leaves, White Band, England, 2 1/4 In. 850.00
Scent Bottle, White Over Pink Floral, Silver-Plated Screw Top, 2 3/4 In. 1350.00
Shade, Blue Cut To Frosted, Bird & Flowering Branch, Regas, 13 1/2 In. 460.00
Vase, Bulbous, Flared Rim, Pink Mottled, Yellow Overlay, Arsall, 5 In. 250.00
Vase, Colored Trailings, Burgun, Schverer & Cie, 1900, 6 In. 4313.00
Vase, Exotic Flower, Plumage, Pale Green, N, 1930, 8 1/4 In. 1495.00
Vase, Female Figures, Frosted, Cazaux, c.1925, 9 In. 920.00
Vase, Fuchsia Floral Branches, Opalescent, Pulled Up Mouth, Pantin, 4 3/4 In. 287.00
Vase, Marguerite Blossoms, Clear, Purple, Cameo, Burgun & Schverer, 7 In. 3163.00
Vase, Molded Greek Frieze Of Hellenic Women, Georges De Feure, 7 In. 575.00
Vase, Orchid, Yellow, Bottle Shape, Etched, Croismare G.V., France, 13 In. 550.00
Vase, Pink & White, England, 9 1/2 In. 2880.00
Vase, Ruby, Green, Gilt Decorations, Etched Pond Lily, France, 10 In. 800.00
Vase, Sailboats On Lake, France, 5 In. 137.00
Vase, Sprays Of Dandelions & Leaves, Fauchard, 1910, 9 3/4 In. 695.00
Vase, Sprays Of Wildflowers & Leaves, Reijmyre, 1916, 11 In. 690.00
Vase, Tricolor, Etched Blossoms, Buds & Leafy Stems, Arsall, 12 In. 550.00
Vase, Trumpet, Etched Polished Blossoms, Frosted, St. Denis, France, 19 In. 165.00
Vase, White Morning Glories, Pale Citron Yellow Ground, England, 5 In. 165.00
Vase, White Opalescent, Amber Layers, Chrysanthemums, France, 13 In. 275.00

CAMPBELL KIDS were first used as part of an advertisement for the
Campbell Soup Company in 1906. The kids were created by Grace Drayton,
a popular illustrator of the day. The kids were used in magazine and
newspaper ads until about 1951. They were presented again in 1966; and in
1983, they were redesigned with a slimmer, more contemporary appearance.

Bowl, Cereal, Alphabet 10.00
Card, Christmas, 15 Different Kids, 1970, 3 1/2 x 9 In. 15.00
Card, Place, Cardboard, Envelope, 1931, 4 1/2 x 7 In., Pair 60.00
Clock 25.00
Dish, Baby, Campbell Soup Kids .... 105.00 to 125.00
Doll, Bicentennial Colonial Outfit, Soft Vinyl, Box, 1976, 5 x 10 In. 65.00
Doll, Composition 90.00
Doll, Dressed Alike, All Composition, 12 In., Pair... 850.00
Doll, Ideal, 15 3/4 In. 95.00
Doll, World, Box, 17 In., Pair 125.00
Doorstop 295.00
Electric Mixer, Mirro Bowl, Battery Operated, 6 In. 90.00
Ornament, Christmas, 1983 .... 10.00
Puzzle, Jigsaw, Frame Tray 15.00
Salt & Pepper, F & F, Plastic, 1950s, 4 In. .... 40.00 to 95.00
Sign, Juice Works, Cardboard, Die Cut, 18 In. 15.00
Spoon, Silver Plated 8.00
Thermometer, Figural, Plaster, 1940s, 7 In. .... *Illus* 202.00

Tile, Tea, 1982 .... 10.00
Toy, Train Car, Box, 1982 .... 20.00
Wall Set, Boy Holds Thermometer, Chalkware, 1950 .... 115.00
Wristwatch, Child's, 1972, Box 150.00

CAMPHOR GLASS is a cloudy white glass that has been blown or pressed. It was made by many factories in the Midwest during the mid-nineteenth century.

Bowl, Long Leaves Swirl Around, Scalloped, Footed, 12 3/4 In. 38.00
Decanter, Hand Painted Cancan Girl, Square Stopper, Says Bourbon 14.00
Powder Box, Cover, Diamond Pattern, Pointed Finial, 4 3/4 In. 35.00

CANDELABRUM refers to a candleholder with more than one arm to hold many candles; a candlestick is designed to hold one candle. The eccentricity of the English language makes the plural of candelabrum into candelabra.

2-Light, Charles X, Ormolu, Mother-Of-Pearl, Turquoise Dots, 1840s, 11 In. 4300.00
2-Light, Figural, Lover, Porcelain & Gilt Bronze, 12 1/2 In., Pair 385.00
2-Light, George III, Cut Glass, Painted Porcelain, Late 1700s, 27 1/2 In., Pair 4600.00
2-Light, Victorian, Sphinx Finials, Chain Swags, 8 In., Pair 330.00
2-Light, Wing-Spread Eagle, Ebonized & Giltwood, 16 1/2 In. 1610.00
3-Light, Crystal, Blue Glass Stem, Early 19th Century, Ireland, 25 In. 303.00
3-Light, Curved Branches, Flame Finial, Bun Feet, 16 3/4 In., Pair 2875.00
3-Light, Dolphin Form, Dolphin-Shaped Standards, 12 3/4 In., Pair 660.00
3-Light, Figural, Crane, Frog & Blackberry, Gilded Bronze, 4 In., Pair 440.00
3-Light, Foliate Cast, Silvered Bronze, c.1900, 19 1/4 In. 2013.00
3-Light, Reticulated Foliate Shape, Bronze, Art Nouveau, 16 In. 1092.00
3-Light, Sterling Silver, Weighted Base, 8 1/4 In., Pair 209.00
3-Light, Sterling Silver, Weighted, 6 In., Pair 88.00
3-Light, Victorian, Cut Glass, Star Finial, Canopy, c.1875, 26 1/2 In., Pair 1495.00
4-Light, Bronze, Baroque, Fire Gilt Finish, 18 In., Pair 330.00
4-Light, Empire, Gilt, Bronze, Winged Victory, c.1820, 22 1/2 In., Pair 7700.00
4-Light, Foliage, Ball Finial, Silver, Handarbeit, Round Base, 1930, 8 In. 1035.00
4-Light, Ormolu, Empire, Stylized Leaf Tips, Tri-Part Concave Base, 22 In. 4890.00
5-Light, Charles X, Patinated Bronze, & Sienna Marble, 27 1/2 In. 4300.00
5-Light, Louis XV Style, Putti Under 5 Scrolled Arms, 19 In., Pair 2330.00
5-Light, Seated Cupid Form, Foliate Arms, Gilt Bronze, 30 In., Pair 1035.00
5-Light, Sterling Silver, 9 1/2 In., Pair 176.00
5-Light, Stylized Leaves, Flowers, Iron, Coberg, c.1925, 13 1/2 In., 3 Piece 460.00
5-Light, Victoria Pattern, Sterling Silver, Convertible, Fisher, 17 x 14 In. 797.00
6-Light, Empire, Gilt, Clustered Columns, France, c.1820, 25 3/4 In., Pair 2310.00
7-Light, Louis XVI Style, Hoof Feet, Gilt & Patinated Bronze, 27 In. 8050.00
7-Light, Neo-Classical Style, Gilt Bronze, Turned Standard, 1 1/2 In., Pair 1870.00
9-Light, Louis XVI Style, Infant Satyr Supports, Wreathed Base, 37 In. 9775.00
Classical Woman, Alabaster, Bronze, Square Base, 19th Century, 26 In., Pair 790.00
Crane & Turtles With Lotus Blossoms, Japan, Edo Period, 22 In., Pair 302.00

CANDLESTICKS were made of brass, pewter, Sandwich glass, sterling silver, plated silver, and all types of pottery and porcelain. The earliest candlesticks, dating from the sixteenth century, held the candle on a pricket (sharp pointed spike). These lost favor because in times of strife the large church candlesticks with prickets became formidable weapons, so the socket was mandated. Candlesticks changed in style through the centuries, and designs range from classic to rococo to Art Nouveau to Art Deco.

Bisque, Griffin, Marbleized Box, Italy, Pair 330.00
Brass, Ace Of Diamonds, Push-Up, England, 14 In., Pair 467.00
Brass, Adams Style, Oval Base, 9 1/2 In., Pair 99.00
Brass, Baluster Shape, 19th Century, 11 In. 44.00
Brass, Beehive, England, 9 In., Pair 140.00
Brass, Circular Form, Turned, Punched Foliate Design, 9 In., Pair 70.00
Brass, Engine-Turned, Bottle Shape, Domed Base, Bird Stamp, 9 In., Pair 132.00
Brass, George III, Round Base, 8 3/4 In., Pair 165.00
Brass, Georgian, Engraved Design, c.1780, 10 In., Pair 1650.00
Brass, Georgian, Square Base, 9 In., Pair 105.00

Brass, Hexagonal Base, 9 5/8 In. 275.00
Brass, Jarvie Style, Nozzle Over Disc, Rod Stem, Disc Base, 12 In. 165.00
Brass, Octagonal Balluster, 10 In., Pair 118.00
Brass, Octagonal Knopped Standard, Domed Base, 18 In., Pair 88.00
Brass, Pricket, Pair 165.00
Brass, Push-Up, Gadrooned Base, Pair 385.00
Brass, Push-Up, Inverted Beehive, Octagonal Base, England, c.1850, 12 In., Pair 66.00
Brass, Queen Anne, Baluster Stems, Square Base, 6 3/4 In., Pair 550.00
Brass, Queen Anne, Scalloped Edge Base, 7 3/4 In. 330.00
Brass, Seamed Construction, French, c.1740, 6 1/2 In. 395.00
Brass, Tapering Shaft, Circular Base, Jarvie, 9 1/2 In., Pair 475.00
Brass, Threaded Stem, Saucer Base, 5 1/2 In. 137.50
Brass, Trumpet Turned Stem, Gadrooned Support, 18th Century, 10 In., Pair. 2185.00
Brass, Turned Form, Baldwin, 8 1/2 In., Pair 80.00
Brass, Victorian, Diamond Prince, Push-Up, 11 3/4 In., Pair 155.00
Brass & Cut Glass, Continental, Foliate Nozzle, Faceted Stem, 13 In., Pair 1380.00
Brass Bobeches, Oak Base, 6 Square Shafts, Charles Rohlfs, 20 1/2 In., Pair 650.00
Bronze, Charles X, Bands Of Fleur-De-Lis, 11 1/2 In., Pair 4600.00
Bronze, Empire Style, Columnar Shafts, 3 Paw Feet, Lion, Mask, 14 In., Pair 605.00
Bronze, Heart-Shaped Pattern, Dark Green Patina, Jarvie, 14 In. 1250.00
Bronze, Monkey Form, Continental, 13 In., Pair 440.00
Bronze, Pricket, 19th Century, 15 1/2 In., Pair 330.00
Bronze, Roman Style, Dark Patina, 8 3/4 In., Pair 165.00
Bronze, Tapered Stem, 8 In., Pair 90.00
Bronzed Zinc, Lead, Buffoon, Musicians, Removable Hats, 11 5/8 In., Pair 875.00
Cast Iron, Dolphin Base, 7 1/2 In., Pair 100.00
Chrome Plated, Balluster & Disc Stem, Footed, 9 3/4 In., Pair 75.00
Copper, Wooden Handle, Iron Spike, Pan, 11 In. 192.00
Gilt Metal, George II Style, Masks Of Seasons, c.1830, 12 1/4 In., Pair 5175.00
Glass, Amber, 12 1/4 x 3 3/4 In., Pair 10.00
Glass, Black, Hexagonal, Round Base, 7 In., Pair 55.00
Glass, Blown, Pressed, Hexagonal Base, Clear, 1835-1845, 6 3/4 In. .... *Illus* 193.00
Glass, Blown, Pressed, Roman Rosette Base, Clear, 1840, 7 1/2 In. .... *Illus* 715.00
Glass, Blown, Pressed, Square Base, New England, 1828-1835, 7 3/8 In. .... *Illus* 220.00
Glass, Blown, Pressed, Stepped Base, Clear, 1830-1840, 10 1/2 In. .... *Illus* 385.00
Glass, Crucifix, Flint, Opaque White, 11 1/4 In. 82.00
Glass, Cut, German Silver Figural Base, 12 3/4 In., Pair 3163.00

Left to Right: Candlestick, Glass, Blown, Pressed, Stepped Base, Clear, 1830-1840, 10 1/2 In.
Candlestick, Glass, Blown, Pressed, Roman Rosette Base, Clear, 1840, 7 1/2 In.
Candlestick, Glass, Blown, Pressed, Square Base, New England, 1828-1835, 7 3/8 In.
Candlestick, Glass, Blown, Pressed, Hexagonal Base, Clear, 1835-1845, 6 3/4 In.

Glass, Dolphin, Cobalt Blue, 4 In.	75.00
Glass, Double, Yellow, Octagonal Bell-Shaped Base, Pair	50.00
Glass, Free-Blown Socket, Stem, Tooled Knop, Pittsburgh, 1845, 8 7/8 In., Pair	435.00
Iron, Bride's, Brass Rings & Insert, S Base, 4 1/2 In., Pair	110.00
Iron, Hog Scraper, Hook, 6 1/2 In.	80.00
Iron, Hog Scraper, Wedding Ring	285.00
Iron, Ivy & Leaf Design, Dark Patina, Cast, 4 5/8 In.	138.00
Iron, Spiral, Signed LM-LN	295.00
Marble, Figural, 2 Putti Holding Urns On Shoulders, Ormolu, 11 In.	330.00
Oak, Georgian, Tilt Top, Tripod Base, Primitive, 1780, 19 x 16 In.	275.00
Paktong, Queen Anne, 18th Century, 10 1/4 In., Pair	1045.00
Porcelain, Figural, Greek God	95.00
Porcelain, Flower Encrusted, Stem Handle, England, c.1835, 4 In.	2010.00
Silver, Female Saint Stem, Rock Crystal Base, Continental, 11 In.	2128.00
Silver Plate, Rococo, Applied Flowers, Leaves, England, c.1890, 10 In., Pair	137.50
Silver Plate, Sabbath, Poland, 12 In.	350.00
Silver Plate, Skyscraper, Stepped Top, Bernard Rice's Sons, c.1925, 8 1/2 In., Pair	920.00
Silvered Bronze, Italian Renaissance Style, Pricket, 45 In., Pair	302.50
Silvered Bronze, Twist Turned Center, Flutes & Scrolls, 12 3/4 In., Pair	5750.00
Silvered Metal, Figural, Maiden, Trees, Bonnefond, 1900, 15 1/2 In., Pair	4600.00
Sterling Silver, Adam Style, Continental, 12 1/2 In., Pair	1210.00
Sterling Silver, Regency Style, 10 In., Pair	155.00
Sterling Silver, Shells & Scrolls, Domed Base, Kiev, c.1885, 14 3/4 In., Pair	3565.00
Sterling Silver, Weighted Base, 10 In., Pair	27.50
Tin & Cast Iron, Serpent, Black, 10 7/8 In.	130.00

CANDY CONTAINERS have been popular since the late Victorian era. Collectors have long favored the glass containers, but now all types, including tin and papier-mache, are collected. Probably the earliest glass container sold commercially was the Liberty Bell made in 1876 for sale at the Centennial Exposition. Thousands of designs were made until the cost became too high in the 1960s. By the late 1970s, reproductions were being made and sold without the candy. Containers listed here are glass unless otherwise described.

Airplane, Spirit Of St. Louis, Clear	65.00
Airplane, Spirit Of St. Louis, Monoplane, Pink	525.00
Alarm Clock, Penny Toy, No. 1	125.00
Apothecary Jar	110.00
Auto, Coupe, Long Hood, Glass Wheels	135.00
Auto, Coupe, Long Hood, No. 3	125.00
Auto, Electric Coupe, No. 1	95.00
Auto, Limousine, 4 Doors	650.00
Auto, Limousine, Glass Wheels	175.00
Auto, Metal Closure, Yellow Paint	65.00
Auto, Model T, Glass	110.00
Auto, Racer, Driver, With Candy	225.00
Auto, Sedan, 4 Doors, Brown Paint, Wheels, Closure	125.00
Auto, Sedan, 4 Doors, Tin Wheels, With Candy	225.00
Bank, Village Building, Insert	150.00
Barney Google, New Paint	325.00
Baseball, Clear, Original Closure	30.00
Baseball Player, With Glove	350.00
Battleship, Black Paint, Tin Snap Closure	40.00
Battleship, On Waves	75.00
Battleship, Victory Closure	40.00
Bear, Circus Tub, Old Wheel	325.00
Belsnickle, Fur Bears, Felt Robe, Papier-Mache, 10 In.	575.00
Belsnickle, Metallic Glitter, Gold Coat, Papier-Mache, 12 3/4 In.	605.00
Belsnickle, Mica Glitter, White Coat, Feather Tree, Papier-Mache, 9 In.	330.00
Belsnickle, White Coat, Red Trim, Feather Tree, Papier-Mache, 8 In.	275.00
Birdcage, Original Closure	200.00
Boat, Queen Mary, M. Baldwin	900.00
Boot, 2 In.	10.00

Bulldog	20.00
Bulldog, Closure, Painted	75.00
Bulldog, Sitting	15.00
Bus, Chicago	325.00
Bus, Victory Lines	40.00
Caboose Lamp	265.00
Camera	300.00
Candlestick, 2 Handles	350.00
Candlestick, Ruby, 2 Handles, Seaside Park, N.J.	300.00
Candlestick, With Candy, Small, Pair	95.00
Candy Cane, Mercury Glass, Red, Small	18.00
Candy Soda Fountain, Blue, Box Of Candy, Box	100.00
Candy Soda Fountain, Red, Box Of Candy, Box	125.00
Cannon, Fanny Farmer	65.00
Carrier, 4 Milk Bottles, Anco, With Candy, Box	275.00
Cash Register	250.00
Cash Register, Original Closure	550.00
Cat, Black, Keystone, 6 In.	375.00
Cat, Black, Large	250.00
Cat, Black, Walking, Removable Head, Composition	160.00
Charlie Chaplin	350.00
Chick, Eggshell Auto, Painted	350.00
Chick, Red Suit, Riding Rooster	155.00
Chicken	35.00
Chicken, Comical, Papier-Mache, Germany	22.50
Chicken In Egg	225.00
Chicken On Nest, Candy	35.00
Chicken On Nest, With Candy, Original Seal	28.00
Chickens, Wood, Cardboard & Papier-Mache, Germany, 3 1/2 In.	50.00
Child, Nude, Original Closure, With Candy	20.00 to 75.00
Child's Face, Mohair, Removable Head	178.00
Circus Wagon, Fanny Farmer	85.00
Clock, Mantel, Gold Trim, Paper Dial	185.00
Clock, Mantel, No. 1, Original Dial	200.00
Clock, Mantel, Octagon, Original Dial	300.00
Clown Dog, With Candy, 2 1/2 In.	4.50
Cornucopia, Cardboard, Fanny Farmer	60.00
Crystal Palace	375.00
Devil, West Germany, 1950s, 7 In.	32.00
Dirigible, Los Angeles, Original Closure	200.00
Dirigible, Los Angeles, Wheels, With Candy	195.00
Dirigible, Runs & Spins Props, Goes Down String	675.00
Dog, Metal Cap, Red Stripes, With Candy	20.00
Dog, Salon, Papier-Mache, White Fur, Swivel Head, France, 1910, 11 In.	800.00
Dog, Terrier, Frosted	15.00
Doll, Baby, Poured Wax Head, Blond Curls, France, 1890, 6 In.	375.00
Doll's Head, 10 In.	425.00
Dough Boy Soldier, Tin Hat	650.00
Drummer Boy, 8 In.	750.00
Duck, Policeman, Papier-Mache	180.00
Duck, Rectangular Basket	110.00
Duck, Round Base	475.00
Duckling	85.00
Easter Egg, Cardboard, W. Germany	15.00
Ed Wynn, Glass	38.00
Elephant, Howdah, Blue	85.00
Elephant, Howdah, Clear	55.00
Elephant, Howdah, Frosted	125.00
Elk's Tooth, Screw-On Cover, Milk Glass, 6 In.	125.00
Engine, Man In Window	125.00
Fat Boy	250.00
Felix, By Barrel, Paint Traces	650.00
Flat Iron Building	150.00

George Washington, Removable Bisque Head, Horse, c.1890, 9 In. 2100.00
Girl, Bisque Head, Seated, Green & White Vest, 2 1/2 In. 245.00
Globe, World, Stand 250.00
Goose, Movable Wooden Neck, Papier-Mache, Germany 85.00
Gun, Cambridge Automatic, Original Closure 225.00
Gun, Straight Grip, Original Closure, With Candy 30.00
Happifats 205.00
Happifats On Drum 150.00
Hat, Tin Brim, Milk Glass 120.00
Hen On Nest, Chalk-Covered Composition, 3 3/4 In. 93.00
Hen On Nest, Woven Wicker Base, Bisque Hen, 4 In. 82.50
Hen Turkey, Papier-Mache, West Germany, 4 1/2 In. 18.00
Horn, Fanny Farmer 48.00
Horn, 3 Valves 250.00
Horse, On Wheels, Plastic, Paper Label 13.00
Horse, Pulling Wagon 80.00
Horse, Spark Plug, Dated 2 3/4 x 3 1/2 In. 195.00
Horse & Cart, 2 Wheels, 9 In. 20.00
House, Cabinet Bank, Emerald Green 150.00
House, Snow Covered, Santa Claus On Roof, 3 x 3 In. 395.00
Independence Hall 325.00
Jack-O'-Lantern, Paper Face, West Germany, 2 1/4 In. 55.00
Jack-O'-Lantern, Paper Face, West Germany, 3 1/4 In. 90.00
Jack-O'-Lantern, Pop-Eyed 500.00
Jackie Coogan, No. 1 .... 300.00
Jackie Coogan, Painted, Original Closure 1275.00
Jitney Bus, Red, Original Closure 350.00
Kettle, Candy, Handle 55.00
Kettle, Ruby Flashed, Gilded Bail Handle, Pennsylvania 45.00
Lamp, Plastic, With Candy 50.00
Lantern, Barn Type, No. 2, Green 85.00
Lawn Swing, Canopy 750.00
Learned Fox 100.00
Liberty Bell, Gold Painted 125.00
Liberty Bell, No. 1, With Candy 175.00
Liberty Bell, No. 3, Amber 55.00
Locomotive 35.00
Locomotive, Double Rectangular Windows 100.00
Locomotive, Double Square Windows 75.00
Locomotive, Pink 13.00
Man On Motorcycle 500.00
Milk Bottle Carrier, 4 Large Bottles, A. Newburg, Kiddies Fancies 120.00
Mother Goose, Ducklings, Papier-Mache, Fanny Farmer Box, 1930s, 7 In. 150.00
Mr. Rabbit, With Hat, Green, White & Blue 2200.00
Mug, Eagle, Atlantic City, Gilded 40.00
Oil Can, Independence Bell Oiler 75.00
Owl, Partial Paint 150.00
Pencil 35.00
PEZ, Airline Pilot, Dark Blue Body 95.00
PEZ, Arlene, Footed 5.00
PEZ, Baseball Glove & Ball, Original Box, 1960s, 4 1/2 In. 299.00
PEZ, Batgirl, Package 75.00
PEZ, Batman 65.00
PEZ, Batman, Batgirl, Soft Head 45.00
PEZ, Betsy Ross 60.00
PEZ, Black Head, Orange Stem 150.00
PEZ, Blue Smurf 40.00
PEZ, Boy, Baseball Cap, Brown Hair, Blue Cap, Red Body 45.00
PEZ, Bozo 50.00
PEZ, Bugs Bunny, Red Stem 4.00
PEZ, Bullwinkle, 1960s 200.00
PEZ, Captain America .... 25.00 to 40.00
PEZ, Charlie Brown, Frowning 6.00

PEZ, Clown, Whistle Head 6.00
PEZ, Clown, Yellow Metal Base 300.00
PEZ, Creature From Black Lagoon, Green & Orange 145.00
PEZ, Crocodile, Orange Body 95.00
PEZ, Daffy Duck 40.00
PEZ, Dalmatian Pup 20.00
PEZ, Daniel Boone 95.00
PEZ, Donkey, On Card 6.00
PEZ, Droopy, Red Stick 7.50
PEZ, Duck, Brown, Whistle Head 15.00
PEZ, Dumbo 35.00
PEZ, Easter Bunny, Yellow Head, Long Ears, Smiling 400.00
PEZ, Elephant, Pink Head, Brown Hair 75.00
PEZ, Elmer Fudd 40.00
PEZ, Flintstones, Pebbles 3.00
PEZ, Foghorn Leghorn 25.00
PEZ, Frankenstein 150.00
PEZ, G.I. Joe Action Pilot, 1964 .... 75.00
PEZ, Garfield, Grinning 6.00
PEZ, Golden Glow 125.00
PEZ, Goofy 12.00
PEZ, Green Hornet .... 155.00 to 250.00
PEZ, Incredible Hulk, Box 10.00
PEZ, Indian Chief, Multicolored Headdress 45.00
PEZ, Little Lion 25.00
PEZ, Make A Face 1800.00
PEZ, Mickey Mouse .... 15.00 to 100.00
PEZ, Mr. Ugly, Black Hair, Green Head 30.00
PEZ, Nurse 45.00
PEZ, Octopus, Orange 50.00
PEZ, Piggy, Pink Stick 6.00
PEZ, Pinocchio 65.00
PEZ, Policeman, Blue Body 38.50
PEZ, Popeye, With Red Hat, Box 45.00
PEZ, Popeye, With White Hat 35.00
PEZ, Rhino Whistle, On Card 6.00
PEZ, Rooster 30.00
PEZ, Rooster, Whistle Head 20.00
PEZ, Sailor, Beard 75.00
PEZ, Santa Claus, Red Suit 175.00
PEZ, Sheik, Black Body 59.50
PEZ, Space Gun, 1982 .... 95.00
PEZ, Space Gun, Red, 1950s 140.00
PEZ, Spaceman .... 50.00 to 80.00
PEZ, Spiderman 65.00
PEZ, Thor 170.00
PEZ, Thumper 55.00
PEZ, Tim 6.00
PEZ, Tuffy Mouse, On Card 10.00
PEZ, Wolfman 165.00
PEZ, Woodstock, Feathered, Footed 5.00
PEZ, Woodstock, With Painted Feathers 10.00
PEZ, Zorro, Embossed 85.00
Phonograph, Glass Horn, With Candy 475.00
Phonograph, Record, With Candy 360.00
Piano, Brown 350.00
Pipe, Open Bowl, Amber 165.00
Pistol, Cobalt Blue 5.50
Pluto, Papier-Mache, 7 In. 180.00
Porch Swing, Tin 450.00
Powder Horn, Original Closure 60.00
Pretty Maid Washing Machine 85.00
Princess Theater, Village Building, Insert 125.00

Pumpkin, Horn Nose, Metal, West Germany, 6 In. 35.00
Pumpkin Head Policeman .... 400.00 to 450.00
Pumpkin Head Witch, Painted, Original Closure 900.00
Pumpkin Head Witch 750.00
Pumpkin Man, Bisque, Germany, 1930s 65.00
Pumpkin Man, West Germany, 1950s, 4 In. 22.00
Purse, Paper Face On Front, Nippon 155.00
Rabbit, Apron, With Candy 950.00
Rabbit, Glass, Millstein 45.00
Rabbit, On All 4 Feet, Papier-Mache, Glass Eyes, Germany, 8 1/2 In. 95.00
Rabbit, Paws Together 95.00
Rabbit, Pushing Cart 375.00
Rabbit, Removable Head, Germany 72.00
Rabbit, Running On Log 350.00
Rabbit, Standing 90.00
Revolver, No. 2, Contents .... 30.00 to 75.00
Rocking Horse 150.00
Rocking Horse, Clown Rider, Blue 275.00
Rocking Settee 475.00
Rolling Pin 95.00
Rooster, Bisque, Spring Feet On Cardboard Box, Germany, 3 3/4 In. 65.00
Rooster, Ceramic, Fanny Farmer 12.00
Rooster, Crowing 200.00
Rooster, Crowing, Candy, Green Glass 250.00
Rubber Boot, Wale's Goodyear, Clear 135.00
Santa Claus, Banded Coat, Original Closure 200.00
Santa Claus, Bell In High Hat, Papier-Mache, 7 In. 65.00
Santa Claus, Cardboard, 1930s, 4 In. 18.00
Santa Claus, Celluloid Face, Clay Hands & Boots, Netting 95.00
Santa Claus, Cloth Coat, Fur Beard, Painted Pants, Papier-Mache, 16 In. 235.00
Santa Claus, Fur Beard, Papier-Mache, 12 In. 25.00
Santa Claus, Head, Plastic, Contents 70.00
Santa Claus, Leaving Chimney 95.00
Santa Claus, Nodder, 11 In. 85.00
Santa Claus, Paneled Coat, Original Closure 175.00
Santa Claus, Papier-Mache, 10 1/2 In. 22.00
Santa Claus, Papier-Mache, West Germany, 1950s, 7 1/2 In. 18.00
Santa Claus, Papier-Mache & Cloth, Lamb's-Wool Beard, 15 In. 1320.00
Santa Claus, Square Chimney, Contents 325.00
Scotty Dog, Contents 45.00
Settee, Rocking 475.00
Ship, Remember The Maine, 2 Piece 75.00
Skookum, Painted, Original Closure 500.00
Snow White & Seven Dwarfs, Curtiss, Candy, Box 425.00
Snow White & Seven Dwarfs, Papier-Mache, Germany, 8 Piece 495.00
Snowbaby 175.00
Snowman, 5 In. 30.00
Snowman, Cap, Papier-Mache, 5 1/2 In. 12.00
Snowman, Carrot Nose, Papier-Mache, 7 1/4 In. 28.00
Snowman, Musical Hat, Papier-Mache, 8 3/4 In. 60.00
Snowman, Snowball, Papier-Mache, 5 In. 38.00
Snowman, With Umbrella, Papier-Mache, 6 1/2 In. .... 28.00 to 36.00
Soldier, German Imperial, Standing, With Sword, 1914 .... 1200.00
St. Nicholas, Papier-Mache, Hollow Body, France, 1890, 12 & 14 In., Pair 1050.00
Straw Hat, Milk Glass 55.00
Submarine, Hull & Superstructure 375.00
Suitcase, Milk Glass 150.00
Suitcase, Westmoreland 65.00
Taxi, 12 Vents 145.00
Teakettle, Bail Handle 245.00
Teddy Roosevelt, Astride Rabbit, Papier-Mache 3000.00
Teddy Windmill, Decals, M. Baldwin 450.00
Telephone, Candlestick, Glass, Contents 65.00

◆ ◆ ◆ ◆ ◆ ◆ ◆ ◆ ◆ ◆ ◆ ◆ ◆ ◆ ◆ ◆ ◆ ◆

Rubber cement solvent, available at art supply and office supply stores, has many uses. Put a few drops on a paper towel and rub off ink smudges, adhesive tape glue, and label glue from glass or porcelains.

◆ ◆ ◆ ◆ ◆ ◆ ◆ ◆ ◆ ◆ ◆ ◆ ◆ ◆ ◆ ◆ ◆ ◆

Candy Container, Uncle Sam, Riding Rabbit, Composition, 15 In.

Telephone, Clear Dial, Yellow Flash, RC	50.00
Telephone, Pewter Top, Redlich's No. 4, Lines Busy	100.00
Telephone, Victory Glass, Receiver	225.00
Tom Turkey, Papier-Mache, West Germany, 4 In.	22.00
Toonerville Trolley, Green Tinted Glass, Paint Traces	675.00 to 900.00
Top, No. 2, Spring Winder	150.00
Truck, Express, Wheels	750.00
Truck, Fire, Double Square Windows, Lithograph	100.00
Truck, Fire, Large Boiler, Red Paint, Clear	95.00
Truck, Fire, Man	55.00
Trumpet, Decals, Milk Glass	200.00
Turkey, Bisque, Toy Packs, Candy	75.00
Turkey, Lying Down, Open Back, Pullout Sack For Candy	100.00
Turkey, Removable Head, Germany, 4 3/4 In.	95.00
Uncle Sam, Movable Arms, Fanny Farmer	75.00
Uncle Sam, Riding Rabbit, Composition, 15 In. .... *Illus*	8250.00
Watch, With Fob, Original Closure	325.00
Watch Fob, All Original, Contents	475.00
Wheelbarrow, Glass	32.50
Windmill	110.00
Windmill, Ruby Flashed, Screw-On Closure	300.00
Witch, Cone Shape, West Germany, 1950s, 7 1/2 In.	32.00
World Globe, On Stand, Our Country On Cap	600.00

CANES and walking sticks were used by every well-dressed man in the nineteenth century, but by World War I the style had changed. Today canes are used by few but the infirm. Collectors prize old canes made with special features, like hidden swords, whiskey flasks, or risqué pictures seen through peepholes. Examples with solid gold heads or made from exotic materials, such as walrus vertebrae, are among the higher priced canes.

Alligator Clinging To Log, Glass Eyes, Snakewood Shaft	605.00
Blowgun, Brass Dog Head, Percussion Cap Inside	2420.00
Brass Top, Removable Swiss-Made Superior Railway Timekeeper	660.00
Carved Head, Abraham Lincoln Style, Staff Carved Our Emancipator	175.00
Cobra, Coiled, Black Paint, Silver Dots, Kentucky	45.00
Eagle, Handle, Carved, Relief Leaves Wind Up Shaft, 32 In.	395.00
Elephant, Rope & Tassel Carvings, Ivory, Gold Collar	605.00
Folding Seat, Canvas Seat	357.50
Glass, Aqua, 2 Blue Shades Threading, White, 47 1/2 In.	137.00
Glass, Corkscrew, Amber & Clear	80.00
Glass, Red, Yellow & Blue, Milk Glass Core	550.00
Glass, Spiraled, Aqua, Mid-19th Century, 46 1/2 In.	66.00
Great Lakes Exposition, Cleveland, Ohio, Wooden, 1936	85.00
Ivory, Handle, Boar's Tusk, Erotic Seminude Woman	660.00
Ivory, Handle, Skull & Crossbones, E.S. Berry, M.D.	880.00
Ivory, Mechanical, Skull, Eyes & Mouth Open, Tongue Sticks Out, 19th Century	1540.00
Ivory, Whale, Curved Handle, Whalebone Shaft, 19th Century	330.00

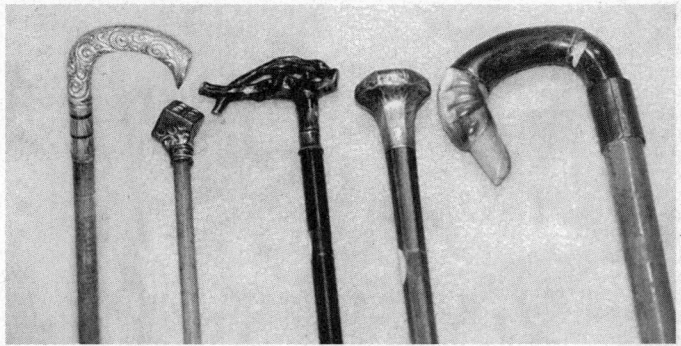

Left to right: ; Cane, Walking Stick, Gold Filled Floral Repousse Handle, 38 In.; Cane, Walking Stick, Dice Cap, Silver, 34 In.; Cane, Walking Stick, Free-Form Root Handle, Silver, 36 In.; Cane, Walking Stick, Etched Gadroon Handle, 34 In.; Cane, Walking Stick, Dog Head, Carved Horn Handle, 35 In.

Ivory, Whale, T-Shaped Top, Whalebone Shaft, 19th Century 550.00
Ivory & Whalebone, Carved Bent Index Finger On Baleen Spacer, 19th Century 550.00
Ivory Knob, Handle, Flexible, Tanned Elephant Tail, Silver Collar 605.00
Ivory Knob, Handle, Reeded Shaft, Ivory Ferrule 110.00
Lion Head, Ball In Mouth, Sterling Silver 330.00
Masonic, Handle Opened To 6 Sections, Inscribed Masonic Symbols 3960.00
Microscope, Williams, Brown & Earle Inc., Entomologist Use 3410.00
Open Hand, Silver Nails, Horseshoe, Face Of Monster, Silver Teeth, 34 1/2 In. 3450.00
Pullout Knife, Scrimshaw, Whale Ivory Diamonds, Rosewood, 1840, 34 1/2 In. 495.00
Schoolmaster's, Alphabet & Numbers Down Length 2500.00
Shillelagh, Dog's Head Handle, c.1860 .... 85.00
Skull, Ivory, Surrounded By 8 Emeralds, Snake With Ruby Eyes 3300.00
Sterling Silver, Handle, Boar's Head, Glass Eyes 440.00
Sterling Silver, Handle, Dog, Sleeping 358.00
Sterling Silver, Handle, Tigress, Ball In Mouth, Glass Eyes 319.00
Sterling Silver, Handle, Tree Stump 193.00
Sword, Bamboo, Ivory Inlaid Faces & Tooth Finial, Oriental, 37 In. 247.00
Sword, Brass Pommel Cap, Concealed Section, French, c.1880 .... 170.00
Sword, Cherry Wood, Concealed Brass Ferrule, Europe, 1850 .... 165.00
Walking Stick, 30 Wavy Faces, Brown 2-Tone Finish, 34 In. 192.50
Walking Stick, Adam & Eve Motif, 1866 Nickel Three-Cent Piece Set In Top 220.00
Walking Stick, Bamboo, Movable Celluloid Ferrule 95.00
Walking Stick, Bone, Silver Plated Handle, Engraved Design, Europe, 32 1/2 In. 770.00
Walking Stick, Carved Bone Handle, Cherry 150.00
Walking Stick, Carved Foliage, Gilded Barrels, c.1917, 37 In. 920.00
Walking Stick, Clenched Fist, Whalebone Knop, 31 1/2 In. 495.00
Walking Stick, Dice Cap, Silver, 34 In. .... *Illus* 66.00
Walking Stick, Dog Head, Carved Horn Handle, 35 In. .... *Illus* 75.00
Walking Stick, Dog Head, Glass Eyes, Carved, Engraved From A Friend, 33 In. 575.00
Walking Stick, Double-Wrapped Serpent, Whale Ivory, 19th Century 4730.00
Walking Stick, Dragon, Carved Ivory Handle 695.00
Walking Stick, Egyptian Face Handle, Ivory 550.00
Walking Stick, Etched Gadroon Handle, 34 In. .... *Illus* 77.00
Walking Stick, Faceted Knob, Ebony Inlay, Whalebone Shaft, 19th Century 880.00
Walking Stick, Faceted Knob, Whale Ivory, Bone Shaft, Painted, 19th Century 1540.00
Walking Stick, Fireman, Seated, Legs Stretched, Carved, 33 5/8 In. 1035.00
Walking Stick, Free-Form Root Handle, Silver, 36 In. .... *Illus* 358.00
Walking Stick, Friendship, Monkey's Knot, Carved, 37 In. 690.00
Walking Stick, Gilded Barrels, Ellipses, Clerical Figure Top, c.1917, 37 In. 920.00
Walking Stick, Gold Filled Floral Repousse Handle, 38 In. .... *Illus* 192.00
Walking Stick, Grand Army Of Republic, Military Motifs, 1860s, 36 3/4 In. 1380.00

Walking Stick, Hand Clenching Snake, Ivory, Whale, 19th Century 880.00
Walking Stick, Hearts Handle, Ivory, Serpent Winding Up Shaft, 19th Century 225.00
Walking Stick, Hermit In Mountain Landscape, Bamboo Carved, Japan, 35 3/4 In. ... 440.00
Walking Stick, Horse Head, Silver, Glass Eyes, Ebony Shaft, 34 In. 310.00
Walking Stick, Indian Heads, Flowers, Animals, Eagle, Carved, 38 In. 225.50
Walking Stick, Ivory Knob, Silver Inlaid 225.00
Walking Stick, Ivory, Lion Mask, Paw Handle, Ivory, 37 In. 205.00
Walking Stick, Ivory, Whale, Mother-Of-Pearl, Whalebone Shaft, 19th Century 770.00
Walking Stick, Martyred Saint, Carved Ivory Handle, Coconut Shaft, 36 1/2 In. 247.00
Walking Stick, Portrait Of Gentleman Handle, Carved, 36 In. 130.00
Walking Stick, Presented To Jefferson Davis, c.1880, 34 1/2 In. 7700.00
Walking Stick, Rosewood, Ivory Finial, Rats, Owl, Japan, 19th Century, 37 In. 770.00
Walking Stick, Six Horse Heads, Rosewood Shaft, Ivory Handle, Carved, 35 In. 1100.00
Walking Stick, Snake Head, Handle, Hand Carved 125.00
Walking Stick, Spherical Marble Handle, Silver Ferrule, Ebony Shaft, 37 In. 220.00
Walking Stick, Stag Horn Handle, Grotesque Head, Chestnut Shaft, 37 In. 275.00
Walking Stick, Totem, Tiki Face, Allegorical Crocodile & Head, Maori, 32 In. 425.00
Walking Stick, Whale's Tooth Handle, Whalebone, 32 In. 440.00
Walking Stick, Whalebone, Carved, Ivory Handle, Initialed A.G., 33 In. 550.00
Walking Stick, Whalebone, Carved, Whale Tooth Handle, 19th Century, 30 1/2 In. .. 330.00
Walking Stick, Whalebone, Flat Top Knob, Hardwood Extender, 19th Century 330.00
Walking Stick, Whalebone, Turned & Incised Knop, 38 1/2 In. 825.00

CANTON CHINA is blue-and-white ware made near Canton, China, from
about 1785 to 1895. It is hand decorated with Chinese scenes.

Berry Bowl, Oval, 8 In. 575.00
Bidet, End Drain, Kidney Shape, 23 1/2 In. 1980.00
Bowl, Cover, Vegetable, Rectangular, 8 In. 292.00
Bowl, Reticulated, Oval, Orange Peel Glaze, 8 1/2 In. 360.00
Bowl, Vegetable, Pinecone Finial Cover, Lozenge Form, 9 3/4 In., Pair 550.00
Candleholder, Elephant, Saddle Blanket, Famille Rose, 5 11/16 In., Pair 2875.00
Cup & Saucer 70.00
Dish, 6 In. 20.00
Dish, Cloud & Rain Border, 1830, 10 In. 165.00
Dish, Shrimp 660.00
Dish, Vegetable, Cover, 9 1/2 In. 192.00
Garden Seat, Sailboats, Barrel Shape, 19 1/4 In., Pair 9200.00
Ginger Jar, 7 In. 165.00
Platter, 12 1/2 In. 385.00
Platter, 8 Sides, 19th Century, 17 1/2 In. 770.00
Platter, Cloud & Rain Border, Oval, 1830, 11 3/4 In. 295.00
Platter, Orange Peel Glaze, 16 3/4 In. 330.00
Platter, Pierced Corners, 15 In. 500.00
Platter, Riverscape, Blue & White, 19th Century, 20 5/8 In. 1725.00
Soup, Dish, 8 1/2 In. 80.00
Sugar, Domed Cover, 1840, 5 3/4 In. 660.00
Tea Caddy, 6 1/4 In., Pair 990.00
Teapot, Pear Shape 395.00
Teapot, Straight Sides 632.50
Tile, Tea, Round, 5 1/4 In. 412.50
Toddy Jug, Cover, Mandarin Women, Iron Red, Barrel Shape, 9 1/2 In. ..... 1380.00 to 1540.00
Tray, Famille Rose, Scene Of Noblemen & Ladies In Garden Of Pavilion, 9 7/8 In. ... 1380.00
Tureen, Cover, Boar's Head Handles, 19th Century, 13 In. 825.00
Tureen, Fruit Finial, Fruit & Foliage Handles, 11 3/4 In. 1980.00
Tureen, Sauce, Cover, Oval, 8 1/2 In. 577.50
Tureen, Soup, Cover, 12 In. 935.00

CAPO-DI-MONTE porcelain was first made in Naples, Italy, from 1743 to
1759. The factory moved near Madrid, Spain, reopened in 1771, and worked
to 1834. Since that time, the Doccia factory of Italy acquired the molds and is
using the N and crown mark. Societe Richard Ceramica is a modern-day firm
often referred to as Ginori or Capo-di-Monte. This company uses the crown
and N mark.

Basket, Applied Flowers, Open Basket Weave, N & Crown Mark, 4 x 4 In.	13.00
Bowl, Cherubs, Capri San Michele, Pierced, N & Crown Mark, 12 In.	68.00
Bowl, Cover, Allegorical Scenes, Molded Figures, Lion Finial, 3 1/ 2 In.	125.00
Bowl, Pierced Cover, Greek Classical Figures & Florals, 6 x 12 3/4 In.	265.00
Box, Armor-Making Scene On Lid, Gilded Brass Fittings, 9 In.	247.50
Box, Classical Scenes, Cherubs, Polychrome & Enamel, Marked, 11 In.	605.00
Box, Classical Scenes, Cherubs, Polychrome & Gilt, Marked, 5 In.	101.00
Cache Pot, Cherubs & Flowers On Lid, Floral & Cherub Handle	55.00
Chocolate Pot, Women Swimming, Pear Finial, 7 In.	225.00
Ewer, Polychrome, Gilt Ground, Boar Hunt Scenes, Neapolitan, c.1850, 9 In.	357.50
Figurine, English Sheep Dog, Raised Flowered Bow, 1950s, 10 In.	65.00
Figurine, Girl Cooking, Boy Making Love To Her, 9 1/2 x 9 In.	395.00
Figurine, Man With Hurdy-Gurdy, Marked, 3 3/8 In.	27.50
Figurine, Young Couple, Musical Instruments, Marked, 8 1/2 x 8 1/2 In.	330.00
Group, Coach, 2 Horses & Coachmen, Woman & Man, 17 1/2 x 9 1/8 In.	165.00
Group, Fancy Ladies, Floral Garlands, N & Crown Mark, 10 In.	590.00
Lamp, Cherubs, Silk Shade, 1930s, 32 In., Pair	975.00
Plaque, Dealer's, Flowers	45.00
Plaque, Seminude Lovers In Garden, Gold Trim, 5 1/2 In.	10.00
Plate, Cherub Rim, Gilt, N & Crown Mark, 8 In., Pair	77.00
Plate, Clusters Of Flowering Branches, Doccia, 1745, 9 In.	805.00
Plate, Neptune & Cherubs, Chariot, Reticulated, N & Crown Mark, 9 In.	35.00
Snuffbox, Portrait Medallions, c.1750, 2 7/8 In.	1150.00
Stein, Classical Scene & Figures, Rampant Lion On Lid, c.1920, 11 In.	365.00
Stein, Hand Painted Chariot Scene, Figural Goat On Lid	660.00
Tureen, Cupid Design, Cover, Black N & Crown Mark, 10 In.	465.00
Urn, Rollicking Cherubs & Sea Gods, Marked, 7 1/4 In., Pair	115.00

CAPTAIN MARVEL was introduced in February 1940 in Whiz comic books. An orphan named Billy Batson met the wizard Shazam, and whenever he said the magic word he was transformed into a superhero. A movie serial was released in 1940. The comic was discontinued in 1954. A second Captain Marvel appeared in 1966, a third in 1967. Only the original was transformed by shouting *Shazam*.

Bank, Magic Dime Saver, Tin Lithograph, 1948, 2 1/2 x 2 1/2 In.	345.00
Car, No. 4, Blue, 1947	100.00
Pennant, Blue Felt, 1940s	85.00
Tie Clip, On Card	90.00
Wristwatch, Box, 1948	375.00
Wristwatch, Mary Marvel, Comic Character, Box, 1948	250.00

CAPTAIN MIDNIGHT began as a radio show in September 1940. The first comic book appeared in July 1941. Captain Midnight was really the aviator Captain Albright, who was to defeat the Nazis. A movie serial was made in 1942 and a comic strip was published for a short time. The comic book Captain Midnight ended his career in 1948. The radio premiums are the prized collector memorabilia today.

Badge, Decoder, Magni-Matic Code-O-Graph, 1945	80.00
Key Chain	150.00
Mug, Ovaltine, 1940s	8.00
Pin, Patrol	20.00
Ring, Flight Commanders	400.00
Ring, Mystic Sun God	1450.00 to 1650.00

CARAMEL SLAG, see Chocolate Glass category

CARDS listed here include advertising cards, greeting cards, baseball cards, playing cards, valentines, and others. Color pictures were rare in the nineteenth century, so companies gave away colorful cards with pictures of children, flowers, products, or related scenes that promoted the company name. These were often collected and stored in albums. Greeting cards are also a nineteenth-century idea that has remained popular. Baseball cards also date from the nineteenth century when they were used by tobacco companies as giveaways. The gum cards were started in 1933, but it was not until after

World War II that the bubble gum cards favored today were produced. Today
over 1,000 cards are issued each year by the gum companies. Related items
may be found in the Postcard category.

Advertising, 7-Up, Oh Brother!, 2 Boys, 1955, 11 x 21 In.	30.00
Advertising, Ayer's Pills, The Little Favorites, Sugar Coated, 1880s	15.00
Advertising, Beach Soap, Kate Greenaway Children, 2 1/2 x 4 1/2 In., 5 Piece	25.00
Advertising, Chase & Sanborn, Color, 2 Sides, 1886, 3 x 5 In.	10.00
Advertising, Corrugated Stove Pipe Elbow Co., Cartoon Type, 1870-1877, 6 In.	15.00
Advertising, Domestic Sewing Machine Silver Anniversary, Elegant, 1863-1888	15.00
Advertising, Dozier Weyl Cracker Co., Parrot Eating Cracker, 1880s, 5 x 3 In.	15.00
Advertising, Drink Hires Root Beer, Put Roses In Your Cheeks, 1891, 3 x 5 In.	30.00
Advertising, Emerson Piano Co., Lady Playing Piano, Angel, 1880s, 4 x 3 In.	7.50
Advertising, Esso Logo, Happy, Standing, Punch-Out, Cardboard, 1950s, 5 x 8 In.	20.00
Advertising, Fairbanks Tom, Dick & Harry Soap, Black Children In Wagon, 1880	22.50
Advertising, Gail Borden Eagle Condensed Milk, Girl & Dog, 1880s, 3 x 5 In.	14.00
Advertising, Havana 5-Cent Cigar, Floral, Bees, Butterfly, 3 x 4 1/2 In., 4 Piece	15.00
Advertising, Heinz, Mama's Favorites, Peanut Butter, 1910, 3 1/2 x 5 1/2 In.	12.50
Advertising, Helpmate Sewing Machine, Building, Columbian Exhibition	4.00
Advertising, Hood's Pills Cure Liver Ills, 2 Sides, 3 x 3 In.	18.00
Advertising, Humphreys' Witch Hazel, Barefoot Girl, 1880s, 5 x 3 In.	15.00
Advertising, Lydia Pinkham, Yours For Health, Black & White, 1880s, 2 1/2 x 4 In.	10.00
Advertising, McLaughlin Coffee	6.00
Advertising, Petrola Hair Restorer, American Indian Women, 1860-1870, 4 3/4 In.	15.00
Advertising, Red Man Chewing Tobacco, Indian Chiefs In American History, 9 In.	45.00
Advertising, Reynolds Brothers Fine Shoes, Ladies, 1880s, 5 x 3 In.	9.00
Advertising, Rising Sun Stove Polish	25.00
Advertising, Smith Bros. Fine Teas, Syracuse, N.Y., Sporting Scene, 3 1/2 x 5 In.	6.00
Baseball, Babe Ruth, Churchman Cigarettes, 1929	175.00
Baseball, Dom DiMaggio, 1952	80.00
Baseball, Hank Aaron, 1958	45.00
Baseball, Jello, Uncut Sheet, 1963	600.00
Baseball, Johnson, Piedmont Cigarettes, c.1910	220.00
Baseball, Mickey Mantle, 1958	85.00
Baseball, Mickey Mantle, Bazooka, 1959	595.00
Baseball, Ty Cobb, Piedmont Cigarettes, c.1910	230.00
Baseball, Whitey Ford, Post, 1961	30.00
Basketball, Wilt Chamberlain, Rookie, Fleer, 1961-1962	1045.00
Business, Beetle Boat Building Co., New Bedford, 1890	145.00
Christmas, Fancy, Original Envelope, 1930, 8 x 10 In.	1.00
Christmas, U.S. Eagle Picking Up Japanese Soldier, 1944, 5 x 4 In.	30.00
Christmas, Pensacola Naval Air Station, Photograph, 1935, 4 x 5 1/2 In.	8.50

Card, Football, Stand-Up,
Spalding's Football Player

◆◆◆◆◆◆◆◆◆◆◆◆◆◆◆◆◆◆◆◆

Leather that crumbles to red
powder has "red rot." It is caused
by absorption of sulphur dioxide
and cannot be stopped.

◆◆◆◆◆◆◆◆◆◆◆◆◆◆◆◆◆◆◆◆

Cigarette, Animals' Heads, British, c.1931, 50 Piece 85.00
Cigarette, Animals Of The Countryside, England, 1930s, 50 Piece 58.00
Cigarette, British Empire Series, Player Cigarettes, c.1904, 50 Piece 200.00
Cigarette, Imperial, Poker Hands, 1920s, 53 Piece 80.00
Cigarette, Lighthouses, British, 1920s, 50 Piece 68.00
Cigarette, Movie Stars, Player Cigarettes, Full Album, 1940s 85.00
Cigarette, School Emblems, British, 1920s, 40 Piece 60.00
Cigarette, Uniforms Of The Territorial Army, British, 1930s, 50 Piece 68.00
Cigarette, Wings, Modern Airplanes, 23 Piece 35.00
Football, Stand-Up, Spalding's Football Player .... *Illus* 345.00
Golf, Arnold Palmer Hologram, 1991 Pro Set 80.00
Gum, Addams Family, Set, 66 Piece 50.00
Hockey, Ray Bourque, No. 140, Rookie, O-Pee-Chee, 1980-1981 .... 125.00
Lobby, Battle Hymn, Rock Hudson, Scene, 1957 .... 10.00
Lobby, Cliff Robertson, In Jeep, 1976 .... 5.00
Lobby, Crimson Skull, Anita Bush, Norman Film Mfg. Co., 1921, 8 Piece 200.00
Lobby, Flame & Flesh, Starring Lana Turner, 1954, 8 Piece 60.00
Lobby, Hi De Ho, Cab Calloway, All American Films, 1947, 14 x 22 In. 300.00
Lobby, Men Of The Night, 1934 .... 35.00
Lobby, Phantom Of The Opera, Claude Rains, 1943 .... 3850.00
Lobby, Tales Of Robin Hood, Lippert Pictures, 1951, 11 x 14 In., 8 Piece 75.00
Lobby, The Outlaw, Jane Russell, 4 Lead Stars, 1950 .... 36.00
Lobby, Virginia Judge, Steppin' Fetchit, Paramount, 1935, 6 Piece 35.00
Lobby, Young Winston, R. Shaw, A. Bancroft, 1972, Set 26.00
Playing, Animals, Gold Edge, Box, Miniature 10.00
Playing, Bicycle, Double Deck, 1910 .... 15.00
Playing, Chesapeake & Ohio Railroad, Double Deck, Sealed 22.00
Playing, CM & St. P RR, Lake Michigan To Puget Sound, Slip Case 45.00
Playing, Congress, 1 Deck Has Fortunes, 2 Sets 45.00
Playing, Great Hagenbeck & Wallace Circus 75.00
Playing, Green Hornet, Photograph Of Van Williams Or Bruce Lee, Ed-U-cards, 1966 32.00
Playing, Historic Boston Souvenir, Chisholm Brothers, 1920s 38.50
Playing, Karl Wallenda Wirewalk Georgia Chasm 20.00
Playing, Marilyn Monroe, 1956, Box 19.00
Playing, New York City Scenes, United Nations, Red Felt Box 6.00
Playing, Norman Rockwell, Double Deck 15.00
Playing, Old Bourbon Supreme 10.00
Playing, Red Cross, World War II 10.00
Playing, Reddy Kilowatt, Logo, Shrink-Wrapped Box, 1950s 38.00
Playing, Southern Pacific Railroad, Scenic, Box 28.00
Playing, St. Luania, Double Deck, 1940s 25.00
Valentine, 54th Battalion, My Love To You On Valentine's Day, 1945, 5 x 4 In. 40.00
Valentine, Aladdin, Movable, 5 1/2 In. 35.00
Valentine, Boy & Girl Boxing, Mechanical, 1940s 2.00
Valentine, Dolly Dingle, Insert, Movable Eyes, 6 x 6 In. 35.00
Valentine, Fold-Out, Pleated, Figure, Hearts & Flowers, Gold Design, 1920s, 8 1/2 In. 15.00
Valentine, Googly-Eyed Child, Wishing Well, Glass Display Frame, 7 1/2 In. 32.00
Valentine, McDonald's, 1974, 4 Piece 12.00
Valentine, Mechanical, Betty Boop Type 14.00
Valentine, Multilayer, c.1880, 7 x 10 In. 15.00
Valentine, Roses, Birds, Cherubs, Crepe Paper, Fold-Out, 1934, 8 In. 32.00
Valentine, Wizard Of Oz Scarecrow, 3 x 5 In. 60.00

CARLSBAD, Germany, is a mark found on china made by several factories in
Germany. Most of the pieces available today were made after 1891.

Bowl, Sauce, Red Flower, Gold Trim, Scrolled, 5 1/2 In. 2.50
Cup, Scenes Of Washington, D.C. 45.00
Plate, Beautiful Woman, Holding Flower, Gold Wooden Frame, Beehive, 18 In. 125.00
Plate, Portrait, Cinq Mars, 7 In. 20.00
Plate, Portrait, Philippe De Orleans, 7 In. 20.00
Platter, Fish, Scalloped, 6 Small Plates 600.00
Platter, Rose & Gold Rim, Fish, Underwater Scene, 25 x 11 In. 750.00
Vase, Multicolor Flowers, Matte Pink Top, Gold Trim, JK Mark, 11 x 5 In. 45.00

CARLTON WARE was made at the Carlton Works of Stoke-on-Trent, England, about 1890. The firm traded as Wiltshaw & Robinson until 1957. It was renamed Carlton Ware Ltd. in 1958.

Bowl, Art Deco, Rouge Royal, 11 In.	125.00
Box, Cover, Black Base, Embossed Iris & Branch Top, 4 x 6 1/2 In.	145.00
Condiment Set, Floral Shape, 4 Piece	65.00
Cup & Saucer, Black & White Silhouette, Demitasse	85.00
Dish, Divided, Flower, Orange & Green Center, 8 1/2 x 9 1/2 In.	165.00
Figurine, Ostrich, My Goodness My Guiness, 4 In.	95.00
Pitcher, Green Basket Weave, Fruit Border, 4 In.	55.00
Pitcher, Ring Handle, Rouge Royale, Gold & Enamel Chinoiserie	250.00
Pitcher, Rouge Royale, 5 1/2 In.	95.00
Sugar & Creamer, Bell-Shaped Flowers, Green	75.00
Toast Rack, Embossed Pink Flower, 3 1/4 x 4 3/4 In.	88.00
Vase, Ducks, Iris, Handles, Crimson, 7 In.	150.00

CARNIVAL GLASS was an inexpensive, iridescent, pressed glass made from about 1907 to about 1925. More than 1,000 different patterns are known. Carnival glass is currently being reproduced. Additional pieces may be found in the Northwood category.

Acanthus, Bowl, Green, 8 In.	85.00
Acanthus, Chop Plate, Marigold 10 In.	165.00
Acorn, Bowl, Crimped, Blue, 7 1/2 In.	55.00
Amaryllis pattern is listed here as Tiger Lily	
American Beauty Roses pattern is listed here as Wreath of Roses	
Apple Tree, Tumbler, Blue	52.50
Apple Tree, Water Set, Marigold, 7 Piece	285.00
April Showers, Vase, Marigold, 11 In.	55.00
Arcs, Bowl, Ruffled, Marigold, 8 1/2 In.	30.00
Battenburg Lace No. 1 pattern is listed here as Hearts & Flowers	
Battenburg Lace No. 2 pattern is listed here as Captive Rose	
Battenburg Lace No. 3 pattern is listed here as Fanciful	
Beaded Cable, Rose Bowl, Aqua Opalescent	200.00
Beaded Cable, Rose Bowl, Footed, Blue	170.00
Beaded Cable, Rose Bowl, Marigold	75.00
Beaded Shell, Berry Bowl, Footed, Amethyst, 8 3/4 In.	165.00
Beaded Shell, Mug, Amethyst	45.00 to 100.00
Beaded Shell, Tumbler, Amethyst	60.00 to 70.00
Big Fish, Bowl, Marigold, 9 3/4 In.	650.00
Birds & Cherries, Bonbon, Blue	75.00
Birds on Bough pattern is listed here as Birds & Cherries	
Blackberry, Compote, Purple	100.00
Blackberry A. pattern is listed here as Blackberry	
Blackberry B. pattern is listed here as Blackberry Spray	
Blackberry Banded, Hat, 4 Sides, Ruffled, Blue	35.00
Blackberry Bramble, Compote, 4 Sides, Blue	110.00
Blackberry Bramble, Compote, Ruffled, Marigold, 6 1/2 In.	42.00
Blackberry Spray, Bowl, Scalloped, Amethyst, 5 In.	95.00
Blackberry Wreath, Bowl, Amethyst, 6 1/4 In.	68.00
Blueberry, Tumbler, Blue	40.00
Bouquet, Water Set, Marigold, 5 Piece	250.00
Broken Arches, Punch Bowl, Amethyst	175.00
Broken Arches, Punch Set, Marigold, 8 Piece	395.00
Broken Arches, Punch Set, Purple, 7 Piece	575.00
Brooklyn Bridge, Bowl, Marigold	350.00
Butterfly, Bonbon, 2 Handles, Amethyst	85.00
Butterfly & Berry, Berry Set, Marigold, 7 Piece	100.00 to 125.00
Butterfly & Berry, Butter, Cover	100.00
Butterfly & Berry, Tumbler, Blue	60.00 to 75.00
Butterfly & Berry, Tumbler, Marigold	35.00
Butterfly & Berry, Vase, Blue, 8 1/4 In.	85.00
Butterfly & Berry, Water Set, Blue, 11 Piece	1150.00

Butterfly & Berry, Water Set, Marigold, 7 Piece 310.00
Butterfly & Cable pattern is listed here as Springtime
Butterfly & Grape pattern is listed here as Butterfly & Berry
Butterfly & Stippled Rays pattern is listed here as Butterfly
Cactus Leaf Rays pattern is listed here as Leaf Rays
Cannon Ball, Pitcher, Marigold 350.00
Captive Rose, Bowl, Candy Ribbon Edge, Amethyst, 8 In. 100.00
Captive Rose, Bowl, Candy Ribbon Edge, Green, 8 In. 65.00
Captive Rose, Bowl, Ruffled, Blue, 9 In. 95.00
Carolina Dogwood, Bowl, Ruffled, Blue Opalescent, 8 In. 300.00
Cattails & Water Lily pattern is listed here as Water Lily & Cattails
Cherries & Holly Wreath pattern is listed here as Cherry Circles
Cherry, Bowl, Footed, Amethyst, 9 In. 135.00
Cherry Chain, Bowl, White, 10 1/2 In. 125.00
Cherry Chain, Plate, Marigold, 6 1/2 In. 60.00
Cherry Circles, Bowl, Handle, Marigold, 7 1/4 In. 37.00
Christmas Cactus pattern is listed here as Thistle
Christmas Plate pattern is listed here as Poinsettia
Chrysanthemum Wreath pattern is listed here as Ten Mums
Coin Dot, Bowl, Amethyst, 8 3/4 In. 52.00
Colonial, Vase, 8-Scalloped Foot, Marigold, 5 1/4 x 7 1/2 In. 38.00
Colonial Lady, Vase, Marigold, 5 1/2 In. 1025.00
Constitution pattern is listed here as God & Home
Cosmos, Bowl, Green, 5 3/4 In. 55.00
Crab Claw, Tumbler, Marigold, 4 1/2 In. 36.00
Crackle, Pitcher Set, Footed Tumblers, 6 Piece 95.00
Daisy & Drape, Vase, Aqua, 6 1/4 In. 600.00
Daisy & Lattice Band pattern is listed here as Lattice & Daisy
Daisy & Plume, Banana Boat, 3 Footed, Peach 130.00
Daisy & Plume, Rose Bowl, Stem, Marigold .... 50.00 to 65.00
Dandelion, Tumbler, Amethyst 72.50
Dandelion Variant pattern is listed here as Panelled Dandelion
Diamond & Daisy Cut, Tumbler, Marigold 40.00
Diamond Band pattern is listed here as Diamonds
Diamond Lace, Tumbler, Purple 82.50
Diamond Lace, Water Set, Purple, 5 Piece .... 425.00 to 450.00
Diamond Point, Vase, Amethyst, 10 In. 75.00
Diamond Point, Vase, Amethyst, 10 1/2 In. 40.00
Diamond Point, Vase, Green, 11 In. 30.00
Diamond Point, Vase, Marigold, 12 In. 28.00
Diamonds, Pitcher, Marigold 140.00
Dogwood & Marsh Lily pattern is listed here as Two Flowers
Double Loop, Sugar, Blue 75.00
Double-Stem Rose, Bowl, Marigold, 9 In. 40.00
Dragon & Lotus, Bowl, 8 Ruffles, Marigold 125.00
Dragon & Lotus, Bowl, Ice Cream, Amber, 8 In. 200.00
Dragon & Lotus, Bowl, Ice Cream, Blue 55.00
Dragon & Lotus, Bowl, Ice Cream, Green, 8 In. 250.00
Dragon & Lotus, Bowl, Marigold, 8 1/2 In. .... 55.00 to 65.00
Drapery, Rose Bowl, Aqua Opalescent, Marigold Overlay 350.00
Egyptian Band pattern is listed here as Round-Up
Elk, Lying Down, Purple, 3 1/2 In. 12.00
Embroidered Mums, Bowl, Ruffled, Aqua Opalescent, 9 In. 475.00
Fan & Arch pattern is listed here as Persian Garden
Fanciful, Plate, Amethyst, 9 In. 245.00
Fantasy pattern is listed here as Question Marks
Fashion, Punch Bowl, Base, Marigold, 8 Piece 175.00
Fashion, Punch Cup, Marigold 22.00
Fashion, Punch Set, Marigold, 13 Piece 235.00
Fashion, Rose Bowl, Marigold 150.00
Fashion, Toothpick, Red 25.00
Fashion, Water Set, Marigold, 7 Piece 292.50
Feathered Scroll pattern is listed here as Feathered Serpent

Feathered Serpent, Bowl, Honeycomb Exterior, Green, 10 In. 55.00
Fenton's Butterfly pattern is listed here as Butterfly
Fine Cut & Roses, Candy Dish, White 165.00
Finecut & Star pattern is listed here as Star & File
Fish & Flowers pattern is listed here as Trout & Fly
Fisherman's Mug, Mug, Purple 125.00
Fisherman's Net pattern is listed here as Tree Bark
Floral & Diamond Point, pattern is listed here as Fine Cut & Roses
Floral & Grape, Water Set, Blue, 6 Piece 340.00
Floral & Grapevine pattern is listed here as Floral & Grape
Flowering Almonds pattern is listed here as Peacock Tail
Four Flowers, Plate, Green, 9 In. 240.00
Fruit & Flowers, Bonbon, Basket Weave Exterior, Blue 300.00
Fruit & Flowers, Bonbon, Handles, Blue .... 200.00 to 225.00
God & Home, Tumbler, Blue 275.00
Good Luck, Bowl, Piecrust Edge, Green, 9 In. 425.00
Good Luck, Bowl, Ruffled, Blue, 8 1/2 In. .... 275.00 to 475.00
Good Luck, Bowl, Ruffled, Ribbed, Marigold, 9 In. 160.00
Grape, Bowl, Marigold, 9 1/2 In. 65.00
Grape, Pitcher, Marigold, 8 1/2 In. 95.00
Grape & Arches, Tumbler, Blue 50.00
Grape & Cable, Banana Boat, Marigold .... 140.00 to 335.00
Grape & Cable, Berry Bowl, Amethyst, 9 In. 78.00
Grape & Cable, Bonbon, Stippled, Amethyst 175.00
Grape & Cable, Bowl, Purple, 10 In. 400.00
Grape & Cable, Bowl, Ruffled, Amethyst, 6 In. 40.00
Grape & Cable, Bowl, Ruffled, Ribbed, Blue, 8 1/2 In. .... 350.00 to 425.00
Grape & Cable, Bowl, Spatula Feet, Marigold, 7 3/4 In. 45.00
Grape & Cable, Butter, Marigold 145.00
Grape & Cable, Candlestick, Marigold, Pair 235.00
Grape & Cable, Compote, Green .... 795.00 to 1100.00
Grape & Cable, Cracker Jar, Marigold 225.00
Grape & Cable, Creamer, Breakfast, Marigold 65.00
Grape & Cable, Creamer, Marigold .... 65.00 to 85.00
Grape & Cable, Hatpin Holder, Amethyst 300.00
Grape & Cable, Hatpin Holder, Marigold 286.00
Grape & Cable, Hatpin Holder, Purple 245.00
Grape & Cable, Orange Bowl, Blue, 10 1/2 In. 600.00
Grape & Cable, Orange Bowl, Green 695.00
Grape & Cable, Pitcher, Marigold 540.00
Grape & Cable, Pitcher, Purple 275.00
Grape & Cable, Plate, Basket Weave, Amethyst, 9 1/2 In. 260.00
Grape & Cable, Plate, Spatula Feet, Green, 9 In. 175.00
Grape & Cable, Powder Jar, Cover, Green 95.00
Grape & Cable, Punch Set, Marigold, 7 Piece 285.00
Grape & Cable, Punch Set, Purple, Master, 14 Piece 3800.00
Grape & Cable, Spooner, Marigold 85.00
Grape & Cable, Sugar & Creamer, Amethyst 350.00
Grape & Cable, Sugar, Cover, Marigold .... 100.00 to 150.00
Grape & Cable, Sweetmeat, Cover, Amethyst 365.00
Grape & Cable, Sweetmeat, Purple 235.00
Grape & Cable, Tumbler, Green 70.00
Grape & Cable, Tumbler, Purple 28.00
Grape & Cable, Water Set, Amethyst, 7 Piece 550.00
Grape & Cable, Water Set, Purple, 7 Piece 625.00
Grape & Gothic Arches, Table Set, Blue, 3 Piece 500.00
Grape & Gothic Arches, Table Set, Blue, 5 Piece 565.00
Grape & Gothic Arches, Tumbler, Purple 75.00
Grape Arbor, Water Set, Marigold, 6 Piece 360.00
Grape Delight pattern is listed here as Vintage
Grapevine & Lattice, Tumbler, Amethyst 60.00
Greek Key, Tumbler, Green 110.00
Heart & Vine, Bowl, 6 Ruffles, Blue 95.00

Hearts & Flowers, Bowl, Ruffled, Blue, 9 In. 425.00
Hearts & Flowers, Compote, Aqua Opalescent 750.00
Hearts & Flowers, Compote, Ruffled, White 210.00
Heavy Iris, Tumbler, Amethyst 50.00
Heron, Mug, Purple 350.00
Heron & Rushes pattern is listed here as Stork & Rushes
Hobnail pattern is listed in this book as its own category
Hobstar & Arches, Bowl, Ruffled, Marigold, 9 x 3 In. 45.00
Holly, Bowl, Marigold, 8 1/4 In. 38.00
Holly, Bowl, Round, Marigold, 9 In. 85.00
Holly, Bowl, Ruffled, Green, 9 In. 70.00
Holly, Compote, Crimped, Blue, 4 1/2 x 4 In. 36.00
Holly, Plate, Marigold, 9 In. 200.00
Holly, Rose Bowl, Blue 250.00
Holly, Sherbet, Marigold, 4 1/4 In. 22.00
Holly & Berry pattern is listed here as Holly Carnival
Holly Carnival, Bowl, Green, Gold Trim, 9 1/2 In. 75.00
Holly Spray pattern is listed here as Holly Sprig
Holly Sprig, Bowl, Ruffled, Amethyst, 10 In. 125.00
Honeycomb, Rose Bowl, Peach Opalescent 250.00
Horseshoe, Bowl, Green, 8 3/4 In. 240.00
Horseshoe, Bowl, Marigold, 8 3/4 In. 195.00
Imperial Crackle, Vase, Car, Marigold 32.00
Imperial Grape, Berry Set, Marigold, 7 Piece 175.00
Imperial Grape, Bowl, Marigold, 9 In. 48.00
Imperial Grape, Goblet, Marigold, 5 1/4 In. 35.00
Imperial Grape, Goblet, Purple 60.00
Imperial Grape, Pitcher, Marigold 48.00
Imperial Grape, Punch Set, Marigold, 10 Piece 235.00
Imperial Grape, Tumbler, Marigold 25.00
Imperial Grape, Wine, Marigold .... 28.00 to 30.00
Imperial Grape, Wine, Purple 30.00
Inverted Strawberry, Sugar, Green 250.00
Iris, Compote, Crystal Base & Stem, Marigold, 5 In. 25.00
Iris, Compote, Marigold, Fenton 45.00
Iris, Sugar & Creamer, Amber 18.00
Irish Lace pattern is listed here as Louisa
Kittens, Bowl, Marigold, 5 1/2 In. 200.00
Kittens, Cup & Saucer, Marigold 230.00
Kittens, Saucer, Marigold 175.00
Kittens, Toothpick, Marigold 295.00
Kookaburra, Bowl, Marigold 400.00
Labelle Poppy pattern is listed here as Poppy Show
Labelle Rose pattern is listed here as Rose Show
Lattice & Daisy, Pitcher, Marigold 225.00
Lattice & Daisy, Tumbler, Marigold 20.00
Lattice & Daisy, Tumbler, Marigold, 6 Piece 150.00
Lattice & Grape, Tankard, Marigold, 11 3/4 In. 260.00
Lattice & Grapevine pattern is listed here as Lattice & Grape
Lattice Grape, Water Set, Blue, 7 Piece 685.00
Leaf & Beads, Candy Dish, 3-Footed, Marigold, 8 1/4 In. 45.00
Leaf & Beads, Rose Bowl, 3-Footed, Amethyst 75.00
Leaf & Beads, Rose Bowl, Aqua Opalescent .... 300.00 to 350.00
Leaf & Beads, Rose Bowl, Blue 250.00
Leaf & Beads, Rose Bowl, Marigold 60.00
Leaf & Beads, Rose Bowl, Olive Green 125.00
Leaf Chain, Bowl, Blue 85.00
Leaf Medallion pattern is listed here as Leaf Chain
Leaf Rays, Nappy, Amethyst .... 24.00 to 34.00
Leaf Rays, Nappy, Marigold 18.00
Lion, Bowl, Marigold, 7 In. 130.00
Little Flowers, Bowl, Blue, 6 In. 40.00
Loop & Column pattern is listed here as Pulled Loop

Lotus & Grape, Bowl, Ruffled, Blue, 8 1/2 In. .... 95.00 to 105.00
Louisa, Rose Bowl, Amethyst, 3-Footed 70.00
Louisa, Rose Bowl, Green 65.00
Lustre Flute, Vase, Hat, Green 36.00
Lustre Rose, Sugar & Creamer, Marigold 45.00
Lustre Rose, Tumbler, Marigold 25.00
Magnolia & Poinsettia pattern is listed here as Water Lily
Many Stars, Bowl, Ruffled, Amethyst, 10 1/2 In. 475.00
Maple Leaf, Bowl, Stemmed, Marigold, 4 1/2 In. 25.00
Maple Leaf, Table Set, Blue, 4 Piece 295.00
Maple Leaf, Tumbler, Marigold 25.00
Maple Leaf, Water Set, Amethyst, 7 Piece 350.00
Marilyn, Tumbler, Amethyst 125.00
Mary Ann, Vase, 2 Handles, Amethyst 165.00
Melinda pattern is listed here as Wishbone
Milady, Tumbler, Blue 25.00
Mums & Greek Key pattern is listed here as Embroidered Mums
Nesting Swan pattern is listed here as Swan, Carnival
Nu-Art, Shade, Lamp, Marigold, 4 1/2 In. 20.00
Oak Leaf & Acorn pattern is listed here as Acorn
Octagon, Goblet, Marigold 40.00
Octagon, Wine, Marigold 37.50
Old Fashion Flag pattern is listed here as Iris
Open Rose, Bowl, Marigold 48.00
Open Rose, Plate, Green, 9 In. 165.00
Open Rose, Plate, Marigold, 9 In. 62.00
Orange Tree, Creamer, Footed, Blue 23.00
Orange Tree, Fruit Bowl, 3-Footed, Marigold 125.00
Orange Tree, Fruit Bowl, White, Gold Rim, 10 In. 200.00
Orange Tree, Jelly Compote, Marigold, 4 1/2 x 3 In. 32.00
Orange Tree, Loving Cup, Blue 345.00
Orange Tree, Mug, Amber 110.00
Orange Tree, Mug, Amethyst 75.00
Orange Tree, Mug, Blue 90.00
Orange Tree, Mug, Marigold 30.00
Orange Tree, Mug, Shaving, Blue 65.00
Orange Tree, Mug, Shaving, Marigold 36.00
Orange Tree, Orange Bowl, Blue .... 225.00 to 245.00
Orange Tree, Orange Bowl, Marigold, 1911 .... 165.00
Orange Tree, Plate, Blue, Smoky Iridescent, 9 In. 300.00
Orange Tree, Powder Jar, Cover, Blue 140.00
Orange Tree, Powder Jar, Cover, Marigold 95.00
Orange Tree, Punch Bowl, Blue 175.00
Orange Tree, Punch Cup, Marigold 10.00
Orange Tree, Punch Set, White, 6 Piece 1000.00
Orange Tree, Tumbler, Blue 38.00
Paneled Bachelor Buttons pattern is listed here as Milady
Panelled Dandelion, Tumbler, Marigold 65.00
Panelled Dandelion, Water Set, Marigold, 7 Piece 595.00
Panther, Berry Bowl, Blue, 9 1/2 In. 270.00
Paperweight, Fish, Apricot Pink 40.00
Peacock & Grape, Bowl, Ruffled, Marigold, 9 In. 95.00
Peacock & Grape, Bowl, Ruffled, Spatula Feet, Marigold 45.00
Peacock & Urn, Bowl, Amethyst, 10 1/2 In. 375.00
Peacock & Urn, Bowl, Ruffled, Amethyst, 9 In. 575.00
Peacock & Urn, Bowl, Ruffled, Green, 8 1/2 In. 325.00
Peacock & Urn, Bowl, White, 9 In. 480.00
Peacock & Urn, Plate, Amethyst 300.00
Peacock & Urn, Plate, Bearded Berry Exterior, 9 In. 450.00
Peacock At The Fountain, Berry Bowl, Marigold 75.00
Peacock At The Fountain, Compote, Blue, 10 In. 165.00
Peacock At The Fountain, Punch Cup, Ice Green 425.00
Peacock At The Fountain, Tumbler, Blue 80.00

Peacock At The Fountain, Water Set, Purple, 7 Piece 450.00
Peacock Eye & Grape pattern is listed here as Vineyard
Peacock on Fence pattern is listed here as Peacocks
Peacock Tail, Compote, Amethyst 90.00
Peacock Tail, Compote, Ruffled, Amethyst, 6 1/4 In. 48.00
Peacock Tail, Plate, Tricornered, Green, 6 In. .... 100.00 to 175.00
Peacock Tail & Daisy, Bowl, Amethyst 425.00
Peacocks, Bowl, Marigold, 8 1/2 In. 305.00
Peacocks, Bowl, Piecrust Edge, Purple 775.00
Peacocks, Plate, Ice Green, 9 In. 500.00
Persian Garden, Bowl, Ice Cream, White 250.00
Persian Medallion, Bowl, Ruffled, Blue, 9 In. 150.00
Persian Medallion, Hair Receiver, Marigold 75.00
Persian Medallion, Plate, Marigold, 6 In. 70.00
Persian Medallion, Rose Bowl, Marigold .... 60.00 to 85.00
Petals, Compote, Ruffled, Amethyst, 7 1/4 In. 60.00
Plain Jane, Bowl, Ruffled, Marigold, 7 In. 55.00
Poinsettia, Bowl, Ruffled, Blue 325.00
Poinsettia, Milk Pitcher, Marigold, 6 In. .... 85.00 to 110.00
Poinsettia & Lattice pattern is listed here as Poinsettia
Poppy Show, Plate, Blue, 9 In. 850.00
Princess Lace pattern is listed here as Octagon
Prisms, Bonbon, Marigold 60.00
Prisms, Bonbon, Purple 90.00
Pulled Loop, Vase, Peach, 10 1/2 In. 60.00
Question Marks, Compote, Marigold 40.00
Raindrops, Bowl, Turned-Up Rim, Peach Opalescent, 7 x 4 1/4 In. 85.00
Raspberry, Milk Pitcher, Marigold .... 95.00 to 150.00
Raspberry, Tumbler, Amethyst 47.50
Raspberry, Tumbler, Green 45.00
Raspberry, Tumbler, White 250.00
Raspberry, Water Set, Marigold, 6 Piece 250.00
Rays & Ribbons, Bowl, Ruffled, Green, 10 In. 85.00
Ripple, Vase, Amethyst, 9 In. 40.00
Rose & Ruffles pattern is listed here as Open Rose
Rose Show, Bowl, Ruffled, White, 8 In. 250.00
Roses & Fruit, Bonbon, Marigold 375.00
Roses & Loops pattern is listed here as Double-Stem Rose
Rosettes, Bowl, Ruffled, 3-Footed, Amethyst, 8 1/2 In. 85.00
Round-Up, Plate, Amethyst, 9 In. 350.00
Round-Up, Plate, White, 9 In. 360.00
Ruffles & Rings, Bowl, White, 8 1/2 In. 95.00
S-Repeat, Punch Cup, Amethyst 110.00
Sailboat & Windmill pattern is listed here as Sailboats
Sailboats, Bowl, Ruffled, Marigold, 6 In. 25.00
Sailboats, Plate, Marigold, 6 In. 335.00
Sailboats, Wine, Marigold 28.00
Singing Birds, Mug, Amethyst .... 95.00 to 125.00
Singing Birds, Mug, Blue 270.00
Singing Birds, Mug, Ice Blue 850.00
Singing Birds, Mug, Marigold .... 110.00 to 185.00
Singing Birds, Mug, Purple 250.00
Singing Birds, Water Set, Marigold, 5 Piece 450.00
Smooth Rays, Bowl, Fluted, Peach Opalescent, 7 3/4 In. 100.00
Smooth Rays, Bowl, Teal Blue, 8 1/2 In. 65.00
Soda Gold, Candlestick, Marigold 40.00
Spider Web pattern is listed here as Soda Gold
Spring Flowers pattern is listed here as Bouquet
Springtime, Berry Bowl, Green, 5 In. 50.00
Springtime, Table Set, Marigold, 4 Piece 500.00
Stag & Holly, Bowl, Ice Cream, Green, Spatula Feet, 8 In. 250.00
Stag & Holly, Bowl, Ruffled, Blue, 11 In. 275.00
Stag & Holly, Bowl, Spatula Feet, Amethyst, 8 In. 210.00

Stag & Holly, Plate, Footed, Marigold, 9 In. 210.00
Star & File, Bowl, Marigold, 5 1/2 In. 24.00
Star & File, Compote, Marigold, 6 3/4 In. 45.00
Star & File, Tumbler, Amber 75.00
Star Medallion, Punch Cup, Marigold, Imperial 20.00
Star Of David, Bowl, Marigold 75.00
Star Of David & Bows, Bowl, Footed, Purple, 8 In. .... 95.00 to 155.00
Star Of David & Bows, Bowl, Ruffled, Amethyst 150.00
Star of David Medallion pattern is listed here as Star of David & Bows
Stipple & Ray, Bowl, Fluted, Green 65.00
Stippled Diamond & Flower pattern is listed here as Little Flowers
Stippled Leaf & Beads pattern is listed here as Leaf & Beads
Stippled Posy & Pods pattern is listed here as Four Flowers
Stippled Rays, Bonbon, Amethyst 55.00
Stippled Rays, Bonbon, Handle, Marigold, 7 In. 55.00
Stippled Rays, Bowl, Ruffled, Amethyst, 9 1/2 In. .... 45.00 to 52.00
Stippled Ribbons & Rays pattern is listed here as Rays & Ribbons
Stork & Rushes, Tumbler, Blue .... 30.00 to 125.00
Stork & Rushes, Tumbler, Marigold 30.00
Stork & Rushes, Water Set, Marigold, 7 Piece 125.00
Strawberry pattern is listed here as Wild Strawberry
Sunflower pattern is listed here as Dandelion
Swan, Carnival, Bowl, Ruffled, Marigold, 10 In. 160.00
Teardrops pattern is listed here as Raindrops
Ten Mums, Tumbler, Marigold 50.00
Thin Rib, Vase, Marigold, 6 1/2 In. 26.00
Thistle, Banana Boat, Amethyst 425.00
Thistle, Banana Boat, Blue 465.00
Thistle, Banana Boat, Footed, Green 465.00
Thistle, Bowl, Amethyst 85.00
Three Fruits, Bonbon, Amethyst, 5 In. 45.00
Three Fruits, Bonbon, Marigold, 7 In. 45.00
Three Fruits, Bowl, Amethyst, 8 1/2 In. 45.00
Three Fruits, Bowl, Ruffled, Amethyst, 5 In. 28.00
Three Fruits, Bowl, Ruffled, Aqua, 9 In. 875.00
Three Fruits, Plate, Purple, 9 In. 275.00
Tiger Lily, Tumbler, Marigold 40.00
Tiger Lily, Water Set, Amethyst, 7 Piece 250.00
Tiger Lily, Water Set, Marigold, 5 Piece 250.00
Tree Bark, Candlestick, Marigold 60.00
Tree Bark, Pitcher, Marigold 45.00
Tree Bark, Pitcher, Marigold, 8 1/2 In. 58.00
Tree Bark, Plate, Marigold, 7 3/4 In. 22.00
Tree Bark, Tankard, Marigold 46.00
Tree Bark, Tumbler, Marigold, 4 1/2 In. 20.00
Tree Trunk, Vase, Funeral, Amethyst 185.00
Tree Trunk, Vase, Marigold, 10 In. 65.00
Tree Trunk, Vase, Purple, 11 In. 75.00
Trout & Fly, Bowl, Ice Cream, Amethyst 385.00
Trout & Fly, Bowl, Marigold 400.00
Trout & Fly, Bowl, Square, Green 675.00
Two Flowers, Bowl, 3-Footed, Blue, 9 In. 85.00
Two Flowers, Bowl, Green, 8 In. 65.00
Two Flowers, Bowl, Marigold, 9 In. .... 110.00 to 135.00
Two Flowers, Bowl, Ruffled, Amethyst, 10 1/2 In. 150.00
Two Flowers, Rose Bowl, Peach, 5 1/2 In. 375.00
Vineyard, Water Set, Marigold, 7 Piece 195.00
Vintage, Bowl, Ice Cream, Blue, 10 In. 200.00
Vintage, Mug, Blue, 5 1/2 In. 110.00
Vintage, Powder Jar, Cover, Marigold 75.00
Vintage, Rose Bowl, 6-Footed, Amethyst, 5 In. 55.00
Vintage Leaf, Berry Set, Light Marigold, 7 Piece 200.00
Waffle Band pattern is listed here as Lustre Flute

Waffle Block, Bowl, Square, Marigold, 7 1/2 In. 36.00
Water Lily, Bowl, 3-Footed, Marigold, 10 In. .... 70.00 to 110.00
Water Lily & Cattails, Butter, Cover, Dark Marigold 125.00
Water Lily & Cattails, Tumbler, Marigold 25.00
Wild Strawberry, Bonbon, Handles, Square, Marigold, 5 1/4 In. 30.00
Wild Strawberry, Bowl, Amethyst, 9 In. 95.00
Wild Strawberry, Bowl, Basket Weave, Ruffled, Green, 9 In. 140.00
Wild Strawberry, Bowl, Piecrust Rim, Purple, 8 1/2 In. 165.00
Wild Strawberry, Bowl, Ruffled, Amethyst, 10 In. 185.00
Wind Flower, Bowl, Marigold, 8 1/2 In. 38.00
Wind Flower, Bowl, Ruffled, Amethyst, 8 1/2 In. 48.00
Wind Flower, Plate, Marigold, 9 In. 65.00
Windmill, Pitcher, Lemonade, Marigold 75.00
Windmill, Water Set, Marigold, 7 Piece 190.00
Windmill Medallion pattern is listed here as Windmill
Wishbone, Plate, Tricornered, Amethyst, 8 1/2 In. 320.00
Wreath Of Roses, Punch Cup, Persian Medallion Interior, Blue 25.00
Wreath Of Roses, Rose Bowl, Marigold 28.00
Zippered Heart, Berry Set, Purple, 6 Piece 270.00

CAROUSEL or merry-go-round figures were first carved in the United States in 1867 by Gustav Dentzel. Collectors discovered the charm of the hand-carved figures in the 1970s, and they were soon classed as folk art. Most desirable are the figures other than horses, such as pigs, camels, lions, or dogs. A jumper is a figure that was made to move up and down on a pole; a stander was placed in a stationary position.

Antelope, Stripped, Illions 7700.00
Bull, Charging, Bayol 5500.00
Chariot Bench, Donna & Ariel Johnson 3500.00
Cow, Bayol 9900.00
Donkey, Germany 5000.00
Donkey, Nodding Head, Bayol 2750.00
Giraffe, Looff 29700.00
Giraffe, Polychrome Paint Traces, 1920s 3737.50
Horse, Center Row, Glass Eyes, Parrot Seat, Looff, c.1880, 58 1/2 In. 8250.00
Horse, Derby Racer, Prior & Church 1760.00
Horse, Jumper, Armored, C.W. Parker 7150.00
Horse, Jumper, Inner Row, Dapple Gray, Spillman 3000.00
Horse, Jumper, Magnolia On Shoulder, Philadelphia Toboggan Co., 1910 .... 8800.00
Horse, Jumper, Middle Row, Spillman 2500.00
Horse, Jumper, Outside Row, Fish-Scale Blanket, Crest On Flank, Spillman 5500.00
Horse, Jumper, Stein & Goldstein 8800.00
Horse, Jumper, Tucked Head, Philadelphia Toboggan Co. 9350.00
Horse, Laminated Construction, Glass Eyes, Horsehair Tail, 43 In. 825.00
Horse, Metal, With Stand, Parker, 1940s 1500.00
Horse, Outside Row, Zebra-Like Paint, Spillman 4000.00
Horse, Park Paint, Illion, c.1910, 54 x 51 In. 6800.00
Horse, Park Paint, Illions, 1920s 6800.00
Horse, Prancer, Dappled Gray, Looff, c.1895, 62 In. 6900.00
Horse, Stander, Carmel, Borelli 8800.00
Horse, Wooden, Herschel Spillman, 5 Ft. 1900.00
Organ, Wurlitzer 150, North Tonawanda, N.Y. 8700.00
Ostriches, 2-Seater, Frederick Savage 2750.00
Panel, Boat Side, Carved Leaves & Flowers, Mirror Roundels, Pine, 75 In. 1840.00
Pig, Dentzel 8250.00
Sleigh, Wooden 962.50
Tiger, Ready To Pounce, Wooden, Orange, 1920s 700.00
Turkey, Hinged Tail Feathers Form Backrest, Frederick Savage 8250.00
Zebra, Jumper, E. Joy Morris 7700.00

CARRIAGE means several things, so this category lists baby carriages, buggies for adults, horse-drawn sleighs, and even strollers. Doll-sized carriages are listed in the Toy category.

Baby Buggy, Bentwood, Woven, Reclining Back, Rolled Tires, Victorian, c.1900 ...... 330.00
Baby Buggy, Victorian, Tan Wicker, Spoke Wheels, Rubber Rims 350.00
Baby Buggy, Wicker, Parasol, Heywood-Wakefield, 1900 .... 1100.00
Baby Buggy, Wicker, Stick & Ball Design, Lace Parasol, Heywood, c.1880 .... 1430.00
Baby Buggy, Wicker, Wooden Spokes 325.00
Baby Buggy, Wicker, Woven, Upholstered, Fringed Parasol, Heywood, c.1890 .... 990.00
Baby Buggy, Worn Leather Hood, Art Deco Wood 150.00
Baby Pony Cart, Wooden, 3 Wheels, Horsehair Pony, Velvet Upholstery, c.1920 ...... 1320.00
Buggy, 1 Seat, Wooden, Painted, Leather Seat 350.00
Buggy, Wooden, Orange Paint, Spoke Wheels, Cloth Fringed Top, J. Ellis 275.00
Perambulator, Child's, Square Top Awning, 4 Large Wheels, Victorian 495.00
Perambulator, Surrey, Original Paint, 2 Large Back Wheels, 1880 .... 1195.00
Perambulator, Upholstered Seat, Cast Aluminum, Italy, c.1930, 35 x 50 In. 6600.00
Sleigh, Blue & Red, Gold Stenciled 1045.00
Sleigh, Green Paint, Gold Trim, Painted Date, 1867 .... 650.00
Sleigh, Open, 1-Horse Type, Late 1800s 2400.00
Sleigh, Push, Handmade, New England, 1880s 535.00
Sleigh, Push, Red, Victorian 345.00
Sleigh, Push, Scene Painted On Seat, Old Red Ground 302.00
Sleigh, Skater's, Blue Striping, Floral Design, Light Blue Paint 350.00
Stroller, Wicker, 1880s, 19 x 48 In. 110.00
Stroller, Wicker, Heart Shape, Early 1900s 1650.00

CASH REGISTERS were invented in 1884 because an eye on the cash was a
necessity in stores of the nineteenth century, too. John and James Ritty
invented a large model that resembled a clock and kept a record of the dollars
and cents exchanged in the store. John Patterson improved the cash register
with a paper roll to record the money. By the early 1900s, elaborate brass
registers were made. About World War I, the fancy case was exchanged for
the more modern types.

National, Model 3, Yellow Brass, 1893 .... 2900.00
National, Model 7 .... 450.00
National, Model 8 .... 400.00
National, Model 211 .... 900.00
National, Model 216, Bronze, Small 750.00
National, Model 250 .... 600.00
National, Model 313, Cigar Store, Brass 695.00
National, Model 317, Candy Store, Side Tape Dispenser, Brass, 16 In. 475.00
National, Model 332 .... 115.00
National, Model 442, Oak Base, Drawer, Tape Dispenser, Brass, 24 In. 325.00
National, No. 226, Candy Store, Bilingual Top Sign, Bronze 700.00
National, Stand, Bombay Sides, Multiple Drawers, Brass Feet, Oak, 4 Ft. 600.00
National, Ustler, Bronze, 1902 .... 125.00

CASTOR JARS for pickles are glass jars about six inches in height, held
in special metal holders. They became a popular dinner table accessory
about 1890. Each jar had a top that was usually silver or silver plate. The
frame, also of a silver metal, had a handle that arched above the jar and a
hook that held a pair of tongs. By 1900, the pickle castor was out of
fashion. Many examples found today have reproduced glass jars in old
holders. Additional pickle castors may be found in the various Glass
categories.

Pickle, 16 Blown-Out Ribs, Cranberry Insert, Meriden Frame, Tongs 495.00
Pickle, Beaded Column, Insert, Tongs 115.00
Pickle, Blue, Enameled, Silver Frame 275.00
Pickle, Blue Swirls On Jar, Tongs, Barbor Bros. Silver Frame, 8 3/4 In. 575.00
Pickle, Cranberry Hobnail Insert, Tufts Frame 450.00
Pickle, Cranberry Insert, Silver Frame & Fork 285.00
Pickle, Cupid & Venus, Silver Plated Holder, Fork .... 135.00 to 155.00
Pickle, Daisy & Button, Blue, Silver Plated Frame 235.00
Pickle, Dragons, Vines, Cranberry Insert, Tufts Frame 325.00
Pickle, Florette Insert, Footed Silver Plated Frame, Tongs 350.00
Pickle, Gold Lines Form Shaped Boxes, Dotted, Enameled Flowers, Tufts Frame 450.00

Pickle, Inverted Thumbprint, Corset Shape, Rubena Verde, Tufts Frame, Tongs 395.00
Pickle, Inverted Thumbprint, Enameled Flowers, Silver Plated Frame, 10 1/2 In. 495.00
Pickle, Leaf Mold, Cranberry & Vaseline Spatter, Silver Plated Frame, Tongs 375.00
Pickle, Oriental Design, Glass Lid 250.00
Pickle, Pressed Glass Insert, Tongs, Pairpoint, 14 In. 350.00
Pickle, Ribbed Pillar Insert, Footed Frame, Northwood 335.00
Pickle, Shell & Tassel, Tufts Frame, Tongs 165.00
Pickle, Square Fuchsia Insert, Crystal, Silver 190.00
Pickle, Vertical Ribbing, Entwined Rigaree, Derby Frame, Tongs 375.00

CASTOR SETS holding just salt and pepper castors were used in the
seventeenth century. The sugar castor, mustard pot, spice dredger, bottles for
vinegar and oil, and other spice holders became popular by the eighteenth
century. These sets were usually made of sterling silver. The American
Victorian castor set, the type most collected today, was made of silver plated
Britannia metal. Colored glass bottles were introduced after the Civil War.
The sets were out of fashion by World War I. Be careful when buying sets
with colored bottles; many are reproductions. Other castor sets may be listed
in various porcelain and glass categories in this book.

2-Bottle, Cut Glass, Octagonal, 8 1/2 In. 190.00
5-Bottle, Cut Glass, Stopper, Cover 95.00
5-Bottle, Inverted Thumbprint, Pairpoint Holder, Cranberry 615.00
5-Bottle, Pewter, Miniature 110.00
5-Bottle, Pewter, Pressed Glass, 19th Century, 9 In. 88.00
6-Bottle, Etched, Reed & Barton 125.00

CAULDON Limited worked in Staffordshire, Great Britain, and went through
many name changes. John Ridgway made porcelain at Cauldon Place,
Hanley, until 1855. The firm of John Ridgway, Bates and Co. of Cauldon
Place worked from 1856 to 1859. It became Bates, Brown-Westhead, Moore
and Co. from 1859 to 1862. Brown-Westhead, Moore and Co. worked from
1862 to 1904. About 1890, this firm started using the words *Cauldon* or
Cauldon ware as part of the mark. Cauldon Ltd. worked from 1905 to 1920,
Cauldon Potteries from 1920 to 1962. Related items may be found in the
Indian Tree category.

Mug, Hires, Boy, Patterned Shirt, Crazed, 4 In. 99.00

CELADON is the name of a velvet-textured green-gray glaze used by
Chinese, Japanese, Korean, and other factories.

Bowl, Central Incised Design, Fluted Body, Ming Dynasty, 15 In. 1760.00
Bowl, Central Incised Design, 12 3/4 In. 330.00
Bowl, Shaped Serpentine Rim, Fluted Body, Ming Dynasty, 13 In. 495.00
Brush Washer, Crackled Glaze, Qing Dynasty, 6 In. 35.00
Jar, Double Cylindrical Handles, Green Crackled Glaze, 9 In. 65.00
Jar, Double Cylindrical Handles, Green, Song Dynasty, 6 In. 175.00
Jardiniere, Wrought Iron & Porcelain Flowers, 17 In., Pair 288.00
Pitcher, Bamboo Handle, 6 In. 125.00
Plate, Figures, Flower & Butterflies 154.00
Vase, Baluster Shape, Scrolling Lotus, Daoguang, 10 1/2 In. 330.00
Vase, Blue & White Birds, Flowers, Chinese, 16 1/2 In. 27.00
Vase, Blue & White Design, Drilled For Lamp, Chinese, 16 3/4 In. 88.00
Vase, Crackled, Baluster Form, Qing Dynasty, 10 In. 198.00
Vase, Raised White Floral & Bird Design, 19th Century, 15 1/2 In. 192.00
Vase, Teardrop Shape, 3 Rams' Heads, Yongzheng, 8 3/8 In. 165.00

CELLULOID is a trademark for a plastic developed in 1868 by John W. Hyatt.
Celluloid Manufacturing Company, the Celluloid Novelty Company,
Celluloid Fancy Goods Company, and American Xylonite Company all used
Celluloid to make jewelry, games, sewing equipment, false teeth, and piano
keys. Eventually, the Hyatt Company became the American Celluloid and
Chemical Manufacturing Company, the Celanese Corporation. The name
Celluloid was often used to identify any similar plastic. Celluloid toys are
listed under Toys.

Box, Cuff	75.00
Box, Handkerchief	45.00
Box, Jewelry, Woman, Child & Dog Hand Painted Scene	85.00
Comb, Leaf Design, 1916	40.00
Dresser Set, Ivory, 5 Piece	20.00
Dresser Set, Ivory, Baskets Of Flowers, Tray, 6 Piece	40.00
Dresser Set, Jewel Design, Salmon Color, Clock, 7 Piece	65.00
Figure, Hula Dancer, Box, Occupied Japan	160.00
Frame, Easel Back, Ivory, Round, 2 In.	15.00
Gavel, Dated 1923	50.00
Glove Box, Victorian	65.00
Manicure Set, Art Deco Design, 4 Piece	22.00
Rattle, Bulldog, Figural, Occupied Japan	20.00
Rattle, Donkey, Figural, Occupied Japan	20.00
Shaving Set, Mirror, Ivory, With China Bowl, Open & Close Positions	55.00
Shoehorn, Horse Head Handle	3.00
Toilet Set, Brush, Comb & Mirror, Candy Pink, Flowers, Box, 1931	95.00

CERAMIC ART COMPANY of Trenton, New Jersey, was established in 1889 by J. Coxon and W. Lenox and was an early producer of American Belleek porcelain. It became Lenox, Inc. in 1906. Do not confuse this ware with the pottery made by the Ceramic Arts Studio of Madison, Wisconsin.

Tile, Central Galleon, Walnut & Marble Shelves, 51 x 34 In.	2500.00
Vase, Gold Design, Mottled Ground, Mayer & Marsh, 7 3/4 In.	260.00

CERAMIC ARTS STUDIO was founded in Madison, Wisconsin, by Lawrence Rabbett and Ruben Sand. Their most popular products were expensive molded figurines. The pottery closed in 1955. Do not confuse these products with those of the Ceramic Art Co. of Trenton, New Jersey.

Bank, Figural, Gangster	45.00
Figurine, Archibald Dragon	145.00
Figurine, Baby Skunk	15.00
Figurine, Becky	80.00
Figurine, Billy Goat	68.50
Figurine, Boy, Balinese Dance	85.00
Figurine, Cat, Green Bow, 3 In.	15.00
Figurine, Couple Kissing, Sitting	40.00
Figurine, Fawn	45.00
Figurine, Girl, Balinese Dance	85.00
Figurine, Lady Rowena, On Charger	145.00
Figurine, Lovebird, Pair	30.00
Figurine, See No Evil	95.00
Figurine, Speak No Evil	95.00
Figurine, Ting-A-Ling & Sung-Tu, Chartreuse, Green, Black, 6 In., Pair	25.00
Figurine, Turtle, With Spots	50.00
Salt & Pepper, Black Boy On Elephant	175.00
Salt & Pepper, Blackamoor	18.00
Salt & Pepper, Blythe & Pensive	285.00
Salt & Pepper, Calico Dog & Cat	65.00
Salt & Pepper, Cat, Stylized, Black	35.00
Salt & Pepper, Chihuahua & Doghouse	85.00
Salt & Pepper, Covered Wagon & Ox	95.00
Salt & Pepper, Elsie & Beauregard	100.00
Salt & Pepper, Eskimos	35.00
Salt & Pepper, Gingham Dog, Calico Cat	55.00
Salt & Pepper, Gypsy Couple	95.00
Salt & Pepper, Kangaroo & Baby	50.00
Salt & Pepper, Leopard	200.00
Salt & Pepper, Monkeys, Nesting	65.00
Salt & Pepper, Mouse & Cheese	28.00
Salt & Pepper, Polar Bear & Baby	53.00
Salt & Pepper, Rabbits, Nesting	85.00
Salt & Pepper, Sheep, Polkadot	60.00

Salt & Pepper, Wee Indians	45.00
Shelf Sitter, Boy, Square Dancer	65.00
Shelf Sitter, Country Kids, Bench	89.50
Shelf Sitter, Girl, Square Dancer	65.00
Shelf Sitter, Jack	22.50
Shelf Sitter, Jill	22.50
Shelf Sitter, Maurice & Michelle	95.00
Shelf Sitter, Pierrot & Pierrette	135.00
Wall Plaque, Zorina	65.00
Wall Pocket, Fu Manchu	160.00
Wall Pocket, Lotus	160.00

CHALKWARE is really plaster of Paris decorated with watercolors. One type was molded from Staffordshire and other porcelain models and painted and sold as inexpensive decorations in the nineteenth century. Figures of plaster, made from about 1910 to 1940 for use as prizes at carnivals, are also known as chalkware. Kewpie dolls made of chalkware will be found in their own category.

Ashtray, Goateed Gentleman, Glenmore Whiskey	22.00
Bank, Piggy, Large	15.00
Cake Topper, Bride & Groom, 1920s	25.00
Figurine, Bulldog, Sitting, Sherlock Holmes Cap & Pipe, 6 In.	15.00
Figurine, Cat, Black & White Paint, Red & Blue Ribbon, 12 In.	165.00
Figurine, Cat, Black Stripes, White Ground, 12 1/4 In.	110.00
Figurine, Cat, Polkadot Tie, Black, Gold Marks, 11 3/4 In.	115.00
Figurine, Cupid, Sitting, Arms Around Knees, Pink Glasses, 10 1/2 In.	95.00
Figurine, Dog, 3 Sides	65.00
Figurine, Dog, Seated, Red, Green, Brown, 6 In.	363.00
Figurine, Dog, Sitting, Large	475.00
Figurine, Dog, Standing	100.00
Figurine, Dog, Yorkie, Sitting On Hind Legs, Begging, 11 In.	20.00
Figurine, Eagle, 10 1/2 In.	65.00
Figurine, Ferdinand The Bull	25.00
Figurine, Floral & Fruits, Large	300.00
Figurine, Parrot	90.00
Figurine, Poodle, Pair	525.00
Figurine, Quaker, With Bible, 4 1/2 In.	5.00
Figurine, Rabbit, Yellow & Brown, White Ground, 10 In.	50.00
Figurine, Rooster, Standing, Painted Marks, 19th Century, 7 3/8 In., Pair	748.00
Figurine, Sheep With Lamb, 19th Century, 7 In.	82.50
Figurine, Southern Boy & Girl, Pair	35.00
Figurine, Squirrel	90.00
Figurine, Uncle Sam	250.00
Incense Burner, Buddha	115.00
Salt & Pepper, Children Eating Melon	45.00
String Holder, Cat, Ball Of Yarn	35.00
String Holder, Shelf Sitter, Yawning Baby	55.00
Thermometer, Woodpecker On Tree Shape, Large	5.00
Vase, Art Nouveau Women, 18 In., Pair	125.00

CHARLIE CHAPLIN, the famous comic and actor, lived from 1889 to 1977. He made his first movie in 1913. He did the movie *The Tramp* in 1915. The character of the Tramp has remained famous, and in the 1980s he appeared in a series of television commercials for computers. Dolls, candy containers, and all sorts of memorabilia picture Charlie Chaplin. Pieces are being made even today.

Candy Container, Gold Paint, Borg	150.00
Candy Container, Smith	400.00
Doll, Vinyl, Cloth, 1972, 8 In.	136.00
Doorstop, Standing, Aluminum, 9 1/2 x 3 In.	410.00
Fabric, To Make Stuffed Doll, British Mfg., 1930s, 13 In.	120.00
Figure, Estolin	98.00
Figure, Porcelain, 8 In.	375.00

Flip Book, Cracker Jack 75.00
Jigger, Musical, Dancing On Stage, Walter Krauss 1775.00
Lobby Card, King In New York, 12 1/2 x 16 In. 45.00
Pencil Box, 1920s 75.00
Slide, Animated, State Senator, Representative, People, G. Wm. Beales 145.00
Toy, Tap Dancer 1650.00
Toy, Tin Lithograph, Articulated, John Distler, Germany, 6 1/2 In. 1210.00
Toy, Waddler, Germany 950.00
Watch, Pocket 325.00
Windup, Hand Painted, 1920s, 8 1/2 In. 1450.00
Wristwatch 48.00

CHARLIE MCCARTHY was the ventriloquist's dummy used by Edgar
Bergen from the 1930s. He was famous for his work in radio, movies, and
television. The act was retired in the 1970s.

Book, A Day With Edgar's Advice On Art Of Ventriloquism, 1938 .... 45.00
Book, Charlie McCarthy Meets Snow White, 1938 .... 55.00
Book, Day With Charlie McCarthy, Whitman, 1938, 8 1/2 x 13 In. 27.00
Bubble Gum Wrapper, 1940 .... 28.00
Car, Charlie & Mortimer Snerd, Tin Lithograph, 1939, 16 In. .... 935.00 to 990.00
Clock, Alarm, 1938 .... 1292.00
Costume, Hat, Coat & Pants, 1930s 85.00
Doll, 28 In. 98.00
Doll, Mortimer Snerd, Composition Head, Clown Face, Ideal, 13 In. 45.00
Doll, Top Hat, Tails, Diamond Stick Pin, All Original, 1930s, 16 In. 625.00
Doorstop, Standing, 9 1/4 x 2 7/8 In. 1100.00
Figure, With Monocle, Composition, 1935, 13 In. 325.00
Figurine, Aluminum Cat, Majestic Radio 75.00
Figurine, Sitting, Chalk, Carnival Prize, Glitter On Hat, 7 In. 85.00
Game, Bingo, Put & Take, Whitman, Box 45.00
Game, Question & Answer, 1938, Box 40.00
Game, Snatch The Hat, Cards, 8 Wooden Hats, Box, 1938 .... 125.00
Game, Topper, With Charlie's Talking Card, 1938, Christmas Box 110.00
Knife 45.00
Paper, Chase & Sanborn Promotion, 20 In. 60.00
Pencil Sharpener, Celluloid, Decal, 1 3/4 In. 85.00
Perfume Bottle 25.00
Pin, Mechanical, Mouth Moves, c.1936, 1 3/8 In. 235.00
Radio, Brown, Majestic 950.00
Radio, Top Hat, Tails 800.00
Spoon, Sleuth 13.00
Toy, Benzine Mobile, Clockwork, Lithographed, Louis Marx, Box, 7 In. .... 500.00 to 880.00
Toy, Charlie & Moritimer Snerd Private Car, Clockwork, 15 In. 990.00
Toy, Drummer, Clockwork, Lithographed, Marx, Box, 8 1/2 In. 1540.00
Toy, Mortimer Snerd Drummer, Tin Lithograph, Clockwork, 7 3/4 In. 1430.00
Toy, Windup, Tin, Marx, 8 1/4 In. 495.00

CHELSEA GRAPE pattern was made before 1840. A small bunch of grapes in
a raised design, colored with purple or blue luster, is on the border of the white
plate. Most of the pieces are unmarked. The pattern is sometimes called *Aynsley*
or *Grandmother*. Chelsea sprig is similar but has a sprig of flowers instead of
the bunch of grapes. Chelsea thistle has a raised thistle pattern. Do not confuse
these Chelsea patterns with Chelsea Keramic Art Works, which can be found in
the Dedham category, or with Chelsea porcelain, the next category.

Bowl, 4 x 6 1/2 In. 35.00
Creamer, 1830s, 5 In. 45.00
Cup & Saucer 18.50

CHELSEA PORCELAIN was made in the Chelsea area of London from about
1745 to 1784. Some pieces made from 1770 to 1784 may include the letter *D*
for *Derby* in the mark. Ceramic designs were borrowed from the Meissen
models of the day. Pieces were made of soft paste. The gold anchor was used
as the mark but it has been copied by many other factories. Recent copies of

Chelsea have been made from the original molds. Do not confuse Chelsea porcelain with Chelsea Grape, the preceding category.

Dish, Botanical, Grapes, Cherries, Plums, Brown Anchor, 9 In., Pair 6610.00
Dish, Cabbage Leaf, Floral Spray, Red Anchor, c.1756, 10 3/4 In. .... 2185.00 to 2875.00
Dish, Cabbage Leaf, Flowering Branch, Puce Anchor, c.1758, 10 3/4 In. 4890.00
Dish, Peach Shape, Three Insects & Celery, Red Anchor, c.1755, 8 In. 7190.00
Dish, Peony, Petal Cluster, Purple & Red Center, c.1757, 7 7/8 In. 4890.00
Figurine, Pantaloon, Black Cap & Coat, Red Anchor, c.1755, 5 1/2 In. 1495.00
Figurine, Rustic Shepherd, Shepherdess, 12 In., Pair 460.00
Mug, Cylindrical, Jabberwocky, S-Scroll Handle, Derby, c.1775, 6 1/4 In. 920.00
Pitcher, Black Transfer, Independent Order Of Odd Fellows, 8 1/4 In. 11.00
Plate, Botanical, Turnips, Carrots, Cherries, Nuts, Brown Anchor, 8 1/2 In. 3740.00
Platter, Oval, Floral Bouquets, Scalloped Rim, Red Anchor, c.1755, 14 1/2 In. 4025.00
Potpourri Vase, Cover, Baluster Shape, Derby, c.1770, 3 Piece 2590.00
Sweetmeat Dish, Two Rosebud Sprays, Red Anchor, c.1755, 5 3/4 In. 2010.00

CHINESE EXPORT porcelain comprises all the many kinds of porcelain made in China for export to America and Europe in the eighteenth and nineteenth centuries. Other pieces may be listed in this book under Canton, Celadon, Nanking, and Rose Medallion.

Basket, Brown, Reticulated, Oval, Fitzhugh, 1815-1820, 8 1/4 In. 1035.00
Basket, Twig, Inclined Pines Pattern, Trellis Border, 1820, 9 5/8 In. 575.00
Bowl, Barber, Famille Rose, 18th Century, 12 In. 1100.00
Bowl, Blanc-De-Chine, Lotus Form, 7 In. 165.00
Bowl, Blue & White, Floral Design, Flat Rim, c.1800, 15 In. 330.00
Bowl, Blue Floral, Gilt Highlights, 9 In. 247.00
Bowl, Famille Verte, Dragons, Flowers, Kangxi Mark, 19th Century, 6 In. 1980.00
Bowl, Peony, 9 1/4 In. 297.00
Bowl, Polychrome Enamel Floral, 8 1/4 In. 495.00
Bowl, Polychrome Enamel Scenes Of Family Life, 8 In. 467.50
Bowl, Salad, Blue, Fitzhugh, 19th Century, 9 3/4 In. 990.00
Box, Cover, Blue, Clobbered, Rectangular, Fitzhugh, 1875, 7 1/4 In. 345.00
Brush Pot, Blue & White, Cylinder Form, 1820, 5 1/2 In. 605.00
Butter Tub, Cover, Black, Floral Sprigs, Fitzhugh, 1810-1820, 5 3/16 In. 4025.00
Cane Handle, Dragon's Head, Salmon To Red, Curved, 4 In. 1380.00
Charger, Famille Rose, Cockerel, 1700, 9 In. 413.00
Charger, French Coat Of Arms, 15 In. 1430.00
Cream Jug, Polychrome, Enamels, c.1810, 3 x 4 1/2 In. 175.00
Cup & Saucer, Fruit & Flowers, Gilt, Handleless 82.50
Cup & Saucer, Gold & Blue, Fitzhugh, 1820-1840, 3 11/16 In. 1035.00
Cuspidor, Chrysanthemums, Interior Peonies, 1740, 4 3/8 In. 1495.00
Dish, Famille Rose, Flowering Branch, Bats, Qianlong, 8 3/8 In., Pair 2090.00
Dish, Shrimp, Fitzhugh, Pair 2200.00
Figurine, Duck, Iron Red, Gilt Eyes, 8 5/8 & 9 In., Pair 1035.00
Figurine, Phoenix, Famille Rose, 19th Century, 19 In., Pair 1650.00
Figurine, Turkish Girl, Turquoise Coat, 1780, 4 15/16 In. 1610.00
Figurine, Woman, Animal At Feet, Basket On Arm, Famille Rose, 14 In. 72.00
Figurine, Woman, Hat, Animal, Famille Rose, 14 1/4 In. 72.00
Fishbowl, Dragons, Clouds, Blue & White, Globular, 17 x 22 In., Pair 440.00
Fishbowl, Famille Verte, 19th Century, 16 In. .... 275.00 to 302.50
Garden Seat, Swimming Ducks, Pale Green, Barrel Shape, 18 In., Pair 3163.00
Ginger Jar, Wooden Cover, Famille Rose, 16 In. 110.00
Jardiniere, Famille Verte, Flowers, Birds, Cartouches, 19th Century, 15 In. 990.00
Mug, Bacchus, Loop Handle, Derby Style, 1790, 3 In., Pair 3163.00
Mug, Double Entwined Handle, Diaper Pattern, 5 In., Pair 715.00
Mug, Household Scene, Floral Designs, Dragon Handle, 4 1/2 In. 187.00
Mustard, Lotus Sprig On Front, Loop Handle, Trellis Diaper Border, 3 In. 800.00
Plaque, Ceremonial, Arms Of Duc De Vendome, 1720s, 9 3/4 In. 4620.00
Plaque, Famille Verte, Monkeys, Deer, Pine Tree, 18 x 14 In. 247.50
Plate, Cherry Pickers, Boy, On Ladder, Tree, 1775-1780, 9 1/8 In. 2013.00
Plate, Famille Rose, Erotic Scene, Cockerels In Love, 9 In. 330.00
Plate, Famille Verte, Landscape, Cobalt Border, 8 1/2 In., 4 Piece 330.00

Plate, Fish Design, Sanskrit Characters, Red, White & Blue, 1800, 10 In. 165.00
Plate, Floral Central Medallion, White Ground, Blue & Gilt Edge, 10 In. 155.00
Plate, Fortune-Teller, Gypsy & Infant, Grisaille, 1740, 9 1/8 In. 1265.00
Plate, People In Rowboat, Rose, Fitzhugh, 1825, 9 11/16 x 9 3/4 In., Pair 2875.00
Plate, Scrolling Acanthus, Egg & Dart Design, 10 In. 115.00
Plate, Seamstress, Woman, Sewing, Window, Grisaille, 1750, 9 In. 920.00
Plate, Tobacco Leaf, 1770-1780, 9 In., Pair 4025.00
Platter, Armorial, Green, Fitzhugh, 19th Century, 17 3/8 x 14 5/8 In. 2090.00
Platter, Auspicious Figures, Central Floral Medallion, 1830s, 12 3/4 In. 635.00
Platter, Chamfered, Peonies In Fenced Garden, 1760, 13 1/2 In., Pair 1035.00
Platter, Famille Rose, Landscape, Men & Horse, 1825, 11 3/4 In. 920.00
Platter, Fish, Blue, Inset Liner, Fitzhugh, 19th Century, 18 In. 880.00
Platter, Hot Water, Fitzhugh, Acorn Knop On Cover, c.1810, 14 3/4 In. 2240.00
Platter, Tobacco Leaf, Oval, 1770-1780, 11 In. 6900.00
Platter, Well & Tree, Talbot's Head Crest, Fitzhugh, 17 1/2 In. 1725.00
Porringer, Famille Rose, Scalloped Triangular Handle, c.1745, 6 In. 1035.00
Punch Bowl, Armorial, Gilt And Floral Surrounds, c.1765, 14 In. 2415.00
Punch Bowl, Blue & White, Fitzhugh Variant, 11 In. 1320.00
Punch Bowl, Diaperwork Panels, Garlands, Gilt Border, c.1785, 21 In. 4890.00
Punch Bowl, Famille Rose, Cobalt Blue, Fruiting Vine Rim, c.1750, 15 1/2 In. 2185.00
Punch Bowl, Peonies, Chrysanthemums, Floral Interior, 1770, 16 In. 4313.00
Punch Bowl, Underplate, Landscape Vignettes 7370.00
Rose Bowl, Cranes In Garden, Flower Spray Interior, c.1760, 10 3/8 In. 460.00
Salt Cellar, Pseudo-Tobacco Leaf, Shell, 1770-1780, 3 5/8 x 3 13/16 In. 6325.00
Sand Shaker, Foliage Design, Late 18th Century, 2 In. 175.00
Sauceboat, Leaf Shape Stand, 1770-1780, 7 7/8 x 8 1/4 In. 3450.00
Table Screen, Famille Rose, 4-Panel, Hardwood Frame 330.00
Table Screen, Famille Rose, Wooden Stand, 31 In. 440.00
Tea Bowl & Saucer, Lotus Petals, Gilt Edged Rim, 1740, 2 11/16 In. 920.00
Tea Caddy, Garden Scenes, Salmon, Black, Gold, Europe, 1720-1730, 4 In. 3450.00
Tea Caddy, Martin Luther, Half Length Portrait, c.1745, 4 3/4 In. 1725.00
Tea Caddy, Tobacco Leaf, Arched, Rectangular, 1775-1785, 4 3/4 In. 3163.00
Teapot, Blue & White Foliage Design, 5 3/4 In. 50.00
Teapot, Figural Landscape Design, Blue & White, 18th Century, 7 In. 247.00
Teapot, Famille Rose, Pink Peonies, Pear Shape, 4 3/4 In. 1610.00
Teapot, Floral & Butterfly, Floral Ground, 1780s, 5 In. 120.00
Teapot, Floral Design, Gilt, Fruit Finial, Grisaille, 5 3/4 In. 192.00
Teapot, Floral Reserves On Relief Pattern, Lion Paw Feet, 6 In. 825.00
Teapot, Fruit Finial, Double Entwined Floral Spray Handle, 5 In. 187.00
Teapot, Landscape Design, Blue & White, Drum Form, 19th Century, 5 In. 247.00
Teapot, Mandarin, Figural Cartouches, Lattice Ground, 18th Century, 9 In. 440.00
Teapot, Salmon, Bird, Flowering Tree, Drum Shape, 18th Century, 6 In. 192.00
Teapot, Wicker Caddy, Famille Rose, Florals, Birds, Butterflies, People 450.00
Toddy Jug, Cover, Rose Peonies, Barrel Shape, 1810-1820, 11 In. 4025.00
Tureen, Cover, Stand, Blue & White Clobbered, 1780-1820, 13 5/8 In. 3739.00
Tureen, Sauce, Undertray, Fitzhugh 2200.00
Tureen, Soup, Cover, Stand, Pseudo-Tobacco Leaf, 13 3/8 In. 4600.00
Tureen, Soup, Rope Twist Border, Floral Sprays, 1830s, 8 x 14 In. 2650.00
Tureen, Vegetable, Acorn Knops, Lakeside Pavilions, Figures, c.1800, Pr. 1955.00
Umbrella Stand, Green, Cylindrical, Fitzhugh, 23 1/2 In. 1450.00
Vase, Blue & White, 6 Character Mark, 8 In. 2100.00
Vase, Buddhist Lions Crouching Amid Plants, Marked, 12 In. 575.00
Vase, Double Gourd, Blue & White, 4 Character Mark, 9 1/2 In., Pair 80.00
Vase, Famille Rose, Bands Of Figure Scenes, Boys At Play, 21 In. 1205.00
Vase, Famille Rose, Figures, Before Seated Dignitary, Hexagonal, 21 1/4 In. 465.00
Vase, Famille Verte, Cartouches, Flowers, Blue Ground, 19th Century, 22 In. 525.00
Vase, Finial Cover, Blue & White Clobbered, Late 17th Century, 15 7/8 In. 2600.00

CHOCOLATE GLASS, sometimes mistakenly called caramel slag, was made
by the Indiana Tumbler and Goblet Company of Greentown, Indiana, from
1900 to 1903. Fenton Art Glass Co. also made chocolate glass from about
1907 to 1915. More recent pieces have been made by Imperial, Heisey, and
others.

Bell,	Bicentennial, Fenton	25.00
Box,	Dresser, Brass Bound	135.00
Butter,	Cactus, Greentown	240.00
Butter,	Cover, Dewey, 4 In.	165.00
Compote,	Cactus, Greentown, 5 1/4 In.	145.00 to 240.00
Compote,	Jelly, Pleat Band	175.00
Creamer,	Cactus, Greentown	45.00
Cruet,	Herringbone Stopper	200.00
Cruet,	Leaf Bracket, Greentown	95.00 to 175.00
Dish,	Cover, Bird With Berry	850.00
Dish,	Dolphin Cover	120.00
Dish,	Lamb Cover, Greentown	350.00
Dish,	Rabbit Cover, Greentown	385.00
Dish,	Santa Claus On Sled Cover	48.00
Figurine,	Cat On Hamper, Greentown	575.00
Mug,	Indoor Drinking Scene, Handleless, Greentown	330.00
Mug,	Outdoor Drinking Scene	165.00 to 175.00
Mug,	Storybook, Imperial	50.00
Nappy,	Leaf Bracket, Handle, Triangular, 3 3/4 x 5 3/4 In.	60.00
Owl,	6 1/2 In., 2 Piece	35.00
Pitcher,	Milk, Windmill	45.00
Pitcher,	Racing Deer, Greentown	570.00
Pitcher,	Water, Squirrel, Greentown	630.00
Plate,	Cactus, Greentown	395.00
Plate,	Lafayette, Fenton	35.00
Powder Box,	Orange Tree	145.00
Rose Bowl,	Orange Tree	338.00
Spooner,	Flying Swan	125.00
Sugar,	Cover, Cactus	150.00
Sugar,	Cover, Dewey	380.00
Sugar,	Cover, Flying Swan	85.00
Sugar,	Leaf Bracket, Greentown	90.00
Sugar & Creamer,	Dewey, Greentown	125.00
Sweetmeat,	Cactus, Pedestal, Greentown	700.00
Tankard,	Cover	85.00
Toothpick,	Cactus	65.00
Tumbler,	Cactus, 5 In.	60.00

CHRISTMAS collectibles include not only Christmas trees and ornaments listed below, but also Santa Claus figures, special dishes, and even games and wrapping paper. A Belsnickle is a nineteenth-century figure of Father Christmas. A kugel is an early, heavy ornament made of thick blown glass, lined with zinc or lead, and often covered with colored wax.

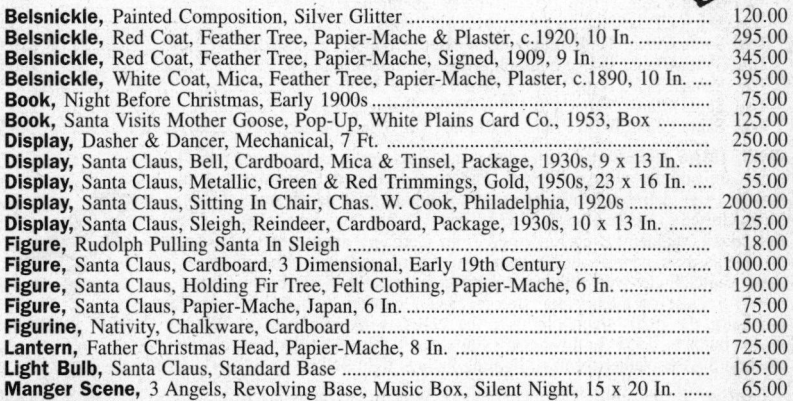

Belsnickle,	Painted Composition, Silver Glitter	120.00
Belsnickle,	Red Coat, Feather Tree, Papier-Mache & Plaster, c.1920, 10 In.	295.00
Belsnickle,	Red Coat, Feather Tree, Papier-Mache, Signed, 1909, 9 In.	345.00
Belsnickle,	White Coat, Mica, Feather Tree, Papier-Mache, Plaster, c.1890, 10 In.	395.00
Book,	Night Before Christmas, Early 1900s	75.00
Book,	Santa Visits Mother Goose, Pop-Up, White Plains Card Co., 1953, Box	125.00
Display,	Dasher & Dancer, Mechanical, 7 Ft.	250.00
Display,	Santa Claus, Bell, Cardboard, Mica & Tinsel, Package, 1930s, 9 x 13 In.	75.00
Display,	Santa Claus, Metallic, Green & Red Trimmings, Gold, 1950s, 23 x 16 In.	55.00
Display,	Santa Claus, Sitting In Chair, Chas. W. Cook, Philadelphia, 1920s	2000.00
Display,	Santa Claus, Sleigh, Reindeer, Cardboard, Package, 1930s, 10 x 13 In.	125.00
Figure,	Rudolph Pulling Santa In Sleigh	18.00
Figure,	Santa Claus, Cardboard, 3 Dimensional, Early 19th Century	1000.00
Figure,	Santa Claus, Holding Fir Tree, Felt Clothing, Papier-Mache, 6 In.	190.00
Figure,	Santa Claus, Papier-Mache, Japan, 6 In.	75.00
Figurine,	Nativity, Chalkware, Cardboard	50.00
Lantern,	Father Christmas Head, Papier-Mache, 8 In.	725.00
Light Bulb,	Santa Claus, Standard Base	165.00
Manger Scene,	3 Angels, Revolving Base, Music Box, Silent Night, 15 x 20 In.	65.00
Manger Scene,	Fold-Out, Die Cut, Germany	20.00

Christmas, Toy, Santa Claus, In Car,
Tin Windup, 1920, 10 In.

◆◆◆◆◆◆◆◆◆◆◆◆◆◆◆◆◆◆◆◆◆

A little damage and wear adds to
the charm of old Christmas ornaments. It indicates an antique
that has seen many holidays of
use. Don't try to restore old ornaments.

◆◆◆◆◆◆◆◆◆◆◆◆◆◆◆◆◆◆◆◆◆

Mold, Candy, Belsnickle, Tin, 8 In. 70.00
Nativity Set, Chalkware, 10 In., 16 Piece 200.00
Pin, Father Christmas, Message 15.00
Plates are listed in the Collector Plate category
Santa Claus, Celluloid Face, Net Bag Body 95.00
Santa Claus, In Airplane, Cotton 95.00
Santa Claus, In Sleigh, Reindeer In Front, Cast Iron, Hubley, 15 In. 1400.00
Santa Claus, On Metal Bicycle, Ringing Bell, 1950s, Package 25.00
Santa Claus, Walking, Ives Hotchkiss 2750.00
Santa Claus, Windup, Arms Move, Rings Bell, Tin Lithograph, 1940s, Box 110.00
Santa's Post Office, Toy Store Display, 1950s, 48 x 7 1/2 x 11 1/2 In. 3500.00
Snow Dome, Santa Claus, Perpetual Calendar, Box 20.00
Toy, Rudolph Pulling Santa Claus In Sleigh 15.00
Toy, Santa Claus, Cycle, Tin, Celluloid, Box 65.00
Toy, Santa Claus, Drummer, Tin Lithograph, Clothes, Battery Operated, Japan 66.00
Toy, Santa Claus, Helicopter, Battery Operated, Box .... 150.00 to 175.00
Toy, Santa Claus, In Car, Tin Windup, 1920, 10 In. .... *Illus* 8500.00
Toy, Santa Claus, In Chimney, Windup 60.00
Toy, Santa Claus, On Roof, Battery Operated, 1960s, Box 225.00
Toy, Santa Claus, On Scooter, Tin Lithograph & Plastic, Battery Operated, Box 44.00
Toy, Santa Claus, On Skis, Windup 85.00
Toy, Santa Claus, Push-Button Puppet 15.00
Toy, Santa Claus, Red & White, Irwin, 4 In. 55.00
Toy, Santa Claus, Reindeer Sleigh, Celluloid, Windup 77.00
Toy, Santa Claus, Ringing Bell & Holding Candy Cane, Box 95.00
Toy, Santa Claus, Ringing Bell, Battery Operated, 1950s, 13 In. 65.00
Toy, Santa Claus, Squeeze, Rempal, Late 1940s 85.00
Toy, Santa Claus, Tin Lithograph, Windup, Chein 220.00
Toy, Santa Claus, Tin Lithograph, Windup, Lindstrom 286.00
Toy, Santa Claus, Walking, Key Wind, Ives, 9 3/4 In. 2750.00
Toy, Santa Claus, Windup, c.1950, 10 In., Box 125.00
Toy, Santa Claus, With Pram, Celluloid, Tin, Windup 44.00

CHRISTMAS TREES made of feathers and Christmas tree decorations of all
types are popular with collectors. The first decorated Christmas tree in
America is claimed by many states, including Pennsylvania (1747),
Massachusetts (1832), Illinois (1833), Ohio (1838), and Iowa (1845). The
first glass ornaments were imported from Germany about 1860. Dresden
ornaments were made about 100 years ago of paper and tinsel. Manufacturers
in the United States were making ornaments in the early 1870s. Electric lights
were first used on a Christmas tree in 1882. Character light bulbs became
popular in the 1920s, bubble lights in the 1940s, twinkle bulbs in the 1950s,
plastic bulbs by 1955. In this book a Christmas light is a holder for a candle
used on the tree. Other forms of lighting include light bulbs.

Feather, Collapsible, Stenciled Bells & Wreath, Germany, 57 In. 355.00

Feather, Red Composition Berries, 22 In. 195.00
Feather, Tricolor, 30 In. 154.00
Fence, Green, Red Picket Gate, Wooden, 2 In. x 8 Ft. 60.00
Fence, Looped Wicker, Green Wooden, A.W. Drake, Gate, Square, 38 In. 265.00
Fence, Twig, Swinging Gate, Germany, 4 In. 128.00
Garland, Bulbs, Tinsel, 5 Ft. 2.00
Light Bulb, Baby In Red Stocking 15.00
Light Bulb, Cat & Mandolin 30.00
Light Bulb, Cone Shape, Box, 1920s, 12 .... 25.00
Light Bulb, Father Christmas, Painted Glass, 6 1/2 In. 286.00
Light Bulb, Father Christmas, Painted Glass, Ochre, Green, Red, Gold, 3 In. 66.00
Light Bulb, Old King Cole 35.00
Light Bulb, Pig With Drum 125.00
Light Bulb, Pinocchio 65.00
Light Bulb, Purple Tinsel, Square, 1 1/2 In. 3.00
Light Bulb, Red Glass, Face On Scrap, 1950s, 5 In. 10.00
Light Bulb, Santa Claus, Japan 150.00
Light Bulb, Santa Claus, Painted Glass, Multicolored, 5 1/2 In. 49.50
Light Bulb, Scrooge, Milk Glass, Red, Green, Blue 40.00
Light Bulb, Swirled Candle Flame, Pointed Tip, Clear, Red Paint 10.00
Light Bulb, Zeppelin, Lantern & Ear Of Corn, Set Of 3, Miniature .... 30.00 to 50.00
Light Bulb Set, Mazda, Display Box, 1930s 245.00
Light Bulb Set, Milk Glass, Painted Santa Claus, 10 Piece 185.00
Ornament, Angel, Waxed, Human Hair, Gold Wings, 5 In. 60.00
Ornament, Ball, Quilted, Gold Indents, 3 1/2 In 15.00
Ornament, Bell, Gold Glass, Flocked Flowers & Leaves, 3 1/2 In. 2.50
Ornament, Bell, Honeycomb, Red & Silver Foil, 9 1/2 In. 35.00
Ornament, Bell, Red Glass, Japan, 2 In. 2.00
Ornament, Cat Face, Painted Glass, Germany 330.00
Ornament, Cello, Painted Glass 60.50
Ornament, Choir Doll, Yarn, Felt, 4 In. 1.25
Ornament, Clown Face, Painted Glass, Germany 88.00
Ornament, Clown, With Crescent Moon 60.00
Ornament, Cockatoo, Glass 75.00
Ornament, Cross Shape, Scrap & Tinsel, 6 In. 18.00
Ornament, Doll, Playing Harp, Composition, Pipe Cleaner Arms, 1950s, 3 In. 1.85
Ornament, Drummer, Hallmark, 1976, Box 55.00
Ornament, Elephant, Painted Glass, Germany 33.00
Ornament, Father Christmas, Head, Painted Glass, Glitter .... 38.50 to 44.00
Ornament, Fish, Blown Glass 15.00
Ornament, French Horn, Teal Blue Glass, 4 In. 6.00
Ornament, Girl's Face, Painted Glass, Glass Eyes, Germany 71.50
Ornament, Grape Cluster, Silver Glass, 4 In. 18.00
Ornament, Kugel, Bunch Of Grapes, Green, Brass Fastener, 5 1/8 In. 440.00
Ornament, Kugel, Green, Brass Hanger, 4 3/4 In. 27.50
Ornament, Mrs. Santa Claus, Head 20.00
Ornament, MultiLoop, Tinsel, Wrapped Wire, 8 In. 20.00
Ornament, Santa Claus, Clip-On, Painted Glass, Multicolored, Snow 44.00
Ornament, Santa Claus, Face, Treetop, Silver Frame, Tin, 1930-1940s 38.00
Ornament, Santa Claus, Face On Pinecone Bulb, Painted Glass 44.00
Ornament, Santa Claus, Head, On Icicle, Painted Glass 88.00
Ornament, Santa Claus, Head, Papier-Mache, Germany, 1930s 25.00
Ornament, Santa Claus, Holding Tree, Red & Silver Glass, 2 In. 8.00
Ornament, Santa Claus, In Chimney, Painted Glass 49.50
Ornament, Santa Claus, In Sleigh, Celluloid 45.00
Ornament, Santa Claus, In Sleigh, Hand Painted, Gold Foil, Dresden 110.00
Ornament, Santa Claus, In Wreath, Painted Glass & Wire 38.50
Ornament, Santa Claus, Mechanical, Hand Painted Tin, Germany 286.00
Ornament, Santa Claus, Painted Glass, Glitter Beard 93.50
Ornament, Santa Claus, Papier-Mache Face, 1930-1940, 3 1/2 In. 15.00
Ornament, Santa Claus, Plastic, 1940s, 3 In., Set Of 6 .... 35.00
Ornament, Snoopy 15.00

Ornament, Treetop, Angel, 1950s 20.00
Ornament, Treetop, Angel, Gold Wings & Stars, Spun Glass, Round, 8 In. 82.00
Ornament, Treetop, Angel, Spun Glass, Gold Wings, 8 In. Diam. 78.00
Skirt, Snow White, Disney 85.00
Stand, Wooden, Musical, Ringling Bros. 4400.00

CHROME items in the Art Deco style became popular in the 1930s.
Collectors are most interested in high-style pieces made by the Connecticut
firms of Chase Brass and Copper Company and Manning Bowman.

Ashtray, Spinning Bucket, Bird Cigarette Grips, Hamilton, 5 3/4 In. 9.50
Candlestick, Baluster & Disc Stem, 9 3/4 In., Pair 75.00
Candy Dish, Cover, Pierced, Glass Insert, Bakelite Finial, Farberware, 7 x 5 1/2 In. .. 42.00
Candy Dish, Nude, Purple, Farber Bros. 135.00
Cocktail Jug, Conical, Wooden Handle, Pull Top, Screw Cap On Spout, Farberware . 28.00
Cocktail Set, Hammered, Black Plastic Handle, Goblets, Farberware, 7 Piece 28.00
Cocktail Shaker, Art Deco, Manning Bowman 25.00
Cocktail Shaker, Cobalt Blue, Chrome Top 65.00
Cocktail Shaker, Penguin 325.00
Cocktail Shaker, Zeppelin Shape, Disassembles, Fitted, Tools, Germany, c.1929 ...... 3300.00
Cocktail Shaker Set, Chase, 6 Piece 115.00
Coffee Set, Art Deco, Farberware, 4 Piece 325.00
Coffeepot, Diplomat, Chase 85.00
Coffeepot, Sugar & Creamer, Westinghouse, Green Bakelite Handles 27.50
Compote, Nude Stem, Scalloped, Grape & Leaf Pierced Bowl, Sferrazza, 8 In. 24.00
Compote, Nude Woman, Cambridge Amber Glass Insert, Farberware 40.00
Dish, Sundae, Vertical Ribbed, Footed, 4 1/4 In., 6 Piece 15.00
Flask, Hip, 1920s, 6 1/2 x 3 3/4 In. 47.50
Golf Ball Corkscrew, Golf Club Bottle Opener, 1950, Partial Box 22.00
Head, Man, Art Deco, Plated, Hagenauer 7500.00
Head, Woman, Art Deco, Plated, Hagenauer 8000.00
Humidor, Rumidor, Art Deco Horizontal Ribbed 28.00
Ice Bucket, Art Deco, Penguin 18.00
Ice Bucket, Penguin, Westbend 15.00
Pitcher, Cocktail, Red Bakelite Handle 23.00
Pitcher, Deco Style, Continental, 8 In. 18.00
Sconce, Dolphin, Chase Brass 50.00
Server, Electric, Chase Brass, Lurelle Guild 145.00
Sugar & Creamer, Footed, High Handles, Farberware, 4 In. 6.00
Tray, Scroll & Lattice, Pierced Medallions Rim, Oval, 16 3/4 x 12 In. 8.00
Tumbler, Juice, Chase 25.00

CIGAR STORE FIGURES of carved wood or cast iron were used as
advertisements in front of the Victorian cigar store. The carved figures are
now collected as folk art. They range in size from counter type, about three
feet, to over eight feet high.

Indian, Maiden, Carved, Painted 605.00
Indian, Maiden, C.H. Monley & Co., Composition, c.1930, 6 Ft. 2800.00
Indian, On Drum, Full Headdress, Leggings, Moccasins, 68 In. 2300.00
Indian, Squaw, Painted, Cast Zinc, 81 x 21 In. 8050.00
Indian, Stand, 46 In. 4250.00
Indian Princess, Feathered Headdress, Cigars In Hand, S. Robb, 77 In. 32200.00

CINNABAR is a vermilion or red lacquer. Pieces are made with tens to
hundreds of thicknesses of the lacquer that is later carved.

Box, China, 3 x 4 In. 55.00
Bracelet 40.00
Lamp, Orange & Red Fringed Victorian Shade, Pair 1100.00
Plaque, Carved Ivory Boat, China, 2 x 4 In. 55.00
Snuff Bottle, Carved Figures 45.00
Snuff Bottle, Carved Figures In Landscape, Red 220.00
Snuff Bottle, Carved Mountain Scenes 45.00
Urn, Cover 395.00

CIVIL WAR mementos are important collector's items. Most of the pieces are military items used from 1861 to 1865.

Badge, Dept. Of Washington & Alaska Annual Encampment, Ribbon, 1904	95.00
Badge, Hat, Musician, Lute Shape	30.00
Banner, GAR, Blue, Yellow, 20 x 30 In.	35.00
Bayonet, Saber, Enfield, 2 Band	75.00
Bottle, Hinged Cap, Tin, Unpainted, 7 3/8 In.	110.00
Box, Candle, Tin, Brass Catch, 8 1/4 x 5 In.	75.00
Box, Cap, Military, Black Leather Belt	247.00
Box, Cartridge, Rifleman's, Oval, U.S. Logo On Flap	135.00
Bugle, U.S. Marine Corps., Wurlitzer	6500.00
Can, Powder & Shot, Tin, 5 3/4 In.	60.00
Canteen, Blue Transfer, Gilding, Pottery, 1870s	395.00
Canteen, Bull's-Eye, Stripes On Reverse, 7 1/2 In.	220.00
Canteen, Pewter Neck, 3 Suspension Bands, Tinned, No Stopper, Standard Issue	95.00
Chest, Apothecary, Doctor's, c.1860	875.00
Drum Sticks	35.00
Epaulet, General's, Gold Bouillon Tassels, Brass Crescent	175.00
Flag, Battle, Confederate, Red Stripes, White Stars, Blue Ground	6500.00
Flag, Signal, Red, White & Blue	200.00
Flask, Whiskey, Pewter Top & Cup, Leather Covered	55.00
Fork & Spoon, Folding, Wood Side Scales, Pair	30.00
Horn, Signal, Confederate Cavalry	395.00
Kepi, Silver & Gold Braid, Philadelphia Label	375.00
Knapsack, Folding, Straps, Brass Hooks, Oil Cloth	175.00
Lamp, Soldier's, Personal Camp Type, Brass, Dated 1863	80.00
Map Case, Heavy Gauge Tin, Black Paint, 6 3/4 x 13 In.	110.00
Medal, Of Honor, Cased, Unissued	2499.00
Mold, Bullet, Brass, 36 Caliber Round Ball & Patch Type	55.00
Musket, Springfield, Bayonet	1100.00
Muster Roll, Co. 1, 66th North Carolina Partisan Rangers, 162, 34 x 20 In.	395.00
Newspaper, Louisville Gazette	25.00
Pouch, Leather Cap	65.00
Saddle, Cavalry, McClellan, 1859	850.00
Shield, Carved, Relief, Henry Cole, Wilton, Me., 6 1/4 x 8 5/8 In.	245.00
Shoulder Boards, Officer's, Pair	65.00
Stirrups, U.S. Watervliet Arsensal, Brass	120.00
Sword, Drummer's, Hand To Hand Combat, Leather Scabbard	325.00
Sword, Foot Officer's, Wire Wrap Sharkskin Grip, 31 1/4 In.	775.00
Sword, Militia, Knight's Head Pommel, Ivory Handle	165.00
Sword, Short, Confederate, Solid Brass Guard & Handle, Rusty, 1885	650.00
Sword, Trooper's, U.S., M1868, Ames Marks, Scabbard	425.00
Torch, Kerosene, 1860s, 9 x 5 In.	90.00
Wrench, Musket, Model 1879	12.50

CKAW, see Dedham category

CLAMBROTH glass, popular in the Victorian era, is a grayish color and is somewhat opaque, like clambroth.

Bowl, Scalloped, 12 x 3 In.	35.00
Epergne, Child's, Lily Insert, Gold Design, Ruffled Base, 6 1/4 In.	225.00
Toothpick, Enameled Red Berries, Green Leaves	125.00
Vase, Black Horizontal Lines, Bulging Shoulder, White Optic Interior, 9 x 5 In	30.00

CLARICE CLIFF was a designer who worked in several English factories after the 1920s. She died in 1972.

Beaker, Sunray, Orange Banding, Marked, 3 In.	230.00
Biscuit Barrel, Bizarre, Bomb Shape, Electroplate Mount, Blue Chintz, 6 In.	538.50
Bone Dish, Tonquin, Brown	11.00
Bone Dish, Tonquin, Green, 6 Piece	50.00
Bowl, Berries, Bizarre, Banded Orange Interior, 2 3/4 In.	370.00
Bowl, Fantasque, Hiawatha, Broth, 9 3/4 In.	420.75

Bowl, Fruit, Goldstone	425.00
Bowl, Inspiration, Stepped, Square, Green, Blue & White, 8 In.	605.00
Bowl, Rhodanthe, Bizarre, 9 1/4 In.	875.00
Bowl, Sliced Fruit, Bizarre, Orange, Yellow, Brown, Black, 9 1/4 In.	404.00
Bowl, Sungleam, Bizarre, Green Banding, 9 1/2 In.	168.00
Bowl, Tonquin, Red, 8 3/4 In.	18.00
Bowl, Woodland, Octagonal Rim, Marked, 6 1/4 In.	255.00
Box, Cover, Fantasque, Abstract Foliage, Orange Scallops, Triangles, 5 1/2 In.	303.00
Butter, Cover, Crocus, Ivory Field, Signed, 2 3/4 x 4 In.	303.00
Cake Set, Ophelia, 18 Piece	1000.00
Candleholder, My Garden, Kneeling Female, Basket, Marked, 7 1/4 In., Pair	403.00
Candleholder, Tonquin	45.00
Centerpiece, Viking Ship, Frog Insert, Bizarre, c.1925, 15 3/4 In., 2 Piece	345.00
Charger, Floral Design, 12 1/2 In.	285.00
Chop Plate, Peacock, Flowers, Lakeside, 12 1/4 In.	65.00
Coffee Can, Saucer, Fantasque, Trees And House Pattern	151.50
Coffee Set, Bonjour, Concentric Circles, 7 1/2-In. Coffeepot, 15 Piece	370.00
Coffee Set, Crocus, Blossoms, Marked, 16 Piece	483.00
Coffee Set, Fantasque, Trees & House, 7-In. Coffeepot, 15 Piece	1683.00
Creamer, Bizarre	350.00
Creamer, Spring Crocus .... 175.00 to	235.00
Cruet, Crocus, Conical	252.00
Cup & Saucer, Autumn Crocus	185.00
Cup & Saucer, Coral Firs, Conical	435.00
Cup & Saucer, Moonlight	365.00
Dessert Set, Aurea, Octagonal, 7 Piece	303.00
Figurine, Cat, Laughing, Bizarre, Orange, Green & Black Spots, 4 1/4 In.	539.00
Figurine, Dutch Man, Hands In Pocket, Pipe In Mouth, Polychrome, 8 1/4 In.	420.00
Honey Pot, Beehive, Cover, Crocus Design, 3 1/2 In.	168.00
Honey Pot, Beehive, Crocus, Flowers & Squares, Bee Mount, 6 In.	247.00
Honey Pot, Fantasque, Bizarre, Beehive, Windbells, 3 3/4 In.	219.00
Jam Jar, Blue Firs, Flat Sides, Marked, 4 1/4 In.	253.00
Jam Jar, Trees & House, Cherry Finial, Marked, 3 1/2 In.	175.00
Jardiniere, Aurea, Ribbed, 8 In.	252.50
Jug, Coral Firs, Lotus, Bizarre, Signed, 7 x 6 In.	770.00
Jug, Delecia Pansy, Lotus, Bizarre, One Handle, 11 3/4 In.	841.50
Jug, Dragon, Bizarre, Green And Orange, 9 In.	437.50
Jug, Fantasque, Red Roofs, Lotus, Bizarre, 11 3/4 In.	1515.00
Jug, Fantasque, Trees & House, 7 In.	437.50
Jug, Gayday, Flowers, Green Foliage, Ivory Ground, Signed, 10 x 7 In.	1210.00
Jug, Liberty Stripe, Lotus, Bizarre, One Handle, 11 3/4 In.	505.00
Jug, Lotus, Garland, 2 Handles, 12 In.	805.00
Jug, Lotus, Nasturtium, Yellow & Orange Band, Handle, Mark, 12 In.	460.00
Jug, Milk, Gilbraltar, Bizarre, Stamford, 4 In.	370.00
Jug, Mountain, Conical, 6 1/2 In.	370.00
Jug, Poppy Delecia, Pear Shape, Angular Handle, Signed, 7 1/4 In.	633.00
Jug, Sunrise, Yellow & Orange Band, 1 Handle, Marked, 12 In.	920.00
Jug, Sunshine, Blue, Orange & Green Flowers, Ivory Ground, 7 In.	660.00
Lamp Base, Rhodanthe, Tapering Ovoid, 10 1/4 In.	219.00
Napkin Ring, Crocus, Bizarre, Square, Green & Yellow Bands, 4 Piece	286.00
Pitcher, Fantasque, Athens, Lily, Orange	770.00
Pitcher, Fantasque, Melon, 1929-1935	715.00
Plaque, Delecia Pansy, Bizarre, Circular, 13 In.	358.00
Plate, Alpine Design, Hexagonal, 1920s	425.00
Plate, Biarritz, Bizarre, Aurea, 9 In.	185.00
Plate, Biarritz, Forest Glen, 10 1/4 In.	437.00
Plate, Dinner, Crocus, Square	285.00
Plate, Fantasque, Bizarre, Hexagonal	365.00
Plate, Fantasque, Bizarre, Melon, Orange Banding, Octagonal, 9 In.	286.00
Plate, Fantasque, Bizarre, Mountain, Orange Banding, 9 In.	640.00
Plate, Fantasque, Bizarre, Orange Chintz, Octagonal, 8 In.	135.00
Plate, Fantasque, Bizarre, Summerhouse, Orange Banding, Square, 9 1/2 In.	303.00
Plate, Fantasque, Trees And House, Five Colors, 10 In.	202.00

Plate, Forest Glen, House On Green Hills, Signed, 9 3/4 In. 550.00
Plate, Forest Glen, Polychrome, Marked, 10 In. 92.00
Plate, Forest Glen, Ribbed, 8 1/2 In. 470.00
Plate, Geometric Flowers, Bizarre, 1920s 345.00
Plate, Geometric Star, Bizarre, Blues & Oranges, 1930s 250.00
Plate, Spoke Design, Bizarre, Orange, Purple, Green, Yellow, 9 In. 135.00
Plate, Sunrise, Scalloped Rim, Marked, 10 1/4 In. 253.00
Plate, Tonquin, Red, 6 In. 5.00
Plate, Umbrellas, Bizarre, Red, Blue, Black, Yellow, Green, 9 In. 590.00
Platter, Tonquin, Red, 11 3/4 In. 25.00
Preserve Pot, Cover, Bonjour, Garden Stile & Flowers, 4 1/4 In. 202.00
Preserve Pot, Cover, Bonjour, Newlyn, 4 1/4 In. 270.00
Rose Bowl, Fantasque, Blue Chintz 467.00
Salt & Pepper, Tonquin 55.00
Soup Dish, Tonquin, Red, 8 In. 12.00
Sugar & Creamer, Bizarre 250.00
Sugar Shaker, Autumn, Conical, 5 1/2 In. 368.00
Sugar Sifter, Crocus, Bizarre, Conical, 5 1/2 In. 404.00
Sugar Sifter, Kelverne, Bizarre, Conical, 5 1/2 In. 236.00
Tea Set, Celtic Harvest, 3 Piece 350.00
Tea Set, Trieste, Green Capri, Bizarre, 5 1/2-In. Teapot, 3 Piece 320.00
Tea Set, Teapot, Sugar & Creamer, Celtic Harvest, 3 Piece 350.00
Tile, Tea, Bizarre .... 120.00 to 160.00
Toby Jug, Man Holding Mug Of Frothing Beer, 6 1/2 In. 118.00
Vase, Bizarre, 2 3/4 In. 175.00
Vase, Bizarre, Patina Tree, Flowering Tree, Blue Splatters, Marked, 6 1/2 In. 600.00
Vase, Bon Jour, Bizarre, Green 440.00
Vase, Delecia, Pansy, Bizarre, Spherical, 6 In. 1094.00
Vase, Delecia Isis, Anemone Pattern, 9 3/4 In. 538.50
Vase, Fantasque, Abstract Geometrics & Scalloped Lines, No. 186, 8 1/2 In. 437.00
Vase, Fantasque, Bizarre, Isis, Nasturtium, 9 3/4 In. 370.00
Vase, Fantasque, Cylindrical, Painted Panels Of Flowers On Sunbursts, 6 In. 404.00
Vase, Fantasque, Red Tree, Oviform, 2 1/4 In. 505.00
Vase, Inspiration, Persian, Turquoise, Yellow, Speckled Blue Ground, 9 In. 370.00
Vase, Isis, Newlyn, Bizarre, One Handle, 9 3/4 In. 1178.00
Vase, Latona Glaze, Bizarre, Stylized Flower, Mushrooms, No. 360, 8 In. 1430.00
Vase, Multicolored Landscape, Stippled Yellow Ground, Marked, 8 1/4 In. 368.00
Vase, My Garden, Cylindrical, 6 In. 100.00
Vase, No. 358, Secrets, Hilly Landscape, Signed, 8 In. 880.00
Vase, Orange, Yellow & Black, 10 In. 750.00
Vase, Trees & House, Ivory Field, Signed, 6 1/4 In. 880.00
Wall Mask, Marlene, Bizarre, 7 1/4 In. 370.00
Wall Pocket, Leaping Scaly Fist, Turquoise Inspiration Glaze, 11 In. 252.00
Wall Pocket, Marlene, Matte Green, Enameled Flowers, 7 In. 404.00
Wall Pocket, Woman's Head, Long Ears, Curly Blue Hair, 9 In. 168.00

CLEWELL ware was made in limited quantities by Charles Walter Clewell of
Canton, Ohio, from 1902 to 1955. Pottery was covered with a thin coating of
bronze, then treated to make the bronze turn different colors. Pieces covered
with copper, brass, or silver were also made. Mr. Clewell's secret formula for
blue patinated bronze was burned when he died in 1965.

Bowl, Bronze, 4 In. 375.00
Candlestick, Bulbous, Brown-To-Verdigris Patina, Copper Clad, 9 1/2 In., Pair 550.00
Mug, Copper Clad, Hammered Effect Near Base, Dark Patina, 5 In. 93.50
Pitcher, Bronze & Brown, 6 1/2 In. 265.00
Vase, Angular Shoulder, Cratered Verdigris Patina, Copper Clad, 8 In. 550.00
Vase, Bronze Clad, 1931, 22 1/2 In. 3190.00
Vase, Bud, 7 1/2 In. 485.00
Vase, Cattail & Dragonfly Design, Oxidized Copper On Natural Copper, 7 In. 475.00
Vase, Copper Clad, Brown & Verdigris Patina, Marked, 7 In. 800.00
Vase, Copper Clad, Patinated In Reddish Brown & Verdigris, 21 1/2 In. 2500.00
Vase, Copper Clad, Raised Design, 6 x 4 3/4 In. 495.00
Vase, Copper Clad, Rust To Verdigris Finish, Marked, 8 1/4 In. 440.00

Vase, Copper Clad, Voluted Handles, 9 1/2 In. 450.00
Vase, Dark Copper & Green Patina, 9 In. 600.00
Vase, Green Patination Around Neck & Shoulder, Copper Red Ground, 7 1/4 In. 517.00

CLEWS pottery was made by George Clews & Co. of Brownhill Pottery, Tunstall, England, from 1806 to 1861. Additional pieces may be listed in the Flow Blue category.

Creamer, Eagle On Urn, Dark Blue 850.00
Cup & Saucer, Corinthian Ornament, Dark Blue 150.00
Cup Plate, Lafayette, 4 3/8 In. 335.00
Pitcher, Landing Of Lafayette, Dark Blue, Baluster, 4 1/2 In. 1850.00
Pitcher, Welcome Lafayette, Nation's Guest, Dark Blue, 6 7/8 In. 2750.00
Plate, Abbey & Fishermen, Dark Blue, 10 In. 165.00
Plate, Blue Transfer, Landing Of Lafayette, 9 In. 192.00
Plate, Dark Blue Transfer, English River Scene, Fisherman, 8 7/8 In. 170.00
Plate, Dark Blue Valentine, 8 7/8 In. 660.00
Plate, Landing Of Lafayette, 7 1/2 In. 200.00
Plate, Landing Of Lafayette, Impressed, 9 In. 385.00
Plate, Medium Blue Transfer, Coronation, 10 In. 180.00
Plate, Oriental, Dark Blue, Scalloped, 10 In. 125.00
Plate, Peace & Plenty, Dark Blue, 8 7/8 In. 350.00
Plate, Winter View Of Pittsfield, Mass., Impressed, 7 3/4 In. 357.50
Platter, Blue Transfer, Letter Of Introduction, Wilkie, 12 3/8 In. 577.00
Platter, Dark Blue, Peace, Plenty, 19 In. 880.00
Platter, Picturesque Scene, Fishkill, Hudson River, Purple Transfer 137.50
Platter, Rabbit On The Wall, Wilkie, Dark Blue, 11 In. 880.00
Tray, Landing Of Lafayette, Dark Blue Transfer, 6 In. 1237.00
Tureen, Soup, Little Falls At Luzerne, Brown 1100.00

CLIFTON POTTERY was founded by William Long in Clifton, New Jersey, in 1905. He worked there until 1908 making a line called *Crystal Patina*. Clifton Pottery made art pottery. Another firm, Chesapeake Pottery, sold majolica marked *Clifton ware*.

Bowl, Blackberry, Footed, 8 1/2 In. 38.50
Bowl, Matte Gunmetal Green, Crystal Patina, 5 3/4 x 2 In. 25.00
Dish, Indian Ware, 2 x 4 1/2 In. 65.00
Humidor, Cover, Indian Ware, Unglazed Terra-Cotta, Black Matte 95.00
Humidor, Incised Indian-Type Design, Sponge Reserve, 5 3/4 In. 375.00
Modernistic Form, Green Semigloss Glaze, 4 x 5 In. 295.00
Mug, Black Indian Designs, Brick Red Matte Ground, 6 In. 55.00
Mug, Indian Art, 4 In. 95.00
Pitcher, Eggplant, Squash & Grapes Pattern, 7 1/2 In. 195.00
Pot, Arkansas, Indian Design, 7 In. 450.00
Teapot, Green, Signed 100.00
Teapot, Indian Ware, Mottled Yellow Luster, Gold Trim, 7 1/2 In. 50.00
Vase, Crane & Exotic Flowers, Burgundy Matte Ground, Marked, 12 1/4 In. 1880.00
Vase, Egg Shape, 2 Ear Handles, Crystalline Glaze, 4 1/2 In. 190.00
Vase, Flaring Neck, Mottled Yellow & Buff Crystalline Glaze, Marked, 7 1/4 In. 275.00
Vase, Green-Gold Speckled Glaze, Green Drips, Bottle Shape, 1906, 8 1/2 In. 225.00
Vase, Indian, Stovepipe Neck, Black & Tan Designs, Terra-Cotta Body, Marked, 4 In. ... 192.00
Vase, Poppy Blossoms On Opening, Green Glaze, No.173, 6 3/4 In. 475.00
Vessel, Matte Green Flambe Over Crystalline Green Glaze, 1906, 4 1/2 x 8 In. 550.00
Vessel, Stylized Lily Pads, Matte Green Glaze, 2 1/2 x 3 1/2 In. 385.00

CLOCKS of all types have always been popular with collectors. The eighteenth-century tall case, or grandfather's clock, was designed to house a works with a long pendulum. In 1816, Eli Terry patented a new, smaller works for a clock, and the case became smaller. The clock could be kept on a shelf instead of on the floor. By 1840, coiled springs were used and even smaller clocks were made. Battery-powered electric clocks were made in the 1870s.

Advertising, 7-Up, Flower, 16 In. 35.00
Advertising, 7-Up, With Sign 60.00
Advertising, American Express Money Orders, Light-Up, Plastic, 1958 .... 125.00

Clock, Ansonia, Regulator, Oak,
Gilt Bronze Mounts, 48 In.

Clock, Lantern, Brass, Bell Chime,
Whittemore Blair & Co. , New Orleans

Advertising, American Legion, Light-Up, 15 In.	95.00
Advertising, Blackwell's Bull Durham Tobacco, Ingraham, 33 In.	231.00
Advertising, Brownies Chocolate	200.00
Advertising, Burkhardt Beer, Electric, Convex Glass, 1950s, 15 In.	160.00
Advertising, Buy St. Joseph Aspirin, Light-Up, 15 In.	235.00
Advertising, Chancellor Cigar, Wooden, Printed Dial, 32 In.	132.00
Advertising, Charlie The Tuna	50.00
Advertising, Chevrolet Time, Neon, Logo, Round, 20 1/2 In.	523.00
Advertising, Clover Dairy, Light-Up	265.00
Advertising, Cool Joe, Camel Cigarettes	50.00
Advertising, Country Club Beer, Stenciled Face, Reverse On Glass, 19 In.	88.00
Advertising, Distler, BMW Sedan, 1939, 8 In.	265.00
Advertising, Dr Pepper, 10-2-4, Light-Up	275.00
Advertising, Dr Pepper, Calendar, Box, 1976	45.00
Advertising, Dr Pepper, Light-Up, Round	275.00
Advertising, Dr Pepper, Red Brick Logo, Round, 1940s, 14 In.	250.00
Advertising, Dr Pepper, Wooden Frame	450.00
Advertising, Ever-Ready Safety Razor, Pendulum	2420.00
Advertising, Ever-Ready, Man With Foaming Beard, 18 x 28 x 3 1/2 In.	3190.00
Advertising, Four Roses, Back Bar, Square, 13 In.	50.00
Advertising, Grant Batteries	100.00
Advertising, Grapette Soda, Bubble-Up	195.00
Advertising, Griesedieck Bros., Electric, 1950s, 14 In.	150.00
Advertising, Gunther Brewing Co., Bottle Cap, Pin-up Girls, Electric	455.00
Advertising, Hamm's Beer, Revolving Waterfall, Campsite Scene, 19 x 60 In.	600.00
Advertising, Heinz Man, Talking, Alarm	400.00 to 450.00
Advertising, Homelite Chain Saws, Pictures Saw, Light-Up	140.00
Advertising, J.P. Hoeltgen Optometrist, Reverse Painted Eye On Door, 33 In.	1485.00
Advertising, Jefferson Golden Hour, Art Deco, Electric	95.00
Advertising, Jolly Tar, Baird Clock Co., Plattsburgh, N.Y., 1895	495.00
Advertising, Keen Kutter, Electric, Light-Up, Square	875.00
Advertising, Keen Kutter, Red Metal Case, Iron Brackets, Logo Center, 18 In.	550.00
Advertising, Keen Kutter, Wall, Round	325.00
Advertising, Kodak Film, Bubble-Up, Square	175.00
Advertising, Little Sprout, Talking Alarm, Box	33.00
Advertising, Lucky Strike Tobacco, Wooden, Molded Composition Panels, 28 In.	220.00
Advertising, Lucky Strike, Wall, Sessions, Key Wind	500.00
Advertising, Mason Root Beer, Electric	125.00
Advertising, Mayo's Tobacco, Figure-8 Shape, Baird, 30 1/2 In.	900.00
Advertising, Melody Time, Neon, Stenciled Metal Dial, 20 In.	275.00

Advertising, Mid-West Ice Cream 85.00
Advertising, Moxie Nerve Food, Lowell, Mass., Baird Clock Co., 1890 .... 5500.00
Advertising, Neathery Credit Jewelry, Sessions, Stenciled, Wooden, 39 In. 165.00
Advertising, New York Clothing House, Papier-Mache 1450.00
Advertising, Nu-Grape, Light-Up 195.00
Advertising, Olbrych's Dairy, Time For Milk 125.00
Advertising, Old Mr. Boston, Metal Case, 1920s, 21 In. 750.00
Advertising, Old Overholt Rye, Light-Up, 4 1/2 x 14 In. 65.00
Advertising, Orange Crush, Light-Up, 1967 .... 60.00
Advertising, Pard Dog Food, Bobbing Head Of Dog, Ticks Seconds, 15 1/2 In. 275.00
Advertising, Pearl Beer, Neon, 1940s 375.00
Advertising, Pepsi-Cola, Cloverdale 500.00
Advertising, Peters Shoes, Ray-Flex Corp., Nickel Plated, Square, 15 In. 66.00
Advertising, Phillips 66, Light-Up 400.00
Advertising, Procter & Gamble, Electric, 1930s 100.00
Advertising, Purina Chows, Light-Up 300.00
Advertising, Purolator, Light-Up, 1960 .... 100.00
Advertising, Red Goose Shoes, Store 150.00
Advertising, Remington, Plaster Sheep Head Top, 150th Anniversary, 1966, 14 In. ... 55.00
Advertising, Ronald McDonald, Prototype, Plastic, Electrified, 12 x 28 x 5 In. 137.00
Advertising, Salem Cigarettes, Figural, Wall, 20 In. 85.00
Advertising, Seagram 7, Backbar 65.00
Advertising, Seiberling Safety Tire, Tire Shape, 1934 .... 50.00
Advertising, Skelly Gasoline, Glass 95.00
Advertising, Snow Crop, Figural, Teddy Bear 75.00
Advertising, Speed Queen, Washer & Dryer, Light-Up 95.00
Advertising, Squirt, Light-Up, Bottle 160.00
Advertising, St. Joseph's Aspirin, Light-Up, Round 175.00
Advertising, Star Brand Shoes, Windup .... 65.00 to 75.00
Advertising, Strauss Bros., America's Leading Trailers, Seth Thomas 1650.00
Advertising, Suncrest, Bottle On Face, Light-Up .... 200.00 to 225.00
Advertising, Sunkist, Electric 15.00
Advertising, Super-Sweet Feeds, Light-Up 250.00
Advertising, Valvoline Oil, Bubble-Up 165.00
Advertising, Vess Cola, Light-Up 350.00
Advertising, White King Soda, Illuminated Dial 1650.00
Advertising, Winston Cigarettes 20.00
Advertising, Wolf's Head, Round, Light-Up 275.00
Advertising, Woolsey Marine Paints, Mermaid Picture 200.00
Advertising, Zodiac Fine Watches, Light-Up, Allentown, Penna., 1940s, 13 In. 175.00
Alarm, Bakelite, Flashing, Electric 85.00
Alarm, Kal-Klock, Tape, Day-Date, With Manual 65.00
Alarm, Repeating Carriage, Swiss, Fitted Case, Henry Capt, 6 In. 880.00
Alarm, Snoopy Playing Tennis, Peanuts, Animated, 1960s 45.00
Alarm, Snoopy, 1958 .... 60.00
Alarm, Star Wars, Talking 100.00
Animated, Blacksmith, Striking Anvil On Hour & Half Hour, Celluloid Dial 1430.00
Animated, Victorian Picture, Round, 1880 .... 1100.00
Animated, Woody Woodpecker 175.00
Ansonia, French Type, Cast Iron, Brass 500.00
Ansonia, Kitchen, Gingerbread, 1870s 350.00
Ansonia, Louis XIV, Cast Iron 350.00
Ansonia, Mantel, Louis XV Style, Gilt Metal, Rocaille Case, c.1890 .... 302.50
Ansonia, Mantel, Red & Yellow Tulips, Royal Bonn Case 650.00
Ansonia, Mantel, Royal Bonn Case, Exposed Escapement, 14 In. 695.00
Ansonia, Mantel, Spelter-Figure Seated Woman, Open Escapement, 14 3/4 x 16 In. ... 305.00
Ansonia, Regulator, Oak, Gilt Bronze Mounts, 48 In. .... *Illus* 3700.00
Ansonia, Steeple, 8-Day 175.00
Ansonia, Wall, Regulator, Brass Trim, Walnut Veneer, 32 In. 302.50
Ansonia, Wall, Regulator, Calendar, Mahogany Veneer, 32 In. 330.00
Art Deco, Dancing Figure, Onyx, Bronze 900.00
Banjo, Federal, Mahogany & Giltwood, New England, c.1820, 32 In. 935.00
Banjo, Mahogany, New England, c.1830, 40 In. 330.00

Banjo, Mahogany, Reverse Glass Panels, 33 3/4 In. 825.00
Banjo, Reverse Painted Glass, 8-Day, Brass Movement 1700.00
Banjo, Rosewood, Black & Gold Eglomise, Tablet Glasses, 19th Century, 29 In. 825.00
Bezancon A. Charny, Hanging, Iron Case, Plowing Scene, Brass Works, 15 1/4 In. .. 275.00
Bigelow Kennard, George III Style, Mahogany, Parcel Gilt, 8 Bells, Mantel 4125.00
Blinking Eye, Dog, Recumbent, Shelf, 30-Hour, Cast Iron, 1860, 8 1/4 In. 2070.00
Blinking Eye, Owl, Hand Carved, Pendulum, Prewar Japan 265.00
Bracket, Louis XV, Foliate Scrolls & Flower Heads, Painted Green, 15 1/4 In. 3450.00
Bracket, Regency, Boulle Marquetry, Allegorical Figures On Door, 42 In. 7475.00
Brewster & Ingrahams, Shelf, Gothic, Mahogany, 1840s, 20 In. 935.00
Burr & Chittenden, Wall, Painted Pillars, Mirror, Original Papers 250.00
C. & L.C. Ives, Triple Decker, Wooden Dial, Original Finish 3300.00
C. Boardman, Steeple, Reverse Painted Door, Balloon Ascension, 20 In. 440.00
C. Jerome, Mantel, Mahogany Veneer, Ogee, 26 x 15 1/2 In. 154.00
Caldwell, Enamel Dial, Drum-Shaped Case, Torch & Quiver, Bronze, 14 In. 1380.00
Canterbury Westminster, Walnut, Auxiliary Movement 120.00
Carey, Sheraton, Mirror Bottom, Frame 8250.00
Carriage, Enamel Dial, Floral Swags, Blue Ground, French, Brass, c.1900, 7 In. 3450.00
Carriage, Glazed Case, French, Brass, 4 1/2 In. 207.00
Carriage, Musical, Enamel Sides, Amethystine Cabochons, Gilt, 7 In. 2070.00
Carriage, Panels Of Figures, Enamel & Brass, French, 5 1/2 In. 1610.00
Carriage, Porcelain Face, Beveled Glass, Brass, 3 3/4 In. 71.50
Carriage, Swing Handle, Brass Case, 7 In. 382.00
Cartel, Edwardian, Inlaid Satinwood, 29 In. 2013.00
Cartel, Enamel Numerals, Figure Of Venus & Cupid On Case, Bronze, 38 In. 5750.00
Cartel, Roman Numerals, Gilt Bronze, Rococo, Pendulum, France, 1760, 27 x 13 In. 7475.00
Chauncey Goodrich, Cottage, Rosewood, c.1845, 15 In. 302.00
Chelsea, Mantel, Ship's Bell Strike, Bronze, c.1926, 33 x 17 In. 9500.00
Chelsea, Ship's, Blue Dolphin, 1926, 29 In. 6050.00
Cloisonne, Oriental Movement, Bronze Rococo Base, 19 3/4 In. 4313.00
Connecticut Clock Co., Ogee, Empire, Mahogany, New York, c.1846, 25 3/4 In. 220.00
Country, Rocking Ship Dial, Mirror, Contrasting Woods 6600.00
Cowboy, Twirling Lariat, Clock Face In Horseshoe, Faux Marble Base 225.00
Cuckoo, Black Forest, Carved Deer Head Crest, 55 x 49 In. 7150.00
Cuckoo, Germany, 1910 .... 175.00
Cuckoo, Musical, Beechwood, Weight Driven, G.G. Berger, 1900, 29 x 21 In. 1610.00
Curtis & Dunning, Banjo, Federal, Giltwood & Eglomise, Vermont, 40 x 10 In. 3220.00
Curtis & Dunning, Banjo, Reverse Painted, Woman, Girl, Gilt, 1830, 34 3/4 In. 575.00
D. Dupuis, Wall, Relief Figures, Dawn, Father Time, Silver Plated, c.1900, 22 In. 1150.00
Desk, Little Black Sambo, Wooden, 3 1/2 x 4 In. 88.00
E. Howard, Banjo, No.1, Paper Instruction Label 5500.00
E. Howard, Banjo, Walnut, Boston, c.1840, 44 In. 1760.00
E. Howard, Marble Face, Wooden Case, Brass Works, Weight, Key & Pendulum, 28 In. .. 1315.00
E. Howard, Regulator, Mahogany, Weight Driven, Pendulum, 1860, 7 Ft. 4600.00
E. & G.W. Bartholomew, Pineapple Finials, Stenciled Face, c.1845 .... 950.00
Eli Terry, Pillar & Scroll, Mahogany & Eglomise, 1816 .... 7150.00
Eli Terry, Pillar & Scroll, Mahogany Veneer, c.1820, 30 1/4 In. 1870.00
Eli Terry, Pillar & Scroll, Reverse Painted Lakeside Scene, Mahogany 3190.00
Elisha Hotchkiss, Reverse Painted River Scene, Eagle At Top, Walnut 895.00
Elliott Westminster, Mantel, Chimes 240.00
Empire, Ebonized Portico, Silvered Dial, Pinwheel Escapement, 23 1/4 In. 6900.00
Figural, 3 Graces, Louis XVI Style, Marble, 1860s, 29 In. 6325.00
Figural, Football Player, With Ball In Hand, Perched Over Round Clock, 1930s 145.00
Figural, Fred Flintstone, Clock In Stomach 775.00
Figural, John Bull, Red, White, Blue, Green & Black Paint, 14 1/2 In. 725.00
Figural, Mystery, Girl, Sphere In Arm, Spelter, Striking, 1900, France, 45 In. 6900.00
Figural, Mystery, Maiden, Holding Sphere, Globe Pendulum, France, 1900, 29 In. 3680.00
Figural, Mystery, Viking, Spelter, Signed G. Omerth, France, 1890, 38 1/2 In. 5750.00
Figural, Putto Riding Dolphin, Louis Philippe, Gilt Bronze, 15 1/2 In. 1265.00
Figural, Salesman With Wagon, Clock On Chest, Painted, Metal, Europe, 16 In. 550.00
Figural, Teddy Roosevelt, Original Paint, c.1915, 10 1/2 x 8 1/2 In. 330.00
Forestville Mfg. Co., Shelf, Acorn 7150.00
French, Nautical, Compass Mounted On Top, 4 Dials 2750.00

Frodsham & Baker, Gothic Castle, Walnut, Quarter Striking, 1850, 20 x 13 In. 4830.00
George Mitchell, Shelf, Classical, Mahogany, Scenic Panel, 1830s, 29 In. 385.00
George Nelson, 12 Metal Rods Around Black Disc, Chromed, 24 In. 690.00
German Gothic, Monk In Doorway Ringing Bell, 28 In. 1760.00
Gilbert, Case, Weight Driven, Glass Side Panels, Wooden, Printed Dial, 51 In. 715.00
Gilbert, Gingerbread, Walnut, 8-Day, Strike Movement, Signed, Paper Dial, 19 In. 120.00
Gilbert, Hanging, Key, Brass Works, Paper Label, Walnut Frame, 16 In. 247.50
Gilbert, Long Branch, Reverse Glass Stencil, Striking, 27 1/2 In. 357.00
Gilbert, Oak, Eastlake 225.00
Gilbert, Queen Bess, Cottage 250.00
Gilbert, Shelf, Reverse Painted Bird, 2 Keys, Walnut, 24 x 14 In. 385.00
Gilbert, Shelf, Walnut, 8-Day 165.00
Gilbert Rohde, Alarm, Black Dots On Face, Wooden Frame, 1933, 8 1/8 In. 3680.00
Gilbert Rohde, Glass Frame, Etched Chapter Ring, Metal Face, 1933, 12 In. 9200.00
Gillett & Johnston, Tall Case, Mahogany, Calendar, Regulator, 1900, 72 In. 4600.00
Globe, Winged Putti, Ormolu, White Marble Base, 1860, 15 x 7 In. 9200.00
H.F. Hewitt, Regulator, Mercury Pendulum, Mahogany, 76 1/2 In.. .... 4600.00
Hahl, Pneumatic, Master, c.1875 .... 2000.00
Handley & Moore, Painted Metal Face, Time & Strike, 1780s, 16 1/2 In. 1100.00
Houdebine, Mantel, Greco Roman Revival, Brass Face, Key, Gilt Metal, 16 In. 4675.00
Houghton, Tall Case, George III, Mahogany, Moon Phase Dial 2310.00
Howard, Regulator, Figure 8 .... 2640.00
Howard, Regulator, Railroad Depot, Model 89 .... 7000.00
Howard & Co., Regulator, Oak, Figure-8 Design, 19th Century, 44 In. 2640.00
I. Hough, 8-Day, Strike & Alarm, Label, With Directions 150.00
Ingraham, Admiral Dewey, Eagle Pendulum 700.00
Ingraham, Banjo, 1890, Large 395.00
Ingraham, Calendar, Lyric, Oak Case 400.00
Ingraham, Date, Printed Dials, Lower Window Day Of Week, 22 In. 468.00
Ingraham, Regulator, Scrolled Bonnet, Brass Pendulum, Wall, 38 x 16 x 5 In. 325.00
Ingraham, Regulator, Stained Wood, Impressed Pattern, Octagonal, 25 In. 231.00
Ingraham, Shelf, Steeple Form, Roman Numerals, Mahogany, 16 1/2 In. 110.00
Ithaca, Carved Walnut, Hanging, 19th Century 5000.00
Ithaca, Double Dial, 1880 .... 575.00
J. & A. Jump, Victorian, Chiming, Bracket, Ebonized, Bronze, London, 26 In. 2590.00
J. Barlow, Calendar, Moon & Sun Phases, Second Hand, Mahogany, c.1750 .... 3200.00
J. Laroije-De Joncheere, Napoleon III, Gilt, Gesso, Wall, 48 In. 605.00
J.L. Mitchell, Sessions, Pendulum, Oak, Paper Dial, Weight Driven, 46 In. 264.00
John Cope, 30-Hour, Day Of Month, Upper Bucks County, Pa., c.1830, 94 In. 1800.00
John Moore, Tall Case, George III, Walnut, c.1750, 92 1/2 In. 4600.00
John Murphy, Tall Case 7500.00
John Pyke, George II, Bracket, Black Japanned, c.1750, 20 1/2 In. 3520.00
John Sawin, Banjo, Full Strike, Gilt & Mahogany, 1840s, 33 1/2 In. 3575.00
John Warry, Tall Case, Painted Dial, Rocking Ship, Mahogany, c.1820, 88 In. 6250.00
Josef Hoffmann, Tall Case, Beechwood, 1906, 76 In. 5175.00
Julien Le Roy, Louis XV, Green Horn, Infant Mask Corners, 27 3/4 In. 9200.00
Junghans, Animated, Man On Trapeze, Oak 990.00
Junghans, Enamel Face, Music Box, Alarm, 7 x 6 1/2 In. 170.00
Kienzle, Red & Black Champleve, 2 1/2 x 2 1/2 In. 245.00
Kitchen, 8-Day, Delft Porcelain Face, Key, Pendulum, Germany 72.00
Kitchen, Mammy, Cast Metal 675.00
L. & J.G. Stickley, Mantel, Exposed Pendulum, Oak, c.1912, 22 x 16 In. 8625.00
L. & J.G. Stickley, No. 85, Beveled Top & Base, Copper Face, 22 x 16 In. 7425.00
L. Bottock, Tall Case, Maple Wood, Astronomical, Striking, 1750, 8 Ft. 4 In. 1610.00
L.W. Noyes, Banjo, Mahogany, New Hampshire, c.1832-1838, 60 In. 3300.00
Lantern, Brass, Bell Chime, Whittemore Blair & Co., New Orleans .... *Illus* 725.00
Le Coultre, Lamppost, Windup, 8-Day, Gold Plated 350.00
Lowell Senter, Tall Case, Astronomical Regulator 2750.00
Lux, Alarm, Open Gear 25.00
Lux, Animated Alarm, Man Sitting At Fireplace, Woman Spinning, 5 In. 65.00
Lux, Animated Black Man Shines Woman's Shoe As Clock Ticks 65.00
Lux, Animated Cat's Eyes & Tail, 1930 .... 275.00
Lux, Animated Church With Bell 325.00

Left to right: Clock, Mantel, Ship's Quarter Deck, Bronzed, France, c. 1900, 11 1/2 In.
Clock, Mantel, Sailors, 8-Day, Marble, Gilt Metal, France, c. 1900, 15 In.
Clock, Mantel, Napoleon, Cannon, Ormolu, France

Lux, Animated, People Drinking Beer, 1930s	200.00
Lux, Blue & White Checkerboard, Pendulette	95.00
Lux, Cuckoo, Linden, Germany	60.00
Lux, Cuckoo, Miniature	40.00
Lux, Happy Face, 1960s	50.00
Lux, Keebler, Bobbing Bird	40.00
Lux, Mack & Jack, 1942	295.00
Lux, Schmoo, Light Blue, 1950s, Box	585.00
Lux, Shoeshine Boy	395.00
Lyre, Oscillating, Giltwood, Stepped Black Marble Plinth, France, 1850, 54 x 18 In. .	5750.00
Mantel, Automaton, Iron-Clad Ship, 8-Day, Gilt Metal, 1900, France, 15 In.	9200.00
Mantel, Automaton, Lighthouse, Silvered & Gilt Metal, France, 1900, 12 In.	3910.00
Mantel, Automaton, Locomotive, Bronze, Barometer, Thermometer, France, 17 In. ...	6325.00
Mantel, Beehive, Metal, Mother-Of-Pearl, Lacquered, 16 x 8 1/2 In.	357.00
Mantel, Beehive, Mother-Of-Pearl, Lacquer, Metal, Terry & Andrews, 16 In.	387.00
Mantel, Brass, Time & Strike, Enameled Face, Pendulum, France, 1900, 11 In.	550.00
Mantel, Calendar, Brass, 4-Glass, Day & Month, Striking, Pendulum, France, 16 In. .	2530.00
Mantel, Canon, Silvered, 8-Day, Red Marble Base, France, 1900, 5 In.	1035.00
Mantel, Cupid & Pysche, Arched Case, Red Marble, Bronze, France, 30 In.	6900.00
Mantel, Dial Within Domed Columnar Case, Porcelain, c.1845, 14 In.	165.00
Mantel, Drum Shape, Patinated Bronze, Classical Bust, Regency, Early 1800s, 12 In.	2300.00
Mantel, Egyptian Revival, Bronze Heads & Trim, 2-Tone Marble	4000.00
Mantel, Egyptian Scenes, Arabs & Camels, Teardrop Case, Restored, 1875	400.00
Mantel, Eiffel Tower, Bronze, Enamel, Japy Freres Movement, 1910s, 41 In.	1840.00
Mantel, Embracing Couple, Gilt Bronze, c.1840, 19 1/2 x 14 1/4 In.	990.00
Mantel, Empire Style, Black Marble, Ormolu, Pendulum, Key, c.1850, 16 In.	440.00
Mantel, Empire, Surround Of Palmettes, Sleeping Child, 1830s, 14 1/2 In.	5463.00
Mantel, Figural Scenes, Continental Style, Enamel, Champleve, 20th Century	550.00
Mantel, Figural, Greek Archer, Laurel Wreath Frame, Bronze, Pons, c.1823, 26 In. ...	1760.00
Mantel, George III, Mahogany, Inlaid, Late 19th Century, 16 1/4 In.	330.00
Mantel, Gilt Bronze, Onyx, Enameled Dial, France, 1900, 16 1/2 In.	880.00
Mantel, Gilt Spelter, Girl, Standing, Conical Pendulum, Marble, 1885, France, 23 In.	5750.00
Mantel, H & L, Cattle Scene, 1890	1250.00
Mantel, Josef Maria Olbrich, Metal, Jugendstil Foliage, Stylized, 1862, 8 In.	3910.00
Mantel, Le Boutillier & Co., Paris, Marble, c.1880, 14 1/2 In.	550.00
Mantel, Mahogany, 4-Glass, Striking, Pendulum, France, 1800, 17 3/4 In.	1610.00
Mantel, Napoleon, Cannon, Ormolu, France .... *Illus*	2860.00
Mantel, Neo-Classical, Patinated, Gilt Bronze, Venus, Scallop Shell, France, c.1840 .	880.00
Mantel, P. Mantin & Luzarche, Gilt Bronze, Maiden At Shrine, Paris, c.1850	605.00
Mantel, Perpetual Calendar, 4-Glass, Striking, Red Marble, France, 1875, 20 In.	9775.00
Mantel, Perpetual Calendar, Black & Red Marble, France, 1880, 13 1/2 x 12 In.	1150.00
Mantel, Perpetual Calendar, Black Marble, Striking, France, 1875, 17 x 28 In.	920.00

Mantel, Porcelain, Floral, Scrolling Shape, Key, Pendulum, France, 12 In. 770.00
Mantel, Portico Form, Restauration, Inlaid Walnut, Ormolu, 19th Century, 19 In. 605.00
Mantel, Raingo, Patinated Bronze, Black Marble, Biblical Prophet, Paris, 24 In. 660.00
Mantel, Regulator, Urn Form Finial, Floral Dial, Brass & Glass, 18 In. 660.00
Mantel, Sailors, 8-Day, Marble, Gilt Metal, France, c.1900, 15 In. .... *Illus* 9200.00
Mantel, Seaman In His Dory, Rock Base, Entitled Rescue, Gilt Metal, 26 1/2 In. 242.00
Mantel, Ship's Quarter Deck, Bronzed, France, c.1900, 11 1/2 In. .... *Illus* 13225.00
Mantel, Silvered Face, Arabic Chapters, Mahogany, 26 x 11 1/2 In. 80.00
Mantel, Windmill, Automaton, 8-Day, Barometer, Thermometer, France, 1900, 16 In. 3220.00
Markwick & Markham, Table, George III, Bob Pendulum, Brass, 7 1/2 In. 1150.00
MasterCrafters, Motion, Falls 90.00
MasterCrafters, Motion, Fire 70.00
Milliken, Tall Case, Chippendale, Mahogany 3800.00
Musical, Apollo In Chariot, Ebonized Mahogany, 1870s, 23 3/4 In. 9200.00
Napoleon III, Dial Within Vase, Flanked By Rams Heads, Gilt Bronze, 27 In. 1725.00
New Haven, Alarm, Gold Bird Design, 8-Day, Oak 200.00
New Haven, Alarm, Gold Flower Vase Design, Oak 200.00
New Haven, Banjo, 8-Day, Gilt Metal Eagle Finial, Label, 24 3/4 In. 88.00
New Haven, Mantel, Chateau, 8-Day, Brass Works, Marbleized Iron, Hour Strike, 10 In. 45.00
New Haven, Mantel, Occidental, 8-Day, Gong Alarm, Walnut, 24 In. 275.00
New Haven, School, Long Drop, Strike & Calendar, Oak Case 450.00
New Haven, Steeple, Alarm, 30-Hour, 8-Day, Reverse Painting 200.00
New Haven, Steeple, Painted Leaf Pattern On Glass 125.00
New Haven, Veined White Onyx Portico, 7 3/4 In. 88.00
Phinney Walker, Travel, Box 8.50
Picture, Woman, With Mandolin, Mechanical, Metal, Pat. 1886, Round, 4 1/4 In. 495.00
Pillar & Scroll, Mahogany, Painted Scene, Probably S.E. Pa., 32 In. .... *Illus* 6800.00
Pratt & Frost, Pillar & Scroll, Mahogany, 35 In. 85.00
Railroad, Pendulum, Bureau Of Standards Certified Railroad Time, 64 In. 2000.00
Regulator, Empire, Brass Trim, Gilded Letters, Standard Time, 66 1/4 In. 962.00
Regulator, Reverse Painted Gold Lettering, Paper Dial, Wooden, 22 In. 121.00
Rotary, 3 Graces Supporting Urn, Putti At Top, Gilt Bronze, 21 In. 4025.00
Rotary, Dial In Urn, 4 Column Supports, Marble Base, Gilt Bronze, 19 In. 4025.00
Rotary, Louis XVI Style, Dial In Urn, Wrapped With Snake, Porcelain, 16 In. 6325.00
S.F. Smith & Son, Mantel, Brass Inlay, Anchor Escapement, Rosewood, 29 1/2 In. .. 1380.00
Samuel Abbot, Lower Mirror, 33 1/2 x 17 1/4 In. 2365.00
Samuel Ritchie, Tall Case, Grandmother Size, 1815 .... 2600.00
Sessions, Banjo, Strikes Bim Bam, Octagonal Top 165.00
Sessions, Kitchen, Chef Shape, c.1940 .... 65.00
Sessions, Kitchen, Teapot Shape, Wall 7.50
Sessions, Mantel, Art Deco, Spelter Eagles 160.00
Sessions, Regulator, Wooden, Stenciled Dial, Second Hand, 38 In. 248.00
Sessions, Tall Case, Dovetailed Bonnet, Wooden Face, Eagle, Walnut, 90 In. 4180.00
Sessions, Wooden Boat Shape, Metal Sails, 1940s 85.00
Seth Thomas, 8-Day, Time & Strike, 1930s 225.00
Seth Thomas, Boat, Blued Steel Hour, Double Wind, Hinged Face, Brass Case 340.00
Seth Thomas, Calendar, Hanging, Mahogany Veneer, Pat. 1876, 30 In. 990.00
Seth Thomas, Calendar, Shelf, Walnut, Striking, 1879, 24 x 15 1/4 In. 920.00
Seth Thomas, Candlestick Timepiece, Under Dome, Porcelain Dial, 10 3/4 In. .... ·330.00
Seth Thomas, Carriage, Glazed Case, Enameled Arabic Dial, 11 In. 315.00
Seth Thomas, Dresser, Windup, Tempus Fugit 25.00
Seth Thomas, Empire Style, 2 Columns, Lion Mask Ring Handles, 10 x 12 1/2 In. .. 45.00
Seth Thomas, Empire, Shelf, Glass & Brass Case, Porcelain Face 495.00
Seth Thomas, Mantel, Marbleized 270.00
Seth Thomas, Pillar & Scroll, Federal, Mahogany, c.1818, 29 In. 4125.00
Seth Thomas, Pillar & Scroll, Glazed Door, Eglomise Panel, Mahogany, 25 In. 287.00
Seth Thomas, Pillar & Scroll, Wooden Works, Reverse Painted Glass, 29 In. 605.00
Seth Thomas, Regulator, Crystal, Brass Case, Hour & Half-Hour Strike, 10 In. 165.00
Seth Thomas, Regulator, Walnut, 19th Century, 36 1/2 In. 715.00
Seth Thomas, Shelf, Mahogany Veneer, Reverse Painting, No Weights, 25 In. 170.00
Seth Thomas, Stained Wood, Finial, Pendulum, Stenciled Dial, 30-Day, 39 In. 286.00
Seth Thomas, Time & Strike, Porcelain Design, Marble, 1887 .... 525.00
Seth Thomas, Time & Strike, Porcelain Dial, Open Escapement, Marble, 1890 .... 525.00

Clock, Pillar & Scroll, Mahogany, Painted
Scene, Probably S. E. Pa. , 32 In.

Clock, Tall Case, Hagey, Cherry,
Night Alarm, 1810, 95 In.

Seth Thomas, Tower, Milk Glass Face, 1890s 6500.00
Seymour Williams & Porter, Pillar & Scroll, Mahogany, 33 In. 258.00
Shreve & Co., Traveling, Chased Silver, Dragon Design, Japan, 5 x 4 x 1 1/2 In. 302.00
Smith Patterson, Tall Case, Painted, Swan Neck, Chiming, 1910, 100 In. 6900.00
Spartus, Electric, Wall, Tiger, Blinking Eyes 45.00
Steeple, Mahogany Veneer, Reverse Painted Scene, Washington's Rock, N.J., 20 In. . 137.00
Sunbeam, Garfield, Electric 20.00
Table, Chiming, Ebonized, Brass Mounted, c.1875, 28 In. 2875.00
Tall Case, Arts & Crafts, Arabic Numerals, Weights, Oak, 1910, 75 In. 585.00
Tall Case, Arts & Crafts, Oak, 8-Day, 1/2 Hour Striking, Cupboard Base, 76 In. 1035.00
Tall Case, Brass Face, Ivory Numerals, Bird Design 325.00
Tall Case, Brass Pull-Up Movement, Walnut, Pennsylvania, c.1750, 91 In. 3025.00
Tall Case, C. Croll, Brass Works, Silvered Face, Inlay, Mahogany, 82 3/4 In. 1870.00
Tall Case, Cherry, Roxbury Style, Bonnet Door, Banded Inlaid, 92 In 6160.00
Tall Case, Fra Della Ball, Mahogany, 18th Century, England 5500.00
Tall Case, Francis Pile, Honiton, George III, Oak, Late 18th Century, 81 In. 1100.00
Tall Case, George III Style, Mahogany, Arched Pediment, Moon Phase Dial 2530.00
Tall Case, George III, Oak, Painted Dial, Hargrave, Sleaford, 76 3/4 In. 1540.00
Tall Case, George IV, Mahogany, Broken Arch Pediment, Moon Phase Dial, 1780 ..... 1540.00
Tall Case, Georges Menard, Limed Oak, Art Moderne, 1940, 82 x 21 x 13 1/2 In. 1725.00
Tall Case, Georgian, Provincial, Painted Dial, 30-Hour, Otelli, Buckingham, 1780 .... 880.00
Tall Case, Gothic Revival, Astronomical Dial, Mahogany, 110 In. 7700.00
Tall Case, Hagey, Cherry, Night Alarm, 1810, 95 In. .... *Illus* 14500.00
Tall Case, Herschede, Musical, Moon Dial, 9 Tubes, 3 Weights, c.1920 .... 6750.00
Tall Case, Jacob Hostell, Molded Overlapping Door, Bonnet, Walnut, 87 In. 3795.00
Tall Case, John Bayley, Painted Dial, Flame Birch 4400.00
Tall Case, John Murphy, Country Chippendale, Painted Case, 30-Hour 3500.00
Tall Case, Jonathan Winslow, Black & Gold Painted, c.1810, 48 In. 7700.00
Tall Case, Mahogany, Broken Arch, 78 In. 3250.00
Tall Case, Mahogany, Gothic Broken Arch Hood, England, 1815, 80 In. 7475.00
Tall Case, Mahogany, Moon Phase, Chas. Campbell, 1780, 85 In. 6600.00
Tall Case, Mahogany, Regulator, Barometer, Thermometer, Scotland, 71 In. 4370.00
Tall Case, Matthew Gemmel, Gothic Revival 6050.00
Tall Case, Michael Strieby, Cherry, 30-Hour, Greensburg, Penn., c.1800, 95 In. 5400.00
Tall Case, Moon Phase Dial, 5 Tubular Chimes, 3 Brass Weights, 1940s, 85 In. 1200.00
Tall Case, Oak, Deer & Floral, Hand Painted Face, England 1430.00
Tall Case, Peter Miller, Walnut, Painted Floral Designed Metal Face 4750.00
Tall Case, Rhode Island, Fluted Columns, Inlaid Base, Brass Moon Phase Dial 4675.00
Tall Case, Riley Whiting, 34-Hour Wooden Movement, c.1830, 88 In. 2200.00
Tall Case, Thomas Jones, George III, Mahogany, Pagoda, Painted Dial 4125.00
Tall Case, Thomas Wagstaff, Walnut, Brass Face, 18th Century 3190.00

Clock, Torpedo, Brass, Automaton, France, c. 1900, 6 x 17 In.

◆◆◆◆◆◆◆◆◆◆◆◆◆◆◆◆◆◆◆◆◆

Clean a clock face
as seldom as pos-
sible. The brass trim
may be coated with
colored lacquer, and
brass polish will re-
move the color.

◆◆◆◆◆◆◆◆◆◆◆◆◆◆◆◆◆◆◆◆◆

Tall Case, Walnut, Quarter Columns, 8-Day, Day Of Month, c.1810, 89 In. 6250.00
Tall Case, Walter Durfee, Chippendale, Mahogany, Columns, 19th Century, 99 In. 4675.00
Tall Case, Wm. Alston, William IV, Fluted Case, Mahogany, 80 In. 5290.00
Telechron, Alarm, Brass Front, Cut Deco Numbers, Second Hand, Electric 11.00
Telechron, Cathedral Style, Cream Colored 45.00
Telechron, Red Plastic Bubble Dome, Spaceship Type 40.00
Terry, Pillar & Scroll, Wooden Works, Mantel, c.1830 .... 650.00
Thomas Hunter, George II, Bracket, Ebonized, Acorn Finials, London, 20 x 11 In. ... 3450.00
Thomas Lindsay, Tall Case, Federal, Inlaid Mahogany, 1810 .... 6050.00
Tiffany clocks are listed in the Tiffany category
Torpedo, Brass, Automaton, France, c.1900, 6 x 17 In. .... *Illus* 3220.00
Travel, Brass, Glass, Time & Strike, Key, France, 20th Century, 5 1/8 In. 385.00
Travel, His & Her, Bakelite 20.00
Travel, Tortoiseshell, Octagonal 132.00
True Time Tellers, Wall, New Haven, 14 x 14 In. 225.00
Van Aken, Tall Case, Dutch Baroque, Automaton Dials, Burl Walnut, 100 In. 6050.00
Vienna Regulator, Enameled Dial, Time & Strike, 3 Weights, Mahogany, 42 In. 3850.00
Wag-On-Wall, Wooden Face, Flowers & House, Brass Gears, 19 1/2 In. 467.50
Wall, Comtoise, 1/4 Hour Striking, 4 Bells, Brass Dial, France, 1820, 17 3/4 x 11 In. 2300.00
Wall, Louis XVI Style, Roman Numerals, Rocaille Molded Frame, Gilded, 35 In. 1210.00
Wall, Walnut, Year-Type, Pendulum, Germany, 1900, 58 1/2 x 21 1/2 In. 2185.00
Waterbury, Mantel, Glass Front & Back, See-Through Base 195.00
Waterbury, Regulator, Jeweler's, Glazed Door, Brass Weight, Pendulum, 80 In. 3300.00
Waterbury, Regulator, Oak, Pressed Design, Printed Dial, 46 In. 176.00
Waterbury, Regulator, Stained Oak, Painted Dial, Date Hand, 31 In. 357.00
Waterbury, Regulator, Stained Oak, Printed Dial, 30-Day, 31 In. 330.00
Waterbury, Regulator, Stained Wood, Replaced Pendulum, Octagonal, 32 In. 176.00
Welch, Dickens, Alarm, 1/2 Hour Striking, 8-Day 200.00
Welch, No. 2, Regulator, Rosewood Veneer, Painted Dial, 19th Century, 55 x 25 In. ... 1540.00
Welton, Ogee, Empire, Mahogany, 26 1/2 In. 145.00
Westclox, Alarm, Art Deco, Light Flashing 55.00
Westclox, Alarm, Yellow Celluloid 55.00
Western Horse, 1950s 45.00
Westinghouse, With Sign, Light-Up, 48 In. 75.00
Westminster Chime, Palladian Style, Anchor Escapement, Oak, 1870s, 23 1/2 In. 1380.00
Whiting, Banjo, Acorn Finial, Reverse Painted, Mt.Vernon, Mahogany, 33 In. 1430.00
Willard, Banjo, Federal, Gilt & Mahogany, Signed, Boston, Mass., c.1815, 41 In. 1100.00
Willard, Banjo, Federal, Mahogany Inlay, Boston, Mass., c.1815, 33 In. 2750.00
Willard, Banjo, Federal, Mahogany, Alarm, 1820s, 29 In. 2530.00
Willard, Banjo, Gilt & Mahogany, c.1815, 33 1/2 In. 1650.00
Willard, Banjo, Painted Dial, Acorn Finial, Eglomise Cottage, Mahogany, 32 In. 1495.00
Willard, Double Case, Arched Hood, Brass Finial, Enamel Dial, Mahogany, 28 In. 4600.00

CLOISONNE enamel was developed during the tenth century. A glass enamel
was applied between small ribbons of metal on a metal base. Most cloisonne
is Chinese or Japanese. Pieces marked *China* are twentieth-century examples.

Ashtray, Red Floral, White Cloud Ground, 2 Rests, China, 4 1/2 In. 26.00

Bowl, Scalloped Rim, 17 1/2 In.	395.00
Bowl, Stylized Flowers, Silver-Gilt, Gustave Klingert, Moscow, 1891, 3 1/2 In.	862.50
Bowl, White Flowers, Leaf Border, Turquoise Interior, Teak Stand, 4 3/8 In.	28.00
Box, Cover, Allover Floral, Black Ground, 3 1/2 x 4 1/2 In.	125.00
Box, Cover, Hen With Chick On Back, China, Late 19th Century, 6 In., Pair	165.00
Box, Cover, Roses On Celadon Ground, Silver, Japan, 1900, 5 1/2 x 4 In.	770.00
Box, Hinged Cover Floral Spray, Yellow Curlicue Ground, Ball Footed, 3 1/2 In.	35.00
Charger, Birds & Prunus Tree, Japan, 19th Century, 25 In.	1870.00
Charger, Peony, Daisy & Lily, Gray Ground, Medallions, 13 In.	275.00
Charger, Raven, Finches, Peonies, Leaves, Japan, Meiji Period, 24 In.	357.50
Compote, Geometric Bands, Stylized Florals, Pedestal, Champleve, 8 1/4 In.	175.00
Drinking Cup, Elephant Head, Dark Green, China, 5 3/8 In.	518.00
Egg, Double-Headed Eagle, Silver-Gilt, N. Zverev, Moscow, c.1900, 5 1/2 In.	1265.00
Figurine, Dragon, Polychrome Scrolls, Coiled Tail, 5-Toed Feet, China, 13 In., Pair	825.00
Figurine, Foo Dog, Peacock Blue, 19th Century, 29 In.	3000.00
Jar, Finial Cover, Dragon, 5 1/4 In.	82.00
Jar, Flowers & Butterfly, 4 1/2 x 3 In.	93.00
Jar, Geometric Floral, Blue Shades, Olive Tan Ground, China, 7 1/2 In., Pair	110.00
Lamp, Elephant Handles, Floral, Rosewood Base, Champleve, 24 In.	120.00
Napkin Ring, Berries, Flowers, Geometric Black Ground, Pair	45.00
Plaque, Fuji Dragon Ascending From Waves, 9 x 14 In.	1950.00
Plaque, Oriental Birds, Black Trim, Pink, 12 In.	395.00
Plate, Floral, Plique-A-Jour, Stand, Fitted Box, 6 In.	71.50
Teapot, Butterflies, Gold Stone, 4 In.	225.00
Teapot, Turquoise Band, Black Ground, c.1910, 6 In.	82.50
Vase, Baluster Form, Birds & Flowers, Black Ground, 7 1/2 In.	330.00
Vase, Baluster Form, Iris & Stork Design, 7 1/2 In.	220.00
Vase, Baluster Form, Writhing Dragon, Green Ground, 7 1/2 In.	145.00
Vase, Chrysanthemums, Foliage, Red Flowers, Japan, 8 5/8 In., Pair	495.00
Vase, Flowers, Black Ground, Fishscale Base, Wooden Stand, 4 x 2 5/8 In.	22.00
Vase, Flowers, Green, 5 1/8 In.	93.00
Vase, Melon Shape, Floral Reserves, Silver Rim, c.1900, 6 In.	247.50
Vase, Peacock Shape, China, 18th Century, 17 1/2 In.	275.00
Vase, Pink Goldfish, Yellow, Sato, 6 In.	275.00
Vase, Polychrome Flowers & Buddhas, Blue Ground, 15 3/4 In.	247.50
Vase, Yellow & Pink Goldfish, Sato, 6 In.	275.00
Wall Pocket, Scrolling Flowers, Turquoise Ground, Qianlong, China, 6 1/4 In.	605.00

CLOTHING of all types is listed in this category. Dresses, hats, shoes, underwear, and more are found here. Other textiles are to be found in the Coverlet, Quilt, Textile, and World War I and II categories.

Apron, Dimity, Pink, Pale Blue Lace, Applied Flowers	6.50
Apron, Hostess, Aqua Silk, White Lace Edge, Souvenir Of France, Patch Pocket	12.00
Apron, Hostess, Crocheted, White, Lace Corners, Ribbon Waistband, Pocket	6.00
Apron, Louis Wethersfield, Vt., Masonic, Silk, Ribbon Bound, 1825, 16 x 13 In.	192.00
Bathrobe, Beacon, Geometric Pattern, Blue, Orange & Black	90.00
Bathrobe, Blanket, Rayon Rope, Tassel Belt, 1930s	50.00
Bed Jacket, Pink Floral, Pink Rayon, Eyelet Lace, Puffed Sleeves, 1940s	8.50
Bed Jacket, Rose, Rayon, Long Sleeves, Ruffled Yoke, Countess Layne, 1940s	8.50
Belt, Gilt & Silver, Rhinestones, Diamonds & Faux Pearl Drops, Chanel	1725.00
Belt, Silver Link Chain, Whiting & Davis	16.00
Belt, Snake Chain, Elasticized, Silver, 27 In.	1.50
Blouse, Aqua, Rayon, Button Down Back, Short Sleeves, Embroidered, 1940s	3.00
Blouse, Beaded, Blue & White, 1912, Size 10	100.00
Blouse, Beaded, Gold Satin, Scoop Neck, Sleeveless, 2-In. Border	32.00
Blouse, Crocheted, Orange, Long Sleeves, Scalloped, See-Thru, Drawstring Neck	10.00
Blouse, Persimmon, Rayon, Long Sleeves, V Neck, Pleated Panels, Wardles, 1940s	5.00
Blouse, Sequins, Pastel, Horizontal Stripes, Sleeveless, Stephen O'Grady, Size 20	16.00
Bonnet, Baby's, White Silk, 1910	3.00
Bonnet, Black, 1850-1860	155.00
Bonnet, Child's, Crocheted, Off White, Fishnet, Scalloped Edge	4.00
Bonnet, Child's, Poke, White, Ruffled	45.00
Bonnet, Velvet, Black, Ruffled, Red Velvet Flowers, Blue Plumes, 1880s	95.00

Boots, Go-Go, Black, Shiny, Unused, Size 5 1/2 .... 25.00
Boots, Go-Go, Calf High, Vinyl, White, Mondrian Pattern, Black, Red & Blue. 403.00
Boots, Woman's, Red, White & Blue Checked, Red Laces, Heels, 1960s, Size 8 .... 35.00
Bra, Ivory Lace & Net, Peach Ribbon, Label, Fem-Lin Brassiere, Pat. 1920 .... 86.00
Bra, Straw Padded, 1860 .... 65.00
Camisole, Crocheted, Off White, Flower & Leaf Pattern, V Neck, 38 x 10 1/2 In. 12.00
Camisole, Peach, Nylon Tricot, Thin Straps, Drawstring Top 2.00
Cape, Crocheted, Light Blue Wool, Checkerboard, Tassel Tie, 1940s 18.00
Cape, Mink, Blond, Arm Slits, Lined, Short 125.00
Cape, Opera, Victorian, Beaded 55.00
Cloche, Beige, Velvet, Pins 75.00
Cloche, Flapper, Crocheted, Purple Banding 35.00
Coat, Baby's, 1902, 25 In. 75.00
Coat, Brocade Velvet, Victorian 150.00
Coat, Evening, Black Velvet, Sequined Hood, c.1920 .... 130.00
Coat, Evening, Liberty & Co., 1920s 747.00
Coat, Evening, Vinyl, Blue, White Knit Lining, White Mink Trim, Gres Label, 1960s   258.00
Coat, Man's, Raccoon, 1920s, Large 350.00
Coat, Morning, Man's, Paisley, 1870s 150.00
Coat, Opera, Black Satin, Black Lace Trim, Worth, 1920s 690.00
Coat, Touring, Beige Linen, Long 45.00
Coat, Velvet, Deep Green, Fitted Waist, Self Belt, Large Lapels 22.00
Collar, Crocheted, Ecru, Fine Thread, Rosettes, 8 In. 2.50
Collar, Crocheted, Fishnet, White, Ruffled, Threaded, Black Velvet Ribbon, 4 x 15 In.   5.00
Collar, Mink, Medium Brown, 16 x 2 1/2 In. 7.00
Collar, Muskrat, Brown, 7 x 34 In. 8.00
Collar, Pearls, Divided Front, Ajustable Hook Closure Back, 13 In. 8.00
Collar, Raccoon, 42 x 6 1/2 x 1/2 In. 10.00
Collar, White Cotton, Crescent, 1-In. Scalloped Lace Edge, 2 Sections 2.00
Collar & Cuffs, Ecru, Knotted & Netted, Unbroken Circle, 17 In. 6.50
Corset, Salesman's Sample 45.00
Crinoline, Nylon Net, 3 Tiers, Ivory On Ivory, Barbizon Pettisweet, 1950s 7.50
Cuff, Crocheted, Off White, 4 In., Pair 2.00
Cuff, Woman's, Victorian, Scenic Box, Dated 1887, 4 Pair 59.00
Dickey, Gold Sequins, Sheet Black, Rayon, Ruffled, V Neck 5.00
Dickey, Nylon Organza, White, Lace Edge, Ruffle 2.50
Dickey, White Eyelet, Bib Front, Long Pointed Collar, Scalloped Lace, 13 In. 3.50
Dress, Baby's, Jacket, Presentation, Embroidery & Ribbon, Box, 1920s 35.00
Dress, Baby's, White Cotton, Scalloped Edge, Eyelet Front, Sleeveless 5.00
Dress, Baby's, White Cotton, Tucks, Cutwork, Pearl Buttons, 21 In. 110.00
Dress, Baby's, White Linen, Lace Hem, 1910 .... 5.00
Dress, Beaded, Black, 1910, Size 12 .... 85.00
Dress, Beaded, Brown, 1912, Size 8 .... 100.00
Dress, Black, Faille, Narrow Skirt, Dolman Sleeves, V Neck, Bow, 1940s 8.00
Dress, Black, Lace Collar, 1920s 25.00
Dress, Black, Rayon Crepe, Boat Neckline, Satin Lining, Cap Sleeves, 1940s 10.00
Dress, Black, Satin, High Scoop, V Back, Side Slips, Floor Length, Size 14 .... 12.00
Dress, Black, Silk Crepe, Red & Ivory Silk Trim, Nina Ricci, 1930s 287.00
Dress, Black, V-shaped Crepe Panels, Fagoting, Vionnet, 1920s 1610.00
Dress, Boutique, Navy Wool, Paddle Shape Flaps, Pierre Cardin, 1960s 3680.00
Dress, Bubble, Black Faille, Elastic & Ribbon Sash, Trigere, 1950s 345.00
Dress, Chiffon, Beige, Face Trim, 1920 .... 55.00
Dress, Child's, Cotton Brocade, Mid-1800s 85.00
Dress, Child's, Maroon & White Calico, 1880-1890 .... 65.00
Dress, Child's, White Organza, Gathered Yoke & Bodice, Lace Collar, France 25.00
Dress, Christening, Civil War Era 55.00
Dress, Country, Figured Cotton, Long Sleeves, 1870 .... 65.00
Dress, Dark Green, Purple Trim At Waist, Dior, Late 1940s 2000.00
Dress, Dinner, Jacket, Navy Wool Knit, Rudi Gernreich, 1972 .... 1725.00
Dress, Dinner, Jewel Embroidered Lace Trim, Black Silk Crepe, Patou, 1930s 1725.00
Dress, Evening, Black Velvet, Train, Traina-Norell, 1930s 1150.00
Dress, Evening, Black Wool, Emerald Green Taffeta, Balenciaga, 1949 .... 7820.00

Dress, Evening, Embroidered, Navy Blue, John Wanamaker 1380.00
Dress, Evening, Matte Jersey, Silver Leather Trim, 1930s 1150.00
Dress, Evening, Short, Embroidered Black Tulle, Camisole Bodice, Sarmi, 1950s 287.00
Dress, Flapper, Lace Over Moire, Floral Design Bottom, 1920s 395.00
Dress, Gaille, E.H. Barrett, 2 Piece, 1880s 315.00
Dress, Gauze, Fortuny, 1910 .... 2760.00
Dress, Girl's, White, Embroidered Flowers Front & Pocket, 1920 .... 4.50
Dress, Green Taffeta & Cut Velvet, 1850s 1725.00
Dress, Jacket, Beaded Floral Neck, Hem & Jacket Edge, 1929 .... 225.00
Dress, Metallic Thread, Sleeveless, Full Skirt, Boat Neckline, 1960s, Size 15 .... 6.00
Dress, Mini, Beaded, Yves Saint Laurent, 1967 .... 6670.00
Dress, Off White Rayon Satin, Slit Slides, Sleeveless, Heart V Neck, Floor Length ... 30.00
Dress, Red, Wool, Pierre Cardin, 1970s 3680.00
Dress, Sheath, Pink, Linen, Sleeveless, Cutwork, Flowers Down Front, Size 18 .... 6.00
Dress, Tea, Gray Pleated Silk, Sleeveless, Glass Beads, Belt, Fortuny 1150.00
Dress, Trapeze, Cherry Red Wool, Slanted Pockets, Yves Saint Laurent, 1950s 405.00
Dress, Velvet Collar & Cuffs, Buttons Down Skirt Front, 1940s 35.00
Dress, Velvet, Embroidered Daisies, Ruffles, Lace, Empire Waist, 1910 .... 85.00 to 120.00
Dress, Wedding, Cream Silk, Lace, Hoop Skirt, 1800s 125.00
Dress, Wedding, Embroidered On Net, Drop Waistline, 1920s, Size 8-10 .... 200.00
Dress, Wedding, Ivory Silk, Lace, Victorian 210.00
Dress, Wedding, Lace, 1911, Size 8-10 .... 250.00
Dress, Wedding, Machine Lace, 1911 .... 250.00
Dress, Wine Red Faille, 1880s, 2 Piece 1725.00
Dress, With 21 Covered Buttons, Gray, Boned Bust, Full Skirt, Bolero Jacket 12.00
Ear Muffs, Child's, Handmade, China, 1800s 25.00
Garters, Men's, Box, 1930s 22.00
Garters, Men's, Leather, Metal & Rubber, Box, 1930s 12.00
Gloves, Crocheted, Lace Trim 20.00
Gloves, Eyelet Cotton, Pink, Embroidered Floral, 10 1/2 In. 2.00
Gloves, Kidskin, Off White, 3 Pearl Buttons, 20 In. 8.50
Gloves, Opera, Silk, Eggshell, Kayser Glove Co., Box & Tissue, 1915 .... 75.00
Gloves, Suede, Black, Washable, Size 6 1/2 .... 5.00
Gown, Ball, Draped Silk, Balmain, 1950s 2300.00
Gown, Ball, Draped Silk, Off-The-Shoulder Straps, Satin Skirt, Balmain, 1950s 2300.00
Gown, Ball, Red Organdy, Lanvin-castillo, 1955 .... 575.00
Gown, Ball, Summer, Organdy, Embroidered Flowers, Jacques Fath, c.1954 .... 1150.00
Gown, Ball, White Faille, Pearls, Rhinestones & Silver Thread, Satin Sash, 1960s 1265.00
Handkerchief, Centennial, Philadelphia Memorial Hall Art Gallery, Frame, 1876 ...... 312.00
Handkerchief, Child's, Embroidered, Children & Day Of The Week, Box, 1930s 25.00
Handkerchief, Embroidered, Scalloped, Box, Switzerland, 1940s 15.00
Handkerchief, Man's, Box, Original Price 10 Cents 10.00
Handkerchief, White, Colored Crocheted Border .... .50
Handkerchief, White, Embroidered Flowers, Fruit Of Loom, Original Card, 2 Piece . 3.00
Hat, Beach 65.00
Hat, Black Feathers Over Felt Form 12.00
Hat, Brushed Beaver, Gold, Brown Leather Banding, Christian Dior 55.00
Hat, Girl's, Black Velvet, Black & Gold Box, 1930s 55.00
Hat, Lace, Black, Velvet Banding, Schiaparelli 55.00
Hat, Man's, Stetson, Leather Hat Band, 1915-1925 .... 265.00
Hat, Picture, Leg Horn, Navy Blue Straw, Apricot Silk Flowers, 1930s 125.00
Hat, Pillbox, Mink, Beige, Allover Swirled Stripes, Sewed On Combs 8.50
Hat, Pull Down, Velvet, Black, Gold Satin Piping, Velvet Flowers, Metallic Lace 120.00
Hat, Ranch Mink 25.00
Hat, Satin, Black, Woven Ribbon, Translucent Flowers, Hattie Carnegie 35.00
Hat, Satin, Pale Orange & Green, On Pale Green Silk, 1920s 125.00
Hat, Sheared Beaver, Black 10.00
Hat, Sombrero, Gold Braid, Stetson, Box 4400.00
Hat, Top, Beaver, Strakburger, Box 125.00
Hat, Top, Collapsible, Silk 64.00
Hat, Top, Spellman Hatter, With Head, Box 750.00
Jacket, Dinner, Black Wool, Gold, Embroidered, Schiaparelli, 1936 .... 4715.00

Jacket, Man's, Pistachio, Herringbone, Pinstripes, Wool, 1950s, Charcross, Size 42 ..   22.00
Jacket, West Point, 1951 ....   50.00
Jeans, 501 Levi 15.00
Muff, Beaver, Brown, Gray Lining & Strap 10.00
Muff, Ranch Mink 35.00
Muff & Mitten Set, Rabbit, White, Satin Lining In Muff 15.00
Nightgown, Child's, White, Embroidered, Tucks 8.50
Nightgown, Cotton, Cap Sleeves, Pink Flowers, Lace V Neck, 1940s 10.00
Over Blouse, Lace, Crepe, Eggshell, 1930s 10.00
Pants, Bell-Bottoms, Leopard Printed, Biba, 1970 ....   373.00
Pants, Toreador, Black Velvet, 1950s, Size 12 .... 12.00 to 15.00
Robe, Child's, Blue & White Homespun Blanket, 1880-1890 ....   85.00
Robe, Court, Embroidered Silk, Salmon Red, Faded, China, 54 In. 137.00
Robe, Green Stamped Velvet, Tan Silk Lining, Fortuny, 1912 ....   2875.00
Robe, Mandarin, Embroidered Panels, Shadowbox Frame, 48 x 40 In. 550.00
Robe, Summer, Woven Dragon Pursuing Pearl & Clouds, Silk, China 920.00
Scarf, Black Lace, Bows, 52 x 13 In. 7.00
Scarf, Black Nylon, Red & White Satin Stitch Flowers, Square, 28 In. 20.00
Scarf, Frontaux Et Cocardes, Horse's Head, Silk, Hermes, 1970s 230.00
Scarf, Light & Dark Purple Plaid, Wool, Open Weave Squares, Fringed, 11 x 47 In. ..   5.00
Scarf, White Silk, Jones Beach, Long Island, Anchor & Sea Horse, 1920s 25.00
Serape, Multicolored Stripes, Hand Woven Wool, Mexican, 1900, 84 x 45 In. 175.00
Shawl, Black Lace, Knotted 5-In. Fringe, 52 x 52 In. 12.00
Shawl, Blue & White, Woven Twill, Checked, Plaid Border 468.00
Shawl, Embroidered, Black, Pink, Yellows, Greens, Long Fringe 95.00
Shawl, Evening, Woven Silver, 1920s 125.00
Shawl, Kashmir, Rosette Center, Surround Of Florals, c.1875, 6 x 6 Ft. 495.00
Shawl, Kashmir, Woven Twill, Patchwork, Square, 75 x 75 In. 467.50
Shawl, Paisley, Hand Embroidered, Rebacked On Black Wool, 63 x 62 In. 220.00
Shawl, Paisley, Red Center, 69 x 69 In. 165.00
Shawl, Paisley, Wool, 67 x 68 In. 77.00
Shawl, Paisley, Wool, Green, Purple, 57 x 128 In. 550.00
Shawl, Paisley, Woven Design, Cream Ground, 60 x 62 In. 104.50
Shawl, Paisley, Woven, Indian, 67 x 68 In. 159.00
Shawl, Piano, Silk, Embroidered Flowers, 1900s 200.00
Shawl, Pierced, Handwoven, Embroidered Borders, Kasmir, c.1860 ....   860.00
Shawl, Silk, Lavender, Green & Gold, Cream Ground, Deep Fringed 165.00
Shawl, Silver Metallic, Large Floral Weave, Triangular, Fringed, 60 x 60 x 76 In. 18.00
Shawl, Silver Strip Embroidered, Egyptian Jewish, 80 In. 120.00
Shawl, Striped Paisley, Kasmir, 1830s 285.00
Shawl, Victorian, Paisley, Red Ground, 120 x 57 In. 185.00
Shirt, Bowling, Ready Kilowatt, Gray 90.00
Shirt, Hawaiian Aloha, Rayon, Coconut Buttons, Multicolor 805.00
Shirt, Hawaiian, Floral, 1950s 35.00
Shoes, Baby's, Black, Pink Leather, High Buttons, 3 Straps 120.00
Shoes, Brown, Lace Up, Heels, 1930s, Small 45.00
Shoes, High Top, Black 24.00
Shoes, High Top, Lace, Brown Leather, Round Cap Toe 28.00
Shoes, Kidskin, Rhinestone Studded, Marcasite Beadwork, c.1920 ....   121.00
Shoes, Open Weave, Black, Heels, 1940s, Medium 65.00
Shoes, Wedding, White Kid, Louis Heel, Instep Button, Size 5 AA 60.00
Shoes, Woman's, Alligator 45.00
Shoes, Woman's, Pumps, Cream Patent Leather, 1950s 110.00
Shoes, Woman's, Silver Lame, Platform, Original Tags, 1960s 50.00
Shoes, Wooden, Heinekin Beer, 1960s, 10 In., Pair 35.00
Slip, Half, White Cotton, Ruffled Lace Edge, Side Button 14.00
Slip, Pink Nylon, Lace, Beige Pleated Edge, Large 3.50
Slippers, Child's, Felt, Unused 20.00
Socks, Baby's, Amish, Pink Wool, Green Stripes, Lancaster County, Pa., 1910 ....   125.00
Socks, Baby's, Amish, Woolen, Yellow Striped Tops, 1940 ....   65.00
Spats, Box 15.00
Spats, Man's, Black Felt, 6 Buttons 6.50

Stockings, Child's, Striped, Blue & Yellow	28.00
Stole, Black Diamond Mink	75.00
Stole, Ranch Mink	125.00
Stole, Silver Fox	100.00
Stole & Muff, Black Fox	75.00
Suit, Ivory Boucle, Wool Braid Trim, Lion's Head Buttons, Chanel, c.1965	805.00
Suit, Navy Wool, Flat Navy Buttons, Adian, 1940s	460.00
Suit, Olive Green, Navy & Yellow Plaid Wool, Mainbocher, 1940s	258.00
Suspenders, Child's, Flame Stitched, Leather Work, 18th Century	750.00
Suspenders, Man's, Evening, White, Rayon Machine Braided Ends	3.00
Sweater, Beaded, Beige Wool, Lined, Flowers at Neck, Waist & Front, Size 42	30.00
Sweater, Beaded, Mother-Of-Pearl Sequined Scrolls, Light Blue, Pearl Buttons	24.00
Sweater, Child's, Wool Crocheted, Pale Blue, Pink, Off White Shells	4.00
Swimsuit, Woman's, Wool, Red & White Striped, 1900s	75.00
Swimsuit, Worsted Wool, Turquoise, 1920-1930	44.00
Tennis Shoes, Man's, Peter Max	575.00
Tie, Man's, Lily Dache	4.00
Tie, Silk, Embroidered Multicolor Flowers, Black, 4 1/2 In. Wide	7.00
Underpants, Blue Nylon-Crepe, Button Side, Appliqued, Lace Trim, Size 34	5.00
Underpants, Child's, White, 1910, Tiny	4.00
Underpants, Pink Silk, Side Button, Lace Edge, Appliqued Chain & Bow	4.00
Uniform, Army, Campaign, Hat, Coat, Trousers, 1890s, 3 Piece	595.00
Vest, Man's, Wedding, Brocade, 1847	150.00
Vest, White Gauze, Fortuny, 1910	2760.00
Vest, Woman's, Battenburg, 1900, Small	75.00

CLUTHRA glass is a two-layered glass with small air pockets that form white spots. The Steuben Glass Works of Corning, New York, made it after 1903. Kimball Glass Company of Vineland, New Jersey, made Cluthra from about 1925. Victor Durand signed some pieces with his name. Related items are listed in the Steuben category.

Vase, Green & White, 4 In.	165.00
Vase, Green & White, Bowl Shape, Green To White, Steuben, 4 1/2 In.	467.50
Vase, Mottled Green, Horizontal Ribs, Flared, Durand & Kimble, 11 3/4 In.	795.00
Vase, Tinted Glass, White Striations, Foil & Bubble, A.J. Couper & Sons, 16 1/4 In.	2070.00
Vase, White, Bubbles, 12 In.	900.00
Vase, White, Pink, 4 1/2 In.	500.00

COALBROOKDALE was made by the Coalport porcelain factory of England during the Victorian period. Pieces are decorated with floral encrustations.

Candlestick, Socket On Horns Of Stag, Square Base, 1980s, 5 1/2 In.	150.00
Urn, Cover, Pierced Lid, Scrolled Handles, 17 In., Pair	880.00
Vase, Raised Flowers, Vignette Of Castle, 12 In.	400.00

COALPORT ware has been made by the Coalport Porcelain Works of England from 1795 to the present time. Early pieces were unmarked. About 1810–1825 the pieces were marked with the name *Coalport* in various forms. Later pieces also had the name *John Rose* in the mark. The crown mark has been used with variations since 1881. The date 1750 is printed in some marks but it is not the date the factory started.

Bough Pot, Gold Ground, Flowers, D Shape, c.1810, 8 3/4 In., Pair	9200.00
Cup & Saucer, Cover, Rosebuds, Yellow Panels, 4 1/2 In.	55.00
Cup & Saucer, Imari Pattern, 6 Sets	275.00
Dessert Set, Gilt Flowers, Cream & Blue Bands, White Ground, c.1850, 50 Piece	605.00
Dessert Set, Kings Pattern, With Silver Demitasse Spoons, 1900, Case	424.00
Fruit Cooler, Cover, Liner, Rock And Tree Pattern, c.1805, 10 1/2 In., Pair	8625.00
Plate, Exotic Birds In Flight, Reticulated, c.1850, 9 1/2 In., 21 Piece	3165.00
Platter, Japan Pattern, Oblong, c.1805, 21 3/8 In.	1495.00
Tea Set, Indian Tree, 19 Piece	185.00
Teapot, Pink & Red Roses, Miniature	85.00
Vase, Church Gresley Pattern, Flaring Cylindrical Neck, c.1805, 8 3/4 In.	1150.00
Vase, Reserves Of Birds & Flowers, Blue Ground, c.1900, 15 In., Pair	632.00

COBALT BLUE glass was made using oxide of cobalt. The characteristic bright dark blue identifies it for the collector. Most cobalt glass found today was made after the Civil War.

Ashtray, Hat, Stippled Border, 4 x 3 In.	7.50
Ashtray, Swirled Rim, 3 Rests, 1 3/4 x 5 In.	12.00
Bowl, Lotus Scallops & Points, Frosted Petals, 7 1/2 x 5 In.	50.00
Bowl, Mica Flecks, Gold Bands, Goblet Shape, 4 5/8 In.	60.00
Box, Cover, Pink Flowers, White Dots, Gold Bands, 2 x 3 In.	55.00
Cheese Plate, Applied Floral Domed Lid, Scalloped, 9 1/4 In.	137.00
Cocktail Shaker, Platinum Rings	100.00
Cruet, Pink Flowers, Green Leaves On Gold, Gold Trim, 6 1/4 In.	85.00
Flask, Roman Emperors, 19th Century, 1/2 Pt., 5 1/2 In.	82.00
Fruit Bowl, Shell Shape, 9 In	55.00
Goblet, Octagonal Footed, Flint, 4 In.	60.00
Holder, Spill, Flutes & Ovals, 2 7/8 In.	27.00
Ice Bucket, Platinum Rings	85.00
Jigger, 6 Panels, 2 1/8 In.	50.00
Jigger, 6 Panels, Pittsburgh, Pa., 2 3/8 In.	30.00
Jigger, 8 Panels, Flint, 2 3/8 In.	60.00
Pitcher, 19 Ribs, Applied Foot & Handle, 4 3/4 In.	302.00
Pitcher, Applied Clear Handle, 8 1/2 In.	189.00
Tankard, Pitcher Shape, Winged Gargoyle Handle, Gold Trim	95.00
Tumbler, 6 Arches & 6 Panels, Flint, 3 3/8 In.	105.00
Tumbler, 8 Panels, Flint, 3 1/4 In.	85.00
Tumbler, Rooster Pattern	100.00
Vase, 5 Blown-Out Horizontal Ribs, Art Deco, 8 1/2 x 5 3/8 In.	68.00
Vase, Cover, Gold Bands & Scroll Designs, 4 1/2 In.	75.00
Vase, Fluted, Footed, 7 x 3 1/4 In.	22.00
Vase, Horizontal Platinum Bands, Flared, 11 5/8 x 6 In.	85.00
Water Set, Robin, 7 Piece	195.00

COCA-COLA was first served in 1886 in Atlanta, Georgia. It was advertised through signs, newspaper ads, coupons, bottles, trays, calendars, and even lamps and clocks. Collectors want anything with the word *Coca-Cola*, including a few rare products, like gum wrappers and cigar bands. The famous trademark was patented in 1893, the *Coke* mark in 1945. Many modern items and reproductions are being made.

Album, Picture, Movies, 1945, 16 Pages, 8 1/2 x 11 In.	47.00
Ashtray, Enjoy Coca-Cola, Gold Lettering, Glass	22.00
Ashtray, Metal Logo Insert, 1950s	22.50
Ashtray, Metal, Red, 1961	6.00
Bag, Insulated, Democratic Convention, Nylon, 1960	40.00
Bag, Stadium, Insulated, Red, 1950s	45.00
Bank, House, 1970s, 5 In.	15.00
Bank, Vending Machine, c.1950, Box	225.00
Banner, 10th Anniversary, 120 x 36 In., 1987	40.00
Barrel, Syrup, Label, 10 Gal.	300.00
Bellhop, Plastic, 6 In., Box	35.00
Billfold, Pigskin, Envelope	138.00
Blotter, 1932, OK, 2 Friends	110.00
Blotter, 1937, Frosty Bottle Picture, Unused	40.00
Blotter, 1938, Policeman, With Bottle, Unused	30.00
Blotter, 1942, Girl On Beach Blanket	35.00
Blotter, 1953, Bottle Cap, Boy With Bottle	15.00
Blotter, 1957, Bottle, 58 Million A Day	10.00
Book, Alphabet, 1928	65.00
Book, Record, Baseball, Schedules, Poem Casey At The Bat, 1910	367.00
Book, When You Entertain, 124 Pages, 1932, 4 x 6 In.	14.00 to 20.00
Bottle, 75th Anniversary, Williamsport, Pa., 1988	20.00
Bottle, 100th Anniversary, Gold Dipped, Velvet Sleeve	175.00
Bottle, 300th Anniversary, Albany, N.Y., 1987	60.00
Bottle, Alexandria, Minnesota, Cola Clan, 1980	70.00

Coca-Cola, Clock, Delicious,
Refreshing, 5 Cents

Coca-Cola, Calendar, 1899,
Cures Headaches, Cardboard,
7 1/4 x 13 In.

Coca-Cola, Sign, Great
Together, Hot Dog, 3-D, 1932

Coca-Cola, Sign, 6-Pack, Die Cut, Tin

Coca-Cola, Tray, 1905, Juanita,
10 x 13 In.

Bottle, Battle Creek, Michigan, Block Letters, Emblem In Center	70.00
Bottle, Birmingham Barons, 1983 Southern League Champs	6.00
Bottle, Birmingham, Alabama, Logo At Base, Clear	20.00
Bottle, Birmingham, Alabama, Straight Sides	30.00
Bottle, Bottling Works, Fall River, Mass., Light Green, 8 Oz.	68.00
Bottle, Brian's Bash, Gilleys, Feb. 1984, Pasadena, Texas	30.00
Bottle, Buffalo, N.Y., Amber	225.00
Bottle, Centerville, Iowa, Raised Star, Square	5.00
Bottle, Everett's Super-Market, Goshen, Ind., 1935-1985	110.00
Bottle, Georgia Bulldog, NCAA National 1 Champions, Athens, 1980	5.00
Bottle, Gold, Scranton, Pa.	25.00
Bottle, Iowa Hawkeyes, Pasadena Tournament Of Roses, 1985	6.00
Bottle, Iowa Hawkeyes, Rose Bowl, Big 10 Champions, 1981	6.00
Bottle, Jacksonville, Florida, Script Logo In Center	35.00
Bottle, Jimmy Carter, 39th President, Ga., 1986	100.00
Bottle, Johnson City, Tennessee, Logo, Dark Amber	50.00
Bottle, Kentucky Derby 110th Run For The Roses, 1984	7.00
Bottle, Montgomery, Ala., New Plant Grand Opening, Red, 1985	30.00
Bottle, Mud Island Park, July 3, 1982, Memphis, Tenn.	7.00

Bottle, Norfolk, Va., Aqua, 6 1/2 Oz. 95.00
Bottle, Paul Bear Bryant, Alabama Crimson Tide, Elephant, 1981 .... 20.00
Bottle, Pittsburgh, Pa., Light Amber 85.00
Bottle, Rochester, N.Y., 8 Sides 40.00
Bottle, Rochester, N.Y., Clear 110.00
Bottle, Salvation Army, Macomb, Ill., July 17-24, 1985 .... 60.00
Bottle, Syrup, Label Under Glass, Red, White & Gold, 1910s 400.00
Bottle, Syrup, Paper Label 202.00
Bottle, Washington Redskins Super Bowl XVII Championship, 1983 .... 30.00
Bottle, Water 125.00
Bottle, Winter Olympic Games, Alpine Skiing, Lake Placid, 1980 .... 6.50
Bottle Cap, Replacement .... .25
Bottle Opener, Drink Coca-Cola, Iron, Pocket 3.50
Bottle Opener, Have A Coke, Drink Coca-Cola, Hand Held, Over-The-Top, 1950 ..... 3.00
Bottle Opener, Wall Mount, Coke, Box 40.00
Bottle Opener, Wall Mount, With Corkscrew, Hanger Hook On Bottom 30.00
Box, Hinged Top, Drink Coca-Cola In Bottles, Wooden, 8 1/2 x 17 1/2 In. 65.00
Buckle, Driver's, Name In Red Enamel, Jim In Center 55.00
Button, Pinback, Drink Coca-Cola In Bottles, Celluloid .... .75
Calendar, 1899, Cures Headaches, Cardboard, 7 1/4 x 13 In. .... *Illus* 4400.00
Calendar, 1910, Hamilton King, 8 3/4 x 11 1/4 In. 650.00
Calendar, 1915, Elaine, June Page, Paper, 13 x 32 In. 2750.00
Calendar, 1917, Constance, With Bottle, Matted, Framed, 26 x 22 In. 578.00
Calendar, 1917, Constance, With Glass 1770.00
Calendar, 1932, Boy On Wall, Holding Coke, Dog, Full Pad 695.00
Calendar, 1935, Boy & Dog, Fishing, Holding Coke, 12 x 24 In. 28.50
Calendar, 1936, N.C. Wyeth, Sailor, Girl, On Boat, 50th Anniversary Cover Sheet 725.00
Calendar, 1937, Farm Boy & Dog, Fishing, Holding Bottles, Full Pad 595.00
Calendar, 1963, Pause That Refreshes 80.00
Calendar Holder, Tin, 1960s 100.00
Camera, Kodak, Happy Times Print, 1970s 150.00
Can, Syrup, Red & Green Label 145.00
Card, Christmas, Toonerville Refreshment Palace, 1930, 3 1/2 x 6 1/4 In. 35.00
Card, Playing, 1939, Red, Box 55.00
Card, Playing, 1958, Box 60.00
Card, Playing, Airplane Spotter, Aircraft Silhouettes, 1943 .... 75.00 to 100.00
Carrier, Aluminum, Red Wooden Handle, Wire Bail 35.00
Carrier, Metal, 6 Pack, 6 Bottles With Contents 48.00
Case, Aluminum, Embossed, 24 Bottle Case 40.00
Chalkboard, 1940, 18 x 26 In. 120.00
Chalkboard, Coke, Fishtail, Logo 225.00
Clock, 1950, Gold Frame, Light-Up, Counter 653.00
Clock, 1960, Light-Up 65.00
Clock, 1970, Berry, Plastic, Battery Operated 30.00
Clock, Delicious, Refreshing, 5 Cents .... *Illus* 35200.00
Clock, Fishtail Logo, Light-Up, Square, 1960s 125.00
Clock, Fluorescent, Drink Coca-Cola, c.1960 .... 95.00 to 125.00
Clock, Light-Up, 1950s, 22 In. 400.00
Clock, Light-Up, Gold Bottle, 1950s 450.00
Clock, Regulator, Coca-Cola In Bottles, 16 x 31 x 5 1/2 In. 1210.00
Clock, Reverse Painted On Glass, Red, White & Yellow 675.00
Clock, The Ideal Brain Tonic, Relieves Exhaustion 6875.00
Clock, Wall, Red & Green, Electric 27.50
Clock, Wood, Reverse Gold Stenciled Lettering, Winsted, Conn., 31 In. 578.00
Coaster, World's Fair, Punch-Out Cardboard, Unused, 1939, 5 x 9 3/4 In. 27.00
Coin-Operated Machine, 10 Cents, Dome Top, Stenciled, 54 In. 743.00
Coin-Operated Machine, Model 39, 10 Cents 1800.00
Coin-Operated Machine, Model 144, Restored, 1950 .... 550.00
Coin-Operated Machine, Vendo 27, Stand 2100.00
Coin-Operated Machine, Vendo 39 .... 600.00
Coin-Operated Machine, Vendo 44 .... 1500.00
Cooler, Airline, Box 245.00
Cooler, Bendon, Round Top, Electrified 385.00

Cooler, Standard, 1939 .... 220.00
Cooler, Under Shelf 175.00
Cooler, Wooden Sliding Doors, English & French Printing, 1923, 28 x 21 x 34 In. 595.00
Cup, Paper, Unused, c.1960 .... 2.00
Dice, Pair 3.50
Dispenser, Cup, Wooden, 1940s 85.00
Display, Frances Dee, Cardboard, Die Cut, 1953 .... 2800.00
Display, Santa Claus, Cardboard, 1948, 7 x 14 In. 40.00
Door Pull, Figural Bottle, Embossed Aluminum, 11 In. 209.00
Door Push, Enjoy Coca-Cola Here, Porcelain 135.00
Earrings, Bottle Cap, Pair 2.50
Fan, Ft. Myers, Fl. 25.00
Fan, San Marcos, Texas, 1950s 50.00
Figurine, Santa Claus, 1987 .... 90.00
Figurine, Santa Claus, Plastic, 5 In., Box 35.00
Flashlight, Miniature Bottle, Box 25.00
Fly Swatter, Advertisement On Handle, Wooden & Mesh, 1942 .... 18.00
Folder, Twas The Night Before Christmas, 1960s, 4 x 8 In. 22.00
Glass, Drink Coca-Cola, Syrup Line, Flared 335.00
Glass, Heritage Series, Spirit Of 1776 .... 5.00
Glass, Tulip, Double Syrup Lines 12.00
Glass, Wimpy, 1975, 6 In. 7.00
Golf Ball, Drink Coca-Cola 23.00
Gum Jar, Lid, Embossed, 4 1/2 x 11 1/2 x 4 1/2 In. 495.00
Handbook, Advertising, 1940s 25.00
Holder, 1 Bottle 18.00
Holder, Shopping Cart, 2 Bottles, 1940s 35.00
Ice Pick 4.00
Ice Scraper, Snowman Shape 1.50
Inkwell, Drawer On Front, Plastic, 3 In. 165.00
Kerchief & Information Folder, Kit Carson, 1950s 105.00
Key Chain, Gold Bottle, 1960s 23.00
Key Chain, Retractable Knife, Red Text & Logo, Kutzig Blades, 1980s, 2 1/4 In. 20.00
Letter Opener, Plastic, 1960s, 8 1/2 In. 4.00
Lighter, Cigarette, Coke 22.00
Lighter, Cooler Shape 36.00
Lighter, Figural, Tin Lithographed Bottle Cap, 1950s 38.00
Lighter, Zippo Style 15.00
Marble, Glass, Bottle On Side, Large 1.50
Match Holder, Beeville Bottling Co. 45.00
Menu Board, Drink Coca-Cola, Metal 175.00
Menu Board, Masonite, 1950s 175.00
Menu Board, With Clock, 1960 .... 65.00 to 75.00
Mirror, Delicious & Refreshing, Pocket, Package 60.00
Mirror, Garden Girl, Photograph Both Sides, 1920s, Pocket 332.00
Mirror, Juanita, 1905, Pocket 275.00
Needle Case, Woman In Fox Stole, Holding Glass, Blue Hat, 1925 .... 85.00
Needle Case, Young Woman, By Pool, Holding Glass, 1924 .... 60.00
Paper Clip, Heart Shape .... .25
Paper Doll, 1950s, Unpunched 8.00
Paperweight, Bottled Purity, Beeville Bottling Co., 1930s 105.00
Paperweight, Coke Is Coca-Cola 250.00
Pencil, Bullet 2.50
Pencil Clip, Coca-Cola In Bottles, Celluloid 1.50
Pencil Holder, Ceramic, 1960s 240.00
Pencil Sharpener, Coke Bottle 45.00
Pencil Sharpener, Figural, Bottle Shape, 1930s, 1 3/4 In. 57.00
Plate, 1931 .... 220.00
Plate, 4 Gold Logos 165.00
Plate, Vienna Art, Nude, 1905, 10 In. 1000.00
Pocket Knife, 1950s 9.00
Pocket Knife, Nickel Silver, 1 Blade, Opener, D. Peres, Germany, 1910 .... 340.00 to 350.00
Pocket Watch, Time For A Cold Bottle Of Coca-Cola, 2 In. 825.00

Poster, Color, 1960, 30 x 25 In. 44.00
Poster, Pause A Minute Refresh Yourself, Girl With Bottle, 1928, 12 x 20 In. 1250.00
Punch Board, 1940s, 7 x 8 In., Unused .... 15.00 to 18.00
Punch Board, Win 6 Bottles, 15 Chances, 1930s, 5 x 4 In. 3.00
Push Bar, Coke, Porcelain, 1950s 75.00
Push Bar, Porcelain, 1950s 65.00
Push Bar, Stenciled, Steel, Adjustable, 24 In. 88.00
Push Plate, Coke, Porcelain, 1950s, Restored 115.00
Radiator Plate, Drink Coca-Cola In Bottles, Metal, 1920s, 17 In. 495.00
Radio, Bottle Shape 30.00
Radio, Bottle Shape, 1930s, 8 x 24 In. 4125.00
Radio, Coke Can, 1970s .... 65.00 to 75.00
Radio, Coke Cooler Shape, Plastic Case, 1940s, 12 x 9 1/2 x 8 1/2 In. .... 660.00 to 725.00
Radio, Cooler, High Gloss Finish, 1950s 980.00
Razor, Travel, Plastic 12.00
Ruler, 1938 .... 40.00
Ruler, A Good Rule, Do Unto Others Etc., Compliments Of, 1950s, 12 In. 5.00
Ruler, Semi-Truck Shape 2.50
Salt & Pepper, Coke Cans 15.00
Scorer, Baseball, Relieves Fatigue, 1907 .... 120.00
Sewing Kit, Plastic Cover, 1960s 5.00
Shade, Rippled, Slag Glass 2970.00
Shade, Slag Glass, Copper Skirt, 13 1/2 x 16 In. 2700.00
Sign, Bottle, 40 x 15 In. 275.00
Sign, Button, 1949, 16 In. Diam. 175.00
Sign, Button, Coke, 24 In. Diam. 45.00
Sign, Cardboard, Aluminum Frame, 60 x 29 In. 150.00
Sign, Coke 6-Pack Shape, Die Cut, Tin, Dated Sept. 1950, 11 x 13 In. 750.00
Sign, Coke 6-Pack, Die Cut, Tin .... *Illus* 515.00
Sign, Coke 6-Pack, Take Home A Carton, 20 x 28 In. 350.00
Sign, Coke Bottle, Porcelain Enameled Steel, 1950s, 6 x 21 In. 21.00
Sign, Coke Headquarters, Girl & Boy At Fridge, 1947, 16 x 27 In. 600.00
Sign, Coke, Porcelain, Flange, Dated 1949, 17 x 19 In. 175.00
Sign, Come In, Have A Coca-Cola, Porcelain, 12 x 4 In. 295.00
Sign, Curb Service, Coca-Cola Sold Here, Stenciled Tin, 1933, 28 x 19 1/2 In. 210.00
Sign, Delicious & Refreshing, Embossed, Tin, Christmas, 1931, 10 x 27 In. 335.00
Sign, Delicious, Refreshing, Porcelain, 24 x 24 In. 550.00
Sign, Drink Coca-Cola 50th Anniversary, 1936, Frame, 13 x 22 1/2 In. 335.00
Sign, Drink Coca-Cola Delicious & Refreshing, Porcelain, 36 x 60 In.. .... 2250.00
Sign, Drink Coca-Cola In Bottles 5¢, Embossed Tin, 1908, 12 x 36 In. 2650.00
Sign, Drink Coca-Cola In Bottles, Red, White, Yellow, 1948, 11 x 24 In. 110.00
Sign, Drink Coca-Cola, Porcelainized Steel, Red, White & Black, 10 x 30 In. 798.00
Sign, Drink Coca-Cola, Tin Lithograph, Christmas Bottle, 1931, 10 x 27 1/2 In. 363.00
Sign, Drink With Ham Salad Sandwich, Cardboard, 1953, 12 x 16 3/4 In. 92.00
Sign, Fishtail Logo, 1960, 20 x 28 In. 115.00
Sign, Flapper Girl, Hat, Holding Bottle, Paper, 12 x 20 In. 385.00
Sign, Fountain & Glass, Double Sided, Porcelain, 1940s, 26 x 25 In. 1870.00
Sign, Great Together, Hot Dog, 3-D, 1932 .... *Illus* 550.00
Sign, Helene Madison, Olympic Swimmer, Heavy Cardboard, 1947 .... 90.00
Sign, In Bottles, Embossed Tin Lithograph, Shonk Works, 6 x 23 1/2 In. 187.00
Sign, Leaf Festoon, Paperboard, Pastel, Envelope, 1927, 20 x 123 In. 2310.00
Sign, Pause A Minute Refresh Yourself, Woman's Profile, Bottle, 20 x 12 In. 440.00
Sign, Sailor Girl, Take Enough Home, Cardboard, 1952, 11 x 12 In. 600.00
Sign, Sold Here Ice Cold Coke, Metal Arrow, Green, Red, White Letters, 9 x 27 In. .. 25.00
Sign, Tin, Frame, 1941, 6 x 3 Ft. 675.00
Sign, Woman Holding Glass Of Coca-Cola, Oval, Tin, Hanging, 1926 .... 6500.00
Sign, Woman In Riding Gear, Cardboard, 1937, 49 x 32 In. 350.00
Siphon, Acid Etched, Marked C. C., Bradford, Pa. 240.00
Straw, 1940s 3.00
String Dispenser, 16 x 12 In. 450.00
String Holder, Tin, Stenciled, Convex, Red, White & Yellow, 16 In. 330.00
Thermometer, Bottle Shape, Embossed Tin, 1950s, 5 x 17 In. 110.00
Thermometer, Bottle Shape, Gold, 1936 .... 150.00

Thermometer, Bottle Shape, Tin Lithograph, 1970s, Box, 16 In. 25.00
Thermometer, Christmas Bottle Shape, Tin, 1930s 53.00
Thermometer, Christmas Bottle, Tin Lithograph, 1937, 16 In. 154.00
Thermometer, Embossed Tin Lithograph, 1941, 16 In. 231.00
Thermometer, Gold Bottle, Round, 1950s 350.00
Thermometer, Refresh Yourself, Stenciled Sheet Metal, Convex Shape, 30 In. 110.00
Thermometer, Silhouette Girl, Porcelain, 1939 .... 250.00 to 300.00
Thermometer, Silhouette Girl, Tin Lithograph, Green, Red & Silver, 1939, 16 In. 198.00
Thermometer, Silhouette Girl, With Mirror, 1947 .... 48.50
Thermometer, Wooden, c.1915 .... 50.00
Thimble, No. 5 .... 85.00
Tie Clasp, 30 Year, Gold Filled 75.00
Tin, Syrup, Fountain, New York 1000.00
Tip Tray, 1901, Hilda Clark, 6 In. .... 1540.00 to 2860.00
Tip Tray, 1903, Girl Holding Fountain Glass & Fan, 6 In. .... 800.00 to 880.00
Tip Tray, 1907, Drink Coca-Cola, 5 Cents, Glass 3200.00
Tip Tray, 1907, Relieves Fatigue .... 700.00 to 965.00
Tip Tray, 1910, Hamilton King .... 450.00 to 660.00
Tip Tray, 1913, Hamilton King 620.00
Tip Tray, 1914, Betty .... 195.00 to 290.00
Tip Tray, 1938, Girl In The Afternoon 165.00
Token, Louisiana 12.00
Toy, Airplane, 600 Vega, No. 5 .... 70.00
Toy, Robot, Box 250.00
Toy, Soda Fountain Dispenser, Miniature, Glasses, 1950s 95.00
Toy, Truck, Tin Lithograph, 1950s 350.00
Toy, Yo-Yo, Red & White, On Card 8.00
Tray, 1903, Delicious & Refreshing, Woman Holding Glass, 9 1/2 In. 440.00
Tray, 1903, Hilda Clark, 15 x 18 1/2 In. 2310.00
Tray, 1905, Juanita, 10 x 13 In. .... *Illus* 3740.00
Tray, 1914, Betty In Bonnet, 12 1/2 x 15 In. .... 389.00 to 560.00
Tray, 1914, Betty, Oval 225.00
Tray, 1920, Garden Girl, Oval 625.00
Tray, 1921, Summer Girl 695.00
Tray, 1922, Autumn Girl, 10 1/2 x 13 1/4 In. .... 90.00 to 575.00
Tray, 1923, Flapper Girl .... 175.00 to 395.00
Tray, 1924, Smiling Girl, 10 1/2 x 13 1/4 In. 425.00
Tray, 1925, Girl At Party, White Fox 20.00
Tray, 1926, Sports Couple, Golfers, 10 1/2 x 13 1/4 In. 295.00
Tray, 1927, Car Hop, 10 1/2 x 13 1/4 In. .... 250.00 to 500.00
Tray, 1927, Soda Jerk, 10 1/2 x 13 1/4 In. .... 495.00 to 750.00
Tray, 1929, Girl In Swimsuit, 10 1/2 x 13 1/4 In. 150.00
Tray, 1930, Bathing Beauty, 10 1/2 x 13 1/4 In. .... 275.00 to 285.00
Tray, 1930, Telephone Girl, 10 1/2 x 13 1/4 In. 225.00
Tray, 1930s, Pretzel 175.00
Tray, 1931, Boy & Dog, Rockwell, 10 1/2 x 13 1/4 In. 525.00
Tray, 1933, Frances Dee, 10 1/2 x 13 1/4 In. 300.00
Tray, 1935, Madge Evans, 10 1/2 x 13 1/4 In. .... 285.00 to 300.00
Tray, 1936, Hostess, 10 1/2 x 13 1/4 In. 250.00
Tray, 1937, Running Girl, 10 1/2 x 13 1/4 In. 165.00
Tray, 1938, Girl In The Afternoon, 10 1/2 x 13 1/4 In. .... 125.00 to 195.00
Tray, 1939, Springboard Girl, 10 1/2 x 13 1/4 In. .... 85.00 to 175.00
Tray, 1940, Sailor Girl, 10 1/2 x 13 1/4 In. 125.00
Tray, 1941, Girl Ice Skater, 10 1/2 x 13 1/4 In. .... 125.00 to 290.00
Tray, 1942, 2 Girls At Car, 10 1/2 x 13 1/4 In. 190.00
Tray, 1948, Girl With Wind In Hair, 10 1/2 x 13 1/4 In. .... 75.00 to 85.00
Tray, 1950, French 75.00
Tray, 1950, Girl With Menu, 10 1/2 x 13 1/4 In. .... 60.00 to 75.00
Tray, 1950, Mexican 160.00
Tray, 1957, Umbrella Girl 125.00
Tray, 1967, Birdhouse, England 100.00
Truck, Buddy L, 1976 .... 50.00
Truck, Model T, 1912 Model, Matchbox, Box, 1970 .... 100.00

Truck, Van, Battery Operated, Tin, Plastic, Big Wheel 75.00
Truck, Yellow, Plastic Cases, Hand Truck, Roller Slide, Buddy L, 15 In. 275.00
Watch, All Star, 1986 .... 28.00
Watch Fob, Delivery Truck, Enameled Brass 10.00
Watch Fob, Motor Girl, Drink Coca-Cola In Bottles, 5 Cents, 1911 .... 825.00
Whistle, Red & White Logo, 2 In. 5.00
Wristwatch, 75th Anniversary, Xantia Watch Co., Tennessee, 17 Jewel 128.00

COFFEE GRINDERS of home size were first made about 1894. They lost
favor by the 1930s. Large floor-standing or counter-model coffee grinders
were used in the nineteenth-century country store. The renewed interest in
fresh-ground coffee has produced many modern electric and hand grinders,
and reproductions of the old styles are being made.

Arcade, Wall Mount, Crystal .... 90.00 to 135.00
Biedermeier, Walnut, Brass 302.00
Bronson-Walton Co., Cleveland, Oh., Tin, Cavalry Officers, Flags, 8 In. 550.00
Cherry Case, Pewter Hopper, Iron Crank, 8 1/2 In. 82.50
Dovetailed Wooden Case, Drawer, Iron Dome Top, Crank Handle, 1850s 70.00
Enterprise, Cast Iron, Painted, Wooden Handles & Drawer, 27 In. .... 850.00 to 935.00
Enterprise, Double Wheels, Small 600.00
Enterprise, Iron, Painted, Design, Philadelphia, U.S.A., 33 In. 880.00
Enterprise, No. 1, Cast Iron, Counter Top 160.00
Enterprise, No. 2, Stenciled, Double Wheels, Large 310.00
Enterprise, No. 5, Black Paint, 15 1/2 In. 302.00
Golden Rule, Wall Mount, Cast Iron, Wooden 235.00
J. Fisher, Dovetailed, Cherry, Iron Handle & Hopper, 6 In. 193.00
Kendrick, No. 1 .... 95.00
Kitchen Aid, Measuring Glass 115.00
Koffee Krusher, S.H. Co., Cast Iron, Wooden Base, Pat. 1901, 12 1/2 In. 550.00
Landers & Frary & Clark, Lap Type 150.00
Peugeot Frenres, Tin, Lap Type, France 50.00
Pine, Dovetailed Pullout Drawer, Lap Type 60.00
Sun Mfg. Co., Wooden, Paper Label, 1 Lb. 45.00

COIN SPOT is a glass pattern that was named by the collectors for the spots
resembling coins which are part of the glass. Colored, clear, and opalescent
glass was made with the spots. Many companies used the design in the 1870-
1890 period. It is so popular that reproductions are still being made.

Pitcher, Amethyst, 1910 .... 395.00
Pitcher, Blue 175.00
Pitcher, Cranberry, Applied Clear Handle, 6 3/4 In. 90.00
Pitcher, Green 110.00
Sugar Shaker, 9 Panels, Blue 195.00
Syrup, Clear 150.00
Water Set, Blue Opalescent, 5 Piece 355.00
Water Set, Blue, 5 Piece 125.00
Water Set, White, 5 Piece 120.00

COIN-OPERATED MACHINES of all types are collected. The vending
machine is an ancient invention dating back to 200 B.C. when holy water was
dispensed in a coin-operated vase. Smokers in seventeenth-century England
could buy tobacco from a coin-operated box. It was not until after the Civil
War that the technology made modern coin-operated games and vending
machines plentiful. Slot machines, arcade games, and dispensers are all
collected.

Candy, Figural, M & Ms, Pull Arm To Dispense, 10 In. 35.00
Cigar, Cigarola, Jennings 2000.00
Crap Game, Buckley, Side Play Handle, 5 Cent, 10 In. 3080.00
Dice, Mills, Operating As Dice Table Game, 25 Cent, 1930s 4125.00
Digger, Gold, 25 Cent 777.00
Digger, Imperial, Exhibit 2500.00
Digger, Oak 1500.00
Dispenser, Cup, Dixie, Globe 250.00

Coin-Operated Machine, Gum, Spearmint, Mills, 5 Cent, 1915

♦♦♦♦♦♦♦♦♦♦♦♦♦♦♦♦♦♦♦♦♦♦♦♦

If you have unopened bottles of drugs or other pharmaceuticals, be sure to check for ether or picric acid. These can explode spontaneously and are dangerous to keep.

♦♦♦♦♦♦♦♦♦♦♦♦♦♦♦♦♦♦♦♦♦♦♦♦

Fortune Teller, Wizard, 1 Cent, 18 1/2 x 14 In.	900.00
Gum, Beeman's, Mirror, Green	230.00
Gum, Bullwinkle, 1 Cent, 1960s, 16 In.	175.00
Gum, Get Your Beatles Buttons Here, Glass Globe	55.00
Gum, National, Aluminum, 15 In.	154.00
Gum, Premiere, Card, Red Painted Metal, 13 In.	264.00
Gum, Pulver, Blue Enamel, 1 Cent	71.50
Gum, Pulver, Mechanical Clown, 1930	500.00
Gum, Roth, Pansy	3200.00
Gum, Roth, Peaches & Cream	5200.00
Gum, Smilin' Sam, Stick, Red Paint Traces, Iron, Tongue Is Gum	2500.00
Gum, Spearmint, Mills, 5 Cent, 1915 .... *Illus*	1800.00
Gum, Tutti-Frutti	4500.00
Gum, Zeno, Clockwork, Porcelain, 7 x 16 1/2 In. .... 400.00 to	600.00
Gumball, 1 Cent Hit The Target, Spaceship & Worlds, Penny Grid	225.00
Gumball, Advance	275.00
Gumball, Columbia Model B, Cast Iron, Dome, 5 Cent, 16 In.	385.00
Gumball, Columbus, Painted Cast Iron & Dome, 1 Cent, 14 1/2 In.	330.00
Gumball, Confection Superior, Nickel Plated, 1 Cent, 14 In.	176.00
Gumball, Empire Vendor, Nickel Plated Face Plate, 16 1/2 In.	286.00
Gumball, Ford, 1 Cent, 1950s .... 60.00 to	75.00
Gumball, Globe, Painted Aluminum & Dome, 1 Cent, 14 1/2 In.	440.00
Gumball, Lark, Gumball & Fortune, Metal, 1 Cent, 10 1/2 In.	165.00
Gumball, Master, Painted Metal, 1 Cent, 16 In.	187.00
Gumball, Poppin' Fresh	150.00
Gumball, Saturn, Northwestern, 72 In..	275.00
Gumball, Silver King, Decals, Lock & Key, 1 Cent	125.00
Gumball, Toy 'n Joy, 1950s	25.00
Gumball, Victor, Halfback	29.95
Gumball, Victor, Model V, Chrome Plated, 1940s, 1 Cent	135.00
Lighter Fluid, Gas Pump, Cast Iron, 1 Cent	650.00
Match, Advance Machine Co., Iron, Painted, Glass Dome, 17 In.	798.00
Match, Albert Pick & Co., Iron, Wooden, 1 Cent, 14 1/2 In.	330.00
Mutoscope, Nature's Beauties, Stand, 14 x 74 In.	1250.00
Peanut, Acorn, Tall Glass Globe, 1950s	75.00
Peanut, Eatem Hot, 1930s	150.00
Peanut, Globe Machine Co., Cast Iron & Dome, 1 Cent, 13 1/2 In.	440.00
Peanut, Hance, White Base, 1 Cent	950.00
Peanut, Hot Nuts, 5 Cents	140.00
Peanut, Northwestern, Frosted Globe, 1 Cent	175.00
Peanut, Silver King, Cast Iron, 1 Cent, 1930s	100.00
Peanut, Verdex, Cast Iron	275.00
Peanut, Victor, Model V, Chrome Plated, Cast Iron, 1 Cent	130.00
Pinball, Fan-Tan, Counter, 5 Balls, 1 Cent	425.00
Pinball, Surf Queen, Bally, Wooden Rail, 1946	175.00

Pinball Table, Little Manhattan, Green Cast Iron, 3 Balls, 1901, 22 In. 495.00
Popcorn, Federal 225.00
Popcorn, Holcomb & Hoke, 1908 .... 3500.00
Popcorn, Holcomb & Hoke, With Peanut Warmer, 5 1/2 Ft. 2000.00
Popcorn, Manley 500.00
Razor Blade, Porcelain 295.00
Shoe Shine, Green Enameled, 5 Cents 66.00
Skill Jump, Ball Flip, Skiers, Groetchen Co., 1 Cent, 1940s, 73 In. 225.00
Slot, Bally, Double Bell, 5 & 25 Cent 3000.00
Slot, Bull Durham, Triple Jackpot 5800.00
Slot, Caille, Cadet, 10 Cent, 1936 .... 1900.00
Slot, Caille, Naked Lady, 5 Cent, 1926 .... 2400.00
Slot, Caille, Silent Sphinx, 5 Cent 2600.00
Slot, Caille, Silver Cup, 1912, 5 Cent 7150.00
Slot, Groetchen, Columbia 750.00
Slot, Jennings, Bull Durham, B.D. Novelties, 5 Cent 3800.00
Slot, Jennings, Dutch Boy, 1929 .... 1800.00 to 1900.00
Slot, Jennings, Governor, 3 Reel, 10 Cent, 1960s, 27 In. 1210.00
Slot, Jennings, Mints Of Quality, Side Vendor 2500.00
Slot, Jennings, Peacock, 3 Reel, 5 Cent, c.1932, 27 In. 5500.00
Slot, Jennings, Standard Chief, Indian Profile, 50 Cent, 28 In. 1100.00
Slot, Jennings, Sun Chief, Illuminated Panels Front, 27 In. 935.00
Slot, Liberty, 1 Cent 450.00
Slot, Mechanical Farm, 60 Moving Figures, 50 Cent 10000.00
Slot, Mills, Aristocrat Money Maker 1095.00
Slot, Mills, Babe Ruth Game 1895.00
Slot, Mills, Baseball, Black Cherry 1455.00
Slot, Mills, Bonus Horsehead, Cast Iron, 5 Cent, 1937 .... 2200.00
Slot, Mills, Bull Durham, 5 Cent 1600.00
Slot, Mills, Bursting Cherry, 10 Cent, 1937 .... 2100.00
Slot, Mills, Cherry, Metal, Wood Side Panels, 26 In. 995.00
Slot, Mills, Chicago, 1 Wheel, Upright, Oak Case, c.1900, 65 1/2 In. 8850.00
Slot, Mills, Extraordinary, Bell, 3 Reel, 1930s, 29 In. 600.00
Slot, Mills, Jackpot, 50 Cent 1595.00
Slot, Mills, Lion's Head, 25 Cent, 1931 .... 1775.00
Slot, Mills, Lion's Head, 5 Cent 1650.00
Slot, Mills, Owl, Music, 5 Cent 9500.00
Slot, Mills, Poinsettia, Gooseneck, Jackpot, 5 Cent, 1929 .... 1145.00 to 2100.00
Slot, Mills, Three Big Jacks 375.00
Slot, Mills, Vest Pocket, 5 Cent .... 300.00 to 475.00
Slot, Mills, War Eagle, 10 Cent 1800.00
Slot, Pulver, Cop & Robber, Red Case 800.00
Slot, Rol-A-Top, Coin Front 3800.00
Slot, War Eagle, 5 Cent 2000.00
Slot, Watling, Gold Seal Award, Twin Jackpot 2500.00
Slot, Watling, Gooseneck, Jackpot, Side Vendor, 5 Cent 2400.00
Slot, Watling, Rol-A-Top, 3 Reel, 5 Cent, 1930s, 26 1/2 In. 3300.00
Slot, Watling, Rol-A-Top, 8 Coin Front, Cornucopia, 26 In. 1980.00
Slot, Watling, Treasury 4500.00
Slot, Williams, Crane 1000.00
Steam Shovel, Arcade, 25 Cent 550.00
Strength Tester, Breath Ball, Cast Iron Base, Decal, 1 Cent 3135.00
Strength Tester, Lift & Twist, c.1890 .... 6500.00
Tissue, Kleenex, Store, Metal, Large 95.00
Trade Stimulator, Caille Doughboy 475.00
Trade Stimulator, Cigar, Oak Base, 1 Cent, 1910, 13 1/2 In. 605.00
Trade Stimulator, Circus, Penny Flip 275.00
Trade Stimulator, Daval, American Eagle 295.00
Trade Stimulator, Gorethen Mercury 250.00
Trade Stimulator, Jennings, Rainbow, 1 Cent, 1930s, 20 In. 1430.00
Trade Stimulator, Klix, 5 Reel 350.00
Trade Stimulator, Midget Baseball, 1 Cent 1980.00
Trade Stimulator, Mills, Puritan Bell 800.00

Trade Stimulator, Roulette Wheel, Cigar, Nickeled 1100.00
Trade Stimulator, Wings, 5 Reel 350.00

COLLECTOR PLATES are modern plates produced in limited editions. Some may be found listed under the factory name, such as Bing & Grondahl, Royal Copenhagen, Royal Doulton, and Wedgwood.

Avon, Christmas, 1971 .... 12.00
Avon, Christmas, Skaters On The Pond, 1975 .... 30.00
Avon, Mother's Day, 1982 .... 8.00
Avon, Tenderness Aware, 1974 .... 15.00
Brackenbury, Cat Tales, A Chance Meeting, Shorthairs, Knowles, 1987 .... 40.00
Brackenbury, Cinderella, Bibbidi-Bobbidi-Boo, Knowles, 1988 .... 89.00
Davis, Cat Tales, Flew The Coop, Schmidt, 1983 .... 330.00
Davis, Christmas, At Red Oak, Schmidt, 1986 .... 180.00
Davis, Christmas, Peter & The Wren, Schmidt, 1989 .... 300.00
Fenton, Christmas, 1970, Carnival Glass 20.00
Fernandez, As Free As The Wind, Fountainhead, 1989 .... 250.00
Gorham, Tiny Tim 25.00
Granget, Freedom & Justice Soaring, 24K Gold On Copper, Box, 1979, 8 In. 30.00
Jensen, Mother's Day, Blue & White, 1974 .... 35.00
Kaatz, Field Puppies, Caught In The Act, Retriever, Knowles, 1987 .... 60.00
Kaiser, Tutankhamen, Box 495.00
Kuck, Days Gone By, Amy's Magic Horse, Reco International, 1983 .... 43.00
Kuck, Days Gone By, Little Tutor, Reco International, 1984 .... 25.00
McClelland, Mother Goose, Little Jack Horner, Reco International, 1982 .... 29.00
McClelland, Mother Goose, Mary, Mary, Reco International, 1979 .... 105.00
Morley, Flowers Of Your Garden, Tulips, W.S. George, 1989 .... 50.00
Rockwell, Family Tree, Gorham 27.50
Rockwell, Toy Maker, Box 85.00
Rogers, Gone With The Wind, Burning Of Atlanta, W.S. George, 1988 .... 80.00
Rogers, Gone With The Wind, Scarlett's Resolve, W.S. George, 1989 .... 50.00
Sports Impressions, Darryl Strawberry, No. 2, Fogarty, 1989 .... 195.00
Sports Impressions, Jackie Robinson, 1956 .... 150.00

COMIC ART, or cartoon art, is a relatively new field of collecting. Original comic strips, magazine covers, and even printed strips are collected. The first daily comic strip was printed in 1907. The paintings on celluloid used for movie cartoons are listed in this book under Animation Art.

Strip, Captain Eddie Rickenbacker, Ace Drummond, 12 Frames, Color, 1935 .... 45.00
Strip, Wimpy, Naughty, 1940s, 2 x 4 In. 35.00

COMMEMORATIVE items have been made to honor members of royalty and those of great national fame. World's fairs and important historical events are also remembered with commemorative pieces. Related collectibles are listed in the Coronation and World's Fair categories.

Bag, Shopping, Queen's Silver Jubilee, Burlap, 14 x 17 1/2 In. 6.50
Mug, Elizabeth II, Silver Jubilee 18.50
Mug, King George, Minton, 8 In. 25.00
Plate, Charles & Diana's Marriage, July 29, 1981, Weatherby, 9 3/4 In. .... 38.00 to 42.50
Spoon, Queen Victoria, 1839-1897, Jubilee Handle, Osmium Silver 24.00
Tin, Queen Elizabeth, Prince Phillip, St.Lawrence Seaway, 1959 .... 28.00

COMPACTS hold face powder. A woman did not powder her face in public until after World War I. By 1920, the beauty parlor, permanent waves, and cosmetics had become acceptable. A few companies sold cake face powder in a box with a mirror and a pad or puff. Soon the compact was being designed by jewelers and made of gold, silver, and precious materials. Cosmetic companies began to sell powder in attractive compacts of less valuable metal or plastic. Collectors today search for Art Deco designs, commemorative compacts from world's fairs or political events, and unusual examples. Many were made with companion lipsticks and other fittings.

14K Gold, 3-Tone Ribbon Clasp With Diamond & Sapphires, 2 7/8 x 2 3/8 In. 1840.00
Aluminum, Birds 295.00

Applied Gold Leaping Gazelle, Black, Flannel Case 150.00
Art Deco, Black, Gold 28.50
Art Deco, Silver Peacock, Black 65.00
Art Deco, Wooden, Enamel, Octagonal 35.00
Babbitt Perfumers, Yellow Brass, Moon & Stars Lid 5.00
Belais, 14K Gold, Enamel Silhouette Of 1920s Woman, Mirror 295.00
Brass, Gilt, Miniature Portrait & Turquoise Stones In Lid, Square, France 50.00
Carlton, Round, Green Enamel Top 20.00
Cloisonne, Art Deco, Sunflowers, Lipstick On Chain 95.00
Dali, Bird Shape, Gold Trim, Signed 250.00
Edgewater Beach Hotel, Chicago, Basket Of Green Flowers, Finger Ring 195.00
Eiffel Tower On Faux Tortoise Cover, Paris 65.00
Elgin, Black Enamel, Paisley Flowers, Square 25.00
Elgin, Checkerboard Design, Mother-Of-Pearl 30.00
Elgin, Square, Black Enamel, Paisley Flowers 25.00
Elgin American, Art Deco, Yellow Enamel, With Chain 80.00
Elizabeth Arden, Harlequin Mask, Black 150.00
Enamel Both Sides, Pink Rose Cover, White 250.00
Evans, Boston Terrier, Enamel 35.00
Evans, Gold Gazell, Black Enamel 195.00
Evans, Goldtone, Watch In Lid 85.00
Evans, Mother-Of-Pearl, Large 75.00
Evans, Top Sift, Art Deco, Silver & Black 45.00
Evans, Trunk Form, Watch In Lid 75.00
Ft. Knox, Ky., Camera Style, Gold Glitter Body, Metallic Eagle 125.00
Georg Jensen, Sterling Silver 375.00
Gold Anchor, Black Enamel, U.S. Navy 115.00
Gold Eagle, Flag, U.S. Army, White, 1940s 150.00
Harriet Hubbard Ayers, Pink Shamrock 18.00
Houbigant, Yellow Brass, Mirror, Round 2.50
Kirk, Floral Chased Design, Sterling Silver 185.00
Langlois, Octagonal 25.00
Lola Montez, Brass, Eye Shadow, Enamel Design, 1920s 30.00
Lydia E. Pinkham, Celluloid, Facsimile Signature & Slogan, Inside Mirror, 2 1/8 In. ... 50.00
Masonic, Islam Temple, San Francisco, 1922 .... 45.00
Mavco, Raspberry Lucite 42.00
Max Factor, Replica Of 1880s Gold Watch, Golden Lark Co., 1960s, 2 1/4 In. 45.00
Mesh, Silver Overlay, Lovebirds 40.00
Morhill, Mother-Of-Pearl, Abalone Pagoda, Black Ground 12.00
Norida, Colonial Woman, 1924 .... 35.00
Olympian, Running With Torch, Black, 1930s 135.00
Powdrette-DuBarry, Copper, 2 In. 5.00
Rex, Art Deco, Black, Gold Embossed Flowers 30.00
Rex 5th Ave., Yellow Brass, Raised Leaf Design, Large 5.00
Richard Hudnut, Art Deco, Pink & Black Enamel 30.00
Richard Hudnut, DuBarry, Pink & Black, Art Deco 30.00
Richard Hudnut, Green & Gold Cloisonne, Attached Lipstick On Chain 250.00
Richard Hudnut, Green & Gold Enameled 15.00
Rockefeller Center, Rhinestones, Green & Gold, Relief Center 165.00
Sailor Kissing Girl Good-Bye, U. S. Navy, World War II, Wooden, Box 110.00
Shield, Woven Silver Chain, 2 3/4 In. 72.00
Silver, Mesh Chain, Gold Trim 50.00
Silver, Mirror, Lipstick In Handle 72.00
Statue Of Liberty, Blue Enamel, Yellow Plastic Cover .... 35.00 to 60.00
Statue Of Liberty, New York, Blue Enamel, Yellow Plastic Lid 60.00
Sterling Silver, Art Deco, Powder, Rouge & Lipstick Compartments, Box 145.00
Sterling Silver, Red Lucite, Doves In Center 125.00
Stratton, Blue Enamel, England 45.00
Stratton, Flowers 35.00
Stratton, Long Stemmed Roses 22.50
Stratton, Peacock & Flowers, Red Enamel 35.00
Tiffany, Chased Rim, 14K Yellow Gold, Octagonal 247.50
U.S. Naval Academy, Art Deco, Lipstick Holder 40.00

◆◆◆◆◆◆◆◆◆◆◆◆◆◆◆◆◆◆◆◆◆◆

To protect your investment in household furnishings, rewire any lamps in your home that are 15 or more years old. Cords crack and are a fire hazard.

◆◆◆◆◆◆◆◆◆◆◆◆◆◆◆◆◆◆◆◆◆◆

Consolidated Glass, Pitcher, Cranberry, White Opalescent, Shell Handle, 9 In.

Victorian Cameo, Woman With Dove, England	195.00
Volupte, Adam & Eve, Gold Tone	110.00
Volupte, Black Enamel Top, Painted Floral Bouquet, Puff Cloth, 3 1/8 x 2 1/4 In.	30.00
Volupte, Brass, Tooled & Enamel Birds, Gazelles, Elephants, Rectangular	12.00
Volupte, Gold Basket Weave, Square Shape, Box, 1930s	30.00
Volupte, Manicured Hand	175.00
Volupte, Music Box, Plays Oklahoma	65.00
Volupte, Piano Keyboard	95.00
Washington, DC, Tin	25.00
Weisner, Pink Rhinestones	25.00
Yardley, Gold Tone	25.00
Zell, Love & Marriage, Courtship, Marriage, Baby Scenes	185.00
Zell, Mother-Of-Pearl, Black & White	35.00

CONSOLIDATED LAMP AND GLASS COMPANY of Coraopolis, Pennsylvania, was founded in 1894. The company made lamps, tablewares, and art glass. Collectors are particularly interested in the wares made after 1925, including black satin glass, Cosmos (listed in its own category in this book), Martele (which resembled Lalique), and colored glasswares. The company closed for the final time in 1967.

Candy Dish, Cover, Pond Lily, Purple	180.00
Lamp, Cockatoos, Blue, Custard Ground, Brass Base & Cap, 9 1/2 In.	295.00
Lamp, Gone With The Wind, Muses, Musical Instruments, 23 In.	985.00
Lamp, Gone With The Wind, Star Burst, 10 1/2-In. Shade	775.00
Lamp, Umbrella Vase, Thistle, Blue, Iridescent White, 25 In.	550.00
Pitcher, Cranberry, White Opalescent, Shell Handle, 9 In. .... *Illus*	2420.00
Plate, Catalonian, Kumquat, Green, 8 1/4 In.	25.00
Plate, Catalonian, Pear Shape, Fruit, Green, 9 1/4 In.	18.00
Plate, Dancing Nymphs, Green, 9 In.	150.00
Shade, Torchiere, Diving Girl	900.00
Sugar & Creamer, Catalonian, Yellow	25.00
Toothpick, Shell & Seaweed, Blue	45.00
Tumbler, Catalonian, Purple, 4 In.	8.00
Tumbler, Catalonian, Yellow, 3 7/8 In.	7.00
Vase, Blue Dancing Nudes, Custard Ground, 11 In.	495.00
Vase, Catalonian, Corset Shape, Green, 11 3/4 x 8 3/4 In.	45.00
Vase, Dancing Girl, Strawberry Opalescent	700.00
Vase, Dancing Nudes With Pan, Frosted Ground, 11 3/4 In.	410.00
Vase, Dancing Nudes, Cobalt Blue, 12 In.	295.00
Vase, Dogwood, Custard, Ecru Ground, 10 5/8 In.	140.00
Vase, Dogwood, Yellow, Brown, Green & White, 10 1/2 In.	135.00
Vase, Lovebird, Crystal	250.00
Vase, Martele, White & Gold, 6 1/2 In.	85.00
Vase, Screech Owl, White, Gold Trim	110.00

CONTEMPORARY GLASS, see Glass-Contemporary

COOKBOOKS are collected for various reasons. Some are wanted for the recipes, some for investment, and some as examples of advertising. Cookbooks and recipe pamphlets are included in this category.

100 Picnic Suggestions, Linda Hull Lomed, 123 Pages, 1915, 5 1/4 x 4 In.	10.00
7-Up Party Recipes, Full Color, 16 Pages, 1961	5.00
Art Of Making Bread At Home, NW Yeast Co., 28 Pages, 1940s, 5 x 7 In.	5.00
Aunt Jemima, 3 1/2 x 5 In.	170.00
Aunt Jemima Recipe Book, 1906	250.00
Authentic Mexican, Illustrated, Hardcover, Large	3.00
Better Homes & Gardens, 1952	15.00
Betty Crocker, Child's, Spiral, 1965	15.00
Bond Bread, Green Cover, 72 Pages, 1935	6.00
Butternut Bread, Lunch Box Menus, 1943	2.50
Calumet, Boy With Dog Cover, 1918	15.00
Carnation, 5-Minute Recipes, 8 Pages, 1930s	2.00
Chiquita Banana, 1950	15.00
Desserts, Cakes To Sweet Breads, 375 Pages, 1956	2.50
Dixie, Mammy, 1935	55.00
Edith Bunker, All In The Family	15.00
Fannie Farmer's Chafing Dish Possibilities, Boston, 1899	50.00
Fish & Game Cookery, Roy Wall, 218 Pages, 1945	10.00
Fish Cookery, 348 Pages, 1921	18.00
Frigidaire Recipe Book, 1931	5.00
Gold Medal Flour, 72 Pages, 1910, 8 x 11 In.	12.00
Heinz Recipe Book, Spiral, 212 Pages	8.00
Helen Corbitt's Potluck, 181 Pages, 1962	8.00
Hood's, Sarsaparilla, 1889	55.00
Iowa Power & Light, Holiday Recipes, 1967	1.50
Jell-O, Bride Cover	15.00
Jell-O, Recipe Book, 1934	5.00
Jell-O & Kewpies, Young Girl Helped By 2 Kewpies Cover, 1915, 4 1/2 x 6 In.	82.00
Joy Of Cooking, 1946-1947	6.00 to 25.00
Junior Crafts, Warren, Ohio, 379 Pages, 1950s, 6 x 8 1/2 In.	5.00
Kerr Glass Co., Home Canning & Recipe, 1948	2.00
Knox Gelatin, 1920s	15.00
Knox Gelatin Dainty Desserts, Black, Unopened Gelatin Envelope, 1924	32.00
Knudsen, Calorie Way To Right Weight & Health, 8 Pages, 1951	1.00
Little Brown Cocoa Book, 1959	39.00
Majestic Stoves, 1890s	19.00
Mazola Salad Bowl, Bowl Shape, 1938	5.00
National Brewing Co., Black Chef Cover	35.00
New Health Cookery, 51 Pages, 1925	12.00
People's Home Library, Medical Cooking, 1910	25.00
Pet Milk, Thrifty Tempting Meals, 33 Pages, 1937	2.00
Pet Springtime Recipes, 31 Pages, 1934	2.00
Piggly Wiggly, 1926	20.00
Pillsbury, 4th Grand National Contest, 96 Pages, 1952	15.00
Poor Man's Rice, Wright Labs, 36 Pages, 1963, 6 x 8 In.	3.00
Pure Food, Woman's Society Of Wadsworth Ave., Baptist Church, NYC	7.00
Ralston Recipe, 24 Pages, 1922, 4 1/4 x 7 3/4 In.	20.00
Rumford, Child Cover, 1913	20.00
Sealtest, 1001 Dairy Dishes, 288 Pages, 1963	5.00
Sealtest, Kitchen 641 Tested Recipes, 1954	5.00
Sego Milk Premium Book, Pictures, 35 Pages, 1937	3.00
Sunny Side Of Life, Kellogg's	5.00
Texas Centennial, 1936	20.00
Thompson Dairy, Cottage Cheese Recipes, 30 Pages, 1940	1.00
Universal Food Chopper, 44 Pages, 1897, 6 1/2 x 4 1/2 In.	6.00
Wilbur's Cocoa, Cocoa Can Shape	5.00
Woman's Favorite, 1906	25.00
Working Girl Must Eat, 1938	10.00

You Can Be A Better Cook Than Mama Was, Hardcover, 322 Pages, 1968 .... 23.00

COOKIE JARS with brightly painted designs or amusing figural shapes became popular in the mid-1930s. Many companies made them and collectors search for cookie jars either by design or by maker's name. Listed here are examples by the less common makers. Major factories are listed under their own names in other categories of the book, such as Abingdon, Brush, Hull, McCoy, Red Wing, and Shawnee. See also the Black and Disneyana categories.

Acorn, Corner, American Bisque	225.00
Agatha Tastesetter, Sigma	50.00
Albert Apple, Pitman-Dreitzer	225.00
Alice In Wonderland, Japan	85.00 to 150.00
Amish Boy, American Bisque	350.00
Apple, California Originals	48.00
Aunt Jemima, Brown Face, Plastic, F & F	325.00
Aunt Jemima, Red Dress, Plastic, F & F	475.00
Bacon & Eggs Hog, Fitz & Floyd	125.00
Barn, Regal China	400.00
Barrel, Spongeware	115.00
Bear, Aramis	150.00
Bear, Ballerina, Metlox	75.00 to 125.00
Bear, Beau, Metlox	80.00
Bear, Blue Ribbon & Bow, Treasure Craft	50.00
Bear, Blue Sweater, Metlox	30.00
Bear, California Originals	25.00 to 35.00
Bear, Hamm	200.00
Bear, On Roller Skates, Metlox	125.00
Bear, Shopper, Mardoux	150.00
Bear, With Visor, American Bisque	45.00
Bear, Yellow Sweater, Holds Cookie, Maurice Of California	50.00
Beau Bear, Metlox	45.00
Big Al, Treasure Craft	110.00
Big Bird, California Originals	100.00
Big Bird On Nest, California Originals	45.00
Big Boy, Kathy Wolfe	395.00
Blackboard Boy, American Bisque	400.00
Blackboard Clown, American Bisque	250.00
Blackboard Girl, American Bisque	375.00
Blackboard Hobo, Remember, American Bisque	375.00
Blue Bonnet Sue	40.00 to 49.00
Buddha, Twin Winton	135.00
Bulldog, Enesco	25.00
Bulldog, Relco	50.00
Bunch Of Grapes, Metlox	150.00
Bunny, California Originals	75.00
Bunny On Lettuce, Metlox	75.00
Calico Cat, Metlox	67.00
Car, Flat Tire, Fitz & Floyd	265.00
Car, Starnes	180.00
Casper, American Bisque	850.00
Casper The Friendly Ghost, Harney Productions, Inc.	*Illus* 650.00
Cat's Head, Metlox	95.00
Cats In Shoe, Maurice Of California	125.00
Century 21, House	800.00 to 1050.00
Cheerleaders, American Bisque	*Illus* 205.00
Cheerleaders, Flasher, American Bisque	280.00 to 475.00
Chef, Entenmann's Thrift-E	250.00
Chef, White, Artistic Potteries	575.00
Chef, With Salad, Orange, Regal	395.00
Chevrolet, Applause, 1957 Model	60.00
Churn Boy, American Bisque	225.00
Cinderella, Regal China	325.00

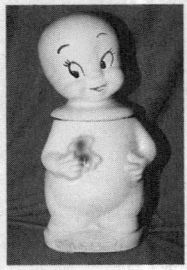

Cookie Jar, Casper The Friendly Ghost, Harney Productions Inc.

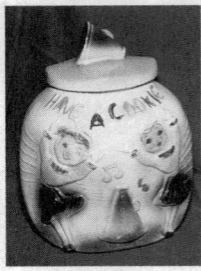

Cookie Jar, Cheerleaders, American Bisque

Cookie Jar, Fred Flintstone, Golfer, American Bisque

Clown, Black & White, Metlox	125.00
Clown, California Originals	55.00
Clown, Flasher, On Stage, American Bisque	395.00
Clown, Pan American Art	45.00
Clown, Sierra Vista	60.00
Clown, White & Black, Metlox	125.00
Clown, Yellow, Metlox	95.00 to 125.00
Coffee Grinder, House Of Webster	30.00
Comical Fish, Yellow	85.00
Cookie Bear, Blue Shirt, Metlox	65.00
Cookie Bus, Disney	525.00
Cookie Monster, California Originals	35.00 to 60.00
Cookie Railroad, American Bisque	85.00
Cookie Truck, American Bisque	95.00
Cookies & Milk, American Bisque	95.00
Corn, Metlox	225.00
Cow, Twin Winton	65.00
Cow Head, Metlox	425.00
Cow Over The Moon, Gold	400.00
Cream Of Wheat Man	20.00
Dalmations, IRC	275.00
Dancing Bunnies, Fitz & Floyd	35.00
Davy Crockett, Regal	675.00
Delicious Cookie Co., 1988	45.00
Diaper Pig, Regal	275.00
Dinosaur, Doranne	45.00
Dog, Brayton	210.00
Dog On Pillow, American Bisque	240.00
Donkey, Sitting, Twin Winton	85.00
Donkey Cart, American Bisque	75.00
Donut Chef, Regal	500.00
Drummer Boy, Metlox	395.00
Dutch Girl, Twin Winton	55.00
Elephant, Baseball Cap, American Bisque	110.00
Elephant, Cumberland Ware	80.00
Elephant, Yellow, Doranne	45.00
Elf, Twin Winton	50.00
Elf Bakery, Twin Winton	42.00
Elves School, Turquoise Tile Roof	50.00
Emmett Kelly Jr., Brayton	295.00
Emmett Kelly Jr., Flambro	275.00 to 350.00
Emmett Kelly Jr., Metlox	650.00
Ernie, California Originals	60.00
Ernie & Bert, Fine Cookies, California Originals	275.00 to 495.00
Famous Amos, Bag Of Cookies, Treasure Craft	150.00

Fi Fi, Regal China 500.00
Figaro, Cookie Jar & Milk Pitcher, American Bisque 695.00
Fish, Metlox 175.00
Flasher, Black Curtains, American Bisque 350.00
Fluffy Cat, Ludowici Celadon 50.00
Football Coach, Treasure Craft 70.00
Fred Flintstone, American Bisque 950.00
Fred Flintstone, Golfer, American Bisque .... *Illus* 1100.00
Fred Flintstone, Vandor .... 125.00 to 265.00
French Baker, Regal 200.00
Friar Tuck, Twin Winton 40.00
Frosty Penguin, Metlox 125.00
Garfield, Enesco .... 45.00 to 65.00
George & Martha Washington, American Bisque .... 85.00 to 200.00
Gingerbread House, Cleminson 200.00
Gingerbread House, Deforest 175.00
Goldilocks, Regal .... 245.00 to 350.00
Grandma, American Bisque 120.00
Granny, Brayton 495.00
Green Frog, Bowtie, California Originals 45.00
Green Giant Sprout .... 35.00 to 79.00
Gypsy Woman, Brayton 495.00
Harpo, Regal 1150.00
Haunted House, Fitz & Floyd 135.00
Helen's Tat-L-Tale, Large 750.00
Herbert The Harris Lion 725.00
Hippo, Pink, Fitz & Floyd, 1980 .... 110.00
Hobby Horse, Hubert 350.00
Homer Simpson 800.00
Hubert The Lion, Regal 850.00
Humpty Dumpty, California Originals 125.00
Humpty Dumpty, Maddux .... 225.00 to 250.00
Humpty Dumpty, Metlox .... 185.00 to 275.00
Humpty Dumpty, Yellow Base, Regal .... 450.00 to 495.00
Humpty-Dumpty, Puriton 425.00
Indian Girl, California Originals 195.00
Indian Lady, American Bisque 250.00
Jack-In-The-Box, American Bisque .... 90.00 to 95.00
Jaguar, N.A.C. 225.00
Jukebox, Vandor 100.00
Kangaroo, Blue 425.00
Katrina, Treasure Craft 625.00
Katy Cat, Metlox .... 95.00 to 120.00
Keebler Elf, Plastic, F & F 235.00
Keebler Elf, Sitting 75.00
Keebler Tree House, 1981 .... 36.00 to 95.00
Keystone Cop, California Originals 125.00
Keystone Cop, Twin Winton .... 190.00 to 300.00
King Of Tarts 450.00
Kitty Kottage, Fitz & Floyd 130.00
Koala Bear, California Originals 295.00
Koala Bear, Cardinal 250.00
Koala Bear, Metlox .... 110.00 to 125.00
Koala In Tree, California Originals 225.00
Kraft T Bear, Regal .... 155.00 to 350.00
Lady, Brayton Laguna 375.00
Lazy Dog, Doranne, Large 45.00
Leisure Frog, California Originals 45.00
Lion, Hubert 995.00
Little Bopeep, Napco .... 150.00 to 250.00
Little Debbie, Glass 35.00
Little Girl, Sears 550.00
Little Red Riding Hood 210.00

Little Red Riding Hood, Pottery Guild .... 95.00 to 145.00
Lucy Goose, Metlox 75.00
M & M's 60.00
Magic Bunny, American Bisque .... 90.00 to 95.00
Majorette, American Bisque 395.00
Majorette, Japan 65.00
Majorette, Regal .... 285.00 to 425.00
Mammy, Artistic Pottery 600.00
Mammy, Blue, Mosaic Tile Co. .... 450.00 to 875.00
Mammy, Brown, Plastic, F & F 365.00
Mammy, Green, Artistic Potteries 675.00
Mammy, Green, Brayton 1295.00
Mammy, Mauve, Metlox 1000.00
Mammy, Pearl China .... 695.00 to 800.00
Mammy, Plum Dress, Brayton 1200.00
Mammy, Yellow Dress, Mosaic Tile Co. 595.00
Mammy, Yellow Rose, Maruhon Ware 1500.00
Mammy, Yellow, Brayton 1295.00
Mammy, Yellow, Metlox 495.00
Man With Chicken, Animals & Co., ... 425.00
Matilda, Brown, Yellow, Brayton Laguna .... 375.00 to 725.00
Maurice Clown, American Bisque 250.00
Miss Muffet, Regal .... 150.00 to 295.00
Mohawk Indian, ABC 440.00
Monk, Thou Shall Not Steal, Treasure Craft 55.00
Mother Goose, Doranne 145.00
Mouse, Chef Pierre, Metlox 120.00
Mouse, Treasure Craft 40.00
Muppets, Sesame Street, Cylinder, California Originals 125.00
Nerd, On Skateboard, Dark Blue, Box, 1984 .... 80.00 to 110.00
Nestle's Toll House Cookies .... 65.00 to 90.00
Noah's Ark, Metlox 125.00
Noah's Ark, On Mt. Ararat 75.00
Nun 250.00
Orange, Blossom Lid, Metlox 120.00
Orange Rooster, California Originals 45.00
Oriental Lady, Regal 500.00
Oscar The Grouch, California Originals .... 65.00 to 125.00
Owl, Brown, Metlox 60.00
Owl, Fitz & Floyd 90.00
Owl, Poppy Trail, Metlox 60.00
Owl, Twin Winton 50.00
Panda, Metlox 155.00
Parrot, Metlox 295.00
Peek-A-Boo, Regal 1350.00
Pelican, California Originals .... 55.00 to 60.00
Pelican, Metlox .... 115.00 to 140.00

Cookie Jar, Puppy, Brayton Laguna

Cookie Jar, Witch, Green Face, Fitz & Floyd

Penguin, Metlox	100.00
Pennsylvania Dutch Boy, Bisque	150.00
Pepperidge Farm	60.00
Peruvian Woman, Brayton	750.00
Peter Pumpkin Eater, Vallona Starr	450.00
Pig, Clemenson	175.00
Pig In Poke, American Bisque	65.00
Pillsbury Doughboy	39.00
Pinecone Coffeepot, American Bisque	55.00
Pineapple, Metlox	70.00
Pinky Lee, Blue Hat, American Bisque	200.00 to 595.00
Pinky Lee, Pink Hat, American Bisque	795.00
Polkadot Kitty, American Bisque	85.00
Polkadot Witch, Fitz & Floyd	195.00 to 295.00
Popeye, American Bisque	775.00 to 925.00
Popeye, Vandor	595.00
Provincial Woman, Brayton Laguna	65.00
Prunella Pig, Lorraine Elam	120.00
Puddles, Metlox	45.00 to 70.00
Puppy, Brayton Laguna	*Illus* 350.00
Purple Cow, Metlox	375.00
Puss In Boots	100.00
Quaker Oats, Regal	95.00 to 145.00
Queen Of Hearts, Fitz & Floyd	130.00
Queen Of Tarts, Maddux	285.00
R2-D2, Roman Ceramics	100.00 to 150.00
Rabbit On Cabbage, Metlox	125.00 to 195.00
Raccoon, Bandit, Metlox	85.00
Raccoon Cookie Bandit, Poppy Trail	115.00
Rag Doll, Starnes	195.00
Raggedy Andy, Maddux	150.00
Raggedy Ann, California Originals	75.00
Raggedy Ann & Andy, Metlox, Pair	385.00
Ranger Bear, Twin Winton	65.00
Red Baron, California Original	500.00
Rio Rita, Vandor	250.00
Roller Bear, Metlox	125.00 to 150.00
Rose, Metlox	525.00
Rubbles House, American Bisque	850.00 to 900.00
Sad Hound, Green, Doranne	55.00
Saddle, ABC	225.00
Sailor Elephant, American Bisque	95.00
Sailor Elephant, Twin Winton	40.00 to 50.00
Sailor Mouse, Twin Winton	50.00
Santa Claus, 1958	95.00
Santa Claus, Ceramic, 1950s	65.00
Santa Claus, Holt Howard, 3 Piece	95.00
Scarecrow, California Originals	165.00
Scarecrow, Yellow, Japan	50.00
Schnauzer, California Originals	325.00
Schoolhouse, With Bell, American Bisque	70.00
Scotty Dog, Black, Metlox	125.00 to 195.00
Seal On Igloo, American Bisque	175.00 to 385.00
Sealy Train	60.00
Sheriff, California Originals	60.00
Sheriff, Lane Potteries	950.00
Snoopy, On Doghouse	200.00
Space Cadet	135.00
Spaceship, American Bisque	250.00
Squirrel, Arnel	25.00
Squirrel, On Pinecone, Metlox	90.00
Squirrel, On Stump, Gilner	65.00
Stagecoach, Sierra	275.00

Stella Strawberry 85.00
Tasmanian Devil, Vandor 300.00
Tasmanian Devil, Warner Bros. 325.00
Tat-L-Tales, Helen Hutula 995.00
Taxi, Gold, California Originals 300.00
Taxi, New York, Fitz & Floyd 325.00
Tin Soldier, Marsh 110.00
Tony The Tiger, Plastic, Kellogg's, 1968 .... 160.00
Tortoise & Hare, Flasher 700.00
Truck, American Bisque 85.00
Turtle, California Originals 35.00
Turtle, Doranne 30.00
Turtle & Hare, USA 60.00
Ugly Pumpkin Witch, Coral Collection 99.00
Umbrella Kids, American Bisque .... 175.00 to 425.00
Victrola, California Originals 150.00
Walrus, Doranne 45.00
Winnie The Pooh, Bee On Lid, American Bisque .... 85.00 to 90.00
Winnie The Pooh, Holding Honey Pot 235.00
Witch, Green Face, Fitz & Floyd .... *Illus* 275.00
Witch, On Broom, Fitz & Floyd 150.00
Woman, Cat Around Neck, Animals & Co. 300.00
Woman In Shoe, Fitz & Floyd 78.00
Woody Woodpecker, California Originals 625.00
Woody Woodpecker, Figural Head, Decal 750.00
Woody Woodpecker, On Barrel, Napco 475.00
Yarn Doll, American Bisque .... 80.00 to 125.00
Yogi Bear, American Bisque .... 275.00 to 450.00

COORS ware was made by a pottery in Golden, Colorado, owned by the Coors Beverage Company. Dishes and decorative wares were produced from the turn of the century until the pottery was destroyed by fire in the 1930s. The name *Coors* is marked on the back. For more information, see *Kovels' Depression Glass & American Dinnerware Price List.*

COORS
U.S.A.

Bowl, Mixing, Maroon, Handle, 3 1/2 Pt. 50.00
Casserole, Cover, Underplate, Rosebud, Blue 35.00
Custard, Rosebud, 4 Colors, 4 Piece 35.00
Honey Pot, Rosebud, Maroon 75.00
Jar, Utility, Rosebud, Green, 2 1/2 Pt. 45.00
Mortar & Pestle, Porcelain 65.00
Platter, Rosebud, Blue, 13 In. 35.00
Saltshaker, Yellow, Barrel Shape 29.95
Urn, Handle, Bulbous, 7 1/2 x 7 In. 68.00
Vase, Blue, 5 In. 30.00
Vase, Turquoise, Handle, 8 1/2 In. 20.00
Vase, Turquoise, Pink, Square Shoulder Handles, 5 3/4 x 8 1/2 In. 45.00

COPELAND pieces listed here are those that have a mark used between 1847 and 1976. See also Copeland Spode and Royal Worcester.

COPELAND

Centerpiece, 2 Women, Holding Basket, Majolica 1760.00
Figurine, Parrot, Polychrome, 7 In. 27.50
Plate, Imari, 10 1/4 In., 12 Piece. 375.00
Plate, Purple Floral Transfer, 10 1/2 In., Pair 44.00
Tea Tray, Maroon Design, White Ground, 21 x 17 In. 165.00
Tile, Cherubs, Relief Molded, White Glaze, 8 x 8 In., Pair 110.00

COPELAND SPODE appears on some pieces of nineteenth-century English porcelain. Josiah Spode established a pottery at Stoke-on-Trent, England, in 1770. In 1833, the firm was purchased by William Copeland and Thomas Garrett and the mark was changed. In 1847, Copeland became the sole owner and the mark changed again. W. T. Copeland & Sons continued until a 1976 merger when it became Royal Worcester Spode. Pieces are listed in this book under the name that appears in the mark. Copeland Spode, Copeland, and Royal Worcester have separate listings.

COPELAND
SPODE
ENGLAND

Bowl, Vegetable, Cover, Landscape 225.00
Coffeepot, Queen Bird .... 100.00 to 150.00
Cup & Saucer, Mulberry Flowers, Scrolls, Gadroon Rim 23.00
Cup & Saucer, Wicker Dell 10.00
Pitcher, Milk, Tower, Blue, 6 In. 75.00
Pitcher, Tower, Blue & White, 6 Qt., 9 1/2 x 10 In. 380.00
Pitcher, Winston Churchill, We Stand For Democracy, 1940s, Large 100.00
Plate, Basket Of Flowers & Fruits, c.1833, 10 1/2 In. 90.00
Plate, Phoenix Bird, Allover Lace, Scalloped, Cream, Pat, 1874, 9 In. 20.00
Plate, Stanford University, 10 1/2 In. 42.00
Plate, Tower, Pink, 10 1/2 In. 23.00
Platter, Florence, 13 In. 70.00
Platter, Turkey, Landscape Center, Floral Boarder, Oval, 23 3/4 In. 410.00
Punch Bowl, Tower, Blue, 15 1/2 In. 200.00
Relish, Chinoiseries, Dark Blue, Leaf Form 110.00
Syrup, Classical Maidens 50.00
Teapot, Classical Figures, Blue & White, 6 In. 121.00

COPPER has been used to make utilitarian items, such as teakettles and
cooking pans, since the days of the early American colonists. Copper became
a popular metal with the Arts & Crafts makers of the early 1900s, and
decorative pieces, like bookends and desk sets, were made. Other pieces of
copper may be found in the Arts & Crafts, Bradley & Hubbard, Kitchen, and
Roycroft categories.

Bed Warmer, Bird Design, Turned Wooden Handle 192.00
Bed Warmer, Engraved Lid, Turned Wooden Handle, 45 1/2 In. 165.00
Bed Warmer, Floral Pinwheel Tooled Brass Lid, 36 1/2 In. 160.00
Bed Warmer, Hinged Lid, No Handle, 12 1/ 2 In. 137.00
Blotter, Rolling, Copper, Mother-Of-Pearl, Burton Hammer Mark 65.00
Bowl, Hammered, Cupped, Scalloped, Gregorian Copper, 8 1/2 x 3 In. 15.00
Bowl, Reticulated, Pedestal, Manning Bowman, 4 x 7 1/2 In. 22.00
Bucket, Iron Handle & Base, 19 1/2 x 18 In. 180.00
Candleholder, Riveted Handle, Hammered, Gustav Stickley, No.74, 10 In. 1380.00
Centerpiece, Hand Hammered, Antelope, Elephant & Camel Medallions, 15 5/8 In. . 40.00
Chafing Dish, Cover, Wooden Handles, With 14 1/4-In. Tray, 3 Piece 48.00
Chafing Dish, On Wooden Tray, Shreve, Crump & Low, 1888, 11 x 16 1/2 In. 440.00
Chamberstick, Hammered, Scroll Handle, Snuffer, 3 1/2 & 5 In., 2 Piece 373.00
Chandelier, Reticulated, Figures, Cylindrical, Part Chain, 13 x 31 In. 373.00
Charger, Stylized Pods, Gustav Stickley, 20 In. 5250.00
Coffee & Tea Set, Hammered, Bronze Warmer, Gorham, 5 Piece 450.00
Coffee Server, Brass Fittings, Finial, Black Wooden Stick Handle 22.00
Coffee Urn, Universal, Early 1900s 250.00
Coffeepot, Percolator, Sterno Inferno, Pat. 2/17/1903 .... 120.00
Coffeepot, Persian Type, Hammered, Gorham, Late 19th Century, 7 3/4 In. 220.00
Coffeepot, Universal, 1913 .... 10.00
Jardiniere, Warty, Wide Mouth, Ovoid, Cylindrical Foot, Dirk Van Erp, 8 x 10 In. 2875.00
Jug, Hammered, Scroll Handle, Short-Waisted Neck, Dirk Van Erp, 9 1/4 In. 1265.00
Kettle, Bail Handle, Dovetailed, Riveted Handle Loops, Lacquered, 5 1/2 In. 60.00
Kettle, Candy, Rounded Bottom, Steel Rim Handles, 8 1/2 x 14 In. 82.50
Kettle, Preserving, 15 In. 175.00
Lamp, Hammered Riveted Conical Shade, Mica Panels, Dirk Van Erp, 20 In. 6250.00
Measures, Graduated, 1/2 Gill To Gal., England, 7 Piece 770.00
Measure, Haystack, 12 In. 115.00
Molds are listed in the Kitchen category
Pan, Tin Lining, Wrought Iron Handle, Rivets, Impressed K.K., 16 1/2 In. 140.00
Saucepan, Wrought Iron Handle, 26 x 12 In. 77.00
Sconce, Hammered, Evergreen Tree Form, Pierced, 17 In. 632.00
Sideboard Set, Copper, Manning & Bowman 115.00
Sugar & Creamer, Flattened Disc Shape Bodies, Craftsman Studios 95.00
Teakettle, 10 1/2 In. 99.00
Teakettle, Brass Finial, Handle, Melon Ribbed, Tin, China, 6 1/2 In. 74.00
Teakettle, Carved Hunt Scenes, Gilt Metal Mount, Stand, Late 1700s, 13 1/2 In. 2300.00
Teakettle, Gooseneck Spout, Acorn Finial, 10 1/2 In. 182.00

Tray, Silver Peacock, Branch, Butterfly, Gorham, 12 x 9 In. 1210.00
Utensil, Candy Maker's, 3 Spouts, Paris Label, 9 1/2 In. 71.50
Vase, 6 Arched Panels, Hammered, Cylindrical, Harry Dixon, 14 3/4 In. 1475.00
Vase, Hammered, Footed, Wide Mouth, Cylindrical, Dirk Van Erp, 1915, 23 In. 7475.00
Vase, Hammered, Painted Stylized Flowers, Cylindrical, Dirk Van Erp, 15 In. 1495.00
Whiskey Still, Cone Top, 1 Gal. 85.00
Wine Cooler, Urn Form, 11 1/2 In., Pair 287.00

CORALENE glass was made by firing many small colored beads on the
outside of glassware. It was made in many patterns in the United States and
Europe in the 1880s. Reproductions are made today. Coralene-decorated
Japanese pottery is listed in the Japanese Coralene category.

Vase, Allover Seaweed Beading, Yellow, 8 In. 325.00
Vase, Beading Of Flowers, Yellow To Burnt Orange, Marked, 4 3/4 In. 345.00
Vase, Blue To White, Ruffled, Crimped Top, 6 In. 525.00
Vase, Leaves & Buds, Gold Outlining, 10 1/2 In. 600.00
Vase, Long Leaves, Gold Outlined Buds, Lavender Ground, Kinran, 1909, 10 In. 650.00
Vase, Peachblow, Opalescent, Gold Beaded Coral Design, 8 3/4 In., Pair 495.00
Vase, Seaweed Design, Yellow Beads, Gold Trim, Mt.Washington, 7 1/2 In. 625.00
Vase, Yellow Seaweed, Pink To White, White Interior, Square Mouth, 10 1/2 In. 905.00
Vase, Yellow, Green & White Flowers, Gold Borders Top & Base, 4 3/4 In. 375.00

CORDEY China Company was founded by Boleslaw Cybis in 1942 in
Trenton, New Jersey. The firm produced gift shop items. In 1969 it was
acquired by the Lightron Corp. and operated as the Schiller Cordey Co.,
manufacturers of lamps. About 1950 Boleslaw Cybis began making Cybis
porcelains, which are listed in their own category in this book.

Box, Cover, Pink Roses, Green Leaves, Gold Trim, 5 x 5 In. 45.00
Bust, Woman 49.00
Clock, Rococo, Scrolled, Bird & Roses, 14 1/2 In. 150.00
Figurine, Ballet Dancer, Pair 170.00
Figurine, Colonial Man & Woman, 16 In. 90.00
Figurine, Man, 16 In. 80.00
Figurine, Woman, Blue Rose At Bodice, Flowers In Hair, No. 5012, 6 In. 55.00
Figurine, Woman, Holding Flowers, 9 1/2 In. 65.00
Figurine, Woman, With Fan, Peach Skirt, Fuchsia Bodice, 16 In. 110.00
Lamp, Bouquet Tulips, No. 532 .... 135.00

CORKSCREWS have been needed since the first bottle was sealed with a
cork, probably in the seventeenth century. Today collectors search for the
early, unusual patented examples or the figural corkscrews of recent years.

Dog's Head, Handle 18.00
Folding, Oct. 16, 1877 .... 25.00
Gnarled Briar Handle, France, 8 In. 22.00
Keen Kutter, Marked 25.00
Lady's Leg, Red & Tan Striped, Germany 125.00
Lady's Leg, Tooled Brass, Striped Celluloid Inlay, 2 5/8 In. 148.50
Opicci Wines, Brass, With Bottle Opener 20.00
Zigzag, Bottle Opener, Instructions, 1951, Paris, Box 16.00

CORONATION souvenirs have been made since the 1800s. Pottery, glass, tin,
silver, and paper objects with a picture of the monarchs and date have been
sold at many coronations. The pieces that mention King Edward VIII, the
king who was never crowned, are not rare; collectors should be sure to check
values before buying. Related pieces are found in the Commemorative
category.

Book, King Edward VII, George VI & Queen Elizabeth, 1937, 176 Pages 150.00
Book, King George VI, Queen Elizabeth, 126 Pages 80.00
Book, Our King, Queen, Royal Princesses, 176 Pages 80.00
Coaster-Ashtray, Center Medallion, Milk Glass, 1953 .... 10.00
Coloring Book, Queen Elizabeth 20.00
Cup & Saucer, Bread Plate, Queen Elizabeth II, 3 Piece 48.00
Fork, George VI, Chrome & Ivory, 1937 .... 38.00

Mug, Queen Elizabeth, June 2, 1953, Tuscan, 3 1/2 In.	24.00
Pin Tray, Queen Elizabeth II	15.00
Tray, Wicker, 1937	25.00

COSMOS is a pressed milk glass pattern with colored flowers made from 1894 to 1915 by the Consolidated Lamp and Glass Company. Tablewares and lamps were made in this pattern. A few pieces were also made of clear glass with painted decorations. Other glass patterns are listed under Consolidated Lamp and also in various glass categories.

Butter, Cover, Pink Band	235.00 to 335.00
Condiment Set, Matching Frame, 3 Piece	310.00
Spooner, Pink Band	95.00
Tumbler, Spooner & Mustard	200.00
Water Set, 5 Piece	425.00

COVERLETS were made of linen or wool during the nineteenth century. Most of the coverlets date from 1800 to 1850. Four types were made: the double weave, jacquard, summer and winter, and overshot. Later coverlets were made of a variety of materials. Quilts are listed in this book in their own category.

Double Weave, Geometric, Cotton, Blues, Reds, Gold Fringe 3 Sides, 78 x 90 In.	135.00
Jacquard, 4 Rose Medallions, Stars, Flora Groton, 1833, 80 x 96 In.	165.00
Jacquard, Blue & Cream, Corner Block Design, 3 Fringed Sides, 1840, 87 x 70 In.	650.00
Jacquard, Boston Town Design, Vintage Border, Navy & White, 62 x 74 In.	385.00
Jacquard, Central Medallion, Floral Border, Wm. Ney, Lebanon, Penna., 78 x 84 In.	330.00
Jacquard, Double Weave, Star Center, Birds, Deer, Red, Navy, Brown, 75 x 82 In.	440.00
Jacquard, Flora Medallions, Colored Border, 74 x 78 In.	330.00
Jacquard, Floral Medallions, H. Wolf, Ohio AD 1854, Blue, Red, Gold, 74 x 82 In.	357.00
Jacquard, Floral Medallions, Michael Franze, Miami County, 1840, 67 x 90 In.	605.00
Jacquard, Floral Medallions, Navy & Red, 81 x 92 In., 2-Piece	440.00
Jacquard, Floral, Bird Border, Made By P. H. For L Eveitt, 1839, 78 x 84 In.	192.50
Jacquard, Floral, Vintage Border, Jacob Daron, 1845, 82 x 84 In.	357.50
Jacquard, Floral Star Medallions, Rose Border, Knox County, Oh., 1848, 69 x 77 In.	465.00
Jacquard, Floral & Star Medallions, Vintage Border, Samuel Dornbach, 82 x 89 In.	440.00
Jacquard, Flowers & Stars, Vining Border, 80 x 86 In.	137.50
Jacquard, Flowers, D. Cosley, Zenia, Ohio, 1857, 86 x 96 In.	137.50
Jacquard, Flowers, Squares, Bouquet Border, House With Date 1848, 90 x 76 In.	275.00
Jacquard, Geometric Floral, 71 x 90 In.	193.00
Jacquard, Geometric Floral, Corners Dated 1841, 76 x 84 In.	85.00
Jacquard, Geometric Floral, Corners Dated 1852, 66 x 86 In.	192.50
Jacquard, Geometric Floral Center, House & Bird Border, 72 x 88 In.	687.50
Jacquard, Hempfield Railroad, Blue & Red, 75 x 88 In.	3520.00
Jacquard, Medallions, Eagle, Buildings, Navy, Red, Olive, Natural, 74 x 86 In.	550.00
Jacquard, Medallions, Roses, John Kittinger, 1839, Salmon, Navy, 72 x 92 In.	550.00
Jacquard, Medallions, Steamship Borders, B.Lichty, 1845, 2-Piece, 71 x 71 In.	577.00
Jacquard, Peter Grimm, Loudenville, Ohio, 1868	1000.00
Jacquard, Railroad Border, Floral, Navy & White, Paper Tag, 2-Piece, 77 x 85 In.	2860.00
Jacquard, Red & White, Bird Design, 19th Century, 90 x 83 In.	198.00
Jacquard, Star & Flower, Bird, Roses, G. Stich, 1839, Red, Natural, 70 x 84 In.	319.00
Jacquard, Star Center, Eagles & Flowers, Fringe, 80 x 90 In.	192.50
Jacquard, Star Center, Flowers, Eagles & Shield Corners, 78 x 80 In.	280.00
Jacquard, Stylized Floral, Bird Border, Corner H. Petry, 1839, 63 x 80 In.	275.00
Jacquard, Turkey & Peacocks, Navy, Natural, 78 x 84 In.	110.00
Jacquard, Urns Of Flowers, Peacocks Feeding Young, 68 x 88 In.	220.00
Made By W. Kuder, N.W. Hall, Lehigh Co., Pa., For Feietta Miller, 1862.	375.00
Overshot, Butternut & Olive, 19th Century, 96 x 45 In.	275.00
Overshot, Optical Design, 64 x 88 In.	125.00
Overshot, Optical Pattern, Red, Navy, Natural, 2-Piece, 62 x 88 In.	115.00
Overshot, Plaid Pattern, 72 x 82 In.	155.00
Overshot, Red & Blue Geometric Design, White Ground, 69 x 74 In.	140.00
Overshot, Star & Circle, Red, Navy, Teal & Natural, 2-Piece, 72 x 90 In.	550.00
Overshot, Star, Diamond & Stripe, Red, Navy, Gold, Olive, White, 74 x 90 In.	165.00
Overshot, Stars, Trees, Floral, Soldiers, Navy, Salmon, White, 2-Piece, 70 x 89 In.	313.00

Overshot, Star Design, 90 x 95 In. 357.50
Overshot, Tomato Red, Navy Blue & White, 72 x 86 In. 330.00
Pine Tree Design, Red, White & Blue, 1830 .... 595.00
Red & Blue Geometric Design, White Ground, 69 x 74 In. 140.00
Single Weave, Geometric Floral, Navy, Teal, Red & Natural, 74 x 82 In ... 82.50
Single Weave, Rose Medallions, Andre Kump, 1839, 87 x 87 In. 357.00
Single Weave, Rose Medallions, Red, Navy, Olive, Natural, 1848, 72 x 94 In. 88.00
Summer & Winter, Geometric, Blue & White, 19th Century, 69 x 86 In. 176.00

COWAN POTTERY made art pottery and wares for florists. Guy Cowan made pottery in Rocky River, Ohio, a suburb of Cleveland, from 1913 to 1931. A stylized mark with the word *Cowan* was used on most pieces. A commercial, mass-produced line was marked *Lakeware.* Collectors today search for the Art Deco pieces by Guy Cowan, Viktor Schreckengost, Waylande Gregory, or Thelma Frazier Winter.

Ashtray, Art Deco Bird, Attached Match Holder 65.00
Bowl, Cream, Apple Green Interior, Scalloped, Footed, 9 1/2 x 4 In. 24.00
Bowl, Footed, Blue Luster, 2 Handles, 6-In. Draped Nude Flower Frog, 12 In. 360.00
Bowl, Footed, Cream, Green Interior, 9 1/4 In. 30.00
Candleholder, Sea Horses, Oblong Base, White Semigloss, 4 In., Pair 66.00
Candlestick, Lavender Luster, 3 1/4 In. 55.00
Candlestick, Orange Luster, Scalloped, 3 3/4 In., Pair 32.00
Candlestick, Purple Luster, 10 1/2 In., Pair 80.00
Console, Birds' Heads, 15 In. 150.00
Console Set, Blue Luster Glaze, Pink & Yellow Highlights, 10-In. Bowl, 3 Piece 95.00
Console Set, Ivory, Nude Woman Shape, Flower Frog, Candleholder, 3 Piece 245.00
Console Set, Nude Woman Flower Frog, Candleholders, 4 Piece 265.00
Figurine, Clown, Kneeling, Holding Bowl, Yellow Glaze, 3 x 4 In. 70.00
Figurine, Dancer, 9 1/4 In. .... *Illus* 350.00
Flower Frog, Dancer Figure, Holding Disc On Swirling Base, 10 x 6 1/2 In. 500.00
Flower Frog, Dancing Woman, Drape, White Glaze, 6 In. 150.00
Flower Frog, Dancing Woman, With Disc, White Glaze, 10 In. 825.00
Flower Frog, Double, Dancing Women With Drapes, White Glaze, 8 In. 525.00
Flower Frog, Nude Dancer, Scarf, 6 1/2 In. 135.00
Match Holder, Sea Horses, Ivory 60.00
Soap Dish, Sea Horse Pedestal, Pink, White, Pair 55.00
Trivet, Art Deco Woman's Face, Scalloped Rim, 6 1/2 In. 125.00
Urn, Cover, 2 Rams' Heads, 2-Handled, Square Base, Turquoise Blue Glaze, 13 In. ... 440.00
Vase, Blue Luster, 3 1/2 x 5 1/2 In. 35.00
Vase, Blue Luster, Bulbous Bottom, Cylindrical Neck, 13 In. 130.00
Vase, Bulbous, Molded Birds, Squirrel, Flowers, Light Green Glaze, 8 1/2 In. 495.00
Vase, Fan, Sea Horses On Base, Crystalline, Green 150.00
Vase, Flared, Flower Frog, Aqua, 7 1/2 In., Pair 100.00
Vase, Flared, Orange Luster, 5 1/2 In. 11.00
Vase, Flared, Sunrise Glaze, Melon Ribbed, 11 In. 225.00
Vase, Green Luster, 7 1/4 In. 65.00

◆◆◆◆◆◆◆◆◆◆◆◆◆◆◆◆◆◆◆◆◆◆◆

Plastic bubble wrap can harm the glaze on old ceramics. If the wrap touches the piece for a long time in a hot storage area, it may damage the glaze.

◆◆◆◆◆◆◆◆◆◆◆◆◆◆◆◆◆◆◆◆◆◆◆

Cowan, Figurine, Dancer, 9 1/4 In.

Cracker Jack, Postcard, Baseball, Bears, 1927, Set of 16

Clean dirty post-cards with a piece of white bread. Be sure to cut the crust off first.

Vase, Lusterware, Blue, 8 x 7 In.	70.00
Vase, Pillow, Exotic Bird, Green & Turquoise Glaze, 11 In.	445.00
Vase, Stick, Ivory, 4 In.	15.00
Vase, Turquoise, 15 In.	150.00

CRACKER JACK, the molasses-flavored popcorn mixture, was first made in 1896 in Chicago, Illinois. A prize was added to each box in 1912. Collectors search for the old boxes, toys, and advertising materials. Many of the toys are unmarked.

Bear, Seated, Rocks Back & Forth	19.00
Book, Drawing, 4 Sheets, Tracing Paper, 1930s, 1 1/4 x 2 1/4 In.	25.00
Book, Drawing, With Tracing Paper, 1930s, 8 Pages, 2 1/2 x 3 1/2 In.	77.00
Book, Riddle	35.00
Book, Uncle Sam's Famous National Songs, 1917, 2 1/4 x 3 /4 In.	48.00
Booklet, Riddles	30.00
Box, Empty, 1923	65.00
Box, Red, White & Blue, Ends Missing, 1930s, 1 1/2 x 3 x 6 1/2 In.	56.00
Bumble Bee, Light Green Plastic	10.00
Coconut Crisp, Tin, 1 Lb...	50.00
Doll, On Card	55.00
Duck, Dark Pink Plastic	10.00
Elephant, Light Green	10.00
Game, Board, Milton Bradley, 1976	45.00
Goat, Pale Gray Plastic	10.00
Hat, Me For Cracker Jack, Paper, Tassels, 1930s, 7 x 14 In.	58.00
Lunch Pail, Metal Carrying Handles, Tin Lithograph, 1970s, 5 x 6 In.	40.00
Marshmallow Wagon	100.00
Ocarina, Celluloid	3.00
Periscope, Box	35.00
Police Badge	20.00
Postcard, Baseball, Bears, 1927, Set Of 16 .... *Illus*	440.00
Postcard, Bears Meeting President Theodore Roosevelt, 1907, 3 x 5 1/2 In.	42.00
Smitty, Stand-Up, Tin	75.00
Whistle, Embossed Tin, 1930s	12.00

CRACKLE GLASS was originally made by the Venetians, but most of the ware found today dates from the 1800s. The glass was heated, cooled, and refired so that many small lines appeared inside the glass. It was made in many factories in the United States and Europe.

Bowl, Beaded Buttons, Flared, Iridescent, 11 3/8 x 3 1/4 In.	45.00
Bowl, Blue, Vally, 2 1/4 x 6 1/2 In.	300.00
Compote, Blue Cast, Applied Foot, 13 x 7 1/2 In.	36.00
Compote, Blue, Eggplant, 2 x 7 In.	275.00
Cruet, Blue, 7 1/2 In.	20.00
Pitcher, Green, Applied Handle, 9 1/2 In.	30.00

Vase, Blue & White, China, 7 1/4 In.	55.00
Vase, Car, Jeanette, Marigold	25.00
Vase, Domed Lid, 19 In.	210.00
Vase, Red To Orange, 7 In.	22.50

CRANBERRY GLASS is an almost transparent yellow-red glass. It resembles the color of cranberry juice. The glass has been made in Europe and America since the Civil War. It is still being made, and reproductions can fool the unwary. Related glass items may be listed in other categories, such as Northwood, Rubena Verde, etc.

Basket, Blown	65.00
Basket, Insert, Ornate Brass Frame	165.00
Biscuit Jar, Gold Flowers & Leaves, Square, 7 /14 In.	295.00
Bottle, Barber, Hobnail, Opalescent	170.00
Box, Hinged, Cut To Clear .... *Illus*	1550.00
Carafe, Forget-Me-Nots, Dotting, Gold Trim, 8 3/4 In.	165.00
Champagne, Panel & Flute, Crystal Stem, Dorflinger	160.00
Compote, Enameled, Cut, Etched, Gold Trim	175.00
Cracker Jar, Inverted Thumbprint	265.00
Creamer, Inverted Thumbprint, Square Mouth, 4 3/4 In.	135.00
Cruet, Inverted Thumbprint .... 60.00 to	150.00
Cruet, Thumbprint, Tricornered, Prism Cut Stopper	125.00
Cruet, Wine, Pewter Frame, 15 In.	325.00
Decanter, Crackle, Pinched Sides	95.00
Decanter, Overlay, Shaded To Clear, Ribbed, Stopper, 12 In.	242.00
Decanter, Wine, 3-Petal Top, Enameled Fans, Dots & Arches, 4 3/4 x 9 In.	235.00
Epergne, Door On Silver Plated Base, Holding Bud Vase	247.00
Hat, White & Opalescent Swirl, 4 In.	75.00
Jar, Cover, Hand Painted, Pam Muller, Fenton	75.00
Lamp, Lily-Of-The-Valley, 7 1/4 In.	1075.00
Perfume Bottle, Blue Forget-Me-Nots, Gold Centers, 3 1/2 In.	185.00
Perfume Bottle, Mary Gregory-Style Girl With Bubble Pipe	350.00
Pitcher, Cream, Clear Glass Handle, 3 1/2 In.	50.00
Pitcher, Inverted Thumbprint, Ruffled, Clear Applied Handle, 8 1/2 In.	95.00
Pitcher, Leaf Mold	450.00
Pitcher, Stars & Stripes, Opalescent, Tankard Shape, 8 1/2 In. .... *Illus*	1650.00
Pitcher, Water, Polkadot, Opalescent, Shoulder Shape, 1950s	295.00
Pitcher, Water, Square Mouth, Raised Swirl, Hobb	335.00
Pitcher Set, Inverted Thumbprint, 6 Piece	450.00

♦♦♦♦♦♦♦♦♦♦♦♦♦♦♦♦♦♦♦♦♦♦♦

Look in your hardware store for the new glues that can fix almost anything. Buy the proper one to fix transparent glass, porous pottery, or non-porous metals. There will be one that will work.

♦♦♦♦♦♦♦♦♦♦♦♦♦♦♦♦♦♦♦♦♦♦♦

Left: Cranberry Glass, Tumble-Up, Cut To Clear, Squares
Upper: Cranberry Glass, Box, Hinged, Cut To Clear
Right: Cranberry Glass, Tumble-Up, Cut To Clear
Lower: Cranberry Glass, Ramekin, Underplate, Cut To Clear

Cranberry Glass, Pitcher, Stars & Stripes,
Opalescent, Tankard Shape, 8 1/2 In.

◆◆◆◆◆◆◆◆◆◆◆◆◆◆◆◆◆◆◆◆◆◆◆◆◆

Think about the problems of
owning a cat and a large collection of ceramics.

◆◆◆◆◆◆◆◆◆◆◆◆◆◆◆◆◆◆◆◆◆◆◆◆◆

Plate, 8 In.	23.00
Punch Set, Child's, Fan & File, 7 Piece	30.00
Ramekin, Underplate, Cut To Clear .... *Illus*	1800.00
Saltshaker, Applied Clear Pedestal, Enameled Floral, Pewter	195.00
Shade, Bull's-Eye, 14 In.	875.00
Stein, Pewter Trim & Lid	90.00
Sugar Shaker, Beaded Cover, Optic Panel	150.00
Sugar Shaker, Leaf Umbrella	345.00
Sugar Shaker, Ribbed Lattice, Opalescent	179.00
Sugar Shaker, Ribbed Opal Lattice	225.00
Toothpick, Inverted Thumbprint	55.00
Tumble-Up, Cut To Clear .... *Illus*	4100.00
Tumble-Up, Cut To Clear, Squares .... *Illus*	3100.00
Tumbler, Daisy & Fern, Opalescent	46.00
Tumbler, Seaweed, Opalescent	100.00
Vase, Bud, White Stripes, Flared, 8 In.	85.00
Vase, Cornucopia, Crystal Thorny Footed, 10 In.	85.00
Vase, Flared, Enameled Lacy Scroll Design, Dots, 14 In.	165.00
Vase, Flared, White Enameled Flowers & Leaves, 10 1/2 In.	95.00
Vase, Mary Gregory-Style Boy, 3 In.	225.00
Vase, Notched Lip, 18 3/4 In.	1540.00
Vase, Swirl, White Rim, 9 1/2 In.	45.00
Vase, Trumpet, Crimped, Clear Footed, 11 1/4 In., Pair	350.00
Vase, White & Cranberry Fused Beads, Flashed White, 11 3/4 In.	175.00
Water Set, Enameled, 7 Piece	450.00
Water Set, Inverted Thumbprint, 6 Piece	275.00

CREAMWARE, or queensware, was developed by Josiah Wedgwood about
1765. It is a cream-colored earthenware that has been copied by many
factories. Similar wares may be listed under Pearlware and Wedgwood.

Bowl, Polychrome Floral, 3 x 7 1/4 In.	220.00
Bowl, Reticulated Design, 3-Footed, 8 3/4 x 2 1/2 In.	27.50
Candlestick, Dolphin Form, Shell Design Base, 10 In., 4 Piece	460.00
Coffeepot, Floral & Foliate Design, Bulbous Body, Multicolored, 12 In.	200.00
Cruet, 18th Century, Pair	4500.00
Cup & Saucer, Twined Handle	132.00
Dish, Quatrefoil, Molded Basket Weave Design, Brown, Green, 8 x 9 In.	121.00
Dish, Reticulated Rim, 6 5/8 In.	93.00
Figurine, Owl, Incised Plumage, Green & Brown Spots, c.1785, 5 1/2 In.	5280.00
Figurine, Peacock, Blue-Green, Staffordshire, c.1770, 3 3/8 In.	1495.00
Figurine, Ram, Clear Glaze With Dark Brown, 3 5/8 In.	120.00
Figurine, Sheep, Brown, Tan & White, 3 In.	192.00
Figurine, Shepherd Carrying Sheep On Shoulders, R. Wood, c.1780, 8 3/4 In.	1265.00
Figurine, Squirrel, Eating Nut, Mound Base, Staffordshire, c.1780, 7 1/8 In.	1380.00
Figurine, St. George And The Dragon, R. Wood, c.1780, 10 7/8 In.	1265.00 to 1380.00

◆◆◆◆◆◆◆◆◆◆◆◆◆◆◆◆◆◆◆◆◆◆◆◆◆

Spray the inside of a glass
flower vase with a non-stick
product made to keep food from
sticking to cooking pots. This
will keep the vase from staining
if water is left in too long.

◆◆◆◆◆◆◆◆◆◆◆◆◆◆◆◆◆◆◆◆◆◆◆◆◆

Creamware, Pitcher, Banded

Inkstand, Blue Spatter, Figural Reclining Roman Soldier Lid, Continental, 8 In.	330.00
Jug, Cream, Trailing Vine, Animal Paw Feet, Staffordshire, c.1760, 5 1/2 In.	1760.00
Medallion, Stuart's George Washington, Gilded Frame, 2 3/4 x 2 1/4 In.	275.00
Mug, Floral Enamel, Blue Transfer Band, Polychrome, 2 1/4 In.	38.50
Pitcher, Banded .... *Illus*	275.00
Pitcher, Black Transfer, Washington & Lafayette, U.S. In Year 1824, 5 1/4 In.	545.00
Pitcher, Floral Enameling, Brown Striping, Polychrome, 5 7/8 In.	115.50
Plaque, Black Transfer, Washington, Oval, c.1800, 5 x 4 In.	1540.00
Plate, Basket Weave, Reticulated Rim, 8 1/4 In.	110.00
Plate, Duke Of Orange, In Dutch, Dated 1785, 9 3/4 In.	99.00
Plate, Scalloped, Allover Leaves & Branches, Staffordshire, 9 3/4 In., Pair	2420.00
Platter, Persia, Ridgway, 18 In.	35.00
Salt Box, Hanging, Windmill, Landscape, Wooden Lid	70.00
Sauceboat, Twisted Handle	875.00
Sugar, Flower Finial, Twined Handles, 4 In.	137.00
Tea Bowl & Saucer, Red & Green Design, 5-In. Saucer, c.1770	285.00
Teapot, Cauliflower Shape, William Greatbatch, 1765, 4 7/8 In.	2185.00
Teapot, Mottled Brown & Green, c.1770, 3 1/2 In.	220.00
Teapot, Transfer Printed Sunflowers, 1870s, 9 In.	105.00
Vase, 5-Finger, Blue Design, Pair .... 990.00 to	1100.00
Vase, Speckled Brown & Blue, Portrait, Neale Porphyry, c.1780, 8 1/4 In.	1100.00
Vase, Spill, Fox, Goose & Tree Trunk, c.1790, 4 3/4 In.	2300.00
Vase, Spill, Lion, Fox & Tree Trunk, c.1790, 5 In.	1955.00

CREDIT CARDS, credit tokens, metal charge plates, and other similar
collectibles are now part of the numismatic collecting hobby.

American Express, Money Card, Expires 3-74	18.50
American Express, Violet, Expires 12-69	85.00
Bank Americard, Expires 9-71	4.50
Bergdorf Goodman, Princess, Violet, Store Drawing	3.00
Carte Blanche, Blue Top, March 1963	11.50
Carte Blanche, Gold, Expires 1-75	6.00
Continental Airlines, 3 Photographs Top, Expires 4-82	7.00
Diners Club, Colored Boxes Near Top, Nov. 73	11.00
Goodyear, Blue Top With 6-Picture Yellow Bottom, Expires 4-80	4.00
Harrods, White On Green, Princess, Full Mailing Address Embossed	9.00
Hertz, Paperboard, Courtesy Card, Expires 7-16-45	24.00
Hotel Corporation Of America, 1956	40.00
I. Magnin, Princess, Tan, Brown Letters	5.00
John Wanamaker, Princess, Light Blue, Eagle On Back	7.00
Kaufmann's, Charge Coin, White Metal, Oval	12.00
Montgomery Ward, Data Punch Hole	12.50
Playboy Club, Gold, Bunny Design, Expires 2-80	7.00
Playboy Club, Gold, Bunny Design, Expires 2-87	5.00
Standard Oil, Calendar Envelope, 1940, 2 1/2 x 3 1/2 In.	7.00
Visa, Finance America, Expires 6-79	4.00
Western Union, Paperboard, Collect, 1924	6.00
Wiebolt's, Green, White Ground	8.00

CROWN DERBY is the name given to porcelain made in Derby, England, from the 1770s to 1935. Pieces are marked with a crown and the letter *D* or the word *Derby*. The earliest pieces were made by the original Derby factory, while later pieces were made by the King Street Partnerships (1848–1935) or the Derby Crown Porcelain Co. (1876–1890). Derby Crown Porcelain Co. became Royal Crown Derby Co. Ltd. in 1890. It is now part of Royal Doulton Tableware Ltd.

Bowl, Cover, Vegetable, Rectangular, 1800 .... 495.00

CROWN MILANO glass was made by Frederick Shirley at the Mt. Washington Glass Works about 1890. It had a plain biscuit color with a satin finish. It was decorated with flowers and often had large gold scrolls.

Biscuit Jar, 3 Smiling Faces, Scrolls Of Gold Frame Each Face, 6 In. 1050.00
Biscuit Jar, Butterfly Over Floral, Silver Plated Lid, Signed, 5 In. 785.00
Biscuit Jar, Gilded Flowers, Silver Plated Rim, Handle & Cover 600.00
Biscuit Jar, Gold Wash Lid, 3 Pansies, 2 Cartouches, Gold Scrolls, 6 x 7 In. 1050.00
Biscuit Jar, Pansies, Butterfly Finial, Silver Plated Lid, Floral Embossed, 5 In. 785.00
Bowl, Cover, Florals, Aladdin Lamp Shape, White Ground, 5 3/4 x 9 In. 1850.00
Bowl, Foliated Sprays, Forget-Me-Nots Rim, 2 1/2 x 4 In. 565.00
Bowl, Pansy Blossoms, 3 Gold Blossoms, 5 1/8 In. 585.00
Box, Trinket, Enamel Pansies On Cover & Base, 3 1/2 In. 275.00
Bride's Basket, Bouquets Of Florals, Allover Enamel, Cupid Stem, 10 In. 495.00
Condiment Set, Gold Chrysanthemums, Ormolu Mounts, Signed, 3 Piece 1100.00
Cracker Jar, Cover, Melon Design 875.00
Dish, Sweetmeat, Floral & Gold Woven On Melon Ribs, Signed 650.00
Dish, Sweetmeat, Stylized Starfish, Silver Plated Collar, Lid & Bail, 6 In. 845.00
Pitcher, Pond Lilies, Serpent Handle, Cream Ground, 8 1/2 In. .... *Illus* 2310.00
Rose Bowl, Enameled Pansies, 3 Gold Blossoms & Design, 5 1/8 In. 585.00
Rose Bowl, Mt. Washington, 6 1/2 In. 95.00
Sugar & Creamer, Lavender Violets, Lusterless White, Pink Rim, Gold Trim 920.00
Sugar & Creamer, Pansies, Brushed Gold, 3 1/2 In. 985.00
Vase, 3 Leaf Handles, Opaque Eggshell Base, Triangular, 8 1/4 In. 1250.00
Vase, Cover, Ivy Leaves & Vines, Gold Outlining, 10 1/2 In. 2295.00
Vase, Fern Design, 5 In. 695.00
Vase, Gold Spider Mums, Cream Ground, Signed, 11 1/2 In. .... 850.00 to 895.00
Vase, Mums, Gold Outlined, Scalloped Gold Rim, 4 1/2 In. 750.00
Vase, Pastel Dots, Melon Ribs, 6 Medallions, 8 1/2 In. 485.00
Vase, Spider Mums In Raised Gold, Shadow Medallions, 11 1/2 In. 875.00
Vase, Yellow Neck & Mouth, 4 Fold-Down Sides, 6 In. 965.00

CRUETS of glass or porcelain were made to hold vinegar, oil, and other condiments. They were especially popular during Victorian times and have been made in a variety of styles since the eighteenth century. Additional cruets may be found in the Castor Set category and also in various glass categories.

Amberina, Baby Thumbprint 95.00
Apple Blossom, Netted, Milk Glass Stopper, Northwood 275.00

Crown Milano, Pitcher, Pond Lilies, Serpent Handle, Cream Ground, 8 1/2 In.

Blue Glass, Hand Painted, Satin Overlay, Wright, Pair 75.00
Cable, Flint 115.00
Cut Glass, Overlay, Opaque White To Clear, Enameled, Gilt, 7 In. 71.00
Cut Glass, Plaid Cut Neck & Waist, Cone Shape, Applied Handle, No Stopper 18.00
Florette, Satin Glass, Pink, Frosted Handle & Stopper 185.00
Oil & Vinegar, Glass, Etched Lines, Lettering, Ball Stopper 18.00
Pressed Glass, Hobstars, Facets, Octagonal Neck, Blown In Mold, No Stopper 6.00
Prize Pattern, Emerald Green, Gold, Original Stopper 225.00
Royal Oak, Clear, Frosted, Original Stopper, Northwood 250.00
Ruby Glass, Bohemian 75.00
Silver Overlay, Cut Green Over Crystal, Star Cut Base, 7 1/4 In. 825.00
Vinegar, Purple Iridescent, Carnival Glass, Stopper, Large 28.00

CT GERMANY was first part of a mark used by a company in Altwasser, Germany, in 1845. The initials stand for C. Tielsch, a partner in the firm. The Hutschenreuther firm took over the company in 1918 and continued to use the *CT.*

C.T.

Bowl, Pink & Gold, Ornate Shape, Shallow, 14 In. 55.00
Cup & Saucer, Lavender & Yellow Floral Sprays, Gold Sponged 12.00
Dish, Serving, Flowers, Gold, Handle 55.00
Plate, Portrait, Louis XVI, 8 In. 85.00
Plate, Wild Rose Sprays, Gold Rim, Scalloped, Marked, 11 Piece 55.00
Plate, Woman, With Roses, Long Brown Hair, Gold Tracery, Handle, 9 3/4 In. 85.00
Ramekin, Pink Roses, Scalloped, Altwasser 5.00
Vase, Portrait, Woman, With Roses, Brown, Twig Shoulder Handles, 10 1/2 In. 95.00

CUP PLATES are small glass or china plates that held the cup while a diner of the mid-nineteenth century drank coffee or tea from the saucer. The most famous cup plates were made of glass at the Boston and Sandwich factory located in Sandwich, Massachusetts. There have been many new glass cup plates made in recent years for sale to the gift shops or the limited edition collectors. These are similar to the old plates but can be recognized as new.

Arched Stone Bridge, Dark Blue, Trefoil Border, Wood 225.00
Battersea Park, Dark Blue Transfer, Staffordshire, 3 5/8 In. 357.50
Cadmus, Dark Blue Transfer, Staffordshire, 3 5/8 In. 264.00
Cadmus, Dark Blue, Trefoil Border, Enoch Wood 350.00
Christmas Eve, Wilkie Series, Dark Blue, Clews 145.00
Eagle, Pale Blue 770.00
Fakeers Rock, Red, Hall 85.00
Garfield, Frosted Intaglio Bust 75.00
Hearts, Flint 25.00
Lacy Glass, Lyre, 3 3/8 In. 71.50
Landing Of Lafayette, Dark Blue 295.00
Log Cabin, Flint 50.00
Plentiful, Honey Amber 45.00
Quadrupeds Series, Dark Blue, Staffordshire, 3 7/8 In. 148.50
Sailboats, Dark Blue, Full Shell Border, Wood 75.00
Sulphide, Bust, Colorless, Lee No. 842 .... 300.00
Sulphide, Bust, Facing Right 220.00
Sulphide, Bust, Man In Uniform, Facing Left 231.00
Windsor Castle, Pink 125.00

CURRIER & IVES made the famous American lithographs marked with their name from 1857 to 1907. The mark used on the print included the street address in New York City, and it is possible to date the year of the original issue from this information. Earlier prints were made by N. Currier and use that name from 1835 to 1847. Many reprints of the Currier or Currier & Ives prints have been made. Some collectors buy the insurance calendars that were based on the old prints. The words *large, small,* or *medium folio* refer to size. Other prints by Currier & Ives may be listed in the Card category under Advertising and in the Sheet Music category.

A Home On The Mississippi, Frame, 17 1/2 x 21 1/2 In. 465.00
American Country Life, May Morning, 1855, Large Folio 1900.00

American Farm Scenes, Autumn, Large Folio 3695.00
American Homestead, Autumn, 13 1/2 x 17 1/2 In. 495.00
American Homestead, Summer, 1868, Small Folio 242.00
American Scenery, Palenville, N.Y., Small Folio 235.00
American Whaler, 9 1/2 x 14 1/2 In. 440.00
American Whalers Crushed In The Ice, 12 x 15 In. 550.00
Among The Pines, A First Settlement, Small Folio 308.00
Arkansas Traveler, Frame, 13 x 17 1/2 In. 165.00
Awful Conflagration Of Steamboat Lexington, Small Folio 2485.00
Battle Of Cedar Creek, Large Folio 275.00
Battle Of Chickamauga, Small Folio 225.00
Beautiful Pair, Small Folio 225.00
Burning Of Clipper Ship Golden Light, Small Folio 455.00
Camping In The Woods, Large Folio 5480.00
Capture Of Atlanta, Georgia, Small Folio 255.00
Caroline, Small Folio 75.00
Catterrskill Fall, Framed, 12 1/2 x 16 1/2 In. 60.50
Celebrated Four In Hand Stallion Team, 1875, Large Folio 1700.00
Celebrated Stallion Trio, Frame, 28 x 34 In. 990.00
Celebrated Trotting Horse Hopeful, 1881, Large Folio 2000.00
Celebrated Trotting Mare Hattie Woodware, Small Folio 1795.00
Celebrated Trotting Mare Lucy, Frame, 13 x 18 In. 220.00
Central Park, The Drive, 1862, Medium Folio 1870.00
Chicago In Flames, Small Folio 435.00
Clipper Ship Dreadnought, Off Sandy Hook, Large Folio 2685.00
Cottage Life, Summer, Framed, 15 1/2 x 18 3/4 In. 275.00
Darktown Elopement, Frame, 14 x 17 1/2 In. 137.50
Darktown Fire Brigade To The Rescue, Frame, 13 1/4 x 17 1/4 In. 357.50
Death Of President Lincoln, 1865 .... 150.00
Discovery Of Mississippi, Large Folio 235.00
Disputed Heat, Claiming A Foul, Frame, 1878, Large Folio 1430.00
Don Juan, Small Folio 95.00
Falls Of Ottawa River, Canada, Small Folio 250.00
Flowers, Walnut Frame, 15 x 12 In. 120.00
Flushing A Woodcock, Small Folio 295.00
Friendship, Love, & Truth, 13 1/2 x 17 1/2 In. 192.00
Frontier Lake, Small Folio 187.00
Frontier Settlement, Medium Folio 467.00
Fruits Of Temperance, 1870, Small Folio 190.00
General Grant & Family, Small Folio .... 75.00 to 90.00
General Tom Thumb's Marriage, Frame, 12 1/2 x 16 1/2 In. 205.00
Good Times On The Old Plantation, Small Folio 595.00
Grandpapa's Cane, 16 x 12 In. 120.00
Great Eastern, Frame, 10 3/4 x 15 1/2 In. 280.00
Great Fight Between Merrimack & Monitor, 9 1/4 x 13 In. 440.00
Great Fire At Boston, Frame, 1872, 9 1/2 x 13 1/4 In. 192.00
Great Race On Mississippi, New Orleans To St. Louis, Large Folio 6525.00
Hiawatha's Wooing, Large Folio 475.00
Home In The Wilderness, Frame, 11 1/2 x 15 3/4 In. 302.50
Hunting On Susquehanna, Medium Folio 545.00
Hush I've A Nibble, Walnut Frame, 13 3/8 x 7 3/8 In. 165.00
Idlewild On Hudson, Small Folio 195.00
John Brown The Martyr, Carte De Visite Photo Frame Corner, 19 x 17 In. 247.00
Last War-Whoop, 1856, Bird's-Eye Maple Frame, Large Folio 1850.00
Life & Age Of Man, Cross Corner Frame, 12 1/2 x 16 1/2 In. 115.50
Life Of A Fireman, Metropolitan System, 1856, Large Folio 4500.00
Life Of A Fireman, Night Alarm, 1854, Frame, Large Folio 1980.00
Lion Hunter, Small Folio 125.00
Little Sarah, Girl Holding Doll, 1876, 12 x 15 In. 395.00
Lookout Mountain, Tennessee, & Chattanooga Rail Road, Large Folio 7850.00
Midnight Race On Mississippi, Large Folio 3450.00
Moosehead Lake, Frame, 12 3/8 x 16 3/8 In. 60.50
Mother's Blessing, Frame, 19 x 15 In. 40.00

Mountain Spring, West Point, Near Cozzen's Dock, 1862, Medium Folio 605.00
My Little White Kittie, After The Goldfish, 12 1/2 x 17 1/4 In. 220.00
My Little White Kitties, Playing Dominoes, Small Folio 125.00
My Love & I, Frame, 17 x 21 In. 22.00
My Pet Bird, Frame, 25 x 21 In. 40.00
My Three White Kittens, Frame, 11 2/3 x 15 1/2 In. 255.00
Naughty Cat, 15 1/2 x 11 3/4 In. 115.00
Naval Bombardment Of Vera Cruz, Small Folio 260.00
Niagara Falls, From Canada Side, Small Folio .... 110.00 to 195.00
Night By The Camp-Fire, Black Frame, 1861, Medium Folio 545.00
O'Sullivan's Cascade, Frame, 11 1/2 x 15 1/2 In. 60.00
Occident, Frame, 1876, Large Folio 990.00
Old Blandford Church, Frame, 13 1/4 x 16 3/4 In. 110.00
Old Farm Gate, Frame, 1864, Large Folio 1980.00
Old Homestead, Bird's-Eye Maple Frame, 1855, Medium Folio 495.00
Old Homestead In Winter, Large Folio 7250.00
Partridge Shooting, Matted, Small 395.00
Peaceful River, Small Folio 165.00
Pleasures Of The Country, Winter, Large Folio 1795.00
Prairie Fires Of Great West, Frame, 10 x 13 1/4 In. 715.00
Presidents Of The United States, Frame, 16 3/4 x 112 1/2 In. 165.00
Quail Shooting, Large Folio 2485.00
Queen Of Clippers, Small Folio 595.00
Rabbit Catching, Trap Sprung, Small Folio 725.00
Rarus, By Son Of Old Abdallah, 1877, Small Folio 285.00
Raspberries, Frame, 12 1/4 x 16 1/4 In. 195.00
Return From The Woods, Medium Folio 440.00
River Side, Shadowbox Frame, 17 3/4 x 21 3/4 In. 72.00
Roses Of May, White, Pink, Red Flowers, Colorful Butterfly 119.00
Sale Of Pet Lamb, Large Folio 495.00
Sinking Of Steamship Ville Du Havre, Small Folio 195.00
Sinking Of The Cumberland 400.00
Sperm Whale, In A Flurry, Small Folio .... 935.00 to 1195.00
Storming Of Fort Donelson, Tenn., Small Folio 495.00
Sunnyside, On The Hudson, Frame, 15 1/2 x 18 3/4 In. 71.50
Surrender Of General Burgoyne At Saratoga, Frame, 1777, Large Folio 2310.00
Surrender Of General Lee, At Appomattox 250.00
Surrender Of Lord Cornwallis, At Yorktown, Va., Small Folio 225.00
Susan, 1846, Small Folio 85.00
To The Rescue, Small Folio 785.00
Tobogganing On Darktown Hill, 12 1/2 x 17 In. 302.50
Top Of The Heap, 1880 .... 330.00
Tree Of Life, Christian, Frame, 16 1/2 x 12 1/2 In. 105.00
Vase Of Flowers, 1847, Frame, 10 x 14 In. 95.00
View Of The Park, Fountain & City Hall, N.Y., 1847, Small Folio 495.00
Village Blacksmith, Medium Folio 525.00
Washington As A Mason, Small Folio 195.00
Washington At Prayer, Small Folio 170.00
Whale Fishery, Sperm Whale In A Flurry, Small Folio 1650.00
William Penn's Treaty With Indians, Small Folio 235.00
Winter Morning, Medium Folio 1985.00
Won By A Neck, Lady Thorn, 1869, Large Folio 1800.00
Woodcock Shooting, 1855, Small Folio 550.00
Yankee Doodle On His Muscle, Small Folio 280.00
Yosemite Falls, Frame, 15 1/2 x 18 1/2 In. 93.50
Young Mother, 1870, 14 x 10 1/8 In. 125.00

CUSTARD GLASS is a slightly yellow opaque glass. It was first made in the
United States after 1886 at the La Belle Glass Works, Bridgeport, Ohio. It is
being reproduced. Additional pieces may be found in the Cambridge, Fenton,
Heisey, and Northwood categories.

Argonaut Shell, Cruet 495.00
Argonaut Shell, Pitcher 450.00

Argonaut Shell, Spooner 160.00
Argonaut Shell, Sugar 225.00
Argonaut Shell, Toothpick .... 160.00 to 200.00
Argonaut Shell, Water Set, 6 Piece 900.00
Argonaut Shell, Water Set, Blue, 4 Piece 400.00
Beaded Circle, Butter, Cover, Green 485.00
Beaded Circle, Creamer, Green 190.00
Beaded Circle, Spooner, Green 190.00
Beaded Circle, Tumbler 45.00
Beaded Swag, Sugar 45.00
Cherry Sprig, Creamer, Blue 295.00
Chrysanthemum Sprig, Berry Set, 11 Piece 975.00
Chrysanthemum Sprig, Butter, Cover 350.00
Chrysanthemum Sprig, Celery Dish 795.00
Chrysanthemum Sprig, Creamer .... 80.00 to 100.00
Chrysanthemum Sprig, Creamer, Blue 385.00
Chrysanthemum Sprig, Cruet 200.00
Chrysanthemum Sprig, Cruet, Blue, 6 1/2 In. 1000.00
Chrysanthemum Sprig, Salt & Pepper 200.00
Chrysanthemum Sprig, Salt & Pepper, Blue 395.00
Chrysanthemum Sprig, Spooner 100.00
Chrysanthemum Sprig, Spooner, Blue, Gold Trim .... 150.00 to 275.00
Chrysanthemum Sprig, Table Set, Gilt Trim, 3 Piece 200.00
Chrysanthemum Sprig, Tray, Condiment 575.00
Chrysanthemum Sprig, Tumbler, 4 In. .... 65.00 to 70.00
Daisy & Drape, Tumbler 80.00
Delaware, Tumbler, Blue Design 50.00
Diamond With Peg, Butter, Cover 250.00
Everglades, Sauce 60.00
Everglades, Spooner 155.00
Everglades, Sugar, Cover 235.00
Everglades, Tumbler 80.00
Fine Cut & Roses, Rose Bowl, Nutmeg Stain 60.00
Fluted Scroll, Cruet 300.00
Geneva, Compote, Jelly 50.00
Geneva, Sugar, Cover 95.00
Geneva, Toothpick 90.00
Geneva, Tumbler 70.00
Georgia Gem, Toothpick 40.00
Grape & Cable, Bowl, 7 In. 40.00
Grape & Cable, Sugar, Nutmeg Stain 60.00
Grape & Gothic Arches, Goblet, Nutmeg Stain 65.00
Grape & Gothic Arches, Tumbler 105.00
Harvard, Toothpick .... 25.00 to 50.00
Intaglio, Butter, Cover, Blue 295.00
Intaglio, Butter, Cover, Green 295.00
Intaglio, Creamer, Blue 140.00
Intaglio, Cruet, Clear Stopper, Blue 335.00
Intaglio, Green, Gold Trim 300.00
Intaglio, Spooner, Blue .... 95.00 to 140.00
Intaglio, Spooner, Green 135.00
Intaglio, Sugar & Creamer 275.00
Intaglio, Sugar, Cover, Green 190.00
Intaglio, Tumbler, Green 85.00
Intaglio, Tumbler, Green, Gold Trim 80.00
Inverted Fan & Feather, Butter, Cover 250.00
Inverted Fan & Feather, Creamer 125.00
Ivorina Verde pattern is in this category under Winged Scroll
Little Gem, see Georgia Gem pattern in this category
Lotus & Grape, Bonbon, Rose Stained Rim, 2 Handles 32.00
Louis XV, Butter, Cover, Gold Trim 190.00
Louis XV, Spooner, Gold Trim 78.00
Louis XV, Sugar & Creamer 250.00

Maize is its own category in this book

Maple Leaf, Compote, Jelly, Gold Rim	350.00
Maple Leaf, Creamer, Green	160.00
Maple Leaf, Sugar, Cover, Green	235.00
Maple Leaf, Tumbler	105.00
Maple Leaf, Tumbler, Green	95.00
Northwood Fan, Bowl, Pansy, Ruffled, 8 In.	250.00
Peacock At Urn, Bowl, Scalloped Rim, 10 In.	225.00
Ribbed Thumbprint, Cup, Krystal Souvenir Centennial, 1911	20.00
Ribbed Thumbprint, Toothpick	75.00
Ring Band, Toothpick, Rosebuds, Leaves	110.00
Tarentum's Victoria, Vase, Bud	450.00
Tiny Thumbprint, Goblet, Roses	60.00
Vermont, Tumbler	80.00
Winged Scroll, Celery Vase	350.00
Winged Scroll, Cruet, Heisey	110.00
Winged Scroll, Toothpick, Gold Trim	120.00

CUT GLASS has been made since ancient times, but the large majority of the pieces now for sale date from the brilliant period of glass design, 1880 to 1905. These pieces have elaborate geometric designs with a deep miter cut. Modern cut glass with a similar appearance is being made in England, Ireland, and the Czech and Slovak republics. Chips and scratches are often difficult to notice but lower the value dramatically. A signature on the glass adds significantly to the value. Other cut glass pieces are listed under factory names.

Banana Bowl, Royal, Hunt	500.00
Basket, Diamond Points, Piecrust Rim, Star Base, 6 x 4 1/4 In.	90.00
Biscuit Barrel, Diamond Star Base, Bail Handle, 5 1/2 x 5 5/8 In.	98.00
Biscuit Barrel, Hob & Lace, Dorflinger, 5 1/2 In.	225.00
Biscuit Box, Diamond Cut, Silver Plated Collar & Cover, England, 7 1/2 In.	488.75
Bishop's Hat, Viscaria Variant, Hobstar Base, 4 x 7 In.	525.00
Bottle, Bitters, Oval & Split, Dorflinger	175.00
Bottle, Cologne, Cranberry To Clear, Hobstar, 5 1/2 In.	850.00
Bottle, Cologne, Parisian, Dorflinger, 8 1/2 In.	375.00
Bottle, Dresser, Crisscross Miters, Round Stopper, Square, 7 In.	60.00
Bottle, Ketchup, Hobstar, Strawberry-Diamond, Handle, Sterling Stopper	225.00
Bottle, Smelling Salts, Sultana, Hinged Silver Top, Dorflinger	250.00
Bottle, Whiskey, Strawberry-Diamond & Fan, 11 x 4 1/4 In.	525.00
Bowl, Butterfly, Dragonfly, 20 In.	350.00
Bowl, Carolyn, J. Hoare, 8 In.	290.00
Bowl, Checkerboard, 8 In.	365.00
Bowl, Cover, Overlay, Cobalt Blue To Clear, 7 x 6 1/2 In.	88.00
Bowl, Crosscut Diamonds & Fan, Wooden Base, Dorflinger, 5 In.	160.00
Bowl, Flower, Faust, Bergen, 5 x 6 3/4 In.	440.00
Bowl, Fruit, Sawtooth Rim, Diamond, Fan & Button, Emerald To Clear, Dorflinger	250.00
Bowl, Fruit, Scalloped Hobstar Foot, Faceted Knob Stem, 7 3/4 x 8 In.	685.00
Bowl, Hobstars Separated By Tusks, Egginton	850.00
Bowl, Hobstars, Miters, Sawtooth & Fans, 3-Footed, 7 3/8 x 4 In.	90.00
Bowl, Lamont, Hawkes, 7 x 1 1/2 In.	175.00
Bowl, Notched Prism & Panel, Silver Sterling Beaded Rim, 12 In.	550.00
Bowl, Nut, Chain Of Hobstars, Miters, Star Bottom, Egginton	95.00
Bowl, Quatrefoil Rosette, 4 x 9 In.	1875.00
Bowl, Royal, Allover Cutting, Oval, Hunt Glass Co., 6 1/2 x 9 1/2 In.	295.00
Bowl, Royal, Hunt, 9 In.	375.00
Bowl, Star & Diamond Miters, Pleated Rays, Piecrust Rim, 6 1/4 x 2 3/4 In.	84.00
Bowl, Swirl & Hobstar, 8 In.	95.00
Bowl, Theodora, 4 x 9 In.	2500.00
Bowl, Underplate, Split Ovals, Gold Sulphide, Dorflinger, 3 x 5 In.	225.00
Box, Candy, Crosscut Diamond, Pedestal, Round, 6 In.	195.00
Box, Dresser, Pearl, Pairpoint, 3 1/2 x 5 1/2 In.	315.00
Box, Glove, Hobstars & Fans, Silver Mounts, 4 x 11 In.	2750.00
Box, Hinged Lid, Expanding Star On Lid & Bottom, 4 1/2 x 3 In.	195.00

Box, Jewelry, Hobstar & Fan, Silver Mount, C.F. Monroe, 7 x 8 1/2 In. 2250.00
Box, Jewelry, Hobstars, C.F. Monroe, 4 x 6 1/2 In. 550.00
Box, Trinket, Hobstar Lid, Corner Fans, Concave Paneled Sides, Square 550.00
Butter Chip, Neptune, Laurel Co., 3 1/2 x 4 In. 65.00
Butter Chip, Russian 60.00
Butter, Hobstar & Cane, Cover 145.00
Cake Plate, Harvard, Giant X in Center, 10 In. 475.00
Cake Plate, Scalloped, Leaf Sprays Alternate Daisy Sprays, Brilliant, 12 1/2 In. 195.00
Candelabrum, 2-Light, Regency, Faceted Prisms, Sunburst Inset, 21 In., Pair 6900.00
Candlestick, Hobstar Cut On Foot, Dorflinger, 10 In., Pair 975.00
Candlestick, Hobstars, Crosshatching & Fans, Rayed Base, 7 1/2 In., Pair 250.00
Candlestick, Notch Cutting, Teardrop Stem, Dorflinger, 6 1/2 In., Pair 75.00
Candy Dish, Hobstar, Paperweight Base, Pedestal, 4 3/4 x 6 1/2 In. 310.00
Canoe, Intaglio Flowers & Hobstars, 8 In. 65.00
Canoe, Iowa, Irving, 9 x 3 1/2 In. 170.00
Carafe, Baker's Gothic, T.B. Clark, 7 1/4 In. 425.00
Carafe, Hobstars, Single Stars, Crosscut Diamonds, Bowling Pin Shape 150.00
Carafe, Water, Brilliant, 8 1/8 In. 200.00
Carafe, Water, Lotus, Egginton, 7 x 6 In. 270.00
Carafe Set, Allover Brilliant, Hobstars, Crosshatching, Fluted Neck, 3 Piece 125.00
Casserole, Cover, Finial, Hobstar & Fan, 8 x 7 In. 2000.00
Celery Boat, Harvard Rim & Base, Band Of Cut Florals & Leaves, 13 1/2 In. 275.00
Celery Boat, Russian, Rayed Buttons, 14 x 4 In. 840.00
Chalice, Double Teardrop Stem, Hobstar Foot, Amethyst To Clear, 12 In. 2500.00
Chalice, Vase, Hobstar Cut Base, 14 x 6 1/2 In. 780.00
Champagne, Parisian, Dorflinger 135.00
Champagne, Parisian, Dorflinger, Set Of 6 .... 695.00
Champagne, Wheel Cut Flowers, Hawkes 65.00
Coaster, Clear Flute, Inverted Notching On Sides 95.00
Compote, Diamond, 6 Sides, Averbeck 700.00
Compote, Diamond, 6 Sides, Hobstar Foot, 9 x 8 1/4 In. 795.00
Compote, Dolphin Shape, Silver Tails, Silver Mount, Late 19th Century, Pair 2300.00
Compote, Geometric, Faceted Stem, Circular Starburst Foot, 8 1/2 In., Pair 440.00
Compote, Hobstar Chain, Step Cut Stem, Hoare, 8 In. 1425.00
Compote, Hobstar Scalloped Base, 5-Sided Notched Stem, 10 x 8 In. 775.00
Compote, Hobstars, Buttons, Crosshatching, Hoare, 6 3/4 x 8 In. 235.00
Compote, Paneled Cone Stem, American Brilliant, J. Hoare, 1853, 6 x 4 1/2 .... 275.00
Compote, Paneled Cone Stem, American Brilliant, J. Hoare, 1853, 8 x 6 3/4 In. 375.00
Compote, Teardrop Stem, Fans Between Hobstars, Pair 475.00
Compote, White Overlay To Clear, Silver Plated Base, 8 x 7 In. 104.00
Cookie Jar, Harvard, Brilliant Blank, 6 1/2 x 5 1/4 In. 480.00
Cordial, Parisian, Hobstar Foot, Dorflinger, 3 5/8 In. 70.00
Cordial Set, Ithaca, Huntley Glass Co., 7 Piece 450.00
Cruet, Prism, Sterling Collar & Lid 275.00
Decanter, Amber To Clear, Heavy Stopper, 15 In. 150.00
Decanter, Banjo Shape, Bands Of Canes, Descending To Cane Foot 850.00
Decanter, Bowling Pin Shape, Bull's-Eye & Notched Neck, Star Stopper, 14 In. 92.00
Decanter, Buzz, Overall Cutting 250.00
Decanter, Cane, Elongated Stars, Fans, Clark, 13 In. 75.00
Decanter, Cordial, Ruby To Clear, Grape Clusters, Stopper, 11 3/4 In. 285.00
Decanter, Crystal, Hobstar, Stopper, J. Hoare, 13 1/4 In. 1150.00
Decanter, Cut Laurel Band Shoulder, Faceted Stopper, 12 In. 45.00
Decanter, Double Gooseneck, 11 x 6 In. 545.00
Decanter, Elongated 8-Point Stars, Cane, Fluted Neck, Clark 200.00
Decanter, Harvard, Double Spout, Pyramid, Steeple Stopper, 16 In. 275.00
Decanter, Hobstar & Cane, Triple-Notched Handle, Stopper, 12 x 5 1/2 In. 435.00
Decanter, Hobstars, Elongated Stars, Miter, Wine Glass Stopper, 17 In. 110.00
Decanter, Hung With Silver Plated Ladle, Allover Diamond, 10 In. 80.00
Decanter, Sherry, Quatrefoil, Sterling Stopper, Cranberry, Dorflinger 575.00
Decanter, Thumbprints, Vertical Fans, Disc Stopper, 10 In. 95.00
Decanter, Triple-Cut Handle, Bars Of Canes, Oval Punties, Fans, Dorflinger, 13 In. 625.00
Decanter Set, Ruby To Clear, Grape Clusters, Miters, Fans, Hobstars, 7 Piece 350.00
Dish, Aberdeen, Jewel Glass Co., 6 In. 315.00

Dish, Carolyn, Napoleon's Hat, J. Hoare, 13 1/2 x 8 3/4 In. 1650.00
Dish, Dessert, Trellis, Egginton, 7 In. 2300.00
Dish, Olive, Royal, Hunt, 7 1/2 x 3 1/2 In. 165.00
Dish, Parisian, Curved Miters, Square, Dorflinger, 7 In. 290.00
Dish, Pickle, Allover Harvard, Boat Shape, 6 1/2 In. 85.00
Dish, Royal, Heart Shape, Hunt Glass Co., 7 In. 345.00
Dish, Russian, Rayed Button, 4 Sides, 19 In. 390.00
Finger Bowl, Underplate, Hobstar, Clear Blanks, Hawkes, 5 x 7 1/4 In. 375.00
Flowerpot, Allover Flowers & Ferns, Rayed Base, 21-In. Middle, 5 1/2 In. 325.00
Frame, Art Nouveau, Lilies, Brass Plated, 8 In. 85.00
Glass, Water, Butterfly & Flower 75.00
Goblet, Kalana Lily, Dorflinger, 5 1/2 In. 75.00
Goblet, Wine, Ruby To Clear, Bohemian, c.1910, 6 In. 358.00
Hat, Napoleon, Dorflinger 550.00
Ice Bucket, Alhambra, Sterling Rim 2250.00
Ice Bucket, Hindu, Hoare 225.00
Ice Bucket, Hobstars, Strawberry & Diamonds, Sawtooth Edge, 6 x 9 In. 475.00
Ice Tub, Russian Tab Handles, Starred Button, 7 x 4 In. 375.00
Jar, Cover, Russian Cut, Cobalt To Clear, 10 Sides, Gilt, 5 In., Pair 995.00
Jar, Horseradish, Rayed Atop Balloon Stopper, 6 In. 265.00
Jar, Marlboro, Matching Stopper, Dorflinger, 9 1/4 In. 1295.00
Jar, Stopper, Brilliant, 5 3/4 In. 258.00
Jug, Claret, Silver Cover & Handles, Heath & Middleton, 1894, 3 Piece 1725.00
Jug, Whiskey, Poppy, Allover Cut, Flute-Cut Neck, Honeycomb Handle, Fry, 8 In. 345.00
Knife Rest, Crosscut Diamonds, 4 3/8 In. 90.00
Knife Rest, Diamond, 4 3/4 In. 25.00
Knife Rest, Hobstars & Single Stars, 4 1/2 In. 85.00
Knife Rest, Notched Prism & Diamond, 4 1/2 In. 35.00
Knife Rest, Zipper, Rayed Ends, 5 In. 40.00
Lamp, 1-Light, Hobstars, Diamond Point, Crosshatching, 20 In. 2350.00
Lamp, Boudoir, Hobstar, Peaked Dome, Replated Metal, 15 In. 985.00
Lamp, Chimney, Gold Ruby, Dorflinger, 11 1/2 In. 150.00
Lamp, Flowers, Stars, Crosshatching, No Shade, 13 In. 70.00
Lamp, Oil, Crosscut Diamond & Fan, Dorflinger, 15 3/4 In. 4850.00
Lamp, Strawberry, Variation Of Expanding Star, 16 1/2 In. 3450.00
Lamp, Table, Cane-Cut Dome Shade, Prisms, Pedestal Skirt Base, 23 In. 880.00
Mug, Coffee, Arcadia, 16-Point Hob Base 250.00
Napkin Ring, Chain Of Hobstars 125.00
Nappy, Hobstar & Vesicas 55.00
Nappy, Sawtooth Rim, Overall Star & Hobstar, Hoare, 6 In. 45.00
Orange Bowl, Blown-Out Hobstars, Completely Cut Foot, 9 1/2 In. 850.00
Orange Bowl, Open Petal, Louis Hinsberger, 11 1/2 x 4 1/2 In. 695.00
Perfume Bottle, Cut Leaf Design, Paperweight Base, Green, 5 1/4 In. 165.00
Pitcher, 2 Large Pinwheels Each Side, Fluted Lip, 10 1/2 In. 260.00
Pitcher, 32-Point Hobstars, Pedestal, Cut Base, 9 1/2 In. 2800.00
Pitcher, Alhambra, Meriden, 12 1/4 In. 5750.00
Pitcher, Champagne, Brilliant Cut, 14 In. 1000.00
Pitcher, Champagne, Strawberry-Diamond & Fan, 11 3/4 In. 325.00
Pitcher, Claret, Sterling Silver Trim, Unger Bros. 350.00
Pitcher, Hobstars, Engraved Poinsettias, Notched Handle & Rim 225.00
Pitcher, Marcella, 11 In. 6000.00
Pitcher, Milk, Hobnail & Fan, Triple Notched Handle, 5 1/4 In. 95.00
Pitcher, Milk, Hobstar Diamond Point, Fan, 6 In. 225.00
Pitcher, Milk, Hobstars & Strawberry-Diamond, 4 1/2 In. 125.00
Pitcher, Milk, Hobstars, Rays & Strawberry-Diamond, Handle, 5 1/2 In. 165.00
Pitcher, Mitered Cane With Honeycomb, Silver Fitting, J. Russel, c.1880 .... 325.00
Pitcher, Parisian, Dorflinger, 8 In. 685.00
Pitcher, Parisian, Hobnail Handle, Dorflinger, 9 1/4 x 6 3/4 In. 975.00
Pitcher, Royal Pattern, Notched Handle, Step-Cut Spout, 10 In. 375.00
Plate, Arcadia With Star, 7 In. 150.00
Plate, Diamond & Hobstars, Hawkes, 10 In. 500.00
Plate, Greek Key, Alhambra, 10 In. 1175.00
Plate, Hob & Lace, Double Miter Cane, Dorflinger, 5 In. 85.00

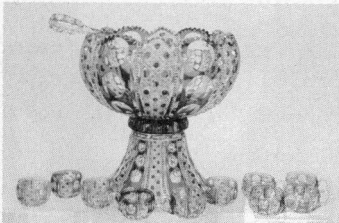

Cut Glass, Punch Bowl Set,
Green Cut To Clear,
Dorflinger, 15 Piece

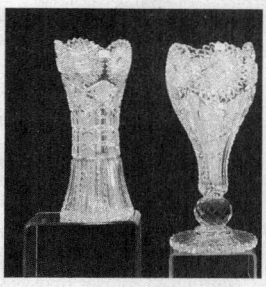

Left: Cut Glass, Vase, Corset
Shape, Zipper Base, 14 In.;
Right: Cut Glass, Vase, Tulip
Shape, 16 In.

Cut Glass, Tray, Festoon, 12 In.

Plate, Hobstar Chain Rim, Engraved Flowers & Ferns, Hobstar Center, 10 In.	325.00
Plate, Intaglio Cherries, Pears & Grapes, Scalloped Rim, 10 In., 3 Piece	375.00
Plate, Notched Sawtooth & Fan, Square, 7 In.	55.00
Plate, Parisian Pattern, Dorflinger, 1886, 7 In.	155.00
Plate, Prism, 24-Point Hobstar Center, J.D. Bergen	225.00
Plate, Seneca, Empire Glass Co., 7 In.	525.00
Plate, Swirls Of Notched Prisms, Hobstars, 7 In.	125.00
Pokal, Overlay Opaque White To Clear, Cranberry Flashing, Worn Gilt, 14 In.	330.00
Powder Box, Arcola, Lift-Off Lid, Faceted Finial, Dorflinger	150.00
Powder Box, Cover, Harvard, 3 Footed, 5 1/2 x 4 In.	175.00 to 325.00
Powder Box, Cover, Vesicas Of Pyramidal Stars, Separated By Fans, Dorflinger	95.00
Punch Bowl, Dorflinger, 1890, Pair	1550.00
Punch Bowl, Elmira, 14 In., 2 Piece	2800.00
Punch Bowl, Hobstars Alternating With Crosshatching, Alford, 5 1/2 x 12 In.	750.00
Punch Bowl, Mercedes, Clark, 14 In.	1000.00
Punch Bowl, Stand, Crosshatched Pointed Ovals, Triangles, Hobstars, 12 In.	440.00
Punch Bowl, Stand, Harvard, 15 In.	715.00
Punch Bowl, Stand, Hobstar & Quilted Design, 12 In.	920.00
Punch Bowl Set, Green Cut To Clear, Dorflinger, 15 Piece .... *Illus*	23000.00
Punch Cup, Star, Cut Allover, Rayed Base, Clear Handle, Dorflinger	55.00
Relish, Allover Hobstar, Cane & Radiants, 6 x 7 1/2 In.	95.00
Rose Bowl, American, Dorflinger, 8 x 10 In.	650.00
Rose Bowl, Notched Prism, Zipper To Cranberry Base, 3 In.	350.00
Salt, Monarch, J. Hoare	95.00
Salt, Diamond Cut, Silver Top, Tray, 2 In.	120.00
Salt, Notched Prism, 6 Piece	75.00
Salt, Russian, Triangular, 3 1/2 In.	60.00
Salt, Single Stars, Crosshatching & Fan, Individual, 6 Piece	120.00
Salt, Strawberry-Diamond, Paperweight Base, Master, 2 x 3 In.	75.00
Salt & Pepper, Floral & Leaf, Nickel Silver Tops	38.00
Salt Dip, Crosscut Diamond, Triangular, 2 In.	35.00
Server, Cookie, Butterflies & Ferns, T Shape Handle, Signed, Round, 10 In.	395.00
Sherbet, Crosscut Diamond, Pinwheels, Taylor	55.00
Spooner, Allover Hobstars & Fans	85.00
Spooner, Harvard, 4 3/4 x 3 3/8 In.	180.00
Spooner, Hobstar Rim, Alternating Panels Of Notched Prism, Serrated, 4 3/4 In.	75.00
Stand, Petit Four, Flashed & Feather Half Stars, Unger Bros., 8 x 7 In.	325.00
Sugar & Creamer, 8-Sided, 2 1/2 x 4 In.	245.00

Sugar & Creamer, Cluster, Egginton 650.00
Sugar & Creamer, Hobstar & Fan, Signed Clark's Leaf 375.00
Sugar & Creamer, Hobstar, Strawberry-Diamond Clusters, 4 1/2 In. 290.00
Sugar & Creamer, Pedestal, Allover Crosscut Diamonds, Rayed Base 325.00
Sugar & Creamer, Prima Donna, Clark, 2 3/4 x 4 1/4 In. 235.00
Sugar & Creamer, Sawtooth Rim, Pinwheel Hobstar & Notched, Fry, 3 In. 65.00
Sugar Shaker, Allover Diamonds, Silver Plated Top, 3 x 5 3/4 In. 72.00
Syrup, Overall Hobstar Cutting, Rayed Base, Sterling Hinged Cover 250.00
Syrup, Zipper, Squat, Metal Lid & Handle 80.00
Tankard, Genoa, Averbeck, 11 In. 295.00
Tankard, Pluto Type, 14 In. 550.00
Tazza, Hobstar, 9 In. 625.00
Tazza, Venetian, Scalloped Hobstar Base, Fry, 8 1/2 x 7 In. 545.00
Toothpick, Allover Branches & Leaves, Notched Rim, Hoare 110.00
Tray, Festoon, 12 In. .... *Illus* 3500.00
Tray, Grecian, Egginton, 14 1/2 In. 8000.00
Tray, Ice Cream, Baker's Gothic, Clark, 15 In. 1500.00
Tray, Ice Cream, Hobstars, Flashed Hobstars, Meriden Co., 17 x 10 1/2 In. 475.00
Tray, Ice Cream, Sunbursts, Hobstars, Crosshatching, Diamonds, 18 In. 685.00
Tray, Imperial, Straus, 14 x 8 3/4 In. 500.00
Tray, Pin, Hobstars, Center Hobstar, 4 Diamonds Of Crosshatching, 4 1/2 In. 125.00
Tray, Pin, Persian, 7 x 4 In. 225.00
Tray, Royal, 6 Fan-Shaped Sections, Oval, Hunt, 16 In. 247.50
Tumble-Up, Allover Panel & Fern, 16-Rayed Star Cut Base, 7 1/2 In. 275.00
Tumble-Up, Hob Diamond & Lace, Dorflinger 3100.00
Tumble-Up, Honeycomb, Dorflinger 1200.00
Tumble-Up, Pinwheel, Dorflinger 725.00
Tumble-Up, Underplate, Vintage, White Cut To Clear, 3 Piece 825.00
Tumbler, Buzz Star, Fans, Cane 20.00
Tumbler, Crosscut Diamond Separated By Fans, Hobstar Base, 3 1/2 In. 110.00
Tumbler, Geometric Cut, Flared Neck, 5 1/4 In., 17 Piece 135.00
Tumbler, Palm Fan, 6 Piece 245.00
Tumbler, Renaissance, Dorflinger, 6 Piece 180.00
Vase, Bowling Pin, Hobstar, Step Cut Neck, 12 x 6 1/2 In. 785.00
Vase, Cobalt Blue To Clear, Crosshatching Stars, Fans, 8 1/4 In. 75.00
Vase, Corset Shape, Zipper Base, 14 In. .... *Illus* 400.00
Vase, Cranberry, 1930, 9 x 8 1/2 In. 66.00
Vase, Crosshatching, Fans & Vesicas, Clear Ovals, Corset Shape, 12 In. 475.00
Vase, Green To Clear, Intaglio Grapes, 9 1/4 In. 295.00
Vase, Green To Clear, Montrose, 16-Pt. Hobstar Base, Dorflinger, 8 In. 3250.00
Vase, Limousine, Hobstars, Fans & Notched, Cone Shape, 8 1/2 In. 325.00
Vase, Out-Turned Rim, Notched Body, Floral Medallion Band, St. Clair, 24 In. 995.00
Vase, Polar Star, Unger Bros. 375.00
Vase, Sultana, Dorflinger, 10 In. 1285.00
Vase, Trumpet, J. Hoare, 12 In. 900.00
Vase, Trumpet, Opalescent To Jade, Fry, 8 x 5 1/2 In. 137.00
Vase, Tulip Shape, 16 In. .... *Illus* 1350.00
Vase, Tulip Shape, Hobstar Base, 6 In. 225.00
Vase, Violet, Pedestal, Daisies & Entwining Leaves, 4 3/4 In. 95.00
Water Set, Lotus, Allen Glass Co., 5 Piece 425.00
Water Set, Royal, Dorflinger, 1890, 7 Piece 880.00
Whiskey, Double, Crosscut Diamonds & Fans, 1 Star On Bottom 80.00
Whiskey, Large Hobstar Faces, Diamond Crosshatching, 1 Oz. 50.00
Whiskey, Monarch, J. Hoare, 1 Oz. 70.00
Whiskey, Renaissance, Cranberry To Clear, Dorflinger 150.00
Wine, Arched Areas Filled With Cane, Stylized Flowers, 7 1/2 In. 70.00
Wine, Chain Of Crosscut Diamonds, Elliptical Punties, Dorflinger 155.00
Wine, Crosscut Diamond, Dorflinger, Green 175.00
Wine, Hob Diamond, Stemmed, Dorflinger 75.00
Wine, Old Colony, Cranberry To Clear, Dorflinger 195.00
Wine, Panel Cut, Green, 6 Piece 225.00
Wine, Renaissance, Cranberry Cut To Clear, Dorflinger 195.00
Wine, Sapphire Blue To Clear, Arched Miters, Cane, Stylized Flowers, 7 1/4 In. 50.00

Wine, Sapphire To Vaseline To Clear, American Single Star, Crosshatching 275.00
Wine, Strawberry-Diamond & Fan, Green, Clear Stem, Dorflinger 275.00

CUT VELVET is a special type of art glass, made with two layers of blown glass, which shows a raised pattern. It usually had an acid finish or a texture like velvet. It was made by many glass factories during the late Victorian years.

Rose Bowl, Diamond Quilted, White Lining, 4-Crimp Top, 4 1/4 In. 165.00
Rose Bowl, Diamond Quilted, White Lining, Egg Shape, 4 1/2 In. 175.00
Rose Bowl, Quilting, 4-Crimp Top, Blue, 3 3/4 In. 165.00
Sugar Sifter, Diamond Quilted, Blue 350.00
Vase, Diamond Quilted, Satin Glass, 6 1/4 In. 72.00
Vase, Flared Top, Satin Glass, 6 In. 125.00
Vase, Frosted Flower, Applied Bellflower & Branch, White Lining, 5 1/2 In. 165.00
Vase, Herringbone, Flared Top, Pink, 6 In. 125.00
Vase, Ribbed, White Lining, 6 1/4 In. 110.00
Vase, Ruffled, Raised Diamond Quilted, Green, 8 1/2 In., Pair 275.00
Vase, Ruffled Top, Diamond Quilted, 6 x 9 In. 625.00

CYBIS porcelain is a twentieth-century product. Boleslaw Cybis came to the United States from Poland in 1939. He started making porcelains in Long Island, New York, in 1940. He moved to Trenton, New Jersey, in 1942 as one of the founders of Cordey China Co. and started his own Cybis Porcelains about 1950. The firm is still working. (See also Cordey.)

Figurine, Ballerina On Cue, White, Wooden Stand, 12 1/2 In. 450.00
Figurine, Bathsheba, No. 452, 14 In. 1500.00
Figurine, Calla Lily, No. 427, 16 In. 850.00
Figurine, Girl, Kneeling With Flowerpot, 6 In. 75.00
Figurine, Girl, Seated, Holding An Apple, 7 1/2 In. 60.00
Figurine, Gray Donkey, 7 In. 98.00
Figurine, Heidi, 8 In. 250.00
Figurine, Jane Eyre, 1970s, 12 In. .... 895.00 to 975.00
Figurine, Lady Macbeth 950.00
Figurine, Lady With Blue Bird 250.00
Figurine, Little Boy Blue, 9 In. 450.00
Figurine, Little Miss Muffet, 7 In. 300.00
Figurine, Little Red Riding Hood, 6 3/4 In. .... 175.00 to 200.00
Figurine, Madame Butterfly, No. 321, 13 1/2 In. 2000.00
Figurine, Madonna With Bird 225.00
Figurine, Magnolia, No. 391, 8 In. 350.00
Figurine, Melissa, 10 In. 80.00
Figurine, Mushroom Jack-O'-Lantern 150.00
Figurine, Owl, 4 1/2 In. .... 20.00 to 65.00
Figurine, Performing Dog, 8 1/4 In. 250.00
Figurine, Pink Flower, Long Stem, Green Leaves, Ladybug, 8 In. 110.00
Figurine, Pollyanna, 7 1/2 In. 350.00
Figurine, Portia 2200.00
Figurine, Priscilla 950.00
Figurine, Queen Esther, No. 98, 13 In. 1100.00
Figurine, Turtle 165.00
Figurine, Wendy, Girl With Teddy Bear .... 175.00 to 350.00
Plaque, Comanche Indian Portrait, Porcelain, Frame, 7 3/4 x 7 3/4 In. 50.00

CZECHOSLOVAKIA is a popular term with collectors. The name, first used as a mark after the country was formed in 1918, appears on glass and porcelain and other decorative items. The name is still used in some trademarks.

Ashtray, Figural, Cowboy, Glass 120.00
Basket, Arched Handles Meet Over Top, Pottery 50.00
Bottle, Dresser, Pink, Mitered Corners, Gold Trim, Square, 4 1/2 In. 30.00
Box, Egg Shape, Blue To Clear, Cut Glass, Geometric, 10 In. 120.00
Box, Stagecoach, Ruby To Clear, Cut Glass, Hinged Top, Rectangular 275.00
Candlestick, Floral Etched Design, Amber, 13 In., Pair 70.00

Candlestick, Luster, Orange & Cream Pottery, Pair 30.00
Candlestick, Turquoise, Cream Interior, Flared Base, Porcelain, 10 x 5 In. 10.00
Candy Basket, Amber, Cobalt Ruffle Top & Handle 90.00
Creamer, Orange Luster, White Iridescent, Pottery 25.00
Decanter, Cordial, Art Nouveau, Round Flared Base, Cork Stopper, 10 3/4 In. 55.00
Decanter, Diamond Facets, Flattened Circle Stopper, 9 1/2 In. 55.00
Dinner Set, Teahouse & Geisha Scene, Demitasse, Victoria China, 12 Piece 90.00
Flower Frog, Basket, Black Handle, Porcelain, 4 1/2 In. 15.00
Mug, Parrot Handle, Yellow, Large, Pottery 125.00
Perfume Bottle, Amber Crystal, Stopper, 9 In. 85.00
Perfume Bottle, Controlled Bubbles, Handmade Flower Stopper, 4 In. 125.00
Perfume Bottle, Cut Glass, Fans, Stars, No Stopper, 3 1/2 In. 50.00
Perfume Bottle, With Dauber, Purse Size, 2 In. 100.00
Pitcher, Black & White Polka Dots, Erphila, Cover, Pottery 22.50
Pitcher, Orange Flowers On Yellow, Blue Handle & Trim, Pottery 42.50
Pitcher, Parrot, Art Deco, Jagged Top Edge, Large, Pottery 205.00
Pitcher, Parrot, Jagged Top Edge, Medium, Pottery 175.00
Planter, Ram's Head, White, Paper Label, Pottery, Pair 120.00
Plate, Bartered Bride, Porcelain 16.00
Salt Box, Red, Wooden Lid, Pottery 50.00
Salt & Pepper, Flower Basket Design, Pottery 2.50
Stagecoach Scene, Yellow, Pottery 12.50
Sugar, Flowers, Handles, Pottery 12.50
Sugar & Creamer, Swan, Iridescent Trim On Lids, Signed, Porcelain 110.00
Vase, Applied Flowers, Orange, Clambroth Interior, Crimped Mouth, Glass 45.00
Vase, Black Glass, Silver Overlay Bird, 9 1/2 In. 110.00
Vase, Black Spider Web Design, Blue Flowers, Yellow, Pottery 75.00
Vase, Cut Flowers, Squatty, Cased Glass Base 60.00
Vase, Dancing Clown, Black, Porcelain, 9 1/2 In. 110.00
Vase, Flower, Brown Glaze, 10 In. 50.00
Vase, Orange Glass, Pulled Blue Windows, 1925, 10 In. 400.00
Vase, Orange, Black Trim, 3 Handles, 12 In. 250.00
Vase, Sculptured Dogwood, Frosted, Phoenix-Type Glass, 10 1/2 In. 42.00
Vase, Stylized Floral, Enameled Outlining, 5 3/8 In. 25.00
Water Set, Grapes & Fruit Design, Pottery, 7 Piece 115.00

D'ARGENTAL is a mark used in France by the Compagnie des Cristalleries de St. Louis. The firm made multilayered, acid-cut cameo glass in the late nineteenth and twentieth centuries. D'Argental is the French name for the city of Munzthal, home of the glassworks. Later they made enameled etched glass.

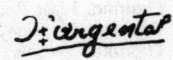

Lamp, Table, Dome Shade, Footed, Yellow, Etched Lake Scene, 23 1/2 In 8150.00
Perfume Bottle, Carnelian, Lavender, Lime, Bell Shape, Cameo, 6 In. 230.00
Vase, Brown Floral Design, Butterscotch & Russet Ground, Cameo, 13 1/2 In. 2295.00
Vase, Cameo, Palm Trees, Volcano, Opalescent Ground, Signed, 8 In. 935.00
Vase, Gray Berries, Vines & Leaves, Cream & Gray Ground, 6 In., Pair 750.00
Vase, Iris, Cream & Pink Ground, Fluted, 11 3/4 In. 2000.00
Vase, Mountains, Stream, Flower Heads, Signed, c.1920, 14 In. 2100.00
Vase, Purple & White Floral, Signed, 7 In. 650.00
Vase, Scenic, Cameo, Bottle Form, Fiery Opal, Green & Brown, 6 7/8 In. 880.00
Vase, Tranquil Forest & Lake Scene, Signed, c.1920, 14 In. 1400.00
Vase, Venetian Scene, Ovoid, Gray, Yellow, Cranberry, c.1920, 7 3/4 In. 1265.00

DANIEL BOONE, a pre-Revolutionary War folk hero, was a surveyor, trapper, and frontiersman. A television series, which ran from 1964 to 1970, was based on his life and starred Fess Parker. All types of Daniel Boone memorabilia are collected.

Book, Wilderness Scout, 1957 .... 8.00
Display, Figural, Plaster, Old Boone Distillery Co., Place For Bottle, 12 In. 100.00
Lunch Box, Fess Parker, 1965 .... 30.00 to 90.00
Ring, Kellogg's 12.00
Shoes, Boy's, Fess Parker, High Top, Daniel Picture, Box, Size 6 .... 90.00
Slate, Fess Parker Super Slate, 1964 .... 17.50

◆◆◆◆◆◆◆◆◆◆◆◆◆◆◆◆◆◆◆◆◆◆

In case of a major theft, keep careful records. You may be able to deduct part of the uninsured loss from your income tax.

◆◆◆◆◆◆◆◆◆◆◆◆◆◆◆◆◆◆◆◆◆◆

Daum, Box, Trinket, Cover, Flowers & Leaves, Cameo, 2 x 3 1/4 In.

T-Shirt, 1950s, Child's Size 8 .... 75.00
Viewmaster Set, 3 Reels, Book, 1965 .... 33.00

DAUM, a glassworks in Nancy, France, was started by Jean Daum in 1875. The company, now called *Cristalleries de Nancy*, is still working. The *Daum Nancy* mark has been used in many variations. The name of the city and the artist are usually both included.

    Ashtray, Circular, Gray, White, Green, Falling Leaves, Cameo, c.1910, 6 1/2 In. 920.00
    Ashtray, Mortar & Pestle Form, Clear, Triangular, Box, 5 In. 175.00
    Bottle, Fitted Stopper, Swarm Of Bees Hovering Over Grasses, Signed, 3 1/2 In. 4620.00
    Bowl, Acid-Etched Bands & Dots, c.1930, 6 1/4 In. 1035.00
    Bowl, Blown-Out Design, Glass & Metal, Pint, 8 x 11 In. 1950.00
    Bowl, Burgundy Blossoms, Olive Vines, Tangerine Opalescent Ground, 8 1/4 In. 1380.00
    Bowl, Cylindrical, Enameled Geranium, Gilding, Green & Raspberry Ground, 6 In. ... 2990.00
    Bowl, Enamel Sprays Of Wildflowers & Leaves, 1910, 11 1/2 In. 2013.00
    Bowl, Enameled, 4-Lobed Rim, Gray, White, Purple, Flowers, Cameo, c.1915, 5 In. .. 1840.00
    Bowl, Enameled, White Shading To Violet, Cut Violets, Cameo, c.1910, 5 3/8 In. 2300.00
    Bowl, Free-Form, 3 Rim Points, Signed 90.00
    Bowl, Fuchsia Blossoms, Shaded Purple & White Ground, Cameo, 2 1/2 x 5 1/2 In. .. 1925.00
    Bowl, Gray, Green, Lavender & Purple, Square Pinch Top, Footed, 3 x 8 3/4 In. 690.00
    Bowl, Mottled Yellow & Orange Body, Green At Raised Foot, Signed, 5 In. 690.00
    Bowl, Opalescent Walls, Red & Gilt Overlay, Pendant Leaves & Berries, Signed, 7 In. 1200.00
    Bowl, Upturned Corners, Etched Lush Trees, Signed, 6 1/2 In. 1840.00
    Bowl, Winter Forest Scene, Gray, Orange, Yellow, Black, Cameo, 1910, 6 In. 3680.00
    Box, 2 Glass Handles, Carved & Enameled Bird Feeding Fox, Signed, 4 3/4 In. 4400.00
    Box, Cover, Fuchsia Buds, Gray & White Opalescent, Cameo, 1900, 2 x 4 3/4 In. 2300.00
    Box, Cover, Yellow Walls, Cameo Iris, Gilt, Signed, Round, 5 1/2 In. 1600.00
    Box, Painted Red Clover, Cover, 4 1/4 In. 1725.00
    Box, Trinket, Cover, Flowers & Leaves, Cameo, 2 x 3 1/4 In. .... *Illus* 1500.00
    Candlestick, Frosted, Rope Twist Standard, Brown Stripe, Footed, 1930, 20 1/4 In. .. 575.00
    Chandelier, 5-Light, Amber Glass, Iron, Gold Foil, E. Brandt, 1925, 41 x 26 In. 8625.00
    Compote, Cameo, Carnation, Ruffled Rim, Stylized Border, 7 1/4 In. 2420.00
    Decanter, Silver Mounting, Green, Crimson, Strawberries, Cameo, c.1900 .... 1495.00
    Decanter, Windmill & Lake Scene, White Opalescent, Original Stopper, 9 1/2 In. 2420.00
    Dish, Change Receiver, Leaf & Berries, Nibbling Mouse On Rim, Signed, 8 1/4 In. .. 3080.00
    Figurine, Striding Maiden, Flowing Cape, Signed, c.1905, 8 5/8 In. 3163.00
    Lamp, Cut Peacock Feathers, Gray, 3-Arm Mount, Signed, c.1910, 16 In. 8050.00
    Lamp, Dome Shade, Wooded Lake Scene, Trailing Ivy Base, Signed, 14 In. 8800.00
    Lamp, Frosted Domed Shade, Etched Irregular Vertical Lines, Signed, 24 3/4 In. 9350.00
    Lamp, Fruiting Grapevines, Flattened Circular Shade, Signed, 21 In. 5750.00
    Lamp, Mottled Yellow Glass, Radiating Vertical Lines, Wrought Iron, 1930, 16 In. 9200.00
    Lamp, Table, Dome Shade, Frosted White, Etched Vertical Pattern, 14 1/2 In. 4025.00
    Lamp, Tapering Shade, Etched Flowering Stems & Leaves, Signed, 14 In. 9775.00
    Lamp Base, Etched Glass Vertical Strips, 3 Metal Arms, c.1925, 7 1/2 In. 1150.00
    Paperweight, Egg Form, Central Lilac, Floral, Signed, 4 In. 80.00
    Perfume Bottle, Dutch Lake Scene, Enamel, Silver Mounted, Signed, 5 1/2 In. 990.00

Perfume Bottle, Enameled, Floral Leafy Stems, Frosted Stopper, Cameo, 10 1/2 In. 2530.00
Perfume Bottle, Etched Snowdrops, Silver Mounted Glass Stopper, Signed, 5 In. 1265.00
Perfume Bottle, Flagon, 4 Colors, Cameo, 1910 .... 1485.00
Perfume Bottle, Green, Oval, Etched, Enamel Mistletoe, Cameo, 8 In. 1210.00
Perfume Bottle, Round, Mottled White, Etched, Black Desert Scene, 1 5/8 In. 1760.00
Toothpick, Winter Scene, Signed 750.00
Vase, Acid-Etched Circles, Cylindrical, Turquoise, c.1930, 6 7/8 In. 800.00
Vase, Acid-Etched Geometric Design, Cylindrical, Orange, c.1925, 6 7/8 In. 925.00
Vase, Acid-Etched Zigzags & Dots, Ovoid, Everted Rim, Topaz, c.1930, 7 7/8 In. 800.00
Vase, Alternating Pattern Of Graduating Disks, Bars, Topaz, Signed, 12 5/8 In. 520.00
Vase, Art Deco, Cross Of Lorraine, 9 In. 2500.00
Vase, Baluster Shape, Amber Flowers Overlay, Peach & Yellow Ground, 9 1/2 In. 2645.00
Vase, Berluze, Gray & Red Mottled Ground, Pinched Sides, 18 1/2 In. .... 975.00 to 1075.00
Vase, Blossoms, Mottled, Dark Leaves, Metal Base, Cameo, 7 1/2 In. 1100.00
Vase, Blossoms & Buds, Ice Blue, Maroon, Cameo, 1910, 11 1/4 In. 4315.00
Vase, Blown-Out Metal Frame, Grays, Pinks, Amber Glass, 8 x 11 In. 2150.00
Vase, Blue Blackberries, Frosted & Blue Ground, Cameo, 15 In. 3740.00
Vase, Blue Opalescent To Frosted Clear, Flowers, Signed, Cameo, 9 3/4 x 3 1/2 In. .. 935.00
Vase, Bulbous, Blown Into Iron Majorelle Frame, Signed, c.1925, 11 1/8 In. 3100.00
Vase, Bulbous, Enamel, Columbine, Foliage, Salmon & Yellow Ground, 11 1/2 In. 3220.00
Vase, Burgundy, Orange & Lavender, Iron Rib Frame, Majorelle, 14 1/2 In. 1150.00
Vase, Butterfly & Flowers, Carved, Signed, 13 In. 440.00
Vase, Carnations, Buds, Red, Emerald, Clear, Cameo, Silver Footed, 1910, 9 3/8 In. . 7475.00
Vase, Clear Yellow & Frosted, Flaring Form, Signed, 8 In. 200.00
Vase, Clematis Blossoms & Leaves, Amethyst, c.1900, 12 1/8 In. 2070.00
Vase, Cobalt & Powder Blue, Wrought Iron Mounted, Louis Majorelle, 10 In. 4600.00
Vase, Continuous Lake Landscape, Cross Of Lorraine, Cameo, 17 In. 2800.00
Vase, Coral Bell Blossoms, Etched, Tangerine Ground, Signed, 9 1/4 In. 1870.00
Vase, Cornflowers, Etched & Enamel, Signed, 3 7/8 In. 1150.00
Vase, Cylindrical, Opalescent, Cut Blackberries, Branches, Cameo, c.1910, 6 3/4 In. . 920.00
Vase, Dark Blue, Blue Green Flecks, Ribbed, Frosted, Ovoid, 1930, 15 1/8 In. 575.00
Vase, Enamel, Etched Roses, Branches, Cased Amber Cylinder, Cameo, 4 5/8 In. 770.00
Vase, Enamel, Spherical, Indented Sides, Landscape, Cameo, c.1915, 3 5/8 In. 1600.00
Vase, Etched Daisies, Frosted White & Yellow Ground, Ovoid, Footed, 14 3/4 In. 4600.00
Vase, Etched Flowering Branch, Pink & Gilt Enamel, Cameo, 7 1/4 In. 550.00
Vase, Etched Smoky Ground, 4 Clear Panels, Ovoid, 1925, 15 1/2 In. 488.00
Vase, Faceted, Art Deco Style, Octagonal, Topaz, 11 1/2 In. 440.00
Vase, Flight Of Herons, Marsh Marigolds, Textured Ground, 18 3/4 In. 5520.00
Vase, Flowering Branches & Leaves Etching, Green & White, Signed, 16 In. 2530.00
Vase, Flowers Rise From Water, Burnt Orange, Green, Signed, 9 1/2 In. 8500.00
Vase, Folded Rim, Topaz Ground, Etched Scrolls & Lozenges, Ovoid, 18 3/4 In. 2875.00
Vase, Forest & Village Scene, Etched, Mottled Ground, 11 In. 2860.00
Vase, Frosted Ground, Leaves & Boysenberries, Signed, 14 1/2 In. 4600.00
Vase, Grape Clusters Amid Foliage, Etched & Enamel, Signed, 8 1/4 In. 4830.00
Vase, Gray Walls, Budding & Blooming Cornflowers, Cameo, Signed, 8 In. 3300.00
Vase, Green Diamonds, Cut Daisies, Cross Of Lorraine, Cameo, c.1900, 7 1/8 In. 800.00
Vase, Internal Tiger Lily, c.1900 .... 6900.00
Vase, Iris Design, 12 In. 6050.00
Vase, Jack-In-The-Pulpit, Spider Web, Enamel, Signed, c.1910, 4 7/8 In. 1725.00
Vase, Lake Scene, Foliage Around Water, Mottled Ground, Signed, 16 In. 4000.00
Vase, Lily-Of-The-Valley Blossoms, Gold Outlined, Frosted, 4 3/4 In. 750.00
Vase, Marquetry, Frosted & Mottled, Poppy Blossoms, Cameo, 20 In. 7150.00
Vase, Martele Ground, 3 Tulips & Leaves, Signed, 19 1/4 In. 5520.00
Vase, Mottled Gray, Trumpet Blossoms, c.1900, 15 7/8 In. 2990.00
Vase, Mottled Ground To Depict Flowering Vines, Handles, Signed, 9 1/2 In. 3220.00
Vase, Mottled Pumpkin & Gray, Lattice Wrought Iron Armature, 9 1/2 x 12 In. 2185.00
Vase, Mottled, Multi-Blossoms, Leafy Stems, Cameo, 8 1/4 In. 3190.00
Vase, Orange & Amethyst, Ovoid Form, Signed, 7 In. 175.00
Vase, Orchid Sprays, Leaves, Gray, White, Lemon, Amber, Cameo, 1910, 9 1/2 In. ... 2070.00
Vase, Ovoid, Orange, Amber, Purple, Cut Grape Clusters, Cameo, c.1900, 6 3/8 In. .. 2015.00
Vase, Ovoid, Pedestal Base, Cut Mistletoe, Emerald, Gilt, Cameo, c.1900, 5 3/8 In. .. 575.00
Vase, Pea Pods & Insects, Ice Blue, Maroon, Cameo, 1910, 11 3/8 In. 4315.00
Vase, Persimmon, Pink & Green Overlay, Fruits, Leafy Branches, Cameo, 15 In. 2750.00

Vase, Pine Trees, Gray, Lemon, Raspberry, Cobalt Blue, Brown, Cameo, 8 In. 3450.00
Vase, Poppy Blossoms, Tangerine, Emerald, Clear, Cameo, 1920, 8 3/8 In. 3450.00
Vase, Poppy Flowers & Foliage, Gilt Foot & Rim, Signed, 4 In. 1380.00
Vase, Prunus Blossoms & Leafage, Gray, Lavender, Teal, Cameo, 1900, 11 1/4 In. 4000.00
Vase, River Landscape, Amber Overlay, Signed, 5 3/4 In. 1150.00
Vase, River Landscape, Brown Cut To Yellow & Red, 8 In. 1155.00
Vase, River Landscape, Gray, Yellow, Orange, Forest Green, Cameo, 1915, 19 In. 2875.00
Vase, Rose Blossoms, Gray, Brown, Orange, Lemon, 1910, 13 1/2 In. 3013.00
Vase, Rust & Tortoiseshell Splotches, Bubbles, Majorelle Wrought Iron, 12 In. 1150.00
Vase, Sailboats, Cloudy Sky, Yellow Ground, Signed, 4 In. 1540.00
Vase, Scenic Landscape, Bulbous, Blue Streaked, c.1910, 6 3/8 In. 2300.00
Vase, Smoky Amber Top & Base, Scrolls, Frosted, Cylindrical, 12 5/8 In. 575.00
Vase, Smoky Amber, Clear Overlapping Square Bands, Bell Shape, 10 1/4 In. 862.00
Vase, Smoky, Horizontally Ribbed, Globular, 1930, 10 In. 690.00
Vase, Sprays Of Wildflowers, Grasses, Signed, c.1910, 6 1/2 In. 2185.00
Vase, Spring Landscape, Trees, Rainstorm, Signed, c.1910, 4 1/2 In. .... 6325.00 to 7475.00
Vase, Stylized Flowers & Leaves, 3 Ridges, Black Patina, Signed, 6 3/8 In. 690.00
Vase, Thistle, Etched, White Satin Glass, 9 In. 600.00
Vase, Triangular Footed, Gray, Yellow, Green, Cut Raspberries, Cameo, c.1910, 4 In. .. 1380.00
Vase, Trumpet Shape, Footed Base, Topaz, Acid-Etched Bands, c.1930, 9 5/8 In. 1150.00
Vase, Trumpet, Woodland Lake Scene, Enamel, Frosted Ground, Signed, 15 3/4 In. ... 3850.00
Vase, Tulips, Leaves, Opalescent, Amber, Emerald Green, Cameo, 1910, 7 3/8 In. 3450.00
Vase, Undulating Rim, Cameo & Enamel 4-Leafed Clovers, Clover Frieze Neck, 3 In. .. 2300.00
Vase, Wheel Carved, Square Body, Cornflower Blossoms, Signed, 6 1/4 In. 3680.00
Vase, Wildflowers & Leaves Enameled, Gray Mottled, Signed, c.1910, 3 1/8 In. 1265.00
Vase, Woodbine Berries & Leaves, Gray, Pink, Emerald, Cameo, 7 1/2 In. 2875.00

DAVENPORT pottery and porcelain were made at the Davenport factory in Longport, Staffordshire, England, from 1793 to 1887. Earthenwares, creamwares, porcelains, ironstone, and other ceramics were made. Most of the pieces are marked with a form of the word *Davenport.*

DAVENPORT
LONGPORT
STAFFORDSHIRE

Dinner Set, Child's, 1836, 34 Piece 350.00
Plate, Japan Pattern, Butterfly, Peony, Foliage, c.1820, 10 1/4 In., 24 Piece 2875.00
Plate, Molded Leaf Design, Green Enameled, 9 In. 38.50
Sugar & Creamer, Rose Design, Polychrome, Marked, 5 In. 258.50
Tureen, Marked, 7 1/2 In. 245.00

DAVY CROCKETT, the American frontiersman, was born in 1786 and died in 1836. He became popular in 1954 with the introduction of a television series about his life. Coonskin caps and buckskins became popular, and hundreds of different Davy Crockett items were made.

Belt, Leather, Fancy Buckle, Tooled, Size 28 .... 47.00
Belt, Metal Buckle 38.00
Bowl, 1950s, Melmac 27.00
Cap Gun, Buffalo Rifle, Plastic & Metal, Hubley, 24 1/4 In., Box 175.00
Coloring Book, 1955 .... 25.00
Cookie Jar, Brush .... 200.00 to 350.00
Cookie Jar, Bust, Regal 325.00
Cookie Jar, Coming Out of Woods, American Bisque .... 850.00 to 975.00
Cookie Jar, Hubert 650.00
Cookie Jar, McCoy 500.00
Cookie Jar, Ransburg 125.00
Coonskin Cap, Polly Crockett, White, 1950s 30.00
Dinner Set, Sears, 1950s, Box 90.00
Doll, Coonskin Cap, Fringed Jacket & Pants, Uneeda Rubber, 1950s 125.00
Figure, Official Davy Crockett As Portrayed By Fess Parker, Marx, 1950s 18.00
Frontier Kit, Leather Powder Horn & Belt, Box 75.00
Game, Bagatelle, Transogram, 1960s, 4 1/2 In. 30.00
Game, Frontierland 35.00
Glass, Holiday Frieze, 1955, Box, 12 Piece 245.00
Gun, Cork, Frontier Fighter, Tin, Wood, Japan, 1950s 65.00
Gun & Holster Set, Box 50.00
Gun Set, Frontier, On Card, 3 Prints, Frame 85.00

Handcuffs & Badge, 1950s	40.00
Lamp, 1950s, 11 In.	75.00
Lamp, Figural, Pottery, Premo Mfg. Co., 1955, 17 In.	195.00
Lunch Box, Holtemp, 1950s	120.00
Lunch Box, Indian Fighter, Metal, Thermos	100.00
Magic Paint Set	125.00
Mug, Brush	50.00
Mug, Milk Glass	13.50
Neckerchief, Silk, Leather Slide, 1950s	30.00
Pistol, Box	80.00
Pitcher, Glass, Ice Lip, Large	45.00
Plate, Webb Oil Promotional, 1955	20.00
Pocket Knife, Tomahawk, Fess Parker, Imperial, 1950s, 4 3/4 In.	75.00
Powder Horn, Compass, Belt, On Card	10.00
Rifle, Buffalo, Hubley	185.00
Ring, On Card	12.00
Stamp Book, King Of The Wild Frontier, c.1950	45.00
Suitcase, Simulated Leather, Cloth Design, Neevel, 1956, 10 x 12 x 4 In.	289.00
Sunglasses, Child's	35.00
Sunglasses, Shatterproof Lenses, Foster Grant, White Frames, c.1955	60.00
Target Set, Wooden, Keystone, Box	45.00
Thermos, Lunch Box, Holtemp, Tall, 1955	45.00
Toy, Pull, Wooden, Metal, 9 x 9 In.	155.00
Toy, Wristwatch, On Card, 1940s	12.00
Tumbler, Davey Was Happy Boy	10.00
Wristwatch, Engraved Powder Horn, No Top	200.00

DE VEZ was a signature used on cameo glass after 1910. E. S. Monot founded the glass company near Paris in 1851. The company changed names many times. Mt. Joye, another glass by this factory, is listed in its own category.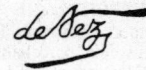

Lamp, Pine Trees, Yellow, Orange, Green, Wrought Iron, 1915, 11 In.	2875.00
Vase, Bird In Blossoms, Island Scene On Reverse, Signed	1995.00
Vase, Venetian Lagoon, Boating, Signed, c.1920, 9 7/8 In.	575.00

DECOYS are carved or turned wooden copies of birds, fish, or animals. The decoy was placed in the water or propped on the shore to lure flying birds to the pond for hunters. Some decoys are handmade, some are commercial products. Today there is a group of artists making modern decoys for display, not for use in a pond.

Beaver, Ice Spearing, Cedar, Leather Tail, Tobacco Tin Legs, Wire Whiskers	495.00
Black Duck, Hollow Block, Glass Eyes, C.W. Black, Bordentown, N.J., 16 3/4 In.	275.00
Black Duck, Hollow Body, G. Gerlach, New York, 16 3/4 In.	38.50
Black Duck, Lowhead, William Kuhn, c.1920	500.00
Black Duck, Original Paint, Wooden Ballast, Wildfowler Decoy Co.	99.00
Black Duck, Sleeping, Cork, McNulty, Oversize	330.00
Black Duck, Turned Head, Carved Tail & Feathers, Painted	357.00
Blackbellied Plover, Shorebird, Original Paint, Spring Plumage, Mason, 1905	2750.00
Blue Heron, Stick-Up, Glass Eyes, Leather Trim, 41 1/2 In.	165.00
Blue-Winged Teal, Balsa Wood, Ward Brothers, 1952, 8 In.	412.00
Blue-Winged Teal, Glass Eyes, C.K. Orser, Paper Label, 10 1/2 In.	143.00
Bluebill, Carved & Painted, Signed F.C.W. '60	75.00
Bluebill, Flying, Tin Wings, Quebec	3600.00
Bluebill Drake, Glass Eyes, Profile, Ontario, 15 1/4 In.	71.50
Bluebill Drake, Hollow Body, Glass Eyes, George Chick Poynton, 25 1/2 In.	38.50
Bluebill Drake, Lincoln, Miniature	650.00
Bluebill Drake, Reggie Culver, c.1920	2000.00
Bluebill Drake, Taunton River Rig, H. Keyes Chadwick, c.1915	300.00
Bluebill Hen, Addie Nichols	850.00
Bluebill Hen, Glass Eyes, Wooden, c.1930	85.00
Bluebill Hen, Hollow Body, Glass Eyes, 13 1/4 In.	27.50
Bluebill Hen, Thomas Chambers, Hollow Carved	2300.00
Brant, Ira Hudson, Original Paint	850.00

Bufflehead, Original Paint, Glass Eyes, Jim VanBrunt, 1950s, Small, Pair 517.00
Bufflehead Drake, F. J. Dubbins, Jonesport, Maine, 10 1/2 In. 165.00
Bufflehead Drake, Hollow Block, Glass Eyes, Original Paint, 13 1/2 In. 357.50
Bufflehead Drake, Martha's Vineyard, c.1920 .... 65.00
Bufflehead Drake, Wildfowler Of Old Saybrook, Cedar, c.1938 .... 70.00
Canada Goose, Balsa Body, Wildfowler Decoy Co., 1950s 121.00
Canada Goose, Captain Clarence Bailey 1980.00
Canada Goose, Cork Body, Wooden Head, Original Paint, Lowell Strayer, 21 In. 55.00
Canada Goose, Cork Body, Wooden Head, Phil Soukup, 21 In. 181.00
Canada Goose, Hissing Position, 25 1/2 In. 1980.00
Canada Goose, Hollow Carved, Ontario, Repainted, 1880 .... 2090.00
Canada Goose, Old Paint, Madison Mitchell, 21 1/2 In. 385.00
Canada Goose, R.D. Laurie, Painted 302.50
Canada Goose, Stick-Up, Cardboard, Folding Head, 5 Piece 49.50
Canada Goose, Swimmer, Nova Scotia, 26 In. 137.50
Canada Goose, Wooden Base, J. Lapham, 6 1/2 In. 209.00
Canvasback, Thom Chambers 4400.00
Canvasback Drake, Carved & Combed Feathers, Dave Hodman, 15 1/4 In. 105.00
Canvasback Drake, Cork, Moody Linn, 1940, 18 1/2 In. 110.00
Canvasback Drake, Glass Eyes, Wildfowler, 16 In. 33.00
Canvasback Drake, Gunning, Ken Anger, c.1948, Pair 2200.00
Canvasback Drake, Jim Baines, Chesapeake Bay 150.00
Canvasback Drake, Original Paint, Glass Eyes, Factory, 15 1/2 In. 209.00
Canvasback Drake, Paper Label, Upper Chesapeake Bay, 8 x 13 In. 126.50
Canvasback Drake, Pratt Decoy Co. 100.00
Canvasback Duck, Captain Harry Jobes 66.00
Coot, Paint Wear, Glass Eyes, Bill Goenne, 11 1/2 In. 82.00
Crayfish, Confidence, Painted, Bud Stewart, 6 1/4 In. 160.00
Crow, Papier-Mache, Large 30.00
Curlew, A.E. Crowell, Paper Label, Miniature 1450.00
Curlew, Captain Savage, Carved & Painted, 10 1/2 x 12 In. 2750.00
Curlew, Herters Decoy Co., Minnesota, c.1960s 88.00
Curlew, On Stand, Crowell, Miniature 1595.00
Curlew, Split Tail, Carved Eye Detail 155.00
Dowitcher, c.1900 .... 110.00
Duck, All Original, Orin Hiltz, 1940, 17 & 18 In., Pair 2000.00
Duck, Glass Eyes, Jack Sweet Of Decoys Unlimited, 17 1/2 In. 44.00
Eider Drake, Nova Scotia, 1920 .... 110.00
Eider Drake, Open Billed, Mike Valley 170.00
Fish, Brook Trout, Wood, Brass Tack Eyes, Metal Fins, 1930s, 12 In. 300.00
Fish, Carved Wooden Tail, Leroy Howell, 7 In. 425.00
Fish, Ice Fishing 70.00
Fish, Muskie, Aluminum & Wood, Bud Stewart, 11 1/2 In. 72.00
Fish, Northern Pike, Ice Spear, Floater, Repainted, Cedar, Tin Fins, 1945, 32 In. 225.00
Fish, Sturgeon, Cylindrical, Carved, Nailhead Eyes, Copper Fins, 20 In. 1150.00
Fish, Trout, D.R. Hammeral, 10 In. 35.00
Fish, Trout, Tarzan Gieselharet, Minn., 5 In. 65.00
Freshwater Coot, Evans Decoy Co. 300.00
Freshwater Coot, Wisconsin, Carved & Painted, 11 In. 220.00
Golden Plover, Morton 1100.00
Goldeneye Drake, Original Paint, Labeled J. Dadd 1976, 12 In. 38.50
Goldeneye Hen, Luther Nickerson, Painted Eyes, Initials On Bottom 125.00
Goose, Sheldon, Outlaw, Opens In Middle To Hide Full Size Duck, c.1920 .... 325.00
Hooded Merganser, Pete Peterson, 1980, Pair 330.00
Mallard, Carved & Painted, Solberg 50.00
Mallard, Stevens Factory 2420.00
Mallard Drake, Original Paint, Glass Eyes, F. Uzee, Louisiana, Signed, 16 In. 165.00
Mallard Drake, Original Paint, Glass Eyes, Nestled Head, T.J.'s Rig, 14 In. 165.00
Mallard Drake, Original Paint, Glass Eyes, Wm. E. Pratt Co., Chicago 1920s, 17 In. 220.00
Mallard Drake, Snakelike Neck, Tack Eyes, Raised Wing Tips, 19 In. 594.00
Mallard Drake, Tucked Head, Papier-Mache 20.00
Mallard Drake, Victor, No. 118 .... 75.00
Mallard Drake, Weighted, Marked Perdew, Henry, Illinois 550.00

Mallard Hen, Balsa Body, Original Keel, Wildfowler Decoy Co., c.1946	88.00
Mallard Hen, Glass Eyes, Yellow Over Varnish, 17 1/2 In.	60.00
Mallard Hen, Inscribed Base, W. Sheerman, 1967	60.00
Mallard Hen, Weighted, Marked Perdew, Henry, Illinois	725.00
Merganser, Carved Tail, Martin Collins, Oval Stamp	220.00
Merganser, Glass Eyes, Original Paint, Folk Art Type, 17 1/2 In.	495.00
Merganser Drake, Benjamin Smith, Branded Top & Bottom, c.1890	3900.00
Merganser Drake, Hollow Block, Glass Eyes, Holloway, 14 1/2 In.	275.00
Merganser Hen, Augustis Aaron Wilson, c.1900, Miniature	775.00
Oldsquaw Drake, Joseph Whiting Lincoln, c.1900	26000.00
Owl, Carrylite, Papier-mache	75.00
Owl, Glass Eyes, Boales Swisher, Decatur, Illinois, Papier-Mache, 12 3/4 In.	275.00
Owl, Great Horned, Cloth, Glass Eyes, Herters Factory, c.1918	627.00
Owl, Papier-Mache, Small	85.00
Owl, Stuffed Canvas, Flapping Wing, Original Papers & Box, J. W. Reynolds Co.	495.00
Owl, Stuffed, Printed Canvas, Herters Company, c.1940s	990.00
Pancake-Bodied Elder, Nova Scotia, c.1900, 17 & 8 In., Pair	800.00
Pigeon, Flying, Mechanical, Lime Green & Brown, Price	1072.00
Pigeon, Original Paint, Pennsylvania Dutch, 1900, Half Size	450.00
Pigeon, Tack Eyes, 13 1/2 In.	165.00
Pintail Drake, Glass Eyes, Paul Arness, 19 In.	82.50
Pintail Drake, Jim Pierce	175.00
Pintail Drake, Paul Gibson, Pair	600.00
Pintail Drake, R. Madison Mitchell, Turned Head, 1958-1960	385.00
Pintail Drake, Sleeping, Downeast Sportcraft Co., c.1940	200.00
Pintail Drake, Turned Head, Glass Eyes, Original Paint, Mike Bonnet, 14 In.	72.00
Pintail Drake, Zeke McDonald, Original Paint, 1910	500.00
Pintail Hen, Heckwhittington, Oglesby, Illinois, 6 x 18 In.	357.50
Plover, Cobb Island, c.1880	260.00
Preener, 9 In.	61.50
Red Breasted Grosbeak, A.E. Cowell, c.1915, Miniature	450.00
Red Breasted Merganser, Ben Smith	4290.00
Red Breasted Merganser Drake, Balsa Wood, Ward Brothers, 8 In.	495.00
Red Breasted Merganser Drake, Capt. P. Wright, Horsehair Crest, 1900 .. 9000.00 to	9900.00
Red Breasted Merganser Drake, Fish In Bill, Paul Casson	100.00
Redhead Drake, Doug Jester	500.00
Ring-Neck Drake, Original Paint, Bill Goening, 15 In.	105.00
Rose Breasted Grosbeak, On Stand, Crowell, Miniature	385.00
Ruddy Duck, On Stand, Crowell, Miniature	605.00
Ruffed Grouse, Wendell H. Gilley, Signed, Miniature	350.00
Shorebird, Black & Grayish Paint, Steel Rod, Driftwood Base, Primitive, 12 In.	55.00
Shorebird, Carved & Painted, Solberg	90.00
Shorebird, Driftwood Base, Contemporary, Herb Paisly Sr., 5 In.	33.00
Shorebird, Shot Scars, Walker, 11 In.	27.50
Shorebird, Stylized, Old Black & Gray Paint, Long Beak, 5 In.	27.50
Shoveler Hen, Dr. Miles Pirnie	400.00
Spoonbill Hen, Balsa Wood, Ward Brothers, 8 In.	412.00
Teal Drake, Green-Winged, Bill Joeckel, Signed, 1968	270.00
Teal Drake, Green-Winged, Glass Eyes, Paul Arness, 11 3/4 In.	50.00
Teal Duck, Green-Winged, Jim Pierce, Pair	140.00
Turkey, Painted Canvas, Wooden	875.00
Widgeon Drake, A.E. Crowell	1000.00
Wood Duck Drake, Original Paint, Glass Eyes, 8 In.	110.00
Woodcock, Carved & Painted, Kach	176.00
Yellowlegs, Boyd, 11 In.	63.50
Yellowlegs, Verity, c.1880	500.00

DEDHAM Pottery was started in 1895. Chelsea Keramic Art Works was established in 1872 in Chelsea, Massachusetts, by members of the Robertson family. The firm used the mark *CKAW*. The factory closed in 1889 and was reorganized as the Chelsea Pottery U.S. in 1891. It became the Dedham Pottery of Dedham, Massachusetts. The factory closed in 1943. It was famous for its crackleware dishes, which picture blue outlines of animals, flowers, and other natural motifs.

Ashtray, Elephant, Pair 660.00
Ashtray, Rabbit, Registered Blue Stamp, 1943, 6 In. 1540.00
Bowl, Heavily Mottled, Oxblood Glaze, Hugh C. Robertson, 2 1/2 x 3 1/2 In. 330.00
Bowl, Rabbit, 5 1/4 In. 275.00
Bowl, Rabbit, Square, 8 1/4 In. 450.00
Bowl, Scalloped, Blue Flowers, White Ground, Crackleware, 8 3/4 In. 600.00
Butter Chip, Pansy, 3 1/2 In. 325.00
Candle Snuffer, Rabbit, 2 In. .... 600.00 to 700.00
Celery, Rabbit, Oval, 8 In. 225.00
Cookie Jar, Elephant, Blue Stamp, Incised DP Co., 6 In. 1750.00
Cookie Jar, Poppy, Blue Stamp, 1931, 6 1/4 In. 3300.00
Creamer, Double Turtle 450.00
Creamer, Rabbit 425.00
Cup & Saucer, Bouillon, Rabbit, 3 1/2 In. 275.00
Cup & Saucer, Elephant, Stamp Mark, 6 In. 775.00
Cup & Saucer, Polar Bear, Blue Stamp, Exhibition Label 357.50
Dish, Bacon, Rabbit 247.50
Eggcup, Attached Saucer, Rabbit, Blue Stamp, Exhibition Label, 4 1/2 In., Pair 445.00
Eggcup, Rabbit 190.00
Flower Frog, Standing Rabbit, Blue Stamp, 1931, 6 1/4 In. 885.00
Humidor, 2 Elephants, Inscribed May 1917, 7 In. 1980.00
Knife Rest, Figural Rabbit, 3 3/4 In. 450.00
Paperweight, Rabbit, Blue Stamp, 1931, 3 In. 425.00
Pitcher, Middle Band Of Rabbits, 8 1/2 In. 8800.00
Pitcher, Milk, Rabbit 418.00
Pitcher, Night & Day, Blue Stamp, 5 In. .... 650.00 to 660.00
Pitcher, Oak Block, Blue Stamp, 5 3/4 In. 660.00
Pitcher, Rabbit, Blue Stamp, Exhibition Label, 8 3/4 In. 550.00
Pitcher, Rabbit, Impressed & Stamp Mark, 8 3/8 In. 1325.00
Plaque, Scenic Landscape, Robertson, Exhibition Label, CKAW, 11 In. 1650.00
Plaque, Translucent Blue Glaze, Muse, Triton, Laurel Crown, CKAW, c.1880, 11 In. ... 445.00
Plate, 8 Vining Ships Border, Sailor & Breaking Wave, 9 3/4 In. 2975.00
Plate, Azalea, 6 1/4 In. 150.00
Plate, Azalea, Blue Stamp, 9 3/4 In. 445.00
Plate, Butterfly Border, 6 In. 300.00
Plate, Chick, Blue Stamp, Double Impressed Rabbit, 6 1/2 In. 2550.00
Plate, Clover, 6 In. 1765.00
Plate, Crab, Blue Stamp, Double Impressed Rabbit, 7 1/2 In. 357.50
Plate, Crab, Wave Design, 7 3/4 In. 850.00
Plate, Crocus & Clover, 9 3/4 In. 3740.00
Plate, Dark Blue Lion & Owl, H.C. Robertson, 1900, 10 In. 1540.00
Plate, Dolphin In Surf, Blue Stamp, Impressed Rabbit, Exhibition Label, 6 In. 335.00
Plate, Dolphins, Marked, 8 3/4 In. 500.00
Plate, Double Turtle, 6 In. 2090.00
Plate, Duck, 8 In. 220.00
Plate, Elephant, 7 5/8 In. 1000.00
Plate, Elephant, Blue Stamp, Double Impressed Rabbit, 7 1/2 In. 440.00
Plate, Elephant, Blue Stamp, Double Impressed Rabbit, 10 In. 715.00
Plate, Golden Gate, San Francisco, M. Sheperd, 10 In. 2750.00
Plate, Grape, Marked, 6 1/4 In. 110.00
Plate, Grape, Marked, 8 1/2 In. 85.00
Plate, Grouse & Haystack, 9 1/2 In. 3300.00
Plate, Grouse, Blue Stamp, Impressed Rabbit, 9 7/8 In. 1450.00
Plate, Grouse, Marked, 8 1/4 In. 165.00
Plate, Horsechestnut, 6 In. 155.00
Plate, Horsechestnut, Marked, 6 1/4 In., 4 Piece 385.00
Plate, Iris, 6 In. 195.00
Plate, Iris, 8 In. 160.00
Plate, Lily Pattern 4180.00
Plate, Lobster, Impressed & Stamped Mark, 8 3/4 In., 5 Piece 1650.00
Plate, Magnolia, 10 In. 175.00
Plate, Magnolia, Marked, 9 In. 95.00
Plate, Peacock, Impressed Rabbit, 6 1/8 In. 1450.00

Plate, Pine Tree Design, Hugh Cornwall Robertson, 8 1/2 In. 5100.00
Plate, Pineapples, 8 3/4 In. 250.00
Plate, Polar Bear Border, 8 1/2 In. 302.00
Plate, Pond Lily, 6 In. 195.00
Plate, Pond Lily, Marked, 8 1/2 In. 110.00
Plate, Pond Lily, Marked, 9 3/4 In. 145.00
Plate, Poppy, Blue Stamp, 6 In. 165.00
Plate, Poppy, Gray Glaze, Blue Stamp, Impressed Rabbit, Exhibition Label, 8 1/4 In. 225.00
Plate, Poppy, Impressed Mark, 8 1/2 In. 495.00
Plate, Rabbit, 8 1/2 In. 198.00
Plate, Rabbit, 10 1/4 In. .... 165.00 to 300.00
Plate, Rabbit, White Ground, Maud Davenport, 10 1/4 In. 1980.00
Plate, Rabbits, Marked, 12 In. 410.00
Plate, Raised Pineapple, Impressed CPUS, EE, X, 8 1/2 In. 275.00
Plate, Reverse Poppy, Blue Stamp, Impressed Rabbit, 8 3/8 In. 495.00
Plate, Scotty In Landscape, 8 1/2 In. 2970.00
Plate, Snowtree Border, Marked, 8 1/2 In. 250.00
Plate, Tapestry Lion, 8 1/2 In. 1650.00
Plate, Tapestry Lion, Blue Stamp, Impressed Rabbit, Blue Heart, 8 1/4 In. 1320.00
Plate, Tree Design, Hugh Cornwall Robertson, 8 1/2 In. 2420.00
Plate, Turtles, Blue Stamp, Impressed Rabbit, 8 3/8 In. 600.00
Plate, Turtles, Blue Stamp, Impressed Rabbit, 9 3/4 In. 935.00
Plate, White Peacock Border, 6 In. 6325.00
Plate, Wild Rose, 8 1/4 In. 7425.00
Platter, Chop, Lobster, 1900, 12 In. 880.00
Platter, Chop, Rabbit, Marked, 12 In. 275.00
Platter, Lobster, Blue Stamp, Double Impressed Rabbit, 12 In. 715.00
Platter, Sailing Ship, C.F. Davenport, Blue Stamp, Exhibition Label, 1927, 12 In. 2650.00
Sherbet, Rabbit, Blue, 3 1/2 In. 1200.00
Soup, Dish, Rabbit, Marked, 9 1/4 In. 145.00
Sugar, Cover, Rabbit 275.00
Sugar & Creamer, Rabbit, Blue Stamp, 3 1/4 In. 357.00
Tankard, Rabbit, 5 1/4 In. 330.00
Teapot, Elephant, Blue Stamp, 5 1/4 In. 1540.00
Tile, Rabbit, Round, 6 In. 235.00
Toothpick, Rabbit, Figural, 4 1/2 In. 110.00
Tureen, Rabbit, Rabbit Handle, Blue Stamp, 5 /12 x 9 In. 935.00
Vase, Colored Volcanic Glaze, Marked, Hugh Robertson, 6 1/2 In. 2800.00
Vase, Crackle Glaze, Butterfly, Flowers, CKAW, c.1888, 5 5/8 In. 1100.00
Vase, Dragon's Blood & Olive Green Iridescent Glaze, CKAW, 9 1/2 In. 1550.00
Vase, Dragon's Blood, Oxblood Streaks, Hugh C. Robertson, CKAW, 8 1/4 In. 3080.00
Vase, Flambe Glaze, Swollen Shoulder, Hugh Robertson, Marked, 9 1/4 In. 1200.00
Vase, Flask Shape, Suspended Rings, Blue-Brown Drip Glaze, Handles, 13 In. 395.00
Vase, Glossy Green, Blue Drip, Beige Mottling, Hugh C. Robertson, 7 1/2 In. 385.00
Vase, Gray Crackle Glaze, 1886, 6 3/4 In. 165.00
Vase, Green Drip, Gray, Sang De Boeuf, Marked HCR, 4 x 3 In. 650.00
Vase, Neoclassicism, Chelsea Keramic Art Works, 7 In. 250.00
Vase, Poppy Blossoms & Pods, Crackleware, White Ground, 8 In. 2600.00
Vase, Rectangle, Translucent, Daisy, Lion's Head, CKAW, c.1878, 7 3/4 In., Pair 1100.00
Vase, Stovepipe Neck, Buff Glossy Glaze, Marked, 3 3/4 In. 195.00
Vase, Stylized Branches & Blossoms, Rabbit Mark, 7 1/4 In. 1800.00
Vase, Tan, Black Pits, Signed HCR, 8 1/2 x 6 In. 1300.00
Vase, Translucent Drip, Hugh C. Robertson, 8 1/2 In. 522.50
Vase, Translucent Matte Brown, High Relief Blossom, J. Day, CKAW, 6 3/4 In. 330.00
Vase, Translucent Yellow, Low Relief Flowers, J. Day, CKAW, c.1880, 4 3/4 In. 440.00
Vase, Volcanic Glaze, Olive & Opalescent Highlights, H.C. Robertson, 7 3/4 In. 2970.00
Vase, Volcanic, Heavily Mottled, Craters, Green, Blue & Red, Robertson, 8 In. 1100.00
Wall Pocket, Rabbits, Azaleas, Blue Stamp, Marked, 6 x 4 3/4 In. 2750.00

DEGENHART is the name used by collectors for the products of the Crystal Art Glass Company of Cambridge, Ohio. John and Elizabeth Degenhart started the glassworks in 1947. Quality paperweights and other glass objects were made. John died in 1964 and his wife took over management and production ideas. Over 145 colors of glass were made. In 1978, after the

death of Mrs. Degenhart, the molds were sold. The D in a heart trademark
was removed, so collectors can easily recognize the true Degenhart piece.

Figurine, Baby's Shoes, Red, Blue & Pink 25.00
Figurine, Owl, Amethyst 35.00
Figurine, Owl, Light Lime 30.00
Mug, Baby's, Red, White & Blue, Signed 25.00
Pitcher, Elizabeth Degenhart Profile, Amethyst 35.00
Plate, Elizabeth Degenhart Portrait 15.00
Toothpick, Daisy & Button, Cobalt Blue, 3 Footed 38.00
Wine, Buzz Saw 25.00
Wine, Cobalt 25.00

DEGUE is a signature found acid-etched on pieces of French glass made in
the early 1900s. Cameo, mold blown, and smooth glass with contrasting
colored rims are the types most often found.

Chandelier, Domed, 4 Side Panels, Molded Foliate, Metal, c.1925, 36 1/2 In. 2530.00
Lamp, Domed Shade, Cut Rose Blossoms, Buds & Leaves, 1920, 14 In. 5175.00
Lamp, Domed Shade, Etched Morning Glories, Iron Mount, Signed, 17 1/4 In. 2300.00
Lamp, Domed Shade, Stylized Sprays Of Flowering Branches, Signed, 18 1/4 In. 8250.00
Planter, Mottled Brown & Orange Floral, Clear Frosted Ground, Cameo, 7 In. 1925.00
Vase, Acid-Etched Arches, Bulbous, Everted Rim, Amethyst, c.1925, 17 In. 1380.00
Vase, Cut Triangle Designs, Ovoid Form, Signed, 17 In. 517.00
Vase, Frosted Yellow, Etched Blossoms & Stems, Cased, 16 1/2 In. 1430.00
Vase, Internal Design, Amethyst Handles, Signed, c.1928, 15 In. 1495.00
Vase, Stylized Bamboo, Gray, Orange, Red, Blue, Cameo, c.1925, 18 3/4 In. 920.00

DELATTE glass is a French cameo glass made by Andre Delatte. It was first
made in Nancy, France, in 1921. Lighting fixtures and opaque glassware in
imitation of Bohemian opaline were made. There were many French cameo
glass makers, so be sure to look in other appropriate categories.

Box, Cover, Bleeding Hearts & Leaves, Signed, c.1920, 3 3/4 In. 1265.00
Vase, Bird, 7 In. 675.00

DELDARE, see Buffalo Pottery Deldare

DELFT is a tin-glazed pottery that has been made since the seventeenth
century. It is decorated with blue on white or with colored decorations. Most
of the pieces sold today were made after 1891, and the name *Holland* appears
with the Delft factory marks. The word *delft* also appears on pottery from
other countries.

Bottle, Rosewater, Branch Of Peony, Liverpool, c.1760, 10 In. 665.00
Bowl, House In Landscape, Trees, Rocks, Lambeth, c.1730, 6 1/2 In. 2650.00
Bowl, Iron Red Flowers, Blue Tendrils, Scalloped Border, c.1730, 8 3/4 In. 2425.00
Bowl, Serving, Floral Design 600.00
Bowl, Stylized Florals, Blue Leaves, Fluted Rim, Lambeth, c.1740, 9 In. 2860.00
Bowl, Stylized Leaf & Scroll, Melon Ribbed, Footed, Tab Handles, 6 1/4 In. 42.00
Bowl, Vegetable, Cover, Blue Parsley, Tab Handles, 8 1/2 In. 40.00
Chamber Pot, Flowering Branches & Rushes, Strap Handle, c.1715, 5 In. 6325.00
Charger, Adam & Eve, Brislington, Striped Fruit, 1690, 13 5/8 In. 2000.00
Charger, Biblical Scene, Polychrome, 18th Century 275.00
Charger, Floral Decoration, Polychrome, 18th Century 335.00
Charger, Floral Urn, 19th Century, 14 In. 600.00
Charger, Landscape Decoration, Continental, 18th Century 415.00
Charger, Oak Leaf, Central Leaf Medallion, Scattered Berries, 1715-1720, 13 In. 1380.00
Charger, Stylized Man, Courtly Dress, 17th Century 290.00
Charger, Tulip, Stylized Carnations, 17th Century, 11 1/2 In. 6900.00
Charger, Tulips & Small Leaves, Exotic Landscape, 18th Century, 12 In. 315.00
Dish, Divided, 8 1/2 In. 55.00
Dish, Flowers In Vase, Wheat Sheaves Rim, Wincanton, c.1745, 13 1/4 In. 1550.00
Dish, Flowers In Vases Center, Rock Work, Reticulated, Dublin, c.1760, 11 1/2 In. 2100.00
Ewer, Floral Design, Pewter Fittings 275.00
Flower Brick, Blue & White, England, 18th Century, 6 1/4 In. 605.00
Flower Brick, Chinamen In Rocky Landscape, Birds, c.1750, 6 In. 2090.00

Flower Brick, Man On River, Buildings, Pierced Top, Bristol, c.1755, 5 13/16 In. 575.00
Loving Cup, Cover, Blue, Red, Yellow, Baluster Shape, Bristol, c.1725, 7 1/2 In. 5175.00
Mug, Seated Oriental, Rocky Landscape, Loop Handle, 17th Century, 4 3/8 In. 9200.00
Plaque, Birdcage, Polychrome, 19th Century, 10 In. 1725.00
Plate, Center Initial, Foliate Wreath, 1712, 8 3/4 In. 1850.00
Plate, Central Seated Oriental, Scene Top & Bottom, 17th Century, 8 5/8 In. 5175.00
Plate, Cockerel Within A Blue & Green Border, Bristol, c.1740, 8 5/8 In. 1540.00
Plate, Dutch Canal Winter Scene, Scalloped, Pierced, Bonneville, 15 In. 80.00
Plate, King Of Prussia, Frederick The Great, Armor, 1756-1763, 8 7/8 In. 4300.00
Plate, Merryman, Winged Cherub's Head, Scrolls, c.1690, 8 9/16 In. 1265.00
Plate, Monogram, Scroll-Edged Cartouche, Cherub's Head, 1693, 8 3/4 In. 1100.00
Plate, Peacock In Landscape, Sponged Trees, Bristol, c.1740, 8 1/4 In. 1760.00
Plate, Pears, Concentric Lines Center, Octagonal, c.1690, 7 7/8 In. 925.00
Plate, Scalloped, Chinese Man, Fluted Rim, Lambeth, c.1750, 8 3/4 In. 575.00
Plate, Seated Oriental, Grasses, Rocky Landscape, 17th Century, 8 7/8 In. 925.00
Plate, Tasseled Cartouche, 1698, 10 1/4 In. 825.00
Plate, Tin Glazed, 9 1/8 In. 225.00
Plate, Two Peacock Pattern, Marked, 18th Century, 12 1/2 In. 550.00
Plate, William & Mary, Royal Portrait, Deep Well, c.1690, 8 1/4 In. 5175.00
Pot, Posset, 3 Seated Chinamen, c.1680, 5 1/8 In. 1840.00
Pot, Posset, Cover, Seated Chinamen, c.1690, 6 3/4 In. 6600.00
Punch Bowl, Blowing Branches, Arched Panels, Lambeth, c.1720, 11 1/2 In. 4620.00
Punch Bowl, Long Eliza, Fenced Garden, Bristol, c.1740, 12 1/4 In. 1320.00
Sauceboat, Double-Lipped, Stylized Flowering Branches, c.1760, 8 7/8 In. 2860.00
Sugar & Creamer, Cover, Blue Parsley, Marked 45.00
Teapot, Gold Castle 50.00
Tile, Bible Verse, Genesis 25:23 .... 145.00
Tile, Bible Verse, Luke 35:20 .... 145.00
Tile, Galleon Vessel, Arts & Crafts, 9 x 5 In. 225.00
Tile, Sailing Ship Scene, Signed, Large 125.00
Urn, Tobacco, Lion Finial, Reeded & Paneled, Birds & Flowers, 14 In. 1650.00
Vase, Blue & White, Van Duyn Mark, 16 1/2 In., Pair 495.00
Vase, Cover, Man Of War, Blue & White, 10 In. 250.00
Vase, Sailboat, Windmill, 4 3/4 In. 60.00
Vase, Scenic, Floral, Flared, Cylindrical, 19th Century, 15 In. 165.00
Wall Pocket, Bearded Mask, Flowering Plants, Liverpool, c.1770, 8 1/8 In. 400.00
Wall Pocket, Fish Shape, Iron Red Spines, Fins, Liverpool, c.1770, 8 In., Pair 8800.00
Wall Pocket, Green Bird, Flowering Branches, Liverpool, c.1760, 8 1/2 In. 4200.00

DENTAL cabinets, chairs, equipment, and other related items are listed here.
Other objects may be found in the Medical category.

Cabinet, 19 Drawers & Doors, Paneled Sides & Back, Oak 450.00
Cabinet, Office, 1915 .... 1500.00
Cabinet, Drawers & Cabinets, Oak 1475.00
Cabinet-Table, Oak, Steel Adjustable Swivel Arm, 1880 .... 500.00
Chair, Camp, Civil War 425.00
Extractor, Brass, T Handle 5.00
Forceps Set, S.S. White, Leather Case, 8 Piece 200.00
Mold, Gold Teeth, Case, Central Tool Co., Box, 4 1/8 x 7 1/2 In. 190.00
Pliers, Pulling Teeth, Iron 10.00

DEPRESSION GLASS was an inexpensive glass manufactured in large
quantities during the 1920s and early 1930s. It was made in many colors and
patterns by dozens of factories in the United States. The name *Depression
glass* is a modern one. For more descriptions, history, pictures, and prices of
Depression glass, see the book *Kovels' Depression Glass & American
Dinnerware Price List.*

Adam, Ashtray, Green, 4 1/2 In. 15.00
Adam, Cake Plate, Pink, 10 In. 20.00
Adam, Candy Dish, Pink 65.00
Adam, Plate, Green, 9 In. 20.00
Adam, Saucer, Pink 6.50
Adam, Sherbet, Pink, 3 In. 8.00

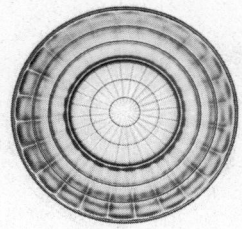

Depression Glass,
American Sweetheart

Depression Glass,
Block Optic

Depression Glass,
Bubble

Adam, Sugar & Creamer, Cover, Pink	50.00
American Pioneer, Lamp, Green, 8 1/2 In.	75.00
American Sweetheart, Berry Bowl, Pink	35.00
American Sweetheart, Bowl, Cereal, Pink	14.00
American Sweetheart, Creamer, Footed, Pink	6.50
American Sweetheart, Plate, Monax, 10 1/4 In.	18.00
American Sweetheart, Plate, Pink, 6 In.	2.50
American Sweetheart, Platter, Oval, Monax, 13 In.	60.00
American Sweetheart, Salver, Pink, 12 In.	8.00
American Sweetheart, Saucer, Pink	2.50
American Sweetheart, Service For 8, Monax, 64 Piece	495.00
American Sweetheart, Soup, Cream, Monax, 4 1/2 In.	85.00
American Sweetheart, Soup, Cream, Pink	90.00
American Sweetheart, Soup, Dish, Monax	73.00
American Sweetheart, Sugar, Cover, Pink	3.00
American Sweetheart, Tidbit, 2 Tiers, Red	220.00
Apple Blossom pattern is listed here as Dogwood	
Aunt Polly, Tumbler, Blue, 3 5/8 In.	20.00
Aurora, Bowl, Cereal, Cobalt Blue, 5 3/8 In.	8.50
Aurora, Bowl, Cobalt Blue, 4 1/2 In.	18.00
Aurora, Cup, Cobalt Blue	7.50
Aurora, Tumbler, Cobalt Blue	17.50
Ballerina pattern is listed here as Cameo	
Banded Rib pattern is listed here as Coronation	
Banded Rings pattern is listed here as Ring	
Basket pattern is listed here as No. 615	
Beaded Block, Bowl, Square, Pink, 5 1/2 In.	4.50
Beaded Block, Plate, Round, Pink, 8 3/4 In.	10.00
Beaded Block, Sugar & Creamer, Green	38.00
Block pattern is listed here as Block Optic	
Block Optic, Berry Bowl, Green, 8 1/2 In.	16.00
Block Optic, Plate, Green, 8 In.	2.50
Block Optic, Saltshaker, Green	12.50
Block Optic, Saucer, Ring, Green, 5 3/4 In.	6.00
Block Optic, Saucer, Ring, Green, 6 1/8 In.	6.00
Block Optic, Sherbet, Green, 3 1/4 In.	3.00
Block Optic, Sugar, Green	10.00
Block Optic, Sugar, Tall, Green	8.50
Block Optic, Vase, Green, 8 1/2 In.	350.00
Bouquet & Lattice pattern is listed here as Normandie	
Bowknot, Sherbet, Low Footed, Green	8.00
Bubble, Plate, Blue, 6 3/4 In.	3.00
Bubble, Plate, Blue, 9 3/8 In.	6.00
Bubble, Plate, Green, 9 3/8 In.	14.00
Bubble, Platter, Oval, Blue, 12 In.	12.00
Bubble, Soup, Dish, Blue, 7 3/4 In.	10.00
Bubble, Sugar & Creamer, Blue	50.00

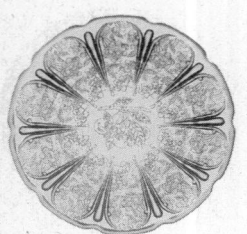

Depression Glass, Cherry Blossom   *Depression Glass, Colonial*   *Depression Glass, Cubist*

Bubble, Tumbler, Red, 16 Oz.	12.00
Bullseye pattern is listed here as Bubble	
Buttons & Bows pattern is listed here as Holiday	
Cabbage Rose pattern is listed here as Sharon	
Cameo, Bowl, Cereal, Green, 5 1/2 In.	18.00
Cameo, Bowl, Oval, Green, 9 In.	18.00
Cameo, Cake Plate, Footed, Green, 10 In.	20.00
Cameo, Candlestick, Green, 4 In., Pair	110.00
Cameo, Console, Footed, Green	57.00
Cameo, Cup, Green	9.00 to 11.00
Cameo, Goblet, Pink, 6 In.	160.00
Cameo, Grill Plate, Yellow, 10 1/2 In.	22.00
Cameo, Pitcher, Juice, Green, 36 Oz.	45.00
Cameo, Pitcher, Water, Green, 56 Oz.	45.00
Cameo, Saltshaker, Green	40.00
Cameo, Sherbet, Stemmed, Green, 4 7/8 In.	15.00
Cameo, Tumbler, Green, 5 In.	12.00 to 15.00
Candlewick pattern is listed in the Imperial Glass category	
Cape Cod, Punch Set, Crystal	250.00
Cape Cod, Sugar & Creamer, Tray, Square	200.00
Cape Cod, Tom & Jerry Set, Crystal	450.00
Caprice pattern is included in the Cambridge Glass category	
Cherry Blossom, Berry Bowl, Pink, 4 3/4 In.	8.00
Cherry Blossom, Berry Bowl, Round, Green, 8 1/2 In.	30.00
Cherry Blossom, Bowl, Pink, 8 1/2 In.	34.00
Cherry Blossom, Bowl, Vegetable, Oval, Pink, 9 In.	25.00
Cherry Blossom, Butter, Cover, Pink	55.00 to 75.00
Cherry Blossom, Cake Plate, Pink, 10 1/4 In.	22.50
Cherry Blossom, Child's Set, Delphite, 14 Piece	240.00
Cherry Blossom, Creamer, Child's, Delphite	30.00

Depression Glass, Doric & Pansy

Depression Glass, Floragold

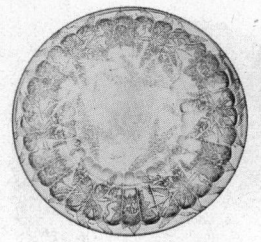 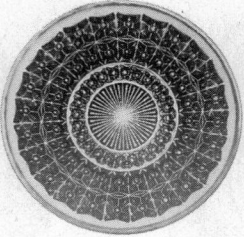 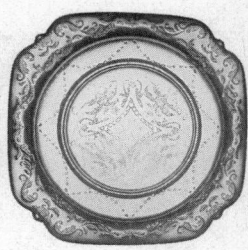

Depression Glass, Floral   *Depression Glass, Holiday*   *Depression Glass, Madrid*

Cherry Blossom, Cup, Green	12.00
Cherry Blossom, Grill Plate, Pink, 10 In.	20.00
Cherry Blossom, Plate, Child's, Delphite	8.00
Cherry Blossom, Plate, Pink, 9 In.	15.00 to 19.00
Cherry Blossom, Platter, Divided, Pink, 13 In.	60.00
Cherry Blossom, Platter, Pink, 13 In.	50.00
Cherry Blossom, Salt & Pepper, Pink	1150.00
Cherry Blossom, Soup, Dish, Pink	68.00
Cherry Blossom, Sugar & Creamer, Cover, Green	28.00
Cherry Blossom, Sugar, Cover, Pink	18.00
Cherry Blossom, Tumbler, Green, 4 1/4 In.	19.00
Cloverleaf, Tumbler, Green, 4 In., 5 Piece	210.00
Cloverleaf, Tumbler, Green, 5 3/4 In.	30.00
Colonial, Butter, Cover, Green	50.00
Colonial, Sugar, Cover	18.00
Colonial Block, Goblet, Claret, Green, 5 1/2 In.	12.00
Colonial Block, Sugar & Creamer, Green, Large	30.00
Colonial Fluted, Berry Bowl, Green, 4 In.	3.00
Columbia, Bowl, 5 In.	12.00
Columbia, Bowl, Salad, 8 1/2 In.	9.00
Columbia, Chop Plate, 11 In.	14.00
Columbia, Cup	4.00
Columbia, Saucer	1.00
Columbia, Soup, Dish, 8 In.	13.00
Coronation, Berry Bowl, Ruby, 7 Piece	45.00
Coronation, Plate, Pink, 8 1/2 In.	5.00
Cremex, Plate, Fired-On Yellow, 12 In.	6.00
Cube pattern is listed here as Cubist	
Cubist, Bowl, Dessert, Pink, 4 1/2 In.	3.00
Cubist, Candy Dish, Cover, Green	24.00
Cubist, Creamer, Pink, 3 In.	2.00 to 3.00
Cubist, Dish, 5 Sections, Handle, 8 x 13 In.	14.00
Cubist, Plate, Pink, 8 In.	3.00
Cubist, Saucer, Pink	2.50
Daisy pattern is listed here as No. 620	
Dancing Girl pattern is listed here as Cameo	
Della Robia, Punch Set, Crystal, 8 Piece	240.00
Diamond Pattern is listed here as Miss America	
Diamond Quilted, Sherbet, Green	4.00
Diana, Creamer, Pink, Oval	6.00
Dogwood, Bowl, Cereal, Pink	40.00
Dogwood, Cup & Saucer, Pink	15.00
Dogwood, Pitcher, 80 Oz.	10.00
Dogwood, Plate, Pink, 8 In.	6.50 to 10.00
Dogwood, Salver, Pink, 12 In.	18.00
Dogwood, Sugar, Flat, Pink	15.00
Dogwood, Tumbler, 5 In.	35.00
Dogwood, Tumbler, Flat, Pink, 4 3/4 In.	40.00

Depression Glass, Mayfair Open Rose

Depression Glass, Miss America

Doric, Candy Dish, Cover, Pink	18.00
Doric & Pansy, Tumbler, Ultramarine	70.00
Dutch Rose pattern is listed here as Rosemary	
English Hobnail, Cup	4.00
English Hobnail, Marmalade, Cover	48.00
English Hobnail, Pitcher, Straight Side, 1/2 Gal.	160.00
English Hobnail, Plate, Square, 9 In.	5.00
Fire-King, Bowl, Measuring, 2 Spouts, Label	24.00
Fire-King, Bowl, Utility, Blue, 10 1/2 In.	14.00
Fire-King, Pie Plate, Blue, 9 In.	8.00
Fire-King, Roaster, Blue, 10 3/4 In.	28.00
Flat Diamond pattern is listed here as Diamond Quilted	
Floragold, Bowl, Ruffled, Iridescent, 5 1/2 In.	5.00
Floragold, Bowl, Ruffled, Iridescent, 9 1/2 In.	4.50
Floragold, Bowl, Salad, Deep, Iridescent, 9 1/2 In.	25.00
Floragold, Bowl, Square, Iridescent, 4 1/2 In.	3.00
Floragold, Butter, Cover, Oblong, Iridescent	7.00
Floragold, Candy Dish, 4 Footed, Iridescent, 5 1/4 In.	3.50
Floragold, Creamer, Iridescent	4.50
Floragold, Pitcher, Ice Lip, Iridescent	18.00
Floragold, Pitcher, Iridescent, 64 Oz.	22.50
Floragold, Plate, Iridescent, 8 1/2 In.	24.50
Floragold, Platter, Iridescent, 11 1/4 In.	13.00
Floragold, Sugar & Creamer, Iridescent	18.00
Floragold, Tray, Indent, Iridescent, 13 1/2 In.	35.00
Floragold, Tumbler, Iridescent, 10 Oz.	15.00
Floragold, Tumbler, Iridescent, 15 Oz.	10.00
Floragold, Water Set, Iridescent, 5 Piece	95.00
Floral, Bowl, Vegetable, Oval, Pink, 9 In.	14.00
Floral, Creamer, Pink	10.00
Floral, Cup & Saucer, Pink	18.00
Floral, Pitcher, Cone Foot, Pink	30.00
Floral, Plate, Pink, 9 In.	30.00
Floral, Platter, Oval, Pink, 10 3/4 In.	20.00 to 22.00
Floral, Shaker, Pink	15.00
Floral, Tumbler, Water, Pink, 4 3/4 In.	13.00
Florentine No. 1, Sherbet, 3 Oz.	7.00
Florentine No. 1, Soup, Cream, Pink, 5 In.	8.00
Florentine No. 1, Sugar, Ruffled, Pink	18.00
Florentine No. 2, Bowl, Vegetable, Cover, Green, 9 In.	42.00
Florentine No. 2, Candy Dish, Cover, Green	100.00
Florentine No. 2, Pitcher, Green, 28 Oz.	25.00

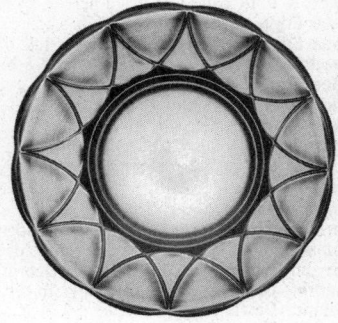

Depression Glass, New Century   *Depression Glass, Newport*

Florentine No. 2, Plate, Green, 10 In. 12.00
Florentine No. 2, Platter, Yellow, 11 1/2 In. 35.00
Florentine No. 2, Salt & Pepper, Green 35.00
Forest Green, Pitcher, 22 Oz. 25.00
Fortune, Bowl, Dessert, Pink, 4 1/2 In. 2.00
Fortune, Bowl, Handle, Pink, 4 1/2 In. 2.00
Fortune, Bowl, Pink, 5 1/4 In. 2.50
Fruits, Saucer, Green 4.00
Georgian, Butter, Cover, Green .... 55.00 to 75.00
Georgian, Sugar & Creamer, Green 30.00
Hairpin pattern is listed here as Newport
Harp, Cake Stand, 9 In. .... 12.00 to 13.00
Heritage, Bowl, Fruit, 10 1/2 In. 8.50
Hex Optic pattern is listed here as Hexagon Optic
Hexagon Optic, Tumbler, Footed, Green, 7 In. 6.00
Hexagon Optic, Whiskey, Green, 2 In. 7.50
Hobnail pattern is listed in the Hobnail category
Holiday, Plate, Pink, 8 1/2 In. 8.50
Holiday, Sugar & Creamer, Pink 28.00
Holiday, Sugar, Cover, Pink 14.00
Honeycomb pattern is listed here as Hexagon Optic
Horizontal Ribbed pattern is listed here as Manhattan
Horseshoe pattern is listed here as No. 612
Iris, Candlestick, Iridescent 12.50
Iris, Cup & Saucer, Iridescent 25.00
Iris, Lampshade, Pink 70.00
Iris, Vase, Iridescent, 9 In. 18.00
Iris, Wine, Iridescent, 4 1/2 In. 15.00
Iris & Herringbone pattern is listed here as Iris
Jamestown pattern is listed here as Tradition
Jane-Ray, Cup & Saucer, Jadite .... 2.50 to 3.00
Jane-Ray, Cup, Jadite 3.00
Jane-Ray, Plate, Jadite, 9 In. 9.00
Jane-Ray, Plate, Jadite, 10 1/2 In. 4.00
Jane-Ray, Sugar & Creamer, Jadite 5.00
Jubilee, Cake Tray, Handles, Yellow, 11 In. .... 38.00 to 45.00
Jubilee, Creamer, Yellow 20.00
Jubilee, Cup & Saucer, After Dinner, Yellow, Set Of 6 .... 75.00
Jubilee, Cup & Saucer, Yellow 20.00
Jubilee, Sugar & Creamer, Yellow 40.00
Jubilee, Sugar, Yellow 20.00
Katy Blue pattern is listed here as Laced Edge

Knife & Fork pattern is listed here as Colonial

Lace Edge, Bowl, Pink, 9 1/2 In. 16.00
Lace Edge, Bowl, Rayed Bottom, Pink, 9 1/2 In. 17.00
Laced Edge, Bowl, Cereal, Blue, 6 3/8 In. 35.00
Laced Edge, Torte Plate, 10 In. 175.00
Laced Edge, Tumbler, Pink, 9 Oz. 12.00
Laurel, Candlestick, Green, 4 In., Pair 30.00
Laurel, Cheese Dish, Cover, Green 40.00
Laurel, Sherbet, Stemmed, Green 7.00

Lorain pattern is listed here as No. 615

Lorain, Cup & Saucer, Crystal 10.00

Lorna pattern is included in the Cambridge Glass category
Louisa pattern is listed here as Floragold
Lovebirds, pattern is listed here as Georgian

Madrid, Bowl, Console, Amber, 11 In. 15.00
Madrid, Bowl, Vegetable, Blue, 10 In. 25.00
Madrid, Butter, Cover, Round, Pink 65.00
Madrid, Candlestick, Amber, 2 1/4 In., Pair 22.00
Madrid, Creamer, Amber .... 5.00 to 8.50
Madrid, Cup & Saucer, Amber 5.00
Madrid, Cup, Amber 3.00
Madrid, Grill Plate, Amber, 10 1/2 In. 22.00
Madrid, Grill Plate, Green, 10 1/2 In. 12.50
Madrid, Plate, Green, 8 7/8 In. 13.00
Madrid, Platter, Amber, 11 1/2 In. 15.00
Madrid, Relish, Pink, 10 1/4 In. 6.00
Madrid, Sugar, Amber 7.50
Manhattan, Berry Bowl, Handles, Pink, 5 3/8 In. 10.00
Manhattan, Cup, Crystal 12.00
Manhattan, Pitcher, Crystal, 24 Oz. 20.00
Manhattan, Plate, Sherbet, Crystal, 6 In. 3.00
Manhattan, Sauce Bowl, Handles, Crystal, 4 1/2 In. 5.00
Manhattan, Sugar, Pink 7.00

Martha Washington pattern is included in the Cambridge Glass category

Mayfair Open Rose, Bowl, Blue, 11 3/4 In. 65.00
Mayfair Open Rose, Bowl, Cereal, Pink, 5 1/2 In. 20.00
Mayfair Open Rose, Bowl, Fruit, Low, Pink 50.00
Mayfair Open Rose, Bowl, Vegetable, Cover, Blue, 10 In. .... 75.00 to 110.00
Mayfair Open Rose, Bowl, Vegetable, Cover, Pink, 10 In. .... 80.00 to 100.00
Mayfair Open Rose, Butter, Cover, Pink 65.00

Depression Glass, No. 612

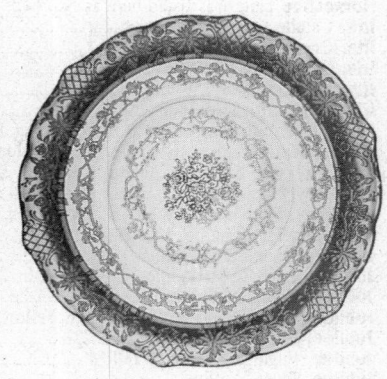

Depression Glass, Normandie

Depression Glass, Petalware

Depression Glass, Princess

Mayfair Open Rose, Candy Dish, Cover, Blue	290.00
Mayfair Open Rose, Celery Dish, 2 Sections, Blue	55.00
Mayfair Open Rose, Cocktail Set, Decanter, Pink, 7 Piece	585.00
Mayfair Open Rose, Cookie Jar, Cover, Blue	290.00
Mayfair Open Rose, Cracker Jar, Blue	265.00
Mayfair Open Rose, Goblet, Wine, Pink, 4 1/2 In.	68.00 to 75.00
Mayfair Open Rose, Plate, Pink, 9 1/2 In.	30.00 to 50.00
Mayfair Open Rose, Relish, 4 Sections, Blue, 8 3/8 In.	60.00
Mayfair Open Rose, Soup, Cream, Pink, 5 In.	38.00
Mayfair Open Rose, Sugar, Blue	75.00
Mayfair Open Rose, Tumbler, Green, 4 1/4 In.	25.00
Mayfair Open Rose, Tumbler, Iced Tea, Footed, Pink, 6 1/2 In.	35.00
Miss America, Berry Bowl, Pink, 6 1/4 In.	15.00
Miss America, Bowl, Deep, Pink, 8 3/4 In.	45.00
Miss America, Cake Plate, Pink, 12 In.	40.00
Miss America, Celery Dish, Oblong, Crystal, 10 1/2 In.	21.00
Miss America, Creamer, Footed, Pink	12.00
Miss America, Cup & Saucer, Pink	32.00
Miss America, Goblet, Wine, Pink, 3 3/4 In.	45.00
Miss America, Grill Plate, Pink, 10 1/4 In.	17.00
Miss America, Plate, Pink, 8 1/2 In.	20.00
Miss America, Platter, Oval, Pink, 12 In.	22.00
Miss America, Relish, 4 Sections, Pink, 8 3/4 In.	20.00
Miss America, Sugar & Creamer, Pink	32.00 to 39.50
Miss America, Tumbler, Green	16.00
Moderntone, Berry Bowl, Cobalt Blue, 8 3/4 In.	55.00
Moderntone, Butter, Cover, Cobalt Blue	105.00
Moderntone, Cup & Saucer, Cobalt Blue	16.00
Moderntone, Cup, Cobalt Blue	9.00
Moderntone, Custard, Cobalt Blue	20.00
Moderntone, Mustard, Cover, Spoon, Cobalt Blue	30.00
Moderntone, Plate, Cobalt Blue, 7 3/4 In.	7.00 to 9.00
Moderntone, Plate, Cobalt Blue, 8 7/8 In.	12.50
Moderntone, Plate, Sherbet, Amethyst	7.00
Moderntone, Salt & Pepper, Cobalt Blue, 2 Sets	46.00
Moderntone, Saltshaker, Cobalt Blue	12.00
Moderntone, Soup, Cream, Amethyst	12.00
Moderntone, Soup, Cream, Cobalt Blue, 4 3/4 In.	20.00 to 22.00
Moderntone, Sugar, Cobalt Blue	6.00
Moondrops, Compote Set, Ruffled, Amber, 3 Piece	80.00
Moondrops, Cup & Saucer, Red	13.00

Depression Glass, Royal Lace

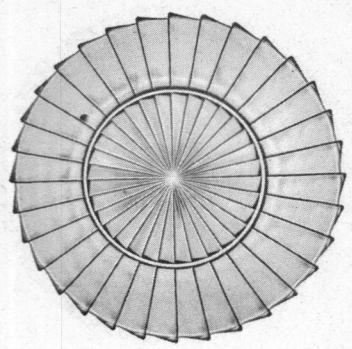

Depression Glass, Sierra

Moondrops, Goblet, Water, Red, 6 1/4 In.	28.00
Moondrops, Sherbet, Red, 4 1/2 In.	20.00
Moonstone, Berry Bowl, Crystal, 5 1/2 In.	12.00
Moonstone, Box, Cigarette Jar, Cover, Crystal	17.00
Moonstone, Cup & Saucer, Crystal	17.00
Moonstone, Goblet, Crystal	18.00
Moonstone, Relish, 3 Sections, Crystal	7.50
Mt. Vernon pattern is included in the Cambridge Glass category	
New Century, Tumbler, Amethyst, 3 1/2 In.	12.00
Newport, Berry Set, Amethyst, 7 Piece	55.00
No. 612, Bowl, Cereal, Yellow, 6 1/2 In.	22.00
No. 612, Creamer, Yellow	15.00
No. 612, Cup & Saucer, Yellow	16.00
No. 612, Pitcher, Yellow, 64 Oz.	295.00
No. 612, Plate, Green, 9 1/2 In.	7.00
No. 612, Tumbler, Yellow, Footed, 4 1/2 In.	18.00
No. 615, Relish, 4 Sections, Yellow, 8 In.	30.00
No. 615, Sugar & Creamer, Yellow	35.00
No. 618, Plate, Crystal, 9 3/8 In.	12.00
No. 618, Relish, 3 Sections, Crystal	16.00
No. 620, Creamer, Footed, Amber	6.50
No. 620, Cup, Amber	5.00
No. 620, Grill Plate, 10 3/8 In.	3.00
No. 620, Plate, Amber, 9 1/2 In.	7.00
No. 620, Saucer, Amber	1.50
No. 620, Soup, Cream, Handles, Amber	7.50
No. 620, Sugar, Cover, Footed, Amber	6.50
No. 622 pattern is listed here as Pretzel	
Normandie, Sugar & Creamer, Amber	15.00
Old Cafe, Bowl, Handles, Pink, 5 In.	5.00
Old Cafe, Bowl, Handles, Pink, 9 In.	6.00
Old Cafe, Candy Dish, Low, Pink, 8 In.	7.00
Old Cafe, Olive Dish, Oblong, Pink, 6 In.	3.00
Old Cafe, Pitcher, Pink, 80 Oz.	50.00 to 68.50
Old Colony pattern is listed here as Lace Edge	
Old Florentine pattern is listed here as Florentine No. 1	
Open Lace pattern is listed here as Lace Edge	
Open Rose pattern is listed here as Mayfair Open Rose	
Oyster & Pearl, Bowl, Pink, 10 1/2 In.	15.00
Oyster & Pearl, Candleholder, Fired-On Pink, 3 1/2 In., Pair	9.00

Oyster & Pearl, Candleholder, Ruby, 3 1/2 In., Pair 35.00
Parrot pattern is listed here as Sylvan
Patrician, Dish, Jam, Amber 17.00
Patrician, Grill Plate, 10 In. 10.00
Petal Swirl pattern is listed here as Swirl
Petalware, Plate, Monax, 11 In. 7.00
Petalware, Platter, Pink, 13 In. 12.00
Petalware, Sugar, Pink 4.00
Pineapple & Floral pattern is listed here as No. 618
Pinwheel pattern is listed here as Sierra
Poinsettia pattern is listed here as Floral
Poppy No. 1 pattern is listed here as Florentine No. 1
Poppy No. 2 pattern is listed here as Florentine No. 2
Pretty Polly Party Dishes, see also the related pattern Doric & Pansy
Pretty Polly Party Dishes, Cup & Saucer, Pink 20.00
Pretzel, Bowl, 7 1/2 In. 10.00
Princess, Bowl, Hat Shape, Green, 9 1/2 In. 30.00
Princess, Cup, Pink 5.00
Princess, Grill Plate, Handles, Pink, 11 1/2 In. 8.00
Princess, Plate, Green, 9 In. 20.00
Princess, Saltshaker, Green 15.00
Prismatic Line pattern is listed here as Queen Mary
Provincial pattern is listed here as Bubble
Queen Mary, Bowl, Cereal, Pink, 6 In. 15.00
Queen Mary, Candy Dish, Cover, Crystal 12.00
Queen Mary, Creamer, Pink 3.50
Queen Mary, Cup & Saucer, Pink 9.00
Radiance, Sugar & Creamer, Amber 30.00
Ribbon, Sugar, 2 Loop Handles, Green 5.00
Ring, Goblet, Crystal, Silver Rings, 7 1/4 In. 7.00
Rope pattern is listed here as Colonial Fluted
Rose Cameo, Bowl, Cereal, Green, 5 In. 7.00
Rose Cameo, Tumbler, Green, 5 In. 11.00
Rosemary, Sugar & Creamer, Amber 17.00
Royal Lace, Berry Bowl, Green, 5 In. 22.00
Royal Lace, Bowl, Vegetable, Oval, Pink, 11 In. 48.00
Royal Lace, Cookie Jar, Cover, Pink 45.00
Royal Lace, Creamer 7.00
Royal Lace, Creamer, Footed, Cobalt Blue 32.00
Royal Lace, Cup & Saucer, Cobalt Blue 45.00
Royal Lace, Pitcher, Cobalt Blue, 68 Oz. 225.00
Royal Lace, Pitcher, Cobalt Blue, Straight Sides, 48 Oz. .... 145.00 to 150.00
Royal Lace, Sherbet, Cobalt Blue, Metal Holder .... 28.00 to 30.00
Royal Lace, Sherbet, Footed 8.00
Royal Lace, Soup, Cream, Cobalt Blue .... 38.00 to 40.00
Royal Lace, Sugar & Creamer, Cobalt Blue 64.00
Royal Lace, Sugar, Cover, Cobalt Blue .... 16.00 to 25.00
Royal Lace, Tumbler, Cobalt Blue, 4 1/8 In. .... 35.00 to 48.50
Royal Ruby, Creamer, Footed, Red 7.00
Royal Ruby, Pitcher, Red, 42 Oz. 35.00
Royal Ruby, Plate, Red, 6 1/2 In. 2.00
Royal Ruby, Sugar & Creamer, Red 10.00
Royal Ruby, Tumbler, 9 1/8 In. 6.00
Royal Ruby, Tumbler, Red, 4 7/8 In. 4.00
Sail Boat pattern is listed here as Sportsman Series
Sandwich, Sugar & Creamer, Tray 10.00
Sandwich Anchor Hocking, Bowl, Oval, 8 1/4 In. 4.00
Sandwich Anchor Hocking, Cup 1.50
Sandwich Anchor Hocking, Saucer 1.00
Sandwich Anchor Hocking, Tumbler, 3 9/16 In. 3.50
Saxon pattern is listed here as Coronation
Sharon, Bowl, Amber, 8 1/2 In. 6.00
Sharon, Bowl, Green, 8 1/2 In. 18.00

Sharon, Bowl, Vegetable, Oval, Pink, 9 1/2 In. 30.00
Sharon, Candy Dish, Cover, Footed, Pink, 8 In. .... 32.00 to 40.00
Sharon, Cheese Dish, Amber 180.00
Sharon, Pitcher, Pink, Ice Lip, 80 Oz. .... 95.00 to 155.00
Sharon, Plate, Amber, 9 1/2 In. .... 8.00 to 10.00
Sharon, Platter, Amber, 12 1/2 In. 18.00
Sharon, Salt & Pepper, Pink 34.00
Sharon, Sherbet, Footed, Amber 7.00
Sharon, Sherbet, Footed 15.00
Sharon, Soup, Cream, Green 32.00
Sharon, Tumbler, Amber, 4 1/8 In. 17.00
Sierra, Bowl, Pink, 5 1/2 In. 7.50
Sierra, Bowl, Pink, 8 1/2 In. 20.00
Sierra, Creamer, Pink 10.00
Sierra, Plate, Pink, 9 In. 10.00
Spiral, Plate, Sherbet, Green, 6 In. 1.00
Spiral, Sherbet, Green 2.00
Spoke pattern is listed here as Patrician
Sportsman Series, Tumbler, Cobalt Blue, 9 Oz. 8.00
Sportsman Series, Tumbler, Iced Tea, Cobalt Blue, 10 Oz. 8.00
Sunflower, Cake Plate, 3-Footed, Green, 10 In. .... 8.00 to 15.00
Swirl, Candy Dish, Footed, Ultramarine 10.00
Swirl, Cup, Ultramarine 8.00
Swirl, Plate, Ultramarine, 7 1/4 In. 7.00
Swirl, Sherbet, Footed, Low, Ultramarine 10.00
Swirl, Sugar, Footed, Ultramarine 8.00
Swirl, Vase, Footed, Ultramarine, 8 1/2 In. 17.00
Sylvan, Creamer, Green 5.00
Sylvan, Grill Plate, Green, 10 1/2 In. 33.00
Sylvan, Plate, Green, 7 1/2 In. 35.00
Sylvan, Platter, Green, 11 1/4 In. 50.00
Sylvan, Sherbet, Footed, Cone, Amber 16.00
Tea Room, Sugar & Creamer, Rectangular, Pink 30.00
Tea Room, Vase, Pink, 9 In. 80.00
Tradition, Goblet, Water, Blue, 5 1/4 In. .... 10.00 to 12.00
Tradition, Goblet, Wine, Blue, 4 7/8 In. 13.00
Tradition, Plate, Amethyst, 8 In. 8.50
Tradition, Sherbet, Blue, 3 3/8 In. 10.00
Twisted Optic, Plate, Green, 8 In. 1.50
Twisted Optic, Plate, Sherbet, Green, 6 In. 1.00
Twisted Optic, Sherbet, Green 3.50
Vertical Ribbed pattern is listed here as Queen Mary
Vesper, Candlestick, Amber, 2 In. 25.00
Waffle pattern is listed here as Waterford
Waterford, Berry Bowl, 8 1/4 In. 5.00
Waterford, Butter, Cover .... 18.00 to 20.00
Waterford, Cup 3.50
Waterford, Goblet, 5 1/4 In. .... 8.00 to 15.00
Waterford, Plate, 7 1/8 In. 2.00
Waterford, Plate, 9 5/8 In. 5.00
Waterford, Plate, Sandwich, 13 3/4 In. 6.00
White Ship pattern is listed here as Sportsman Series
Wild Rose pattern is listed here as Dogwood
Windsor, Bowl, Handles, 8 In. 4.00
Windsor, Bowl, Oval, Pink, 9 1/2 In. 9.00
Windsor, Compote, Cover, 6 1/2 In. 18.00
Windsor, Creamer, Pink 9.00
Windsor, Plate, Sandwich, Handles, Pink, 10 1/4 In. 13.50
Windsor, Relish, Divided, 11 1/2 In. 6.00
Windsor, Sugar & Creamer, Green 27.00
Windsor, Tumbler, 3 1/4 In. 4.00
Windsor, Tumbler, Pink, 5 In. 16.00
Windsor Diamond pattern is listed here as Windsor

DERBY has been marked on porcelain made in the city of Derby, England, since about 1748. The original Derby factory closed in 1848, but others opened there and continued to produce quality porcelain. The Crown Derby mark began appearing on Derby wares in the 1770s.

Coffeepot, Cover, Birds, Peacock, Insects On Cover, c.1760, 8 1/2 In.	1150.00
Cup, Satyr, Molded Bacchant Masks, Grape Laurel, 4 In., Pair	343.00
Cup & Saucer, Imari	165.00
Dish, Oval, Floral Sprays, Pink Grapes, Rococo Scrolls, c.1760, 10 3/4 In.	800.00
Figurine, Actor, Bearded, Long Cloak, Hands Behind Back, 1780s, 8 1/2 In.	465.00
Figurine, Bullfinch, Salmon, Black, Blue, On Flower Cluster, c.1820, 2 1/2 In.	690.00
Figurine, Canary, Yellow Plumage, Tan Beak, Tree Stump Base, c.1820, 2 1/2 In.	690.00
Figurine, Goldfinch, Tan, Brown, Yellow Spotted Wings & Tail, c.1800, 2 1/2 In.	690.00
Figurine, Harlequin, Pink Hat, White Plume, Black Mask, c.1770, 6 In.	2300.00
Figurine, Sheep, Sitting, White Fleecy Ewe, Gray-Horned Ram, c.1775, 4 In., Pair	1380.00
Figurine, Spring, Winter, Mythological Child, Model 64, c.1775, 5 1/2 In., Pair	690.00
Garniture, Shield Shape, Japan Pattern, Cobalt Blue Panel, c.1820, 3 Piece	2590.00
Plate, Botanical, Moss Roses, Gilt Edge, Cobalt Blue Rim, c.1810, 9 1/4 In.	1150.00
Plate, Imari, 8 In.	175.00
Platter, Oval, Center Floral Motif, Imari Colors, Gilt, c.1820, 10 1/2 In., Pair	880.00
Stirrup Cup, Hound's Head, Brown & Black Coat, Stevenson & Hancock, 5 1/2 In.	1380.00
Urn, Garden Flowers, Cobalt, Gilt Scrollwork, Early 19th Century, 6 3/4 In., Pair	240.00
Vase, Floral Reserves, Cobalt Blue Ground, Campana Form, 1880s, Pair	715.00

DICK TRACY, the comic strip, started in 1931. Tracy was also the hero of movies from 1937 to 1947 and again in 1990, and starred in a radio series in the 1940s and a television series in the 1950s. Memorabilia from all these activities is collected.

Badge, 2nd Year Membership, Wheaties Premium, 1939	45.00 to 50.00
Badge, Crime Stopper, ID Card, Unused	18.50
Book, Ace Detective, 1943	15.00
Book, Big Little Book, Dick Tracy, Larceny Lu	35.00
Book, Code, 1939	95.00
Book, Comic, Puffed Wheat Premium, 1938	15.00
Book, Dick Tracy Meets The Night Crawler, Chester Gould, Whitman, 1945	30.00
Box, Aurora, 1968, Sealed	225.00
Car, Marx, 11 In.	155.00 to 175.00
Car, Marx, Box	475.00
Car, Police, Battery Operated, Marx, 11 In.	210.00
Car, Police, Windup, Tin, Battery Operated	235.00
Car, Squad, Green, Marx, 1950	125.00 to 190.00
Car, Squad, Windup & Battery Operated, Marx, Tin, Box	265.00
Car, Tin, Battery & Friction	275.00
Card, Valentine, Moveable, 5 3/4 In.	55.00
Card Game, 1938	75.00
Dart Board, 1930s	110.00
Doll, Sparkle Plenty	150.00
Figurine, Resin, Applause, 7 In.	40.00
Figurine, The Tramp, Card	10.00
Flashlight, Pocket, Bullet Shape, Chrome Bands, 1939	125.00
Flashlight, Secret Service	60.00
Game, Crime Stopper, 1963	40.00
Getaway Car, Playmate, Box	40.00
Handcuffs, 1930s	50.00
Handcuffs, Junior, John-Henry Products, On 3 1/2 x 9-In. Card, 1940s	20.00
Hat, 1950s	85.00
Kit, Crime Stoppers, 1961	65.00 to 75.00
Knife, Pocket, Profile On Celluloid Handle, c.1930	200.00
Lobby Card, Neuvas Aventuras De Dick Tracy, 12 x 15 In.	45.00
Lunch Box, Canada, 1967	95.00
Pinback, Secret Service Patrol Member, 1939	40.00
Pistol, Siren	77.00
Puppet, Hand, 1961	35.00 to 75.00

Puzzle, Bonnie Braids 30.00
Puzzle, Dick Tracy Reviewing Police Line-Up, Jaymar, 1961 .... 22.00
Puzzle, Pictures Different Things, Golden, Box, 200 Piece 4.00
Radio Set, Wrist Straps, Wire Joined, Battery, Remco, 1950s, 13 x 9 x 3 In. .. 80.00 to 100.00
Ring, Hat 185.00
Ring, Secret Compartment, Radio Premium 550.00
Salt & Pepper, Tracy & Junior, 3-D, Ceramic, Late 1930s, 2 x 2 1/2 In. .... 50.00 to 65.00
Toy, Target, Metal Gun, 2 Darts, Tin, 1941, Marx 175.00
Wrapper, Candy 15.00

DINNERWARE, see American dinnerware

DIONNE QUINTUPLETS were born in Canada on May 28, 1934. The publicity about their birth and their special status as wards of the Canadian government made them famous throughout the world. Visitors could watch the girls play; reporters interviewed the girls and the staff. Thousands of special dolls and souvenirs were made picturing the quints at different ages. Emilie died in 1954, Marie in 1970. Yvonne, Annette, and Cecile still live in Canada.

Bowl Set, Cereal, 5 Piece 200.00
Calendar, 1939, Commercial Bank, Chilton, Wis., Elvgren, 11 1/2 x 16 In. 23.00
Calendar, 1940 .... 45.00
Calendar, 1940, D.W. Coulter, 15 x 12 In. 35.00
Calendar, 1948 .... 20.00
Doll, Baby, Diaper, Gerling Creation, 1935, 7 In., 5 Piece 795.00
Doll, Emilie, Composition, Toddler Body, Alexander, 1935, 17 In. 575.00
Magazine, Life, May 17, 1937 .... 50.00
Mirror, Pocket 15.00
Photograph, Quintuplets & Dr. DeFoe, Signed Allan Roy DeFoe, 1938 .... 395.00
Pinback, Calendar 25.00
Radio 595.00
Spoon, Figural, Silver, With Framed Print, 7 Piece 160.00
Spoon, Marie & Annette, Pair 35.00
Spoon Rack, 5 Silver Spoons, Print In Frame 145.00
Spoon Rack, Figural, Set Of 5 .... 100.00 to 135.00

DISNEYANA is a collector's term. Walt Disney and his company introduced many comic characters to the world. Collectors search for examples of the work of the Disney Studios and the many commercial products modeled after his characters, including Mickey Mouse, Donald Duck, and recent films, like *Beauty and the Beast* and *The Little Mermaid*.

Applique, Cloth, Lady & The Tramp, Uncut, McCall, 1959, 8 x 10 In. 20.00
Baby Rattle, Snow White & Seven Dwarfs, Celluloid, 1938, 6 1/2 In. 150.00
Badge, Mickey Mouse Club Member, Cloisonne 4.00
Badge, Mickey Mouse, Audience Gift, 1950s 18.00
Bank, Donald Duck Head, Ceramic, Enesco, 1960s, 5 1/2 In. 85.00
Bank, Donald Duck, 1950s, 10 In. 30.00
Bank, Donald Duck, Head, Figural, Vinyl 40.00
Bank, Mechanical, Mickey Mouse, Cast Aluminum 950.00
Bank, Mickey Mouse, Nabisco Wheat Puffs, 1966 .... 20.00
Bank, Mickey Mouse, Smoked Glass, Mickey Mouse Club, 6 3/4 In. 30.00
Belt, Mickey Mouse Bronze Buckle, Mickey Mouse 60th Anniversary, Elastic 16.50
Blocks, Wood, 1930s, Wood Box, 6 Piece 300.00
Book, Babes In Toyland, Big Golden Book, 1961 .... 9.00
Book, Donald Duck And His Cat Troubles, Whitman, 1948 .... 35.00
Book, Donald Duck, Big Little Book, 1926 .... 36.00
Book, Funny Stories About Mickey And Donald, 1938 .... 45.00
Book, Johnny Appleseed, Little Golden Book, 1949 .... 6.00
Book, Mickey Mouse & Donald Duck, Pie-Eyed, 1937, 10 1/2 x 15 In. 150.00
Book, Mickey Mouse And The Lectro Box, Big Little Book, c.1946 .... 49.00
Book, Mickey Mouse Has A Busy Day, No. 1077, Whitman, 1937 .... 90.00
Book, Mickey Mouse Mother Goose, Pie-Eyed, 1930s, 140 Pages 185.00
Book, Mickey Mouse Runs His Own Newspaper, Big Little Book, Whitman, 1937 .... 60.00

Disneyana, Doll, Mickey Mouse, 2 Gun,
Stuffed, Knickerbocker, 12 In.

◆◆◆◆◆◆◆◆◆◆◆◆◆◆◆◆◆◆◆◆◆◆◆

Date Mickey Mouse from his appearance. He has changed in the 60 years since his introduction in "Steamboat Willie." Originally, he didn't have pupils in his eyes. His legs were like pipe cleaners, now they have shape. He had a neck and white inside his ears in his middle years, but none when young or old. His nose has gotten shorter and more tilted.

◆◆◆◆◆◆◆◆◆◆◆◆◆◆◆◆◆◆◆◆◆◆◆

Book, Mickey Mouse Sails For Treasure Island, Big Little Book, 1935	85.00
Book, Mickey Mouse, Pop-Up	295.00
Book, Minnie Mouse, Pop-Up, Blue Ribbon Books, 1933	145.00
Book, Snow White & Seven Dwarfs, Line Type, Movie Version, 1938, 9 1/2 x 13 In.	125.00
Book, Snow White & Seven Dwarfs, Punch-Out Masks, Whitman, 1938	275.00
Book, Snow White, Pop-Up, 1961	30.00
Book, Walt Disney Magic Moments, 50th Anniversary, 191 Pages, 1973	80.00
Book, Walt Disney's Golden Touch Book, Hardcover, 1937	125.00
Book, Walt Disney's Guide To Disneyland, 28 Pages, 1953, 8 x 11 1/2 In.	25.00
Bookmark, Winnie The Pooh, Charpentere, 14 In., Pair	92.50
Bottle, Donald Duck Soda, 6 Pack	150.00
Bottle, Mickey Mouse, NSDA Convention, 1977	25.00
Bottle, Mickey Mouse, Soaky	28.00
Bottle Cap, Clarabell Cow, 1930s	50.00
Bottle Cap, Mickey Mouse, 1930s, Unused	45.00 to 50.00
Bottle Cap, Pluto, 1930s, Unused	45.00
Bowl, Cereal, Donald Duck, Yellow, Beetleware, Alphabet Rim, 1930s	50.00
Bowl, Cereal, Mickey Mouse, Post Cereal, Beetleware, Yellow	20.00 to 30.00
Bowl, Three Little Pigs, Divided, Blue Trim, Patriot China, 1930s, 7 3/4 In.	100.00
Box, Paint, Mickey Mouse, Donald Duck, Nephews, Tin Lithograph, Transogram	40.00
Box, Pencil, Mickey Mouse, Composition, 1930s	265.00 to 350.00
Box, Soap, Mickey Mouse My Pal Pluto, Empty, 1930s	35.00
Brush, Clothes, Mickey Mouse, Wooden	19.00
Bus, Mickey Mouse, Walt Disney Stars, Paper Lithograph On Wood, 19 In.	375.00
Camera, Donald Duck, 1950	85.00
Camera, Donald Duck, Raised Figures, Donald & 3 Nephews, 1946	85.00
Can, Watering, Donald Duck, Ohio Art, 3 In.	125.00
Car, Crazy, Mickey Mouse, Battery Operated, Marx, Box	225.00
Card, Mickey Mouse, Bell Bread Premium, c.1930	35.00
Card, Valentine, Mechanical, Dopey, 1938, 3 x 4 1/2 In.	60.00
Card, Valentine, Pinocchio, Heart Shape, Mechanical, 1939	22.00
Case, Model, Cinderella, Round, 1950s	45.00
Cel, see Animation Art category	
Chair, Club, Snow White & Dwarfs, White Leather, Lithograph, 1938	650.00
Charm Bracelet, Snow White & Seven Dwarfs	50.00
Christmas Lights, Mickey Mouse, Noma, 1930s, Box	250.00
Circus Train, Mickey Mouse, Wells-Brimtoy, Box	2095.00
Clock, Alarm, Cinderella, Travel, Bradley, Germany, Box	90.00
Clock, Alarm, Goofy & Mickey Mouse	135.00
Clock, Alarm, Mickey Mouse & Donald Duck, Phinny-Walker	75.00

Clock, Alarm, Mickey Mouse, Bradley, 1980s 50.00
Clock, Alarm, Minnie Mouse, Travel, Bradley, Box 90.00
Clock, Castle, Animated 295.00
Clock, Donald Duck, Glen 395.00
Clock, Mickey Mouse, Feet Move, Bradley 95.00
Clock, Mickey Mouse, Wagging Head 175.00
Clock, Pluto, Animated, Plastic, 1950s 475.00
Clock, Tramp, Eyes Move, Wall, 1960s 95.00
Clock Radio, Mickey Mouse On Dial, 1950s 175.00
Clock Radio, Tinker Bell, Lithograph Characters, Pointer, GE, 1950s, 11 x 6 In. 95.00
Coloring Set, Pencil, Numbered Coloring Sheets, Walt Disney, 1950s, Box 55.00
Cookie Cutters, 4 Characters, Loma Plastics Inc., 1940s, Set Of 4 .... 45.00
Cookie Jar, Alice In Wonderland, Signed 195.00
Cookie Jar, Donald Duck, Walt Disney USA 350.00
Cookie Jar, Dumbo, Mouse Finial, Walt Disney 90.00
Cookie Jar, Ludwig Von Drake, American Bisque 895.00
Cookie Jar, Ludwig Von Drake, Felt Tongue, American Bisque 1450.00
Cookie Jar, Mickey & Minnie Mouse 190.00
Cookie Jar, Mickey Mouse & Pluto 165.00
Cookie Jar, Mickey Mouse, Minny Mouse, Turnabout, Leeds China, 13 1/2 In. 31.00
Cookie Jar, Pinocchio, Metlox .... 300.00 to 600.00
Cookie Jar, Snow White 975.00
Costume, Official Mouseketeers Play Outfit, Cooper 165.00
Creamer, Minnie Mouse, Pearlized, Cobalt Handles 125.00
Dish, Child's, Feeding, Donald Duck, Divided, Head Removes To Fill Water, 1940s .. 85.00
Doll, Donald Duck, Cowboy, Composition, Knickerbocker, 1930s, 8 3/4 In. 660.00
Doll, Donald Duck, Dakin, 8 In. 20.00
Doll, Grumpy, Snow White & Seven Dwarfs, Cloth, Japan, 7 In. 9.00
Doll, Mary Poppins, Yarnlike Hair, Accessories, Gund Mfg., 1964, 11 1/2 In. 40.00
Doll, Mickey Mouse, 2 Gun, Stuffed, Knickerbocker, 12 In. .... *Illus* 3500.00
Doll, Mickey Mouse, Cloth, Early 1930s, 20 In. 175.00
Doll, Mickey Mouse, Felt, Velvet, 1930s, 17 In. 875.00
Doll, Mickey Mouse, Musical, Velveteen, Knickerbocker 30.00
Doll, Mickey Mouse, Velvet, 1930s, 4 In. 150.00
Doll, Mickey Sorcerer's Apprentice, Bisque, 50th Anniversary 85.00
Doll, Minnie Mouse, Deans, 6 In. 575.00
Doll, Minnie Mouse, Wooden Face, Plush Body, Certificate, Applause, 16 In. 45.00
Doll, Peter Pan, Sun Rubber 20.00
Doll, Pinocchio, Cloth, Mask Face, Sutton Co., 36 In. 250.00
Doll, Pollyanna, Vinyl, Sleep Eyes, Checked Dress, Uneeda Mark, 31 In. 100.00
Doll, Seven Dwarfs, Stuffed, Velvet Costumes, Painted Faces, 1938, 11 In., Set 3250.00
Doll, Snow White & Seven Dwarfs, Wrist Tags, 21 & 11 1/2 In., 8 Piece 3000.00
Doll, Snow White, Composition, Original Outfit, Knickerbocker, 1938, 12 In. 275.00
Drum, Mickey Mouse, Ohio Art, 1930s, 6 1/2 In. .... 150.00 to 275.00
Fan, Silly Symphonies Characters Picnicking, 1930s 175.00
Fan, Snow White & Seven Dwarfs, Expandable, Illustrations 125.00
Figurine, Bashful, Rubber, Seiberling, Needs Paint, 5 3/4 In., Pair 110.00
Figurine, Cinderella, American Pottery 325.00
Figurine, Donald Duck, Admiral, Purple Uniform, Bisque, 1930s, 3 In. 175.00
Figurine, Donald Duck, Chalkware, 13 1/2 In. 250.00
Figurine, Donald Duck, Composition, Knickerbocker Toy Co., 1930s, 9 In. 1500.00
Figurine, Donald Duck, Sailor Suit, Yellow Scooter, Bisque, 1930s, 3 1/4 In. 175.00
Figurine, Dopey, Bisque, 1930s, 2 In. 35.00
Figurine, Ferdinand The Bull, Bisque, 1930s, 3 In. 43.00
Figurine, Happy, Brayton Sticker, 1938 .... 165.00
Figurine, Jiminy Cricket, Composition, W. Disney Pro KNT, 10 In. 595.00
Figurine, Mickey & Minnie, Day-Glo, Marx, 6 In., Pair 20.00
Figurine, Mickey & Minnie, Hands On Hips, Bisque, 1930s, 2 1/2 In., Pair 75.00
Figurine, Mickey Mouse, Boxing Gloves, Pointed Ears, Nose, Composition, 10 In. 395.00
Figurine, Mickey Mouse, Chalkware 45.00
Figurine, Mickey Mouse, Cloth Yellow Shirt, Red Shorts, Dakin, 1970s, 8 In. 12.00
Figurine, Mickey Mouse, Composition, Mexican Outfit, Sombrero, 9 In. 1495.00
Figurine, Mickey Mouse, Fun-E-Flex, Wood Jointed Body, 1930s, 9 In. 1035.00

Figurine, Mickey Mouse, Holding Drum, Bisque, Japan 180.00
Figurine, Mickey Mouse, Pie-Eyed, Label, Enesco, 1960s, 5 In. 75.00
Figurine, Mickey Mouse, Plastic Flexible, Cloth Outfit, Marx, 1960s, 4 x 5 In. 28.00
Figurine, Mickey Mouse, Riding On Pluto, Painted, Bisque, 1940s, 3 In. 150.00
Figurine, Mickey Mouse, Saxophone Player, Pie-Eyed, Bisque, 1928, 3 1/2 In. 525.00
Figurine, Minnie Mouse, Bisque, 3 1/2 In. 55.00
Figurine, Minnie Mouse, Lead, Germany, 2 1/2 In. 250.00
Figurine, Peter Pan & Captain Hook, Plastic, Pair 75.00
Figurine, Pinocchio, Bisque, 1930s, 5 In. 225.00
Figurine, Sleepy, Bisque, 1930s, 3 In. 25.00
Figurine, Sleepy, Brayton, 1938 .... 125.00
Figurine, Snow White & Seven Dwarfs, Chalkware, 1941, 8 Piece 425.00
Figurine, Snow White, Bisque, 1930s, 3 1/2 In. 55.00
Figurine, Thumper, American Pottery, 1940s, 4 In. 60.00
Flashlight, Mickey Mouse, Tin Lithograph 395.00
Fork, Mickey Mouse, Sterling Silver 40.00
Fork & Spoon, Mickey Mouse, Bonny 50.00
Game, Adventureland, Walt Disney, 1956 .... 20.00
Game, Disneyland Express, Card, c.1950, 7 Piece 125.00
Game, Donald Ducks Party Game For Young Folks, Parker Bros., 1938 .... 65.00
Game, Frontierland, Official, Complete, Parker Bros., c.1955 .... 130.00
Game, Mickey Mouse Funny Rummy, Card, Russel, c.1952 .... 18.00
Game, Peter Pan, Game Of Adventure, Transogram, 1952 .... 30.00
Game, Pin The Nose On Pinocchio, Parker Bros., 1939 .... 40.00
Game, Pin The Tail On Mickey, 1930s, Box 185.00
Game, Robin Hood, Display Box, Parker Bros., 1973 .... 25.00
Game, Silly Symphony Mickey Snap, Card, England, 1930s 110.00
Game, Sleeping Beauty, Parker Brothers, 1959 .... 50.00
Game, Sleeping Beauty, Parker Brothers, 1958, Box 35.00
Game, Snow White & Seven Dwarfs, Cadaco, 1977 .... 25.00
Game, Snow White, Cadaco, 1977 .... 10.00
Game, Swamp Fox, Board 65.00
Game, Three Little Pigs, Board, 1933 .... 45.00
Game, Tomorrowland Rocket To The Moon, Box, 1956 .... 75.00
Glass, Ferdinand The Bull, 1938 .... 39.00
Glass, Mickey Mouse, Bosco, 1930s, 3 1/4 In. 18.00
Holder, Pencil, Doc 65.00
Holder, Toothbrush, Dumbo, Bisque, Painted, 1940s .... 425.00 to 500.00
Holder, Toothbrush, Happy 65.00
Holder, Toothbrush, Mickey & Minnie Mouse, Bisque 250.00
Holder, Toothbrush, Mickey & Minnie Mouse, Bisque, 1930s, 4 1/2 In. 200.00
Holder, Toothbrush, Mickey & Pluto, Bisque 400.00
Holder, Toothbrush, Minnie & Mickey Mouse, Bisque, Moveable Arms, 1930s 900.00
Holder, Toothbrush, Three Little Pigs, Bisque, Japan, 4 In. 698.00
Holder, Toothbrush, Three Little Pigs, With Instruments, Bisque, Painted, 1930s 100.00
Kaleidoscope, Mickey Mouse .... 135.00 to 250.00
Lamp, Dopey, Figural Base, Plaster, 1938 .... 365.00
Lamp Base, Mickey Mouse, Tin, Soreng Mane Gold, 1930s 300.00
Lawn Sprinkler, Mickey Mouse, Arco 55.00
Lunch Box, Disney On Parade, Plastic, Thermos, Glass, 1970 .... 20.00
Lunch Box, Disney School Bus, Thermos, Steel, Glass, 1960s 22.00
Lunch Box, Disney World, With Thermos 15.00
Lunch Box, Disneyland Castle, 1957 .... 155.00
Lunch Box, Disneyland, 1960 .... 920.00
Lunch Box, Mickey Mouse & Donald Duck, Thermos, 1954 .... 403.00
Lunch Box, Snow White & Seven Dwarfs, Tin Lithograph, Double Handle, Belgium ... 395.00
Lunch Box, Snow White, Thermos, 1975 .... 35.00
Lunch Box, Walt Disney World 20.00
Lunch Box, Winnie The Pooh, Thermos, 1967 .... 322.00
Lunch Kit, Mickey Mouse, Geuder, Paeschke & Frey 3025.00
Lunch Pail, Pinocchio, 1940s 125.00
Magic Slate, Mickey Mouse, Box 125.00
Marionette, Geppetto, England, Box 125.00

Marionette, Jiminy Cricket, Gund, 1950s 75.00
Marionette, Pinocchio, England, Box 135.00
Mask, Mickey Mouse, Delta Airlines 12.50
Mask Set, Pinocchio, Geppetto & Figaro, Gillette Blue Blades, 1939, 3 Piece 60.00
Mirror, Mickey Mouse, Celluloid, Black & Red, Ivory Ground .... 3.00 to 15.00
Movie Film, Mickey's Canary, 16 mm, Box, 1930s, Disney 60.00
Mug, Donald Duck & Ludwig, Pair 40.00
Music Box, Mickey & Minnie, Pluto 650.00
Music Box, Mickey Mouse, On Ice, Top Hat & Cane, c.1960 .... 65.00
Napkin Ring, Mickey Mouse, Bakelite, Decal, 1930s, 2 3/4 In. .... 90.00 to 95.00
Night-Light, Donald Duck, Figural 100.00
Night-Light, Mickey Mouse, Glo-Worm Products, London, Eng., Box, 8 In. 185.00
Nodder, Mickey Mouse, Top Hat, Plastic, Marx, 2 In. 15.00
Organ, 15 Keys, Walt Disney, Box 33.00
Pail, Jungle Book, Chein 145.00
Pail, Mickey Mouse, Chein 155.00
Pail, Mickey Mouse, Red, Tin Litho Handle, Marx, 1950s, 4 In. 25.00
Pail, Minnie Mouse, Donald Duck & Pluto 135.00
Pencil, Mechanical, Mickey Mouse, Inkograph, 1930s 135.00
Pencil Sharpener, Bambi, Bakelite, 1940s 75.00
Pencil Sharpener, Mickey Mouse, Figural, Red Bakelite, 1930s 125.00
Perfume Bottle, Grumpy, 1940s 35.00
Phonograph, Alice In Wonderland, Disney, 1951 .... 100.00
Phonograph, Mickey Mouse, Hand Plays Records 45.00
Picture, Alice In Wonderland, Reverse On Glass, No. 425, c.1935, 12 x 8 In. 90.00 to 130.00
Pillow Case, Mickey Mouse, 1930s 85.00
Pin, Enameled, The Mighty Ducks, NHL Hockey Team Logo, 1993 .... 15.00
Pin, Pinocchio, Walking, With Books In Hand, Plastic, Painted, Brier Mfg.Co. 25.00
Pinback, Mickey Mouse, Southern Dairies Ice Cream, 1930s 1580.00
Pincushion, Tinker Bell, Box 65.00
Planter, Dopey, Walt Disney Productions .... 45.00 to 55.00
Planter, Mickey Mouse, Cowboy, 1940s 32.00
Planter, Snow White, Figural, Leeds Pottery, 6 1/2 In. 45.00
Plaque, Donald Duck, Jewelry Co., Tile Shape, Square, 1950s, 4 In. 60.00
Plate, Fantasia 29.00
Plate, Mickey Mouse, China, 1930s, 7 In. 45.00
Plate, Three Little Pigs, Dancing, Playing Instruments, Patriot China, 6 1/4 In. 65.00
Pocket Watch, Donald Duck, Chrome Case, W.D. Prop., c.1939 .... 330.00
Pocket Watch, Mickey Mouse, Fob, Ingersol, 1933 .... 725.00
Postcard, Pinocchio, 3-D, Moving, 3 Piece 15.00
Poster, Pinocchio, Color, 1 Sheet, 40 x 78 In. 3000.00
Poster, Pinocchio, Walt Disney, 1940 .... 3300.00
Program, Fantasia, Ice Capades, 1957 .... 20.00
Program, Mickey Mouse, Minnie Mouse & Donald Duck, Armed Forces, 1940s 15.00
Program, Snow White & Seven Dwarfs, Ice Capades, 1949 .... 25.00
Program, Snow White, Radio City, Showplace Magazine, Vol. 2, No. 4, 1938 .... 75.00
Projector, Donald Duck, Walt Disney, Box 85.00
Projector, Mickey Mouse, Keystone 200.00
Projector, Mickey Mouse, Talking 695.00
Punch-Out Set, Snow White, Box, 1961 .... 25.00
Puppet, Hand, Donald Duck, Gund, 1950s, 12 In. 29.00
Puppet, Hand, Jiminy Cricket, Gund, 1950s 45.00
Puppet, Hand, Mickey Mouse, Gund, 1950s, 12 In. 29.00
Puppet, Hand, Minnie Mouse, Hard Rubber, 1952 .... 35.00
Puppet, Hand, Pluto, Gund 30.00
Puppet, Mickey Mouse, Checker Cloth Outfit 14.00
Puppet, Minnie Mouse, Pelham, Box 395.00
Puppet, Peter Pan 20.00
Puppet, Pluto, Paddle, Wooden Jointed, Decal, Fisher-Price, 1930s .... 55.00 to 75.00
Purse, Snow White, 1938 .... 65.00
Puzzle, Cinderella, Harter Co., 1931, 4 Complete Puzzles 45.00
Quilt, Snow White & Seven Dwarfs, Hand Sewn, McCall Pattern, Walt Disney Ent. .. 135.00
Radio, Mickey Mouse, Emerson, Front & Back Brass Plates, Pinback Button 1950.00

Radio, Mickey Mouse, Emerson, Table-N, 1933 .... 2500.00
Rattle, Mickey Mouse, Bell Hands, Wooden Bead Legs, Celluloid, 1930s 100.00
Record, Snow White & Seven Dwarfs, Mickey Mouse, 45 RPM 7.50
Record, Snow White, Storybook, 33 1/3 RPM 25.00
Ring, Donald Duck, Sterling Silver, Square, Osbee, 1940s 35.00
Rug, Game, 6 x 12 Ft. 350.00
Salt & Pepper, Bambi 22.00
Salt & Pepper, Dumbo, American Pottery 20.00
Salt & Pepper, Figaro, Yellow, National Porcelain, 1940s, 2 1/2 In. 65.00
Salt & Pepper, Pluto, Leeds 40.00
Saltshaker, Kaa The Snake, Jungle Book, Enesco, 1960s 150.00
Sheet Music, Blue Shadows On The Trail, Disney's Melody Time 18.00
Sheet Music, Heigh-Ho & One Song, Snow White & Seven Dwarfs, 1937 .... 25.00
Sheet Music, Mickey Mouse Birthday Party, 1936 .... 5.00
Sheet Music, Song Of The South, Zippity Doo Dah, 1946 .... 12.00
Sheet Music, Who's Afraid Of The Big Bad Wolf, 1933 .... 20.00
Sneakers, Mickey Mouse Club 125.00
Soap, Character, Box, 1950s, 24 Piece 90.00
Soap Dish, 3 Dwarfs 175.00
Soap Set, Mickey Mouse 25.00
Soundtrack & Storybook, Pinocchio, 1939 .... 95.00
Spoon, Mickey Mouse, Silver Plated, Wm. Rogers & Son, 1930s .... 7.00 to 15.00
Spoon, Sterling Silver, Porcelain Top Piece With Castle, 4 1/2 In. 35.00
Tea Set, Disneyland, Mickey Mouse, Box 650.00
Tea Set, Mickey & Minnie Mouse, Blue Luster, George Borgfeldt, 1930s, Box 950.00
Tea Set, Mickey Mouse, Blue Luster, Box 775.00
Tea Set, Plastic, Wolverine, Box 48.00
Teapot, Mickey Mouse Face 40.00
Teapot, Mickey's Ears, Disney 28.00
Telephone, Mickey Mouse, Original Box, Late 1970s 325.00
Thimble, Mickey & Minnie Mouse, Pair 25.00
Toothbrush, Mickey Mouse, Talking .... 70.00 to 85.00
Toy, Action Arcade, Walt Disney, 1960s, Box 35.00
Toy, Battling Donald Duck, Celluloid, Windup 1450.00
Toy, Car, Parade Roadster, Windup, Disney, Box 1300.00
Toy, Car, Playing, Three Little Pigs, 1930s, Box 100.00
Toy, Christmas, Ornament, Donald Duck, On Fire Truck, Hard Plastic 12.00
Toy, Cinderella, Prince, Dancing, Windup, Irwin, 1950s 165.00
Toy, Disney Express, Train Set, Lionel, Boxes 1815.00
Toy, Disney Express, Train, Tin, Linemar, Box 315.00
Toy, Disneyland, Ferris Wheel, Chein 400.00
Toy, Disneyland, Train, Windup, Tin Lithograph, Marx, 1962 .... 125.00 to 135.00
Toy, Donald Duck & Pluto, Car, Sun Rubber, 1940s .... 60.00 to 95.00
Toy, Donald Duck & Pluto, Handcar, Windup, Lionel .... 700.00 to 725.00
Toy, Donald Duck Drummer, Tin 595.00
Toy, Donald Duck, Bubble Blower, Soap Powder & Spoon, 1950s, Box 45.00
Toy, Donald Duck, Car, Racing, Sun Rubber 185.00
Toy, Donald Duck, Drum Major, Pull Toy 195.00
Toy, Donald Duck, Fisher-Price, No. 450, 1940 .... 1275.00
Toy, Donald Duck, Handcar, With Track, Lionel 450.00
Toy, Donald Duck, Krazy Cart, Marx 400.00
Toy, Donald Duck, Motorcycle, Marx, 4 In. 135.00
Toy, Donald Duck, On Trapeze, Gym Toys 425.00
Toy, Donald Duck, On Trapeze, Linemar 450.00
Toy, Donald Duck, Pull, Fisher-Price, No. 400 .... 67.50
Toy, Donald Duck, Pulltop, Bells On Wheels Ring, Wood & Paper, 12 In. 235.00
Toy, Donald Duck, Rail Car, Original Box 1072.00
Toy, Donald Duck, Ramp Walker, Pushing Wagon 35.00
Toy, Donald Duck, Talker, Pull String, Mattel 15.00
Toy, Donald Duck, Walker, Wheelbarrow, Marx 85.00
Toy, Donald Duck, Xylophone, Fisher-Price, Wood & Paper, 13 x 11 In. 550.00
Toy, Fantasia, Elephant, Dancing, American Pottery, c.1940, 5 1/2 In. 350.00
Toy, Ferdinand The Bull, Windup, Tail Spins, Tin Lithograph, Marx, 1938 ..... 145.00 to 185.00

Toy, Frontierland, Logs, Halsam	85.00
Toy, Goofy, Dancer, Donald Plays Drum, Windup	895.00
Toy, Goofy, Windup, Tin, Linemar, Box, 5 1/2 In.	850.00
Toy, Jeep, Disneyland, Tin, Marx, Box	595.00
Toy, Mickey & Minnie Mouse, Handcar, Wells	2500.00
Toy, Mickey Mouse & Donald Duck, Fire Engine, Sun Rubber	60.00
Toy, Mickey Mouse & Donald Duck, Handcar, Wells	1250.00
Toy, Mickey Mouse & Donald, Handcar, Tin Lithograph, Clockwork, Marx	440.00
Toy, Mickey Mouse & Minnie Mouse, Acrobats, Original Tag & Price, Japan	1695.00
Toy, Mickey Mouse & Minnie Mouse, Handcar, Windup, Lionel	825.00
Toy, Mickey Mouse, Acrobat, Walt Disney, 1930s	95.00
Toy, Mickey Mouse, Airplane, Rubber, Blue, Sun Rubber, 1930s	200.00
Toy, Mickey Mouse, Circus Train, Lithograph, Painted, Lionel, Box, 7 Piece	4290.00
Toy, Mickey Mouse, Driver, Linemar	1295.00
Toy, Mickey Mouse, Drummer, Battery Operated, Box	1500.00
Toy, Mickey Mouse, Drummer, Pull, Paper On Wood, Fisher-Price, 7 1/2 In. . 185.00 to 525.00
Toy, Mickey Mouse, Express Caboose, Lionel, No. 6, 1978, Box	95.00
Toy, Mickey Mouse, Gun, Bubble Buster	200.00
Toy, Mickey Mouse, Handcar, Clockwork, Tin Plate, Track, Wells, Box	978.00
Toy, Mickey Mouse, Handcar, Speedy, Windup, Red Lionel	1450.00
Toy, Mickey Mouse, Hurdy-Gurdy, Tin Plate, Key Wind, Distler, 1930	2500.00
Toy, Mickey Mouse, In Car, Pull Toy, 1965	60.00
Toy, Mickey Mouse, Krazy Kar, Battery Operated	145.00
Toy, Mickey Mouse, Locomotive, Western, Battery Operated, Durham, Box, 1970s	35.00
Toy, Mickey Mouse, Loop The Loop, Battery Operated, Box	175.00
Toy, Mickey Mouse, Meteor, Train Set, Clockwork, Marx, 4 Piece	484.00
Toy, Mickey Mouse, On Tricycle, Windup, Marline	80.00
Toy, Mickey Mouse, Plane, Rubber	175.00
Toy, Mickey Mouse, Puddle Jumper, Pull, Wooden, Fisher-Price, 1940s	300.00
Toy, Mickey Mouse, Rubber Band Action, 1970s, Box	30.00
Toy, Mickey Mouse, Safety Patrol, Fisher-Price No. 733	45.00
Toy, Mickey Mouse, Saxophone, Tin, Haro, 1935, 16 In.	500.00
Toy, Mickey Mouse, Talker, Pull String, Mattel	15.00
Toy, Mickey Mouse, Tractor, Sun Rubber	185.00
Toy, Mickey Mouse, Train, Lionel, 1930s	1485.00
Toy, Mickey Mouse, Trapeze, Wooden, Milton Bradley, 1930s, 2 x 8 In.	45.00
Toy, Mickey Mouse, Typewriter, Tin, c.1950, Box	150.00
Toy, Mickey Mouse, Xylophone, Tin	225.00
Toy, Minnie Mouse, Knitting, Rocking Chair, Windup, Tin, Linemar	425.00 to 480.00
Toy, Minnie Mouse, Shopping Cart, Battery Operated, Box	150.00
Toy, Periscope, 20,000 Leagues Under The Sea, 1960s	125.00
Toy, Pinocchio, Cymbal Player, Tin, Vinyl Head, Cloth Body, Box, Japan	150.00
Toy, Pinocchio, On Donkey, Pull Toy	350.00
Toy, Pinocchio, Pool, Submarine, 1960s	25.00
Toy, Pinocchio, Ramp Walker, Marx	225.00
Toy, Pluto, Drum Major, Marx	650.00
Toy, Pluto, Motorized, Push Tail To Start, Tin, 1939	275.00
Toy, Pluto, On Motorcycle, Friction, Tin, Linemar	195.00
Toy, Pluto, Plastic, Windup, Marx	85.00
Toy, Pluto, Pull Toy, Fisher-Price	50.00
Toy, Pluto, Push Tail Down, He Rolls Along, Marx	350.00
Toy, Pluto, Roll-Over, Marx, Box	540.00
Toy, Pluto, Tin, Windup, Slinky Type Body, Marx, c.1940	255.00
Toy, Pluto, Walker, Marx	85.00
Toy, Pluto, Windup, Plastic, Replaced Ears, Marx	325.00
Toy, Rifle, Training, Disney, No. 960	20.00
Toy, Robin Hood, Wind Up, 1971, 5 In.	85.00
Toy, Rocket Ship Control Board, Disneyland, Box	250.00
Toy, Snow White, Ironing Board, Metal, Wolverine, 8 x 27 x 21 In.	145.00
Toy, Tambourine, Mickey Mouse & Donald Duck, Disney On Parade, 1970s	35.00
Toy, Train, Disneyland Express, Windup, Marx	165.00
Toy, Xylophone, Donald Duck & Daisy, Fisher-Price	140.00
Toy, Xylophone, Mickey Mouse, Clockwork, Tin Lithographed, Linemar	302.00

Tray, Fantasia, Glass, 1961, 4 Piece 225.00
Tray, Mickey Mouse Club, Disney Characters, Tin, 1950s, 12 x 17 In. 65.00
Umbrella, Mickey & Minnie Picture, Cloth, Disney, 1930 .... 150.00
Wall Pocket, Mickey & Minnie Mouse, Gold Luster, c.1930 .... 225.00
War Bond, Seven Dwarfs, Mickey Mouse, Donald Duck, 1944 .... 65.00
Watch, Daisy Duck 350.00
Watch, Donald Duck, Pocket, Box, 1939 .... 695.00 to 1800.00
Watch, Goofy, Backwards, Pedre, Gold Tone 400.00
Watch, Mickey Mouse, Ingersoll, Pocket, 1930s 250.00
Watch, Mickey Mouse, Leather Band, 1933 .... 400.00
Watch, Mickey Mouse, Pocket, Box 775.00
Watch, Mickey Mouse, Pocket, Fob, Ingersoll, 1933 .... 725.00
Watch, Mickey Mouse, Pocket, Tall Stem, New Crystal, Ingersoll, 1933 .... 437.00
Watch, Three Little Pigs, Pocket, Pictures Wolf, Ingersoll, Box 1400.00
Watch Holder, Cinderella Form, Porcelain, Disney 35.00
Whirligig, Mickey Mouse, Borgfeldt, Box .... 5500.00 to 7770.00
Wristwatch, 101 Dalmatians, For Employees Only 175.00
Wristwatch, Cinderella's Slipper, Box 375.00
Wristwatch, Daisy Duck, 1930s 350.00
Wristwatch, Donald Duck, Bradley, Case 100.00
Wristwatch, Mickey Mouse & Donald Duck, Portraits, Lorus, Box 95.00
Wristwatch, Mickey Mouse, Birthday, Square, 1978 .... 345.00
Wristwatch, Mickey Mouse, Box, 1948 .... 475.00
Wristwatch, Mickey Mouse, Bradley, Box, 1973 .... 145.00 to 245.00
Wristwatch, Mickey Mouse, Chrome Case, Red Vinyl Band, Ingersoll, 1947, Box 345.00
Wristwatch, Mickey Mouse, Helbros, 17 Jewel, 1971 .... 180.00
Wristwatch, Mickey Mouse, Ingersoll, 1949 .... 115.00
Wristwatch, Mickey Mouse, Ingersoll, Leather Band, Case, 1933 .... 225.00
Wristwatch, Mickey Mouse, Metal Link Band, Ingersoll, 1930s, Box 700.00
Wristwatch, Mickey Mouse, Metal Silhouettes, Leather Strap, Ingersoll, 1940s 665.00
Wristwatch, Mickey Mouse, Plastic, 1977 .... 8.00
Wristwatch, Mickey Mouse, Pluto Wagging Head, Bradley 795.00
Wristwatch, Mickey Mouse, Red Vinyl Band, WDP-Timex, 1960s, Large 125.00
Wristwatch, Mickey Mouse, Timex, Electric, Box, 1968 .... 225.00 to 450.00
Wristwatch, Mickey Mouse, Wagging Head, Bradley .... 175.00 to 295.00
Wristwatch, Minnie Mouse, Wagging Head, Bradley .... 225.00 to 395.00
Wristwatch, Minnie Mouse, Winking & Blinking Eyes, Instructions, Disney 195.00
Wristwatch, Pluto, Wagging Head 595.00
Wristwatch, Snow White Magic Mirror, Box 395.00

DOCTOR, see Dental; Medical

DOLL entries are listed by marks printed or incised on the doll, if possible. If
there are no marks, the doll is listed by the name of the subject or country.

A. & B., Susan Hayworth, Suit, Movie, I Can Get It For You Wholesale, 27 In. 1695.00
A.M., 17, Fixed Eyes, Jointed Wood & Composition Body, Silk Dress, 37 In. 660.00
A.M., 200 3/0, Googly Eyed, Bisque Head, Blue Sleep Eyes, 1915, 9 1/2 In. 805.00
A.M., 200, Googly, Toddler Body, Watermelon Smile, Pixie Clothes, 9 1/2 In. 2100.00
A.M., 210, Campbell Kid, Googly, 6 1/2 In. 575.00
A.M., 210, Painted Googly Eyes, 5-Piece Body, 7 In. 325.00
A.M., 241, Googly, Toddler, Chubby, Sleep Eyes, Watermelon Mouth, 10 1/2 In........ 1850.00
A.M., 251/248, Baby, Closed Mouth, Bisque, Sleep Eyes, Mohair, 11 In. 1425.00
A.M., 341, Bisque Flange Head, Cloth Body, Baby Dress, In Wicker Carriage, 8 In. .. 65.00
A.M., 351, Baby, Bisque, Molded Curls, Sleep Eyes, Crocheted Socks, 24 In. 950.00
A.M., 351, Baby, Stockinet, Brown Sleep Eyes, 20 1/2 In. 695.00
A.M., 351, Dream Baby, Black, Sleep Eyes, Bent Knee, 11 In. 595.00
A.M., 351, Dream Baby, Glass Sleep Eyes, Bent Knee Body, 11 In. 600.00
A.M., 353, Googly Sleep Eyes, Ball-Jointed Body, 12 In. 995.00
A.M., 353, Oriental, Olive Tint Body, Period Kimono, 17 In. 1795.00
A.M., 370, Bisque Head, Kid Body, Brown Curls, Teeth, Dressed, 19 In. 395.00
A.M., 370, Dainty Dorothy, Bisque, Kid Body, Human Hair Wig, Dressed, 20 In. 235.00
A.M., 390, Bisque Head, Mohair Eye Brows, Composition Body, Lace Dress, 17 In. . 220.00
A M., 390, Bisque Head, Mohair Wig, Sleep Eyes, Old Dress, 14 In. 175.00
A.M., 390, Bisque Socket Head, Sleep Eyes, Lashes, Open Mouth, Jointed, 18 In. 245.00

◆◆◆◆◆◆◆◆◆◆◆◆◆◆◆◆◆◆◆◆◆◆◆◆

Don't wash, set, comb, or change
the original hair on a vinyl doll. It
lowers the value.

◆◆◆◆◆◆◆◆◆◆◆◆◆◆◆◆◆◆◆◆◆◆◆◆

Doll, Advertising, Dutch Boy, Cloth,
Plastic Head, 14 In.

A.M., 390, Bisque, Brown Sleep Eyes, Human Hair Wig, Antique Clothing, 31 In. 895.00
A.M., 390, Red Wig, Brown Eyes, Silk Dress, Bonnet, 28 In. 995.00
A.M., 390, Sleep Eyes, Ball-Jointed Body, 25 In. 190.00
A.M., 500, Googly, Fat Chunky Toddler Body, Original Clothes, 11 In. 2500.00
A.M., 985, Character, Baby, Blue Sleep Eyes, Bisque, Repainted, Gown, Bonnet, 18 In. 650.00
A.M., Bisque, Glass Sleep Eyes, Open Mouth, Jointed, Composition Body, 30 In. 330.00
A.M., Floradora, Bisque Head & Arms, Kid Body, Label, Box, 16 In. 400.00
A.M., Florodora, Blue Sleep Eyes, Fur Eyebrows, Ball-Jointed, Clothes, 23 1/2 In. 575.00
A.M., Florodora, Kid Body, Original Clothes, 16 In. 300.00
A.M., Googly, Watermelon Mouth, Romper Suit, c.1915, 9 3/4 In. 660.00
A.M., Indian, Bisque, Composition Body, 11 In. 200.00
A.M., Infant, Bisque Head, Painted Hair, Hard Stuffed Body, 10 In. 175.00
A.M., Infant, Bisque Head, Painted Hair, Cloth Body, Antique Gown, 17 In. 450.00
Advertising, Allied Van Lines, Girl, Cloth 25.00
Advertising, Buddy Lee, Composition 235.00
Advertising, Burger King, 1980, 21 In. 30.00
Advertising, Burger King, Cloth, 1973, 15 In. 15.00
Advertising, Burger King, Stuffed, 1973, 14 In. 20.00
Advertising, Chiquita Banana, With Recipe Book 20.00
Advertising, Dolly-Gram, Western Union, Box, 1975 .... 15.00
Advertising, Dutch Boy, Cloth, Plastic Head, 14 In. .... *Illus* 70.00
Advertising, Eskimo Pie, Cloth, 16 1/2 In. 20.00
Advertising, Eskimo Pie, Cloth, 1970s, 15 In. 12.00
Advertising, Freckles The Frog, Kellogg's, Uncut 30.00
Advertising, General Electric, Maxfield Parrish Soldier, Wooden Jointed 925.00
Advertising, Gerber Baby, Box, 1979 .... 50.00
Advertising, Green Giant, Cloth, 1966, 16 In. 15.00
Advertising, Hawaiian Punch, Stuffed 25.00
Advertising, Irish Spring Soap, Stuffed Body, Rubber Face, 20 In. 110.00
Advertising, Kellogg's Snap, Crackle & Pop, Cloth, Uncut, Dated 1948, 3 Piece 175.00
Advertising, Kellogg's Snap, Crackle & Pop, Vinyl, 3 Piece 110.00
Advertising, Little Sprout, Green Giant, Green Fleece, Plastic Eyes, 1980, 12 In. 12.00
Advertising, McDonald's, Hamburglar, c.1950 .... 65.00
Advertising, McDonald's, Kermit, Christmas 10.00
Advertising, Miss Curity, Composition, Blond, 5-Piece Body, 1940, 20 In. 500.00
Advertising, Miss Debbie, Horsman, 1984 .... 25.00
Advertising, Nestle, Little Hans, Vinyl, 12 In., 1969 .... 75.00
Advertising, Northern Toilet Tissue 35.00
Advertising, Pillsbury, Poppin' Fresh, Vinyl, 1971, 7 In. 12.00
Advertising, Quaker Oats, Boy, Cloth, 16 In. 35.00
Advertising, RCA Radiotron, Wooden, Composition, Ball-Jointed, Parish, 17 In. 950.00
Advertising, Rice Krispies, Pop, Cloth, 1945, 14 In. 65.00
Advertising, Ronald McDonald, Stuffed, Sealed Bag, 1980, 16 In. 24.00
Advertising, Ronald McDonald, With Whistle, Hasbro, 1978, 18 In. .... 30.00 to 50.00
Advertising, Swift & Co., Vinyl, 7 1/2 In. 300.00
Advertising, Tony The Tiger, Inflatable, 5 Ft. 50.00
Advertising, Twinkle, Tin Flirty Eyes, Original Felt Clothes, Shoes 145.00

Doll, Automaton, Black Flutist, Papier-Mache,
Gustave Vichy, 1870, 34 In.

Doll, Automaton, Drunken Clown, On Stilts,
Roullet & Decamps, 1910, 28 In.

Advertising, Uncle Ben's Rice Man	25.00
Advertising, Uneeda, Plumpees, Rubber, 1969	15.00
Advertising, Uneeda, Pong Boy, Unused, Original Package	5.00
Advertising, Weatherbird Shoe, 1911-1914, 25 In.	100.00
Advertising, Wrigley's Gum, Talking, Multicolor Lithograph	150.00
Alabama Baby, Pink Shoes	1500.00
Alexander dolls are listed in this category under Madame Alexander	
Alfred E. Neuman, What Me Worry, MAD Magazine, 1961	2595.00
Alice In Wonderland, Cloth, 1930s, 30 In.	135.00
Alt, Beck & Gottschalk, 1008, Cloth Body, Bisque Arms, Silk Dress, 1890, 26 In.	440.00
American Character, Petite, Composition Arms & Legs, Stuffed Cloth Body, 13 In.	195.00
American Character, Tiny Tears, Hard Plastic Head, Rubber Body, 13 In.	95.00
Amish, Heavy Cotton Body, Coarse Cotton Dress, 1930-1940, 14 In.	140.00
Amish, Rag Stuffed Cotton, Black Cotton Bonnet, Brown Dress, Apron, 1940, 13 In.	115.00
Amish, Rag, Green Dress, 17 1/2 In.	33.00
Annalee, Mr. & Mrs. Santa Claus, 24 In., Pair	150.00
Annalee, Santa Claus, With North Pole, 7 In.	70.00
Annalee, Santa Claus, With Skis, 7 In.	70.00
Applause, E.T., 8 In.	10.00
Applause, Snow White, Lever Bros. Premium, Box, 12 In.	50.00
Applehead, In Ladder-Back Armchair	65.00
Armand Marseille dolls are listed in this category under A.M.	
Arranbee, Debu'teen, Composition, Pageboy Hair, 5-Piece Body, 14 In.	450.00
Automaton, Bisque Head & Hands, Music, Turns Globe With Foot, 7 1/2 x 14 In.	5800.00
Automaton, Black Flutist, Papier-Mache, Gustave Vichy, 1870, 34 In. .... *Illus*	16500.00
Automaton, Cat Band, Paper, Cloth, Manivelle, c.1900, 11 x 12 In. .... *Illus*	1000.00
Automaton, Drunken Clown, On Stilts, Roullet & Decamps, 1910, 28 In. .... *Illus*	19800.00
Automaton, Felt, Walks, Waves & Turns Head, Italy, Box, 19 In.	950.00
Automaton, Garden Tea Party, Manivelle, c.1900, 11 1/4 x 12 In. .... *Illus*	2800.00
Automaton, Goat Pulling Cabriolet, Papier-Mache, France, 1885, 17 In.	3500.00
Automaton, Happy Baker & Kitten, France ....*Illus*	24000.00
Automaton, Little Boy With Balloons, Bisque, Vichy, 1875, 10 In.	3200.00
Automaton, Pierrot, Serenading The Moon, 1890, 20 x 22 In. .... *Illus*	27500.00
Automaton, Precious Sailor Boy, Clashes Cymbals, Germany, 10 In.	575.00
Automaton, Violinist, Dickens' Christmas Carol Figure, 1930s	4500.00
Autoperipatetikos, Walking, Mechanical, Box	1375.00
Averill, American Indian Girl, Cloth, 1930	65.00
Averill, Bonnie Babe, Bisque Head, Sleep Eyes, Cloth Body, 1920s, 15 1/4 In.	575.00
Averill, Bonnie Babe, Bisque Head, Smiling Mouth, 2 Teeth, c.1926, 22 In.	660.00
Averill, Bonnie Babe, Bisque, Sleep Eyes, Happy Face, Cloth Body, 17 In.	995.00

Doll, Automaton, Happy Baker & Kitten, France

Doll, Automaton, Garden Tea Party, Manivelle, c.1900, 11 1/4 x 12 In.; Doll, Automaton, Cat Band, Paper, Cloth, Manivelle, c.1900, 11 x 12 In.

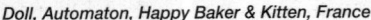

Averill, Bonnie Babe, Crooked Smile, Wax Lids, Tongue, Fancy Clothes, 22 In. 1495.00
Averill, International Girl 110.00
B.J. & Co., Bisque Head, My Sweetheart, Cotton Dress, Lace Trim, 20 In. 245.00
Baby, Poured Wax, Rooted Hair, Glass Eyes, Old Clothes, England, 18 In. 1500.00
Baby, Solid Dome, Blue Sleep Eyes, Open Mouth, Composition, Blue Romper, 10 In. ... 175.00
Babyland, Rag, Pink & Cream Costume, 15 In. 750.00
Babyland, Rag, Silk Face, Original Clothes, 14 1/2 In. 850.00
Bahr & Proschild, 204, 16 In. 850.00
Bahr & Proschild, Character Baby, Bisque, Composition Body, 14 In. 550.00
Ballplayer, Cincinnati Reds Uniform, 1911 .... 3000.00
Barbie dolls are listed in this category under Mattel
Bebe, Gaultier, Stiff Wrists, Open Mouth, Antique Laces, 18 In. 1895.00
Bebe, Oily Sheen, Paperweight Eyes, 6 Teeth, Lace Dress, 18 In. 1895.00
Belton, 137, Blue Paperweight Eyes, Blond Mohair Wig, Closed Mouth, 20 In. 3150.00
Belton, 1044, Dressed, 9 1/2 In. 550.00
Belton, Bisque, Blue Eyes, Stiff Wrist, Tailored Dress, Button Boots, 17 1/2 In. 3200.00
Belton, Closed Mouth, Composition Body, French Style Clothes, 12 In. 1400.00
Belton, Closed Mouth, French Jointed Body, Taffeta Costume, 11 In. 1650.00
Belton, Closed Mouth, Painted Features, Blue Paperweight Eyes, 14 In. 1450.00
Belton, Kid Body, Clothes, 13 In. 1500.00
Belton, Paperweight Eyes, Closed Mouth, Human Hair Wig, Dressed, 12 In. 1400.00
Bergmann dolls are also in this category under S & H and Simon & Halbig
Bergmann, Bisque, Stavenger, Norway Costume, 26 In. 850.00
Bergmann, No. 1916, Sleep Eyes, Ball-Jointed, 17 In. 275.00
Bionic Man 40.00
Bionic Woman, Box, 12 In. 45.00
Bisque, Composition, 5 Piece, Blue Glass Eyes, Open Mouth, Germany, 11 In. 210.00
Bisque, Glass Eyes, Bobbed Wig, Incised 540-3, 5 1/2 In. 295.00
Bisque, Highland Mary Type, German, Glass Eyes, 14 In. 615.00
Bisque, Kid Body, Male Clothing, German, 15 In. 525.00
Black dolls are included in the Black category
Borgfeldt, Baby, Gray Eyes, Original Wig, Period Clothes, 26 In. 1450.00
Boudoir, Composition & Cloth, 1920s, 28 In. 95.00
Boudoir, Smoker, Cloth, 1930s 185.00

Boudoir, Smoking, Man & Woman, France, Pair 285.00
Boy, Holland American Line, Sailor 29.00
Brenda Starr, Baby, Original Clothes, 1975 .... 125.00
Bru Brevete, Bisque, Blue Eyes, Shaded Lids, Earrings, Signed Shoes, 19 In. 14500.00
Bru Jne, Bisque Head, Blue Eyes, Human Hair Wig, Jointed Body, Silk Dress, 12 In. 2500.00
Bru Jne, Bisque Head, Stationary Eyes, Open Mouth, Teeth, Dressed, 22 In. 9000.00
Bru Jne, Fashion, Blond Mohair Wig, Cobalt Blue Eyes, 15 In. 3950.00
Bru Jne, Kissing, Bisque, Paperweight Eyes, Dressed, Molded Shoes, Box, 23 In. 7500.00
Bruckner, Girl, Dressed As Red Riding Hood, 13 In. 175.00
Bruckner, Topsy-Turvy, Cloth, Black & White Mask Faces, Original Clothes, 13 In. . 105.00
Bye-Lo, Baby, Bisque Head, Molded Hair, Cloth Body, 14 In. 450.00
Bye-Lo, Baby, Bisque Head, Molded Hair, Sleep Eyes, Signed Grace Putnam, 13 In. . 455.00
Bye-Lo, Baby, Bisque, Celluloid Hands, Christening Gown 675.00
Bye-Lo, Baby, Bisque, Sleep Eyes, Cloth Body, Celluloid Hands, 1920s, 15 In. 330.00
Bye-Lo, Baby, Sleep Eyes, Cloth Body, Composition Hands, 12 In. 525.00
Bye-Lo, Bisque, Painted Eyes, In Basket, Antique Wardrobe, Quilt, 5 1/2 In. 400.00
Bye-Lo, Blue Sleep Eyes, Slip & Diaper, 11 In. 595.00
Bye-Lo, Cloth Body, Composition Hands, Blue Sleep Eyes, 12 In. 525.00
Bye-Lo, Dream Baby, Sleep Eyes, Celluloid Hands, 14 In. 375.00
Bye-Lo, Period Clothes, Miniature 495.00
Bye-Lo, Sleep Eyes, Swivel Neck, Gown, Wicker Bassinet, 5 In. 895.00
Bye-Lo, Wax, Sleeping, Celluloid Hands, Baby Clothes 5500.00
Cabbage Patch, Della Frances, Box 150.00
Cabbage Patch, Leslie Ellen, Box 150.00
Cameo, Kewpie, 6 In. 20.00
Cameo, Kewpie, Jointed, Vinyl, 16 In. 55.00
Canadian Air Force Man, Composition, Painted Brown Eyes, Cloth Body, 17 In. 65.00
Celluloid, Flirty Eyes, Original Outfit, 20 In. 450.00
Celluloid, Girl, Original Clothes, Germany, 14 In. 85.00
Celluloid, Hula Dancer, Occupied Japan, Box 160.00
Celluloid, Triplets, Glass Eyes, Blue, Turtle Mark, 19 In. 150.00
Celluloid, Windup, Original Clothes, Germany, Box, 6 In. 238.00
Chad Valley, Guard 85.00
Chad Valley, Royal Family Princess, Cloth, Glass Eyes 1500.00
Charlie's Angel, Hasbro, Box, 8 1/2 In. 16.00
Charming Chatty, Original Clothes, 1961 .... 65.00
Chase, Baby, Big Cheeks, Dimples, 20 In. 540.00
Chase, Baby, Painted Eyes, Cloth Body, Jointed, 23 In. 550.00
Chase, Cloth, Brown Eyes, 27 In. 1800.00
Chase, Cloth, Side-Part Hair, 17 In. 1300.00
Chase, George Washington, 26 In. 4875.00
Chase, Stockinet, Black, Molded & Painted Head, 20th Century, 24 In. 3630.00

◆ ◆

The 1961 Brownette Barbie is often a "greasy face." An ingredient used in the vinyl is slowly being rejected and a greasy film appears on the face while the head slowly shrinks. Remove the head. Wipe it inside and out with alcohol, then fill the head with baking soda. It will soak up any future grease. Return the filled head to the doll.

◆ ◆ ◆ ◆ ◆ ◆ ◆ ◆ ◆ ◆ ◆ ◆ ◆ ◆ ◆ ◆ ◆ ◆ ◆ ◆

Doll, Automaton, Pierrot, Serenading The Moon, 1890, 20 x 22 In.

Chase, Stockinet, Molded & Painted Hair & Features, 1920s, 20 In.	305.00
Chase, Toddler, Boy, 14 In.	595.00
Cher, Growhair, Box	35.00
Child, Closed Mouth, Brown Paperweight Eyes, Bisque, Heirloom Clothes, 12 In.	850.00
Child, Felt Face, Velvet Body, Glass Eyes, Organdy Dress, 14 In.	495.00
Child, Queen Louise, Sleep Eyes, Ball-Jointed Body, Human Hair Wig, 30 In.	895.00
Child, Turned Head, Closed Mouth, Bisque, Kid Jointed Body, 24 In.	2200.00
China, Pink Luster, Civil War Period, 27 In.	850.00
Chucky, Child's Play, Movie, 10 In.	25.00
Clark Gable, Bisque, Ball-Jointed, Gone With The Wind Clothes, 26 1/2 In.	495.00
Cloth, Cut & Sew, Flour Sack, 1940s, Uncut	48.00
Cloth, Diana, Aunt Jemima's Little Girl, 1924	120.00
Cloth, Flat Face, Ruffled Bonnet, Printed Cloth Covers Arms & Legs, 16 In.	622.00
Cloth, Oil Painted Head & Flat Features, 17 In.	110.00
Cloth, Satin Face, Sweetheart Mouth, Felt Clothes, Painted Details, 1920s, 10 In.	35.00
Connie Lynn, Baby, From Terri Lee Family	350.00
Dan Astronaut, Red Hair, 1964, 12 In.	90.00
Dancing, Key Wind, Silk Face & Clothes, 1940s, Box, 6 In.	65.00
Demacol, Googly, Original Clothes, 9 In.	895.00
DEP, Blue Earrings & Necklace, Solid Wrist, 16 1/2 In.	6600.00
Dick Clark, Vinyl Hands & Head, Painted Features, Cloth Body, Early 1950s, 28 In.	195.00
Dollhouse, Grandma, 5 1/2 In.	150.00
Dollhouse, Great Aunt Cissy, Wig, 5 1/4 In.	175.00
Dr. John Littlechap, Wears Blue & White Towel, Stand, Box	55.00
Dracula, Death Certificate, Coffin Box, 1985, 19 In.	40.00
Dracula, Talking, Early 1960s, Box	375.00
Dream Baby, Bisque, Blue Sleep Eyes, 14 In.	475.00
Dream Baby, Composition Body, Vintage Clothes, 14 In.	450.00
Dream Baby, In Basket	300.00
Dresser, Blue, Noritake	200.00
Effanbee, Anne Shirley, Dressed, 21 In.	350.00
Effanbee, Baby Dainty, Cloth & Composition	145.00
Effanbee, Baby Grumpy, 18 In.	50.00
Effanbee, Baby Tinyette, Pink Organdy Outfit, Pink Stick Cradle, 7 In.	195.00
Effanbee, Bethany, Bride, Jerusalem	30.00
Effanbee, Bride, Blond, Vinyl, 14 In.	70.00
Effanbee, Bubbles, Composition, Antique Clothes, 18 In.	100.00 to 175.00
Effanbee, Bubbles, Composition, Blond Baby Curls, Bent Arms, 1924, 26 In.	850.00
Effanbee, Bubbles, Toddler, Pink Taffeta Dress, Shoes, Tagged, 16 In.	275.00
Effanbee, Candy Kid, Composition, Blue Sleep Eyes, Molded & Painted Hair, 13 In.	125.00
Effanbee, Candy Kid, Prizefighter Costume, 1946	495.00
Effanbee, Candy Kid, Red & White Clothes, 13 In.	350.00
Effanbee, Cinderella & Prince Charming, Glass Slippers, 1952, 15 In., Pair	650.00
Effanbee, Dimples, Original Clothes	195.00
Effanbee, Dye-Dee Baby, Plastic Head, Rubber Body, Original Clothes, 21 In.	225.00
Effanbee, Girl, Peignoir, Composition, 9 In.	110.00
Effanbee, Honey, 15 In.	250.00
Effanbee, Honey, 16 In.	250.00
Effanbee, Honey Tint Hair, Hair Supplies, Box	950.00
Effanbee, Little Lady, Composition, 14 In.	295.00
Effanbee, Little Lady, Composition, Wrist Tag, Box	325.00
Effanbee, Lovums, Composition, Red Skin Wig, Windup, Honograph, 18 In.	315.00
Effanbee, Mae West, Box	50.00
Effanbee, Patsy Ann, Composition, Tin Sleep Eyes, Painted Hair, 18 In.	185.00
Effanbee, Patsy Baby, In Bassinet, Sleep Eyes, Molded Hair, Bent Limb, 1928, 10 In.	270.00
Effanbee, Patsy Joan, Wrist Bracelet, 16 In.	325.00
Effanbee, Patsy Jr., Sleep Eyes, Wig, 12 In.	130.00
Effanbee, Patsy, Red Dress, Coat & Hat	225.00
Effanbee, Patsy, Sleep Eyes, Pink Outfit, Composition, 14 In.	220.00
Effanbee, Patsyette, Long Dotted-Swiss Dress & Hat, 9 1/2 In.	275.00
Effanbee, Rosemary, Original Dress, 18 In.	225.00
Effanbee, Sugar Plum, Black, Wrist Tag, 1969	52.00
Effanbee, Susie Sunshine, Blonde, Blue Dress, 16 In.	45.00

Effanbee, Sweetie Pie, Flirty Eyes, Caracul Wig, 1942, 17 In. 85.00
Effanbee, Sweetie Pie, Moving Eyes, Composition, Skin Wig, 19 In. 250.00
Effanbee, Tommy Tucker, Flirty Eyes, 20 In. 350.00
Effanbee, W.C. Fields, Box 195.00
Emma Clear, Gibson Girl, Bisque Shoulder Head, Cloth Body, 1944, 19 In. 150.00
Emma Clear, Margaret Rose, Bisque Shoulder Head, Painted Hair, Cloth Body, 24 In.   75.00
F.G., Bebe, Bisque Socket Head, Brown Paperweight Eyes, Ball-Jointed, 15 In. 850.00
F.G., Bisque, Mohair Wig, Silk & Lace Dress, 13 In. 4675.00
Fashion, Bisque Head, All Wood Articulated Body, Original Clothes, 12 In. 5500.00
Fashion, Smiler, Kid Body, Dressed, 15 In. 3995.00
Felix The Cat, Jointed, Arms, Legs, Head & Tail Move, 4 In. .... 265.00 to 310.00
Franz Schmidt, Baby, Breather, 2 Molded Upper Teeth, 13 In. 595.00
Freddie Krueger, Talking, Box .... 45.00 to 50.00
French, Boudoir, Cloth Face, Silk Hair, 20 1/2 In. 225.00
French, Composition, Sleep Eyes, Paper Tongue, Wood & Composition, Nude, 25 In.   95.00
· French, Fashion, Bisque Socket Head, Kid Body, Mohair Wig, Redressed, 17 In. 550.00
French, Fashion, Merry Widow, Gray Eyes, Original Clothes, 16 In. 3800.00
French, Fashion, Paperweight Eyes, Original Clothes, 14 1/2 In. 2200.00
French, Fashion, Woman, Papier-Mache, Black Glass Eyes, Human Wig, 21 In. 6200.00
French, Flirty Eyes, Original Outfit, Celluloid, 20 In. 450.00
Frozen Charlotte, Pink Luster Feet, Dressed, c.1860, Small 165.00
Fulper, Toddler, Bent Limb Body, Swivel Wrists, 17 In. 550.00
Fulper, Toddler, Bisque, 21 In. 750.00
Furga, Mohair Wig, Hard Plastic, Flirty Eye, Clothes, 28 In. 250.00
Furga, Sleep Eyes, Blue & White Dress, Parasol, Box, 12 In. 85.00
G.I. Joe figures are listed in the Toy category
G.K., 1891, Carved Teeth, Long Face, Heirloom Clothes, 19 In. 750.00
Gebruder Heubach dolls are also in this category under Heubach
Gebruder Heubach, 5636, Laughing Child, Glass Sleep Eyes, Mohair Wig, 16 In. 3500.00
Gebruder Heubach, 8192, Bisque, Brown Sleep Eyes, 16 In. 1100.00
Gebruder Heubach, 8192, Sleep Eyes, Composition Flapper Body, 12 In. 490.00
Gebruder Heubach, 8192, Twins, Sleep Eyes, Open Mouth, 8 In., Pair 1200.00
Gebruder Heubach, 9191, Winker, Intaglio Eyes, 7 In. 1350.00
Gebruder Heubach, Girl, Bisque, Molded Shoes, Original Clothes, Box 850.00
Gebruder Heubach, Large Eyes, Replaced Hair, Blue & White Dress, 1910, 31 In. ... 1495.00
Gebruder Koch, Character, Boy, Laughing, Blue Intaglio Eyes, 18 In. 695.00
Georgene, Oriental, Cloth, All Original, 13 In. 75.00
German, Bisque Head, Set Brown Eyes, Composition, Long Curl Wig, 17 In. 450.00
German, Bisque, Turned Head, Smile, Silken Wig, Bustled Gown, 1880s, 14 In. 875.00
German, Child, Bisque, Sleep Eyes, Sonneberg-Type, Composition, 1890, 11 In. 500.00
German, Dressmaker, Paperweight Eyes, Swivel Head, Dressed, 16 1/2 In. 1495.00
German, Papier-Mache Shoulder Head, Cloth Body, Painted Eyes, 16 1/2 In. 175.00
German, Scottish Character, Bisque, Jointed Body, Costume, 1920, 11 In. 2100.00
Gilbert, Man From U.N.C.L.E., Box 125.00
Ginny, Indian Maid, Papoose, Leather Dress, 8 In. 75.00
Ginny, Walker, Painted Lash, All Original 275.00
Golliwog, 1942 .... 65.00
Googly, 173, Toddler Body, Teddy Bear On Sleeve, 16 In. 2750.00
Googly, Biskaloid Head, Barcelona, Spain, 14 In. 895.00
Googly, Bisque, Germany, Tiny 375.00
Googly, Composition, Pink Felt Body, Jointed, Eye Mechanism, 8 1/2 In. 400.00
Googly, Little Bright Eyes, Mask Face, Glass Eyes To Side, Original, 12 1/2 In. 895.00
Gracy Corry, Rockwell Character, Composition, Original Clothes, Crazed, 14 In. 395.00
Greiner, Blond Hair, Blue Eyes, Calico Dress, 22 In. 375.00
Greiner, Dark Blue Eyes, Paper Label, 22 In. 550.00
Greiner, Papier-Mache, Blond Curly Hair, Muslin Body, Leather Arms, 1872, 30 In. .. 850.00
Grizzly Adams, Box, 1978 .... 40.00
Gulliver, Painted Eyes, Deanna Durbin Mold, Wig & Boots, 20 In. 800.00
Gumby, Plush, 15 In. 15.00
Handkerchief, Victorian, Wooden Head, Price Sticker, Neiman-Marcus 20.00
Handwerck, 16 1/2, Brown Sleep Eyes, Human Hair, Clothes, 35 In. 1500.00
Handwerck, 79, Smile, Long Cheeks, Victorian Whites, Shoes, 30 In. 1595.00
Handwerck, 99, Almond Eyes, Ball-Jointed, Antique Clothes, 21 In. 750.00

Handwerck, 99, Bisque, Sleep Eyes, Mohair Wig, Dress & Boots, 32 In. 1450.00
Handwerck, 109, Bisque, Blue Eyes, Brown Wig, Original Dress, 28 In. 1500.00
Handwerck, 109, Child, Jointed Wood & Composition, Sleep Eyes, Nude, 22 In. 325.00
Handwerck, 119, Brown Sleep Eyes, Ball-Jointed, Ethnic Costume, 27 In. 1200.00
Handwerck, 189, Child, Almond-Shaped Eyes, Antique Lawn Dress, 23 In. 950.00
Handwerck, 421, Ball-Jointed, Bisque, Wax Lids, Original Wig, 35 In. 1750.00
Handwerck, Baby Elite, Blue Sleep Eyes, Lashes, Human Hair, Clothes, 17 In. 495.00
Handwerck, Bisque Head, Brown Eyes, Pierced Ears, Human Hair, 1910, 34 In. 1265.00
Handwerck, Bisque Head, Sleep Eyes, Mohair Wig, Composition Body, 22 In. 550.00
Handwerck, Child, Bisque, Brown Eyes, 38 In. 3400.00
Handwerck, Child, Sleep Eyes, Brunette, Ball-Jointed, Silk Dress, 1890, 41 In. 4300.00
Hartman, Bisque, Brown Eyes, Open Mouth, 4 Teeth, Human Hair, 20 In. 375.00
Heebee Shebee, Jointed, Dressed, Stand, 10 1/2 In., Pair 950.00
Hendren, Florodora, Kid Body, 19 In. 225.00
Hendren, Tin Eyes, Mohair Wig, Composition, 19 In. 165.00
Henri Alexandre, Phenix Steiner, Bisque, Blue Paperweight Eyes, 21 In. 4875.00
Hertel Schwab, 136, Bisque, Sleep Eyes, Jointed Body, Dressed, 24 In. 1375.00
Hertel Schwab, 151, Character, Bisque Head, Glass Eyes, Bent Knee, 14 In. 525.00
Hertel Schwab, 152, Baby, 20 In. 675.00
Hertel Schwab, 165, Googly, Sleep Eyes, Watermelon Mouth, Dressed, 12 In. 4100.00
Hertel Schwab, 173, Toddler, Composition Body, 11 In. 3450.00
Hertel Schwab, Baby, Open Close Smile, Molded Tongue, Lace Gown, 12 In. 495.00
Hertel Schwab, Bald Head, Dimples, 12 In. 375.00
Hertel Schwab, Googly, Bisque Head, Smiling Mouth, Bent Limb, c.1914, 16 In. 4400.00
Heubach dolls are also in this category under Gebruder Heubach
Heubach, 302, Ball-Jointed Trunk, Original Dress, 25 In. 750.00
Heubach, 6692, Pouty, Bisque, Fat Cheeks, Intaglio Eyes, 12 In. 1495.00
Heubach, 7054, Character, 2 Teeth, Protruding Ears, Jointed Body, 12 In. 795.00
Heubach, 7602, Bisque, Pouty Character, Intaglio Eyes, Marked, 10 In. 395.00
Heubach, 7788, Coquette, Bisque, Jointed Body, 12 In. 895.00
Heubach, 7851, Singing, Kid Body, Bisque Arms, 18 In. 2495.00
Heubach, 8192, Glass Eyes, Dolly Face, Painted Shoes & Socks, 12 In. 595.00
Heubach, 8550, Character, Bisque Head, Wicker Basket, 3 Outfits, 13 In. 1295.00
Heubach, 9141, Googly, Winker, 5-Piece Body, Dressed 1495.00
Heubach, Baby, Bisque Head, Pouty, Fat Cheeks, Intaglio Eyes, Bent Knee, 12 In. ... 1295.00
Heubach, Bisque, Boy, Lavender Suit, Holding Monkey, 13 In. 375.00
Heubach, Black, Bisque, Painted Hair, Cloth Body, Composition Limbs, 13 In. 1100.00
Heubach, Character, Front Teeth, Protruding Ears, Dressed, 12 In. 795.00
Heubach, Fifi O'Toole, Mechanical, Signed 2800.00
Heubach, Glass Eyes, Dolly Face, 5-Piece Body, Painted Shoes & Socks, 12 In. 595.00
Heubach, Googly, Bisque, Socket Head, Molded Blond Hair, 9 In. 1795.00
Heubach, My Coquette, Bisque, Jointed Body, 12 In. 895.00
Heubach, Pouty, Cloth Body, Composition Arms, Intaglio Eyes, 18 In. 995.00
Heubach, Sanro, Bisque, 24 In. 4500.00
Heubach, Toddler, Bisque, Flirty Eyes, Playsuit, 15 In. 495.00
Heubach, Young Lady, Upswept Hair, Doing Curtsy, Marked, 10 In. 275.00
Heubach Koppelsdorf, 32, Painted Bisque, Blue Glass Sleep Eyes, 12 1/2 In. 250.00
Heubach Koppelsdorf, 267, Blue Sleep Eyes, Human Hair, 15 In. 425.00
Heubach Koppelsdorf, 300, Blue Sleep Eyes, Braids, Ball-Jointed, 10 In. 425.00
Heubach Koppelsdorf, 342, Toddler, Flirty Eyes, 21 In. 850.00
Heubach Koppelsdorf, 444 3/4, Character, Sleep Eyes, Bobbed Wig, 1915, 13 In. 650.00
Heubach Koppelsdorf, Baby, Molded Hair, Intaglio Eyes, 9 In. 375.00
Hilda, Blue Sleep Eyes, Old Clothes, Ges Gesch, 11, 14 In. 3200.00
Hilda Baby, Bisque, Sleep Eyes, Baby Clothes, 18 In. 4700.00
Horsman, Baby Dimples, 18 In. 175.00
Horsman, Belted Short Skirt, Matching Hat, c.1910, 18 In. 275.00
Horsman, Black, Painted Eyes, Cloth Body, Original Clothes, 15 In. 250.00
Horsman, Cindy, Ball Gown, Box, 1950 .... 60.00
Horsman, Dimples, Composition & Cloth, Tagged, 21 In. 325.00
Horsman, Rosebud, Tin Eyes, Original Wig & Underwear, 18 In. 100.00
Horsman, Shirley, 20 In. 350.00
Horsman, Simon Says, Case, 1973 .... 45.00

Horsman, Twins, Pink Dress, Blue Romper, Hat, Satin Pillow, Box, 13 In., Pair 85.00
Hoss, Bonanza, Horse & Accessories, 1966 ....   90.00
Huckleberry Hound, Plush, Tag 50.00
I Love Lucy Baby, Accessories, 1952, Box 375.00
Ideal, Baby Snooks, Composition, Painted Eyes, Hair, Wooden Body, Clothes, 13 In.   85.00
Ideal, Deanna Durbin, Brown Eyes, Human Hair Wig, Original Dress, 21 In. 675.00
Ideal, Dorothy, Tin Man, Lion, Scarecrow, Wizard Of Oz, Boxes, 10 In., 4 Piece 250.00
Ideal, James Bond, Swim Trunks 75.00
Ideal, Joey Stivic, Archie Bunker's Grandson, 1976, 14 In. 40.00
Ideal, Little Honey Moon, Box, 15 In. 185.00
Ideal, Little Lost Baby, 3 Faces, 1968 .... 85.00 to 185.00
Ideal, Magilla Gorilla, Vinyl, Felt, 8 In., Early 1960s 75.00
Ideal, Miss Curity Toni 145.00
Ideal, Miss Revlon, Cherries A La Mode Dress, Tag, 20 In. 145.00
Ideal, Petite Patty Playpal, Original Clothes, 18 In. 150.00
Ideal, Sara Ann, 14 In. 200.00
Ideal, Snow White, Box, 15 In. 1100.00
Ideal, Tammy, The Teenage Doll, 1965, 12 In., Box 45.00
Ideal, Thumbelina, 1971 ....   45.00
Ideal, Tiffany Taylor, Box, 1973 ....   35.00
Ideal, Toddler, Hard Plastic, 15 In. 195.00
Ideal, Wonder Woman, Super Queens Posin' Doll, 1967, 11 1/2 In. 1200.00
Illfelder, Bisque Head, My Sweetheart, Jointed Wood, Composition, 1915, 23 In. 345.00
Incredible Hulk, Action Figure, Poseable, Vinyl, Marvel, 18 In. 25.00
Indian dolls are listed in the Indian category
J.D.K. dolls are also listed in this category under Kestner
J.D.K., 214, Bisque Head, Blue Eyes, Open Mouth, Replaced Wig, Jointed, 23 In. 748.00
J.D.K., 214, Character, Baby Face Curls, Period Clothes, 31 In. 1795.00
J.D.K., 226, Pleated Lacy Gown, Ribbon Inserts, Bonnet, 16 In. 850.00
J.D.K., 237, Toddler, Hilda, 27 In. 4000.00
J.D.K., 243, Baby, Oriental, 13 In. 4500.00
J.D.K., 247, Hilda, Skin Wig, Christening Dress, 20 In. 4200.00
J.D.K., 260/63, Character, Flirty Blue Eyes, Molded Tongue, 1916, 25 In. 1093.00
J.D.K., Baby Jean, 21 In. 1500.00
J.D.K., Boy, Jointed Composition Body, Painted Hair, Set Eyes, 20 In. 750.00
J.D.K., Character, Baby, Blue Glass Eyes, Upper Teeth, Red Mohair Wig, 18 In. 633.00
J.S. Sutton & Sons, Scooby Doo, Stuffed, Illustrated Tag, 1970, 14 In. 60.00
Jane Withers, 15 1/2 In. 950.00
Japanese, Dairi-Bina, Wooden Heads, Brocade Costume, Jeweled Coronet, 8 In., Couple 100.00
Japanese, Dairi-Bina, Wooden Hands & Feet, Padded Robe, Gilt Platform, 6 In. 300.00
Japanese, Gonin-Bayashi, Purple & Red Brocade Robe, Wooden Box, 4 & 5 In., Pr. ..   75.00
Japanese, Shicho, Cross-Legged Man, Black Hair, Aqua Silk Trousers, 4 In. 275.00
Japanese, Shicho, Cross-Legged Man, White Hair, Pink Silk Robe, 4 In. 50.00
Japanese, Yusoku Hina, Black Dots At Forehead, Brocade Costume, Paper Wings, 6 In. 100.00
Japanese, Zuishin, Aged Man & Young Man, Tapestry Costume, Bow & Arrows, 14 In. 300.00
Japanese, Zuishin, Wooden Heads, Enamel Eyes, Brocade Costume, 7 In., Pair 125.00
Jenny Lind, Portrait, Porcelain, Brush Marks, Coiled Bun, Original Clothes, 21 In. 1100.00
Jerri Lee, Blond Caracul Wig, Shirt, Jeans, Boots, 16 In. 295.00
Jerri Lee, Suit, Skin Wig, 16 In. 250.00
Jessica, Flat Top, Translucent Glaze, Cloth Body, Leather Boots, 35 In. 895.00
Julia, Brunette, Bend Knees, Nurse Uniform, Box 75.00
Jullien, Boy, Marked Shoes, Original Wig, 29 In. 4000.00
Jumeau, Bebe, Cork Pate, Replaced Hair, Jointed, 1900, 13 1/4 In. 1265.00
Jumeau, Bebe, Paperweight Eyes, Cork Pate, Wood & Composition Body, 22 In. 2475.00
Jumeau, Bisque Head, Fixed Paperweight Eyes, Wood, Composition, c.1890, 21 In. .. 715.00
Jumeau, Bisque Head, Human Hair, Jointed Wood, Composition, White Dress, 28 In. 1400.00
Jumeau, Bisque, Closed Mouth, Brown Almond-Shaped Eyes, 18 In. 5750.00
Jumeau, Bisque, Closed Mouth, Chunky Body, Long Curls, Sailor Clothes, 28 In. 5500.00
Jumeau, Bisque, Closed Mouth, Paperweight Eyes, France, 15 In. 6700.00
Jumeau, Bisque, Closed Mouth, Signed Costume & Shoes, 10 In. 4750.00
Jumeau, Bisque, Medaille D'Or Paris, Socket Head, 19 In. .... *Illus* 5500.00
Jumeau, Bisque, Open Mouth, Signed Costume & Shoes, 10 In. 3600.00

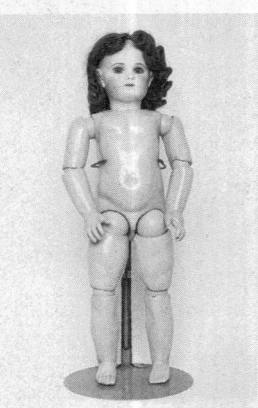

Doll, Jumeau, Bisque, Medaille D'Or Paris,
Socket Head, 19 In.

Doll, Jumeau, Brevette, 19 In.

Doll, Jumeau, Triste, Long Face,
Costume, 29 In.

Doll, Kathe Kruse,
Character, Boy,
Cloth, Box, 17 In.

Doll, Kathe Kruse,
Character, Girl,
Cloth, Box, 17 In.

Jumeau, Bisque, Straight Wrists, Mohair Wig & Pate, Marked Shoes, 20 In. 8700.00
Jumeau, Blue Eyes, Human Hair, Ball-Jointed, 18 In. 1950.00
Jumeau, Blue Sleep Eyes, Ball-Jointed, Human Hair, Clothes, 28 In. 3000.00
Jumeau, Brevette, 19 In. .... *Illus* 10450.00
Jumeau, Child, Bisque Head, Jointed Composition Body, Open Mouth, 24 In. 900.00
Jumeau, Child, Bisque, Human Hair Wig, Glass Eyes, Antique Clothes, 27 In. 550.00
Jumeau, Cloth, Bisque Head & Hands, Original Dress, 19 1/2 In. 5500.00
Jumeau, Fashion, Bisque, Dressed, 14 In. 3200.00
Jumeau, Lady, Portrait Head, Ball-Jointed Body, 19 1/2 In. 5900.00
Jumeau, Luminous Bisque, Paperweight Eyes, Chunky Body, Dress, Bonnet, 25 In. .. 6900.00
Jumeau, Paperweight Eyes, Mohair Wig, 11 In. 7000.00
Jumeau, Paperweight Threaded Eyes, Blue, 8-Ball Body, Exquisite, Bisque, 16 In. 6975.00
Jumeau, Phonograph, Record In Stomach, Key Wind, 25 In. 7350.00
Jumeau, Portrait Bebe, Bisque Head, Paperweight Eyes, 8 Ball-Jointed Body, 20 In. . 5500.00

Jumeau, Portrait, Blond Mohair Wig, Paperweight Eyes, Twist Wrists, 14 In. 3800.00
Jumeau, Portrait, Blue Almond Eyes, Ball-Jointed, 11 1/4 In. 6500.00
Jumeau, Portrait, Long Curls, Dressed, 15 In. 3500.00
Jumeau, Stiff Wrist Body, Applied Ears, Boots, Silk Drop-Waist Dress, 20 In. 2200.00
Jumeau, Toddler Body, Laughing, Blue Eyes, Lashes, Mohair Wig, 14 In. 1595.00
Jumeau, Triste, Long Face, Costume, 29 In. .... *Illus* 17000.00
Juro, Dick Clark, 27 In. 450.00
Juro, Pinkie Lee, Molded Hat, 23 1/2 In. 395.00
Just Me, Bisque, Blue Googly Eyes, 9 In. 1600.00
Just Me, Bisque, Mohair Wig, Blue Flirty Eyes, Pompom Shoes, Bonnet, 8 In. 1600.00
Jutta, Character Baby, Movable Tongue, Knitted Outfit, 1914, 19 In. 775.00
K * R, 36, Child, Blue Sleep Eyes, Blond, Composition, Wooden Ball-Jointed, 14 In. 1100.00
K * R, 100, Baby, Bent-Knee Body, Christening Gown, 12 In. 575.00
K * R, 100, Character Boy, Jointed Composition Body, Shirt, Red Pants, 18 In. 750.00
K * R, 101, Marie, Pouty Expression, Painted Eyes, Braided Mohair Wig, 9 In. 2375.00
K * R, 112, Elsa, Character, Painted Eyes, Open Close Mouth, Composition, 7 In. 3500.00
K * R, 114, Gretchen, 11 In. 3500.00
K * R, 114, Gretchen, Bisque, Pouty Mouth, Braids, Crocheted Dress, 11 In. 3000.00
K * R, 114, Hans, Character, Pouty, Ball-Jointed, Mohair Wig, 8 In. 1750.00
K * R, 114/46, Sleep Eyes, Dimpled, Curly Wig, Wood, Composition, c.1909, 16 In. 7975.00
K * R, 115A, Toddler, Pouty, Layered Costume, 16 In. .... 5875.00 to 6875.00
K * R, 117, Mein Leibling, Bisque, Old Shoes, 22 In. 6900.00
K * R, 117/N, Mein Leibling, Flirty Sleep Eyes, Lashes, 28 In. 2500.00
K * R, 117A, Mein Leibling, Character Child, Antique Clothes, 32 In. 7500.00
K * R, 121, Baby, Dimples, All Original, 15 In. 1275.00
K * R, 121, Jointed Toddler Body, Blue Eyes, Chubby Cheeks, 27 1/2 In. 2300.00
K * R, 121, Toddler Body, Fully Jointed, 27 In. 2950.00
K * R, 121, Toddler, Bisque, Sleep Eyes, Original Wig, Jointed, 19 In. 2150.00
K * R, 121, Toddler, Jointed, Original Clothes 1450.00
K * R, 121/26, Boudoir, Manuelita, Flamenco-Style Dress, 1920s, 24 1/2 In. 1760.00
K * R, 122, Baby, Bisque, Dimples, Tongue, Blue Eyes, Chunky Body, Gown, 25 In. .. 1795.00
K * R, 122, Baby, Blond Wig, Antique Clothing, 22 In. 1650.00
K * R, 122, Toddler, Fully Jointed, Dimples, Blue Eyes, 16 In. 2000.00
K * R, 126, Baby, Chubby, Original Wig 895.00
K * R, 126, Child, Bisque, 28 In. 1200.00
K * R, 126, Toddler Body, 9 In. 850.00
K * R, 126, Toddler, Brown Sleep Eyes, Human Hair Wig, 19 In. 895.00
K * R, 126, Toddler, Character, Voice Mechanism, Open Mouth, Jointed, 13 1/2 In. ... 485.00
K * R, 126, Toddler, Flirty Eyes, Wobble Tongue, 23 In. 1400.00
K * R, 192, Sleep Eyes, Bisque, Human Hair Wig, Spring Strung Body, 30 In. 2200.00
K * R, 225, Toddler, Blue Eyes, 16 In. 4500.00
K * R, 406, Girl, Original Outfit, Celluloid, Ball-Jointed Body, 21 In. 375.00
K * R, Baby, Bisque, Brown Eyes, Bent Knee, 14 In. 995.00
K * R, Baby, Bisque, Sleep Eyes, Original Gown, 26 In. 1300.00
K * R, Black Child, In Trunk, Extra Garments, Straw Hat, Blue Shoes, 21 In. 1850.00
K * R, Child, Bisque Head, Sleep Eyes, Composition, Ball-Jointed, 33 In. 1600.00
K * R, Child, Bisque, Gray Sleep Eyes, Pleated Dress, Silk Sash, 20 In. 895.00
K * R, Chunky Body, Blue Sleep Eyes, Human Hair Wig, Dressed, 36 In. 2300.00
K * R, Elise, All Original, 9 In. 6900.00
K * R, Girl, Blue Sleep Eyes, Jointed Wood & Composition, No Wig, Nude, 20 In. ... 425.00
K * R, Gretchen, Pouty, Original Wig & Clothes, 11 In. 2875.00
K * R, Hans, Bisque, Socket Head, Glass Eyes, Ball-Jointed Body, 1912, 17 In. 11000.00
K * R, Hans, Scotch Outfit, 18 In. 5460.00
K * R, Mein Leibling, Bisque, Glass Sleep Eyes, Composition, Costume, 23 In. 8800.00
K * R, Mein Leibling, Bisque, Sleep Eyes, Blond, Ball-Jointed, 15 In. 7200.00
K * R, Toddler, 5 Piece Body, 12 1/2 In. 225.00
Kaiser, Child, Jointed Child Body, Painted Hair, 16 In. 1250.00
Kamkin, Child, Cloth, Dress, Undies, Coat, Leatherette Shoes, 20 In. 1600.00
Kamkin, Child, Original Wig, Vintage Attire, 20 In. 1600.00
Kathe Kruse, 8, Swivel Head, 20 In. 1300.00
Kathe Kruse, Character, Boy, Cloth, Box, 17 In. .... *Illus* 4000.00
Kathe Kruse, Character, Girl, Cloth, Box, 17 In. .... *Illus* 4600.00

*Doll, Kestner, Character, Boy, Bisque Head,
Austrian Clothes, 18 In.*

*Doll, Lenci, Googly Eyes,
Cloth Clothes*

*Left to Right: Doll, Skookum, Squaw & Papoose,
Beadwork, Original Clothes, 1920, 15 In.; Doll,
Skookum, Chief, Original Clothes, 1920, 13 In.*

Doll, Uncle Sam, Cloth, 1900, 15 In.

Kathe Kruse, Cloth, 6456, Original Clothes, Hand-Knitted Accessories, 16 In. 660.00
Kathe Kruse, Cloth, Painted Brown Hair & Eyes, F635, 17 In. 440.00
Kathe Kruse, Girl, Painted Hair & Face, Wide Hips, Original Dress, Style 1, 17 In. . 3500.00
Kathe Kruse, Swivel Head, Blond Mohair Wig, Canvas Body & Limbs, 20 In. 270.00
Keebler, Elf, 1981, 26 In. 40.00
Kelley, Quick Curl, Green & White Polka-Dot Dress, Box 75.00
Kenner, Alien, Spring-Action Mouth, 20th Century Fox, 1979, 7 x 19 x 8 In. 40.00
Kenner, Terminator, Talking, 12 In. 45.00
Kestner dolls are also in this category under J.D.K.
Kestner, 11, Kid Body, 25 In. 550.00
Kestner, 143, Ball-Jointed, Antique Clothing, 19 In. 1500.00
Kestner, 143, Brown Sleep Eyes, Ball-Jointed Body, Old Clothes, 14 In. 950.00
Kestner, 143, Brown Sleep Eyes, Ball-Jointed, Square Teeth, Clothes, 9 In. 850.00
Kestner, 143, Brown Sleep Eyes, Bisque, 18 In. 1395.00

Kestner, 143, Brown Sleep Eyes, Bowed Upper Lip, Dimpled Chin, 24 In. 2950.00
Kestner, 143, Toddler, Square Teeth, Ball-Jointed, 13 1/2 In. 950.00
Kestner, 147, Blue Sleep Eyes, Bisque, Kid Riveted Body, 27 1/2 In. 895.00
Kestner, 154, 22 In. 425.00
Kestner, 154, Bisque, All Original, 19 In. 750.00
Kestner, 154, Bisque, Period Dress, 23 In. 595.00
Kestner, 154, Human Hair Wig, Kid Arms, Body, Jointed At Hips, 25 In. 595.00
Kestner, 154, Original Wig & Dress, 1892, 28 In. 950.00
Kestner, 162, Bisque, Bosomed Body, Gibson Blond Wig, Walking Suit, 22 In. 2500.00
Kestner, 162, Bisque, Stiff Wrists, Leather Shoes, Dress, Straw Hat, 16 In. 1595.00
Kestner, 164, Ball-Jointed Body, Blue Sleep Eyes, Antique Clothes, 29 In. 1000.00
Kestner, 164, Ball-Jointed, Brown Sleep Eyes, Brown Wig 1490.00
Kestner, 168, Child, Bisque, Original Wig & Dress, Marked, 18 1/2 In. 875.00
Kestner, 171, Child, Bisque Head, Human Hair, Jointed Wood, Composition, 24 In. .. 270.00
Kestner, 171, Daisy, Ball-Jointed, Cream Silk Dress, Human Hair Wig, 27 In. 1000.00
Kestner, 171, Daisy, Bisque, Human Hair Wig, Old Dress, Marked, 31 In. 1995.00
Kestner, 171, Daisy, Sleep Eyes, Bisque, Antique Dress & Shoes, 25 In. 1195.00
Kestner, 186, Ball-Jointed, Composition Body, Low-Waisted Dress, 14 In. 695.00
Kestner, 208, Bisque, Sleep Eye, Original Clothes, 7 1/2 In. 500.00
Kestner, 211, Character, Sleep Eyes, Burly Wig, 27 In. 825.00
Kestner, 221, Googly Eyes, Watermelon Mouth, Jointed Composition Body, 12 In. ... 3800.00
Kestner, 257, Baby, Bisque, Brown Sleep Eyes, Tremble Tongue, 23 In. 1350.00
Kestner, 257, Ball-Jointed Body, Gray-Green Eyes, 26 In. 195.00
Kestner, 257/57, Bisque Head, Sleep Eyes, 2 Teeth, Composition, 1920, 22 In. 990.00
Kestner, 602, Bisque, Blue Sleep Eyes, Swivel Head, 6 In. 645.00
Kestner, 1143, Bisque, Brown Sleep Eyes, Bowed Upper Lip, 24 In. 2750.00
Kestner, Bisque, Blue Sleep Eyes, Open Mouth, Kid Body & Legs, 26 In. 440.00
Kestner, Bisque, Child, Closed Mouth, Pensive Expression 3800.00
Kestner, Bisque, Child, Light Complexion, Closed Mouth, 20 In. 3750.00
Kestner, Bisque, Open Mouth, Sleep Eyes, Kid Body, Jointed, 19 In. 335.00
Kestner, Bisque, Turned Head, Teeth, Sleep Eyes, Linen Dress, 1880s, 22 In. 850.00
Kestner, Character, Boy, Bisque Head, Austrian Clothes, 18 In. .... *Illus* 3700.00
Kestner, Child, Closed Mouth, 15 In. 2600.00
Kestner, Child, Open Mouth, Sleep Eyes, Dress & Underwear, Parasol, 26 In. 1350.00
Kestner, Gibson Girl, Original Wig & Clothes, 20 In. 4000.00
Kestner, Googly Eyes, Bisque Socket Head, Mohair Wig, Composition, 12 In. 4000.00
Kestner, Hilda, Baby, Blond Mohair, Antique Gown, 19 In. 5700.00
Kestner, L-15, Bisque, Blue Sleep Eyes, Original Wig & Pate, Old Shoes, 29 In. 1175.00
Kestner, Oily Sheen, Upturned Paperweight Eyes, Vintage Clothes, 18 In. 650.00
Kestner, Satin Bisque, Platinum Wig, Kid Body, Leather Shoes, Dressed, 17 In. 950.00
Kestner, Turned Head, Brown Eyes, Square, Kid Body, Human Hair, 24 In. 950.00
Kestner, XII, Pouty, Brown Eyes, Straight Wrists, 19 In. 3495.00
Kewpie dolls are listed in the Kewpie category
Keystone Cop, Papier-Mache, Wooden Base, Movable Arms, 5 In., 5 Piece 375.00
Kley & Hahn, 167-17, Character, Bisque, Blue Sleep Eyes, Vibrating Tongue 1100.00
Kley & Hahn, 546, Schoolgirl Clothes, 16 In. 5700.00
Kley & Hahn, Dad, 16 In. 1200.00
Kley & Hahn, Son, 10 1/2 In. 850.00
Kley & Hahn, Walker, Bisque, Sleep Eyes, 4 Teeth, Ball-Jointed, 32 In. 950.00
Kley & Hahn, Walker, Bisque, Sleep Eyes, Human Hair Wig, 28 In. 1100.00
Kling, 220, Wide Eyes, Heirloom Clothes, 33 In. 995.00
Kling, Boy, Bisque Arms, Molded Hair, Feathered Brows, 21 In. 590.00
Kling, Pink Luster Body, 27 In. 595.00
Kling, Wavy Hair, Happy Look, 25 In. 695.00
Knickerbocker, Andy, 31 In. 60.00
Knickerbocker, Baba Looey, Vinyl Head, 1959, 7 1/2 x 14 In. 60.00
Knickerbocker, Dopey, Accurately Costumed, 9 In. 198.00
Knickerbocker, Huckleberry Hound, 1959 .... 35.00
Knickerbocker, Jiminy Cricket, Movable Head, 10 In. 500.00
Knickerbocker, Little Miss Muffet, Jointed Legs 125.00
Knickerbocker, Raggedy Andy, 15 1/2 In. 20.00
Knickerbocker, Raggedy Andy, 1960s, 19 In. 80.00
Knickerbocker, Raggedy Andy, 31 In. 60.00

Knickerbocker, Raggedy Ann & Andy, 36 In., Pair 215.00
Knickerbocker, Raggedy Ann, 23 In. 50.00
Knickerbocker, Raggedy Ann, 42 In. 125.00
Knickerbocker, Raggedy Ann, Clothes Bag 95.00
Knit, Blue Knit Shirt, Brown Striped Pants, Red Cap, 19th Century, 17 In. 750.00
Kohner, Puppet, Casper The Friendly Ghost, Push Button 25.00
Konig & Wernicke, Blue Glass Flirty Eyes, Composition, 16 In. 250.00
Konig & Wernicke, Child, Painted Bisque, Sleep Eyes, Jointed, Dressed, 16 In. 225.00
Konig & Wernicke, Flirty, Tremble Tongue, Breather Nostrils, Old Clothes, 27 In. ... 1750.00
Koppelsdorf, 312, Child, Auburn Mohair Wig, Socks & Shoes, 24 In. 775.00
Krauss, Bisque Head, Jointed, Teeth, Sleep Eyes, Composition Body, 28 In. 385.00
Krazy Kat, Cloth, Stuffed, 1915 .... 1297.00
Kreuger, Baby, Molded Face, Cloth, Original Clothes, New York, 12 In. 125.00
Lady, China, Glazed Arms, Period Crepe Silk, 32 In. 795.00
Laurel & Hardy, Original Clothes, 20 In., Pair 75.00
Lawton, Shirley Temple 750.00
Leather, Stuffed, Molded Features, Black Painted Eyes & Hair, 12 In. 99.00
Lenci, 109, Patchwork Felt Outfit, 22 In. 775.00
Lenci, African Man, Sword & Shield, 17 In. 1850.00
Lenci, Alice, Felt, Box 250.00
Lenci, Boy, Sideburns, 3-Piece Suit, Leggings & Hat, 14 In. 895.00
Lenci, Child, Character Face, All Original, 18 In. 1250.00
Lenci, Child, Felt, Painted Brown Eyes, Jodhpurs, 1920-1930, 21 1/2 In. 978.00
Lenci, Clown, Tags, 9 In. 325.00
Lenci, Googly Eyes, Cloth Clothes .... *Illus* 6800.00
Lenci, Jackie Coogan, Original Clothes, 19 In. 2200.00
Lenci, Lucia, Felt Chickens On Skirt, Holding Basket Of Oranges, 14 In. 750.00
Lenci, Molded Felt Face, Human Hair Wig, Checked Pink & White Dress, 20 In. 200.00
Lenci, Monk, Felt Robe, Rope Belt, Red Hair, 16 In. 2000.00
Lenci, Schoolgirl, Book Bag, Box, 9 In. .... 950.00 to 1650.00
Lenci, Sonia, Peasant, Open Mouth, Felt Pinafore, Jacket, 1920s, 26 1/2 In. 2530.00
Li'l Abner, Baby Barry Toy Co., 18 In. 125.00
Limoges, Bisque Head, Open Mouth, Blond Curls, Print Dress, 19 In. 595.00
Limoges, Character, Caprice, Open Close Mouth, 27 In. 2000.00
Little Lulu, Cloth 175.00
Little Red Riding Hood, Vinyl Plastic, Movable, Fairyland Toys, 1950s, 11 In. 40.00
Liza, Black Money, Cabaret Clothes, 27 In. 2500.00
Lurch, Addams Family 95.00
Madame Alexander, Agatha, Auburn Hair, Blue Eyes, Lavender Dress, Box, 21 In. . 80.00
Madame Alexander, Alice In Wonderland, Cloth, 1930s, 20 In. 295.00
Madame Alexander, Alice In Wonderland, Margaret, 1948 .... 500.00
Madame Alexander, Alice, Storyland, Blond Hair, Blue & White Clothes, Box, 8 In. 30.00
Madame Alexander, Amy, Walker, Blond, 8 In. 75.00
Madame Alexander, Baby Brother 50.00
Madame Alexander, Baby Brother, 6550, Box, 21 In. 135.00
Madame Alexander, Baby Genius, Composition, Tagged, 21 In. 350.00
Madame Alexander, Ballerina, All Original, 1964, 16 In. 325.00
Madame Alexander, Beth, Little Women, 1956, 15 In. 225.00
Madame Alexander, Betty, Flirty Eyes, 30 In. 425.00
Madame Alexander, Bolivia, Bent-Knee Walker, Wrist Tag 400.00
Madame Alexander, Cinderella, Blue Ball Gown, Crown, 14 In. 60.00
Madame Alexander, Cinderella, Hard Plastic, Original Gown, 17 In. 275.00
Madame Alexander, Cinderella, Pink Ball Gown, Box 75.00
Madame Alexander, Cissette Daisy, Yellow Dress, Lace Overlay, Hat, Box, 9 In. 30.00
Madame Alexander, Cissette Mary Rose, Bride, Bridal Wreath Gown, 1958 .... 265.00
Madame Alexander, Cissette Melinda, Plastic, Jointed, Lace Dress, 10 In. 200.00
Madame Alexander, Cissy, Pink Long-Torso Gown 495.00
Madame Alexander, Cissy, Queen Elizabeth, White Brocade, Blue Sash, 1955 .... 450.00
Madame Alexander, Confederate Soldier, Blond, Uniform, Gold Trim, Box, 12 In. .. 35.00
Madame Alexander, Croquet Set, Queen Of Hearts, Flamingo & Hedgehog 450.00
Madame Alexander, Davy Crockett, Hard Plastic, 1955, 8 In. 650.00
Madame Alexander, Elise Bride, Box 130.00
Madame Alexander, Eliza, Peacock Blue Jacket, Multicolored Skirt, 14 In. 45.00

Madame Alexander, Fairy Godmother, 14 In. 125.00
Madame Alexander, Fairy Princess, 15 In. 600.00
Madame Alexander, Fairy Queen, Composition, Box, 14 In. 250.00
Madame Alexander, Funny, Cloth, Box 90.00
Madame Alexander, Ginny, Walker, Blond Braids, 7 1/2 In. 62.00
Madame Alexander, Goldilocks, Blond Ponytails, Plaid Dress, Apron, Box, 14 In. ... 40.00
Madame Alexander, Goya, Black Hair, Brown Eyes, Pink, Black Lace, Box, 21 In. . 110.00
Madame Alexander, Hansel & Gretel, Bent Knee, 8 In., Pair .... 125.00 to 250.00
Madame Alexander, Hawaii, 1962 .... 375.00
Madame Alexander, Indian, Bent-Knee Walker, Wrist Tag, 1965 .... 225.00
Madame Alexander, Irish, 8 In. 60.00
Madame Alexander, Jackie Kennedy, Yellow Taffeta Dress, Cape, Box, 14 In. 55.00
Madame Alexander, Jeannie Walker, Composition, 13 1/2 In. 450.00
Madame Alexander, Jenny Lind, 1970, 21 In. 1600.00
Madame Alexander, Jo, Little Women, All Original, Hat Box, 1950s 295.00
Madame Alexander, Kathy, Pigtails, Green & Pink Pinafore, 1950s, 22 In. 675.00
Madame Alexander, Lissy, 1957 .... 200.00
Madame Alexander, Little Bo Peep, 8 In. 32.00
Madame Alexander, Little Genius, Original Clothes, 8 In. 320.00
Madame Alexander, Little Genius, Plastic Head, Vinyl Body, Clothes, 7 1/2 In. 195.00
Madame Alexander, Little Shaver, Tagged Dress 85.00
Madame Alexander, Little Women Set, Bent Knee, 8 In., 4 Piece 115.00
Madame Alexander, Little Women, Rosy Cheeks, Box, 6 Piece 390.00
Madame Alexander, Maggie, Walker, Coat, Hat, Shoes & Socks, 18 In. 200.00
Madame Alexander, Mary, Mary, 8 In. 32.00
Madame Alexander, McGuffey Ana, 20 In. .... 140.00 to 550.00
Madame Alexander, McGuffey Baby, 5266, Box, 20 In. 135.00
Madame Alexander, Meg, Little Women, 1956, 15 In. 225.00
Madame Alexander, Melanie, Blond Hair, Blue Eyes, White Dress, Box, 21 In. 95.00
Madame Alexander, Mimi, Box 70.00
Madame Alexander, Morisot 285.00
Madame Alexander, Morocco, Bent Knee 350.00
Madame Alexander, Napoleon, 12 In. 65.00
Madame Alexander, Peter Pan Set, Wrist Tag, Box, 4 Piece 710.00
Madame Alexander, Polish, Bent-Knee Walker, Wrist Tag, Box 200.00
Madame Alexander, Princess Margaret Rose, Composition, 18 In. 450.00
Madame Alexander, Priscilla, Bent-Knee Walker, Wrist Tag, 1966 .... 485.00
Madame Alexander, Scarlett O'Hara, 1969, 10 In. 195.00
Madame Alexander, Scarlett O'Hara, 1986, Box 125.00
Madame Alexander, Scarlett O'Hara, Green Taffeta, 12 In. 55.00
Madame Alexander, Scarlett O'Hara, Original Clothes, 15 In. 695.00
Madame Alexander, Scarlett O'Hara, Plastic, Bent-Knee, Print Dress, 1971, 8 In. 350.00
Madame Alexander, Scarlett O'Hara, Red Velvet Dress, Coat & Hat, 18 In. 350.00
Madame Alexander, Scarlett O'Hara, White Ruffles, 8 In. 65.00
Madame Alexander, Sergeant, Box 65.00
Madame Alexander, Sleeping Beauty, Original Clothes, 13 In. 35.00
Madame Alexander, Sleeping Beauty, Walt Disney Edition, 1972, 10 In. 425.00
Madame Alexander, Sonja Henie, Composition, 5-Piece Body, 1940, 18 In. 1000.00
Madame Alexander, Sonja Henie, Composition, Sleep Eyes, Ballerina Dress, 13 In. 155.00
Madame Alexander, Spanish, Bent-Knee Walker, Wrist Tag 200.00
Madame Alexander, Sweet Sue, Hard Plastic, 17 In. 40.00
Madame Alexander, Sweet Tears, Pink Dress & Panties, Layette, 14 In. 40.00
Madame Alexander, Thumbelina, 20 In. 85.00
Madame Alexander, Trapeze Artist, Red Lame Clothes, Cape, Box, 10 In. 45.00
Madame Alexander, Walker, Straight Leg, Panties, Shoes & Socks, 8 In. 195.00
Madame Alexander, Welcome Home Boy, Camouflage Clothes, Blond, Box, 8 In. ... 35.00
Mammy Yokum, Al Capp, 1940s, Box 250.00
Marilyn Monroe, Musical, Plays Diamonds Are Girl's Best Friend, 8 1/2 In. 50.00
Marilyn Monroe, Tri Star, 11 1/2 In. 95.00
Marionette, Black, Civil War Officer, Cloth Body, Uniform, 1900, 25 In. 800.00
Marionette, Dagwood Bumstead, Hazelle, c.1940, Box 295.00
Marionette, Jack & Jill, Hand-Painted, Instructions, Hazelle, 1950s, Box, Pair 325.00
Marionette, Soldier, In Armor, 19th Century, Continental, 44 In. 935.00

Mary Hartline, Character, Sleep Eyes, Original Clothes, 7 3/4 In. 55.00
Mary Hartline, Skater, Blue Eyes, 15 In. 250.00
Mary Hoyer, Long Gown, Umbrella 375.00
Mary Hoyer, Toddler, Vinyl 150.00
Mattel, Barbie, American Girl 185.00
Mattel, Barbie, Benefit Ball 40.00
Mattel, Barbie, Blond Ponytail, Evening Splendor 225.00
Mattel, Barbie, Blond, Lime Green, Pink & Black Swimsuit, Box 35.00
Mattel, Barbie, Blond, Swimsuit, Glasses, Earrings, Box 335.00
Mattel, Barbie, Blue Rhapsody, Porcelain 850.00
Mattel, Barbie, Bride, Porcelain 450.00
Mattel, Barbie, Brunet Ponytail, 1962, Box 295.00
Mattel, Barbie, Brunet Ponytail, 2nd Issue, 1959, Box 5175.00
Mattel, Barbie, Brunet, Bend Knees, Original Swimsuit & Net Cover 53.00
Mattel, Barbie, Bubble Cut, Blond, 1962, Box .... 140.00 to 175.00
Mattel, Barbie, Bubble Cut, Case, Clothes 95.00
Mattel, Barbie, Bubble Cut, Titian, Red Swimsuit 25.00
Mattel, Barbie, Color 'n Curl, Box 550.00
Mattel, Barbie, Dark Brunet, Hot Pink Bow, Box 359.00
Mattel, Barbie, Empress Bride 160.00
Mattel, Barbie, Enchanted Evening, 10 In. 65.00
Mattel, Barbie, First Holiday, Red Dress, Box 275.00
Mattel, Barbie, Happy Holiday, USA, 1988 .... 450.00 to 550.00
Mattel, Barbie, Mardi Gras 60.00
Mattel, Barbie, Mardi Gras, Blond, Purse, Hat, Shoes, Mask & Stand, Box 65.00
Mattel, Barbie, No. 2, Box 200.00
Mattel, Barbie, No. 2, Ponytail 2450.00
Mattel, Barbie, No. 3, Swimsuit, Shoes 400.00
Mattel, Barbie, No. 5, Box 275.00
Mattel, Barbie, No. 6, Ponytail 300.00
Mattel, Barbie, Poodle Parade Dress 475.00
Mattel, Barbie, Silken Flame 160.00
Mattel, Barbie, Solo In Spotlight 135.00
Mattel, Barbie, Sophisticated Lady 125.00
Mattel, Barbie, Sun Gold, Box, 1983 .... 20.00
Mattel, Barbie, Swirl Ponytail 300.00
Mattel, Barbie, Swirl Ponytail, Blond, Box 225.00
Mattel, Barbie, Talking, 1970 .... 46.00
Mattel, Barbie, Transitional Ponytail 800.00
Mattel, Barbie, Twist 'n' Turn, Light Brown, 1966, Box 300.00
Mattel, Cat In The Hat, Talks, Pull-String, Cloth, Plastic Head, 1970, 10 In. 90.00
Mattel, Chatty Cathy, Original Dress, Mute, Box 125.00
Mattel, Chatty Cathy, Talks 100.00
Mattel, Cheerful Tearful 16.00
Mattel, Christie Brinkley, Accessories, Box, 1989, 12 In. 22.00
Mattel, Dancerina, 1972 .... 24.00
Mattel, Donny Osmond, Box, 1976 .... 22.00
Mattel, Dr. Doolittle, Talking, 1964, Box 110.00
Mattel, Ken, Blond Crewcut, Pak Jacket, Pants, Shoes & Socks 50.00
Mattel, Ken, Blond Flocked Hair, Pak Clothes 58.00
Mattel, Ken, Blond, Flocked Hair 40.00
Mattel, Ken, Brunet, Dinner Date Clothes 58.00
Mattel, Ken, Carrying Case, 12 Outfits & Accessories, 1960 .... 150.00
Mattel, Ken, Summer Suit, 1968 .... 25.00
Mattel, Midge, 2-Piece Swimsuit, Curly Blond Hair, Stand, Shoes, Box, 1963 .... 110.00
Mattel, Midge, 30th Anniversary, Porcelain 198.00
Mattel, Midge, Bendable Legs, Box, 1965 .... 400.00
Mattel, Midge, Red Hair, 1963, Box 100.00
Mattel, Mork & Mindy, Box 65.00
Mattel, Skipper, Straight Leg, Blond, Box 110.00
Mattel, Wayne Gretzky, Vinyl, Box, 12 In. 200.00
McCelland, Tommy The Clown 50.00
Mego, Cyrl Dragon, Box, 12 1/4 In. 20.00

Mego, Diana Ross, 1970s, 12 In. 55.00
Mego, Good Witch From Wizard Of Oz, 1974, Box 45.00
Mego, Muhammad Ali 15.00
Mego, Toni Tennille, Box, 12 1/4 In. 20.00
Mego, Wonder Woman, Superhero, Bendable, 1970s 100.00
Michael Jackson, Thriller Outfit, Box 35.00
Mignonette, Swivel Head, Kid-Lined Bisque Body, Blond, Jointed, 7 1/2 In. 1700.00
Milliner's Model, Wooden Arms & Legs, Original Costume, 10 In. 875.00
Minerva, Baby, Bent Limb, Black Painted Eyes, Celluloid, 3 In. 50.00
Minerva, Bent Limb, Blue Painted Eyes, Celluloid, 6 In. 65.00
Minerva, Blue Painted Eyes, Celluloid, 12 In. 95.00
Montanari, Baby, Wax, Rooted Hair, Glass Eyes, Original Clothes, 23 In. 1500.00
Montanari, Wax, Original Clothes & Shoes, 24 In. 2600.00
Morimura, Baby, Blue Sleep Eyes, Mohair Wig, Bent Limb, Baby Dress, 20 In. 275.00
Motchman, Baby, Wax, Papier-Mache, Glass Eyes, Mid-19th Century, 11 In. 600.00
Mutt & Jeff, Composition, Ball-Jointed, Felt Cloth, 8 In. 550.00
Nancy Ann, Storybook, Miss Muffet 52.00
Napoleon Solo, Badge, Envelope 235.00
Native Girl, 16 In. 150.00
New Born Babe, Crier, 17-In. Gown, 8 In. 450.00
Nippon, Baby, Bisque Socket Head, Brown Sleep Eyes, No Wig, Nude, 13 In. 125.00
Nippon, Baby, Bisque Socket Head, Open Mouth, Bent Limb, Antique Dress, 21 In. .. 250.00
Nippon, Baby, Hilda, Blue Sleep Eyes, 19 In. 895.00
Nippon, Boy, Blue & White Swimsuit, Bisque, 55, 3 3/4 In. 125.00
Oriental, Intricate Hair Style, Marked Kestner Body, 13 1/2 In. 1700.00
Otto Reinicke, Baby, 14 In. 350.00
Paper dolls are listed in their own category
Papier-Mache, Blond Molded Curls, Original Clothes & Boots, 28 In. 1500.00
Papier-Mache, Florodora Body, 23 In. 115.00
Papier-Mache, Glass Eyes, Closed Mouth, Skin Wig, Cloth Body, Rose Dress, 14 In. 45.00
Papier-Mache, Jester, Set Eyes, Ball-Jointed Body, 27 In. 650.00
Papier-Mache, Kid Body, French Moroccan Costume, 15 In. 1100.00
Papier-Mache, Lady, Kid Body, Wooden Limbs, 1840s, 12 In. 330.00
Papier-Mache, Molded Curls, Fancy Hairdo, 27 In. 1500.00
Papier-Mache, Santa, Cloth, Felt Outfit, Rabbit Fur Beard, Germany, 9 1/2 In. 522.00
Papier-Mache, Silk Gown, Hoop, France, 1840s, 22 In. 2500.00
Pappy Yokum, Baby Barry Co., 1950s, 13 In. 225.00
Parian, Blue Painted Eyes, Elaborate Hairdo, Silk Taffeta Dress, 1850s, 13 In. 500.00
Parian, Cloth Body, Bisque Head & Arms, 23 In. 695.00
Parian, Hair Ornaments, Snood, Leather Body, Underwear, 12 In. 595.00
Parian, Soldier Boy, 17 In. 475.00
Pebbles, Flintstones, 1961, 15 In. 48.00
Pee Wee Herman 30.00
Peter Scherf, Bisque, Kid Body, 18 In. 195.00
Phoenix, Baby, Composition, Blue Eyes, 23 In. 4500.00
Pierotti, Blond Mohair Wig, Blue Eyes, Layette, Hand Signed, 18 In. 1900.00
Pierotti, Wax, Fashion, Blond Mohair Wig, Blue Eyes, 15 1/2 In. 1250.00
Pincushion dolls are listed in their own category
Play Doll, Flagg Flexible, Male Ballet Dancer, Box, 1940s 10.00
Pocketbook, Heidi 18.00
Pocketbook, Spunky 18.00
Poor Pitiful Pearl, Horsman, 1963, 11 In. 35.00
Poor Pitiful Pearl, Horsman, 1963, 17 In. 45.00
Poor Pitiful Pearl, Sleep Eyes, Long Hair, 17 In. 65.00
Puppet, Beany & Cecil, Dishonest John, 1962 .... 125.00
Puppet, Bugs Bunny, Push Button, Jointed, Mechanical, Kohner, 1964, 3 In. 24.00
Puppet, Carved Wood, Cloth, Folk Art Type, New York, 9 In. 135.00
Puppet, Charlie Brown & Lucy, Finger, Pair 8.00
Puppet, Danny O'Day, Ventriloquist, Records 85.00
Puppet, Face, Dick Tracy 75.00
Puppet, Fred Flintstone, Push Button, Jointed, Mechanical, Kohner, 1964, 3 In. 24.00
Puppet, Hamburglar, McDonald's, Plastic, 1979 .... 5.00
Puppet, Hand, Bamm-Bamm, Ideal, 1963, 12 In. 39.00

Puppet, Hand, Barney Google, Gund, 1960s 30.00
Puppet, Hand, Cat, Steiff 45.00
Puppet, Hand, Cookie Monster, Sesame Street, 1969, 12 In. 24.00
Puppet, Hand, Curly, 3 Stooges, Cloth Body, 1950-1960, 10 In. 68.00
Puppet, Hand, Dr. Doolittle, Talking, Mattel, 1967 .... 40.00
Puppet, Hand, Jimmy Carter, 1970s 20.00
Puppet, Hand, Mr. Ed, Talking, Mattel, 1962 .... 65.00
Puppet, Hand, Olive Oyl, Vinyl Head, Rooted Hair 25.00
Puppet, Hand, Oscar The Grouch, Sesame Street, 1969, 12 In. 29.00
Puppet, Hand, Porky Pig, Talking, Pull String, Mattel, 1962, 12 In. 36.00
Puppet, Hand, Squirrel, Steiff 195.00
Puppet, Hand, Stingray, Troy Tempest, 1966 .... 45.00
Puppet, Larry, 3 Stooges, 1960s 115.00
Puppet, Monkey, Talking, Box 350.00
Puppet, Mr. Green Jeans, Capt. Kangaroo, 1950s 38.00
Puppet, Patty & Peter, Composition Head, Hands & Feet, Patty's Box, Pair 95.00
Puppet, Rabbit, Ear Tag, Steiff 135.00
Puppet, String, Dapper Dan The Minstrel Man, Box Back, Side Panels, Kix Cereal .. 49.95
Puppet Show, TV, Dean Martin & Jerry Lewis, 1952 .... 425.00
Puppets, Hand, Flour Sack, Black & White, Uncut 45.00
Queen Louise, Composition, Bisque Socket Head, Mohair Wig, 25 In. 260.00
Quickdraw McGraw, Stuffed Body, Rubber Face, Allied Toys, 17 In. 15.00
R & B, Little Bo Peep, Composition, 8 In. 175.00
R & B, Walking, Plastic, Braids, Sleep Eyes, Plaid Dress, Extra Outfit, 17 In. 225.00
Rabery & Delphieu, Bisque Head, Paperweight Eyes, Cork Pate, 1890, 23 In. 1840.00
Rabery & Delphieu, Bisque, Straight Wrists, Paperweight Eyes, Dressed, 15 In. 4975.00
Rabery & Delphieu, Child, Open Mouth, Mohair Wig, 26 In. 1495.00
Rag, Embroidered Face, Blue Calico Dress, Cotton Body, 1910-1915, 14 In. 220.00
Rag, Handmade, Caracul Wig, Painted Face, Challis Dress, 19th Century, 16 In. 550.00
Rag, Plaid Long Dress, Red Rickrack Trim, Embroidered Face, Yarn Hair, 22 In. 50.00
Ravca, Old Woman & Old Man, Wooden Shoes, 1938, Pair 895.00
Raynal, Cloth, France, 1922-1930, 15 In. 650.00
Reliable, Barbara Ann Scott, Skating Costume, Box, 15 In. 395.00
Remco, Lyndon Johnson, Cowboy Hat, Complete, 1964, 6 In. 20.00
S & H dolls are also listed here as Bergmann and Simon & Halbig
S & H, 749, Blue Sleep Eyes, Lashes, Fully Jointed Body, 9 In. 995.00
S & H, 1079, Brown Sleep Eyes, Human Hair, Silk Dress, 31 In. 1425.00
S & H, 1329, Oriental Child, Tawny Color, Clothes, Ornaments In Wig, 24 In. 5000.00
S.F.B.J., 60, Bisque Head, Set Eyes, Open Mouth, Long Curls, Velvet Dress, 18 In. .. 550.00
S.F.B.J., 236, Boy, Bisque Head, Jointed Wrists, Open Close Mouth, 19 1/2 In. 1800.00
S.F.B.J., 236, Laughing, Blue Sleep Eyes, Human Hair, Baby Body, 13 1/2 In. 1595.00
S.F.B.J., 236, Toddler, Bisque Head, Open Close Eyes & Mouth, Silk Dress, 17 In. ... 1350.00
S.F.B.J., 236/12, Fixed Eyes, Toddler Body, Jointed, c.1910, 28 In. 385.00
S.F.B.J., 252, Character, Bisque, Inset Eyes, Pouty, Blond, Bent-Limb Baby, 10 In. ... 3100.00
S.F.B.J., 301, Bebe Jumeau, Bisque, Sleep Eyes, Wooden Jointed, 1900, Box, 20 In. . 3900.00
S.F.B.J., 301, Child, Blue Paperweight Eyes, Composition, Human Hair, 26 In. 1700.00
S.F.B.J., 301, Jointed, Brown Sleep Eyes, Lashes, 20 1/2 In. 695.00
S.F.B.J., 301, Paperweight Eyes, 27 In. 695.00
S.F.B.J., 401, Mechanical, Walks, Talks, Blows A Kiss, 22 1/2 In. 1695.00
S.F.B.J., Blue Paperweight Eyes, French Clothes, Human Hair Curls, 23 In. 1750.00
S.F.B.J., Character Toddler, Laughing, Smiling, 20 In. 1700.00
S.M. 370, Bisque Shoulder Head, Kid Body, Jumper & Blouse, 20 In. 75.00
Santa Claus, Cloth, 11 In. 10.00
Santa Claus, Rubber, 8 In. 10.00
Scarecrow, Wizard Of Oz, 1920s 1735.00
Schmidt, Bisque Head, Weighted Eyes, Jointed Wood, Composition, 1910, 14 In. 403.00
Schoenau & Hoffmeister, 914, Bisque Head, Open Mouth, Human Hair, 26 In. 365.00
Schoenau & Hoffmeister, Ball-Jointed Body, Sleep Eyes, Red Dress, 1909, 24 In. 550.00
Schoenau & Hoffmeister, Bisque Head, Weighted Blue Eyes, Open Mouth, 23 In. 316.00
Schoenau & Hoffmeister, Child, Box, 1901, 33 In. 1400.00
Schoenhut, Ash Blond Mohair Wig, Brown Eyes, Original Dress, Shoes, 15 In. 1395.00
Schoenhut, Baby, Caracul Wig, Antique Dress, 19 In. 475.00
Schoenhut, Boy, Carved Hair, Spring-Jointed Body, Wooden, 1930s, 15 In. 660.00

Schoenhut, Boy, Pouty, Caracul Wig, Sailor Outfit, 18 In. 1200.00
Schoenhut, Boy, Pouty, Intaglio Eyes, Red & White Striped Suit, 16 1/2 In. 2250.00
Schoenhut, Clown, Wooden Face, Glass Eyes, Costume 135.00
Schoenhut, Felix The Cat, Wooden, Jointed, 4 In. 145.00
Schoenhut, Girl, Carved Bonnet, Painted Hair, Spring-Jointed Body, c.1910, 14 In. ... 1320.00
Schoenhut, Girl, Character, Carved Hair, Intaglio Eyes, Original Dress, 14 In. 1975.00
Schoenhut, Girl, Character, Intaglio Eyes, Mohair Wig, 15 In. 995.00
Schoenhut, Girl, Character, Mohair Wig, Intaglio Eyes, 19 In. 220.00
Schoenhut, Girl, Dolly Face, Open Close Mouth, Teeth, Blond Mohair Wig, 15 In. ... 192.00
Schoenhut, Girl, Intaglio Eyes, Character Face, 15 In. 1500.00
Schoenhut, Girl, Intaglio Eyes, Embroidered Dress, 19 In. 1695.00
Schoenhut, Girl, Painted, Red & White Dress, Pinafore, Crazing, 19 In. 850.00
Schoenhut, Girl, Pouty, Mohair Wig, Intaglio Eyes, 16 1/2 In. 1995.00
Schoenhut, Lion Tamer, Turk Hat, Blue Coat 325.00
Schoenhut, Max, Clothes 550.00
Schoenhut, Pouty, Carved Braided Hair, Painted Eyes, Dressed, 14 In. 1800.00
Schoenhut, Pouty, Original Paint & Wig, 21 In. 1200.00
Schoenhut, Ringmaster, Black Hat, Green Coat 325.00
Schoenhut, Rolly-Dolly, Papier-Mache, Paperweight Head, Egg-Shaped Body, 10 In. 1100.00
Schoenhut, Sleep Eyes, Brown Mohair Wig, 21 In. 895.00
Schuco, Clown, Windup 125.00
Schusmeister & Quendt, Bisque Body, 23 In. 650.00
Shindans Toys, Flip Wilson, Talking, Geraldine Character One Side, 1970, 15 In. 40.00
Shirley Temple dolls are included in the Shirley Temple category
Simon & Halbig dolls are also listed here under Bergmann and S & H
Simon & Halbig, 121, Bisque, Sleep Eyes, Jointed Body, Baby Clothes, 17 In. 775.00
Simon & Halbig, 156, Toddler Body, Blond Mohair Wig, Blue Flirty Eyes, 25 In. 1750.00
Simon & Halbig, 156, Toddler, Flirty Blue Eyes, Chubby, Knit Clothes, 15 In. 750.00
Simon & Halbig, 905, Child, Bisque, Paperweight Eyes, Kid Body, 1890, 12 In. 1500.00
Simon & Halbig, 1000, Bisque Head, Long Curls, Jointed Body, 30 In. 1250.00
Simon & Halbig, 1009, Fashion Lady, Native Costume, All Original, 12 In. 1200.00
Simon & Halbig, 1039, Flirty Eyes, Brown, 18 In. 2300.00
Simon & Halbig, 1078, Composition Body, Trunk With Extra Clothes, 8 1/2 In. 900.00
Simon & Halbig, 1078, Jointed, Composition, Blond, Antique Clothes, 28 In. 1400.00
Simon & Halbig, 1079, Bisque Head, Sleep Eyes, Wood, Composition, Nude, 25 In. 625.00
Simon & Halbig, 1079, Bisque, Sleep Eyes, Human Hair Wig, 30 In. 1400.00
Simon & Halbig, 1079, Bisque, Sleep Eyes, Original Silk & Lace Dress, 27 In. 1275.00
Simon & Halbig, 1079, Cat's Eyes, Antique Clothes, 23 In. 875.00
Simon & Halbig, 1079, Character, Clothes, Long Human Hair Curls, 27 In. 1000.00
Simon & Halbig, 1079, Walker, Cotton & Lace Dress, Key Wind, 13 1/2 In. 1395.00
Simon & Halbig, 1080, Glass Eyes, Mohair Wig, Kid Body, Cloth Legs, 26 In. 475.00
Simon & Halbig, 1129, Oriental Child, Silk Embroidered Clothes, Composition 5500.00
Simon & Halbig, 1129, Oriental, Silk Outfit, 16 In. 2750.00
Simon & Halbig, 1159, Fashion Lady, Molded Bosom, Old Clothes, 22 In. 2300.00
Simon & Halbig, 1199, Oriental, Bound Feet, Silk Kimono, 14 In. 3100.00
Simon & Halbig, 1249, Santa, Bisque, Blue Sleep Eyes, Blond Mohair, 25 In. 2175.00
Simon & Halbig, 1279, Bisque Head, Composition Body, Sleep Eyes, Open Mouth .. 1540.00
Simon & Halbig, 1294, Baby, Clockwork, Eyes Flirt, 25 In. 3850.00
Simon & Halbig, Acrobat, Bisque Hands, Key, Chains, Silk Costume, 13 In. 1800.00
Simon & Halbig, Baby, Bisque Head, Sleep Eyes, Crocheted Outfit, 13 In. 1000.00
Simon & Halbig, Bead-Filled Gypsy Costume, 40 In. 4200.00
Simon & Halbig, Bisque, Flirty Eyes, Jointed Body, Dressed, 17 In. 595.00
Simon & Halbig, Bisque, Strawberry Blond Wig, Composition Body, 24 In. 1000.00
Simon & Halbig, Character, Oily Bisque, Wistful Facial Features, 21 In. 850.00
Simon & Halbig, Eleanore, 29 In. 1500.00
Simon & Halbig, Oriental, Silk Outfit, 16 In. 2750.00
Simon & Halbig, Santa, Bisque Head, Blue Eyes, Painted Mouth, 1914, 33 In. 1380.00
Simon & Halbig, Santa, Sleep Eyes, Fully Jointed, 14 In. 975.00
Simon & Halbig, Santa, Sleep Eyes, Human Hair Wig, Ball-Jointed, 27 In. 1700.00
Simon & Halbig, Sleeping Glass Eyes, Blond Wig, Jointed, Composition, 15 In. 715.00
Simon & Halbig, Walker, Stationary Eyes, Cotton & Lace Dress, 13 1/2 In. 1395.00
Skookum, Chief, Original Clothes, 1920, 13 In. .... *Illus* 290.00
Skookum, Papoose, 14 In. 150.00

Skookum, Squaw & Papoose, Beadwork, Original Clothes, 1920, 15 In. .... *Illus*   165.00
Skootles, Composition, Rose O'Neil, 15 1/2 In. 595.00
Snoopy, Astronaut, & Belle, Pair 34.00
Snoopy, Astronaut, 1960s 50.00
Snoopy, Rag, Box, 1965, 14 In. 25.00
Sonja Henie, 14 In. 465.00
Sonneberg Taufling, Composition, Set Brown Glass Eyes, Cloth Body, Wood 225.00
Steiff, Soldier, Navy & Red Uniform, Metal Sword, Black Shoes, 11 In. 3100.00
Steiner, 133, Googly, Mischievous Expression, 7 In. 595.00
Steiner, Bisque Head, Composition Body, Squeaker, 9 In. 5500.00
Steiner, Bisque, Gray Paperweight Eyes, All Original, 15 In. 6000.00
Steiner, Bisque, Mohair Wig, Silk Dress, Shoes, Marked, 19 In. 6200.00
Steiner, Infant, 7 In. 185.00
Steiner, Key Wind, Legs Kick, Arms Go Up & Down, Says Mama, 17 1/2 In. 2900.00
Steiner, Pale Bisque, Closed Mouth, Painted Eyes, Human Hair Wig, 25 1/2 In. 6500.00
Steiner, Paperweight Eyes, Closed Mouth, Wig, Clothes, Fire A Series, 8 In. 5100.00
Steiner, Paperweight Eyes, Original Wig, 14 In. 2995.00
Stockinet, Boy & Girl, Embroidered Features, Knit Outfits, 6 1/4 In., Pair 95.00
Sukey, Black, Composition Head, Cloth Body, 17 In. 247.50
Superior, Papier-Mache, Shoulder Head, Cloth Body, Black Taffeta Dress, 26 In. 85.00
Swaine, Character Baby, Blue Eyes, Closed Mouth, Painted Hair, 1910, 9 In. 978.00
Sweet Pea, 13 In. 35.00
Sweet Sue, Walker, White & Red Dress, Hat, Box 375.00
Tee Wee, On Pillow, Bisque Head, Blue Sleep Eyes, Closed Mouth 595.00
Terri Lee, Girl Scout 250.00
Terri Lee, Original Dress & Pants, 16 In. 250.00
Terri Lee, Pale Orange Formal, Net Scarf, 16 In. 350.00
Terri Lee, Vinyl, Original Clothes, 16 In. 300.00
Tete Jumeau, Ball-Jointed, Blue Paperweight Eyes, 20 In. 4800.00
Tete Jumeau, Bisque, Paperweight Eyes, Blond Mohair Wig, Composition, 15 In. 1760.00
Tete Jumeau, Bisque, Paperweight Eyes, Dress & Shoes, 23 In. 6500.00
Tete Jumeau, Black Mohair Wig, Blue Paperweight Eyes, Bisque, 17 In. 4800.00
Tete Jumeau, Blue Eyes, Closed Mouth, Mohair Wig, Silk Dress, Signed, 11 In. 3300.00
Tete Jumeau, Blue Paperweight Eyes, Ball-Jointed, Mama & Papa Strings, 22 In. 2900.00
Tete Jumeau, Blue Paperweight Eyes, Box, 29 In. 9500.00
Tete Jumeau, Blue Paperweight Eyes, Human Hair, Dress & Shoes, 24 1/2 In. 3750.00
Tete Jumeau, Closed Mouth, Marked, 14 In. 3500.00
Tete Jumeau, Paperweight Eyes, 8-Ball-Jointed Body, 11 In. 4000.00
Tete Jumeau, Paperweight Eyes, Ball-Jointed, 20 In. 4800.00
Tin Head, Blue Sleep Eyes, Original Clothes, 9 In. 250.00
Toddler, Solid Dome, Blue Sleep Eyes, Brushstroke Hair, 22 In. 23.00
Tomy Kimberley, Skater, 1979 ....   32.00
Topsy-Turvy, Papier-Mache Head, Cloth Body, Silk Dress, 18 1/2 In. 240.00
Tretl, Chalk Type, From Hansl & Gretl, French Comic Strip, 1920s, 9 In. 350.00
Troll, Voodoo, Black Plastic, Cloth Outfit, White Fuzzy Hair, Red Eyes, 1960s 15.00
Troll, Witch Doctor, Black Plastic, Simulated Ruby Eyes, White Hair, 1960s, 3 In. 20.00
Turkish Princess, Child, Bisque, Turkish Royalty Costume, 17 In. 450.00
Turnabout, Little Red Riding Hood, Wolf & Grandma 25.00
Uncle Sam, Cloth, 1800, 15 In. .... *Illus*   220.00
Unis France 60, Brown Bisque Head, Set Brown Eyes, 5-Piece Body, 12 In. 300.00
Universal, Monsters, Box 40.00
Valentine, Mona Lisa, 20 In. 75.00
Ventriloquist, Danny O'Day, Pull String, Book, Record, Box 135.00
Ventriloquist, Dressed As Farmer, Wooden Head 695.00
Ventriloquist, W.C. Fields 50.00
Vogue, Baby, Crib Crow, All Original 650.00
Vogue, Ginny Baby, Original Dress, 1962, 16 In. 25.00
Vogue, Ginny, 1970s 30.00
Vogue, Ginny, Black, Wedding Gown, 1977, 15 In. 35.00
Vogue, Ginny, Hard Plastic, Jointed, With Red Metal Trunk, 1940s, 10 In. 150.00
Vogue, Ginny, Molded Lashes, Walker, Hard Plastic 75.00
Vogue, Ginny, Plastic, Blond Wig, Jointed, Clown Clothes, 7 In. 75.00

Vogue, Ginny, Porcelain, Trunk & Clothes, 1982 .... 100.00
Vogue, Ginny, Toddles, Composition, Mohair Wig, 8 In. 75.00
Vogue, Ginny, Walker, Molded Lashes, Jointed Knees, Original Clothes, 1957 .... 125.00
Vogue, Jan, Tagged Skirt & Blouse, High Heels, 11 In. 75.00
Vogue, Jill, High Heels, 11 In. 85.00
Vogue, Littlest Angel, Original Dress, 1964, 12 In. 25.00
Walker, Paperweight Eyes, Original Clothes, France, Pre-1900, 14 In. 795.00
Walkure, Long Curled Wig, Ball-Jointed, Original Clothes & Shoes, 24 In. 795.00
Wax, Blond Mohair Wig, Blue Eyes, Pierced Ears, England, 1860s, 23 In. 2500.00
Wax, Glass Eyes, Inset Hair, Billowing Ensemble 1500.00
Wax, Infant, Cloth Body, Wax Limbs & Face, Jewel Eyes, 18 In. 1500.00
Wax, Lady, Dressed, English, 20 In. 3250.00
Wax, Shoulder Head, Blue Eyes, Mohair Wig, Cloth Body, Velvet Dress, 23 In. 30.00
Wax, Stationary Eyes, Blond Hair, Cloth Body, Wax Arms, Legs, Dressed, 17 In. 725.00
Whimsey, Pigtails, 1960 .... 45.00
Wislizenus, 110, Boy, 12 In. 800.00
Wooden, Articulated Limbs, Worn Original Paint, 11 3/4 In. 60.50
Wooden Head, Cloth Body, Original Shoes, Black Painted Eyes, 13 In. 175.00
Wooden Peg, Old Woman's Face, Clothes, Black Bonnet, Mid-19th Century, 12 In. . 525.00
Wrestler, Bisque, Human Hair, Brown Sleep Eyes, Painted Boots, 8 1/2 In. 895.00

DOORSTOPS have been made in all types of designs. The vast majority of the doorstops sold today are cast iron and were made from about 1890 to 1930. Most of them are shaped like people, animals, flowers, or ships. Reproductions and newly designed examples are sold in gift shops.

3 Geese, Hubley 225.00
Ann Hathaway's Cottage, Hubley, 6 3/8 x 8 3/8 In. 685.00
Aunt Jemima, Flat Back, Litco, 13 1/4 In. .... 350.00 to 390.00
Aunt Jemima, Full Figure, Green Dress, White Apron, Hubley, 12 1/4 In. 275.00
Bank, Cat, Seated, Cast Iron, 9 1/4 In. 38.50
Basket Of Flowers, Cast Iron, 6 In. 85.00
Basket Of Flowers, Colorful, Cast Iron, 5 1/4 In. 92.00
Basket Of Flowers, Greenblatt Studios, Boston, Cast Iron, 1927, 9 In. 99.00
Basket Of Flowers, Nasturtiums, Painted, Cast Iron, 7 In. 71.00
Basket Of Kittens, Cast Iron, 10 x 7 In. .... 500.00 to 633.00
Basket Of Poppies & Snapdragons, Hubley 85.00
Basket Of Puppies, Cast Iron 175.00
Bathing Beauties, Signed Fish, Hubley, 10 7/8 x 5 1/4 In. 1375.00
Bathing Girls 625.00
Bear, Climbing Tree, Warwick 250.00

  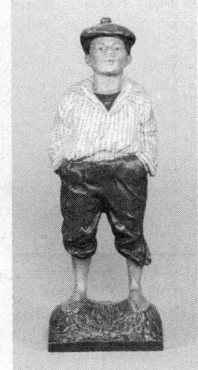

Left to Right: Doorstop, Bear, With Honey, Full Figure, 15 In.; Doorstop, Dog, Pekingese, Full Figure, Hubley, 14 1/2 x 9 In.; Doorstop, Whistling Jim, Bradley & Hubbard, Iron, 16 1/4 x 5 1/2 In.

Bear, With Honey, Full Figure, 15 In. .... *Illus* 3080.00
Bellhop, Cast Iron .... 195.00 to 925.00
Billiken, Full Figure, Painted, 7 1/2 x 5 1/8 In. 220.00
Bird, Long Bead, Polychrome, Full-Bodied, 4 In. 325.00
Bird Of Paradise, 13 3/8 x 7 In. 880.00
Blowfish, On Base, Full Figure, Hubley, 8 x 7 1/4 In. 1210.00
Bobby Blake, Grace Drayton Design, Hubley, 9 1/2 x 5 1/4 In. 465.00
Boot, High Button, Blue/Gray, Original Paint, 7 In. 42.00
Boot, Man's, Cast Iron 125.00
Boston Terrier, Bradley & Hubbard, 9 5/8 x 11 3/4 In. 853.00
Bulldog, Erect Ears, Twisted Tail, Cast Iron .... 165.00 to 180.00
Butler, Hands At Sides, 12 1/2 x 6 In. 470.00
Car, Open Touring Auto, Painted, Cast Iron, 12 In. 240.00
Car, Touring, Cast Iron 45.00
Cat, Black, Cast Iron, Hubley 85.00
Cat, Comic, Seated, Greenblatt 275.00
Cat, Full Body, Black Paint, Yellow Eyes, Cast Iron, 6 3/4 In. 115.50
Cat, Hunchback, Cast Iron 125.00
Cat, Lying, White Repaint, Hubley, Cast Iron, 10 3/4 In. 82.50
Cat, On Pillow, Black, Hubley 175.00
Cat, Seated, White, Hubley 140.00
Cat, Sitting, Original Paint, Cast Iron, 12 1/2 In. 135.00
Cat, White Paint, Pink, Green & Black, Cast Iron, 10 1/4 In. 93.00
Cat, With Bow 75.00
Charleston Dancers, Cast Iron 685.00
Children Kissing, Cast Iron, Hubley 65.00
Clipper Ship, Patina, Cast Iron .... 85.00 to 95.00
Coach, London Mail, Cast Iron 185.00
Cockatoo, Cast Iron 395.00
Cottage, Polychrome Paint, Cast Iron, 8 3/4 In. .... 85.00 to 104.50
Couple Dancing, Original Paint, Art Deco, Fish, 1920s, 8 1/2 In. 185.00
Dog, Airedale, Black & White Paint, Cast Iron, 8 1/2 In. 82.50
Dog, Airedale, Full Figure, Cast Iron, 8 1/2 In. 66.00
Dog, Bird Dog, Painted, Cast Iron, 7 In. 253.00
Dog, Boston Terrier, Original Paint, Cast Iron, Hubley, 10 x 10 In. 135.00
Dog, Boston Terrier, Painted, Cast Iron, 9 In. .... 99.00 to 110.00
Dog, Boxer, Cast Iron 425.00
Dog, English Bulldog, Avery Tractor 180.00
Dog, Fox Terrier, Painted, Cast Iron, 9 In. 148.00
Dog, German Shepherd Pair, Cast Iron, 15 In. 135.00
Dog, German Shepherd, Cast Iron, Original Paint 75.00
Dog, Pekingese, Full Figure, Hubley, 14 1/2 x 9 In. .... *Illus* 4510.00
Dog, Pointing Setter, Hubley 155.00
Dog, Russian Wolfhound, Black & Tan, Cast Iron .... 325.00 to 350.00
Dog, Russian Wolfhound, Standing, 9 x 16 In. 440.00
Dog, Scotty, Cast Iron, c.1920 .... 275.00
Dog, Scotty, Full Figure, Red Lips & Nose, Cast Iron, 8 1/2 x 11 In. 225.00
Dog, Scotty, Standing, Full Figure, White Tail Tip & Neck Hair, Black, Hubley 285.00
Dog, Seated, Glass Eyes, Black Paint, Red & Gold Collar, Cast Iron, 14 In. ... 125.00
Dog, Setter, Cast Iron 265.00
Dog, Setter, Full Figure 110.00
Dog, Spaniel, Black, Cast Iron, 15 In. 66.00
Dog, Springer Spaniel, Cast Iron, 6 3/4 x 7 In. 230.00
Dog, Wire-Haired Terrier, Hubley 425.00
Dolly Dingle, Cast Iron 245.00
Drum Major, Blue & White Uniform, Cast Iron 375.00
Drum Major, Standing, Cast Iron, 13 1/2 x 6 1/2 In. 165.00
Dutch Windmill, Painted, Cast Iron, 7 In. 88.00
Elephant, Art Deco, Brass 80.00
Elephant, By Palm, Cast Iron 385.00
Elephant, Cast Iron 95.00
English Man, In Chair 275.00

Fantail Fish, Hubley, 9 3/4 x 5 7/8 In. 175.00
Fireplace, With Kettle, Andirons & Fire, Painted, Cast Iron, 6 In. 93.00
Flower Vase, Hubley 75.00
Football Player, Cast Iron 325.00
Fort Dearborn, Cast Iron 150.00
Fox Head, Foliage, Cast Iron, 11 1/2 In. 126.00
Frog, Cast Iron, 5 1/4 In. 135.00
Frog, Full Figure, 14 x 7 In. 2970.00
Frog, With Black Boy, Full Figure, 5 1/2 x 6 1/2 In. 465.00
Fruit Bowl, Painted, Cast Iron, 7 In. 88.00
Geese, Cast Iron 425.00
George Washington, Cast Iron 100.00
Giraffe, Hubley, 12 1/2 x 9 In. 4070.00
Girl, Holding Dress, Bradley & Hubbard, 13 x 7 3/4 In. 688.00
Girl, With Parasol, 6 7/8 x 4 1/8 In. 275.00
Gladiolus, Cast Iron 250.00
Gnome, With Barrel 425.00
Gnome, With Keys, Cast Iron 400.00
Golfer, Knickers 300.00
Golfer, Overhead Swinging, Hubley, 10 x 7 In. 795.00
Golfer, Putting, Cast Iron 450.00
Heron, Cast Iron, 7 1/2 In. .... 130.00 to 145.00
Horse, Brown, Black Detail, Cast Iron, 10 In. 180.00
Horse, Jumping Fence, Eastern Specialty Co., 7 7/8 x 11 3/4 In. 550.00
Horse, Original Paint, Cast Iron 225.00
Huckleberry Finn, Littco Products, 12 1/2 x 9 1/2 In. 495.00
Kitten, Black, Blue Ribbon, Cast Iron, 8 In. 99.00
Kitten, With Yarn, Cast Iron 155.00
Kittens, Twin 200.00
Lighthouse, National Foundry 250.00
Lighthouse & House, Cast Iron, Unpainted, 6 In. 165.00
Lion, Full Body, Brown & Black Paint, Cast Iron, 9 1/2 In. 82.50
Lion Head, Black & Gold Paint, Cast Iron, 5 1/2 In. 71.50
Little Black Sambo, Aluminum, 8 5/8 x 4 1/2 In. 440.00
Little Black Sambo, Iron, 8 5/8 x 4 1/2 In. 605.00
Little Red Riding Hood, Grace Drayton Design, Hubley, 9 1/2 x 5 In. 550.00
Little Red Riding Hood, Nuyde 1350.00
Little Red Riding Hood & Wolf, Cast Iron, Brown Paint, 7 1/2 In. 137.00
Little Red Riding Hood & Wolf, Nuyde 985.00
London Royal Mail Coach, Original Paint, Cast Iron 135.00
Mad Hatter, Full Figure, 6 5/8 x 2 7/8 In. 330.00
Mammy, Cast Iron 120.00
Mammy, Hubley, 10 In. 200.00
Man, Flowers In Each Arm, Standing, Painted, 9 x 5 3/4 In. 688.00
Man, Sou'wester & Oil Skins, Cast Iron, 6 In. 132.00
Mary Quite Contrary, Littco Products, 11 3/8 x 9 5/8 In. 1250.00
Monkey, Full Figure, Cast Iron 12.00
Napoleon, Lead, 8 1/8 In. 160.00
Old Crow, Cast Iron 325.00
Old Salt, Cast Iron, 11 In. 235.00
Old Salt, Cast Iron, 14 1/2 In. 400.00
Organ Grinder, Cast Iron 300.00
Ostrich, Wedge, 8 1/2 x 9 In. 120.00
Owl, Cast Iron 450.00
Owl, On Stump, Bronze 130.00
Owl, Standing, Green Slag Glass 35.00
Owl On Books, 9 1/4 x 6 1/2 In. 715.00
Pan & Nymph, Cast Iron .... 1200.00 to 2000.00
Pan & Nymph, On Toadstool, 9 1/4 x 14 In. 935.00
Parrot, Cast Iron, Original Paint, 8 In. .... 95.00 to 145.00
Parrot On Branch, Metallic Polychrome, Lacs 711, 8 1/2 In. 380.00
Peacock, Cast Iron, Painted, 6 3/4 In. 165.00

Penguin 100.00
Peter Rabbit, Grace Drayton Design, Cast Iron, 9 1/2 x 4 3/4 In. .... 475.00 to 495.00
Peter Rabbit, With Carrot, Flat Back, Cast Iron, 9 1/4 In. 605.00
Petunias & Asters, Cast Iron 215.00
Pirate On Chest, Cast Iron 75.00
Pirate With Sack, 11 7/8 x 9 5/8 In. 660.00
Police Boy, White Repaint, Cast Iron 10 1/2 In. 187.00
Policeman, LeMur Light Co., Partial Overpainted, 7 7/8 x 4 In. 440.00
Popeye, Cast Iron 2200.00
Pumpkin, Top Hat, Cast Iron 225.00
Rabbit, Eating Carrot, Red Sweater, Cast Iron, 9 1/4 In. .... 210.00 to 220.00
Rabbit, Top Hat, Gold Jacket, Red Vest, Black Pants, Cast Iron 200.00
Race Horse, Virginia Metalcrafters, Cast Iron, 1949 .... 145.00 to 150.00
Ram, Cast Iron 110.00
Retriever, Black & White, Full-Bodied, 8 1/2 In. 17.00
Rooster, Cast Iron 12.00
Rumba Dancer, 11 1/8 x 6 5/8 In. 935.00
Santa Claus, Cast Iron 295.00
Ship, Polychrome Paint, Cast Iron, 11 3/4 In. 82.50
Snow White & Seven Dwarfs, 16-In. Snow White, 8 Piece 4400.00
Soldier, Revolutionary, Cast Iron, 1940 .... 48.00
Squirrel, Cast Iron, Black Paint, 7 In. 50.00
Squirrel With Nut, Hubley, 8 1/2 x 7 In. 220.00
Stork, Standing, Hubley, 12 1/4 x 7 In. 660.00
Sunbonnet Girl, Cast Iron 185.00
Tulips, Cast Iron 115.00
Whistling Jim, Bradley & Hubbard, Iron, 16 1/4 x 5 1/2 In. .... *Illus* 7150.00
White Rabbit, Flat Figure, Cast Iron, 10 In. 203.50
White Rabbit, Red Vest, Cast Iron 525.00
Woman, Nude, Iron, Art Deco .... 99.00 to 125.00
Yawning Child, Cast Iron, Original Paint .... 225.00 to 575.00
Young Black Boy, On Back Of Frog, Cast Iron, 6 1/2 In. 175.00
Zinnias, No. 267 .... 150.00

DOULTON pottery and porcelain were made by Doulton and Co. of Burslem,
England, after 1882. The name *Royal Doulton* appeared on their wares after
1902. Other pottery by Doulton is listed under Royal Doulton.

Ashtray, Parson Brown 95.00
Biscuit Jar, Arundel, Flow Blue 265.00
Biscuit Jar, Ferns, Plants, Gold Leaves, Blue & Beige Ground, Lambeth, 5 1/2 In. ... 300.00
Bowl, Earth Floral Colors, Silver Plated Rim & Handles, Lambeth, 5 1/2 In. 440.00
Candlestick, Incised & Enamel Design, Lambeth, 9 1/2 In., Pair 1200.00
Candlestick, Woodlands, 7 In., Pair 85.00
Chop Plate, Under The Greenwood Tree, 13 1/2 In. 270.00
Creamer, Floral, Browns & Blues, Lambeth, 4 3/16 In. 220.00
Dish, Nut, Plowing 55.00
Ewer, Burslem, 6 1/2 In. 225.00
Jar, Cylindrical, Incised & Enamel Design, Lambeth, 4 In. 120.00
Jar, Tobacco, Blue & Brown Glazed Leaves 20.00
Jug, Brown, Molded Design, Handle Initialed I.W. & S.W., Lambeth, 7 3/4 In., Pair .. 450.00
Jug, Hard Cider, c.1890, 9 1/2 In. 150.00
Pitcher, Babes In The Woods, Woman With Guitar, 6 In. 285.00
Pitcher, Caprice 1200.00
Pitcher, Don Quixote, 4 1/2 In. 90.00
Pitcher, Madras, Flow Blue, 6 In. 155.00
Pitcher, Milk, Ophelia, 7 In. 90.00
Pitcher, Portrait Medallions, Lambeth, Signed 295.00
Pitcher, Watteau, Flow Blue, 8 In. 395.00
Plaque, Babes In Woods, 7 3/4 x 9 3/4 In. 795.00
Plate, Madras, Flow Blue, 6 1/2 In. 65.00
Plate, Madras, Flow Blue, 7 In. 45.00
Plate, Madras, Flow Blue, 8 5/8 In. 60.00

Plate, Melrose, Flow Blue, 10 In.	95.00
Plate, Persian Spray, Flow Blue	75.00
Platter, Madras, Flow Blue, 17 In.	325.00
Platter, Watteau, Flow Blue, 13 1/2 x 11 In.	195.00
Saucer, Indian, Flow Blue, 5 3/4 In.	33.00
Umbrella Stand, Blue & White, Fan-Shaped, Chinoiserie, 19th Century, 24 In.	715.00
Urn, Water, Floral Glazed, Brass Spigot, Lambeth	350.00
Vase, Beige Tapestry, Moss Green, Blue Interior Collar	175.00
Vase, Blue, Brown, Lambeth, 4 1/2 In.	80.00
Vase, Cylinder, Multicolored Glaze, Earthenware, Crown Mark, 7 1/4 In.	60.00
Vase, Flowers, Gold Outlining, 2 Handles, Burslem, 11 1/2 In.	190.00
Vase, Peonies, Carnations, Matte Finish, Gold Tracery, Burslem, c.1880, 10 1/2 In.	275.00
Vase, Silicon Pottery, Animals, Tan Ground, 9 1/4 In.	325.00

DRAGONWARE is a form of moriage pottery. Moriage is a type of decoration on Japanese pottery. Raised white designs are applied to the ware. White dragons are the major raised decorations on the moriage called *dragonware*. The background color is gray and white, orange and lavender, or orange and brown. It is a twentieth-century ware.

Condiment Set, Cruet, Salt & Pepper, Mustard, Tray, 10 x 6 In.	58.00
Cup & Saucer, Gray & White	75.00
Cup & Saucer, Lithophane Geisha Head, Green & White Ground, Demitasse .. 10.00 to 24.00	
Dish, Lemon, White Dragons, Blue Trim, Loop Handle, Square, 5 1/2 In.	14.00
Lighter, Cigarette, 7 In.	32.00
Plate, Black, Pink & Gray Ground, Gold Rim, 7 1/2 In.	12.00
Pot, Incense	18.00
Saki Set, With Bird Whistle, Lithophane Geisha, Bottom Cup, Gray, 5 Piece	65.00
Sugar, Cover, Pale Blue Highlights, Gold Trim, Japan	15.00
Sugar & Creamer, Niagara Falls, Slipware, Gray-Green Luster, Japan, 4 In. .... 22.00 to 25.00	
Tea Set, Fairyland, Occupied Japan, 15 Piece	125.00
Tea Set, Jeweled, Brown Trim, White Beading, 11 Piece	165.00
Tea Set, Pastel, Brown Trim, 3 Piece	55.00
Vase, Orange Luster Interior, Shoulder Handles, Hinode, 6 x 9 In.	80.00
Vase, Shoulder Handles, 9 In., Pair	160.00
Vase, White Dragon, Orange Luster Interior, Flared, Hinode, 8 3/4 In., Pair	160.00

DRESDEN china is any china made in the town of Dresden, Germany. The most famous factory in Dresden is the Meissen factory. Figurines of eighteenth-century ladies and gentlemen, animal groups, or cherubs and other mythological subjects were popular. One special type of figurine was made with skirts of porcelain-dipped lace. Do not make the mistake of thinking that all pieces marked *Dresden* are from the Meissen factory. The Meissen pieces usually have crossed swords marks, and are listed under Meissen. Some recent porcelain from Ireland, called *Irish Dresden*, is not included in this book.

Candelabra, 3 Scrolled Arms, Applied Flowers, 7 x 9 In., Pair	187.00
Candelabra, 3-Light, Louis XV, Painted Parrot, Among Flowers, Ormolu, 15 1/2 In.	880.00
Candelabra, 6-Light, Frolicking, Putti On Bobeches, 1870s, 22 In., Pair	1320.00
Candelabrum, Ornate Cherubs, 24 In.	850.00
Candelabrum, Pink & Yellow Roses, White Ground, 10 In., Pair	395.00
Celery, Flowers Allover, Gold Accents, Scalloped, c.1881, 5 x 13 In.	195.00
Charger, Pastel Flowers, White Ground, c.1893, 11 1/2 In.	395.00
Compote, Figural, Peasant Figures, Openwork Floral Bowl, 12 1/4 In.	605.00
Couple, Woman Sitting In Chair, Man Standing, Mandolin, Crown Mark, 4 x 4 In.	275.00
Cup & Saucer, Portrait	45.00
Figurine, Angel, Marked, 1900, 5 1/2 In., 3 Piece	225.00
Figurine, Ballerina, Flirting With Fan, c.1920, 10 In.	305.00
Figurine, Ballerina, Girl With Tiered Skirt, Oval Base, 9 In.	395.00
Figurine, Ballerina, Lace & Flowers, Marked, 1890, 11 In.	525.00
Figurine, Boy & Girl, c.1920, 7 In., Pair	220.00
Figurine, Bride, 9 In.	350.00
Figurine, Courting Couple, 6 In.	250.00

Figurine, Flamenco Dancer, 7 1/4 In. 40.00
Figurine, Horned Owl, On Stump, 14 In. 330.00
Figurine, Nymph, Seated, Applied Bisque Flowers, 19th Century, 8 In. 77.00
Figurine, Spanish Dancer, Pink Lace Dress, White Ruffles, Flowers, Crown Mark 350.00
Figurine, Spanish Dancing Lady, Holds Fan, Porcelain Lace, 7 In. 125.00
Figurine, Woman, Brown Hair, Holding Pink Bonnet, White Ruffles, 6 In. 250.00
Group, Imperial Coach, 2 Horses, 1900, 24 In. 2900.00
Jardiniere, Porcelain, Ram's Head Handle, 7 In., Pair 1450.00
Lamp, Cupids Holding Birds, Overall Flowers, Electric, c.1920, 16 In. 450.00
Lamp, Floral Nosegays, White Opaque Base, 10 1/2 In. 845.00
Pitcher, Cover, Floral Sprays, Yellow Ground, 7 1/2 In. 210.00
Plate, Fairy Design, Signed, 9 In. 115.00
Plate, Floral Center, Ivory, Green Border, Marked, 8 3/8 In., 14 Piece 320.00
Plate, Victorian Couple, Cobalt & Gold Border, 9 In. 195.00
Shoe, High Heel, Hand Painted Flowers, Gold Trim, Ruffle, Applied Rose, 5 In. 125.00
Tea Set, Green & Black, Allegorical Portrait Tray, Service For 2 .... 1500.00
Tureen, Soup, Allover Floral, Handles 795.00

DUNCAN & MILLER is a term used by collectors when referring to glass made by the George A. Duncan and Sons Company or the Duncan and Miller Glass Company. These companies worked from 1893 to 1955, when the use of the name *Duncan* was discontinued and the firm became part of the United States Glass Company. Early patterns may be listed under Pressed Glass.

American Way, Plate, 15 In. 45.00
Canterbury, Ashtray, Rectangular, 3 1/2 x 2 3/4 In. 6.00
Canterbury, Basket, 8 x 9 In. 40.00
Canterbury, Bowl, Blue Opalescent, Ruffled, 10 In. 52.00
Canterbury, Bowl, Pink Opalescent, Crimped, 9 1/2 x 4 1/4 In. 38.00
Canterbury, Bowl, Ruffled, 10 x 6 x 4 1/2 In. 22.00
Canterbury, Candy Compote, 7 x 5 3/8 In. 20.00
Canterbury, Celery, 11 In. 16.00
Canterbury, Compote, Green, 7 1/8 x 5 1/2 In. .... 29.50 to 32.00
Canterbury, Cruet, Oil, Stopper, 3 Oz. 15.00
Canterbury, Plate, 2 Handles, 11 In. 22.50
Canterbury, Plate, Handles, 7 1/2 In. 12.00
Canterbury, Relish, 3 Sections, 7 In. 25.00
Canterbury, Relish, 4 Sections, 12 In. 45.00
Canterbury, Salt & Pepper, Copper Tops 15.00
Canterbury, Sherbet, Crimped, 5 1/2 In. 12.00
Canterbury, Vase, Cloverleaf, 4 In. 15.00
Canterbury, Vase, Crimped, 5 In. 15.00
Caribbean, Tumbler, Footed, Blue, 5 1/2 In. 35.00
Cosmos, Lamp, Clear, Enameled, Miniature 75.00
Donkey 165.00
Fat Goose, Blue Cast, 6 x 6 In. 245.00
First Love, Cocktail, Oyster 20.00
Hobnail, Basket, Pink Opalescent, 10 1/2 In. 150.00
Hobnail, Bowl, Crimped, 9 In. 22.00
Hobnail, Compote, Crystal 25.00
Hobnail, Goblet, 5 3/4 In. 13.00
Hobnail, Goblet, 9 Oz. 6.00
Hobnail, Hat, Blue Opalescent, 4 1/2 In. 25.00
Hobnail, Plate, 8 1/2 In. 12.00
Hobnail, Sherbet, Low 9.00
Hobnail, Tumbler, 5 In. 12.00
Hobnail, Vase, Blue Opalescent, Crimped, 4 1/2 In. 30.00
Indian Tree, Candy Dish, Cover, 3 Sections, 8 In. 25.00
Mardi Gras, Toothpick 30.00
Murano, Bowl, Milk Glass 95.00
Murano, Bowl, Opalescent Pink, 10 3/4 In. 75.00
Pall Mall, Ashtray, Duck, 4 3/4 In. 18.00
Pall Mall, Figurine, Swan, Ruby, 7 1/2 In. 45.00
Puritan, Cup & Saucer, Footed 6.00

Puritan, Vase, Pink, Cut 95.00
Quartered Block, Syrup, Silver Plated Top 60.00
Quartered Block With Diamonds, Toothpick 20.00
Ruby Glass, Plate, Sandwich, 16 In. 1750.00
Sandwich, Condiment Set, 5 Piece 80.00
Sandwich, Cruet, 3 Oz. 35.00
Sandwich, Deviled Egg Tray, Large 75.00
Sandwich, Epergne, 12 In. 160.00
Sandwich, Goblet, 9 Oz. 9.00
Sandwich, Syrup 90.00
Sanibel, Floating Garden, Candle Holes, Blue Opalescent 69.00
Sanibel, Relish, 3 Sections, Blue Opalescent 35.00
Sanibel, Relish, Peach Opalescent, 2 Sections, 8 1/2 In. 38.00
Spiral Flutes, Cup & Saucer, Pink 12.00
Spiral Flutes, Plate, Green, 7 1/2 In. 5.00
Spiral Flutes, Plate, Green, 9 3/8 In. 12.50
Swans, Candle Bowl, Green Head 600.00
Swans, Milk Glass, Green Beak & Neck, Sticker, 7 In. 300.00
Sylvan, Bowl, Mayonnaise Section, Ladle, Leaf Shape, 11 In. 48.00
Sylvan, Relish, Leaf, 2 Sections, 7 1/2 In. 15.00
Teardrop, Dish, Nut, Divided, 6 In. 7.00
Teardrop, Plate, 6 1/4 In. 6.00
Teardrop, Plate, 8 1/2 In. 18.00
Teardrop, Sugar & Creamer 35.00
Teardrop, Tumbler, Juice, 3 1/2 In. 8.00
Teardrop, Whiskey, Footed, 3 In. 16.50
Terrace, Bonbon, 6 In. 12.00
Terrace, Console, 11 1/4 In. 38.00
Terrace, Plate, 2 Handles, 9 3/4 In. 22.00
Terrace, Plate, Lemon, Amber, 2 Handles, 5 In. 10.00
Three Feathers, Relish, 3 Sections, 7 In. 25.00

DURAND glass was made by Victor Durand from 1879 to 1935 at several factories. Most of the iridescent Durand glass was made by Victor Durand, Jr., from 1912 to 1924 at the Durand Art Glass Works in Vineland, New Jersey.

Compote, Baluster Stemmed Foot, Stretched Surface, 7 1/2 In., Pair 660.00
Compote, White Pulled Feather, Red, Signed, 6 1/4 x 7 1/2 In. 1150.00
Lamp, King Tut, Applied Glass Stringing, Bronze Mounts, 24 In. 690.00
Vase, Amethyst, Trumpet Form, Signed, 14 In. 80.00
Vase, Blue, 9 1/2 In. 475.00
Vase, Blue, No. 20154-10, 10 1/2 In. 500.00
Vase, Cover, Opal, Swirled & Crackled, Berry Finial, 10 In. 990.00
Vase, Cut Neck Band, Blue & White Pulled Feather Design, 6 1/4 In. 500.00
Vase, Cylindrical, Flared Lip, Amber, No. 12011-14, c.1925, 14 3/8 In. 345.00
Vase, Cylindrical, Squared Lip, Amber, Heart-Shaped Leaves, c.1925, 11 7/8 In. 515.00
Vase, Flared & Ruffled Lip, Iridescent, Gold Leaves & Vines, 10 In. 575.00
Vase, Gold Iridescent, Round Neck, Globular Body, Signed, 6 1/2 In. 120.00
Vase, Green Heart & Vine Decoration, Flared Amber Body, Iridescent, 5 3/4 In. 525.00
Vase, Green Iridescent Leaves, Flaring Cylinder, Signed, 7 7/8 In. 690.00
Vase, Heart & Vine, Blue, 9 1/2 In. 935.00
Vase, Heart & Vine, Cobalt Blue To White, Signed, 9 1/4 In. 1100.00
Vase, King Tut, Green Scrolling Lines, Peach Ground, Signed, 9 1/2 In. 1760.00
Vase, King Tut, Ovoid, Amber, Blue-Green Scrolls, c.1925, 7 In. 575.00
Vase, King Tut, Pyriform, Amber, Lime Green Loopings, c.1925, 8 1/4 In. 690.00
Vase, Opalescent Heart & Vine Design, Gold Ground, 9 In. 1320.00
Vase, Ovoid, Amber Iridescent, Pale Green Leaves, No. 1968-6, c.1920, 6 3/16 In. 575.00
Vase, Ovoid, Amber, Blue Feathering, c.1925, 12 3/8 In. 920.00
Vase, Ovoid, Bright Amber, Blue-Green Feathering, No. 1812-10, c.1925, 9 5/8 In. ... 515.00
Vase, Ovoid, Everted Rim, Amber, Heart-Shaped Leaves, No. 1710-9, c.1920, 7 In. .. 750.00
Vase, Ovoid, Flaring Lip, Amber-Orange, Green Leaves, No. 2011-12, c.1925, 12 In. 800.00
Vase, Ribbed, Amethyst & Crystal, Signed, 6 1/2 In. 275.00
Vase, Swirly & Twisted Light Blue Design, Gold Interior, 11 In. 1380.00

Vase, Trumpet Shape, Silver-Blue Iridescent, No. 1986-8, c.1925, 7 3/4 In. 520.00
Vase, Wavy Green, No. 1712, 8 1/2 In. 1595.00

ELFINWARE is a mark found on Dresden-like porcelain that was sold in dime stores and gift shops. Many pieces were decorated with raised flowers. The mark was registered by Breslauer-Underberg, Inc. of New York City in 1947. Pieces marked *Elfinware Made in Germany* had been sold since 1945 by this importer.

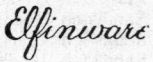

Figurine, Poodle, Pottery 40.00
Salt, Basket, Open 15.00

ELVIS PRESLEY, the well-known singer, lived from 1935 to 1977. He became famous by 1956. Elvis appeared on television, starred in twenty-seven movies, and performed in Las Vegas. Memorabilia from any of the Presley shows, his records, and even memorials made after his death are collected.

Album, Signed & Inscribed To Felton Jarvis, July 1977 .... 2200.00
Bracelet, Photo Pendant, Gold, Package 6.50
Calendar, 1963, Color, RCA 22.00
Card, Gum, Topps, 1956, 64 Piece 895.00
Case, Overnight, Guitar Pose, Signed, 1956, 12 x 8 In. ...: 750.00
Clock, Figural, Guitar, Elvis' Photograph, Quartz Movement 40.00
Decanter, Love Me Tender, Hand Painted, 1977 Commemorative, Box 350.00
Dog Tag, Anklet, Etched Image & Tag Number, 1956 .... 35.00
Dog Tag, On Neck Chain, Elvis Presley Fan Club, Metal, 1956 .... 6.50
Doll, Bisque, Ball-Jointed, Jump Suit, Buckle, 26 1/2 In. 495.00
Doll, Box, 12 In. 75.00
Doll, Plaid Shirt, Pants, Blue Suede Shoes, Rubber & Vinyl, 1957, 23 In. 1500.00
Doll, White Suit, Standing, Box, 1950s 165.00
Game, Board, Teenage Games, 1957 .... 1000.00
Guitar, Black Plastic, Elvis Presley Enterprises, Pictures, 1984 .... 15.00
Key Chain, Portrait, Record Shape, Advertising The Bread Box, 1960s, 3 In. 20.00
Knife, Pocket .... 8.00 to 12.00
Magazine, Elvis The King, Memorial, 1977 .... 10.00
Magazine Cover, TV Guide, May 7, 1960 .... 35.00
Menu, Sahara Tahoe Hotel, 1973, 8 1/2 x 11 In. .... 68.00 to 70.00
Movie Poster, Kissin' Cousins, 3 Sheets, 40 x 81 In. 145.00
Music Box, Love Me Tender, Elvis Figure With Guitar 125.00
Perfume Bottle, Bear, Gold Cap, Dated 1957 .... 38.00
Pinback, Elvis In Concert, Picture 2.00
Pinback, Flasher 20.00
Poster, Double Trouble 275.00
Poster, Easy Come Easy Go 85.00
Poster, In Las Vegas, White Flowery Outfit, 24 x 36 In. 16.00
Poster, Love Me Tender, 1956, 1 Sheet 300.00
Radio, Figural, AM, Transistor, Box, 1977 .... 75.00 to 85.00
Record, Album, Blue Hawaii, RCA 10.00
Record, Album, Christmas, Elvis In Blue Jacket, Pink Stripes 15.00
Record, Elvis Sings The Wonderful World Of Christmas, RCA, 1971 .... 10.00
Record, Girls! Girls! Girls! 40.00
Record, Heartbreak Hotel/I Was The One, RCA Victor, 78 RPM, 1950s 125.00
Sheet Music, All Shook Up, Photograph Of Elvis, 1957 .... 9.00
Teddy Bear, Plays 18 Christmas Songs, 20 In. 100.00
Toy, Jeep, Pink, Fringe Top, Tonka, c.1962 .... 95.00
Watch, Pocket 65.00

ENAMELS listed here are made of glass particles and other materials heated and fused to metal. In the eighteenth and nineteenth centuries, workmen from Russia, France, England, and other countries made small boxes and table pieces of enamel on metal. One form of English enamel is called *Battersea* and is listed under that name. There was a revival of interest in enameling in the thirties and a new style evolved. Graniteware is a separate category and enameled metal kitchen pieces may be included in the Kitchen category.

◆◆◆◆◆◆◆◆◆◆◆◆◆◆◆◆◆◆◆◆◆◆◆◆

Repairs on standing fig-
ures or pitchers should
be made from the bot-
tom up.

◆◆◆◆◆◆◆◆◆◆◆◆◆◆◆◆◆◆◆◆◆◆◆◆

*Left to Right: Erphila, Pitcher, Ram,
Cream, Red & Black, 8 1/2 In.
Erphila, Pitcher, Goat, Cream,
Red & Black, 8 1/2 In.*

Bookends, Panels, Colored Fish, Brass, Rokesley Shops, 6 x 6 In.	1400.00
Bottle, Water, Blue, Cone Top, Porcelain Stopper, 1 Qt.	14.00
Bowl, Juggler, Circus Horse, Copper, Speckled Under, Karl Drerup, 1940s, 7 In.	290.00
Bowl, St. George, Dragon, Copper, Speckled Under, Karl Drerup, 1955, 6 3/4 In.	290.00
Box, Form Of Female Bust Top, Flowered Headdress, Continental, 5 1/8 In.	1840.00
Box, Hinged Cover, Girl, Flower, Silver, Sarcophagus, Wiener Werkstatte, 5 In.	4025.00
Cigarette Case, Silver, Geometric Strips, Monogram, Silver, J. Sedlicky, 3 3/8 In.	4025.00
Dish, Domed Cover, Stylized Brown Branches, Pink Buds, Mabel A. French, 4 In.	357.00
Pitcher & Wash Bowl, Ribbed Body, Brown & Gold, 12 1/2 x 15 In. Diam.	2070.00
Plaque, Round, Portrait Of Young Woman, Limoges, 1880s, 7 1/2 In., Pair	990.00
Portrait, Gaston De Foix Portrait, Man In Armor, Brass Frame, France, 4 1/4 In.	3500.00
Salt, Berry Finial, Stylized Flowers, Silver Gilt, Khlebnikov, c.1910, 3 1/2 In.	690.00
Spoon Set, Twisted Handles, Gustav Klingert, 1890-1895, Demitasse, 6 Piece	640.00
Sugar Scoop, Russian, Klingert, 1891, 5 In.	650.00
Vase, 4 Stylized Male Profiles, Copper, Sarlandie, 1930, 10 5/8 In.	2875.00
Vase, Bud, Baluster Shape, Butterflies, Leaves, Moscow, c.1910, 5 In.	1380.00
Vase, Champleve, Ovoid, Lotus Designs, China, c.1800, 18 In.	220.00
Vase, Ovoid, Red Translucent Body, Ando Jubei, Japan, 15 In.	412.50

ERPHILA is a mysterious mark found on 1930s Czechoslovakian pottery and
porcelain. It is thought that the mark was used on items imported by Eberling
& Reuss, Philadelphia, a giftware firm which is still operating in
Pennsylvania. The mark is a combination of the letters *E* and *R* (Eberling &
Reuss) and the first letters of the city, Phila(delphia). Many whimsical figural
pitchers and creamers, figurines, platters, and other giftwares carry this mark.

Box, Dresser, Cover, Madame Pompadour, Yellow Dress	90.00
Creamer, Green & White, 3 1/2 In.	28.00
Dish, Silhouette In 4 Sections, Czechoslovakia	45.00
Figurine, Fox Terrier	20.00
Pitcher, Goat, Cream, Red & Black, 8 1/2 In. .... *Illus*	165.00
Pitcher, Ram, Cream, Red & Black, 8 1/2 In. .... *Illus*	165.00
Plate, Black Forest, Grapes & Leaves, Majolica, 7 1/2 In.	65.00
Vase, Bud, Triple, Stylized Trumpet Flowers, Ivory, 7 1/2 In.	25.00

ES GERMANY porcelain was made at the factory of Erdmann Schlegelmilch
from 1861 to 1925 in Suhl, Germany. The porcelain, marked *ES Germany* or
ES Suhl, was sold decorated or undecorated. Other pieces were made at a
factory in Saxony, Prussia, and are marked *ES Prussia*. Reinhold
Schlegelmilch made the famous wares marked *RS Germany*.

Bowl, Portrait, Pale Green Ground, Gold Scallops, 9 In.	185.00
Celery, Apples, Multicolor Trim, 12 In.	95.00
Celery, Bird Of Paradise, 10 1/2 In.	195.00
Celery, Chief Spotted Horse, 12 x 5 1/2 In.	225.00
Plate, Queen Josephine, 8 1/2 In.	125.00
Shaving Mug, Swallows Over Mountain Lake	85.00
Tankard, Yellow Roses, Hand Painted, 11 1/2 In.	495.00

Tea Set, Romantic Serenade, Child's 795.00
Urn, Cover, Cupids, Pink Ground, Floral Base, 12 1/2 In. 195.00
Vase, Swallows, Cream Ground, Gold Highlights, 10 1/2 In. 165.00

ESKIMO artifacts of all types are collected. Carvings of whale or walrus teeth
are listed under Scrimshaw. Baskets are in the Basket category. All other
types of Eskimo art are listed here.

Amulet, Walrus Tooth, Male Figure 475.00
Basket, Baleen, Ivory Seal's Head On Lid, Ivory Disk In Base, 3 1/2 In. 1320.00
Basket, Ivory Polar Bear On Top, Baleen Whale, 1940, 3 x 4 In. 850.00
Basket, Lid, Polychrome Cross Design, 1920, 10 x 10 In. 250.00
Bookends, Walrus, Driftwood, Ivory Tusks, 1920, 4 x 6 In. 275.00
Bowl, Carved From Single Piece Of Wood, c.1900, 2 x 15 In. 45.00
Box, Cover, Baleen & Ivory, Basketry, Seal Finial, 20th Century, 4 x 3 In. 550.00
Bracelet, Link, Ivory, Figural Polar Bears 412.50
Button, Figural Animal Form, Inlaid Features, 1 3/4 In., 6 Piece 1045.00
Carving, Inuit, Mythological Figure, Green Stone 325.00
Charm, Hunter's, Walrus Ivory, Stone Age Ax, 3 3/4 In. 85.00
Doll, Carved & Incised Face, 1 3/4 In., Pair 1320.00
Doll, Carved Ivory, Traditional Fur Costume, 5 1/8 In. 319.00
Figurine, Dancer, Whalebone, Finger Fans 605.00
Figurine, Dog Sled, Antler Base, Ivory, 12 In. 245.00
Figurine, Loon, Stone, Signed, 7 5/8 In. 220.00
Figurine, Man, With Seal, Stone, Adamie Amm, 4 In. 275.00
Figurine, Whalebone, Bear, Inlaid Eyes & Claws 440.00
Harpoon, Bone & Ivory Ends, Rawhide Wrapped, 1920, 7 Ft. 325.00
Harpoon, Ivory Ends, Wooden Handle, 1930, 49 In. 110.00
Ivory, Whale's Tooth, Mounted With Walrus, 4 In. 154.00
Kayak, Ivory, Skin, Wooden Figure, 15 1/2 In. 253.00
Lamp, Oil, Soapstone, Wedge Shape 225.00
Mask, Skin & Fur, George Paneak, 9 In., Pair 716.00
Moccasins, Child's, 2-Piece Top, Divided By Rabbit Fur, Seal Fur 120.00
Model, Kayak, Skin & Whalebone, 19th Century, 23 In. 247.00
Mukluks, Sealskin, Pair 44.00
Parka, Squirrel, Wolverine, Beaver, Wolf, N. Anawrock, Mittens, Mukluks, 1950 ...... 660.00
Pipe, Caribou Bone, Caribou Design, Wooden Mouth Piece 77.00
Print, Eskimo Western Arctic, 1975, String Game, Nanogak, Framed, 23 x 28 In. 60.00
Spoon, Figural, Cow Horn 220.00

ETLING glass is very similar in design to Lalique and Phoenix glass. It was   ETLING
made in France for Etling, a retail shop. It dates from the 1920s and 1930s.   FRANCE

Bowl, Opalescent, 6 High-Relief Roses, Chrome Base, No. 210, 11 3/4 In. 825.00

FABERGE was a firm of jewelers and goldsmiths founded in St. Petersburg,   ФАБЕРЖЕ
Russia, in 1842, by Gustav Faberge. Peter Carl Faberge, his son, was jeweler
to the Russian Imperial Court from about 1870 to 1914. The rare Imperial   КФ
Easter eggs, jewelry, and decorative items are very expensive today.

Ashtray, Imperial Eagle Center, Copper, c.1914, 14 In. 2300.00
Bellpush, Silver Gilt & Nephrite, Acanthus Leaves, c.1900, 1 3/4 In. 6900.00
Bowl, Ribbon-Tied Silver Rim, Silver Mounted, c.1900, 8 3/4 In. 5750.00
Buckle, Mauve Enameled Over Guilloche Ground, Silver & Gold, c.1900, 2 1/4 In. .. 3163.00
Cake Dish, Shell Form, Scroll Border, Moscow, 1894, 10 In. 1610.00
Case, Cigarette, Embossed Imperial Eagle On Cover, Copper, c.1915, 3 3/4 In. 2070.00
Case, Cigarette, Horse's Head On Lid, 2 Sapphires, 1913, 4 7/8 In. 5750.00
Case, Toothpick, Blue Enameled, Border Of Leaf Tips, Gold, c.1900, 2 3/4 In. 4025.00
Cuff Links, Sapphire Center, Flanked By Diamonds, Gold, c.1910, 3/4 In. 3450.00
Cup & Saucer, Multicolored Foliage, Geometric Borders, After Dinner, c.1900 .... 2875.00
Decanter, Wine, Silver Fruiting Tree Overlay, Silver Ruble Finial, c.1890, 14 In. 5463.00
Flask, Perfume, Blue Enameled, Red Stone Cabochon Finial, c.1900, 1 3/4 In. 6900.00
Handle, Parasol, Bowenite, Enamel Collar, Diamond & Ruby Borders, 2 In. 5750.00
Handle, Parasol, Nephrite, Gold & Diamond, c.1905, 2 7/8 In. 4600.00
Holder, Tea Glass, Copper, Imperial Eagle, War, 1914-1915, 3 1/4 In. 1150.00
Holder, Tea Glass, Peasants & Cattle, Rural Landscape, K.F., c.1892, 4 In. 2645.00

*Faience, Tureen, Soup, Cover, Stand,
Nidierviller, 1760, 3 Piece*

◆◆◆◆◆◆◆◆◆◆◆◆◆◆◆◆◆◆◆◆◆

Quick cure for a leaking flower
vase: Coat the outside and inside with clear silicone household glue. Coat again if it still
leaks.

◆◆◆◆◆◆◆◆◆◆◆◆◆◆◆◆◆◆◆◆◆

Jug, Claret, Hinged Cover, Silver Neck, Ribbon-Tied Handle, 10 1/2 In. 8050.00
Jug, Hinged Cover, Swirl Fluted, Silver Leaves, Scroll Handle, c.1895, 8 1/2 In. 4313.00
Kovsh, Colored Stones, Translucent Enamel, c.1890, 4 1/2 In. 8050.00
Kovsh, Enameled Vegetable Forms, High Handle, Silver-Gilt, c.1910, 2 5/8 In. 2070.00
Kovsh, Silver Leaves, Chrysoprase Cabochons, c.1910, 7 In. 2875.00
Letter Opener, Nephrite, Engraved Gold Royal Crest Set, Marks 5000.00
Locket, Diamond & Sapphire Spray, Gold, c.1890, 2 1/8 In. 5463.00
Pen, Neo-Rococo Scrolls, Flower Heads, Silver, c.1900, 8 In. 1840.00
Pendant, 2 Jewel-Set Flower Sprays, Gold Leaves, c.1900, 1 1/2 In. 2300.00
Pendant, Easter Egg, Diamond-Set Flower, Gold & Enamel, c.1900, 5/8 In. 5463.00
Pendant, Flower Spray Form, Peridots, Diamonds & 1 Ruby, c.1910, 1 1/2 In. 1725.00
Perfume Bottle, Whistle, On Long Chain, Box 45.00
Pin, Diamond Center, Border Chased With Leaf Tips, c.1910, 1 1/2 In. 1725.00
Pin, Diamond-Set Imperial Crown, Corner Diamonds, c.1890, 1 1/2 In. 4600.00
Pin, Gold & Amethyst, Ribbon Form Set With Diamonds, c.1900, 1 3/4 In. 4600.00
Pin, Imperial Eagle Set With Diamonds, c.1913, 1 3/4 In. 3163.00
Pin, Lily-Of-The-Valley Shape, 6 Pendant Diamonds, c.1890, 2 1/8 In. 8050.00
Pin, Scarf, Center Sapphire, Border Of Diamonds, c.1900, 1 1/4 In. 3450.00
Pin, Star Sapphire Surrounded By Diamond-Set Flowers, c.1900, 1 1/4 In. 8625.00
Powder Bowl, Hinged Silver Cover, Bombe Cut Glass, c.1890, 4 3/8 In. 2185.00
Salt Cellar, Enameled Vegetables, Rooster's Head Handle, c.1910, 2 1/4 In. 2300.00
Stickpin, Double Loop Centered By Sapphire, c.1900, 3 In. 4255.00
Thermometer, Red Marble Base, Pine Cone Finial, c.1900, 8 1/4 In. 12650.00
Tray, Tea, Scrolls, Scroll Handles, 1893, 26 In. 7475.00
Vase, Enameled Flowers, Gilded Silver Ground, Handles, c.1900, 2 1/4 In. 3335.00
Vase, Silver Rim Set With Cabochons, Cut Glass, 3 Handles, c.1890, 8 In. 8050.00

FAIENCE refers to tin-glazed earthenware, especially the wares made in
France, Germany, and Scandinavia. It is also correct to say that faience is the
same as majolica or Delft, although usually the term refers only to the tin-
glazed pottery of the three regions mentioned.

Bottle, Snake & Cathedral, Painted, Italy 85.00
Bowl, Barber's, Basket Of Flowers Center, Iron Red Hatchwork, 1740, 12 3/16 In. 460.00
Bowl, Barber's, Blue Feathered Border, Inscribed Verse, Oval Form, 11 In. 135.00
Caster, Polychrome, Egg & Dart Border, Pewter Mounted, 1730s, 5 3/4 In. 288.00
Cup, Posset, Landscape Design 550.00
Ewer, Girl Holding Pitcher For Spout, Blues & Yellow, 12 1/2 In. 225.00
Jar, Cover, Enameled, Castelli, Italy, 11 In. 203.00
Jar, Fisherman, Enameled, White Ground, Craquelle, Iran, Square, 9 1/2 In. 22.00
Mustard, Double Gourd, 6 1/2 x 4 In. 300.00
Pitcher, Pewter Mounts, 10 In. 130.00
Plate, Joan Of Arc, Florie, Honneur Libertie, Partie, 8 1/2 In. 50.00
Plate, Polychrome Portrait Of 2 Monks, Pierced Rim, 5 In. 26.50
Plate, Stenciled Domed Building, Palm Trees, Red Border, 8 In. 55.00
Stein, Coin Design Of Hunter & Deer, Pewter Base, c.1820 .... 415.00
Tile, Alternating Pink Flowers, Leaves, Each Section, Hexagonal, 6 1/2 In. 250.00

Fan, Jeweled, Enameled, Mezzotint, No. 81,
Bertrand, Box, Opens to 20 In.

Tureen, Pheasant & Floral Decoration, Ladle, Underplate, 12 1/2 In., 3 Piece	88.00
Tureen, Soup, Cover, Stand, Niderviller, 1760, 3 Piece .... *Illus*	2185.00
Vase, Trumpet, Flowers & Dragonfly, Footed, 2 Handles, 11 x 6 In.	880.00

FAIRINGS are small souvenir china boxes and figurines that were sold at country fairs during the nineteenth century. Most were made in Germany. Reproductions of fairings are being made, especially of the famous *twelve months of marriage* series.

Figurine, Welsh Tea Party, Present From Rhyl Inscription, Germany	145.00
Pin Box, 2 Cherubs On Lid, Staffordshire, 2 5/8 In.	77.00
Pin Box, Child On Bureau, Pastel, Gilt, Staffordshire, 4 1/2 In.	71.00

FAMILLE ROSE, see Chinese Export category

FANS have been used for cooling since the days of the ancients. By the eighteenth century, the fan was an accessory for the lady of fashion and very elaborate and expensive fans were made. Sticks were made of ivory or wood, set with jewels or carved. The fans were made of painted silk or paper. Inexpensive paper fans printed with advertising were giveaways in the late nineteenth and early twentieth centuries. Electric fans were introduced in 1882.

Advertising, Bissell's Carpet Sweeper, Paper	20.00
Advertising, Cardboard, Putnam Dye	18.00
Advertising, Children Praying	21.00
Advertising, Dr Pepper, Man, Top Hat, 1920s Woman, Earl Moran, 14 In.	66.00
Advertising, Drink Moxie, Cardboard, Blue, Yellow & Red, 1922, 7 x 8 In.	157.00
Advertising, Drink Moxie, Muriel Ostriche, Cardboard, 1920, 5 1/2 x 8 1/2 In.	34.00
Advertising, Farm Service Co., Pretty Woman, Paper, Folding	2.50
Advertising, Fidelity Bank, Dunmore, Penna., Cardboard, Dogs, Babies, 1920s	20.00
Advertising, Frisco System, A Popular Highway, Paperboard, Wood, Handle, 15 In.	143.00
Advertising, Garret's Snuff, Calendar On Reverse, Railroad Scene, 1935	25.00
Advertising, Grand Hotel, Mackinack Island, Gardens, Silk Screened, c.1890	145.00
Advertising, Honest Snuff, Calendar On Reverse, 1934	25.00
Advertising, Kool Cigarette, Penguin, Cardboard, Wooden Handle, 1937, 8 x 10 In.	30.00
Advertising, Merry Widow Postcard, Lehar's Opera, Boston, 1930, 7 In.	45.00
Advertising, Moxie, Muriel Ostriche, Cardboard, 1916, 6 x 8 In.	49.00
Advertising, Natures Remedy	12.00
Advertising, Palace Shoes, Jersey Shore, Child, Horseshoe, Paddle Type, 1900s	8.00
Advertising, Rexall Drug, 8 In.	20.00
Advertising, SAS Airline, Black Silk, White Marigold, 1940s	25.00
Advertising, Staley Feeds, Comical Chickens & Pigs, Wooden Handle	3.50
Advertising, Tip Top Bread, Cardboard	10.00

Advertising, Women On Front, Children On Back, 3 Section 45.00
Black Face, Cardboard 39.00
Celluloid, Black, Lacy Design, Folding 3.50
Electric, Ceiling, Adams Bagnall, Brass Blades & Cages, Restored, 1909 .... 4500.00
Electric, Ceiling, Adams Bagnall Gyro, 6 Brass Blade Motors & Cages, 1909, 16 In. 5250.00
Electric, Century, Skeletal Motor, 12 In. 165.00
Electric, Dayton Fan & Motor Co., Oscillating, 10 In. 145.00
Electric, Dayton, Fan & Motor Co., Oscillating, 12 In. 125.00
Electric, Diehl, Oscillating, Brass Blade & Cage, 16 In. 200.00
Electric, Diehl, Wall Mount, 30 Volt, 9 In. 550.00
Electric, Emerson, Art Deco, Seagull 75.00
Electric, Emerson, Brass & Steel, 6 Blade, Oscillating, 12 In. .... 125.00 to 200.00
Electric, Emerson, Brass Blade & Cage, 6 Blades, Step Base, 12 In. 300.00
Electric, Emerson, No. 24646, Brass, 12 In. 45.00
Electric, Emerson, Silver Swann 195.00
Electric, Emerson, Step Base, 6 Blades, 12 In. 250.00
Electric, Emerson, Step Base, Brass, 8 In. 150.00
Electric, General Electric, 4 Blades, Chrome, Oscillating, 1920s, 16 In. 110.00
Electric, General Electric, 4 Brass Blades, Brass Cage, 1910s, 16 In. 125.00
Electric, General Electric, 4 Brass Blades, Steel Cage, 1916, 12 In. 80.00
Electric, General Electric, 4 Brass Blades, Pancake, Brass Cage, 1908, 12 In. 175.00
Electric, General Electric, Brass & Steel Ring, Oscillating, 8 In. 80.00
Electric, General Electric, Kidney, Oscillating, Brass Blade & Cage, 12 In. 175.00
Electric, General Electric, Pancake, 1/2 Fluted, No Cage, 12 In. 150.00
Electric, General Electric, Trunnion, Brass, Small Motor, 12 In. 75.00
Electric, General Electric, Votalex, Oscillator, 8 In. 50.00
Electric, General Electric, Wizz, 10 In. 70.00
Electric, Hamilton Beach, 4 Legs, 6 In. 145.00
Electric, Hawthorn, Brass Blades & Cage, 12 In. 275.00
Electric, Lake Breeze, Table, Model C, 16 In. 2000.00
Electric, Marelli, Brass Blades & Cage, 12 In. 250.00
Electric, Polar Cub, All Steel, 1920s, 8 In. 125.00
Electric, Robbins & Myer, Oscillating, Brass Blades, 12 In. .... 65.00 to 75.00
Electric, Savory, Bank Teller, Steel Cage 750.00
Electric, Sears & Roebuck, Coldspot, Oscillating, 12 In. 75.00
Electric, Tuerk Type C, Wooden Paddle, 56 In. 250.00
Electric, Vornado, Plastic Top, Iron Rod Legs, Cowl Fan On Bottom 150.00
Electric, Vornado, Two Guys, Oscillating, 12 In. 30.00
Electric, Western Electric, 4 Brass Blades, Brass Cage, 1920s, 12 In. 110.00
Electric, Western Electric, Bi-Polar, 16 In., c.1897 .... 90.00
Electric, Westinghouse, Brass Blades & Cage, 12 In. 125.00
Electric, Westinghouse, Military Badge, Oscillating, Micarta Blades, 16 In. 40.00
Electric, Westinghouse, No. 987361, Brass Blades & Cage, 3 Speed 115.00
Feather, Pink, Celluloid Splines, 15 x 20 In. 65.00
Feathers, Celluloid 10.00
Fold-Away, Purse Size, Box, 1940s 8.00
Friendship, All Wood, Split Poplar, Inscriptions, Folding, Dated 1876 .... 110.00
Fulton, Auto, Attaches To Fan Belt, Instructions & Parts, Box, c.1937 .... 125.00
Hand-Painted, Oriental, Ebonized Box, 34 1/2 In. 187.00
Ivory Rib, Carved, Watercolor Canton Scenes, China, 17 In. 1320.00
Jeweled, Enameled, Mezzotint, No. 81, Bertrand, Box, Opens To 20 In. .... *Illus* 2530.00
Lace, China 10.00
Lace & Mother-Of-Pearl, Papier-Mache Frame 475.00
Luminaire, Cast Iron, Brass Color, Reticulated, Tripod, With Light, 59 In. 688.00
Paper, Hand Painted Woodland Scene, Ivory 500.00
Paper, Printed, Hand Colored Cover, Gilt Frame, 17 x 26 1/4 In. 242.00
Paper, Wooden, Pinocchio, Treasure Island Scene, Expandable 45.00
Paper, Wooden, Snow White & Seven Dwarfs, Expandable, Lithograph 85.00
Silk, Bamboo, 39 Ribs, Pagoda, Cherry Blossoms, Fuki, 14 1/4 In. 28.00
Silk, Silver, Black Lacquer, Black Silk Tassels, Box, 1920s 38.00
Tortoiseshell, Sequins, Black 55.00
Wooden Carved, Painted & Gilt Design, Frame, 12 x 18 In. 50.00

FEDERZEICHNUNG is the very strange German name for a pattern of mother-of-pearl satin glass. The pattern had irregularly shaped sections of brown glass covered with a pattern of gold squiggle lines. It was first made in the late nineteenth century.

Vase, Mother-Of-Pearl, White Lining, Fancy Mouth, 3 In.	285.00

FENTON Art Glass Company, founded in Martins Ferry, Ohio, by Frank L. Fenton, is now located in Williamstown, West Virginia. It is noted for early carnival glass produced between 1907 and 1920. Some of these pieces are listed in the Carnival Glass category. Many other types of glass were also made.

Apple Tree, Tumbler, Marigold	110.00
Aqua Crest, Epergne, 4 Horn	350.00
Aqua Crest, Mayonnaise Set, 3 Piece	60.00
Aqua Crest, Vase, 3 Lobed, Crimped, 4 1/4 In.	16.00
Aqua Crest, Vase, 4 In.	20.00
Aqua Crest, Vase, Crimped, Aqua, 8 In.	75.00
Banana Boat, Milk Glass	25.00
Basket, Milk Glass, 4 1/2 In.	18.00
Basket, Milk Glass, 10 In.	38.00
Bell, Christmas, 1983	15.00
Black Rose, Vase, Tulip, 8 1/2 In.	100.00
Blue Roses On Blue Satin, Fairy Light, 2 Piece	30.00
Blue Roses On Blue Satin, Vase, 4 1/2 In.	30.00
Bowl, Sailboats Inside, Orange Tree Outside, Ruffled, 5 In.	45.00
Box, Candy, Milk Glass, Oval	18.00
Bubble Optic, Vase, Gold, 11 1/2 In.	115.00
Burmese, Hat, Daisy & Button, 1 In.	25.00
Burmese, Rose Bowl, 1970s	55.00
Burmese, Tumbler, Rose	50.00
Burmese, Vase, Blue, Peloton, 1984 Convention	60.00
Burmese, Vase, Dogwood, Pink, 5 1/2 In.	60.00
Burmese, Vase, Dogwood, Ruffled, 5 In.	55.00
Burmese, Vase, Rose, Pinched, 7 In.	55.00
Burmese, Vase, Roses, 4 x 5 In.	68.00
Burmese, Water Set, Raspberries, 1990, 7 Piece	375.00
Butter, Milk Glass, Oval, 1/4 Lb.	18.00
Butterflies, Bonbon, Rosalene	40.00
Butterflies, Candy Box, Cover, Lime Sherbet, Marshall Fields Logo	65.00
Cactus, Sugar & Creamer, Cover, Topaz	105.00
Cactus, Toothpick, White	20.00
Coin Dot, Candy Dish, Cover	45.00
Coin Dot, Cruet, Cranberry, 7 In.	125.00
Coin Dot, Cruet, Vaseline	90.00
Coin Dot, Fairy Light, Cranberry Opalescent, 3 Piece	200.00
Coin Dot, Lamp, Milk Glass Base, Yellow, 18 In.	250.00
Coin Dot, Lamp, Student, Honeysuckle, 20 In.	225.00
Coin Dot, Vase, Cranberry, 9 In.	85.00
Coin Dot, Vase, Jack-In-The-Pulpit, Cranberry, 11 In.	175.00
Coin Dot, Vase, Jack-In-The-Pulpit, Pink To Cranberry, 10 1/4 In.	85.00
Coin Dot, Water Set, French Opal, No. 1353, 7 Piece	275.00
Colonial, Cruet, Acorn Stopper, Amber	65.00
Daisies On Custard, Basket, No. 7437	45.00
Daisy & Button, Basket, Bamboo Handle, Blue Opalescent, 7 In.	95.00
Daisy & Button, Bell, Ruby Iridescent	22.00
Daisy & Button, Celery, 14 In.	225.00
Daisy & Button, Cornucopia Vase, Blue	35.00
Daisy & Button, Cornucopia Vase, Crystal	20.00
Daisy & Button, Cup & Saucer, Blue	25.00
Daisy & Button, Cup & Saucer, Vaseline	25.00
Daisy & Button, Sugar & Creamer, Tray, Rose Pastel	45.00

Daisy & Button, Vase, Fan, Turquoise, 8 1/4 x 9 1/4 In. 20.00
Daisy & Fern, Lamp, Satinized, Cranberry Opalescent, 20 In. 395.00
Daisy & Fern, Pitcher, Cranberry, 80 Oz. 175.00
Daisy & Fern, Pitcher, Vaseline 195.00
Daisy & Fern, Water Set, Cranberry Opalescent, 5 Piece 375.00
Diamond Lace, Epergne Set, Green, 4 Piece 145.00
Diamond Lace, Epergne, 3-Light, White, 1948 .... 50.00
Diamond Lace, Epergne, 3-Lily, Milk Glass 50.00
Diamond Optic, Basket 75.00
Dot Optic, Opalescent, Pitcher, Cream, 1944 .... 55.00
Dot Optic, Top Hat, Blue, Opalescent, 4 1/2 x 5 1/2 In. 90.00
Emerald Crest, Cake Plate, Footed 65.00
Emerald Crest, Candy Dish, Heart Shape, 1951-1955 .... 45.00
Emerald Crest, Compote, Footed, 7 x 3 5/8 In. 35.00
Empress, Vase, Jade Green 65.00
Fenton's Basket, Blue, Overlay, 7 In. 35.00
Fenton's Drapery, Pitcher, Blue Opalescent 350.00
Georgian, Cup Set, Ruby, 8 Piece 60.00
Georgian, Goblet, Pink, 5 1/2 In. 15.00
Georgian, Goblet, Ruby, 5 5/8 In. 7.50
Georgian, Tumbler, Green, 2 1/2 In. 18.00
Georgian, Tumbler, Green, 3 1/4 In. 16.00
Georgian, Tumbler, Ruby, 4 In. 6.50
Grape & Cable, Bowl, Ruffled, Ball Footed, Blue 90.00
Hanging Heart, Rose Bowl, 5 In. 55.00
Hanging Heart, Vase, Turquoise, 7 In. 85.00
Hobnail, Banana Boat, Opalescent, Plum 240.00
Hobnail, Banana Boat, White 28.00
Hobnail, Basket, Blue Opalescent, 7 In. 65.00
Hobnail, Basket, Cranberry Opalescent, 10 In. .... 135.00 to 145.00
Hobnail, Basket, French Opalescent, No. 3837, 7 In. 55.00
Hobnail, Basket, Handle, Topaz, 4 1/2 In. 95.00
Hobnail, Bonbon, Double Crimped, Blue Opalescent, 6 In. 15.00
Hobnail, Bowl, Deep, Topaz Opalescent, 9 1/2 In. 65.00
Hobnail, Candleholder, Blue Opalescent, 4 1/2 In., Pair 55.00
Hobnail, Candleholder, Milk Glass, Pair 47.50
Hobnail, Candleholder, Topaz Opalescent, Pair 45.00
Hobnail, Candy Jar, Footed, Plum Opalescent 145.00
Hobnail, Cruet, Blue .... 28.00 to 75.00
Hobnail, Cruet, Cranberry, 4 In. 35.00
Hobnail, Epergne, White, 3-Lily 38.00
Hobnail, Fruit Bowl, Twisted Stem, White 45.00
Hobnail, Goblet, Blue 25.00
Hobnail, Jam Set, Cranberry Opalescent, 4 Piece 150.00
Hobnail, Jug, Blue, 5 1/2 In. 60.00
Hobnail, Mayonnaise Set, Cranberry Opalescent, 3 Piece .... 110.00 to 115.00
Hobnail, Nut Dish, Milk Glass 22.00
Hobnail, Perfume Bottle, Flat Stopper, French Opalescent .... 30.00 to 35.00
Hobnail, Pickle, Milk Glass 17.50
Hobnail, Pitcher, Cranberry Opalescent, 5 1/2 In. 65.00
Hobnail, Powder Box, Flat Lid, Cranberry Opalescent 65.00
Hobnail, Punch Set, Milk Glass, 15 Piece 250.00
Hobnail, Rose Bowl, Cranberry Opalescent 95.00
Hobnail, Salt & Pepper, Cranberry Opalescent 56.00
Hobnail, Squat Vase, Topaz Opalescent, No. 3854, 4 1/2 In. 30.00
Hobnail, Sugar & Creamer, Milk Glass 27.50
Hobnail, Sugar & Creamer, White, Individual 6.00
Hobnail, Toothpick, Blue 28.00
Hobnail, Tumbler, Cranberry Opalescent, 12 Oz. 45.00
Hobnail, Tumbler, Topaz, 12 Oz. 45.00
Hobnail, Vase, Blue Opalescent, Crimped 25.00
Hobnail, Vase, Blue Opalescent, No. 3858, 8 In. 68.00

Hobnail, Vase, Cranberry Opalescent 80.00
Hobnail, Vase, Fan, Blue, 4 In. 30.00
Hobnail, Vase, White Opalescent, Flared, 5 1/2 In. 16.00
Hobnail, Water Set, Blue, 6 Piece 250.00
Hobnail, Wine Decanter, Ruby Red, No. 3761 .... 65.00
Iris, Goblet, Marigold 85.00
Ivory Crest, Epergne Set, 6 Piece 150.00
Ivy, Vase, Beaded Melon, Green, 1950, 4 1/2 In. 28.00
Jefferson, Compote, Red 165.00
Jug, Ice Lip, Milk Glass, 70 Oz. 55.00
Lily-Of-The-Valley, Candleholder, Topaz Opalescent, Pair 50.00
Lily-Of-The-Valley, Candy Dish, Cover, Footed, Topaz 55.00
Lily-Of-The-Valley, Compote, Cover, Topaz Opalescent 60.00
Log Cabin, Bell 35.00
Log Cabin, Lamp, Colonial 150.00
Log Cabin, Vase, 7 In. 40.00
Lotus, Ashtray, Jade, 3-Footed 5.00
Lotus, Candleholder, Black, 3-Footed 15.00
Lotus, Candleholder, Ruby, 3-Footed, Pair 25.00
Mandarin Red, Basket 95.00
Mandarin Red, Cookie Jar, 1933, 10 1/2 In. 175.00
Paperweight, Fish 37.00
Paperweight, Neil Armstrong 55.00
Peach Crest, Basket, 7 In. 65.00
Peach Crest, Basket, Blue, 4 1/2 In. 45.00
Peach Crest, Bowl, 10 In. 60.00
Peach Crest, Bowl, Triangle, 6 1/2 In. 35.00
Peach Crest, Cornucopia Vase, No. 1523 .... 65.00
Peach Crest, Vase, 9 In. 48.00
Peach Crest, Vase, Triangle, Narrow Neck, c.1940, 8 In. 65.00
Peacock, Vase, Flared, Red 125.00
Persian Medallion, Plate, Amethyst, 9 1/2 In. 25.00
Plymouth, Goblet, Water, Ruby 20.00
Poinsettia, Console Set 75.00
Poinsettia, Plate, 1974 .... 20.00
Polka Dot, Cruet, Crown Stopper, Cranberry 145.00
Polka Dot, Vase, Cranberry, 6 In. 85.00
Poppy, Vase, Custard, 7 In. 38.00
Rib Optic, Vase, Pinch, Blue Satin 55.00
Rib Optic, Wine Bottle, Cranberry, 13 1/2 In. .... 125.00 to 130.00
Rosalene, Basket 250.00
Rosalene, Basket, 9 In. 80.00
Rosalene, Basket, Empress 65.00
Rosalene, Bell 50.00
Rosalene, Candy Box, Cover 95.00
Rosalene, Figurine, Bird, Happiness, Long Tail, Sticker 24.00
Rosalene, Fish 30.00
Rosalene, Vase, Bud, 8 In. 45.00
Rosalene, Vase, Tulip, 10 In. 100.00
Rose Crest, Bowl, Double Crimped, 10 1/2 In. 65.00
Rose Crest, Hat, Ruffled, 4 x 4 3/8 In. 35.00
September Morn, Bowl, Flower Frog, Candlestick, Ruby, 4 Piece 195.00
September Morn, Nymph & Flower Frog 100.00
Silver Crest, Banana Bowl 26.00
Silver Crest, Banana Stand 65.00
Silver Crest, Basket, 7 In. 25.00
Silver Crest, Basket, 13 In. 65.00
Silver Crest, Basket, Melon Shape, 10 In. 95.00
Silver Crest, Basket, Ruffled, Clear Handle, 10 1/4 x 9 In. 35.00
Silver Crest, Basket, White, Ruffled, 7 3/8 In. 32.00
Silver Crest, Bowl, Double Crimped, 7 x 3 3/4 In. 17.00
Silver Crest, Bowl, Footed, 8 In. 28.00

Silver Crest, Cake Stand, Crimped, 13 x 5 In. 30.00
Silver Crest, Candleholder, 3 1/2 In., Pair 30.00
Silver Crest, Candy Box, Cover, Footed 39.00
Silver Crest, Compote, Low, Footed 25.00
Silver Crest, Cup & Saucer 20.00
Silver Crest, Epergne, 2 Piece 55.00
Silver Crest, Epergne, 4 Piece 125.00
Silver Crest, Hat Basket, 5 In. 45.00
Silver Crest, Mayonnaise, Underplate & Ladle, 3 Piece 35.00
Silver Crest, Plate, 8 1/2 In. .... 15.00 to 20.00
Silver Crest, Plate, 9 1/2 In. 40.00
Silver Crest, Plate, 12 1/2 In. 32.00
Silver Crest, Salt & Pepper 45.00
Silver Crest, Server, 3 Tiers, 13, 8 1/2 & 6 In. 55.00
Silver Crest, Tidbit, Chrome Fittings, 12 1/2 In. 38.00
Silver Crest, Vase, 12 In. .... 45.00 to 75.00
Silver Crest, Vase, Crimped, 6 1/2 In. 15.00
Silver Crest, Vase, Fan, 12 In. 95.00
Snow Crest, Vase, Amber 35.00
Snow Crest, Vase, Cranberry 50.00
Snow Crest, Vase, Pinched, Emerald Green, 8 1/2 In. 75.00
Spanish Lace, Basket, Silver Crest, 8 1/2 In. 45.00
Spanish Lace, Cake Plate, Silver Crest 35.00
Spanish Lace, Cake Stand, Turquoise, 13 x 5 In. 60.00
Spanish Lace, Candlestick, Silver Crest, Pair 22.00
Spanish Lace, Salt & Pepper, Silver Crest 50.00
Spiral Optic, Pitcher, 6 In. 65.00
Swan, Bonbon, Pink 20.00
Teal Feather, Lamp 145.00
Temple, Jar, Jade Green 55.00
Threaded Diamond Optic, Basket, 7 In. 50.00
Thumbprint, Cake Plate, Footed 35.00
Two Flowers, Bowl, Footed, Blue, 10 In. 140.00
Valencia, Candy Box, Colonial Blue 35.00
Vasa Murrhina, Basket, Green, Blue, White Cased, 11 In. 120.00
Velva Rose, Basket, Footed 65.00
Vintage, Compote, Marigold 45.00
Violets In The Snow, Basket, No. 7437 .... 55.00
Violets In The Snow, Fan Vase, 6 In. .... 22.00 to 38.00
Violets In The Snow, Vase, Spanish Lace, 8 In. 40.00
Water Lily, Pitcher & Bowl, 9 In., 2 Piece 85.00

FIESTA, the colorful dinnerware, was introduced in 1936 by the Homer
Laughlin China Co., redesigned in 1969, and withdrawn in 1973. It was
reissued again in 1986 in different colors and is still being made. The simple
design was characterized by a band of concentric circles, beginning at the
rim. Cups had full-circle handles until 1969, when partial-circle handles were
made. Harlequin and Riviera were related wares. For more information and
prices of American dinnerware, see the book *Kovels' Depression Glass &
American Dinnerware Price List.*

Ashtray, Cobalt Blue 40.00
Ashtray, Gray .... 75.00 to 80.00
Ashtray, Turquoise 33.00
Ashtray, Yellow .... 33.00 to 35.00
Bowl, Dessert, Ivory, 6 In. 15.00
Bowl, Fruit, Cobalt Blue, 4 3/4 In. 26.00
Bowl, Fruit, Turquoise, 11 3/4 In. 150.00
Bowl, Fruit, Yellow, 11 3/4 In. 150.00
Bowl, Green 15.00
Bowl, Medium Green, 5 1/2 In. 50.00
Bowl, Mixing, No. 2, Light Green 65.00
Bowl, Mixing, No. 3, Light Green 70.00

Bowl, Mixing, No. 6, Gray, Kitchen Kraft, 10 In. 100.00
Bowl, Mixing, No. 6, Green, 10 In. 55.00
Bowl, Mixing, No. 7, Green 275.00
Bowl, Salad, Red, Individual, 7 1/2 In. 60.00
Bowl, Yellow, 8 1/4 x 2 3/4 In. 45.00
Cake Server, Green 65.00
Candleholder, Bulb, Red, Pair 70.00
Carafe, Cobalt, 3 Pt. 200.00
Carafe, Light Green, 3 Pt. 175.00
Carafe, Red, 3 Pt. .... 125.00 to 190.00
Carafe, Turquoise, 3 Pt. 250.00
Carafe, Yellow, 3 Pt. 145.00
Casserole, Cover, Chartreuse 150.00
Casserole, Cover, Green 115.00
Casserole, Cover, Turquoise 125.00
Casserole, French, Turquoise, Handle 135.00
Casserole, French, Yellow 235.00
Casserole, Red 135.00
Casserole, Yellow, Kitchen Kraft, Individual 90.00
Chop Plate, Cobalt Blue, 13 In. 25.00
Chop Plate, Medium Green, 13 In. 200.00
Chop Plate, Red, 13 In. 25.00
Chop Plate, Red, 15 In. 45.00
Chop Plate, Yellow, 15 In. 30.00
Coffeepot, Gray 200.00
Coffeepot, Ivory 125.00
Coffeepot, Red, After Dinner 225.00
Coffeepot, Rose 200.00
Coffeepot, Yellow, After Dinner 250.00
Compote, Fruit, Ivory, 12 In. 115.00
Compote, Green, 12 In. 105.00
Creamer, Chartreuse 15.00
Creamer, Stick Handle, Light Green 35.00
Creamer, Stick Handle, Turquoise 30.00
Creamer, Yellow, Individual 50.00
Cup, Light Green, After Dinner 32.00
Cup, Turquoise 10.00
Cup & Saucer, Amberstone 5.00
Cup & Saucer, Medium Green 35.00
Cup & Saucer, Turquoise 24.00
Cup & Saucer, Yellow 22.00
Eggcup, Cobalt Blue .... 45.00 to 50.00
Eggcup, Gray 95.00
Eggcup, Light Green, Drippy Glaze 25.00
Eggcup, Red 50.00
Fork, Red, Kitchen Kraft 90.00
Gravy Boat, Medium Green 125.00
Gravy Boat, Red .... 40.00 to 95.00
Grill Plate, Cobalt Blue 20.00
Grill Plate, Green 15.00
Jam Jar, Rose, Yellow 250.00
Jam Jar, Turquoise 101.00
Jam Jar, Yellow .... 250.00 to 275.00
Jar, Cover, Cobalt Blue, Kitchen Kraft 275.00
Jar, Cover, Green, Kitchen Kraft, Small 200.00
Jar, Cover, Yellow, Kitchen Kraft .... 250.00 to 275.00
Jar, Stacking, Red, Kitchen Kraft 32.00
Mug, Red 40.00
Mug, Tom & Jerry, Chartreuse 55.00
Mug, Tom & Jerry, Forest Green 55.00
Mustard, Green 95.00
Nappy, Green, 8 1/2 In. 135.00

Nappy, Red, 8 1/2 In. 40.00
Pitcher, Cobalt Blue, 2 Pt. .... 75.00 to 95.00
Pitcher, Cover, Disk, Medium Green 900.00
Pitcher, Disk, Chartreuse 145.00
Pitcher, Disk, Cobalt Blue 85.00
Pitcher, Disk, Gray .... 170.00 to 200.00
Pitcher, Disk, Light Green 85.00
Pitcher, Disk, Medium Green 90.00
Pitcher, Disk, Red .... 140.00 to 150.00
Pitcher, Disk, Rose 145.00
Pitcher, Disk, Turquoise 85.00
Pitcher, Disk, Yellow .... 55.00 to 80.00
Pitcher, Ice Lip, Green .... 75.00 to 85.00
Pitcher, Ice Lip, Light Green 90.00
Pitcher, Ice Lip, Red 110.00
Pitcher, Ice Lip, Yellow 150.00
Pitcher, Juice, Disk, Yellow 30.00
Pitcher, Juice, Light Green 135.00
Pitcher, Juice, Red 400.00
Pitcher, Juice, Yellow 25.00
Pitcher, Milk, Yellow 45.00
Plate, Chartreuse, 6 In. 7.00
Plate, Chartreuse, 9 In. 10.00
Plate, Cobalt Blue, 6 In. 8.00
Plate, Cobalt Blue, 10 In. 20.00
Plate, Divided, Green, 11 5/8 In. 45.00
Plate, Forest Green, 10 In. 32.00
Plate, Gray, 7 1/2 In. 6.00
Plate, Medium Green, 9 In. 35.00
Plate, Medium Green, 10 In. .... 75.00 to 80.00
Plate, Red, 6 In. .... 6.00 to 8.00
Plate, Red, 9 In. 12.00
Plate, Rose, 9 In. 12.00
Plate, Turquoise, 6 In. 3.50
Plate, Turquoise, 7 In. 22.00
Plate, Yellow, 6 In. .... 4.00 to 29.00
Plate, Yellow, 8 In. 7.00
Plate, Yellow, 9 In. .... 6.50 to 9.00
Platter, Forest Green, 12 1/2 In. 45.00
Platter, Medium Green, Oval 115.00
Platter, Red, Oval, 12 In. 22.00
Relish, 5 Colored Inset Dishes, White, Round, 11 In. .... 130.00 to 195.00
Relish, Cobalt Blue 185.00
Salt & Pepper, Red, Kitchen Kraft, Decal 60.00
Saltshaker, Turquoise 12.00
Sauceboat, Yellow 38.00
Saucer, Aqua 2.50
Saucer, Chartreuse, After Dinner 45.00
Saucer, Gray, After Dinner 90.00
Saucer, Red, After Dinner 15.00
Saucer, Rose 2.50
Soup, Cream, Cobalt Blue 45.00
Soup, Cream, Gray 55.00
Soup, Cream, Red 50.00
Soup, Cream, Turquoise 30.00
Soup, Onion, Cover, Green 425.00
Soup, Onion, Cover, Red 500.00
Soup, Onion, Cover, Yellow 150.00
Spoon, Red, Kitchen Kraft 95.00
Sugar, Cover, Ivory 25.00
Sugar, Cover, Red 40.00
Sugar, Cover, Turquoise, 1930s 30.00

Sugar & Creamer, Cover, Red 65.00
Syrup, Cover, Green 220.00
Syrup, Red.. 190.00 to 300.00
Syrup, Turquoise .... 225.00 to 275.00
Teapot, Chartreuse .... 185.00 to 200.00
Teapot, Green 135.00
Teapot, Ivory, Large 135.00
Teapot, Light Green, 6 Cup 90.00
Teapot, Medium Green 750.00
Teapot, Turquoise 105.00
Tumbler, Juice, Cobalt Blue 23.00
Tumbler, Juice, Gray 250.00
Tumbler, Juice, Rose 75.00
Tumbler, Juice, Turquoise 25.00
Vase, Cobalt Blue, 8 In. 300.00
Vase, Cobalt Blue, 12 In. 525.00
Vase, Red, 10 In. 650.00
Vase, Turquoise, 8 In. 375.00
Vase, Yellow, 8 In... 365.00

FINCH, see Kay Finch category

FINDLAY ONYX AND FLORADINE are two similar types of glass made by
Dalzell, Gilmore and Leighton Co. of Findlay, Ohio, about 1889. Each piece
was made using three layers of glass. Onyx is a patented yellowish white
opaque glass with raised silver daisy decorations. A few rare pieces were
made of rose, amber, orange, or purple glass. Floradine is made of raspberry
or tan colored opaque glass with opalescent white raised floral pattern. The
same molds were used for both types of glass.

Berry Bowl, Raised Platinum Design, Opaque, 2 3/4 x 8 In. 850.00
Bowl, Platinum Trim, Opaque Glass Ground, Circles, 8 x 2 3/4 In. 765.00
Celery Vase, White, Silver Trim, 6 1/2 In. 185.00
Creamer, Platinum Trim, 4 1/2 In. 285.00
Muffineer, Silver Trim, 5 1/2 In. 485.00
Pitcher, Platinum Trim, 4 1/2 In. 240.00
Pitcher, White Molded Body, Blossoms & Branches, Platinum Trim, 8 In. 935.00
Spooner, Platinum Trim 195.00
Sugar Shaker, Cinnamon 995.00
Sugar Shaker, Platinum Trim 335.00
Tumbler, Barrel Shape, Platinum Trim Flowers, 3 3/4 In. 325.00

FIREFIGHTING equipment of all types is wanted, from fire marks to
uniforms to toy fire trucks. It is said that every little boy wanted to be a
fireman or a train engineer 75 years ago and the collectors today reflect this
interest.

Alarm, Fire Station, Brass Bell, Coil, On Red Board, Old Ports., N.H., 10 In. 245.00
Alarm Box, Center Wound Gongs, Screw-In Key, Brass 260.00
Alarm Box, Gamewell, Aluminum, Made 1928 To 1951 .... 160.00
Alarm Box, Gamewell, Cottage Style, Pull At Front Opening, 6 1/4 In. 195.00
Alarm Box, Gamewell, Watchman Patrol Station, Key In Door, 11 x 15 In. 145.00
Badge, Cohoes Fire 657 Department, Brass, 1 7/8 In. 65.00
Badge, E.B. Water Co., East Bridgewater, Mass., Nickel, 1 5/8 In. 210.00
Badge, Engineer, Fargo Fire Dept, Williamson, Minn. 65.00
Badge, Hose 1, Ipswich F.D., Silver Plated, Depicting Hose Reel, T-Bar Clasp 137.00
Badge, Lapel, Herkimer 1891, Encircling Hose, 1 7/8 In. 27.00
Badge, Stonington, Steam Fire Engine Co., 2 In. 95.00
Ball, Extinguisher, Electric Blue, 6 1/2 In. 104.00
Belt, Fireman's, Leather, Ladder Hook, Hose Spanner Wrench 45.00
Belt, Staff Boston VFA, Red, Black & White, 19th Century 250.00
Boots, Salesman's Sample, 1920s, 3 In. 75.00
Bucket, Brass Riveted Rim, Seam & Base, Leather, Tulip Shape 350.00
Bucket, Champlost, Leather, Pair 695.00
Bucket, Charlestown, Massachusetts 9500.00

*Firefighting, Horn, Parade, Silver Plated,
Dated July 3/4, 1888, 19 In.*

*Firefighting, Oil Can, American Fire Engine Co.,
Brass, Pair*

Bucket, Connecticut 6050.00
Bucket, E.W.W.N. Starr, No. 1 & 2, Leather, Pair 450.00
Bucket, Firemen Rescuing Woman & Child, Fire-Hose Co, 2, 9 1/2 x 7 In. 880.00
Bucket, Gold On Green Leather, No. 1 Callyin Haven, 1821, 20 In. 1045.00
Bucket, Leather, Brass Hardware, Emblem On Front, 5 x 5 x 4 In. 192.00
Bucket, Leather, Green Repaint, No. 4, N. Tibbets 1843, 13 In. 412.00
Bucket, Leather, Haverhill In Red & Green Banner, 12 1/2 In. 467.00
Bucket, Leather, Mutual Relief, 1801 G.B. Mitchell, Black Paint, 11 In. 467.00
Bucket, Leather, Painted, Lacquered Certificate, Dated July 2, 1787, 11 In. 247.00
Bucket, Leather, Riveted Seam & Strap Handle, Red, Black Trim 185.00
Bucket, Leather, Royal Seal, England, 13 x 8 In. 325.00
Bucket, Leather, Sunburst Design, A. Fish, 12 1/2 In. 385.00
Bucket, Number 1 & Circle In Red, Gold & Black, Black Paint, 12 In. 275.00
Bucket, Scroll Decoration, Red Paint, Charles W. Eliot, 8 1/2 In. 880.00
Cap, Parade, Pillbox Style, Black Felt, Removable Torch 200.00
Catalog, General Fire Extinguisher, Atlanta, Ga., 1930, 668 Pages, 5 x 7 In. 29.00
Certificate, Gilt Frame, Fireman In Troy, New York, 1848, 22 3/4 x 19 1/2 In. 220.00
Certificate, Joseph Chadwick, Fireman, New York City, 1807, Frame, 14 x 10 In. 357.00
Extinguisher, Betz, Yellow, Black & Orange 73.00
Extinguisher, Copper & Brass, Foam Type, 23 1/2 In. 70.00
Extinguisher, Eclipse, Chicago, Silver On Red 40.00
Extinguisher, Elkhart, Copper, Brass, 24 In. 80.00
Extinguisher, Excelsior, 22 In. 40.00
Extinguisher, Firezist, Metal, Red, Black Lettering, 10 x 2 1/2 In. 35.00
Extinguisher, Fyrich, Red, Silver 46.00
Extinguisher, Grecal, Copper, Torpedo Fan, Westinghouse, Cage, 11 In. 65.00
Extinguisher, Mystic, Black, Gold 56.00
Extinguisher, Phillex, Lithograph Of Early Auto On Fire, 10 1/4 In. 95.00
Extinguisher, Pioneer, White & Black, Copper 47.00
Fire Horn, Federal Vibratone, Bow-Tie Shape, 12 In. 22.00
Fire Mark, Cast Iron, F.A., Oval, 11 1/2 x 7 1/4 In. 110.00
Gong, Alarm, Gamewell, Oak Case, 6 In. 725.00
Gong, Faraday, Chrome Bell, Gray Case, 11 In. 90.00
Grenade, Clyde Glass Works 75.00
Grenade, Diamond, Labels 130.00
Grenade, Fire-King, Box 50.00
Grenade, Harden Star, Green, Contents 195.00
Grenade, Harden, Footed, Contents 125.00
Grenade, S.F. Hayward, Cobalt Blue Glass, Patent 1871 .... 250.00
Grenade, Shur-Stop, Wall Mount, c.1930 .... 125.00
Hat, Assistant Fire Chief, Leather, White 250.00
Hat, Blue, Black Visor 65.00
Hat, Fireman's, Red, 1940s 35.00
Hat, Oregon New Bedford XI Within Shield, Cloth Liner, 8 In. 1650.00
Helmet, 1st Assistant Chief's, Leather, 1920s 175.00

Helmet, Cairn, Leather, Brass Eagle, Shield 375.00
Helmet, Fireman's, Leather, Carines EPFD, Brass Eagle 315.00
Helmet, Running Fireman Finial, Leather, Chief Sullivan 358.00
Helmet, Shield, Fireman Aux. Weehawken, Ear Flaps, Size 7 1/8 .... 110.00
Helmet, War Baby Crown, Leather, Black Shield, Dayton, Ohio, 7 In. 160.00
Horn, Parade, Silver Plated, Dated July 3/4, 1888, 19 In. .... *Illus* 1200.00
Lamp, Engine, 6-Sided Colored Glass Front Panel, Marked Orient 5 .... 2300.00
Lantern, Dietz King, Nickel Over Brass 250.00
Lantern, Dietz, Fire King, For White Truck Co. 850.00
Lantern, Dietz, Nickeled Brass 295.00
Machine, Blasting, Oak, Brass 110.00
Nozzle, Embossed With Roses & Santa Rosa 30.00
Nozzle, Fire Hose, Elkart Brass Mfg. Co., No. 211 .... 175.00
Oil Can, American Fire Engine Co., Brass, Pair .... *Illus* 950.00
Plaque, Elmira Exempt Fire Association, Cast Iron 225.00
Telephone, Fire Alarm Box, Red, Metal, Lock & Key, 1920s 400.00
Trumpet, Fire, Good Will Engine Co., Colored Women, G. Bard, 1856, 22 In. 5500.00
Trumpet, Speaking, Nickel Plated, Presentation, Aug. 27, 1901 .... 650.00

FIREPLACES were used to cook and to heat the American home in past
centuries. Many types of tools and equipment were used. Andirons held the
logs in place, firebacks reflected the heat into the room, and tongs were used
to move either fuel or food. Many types of spits and roasting jacks were made
and may be listed in the Kitchen category.

Andirons, Bel Metal, Lemon Top, Slipper Feet 220.00
Andirons, Brass & Iron, Ball Top, Spurs On Legs, 15 1/4 In. 192.50
Andirons, Brass & Iron, Double Lemon Top, Belted, Spurs, Ball Feet, 31 In. 275.00
Andirons, Brass & Iron, Urn Top, 19th Century, 23 In. 665.00
Andirons, Brass & Wrought Iron, Federal, Spurred Supports, 21 1/2 In. 690.00
Andirons, Brass, Acorn Finials, Tapered Columns, 1790-1800, 24 In. 1725.00
Andirons, Brass, Acorn Top, 22 1/2 x 23 In. 1435.00
Andirons, Brass, Ball & Claw Foot, Rostand, 19 1/2 In., Pair 450.00
Andirons, Brass, Ball & Ring Finial, Sphere On Flaring Support, 19 1/2 In. 9200.00
Andirons, Brass, Ball Finial, Fire Dogs, 17 In. 445.00
Andirons, Brass, Ball Top, Snake Feet, c.1810, 18 In. 550.00
Andirons, Brass, Ball Top, Spurred Snake Footed, 15 In. 385.00
Andirons, Brass, Ball Top, Turned Shafts, Arched Spurred Legs, 14 1/2 In. 195.00
Andirons, Brass, Baluster Form, 19 In. 1000.00
Andirons, Brass, Banded Lemon Finial, Spurred Legs, 21 In. 460.00
Andirons, Brass, Bulbous Turned Standard, Spurred Legs, 1830s, 21 In. 525.00
Andirons, Brass, Chippendale Style, Urn Form, Scrolled Legs, 29 1/2 In., Pair 220.00
Andirons, Brass, Double Lemon Top 525.00
Andirons, Brass, Double Lemon Top, 26 x 21 In. 1435.00
Andirons, Brass, Double Lemon Top, Ball Feet, 1800-1810 .... 850.00
Andirons, Brass, Double Urn Finial, 20 In., Pair 445.00
Andirons, Brass, Faceted & Turned Baluster Form, 24 3/4 In. 198.00
Andirons, Brass, Federal Style, Paneled Finial, Scrolling Legs, 20 In. 460.00
Andirons, Brass, Federal, Acorn Finial, Spurred Legs, 20 In. 545.00
Andirons, Brass, Federal, Faceted Turned Shaft, Arched Legs, 5 1/4 In. 517.00
Andirons, Brass, Fluted Column & Ball, Finial, Solid Footed, 20 1/2 In. 80.00
Andirons, Brass, Griffiths & Morgan, 20 In. 440.00
Andirons, Brass, Knob Finial, Ring-Turned Standard, Splayed Feet, 17 In. 770.00
Andirons, Brass, Lemon Top, 18 1/2 x 19 In. 445.00
Andirons, Brass, Lemon Top, Turned Shaft, Spurred Slipper Feet, Signed, 17 In. 495.00
Andirons, Brass, Tapering Spear, Iron Support, c.1960, 18 3/4 In. 370.00
Andirons, Brass, Turned Finial, Ball Footed, 1800-1820, 20 In. 700.00
Andirons, Brass, Urn Top, 25 In. 260.00
Andirons, Brass, Woodington Type, Ball & Urn Finial, 21 In. 460.00
Andirons, Brass Screws, 4-Sided Shaft, Prairie School, 19 1/2 In. 1600.00
Andirons, Bronze, Columnar, Lion Finials, Continental, 50 In., Pair 550.00
Andirons, Bronze, Louis XVI Style, Pine Cone Finial, 32 In. 750.00
Andirons, Bronze, Putti Playing Musical Instruments, Vine Base, 18 In. 5290.00

Andirons, Bronze, Putto, On Ornate Base, France, Pair 2500.00
Andirons, Bronze, Vase Terminals, Acorn Finials At Rear, 16 1/2 In. 1320.00
Andirons, Brushed Aluminum, Glass Columns, c.1935, 17 In. 1050.00
Andirons, Cast Iron, Ducks, c.1890, 27 In. 5700.00
Andirons, Cast Iron, Greek Goddesses, Flowing Dresses, Lighted Torch, 1850 .... 325.00
Andirons, Cast Iron, Half-Round Owl, Orange Glass Eyes, 15 In. 1725.00
Andirons, Cast Iron, Woman, Shell Feet 675.00
Andirons, Chippendale Style, Ball Finial, Ball & Claw Feet, 27 1/2 In. 690.00
Andirons, George Washington Form, Continental Army Uniform, 21 In. 575.00
Andirons, Iron, Brass, Spit Rests, 13 1/2 In. 412.00
Andirons, Iron, Floral Finials, Ring Handles, 19th Century, 28 In. 125.00
Andirons, Iron, George Washington Form, Painted, Pat. Desig'd 1837, 15 x 8 In. 335.00
Andirons, Iron, Gooseneck, Faceted Finials 195.00
Andirons, Iron, Gryphon Form, 17 In., Pair 495.00
Andirons, Iron, Hessian Soldier, c.1920 .... 275.00
Andirons, Iron, Hessian Soldiers, Paint Traces, 20 x 20 In. 220.00
Andirons, Iron, Knife Blade, Brass Ball Finials ....:............... 385.00
Andirons, Iron, Knife Blade, Brass Urn Finial 715.00
Andirons, Iron, Palmer Cox's Brownie Form, 18 1/2 In. 550.00
Andirons, Iron, Salmon, 20 In. 2860.00
Andirons, Iron, Sea Horse, Roycroft, 1902 .... 8800.00
Andirons, Iron, Stylized Dogs, Flared Ears, E. Schenck, c.1932 .... 3450.00
Andirons, Ormolu, Regency, Acorn Finial, Rams' Heads, Center Mask, 11 1/2 In. 6340.00
Andirons, Silvered Metal, 3 Scroll Feet, Applied Acanthus, Urn Finials, 27 In. 6325.00
Andirons, Stylized Floral Design Front, 10 1/4 x 8 In. 220.00
Andirons, Wrought Iron, Pierced Brass Medallion Finials, 20th Century, 27 1/2 In. 137.50
Bellows, Brass, England, c.1780, 23 1/2 In. 1250.00
Bellows, Grain Painted & Stenciled, 19th Century, 17 1/4 In. 165.00
Bellows, Hand Painted Floral, Mustard Ground, 18 1/2 In. 100.00
Bellows, Painted Landscape, Woods Scene, Brass Nozzle, Wooden, 11 1/2 In. 40.00
Bellows, Stenciled & Freehand Fruit & Flowers, Brass Nozzle, 18 In. 275.00
Bellows, Turtle Back, Red Paint, Black Striping, Cornucopia With Fruit, 36 1/2 In. ... 71.50
Bellows, Turtle Back, Stenciled Gilded Basket Of Flowers, 17 1/2 In. 105.00
Bellows, Turtle Back, Yellow Paint, Striped, Stencil, Brass Nozzle, 17 In. 214.00
Bellows, Wood & Brass, Fly Wheel Action, 19th Century, 25 5/8 In. 165.00
Broiler, Adjustable, Heart-Shaped Rack, Iron 1100.00
Coal Hod, Black Metal 100.00
Coal Hod, Brass Footed, Lion's Head Sides, Victorian 140.00
Coal Hod, Inlaid Mahogany, Metal Liner & Shovel, 12 In. 245.00
Coal Scuttle, Brass, Floral & Oval Repousse Design, 19 In. 220.00
Coal Scuttle, Copper & Brass, Mid-19th Century, A.D., Richmond, 20 In. 775.00
Coal Scuttle, Copper, Swing Handle, D.E. Delven & Bros., 10 In. 660.00
Coal Scuttle, Oak, Brass Arched Handle, Slant Front, Hinged, 13 In. 110.00
Crane, Swing-Out Stand For Pot, Hand Wrought, Spanish, 1920, 33 In. 200.00
Fender, Ball Finials, Stylized Brass Paw Feet, Brass & Wire, c.1810, 47 1/2 In. 4600.00
Fender, Bowed Form, Pierced Etched Design, Brass, 19th Century, 48 In. 330.00
Fender, Brass & Wire Mesh, 19th Century, 12 x 54 x 14 In. 550.00
Fender, Brass & Wire, Serpentine Form, 3 Ball Finials, 19th Century, 59 1/2 In. 1955.00
Fender, Brass & Wire, Urn Finial, Paw Footed, 19th Century, 14 x 60 x 11 In. 176.00
Fender, Brass, Pierced & Footed, 8 x 42 x 12 In. 137.00
Fender, Brass, Pierced & Footed, 9 x 54 x 14 In. 192.00
Fender, Brass, Turned Supports, 9 x 55 In. 165.00
Fender, George III, Pierced Foliate Design, 9 1/2 x 36 In. 440.00
Fender, Green Painted Interior Panel, Pierced Design, 19th Century, Brass 235.00
Fender, Kettle Shelf, Brass, 6 1/2 x 47 1/2 In. 165.00
Fender, Lion Head Feet, Brass, 25 1/2 In. 115.50
Fender, Pierced Foliate Design, Brass, 1890s, 66 In. 517.00
Fender, Pierced, Brass & Iron, 19th Century, England, 8 1/2 x 39 x 12 In. 110.00
Fender, Stylized Egrets, Openwork Wings, Iron, 1925, 41 1/2 In. 4600.00
Fender, Wire Grill, Brass Rail, Steel, 37 In. 358.00
Fender, Wire, Brass Rail, Scrolled Wire Design, 56 x 23 x 24 In. 357.00
Fender, Wire, Iron Frame, Brass Rail, 2 Finials, 42 1/2 In. 605.00

Fireback, Agere & Patiforpia, Iron 495.00
Fireback, Flower & Heart, George Ross, George Steven, Iron, 1762, 24 x 26 In. 1035.00
Fireback, Hunting Scene, Iron, 1890, 32 x 26 In. 110.00
Fireback, Wreath & Fleur-De-Lis Design 550.00
Firefront, Cast Iron, United States Capitol Center Relief, Built Before 1812 .... 4500.00
Grate, Cast Iron, Neo-Classical, Arched Crest, Sun King, France, 36 1/2 In. 550.00
Holder, Kettle, Iron 125.00
Kindling Box, Interior Scenes, Embossed Brass Clad, 12 1/4 x 18 In. 55.00
Log Holder, Curved Brass Basket, Curved Tube Legs, 14 x 21 1/2 In. 650.00
Rack, Hanging Cooking Pots, Curved Legs, Wrought Iron, 23 1/2 x 54 In. 247.50
Rack, Spit, Iron, 21 1/2 In. 137.50
Screen, 4 Hinged Panels, Cranes Amid Water Grasses, Iron, 1925 .... 2760.00
Screen, Brass, 3 Sections, Folding, Herringbone Mesh, 13 x 22 In. 125.00
Screen, Brass, Folding, Peacock Shape, 25 In. 135.00
Screen, Brass, Mesh, 3 Sections, Folding, Brocade Panels, 40 x 25 In. 115.00
Screen, Brass, Wire, Folding Sides, Late 18th Century, 25 x 34 x 10 In. 550.00
Screen, Flowers, Brown Ground, Iron Stand, Pressed Board, 1860s, 30 x 20 In. 700.00
Screen, Folding Fan Form, Gilt Bronze, 27 1/2 x 40 In. 145.00
Screen, Louis XV-Style, Acanthus & Foliage Over Needlepoint Panel, Walnut 220.00
Screen, Louis XVI, Framed Tapestry, Giltwood, 47 1/2 x 34 1/2 In. 2320.00
Screen, Needlepoint Panel, Beaded Frame, Mahogany, Carved Legs, 56 1/2 In. 245.00
Screen, Oil On Canvas, Colonial Hearth Scene, Bamboo 235.00
Screen, Openwork, Stylized Maiden, Border Of Arches, Iron, 30 1/2 In. 8625.00
Screen, Painted Scene Of Cavalier & His Lady, Mahogany, 49 x 28 In. 575.00
Screen, Pole, Federal Style, Inlaid Compass Star, Arched Legs, 86 1/4 In. 1895.00
Screen, Pole, George II Style, Needlework, Mahogany, 5 Ft. 1 In. 2875.00
Screen, Pole, George III, Needlework Flower-Filled Vase, England, Mahogany 3520.00
Screen, Pole, Georgian, Petit Point, Tripod 315.00
Screen, Pole, William & Mary, Stitched, Rectangular 2750.00
Screen, Pole, William IV, Floral Painted Velvet, Metal Frame, 43 1/2 In., Pair 6900.00
Screen, Regency Style, Mahogany, Giltwood, Leaf-Carved Splayed Legs, 50 In. 385.00
Screen, Reverse Painted, Verre Eglomise, Toleware Frame, 1850, 23 x 22 In. 330.00
Screen, Sailing Ship, Brass, 27 x 19 In. 60.00
Screen, Sheraton, Mahogany, Rosewood Grained, Petit Point Floral, 40 In. 220.00
Screen, Silk Embroidered Panel, Florals & Reserves, A. Morris & Co., 40 1/4 In. 1035.00
Screen, Silvered Brass, Art Nouveau, Repousse Daffodils, Leaf Footed, 32 In. 920.00
Screen, Slide-Out Panel, Shoe Feet, Mahogany, 38 1/2 x 29 In. 110.00
Screen, Stick & Ball Frame, Oak 250.00
Screen, Stuffed Humming Birds, Barley Twist Supports, Walnut, 45 In. 3450.00
Screen, Stylized Flowers & Leaves, Brass, Painted Black, 42 1/2 In. 800.00
Screen, Stylized Fountain, Iron, Bronze, Brass, 1925, 42 In. 8050.00
Screen, Stylized Sailing Ship, Iron, Oscar Bach, 1925, 37 x 44 In. 3450.00
Screen, Tabletop, Beadwork, Black, White, Brass Stand, Victorian, 21 In., Pair 385.00
Screen, Tole, Oval Sheet Metal Shield, Flower Basket, Black Repaint, 53 In. 245.00
Screen, Wire Mesh, Applied Wrought Sheet-Iron Tree & Deer, 37 x 56 In. 575.00
Screen, Wire Mesh, Brass Handles, 31 x 37 In. 55.00
Skimmer, Brass, Wrought Iron Handle, F.B.S., Canton, O., '86, 20 In. 82.50
Spark Guard, Brass, Wire, Large 295.00
Spit, Forged Iron, Embossed Floral Door, Small 200.00
Toaster, Rotating Handle, 13 3/4 In. 140.50
Tongs, Ember, Wrought Iron, 18th Century, 18 1/8 In. 715.00
Tool, Brass, Lemon Top, Tongs & Shovel, Pair 155.00
Tool Set, 4 Tools & Fender, Brass & Steel, 20th Century, 47 In. 355.00
Tools, Brass, Iron Ball Top, Tongs & Shovel, Pair 100.00
Trammel, Sawtooth, Lollipop Finial, Wrought Iron, 35 In. 165.00
Trivet, Penny Feet, Tin & Iron, c.1800, 13 1/2 x 13 1/4 In. 185.00

FISCHER porcelain was made in Herend, Hungary, by Moritz Fischer. The
factory was founded in 1839 and continued working into the twentieth
century. The wares are sometimes referred to as *Herend* porcelain.

MF

Bookends, Tray Horses, 7 x 8 In. 195.00
Bowl, Blue Garden, 4 x 7 1/2 In. 65.00
Bowl, Butterflies & Insects, Interior Basket Weave, 11 1/2 x 1 7/8 In. 175.00

◆◆◆◆◆◆◆◆◆◆◆◆◆◆◆◆◆◆◆◆◆◆

To remove an unwanted gummed price sticker try heating it with a hair dryer. The glue will melt a bit and it will be easier to peel off the sticker.

◆◆◆◆◆◆◆◆◆◆◆◆◆◆◆◆◆◆◆◆◆◆

Fishing, Reel, Drummed Crank Wind, Silver, London, 1851, 1 5/8 x 2 In.

Coffeepot, Birds, Hand Painted, Bird Form Finial, 6 1/2 In. 330.00
Ewer, Reticulated Handle, White, Blue & Rose, Gold Trim, 17 In. 395.00
Figurine, Bird, No. 5123, 3 1/2 In. .... 70.00 to 95.00
Figurine, Boy, No. 3467, 7 In. 150.00
Figurine, Dancer, No. 3467 .... 200.00
Figurine, Fiddle & Drunk, No. 5512, 12 In. 400.00
Figurine, Folk Dancer, No. 5512/2, 8 1/2 In. 300.00
Figurine, Goose, Polychrome Decoration, 5 In. 50.00
Sugar & Creamer, Butterflies, Yellow Rose Finial, Small 45.00
Teapot, Birds, Hand Painted, Bird Form Finial, 8 1/2 In. 245.00
Teapot, Flowers, Butterflies, Yellow Rose Finial, Ball Shape, 6 In. 180.00
Wine Cooler, Floral Sprays, Scrolling, Gilt, Herend, 6 In., Pair 465.00

FISHING reels of brass or nickel were made in the United States by 1810. Bamboo fly rods were sold by 1860, often marked with the maker's name. Metal lures, then wooden and metal lures were made in the nineteenth century. Plastic lures were made by the 1930s. All fishing material is collected today and even equipment of the past thirty years is of interest if in good condition with original box.

Bait Bucket, Hinged Lid, Copper, Large 135.00
Box, Reel, Pflueger 8.00
Creel, Leather Hinges & Strap 50.00
Creel, Trout, Large 135.00
Fly Reel, Orvis, 1874 .... 450.00
Fly Reel, Trout, Multiplier, Leather Case, St. George, 1930s 750.00
Fly Safe, Wye Reservoir, 6 Drawers 247.00
License, Arkansas, 1937 .... 12.00
License, New Jersey, Celluloid, 1937 .... 40.00
License, Ohio, Metal, 1942 .... 25.00
License, Pennsylvania, 1945 .... 15.00
Lure, Bass-Oreno, Glass Eyes, Arrow Design On Head, South Bend, 1932, 4 In. 25.00
Lure, Cast-A-Lure, Gibbs, Buzzards Bay, Wooden, Box, 4 1/2 In. 30.00
Lure, Crazy Crawler, Heddon, Box 35.00
Lure, Double Barb Hook, Cast Lead, 8 In. 16.50
Lure, Evolution, Shakespeare, Green Back 220.00
Lure, Fish, John Plachner, 8 In. 125.00
Lure, Fish, St. Claire, Green, 10 1/2 In. 125.00
Lure, Fish-Oreno, South Bend, Red & White, Original Box 45.00
Lure, Florida Shiner, Hand Made, Unused, Box 355.00
Lure, Frog, 6 1/2 In. 110.00
Lure, Giant Musky Pikie Minnow, Creek Chub Co., Box, 11 In. 60.00
Lure, Heddon King Weedless Spoon, Brass 25.00
Lure, Heddon Queen Weedless Spoon, Silver 25.00
Lure, Heddon, No. 300, Green Crackle Back, Glass Eyes 135.00
Lure, Hungry Jack, Silver Scale 165.00
Lure, Jumping Jo, Tin, Hollow, Original Box 45.00

Lure, Lane's Wagtail Minnow, Green Scale Finish, 1920 .... 320.00
Lure, Liv Minnow, Haas, Dark Green Back, Silvery Belly, 5 In. 165.00
Lure, Midget, Shakespeare, Underwater, Yellow Body, Red Head 120.00
Lure, Minnow, Rhodes, Underwater, White, Nail Eyes, Staple Rigs 137.00
Lure, Mud Puppy, Red & White Wood, Box, Catalog 65.00
Lure, Multi-Wobbler, Winchester, c.1925, 3 1/2 In. 300.00
Lure, Muskrat, 6 3/4 In. 95.00
Lure, Pat-En Minnow, Dick & Burt's, Phantom-Type, On Card, 3 In. 40.00
Lure, Paw Paw Wotta-Frog, Wooden Jointed 48.00
Lure, Radiant Minnow, Pontiac, Luminous Paint Traces 145.00
Lure, Salamander, 9 In. 95.00
Lure, Striped Fish, 8 In. 75.00
Lure, Triple Hook, Vamp, Heddon 28.00
Lure, True Temper Speed Shad, Original Box 45.00
Lure, Whalebone, Half-Round, Double Hooks, Brass Ring 80.00
Lure, Winchester Spinner, No. 9682 .... 50.00
Lure, Wooden Bucktail, Shakespeare, Patent Applied For 175.00
Model, Flatfish, Silver Body, Red Spot Top, 11 In. 120.00
Plaque, Flattened & Dried Skin Of Brook Trout, Maple Plaque, Oval, 34 In. 725.00
Poster, T.H. Bates' Fish Hooks, Velvet Flocked, Frame, 1855, 21 x 16 1/2 In. .. 8500.00
Print, Biggest Ones Always Get Away, Frame, 14 x 10 In. 35.00
Reel, ABU Ambassadeur, No. 5000s, 1950 .... 110.00
Reel, Ambassadeur, Deluxe Model, Black, Gold Plated, White Knobs, Unused 415.00
Reel, Brass, English, 1870-1880, 2 1/2 In. Diam. 150.00
Reel, Drummed Crank Wind, Silver, London, 1851, 1 5/8 x 2 In. .... *Illus* 7600.00
Reel, Hardy Featherweight, 2 7/8-In. Diam. Silent Check 165.00
Reel, Meek, No. 33, Blue Grass, 1904 .... 275.00
Reel, Meteor, Fishing, Reel, Salmon, Vom Hofe, Single Action, Pat. Jan. 23, '83 .... 495.00
Reel, Nottingham, Brass Backplate, Walnut & Brass 100.00
Reel, Nottingham, Brass Spool Plate, Line Guide 140.00
Reel, Ocean City, No. 1040, Garcia Mitchell 190.00
Reel, Pfleuger, No. 1355 .... 35.00
Reel, Pflueger, Akron, No. 1895 .... 18.00 to 35.00
Reel, Shakespeare, No. 1912 .... 25.00
Reel, Shakespeare, No. 1960 .... 20.00
Reel, Trout, Julius Vom Hofe 3800.00
Reel, Trout, Philbrook & Paine, c.1877 .... 7500.00
Reel, William H. Talbot Reel Co., Pat. Jan. 22, 1901, Leather Case 275.00
Rod, Fly, Battenkill, 2 Piece, 2 Tip, 7 Ft. 467.00
Rod, Fly, Cortland, Hand Crank Reel 35.00
Rod, Fly, Heddon, Split Bamboo, No. 115, Bag, Aluminum Tube, c.1930, 9 Ft. 650.00
Rod, Fly, Lightest Model Trout, Payne, 8 Ft., 2 Piece 1375.00
Rod, Fly, Orvis Battenkill, Bamboo, Cloth Rod Sack, Metal Rod Tube, 3 7/8 Oz. 750.00
Rod, Fly, Split Bamboo, Herter, 9 Ft. 90.00
Rod, Fly, Split Bamboo, Orvis, 7 Ft. 400.00
Rod, Fly, Steel, Winchester, 7 Ft. 125.00
Rod, Fly, Winchester, Split Bamboo, Case 425.00
Rod, Gus Neveros, Extra Midsection & Tip, Gold Inlay, 1983, 8 1/2 Ft. 1550.00
Rod, Jim Payne, 1952, 8 Ft. 1150.00
Rod, Split Bamboo, WJ, 6 Piece 75.00
Rod, Walt Carpenter, Browntone 1300.00
Rod, Winchester Repeating Arms Co., Bamboo, No. 6080 .... 165.00
Rod Case, Wooden, Edward Smith, Pittsford, Vermont 85.00
Trap, Minnow, Glass .... 125.00 to 225.00
Trap, Wicker, 57 In., Pair 275.00

FLASH GORDON appeared in the Sunday comics in 1934. The daily strip started in 1940. The hero was also in comic books from 1930 to 1970, in books from 1936, in movies from 1938, on the radio in the 1930s and 1940s, and on television from 1953 to 1954. All sorts of memorabilia are collected, but the ray guns and rocket ships are the most popular.

Arresting Ray Clicker Gun, Marx 225.00
Board, Dart, Tin 60.00

Book, Big Little Book, Flash Gordon & Witch Queen Of Mongo, 1936	75.00
Book, Big Little Book, Flash Gordon And The Power Men Of Mongo	30.00
Book, Big Little Book, In The Water World Of Mongo, Whitman, 1937	55.00
Book, Big Little Book, Planet Mongo	60.00
Book, Treasure, No. 905, 1956	8.00
Coloring Book, 100 Pages, Whitman, 1952, 8 x 10 In.	80.00
Figure, On Card, 5 In.	25.00
Game, Board, Adventure On The Moons Of Mongo, Waddington, 1977	25.00
Gun, Click	195.00
Lunch Box, 1979	75.00
Model Kit, With Martian, Plastic, Moon Crater Style Base, Revell, Box, 1965	190.00
Model, Revell, Box	150.00
Pinback, Tin Lithograph, 1930s	80.00
Pistol, Click	195.00
Play Set, Mego, Box	95.00
Poster, Flash Gordon, Timothy Dalton, 1980, 27 x 41 In.	5.00
Puzzle, Inlaid, 1951, 14 x 10 In.	60.00
Toy, Rocket Spider	400.00

FLORENCE CERAMICS were made in Pasadena, California, from World War II to 1977. Florence Ward created many colorful figurines, boxes, candleholders, and other items for the giftshop trade. Each piece was marked with an ink stamp that included the name *Florence Ceramics Co.* The company was sold in 1964 and although the name remained the same the products were very different. Mugs, cups, and trays were made.

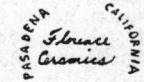

Bowl, Flower, Free Form, Mauve, Green Rim, 15 x 9 In.	75.00
Figurine, Abigail	75.00
Figurine, Ann	70.00
Figurine, Catherine	145.00
Figurine, Catherine, Seated On Settee, 8 x 7 In.	115.00
Figurine, Chinese Boy & Chinese Girl, Pair	45.00
Figurine, Clarissa, Gray Dress, Mauve Hat & Purse, 7 1/2 In. .... 90.00 to 100.00
Figurine, Colonial Gentleman	135.00
Figurine, David, 7 1/2 In.	80.00
Figurine, Delia, White, Gold Trim, 8 In. .... 50.00 to 125.00
Figurine, Edward	125.00
Figurine, Elaine, White Gown, Gold Trim, 6 In. .... 50.00 to 65.00
Figurine, Elizabeth, Maroon Dress, Gray Couch, 9 x 7 In. .... 175.00 to 190.00
Figurine, Ellen	115.00
Figurine, Eugenia, Little Ole Ladies From Pasadena	100.00
Figurine, Georgette	210.00
Figurine, Gloria, Sitting On Couch	275.00
Figurine, Irene, 5 1/2 In.	65.00
Figurine, Jennifer, 8 In.	100.00
Figurine, Jim, 6 1/4 In.	55.00
Figurine, Joy	60.00
Figurine, King Louis XV	200.00
Figurine, Lillian, 7 1/2 In.	30.00
Figurine, Linda Lori .... 115.00 to 120.00
Figurine, Louise, Label, 8 In.	75.00
Figurine, Madame Pompadour	200.00
Figurine, Madeline	100.00
Figurine, Mary, On Chair	150.00
Figurine, Matilda .... 75.00 to 100.00
Figurine, Melanie .... 55.00 to 110.00
Figurine, Oriental Boy, 10 In.	75.00
Figurine, Oriental Girl, 8 1/2 In.	40.00
Figurine, Oriental Girl, 10 In.	150.00
Figurine, Oriental, Woman & Man, 8 In., Pair	115.00
Figurine, Prima Donna	125.00
Figurine, Rebecca	115.00
Figurine, Rhett Butler	125.00
Figurine, Sarah .... 80.00 to 90.00

Figurine, Scarlett, Green Dress .... 105.00 to 125.00
Figurine, Storybook Hour 80.00
Figurine, Sue 65.00
Figurine, Three Choir Boys 150.00
Figurine, Vivian, Little Ole Ladies From Pasadena .... 100.00 to 120.00
Figurine, Winkum 65.00
Head Vase, Oriental Man 55.00
Lamp, Male Figure, 15 In. 75.00
Planter, Blossom Girl 50.00
Planter, Chinese Girl 25.00
Planter, Emily 45.00
Planter, June 40.00
Planter, Kay 45.00
Planter, Lantern Boy 50.00
Planter, Man & Wheelbarrow 80.00
Planter, Mimi 45.00
Planter, Patsy 38.50
Planter, Polly 38.50
Planter, Suzette, Holds Basket Weave Vase, 6 3/4 In. 58.00
Planter, Woman, Pink Coat Dress, Green Hat, 5 3/4 In. 45.00
Planter, Young Boy 40.00
Sign, Dealer's, Embossed Roses, Gold Outlined Scrolls, 8 1/2 In. 195.00
Vase, Girl Holding Skirt, Next To Vase, 7 In. 38.00

FLOW BLUE, or flo blue, was made in England about 1830 to 1900. The
plates were printed with designs using a cobalt blue coloring. The color
flowed from the design to the white plate so that the finished plate has a
smeared blue design. The plates were usually made of ironstone china.

Banana Boat, La Belle 595.00
Berry Bowl, Gironde, Grindley, 5 1/4 In. 35.00
Berry Bowl, Savoy, Johnson Bros., 5 1/8 In. 35.00
Berry Dish, Kelvin, 5 In. 20.00
Biscuit Jar, La Belle 425.00
Bone Dish, Cambridge, Meakin 75.00
Bone Dish, Clayton, Johnson Bros. 45.00
Bone Dish, Fairy Villas, Adams 110.00
Bone Dish, Grace, Grindley 60.00
Bone Dish, Lorne, Grindley 65.00
Bone Dish, Marechal Niel, Grindley 60.00
Bowl, Amoy, Davenport, 5 In. 75.00
Bowl, Argyle, 9 3/8 x 8 3/8 In. 185.00
Bowl, Blue Rose, Grindley, 6 1/2 In. .... 38.00 to 45.00
Bowl, Chinese, Dimmock, 6 x 8 1/4 In. 295.00
Bowl, Chinese, Dimmock, 8 1/2 x 6 In. 275.00
Bowl, Clarence, 10 In. 125.00
Bowl, Clarence, Grindley, 10 In. 150.00
Bowl, Conway, New Wharf Pottery, 9 In. .... 85.00 to 125.00
Bowl, Fairy Villas, 6 1/4 In. 65.00
Bowl, Fairy Villas, W. Adams, Cover 425.00
Bowl, Gainsborough, Ridgway, 10 In. 160.00
Bowl, Grenada, Alcock, Cover, 10 In. 220.00
Bowl, Hamilton, Oval, Maddock, Cover, 11 In. 215.00
Bowl, Holland, Johnson Bros., Oval, 10 In. 125.00
Bowl, Humphrey's Clock, Ridgway, Cover, 10 In. 345.00
Bowl, La Belle, Flower Form Handles, 12 x 9 1/2 In. 200.00
Bowl, La Belle, Scalloped, Loop Handles, 11 1/4 In. 340.00
Bowl, Lorne, Grindley, 10 In. 325.00
Bowl, Lusitania, Wood & Sons, 10 In. 125.00
Bowl, Madras, Doulton, Cover 295.00
Bowl, Manilla, 12 1/4 In. 1250.00
Bowl, New Wharf Pottery, Pair, Cover 395.00
Bowl, Orgia, Oval, Cover, 10 In. 325.00
Bowl, Osborne, Ridgway, Clover Shape, Cover 225.00

Bowl, Oxford, Oval, 7 x 9 1/2 In. 100.00
Bowl, Oyster, Argyle, Grindley, 6 In. 85.00
Bowl, Sunflowers, Scalloped, 7 3/4 In. 60.00
Bowl, Touraine, Oval, 9 In. 125.00
Bowl, Vegetable, Cover, Charleston Exchange, Blue, Staffordshire, Stevenson 2400.00
Bowl, Verona, 7 1/2 x 10 In. 75.00
Bowl, Waldorf, New Wharf Pottery, 9 In. 85.00
Bowl, Waldorf, Round, New Wharf Pottery, 9 In. 125.00
Butter, Cover, Drain, Oxford 295.00
Butter, Cover, Kyber, Adams 475.00
Butter, Cover, Touraine 575.00
Butter Chip, Argyle, Grindley 55.00
Butter Chip, Georgia, Johnson Bros. 42.00
Butter Chip, Grace, Grindley 40.00
Butter Chip, Haddon 35.00
Butter Chip, Manhattan 38.00
Butter Chip, Melborne, Grindley, Round, 3 In. 20.00
Butter Chip, Portman, Grindley 25.00
Butter Chip, Touraine, Stanley 60.00
Cake Plate, Cashmere, Pair 895.00
Cake Plate, Colonial, J. & G. Meakin, 10 In. 75.00
Capitol At Washington, Dark Blue, Wood, Staffordshire, 6 1/2 In. 650.00
Casserole, Cover, Marie, Grindley 250.00
Charger, La Belle, 14 In. 280.00
Chocolate Pot, La Belle 695.00
Chocolate Pot, Warwick Pansy, 9 3/4 In. .... 795.00 to 985.00
Coffeepot, Temple, Podmore, Walker & Co. 975.00
Compote, Raleigh, 5 x 9 In. 295.00
Compote, Tulips, 5 3/4 x 9 In. 250.00
Creamer, Arabesque, Diamond Cut 350.00
Creamer, Bentick, Cauldon 162.50
Creamer, Carlton, Alcock 395.00
Creamer, Clayton 175.00
Creamer, Hindustan 275.00
Creamer, Kaolin 325.00
Creamer, Kyber 350.00
Creamer, Manhattan 40.00
Creamer, Nonpareil .... 195.00 to 225.00
Creamer, Osborne, Ridgway 160.00
Creamer, Oxford 265.00
Creamer, Shell 395.00
Creamer, Temple 550.00
Creamer, Tonquin 395.00
Creamer, Waldorf, New Wharf Pottery 145.00
Creamer, Wild Rose 175.00
Cup, Cashmere 135.00
Cup, Kyber 40.00
Cup, Possit, Kaolin, Handle 185.00
Cup & Saucer, Agra 75.00
Cup & Saucer, Alaska, Grindley 110.00
Cup & Saucer, Amoy, Handleless, 24 Piece 1295.00
Cup & Saucer, Beaufort .... 70.00 to 75.00
Cup & Saucer, Byzantium 65.00
Cup & Saucer, Chain Of States .... 75.00 to 85.00
Cup & Saucer, Chapoo 165.00
Cup & Saucer, Clayton, Johnson Bros. 90.00
Cup & Saucer, Crumlin, Myott 75.00
Cup & Saucer, Fern & Teaberry, Handleless 145.00
Cup & Saucer, Formosa, Mayer 140.00
Cup & Saucer, Grace, Grindley .... 50.00 to 70.00
Cup & Saucer, Grenada, Alcock 68.00
Cup & Saucer, Indian Jar 125.00
Cup & Saucer, Lakewood 85.00

Cup & Saucer, Maltese	60.00
Cup & Saucer, Manilla, Podmore & Walker, Handleless	135.00
Cup & Saucer, Morning Glory	125.00
Cup & Saucer, Normandy	60.00
Cup & Saucer, Oxford	65.00
Cup & Saucer, Phoebe	85.00
Cup & Saucer, Portman, Grindley	115.00
Cup & Saucer, Rhoda Gardens, Handleless	165.00
Cup & Saucer, Scinde, Handleless	185.00
Cup & Saucer, Spinach, Libertas	230.00
Cup & Saucer, Temple, Handleless	165.00
Cup & Saucer, Touraine	70.00 to 95.00
Cup & Saucer, Venetian Scenery, Adams	75.00
Cup & Saucer, Verona, Wood	95.00
Cup & Saucer, Wagon Wheel	95.00
Cup & Saucer, Waldorf	85.00
Cup & Saucer, Wild Rose	75.00
Cup Plate, Amoy	105.00 to 110.00
Cup Plate, Hong Kong	80.00
Drainer, Meat, Ovando	450.00
Eggcup, Burleigh	70.00
Eggcup, Dainty, Maddox	115.00
Eggcup, Delft, Minton	55.00
Eggcup, Nonpareil	195.00
Game Set, LaFrancais, Border, 15-In. Platter, 9 1/2-In. Plate, 7 Piece	650.00
Gravy Boat, Argyle, Grindley	125.00
Gravy Boat, Colonial, Undertray	140.00
Gravy Boat, Dainty, Maddock	125.00
Gravy Boat, Dainty, Undertray, Maddock	95.00
Gravy Boat, Duchess, Grindley	85.00
Gravy Boat, Grace	145.00
Gravy Boat, Hong Kong	395.00
Gravy Boat, Mongolia, Johnson Bros., 8 x 4 In.	70.00
Gravy Boat, Scinde	575.00
Gravy Boat, Tillenberg	175.00
Holder, Egg, Briar Rose	295.00
Jar, Indian, Furnival, 8 1/2 In.	120.00
Ladle, Acme, Hancock	195.00
Ladle, Chatsworth, Keeling	200.00
Ladle, Scinde	3520.00
Loving Cup, Watteau, Doulton	450.00
Mug, Child's, Dahlia, Luster Trim	115.00 to 150.00
Pie Plate, Orchid, J. Maddock & Sons	30.00
Pitcher, Ashburton, 2 Qt.	495.00
Pitcher, Athens, 8 In.	495.00
Pitcher, Baltic, Grindley, 8 In.	390.00
Pitcher, Blue Danube, Johnson Bros., 7 1/4 In.	250.00
Pitcher, Candia, Melon Rib, Cauldon, 5 3/8 x 5 In.	165.00
Pitcher, Cider, Pansy Pattern, Gold Trim, Warwick, 7 1/2 In.	235.00
Pitcher, Clarence, 5 1/2 In.	395.00
Pitcher, Coburg, 8 In.	795.00
Pitcher, Floral & Leaf Sprays, Lattice & Scroll Band, Handle, 6 3/4 In.	145.00
Pitcher, Formosa, 7 In.	700.00
Pitcher, Hong Kong, 2 Qt.	1175.00
Pitcher, Mandarin	595.00
Pitcher, Milk, Amoy	695.00
Pitcher, Milk, Ashburton, 2 Qt.	450.00
Pitcher, Milk, Eclipse, Johnson Bros.	110.00
Pitcher, Milk, Idris, Grindley	185.00
Pitcher, Milk, La Belle	450.00
Pitcher, Milk, Victoria	140.00
Pitcher, Nonpareil, 6 In.	275.00
Pitcher, Nonpareil, 8 In.	325.00

Pitcher, Oregon, 1 1/2 Qt. 225.00
Pitcher, Persian Spray, Doulton, 8 1/2 In. 150.00
Pitcher, Peru, England 75.00
Pitcher, Shell, 8 In. 465.00
Pitcher, Temple, 9 In. 850.00
Pitcher, Touraine, 6 In. 425.00
Pitcher, Touraine, 7 7/8 In. .... 695.00 to 750.00
Pitcher, Verona, 2 Qt. 295.00
Pitcher, Warwick, 2 Qt. 625.00
Pitcher, Watteau, New Wharf Pottery, 5 1/4 In. 365.00
Pitcher & Bowl, Kyber .... 1975.00 to 2250.00
Pitcher & Bowl, Whampoa 2250.00
Plate, Albany, 10 In. 90.00
Plate, Amoy, 1840s, 9 3/4 In. 130.00
Plate, Amoy, Davenport, 10 1/2 In. 145.00
Plate, Argyle, Grindley, 7 In. 37.00
Plate, Argyle, Grindley, 9 In. 75.00
Plate, Argyle, Grindley, 10 In. 95.00
Plate, Bolingbroke, Ridgway, 10 In. 85.00
Plate, Cambridge, Meakin, 9 In. 87.50
Plate, Canton, Edwards, 10 1/2 In. 130.00
Plate, Carlton, Alcock, 9 1/2 In. 125.00
Plate, Chain Of States, 9 In. 65.00
Plate, Chapoo, 9 1/2 In. 150.00
Plate, Clarence, 9 In. 65.00
Plate, Clover, Grindley, 8 In. 45.00
Plate, Coburg, c.1860, 10 1/2 In. 110.00
Plate, Conway, 9 In. .... 68.00 to 80.00
Plate, Cows, 10 In. 75.00
Plate, Crumlin, Myott, 7 In. 45.00
Plate, Delamere, Alcock, 6 1/4 In. 30.00
Plate, Delamere, Alcock, 8 In. 45.00
Plate, Delamere, Alcock, 9 In. 60.00
Plate, Delft, Minton, 10 1/2 In. 65.00
Plate, Dinner, Lorne, Grindley, 10 In. 90.00
Plate, Duchess, 8 In. 65.00
Plate, Dundee, Ridgway, 10 In. 75.00
Plate, Florida, Grindley, 9 In. 100.00
Plate, Florida, Johnson, 7 In. 48.00
Plate, Gironde, Grindley, 8 3/4 In. 76.00
Plate, Grace, 7 In. 45.00
Plate, Grace, 8 7/8 In. 58.00
Plate, Hong Kong, 10 3/8 In. 175.00
Plate, Janette, 10 In. 90.00
Plate, Kelvin, 8 In. 30.00
Plate, Kenworth, Johnson Bros., 7 1/8 In. 45.00
Plate, Kyber, 9 In. 85.00
Plate, Kyber, Adams, 8 In. 80.00
Plate, La Belle, Turkey, 10 In. 175.00
Plate, Lorne, Grindley, 10 In. 75.00
Plate, Lugano, 8 In. 38.00
Plate, Madras, 9 In. 90.00
Plate, Manilla, Podmore & Walker, 9 7/8 In. 135.00
Plate, Manilla, Podmore & Walker, 10 1/2 In. 145.00
Plate, Marguerite, Grindley, 10 In. 90.00
Plate, Marie, Grindley, 10 In. 95.00
Plate, Melbourne, Grindley, 10 In. 80.00
Plate, Nonpareil, Burgess & Leigh, 8 3/4 In. 75.00
Plate, Oregon, c.1840, 9 3/4 In. 130.00
Plate, Oregon, Johnson Bros., 10 In. 95.00
Plate, Oxford, 9 In. 50.00
Plate, Oxford, 10 In. 55.00
Plate, Pelew, 1840s, 9 3/4 In. 130.00

Plate, Pelew, 8 5/8 In. 82.00
Plate, Portman, Grindley, 8 In. 48.00
Plate, Portman, Grindley, 9 In. 70.00
Plate, Scinde, 10 1/2 In. .... 165.00 to 225.00
Plate, Shanghai, 10 In. 565.00
Plate, Shapoo, T & R, 7 1/2 In. 115.00
Plate, Sobraon, 10 1/2 In. 125.00
Plate, Sydney, 10 In. 95.00
Plate, Touraine, 8 3/4 In. .... 50.00 to 55.00
Plate, Touraine, 10 In. 90.00
Plate, Vermont, Burgess & Leigh, 9 In. 85.00
Plate, Waldorf, 10 In. 90.00
Plate, Waldorf, New Wharf Pottery, 6 In. 35.00
Plate, Watteau, 7 In. 75.00
Plate, Wild Rose, George Jones, 10 1/2 In. .... 60.00 to 85.00
Plate, Yedo, Ashworth, 1862, 10 3/8 In. 95.00
Platter, Amoy, 15 1/2 In. 500.00
Platter, Arabesque, 18 In. 795.00
Platter, Argyle, Grindley, 12 x 17 In. 375.00
Platter, Argyle, Grindley, 15 In. 275.00
Platter, Athens, Oval 200.00
Platter, Bacon, Waldorf, New Wharf Pottery 125.00
Platter, Beaufort, 14 In. 175.00
Platter, Brazil, 8 x 10 In. 135.00
Platter, Cecil, Till & Sons, 14 In. 250.00
Platter, Chapoo, 13 1/2 x 10 1/2 In. 350.00
Platter, Chapoo, 18 In. 895.00
Platter, Chapoo, 26 In. 400.00
Platter, Chusan, Morley, 13 1/4 x 10 1/8 In. 265.00
Platter, Clover, Grindley, 16 1/2 In. 160.00
Platter, Conway, 10 3/4 x 7 1/2 In. .... 70.00 to 100.00
Platter, Davenport, Wood & Sons, 16 In. 350.00
Platter, Delamere, 16 In. 295.00
Platter, Dundee, Ridgway, 13 x 8 1/2 In. 115.00
Platter, Dundee, Ridgway, 16 x 11 In. 175.00
Platter, Fulton, Johnson Bros., 12 1/2 In. 210.00
Platter, Georgia, Johnson Bros., 16 In. 395.00
Platter, Gironde, 18 In. 400.00
Platter, Gothic, J. Furnival, 8 x 10 In. 285.00
Platter, Hamilton, 15 x 10 1/2 In. 225.00
Platter, Hong Kong, 16 In. 350.00
Platter, India Ashworth, 1870, 15 In. 395.00
Platter, Indian Jar, 12 In. 215.00
Platter, Kyber, 10 x 7 3/8 In. 100.00
Platter, Kyber, 18 x 14 In. 445.00
Platter, La Belle, 14 5/8 x 10 5/8 In. 325.00
Platter, La Belle, 18 In. .... 495.00 to 595.00
Platter, Lorne, Grindley, 12 In. .... 145.00 to 165.00
Platter, Lorne, Grindley, 14 In. 185.00
Platter, Lorne, Grindley, 16 In. 335.00
Platter, Lorne, Grindley, 18 In. 395.00
Platter, Luzerne, 19 In. 435.00
Platter, Madras, 13 3/4 In. 150.00
Platter, Madras, 15 3/4 In. 255.00
Platter, Manilla, Podmore & Walker, 16 In. 795.00
Platter, Manilla, Podmore & Walker, 18 In. 895.00
Platter, Marechal Niel, Grindley, 14 1/2 In. 295.00
Platter, Melbourne, 16 In. 275.00
Platter, Melbourne, Oval, 14 1/4 In. 140.00
Platter, Mentone, Gold Trim, Johnson Bros., 16 In. 175.00
Platter, Ning Po, 12 In. 225.00
Platter, Nonpareil, 18 In. 795.00

Platter, Oregon, 10 3/4 x 8 1/8 In. 235.00
Platter, Oregon, 13 3/8 In. 375.00
Platter, Ormonde, 18 In. 200.00
Platter, Osborne, 13 x 17 In. 185.00
Platter, Peking, 16 In. 495.00
Platter, Pelew, 13 3/8 In. 302.50
Platter, Portman, Grindley, 12 In. .... 150.00 to 197.00
Platter, Richmond, Johnson, 12 In. 150.00
Platter, Scinde, 13 1/4 In. 495.00
Platter, Scinde, 16 In. 625.00
Platter, Scinde, 20 In. 7700.00
Platter, Scinde, Alcock, 18 In. 850.00
Platter, Shanghai, 20 In. 750.00
Platter, Togo, H. & K., 17 In. 395.00
Platter, Touraine, 15 In. .... 235.00 to 325.00
Platter, Touraine, Stanley Potteries, 12 In. 200.00
Platter, Touraine, Stanley, 10 In. 115.00
Platter, Trent, A.D.J. & Co., 12 In. 195.00
Platter, Trent, A.D.J. & Co., 14 In. 250.00
Platter, Troy, Meigh, 19 1/2 In. 1250.00
Platter, Victoria, Grindley, 12 In. 140.00
Platter, Waldorf, New Wharf Pottery, 9 x 10 In. 197.50
Relish, Argyle 48.00
Relish, Bute, 3 Sections 395.00
Relish, Canton, Edwards 175.00
Relish, Coburg 220.00
Relish, La Belle, 4 3/4 x 13 3/4 In. 275.00
Relish, Melbourne, Oval, 8 x 5 1/ 2 In. 38.00
Relish, Tonquin 270.00
Saucer, Scinde, 5 1/2 In. 35.00
Service For 8, Delaware, Meakin, 106 Piece 5000.00
Service For 8, Touraine, 64 Piece 3000.00
Soup, Dish, Amoy, 10 1/2 In. 175.00
Soup, Dish, Argyle, Grindley, 8 3/4 In. 75.00
Soup, Dish, Candia, 7 1/2 In. 26.00
Soup, Dish, Canton, Maddock, 9 1/4 In. 115.00
Soup, Dish, Conway, Flanged, 9 1/4 In. 88.00
Soup, Dish, Fairy Villas 75.00
Soup, Dish, Geneva 75.00
Soup, Dish, Gothic, 9 1/4 In. 80.00
Soup, Dish, Martha 55.00
Soup, Dish, Melbourne, 7 1/2 In. 35.00
Soup, Dish, Nonpareil 60.00
Soup, Dish, Normandie, Johnson Bros., 7 1/2 In. 75.00
Soup, Dish, Paris 35.00
Soup, Dish, Touraine, Rimless, Stanley 95.00
Soup, Dish, Verona, Wood 85.00
Soup, Dish, Versailles 55.00
Soup, Dish, Waldorf, Flanged, New Wharf Pottery 110.00
Soup, Dish, Watteau, Doulton, 7 1/2 In. 60.00
Sugar, Albany, Cover, Grindley 175.00
Sugar, Amoy, Cover .... 495.00 to 595.00
Sugar, Arabesque, Cover 595.00
Sugar, Arabesque, Diamond Cut 325.00
Sugar, Indian, Cover 495.00
Sugar, Kyber, Cover 350.00
Sugar, Lobelia, Cover 385.00
Sugar, Lorne, Cover 250.00
Sugar, Manilla, Cover, Podmore & Walker 850.00
Sugar, Nonpareil 265.00
Sugar, Normandy, Cover 140.00
Sugar, Oxford 250.00

Sugar, Temple, Cover, Lion's Head Handle 415.00
Sugar & Creamer, Touraine, Alcock .... 480.00 to 495.00
Syrup, Warwick 375.00
Tankard, Copper Luster Trim, Charles Allerton & Sons, 7 In. 175.00
Tea Service, Temple, Podmore & Walker, 47 Piece 7300.00
Tea Set, Arabesque, 3 Piece 1300.00
Teapot, Amoy .... 695.00 to 1985.00
Teapot, Arabesque 895.00
Teapot, Chapoo 1195.00
Teapot, Delft, Minton 395.00
Teapot, Formosa, Mayer 800.00
Teapot, Hong Kong 800.00
Teapot, Indian Jar, Furnival .... 800.00 to 950.00
Teapot, Indian, Pratt .... 595.00 to 800.00
Teapot, Japan 1195.00
Teapot, Nonpareil, Bridges & Leigh 375.00
Teapot, Nonpareil, Podmore, Hall 495.00
Teapot, Oregon, Mayer 795.00
Teapot, Rhine, Dimmock .... 650.00 to 800.00
Teapot, Rhone, Furnival 775.00
Teapot, Scinde .... 775.00 to 985.00
Teapot, Sterling 150.00
Teapot, Touraine 1195.00
Toothbrush Holder, Argyle, Grindley 295.00
Tray, Calcutta, Octagonal 270.00
Tureen, Brazil, 4 Piece 395.00
Tureen, Sauce, Crumlin, Myott 275.00
Tureen, Sauce, Haddon, Cover, Underplate & Ladle, Grindley 440.00
Tureen, Sauce, Hamilton, Ladle, Maddock 275.00
Tureen, Sauce, Jeddo, Tray, Double Leaf-Shaped Handles, 9 In. 125.00
Tureen, Sauce, Kelvin, Ladle 265.00
Tureen, Sauce, Melbourne, Cover, Tray 325.00
Tureen, Sauce, Warwick, Ladle, 5 x 8 In. 335.00
Tureen, Soup, Argyle 595.00
Tureen, Soup, Bamboo, Cabbage Rose Finial, Alcock 2000.00
Tureen, Soup, Clarence 495.00
Tureen, Soup, Georgia 495.00
Tureen, Soup, Gironde 300.00
Tureen, Soup, Messina .... 1195.00 to 1475.00
Tureen, Soup, Waverly 575.00
Tureen, Soup, Waverly, Cover 500.00
Tureen, Vegetable, Athens, Adams 600.00
Undertray, Sauce, Yedo, Tab Handles, 10 1/4 x 91/4 In. 115.00
Vase, Floral Sprays, Shoulder Handle, Crimped, Gold Trim, 12 x 6 In. 225.00
Wash Basin, Formosa, T. J. & J. Mayer 2100.00
Washbowl, Trilby 200.00
Waste Bowl, Chapoo 275.00
Waste Bowl, Manilla .... 140.00 to 175.00
Waste Bowl, Normandy, Johnson Bros. 5 7/8 In. 150.00
Waste Bowl, Scinde, Walker 225.00

FLYING PHOENIX, see Phoenix Bird category

FOLK ART is also listed in many categories of this book under the actual
name of the object. See categories such as Box, Cigar Store Figure, Weather
Vane, Wooden, etc.

Alligator, Carved Wood, Original Varnish, 8 1/2 In. 27.50
Ashtray, Cat, Wooden Silhouette, Worn Red & Black Paint, Glass Insert, 24 In. 27.50
Basket, Made Of Bottle Caps 165.00
Bird House, Replica Of Spite House, Square, 35 In. 2650.00
Birdhouse, 3 Story, Shingled Roof 175.00
Birdhouse, Beach Cottage Shape, Green & White, Large 875.00
Birdhouse, From Gourd 38.00

Birdhouse, Log Cabin, 1930s 365.00
Birdhouse, Plywood, Cutout Bamboo Sections, Valley Of Virginia, 5 1/2 x 7 1/2 In. .. 115.00
Birdhouse, Steepled Church Shape, 19th Century 1350.00
Birdhouse, Stove Pipe Hat Form, c.1930 .... 295.00
Birdhouse, Wooden, 4 Holes, Blue & White, 6 Ft. Pole 295.00
Birdhouse, Wooden, Red Roof, 1880 .... 125.00
Bulldog, Pyrography, Oval, 18 x 22 In. 45.00
Busk, Chip Carved, Blue Calamanco Corset, Wooden, Dated 1779 .... 522.50
Caboose, Painted Red & Black, 19th Century, 116 In. 1540.00
Caddy, Sewing, Cigar Box 95.00
Chain, Bottle Caps, 1940s, 60 Ft. 1150.00
Chicken, Carved Wood, Dark Paint, Red & Yellow Trim, Himmelreicht, 6 1/2 In. 1815.00
Chicken, Wooden Base, Papier-Mache, Polychrome Paint, 5 1/8 In. 60.50
Church, Wooden, Blue & White Paint, 17 In. 55.00
Church, Wooden, Zigzag Edge, 2 Chimneys, Painted, 6 x 4 In. 160.00
Clock Case, Cathedral, Scroll Work Cutouts, 4 Spires, 26 x 20 In. 425.00
Doll, Black Man & Woman, Walnut Heads, Man, Bag Of Cotton, 11 In., Pair 300.00
Doll, Hand Carved, Jointed, Crocheted Dress & Hat, Penciled Features, 1948, 8 In. ... 17.50
Figural Scene, Shotgun Wedding, Maid, Not Wise, Wooden, 1920-1930, 7 Piece 475.00
Figure, Black Woman, Wax, Carrying Bag Of Cotton, Fabric Clothes 365.00
Figure, Blacksmith, Mechanical, Iron 1925.00
Figure, Bottle Cap Man, 3 In. 18.00
Figure, Lady Liberty, Polychromed Carved Wood, 1840, 16 x 29 In. 5000.00
Figure, Sailor, Black Shirt, Red Pants, Carved, Painted, 1840-1860, 10 In. 115.00
Flowers, Shellwork, Glass Dome Cover, Large 650.00
Frame, Acorn Pattern Corners, Button Like Circles Join Sides 20.00
Frame, Crown Of Thorns 1200.00
Frame, Eagle Shape, Spread Wings, Tin On Wood, Blue Paint 850.00
Frame, Mirror, Tassel & Ribbon, Frank Moran, Walnut, 14 In. 150.00
Frame, Zigzag Style, Wooden, 7 Layers, 8 x 10 In 40.00
Grave Wreath, Tiny Glass Beads On Wires, Flower & Leaf Forms, Victorian 225.00
Head, Unglazed Buff Clay, 20th Century, 8 In. 104.00
Horse, Wooden, Papier-Mache, Palomino Paint, 5 In. 27.50
House, Wooden, Red & Green, From Cheese Box, 1920s, 12 In. 95.00
Lamp, Popsicle Sticks, Applied Ceramic Leaves, Table 95.00
Letter Box, Wooden, Painted Design, Bird, To My Love, Dated '43 .... 1200.00
Log Cabin, Carved Stone, Frog Inside, 7 3/8 In. 330.00
Log Cabin, Tin, Pennsylvania 495.00
Man, Carved Wood, Mechanical, Push On Head & Private Part Pops Up, Pair 45.00
Necklace, Woman's, Apple Seeds, Long 1.00
Noah's Ark, Cardboard, 60 Pairs Of Wooden Animals 3850.00
Parrot Cage, Painted Tin, Wooden Parrot Perched Outside 285.00
Parrot, Carved, Glass Eyes, Original Paint, Ohio, 11 1/2 In. 330.00
Pipe, Black Child, Riding Alligator, 11 1/2 In. 440.00
Road Runner, Carved, Original Paint, Glass Eyes, Ohio, 30 In. 550.00
Rooster, Carved, Weathered Paint, 14 1/2 In. 1155.00
Sailboat, Made From Burnt Matchsticks, 20th Century, 12 In. 1200.00
Smoking Pipe-Whistle, Man, Kneeling, Human & Animal Faces, 18th Century 880.00
Toy, Cider Mill, 1910-1925, 26 x 10 x 13 In. 275.00
Toy, Dory, Wooden, Weathered Gray & Green Paint, Oars, 1900, 6 1/2 x 22 1/2 In. 475.00
Toy, Steamroller, Cans & Bottle Caps, Depression Era, 11 In. 247.00
Toy, Train, Tin & Wooden 350.00
Toy, Train, Union Pacific Engine 90.00
Vase, Floral, Wax, Glass Dome Cover, Victorian, Large 275.00
Whirligig, 2 Black Musicians, 1940 .... 125.00
Whirligig, 2 Indians, Paddling Canoe, Full-Headdress, Carved, Painted, 13 x 22 In. ... 3680.00
Whirligig, 3 Figures Sawing Log, 1930s, American, 24 1/2 In 800.00
Whirligig, Black Man, Protecting Himself From Bee, E.M. Carey, 1985, 30 In. 550.00
Whirligig, Boy With Cap, Wooden, Worn Paint, 19 In. 1100.00
Whirligig, Canoe & Two Indians, Polychrome, c.1900, 11 x 21 In. 606.00
Whirligig, Gentleman, Double-Sided, Black Bowler, Striped Pants, Pine, 15 3/4 In. ... 2600.00
Whirligig, Indian Paddling Canoe 250.00
Whirligig, Lumberjack, Carved & Painted, 2 Silhouettes Of Buildings, 16 x 20 In. 345.00

Whirligig, Man With Top Hat, Spoon-Shaped Paddles, 19th Century, 12 1/2 In. 1150.00
Whirligig, Man On Boneshaker Bicycle, Pine & Metal, American, 1910s, 40 In. 5175.00
Whirligig, Man, Standing With Fish Between Legs, Erotic, Weathered 1400.00
Whirligig, Policeman, Green Uniform, 1930s 750.00
Whirligig, Sailor Wearing Tin Cap, Swinging Arms, 19th Century, 15 In. 690.00
Whirligig, Soldier, Tin Belt, Sword, Hat, Prince Albert Ad., 31 In. .... 1050.00 to 1155.00
Whirligig, Upright Figure, Marching, Military Dress, Painted, 22 x 24 In. 1725.00
Whirligig, Woman, Pumping Water, 1900s 225.00
Windmill, Yard, Wooden, Red & White Paint, Metal Trim, Calif. 975.00
Witch, Brooms, Black, Orange, 3 Ft. 4850.00

FOOT WARMERS solved the problem of cold feet in past generations. Some
warmers held charcoal, others held hot water. Pottery, tin, and soapstone were
the favored materials to conduct the heat. The warmer was kept under the
feet, then the legs and feet were tucked into a blanket, providing welcome
warmth in a cold carriage or church.

Buggy, Pair 50.00
Floral Tooled Lid, Red & Black Graining, Brass, 42 1/2 In. 385.00
Punched Diamonds & Circles, Tin, Wooden Frame, 7 1/2 x 9 In. 215.00
Punched Heart & Circle Top, Tin, Mortised Walnut Frame 300.00
Turned Corner Posts, Punched Tin, Cherry Frame, 8 x 9 In. 193.00
Whale Oil Burner, Tin & Wood, 6 3/4 x 7 3/4 In. 50.00

FOSTORIA glass was made in Fostoria, Ohio, from 1887 to 1891. The factory
was moved to Moundsville, West Virginia, and most of the glass seen in
shops today is a twentieth-century product. The company was sold in 1983;
new items will be easily identifiable, according to the new owner, Lancaster
Colony Corporation. Additional Fostoria items may be listed in the Milk
Glass category.

Alexis, Jar, Horseradish 65.00
American, Bowl, Footed 30.00
American, Butter, Cover, 1/4 Lb. 15.00
American, Butter, Cover, Round 160.00
American, Cake Salver, Round 79.00
American, Cake Salver, Square 159.00
American, Cake Stand, Square, 10 In. 75.00
American, Candlestick, 2-Light, Round Foot, 4 3/8 In., Pair .... 30.00 to 50.00
American, Console 30.00
American, Cookie Jar 265.00
American, Cup & Saucer 20.00
American, Decanter, Stopper, Word Scotch Imprinted, 24 Oz. 58.00
American, Dish, 3 Sections, Oblong, 9 1/2 x 6 In. 25.00
American, Fruit, Stand, 16 In. 175.00
American, Fruit, Stand, 18 In. 225.00
American, Goblet, Low, Footed 18.00
American, Humidor, Large 450.00
American, Ice Bucket, Tray 80.00
American, Jam Pot, Hat Shape 20.00
American, Nappy, Tri-Corner 12.00
American, Pitcher, Ice Lip 200.00
American, Pitcher, Straight Side 325.00
American, Plate, 6 In. 5.50
American, Plate, Torte, Round, 18 In. 79.00
American, Punch Bowl, 14 In. 95.00
American, Punch Bowl, 18 In. 150.00
American, Punch Cup, Glared 8.00
American, Punch Set, 3 3/4 Gal., 14 Piece 425.00
American, Punch Set, Underplate, Ladle, 14-Inch Bowl, 3 Piece 190.00
American, Salt, 3 1/2 x 2 3/4 In. 5.00
American, Sherbet 8.00
American, Sugar & Creamer 29.00
American, Tumbler, Footed, 5 Oz. 12.00
American, Vase, Flared, 6 1/2 In. 58.00

American, Vase, Straight, 8 In. .... 32.00 to 45.00
Arcady, Goblet, 9 Oz. 14.00
Arcady, Tumbler, Footed, 12 Oz. 25.00
Baroque, Cup & Saucer, Topaz 23.00
Baroque, Tumbler, Topaz, 3 In. 10.00
Baroque, Vase, Blue, 7 In. 120.00
Baroque, Vase, Topaz, 7 In. 50.00
Bookends, Rearing Horses 85.00
Caprice, Bowl, Silver Overlay, 13 In. 45.00
Century, Cruet .... 40.00 to 45.00
Century, Pitcher, Ice Lip, Pink 80.00
Century, Sugar 8.00
Century, Sugar & Creamer 12.00
Chintz, Cordial 35.00
Chintz, Cup & Saucer 27.00
Chintz, Ice Bucket 90.00
Chintz, Plate, 10 1/2 In. 53.00
Chintz, Sugar & Creamer, Tray, Miniature 60.00
Coin, Ashtray, Emerald, 4 Coins, 10 In. 80.00
Coin, Bowl, Red, 7 1/2 In. 50.00
Coin, Cake Plate, Blue 200.00
Coin, Candleholder, Blue, Pair 65.00
Coin, Candy Dish, Cover, Blue 65.00
Coin, Console, Blue 55.00
Coin, Cruet 45.00
Coin, Cruet, Blue 125.00
Coin, Decanter, Emerald Green 350.00
Coin, Salt & Pepper, Red 40.00
Coin, Sugar & Creamer, Blue 60.00
Coin, Urn, Frosted, Emerald Green, Cover, 12 In. 200.00
Coin, Vase, Bud, Blue, 8 In. 50.00
Coin, Vase, Bud, Red, 8 In. 50.00
Coin, Wedding Bowl, Marigold 55.00
Colonial Dame, Tumbler, 12 Oz. 20.00
Colony, Bonbon, 3-Footed 10.00
Colony, Bowl, Footed, 10 In. 70.00
Colony, Butter, 1/4 Lb. 35.00
Colony, Candlestick, 8 In. 25.00
Colony, Compote, Cover, 6 1/2 In. 35.00
Colony, Cup & Saucer 6.00
Colony, Glass, Juice 16.00
Colony, Goblet 10.00
Colony, Ice Basket 275.00
Colony, Plate, Torte, 13 In. 45.00
Colony, Relish, 3 Sections 20.00
Colony, Sugar & Creamer 14.00
Colony, Sugar & Creamer, Tray 32.00
Colony, Tray, Handles, 11 In. 45.00
Colony, Tray, Sandwich, Center Handle 28.00
Colony, Tumbler, Footed, 5 1/2 In. 9.00
Colony, Tumbler, Juice 16.00
Contour, Goblet, Pink 30.00
Corsage, Goblet, 7 3/8 In. 20.00
Corsage, Pitcher 295.00
Corsage, Wine, 5 1/2 In. 17.50
Cynthia, Cordial, 3/4 Oz. 18.00
Diana, Bell, Dinner 80.00
Dolly Madison, Goblet 15.00
Dolly Madison, Sherbet 9.00
Dolly Madison, Tumbler, Footed 15.00
Dolly Madison, Wine 20.00
Edgewood, Toothpick .... 25.00 to 35.00
Fairfax, Gravy Boat, Green 28.00

Fairfax, Ice Bucket, Topaz 60.00
Fairfax, Pitcher, Amber 120.00
Fairfax, Plate, Azure, 9 In. 11.00
Fairfax, Plate, Topaz, 10 In. 18.00
Fairfax, Relish, 3 Sections, Amber, 11 1/2 In. 15.00
Fairfax, Tumbler, Blue, 12 Oz. 20.00
Figurine, Horse, Rearing, 6 x 7 1/2 In. 55.00
Figurine, Mermaid, 10 1/2 In. 120.00
Grape, Centerpiece 45.00
Hartford, Toothpick 45.00
Heavy Drape, Toothpick 80.00
Heirloom, Candy Bowl Set, Light Green Opalescent, 3 Piece 135.00
Iris, Vase, Gold Hearts, Vines On White Ground, 6 1/2 In. 800.00
Jamestown, Bowl, Dessert, Pink 18.00
Jamestown, Butter 70.00
Jamestown, Goblet, Amber 8.00
Jamestown, Ice Jug, Amber 35.00
Jamestown, Plate, Pink, 8 In. 18.00
Jamestown, Shaker 15.00
Jamestown, Sherbet 6.00
Jamestown, Sherbet, Pink 7.00
Jamestown, Sugar 22.00
Jamestown, Sugar & Creamer 45.00
Jamestown, Tumbler, Footed, Brown, 6 In. 11.00
Jamestown, Tumbler, Iced Tea, Amethyst 11.00
Jamestown, Tumbler, Iced Tea, Pink, 12 Oz. 22.00
Jamestown, Tumbler, Juice, Pink 14.00
Jamestown, Wine, 4 Oz. 22.00
June, Salt & Pepper, Footed 40.00
June, Tumbler, Footed, 6 In. 22.00
Lido, Goblet 22.00
Lido, Oyster Cocktail 5.00
Lido, Wine, 3 Oz. 20.00
Madonna, Paper Sticker 82.00
Mayfair, Ashtray, Silver Mist 10.00
Meadow Rose, Champagne, 6 Oz. 18.00
Meadow Rose, Goblet, 10 Oz. 20.00
Midnight Rose, Champagne, 5 1/2 Oz. 20.00
Navarre, Bowl, Oval, 12 1/2 In. 50.00
Navarre, Champagne, Blue 70.00
Navarre, Claret, Blue, Large 50.00
Navarre, Cordial, 1 Oz. .... 30.00 to 50.00
Navarre, Goblet, Water 19.00
Oak Leaf, Plate, 8 1/2 In. 8.00
Persian, Toothpick 45.00
Plymouth, Goblet 19.00
Priscilla, Toothpick 115.00
Queen Anne, Goblet, Stemmed, 10 Oz. 18.00
Queen Anne, Pitcher, Etched, 60 Oz. 135.00
Queen Anne, Sugar & Creamer 28.00
Queen Anne, Tumbler, 10 Oz. 14.00
Romance, Bowl, Salad, 10 In. .... 30.00 to 33.00
Romance, Plate, 7 1/2 In. 7.00
Romance, Sherbet 10.00
Seascape, Bowl, Square, Blue Opalescent, 8 3/4 In. 39.00
Seville, Plate, Amber, 10 In. 12.00
Shirley, Goblet, Water 19.00
Spool, Bowl, Flared, Topaz, 9 1/2 In. 27.00
Spool, Compote, Low, 6 In. 11.00
Trojan, Cordial, Topaz, 4 Piece 55.00
Verona, Candlestick, Amber, Pair 37.50
Versailles, Ice Bucket, Bail, Tongs, Blue 100.00
Versailles, Pail, Whipped Cream 125.00

Versailles, Pitcher, Pink	285.00
Versailles, Relish, 2 Sections, Oval, Green, 8 3/4 In.	26.00
Versailles, Sugar & Creamer, Blue	50.00
Versailles, Tumbler, Blue, 12 Oz.	30.00
Versailles, Tumbler, Green, 5 1/4 In.	25.00
Vesper, Ice Bucket, Amber	50.00
Vesper, Pitcher, Amber	285.00
Victoria, Rose Bowl, Large	125.00
Vogue, Toothpick	50.00
Wheel Star, Cocktail, Red, Footed	90.00
Willowmere, Sugar & Creamer	30.00
Willowmere, Tumbler, Footed, 5 3/4 In.	20.00

FOVAL, see Fry category

FRANCISCAN is a trademark that appears on pottery. Gladding, McBean and Company started in 1875. The company grew and acquired other potteries. They made sewer pipes, floor tiles, dinnerwares, and art pottery with a variety of trademarks. In 1934, dinnerware and art pottery were sold under the name Franciscan Ware. They made china and cream-colored, decorated earthenware. Desert Rose, Apple, El Patio, and Coronado were best sellers. The company became Interpace Corporation and in 1979 was purchased by Josiah Wedgwood & Sons. The plant was closed in 1984 but a few of the patterns are still being made. For more information, see *Kovels' Depression Glass & American Dinnerware Price List.*

Ashtray, Apple & Rose	2.20
Ashtray, Coral, Individual	12.00
Bowl, Desert Rose, 6 In.	6.00
Bowl, Salad, Desert Rose	95.00
Bowl, Vegetable, Starburst, 2 Sections	16.00
Butter, Apple & Rose, Cover	40.00
Butter, Country Garden	35.00
Butter, Madiera, Cover	25.00
Butter, Stardust, Cover	35.00 to 45.00
Candy Dish, Desert Rose	199.00
Canister, Tea, Desert Rose	120.00
Casserole, Desert Rose, 1 1/2 Qt.	95.00
Chop Plate, Coronado, Turquoise, 14 In.	28.00
Coffeepot, Cosmopolitan	60.00
Coffeepot, Desert Rose	125.00
Compote, Desert Rose, Large	125.00
Cookie Jar, Desert Rose, 11 In.	230.00 to 250.00
Cup, Desert Rose, 10 Oz.	6.50 to 25.00
Cup & Saucer, Apple & Rose	13.00
Cup & Saucer, Apples, Leaves, Twig Rim & Handle	12.00
Cup & Saucer, Desert Rose	8.00 to 35.00
Cup & Saucer, Meadow Rose	12.00
Cup & Saucer, Starburst	7.00
Dinner Set, Apple, 1940s, 20 Piece	60.00
Eggcup, Desert Rose	30.00
Gravy Boat, Apple, Attached Underplate	20.00
Mixing Bowl, Nesting, Apple, 9, 7 1/2 & 5 1/2 In., 3 Piece	250.00
Mug, Desert Rose, Barrel Shape, 12 Oz.	20.00 to 26.00
Mug, Ivy, 12 Oz.	12.00 to 45.00
Mug, Starburst	15.00
Pitcher, Water, Desert Rose	120.00
Plate, Apple, 8 In.	7.00
Plate, Apple, 9 1/2 In.	9.00 to 20.00
Plate, Apple, 10 1/4 In.	12.00
Plate, Desert Rose, 6 1/2 In.	6.00
Plate, Desert Rose, 8 In.	5.00 to 12.00
Plate, Desert Rose, 9 3/4 In..	14.00
Plate, Desert Rose, 10 1/2 In.	12.00 to 75.00

Plate, Fresh Fruit, 10 1/4 In. 14.00
Plate, Ivy & Fresh Fruit, 8 1/2 In. 8.00
Plate, Ivy & Fresh Fruit, 9 3/4 In. 18.00
Plate, Ivy, 8 In. ...... 15.00 to 16.00
Plate, October, 10 1/4 In. 12.00
Plate, Starburst, 8 In. 5.00
Plate, Wild Flower, 7 In. 75.00
Platter, Apple, 12 1/2 In. 28.00
Platter, Apple, 14 In. 29.00
Platter, Desert Rose, Oval, 19 In. 250.00
Platter, Desert Rose, Round, 12 In. 30.00
Platter, Fresh Fruit, 14 In. 38.00
Platter, Meadow Rose, 14 In. 38.00
Platter, Rose, 14 In. 32.00
Platter, Starburst, Oval, 15 In. 45.00
Platter, Wild Flower, 14 In. 60.00
Salt & Pepper, Apple & Rose 25.00
Salt & Pepper, Desert Rose 30.00
Salt & Pepper, Madiera 10.00
Salt & Pepper, Rosebud 10.00
Salt & Pepper, Starburst, Large 35.00
Salt & Pepper Mill, Apple Shape, Wooden Base & Top 450.00
Saltshaker, Coronado, Gray 8.00
Saucer, Desert Rose 3.00
Sherbet, Apple & Rose 30.00
Sherbet, Ivy 25.00
Soup, Cream, Coronado, Turquoise 8.00
Soup, Onion, El Patio 18.00
Sugar, Coronado, Cover, Yellow 12.00
Sugar, Desert Rose, Cover 14.00
Sugar & Creamer, Apple 30.00
Sugar & Creamer, Desert Rose ...... 18.00 to 30.00
Sugar & Creamer, Ivy 40.00
Sugar & Creamer, Meadow Rose 35.00
Teapot, Apple 55.00
Thimble, Desert Rose 30.00
Tidbit, Apple, 3 Tiers 125.00
Tidbit, Desert Rose, 2 Tiers 75.00
Tile, Apple 25.00
Tumbler, Apple 18.00
Tumbler, Desert Rose, 6 Oz. 18.00
Tumbler, Ivy ...... 28.00 to 30.00
Tumbler, Poppy 35.00
Tureen, Soup, Apple, Cover ...... 425.00 to 450.00

FRANCISWARE is the name of a glassware made by Hobbs, Brockunier and Company of Wheeling, West Virginia, in the 1880s. It is a clear or frosted hobnail or swirl pattern glass with amber-stained rim. Some pieces were made by a pressed glass method, others were mold blown.

Berry Bowl, Square, Large 135.00
Syrup, Hobnail, Frosted 395.00
Toothpick, Hobnail 55.00
Water Set, Hobnail, 7 Piece 220.00

FRANKART, Inc., New York, New York, mass-produced nude *dancing lady* lamps, ashtrays, and other decorative Art Deco items in the 1920s and 1930s. They were made of white lead composition and spray-painted. *Frankart Inc.* and the patent number and year were stamped on the base.

Ashtray, Hunter, Green 135.00
Ashtray, Nude, Kneeling, Pottery 150.00
Ashtray, Nude, Pearlized 259.00
Ashtray, Nude, Reclining, 1922 ...... 350.00
Bookends, Boy Sailor And His Dog, c.1930 ...... 150.00

Bookends, Dog, Scotties 140.00
Bookends, Dog, Terrier, Bronzed 35.00
Bookends, Dutch 90.00
Bookends, Eagle .... 60.00 to 75.00
Bookends, Elephant 75.00
Bookends, Horsehead 122.00
Bookends, Nude On Book 75.00
Bookends, Puppies Playing 145.00
Bookends, Sailor Boy With Scotty 75.00
Box, Cigarette, 2 Nude Figures Holding Green Glass Box 450.00
Flower Frog, Nude, Holding Ceramic Tray 150.00
Lamp, 2 Kneeling Women, Brown Glass Globe Between, Gray, 14 In. 1100.00
Lamp, Black Nude Kneeling, Arms Out To Side, Holding Tray 500.00
Lamp, Elephant 225.00
Lamp, Fan 235.00
Lamp, Nude, Seated 250.00
Lamp, Nude, Silhouetted Against Frosted Plate Glass, Rear Light 650.00
Lamp, Nude, Standing On Frosted Plate Glass, Light Beneath 350.00
Lamp, Woman, Seated, Crackled Brown Glass Globe In Lap, Gray, Signed ... 900.00
Wall Pocket, Woman's Head, 7 In., Pair 300.00

FRANKOMA POTTERY was originally known as The Frank Potteries when
John F. Frank opened shop in 1933. The factory is now working in Sapulpa,
Oklahoma. Early wares were made from a light cream-colored clay, but in
1956 the company switched to a red burning clay. The firm makes
dinnerwares, utilitarian and decorative kitchenwares, figurines, flowerpots,
and limited edition and commemorative pieces.

Ashtray, Broadmoor 20.00
Ashtray, Dog, Sprawled On Edge, Blue-Green Glaze, 7 1/4 x 5 1/2 In. 20.00
Bookends, Bucking Bronco 225.00
Bowl & Pitcher, Blue, Brown, 4 1/2 & 6 In. 10.00
Bust, Indian, Frankoma Textile Co., Bronze 55.00
Candlestick, Christ The Light Of The World, Oral Roberts, Pair 18.00
Candlestick, Double, Green-Brown Scrolls, Pair 22.00
Cup & Saucer, Jubilee 19.00
Cup & Saucer, Wagon Wheel, Green, Brown 6.00
Dish, Leaf, Prairie Green, 12 1/2 In. 12.00
Dish, Plainsman, 4-Leaf Clover, Bronze, 6 1/2 In. 6.50
Figurine, Indian Chief, 8 In. 75.00
Figurine, Indian, Headdress, Arrowhead Label, 8 1/2 In. 140.00
Flask, Mayan Aztec, Leather Thong Through Loops, 6 1/2 In. 18.00
Mug, Donkey, Celery Green, 1981 .... 25.00
Mug, Elephant, Nixon, Agnew, Desert Gold, Orange, 1973 .... 45.00
Mug, Plainsman, Desert Gold, 5 3/8 In. 6.00
Mug, Road Runner 25.00
Mug, Woodland Moss, 3 3/4 In. 5.00
Planter, Duck, Brown, 9 1/2 In. 15.00
Planter, Elephant, Nixon, Agnew 25.00
Planter, Lady Head, Ada Clay, Blond, Wall 100.00
Plate, Christmas, 1965 .... 275.00
Plate, Easter, White, 1972 .... 15.00
Plate, Flight Into Egypt 28.00
Plate, Plainsman, Woodland Moss, 6 1/2 In. 2.50
Plate, Wagon Wheel, Green, 10 In. 8.00
Salt & Pepper, Lazybones, Brown, Blue, 1 Piece 10.00
Stein Set, Falstaff, 7 Piece 200.00
Sugar & Creamer, Mayan Aztec, Cover, 3 5/8 In. 15.00
Tea Set, Plainsman, Gold Bronze, 3 Piece 32.00
Teapot, Wagon Wheel, Green 10.00
Trivet, Commemorative, Oklahoma, Arrows To Atoms, 1957 .... 25.00
Vase, Fan, Green Bronze Leaf Form, 9 x 8 x 3 1/2 In. 30.00
Vase, Green, Rose Bowl Shape 20.00
Vase, Leaf Handle, Brown, 10 In. 45.00

Wall Pocket, Acorn, Pair 45.00
Wall Pocket, Cowboy Boot, White 10.00

FRATERNAL objects that are related to the many different fraternal organizations in the United States are listed in this category. The Elks, Masons, Odd Fellows, and others are included. Furniture is listed in the Furniture category. Shaving mugs decorated with fraternal crests are included in the Shaving Mug category.

Elks, Ashtray, Louisiana, 1929 .... 20.00
Elks, Badge, Trustee's, Ornate 90.00
Elks, Baton, Brass, 1911 .... 110.00
Elks, Booklet, Constitution & Statutes Book For Elks, 1938-1939, 150 Pages 6.00
Elks, Buckle, Belt, Brass 15.00
Elks, Buckle, Belt, Pewter 20.00
Elks, Flask, Milk Glass 30.00
Elks, Flask, Roseville 40.00
Elks, Glove, Softball, Des Moines Glove & Mfg. Co., 1940s 13.00
Elks, Match Safe, Copper 10.00
Elks, Match Safe, Sterling Silver 100.00
Elks, Medallion, Inner Guard, Bronze, Enameled 55.00
Elks, Mug, Brown 45.00
Elks, Mug, Brunt Art Ware 50.00
Elks, Pin, Rochester, Enameled, Brass 25.00
Elks, Postcard, Convention, Philadelphia, 1907 .... 10.00
Elks, Postcard, Denver Lodge, Billiard Room, 1920s 10.00
Elks, Postcard, Denver Lodge, Smoking Room, Color 10.00
Elks, Postcard, Denver Street Scene, Early 1900s 8.00
Elks, Postcard, Memorial Hall, Temple, La., 1899 .... 5.00
Elks, Program, Charity Fund, Galveston Lodge 126, Jan. 1905, 10 x 6 1/2 In. 35.00
Elks, Program, Cruise, Indies & Caribbean, 1926 & 1927 .... 20.00
Elks, Program, Flag Day, Galveston Lodge, 4 Pages, 5 1/4 x 8 In. 20.00
Elks, Shaving Mug, Barber's Furniture & Supplies, Gold 24.00
Elks, Timetable, Railroad, Pacific Northwest, Elks Excursion, Summer, 1912 .... 20.00
Elks, Tooth, White Gold 45.00
Elks, Uniform, Softball, Blue & Gold 13.00
Elks, Watch Fob, Elk's Club, Albany, N.Y., Red Star, Oval, 1919 .... 14.00
Knights Templar, Book, Pilgrim Commandery No. 9, Roster, Lowell, Mass., 1932 .... 5.00
Knights Templar, Uniform, 19th Century 125.00
Mason, Mug, Baltic Craftman's Club, Logo, February 5, 1916, White Interior 15.00
Masonic, Apron, Early 19th Century, 15 x 71 In. .... 95.00 to 110.00
Masonic, Box, Blanket, Symbols, Brown, 1850s, Miniature 285.00
Masonic, Button, Imperial Session, Pinback, 1937 .... 10.00
Masonic, Champagne, 1905 .... 85.00
Masonic, Coverlet, Eagles, 1825 .... 340.00
Masonic, Cup, Syria Shrine, 3 Handles, 1905 .... 85.00
Masonic, Emblem, Enameled, Diamond-Set Crown, E.J. Warwick, 14K Gold, 1954 .. 550.00
Masonic, Encyclopedia Of Freemasonry, Mackey, 2 Vol. 60.00
Masonic, Jug, Stoneware, Brown Glaze, Blue Masonic Design, Ovoid, 14 In. 1210.00
Masonic, Match Holder, Emblem Top, Aluminum, 2 Sections, 5 1/2 x 8 1/2 In. 98.00
Masonic, Paperweight, Masonic Temple, Boston, Nov. 29, 1892, 4 In. 22.00
Masonic, Pin, Lapel, 14K Gold 16.00
Masonic, Platter, Butter Chip, Allegheny, KTK, 7 Piece 150.00
Masonic, Sword, Masonic Emblems On Blade, Cross Pommel, Leather Scabbard 190.00
Masonic, Walking Stick, Carved, Painted, 1888, 35 In. 1380.00
Masonic, Watch Fob, Shrine Jerusalem 50.00
Masonic, Watch, 15 Jewel, Mother-Of-Pearl Dial, Sterling Silver, Tempor W. Co. 2200.00
Masonic, Watch, 19 Jewel, Open Face, No. 547, Dudley Watch, Lancaster, Penn... 1650.00
Odd Fellows, Badge, Rebekah Lodge, No. 33, Cuba, Black Ribbon 10.00
Odd Fellows, Badge, Rochester, Bronze, 1912, 2 Piece 24.00
Odd Fellows, Book, The Brotherhood, Rev. Thomas Beharrel, 1875, 7 1/2 x 5 In. 15.00
Odd Fellows, Valentine, Signed F. O'Neill, 1909 .... 10.00
Odd Fellows, Watch Fob, Taunton, Maine, 1914 .... 18.00
Shriner, Badge, World's Fair, 1893, Chicago, Hanger 36.00

Shriner, Book, Mecca Temple N.Y., Ancient Arabic Order, 176 Pages, 6 x 3 In. 12.00
Shriner, Champagne, Rochester & Pittsburgh, Clear, 1911 .... 100.00
Shriner, Fez, Sword Pin 35.00
Shriner, Goblet, Convention, St. Paul, Minn., 1908, 5 1/4 In. 95.00
Shriner, Nodder, Full Figure, 1965 .... 45.00
Shriner, Tumbler, Atlantic City, Woman, With Sword, Fish Handles, 1904 .... 27.00
Shriner, Tumbler, Rochester, N.Y., Man On Camel, Photographer, 1911 .... 42.00
Shriner, Tumbler, San Francisco, Double Column Base, Bear Decal 25.00
Shriner, Tumbler, Saratoga, N.Y., Indian Design, 1903 .... 42.00
Shriner, Tumbler, Washington, D.C., 3-Sword Triangular Base, 1900 .... 30.00
Shriner, Wine, Washington, D.C., 3-Sword Base, 1900 .... 110.00

FRY GLASS was made by the H. C. Fry Glass Company of Rochester,
Pennsylvania. The company, founded in 1901, first made cut glass and other
types of fine glasswares. In 1922, they patented a heat-resistant glass called
Pearl Oven glass. For two years, 1926–1927, the company made Fry Foval,
an opal ware decorated with colored trim. Reproductions of this glass have
been made. Depression glass patterns made by Fry may be listed in the
Depression Glass category. Some pieces of cut glass may also be included in
the Cut Glass category.

FRY FOVAL, Coffeepot, Green Handle & Finial, 6 1/2 In. 225.00
   Cup & Saucer, Clear Handle 30.00
   Cup & Saucer, Green Handle 60.00
   Mug, Iridescent Green, Cobalt Blue Handle 35.00
   Pitcher, Green Handle, Opalescent, 8 In. 275.00
   Teapot, Opalescent Blue 45.00
FRY, Cake Server, Cover, Russian, Strawberry-Diamond Buttons, 9 1/2 x 12 1/2 In. 880.00
   Compote, Amber, 4 In. 30.00
   Cup & Saucer, Opalescent, 6 Sets 225.00
   Dish, Mint, 3-Footed, 3 x 6 1/4 In. 170.00
   Ivy Bowl, Azure Blue 90.00
   Plate & Goblet, Luncheon, Diamond Optic Crystal, Black Reeding, Pair 150.00
   Platter, Engraved Flowers & Ferns, Oval, 12 1/2 x 9 In. 65.00
   Sugar & Creamer, Art Glass 125.00
   Tray, 8 Sided, 9 1/2 In. 1800.00
   Vase, Diamond Optic Crystal, Azure Blue Reeding, 7 1/2 In. 150.00
   Wine, Royal Blue, Twisted Crystal Stem 20.00

FULPER is the mark used by the American Pottery Company of Flemington,
New Jersey. The art pottery was made from 1910 to 1929. The firm had been
making bottles, jugs, and housewares from 1805. Doll heads were made
about 1928. The firm became Stangl Pottery in 1929. Fulper art pottery is
admired for its attractive glazes and simple shapes.

Bookends, Block, Incised Lion Heads, Crystalline Flambe Glaze, Marked, 5 1/2 In. .. 305.00
Bookends, Open Book On Closed Book, Green and Cream Flambe Glaze, 5 In. 330.00
Bookends, Rameses II, Matte Green Glaze, 10 In. 850.00
Bowl, Brown, Green Trim, 9 In. 165.00
Bowl, Cutouts In Base, Green, 9 In. 400.00
Bowl, Dark Blue Crystals, Gold Crystals At Handles, Blue High Glaze, 5 x 7 In. 275.00
Bowl, Effigy, 7 x 10 In. .... 675.00 to 900.00
Bowl, Everted Rim, Flowing Glazes, 6 3/4 In. 215.00
Bowl, Fish Swimming On Interior, Caramel To Sea-Green Flambe Glaze, 11 1/2 In. .. 825.00
Bowl, Green Crystalline Glaze, 11 1/2 In. 250.00
Bowl, Green Crystalline Glaze, Marked, 3 x 11 In. 350.00
Bowl, Green, Crystalline Drip Glaze, 6 1/2 x 12 In. 295.00
Bowl, Inturned Rim, Flambe Glaze, 3 1/4 x 7 1/4 In. 275.00
Bowl, Lotus Leaf, Footed, Black Glaze, 6 1/4 In. 550.00
Bowl, Peacock, Flambe, 10 In. 795.00
Bowl, Scalloped Flower, Built-In Frog, Chinese Blue, 11 1/2 In. 200.00
Candleholder, Many Colored Glazes, Pair 175.00
Candlestick, Cat's-Eye Mirror, Black Glaze, Caramel Flambe, Signed, 10 1/2 In. 303.00
Candlestick, Crystal Patina Glaze, Twist Stem, Signed, 11 In., Pair 165.00
Candlestick, Pink, Blue & Green, Handles, 3 In. 110.00

Chamberstick, Flambe Glaze, Eccentric Shape, 2 2/4 x 6 In. 195.00
Compote, Blue Flambe & Crystalline Glaze Over Chocolate Glaze, 6 x 11 In. 650.00
Console Set, Rose Glazes, Bowl, 9 In., 3 Piece 600.00
Crock, Eared Handles, Cobalt Blue Bird, Perched On Leaf, 11 1/4 x 11 1/2 In. 460.00
Dish, Scallops & Hairpin Ribs Around Bowl, Green Crystalline Glaze, 7 In. 325.00
Flower Frog, Egyptian, 7 1/2 In. 68.00
Flower Frog, Scarab Form, Ocher & Green Glaze 75.00
Jug, Blue Periwinkle, Crystalline Glaze, Flaring Neck, Signed, 10 3/4 In. 247.00
Jug, Musical, Brown, 3 Silver Athletes, Silver Stopper, Little Brown Jug, 10 In. 357.00
Jug, Musical, Ivory Glossy Glaze Over Mustard Matte Glaze, Marked, 9 1/2 In. 305.00
Jug, Musical, Pinch, How Dry I Am, 9 In. 250.00
Lamp, Black To Flemington Green, Mirrored, Flambe Glaze, 15 x 9 In. 1980.00
Lamp, Boudoir, Germanic, 16 1/2 In. 7000.00
Lamp, Brown Metallic Glaze, 10 In. 7700.00
Lamp, Perfume Lamp, Ballerina, Figural, Black & White 450.00
Lamp, Perfume, Ballerina, Figural, Pink 325.00
Lamp, Perfume, Woman, Large Hat, Figural, Holding Fan 395.00
Mug, Cider, Green Leopard Spot Glaze 75.00
Mug, Frogskin Glaze .... 80.00 to 90.00
Pitcher, Ice Lip, Cat's-Eye Glaze 375.00
Pitcher, Mirror Glaze 150.00
Powder Box, Art Deco Woman 135.00
Powder Box, Woman, Yellow Hat, Holds Fan, Bisque, Cover 140.00
Vase, 2 Handles, Green Crystalline Glaze, 10 In. 330.00
Vase, 4 Sides, Mirrored Black To Moss Flambe Glaze, 8 3/4 In. 350.00
Vase, Baluster Shape, Mirror Black To Ivory Flambe Glaze, 9 1/2 x 6 In. 495.00
Vase, Basket, Matte Blue Glaze, 10 In. 495.00
Vase, Berries & Leaves, Mottled Green Ground, Signed, 8 1/2 In. 495.00
Vase, Basket, Matte Blue Glaze, 10 In. 495.00
Vase, Black To Copper Dust Glaze, Barrel Shape, Cover, 5 In. 355.00
Vase, Blue & Tan Crystalline Glaze, Scrolled Handles, Signed, 9 In. 467.00
Vase, Blue Crystalline Glaze, 7 In. 400.00
Vase, Brown & Blue Crystalline Glaze, 3 In. 135.00
Vase, Brown To Chinese-Blue Crystalline Flambe Glaze, Egg-Shaped, Footed, 16 x 8 In. 715.00
Vase, Caramel & Crystalline Glaze, Green Flambe, Handles, 10 1/2 x 4 3/4 In. 465.00
Vase, Caramel Crystalline Glaze, 4 1/2 In. 185.00
Vase, Cat's-Eye Flambe Glaze, Iridescent Surface, 7 In. 350.00
Vase, Cat's-Eye Glaze, 6 x 8 In. .... 115.00 to 200.00
Vase, Cat's-Eye Glaze, Bulbous, Signed, 9 x 8 1/2 In. 275.00
Vase, Closed-In Rim, Green Crystalline Glaze, Ink Mark, 8 1/2 In. 400.00
Vase, Copper Dust Glaze, Marked, 5 1/2 In., Pair 425.00
Vase, Corseted, Buff-Colored Glossy Glaze, Marked, 7 1/4 In. 165.00
Vase, Crystalline Flambe, Blue-Gray Glaze, 13 1/2 x 6 1/2 In. 770.00
Vase, Cucumber Crystalline Glaze, Elephant Handles, 5 1/2 In. 95.00
Vase, Feathered Gray & Purple Flambe Glaze, Ink Mark, 12 In. 180.00
Vase, Flemington, Green Flambe Glaze, Signed, 11 3/4 In. 825.00
Vase, Flemington, Gun Powder Black Drip, Green, 8 In. 350.00
Vase, Globular Body, Tapering To Circular Foot, Blue, Marked, 4 3/4 In. 172.50
Vase, Green & Blue, Paper Label, Pan-Pacific Exposition, 1915, 10 In. 2500.00
Vase, Green & Cream Flambe Glaze, Rolled Rim, 8 x 4 1/2 In. 385.00
Vase, Green Flambe Glaze, 7 In. 145.00
Vase, Green Flambe Glaze, Urn Form, 3 Handles, 6 1/2 In. 300.00
Vase, Green Over Gray Glaze, Squat, Handles, 5 In. 275.00
Vase, Green, Handled, 6 1/2 x 6 In. 175.00
Vase, Gunmetal Drip, Green, 5 In. 125.00
Vase, Indented Shoulder, Flambe Crystalline Glaze, Marked, 10 In. 450.00
Vase, Ivory Drip Glaze, Over Mustard Matte Glaze, Egg-Shape, Marked, 12 In. 850.00
Vase, Ivory To Blue & Green Flambe Glaze, Corset Shape, Signed, 7 1/2 In. 200.00
Vase, Ivory To Periwinkle-Blue Flambe Glaze, Marked, 10 In. 220.00
Vase, Leopard Skin Glaze, Handles, No. 27, 11 x 4 3/4 In. 550.00
Vase, Lustered Cobalt Blue Flambe Glaze, Crystalline Base, Marked, 9 1/2 In. 375.00
Vase, Lustered Olive Green To Blue Flambe Glaze, No. 20, Marked, 13 3/4 In. 500.00

Vase, Matte Mauve, 7 x 6 In.	275.00
Vase, Matte Rose, Green Matte Over Glaze, 9 In.	195.00
Vase, Mirrored Black Glaze, 2 Handles, Marked, 12 3/4 In.	500.00
Vase, Mission Matte Brown Glaze, 5 x 7 In.	325.00
Vase, Mission Matte Brown Glaze, 8 In.	575.00 to 650.00
Vase, Moss To Rose Flambe Glaze, Ring Handles, 13 In.	330.00
Vase, Moss To Chinese-Blue Flambe Mirrored Glaze, 4 Handles, 13 In.	850.00
Vase, Mottled Green Semi-Matte Glaze, Marked, 11 In.	375.00
Vase, Mottled Matte Purple Glaze, Signed, 11 1/2 In.	275.00
Vase, Mottled Purple Wisteria Glaze, Gray Ground, Angular Handles, 6 x 8 In.	715.00
Vase, Pink & Green Flambe, 4 In.	95.00
Vase, Squat, Chinese-Blue Flambe Glaze, 2 Buttressed Handles, 6 1/2 In.	467.00
Vase, Turquoise Crystalline Glaze, 8 3/4 In.	145.00
Vase, Turquoise Crystalline Glaze, Ink Mark, 9 In.	225.00
Vase, Twin Buttressed Handles, Blue Crystalline Glaze, Signed, 11 In.	330.00
Vase, Urn, Dark Blue Dripped Over Brown Glaze, Flared, Side Handles, 7 1/4 In.	170.00
Vase, Vasekraft, Crystalline Green, Hand Thrown, Drilled, Stamp, 1909, 17 In.	357.00
Vase, Wisteria, Turquoise Rim Over Green Flambe Glaze, 7 In.	450.00

FURNITURE of all types is listed in this category. Examples dating from the seventeenth century to the 1950s are included. Prices for furniture vary in different parts of the country. Oak furniture is most expensive in the West; large pieces over eight feet high are sold for the most money in the South, where high ceilings are found in the old homes. Condition is very important when determining prices. These are NOT average prices but rather reports of unique sales. If the description includes the word *style*, the piece resembles the old furniture style but was made at a later time. It is not a period piece.

Armchairs may also be listed under Chair in this category.

Armchair, American Classical, Mahogany, Slip Seat, Early 19th Century, Pair	935.00
Armchair, Arts & Crafts, Oak, Sling Leather Seat, Square Posts	805.00
Armchair, Baker, French Style, Fruitwood	250.00
Armchair, Banister Back, Maple & Ash, c.1780, 46 1/2 In.	1320.00
Armchair, Banister Back, Rush Seat, New England, 18th Century	880.00
Armchair, Belter, Henry Clay Pattern, Pair	7150.00
Armchair, Belter, Scroll Pattern	3190.00
Armchair, Biedermeier, Cherry, Saber Legs, Upholstered	1650.00
Armchair, Carved Back, Velvet Upholstered, Walnut Frame, Victorian	125.00
Armchair, Chinese Export, Brighton Pavilion, Bamboo, Fretwork, 1830s	1150.00
Armchair, Chippendale, Mahogany, Floral Brocade, 19th Century, England	176.00
Armchair, Chippendale, Mahogany, Pierced Splat, Linenfold Legs, Needlework	990.00
Armchair, Chippendale, Walnut, Scalloped Apron, Potty, 18th Century, 18 In.	3700.00
Armchair, Chippendale, Wing Back, Fruitwood, Tan Upholstered, Pair	525.00
Armchair, Chippendale, Wing Back, Mahogany, Square Legs, Upholstered	4750.00
Armchair, Classical, Walnut, Ebonized, Cabriole Legs, American, c.1855	525.00
Armchair, Comb Back, George III, Saddle Seat, Ash & Elm, c.1760	3070.00
Armchair, Cromwellian, Barley Twist, Leather Upholstered, Pair	950.00
Armchair, Drummon, Angled Armrests, Leather, Cherry, Pine, Pair	8050.00
Armchair, Eames, Classic, Plastic, Wire, Herman Miller Co., Early 1950s	460.00
Armchair, Eastlake, Walnut, Gold Upholstered	200.00
Armchair, Egyptian Revival, Ivory Inlaid Rosewood, 1926	8625.00
Armchair, Empire Style, Cherry, Urn Form Splat, Upholstered	2090.00
Armchair, Empire, Arched Rail, Lion's Head Supports, Mahogany, Parcel Gilt	5470.00
Armchair, Empire, Low Back, Paw Feet, Lyre Arms, Early 20th Century, 31 In.	65.00
Armchair, English Style, Beechwood, Trellis Cartouche Back, Upholstered	2875.00
Armchair, Flemish, Fruitwood, Needlepoint Upholstered, 44 x 25 x 27 In., Pair	1760.00
Armchair, Folding, Hunzinger Patent, Upholstered, 1876	725.00
Armchair, Foliate Carved Top Rail, Upholstered Seat, Beechwood	1495.00
Armchair, Footstool, Bruno Mathsson, Bent Laminated Birch, 1950	1210.00
Armchair, Footstool, Widdicomb Co., Robsjohn-Gibbings, Shaped Frame, 1953	1380.00
Armchair, Frank Lloyd Wright, Aluminum, Swivel, Red Leather, 1953	10925.00
Armchair, French Provincial, Fruitwood, Carved, Rush Seat	305.00
Armchair, Gentleman's, Medallion Back, Cabriole Legs, Carved Mahogany, 41 In.	440.00

Armchair, George I, Walnut, Vase-Shaped Splat, Upholstered Seat, 19th Century 440.00
Armchair, George II Style, Mahogany, Vase-Shaped Splats, Cabriole Legs, Pair 770.00
Armchair, George II, Mahogany, Needlepoint Upholstered, Carved Supports 3740.00
Armchair, George II, Painted, Square Back, Faux Tortoiseshell, c.1800, Pair 2990.00
Armchair, George III, Mahogany, Fret-Carved Rectangular Supports, Pair 9775.00
Armchair, George III, Mahogany, Serpentine Crest, Pierced Back, Late 1700s 3165.00
Armchair, George III, Mahogany, Upholstered Seat, Mid-19th Century, Pair 1760.00
Armchair, Georgian, Mahogany, Vasiform Splat, Round, Slip Seat, Ireland, 1750 .... 1210.00
Armchair, Gustav Stickley, 5 Slats, V Back, Original Leather, No. 354, Pair 2400.00
Armchair, Gustav Stickley, Back Slats, Leatherette Seat, No. 344, Child's 375.00
Armchair, Gustav Stickley, Oak, 3 Slats, Later Upholstered Seat, 1907 .... 200.00
Armchair, Gustav Stickley, Oak, 11 Spindles, 9-Spindle Arms, No. 386, 1907 .... 4390.00
Armchair, Gustav Stickley, V Back, Decal, No. 312 1/2, 36 x 25 3/4 In. 750.00
Armchair, H. Hamm, Peacock Feathers At Corners, Mahogany, c.1900 .... 3450.00
Armchair, Harden Co., Oak, Bent Arm, 4 Slats, Spring Cushion Seat 715.00
Armchair, Hepplewhite, Mahogany, Boardman, Mahogany, Pair 4950.00
Armchair, Horn, Steer, Leather Upholstered, Late 19th Century, 41 x 29 In. 467.00
Armchair, Huang Huali, Gilin Back, China, 39 In. 525.00
Armchair, Huang Huali, Yoked Crest, Row Of Stiles, China, 18th Century, 36 In. 385.00
Armchair, James II, Walnut, Caned Back, Pierced Leaf Cresting, c.1685 .... 9360.00
Armchair, Josef Hoffmann, Bentwood, Laminated Back Splat, Upholstered, 1910 ...... 1150.00
Armchair, Jules Leleu, U-Shaped Back, Floral Tapestry Upholstered, Pair 6325.00
Armchair, Ladder Back, 4 Slats Of Different Shapes, Gray Repaint, 41 In. 75.00
Armchair, Ladder Back, Added Rockers, Dark Finish, Rush Seat, Country 93.00
Armchair, Ladder Back, Country English, Rush Seat, Out-Turned Feet, 42 In. 250.00
Armchair, Leather-Covered Writing Arm, 2 Drawers, Seat Drawer, Black, 47 In. 220.00
Armchair, Limbert, 9 Vertical Back Slats, Oak 220.00
Armchair, Lion's Mask & Palmettes Crest, Painted & Parcel Gilt 2875.00
Armchair, Louis XV, Caned Back, Carved Shell & Wave Design, Beechwood 8050.00
Armchair, Mahogany, Art Nouveau, Parcel Gilt, Brown Plush, France, 1900, Pair 9200.00
Armchair, Mahogany, Leather Seat, Tooled Leather Back, c.1900 .... 160.00
Armchair, Mahogany, Shaped Top Rail, Outscrolled Supports, Russia 4025.00
Armchair, Majorelle, Mahogany, Carved Pinecones, Silk Upholstered, 42 In. 4025.00
Armchair, Majorelle, Mahogany, Pierced Crest Rail, Velvet Upholstered 4600.00
Armchair, Maple Rush Seat, 5 Wavy Splats, Turned Legs & Finial 495.00
Armchair, Neoclassical, Giltwood, Italy, c.1800, 42 In. 1210.00
Armchair, Norman Cherner, Curved Back, Tapered Legs, Ply Craft, 1958 .... 800.00
Armchair, Open Carved Frame, Floral Brocade Upholstered, 32 In., Pair 385.00
Armchair, Queen Anne, Maple, Spanish Foot, England, c.1730, 42 In. 5500.00
Armchair, Queen Anne, Upholstered Back & Seat, Carved Knees, Pair 1045.00
Armchair, Reclining, Hongmu, 19th Century, China, 39 In. 467.00
Armchair, Reclining, Rope & Pulley, Walnut, Victorian, 41 x 24 In. 220.00
Armchair, Regency, Black Paint, Parcel Gilt, Caned, Open Arms, 19th Century 690.00
Armchair, Regency, Colonial, Mahogany, Caned, Saber Legs, Open Arms, Pair 4025.00
Armchair, Regency, Double Horizontal Caned Back Splat, Cane Seat, 4 .... 5470.00
Armchair, Regency, Mahogany, Trapezoidal Seat, Hinged Front Opens, 4 Steps 2300.00
Armchair, Renaissance Revival, Carved Walnut, Ebonized Backrest, Phila., Pair 1870.00
Armchair, Renaissance Revival, Walnut, Burl Walnut, 42 x 28 x 22 In., Pair 495.00
Armchair, Robsjohn-Gibbings, Carved Fruitwood, Leather, 1937 .... 1150.00
Armchair, Robsjohn-Gibbings, Stained Ash Frame, Leather Seat & Back, Pair 1035.00
Armchair, Robsjohn-Gibbings, Walnut, Silk Plaid Upholstered, 1936, Pair 2875.00
Armchair, Rococo Revival, Mahogany, Laminated Back, 34 In. 315.00
Armchair, Round Upholstered Back & Seat, Outset Corners, Beechwood 1495.00
Armchair, Roycroft, Leather Seat, Grove Park Inn 1600.00
Armchair, Sausage Turned, Splint Seat 575.00
Armchair, Serpentine Crest, Scrolled Hand Grips, Birch, 1770, 38 In. 2760.00
Armchair, Sheraton, New Rush Seat, Old Dark Varnish, 32 1/2 In., Pair 330.00
Armchair, Slat Back, Painted, England, 51 In. 1045.00
Armchair, Thonet, Bentwood, Upholstered Seat & Back, Gustav Siegel, c.1905 .... 715.00
Armchair, Triangular Solid Seat, Ash Turners, 17th Century 9360.00
Armchair, Tyrolean Style, Paw Feet 165.00
Armchair, Upholstered Back Rest, Foliate Carved Rail & Knees, Drop Seat 5460.00

Furniture, Armoire, French Provincial,
Inlaid, 2 Doors, 1 Drawer

Furniture, Bed, Half-Tester,
Rococo Revival, 101 x 63 In.

Armchair, Victorian Renaissance, Carved Rosewood, c.1880, Pair 1035.00
Armchair, Victorian, Carved Rosewood, New White-On-White Brocade Tufted 595.00
Armchair, Victorian, Oval Upholstered Back, Carved Frame, Rosewood, 42 In. 715.00
Armchair, Warren McArthur, Club Style, 1930s 2600.00
Armchair, Warren McArthur, Upholstered Aluminum, 1935 .... 8060.00
Armchair, William & Mary, Banister Back, Early 18th Century, 49 In. 880.00
Armchair, William & Mary, Caned Back & Seat, Walnut, c.1690 .... 2090.00
Armchair, William IV, Caned Back & Seat, Mahogany, Child's, c.1830 .... 1250.00
Armchair, Windsor, 11 Spindles, Bamboo Turned, Knuckle Arms, S.E. Penn. 2000.00
Armchair, Windsor, Birdcage, Bamboo Legs 325.00
Armchair, Windsor, Bow Back, 9 Spindles, Splayed Base, Bamboo Turnings, 35 In. .. 385.00
Armchair, Windsor, Bow Back, New England, c.1780, 33 1/2 In. 330.00
Armchair, Windsor, Bow Back, Saddle Seat, Splayed Base 550.00
Armchair, Windsor, Comb Back Birdcage, New England, c.1815 .... 4800.00
Armchair, Windsor, Comb Back, 9 Spindles, Blunt Arrow Feet, c.1775 .... 3450.00
Armchair, Windsor, Comb Back, Ash & Maple, 46 1/2 In. 6600.00
Armchair, Windsor, Continuous Arm, Bamboo Turned Legs, 1785-1800, 36 In. 975.00
Armchair, Windsor, High Back, Medallion On Back, Cutout For Potty, 46 3/4 In. 110.00
Armchair, Windsor, Knuckle Arm, Brown Finish 3080.00
Armchair, Windsor, Rod Back, New England, 19th Century, 31 1/2 In., Pair 495.00
Armchair, Windsor, Sack Back, 7 Spindles, Shaped Handholds, Red Paint, 1810 .... 1320.00
Armchair, Windsor, Sack Back, Painted, c.1780, 39 x 18 In. 4400.00
Armchair, Windsor, Saddle Seat, Arm Supports, 36 3/4 In. 7150.00
Armchair, Wing, Carved Frame, Green & Gold Floral Upholstered, 45 In. 195.00
Armchair, Wing, Chippendale, Upholstered, Mahogany, 47 In. 4730.00
Armchair, Wing, Eagles Heads At Knees, Floral Brocade Upholstered, Walnut 440.00
Armchair, Wing, George I, Padded Back, Cushion Seat, Walnut, 1720 .... 7150.00
Armchair, Wing, George II, Handles, Leaf Carved Legs, Walnut, c.1750 .... 6800.00
Armchair, Wing, George III, Mahogany, Leather, Loose Cushion, 1800 .... 9200.00
Armchair, Woman's, Rococo, Walnut, Ebonized, Medallion Back, American, c.1855 .. 412.00
Armoire, Adams Style, Carved Mahogany, Fitted, 19th Century, 69 x 54 x 22 In. 880.00
Armoire, Bamboo Accents, Mirror, Drawer, Bun Feet, Cherry, c.1870, 89 x 38 In. 1650.00
Armoire, Continental, Doors, Flowered Panels, Finger Design, Painted, c.1885 .... 415.00
Armoire, Daniel Pabst, Aesthetic, 1 Door & 1 Base Drawer 2530.00
Armoire, Dutch Baroque Style, Paneled Doors, Mahogany, 90 x 69 In. 1840.00
Armoire, Eastlake Style, Mirrored, c.1890, 107 x 21 1/4 x 84 In. 6000.00
Armoire, Edwardian, Satinwood, 2 Doors, c.1890, 74 x 48 In.. .... 385.00
Armoire, French Provincial, Inlaid, 2 Doors, 1 Drawer .... *Illus* 3300.00
Armoire, Linen Press, William IV, Mahogany, c.1835, 86 x 9 1/2 x 23 In. 5500.00

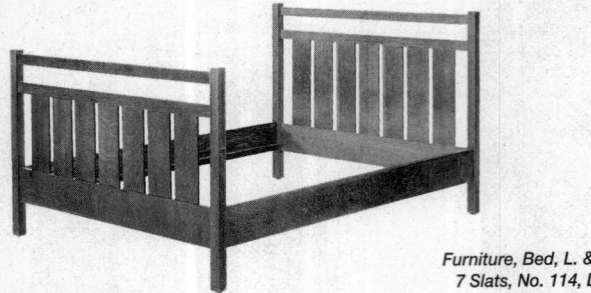

Furniture, Bed, L. & J. G. Stickley, Oak,
7 Slats, No. 114, Double, 44 x 57 In.

Armoire, Louis XV Style, Scrolled Arched Crest, Mirrored Doors, Walnut, 110 In. 360.00
Armoire, Louis XV, Inlaid Walnut, Fruitwood 4750.00
Armoire, Oak, 19th Century, France 4125.00
Armoire, Victorian, 2 Paneled Doors, 2 Drawers, Walnut, 75 In. 440.00
Armoire, Victorian, Mahogany Veneer, 2 Doors, Fluted Columns, 81 x 57 In. 359.00
Armoire, Victorian, Rosewood, Arched Pediment, 1 Door, American, 100 In. 1870.00
Armoire, Walnut, 3 Cabinets, Beveled Mirrored Doors, France, 80 In. 2145.00
Armoire, William IV, Grained Mahogany, 108 In. 5500.00
Aviary Stand, Gothic Revival, Mahogany, Parcel Gilt, Circular Feet, 69 In. 1840.00
Banquette, Frank Lloyd Wright, Curved End, Oak, 1937, 77 In. 2875.00
Bed, Arched Crest, Carved, Walnut & Mahogany, Victorian, 74 x 63 In. 2530.00
Bed, Brass, Curvilinear, Foliate Scrolls, Floral Frieze, 78 1/4 In. 550.00
Bed, Brass, French Style, Flower Basket Inlay, Garlands, 1920, 52 x 44 In. 935.00
Bed, Brass, Victorian, Vian, Paris, Pair 3300.00
Bed, Campaign, Iron, Painted, Collapsible, Finial & Crest, France, 48 In. 880.00
Bed, Cannonball, Maple, Pine, Custom Made Box Springs, 47 x 34 In., Pair 355.00
Bed, Cannonball, Rope, Birch & Pine, Honey Refinished, 53 x 74 x 48 In. 250.00
Bed, Captain's, 3 Lower Drawers, Side Drawers, Cherry, 81 In. 385.00
Bed, Clematis Vines At Head & Foot, Burl Maple, c.1900, 81 In., Pair 6900.00
Bed, Continental, Black Paint, Parcel Gilt Metal, Pierced Scrolling, 48 In.. .... 4310.00
Bed, Eastlake, Carved Walnut & Burl, Tall Fern & Floral Crest Headboard 2200.00
Bed, Empire, Flame Mahogany, Child's, 60 In. 2185.00
Bed, European, Landscapes, Mother-Of-Pearl Inlay, Sheet Iron, 67 x 80 In. 1400.00
Bed, Federal, Ring-Turned Posts, Leaf Carving, Mahogany, 1800s, 96 x 67 In. 9200.00
Bed, Four-Poster, Cannonball, 1840 .... 300.00
Bed, Four-Poster, Canopy, Fluted Posts, Mahogany, 92 In. 715.00
Bed, Four-Poster, Carved Mahogany, Cornucopia, Pineapple, 90 x 60 x 9 In. 7425.00
Bed, Four-Poster, Classical, Mahogany, Double Headboard, c.1820, 59 3/4 In. 5060.00
Bed, Four-Poster, Walnut, Carved, Canopy, Late 19th Century 1400.00
Bed, Gustav Stickley, Oak, Vertical Slats, Tapered Posts, No. 917, 47 x 45 In. 775.00
Bed, Gustav Stickley, Vertical Slats, 5 Wide Slats, c.1907, Double Size 725.00
Bed, Half-Tester, Carved Mahogany, Sunburst, New Orleans, c.1855, 52 x 84 In. 4950.00
Bed, Half-Tester, Rococo Revival, 101 x 63 In. .... *Illus* 6600.00
Bed, Half-Tester, Rococo, Mahogany, New Orleans, Child's, c.1855, 55 x 30 In. 4950.00
Bed, Hired Hand's, Federal, Turned Posts, American 138.00
Bed, J.L. Pallisander, Mother-Of-Pearl & Ebony Marquetry, 1937, 6 Ft. 5 In. 3450.00
Bed, Jacobean Style, Paneled, Turned-Foot Posts, Oak, 20th Century 110.00
Bed, L. & J.G. Stickley, Oak, 7 Slats, No. 114, Double, 44\ x 57 In. .... *Illus* 2760.00
Bed, L. & J.G. Stickley, 5 Vertical Slats, 56 x 78 In. 3100.00
Bed, Louis XV Style, Cartouche Of Figures, Painted Wood, 1770s, 50 In. 315.00
Bed, Louis XV, Upholstered Head & Foot, Carved Flower Heads, Oak, 1750s 8625.00
Bed, Majorelle, Carved Mahogany, Burl Walnut Inlays, 63 x 66 x 84 In. 4600.00
Bed, Majorelle, Pierced Panel, Carved Clematis Vines, Mahogany, 62 x 65 In. 3850.00
Bed, Oak, Carved, Stripped & Refinished, Belgium, 1910 .... 650.00
Bed, Oak, Hand Carved Head & Foot, 72 In. 1250.00

Bed, Opium, Figural Reserves, Canopy, Carved Hardwood 460.00
Bed, Panel, Walnut, Carved, Pierced Crest, c.1860, 78 x 61 In. 1100.00
Bed, Pencil Post, Bell-Shaped Canopy, Original Paint, 1770 .... 5600.00
Bed, Plantation, C. Lee, Mahogany, Stamped 7000.00
Bed, Plantation, James McCracken, Mahogany, Label 5000.00
Bed, Poplar, Knob Finials, Peaked Head & Footboards, Rope, 75 In. 138.00
Bed, Post, Federal, Ring Turned, Square Head Posts, Red Paint, 61 3/4 In. 3850.00
Bed, Post, Turned, Maple, Bottle Finial, Rope, Footboard, 56 x 74 x 52 In. 990.00
Bed, Poster, Victorian, Mahogany, 50 x 48 In. 125.00
Bed, Renaissance, Walnut, Convex Burl-Faced Panels, Refinished, 1860 .... 6150.00
Bed, Rococo Revival, Prudent Mallard, Mahogany 7125.00
Bed, Serpentine Headboard, Tobacco Leaf Carving, Mahogany, c.1795, 96 In. 9200.00
Bed, Shaker, Sister's, New Lebanon, Maple & Pine, 1840s, 66 In., Pair 3900.00
Bed, Sheraton, Four-Poster, Cherry, Reeded, Mattress, Canopy, Spring 1540.00
Bed, Sheraton, Four-Poster, Maple, Mahogany Finish, Pine, 72 x 37 In., Pair 715.00
Bed, Sheraton, Reeded Post, Original Red Wash, Side Rails, Beaded End, Rope 975.00
Bed, Sleigh, French Provincial, Walnut, 1850, Extended Length 495.00
Bed, Sleigh, Mahogany, Bronze Sunburst Head End, c.1840, Double Size 2750.00
Bed, Sleigh, Rolled Head & Footboard, Wood Grain Painted, Pine, 42 In. 316.00
Bed, Spool, Four-Poster, Tapered Baluster Feet, Mahogany, 62 x 60 In. 440.00
Bed, Square Posts, Shield Finial, Walnut, Victorian, 42 x 51 In. 77.00
Bed, Tall Post, Federal, Mahogany & Veneer, Massachusetts, c.1820, 90 x 52 In. 1980.00
Bed, Tall Post, Mahogany, Carved & Fluted, 81 3/4 x 56 3/4 In. 3300.00
Bed, Tall Post, Walnut, Carved, Turned, c.1825, 93 In. 3575.00
Bed, Tester, Continental, Marquetry 5250.00
Bed, Tester, George III, Square Canopy, Central Finial, Upholstered Back 8050.00
Bed, Tester, Regency, Foliate Supports, Carved Mahogany, 90 x 82 In. 1650.00
Bed, Tester, Sheraton, Cherry, Arched, American 495.00
Bed, Tester, Victorian, Walnut, Burl Walnut, Broken-Arch Crest, 73 x 54 In. 2420.00
Bed, Tiger Maple, Iron Brackets, 18th Century 825.00
Bed, Trundle, Rope, Short Turned Posts, Wooden Wheels, Old Red 83.00
Bed, Trundle, White Paint Over Curly Maple Graining, Rope, 60 1/2 In. 176.00
Bed, Tubular Iron & Cane Look, Brown Paint, Child's 170.00
Bed, Tulip Post, Red Over Mustard Feather Graining, c.1840, 69 3/4 x 54 In. 500.00
Bed Steps, Louis XV Style, 2 Upholstered Steps, Giltwood, 17 1/4 In. 7475.00
Bedroom Set, Art Nouveau, 84 x 58 In. Wardrobe, Cheval Dresser, Bed, 3 Piece. 2500.00
Bedroom Set, Burl Head & Footboard, Marble Top, Victorian, 3 Piece 4400.00
Bedroom Set, Danish Modern, 1950s, 4 Piece 120.00
Bedroom Set, Eastlake, Marble Top, 3 Piece 5000.00
Bedroom Set, Marble Top, Bowfront, Queen-Size Bed, Walnut, 3 Piece 9000.00
Bedroom Set, Victorian, Walnut, Marble Top, c.1880, Full-Size Bed, 2 Piece 1275.00
Bedroom Set, Walnut, Marble Top, Ornately Carved, 2 Piece 5545.00
Bench, 3 Back, Painted Design, Arms, Lancaster County 2400.00
Bench, Amish, Pine, Red, Primitive, 80 In. 110.00
Bench, Baroque Style, Oak, Tapestry Upholstery, 57 x 47 In. 550.00
Bench, Baroque Style, Upholstered Seat, Walnut, 16 x 28 In. 300.00
Bench, Bertoia, Redwood Slat Top, Painted Steel Rod Base, 71 1/2 In. 460.00
Bench, Black Slats, Slats Seat, c.1946, 62 In. 1380.00
Bench, Bucket, Green, Rounded Bootjack Ends 325.00
Bench, Bucket, Mahogany, c.1850, 11 3/4 x 8 1/2 In. 395.00
Bench, Bucket, Mustard Paint, New Jersey 1450.00
Bench, Bucket, Old Red Paint 1300.00
Bench, Bucket, Pine, 1870 .... 170.00
Bench, Church, Paneled, Pennsylvania, Pair 275.00
Bench, Deacon's, Federal, Arrow-Back, Stained Hardwood, 81 In. 460.00
Bench, Deacon's, Pine, Maple, Old Paint, Arms, 33 x 83 In. 275.00
Bench, Deacon's, Pine, 1-Board Seat, Pennsylvania, 21 1/2 In. 300.00
Bench, Double Seating, Pegged Construction, England, 27-In. Seat 2500.00
Bench, Dresser, Louis XVI Style, Carved Frame, Brocade Seat, 41 1/2 In. 200.00
Bench, Eugene Schoen, Upholstered Seat, Curbed Sides, 1935, 50 In. 2300.00
Bench, Floral Needlework Upholstered, Rosewood, Victorian, 16 x 26 In. 1200.00
Bench, Frank Lloyd Wright, Cypress, 4 Short Legs, Plank Stretcher, 1951, 73 In. 2990.00
Bench, French Style, Rush Seat & Sides, Fruitwood, 50 1/2 In. 200.00

Bench, George Nelson, Black Slats, Slats Seat, c.1946, 56 In. 1495.00
Bench, Hall, Panel Carved Seat, Rounded Sides, Mahogany, c.1800, 48 In. 9775.00
Bench, Harden, 13 Arrow Vertical Slats, 4 Under Each Arm, Label, 48 In. 900.00
Bench, Jugendstil, Carved Medallion Over Seat, Beechwood, Austria, 31 1/2 In. 65.00
Bench, Lifetime, Tudor Oak, Carved Gothic Style Top, 19 x 48 x 13 In. 825.00
Bench, Lift Top, Hanging Mirror, Double Rope Twist Legs, Oak 405.00
Bench, Lift-Up Seat, Lion's Heads, Carved Panel Back, Oak, Victorian 825.00
Bench, Louis XIII, Walnut, Upholstered, Late 17th Century, 14 x 19 x 15 In. 440.00
Bench, Louis XV, Walnut, Serpentine, Tufted Upholstered Seat, 50 In. 575.00
Bench, Louis XVI Style, Giltwood, Carved Apron, Upholstered Seat, 19 x 30 In. 660.00
Bench, Louis XVI, Painted, Upholstered Seat, Stop-Fluted Legs, 15 x 30 x 17 In. 1725.00
Bench, Lyre Shape, Mahogany Frame, Velvet Upholstered, 36 In. 330.00
Bench, Mammy's, High Back At 1 End, Half Arrow-Backs, Poplar, 57 In. 1045.00
Bench, Meetinghouse, Amish, Paint Traces 495.00
Bench, Mirrored, Oak, Victorian, 76 x 48 In. 747.00
Bench, Nakashima, Spindle Back, Slab Seat, Walnut, c.1958, 89 In. 6900.00
Bench, Nakashima, Spindle Back, Walnut & Hickory, 1977, 60 In. 4600.00
Bench, Neoclassical Style, Painted, Giltwood, Floral Scrolls, Italy, 25 In. 550.00
Bench, Paneled Back, Plank Seat, Walnut, England, 93 In. 100.00
Bench, Queen Anne, Carved, Cabriole Legs, Walnut, Needlepoint Seat, 19 x 40 In. ... 220.00
Bench, Rectangular Form, Rush Seat & Sides, Fruitwood, 50 1/2 In. 200.00
Bench, Rectangular Top & Sides, Pierced Apron, Hardwood, China, 71 In. 495.00
Bench, Regency, Giltwood, Cabriole Legs, 19th Century, 16 1/4 x 39 x 15 In. 550.00
Bench, Split Woven Seat, Pine, Child's, 19th Century 3000.00
Bench, Traditional, Dark Mahogany, Petit Point, Needlepoint, 14 x 36 x 18 In. 247.00
Bench, Triple Chair Back, Lester & Fee, Cast Iron, Victorian, 46 1/2 In. 1850.00
Bench, Walnut, Saber Legs, Rosette Detailing, Hand Carved, Cushion, 34 x 27 In. 1750.00
Bench, Water, 3 Shelves, Bootjack Ends, 13 x 43 x 13 In. 195.00
Bench, Water, Pine, Paneled Doors, Crest, Refinished, Country, 42 x 18 x 54 In. 1760.00
Bench, William IV, Celadon & Silver Damask Upholstered Seat, 24 In. 5750.00
Bench, Window, Regency, Mahogany, Gilt, Pair 4200.00
Bench, Windsor, Birch, Bamboo Turned Legs, H Stretcher, American 4800.00
Bench, Windsor, Spindle Back, Bamboo Turnings, Plank Seat, Medallions, 75 In. 1595.00
Bench Bed, Biedermeier, Flame Birch, Sweden, c.1850 .... 3800.00
Bergere, Empire, Mahogany, Striped Silk Upholstered, 19th Century, 30 In. 225.00
Bonheur Du Jour, Louis XV, Bombe Lid, Ormolu Mounted, 1900 .... 415.00
Bookcase, 2 Drawers, Block Feet, Cherry, France, 30 1/2 x 78 In. 1955.00
Bookcase, 2 Glass Doors Over 2 Drawers, Walnut, Burl, Carved Pediment 2600.00
Bookcase, 2 Leaded Glass Doors, Walnut, Carved Winged Griffins, Paw Footed 2500.00
Bookcase, 3 Doors, Carved Pediment Top, Walnut, 110 In. 5500.00
Bookcase, 4 Drawers, 2 Doors Of 8 Panes, Walnut 4200.00
Bookcase, 4 Tiers, Magazine Rack, Black Wood, China, 64 3/4 In. 90.00
Bookcase, Art Deco, Stepped Case, Walnut, 64 In., Pair 5290.00
Bookcase, Carved Mahogany, Victorian, 19th Century, 56 x 60 x 18 In. 2750.00
Bookcase, Chippendale, 3 Lower Drawers, Cherry, c.1800, 86 x 72 x 19 In. 6100.00
Bookcase, Chippendale, Carved Mahogany, 2 Parts, Glazed Doors, c.1780, 98 In. 5175.00
Bookcase, Cylinder Top, Aqua Colored Glass Panels, Adjustable Shelves 2600.00
Bookcase, Danner, Revolving, Oak, Bucyrus, Ohio 525.00
Bookcase, Eastlake, Walnut, 3 Sections, 1870-1880, 132 In. 1650.00
Bookcase, Empire, Brass Mounted Feet, Bleached Mahogany, 1820s, 70 In. 4888.00
Bookcase, Empire, Floral Carved Cornice Over Shelves, Oak, 89 x 52 In. 625.00
Bookcase, Empire, Mahogany, 2 Glazed Doors, 19th Century, 57 x 48 In. 1550.00
Bookcase, George III Style, Mullion Doors, Chinoiserie, Japanned, 79 In. 1100.00
Bookcase, Gothic, 2 Doors, Carved Heads At Corners, Mahogany, 60 In. 1200.00
Bookcase, Gustav Stickley, 16 Panes, No. 715, Paper Label, 56 x 35 In. .. 3500.00 to 6000.00
Bookcase, Gustav Stickley, 2 Doors, 16 Panes 3900.00
Bookcase, Hepplewhite, 4 Dovetailed Drawers, Walnut, Country, 84 In. 4625.00
Bookcase, L. & J.G. Stickley, Oak, 2 Doors, No. 645, c.1910, 55 x 52 In. 3575.00
Bookcase, Lifetime, 2 Shelves, Overhanging Gallery, 52 x 39 x 11 1/2 In. 1000.00
Bookcase, Louis Philippe, 1 Glazed Door, Mirrored Back, Fruitwood, 66 In. 8000.00
Bookcase, Mission, Oak, 2 Glass Doors 400.00
Bookcase, Mission, Oak, 3-Paneled Glass Door, Small 1000.00
Bookcase, Quartersawn Oak, 5 Lions Faces, Glass Door & Pulls 1100.00

Furniture, Cabinet, China, L. & J. G. Stickley,
Oak, No. 746, 62 x 44 x 16 In.

Furniture, Cabinet, China, L. & J. G. Stickley,
Oak, No. 729, 1906-1912

Bookcase, Regency, Mahogany, 2 Glazed Doors, Columns, Plinth, 96 x 50 In. 660.00
Bookcase, Revolving, Walnut, Victorian 600.00
Bookcase, Rococo Style, Carved, Pineapple Finial, England 7700.00
Bookcase, Roycroft, Oak, Tabard Inn Library, 4 Sides, 1910 .... 2850.00
Bookcase, Step Back, Burl Walnut, 2 Glass Doors, 2 Side-By-Side Drawers 4000.00
Bookcase, William IV, Veined Marble Top, 2 Open Shelves, Mahogany, 43 In. 8100.00
Bookcase Cabinet, 4 Glazed Doors Over 2 Doors, 18th Century, 78 x 36 In. 600.00
Bookcase Cabinet, Mahogany, 2 Glazed Doors, Single Drawer Stand, 82 x 36 In. ... 550.00
Bookshelf, L. & J.G. Stickley, 4 Shelves, Oak, No. 345, c.1910, 45 x 19 In. 1955.00
Bookshelf, Pierced Gallery Over 2 Drawers, Shelves, Painted, 38 x 48 In. 495.00
Bracket, Wall, Pierced Frieze, Pair Of Candle Branches At Side, 31 In. 5000.00
Breakfast Set, Wicker, Early 1900s, 5 Piece 425.00
Breakfront, 4 Brass Latticework Doors, 3 Lower Drawers, Rosewood, 87 In. 4625.00
Breakfront, Georgian Style, Arched Crest, 3 Mullion Doors, Satinwood, 79 In. 770.00
Breakfront, Mahogany, Glass Doors, Pullout Desk, England, 2 Piece, 94 In. 7500.00
Breakfront, Mahogany, Table Base, Mass., c.1829 .... 7500.00
Breakfront Bookcase, Ebonized, Inlaid Brass, Arched Crest, Victorian, 115 In. 3300.00
Breakfront Bookcase, Mahogany, 4 Doors, Glazed, 78 x 86 In. 2650.00
Bucket, Plate, George III, Brassbound, Mahogany, c.1800, 16 In. 2600.00
Bucket, Plate, George III, Brass Liner, Octagonal, Mahogany, 1890s, 11 3/4 In. 3750.00
Bucket, Plate, George III, Brass Mounted, Mahogany, 1890s, 15 In. 2875.00
Buffet, American Empire, Fitted Half Columns, Mahogany, 50 In. 1250.00
Buffet, Arts & Crafts, Marble Countertop, Brass Fittings, Walnut, c.1910 .... 3900.00
Buffet, Bracket Feet & Stretchers, Tulipwood, 53 In. 550.00
Buffet, Diot, Walnut, Glass & Marble, c.1900, 50 In. 1955.00
Buffet, Prairie School, Beveled Mirror, Panels Of Urn-Shaped Finials 2900.00
Buffet, White Marble Top, Walnut & Mahogany, 32 1/2 x 50 1/2 In. 900.00
Bureau, Biedermeier, Cylinder, Ash Wood 3100.00
Bureau, Biedermeier, Cylinder, Mahogany, Exotic Wood Interior 5775.00
Bureau, Bonnet Drawer Over 3 Recessed Drawers, Cherry Veneer, 1840s 225.00
Bureau, Chippendale, 4 Graduated Drawers, Mahogany, 18th Century 1100.00
Bureau, Federal, Bird's-Eye & Mahogany Veneer, c.1810, 33 3/4 In. 2200.00
Bureau, Federal, Bowfront, Cherry, c.1800, 37 1/2 x 39 x 21 In. 2750.00
Bureau, Federal, Bowfront, Mahogany Veneer, 4 Drawers, c.1815, 38 x 37 In. 885.00
Bureau, Federal, Cherry & Tiger Maple Veneer, c.1810, 38 1/2 x 41 1/2 In. 1885.00
Bureau, Federal, Cherry, c.1800, 35 1/4 x 40 1/2 x 19 1/2 In. 1100.00
Bureau, Federal, Mahogany & Veneer, 4 Drawers, c.1800, 35 x 40 In. 2865.00
Bureau, Hepplewhite, 4 Tiger Maple Drawers, Oval Brasses, 39 x 41 x 19 In. 2000.00
Bureau, Mahogany, 4 Drawers, Bracket Base, Ring Pulls, England, 38 x 36 x 18 In. . 665.00
Bureau, Roll-Back Cover, Leather Surface, Mahogany, 60 In. 8100.00
Bureau, Sheraton, 4 Bird's-Eye Drawers, Mahogany, 19th Century, 40 x 44 In. 550.00

Bureau, Sheraton, 4 Bird's-Eye Maple Drawers, Mahogany, 36 x 41 x 19 In. 800.00
Bureau, Sheraton, 4 Drawers, Pine, Turret Corners, Peg Footed, 42 x 41 x 19 In. 715.00
Bureau, Slant Front, George III, Mahogany, Oak, 1800s, Miniature, 13 x 13 x 8 In. .. 1600.00
Bureau, Slant Front, George III, Oak, Bracket Footed, Miniature, 10 x 9 x 4 In. 925.00
Bureau Bookcase, George III, England, 2 Piece 9500.00
Bureau Bookcase, Queen Anne Style, 4 Drawers, Burl Walnut, 85 In. 4125.00
Bureau Plat, Louis XV, Ormolu Mounted, Kingwood, 19th Century, 30 x 42 In. 1650.00
Cabinet, Art Deco, Burl Amboyna, France, c.1926, 38 1/2 x 71 x 16 In. 2750.00
Cabinet, Baker's, Leaded Glass Doors, Mirror 650.00
Cabinet, Baker's, Oak, 3 Drawers Top, Towel Racks 450.00
Cabinet, Bar, Burl Wood, Etched Glass, Parcel Gilt, Fitted, England, 44 In. 4600.00
Cabinet, Belter, Marquetry, Bird's-Eye Maple Interior, Rosewood, Pair 8000.00
Cabinet, Biedermeier, Stepped Cornice, Divided Glazed Doors, Walnut, 66 In. 4025.00
Cabinet, Burl Fruitwood, Ivory, Marble, Shelves, 2 Side Doors, France, 80 In. 8600.00
Cabinet, China, Bowfront, Lion's Head 1100.00
Cabinet, China, Curved Glass, Carved Oak, Paw & Ball Feet, Victorian 715.00
Cabinet, China, Glazed Doors, Mirrored, Mahogany, Austria, 1900, 87 In. 3200.00
Cabinet, China, L. & J.G. Stickley, Oak, No. 729, 1906-1912 .... *Illus* 10350.00
Cabinet, China, L. & J.G. Stickley, Oak, No. 746, 62 x 44 x 16 In. .... *Illus* 3225.00
Cabinet, China, Mirror Back, Brass Trim, Beveled Glass, France 2000.00
Cabinet, China, Mission, Oak, 1 Glass Door, 3 Shelves 475.00
Cabinet, China, Oak, Applied Carving, Mirror, Sturgis, Michigan 2800.00
Cabinet, China, Serpentine Front, Glass Door & Sides, Oak, 42 x 15 x 65 In. 350.00
Cabinet, China, Serpentine Glass Front, Winged Griffin Gallery, Oak 5450.00
Cabinet, China, Step Back, Cherry, Mid-18th Century, Pennsylvania 10000.00
Cabinet, Collector's, Pine, 19 Top Drawers, 1 Long Drawer, 57 In., 2 Sections 1550.00
Cabinet, Corner, Galle, Marquetry Door, Signed, Mahogany, c.1890, 30 In. 2015.00
Cabinet, Corner, George III, Mahogany, Hanging, Doors, Shelves, Drawers, 41 In. ... 360.00
Cabinet, Corner, Hepplewhite, Inlaid Mahogany, Fretwork, String & Shell Inlay 800.00
Cabinet, Corner, Oak, Curved Glass, Paw Footed, c.1900 .... 1895.00
Cabinet, Corner, Paneled Door, Shell Carved Knees, Fruitwood, 100 In. 2875.00
Cabinet, Corner, Pine, Scandinavia, 20 x 15 In. 275.00
Cabinet, Corner, Regency, Reverse Painted Panels, Mahogany, 74 In., Pair 5100.00
Cabinet, Corner, Venetian Style, Painted Scenes, Short Cabriole Legs, Pair 715.00
Cabinet, Curio, Carved Rosewood Dragons, Glass, Victorian 4850.00
Cabinet, Curio, Corner, Lacquered, Gold, Silver, Red, Occupied Japan, 19 x 7 In. 95.00
Cabinet, Curio, Double Doors, Drawers, Oak, 1900, 70 x 50 In. 725.00
Cabinet, Curio, French Style, Marble Top, Lighted, Mahogany, 63 3/4 In. 415.00
Cabinet, Curio, Middle Drawer, Stick & Ball Beveled Glass, Victorian, c.1870 .... 7450.00
Cabinet, Danish, 3 Drawers, Flanked By Sliding Door, Teak, 1950s, 156 In. 575.00
Cabinet, Display, Edwardian, Fretwork, Crest, 1 Frieze Drawer, 72 x 36 In. 665.00
Cabinet, Domed Glazed Doors, 2 Cupboards, Fruitwood, Germany, c.1930, 73 In. 445.00
Cabinet, Doors, Inner Shelves, Mahogany, c.1880, 57 In., Pair 8600.00
Cabinet, Dutch Baroque, Marquetry, 2 Glazed Doors, 1 Long Drawer, 96 In. 9350.00
Cabinet, Empire, 2 Drawers, Cupboard Doors, Mahogany, 36 1/2 In. 2185.00
Cabinet, French Ormolu, Walnut, Glass, Bronze Design, 19th Century 1700.00
Cabinet, Hanging, Walnut & Cherry, Shelves, Drop Pendants, 26 x 18 In. 275.00
Cabinet, Hanging, Walnut, Victorian, Ball Drop Finials 265.00
Cabinet, Italian Renaissance Style, Ebonized, Inlaid Ivory, c.1880, 44 In. 3630.00
Cabinet, Italian Renaissance, Walnut, 2-Section Top, Doors, Cornice, 76 In. 1100.00
Cabinet, Italian Renaissance, Walnut, Slant Front, Fitted, Stand, 56 x 28 In. 770.00
Cabinet, Kitchen, Boone, 2 Frosted Glass Doors, Center Mirror, 2 Piece 400.00
Cabinet, Library, Carved Pinecones, Art Nouveau, France, c.1900, 81 x 61 In. 1725.00
Cabinet, Music, Carved Rosewood, Romeo & Juliet Textile Scene, Gallery 5200.00
Cabinet, Music, Galle, Marquetry Insects, Landscape, 1895, 53 In. 4900.00
Cabinet, Music, Herter Bros., Marquetry, Faux Bamboo, Rosewood 6600.00
Cabinet, Music, Rococo, Rosewood, Fretwork, Woolwork Scene, c.1840, 28 In. 5720.00
Cabinet, Papier-Mache, Mother-Of-Pearl, Parcel Gilt, Victorian, 13 x 14 In. 920.00
Cabinet, Pierced Cornice, Giltwood Dragon, 3 Doors, Red Lacquer, 69 In. 305.00
Cabinet, Queen Anne, Double, 4 Doors, Short Cabriole Legs, 65 x 31 x 16 In. 605.00
Cabinet, Regency, Stone Top, Silk Panel-Inset Doors, Satinwood, 37 1/2 In. 8050.00
Cabinet, Renaissance Revival, Ebonized, Gilt Metal, Plaques, 42 x 19 In. 770.00
Cabinet, Renaissance Style, Inlaid Walnut, Cornice, c.1880, 54 1/2 In. 1320.00

Cabinet, Robsjohn-Gibbings, Fruitwood, 2 Doors, Fitted, c.1936, 36 x 60 In. 4900.00
Cabinet, Side, Edwardian, Painted Satinwood, Demilune, c.1900, 37 x 45 In. 6900.00
Cabinet, Side, Regency Style, Rosewood, Brass Inlay, 3 Drawers, 2 Doors, 36 In. 1430.00
Cabinet, Side, Regency, Rosewood, Marble, Bronze Mounted, c.1810, 63 x 71 In. 9200.00
Cabinet, Smoker's, Mission, Oak, Pipe Rests Mounted On Sides 220.00
Cabinet, Smoker's, Stickley, Iron Strap Hardware, 1 Drawer, No. 89 .... 9500.00
Cabinet, Stand, Eames, Formica, Wood, Black, Orange, c.1950, 32 x 72 In. 920.00
Cabinet, Teak, Carved Dragons, Flowers, 1 Drawer, Shelves, China, 40 x 72 In. 605.00
Cabinet, Utility, Oak, Poplar, Pine, 1930-1940 .... 425.00
Cabinet, Watchmaker's, 31 Vials, 20 Drawers, Imperial Mainsprings, 15 x 8 In. 290.00
Cabinet, Watchmaker's, 166 Small Drawers, 72 In. 525.00
Cabinet, Wedding, Grain Painted, 1829 Inscription, Austria 5900.00
Candlestand, Birch, New Hampshire, 19th Century, 28 x 16 In. 2640.00
Candlestand, Cherry, Tripod, Snake Feet, Serpentine Top, Country, 16 x 20 In. . 275.00 to 385.00
Candlestand, Chippendale, Cherry, Black, Tripod, 1 Drawer, 1-Board Top, 16 In. 660.00
Candlestand, Chippendale, Cherry, Snake Feet, 2-Board Top, 27 In. 710.00
Candlestand, Chippendale, Cherry, Square Top, Shaped Corners 300.00
Candlestand, Chippendale, Cherry, Tripod, 1-Board Scalloped Top, 15 3/4 In. 2700.00
Candlestand, Chippendale, Cherry, Walnut, Tripod, Snake Feet, 17 x 18 In. 605.00
Candlestand, Chippendale, Dish Top, Walnut, c.1770, 27 x 18 1/4 In. 1045.00
Candlestand, Chippendale, Tiger Maple, New England, 18th Century 715.00
Candlestand, Chippendale, Tilt Top, Mahogany, Tripod, 22 x 28 In. 415.00
Candlestand, Chippendale, Vase-Turned Pedestal, 26 x 17 1/2 In. 385.00
Candlestand, Chippendale, Walnut Inlaid, 18th Century 825.00
Candlestand, Empire, Cherry, Tripod, 1-Board Top, Cut Corners, Country, 20 In. 140.00
Candlestand, Federal, Cherry, Baluster Pedestal, Saber Legs, 28 x 18 x 21 In. 185.00
Candlestand, Federal, Cherry, Curved Legs, American 330.00
Candlestand, Federal, Painted, Connecticut, 19th Century 415.00
Candlestand, Federal, Slant Front, Mahogany, New England, c.1800, 28 x 20 In. 385.00
Candlestand, Federal, Tilt Top, Arched Tripod Base, Red Paint, 20 In. 430.00
Candlestand, Federal, Tilt Top, Cherry, Rosewood Inlay, c.1800, 27 x 21 x 15 In. 1100.00
Candlestand, Federal, Tilt Top, Mahogany, New York State, c.1815, 28 x 23 In. 275.00
Candlestand, Federal, Tilt Top, Mahogany, Oval, Spider Legs, c.1795, 28 x 22 In. 1870.00
Candlestand, George III, Mahogany, Piecrust Top, Tripod, 23 x 14 3/4 In., Pair 385.00
Candlestand, George III, Tilt Top, Japanned, 27 x 21 1/2 In. 330.00
Candlestand, Grain Painted, Red & Yellow, Green Trim, 3 Legs, Octagonal Top 325.00
Candlestand, Hepplewhite, Tilt Top, Birch, Curly Maple, Tripod, 12 x 20 In. 385.00
Candlestand, Hepplewhite, Tilt Top, Tiger Maple, Spider Legs, New Hampshire 1375.00
Candlestand, Hepplewhite, Tilt Top, Tripod, Spider Legs, Country, 22 x 27 In. 330.00
Candlestand, Mahogany, Spade Feet, Urn Tripod 745.00
Candlestand, Maple, Adjustable, Double Candlestick, 37 In. 275.00
Candlestand, Maple, Ash, Screw Top, 35 1/2 In. 1265.00
Candlestand, Octagonal Incurved Top, Vase-Shaped Pedestal, Cherry, c.1795 .... 2530.00
Candlestand, Oval Tilt Top, Spade Feet, Cherry, 1785, 30 In. 1495.00
Candlestand, Queen Anne, Serpentine Top, 19th Century 990.00
Candlestand, Round Marble Top, Victorian 450.00
Candlestand, Shaker, 2 Directional Drawers, Cherry, 1820s, 24 1/2 In. 4600.00
Candlestand, Shaker, Harvard, Cherry 5500.00
Candlestand, Smoke Design, Original Red Paint, 3 Feet, Maine 1895.00
Candlestand, Square Top, Cabriole Legs, Snake Feet, Birch, c.1785, 27 In. 920.00
Candlestand, Square Top, Vase-Shaped Post, Cherry, c.1780, 26 In. 880.00
Candlestand, Tiger Maple Top, Cherry Base, Spider Legs 1600.00
Candlestand, Tilt Top, Mahogany, Veneer, Spider Legs, Octagonal, c.1790 .... 1155.00
Candlestand, Tilt Top, Oval, Mahogany, 28 In. 495.00
Candlestand, Tilt Top, Tiger Maple, Drawers, Spider Legs 1600.00
Candlestand, Tripod, Red, Late 18th Century, 26 1/2 x 16 x 15 3/4 In. 2500.00
Candlestand, Turned Post & Cross Base, Birch & Cherry, Painted, 1780 .... 415.00
Candlestand, Windsor, Alligatored Dark Green Paint, 31 1/2 In. 1870.00
Canterbury, 1 Drawer, Rosewood, 16 x 20 x 21 In. 1400.00
Canterbury, Bamboo, Spindle Form, 1880s, 29 3/4 In. 400.00
Canterbury, Chinoiserie, Lacquered, Bamboo, 16 In. 175.00
Canterbury, Lyre Form, Brass Spindles, 5 Sections, Faux Rosewood, 21 In. 1086.00
Canterbury, Regency, Mahogany, Brass Handle, Frieze Drawer, 1810, 21 x 18 In. 3750.00

Canterbury, Rosewood, 1 Drawer, 16 1/2 x 20 1/2 x 21 In. 1400.00
Canterbury, William IV, Mahogany, Pierce Carved Wreaths, M. Munn, 1835, 20 In. ... 990.00
Canterbury, William IV, Rosewood, Parcel Gilt, Lyre Shape, c.1825, 16 In. 1380.00
Cart, Serving, 2 Levels, Black & Gold, Surrealistic Horse & Rider Each Tray 1800.00
Case, Comb, Hanging, Holes For Mirror, Frogs, Fox, Raccoon, 11 1/4 In. 110.00
Cellarette, Converts To Small Bar, Lakeside Craft Shop, Mission Oak 440.00
Cellarette, Hepplewhite, Hinged Lid, Dove & Peace Iron Lick, 30 1/4 In. 3905.00
Cellarette, Sarcophagus Form, Fitted Interior, Mahogany, 21 x 30 In. 1840.00
Chair, Aesthetic, Gilded, Ebonized, Tapestry Upholstered, Painted Crane Back 605.00
Chair, Aesthetic, Satinwood, Mother-Of-Pearl, Brass, Exotic Woods, Pair 1870.00
Chair, Anthropomorphic Arms, Hardwood, 19th Century 690.00
Chair, Arne Jacobsen, Egg Style, Wool Upholstered, Steel Base, c.1955 .... 70.00
Chair, Arrow-Back, Plank Seat, Turned Legs, Pine, Pair 90.00
Chair, Arrow-Back, Yellow & Green Design, Thumb Back 1265.00
Chair, Arts & Crafts, Heywood-Wakefield Label, Oak, Pair 250.00
Chair, Balloon Back, Cabriole Legs, Mahogany, Upholstered, Victorian, 42 In. 330.00
Chair, Banister Back, Carved, New England, 1705-1730, 45 In. 1430.00
Chair, Banister Back, Old Paint, Rush Seat, Spanish Footed 1450.00
Chair, Barrel, George III, Brassbound, Mahogany, Loop Handles, c.1770, 22 In. 7145.00
Chair, Belter, Cornucopia Carved, Upholstered, Pair 9900.00
Chair, Belter, Henry Clay Pattern, Pair 3850.00
Chair, Belter, Laminated Rosewood, Rosalie-Like Carved Crest, Upholstered 2000.00
Chair, Belter, Lincoln Pattern, Laminated Rosewood 1400.00
Chair, Bentwood, Green Paint, Clublike End Arms 1200.00
Chair, Biedermeier Style, Marquetry, Rosewood, 19th Century 200.00
Chair, Biedermeier, Fruitwood, Balloon Back, Upholstered, 1840s, Pair 2450.00
Chair, Biedermeier, Straddle, English Cockfighting 395.00
Chair, Billiard, Limbert, Saddle Seat, Back Posts, Footrest, Marked, 45 In. 2700.00
Chair, Billiard, Mission, Oak, Leather Seat, Pair 895.00
Chair, Bishop's, Hooded, Chestnut, Pine, Drawer, Paneled Back, 27 x 15 x 61 In. 1980.00
Chair, Bishop's, Oak, Ornately Carved, Mass. Convent, Large 3300.00
Chair, C. Rohlfs, Octagonal Stiles, Cutout Seat, Oak, c.1902, 46 3/4 In. 5175.00
Chair, Campaign, Fold Up, Regency, Canework Back & Seats, c.1820, Pair 800.00
Chair, Caned Open Arms, Demilune Caned Back, Lion Mask Center, Painted 4315.00
Chair, Carved & Laminated Mahogany, Fleur-De-Lis, Victorian, 36 In. 330.00
Chair, Carved Cornucopia Slat, Saber Legs, Slip Seat, Mahogany, 31 1/2 In. 85.00
Chair, Carved Crest, Inlaid Mountain Goat Scene, 19th Century 165.00
Chair, Carved Teak, Worn Brown Finish, Signed, India, 42 In., Pair 550.00
Chair, Chinese Style, Parcel Gilt, Continuous Arms, 19th Century, Child's 1150.00
Chair, Chippendale, Cherry, Arched Crest, Pierced Splat, Trapezoidal Seat, c.1760 ..... 920.00
Chair, Chippendale, Gilt Vine Design, Rush Seat, Painted, c.1800, 37 x 16 In. 385.00

◆◆◆◆◆◆◆◆◆◆◆◆◆◆◆◆◆◆◆◆◆◆◆◆

Rub colored furniture wax on
old wooden pieces, let dry for 15
minutes to 8 hours, then buff
with a terry cloth rag. Wait a few
days then apply clear furniture
wax and buff. Be sure the colored wax is just slightly darker
than the original wood finish.

◆◆◆◆◆◆◆◆◆◆◆◆◆◆◆◆◆◆◆◆◆◆◆◆

Furniture, Chair, Circumcision, Carved,
19th Century, Arms

Furniture, Chair, Corner, Chippendale,
Maple, Square Seat

Furniture, Chair, Pennsylvania
Moravian, Cherry, Walnut,
Pierced Heart Splat

Furniture, Chair, Morris, L. & J. G.
Stickley, Ottoman, Oak,
Adjustable Back, No. 412

Chair, Chippendale, Mahogany, 4 Pierced Carved Back Splats, 18 1/2 In., Pair 275.00
Chair, Chippendale, Mahogany, Boston, c.1780, 36 1/2 In., Pair 1045.00
Chair, Chippendale, Mahogany, Carved Side, Boston, 1770s, 38 In. 4070.00
Chair, Chippendale, Mahogany, Square Stop-Fluted Legs, Pair 8800.00
Chair, Chippendale, Maple, New England, c.1780, 37 3/4 In., Pair 660.00
Chair, Chippendale, Ocher & Orange Swirled Paint Design, c.1785 .... 600.00
Chair, Chippendale, Walnut, Cabriole Legs, Slip Seat, Old Refinish 440.00
Chair, Chippendale, Walnut, Serpentine Crest Rail, Vase-Shaped Splat 2530.00
Chair, Chippendale, Walnut, Serpentine Crest Rail, Slip Seat, Matched Rails 2760.00
Chair, Circumcision, Carved, 19th Century, Arms .... *Illus* 2200.00
Chair, Club, Art Moderne, Satin Upholstered, c.1930, Pair 800.00
Chair, Club, Dominique, Upholstered, 1940, Pair 5750.00
Chair, Club, Shaped Back, Rolled Arms, Leather, Art Deco, c.1930, Pair 1600.00
Chair, Commode, Chippendale, Pierced Splat, Walnut, c.1760, 33 1/2 In. 1430.00
Chair, Corner, Art Deco, Arched Upholstered Back, Germany, c.1930 .... 440.00
Chair, Corner, Bamboo, Pair 195.00

White rings on furniture can
sometimes be removed with liquid metal polish or auto paint
cleaner. Apply the cleaner to a
soft cloth and rub until the ring is
gone. Then repolish the surface
with furniture polish.

Furniture, Chair, Silver Gilt, 19th Century, India

Chair, Corner, Chippendale, Cherry, Carved, c.1770, 31 In.	2200.00
Chair, Corner, Chippendale, Mahogany, New England, c.1780	1760.00
Chair, Corner, Chippendale, Maple, Square Seat .... *Illus*	1100.00
Chair, Corner, Mahogany, Shaped Splat, Carved Knee, Ball & Claw Footed	1540.00
Chair, Corner, Maple & Ash, Rush Seat	900.00
Chair, Corner, Queen Anne, 2 Pierced Splats, Mahogany, c.1765	8625.00
Chair, Corner, Queen Anne, Walnut, Mass., 1740-1765	11000.00
Chair, Corner, Turned, Maple & Ash, 32 In.	770.00
Chair, Curved Paneled Back & Side, Orkney Pine, Scotland, 19th Century	465.00
Chair, Cutout Metal, Anaconda, Mont., Dated April 1899	325.00
Chair, Directoire Style, Ribbon Back, Mahogany, c.1860, Pair	5750.00
Chair, Duncan Phyfe, Mahogany, Striped Upholstered Seat, Pair	6875.00
Chair, Eames, DCM, Plywood, Chromed Steel, c.1946	1150.00
Chair, Eames, Eiffel Tower, Plastic, Wire, Herman Miller Co., Early 1950s	1000.00
Chair, Eames, Fiberglass & Chrome, 1960s	150.00
Chair, Eames, LCW, Laminated Molded Plywood, c.1946	690.00
Chair, Eames, Lounge, Laminated Rosewood, Swivel, Leather, Aluminum	550.00
Chair, Eames, Lounge, Molded Plywood	415.00
Chair, Eames, Lounge, Molded Rosewood, Plywood Shell, Leather Upholstered	65.00
Chair, Eames, Lounge, Red Stained Ash Plywood, 1945, Pair	1300.00
Chair, Eames, Molded Plywood, Child's, c.1945	6900.00
Chair, Eastlake, Hip-Hugger, Cane Seat, Pair	175.00
Chair, Easy, Chippendale, Silk Damask Upholstered, 1760s, 45 1/4 In.	3850.00
Chair, Empire, High Scrolled Back, Round Seat, Paw Feet	65.00
Chair, Empire, Mahogany Veneer, Slip Seat, 31 In.	60.00
Chair, Federal, Arch & Point Crest, Rush Slip Seat, Cherrywood, 1780s	1840.00
Chair, Federal, Arched Crest, Pierced Splat, Mahogany, 38 1/2 In.	1380.00
Chair, Federal, Carved Crest, Vase-Shaped Splat, Caned Seat, Tiger Maple	325.00
Chair, Federal, Mahogany, Providence, Rhode Island, 39 In., Pair	770.00
Chair, Fiddleback, Maple, Duck Feet	360.00
Chair, Fornasetti, Black & Gold Lacquer	2200.00
Chair, Frank Lloyd Wright & George Niedecken-Wallbridge, Spindle, 1908	4600.00
Chair, Frank Lloyd Wright & Niedecken, 9 Spindles Join Crest Rail, Oak, c.1908	7475.00
Chair, Frank Lloyd Wright, Upholstered Back & Seat, Painted Steel, c.1904	1840.00
Chair, Frank Lloyd Wright, Usonian, Plywood, c.1938, Pair	4025.00
Chair, Geometric Design, Needlepoint Back & Seat, Walnut, Cabriole Legs	130.00
Chair, George II, Gainsborough, Mahogany, Square Legs	250.00
Chair, George II, Parcel Gilt, Scarlet Japanning, Cane, Foliate Scrolls	3400.00
Chair, George II, Walnut, Lobed Crest, Carved Back Splat, Ball & Paw Feet	6900.00
Chair, George III, Giltwood, Padded Backrest, Seat & Open Arms, c.1775	8050.00

Chair, George III, Mahogany, Cabriole Legs, Ball & Claw Footed, Pair 990.00
Chair, George III, Mahogany, Crest, Pierced Splat, Ring-Turned Feet, c.1770 .... 3740.00
Chair, George III, Mahogany, Open Arms, Foliate Carved, Leather Seat 6900.00
Chair, George III, Mahogany, Shield-Shaped Back, Slip-In Seat, c.1785, Pair 3400.00
Chair, George III, Mahogany, Upholstered Back, Curved Rail, Pair 1320.00
Chair, George IV, Ebonized, c.1810, Pair 135.00
Chair, George Nelson, Coconut, Original Fabric & Foam 3750.00
Chair, George Nelson, Pretzel, Dished Seat, Laminated Wood, 1952 .... 4900.00
Chair, Georgian, Mahogany, Ladder Back, 1780 .... 165.00
Chair, Georgian, Mahogany, Tapestry Upholstered, Pair 770.00
Chair, Gilbert Rohde, U-Form Back & Arms, Velvet Upholstered, 1940s 2530.00
Chair, Gothic, Ebonized, Pierce-Carved Trefoils & Quatrefoils, c.1840 .... 220.00
Chair, Gustav Stickley, Ladder Back, Upholstered Seat, No. 306 1/2, 36 In., Pair 440.00
Chair, Gustav Stickley, Oak, Sling Back & Seat, Replaced Leather, Nail Studded 285.00
Chair, Gustav Stickley, Riveted Leather Back & Seat, No. 364 .... 550.00
Chair, Gustav Stickley, Spindled Cube, Oak, No. 391 .... 8625.00
Chair, H. Jacob, Horseshoe-Shaped Backrest, Upholstered Back, Painted, Pair 6325.00
Chair, Harden, Arched Crest, 5-Slat Back, Curved Apron 605.00
Chair, Hepplewhite, Cherry, Pierced Urn Back, Upholstered Seat, American 330.00
Chair, Hepplewhite, Mahogany, X-Back 165.00
Chair, Herman Miller, Pretzel, Laminated Wood, 1952 .... 4265.00
Chair, Herter Bros., Renaissance Revival, Plum, Silver Inlaid, Pair 3200.00
Chair, Hitchcock, Dark Paint, Yellow Striping, Floral, Balloon Seats, Pair 145.00
Chair, Hunzinger, Ebonized, 34 In. 165.00
Chair, Ice Cream, Wire, Heart Back, Padded Seat 20.00
Chair, Italian Rococo, Walnut, Mid-18th Century 330.00
Chair, J. & J. Kohn, Horseshoe Shape, Green Leather, J. Hoffman, c.1902, 31 In. 6325.00
Chair, Jacobean, Oak, Arch Top, 18th Century 135.00
Chair, Josef Hoffmann, Scalloped Pierced Back, Laminated Seat, 1910 .... 2300.00
Chair, Josef Hoffmann, U-Form Back & Arms, Paper Label, c.1904, Pair 2875.00
Chair, L. & J.G. Stickley, Dining, No. 384 .... 1045.00
Chair, L. & J.G. Stickley, Reclining, Spring Cushion Seat, No. 830, c.1912 .... 770.00
Chair, Ladder Back, 3 Slats, Splint Seat, Turned Finials, 27 In. 330.00
Chair, Ladder Back, 3 Slats, Turned Feet, Paper Rush Seat, 39 In. 135.00
Chair, Ladder Back, 4 Arched Slats, Splint Seat, Finials, 41 1/2 In. 415.00
Chair, Ladder Back, 4 Graduated Arched Slats, Painted, Rush Seat, 43 In. 1100.00
Chair, Ladder Back, Brown Over Red, Paper Rush Seat, 30 In. 120.00
Chair, Ladder Back, Chapin, Chippendale, Cherry, Connecticut, 37 In. 468.00
Chair, Ladder Back, Federal, 5 Arched Splats, Rush Seat, 1840s 1035.00
Chair, Ladder Back, Urn Finial, Taped Seat, 27 In. 165.00
Chair, Le Corbusier, Cube, Pair 5600.00
Chair, Library, Metamorphic, Oak, c.1900 .... 3000.00
Chair, Limbert, Revolving & Tilting, Splayed Legs, No. 535, 39 1/2 In. 1045.00
Chair, Lloyd Loom Products, Steel Spring, Chrome Plated, Wooden Arms, c.1917 ..... 200.00
Chair, Lolling, Federal, Mahogany Inlay, New England, c.1800, 49 x 15 1/2 In. 3025.00
Chair, Lolling, Federal, Molded Arm Terminals, Mahogany, c.1815, 47 In. 2860.00
Chair, Lolling, Federal, Upholstered Back, Damask Seat, Mahogany 1495.00
Chair, Lolling, Shaped Arms, Upholstered Seat, Mahogany, c.1800 .... 6050.00
Chair, Lolling, Sheraton Style, Silk Brocade Upholstered, Mahogany, 48 In. 715.00
Chair, Lolling, String Outlined Legs, c.1800, 44 1/2 In. 1320.00
Chair, Louis XV, Upholstered Backrest & Armrest, Beechwood, Pair 2300.00
Chair, Louis XVI Style, Tapestry Seat, Gilt, Carved Wood 1495.00
Chair, Louis XVI, Oval Upholstered Back, Padded Armrests, Painted, Pair 9200.00
Chair, Louis XVI, Upholstered Backrest & Arms, White Paint, Pair 2875.00
Chair, Louis XVI, Upholstered Backrest & Seat, Carved Borders, Painted 5780.00
Chair, Lounge, Footstool, Vladimir Kagan, Walnut, Teal Leather, 1955 .... 4025.00
Chair, Mackintosh Style, Geometric Back Splat, Ebonized Wood, 55 In., Pair 305.00
Chair, Mahogany, Lotus & Palmetto Splat, Boston, c.1820, 18 In. 880.00
Chair, Majorelle, Cast Leaves, Velvet Upholstered, Mahogany, c.1900 .... 8625.00
Chair, Majorelle, Desk, Gilt-Bronze Capped Arms, Mahogany, c.1900 .... 7475.00
Chair, Majorelle, Flowering Clematis Vines On Head Rail, Pair 770.00
Chair, Majorelle, Rolled Upholstered Arms, Pierced Sides, Mahogany, c.1900 .... 3450.00
Chair, Marcel Breuer, Shaped Laminated Arms, Leather Seat, 1945 .... 3165.00

Chair, Morris, Arts & Crafts, Oak, Adjustable Back, 4 Horizontal Slats, Arms 2070.00
Chair, Morris, Gustav Stickley, 5 Side Slats, Upholstered Seat & Back, c.1912 .... 5750.00
Chair, Morris, Gustav Stickley, Bow Arms, No. 336 .... 4250.00
Chair, Morris, Gustav Stickley, Bow Arms, No. 2340, c.1902 .... 5750.00
Chair, Morris, L. & J.G. Stickley, Oak, Medium Finish, No. 448, c.1910 .... 1540.00
Chair, Morris, L. & J.G. Stickley, Ottoman, Oak, Adjustable Back, No. 412 .... *Illus* 3450.00
Chair, Morris, Limbert, Reclining, Oak, c.1910, 37 1/2 x 31 In. 2750.00
Chair, Morris, Mission, Oak, Slant Arms, Casters, c.1910, 42 In. 880.00
Chair, Morris, Oak, Claw Footed, 1910 .... 385.00
Chair, Morris, Royal Furniture, Oak, Adjustable Back, Retractable Footrest, c.1915 ... 330.00
Chair, Mythological Birds, Upholstered Seat, Walnut, Italy, Pair 5120.00
Chair, Nursing, Mahogany, Victorian, c.1880 .... 175.00
Chair, Nursing, Petit Point Upholstered, Reclining Position, 1800s 850.00
Chair, O. Robertson, Balloon Back, Floral Design, Yellow Striping, 34 In. 105.00
Chair, Oak, Leather Upholstered, Arms, c.1890, Pair 925.00
Chair, Onondaga, 8 Slats Under Each Arm, Upholstered Back, No. 782 .... 950.00
Chair, Paul Follot, Gilt Crest Rail, Silk Brocade Upholstered Seat, 1920, Pair 9200.00
Chair, Pennsylvania Moravian, Cherry, Walnut, Pierced Heart Splat .... *Illus* 1650.00
Chair, Piano, 5 Spindles 500.00
Chair, Pierced Backrest, Trellis Splats, Brass Mounted, Mahogany, Pair 8050.00
Chair, Plank Seat, Painted, Rose Crest, 9 1/4 In. 385.00
Chair, Planter's, Colonial, Canted & Caned Back, Seat Rest, West India, 46 In. 1100.00
Chair, Potty, Primitive, Blue-Green Paint, 19th Century, 8 x 17 x 14 In. 125.00
Chair, Praying, Italy 600.00
Chair, Pressed Back, Oak 125.00
Chair, Pressed Back, Old Man Of The North, Cane Seat 45.00
Chair, Pressed Back, Spindles 100.00
Chair, Prudent Mallard, Original Upholstered, Victorian, Pair 1200.00
Chair, Queen Anne, Banister Back, Rush Seat, Maple, 18th Century 230.00
Chair, Queen Anne, Black, Gold Striping, Chinoiserie, Rush Seat, Country 220.00
Chair, Queen Anne, Cabriole Legs, Pad Feet, Carved Ears On Bow Crest 3250.00
Chair, Queen Anne, Mahogany, Serpentine Crest, Slip Seat, 1750s, 41 In. 4025.00
Chair, Queen Anne, Maple, Slip Seat, Vase-Shaped Splat, H Stretcher, Refinished 990.00
Chair, Queen Anne, Scalloped Apron, Turned Stretchers, Walnut, 1750s 3500.00
Chair, Queen Anne, Spanish Footed, Maple, 18th Century 300.00
Chair, Queen Anne, Spanish Footed, New England, c.1750, 39 1/2 In. 365.00
Chair, Queen Anne, Spanish Footed, Painted, New England, 18th Century, 39 In. 1100.00
Chair, Queen Anne, Spanish Footed, Vase-Shaped Back, c.1780, 41 In. 360.00
Chair, Queen Anne, Vase Splat, Yoke Crest, Rush Seat, 36 3/4 In. 195.00
Chair, Queen Anne, Vase-Shaped Splat, Balloon Seat, Walnut, c.1715, Pair 3450.00
Chair, Queen Anne, Walnut, Marquetry, Yoke Crest, Drop-In Upholstered Seat 805.00
Chair, Queen Anne, Yoke Back, Delaware Valley, Arms 1485.00
Chair, Regency, Mahogany Veneer, Carved Back, Ribbed Legs, Pair 685.00
Chair, Regency, Swan Back, Upholstered Seat, Pair 2850.00
Chair, Rocker, look under Rocker in this category.
Chair, Rosewood, Pierced Crest, Balustered Backrest, Victorian, American, Child's 965.00
Chair, Roundabout, Queen Anne, Walnut & Mahogany, 32 1/2 x 17 In. 6600.00
Chair, Saber Leg, Philadelphia, c.1840, Pair 1100.00
Chair, Serpentine Crest, Urn-Shaped Splat, Cane Seat, Tiger Maple, Pair 200.00
Chair, Shaker, Cherry & Tiger Maple, 1840-1850, 41 1/2 In. 880.00
Chair, Shaker, Ladder Back 3575.00
Chair, Shaker, Tilting Slat Back, Maple, 41 In. 4675.00
Chair, Sheraton, Hardwood, Curly Maple, Rush Seat, Country, Pair 385.00
Chair, Sheraton, Harp-Form Back Splat, Rush Seat, Painted Wood, Pair 550.00
Chair, Sheraton, India, Mid-19th Century, Pair 7150.00
Chair, Sheraton, Turtle Back, Stencil, Rush Seat, 34 In., Pair 200.00
Chair, Shield-Shaped Upholstered Back, Carved Tassels, Oak, 1890s 2600.00
Chair, Silver Gilt, 19th Century, India .... *Illus* 7475.00
Chair, Slipper, Arched Back Rail, Carved, Cabriole Legs, Rosewood 185.00
Chair, Slipper, Belter, Laminated Rosewood, Upholstered Seat 2475.00
Chair, Slipper, Black Lacquer, Mother-Of-Pearl Inlay, Cane Seat, 32 In. 165.00
Chair, Slipper, Out-Scrolled Top Rail, Castors, Giltwood, Victorian, 1870s 5175.00
Chair, Slipper, Plush Upholstered, Short Turned Feet, 29 1/2 In. 66.00

Chair, Slipper, Rococo, Rosewood, Pierced Carved Crest, Cabriole Legs, Pair 2200.00
Chair, Slipper, Transitional, Vase-Shaped Back, New England, c.1750, 36 In. 660.00
Chair, Splint Seat, 19th Century, 24 In. 240.00
Chair, Spoon Back, Carved, New Hampshire, 18th Century 935.00
Chair, Stickley Bros., 5 Vertical Slats, Copper Ornaments Front & Sides 1095.00
Chair, Stickley Bros., Oak, Maiden's Bust, Art Nouveau Style, Shaped Seat 460.00
Chair, Swivel, Floral & Scroll, Cast Iron, 32 1/2 In. 550.00
Chair, Swivel, Rosewood, Steel, Art Nouveau, 1950s 635.00
Chair, Table, 3 Boards, Raised Shoe Feet, Red Paint 3960.00
Chair, Throne, Eagle Back, Viking Figurehead Arms 2915.00
Chair, Throne, Jacobean Style, Carved Squirrel, Figures, Winged Arms, Walnut 605.00
Chair, Thumb Back, Arrow-Back, Yellow & Green Design, Grained Ground 1265.00
Chair, Thumb Back, Plank Seat, Painted & Stenciled, Pennsylvania, 33 In. 300.00
Chair, Van Der Rohe, Chromium Plated, Tubular, Model MR10, c.1931, Pair 800.00
Chair, Wainscot, Black Paint, Hardwood, 41 1/2 In. 275.00
Chair, Wicker, Brown, Arms, Partial Wakefield Label 467.00
Chair, William & Mary, Banister Back, Splint Seat, 41 1/2 In. 330.00
Chair, William & Mary, Carved Maple, Leather Seat & Back, Boston 1870.00
Chair, William & Mary, Split Baluster Back, Rush Seat, 18th Century 230.00
Chair, Windsor, Bamboo, Birdcage Back With Medallion, 33 1/2 In. 100.00
Chair, Windsor, Bamboo, Painted, Birdcage Back, Medallion, 35 1/2 In. 330.00
Chair, Windsor, Bamboo, Plank Seat, Birdcage Back, Refinished, Pair 385.00
Chair, Windsor, Bamboo, Shaped Seat, Scrolled Arms, Spindles, Black Paint 880.00
Chair, Windsor, Bamboo, Yellow Striping, Stenciled Flowers On Crest, Child's 250.00
Chair, Windsor, Birdcage, Square Plank Seat, American 110.00
Chair, Windsor, Bow Back, 9 Spindles, Gold Striping, Saddle Seat 770.00
Chair, Windsor, Bow Back, Black, Gold Striping, Bamboo Turned, H Stretcher 275.00
Chair, Windsor, Bow Back, Spindle Back, Bamboo Turning, Painted, 34 In. 165.00
Chair, Windsor, Bow Back, Vase-Turned Legs, Saddle Seat, c.1790, 37 1/2 In. 450.00
Chair, Windsor, Brace Back, Continuous Arm, England, 18th Century, 42 In. 935.00
Chair, Windsor, Brace Back, Saddle Seat, 9-Spindle Back, Green Paint, 38 In. 220.00
Chair, Windsor, Cutter & Power, Pine, Maple & Other Woods, Rod Back, Pair 275.00
Chair, Windsor, E. Tracy, Sack Back, Arms 1250.00
Chair, Windsor, Fanback, Arched Crest, 9 Spindles, Saddle Seat 400.00
Chair, Windsor, Fanback, Arched Crest, 9 Banisters, 1765-1780, 35 1/2 In. 1380.00
Chair, Windsor, Fanback, Black Paint, Gilt Pinstriping, c.1780, 44 x 18 In. 2420.00
Chair, Windsor, Fanback, Brace Back Maple & Ash, 1770s, 37 1/2 In. 1320.00
Chair, Windsor, Fanback, Brace Back, New England, 18th Century 415.00
Chair, Windsor, Fanback, Painted, New England, 19th Century, 36 In. 880.00
Chair, Windsor, Fanback, Pine, Other Woods, Yellow Paint, 35 In. 385.00
Chair, Windsor, Fanback, Saddle Seat, Spindle Back, Yoke Crest, Black Paint 495.00
Chair, Windsor, Frank Kendall, Continuous Arm, Signed 1050.00
Chair, Windsor, Knuckle, Tortoiseshell Painted Design Seat 3900.00
Chair, Windsor, Moravian, Salmon Paint, c.1815 .... 400.00
Chair, Windsor, Nutting, Fanback, Early 20th Century, Paper Label 1075.00
Chair, Windsor, Rod Back, Painted, Upholstered Seat, 26 In. 1045.00
Chair, Windsor, S.J. Stucke, Bow Back, 7 Spindles, Leather Seat, Black Paint 435.00
Chair, Windsor, Sack Back, Brown Varnish Over Original Green, c.1790 .... 3800.00
Chair, Windsor, Step-Down, Painted Yellow, Leaf Stencil On Crest, Pair 330.00
Chair, Windsor, Writing Arm, Drawer Under Seat, Painted, 18th Century 6500.00
Chair, Wing, French Style, Brocade Upholstered, 20th Century, 43 In. 200.00
Chair, Wing, George I, Out-Scrolled Sides, Loose Cushion, Walnut, 1740s 8050.00
Chair, Wing, Georgian Style, Walnut, Damask, Carved Ball & Claw Feet, 44 In. 660.00
Chair, Wing, Hepplewhite, Mahogany, Damask Upholstered 2300.00
Chair, Wing, Provincial Louis XIV, Walnut 3080.00
Chair, Wing, Queen Anne, Mahogany, Cabriole Legs, 1900s, 35 1/2 In. 660.00
Chair, Wing, Sheraton, Mahogany, Upholstered, 1800-1815 .... 2750.00
Chair, Wing, William & Mary Style, Walnut, Petit Point, 18th Century, 49 In. 3850.00
Chair & Ottoman, Eero Saarinen, Womb, Orange 1350.00
Chair & Ottoman, Eames, Lounge, Rosewood Veneer, Upholstered, 1956 .... 1760.00
Chair Set, Arrow-Back, Dark Brown Paint, Yellow Striping, Floral Crest, 6 .... 1485.00
Chair Set, Arrow-Back, Grained, Line Design, New England, 1820-1840, 4 .... 1550.00
Chair Set, Arrow-Back, Painted, Polychrome Stencil, c.1830, 34 In., 7 .... 1760.00

Furniture, Chair Set, Federal, Mahogany, New England, 1800, 35 1/2 In. , 4

Chair Set, Balloon Back, Fruitwood, Victorian, Late 19th Century, 6 .... 385.00
Chair Set, Barrel, Rosewood Veneer, Upholstered Seat, Mahogany, 1930, 4 .... 4600.00
Chair Set, Biedermeier, Inlay, Drop Seat, Mahogany, Ebony & Fruitwood, 4 .... 6325.00
Chair Set, Black & Red Grained, Stenciled, Rush Seat, 8 .... 2800.00
Chair Set, Brown Paint, Design, Pennsylvania, 6 .... 2200.00
Chair Set, Carved Slats, Saber Legs, Cane Seat, Tiger Maple, 11 .... 6600.00
Chair Set, Chippendale Revival, Mahogany, Carved, 2 Armchairs, 1880, 8 .... 5775.00
Chair Set, Chippendale, Ladder Back, Mahogany, 18th Century, 3 .... 2200.00
Chair Set, Chippendale, Mahogany, 1 Arm, 2 Side, Carving, 3 .... 2860.00
Chair Set, Chippendale, New England, 18th Century, 41 In., 6 .... 2530.00
Chair Set, Classical, Mahogany Veneer, 1835-1845, 31 1/2 In., 6 .... 1760.00
Chair Set, Classical, Tiger Maple, Caned Seat, Saber Legs, American, 18 x 20 In., 3   690.00
Chair Set, Cort Zingelman, Seignouret Style, Carved, Mahogany, 1940, 8 .... 1155.00
Chair Set, Dining, Art Deco, Black Paint, France, 2 Armchairs, 1940s, 12 .... 7475.00
Chair Set, Dining, Arts & Crafts, Oak, 1 Splat, Upholstered, John Cave, 1900, 4 ...... 1380.00
Chair Set, Dining, Cartouche-Shaped Back, Victorian, Philadelphia, 8 .... 4125.00
Chair Set, Dining, Carved & Upholstered Back Splat, Carved Apron, Italy, 8 .... 400.00
Chair Set, Dining, Chippendale, Mahogany, Interlaced Splats, Slip Seat, c.1850, 8 ... 5225.00
Chair Set, Dining, Empire, Mahogany, Dark, Horsehair Upholstered, 2 Arm, 8 .... 2685.00
Chair Set, Dining, French Provincial, Rush Seat, 19th Century, 4 .... 415.00
Chair Set, Dining, From Normandie Ocean Liner, Fluted Skirt, Mahogany, 4 .... 500.00
Chair Set, Dining, George I, Walnut, Upholstered Seats, 2 Armchairs, 10 .... 8250.00
Chair Set, Dining, George II, Walnut, Cabriole Legs, Paw Footed, 1 Armchair, 8 ...... 6900.00
Chair Set, Dining, George III Style, Mahogany, Carved Crest, 1 Armchair, 5 .... 1540.00
Chair Set, Dining, George III Style, Mahogany, Reeded Crest & Legs, 8 .... 9200.00
Chair Set, Dining, George III Style, Vase-Shaped Splat, Mahogany, 8 .... 4830.00
Chair Set, Dining, George III, Carved Foliage, 2 Armchairs, 1800, 8 .... 8050.00
Chair Set, Dining, George III, Curved Back, Molded Crest, c.1800, 6 .... 4600.00
Chair Set, Dining, George III, Mahogany, 38 In., 6 .... 3025.00
Chair Set, Dining, Georgian, Burl Wood, 10 .... 7150.00
Chair Set, Dining, Georgian, Mahogany, Interlaced Splat, Drop-In Seats, 1780, 4 ...... 415.00
Chair Set, Dining, Louis XVI Style, Needlepoint Seat & Back, 10 .... 4370.00
Chair Set, Dining, Queen Anne, Walnut, Vase-Shaped Splat, Upholstered Seat, 6 .... 2475.00
Chair Set, Dining, Regency Style, Oak, Gilt, Tooled Leather, 2 Armchairs, 8 .... 3740.00
Chair Set, Dining, Regency, Mahogany, Concave Crest, Saber Legs, c.1825, 6 .... 3680.00
Chair Set, Dining, Regency, Reeded Legs, 2 Armchairs, 1720s, 6 .... 9200.00
Chair Set, Dining, Ribbon Back, Upholstered Seats, Square Legs, Mahogany, 6 .... 1760.00
Chair Set, Dining, William IV, Mahogany, Rectangular Crest Rail, 2 Armchairs, 6 .... 1045.00
Chair Set, Dutch Baroque, Walnut, Back Splat, Scroll Legs, Late 19th Century, 8 ..... 2530.00
Chair Set, Eames, Birch Backs & Seats, Steel Rods, 1950s, 5 .... 1210.00
Chair Set, Eames, Eiffel Tower, Painted Wire Rod Construction, 4 .... 500.00
Chair Set, Empire, Olive Brown Paint, Angel Wing Crests, Cane Seat, 34 In., 6 .... 400.00
Chair Set, Face Carved On Back, Paw Footed, 1 Armchair, 3 .... 550.00
Chair Set, Federal, Ebony Inlay, Saber Feet, Mahogany, c.1815, 6 .... 8625.00
Chair Set, Federal, Mahogany, New England, 1800, 35 1/2 In., 4 .... *Illus* 2200.00
Chair Set, Federal, Mahogany, Rope-Turned Spindle Back, Saber Legs, 6 .... 1430.00

Chair Set, Fiddleback, Bird's Eye Maple, 8 .... 500.00
Chair Set, George III Style, Pierced Splat, Marlborough Legs, Mahogany, 4 .... 525.00
Chair Set, George III, Carved Mahogany, Shaped Back Rails, c.1820, 4 .... 2420.00
Chair Set, George IV, Dining, Mahogany, Upholstered Seat, c.1800, 6 .... 825.00
Chair Set, Gothic Revival, Oak, Carved Back Splat, Plank Seat, c.1850, 6 .... 5465.00
Chair Set, Gustav Stickley, Experimental Design, No. 352, 6 .... 6000.00
Chair Set, Gustav Stickley, Leather Seat, 6 .... 3400.00
Chair Set, Gustav Stickley, Oak, Upholstered Seat, No. 349 1/2, 6 .... 3450.00
Chair Set, Hongmu, Scroll Carved, Open Arms, Chamfered Inset, China, 6 .... 5175.00
Chair Set, Jacobean, Oak, Barley Twist, Cane Seat, 6 .... 830.00
Chair Set, L. & J.G. Stickley, No. 323, 6 .... 3850.00
Chair Set, Ladder Back, 3 Slats, Turned Finial, Woven Splint Seats, 4 .... 550.00
Chair Set, Ladder Back, Shaker, c.1870, 36 In., 6 .... 770.00
Chair Set, Ledell, Windsor, Bamboo, Gold Striping, Branded, 35 In., 6 .... 2805.00
Chair Set, LeMaire, Upholstered Back & Seat, Black Lacquer, Metal, 6 .... 1380.00
Chair Set, Limbert, Oak, Medium Finish, c.1910, Branded Mark, 6 .... 1980.00
Chair Set, Louis XVI, Upholstered Backrest, Padded Arms, Beechwood, 4 .... 7475.00
Chair Set, Majorelle, Mahogany, Les Clematites, c.1900, 4 .... 5750.00
Chair Set, Nakashima, Spindle Back, Hickory & Walnut, 1955, 36 In., 6 .... 4850.00
Chair Set, Neoclassical, Walnut, Parcel Gilt, Lyre Splat, Rush Seat, Italy, c.1800, 2 .. 330.00
Chair Set, Neoclassical, Walnut, Spindle Back, Leather Upholstered, 35 In., 4 .... 3025.00
Chair Set, Pierced C-Scroll Splat, Leather Seat, Rosewood, Victorian, 4 .... 1380.00
Chair Set, Plank Bottom, Bird & Floral Design Crest, Brown Ground, 5 .... 600.00
Chair Set, Pressed Back, Oak, Cane Seat, 4 .... 650.00
Chair Set, Provincial Louis XVI, Caned Back Fauteuils, 4 .... 4400.00
Chair Set, Queen Anne, Turned, Maple, 18th Century, 4 .... 1980.00
Chair Set, Regency Style, Reeded Slats, Trapezoidal Seat, Mahogany, 9 .... 2100.00
Chair Set, Regency, Mahogany, Brass Inlaid, Caned Seats, Saber Legs, 6 .... 3575.00
Chair Set, Regency, Pierced Crossbar, Saber Legs, Mahogany, 4 .... 1210.00

Furniture, Chair Set, Windsor, Bow Back, New England, 19th Century, 4

Furniture, Chair Set, Windsor, Fanback, New England, 19th Century, 4

Chair Set, Regency, Rosewood, Carved Lyre Back, Caned Seat, Tapered Legs, 3 .... 2090.00
Chair Set, Rosewood, Velvet Upholstered, Block Footed, Art Deco, France, c.1935, 6 . 2875.00
Chair Set, Saarinen, Laminated Bent Birch, Upholstered, Knoll, 1948, 4 .... 522.00
Chair Set, Sheraton, Empire Back, Mahogany, New Seat, 1830s, 6 .... 1800.00
Chair Set, Sheraton, Maple, Rush Seat, New England, c.1820, 33 1/2 In., 6 .... 1045.00
Chair Set, Sheraton, Red Paint, Gilt Design, 4 .... 3150.00
Chair Set, Stickley Bros., Oak, Brass Tags, No. 479 1/2, c.1905, 6 .... 935.00
Chair Set, Stickley, Windsor, Cherry, 6 .... 650.00
Chair Set, Thonet, Ballroom, Green, Lyre Back, Reeded Legs, 6 .... 2200.00
Chair Set, Vladimir Kagan, Walnut, Chartreuse Vinyl, 1955, 8 .... 2875.00
Chair Set, Windsor, 4 Spindles, Yellow, New England, Early 1800s, 6 .... 1650.00
Chair Set, Windsor, 9 Spindles, Bow Back, Saddle Seat, New England, 6 .... 6600.00
Chair Set, Windsor, Bamboo, Brown Finish, Country, 6 .... 630.00
Chair Set, Windsor, Bow Back, New England, 19th Century, 4 .... *Illus* 880.00
Chair Set, Windsor, Fanback, New England, 19th Century, 4 .... *Illus* 2530.00
Chair Set, Windsor, Green Paint Over Original Finish, 4 .... 720.00
Chair Set, Windsor, Oak, Bow & Spindle Back, Saddle Seat, 4 .... 200.00
Chair Set, Windsor, Spindle Back, Floral Spray Crest, Original Finish, 6 .... 975.00
Chair Set, Windsor, Thumb Back Birdcage, Black Paint, Gold & Red Trim, 6 .... 7700.00
Chair-Table, 1-Board Top, Gray Paint, 31 x 41 1/2 In. 3025.00
Chair-Table, 3 Boards, Raised Shoe Feet, Red Paint 3960.00
Chair-Table, Chippendale, Pine & Birch, Red Paint, Scrubbed 4290.00
Chair-Table, Gray Paint, Thick 1-Board Top, 31 x 41 In. 3025.00
Chair-Table, Pine, Mustard Paint, New England, c. 1825, 38 x 48 In. .... *Illus* 4312.00
Chaise Lounge, Campaign, Adjustable Back & Footrest, Teakwood, 72 3/4 In. 1165.00
Chaise Lounge, Chromium Plated, Pony Skin, Leather Upholstered, 59 In. 3105.00
Chaise Lounge, E. Wormley, Listen To Me, Upholstered, Wood, Metal, 72 In. 5175.00
Chaise Lounge, Eames, 2 Loose Cushions, 78 In. 1150.00
Chaise Lounge, Egyptian Revival, Wooden, Egyptian Paintings, c.1925, 72 In. 8050.00
Chaise Lounge, Louis XV, Walnut, Velvet Upholstered, 51 In. 220.00
Chaise Lounge, Out-Scrolled Upholstered Backrest, Giltwood, c.1930, 61 In. 9775.00
Chaise Lounge, Pierre Deux Fabric Cover, Green Wicker, c.1890, Child's 2800.00
Chaise Lounge, Regency, Padded Back, Cushion Seat, Gilt Stenciled, c.1810 .... 6900.00
Chaise Lounge, Upholstered Backrest & Seat, Scrolled Toes, Giltwood, Pair 3165.00
Chaise Lounge, Victorian, Rococo, Damask Upholstered 5800.00
Chaise Lounge, William IV, Serpentine Armrest, Mahogany, 82 1/2 In. 1495.00
Chest, 2 Drawers, Queen Anne, Painted, Pine, 36 1/4 x 34 1/2 In. 1540.00
Chest, 2 Drawers, Raised Panels, 17th Century, 41 1/2 x 19 1/2 In. 4125.00
Chest, 3 Dovetailed Drawers, Walnut, Curly Maple, Refinished, 13 x 13 x 14 In. 330.00
Chest, 3 Drawers, Serpentine Parquetry Stripped Borders, Fruitwood, 32 In. 3450.00
Chest, 3 Drawers, Stenciling, Scalloped Apron, Poplar, 18 x 18 x 11 In. 530.00
Chest, 3 Graduated Drawers, Marble Top 990.00
Chest, 3 Graduated Drawers, Ogee Bracket Footed, Cherry, 36 x 39 1/2 In. 2760.00
Chest, 4 Drawers, Backsplash, Sandwich Glass Pulls, Maple, 44 x 22 x 53 In. 1000.00
Chest, 4 Drawers, Batwing Brass Pulls, Writing Slide, Mahogany, 1940, 32 In. 467.00
Chest, 4 Drawers, Federal, Cherry & Mahogany Veneer, Rope Carved, 41 x 38 In. 605.00

Furniture, Chair-Table, Pine, Mustard Paint,
New England, c.1825, 38 x 48 In.

◆◆◆◆◆◆◆◆◆◆◆◆◆◆◆◆◆◆◆◆◆◆◆

Use an old nylon stocking
bunched into a ball to clean a
rough-surfaced mirror frame,
carved wooden piece, or other
irregular surface.

◆◆◆◆◆◆◆◆◆◆◆◆◆◆◆◆◆◆◆◆◆◆◆

Chest, 4 Drawers, Federal, Mahogany, c.1810, 40 x 41 x 21 In. 1540.00
Chest, 4 Drawers, Hepplewhite, Country, c.1830, 37 1/2 x 17 1/2 x 39 In. 925.00
Chest, 4 Drawers, Oak, Thumb Molded Top, c.1665, 36 3/8 In. 6325.00
Chest, 4 Drawers, Paint Decorated, Pine, c.1825, 41 1/2 x 44 x 17 In. 2750.00
Chest, 4 Drawers, Painted Mirror, Eastlake 425.00
Chest, 4 Drawers, Pennsylvania, Walnut, Reeded Columns, Ogee Feet, c.1800, 42 In. 3250.00
Chest, 4 Graduated Drawers, Reverse Serpentine, Cherry, c.1770, 35 3/4 In. 8625.00
Chest, 5 Drawers, George II, Walnut, Crossbanded Inlaid Top, 34 x 38 x 22 In. 3960.00
Chest, 5 Drawers, Georgian, Mahogany, Bracket Footed, Late 18th Century, 36 In. ... 1210.00
Chest, 5 Drawers, Hepplewhite, Bowfront, Mahogany, England, 42 x 42 x 20 In. 2000.00
Chest, 5 Drawers, Mahogany Veneer Outlining, Tiger Maple, Maple Columns 1650.00
Chest, 6 Drawers, Chippendale, Maple, New England, c.1780, 54 x 36 In. 1980.00
Chest, 8 Drawers, Federal, Cherry, Rope Twist Columns, Beaded Drawers, 66 In. 3600.00
Chest, A. Kjersgaard, 3 Drawers, Teakwood, Denmark, c.1950, 23 x 31 In. 700.00
Chest, Bachelor's, 4 Graduated Drawers, Hinged Top, 30 x 30 In. 715.00
Chest, Bachelor's, George III, Pullout Slide, Mahogany, 30 x 33 In. 3300.00
Chest, Bachelor's, Georgian, 4 Drawers, Bracket Footed, Walnut, 30 x 17 In. 850.00
Chest, Biedermeier, 2 Drawers, Satinwood, Brass Pulls, Key, 32 x 21 In., Pair 3190.00
Chest, Bird's-Eye Maple Drawer Fronts, Birch & Poplar 935.00
Chest, Blanket, 1 Drawer, Bracket Base, Pine 770.00
Chest, Blanket, 2 Drawers, Grain Painted, Lift Top, Putty & Brown 2310.00
Chest, Blanket, 2 Drawers, Lift Top, Connecticut, Ball Footed, 18th Century 2500.00
Chest, Blanket, 2 Drawers, Lift Top, Painted, Vermont, 35 3/4 x 36 In. 500.00
Chest, Blanket, 2 Drawers, Original Brasses, Painted, N.H., 18th Century 4600.00
Chest, Blanket, 2 Drawers, Pine, Grain Painted, New England, c.1820, 33 x 40 In. ... 1320.00
Chest, Blanket, 2 Drawers, Pine, Old Grain Traces, Bracket Base, 39 x 43 x 18 In. ... 575.00
Chest, Blanket, 2 Drawers, Pine, Red Paint, Massachusetts 6325.00
Chest, Blanket, 3 Drawers, Lift Top, Snip Hinges, Oliver Swan, 1808 .... 7425.00
Chest, Blanket, 6 Board, Pine, Child's, 14 1/2 x 25 In. 360.00
Chest, Blanket, Blind Dovetailing, Bun Footed, Poplar 395.00
Chest, Blanket, Brown Comb Graining Over Blue, Till, Pine, 42 3/4 In. 440.00
Chest, Blanket, Chippendale, Maple, 18th Century, 38 1/2 x 38 x 17 In. 1320.00
Chest, Blanket, Chippendale, Walnut, 2 Cock-Beaded Drawers, 44 x 21 x 28 In. 2035.00
Chest, Blanket, Chippendale, Walnut, 3 Drawers, Till, Country, 50 x 22 x 28 In. 1100.00
Chest, Blanket, Decals, Red & Black Base, W. Va., L. T. & 1879 On Front 4950.00
Chest, Blanket, Grain Painted, Bun Footed, 1860 .... 450.00
Chest, Blanket, Grain Painted, Dovetailed Case, Till, 23 1/2 x 43 1/2 In. 255.00
Chest, Blanket, Grain Painted, Lift Top, Pine, Ditty Box Interior, Peg Footed 440.00
Chest, Blanket, Grained, Poplar, Red Flame, Lock Removed, 12 3/4 In. 305.00
Chest, Blanket, Green Paint, 19th Century, 4 3/4 x 9 3/4 In. 440.00
Chest, Blanket, Hepplewhite, Inlaid Walnut, Eagle, c.1800, 30 x 52 x 23 In. 2000.00
Chest, Blanket, Lift Top, Ditty Box Interior, Bootjack Base, 25 x 46 x 19 In. 330.00
Chest, Blanket, Lift Top, Lower Drawer, Oak & Pine, c.1670, 48 In. 6900.00
Chest, Blanket, Lift Top, Pine, 2 Base Drawers, 29 x 50 In. 315.00
Chest, Blanket, Maple, New England, 18th Century, 32 1/2 x 44 1/2 x 18 In. 330.00
Chest, Blanket, Oak, Painted, Applied Design Panels & Molding, Massachusetts 2750.00
Chest, Blanket, On Frame, Dome Top, Grained, Strap Hinges, c.1861, 28 x 54 In. 1500.00
Chest, Blanket, Painted, 6 Board, Early 19th Century, 20 1/2 In. 1100.00
Chest, Blanket, Painted, Pine, 19th Century, Child's, 21 x 20 1/2 x 9 In. 770.00
Chest, Blanket, Painted, Red Strap Handles, Molding, T-Head Nails, 18th Century 775.00
Chest, Blanket, Painted, Red, 19th Century, 21 x 13 x 11 In. 245.00
Chest, Blanket, Pine, Drawers, Original Paint, 18th Century, 32 x 42 x 20 In. 935.00
Chest, Blanket, Pine, Mottled Red, Cathrina Schofern, Anno 1818, 49 In. 880.00
Chest, Blanket, Pine, Turned Feet, Paneled Sides, 14 x 24 x 19 In. 935.00
Chest, Blanket, Polychrome Painted, Bun Footed, Scandinavia, 26 x 62 x 28 In. 440.00
Chest, Blanket, Red Sponged With Black, Pine, Till, New England 1000.00
Chest, Blanket, Salmon, Blue, White, Shoe Footed, Hudson River, Lock, Key 3520.00
Chest, Blanket, Shaker, Red Stain, 1 Drawer, Child's 8250.00
Chest, Blanket, Sheraton, Carved Fans, Sunbursts, Walnut, 31 3/4 In. 2970.00
Chest, Blanket, Vinegar Grained, Pine, 6 Board, 48 x 20 x 30 In. 715.00
Chest, Blanket, William & Mary, Red Paint, Pine, 18th Century, 40 x 37 In. 935.00
Chest, Blanket, William & Mary, Snipe Hinges, Painted, Red, Pine 1000.00
Chest, Blanket, Yellow Grained, Painted, 19th Century, 22 x 36 x 27 1/2 In. 450.00

Chest, Bowfront, 12 Panels, Spooner-Type Turned Legs 3750.00
Chest, Bowfront, 4 Drawers, Mahogany Veneer, Bird's-Eye Maple, c.1805 .... 5175.00
Chest, Bowfront, Charack Furniture Co., 4 Drop Shell Carved Drawers, 1930 .... 1100.00
Chest, Bowfront, George III, Mahogany, 4 Drawers, c.1800, 36 In. 1150.00
Chest, Bowfront, N. Joyt, Mahogany, 4 Graduated Drawers, 40 1/2 In. 880.00
Chest, Bowfront, Regency, Inlaid Mahogany, c.1810, 8 1/4 x 12 1/4 x 5 1/2 In. 920.00
Chest, Bride's, Grained Surface, Stenciled Basket Of Flowers, c.1815 .... 2250.00
Chest, Bride's, Initials A.C.M., Schoharie County, c.1815 .... 1400.00
Chest, Bride's, Roycroft, Hinged Lid, Copper Strap Hinges, No. 097, 40 In. 8625.00
Chest, Butler's, Chippendale, Cherry, 3 Overlapping Drawers, 38 x 41 In. 1575.00
Chest, Campaign, Camphorwood, Bracket Footed, China, 1800s, 41 x 37 x 19 In. 2000.00
Chest, Campaign, Mahogany, 2 Short Over 3 Drawers, Victorian, 1860 .... 880.00
Chest, Chippendale, 2 Over 3 Drawers, Walnut, Fluted Columns, 45 In. 3200.00
Chest, Chippendale, 2 Over 4 Drawers, Tiger Maple 3520.00
Chest, Chippendale, 4 Dovetailed Drawers, Serpentine, Cherry, 38 x 19 x 40 In. 3300.00
Chest, Chippendale, 4 Drawers, Cherry, Dovetail Case, Ogee Footed, 41 x 38 In. 3520.00
Chest, Chippendale, 4 Drawers, Mahogany, Ogee Bracket Footed, Pennsylvania 1430.00
Chest, Chippendale, 4 Drawers, Walnut, Ogee Bracket Base, 40 x 39 x 22 In. 2970.00
Chest, Chippendale, 4 Graduated Drawers, Philadelphia, c.1780 .... 4800.00
Chest, Chippendale, 4 Graduated Drawers, Walnut, Thumb Molded, 33 x 40 In. 3680.00
Chest, Chippendale, 5 Graduated Drawers, Maple, Wooden Pulls, 42 x 39 In. 2970.00
Chest, Chippendale, 6 Drawers, Walnut, Dovetailed Case, 21 x 42 x 64 1/2 In. 7260.00
Chest, Chippendale, 6 Graduated Drawers, Cherry, Rhode Island, 18th Century 4125.00
Chest, Chippendale, 6 Graduated Drawers, Curly Maple, Molded Cornice, 53 In. 3520.00
Chest, Chippendale, 7 Graduated Drawers, Maple, c.1770, 63 x 35 1/2 In. 4125.00
Chest, Chippendale, 8 Overlapping Drawers, Walnut, 63 1/4 In. 3190.00
Chest, Chippendale, 9 Drawers, Walnut, Pennsylvania, c.1780, 62 x 39 In. 2310.00
Chest, Chippendale, Drawers, Birch, New England, 18th Century, 35 x 39 In. 1045.00
Chest, Classical, 5 Bowfront Drawers, Carved Mahogany, Phila., c.1830, 46 In. 1980.00
Chest, Dauphin Co., Cherry, 2 Over 4 Drawers, c.1830, 47 1/2 x 39 In. 1600.00
Chest, Domed Cover, Pine, Brass Nails Form J.B., Brighton Label, c.1850, 32 In. 137.00
Chest, Dower, Hinged Domed Top, Painted Floral Medallions, Scandinavia 475.00
Chest, Dower, Mustard, Orange, White, Flowers, Hearts, Berks Co., 28 x 48 In. 4700.00
Chest, Dower, Painted Design, Scandinavia, 18th Century, 52 In. .... *Illus* 2640.00
Chest, Dressing, George III, Mahogany, Serpentine, Crossbanded, c.1775, 38 In. 4025.00
Chest, Empire, 2 Over 4 Large Drawers, Cherry 255.00
Chest, Empire, 4 Drawers, Mahogany, 43 x 45 In. 345.00
Chest, Empire, 7 Drawers, Tiger Maple, Cherry, Twisted Pilasters, Glass Knobs 1295.00
Chest, Faux Bamboo, 2 Short Over 2 Long Drawers, Victorian, 34 x 36 In. 1650.00
Chest, Federal, 4 Graduated Drawers, Reeded Columns, Cherry, 38 x 18 x 36 In. 650.00
Chest, Federal, 6 Graduated Drawers, Walnut, Pennsylvania, c.1790, 46 x 36 In. 2420.00
Chest, Federal, Lift Top, Oyster Grained Panels, 20 x 37 In. 345.00
Chest, Gentleman's, Walnut, Ornate, Germany, 1860s 2700.00
Chest, George I Style, Inlaid Burl Walnut, Shaped-Skirt Stand, 12 x 9 x 5 In. 3165.00
Chest, George II, 2 Short Over 3 Long Drawers, Crossbanded Walnut, 37 In. 2010.00
Chest, George III, 3 Drawers, Mahogany, Slide-Out Writing Surface, 32 x 38 In. 1210.00

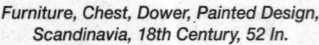

*Furniture, Chest, Dower, Painted Design,
Scandinavia, 18th Century, 52 In.*

*Furniture, Chest, Grain Painted, Lidded Till, New
England, 18th Century, 40 In.*

Chest, George III, 4 Cock-Beaded Drawers, Mahogany, c.1775, 36 In. 2875.00
Chest, George III, 4 Drawers, Crossbanded Rosewood , Satinwood, 32 1/2 In. 5465.00
Chest, George III, 5 Cock-Beaded Drawers, Mahogany, c.1770, 34 x 38 x 21 In. 2070.00
Chest, George III, 5 Drawers, Mahogany, Bowfront, c.1780 .... 1320.00
Chest, George III, 5 Drawers, Mahogany, Bracket Footed, c.1780, 44 x 42 x 22 In. ... 1155.00
Chest, George III, 6 Drawers, Mahogany, Splay Footed, c.1790, 50 x 42 x 21 In. 990.00
Chest, George III, Mahogany, Swan Neck Handles, 45 x 44 x 24 In. 1430.00
Chest, Georgian, 5 Graduated Drawers, Oak, 39 In. 770.00
Chest, Georgian, Mahogany, Splay Footed, c.1800, 33 x 38 x 18 1/2 In. 660.00
Chest, Georgian, Serpentine, Mahogany, Marble Top 1760.00
Chest, Grain Painted, Lidded Till, New England, 18th Century, 40 In. .... *Illus* 1870.00
Chest, Gustav Stickley, Oak, 2 Over 3 Drawers, No. 901, 40 x 36 In. 4315.00
Chest, Gustav Stickley, Oak, 2 Over 4 Drawers, Decal, 48 x 36 In. 2875.00
Chest, Henredon, 2 Drawers, Brass Mounts, 20 x 38 In. 80.00
Chest, Henredon, 2 Drawers, Brass Mounts, Oak, 38 x 18 x 20 In. 80.00
Chest, Hepplewhite Style, 4 Drawers, Bowfront, Mahogany, c.1820 .... 3995.00
Chest, Hepplewhite Style, 4 Drawers, Cherry, Scalloped Apron, 30 In. 495.00
Chest, Hepplewhite, 3 Over 3 Drawers, Cherry, Round Brass Pulls............................ 1100.00
Chest, Hepplewhite, 4 Dovetailed Drawers, Cherry, Inlaid, 37 x 20 x 43 In. 2200.00
Chest, Hepplewhite, 4 Drawers, Inlay, Oval Lion Brasses 2530.00
Chest, Hepplewhite, 4 Graduated Dovetailed Drawers, Cherry, 45 In. 1760.00
Chest, Hepplewhite, 4 Graduated Drawers, Bowfront, Mahogany, Banded Inlay 3410.00
Chest, Hepplewhite, 4 Graduated Drawers, Cherrywood, c.1800, 35 x 42 x 22 In. 4550.00
Chest, Hepplewhite, 5 Dovetailed Drawers, Cherry, 40 x 19 x 40 In. 910.00
Chest, Hepplewhite, 9 Cock-Beaded Drawers, Cherry, Brasses, 42 x 75 In. 3850.00
Chest, Hepplewhite, Beaded Graduated Drawers, Bracket Footed, 39 1/2 x 22 In. 1400.00
Chest, Hepplewhite, Bowfront, Figured Mahogany Veneer, England, 41 x 35 In. 1705.00
Chest, Hepplewhite, Grain Painted, New England, c.1830 .... 770.00
Chest, Hepplewhite, Pine, Oak Grain Painted, Bracket Base, Country 1430.00
Chest, Immigrant's, 2 Drawers, Till, Iron Strap Hinges, Pine, 38 In. 85.00
Chest, J. & J. Kohn, 6 Drawers, Bentwood, Gallery, Brown, Maroon, 1900, 60 In. 2875.00
Chest, Lift Top, Grain Painted, 1830s, 22 x 37 1/2 In. 315.00
Chest, Liquor, Mahogany, With 6 Gilt Glass Decanters, Victorian, 9 1/2 x 12 In. 715.00
Chest, Louis XV, Serpentine Marble Top, Carved Apron, 35 x 52 In. 7105.00
Chest, Mahogany, Ormolu, Brass Molding Around Drawers, Mirror, 62 In. 2500.00
Chest, Mahogany, Tagged & Labeled, Salesman's Sample, 19 x 11 x 7 In. 325.00
Chest, Military, 2 Over 3 Drawers, Mahogany, Anglo-Indian, 19th Century 1650.00
Chest, Military, Top Drawer Secretary, Teak, England, c.1870 .... 6810.00
Chest, Mule, Butternut, Red Stain, Blue Interior, Lift Top, Country, 43 x 20 In. 2035.00
Chest, Mule, Chippendale, 2 Drawers, 2 False Drawers, Cherry, Lift Top, 42 In. 2200.00
Chest, Mule, Chippendale, 2 Drawers, Dovetailed, Lift Top, 42 x 42 In. 2300.00
Chest, Mule, Chippendale, 3 Drawers, 2 False Drawers, Lift Top 1200.00
Chest, Mule, Chippendale, 3 Drawers, Lift Top, Pine, Yellow Grained, 41 In. 1320.00
Chest, Mule, Pine, Flame Grained, 6 Board, Lift Top, Country, 44 3/4 In. 1100.00
Chest, Mule, Poplar, 2 Dovetailed Drawers, Lift Top, Country, 41 x 43 In. 330.00
Chest, Oak, Carved, Panel Construction, Till, 17th Century, 27 x 48 x 23 In. 2700.00
Chest, Oak, Carved, Scandinavia, 18th Century, 28 x 53 x 19 In. 935.00
Chest, Oxbow, Chippendale, 4 Serpentine Drawers, Mahogany, 32 In. 9200.00
Chest, Painted, 6 Board, Molded Top, Lidded Till, 19th Century, 24 x 44 x 19 In. 660.00
Chest, Paneled, Carved, Oak, c.1648, 26 In. 770.00
Chest, Queen Anne, 5 Drawers, Walnut, Veneered, c.1700, 34 x 39 x 27 In. 4400.00
Chest, Queen Anne, 8 Drawers, Oak, 19th Century, 60 x 36 1/2 In. 1760.00
Chest, Queen Anne, 9 Dovetailed Drawers, Walnut, 21 3/4 x 42 1/4 x 69 1/4 .... 550.00
Chest, Queen Anne, Birch, Portsmouth, c.1760, 59 In. 9500.00
Chest, Queen Anne, Cabriole Legs, Trifid Feet, Scalloped Apron, Walnut 5000.00
Chest, Queen Anne, Maple, Drawers, New England, c.1740, 45 x 36 x 18 In. 880.00
Chest, Queen Anne, Maple, Walnut Veneer, Massachusetts, c.1750, 72 x 37 In. 2970.00
Chest, Regency, 3 Short Over 3 Long Drawers, Mahogany, c.1820, 46 In. 990.00
Chest, Regency, 3 Drawers, Mahogany, Bowfront, Reeded Edge, 1825, 38 In. 7475.00
Chest, Seaman's, Painted Western Scenes, Pine & Poplar, Iron Handles, 38 In. 1010.00
Chest, Seaman's, Pine, Original Blue Paint, c.1820, 14 1/2 x 36 x 16 In. 1045.00
Chest, Serpentine, 4 Drawers, Mahogany, Hartford, Conn., Inscription, 38 In. 1200.00
Chest, Serpentine, Thomas Needham, Mahogany, 1811-1815 .... 13800.00

Chest, Shaker, 6 Drawers, Flame Grained Drawer Fronts, Groveland, c.1790 .... 3750.00
Chest, Shaker, 7 Drawers, Cutout Feet, New Hampshire 4400.00
Chest, Shaped Iron Fittings, Hinges, Latch & Prunts, Korea, 18th Century, 35 In. 440.00
Chest, Sheraton, 4 Drawers, Bowfront, 12 Panels, Spooner Type Legs 3750.00
Chest, Sheraton, 4 Drawers, Cherry, String Inlay, Cock-Beaded, c.1840 .... 1700.00
Chest, Sheraton, 4 Drawers, Mahogany, Banded Tiger Maple Drawer Fronts 935.00
Chest, Sheraton, 4 Drawers, Reeded Post Front & Back, Mahogany 900.00
Chest, Sheraton, 5 Drawers, Cherry, Curly Maple, Refinished, 14 x 11 x 17 In. 770.00
Chest, Sheraton, 5 Drawers, McCormack, Cadiz, Ohio, Cherry, 43 1/4 In. 1350.00
Chest, Sheraton, Bowfront, Mahogany, 39 x 42 x 23 1/2 In. 1700.00
Chest, Sheraton, Tiger Maple, Backsplash, Carved Columns 1650.00
Chest, Spice, Cherry & Mahogany, c.1820, 17 x 12 In. 1475.00
Chest, Spice, Oak & Pine, c.1700, 14 1/4 x 14 1/2 In. 990.00
Chest, Sugar, Lift Top, 3 Inside Sections, Tapered Legs, c.1820, 28 In. 3600.00
Chest, Tall, Chippendale, Painted, New England, c.1800, 61 x 41 In. 1100.00
Chest, Walnut, Inlaid Ebony, Satinwood, Stars & Bands, Ormolu Handles, 32 In. 3080.00
Chest, Walnut, Porcelain Button Pulls, Pierced Acorn Crest, Maine, Miniature 275.00
Chest, William & Mary, 4 Drawers, Applied Geometric Moldings 4070.00
Chest, William & Mary, 4 Graduated Drawers, Oak, 33 1/2 In. 2090.00
Chest, William & Mary, Drawers, Oak, Paneled & Jointed, 17th Century, 37 In. 1430.00
Chest, William & Mary, Oyster Veneer, Inlaid Walnut, c.1700, 35 x 38 x 22 In. 3740.00
Chest-On-Chest, 7 Drawers, Rectangular Molded Top, Bracket Footed, 76 3/4 In. 1870.00
Chest-On-Chest, Chippendale, 5 Upper & 3 Lower Drawers, Maple, 1785 .... 3450.00
Chest-On-Chest, Chippendale, Short & Long Drawers, Mahogany, 36 x 43 In. 6900.00
Chest-On-Chest, George I, 6 Drawers, Inlaid Walnut, 69 In. 6325.00
Chest-On-Chest, George I, Walnut, Brush Slide, Bracket Footed, c.1725, 69 In. 4840.00
Chest-On-Chest, George II, Walnut, 2 Over 3 Graduated Drawers, 69 In. 3300.00
Chest-On-Chest, George III, 2 Over 3 Long Drawers, Mahogany, 62 x 41 In. 825.00
Chest-On-Chest, George III, 2 Over 3 Long Drawers, Mahogany, c.1780, 79 In. 9200.00
Chest-On-Chest, George III, 8 Drawers, Mahogany, c.1770, 66 x 42 In. 2875.00
Chest-On-Chest, George III, 8 Drawers, Mahogany, Replaced Brasses, 72 In. 1870.00
Chest-On-Chest, George III, Mahogany, 18th Century, 66 x 45 x 20 In. 2530.00
Chest-On-Chest, George III, Pullout Side, Mahogany, 72 In. 2530.00
Chest-On-Chest, Georgian, Mahogany, Bracket Footed, Swan Handles, 1780 1850.00 to 2035.00
Chest-On-Chest, Georgian, Mahogany, c.1780, 21 x 42 1/2 x 79 In. 3300.00
Chest-On-Chest, Georgian, Mahogany, Inlaid Satinwood, c.1820, 72 In. 3300.00
Chest-On-Frame, 3 Over 4 Graduated Drawers, Walnut, Penna., Jos. Wilcox 7975.00
Chest-On-Frame, Silver, 4 Drawers, Mahogany, Presentation Plate, C.E., 1846 .... 495.00
Chest-On-Frame, William & Mary, 3 Over 3 Drawers, Japanned, 62 In. 5500.00
Chiffonier, Louis XV Style, Drawers, Marble, Marquetry, Cupboards, 61 In. 805.00
Chiffonier, Louis XVI, 6 Drawers, Fruitwood, Brass Mounted, 56 In. 4025.00
Chiffonier, Serpentine Front, Beveled Mirror, Mahogany 775.00
Coat Rack, 2 Rings With Hooks, Wrought Iron, c.1915, 78 In. 920.00
Coat Rack, Art Deco, Bronze & Painted Steel, c.1930, 80 In. 5175.00
Coat Rack, Corner, Bentwood, 5 Scrolled Hooks, Austria 305.00
Coat Rack, Mouchet, Wrought Iron, Beveled Mirror, France, c.1925, 24 x 33 In. 1840.00
Coffer, Charles II, Hinged Paneled Lid, Stile Feet, Oak, c.1660, 36 In. 8850.00
Coffer, Jacobean, Oak, 2 Lower Drawers, c.1700, 33 x 37 In. 660.00
Coffer, Oak Plank, c.1670, Small 1650.00
Commode, 1 Drawer, Mahogany, Marble Lined Cabinet & Top, c.1900, 35 In. 1725.00
Commode, 1 Frieze Drawer Over Cupboard Door, Marquetry, 36 x 42 In. 1265.00
Commode, 2 Drawers, Marble Top, Gilt Metal Handles, Green Paint, 33 1/2 In. 6325.00
Commode, 3 Drawers, Brass Knobs, Circular Feet, Fruitwood, 50 In. 4025.00
Commode, Baroque, Walnut, Inlaid, Cabriole Legs, Germany, 30 x 25 x 15 In. 1650.00
Commode, Bed, Louis XV, Walnut, Marble Inset, Raised Backsplash, c.1860 .... 165.00
Commode, Bombe, 3 Over 2 Drawers, Green Marble Top, 34 x 40 In. 2070.00
Commode, Empire, Mahogany, Marble Top, Gilt Mounts, c.1825, 37 x 52 .... 3450.00
Commode, Georgian, Tray Top, Drawer, Tamboured Cupboard, Mahogany, 32 In. 550.00
Commode, Inlaid, Half-Round Marble Top, Gilt Brass Mounting, Paul Surmani 4125.00
Commode, Louis XV, 3 Drawers, Burl Walnut & Walnut, Inlaid Top, 34 5/8 In. 6325.00
Commode, Louis XV, Kingwood, Parquetry, Inlaid Gilt, Bronze Mounted, Pair 4400.00
Commode, Louis XVI Style, 3 Drawers, Mahogany, 36 x 55 In. 400.00
Commode, Louis XVI Style, Gilt Bronze, Marquetry, Parquetry, 36 In. 5225.00

Commode, Louis XVI Style, Kingwood, Mahogany, Gilt Bronze, Marble, 61 In. 6050.00
Commode, Louis XVI, 1 Frieze Drawer, Marble Top, Mahogany, 33 1/4 In. 6900.00
Commode, Louis XVI, 3 Long Drawers, Fruitwood, Inlaid, 34 x 48 x 20 In. 1980.00
Commode, Rococo Style, Serpentine, Cabriole Legs, Dutch, 24 In., Pair 1430.00
Commode, Venetian Rococo, Red Lacquer, Gilt, Carved, 41 1/2 x 19 In. 3080.00
Console, Continental, White Carrara Marble Top, Gilt Inlay, Italy, 1920s 8200.00
Console, D. Deskey, Black Formica, Chrome, Circular Ends, c.1930, 54 In. 5750.00
Console, Edgar Brandt, Wrought Iron, Black Marble, c.1925, 36 x 25 x 12 In. 5750.00
Console, Empire, Mahogany, Ebonized, Green Marble Top, 34 x 31 x 17 In. 2875.00
Console, Louis XV Style, Giltwood, Marble Top, c.1850, 37 x 37 In., Pair 2320.00
Console, Louis XV Style, Giltwood, Marble Top, Floral & Acanthus, 41 In. 1320.00
Console, Louis XV, Serpentine Front, Marble Top, Garland Frieze, 44 1/2 In. 3450.00
Console, Marble Top, Serpentine Front & Sides, Italy, 1850s, 50 In. 6325.00
Console, Marcel Bergue, Metal Base, Marble Demilune Top, c.1925, 33 In. 8050.00
Console, Oscar Bach, Wrought Iron, Marble Top, c.1925, 45 x 13 In. 6050.00
Console, Paul Kiss, 3 Hammered Scrolling Leaves, Iron, Marble, 1925, 35 In. 5750.00
Costumer, Gustav Stickley, Double, Shoe Footed, 6 Hooks, No. 53, 72 In. 1600.00
Couch, Fainting, Mahogany, Upholstered, Victorian 385.00
Cradle, Amish, Dovetailed, Blue 425.00
Cradle, Bonnet Top, Rocking, Heart Cutout Handles, Mahogany, 39 In. 250.00
Cradle, Curved Front Bracket Hood, Walnut & Curly Walnut, 42 1/2 In. 550.00
Cradle, Cutout Edge, Dovetailed, Walnut, 39 1/2 In. 330.00
Cradle, Cutout Rockers, Scrolled Sides, Poplar, 42 In. 385.00
Cradle, Cutout Sides & Rockers, Old Red Paint, Poplar, 46 In. 385.00
Cradle, Field, Slave, Lightweight, c.1860 .... 465.00
Cradle, Heart Cutouts Each Side, Pine, 42 1/2 In. 165.00
Cradle, Hooded, Green Paint, Pine, 19th Century 220.00
Cradle, Hooded, Mahogany, 29 x 45 In. 220.00
Cradle, Mortised & Pinned Construction, Pine, Dark Red Finish, 39 In. 220.00
Cradle, On Stand, Heart-Shaped Supports, Wrought Iron, Canada 325.00
Cradle, Pine, 19th Century, 41 In. 145.00
Cradle, Pine, Primitive, Hardwood Spindles, Brown Paint Traces, 39 In. 95.00
Cradle, Scrolled Head & Footboards, Mahogany Ball Finial 330.00
Cradle, Scrolled Headboard, Footboard & Sideboard, Tiger Maple 375.00
Cradle, Shell Form, Silk Upholstered, Giltwood Panels, Trestle Frame, 48 In. 5175.00
Cradle, Swinging, Cherry, 20th Century 85.00
Cradle, Walnut, Dr. Ellingwood, Fortville, Ind., Primitive, c.1870 .... 160.00
Cradle, Wicker Sides, Acorn Finials 120.00
Cradle, Windsor, Painted, Molded Railing, Spindles, 13 x 17 x 37 In. 345.00
Credenza, Burl Walnut, Backplate Mirror, Carved Fruit, Victorian, England 1595.00
Credenza, Burl Walnut, D-Shape, 3 Doors, Victorian, 53 x 60 x 17 In. 1650.00
Credenza, George Nelson, Black Ebonized Legs, Primavera Finish 2300.00
Credenza, Inlaid Musical Grouping, 46 1/2 In. 3850.00
Credenza, Louis XVI Style, Bowfront, Figured Veneer, Marble Top, 34 3/4 In. 1375.00
Credenza, Mahogany, Marble Top, Victorian, 19th Century, 36 x 45 x 20 In. 1100.00
Credenza, Renaissance Revival, Rosewood, Marquetry, Door, 44 x 46 x 20 In. 2200.00
Credenza, Renaissance, Burl Walnut, Marble & Bronze Center, 1870 .... 2650.00
Crib, Canopy, Curly Maple 1500.00
Crib, Tester, Prudent Mallard 7700.00
Cupboard, 1 Glass Door, Pie Shelf, Spoon Racks, Painted Red, c.1820, 82 In. 6750.00
Cupboard, 1 Glass Door, Red Graining, Lancaster Co., c.1830, 80 x 51 x 18 In. 5000.00
Cupboard, 1 Paneled Door, Curly Oak, Worn Finish, England, 17 x 18 x 41 In. 250.00
Cupboard, 1 Top & 1 Base Door, Red Paint, Slant Top, 71 In. 7040.00
Cupboard, 2 Base Doors, 3 Open Shelves, Scalloped Crest, Walnut, 65 1/2 In. 375.00
Cupboard, 2 Carved Drawers, Walnut, 39 x 20 x 41 In. 275.00
Cupboard, 2 Glass Doors, 2 Drawers, Rolled Crown 750.00
Cupboard, 4 Doors, 2 Drawers, Old Red Paint, Scalloped Apron, Holland, c.1850 ..... 1500.00
Cupboard, Amish, 2 Drawers, Oak, Pressed Design, New Back 1150.00
Cupboard, Apothecary, Top Cutouts, Pine 935.00
Cupboard, Baker's, Birch, 2 Piece, Original Finish, Dated 1905 .... 895.00
Cupboard, Baker's, Upper Glass Doors, Mixed Woods, Oak Frame, c.1850 .... 795.00
Cupboard, Blue-Green Paint, 2 Glass Doors, 74 In. 1900.00
Cupboard, Brown Over Yellow Grain Panels, Simulated Natural Wood Grain 1500.00

Furniture, Cupboard, Corner, 2 Glazed Doors, Pine, 83 x 58 x 32 In.

Furniture, Cupboard, Corner, Orange, Yellow Stripes, Turn Footed, 72 In.

Cupboard, Bucket Bench, 1 Drawer, Slide Brass Catches, Rail Footed, Painted 1150.00
Cupboard, Chimney, Blue Paint, 77 x 14 x 14 In. 195.00
Cupboard, Chimney, Grayish Green Repaint, Cherry & Poplar, 84 In. 310.00
Cupboard, China, Corner, Oak, Curved Glass 1650.00
Cupboard, Corner, 2 Curly Maple Drawers, 12-Pane Upper Door, Cherry 5940.00
Cupboard, Corner, 2 Glazed Doors, Pine, 83 x 58 x 32 In. .... *Illus* 1650.00
Cupboard, Corner, 5 Drawers, 16 Panes, Cherry, Refinished, Ohio 3600.00
Cupboard, Corner, 9-Pane Over 2-Plate Door, Maryland, 19th Century 3500.00
Cupboard, Corner, 9-Pane Top Door, Pine, Dark Finish, 44 1/2 x 74 1/2 In. 2090.00
Cupboard, Corner, 9-Pane, Cherry, Waist Molding, Bracket Footed, 74 x 30 In. 3600.00
Cupboard, Corner, 12-Pane Door, 1 Paneled Door, Walnut, 30 x 81 In. 3960.00
Cupboard, Corner, 12-Pane Door, Pine, 19th Century, 82 In. 3850.00
Cupboard, Corner, Barrel Back, Cherry, Full Panel Doors, Cornice, 56 x 84 In. 990.00
Cupboard, Corner, Bittersweet Paint, All Original, Pennsylvania, 1800s 1975.00
Cupboard, Corner, Cherry, Broken Arch Pediment, Early 1800s, 95 1/2 x 34 In. 6500.00
Cupboard, Corner, Cherry, Walnut Veneer, Arched Door Lights, Pennsylvania, 81 In. 6875.00
Cupboard, Corner, Cherry, White Enameled, Painted Interior, 96 In. 1600.00
Cupboard, Corner, Chippendale, 3 Shaped Shelves, Painted, Pine, c.1750, 101 In. 5500.00
Cupboard, Corner, Doors, 3 Shelves, Cherry, 82 In. 1320.00
Cupboard, Corner, Federal, Poplar, c.1810, 82 x 37 x 23 In. 1430.00
Cupboard, Corner, Figured Woods, Glass Door, c.1830, 2 Piece, 85 In. 2700.00
Cupboard, Corner, Glazed Doors, Spoon Slots, Tiger Maple, 83 In. 8600.00
Cupboard, Corner, Grain Painted, John Rupp, c.1840, 90 x 50 In. 7800.00
Cupboard, Corner, Hanging, Drawer, Fluted Pilasters, Pine, Poplar, 31 1/4 In. 660.00
Cupboard, Corner, Hanging, Mustard Grained, Ohio, Mid-1800s, 31 1/2 In. 1050.00
Cupboard, Corner, Hanging, Pine, Worn Brown Graining Over Red, 26 x 41 In. 675.00
Cupboard, Corner, Hanging, Refinished Walnut, Paneled Door, 34 x 43 In. 220.00
Cupboard, Corner, Hudson Valley, 12-Pane Door, Original Blue Paint 2450.00
Cupboard, Corner, Orange, Yellow Stripes, Turn Footed, 72 In. .... *Illus* 2200.00
Cupboard, Corner, Pine, 1 Piece, Old Red Flame Grained, 31 x 54 In. 925.00
Cupboard, Corner, Pine, 2 Piece, Pennsylvania, c.1820 .... 2575.00
Cupboard, Corner, Poplar, Cherry, Yellow-Gray Grained, Country, 48 x 80 In. 1540.00
Cupboard, Corner, Queen Anne, Barrel Back, Red Paint 6700.00
Cupboard, Corner, Sunburst Design Lower Doors, Cherry & Maple, 1860s 4200.00
Cupboard, Corner, White Paint, England, 18th Century, 90 1/2 In. 1870.00
Cupboard, Court, 2 Etched Glass Top Doors, Oak, England 1375.00
Cupboard, Dala, Hanging, Original Paint, Gold Leaf 2600.00
Cupboard, Empire, Walnut, Poplar, Paint Grained, Drawer & Door, c.1847, 58 In. 1710.00
Cupboard, Flat Back, 4-Pane Door, 1 Paneled Lower Door, Pine, 69 In. 2300.00
Cupboard, French Provincial, Molded Cornice, 2 Doors, Fruitwood, Pine, 78 In. 2015.00
Cupboard, Glass Door, Pie Shelf, Spoon Racks, Green, Holland, c.1820, 82 1/2 In. ... 7000.00

Cupboard, Hanging, 2 Drawers, Mustard Grained, c.1850, 29 x 30 In. 525.00
Cupboard, Hanging, Glazed, Walnut, 34 x 24 In. 470.00
Cupboard, Hanging, Original Blue Paint 1430.00
Cupboard, Hanging, Single Raised Door, Wooden Pegs, c.1800, 25 1/2 x 19 In. 775.00
Cupboard, Jelly, 1 Divided Drawer, 1-Board End, Walnut, 57 x 36 In. 605.00
Cupboard, Jelly, 1 Door, Turned Feet, Painted, 19th Century, 58 x 35 In. 550.00
Cupboard, Jelly, 1 Paneled Door, Beaded Frame, Wooden Pegs, 53 1/2 In. 1595.00
Cupboard, Jelly, 2 Dovetailed Drawers, Poplar, Stripped Finish 250.00
Cupboard, Jelly, 2 Dovetailed Drawers, Walnut 900.00
Cupboard, Jelly, Original Red Wash, Pine & Poplar, c.1840, 48 x 41 In. 1500.00
Cupboard, Jelly, Scalloped Backsplash, c.1850, 44 x 29 x 14 In. 1400.00
Cupboard, Jelly, Shelves, Zinc Lined, Ocher Grained 550.00
Cupboard, Jelly, Square Nail Construction, 1-Board Shelves, Pine, 63 In. 850.00
Cupboard, Kitchen, Boone, Lebanon, Ind. 250.00
Cupboard, Kitchen, Step Back, Pine 595.00
Cupboard, Milk, 2 Doors Over 2 Shelves, Red, Early 1800s, 69 x 49 x 16 In. 4100.00
Cupboard, Mustard Paint, 9-Light Door 5200.00
Cupboard, Pewter, Original Blue Paint, Early 19th Century 4500.00
Cupboard, Pewter, Walnut, Paneled Doors, Open Top, 47 x 22 x 86 In. 2530.00
Cupboard, Pine, 1 Door, Old Finish, Open Top, 24 x 15 x 84 In. 525.00
Cupboard, Pine, 2 Piece, 4 Doors, 2 Drawers, High Pie Shelf, Refinished, Holland ... 1995.00
Cupboard, Pine, Paneled Doors, Cornice, England, 54 x 58 x 90 In. 495.00
Cupboard, Raised Paneled Doors, 3 Drawers, Porcelain Knobs, Pine, 76 1/4 In. 1430.00
Cupboard, Raised Paneled Doors, Rattail Hinges, c.1760 .... 6500.00
Cupboard, Scandinavia, Painted Rose Bouquets, Pine, 62 x 41 x 22 In. 1045.00
Cupboard, Screened Doors, Scalloped Top, Blue-Green Paint 1100.00
Cupboard, Shaker, Over 4 Graduated Drawers, Canterbury, 96 In. 11000.00
Cupboard, Spice, 6 Drawers, Door, Red Paint, Primitive, 19th Century, 20 1/2 In. 850.00
Cupboard, Step Back, 3 Shelves, Panel Door, Painted, 80 x 34 x 18 In. 1870.00
Cupboard, Step Back, 4 Doors, Chamfered Back, Leesburg, Child's 1750.00
Cupboard, Step Back, Glass Top Doors, Pennsylvania, 19th Century, Child's, 28 3/4 In. . 600.00
Cupboard, Step Back, Paneled, Pine, New England, c.1795, 78 1/2 x 43 In. 1045.00
Cupboard, Step Back, Shaker, 2 Doors, Pine, Red Stain, Drawer Base 6050.00
Cupboard, Wainscot, 4 Doors, 2 Drawers, Illinois, 1890 .... 1395.00
Cupboard, Wales, 3 Base Drawers, Open Top, Oak, 79 3/4 In. 875.00
Cupboard, Wall, 2 Blind Doors, 1 Drawer, Grain Painted, Mid-1800s, 37 x 38 In. 350.00
Cupboard, Wall, 2 Doors, Salmon Paint, Geometric Design, 19th Century 1760.00
Cupboard, Wall, Leather Floral Art Deco, Blue Wallpaper Interior 1540.00
Cupboard, Wall, Paneled Doors, 2 Drawers Base, Poplar, Country, 43 x 26 x 79 In. .. 330.00
Cupboard, Walnut, 2 Piece, 12-Pane Top Doors, Raised Diamond Panels Doors 8250.00
Cupboard, Walnut, 2 Piece, Sheet Glass Top Doors, 2 Drawers 1050.00
Daybed, Biedermeier, Carved Swans, Birch 3080.00
Daybed, Carved Back, New Upholstery, Scandinavia, 1850 .... 1095.00
Daybed, Empire Style, Allegorical Mount, Mahogany, 79 In. 5750.00
Daybed, Empire, Carved, Upholstered, c.1830 .... 2950.00
Daybed, Empire, Turned Legs, Dark Paint Traces, Design, Country, 78 In. 55.00
Daybed, Figured Mahogany Head & Footboard, Brass Paw Feet, American, c.1830 ... 2310.00
Daybed, French Provincial Style, Wrought Iron, 45 x 73 In. 935.00
Daybed, George Nelson, Metal Springs & Legs, Back Cushions, 1955, 72 In. 3165.00
Daybed, Mahogany, Gilt Bronze Mounted, Downcurved Back, Wreaths 2860.00
Daybed, Queen Anne, Rhode Island, c.1740 .... 3850.00
Daybed, Spirals With Acanthus Leaves, Beading, Silvered Iron, 88 1/2 In. 6900.00
Daybed, Tufted Loose Seat, Out-Scrolled Ends, 94 In. 1725.00
Daybed, Walnut, Rope Carved Legs, Posts, England, 22 x 67 In. 1100.00
Desk, 4 Drawers, Walnut, Twisted Rope Half Columns, Country, 45 x 40 In. 1300.00
Desk, Accountant's, 2 Drawers, Original Hardware, c.1780 .... 2350.00
Desk, Accountant's, Plantation, Butternut, c.1850 .... 650.00
Desk, Architect's, Chinese Chippendale Style, 2 Easels & Candle Slide Sides 7500.00
Desk, Architect's, Regency, Mahogany, 2 Pedestals, Leather, Bookrest, c.1825 .... 6325.00
Desk, Arts & Crafts, Oak, Marquetry 1210.00
Desk, Baroque Style, Slant Front, Bombe Case, Marquetry, Holland, 42 3/4 In. 660.00
Desk, Biedermeier, Kneehole, 3 Drawers Each Side, Ash, 31 x 39 In. 2990.00
Desk, Block Front, Shell Carved, Quartered Oak, c.1900 .... 2990.00

Desk, Butler's, 3 Drawers, Mahogany, Fitted Writing Surface, 41 1/2 In. 660.00
Desk, Butler's, 3 Glove Drawers Over Fitted Drawer, Mahogany Veneer 330.00
Desk, Butler's, 3 Overlapping Drawers, Pigeonholes, Walnut, 42 3/4 In. 1210.00
Desk, Butler's, Breakfront, Mahogany 1095.00
Desk, Butler's, Federal, Cherry, Mahogany Veneer, Drawers, 45 x 50 In. 660.00
Desk, Butler's, Hepplewhite, 3 Drawers, Fitted Interior, Mahogany Veneer 650.00
Desk, Butler's, Hepplewhite, 3 Drawers, Mahogany Veneer, England, 40 3/4 In. 715.00
Desk, Butler's, Hepplewhite, Mahogany, Cherry Veneer, New York, 1800s 2500.00
Desk, C Roll Top, Drawers, Pullout Writing Shelves, Oak 700.00
Desk, C Roll Top, Mahogany, 66 In. 1350.00
Desk, Campaign, Fall Front, Pine, Brass Mounted, 19th Century, 46 x 24 x 11 In. 1210.00
Desk, Carlton House, Adam Style, Stepped Case, Garlands, Painted, 48 In. 5100.00
Desk, Center Drawer, 2 Side Banks Of Drawers, Satinwood, c.1900, 51 In. 870.00
Desk, Chippendale, Oxbow Serpentine, Slant Front, Mass., c.1780, 45 x 42 In. 2300.00
Desk, Chippendale, Serpentine Front, Claw Feet, Walnut 320.00
Desk, Chippendale, Slant Front, 3 Drawers, Maple, Fitted 6500.00
Desk, Chippendale, Slant Front, 4 Drawers, Maple, 9 Pigeonholes, 36 x 42 In. 7700.00
Desk, Chippendale, Slant Front, 4 Drawers, Tiger Maple, 43 In. 2200.00
Desk, Chippendale, Slant Front, 4 Drawers, Tiger Maple, c.1770, 45 x 36 3/4 In. 3575.00
Desk, Chippendale, Slant Front, Cherry, 8 Pigeonholes, 36 x 19 x 46 In. 6600.00
Desk, Chippendale, Slant Front, Document Drawers, Mahogany, c.1760, 42 In. 3680.00
Desk, Chippendale, Slant Front, Drawers, Pigeonholes, Cherry, 41 1/2 In. 4675.00
Desk, Chippendale, Slant Front, Maple, c.1770, 44 x 36 1/4 x 17 1/4 In. 3575.00
Desk, Chippendale, Slant Front, Maple, New Hampshire, 36 In. 7200.00
Desk, Chippendale, Slant Front, Maple, Northern New York State, 41 x 36 In. 2530.00
Desk, Chippendale, Slant Front, Original Brass Hardware, Mahogany, c.1780 .... 3800.00
Desk, Chippendale, Slant Front, Tiger Maple, 18th Century, 43 x 38 In. 8750.00
Desk, Clerk's, Slant Front, 3 Drawers, Pedestal, Walnut, 34 x 57 1/2 x 27 In. 935.00
Desk, Counter Top, Vick's Seeds 925.00
Desk, Davenport, Harlequin, Burl Walnut 5500.00
Desk, Davenport, Leather Slant Front, 4 Drawers, Walnut, 33 1/2 In. 935.00
Desk, Davenport, Slant Front, Carved, Walnut, Victorian, 37 x 36 x 25 In. 990.00
Desk, Dominique, Center Shagreen Panel, Bleached Mahogany, 54 In. 8625.00
Desk, Edwardian, Charlton House, Satinwood, Painted 6600.00
Desk, Edwardian, Cylinder, Mahogany, Inlaid, Tambour, 2 Drawers, 39 x 33 In. 1450.00
Desk, Fall Front, 3 Drawers, Pigeonholes, Mirrored Back, Rosewood, c.1870 .... 315.00
Desk, Fall Front, Gustav Stickley, Paneled Front, No. 706, Decal, 44 x 30 In. 1900.00
Desk, Fall Front, Lundstrom, With Bookcase, Stackable, 5 Sections 500.00
Desk, Federal, Inlaid Mahogany, Brass, Massachusetts, c.1800, 51 1/2 x 41 In. 2970.00
Desk, Federal, Slant Front, 4 Graduated Drawers, Maple, c.1790, 42 x 40 In. 4675.00
Desk, Federal, Slant Front, Cherry, Turned Feet, Pennsylvania, c.1820, 45 x 39 In. 770.00
Desk, George III, Kneehole, Pullout Slide, Center Cupboard Door, Walnut 2990.00
Desk, George III, Satinwood, Rounded Tambour Top, Fitted, 54 In. 6050.00
Desk, George IV, Mahogany, 2 Pedestals, Leather, Cupboard, c.1820, 60 In. 3850.00
Desk, Georgian, Double Pedestal, 1 Long & 8 Short Drawers, 48 x 24 In. 275.00
Desk, Georgian, Inset Leather Panel, 2 Drawers, Mahogany, 54 x 27 x 30 In. 750.00
Desk, Governor Winthrop, Mahogany, 4 Drawers 675.00
Desk, Gustav Stickley, Fall Front, Mahogany, Safe Craft, 51 x 35 In. 4950.00
Desk, Heywood-Wakefield, Oak, Wicker, With Chair 650.00
Desk, Lap, Brass Inlaid Lid, Mother-Of-Pearl Center, Victorian, 13 In. 690.00
Desk, Lap, Mahogany, Brass Trim, Secret Compartments 400.00
Desk, Lap, Mahogany, Fitted With Writing Implements, 19 In. 330.00
Desk, Lap, Mahogany, Mother-Of-Pearl Design, c.1890, 16 x 10 x 6 In. 475.00
Desk, Lap, Mother-Of-Pearl & Silver Inlay, Rosewood, 3 7/8 x 12 In. 195.00
Desk, Lap, Partitioned Interior, Leather Surface, Birch, 6 3/4 x 15 In. 1955.00
Desk, Lap, Rosewood, Mother-Of-Pearl, Brassbound, Victorian, 12 In. 235.00
Desk, Lap, Walnut, 6 Compartments, Lock & Key, Early 1900s 185.00
Desk, Lap, Walnut, 6 Compartments, Original Key, c.1890 .... 145.00
Desk, Lap, Walnut, Brassbound, Later Stand, Victorian, 20 In. 248.00
Desk, Larkin, Oak, Mirrored Back 340.00
Desk, Louis XVI, Marble Top, Brass Trim 3600.00
Desk, Mahogany, Original Brasses, Blocked Interior, Inlaid Corners, American 2200.00
Desk, Mahogany, Twin Banks Of Drawers, Kidney Shape, 28 x 42 In. 295.00

Desk, Marble Top, Brass Gallery, Pullout Surface, Parquetry, 53 x 27 In. 975.00
Desk, Melodeon, Hinged Top, Inside Compartments, Oak, Child's, 28 1/2 In. 90.00
Desk, Mirrored Top, Mahogany & Black Lacquer, J. Urban, 1929, 59 In. 8050.00
Desk, Mission, Oak, Victorian 175.00
Desk, Oak, Aesthetic Movement, Top Above Plain Apron, Victorian, c.1880 .... 1035.00
Desk, Oak, Carved, Ornate, Gold Embossed Leather Inset Top 1780.00
Desk, Partner's, Drawers, Lyre-Form Trestle, Mahogany, 30 x 62 In. 935.00
Desk, Partner's, George III, Mahogany, 3 False Drawers, 29 x 48 x 33 In. 385.00
Desk, Partner's, George IV, Leather Top, 8 Drawers, Mahogany, 54 In. 5280.00
Desk, Partner's, Mahogany, 2 Drawers, Winged Griffins Legs & Sides, Paw Feet 2800.00
Desk, Partner's, Walnut, Leather Inset, Plinth, Victorian, c.1875, 72 x 47 x 31 In. 9200.00
Desk, Pedestal, Gilbert Rohde, Mahogany, Leatherette, Kidney Shape, 1930, 56 In. ... 925.00
Desk, Pedestal, Walnut, Leather, Rotary Sections, Victorian, American, 60 In. 1155.00
Desk, Piano, Wirework Doors, Pullout Surface, Rosewood, Mahogany, 76 In. 1100.00
Desk, Pine, Birch, Grain Painted, Red Wash, Smoke Design Interior, Maine 4840.00
Desk, Plantation, 2 Drawers, Ash, Pigeonholes, Glass Doors, 2 Piece 895.00
Desk, Plantation, 3 Graduated Drawers, 2-Door Top, Cherry 2000.00
Desk, Postmaster's, Fall Front, Bird's-Eye Drawers, Cherry & Maple, 56 In. 1150.00
Desk, Postmaster's, Fall Front, Compartment Interior, Mahogany, 59 In. 430.00
Desk, Queen Anne, Slant Front, Mirrored Door, Baize Surface, Walnut, 60 In.. .... 4600.00
Desk, Roll Top, Center Drawer, 3 Side Drawers, Delphos Label, 1940s, Child's 170.00
Desk, Roll Top, Paris Mfg., Child's 250.00
Desk, S Roll Top, Oak, 12 Drawers, Wheels 3000.00
Desk, S Roll Top, Oak, 1900s, 54 In. 1650.00
Desk, Schoolmaster's, Drop Front, Pine, Original Paint Traces, Modern Legs 135.00
Desk, Schoolmaster's, Hepplewhite, Slant Front, Poplar, Pigeonholes, 36 x 32 In. 880.00
Desk, Schoolmaster's, Red Paint Interior, Pine, 30 x 26 In. 525.00
Desk, Schoolmaster's, Slant Front, Fitted Interior, Pine, 35 In. 385.00
Desk, Schoolmaster's, Slant Front, Interior Pigeonholes 550.00
Desk, Schoolmaster's, Slant Front, Painted, Square Tapered Legs, 34 In. 190.00
Desk, Schoolmaster's, Slant Front, Pine, Yellow Graining Over Red, 28 x 34 In. 195.00
Desk, Secretary, Tyrolean, Fruitwood, 18th Century, Europe 3500.00
Desk, Sewing, Walnut, Bird's-Eye Maple Interior, Vanity, 19th Century 1295.00
Desk, Shaker, Sewing, Mid-19th Century, Alfred, Maine 1600.00
Desk, Side-By-Side, Larkin, Oak, Glass Cabinet 725.00
Desk, Slant Front, 4 Drawers, Interior Pigeonholes, Maple, c.1760, 42 In. 6900.00
Desk, Slant Front, 4 Drawers, Mahogany Veneer On Apron, Birch, 40 1/2 In. 1100.00
Desk, Slant Front, 4 Drawers, Secret Drawer, Walnut & Cherry, 46 3/4 In. 660.00
Desk, Slant Front, 4 Graduated Dovetailed Drawers, Walnut, Fitted, 39 x 43 In. 1925.00
Desk, Slant Front, 4 Graduated Drawers, Tiger Maple, New England, c.1770 .... 9500.00
Desk, Slant Front, 4 Graduated Drawers, Cherry, 40 1/4 x 47 1/2 In. 1700.00
Desk, Slant Front, 4 Graduated Drawers, Cherry, Original Brasses 3900.00
Desk, Slant Front, 4 Graduated Drawers, Maple, Fitted, 40 x 36 x 18 In. 2090.00
Desk, Slant Front, Beaded Drawers, Cherry, c.1800, 43 x 29 x 38 In. 3600.00
Desk, Slant Front, Chippendale, Mahoganized Surface, 38 3/4 x 35 1/2 In. 1430.00
Desk, Slant Front, Chippendale, Maple Grain Painted, c.1780, 40 x 36 In. 3850.00
Desk, Slant Front, Chippendale, Oxbow, Mahogany, c.1780, 45 x 42 x 22 1/2 In. 4400.00
Desk, Slant Front, George II, Walnut, Feather Banded Top, c.1750, 39 In. 6325.00
Desk, Slant Front, Hepplewhite, 4 Cock-Beaded Drawers, Cherry, Inlaid, 43 In. 1100.00
Desk, Slant Front, Oak, England, 18th Century 5000.00
Desk, Slant Front, William & Mary Style, 2 Drawers, Oak, 39 x 29 In. 330.00
Desk, Station Master, Oak 575.00
Desk, Student, Lift Top, 6 Drawers, Oak, South Paris, Maine 200.00
Desk, Traveling, Fold Down, Rosewood, Metal Inlaid, 1840s, 22 x 13 x 9 In. 950.00
Desk, Traveling, George I Style, Slant Front, 1 Drawer, Walnut, 11 x 13 1/2 In. 1600.00
Desk, Walnut, Inlaid, Brass, Later Stand, Victorian, 14 In. 250.00
Desk, Walnut, Marquetry, Frieze Drawer Between Doors, Germany, 60 x 31 In. 880.00
Desk, Woman's, Carved Rosewood, Reeded & Turned Legs, 32 x 21 In. 1430.00
Desk, Woman's, Drawers, Side Tambour Compartments, Mahogany, 44 In. 1540.00
Desk, Woman's, Kidney Shape, Mahogany 545.00
Desk, Woman's, Roll Top, Oak, Carved, Over Slide & Drawer, 38 x 32 In. 770.00
Desk Bookcase, Federal, Glazed Doors, 2 Drawers, Mahogany, c.1815, 89 In. 5475.00
Desk Bookcase, Federal, Glazed Doors, 2 Shelves, Line Inlay, Cherry, 80 In. 4830.00

Dinette Set, Chrome, Blue Plastic, Leaf, 1950s, 5 Piece 160.00
Dining Set, Art Deco, Bird's-Eye Maple & Australian Walnut, c.1935, 7 Piece 3250.00
Dining Set, Berkey & Gay, Ornate, 1920s, 10 Piece 3850.00
Dining Set, Bistro, Dark Wood, Round Table, 4 Chairs, 5 Piece 200.00
Dining Set, Chippendale Style, 3 Leaves, 2 Host Chairs, Mahogany, 7 Piece 1925.00
Dining Set, Harden, Colonial Style, Cherry, Hutch, Table & 6 Chairs 860.00
Dining Set, Heywood-Wakefield, Wheat, Buffet, 6 Chairs, 1953, 8 Piece 3000.00
Dining Set, Kitchen, Enameled Top, 5 Piece 110.00
Dining Set, Marble Top Table, 2 Benches, Padded Seats, Wrought Iron, 3 Piece 7150.00
Dining Set, Table, Limbert, 8 Matching Chairs, 60 In. Table, 9 Piece 9400.00
Dining Set, Wrought Iron, Marble Top Table, 1920s, 7 Piece 850.00
Dresser, Aesthetic, Modern Gothic, Cherry 605.00
Dresser, Charles II, 2 Drawers, Geometric Moldings, Oak, 60 In. 3165.00
Dresser, Drop Front, Carved, Walnut & Burl Walnut, Victorian, 76 x 50 In. 1045.00
Dresser, French Provincial, Applewood, 3 Frieze Drawers, c.1800, 90 In. 2570.00
Dresser, George III, Oak, Central Clock, Thos. Legett, Welsh, 80 x 60 x 19 In. 2300.00
Dresser, Grain Painted, 2 Side & 3 Center Drawers, New England, c.1840, 53 In. 4000.00
Dresser, Gustav Stickley, Hammered Copper Oval Pulls, No. 626, 53 x 36 In. 3520.00
Dresser, Inset Marble Top, Burl Insets, Walnut 425.00
Dresser, Jordon & Harsh, Bombe, 3 Drawers Over 2, Attached Mirror 800.00
Dresser, Marble Top, Candle Sconces, Mirror, Mahogany, Carved, c.1860, 83 In. 1550.00
Dresser, Mirror, Side Drawers, 3 Drawers, Leaf Pulls, Mahogany, 73 x 41 In. 495.00
Dresser, Pewter, Slant Back, Painted, Red Stain, Pine, c.1790, 78 1/2 In. 9900.00
Dresser, Pierce-Carved Frame, Marble Top, Swivel & Tilt Mirror, Rosewood 2420.00
Dresser, Rosewood, Marble Top, Serpentine Front, Victorian, American., 90 In. 1200.00
Dresser, Roycroft, 3 Drawers, Chestnut, Half-Moon Pulls, 38 1/2 x 44 x 21 In. 2200.00
Dresser, Serpentine, 2 Over 2 Drawers, Mirror, Oak 450.00
Dresser, Victorian, Glove Box, Mirror, Child's, 36 In. 585.00
Dresser, Walnut, Drop Center, Marble Top, Victorian 495.00
Dresser, Welsh, 3 Drawers, Paneled Doors, Elm, Fruitwood, 70 In. 4600.00
Dresser, Welsh, Oak, Crossbanded, Shelves, 7 Drawers, Victorian, 80 x 86 In. 7475.00
Dresser, Woman's, 3 Over 2 Full Drawers, Painted, Cream, 39 1/2 In. 430.00
Dry Sink, 2 Doors, 2 Drawers, New England 450.00
Dry Sink, Drawer, Well, Cherry, Butternut & Poplar, 29 3/4 x 32 In. 935.00
Dry Sink, Open, Green Paint, Zinc Liner 425.00
Dry Sink, Paneled Doors, 1 Drawer, Well & Hutch Top, Shelf, Poplar, 54 In 375.00
Dry Sink, Paneled, Tin Lining, Clinton, Conn., c.1840, Small 600.00
Dry Sink, Walnut, Red Painted, Pennsylvania 1100.00
Dry Sink, Wood Pinned Doors, 3-Nailed Spice Drawers Top, Gallery 1500.00
Dumbwaiter, 3 Graduated Tiers, Mahogany, Victorian, 51 x 24 In. Largest 770.00
Dumbwaiter, 3 Tiers, Retractable, Mahogany, Raised, 40 1/2 x 22 1/2 In. 3738.00
Dumbwaiter, George III Style, 2 Tiers, Drop Leaves, 37 In. 990.00
Easel, White Wicker 110.00
Etagere, 4 Tiers, 1 Short Drawer, Mahogany, 63 In. 1100.00
Etagere, 4 Tiers, 3 Drawers, Gilt Design, Black Lacquer, Japan, 70 In. 6325.00
Etagere, 5 Oak Shelves, Rattan, 1920s, 41 In. 140.00
Etagere, Cherry, Mirror, Woman's Bust On Lower Door, Rope Turned Posts 2100.00
Etagere, Corner, Carved Oak, 19th Century, 84 x 36 In. 525.00
Etagere, Cupboard Base, Walnut 750.00
Etagere, George IV, 3 Tiers, Mahogany, Rectangular, Ring Turned, 60 In. 1430.00
Etagere, Hall Mirror, Renaissance Revival, Walnut, Marble Base, 101 In. 2860.00
Etagere, Marble Top, Black Walnut 2250.00
Etagere, Marble Top, Mirror-Backed Shelves, Mahogany, Victorian 1300.00
Etagere, Oriental, 6 Open Shelves, Carved Rosewood, Cabinet Base, c.1880 .... 330.00
Etagere, Papier-Mache, Parcel Gilt, Open Shelves, Russia, 38 In. 1100.00
Etagere, Regency Style, 4 Fabric Lined Shelves, Leather Covered, 36 In. 3680.00
Etagere, Rococo Revival, Rosewood, c.1860 .... 8250.00
Etagere, William IV, 4 Tiers, Brass Gallery, Castors, Rosewood, c.1835, 47 In. 8625.00
Etagere, William IV, Hinged Top, Ledge, Lower Drawer, Rosewood, 42 In. 6900.00
Footrest, William & Mary, Unpainted Frame, Turned & Pinned Construction 4070.00
Footstool, Carved, Needlepoint Upholstered, Walnut 165.00
Footstool, Floral Hooked Rag, Green Paint, Brown Fringe, 12 1/2 In. 365.00
Footstool, French Provincial, Walnut, Needlepoint Top, 12 1/2 x 9 In. 165.00

Furniture, Highboy, Queen Anne, 11 Drawers,
Tiger Maple, 74 x 37 In.

Furniture, Highboy, Queen Anne, 8 Drawers,
Maple, Cabriole Legs, 66 x 38 In.

Footstool, Gustav Stickley, Rush Top, Decal, No. 301, 17 1/2 x 19 3/4 In. 605.00
Footstool, Gustav Stickley, Spindles, Leather Top, No. 395, c.1906, 15 x 20 In. 2900.00
Footstool, Gustav Stickley, Tacked Leather Top, 15 x 20 x 16 In. 412.00
Footstool, Hand Painted Floral Design, New England, 14 x 7 1/2 x 7 1/2 In. 155.00
Footstool, L. & J.G. Stickley, Oak, Decal, No. 394, 1915, 16 x 19 x 15 In. 310.00
Footstool, Louis XV Style, Beechwood, Serpentine Apron, 7 x 20 In. 330.00
Footstool, Neoclassical, Needlepoint Top, Curule Legs, Hoof Feet, 21 In. 440.00
Footstool, Poplar, Stylized Floral, Dark Ground, 7 x 13 3/4 In. 105.00
Footstool, Regency, Rosewood, Inlaid Brass, Padded Top, c.1810, 8 x 16 x 11 In. 1150.00
Footstool, Regency, Velvet Upholstered, Down Sloping, Ebonized, c.1813, Pair 5175.00
Footstool, Serpentine Shape, Ogee Footed, Mahogany, Victorian, 15 x 18 In. 175.00
Footstool, Stickley Bros., Oilcloth Upholstered, Oak, Square, 11 3/4 In. 200.00
Footstool, Turned, Fruit Design Tapestry, England, Victorian, 22 x 14 1/2 In. 175.00
Footstool, Upholstered, Cast-Iron Base, 10 1/2 x 14 In. 250.00
Footstool, Walnut, Carved Frame, Cabriole Legs, Victorian, American, 18 In. 305.00
Footstool, Wicker, Gold Paint, Scroll-Type Top 175.00
Footstool, Windsor, Oval, Pine, Turned Legs, 7 1/2 x 11 1/2 x 7 1/2 In. 95.00
Hall Seat, Round Beveled Mirror, Oak 465.00
Hall Stand, 5 Brass Coat Hangers, Umbrella Stand, Mirror, 85 In. 985.00
Hall Stand, 5 Figural Hooks, Oval Mirror, Victorian, 81 1/2 In. 1430.00
Hall Stand, Carved Deer's Head, Antlers, 1 Drawer, Marble Top Stand, Mirror 3000.00
Hall Stand, Carved Floral & Nut Back, Mirror, 2 Umbrella Holders, Oak 800.00
Hall Stand, Empire Style, Beveled Mirror, Claw Footed, Oak 885.00
Hall Stand, Paul Kiss, Wrought Iron, Mirror, Umbrella Holder, 84 x 60 In. 4025.00
Hall Stand, Scrolled Hooks, Oval Mirror, Wrought Iron, c.1890, 72 In. 1265.00
Hall Tree, Black Forest, Bear, J. Grossman, 91 In. 3850.00
Hall Tree, Black Forest, Carved Walnut, Bear, Standing, Antler Top 4675.00
Hall Tree, Black Forest, Walnut, Carved, 19th Century, 93 1/2 In. 4675.00
Hall Tree, Carved Owls At Arm Terminals, Walnut 2750.00
Hall Tree, Eastlake Style, Carved Boar's Head, Oak, 96 In. 850.00
Hall Tree, Foliate Form, Griffin Hooks, Umbrella Holder, Cast Iron, 66 In. 330.00
Hall Tree, Hardwood, Brass Hooks, Old Finish, 72 In. 150.00
Hall Tree, Mahogany, Ball & Stick, Leather Bench, Waterbury Clock, Victorian 4400.00
Hall Tree, Trailing Vines, Wrought Iron, 19th Century, 78 In. 525.00
Hamper, Oriental, 1940s 40.00
Hat Rack, Wall, Walnut, Porcelain Knobs, 6-Pointed Star, Expands To 35 In. 115.00
High Chair, Arrow-Back, 3 Arrow Spindles, 1880s, 35 3/4 In. 440.00
High Chair, Art Deco, Porcelain Top 175.00
High Chair, Ash, Late 18th Century, 34 In. 100.00
High Chair, Bamboo, Red & Black Striping, Floral Crest, 34 3/4 In. 220.00

High Chair, Bow Back, 6 Spindles 245.00
High Chair, Cane Seat, Tray, Back Wheels, Converts To Stroller 1000.00
High Chair, Ladder Back, Maple & Ash, 18th Century, 34 In. 825.00
High Chair, Ladder Back, Turned Finials, 18th Century, Child's, 34 In. 1210.00
High Chair, New England, Maple, c.1795, 36 1/4 In. 660.00
High Chair, Slat Back, Arms, 18th Century 1850.00
High Chair, Spindle Back, Varnish Over White Paint, 34 1/2 In. 95.00
High Chair, Splayed Legs, Spindle Back, Varnish Over White Paint, 14 1/2 In. 95.00
High Chair, Stroller, Convertible, 4 Metal Wheels, 41 x 17 In. 275.00
High Chair, Tray Latch, Bent Legs, Oak, c.1900 .... 245.00
High Chair, Tray, Pressed Back, Cane Seat, Oak 225.00
Highboy, Crotch Veneer, Carved Pediment & Knees, 20th Century, 80 x 36 In. 2300.00
Highboy, Georgian Style, Carved Mahogany, 86 x 42 In. 3450.00
Highboy, Queen Anne Style, Mahogany, 20th Century, 85 1/4 In. 660.00
Highboy, Queen Anne, 8 Drawers, Maple, Cabriole Legs, 66 x 38 In. .... *Illus* 4290.00
Highboy, Queen Anne, 11 Drawers, Tiger Maple, 74 x 37 In. .... *Illus* 14850.00
Highboy, Queen Anne, 4 Top Drawers, 2 Base Drawers, Duck Feet 8500.00
Highboy, Queen Anne, 4 Top Drawers, Maple, Sunburst, 72 3/4 In. 9350.00
Highboy, Queen Anne, Fan Carved, Concealed Document Drawer, Maple 4620.00
Highboy, Queen Anne, Maple & Cherry, 18th Century, 67 x 38 x 21 In. 3190.00
Hoosier Cabinet, Child's, Oak 175.00
Hoosier Cabinet, Child's, Roll-Down Door, Frosted Panes 775.00
Hoosier Cabinet, Maple, With Sifter 795.00
Hoosier Cabinet, Oak, Sellers 700.00
Hoosier Cabinet, Oak, With Sifter & Spice Rack 995.00
Hoosier Cabinet, Porcelain Top, Apartment Size 525.00
Hoosier Cabinet, Zinc Pullout Work Surface, Oak 750.00
Huntboard, 2 Drawers, Black & Gold Painted Design, Pullout Shelf 2000.00
Huntboard, Hepplewhite, 2 Drawers, Pine, Marbleized, Country, 38 In. 2200.00
Huntboard, Southern Pine, Stenciled Horses On Sides, c.1860 .... 3800.00
Hutch, Peter Hunt, Floral Urn Design, Signed & Dated, 1938, 68 x 42 In. 1985.00
Hutch-Chair-Table, Red Paint, c.1830 .... 1980.00
Kas, Mahogany Color, 2 Drawers, Bowl Footed, Hudson River, 52 x 73 In. 2640.00
Kas, Raised Panel Doors, Wrought-Iron Hinges, Walnut, 51 x 46 3/4 In. 1980.00
Kas, Tulipwood, Ebonized Panels, Hudson River, 60 x 78 In. 6875.00
Kitchen Set, Chrome, Table & 4 Chairs, 1950s 400.00
Library Steps, Georgian, 2-Hinged Top, Mahogany & Leather, 26 x 27 In. 660.00
Linen Press, 2 Doors, 3 Graduated Base Drawers, J.T. Owens, 1855, 2 Sections 2700.00
Linen Press, 2 Doors, 4 Cock-Beaded Drawers, Shelves, Pine, 79 1/2 In. 990.00
Linen Press, 2 Doors, White Paint, Green Panels, North Georgia 2400.00
Linen Press, 2 Drawers, Cornice Above Paneled Doors, Pine, Ireland, 80 In. 2420.00
Linen Press, 3 Base Drawers, Paneled Doors, Bleached Pine, 81 1/2 In. 685.00
Linen Press, 4 Base Graduated Drawers, Walnut, Pennsylvania, c.1750 .... 3300.00
Linen Press, Federal, Shaped Pediment, 3 Finials, American, c.1820, 95 x 40 In. 3850.00
Linen Press, George III, 2 Cupboard Doors, 3 Drawers, Mahogany, 70 In. 4660.00
Linen Press, George III, 2 Doors Over 6 Drawers, Mahogany, c.1780, 83 x 48 In. 1980.00
Linen Press, George III, Grillwork Doors, 4 Drawers, Mahogany, 76 In. 3300.00
Linen Press, George III, Mahogany, Bracket Feet, 1700s, 82 x 53 In. 9775.00
Linen Press, Georgian, 3 Base Drawers, Mahogany, Brush Slide 1430.00
Linen Press, Georgian, 5 Lower Drawers, Mahogany, 86 x 46 x 20 In. 2300.00
Linen Press, Grillwork Doors, 4 Drawers, French Feet, Mahogany, 76 In. 2200.00
Linen Press, Regency, 2 Doors, 3 Drawers, Mahogany, c.1825, Ireland, 84 In. 2530.00
Linen Press, Regency, 4 Doors, Mahogany, c.1820 .... 220.00
Linen Press, Regency, 4 Drawers, Mahogany, Ebony Inlaid, c.1800, 90 x 49 In. 2200.00
Linen Press, Regency, Mahogany, Bowfront, 19th Century, Cedar Drawer Base 8500.00
Love Seat, 2-Chair Back, Upholstered, Arms, Simple Design, 1910 .... 1400.00
Love Seat, Beehive & Floral Carvings 155.00
Love Seat, Double Curved Back, Upright Slats, Turned Legs, Casters, France 275.00
Love Seat, French Gilt, 19th Century 1650.00
Love Seat, Majorelle, Mahogany, Clematis, Satin Upholstered, 48 In. 6900.00
Lowboy, 1 Long Over 3 Short Drawers, Shell Knees, Drake Footed, Mahogany 650.00
Lowboy, George I, Mahogany, 3 Drawers, Cabriole, Pad Footed, c.1725, 31 x 39 In. .. 1320.00

Furniture, Mirror, Federal,
Inlaid Mahogany, Giltwood,
c. 1800, 48 x 23 In.

Furniture, Mirror, Girandole,
Giltwood, c. 1800, 36 x 29 1/2 In.

Furniture, Mirror, Louis XVI,
Giltwood, Pierced Crest, Insert,
24 x 37 In.

Lowboy, George I, Walnut, Long Over Short Drawer, Cabriole Legs, 28 x 30 In. 4025.00
Lowboy, Queen Anne, Maple & Birch, c.1740 .... 6600.00
Lowboy, Queen Anne, Oyster Walnut, Mirror, Shaped Front, Cabriole Legs 475.00
Lowboy, Queen Anne, Walnut, 5 Drawers, 44 In. 195.00
Mirror, Acanthus & C-Scroll Crest, Carved Gesso & Giltwood, 60 x 43 In. 2850.00
Mirror, Adam Style, Ornate Gilt Frame, Urn Crest, 20th Century, 47 x 26 In. 440.00
Mirror, Arched Top, Scrolling Cartouche Top, 19th Century, 61 x 27 In. 50.00
Mirror, Architectural, Pine, Red Stain, Reverse Glass Painting, 21 1/2 x 13 1/2 In. 165.00
Mirror, Art Deco, Silvered Mount, Cornucopias, France, c.1925, 32 x 30 In. 8970.00
Mirror, Beechwood, Brass Mounted, Wallpaper Panel, Continental, 50 x 22 In. 1445.00
Mirror, Beveled Glass, Carved & Gilded Frame, 28 x 32 In. 240.00
Mirror, Biedermeier, Ebonized Capitals, Peaked Pediment, Elm, 55 x 30 In. 4900.00
Mirror, Biedermeier, Tiger Maple, Burl, 1940s, 17 1/2 x 56 In. 695.00
Mirror, C. Bugatti, Ebonized, Fruitwood, Ivory, Copper, Parchment, 36 x 29 In. 4900.00
Mirror, Carved & Gilded Ribbon Crest, Oval, 1840s, 36 x 25 In. 330.00
Mirror, Carved & Gilded, Cherubs Across Top, 48 x 37 In. 6600.00
Mirror, Cheval, Beveled, Shield Shape, 72 3/4 In. 395.00
Mirror, Cheval, Carved Acanthus 1350.00
Mirror, Cheval, Carved Mahogany, Victorian, 1900 .... 1485.00
Mirror, Cheval, Regency, Mahogany, Inlay Trestle Stand, Brass, Rectangular, 1825 .... 935.00
Mirror, Chip Carved Poplar Frame, Red Finish, 12 1/2 x 10 3/8 In. 75.00
Mirror, Chippendale, Carved Giltwood, Rococo C-Scrolls, c.1770, 47 x 37 In. 2100.00
Mirror, Chippendale, Eagle Finial, Carved Rosettes, Gilded 1320.00
Mirror, Chippendale, Fretwork, Gilded Phoenix, 19th Century, 37 x 20 In. 410.00
Mirror, Chippendale, Mahogany On Pine, Frame, Gilded Crest, 37 x 20 .... 3960.00
Mirror, Chippendale, Mahogany, Gilt Eagle Design, 14 x 25 In. 150.00
Mirror, Chippendale, Mahogany, Gilt, Carved, Arched, Scrolled Ears, 45 x 24 In. 1600.00
Mirror, Chippendale, Mahogany, Scroll, Dark Finish, Crest, Country, 29 x 15 In. 990.00
Mirror, Chippendale, Mahogany, Scroll-Cut Frame, 50 x 24 In. 500.00
Mirror, Chippendale, Scroll, Mahogany Veneer, Gilded Liner, 44 x 23 In. 495.00
Mirror, Chippendale, Spread-Winged Eagle, Pendant, Mahogany, c.1800, 43 In. 2070.00
Mirror, Chippendale, Walnut Veneer & Giltwood, 1760-1780, 37 1/2 In. 495.00
Mirror, Classical, Tubular Moldings, Diamond Design, American, c.1825, 41 In. 2300.00
Mirror, Convex, Gilded Border, Eagle On Rock Work Base, Giltwood, 30 In. 920.00
Mirror, Convex, Regency, Giltwood, Ball Design, c.1820, 23-In. Diam. 357.00
Mirror, Cornucopia, Pierce-Carved Flowers, Shell, Oval, Victorian, 35 In. 1320.00
Mirror, Courting, Reverse Painted Portrait, 18th-Century Man, Holland 415.00

Mirror, Dresser, Chippendale, Mahogany, 1 Drawer, Ogee Bracket, 18 x 14 In. 180.00
Mirror, Dressing, Carved, Spiral Columns, Bun Feet, Mahogany, 22 x 24 In. 180.00
Mirror, Dressing, George III, Shield Shape, Adjustable, Mahogany, c.1790 .... 1710.00
Mirror, Dressing, Triple Beveled Mirrors, Sides Pivot, Oak, c.1900 .... 1375.00
Mirror, Eagle Top, Ebonized Ball Finials, Mahogany, Fruitwood, Painted, 45 In. 1600.00
Mirror, Eglomise Landscape Panel, Mahogany, 24 x 15 In. 175.00
Mirror, Empire, Black & Gold, Half Turnings, Reverse Painted, 29 x 14 In. 220.00
Mirror, Empire, Convex, Carved Acanthus Leaves, Eagle, 2 Candle Arms, 32 In. 1650.00
Mirror, Empire, White Paint, Gilt, Floral Gesso, 23 x 35 In. 300.00
Mirror, Federal, Gilded Frame, Semicircular Crest, Eagle Shield, 40 x 27 In. 1650.00
Mirror, Federal, Gilt, Girandole, Carved Eagle, 1810-1815, 35 x 20 In. 2990.00
Mirror, Federal, Inlaid Mahogany, Giltwood, c.1800, 48 x 23 In. .... *Illus* 10350.00
Mirror, Federal, Reverse Painted, Ships & Houses, Mahogany, 44 x 23 In. 265.00
Mirror, Federal, Spread-Winged Eagle, Flower Heads, Giltwood, 1820s, 35 In. 3450.00
Mirror, Federal, Tabernacle, Giltwood, 19th Century, 43 x 22 In. 825.00
Mirror, Ferrobrandt, Art Deco, Bronze, Leaded, 2 Sconces, c.1925, 40 x 23 In. 7475.00
Mirror, Fun House, Double Wood Cased, 73 1/2 x 32 In. 600.00
Mirror, George I, Beveled Plate, Candle Arms, Gilt Gesso, 38 x 20 1/2 In. 8625.00
Mirror, George II, Carved Crest, Floral Spray Pendant, Walnut, 38 1/2 In. 690.00
Mirror, George II, Giltwood, Broken Arch Pediment, Flower Basket, 40 x 20 In. 1320.00
Mirror, George III Style, Fleur-De-Lis Crest, Shell Medallion, 45 x 25 In. 425.00
Mirror, George III Style, Giltwood, Beaded Border, 19th Century, 40 x 30 In. 1725.00
Mirror, George III Style, Mirrored Border, Ram's Head Terminals, 71 In. 1760.00
Mirror, George III Style, Pierced Crest, Grape & Vine Frame, Gilt, 40 x 21 In. 220.00
Mirror, George III Style, Stylized Column Dividers, Carved Frame, 60 x 48 In. 2090.00
Mirror, George III, Acanthus Carved Frame, Giltwood, c.1760, 41 x 27 In. 4600.00
Mirror, George III, Giltwood, Pierced Frame, C-Scrolls, 51 x 25 In. 5465.00
Mirror, George III, Giltwood, Regilt, 59 1/2 x 29 1/4 In. 1760.00
Mirror, Gilded Cast Metal, Wood, Beveled 1 Side, Concave Other, Oval, 20 In. 85.00
Mirror, Giltwood, Bull's-Eye, Convex, England, Round, 47 In. Diam. 6875.00
Mirror, Girandole, Giltwood, c.1800, 36 x 29 1/2 In. .... *Illus* 2310.00
Mirror, Gustav Stickley, Pegged Construction, Oak, c.1902, 32 3/4 x 47 In. 5175.00
Mirror, Hagenauer, Brass, Surmounted With Female Nude On Horse, 18 3/4 In. 2530.00
Mirror, Hammond, Convex, Giltwood, London, 47 In. 6875.00
Mirror, Hepplewhite, Crossbanded Veneer, Mahogany, 24 1/2 x 14 1/2 In. 200.00
Mirror, Louis Philippe, Carved, Cherubs Holding Wreaths, Birds, 78 x 53 In. 6600.00
Mirror, Louis Philippe, Carved, Gilded, Scrolled Crest, Beaded Edge, 67 In. 2750.00
Mirror, Louis XV, Divided Plate, Serpentine Edges, 1850s, 72 x 29 1/2 In. 8050.00
Mirror, Louis XVI, Giltwood, Pierced Crest, Insert, 24 x 37 In. .... *Illus* 1210.00
Mirror, Louis XVI, Grisaille, Parcel Gilt, Trumeau, 18th Century, 60 x 21 In. 445.00
Mirror, Louis XVI, Ribbon-Tied Medallion Top, Giltwood, 1760s, 50 1/2 In. 5750.00
Mirror, Mahogany Veneer, 4-Leaf Scroll Ornaments, Ogee Frame, 48 x 27 In. 195.00
Mirror, Mahogany, Original Ears, Backboards & Glass, 42 3/4 In 1300.00
Mirror, Molded Frame, Red, Reverse Painted, Country, 2 Piece, 20 x 11 1/4 In. 220.00
Mirror, Mother-Of-Pearl Inlay, Carved Bats & Medallions, China, 63 x 21 In. 495.00
Mirror, Neoclassical, Egg & Dart, Flower Finials, France, c.1880, 69 In. 2750.00
Mirror, Neoclassical, Mahogany, Parcel Gilt, Winged Cherub, 28 x 15 1/2 In. 250.00
Mirror, Nude Maiden In Lily Pond, Bronze Frame, c.1900 21 3/4 x 11 In. 2015.00
Mirror, Oak, Art Nouveau, Pierced Crest, Square Post Finial, Belgium, 60 x 48 In. 865.00
Mirror, Oak, Pierce-Carved Flowers & Scrolls, c.1880, 52 1/2 In. 715.00
Mirror, Over Mantel, 3 Sections, Acanthus Corner Blocks, Gilt, 59 1/2 In. 290.00
Mirror, Over Mantel, Classical Style, Urn & Swag Crest, 33 x 48 3/8 In. 2310.00
Mirror, Over Mantel, Empire, 3 Sections, Acorn Drops, 28 1/2 x 65 In. 660.00
Mirror, Pier, Arched Top, Scrolling Cartouche Top, 60 3/4 In. 50.00
Mirror, Pier, Empire, Rope Columns, Lions, Eagle, Wood & Gesso Frame, 58 In. 5610.00
Mirror, Queen Anne Style, Curly Maple, Prince Of Wales Plume, 38 x 21 In. 415.00
Mirror, Queen Anne, Black Japanned, Beveled Plate, c.1700, 31 1/2 x 42 In. 2185.00
Mirror, Queen Anne, Pine, Dark Finish, Scrolled Crest, Country, 14 x 8 In. 380.00
Mirror, Queen Anne, Scroll, Mahogany Veneer, Varnish, Regilded, 15 x 10 1/2 In. 330.00
Mirror, Queen Anne, Walnut, Molded & Scrolled Crests, 14 1/2 x 8 3/8 In. 80.00
Mirror, Regency Neoclassical, c.1810, 68 x 46 In., Pair 2310.00
Mirror, Regency Style, Arched Crest, Faux Tortoiseshell, 42 x 26 In. 550.00
Mirror, Regency, Giltwood, Convex, Trumpet-Shaped Urn Top, c.1820, 66 In. 3850.00

Mirror, Regency, Girandole, Giltwood, Eagle, 19th Century, 38 x 22 In., Pair 3300.00
Mirror, Renaissance Revival, Ebonized & Parcel Gilt, 19th Century, 75 x 42 In. 990.00
Mirror, Renaissance, Cottage Style, Green, Black Trim 145.00
Mirror, Reverse-Cut Convex Circles, Black & Gilt Repaint, 11 1/4 x 9 In. 415.00
Mirror, Rococo Style, C-Scroll Acanthus & Foliate Frame, Oak, 54 x 51 In. 1150.00
Mirror, Rococo, Giltwood, Rectangular, Floral Vine Border, 59 In. 2200.00
Mirror, Scallops & Curlicues, Standing Sheep On Top, Mahogany, 8 1/2 In. 4600.00
Mirror, Scroll, Chippendale, Gilded Phoenix In Crest, 36 1/2 x 20 1/2 In. 1320.00
Mirror, Scrolled Vine Border, Putti Masks, 1870s, 39 1/2 x 54 In. 8050.00
Mirror, Shaving, 5 Dovetailed Drawers, Mahogany Veneer, Frame, 31 x 26 In. 385.00
Mirror, Shaving, Arched Plate, Mahogany, Victorian, 15 In. 115.00
Mirror, Shaving, Empire, Scrolled Supports, Mahogany Veneer 110.00
Mirror, Shaving, Hepplewhite, Bowfront, 5 Drawers, Swirled Pulls, Mahogany 800.00
Mirror, Shaving, Stickley, Stand, Swivel, Cast-Iron Pulls, 21 1/2 x 24 In. 1540.00
Mirror, Shaving, Walnut, Pressed Back Design, Roll Drawer, Victorian, 21 In. 265.00
Mirror, Sheraton, Architectural, Reverse Painted, Gilt Split Turnings, 17 x 33 In. 305.00
Mirror, Sheraton, Tabernacle, Mahogany, Reverse Painted Top, 12 1/2 x 27 In. 125.00
Mirror, Split Baluster, New England, Painted & Gilded, c.1830, 27 3/4 In. 330.00
Mirror, Stickley Bros., 3 Sections, Double Hooks, No. 7308, 21 1/2 x 37 1/2 In. 850.00
Mirror, Surround Of 4 Mirrored Panels, Beveled, Holland, 26 x 23 In. 565.00
Mirror, Surround Of Spherules, Garlands, Candle Arms, Giltwood, 21 In. 4600.00
Mirror, Table, B & H, Gilt, Ornate, 12 x 8 1/2 In. 300.00
Mirror, Triangular Pine Frame, 1740s, 6 1/2 x 10 1/4 In. 605.00
Mirror, Urn Finial, Leafy Vines, Italian, Gesso & Giltwood, 22 x 10 In. 210.00
Mirror, Wooden, Rectangular, Arched Top, Art Nouveau, France, c.1900, 35 In. 1725.00
Mirror, Wrought Iron, Rectangular, Art Deco, France, c.1925, 35 1/4 x 29 1/4 In. 1610.00
Mirror & Coat Rack, Remember The Maine, 1893 .... 350.00
Ottoman, Slip Upholstered Seat, Carved Knees, Ball & Claw Feet 305.00
Ottoman, Tufted Shape, Trefoil Shape, Velvet Upholstered, 18 x 44 In. 1380.00
Parlor Set, Chippendale, Mahogany, 3 Piece 1700.00
Parlor Set, J. Hoffmann, U-Shaped Backs, Upholstered, Bentwood, c.1906, 3 Piece .. 5750.00
Parlor Set, Limbert, Ash, Caned, Rocker, Settee, Armchair, 3 Piece 4025.00
Parlor Set, Rococo, Rosewood, Out-Curved Arms, Serpentine Skirts, 7 Piece 7040.00
Parlor Set, Wicker, Dark Brown, Green Diamond Back, Spring Cushions, 5 Piece 600.00
Pedestal, American Empire, Mahogany, Marble Top, 1 Door, Shelf, 21 x 30 In. 715.00
Pedestal, E. Andre, Art Nouveau, Mahogany, c.1900, 52 In., Pair 4600.00
Pedestal, E. Andre, Triangular Top, 3 Arching Legs, 2 Tiers, c.1903, 63 1/2 In. 4025.00
Pedestal, Empire, Marble Top, 3 Columns, 3 Claw Feet, Mahogany, 15 x 35 In. 375.00
Pedestal, J. Gruber, Revolving, 3 Curved Buttresses, Mahogany, 1900, 4 1/2 Ft. 6900.00
Pedestal, Louis XVI Style, Rouge Royale Marble, Fluted, 43 In, Pair 4315.00
Pedestal, Painted Foliage, Parcel Gilt, Ebonized, c.1870, 43 In., Pair 5465.00
Pedestal, Pine, Brass, Square, 4 Cylindrical Columns, Austria, c.1900, 43 x 12 In. ... 460.00
Pedestal, Revolving, Lower Shelf, Mahogany, France, c.1900, 45 In. 5000.00
Pedestal, Twist Carved Support, Mahogany, Victorian 265.00
Pew, Church, Wooden, Original Paint, Virginia, 1890 .... 550.00
Pie Safe, 3 Punched Tin Panels, Double Doors, Tapered Legs, Walnut, 39 x 41 In. 990.00
Pie Safe, 6 Punched Tin Panels, Drawer, Walnut, 1900s 650.00
Pie Safe, 8 Tin Panels, Original Yellow Paint, Square Nails, 1 Drawer, 2 Doors 675.00
Pie Safe, 8 Tin Panels, Walnut, Ohio, Large 1450.00
Pie Safe, 12 Punched Tin Panels, Pinwheel Pattern, Virginia 2200.00
Pie Safe, 12 Tin Panels, Poplar, Refinished Dark Brown, 1 Drawer, 39 x 54 In. 385.00
Pie Safe, Federal, Twin Banks Of Paneled Doors, Pine, 63 1/2 In. 1095.00
Pie Safe, Mustard Paint, 2 Drawers Above 2 Blind Doors 500.00
Pie Safe, Nail Punched Sides & Doors, 5 Shelves, 1 Drawer, Pine 800.00
Pie Safe, Nantucket, Grain Painted, Made By Folger, Feb. '85, 55 x 31 x 22 In. 440.00
Pie Safe, Oak, Masonic Tins, 1870 .... 1600.00
Pie Safe, Poplar, Walnut, 2 Drawers Over Scalloped Doors, Mid-1800s 675.00
Pie Safe, Punched Tin Panels, 2 Doors, Maple, 41 x 56 x 17 1/2 In. 650.00
Pie Safe, Tins, Worn Apple Green Paint, 1860 .... 1795.00
Planter, Frank Lloyd Wright, Stepped Feet, Copper Paint, c.1955, 22 5/8 In. 1725.00
Podium, Renaissance Revival, Oak, Walnut, Columns, 35 x 38 x 33 In. 365.00
Rack, Baker's, Scrolled Design, Glass Shelves, Iron & Brass, 42 1/2 In. 305.00
Rack, Blanket, Oak, Late 19th Century, 32 x 35 In. 135.00

Furniture, Rocker, Adirondack,
Twig, Arms, Pair

◆◆◆◆◆◆◆◆◆◆◆◆◆◆◆◆◆◆◆◆◆◆
When buying a table, study the bottom. Look underneath the top and see if the legs are original, if the top seems to be in one piece, and if there are any unexpected screw or nail holes that indicate changes in the use of the wood.
◆◆◆◆◆◆◆◆◆◆◆◆◆◆◆◆◆◆◆◆◆◆

Rack, Magazine, Gustav Stickley, 4 Tiers, No. 45, c.1910, 45 x 19 x 12 In. 1875.00
Rack, Magazine, Hanging, Golden Oak, Scroll Cut Sides, 30 x 15 x 8 In. 145.00
Rack, Magazine, Oak, Open Shelves, Michigan Chair Co., c.1910 .... 475.00
Rack, Magazine, V Shape, Mahogany, 21 x 18 x 13 1/2 In. 50.00
Rack, Music, Gustav Stickley, Oak, No. 670, c.1912, 39 1/4 x 22 x 15 In. 1980.00
Rack, Plate, Gustav Stickley, Mission Oak, c.1901 .... 5380.00
Rack, Plate, Pine, Mahogany Finish, 3 Tiers, Wall Mount, Pierced Cornice, 53 In. 585.00
Rack, Towel, Mahogany, Folding, 2 Piece, 22 1/4 x 32 1/4 In. 220.00
Recamier, Anglo-Indian, Regency, Rosewood, Scroll Ends, c.1825, 96 In. 3300.00
Recamier, Child's, c.1870 .... 2050.00
Recamier, Louis XV Style, Walnut, 19th Century 2500.00
Recamier, Out-Scrolled Arms, Mahogany, c.1825, 74 In., Pair 6045.00
Recamier, Regency, Giltwood, Silk Damask Upholstered, Pair 3850.00
Rocker, Adirondack, Twig, Arms, Pair... *Illus* 825.00
Rocker, Antonio Volpe, Continuous Oval Legs, Widening, Arms, c.1922 .... 4400.00
Rocker, Arts & Crafts, Spindle Back, Open Arms, Cushion Seat, 33 x 26 In. 220.00
Rocker, Bentwood, Arched U-Shaped Crests, 7 Uprights, Upholstered Seat 1035.00
Rocker, Boston, Cane Seat, Stenciled, Black Paint 260.00
Rocker, Carved Fruit Crest, Mahogany, Victorian, 37 In. 250.00
Rocker, Child's, Adirondack, Blue Paint, Silver, Red & Green Daubs, Arms, 20 In. ... 95.00
Rocker, Child's, Bentwood, Woven Seat & Back 125.00
Rocker, Child's, Caned Back & Seat, Victorian 185.00
Rocker, Child's, Ladder Back, Rush Seat, Red Paint, Late 19th Century 20.00
Rocker, Child's, Limbert, 5 Back Slats, Drop-In Seat, No. 1674, 24 1/2 In. 250.00
Rocker, Child's, Red Paint, Black Graining, 19th Century, 18 1/2 In. 185.00
Rocker, Child's, Shaker, Shawl Bar, No. 0, Arms 7500.00
Rocker, Cottage, Upholstered Seat & Back 200.00
Rocker, Eames, Eiffel Tower, Plastic, Wire, Herman Miller Co., Early 1950s 460.00
Rocker, Eames, Fiberglass Shell Seat, Steel Rod Base, Birch Runners, 1950 .... 470.00
Rocker, Eames, Molded Fiberglass Shell, Leather Cover, Ash Runners 185.00
Rocker, Eastlake, Platform, Walnut, Upholstered 200.00
Rocker, Federal, Comb Back, Yellow Repaint, Stenciled 230.00
Rocker, Federal, Platform, Leather Back Inset & Seat 750.00
Rocker, Greene & Greene, Flared Ladder Back, Carved Base & Apron, c.1907 .... 4830.00
Rocker, Gustav Stickley, Arms, Oak 1650.00
Rocker, Gustav Stickley, No. 303, Oak, Cane Seat Rail, c.1907, 33 In. 220.00
Rocker, Gustav Stickley, No. 311, V-Back, Arms, Red Decal, c.1903, 35 1/4 In. 605.00
Rocker, Gustav Stickley, No. 373, Oak, Spindle, Red Decal, 41 x 19 In. 880.00
Rocker, Gustav Stickley, No. 2597, V-Back, Leather Upholstered, Red Decal 715.00
Rocker, Gustav Stickley, No. 2617A, Open Arm, Rush Seat, 32 1/2 x 25 x 27 In. 440.00
Rocker, Harden Co., 5 Vertical Back Slats, 4 Under Each Arm, Spring Seat, 36 In. 450.00
Rocker, Harden Co., Oak, 3 Slats Under Arm, Paper Label, 38 x 28 In. 330.00
Rocker, Harden Co., Oak, Arms, 20th Century 165.00

Rocker, Hickory, Taped Seat & Back, Paddle Arms 35.00
Rocker, Iron, Leather, Victorian, Mid-19th Century 1650.00
Rocker, Ladder Back, 3 Slats, Splint Seat, Turned Arm Posts, 39 In. 245.00
Rocker, Ladder Back, 3 Slats, Turned Finials, Splint Seat, 38 In. 170.00
Rocker, Ladder Back, 4 Arched Slats, Woven Seat, Maple, Arms 250.00
Rocker, Ladder Back, Cloth Seat, Maple, Arms, 43 1/2 In. 105.00
Rocker, Ladder Back, Sausage Turnings, c.1780 .... 600.00
Rocker, Lifetime, High Back, 5-Slat Back, 4 Slats Under Arms, No. 675, 40 In. 600.00
Rocker, Limbert, Ladder Back, Open Arms, Drop-In Spring Cushion 150.00
Rocker, Lincoln, Pressed Back, Floral, Cane Seat 90.00
Rocker, Musical, Cowboy, Wooden 95.00
Rocker, Nursing, Stenciled, Pennsylvania, c.1835 .... 295.00
Rocker, Oak, Leather Upholstered, Wide Straight Arms 195.00
Rocker, Parlor, Oak, Carved, c.1900 .... 375.00
Rocker, Platform, Oak, Spiral & Reed Supports, Victorian, 39 x 26 In. 275.00
Rocker, Platform, Spindle Design, Upholstered Back & Seat, Walnut 70.00
Rocker, Provincial, Rush Seat, Georgian Oak 315.00
Rocker, Sewing, Cane Seat 40.00
Rocker, Sewing, Floral On Crest, White Striping, Brown Paint, 35 1/2 In. 95.00
Rocker, Sewing, Gustav Stickley, H Back, No. 307, 36 x 14 x 24 1/2 In. 195.00
Rocker, Sewing, Gustav Stickley, High Back, Spindles, No. 373, 39 In. 770.00
Rocker, Sewing, Gustav Stickley, No. 06, 33 x 18 x 25 In. 250.00
Rocker, Shaker, Armless, 1830s, 40 1/2 In. 440.00
Rocker, Shaker, Armless, Canterbury, Maple, 33 1/2 In. 330.00
Rocker, Shaker, Cylindrical Stiles, Acorn Finials, Woven Seat, 28 1/2 In. 345.00
Rocker, Shaker, Ladder Back, 5 Slats, Old Red Paint Traces, Arms, Pair 350.00
Rocker, Shaker, Ladder Back, 6 Arched Slats, Arms, 41 3/4 In. 715.00
Rocker, Shaker, Mt. Lebanon, Bird's-Eye Maple 9500.00
Rocker, Shaker, Mt. Lebanon, Shawl Back, Maple, Tape Seat, No. 7, Refinished 415.00
Rocker, Shaker, Mt. Lebanon, Tape Seat, No. 7, Arms, c.1870 .... 660.00
Rocker, Shaker, New Lebanon, Maple 4950.00
Rocker, Shaker, Slat Back, Enfield, Red Stain, Maple, 39 1/2 In. 3575.00
Rocker, Shaker, Spindle Back & Arms 1200.00
Rocker, Spindle Back, Brown Paint, Orange Striping, Plank Seat 45.00
Rocker, Spindle Back, Farm Style, Oak 75.00
Rocker, Spindle Back, Mule Ears, Oak 60.00

Furniture, Screen, 4-Panel, Burma, Teak,
Carved, 20th Century

◆◆◆◆◆◆◆◆◆◆◆◆◆◆◆◆◆◆◆◆◆◆◆◆◆

Look at the pegs on old furniture when you can. Old pegs are usually straight and sometimes have a small notch at the top to let excess glue escape. Modern machine-made pegs usually have spiral grooves.

◆◆◆◆◆◆◆◆◆◆◆◆◆◆◆◆◆◆◆◆◆◆◆◆◆

Rocker, Steer Horn, Woman's, Arms 1800.00
Rocker, Wicker, Red, Upholstered Spring Seat 40.00
Rocker, Windsor, Bamboo, Shaped Seat, Scrolled Arms, 40 1/2 In. 220.00
Rocker, Windsor, Birdcage, Arms 895.00
Rocker, Windsor, Comb Back, Bamboo, Worn Black Paint, Gold Striping, Arms 495.00
Rocker, Windsor, Comb Back, Rod Back, Arms, Painted 165.00
Rocker, Windsor, Comb Back, Step Down Rails, Arrow-Back Splats, 14-In. Seat 275.00
Rocker, Windsor, Gold Stenciling, Old Green Paint, Arms 435.00
Rocker, Windsor, John Saxton, Double Comb Back 1700.00
Rocker, Writing Arm, Old Green Paint 225.00
Safe, Parlor, Egyptian Revival, Sphinx Heads At Knees, Cast Iron, 1880s 7500.00
Screen, 2-Panel, Floral, Oriental, Worn Red & Black Lacquer, 20 x 39 In. 125.00
Screen, 2-Panel, Geese & Lotus, On Paper, c.1900, 66 x 50 In. 220.00
Screen, 2-Panel, Young Woman Getting Dressed, Green Ground, Canvas 1950.00
Screen, 3-Panel, Arched, Paint Over Silver Leaf, Wooden, 84 x 52 In. 3910.00
Screen, 3-Panel, Charles & Louise Keeler, Mystical Figures, Redwood, 6 x 6 Ft. 3165.00
Screen, 3-Panel, China, Hand Painted Wallpaper, Giltwood Border, 76 x 78 In. 865.00
Screen, 3-Panel, Dressing, Oak, Art Nouveau, Inlaid 400.00
Screen, 3-Panel, F. Barbedienne, Bronze Panels, Walnut, Foundry, c.1910 .... 3900.00
Screen, 3-Panel, Folding, Painted, Landscape, River & Village, 68 In. 320.00
Screen, 3-Panel, Jean-Michel Frank, Straw Marquetry, 59 3/8 In. 9200.00
Screen, 3-Panel, Joined Spindles, Acorn Finials, Mahogany, 64 In. 4600.00
Screen, 3-Panel, Leather, Polychrome Painted Putti & Flowers, 71 x 57 .... 935.00
Screen, 3-Panel, Pleated Fabric Inserts, Fruitwood, Victorian, 54 x 24 In. 230.00
Screen, 3-Panel, Pyrographic & Polychrome Poppies, 65 3/4 x 48 1/2 In. 770.00
Screen, 3-Panel, Wallpaper Covered, Country Estate Garden Scene, 63 x 21 In. 1760.00
Screen, 4 Panel, China, Carved, Red, Gold Highlighting 840.00
Screen, 4-Panel, Atomic Chain, All Wooden, 20th Century 900.00
Screen, 4-Panel, Birds In Floral Landscape, 48 x 11 In. 80.00
Screen, 4-Panel, Burma, Teak, Carved, 20th Century .... *Illus* 8050.00
Screen, 4-Panel, China, Inlaid Hardstone, Figures, Pavilions, 19th Century, 72 In. 825.00
Screen, 4-Panel, China, Ivory, Children, Courtyard, Lacquer, 19th Century, 72 In. 880.00
Screen, 4-Panel, China, Lacquer, Carved, Flowers, Beetles, People, 19th Century 2860.00
Screen, 4-Panel, China, Lacquer, Landscape With Figures, Wooden Frame, 35 In. 475.00
Screen, 4-Panel, Chinese-Style, Paper, Flowers, Birds, Insects, 90 x 72 In. 2530.00
Screen, 4-Panel, Ferguson Co., Aesthetic Floral, Beige Ground, 67 1/2 x 79 In. 165.00
Screen, 4-Panel, Floral Fabric, Reeded Frame, Victorian, England, 73 In. 1760.00
Screen, 4-Panel, Flowers & Fruit, Painted & Gilt Leather, 68 In. 3450.00
Screen, 4-Panel, Fornasetti, Trompe L'oeil Transfer, Landscape, 72 In. 3850.00
Screen, 4-Panel, Fornesetti, Trompe L'oeil Butterflies, House Of Cards 3850.00
Screen, 4-Panel, Japan, Figural & Floral, Lacquer, Mother-Of-Pearl, 68 In. 770.00
Screen, 4-Panel, Japan, Flowering Sakura, Flowers, Late 19th Century, 60 In. 440.00
Screen, 4-Panel, Korea, Court & Battle Scenes, 72 1/2 x 86 In. 2200.00
Screen, 6-Panel, China, Lacquer, Inlaid Ivory & Hardstone, Deities, 73 x 96 In. 605.00
Screen, 6-Panel, Japan, Lake Landscape, 18th Century, 61 x 24 In. 2070.00
Screen, 6-Panel, Korea, Landscapes, Ink & Color On Paper, 65 1/2 x 114 In. 1100.00
Screen, 6-Panel, Landscape Within Greek Key Border, 78 In. 6900.00
Screen, 8-Panel, China, Red Lacquer, Gilt, Birds, Flowers, 86 x 128 In. 660.00
Screen, 8-Panel, Soldiers & Huntsmen, Canvas, 1830s, 62 In. 3738.00
Screen, 10-Panel, Korea, Landscapes, Ink & Color On Silk, 1800s, 70 x 165 In. 1100.00
Screen, 10-Panel, Korea, Sages, Ink & Color On Cotton, 1800s, 47 x 135 In. 3300.00
Screen, 12-Panel, China, Figures, Pagodas, Carved & Painted, 90 x 14 In. 770.00
Screen, 12-Panel, China, Tete De Negre Coromandel, Landscape, 114 In. 8050.00
Screen, Table, Bigelow Kennard White Rabbit, Pink Ears 425.00
Screen, Tambour, A. Mack, Flexible Slats, Rolled For Storage, 69 In. 1610.00
Seat, Theater, Leather Covered, Cast Iron, Walnut, 1930s 125.00
Secretaire a Abattant, Biedermeier, Black Lacquer, 2 Base Doors 8800.00
Secretary, Biedermeier, Fall Front, Center Door, Drawers, Birch, 56 In. 4600.00
Secretary, C. Stetson, Sheraton, Mahogany, 3 Cock-Beaded Drawers, 61 x 41 In. 3410.00
Secretary, Cherry, 4 Bird's-Eye Maple Drawer Fronts, Ohio, Late 1800s 2640.00
Secretary, Chippendale, Butler's Lower, Oak, Brass Bail Pulls, England 8800.00
Secretary, Chippendale, Cherry, 18th Century 5170.00
Secretary, Cylinder, Maiden Crest, Burl Walnut, 108 In. 8800.00

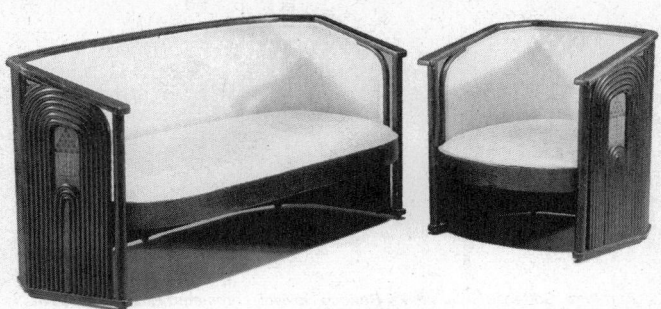

Furniture, Settee, Josef Hoffmann, Art Deco, Bentwood, Chair, 1907, 2 Piece

Secretary, Cylinder, Pinwheel Chip Carved, Walnut, Victorian 3750.00
Secretary, Fall Front, Superior Furniture, Lowell, Mich., Mahogany 375.00
Secretary, Fall Front, Walnut, 1 Drawer Over 2 Doors, Burl Crest, Spindles 1900.00
Secretary, Federal, Mahogany & Veneer, New England, c.1820, 63 x 38 1/2 In. 715.00
Secretary, George III, Mahogany, Blind Door Over Slant Front, Fitted, c.1780 .... 2910.00
Secretary, George III, Mahogany, Glazed Doors, 5 Drawers, 78 x 51 x 19 In. 1650.00
Secretary, Hepplewhite, Inlaid Walnut, Inlaid Doors & Drawers, c.1810, 82 In. 3000.00
Secretary, L. & J.G. Stickley, 12-Panel Top, Copper Hardware, No. 662 .... 4500.00
Secretary, Limbert, Fall Front, Oak, Caned Sides, No. 514, 52 x 27 In. 1150.00
Secretary, Louis XV, Fall Front, Lower Doors, Marquetry, 56 In. 4600.00
Secretary, Spoon Rack On Top Shelf, Butternut & Pine, c.1860 .... 4800.00
Secretary, Tambour, Hepplewhite, Mahogany, Satinwood, 47 x 35 In, 2 Piece 2970.00
Secretary-Bookcase, 4 Glazed Doors, Pullout Surface, Mahogany, 78 In. 1265.00
Secretary-Bookcase, Classical, Mahogany, Ball Feet, 78 In. 5775.00
Secretary-Bookcase, Classical, Mahogany, c.1840, 60 x 47 1/2 x 19 1/2 In. 715.00
Secretary-Bookcase, Double, Beveled Mirror, Oak, 65 1/2 x 55 In. 1500.00
Secretary-Bookcase, Edwardian, Mahogany, Inlay, 88 1/2 x 42 In. 1870.00
Secretary-Bookcase, George III, Mahogany, Glazed Doors, c.1775, 86 In. 9200.00
Secretary-Bookcase, George III, Mahogany, Mullioned Doors, 1770s, 84 In. 5750.00
Secretary-Bookcase, Gothic, c.1840 .... 6500.00
Secretary-Bookcase, Regency, Mahogany, Inlaid, Ormolu Mounted, 105 In. 7975.00
Secretary-Bookcase, Slant Front, 2 Wirework Doors, Oak, 87 x 65 In. 3450.00
Secretary-Bookcase, Turned Columns, Inlaid Mahogany, Brasses, c.1880 .... 3950.00
Secretary-Cupboard, Bamboo Molding, Child's, Victorian, 47 x 23 In. 750.00
Server, Berkey & Gay, Bowfront, Mahogany, Inlaid 585.00
Server, Frieze Drawer Over 3 Drawers In Doors, Mahogany, 1920s, 71 In. 690.00
Server, Hepplewhite, Mahogany, Veneered, 2 Doors, Wine Drawers, 43 x 34 In. 1650.00
Server, Mahogany Veneer, Birch, Rope Legs, Vermont, Country 1400.00
Server, Marble Top, Frieze Drawer, 2 Side Drawers, Rosewood, 93 In. 2070.00
Server, Oak, Beveled Glass, Early 19th Century, 60 In. 2000.00
Server, Stickley Bros., Backsplash, Stretcher Shelf, No. 92, 36 x 36 In. 825.00
Settee, 3-Section Back, Mother-Of-Pearl Portrait Crest, Rosewood, c.1880 .... 1095.00
Settee, 3 Splats, Fruit Design Back, Arms 2200.00
Settee, American Empire, Carved Mahogany, Floral Upholstered 4600.00
Settee, Arched Back, Shaped Seat, Tapered Legs, Spade Footed, Mahogany, 53 In. .. 500.00
Settee, Art Deco, Josef Hoffmann, Bentwood, Chair, 1907, 2 Piece .... *Illus* 11500.00
Settee, Biedermeier, Upholstered Bowed Back, Fruitwood, c.1820, 54 In. 935.00
Settee, Brighton Pavilion, Bamboo, Chinese Export, 73 In. 6325.00
Settee, Burden, Rod Back, Maple, Ash & Pine, 1830s, 77 In. 3740.00
Settee, Carved Antiqued Ivory & Green, Silk Upholstered, France, 51 In. 360.00
Settee, Carved Grapes & Leaves, Needlepoint, Walnut, Victorian, 38 x 54 In. 440.00
Settee, Chair Back, French Provincial, Fruitwood, Rush Seat, Arms, 19th Century 770.00
Settee, Chippendale, Camelback, 4 Ball & Claw Front Feet 1175.00

Furniture, Settee, J. & J. Meeks, Rococo Revival, Laminated Rosewood, 66 In.

Settee, Chippendale, Camelback, Fluted Square Legs, Mahogany, 78 In. 1320.00
Settee, Chippendale, Camelback, Scrolled Arms, Marlborough Legs, 83 In. 1610.00
Settee, Eastlake, Moire Cut Velvet Upholstered, 1880-1890 .... 1400.00
Settee, Eastlake, Walnut, Brocade Upholstered 600.00
Settee, Edwardian, Triple Chair Back, Painted Satinwood, c.1900, 60 In. 4025.00
Settee, Empire, Out-Curved Arms, Ogee Molded Seat Rail, Mahogany, 92 In. 300.00
Settee, Federal, Moire Trim, Welting, Cherry, 82 In. 3575.00
Settee, George II, Walnut, Upholstered, Padded Arms, Carved Legs, 1800s, 66 In. ... 6610.00
Settee, George III Style, Camelback, Rolled Arms, 1880s, 75 In. 500.00
Settee, George III Style, Double Chair Back, Carved Walnut, Leather, 47 In. 2640.00
Settee, George III Style, Mahogany, Camelback, Square Molded Legs, 35 x 80 In. ... 605.00
Settee, George III, Mahogany, Camelback, Out-Scrolled Arms, 80 In. 2300.00
Settee, George III, Needlepoint Upholstered, Walnut, 55 In. 5000.00
Settee, George III, Serpentine Cresting, Parcel Gilt & Painted, 62 In. 8625.00
Settee, Georgian, Scrolled, Cabriole Legs, Silk Damask, Mahogany, 36 x 47 In. 420.00
Settee, Georgian, Shaped Back & Seat, Scrolled Arms, Mahogany, 78 In. 1540.00
Settee, Gustav Stickley, 1 Horizontal Slat, Pillow, No. 215, Child's, 38 In. 850.00
Settee, Half-Spindle, Bird, Butterfly & Flower Design, Green, c.1820, 71 In. 2800.00
Settee, Hepplewhite, Reeded Crest, Leaf Carved Panel, Mahogany, 40 In. 2415.00
Settee, J. & J. Meeks, Rococo Revival, Laminated Rosewood, 66 In. .... *Illus* 5000.00
Settee, Josef Hoffmann, Bentwood, 3 Upholstered Panels, Serpentine, 45 In. 1725.00
Settee, Josef Hoffmann, Bentwood, Suede Upholstered, c.1910, 45 In. 1600.00
Settee, Lift Seat, High Back, Mahogany, Carved Griffin Arms, 1880s, 72 In. 2200.00
Settee, Limbert, 3 Slats Under Each Arm, Upholstered Back, No. 673-9, 76 In. 1200.00
Settee, Louis XIV Style, Serpentine Seat, Upholstered, Rolled Arms, 82 In. 605.00
Settee, Louis XV Style, Carved Fruitwood, 40 In. 525.00
Settee, Majorelle, Carved Clematis Vines, Velvet Upholstered, 51 1/2 In. 3450.00
Settee, Original Paint, Birds On Crest Rail, Pennsylvania, Arms 3200.00
Settee, Red & Black Grained, Converts To Bed, Arrow-Back, Arms 1430.00
Settee, Regency, 4-Chair Back, Ebonized Beechwood, Painted, 1800s, 75 In. 3450.00
Settee, Regency, Rosewood, Padded Back, Ring-Turned Legs, 82 In. 8625.00
Settee, Renaissance Revival, Maple, Upholstered, Parcel Gilt, Armchair, 2 Piece 6050.00
Settee, Rocking, Gold Outlined Splats, Grain Painted, 1830, 50 1/2 In. 9900.00
Settee, Rococo Revival, Giltwood, Upholstered Back & Seat, Arms, 49 x 57 In. 770.00
Settee, Rolled Crest, Cornucopia Arm Supports, Mahogany, c.1830, 76 In. 1110.00
Settee, Rose Carved Crest, Upholstered Back & Seat, Giltwood, 58 In. 935.00
Settee, Sheraton Style, Mahogany, Painted Satinwood, Back Rail, 48 In. 1760.00
Settee, Triple Back, Carved & Ebonized Rosewood, Victorian, American, c.1850 ..... 935.00
Settee, Triple Curved Back, Curved Back Legs, Rosewood, Victorian, 72 In. 550.00
Settee, Wicker, 2 Large Flowers on Back, White Paint, Arms 1200.00
Settee, Windsor, Bamboo Turned, 19 Spindles, New England, Early 1800s, 64 In. 2150.00
Settle, Angel Wing, Fruit & Foliage Design On Crest, S-Scroll Seat, 81 In, ... 1375.00
Settle, Arrow-Back, Poplar, Plank Seat, Country, Refinished, 72 In. 330.00
Settle, Brown Paint, Pine, Canada, c.1800, 66 1/2 In. 880.00
Settle, Charles Stickely, Even Arm, 22-Slat Back, Oak, Chair, 2 Piece 5000.00
Settle, George III, Elm, Molded Cornice, Doors, c.1800, 77 x 70 x 26 In. 4600.00

Settle, Green Repaint, Striping, Crest, Late 18th Century, 36 In. 395.00
Settle, Gustav Stickley, 8 Slats, No. 208, c.1912 .... 9200.00
Settle, Gustav Stickley, Bungalow, No. 173 .... 7000.00
Settle, Gustav Stickley, Crib, Slats At Back & Sides, No. 208, 76 In. 6050.00
Settle, Gustav Stickley, Crib, Vertical Slats Under Side Rails, No. 225, Decal 4750.00
Settle, Gustav Stickley, Even Arm, No. 208 .... 8000.00
Settle, Gustav Stickley, Oak, No. 221, c.1905, 39 x 75 1/2 x 28 3/4 In. 3850.00
Settle, Gustav Stickley, Willow, No. 70 .... 4125.00
Settle, Hinged Seat, Pine, Painted, New England, 19th Century, 55 x 54 In. 3025.00
Settle, L. & J.G. Stickley, 16 Slats, Tapered Posts, Leatherette, No. 221 .... 7500.00
Settle, Lattice Back, Mahogany, Spiral Spreader, Claw & Ball Feet 1500.00
Settle, Oak, Sage Green Wash, Carved Animals, Gargoyle Arms, c.1723, 87 In. 1650.00
Settle, Pine, Lift Seat, Paneling, Bracket Feet 1100.00
Settle, Pine, Maple & Oak, Lift Seat, Wide Arms, c.1760 .... 1875.00
Settle, Pine, Paneled, Orange, Gold & Green Paint, 18th Century, 44 x 52 In. 1870.00
Settle, Pine, Worn Finish, Shaped Arms, Country, 60 x 16 x 55 In. 2420.00
Settle, Rosemaling, 3-Chair Back, Rush Seat, Arms, 1830 .... 1200.00
Settle, Stickley Bros., 12 Slats, Open Arms, Cushion, No. 3504, 49 1/4 In. 750.00
Settle, Stickley Bros., Oak, Leather, Slatted Arms, No. 119, 77 In. 1540.00
Settle, Stickley Bros., Oak, No. 3719, 35 x 84 x 31 1/2 In. 2420.00
Settle, Stickley Bros., Vertical Slats, No. 216, 36 x 72 x 26 In. 3190.00
Shelf, 3 Shelves, Green Paint, 32 x 25 1/4 In. 165.00
Shelf, 6 Graduated Shelves, Turned Posts, Cherry, 55 x 36 In. 935.00
Shelf, Free Standing, Red Wash, 2 Plate Rails, Cutout Base 600.00
Shelf, Galle, Inlaid Forest Scene, Mahogany & Fruitwood, c.1900, 26 In. 5750.00
Shelf, Hanging, 3 Graduated Shelves, Pine, Old Paint, Country, 20 x 7 x 22 In. 150.00
Shelf, Hanging, Chestnut & Poplar, Whale End, 28 x 7 1/4 x 39 In. 915.00
Shelf, Hanging, Rococo, 4 Shelves, Pine, Parcel Gilt, Swan's Crest, 48 x 52 In.. .... 4025.00
Shelf, Hanging, Walnut, Masonic Cutouts, 16 1/2 In. 40.00
Shelf, Whatnot, Hanging, Folding, Pierced Sides 50.00
Sideboard, American Classical, Mahogany, Inlaid Flame Grain Veneer, 78 In. 990.00
Sideboard, Beveled Central Mirror, Oval Side Mirrors 2530.00
Sideboard, Biedermeier, Cupboard Doors, 3 Drawers, Shelves, Walnut, 6 1/2 Ft. 6325.00
Sideboard, Bowed Top, Cupboard Doors, Fan Inlay, Mahogany, 36 x 42 In. 5720.00
Sideboard, Bowfront, String & Bead Inlay, Mahogany, Victorian, 48 x 23 In. 2900.00
Sideboard, Burl Walnut, Marble Top, Carved, 88 In., 2 Piece 5500.00
Sideboard, Classical, Mahogany & Birch Veneer, Carved, c.1825, 50 x 46 In. 1320.00
Sideboard, Ellis & G. Stickley, Center Drawer, Short Side Drawers, c.1903 .... 6900.00
Sideboard, Empire, Cherry, Mahogany, 3 Doors, 3 Drawers, 60 1/2 x 46 In. 550.00
Sideboard, Empire, Cherry, Mahogany, Doors, Drawers, 70 x 25 x 43 In. 935.00
Sideboard, Empire, Chestnut, Chamfered Door Fronts, 1830-1840 .... 2395.00
Sideboard, English Traditional, Mahogany, Ring Brasses, 20th Century, 72 In. 330.00
Sideboard, Federal, 5 Drawers, Convex Doors, Mahogany, c.1800, 72 In. 8050.00
Sideboard, Federal, Flame Veneer, Turned & Rope-Carved Feet 1760.00
Sideboard, Federal, Line Inlay, Bottle Drawer, Mahogany, c.1795, 38 1/4 In. 4600.00
Sideboard, Federal, Mahogany, Wavy Birch, Carved, c.1815, 39 x 69 In. 3025.00
Sideboard, George I, 2 Drawers, 2 Cabinet Doors, Walnut, 35 x 66 x 23 In. 770.00
Sideboard, George III, 3 Center Drawers, Spade Feet, Mahogany, 67 1/2 In. 4400.00
Sideboard, George III, Arched Recess, Drawers, Inlaid Mahogany, 50 In. 4025.00
Sideboard, George III, Bowed Top, 3 Drawers, Inlaid Mahogany, 30 x 43 In. 2640.00
Sideboard, George III, Bowfront, Mahogany, Inlaid Satinwood, 33 x 45 In. 3165.00
Sideboard, George III, Bowfront, Side Drawers, Mahogany, 1780s, 66 In. 8625.00
Sideboard, George III, Crossbanded Inlaid Mahogany, 36 x 71 In. 2420.00
Sideboard, George III, Demilune, 2 Drawers, Inlaid Mahogany, 32 x 44 In. 2530.00
Sideboard, George III, Mahogany, Serpentine, Square Legs, Scotland, c.1800 .... 2475.00
Sideboard, George III, Serpentine Top, 4 Drawers, Mahogany, 76 In. 4025.00
Sideboard, George III, Serpentine, Inlaid Mahogany, Square Legs, 1700s, 84 In. 7475.00
Sideboard, George IV, Mahogany, 3 Drawers Over 3 Doors, c.1810, 59 In. 1045.00
Sideboard, Grapes, Vines, Cellarette, Mahogany, Victorian, 85 1/2 In. 3150.00
Sideboard, Gustav Stickley, 2 Doors, 3 Drawers, Copper Hinges, No. 814, 55 In. 3300.00
Sideboard, Gustav Stickley, Oak, Arts & Crafts, 56 In. 1980.00
Sideboard, Hepplewhite, Kittinger, Demilune, Mahogany, 72 x 26 x 36 In. 315.00
Sideboard, Hepplewhite, Satinwood Line & Fan Inlay, Mahogany, 66 In. 3960.00

Furniture, Sofa, Federal, Mahogany, 19th Century, Upholstered, 76 In.

Sideboard, Hepplewhite, Serpentine, Mahogany Veneer, Fitted Center, 67 In. 7150.00
Sideboard, Lifetime, Mirrored, Iron Hardware, Decal Label, Oak, No. 5452, 54 In. 1210.00
Sideboard, Limbert, Drawers, Doors, No. 1453 3/4, 54 x 54 x 22 In. 1540.00
Sideboard, Mahogany, 4 Doors, 3 Drawers, Brass Gallery, 19th Century, 72 In. 440.00
Sideboard, Marble Top, 3 Drawers, Mythological Insets, c.1810, 43 1/2 In. 4315.00
Sideboard, Molded Gallery, 2 Drawers, 2-Door Cabinet, Pine, 61 x 23 In. 325.00
Sideboard, Oak, Paneled Doors, England, 72 x 21 1/2 x 45 In. 440.00
Sideboard, Rectory, Jacobean Style, Carved 3000.00
Sideboard, Regency, Mahogany, 2 Doors, 3 Center Drawers, England, 67 x 35 In. 330.00
Sideboard, Regency, Mahogany, Satinwood Crossbanding, c.1825, 37 x 84 In. 7475.00
Sideboard, Serpentine, Convex Drawer & Doors, Mahogany, 72 1/2 In. 6900.00
Sideboard, Sheraton, Bowfront, Maple, 5 Beaded & Banded Drawers 6500.00
Sideboard, Sheraton, Center Kneehole Tambour, England 6710.00
Sideboard, Stickley Bros., Oak, Hammered Brass, No. 8868, 44 x 54 x 22 In. 1210.00
Sideboard, William IV, Mahogany, c.1830, 70 x 50 x 22 In. 1320.00
Sitzmachine, J. & J. Kohn, Bent Beechwood & Cane, Adjustable, 1905 .... 8915.00
Sofa, American Empire, Mahogany Lyre Frame, Crewel Upholstered, 84 In. 660.00
Sofa, Angled Arms, Leather Upholstered, W.E. Drummond, Cherry, Pine 9200.00
Sofa, Biedermeier, Birch, Flame Veneer, Straight Back, Upholstered, 84 In. 1430.00
Sofa, Camelback, Rosewood, 1840s 500.00
Sofa, Carved Walnut, Crest, Reupholstered Velvet, Victorian, 65 In. 525.00
Sofa, Carved Walnut Frame, Mohair Upholstered, c.1920 .... 800.00
Sofa, Chinese Chippendale, Camelback, Mahogany, Oriental Tapestry, 96 In.. .... 2850.00
Sofa, Chippendale Style, Mahogany, England, 36 x 81 x 26 In. 2310.00
Sofa, Chippendale, Camelback, Mahogany Base, Floral Damask, 85 In. 855.00
Sofa, Chippendale, Rolled Arms, Serpentine Seat Rail, c.1780, 75 1/2 In. 7700.00
Sofa, Classical, Mahogany Veneer, Carved, New England, c.1835, 48 x 36 1/2 In. 1320.00
Sofa, Classical, Mahogany, Straight Back Rail, Scrolled Arms, American, 71 In. 880.00
Sofa, Depression Modern, Velvet Upholstered, Lacquered, Chair, 1930s, 2 Piece 4200.00
Sofa, Duncan Phyfe-Type Legs, Scroll Arms, Brass Paw Feet, Mahogany 2300.00
Sofa, Empire, Lyre Mahogany Frame, Silk Brocade Upholstered 2310.00
Sofa, Empire, Mahogany, Scrolled Arms, Carved Footed, Phila., 72 In. 2000.00
Sofa, Empire, Scrolled Arms, Upholstered Back & Seat, American, 77 In. 1540.00
Sofa, Federal, Carved Frame, Mahogany, c.1815, 77 In. 1870.00
Sofa, Federal, Mahogany, 19th Century, Upholstered, 76 In. .... *Illus* 12000.00
Sofa, Federal, Mahogany, Inlaid, Mass., c.1810, 35 x 71 x 24 In. 4125.00
Sofa, Federal, Thunderbolts & Ribbon Crest, Mahogany, c.1815, 78 In. 5750.00
Sofa, Finger Carved, Reupholstered, Victorian, Small 550.00
Sofa, Frame, American Empire, Mahogany, Lyre, Old Refinishing, 105 In. 715.00
Sofa, Georgian, Camelback, Red Leather, Button Down, Square Legs 990.00
Sofa, Grape Cluster Carved Crest, Upholstered, Victorian 1300.00
Sofa, John Belter, Laminated Meridienne, Rosalie With Grapes, Rosewood 5800.00
Sofa, Meeks, Stanton Hall Pattern 4125.00
Sofa, Oak, Leather, Brass Nailheads, Fitted Rectangular End Tables, 156 In. 6900.00
Sofa, Rococo, Triple Arch, Rosewood 1800.00
Sofa, Rococo, Triple Back, Carved Rosewood, Foliate Crests, c.1855, 47 In. 1210.00

Sofa, Rococo, Triple Shield, Rosewood, Cabriole Legs, American, c.1852, 69 In. 3740.00
Sofa, Rolled Crest, Scrolling Arms, Padded Back & Seat, Mahogany, 100 In. 3100.00
Sofa, Rosewood, Adam & Eve Top Crest, Cyma Curves, 94 In. 3575.00
Sofa, Sheraton Style, c.1940, 72 In. 650.00
Sofa, Slipper, Flame Grained Veneer, Mahogany 450.00
Sofa, Studio 65, Marilyn, Red Stretch Nylon, Gufram Of Italy, 81 x 33 x 35 In. 2100.00
Sofa, Texas Pine, Scrolling Arms, c.1860 .... 3430.00
Sofa, Triple Back, Serpentine Rails, Gros Point Upholstered, 83 In. 6600.00
Sofa, Victorian, Medallion Back, Carved, Walnut, 19th Century, 36 x 67 In. 715.00
Sofa Set, Heywood-Wakefield, Wicker, Rocker, Chair, 3 Piece 1000.00
Stall, Choir, Renaissance Style, Walnut, 54 In., Pair 1035.00
Stand, 1 Drawer, Tiger Maple 1100.00
Stand, 5 Graduated Tiers, Turned Spindles, Black Paint, 46 In. 195.00
Stand, Basin, Corner, Simulated Drawers, 1 Drawer, Mahogany Veneer, 33 In. 935.00
Stand, Basin, Paneled Door, Carrying Handles, Mahogany, c.1820, 37 In. 1840.00
Stand, Black, Lacquer, Red, Green & Yellow Floral, Octagonal, China, 25 1/4 In. 220.00
Stand, Cane, 3 Sections, Leather Strap Bound, British Royal Arms, 20 In. 230.00
Stand, Carved Teak, Dark Finish, Side Shelves, Indian, 15 x 21 x 28 In. 305.00
Stand, Cherry, 2 Dovetailed Drawers, 2-Board Top, Refinished, 18 x 23 x 29 In. 500.00
Stand, Cherry, 2 Dovetailed Drawers, Turned Legs, 28 x 18 x 20 In. 475.00
Stand, Cherry, Cock-Beaded Drawer, 29 In. 330.00

Furniture, Stand, Federal, 3 Drawers, Mahogany, c. 1820, 27 x 21 x 19 In.

Furniture, Stand, Hepplewhite, 1 Drawer, Cherry, c. 1870, 27 x 17 In.

Furniture, Table, Card, Federal, Cherry, Inlaid, New England, c. 1820, 29 In.

Furniture, Table, Card, Federal, Mahogany, Serpentine, 29 x 37 x 17 In.

Stand, China, Scalloped Inset, Marble Top, Hardwood, 24 In. 250.00
Stand, Chippendale, Octagonal Tilt Top, Mahogany, 1765, 29 1/4 In. 1725.00
Stand, Corner, 2 Tiers, 1 Drawer, Mahogany, 21 x 16 x 37 In. 250.00
Stand, Corner, 2 Tiers, 1 Lower Drawer, Mahogany, England, 37 1/2 In. 250.00
Stand, Crock, Oak, 3 Tiers, Green Repaint, Country, 39 x 19 x 43 3/4 In. 375.00
Stand, Dictionary, Baker, Regency Style, Faux Bamboo 300.00
Stand, Federal, 3 Drawers, Mahogany, c.1820, 27 x 21 x 19 In. .... *Illus* 1075.00
Stand, Federal, Figured, Maple, 1 Drawer, Conical Feet, Rectangular, 30 x 20 In. 1500.00
Stand, Federal, Tripod, Inlaid Cherry, c.1795, 28 In. 2300.00
Stand, Fern, Carved, Ebonized, Bird Supports, Victorian, 28 x 21 In. 150.00
Stand, Fern, Rope Twist Support, Bun Feet, Mahogany, Victorian, 35 x 16 In. 285.00
Stand, Folio, Trestle Supports, Rosewood & Walnut, Victorian, 44 In. 5175.00
Stand, Hardwood, Marble Top, Burma, 15 In. 165.00
Stand, Hepplewhite, 1 Drawer, Cherry, c.1870, 27 x 17 In. .... *Illus* 385.00
Stand, Hepplewhite, Birch, Red Traces, Spider Legs, Square Top, Country, 17 In. 305.00
Stand, Hickory, Fence With Fir Trees Around, Rustic, 1920s 550.00
Stand, Humidor, George III, Hinged Lid, Inlaid Mahogany, 18th Century, 26 In. 3175.00
Stand, Kettle, George II, Removable Dished Top, Mahogany, 22 1/2 In. 8050.00
Stand, Light, Federal, Cherry, New England, c.1810, 29 x 19 3/4 x 18 In. 330.00
Stand, Magazine, Cutout Handles, Arch Footed, 4 Tiers, 40 x 14 In. 440.00
Stand, Magazine, Gustav Stickley, Christmas, No. 79 .... 1500.00
Stand, Magazine, Gustav Stickley, Harvey Ellis, Arches At Bottom, No. 79 .... 2420.00
Stand, Magazine, L. & J.G. Stickley, 4 Shelves, No. 46, 41 3/4 In. 1610.00
Stand, Magazine, L. & J.G. Stickley, Oak, Medium Finish, No. 47, 42 x 26 In. 715.00
Stand, Magazine, Limbert, 4 Shelves, Toeboard, Slanted Sides, No. 304, 42 In. 990.00
Stand, Magazine, Stickley Bros., 4 Shelves, Slatted Sides, 35 1/2 In. 660.00
Stand, Magazine, Stickley Brothers, Oak, Gallery, 2 Shelves, No. 4600, 30 x 16 In. .. 575.00
Stand, Mahogany, Brassbound, Side Handles, c.1800, 28 1/2 In. 1955.00
Stand, Mahogany, Veneer, 2 Drawers, Drop Leaf, Rope Carved Legs 1155.00
Stand, Music, Galle, Marquetry Top, Bird, Fruitwood, c.1900, 30 3/4 In. 4025.00
Stand, Music, Triangular, Sheet Music Under Doors That Fold Down, Carved 1980.00
Stand, Night, Drawer, Lower Cupboard, Marble Top, Walnut & Burlwood 600.00
Stand, Night, Frank Lloyd Wright, 2 Doors, Greek Key Border, Pair 2860.00
Stand, Night, Mahogany, Marble Top, China 695.00
Stand, Night, Majorelle, Top Shelf, 1 Drawer, Open Bays, Mahogany, 43 In. 1320.00
Stand, Night, Sheraton, 2 Bird's-Eye Maple Drawer Fronts, Red Wash, Maine 1870.00
Stand, Octagonal Top & Column, Lamb's Tongue Stops, Maple, 24 In. 1210.00
Stand, Pine & Poplar, 1 Nailed Drawer, Refinished, Country, 20 1/2 x 21 x 29 In. 195.00
Stand, Plant, Gustav Stickley, 4 Post Legs, Inset Grueby Tile, 29 3/4 In. 6600.00
Stand, Plant, Gustav Stickley, Overhanging Top, Wide Apron, No. 660, Square 1200.00
Stand, Plant, L. & J.G. Stickley, Plain Frieze, Square, Square Legs, 28 x 15 In. 290.00
Stand, Plant, Light Green, Nova Scotia, c.1870 .... 850.00
Stand, Plant, Marble Shaft, Square Plant Holder, Brass Mounted, 44 In. 2185.00
Stand, Plant, Onyx Top, Brass Plated Steel & Brass, 29 3/4 In. 77.00
Stand, Plant, Stickley Bros., Oak, Square, Splayed Legs, No. 131, c.1910, 34 In. 825.00
Stand, Plant, Twig 30.00
Stand, Plant, Wire, 3 Tiers, Heart Designs, Birdcage Top, Victorian 400.00
Stand, Plant, Wrought Iron 195.00
Stand, Queen Anne, Tilt Top, Chip Carved Base, Mahogany, c.1775, 27 3/4 In. 2530.00
Stand, Reading, Regency, Candle Slides, Adjustable, Mahogany, 38 In. 1980.00
Stand, Saddlemaker's, For Making & Repairing Saddles, c.1900 .... 250.00
Stand, Sewing, Biedermeier, Fitted Interior, Pedestal 2750.00
Stand, Sewing, Eastlake, Needlepoint Lift Top 285.00
Stand, Sewing, Empire, Pedestal 260.00
Stand, Sewing, Heywood-Wakefield, Wicker, Label 150.00
Stand, Sewing, Hinged Octagonal Top, Satinwood, England, 28 In. 500.00
Stand, Sewing, Oak, 2 Drawers, Spiral Pillar Legs, Ball & Claw Feet 800.00
Stand, Shaker, Breadboard Ends, 1 Drawer 9350.00
Stand, Shaving, Georgian Style, Swing Mirror, Mahogany, 70 In. 745.00
Stand, Shaving, Inlaid Mahogany, Twist Carving, Marquetry, Holland, 63 In. 1980.00
Stand, Shaving, Pivoting Plate, Bird-Shaped Standards, Hardwood, 19 x 25 In. 230.00
Stand, Sheraton, Cherry, 1 Dovetailed Base Drawer, Dark Finish, 18 x 30 In. 140.00
Stand, Sheraton, Tilt Top, Mahogany, Pedestal, Tripod Spider, 1810, 29 x 22 In. 685.00

Stand, Shoeshine, Cast-Iron Footrest, Horse Pedestal, Pine, 20 In. 100.00
Stand, Smoking, Art Deco, Dragon Handle, Iron, Jadite Base, No Tray, 27 In. 45.00
Stand, Smoking, Arts & Crafts, Copper Lined, Carved Door & Trim, Oak, 25 In. 150.00
Stand, Smoking, Mission Oak, Label, Square, 9 1/2 In. 85.00
Stand, Table, Georgian, Scroll Frieze, Tapered Legs, Mahogany, 24 x 17 x 27 In. 450.00
Stand, Telephone, Gustav Stickley, Matching Stool, Paper Label, c.1912 .... 1375.00
Stand, Telephone, Stickley Brothers, 2 Tiers, Arched Rails, 32 x 14 x 14 In. 465.00
Stand, Thomas Hammond Jr., Cherry, c.1883, 27 x 17 In. 5500.00
Stand, Tiger Maple, 2 Drawers, Period Glass Knobs, Wis. 700.00
Stand, Tilt Dish Top, Tripod Base, Cherry, 1780s, 28 In. 935.00
Stand, Tilt Top, Cherry, Mahogany Finish, Urn Pedestal, Spider Leg, 28 x 16 In. 110.00
Stand, Tilt Top, Federal, Mahogany, Octagonal Top, 1790s, 28 x 15 In. 1150.00
Stand, Turned Pulls, Bird's-Eye Maple & Mahogany Veneer, 1830s, 31 In. 1430.00
Stand, Turtle Top, Walnut, Maple, Vermont, 1870s 950.00
Stand, Umbrella, Stickley Brothers, Oak, 6 Supports, Bentwood Rings, 27 x 11 In. ... 115.00
Stand, Walnut, 1 Drawer, Square Tapered Legs, 28 x 18 In. 215.00
Stand, Wig, George III, Mahogany, Pewter Insert, 31 x 13 1/2 In., Pair 935.00
Steps, Bed, Georgian Style, Mahogany, 3 Tiers, Gilt Tooled Leather, 27 1/2 In. 550.00
Steps, Bed, Needlepoint Covered, Mahogany, England, 16 In. 195.00
Stool, Bar, Jugendstil, Adjustable Top, Beechwood, Austria 45.00
Stool, Cricket, Windsor, Yellow Paint 125.00
Stool, Dressing, Dual, Mahogany, Carved Lions' Heads 4 Corners 225.00
Stool, George II, Over Upholstered Seat, Leaf Carved Legs, Walnut, 20 In. 1725.00
Stool, George II, Walnut, Drop-In Seat, Shaped Frieze, c.1750, 17 x 19 In. 4025.00
Stool, George III Style, Mahogany, Drop-In Seat, Cabriole Legs, Scroll Feet, Pair 3450.00
Stool, George III Style, Serpentine Shaped Seat, Carved Knees, Mahogany 825.00
Stool, George III, Floral Needlework Cover, Mahogany, c.1760, 20 In., Pair 8850.00
Stool, Gout, Straight Handles, Paw Feet, Victorian, Mahogany, 9 1/2 x 17 In. 110.00
Stool, Gout, Walnut, 13 x 25 x 17 In. 100.00
Stool, Isamu Noguchi, Rocking, Strut Supports, Birch & Chromed Steel, 1955 .... 9200.00
Stool, James I, Carved Arched Back, Stop-Fluted Pillars, Oak, c.1620 .... 3250.00
Stool, Joint, Charles II, Molded Top, Square Columnar Legs, Oak, 1680, 21 In. 2900.00
Stool, Joint, Commonwealth, Oak, Child's, c.1650, 13 1/2 In. 6800.00
Stool, Lion Supports, Center Rosette, Paw Feet, Painted, Parcel Gilt, 18 In. 9200.00
Stool, Louis XV Style, Giltwood, Serpentine Cushion Seat, Carved, 18 x 20 In. 475.00
Stool, Louis XVI, Upholstered Top, Giltwood, 1870s, 16 1/2 x 17 In., Pair 8625.00
Stool, Mahogany, Art Nouveau, Leather, c.1900, 22 x 23 x 15 In. 4600.00
Stool, Mahogany, Carved, Damask Seat, Continental, 18 In. 330.00
Stool, Mahogany, Turned Legs, Upholstered Top, Dark Finish, 17 x 17 x 20 In. 115.00
Stool, Milking, 3 Legs, 18th Century 145.00
Stool, Ogee Shape, Bootjack Legs, Yellow, Poplar, 3 3/4 x 8 3/4 In. 1725.00
Stool, Organ, Ball & Claw Footed 60.00
Stool, Piano, Louis XV Style, Carved Wood, 18 In. 1035.00
Stool, Piano, Maple, 4 Legs, Boston 1100.00
Stool, Piano, Regency, Rosewood, Inlaid Brass, Lyre Splat, 35 In. 1540.00
Stool, Piano, Rosewood, Scalloped Seat, Pedestal, American, c.1840 .... 500.00
Stool, Regency Style, Rail Flower Heads, Walnut & Parcel Gilt, 18 In., 4 Piece 5750.00
Stool, Robin's-Egg Blue Paint, Late 19th Century 135.00
Stool, Upholstered Needlepoint Seat, Carved Apron, Giltwood, England, 20 In. 2600.00
Stool, Venetian Baroque, Giltwood, 18th Century, 20 x 15 In. 3080.00
Stool, Vladimir Kagan, Triangular Vinyl Upholstered Seat, 1955 .... 805.00
Stool, William & Mary, Arched, Carved With Foliate Designs, Oak, c.1690 .... 3400.00
Swing, Porch, Limbert, Hanging, Slat Back & Seat, No. 42/7, 23 x 84 x 25 In. 1870.00
Table, 1 Drawer, Original Red, Pine, N.H., c.1790, 29 In. 990.00
Table, 2 Level, Mahogany, Chrome Legs, American, c.1930 .... 900.00
Table, 3 Tier Base, Walnut, Scroll Footed, Octagonal, 30 1/4 In. 350.00
Table, 12 Sides, Vase-Shaped Support, Scroll Footed, Mahogany, 27 3/4 In. 500.00
Table, Adam Style, Oval Top, Figural Medallion, Painted Satinwood, 28 In. 465.00
Table, Aesthetic, Ebonized, 1 Drawer 2750.00
Table, Alvar Aalto, 4 Curved Legs, Laminated Birch, Round, 1935, 17 3/4 In. 1150.00
Table, American Aesthetic, Octagon, Pierced Rim, Tassels, c.1885, 15 1/4 In. 825.00
Table, American Empire, Drop Leaf, Rope Carved Legs, Mahogany, 45 1/2 In. 500.00
Table, Art Moderne, Mirrored Top, Molded Legs, Shelf, Italy, c.1930, 23 x 29 In. 575.00

Table, Baker's, French Provincial, Marble Top, Carved Oak, 30 x 35 1/2 In. 1980.00
Table, Baker's, Marble Top, Wrought Iron Base, Brass Trim, c.1860, 48 In. 5200.00
Table, Banquet, Empire, Drop Leaf, Walnut, Swing Legs, 3 Part, 46 x 114 In. 1485.00
Table, Banquet, George III, Mahogany, D-Shaped Ends, 1800, 70 x 48 In. 1720.00
Table, Barcelona, Stainless Steel, Glass, Square Top, X-Base, 17 x 48 In. 2600.00
Table, Berkey & Gay, Marquetry Top, Carved Base, Walnut, Round, 32 In. 4500.00
Table, Bible, Federal, Hinged Top, Barber Pole String Inlay, c.1800, 29 3/4 In. 7475.00
Table, Biedemeier, Paneled Baluster Support, Fruitwood, 1870s, 32 x 35 In. 2300.00
Table, Breakfast, Carved Claw Footed, New Jersey History In Drawer 1550.00
Table, Breakfast, Classical, Mahogany, Drop Leaves, 1 Drawer, Acanthus, 46 In. 825.00
Table, Breakfast, Drop Leaf, 1 Drawer, Spiral Carved Columns, Mahogany, 49 In. 5750.00
Table, Breakfast, Federal, Drop Leaves, Drawers, Mahogany, c.1830, 41 1/2 In. 805.00
Table, Breakfast, George IV, Mahogany, Square Top, Quadruped Base, 1800 .... 715.00
Table, Breakfast, Georgian Style, Mahogany, Curved, Molded Edge, 54 3/4 In. 1100.00
Table, Breakfast, Queen Anne, Arched Skirt, Spanish Footed, Walnut, 32 In. 5175.00
Table, Breakfast, Regency, Inlaid Mahogany, Border, 29 x 68 In. 4025.00
Table, Breakfast, Regency, Mahogany & Calamander, Fluted Legs, 63 In. 1650.00
Table, Breakfast, Regency, Rosewood, Brass Inlaid, Paw Footed, 49 In. Diam. 8800.00
Table, Breakfast, Regency, Rosewood, Trefoil Base, Scroll Footed, 1825, 50 In. Diam. . 9200.00
Table, Breakfast, Tilt Top, Curved Legs, Mahogany 770.00
Table, Breakfast, Tilt Top, George III, Mahogany, c.1800, 28 x 58 In. 6900.00
Table, Breakfast, Victorian, Rosewood, Turned Stem, French Scroll Toes, c.1835 .... 1320.00
Table, Breakfast, William IV, Burl Wood, England, Round 4125.00
Table, Breakfast, William IV, Octagonal, Rosewood, c.1830, 54 In. 9200.00
Table, Butterfly, Birch, 18th Century, 44 x 49 1/2 In. 825.00
Table, Card, 1 Cock-Beaded Drawer, Fretwork Brackets, c.1760, 30 In. 7475.00
Table, Card, 5 Legs, Serpentine Front, Late 18th Century 5900.00
Table, Card, Chinese Chippendale, Mahogany 14300.00
Table, Card, Chippendale, Demilune, Beaded Edge Of Apron, 29 In. 2860.00
Table, Card, Classical, Mahogany, Carved, Massachusetts, c.1820, 36 x 18 In. 1045.00
Table, Card, Demilune, 1 Drawer, Mahogany 275.00
Table, Card, Federal, Beaded Edge, Reeded Legs, Mahogany, c.1810, 29 x 35 In. 880.00
Table, Card, Federal, Cherry, Double Inlay & Crossbanding, c.1790, 40 In. 3220.00
Table, Card, Federal, Cherry, Inlaid, New England, c.1820, 29 In. .... *Illus* 550.00
Table, Card, Federal, Cherry, Painted, Brass Pull, c.1790, 27 1/2 x 36 In. 2310.00
Table, Card, Federal, Inlaid Mahogany, 16-Section Fan Design, 29 x 36 x 18 In. 4125.00
Table, Card, Federal, Inlaid Mahogany, c.1810, 28 1/2 x 34 1/2 x 17 In. 1760.00
Table, Card, Federal, Mahogany Veneer, c.1800, 30 x 36 x 17 1/2 In. 1045.00
Table, Card, Federal, Mahogany, Hollow Front, Inlay, c.1805, 29 3/4 In. 3450.00
Table, Card, Federal, Mahogany, Lift Top, String Inlay, 1790-1810 .... 6000.00
Table, Card, Federal, Mahogany, Lyre Base, Carved Gilded Eagle 2600.00
Table, Card, Federal, Mahogany, Serpentine, 29 x 37 x 17 In. .... *Illus* 1540.00
Table, Card, Federal, Serpentine Sides, Elliptical, Curly Maple & Cherry, Pair 8050.00
Table, Card, Federal, Skirt Line Inlay, Mahogany Veneer, c.1800, 28 1/2 In. 880.00
Table, Card, Folding, For Mah-Jongg, Red, Chinoiserie, 5 Piece 500.00
Table, Card, Foliate Pedestal, Hairy Paw Legs, c.1830 .... 3800.00
Table, Card, Hepplewhite, Console, Walnut, 1 Drawer, 30 x 38 x 18 1/2 In. 1210.00
Table, Card, Hepplewhite, Demilune Top, Inlaid Mahogany, 28 1/4 In. 1000.00
Table, Card, Inlaid Mahogany, Satinwood & Tulipwood, c.1790, 30 In. 4025.00
Table, Card, Mahogany & Mahogany Veneer, Carved, c.1820, 29 x 36 In. 550.00
Table, Card, Mahogany, Satinwood Banding & Inlay 5450.00
Table, Card, Sheraton, Flame Birch, c.1820, 29 x 36 In. 3800.00
Table, Card, Sheraton, Mahogany, Bowed Sides & Front 1980.00
Table, Card, Sheraton, Mahogany, Philadelphia, c.1810 .... 2200.00
Table, Card, Sheraton, Mahogany, Shaped Front, Reeded Legs & Top, 36 x 18 In. 650.00
Table, Card, Sheraton, Mahogany, Shaped Front, Reeded Legs, 26 x 36 x 29 In. 550.00
Table, Card, Sheraton, Maple Veneer Over Mahogany, 1800-1815 .... 2200.00
Table, Card, Swing Legs, Inlaid, Curly Mahogany, 28 1/2 x 38 In. 715.00
Table, Card, Turned Baluster Pedestal, Mahogany, 19th Century 825.00
Table, Carlo Bugatti, Parchment Top, Copper Ends, Inlaid Wood, 46 In. 4370.00
Table, Carved, Pierced Foliage, Cabriole Legs, Burma, 19 In. 275.00
Table, Carved Teak, Pedestal, Revolving Top, Animals Legs, Round, India, 50 In. 440.00

◆◆◆◆◆◆◆◆◆◆◆◆◆◆◆◆◆◆◆◆

To remove white rings on wooden table tops use paste wax and 0000 steel wool. Rub with the grain. Buff with a wad of cheese cloth.

◆◆◆◆◆◆◆◆◆◆◆◆◆◆◆◆◆◆◆◆

Furniture, Table, Dining, Oak, Pedestal, 4 Leaves,
c.1915, 48 In. Diam.

Table, Center, Aluminum, Black & Green Marble Top, 1930, 29 x 29 In.	4600.00
Table, Center, France, Pickled Oak, Marble, Cabriole Legs, c.1900, 48 x 28 In.	1430.00
Table, Center, George III, Mahogany, Molded Edge, 1 Drawer, c.1780, 31 x 34 In.	715.00
Table, Center, Louis XVI, Kingwood, Marquetry, Brass Sabots, 29 x 24 1/2 In.	1870.00
Table, Center, Modified Mission, Oak, Hidden Pullout Desk	570.00
Table, Center, Napoleon III, Ormolu, Marquetry, Fluted Legs, 55 x 31 x 31 In.	4675.00
Table, Center, Rococo, Carved Rosewood, Marble Top, American, c.1855, 45 In.	3300.00
Table, Center, Rococo, Rosewood, Turtle-Shaped Marble Top, c.1855, 47 In.	4235.00
Table, Center, Rosewood, Plinth Base, Oval, Marble Top, Victorian, 38 In.	1430.00
Table, Center, Walnut, Turtle-Shaped Marble Top, Gothic Pedestal, 45 In.	4125.00
Table, Cherry, Shelf, Ball & Stick Gallery, Round, Victorian, 28 1/2 In.	825.00
Table, China, Rectangular Top, Abalone Floral Inlaid, Rosewood, 27 In., Pair	440.00
Table, China, Rosewood, Teak, Abalone Shell Inlaid, 18 x 48 x 16 In.	110.00
Table, Chippendale, Drop Leaf, Walnut, Cabriole Legs, Claw Footed, c.1760, 27 In.	2750.00
Table, Chippendale, Mahogany, 36 x 43 1/2 x 28 1/2 In.	275.00
Table, Chippendale, Mahogany, Tripod, Scroll Toes, c.1750, 36 In.	1025.00
Table, Classical, Mahogany, Marble Top, Hexagonal, American, c.1830, 32 In.	1100.00
Table, Coffee, Arched Section, 1 Straight Side, 3 Tiers, Black Lacquer, 23 In.	575.00
Table, Coffee, Chippendale, Mahogany, Leather Inset Top, 17 x 19 3/4 In.	125.00
Table, Coffee, Dominique, Macassar Ebony, Bronze, Shelf, 1940, 33 x 14 In.	6325.00
Table, Coffee, Eames, Plywood, Dished Top, 1946	460.00
Table, Coffee, Empire, Mahogany, 1 Drawer, Columns, Oval, 47 x 29 x 19 In.	95.00
Table, Coffee, Nakashima, Walnut & Rosewood, Slab Top, Butterfly Key, 69 In.	2760.00
Table, Coffee, Queen Anne, Serpentine, Cabriole Legs, 29 x 20 In.	94.00
Table, Coffee, Tapio Wirkkala, Teak Inlaid, Chromed Metal, 1955, 49 In.	2015.00
Table, Conference, Eames, Rosewood, Aluminum & Steel, 96 In.	5000.00
Table, Conference, Saarinen, Laminated Top, Painted Cast Metal Base, 77 In.	345.00
Table, Conference, Sam Maloof, Walnut, 3 Pedestals, 1970, 4 Ft x 21 Ft.	3280.00
Table, Console, Cast Iron, Marble Top, Entwined Flowers & Vines, 34 x 52 In.	475.00
Table, Console, Donald Desky, Black Laminate, Chrome, c.1935, 27 x 42 x 12 In.	1725.00
Table, Console, Louis XVI Style, Marble Top, Center & Side Drawers, 41 In.	2300.00
Table, Console, Louis XVI, Marble Top, Ormolu & Inlaid	3000.00
Table, Console, Paul Frankl, Cork Top, Oak Supports, 1940, 40 x 20 In.	575.00
Table, Console, Regency, Mahogany, Black Marble Top, Paw Footed, c.1810	5250.00
Table, Console, Venetian, Faux Marble Top, Floral Reserves, Painted, 46 In.	1110.50
Table, Console, William Kent, George II, Palladian, Gilt Shell, 48 x 72 In., Pair	3980.00
Table, Corner, Queen Anne Style, Drop Leaf, Maple, Scrolled Skirt, 41 x 40 In.	1210.00
Table, Cricket, Scalloped Apron, Red Paint, c.1790, 30 In.	1650.00
Table, Dining, 2 Pedestals, Downswept Legs, Mahogany, 1870s, 98 In.	5175.00
Table, Dining, 2 Sections, Pierced Brackets, Mahogany, c.1780, 78 In.	9775.00
Table, Dining, Art Moderne, Black Lacquer, Pedestal, 1940, 84 x 48 In.	4600.00
Table, Dining, Carved Top Split Pedestal, Mahogany, 4 Leaves, 54 In.	2650.00
Table, Dining, Circular, Carved With Fruit Base, Oak, Victorian, 19th Century	1155.00
Table, Dining, Classical, Mahogany, 2 Parts, Maryland, c.1820, 73 1/2 In.	6325.00
Table, Dining, Colonial Revival, Mahogany, 9 Leaves, 54 In.	4675.00
Table, Dining, Divided Pedestal, Rope Apron, 4 Leaves, Mahogany, 60 In.	3025.00
Table, Dining, Drop Leaf, Bakelite Veneer Over Wood, 3 Leaves, 68 3/4 In.	3500.00

Table, Dining, Drop Leaf, Cherry, New England, 1830s, 29 1/4 x 52 x 66 1/2 In. 770.00
Table, Dining, Drop Leaf, Mahogany, 3 Extra Leaves, Oval, 48 In. 5175.00
Table, Dining, Drop Leaf, Mahogany, Leaf Pedestal, Paw Footed, New York 1850.00
Table, Dining, Eames, Molded Plywood, Knockdown, c.1945 .... 4600.00
Table, Dining, Empire, Mahogany, Pedestal, 2 Leaves, Extends 60 x 72 In. 1155.00
Table, Dining, Federal, Drop Leaf, Cherry, 1830s, 29 1/2 x 44 In. 550.00
Table, Dining, France, Mahogany, Marquetry, Art Nouveau, Gilt, 60 x 45 In. 8050.00
Table, Dining, G. Nelson, Drop Leaf, Blond, Gateleg Base, 1955, 64 x 40 In. 1380.00
Table, Dining, George I, Walnut, Frieze Top, Cabriole Legs, 19th Century, 70 In. 1210.00
Table, Dining, George III Style, 3 Pedestals, Mahogany, 4 Leaves, 102 In. 2640.00
Table, Dining, Georgian, Mahogany Banding, 2 Pedestals, Yew Wood, 65 In. 3740.00
Table, Dining, Gustav Stickley, 4 Leaves, No. 632, 30 1/4 x 48 In. 3300.00
Table, Dining, Gustav Stickley, Experimental Design 7500.00
Table, Dining, Gustav Stickley, Flaring Pedestal, 4 Leaves, No. 656, 48 In. 2750.00
Table, Dining, Gustav Stickley, Oak, Round, 4 Leaves, No. 634, 1910 .... 7475.00 to 8250.00
Table, Dining, Hepplewhite, Drop Leaf, Mahogany, D Ends, Opens To 114 In. 4510.00
Table, Dining, Limbert, Circular Top, Octagonal Section Base, Oak, 54 In. 1100.00
Table, Dining, Limbert, Oak, Medium Finish, 5 Square Legs, Corbels, 1910, 48 In. ... 1980.00
Table, Dining, Louis XVI, Fruitwood, Walnut, Hinged, 1 Drawer, Casters, 50 In. 2300.00
Table, Dining, Mahogany, 3 Pedestals, Downswept Legs, Brass Casters, 105 In. 8625.00
Table, Dining, Mahogany, Gadroon Edge, 2 Leaves, c.1860, Open 72 x 46 In. 1430.00
Table, Dining, Oak, Pedestal, 4 Leaves, c.1915, 48 In. Diam. .... *Illus* 990.00
Table, Dining, Oval, Carved Apron, 2 Leaves, Fruitwood, 57 In. 520.00
Table, Dining, Oval, Shaped Apron, Elongated Ball & Claw Footed, Mahogany 7500.00
Table, Dining, Pedestal, Knee Paw Footed, Leaf Carved, Mahogany 1850.00
Table, Dining, Pembroke, Drop Leaf, Mahogany, X Brace, Eagle Brasses 1540.00
Table, Dining, Pierre Martin, Brass, Painted Black, Leather Top, c.1956, 43 In. 2070.00
Table, Dining, Queen Anne, Drop Leaf, Cherry, New England, 51 3/4 In. 1760.00
Table, Dining, Queen Anne, Drop Leaf, Walnut, c.1760, 48 1/2 In. 2300.00
Table, Dining, Regency Style, Mahogany, 2 Pedestals, Reeded Edge, 1800s, 85 In. 8050.00
Table, Dining, Regency, 3 Pedestals, Mahogany, Extends To 112 In. 5060.00
Table, Dining, Regency, Mahogany, 2 Pedestals, 2 Leaves, 66 x 43 In. 1210.00
Table, Dining, Renaissance Style, Carved Mahogany, 1 Leaf, 48 x 79 In. 575.00
Table, Dining, Robsjohn-Gibbings, Pearwood, 2 Leaves, Pierced Sides, 1936 .... 5000.00
Table, Dining, Sheraton, Drop Leaf, Cut Corners, Tiger Maple 1250.00
Table, Dining, Sheraton, Drop Leaf, Ebony, Satinwood Apron, Mahogany, 43 In. 1610.00
Table, Dining, Sheraton, Drop Leaf, Maple, 30 x 48 In. 925.00
Table, Dining, Stickley Brothers, Split Pedestal, Round, 55 In. 1450.00
Table, Dining, William IV, Segmented Top, Quatrefoil Base, c.1825, 58 In. Diam. 2090.00
Table, Dressing, 3 Frieze Drawers, 2 Cupboards, Marble Top, Mahogany, 51 In. 450.00
Table, Dressing, 3 Tiers Of Drawers, Painted Yellow, Stenciled Fruit, 1830s 9900.00
Table, Dressing, Allover Sponge Painted, Pine, c.1810, 36 1/4 In. 1725.00
Table, Dressing, Black Paint, Stencil, Rounded Drawers 750.00
Table, Dressing, Chair, Dominique, Mahogany, Parchment, Bronze, 1940 .... 4600.00
Table, Dressing, Classical, 3 Drawers, Carved, Mahogany, Mirror, 62 x 40 In. 4025.00
Table, Dressing, Classical, Mahogany, Candle Slide Side, Walnut Overlay, c.1825 ...... 3300.00
Table, Dressing, Federal, 1 Drawer, Turned Legs, Tiger Maple, c.1815, 30 x 37 In. 2200.00
Table, Dressing, Fitted Drawers, Bird's-Eye Veneer, Mahogany, c.1810, 35 In. 2530.00
Table, Dressing, French Style, Satinwood, Mirror, Pullout Writing Drawer, Fitted 8800.00
Table, Dressing, George II, 2 Short & 1 Long Drawer, Oak, 1730s, 30 1/2 In. 3450.00
Table, Dressing, George II, Kneehole, Walnut, Crossbanding, c.1850, 31 x 30 In. 7475.00
Table, Dressing, Mahogany, Gadrooned Collar, Shaped Plinth, c.1820, 63 In. 1100.00
Table, Dressing, Man's, Fruitwood Parquetry Panel, Mirror In Well, Satinwood 6325.00
Table, Dressing, Paul Surmani, Walnut, Hinged Top, Inlaid, 19th Century 3630.00
Table, Dressing, Queen Anne, Walnut, Original Brass, c.1760, 31 x 30 In. 6600.00
Table, Dressing, Rococo Revival, Prudent Mallard 8250.00
Table, Dressing, Victorian, Drawer, Carved, Mahogany 440.00
Table, Dressing, Woman's, Louis XV, Hinged Mirror, Marquetry, Fruitwood, 29 In. ... 385.00
Table, Dressing, Woman's, Rococo Revival, Spindled Shelf Supports 8250.00
Table, Dressing, Yellow Painted, Green & Gold Floral 6750.00
Table, Drop Leaf, Cherry, Center Leg, Opens To 96 In. 295.00
Table, Drop Leaf, Chippendale Legs, Red Stain Remnants, Mass., 1780 .... 4200.00
Table, Drop Leaf, Classical, Mahogany, Shaped Leaves, N.Y., c.1880, 39 x 25 In. 935.00

*Furniture, Table, Federal, Tiger Maple &
Mahogany Veneer, New England, 1810-1815*

*Furniture, Table, Hepplewhite, Tiger Maple,
c.1850, 28 x 29 x 18 In.*

Table, Drop Leaf, Federal, 1 Drawer, Walnut, Pa., c.1810, 29 1/2 In. 880.00
Table, Drop Leaf, Federal, Double Cyma Skirt, Maple, 1790s, 28 x 42 In. 1265.00
Table, Drop Leaf, George I, Bowed Ends, Cabriole Legs, Walnut, 29 In. 1150.00
Table, Drop Leaf, George II, Walnut, Cabriole Legs, c.1750, 28 x 48 In. 4600.00
Table, Drop Leaf, Goddard-Townsend, Cherry, Narrow, Stop Fluted Legs, Small 5500.00
Table, Drop Leaf, Gustav Stickley, Round Top, No. 671, 29 x 32 In. 1400.00
Table, Drop Leaf, Queen Anne, Mahogany, Cabriole Legs, Hoof Feet, 42 x 39 In. 2200.00
Table, Drop Leaf, Queen Anne, Swing Leg, Mahogany, c.1770 .... 1340.00
Table, Drop Leaf, Regency, Warming, 2 & 1 Drawer Each End, 1820, 28 In. 475.00
Table, Drum, George III, Mahogany, Gilt Tooled Leather Inset, Round, c.1800 .... 6900.00
Table, Drum, George III, Mahogany, Leather Insert, Quadruped Base 715.00
Table, Drum, Inlaid Figures In Landscape & Geometric, Fruitwood, 30 In. 1870.00
Table, Drum, Regency, Mahogany, 4 Drawers, Concave Plinth, Round, 52 In. 2760.00
Table, Drum, Rosewood, Veneered Revolving Top, 4 Frieze Drawers, 56 In. 1430.00
Table, Eames, Molded Plywood, T-Shaped Back, Molded Seat, Child's, 1945 .... 6900.00
Table, Eames, Rectangular Top, Plywood, Child's, 1945 .... 4600.00
Table, Edwardian Style, Drop Leaf, Inlaid Mahogany, 22 x 22 In. 660.00
Table, Empire, Acanthus Column, Tripod Base, Rosewood, 20 1/2 x 23 In. 110.00
Table, Empire, Maple & Pine, Pedestal, Scrolled Legs, Replaced Top, 28 x 28 In. 165.00
Table, Empire, Pillar Pedestal, Scroll Feet, Mahogany, 33 1/2 In. 500.00
Table, Empire, Round Threaded Top, Country 450.00
Table, Empire, Swing Top, 1 Drawer, Mahogany, 23 1/4 x 43 3/4 In. 440.00
Table, End, Stickley Bros., 2 Tiers, Flared Legs, 32 x 18 x 18 In. 715.00
Table, England, Planked Top, Straight Legs, Pine, 28 1/2 x 83 x 35 In. 525.00
Table, Envelope, George II, Semi-Elliptical Drop Leaves, Mahogany, c.1740 .... 5445.00
Table, Extension, Paw Feet, Mahogany, 9 Leaves, Round, Extends To 18 Ft. 3300.00
Table, Federal, Drawer, Grain Painted, Pennsylvania, 30 1/2 x 28 In. 475.00
Table, Federal, Tiger Maple & Mahogany Veneer, New England, 1810-1815 ...... *Illus* 715.00
Table, Flip Top, Queen Anne, Round 100.00
Table, Frank Lloyd Wright, Rectangular Slab Legs, Cypress, 1940, 27 3/4 In. 2070.00
Table, Galle, 2 Tiers, Carved Mahogany, Marquetry, Rectangular, 29 1/2 In. 2300.00
Table, Galle, 2 Tiers, Inlaid Flowering Narcissus, Mahogany, 29 x 30 In. 2990.00
Table, Galle, 3 Tiers, Marquetry Leaves & Butterfly, Fruitwood, c.1900, 33 In. 2300.00
Table, Galle, Inlaid Reclining Cat Grooming Kittens, Mahogany, 29 1/4 In. 1610.00
Table, Galle, Inlaid Spray Of Apple Blossoms, Fruitwood, c.1900, 24 1/2 In. 2875.00
Table, Galle, Marquetry Tiger Lily Spray, Fruitwood, c.1890, 30 In. 2300.00
Table, Galle, Marquetry, Triangular, Rounded Sides, c.1900, 30 1/4 x 20 3/4 In. 1265.00
Table, Game, 8 Drawers, Ball Feet, Walnut, Round, 1840s 550.00
Table, Game, Arts & Crafts, Oak, Round, American, c.1910, 30 x 29 1/4 In. 460.00
Table, Game, Biedermeier Style, Maple, Tapered Legs, Round, 36 x 29 In. 700.00
Table, Game, Carved Lyre Supports, Satinwood Band, Mahogany, 29 x 34 In. 1100.00
Table, Game, Classical, D-Shaped Top, Inlaid Satinwood, American, c.1820 .... 2310.00
Table, Game, Classical, Mahogany, Reeded, Trestle Base, Boston, c.1820, 36 In. 1870.00
Table, Game, Demilune, 3 Arches, 1 Flap, Frieze Drawers, 19th Century 440.00
Table, Game, Empire, Serpentine Top, Revolving, Trestle Base, 34 x 18 In. 300.00
Table, Game, Galle, Inlaid Blossoming Clover, Twisted Legs, Signed, 35 In. 3450.00

Table, Game, George II, Mahogany, Outset Corners, Polished, c.1850, 40 In. 3450.00
Table, Game, George III, Baize-Lined Surface, Walnut, c.1740, 28 3/4 In. 4620.00
Table, Game, George III, Mahogany, Satinwood, Felt-Lined Top, 35 x 18 In. 1100.00
Table, Game, George III, Triple Top, Shell Carved Legs, Mahogany, 28 In. 3080.00
Table, Game, Georgian, Oak, Square Legs, c.1780 .... 365.00
Table, Game, Inlaid Banded Rosewood, Mahogany 650.00
Table, Game, Inlaid Sliding Board, Over Backgammon Surface, Rosewood, 29 In. 370.00
Table, Game, Oxbow Front, Inlaid Center Star, c.1800, 36 x 29 1/2 In. 4950.00
Table, Game, Regency, Inlaid Rosewood, Chessboard, Work Basket 3450.00
Table, Game, Walnut, Satinwood, Victorian, c.1880 .... 975.00
Table, Game, William IV, Mahogany, Rosewood Bands, c.1840, 30 x 36 In. 1870.00
Table, Gateleg, Birch & Tiger Maple, New England, 18th Century 1540.00
Table, Gateleg, Jacobean, Oak, 1 Leaf, 26 1/2 x 30 x 12 In. 715.00
Table, Gateleg, William & Mary, 2 Leaves, 2 Swing Legs, Maple, c.1720, 36 In. 4600.00
Table, Gateleg, William & Mary, Oak, 1 Frieze Drawer, 28 1/2 x 35 In. 825.00
Table, George I Style, Giltwood, Marble Top, Carved Foliage, 30 x 51 In. 9200.00
Table, George III, Birdcage Support, Carved Baluster, Tripod, c.1760, 24 In. 2725.00
Table, George III, Flap Top, Spider Legs, Mahogany, c.1760, 31 In. 4085.00
Table, George III, Pembroke, Inlaid Mahogany, Serpentine, c.1775, 28 x 43 In. 2300.00
Table, George III, Ring-Turned Baluster Stem, Tripod, Mahogany, c.1760 .... 6800.00
Table, Georgian, Mahogany, 1 Drawer, Square Tapering Legs, 35 x 47 x 19 In. 440.00
Table, Gio Ponti, Glass Top, Butterflies, Flowers, Fruits, c.1950, 63 In. 3520.00
Table, Gustav Stickley, Oak, Square Legs, No. 658, Child's, c.1910, 20 x 24 In. 330.00
Table, Hall, Sheraton, Mahogany, Center Drawer, Ebony Inlay, c.1800, 48 In. 1045.00
Table, Harvest, 1 Center Drawer, Walnut, 30 1/2 x 134 In. 660.00
Table, Harvest, Bird's-Eye Maple & Ash, New England, 28 3/4 x 60 1/2 In. 915.00
Table, Harvest, End Drawers, 144 In. 5500.00
Table, Harvest, Pine, Poplar, Grained Repaint, 1 Drawer, 2-Board Top, 25 x 144 In. .. 210.00
Table, Harvest, Tapered Legs, Birch, 58 In. 400.00
Table, Hepplewhite, Drop Leaf, Cherry, Cutout Corners, Refinished, 35 x 37 In. 440.00
Table, Hepplewhite, Drop Leaf, Swing Legs, Mahogany, 17 x 41 1/4 In. 660.00
Table, Hepplewhite, Pembroke, Mahogany, Inlaid, 32 x 41 x 28 In. 500.00
Table, Hepplewhite, Tiger Maple, c.1850, 28 x 29 x 18 In. .... *Illus* 440.00
Table, Hinged Top, Baize Lined, Patience, Mahogany, c.1790, 28 1/2 Ft. 2725.00
Table, Hollowed Out Logs, Primitive, 2 Chairs, 3 Piece 595.00
Table, Hutch, Flame Mahogany, Chamfered Arms & Legs, Molded Edge 2530.00
Table, Hutch, Pine, Breadboard Top, Square Tapered Legs, 29 x 46 x 32 In. 600.00
Table, Hutch, Poplar, Red Paint, 3-Board Top, Cutout Feet, 19th Century 2900.00
Table, Hutch, Scribed Top, Red Base, Pine, c.1800, 48 1/4 In. 2750.00
Table, Hutch, Shoe Foot, Pine, Original Varnish 1200.00
Table, Isamu Noguchi, Rudder, Crossed Support Steel Rod, c.1959 .... 9350.00
Table, Italian Baroque, Painted Simulated Tortoiseshell, 18 1/2 x 54 In. 5175.00
Table, J. Hoffmann, Leather Inserts, Stained Bentwood, c.1904, 26 In. 1725.00
Table, J. Hoffmann, Mahogany, Beechwood, Fledermaus, c.1905, 28 x 23 In. 1600.00
Table, L. & J.G. Stickley, Oak, Crossed Stretchers, c.1918, 29 x 30 In. 660.00
Table, Lamp, Queen Anne, Drop Leaf, Mahogany, Tripod Base, 55 In. 90.00
Table, Lamp, Rose Marble Top, Victorian 240.00
Table, Leather Top, Foliate Carved Trestle, Bird's-Eye Maple, 49 In. 4025.00
Table, Library, 3 Drawers, Original Brasses, Leather Top, Mahogany, 56 In. 3300.00
Table, Library, Arts & Crafts, 1 Drawer, Bookshelf Sides, Slats, 29 x 48 x 30 In. 715.00
Table, Library, Arts & Crafts, Oak, Rectangular, Bowed Sides, 70 In. 460.00
Table, Library, Federal, Mahogany, 2 Drawers, Finials, Philadelphia Style 4300.00
Table, Library, Gustav Stickley, No. 619, c.1907 .... 4950.00
Table, Library, Harden, 1 Drawer, 3 Slats, 29 x 42 x 26 In. 935.00
Table, Library, Jacobean, Oak, 3 Frieze Drawers, Trestle Base, 30 x 59 x 29 In. 440.00
Table, Library, L. & J.G. Stickley, 2 Drawers, Oak, 29 1/2 x 48 In. 2185.00
Table, Library, L. & J.G. Stickley, Hexagonal Nail Leather Top, No. 563, 48 In.. .... 3745.00
Table, Library, Lifetime, No. 932, Tiger Oak Grained Top, 29 x 30 In. 605.00
Table, Library, Limbert, Recessed Top, 1 Drawer, Brass Hardware, 29 x 37 x 24 In. .. 330.00
Table, Library, Renaissance, Oak, 2 Frieze Drawers, Twisted Legs, 51 x 29 In. 605.00
Table, Library, Scalloped Skirt, Drawers Both Ends, Walnut, c.1700, 33 x 57 In. 6750.00
Table, Library, Stickley Bros., Oak, 1 Drawer, No. 2696 1/2, 36 x 50 In. 1650.00
Table, Library, William IV, Leather Inset, Turned Legs, Castors, Oval, c.1835 .... 1320.00

Furniture, Table, Neoclassical,
Rosewood, Holland, 39 In. Diam.

Furniture, Table, Queen Anne,
Drop Leaf, Mahogany, New
England, 18th Century

Furniture, Table, Renaissance
Revival, Walnut, Mosaic &
Marble Top, Italy

Table, Limbert, Flaring, Paneled Legs, Oval Top, No. 146, 45 x 30 In.	1800.00
Table, Limbert, Oak, Oval, No. 146, c.1910, 28 3/4 x 45 x 30 In.	2420.00
Table, Limbert, Pierced Legs, Square Cutouts, Oak, 29 x 44 In.	1955.00
Table, Lion Pedestal Base, Oak, Round	2100.00
Table, Louis XV Style, Bronze & Onyx, 19 x 40 In.	1500.00
Table, Louis XV, 3 Drawers, Floral Bouquets Veneer, Kingwood & Fruitwood	8050.00
Table, Louis XV, Provincial, Beechwood, Dished Liver-Marble Top, 33 x 25 In.	2300.00
Table, Louis XVI Style, 2 Tiers, Marquetry, 34 x 36 In.	525.00
Table, Louis XVI Style, Brassbound Top, Inlaid, Oriental Scene, Walnut, 30 In.	825.00
Table, Louis XVI, Mondon, Tulipwood & Purplewood Parquetry, 29 In.	9200.00
Table, Mahogany Top, Lyre Base, Victorian, 29 1/2 x 22 In.	125.00
Table, Mahogany, Flame Grained, Tapering Legs, France, Round, 22 x 29 In.	1150.00
Table, Majorelle, 2 Tiers, Marquetry Lozenge Devices, Mahogany, c.1900	2300.00
Table, Majorelle, 2 Tiers, Twisted Vine Legs, 18 1/2 In.	5500.00
Table, Majorelle, Gilt-Bronze Mounted, Rosewood & Mahogany, c.1900, 30 In.	8050.00
Table, Majorelle, Marquetry Nicotiana Blossoms Rim, Fruitwood, 28 1/4 In.	3745.00
Table, Majorelle, Marquetry Top, Fruitwood, c.1900, 29 1/4 In.	3165.00
Table, Marble Top, Double Pedestal, Cast-Iron Base, 28 x 36 In., Pair	2200.00
Table, Marble Top, Friezes Of Foliage, Wrought Iron, France	1955.00
Table, Marble Top, Rams' Heads, At Top Of Supports, Round Stretcher, 27 In.	5150.00
Table, Memphis, Peter Scheier, Painted Metal & Glass, c.1980, 29 x 52 In.	2875.00
Table, Nakashima, Irregular Top, Butterfly Keys, Walnut & Rosewood, Pair	7875.00
Table, Neoclassical, Cast Iron, Pietra Dura, Marble Top, Eagles' Heads, 24 In.	3575.00
Table, Neoclassical, Rosewood, Holland, 39 In. Diam. .... *Illus*	3850.00
Table, Nesting, Galle, Inlaid Flowers & Leaves, Fruitwood, c.1900, 4 Piece	5750.00
Table, Nesting, Galle, Marquetry, 3 Kittens, 2 Parakeets, 22 x 12 In., 2 Piece	4600.00
Table, Nesting, Galle, Marquetry, Blossoms, Leaves, Signed, c.1900, 21 1/2 In.	5300.00
Table, Nesting, Galle, Marquetry, Iris Blossoms, Fruitwood, c.1900, 3 Piece	3450.00
Table, Nesting, Teak, Dark Finish, China, 14 x 19 x 27 1/2 In., 4 Piece	195.00
Table, Nesting, Triangular, Graduated, Gilt Design, Green Lacquer, Japan, 5 Piece	690.00
Table, Nesting, Mother-Of-Pearl Inlay, Black Lacquer, 1860s, 4 Piece	5750.00
Table, Nesting, Regency, Lacquer, Chinoiserie, Dragon Footed, c.1920, 3 Piece	220.00
Table, Night, Majorelle, Clematis, Marble Top, 1 Drawer, 3 Shelves, 41 1/4 In.	1495.00
Table, Night, Robsjohn-Gibbings, Shelf, 1 Door, c.1936, 28 x 22 x 18 In.	2300.00
Table, Oak, 2-Board Top, Square Tapered Legs, English Country, 17 x 33 x 28 In.	145.00
Table, Oak, Art Nouveau, Carved Tendrils, Platform Stretcher, c.1900, 35 3/4 In.	1035.00
Table, Oak, Round, Child's, c.1910	375.00
Table, Oriental Design, Glass Top, Brass, 28 x 60 In.	300.00
Table, Oriental, Black Lacquered Mother-Of-Pearl, Ivory Inlay, 21 1/2 In.	550.00
Table, Ormolu Gallery, 1 Drawer, Parquetry, Fruitwood & Tulipwood, 27 1/4 In.	9200.00
Table, Ormolu Mounted, Veined Marble Top, Steel Supports, 16 1/2 x 42 In.	7475.00
Table, Oval Glass Top, Bronze Figural Base, 2 Angels Back To Back, 1930	4000.00
Table, Painted Chinoiserie Scene, Black Ground, Tole, 26 x 18 In.	330.00
Table, Papier-Mache, Mother-Of-Pearl, Victorian, Late 19th Century, 29 x 23 In.	330.00

Table, Parlor, Eastlake Style, Ball & Stick, Rose Marble Top 320.00
Table, Parlor, Eastlake, Marble Top, Spindle Carved Apron, Victorian, 28 x 31 In. 300.00
Table, Parlor, Neoclassical, Walnut, Inlaid Mother-Of-Pearl, Round, 39 In. 4125.00
Table, Parlor, Walnut, Turtle Shape, Marble Top 650.00
Table, Parquetry, Leather Slide, 1 End Drawer, Tulipwood, 28 1/4 In. 3745.00
Table, Pembroke, 1 Drawer, Oval Inlays, Mahogany, c.1805, 28 1/4 In. 1840.00
Table, Pembroke, Cherry, 4-Board Top, Square Tapered Legs, 10-In. Leaves, 34 In. ... 165.00
Table, Pembroke, Federal, D-Shaped Leaves, 1 End Drawer, Mahogany, 29 In. 575.00
Table, Pembroke, George II, Mahogany, Rectangular, Marlborough Legs, 30 1/2 In. .. 660.00
Table, Pembroke, George III, Demilune Flaps, Medallion, Painted, 27 In. 9200.00
Table, Pembroke, George III, Mahogany, Crossbanded Kingwood, c.1780, 41 In. 6900.00
Table, Pembroke, Georgian, Mahogany, Square Tapering Legs, c.1780 .... 325.00
Table, Pembroke, Hepplewhite, Drop Leaf, 1 Drawer, Cherry, 28 In. 825.00
Table, Pembroke, Hexagonal Leaves, 1 Drawer, Mahogany, c.1815, 29 1/4 In. 1725.00
Table, Pembroke, Sheraton, Mahogany, 1 Drawer, 35 1/2 x 36 x 28 3/4 In. 525.00
Table, Pier, Classical, Mahogany, Bronze Mounted, Marble, N.Y., c.1825, 48 In. 4950.00
Table, Pier, Continental, Painted Classical Design, Composition, 69 x 20 In. 1320.00
Table, Pier, French Marble Top, Ormolu & Stenciled Mounts, New York 8500.00
Table, Pier, Marquetry, Holland, 18 1/2 x 14 1/2 In. 3800.00
Table, Pietra Dura, Giltwood, Italy, Late 19th Century, 31 x 24 1/2 x 18 In. 1760.00
Table, Poker, Fitted Dealer's Drawer, Reversible Top, Oak, c.1900 .... 2200.00
Table, Queen Anne Style, Lamp, Drop Leaves, Mahogany, 55 In. 90.00
Table, Queen Anne, 3 Drawers, England, 18th Century, 58 x 32 In. 2200.00
Table, Queen Anne, Drop Leaf, Chip-Carved Feet, Poplar, 43 1/2 In. 2200.00
Table, Queen Anne, Drop Leaf, Mahogany, New England, 18th Century .... *Illus* 19800.00
Table, Queen Anne, Drop Leaf, Maple, 18th Century, 26 1/2 In. 935.00
Table, Queen Anne, Drop Leaf, Maple, Swing Legs, 15 x 52 x 27 In. 1650.00
Table, Queen Anne, Drop Leaf, Poplar, Worn Red Repaint Base 2200.00
Table, Queen Anne, Walnut, Kidney Shape, 5 Drawers, 30 x 47 In. 605.00
Table, Raymond Subes, Marble Top, Iron Frame, Scrolling Legs, 92 In. 9350.00
Table, Refectory, England, Carved, Oak, 19th Century, 30 x 96 x 28 In. 935.00
Table, Refectory, Italian Renaissance, Walnut, 2 Frieze Drawers, Trestle, 90 In. 2100.00
Table, Refectory, Jacobean Style, Floral Frieze, Rope Turned Legs, 89 In. 1200.00
Table, Refectory, Oak, Spain, c.1680 .... 5775.00
Table, Refectory, Planked Top, Stylized Foliate Frieze, Oak, 74 In. 6900.00
Table, Refectory, Tudor Style, Oak, Elm, Frieze, Leaf Carved Legs, 102 In. 2875.00
Table, Refreshment, Louis XVI, 2 Wine Coolers, 1 Drawer, Mahogany, 29 1/4 In. 6900.00
Table, Regency, Drop Leaf, 1 Drawer, Mahogany, 29 x 48 In. 525.00
Table, Regency, Elm, Parcel Gilt, Round, Triangular Base, c.1825, 29 x 50 In. 9200.00
Table, Renaissance Revival, Herter Brothers, Marble Top, c.1865 .... 1430.00
Table, Renaissance Revival, Walnut, Mosaic & Marble Top, Italy .... *Illus* 3960.00
Table, Renaissance Style, Carved Walnut, Onyx, Late 19th Century, 42 x 26 In. 770.00
Table, Revolving, Russel Wright, Plywood & Chromed Steel, 1934, 42 In. 2875.00
Table, Robsjohn-Gibbings, Walnut, 2 Doors, 1936, 21 x 18 In. Diam. 3738.00
Table, Rococo, Carved Rosewood, Turtle-Shaped Marble, New Orleans, 42 In. 1760.00
Table, Rosewood, Glass Inset, Art Deco, Round, France, c.1935, 22 x 29 1/2 In. 1445.00
Table, Rosewood, Radiating Veneers, Art Deco, Round, France, 1935, 23 x 43 In. 2875.00
Table, Roycroft, Little Journeys', Oak, 2 Tiers, Trestle Base, Metal Tag, 26 In. 650.00
Table, Salon, Louis XV, Carved, Gilt, Large 4950.00
Table, Sawbuck, Oak, Grain Paint, England, c.1820 .... 2500.00
Table, Sawbuck, Pine, Paint Traces Under Red Wash, 2-Board Top, 23 x 31 In. 415.00
Table, Sawbuck, Turned Out Feet, Pine, 28 3/4 x 68 In. 1175.00
Table, Scalloped Top, Tripod Pedestal Base, Victorian, Mahogany, Round, 36 In. 175.00
Table, Serving, 3 Tiers, Tulipwood & Purplewood Parquetry, 1880s, 35 1/2 In. 9200.00
Table, Serving, George III, Mahogany, 3-Drawer Apron, c.1800, 84 In. 9200.00
Table, Serving, George III, Mahogany, Serpentine, Fluted Legs, 1700s, 34 x 60 In. 4600.00
Table, Sewing, 1-Board Top, Rounded Edges, 1 Drawer, H Stretcher 9800.00
Table, Sewing, 1 Convex Drawer Over 2 Long Drawers, Mahogany, 1815, 30 In. 2300.00
Table, Sewing, 1 Drawer, Candle Slide, Curly Maple Panels, Cherry, 33 In. 3000.00
Table, Sewing, 1 Drawer, Lyre-Shaped Base, Mahogany, 31 In. 475.00
Table, Sewing, 1 Drawer, Pine, 2-Board Top, English Country, 29 x 72 In. 330.00
Table, Sewing, 2 Drawers, Mahogany, Rope & Ring Turned Legs, 29 x 21 In. 1840.00
Table, Sewing, 2 Drawers, Pine Top, Turned Legs, Walnut, c.1848 .... 2150.00

Furniture, Table, Sewing, Hepplewhite, Inlaid,
Scalloped Shelf, New Hampshire

Furniture, Table, Sewing, Sheraton,
Drop Leaf, 2 Drawers, Refinished

Table, Sewing, 2 Drawers, Rounded Fronts, Hinged Top, Cherry, 29 In. 385.00
Table, Sewing, 2 Drawers, Tiger Maple, Cherry Legs, 1830 .... 425.00
Table, Sewing, American Empire, Hinged Top, Fitted Interior, Mahogany, 29 In. 330.00
Table, Sewing, Classical, Mahogany, Crossbanded Rosewood, Brass, c.1820, 32 In. ... 880.00
Table, Sewing, Divided Drawer, Cherry, Poplar, 27 1/2 In. 715.00
Table, Sewing, Drop Leaf, Carved Columns, Pineapple Stretcher, Mahogany, 29 In. .. 525.00
Table, Sewing, Empire, Duncan Phyfe, Mahogany Pedestal, Claw Footed 500.00
Table, Sewing, Farm, Pine Top, Traces Of Paint, 55 1/2 x 32 1/2 In. 785.00
Table, Sewing, Federal, 1 Drawer, Mahogany & Mahogany Veneer, 29 x 18 In. 715.00
Table, Sewing, Federal, 1 Drawer, Mahogany, Side Lift Top, Candle Shelves 6400.00
Table, Sewing, Federal, 1 Drawer, Tiger Maple 525.00
Table, Sewing, George II, Mahogany, Cabriole Legs, 1700s, 29 x 36 In. 1725.00
Table, Sewing, Hepplewhite, 2 Drawers, Walnut, Tapered Legs, Country, 33 x 59 In.. 660.00
Table, Sewing, Hepplewhite, Inlaid, Scalloped Shelf, New Hampshire .... *Illus* 4675.00
Table, Sewing, Hinged Top, Drop Leaf, Divided Drawer, Mahogany, 28 In. 6325.00
Table, Sewing, Lacquer, Lift Top, Basket Drawer, 19th Century, 28 x 25 In. 550.00
Table, Sewing, Lift Top, Pigeonholes, Flame Grained Mahogany Facade, 29 1/2 In. ... 365.00
Table, Sewing, Mahogany Veneer, Classical, New England, c.1820, 29 x 21 In. 1210.00
Table, Sewing, Mahogany, 4 Columns, Glass Knobs, New York, c.1830 .... 5800.00
Table, Sewing, Paris Mfg., Laminated Maple, Collapsible 50.00
Table, Sewing, Regency, Center Drop Bag, Satinwood, c.1790 .... 2600.00
Table, Sewing, Regency, Oak, Burl Wood, Mahogany, Ormolu, Gameboard, 35 In. 9625.00
Table, Sewing, Shaker, Drawer, Red Painted Pine, 29 1/4 x 18 1/8 In. 2530.00
Table, Sewing, Sheraton, 2 Drawers, Mahogany, Veneer, 28 x 16 x 18 In. 305.00
Table, Sewing, Sheraton, Drop Leaf, 2 Drawers, Refinished .... *Illus* 500.00
Table, Sewing, Sheraton, Sandwich Glass Knobs, Tiger Maple, 1830s 2500.00
Table, Sewing, Walnut, Pedestal, c.1835 .... 900.00
Table, Sewing, William IV, Parquetry, Parcel Gilt, Ebonized, 30 x 17 x 17 In. 2875.00
Table, Shaker, 1 Drawer, Canterbury, Maple & Birch, 26 x 30 In. 2420.00
Table, Shaker, Cherry, 1 Drawer, E.B.K Chalk Mark Underside 7700.00
Table, Sheraton, Drop Leaf, Mahogany, Acanthus Legs, Casters, 39 x 50 In. 500.00
Table, Sheraton, Drop Leaf, Mahogany, Reeded Legs, c.1820, 49 x 36 x 29 In. 775.00
Table, Sheraton, Mahogany, Concave Ends, Fake Drawers, 45 3/4 x 23 In. 2090.00
Table, Side, 1 Long Drawer, Turned Legs, Curly Maple, 19 x 19 x 28 In. 225.00
Table, Side, Burl Wood, 3 Tiers, Inlaid Ebony Top, c.1930, 23 x 29 In. 1275.00
Table, Side, Chinese Export, Marble Inset, Pierced Frieze, 32 x 48 In., Pair 6900.00
Table, Side, George III, Mahogany, 2 Drawers, Square Legs, 36 x 46 In., Pair 777.00
Table, Side, Italian Neoclassical, Walnut, Crossbanding, Square Legs, 66 In. 3450.00
Table, Side, Regency, Mahogany, Faux Bamboo Legs, X Stretcher, c.1840 .... 365.00
Table, Side, Regency, Mother-Of-Pearl, Japanned, Painted Landscape, 34 In. 9775.00
Table, Silver, George I, Mahogany, 1 Frieze Drawer, Apron, Dish Rim, 1750 .... 1540.00
Table, Smoking, Robsjohn-Gibbings, Carved Rim, Fruitwood, 1937, 23 In., Pair 5175.00
Table, Sofa, Calamander, Maple, Inlaid Satinwood, Victorian, c.1850, 58 In. 4025.00
Table, Sofa, Drop Leaf, 2 Short & 2 False Drawers, Mahogany, 31 In. 275.00
Table, Sofa, Regency Style, Drop Leaf, Mahogany, 2 Drawers, 30 x 60 In. 1725.00
Table, Sofa, Regency, 2 Drawers, 2 False Drawers, Inlaid Mahogany, 29 1/4 In. 2070.00

Furniture, Table, Sunderland, Lyre Pedestal,
Victorian, 40 In. Diam.

Furniture, Table, Tea, Tilt Top, Chippendale,
Mahogany, 1760-1780, 27 x 30 In.

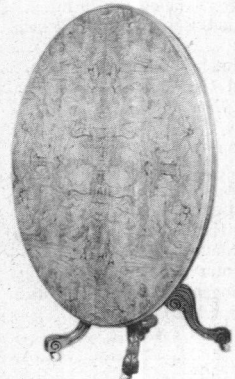

Furniture, Table, Tilt Top, Burl Walnut,
Mid-19th Century, 53 x 39 x 28 In.

Furniture, Table, William IV, Rosewood, Pedestal,
c. 1835, 47 In. Diam.

Table, Sofa, Regency, Rosewood, Inlaid Satinwood	4950.00
Table, Sofa, William IV, Mahogany, Gilt, 2 Frieze Drawers, Trestle, c.1840	1550.00
Table, Stickley Bros., Bulbous Turnings, Cross Stretchers, 29 x 40 In.	1450.00
Table, Sunderland, Lyre Pedestal, Victorian, 40 In. Diam. .... *Illus*	11000.00
Table, Supporting Spheres, Black & Silver Lacquered Wood, c.1915, 44 1/2 In.	1725.00
Table, Tavern, 1 Drawer, Turned Legs, Maple, New England, 27 x 43 1/2 x 29 In.	525.00
Table, Tavern, 1-Board Top, 22 1/2 x 31 In.	3850.00
Table, Tavern, Birch, New England, 18th Century, 26 1/2 In.	1100.00
Table, Tavern, Breadboard Top, 1 Drawer, Stretcher Base	1870.00
Table, Tavern, Chippendale, Square Legs, Painted	275.00
Table, Tavern, Federal, Maple & Pine, New England, c.1800, 27 x 30 In.	500.00
Table, Tavern, Mortised & Pinned Apron, 2-Board Top, Pine, 26 In.	330.00
Table, Tavern, New England, Cherry & Pine, c.1810, 27 1/2 In.	770.00
Table, Tavern, Painted, Maple & Pine, Massachusetts, 24 x 27 1/2 In.	8800.00
Table, Tavern, Pilgrim Century, Butterfly Support For Missing Drop Leaf	1980.00
Table, Tavern, Queen Anne, 2-Breadboard Top, Drawer, Hardwoods, 26 x 41 In.	1540.00
Table, Tavern, Queen Anne, Oval Top, Maple, New England, 18th Century	365.00
Table, Tavern, Scrubbed Top, Red Base, Pine, 29 x 42 In.	2310.00
Table, Tavern, Walnut, 2 Drawers, 4-Board Top, Box Stretcher, 29 x 52 x 30 In.	1265.00

Table, Tavern, William & Mary, Drawer, Turned Legs, c.1760, 31 x 35 1/2 In. 385.00
Table, Tavern, William & Mary, Massachusetts, Maple, c.1730, 23 3/4 In. 8800.00
Table, Tea, 2 Tiers, Mahogany, Art Nouveau, France, 1900, 36 x 31 In. 920.00
Table, Tea, 3 Flat Legs, 3 Stretchers, Dark Finish, 30 1/2 x 24 In. 220.00
Table, Tea, Button Footed, Oval Top, Cupid's Bow & Crown Cutout Skirt 3630.00
Table, Tea, Cherry, Snake Feet, Connecticut, c.1780, 36 In. Diam. 3250.00
Table, Tea, Chippendale Style, Tilt Top, Cherry, 28 x 34 In. 440.00
Table, Tea, Chippendale, Birdcage, 2-Board Top, Walnut, 29 1/2 In. 6875.00
Table, Tea, Chippendale, Mahogany, Tripod, Snake Footed, England, 32 x 27 In. 990.00
Table, Tea, Chippendale, Pierced Supports, Mahogany, 1770s, 27 1/2 In. 1840.00
Table, Tea, Galle, 2 Tiers, Marquetry Top, Fruitwood & Mahogany, c.1900, 32 In. 1725.00
Table, Tea, Galle, 2 Tiers, Marquetry Trefoil Top, Fruitwood, c.1900, 29 x 21 In. 1840.00
Table, Tea, Galle, Marquetry Iris Blossoms, Folding, Fruitwood, c.1900, 28 In. 2185.00
Table, Tea, Galle, Marquetry Landscape, Daffodils, Fruitwood, c.1900, 29 1/4 In. 3450.00
Table, Tea, George III, Mahogany, Square Legs 415.00
Table, Tea, Gustav Stickley, Arched Cross Stretchers, No. 604, Decal 750.00
Table, Tea, L. & J.G. Stickley, Arched Cross Stretchers, Black Finish, No. 381 .... 1500.00
Table, Tea, Queen Anne, Maple, 18th Century, 27 3/4 x 27 1/2 x 19 1/4 In. 3740.00
Table, Tea, Queen Anne, Maple, c.1770, 25 1/2 In. 1430.00
Table, Tea, Queen Anne, Mustard & Gray Paint, Country 2640.00
Table, Tea, Queen Anne, Rectangular Top, Pedestal, Mahogany, 30 x 24 1/2 In. 235.00
Table, Tea, Tilt Top, Birdcage, Tiger Maple, c.1800, 27 1/2 x 32 In. 1045.00
Table, Tea, Tilt Top, Birdcage, Tiger Maple, Snake Feet, 1-Board Top 2700.00
Table, Tea, Tilt Top, Chippendale, Carved Mahogany, 1770-1790 .... 3025.00
Table, Tea, Tilt Top, Chippendale, Cherry & Maple, Birdcage, 18th Century, 28 In. ... 550.00
Table, Tea, Tilt Top, Chippendale, Mahogany, 1760-1780, 27 x 30 In. .... *Illus* 1725.00
Table, Tea, Tilt Top, Chippendale, Mahogany, New England, 1760-1785, 28 In. 825.00
Table, Tea, Tilt Top, Chippendale, Walnut, Birdcage, 32 1/2 x 29 In. 2200.00
Table, Tea, Tilt Top, Country Scene, Papier-Mache, Victorian, 26 x 27 x 23 In. 445.00
Table, Tea, Tilt Top, Dish Top, Tripod Base, Snake Feet 775.00
Table, Tea, Tilt Top, Mahogany, 1940s, 26 In. 250.00
Table, Thomas Brooks, Marble Top, Oval 1500.00
Table, Tilt Top, Biedermeier, Octagonal Pedestal Base 2250.00
Table, Tilt Top, Burl Walnut, Mid-19th Century, 53 x 39 x 28 In. .... *Illus* 1650.00
Table, Tilt Top, Chest In Seat, Pine, c.1820 .... 600.00
Table, Tilt Top, Chippendale, Tripod Base, 33 x 27 In. 1540.00
Table, Tilt Top, Chippendale, Walnut, Turned Column, Snake Feet, 32 x 28 In. 1155.00
Table, Tilt Top, Classical, Mahogany, Shaped Top, Carved, American, 27 In. 400.00
Table, Tilt Top, Empire, Mahogany, Spider Legs, Rectangular Top, 17 x 24 x 29 In. .. 275.00
Table, Tilt Top, England, Painted Floral Spray, Gilt Scrollwork, Tripod, Victorian 990.00
Table, Tilt Top, Federal, Mahogany, Massachusetts, c.1790, 29 x 17 In. 1200.00
Table, Tilt Top, Federal, Walnut & Curly Maple, 26 In. 660.00
Table, Tilt Top, George II, Mahogany, Tripod, Round, Mid-1700s, 27 x 35 In. 6900.00
Table, Tilt Top, George III, Carved Mahogany, Tripod, Scalloped, 28 x 38 In. 1050.00
Table, Tilt Top, Georgian Style, Mahogany, 8 Round Recesses, 29 3/4 In. 2000.00
Table, Tilt Top, Herter Bros., Marble Top, Glass Door, Claw Feet, Rosewood 6600.00
Table, Tilt Top, Papier-Mache, Wood, Black, Gold, Horse Scene Top, 23 x 32 In. 220.00
Table, Tilt Top, Piecrust, Tripod Base, Mahogany, 28 x 27 In. 135.00
Table, Tilt Top, Queen Anne, Mahogany, Tripod, Birdcage, 28 1/2 x 34 In. 1265.00
Table, Tilt Top, Regency, Mahogany, 4 Downswept Legs, c.1825, 53 x 46 In. 2300.00
Table, Tilt Top, Regency, Mahogany, Walnut Parquetry, Tripod, c.1825, 28 In. 6900.00
Table, Tilt Top, Spider Leg, Cherry, Urn Form Pedestal, 28 In. 110.00
Table, Tilt Top, Tripod, Mahogany, 28 x 31 In. 1500.00
Table, Trellis Parquetry, Brass Stringing, Zephyrs' Masks, Mahogany, 29 1/2 In. 7475.00
Table, Trestle, L. & J.G. Stickley, Tenon & Key, No. 593, 48 x 30 In. 880.00
Table, Tric Trac, Leather Lined, Reverse Chessboard, Cherry, Mahogany, 1875 .... 6900.00
Table, Tripod, Inlaid Gallery & Flower Head, Mahogany & Birch, 28 3/4 In. 5175.00
Table, Tuckaway, Spiral Turned Legs, Oak, 19th Century 250.00
Table, Tuckaway, William & Mary, Shoe Feet 6325.00
Table, Turtle Top, Grape Carving, Victorian 1300.00
Table, Turtle Top, Marble Top, Mahogany, Europe, 19th Century, 37 1/2 In. 525.00
Table, Vanity, Hinged Mirror, 2 Compartments, Drawers, Parquetry, 29 1/2 In. 550.00
Table, Vanity, Shield-Shaped Mirror, Burl Inlaid, Mahogany, 54 In. 1155.00

Table, Walnut, Continental, Tilt & Fold, Round Top, 31 1/2 In. Diam. 2015.00
Table, Walnut, Inlaid Parcel Gilt, 3 Drawers, Early 19th Century, 20 1/4 In. 2000.00
Table, Walnut, Inlaid, 1 Frieze Drawer, Curved Legs, Shelf, Germany, 33 x 23 In. 880.00
Table, William & Mary, Frieze Drawer, Ball Feet, 17th Century, 26 x 29 In. 1320.00
Table, William & Mary, Gateleg, Maple, 1 Dovetailed Drawer, 18 x 52 x 28 In. 990.00
Table, William IV, Leaf Carved Trestle, Mahogany, 1850s, 65 In. 4025.00
Table, William IV, Rosewood, Pedestal, c.1835, 47 In. Diam. .... *Illus* 3080.00
Table, Wine, Biedermeier, Tilt Top, Mirror, Oyster Walnut, 42 x 18 In. 2860.00
Table, Wine, Walnut, Mirror Top, 19th Century 2860.00
Table, Writing, Arts & Crafts, Oak, Shelves, H Stretcher, 45 In. 750.00
Table, Writing, Arts & Crafts, 2 Drawers, Oak, Scrolls, Flower Heads, 54 In. 975.00
Table, Writing, George III Style, Walnut, Burl, Inlaid Satinwood, 41 1/2 In. 4950.00
Table, Writing, Kingwood Parquetry, Drawer At Ends, Leather Top, 70 In. 9775.00
Table, Writing, Louis XVI, Leather Surface, Slides, Drawers, Mahogany, 51 In. 5750.00
Table, Writing, Lyre Ends, Fitted Interior, Paw Feet, Rosewood Veneer, 29 In. 660.00
Table, Writing, Paris Mfg., Trestle Base, Child's 150.00
Table, Writing, Partner's, Mahogany, Adjustable Slope Each Side, Gallery 4950.00
Table, Writing, Regency, Calamander, Brass Mounted, Rosewood, c.1810, 29 In. 6900.00
Table, Writing, Regency, Calamander, Crossbanded Mahogany, c.1825, 29 In. 5465.00
Table, Writing, Regency, Ebony, Inlaid Mahogany, c.1810, 29 x 34 In. 2875.00
Table, Writing, Regency, Mahogany, Leather Inset, Splayed Legs, c.1800, 44 In. 8625.00
Table, Writing, Regency, Mahogany, Leather Inset, Trestle Base 1100.00
Table, Wrought Iron, Bronze, Gray & White Marble Top, c.1925, 60 x 26 In. 8625.00
Table, Wrought Iron, Circular Glass Top, Scroll Legs, Art Deco, c.1925, 19 In. 920.00
Table & Chair, Combination, Mission, Oak, Brown Leather 880.00
Tabouret, Harden, Square, 18 1/4 x 16 In. 330.00
Tea Cart, Stickley Bros. 500.00
Tea Cart, Wicker 200.00
Teapoy, Regency, Rosewood, Inlaid Mother-Of-Pearl, Fitted, c.1825 .... 1925.00
Tray, Butler's, George III, Mahogany, Pierced Handholds, Square, 16 1/2 In. 1150.00
Tray, Chippendale, Gertrude Rose, Insects, Birds, Frogs, 25 In. 185.00
Tray, Tea, Inlaid Center Urn-Shaped Medallion, Brass Handles, American 120.00
Trolley, Cocktail, Art Deco, 1940-1950 .... 500.00
Umbrella Stand, Hammered Iron, Riveted Band, Applied Medallion, 24 1/2 In. 440.00
Umbrella Stand, Scalloped Pan, 6 Holes, Green Paint, Cast Iron, 39 1/2 In. 415.00
Urn, Knife, Mahogany Inlay, Holds 50, Pair 2420.00
Vanity, Gustav Stickley, Maple Knobs, Curly Maple, No. 914, 55 x 36 1/4 In. 2310.00
Vitrine, Allegorical & Landscape Vignettes, Gilt Bronze, 56 x 24 In. 985.00
Vitrine, Art Nouveau, Clematis Blossoms, Leaves, 1 Door, Walnut, 1900, 60 In. 5463.00
Vitrine, Biedermeier, Mahogany & Fruitwood Marquetry, Silk Backed, c.1833 .... 6325.00
Vitrine, Cabriole Legs, Paw Feet, Marquetry, 29 x 24 In. 575.00
Vitrine, Empire Style, Gilt Bronze Mounted, Mahogany, 19th Century 9775.00
Vitrine, Louis XV, Mahogany, Brass Ormolu Mount, Marble Top 825.00
Vitrine, Louis XVI, Blue Paint, Wire Top, 2 Doors, 88 x 38 In., Pair 6325.00
Vitrine, Stand, Edwardian, Painted Satinwood 6600.00
Wardrobe, Arts & Crafts, Mahogany, Floral Inlaid, Mirrored, 3 Doors, 72 x 60 In. 975.00
Wardrobe, Crotched Mahogany Veneer, Rope Twist Swirls, c.1860 .... 2000.00
Wardrobe, George II, Yew Wood, 2 Upper Doors, Cabriole Legs, 75 x 40 In. 1980.00
Wardrobe, Oak, Base Drawer, Applied Design Top, Knockdown 995.00
Wardrobe, Renaissance Revival, Walnut Parquetry, c.1870, 81 In. 1265.00
Washstand, 1 Convex Drawer, Medial Shelf, Curly Maple, c.1825, 36 1/2 In. 2415.00
Washstand, Cherry, 2 Drawers, 2 Doors, Backsplash, c.1890 .... 275.00
Washstand, Corner, Mahogany, England, c.1840 .... 280.00
Washstand, Corner, Federal, Signed M.M. Cody, 1795 .... 1300.00
Washstand, Corner, George III, Drawer In Shelf, Mahogany, 41 In. 385.00
Washstand, Corner, Hepplewhite, Mahogany, Inlaid, Scalloped Frieze, 31 1/4 In. 550.00
Washstand, Corner, String Inlay, 1 Drawer, Outward Curving Legs, Mahogany 1150.00
Washstand, Empire, Gold Striping, Shelf, 1 Oval Drawer, Pine, 39 In. 275.00
Washstand, Empire, Walnut, Shelf, 1 Dovetailed Drawer, 25 x 21 x 35 1/4 In. 305.00
Washstand, Federal, Base Shelf, Butternut & Maple, 30 x 32 1/2 In. 345.00
Washstand, George III Style, 2 Drawers, Mahogany, Round Frame, 33 3/4 In. 250.00
Washstand, George III, 2 Drawers, Mahogany, 30 1/2 In. 275.00
Washstand, George III, Mahogany, Inlaid, Triangular Top, Arched Front, 40 In. 305.00

Washstand, George III, Three-Quarter Gallery, Mahogany, 40 In. 460.00
Washstand, Lift Top Compartment, Backsplash, Walnut, c.1840, 33 In. 590.00
Washstand, Lift Top, Zinc Lined, Cabinet Base, Pine, Victorian, 31 In. 265.00
Washstand, Marble Top, Pine & Walnut, Victorian 365.00
Washstand, Paint Design, Yellow & Green, Massachusetts, c.1830, 39 x 18 In. 275.00
Washstand, Pine, Turned Legs, 1 Drawer, Gallery, Shelf, 35 x 16 1/2 x 37 In. 275.00
Washstand, Shaker, Yellow Wash, Pine, c.1850, 38 x 45 1/4 In. 6050.00
Washstand, Sheraton, Walnut, 1 Drawer, Gallery, Country, 24 x 30 In. 195.00
Washstand, Stenciled Flowers, Leaping Deer, Yellow Paint, 31 x 16 In. 385.00
Washstand, Walnut, 3 Drawers, 1890s 350.00
Wastebasket, Stickley Brothers, Slatted, Cutout Pulls, 18 x 14 In. 415.00
Whatnot, Bamboo, 3 Upper Shelves 2400.00
Whatnot, Corner, 5 Shelves, Pierced Sides 125.00
Window Seat, George I, Walnut, Scrolled Arms, Gilt Trim, Upholstered 990.00
Window Seat, George III, Upholstered Scrolled Ends, Mahogany, c.1775, 41 In. 6465.00
Window Seat, Gustav Stickley, Oak, Leather, No. 178, c.1902, 26 x 36 In. 1210.00
Window Seat, Louis Philippe Style, Upholstered Sides, Hoof Feet, Cherry 1045.00
Wine Cooler, Georgian, Brass Trim, 3 Legs, Hexagonal Case, Mahogany, 27 In. 2200.00

G. ARGY-ROUSSEAU is the impressed mark used on a variety of objects in
the Art Deco style. Gabriel Argy-Rousseau, born in 1885, was a French glass
artist.

G-ARGY-
ROUSSEAU

Bowl, Clusters Of Stephanotis, White & Green Ground, Signed, 4 In. 3680.00
Bowl, Long-Legged Birds, Blue, Purple, Green, Pate-De-Verre, 10 In. 6600.00
Bowl, Molded Vines & Leaves, c.1925, 10 In. 5750.00
Bowl, Overlapping Stephanotis Flower Heads, c.1924, 4 In. 4830.00
Bowl, Papillons, 4 Butterflies, Signed, c.1915, 4 1/4 In. 9775.00
Bowl, Streaked Sides, Roundels Of Pine Cones, c.1922, 4 In. 5750.00
Buckle, Faun Amid Swirling Foliage, Silver Mount, 1925, 4 In. 2013.00
Night Light, 3 Satyrical Masks, Wrought Iron Stand, 6 In. 3680.00
Pendant, Berry Cluster, Gray, Red, Purple, Black, Pate-De-Verre, 3 In. 1725.00
Pendant, Brown Pine Cone Amid Orange Needles, Signed, 2 1/4 In. 1430.00
Pendant, Butterfly, In Reserve, Gray, Pate-De-Verre, 1924, 2 1/4 In. 1725.00
Pendant, Cicada, Gray, Purple, Orange, Red, Pate-De-Verre, 2 1/2 In. 1495.00
Pendant, Conifer, Red Pine Cone, Violet Leaves, Signed, 2 1/2 In. 1150.00
Pendant, Daisy Blossoms, Orange Petals, 1 3/4 In., Pair 920.00
Pendant, Violets, Green Stems, Pate-De-Verre, Signed, 2 1/4 In. 1100.00
Pendant, White Trumpet Blossom, Green Stems, Signed, 2 5/8 In. 2310.00
Shade, Allover Asymmetrical Pattern, Oviform, Signed, 7 In. 5290.00
Tray, Pink & Purple, Molded Leaf Border, Pate-De-Verre, 12 1/4 In. 1320.00
Vase, Green Crabs, Frosted Opaque Ground, Signed, 6 1/2 In. 7475.00
Vase, Libations, Egyptian Slave Girl, Brown, Pate-De-Verre, 12 In. 7475.00
Vase, Scrolled Handles, Flowers & Leaves, Pate-De-Verre, 8 1/4 In. 5175.00
Vase, Stylized Foliage, Gray, 2 Handles, Pate-De-Verre, 9 In. 4600.00
Veilleuse, Flower Heads, Gray Mottled, Pate-De-Verre, Iron, 8 3/4 In. 5750.00

GALLE was a designer who made glass, pottery, furniture, and other Art
Nouveau items. Emile Galle founded his factory in France in 1874. After
Galle's death in 1904, the firm continued to make glass and furniture until
1931. The name *Galle* was used as a mark, but it was often hidden in the
design of the object. Galle Pottery is listed below and his furniture is listed in
the Furniture category.

Bottle, Iris Blossoms, Opalescent Gray, Purple, Cameo, Stopper, 9 1/2 In. 3750.00
Bottle, Pilgrim, Purple Wisteria Blooms, Handles, Signed, 12 1/2 In. 2070.00
Bottle, Stopper, Cylindrical, Ice Blue Crackle, Gilded Grasshopper, Fly, 6 1/2 In. 3450.00
Bottle, Stopper, Heraldic Shields, Medieval Princess, Coats Of Arms, Signed, 9 In. .. 9350.00
Bowl, Candy, Enamel Spider Chrysanthemum Blossoms, Blue, c.1890, 5 1/2 In. 750.00
Bowl, Enamel, Wheel-Carved, Shield Outline, Burgundy, Hunting Vignettes, 4 3/4 In. 2875.00
Bowl, Gray, Green, Overlaid & Cut Ferns, Cameo, c.1900, 4 5/8 In. 800.00
Bowl, Gray, Mottled Yellow, Blue & Purple Cut Blossoms, Cameo, c.1900, 8 In. 1840.00
Bowl, Leaves & Berries, Red Cut To Yellow, 4 x 10 1/2 In. 875.00
Bowl, Olive & Lime, Box Elder Leaves & Seed Pods, Cameo, 2 1/4 x 6 1/2 In. 435.00
Box, Bulbous Base, Gray, Mottled Pink, Rust Overlay, Grapes, Cover, c.1900, 4 In. .. 1265.00

Box, Bulbous Base, Gray, Mottled Pink, Green Floral Overlay, Cover, c.1900, 6 In. ... 1035.00
Box, Hydrangea Blossoms & Leaves, Mottled Colors, Signed, 1904, 3 3/8 In. 1380.00
Box, Purple Floral, Cream & Yellow Ground, Cover, 2 x 4 1/4 In. 2000.00
Candy Dish, Enamel Designs, Mosquito, Topaz, Signed, 4 1/4 In. 475.00
Centerpiece, Canoe Shape, Gray, Yellow, Crimson, Poppies, c.1900, 9 1/4 In. 2070.00
Coupe, Opaque Pink To Clear To Pink, Carved Flowers, Signed, 4 x 5 1/2 In 445.00
Cruet, Fern & Flower, 2-Tone Amber, 7 3/4 In. 1200.00
Cup, Red Leaves, Silver Handles Rising From Silver Leaves, c.1900, Pair 3750.00
Ewer, Applied Lotus Blossoms, Buds, Handle, Pale Champagne, 1900, 9 5/8 In. 2600.00
Ewer, Enameled Front Window, Outdoor Scene, Signed, 8 In. 900.00
Inkwell, Cone Shape, Gray, Yellow, Red Overlaid Blossoms, Cameo, c.1900, 3 In. 575.00
Lamp, Art Nouveau Bronze Base, Etched Grape Clusters & Vines, Cameo, 15 In. 4950.00
Lamp, Dancing Putti At Base, Tree Trunk Standard, Signed, 1904, 20 In. 4900.00
Lamp, Gazebo Enclosing 6 Figures, Domed Shade, Signed, c.1900, 20 1/2 In. 9775.00
Lamp, Hanging, 3 Colors, Original Hardware, 10 In. 9000.00
Lamp, Hanging, Hydrangea Blossoms, Opalescent Gray, Cameo, 15 5/8 In. 6900.00
Lamp Shade, Floral, 2 Women Holding Shade, Podany, 17 In. 6875.00
Perfume Bottle, Atomizer, Deep Amber Leaves & Vines, White Frosted, 3 3/4 In. ... 600.00
Perfume Bottle, Atomizer, Flowers, Yellow & Frosted Ground, Cameo, 8 In. 1375.00
Perfume Bottle, Atomizer, Purple Floral, White Frosted, Signed, 7 3/4 In. 875.00
Perfume Bottle, Berries, Leafage, Gray, Teal, Floriform Stopper, Cameo, 3 3/4 In. .. 3163.00
Perfume Bottle, Etched Wooded River Scene, Metal Mounted, Signed, 8 1/2 In. 1850.00
Perfume Bottle, Forested Landscape, Boater, Gray Glass, Signed, 4 3/4 In. 1265.00
Perfume Bottle, Stopper, Enameled, Thistles, White, Rose, c.1900, 5 5/8 In. 1150.00
Perfume Bottle, Undulating Blossoms, Signed, c.1910, 7 5/8 In. 1093.00
Pitcher, Enameled, Bulbous, Amber, Red, Black, Green, Poppies, c.1890, 3 1/4 In. ... 1265.00
Sconce, Double Overlay, Etched, Yellow Ground, Blue & Umber Overlay, 21 1/2 In. 6325.00
Tumbler, Blue & Violet Flowers, Pink Frosted 950.00
Vase, Alsatian Mountain Landscape, Gray, Lemon, Purple, Cameo, 1900, 16 In. 4600.00
Vase, Amber & Green Honeysuckle, Signed, 19 1/2 In. 2300.00
Vase, Amber Glass, Enameled Ferns & Flowers In Ribs, Ruffled, 10 3/4 In. 805.00
Vase, Baluster Shape, Gray, Yellow, Purple Overlay, Cameo, 1900, 14 1/8 In. 920.00
Vase, Banjo, Brown Branches & Berries, Frosted Yellow-Green Ground, 5 1/2 In. 850.00
Vase, Banjo, Brown Lakeside Scene, Yellow & Frosted Ground, 6 1/2 In. 1155.00
Vase, Banjo, Light Brown Floral, Frosted White Ground, Cameo, 6 1/2 In. 660.00
Vase, Banjo, Pink Floral, Yellow & Frosted White Ground, Cameo, 6 1/2 In. 1210.00
Vase, Banjo, Violet-Brown Leaves & Blossoms, Flared, Frosted Ground, 5 1/2 In. 850.00
Vase, Berried Branches, Frosted Yellow Ground, Goblet Shape, Signed, 17 In. 6050.00
Vase, Blossoms, Cicada, Veiny Leaf Interior, Marine Blue, Cameo, 1890, 7 1/8 In 2875.00
Vase, Blown Out, Oval, Amber, Brown, Leaves & Seed Pods, Cameo, 7 1/2 In. 6600.00
Vase, Blue-Green Eucalyptus Branches, Green & White Frosted, Cameo, 23 1/4 In. .. 2300.00
Vase, Bottle Neck, Pastel Florals, 4-Color, 15 1/2 In. 4500.00
Vase, Branches, Leaves & Berries, Yellow-Orange Frosted Ground, Cameo, 5 1/2 In. 850.00
Vase, Brown Floral Design, Coral & Frosted Ground, Cameo, 15 In. 2950.00
Vase, Brown Flowers, Banjo Shape, Yellow, 5 1/2 In. 1050.00
Vase, Brown Flowers, Yellow Buds, Frosted Clear Ground, Waisted, Cameo, 15 In. .. 2585.00
Vase, Brown Fuchsias, Yellow-Brown Ground, Cameo, 6 1/2 In. 578.00
Vase, Brown Leaves & Blossoms, Yellow-Green Frosted Ground, Cameo, 5 1/4 In. ... 850.00
Vase, Brown Leaves & Stalks, Rose & Yellow Overlay, Cameo, 1910, 8 1/2 In. 1092.00
Vase, Brown Leaves, Berries, Gold Frosted Ground, Bulbous, Signed, 10 1/4 In. 1400.00
Vase, Bud, Banjo, Gray, Yellow, Red Overlaid Blossoms, Cameo, c.1900, 6 3/4 In. ... 1495.00
Vase, Bud, Brown Scrolling Branches, Gold Frosted, Ovoid, Footed, 5 3/4 In. 546.00
Vase, Bud, Gray, Olive Green Cut Branches, Cameo, c.1900, 6 3/4 In. 1035.00
Vase, Bud, Lemon Yellow, Blue & Purple Cut Wildflowers, Cameo, c.1900, 6 3/4 In. 1495.00
Vase, Bud, Lime & Olive Box Elder Branches, Pink & Gray, Cameo, 8 1/8 In. 747.00
Vase, Bud, Lime Star-Shaped Thistles, Apricot Interior, Cameo, 8 1/4 In. 690.00
Vase, Bud, Purple Flower Design, Bottle Shape, Frosted Pink, Cameo, 4 1/2 In. 880.00
Vase, Bulbous, Gray Shaded With Rose, Green Blossoms, Cameo, c.1900, 5 3/4 In. .. 345.00
Vase, Bulbous, Green, Red-Brown, Trees, Riverside, Cameo, 6 1/2 In. 1210.00
Vase, Caramel & Light Green Acanthus Leaves, Amber Foot, Cameo, 27 1/2 In. 2587.00
Vase, Carnation Pink Mottling, Frosted White, Bulbous, Signed, 3 5/8 In. 975.00
Vase, Chestnut Swirling Marine Grasses, Orange, White, Cameo, Ovoid, 6 In. 747.00
Vase, Cranberry Lilies, Frosted Gray, Silvered Metal Mount, Ovoid, 15 1/4 In. 977.00

Vase, Cylindrical Neck, Bulbous Base, Gray, Poppies, Cameo, 1900, 8 1/2 In. 1380.00
Vase, Cylindrical, Bulbous Base, Rose, Green Overlay, Cameo, 1900, 6 In. 575.00
Vase, Enamel Painted Anemones, Gilt Highlights, 10 1/4 In. 1610.00
Vase, Enameled, Brown, Green, White, Wild Flowers, Cameo, c.1900, 17 1/4 In. 1495.00
Vase, Enameled Chrysanthemums, Buds, Champagne, Gilded, 1900, 12 1/2 In. 2013.00
Vase, Enameled Dragonflies, Stars, Bubbles, Turquoise, Baluster, 6 1/2 In. 9775.00
Vase, Enameled Wild Flowers & Leafage, Champagne, Gilded, 1900, 12 7/8 In. 2875.00
Vase, Etched Acorns & Oak Leaves, Pink To Green, Cameo, 13 In. 1210.00
Vase, Etched Aquatic Flowering Plants, Frosted Ground, Signed, 10 1/8 In. 1540.00
Vase, Etched Fruiting Vine & Foliage, Pink Over Amber, Signed, 3 1/2 In. 460.00
Vase, Etched Lily Blossoms, Double Overlay, Signed, 11 1/2 In. 4600.00
Vase, Etched, Enameled, Oviform, Amber Honeycomb, Branches & Bees, 5 3/4 In. ... 4830.00
Vase, Flaring Lip, Bulbous Base, Blue Blossoms, Cameo, 1900, 10 1/2 In. 1150.00
Vase, Floral & Foliate Design, Sang De Boeuf, Pink Ground, Signed 330.00
Vase, Floral Decoration, Navy To Opaque Glass, Signed, Cameo, 9 In. 1100.00
Vase, Floral Design, Red Cut To Frost, 6 1/4 In. 450.00
Vase, Floral, Purple, Green, Frosted Ground, Cameo, Banjo Shape, 6 1/2 In. 1295.00
Vase, Floral, Single Cut, Orange To Frost, Signed, 6 3/4 In. 575.00
Vase, Flower Buds, Vines, Leaves, Cream & Blue Ground, Fluted, 12 In. 3000.00
Vase, Flowering Clematis, Pink Overlaid In Plum Red, Signed, 6 In. 670.00
Vase, Flowers, Greenish White Overlaid With Blue, Signed, 24 In. 3737.00
Vase, Flowers, Rose Overlaid With Cranberry, Signed, 5 In. 460.00
Vase, Frosted White Ground, Crimson Flower Overlay, Oviform, 7 1/2 In. 2550.00
Vase, Fuchsia Blossoms & Leaves, Inverted Rim, Signed, 11 7/8 In. 8800.00
Vase, Fuchsia On White, Frosted, Signed, 16 In. 4250.00
Vase, Fuchsia, Foliage, Mold Blown, Double Overlay, Oviform, Periwinkle, 12 In. ... 7820.00
Vase, Geranium, Frosted, Pink, Blue, Green Etched Blossoms, Cameo, 13 1/4 In. 1320.00
Vase, Gray Walls, Cameo Carved Mountainous Landscape, Signed, 9 In. 1400.00
Vase, Gray Walls, Mottled Pink, Green Cameo Hydrangea, Signed, 6 In. 425.00
Vase, Grapevine, Pink, Yellow, Oval Layers, Polished Grapes & Vines, Cameo, 6 In.   990.00
Vase, Green Carved Leaves, White Frosted Ground, Cameo, 6 x 11 In. 3300.00
Vase, Green Ferns & Fronds, Pink Frost, 15 1/2 In. 2200.00
Vase, Green Leaves, Frosted, Cameo, 5 1/4 In. 750.00
Vase, Green Overlaid In Caramel, Maple Leaves & Acorns, Signed, 10 In. 2875.00
Vase, Hummingbird, Mouth-Blown, 11 In. 350.00
Vase, Iris Blossoms, Clear, Mustard & White, Marqueterie-Sur-Verre, 7 1/4 In. 6325.00
Vase, Lake & Forest Scene, Green To Deep Chocolate, Birds, Banjo Shape, 6 1/2 In. 1350.00
Vase, Lake & Mountains, Trees In Foreground, Signed, c.1900, 11 3/8 In. 5750.00
Vase, Lake Como Landscape, Gray, Lemon, Blue, Purple, Cameo, 1900, 11 In. 6325.00
Vase, Leaves & Blossoms, Green, Yellow, Frosted Ground, 2 Handles, Cameo, 5 In. . 1400.00
Vase, Leaves & Blossoms, Orange, Brown, Signed, Cameo, 6 1/2 x 2 In. 850.00
Vase, Lilac & Foliate Design, Pink Ground, 17 1/4 In. 1980.00
Vase, Lilies-Of-The-Valley, Dragonfly, Enameled, Gilded, Signed, 1900, 4 1/2 In. 2000.00
Vase, Lily Pads, Lotus Blossoms, Gray, Red, Cameo, 1900, 24 3/4 In. 2875.00
Vase, Lime Poppy Leaves, White Frosted, Bottle Shape, Cameo, 1910, 12 1/8 In. .. 1265.00
Vase, Lime Scrolling Ferns, White, Bottle Shape, Cameo, 1910, 12 1/4 In. 1495.00
Vase, Mountains, Lake, Trees, Sun Rays, 14 In. 3400.00
Vase, Mountains, Lake, Double Overlaid, Signed, 18 In. 6670.00
Vase, Nasturtium, Bulbous, Dimpled, Blossoms & Buds, Vines, Cameo, 11 1/2 In. 990.00
Vase, Naturalistic Scene With Lake, Banjo Form, Signed, 6 1/2 In. 805.00
Vase, Olive & Lavender Hydrangea, Rose To White Frosted, Waisted, Cameo, 22 In. 3750.00
Vase, Opalescent Yellow, Molded, Oviform, Cameo, 1920 .... 5000.00
Vase, Oval, Mottled Yellow, Pink Frosted, Ruby Flower Overlay, Cameo, 7 In. 770.00
Vase, Overlaid Flowering Buddleia, Butterflies, Signed, 29 1/2 In. 4400.00
Vase, Overlaid In Lime Green & Umber, Wooded Lake Scene, Signed, 6 In. 1725.00
Vase, Overlay Of Brick & Amber, Depicts Flowers, Signed, 19 1/4 In. 2300.00
Vase, Overlay, Squat, Yellow & Blue Ground, Caramel Etched Seaweed, 11 In. 8625.00
Vase, Pilgrim, Frosted Ground, Wooded River Landscape Overlay, Signed, 10 3/4 In. 1725.00
Vase, Pilgrim Hydrangea Blossoms, Gray, Pink, White, Green, Lavender, 11 1/4 In. .. 8000.00
Vase, Pilgrim Shape, Handles, Gray, Amber, Leaf Clusters, Cameo, c.1900, 5 1/4 In. 1035.00
Vase, Pilgrim, Wildflowers & Leaves, Signed, c.1900, 5 3/8 In. 1600.00
Vase, Pine Boughs & Cones, Gray, Blue, Amber, Cameo, 1900, 7 1/8 In. 4600.00
Vase, Pink Ground, Green Overlay, Budding Clematis Vines, Signed, 8 1/2 In. 925.00

Vase, Plum Flowers, Carved, Green To Frosted Ground, 4 x 4 In. 600.00
Vase, Pond Lily, Green, Amethyst Etched Lily Blossoms, Oval Layers, Cameo, 8 In. 935.00
Vase, Poppies, White Overlaid With Cranberry, Signed, c.1900, 12 In. 6325.00
Vase, Purple Berry & Floral Design, Coral & Carnation Ground, Signed, 4 3/8 In. 1175.00
Vase, Purple Iris, Cream & Gold Ground, 15 3/4 In. 4000.00
Vase, Purple Irises, Signed, Cameo, 12 In. 350.00
Vase, Purple Landscape, Gray & Lemon Overlay, Cameo, 1900, 14 1/4 In. 3450.00
Vase, Purple Lilies, Cream & Yellow Ground, 11 1/4 In. 3000.00
Vase, Raised & Flared Rim, Mottled, Leaves, Seed Pods, 3 Layers, Cameo, 16 In. 3300.00
Vase, Red Cherries, Frosted Ground, Yellow, Cameo, 6 3/4 In. 850.00
Vase, Red Flowers, Maroon Leaves, Golden Ground, Signed, 8 1/4 In. 3500.00
Vase, Red Leaf & Berry Design, Yellow Ground, Cameo, Signed, 4 3/8 In. 975.00
Vase, Red Roses, Citron, Yellow & Clear Ground, 8 x 6 1/2 In. 4400.00
Vase, Relief Stems & Blossoms, Baluster Form, Signed, 5 7/8 In. 1380.00
Vase, Seascape, Flattened Egg Shape, Yellow Ground, Signed, 10 1/4 In. 1725.00
Vase, Silver-Plated Rim, Etched River Scene, Amber, Brown, 3 3/4 In. 825.00
Vase, Spider Chrysanthemum Blossoms, Enameled, Signed, 1890, 8 5/8 In. 4600.00
Vase, Squash & Foliage, Amber Ground, Signed, 7 1/8 In. 4625.00
Vase, Squash, Mold Blown, Double Overlay, Lime Green, Brown, 7 3/4 In. 5175.00
Vase, Stick Shape, Orange Layers, Stemmed Chrysanthemums, Cameo, 23 1/2 In. 2640.00
Vase, Tapered Cylinder, Gray, Pink, White Overlay, Blossoms, Cameo, 1905, 10 In. .. 1265.00
Vase, Thistle Blossoms, Leaves, Frosted Ground, Pink & Yellow Tones, 2 1/4 In. 450.00
Vase, Trailing Hops, Leaves, Gray Glass, Signed, c.1900, 7 1/4 In. 925.00
Vase, Trefoil Rim, Double Overlay, Blossoms & Leaves, Cameo, 8 1/2 In. 990.00
Vase, Trumpet, Mottled Orange, Frosted, Etched Orange Flowers, Cameo/, 12 1/4 In. 825.00
Vase, Tulips, Cream & Pink Ground, 11 1/2 In. 4000.00
Vase, Tulips, Grasses, Opalescent Lemon, Blue, Purple, Cameo, 1900, 6 1/4 In. 2300.00
Vase, Umber River Landscape, Signed, 13 In. 2530.00
Vase, Violet Hanging Fuchsias, Yellow Frosted Ground, 4 1/2 In. 1295.00
Vase, Violet-Brown, Frosted Ground, Banjo, Flared, Cameo, 5 1/2 In. 850.00
Vase, White & Pink Frosted Ground, 4 1/2 x 5 In. 675.00
Vase, Wide Mouth, Gray, Mottled Yellow, Purple Blossoms, Cameo, c.1900, 5 In. 1265.00
Vase, Wild Flowers, Opalescent Yellow, Maroon, Raspberry, Cameo, 9 1/8 In. 2875.00
Vase, Winter Landscape, Opalescent Yellow, Orange, Gray, Blue, Cameo, 10 In. 3200.00
Vase, Wisteria Blossoms, Buds, Gray Mottled, Lime, Purple, Cameo, 21 5/8 In. 3750.00
Vase, Wisteria, Gray Top, Violet, Rose, Amber Base, Cameo, 1900, 14 In. 4600.00
Vase, Yellow Walls, Purple Shading To Brown, Cameo Blossoms, Signed, 5 In. 400.00

GALLE POTTERY was made by Emile Galle, the famous French designer, after 1874. The pieces were marked with the initials *E. G.* impressed, *Em. Galle Faiencerie de Nancy*, or a version of his signature. Galle is best known for his glass, listed above.

Basket, Scenic, 14 In. 2500.00
Bowl, Figural, 3 Geese With Necks Intertwined, Backs Form Bowls, 15 In. 2100.00
Owl, Enameled, On Circular Socle, Green Glass Eyes, 13 1/4 In. 4025.00
Pin Tray, Allover Bachelor Buttons, White, 6 x 3 In. 220.00
Tureen, Domed Cover, Blue, Landscape Scenes, Handles, 1890, 10 1/4 In. 920.00
Vase, 3 Sections, Ivory Ground, Gold & Blue Pattern, Signed, 9 3/4 In. 1100.00
Vase, Bamboo Shoots, Black Outlining, Ivory Ground, 3 Sections, 9 3/4 In. 1100.00
Vase, Ewe, Man With Bagpipe Scene, Handle, Blue Ground, 8 x 6 In. 900.00
Vase, Gold & Blue Bamboo Shoots, Black Outlining, Ivory Ground, 10 In. 1100.00

GAME collectors like all types of games. Of special interest are any board games or card games. Transogram and other company names are included in the description when known. Other games may be found listed under Card, Toy, or the name of the character or celebrity featured in the game.

$64,000 Question, Lowell Toy, 1956 .... 40.00
12 O'clock High, Card, Milton Bradley, 1965 .... 35.00
12 O'clock High, Ideal, 1965 .... 45.00
1964 World's Fair, Milton Bradley 20.00
3 Musketeers, Milton Bradley, 1958 .... 32.00
Abbott & Costello, Who's On First, Box 25.00
Across The Continent, Parker Brothers, 1952 .... 45.00 to 100.00

Addams Family, Milton Bradley, 1974 .... 57.00
ADT Delivery Box, Milton Bradley, 1890 .... 125.00
Adventures Of Robin Hood, Milton Bradley, 1938 .... 45.00
Alfred Hitchcock's Why?, Milton Bradley, 1957 .... 35.00
All-Star Baseball, Cadeco, 1962 .... 50.00
All-Star Basketball, Whitman, 1935 .... 28.00 to 60.00
Alley Oop, Lithograph Label, Stephen Slesinger, 1937 .... 60.00
Annie Oakley, Board, Milton Bradley, 1955 .... 60.00 to 85.00
Aquanauts, Transogram, 1961 .... 100.00
Archie Bunker, Card 19.00
Archie Game, Whitman, 1964 .... 60.00
Around The World In 80 Days, Board 30.00
Assembly Line, Selchow & Righter, 1953 .... 75.00
Automatic Racing, With Garage, Lithograph Tin, Box, 6 1/2 x 6 1/2 In. 225.00
Babe Ruth, Baseball, 1920s 1750.00
Babes In Toyland, Parker Bros., 1961 .... 40.00
Babysitter, Ideal, 1966 .... 45.00
Backgammon, Counters, Matching Dice Shakers, Ivory, 19th Century 265.00
Bagatelle, Atlas, Tin, Wood, 1930s 175.00
Bagatelle, Lithograph Covering, Oriental Scene, Clay Marbles, 17 x 7 In. ... 145.00
Bagatelle, Nutty Mad, Marx, 1963 .... 45.00
Bagatelle, Tom & Jerry, Marx, Box 75.00
Bambino Baseball, 1940s 75.00
Banana Tree, Marx, 1977 .... 10.00
Barbie, Queen Of The Prom, Mattel, 1960 .... 30.00 to 40.00
Barbie, World Of Fashion, 3-D On Carnaby Street 125.00
Barney Google, Board, 1923 .... 45.00 to 50.00
Barney Google & Spark Plug, Board, 1923 .... 175.00 to 195.00
Baron Munchausen, 1933 .... 25.00
Baseball, Milton Bradley, 1941 .... 45.00
Baseball, Parker Brothers, Box 195.00
Basket Making, 1940s 18.00
Bat Masterson, Lowell, 1959 .... 95.00
Batman, 1966 .... 35.00
Battle Line, 1964 .... 65.00
Battle-Cry, Milton Bradley, 1962 .... 35.00
Battlestar Galactica, Milton Bradley, 1976 .... 18.00
Battlestar Galactica, Parker Bros., 1978 .... 20.00 to 25.00
Beachhead Invasion Game, Built-Rite, 1950s 75.00
Beany & Cecil Jumping DJ 22.00
Beaver Money-Making Game, Hasbro, 1959 .... 35.00
Beetle Bailey, Soldiers, Jaymar, 1956 .... 69.00
Ben Casey MD, Transogram, 1961 .... 28.00 to 29.00
Benny Goodman Swings Into A Game Of Musical Information, 1930s 70.00
Bewitched, 1965 .... 90.00
Bible Rhymes, Goodenough & Weglem, New York, 1930s 70.00
Big Business, Board, Transogram, 1937 .... 140.00
Bing Crosby's Call Me Lucky, 1954 .... 50.00
Bingo Cage, Board, Numbered Balls 165.00
Bingo-Matic, Card, Transogram, Number Dispenser, 1954, Box 35.00
Black Beauty, Transogram, 1958 .... 22.00
Blacks & Whites, Board, 1970s 95.00
Blast Off!, Selchow, 1953 .... 95.00
Blocks, 6 Victorian Scenes, Wooden, France, Box, 8 x 7 In., 20 Piece 325.00
Blondie Goes To Leisureland, Send-Away, Package, 1935 .... 35.00
Board, 2-Sided, Parqueted Walnut, Bird's-Eye Maple & Mahogany 195.00
Board, Carved & Painted Each Side, Pine, 18 x 19 1/2 In. 275.00
Board, Cribbage, Carved, Quillwork, Portrait Center, 5 Original Pegs, Case, 8 In. 400.00
Board, Double Sided, Checkers & Chinese Checkers, Christmas 1884, 22 x 15 In. 1610.00
Board, Junior Combination Board 65.00
Board, Lash's Bitters, Wooden, 4 1/2 x 13 In. 65.00
Board, Primitive Landscape In Center, Folding, 21 1/2 x 20 1/4 In. 357.00
Board, Red & Black Paint, Pine, 17 1/2 x 17 1/2 In. 236.50

Board, Stone, Faux Marble Paint, 20 3/4 x 20 3/4 In. 313.00
Bob Feller's Big League Baseball Game, 1963 .... 165.00
Bomber Ball, Game Makers, 1940 .... 75.00 to 100.00
Bonanza Rummy, Parker Bros., 1964 .... 35.00
Booby Trap, Parker Bros., 1965 .... 39.00
Box, Checkerboard Exterior, Backgammon Inside, Green Paint, 16 x 16 1/2 In. 165.00
Branded, Milton Bradley 85.00
Break Par Golf, Warren Built-Rite, 1940s 15.00
Break-A-Plate, Carnival Pitch, Hanna-Barbera, 1961 .... 70.00
Bridge Lotto, Card, Jean Harlow, 1930s 38.00
Buckaroo, The Cowboy Roundup Game, Milton Bradley, 1947 .... 60.00
Bull In A China Shop, Milton Bradley, 1930 .... 55.00
Cage, Chug-A-Lug, Nome, Alaska 400.00
Calling All Cars, Fox, 1938 .... 45.00
Calling Superman, Transogram, 1954 .... 100.00
Calypso, 1955 .... 48.00
Camelot, Parker Bros., Box, 1931, 10 x 20 In. .... 20.00 to 50.00
Camp Granada, Milton Bradley, 1965 .... 45.00
Capt. Kangroo Kangadoodles Game, Hasbro, 1956 .... 40.00
Captain Video, Stand-Up Control Panel, Instrument Panel, 1950s 98.00
Careers, Parker Bros., 1957 .... 38.00
Carl Hubbell Strike 3 Baseball, Autographed Cover, Box 650.00
Carrier Strike, War, Milton Bradley, 1977 .... 32.00
Carroway's Game Of Possession, NBC, 1955 .... 40.00
Casper The Friendly Ghost, Glow In The Dark, 1974 .... 25.00
Casper The Friendly Ghost, Milton Bradley, 1959 .... 10.00
Charlie Chan Detective, Milton Bradley 90.00
Checkerboard, 1 Side, Parcheesi Other, Painted, 16 x 16 In. 550.00
Checkerboard, 2-Tone Pattern, Hardwood, 27 x 29 1/2 In. 182.00
Checkerboard, Black & Natural, Gallery, 14 1/2 x 14 3/4 In. 247.00
Checkerboard, Black Paint, Pine, 17 3/4 x 18 In. 137.50
Checkerboard, Black & Yellow Cardboard, Pine Back, Walnut Edge, 13 x 13 In. 137.50
Checkerboard, Lithograph Paper Cover, Chess India, Tokalon, 18 x 18 In. 1.10
Checkerboard, Red & Black, Yellow, Green & Blue Striping, Poplar, 18 3/4 x 19 In. 385.00
Checkerboard & Backgammon, Raised Buttons On Edge, 17 3/4 x 18 3/4 In. 440.00
Checkerboard & Parcheesi, Painted, 36 3/4 x 36 3/4 In. 1100.00
Checkers, Holson, Box, 30 Piece 15.00
Chess, World Figure Pieces, F.D.R., Eleanor, Etc., Myma Gorden Design, 1940s 2850.00
Chess & Backgammon, Fold-Out Box, Hardwood 10.00
Chess Set, Bears In Medieval Costumes, Painted Wood, King-4 In. 286.00
Chess Set, Box, Opens To Board, Backgammon, Mother-Of-Pearl Inlay, India 520.00
Chess Set, Camelot, King Arthur, Guenivere, Merlin, Board 150.00
Chess Set, Each Piece On Puzzle Ball, Ivory, China, Late 19th Century 1650.00
Chess Set, Europeans Versus Africans, Porcelain, Germany, Box, 32 Piece 1150.00
Chess Set, Gilt & Silvered White Metal, King-4 1/2 In. 825.00
Chess Set, Ivory, 5 In. Figures 3000.00
Chess Set, Ivory, Elephants, Mahouts As Rooks, Horsemen As Knights, China 1100.00
Chess Set, Lord Howe Versus George Washington, England, c.1976, 32 Piece 3565.00
Chess Set, Medici Dynasty Theme, Gilt & Silvered Metal, Italy, Early 20th Century 1100.00
Chess Set, Miniature Teacup & Samovar Pieces, Russia, Board, Box, King-1 3/8 In. 220.00
Chess Set, Red & Natural Ivory, Fitted Box With Board 600.00
Chess Set, Traveling, Celluloid Pieces, Catlin 90.00
Chess Set, Traveling, Leather Pocket With Pin-In Ivory Pieces 70.00
Chess Set, Whale, Red Lines, Ivory, 19th Century 4400.00
Chessboard, Leather, Square, 19 In. 88.00
Chinese Checkers, Wooden Frame, 1958 .... 12.00
Chitty Chitty Bang Bang, Electric Quiz Game, Remco, 1968 .... 100.00
Chitty Chitty Bang Bang, Milton Bradley, 1968, Box 28.00
Chromagica, McLoughlin, Complete & Working, 1875 .... 650.00
Chuggedy Chug, Milton Bradley, 1955 .... 75.00
Chutes & Ladders, Milton Bradley, 1943 .... 35.00
Chutes & Ladders, Milton Bradley, 1956 .... 35.00
Citadel, Parker Bros., 1940 .... 100.00

Civil War, Parker Bros., 1961 .... 32.00
Clipper Race, Samuel Gabriel & Sons, 1930-1940 .... 190.00
Coke Game Of Health, Envelope, 11 x 26 In. 110.00
Combat, Ideal, 1963 .... 30.00 to 50.00
Cowboy Roundup, 1952 .... 12.00
Crime Stoppers, Dick Tracy, Box 50.00
Croquet Set, Table, Victorian, Box 120.00
Cross-Country, 1941 .... 36.00
Crow Shoot, Cardboard, Box 4.00
Crown Checkers, Whitman, Box 1.00
Dark Shadows, 1960s .... 30.00 to 75.00
Dart, Space Station, Periscopic Viewer, Rocket Launcher, Amsco, 1950s, 15 In. 65.00
DC-3 Airline, Parker Bros., 1941 .... 125.00
Deputy Dawg, Milton Bradley, 1961 .... 120.00
Disko Un Taraget, Parker Bros. 35.00
Dixie Land, Card, Pictures Blacks, Fireside Game Co., 1897 .... 220.00
Doc Holliday, 1960 .... 45.00
Dogfight, Milton Bradley, 1962 .... 40.00
Dominoes, Good Roads Machinery, Smith & Sons Mfg., Celluloid, Box 298.00
Dominoes, Woody Woodpecker, Whitman, 1961 .... 35.00
Dondi Potato Race Game, Massenfeld Bros., 1950s 40.00
Donkey Party, Whitman 30.00
Double 9 Domino Set, English Crown & White House Etched, Leatherette Box 45.00
Down You Go, Selchow & Righter, 1954 .... 22.00
Dr. Busby, Hand Colored Lithographed Cards, Busby Family, Ives, 1830s 240.00
Dr. Busby, No. 4379, Milton Bradley, 1905 .... 50.00
Dr. Daniels Veterinarian Dice Game, Don't Gamble Use Dr. Daniels Remedies 385.00
Dr. Doodle's Dog, Selchow & Righter, Junior Edition, 1940 .... 40.00
Dr. Kildare, Ideal, 1962 .... 35.00
Duck Shooting, Parker Bros., 1930s 120.00
Dukes Of Hazzard, Board, Ideal, 1981 .... 10.00 to 15.00
Earth Satellite, Gabriel, 1956 .... 150.00
Easy Money, Milton Bradley, 1956 .... 4.50
Electric Baseball, Jim Prentice, Electric Game Co., Late 1940s, Box 65.00
Elsie's Milkman, Illustrated Board, Truck, Town, Instructions, Smith-Edwards, 1963 ..... 87.00
F.B.I., Transogram, 1960s, 20 x 10 x 2 In. 25.00
Fall Guy, Milton Bradley, 1982 .... 28.00
Famous Authors, Parker Brothers, c.1910 .... 55.00
Fashionable English Game Sorry, Board, Parker Bros., 1934 .... 185.00
Fish Pond, Folding Pond, 33 Fish, 6 Poles, Magnetic, McLoughlin, 1891, 14 In. 220.00
Fish Pond, National Games, Inc., 1950s 70.00
Fishing, 2 Fishing Rods & Metal Magnets, 6 Tin Fish, 1930s, On Card 10.00
Flash Cards, Dr. Kildare Jr., Medical School, 1963 .... 20.00
Flight Top, Louis Marx 10.00
Flip Your Wig 110.00
Flivver, Car Pieces, 1920s 185.00
Flying Nun, Milton Bradley, 1968 .... 25.00
Flying The Beam, 4 Metal Planes, Instructions, Box, 1941 .... 70.00
Football, Foto-Electric, Cadaco, 1962 .... 50.00
Football, Stars On Stripes, Graphic Box 65.00
Football, Tudor, Electric 36.00
Football, Tudor, Electric, 1955, Box 85.00
Fortune Telling, Card, Gypsy Witch & Cake Set, c.1930 .... 12.50
Fortune Telling, Je Vois Tout, Interior Playing Surface, Box, 10 3/4 x 8 3/4 In. 180.00
Fox & Geese, Wooden, Ivory Pegs, Container, Directions, 7 3/4 In. 170.00
G.I. Joe Adventure, Hasbro, 1982 .... 15.00
Game Of Airmail, Marble, Milton Bradley, 1927 .... 150.00
Game Of Birds, Cincinnati Card Game Co., 1899 .... 35.00
Game Of Dixie, Parker Bros., 1954 .... 20.00
Game Of Flowers, Cincinnati Game Co., Card, 1899 .... 45.00
Game Of Fox Hunting, Lead Figures, Spear Bavaria 247.00
Game Of Hollywood Stars, 1955 .... 20.00
Game Of Letters, Parker Bros., Box 35.00

Game Of Life, Board, 4 Spinners, March, 1866 .... 300.00
Game Of Moon Tag, Parker Bros., 1957 .... 130.00
Game Of State Capitals, Parker Bros., 1952 .... 18.00
Game Of Venetian Fortune Teller, Card, Parker Bros., 1898 .... 80.00
Game Of Who, Parker Bros., 1951 .... 50.00
Gee-Whiz, Racing Game Sensation, Wolverine Supply & Mfg., 1929, Box 225.00
Get Smart, 1965 .... 30.00
Giant Step, 1950s, Box 25.00
Giant Wheel Horse Race Game, Remco, 1950s 135.00
Gidget Fortune Telling, Cards & Fold Out Mat, Milton Bradley, 1965 .... 12.00
Gil Hodges Pennant Fever 145.00
Go To The Head Of The Class, 1949 .... 12.00
Goldfinger, Milton Bradley, 1966 .... 55.00
Golf, Kargo, England, 1930s 40.00
Gomer Pyle, Transogram, 1965 .... 32.00
Ol' Charlie Brown, 1971, Box 55.00
Great American Flag Game, Parker Bros., 1943 .... 75.00 to 100.00
Green Ghost, Transogram, 1965, Box 95.00
Green Hornet, Card, Box, 1966 .... 25.00
Groucho's TV Quiz, Pressman, 1954 .... 90.00
Groucho's You Bet Your Life, Lowell, 1955 .... 70.00
Gunsmoke, Lowell Games, 1958 .... 20.00 to 40.00
Gypsy Fortune Telling, Milton Bradley, 1895 .... 215.00
Harlem Globe Trotters 20.00
Haunted House, Ideal 300.00
Have Gun Will Travel, Parker Bros., Canada, 1959 .... 38.00
Hawaiian Punch, Box 15.00
Hendrik Van Loon's Wide World, Parker Bros., 1933 .... 25.00 to 30.00
Home In Center, Checkers On Reverse, 21 x 21 In. 605.00
Hoop-O-Loop, Wolverine, 1925 .... 75.00
Hop Ching Chinese Checkers, Pressman, Co. 29.00
Horse Racing, Escalado Deluxe, Chad Valley, England 250.00
Horse Racing, Lead Horses, England, Box 95.00
Horse Racing, Eddie Arcaro Sweepstakes, Board Game, 1945 .... 75.00
Horseshoe, Auburn Rubber, Box 32.00
How Silas Popped The Question, c.1915 .... 25.00
Hungry Pup, Bones On Copper Platter, Gilbert Co., 1940s, 3 3/4 x 4 3/4 In. 20.00
I Dream Of Jeannie, Milton Bradley, 1965 .... 45.00
I Spy, 1965 .... 40.00
In Dixie Land, Card 95.00
Interchangeable Combination Circus, Milton Bradley 242.00
It, Card, Parker Bros., 1904 .... 40.00
Jack & Beanstalk Adventure, Transogram, 1957 .... 15.00
Jackie Gleason, Transogram, 1956 .... 50.00
Jacks, Metal, Rubber Ball, 1930-1940, Illustrated Package 15.00
James Bond, Box, 1964 .... 75.00
Jollie Darkie Target Game, 1890 .... 395.00
Jolly Clown Party Game, 3 Wooden Balls, Milton Bradley, Box, 1932 .... 45.00
Jungle Hunt, Marble, Gotham 85.00
Kentucky Derby Racing, Whitman, Box, 1938 .... 25.00 to 35.00
King Kong, Ideal, 1976 .... 25.00
Kissing, Masters, 1928 .... 55.00
Knitting Spool Family, Box, 1940s 15.00
Knock Hockey, 1960s 65.00
Kukla & Ollie, Parker Bros., 1962, Box, 10 x 13 In. 39.00
Lame Duck, Parker Bros. 150.00
Laverne & Shirley, Board, Parker Brothers, 1977 .... 20.00
Lawn Croquet Set, Hand Carved 375.00
Leaning Tower, Wooden, Game Of Skill, 1940s, Box, Miniature 13.00
Lee Vs. Meade; Battle Of Gettysburg, Game Of Games, 1974 .... 50.00
Lindy Hop Off, Parker Bros., 1920 .... 125.00
Lippy The Lion, Transogram, 1963 .... 120.00
Lost In Space, Milton Bradley, 1965 .... 65.00 to 75.00

Lotto, Milton Bradley, 1939 .... 12.00
Magic Set, Conjures, Wood & Metal Tricks, Box, 1850s, 3 1/8 x 9 x 7 In. 515.00
Magilla Gorilla, Box, Ideal, 1964, 10 x 20 In. 98.00
Mah-Jongg, Cone Over Bamboo, Instructions, Wooden Box, 1923 .... 195.00
Make A Million, 1945 .... 25.00
Man From U.N.C.L.E., Pinball 145.00
Man From U.N.C.L.E., Board, Box 65.00
Marble Mugins, 15 Small Clay Marbles 285.00
Mardi Gras, Card, 1933, 60 Piece 95.00
Margie, Milton Bradley, 1961 .... 40.00
Maypole, Paper On Wood, Bliss, Directions, c.1900, 12 x 12 In. 2530.00
McDonald's, Bradley, 1975 .... 12.50
McHale's Navy, Board, Transogram, 1962 .... 25.00 to 45.00
Meet The Missus, Radio Premium, Big Jack Laundry Soap, Board, 1937 .... 110.00
Men In Space, Milton Bradley, 1960 .... 130.00
Message From M, James Bond, 1966 .... 75.00
Mighty Mouse Skill Roll, 1950s 200.00
Million Dollar Man, Board 20.00
Mission Impossible, England, 1975, Box 75.00
Monopoly, Board, Parker Bros., 1935 .... 170.00
Monster Madness, American Publishing 15.00
Monster Madness, Universal Studios 10.00
Monster Squad, Box, 1977 .... 25.00
Mother Goose, Pop-Up, Paper On Wood, Bliss, c.1890 .... 978.00
Mother Hubbard's Party, Paper Lithograph, Balls Attached, Forbes & Co. 1500.00
Motor Race, 1920s 80.00
Motoreeno, Auto License, 1918, Box, 15 x 6 In. 95.00
Motorific Speed Trial Mark II, Racing Set, Ideal, Box, 1969 .... 15.00
Mouse Trap, Ideal, 1961 .... 45.00
Movie Land Keeno, 1929 .... 60.00
Mr. Machine, Plastic Robot Figure Acts As Spinner, Ideal, 1961 .... 79.00
Mr. Novak, Transogram, 1963 .... 29.00
Mr. Ree, Selchow & Righter, Glue Like, 1957 .... 32.00
Mummy Mystery, Hasbro, 1963 .... 350.00
Munsters, Card 35.00
My Favorite Martian, Transogram, 1960s 75.00
Parcheesi, Paint Decorated, 19th Century, Square, 18 In. 880.00
Park And Shop, Milton Bradley, 1960 .... 25.00
Peter Coddle Tells Of His Trip To Chicago, Parker Bros. 25.00
Peter Pan, Board, Selchow & Righter, 1926, 21 x 12 In. 125.00
Peter Pan, Transogram, 1953 .... 18.00
Petticoat Junction, Board 45.00
Pick-Up Sticks, Schoenhut, Box 35.00
Pin The Que On The Chinaman, Anti-Asian 120.00
Pin The Tail On The Donkey, Milton Bradley, 1932 .... 30.00
Pin The Tie On Buster Brown, Cloth, Selchow & Righter 235.00
Pinball, Blue Ribbon, 1933 .... 600.00
Pinball, Clowns & Circus Characters, Marbles Enclosed, Metal, Glass, 8 1/2 x 16 In. ... 57.00
Pinball, Electric, Marx, 1965 .... 100.00
Pinball, Poosh-M-Up Jr., Baseball & Clown, 1940s, 14 x 10 In. 29.00
Pinball, Sweepstakes, Electric, Marx, 1965 .... 100.00
Pirate & Traveler, Milton Bradley, 1953 .... 25.00
Pirate And The Traveler, Milton Bradley, 1936 .... 38.00
Pirate's Island, Corey Games, 1942 .... 220.00
Planet Of The Apes, Milton Bradley, 1974 .... 15.00 To 25.00
Planet Patrol Space Game, Board 39.00
Play-A-Tune-Box, Tony Sarg, 1942 .... 190.00
Play Golf, Windup Lithographed Metal Golfer, Box, Strauss, 1920s, 12 In. 513.00
Poker Chips, 4 Colors Marbled Plastic, Oak Case, Lift Out Rack 75.00
Poker Chips, Catlin, Mustard Colored Holder, 192 Piece 250.00
Poker Chips, Clay Composition, Plane Stamped, 42 Piece 30.00
Poker Dice, Marlboro Cigarettes, Leather Pouch, Box 35.00
Pollyanna, The Glad Game 35.00

Pope & Pagan, Board 495.00
Prince Valiant, Transogram, 1958 .... 50.00
Pro-Quarterback, Championship Games, Inc., 1965 .... 38.00
Professor Quiz Radio Game, Proctor & Gamble, 1939 .... 65.00
Punchboard, Yellow Kid, Kid Holding Umbrella 195.00
Puzzle, 1897 Locomotive, Original Box, McLoughlin Brothers 325.00
Puzzle, 1964 World's Fair, Milton Bradley 20.00
Puzzle, Allis-Chalmers Tractor Co., Original Envelope, 1930s 67.50
Puzzle, Baby Huey, Eating Pies, Built-Rite, 1961 .... 29.00
Puzzle, Barbie & Ken, Whitman, 1963, 100 Piece 66.00
Puzzle, Barbie Twins, Playboy, 1968, Unopened 20.00
Puzzle, Bee Bee, Comic Picture, Paper, Celluloid, Japan, 1950s 25.00
Puzzle, Ben & Jerry's Ice Cream, Box, 1987, 60 Piece 8.00
Puzzle, Brooklyn Bridge Block & Ball, Litho Paper-Over-Wood, Patented 1880s 770.00
Puzzle, Brownies, Paper On Wood 65.00
Puzzle, Buffalo Bill, Advertising Cocoa Malt 65.00
Puzzle, First Ringing Of Liberty Bell, Wooden, c.1880, 200 Piece, Box 85.00
Puzzle, Folger's Coffee, In Can 50.00
Puzzle, Gunsmoke, Whitman, 1950s, Box 35.00
Puzzle, Horse Scroll, McLoughlin, 1898 .... 295.00
Puzzle, Jetsons, Jet-In, Whitman, 1962, 14 x 18 In. 22.00
Puzzle, Jigsaw, Chromolithographed Paper On Wood, France, Box, 15 3/8 x 11 1/4 In. .. 210.00
Puzzle, Jigsaw, Columbia Space Shuttle, Jamor, Box 20.00
Puzzle, Jigsaw, Dissected Map Of World, Wooden, Box 425.00
Puzzle, Jigsaw, Jesse James & His Gang, Milton Bradley, Box, 1965 .... 32.00
Puzzle, Jigsaw, Mr. I. Magination, 400 Pieces, Jaymar, Box, 1951, 7 x 10 In. 60.00
Puzzle, Jigsaw, Planet Of The Apes, HG Toys, Box, 1972, 9 x 8 In. 12.00
Puzzle, John Wayne, Frame Tray, Saalfield, 1951 .... 40.00
Puzzle, Locomotive, Mounted, McLoughlin, 1887 .... 440.00
Puzzle, Marlin Perkins Wild Kingdom, Marlin With Hawk, Box, 1971 .... 10.00
Puzzle, Monkee's Hey-Hey, Box 35.00
Puzzle, Paine's Puzzle Blocks, 1890 .... 44.00
Puzzle, Party, AC Gilbert, Box & Gift Card, 1920s, Box 125.00
Puzzle, Pluto 17.00
Puzzle, Queen Page, Parrish, Box 155.00
Puzzle, Snow White, Jaymar, Box, 1940s 22.00
Puzzle, Trailways Bus, Box, 1948 .... 40.00
Puzzle, Train, Makes A Nine Foot Train, Milton Bradley 350.00
Puzzle, U.S. Map, Milton Bradley, Box 12.00
Puzzle, Uncle Scrooge 4.00
Puzzle, Underdog, Fairchild 95.00
Puzzle, Venetian Afternoon, Arthur Kieht, Lux Toilet Soap, 150 Piece 9.00
Puzzle, Whimsey, Wooden, Early Form Of Cube 35.00
Puzzle, Woozy-Jig, Brundage, No. 6 .... 45.00
Puzzle, Zorro, Duel With Mexican Soldier, Whitman, 1965, 14 x 18 In. 15.00
Puzzle Cube, Aunt Louisa's Visit Of St. Nicholas, McLoughlin 3500.00
Puzzle Peg, Lubbers & Bell Mfg. Co., Rules Book, 1923 .... 17.00
Puzzle Set, Modern Airplanes, Platt Munk, Artist Holcombe, 1941, Box, 6 ...... 45.00
Queen Of Prom, Board 5.00
Quick Draw McGraw Private Eye, Milton Bradley, 1960 .... 25.00 to 45.00
Quiz Kids Radio Question Bee, Whitman, 1941 .... 25.00
Quoits Ahoy, Ring Toss, Wartime American Toy, 3 Sailors, Box 28.00
Race Horse, Wooden, Primitive, Maine 150.00
Rack-O, Card, Racks, Milton Bradley, Box 20.00
Radio Amateur Hour Game, Milton Bradley, 1930s 110.00
Ranger Commandos, Parker Bros., 1942 .... 85.00
Ray's Track, 9 Horses, Coin-operated, Bally, 1936 .... 3025.00
Rebel, Nick Adams, TV Program, Ideal, 1961 .... 85.00
Replogle Globe, Blast Off Space, Tin World Globe, Box, 1950s 100.00
Restless Gun, Milton Bradley 85.00
Rich Uncle From The States, Board, Cards, Dice, John Waddington Ltd., Box, 1930s   48.00
Rich Uncle Stock Market, Board, Parker Bros., 1955 .... 32.00

Rifleman, Milton Bradley, 1959 .... 130.00
Rin Tin Tin, Transogram, 1955, 9 x 18 In. .... 32.00 to 57.00
Ring My Nose, Clown Face, Milton Bradley, 1920s, Box 65.00
Ring Toss, Bliss, c.1895 .... 350.00
Ring Toss, Parker Bros., Box 8.50
Rings On Cat's Tail, Glass Front, Gilbert Co., 1940s, 3 3/4 x 4 3/4 In. 20.00
Road Runner, Looney Tunes, Whitman, 1969 .... 25.00
Road Runner, Coyote, Tweety & Sylvester, Box, Milton Bradley 50.00
Robot Sam The Answer Man, Battery Operated, 1950s 35.00
Rocket To The Moon Space Game, Leave It To Beaver, Hasbro, 1959 .... 65.00
Roger Maris, Baseball .... 65.00 to 85.00
Roll-A-Ball, 2 Sides, Key Chain 20.00
Rootie Kazootie, Card, Box, 1953 .... 20.00
Round The World Fliers, Tin, Box 100.00
Royal Game Of Somer, Selchow & Righter, Box, 1977 .... 15.00
S.O.S. Marble Game, Lithographed Steel, 1930s 125.00
Sambo, Target Board, Wyandotte 100.00
Saratoga, 1777, Military, Board, 1974 .... 50.00
Scat, Card, Home & Industry, Mandor Platnik, c.1880, 32 Piece 38.50
Scavenger Hunt, Box, 1933 .... 25.00
Scooby-Doo & Scrappy Doo, Milton Bradley, 1983 .... 30.00
Scoop, Reporters, John Waddington 100.00
Scrabble, Hebrew Instructions, Box 225.00
Sergeant Preston, c.1950 .... 45.00
Sharp Shooters, Milton Bradley 125.00
Shuffleboard, Tavern Style, Hardwood Construction, Metal Disks, 30 x 22 In. 450.00
Skill Ball, Marble, Marx 25.00
Skittles, 3 Dogs, 3 Cats, 3 Japanese Women, Cloth Covered, c.1895 .... 690.00
Skittles, 9 Wooden Pins, Figural With Dark Faces, 7 In. 70.00
Skittles, Chief, Nine Braves, 1890 .... 4900.00
Skittles, Painted Indian Head Portraits, 10 Piece 363.00
Smashed Up Locomotive, Milton Bradley 100.00
Snagglepuss, Transogram, 1961 .... 90.00
Snake Eyes, Dice, Card 70.00
Snap, Parker Bros., Card, Roosevelt Bears Picture, 1900s 35.00
Snatch The Hat, Charlie McCarthy, Puppet Characters, Box, 1938 .... 125.00
Snoopy, Selchow & Righter, Board 35.00
Sociable Snake, Board, Tokens, Dice, McLoughlin, 1893, 10 x 21 In. 357.00
South American Blow-Gun, Target, Parker Bros., 1930s 17.00
Space Chess, 4th Dimensional, 1970 .... 20.00
Space Race, Card, Box, 1952 .... 45.00
Space Shuttle 101, Media/Ungame, 1978 .... 32.00
Speedway Auto Racing, Parker Bros., 1920s 135.00
Spider Woman, Hasbro, 1977 .... 15.00
Spiro Agnew History Challenge, 1971 .... 20.00
Stagecoach West, Transogram, 1961 .... 110.00
Star Reporter, Parker Bros., 1954 .... 45.00
Star Trek, 1979 .... 20.00 to 50.00
Star Trek, Hasbro, 1974 .... 20.00
Star Wars, Escape From Death Star, 1977 .... 10.00
Star Wars, Kenner, Box, 1977 .... 55.00
Starsky & Hutch, Milton Bradley, 1977 .... 25.00
Stingray, Transogram, 1965, Box 250.00
Stocks & Bonds, Board, 1964 .... 10.00
Sunken Treasure, Parker Bros., 1948 .... 50.00
Superman Pinball, Mattel, Box 75.00
Surf Side Six, Lowell, 1960 .... 98.00
Target, Burke's Law, Transogram 275.00
Table, Craps, With Chips, Chip Rack, Stick & Dice 1500.00
Target, Coast Defense, World War II 20.00
Target, Crow Hunt, Parker Bros. 25.00
Target, Mighty Mouse, Terry Toon 60.00

Target, Shooting Gallery, Bear, Cast Iron, 5 In. 55.00
Target, Shooting Gallery, Indian In Canoe, Cast Iron, 9 In. 75.00
Target, Shooting Gallery, Rabbit, Cast Iron, 11 1/2 In. 60.00
Target Shooting, Gabby Hayes, Box 275.00
Tarzan, Board, Milton Bradley, 1977 .... 25.00
Telepathy, Cadaco-Ellis, 1930 .... 105.00
Tell It To The Judge, Eddie Cantor, Board 75.00
There's A Goat On The Roof, Parker Bros., 1966 .... 16.00
This Is Your Life, Lowell, 1955, Box, 13 x 18 In. 59.00
Tiddlywinks, Ally Oop 28.00
Tootsie Roll Rocket, Paper Gameboard, Plastic Rocket, Original Mailer, 1962 .... 26.00
Tortoise & Hare, Russell Mfg. Co., 1922 .... 140.00
Touchdown, Milton Bradley, 1930s 250.00
Touring, Card, Parker Bros., Box, 1927 .... 20.00
Tru Action Basketball, Electric, Metal Pieces, Tudor 23.00
Tru Action Football, Electric, Metal Pieces, Tudor 23.00
Turn Horse Racing, Delmar Derby, 1949 .... 15.00
Twelve O'Clock High, Aircraft On Cards, Milton Bradley, Box, 1965 .... 35.00
Twelve O'Clock High, Ideal, 1964 .... 55.00
Twiggy, Milton Bradley, 1967, 19 x 9 1/2 In. 40.00
Twilight Zone, Ideal, 1963 .... 185.00
Uncle Remus Bagatello, Box, 1946, 17 x 10 In. 195.00
Uncle Sam's Mail, 4-fold United States Map, 4 Dice, McLoughlin Bros., Box, 1893 ... 210.00
Uncle Tom's Cabin, W. & S.B. Ives, Cards 330.00
Uncle Wiggily, Board, 1934 .... 35.00
Uncle Wiggily, Milton Bradley, 1949 .... 45.00
Under Sea World Of Jacques Cousteau, Parker Bros., 1968 .... 35.00
Varsity Football, Cadaco, 1953 .... 35.00
Varsity Scientific Football, 1940s 65.00
Voyage To The Bottom Of The Sea, 1964 .... 60.00 to 70.00
Wagon Train, Milton Bradley, Box 55.00
Wells Fargo, Milton Bradley, 1959 .... 55.00
West Point Story, Transogram, 1961 .... 25.00
What's My Line, 1950s 22.00
Wheel Of Chance, Carnival, Red & Yellow 195.00
Wheel, Racing, Carnival, 20th Century, 46 x 33 In. 990.00
Whirl-O-Stunt, Board 28.00
Whirst Music, Flash Cards, 1936, Box 25.00
Who's Afraid Of The Big Bad Wolf, Parker Bros., 1933 .... 95.00
Who's On First? Abbott & Costello, Board, 1978 .... 70.00
Wicket The Ewok, Star Wars, Parker Bros., 1983 .... 15.00
Wide World Travel Game, Parker Bros., c.1957, Box 150.00
Wild Kingdom, Marlin Perkins & A Cheetah, Teaching Concepts, 1977 .... 35.00
Wildlife, E.S. Lowe, 1971 .... 70.00
Winnie The Pooh, 1958 .... 30.00
Wizard Of Oz, 1974 .... 19.00
Wizards Quest, Board 10.00
Wolverine Car Race 135.00
Wonderful Game Of Oz, Parker Bros., 1921 .... 350.00
World Educator, W.S. Reed, Learn About History, Geography, Wooden Box, 1887 .... 225.00
Wrigley's Zoo, Pop-Up, Animals, 1950s, 6 x 10 In., 6 Piece 47.00
Yacht Race, Parker Bros., 1961 .... 100.00
Yankee Trader, Ives 60.50
Yogi Bear, Milton Bradley, 1971 .... 50.00
You'll Never Get Rich, Phil Silvers, Sgt. Bilko, Gardner Games, 1950s 85.00
Zorro, Parker Bros., 1966 .... 100.00

GAME PLATES are plates of any make decorated with pictures of birds, animals, or fish. The game plates usually came in sets consisting of twelve dishes and a serving platter. These sets were most popular during the 1880s.

Bird, Gold Handles, Pastel Ground, Limoges, Platter-14 1/2 In., Pair 450.00
Bird, Gold Rim, Flowers, Grain, Limoges, 10 1/8 In., Pair 265.00

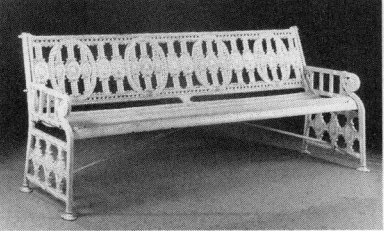

Garden Furnishings, Bench, Cast Iron,
Roundels Back, Painted, 76 In.

Left: Garden Furnishings, Bench, Cast Iron,
Painted, Peter Timmes Son, Late 19th Century

Fish, Seaweed, Mollusk Designs, Gold Rim, Limoges, 1885, 8 1/2 In., 12 Piece 350.00
Fowl & Chick, Gold Rim, Limoges, Duvay, 19 x 12 x 2 1/4 In. 225.00
Mallard Duck, Hand Painted, Coronet, 10 In. 50.00
Olden Pheasant, Shadow Ferns, Gold Border, Limoges, Signed, 9 In. 165.00
Pheasants Scene, Pierced, Reticulated Border, Bavaria 60.00
GAME SET, 2 Bowls, 11 Plates, Platter-19 1/2 In., Limoges, 14 Piece 1150.00
Bird, Limoges, Platter-18 In., 6 Piece 550.00
Bird, Limoges, Scalloped Rim, Gold Trim, 5 Plates 9-In., Platter-18 In. 995.00
Fish, Hand Painted Fish, Gold Scalloped Rim, Limoges, Platter-23 In., 13 Piece 475.00
Fish, Limoges, 13 Piece 1295.00
Fish, Platter, Gravy Boat, Underplate, Limoges, 1800, 13 Piece 2700.00
R.K. Beck, Buffalo, 7 Piece 275.00

GARDEN FURNISHINGS have been popular for centuries. The stone or
metal statues, wire, iron, or rustic furniture, urns and fountains, sundials, and
small figurines are included in this category. Many of the metal pieces have
been made continuously for years.

Arbor Seat, Trellises Either Side 1500.00
Armchair, Cast Iron, Limb Design, Oak Leaves & Acorns, 30 1/2 In. 715.00
Bench, Cast Iron, Basket Of Flowers, Female Mask Under Urn, 45 x 16 In. 2310.00
Bench, Cast Iron, Fish Scale Grate Back, James W. Carr, 46 In. 1100.00
Bench, Cast Iron, Gothic, Quatrefoil Design, Pair 2185.00
Bench, Cast Iron, Limb Design, Oak Leaves & Acorns, 32 x 38 In. 660.00
Bench, Cast Iron, Painted White, Late 19th Century, 38 x 44 In. 275.00
Bench, Cast Iron, Painted, Peter Timmes Son, Late 19th Century .... *Illus* 1150.00
Bench, Cast Iron, Roundels Back, Painted, 76 In. .... *Illus* 1150.00
Bench, Cast Iron, White Paint, 46 In. 544.00
Bench, Fern Design, Kramer Bros., Dayton, Ohio, 58 In. 880.00
Bench, James W. Carr, Cast Iron, Arms, Richmond, Va. 1100.00
Bench, Rustic Limbs, Oak Leaves & Acorns, Cast Iron, Arms 1155.00
Bench, Stone, Scroll Supports, 33 1/2 In. 2300.00
Bench, Wrought Iron, Foliate Backrest, Pierced Seat, 1890, 34 1/2 In., Pair 2300.00
Birdbath, Encrusted In Seashells 475.00
Birdbath, Shell Form, 4 Perched Birds, 44 In. 155.00
Chair, Barrel Back, Terra-Cotta 302.50
Chair, Cast Iron, Berried Oak Leaves, Animal Form Legs, Painted 2645.00
Chair, Cast Iron, Honeysuckle Pattern 300.00
Chair Set, Bamboo Style, Metal, 4 .... 560.00
Chair Set, Cast Iron, Oval Back, Centered Boy, Legs Headed By Mask, 4 .... 2875.00
Figure, Cat, Sitting, Terra-Cotta, White Tin Glaze, France, 1930, 21 In. 750.00
Figure, Cherublike Child With Bird, Cast Lead, 22 In. 495.00
Figure, Crane, Standing, Repainted, 40 x 16 In. 605.00

*Garden Furnishings, Topiary, Statue Of Liberty,
Wirework, Green, Platform, 1960*

Figure, Cupid Stretching Bow, Zinc, 20 In. 275.00
Figure, Dog, Dalmatian, Sitting, Composition, 1950, 33 In. 850.00
Figure, Duck, Marble, 11 In., Pair 1035.00
Figure, Frog, Green, Spots, Cream Highlights, Brush McCoy, 16 x 9 In., Box 522.50
Figure, Horse, Recumbent, Terra-Cotta, 35 In., Pair 4025.00
Figure, Immortal Figure, Marble, 5 Ft. 5 In. 1380.00
Figure, Limestone, Nude Woman, Drapery, Holding Foliage, 6 Ft. 5 In. 7475.00
Figure, Rabbit, Cast Iron, 12 x 12 In. 375.00
Figure, Rabbit, Full-Figure, White Paint, 15 In. 275.00
Figure, Rabbit, White Paint, 12 In. 302.50
Figure, Winged Victory, Sandstone Base, Bronze, 42 In. 825.00
Fountain, 2 Children Under Umbrella, Frogs, Turtles, Cast Iron, 4 Ft. 5 In. 3735.00
Fountain, 3 Swans Surmounted By Well, Child With Duck, Lead, 5 Ft. 1 In. 2760.00
Fountain, Boy Riding Hound, Marble, 32 In. 6325.00
Fountain, Fisherboy, Water-Spouting Fish, Mottled Glaze, Ceramic 1600.00
Fountain, Goose, Outstretched Neck, Lead, 18 In. 920.00
Fountain, House Shape, Random Colored Glass Chips, Cement 475.00
Fountain, Iron, Flowers & Foliage At Base, Thomas Griffith, 80 x 70 In. 7975.00
Fountain, Neptune, Lead, Wheeler Williams, 1939, 33 In. 3450.00
Fountain, Nude Holding Urn, Lead, C.S. Paolo, 1955, 3 Ft. 7 In. 1725.00
Fountain, Partially Nude Female, Putti At Feet, Zinc, J.W. Fiske, 5 Ft. 3 In. 6900.00
Fountain, Tri-Form Cast With Swans, 3 Tiered, Lead, 42 In. 2587.00
Gate, Renaissance Style, Scrolls, Wrought Iron, 72 x 39 In. 1380.00
Gate, Totem Finials, Abutting Bars, Frank Lloyd Wright, 1956, 51 In., Pair 4830.00
Gazebo, Arched Sides, Domed, Scrolled Finial, Wrought Iron, 6 Ft. 10 In. 3450.00
Glider Set, Porch, 2 Chairs, Table, Original Paint, White, Aqua, 1950s, 3 Piece 275.00
Hitching Post, Dog Head, Grasping Ring Handle In Mouth, Iron, 16 In. 1495.00
Jardiniere, Rope Twist Rim, Carved Roundels, Sandstone, 44 In. 6325.00
Lion, Cast Iron, Crouched Position, Rectangular Base, 29 In. 357.00
Ornament, Pigeon, Cast Lead, 19th Century, 10 1/2 In. 357.50
Ornament, Rabbit, Holding Egg, Hammered Metal, England, 1890s, 24 In. 275.00
Planter, Carved Frolicking Putti Holding Swags, Marble, 33 x 40 In. 1475.00
Planter, Lead, Paneled, Cast Acorns & Leaves, 47 1/2 In. 2875.00
Seat, Barrel Shape, Figures, China, Pair 4200.00
Seat, Earthenware, Barrel Shape, Transfer Printed, Minton, 1865, 18 In., Pair 2875.00
Seat, Ironstone, Hexagonal, Ashworth & Bros., Late 1800s, 18 7/8 In., Pair. 2875.00
Seat, Porcelain, Blue & White, China, 19 In., Pair 357.50
Set, Iron, Fern Pattern, Settee & 2 Armchairs, Painted 1380.00
Set, Iron, 3 Tables, Plant Stand, 5 Chairs, Woodard, White Repaint 522.50
Set, Iron, Grapevine, 4 Section Tree Surround, Settee, Chair, Benches 650.00
Set, Iron, Painted White, Late 19th Century, 44 1/2 In. Bench, 2 Chairs 1045.00
Set, Iron, Table, 2 Armchairs, Garden Urn, West Point Foundry, 4 Piece 2750.00
Set, Settee, Armchair, Chair & Table, Vintage, White Repaint, 4 Piece 265.00
Settee, Cast Iron, Geometric Seat & Back, 32 x 33 In. 165.00
Statue, Neptune, Trident, Straddling Fountain, Horse Supports, Bronze 3740.00

Sundial, Metal Gnome, Painted Wood, Square, 19th Century, 7 1/8 In. 440.00
Swing, Teak, Flip Back, Faces Either Way, Floral Ceramic Inserts, 1900 .... 1200.00
Table, Cast Iron, Plate Glass Top, Yellow Paint, Round, 17 3/4 x 18 In. 71.50
Table, Round, Glass Top, 4 Chairs, Steel, Woodard, Sage Green Paint 357.50
Table & Chaise, Cast Iron, Leaf Design, Cushions, Woodward, 7 Piece 605.00
Table Set, Bamboo, Victorian, 3 Piece 295.00
Topiary, Statue Of Liberty, Wirework, Green, Platform, 1960 .... *Illus* 2420.00
Urn, Cast Iron, Floral Detail, Walbridge & Co., Buffalo, N.Y., 34 In., Pair 649.00
Urn, Cast Iron, Fluted, Ribbed, Egg & Dart Detail, 29 3/4 x 29 In. 385.00
Urn, Cast Iron, Green, 1870 .... 250.00
Urn, Cast Iron, Stork Pedestal, J.W. Fiske, 52 x 39 In. 2250.00
Urn, Iron, 2 Ornate Handles, J.W. Fiske, N.Y., Pair 6050.00
Urn, Iron, Buffalo, White Repaint, Ears, C.E. Walbridge, 21 x 36 In. 357.00
Urn, Iron, Campana Form, Scrolled Griffin Handles, c.1850, 48 In., Pair. 3850.00
Urn, Kramer, Cast Iron, 36 x 21 1/2 In. 440.00
Urn, Kramer Bros., Dayton, Ohio, 2 Ornate Handles, Pair 7920.00
Urn, Lead, Neoclassical Style, 22 In., Pair 990.00
Urn, Marble, Continuous Carved Busts, Lion Pelts Band, Warwick, 23 In. 7475.00
Urn, Marble, Cupid Faces On Lid & Base, Dolphin Handles, 3 x 3 Ft. 7150.00
Urn, Mermaids Holding Up Sea Horses, Scalloped Bowl, 3 Ft. 4125.00
Urn, White, Weathered, Campana Shape, Gadrooned Body, 40 x 28 In. 1980.00
Urn, Wm. Adams & Co., Victorian, 36 In.. .... 880.00

GARDNER Porcelain Works was founded in Verbiki, outside Moscow, by the
English-born Francis Gardner in 1766. The Gardner family retained
ownership of the factory until 1891 and produced porcelain tablewares,
figurines, and faience.

ГАРДНЕРЪ

Cup & Saucer, Fuchsia, Blue & Green Flowers, 1870, Marked, 6 Sets 400.00
Inkstand, 2 Wells, Center Candleholder, Porcelain, 13 1/4 In. 1380.00
Tankard, Turk's Head Shape, Porcelain, 19th Century, 8 In. 1200.00

GAUDY DUTCH pottery was made in England for America from about 1810
to 1820. It is a white earthenware with Imari-style decorations of red, blue,
green, yellow, and black. Only sixteen patterns of Gaudy Dutch were made:
Butterfly, Carnation, Dahlia, Double Rose, Dove, Grape, Leaf, Oyster,
Primrose, Single Rose, Strawflower, Sunflower, Urn, War Bonnet, Zinnia,
and No Name. Other similar wares are called *Gaudy Ironstone* and *Gaudy
Welsh.*

Cup & Saucer, Handleless, Urn Pattern 247.00
Cup & Saucer, Handleless, War Bonnet Pattern 412.50
Cup & Saucer, Single Rose 450.00
Plate, Butterfly Pattern, 7 1/2 In. 385.00
Plate, Carnation Pattern, 8 1/2 In. 550.00
Plate, Dove Pattern, 8 /12 In. 715.00
Plate, Single Rose, 6 3/4 In. .... 300.00 to 385.00
Plate, Single Rose, 8 1/2 In. 450.00
Plate, Toddy, Grape Pattern, 5 3/8 In. 220.00
Plate, Urn Pattern, 10 In. 795.00
Soup Dish, War Bonnet Pattern, 8 1/8 In. 715.00
Teapot, War Bonnet Pattern 2500.00
Waste Bowl, Single Rose, 5 1/2 In. 500.00

GAUDY IRONSTONE is the collector's name for the ironstone wares with the
bright patterns similar to Gaudy Dutch. It was made in England for the
American market. There may be other examples found in the listing for
Ironstone or under the name of the ceramic factory.

Cup & Saucer, Handleless, Polychrome Floral Design, Blue Underglaze 93.00
Cup & Saucer, Morning Glory & Berries, Handleless 93.00
Cup & Saucer, Urn, Handleless 192.00
Mug, Black Transfer, Rabbits & Frogs, 5 3/8 In. 1320.00
Pitcher, Geometric Pattern, 8 In. 220.00
Plate, Blue Urn, Underglaze, Polychrome Enamel & Luster, 9 In. 193.00

Plate, Floral Design, Blue Underglaze, Polychrome Enamel, 8 1/2 In. 126.00
Plate, Floral, Cornucopias, T. Walker, 8 3/4 In. 203.00
Plate, Morning Glory, Red, 2 Shades Of Green Enameling, 8 5/8 In. 105.00
Plate, Strawberry, 14-Sided, 8 1/2 In. 78.00
Plate, Strawberry, Enameled, 8 1/2 In. 148.00
Platter, Floral, Green Enamel & Luster, 13 1/2 In. 55.00
Platter, Floral With Strawberries, 15 3/4 In. 715.00
Platter, Imari Floral Design, Underglaze Blue, Red & Gilt, 10 3/4 In. 220.00
Platter, Urn, 12 1/2 In. 550.00
Platter, Vintage Design, 12 1/4 In. 275.00
Sugar Bowl, Stick Roses, Blue, 8 1/4 In. 220.00
Tea Set, Floral Design, 3 Piece 495.00

GAUDY WELSH is an Imari-decorated earthenware with red, blue, green, and gold decorations. Most Gaudy Welsh was made in England for the American market. It was made after 1820.

Bowl, Floral, Cornucopias, Polychrome, Gilt, 8 3/4 x 8 3/4 In. 104.00
Cake Plate, Pansy, Square 135.00
Creamer, Columbine, 3 1/2 In. 120.00
Creamer, Davenport Stone China, Serpent Handle, 4 In. 115.00
Creamer, Floral, Serpent Handle, Mason's Ironstone, 4 In. 148.00
Creamer, Lotus, Luster Trim, 4 3/4 In. 121.00
Creamer, Oyster, Luster Trim, 4 1/2 In. 105.00
Cup & Saucer, Buckle, Luster Trim, 6 Sets 100.00
Cup & Saucer, Copper Luster, Stylized Urn, Pink Berries, Fluted 56.00
Cup & Saucer, Flower Basket 75.00
Cup & Saucer, Hexagon, Luster Trim, Oversize 82.00
Cup & Saucer, Pansy 75.00
Cup & Saucer, Pedestal Bowl With Flowers, Cobalt Blue 55.00
Cup & Saucer, Rainbow, Luster Trim, 6 Sets 230.00
Cup & Saucer, Tulip 85.00
Inkwell, Hinged Lid, Blue Underglaze, Porcelain, Brass Fittings 330.00
Mug, Floral, Serpent Handle, Pink Luster, 3 7/8 In. 269.00
Pitcher & Bowl, Tulip Design, Miniature 330.00
Pitcher, Dragon Handle, Green Enamel, 6 3/8 In. 192.50
Pitcher, Gargoyle Handle, Ironstone, 6 1/2 In. 71.50
Pitcher, Imari Design, Dragon Handle, 5 3/4 In. 203.00
Pitcher, Serpent Handle, 6 1/4 In. 192.50
Plate, Feather, 6 3/4 In. 55.00
Plate, Grapes, 6 1/2 In. 40.00
Plate, Lotus, Luster Trim, 9 In., Pair 187.00
Plate, Oyster, Luster Trim, 8 1/2 In. 105.00
Sauce Bowl, Matching Ladle, Cover, Wedgwood, 8 1/2 In. 137.50
Sugar, Tulip, Luster Trim, 7 In. 210.00
Tea Set, Peppermint, Luster Trim, Waste Bowl, No Sugar, 14 Piece 765.00
Teapot, Peach Design, Luster Trim, 6 In. .... 300.00 to 335.00
Teapot, Sadler, 5 3/4 In. 30.00
Tray, Floral, Gilt, Brass Frame, Oval, 14 1/2 In. 27.50
Tureen, Sauce, Undertray, Imari Design, Crown Finial, Gilt, 6 1/2 In. 192.00
Vegetable, Cover, Floral, Flower Finial, Minton, 10 1/4 In. 95.00
Waste Bowl, Grapes 120.00

GEISHA GIRL porcelain was made for export in the late nineteenth century in Japan. It was an inexpensive porcelain often sold in dime stores or used as free premiums. Pieces are sometimes marked with the name of a store. Japanese ladies in kimonos are pictured on the dishes. There are over 125 recorded patterns. Borders of red, blue, green, gold, brown, or several of these colors were used. Modern reproductions are being made.

Chocolate Pot, Cobalt Blue 70.00
Cup & Saucer, Art Show, Red 60.00
Hair Receiver, Red & Orange 40.00
Sugar & Creamer, Royal Naga 55.00

GENE AUTRY was born in 1907. He began his career as the *Singing Cowboy* in 1928. His first movie appearance was in 1934, his last in 1958.

Badge, Merit, Sharpshooters	175.00
Belt, Leather, Brown	85.00
Book, Better Little Book, Gene Autry Cowboy Detective, Whitman, 1940	20.00
Book, Coloring, 1940s, 11 x 14 In.	85.00
Book, Coloring, Cowboy Adventures To Color, Merrill, 1941	48.00
Book, Gene Autry & The Big Valley Grab, Whitman, 1954	7.00
Book, Little Golden Book, Champion Rearing, 1955	25.00
Cap Gun, 44, Box	495.00
Cap Gun, 9 In.	55.00
Cap Gun, Cast Iron, Name On Grips, Gene Autry Impressed, 6 1/2 In.	115.00
Cap Gun, Copper Barrel	125.00
Cap Gun, Inlaid Grips, Box, 7 1/2 In.	250.00
Cap Gun, Kenton, Cast Iron	140.00
Cap Gun, Scroll Grip, Lenton, 6 1/2 In.	150.00
Cap Gun, Smoker, Copper Colored, Box	325.00 to 425.00
Cap Gun, Swing-Out Loading Action, 6 Metal Bullets, 1950s, 11 In.	275.00
Card, Playing, Melody Ranch	8.00
Charm, Photo In Frame, Bubble Gum Machine, 1/2 In., c.1950	15.00
Comic Book, Champion, Dell, 1958	10.00
Flashlight, Pencil	125.00
Game, Badmen Of Broken Bow, Board, 18 x 18 In.	32.00
Guitar, Box	195.00
Guitar, Wooden, Case	295.00
Gun & Holster, Name On Holster, Left-Handed	225.00
Hat, Cowboy	150.00
Label, Cowboy Boot	20.00
Lobby Card, Trail To San Antoine, 1947, 11 x 14 In.	25.00
Lunch Box, Autry On Horse	500.00
Paint Book, Cowboy, Merrill Pub. Co., 1940	48.00
Pencil Sharpener	65.00
Pennant, Back In The Saddle Again, Cloth	65.00
Photographokeh Records, Color, Wooden Frame, 20 x 15 1/2 In.	230.00
Pop Gun, Cardboard, 1950s	22.00
Poster, Hills Of Utah, 1956	68.00
Puzzle, Frame Tray, Whitman, 1950	30.00
Puzzle, Tray, 1950s	35.00
Record, Gene Autry's West, Classics, 78 RPM	40.00
Record, Wild Cat Mama, 78 RPM	75.00
Record Player, Flying A, Box	500.00
Ring, Bust Portrait, Sterling Silver	250.00
Ring, Horseshoe Nail, On Card	125.00
Ring, Magnifying, 1950s	85.00
Ring, Portrait, Metal	175.00
Scarf, 20 x 20 In.	125.00
Sheet Music, At Mail Call Today, Gene In WWII Sergeant Uniform, 1945	15.00
Vest, Green On 1 Side, Autry On Other	175.00
Viewmaster, Gene & Champion, 1950	10.00
Wristwatch, Always Your Pal, New Haven, 1948	300.00
Wristwatch, Moving Gun, Box	500.00

GIBSON GIRL black-and-blue decorated plates were made in the early 1900s. Twenty-four different 10 1/2-inch plates were made by the Royal Doulton Pottery at Lambeth, England. These pictured scenes from the book *A Widow and Her Friends* by Charles Dana Gibson. Another set of twelve 9-inch plates featuring pictures of the heads of Gibson Girls had all-blue decoration. Many other items also pictured the famous Gibson Girl.

Plate, A Quiet Dinner With Dr. Bottles	105.00
Plate, Miss Babbles, The Authoress, Doulton	110.00 to 125.00
Plate, She Contemplates The Cloister	100.00

Plate, They All Go Skating, 10 1/2 In. 125.00
Plate, They Take A Morning Run, 10 1/2 In. 110.00
Set, Widow Series, 1901, 24 Piece 2250.00

GIRL SCOUT collectors search for anything pertaining to the Girl Scouts, including uniforms, publications, and old cookie boxes. The Girl Scout movement started in 1912, two years after the Boy Scouts. It began under Juliette Gordon Low of Savannah, Georgia. The first Girl Scout cookies were sold in 1928.

Box, Medals 35.00
Catalog, New York, N.Y., 284 Pages, 1938 .... 11.00
Dress, Doll's, Box 20.00
Dress, Khaki, 1920s 50.00
Dress & Hat, Green, 1930s 30.00
Outfit, Indian, Ribbon, 1927 Conference 75.00
Uniform, Belt, 1940s 225.00

GLASS-ART. Art glass means any of the many forms of glassware made during the late nineteenth or early twentieth century. These wares were expensive and production was limited. Art glass is not the typical commercial glass that was made in large quantities, and most of the art glass was produced by hand methods. Later twentieth-century glass is listed under Glass-Contemporary, Glass-Midcentury, or Glass-Venetian. Even more art glass may be found in categories such as Burmese, Cameo Glass, Tiffany, Venini, and other factory names.

Bottle, Internal Air Bubbles, Mossy Gray Inclusions, Maurice Marinot, 4 1/4 In. 2300.00
Bowl, Allegorical Scenes, Chalice Form, Lobmeyer, 7 1/2 In. 690.00
Bowl, Amber, Acid-Etched Triangles, Jean Luce, c.1930, 7 1/4 In. 690.00
Bowl, Black Threading, Green Iridescent, Silver Rim, Pallme Konig, 9 In. 225.00
Bowl, Black, Green Rim & Foot, Polished Pontil, 12 1/2 In. 75.00
Bowl, Etched Alternating Design On Rim, Horizontal Waves, Jean Luce, 4 In. 920.00
Bowl, Figural Scene, Sand Blasted, Signed B.Vallien 3450.00
Console Set, Painted Flowers, Pink, Cased Lavender Under Wide Rim 100.00
Cordial Set, Enamel Blue Berries, Exotic Bird In Medallion, M. Goupy, 5 Piece 805.00
Goblet, Alexandrite 1100.00
Jar, Black Threading, Green, Brown, Purple Iridescent Ground, Pallme Konig 250.00
Lamp, Table, 6 Panels, Caramel To Blue, Cottage & Tree Motif, c.1910 .... 825.00
Lampshade, Mushroom Shape, Amber, Random Threading, Austria, 7 In. 330.00
Pitcher, Blue Shaded To Orange-Red, Globular, Handle, Georges De Feure, 7 In. 230.00
Tumbler, Raised Gold Swags Of Blossoms, Ribbons, 3 3/4 In. 745.00
Vase, Black Threading, Olive Green Iridescent, Freeform, Pallme Konig, 13 In. 375.00
Vase, Clear, Panels, Spattered Primary Colors, Baluster Shaped 55.00
Vase, Cranberry Over White Cased, Basket Weave Silver Overlay, 5 1/2 In. 83.00
Vase, Enameled Pink Flowers, Green Textured Ground, France, 3 1/2 In. 137.00
Vase, Finches Amid Stylized Foliage, Aristide Colotte, 13 3/4 In. 6325.00
Vase, Flared, Transparent Blue, Tapered Bowl, Green Foot, 10 In. 66.00
Vase, Goldfish Pattern, Barolac, 1930s 1000.00
Vase, Hanging, Iridescent Green, Maroon, Bronzed Hanger, Austria, 8 x 18 In. 440.00
Vase, Intaglio, Crackled, Swirling Bands, Gold Foil, Leveille, 1900, 8 1/2 In. 4025.00
Vase, Oval, Art Deco, Maroon Enameled & Metallic Blossoms, Moda, 12 In. 275.00
Vase, Overlapping Graduated Rectangles, Monogram, Jean Luce, 7 1/2 In. 575.00
Vase, Oyster White, Iridescent, Maroon & Red Swirled Pull-Ups, Europe, 14 In. 275.00
Vase, Peacock, Pink Opalescent, Pulled Gold Iridescent Feathers, 14 In. 330.00
Vase, Purple, Iridescent, Art Nouveau Silver Overlay Design, Europe, 5 1/2 In. 220.00
Vase, Stylized Snake, Mother-Of-Pearl Interior, Krauk, 8 In. 425.00
Vase, Swelled Gray Glass, Corroded Finish, Barovier & Toso, 14 In. 1725.00
Vase, Threaded, Opalescent Amber, Applied Handles, Oil Spot, Austria, 6 3/4 In. 330.00
Vase, Trumpet, Alexandrite, 8 1/4 In. 2800.00
Vase, Yellow Mottled, Brown, Satin Finish, Footed, Ovoid, 1920, 14 1/4 In., Pair 402.00
Water Set, Inverted Thumbprint, Honey Amber, Enameled Flowers, 5 Piece 375.00
Whimsy, Sock Darner, 1900, 7 In., Pair... 385.00

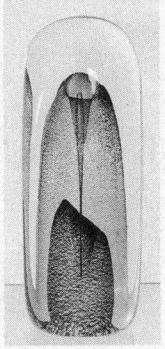

Glass-Midcentury, Sculpture, Fountain, Blue, Pink, Gold Veil Interior, Labino, 6 In.

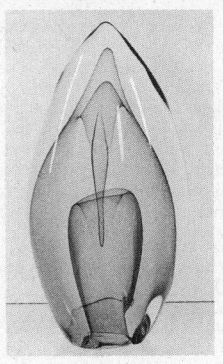

Glass-Midcentury, Sculpture, Gold Iridescent, Blue Veiling, Labino, 9 x 4 In.

Glass-Midcentury, Vase, Cobalt Streaks, Air Traps, White Interior, 13 In.

GLASS-CONTEMPORARY includes pieces by glass artists working after 1975. Many of these pieces are free-form, one-of-a-kind sculptures. Paper-weights by contemporary artists are listed in the Paperweight category. Earlier studio glass may be found listed under Glass-Midcentury or Glass-Venetian.

Figurine, Dolphin, Rock Type Pedestal, Clear, Labino, 1981, 6 1/2 In.	400.00
Figurine, Female Torso, Cobalt Blue, Labino, 1969, 5 1/2 In.	450.00
Figurine, Fish, Copper Schmelzglass, Blue Eyes, Labino, 5 1/2 In.	550.00
Jar, Stopper, Interior White & Ivory Folds, E. Wright, 1979, 7 3/4 In.	82.00
Jar, Stopper, Opalescent Swirls, Clear, E. Wright, 1979, 4 1/4 In.	60.00
Sculpture, Building Shape, Oxblood, Navy, Clear, D. Navarra, 10 In.	402.00
Sculpture, Cone Over Sphere, Clear & Amber, Kochrda, 7 In.	373.00
Sculpture, Stepped Geometric, Vaclav Cigler, 7 x 9 3/4 In., 2 Piece	3162.00
Vase, Blue Glass, Labino, 1964, 5 In.	250.00
Vase, Bowl Form, Cadmium Orange Designs, Labino, 1985, 5 1/2 In.	500.00
Vase, Elongated Prunts, Amber To Aqua, Labino, 1968, 7 1/2 In.	550.00
Vase, Floral, Gold Ground, Multi Flora, Charles Lotton, 1977, 8 3/4 In.	632.00
Vase, Internal Swag Pattern, Ovoid, Labino	900.00
Vase, Looping Swirls, Smoke Colored Glass, Labino, 1978, 10 3/4 In.	700.00
Vase, Pink Abstract Design, Red, Signed, Lotton 1991, 10 In.	230.00
Vase, Silver Schmelzglass, Labino, 1978, 7 In.	750.00

GLASS-MIDCENTURY refers to art glass made from the 1950s to the 1980s. Some glass factories, such as Baccarat or Orrefors, are listed under their own categories. Earlier glass may be listed in the Glass-Art and Glass-Contemporary categories. Italian glass may be found under Venini and Glass-Venetian.

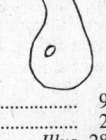

Dish, Opposing Parallel Lines, Tapio Wirkkala, 1955, 10 In.		920.00
Platter, Radiating Design, Platinum Luster, Higgins, 1950s, 15 In.		288.00
Sculpture, Fountain, Blue, Pink, Gold Veil Interior, Labino, 6 In.	*Illus*	2800.00
Sculpture, Gold Iridescent, Blue Veiling, Labino, 9 x 4 In.	*Illus*	4700.00
Vase, Bark, Finlandia Series, Clear, Gray, 10 1/2 In.		365.00
Vase, Bird Form, Aureliano Toso, Dino Martens Design		4800.00
Vase, Cobalt Streaks, Air Traps, White Interior, 13 In.	*Illus*	325.00
Vase, Cordonato D'Oro, Pinched Sides, Loop Handles, Barovier Toso, 6 In.		500.00
Vase, Gray, Gold Foil Inclusions, Ribbed, Barovier & Toso, 1950, 20 In.		1725.00
Vase, Opaque Blue, Iridescent, Mark Peiser, 2 7/8 In.		247.00
Vase, Well-Oiled Machine, Etched, Enameled, Black, Stuart Davis, 1950		1200.00
Vase, White & Amber Threads, Stripes, Lino Tagliapietra, 13 In.		316.00

GLASS-VENETIAN. Venetian glass has been made near Venice, Italy, since the thirteenth century. Thin, colored glass with applied decoration is favored, although many other types have been made. Collectors have recently become interested in the Art Deco and fifties designs. Glass was made on the Venetian island of Murano from 1291. The output dwindled in the late seventeenth century, but began to flourish again in the 1850s. Some of the old techniques of glassmaking were revived and firms today make traditional designs and original modern glass. Since 1981, the name *Murano* may only be used on glass made on Murano Island. Other pieces of Italian glass may be found in the Glass-Contemporary, Glass-Midcentury, and Venini categories of this book.

Ashtray, Cranberry To Clear, Controlled Bubbles, 3 Cigarette Rests, 5 1/2 In.	18.00
Bowl, Canes & Foil, Amethyst, Murano, 10 In.	45.00
Bowl, Cover, Pink Glass, Gold Dust Overlaid	1500.00
Bowl, Dessert, Leaf Shaped, Gold Flecks, Pink, Set Of 10	88.00
Bowl, Fruit, Cover, Amber, Pear-Shaped Handles, Murano, c.1960, 7 3/4 In.	700.00
Bowl, Pale To Electric Blue, Gold Swirls, Freeform Scallops, 17 1/2 In.	245.00
Bowl, Ribbed, Gold Leaf, Grape Handles, Barovier & Toso, c.1940, 9 3/4 In.	690.00
Bowl, Ruby, Freeform, Metal Bubbles, Hexagonal, 11 x 3 In.	26.00
Candlestick, Aqua Edged Bobeche & Foot, 12 In.	247.00
Centerpiece, 2 Fish On Rocks, Controlled Bubbles, Label, 12 In.	450.00
Centerpiece, Freeform, Foil Inclusions, 21 In.	60.00
Chandelier, 6-Light, Crystal Prisms, 27 x 20 In.	750.00
Chandelier, 6-Light, Daffodils, Gold & Red.	895.00
Chandelier, Brevattati, Opalescent Disks, Chrome Frame, c.1958, 25 In.	2760.00
Cordial Set, Cobalt Blue, Raised Gold, Pastel Flowers, Bell Shape, Italy	45.00
Decanter, Clown, 13 In.	60.00
Dish, Heart, Gold Flecks, Murano, Label, 5 1/2 In.	12.00
Figure, Stylized Maiden, Floral, Clear, Pale Shades, Murano, 1935, 15 5/8 In.	1725.00
Figurine, Bird, Green, Gold Flecked, 15 In.	75.00
Figurine, Bird, Smoky, White Beak & Eyes, A. Seguso, c.1960, 8 In., Pair	920.00
Figurine, Clown, Baggy Outfit, Red & Blue, Murano	90.00
Figurine, Clown, Fat, 13 1/2 In.	150.00
Figurine, Clown, Holding Ball, 11 3/4 In.	125.00
Figurine, Clown, Holding Guitar, 8 3/4 In.	70.00
Figurine, Clown, Holding Umbrella, 8 1/2 In.	90.00
Figurine, Clown, Kneeling, 8 In.	75.00
Figurine, Fish, Cobalt & Red Cased, Archimede Seguso, c.1955, 14 In.	1840.00
Figurine, Woman, Blue Gown, Large Hat, Gold Dust In Hands, 12 In.	235.00
Figurine, Woman, Period Costume, Zanfirico Trim, Bianconi, 1948, 9 3/8 In.	460.00
Garniture, Dolphin Handles, Pink, Salviati, c.1925, 7 Piece	800.00
Mirror, Rectangular, Foliate Crest, 55 x 32 In.	550.00
Perfume Bottle, Blue, Pink Floral Stopper, 10 3/4 In.	55.00
Sconce, Triangular Chrome Backplate, 13 Disks, Purple, c.1958, 17 In.	1840.00
Shell, Raised Dotted Surface, Black Amethyst, 4 In.	357.50
Swan, Ruby, Inverted Thumbprint Body, Gold Flecked Wings, 4 1/2 In.	65.00
Swizzle Stick, Horse & Jockey Motif, 8 In., 5 Piece	30.00
Vase, 5 Square Sections, Barovier & Toso, 1960, 13 3/4 In.	690.00
Vase, Blue, Green, & Gold, Triangular Form, 13 In.	55.00
Vase, Bottle Shape, Brown, Incised Texture, c.1960, 18 3/4 In.	690.00
Vase, Bud, Green, Gold Lattice & Scrolls, Floral, 8 In.	18.00
Vase, Colored Fish Amid Seaweed & Dragonfly, Johnolyth, 5 1/8 In.	435.00
Vase, Cylindrical, Horizontal Ribs, Air Bubbles, Opalescent, c.1950, 12 3/4 In.	690.00
Vase, Flat Ovoid, Red-Cased, Archimede Seguso, Plexiglas Stand, 9 1/2 In.	1265.00
Vase, Green, Foil Label, Signed, Murano, 12 In.	50.00
Vase, Latticinio Purple Design	150.00
Vase, Murrina, Crystal, Blue & Red Triangles, Barovier & Toso, 1961, 11 In.	5175.00
Vase, Oriente, Overlapping Layers, Silver Foil Inclusions, E. Barovier, 1940	2645.00
Vase, Pale Amber, Carlo Scarpa, 1936, 8 1/4 In.	1150.00
Vase, Pale Turquoise, Scorroso, Carlo Scarpa, 1936, 7 3/4 In.	1725.00
Vase, Rialto Bridge Scene, Cobalt Blue, 7 In.	42.00
Vase, Urn Shape, White Spirals, Gold Leaf, Murano, c.1960, 18 3/4 In.	1725.00

Whimsy, Pink, Clear & Gold Flecks, 5 3/4 In. 77.00

GLASSES for the eyes, or spectacles, were mentioned in a manuscript in 1289 and have been used ever since. The first eyeglasses with rigid side pieces were made in London in 1727. Bifocals were invented by Benjamin Franklin in 1785. Lorgnettes were popular in late Victorian times. Opera glasses are listed in their own category.

Benjamin Franklin, Advertising Cloth, Case	200.00
Goggles, Wellaworth, Wire Frame, Tinted Lenses, Box, Early 1900s	25.00
J. Hyde, Sterling, c.1815	585.00
Lorgnette, 14K White Gold, Folding, Leather Case	110.00
Lorgnette, Black Bakelite, Folding	75.00
Lorgnette, Center Diamond, Geometric Onyx & Diamond Mount, Platinum	5775.00
Lorgnette, Diamond Bail & Bridge, Sapphire Ring, Platinum & White Gold	920.00
Lorgnette, Diamonds, Black Enamel, Cord, Diamond Handle, Cartier, Art Deco	3850.00
Lorgnette, Folding, Pin, Sterling Silver	82.00
Lorgnette, Gilded Brass Handle, 8 In.	605.00
Lorgnette, Heart-Shaped Handle, 10K Gold	175.00
Lorgnette, Onyx & Diamond Handle, Seed Pearl Chain, 41 In.	1760.00
Lorgnette, Scroll Work Handles & Top, Yellow Gold	440.00
Opera, Attached To Gold Plated Holder, Folding, Case, 1880s......................	150.00
Pince-Nez, Folding, Leather Case	35.00
Sun, Cher, Space Age Design, Black & White, Deep Harlequin Frame, Case	65.00
Wire, Round, Small	18.00
Woman's, Attached To Fine Gold Chain & Hairpin	45.00

GOEBEL is the mark used by W. Goebel Porzellanfabrik of Oeslau, Germany, now Rodental, Germany. Many types of figurines and dishes have been made. The firm is still working. The pieces marked *Goebel Hummel* are listed under Hummel in this book.

Ashtray, Little Hiawatha, Full Bee, 4 x 4 In.	415.00
Bank, Penguin, 4 1/2 In.	85.00
Bell, 1983	25.00
Bookends, Dutch Boy & Girl, Kissing, Crown Mark	65.00
Bottle Stopper, Man & Woman, Yellow Holder, Label, No. X247	75.00
Bowl, Cereal, With Eggcup, Chick, Crown Mark	75.00
Condiment Set, Tray, Monks, Brown, Full Bee, 4 Piece	125.00
Cookie Jar, Friar Tuck	400.00
Cookie Jar, Owl	165.00
Creamer, Cow, Standing, Tan & Brown, Bee-V Mark, 4 x 6 In.	25.00
Creamer, Friar Tuck, 2 1/2 In. .... 28.00 to 40.00
Creamer, Monk	35.00
Creamer, Monk, Full Bee, 5 In.	70.00
Figurine, 3 Birds In Tree, Cream Finish	90.00
Figurine, 3 Owls, Brown	50.00
Figurine, A Gentle Glow	66.00
Figurine, Autumn Harvest	75.00
Figurine, Baby Zebra, Standing, 4 In.	50.00
Figurine, Bear Cub, Seated, Brown	25.00
Figurine, Bird, Blue Jay, 9 In.	85.00
Figurine, Bird, Nesting, Brown	15.00
Figurine, Bird, Pigeon, 7 In.	85.00
Figurine, Birds In Tree, Cream	90.00
Figurine, Cat, Seated, Gray, 11 In.	200.00
Figurine, Child, Ice Skating, White...	40.00
Figurine, Child, Picking Berries, White	40.00
Figurine, Child, With Butterfly, White	40.00
Figurine, Clown, Light Glaze, 6 In.	55.00
Figurine, Dog, Pointing, 11 In.	300.00
Figurine, Dog, Pomeranian, 12 In. .... 225.00 to 250.00
Figurine, Dog, Schnauzer, Seated, 11 In.	225.00
Figurine, Flower Vendor	121.00
Figurine, Hear Ye, Hear Ye	100.00

Figurine, Hedgehog 40.00
Figurine, Koala, Climbing, With Young 50.00
Figurine, Lion, Prestige, 19 In. .... 275.00 to 300.00
Figurine, Maiden, Standing, No. 283/500, 11 3/4 In. 70.00
Figurine, Make A Wish 88.00
Figurine, Mountaineer 88.00
Figurine, Mouse, On Rock 50.00
Figurine, Nativity, Stable, Vee Over Gee, 10 Piece 325.00
Figurine, Panda & Cub 85.00
Figurine, Parrots, On Trunk 100.00
Figurine, Poodle, Black, 1968, 7 In. 85.00
Figurine, Porcupines, Mother With 4 Young 35.00
Figurine, Rabbit, Sitting 40.00
Figurine, Rise & Shine 65.00
Figurine, Snowgirl, White, Blond 25.00
Figurine, Tiger, On Rock, 17 In. 300.00
Figurine, Tiger, Prestige, 19 In. 275.00
Flower Frog, Bird, Marked 40.00
Flower Frog, Maiden, Standing, Marked 125.00
Plate, Happy Anniversary, Crystal .... 50.00 to 75.00
Plate, Mother's Series, Seals 75.00
Plate, Trakenhner, Persian Arab 45.00
Salt & Pepper, Cardinal Tuck, Red 225.00
Salt & Pepper, Friar Tuck With Books 125.00
Salt & Pepper, Friar Tuck, Full Bee, 2 1/4 In. 32.00
Salt & Pepper, Poodles 30.00
Stein, Flight Into Egypt, 3 Liter 75.00
Tumbler, Blown-Out Face Of Santa Claus 35.00

GOLDSCHEIDER has made porcelains in three places. The family left Vienna in 1938 and started factories in England and in Trenton, New Jersey. The New Jersey factory started in 1940 as Goldscheider-U.S.A. In 1941 it became Goldscheider-Everlast Corporation. From 1947 to 1953 it was Goldcrest Ceramics Corporation. In 1950 the Vienna plant was returned to Mr. Goldscheider and the company continues in business. The Trenton, New Jersey, business, now called *Goldscheider of Vienna*, imports all of the pieces.

Box, Figural, German Shepherd Head On Lid, 5 1/2 x 4 In. 85.00
Bust, Katherine The Great, Signed, 16 1/2 In. 675.00
Bust, Madonna, Praying 75.00
Bust, Mongol, Liedhoff 50.00
Figurine, African Girl, Late-19th Century Clothes, 1900, 10 & 10 1/4 In., Pair 1265.00
Figurine, Black Sailor & Girl, Pair 850.00
Figurine, Cat, Yellow Salt Glaze 45.00
Figurine, Chinese Teahouse, Kneeling Orientals, 7 x 5 In. 60.00
Figurine, Colonial Couple 75.00
Figurine, Dancer, Woman, Arabian Costume, 1925, 17 7/8 In. 2300.00
Figurine, Dog, Spaniel, No. 680 .... 105.00
Figurine, Exotic Dancer, Art Deco 1430.00
Figurine, Girl, Sailor Suit, No. 6748, 12 1/2 In. 1050.00
Figurine, Girl, Summer Hat, No. 6940, 12 In. 1050.00
Figurine, Head, Red Hair & Lips, Yellow Blossom, Marked, c.1925, 8 In. 357.00
Figurine, Juliet With Doves, Rose, Gray, Cobalt, Pale Blue, 12 1/4 In. 225.00
Figurine, Lady As A Page, 14 1/2 In. 990.00
Figurine, Lady Caller 75.00
Figurine, Madonna & Child 250.00
Figurine, Nude Female Dancer, c.1925, 11 In. 805.00
Figurine, Sing Lo, Oriental Holds Bird & Bird House, 7 1/4 In. 32.00
Figurine, Woman, Green Ruffled Skirt, Signed, 12 In. 145.00
Mask, Wall, Medusa Style Hair, 11 1/2 In. 1250.00
Plaque, Madonna & Child, Gold Sticker, 15 In. 695.00
Plaque, Woman's Sinister Head, Holding Rose, c.1925, No. 4490, 10 1/2 In. 700.00
Vase, Lobed, Painted Panels, Yellow Interior, c.1930, 17 3/4 In., Pair. 3163.00
Vase, Village Scene, Baluster Form, 8 1/4 In. 65.00

GOLF, see Sports category

GONDER Ceramic Arts, Inc., was opened by Lawton Gonder in 1941 in Zanesville, Ohio. Gonder made high-grade pottery decorated with flambe, drip, gold crackle, and Chinese crackle glazes. The factory closed in 1957. From 1946 to 1954, Gonder also operated the Elgee Pottery, which made ceramic lamp bases.

Console Set, Mottled Green, Leaf-Shape Basket, Scalloped Candleholder, 3 Piece	45.00
Ewer, Mottled Beige Over Gray, Pink Interior, 5 1/2 x 7 1/2 In.	15.00
Pitcher, Green	10.00
Planter, Gondola	40.00
Planter, Swan, Figural, Yellow, Pink Mottling, 5 In.	16.00
Vase, Gray, 7 In.	20.00
Vase, Lime Green, White Drizzled Top, Square, 6 In.	25.00
Vase, Mottled Turquoise, Gray, Pink, Twisted Handles, 8 3/4 In.	15.00
Vase, Pink, 9 1/2 In.	20.00
Vase, Violet, 2 Handles, 9 In.	15.00

GOOFUS GLASS was made from about 1900 to 1920 by many American factories. It was originally painted gold, red, green, bronze, pink, purple, or other bright colors. Many pieces are found today with flaking paint and this lowers the value.

Berry Bowl, 9 In.	22.00
Chop Plate, Bird & Strawberry, 12 In.	110.00
Plate, 13 1/2 In.	20.00
Plate, Rose & Lattice, 5 3/4 In.	17.50
Wall Pocket, Bird & Grapes, 7 3/4 In.	55.00

GOUDA, Holland, has been a pottery center since the seventeenth century. Two firms, the Zenith pottery, established in the eighteenth century, and the Zuid-Hollandsche pottery, made the brightly colored wares marked *Gouda* from 1880 to about 1940. Many pieces featured Art Nouveau or Art Deco designs.

Bowl, Black Glaze, Spots Of Enamel Eyelike Design, 4 x 7 In.	175.00
Creamer, Enamel Highlights, Black, 2 1/2 In.	45.00
Dish, Cover, Flowers, Leaves, Anjer House, 6 In.	73.00
Pitcher, Floral Design, 6 In.	225.00
Pitcher, Green, 2 1/2 In.	25.00
Vase, 2 Handles, Zigzags & Circles, 4 In.	65.00
Vase, Butterflies On Flowers, 2 Handles, Polychrome, 15 1/2 In.	525.00
Vase, Polychrome Landscape, Windmills, Trees, Signed, 9 1/4 In.	137.00
Vase, Stick, Colorless Glaze Over Green, Gold & Orange, 8 1/2 In.	210.00
Vase, Stylized Dandelions, Cream Ground, 6 1/4 In.	345.00
Vase, Stylized Poppies, Handle Looping From Shoulder, Ovoid, 9 5/8 In.	405.00
Vase, White Circles, Outlined In Gold, Burgundy, Pair	75.00

GRANITEWARE is an enameled tinware that has been used in the kitchen from the late nineteenth century to the present. Earlier graniteware was green or turquoise blue, with white spatters. The later ware was gray with white spatters. Reproductions are being made in all colors.

Basin, Gray, 11 In.	9.00
Bath Set, Baby's, Pink, Pitcher & Soap Dish, 4 Piece	500.00
Boiler, Coffee, Gray, Tin Lid	50.00
Bottle Cooler, Attached Lid, 7 Bottles, Universal Container, Green & White	245.00
Box, Salt, Mottled Gray, L. & G. Mfg., 11 In.	400.00
Box, Salt, Yellow	65.00
Bucket, Berry, Marbled Blue & White	40.00
Bucket, Field Worker's, Light Blue, 8 x 10 In.	165.00
Bucket, Tin Lid, Blue & White Swirl, 6 In. Diam.	135.00
Cake Saver Cover, Solid Green	25.00
Can, Milk, Blue & White Swirl, Wooden Handle, 7 1/2 In.	195.00
Can, Milk, Gray, Bail Handle, Gal.	90.00

Canister Set, Cobalt Blue, White Plaid, 6 Piece 195.00
Canteen, Metal Closure, Porcelain Stopper, Cobalt Blue 48.00
Carrier, Dinner, Stacked, 4 Sections, Cream & Green 145.00
Coffeepot, Blue & White 85.00
Coffeepot, Blue Swirl 75.00
Coffeepot, Flower On White, Pewter Trim 175.00
Coffeepot, Gray 35.00
Coffeepot, Medium Blue, Gooseneck, 8 1/2 In. 62.00
Coffeepot, Orange 35.00
Coffeepot, Solid Beige 35.00
Coffeepot, Solid Cream, Black Trim 30.00
Coffeepot, White, Pewter Trim, Castle Scene, German 210.00
Coffeepot, Yellow & White Swirl, 1930s 75.00
Colander, Brown Swirl 165.00
Colander, Gray 25.00
Colander, Purple, Shaded 36.00
Cooker, Tabletop, Mottled Blue, Beatrice, England 150.00
Cup, Hinged Lid, Paper Label, White 32.00
Cuspidor, Cobalt Blue, White Speckles 45.00
Eggcup, Light Blue Checked, Pair 69.00
Fruit Jar Filler, Mottled Gray 10.00
Funnel, Blue Swirl, White Interior 260.00
Funnel, White, Black Trim, 4 1/2 In. 19.00
Grater, Child's, Gray Speckled 65.00
Grater, Snow On Mountain 200.00
Kettle, Yellow & White Swirl, 1930s 95.00
Ladle, Apple Green, Speckled 50.00
Loaf Pan, Blue & White Mottled, Folded Corners 80.00
Lunch Pail, Blue Swirl 240.00
Lunch Pail, Miner's, Gray 165.00
Measure, Gray, 3 1/3 In. 45.00
Mold, Child's, Gray Speckled, Ruffled 55.00
Mold, Fish, Solid White, Hanging Ring 180.00
Mold, Melon Shape, Large 85.00
Mug, Mottled Gray, Red 12.00
Mug, Red, Black Trim 10.00
Pail, Milk, Tin Cover, Gray, 1 Qt. 55.00
Pail, Soup, Gray, 3 1/2 In. 55.00
Pail, Water, Brown & White 95.00
Pan, Baking, Oblong, Gray, 9 1/2 x 15 In. 20.00
Pan, Blue Swirl, Oblong 195.00
Pan, Cake, Tube, Gray 45.00
Pan, Double Boiler, Medium Blue, 6 In. 115.00
Pan, Knudsen Cottage Cheese 48.00
Pan, Pudding, Mottled Blue, Elite, Austria, 12 In. 20.00
Pan, Sauce, Blue Swirl, 8 1/2 In. 40.00
Pan, Tube Cake, Gray 45.00
Perculator, Pear Shape, Gooseneck Spout, Medium Green 50.00
Pie Plate, Blue & White 35.00
Pie Plate, Cobalt Blue Swirl 70.00
Pitcher, Molasses, White, Blue Trim 75.00
Pitcher, Solid Blue, 5 In. 27.00
Pitcher, Water, Gray Mottled 85.00
Pitcher, Water, White, Large 27.50
Platter, Blue & White Mottled, 14 In. 59.00
Pot, Cover, Spattered Cobalt Blue, 5 1/2 In. 40.00
Potty, Blue & White Speckled 15.00
Potty, Cobalt Blue & White Swirl 80.00
Potty, White & Black, Handle, 8 1/2 x 4 In. 16.00
Roaster, Blue & White Swirl, Iris 70.00
Roaster, Child's, Gray Speckled 65.00
Roaster, Cover, Green & Ivory 25.00
Roaster, Cover, Solid Blue 42.00

Roaster, Hood, Patent 1911 .... 25.00
Roaster, White, Black Specks, Savory 49.00
Sauce Pan, Red & White Swirl, 1930s, 6 In. 69.00
Skillet, Poached Egg, Child's, Gray Speckled 85.00
Spoon, White, Cobalt Blue Handle, 16 In. 20.00
Strainer, Gray, Handle 35.00
Strainer, Tea, Gray 25.00
Syrup, Brown & White Mottled 395.00
Tea Set, Border Design, Blue, Germany, Box, 8 Piece 575.00
Tea Set, Child's, Blue & White, 13 Piece 385.00
Teakettle, Cream, Red Trim 25.00
Teapot, Apple, Mottled Green 40.00
Teapot, Blue Mottled 110.00
Teapot, Blue, Glass Dome 35.00
Teapot, Gooseneck, Cream & Green, 8 1/2 In. 69.00
Teapot, Gooseneck, Dutch Scene 145.00
Teapot, Gooseneck, Red & White, Checkered Trim, 8 3/4 In. 165.00
Teapot, Gray Mottled, Pewter Trim, Dated 1886 .... 245.00
Teapot, Gray, Small 225.00
Teapot, Green, 1 Cup 30.00
Teapot, Light Green 35.00
Teapot, Mottled Apple Green 40.00
Washboard, Soap Saver 45.00

GREENTOWN glass was made by the Indiana Tumbler and Goblet Company of Greentown, Indiana, from 1894 to 1903. In 1899, the factory name was changed to National Glass Company. A variety of pressed, milk, and chocolate glass was made. Additional pieces may be found in other categories, such as Chocolate Glass, Custard Glass, Holly Amber, Milk Glass, and Pressed Glass.

Berry Set, Fleur-De-Lis, Blue, 7 Piece 95.00
Bowl, Beveled Star 37.50
Bowl, Corded Drapery, Footed, 6 In. 95.00
Bowl, Herringbone Buttress, Gold Trim, 7 In. 70.00
Butter, Cover, Teardrop & Tassel, Blue 130.00
Compote, Pleat Band, Clear, Etched 47.50
Cordial, Shuttle, Pair 35.00
Cruet, Cord & Tassel 115.00
Cruet, Cord Drapery, Amber 290.00
Dish, Cover, Rabbit, Teal Blue 185.00
Goblet, Diamond Prism, Clear 67.50
Mug, Drinking Scene, Chocolate Glass, 5 In. 125.00
Mug, Elves, Green 95.00
Mug, Serenade Scene, Green, 4 In. .... 85.00 to 125.00
Nappy, Austrian, 2 Handles 85.00
Pitcher, Austrian, Canary, 3 In. 110.00
Pitcher, Fleur-De-Lis 35.00
Pitcher, Squirrel, Clear 160.00
Pitcher, Wild Rose & Bowknot, Satin, Red & Gold Flashed 200.00
Salt & Pepper, Austrian, Silver Plated Tops 175.00
Spooner, Blue 175.00
Spooner, Holly Amber 625.00
Spooner, Pleat Band, Clear 20.00
Sugar, Cover, Austrian, Pedestal 85.00
Tumbler, Brazen Shield, Blue 60.00
Tumbler, Dewey, Amber 65.00
Vase, Austrian, 8 In. 85.00
Vase, Herringbone Buttress, Green, 6 In. 175.00

GRUEBY Faience Company of Boston, Massachusetts, was incorporated in 1897 by William H. Grueby. Garden statuary, art pottery, and architectural tiles were made until 1920. The company developed a matte green glaze that was so popular it was copied by many other factories making a less expensive type of pottery. This eventually led to the financial problems of the pottery.

Bowl, Doughnut, Blue-Green Glaze, Textured Surface, 4 In. 350.00
Bowl, Incised Overlapping Leaves, Wilhelmina Post, Bisque Form, 8 In. 825.00
Bowl, Italian Green, 8 1/2 In. 300.00
Bowl, Matte Green, Low Relief Decorations, 1906, 2 1/4 In. 467.00
Bowl, Tooled & Applied Leaves, Organic Green Glaze, Green Interior, 7 1/4 In. 600.00
Frieze, 4 Tile, Sailing Ship, Blue Sky, Seagulls, Frame, 8 3/4 x 27 In. 1900.00
Lamp Base, Curly Leaves Under Veined Green Glaze, 5 1/2 x 5 In. 715.00
Lamp Base, Tooled & Applied Leaves, Matte Green Glaze, 12 1/4 In. 3000.00
Paperweight, Scarab, Light Green Matte Glaze, Marked, 1 1/2 x 4 In. 410.00
Paperweight, Scarab, Matte Green Glaze, Sterling Silver Band Base, 4 In. 1650.00
Plant Stand, Square Green Textured Glaze Tile, Oak Stand, c.1900, 29 3/4 In. 5750.00
Pot, Incised Rings, Matte Green Glaze, Impressed Mark, 3 1/4 In. 300.00
Tile, Blue Cracked Design, Black High Glaze Ground, 4 In. 40.00
Tile, Cherub, With Cornucopia, 2 Colors, 6 In. 285.00
Tile, Galleon Ship, 8 x 8 In., Pair 1760.00
Tile, Galleon, Ivory Sails, Green Ground, Square, 6 In. 495.00
Tile, Geometric Relief Design, Green, Square, No. 5005, A.F., Faience, 8 1/4 In. 445.00
Tile, Kelsey Ranch, Lexington, Supplying Waldorf Lunches, 6 Piece 825.00
Tile, Knight On Horseback, Green Organic Glazes, 6 x 6 In. 357.00
Tile, Lily Pad, 6 x 6 In., 7 Piece 2200.00
Tile, Medieval Knight On Horseback, 6 x 6 In., 3 Piece 1000.00
Tile, Scenes From Alice In Wonderland 3080.00
Tile, Seascape, Matte Blue, Green, Ivory & Brown, Faience, 8 1/2 In., 3 Piece 1775.00
Tile, Yellow Matte Glaze, Red Clay Body, Square, 4 In., Pair 75.00
Tile, Yellow Tulip, Green Leaves, 6 x 6 In. 500.00
Vase, 4 Full-Length Leaves, Matte Glaze, Green, Signed, 7 3/4 In. 1200.00
Vase, 7 Buds, Avocado & Yellow, Leaf Molded, Ovoid, Artist E.R., 12 1/4 In. 3050.00
Vase, Alternating Small & Large Leaves, Green Glaze, Signed, 7 1/4 In. 1200.00
Vase, Broad Layered Leaves, Mustard Glaze, Matte, Marie S. Seaman, 7 1/2 In. 1775.00
Vase, Bud & Stem Alternate With Leaf, Matte Green Glaze, Impressed Mark, 7 In. ... 665.00
Vase, Corset, 8 1/4 In. 750.00
Vase, Gourd Shape, Clear Glaze Over Curdled Cobalt Dripping, 13 In. 6150.00
Vase, Incised Alternating Floral & Leaf, Navy Blue, Gertrude Stanwood, 6 In. 1000.00
Vase, Incised Lines, Deep Blue Mottled Glaze, 9 x 4 In. 1450.00
Vase, Incised Repeating Design, Matte Green Glaze, Ruth Erickson, 7 In. 770.00
Vase, Iris Leaf, 11 3/8 In. 2300.00
Vase, Leaves & Buds, Cucumber Green Glaze, 7 3/4 x 3 3/4 In. 1550.00
Vase, Leaves & Flowers, Yellow, Matte Green, 13 1/4 In. 2970.00
Vase, Long Flared Neck, Buds On Stems, Whilhelmina Post, 7 x 4 1/2 In. 450.00
Vase, Matte Dark Green Glaze, Impressed Mark, 13 In. 600.00
Vase, Matte Green Stylized Design, 7 In. 1475.00
Vase, Matte Green, 8 In. 600.00
Vase, Matte Turquoise, Ribbed, Wilhelmina Post, 7 3/4 In. 357.00
Vase, Model Leaves, 5 Scrolled Handles, Matte Green Glaze, 11 1/4 In. 7150.00
Vase, Mustard Colored, Globular, 3 1/2 In. 1250.00
Vase, Red Water Lilies 7700.00
Vase, Spherical, Veined Green-Brown Glaze, 3 1/4 x 3 1/4 In. 300.00
Vase, Tooled & Applied Leaves, Buds On Stems, Ruth Erickson, 7 1/2 In. 1400.00
Vase, Tooled Leaves & Buds, Star-Shaped Rim, Florence Liley, 7 1/2 In. 950.00
Vase, Tooled Wide Leaves, Curled White Glaze, Marked, 9 1/2 In. 1600.00
Vase, Yellow Matte Glaze, 4 1/2 In. 330.00
Vessel, Bulbous, Blossoms, Watermelon-Green Veined Glaze, W. Post, 5 x 8 In. 3525.00
Vessel, Closed-In Rim, Allover Leaves, Matte Green, 5 3/4 x 6 3/4 In. 885.00

GUN is the name used for this category, which includes shotguns, pistols, and
other antique firearms. Rifles are listed in their own category. Be very careful
when buying or selling guns because there are special laws governing the sale
and ownership. A collector's gun should be displayed in a safe manner,
probably with the barrel filled or a part missing to be sure it cannot be
accidentally fired.

BB, Benjamin, Barrel Model, Steel-Chrome 200.00
BB, Benjamin, Brass, 25-Shot Repeater, Early 1900s 600.00
BB, Daisy, Model 40, Copper Bandit, Red Ryder, 1940 .... 250.00

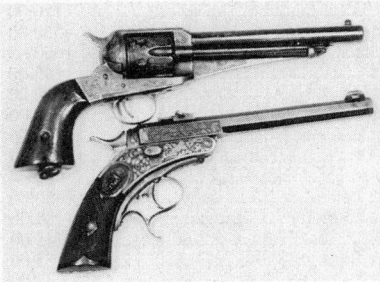
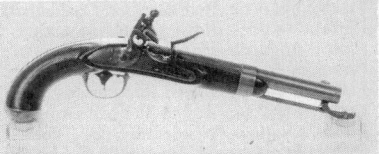

Above: Gun, Pistol, Flintlock, U. S. R. Johnson, Model 1836, 1841

Left, top to bottom: Gun, Revolver, Colt Navy Dragoon, Model 1850, Brass Trigger, Ships; Gun, Revolver, Navy Dragoon Style, Floral Engraving

BB, Daisy, Model 40, Military, Bayonet, Sling 450.00
BB, Daisy, Model 104, Double Barrel 990.00
BB, Daisy, Model 111, Red Ryder 85.00
BB, Daisy, Model 118, Targeteer, Nickel Plated 75.00
BB, Daisy, No. 96 .... 75.00
BB, Daisy, Red Ryder 80.00
BB, Hahn, No. 45, Repeater, Six-Gun Style, Box 37.00
Colt, Lightning, Pump Action, 1887 .... 500.00
Daisy, No. 220, Scotland 25.00
Derringer, Double Barrel, 36 Caliber, Pearl Grips, Brass, c.1860 .... 225.00
Derringer, Rim Fire, Iron Frame, 41 Caliber, Southern, 1860s 210.00
Double Barrel, Hammer, Damascus Barrel, Belgium, c.1885 .... 250.00
Flintlock, Dag Blunderbuss, 12 3/4-In. Iron Barrel 330.00
Flintlock, John Murdoch, Doune, Scotland, c.1750, 12 1/4 In. 5750.00
Fowling, Silver Inlay, Inscribed A. Manley, Vt., 1803, 68 In. 1980.00
Luger, 9 mm, World War I, 1917 .... 1400.00
Luger, American Eagle, 30 Caliber, 1900 .... 2310.00
Luger, German, No. 5067, 8-Shot, Shoulder Holster 770.00
Marking, Crosman, 1400, 50 Caliber, Forestry Service, Barrel Muzzle Load 140.00
Musket, Flintlock, Canton, Mass., 1810 .... 810.00
Pistol, Air, Beeman, P-1, Holster, 177 Caliber, Box 150.00
Pistol, Air, Benjamin Target, No. 130, Pump-Up, Box 100.00
Pistol, Air, Benjamin, No. 117, Long Stroke, Pump-Up, Nickel 100.00
Pistol, Air, Benjamin, No. 132, Black Nickel, Translucent Grips, Box 58.00
Pistol, Air, Benjamin, No. 250, Black Nickel, Box 77.00
Pistol, Air, Brass, Model 115, Can Of Pellets, Air Bottle, Book, Box 225.00
Pistol, Air, BSA Scorpion, 22 Caliber, Box 125.00
Pistol, Air, Bull's-Eye, 177 Caliber, Box, Italy 30.00
Pistol, Air, Crosman 118, 22 Caliber, Repeater 325.00
Pistol, Air, Crosman 600, 22 Caliber 90.00
Pistol, Air, Crosman, 112, 22 Caliber, Gray Grips 115.00
Pistol, Air, Crosman, Model 130, Pump-Up 50.00
Pistol, Air, Crosman, No. 622, Pump Action, Repeater, Box 120.00
Pistol, Air, Daisy, No. 790, Box 50.00
Pistol, Air, Healthways, Plainsman 175 .... 18.00
Pistol, Air, Hy-Score, 802, 177 Caliber, Repeater, Wooden Grip 100.00
Pistol, Air, Schimel, GP22, 22 Caliber 175.00
Pistol, Air, Walther, LP53, Accessories, Papers, Box 225.00
Pistol, Army, Center Fire, Elephant Head & Winged Lizard, 44 Caliber, 1970 .... 195.00
Pistol, Browning, Automatic, 6 Mm Caliber, 8 Shot 165.00
Pistol, Crosman, No. 106, Skeleton Pump-Up, 22 Caliber., Box 85.00
Pistol, Damascus, Double Barrel, Engraved, 1830 .... 225.00
Pistol, Dragoon Flintlock, Brass Mounted, England, Engraved Farmer, 1744 .... 1650.00
Pistol, Dueling, Flintlock, H.W. Mortimore & Co., Late 18th Century, 10 1/4 In. 1750.00
Pistol, Dueling, Georgian, Turvy, London, Case, 1794-1810, Pair 1540.00
Pistol, Dueling, Leather Case, Turvy, London, 1794-1810, Pair 1435.00
Pistol, Flintlock, Folding Trigger, England 275.00

Pistol, Flintlock, Ball Hammer, Dated 1810 .... 170.00
Pistol, Flintlock, Holster, Brass Mountings & Barrel, England, 14 In. 550.00
Pistol, Flintlock, Johnson, U.S.Military, 1837 .... 1650.00
Pistol, Flintlock, Military, Brass, 9-In. Barrel 145.00
Pistol, Flintlock, U.S.R. Johnson, Model 1836, 1841 .... *Illus* 3500.00
Pistol, Flintlock, Walnut Stock & Grip, 50 Caliber, France, 18 In. 800.00
Pistol, Flintlock, Wooden & Brass Tinder 495.00
Pistol, Iver Johnson, Tip-Up, 22 Caliber, Late 1800s 55.00
Pistol, Luger Automatic, 8 Shot, Germany, c.1939 .... 935.00
Pistol, Muff, Continental, Ivory Handles, 4 1/2 In., Pair 1450.00
Pistol, Pepperbox, Muzzle Loading, Allens, Engraved Frame 285.00
Pistol, Percussion, Boot, England, Single Shot 245.00
Pistol, Percussion, Double Barrel, B. Woodward & Sons, c.1850 .... 625.00
Pistol, Signal, ST/R Tr., Walnut Grip, 6 1/4 In. 245.00
Pistol, Stevens, Tip-Up, 22 Caliber, Single Shot 145.00
Pistol, Target, Percussion, Octagonal Barrel, Walnut Stock, 9 In. 575.00
Pistol, Tiger Maple Stock, Inlaid Metal Hearts & Diamonds, J. Brown & Sons 1300.00
Pistol, Walther, Automatic P-38, 8 Shot, Germany 825.00
Revolver, 45 Caliber, Germany, 1882 .... 500.00
Revolver, Army, 45 Caliber, Civil War 2200.00
Revolver, Colt 1877, 38 Caliber, Horn Bird's Head Grip, Serial No. 48327 .... 275.00
Revolver, Colt 36, Naval, Accessories & Flask, c.1851 .... 1750.00
Revolver, Colt 38 RF, Pocket, 4 1/2 In. Octagonal Barrel, 5 Shot 550.00
Revolver, Colt Navy Dragoon, Model 1850, Brass Trigger, Ships .... *Illus* 2475.00
Revolver, Colt, Dragoon, 44 Caliber, S/N 17299 .... 4000.00
Revolver, Colt, Harbor Scene Cylinder, 5-In. Barrel 300.00
Revolver, Colt, Line Engraved Frame, Bone Grips, 4 3/4-in. Barrel 300.00
Revolver, Colt, Model 3, Navy, Ivory Handle, Silver, 1851 .... 4400.00
Revolver, Colt, Model 1849, Mahogany Case 2150.00
Revolver, Colt, Model 1849, Pocket, Serial No. 52164 .... 357.00
Revolver, Colt, Model 1875, 6 Shot 770.00
Revolver, Colt, Model 1877, 38 Caliber, Rosewood, Leather Holster 255.00
Revolver, Colt, SA, 45 Caliber 700.00
Revolver, Forehand, 32 Caliber, Hammerless, Leather Holster 50.00
Revolver, Harrington & Richardson, 22 Caliber, Walnut Grips, Dated 1886 .... 30.00
Revolver, Hidden Trigger, 7.65 Caliber 65.00
Revolver, Hopkins Allen X, No. 4, 38 Caliber, Spur Trigger, 1871 .... 75.00
Revolver, Merwin & Hulbert, 44-40, Nickel, Barrel 7 In. 850.00
Revolver, Meyers Brevete, Pin Fire 2200.00
Revolver, Model 1900, Double Action, Nickel Plated 130.00
Revolver, Navy Dragoon Style, Floral Engraving .... *Illus* 770.00
Revolver, Pin Fire, Fold-Up Trigger, 6 Shot, 32 Caliber, 1870 .... 150.00
Revolver, Smith & Wesson, 22 Caliber, K-22 Masterpiece, 6-Shot, Box 440.00
Revolver, Smith & Wesson, 32 Caliber, Baby Russian, Serial No. 6635 .... 220.00
Revolver, Smith & Wesson, 32 Caliber, Spur Trigger, 1877 .... 85.00
Revolver, Smith & Wesson, 38 Caliber, 1938, Box 440.00
Revolver, Smith & Wesson, Model 1 1/2, 32 Caliber, Rim Fire, Civil War 110.00
Revolver, Smith & Wesson, No. 3, 44 Caliber, Russian Model, Serial No. 7900 .... 605.00
Revolver, Smith & Wesson, Schofield, Single Action, c.1876 .... 965.00
Revolver, Starr Arms, 44 Caliber, Army, 1858 .... 605.00
Revolver, Winchester, Cartridge, Frontier, 44 Caliber, Belgium 245.00
Shotgun, Double Barrel, No. 1524, W. Richards, 19th Century 110.00
Shotgun, Double Barrel, Percussion, 12 Gauge, Fisher & Long, 29 1/2 In. 150.00
Shotgun, Eclipse Arms, 12 Gauge, Double Barrel Hammer 115.00
Shotgun, Henry Arms, 12 Gauge, Double Barrel 100.00
Shotgun, Ithaca, 12 Gauge 203.00
Shotgun, Ithaca, 12 Gauge Field Grade, NID, 30 In. Barrel 467.00
Shotgun, Ithaca, 12 Gauge Grade III, 26 In. Barrel 990.00
Shotgun, Ithaca, Mag 10 Supreme, 32 In. Rib Barrel 825.00
Shotgun, NR Davis, 410 Gauge, Double Barrel 700.00
Shotgun, Over-And-Under, Extra Barrel, Soft & Hard Cases 1650.00
Shotgun, Parker, 12 Gauge 375.00
Shotgun, Parker, 20 Gauge, Double Barrel 2750.00

Shotgun, Parker, DHE, 20 Gauge, 28 In. Barrel 3300.00
Shotgun, Parker, Double Barrel 1500.00
Shotgun, Watson, Sidelock Ejector, 30 In. Barrel 2860.00
Shotgun, Winchester, M70, 7 mm 841.00
Whaling, Christopher Brand, Ledyard, Conn. 990.00

GUNDERSON glass was made at the Gunderson-Pairpoint Glass Works of
New Bedford, Massachusetts, from 1952 to 1957. Gunderson Peachblow is
especially famous.

Hat, Burmese, Diamond Quilted 300.00
Jug, Peachblow, Loop Handle, Acid Finish, Bulbous, 4 1/2 x 4 In. 450.00
Toothpick, Burmese, 2 3/4 In. 450.00

GUSTAVSBERG ceramics factory was founded in 1827 near Stockholm,
Sweden. It is best known to collectors for its twentieth-century art wares,   **Gustafsberg**
especially a green stoneware with silver inlay called *Argenta*.

Ashtray, Domino, Radiating Circles, c.1955, 8 x 6 In., Pair 403.00
Ashtray, Flowers On Vine, Argenta, Square, 8 In. 185.00
Bouillon Cup & Saucer, Yellow & Green Floral, Porcelain, 8 Piece 33.00
Dish, Fish Shape, 13 In. 75.00
Dish, Port Scene, Green, Argenta, 5 1/2 In. 68.00
Figurine, Girl, Holding Cat 175.00
Vase, Fish Design, Green, 6 In. 150.00
Vase, Floral, Green, Argenta, 5 In. 275.00
Vase, Silver Overlay Flowers, Green, 5 In. 145.00
Vase, Surrea, Flattened Planes, White Crackle Glaze, 1940, 12 3/4 In. 2760.00
Vase, WASA Ship, Green Argenta, 7 In. 275.00
Vase, White Floral, Green, Blue-Green Ground, Signed, 16 In. 650.00

GUTTA-PERCHA was one of the first plastic materials. It was made from a
mixture of resins from Malaysian tress. It was molded and used for
daguerreotype cases, toilet articles, and picture frames in the nineteenth
century.

Brush & Mirror, Child's, Pale Green 140.00
Case, 4 Figures & Horse, Brown, 4 x 4 7/8 In. 93.00
Case, Daguerreotype, Bartering Soldiers On Both Sides, 4 x 5 In. 302.50
Case, Daguerreotype, Landing Of Columbus, 9 1/4 In. 2475.00
Case, Daguerreotype, Little Boy 72.00
Case, Daguerreotype, Profile Bust Of Washington, 3 3/8 x 3 3/4 In. 330.00
Case, Deer & Cherub, Black, 4 7/8 In. 159.00
Case, Ferrotype, Civil War Soldier 165.00
Case, Landing Of Columbus, Niagara Falls Tintype, 7 x 9 In. 2475.00
Case, Military Figures Bartering, Black, 4 x 4 7/8 In. 104.00
Case, Washington Monument, Richmond, Va., 5 x 6 1/4 In. 632.00
Case, Woman On Horse, Boy, Dog, Black, 4 x 4 7/8 In. 82.00
Match Safe, Figural, Book 75.00

HAEGER Potteries, Inc., Dundee, Illinois, started making commercial art
wares in 1914. Early pieces were marked with the name *Haeger* written over   **Haeger**
an *H*. About 1938, the mark *Royal Haeger* was used. The firm is still making
florist wares and lamp bases.

Ashtray, Advertising, Craftsmen For A Century, 1871-1971 .... 30.00
Bowl, Centerpiece, Leaf Form, Applied Fruit Cluster, Green & Black, 20 x 6 In. 32.00
Bowl, Cover 20.00
Bowl, Cream, Free Form, Oval, 11 x 6 In. 12.00
Bowl, Daisy, Low 20.00
Bowl, Flower Frog, Nude, Mauve Agate 125.00
Candlestick, Trumpet Flowers, Leaf Form, Black, 8 x 5 1/2 In., Pair 22.00
Console Set, Green, Oval Bowl, Candlesticks, Oval Thumbprints 35.00
Console Set, Pea Green, Ocean Waves, 2 Swans, 3 Piece 28.00
Figurine, Ballerina, Cream, Speckled Flower, 9 1/2 In. 38.00
Figurine, Black Panther, 25 In. 100.00
Figurine, Egyptian Cat, Orange, 16 In. 65.00

Lamp, Aladdin Shape, 1950s	27.00
Lamp, Panther, Green Base	35.00
Lamp, TV, Black Panther	50.00
Lamp, TV, Lion	65.00
Planter, Girl, Holds Basin In Lap, Figural, 11 1/4 x 9 x 9 3/4 In.	25.00
Planter, Sailfish	25.00
Vase, Figural Gazelle, Brown & Green, Royal Hickman, 13 In.	65.00
Vase, Figural Swan, Dark Green & Gunmetal, Mottled, 13 In.	35.00
Vase, Ram Figurine, Blue, 3 Piece	95.00
Vase, Standing Gazelles On Side, Dark Green, 15 1/2 In.	100.00
Vase, Yellow, Ovoid, 7 x 5 x 8 In.	15.00
Window Box, Mottled Green, Label, 13 x 6 x 4 1/2 In.	8.00

HALF-DOLL, see Pincushion Doll category

HALL CHINA Company started in East Liverpool, Ohio, in 1903. The firm made many types of wares. Collectors search for the Hall teapots made from the 1920s to the 1950s. The dinnerwares of the same period, especially Autumn Leaf pattern, are also popular. The Hall China Company is still working. For more information, see *Kovels' Depression Glass & American Dinnerware Price List.* Autumn Leaf pattern dishes are listed in their own category in this book.

Ashtray, Missouri Pacific Lines, Cobalt & Gold	75.00
Ashtray, With Match Holder, Red	45.00
Ball Jug, Red	30.00
Bean Pot, New England No. 4, Green-Yellow	30.00
Bean Pot, Rose Parade, Tab Handle	35.00
Berry Bowl, Springtime, 5 1/2 In.	3.00
Berry Bowl, Wildfire, 5 1/2 In.	2.50
Bowl, Fantasy, Eva Zeisel, 9 In.	40.00
Bowl, Fantasy, Square, Eva Zeisel, 8 3/4 In.	28.00
Bowl, Poppy, 9 In.	15.00
Bowl, Vegetable, Mt. Vernon, Oval	9.00
Butter, Cover, Fern, Eva Zeisel	120.00
Butter, Westinghouse, General, Dark Green	40.00
Butter, Westinghouse, Hercules, Yellow	40.00
Cake Plate, Springtime	12.00
Canister Set, Poppy, 3 Piece	1200.00
Casserole, Blue Garden, Sundial, Blue Trim	60.00
Casserole, Cover, Rose Parade, Tab Handles, Blue	28.00
Casserole, Cover, Rose White	35.00
Casserole, Cover, Royal Rose	20.00
Casserole, Cover, Tritone, Oval, 11 1/2 In.	45.00
Casserole, Pinecone, Eva Zeisel, Large	115.00 to 125.00
Casserole, Sundial, Red	25.00
Casserole Set, Bird Top, Green-Yellow, 3 Piece	60.00
Coffeepot, Bouquet, Electric	85.00
Coffeepot, Buchanan, Tricolator, Green	60.00
Coffeepot, Diver, Tricolator, Floral, White	50.00
Coffeepot, Drip-O-Lator, Pasture Rose, Step-Down	26.00
Coffeepot, Hallcraft, Golden Glo, Eva Zeisel	170.00
Coffeepot, Red, Medallion Band, 3 Piece	175.00
Coffeepot, Ritz, Black, Red Top	75.00
Coffeepot, Sash, Drip-O-Lator, White, Red	95.00
Coffeepot, Serenade	35.00
Coffeepot, Terrace, Red, White	65.00
Coffeepot, White Rose, Electric	80.00
Cookie Jar, Saf-Handle, Red	125.00
Cookie Jar, Sundial, Red	400.00
Creamer, Mt. Vernon	5.00
Creamer, Poppy	6.50
Creamer, Red Poppy	8.00
Creamer, Wild Poppy, Radiance, Large	40.00

Creamer, Wildfire 8.00
Cup & Saucer, Fantasy, Eva Zeisel 15.00
Cup & Saucer, Fern, Eva Zeisel 18.00
Cup & Saucer, Red Poppy 7.50
Cup & Saucer, Wildfire .... 5.00 to 15.00
Dispenser, Iced Tea, Lipton, Large 300.00
Gravy Boat, Spring, Eva Zeisel 20.00
Jar, Cover, Green, Round, 3 1/2 x 3 In. 20.00
Jug, Ball, Poppy 75.00
Leftover, Hotpoint, No. 4, Daffodil, Square, 6 3/4 In. 22.00
Leftover, Hotpoint, Square, Gray, 4 3/4 In. 40.00
Leftover, Montgomery Ward, Rectangular, Ivory 60.00
Leftover, Westinghouse, General, Orange 30.00
Leftover, Westinghouse, Hercules, Ivory 30.00
Leftover, Westinghouse, Phoenix, Blue 30.00
Mug, Hires Root Beer, Toasting Boy, With Bib, 4 1/4 In. 33.00
Pitcher, Maroon, 5 1/2 In. 20.00
Pitcher, Miniature, Yellow, 2 x 2 In. 15.00
Pitcher, Seagram's, Cobalt, Gold 20.00
Pitcher, Tea, Ivory, Individual 15.00
Pitcher, Water, St. Francis, Cobalt, Gold 45.00
Pitcher, Water, Wildfire 75.00
Pitcher, Wildfire, No. 85, Sani-Grid 23.00
Planter, Dachshund, Black, 14 In. 110.00
Plate, Fantasy, Eva Zeisel, 6 In. 6.00
Plate, Fantasy, Eva Zeisel, 9 3/4 In. 15.00
Plate, Mt. Vernon, 10 In. 6.50
Plate, Poppy, 7 In. 8.00
Plate, Red Poppy, 9 In. 6.00
Plate, Red Poppy, 10 In. 10.00
Plate, Wildfire, 6 1/4 In. 5.00
Plate, Wildfire, 9 In. 4.50
Punch Set, Old Crow, Ladle, 12 Cups, Bowl 150.00
Punch Set, Tom & Jerry, Ivory, Gold, 12 Piece 80.00
Salad Bowl, Silhouette, 9 In. 14.00
Server, Water, Cover, Hercules, Tan .... 25.00 To 75.00
Shaker, Pepper, Wildfire, Handle 8.00
Soup, Dish, Wildfire, 8 1/2 In. 18.00
Strainer, Tea, Twin-Tee, Green, Aluminum 60.00
Sugar, Cover, Red Poppy 12.00
Sugar, Cover, Sundial, Yellow 7.00
Sugar, Philadelphia, Black 15.00
Sugar & Creamer, Fern, Eva Zeisel 54.00
Sugar & Creamer, Morning Set, Red 70.00
Sugar & Creamer, Philadelphia, Daffodil Yellow, Gold 40.00
Syrup, Sundial, Red 70.00
Teapot, Airflow, Blue 100.00
Teapot, Airflow, Canary Yellow, Gold, 6 Cup 55.00
Teapot, Airflow, Daffodil Yellow, Gold 55.00
Teapot, Aladdin, Black Matte, White Top & Handle, Gold 75.00
Teapot, Aladdin, Black, Gold Trim 35.00
Teapot, Aladdin, Black, Gold, Infuser, 6 Cup 60.00
Teapot, Aladdin, Cobalt Blue, Infuser 60.00
Teapot, Aladdin, Strainer 65.00
Teapot, Aladdin, Yellow, Infuser 45.00
Teapot, Albany, Green, Gold 55.00
Teapot, Automobile, Canary 775.00
Teapot, Basket, Canary Yellow, Gold 375.00
Teapot, Basket, Turquoise 150.00
Teapot, Basketball, Red 800.00
Teapot, Birch, Light Blue 45.00
Teapot, Birdcage, Maroon 295.00
Teapot, Birdcage, Maroon, Gold 325.00

Teapot, Boston, Brown 10.00
Teapot, Boston, Cobalt Trailing Aster, 6 Cup 25.00
Teapot, Boston, Cobalt, Gold, 2 Cup 20.00
Teapot, Boston, Light Blue, Gold, 6 Cup 40.00
Teapot, Bowling Ball, Turquoise 1200.00
Teapot, Car, Maroon, Gold Trim, c.1938 .... 225.00
Teapot, Connie, Light Green 45.00
Teapot, Coverlet, Yellow, Silver Cover 40.00
Teapot, Donut, Chinese Red 325.00
Teapot, Doudecagon, Chrysler Decal 40.00
Teapot, Football, Yellow 650.00
Teapot, Forman 45.00
Teapot, French Flower, Black 40.00
Teapot, French Rose 45.00
Teapot, French, Matte Black, Gold 55.00
Teapot, Globe, Canary Yellow, Dripless 70.00
Teapot, Globe, Light Green 65.00
Teapot, Gold Flowers, Blue, Hook Cover 25.00
Teapot, Hollywood, Dark Green, 8 Cup 40.00
Teapot, Hollywood, Maroon 45.00
Teapot, Los Angeles, Cobalt Blue, Gold 65.00
Teapot, Los Angeles, Yellow, Gold Trim 22.00
Teapot, Manhattan, Stock Brown, 3 Cup 25.00
Teapot, Maroon, Gold Trim, 6 Cup 475.00
Teapot, McCormick, Maroon, Infuser 30.00
Teapot, McCormick, White 30.00
Teapot, Melody, Emerald Green, 6 Cup 400.00
Teapot, Moderne, Canary Yellow, Gold 40.00
Teapot, Nautilus, Daffodil Yellow, Gold 240.00
Teapot, Nautilus, Green 115.00
Teapot, New York, Red Poppy 65.00
Teapot, New York, Yellow, Gold Label 25.00
Teapot, Parade, Canary Yellow, Gold 35.00
Teapot, Parade, Cobalt Blue, Gold Trim 55.00
Teapot, Parade, Daffodil Yellow, Gold 45.00
Teapot, Pert, Yellow, 6 Cup 65.00
Teapot, Philadelphia, Green, Gold 45.00
Teapot, Red Poppy 50.00
Teapot, Ronald Reagan, White 85.00
Teapot, Rose Parade 48.00
Teapot, Sani-Grid, White, Blue Roses, 6 Cup 50.00
Teapot, Sanka, White, Small 15.00
Teapot, Star, Emerald Green, Gold 45.00
Teapot, Streamline, Blue, Gold 45.00
Teapot, Streamline, Ivory, Gold 55.00
Teapot, Streamline, Red 35.00
Teapot, Sundial, Canary Yellow 55.00
Teapot, Sundial, Turquoise, Gold Trim 95.00
Teapot, T-Ball, All Silver 150.00
Teapot, T-Ball, Canary Yellow, Square 60.00
Teapot, Tea Taster, Dark Green 90.00
Teapot, Tea Taster, Maroon, Gold 115.00
Teapot, Twin Spout, Cobalt Blue 115.00
Teapot, Twin Spout, Ivory 80.00
Teapot, Twin-Tea, Green 60.00
Teapot, Windshield, Maroon, Gold 60.00
Tile, Tea, Wild Poppy, Round, 6 In. 70.00
Water Server, General Electric, Gray, Yellow 45.00

HALLOWEEN is an ancient holiday that has been changed in the last 200 years. The jack-o'-lantern, witches on broomsticks, and orange decorations seem to be twentieth-century creations. Collectors started to become serious about collecting Halloween-related items in the late 1970s. The papier-mache decorations, now replaced by plastic, and old costumes are in demand.

Bag, Trick Or Treat, Witch On Broom, Full Moon, Orange Ground, 1930s 3.50
Bucket, Trick Or Treat, Frankenstein Head, Plastic, 1960s, 7 1/2 In. 175.00
Candleholder, Jack-O'-Lantern, Tin, Painted, Victorian, 7 In. Diam. 750.00
Candy Container, Frog, German 875.00
Clapper, Witch On Broom, Long Handle, Metal, 4 1/2 x 4 In. 30.00
Clicker, Peters Weather Bird Shoes, Tin Lithograph, 1930s, 2 In. 30.00
Cookie Cutter, Trick Or Treat, Metal, Box 35.00
Costume, Alfred E. Neuman 175.00
Costume, California Raisins, On Header Card, Collegeville, 1988 .... 25.00
Costume, Captain Kangaroo, 1950s, Box 65.00
Costume, Casper, Ben Cooper, 1961, Box 24.00
Costume, Charlie McCarthy 75.00
Costume, Cinderella 15.00
Costume, Close Encounters Of The Third Kind, Graphics Box 25.00
Costume, Cornhusk, From Iowa, 1920s, Pair 225.00
Costume, Darth Vader, Empire Strikes Back, Box, 1980 .... 25.00
Costume, Donny Osmond, Box 5.00
Costume, Dracula, 1963 .... 55.00
Costume, Dr. Jekyll-Mr. Hyde, Mask With 2 Faces, Ben Cooper, 1964 .... 98.00
Costume, Flipper, Box, Collegeville, 1966 .... 59.00
Costume, Frankenstein, 1963 .... 65.00
Costume, Green Hornet, Body Suit, 1966 .... 75.00
Costume, Howdy Doody, 1970s 28.00
Costume, Jane Jetson, Space Dress, Mask, Austin Art, 1972, 8 x 11 In. 50.00
Costume, Kukla, From Kukla, Fran & Ollie Show, Box 45.00
Costume, Lamb Chop, Shari Lewis, Box, Halco, 1961 .... 39.00
Costume, Monkees, Mickey Dolenz, Raybert Products, 1960s, Box 70.00
Costume, Mummy, Sealed, Ben Cooper, 1963 .... 59.00
Costume, Paper Nose, On Tin Eyeglasses 5.00
Costume, Pee Wee Herman, Box, Adult Size 85.00
Costume, Rat Patrol, Desert Patrol Outfit, Ben Cooper, 1967 .... 59.00
Costume, Shazzan, Box, 1967 .... 65.00
Costume, Space Ghost, Unused, Ben Cooper, 1965 .... 62.00
Costume, Star Wars Return Of The Jedi, Box 20.00
Costume, T.H.E. Cat, Collegeville, Box, 1966 .... 89.00
Costume, Wonder Woman, Super Hero, Box 45.00
Costume, Zorro, Mask, Box 95.00
Costume & Mask, E.T. 35.00
Display, Owl & Moon, Die-Cut Paper, Round 38.00
Display, Wall, Scarecrow, Jack-O'-Lantern Head, Cardboard, 1940s, 28 In. 30.00
Flute, Pump, Tin, Wooden, Eerie Sound Is Emitted, 1930s, 10 In. 15.00
Hat, Black Cat, Beeline, 11 In. 25.00
Hat, Cat, Orange Crepe-Paper Tassels, 13 In. 38.00
Hat, Pumpkin Face On Front, Honeycomb Tissue, 8 In. 46.00
Hat, Raven, Beeline, 10 In. 22.00
Hat, Spider, Beeline, 8 1/2 In. 22.00
Hat, Witch, Beeline, 10 In. 24.00
Horn, Pumpkin Head, Germany 135.00
Jack-O'-Lantern, 2 Faces, Cardboard 68.00
Jack-O'-Lantern, Cardboard, Papier-Mache, Germany, 8 In. .... *Illus* 275.00
Jack-O'-Lantern, Cardboard, Surprise Expression, 1930-1940, 25 In. 65.00
Jack-O'-Lantern, Papier-Mache, 3 Piece 250.00
Jack-O'-Lantern, Papier-Mache, With Paper Inserts 125.00
Jack-O'-Lantern, Tin, Box, Small 55.00
Jack-O'-Lantern, Venetian Beads, Orange, Germany, 5 In. 285.00
Lantern, Cardboard, Black, Witch, Owl, Cat, Pumpkin, 2 1/2 x 3 1/2 x 6 In. 56.00
Lantern, Cat Face 65.00
Lantern, Cat Shape, Orange Paint 175.00
Lantern, Cat, Candy Container, German 575.00
Lantern, Devil, Cardboard, Papier-Mache, Germany, 1900s, 4 In. .... *Illus* 495.00
Lantern, Devil, Pulp, Paper Insert, 1930s, 7 In. .... *Illus* 475.00
Lantern, Owl Face 65.00
Lantern, Pumpkin Shape, Arms & Legs, Celluloid 145.00

Lantern, Pumpkin, Germany, Small 85.00
Lantern, Skull, Cardboard & Tissue 55.00
Lantern, Witch Head, Celluloid Globe, Metal, Black Paint, Late 1940s, 2 x 5 In. 65.00
Light Set, Pumpkin, Noma 150.00
Mask, Alfred E. Neuman, 1960 .... 50.00
Mask, Banana Splits 40.00
Mask, Black Man, Cloth 45.00
Mask, Bo-Bo The Clown, Back & Side Panels, Wheaties 20.00
Mask, Bruno The Dog, Box Back & Side Panels, Wheaties 30.00
Mask, Clown, Papier-Mache, 5 1/2 x 8 In. 55.00
Mask, Devil, Accordion Paper Hat 38.00
Mask, Dr Pepper, Envelope Turns Into Mask, 1950s 12.00
Mask, E.T., Full Head, Latex 65.00
Mask, E.T., Rubber 25.00
Mask, Herman Munster, 1960s 50.00
Mask, Hobo, Rubber 30.00
Mask, Mammy 150.00
Mask, Pumpkin, Honeycomb 35.00
Mask, RoboCop 10.00
Mask, Skull, Mounted, Black Outlined 195.00
Mask, Witch, Honeycomb Crown 35.00
Mask, Zorro, Disney, 1950s 45.00
Mask Set, Pinocchio, 5 Characters, Gillette Blades Premium 70.00
Noisemaker, Black Cat, Kirchoff 20.00
Noisemaker, Devil Head 375.00
Noisemaker, Jack-O'-Lantern, Tin, 5 In. 65.00
Noisemaker, Tin Lithograph, Germany 1930s 75.00
Owl, Embossed, Die Cut, Germany 45.00
Pail, Casper 6.00
Pin, Witch, Composition, Spring Legs & Arms 40.00
Postcard, Witch, Owl, Pumpkin, Winsch, 1914 .... 50.00
Pumpkin, Horn Nose, Metal, 6 In. 35.00
Sconce, Pumpkin, Tin, Orange Paint, On Pole, Villainous Mustache & Eyebrows 495.00
Sparkler, Black Cat Picture, Red, White & Blue, 1950s 5.00
Sparkler, Black Cat, Tin, Chein, Box, 5 In. 275.00
Sparkler, Jack-O'-Lantern, Chein, Box 140.00
Sparkler, Old Witch, On Display Card, 1950s .... *Illus* 125.00
Tambourine, Banana Splits, Tin 35.00
Tambourine, Black Cat Face 40.00
Tambourine, Cat, Tin 65.00
Toy, Cat Shape, Squeak, 4 In. 75.00
Toy, Wagon, Pull Toy, Witch, Wheel, Cardboard 135.00

Left to Right: Halloween, Jack-O'-Lantern,
Cardboard, Papier-Mache, Germany, 8 In.;
Halloween, Lantern, Devil, Cardboard,
Papier-Mache, Germany, 1900s, 4 In.;
Halloween, Lantern, Devil, Pulp, Paper
Insert, 1930s, 7 In.; Halloween, Sparkler,
Old Witch, On Display Card, 1950s

Whirligig, Witch, Wooden 145.00
Witch, Cardboard, Crepe Paper, Hanging 40.00
Witch, Orange, White & Black, Die Cut, Germany, 15 1/2 In. 125.00

HAMPSHIRE pottery was made in Keene, New Hampshire, between 1871
and 1923. Hampshire developed a line of colored glazed wares as early as
1883, including a Royal Worcester-type pink, olive green, blue, and
mahogany. Pieces are marked with the printed mark or the impressed name
Hampshire Pottery or *J.S.T. & Co., Keene, N.H.* Many pieces were marked
with city names and sold as souvenirs.

Bowl, Swastika Design, 7 In. 285.00
Chamberstick, Leaf Shape, Matte Green 75.00
Lamp, Leaves & Stems, Flared Top, Dark Blue Glaze, 19 x 17 1/2 In. 385.00
Lamp, Matte Green Glaze, Green Slag Shade, C. Robertson, 19 In. 600.00
Lamp Base, Long Leaves, Smooth, Matte Green Glaze, Marked, 15 In. 900.00
Lamp Base, Matte Green, Electric Canister Insert, c.1907, 7 1/2 In. 330.00
Mug, Souvenir, Oshkosh, Wisconsin, Green, 5 1/2 In. 45.00
Pitcher, Cover, Purple Iris, Black Trim, Shaded Green, 9 In. .... 195.00 to 225.00
Pitcher, Milk, Embossed White Blackberry Sprays, Twig Handle, 4 1/2 In. 45.00
Vase, Alternating Buds & Leaves, Matte Green, 7 In. 280.00
Vase, Bottle Shape, Crackled Green Glaze, 6 1/2 In. 175.00
Vase, Conical, Blue Volcanic Glaze On White Clay, 3 1/2 In. 250.00
Vase, Curdled & Marbleized Blue-Green Glaze, Signed, 6 3/4 In. 375.00
Vase, Dark Green Glaze, Handles, 5 In. 225.00
Vase, Elongated Leaves, Veined Taupe Glaze, Oval, Signed, 9 In. 275.00
Vase, Geometric Naturalistic Design, Yellow-Green Glaze, 7 3/4 In. 895.00
Vase, Matte Blue Glaze, Stylized Leaves, 8 In. 450.00
Vase, Matte Green Glaze, Double Handled, 5 In. 250.00
Vase, Matte Green Glaze, Flaring Base, Marked, Handles, 7 In. 165.00
Vase, Mottled Green Glaze, Globular, 5 1/2 In. 285.00
Vase, Stylized Flowers All Around, Mottled Blue Glaze, Marked, 7 1/4 In. 360.00
Vase, Stylized Leaves All Around, Brown Matte, Marked, 9 In. 275.00
Vase, Vertical Leaves, Matte Green, 7 In. 425.00

HANDEL glass was made by Philip Handel working in Meriden, Connecticut,
from 1885 and in New York City from 1893 to 1933. The firm made art glass
and other types of lamps. Handel shades were made not only of leaded glass
in a style reminiscent of Tiffany but also of reverse painted glass. Handel also
made vases and other glass objects.

Ceiling Fixture, Geometric Design, 6 Slag & Brass Shades, Marked, 20 1/4 In. 1100.00
Chandelier, Conical Shade, Green Mottled Glass, Fruits On Apron, 25 1/2 In. 3680.00
Chandelier, Leaded Glass, Conical Shade, Fruit On Apron, 25 1/4 In. 4950.00
Chandelier, Reverse Painted Perched Parrots On Shade, Signed, 33 In. 2530.00
Hawaiian Palms Overlay Scene, Hanging, 23 In. 4000.00
Humidor, Horse & Dog Head, Brown-Green Base, Metal Lid & Pipe 950.00
Humidor, Teroma, 7 1/4 In. 995.00
Lamp, 3-Light, Reverse Painted, Parrots, Bronze Base, 24 1/2 In. .... 8250.00 to 9900.00
Lamp, 9-Paneled Domed Shade, Geometric Border, Bronzed Base, Signed, 18 In. 2000.00
Lamp, Boudoir, Allover Wild Rose Blossoms, Signed, Bronze, c.1917, 16 In. 1840.00
Lamp, Boudoir, Chipped Shade, Painted Interior, c.1915, 13 3/4 In. 3738.00
Lamp, Boudoir, Cottage, Boat Pond & Trees Shade 200.00
Lamp, Boudoir, Metal, Reverse Painted, Sailing Ships Conical Scene, 12 1/2 In. 575.00
Lamp, Boudoir, Metal, Reverse Painted, Landscape, Cylindrical Shade, 15 In. 575.00
Lamp, Boudoir, Poppy, Domed Teroma Glass Shade, Yellow Interior, 14 In. 3190.00
Lamp, Boudoir, Reverse Painted, Floral, Chipped Ice Shade, Signed 1850.00
Lamp, Boudoir, Reverse Painted, Squared Shade, Scalloped Rim, Landscape, 15 In. .. 1760.00
Lamp, Boudoir, Reverse Painted, Windmill & Village Scene 3025.00
Lamp, Boudoir, Reverse Painted, Winter Snow Scene 3575.00
Lamp, Boudoir, Snow Scene, Square, 7 In. 2530.00
Lamp, Boudoir, Treasure Island, Reverse Painted, Shade, Signed, 14 In. 2310.00
Lamp, Brass, 3 Candle Arms, Enameled Cameo Glass Shade, Loop Handle, 26 In. 1265.00
Lamp, Brass, Reverse Painted, Palm Trees Scene, Hexagonal Domed Shade, 24 In. ... 2185.00

Lamp, Bronze, 3 Opposed Winged Lions, 5 Cylindrical Stems, 39 1/2 In. 1380.00
Lamp, Brown Patina, Sockets & Pulls, Signed, 22 In. 250.00
Lamp, Cased, Pine Needle, Acid Etched, Mosserine 6202, Bronze Base, 22 1/2 In. 2200.00
Lamp, Chinese Design, Reverse Painted, Shade, Marked, 21 1/4 In. 1100.00
Lamp, Desk, Rose Blossom Rectangular Shade, 2 Arms, Circular Base, 13 7/8 In. 4600.00
Lamp, Floor, Reverse Painted, Floral Shade, Signed 3995.00
Lamp, Floor, Swing-Out, Leaded Phlox Design Shade, Signed 2850.00
Lamp, Floral Border, Yellow, Orange & Green, 16 In. Shade 2350.00
Lamp, Hanging, Grape Shade, 14 In. 750.00
Lamp, Hawaiian Scenic, No. 6310, Brown Patina, 15 In. 3950.00
Lamp, Leaded Dogwood Design, Bulbous Base, Signed, 16 In. 3250.00
Lamp, Leaded Geometric & Phlox Design Shade, Signed, 18 In. 3250.00
Lamp, Leaded Glass, Conical Shade, Flower Border, Paneled, c.1915, 10 In. 1380.00
Lamp, Leaded Slag Shade, Foliage Pointing Down, Bronze Base, Marked, 27 In. 2000.00
Lamp, Lotus Blossom Slag Glass Shade, Lily Pad Base, 13 1/2 In. 646.00
Lamp, Mantel, Teroma, Hand Painted, Mountains, 15 1/2 In., Pair 2310.00
Lamp, Metal Filigree, Butterscotch & White Domed Octagonal Shade, 21 In. 862.00
Lamp, Mantel, Teroma, Pair 2310.00
Lamp, Painted Pine Tree Shade, Signed & Numbered, 18 In. 5975.00
Lamp, Peach, With Art Nouveau Border, Painted Gold Base, 14 In. 1495.00
Lamp, Piano, Etched Shade, Reverse Painted, Brown, Metal Base, Marked, 8 In. 750.00
Lamp, Piano, Flower Border On Shade, Bronze, Signed, c.1916, 14 1/2 In. 1035.00
Lamp, Piano, Zigzag Pattern On Shade, Green Ground, Pivoting Base, 8 In. 1700.00
Lamp, Reverse Painted, Apple Blossom, Bronzed Metal, Signed, 23 In. 3300.00
Lamp, Reverse Painted, Band Of Dogwood, Green To Tan, 1920, 22 1/4 In. 4313.00
Lamp, Reverse Painted, Floral & Foliate Domed Shade, Chipped Ice, 24 In. 2597.00
Lamp, Reverse Painted, Narcissi Band Shade, Chipped Ice, 14 3/4 In. 2300.00
Lamp, Reverse Painted, Shade, Daffodils & Foliage, Signed, 24 In., ... 8625.00
Lamp, Reverse Painted, Stylized Palmettes Domed Shade, 22 3/4 In. 2300.00
Lamp, Reverse Painted, Vine & Berries Domed Shade, 22 1/2 In. 2300.00
Lamp, Reverse Painted, Winter Landscape Shade, Chipped Ice, 14 In. 2185.00
Lamp, Rose Bordered Shade, Signed, 18 In. 3450.00
Lamp, Slag Glass, Lotus Blossom Shade, Lily Pad Base, Cloth Label, 13 In. 546.00
Lamp, Table, Full Rose Pattern, Signed 6850.00
Lamp, Table, Hexagonal Opaline Glass Shade 2530.00
Lamp, Table, Orange & Purple Flower Clusters 2530.00
Lamp, Table, Reverse Painted, Shade, Sunset Palm 4125.00
Night-Light, Egg Shape Shade, Enameled Exterior Birds, No. 7098, c.1915, 7 1/2 In. .. 400.00
Shade, Leaded Hydrangea, Pink & Green, 21 1/2 In. Diam. 2200.00
Tobacco Jar, Woodland Scene, Elk, Smokers Pipe Finial, Signed 1795.00
Torchere, Metal, Reverse Painted, Trees & Water Scene, Stepped Base, 15 3/4 In. 1150.00
Vase, Tazza, Opal, Art Nouveau Floral, Cream Ground, Signed, 7 1/2 x 6 In. 995.00
Vase, Teroma, Birds In Flight, Autumn Foliage, Signed, 10 1/2 In. 2950.00

HARDWARE, see Architectural category.

HARKER Pottery Company of East Liverpool, Ohio, was founded by
Benjamin Harker in 1840. The company made many types of pottery but by
the Civil War was making quantities of yellowware from native clays. They
also made Rockingham-type brown-glazed pottery and whiteware. The plant
was moved to Chester, West Virginia, in 1931. Dinnerwares were made and
sold nationally. In 1971 the company was sold to Jeannette Glass Company
and all operations ceased in 1972. For more information, see *Kovels'
Depression Glass & American Dinnerware Price List*.

Bowl, Petit Point, Stacking, 3 Piece 65.00
Bowl, Vegetable, Cameoware 20.00
Cake Lifter, Colonial Lady 22.00
Cake Plate, Green & White, Tab Handles 6.00
Cake Plate, Wild Rose 10.00
Cake Set, Wild Rose, With Lifter 30.00
Casserole, Cover, Petit Point 35.00
Coffeepot, Drip, Cameoware, White Rose, Pink 60.00

Dessert Set, Fruit Center, Gold Fluted Rim, 7 Piece 35.00
Drip Jar, Cover, Petit Point 25.00
Dripolator, Petit Point 55.00
Pitcher, Cover, Petit Point 35.00
Pitcher, Disc, Shepherd & Shepherdess, Lamb, Gold Trim, 7 5/8 In. 18.00
Place Setting, Cameoware, Provincial Tulip, Box, 6 Piece 25.00
Rolling Pin, Petit Point 115.00
Service For 8, Cameoware, Yellow, Rooster, 45 Piece 225.00
Stein, Hound Handle, 1960s 20.00
Teapot, Apple & Nuts 30.00
Teapot, Petit Point .... 22.00 to 30.00

HARLEQUIN dinnerware was produced by the Homer Laughlin Company
from 1938 to 1964, and sold without trademark by the F. W. Woolworth Co.
It has a concentric ring design like Fiesta, but the rings are separated from the
rim by a plain margin. Cup handles are triangular in shape. For more information, see *Kovels' Depression Glass & American Dinnerware Price List.*

Bowl, Medium Green, 5 1/2 In. 20.00
Casserole, Cover, Spruce Green 40.00
Creamer, Gray 10.00
Creamer, Individual, Yellow 18.00
Cup & Saucer, Medium Green 18.00
Dish, Nut, Spruce Green 18.00
Eggcup, Double, Forest Green 20.00
Eggcup, Mauve 20.00
Figurine, Donkey, Maroon 85.00
Figurine, Duck, Maroon 95.00
Figurine, Duck, Mauve .... 95.00 to 100.00
Figurine, Fish, Mauve 110.00
Figurine, Penguin, Maroon 100.00
Gravy Boat, Rose .... 25.00 to 30.00
Jug, Maroon, 22 Oz. 45.00
Pitcher, Ball, Burgundy 50.00
Pitcher, Water, Spruce Green 85.00
Pitcher, Water, Yellow 65.00
Plate, Gray, 10 In. 28.00
Plate, Salad, Gray, Individual 26.00
Saltshaker, Yellow 4.00
Sugar & Creamer, Cover, Yellow 29.00
Teapot, Chartreuse 110.00
Teapot, Hall 195.00
Teapot, Turquoise 75.00
Teapot, Yellow 75.00
Tumbler, Mauve .... 40.00 to 45.00

HATPIN collectors search for pins popular from 1860 to 1920. The long pin,
often over four inches, was used to hold the hat in place on the hair. The tops
of the pins were made of all materials, from solid gold and real gemstones to
ceramics and glass. Be careful to buy original hatpins and not recent pieces
made by altering old buttons.

Art Nouveau, Silverplate Shield, Woman's Profile, Hat, 8 In. 115.00
Articulated Flowers, Woven Design, Gem-Set Tips, 18K Gold, Italy 275.00
Blackbird Head, Art Deco, Charles Horner 110.00
Carnival, Blue Curves & Raised Dots, Button Style, 1 1/2 In. 22.00
Cartier Logo, 18K Gold On Sterling Silver 165.00
Conch Shell, Wire Mount, 8 In. 40.00
Flat Topped Medallion, Art Nouveau, Gold Plated, 8 1/2 In. 220.00
Glass, Faceted, 8 1/2 In. 25.00
Gold, Charles Horner 225.00
Golf Club, Sterling Silver, Charles Horner 68.00
Iron, Round Black Glass Fob 2.50
Knob Design, Art Deco, Brass, 8 1/2 In. 95.00

Mayflower, Figural, Sterling Silver 30.00
Moonstone, Diamonds, Rubies, 14K Gold Wire Mount, Victorian, Austria, Pair 1650.00
Patriotic, Iron, Large Brass Fob, Civil War 15.00
Petal, Gold Plated, Amethyst Glass, Cameo Bust, 9 In. 88.00
Prism Design, Gold Plated, Blue Cut Glass, 8 In. 55.00
Queen Alexandra Photo, Tinted, Mother-Of-Pearl & Vermeil, Charles Horner 145.00
Ram's Horn, Art Nouveau, Gold Plated, 8 1/2 In. 22.00
Rooster, Bronze Color, Red Comb, Wattles 22.00
Shaggy Dog Head, Brass, 9 In. 65.00
Spiral Tear Shape, Gilded, Tiny Blue Stones, 8 1/2 In. 55.00
Sterling Silver, Charles Horner 135.00

HATPIN HOLDERS were needed when hatpins were fashionable from 1860 to 1920. The large, heavy hat required special long-shanked pins to hold it in place. The hatpin holder resembles a large saltshaker, but it often has no opening at the bottom as a shaker does. Hatpin holders were made of all types of ceramics and metal. Look for other pieces under the names of specific manufacturers.

Geisha Pattern, Short 32.00
Porcelain, Hand Painted Floral, Marked RS 18.00
Red Rose 45.00
Silver Frame, Velvet, Purple, England 100.00

HAVILAND china has been made in Limoges, France, since 1842. The factory was started by the Haviland Brothers of New York City. Pieces are marked *H & Co.*, *Haviland & Co.*, or *Theodore Haviland*. It is possible to match existing sets of dishes through dealers who specialize in Haviland china. Other factories worked in the town of Limoges making a similar chinaware. These porcelains are listed in this book under Limoges.

HAVILAND & CO.

Bowl, Vegetable, Athena 135.00
Cake Set, Birds, Pink Flowers, Scalloped Gold Rim, 12 Piece 340.00
Casserole, Cover, White, Gold Rope Braid, Large 200.00
Chocolate Set, Baltimore Rose, 13 Piece 1500.00
Cup & Saucer, Plate, Pale Asters, Porcelain, Demitasse 30.00
Match Holder & Ashtray, Advertising, Early 1900s 90.00
Oyster Plate, Floral, 9 In., Pair .... *Illus* 120.00
Plate, Christmas, Three French Hens 25.00
Plate, Christmas, Twelve Drummers 40.00
Plate, Drop Rose, 11 1/2 In. 275.00
Platter, Apple Blossom, Gold Rim, 21 x 14 1/2 In. 165.00
Platter, Athena, 14 In. 195.00
Service For 6, Chanson Pattern 100.00
Tea Service, Anneau D'or, 17 Piece 330.00
Tureen, Soup, Cover, Blackberry 175.00
Tureen, Soup, Pink Roses, Blue Forget-Me-Nots, 12 Soup Dishes 340.00
Vase, 2 Wild Fowl, Mottled Ground 1300.00

Haviland, Oyster Plate, Floral, 9 In.

◆◆◆◆◆◆◆◆◆◆◆◆◆◆◆◆◆◆◆◆◆◆

Shallow nicks and rough edges on glass can sometimes be smoothed off with fine emery paper.

◆◆◆◆◆◆◆◆◆◆◆◆◆◆◆◆◆◆◆◆◆◆

HAWKES cut glass was made by T. G. Hawkes & Company of Corning, New York, founded in 1880. The firm cut glass blanks made at other glassworks until 1962. Many pieces are marked with the trademark, a trefoil ring enclosing a fleur-de-lis and two hawks. Cut glass by other manufacturers is listed under either the factory name or in the general Cut Glass category.

Ashtray, Engraved Border, Sterling Silver Center Stand To Hold Cigar	150.00
Ashtray, Flat Knob In Center, Engraved, Signed	160.00
Bottle, Cologne, Brazilian, 7 1/2 In.	375.00
Bottle, Whiskey, Gladys, 13 1/4 In.	840.00
Bottle, Worcestershire, Brazilian, Signed, 7 3/4 In.	345.00
Bowl, Alternating Panels Of Hobstars & Pears, Sawtooth Rim, 10 In.	185.00
Bowl, Centaur, 8 In.	325.00
Bowl, Russian, Canoe, Rayed Buttons, 14 1/2 In.	850.00
Bowl, Snowflake, Blown-Out, 10 1/2 In.	1700.00
Bowl, Strawberry Diamonds & Miters, Signed, 6 3/4 In.	50.00
Box, Handkerchief, Hinged Top With Hobstars & Miters, Signed, Square, 6 3/4 In.	320.00
Candlestick, Teutonic, Signed, 9 1/4 In.	385.00
Candy Dish, Etched, Gold Trim, Pedestal, 5 1/2 In.	165.00
Candy Stand, Devonshire, Pedestal, Signed	245.00
Carafe, Cypress, Large Hobstars Between Fans & Hobstars, Signed	145.00
Compote, Candy, Floral Swags, Signed, 5 x 7 In.	165.00
Compote, Sheraton, St. Louis Diamond Cut Stem, 7 1/2 In.	225.00
Cordial, Fluted, 50 Ray Star Base, Signed	30.00
Decanter, Basket Weave, Sterling Silver Stopper, 12 1/2 In.	1490.00
Decanter, Brunswick, 13 x 3 In.	530.00
Decanter, Intaglio Thistles, Shot Glass Top, Signed	275.00
Decanter, Paneled Baluster Form, Trailing Flowers, Silver Stopper, 13 1/2 In.	220.00
Dish, Blown-Out Form, 6 Petals, Signed, 6 x 1 3/4 In.	495.00
Dish, Dessert, Hobstar Wedges Alternate With Strawberry Diamond, 5 In.	80.00
Dish, Ice Cream, Leaf Shape, Hobstars & Zipper	1000.00
Flower Center, Kings Pattern, 6 x 9 In.	1850.00
Frame, Etched, Sterling Silver, Signed, Oval, 7 In.	295.00
Goblet, Engraved, Signed	125.00
Goblet, Russian, Clear Buttons, Full Teardrop, 6 1/2 In., 6 Piece	750.00
Knife Rest, Hobstars, Notched Prism, 4 3/4 In.	65.00
Match Holder, Strike Panel, 2 1/4 x 2 1/4 In.	115.00
Nappy, Canton, Bands Of Hobstars To Center, Step Cutting, 4 In.	125.00
Nappy, Corinthian, Signed, 1890, 6 In.	170.00
Perfume Bottle, Steeple Stopper, 8 x 2 1/4 In.	215.00
Perfume Bottle, Venetian, Signed, 6 1/4 In.	375.00
Pitcher, Marion, Signed, 7 In.	295.00
Pitcher, Queens, Signed	1200.00
Pitcher, Queens, Triple Notched Handle, Signed, 8 /34 In.	980.00
Pitcher, Venetian, Triple Cut Handle, c.1889, 8 /12 In.	650.00
Plate, Chain Of Hobstars Around Bottom, Signed, 7 In.	220.00
Plate, Chain Of Hobstars, Signed, 10 In.	575.00
Plate, Gladys, Signed, 7 1/4 In.	175.00
Plate, Hobstars, Fans & Cane, Signed, 7 In.	145.00
Plate, Panel, 8 3/4 In.	1800.00
Plate, Portland, 7 In.	215.00
Plate, Russian & Pillar, 9 In.	685.00
Plate, Russian, 1882, 7 In.	135.00
Plate, Strawberry, Signed, 8 In.	75.00
Spooner, Hobstars & Strawberry Diamonds, Signed, 7 1/2 In.	80.00
Sugar & Creamer, Milton, 4 & 5 In.	250.00
Sugar & Creamer, Venetian, 1890, 2 3/4 x 4 1/2 In.	415.00
Syrup, Holland, String Silver Top, 4 1/4 In.	415.00
Tray, Celery, Festoon, 11 3/4 In.	250.00
Tray, Chrysanthemum, Oval, Signed, 11 x 7 1/2 In.	585.00
Tray, Dresser, Carnation, Oval, Signed, 10 1/4 x 7 In.	425,00

Tray, Floral Urns & Cornucopia, Oval, Signed, 10 1/2 In. 100.00
Tray, Ice Cream, Gladys, 16 In. 850.00
Tray, Kensington, 10 In. 985.00
Tray, Middlesex, Hobstar, 16 Star Base, Fans & Hobstars Rim 135.00
Tray, Russian, Handles, 8 x 15 In. 775.00
Tray, Russian, Handles, Rectangular, 11 1/2 In. 850.00
Tray, Venetian, Signed, 12 In. 1245.00
Tumble-Up, Florence, Signed 1050.00
Tumble-Up, Underplate, Engraved Flowers, Handle, Signed 500.00
Tumbler, Gladys, 4 In. 67.50
Vase, Brunswick, Signed, 12 In., Pair 450.00
Vase, Engraved Flowers & Vines, Ice Bucket Shape, Light Green, 8 In. 295.00
Vase, Fan Form, Carnation, 12 In. 500.00
Vase, Flowers, Swags & Ribbons, Gold Design On Rim, Signed, 8 1/2 In. 195.00
Vase, Harvard, Floral, 6 In. 85.00
Vase, Lorraine, Signed, 18 In. 1300.00
Vase, Navarre, Signed, 18 In. 1275.00
Vase, Pheasant & Tree, Black Ground, Signed, 12 1/2 In. 750.00
Vase, Queens, Cylindrical, 12 In. 535.00
Vase, Queens, Trumpet, Signed, 15 1/2 In. .... 1200.00 to 1400.00
Vase, Tulip Shape, Cut Foot, Signed, 16 In. 1350.00
Water Set, Brunswick, 9 Piece 775.00
Water Set, Iris, 5 Piece 575.00
Wine, Grecian, Cranberry Cut To Clear, 4 3/4 In., 8 Piece 6600.00

HEAD VASES, generally showing a woman from the shoulders up, were used
by florists primarily in the 1950s and 1960s. Made in a variety of sizes and
often decorated with imitation jewelry and other lifelike accessories, the
vases were manufactured in Japan and the U.S.A. Less elaborate examples
were made as early as the 1930s. Religious themes, babies, and animals are
also common subjects.

Barbie & Bonnie, Ceramic Arts Studio 165.00
Betty Grable 35.00
Black Man, Royal Copley .... 15.00 to 28.00
Black Native, 6 1/2 In. 24.50
Black Woman, Occupied Japan 15.00
Black Woman, Royal Copley 27.00
Blond, Pageboy Hair Set, 5 In. 25.00
Blond, Pearl Necklace, Leaf Pin 25.00
Boy & Girl, Chef's Hat, Pair 70.00
Boy Golfer 18.00
Buxom Bathing Suit, Vcagco 65.00
Christmas Girl, Pearls, Holly Sprigs, Red Dress, Napco, 7 1/2 In. 100.00
Clown 15.00
Dagwood Bumstead 95.00
Girl, Holding Raggedy Ann, Pigtails 45.00
Hussar 95.00
Jackie Kennedy .... 110.00 to 125.00
Madonna, Praying 15.00
Manchu 75.00
Marilyn Monroe 275.00
Peasant Girl, Hull 30.00
Toy Soldier 42.00
Woman, Applied Hand, Faux Pearls 50.00
Woman, Art Deco, 7 1/2 In. 45.00
Woman, Green Hat, Curls, Large 55.00
Woman, Hat With Bow, Pearls, Blues 130.00
Woman, Hat, Floppy Brim, Bow, Pearls, Greens 130.00
Woman, Maroon Hat, Earrings 25.00
Woman, Pearl Earrings 25.00
Woman, Peasant, Blue, Catalina 75.00
Woman, Pouty, Bow & Hat 65.00
Woman, With Fan 12.00

HEDI SCHOOP Art Creations, North Hollywood, California, started about 1945 and was working until 1954. Schoop made ceramic figurines and lamps.

Hedi Schoop s (handwritten)

Ashtray, Floral, Pottery	20.00
Candleholder, Peasant Woman, Blue-Green Tones, Double, 12 1/2 In.	35.00
Console, Oriental Couple, Yellow & Black	98.00
Cookie Jar, Queen Of Hearts	425.00 to 550.00
Cookie Jar, Woman, Pottery	795.00
Figurine, Cander	85.00
Figurine, French Man & Woman, Pottery, Pair	145.00
Figurine, Masked Dancer, Pottery, Pair, 12 In.	75.00
Figurine, Peasant Girl, Holding Bowl Over Head, 14 In.	60.00
Planter, Basket Weave, Handles, Green, 11 In.	18.00
Planter, Dancing Woman, Basket On Head, Pottery, 13 In.	45.00
Planter, Girl, Eyes Open, Pottery, 8 In.	65.00
Planter, Horse, White With Lavender, Pottery, 7 x 8 In.	65.00
Vase, Crowing Cock, 5-Color Glaze, 14 In.	85.00
Vase, Figural, Woman In Long Dress, Holding Basket Of Flowers, 12 1/2 In.	70.00
Vase, Gray & Pink	65.00

HEINTZ ART Metal Shop made jewelry, copper, silver, and brass in Buffalo, New York, from 1906 to 1935, when a new company name was taken and the mark became *Silvercrest.* The most popular items with collectors today are the copper desk sets and vases made with applied silver designs.

Box, Silver Crest, 3 x 4 In.	95.00
Candlestick, 5 1/2 In., Pair	175.00
Humidor, Hunting Scene On Cover, Cedar Lined, Silver On Bronze, 10 In.	400.00
Lamp, Jonquils, Mica Panels, Silver Overlaid Flowers, Marked, 14 3/4 In.	600.00
Lamp, Mushroom Shape, Sterling On Bronze, 10 In.	450.00
Pin, Bar, Sterling On Bronze, Pair	90.00
Vase, Bronze, Silver Overlay Floral Design, Inscribed MAA, 11929 Man's 4th, 4 In. ...	165.00
Vase, Cherry Blossom Branches, Silver On Bronze, Marked, 8 In.	250.00
Vase, Everted Rim, Applied Silver Orchid, Bronze, Marked, 7 15/16 In.	138.00
Vase, Overlaid Stylized Weeds, Silver On Bronze Body, Marked, 11 In.	450.00
Vase, Overlaid Swamp Grass, Silver On Bronze, Marked, 12 1/2 In.	350.00

HEISEY glass was made from 1896 to 1957 in Newark, Ohio, by A. H. Heisey and Co., Inc. The Imperial Glass Company of Bellaire, Ohio, bought some of the molds and the rights to the trademark. Some Heisey patterns have been made by Imperial since 1960. After 1968, they stopped using the *H* trademark. Heisey used romantic names for colors, such as *Sahara.* Do not confuse color and pattern names. The Custard Glass and Ruby Glass categories may also include some Heisey pieces.

Acorn & Leaves, Plate, Flamingo, 8 In.	25.00
Aqua Caliente, Cocktail, Golfer Etch	135.00
Aristocrat, Candlestick, Marked, 9 In., Pair	190.00 to 195.00
Banded Flute, Dish, Nut, Oval, Marked, 5 In.	55.00
Banded Flute, Punch Bowl, Base	225.00
Banded Flute, Toothpick, Marked	85.00
Banded Flute, Tray, Round, 13 In.	95.00
Baroque, Candelabra, 3-Light, Pair	130.00
Beaded Panel & Sunburst, Punch Bowl, Base, Marked	150.00 to 155.00
Beaded Swag, Pitcher, Lemonade	185.00
Beaded Swag, Toothpick, Floral, Opaque	85.00
Beaded Swag, Tumbler, 6 Piece	200.00
Bob White, Goblet, Peacock Etch, 7 Oz., 6 Piece	225.00
Bonnet, Basket, 16 In.	345.00
Cabochon, Sugar & Creamer, Moonglo Cut, Marked	50.00
Carcassonne, Flagon, Moongleam Stem & Foot	195.00
Carcassonne, Goblet, Ice Tea, 12 Oz.	100.00
Carcassone, Soda, Classic Etch, Sahara, 12 Oz.	17.50
Cascade, Candlestick, 3-Light, Orchid Etch	60.00
Cascade, Candlestick, 3-Light, Pair	185.00

Charter Oak, Compote, Floral Cut, Silver Overlay, 7 In. 95.00
Charter Oak, Goblet, Flamingo, Marked, 8 Oz. 34.00
Charter Oak, Tumbler, Flamingo 25.00
Chintz, Sugar & Creamer. 38.00
Chintz, Tumbler, Sahara, Footed 20.00
Circle Pair, Jug, Flamingo, 1/2 Gal. 185.00
Coarse Rib, Bowl, Crimped, Footed, Marked, 9 In. .... 75.00 to 89.50
Coarse Rib, Mustard, Cover, Amber Stain, Marked 60.00
Colonial, Punch Set, 13 Piece 225.00
Colonial, Syrup, Flora Cut, 7 Oz. 47.50
Colonial Panel, Jug, Marked, 2 Qt. 155.00
Continental, Compote, Cover, Marked, 8 1/2 In. 235.00
Continental, Toothpick 140.00
Coronation, Slim Jim, Tavern Etch, 12 Oz. 100.00
Crocus, Candleholder, 2-Light, Star Cut, 7 1/2 In., Pair 395.00
Crystolite, Cup & Saucer 25.00
Crystolite, Goblet, 10 Oz. 25.00
Crystolite, Jam Jar, Cover 55.00
Crystolite, Mustard, Cover, Individual 20.00
Crystolite, Punch Set, 15 Piece 325.00
Crystolite, Relish, 4 Sections, 9 In. 20.00
Crystolite, Sugar & Creamer 65.00
Danish Princess, Goblet 25.00
Decanter, Girl, Head, Stopper, Amber 900.00
Diamond Optic, Tankard, Flamingo 145.00
Double Rib & Panel, Basket, Flamingo, 8 In. 195.00
Eagle, Plate, 8 In. 15.00
Empress, Ashtray, Flamingo, Marked 185.00
Empress, Bowl, Footed, Aqua, 11 In. 795.00
Empress, Bowl, Sahara, 7 In. 65.00
Empress, Candlestick, Sahara, 6 In. 165.00
Empress, Compote, Flamingo, 6 In. 55.00
Empress, Cruet, Yellow 135.00
Empress, Cup & Saucer, Miniature 65.00
Empress, Ice Bucket, Orchid Etch 225.00
Empress, Mayonnaise, Sahara 55.00
Empress, Plate, Formal Chintz, Sahara, Square, 10 1/2 In. 110.00
Empress, Plate, Square, 8 In. 155.00
Empress, Plate, Square, Tangerine, 8 In. 150.00
Empress, Relish, 3 Sections, Alexandrite, Marked 295.00
Empress, Salt & Pepper, Alexandrite 850.00
Empress, Salt & Pepper, Sahara 135.00
Essex, Candlestick, 1-Light, 9 In. 110.00
Fairacre, Jug, Footed, Flamingo, Marked 185.00
Fancy Loop, Punch Cup 15.00
Fancy Loop, Rose Bowl, Marked, 4 In. 120.00
Fancy Loop, Rose Bowl, Small 65.00
Fancy Loop, Salt Dip 15.00
Fancy Loop, Syrup 135.00
Fancy Loop, Toothpick .... 55.00 to 65.00
Fancy Loop, Toothpick, Green, Gold Trim 80.00
Fandango, Creamer, Individual 22.00
Fandango, Cruet 125.00
Fandango, Mustard, Gold Design 27.50
Fandango, Tray, Ice Cream, 13 x 8 In. 100.00
Fern, Sugar & Creamer, Belvidere Cut, Marked 60.00
Figurine, Angelfish 120.00
Figurine, Asiatic Pheasant, 10 1/2 In. .... 200.00 to 425.00
Figurine, Bunny, Head Up, 2 3/8 In. 295.00
Figurine, Clydesdale, 7 1/4 In. 120.00
Figurine, Clydesdale, Verde Green 130.00
Figurine, Colt, Balking 295.00
Figurine, Colt, Kicking, 3 3/4 In. .... 175.00 to 295.00

Figurine, Cygnet, 2 1/8 In. 295.00
Figurine, Donkey, 6 1/2 In. .... 385.00 to 450.00
Figurine, Elephant, Medium, 4 In. 348.00
Figurine, Filly, Head Forward, 8 1/4 In. 2500.00
Figurine, Flying Mare, 8 7/8 In. 3200.00
Figurine, Giraffe, Head Turned, Amber, 11 In. 500.00
Figurine, Goose, Wings Down, 2 3/4 In., Pair 315.00
Figurine, Hen, 4 1/4 In. 450.00
Figurine, Mallard, Wings Halfway, 5 In. 125.00
Figurine, Mallard, Wings Up, 6 3/4 In. 240.00
Figurine, Pheasant, Ring Necked, 4 3/4 In. 145.00
Figurine, Plug Horse, Pink, 1978, 4 In. 40.00
Figurine, Pouter Pigeon, 6 1/4 In. 495.00
Figurine, Rooster, Fighting, Pink, Sticker, 8 In. 235.00
Figurine, Scotty, 3 1/2 In. 95.00
Figurine, Show Horse, 7 3/8 In. 1175.00
Figurine, Show Horse, Amber, 7 3/8 In. 450.00
Figurine, Sow 950.00
Fish, Bookends 165.00
Grape Cluster, Candlestick, 1-Light, Prisms, Marked, Pair 315.00
Grape Leaf Square, Ashtray, Moongleam 65.00
Grecian Border, Nappy, Marked, 8 In. 50.00
Greek Key, Bowl, 8 In. 95.00
Greek Key, Bread Tray, 12 In. 115.00
Greek Key, Dish, Banana Split 100.00
Greek Key, Eggcup, Marked 45.00
Greek Key, Pitcher 70.00
Greek Key, Punch Bowl 495.00
Greek Key, Punch Bowl, Cupped, Base 300.00
Hexagon, Plate, Moongleam, 8 In., 8 Piece 45.00
Horn Of Plenty, Candlestick, Pair 40.00
Horn Of Plenty, Vase, Sahara, 9 In. 140.00
Horsehead, Box, Cigarette 70.00
Horsehead, Sherry, Cut Star Base 500.00
Ipswich, Console Set, Crystal, 3 Piece .... 225.00 to 250.00
Ipswich, Cruet, Green, 2 Oz. 85.00
Ipswich, Plate, Square, 7 In., 4 Piece 68.00
Ipswich, Sherbet, 8 Piece 144.00
Iris, Candlestick, Crystal, Pair 28.00
Jack-Be-Nimble, Candlestick, Child's 60.00
Jamestown, Goblet 15.00
Jamestown, Sherbet 6.00
Kalonyal, Cake Tray, Marked 225.00
Kalonyal, Sherbet, Flared, Marked, 3 1/2 In. 75.00
Kohinoor, Ashtray, Zircon, Marked, 3 In. 75.00
Kohinoor, Soda, 12 Oz. 15.00
Lady Leg, Goblet, Crusader Cut, Marked 28.00
Lariat, Basket, Bonbon, 7 1/2 In. 95.00
Lariat, Bonbon, Crimped, 8 1/2 In. 40.00
Lariat, Butter 125.00
Lariat, Candlestick, 2-Light, Pair 75.00
Lariat, Candy Dish, Cover, 12 Oz. 40.00
Lariat, Punch Set, Bowl, Underplate, 12 Cups .... 225.00 to 395.00
Lariat, Relish, 3 Sections 25.00
Liberty, Candleholder, 1-Light, Moongleam, 4 In., Pair 85.00
Lion Head, Bowl, Flared 250.00
Locket On Chain, Cruet 150.00
Locket On Chain, Wine .... 110.00 to 150.00
Locket On Chain, Wine, Ruby, Gold Trim 225.00
Lodestar, Bowl, 8 In. 90.00
Mahabar, Box, Cigarette, Clear, Brass Filigree, Marked Apollo 35.00
Mercury, Candlestick, 1-Light, Orchid Etch 32.00
Minuet, Champagne 38.00

Minuet, Pitcher, 2 Qt. 295.00
Minuet, Plate, Toujours, 8 In. 35.00
Minuet, Tumbler, Ice Tea 38.00
Minuet, Wine, 3 1/2 Oz. 75.00
Moongleam, Jug, 3 Pt. 225.00
Mt. Pleasant, Mayonnaise, Cobalt Blue 22.00
Mt. Pleasant, Rose Bowl, Cobalt Blue, 4 In. 25.00
Narrow Flute, Goblet, Marked, 9 Oz. 20.00
Narrow Flute, Jug, Marked, 1/2 Gal. .... 75.00 to 85.00
Narrow Flute, Nut Dish, 6 Piece 48.00
Narrow Flute, Tray, Sugar Cube, Individual 35.00
National, Soda, Tally Ho Etch, 3 Oz. 55.00
New Era, Claret, 4 Oz., 8 Piece 100.00
New Era, Cocktail, Marked, 3 1/2 Oz. 22.00
New Era, Goblet, 10 Oz. 22.00
New Era, Relish, Normandie Etch, 13 In. 50.00
New Era, Wine, Burgundy Bands, Gold Trim 18.00
Newport, Berry Bowl 8.00
Oak Leaf, Candlestick, Frosted, Signed, Pair 150.00
Oak Leaf, Console Set, Flamingo, Frosted Leaves 220.00
Octagon, Nut Cup, Moongleam, Individual, Marked 18.00
Octagon, Sugar & Creamer, Sahara, Marked 70.00
Octagon With Floral Cut, Plate, Frozen Desert, Green 17.00
Old Dominion, Goblet, Empress Etch 22.50
Old Dominion, Goblet, Sahara, 10 Oz. 30.00
Old Glory, Cordial, Renaissance Etch 75.00
Old Sandwich, Ashtray, Marked, Sahara, Individual 35.00
Old Sandwich, Compote, Moonbeam, Marked, 6 In. 155.00
Old Sandwich, Cruet, Sahara 225.00
Old Sandwich, Goblet, Flamingo 45.00
Old Sandwich, Mug, Beer, Cobalt Blue, Marked, 12 Oz. 285.00
Old Sandwich, Mug, Beer, Marked, 12 Oz. 48.50
Old Sandwich, Pitcher, Ice Lip, Sahara 128.00
Old Sandwich, Sugar & Creamer, Marked, Oval .... 35.00 to 45.00
Old Sandwich, Tumbler, Iced Tea, Sahara, Footed, 12 Oz. 24.00
Old Williamsburg, Candelabra, 3-Light, Prisms, Pair 575.00
Old Williamsburg, Candlestick, Prisms, 9 In. 90.00
Old Williamsburg, Goblet, Marked 27.50
Old Williamsburg, Wine, Marked, 1 1/2 Oz., 8 Piece 90.00
Orchid Etch, Creamer, Individual .... 20.00 to 25.00
Orchid Etch, Jug, 73 Oz. 385.00
Orchid Etch, Plate, Salad, 8 In. 22.00
Orchid Etch, Sherbet, Tyrolean 18.00
Orchid Etch, Sugar & Creamer, 4 In. 68.00
Orchid Etch, Wine 65.00
Paneled Cane, Toothpick 40.00
Paperweight, Rabbit Shape .... 125.00 to 175.00
Paperweight, Tiger Shape 130.00
Park Lane, Goblet, Briarcliff Cut 30.00
Patrician, Candleholder, 7 5/8 In., Pair 125.00
Peacock, Goblet, Etched 33.00
Peacock, Tumbler 33.00
Peerless, Water Set, 3 Part Pitcher, 4 Tumblers, Marked 150.00
Peerless, Water Set, 5 Piece 160.00
Pembroke, Candlestick, Prisms, Flamingo, 7 In., Pair 200.00
Pembroke, Candlestick, Prisms, Moongleam, 9 In., Pair 225.00
Penn Charter, Champagne, 6 Oz. 60.00
Petal, Sugar & Creamer, Moongleam .... 65.00 to 85.00
Pied Piper, Tankard, Etch 135.00
Pied Piper, Water Set, 7 Piece 500.00
Pillows, Ice Tub, Marked 595.00
Pillows, Punch Cup 30.00

Pillows, Rose Bowl, 7 In 95.00
Pillows, Spooner 95.00
Pineapple & Fan, Cracker Jar, Green, Gold Trim 225.00
Pineapple & Fan, Cruet, Green 125.00
Pineapple & Fan, Spooner, Emerald, Gold Trim .... 45.00 to 55.00
Pineapple & Fan, Toothpick 50.00
Pineapple & Fan, Water Set, Emerald, Gold Trim, 6 Piece 595.00
Pinwheel & Fan, Nappy, Marked 55.00
Pinwheel & Fan, Sugar & Creamer, Marked 75.00
Plantation, Cruet, Stopper 100.00
Plantation, Dish, Jelly, Handle, Marked, 6 1/2 In. 45.00
Plantation, Goblet, Ivy Etch 15.00
Plantation, Jam Jar, Ivy Etch, Marked, 6 In. 45.00
Plantation, Punch Set, Bowl, Plate, 8 Cups 650.00
Plantation, Tumbler, Iced Tea, 12 Oz. 47.00
Plantation, Vase, Flared, Footed, 5 1/2 In. 75.00
Plateau, Goblet 30.00
Pleat & Panel, Compote, Cover, Marked, 6 In. 57.50
Pleat & Panel, Decanter 285.00
Pleat & Panel, Marmalade, Flamingo Footed, Handle 35.00
Pleat & Panel, Plate, 8 3/8 In. 18.50
Pleat & Panel, Plate, Sandwich, Moongleam, 14 In. .... 58.00 to 65.00
Prince Of Wales Plumes, Cake Plate, High Standard, 10 In. 90.00
Prince Of Wales Plumes, Tankard, Marked 165.00
Prince Of Wales Plumes, Toothpick, Gold 175.00
Priscilla, Sherbet, 3 Piece 45.00
Priscilla, Toothpick, Marked 30.00
Priscilla, Vase, Sweet Pea, Flared, Marked, 3 1/2 In. 35.00
Prison Stripe, Cake Tray, Marked 225.00
Prison Stripe, Toothpick 200.00
Puritan, Candy Dish, Cover, 2 Lb. 495.00
Puritan, Jug, Squat, 3 Qt. 140.00
Puritan, Oyster Cocktail, 10 Piece 130.00
Puritan, Pitcher, 3 Qt. 115.00
Puritan, Pitcher, Marked, 1 Qt. 125.00
Puritan, Punch Bowl, Vase, Marked, 15 In. 150.00
Puritan, Sherbet 75.00
Puritan, Toothpick, Silver Overlay 225.00
Pussy Willow, Vase, Marked, 16 In. 290.00
Queen Ann, Cruet, Everglades Cut, 4 Oz. 85.00
Queen Ann, Ice Bucket, Plated Handle, Marked 105.00
Queen Ann, Plate, Old Colony Etch, Square 60.00
Queen Ann, Plate, Sahara, 7 1/2 In. 25.00
Raised Loop, Pitcher, Milk, 20 Oz. 195.00
Recessed Panel, Candy Dish, Cover, 3 Lb. 195.00
Recessed Panel, Candy Dish, Cover, Cut, 1 Lb. 85.00
Regency, Candy Dish, Cover, Divided, 7 In. 145.00
Revere, Compote, Moongleam Stem & Foot, Marked, 6 In. 25.00
Ridgeleigh, Bowl, Underplate, 5 In. 22.00
Ridgeleigh, Cruet 25.00
Ridgeleigh, Cup & Saucer 22.00
Ridgeleigh, Pitcher 225.00
Ridgeleigh, Relish, Divided, Oval, Marked, 7 In. 47.50
Ridgeleigh, Sherbet, 6 Piece 108.00
Ridgeleigh, Sugar & Creamer, Marked, Individual 25.00
Ring Band, Syrup, Custard 350.00
Ring Band, Table Set, Rose Design, Custard Glass 470.00
Ring Band, Tumbler, Waukeska, Wisconsin, Custard, Marked 40.00
Rococo, Candlestick, 2-Light 150.00
Rooster, Cocktail Shaker .... 90.00 to 125.00
Rooster, Cocktail, Martini, Tail Up, 5 3/4 In. 75.00
Rooster, Cocktail, Moonglo, Pair 125.00

Rooster, Vase, 6 1/2 In. 98.00
Rose, Cake Stand, 14 In. 310.00
Rose, Candlestick, 3-Light, 7 1/2 In., Pair 225.00
Rose, Goblet 45.00
Rose, Goblet, 9 Oz. 33.00
Rose, Jelly, Footed, 6 3/4 In. 40.00
Rose, Plate, Salad 20.00
Rose, Salt & Pepper 85.00
Rose, Sherbet .... 22.00 to 27.50
Rose, Tumbler, Iced Tea, Footed, 12 Oz. 38.00
Rose, Tumbler, Juice, Footed, 5 Oz. 35.00
Rose Etch, Champagne 22.00
Rose Etch, Cruet, Plum Stopper, Waverly, 3 Oz. 225.00
Rose Etch, Iced Tea, 12 Oz. 35.00
Rose Etch, Mayonnaise, Liner 50.00
Sahara, Relish, Etched, Oblong 35.00
Satellite, Bowl, 8 1/2 In. 25.00
Saturn, Bonbon, Marked 38.50
Saturn, Champagne, Moongleam 85.00
Saturn, Salt & Pepper, Marked 60.00
Sawtooth, Butter, Cover, Child's 295.00
Sawtooth Band, Wine, Ruby Stained 18.00
Sign, Dealer, Logo, Cobalt Blue 150.00
Spanish, Champagne, Cobalt Blue 85.00
Spanish, Champagne, Tangerine .... 300.00 to 375.00
Spanish, Cocktail, Cobalt Blue 120.00
Spanish, Cocktail, Tangerine 300.00
Spanish, Goblet, Killarney Cutting 25.00
Spanish, Goblet, Tangerine .... 325.00 to 375.00
Spanish, Tumbler, Cobalt Blue, 10 Oz. 75.00
Star Colonial, Pitcher 60.00
Sunburst, Flower Frog 90.00
Sunburst, Pitcher, Milk, 28 Oz. 250.00
Sussex, Sherbet, Flamingo Bowl, Crystal Stem, Marked 80.00
Symphony, Champagne, Crinoline Etch 16.00
Symphony, Soda, Footed, Minuet Etch, 12 Oz. 42.00
Thumbprint & Panel, Bowl, Floral, Cobalt Blue, 11 In. 275.00
Tudor, Cruet, Stopper, 6 Oz. 37.50
Tudor, Dish, Mint, Handle, Marked, 6 In. 35.00
Twist, Candlestick, Moongleam 55.00
Twist, Celery, Sahara, Marked, 13 In. 2.50
Twist, Compote, Pink 50.00
Twist, Cup & Saucer, Flamingo 35.00
Twist, Dish, Pickle, Moongleam, Marked, 7 In. 27.50
Twist, Mayonnaise, Footed, Etched, Moongleam 75.00
Victorian, Claret, Marked, 4 Oz. 20.00
Victorian, Compote, 6 In. 55.00
Victorian, Goblet, Footed, 9 Oz. 25.00
Victorian, Plate, 7 In. 20.00
Victorian, Punch Cup 9.00
Victorian, Sherbet, Marked, 5 Oz. 11.00
Victorian, Sugar & Creamer, Marked 47.50
Victorian, Tumbler, 10 Oz. 20.00
Waldorf-Astoria, Toothpick .... 77.00 to 125.00
Warwick, Cornucopia, 7 In. 27.50
Warwick, Vase, Cornucopia, Sahara, Marked, 9 In. 195.00
Waverly, Butter, Cover, Horsehead Finial 195.00
Waverly, Candleholder, Double, 6 1/2 x 6 1/2 In., Pair 60.00
Waverly, Candy Dish, Sea Horse Handles, Rose 165.00
Waverly, Relish, 3 Sections, Orchid Etch 75.00
Waverly, Salt & Pepper 85.00
Waverly, Sugar & Creamer 45.00

◆ ◆ ◆ ◆ ◆ ◆ ◆ ◆ ◆ ◆ ◆ ◆ ◆ ◆ ◆ ◆ ◆ ◆ ◆ ◆

Pet doors should be less than
six inches across to keep out
small children who might then
open a regular door for a burglar.

◆ ◆ ◆ ◆ ◆ ◆ ◆ ◆ ◆ ◆ ◆ ◆ ◆ ◆ ◆ ◆ ◆ ◆ ◆ ◆

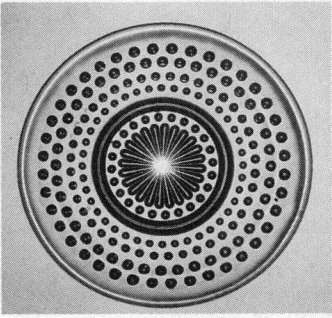

Hobnail, Plate, Pink, 8 In.

Waverly, Tray, Center Handle, 14 In.		175.00
Whirlpool, Cruet, 4 Oz.		50.00
Whirlpool, Nappy, 5 1/2 In.		5.00
Whirlpool, Sherbet		6.00
Whirlpool, Tumbler, Iced Tea, Footed		25.00
Windsor, Candlestick, 7 In., Pair		125.00
Winged Scroll, Cigarette Holder		95.00
Winged Scroll, Spooner, Gold Trim		50.00
Yeoman, Compote, Flamingo, 6 In.		35.00
Yeoman, Compote, Mint, Moongleam Stem & Foot, Marked		43.00
Yeoman, Compote, Moongleam, Marked, 6 In.		45.00
Yeoman, Cruet, Sahara, Signed		65.00
Yeoman, Plate, Empress Etch, 9 1/2 In.		67.50
Yeoman, Plate, Empress Etch, Marigold, 8 In.		25.00
Yeoman, Plate, Marigold, 7 In.		15.50
Yeoman, Plate, Sahara, 8 In.		15.00
Zircon, Rose Bowl, Saturn, 6 1/2 In.		395.00
Zircon, Sherbet, Kohinoor, 5 1/2 Oz.		60.00
Zodiac, Cocktail, Oyster, Marked		15.00
Zodiac, Relish, 2 Sections		48.00

HEREND, see Fischer category

HEUBACH is the collector's name for Gebruder Heubach, a firm working in Lichten, Germany, from 1840 to 1925. It is best known for bisque dolls and doll heads, their principal products. They also manufactured bisque figurines, including piano babies, beginning in the 1880s, and glazed figurines in the 1900s. Piano babies are listed in their own category. Dolls are included in the Doll category under *Gebruder Heubach* and *Heubach*. Another factory, Ernst Heubach, working in Koppelsdorf, Germany, also made porcelain and dolls. These will also be found in the doll category under Heubach Koppelsdorf.

Bank, Girl		150.00
Figurine, Baby Girl, Tilted Head, Bonnet, Pink Ribbons & Bows, 5 In.		195.00
Figurine, Baseball Players, Bisque, 1890s, 24 In., Pair		8000.00
Figurine, Bust, Victorian Girl Leaning On Log, Chin In Hand, 6 In.		595.00
Figurine, Dove, Fanned Tail, Marked, 6 In.		350.00
Figurine, Girl & Boyfriend, Seated On Chair, 7 1/2 In., Pair		225.00
Figurine, Girl, Green Pleated Skirt, 6 1/4 In.		165.00
Figurine, Man & Woman, Feeding Chickens, Marked, 13 1/2 In., Pair		895.00
Figurine, Man With Ax, Woman Holding Baby, Impressed Mark, 12 1/2 In., Pair		750.00
Humidor, Indian, Full Headdress Cover, Peace Pipe Base, 5 In.		225.00
Pincushion Doll, On Glass Jar, Ribbon Dress, 1920s		250.00
Vase, White Iris, Dark Mottled Blue-Green Ground, Monogram, 5 x 3 1/2 x 3 In.		50.00

HIGBEE glass was made by the J. B. Higbee Company of Bridgeville, Pennsylvania, about 1900. Tablewares were made and it is possible to assemble a full set of dishes and goblets in some Higbee patterns. Most of the glass was clear, not colored. Additional pieces may be found in the Pressed Glass category by pattern name.

Butter, Cover, Fashion	115.00
Wine, Plain Panels	9.00

HISTORIC BLUE, see factory names, such as Adams, Clews, Ridgway, and Staffordshire

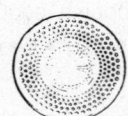

HOBNAIL glass is a style of glass with bumps all over. Dozens of hobnail patterns and variants have been made. Clear, colored, and opalescent hobnail have been made and are being reproduced. Other pieces of hobnail may also be listed in the Duncan & Miller, Fenton, and Francisware categories.

Bottle, Barber's, Blue, 7 In.	30.00
Bottle, Oil, Cranberry Opalescent, 1940, 9 In.	68.00 to 90.00
Bowl, Flared, 11 In.	12.00
Candleholder, Blue Opalescent, 1940-1945, 4 1/2 In., Pair	60.00
Cruet, Clear Stopper, Blue, Opalescent, 4 1/2 In.	25.00
Cuspidor, Amethyst, Carnival Glass	1025.00
Cuspidor, Red	75.00
Decanter, White Disc Stopper, Opalescent, 12 In.	165.00
Dish, 2 Sections, Loop Handle, 6 In.	8.50
Goblet, Electric Blue, 5 5/8 In.	11.00
Hat, Blue-White Opalescent, 2 1/2 In.	14.00
Jug, Cranberry Opalescent, 4 1/2 In.	65.00
Pitcher, Clear Threaded Handle, Opalescent Blue, 5 1/2 In.	45.00
Pitcher, Cranberry, Opalescent	275.00
Plate, Pink, 8 In. *Illus*	3.00
Plate, Square, 8 1/4 In.	6.00
Rose Bowl, Amethyst	110.00
Server, 2 Tiers, White	55.00
Sugar & Creamer, Blue Opalescent	35.00
Toothpick, Vaseline	30.00
Vase, Green Opalescent, 1940, 3 1/2 In.	22.00
Vase, Green, 6 In., Pair	90.00
Vase, Jade Green, 3 1/2 In.	20.00
Vase, Lime Opalescent, 1952-1954, 6 In.	60.00
Vase, Lime Opalescent, 4 1/2 In.	48.00
Vase, Ruffled, Topaz, 1941, 8 1/2 In.	135.00
Water Set, Blue Opalescent, 7 Piece	200.00
Water Set, Child's, Opalescent, Carnival Glass, 5 Piece	35.00

HOCHST, or Hoechst, porcelain was made in Germany from 1746 to 1796. It was marked with a six-spoke wheel. Be careful when buying Hochst; many other firms have used a very similar wheel-shaped mark.

Dish, Saucepan, Cover, Sprays Of Flowers, Scrolling Legs, Marked, 9 3/8 In.	3750.00
Figurine, Chinese Boy, Dressed As Harlequin, Marked, c.1770, 5 3/8 In.	1850.00
Figurine, Girl, Ruched Bonnet, Plaid Skirt, Orange Shoes, Marked, 5 9/16 In.	2300.00

HOLLY AMBER, or golden agate, glass was made by the Indiana Tumbler and Goblet Company of Greentown, Indiana, from January 1, 1903, to June 13, 1903. It is a pressed glass pattern featuring holly leaves in the amber-shaded glass. The glass was made with shadings that range from creamy opalescent to brown-amber.

Butter, Cover, 1903	1250.00 to 1500.00
Butter, Cover, Pedestal, Greentown	725.00
Cruet, Conforming Stopper, 6 1/4 In.	825.00
Pitcher, Greentown, 9 In.	2500.00 to 2950.00
Spooner, 4 In.	485.00
Toothpick, 2 1/2 In.	685.00

Tumbler, 4 In.	210.00
Tumbler, Greentown	500.00

HOPALONG CASSIDY was named William Lawrence Boyd when he was born in Cambridge, Ohio, in 1895. His first movie appearance was in 1919, but the first Hopalong Cassidy film was not until 1934. Sixty-six films were made. In 1948, William Boyd purchased the television rights to the movies, then later made fifty-two new programs. In the 1950s, Hopalong Cassidy and his horse, named *Topper*, were seen in comics, records, toys, and other products. Boyd died in 1972.

Badge, 1930s	35.00
Badge, 6-Pointed Star, Raised Picture, 1950s	15.00 to 28.00
Badge, Bond Bread, Black & Silver, 3 In.	15.00
Badge, Post Raisin Bran	35.00
Bedspread, Chenille, Hoppy & Topper, Full Size	225.00
Belt, Western, Gun & Holster Buckle, On Card	265.00 to 270.00
Bicycle, Boy's, Restored, Leather Saddle Bags, Display Card, 24 In.	4800.00
Book, Hopalong Cassidy's Private War, Clarence Mulford	12.00
Book, Two Young Cowboys, Cozy Corner, 1951	18.00
Book Cover, Bond Bread, Unused	8.00
Button, Savings Club, c.1950, 3 1/2 In.,	35.00
Camera, Galter Products Co., Original Box, 1940	275.00
Camera, Hoppy On Topper, Tin Flash Attachment	175.00
Card, Bond Bread, 1950s	20.00
Card, Hopalong Cassidy & Metal Boots	18.00
Card, Trading, Post Cereal Premium, 1959, 25 Piece	230.00
Charm, Figural, Metal, Silver Finish, 1950s, 1 1/2 In.	35.00
Coaster, Spun Honey Sandwich Spread, Round, 4 In.	6.00
Coat Rack, Northland Milk, Wooden	195.00
Coloring Book, Trouble Shooter, 1950	35.00
Coloring Book, William Boyd And His Friend Danny, Lowe, 1951	25.00
Container, Ice Cream, 1950s, 6 x 4 In.	58.00
Container, Milk	8.00
Display, Hopalong Cassidy Holding 12 Pocket Knives, 1950	1654.00
Flashlight, Morse Code, Box	350.00
Game, Shooting Gallery, Box	250.00 to 350.00
Glass, Plastic, 1948	32.00
Ice Cream Lid, Dixie	25.00
Kit, Wood Burning, Box	275.00
Knife, Sheath	45.00
Knife & Fork	33.00
Lamp, Bullet Shape, Milk Glass, Decal	250.00
Lamp, Hoppy Holster	55.00
Lapel Stud, Figural, Silver, Round	2.50
Lunch Box, Decal Of Hoppy, 1954	110.00 to 225.00
Magazine Cover, Life, June 12, 1950	15.00
Mug, Milk Glass, Green Decal	17.50 to 35.00
Napkin, 126 Piece	126.00
Night-Light, Gun In Holster Shape, Aladdin, 1950s	300.00 to 550.00
Penknife, Black, Hoppy On Topper, 1950s, 2 In.	125.00
Photograph, 1950s, 5 x 7 In.	15.00
Pin, Gun Hanging From Ribbon	25.00
Plate, Ceramic, W.S. George, 1950s, 9 In.	45.00
Popcorn Tin	85.00
Postcard, Promotional Photo, 1950s, 3 1/2 x 5 1/2	25.00
Poster, Movie, False Colors, 1943	350.00
Poster, Movie, Revenge Of The Sioux, Full Color, 1940s	125.00
Poster, Sunny Spread, Black & White	10.00
Puppet, Hand, Rubber Head, Composition Hands, Cloth Body	225.00
Radio, Hoppy On Topper, Red, Arvin	785.00
Radio, Rearing Topper, Black	550.00 to 690.00
Record, Album, Hopalong Cassidy & The Singing Bandit, 1950	95.00 to 135.00

Howdy Doody, Phono Doodle, Electric, Shura-Tone, Kargan, 1951-1956, Box

We hung a 1950s L'il Abner game board on the wall near a window. The sun removed all of the yellow color in a year. The grass in the print is now blue.

Sleeping Bag, 1950s 225.00
Two Badges, Display Card, 1950s 195.00
View-Master Reel, 1954 .... 10.00
Wristwatch, Large Flat Box 450.00
Wristwatch, Saddle-Shaped Holder, Box 425.00

HOWARD PIERCE has been working in southern California since 1936. In 1945, he opened a pottery in Claremont. His contemporary-looking figurines are popular with collectors. Pieces are marked with his name. He stopped making pottery in 1991.

Howard Pierce

Figurine, Duck, 13 In. .... 35.00 to 45.00
Figurine, Goose, Black, Gray Speckled, 8 1/4 In. 25.00
Figurine, Quail & Chick 25.00

HOWDY DOODY and Buffalo Bob were the main characters in a children's series televised from 1947 to 1960. Howdy was a redheaded puppet. The series became popular with college students in the late 1970s when Buffalo Bob began to lecture on campuses.

Bank 20.00
Barrette, Clarabell 20.00
Belt Buckle, 1950s, 2 1/2 In. .... 25.00 to 35.00
Billfold 40.00
Book, Activity, Child Life, 1950s 30.00
Book, Golden Book, Howdy Doody In Wild West 35.00
Book, Howdy & Clarabell, Little Golden Book 21.00
Book, Howdy Doody's Lucky Trip, Little Golden Book, 1st Edition, 1953 .... 22.00
Book, Sticker Fun, 1951 .... 25.00
Bottle, Welch's Grape Juice, Picture, 1946 .... 100.00
Box, Pudding, Royal, Original Contents, Trade Card No. 9 On Back, 1950s 45.00
Cake Decoration, Birthday, Plastic, Box, 1950s 39.00
Camera, Sun Ray 70.00
Cap, Red Felt, 1950s 35.00
Cookie Jar, Purinton .... 450.00 to 495.00
Display, Key Chain, Mark Brand, Late 1950s, On Card 175.00
Doll, Bean Bag 30.00
Doll, Composition, c.1950 .... 145.00
Doll, Plastic Head & Hands, Cotton Body, Eegee Co., NBC, 19 1/2 In. 16.00
Doll, Ventriloquist, Box, 1971, 30 In. 65.00
Doll, Ventriloquist, Composition, 24 In. 175.00
Earmuffs, Colorful, Blown-Out Plastic Howdys 110.00
Figure, Jointed, Wonder Bread Premium 30.00
Figurine, Mr. Bluster, 1950s, 4 In. 18.00
Flashlight, On Card, 1980s 12.00
Game, Bowling, Parker Bros., Box, 1949 .... 75.00 to 120.00
Game, Card 17.00

Game, Dominos, 1950s 145.00
Game, Howdy Doody's Own Game, Parker Brothers 85.00
Glass, Howdy On A Picnic, Red, Welch's Jelly, 1953 .... 12.00
Holder, Pencil, Face 120.00
Howdy Doody Catalog, 1955 .... 10.00
Key Puzzle, Instructions 15.00
Lamp, Figural, 1950s, 24 In. 385.00
Lamp, Figural, Plastic, Wooden Base, 1950, 9 1/2 In. 379.00
Lunch Box, 1954 .... 100.00
Lunch Box, 1977 .... 95.00
Marionette, Clarabell The Clown, Composition .... 150.00 to 175.00
Marionette, Composition Head & Hands, Original Clothes, 19 In. 100.00
Marionette, Composition, 17 In. 175.00
Marionette, Peter Puppet Playthings, Box .... 365.00 to 395.00
Marionette, Princess Summerfall Winterspring, Composition 150.00
Mask, Premium, 1950s, 17 x 13 In. 75.00
Mug, Bob Smith, Ovaltine 50.00
Neckerchief, Bob Smith, 1949 .... 35.00
Night-Light, Nodder, 1950s 65.00
Night-Light, Plastic Body, Wooden Stand .... 165.00 to 195.00
Nodder, Ceramic, 1980s, 6 In. 18.00
Nodder, Japan, 1950 .... 85.00
Paper Napkin, 1950s 16.00
Phono Doodle, Electric, Shura-Tone, Kargan, 1951-1956, Box .... *Illus* 570.00
Pinback, 1 In. 8.00
Pinwheel, Plastic, Blue, 1950s 51.00
Place Mat, Unused, 4 Piece .... 20.00 to 45.00
Pocketbook, Shoulder Strap, Raised Face On Front 145.00
Prize Doodle List 16.00
Pump-Mobile, Windup, Nylint .... 450.00 to 575.00
Puppet, Cloth Body, String-Pull Mouth 80.00
Puppet Show, Cardboard, Punch-Outs 265.00
Purse, Raised Face On Front, Shoulder Strap 145.00
Puzzle, Frame Tray, 1953 .... 25.00
Record, 45 RPM, 1950s 18.00
Record, Storybook, Air O Doodle, RCA Victor, 1949 .... 50.00
Record Album, It's Howdy Doody Time, 78 RPM, 1952 .... 25.00
Ring, Flasher, 8 Piece 75.00
Ring, Flashlight 95.00
Salt & Pepper, Figural Head, Bandannas, Plastic, 1950s 225.00
Sign, Display, Colgate Dental Cream, Cardboard, 1950, 4 x 7 In. 50.00
Sign, Palmolive Soap, With Howdy, Die-Cut Cardboard 45.00
Spoon, Ice Cream 20.00
Stationery, It's Howdy Doody, Box .... 15.00 to 26.00
Swim Tube, Inflatable, TV Characters 75.00
Tin, Cookie Go Round, Lithograph, 1950s 195.00
Toy, Bob Smith At Piano, Standing, Tin, Windup, Unique Art 1550.00
Toy, Howdy Doody On Trapeze, Windup, Tin, Arnold, Large 210.00
Toy, Top, Tin, W. Germany, 1970s 75.00
Truck, Plastic, Green, 4 In., 1950s 40.00
Tumbler, Clarabell Gets A Kick Out Of Circus Mule, Orange 12.00
Tumbler, Here Comes Music For Doodyville Circus, Yellow 12.00
Tumbler, Hey Kids On Land Or Sea, Clarabell Bottom, Yellow, 1953 .... 12.00
Tumbler, Howdy, 1953 .... 20.00 to 30.00
Ukulele, Box .... 125.00 to 145.00
Ukulele, Yellow, Portrait, Emenee .... 65.00 to 75.00
Wristwatch, Stand-Up Display, Box 850.00

HULL pottery was made in Crooksville, Ohio, from 1905. Addis E. Hull
bought the Acme Pottery Company and started making ceramic wares. In
1917, A. E. Hull Pottery began making art pottery as well as the
commercial wares. For a short time, 1921 to 1929, the firm also sold pottery
imported from Europe. The dinnerwares of the 1940s, including the Little

Red Riding Hood line, the high gloss artwares of the 1950s, and the matte wares of the 1940s, are all popular with collectors. The firm officially closed in March 1986.

Ashtray, Ebb Tide, With Mermaid, 8 In. .... 100.00 to 160.00
Ashtray, House & Garden 15.00
Ashtray, Serenade, Yellow, 13 x 10 1/2 In. .... 80.00 to 85.00
Bank, Little Red Riding Hood .... 675.00 to 695.00
Basket, Blossom Flite, Pink & Blue, 8 1/2 In. 125.00
Basket, Butterfly, Matte, 10 1/2 In. 325.00
Basket, Butterfly, Matte, 8 In. 125.00
Basket, Capri, Coral 37.00
Basket, Capri, Sea Green, 12 1/4 x 5 1/2 In. 50.00
Basket, Dogwood, Pink & Blue, 7 1/2 In. .... 210.00 to 265.00
Basket, Ebb Tide, Chartreuse & Wine, 9 1/2 In. 95.00
Basket, Fiesta, Squirrel, Red, Cream, 7 x 6 1/2 In. 30.00
Basket, Imperial, Green Over Dark Brown, 7 1/2 In. 25.00
Basket, Mardi Gras, Paper Label, 8 In. 90.00
Basket, Parchment & Pine, 6 In. 45.00
Basket, Rosella, Ivory, 7 In. 140.00
Basket, Serenade, Yellow, 12 In. 300.00
Basket, Sun Glow, Pink, 6 1/2 In. 35.00
Basket, Sun Glow, Yellow, 6 1/2 In. 75.00
Basket, Tokay, Moon, White & Green, 10 1/2 In. 80.00
Basket, Tokay, Pink & Green, 12 In. .... 75.00 to 175.00
Basket, Water Lily, Tan & Brown, 10 1/2 In. 240.00
Basket, Wildflower, Pink & Blue, 10 1/2 In. 185.00
Basket, Woodland, Pink 10 1/2 In. 175.00
Bean Pot, Cover, Nuline, Pale Blue, Fish Scale 16.00
Bowl, Blossom Flite, 16 1/2 In. .... 80.00 to 95.00
Bowl, Calla Lily, 8 In. 75.00
Bowl, Fruit, Serenade, Blue, Footed, 11 1/2 In. .... 95.00 to 120.00
Bowl, Imperial, Dark Green, 9 In. 12.00
Bowl, Imperial, Leaf, Scalloped, Dark Green, 10 1/2 x 9 x 2 1/2 In. 20.00
Bowl, Imperial, Pink, Oval, 8 1/2 x 6 1/2 In. 12.00
Bowl, Sun Glow, Pink, 5 1/2 In. 16.00
Bowl, Vegetable, House & Garden, Divided 15.00
Butter, Cover, Little Red Riding Hood .... 350.00 to 375.00
Candleholder, Blossom Flite, Pink & Blue, 3 1/4 In., Pair 75.00
Candleholder, Bow Knot, Blue, 4 In., Pair 165.00
Candleholder, Open Rose, Dove, 6 1/2 In., Pair 250.00
Candleholder, Serenade, Blue, 6 1/2 In., Pair 60.00
Candleholder, Water Lily, Tan & Brown, 4 In., Pair 50.00
Candy Dish, Imperial, Pink, White Interior, Pedestal 15.00
Candy Dish, Serenade, Pink, 5 3/4 In. 115.00
Canister, Cereal, Little Red Riding Hood .... 1100.00 to 1250.00
Canister, Coffee, Little Red Riding Hood 700.00
Canister, Flour, Little Red Riding Hood .... 595.00 to 700.00
Canister, Sugar, Little Red Riding Hood 700.00
Canister, Tea, Little Red Riding Hood 700.00
Casserole, House & Garden, Hen On Nest .... 50.00 to 65.00
Clock, Bluebird 175.00
Clock, Cherries 175.00
Console, Bow Knot, Pink & Blue, 13 1/2 In. .... 285.00 to 300.00
Console, Parchment & Pine, 16 In. 55.00
Console, Water Lily, Pink & Blue, 13 1/2 In. 115.00
Console, Woodland, Chartreuse & Pink, 14 In. .... 75.00 to 80.00
Console Set, Blossom Flite, 3 Piece 85.00
Cookie Jar, Barefoot Boy .... 350.00 to 450.00
Cookie Jar, Gingerbread Boy 110.00
Cookie Jar, Little Red Riding Hood, Closed Basket .... 250.00 to 395.00
Cookie Jar, Little Red Riding Hood, Open Basket .... 350.00 to 395.00
Cookie Jar, Little Red Riding Hood, Open Basket, Gold Stars On Apron ...... 375.00 to 425.00

Cornucopia, Blossom Flite, Pink & Blue, 10 1/2 In. 75.00
Cornucopia, Butterfly, White, 6 In. 22.00
Cornucopia, Double, Bow Knot, Pink & Blue 185.00
Cornucopia, Double, Magnolia, 12 In. 135.00
Cornucopia, Double, Water Lily, Tan & Brown, 12 In. 44.00
Cornucopia, Ebb Tide, With Mermaid, Chartreuse & Wine, 7 1/2 In. 175.00
Cornucopia, Magnolia, Glossy White, 8 1/2 In. 50.00
Cornucopia, Magnolia, Pink & Blue, 8 1/2 In. 95.00
Cornucopia, Magnolia, Pink & Blue, 12 In. 40.00
Cornucopia, Parchment & Pine, 12 In. 165.00
Cornucopia, Rosella, Pink, 8 1/2 In. 45.00
Cornucopia, Water Lily, Tan & Brown, 6 1/2 In. .... 25.00 to 50.00
Cornucopia, Wildflower, 7 1/2 In. 70.00
Cornucopia, Wildflower, 8 1/2 In. 75.00
Cornucopia, Woodland, Chartreuse, Pink, 11 In. .... 40.00 to 45.00
Cracker Jar, Little Red Riding Hood 575.00
Creamer, Bow Knot, Pink & Blue 85.00
Creamer, Cinderella Blossom, Pink Flowers 18.00
Creamer, House & Garden, Brown 7.00
Creamer, Little Red Riding Hood, Side Pour 195.00
Creamer, Little Red Riding Hood, Tab Handle 265.00
Creamer, Magnolia 25.00
Creamer, Royal Woodland, Blue Speckled 15.00
Cuspidor, White, 7 In.. .... 85.00
Dish, Leaf, Brown, 13 1/2 In. 22.00
Dish, Tokay, Leaf Shape 40.00
Figurine, Accordion Player, Swing Band 60.00
Figurine, Goose, Gold Trim 35.00
Figurine, Madonna & Child, Standing, 11 1/2 In. 30.00
Figurine, Rooster 25.00
Flowerpot, Bow Knot, Saucer, Pink, 6 1/2 In. .... 150.00 to 195.00
Flowerpot, Saucer, Bow Knot, Pink 150.00
Flowerpot, Tulip, Saucer, 6 In. .... 125.00 to 150.00
Flowerpot, Water Lily, Saucer, 5 1/4 In. 60.00
Goblet, Capri, Lion Head, Footed, Green, 5 3/4 In. 30.00
Goblet, Imperial, White Spiral Bowl, Beaded Stem 7.50
Grease Jar, Basket, Yellow & Peach, Gold Trim, No. 982 .... 1800.00
Grease Jar, Heritageware, Blue, 5 3/4 In. 35.00
Grease Jar, Sun Glow 30.00
Honey Jar, Blossom Flite, 6 In. .... 32.00 to 45.00
Jar, Grease, Floral, Cover, 5 3/4 In. 20.00
Jardiniere, Bow Knot, 9 3/8 In. 650.00
Jardiniere, Orchid, 9 1/2 In. 400.00
Jardiniere, Stoneware, Art, Honeycomb, 7 1/4 x 6 In. 58.00
Jardiniere, Woodland, 5 1/2 In. 90.00
Lamp, Rosella, Ivory, 6 3/4 In. 225.00
Lamp, Supreme, Green, 12 1/2 In. 195.00
Lavabo, Butterfly, 2 Piece 125.00
Matchbox, Little Red Riding Hood 495.00
Mug, House & Garden 9.00
Mug, Old Spice .... 20.00 to 25.00
Mug, Stoneware, Happy Days Are Here Again, 4 3/4 In. 30.00
Mustard, Little Red Riding Hood, Spoon 395.00
Pie Baker, House & Garden .... 20.00 to 30.00
Pillow Vase, Calla Lily, 8 1/4 In. 95.00
Pitcher, Batter, Little Red Riding Hood .... 400.00 to 450.00
Pitcher, Bow Knot, Blue, 5 1/2 In. .... 125.00 to 175.00
Pitcher, Butterfly, White, 8 1/4 In. 65.00
Pitcher, Cinderella Blossom, Yellow Flower 30.00
Pitcher, Classic, Pink, 6 In. 17.00
Pitcher, Dogwood, Turquoise & Peach, 7 In. .... 195.00 to 220.00
Pitcher, Ebb Tide, 8 1/4 In. 50.00
Pitcher, Ebb Tide, Chartreuse & Wine, 13 In. .... 75.00 to 100.00

Pitcher, Granada, Cream & Pink, 10 In. .... 85.00 to 100.00
Pitcher, Heritageware, Pitcher, Blue 45.00
Pitcher, House & Garden, 9 1/2 In. 25.00
Pitcher, Iris, Pink & Cream, 8 In. 195.00
Pitcher, Little Red Riding Hood 240.00
Pitcher, Magnolia, Cream With Yellow Flowers, 13 1/2 In. 240.00
Pitcher, Magnolia, Pink & Blue, 13 In. 325.00
Pitcher, Mardi Gras, Pink, 10 In. 90.00
Pitcher, Milk, Little Red Riding Hood .... 275.00 to 300.00
Pitcher, Open Rose, 13 In. 450.00
Pitcher, Open Rose, Pink & Blue, 7 In. .... 150.00 to 195.00
Pitcher, Parchment & Pine, Green, 13 1/2 In. 135.00
Pitcher, Rosella, Pink, 7 In. 65.00
Pitcher, Serenade, 6 In. 35.00
Pitcher, Sun Glow, 24 Oz. 40.00
Pitcher, Tokay, White & Green, 12 In. 150.00
Pitcher, Wild Flower, 5 1/2 In. .... 35.00 to 60.00
Pitcher, Wind Flower, Pink & Blue, 8 1/2 In. 140.00
Pitcher, Woodland, Glossy Chartreuse & Rose, 13 1/2 In. .... 140.00 to 195.00
Pitcher, Woodland, Green, 5 1/2 In. 60.00
Planter, Clown 25.00
Planter, Dancing Lady .... 20.00 to 50.00
Planter, Double Swan 55.00
Planter, Duck .... 25.00 to 30.00
Planter, Geese, Green, Yellow, 7 1/4 In. 40.00
Planter, Imperial, Bucket, Tan, Bail Handle, 5 In. 12.00
Planter, Imperial, Dark Green, Vertical Ribbed, 7 1/4 In. 8.50
Planter, Kitten 30.00
Planter, Pheasant 24.00
Planter, Poodle, Pink .... 45.00 to 95.00
Planter, Swan 25.00
Pretzel Jar, Stoneware, Alpine, 9 1/2 In. 275.00
Salt & Pepper, Floral, 3 1/2 In. 15.00
Salt & Pepper, Little Red Riding Hood, 3 1/2 In. 125.00
Salt & Pepper, Little Red Riding Hood, 4 1/2 In. .... 1200.00 to 1250.00
Salt & Pepper, Little Red Riding Hood, 5 1/2 In. 150.00
Salt & Pepper, Sun Glow 30.00
Spice Jar, Nutmeg, Little Red Riding Hood 695.00
String Holder, Little Red Riding Hood .... 2800.00 to 3200.00
Sugar, Cover, Blossom Flite, Pink & Black 35.00
Sugar, Cover, Crescent, 4 1/2 In. 12.00
Sugar, Cover, Little Red Riding Hood Crawling 265.00
Sugar & Creamer, Little Red Riding Hood, Head Pour 700.00
Sugar & Creamer, Little Red Riding Hood, Side Pour .... 195.00 to 250.00
Sugar & Creamer, Serenade, Pink 75.00
Tankard, Stoneware, Alpine, 9 1/2 In. 250.00
Tea Set, Blossom Flite, Pink, Black & Gold, 3 Piece 195.00
Tea Set, Butterfly, Glossy, 3 Piece 235.00
Tea Set, Water Lily, Tan & Brown, Gold Trim, 3 Piece 200.00
Teapot, Bow Knot 450.00
Teapot, Dogwood 225.00
Teapot, Little Red Riding Hood .... 275.00 to 365.00
Teapot, Magnolia, Pink Gloss 70.00
Teapot, Open Rose, Pink 295.00
Teapot, Serenade, Pink 150.00
Teapot, Woodland, 1950s 110.00
Vase, Blossom Flite, Pink & Black, 10 1/2 In. .... 50.00 to 75.00
Vase, Bow Knot, 6 1/2 In. 150.00
Vase, Bow Knot, 8 1/2 In. .... 200.00 to 225.00
Vase, Bow Knot, Pink & Blue, 11 In. 275.00
Vase, Bud, Tulip, 6 In. 65.00
Vase, Bud, Woodland, Matte Cream To Rose, Double 100.00

Vase, Butterfly, Scalloped, 3 Footed, 7 In. 26.00
Vase, Calla Lily, 5 In. 75.00
Vase, Calla Lily, 8 In. 140.00
Vase, Calla Lily, Brown, Turquoise, 6 1/2 In. 38.50
Vase, Continental, 15 In. 85.00
Vase, Continental, Persimmon, 12 1/2 In. 42.00
Vase, Crab Apple, Blue, 5 In. .... 75.00 to 100.00
Vase, Crab Apple, White, 8 In. .... 155.00 to 175.00
Vase, Dogwood, 8 1/2 In. 90.00
Vase, Double Bud, Woodland, Chartreuse, 8 1/2 In. .... 32.00 to 45.00
Vase, Fan, Magnolia, Gold Side Handles 55.00
Vase, Fan, Mardi Gras, Pink To Blue, Side Handles, 9 1/4 In. 28.00
Vase, Fan, Wild Flower, 10 1/2 In. 135.00
Vase, Imperial, Dark Green, Light Green Mottled Rim, Square, 9 1/4 In. 17.00
Vase, Imperial, Rose, White, Footed, Flared, 9 3/4 In. 15.00
Vase, Iris, 10 1/2 In. 200.00
Vase, Magnolia, 6 1/2 In. .... 35.00 to 50.00
Vase, Magnolia, 8 1/2 In. .... 25.00 to 35.00
Vase, Magnolia, 12 1/2 In. .... 95.00 to 115.00
Vase, Magnolia, Pink, Blue Flower, 13 In. 90.00
Vase, Magnolia, Pink, Pink Flowers, Base Handles, 7 3/4 In. 45.00
Vase, Magnolia, Yellow Flowers, 15 In. 300.00
Vase, Mardi Gras, 9 In. 65.00
Vase, Morning Glory, White, Blue & Pink Flower, 8 1/2 In. 195.00
Vase, Open Rose, 4 3/4 In. 30.00
Vase, Open Rose, Pink, 8 1/2 In. 145.00
Vase, Orchid, Blue & Pink, 6 1/2 In., Pair 175.00
Vase, Orchid, Pink & Cream, Long Side Handles, 5 1/2 In. 85.00
Vase, Parchment & Pine, 10 In. .... 60.00 to 70.00
Vase, Parchment & Pine, Green, 7 In. 26.00
Vase, Pillow, Calla Lily, 8 In. 95.00
Vase, Pillow, Orchid, Blue, Pink Flowers, 6 1/2 In. 95.00
Vase, Pine Cone, Blue, 6 1/2 In. 140.00
Vase, Pitcher, Morning Glory, Cream, Blue Flower, 9 1/2 In. 375.00
Vase, Rosella, Coral, 5 In. 80.00
Vase, Rosella, Pink, White Flowers, Rectangular, 8 3/4 In. 45.00
Vase, Royal Woodland, Blue Speckled, Shoulder Handles, 6 3/4 In. 23.00
Vase, Stoneware, Art, Mottled Green 20.00
Vase, Sun Glow, Flamingo, 9 In. 35.00
Vase, Swan, Open Rose, Pink & Blue, 6 1/2 In. 115.00
Vase, Thistle, Pink, 6 In. 110.00
Vase, Thistle, Turquoise, 6 1/2 In. 95.00
Vase, Tokay, 6 In. 18.00
Vase, Tokay, Pink & Green, High Shoulder Handles, 6 In. 35.00
Vase, Tropicana, 12 1/2 In. 400.00
Vase, Tropicana, Hanging, 14 1/2 In. 650.00
Vase, Tulip Suspended, 6 In. 150.00
Vase, Tulip, 10 In. 200.00
Vase, Water Lily, Paper Label, 9 In., Pair 140.00
Vase, Water Lily, Pink & Blue, 6 1/2 In. 22.00
Vase, Water Lily, Tan & Brown, 6 1/2 In. 33.00
Vase, Water Lily, Tan & Brown, 12 1/2 In. 155.00
Vase, Wild Flower, 6 1/2 In. 45.00
Vase, Wild Flower, 7 1/2 In. 50.00
Vase, Wild Flower, Pink & Blue, 10 1/2 In. 135.00
Vase, Wild Flower, Pink & Blue, Label, 8 1/2 In. 65.00
Vase, Wild Flower, Pink & Blue, Side Handles 55.00
Vase, Wild Flower, Tan & Brown, 5 1/2 In. 30.00
Vase, Woodland, Blue & Green, 6 1/2 In. .... 35.00 to 50.00
Vase, Woodland, Cream & Rose, 12 1/2 In. 310.00
Vase, Woodland, Rose Matte, Yellow, 5 1/2 In. 90.00
Wall Pocket, Bow Knot, Cup & Saucer, 6 In. 275.00

Wall Pocket, Bow Knot, Pitcher, 6 In.	225.00
Wall Pocket, Bow Knot, Whisk Broom, 8 In.	150.00
Wall Pocket, Flying Duck	75.00
Wall Pocket, Little Red Riding Hood	395.00 to 485.00
Wall Pocket, Open Rose, White, 8 1/2 In.	275.00
Wall Pocket, Royal Woodland	40.00
Wall Pocket, Sun Glow, Cup & Saucer	28.00
Wall Pocket, Sun Glow, Iron Shape	45.00 to 75.00
Wall Pocket, Sun Glow, Whisk Broom	50.00
Wall Pocket, Whisk Broom, Bow Knot	110.00
Window Box, Imperial, Fantasy, Scalloped, Blue, 12 In.	25.00
Window Box, Woodland, Blue & Green, 10 In.	45.00

HUMMEL figurines, based on the drawings of the nun Berta Hummel, are made by the W. Goebel Porzellanfabrik of Oeslau, Germany, now Rodenthal, Germany. They were first made in 1934. The mark has changed through the years. The following are the approximate dates for each of the marks: *Crown* mark, 1935 to 1949; *U.S. Zone, Germany,* 1946 to 1948; *West Germany,* after 1949; *full bee* with variations, 1950 to 1959; *stylized bee,* 1960 to 1972; *three line mark,* 1968 to 1979; *vee over gee,* 1972 to 1979; *new mark, West Germany* 1979 to 1990; *G Mark, Goebel,* 1979 to 1991; and the *Goebel, Germany,* mark introduced in 1991. Other decorative items and plates that feature Hummel drawings have been made by Schmid Brothers, Inc., since 1971.

Ashtray, No. 33, Joyful, Full Bee	205.00
Ashtray, No. 34, Singing Lesson, New Mark	130.00
Ashtray, No. 114, Let's Sing, Full Bee	400.00
Bank, No. 118, Little Thrifty, Full Bee	350.00
Bell, Annual, 1978, Let's Sing	85.00 to 100.00
Bell, Annual, 1979, Farewell	75.00
Bell, Annual, 1980, Thoughtful	75.00
Bell, Annual, 1983, Knit One	50.00
Bell, Annual, 1985, Sweet Song	75.00
Bell, Annual, 1987, With Loving Greetings	125.00
Bell, Annual, 1992, Whistler's Duet	100.00
Bookends, No. 14A, Bookworm, Full Bee	375.00
Calendar, 1967	25.00
Candleholder, No. 193, Angel Duet, Three Line Mark	125.00
Candy Dish, No. 111/57, Chick Girl, Round, Stylized Bee	135.00
Clock, No. 441, Call To Worship	495.00
Doll, Bertl & Wanderbub, Box, Full Bee	385.00
Doll, Sister	65.00
Figurine, Boy, Playing Guitar, Dog	149.00
Figurine, No. 1, Puppy Love, Stylized Bee	250.00 to 330.00
Figurine, No. 4, Little Fiddler, Stylized Bee	140.00 to 200.00

Hummel, Figurine, No. 142/X, Apple Tree Boy, Jumbo, Full Bee

• •

Hummel figurines should be cleaned by washing in liquid detergent and water, half and half. Never put them in the dishwasher.

• •

Figurine, No. 5, Strolling Along, Full Bee 290.00
Figurine, No. 6/0, Sensitive Hunter, Stylized Bee 100.00
Figurine, No. 6/0, Sensitive Hunter, Vee Over Gee 85.00
Figurine, No. 7/I, Merry Wanderer, Stylized Bee 500.00
Figurine, No. 8, Bookworm, Missing Bee, 4 In. 137.00
Figurine, No. 10/I, Flower Madonna, New Mark 220.00
Figurine, No. 10/I, Flower Madonna, Vee Over Gee 330.00
Figurine, No. 10/III, Flower Madonna, Full Bee 330.00
Figurine, No. 13/0, Meditation, Full Bee 169.00
Figurine, No. 13/II, Meditation, Vee Over Gee .... 360.00 to 365.00
Figurine, No. 15/0, Hear Ye, Full Bee 125.00
Figurine, No. 16/I, Little Hiker, Stylized Bee 120.00
Figurine, No. 17/0, Congratulations, Stylized Bee 150.00
Figurine, No. 23, Adoration, 6 1/4 In., Stylized Bee 440.00
Figurine, No. 23/I, Adoration, Full Bee 270.00
Figurine, No. 28/II, Wayside Devotion, Full Bee 325.00
Figurine, No. 43, March Winds, Stylized Bee 85.00
Figurine, No. 47/0, Goose Girl, Stylized Bee .... 100.00 to 150.00
Figurine, No. 47/3/0, Goose Girl, Full Bee .... 175.00 to 195.00
Figurine, No. 51, Village Boy, Full Bee 115.00
Figurine, No. 52/0, Going To Grandma's, Full Bee 200.00
Figurine, No. 52/I, Going To Grandma's, Vee Over Gee 372.00
Figurine, No. 55, St. George, Stylized Bee 295.00
Figurine, No. 56/A, Culprits, Stylized Bee 175.00
Figurine, No. 56/B, Out Of Danger, Stylized Bee 200.00
Figurine, No. 57, Chick Girl, Stylized Bee 100.00
Figurine, No. 57/0, Chick Girl, Vee Over Gee 120.00
Figurine, No. 58, Playmates, Full Bee .... 140.00 to 175.00
Figurine, No. 58, Playmates, Stylized Bee 125.00
Figurine, No. 59, Skier, Full Bee 149.00
Figurine, No. 59, Skier, Stylized Bee 155.00
Figurine, No. 65, Farewell, Full Bee 275.00
Figurine, No. 66, Farm Boy, Full Bee 275.00
Figurine, No. 66, Farm Boy, Vee Over Gee 220.00
Figurine, No. 67, Doll Mother, Vee Over Gee .... 150.00 to 280.00
Figurine, No. 68/0, Lost Sheep, Vee Over Gee 180.00
Figurine, No. 68/2/0, Lost Sheep, Vee Over Gee 125.00
Figurine, No. 69, Happy Pastime, Stylized Bee .... 125.00 to 140.00
Figurine, No. 71, Stormy Weather, Full Bee .... 350.00 to 575.00
Figurine, No. 71, Stormy Weather, Stylized Bee 350.00
Figurine, No. 72, Spring Cheer, Full Bee 100.00
Figurine, No. 74, Little Gardener, Missing Bee 100.00
Figurine, No. 79, Globe Trotter, Full Bee 297.00
Figurine, No. 79, Globe Trotter, Stylized Bee 185.00
Figurine, No. 80, Little Scholar, Full Bee .... 150.00 to 225.00
Figurine, No. 81, School Girl, Crown Mark 375.00
Figurine, No. 81, School Girl, Full Bee 150.00
Figurine, No. 85/0, Serenade, Full Bee 100.00
Figurine, No. 85/II, Serenade, Stylized Bee 315.00
Figurine, No. 86, Happiness, Crown Mark 200.00
Figurine, No. 86, Happiness, Stylized Bee 100.00
Figurine, No. 87, For Father, Full Bee 240.00
Figurine, No. 87, For Father, Stylized Bee 225.00
Figurine, No. 89/I, Cellist, Crown Mark 360.00
Figurine, No. 94, Surprise, Full Bee 149.00
Figurine, No. 94/I, Surprise, Stylized Bee .... 90.00 to 140.00
Figurine, No. 95, Brother, Stylized Bee 135.00
Figurine, No. 98, Sister, Stylized Bee 140.00
Figurine, No. 109/0, Happy Traveler, Stylized Bee 140.00
Figurine, No. 110, Let's Sing, Vee Over Gee 75.00
Figurine, No. 111, Wayside Harmony, Stylized Bee 100.00
Figurine, No. 112/I, Just Resting, Three Line Mark 150.00

Figurine, No. 114, Let's Sing Ashtray, Full Bee 450.00
Figurine, No. 123, Max & Moritz, Three Line Mark 100.00
Figurine, No. 127, Doctor, Full Bee .... 150.00 to 190.00
Figurine, No. 127, Doctor, Stylized Bee 120.00
Figurine, No. 127, Doctor, Vee Over Gee 185.00
Figurine, No. 128, Baker, Vee Over Gee 270.00
Figurine, No. 129, Band Leader, Vee Over Gee 180.00
Figurine, No. 130, Duet, Stylized Bee 150.00
Figurine, No. 133, Mother's Helper, Full Bee.. 150.00
Figurine, No. 141/3/0, Apple Tree Girl, Stylized Bee, 4 In. 75.00
Figurine, No. 142/I, Apple Tree Boy, New Mark 120.00
Figurine, No. 142/V, Apple Tree Boy, Vee Over Gee 600.00
Figurine, No. 142/X, Apple Tree Boy, Jumbo, Full Bee .... *Illus* 6500.00
Figurine, No. 144, Angelic Song, Crown Mark 225.00
Figurine, No. 152/0 A, Umbrella Boy, Three Line Mark 325.00
Figurine, No. 152/II A, Umbrella Boy, Goebel Bee 715.00
Figurine, No. 152/II B, Umbrella Girl, Full Bee... 850.00
Figurine, No. 153, Auf Wiedersehen, Vee Over Gee 270.00
Figurine, No. 153/0, Auf Wiedersehen, Stylized Bee 150.00
Figurine, No. 157, Doctor, Full Bee.. 165.00
Figurine, No. 171, Little Sweeper, Vee Over Gee 75.00
Figurine, No. 175, Mother's Darling, Vee Over Gee 100.00
Figurine, No. 176/I, Happy Birthday, New Mark 150.00
Figurine, No. 177/I, Schoolgirls, Three Line Mark 715.00
Figurine, No. 178, Photographer, Full Bee 175.00
Figurine, No. 184, Latest News, Full Bee 595.00
Figurine, No. 185, Accordion Boy, Stylized Bee 100.00
Figurine, No. 185, Accordion Boy, Vee Over Gee .... 100.00 to 180.00
Figurine, No. 186, Sweet Music, Stylized Bee 150.00
Figurine, No. 192, Candlelight, Full Bee 305.00
Figurine, No. 196, Telling Her Secret, Stylized Bee 195.00
Figurine, No. 197, Be Patient, Full Bee 275.00
Figurine, No. 197/I, Be Patient 150.00
Figurine, No. 198, Home From Market 285.00
Figurine, No. 199/0, Feeding Time, Three Line Mark 125.00
Figurine, No. 199/1, Feeding Time, Small Bee 110.00
Figurine, No. 200/II, Little Goat Herder, Full Bee 300.00
Figurine, No. 201/2/0, Retreat To Safety, Full Bee 300.00
Figurine, No. 203/I, Signs Of Spring, Stylized Bee .... 250.00 to 292.00
Figurine, No. 203/I, Signs Of Spring, Three Line Mark .... 192.00 to 220.00
Figurine, No. 203/I, Signs Of Spring, Vee Over Gee 120.00
Figurine, No. 214/A & B, Holy Family, Full Bee 535.00
Figurine, No. 214/E, We Congratulate, New Mark 87.00
Figurine, No. 217, Boy With Toothache, Full Bee 175.00
Figurine, No. 217, Boy With Toothache, Vee Over Gee 200.00
Figurine, No. 218/0, Birthday Serenade, Full Bee 300.00
Figurine, No. 226, Mail Is Here, Full Bee 595.00
Figurine, No. 226, Mail Is Here, Three Line Mark .... 310.00 to 400.00
Figurine, No. 226, Mail Is Here, Vee Over Gee 355.00
Figurine, No. 238/A, Angel, Playing Lute 77.00
Figurine, No. 258, Which Hand, Vee Over Gee 180.00
Figurine, No. 305, Builder, Three Line Mark 140.00
Figurine, No. 307, Good Hunting, Bee Mark 150.00
Figurine, No. 311, Kiss Me, Three Line Mark 275.00
Figurine, No. 321, Wash Day, Stylized Bee 130.00
Figurine, No. 327, Runaway, Vee Over Gee 225.00
Figurine, No. 331, Crossroads, Vee Over Gee .... 380.00 To 500.00
Figurine, No. 340, A Letter To Santa, Stylized Bee 225.00
Figurine, No. 340, Letter To Santa, Three Line Mark 450.00
Figurine, No. 344, Feathered Friends, Vee Over Gee 160.00
Figurine, No. 345, A Fair Measure, Vee Over Gee 180.00
Figurine, No. 346, Smart Little Sister, New Mark 200.00

Figurine, No. 346, Smart Little Sister, Three Line Mark 125.00
Figurine, No. 348, Ring Around The Rosie, Three Line Mark 1430.00
Figurine, No. 353/I, Spring Dance 250.00
Figurine, No. 363, Big Housecleaning, Vee Over Gee 160.00
Figurine, No. 367, Busy Student, Vee Over Gee .... 85.00 to 125.00
Figurine, No. 386, On Secret Path, Vee Over Gee 235.00
Figurine, No. 387, Valentine Gift, Vee Over Gee 400.00
Figurine, No. 396, Ride Into Christmas, Vee Over Gee .... 220.00 to 350.00
Figurine, No. 406, Pleasant Journey, New Mark .... 1400.00 to 1525.00
Figurine, No. 408/O, Smiling Through, New Mark 180.00
Figurine, No. 414, In Tune, New Mark 138.00
Figurine, No. 479, I Brought You A Gift, New Mark 80.00
Lamp, No. 44B, Out Of Danger 230.00
Lamp, No. 224, Wayside Harmony, Full Bee 395.00
Lamp, No. 227 & 228, Full Bee, Pair 550.00
Plaque, No. 134, Quartet, Full Bee 495.00
Plaque, No. 168, Standing Boy, Gee Mark 135.00
Plate, Anniversary, 1975, Stormy Weather 100.00
Plate, Anniversary, 1980, Spring Dance 90.00
Plate, Annual, 1971, Heavenly Angel .... 485.00 to 500.00
Plate, Annual, 1972, Hear Ye, Hear Ye 50.00
Plate, Annual, 1974, Goose Girl 65.00
Plate, Annual, 1976, Apple Tree Girl 65.00
Plate, Annual, 1977, Apple Tree Boy .... 55.00 to 65.00
Plate, Annual, 1979, Singing Lesson 65.00
Plate, Annual, 1983, Postman 125.00
Plate, Annual, 1985, Chick Girl 50.00
Plate, Christmas, 1971, Angel With Candle 660.00
Plate, Christmas, 1972, Angel With Flute 39.00
Plate, Christmas, 1973, Nativity 50.00

HUTSCHENREUTHER Porcelain Company of Selb, Germany, was established in 1814 and is still working. The company makes fine quality porcelain dinnerwares and figurines. The mark has changed through the years, but the name and the lion insignia appear in most versions.

LORENZ
HUTSCHEN REUTER

GERMANY

Celery, Hand-Painted Blackberries, Blossoms, Leaves, Gold Trim, 1912 .... 58.00
Creamer, Magnolia 50.00
Cup, Bouillon, Underplate, 5 In., 4 Sets 517.00
Cup & Saucer, Magnolia 40.00
Figurine, Boxer, 10 In. 90.00
Figurine, Child & Cockatoo, c.1930, 14 In. 575.00
Figurine, Clown 150.00
Figurine, Elephant 65.00
Figurine, Nude Little Girls Dancing, White, 4 In. 250.00
Figurine, Pan With Fawn, No. 4503 .... 140.00
Figurine, Panda 70.00
Figurine, Tiny Birds 30.00
Figurine, Two Geese In Flight, 13 In. 355.00
Flower Frog, Cupid Standing, 11 x 12 In. 350.00
Flower Frog, Harem Girl, 10 In. 275.00
Gravy Boat, Magnolia 95.00
Group, Nymph Riding Stag, 9 1/4 In. 150.00
Luncheon Set, Audubon Birds, 23 Piece 275.00
Plaque, Female Holding Flowers, Framed, Signed, 16 x 14 In. 935.00
Plate, Magnolia, 6 1/4 In. 16.00
Plate, Magnolia, 8 1/2 In. 22.00
Plate, Magnolia, 9 3/4 In. 30.00
Platter, Magnolia, Oval, 12 In. 75.00
Platter, Magnolia, Oval, 15 In. 95.00
Relish, Magnolia, 10 In. 50.00
Sugar, Cover, Magnolia 60.00
Sugar Sifter, Blackberries, Blossoms, Leaves, Gold Trim 42.00

Vase, Stylized Birds & Ferns, Red Luster, 6 In. 110.00

ICONS, special, revered pictures of Jesus, Mary, or a saint, are usually Russian or Byzantine. The small icons collected today are made of wood and tin or precious metals. Many modern copies have been made in the old style and are being sold to tourists in Russia and Europe.

Akhtirskaya Mother Of God, Moscow, 1806, 12 1/4 x 10 1/4 In. 2530.00
Coronation Of The Mother Of God, Russian Provincial, Framed, 12 x 9 In. 165.00
Crucifixion, Brass & Enamel, Russia, 19th Century, 21 x 19 In. 1840.00
Descent Into Hell, Chased Vines, Russia, 17th Century, 12 1/2 x 10 1/2 In. 3910.00
Dormition Of Holy Virgin, Russia, 18th Century, 12 1/4 x 10 1/2 In. 1035.00
Hodigitria Mother Of God, Silver & Enamel, Russia, 1895, 8 3/4 x 7 In. 2300.00
Kazan Mother Of God, Egg Tempera On Wood, 19th Century, Russia, 12 x 10 In. 413.00
Madonna & Child, Oil On Board, Russia, 19th Century, 9 x 9 Ft. 101.00
Madonna & Child, Red Ground, Silver Border, Russia, 7 x 5 3/4 In. 165.00
Mother Of God, Feodorovskaya, 19th Century, 12 x 10 In. 1035.00
Mother Of God, Fruiting Vine Border, Russia, c.1910, 8 3/4 x 7 1/2 In. 1495.00
Mother Of God, Gilt Ground, Christ Pantocrator, Early 18th Century, 14 x 11 In. 1725.00
Mother Of God Of Joy To Those Who Sorrow, Russia, 12 x 11 In. 11150.00
Resurrection & Descent Of 12 Major Feasts, Russia, 15 x 17 7/8 In. 1925.00
Saint, Vision Of Christ, Egg Tempera On Wood, 19th Century, Russia, 17 x 13 In. 220.00
Saints, 3 At Table, Silver Inlaid, Red & Blue Stones, Russia, 11 3/4 x 13 1/4 In. 110.00
Saints, Group, Painted Wood, Russia, 12 7/8 In. 330.00
St. Alexander Nevskky, Silver Gilt Frame, Moscow, 10 1/2 x 8 3/4 In. 1495.00
St. Dimitrius, Greece, 19th Century, 12 1/4 x 9 1/2 In. 440.00
St. John The Evangelist, Silver Robe, 19th Century, 12 1/2 x 11 1/4 In. 2013.00
St. Nicholas, Mico-Mosaic, Silver Gilt Border, Sazikov, 1858, 7 1/8 x 5 3/8 In. 4370.00
Virgin Of Kazan, Russia, 1900, 8 3/4 x 7 In. 220.00
Virgin Of Tenderness, Silver Filigree Robes, Russia, c.1900, 7 x 5 5/8 In. 1265.00
Virgin Of The Sign, Egg Tempera On Wood, Tin, 18th Century, Russia, 12 x 10 In. .. 467.00
Vladimir Mother Of God, Brass Frame, Russia, 1780s, 16 1/2 x 19 3/4 In. 2185.00
Vladimir Mother Of God, Gilded Silver Frame, Russia, c.1900, 10 x 8 1/4 In. 1150.00

IMARI patterns are named for the Japanese ware decorated with orange and blue stylized flowers. The design on the Japanese ware became so characteristic that the name *Imari* has come to mean any pattern of this type. It was copied by the European factories of the eighteenth and early nineteenth centuries.

Bowl, Flared, 19th Century, 4 x 9 1/2 In. 286.00
Bowl, Mounted, Wood Stand, 3 1/4 x 2 3/4 In. 25.00
Bowl, Octagonal, Fukagawa, 19th Century, 5 In. 193.00
Bowl, Polychrome, 9 1/2 In. 176.00
Bowl, Potted Flowers Center, Alternating Flowers & Birds, 10 In. 165.00
Bowl, Soup, Flowers & Butterflies, Blue Border, Gilt Rim, 9 In., Pair 330.00
Charger, Birds, Flowers, Shaped Panels, Red Background, Meiji Period, 18 1/4 In. ... 440.00
Charger, Multicolored Carp, Enameled, Gilt, 19th Century, Signed 4290.00
Charger, Pomegranate Center, 6 Bird Alternating Flowers Panels 90.00
Fruit Bowl, Shell Shape, 10 In. 230.00
Jar, Temple, 32 1/2 In. 1000.00
Jardiniere, Blue, Orange & Yellow, 19th Century, 9 1/2 In. 798.00
Jardiniere, Oriental Design, 8 In. 400.00
Plate, 8 1/2 In. 37.00
Plate, 11 In. 50.00
Plate, Pierced Edge, 9 In. 127.00
Plate, Polychrome, 11 5/8 In. 236.00
Plate, Scenic, Blue, White, Red, Octagonal, 10 1/4 In. 66.00
Platter, Polychrome, Japan, 7 1/4 In. 104.00
Punch Bowl, Ho-O Birds & Blossoms, Brocade Border, Scalloped, 14 In. 880.00
Punch Bowl, Polychrome, 13 3/4 In. 715.00
Sauce, Tree Design, Rectangular, 7 In. 33.00
Sugar, Polychrome, Gilt, Japan, 4 3/4 In. 65.00
Tea Caddy, Insert 260.00
Tureen, Peach Sprig Finial Cover, Blue Loop Handles, 1750, 9 3/16 In. 4025.00

Umbrella Stand, Blue & White, 24 In. 165.00
Vase, Blue, White, Red, Frilly Rim, 15 In., Pair 193.00
Vase, Cover, Hexagonal, 19th Century, 13 1/2 In. 633.00
Vase, Floor, Peacock Design 4800.00
Vase, Gilt Bronze Lion Figural Mounts, 22 1/4 In. 2750.00
Vase, High Shoulder, Japan, 19th Century, 23 In. 605.00
Vase, Ovoid, Fan Design, 22 In. 880.00
Vase, Temple, Ruffle Top, Pair 1150.00

IMPERIAL GLASS Corporation was founded in Bellaire, Ohio, in 1901. It
became a subsidiary of Lenox, Inc., in 1973 and was sold to Arthur R. Lorch
in 1981. It was sold again in 1982, went bankrupt that same year, and some of
the molds and assets were sold to other companies. The Imperial glass
preferred by the collector is stretch glass, art glass, carnival glass, and the
top-quality tablewares.

Beaded Block, Plate, Amber, 7 3/4 In. 8.00
Beaded Block, Sugar, Cover 15.00
Candlewick, Ashtray, 6 In. 8.00
Candlewick, Ashtray, Eagle 45.00
Candlewick, Basket, Handle, 6 1/2 In. 85.00
Candlewick, Berry Bowl, Set 70.00
Candlewick, Bowl, 2 Handles, 12 In. 65.00
Candlewick, Cake Plate, Silver Pedestal, 11 1/2 In. 75.00
Candlewick, Celery Tray, 13 1/2 In. .... 35.00 to 55.00
Candlewick, Cheese & Cracker Set 55.00
Candlewick, Cigarette Set, 6 Piece 80.00
Candlewick, Compote, Gold Beads, 5 1/2 In. 55.00
Candlewick, Compote, Low, 5 1/2 In. 25.00
Candlewick, Cordial 22.00
Candlewick, Cruet Set, Oil & Vinegar 50.00
Candlewick, Cruet, Etched 45.00
Candlewick, Cup & Saucer 11.00
Candlewick, Epergne Set, 2 Piece 240.00
Candlewick, Goblet, 4-Bead Stem, 9 Oz. .... 15.00 to 18.00
Candlewick, Jam Jar, Cover, Spoon 25.00
Candlewick, Mayonnaise Set, Blue, 2 Piece 75.00
Candlewick, Nappy 37.00
Candlewick, Pitcher, 80 Oz. 150.00
Candlewick, Pitcher, Pint 175.00
Candlewick, Pitcher, Star Cut 190.00
Candlewick, Pitcher, Water 165.00
Candlewick, Plate, Birthday Candle 495.00
Candlewick, Plate, Crimped, 8 1/2 In. 20.00
Candlewick, Plate, Deviled Egg 98.00
Candlewick, Plate, Torte, 14 In. 55.00
Candlewick, Platter, Oval, 16 In. 195.00
Candlewick, Punch Bowl 70.00
Candlewick, Punch Bowl, Underplate, Ladle, Crystal 125.00
Candlewick, Punch Set, Crystal, 9 Piece 400.00
Candlewick, Relish, 2 Sections, Handles, 6 1/2 In. 18.00
Candlewick, Relish, 5 Sections, Gold Beads, 10 1/2 In. 75.00
Candlewick, Sherbet 20.00
Candlewick, Tidbit, 2 Tiers, Green 550.00
Candlewick, Tray, 9 In. Diam. 40.00
Candlewick, Tray, Fruit, Center Handle 150.00
Candlewick, Tray, Pastry, Center Heart Handle, 11 1/2 In. 45.00
Candlewick, Tray, Round 50.00
Candlewick, Tumbler, Iced Tea, 12 Oz. 22.00
Candlewick, Tumbler, Juice, 5 Oz. 3.00
Candlewick, Tumbler, Water, 10 Oz. 15.00
Candlewick, Vase, Crimped, 8 In. 45.00
Candlewick, Vase, Fan, Side Handles, 8 1/2 In. 45.00
Candlewick, Vase, Star Engraving, 8 1/2 In. 40.00

Cape Cod, Cake Plate, Footed, Square 80.00
Cape Cod, Cake Stand, Footed, 11 In. 60.00
Cape Cod, Goblet 16.00
Cape Cod, Plate, 7 In. 10.00
Cape Cod, Plate, 10 In. .... 20.00 to 35.00
Cape Cod, Plate, 16 In. 35.00
Cape Cod, Plate, 8 In. 8.00
Cape Cod, Punch Set, 15 Piece 110.00
Cape Cod, Punch Set, Undertray, 12 Cups, Ladle 150.00
Cape Cod, Relish, 3 Sections 30.00
Cape Cod, Salt & Pepper 90.00
Cape Cod, Sherbet 12.00
Cape Cod, Wine, 4 1/2 In. .... 7.00 to 8.00
Diamond Quilted, Bowl, Green, 5 1/2 In. 6.00
Diamond Quilted, Bowl, Green, 7 In. 8.00
Figurine, Bulldog, Parlor Pup, Dark Blue, Carnival Glass, 3 3/4 In. 38.00
Figurine, Colt Set, Blue, 5 1/4, 4 1/4 & 3 1/4 In., 3 Piece 200.00
Figurine, Colt, Standing, 5 1/8 In. 100.00
Figurine, Mallard, Wings Up, Caramel Slag, 5 3/4 In. 45.00
Figurine, Swan, Green Iridescent, 4 1/2 In. 28.00
Figurine, Terrier, Champion, Caramel Slag, 6 1/2 In. 110.00
King's Crown, Cake Stand, 12 In. 35.00
Match Holder, Fish, Yellow 24.00
Mt. Vernon, Bowl, Ruffled, 13 x 3 In. 23.00
Mt. Vernon, Console, Flared, 12 In. 20.00
Old English, Candlestick, Ruby, Pair 38.00

INDIAN art from North America has attracted the collector for many years.
Each tribe has its own distinctive designs and techniques. Baskets, jewelry,
pottery, and leatherwork are of greatest collector interest. Eskimo art is listed
in another category in this book.

Apron, Hopi, Dancer 90.00
Arrow, Pawnee, Flint Point, c.1880 .... 99.00
Awl Case, Southern Plains, Beaded, Red, Blue, White, c.1890, 8 In. 300.00
Ax, Missouri, Stone Grooved, Black, 5 In. 42.00
Ax Head, Iron, 18th Century, Trade, 4 1/8 In. 90.00
Bag, Arapaho, Allover Beaded 4125.00
Bag, Beaded Floral Design, Hide, c.1930, 10 x 12 In. 175.00
Bag, Beadwork, Multicolored, Star Pattern, Beaded Fringe, 15 In. 475.00
Bag, Corn Husk, Nez Perce, Yarn Geometric Design, Leather Handle, 9 x 8 In. 385.00
Bag, Crow, Teepee, Sinew Sewn, Mountain Sheepskin 4000.00
Bag, Medicine, Wool Felt, Glass Beadwork Both Sides, Strap Handle, 9 x 4 In. 185.00
Bag, Nez Perce, Beaded, Deer Head, c.1940, 9 x 12 In. 125.00
Bag, Nez Perce, Beaded, Parrot 1 Side, Indian On Other, c.1960, 8 In. 225.00
Bag, Nez Perce, Corn Husk, Hide Handles, Wool Arrow Design, 8 x 9 1/2 In. 475.00
Bag, North Woodlands, Tobacco, Beaded 660.00
Bag, Pipe, Cheyenne, Beaded, Quilled, Fringed 4100.00
Bag, Pipe, Northern Plains, Tab Topped, Ocher, Beaded 7800.00
Bag, Pipe, Plains, Beaded, Cut Steel Beads, Hide, Quilled Fringe 4950.00
Bag, Plateau, Beaded, Fringed 3950.00
Bag, Sioux, Beaded, Sinew Star Design, Beaded Ground, 13 x 19 In., Pair 6600.00
Basket, Algonquin, Rectangular, Blue Decoration, Eastern 85.00
Basket, Apache, Checkerboard Band, Men & Dog Figures 12 In. 1300.00
Basket, Apache, Connecting Diamond Design, Dogs, c.1930, 3 x 14 In. 2450.00
Basket, Apache, Gambling, Dish Shape, Brown Geometric, 19th Century, 14 In. 715.00
Basket, Apache, Olla, Geometric Diamonds, Martynia & Willow, 17 x 13 In. 3850.00
Basket, Apache, Pinyon Water Storage, Horsehair Handles, 1940, 14 x 17 In. 250.00
Basket, Apache, Positive & Negative Dogs, Horses, 1920, 4 x 13 In. 1450.00
Basket, Apache, Star With Dogs & Cross Design, c.1920, 2 x 12 In. 700.00
Basket, California, Hourglass Design, Brown & Orange, 4 In. 250.00
Basket, Cherokee, Handle, Earth Colors 55.00
Basket, Hopi, Butterfly Design, Wicker, 11 In. 125.00
Basket, Hopi, Peach Gathering, Wicker, c.1930, 11 x 15 In. 325.00

Indian, Pot, Zuni, Red & Black Animal
Design, White Ground

Indian, Doll, Apache, Beaded Hide, 12 In.

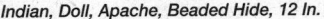

Basket, Hupa, Geometric Design, c.1920, 9 In.	175.00
Basket, Klikitat, Berry, Cedar Root, No Design, 10 In.	395.00
Basket, Navajo, Wedding, c.1970, 12 In.	80.00
Basket, Navajo, Wedding, 6-Banded Mountain & Geometric Design, 16 In.	935.00
Basket, Navajo, Wedding, Geometric, 10 In.	99.00
Basket, Navajo, Wedding, Sumac Design, Brown, Russet, 13 In.	192.00
Basket, Northwest Coastal, Black & Red Design, Oval, 4 1/2 In.	525.00
Basket, Paiute, Butterfly Design, Polychrome, 4 x 9 In.	150.00
Basket, Papago, Birds, Horse, Men, Women Figures, Yucca, Martynia, 9 x 12 In.	577.00
Basket, Papago, Bowl, Martynia Cactus, Geometric Fret Design, Yucca, 6 x 13 In.	325.00
Basket, Papago, Dark Brown Lizards	200.00
Basket, Papago, Stair-Step Design, Devil's Claw, Yucca Field, 9 x 10 In.	100.00
Basket, Pima, Bowl, Geometric Fret Design, Martynia & Willow, 6 x 11 In.	335.00
Basket, Pima, Duckwing Design, 10 In.	357.00
Basket, Pima, Olla, Geometric Fret Design, Martynia & Willow, 15 x 14 In.	1980.00
Basket, Pima, Spiraling Stair-Step Design, 1920, 14 In.	300.00
Basket, Pima, Stair-Step Design, Negative Pattern, c.1930, 13 In.	250.00
Basket, Pima, Stair-Step Whirlwind Design, 1920, 4 x 15 In..	650.00
Basket, Pima, Stair-Step, Martynia, With Willow, 2 1/2 x 6 In.	82.00
Basket, Pima, Whirling Fret Design, Martynia & Willow, 5 x 17 In.	1100.00
Basket, Pima, Willow, Slant Sides, 5 Male Figures, Hanging Holes, 10 7/8 In.	825.00
Basket, Pomo Bam Tush, Storage, 12 1/2 x 18 In.	4125.00
Basket, Pompona, Earth Tones, Red & Blue Beaded, 5 x 2 In.	1350.00
Basket, Shoshone, Geometric Design, Rim Ticking, 1920, 3 x 6 In.	100.00
Belt, Navajo, 7 Conchas, Silver Sterling, Blue Turquoise	415.00
Belt, Navajo, Concha, Spoke Shaped Buckle, Sterling Silver, Turquoise, Signed	250.00
Belt, Navajo, Silver & Turquoise Concha, Signed	750.00
Belt, Northern Plains, Beaded, Harness Leather, Brass Tack Design, 54 In.	236.00
Belt, Northern Plains-Plateau, Lazy Stitch Beading, Pink Ground, 40 1/ 2 In.	250.00
Belt, Plains, Beaded, Ornamented Hanging End, 1888, 62 In.	400.00
Belt Buckle, Navajo, Silver & Turquoise Between Red Stone, 3 3/4 In.	125.00
Blanket, Chilkat, Northwest Coast Pattern, Cedar Bark Wrap, 1890, 58 x 33 In.	2970.00
Blanket, Navajo, Browns, Red, White, Border, c.1910, 91 x 52 In.	450.00
Blanket, Navajo, Chief's Type, Moki Field, Brown & Indigo, 4 Ft. 8 In. x 8 Ft.	6100.00
Blanket, Navajo, Saddle, Striped Design, 1950s, 55 x 55 In.	27.00
Blanket, Navajo, Wool, Concentric Diamonds & Hourglass Design, 54 x 37 In.	1320.00
Bow, Plains, Buffalo Horn Back, 39 1/2 In.	71.00
Bow Case, Plains, Quiver, Beaded Ends, Blue Ground, Quilled Strips, Fringe, 31 In.	8250.00
Bowl, Apache, Basketry, Geometric, Martynia & Willow, 1890, 11 3/4 In.	575.00
Bowl, Basketry, Mission, Coiled, Shiny Variegated Juncus & Rush, 14 1/2 In.	522.50
Bowl, Dough, Pottery, Red & Black Crescent, White Ground, 12 3/4 In.	1650.00
Bowl, Hopi, Dough, 4 Directional Parrot Design, c.1940, 6 x 14 In.	550.00
Bowl, Hopi, Indian Warrior, Polychrome, 2 1/4 x 6 1/4 In.	2400.00
Bowl, Hopi, Polychrome, Kachina, 7 1/2 In.	1650.00
Bowl, Hopi, Thunderbird Design, c.1940, 7 In.	100.00
Bowl, Pima, Basketry, Coiled, Flaring Sides, Devil's Claw On Foundations, 16 In.	935.00
Bowl, Pima, Basketry, Martynia & Willow, Fret Design, 18 In.	775.00

Bowl, Pima, Basketry, Whirling Fret Design, Martynia & Willow, Holes, 10 1/4 In. ... 360.00
Bowl, Pima, Basketry, Woven Devil's Claw Over Willow Foundation, 3 1/2 In. 360.00
Bowl, San Ildefonso, Bowl, Black On Black, Pottery, Yakutu, 6 In. 137.00
Bowl, San Ildefonso, Matte On Black Design, Marie & Julian, 1940, 5 In. 500.00
Bowl, San Ildefonso, Raised Serpent Design, Signed Blue Corn, 6 In. 400.00
Bowl, Santa Clara, Thundercloud, Lightning, Animal Handles, Faustina, 1950, 5 In. .. 1450.00
Bowl, Santana & Adam, Feather Design, Signed, 5 1/2 x 8 In. 3000.00
Bowl, Southwest, Pipe, Deep Oval Cavity, Green Stone, 2 1/2 In. 185.00
Bowl, Washo, Basketry, Redbud, Bracken Fern Root, Willow Foundation, 11 1/4 In. ... 1100.00
Box, Chippewa, Cover, Birchbark, Quill & Sweet Grass, Small 80.00
Box, Chippewa, Star Design, Quilled, Birchbark, c.1930, 3 x 4 In. 65.00
Box, Micmac, Birchbark, Incised Design Of Horses & Flowers, c.1890 .... 275.00
Box, Woodland, Plant Fiber Hinge, Birchbark, 2 3/4 In. 120.00
Bracelet, Navajo, Turquoise Nuggets, Coral, Sterling Silver, Inscription '77 .... 60.00
Bracelet, Navajo, Turquoise, Sterling Silver, Tooled Feather 70.00
Bracelet, Zuni, Petit Point, Sterling Silver, Stamped V.M.B. 105.00
Bracelet, Zuni, Silver & Turquoise Cluster Work, Braided Wire Cuff, 2 1/2 In. 275.00
Breech Cloth, Woodlands, Beaded Floral Design, Black Trade Cloth, 61 x 16 In. 125.00
Candlestick, Santa Clara, Redware, Sepia, 5 1/4 In., Pair 250.00
Canoe, Cree, Birchbark, 1910, 13 Ft. 7 In. x 12 In. x 36 In. 2800.00
Canteen, Acoma, Birds, Large 250.00
Canteen, Water, Flowers, Polychrome, Pair 700.00
Cap, Iroquois, Man's, Beaded, 1880s 750.00
Carrier, Baby, Nez Perce, Contour Beaded 6875.00
Carving, Northwest, Totem, Pacific, Argilite, 11 In. 715.00
Case, Knife, Tin Cone, Porcupine Quill & Bead-Wrapped Hide Thong, 10 In. 1760.00
Club, Plains, Stone Head, Rawhide Wrapped, 20 In. 115.00
Collar, Sioux, Dance, Otter Skin, Wrapped Porcupine Quill Trim, Red Ground 3080.00
Comb, Algonquin, Bone, Geometric Wolf Head 1980.00
Cradle, Apache, Yellow Canvas Over Wood, Doll, c.1960, 12 x 28 In. 600.00
Cradle, Hupa, Basketry, c.1920, 21 x 8 In. 80.00
Cradle Board, Cherokee, 1920s 625.00
Cradle Board, Cover, Sioux, Geometric, Rosebud Indian Agency, 1900, 27 In. 6600.00
Cradle Board, Desert Paiute, Basketry, Rawhide Anchors, Early 19th Century, 36 In. 335.00
Cushion, Woodland, Beaded, Buckskin, 7 x 6 In. 125.00
Dance Bow, Hupa, Beaded, Red, White & Blue, 2 American Flags, 47 In. 550.00
Dance Stick-Rattle, Plains, 1 Side Green Stain, Other Striped Diagonally, 26 In. 2650.00
Dish, Acoma, Red Flowers, 1 1/2 x 5 1/2 In. 300.00
Doll, Apache, Beaded Hide, 12 In. .... *Illus* 4290.00
Doll, Cheyenne, Beaded Belt, Moccasins, 10 In. 95.00
Doll, Hide, Beaded, Quill Earrings, 11 In. 350.00
Doll, Hopi, Kachina, Laguna Gambler, c.1960, 11 In. 600.00
Doll, Hopi, Kachina, Thundercloud Symbols On Back Of Head, 5 3/4 In. 495.00
Doll, Hopi, Kachina, Yellow-Green Face, Striped Kilt, 8 3/4 In. 885.00
Doll, Kachina, Hopi, Corn Maiden, c.1950, 9 In. 95.00
Doll, Kachina, Hopi, Talavai, C. Honanwaima, 1980, 10 In. 70.00
Doll, Kachina, Worn Cottonwood Root Figure, Wearing Manta, 12 1/4 In. 475.00
Doll, Seminole, Patchwork Dress, 15 In. 165.00
Doll, Sioux, Pony Boy, In Uniform 90.00
Doll, Zuni, Woman, Movable Arms, c.1940, 10 In. 150.00
Drum, Plains, Rawhide Over Wooden Hoop, Green Paint, Ribbon & Beads, 14 In. 192.00
Drum, Seminole, Child's, Carved Wood, 6 7/8 x 5 3/8 In. 225.00
Drum, Southwestern, Painted Cottonwood 660.00
Earrings, Zuni, Green Turquoise, 3 1/4 In. 125.00
Envelope, Crow, Painted Parfleche, 1890s 750.00
Fetish, Zuni, Badger, Arrowhead On Back, Lena Boone, 3 In. 35.00
Figurine, Bear, Seated, Carved Wood, Natural Finish, Black Beaded Eyes, 3 1/2 In. .. 55.00
Figurine, Bearded Musician, Wooden Base, 7 In. 71.00
Figurine, Woman Balancing Pot, Wooden Base, 8 1/4 In. 93.00
Flag, Cheyenne, Clan, Wooden Spear, Red Cloth, Bells & Feathers, 63 In. 60.00
Gloves, Child's, Teddy, Fringed Leather, 1910, 7 1/4 In. 125.00
Group, Northwest Coastal, Beast, Bird On Back, Carved Soapstone, 6 In. 3750.00

Hair Ties, Loom Beaded, Geometric Design, 36 In., Pair 265.00
Headband, Apache, Geometric Design, Riker Mount, c.1940 .... 90.00
Headband, Ute, Beaded 30.00
Jacket, Sioux, Hide, Beaded, Fringed, European Style, American Flags Back, 1890 .. 3100.00
Jar, Acoma, Pottery, Geometric, Ocher & Umber, White Ground, 5 x 6 3/8 In. 60.00
Jar, Acoma, Water, Pottery, Polychrome Design, White Slip Body, 10 1/8 x 11 In. 8600.00
Jar, Acoma, Water, Red Ocher, Umber, Bird & Flower, 1900, 6 1/2 x 7 3/4 In. 687.00
Jar, Apache, Water, Basketry, Pitched, 10 5/8 x 6 3/4 In. 195.00
Jar, Hopi, Geometric Design, Yenora Silas, 9 x 8 In. 450.00
Jar, Hopi, Seed, Polychrome Geometric Design, Stella Luma, 1970, 10 In. 500.00
Jar, Hopi, Stylized Butterflies & Checkered Geometrics, 5 1/4 x 9 In. 357.00
Jar, San Ildefonso, Pottery, Blackware, Geometric, Gunmetal, 1960s, 4 x 5 In. 286.00
Jar, Santa Clara, Blackware, Elaine Salazar, 4 x 3 In. 50.00
Jar, Santo Domingo, Black Floral, Creamy Slip Ground, Pottery, 1900, 5 1/4 In. 250.00
Jar, Southwestern Pueblo, Pottery, Sunflower Design, 1900-1910, 6 3/4 In. 360.00
Jar, Zuni, Seed, Frog Effigy On Side, H.A. Teyneetsa, 3 x 3 In. 50.00
Kilt, Pueblo, Dance, Image Of Water Serpent, 23 x 30 In. 775.00
Knife, Skinning, Buffalo, 1870s 35.00
Leggings, Sioux, Girl's, Green Dyed Tops, Beaded Geometric Design, 1890 .... 525.00
Mask, Cherokee, Snake Head, Pierced Eyes, Nostrils & Mouth, 11 1/2 In. 1650.00
Mat, Cherokee, River Cane, Rust, Brown & Tan 48.00
Mat, Navajo, Woven, 58 x 38 In. 60.00
Moccasins, Apache, Deerskin, Edge-Beaded Tongues & Cuffs, Parfleche Soles 665.00
Moccasins, Cheyenne, Sinew Stitched, Multicolored Beaded Design, Hard Soles 1550.00
Moccasins, Child's, Beaded, Plain Scalloped Cuff, 5 1/2 In. 295.00
Moccasins, Cree, Beaded, Floral, Hide, Cloth Tops, c.1890 .... 300.00
Moccasins, Delaware, V Shaped, Beaded Design, On Toe, c.1880, 10 In. 700.00
Moccasins, Floral Beaded, Waterproof Sole, Muslin Cuffs, 11 3/4 In. 300.00
Moccasins, Iroquois, Floral Padded Beading, Black Velvet, 1885, 11 In. 302.00
Moccasins, Northern Plains, Floral Beaded, Leather, Clara Crazy, 1888, 10 In. 1700.00
Moccasins, Northern, Hard Soles, Beaded Uppers, Sinew Stitched, 9 3/4 In. 1450.00
Moccasins, Plains, Hide Bottoms, Buckskin Tops, 4 Bands Of Beading 220.00
Moccasins, Ponca, Spot Beaded, Daughter Of White Eagle, 1910, 6 3/8 In. 415.00
Moccasins, Sioux, Burial, Full Beaded, Geometric Design, c.1890, 9 In. 2200.00
Moccasins, Sioux, Geometric Beading, Metallic Design, Tab Tongue, 1900, 11 In. ... 440.00
Necklace, Apache, Loom Beaded, Ricer Mount, c.1930 .... 75.00
Necklace, Cherokee, Beaded Rope & End Fringe, Red, White, Black On Satin, 1930 125.00
Necklace, Heishi, Nugget Turquoise & Shell 60.00
Necklace, Navajo, Leaf Ornaments, Silver, Brown Veined Turquoise, Bear Claws 275.00
Necklace, Navajo, Squash Blossom, Earrings, Polished Black Stones, Silver 297.00
Necklace, Navajo, Squash Blossom, Sterling Silver 300.00
Necklace, Santo Domingo, Fetish, Various Carved Colored Stones 126.00
Olla, Acoma, Pottery, Red & Brown, Cream, Ground, Scalloped Rim 1815.00
Olla, Apache, Dogs, Geometric, Numbers Add To 21, c.1930, 11 x 8 In. 2650.00
Olla, Apache, Geometric Step Design, Leather Handles, 12 1/2 x 11 In. 995.00
Olla, Papago, Banded Geometric, Human & Lizard Figures, 16 In. 385.00
Olla, Papago, Basketry, Yucca, Martynia, Terrace Design, Arrowheads, 12 x 9 1/2 In. 775.00
Olla, Papago, Geometric Pattern, Double Half-Diamond Band, 9 x 15 In. 250.00
Ornament, Arapaho, Leather Wrapped, Dyed Fiber, Red Trade Cloth, 8 3/4 In. 126.00
Ornament, Hair, Navajo, Silver & Turquoise, Stamped Elizabeth A 88.00
Painting, Casein, Frolicking Colts, Begay, Matted, Framed, 25 5/8 x 27 In. 176.00
Painting, Casein, Navajo, Girl, Riding Horse, Begay, Matted, Framed, 19 x 23 In. 180.00
Painting, Casein, Navajo, Warrior, Releasing Earth Spirit, Chee, Frame, 23 x 27 In. .. 110.00
Painting, Oil On Board, Indian Camp, Mt.Tacoma, Puget Sound, 1886, Frame, 16 In. 715.00
Pillbox, Navajo, Turquoise Stones, Engraved, Hand Crafted 165.00
Pin, Zuni, Mudhead Form, Mosaic Pattern Of Wheel, Turquoise, 6 1/2 In. 335.00
Pipe, Catlinite, Carved Wooden Stem, 19 1/2 In. 125.00
Pipe, Central Plains, Wood, Brass Bowl, 9 7/8 In. 375.00
Pipe, Effigy, Burial 200.00
Pipe, Northwest, Soapstone, Carved, Crude, 10 3/4 In. 190.00
Pipe, Plains, Tomahawk Form, Cast Head, Brass Bowl, Wooden Stem, 16 In. 375.00
Pipe, Woodland, Incised Turtle, Small 245.00

Pipe Bag, Plains, Beaded, Fringed, 20 In. 935.00
Pipe Bag, Plains, Porcupine Quill Wrapped Rawhide, Beaded, 17 In. 6100.00
Plate, San Ildefonso, Marie & Julien, 5 3/4 In. 550.00
Pot, Acoma, Brown & Black Geometric, White Ground, Pottery, 3 x 4 In. 145.00
Pot, Acoma, Goats, Polychrome, Signed, 1 1/4 In. 60.00
Pot, Hopi, Geometric Design, Red Polychrome, 5 1/2 x 8 1/2 In. 375.00
Pot, Santa Clara, Black On Black, Geometric Design, Signed, 3 1/2 x 4 1/2 In. 200.00
Pot, Zuni, Pinched Ruffled Tim, 2 1/2 x 4 3/4 In. 150.00
Pot, Zuni, Polychrome, Ruffled Rim, 3 1/4 x 4 1/4 In. 150.00
Pot, Zuni, Red & Black Animal Design, White Ground .... *Illus* 7000.00
Pouch, Chippewa, Multicolored Floral Beads, Velvet Body 225.00
Pouch, Ottawa, Beaded Heart & Surround, Semicircular Form 115.00
Pouch, Plains, Tobacco, Beaded Design, Fringed, 9 In. 715.00
Pouch, Woodlands, Drawstring Cuff, Foliage Beaded Panel, 6 1/2 In. 275.00
Purse, Yurok, Antler, Fitted Lid, Black Paint, Engraved, California 1320.00
Rake, Northwest, Clam/Moss, Carved Wood, Iron, Mountain Ram Horn, 1800, 12 In.   285.00
Rattle, Hopi, Gourd, Butterfly Design, R. Sammie, 1980, 8 x 3 In. 100.00
Rattle, Navajo, Turquoise Stones, Beadwork, Sterling Silver, c.1960, 14 In. 325.00
Rattle, Tlingit, Shaman's, Carved, Oyster-Catcher Form, Human Face, 13 In. 5200.00
Ring, Zuni, Inlaid Turquoise, Sterling Silver 11.00
Ring, Zuni, Needlepoint, Sterling Silver, 15 Blue Turquoises 95.00
Rug, Navajo, 2 Gray Hills, Natural, Hand Woven, 46 1/2 x 72 In. 1600.00
Rug, Navajo, Black, Red & Brown, Natural Ground, 24 x 40 In. 75.00
Rug, Navajo, Black, Red, Gray & White Geometric Design, 2 Ft. 10 In. x 4 Ft. 10 In.   825.00
Rug, Navajo, Central Diamonds, Tan, Brown, Natural Wool, 62 x 74 In. 935.00
Rug, Navajo, Crystal Style, Airplanes, Swastikas, 29 x 49 In. 550.00
Rug, Navajo, Ganado Pattern, Black, Red Gray & White, 2 Ft. 10 In. x 5 Ft. 2 In. 450.00
Rug, Navajo, Geometric Pattern, 1900s, 58 x 89 In. 2200.00
Rug, Navajo, Gray-Brown, Geocentric Bands, Geometric Design, 137 x 88 In. 7150.00
Rug, Navajo, Legado Type, Geometric Design, Gray Ground, 52 x 108 In. 495.00
Rug, Navajo, Pictorial, Map Of United States, Western States Oversized 6325.00
Rug, Navajo, Serrate Design, Hand-Carded Wool, Red, Brown, Natural, 33 x 59 In. ..   357.00
Rug, Navajo, Serrate Diamond Design, 39 x 46 In. 385.00
Rug, Navajo, Stepline & Geometric Design, 6 Borders, 94 x 146 In. 3000.00
Rug, Navajo, Stripe Pattern, Geometric, c.1960, 29 x 49 In. 250.00
Rug, Navajo, Wide Ruins, White, Black & Red, 3 Ft. 1 In. x 4 Ft. 9 In. 500.00
Rug, Navajo, Wool, Analine Dye, Bleeding To White, Part Fringe, 55 x 69 In. 385.00
Rug, Navajo, Wool, Natural, Native Dyes, Rabbit Brush, 47 x 71 In. 220.00
Rug, Navajo, Yei, Polychrome Figures, Red Ground, 35 x 42 In. 410.00
Rug, Red & Tan Medallions, Brown Field, 5 Ft. 2 In. x 8 Ft. 3 In. 100.00
Rug, Tec Nos Pos, Tight Weaving, c.1960, 30 x 50 In. 900.00
Rug, Yeibichai, Red, Yellow & Brown Clothed Figures, Ivory Ground, 37 x 50 In. 495.00
Saddle, Plains, Rawhide, Wooden Frame, Stitched, 23 1/2 x 15 In. 275.00
Saddle, Woman's, Plains, Sinew-Laced Rawhide, Stirrups, 12 x 17 In. 1950.00
Sash, Woodlands, Braided Wool Panel, Beaded, Fringe At Either End 1325.00
Sheath, Great Lakes, Knife, Woman's, Floral Beaded Squares, 10 1/2 In. 445.00
Sheath, Plains, Knife, Beaded & Tacked Hide, Utility Knife, 1880 .... 5500.00
Sheath, Ute, Knife, Multicolored Beading, 10 In. 1000.00
Shirt, Scout's, Fringed Hide, Yellow, Red & Orange, Bone Buttons, Epaulets 1650.00
Sling, Stone, Inca, 6 Strands, Braided Suspension Cord, c.1200, 70 In. 525.00
Snowshoes, Bear Paw, Canada, Miniature 275.00
Tile, Hopi, Kachina Face, Brown On Red, Bonnie Nampeyo, 4 x 4 In. 100.00
Toboggan, Micmac, Birch Bark, Small 55.00
Tools, Navajo, Weaving, Combs, Beater & Spacers, Oak, 24 In. 75.00
Tray, Apache, Basketry, 5 Human Figures, Central Star 1100.00
Tray, Pima, Coiled Basketry, Flaring Sides, Brown Devil's Claw, 15 In. 600.00
Vase, Acoma, Polychrome, 6 1/2 x 8 1/2 In. 350.00
Vase, Navajo, Black Ware, Abstract Design, Round, Signed Pat Martinez, 8 In. 350.00
Vase, Santa Clara, Black Glaze, Pottery, Lupita Martinez, 3 In. 195.00
Vase, Santa Clara, Black On Black, Pottery, Cresencia Tafoya, 7 3/4 x 4 1/2 In. 60.00
Vase, Wedding, Santa Clara, Black On Black, Snake Motif, Signed, 8 1/4 In. 500.00
Vase, Wedding, Tesuque Pueblo, Pottery, Poster Paint, 1940s, 19 1/2 x 12 In. 50.00
War Club, Plains, Stone, Red & Turquoise Beaded Bands, Head & Handle, 28 In. 665.00

Flea Market Finds

Shopping at the Flea Market

Flea market shopping is fun! It has become the the number one recreational activity in most parts of the country. More people go to flea markets than to baseball games, concerts, or golf courses. Go alone, take your family, or join friends for fun, find a treasure and begin a collection. Children are welcome and enjoy the search for a collectible of their own, or for you. But be sure you and the children understand the rules, especially the major rule: If they break it, they own it.

Flea market outings are good for your health. Walking is good exercise, and if you go up and down the aisles at a large market, you may walk more than five miles. Most flea markets are also wheelchair friendly. Searching in a flea market is the perfect way to reduce stress. A good flea marketer will focus on the objects, the weather, and the crowd and block out the problems of life outside the flea market. It takes concentration to shop well.

Prepare for your jaunt. Check the local papers each week. Every big city has a few permanent markets set up at an old drive-in theater or on the fairground tracks or in buildings. These sales attract a variety of dealers. Some sell only discounted new merchandise and food products. Many sell new jewelry, T-shirts, crafts, hubcaps, and other useful and useless items. But among the

"What's-it" appeal adds to the value of collectibles. This 10-inch high pottery woman held toothpicks in her tray and had napkins in her skirt and salt and pepper shaker girls beside her. The 1950s set is marked Kneiss Co., New York. Few paper napkin holders are to be found, and this set could sell for $50.

"Pyro" (enamel painted) label bottles are a hot new collecting item. Ten years ago these soda bottles were virtually ignored. Today they are in demand and prices are rising. The Kayo Drink bottle pictures Kayo the comic strip character, still used as a trademark for chocolate drink. The picture of a comic book character adds value. The green "Pep-Up" bottle has collector interest because of the graphics and the interesting name. Each bottle in good condition costs $10 to $15.

booths are part-time dealers who sell collectibles and a few antiques. You never know what might appear. We have purchased museum-quality folk art, mourning pictures, art pottery, rare English ceramics, printed textiles, old toys and games, and most of our collection of early advertising. If you are going to a weekly flea market, try to get there when it opens, even if it is 6:00 A.M. The most interesting pieces are often bought and sold by dealers as they unpack to set up their booths. Some dedicated collectors go early and offer to help dealers to unpack. Many of these weekly markets are closed before noon.

Seasoned collectors know the best time to buy is the first day the shop or flea market stand opens. Often the items for sale are overflow from a collection the dealer has had for years. Prices are low at times because the seller remembers the purchase price, not today's value. This happy circumstance does not last long. Watch for new dealers. They may have bargains.

There are large, primarily "antiques" flea markets. These are also advertised in local papers. Some papers have a section devoted to art and antiques where ads for shows and flea markets appear once a week. If you don't find a listing of nearby flea markets, go to the library and find the ads in the community weekly paper or farm paper. But best of all are antiques publications. These are national, regional, and local papers devoted to collecting. Each issue lists flea markets for the next few months. Send for a sample issue, then subscribe to keep informed.

Ask fellow collectors about the size and scope of a specific flea market before you plan a long trip. At least two dozen mammoth flea markets are held in the United States each year. They are gatherings of more than 500 dealers. Some last more than a week. Any serious collector or dealer can

Snow domes, paperweights filled with liquid and artificial "snow," have gained in popularity since 1985. Some dating back to 1878 were made of glass, while recent ones are plastic. Some new domes have "snow" shaped like hearts or bats or money. Snow domes pictured are (L to R) Alaska with a totem pole, Christmas tree scene, 1982 World's Fair with space needle, London skyline, and Virginia with bird scene. In good condition, with all of the liquid, these paperweights sell for $15 to $95.

tell you what to expect if you go. Many collectors plan vacations around the dates of these events.

Dressing for the Flea Market

Every "sport" has a uniform. Dress for all kinds of weather. Keep a raincoat or large garbage bag in the car to use in case of a storm. Use suntan lotion. Wear comfortable shoes. The flea market may be on rocky hills, muddy track, or slippery grass. Dress in layers. It is often cool in the morning but hot by noon. A high collar or scarf on the back of the neck prevents sunburn. A hat is important too. It keeps off sun and rain. We always wear bright scarves or hats to make it easier for companions to spot us.

Keep sunglasses on a chain. Take a light purse or fanny pack. Be sure your money is safely zipped away. We like to wear a jacket or pants with pockets for small bills and change, and we keep large bills out of sight. Do take cash. Dealers have a right to be suspicious of checks, and very few accept credit cards. Women should take a small wallet-type purse that can be put in a tote bag or a zipper-closed shoulder bag. Men should carry a wallet in a secure pocket or fanny pack. A hunting vest or jacket with pockets is good.

Carry a large backpack or tote bag for your purchases. Take another bag

Fast food restaurant glasses are an up-and-coming collectible. Prices range from 50¢ to $50 for rarities that date before 1985. These McDonald's glasses are (L to R) the Great Muppet Caper, 1981, $4 to $6; Camp Snoopy, Civilization is Overrated, 1971, $3.50 to $5; and Camp Snoopy, The Struggle for Security Is No Picnic, 1965, $4 to $6.

folded away for even more buys. At some flea markets, arrangements can be made to haul large dressers or beds to a location near a road open to cars. If you buy something too large or heavy to carry, ask how it can be moved.

Carry a magnifying glass (best hung on a chain around your neck), tape measure, magnet, small knife, and long corsage pin. The magnifying glass helps you read the marks on silver or china. The tape measure is needed for furniture. Is that bureau small enough to fit in your room? Beware of anything more than eight feet high. (Should you forget the tape measure, remember a dollar bill is six inches long.) The magnet identifies iron and the pin can tell you if the "worm holes" in wood are crooked or are straight, man-made drill holes. With permission from the dealer, use the knife to scrape off bits of paint or to scratch the bottom of a metal statue to see if it is all-bronze or bronze finish. Take a pencil and paper to keep track of your purchases. Many dealers do not

Anything that belongs to Barbie is collectible, but be sure the clothes and dolls are in good condition. Best are MIB (mint in the box) or NRFB (never removed from box). This Bubble-Cut Barbie came in the striped swimsuit in 1961. The doll is worth $150 in mint condition. When buying accessories and clothes, be sure to have all of the set, like the eyeglasses and tennis racket.

give receipts or do not have their names and addresses on the receipts. Keep handy a copy of Kovels' price book!

Take premoistened towelette packets. You might need them to clean up enough to handle a sandwich. Carry tissues for little necessities. If you are going with friends, you may want a walkie-talkie. It's easy to get separated. Plan ahead and pick a place to meet in case of emergency. We always arrange to "meet at the grandstand at one o'clock." At one o'clock we decide about lunch and how many more hours of walking and buying are left.

When buying at flea markets remember: "Buyer beware." There are no returns, no guarantees. And you must decide quickly. If you wait to purchase later in the day, your treasure might be sold. It is acceptable to ask for a lower price, but remember to be courteous. Point out defects and ask if these were noticed before pricing. There are many ways to negotiate a lower price, but the best seems to be a variation of the simple "Is that the best price?" Some buyers claim it helps to be holding the cash when you ask. Some like to make a low offer and negotiate a satisfactory compromise. If you want more than one collectible, pile them on the table and ask for a lower price to buy all of them.

At the End of the Trip

The best part of the day is when you show off your treasures. Take everything home or to your motel room. Unpack and wash off the surface grime. Do not bring live bugs into the house. Small paper pieces may need to be zapped in a microwave to kill mold and eggs. If you suspect there are living creatures residing in your treasures, keep them outside until you can spray and disinfect. Invite other collectors to admire your purchases. Have a pizza sent in so you can all relax and brag about the great buys. Half the fun is knowing you *did* find a treasure.

Autumn Leaf pattern has been collected ever since it was first offered for sale in 1933. This 7-inch Hall Pottery ball jug is worth $30 at a Depression Glass and pottery show. If the Autumn Leaf pieces are already out of your range, choose another 1930s–1950s dish pattern like Bittersweet, Cameoware, or Mexicana, and start your own set.

Cast-iron bookends sold for $5 a set in the 1980s. Today they are $30 to $150 at antiques shows. Prices will go up because they have the same appeal as the now expensive iron doorstops. Many bookends were made in the 1930s and 1940s by the companies that made doorstops and toys. Both the 4 $^3/_4$-inch log cabin scene and fireplace with hanging kettle are made of painted cast iron.

Black collectibles have been rising in price steadily since the 1980s. Especially popular are the small bisque figures. (L to R) Man riding a frog flower holder, 5 inches high, $35; black and white children sitting on potty, c. 1900, $50; cakewalk dancing couple, c. 1890, $75. More recent black figures can be found at bargain prices.

Buy a children's meal at a fast food restaurant and get a collectible toy. Flea market dealers often price these toys $1 to $3. A knowing collector can probably find a bargain because the fast food collector price books list the toys for 50¢ to $3. Toys shown here (L to R): Wendy's milkshake car, Burger King chicken tenders box, Wendy's car with man, lettuce, and tomato, and Wendy's hamburger, fries, and drink car.

First it was Christmas, then Easter, now it is Halloween collectibles that are in demand. Look for papier-mâché pumpkins, masks, decorations, or figures. These came from a store that specializes in "fun stuff" from old drugstores and warehouses. The cardboard dancing cat, 12 inches, and witch, $14^1/_2$ inches, each cost $6. The orange candy container with the man's face was $5 and the small pumpkin was $25.

It seems as if an endless supply of salt and pepper shakers is to be found in shops, shows, and yard sales. Look for unusual shapes, comic figures, and huggers by Van Tellingen, like these 1947 bear cubs worth $20. The broken gold hearts are worth as much as $10.

Tin collectors divide into groups; some like tobacco tins, some coffee tins, and some talcum powder tins. These are 1930s examples of talcum tins: Spencer Narcissus Talcum, 6 inches; Talc Egyptian by Palmolive Company; and Cleopatra Rose by Palmolive. The Egyptian graphics bring a value of $40 to the Palmolive cans; the other tin is worth about $25.

Advertising cards were sold in box lots, or sometimes for a nickel apiece in the 1970s. They gradually gained in value and now are seen carefully displayed in plastic holders with prices of $2 and up. In 1994 the record price for a trade card was $7,000 for a baseball bank ad. Banks and sports figures add value to the cards. Look in the scrapbooks and stacks of paper items at church sales and yard sales. Old cards are often bargains.

Miniature jugs are hard to find but seem to have been made in many varieties. (L to R) Duray Wine Co., Cleveland, Ohio, 2 $^{3}/_{4}$ inches, $60; J. Fries, Cleveland, Ohio, $65; and Benton, Meyers & Co., Cleveland, Ohio, $65. These early 20th-century bottles were given to special customers.

Old lithographed tins have been seriously collected since the 1970s, and prices have gone up. A new group of collectors is searching for the modern lithographed tins that resemble the old, expensive examples. (L to R) World's Greatest, 5 inches high, made in 1983; the chef with mixing bowl is 6 $^{3}/_{4}$ inches high, made in 1980; the 4 $^{1}/_{4}$-inch chef in a hat was made by Dahler in the late 1980s. The original Singing Waiter was made in 1912 by Tindeco, but this reproduction was made in 1983. The three large tins were made by Bristol Ware, Chein & Co. Today these tins sell for about $25 each.

These common telephone insulators were found buried near a telephone pole. The dark aqua Hemingray No. 42 is 4 inches high and the aqua W. Brookfield, 3 1/2 inches. These sell for about $1 to $6, while rarities go for up to $275.

Old bottles can be valuable. The record price is $66,000 (set in 1993) for a historic flask with the name Jared Spencer in the olive yellow glass. This flask was made about 1815–1830. But inexpensive 20th-century copies can be found. The $7 \frac{1}{2}$-inch turquoise log cabin–shaped bottle (L) has a picture of Paul Revere on the side. It was filled with Wheaton maple syrup for the 1976 centennial. The amber bottle (CTR) pictures Jefferson Davis and Robert E. Lee. It too

was filled with maple syrup in the 1970s. The cobalt blue Jenny Lind bottle (R) says American Glass Works and is a copy of an early flask. These machine-made bottles are priced under $15 each.

Ever go on a trip and buy a pillow with Niagara Falls pictured on the silk, or a shell-covered jewelry box? These souvenirs are being bought by a few pioneering collectors. Prices are low, even at shows. Will prices go up? Probably. Look for "kitsch" pieces like this $6 \frac{1}{2}$-inch stuffed alligator with suitcase (flea market price $3) or the miniature crate of oranges (50¢).

Ask a World's Fair collectibles buff—some pieces are easy to spot; others are found at bargain prices because they are unrecognized souvenirs of the fairs. The Expo '67 plastic ashtray from the Montreal Canada Fair (L) is 5 inches across. It is easy to identify but worth under $15. The green

pottery ashtray from the same Expo can be identified only by the circle of treelike symbols used at the fair. It was bought at a garage sale for a quarter.

Cloth advertising dolls have been made since the 1890s and the old ones sell for $75 to $300. But new dolls are offered each year, usually available for a package label and a small check. The dolls seem to migrate to flea markets, where they are sold for under $10—an inexpensive collectible that will probably become more valuable with age. Both advertising and doll collectors want them. Pictured here (L to R): 14-inch high Ovaltine doll, Burger King, and Dr Pepper animal.

Clean up with old cleanser cans you found for bargain prices at house sales. Flea market dealers and advertising show dealers get from $25 for the 1940s Gold Dust can to $4 for the Octagon can. The peasant figures add to the interest in the Kirkman cleanser. It was found at a house sale for a bargain $1.

Tip trays were about 25¢ to $2 in the 1970s, $5 to $25 in the 1980s, and are $12 to $400 in the 1990s. A Fairy Soap tray (L) sells for $45 to $75 today. The Schmauss Garden and Cafe, Milwaukee, Wisconsin, tray with the unusual restaurant scene was a bargain $25 at a flea market.

Fisher-Price toys and other wooden toys have gained in popularity and price since 1987 when the first book about the toys was published. Look for toys in good condition with complete decoration. Plastic parts indicate later models. Teddy Zilo (L), 11 x 9 inches, was made from 1946 to 1950 and is worth over $250. The grasshopper with wooden wheels sells for $100.

One of the newest collectibles could be free. Save your old credit cards instead of cutting them in half and discarding them. The first green paper American Express card from 1959 sells today for $500. The platinum American Express card is worth up to $100 because relatively few are distributed. Look for gas cards, department store cards, and phone cards. They probably won't be seen at flea markets, but perhaps friends will contribute their old cards to your collection.

Toys of all sorts are collected. Sometimes important toys are unrecognized at flea markets. These 4-inch high Wilson Walkies were made in the 1930s. The nurse, mammies, and soldier have moveable legs. Put them at the top of a ramp and they "walk" to the bottom. The original clothing and arms are important. A soldier with no arms was being offered at a show for $10; the complete toy is worth $25. Other Wilson Walkies include Disney and Popeye characters, political elephants and donkeys, brides, bridesmaids, Santa Clauses, penguins, and soldiers from World War II. The company stopped making this type of toy in 1952.

Dark green, red, and cobalt blue Depression Glass is gaining in value. The hobnail creamer sells for $10, the Forest Green handleless cup and saucer are $5.

It's easy to know what to buy if you are a Blue Willow collector—anything with the familiar design. Look for the weeping trees, pagoda, bridge, Oriental figures, birds, fishermen, and distinctive borders. The Buffalo pottery sugar bowl and 5-inch bowl are expensive Willow pieces because Buffalo pottery collectors also look for them. But similar, newer bowls can be found for under $20 at garage sales. Flea market dealers know about the popularity of the pattern, so prices are higher. You may find paper plates, magazine ads, plastic tablecloths, even dresses decorated with the Willow design first used in the 1780s.

Big Little Books were made to encourage young readers. The small pages and thick books made even a short story seem as important as a huge novel. Collectors today remember these books published from 1932 to 1949 and search for them as well as Bigger Little Books, Big Big Books, and others. Look in boxes at church rummage sales, garage sales, and book sales. Prices will be low. In excellent condition, Zane Grey's *King of the Royal Mounties* (1938) is worth about $20, *Buck Jones and the Two-Gun Kid* (1937) is $25, and *Barney Baxter in the Air* (1938) is $12. The books shown here are in good, not excellent, condition.

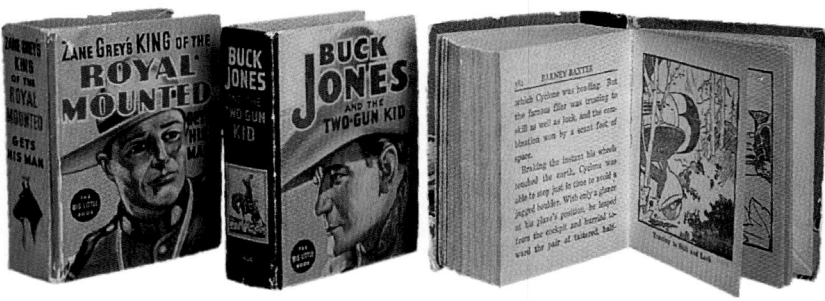

One of the hot new fads is cereal box collecting. Old boxes sell for as much as $1,540 for a 1937 Joe DiMaggio Wheaties Box. But old boxes are rare and those with sports, comic, or TV or radio personalities pictured are most valuable. Get free boxes and wait for the prices to climb. Check the supermarket cereal aisle for boxes that can be dated by the design and the special features. (L to R) The Kellogg's Rice Krispies commemorative box from 1990 is a copy of the 1920s box. The Kellogg's Toasted Corn Flakes 85th anniversary box from 1984 is a copy of the original Kellogg's girl box. The Trix box with Arabic name was found filled with cereal at a discount store in 1988.

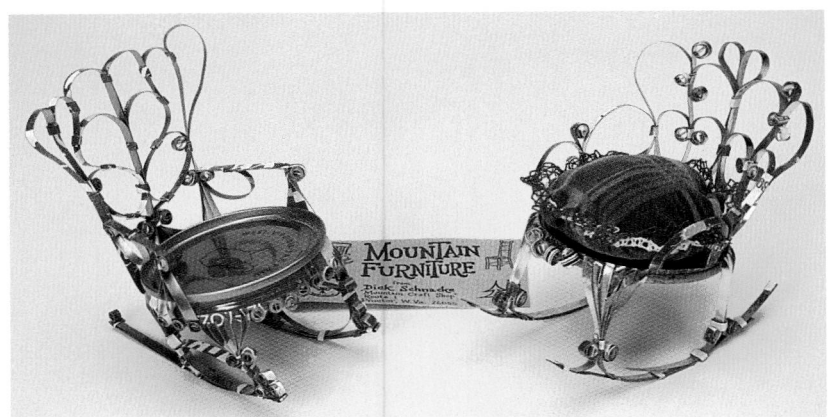

Not all cans are recycled as trash or scrap aluminum. A few become folk art tinware made from cut cans. The chair on the left was made from a Coca-Cola can about 10 years ago; the chair on the right is by Dick Schnacke of Proctor, West Virginia, who sells "Mountain Furniture." Cut tin cans from the early 1900s were made into similar "Victorian" chairs. Look for these for under $10.

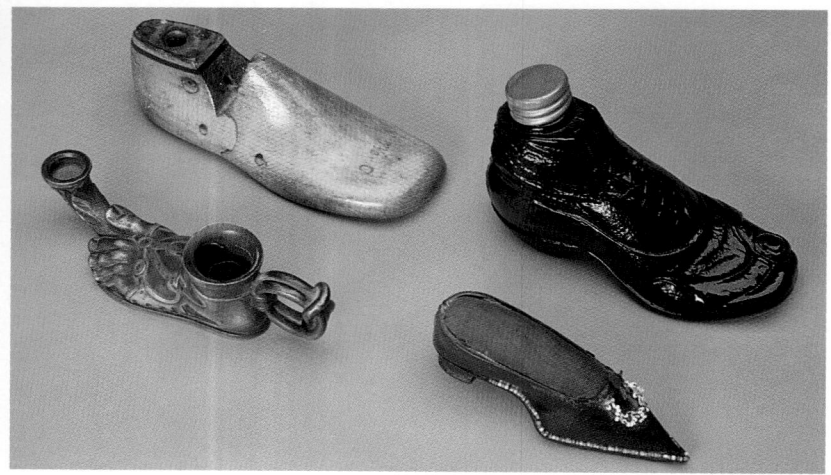

Replicas of shoes have long been popular with collectors. Flea markets are full of examples from the past 200 years. (Back row) A size 7 $^1/_2$ wooden last for a child's shoe, made about 1900, is worth $15; the 5 $^1/_2$-inch-high black glass bottle molded like a shoe with the toes exposed costs $75. (Front row) The bronze Roman foot lamp is a Victorian copy of an ancient lamp. It was found in a London flea market 5 years ago for $15. Today it is worth over $100. The pointed slipper is an 1870 pincushion purchased for $10 but worth $95 in a city antiques shop.

Trolls are "in." This 6 $^1/_2$-inch 1960s troll sold in the original box for $2.49. Today at a toy show the boxed troll brings $50. One lucky collector found 10 cases of these dolls in a warehouse when his company moved to a new location. They were the leftovers from a 1960s promotional giveaway.

Inkstand, Hunting Dog, Porcelain,
Side Inkwells, Jacob Petit

INDIAN TREE is a china pattern that was popular during the last half of the
nineteenth century. It was copied from earlier Indian textile patterns that were
very similar. The pattern includes the crooked branch of a tree and a partial
landscape with exotic flowers and leaves. Green, blue, pink, and orange were
the favored colors used in the design.

Cup & Saucer, Coalport	65.00
Dinner Set, Nasco, 59 Piece	295.00
Dinner Set, Service For 6, Plus Serving Pieces, Syracuse	295.00
Planter, 14 In.	38.00
Plate, Maddock, 8 In.	4.50
Plate, Minton, 10 In.	35.00
Platter, Maddock, 14 In.	32.00

INKSTANDS were made to be placed on a desk. They held some type of
container for ink, and possibly a sander, a pen tray, a pen, a holder for pounce,
and even a candle to melt the sealing wax. Inkstands date to the eighteenth
century and have been made of silver, copper, ceramics, and glass. Additional
inkstands may be found in these and other related categories.

18th-Century Couple, Dog, Porcelain, c.1875, 6 1/4 In.	121.00
Children At A Pond, Frogs, Porcelain, M. Blondat For E. Decoeur, c.1900, 15 In.	1840.00
Crystal, Silver Plate, Square Galleried Stand, England, c.1890, 5 x 6 3/4 In.	220.00
George III, Sheffield Plate, Mathew Boulton	1100.00
Glazed Drabware, Early 19th Century, Wedgwood, 8 1/4 In.	220.00
Griffin Head, Bronze, Pen Trays, Scrolling Feet, 2 Wells, 13 x 8 1/2 x 5 1/2 In.	350.00
Hunting Dog, Porcelain, Side Inkwells, Jacob Petit .... *Illus*	3400.00
Lion, Bronze, Marble Base Carved As Rock, 17 1/2 x 8 In.	660.00
Napoleon's Hat Opens To Well, Sarcophagus Form, Bronze, 4 x 4 1/2 In.	198.00
Nude Women In Surf, Crab Form Lid, Gilt Bronze, France, c.1900, 6 7/8 In.	522.00
Papier-Mache, Jennens & Bettridge, Mother-Of-Pearl, England, c.1860, 13 In.	121.00
Rosso Antico, Black Basalt, Leaf & Berry, Wedgwood, Early 19th Century, 4 In.	523.00
Sheffield Silver, Burl Walnut, Regency, 19th Century, 12 In.	770.00
Tortoiseshell, Napoleon III, 2 Bottles, 19th Century, 9 1/4 x 6 1/4 In.	302.00
Viking Head, Creamware, Gilt Decorated, Wedgwood, 10 1/4 In.	468.00
William IV, Bronze Handle, 2 Glass Bottles, Tortoiseshell, 1860s, 15 3/4 In.	3163.00

INKWELLS, of course, held ink. Ready-made ink was first made about 1836
and was sold in bottles. The desk inkwell had a narrow hole so the pen would
not slip inside. Inkwells were made of many materials, such as pottery, glass,
pewter, silver. Look in these categories for more listings of inkwells.

Art Glass, Round, Loetz Type	350.00
Bear, Gilt Bronze, Malachite Base, Russia	600.00
Bell, Brass, Onyx Glass Base	85.00
Bird On Nest, Staffordshire	295.00

Blown Glass, 3-Mold, Mt. Vernon 2860.00
Brass, Ornate, Footed Base, Large 65.00
Brass, Slotted Underplate, Round, 1870-1880 .... 350.00
Bronze, Boar With Her Young, Head Lifts, 5 3/4 In. 195.00
Buffalo, Cast Metal, c.1900 .... 665.00
Bulldog, Victorian, Fruitwood, 6 In. 770.00
Bulldog Head, Milk Glass, Cast Iron, Self-Closing, 4 1/2 In. 275.00
Camel, Lying Down, Polychromed, 9 x 6 In. 120.00
Cat, Iron 275.00
Cherubs, Grapevines, Bronze, Center Canister, Cut Glass Cube Wells, 7 x 10 In. 300.00
Cheshire Cat, Cast Iron, White Paint, 7 In. 145.00
Chickens & Chicks On Top, 2 Wells, 4 x 4 In. 300.00
Cover, Black Basalt, 3 Dolphin Feet, Etruria, Wedgwood, c.1895, 5 1/4 In. 523.00
Cover, Pearlware; Glow Blue Decorations, Wedgwood, c.1850, 3 1/2 In. 275.00
Crystal, Brass Mounted, Onyx Base, England, c.1900 .... 155.00
Crystal, Gilt Sterling, Amethyst Top 335.00
Cut Glass, Brass Top, Hexagon 79.00
Cut Glass, Cube, Filigree, Silver Plated Hinged Lid, 4 1/2 In. 50.00
Devil's Head, Bisque 150.00
Double, Bakelite Top, Patent 1914 .... 45.00
Eagle, Spread Wing, Yellow Marble, Bronze & Gilt, France 1250.00
Eiffel Tower, White Metal 45.00
Frosted Black & White Enameled Man, Deer, Tree, Hexagonal, 4 x 3 In., Pair 185.00
Girl On Gate, Staffordshire 400.00
Glass Hinged Top, Red Controlled Bubbles, Brass Mountings, 3 3/4 In. 265.00
Glass Well, French Champleve, Onyx Base, Acorn Finial 295.00
Green Glass, Silver Overlay Rose & Scroll, Cover, Monogram E, 3 3/4 x 3 In. 715.00
Hinged Dome, Silver Plated Cover, Pen Rest, 4 1/2 In. 56.00
Hinged Top, Pyramid Shape, Cut Glass, Vaseline, 3 1/4 x 3/ 1/4 In. 195.00
Horse Hoof, Sterling Silver, London, 1905 .... 302.50
Hunting Dogs, Bronze, Onyx Base, With Blotter, & Duck Tray, 3 Piece 3850.00
Kate Greenaway Boy & Girl Standing On Tray, Silver Plate, Hammered, 1890 ...... 295.00
Labino Glass, Clear Blue, 1972, 2 x 3 In. 130.00
Louis XV, Traveling, Sterling Silver, Baradell, 1753, 1 1/4 In. 2875.00
Majolica, Cobalt & Multicolored, 2 Part, 5 x 13 In. 415.00
Mother Hen & 4 Chicks Against Log Box, Bronze, Original Insert, 4 In. 350.00
Mounted Horse Hoof, Victorian, 1898, 5 1/2 In. 115.00
Napoleon's Tomb Shape, Figure Of Napoleon In Repose Inside, 4 1/2 In. 412.50
Nut, 1895 .... 95.00
Perthshire, Millefiori, Signed, 6 In. 325.00
Pottery, Art Nouveau, Blossoms, Pewter Mounted, Reg DeBigot, 3 7/8 In. 2300.00
Pottery, Torquay, Embossed Irish Saying 75.00
Putto Drummer, Bronze, Ormolu, Double, 1800, France 700.00
Queen Victoria, Jubilee Year, Hinged Back, Marked, 7 1/4 x 6 In. 350.00
Rockingham Glaze, 19th Century 165.00
Rustic Fisherman On Brass Base, Barrel Form Inkwell, Copper, 7 In. 245.00
Sengbusch Self-Closing Inkstand Co., Gutta-Percha Lid, Glass 75.00
Shamrocks Hold Pewter Hinged Top, Marble Base, 6 1/4 x 5 1/4 In. 110.00
Silver, Rococo, Victorian, London, 1896-1897, 4 In. 660.00
Skull & Crossbones, Bronze, 2 1/2 In. 70.00
Stoneware, M. Tyler, Brushed Flowers At Top, Blue Accent Over Name 1870.00
Turtle, J. & E.M., Aqua, 1865 .... 35.00
Whimsy, Blown Glass, Applied Foot, Bauster Stem, 2 Ink Pots, Gallery 1850.00
Whippet, Gold Stripe On Tan Enamel, Staffordshire, 6 1/2 In. 247.50
Wolf, Feeding Twins, Brass, Rome 110.00
Woman's Bust, With Red Feather, Art Deco, France 300.00
Woman's Face, Long Hair, Brass, Art Nouveau, 1910, 8 3/4 In. 175.00

INSULATORS of glass or pottery have been made for use on telegraph or
telephone poles since 1844. Thousands of different styles of insulators have
been made. Most common are those of clear or aqua glass; most desirable are
the threadless types made from 1850 to 1870.

American, Green Aqua 8.00

AT&T, Aqua	5.00
B.T.C., Aqua, Canada	3.00
Brookfield, B & O, Aqua	8.00
Brookfield, Dark Green, Amber, Rear Aqua	7.00
Brookfield, No. 9, Aqua	5.00
C.D. & P. Tel. Co., Light Aqua, Amber Swirls	9.00
California, Plum Purple	15.00
Canadian National Railway, Green	18.00
Canadian Pacific Railway, Royal Purple	30.00
Chicago, Diamond Groove, Dome Embossed, Blue	50.00
Civil War Egg, Dark Green	375.00
Diamond, Dark Amber	5.00
Diamond, No. 5, SCA	15.00
Diamond, Olive Amber	12.00
Dominion, No. 42, Yellow	65.00
E.C. & M., Extended Skirt, Aqua	65.00
Electric Supply, Aqua	10.00
F.M. Locke, White	100.00
Fogbowl, Glazeweld, Brown	25.00
H.G. Co., Petticoat, Lime Green	365.00
H.G. Co., Royal Purple	145.00
H.G. Petticoat, Aqua	8.00
Hawley, Aqua	6.00 to 60.00
Hemingray, Big Mouth, Clear	40.00
Hemingray, No. 3, Embossed	35.00
Hemingray, No. 4, Aqua, 1871	25.00
Hemingray, No. 4, Green-Aqua, Amber Hint	15.00
Hemingray, No. 8, Aqua	25.00
Hemingray, No. 9, 7-Up Green	8.00
Hemingray, No. 9, Dark Green, Small	2.50
Hemingray, No. 16, Olive Green	10.00
Hemingray, No. 25, Aqua	16.00
Hemingray, No. 40, Green With Amber Swirls	10.00
Hemingray, No. 40, Olive	10.00
Hemingray, No. 56, Clear, Large	2.00
Hemingray, No. 95, Blue	75.00
Hemingray, No. TS2, Carnival	15.00
Hemingray, Telegraph, Green Glass, 1893, Small	3.00
Imperial, White	125.00
Knowles, Aqua, Tall Style	15.00
Knox, Brown Glazed Pottery, Large	2.00
Locke, Aqua, Milky Streaks	25.00
Lynchburg, No. 44, Aqua	3.00
Maydwell, Green Milk Glass, Gold Swirls	25.00
Maydwell, No. 14, Light Pink	7.00
Maydwell, No. 16, Straw	17.00
McLaughlin, No. 16, Steel Blue	15.00
McLaughlin, No. 20, Emerald Green	12.00
McLaughlin, Olive Black	14.00
N.A.T. Co., Peacock Blue	285.00
N.E.G.M., Blue Aqua, Bubble	8.00
N.E.G.M., Lime Green, Snow & Bubbles	75.00
N.E.G.M., Straight Side, Green	150.00
Oakman, Light Aqua	275.00
Petticoat, Dark Purple	650.00
Pyrex, No. 662, Carnival	20.00
Star, Green	3.00
Star, Yellow Olive	9.00
Tillotson, Aqua	225.00
W. Brookfield, 55 Fulton, 3-Date, Blue Aqua With White Swirls	20.00
W. Brookfield, Light Aqua, 3 Piece Mold	20.00
W.E. Mfg. Co., Dark Aqua, 1871	15.00
Westinghouse, Blue	5.00

Whitall Tatum Co., No. 1, Light Blue 5.00
Whitall Tatum Co., No. 1, Medium Purple 15.00

IRISH BELLEEK, see Belleek category

IRON is a metal that has been used by man since prehistoric times. It is a popular metal for tools and decorative items like doorstops that need as much weight as possible. Items are listed here or under other appropriate headings, such as Bookends, Doorstop, Kitchen, Match Holder, or Tool. The tool that is used for ironing clothes, an iron, is listed in the Kitchen category under Iron and Sadiron.

Ashtray, Skillet Shape, Brown Stove Works, Cleveland, Tenn., Miniature 14.00
Ashtray, Skillet, Ace Hardware Stores, Miniature 6.00
Ashtray, Skillet, Majestic Fireplace, Miniature 12.00
Belaying Pin, c.1890, 18 In. 65.00
Bill Hook, Scrolled 10.00
Boot Scraper, Boxer Dog 825.00
Boot Scraper, Cat, 10 1/4 x 10 1/4 In. 190.00
Boot Scraper, Dachshund, Green, Cast Iron, 21 In. .... 225.00 to 280.00
Boot Scraper, Dachshund, Open Mouth, Curled Tail, Old Black Paint, 21 In. 95.00
Boot Scraper, Double Griffin, 18 1/2 In. 750.00
Boot Scraper, Dragon, 12 3/4 In. 215.00
Boot Scraper, Floral, 6 3/4 x 7 In. 70.00
Boot Scraper, Stone Base, 11 1/2 In. 148.00
Boot Scraper, Witch On Broom, 7 1/8 x 10 3/8 In. 245.00
Bootjack, Cricket 85.00
Buggy Seat, Child's, Hand Forged, Fold Up 17.50
Candleholder, Sawtooth Trammel, 15 1/2 In. 412.00
Candleholder, Tommy, Sticking, 8 1/2 In. 137.00
Candleholder, Wooden, Spiral Push-Up, 7 In. 77.00
Cauldron, Swing Handle, 10 x 9 1/2 In. 44.00
Cigar Cutter, Figural, Elf On Top Of Hand Lever, 12 In. 65.00
Cigar Cutter, Master Cigars, Key Wind, 6 x 3 1/2 In. 150.00
Cigar Cutter, Plug, Spearhead 95.00
Cigar Cutter, Violin Shape, 2 In. .... 90.00 to 125.00
Cigar Cutter, Wise Man's Choice Cigars, Turning Display, 14 1/2 In. 335.00
Cigarette Dispenser, Elephant 50.00
Cuspidor, Turtle, Original Pan 375.00
Cuspidor, Turtle, Tin Back & Inserts, Royal Products, Chicago, 4 1/4 x 14 In. 465.00
Cuspidor, Turtle, Tin Lid, Royal Products, Chicago, 13 1/2 In. 82.50
Door Knocker, Basket Of Flowers, Painted 110.00
Door Knocker, Flower Basket, Oval Plate, 4 In. 55.00
Door Knocker, Parrot, Painted 145.00
Figure, Bird, White Paint Traces, 50 In. Wingspan 2970.00
Figure, Bulldog, Painted, 12 x 26 In. 8580.00
Figure, Dalmatian, Painted, Freestanding, 29 1/2 x 43 In. 6325.00
Figure, Eagle, 31-In. Wingspan 302.50
Figure, Eagle, On Sphere, Outstretched Wings, Gold Repaint, 14 In. 220.00
Figure, George Washington, Standing, 3 Ft. 4400.00
Figure, Running Horse, American, c.1900, 30 x 23 1/2 In. 2640.00
Figure, Woman, Columbia, 4 Ft. 3960.00
Figurine, Frog, Old Green Traces, 5 1/2 In. 60.50
Figurine, Lion, 5 In. 60.00
Figurine, Owl, Black Paint, 2 3/8 In. 10.00
Footscraper, Spaniel Each End, Painted, 13 x 19 x 12 In. 495.00
Gate, Victorian, No. 235, Dated 1856, 45 In. 385.00
Hinges, Strap, Y Ends, Wrought, 24 In., Pair 138.00
Hitching Post, Black Boy, Square Base, 46 In. 3300.00
Hitching Post, Dog's Head 550.00
Hitching Post, Fluted Column, Ring In Mouth, 45 In. 775.00
Hitching Post, Horsehead, Pair .... 600.00 to 1400.00
Hitching Post, Horsehead, Tapered Fluted Column, 67 1/2 In. 1100.00
Hitching Post, Jockey, Polychrome Repaint, 48 In. 410.00

Hitching Post, Jockey, Square Base, Champion Iron Fence Co., Ohio, 50 In.	715.00
Hitching Post, Tree Trunk Form Vine Design, 67 In., 4 Piece	1325.00
Hook, Trammel, Ratcheting Adjustment, Extends To 68 In.	77.00
Horse Tie, Acorn, Black Paint, 4 1/2 x 9 1/4 In.	140.00
Horse Tie, Ball Finial, 6 3/4 In., Pair	155.00
Horse Trough, J.L. Mott Iron Works, N.Y.	1430.00
Horse Trough, Oblong Basin, Drain Hole, J.L. Mott, 20 3/8 x 45 1/2 In.	1430.00
Incense Burner, Foo Dog	85.00
Key, Fancy Shape, England, 11 In.	34.00
Lamppost, Used In Baltimore, 105 In.	275.00
Letter Holder, Coiled Spring, 5 1/2 In.	5.00
Lid Lifter, Estate Wood Stove, Cutout Lettering On Handle	5.00
Mailbox, Griswold	65.00
Planter, Bulb, Bronze Plated, 11 3/4 x 7 3/4 In.	25.00
Rushlight, Candlesocket Weight-Balance, Wrought, 16 1/2 In.	1165.00
Sconce, Pumpkin Paint, Late 19th Century, 7 1/2 In., Pair	70.00
Snow Eagles, Outspread Wings, 5 In.	110.00
Tiebacks, Parrots On Oval Medallion, Worn Polychrome, 2 1/4 x 3 5/8 In., 4 Piece	242.00
Tray, Pin, Figural, Parrot, Painted, 2 1/2 In.	35.00
Umbrella Stand, Nautical Design	1650.00
Windmill Weight, Buffalo	1700.00
Windmill Weight, Eagle	1200.00
Windmill Weight, Eclipse, Fairbanks Morse	175.00
Windmill Weight, Horse, Black & White	200.00 to 295.00
Windmill Weight, Horse, Long-Tailed	400.00 to 1000.00
Windmill Weight, Rooster, 15 3/4 In.	495.00
Windmill Weight, Rooster, Standing, Paint Traces, 6 1/2 x 6 3/4 In.	240.00

IRONSTONE china was first made in 1813. It gained its greatest popularity during the mid-nineteenth century. The heavy, durable, off-white pottery was made in white or was decorated with any of hundreds of patterns. Much flow blue pottery was made of ironstone. Some of the decorations were raised. Many pieces of ironstone are unmarked, but some English and American factories included the word *Ironstone* in their marks. Additional pieces may be listed in other categories, such as Chelsea Grape, Chelsea Sprig, Flow Blue, Gaudy Ironstone, Moss Rose, Staffordshire, and Tea Leaf Ironstone.

Basin, Wash, Blue, Dunn Bennett & Co.	185.00
Basin, Wash, White, Meakin, 12 In.	105.00
Bowl, Japanese Pattern, Kakiemon Style, Turner's Patent, c.1800, 11 In.	1840.00
Bowl, Vegetable, Victoria Pattern, Polychrome Enameling, Gilt, 11 1/2 In.	95.00
Butter, Cover, Sharon Arch, White, 3 Piece	195.00
Cheese Dome, Ferns, Overlay Of Rope Pattern, 1860s, 10 In.	517.00
Chop Plate, Molded Floral, Enameled Floral Design, 12 3/8 In.	71.50
Coffeepot, Black Transfer, Abbey, Paneled, 10 1/4 In.	82.00
Coffeepot, Powell, Bishop & Stonier, 2 Qt.	65.00
Condiment Server, 2 Bowls, Hinged Lid, Over Top Handle	150.00
Dinner Set, Watteau, Mason's, 88 Piece	6000.00
Dish, Warming, Flower & Bird Design, Davenport, c.1850, 9 1/2 In.	220.00
Dish, Wheat & Berry, White, Meakin	88.00
Fruit Basket, Footed, Mason's Patent Ironstone China, 19th Century, 9 In.	247.00
Jug, Boar & Stag Hunt, Green, Mason's	80.00
Pitcher, Lion's Head & Sea Serpent's Body Handle, Mason, c.1830, 7 In.	395.00
Pitcher, Octagonal, Serpent Handle, Mason's, Late 19th Century, 11 1/4 In.	220.00
Pitcher, White, Henry Alcock, 7 In.	25.00
Plate, Brown Transfer, Spelling Bee, Molded Border, 6 3/4 In.	38.00
Plate, Imari, Mason's, 10 1/2 In., 12 Piece	1150.00
Plate, Landscape Scene, Gilt, Ivory Ground, Mason's, 10 1/2 In., 12 Piece	175.00
Plate, Light Blue Oriental Transfer, Mason's, 8 In.	27.00
Plate, Persiana, Magenta Transfer, Mason's, 10 1/4 In., 6 Piece	115.00
Plate, Transfer, Rural England, Blue Rim, Pratt & Co., 8 3/4 In.	27.00
Plate, White, Davenport, 1856, 11 In.	55.00
Plate, White, Davenport, 9 In.	45.00
Platter, Architectural Landscape, Figures, Imari Colors, 20 1/2 x 16 In.	495.00

Platter, Black Floral Transfer, Enamel, 19 1/4 In. 165.00
Platter, Black Transfer, Athens, 13 3/4 In. 27.00
Platter, Blue Feather Edge 145.00
Platter, Friburg, G. Phillips, Longport, c.1846, 14 x 18 In. 110.00
Platter, Imari Pattern, Painted & Parcel Gilt, 20 3/8 In. 302.00
Platter, Light Blue Transfer, Columbian Star, 15 In. 258.50
Platter, Medina, Blue Transfer, 15 1/2 In. 104.00
Platter, Paneled, Octagon, 21 In. 160.00
Platter, Red & Cobalt Blue, Flowers, 19 In. 287.00
Platter, Well & Tree, Blue & Orange Glaze, England, 19 In. 302.00
Punch Bowl, Chinoiserie, Transfer Printed, Mason's, c.1820, 13 1/2 In. 460.00
Sugar, Cover, Canton Style, Blue & White, 2-Handled, Mason's, 5 3/4 x 6 In. 60.00
Teapot, Canton Style, Blue & White, Mason's, 6 x 9 1/2 In. 80.00
Tureen, Powell & Bishop, 16 x 12 In., 4 Piece 235.00
Tureen, Soup, Cover, Stand, Hexagonal, Japanese Pattern, c.1820, 12 In., Pair 6325.00
Tureen, Soup, Cover, Underplate, Ladle, Blue & White Transfer, Mason's 275.00
Tureen, Underplate, Balmoral, Venables, Mann & Co., c.1850, 11 In. 275.00
Tureen, Underplate, Cover, Imari Pattern, Demon Mask Handles, Mason's, 13 In. 2400.00
Vase, Cover, Octagonal Baluster Shape, Dragon Scroll Handles, 1840, 30 1/2 In. 2000.00

IVORY from the tusk of an elephant is thought by many to be the only true
ivory. To most collectors, the term *ivory* also includes such natural materials
as walrus, hippopotamus, or whale teeth or tusks, and some of the vegetable
materials that are of similar texture and density. Other ivory items may be
found in the Scrimshaw and Netsuke categories. Collectors should be aware
of the recent laws limiting the buying and selling of elephant ivory and
scrimshaw.

Box, Figural, Duck, Stylized, 19th Century, China, 7 In. 1025.00
Box, Quail Shape, Recumbent Bird, Teak Stand, c.1800, 4 1/2 In., Pair 1540.00
Card Case, Dragon & Cloud Design, Japan, Signed, 4 1/4 x 2 1/2 In. 467.00
Carving, Figurine, Woman With Stringed Instrument, 6 1/2 In. 247.00
Casket, Jewelry, Scrolling Penwork Design, Handle On Cover, 14 In. 715.00
Column, Thermometer On Side, Compass Sundial Top, 6 3/8 In. 330.00
Cribbage Board, Eskimo Engraved, 30 In. 1430.00
Cup, Cover, Frieze Of Neptune And Tritons, Silver Mounted, 19th Century, 15 In. 5463.00
Dominoes Set, Ivory Box, Sliding Lid, 3 5/8 In. 110.00
Figurine, Bearded Sage Holding Turtle, 19th Century, 5 In. 192.00
Figurine, Chinese Emperor, Seated, Signed, Teak Stand, 7 1/2 In. 357.00
Figurine, Cupid, Marble Base, 19th Century, Germany, 10 In. 1210.00
Figurine, Deity, Seated, Oriental, 15 In. 93.00
Figurine, Eagle, Spread Wings, Wooden Stand, 23-In. Wingspan 3080.00
Figurine, Egyptian, Standing, 9 In. 220.00
Figurine, Elephant, Kuan Yin, 19th Century 1195.00
Figurine, Emperor & Empress, Seated, Wooden Stand, China, 9 1/2 In., Pair 990.00
Figurine, Female Acrobat Bent Backwards, Whale, 19th Century, 2 1/4 In. 2035.00
Figurine, Fukurokuju, Teak Stand, Signed, 12 In. 302.00
Figurine, Gazelle, Leaping, With Hanger, 4 1/2 In. 60.00
Figurine, Japanese Fisherman Feeding Pelican, 19th Century, 6 In. 440.00
Figurine, Japanese Peddler, Carrying Wares, 9 1/2 In. 495.00
Figurine, Kneeling Nude, Green Marble Vase, Late 19th Century, 12 In. 4600.00
Figurine, Lady With Broom & Rooster, Carved, Signed, Teak Stand, 8 In. 192.00
Figurine, Madonna, With Rosary, 5 1/2 In. 195.00
Figurine, Okimono, Fisherman, Basket Of Mollusks, 19th Century, 10 In., Pair 715.00
Figurine, Open Hand, 19th Century, 1 In. 137.00
Figurine, Rabbit, Eskimo, Walrus Ivory, 19th Century 495.00
Figurine, Ryugu, Holding Sword, Dragon Looking Up, 11 1/4 In. 195.00
Figurine, Sage Holding Peach & Staff, 19th Century, 5 1/2 In. 330.00
Figurine, Woman, Bird & Flowering Branch, With Stand, Oriental, 9 In. 258.00
Group, Fishermen, Oriental, 6 In. 300.00
Group, Man & Lady Carrying Baby On Her Back, Signed, 6 In. 330.00
Holder, Cigarette, Solid Gold Ferrule, 5 1/2 In. 40.00
Holder, Oriental Figural, Holding Crystal Ball, 7 In. 160.00

Incense Burner, Phoenix Figures, 19th Century, Pair	935.00
Inkwell & Sander, Red & Black Lines, 19th Century	770.00
Letter Opener, 3-Layer Handle, Mother-Of-Pearl Inserts	125.00
Manicure Set, Velvet, Satin, Leatherette Case, France, 15 Piece	55.00
Miniature, Gentleman, Mid-19th Century, Frame, 4 1/2 x 3 1/2 In.	550.00
Mirror, Hand, Gold Ormolu, Large Hand-Painted Woman Portrait	265.00
Mirror, Pocket, Scissor Action, Young Woman Painted On Ivory, 3 1/2 In.	120.00
Picture Frame, Inlaid Abalone, Baleen-Wrapped Oval Cutout, 5 1/4 x 3 1/2 In.	880.00
Pipe, Tamper, Handle, Brass Base, 2 3/8 In.	70.00
Pipe, Tamper, Lady's Leg, High-Heeled Shoe, Early 1800s	125.00
Pipe, Tamper, Wooden, 1810s, 2 7/8 In.	75.00
Plaque, Hand-Painted Woman, Ebonized Frame, Artist Signed, Pair	345.00
Puzzle Ball, Pierced & Dragon Carved, 11 In., Pair	358.00
Saber, Carved, Silver Filigree Inlay, c.1900, 2 In. x 2 Ft.	950.00
Scale, Whalebone, Copper Pans, Weights, Wooden Stand, c.1850, 15 1/2 In.	1540.00
Scene, Oriental Interior	550.00
Swift, Barrel-Shaped Clamp, Whalebone Ribs, 19 1/4 In.	3300.00
Sword, Carved Samurai Scenes, Japan, 19th Century, 20 In.	247.00
Tusk, Gods, Climbing Among Foliage, 19th Century, India, 9 1/4 In.	165.00
Vase, Bottle, Women's Heads, 9 In.	95.00
Vase, Double Gourd, Carved, China, Qianlong Mark, 19th Century, 11 In., Pair.	660.00

JACK ARMSTRONG, the all-American boy, was the hero of a radio serial from 1933 to 1951. Premiums were offered to the listeners until the mid-1940s. Jack Armstrong's best-known endorsement is for Wheaties.

Game, Football, Big Ten, Mailer	49.00
Secret Bomb Sight, 1942, 2 1/2 x 3 1/2 x 1 In.	325.00
Telescope, Explorer, 1937	65.00

JACK-IN-THE-PULPIT vases, oddly shaped like trumpets, resemble the wild plant called jack-in-the-pulpit. The design originated in the late Victorian years. Vases in the jack-in-the-pulpit shape were made of ceramic or glass and the complete list of page references can be found in the index.

Vase, Burmese, Lemon, Pink Blush Interior, Mt. Washington, 7 1/4 In.	345.00
Vase, Burmese, Pink To Yellow Floriform, 9 1/4 In.	440.00
Vase, Cranberry & White Spangled Top, Vaseline, 9 In.	125.00
Vase, Pink Petals, Thorn Handles, Green	250.00
Vase, Pink To Crystal Petals, Twig Handle	350.00
Vase, Scattered Florals, Raised Gold Outlining, 9 1/2 In.	485.00
Vase, White Satin Glass, Shaded Cranberry, 7 In., Pair	250.00

JACKFIELD ware was originally a black glazed pottery made in Jackfield, England, from 1750 to 1775. A yellow glazed ware has also been called Jackfield ware. Most of the pieces referred to as *Jackfield* today are black-glazed, red-clay wares made at the Jackfield Pottery in Shropshire, England, in Victorian times.

Creamer, Cow	295.00
Creamer, Cow, Black, Gold Accents	195.00
Figurine, Spaniel, 13 In.	375.00
Inkwell, Floral Baroque Form, 3 3/4 In.	250.00

JADE is the name for two different minerals, nephrite and jadeite. Nephrite is the mineral used for most early Oriental carvings. Jade is a very tough stone that is found in many colors from dark green to pale lavender. Jade carvings are still being made in the old styles, so collectors must be careful not to be fooled by recent pieces. Jade jewelry is found in this book under Jewelry.

Bowl, Cover, Foo Dragon, Loose Ring Handles, Qianlong, 6 In.	3960.00
Bowl, On Stand, Carved, China, 7 In.	100.00
Brush Washer, Late Ming Dynasty, 3 1/2 In.	2640.00
Bunch Of Grapes, Oriental, 6 In.	16.00
Figurine, 2 Horses, Wooden Base, 4 1/2 x 6 1/2 In.	250.00
Figurine, Cat, With Kitten, Ching Dynasty, 3 In.	1540.00

♦ ♦

To remove verdegris (the green mold that forms on metal) from costume jewelry mix mayonnaise and catsup in equal amounts. Rub it on and quickly remove it. Wash. Try again and leave it longer if the first treatment didn't work. Don't use on pieces with pearls.

♦ ♦

Bracelet, Charm, Silver, Diamonds, 14K White Gold Chain, 7 In.; Bracelet, Charm, Silver, Edwardian, 18K White Gold Chain

Figurine, Finger Citron, Grayish-White, 18th Century, 4 1/2 In.	2310.00
Figurine, Foo Lion, Kangxi, Yellow, 5 In.	2640.00
Figurine, Foo Lion, Qianlong, 2 In.	1320.00
Mirror, Handle, Silver Back & Fittings, Oriental, 8 1/2 In.	72.00
Plaque, Carved Peaches & Bats, Greenish White, 19th Century, 4 3/4 In.	220.00

JASPERWARE can be made in different ways. Some pieces are made from a solid colored clay with applied raised designs of a contrasting colored clay. Other pieces are made entirely of one color clay with raised decorations that are glazed with a contrasting color. Additional pieces of jasperware may also be listed in the Wedgwood category or under various art potteries.

Cheese Dish, Cover, Blue & White, 19th Century	2450.00
Hair Receiver, Dark Blue, Horse & Hunt Design, Adams	50.00
Plaque, Beethoven, Green, White, Germany, 5 x 6 In.	75.00
Plaque, Cupid, Holds Broken Bow, Green & White, German, 5 3/8 In.	65.00
Plaque, Indian Bust, Crucifix In Headdress, Green, 6 1/2 x 5 In.	135.00
Plaque, Lohengrin & Elaine, Flower Border, Blue & White, 5 7/8 In.	85.00
Plaque, Richard Wagner, Green, White, Germany, 5 x 6 In.	75.00

JEWELRY, whether made from gold and precious gems or plastic and colored glass, is popular with collectors. Values are determined by the intrinsic value of the stones and metal and by the skill of the craftsmen and designers. Victorian and older jewelry has been collected since the 1950s. More recent interests are Art Deco and Edwardian styles, Mexican and Danish silver jewelry, and beads of all kinds. Copies of almost all styles are being made. Indian jewelry is listed in the Indian category.

Box, Pill, Diamond Ruby & Sapphire On Lid, 14K Gold	285.00
Bracelet, 2 Strands Pink Enamel Beads, Evans	35.00
Bracelet, 3 Green Onyx Rings, 3 Black Onyx Sugar Loaves, 14K Yellow Gold	1092.00
Bracelet, 3 Strands Of Pearls, Diamond Bar Spacers, Gold Clasp	2420.00
Bracelet, 6 Oval Carved Jade Disks, Flexible, Gold	2070.00
Bracelet, Bakelite Cone Beads, Black, Orange, Caramel, Brown, Strung On Elastic	27.00
Bracelet, Bakelite, Red, Expansion	30.00
Bracelet, Bakelite, Rope Design, Persimmon Orange	18.00
Bracelet, Bangle, Bakelite, Dark Caramel, Carved Stylized Leaf Flowers, 1/2 In.	27.00
Bracelet, Bangle, Center Mine Diamonds, Rose-Cut Diamonds, 14K Yellow Gold	1610.00
Bracelet, Bangle, Diamond-Mounted Bow Design, 59 Diamonds, 14K Gold	517.00
Bracelet, Bangle, Diamonds & Sapphires, Hinged, Safety Chain, 14K Gold	395.00
Bracelet, Bangle, Hinged, Wire Twist Edge, Beaded Top, 15K Gold, Victorian	880.00
Bracelet, Bangle, Orange Bakelite, Floral Carving, 1 In. Wide	85.00

Bracelet, Bangle, Pave-Set Garnets, Silver Gilt Mount 357.00
Bracelet, Bangle, Poodle Charm, Cartier, 18K Gold 165.00
Bracelet, Bangle, Rectangular Onyx Plaques, 14K Pink Gold Mount, Victorian 935.00
Bracelet, Bangle, Rows Of Cultured Pearls, 22 Sapphires, 14K Gold 402.00
Bracelet, Bangle, Sterling, Baltic Amber Cabochon Plaque, Hinged, Hallmark, 1890 .. 190.00
Bracelet, Beaded V-Links, Polished Edges, 18K Gold, 7 1/2 In. 1320.00
Bracelet, Bright Orange, Bakelite, 1920s, 1 1/2 In. 9.00
Bracelet, Charm, 18 Venezuelan Coins & Charms, 12K Gold 412.00
Bracelet, Charm, Silver, Diamonds, 14K White Gold Chain, 7 In. .... *Illus* 1870.00
Bracelet, Charm, Silver, Edwardian, 18K White Gold Chain .... *Illus* 3575.00
Bracelet, Child's, Bangle, Gold Filled, 1940s 65.00
Bracelet, Cuff, 6 Diamonds, Sapphire Charms, 14K Yellow Gold, 1940s 4750.00
Bracelet, Cuff, Black Beads, Lesage 100.00
Bracelet, Damascene, Hinged Panels, Silver & Gold, Etched Back 125.00
Bracelet, Edwardian, Flexible Double Row Diamond Band, Emeralds, Platinum 6325.00
Bracelet, Engraved, 14K Gold 275.00
Bracelet, Filigree, Center Diamond, 4 Emeralds, 14K White Gold, c.1920 .... 285.00
Bracelet, Flexible Band, Center Marquise Cut Diamonds, Platinum 7187.00
Bracelet, Floral Engraved Oval Discs, Flexible, Hinged, 22K Gold 575.00
Bracelet, Gold Mesh Center, Twisted Rope, Gold Beads, 14K Gold 550.00
Bracelet, Hard Stone Cameo, Man's Profile, Woven Wire Twist Frame, 15K Gold 1320.00
Bracelet, Hinged, 37 Turquoise Beads, 18K 375.00
Bracelet, Jade, Yellow & Russet, 3 1/2 In. 275.00
Bracelet, Link, 5 Diamonds, 6 Emeralds, 14K Gold 650.00
Bracelet, Link, Aventurine Quartz, 14K Yellow Gold, Seaman Schepps 1150.00
Bracelet, Link, Flexible Band, 18K Yellow Gold 977.00
Bracelet, Link, Flexible Honeycomb, Diamond Buckle, 18K Gold 1650.00
Bracelet, Link, Fluted & Triangular, 14K Gold, 1940s 1540.00
Bracelet, Link, Gold Double Leaf, Textured, Trifari 10.00
Bracelet, Link, Gold, Set In Rose Stones, Chain Guard, Freirich 14.00
Bracelet, Link, Harlequin-Shaped, Chased & Polished, 18K Gold, Italy, 7 1/4 In. 1100.00
Bracelet, Link, Interlocking Curb, 14K Gold, Italy, 8 1/2 In. 385.00
Bracelet, Link, Reeded Pierce, 18K Pink Gold 550.00
Bracelet, Link, S Shaped, Round Diamonds, Platinum, France 9350.00
Bracelet, Link, Scarab, 6 Different Stones, 14K Gold 295.00
Bracelet, Link, Textured & Smooth Square, 14K Gold, Victorian, 7 In. 385.00
Bracelet, Ornate, Mazer 85.00
Bracelet, Panther, Enamel, Emerald Eyes, Diamonds, Onyx, 18K Gold, France 2750.00
Bracelet, Pearl, Rhinestone & Sterling Silver, Da Rosa 175.00
Bracelet, Pearl, Single Strand, Butterfly Clasp, 1 Dangling Pearl, Haskell 75.00
Bracelet, Pearls, Diamonds, 3 Strands, Platinum & Diamond Clasp, 7 1/4 In. 2000.00
Bracelet, Pin & Earrings, Orientals In Garden, German Silver, 3 Piece 150.00
Bracelet, Red Rhinestones, Hattie Carnegie 65.00
Bracelet, Rhinestone, Aurora Borealis, Weiss 40.00
Bracelet, Rhinestone, Bakelite 45.00
Bracelet, Rhinestone, Weiss, 3/4 In. 25.00
Bracelet, Slide, Cameo, Enamel Slide, Large Precious Stones, 14K Gold 850.00
Bracelet, Slide, Rubies, Garnets, Sapphires, 12 Slides 850.00
Bracelet, Slide, Victorian Style, 14K Gold 850.00
Bracelet, Slide, White Gold, Diamonds, 14K, Tiffany & Co. 1980.00
Bracelet, Slide, Woman, Surround Of Rubies & Diamonds, 14K Gold 1650.00
Bracelet, Snake, Abstract, French-Link Chain, 18K Gold 770.00
Bracelet, Snake, Coiled, Emerald Eyes, 18K Gold, Pair 2750.00
Bracelet, Woven Design, 14K Yellow Gold 747.00
Bracelet & Earrings, English Half-Sovereigns, 1902 .... 1500.00
Bracelet & Earrings, Hinged Panels, Dancing Orientals, Siam, Sterling Silver 50.00
Buckle, Belt, Elk Antler Rosette, Silver Inlaid, Turquoise, Hawaiian, 3 In. 295.00
Buckle, Belt, Jacques Seeds, Advertising 15.00
Buckle, Belt, Woman's, Butterfly Shape, Silver, Beaded 2.00
Buckle, Blue Enameling, Gilded Silver, England, 2 1/4 In. 27.50
Buckle, Ivory Celluloid, Curved, Rectangular, Musi 3.00
Buckle, Lamb Form, Silver, Copper & Garnet, Ed Wiener, c.950, 2 1/4 In. 460.00
Buckle, Metal, Bronze Color, Concentric Beaded, Rectangular, 2 3/8 x 1 7/8 In. 4.00

Jewelry, Pin, Cameo, Mythological
Scene, 18K Gold Frame

Jewelry, Cuff Links, Onyx, Warrior's
Profile, 15K Yellow Gold

Buckle, Rhinestone, 2 x 2 In. 25.00
Buckle, Square, Diamond, 1950s, Pair 25.00
Buckle, Victorian, Lace Gold Over Brass, Amethyst Colored Stones 48.00
Buckle, Woman's, Chinese Imperial Dragon, Sterling Silver, 2 Piece 200.00
Chain, Curb Link, Alternating With Letter, Tiffany, 18K Gold, 26 In. 330.00
Chain, Paper Clip, Citrine Cabochons, Floral Mounts, Arts & Crafts, Silver, 44 In. 3300.00
Chain, Paper Clip, Dyed Green Onyx Cabochons, Arts & Crafts, Silver, 50 In. 605.00
Chain, Rope, 14K Yellow Gold, 34 In. 747.00
Chain, Slide, Victorian, 2 Opal Sides, Etruscan Work, 26 In. 200.00
Chain, Textured & Polished Links, 14K Gold, 65 In. 385.00
Chatelaine, Art Nouveau Animal Design, Gold Plated, 3 1/2 In. 66.00
Chatelaine, Mesh, Sterling Silver 350.00
Choker, Faux Pearl & Crystal Beads, Rhinestone Medallion, Miriam Haskell 55.00
Cigarette Holder, 14K Gold Bands, Amber, Case 65.00
Clip, Clear Rhinestones, Eisenberg 50.00
Clip, Dress, Bakelite, Grapes 45.00
Clip, Fur, Clear Stone Floral, Gold, Eisenberg 225.00
Clip, Fur, Crown, Moonstones & Rhinestones, Trifari 200.00
Clip, Fur, Earrings, Sterling Silver, Floral, Red Cabochons, Trifari 125.00
Clip, Fur, Faux Rubies & Diamonds, Turquoise, Trifari, 1 11/16 In. 125.00
Clip, Fur, Lavender Stones, Leaf Shape, Boucher 65.00
Clip, Fur, Moonstone & Enamel, Trifari 85.00
Clip, Fur, Sterling Silver, Gold Wash, Colored Stones, Eisenberg 450.00
Clip, Fur, Sterling Silver, Pair 250.00
Clip, Glove, Textured Leaf, Chain, Trifari 4.00
Clip, Rhinestone Lily, Enameled, Trifari, 2 1/2 In. 20.00
Clip, Shield Shape, Box, Eisenberg, 2 /3 x 2 1/2 In. 230.00
Clip, Shield Shape, Varied Rhinestones, Eisenberg, 1940s 150.00
Comb, Art Nouveau, Faux Tortoiseshell, Gold-Plated Band, Blue Glass Stone, 4 In. .. 22.00
Comb, Faux Tortoiseshell, Ormolu Rose, Seed Pearls, Horseshoe Shape, 4 In., Pair ... 22.00
Comb, Faux Tortoiseshell, Painted Floral, Rhinestones, 4 1/2 In. 30.00
Comb, Faux Tortoiseshell, Scalloped, Gilt, Rhinestone Band, 4 1/2 In. 44.00
Comb, Oval Shell Cabochon, Abalone, Sterling Silver, Sam Kramer, 1950 .... 1035.00
Cross, Rose-Cut Diamonds, Pearl Centers, Oval Link Chain, 18K Gold, 22 In. 880.00
Crucifix, Gold Plated, Design, 7 In. 125.00
Cuff Links, 14K Gold, Row Of Sapphires, 1940 .... 295.00
Cuff Links, Diamonds, Coral Bead Terminals, Ribbed Barrel Bar Link, 14K Gold 990.00
Cuff Links, Double Oval, Mother-Of-Pearl, Gold, Fleur-De-Lis Motif 275.00
Cuff Links, Dumbbells, Malachite Bead Terminals, Gold Bars 460.00
Cuff Links, Gold Coin, Form Of 2 1/2 Mexican Pesos 185.00
Cuff Links, Head Of Egyptian & Nordic, Lalique, 1920s, 1/2 In. 2875.00

Cuff Links, Onyx, Warrior's Profile, 15K Yellow Gold .... *Illus*   605.00
Cuff Links, Open Reeded Top, Shaped Concave Back, 18K Gold, Egypt 220.00
Cuff Links, Reverse Painted, Horses, 14K Gold Mounts, Diana 440.00
Cuff Links, Sapphire & Diamond Centers, Platinum 495.00
Cuff Links, Sterling Silver, 1/2 In. Squares, Design, Taxco 10.00
Cuff Links, Sterling Silver, Gold Washed, Pearl 7.00
Cuff Links, Tourmaline, Sapphires, 18K Yellow & White Gold, Buccelletti 2750.00
Cuff Links, White Textured Oval Plaque, Mine-Cut Diamond, 14K Gold Backs 165.00
Earrings, 19 mm. Textured Ball, Screw Backs, 14K Gold 110.00
Earrings, Aurora Borealis, Kidney-Bean Shape, Clip-On, 1 1/4 In. 18.00
Earrings, Blue Button, Art Deco, Gold, 3-Tiered Circle, Monet 9.00
Earrings, Carved Flower, Pearl Center, 14K Gold Mount 247.50
Earrings, Center Diamond, Round & Baguette Diamond Surround, 14K Gold 1870.00
Earrings, Circle & Rectangle Mobiles, Silver, Ed Wiener, c.1955 ....   575.00
Earrings, Clip, Blue Rhinestone, Weiss 20.00
Earrings, Clip, Gold Leaf, Trifari 8.00
Earrings, Clip, Marcasite Flower, Weiss 37.00
Earrings, Clip, Marcasite, Sterling Silver, Stylized Free-Form Fans 48.00
Earrings, Clip, Rosebud, Gold Tone, Trifari 18.00
Earrings, Clusters Of Rose-Cut Diamonds, 14K Gold Disc, Chased Border 440.00
Earrings, Dangling Lanterns, Rose Gold, 1 1/2 In. 245.00
Earrings, Diamonds Around Center Sapphire, Screw Backs 2530.00
Earrings, Diamonds, Cultured Pearls, 18K White Gold Mount 1540.00
Earrings, Double Loop, Clustered Rays Of Diamonds, 14K Gold 3450.00
Earrings, Dragon Heads, Diamond Collars Of White Gold, 18K Gold 920.00
Earrings, Flat Discs, Reeded Edges, Screw Backs, 14K Gold, c.1950 ....   110.00
Earrings, Flower-Head Style, Round Diamond, Yellow Gold 2990.00
Earrings, Fluted Half-Hoop, Row Of Diamonds, 18K Gold, Chaumet 990.00
Earrings, Garnet Cabochons, Sterling Silver, Ed Wiener, c.1955 ....   460.00
Earrings, Gold Circle, Cascading Tassels, Ruby Bead Terminals, 14K Gold 1650.00
Earrings, Heart, Bands Of Small Diamonds, 18K Yellow Gold 545.00
Earrings, Hoop, Diamonds Encased In Lucite, 18K Gold, France 1760.00
Earrings, Hoop, Polka Dot, Brown & Yellow, Bakelite 95.00
Earrings, Horn Shape, Taxco 55.00
Earrings, Jadeite, Pear Shapes, Sterling Silver Mounts 330.00
Earrings, Love Knots, Rosettes Of 36 Rubies, 6 Small Diamonds, 18K Gold 1610.00
Earrings, Mabe Pearl, Diamonds, 14K Gold 605.00
Earrings, Mabe Pearl, Twisted 18K Gold Frame, Tiffany & Co. 1100.00
Earrings, Moonstone, Sterling Silver, Georg Jensen 105.00
Earrings, 3 Moonstones, Sterling Silver, Georg Jensen 145.00
Earrings, Onyx Discs, Diamond Centers, Platinum, 18K Gold Backs 522.00
Earrings, Onyx, Cameo, Pearls, Diana Heads, 14K, 1860s 550.00
Earrings, Opalescent Blue, Bravia 25.00
Earrings, Oval Green Quartz Cabochon, 14K Yellow Gold 230.00
Earrings, Pearl, Enamel, Floral Design, 14K Yellow Gold 55.00
Earrings, Red Stone, Wing Back, Marvella 15.00
Earrings, Reeded Pinwheels, Sapphire & Diamond Centers, 18K Gold, c.1950 ....   990.00
Earrings, Reeded Stylized Ovals, Emeralds, 14K Gold, c.1950 ....   935.00
Earrings, Repousse Hoop, Large, 14K Yellow Gold 90.00
Earrings, Rhinestone, Weiss 30.00
Earrings, Roman Coin, Cabochon Amethyst, Ruby Terminals, 18K Gold, Bulgari 2860.00
Earrings, Textured Elephants, Ruby Eyes, Ruser, 14K Gold 247.00
Earrings, Turquoise & Silver, Screw Back, c.1930 ....   85.00
Earrings, Turquoise Heart, Textured Gold, Pearl & Rhinestone, Hattie Carnegie 14.00
Earrings, Victorian, Black Enamel, Floral, 14K Gold 275.00
Earrings, Yellow Sapphires, 18K Gold Beads, Sabbidini, Milano 2090.00
Enhancer, Amethyst, Oval, 14K Gold Frame 220.00
Hair Clip, Large Smoky Rhinestones, 1960s 70.00
Hair Pin, Onyx, Rose-Cut Diamonds, Platinum, Yellow Gold, B.B. & B., Art Deco ...   990.00
Hatpins are listed in this book in the Hatpin category
Lavaliere, 3 Yellow-Brown Diamonds, 3.6 Cts. Total Wt., Platinum Chain 4675.00
Lavaliere, Diamond Drop, Platinum Chain, 17 In. 1320.00

Lavaliere, Victorian, Cupid, 2 Hanging Garnets 225.00
Locket, Hinged Heart, Diamond Leaf, c.1920 .... 150.00
Locket, Horseshoe, Textured Hoof, 5-Leaf Clover, 15K Gold, Victorian, Pierret 1320.00
Locket, Interwoven Horseshoes, Half-Pearls & Pink Coral, 15K Gold 488.00
Locket, Oval, Engraved, 14K Gold Chain, Victorian, 34 In. 165.00
Locket, Porcelain, Putti Within Mount, 14K Gold Rope Chain 357.00
Locket, Turquoise Within Wire Twist & Bead Frame, Gold Chain 385.00
Necklace, Amber, Inclusions, Large Cubes, 31 In. 150.00
Necklace, Amethyst Nuggets, Silver Links, 38 In. 24.00
Necklace, Amethyst, Agate, Aquamarine, Cat's-Eye, 18K Gold Cable Link, France ... 2200.00
Necklace, Aurora, Double Strand, 14 In. 13.00
Necklace, Basket Weave, Chain Tassel Pendant, Gold Link Chain, Monet, 20 In. 12.00
Necklace, Beads, 5.5-Mm., 14K Gold, 14 1/2 In. 1210.00
Necklace, Beads, Persian Turquoise, Carved Turquoise Pendant 450.00
Necklace, Bib, Oval Faux Pearls, Yellow & Lavender Rhinestones, 1950s 285.00
Necklace, Blue & Green Rhinestones, Weiss 120.00
Necklace, Book Chain, Cameo Pendant, Gold Wash Link Tassels, Victorian 125.00
Necklace, Book Chain, Cameo, Large Slide, Victorian 120.00
Necklace, Book Chain, Locket, c.1860 .... 95.00
Necklace, Boys & Girls, Flat Linked Chain, Ilya Schor, 22 3/4 In. 4180.00
Necklace, Bracelet & Earrings, Green & Clear Rhinestones, Trifari, 3 Piece 40.00
Necklace, Choker, Carved Amethyst Pendant, 14K Gold 275.00
Necklace, Choker, Center 3 Full-Cut Diamonds, 18K Gold, 14 1/2 In. 3220.00
Necklace, Choker, Glass Beads, Rhinestone & Pate-De-Verre Medallion, Gripoix 1035.00
Necklace, Choker, Pearl, Haskell 80.00
Necklace, Choker, Semi-Flexible, Polished Finish, 14K Gold 247.00
Necklace, Coral, Hand Carved, 1780 .... 2800.00
Necklace, Crystal, Faceted, Graduated, Separated By Small Beads, 14 In. 10.00
Necklace, Faceted Crystals & Rhinestones, Haskell, 35 In. 60.00
Necklace, Flexible Band, Brickwork, 14K Yellow Gold, 14 In. 400.00
Necklace, Gilded Silver, Cameo, Victorian 82.00
Necklace, Gold & Pearl, 16 Strands, Kramer 35.00
Necklace, Gold Textured Links, 1 1/8 In., Blue Rhinestones, Coro, 14 In. 14.00
Necklace, Green Crystal & Crystallite, Miriam Haskell 155.00
Necklace, Green, Red & Blue Pate De Verre, Gripoix, 1960s 2070.00
Necklace, Ivory Beads, Screw Closure, 15 In. 15.00
Necklace, Jade Beads, Graduating, 14K Gold Clasp, 19 3/4 In. 1150.00
Necklace, Knot, Etched Interlocking Circles, Hinged Bangle, 14K Pink Gold 330.00
Necklace, Links, Suspended Citrine Flower, 14K Gold, W.A.B. Wordley, 16 In. 275.00
Necklace, Mesh, Winding Snake 25.00
Necklace, Micro Mosaic, Venetian Glass, Hand-Set In Italy, 1900 .... 365.00
Necklace, Mother-Of-Pearl Beads, 24 In. 10.00
Necklace, Mother-Of-Pearl Dyed Sea Green Nuggets, 4 Strands, 17 In. 7.00
Necklace, Opal Beads, Faceted Crystal Rondels, 36 In. 715.00
Necklace, Oval Cherry Amber, Venetian Glass Beads 185.00
Necklace, Pearl, Cultured, 14K White Gold Filigree Clasp 605.00
Necklace, Pearl, Cultured, Graduated, Diamond Clasp, 20 In. 6000.00
Necklace, Pearl, Cultured, 4 Strands, Box Clasp, 14K Yellow Gold 6500.00
Necklace, Pearl, Cultured, 58 Graduated, Pearl Clasp, 21 In. 3850.00
Necklace, Pearl, Cultured, Double Strand, 14K White Gold Clasp, 18 In. 715.00
Necklace, Pearl, Cultured, Graduated, Diamond Clasp, 21 In. 690.00
Necklace, Pearl, Cultured, Graduated, Double Strand, Gold Clasp, 18 In. 925.00
Necklace, Pearl, Freshwater, Alternating Diamonds, Gold & Platinum, 28 In. 6050.00
Necklace, Pearlized Yellow Glass Pendant, White Metal, Czechoslovakia 50.00
Necklace, Rhinestone, Triple Swag & Drops, 6 1/2 x 16 1/2 In. 16.00
Necklace, Roman Coin, Double Oval Links, 18K White Gold, Italy 1320.00
Necklace, Rose Melon Beads & Rhinestones 1840.00
Necklace, Silver Links, Turquoise Beads, Ceramic Beetle, Ed Wiener, 1950 .... 575.00
Necklace, Snake, Cabochon Garnet, Chased 15K Gold Mount, Victorian 1980.00
Necklace, Tassel, Enameled, Seed Pearls, 15K Gold, Victorian 1000.00
Necklace, White & Pink Freshwater Pearls, Diamond Bezel 1650.00
Necklace, White Nephrite Jade Medallion, Grape Tassels, F.G. Hale, 41 In. 7150.00

*Jewelry, Pin, Cameo, Pendant,
Virgin Mary, Agate, 36 Pearls*

◆◆◆◆◆◆◆◆◆◆◆◆◆◆◆◆◆◆◆◆◆◆

Never soak rhinestone jewelry in
water. The moisture seeps behind the stones and will cause
discoloration.

◆◆◆◆◆◆◆◆◆◆◆◆◆◆◆◆◆◆◆◆◆◆

Necklace, White Plastic Braided Links, Separated By Gold Discs, Trifari 12.00
Necklace, Woven, Bead & Wire Twist, 18K Gold, Etruscan Revival, J. Brogden 7150.00
Necklace, X & O Design, Florentine Finish, 14K Gold, 16 In. 302.00
Necklace & Bracelet, Child's, Lord's Prayer Engraved, 18K Gold Plate, 1940s 25.00
Necklace & Bracelet, Pearls, Red Crystal Beads, Rhinestones, Trifari 165.00
Necklace & Earrings, Stones, Freshwater Pearls, Woven Goldtone, Boucher 115.00
Pendant, Abalone Shell, Sterling Silver Mount, Arts & Crafts, Kalo, 15 In. 715.00
Pendant, Abstract, Sterling Silver, c.1950, Georg Jensen, No. 342 .... 192.00
Pendant, Amethyst, Carved Warrior Intaglio, Diamonds, 14K Gold, J.E. Caldwell 1100.00
Pendant, Anchor Form, Diamond, Gold, 14K 125.00
Pendant, Baroque Pearl, Abstract Shape, Diamond Cap, Silver Count 715.00
Pendant, Dragonfly Amid Leaves, Frosted Blue Drop, Bronze 45.00
Pendant, Dragonfly, Bronze Filigree Wings, Jewels At Bottom, 6 1/2 x 10 In. 3000.00
Pendant, Dragonfly, Outstretched Wings, Bronze Openwork, 10 In. 2070.00
Pendant, Enamel, Opal, Diamonds, Paper-Clip Chain, Arts & Crafts, 20 In. 2860.00
Pendant, Filigree, Six Round Cut Sapphires, 14K Gold 154.00
Pendant, Floral Frame18K Gold, 3 Aquamarines, Citrine, F.G. Hale, 23 In. 2970.00
Pendant, Flower, Pink & Green Enamel, C. & A. Giuliano, c.1886, Leather Box 1210.00
Pendant, Flower, Seed Pearls, Cabochon Garnets, Sterling Silver 715.00
Pendant, Heart, Diamond Border, 1 Ct. Total Weight, 14K White Gold Chain 495.00
Pendant, Indian Child, Leather Thong Necklace, De Grazia 27.00
Pendant, Jade, Carved, Pierced, Diamonds, Platinum & Gold, Allsopp & Allsopp 1210.00
Pendant, Jade, Seed Pearl Necklace, 18 In. 1320.00
Pendant, Lady Liberty Coin, Gold Holder, 1881 .... 105.00
Pendant, Lion Form, Diamond, Ruby & Emerald, 14K Yellow Gold 1087.00
Pendant, Lion, Jeweled Frame, Diamonds, Rubies, Pearls, 18K Gold, c.1950 .... 550.00
Pendant, Moonstone, Sterling Silver, Ed Wiener, 1955, 1 1/4 In. 173.00
Pendant, Opal, Filigree, Black & White Enamel, Diamond, Giuliano, 18K Gold 550.00
Pendant, Opal, Heart Shape, Round Diamonds, 18K Gold Mount, 14K Gold Chain .. 715.00
Pendant, Pencil, Lapis Bead Dividers, Pharaoh Form Pencil, Chain, 36 In. 1100.00
Pendant, Pink Tourmaline Cameo, Pharaoh, 14K Gold Frame, Egyptian Revival 1760.00
Pendant, Platinum, Emerald & Diamond 3960.00
Pendant, Sapphire In Floral & Leaf Design, Georg Jensen, 18K Gold 660.00
Pendant, Teardrop Form, 2 Diamonds, Link Chain, Platinum 8912.00
Pendant, Twenty Dollar Piece, U.S., 1895, 12 Cut Rubies, 14K Gold 650.00
Pendant, Yellow Sapphire, Diamond Border, Ribbon Bow, c.1900, 1 In. 3565.00
Pin, 3 Swallows, Silver, Diamonds, 18K Gold Branch 990.00
Pin, 5 Cabochon Stones, Gold Over Sterling, 14K Gold 125.00
Pin, 8 Spheres, Curled Edges, Jean Despres, 2 3/4 In. 1200.00
Pin, Abstract Design, Enamel, Opals, Silver, Arts & Crafts, T. Fahrner 632.00
Pin, Abstracted Eye Center, Sam Kramer, c.1950, 3 In. 2185.00
Pin, Amber, Bird & Flowers, Silver Mounting, Enameled, 2 1/4 x 2 3/4 In. 185.00
Pin, American Women's Voluntary Services, Bronze Eagle, Enamel 10.00
Pin, Amethystine, Radiating Scrolls, Sterling, Reticulated, Kalo Shop, 1 1/4 In. 605.00
Pin, Angelfish, Pave Diamond Head, Tail & Fins, Enamel, 18K Gold 1650.00
Pin, Bar, 19 Diamonds, Pearl Terminals, Platinum Mount, Cartier 3850.00

Pin, Bar, 6 Cherries, Bakelite 185.00
Pin, Bar, Carved Jade Angelfish, 14K Gold 495.00
Pin, Bar, Diamond, Curved, 14K White & Yellow Gold 1265.00
Pin, Bar, Diamonds, Seed Pearls, Openwork Mount 357.00
Pin, Bar, Four 6.5 mm. Pearls, Cultured, 18K Gold, Italy 275.00
Pin, Bar, Rubies, Pearls, Diamonds, 14K Gold Mount 522.00
Pin, Bar, Sapphires In Openwork Diamond Set Foliate Mount, 14K Gold 687.00
Pin, Bird, Blue & Green Enamel, Diamonds, 18K Textured Gold, Italy 2420.00
Pin, Bird, Lapis, Green Stone Eye, 18K Gold, France 880.00
Pin, Bird, Textured 18K Gold Body, Polychrome Enamel Head, Wings, Tail, France .. 247.00
Pin, Black & White Ceramic Cameo, Sterling Silver, Box, 1 3/4 In. 33.00
Pin, Blooming Bluebells, Gold Branch, Lapis Flowers, Diamond Pistils, Gold 430.00
Pin, Bouquet Of Blooming Quartz Peonies, Nephrite Leaves, Diamond Pistil 805.00
Pin, Bow, 18K Gold Nugget, Dawson, Mendham 440.00
Pin, Bow, Diamond & Platinum, European-Cut Diamonds, Edwardian 4400.00
Pin, Bow, Diamonds & Rubies, 14K Bicolor Gold, Eckfeldt & Ackley, c.1940 .... 415.00
Pin, Bow, Fan Shape, Foliate Center, 14K Bicolor Gold, Mossalone 302.50
Pin, Bow, Tiffany, 14K Gold 350.00
Pin, Broken Circle, Entwined Gold On Half, Gunmetal Gray, Monet, 1 1/2 In. 10.00
Pin, Bunny, Ruby, Sapphire & Enamel, 18K Yellow Gold, 2 3/4 In. 825.00
Pin, Butterfly, Acid Finish, Diamonds, Ruby Body, HAN No. 5989, 14K Gold 1540.00
Pin, Butterfly, Azurmalachite Wings, 14K Gold Body, Macefield 385.00
Pin, Butterfly, B. David, Box 20.00
Pin, Butterfly, Enameled, Silver, Margot De Taxco, 2 In. 275.00
Pin, Butterfly, Gold Wash, Faux Emerald, Blue Topaz & Diamonds, Trifari, 2 1/4 In. .. 95.00
Pin, Butterfly, Ruby & Sapphire Wings, Diamond & Pearl Body 1650.00
Pin, Butterfly, Sterling Silver, Enameled, Filigree 25.00
Pin, Butterfly, Tourmaline, Diamonds, Rubies, 14K Gold, 1940, Lester & Co. 825.00
Pin, Cactus, Prickly Gold Body, 45 Single-Cut Diamonds, 14K Gold 805.00
Pin, Cameo, 4 Layers Of Stone, 14K White Gold With Seed Pearls, c.1890 .... 1450.00
Pin, Cameo, Agate, Horses & Chariot, 14K Gold Filigree Mount 350.00
Pin, Cameo, Hard Stone Agate, Mine-Cut Diamonds, Shell Accents, 14K Gold 3300.00
Pin, Cameo, Hard Stone, Pendant, Woman's Profile, 14K Gold, Mount, Victorian 935.00
Pin, Cameo, Lava, Angel, Cherubs, 15K Beaded Frame 330.00
Pin, Cameo, Mythological Scene, 18K Gold Frame .... *Illus* 545.00
Pin, Cameo, Onyx, Zeus Head, 14K, 1880s 275.00
Pin, Cameo, Pendant, Virgin Mary, Agate, 36 Pearls .... *Illus* 2530.00
Pin, Cameo, Rebecca At The Well, Gold-Filled Mount 135.00
Pin, Cameo, Shell, 24K Gold Rope-Turned Frame 275.00
Pin, Cameo, Shell, Drop Earring, Flowers On Shoulder, c.1900, 1 1/2 In. 160.00
Pin, Cameo, Shell, Scene, 18K Gold, Etruscan Revival, C. Giuliano, Box 7700.00
Pin, Cameo, Shell, Woman With Dove, Turquoise, 15K Gold Frame, Victorian 660.00
Pin, Cameo, Shell, Woman's Head, Seed Pearls Around, 14K Gold Back 500.00
Pin, Cameo, Shell, Woman, With Tree Scene, Oval 250.00
Pin, Carved Jadeite Plaque, Wire Scrollwork Frame, J. Kohn 600.00
Pin, Caterpillar, Gold Ribs & Head, Nephrite, 14K Yellow Gold 375.00
Pin, Center Set Blue Chalcedony Cabochon, 2 Half-Pearls, 14K Gold 415.00
Pin, Chatelaine Bow, Double Row Of Seed Pearls, Edwardian, 14K Gold 550.00
Pin, Cherubs, Diamond Frame, Enamel Flowers, Maison Louis Aucoc, c.1899 .... 6325.00
Pin, Christmas Tree, DeNicola 35.00
Pin, Christmas Tree, Ice, Eisenberg 65.00
Pin, Chrysoberyl & Ruby, Fish Design, 18K Yellow Gold, Tiffany 5230.00
Pin, Circle, 2 Rams Kissing, Sterling Silver 30.00
Pin, Circle, Bow, Onyx, Diamonds, 2.25 Cts. Total Wt., Platinum, Art Deco 2860.00
Pin, Circle, Diamonds, Emeralds, 18K White Gold Mount 2530.00
Pin, Circle, Diamonds, Pearls, Rubies, 14K White Gold, Fisher & Co. 1045.00
Pin, Citrine, Oval, Cherubs, Diamonds, 14K Gold Ribbon Mount, Art Nouveau 1980.00
Pin, Citrine, Rose-Cut Diamonds, 14K Gold Geometric Mount 275.00
Pin, Clover, Heart-Shaped Amethysts, Diamonds, 14K White Gold 1210.00
Pin, Commemorative, Round Rubies, 32 Diamonds, Platinum & Gold 6325.00
Pin, Coral Cameo, Woman's Profile, Floral Border, 14K Gold, Arts & Crafts 550.00
Pin, Crescent Hat, Silver, Rhinestones, 1920s, Large 5.00

Pin, Cross, Pearls, Rhinestones, Trifari, Large 20.00
Pin, Crown, Sterling Silver, Trifari 100.00
Pin, Crown, Trifari, Large 175.00
Pin, Cyclist, Bicycle, Movable Wheels, Coat, Tails, Top Hat, Brass, Silver, 1920s 65.00
Pin, Dog, Rose-Cut Diamond Collar, Box, 18K Yellow Gold 1650.00
Pin, Door Knocker, Coro 35.00
Pin, Doughnut Shape, Amber, Engraving, Bakelite 25.00
Pin, Dragonfly, Marcasite, Sterling Silver 125.00
Pin, Elephant, Gold Tone, Aqua Body, 2 In. 65.00
Pin, Elephant, Rhinestone, Marked, Large 20.00
Pin, Exotic Bird, Sterling Silver, Coro 30.00
Pin, Feather, 2 Layers, Eisenberg 32.00
Pin, Figures Seated At Table Under Tree, Schor 1650.00
Pin, Fish, Copper Stringing, Amethyst Eye, Ed Wiener, 1955, 2 1/2 In. 690.00
Pin, Flags Of 4 Countries, Enameled, Sterling Craft, Coro 50.00
Pin, Floral Spray, Blue Faceted Stones, Textured Gold, 2 1/4 In. 10.00
Pin, Floral, 8 Small Full-Cut Diamonds, 18K Gold 350.00
Pin, Floral, Aurora Borealis, Enamel, 3 In. 20.00
Pin, Floral, Sterling Silver, F. Davis, 2 3/4 x 3 3/4 In. 545.00
Pin, Floral, Yellow, Green & Brown Diamonds, 7.5 Cts, Total Wt., 18K Gold 5500.00
Pin, Florentined Tree Branch, 3 Birds, Ruby, Emerald & Sapphire Bodies 360.00
Pin, Flower, 11 Round Diamonds, Textured Petals, 18K Gold, Cellino 1045.00
Pin, Flower, Bow Shape, Sterling Silver, Hobe 100.00
Pin, Flower, Pink Coral Roses, 14K Gold Leaves 330.00
Pin, Flower, Rose-Cut Diamond, Engraved Leaves, Stem, 14K Bicolor Gold 550.00
Pin, Flower, Ruby, Green Gold Leaves & Stem, 14K Bicolor Gold, Tiffany & Co. 880.00
Pin, Flower, Sapphires, Rubies, Diamonds, Textured Branch & Leaves, 18K Gold 2090.00
Pin, Flower, White Enamel Petals, Pink Sapphire Center, c.1900 .... 385.00
Pin, Free Form, Baroque Pearls, Marquise Cut Diamonds, 4 Round Diamonds 355.00
Pin, Frog, Goldtone, Textured Skin, Trifari, 2 In. 22.00
Pin, Frog, Hollycraft, Enamel 30.00
Pin, Garnet, 10K Gold, Pegasus, Marked 500.00
Pin, Garnet Cluster Center, Openwork Design, 14K Yellow Gold 335.00
Pin, Gold Flower, White Petals, Trifari 5.00
Pin, Gold Looped Oval, Monet, 2 1/4 In. 9.00
Pin, Grape Design, Micro-Mosaic, Gold Case, 2 In. 160.00
Pin, Guitar, Pave-Set Diamonds, Rubies & Gold Strings, 18K Gold 1100.00
Pin, Heart Leaf & Scroll, Sterling Silver, 1 3/4 In. 10.00
Pin, Heart, Faceted, Red, Bakelite 95.00
Pin, Horse, Carved, Butterscotch, Bakelite, 3 In. 65.00
Pin, Horsehead, Bakelite 150.00
Pin, Horseshoe, 18K Gold, Brogden 1100.00
Pin, Horseshoe, Engraved Floral Decoration, Amethysts, 14K Gold 275.00
Pin, Ice Capades, Script With Ice Skates Dangling, On Original Card, 1953 .... 18.00
Pin, Jockey, Diamond Set, Silver & Enamel 660.00
Pin, King Tut, Eisenberg 50.00
Pin, Knot, Light Blue Cabochons, 18K Gold 192.50
Pin, Ladybug, Coro 20.00
Pin, Lapis Lazuli, Silver Mount, Oval, 1 1/2 In. 137.00
Pin, Leaf, Cultured Pearl Center, 14K Yellow Gold 85.00
Pin, Leaf, Rhinestone & Pearl, Coro, 1 3/4 In. 15.00
Pin, Leaf, Round Diamonds,.75 Ct. Total Wt., 18K Gold 770.00
Pin, Leaf, Textured Design, Rubies, 18K Gold, Tiffany & Co. 495.00
Pin, Lilies, Pearls, Enamel On Gold, Lalique 375.00
Pin, Moonstone, Diamond & Yellow Gold, Georges Fouquet, 3 1/4 In. 9775.00
Pin, Moonstone, Sapphires, Sterling Silver, 1910-1920 .... 325.00
Pin, Moonstone, Silver, Georg Jensen 385.00
Pin, Mourning, Geo. Washington, 14 Dec. 1799, 10K Gold Frame, Glass Cover 3250.00
Pin, National Congress Of Parents & Teachers, 1897 .... 10.00
Pin, Nautical, Silver, Spratling 200.00
Pin, Needlepoint, Butterfly, Black Ground, Oval, 1 1/2 x 1 1/4 In. 30.00
Pin, Nude, Sterling Silver, Margot De Taxco 75.00

Pin, Nymph & Iris Design, Yellow Gold, Pasteyer, 1 3/8 In. 1650.00
Pin, Oval Opal, Gold Finish, Pendant Freshwater Pearl, Art Nouveau 440.00
Pin, Owl, Hattie Carnegie 45.00
Pin, Owl, Sapphire, Textured Wings, Ruby Eyes, Pave-Set Diamonds, 18K Gold 1980.00
Pin, Paperweight Type, Horse & Carriage, Iridescent, Box, 1800s, 1 1/2 In. 45.00
Pin, Parrot, Enameled, Hattie Carnegie 24.00
Pin, Pave Clear Swirl Stones, Trifari, Sterling Silver 60.00
Pin, Peacock, Diamond Collar, Enamel, Silver Back 990.00
Pin, Pendant, 18K Yellow Gold, Ivory, 10 Emeralds, Openwork, 2 x 3 In. 635.00
Pin, Pendant, Large Baroque Pearl Drop, Surrounded By Rhinestones, Weiss 60.00
Pin, Pink Sapphire & Diamond 7425.00
Pin, Portrait, Woman In 3/4 Profile, Diamond Frame, Silver & Gold 775.00
Pin, Pullout Chain, Attached Pen, February 24, 1903 .... 20.00
Pin, Rectangle, Twisted Wire & Beadwork, 14K Bicolor Gold, Victorian 247.00
Pin, Red Arrow, Hanging Letters, Gladys, Bakelite 22.00
Pin, Red Hair & Gray Hair, Bezeled Glass, Gold Filled, 7/8 In. 75.00
Pin, Rhinestones & Rose Glass, Gripoix, 1950s 2300.00
Pin, Rhinestones Set In Silver Metal, Stylized Branch, Trifari, 1950s 145.00
Pin, Rhinestones, Eisenberg 150.00
Pin, Rooster, Rubies, Diamond Accents, 18K Gold, Tiffany & Co. 3080.00
Pin, Rose Spray, Sterling Silver, Corocraft 22.50
Pin, Rose, Textured Leaves, 14K Bicolor Gold, Krementz 137.50
Pin, Round & Baguette Diamonds, 8 Emeralds, Platinum 4830.00
Pin, Round, Gold Lead Pencil Attached, Gold Chain, Engraved 25.00
Pin, Scotty Dog Head, Polka Dot Bow, Celluloid, Hand Painted, Occupied Japan 9.00
Pin, Scotty Dog, Celluloid, Hand Painted, Full Figure, Occupied Japan 9.00
Pin, Sea Horse, Pewabic, Signed 125.00
Pin, Sea Urchin, Movable Spines, Hungry Starfish About To Feast, 18K Gold 1150.00
Pin, Seal, Balancing Pearl Ball, Diamond On Tail, 18K Yellow Gold 517.00
Pin, Seated Woman, Pierced Silver & Gold Frame, Seed Pearls 440.00
Pin, Set, Angel Skin Coral, 14K Gold, Lavaliere, Earrings, Bar Pin 5225.00
Pin, Silver, Brass & Copper, c.1955, Pater Macchiarni, 3 1/2 In. 575.00
Pin, Snowflake, Enamel Borders, 7 Round Diamonds, 14K Yellow Gold 747.00
Pin, Snowman, Rhinestone, Hobe 25.00
Pin, Sphere Joined To A Parabola, Silver, Betty Cooke, 1955, 5 In. 230.00
Pin, Spider, Wire Legs, 14K Gold 412.00
Pin, Spray Of Leaves & Flowers, Rubies, 14K Gold, c.1950 .... 605.00
Pin, Spray Of Marquise Rhinestone Leaves, Adele Simpson, 1950s 315.00
Pin, Star Burst, Green & Blue Cabochon, Rhinestones, Jomaz, 1960s 258.00
Pin, Star Burst, Seed Pearls, Diamond Cluster Center, 14K Gold, Edwardian 302.00
Pin, Sterling Silver, Flowers & Leaves, Faceted Stone Center, Bow, 2 1/2 In. 14.00
Pin, Sterling Silver, Georg Jensen 250.00
Pin, Stylized Flower, Sterling Silver, Georg Jensen No. 97 .... 275.00
Pin, Sunburst, 3-D, Twisted Gold Wire Rays, 2 3/8 In. 9.00
Pin, Terrier, Pave, 60 Small Diamonds, Ruby Eye, 18K White Gold 2300.00
Pin, Tiger, Enamel, Diamonds, Emerald Eyes, 18K Gold, Kutchinsky, England 3025.00
Pin, Turquoise, Miniature Pearls Flanked, Gold Finish, Merl Bennett, 1900 .... 990.00
Pin, Turtle, Ruby Shell, Diamonds, Emerald Eyes, Movable Parts, 2 In. 1870.00
Pin, Wedgwood Medallion, 14K Gold 200.00
Pin, Winged Nymph, Diamonds On Wings, Cressarrow, 1 5/8 In. 4950.00
Pin, Wishbone Form, Small Sapphire, 14K Yellow Gold 55.00
Pin, Woman & 3 Children, Silver, Ilya Schor, 1950s, 2 1/2 x 1 1/4 In. 3520.00
Pin, Woman & Man Seated, Garden Scene, I. Schor, Sterling, Judaica, 1 1/4 In. 1650.00
Pin, Woman's Profile, Snake Frame, William Link, Arts & Crafts, Silver, c.1902 .... 412.00
Pin, Woman, Picking Flowers, Art Nouveau, Papier-Mache 125.00
Pin & Earrings, Autumn Leaves, Weiss 20.00
Pin & Earrings, Flower On Stem, Sterling Silver, Les Bernard 110.00
Pin & Earrings, Ice, Black Pearl, Smoky Crystal, Eisenberg, Box 175.00
Pin & Earrings, Tortoiseshell, Carved, 1880, 3 Piece 1250.00
Pin & Earrings, Victorian, White Pave, 16K Gold 2000.00
Pin-Pendant, Putti, Peridot, Emeralds, Polished & Matte Finish, 18K Gold, Branson 220.00
Ring, Abstract Design, Thick Silver Band, Sam Kramer, c.1955 .... 575.00

Ring, Amethyst & Seed Pearls, 14K Gold 80.00
Ring, Amethyst, Carved Woman's Profile, Diamonds, Platinum, 14K Gold 1870.00
Ring, Amethyst, Oval, Pave-Set Diamond Shoulders, Yard 2310.00
Ring, Aquamarine, Rectangular, Step-Cut, 30 Cts., 18K White Gold Mount 2090.00
Ring, Archer's, Streaked Jadeite, Chinese, 1 In. 545.00
Ring, Blue Sapphire, Surrounded By Diamonds, Platinum, 18K Yellow Gold 7700.00
Ring, Blue Topaz, 4 Diamonds, 14K Gold 95.00
Ring, Bow, Round Diamond Center, 24 Diamonds Surround, Platinum 605.00
Ring, Buckle, Diamond & Ruby, 14K Pink Gold 85.00
Ring, Buckle, Flexible Brick Work, Diamond Buckle, Cartier, 14K Gold 1210.00
Ring, Buckle, Ruby, Diamond, 14K Pink Gold 467.00
Ring, Carnelian Intaglio, Roman Warrior, 18K Gold Mount, Column Shoulders 660.00
Ring, Cat's Eye Chrysoberyl, 14 Mine-Cut Diamonds, .5 Ct. Total Weight 1045.00
Ring, Center Ruby, Surrounded By Round Diamonds, 14K Yellow Gold 385.00
Ring, Cluster, 13 Full-Cut Diamonds, 10 Sapphires, Platinum 3680.00
Ring, Cluster, Mine-Cut Diamonds, 3 Cts. Total Wt., Platinum Mount 1550.00
Ring, Diamond Center, 6 Sapphires, 8 Star-Set Diamonds, 18K Gold, France 522.00
Ring, Diamond Solitaire, 1 Ct., European-Cut, 14K Gold Mount, Tiffany & Co. 3300.00
Ring, Diamond Solitaire, 1.3 Cts., Platinum Mount 5500.00
Ring, Diamond Solitaire, Bezel Set, European-Cut, .7 Ct., 18K, Tiffany & Co. 1775.00
Ring, Diamond Solitaire, Emerald-Cut, .75 Ct., 18K White Gold Mount 1100.00
Ring, Diamond Solitaire, European Cut, .9 Ct., 14K Gold Mount 935.00
Ring, Diamond Solitaire, Round, .75 Ct., 14K Gold Mount 467.00
Ring, Diamond, 1.25 Cts., Triangular Baguettes, 14K Gold Mount 2475.00
Ring, Diamond, 6 Tapered Baguettes, 18 Round, .75 Ct. Total Wt., Platinum Mount .. 665.00
Ring, Diamond, Emerald Cut, .5 Ct., 14K Textured Gold Mount 440.00
Ring, Diamond, Man's, 5 Channel-Set, Princess-Cut, 18K Gold 880.00
Ring, Diamond, Mine-Cut, Collet Setting, .5 Ct., Platinum Top, 14K Gold Mount 385.00
Ring, Diamond, Oval, 1.25 Ct., Pear-Shaped Emeralds, Platinum & Gold Mount 2750.00
Ring, Diamond, Triangular Emeralds, .6 Ct., 14K Gold Mount 935.00
Ring, Diamonds & Rubies, Animal Figure, 18K Yellow & White Gold, Signed 302.00
Ring, Diamonds, 3 Rows, .6 Ct. Total Weight, Navette-Shaped 14K Gold Mount 412.00
Ring, Diamonds, Rubies & Emeralds, Center Motif, Silver-Topped, 14K Gold 1045.00
Ring, Dinner, 3 Emeralds, Seed Pearls, 14K Pink Gold 100.00
Ring, Dome, Turquoise, 14K Textured Gold Mount 110.00
Ring, Double Snake, Heads Set With Table-Set Diamond, 18K Gold 247.00
Ring, Edwardian, Center Diamond, Small Diamonds At Side, c.1915 .... 9900.00
Ring, Egyptian Scarab, Figure, Beadwork, Chasing, 18K Gold Mount 2650.00
Ring, Emerald, 2 Rows Of Diamonds, 14K White Gold 440.00
Ring, Emerald, 4 Cts., Diamond Shoulders, 18K White Gold, France 2750.00
Ring, Enamel Band, Bull's Heads, Wire Twist, 18K Gold, Elizabeth Gage, England ... 2000.00
Ring, Eternity Band, 23 Diamonds, 1.75 Cts. Total Wt., 14K White Gold Mount 990.00
Ring, Eternity Band, 64 Diamonds In 2 Rows, 1 Ct. Total Wt., 14K Gold Mount 880.00
Ring, Eternity Band, Diamonds, 3 Cts. Total Wt., Platinum, Tiffany & Co. 3080.00
Ring, Eternity, Band, 20 Diamonds, Platinum, Size 8 .... 300.00
Ring, Eternity, Band, 7 Full-Cut Diamonds, Platinum 115.00
Ring, Eternity, Band, Diamonds & Rubies, 14K Gold 715.00
Ring, European Cut Round Diamond, Platinum 980.00
Ring, Fish, Pave Rubies & Round Diamonds, 14K Gold 3737.00
Ring, Flower Shape, Marquis Cut Sapphires, Diamonds, 14K White Gold 495.00
Ring, Freshwater Pearls, 3, 15K Gold 192.00
Ring, Graduated Natural Pearls, Rose-Cut Diamonds, 18K Gold 1035.00
Ring, Gray Star Sapphire, Amethysts, Peridots, Citrines, Silver Mount, Arts & Crafts 275.00
Ring, Jade, Carved Buddha, 22K Chased Gold Mount 192.00
Ring, Jade, Carved Floral, 14K Gold, c.1930s 900.00
Ring, Knot, Diamond, 3 Rows Of Gray Pearls, 14K Gold Mount 605.00
Ring, Man's, 11 Full-Cut Diamond Horseshoe, 14K White Gold 345.00
Ring, Man's, Bacchanalian Head, Diamond Eyes, 14K Gold 338.00
Ring, Man's, Cameo, 10K Gold 135.00
Ring, Man's, Florentined Mounting, Round Diamond, 14K White Gold 4830.00
Ring, Man's, Horse In Horseshoe, Diamonds 145.00
Ring, Man's, Round Diamond, .75 Ct., Box Setting, 14K Gold Mount 1050.00

Ring, Man's, Ruby, 14K Gold Textured Mount 137.00
Ring, Man's, Star Sapphire, Collet-Set Round Diamonds, 14K White Gold 412.00
Ring, Marquise Shape, 25 Assorted Rose Diamonds, Yellow Gold 1610.00
Ring, Marquise Shape, Filigree, White Gold 325.00
Ring, Mobe Pearl Surrounded By Pearls, 14K Gold 350.00
Ring, Opal, Boulder, 14K Gold Foliate Mount, Arts & Crafts, Kalo 2650.00
Ring, Opposing Leaves, Sterling Silver, Margaret De Patta, c.1938 .... 575.00
Ring, Oval Cabochon Opal, Framed By Full-Cut Diamonds, 14K Yellow Gold 865.00
Ring, Oval Carnelian Plaque, 18K Gold Foliate Mount, England 440.00
Ring, Oval Turquoise Surrounded By Diamonds, 18K White Gold 412.00
Ring, Pearl, Rhinestones, Avon 8.00
Ring, Pearls At Shoulder, 6 Rose Diamonds, Platinum 517.00
Ring, Peep-In, Nude Woman, On Bicycle 95.00
Ring, Pink Tourmaline, Collet Setting, 18K Pierced Gold, Art Nouveau 660.00
Ring, Platinum, 1.4 Ct Diamonds & Sapphires, Art Deco 1850.00
Ring, Reverse Crystal, Black Terrier, 14K Gold Buckle-Shaped Mount 605.00
Ring, Rose-Cut Diamond, 14K Yellow Gold 550.00
Ring, Round Cabochon Amethyst, Heart, 14K Pink Gold 65.00
Ring, Round Diamond Surrounded By 32 Smaller Round Diamonds, 18K Gold 550.00
Ring, Sapphire, 3.25 Cts., Oval Diamonds, 18K Gold Mount 4400.00
Ring, Sapphire, Oval, Collet- And Bead-Set Diamonds, 18K Gold 1875.00
Ring, Sapphires & Diamonds, Van Cleef & Arpels, 1940s 8250.00
Ring, Silver, 3 Lapis Beads, Foliate Mount, Arts & Crafts, Georg Jensen 385.00
Ring, Solitaire, Bezel Set, Etched 14K Gold Mount 467.00
Ring, Star Sapphire, Gray, Bead-Set Rose-Cut Diamonds, 14K Gold Mount 605.00
Ring, Topaz, Ribbon-Type Setting, 14K Gold 275.00
Ring, Two Enameled Fish Holding Diamond In Mouths, 18K Gold 880.00
Ring, Victorian, Gingerbread, Ruby, 2 Diamonds, 14K Pink Gold 85.00
Ring, Victorian, Sapphires, Seed Pearls, Pink Gold 68.00
Ring, Wedding Band, 22 Marquise-Cut Diamonds, Platinum 3450.00
Ring, Wedding Band, Twisted Rope Borders, 3 Cabochon Emeralds, 22K Gold 805.00
Ring, Wedding, 3 Rows Of Full-Cut Diamonds, Platinum 1610.00
Rosary, Mother-Of-Pearl, Sterling Silver 75.00
Rosary, Sterling Silver 25.00
Stickpin, Cameo, Woman's Head, Pink-Coral 92.00
Stickpin, Dancing Girl, Chicago Tailoring, Celluloid 55.00
Stickpin, Gargoyle Holding Cultured Pearl In Mouth, Whiteside & Ablank 3300.00
Stickpin, Indian Chief, Figural, Silver Sterling 26.00
Stickpin, Initial M, Silver Sterling, Case 15.00
Stickpin, Jade, Diamond, 14K Gold, .15 Ct. 175.00
Stickpin, Old Dutch Cleanser, Enamel 50.00
Stickpin, Panther's Head, Ruby Eyes, 15K Gold 350.00
Stickpin, Sapphire & Diamond, 18K Gold & Platinum, Cartier 3575.00
Stickpin, Sapphire, Blue Enamel, 14K Gold, Arts & Crafts 220.00
Stickpin, Sculpted Female Nude, Celedon Enamel Ground, Lalique, 3 5/8 In. 7150.00
Stickpin, Teddy Bear, Celluloid, Teddy Bear Bread 42.00
Stud Set, Black Pearl, Yellow Gold Cufflinks, White Gold Studs 245.00
Stud Set, Cuff Links & Studs, Black Onyx, Seed Pearl Centers, Larter 550.00
Stud Set, Man's, White Mother-Of-Pearl, Pearl, Platinum & 14K Gold, Krementz 302.00
Stud Set, Mother-Of-Pearl, Cuff Links, 3 Shirt Studs, Larter & Co., 14K Gold 357.00
Tie Tack, Scotty Dog, Swank 15.00
Watches are listed in their own category
Watch Band, Gold-Filled Caps, Expandable, Speidel 4.00
Watch Chain, Alternating Round & Oval Links, 15K Gold, 14 In. 660.00
Watch Chain, Curb Link Chain, 18K Yellow Gold 302.00
Watch Chain, Hair, 15 In. 100.00
Watch Chain, Links, Matching Fob, Swivel Clasp, 14K Gold, Victorian, 15 In. 440.00
Watch Chain, Reeded & Open Platinum Links, 14K Gold Swivel, 14 In. 302.00
Watch Chain, Round Reeded Links, 14K Yellow Gold 220.00
Watch Pin, Four-Leaf Clover, Enamel, Gold, European-Cut Diamonds 1430.00
Watch Pin, Rose-Cut Diamonds, Enamel Dial, 18K Gold, Edwardian, France 1650.00
Wristwatches are listed in their own category

JOHN ROGERS statues were made from 1859 to 1892. The originals were bronze, but the thousands of copies made by the Rogers factory were of painted plaster. Eighty different figures were created. Similar painted plaster figures were produced by some other factories. Rights to the figures were sold in 1893 and they were manufactured for several more years by the Rogers Statuette Co. Never repaint a Rogers figure because this lowers the value to collectors.

Group, Challenging The Union Vote	785.00
Group, Checkers Up At The Farm	360.00
Group, Coming To The Parson	300.00
Group, Council Of War	950.00 to 3575.00
Group, Courtship In Sleepy Hollow	423.00
Group, Faust & Marguerite	513.00
Group, Favored Scholar	365.00
Group, First Love	400.00
Group, Frolic At The Old Homestead	575.00
Group, Parting Promise	480.00
Group, Taking The Oath And Drawing Rations, White, 24 In.	200.00
Group, Tap On The Window	545.00
Group, Union Refugees	575.00
Group, We Boys	453.00
Group, Weighing The Baby	550.00 to 605.00
Group, Wounded Scout	990.00

JUDAICA is any memorabilia that refers to the Jews or the Jewish religion. Interests range from newspaper clippings that mention eighteenth- and nineteenth-century Jewish Americans to religious objects, such as menorahs or spice boxes. Age, condition, and the intrinsic value of the material, as well as the historic and artistic importance, determine the value.

Bible, Engraved Border, Magnifying Glass, Gold Case, c.1890, 1 1/2 x 1 In.	3950.00
Binder, Torah, Painted Hebrew Inscriptions, Linen, German, 8 1/4 x 136 In.	330.00
Box, Charity, Images Of 2 Institutions, Tin, 1940s, 3 In.	120.00
Box, Hebrew Inscription, Bronze, 4 Footed, 3 x 4 In.	30.00
Candelabra, 3-Light, 2 Rampant Lions Support Star Of David, Brass, 14 In., Pair	522.00
Candelabra, 7-Light, Birds & Blossoms, Poland, Brass, 20 1/2 In., Pair	770.00
Cover, Hallah, Blessings For Sabbath & Festivals, c.1900, 18 1/4 x 21 In.	220.00
Dreidel, Hebrew Letters, Signed Schor, Silver, c.1960, 2 In.	3520.00
Etrog Container, Hinged Lid, Repousse Star Of David, Sterling Silver, 18th Century	440.00
Goblet, Kiddush & Havdalah, Engraved Exterior & Interior, Pair	9350.00
Goblet, Kiddush, Flowers Alternating With Scroll, Hebrew, Silver, 5 In.	302.00
Haggadah, Passover, Hebrew, Marathi Translation	3750.00
Ketubah, Marriage Contract, Peacock, Lions, Foliate, Framed, 1865	680.00
Ketubah, Rabbinic Script, Relevant Blessings, Handwritten	225.00
Kiddush Cup, Chased Scene, Moses With Tablets, Sterling Silver, 7 1/2 In.	885.00
Menorah, Repousse Florals & Lions, Lion Form Fonts, Sterling Silver, 13 In.	1850.00
Mezuzah, Beaded Windows, Tiled Roof, Hebrew Shin, Ebony & Silver, 6 1/4 In.	770.00
Plate, Passover, Celebration Of Faith, Royal Doulton	500.00
Plate, Passover, Hebrew, 4 Questions, Symbolic Foods, Silver, 1920s, 13 In.	715.00
Plate, Rosh Hashonah, No. 4, Celebration Of Faith, Royal Doulton,	500.00
Plate, Yom Kippur, No. 3, Celebration Of Faith, Royal Doulton	500.00
Platter, Moses Found In Nile, Oval, Sterling Silver, c.1900, 20 x 15 1/2 In.	550.00
Postcard, Bezalel School Of Arts, Museum, Professor Schatz, 15 Piece	385.00
Postcard, Scenes Of Jews Praying At Western Wall, 40 Piece	195.00
Prayer Book, For American Immigrants, Pocket Size, Gusdorfer, 1860	1320.00
Prayer Book, Laws, Hebrew Text, 220 Pages, Chicago, 1840s, Miniature	470.00
Prayer Book, New Year, Day Of Atonement, Passover, French & Hebrew, 1797	885.00
Prayer Book, Passover, Hebrew Quotations, Calf Cover, Venice, 1664	4400.00
Salt Dish, Hebrew Characters On Rim, Claw & Ball Feet, Russian Silver	330.00
Sampler, Legend, Holy Places, Hebrew Titles, Wool, 1925, 18 x 21 In.	300.00
Spice Box, Hebrew Inscription, Sterling Silver, Contemporary, 4 In.	195.00
Spice Box, Silver, Globe Shape, Shells, Lion Finial, Rome, c.1800, 8 1/2 In.	4885.00

Spice Box, Vase Of Flowers Finial, Sterling Silver, 11 1/4 In. 1875.00
Spice Container, Basket Form, Latticework Top, Oval, Dutch Silver, 18th Century .. 445.00
Spice Container, Fish Form, Engraved Head, Garnet Eyes, Silver, 7 1/2 In. 550.00
Spice Tower, Center Doors, Pennants, Wirework Stem, Silver, Austria, 1868, 7 In. 360.00
Spice Tower, Filigree Silver, Ball & Pennant, Austro-Hungarian, 10 1/4 In. 885.00
Spice Tower, Pomegranate Form, 2 Sections, Silvered, 3 3/4 In. 225.00
Torah Shield, Silver, Continental, Rococo Border, Lions, Crown, Chain, 17 In. 4315.00

JUGTOWN Pottery refers to pottery made in North Carolina as far back as the 1750s. In 1915, Juliana and Jacques Busbee set up a training and sales organization for what they named *Jugtown Pottery.* In 1921, they built a shop at Jugtown, North Carolina, and hired Ben Owen as a potter in 1923. The Busbees moved the village store where the pottery was sold to New York City. Juliana Busbee sold the New York store in 1926 and moved into a log cabin near the Jugtown Pottery. The pottery closed in 1958. It reopened and is still working near Seagrove, North Carolina.

Bowl, Mottled Ocher, Tea Bowl Form, 1920s, 5 1/2 In. 75.00
Candlestick, Massive, 12 In. 65.00
Pitcher, Frog-Skin Glaze, 9 In. 110.00
Pitcher, Speckled Brown, Bulbous, 8 1/2 In. 57.00
Plate, Tobacco Brown, 10 In. 11.00
Vase, 4 Strap Handles, Opaque White Glaze, Marked, 8 1/2 In. 400.00
Vase, Bulbous, Chinese, Black, 10 In. 700.00
Vase, Chinese Blue, Glossy Red & Turquoise, Marked, 5 x 5 In. 425.00
Vase, Chinese Blue, Ovoid, 6 In. 688.00
Vase, Glossy Black Glaze, Cover, Marked, 3 3/4 In. 135.00
Vase, Green & Brown, 5 1/2 In. 65.00
Vase, Green, 4 In. 50.00
Vase, Greenish Brown Glaze, Referred To As Tobacco Spit 75.00
Vase, Ovoid, Frog-Skin, 4 In. 135.00
Vase, Pear Shape, Red Glossy Glaze, Marked, 6 1/4 In. 357.00
Vase, Speckled Dark Green, 6 In. 50.00
Vase, Speckled Green, 4 Handles, 7 In. 150.00

JUKEBOXES play records. The first coin-operated phonograph was demonstrated in 1889. In 1906 the *Automatic Entertainer* appeared, the first coin-operated phonograph to offer several different selections of music. The first electrically powered jukebox was introduced in 1927. Collectors search for jukeboxes of all ages, especially those with flashing lights and unusual design and graphics.

Mills, Ferris Wheel, 78 Rpm .... 1200.00 to 2300.00
Mills, Model 801, 1927, Records 4750.00
Mills, Panoram, c.1940 .... 1200.00
NSM Prestige, 60 Records, 1960s, Dinky Size 1250.00
Rock-Ola, Model 1422, 20 Tunes, Flashing Lights, 1940s, 60 In. .... 2150.00 to 4000.00
Seeburg, Beveled Glass Mantle, Oak 995.00
Seeburg, Record Selector, Wall-O-Matic, 5 Cent, 1950s 48.00
Wurlitzer, Model 600 .... 3000.00
Wurlitzer, Model 600a, Multi-Selector, 56 x 30 In. 1760.00
Wurlitzer, Model 700 .... 4900.00
Wurlitzer, Model 750, Original Records, Bubbles, Light & Music, 1941 .... 9500.00
Wurlitzer, Model 1015, 24 Song Selections, 1940s, 58 In. .... 6900.00 to 8500.00
Wurlitzer, Model 1050 .... 5800.00
Wurlitzer, Model 1100, 45 RPM Records 6500.00
Wurlitzer, Simplex 750.00

KATE GREENAWAY, who was a famous illustrator of children's books, drew pictures of children in high-waisted Empire dresses. She lived from 1846 to 1901. Her designs appear on china, glass, and other pieces. Figural napkin rings depicting the Greenaway children may also be found in the Napkin Ring category under Figural.

Almanac, Color, 1929 .... 55.00
Figurine, Boy & Girl, Pair 85.00

Illustration, Little Ann 65.00
Napkin Ring, Girl Pushing Ring 150.00
Napkin Ring, Boy Standing Before 6-Sided Eing, Silver Plate 185.00
Paperweight, Sitting Girl In Large Bonnet, Iron, 3 x 3 In. 110.00

KAY FINCH Ceramics were made in Corona Del Mar, California, from 1935 to 1963. The hand-decorated pieces often depicted whimsical animals and people. Pastel colors were used. *Kay Finch* CALIFORNIA

Console Set, 2 Oriental Ladies & Vase, Green, 10 In. 145.00
Cup & Saucer, Blue Daisy 25.00
Cup & Saucer, Briar Rose 25.00
Figurine, Angel, 4 In. 38.00
Figurine, Butch & Biddy, 4 In., Pair 85.00
Figurine, Cat, Pink, 4 In. 40.00
Figurine, Cocker Spaniel, 11 3/4 In. 95.00
Figurine, Duck, 4 In. .... 35.00 to 165.00
Figurine, Duck, Peep 40.00
Figurine, Godey Couple 155.00
Figurine, Owl, Toot 65.00
Figurine, Pig, Smiling, 9 In. 125.00
Figurine, Tyrolean 120.00
Head Vase, Mermaid 75.00
Plate, Multicolored Prancing Horse, Square, Signed, 10 In. 125.00
Salt & Pepper, Ducks, White & Green 65.00
Salt & Pepper, Owls, White, Blue Trim 70.00
Wall Pocket, Girl, Green, Gold Trim, 15 In., Pair 120.00

KAYSERZINN, see Pewter category

KELVA glassware was made by the C. F. Monroe Company of Meriden, Connecticut, about 1904. It is a pale, pastel-painted glass decorated with flowers, designs, or scenes. Kelva resembles Nakara and Wave Crest, two other glasswares made by the same company. **KELVA**

Box, Blue & Pink Flowers, Round, 6 In. 695.00
Box, Hinged Cover, White Flowers, Red Mottled Ground, Signed, 3 1/2 x 6 In. 525.00
Box, Jewelry, Hinged Cover, Dark Green Enamel Floral, 5 x 5 1/2 In. 350.00
Box, Mirror In Lid, Pink Flowers, 4 1/2 In. 515.00
Box, Red & Gray Flowers, Round, 6 In. 695.00
Box, White Floral Beading, Green, Rose, 5 3/4 In. 500.00

KEW BLAS is the name used by the Union Glass Company of Somerville, Massachusetts. The name refers to an iridescent golden glass made from the 1890s to 1924. The iridescent glass was reminiscent of the Tiffany glass of the period. *KEW-BLAS*

Candlestick, Gold Iridescent, Column Shape, 8 1/4 In. 247.50
Vase, Flared Oval, Diagonal Green Stripes, Marked, 7 In. 605.00

KEWPIES, designed by Rose O'Neill, were first pictured in the *Ladies' Home Journal.* The figures, which are similar to pixies, were a success, and Kewpie dolls started appearing in 1911. Kewpie pictures and other items soon followed. Collectors search for all items that picture the little winged people.

Booklet, Jell-O & The Kewpies, Rose O'Neill, 1915, 4 1/2 x 6 In. 82.00
Bowl, Dome Cover, 3 Hand-Painted Action Kewpies, J.C. Bavaria 135.00
Camera, Box 185.00
Candy Container, Kewpie Next To Barrel 125.00
Candy Container, Painted, E & A 200.00
Display, Santa Claus, Standup, Rose O'Neill, 1913, 5 x 11 In. 45.00
Doll, 12 In. 1050.00
Doll, Action, Arms Up, 2 In. 125.00
Doll, All Bisque, Black Painted Eyes, 6 In. 165.00
Doll, Aubis, O'Neill, 1 1/2 In. 950.00
Doll, Bisque Head, Blond Topknot, 5 Piece Composition Body, Kestner, 15 In. 5400.00
Doll, Bisque, 5 1/4 In. .... 60.00 to 85.00

Kewpie, Doll, Bisque, Hottentot,
Gluck-Kind Label, Germany

♦ ♦ ♦ ♦ ♦ ♦ ♦ ♦ ♦ ♦ ♦ ♦ ♦ ♦ ♦ ♦ ♦ ♦ ♦ ♦

If wooden nesting dolls stick, try putting a few drops of baby oil into the space between the dolls. Then try separating the dolls.

♦ ♦ ♦ ♦ ♦ ♦ ♦ ♦ ♦ ♦ ♦ ♦ ♦ ♦ ♦ ♦ ♦ ♦ ♦ ♦

Doll, Bisque, Hottentot, Gluck-Kind Label, Germany	*Illus*	6000.00
Doll, Bisque, Jointed Arms, Paper Chest Label, 5 In.		185.00
Doll, Bisque, Kuddles, Tagged, 8 1/2 In.		225.00
Doll, Bisque, Lying On Back, Hands Down, Head Up, Rose O'Neill, 3 In.		350.00
Doll, Bisque, Movable Legs, 6 In.		500.00
Doll, Bisque, Signed, Rose O'Neill, Heart Sticker, Germany, 1900, 8 1/2 In.		352.00
Doll, Bisque, Signed, Rose O'Neill, 12 In.		1250.00
Doll, Bisque, Signed, Rose O'Neill, 7 1/2 In.		195.00
Doll, Bisque, Sitting, Hand To Mouth, Rose O'Neill, 3 1/2 In.		350.00
Doll, Celluloid, 5 In.		75.00
Doll, Composition, Jointed, Rose O'Neill, 13 In.		225.00
Doll, Composition, Painted Eyes, Molded & Painted Hair, Rose O'Neill, 1913, 13 In.		30.00
Doll, Composition, Swimsuit, 12 1/2 In.		250.00
Doll, Hugger, 3 1/2 In.		295.00
Doll, Kewpiesta, Ceramic, Painted Blue Side Eyes, Blue Base, 1983, 11 In.		15.00
Doll, Reclining, On 1 Arm, 5 In.		50.00
Doll, Rubber, Rose O'Neill, 8 In.		40.00
Doll, Scootles, Composition, Cameo		400.00
Doll, Sweeper, Attached Broom & Dust Bin, 4 1/4 In.	395.00 to	450.00
Doll, Traveler		350.00
Figurine, Bride & Groom, Bisque		375.00
Figurine, Legs In Air, Propped Up On Hands, Bisque		12.00
Figurine, Sitting, Sucking Thumb, Bisque, 4 1/2 In.		15.00
Figurine, Thinker, Seated, Cameo, Vinyl, Rose ONeill, 3 3/4 In.		25.00
Flannel, Carrying American Flag, Dated 1914, 4 x 5 In.		100.00
Magazine Cover, Santa's Head, Surrounded By Busy Kewpies, 1927		37.00
Paperweight, Glass, Joe St. Clair		35.00
Paperweight, Kewpie & Purdue Foundry, Cast Iron		110.00
Paperweight, Purdue Foundry		120.00
Placecard, Posy Holder, Rose O'Neill		325.00
Postcard, Kewpie Suffragette, Vote For Our Mothers, Rose O'Neill		600.00
Santa Claus, Cameo		50.00
Sugar Shaker, 14 Action Kewpies Around, Bavaria		165.00
Tin, Kewpie Klenser, Australia, 4 3/4 In.		150.00
Vase, Baby's Head, 1974		20.00

KIMBALL, see Cluthra category

KING'S ROSE, see Soft Paste category

KITCHEN utensils of all types, from eggbeaters to bowls, are collected today. Handmade wooden and metal items, like ladles and apple peelers, were made in the early nineteenth century. Mass-produced pieces, like iron apple peelers and graniteware, were made in the nineteenth century. Other kitchen wares are listed under manufacturers' names or under Advertising, Iron, Tool, or Wooden.

Apple Corer, White Mountain	20.00
Apple Parer, Goodell, Mechanical, Cast Iron, 1898	70.00

Basket, Egg, Wire, 1/2 Bushel 35.00
Basket, Egg, Wire, Collapsible 12.50
Beater, Pillow, Metal, Wooden 20.00
Beater Jar, Wesson Oil, Blue Band 90.00
Board, Bread, Wooden, Natural, Handle, 5 1/4 x 12 1/2 In. 42.00
Board, Bread, Pine, Applied Ends, Red Back, 17 1/2 x 23 1/2 In. 50.00
Board, Pastry, Slate, Round, 17 3/4 In. 192.50
Bottle, Sprinkler, Dutch Girl 45.00
Bottle, Sprinkler, Siamese Cat 30.00
Bowl, Mixing, Cattail, Universal, 6 In. 20.00
Bowl, Mixing, Petit Point House, Crooksville, 9 In. 40.00
Box, Dough, Dovetailed, Poplar Base, Walnut Lid, 22 3/4 x 47 In. ... 1540.00
Box, Spice, Hanging, 5 Drawers, Embossed Labels, Beech, 8 3/8 In. 55.00
Bread Rack, Cooling, Brass, For Table Use, 1800s, 2 x 3 x 10 In. 140.00
Bucket, Sugar, Wooden Staves, Worn Dark Finish, 9 1/2 In. 50.00
Butter Mold, look under Mold, Butter in the Kitchen category
Butter Paddle, Curly Maple, Bird-Head Hook, 11 In. 99.00
Butter Paddle, Maple, Natural, 10 1/2 In. 71.50
Butter Stamp, 4 Hearts & Compass Star, Poplar, Rectangular, 3 1/2 x 5 In. 165.00
Butter Stamp, Acorn 145.00
Butter Stamp, Acorn & Oak Leaf, Round, 3 3/4 In. 220.00
Butter Stamp, Basket Of Fruit, Round, Elongated Handle, 4 In. 330.00
Butter Stamp, Cow, 4 1/2 x 4 1/2 In. 275.00
Butter Stamp, Cow, Turned Threaded Handle, Wooden, 3 5/8 In. 220.00
Butter Stamp, Eagle, Round, Turned Handle, 4 3/8 In. 220.00
Butter Stamp, Fish Design, Hardwood, Elongated Turned Handle, 3 x 5 In. 193.00
Butter Stamp, Floral Design, Round, Turned Handle, 3 1/2 In. 110.00
Butter Stamp, Flower Pattern, 19th Century 85.00
Butter Stamp, Half Moon Wheat, Turned Handle 215.00
Butter Stamp, Lollipop With Star Flower .... 275.00 to 300.00
Butter Stamp, Pineapple, 1-Piece Turned Handle, 4 1/4 In. 101.00
Butter Stamp, Pomegranate & Foliage, Round, Concave Surface, 5 1/8 In. 247.00
Butter Stamp, Sheaf Of Wheat, Round, Turned Handle, 4 1/4 In. 335.00
Butter Stamp, Sheaf, Wooden, Turned Handle, 7 In. 82.00
Butter Stamp, Star Flower, Round, Turned Handle, 5 1/2 In. 127.00
Butter Stamp, Star Flower, Wooden, 3 3/4 In. 110.00
Butter Stamp, Strawberry & Leaf, Inserted Turned Handle, 3 1/2 In. 165.00
Butter Stamp, Stylized Eagle, Round, Wooden, Turned Handle, 4 1/2 In. 220.00
Butter Stamp, Stylized Pineapple, Round, Turned Handle, 4 1/2 In. 165.00
Butter Stamp, Stylized Pineapple, Wooden, Round, Handle, 3 3/4 In. 38.50
Butter Stamp, Stylized Tulip & Star, Rectangular, 3 1/4 x 4 7/8 In. 182.00
Butter Stamp, Sunburst, Wooden, 4 3/4 In. 192.50
Cake Pan, Baker's Chocolate, Professional Size 195.00
Cake Pan, Hetty Harper Mixes 6.50
Cake Pan, Pillsbury Boy 13.00
Cake Pan, Swansdown, With Knife 12.50
Can Opener, Dazey Churn Co., Wall 20.00
Can Opener, Edlund, Wooden Handle 2.50
Can Opener, Iron, Sprague 9.00
Can Opener, Movable Wheel, Vaughan 9.50
Can Opener, Winchester 35.00
Carrying Case, Egg, Wooden, 12 Dozen 20.00
Cheese Keeper, Sanitary, Crystal Glass, Embossed Instructions 45.00
Cherry Pitter, Enterprise Mfg., No. 16 .... 45.00
Cherry Pitter, Enterprise, 1903 .... 65.00
Cherry Pitter, Enterprise, Cast Iron, Hand Crank, 1883 .... 18.00 to 25.00
Chopper, Food, Bone & Composition Inlaid Handle, 7 In. 357.50
Churn, Barrel, Midding Crank, 1900s 90.00
Churn, Crown, Wooden Lid & Dasher, 3 Gal. 52.50
Churn, Davis Swing Churn No. 3, Swinging, Yellow Paint 375.00
Churn, Dazey, Glass, 1 Qt. 175.00
Churn, Dazey, Glass Barrel 165.00
Churn, Dazey, No. 8, Steel Blades, Glass Body, 1 Gallon 50.00

Churn, Dazey, No. 408, Glass, Wooden Paddle 65.00
Churn, Elgin, 2 Gal. 100.00
Churn, Funk's Folding Dash Churn, Original Stenciling 280.00
Churn, Stenciled Red Cow, Wooden 225.00
Churn, Taylor Bros. Churn Co., Stone Dasher, Hand Crank 45.00
Churn, Wooden, Crank Handle 105.00
Clothes Dryer, Wall, Collapsible Wooden Arms 35.00
Clothes Sprinkler, Figural, Elephant, Metal Top 45.00
Clothes Sprinkler, Hand Iron Shape 35.00
Clothes Sprinkler, Siamese Cat 75.00
Coffee Grinders are listed in their own category
Coffee Maker, Universal, Aluminum, Stove Top, Wooden Handle, Gooseneck Spout   25.00
Coffee Mill, Double Wheel, 10 In. 450.00
Coffee Mill, Griswold Grand Union 345.00
Coffee Mill, Job King, Taunton, Mass. 69.00
Coffeepot, Percolator, Thomas Edison, Art Deco 150.00
Cookie Board, 2 Designs, Urn Of Flowers & Dog With Tree, Wooden, 3 x 5 In. 192.00
Cookie Board, 2 Sheep, Chestnut, 12 In. 77.00
Cookie Board, 4 Oval Designs, Cherry, 3 x 5 In. 165.00
Cookie Board, 6 Rectangular Designs, Basket, Bird, Ship, Wooden, 3 x 5 In. 165.00
Cookie Board, 6 Round Designs, Woman, Fruit, Animals, Birds, Wooden, 4 x 6 In. .. 275.00
Cookie Board, 8 Rectangular Designs, Poplar, 3 x 7 In. 110.00
Cookie Board, 11 Carved Animals, Fish, Basket, People, 4 x 27 1/2 In. 550.00
Cookie Board, Bird On Branch, Cast Iron, Oval, 3 x 4 7/8 In. 165.00
Cookie Board, Carved Animal, Refinished, Round, 14 1/2 In. 49.50
Cookie Board, Carved Beech, Metal Edge, Figural Man, 6 3/4 x 18 In. 357.00
Cookie Board, Fish, Basket, House, Pineapple, Rectangular Designs, 3 x 4 In. 148.00
Cookie Board, Hearts, Clubs, Spades, Diamonds, Steel, Art Deco Box, 1920s 25.00
Cookie Board, Pineapple On Oblong, Cast Iron, 4 1/2 x 6 In. 150.00
Cookie Board, Seated Cat, Carved, Wooden, 14 1/2 x 9 1/4 In. 55.00
Cookie Board, Springerle, 6 Designs, c.1830, 7 x 3 1/2 In. 325.00
Cookie Board, Swan In Circle, Dots In Oval, Cast Iron, 4 3/4 x 5 3/4 In. 170.00
Cookie Cutter, Animal With Long Ears, Stylized, Tin, 6 3/4 In. 214.00
Cookie Cutter, Bird With Long Tail, Stylized, Tin, 6 1/2 In. 27.00
Cookie Cutter, Dagwood, Blondie, Alexander, Plastic, 1940s, 3 In., Set Of 3 .... 42.00
Cookie Cutter, Dancing Dutchman, Tin 205.00
Cookie Cutter, Dancing Dutchman, Tin, Dark Patina, 7 In. 225.00
Cookie Cutter, Duck, Early 1900s 22.00
Cookie Cutter, Figure With Boots, Tin, 8 In. 82.50
Cookie Cutter, Fish, Tin, 5 1/2 In. 33.00
Cookie Cutter, Heart-In-Hand, Tin 475.00
Cookie Cutter, Heart, Flower, Star & Tulip, Tin, Set Of 4 .... 27.50
Cookie Cutter, Horse, Tin, 6 1/2 In. 55.00
Cookie Cutter, Horse, Tin, 9 1/2 In. 150.00
Cookie Cutter, Man, Outstretched Hand, Tin, 9 3/4 In. 395.00
Cookie Cutter, Nagley, Noah's Ark Cake Cutters, Box, Set Of 9 .... 38.50
Cookie Cutter, Punched Star Design On Back, Animal Shapes, Set Of 5 .... 27.50
Cookie Cutter, Razorback Pig, Tin, 4 1/4 In. 41.00
Cookie Cutter, Reddy Kilowatt 10.00
Cookie Cutter, Santa Claus With Tree, Tin, 10 1/4 In. 56.00
Cookie Cutter, Silhouette Of Man With Coat Tails, Tin, 6 1/4 In. 66.00
Cookie Cutter, Tin, Animal Shapes, Set Of 6 .... 55.00
Cookie Cutter, Tin, Hatchet, 7 In. 55.00
Cookie Cutter, Tweety Bird 10.00
Cookie Cutter, Woman With Dress, Tin, 6 In. 22.00
Cookie Cutter, Woman, Full Dress, Arms Akimbo 43.00
Cookie Mold, Cornucopia With Fruit, Cast Iron, 5 5/8 In. 50.00
Cover, Food, Fly Net, Gauze 22.00
Cover, Food, Screen 28.00
Cover, Toaster, Black Doll 3500.00
Cream Whip Spoon, Bent Wire, Red Wooden Handle 2.50
Cup, Measuring, Glasbake, 1 Cup 8.00
Cutter, Cabbage, Cherry & Walnut, Curved Crest, Heart Cutout, A.J. Kuhn, 26 In. 110.00

Cutter, Cabbage, Disston & Morse 45.00
Cutter, Cabbage, Tee-Dee, Indianapolis, Wooden, 27 x 9 In. 65.00
Cutter, Cabbage, Walnut, Heart Cutout Crest, Ex Ellie Hoover, 16 3/4 In. 175.00
Cutter, Doughnut, Rumford, Tin 15.00
Cutter, Noodle, Green Handle 5.00
Cutter, Noodle, Red Wooden Handle 6.00
Dough Box, 1-Board Lid, Poplar, 27 x 16 x 32 1/2 In. 137.50
Dough Box, Napoleonic Scene Medallion, Chestnut, France, c.1810 .... 975.00
Dough Box, Slant Sides, Notched Handles In Lift Lid, 1820s, 8 x 13 x 27 In. 250.00
Dough Table, H Stretcher, Cherry Stained, c.1800, 29 x 48 x 27 1/2 In. 650.00
Dutch Oven, Griswold, No. 9, Erie, 1920, 4 1/4 x 9 3/4 In. 110.00
Dutch Oven, Griswold, No. 11 .... 450.00
Dutch Oven, Tite-Top 35.00
Egg Coddler, 1870s 55.00
Egg Poacher, Copper, Iron Rattail Handle, Round 38.00
Egg Separator, Puritan Meats, Tin 12.00
Egg Separator, Tin, Fanchon Flour 5.00
Egg Strainer, South Bend Malleable Range 15.00
Egg Timer, Monk, Goebel 35.00
Egg Warmer, Rooster & Hen, Steiff Button, 1913, Pair 385.00
Eggbeater, A & J, Iron, Red Wooden Tee Handle 6.50
Eggbeater, A. & J., Green Glass Bowl, 1923 .... 77.00
Eggbeater, A. & J., Green Handle 6.00
Eggbeater, A. & J., Pat. 1923 .... 12.00
Eggbeater, Beats Anything In A Cup Or Bowl, Green Wooden Handle, A & J 17.00
Eggbeater, Betty Taplin, Tin, 5 1/2 In. 25.00
Eggbeater, Cassidy Fairbanks, Turbine 20.00
Eggbeater, Child's, Taplin 19.00
Eggbeater, Dover, 1891 .... 20.00
Eggbeater, Dover, Cast Iron, 1904 .... 28.00
Eggbeater, Dunlap Sanitary, Cream & Egg 20.00
Eggbeater, Ekco, Hand Crank, Iron, Odd Top Handle 4.00
Eggbeater, Holt, Side Handle, Cast Iron 95.00
Eggbeater, Nut Brown, Vacuum, Whiskey, England, Instructions & Box 60.00
Eggbeater, Quarter, Hand Held, Germany 550.00
Eggbeater, Taplin, Iron, Wooden Handle 4.00
Eggbeater, Washburn Co., Turbine 25.00
Extract Kit, Flavoring, California Perfume Co., 7 Piece 125.00
Firkin, Red Over Green Paint, Copper Tacks, 11 x 11 1/2 In. 195.00
Firkin, White, 19th Century, 13 x 14 In. 195.00
Flop Griddle, C. Mfg. Co., Connecticut, Raised Letters 150.00
Flue Cover, Child Reading Story Book 65.00
Flue Cover, Dutch Windmill Scene 60.00
Flue Cover, Peaches, Twisted Rim, Germany, 9 1/2 In. 27.50
Food Mill, Universal L.F.C., Pat. 1897 .... 35.00
Fork, Toasting, Brass, Weighted Conical Base, Adjustable, Stamped Patent Number 165.00
French Waffle Iron, Griswold, No. 7 .... 750.00
Funnel, Inner Sieve, 4 1/2 In. 9.00
Grater, Fels Naptha 6.50
Grater, Nutmeg, Bogar, c.1896 .... 110.00
Grater, Nutmeg, Edgar, 1891-1896 .... 75.00
Grater, Nutmeg, Hinged Lid, Cast Iron, Patented June 7, 1870, 6 In. 258.00
Grater, Nutmeg, Hinged Top, Kramer, 6 1/4 In. 15.00
Grater, Sliding Compartment, Hand Punched Tin, Wood, 16 x 9 In. 325.00
Grater, Vegetable, Griseu, Cast Iron, Hand Crank, 1922 .... 15.00
Griddle, Griswold, No. 9, Oval 100.00
Griddle, Sultana, Cast Iron, Oval, 8 In. 40.00
Griddle, Wagner, Cast Iron, Round 20.00
Grinder, Cheese, Mouli, Red Wooden Handle 10.00
Grinder, Food, Baby, Cast Iron, 4 In. 45.00
Grinder, Food, Keen Kutter, No. 22 1/2 .... 18.00
Grinder, Food, Keystone, No. 5, Cast Iron, Small 5.00
Grinder, Food, Winchester, Model W12 .... 75.00

Grinder, Food, Winchester, No. 13, Cast Iron, Hand Crank	60.00
Grinder, Meat, White Metal, Salesman's Sample, 7 In.	195.00
Grinder, Meat, Winchester, Model 31	75.00
Grinder, Nut, Anchor Hocking	10.00
Grinder, Square Nail Teeth, Sheet Metal Blades, Wooden, 24 In.	132.00
Hanger, Fold-Up, Traveling, Silver, Germany, Folds To 4 In.	12.00
Holder, Straw, Green	490.00
Hors D'oeuvre Fork Set, Bakelite & Brass, 8 Piece	35.00
Huller, Strawberry, Nip-It, Iron, 1906	3.00
Ice Chest, Wooden, Primitive	195.00
Ice Cream Freezer, White Mountain	25.00
Ice Cream Freezer, White Mountain, Jr., Small	400.00
Ice Cream Paddle, Rubberized Handle, Hamilton Beach	25.00
Ice Crusher, Brass, Mounted On Marble	600.00
Ice Pick, Yankee, Cast Iron, Wooden Handle	3.00
Ice Tongs, Iron, Chain Handle	12.00
Icebox, 6 Doors, Mirror, 6 1/2 x 7 x 2 1/2 Ft.	2500.00
Icebox, Eastlake, Ash & Elm, c.1880	1200.00
Icebox, Oak, 1915	325.00
Icebox, Oak, 2 Doors, Commercial Type, 60 In.	1400.00
Icebox, Oak, 3 Doors, Refinished	550.00
Icebox, Oak, 6 Doors, 2 Have Leaded Glass, Large	1500.00
Icebox, Oak, 6 Doors, 87 x 74 x 32 In.	1000.00
Iron, American Beauty, Amber Handle	42.50
Iron, American Beauty, Electric	110.00
Iron, American Beauty, Red Bakelite Handle	20.00
Iron, Charcoal, Original Grate	75.00
Iron, Coleman, Instructions, Pump, Wrench	95.00
Iron, Crown Mfg. Co., Electric, 1930s	25.00
Iron, Durabilt, Travel, Folding Wooden Handle, Leather Case	7.50
Iron, Electric, Winchester	95.00
Iron, Flat, Monitor, Cast Iron	35.00
Iron, Fluting, 1866	48.00
Iron, Fluting, Geneva, 1871, 2 Piece	75.00
Iron, Gas, Coleman, Blue Enamelware	38.00
Iron, Hand, The Monitor, Key	33.00
Iron, Hotpoint, Chrome, Bakelite Thumb Rest	28.00
Iron, Neutered Alcohol	50.00
Iron, Sunbeam, Electric, Metal Case, 1930	40.00
Iron, Traveling, Fiery Feather, Folding, Wooden Handle, Original Case, 1920s	5.00
Ironing Board, Wooden	35.00
Jar Opener, Anchor, Iron	1.00
Jar Opener, Speedo, Iron	18.00
Jigger, Nickel Plate, Folding Handle, Leather Case, US Germany, 3 Piece	10.00
Juicer, Dazey, Metal, Wall Mount, Handle	35.00
Juicer, Juistractor, Metal Screw	2.75
Juicer, Soda Fountain, Sunkist, Electric	75.00
Juicer, Sunkist, Yellow Slag Glass Top, All Attachments, Electric	50.00
Kettle, Bowl Type, Iron, Wire Bale Handle, Erie, Pa., 11 1/2 In.	22.00
Kettle, Candy, Iron Handles, Dovetailed Copper, 15 x 19 1/2 In.	105.00
Kettle, Griswold, Erie, Cast Iron	50.00
Kettle, Jelly, Brass, Medium Size	45.00
Kettle, Tin Lid, Safety, No. 8	200.00
Knife & Fork, Keen Kutter, Oak Dovetailed Box	225.00
Knife & Fork Set, Bone Handled Pistol Grip, Civil War Period, 12 Piece	1340.00
Lemon Squeezer, Drum, Newman, Pat. 1883, 9 In.	75.00
Lid Lifter, Spiral Loop Handle, Steel, 8 In.	12.00
Lid Lifter, Spiral Twist Handle, Steel, 8 In.	8.00
Lifter, Fruit Jar, Wire, Wooden Handle	3.50
Masher, Tiger Maple	40.00
Match Safes can be found in their own category	
Meat Hook, Crown Hanger, 5 Hooks, 3 Prongs Each, Wrought Iron, 22 In.	275.00
Meat Jack, Brass, Mechanical, 19th Century	88.00

Milk Shake Machine, Hamilton Beach, 3-Shake, Cast Iron, 1950s .... 550.00 to 750.00
Milk Shake Machine, Arnold, Green Porcelain 165.00
Mixer, Cake, Iron Crank, Clamps To Table 75.00
Mixer, Gilchrist, No. 22 .... 100.00
Mixer, Glass Bottom, Tin Cover, Keystone 110.00
Mixer, Jaguar, Drink, Mechanical, Battery Operated, Red Lucite, Chrome, 6 In. 75.00
Mixer, Juicer, Samson, Electric, Jadite Bowl, 1940s 40.00
Mixer, Mayonnaise, Hutchinson 425.00
Mixer, Mayonnaise, Universal 395.00
Mixer, Soda Fountain, Green Granite, Machine Craft, California 295.00
Molds may also be found in the Pewter and Tinware categories
Mold, Butter, Cow, Screw Handle, Round, 2 5/8 In. 165.00
Mold, Butter, Double Star, Plunger, 4 1/2 x 5 1/4 In. 148.50
Mold, Butter, Eagle, Handle 195.00
Mold, Butter, Flower, Turned Handle, Round, 3 3/4 In. 105.00
Mold, Butter, Hearts With Initials H.R., Turned Handle, Round, 4 In. 270.00
Mold, Butter, Leaf Shaped, Turned Handle, 2 3/4 In. 215.00
Mold, Butter, Pineapple Design, Turned Handle, Semi-Circular, 7 In. 215.00
Mold, Butter, Pineapple, Turned Handle, Round, 4 1/2 In. 66.00
Mold, Butter, Primitive Tulip, Round, Turned Handle, 4 1/2 In. 110.00
Mold, Butter, Sheaf Carved, Turned Handle, Round, 4 5/8 In. 247.00
Mold, Butter, Stylized Flower, Turned Handle, Round, 4 5/8 In. 94.00
Mold, Butter, Stylized Tulip, Round, 4 1/2 In. 55.00
Mold, Butter, Swan, Screw Handle, Round, 2 7/8 In. 83.00
Mold, Cake, Lamb, Iron, 13 In., 2 Piece 93.00
Mold, Cake, Lamb, Iron, 15 In., 2 Piece 65.00
Mold, Cake, Rabbit, Griswold 275.00
Mold, Cake, Redware, 11 In. 125.00
Mold, Cake, Santa Claus, Griswold 475.00
Mold, Cake, Santa Claus, Griswold, Cast Iron 250.00
Mold, Cake, Santa Claus, Says Hello Kiddies, Griswold, 12 In. .... 275.00 to 295.00
Mold, Candle, see Tinware category
Mold, Candy, 2 Rabbits, Either Side Of Nest Of Eggs, 5 1/4 In. 165.00
Mold, Candy, 2-Part, Leaf-Like Designs, Wooden, 12 In. 27.50
Mold, Candy, 3 Eagles With Shield, Cast Iron, 8 1/4 In. 181.50
Mold, Candy, 3 Uncle Sam Figures, 3 In. 110.00
Mold, Candy, Bird, Wooden, 5 1/2 x 9 1/2 In. 5.50
Mold, Candy, Kewpie, Arms Down, 5 In. 110.00
Mold, Candy, Kewpie, Finger At Mouth, 11 In. 170.50
Mold, Candy, Kewpie, Germany, 4 In. 125.00
Mold, Candy, Rabbit With Sack, Riding Rooster, 10 In. 70.00
Mold, Candy, Rabbit, Holding Basket, 5 1/4 In. 165.00
Mold, Candy, Zeppelin Hindenburg, 11 1/2 In. 121.00
Mold, Chocolate, 3 Rabbits, Tin Plated Steel, Folding, 10 1/2 In. 44.00
Mold, Chocolate, 4 Rabbits, Tin, Hinged Steel Frame, 4 x 7 In. 33.00
Mold, Chocolate, Airship, c.1910 .... 70.00
Mold, Chocolate, Father Christmas, Cast Iron, Makes 4 .... 80.00
Mold, Chocolate, Father Knickerbocker, Pewter 75.00
Mold, Chocolate, Pipe, Tin 40.00
Mold, Chocolate, Rabbit Face, Bow Tie, 2 Rows Of 8 Each, Frame, 11 1/4 x 12 1/2 In. 65.00
Mold, Chocolate, Rabbit, 10 In. 130.00
Mold, Chocolate, Rabbit, Seated, Clamps, Van Emden, 11 x 10 In. 60.00
Mold, Chocolate, Rabbit, Standing, Basket On Back, Hinges, Clips, 5 1/2 x 16 In. 110.00
Mold, Chocolate, Rabbit, With Basket On Back, 27 In. 1250.00
Mold, Chocolate, Santa Claus, Copper, Tin Wash, 10 In. 495.00
Mold, Chocolate, Standing Lion Each Section, Copper Over Metal, 6 Panels 145.00
Mold, Food, Lion, Oval, Tin, 5 1/4 In. 44.00
Mold, Food, Lion, Oval, Tin, 7 In. 82.50
Mold, Food, Turk's Head, Olive Amber Glaze Pottery, 11 In. 38.50
Mold, Food, White, Elephant, 5 In. 165.00
Mold, Food, White, Shell, 5 In. 65.00
Mold, Gelatin, Melon Shape, Tin 15.00
Mold, Ice Cream, see Pewter category

Mold, Maple Sugar, Bellows Falls, Vermont, 13 x 27 In. 70.00
Mold, Maple Syrup, 5 Cavities, Handle, Fruitwood, 16 x 5 1/2 In. 150.00
Mold, Muffin, Heart, Cast Iron 45.00
Mold, Pudding, Cover, Melon Shape 20.00
Mold, Turk's Head, Pennsylvania, Redware, 9 1/2 In. Diam. 95.00
Mold, Turk's Head, Scalloped Rim, Brown Sponged, Redware, 2 3/4 x 7 1/4 In. 95.00
Mold, Turk's Head, Scalloped Rim, Swirled Flutes, Brown, Redware, 11 x 4 In. 71.00
Mold, Turk's Head, Scalloped Rim, Swirled Flutes, Brown Sponging, Redware, 9 In. 11.00
Mold, Turk's Head, Swirled Ribs, White Slip Rim, Brown Line, Redware, 12 In. 72.00
Mold, Turk's Head, Yellow Slip, Wavy Line & Polka Dot, Redware 1567.00
Muffin Pan, G.F. Filley, No. 7 .... 425.00
Oven, Reflector, Tin, Hinged Door, 14 x 19 In. 110.00
Pan, Breadstick, Griswold, No. 23, Divided 85.00
Pan, Brownie, Griswold, No. 19, Full Writing 175.00
Pan, Corn Stick, Duraware, 5 Ears 30.00
Pan, Corn Stick, Griswold No. 262, Iron 75.00
Pan, Corn Stick, Griswold, 5 Ears 50.00
Pan, Corn Stick, Griswold, July 6, 1920 .... 46.00
Pan, Corn Stick, Miracle Maize Glass 20.00
Pan, Corn Stick, Wagner Ware, Krusty Korn Kobs, Iron, Pat'd. July 6, 1920 .... 75.00
Pan, Crispy Corn, Griswold, No. 273 .... 40.00 to 50.00
Pan, Krusty Korn Kobs, Wagner Ware, Cast Iron .... 75.00 to 125.00
Pan, Muffin, 6 Fruit-Shaped Pans, Cast Iron, 6 3/4 x 9 1/2 In. 77.00
Pan, Muffin, Circle & Scalloped Circles Pans, Iron, Reids Pan, 1870, 9 x 16 In. 159.50
Pan, Muffin, Filley, No. 5 .... 125.00
Pan, Muffin, Griswold, Ear Of Corn, Iron, Miniature 35.00
Pan, Muffin, Griswold, No. 10 .... 55.00
Pan, Popover, Griswold, No. 10 .... 45.00 to 55.00
Pan, Popover, Griswold, No. 18 .... 55.00
Pan, Roll, Griswold, No. 26, Cast Iron 45.00
Pastry Wheel, Tin, Red Wooden Handle, England 15.00
Pea Sheller, Iron, Crank 25.00
Peeler, Apple, Bench Mounted, Adjustable Candleholder 400.00
Peeler, Apple, Goodell 75.00
Peeler, Apple, No. 78, Reading Hardware Co. 70.00
Peeler, Apple, White Mountain, Iron, Instructions, Box 45.00
Peeler, Ram's Horn Handle, Wrought Iron, 43 In. 143.00
Pie Bird, Black Girl Praying, Pottery 15.00
Pie Bird, Bull, Standing, England 50.00
Pie Bird, Indian Princess, Figural, Pottery 14.00
Pie Bird, Mammy Holding Rolling Pin, England 60.00
Pie Bird, Witch Holding Pie, England 50.00
Pie Crimper, Ivory Lady's Leg Handle, Engraved Flowers, 6 In. 330.00
Pie Crimper, Whale Ivory, Hearts On Handle, c.1850, 6 In. 1790.00
Pie Crimper, White Pottery Blade, Wooden Handle, 7 In. 71.50
Pie Pan, Jane Parker, Tin, Embossed 2.00
Pie Pan, Metal, Embossed, Mrs. Marshall's Pies For The ApPIEtite 5.00
Pie Pan, Return To Tender Crust Pie Co., Round 2.50
Pie Plate, Mrs. Wagner's Pies, Tin Plate 4.00
Pie Rack, Wire, 4 Shelves 52.00
Pot Holder, Reddy Kilowatt 18.00
Pot Stand, A. Kenrick & Sons, Cast Iron, 19th Century, 64 In. 500.00
Potato Cutter, Yellow Paint, Stenciling, Iron & Wood, Champion, 1870s 195.00
Potato Ricer, Green Iron Handle 4.00
Press, Cheese, Large 395.00
Prototoaster, White Porcelain Base, 1908 .... 250.00
Rack, Broom, Blu-J, Sign Each End, Holds 12, 1920s 495.00
Rack, Spoon, Green Paint, Carved Pine, c.1800, 21 1/2 In. 4950.00
Rack, Utensil, 7 Iron Hooks, Scrolled Edge Board, 30 1/2 In. 60.50
Reamers are listed in their own category
Refrigerator, General Electric, Top Motor, 1930s, 64 In. .... 245.00 to 425.00
Roaster, Chestnut, Iron, Brass, Pierced Lid, 33 In. 66.00
Roaster, Coffee, Family, Iron, Pat. 1881 .... 250.00

Roaster, Coffee, Globe, Patent Date 1849, Iron 695.00
Roaster, Coffee, Royal, No. 4, Top Light 7000.00
Rolling Pin, Cobalt Blue, Glass, 15 In. 175.00
Rolling Pin, Columbian 100.00
Rolling Pin, Custard Glass, Green Wooden Handles 350.00
Rolling Pin, Floral & Fruit Basket, Harker, Cork Closure 95.00
Rolling Pin, Fruits 85.00
Rolling Pin, Harker 100.00
Rolling Pin, J.H. Haley, One Price Grocery, Carbondale, Illinois 350.00
Rolling Pin, Maple, 16 In. 38.50
Rolling Pin, Movable Handles, Maple, 18 In. 30.00
Rolling Pin, Oak, 1-Piece, 17 1/2 In. 35.00
Rolling Pin, Obey & Son Whiskey Gin, Stoneware 495.00
Rolling Pin, Praire Du Chien, Advertising 265.00
Rolling Pin, Stoneware, A.G. Armes General Merchandise 250.00
Rolling Pin, Yellowware 365.00
Rolling Pin & Pastry Board, Tin 350.00
Rosette Iron, Iron, Directions, Box 8.00
Rotisserie, Forged Iron, Fancy 275.00
Sadiron, American Foundry, St. Louis 2.50
Sadiron, Child's, Iron, Wooden Handle, With Trivet 50.00
Sadiron, Child's, Sensible No. 6 .... 175.00
Sadiron, Colebrookdale Iron Co., Marked 2.50
Sadiron, Ruffle, 3 1/2 x 6 1/2 In. 10.00
Salt & Pepper Shakers are listed in their own category
Scoop, Apple Butter, Large-Handled 330.00
Scoop, Butter, Bird's-Eye Maple, 8 1/2 In. 45.00
Scoop, Flour, Brass, Dated December 8, 1868 .... 38.00
Scoop, Gilchrist No. 31, Nickel Over Brass, 10 1/2 In. 62.50
Scoop, Ice Cream, Banana Split, Griswold 475.00
Scoop, Ice Cream, Cone Shape, Gilchrist, No. 33 .... 90.00
Scoop, Ice Cream, Cone Shape, Key Turn On Top 25.00
Scoop, Ice Cream, Conical, Turnknot, No. 8 .... 20.00
Scoop, Ice Cream, Diplomis, Eskimo, Gray Metal 20.00
Scoop, Ice Cream, Gilchrist No. 30 .... 30.00
Scoop, Ice Cream, Hamilton Beach 25.00
Scoop, Ice Cream, Hamilton Beach, Large 40.00
Scoop, Ice Cream, Kerr-McGee, Triangular, 1905 .... 25.00
Scoop, Ice Cream, Nickel Over Brass 42.50
Scoop, Ice Cream, Shortening & Ice Cream Spoons, Aluminum 7.50
Scoop, Ice Cream, Size 20, Gilchrist, 11 In. 50.00
Scoop, Ice Cream, Wafer, Magic 250.00
Scoop, Ice Creamer, Gilchrist, Model 31, Brass 29.00
Scraper, Dough, Wrought Iron, Heart Cutout In Blade, Iron Handle, 4 In. 110.00
Seeder, Raisin, Landers Frary Clark, Clamp-On 50.00
Shaker, Paprika, Round, Delphite 128.00
Shelf, Kettle, Bird Heads, Baluster Legs, Brass, 6 1/4 x 10 In. 33.00
Sieve, Horsehair, 19th Century, 6 1/2 In. Diam. 24.00
Sifter, Corn Meal, Oak, Screen, 17 1/2 In. 20.00
Sifter, Flour, Double-Ended, Duplex 18.00
Sifter, Flour, Sifter Squeeze Action Handle 10.00
Sifter, Flour, Tole Painted, Floral, Red 137.00
Sifter, Flour, Wooden Frame, Partial Label, Pat. 1861, 9 x 10 3.4 In. 192.50
Skillet, Egg, Enameled Cast Iron, Speckled White & Black 20.00
Skillet, Forged Handle, Wrought Iron, Whitfield Z, 11 1/2 In. 38.50
Skillet, Griswold, No. 3 .... 15.00 to 16.00
Skillet, Griswold, No. 3, Hammered Cover 85.00
Skillet, Griswold, No. 7, Cast Iron 20.00
Skillet, Griswold, No. 9, Marked Lid 125.00
Skillet, Griswold, No. 12 .... 76.00
Skillet, Griswold, Spider Logo 1200.00
Skillet, Hotel, Griswold, No. 20 .... 350.00
Skillet, Miami, No. 8, Cast Iron 26.00

Skillet, Victor, No. 9 .... 38.00
Skillet, Wagner Ware, No. 1101A, Cast Iron, Square 20.00
Skillet, Wagner, No. 0, Cast Iron 20.00
Skimmer, Cast Iron Handle, Perfection Skimmer, Cleveland, Ohio, 9 1/4 In. 60.50
Skimmer, Heart-Shaped Handle, Brass, Wrought Iron 330.00
Slicer, Vegetable, Yellow Pine, Forged Steel Blade, 19th Century, 23 In. 104.00
Smoother, Feather Bed, Dated 1897 .... 125.00
Soap Saver, Slotted, Aluminum 15.00
Spice Box, Grinder Insert, Old Red, Tin, 6 3/8 x 8 3/8 In. 75.00
Spice Chest, Raised Panel Door, Iron Butterfly Hinges, 10 Drawers, Oak, 19 1/2 In. 990.00
Spice Chest, Walnut, 3 Drawers, Porcelain Knobs, Late 19th Century, 12 x 10 In. 150.00
Spoon, For Cream-Top Milk Bottle, Pat. Mar. 3, 1925 .... 25.00
Spoon, Mixing, Slotted & J, Iron, Wooden Handle, Large 1.50
Spoon Rest, Head, Gilner 285.00
Spoon Rest, Mammy, Polka Dots 1100.00
Strainer, Porcelain, Blue & Black, 12 In. 15.00
Strainer, Separator, National Stoves & Ranges, Excelsior Stove Co. 35.00
String Dispenser, Head Of Black Bellhop, Ceramic, 6 In. 98.00
String Holder, Beehive, Cast Iron 65.00
String Holder, Beehive, Cast Iron, 4 3/4 In. 82.50
String Holder, Cat, Chalkware 28.00
String Holder, Chef, Chalkware 28.00
String Holder, Mammy Holding Flowers, California Originals 290.00
String Holder, Mammy Holding Flowers, Ceramic Arts 258.00
String Holder, Mammy, Red Turban, Orange Dots, 6 3/4 In. 110.00
String Holder, Spherical, Brass Ball Feet, Wooden, Victorian, Pair 145.00
String Holder, Strawberry, Chalkware 20.00
String Holder, Windmill, Dutch People 30.00
Sugar Shaker, Green Glass, Removable Bottom 225.00
Teakettle, Wooden Handle, Porcelain Knob, Copper, c.1875. 4 x 8 In. 52.00
Thermometer, Oven, Cream & Green 40.00
Timer, Clock, Bakelite 25.00
Toast Rack, White Porcelain, Czechoslovakia 35.00
Toaster, Blue Willow 2000.00
Toaster, Flip-Down Sides, Seneca 20.00
Toaster, General Electric, Model D12, 8 In. 165.00
Toaster, Hot Point, General Electric, 1928 .... 275.00
Toaster, Hotpoint, Art Deco, Running Animal Embossed Sides, Plastic Base, 7 In. 65.00
Toaster, Iron, Double Jaws, 26 In. 137.00
Toaster, Iron, Hand Held, Mid-19th Century, 36 1/2 In. 150.00
Toaster, Reverso 60.00
Toaster, Star-Rite, Electric, Reversible Box 50.00
Toaster, Toast-O-Later, Model J 80.00
Toaster, Universal, 1906 .... 50.00
Toaster, Westinghouse, Turquoise Enameled, 1950s 125.00
Toaster-Oven-Griddle, Toastmaster Breakfast 85.00
Tongs, Ice, Hand Forged Iron, 1820s, 16 In. 23.00
Trencher, Maple, 24 In. 99.00
Trencher, Wooden, 24 x 10 In. 220.00
Wafer Maker, For Communion Bread, 1881 .... 65.00
Waffle Iron, Child's, Stover Jr., No. 08, Cast Iron 225.00
Waffle Iron, Cruso, Embossed Rooster 115.00
Waffle Iron, E.G. Simmons, Wooden Handles, Cast Iron 225.00
Waffle Iron, Griswold, No. 8, High Stand 100.00
Waffle Iron, Griswold, No. 11, Square 45.00
Waffle Iron, Griswold, No. 18, Hearts & Star 155.00
Waffle Iron, Hearts & Stars, Griswold 200.00
Waffle Iron, Keen Kutter, Miniature 120.00
Waffle Iron, Piqua Ware, No. 9 .... 70.00
Waffle Iron, Porcelain Bird Of Paradise Cover, Royal Rochester 145.00
Waffle Iron, Puritan, No. 8 .... 65.00
Waffle Iron, Square, Stand, Feb. 22, 1910, Wagner 110.00
Waffle Iron, Stand, Hearts & Diamonds, No. 7 Center, 6 3/4 In. .... 138.00 to 158.00

Waffle Iron, Star-Burst Pattern, Marked 8 & 9 .... 50.00
Waffle Iron, Wagner, No. 8 .... 100.00
Waffle Iron, Winchester 175.00
Washboard, Blue Graniteware 50.00
Washboard, Champion Silver 12.00
Washboard, Graniteware, Soap Saver, National Washboard, 1897 .... 9.00
Washboard, National No. 701, Wooden, Glass, 24 In. 45.00
Washboard, Shapleigh, Brass 38.00
Washboard, Stenciled National 30.00
Washer, Handy Washer, Warren Mfg. Co., Warren, Ind., Red Paint, Wooden 70.00
Washing Machine, Boss, Hand-Operated, E.H. Huenefeld 225.00
Washing Machine, Maytag, Wooden, 1915 .... 850.00
Washing Machine, WashKosh, Oshkosh, Wis. 110.00
Wringer, Cast Iron, Composition Rollers, Sample 120.00
Wringer, Gem, American Wringer Co., Iron, Wooden, Salesman's Sample, 16 In. 88.00

KNIFE collectors usually specialize in a single type. In the 1960s, the United
States government passed a law that required knife manufacturers to mark
their knives with the country of origin. This seemed to encourage the
collectors, and knife collecting became an interest of a large group of people.
All types of knives are collected, from top quality twentieth-century
examples to old bone- or pearl-handled knives in excellent condition.

Alamo Bowie, Stag Hilt, 15 1/4 In. 320.00
Army, Survival, Sheath, Camillus, 12 In. 40.00
Autocrat, Morton Foods 11.00
Babe Ruth, Bat Shape .... 100.00 to 115.00
Bouka, Baluster Base, Sweden, 4 3/4 In. 90.00
Bowie, 2-Piece Antler Grip, Leather Scabbard, Civil War, 6 1/8 In. 245.00
Bowie, Brass Tacked Grip, Rio Grande Etched On Blade, 7 1/2 In. 350.00
Bowie, Civil War, Blacksmith Made From Wagon Wheel Tire 1380.00
Bowie, Cutlery Hilt, Civil War Period, 6 3/4-In. Blade 475.00
Bowie, Hand Made, Brass Haft, Wooden Scabbard, 9 In. 110.00
Bowie, Horn Handle, Tooled Leather Sheath, Mexico, 14 In. 110.00
Bowie, Stag Haft, 9 1/2 In. 210.00
Bowie Form Blade, Chiseled Zoomorphic Figures, Spain, Large 475.00
Butcher's, Shapleigh's Hammer Forged, 1843 .... 20.00
Case, 2 Blades, Pocket, 4 In. 45.00
Case, Pocket, XX 9-Dot Sod Buster, 1 Blade, 4 3/4 In. 60.00
Cittaraugus, Sheath, Bone Handle 165.00
Combat, Case, 6 In. 60.00
Dagger, Nazi, Scabbard, Ornate Chain 2200.00
Dagger, Peasant, Pierced, Horn & Brass Scales Handle, Spain, 1800, 6 1/4 In. 190.00
Dagger, Renaissance, Ivory Cased, 19th Century, 13 1/2 In. 550.00
Display, Antler Handle, On Stand, 1835-1852, Large 895.00
Draw, Keen Kutter 29.00
File, Brass, Wooden Haft, Copper Guard, 10 3/4 In. 140.00
Gerber Commando, Original Sheath 45.00
Harness Maker's, Iron Crescent Blade, Brass Bound, Wooden Handle 9.50
Horse Hoof, Wooden Handle, Iron 6.50
Hunter, Bicentennial 1976, Folding, Under Glass Dome 210.00
Hunting, Copper Head, Leather Case, Folding 95.00
Hunting, Remington, Leather Sheath 45.00
KaBar, U.S. Navy, Leather Sheath 50.00
Knuckle, Military Type, Brass Handle, Eagle Head 895.00
Kuba Warrior's, Hourglass Shaped Blade, Inlaid Wooden Hilt, 9 3/8 In. 240.00
Marbles, Ideal, Leather Sheath 100.00
Moro Borong, Ebony Handle, Wooden Sheath, 13 3/4 In. 175.00
Pal, Combat, Leather Sheath 60.00
Pattern, Knife Maker's, 9 1/4 To 17 In., 8 Piece 85.00
Pen, Panther, Saguaro Cactus, Eagle 22.00
Pen, Russia 22.50
Pen, Woman's, Nickled Steel Blade, Chain Loop, 14K Gold, 2 1/2 In. 125.00
Pistol Grip, Hand Forged & Engraved Steel, Calf & Deerskin Holster, 8 In. 220.00

Pocket, 2 Blades, 3 In. 30.00
Pocket, Abalone Grips, 14-In. 14K Gold Filled Watch Chain Attached 25.00
Pocket, Barlow 8.00
Pocket, Camco USA, 3 Blades 25.00
Pocket, Case, 2 Blades, 3 In. 30.00
Pocket, Combination, 2 Blades, Bottle Opener, Screwdriver, Black, 3 In. 5.00
Pocket, Imperial, Boy Scout Style, 4 Blades, Black End Ring, 3 1/2 In. 8.00
Pocket, Imperial, Empire State Building, Plastic Mother-Of-Pearl, IK Co. 8.00
Pocket, Imperial, Fish Scaling Blade, Bottle Opener, Ivory Celluloid, 4 1/4 In. 10.00
Pocket, Purina 12.50
Pocket, Reddy Kilowatt 25.00
Pocket, Schrade, French Ivory, 2 Blades, Pat. Feb. 12, '06, 3 5/8 In. 45.00
Pocket, Sunshine Biscuits 20.00
Pocket, Tombstone Casket Co., Brass Handle 6.50
Pocket, Travelers Insurance, Sterling Silver 35.00
Pocket, Winchester 8.00
Purina, Checkerboard, 12 In. 22.00
Remington, Patent 1937 .... 98.00
Sanfax Company, Folding, Stainless Steel Blade, Ivory Handle, 4 1/2 In. 6.00
Shell Gasoline, Pocket 20.00
Silver, Folding, Kearney Livestock Co. 7.00
Space Ship, Morse Code & Space Scenes 65.00
Throwing, Crescent Head, Fur-Wrapped Grip, Congo 475.00
Tomato, Bakelite, Butterscotch, Original Wrapper 4.00
Utility, USMC 35.00
Winchester, 1 Blade, Pocket 35.00
Winchester, Advertising, 1950s, Pair 75.00
Woodcraft, Marbles, Leather Sheath 65.00
Zippo, Star Hardware, 2 x 1 In. 25.00

KOREAN WARE, see Sumida

KOSTA, the oldest Swedish glass factory, was founded in 1742. During the 1920s through the 1950s, many pieces of original design were made at the factory. The firm is still working.

Bowl, Green Over Clear Casing, Warff 1350.00
Dish, Candy, Fish Shape, Signed 50.00
Figurine, Hedgehog 80.00
Figurine, Moon Landing, Signed, 9 In. 690.00
Figurine, Owl 68.00
Figurine, Swimming Polar Bear, Signed, 6 In. 317.00
Sculpture, Engraved Cowboy & Reindeer, Vicke Lindstrand, 1948, 6 In. 315.00
Vase, Blue Stripe Fishnet, Black Base 350.00
Vase, Blue Vertical Trailings Interior, Clear, Vicke Lindstrand, c.1955, 15 In. 690.00
Vase, Bud, Faceted Apple Blossom, Prism Cut, 5 In. 935.00
Vase, Etched Female Guitar Player, Flattened Form, 10 In. 287.50
Vase, Frosted Nude Female, Signed, 12 1/2 In. 1200.00
Vase, Molding Of Nude Maiden, Pale Amber, c.1935. 10 3/4 In. 805.00

KPM refers to Berlin porcelain, but the same initials were used alone and in combination with other symbols by several German porcelain makers. They include the Konigliche Porzellan Manufaktur of Berlin, initials used in mark, 1823–1847; Meissen, 1723–1724 only; Krister Porzellan Manufaktur in Waldenburg, after 1831; Kranichfelder Porzellan Manufaktur in Kranichfeld, after 1903; and the Kister Porzellan Manufaktur in Scheibe, after 1838.

Basket, Applied Flowers & Cherub Handle, Blue & White, 7 1/2 In. 55.00
Charger, Vignettes Of Cupids, Grotesque Heads, 18 In. 1380.00
Cup & Saucer, Green Grapes, Brown Eagle Mark & Blue Scepter 247.00
Cup & Saucer, Paneled 1540.00
Dinner Set, Beverly, Fruit Basket Medallions, Green Crown, 43 Piece 160.00
Dish, Double Shell, Lobster Handle, 12 In. 150.00
Figurine, Polar Bear, 10 In. 495.00
Lithophane see also Lithophane category
Panel, Christ, Teach The Pharisees, Porcelain, 12 x 15 In. 6325.00

Plaque, 2 Children, Reading A Book, Frame 9020.00
Plaque, Beautiful Woman 3/4-Length Portrait, Keller 8250.00
Plaque, Female Saint At Prayer, 12 x 9 3/4 In. 4025.00
Plaque, Game Birds, Gilt Designed Border, Oval, 15 In. 460.00
Plaque, Girl With Hat, Oval, Scepter Mark, Signed, 10 x 7 1/4 In. 1430.00
Plaque, Monk Despairing Over Dead Nude Woman, 8 1/2 x 11 1/2 In. 2415.00
Plaque, Portrait Of Young Woman, F. Fauer, 10 3/4 x 8 1/2 In. 2940.00
Plaque, Queen Louis Portrait 2860.00
Plaque, Ruth, Pierced Foliate Frame, Late 19th Century, 8 1/2 x 5 1/2 In. 1210.00
Plaque, Semi-Nude, Gilded Rectangular Frame, Wagner, 6 1/2 x 4 1/2 In. 2400.00
Plaque, Turkish Girl, Scepter Mark, Gilt Florentine Frame, 7 x 4 1/2 In. 1870.00
Plate, Fuchsia Scrollwork Edge, Floral Center, c.1880, 10 1/8 In., 10 Piece 385.00

KTK are the initials of the Knowles, Taylor & Knowles Company of East Liverpool, Ohio, founded by Isaac W. Knowles in 1853. The company made many types of utilitarian wares, hotel china, and dinnerwares. They made the fine bone china known as Lotus Ware from 1891 to 1896. The company merged with American Ceramic Corporation in 1928. It closed in 1934. Lotus Ware is listed in its own category in this book.

K.T.& K.
CHINA

Bowl, Swirls, Art Deco, Mottled Rose, Green, Turned In, 8 x 3 In. 15.00
Pitcher, Fishnet Design, Knotted Handle, 3 1/4 In. 285.00

KU KLUX KLAN items are now collected because of their historic importance. Literature, robes, and memorabilia are available. The Klan is still in existence, so new material is found.

Certificate, Membership, Raised Seal & Signed 75.00
Figure, Klansman, Hooded, Plaster, Black & Red, 8 In. 125.00
Lamp, Figural, Hooded Klansman 450.00
Mirror, Celluloid, Pocket 5.00
Record, 78 RPM 100.00
Robe & Hat 350.00
Token, Brass, Convention Of The Order, Bristol, Tenn., May 11, 1907 .... 45.00

KUTANI ware is a Japanese porcelain made after the mid-seventeenth century. Most of the pieces found today are nineteenth-century. Collectors often use the term *kutani* to refer to just the later, colorful pieces decorated with red, gold, and black pictures of warriors, animals, and birds.

Bowl, Fluted Corners, Gold Designs, c.1930 .... 48.00
Charger, Red, Blue & White, Imari, 1850, Large 1650.00
Dish, Pine Tree, Figures, Fuku Mark, 19th Century, 15 In. 1430.00
Dish, Vines, Tendrils, Patterned Background, 19th Century, 14 1/2 In. 2310.00
Platter, Peacocks & Flowers, 19th Century, 16 In. 220.00
Vase, Birds, Trees, Red & Gold Border, Mounted As Lamp, c.1900, 28 In., Pair 660.00
Vase, Orange Flower, Cobalt & Black, White Ground, 2 1/2 In. 5.00

LACQUER is a type of varnish. Collectors are most interested in the Chinese and Japanese lacquer wares made from the Japanese varnish tree. Lacquer wares are made from wood with many coats of lacquer. Sometimes the piece is carved or decorated with ivory or metal inlay.

Basin, Water Plants, Nashiji Ground, Silver Handles, Japan, 1900, 11 In. 2640.00
Box, Carp Scene On Cover, 19th Century, 12 x 8 1/2 In. 247.50
Box, Document, Gold Pine Branches, Ro-Inro Interior, 19th Century, 17 3/4 In. 220.00
Box, Rectangle, Landscape, Boats, Mountains, Interior Tray, Meiji Period, 4 7/8 In. .. 467.50
Box, Tea, 1 Drawer, Japan, 10 In. 110.00
Box, Writing, 2 Tiers, Floral Spray On Cover, Kiriwood, 19th Century, 10 x 8 In. 440.00
Candlestick, Gold Tokugawa Mon, Black Ground, Japan, Edo Period, 19 In., Pair 522.50
Coffer, Mother-Of-Pearl Borders, Gilt Metal Clasp, Handle, 10 x 14 In. 2588.00
Cosmetic Stand, Mirror Stand Above 2 Drawers, Floral, 19th Century, 26 1/2 In. 440.00
Crumb Scoop, Tray, Pair 138.00
Figurine, Guandi, Polychrome, Dynasty, 35 In. 412.50
Lunch Box, Tiered Compartments, Overall Gilt Design, Japan, 14 In. 55.00
Tray, On Stand, Red, Round, 24 In. 440.00

LADY HEAD VASE, see Head Vase

LALIQUE glass was made by Rene Lalique in Paris, France, between the 1890s and his death in 1945. The glass was molded, pressed, and engraved in Art Nouveau and Art Deco styles. Pieces were marked with the signature *R. Lalique*. Lalique glass is still being made. Pieces made after 1945 bear the mark *Lalique*. Jewelry made by Rene Lalique is listed in the Jewelry category.

LALIqve

Ashtray, Medicis, Opalescent Rim, Nude Women, Navy Blue, c.1924, 5 7/8 In.	925.00
Bonbon, Cigales, Opalescent Cover, 12 Cicadas, Satin-Lined Box, 10 In.	1100.00
Bonbon, Vallauris, Berry & Leaves Cluster Finial Cover, Frosted, 6 x 4 1/2 In.	895.00
Bookends, Chrysis, Arched Nudes, Flowing Hair, Marked, 6 1/2 In.	775.00
Bookends, Reverie, Kneeling Maiden, Signed, 8 In.	1850.00
Bowl, Aries, Signature, 7 5/8 x 8 5/8 In.	500.00
Bowl, Calypso, 5 Swimming Mermaids, Frosted Opalescent, 1930, 14 1/2 In.	2875.00
Bowl, Calypso, Molded Mermaids, Gray, 13 7/8 In.	1035.00
Bowl, Calypso, Nude Maidens In Surf, Signed, 11 3/4 In.	3225.00
Bowl, Coquille, Blue Opalescent, Overlapping Shells, No. 3200, 9 3/8 In.	715.00
Bowl, Nemours, Black Enamel Blossoms, Frosted, 10 In.	385.00
Bowl, Perruches, Foliate & Branch Ground, Signed, 9 In.	2550.00
Bowl, Phalenes, Overlapping Gypsy Moths, Blue, 1929, 15 1/4 In.	6050.00
Bowl, Pissenlit, Dandelion Leaves, Enameled, Sepia, Flattened Base, 3 x 9 1/2 In.	290.00
Bowl, Pissenlit, Dandelion Leaves, Signed, 13 In.	495.00
Bowl, Poissons, Excised Fish On Entire Surface, Signed, 9 1/2 x 10 In.	1600.00
Bowl, Sirenes, Flattened Flared Rim, 8 Nude Women In Different Poses, 14 1/4 In.	1320.00
Bowl, Soucis, Flowers, Frosted, Blue Patina, c.1931, 9 3/8 In.	1150.00
Bowl, Undulating Linear Design, Flaring Form, Signed, 9 1/2 In.	345.00
Box, 3 Dahlias, Opalescent, Blue Satin Base, 8 1/2 x 2 In.	1000.00
Box, Cover, Frosted, Raised Clusters Of Florets, Floret Handle, 6 1/4 x 4 In.	850.00
Box, Dresser, Fern Design, Satin Base, Signed, 5 1/2 In.	450.00
Box, Emiliane, Clear & Amber Cover, Allover Blossoms, D'Orsay, 4 x 1 1/2 In	500.00
Box, Powder, 4 Scarabees, 5 Scarabs, Black, 2 1/4 In.	3300.00
Box, Sea Nymphs Inside Cover, 2 Sirenes, Signed, 10 1/4 In.	3680.00
Bracelet, 18 Glass Cylindrical Beads, Stepped Pyramid Ends, Blue	2070.00
Brooch, Flowering Stems, Teal Foil Backed, Signed, 2 3/4 In.	1725.00
Brooch, Serpent, Yellow Foil Back, Brass Backing, Stamped, 1 1/2 In.	1495.00
Candelabra, Hanging, 4-Light	3500.00
Chandelier, 6-Arm, Champs Elysee, Gilt Metal Frame, 28 In.	4325.00
Chandelier, Hanging, Candle Lit, Stained	3500.00
Chandelier, Madagascar, Domed Shade, Band Of Monkey Heads, 11 3/8 In.	9350.00
Chandelier, Villeneuve, Domed Shade, Floral Relief, Opalescent, 12 1/2 In.	2760.00
Clock, 6 Swimming Mermaids, Centered Clock, 1926, 4 1/2 x 4 3/8 In.	3450.00
Clock, Deux Colombes, Opalescent, 8 x 6 In.	4400.00
Clock, Moineaux, Frosted, Dome Case, Molded Birds & Berries, 6 x 8 1/2 In.	1345.00
Cordial, Panels Of Draped Maidens, Signed, 6 Piece	3450.00
Cup & Plate, Jaffa, Deep Amber Wash, Frosted, Glass Handle, 7 1/4 In.	175.00
Cup & Plate, Jaffa, Green Wash, Frosted, Glass Handle, 7 1/4 In.	175.00
Decanter, Sirenes, Et Grenouilles, Mermaids, Frog Heads, Green, Stopper, 15 In.	6900.00
Decanter, Stopper, 6 Tetes, Frosted, 6 Enameled Masks Band, Ovoid, 15 1/8 In.	3450.00
Figurine, Avec Guirlande De Fruits, Frosted, 1913, 8 1/2 In.	5750.00
Figurine, Cat, Frosted, Signed, 8 In.	1250.00
Figurine, Grande Nue Bras Leves, Nude Female, Arms Up, Signed, 23 In.	5980.00
Figurine, Maiden Moyenne Voilee, Standing, Frosted, Enameled, Signed, 5 1/2 In.	975.00
Figurine, Turtle, Amber, Signed	295.00
Holder, Placecard, Basket Of Flowers, Frosted, Signed, 2 x 2 In., 4 Piece	500.00
Hood Ornament, Falcon Hawk, c.1932, 5 7/8 In.	1265.00
Hood Ornament, Grande Libellule, Dragonfly, Wings Open, Gray, 8 1/4 In.	4400.00
Hood Ornament, Petite Libellule, Dragonfly, Closed Wings, Signed, 6 1/4 In.	1150.00
Hood Ornament, Tete D'Aigle, Eagle's Head, Signed, 4 5/16 In.	920.00
Hood Ornament, Tete D'Epervier, Kestrel Head, Signed, 2 5/8 In.	690.00
Hood Ornament, Tete De Belier, Head Of Ram, 1928, 3 3/4 In.	1100.00
Hood Ornament, Victoire, Woman's Head, Streaming Hair, Signed, 6 1/8 In.	7700.00
Incense Burner, Mermaids, Blue Patina, Signed, 5 1/4 In.	450.00

Lamp, Camellia, Nickeled Bronze, Gray Frosted Shade, 1928, 15 7/8 In. 8050.00
Lamp, Feuilles De Murier, Overlapping Leaf Frosted Glass Shade, 1927, 14 1/2 In. ... 7475.00
Lemonade Set, Setubal, Amber, Molded Branches, 18 1/8-In. Tray, 10 Piece 4850.00
Lighter, Double-Headed Lion, Gold & Crystal 225.00
Liquor Set, Clear & Frosted Carafe, Raised Scroll Rolls, 5 Piece 1000.00
Liquor Set, Clear & Frosted, Stopper, Pedestal Liquors, 7 3/4 In. 5 Piece 1000.00
Mirror, Eglantines, 6 Curved & Molded Glass Sections, Metal Dividers, 17 1/8 In. 5175.00
Mirror, Hand, 2 Oiseaux, Phoenix, Grape Clusters, Frosted & Clear, 1932, 6 3/8 In. .. 1500.00
Necklace, 11 Fuchsia Beads, Modeled As Flower Blossoms, 18 In. 2070.00
Necklace, Feuilles De Lierre, 18 Frosted & Molded Ivy Leaves, Green 3220.00
Paperweight, Chouette, Owl 125.00
Paperweight, Deux Aigles, Amber, 2 Eagle Heads Holding Jewel, 3 In. 2530.00
Paperweight, Horse's Head, Molded, Longchamps, 5 In. 2300.00
Paperweight, Raised Blossoms & Leaves, Dome Shaped, Frosted, Signed, 2 In. 350.00
Pendant, Floret, Green Wash, 1 5/8 In. 950.00
Pendant, Floret, Molded Nude Sitting Among Flowers, Rose, Pierced For Silk Cord . 385.00
Pendant, Graines, Rounded Triangle, Turquoise Blue, Branches, Silk Cord, c.1920 ... 1150.00
Pendant, Graines, Triangular, Frosted Amber, Signed, 1 7/8 In. 1540.00
Pendant, Libellules, Tapered Cross, Relief Dragonflies, Green, 2 1/8 In. 2300.00
Pendant, Sauterelles, Oval, Molded Lilies & Grasshoppers, Green Foil, 3 In. 1320.00
Pendant, Scrolled, Curvilinear Motif, Sienna, Pierced For Silk Cord 415.00
Perfume Bottle, 4 Faces At Corners, Frosted, 4 In. 385.00
Perfume Bottle, A Cotes Bouchon Papillons, Signed, 2 1/4 In. 1840.00
Perfume Bottle, Air Du Temps, Double Dove Stopper, Signed, 14 In. 1150.00
Perfume Bottle, Ambre D'Orsay, Black, Frosted Caryatids, Floral Stopper, 5 1/2 In. 1325.00
Perfume Bottle, Ambre D'Orsay, Maidens, Daisies, Brown Patina, 5 1/8 In. 2530.00
Perfume Bottle, Ambre D'Orsay, Square, Robed Figures At Corners, 5 1/2 In. 1200.00
Perfume Bottle, Anemones, 2 Large Flowers 350.00
Perfume Bottle, Calendal, Floral Stopper, Green, Signed, 4 5/8 In. 2415.00
Perfume Bottle, Cicada Form, Frosted, 2 1/2 In. 1700.00
Perfume Bottle, Corday, Tzigane, Frosted, R. Lalique, 1930s, 3 3/4 In. 435.00
Perfume Bottle, Cupid Set Within Heart, Brown Patina, Signed, 4 In. 800.00
Perfume Bottle, Dans La Nuit, Labeled Box, Signed, 1945, 3 In. 635.00
Perfume Bottle, Deux Fleurs, Engraved, 3 3/4 In. 210.00
Perfume Bottle, Double Dahlia 195.00
Perfume Bottle, Elegance, 2 Nude Women, Flowering Branches, Signed, 3 3/4 In. ... 2760.00
Perfume Bottle, Fleurs De Pommier, Reticulated Apple Blossoms, 5 3/8 In. 4400.00
Perfume Bottle, Fougeres, Square, Molded Ferns, Portrait Medallions, 3 1/2 In. 4675.00
Perfume Bottle, Frosted Apple, Veined Apple Leaves Top, Signed 185.00
Perfume Bottle, Frosted, Quatre Coeurs, Gilt Screw Cap, Blue Leather Pouch, 4 In. 190.00
Perfume Bottle, Habanita 10.00
Perfume Bottle, Les Sylvies, Dragonflies, Black, Turquoise, Box, c.1925 .... 2300.00
Perfume Bottle, Les Temps Des Lilas, Vertical Ribs & Scrolls, c.1922, 3 3/8 In. 800.00
Perfume Bottle, Molded Doves On Branches, Butterfly Stopper, 4 5/16 In. 1150.00
Perfume Bottle, Molinard, 12 Nude Women Dancers, La Provencal, 5 In. 225.00
Perfume Bottle, Nina Ricci, Frosted Bird Stopper, c.1950s 150.00
Perfume Bottle, Nina Ricci, Signoricci, Contents 125.00
Perfume Bottle, Poesie D'Orsay, Dancing Maidens, Floral Ground, Umber 5 3/4 In. 2875.00
Perfume Bottle, Requete, 3 1/2 In. 395.00
Perfume Bottle, Rose, Radiating Bands, Frosted Stopper, Signed, 4 In. 3080.00
Perfume Bottle, Samoa 275.00
Perfume Bottle, Scarabee, Molded Flower Stopper, Light Brown Patina, 3 1/2 In. 1725.00
Perfume Bottle, Single Dahlia 175.00
Perfume Bottle, Sirenes, Frosted Mermaids, Gray, 5 1/2 In. 250.00
Perfume Bottle, Spherical, Etched, Draped Woman Stopper, 4 In. 1650.00
Perfume Bottle, Toutes Les Fleurs, Flask Form, Signed, 4 In. 2550.00
Perfume Bottle, Worth, Dans La Nuit, Star Motif, Quarter-Moon Stopper, 4 In. 715.00
Perfume Bottle, Worth, Je Reviens, Blue, Turquoise Stopper, 5 In. 95.00
Perfume Burner, Cover, Sirenes, 10 Green Mermaids, Waves, 6 3/4 In. 1325.00
Plaque, Vierge A L'enfant, Mother & Child, Wooden Base, Signed, 13 1/2 In. 1150.00
Plate, Burning Bush, Black Lead Crystal, Signed, 7 7/8 In. 180.00
Plate, Ondines, Nude Women Amidst Surf, Marked, 10 3/4 In. 1200.00

Plate, Ormeaux No. 2, Bands Of Leaves, Green, 1931, 13 3/4 In. 925.00
Plate, Oursins, Opalescent, 16-Ray Design, 11 In., Pair 250.00
Plate, Swimming Sirens, Original Velvet & Silk Lined Box, c.1919, 10 In. 2645.00
Powder Box, 3 Dancing Nudes On Cover, Signed, 3 3/4 In. 325.00
Powder Box, Chantilly, Central Cabochon On Lid, Deer Amid Foliage, 3 5/8 In. 575.00
Powder Box, Dans La Nuit, Blue Enameled, Stars & Moon, Cover, 5 In. 1265.00
Salt, Embossed Birds On Rim, 3 1/2 In. 125.00
Tray, 2 Sections, Raised Blossoms, Stand-Out Centers, Signed, 3 1/2 x 4 1/2 In. 250.00
Tray, Enamel Leaf Border, Marked, 12 In. 300.00
Tray, Frosted Raised Blossoms, 2 Sections, 3 1/2 x 4 1/2 x 1 In. 250.00
Vase, Albert, Falcon Head Handles, Deep Blue To Purple, 6 3/4 In. 9200.00
Vase, Archers, Smoky Topaz, 10 Male Hunters With Bows, Bird Border, 10 1/2 In. ... 4675.00
Vase, Avallon, Birds Perched On Berried Branches, Signed, 6 In. 1150.00
Vase, Avallon, High Relief Birds & Berries, Frosted, Green Patina, c.1927, 5 5/8 In. .. 1955.00
Vase, Bacchantes, Frosted, 10 Full-Length Nudes, 1950s, 9 3/4 In. 4950.00
Vase, Bacchantes, Procession Of Nudes On Sides, Signed, 10 In. 1955.00
Vase, Beliers, Crouching Ram Handles, Frosted, Smoky, Short Stem, 7 3/8 In. 1495.00
Vase, Birches, Deer Among Trees, Marked, 1940s, 6 1/2 In. 600.00
Vase, Camaret, Blown-Out Fish, Frosted, Signed, 5 1/2 x 5 In. 850.00
Vase, Ceylon, Lovebirds, Branches, Frosted Pale Blue, 1924, 9 1/4 In. 4100.00
Vase, Charmilles, Charcoal Gray Overlapping Leaves, Frosted, 14 1/4 In. 6325.00
Vase, Chevaux, Frosted, Flared Shape, 5 Molded Horses, 7 1/4 In. 2200.00
Vase, Coqs Et Raisins, Frosted, Enameled, Roosters, Stylized Branches, 6 In. 975.00
Vase, Danaides, Water Maidens, Frosted Opalescent, Blue, 1926, 7 1/4 In. 3175.00
Vase, Erimaki, Mounted With Amber Lizards, Marked, 9 1/2 In. 1580.00
Vase, Eucalyptus, Frosted, Bell Shape, Berry Feet, Blue Patina, c.1925, 6 3/ 8 In. 2100.00
Vase, Formose, Spherical, Etched Fish, Green, 7 In. 5175.00
Vase, Graines, Alexandrite, Seed Pods, 7 1/2 In. 2875.00
Vase, Graines, Applied Spherical Designs At Base, Signed, 8 In. 1100.00
Vase, Grasshopper, Emerald Green, 10 1/2 In. 7700.00
Vase, Gui, Mistletoe Branches, Berries, Opalescent, Blue Enameled, 6 3/4 In. 800.00
Vase, Jade Green, Signed, 1932, 7 In. 3000.00
Vase, Languedoc, Serrated Leaf Bands, Frosted Gray, 1929, 9 In. 5750.00
Vase, Luxembourg, Signed, Paper Label, 8 1/2 x 12 1/2 In. 1700.00
Vase, Marguerites, Oviform, Molded Daisies, Black Enamel, 9 In. 3000.00
Vase, Milan, Spherical, Green Patina, Leaf Design, 11 1/4 In. 3575.00
Vase, Moissac, Frieze Of Stylized Leaves, Signed, 5 1/8 In. 1725.00
Vase, Molded Relief Of Birds Amid Foliage, Signed, 7 In. 300.00
Vase, Monnaie Du Pape, Amber, Frosted & Polished Leaves, 9 1/4 In. 3850.00
Vase, Monnaie Du Pape, Oviform, Amber Overlay, Signed, 9 1/2 In. 7150.00
Vase, Mures, 8 In. 3000.00
Vase, Ormeaux, Overlapping Leaves, Veins In High Gloss, Signed, 6 1/2 In. 850.00
Vase, Ormeaux, Red Amber, Overlapping Elm Leaves, 6 5/8 In. 2550.00
Vase, Ornis, Bird Handles, Opalescent, Gray Enameled, Footed, 7 1/2 In. 1725.00
Vase, Parrot Motif, Frosted Opalescent, Drilled For Lamp, 10 x 9 In. 3000.00
Vase, Perigord, Frosted Gray, Overlapping Sides, 1928, 5 3/4 In. 1450.00
Vase, Pierrefonds, Scrolled Thorny Strap Handles, Amber, Signed, 6 1/4 In. 8625.00
Vase, Pierrefonds, Scrolled Throny Strap Handles, Frosted, 6 1/8 In. 5775.00
Vase, Poissons, Spiny Fish, Signed, 9 1/4 In. 1610.00
Vase, Raisins, Frosted, Stylized Grape Clusters, Curved Vines, 6 1/4 In. .... 330.00 to 700.00
Vase, Rampillon, Conical, Amber, Molded Protrusions, Floral Surround, 5 1/4 In. 2425.00
Vase, Rennes, Stylized Antelopes, Foliage, Frosted, Blue Patina, c.1933, 4 7/8 In. 925.00
Vase, Rennes, Stylized Antelopes, Frosted, Ovoid, c.1933, 4 7/8 In. 400.00
Vase, Ronces, Entwined Brambles, Amber, 9 In. 2500.00
Vase, Ronces, Entwined Brambles, Cranberry Red, 9 1/4 In. 5750.00
Vase, Ronces, Entwined Brambles, Frosted, Brown Patina, c.1921, 9 1/2 In. 1150.00
Vase, Ronces, Entwined Brambles, Signed, 9 1/4 In. 885.00
Vase, Saint-Francois, Finches, Foliage, Frosted, 1930, 6 7/8 In. 300.00
Vase, Sauterelles, Allover Grasshoppers, Marked, 11 In. 3225.00
Vase, Serpent, Modeled As Coiled Snake, Signed, 10 1/2 In. 5500.00
Vase, Six Figurines Et Masques, Nude Maidens Amid Foliage, Signed, 10 In. 6325.00
Vase, Soaring Birds Above Hunters, Raised Bows, Signed, 1921, 10 3/8 In. 3450.00
Vase, Sophora, Gray, 6 Stylized Leaves In Frosted Recesses, 10 1/8 In. 4400.00

Vase, Thistle Molded, Tapered Sides, Green Highlights, Signed, 8 1/2 In. 1100.00
Vase, Upright Stylized Thistle Leaves, Signed, 1922, 7 3/8 In. 2013.00

LAMPS of every type, from the early oil-burning Betty and Phoebe lamps to the recent electric lamps with glass or beaded shades, interest collectors. Fuels used in lamps changed through the years; whale oil (1800–1840), camphene (1828), Argand (1830), lard (1833–1863), turpentine and alcohol (1840s), gas (1850–1879), kerosene (1860), and electricity (1879) are the most common. Other lamps are listed by manufacturer or type of material.

Aladdin, Alacite Swirl, Electric, Finial, 30 In., Pair	110.00
Aladdin, Alacite, Boudoir, Whip-O-Lite Shade	150.00
Aladdin, Alacite, Swirled Acanthus Leaves, Bulbous, 7 3/4 In.	35.00
Aladdin, B-11, Green	185.00
Aladdin, B-25, Victoria & B-26, Decalmania, Pair	650.00
Aladdin, B-27, Alacite, Simplicity, Gold Luster	325.00
Aladdin, B-62, Ruby Crystal, Short Lincoln Drape	450.00
Aladdin, B-75, Alacite, Scalloped Foot	400.00
Aladdin, B-75, Alacite, Tall Lincoln Drape	115.00
Aladdin, B-77, Ruby Crystal, Tall Lincoln Drape	495.00
Aladdin, B-80, Beehive, Clear Crystal	65.00
Aladdin, B-81, Beehive, Green Crystal	55.00
Aladdin, B-82, Beehive, Dark Amber	95.00
Aladdin, B-85, Quilt, White Moonstone	250.00 to 275.00
Aladdin, B-87, Rose	200.00 to 360.00
Aladdin, B-87, Vertique, Rose Moonstone	295.00
Aladdin, B-88, Yellow Moonstone	425.00 to 525.00
Aladdin, B-91, White, Font, Rose Foot	250.00
Aladdin, B-92, Green	225.00
Aladdin, B-98, Queen, Rose Moonstone	170.00
Aladdin, B-105, Corinthian, Clear Green	75.00
Aladdin, B-110, Old Chimney	275.00
Aladdin, B-111, Cathedral, Green Moonstone	190.00
Aladdin, B-112, Cathedral, Rose Moonstone, 1935	225.00 to 330.00
Aladdin, B-112, Rose	200.00
Aladdin, B-115, Corinthian, Green Moonstone	110.00
Aladdin, B-116, Rose Moonstone	160.00
Aladdin, B-120, Majestic, White Moonstone	300.00
Aladdin, B-124, Corinthian, White Moonstone	140.00
Aladdin, Brass Burner, Jade Green	115.00
Aladdin, Caboose	65.00
Aladdin, G-16, Opalique, Alacite	4500.00
Aladdin, G-21, Alacite, Boudoir, Shades, Pair	95.00
Aladdin, G-130, Lady In Cape, Amber Opalique	6200.00
Aladdin, G-163, Double Nude, New Metal Base, Opalique	1350.00
Aladdin, G-237, Electric, Ruby Bowl	90.00
Aladdin, G-253, Electric, Table, Flowers In Vase	140.00
Aladdin, G-291d, Alacite, Lighted Base, Pair	55.00
Aladdin, G-309, Alacite, Coral Illuminated, Base, Shade & Finial	85.00
Aladdin, G-311, Vase, Blue Pedestal, Electric	40.00
Aladdin, G-331, Forest Green, Precision Finials, Electric	100.00
Aladdin, G-375, Dancing Ladies, Urn	800.00
Aladdin, Gun In Holster, Pin-Up	110.00
Aladdin, Model B, Floor, 16 In. Parchment Shade	370.00
Aladdin, No. 11, Kerosene, Table, Complete	125.00
Aladdin, No. 12, Table	60.00
Aladdin, No. 413, 75th Anniversary, Student	425.00
Aladdin, No. 1240, Variegated Verde, No. 455 Parchment 20 1/2 In. Shade	275.00
Aladdin, No. 3982, Floor, Night-Light, 18 In. Whip-Off-Lite Shade	200.00
Aladdin, Student, Brass, 20 In.	605.00
Alcohol, Black, Starr & Frost, Sterling Silver, 1886	1295.00
Argand, Bronze, Cut Glass Shade, Lewis Vernon & Co., 14 1/4 In., Pair	990.00
Argand, Double Arm, Engraved Shades, Brass	725.00
Argand, Gilt & Patinated Bronze, Artichoke Finial, Cox, N.Y., c.1830, 22 In., Pair	4125.00

Lamp, Chandelier, 6-Light, Brass

◆◆◆◆◆◆◆◆◆◆◆◆◆◆◆◆◆◆◆◆◆◆◆

Chandeliers can be cleaned in place with a new spray cleaner made for that purpose. Cover the floor with paper or cloth to catch the drips. Then spray the chandelier. It will clean and drip dry.

◆◆◆◆◆◆◆◆◆◆◆◆◆◆◆◆◆◆◆◆◆◆◆

Argand, Single Arm, Clark & Cargill, 18 3/4 In., Pair 1320.00
Argand, Stylized Pilasters, Prisms, Etched Glass Shade, 18 In., Pair 1840.00
Astral, Brass, Column & Font, Cornelius & Co., Cut Prisms, 21 1/4 In. 605.00
Astral, Brass, Corinthian Column, White Marble Base, Electrified, c.1830, 33 In. 154.00
Astral, Brass, Prisms, Blossom-Shaped Shade, Electrified, c.1845, 20 In. 412.50
Astral, Bronze, Double Burner, Frosted & Etched Shades, Electrified, Pair 1650.00
Astral, Frosted & Cut Shade, Brass, Electrified, 22 In. 357.50
Astral, Ionic Capital, Brass, Prism Band, Marble Base, 17 In. 253.00
Astral, Messenger & Son, London & Birmingham, Bronze, c.1830, 17 In. 1210.00
Astral, Prisms, Frosted Cut Shade, Brass, Marble Base, Corneallius & Co., 22 1/2 In. 605.00
Barn, Black Paint, Tin, C.1800, 18 x 9 In. 185.00
Betty, Cast Iron, Crescent Shield, Hammers & Heart Finial, Font Lid, 3 1/2 In. 170.00
Betty, Copper, 6 In. 55.00
Betty, Hinged Brass Lid, Iron Finial, Wrought Iron, 5 1/4 In. 155.00
Betty, Iron, 4 1/2 In. 71.50
Betty, Tin, Stand, Crimped Edge, Shelf & Round Pan, 7 In. 357.00
Betty, Wooden, Trammel, Red Paint 1072.00
Betty, Wrought Iron, Spout, Swivel Font Cover, 4 In. 220.00
Betty, Wrought Iron, Swivel Font Cover, Chain, Hanger, 3 1/2 In. 137.00
Bradley & Hubbard, lamps are included in the Bradley & Hubbard category
Candle, Carriage, With Bracket, Beveled Glass 210.00
Candle, Cranberry Cylinder Shade, Brass Holder, 6 3/4 In. 245.00
Carbide, Auto-Lite 17.50
Carbide, Miner's, Brass 80.00
Carbide, Miner's, Floodlight, Oxweld, Carbic 165.00
Carbide, Miner's, Hat Mounted .... 20.00 to 40.00
Chandelier, 3-Light, Bronze, Russia 330.00
Chandelier, 3-Light, Cast Iron, Lomax Frosted Star Fonts, 10 In. Shades, 46 In. 467.00
Chandelier, 3-Light, Central Globe, Bronze 1870.00
Chandelier, 3-Light, Silvered Bronze, Blue Opaline, Russia, 22 In. 6325.00
Chandelier, 5-Light, Charles X, Acanthus Branches, Font Form, 25 1/2 In. 2875.00
Chandelier, 5-Light, Drip Pans, Turned Finial, Brass, Dutch, 1680s, 31 In. 4765.00
Chandelier, 6-Light, Blown Glass, Glass Rods With Drop Lustres, Italy, 25 In. 330.00
Chandelier, 6-Light, Brass .... *Illus* 2750.00
Chandelier, 6-Light, Brass, Scroll Arms, Electrific, England, 18th Century, 28 In. 3450.00
Chandelier, 6-Light, Cut Glass, Teardrop Bobeche, Late 19th Century 165.00
Chandelier, 6-Light, Dutch Baroque, Brass, 18 x 27 In. 880.00
Chandelier, 6-Light, Maria Theresa Style, Crystal Pendant Drops, 90 In. 1610.00
Chandelier, 6-Light, Wrought Iron, Scrollwork, Curved Arms, 38 x 39 1/2 In. 3520.00
Chandelier, 8-Light, Baroque Style, Brass, Scrolled Arms, Stylized Fans, 26 x 23 In. .. 3450.00
Chandelier, 8-Light, Crimped Drip Plates, Wood & Tin, 22 1/4 In. 575.00
Chandelier, 8-Light, Rococo Style, Warrior Maiden Figure, Bell Drop, 32 x 30 In. 308.00
Chandelier, 9-Light, Cascading Form, Silver Plated & Crystal, 42 x 21 1/2 In. 880.00
Chandelier, 9-Light, Leafy Branch, Lilies, Floral Arms, Brass, 32 x 20 In. 825.00
Chandelier, 9-Light, Louis XV Style, Rock Crystal & Cut Glass, Electrified 8625.00
Chandelier, 9-Light, Louis XV, Crystal, 1700, 48 In. 7425.00
Chandelier, 12-Light, 2 Tiers Of Scrolled Arms, 19th Century, 32 In. 5750.00

Chandelier, 12-Light, Dutch Baroque Style, Removable Arms, 40 In. 5463.00
Chandelier, 12-Light, George I Style, Giltwood, 1800s, 42 x 45 In. 9200.00
Chandelier, 15-Arm, Wire, Tin, Wooden Center, Mid-19th Century, 36 x 36 In. 1975.00
Chandelier, 16-Light, Cage Form, Flowerhead Pans, Wrought Iron, 48 In. 2875.00
Chandelier, 16-Light, Painted Tin, Prisms, 1870s, 32 In. 1500.00
Chandelier, 18-Light, Open Cage, 6 Curved Branches, Brass, Cut Glass, 52 In. 9200.00
Chandelier, 48-Light, Marie Theresa Style, 12 Bracket Arms, 4 Lights Each, 45 In. .. 3520.00
Chandelier, Fluted, Foliate Carving, Swan Supports, Bronze & Alabaster, 27 In. 3335.00
Chandelier, Gas, Rococo Revival, Central Woman Statue 7425.00
Electric, 2 Four-Sided Leaded Shades, Hunter, 28 1/2 In. 5225.00
Electric, 3 Dogs, Around Lamp Post, China, 1930s 37.50
Electric, 3-Light, Hanging, Butterscotch Slag Glass, Brass Frame, Octagonal, 20 In. . 400.00
Electric, 3-Light, Louis XVI Style, Rock Crystal & Gilt Bronze, 18 1/2 In. 1150.00
Electric, 3 Tulips, Alabaster Shades, Leaf Base, Bronze, Albert Cheuret, 14 1/2 In. ... 8625.00
Electric, 4 Flower Baskets Shade, Bronze, Duffner & Kimberly, c.1915, 23 In. 4888.00
Electric, Airplane, Figural, Art Deco, Molded Teal Glass, Silver Platform 875.00
Electric, Airplane, Tall Fins, 1930 .... 575.00
Electric, Architectural Capital, Contemporary Base & Shaft, Shade, 27 1/2 In., Pair .. 995.00
Electric, Aroos, Gilt-Metal, Reverse-Painted Winter Scene Domed Shade, 20 In. 431.00
Electric, Art Deco, Figural, Ballroom Dancers 125.00
Electric, Art Deco, Marble Carved, Nude Woman, Sitting, Looking Into Large Pool .. 495.00
Electric, Art Nouveau, Mermaid, Seashell, Blue & White Slag Glass Shade, Metal 195.00
Electric, Baby Face, Green Satin Glass, Consolidated 1975.00
Electric, Bamboo, Pedestal, 1950s, Pair 85.00
Electric, Banker's, Amronlite, Square Base, Rotates, Curved Stem, 13 1/2 In. 193.00
Electric, Banker's, Verdelite, Square Base, Column Stem, 17 3/4 In. 193.00
Electric, Big Boy, Figural, Vinyl, 6 1/2 In. .... *Illus* 96.00
Electric, Bisque, Ewer, Multicolored Flowers, Gold Handles, SF & Co., 12 In., Pair . 135.00
Electric, Boudoir, Blue Sea Gulls, Frosted Olive Ground, A. Delatte, 17 In. 220.00
Electric, Bouillotte, 2 Candle Arms, Swan Form, Bronze, Electrified, 24 x 13 In. 770.00
Electric, Brass, Persian Style Enameled Ceramic Insert, 22 In. 93.00
Electric, Bridge, Iron, Leaf Design, 63 In. 82.00
Electric, Bronze, Figural, Arab Street Musician, Palm Trees, 10 In. 550.00
Electric, Bronze, Nude Woman, Beaded Shade, Austria, 1900, 24 In. 4025.00
Electric, Catalin, Amber Plastic, Art Deco, Pair 150.00
Electric, Champleve, Stylized Florals, Elephant Handles, Rosewood Base, 24 In. 120.00
Electric, Classical Revival, Marble Pedestal, Gilt-Bronze, No Shade, 26 In., Pair 550.00
Electric, Classique, Boudoir, Reverse-Painted, Woodland Scene, Brass Base 1450.00
Electric, Cliftwood, Drip Glaze, Pink-Lavender, Bulbous 75.00
Electric, Coach, Copper & Steel, 1860, 3 1/2 In., Pair 4500.00
Electric, Copper Foot, L Shape Standard, Copper & Glass Shade, Kurt Versen, 13 In. 1150.00
Electric, Couple, Figural, Period Costume, Porcelain, Vanity, Pair 55.00
Electric, Damon, Chromed Metal, Adjustable, Round, Art Deco, 1928, 13 x 11 In. 3163.00
Electric, Desk, Adjustable Shade, Painted Metal, 1955, 28 In. 1035.00
Electric, Desk, Art Nouveau, Nautilus Shell Frosted Glass Shade, Adjustable Base 1250.00
Electric, Desk, Bronze, Bell-Shaped Shade, France, c.1900, 17 3/8 In. 1150.00
Electric, Desk, Donald Deskey, Copper Standard, 4 Glass Squares, 1930, 17 In. 2875.00

Lamp, Electric, Big Boy, Figural, Vinyl, 6 1/2 In.

Electric, Desk, Gilbert Rohde, Chrome Plated Supports, Tubular Shade, 1933, 14 In. 1035.00
Electric, Dominique, Nickeled Bronze, Parchment Ringed Top, 1940, 5 Ft. x 18 In. .. 5750.00
Electric, Don Juan, Bronze Finish, Vaseline Shades 400.00
Electric, Duffner & Kimberly, Louis XV Style, Leaded Glass, Bronze Base, 29 In. ... 9900.00
Electric, Duffner & Kimberly, Metal, Pottery, Arts & Crafts 3800.00
Electric, Dutch Boy Paints, Figural, 9 1/2 In. ....,....... 300.00
Electric, Econolite, Fountain Of Youth, Heat Motion, Tag 75.00
Electric, Econolite, Heat Motion, Fireplace With Dog & Cat 80.00
Electric, Econolite, Heat Motion, Mill Scene 80.00
Electric, Econolite, Water-Skiers, Heat Motion 125.00
Electric, Edgar Brandt, Wrought Iron, Stylized Foliage, 1925, 20 1/2 In. 5175.00
Electric, Etched Arched Columns & Lake Scene, Michel, 15 1/2 In. 1095.00
Electric, Fairy & Snail, Nautilus Shell Shade, Germany, c.1900, 11 1/2 In. 2300.00
Electric, Floor, Rattan, Onion Skin Shade 135.00
Electric, Floor, Wicker, Eiffel Towers, ... 1200.00
Electric, Frankart, 2 Nudes, Feet Holding Original Glass Shade, Signed 1350.00
Electric, Gustav Stickley, Basketweave Shade, Copper Finial, No. 504, 24 In. 2185.00
Electric, Gustav Stickley, Hammered Copper, Original Wicker Shade, 1909 .... 4785.00
Electric, Gustav Stickley, Hammered Copper, Wicker Shade, No. 500, Oak, 57 In. ... 2090.00
Electric, Hall, Hanging, Dark Pink To Light Satin Glass Shade, Brass Frame 50.00
Electric, Hammered Copper, 4 Mica Panels, Strap Handle, 11 x 15 In. 1035.00
Electric, Hammered Copper, Baluster Form, Band Of Rivets, No Shade, 22 In. 747.00
Electric, Hammered Copper, Dark Patina, 3 Lights, 25 In. 1100.00
Electric, Hammered Copper, Oriental Enameled Bronze Base, 19 In. 3162.00
Electric, Hand Painted Pansy, China Stem, Glass Font 350.00
Electric, Hikers At Campfire, Heat Motion 125.00
Electric, Horn Of Plenty, Green 38.00
Electric, Hula Girl, Hips Move 750.00
Electric, Iron, Enameled White Slag Glass, 24 1/2 In. 402.00
Electric, Jar, Celadon, White Silhouetted Figures, Gilt, No Shade, 24 1/2 In., Pair 99.00
Electric, Jefferson, Fountain, Hand-Painted Landscape Slag Glass Shade, 25 In. 1100.00
Electric, Jefferson, Metal, Chipped Sanded Glass Domical Shade, 22 1/4 In. 1610.00
Electric, Jefferson, No. 1641, Reverse Painted Landscape Shade, V. Beck 2200.00
Electric, Jefferson, Reverse Painted, Hibiscus Shade, Art Nouveau Base, 16 In. 1775.00
Electric, Lacquer On Metal, Gold Trim, Occupied Japan, 14 In. 385.00
Electric, Lady With Dog, Figural, Chalkware 8.00
Electric, Lipton Ice Tea, Counter, Gooseneck Base, Painted Globe 495.00
Electric, Merry-Go-Round, Children On Horses, Heat Motion, Rotating, Cylinder 175.00
Electric, Metal, Reverse Painted, Trees & Lake Domed Shade, 1900, 24 In. 690.00
Electric, Millefiori, Flowers, Boudoir, 14 In. 880.00
Electric, Moe Bridges, Bell Shade 460.00
Electric, Moe Bridges, Ceiling, 5-Light 150.00
Electric, Moe Bridges, Flight Of Geese, 2-Handled Base, Signed, 18 In. 4450.00
Electric, Moe Bridges, Lake, Rolling Valleys & Hills, Table 1975.00
Electric, Moe Bridges, Reverse Painted, Autumn Scene, Signed, Table 1950.00
Electric, Moe Bridges, Reverse Painted, Floral Shade, Boudoir 750.00
Electric, Moe Bridges, Reverse Painted, Landscape, Blue, Green, No. 186H, 23 In. .. 2200.00
Electric, Moe Bridges, Reverse Painted, Nasturtiums Around Shade, 15 In. 2250.00
Electric, Moe Bridges, Yellow Chrysanthemum, No. 190, Signed, 18 In. 3850.00
Electric, Oil, Stand, Trapezoidal Pink & Green Glass Panels, 5 Ft. x 19 In. 460.00
Electric, Pantin, Embossed Swirl Base, Pink Square Shade, Monot Stumpf, 10 In. 850.00
Electric, Peacock, Bronze, Green & Blue Glass Pea Eyes, Europe, 1900, 21 In. 4888.00
Electric, Piano, Bronze Bats On Domical Shade, Adjustable, c.1900, 13 1/2 In. 3163.00
Electric, Phoenix, Hawaiian Scenes, Palm Trees & Foliage, 18 In. 1975.00
Electric, Phoenix, Nighttime Camp On Water, Owl Base 2450.00
Electric, Phoenix, Scene, Tree Lined Lane, 2-Handled Copper Tone Base, 18 In. 1475.00
Electric, Pittsburgh, Metal, Sailboats Continuous Scene Domical Shade, 1900, 22 In. 488.00
Electric, Poodle, Figural, Ceramic, Lacy Shade, 1950-1960 .... 55.00
Electric, Porcelain, Baluster Shape, Floral, Gold Ground, Silk Shade, 13 In., Pair 605.00
Electric, Pottery, Teal, White Cherubs, Gilded Fittings, No Shade, 28 In., Pair 759.00
Electric, Rainaud, Reverse Painted, Table 850.00
Electric, Revere Studio, 7 Grapevine Panels, Green Marbleized Glass, 29 In. 3162.00
Electric, Siamese Cat, Figural, Lighted Eyes 65.00

Electric, Skeleton, White Bisque, Blue & Orchid Trim, Green Glass Eyes, 6 1/2 In. .. 5500.00
Electric, Slag Paneled, Metal Overlay, Table 500.00
Electric, Soldier, Figural, Pot Metal, 1920 .... 225.00
Electric, Stage, Heat Motion, Metal, Revolving 75.00
Electric, Stagecoach, Cowboy, 9 x 6 In., Pair 65.00
Electric, Statue Of Liberty, Light-Up Torch, Eagle Finial 225.00
Electric, Student, Brass, Applied Fleur-De-Lis Type Designs, 21 In. 275.00
Electric, Student, Brass, Green Metal Shade, 19th Century 275.00
Electric, Student, Brass, Milk Glass Shade, 22 1/2 In. 60.00
Electric, Student, Brass, Venetian Scenes, 19th Century, 20 1/2 x 16 In. 1750.00
Electric, Student, Cranberry & White Swirl Font & Shade, Brass Fittings 850.00
Electric, Student, Milk Glass, Amethyst, 33 In. 250.00
Electric, Student, Yellow Brass, Green Cased Shades, Double, 27 x 22 1/2 In. 440.00
Electric, Student, Yellow Ribbed Glass Shades, 56 In. 285.00
Electric, Television, Panther, 1950s 26.00
Electric, Television, Sailing Ship, Metal Sails, 1950s 60.00
Electric, Umbrella-Shaped Shade Held By Frog, Bronze, Germany, 1900, 14 1/4 In. . 2875.00
Electric, Van Erp, Flattened Round Shade, Mica Panels, Copper Cut-Outs, 18 1/2 In. 9200.00
Electric, Wall, Venetian Style, Masked Lady, Gondola, Carved Wood, 1920s, 36 In. .. 365.00
Electric, Wannopee, Iridescent Glaze Base, Wicker Shade, 1903, 18 In. 715.00
Electric, Water Lily Shape, Brass, Gold Wash, Free Form 235.00
Electric, Western Union Triangular Shade, Cast Metal, 26 In. 1590.00
Electric, Wilkinson, Leaded Glass, Patina, Drum-Shaped Shade, 1910, 21 In. 2760.00
Electric, Windmill & Sailboat Design, Yellow Brown, Cameo, Peynaud, 10 In. 385.00
Electric, Winged Maiden, Holding Openwork Shade, Bronze, E. Lias, 30 In. 3520.00
Electric, Winnie The Pooh, Matching Shade, 1977, 16 In. 24.50
Electric, Woman, Figural, Standing, Arm Pointing To Shade, Metal, Slag Glass Shade 1100.00
Electric, Zeppelin, Clock Combination, Art Deco, Cobalt Blue Glass, Chrome 850.00
Fairy, Blue & Opalescent Strip, Clarke Base .... 160.00 to 175.00
Fairy, Blue Mother-Of-Pearl, Satin Glass, Diamond-Quilted, 4 1/2 In. 225.00
Fairy, Diamond Quilted Mother-Of-Pearl, Swirled Shade, Clarke Inset, 5 7/8 In. 375.00
Fairy, Diamond-Cut Pyramid, Clarke Base, Amber 80.00
Fairy, Doll Head, Boy, Brown Eyes, 3 1/4 In. 425.00
Fairy, Foliage Design On Shade, Herringbone Mother-Of-Pearl Ground, 5 1/4 In. 1750.00
Fairy, Frosted Embossed Swirl, Burglar's Horror Candle, Clarke, 3 3/4 In. 150.00
Fairy, Frosted, Applied Rigaree, Pink, Matching Base, 5 3/4 In. 375.00
Fairy, Lighthouse Shape, Ivory Ring Handle, Pantin, 8 1/2 In. 345.00
Fairy, Lighthouse, Satin Glass, Clarke Base 125.00
Fairy, Lithophane, 2 Scenic Panels, Glazed Porcelain Base, White, 4 1/4 In. 550.00
Fairy, Moire Glass, Blue, Matching Base, Ruffled Rim, Clarke Candleholder, 8 In. 350.00
Fairy, Moire Glass, Pink, Matching Base, Clarke Clear Candleholder, 6 x 6 In. 450.00
Fairy, Mother-Of-Pearl, Satin Glass, Clarke Base, Blue 195.00
Fairy, Prunus Flower, Burmese Clear Shade, Clarke & Taylor-Tunnecliff, 6 1/4 In. 1430.00
Fairy, Stacked Seashell Design, Matching Base, White Porcelain, 4 3/4 In. 175.00
Fairy, Verre Moire, Ruffled Base, White Loopings, Clarke Insert, 5 In. 650.00
Fairy, Verre Moire, White Loopings, Clarke Cup, Citron Shade, 5 3/4 In. 845.00
Gasoline, Brass, 6 Panel Lithophane Shade, Name Of Scene On Each, 20 3/4 In. 1540.00
Gasoline, Table, Frosted & Etched Shade, 20 In. 595.00
Girandole, 1-Light, Boy & Dog, Pair 150.00
Girandole, 3-Light, Paul & Virginia, 2-Toned Gilding 100.00
Girandole Set, Gilt Brass, Marble Base, H.N. Hopper, Boston, c.1850, 3 Pc. 385.00
Gone With The Wind, Blown-Out Poppies, Stippled, Brass Fittings, c.1890, 25 In. .. 795.00
Gone With The Wind, Draped Red Satin 525.00
Gone With The Wind, Milk Glass, Lion Head 350.00
Gone With The Wind, Painted Milk Glass, Artichoke Pattern, Electrified, 24 In. 275.00
Gone With The Wind, Pink, Floral, Electrified, 22 In., Pair 375.00
Gone With The Wind, Red Bead & Drape 825.00
Gone With The Wind, Red Bull's-Eye 495.00
Gone With The Wind, Red Satin Glass Base & Shade, Brass 220.00
Gone With The Wind, Red Satin Glass, Miniature 395.00
Gone With The Wind, Red Satin, Victoria Patter, Electrified, 27 In. 523.00
Handel lamps are included in the Handel category
Hanging, Acorn Leaf & Nut, Hand Painted Shade, Brass, Glass 425.00

Hanging, Double Angle, Grape, Copper Bellflowers Elbows, Amberina Chimney 2800.00
Hanging, Great Plains, Flying Saucer, Chain, 1960s 125.00
Hanging, Iron Horse, Black Frame, White Milk Glass Shade 303.00
Hanging, Store, Signed Rochester, Yellow Brass, 27 In. 110.00
Head, Cord, Belt Hook, Battery Case, Winchester, Pat. Date, 1920 & 1923 .... 80.00
Kerosene, 3 Animal Heads In Stem, Clear, 11 3/4 In. 137.00
Kerosene, Acanthus Leaf, Blue Clambroth Font, White Base, 11 In. 440.00
Kerosene, Adlake, Pennyslvania R.R. 55.00
Kerosene, Advance Knob, Garden, French, Brass, 9 In. 214.50
Kerosene, Angle, Brass Plated Tin, Wall Mount, Ruby To Light Tulip Shade 880.00
Kerosene, Apple Sauce, Crystal, Fruit Bowl Cup, 21 In. 330.00
Kerosene, Aquaris, Amber 165.00
Kerosene, Climas, Brass, 1906 .... 55.00
Kerosene, Daisy & Button, 1 Piece, Amber Glass, Stem, 10 1/4 In. 137.00
Kerosene, Finger, Amber Glass, Ruffled Bulls-Eye Pattern, Footed, 4 In. 94.00
Kerosene, Finger, Blue Glass, Janice Pattern, Footed, 5 1/2 In. 132.00
Kerosene, Finger, Clear Opalescent, Polka Dot, Footed, O Burner & Chimney, 5 In. . 495.00
Kerosene, Finger, Cobalt Blue Base, Corning Chimney 140.00
Kerosene, Finger, Cranberry Glass, Optic Ribbed, Applied Clear Handle, 4 1/4 In. ... 94.00
Kerosene, Finger, Diamond Sunburst, Amber 140.00
Kerosene, Finger, Marigold Carnival, Zipper Loop Pattern, Footed, 5 1/4 In. 330.00
Kerosene, Finger, Night Clock, Brass Base, Etched Numerals, Tin Can Movement.... 495.00
Kerosene, Finger, Pink Cased Base, Grapevine Design, Chimney 120.00
Kerosene, Finger, Ribbed Cranberry Base, Miller Chimney 145.00
Kerosene, Finger, Sapphire Blue Glass, Applied Handle, 3 1/4 In. 198.00
Kerosene, Finger, Zigzag, Diamond, Cast Iron Base, Brass Ferule 37.50
Kerosene, Finger, Zipper Loop, Pedestal 45.00
Kerosene, Furnace, Taylor & Boggie, Cast Iron 37.50
Kerosene, Hanging, Hand Painted Milk Glass Shade & Globe, Prisms 225.00
Kerosene, Heart, Opaque Green Glass, Stem, 9 3/4 In. 193.00
Kerosene, Hobb's Blackberry Pattern, Clear Glass, Opalescent, Stem, 8 5/8 In. 275.00
Kerosene, Hobb's Snowflake, Blue Opalescent, Stem, 8 3/4 In. 330.00
Kerosene, Painted Owl Stem, Owl Chimney 125.00
Kerosene, Peacock Feather, Amber Glass, Stem, 9 1/2 In. 247.00
Kerosene, Pink Looping, Opaque White Font, Brass, Marble Foot, Stem, 9 In. 413.00
Kerosene, Princess Feather, Cobalt Blue, Stem, 8 1/4 In. 330.00
Kerosene, Princess Feather, Opaque Green Glass, Stem, 9 3/4 In. 220.00
Kerosene, Ripley Double Loop, 1868 .... 135.00
Kerosene, Sandwich Glass, Bronze Base 325.00
Kerosene, Three Face, Frosted 240.00
Kerosene, Thuro, Erin Fan, Clear 45.00
Kerosene, Turquoise Font, France, 19th Century, 13 In. 44.00
Kerosene, Webster, Brass Ferrule, Cast Iron Base 37.50
Lace Maker's, Clear Font, Cobalt Blue Base, Pair 4070.00
Lace Maker's, Diamond Quilted, Cranberry, Victorian 850.00
Lace Maker's, Hollow Baluster Stem, Opening For Drop Burner, 6 1/2 In. 330.00
Lard, Kinnear Patent Type, Tin, 7 1/4 In. 220.00
Lard, Saucer Base, Tin, 6 3/4 In. 120.00
Oil, 4-Spout, Lucerna, Adjustable Height, Brass, c.1750, 13 1/4 In. 220.00
Oil, Banquet, Cupid, 24 In., Pair 295.00
Oil, Banquet, Glass Font, Brass Pedestal, Raised Birds, Sherwood Victorian Style 195.00
Oil, Banquet, Porcelain, Hand Painted Glass Globe, Germany, 1870s, 37 In. 850.00
Oil, Beaded Base, Opalescent Striped Font, Jensen 425.00
Oil, Beaded Drape, Frosted, Ornate 80.00
Oil, Block & Dot, Shade, Miniature 70.00
Oil, Blown-Out Roses, Brass Base, Etched Shade 165.00
Oil, Blue Bristol Base, Floral Enameling On Glass, Cast Iron, 11 1/2 In. 77.00
Oil, Blue Font, Bras Sucer, Miniature 125.00
Oil, Brass Base & Burner, Enamel Glass Font, Falk's British, 19 In. 150.00
Oil, Brass, Eagle Finial, Double Amethyst Font, Onyx Base, 18 In. 220.00
Oil, Bristol Stem, House Scene, Brass Trim, Flags On Font, Tin Top, 20 3/4 In. 192.50
Oil, Canary Glass, Hexagonal, Ellipse Panel Font, Pewter Collar, Flint, 9 In. 467.00
Oil, Clear Flint, Square Base, Double Baluster Stem, Bigler Font, 9 5/8 In., Pair 385.00

Oil, Clear Swirled Font, White Loops, Marble Base, Brass Collar, 8 In. 412.00
Oil, Cobalt Blue, Little Buttercup, Applied Handle, 3 1/4 x 2 1/2 In. 75.00
Oil, Copper, Classical Style, Handle, Snuffer With Chain, Dirk Van Erp, 3 x 10 In. 747.00
Oil, Cranberry Opalescent, Reverse Swirl, Brass Base, Chimney, 21 In. 550.00
Oil, Cranberry Shade, White Leaves & Berries, Prisms, Brass Base, 19 In., Pair 325.00
Oil, Cranberry Swirl Base & Shade, 8 1/4 In. 695.00
Oil, Cut Overlay, Stepped Brass, Marble Base, White To Cobalt Blue, 12 In. 357.00
Oil, Dark Blue Cut To Clear Font, Brass, Double Step Marble Foot, 11 1/2 In. 770.00
Oil, Empire Style, Dore Bronze, Suspended Font, Swan Support, 9 x 4 1/2 In. 715.00
Oil, Flint, Bull's-Eye & Sawtooth Font, Brass Collar, 9 1/4 In. 104.50
Oil, Frosted Globe, Cut Lustres, Brass Column, Marble Base, Victorian, 25 In. 303.00
Oil, Green Glass, Daisy, Acorn Burner, 4 3/4 In. 105.00
Oil, Greentown, Wild Rose, Chocolate Glass, 9 1/4 In. 660.00
Oil, Hall, Brass, Clear Beveled Glass, Jewels Set In Chamfered Corners, 17 1/2 In. 192.00
Oil, Hanging, 12 Slag Glass Panels, Royal, Patent 1895 .... 500.00
Oil, Hurricane, Double, Patinated Brass & Ormolu, Pair 2200.00
Oil, Ice Skater, Dated 1864-1867 .... 625.00
Oil, Liberty, Nickel Over Brass, Leaf Emboss Font & Base, Pair 250.00
Oil, Little Banner, Clear, Miniature 55.00
Oil, Loops & Beading Font, Milk Glass Base, 25 In. 145.00
Oil, Louis Philippe, Patinated Bronze, Electrified, c.1840, 33 In., Pair 1100.00
Oil, Meissen Onion Pattern, Etched Glass Shade, Porcelain, 30 In. 575.00
Oil, Mercury Glass, Shade, Permaflector 35.00
Oil, Mission Design, Matching Shade, 6 1/2 In., Pair 100.00
Oil, Molded Design, Matching Shade, Clear Glass Chimney, 6 3/4 In. 100.00
Oil, Molded Satin Glass, Pink Frosted, Miniature 60.00
Oil, Nellie Bly, Miniature 55.00
Oil, Overlay, Cobalt Blue Cut To Clear Font, Brass, Double Stepped Marble, 22 In. ... 990.00
Oil, Overlay, White Cut To Clear Floral Font, Mercury Glass Stem, 8 1/2 In. 467.00
Oil, Overlay, White Cut To Clear, Punty Pattern, Brass Stem, Marble Foot, 9 In. 275.00
Oil, Painted White Milk Glass, Duck Scene, Fringed Design, 20 1/2 In. 275.00
Oil, Pharaoh Figure In Desert Hood, Terra-Cotta, Egypt 375.00
Oil, Pink Roses & Green Leaves, Matching Shade, 8 3/4 In. 100.00
Oil, Plume & Atwood Burners, Clear, Miniature, Pair 125.00
Oil, Pressed Glass Base, Blown Hollow Stem & Font, Pewter, Pair 4015.00
Oil, Pressed Glass, Opalescent, Flowers, Lion Heads, White Blown Font, 10 In. 605.00
Oil, Puffy Shade, Satin Glass, Reverse, 10 1/2 In. 100.00
Oil, Quad Loop Font, Milk Glass Base, Electrified 320.00
Oil, Rayo, Original Chimney, Signed, 21 In. 145.00
Oil, Rhead Faience, Marching Ducks, Glossy Glaze, Electrified, 21 In. 1320.00
Oil, Skater's, 1860s, 9 1/8 In. 260.00
Oil, Star & Dot Cutting, Mushroom Shade, Cranberry Cut To Clear, 15 In. 165.00
Oil, Tulip, Red Satin Glass, Shade, Miniature 135.00
Oil, White Diamond Quilted, Mother-Of-Pearl, Ribbed Font, Brass Stem, 16 1/4 In. ... 2000.00
Oil, William IV, Messenger & Sons, Bronze, 1840s, 9 1/2 In. 3163.00
Oriental Group, Painted Metal, Austria, 15 1/2 In. 2750.00
Oscar Bach, Bronze, Filigree, Amber Iridescent Glass Globe, 1925, 25 1/2 In. 2875.00
Oscar Bach, Bronze, Nude Woman Steuben Shade, 1925, 79 In. 6325.00
Oscar Bach, Gilt-Bronze, Pierced, Mica Fringed Shade, 1925, 42 In. 2300.00
Pairpoint lamps are in the Pairpoint category
Peg, Allover Stippled Design, Gold Leaves, Cherries On Shade, 11 In. 550.00
Peg, Clear Cut, Brass Kerosene Burner 27.50
Peg, Cut Glass, Diamond & Sawtooth 95.00
Peg, Satin Font Shades, Deep To Pale Yellow, Brass Fittings, 4 1/2 In. 170.00
Perfume, Belova, Pink, Enameled Flowers 200.00
Perfume, Oriental, Robj 325.00
Rush, Candle Socket, Wrought Iron, Counter Weight, Wooden Base, 11 1/4 In. 253.00
Rush, Wrought Iron, 1750 .... 785.00
Sconce, 1-Light, Concave Backplate, Paved Mirror Tiles, Tin, 9 1/2 In., Pair 1610.00
Sconce, 1-Light, Water Gilt, Mirror, Italy, 19th Century, 36 x 14 x 12 In. 325.00
Sconce, 2-Light, Brass Scroll Arm, Glass Shade, Pair 690.00
Sconce, 2-Light, Leaf-Tip Carved Backplate, Italy, 16 1/2 x 10 3/4 In., Pair 2013.00
Sconce, 2-Light, Louis XVI Style, Carved Gesso, Horn Backplate, 31 In., Pair 825.00

Sconce, 2-Light, Louis XVI, Mirrored, Dolphin Finial, 23 1/2 In., Pair 440.00
Sconce, 2-Light, Louis XVI, Scrolled Branches On Back Plate, 30 In., Pair 2990.00
Sconce, 2-Light, Parcel Gilt, Stylized Thistle, Electrified, Scotland, 9 In., Pair 1035.00
Sconce, 2-Light, Tole & Porcelain Backplate, Silvered Bronze, 12 3/4 In., Pair 7188.00
Sconce, 3-Light, Cupid Blowing Horn On Dolphin, Standard, Bronze, 15 In. 2070.00
Sconce, 3-Light, Rococo Style, Giltwood, Wrought Iron, Flowers, 30 x 21 In., Pair .. 385.00
Sconce, 3-Light, Wall, Louis XV Style, Gilt Bronze, Acanthus Leaves, 17 In., Pair ... 330.00
Sconce, 5-Candle, Vine & Floral Design, Iron, 30 1/2 x 54 In. 70.00
Sconce, 5-Light, Napoleon III, Gilt Bronze, 17 In., Pair 412.50
Sconce, 6-Candle, Brass, Mirror, Electrified, 1870, Pair 3500.00
Sconce, Art Deco, Chrome, 1932 .... 350.00
Sconce, Blackamoor Arm, Pair 3300.00
Sconce, Candle, Crimped Crest, Tin, 5 3/4 In. 165.00
Sconce, Candle, Mirror Back, Prisms, Glass Beads, 23 In., Pair 253.00
Sconce, Cobra Form, India, 29 1/2 In., Pair 440.00
Sconce, Gilded Brass, 8 1/4 In., Pair 77.00
Sconce, Leaded Glass Panel, Angled Arm, Frank Lloyd Wright, Bronze & Oak 4025.00
Sconce, Mary Gregory Cranberry Shade, Bronze Back, Pair 1980.00
Sconce, Overlapping Triangles, Alabaster Panels, Albert Cheuret, 13 In., Pair 7475.00
Sconce, Tin, 14 7/8 In., Pair 1760.00
Semi-Nude, Holding Arch Of Light Flowers Overhead, Bronze, 44 1/2 In. 4025.00
Skater's, Brass, Nantucket 120.00
Skater's, Brass, Orion, 6 1/2 In. 126.00
Skater's, Brass, Tin, Clear Globe, 7 3/4 In. 38.50
Skater's, Tin, Jewel, Clear Globe, 7 In. 49.50
Skater's, Tin, Red Stained Globe, 7 In. 27.50
Sparking, Blown Glass, Open Font, Drop Burner, 3 1/4 In. 170.00
Sparking, Flint, Miniature 48.00
Tiffany lamps are listed in the Tiffany category
Torchere, 6-Light, Venetian Style, Nubian Figure Supporting Cage, 97 In. 5750.00
Torchere, Art Deco, Wire Bound Bamboo Rods, Russel Wright, c.1960, 64 1/2 In. 115.00
Torchere, Baroque Style, Carved, Gilded, 66 1/4 In. 935.00
Torchere, Fluted Column, Tripod Base, Paw Feet, Mounted As Lamp, 54 3/4 In. 1380.00
Torchere, George III Style, Giltwood, Carved Legs, Hoof Feet, Glass Shade, 68 In. .. 9200.00
Torchere, George III, Carved Leaves & Flowers, Gilt, c.1765, 47 In. 6467.00
Torchere, Overlapping Leaves, Plaster, Serge Roche, 1935, 5 Ft. 10 In. 9775.00
Whale Oil, Argus Pattern, Wafer Attachment, Colorless, 1800s, 9 In. 165.00
Whale Oil, Block Pattern, Wafer Attachment, 1840-1860, 11 1/2 In. 137.50
Whale Oil, Blown & Molded, Etched Pontil, Milk Glass, 11 In. 99.00
Whale Oil, Bulb-Shaped, Pressed & Blown, 1830s, 7 1/4 In., Pair 165.00
Whale Oil, Dietz, Buggy, Font 95.00
Whale Oil, Gimballed, Tin, Painted Black, 7 1/2 In. 165.00
Whale Oil, Globular, Cast Iron, 10 In. 66.00
Whale Oil, Hexagonal Paneled, Leaf & Flower Cutting, 9 1/2 In. 35.00
Whale Oil, Holder, Glass Shade, Tin, 10 3/4 In. 385.00
Whale Oil, Moon & Star, c.1850, 11 In., Pair 325.00
Whale Oil, Pressed Glass, Handle, Brass Collar, 4 1/4 In. 500.00
Whale Oil, Smith & Co., 8 In. 440.00
Whale Oil, Thumbprint Variant Font, Milk Glass Globe Shade, Cyma Tiered, 18 In. .. 302.00
Whale Oil, Waffle & Thumbprint, Glass, Clear, Pewter Collar, 6 In. 99.00
Woman Lighting Lamppost, Figural, Bronze, Japan, c.1900, 24 In. 550.00

LANTERNS are a special type of lighting device. They have a light source,
usually a candle, totally hidden inside the walls of the lantern. Light is seen
through holes or glass sections.

Adams & Westlake, Model 39, Clear Globe, Patent 1864 .... 470.00
Ash, Leaded Glass, Wall, Oriental Type, Dowel Corners, Greene & Greene, 13 In. 1512.00
B & R, Changeable Lenses 70.00
Barn, Black Paint, Unusual Tipping Shade, 19th Century, 18 In. 88.00
Barn, Ham's, Brass Font 60.00
Black Out, Copper Band, Spring Loaded Candle Tube, Tin, 9 1/2 In. 192.50
Candle, Semi-Circular, Hinged Door, Ring Handle, Tin, 11 In. 265.00
Candle, Tin, 6 Glass Sides, Black Paint, Ring Handle, 11 1/4 In. 220.00

Candle, Tin, Old Black Paint, Hinged Door, 13 In. 139.00
Dietz, Buggy Dashboard, Whale Oil, Tin 125.00
Dietz, Crystal, Hand, With Green Globe 165.00
Dietz, Crystal, Kerosene, Glass Fuel Tank 28.00
Dietz, Little Wizard, Kerosene, Tin 14.00
Dietz, Pocket, Man Reading, Patent 1875 .... 250.00
Dietz, Queen, Green Globe, Brass 1125.00
Dietz, Skater's, Candle, Tin, 5 In. 60.00
Dietz King, Fire Dept., Copper Font, Slide Off Cage 175.00
Dietz Sport, Skater's, Reprinted 45.00
Dirk Van Erp, Copper, Drum Form, 5 Mica Panels, Rings, 22 1/3 x 16 1/2 In., Pair ... 2875.00
Electric, Metal, 5-Lozenge Form, Mica Interior, Hinged Door, 15 In. 345.00
Electric, Metal, Oak-Tree Panels, Mica Underneath, Hanging, Chain, 34 In. 620.00
Electric, Metal, Wall, Mica Shade, Loop Handle, 20 In. 201.00
Folding, Brown Japanning, Gold Design, 2 Mica Panels, 1/ 4 In. 71.50
Frank Lloyd Wright, Peaked Top, Textured & Frosted Panels, 1911, 8 5/8 x 9 In. 1955.00
Gas, Cast Iron, Oval Glass, 12 In. Square 75.00
Gustav Stickley, Heart-Shaped Cutouts, Riveted Straps, No. 205, 8 1/2 In., Pr. 1500.00
Hanging, Gustav Stickley, Grid Design On Amber Glass Panels, 11 In. 550.00
Hanging, Gustav Stickley, No. 671, Hammered Copper, Pair 3630.00
Hanging, Gustav Stickley, Spade Cutouts, Amber Glass Liner, Brass, 25 x 6 In. 1700.00
Hanging, Pierced Tin, Candle-Lighting Holder, Double Lens 295.00
Iron, Brass, Fitted For Gas, England, 14 In. 44.00
Kerosene, Pagoma Cold Blast, Tin, Large 14.00
Kerosene, Works Progress Administration Of Ohio, Red Globe, Brass Fount 150.00
Long Spout, Chain & Hook, Pennsylvania, Tole 145.00
Miner's, Peterson, Round Glass Globe, Brass, 9 In. 95.00
Oil, Chicken Coop, England 45.00
Pierced Tin, No Door, Legend Jackson Forever, 13 In. 900.00
Post, Tin, Painted, 5 Sides, Floral, Victorian, 25 In. 275.00
Punched Tin, Revere-Type, Hearts, Compass, Flowers, Ring Handle, 12 In. 495.00
Signal, Kerosene, Tin, Red Lens, Primitive, Civil War 35.00
Skater's, Tin, Battery Operated 27.50
Tin, Removable Oil Burner, 8 3/4 In. 126.50
Wagon, Bull's-Eye Globe, Japanned Finish 75.00

LE VERRE FRANCAIS is one of the many types of cameo glass made in
France. The glass was made by the C. Schneider factory in Epinay-sur-Seine
from 1920 to 1933. It is a mottled glass, usually decorated with floral designs,
and bears the incised signature *Le Verre Francais.*

Compote, Mottled Yellow & Pink, Art Deco Floral, Brown Overlay, 5 In. 360.00
Ewer, Cameo Cut Rose, Flaring Lip, Arched Handle, Signed, 12 In. 715.00
Ewer, Cameo, Pedestal, Brown & Orange, Yellow Ground, 12 In. 880.00
Lamp, Boudoir, Deco Designs, Mottled White, Blue, Amethyst, 14 x 6 In. 1650.00
Lamp, Table, Domed Shade, Gray, Orange, 3-Arm Iron Base, c.1925 .... 690.00
Pitcher, Art Deco, Yellow, Blue & Orange, Charder, 13 In. 1500.00
Punch Bowl, Thorny Apples, Thorny Stems, Pedestal, 12 1/2 x 15 In. 1975.00
Vase, Bulbous Body, Purple To Pink Florals, Signed, 25 1/2 In. 2200.00
Vase, Cameo, Mottled Brown & Orange, Yellow Ground, 14 In. 935.00
Vase, Double Gourd, Berries, Leaves, 2 Handles, Orange, 17 3/4 In. 1485.00
Vase, Etched Stylized Flowers & Foliage, Gourd Shape, 11 In. 138.00
Vase, Ming Tree, Amber, Brown, Yellow, Green, Art Deco Design, 16 In. 1870.00
Vase, Oval, Footed, Mottled Yellow, Blue Overlay, Seed Pods, 15 In. 825.00
Vase, Stylized Blossoms, Leaves, Signed, c.1925, 23 In. 1610.00
Vase, Stylized Pendent Berried Leaves, Signed, c.1920, 16 In. 460.00
Vase, Yellow, Orange, Amethyst, Art Deco Flowers, Charder, 18 1/2 In. 1320.00

LEATHER is tanned animal hide and it has been used to make decorative and
useful objects for centuries. Leather objects must be carefully preserved with
proper humidity and oiling or the leather will deteriorate and crack. This
damage cannot be repaired.

Belt, Allover Metal Eyelets, 9 Octagonal Metal Studs, 40-46 In. 10.00
Book Cover, Florentine, Tooled, Gold, Blue, Red & White, 16 x 11 In. 15.00

Book Safe, Calfskin, Over Wood, Paper Edges, Felt Liner, 7 3/8 x 6 3/4 In. 160.00
Boots, 9-Stitch Design, Blue, c.1960, Size 9 1/2 .... 55.00
Boots, Eagle Design, Acme 300.00
Boots, Inlaid Floral Design, Brown, c.1960, Size 9 1/2 .... 65.00
Boots, Man's, Alligator, Pointed Toe 137.50
Boots, Salesman's Sample, 4 1/2 In. 99.00
Boots, Woman's, Acme, Pointed Toe 52.50
Bridle & Bit, Silver Roundels, Yuma, Arizona 55.00
Buckle, Belt, Davis, Embossed, Oval 2.50
Chaps, Batwing, 2100 Nickel Studs, Pair 5600.00
Chaps, Batwing, Outside Pockets, Conches, Colorado Saddlery, Denver, 1930s 375.00
Chaps, Cowhide, 12 Aluminum Conches, Powder River, 1940s 250.00
Chaps, Pick-Up, Black, White Strings & Circle Star, Tooled Belt, 1930s, Large 650.00
Chaps, Rodeo, White Stars On Red Borders, Blue, Rusty Allee, Montana, 1960s 395.00
Chaps, Shotgun, Territorial Fringed, A.J. Stevenson, Helena, Mont., Pair 440.00
Crop, Sterling Silver Handle, Victorian 95.00
Dog Collar, Bunk Engraved On Metal Plate, Metal Studs, 1920 Dog Tag 80.00
Holster, Half Flap Style, Spangenburg, Tombstone, Ariz. 4500.00
Holster, Slim Jim, For 1849 Colt Revolver, Tooled 40.00
Jacket, Motorcycle, 1950s 100.00
Jacket, Western, Fringed, Deming, New Mexico, Early 1900s 45.00
Mail Bag, Post Office 75.00
Pouch, Mayo Tobacco, Metal Frame 22.50
Saddle, Child's, Nickel Horn & Taps, c.1930, 12-In. Seat 247.50
Saddle, Cowboy, Nickel Plated Stars 375.00
Saddle, Half-Seat, Unmarked 950.00
Saddle, Heiser 800.00
Saddle, Mule Pack, Prospector's 95.00
Saddle, Presentation, Tooled, Silver & Gold Embroidery, 1900-1905 .... 9900.00
Saddle, Roping, Hand Tooled, 1950s 395.00
Saddle, Tooled High Back, Moderate Swells, 8 Strings, Texas Skirt, 1905-1915 .... 650.00
Sheath, Cigar, Indian Design 35.00
Shot Flask, Bag 38.50
Suitcase, Louis Vuitton, Marshall Field's Metal Tags 1000.00
Suitcase, Stagecoach, 1910s 40.00
Valise, Grand Army Of Republic Encampment, Akron, Ohio, 1917 .... 895.00
Wallet, Lizard, Sterling Silver Mount, Pierced Design Of Gargoyle & Floral 200.00
Wardrobe, Vuitton 1870.00
Wastebasket, Greek Key & Foliate Scrolls, Paw Feet, Dark Green, 14 1/4 In. 1725.00

LEEDS pottery was made at Leeds, Yorkshire, England, from 1774 to 1878.
Most Leeds ware was not marked. Early Leeds pieces had distinctive twisted **LEEDS POTTERY,**
handles with a greenish glaze on part of the creamy ware. Later ware often
had blue borders on the creamy pottery.

Cookie Jar, Mickey Mouse, Turnabout 225.00
Pepper Pot, Triangular Base, Creamware, 4 1/4 In. 60.00
Sugar, Brown Floral Design, Swags, Pearlware 38.00
Sugar, Floral, Silver Luster, Intertwined Handles & Floral Finial, 4 1/2 In. 577.00
Sugar, Gaudy Floral Design, Pearlware, 4 1/2 In. 110.00
Sugar Bowl, Flower Finial, Silver Luster, Intertwined Handles, Marked 525.00
Waste Bowl, Red Transfer, Woman & Child 275.00

LEFTON is a mark found on many pieces. The Geo. Zoltan Lefton Company
has imported porcelains to be sold in America since 1940. The firm is still in
business. The company mark has changed through the years; but because
marks have been used for long periods of time, they are of little help in dating
an object.

Bank, Hubert Lion 55.00
Cookie Jar, Bluebonnet Sue 40.00
Cookie Jar, Cat's Head 75.00
Cookie Jar, Chick, With Butter 95.00
Figurine, Bride & Groom, Cake Topper, 5 In. .... 22.50 to 25.00
Salt & Pepper, Bunch Of Carrots 20.00

Salt & Pepper, Pink Roses 10.00
Salt & Pepper, Snowmen 15.00
Sugar & Creamer, Moss Rose 12.00

LEGRAS was founded in 1864 by Auguste Legras at St. Denis, France. It is best known for cameo glass and enamel-decorated glass with Art Nouveau designs. Legras merged with Pantin in 1920 and became the Verreries et Cristalleries de St. Denis et de Pantin Reunies.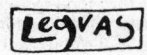

Compote, Stylized Foliage, Etched Irregular Design, Signed, 10 1/4 x 16 In. 1150.00
Lamp, Electric, Deep Purple, Grapevine & Leaf Design, Frosted Ground, 19 In. 1650.00
Lamp, Winter Scene, Metal Branches Hold Shade, 16 In. 4000.00
Tray, Pine Trees, Island & Mountains Around Lake, 3 1/4 x 8 3/4 In. 500.00
Tray, Purple Grapes, Hanging Vine, Cream & Peach Ground, 3 1/4 x 8 In. 500.00
Vase, Aquatic Scene, 6 In. 675.00
Vase, Brownish Green, Leaf Decoration, 9 1/2 In. 600.00
Vase, Cut Back Blossoms, Flarec Oval, Enamel, 12 1/2 In. 825.00
Vase, Enameled Red Leaves & Vines, Cameo, 9 In. 625.00
Vase, Etched & Engraved Birds, Art Deco Border, Cameo, 16 1/4 In. 935.00
Vase, Flowers & Leaves, White With Cranberry & Green, Signed, 25 In. 1840.00
Vase, Frosted Oval, Maroon Etched & Enamel Prunus Blossoms, Cameo, 8 In. 550.00
Vase, Leaves, Pink Ground, Cameo, 8 In., Pair 1250.00
Vase, Mountain Landscape, Shepherd & Flock, Signed, 4 In. 575.00
Vase, Poppies, 9 In. 450.00
Vase, Raspberries & Foliage, Shades Of Raspberry, Signed, c.1920, 25 1/2 In. 690.00
Vase, Rose & Purple Grapes, Beige Ground, Signed, 8 In. 550.00
Vase, Scenic, 4-Color Enamel, Cameo, 10 1/4 In. 750.00
Vase, Stylized Geometric Band At Shoulder, Burgundy, Signed, 8 3/8 In. 460.00
Vase, Underwater Scene, Earth Tones, Cameo, Signed, 8 In. 1095.00
Vase, Underwater Scene, Earth Tones, Tri-Corner, 10 1/2 In. 1150.00
Vase, Water Fountain, Pink & Maroon, 14 1/2 In. 1250.00
Vase, Winterscape, Hand Painted, & Enamel, Cylindrical, 16 In. 275.00
Vase, Yellow Walls, Cameo Coral & Shell Design, Signed, 7 In. 150.00

LENOX is the name of a porcelain maker. Walter Scott Lenox and Jonathan Cox founded the Ceramic Art Company in Trenton, New Jersey, in 1889. In 1906, Lenox left and started his own company called *Lenox*. The company makes a porcelain that is similar to Irish Belleek. The marks used by the firm have changed through the years and collectors prefer the earlier examples. Related pieces may also be listed in the Ceramic Art Co. category.

Bowl, Blue, Green Mark 35.00
Chamberstick, Windshield, 8 In. 25.00
Coffee Set, Deep Cobalt Blue, Sterling Silver Overlay, Wooden Handle, 3 Piece 330.00
Cup & Saucer, Cobalt Blue, After Dinner 12.00
Cup & Saucer, Solitaire 30.00
Cup & Saucer, Tuxedo, 24 Piece 200.00
Dish, 3 Lobed Grape Leaf, 24K Gold Rim, Gold Mark, 8 1/2 In. 22.00
Figurine, Bird, American Goldfinch 75.00
Figurine, Bird, Blue Jay .... 70.00 to 75.00
Figurine, Bird, Chipping Sparrow 75.00
Figurine, Bird, Downey Woodcock 70.00
Figurine, Bird, Eastern Bluebird, Atte 75.00
Figurine, Bird, Hummingbird 70.00
Figurine, Bird, Owl, Saw Whet 75.00
Figurine, Bird, Red Breasted Nuthatch 65.00
Figurine, Rapunzel 200.00
Figurine, Shoe, Floral Design, Ivory 75.00
Figurine, Sleeping Beauty 200.00
Figurine, Snow Queen 200.00
Figurine, Swan, Pink, Green Mark 60.00
Figurine, Tea At The Ritz 150.00
Gravy Boat, Solitaire 95.00
Lamp, Floral Design, Multicolored, 33 1/2 In. 85.00
Lamp, Olive Leaf Border, Pink Finial, Scroll Handles, 26 In., Pair 400.00

Letter Rack, 3 Sections, Cobalt Blue & Gold 115.00
Mug, Atlantic City Shrine Temple, Green Mark 85.00
Mug, William Penn 225.00
Pitcher, Lemonade, Belleek, 1906 .... 410.00
Plate, Floral Design, Pink Rim, 10 In., 6 Piece 33.00
Plate, Gilt With Floral Swags, Green Border, 8 In., 12 Piece 460.00
Plate, Pembrook, 10 1/2 In., 12 Piece 300.00
Salt & Pepper, Nipper, His Master's Voice 50.00
Service For 12, Autumn, 53 Piece 1385.00
Service For 14, Rondelle, 71 Piece 750.00
Sugar & Creamer, Shell Spout, Swirl Ribbed, Green Wreath, 3 1/2 In. 30.00
Tea Set, Pale Cream, Monogram, Silver Overlay, 3 Piece 225.00
Teapot, Sterling Silver Overlay 350.00
Vase, Black Spider Webs, Butterflies, c.1906, 10 In. 225.00
Vase, Ivory, Flared, Scalloped Neck, Bulbous Base, Green Wreath, 7 3/4 In., Pair 55.00
Vase, Pink, Green Mark, 7 In. .... 50.00 to 90.00
Vase, Queen's Garden 95.00
Vase, Saxony, Flowers & Birds, 11 In., Pair 295.00
Vase, White Birds, Tree Florals, Celadon Ground, 9 1/2 x 4 In. 145.00
Water Set, Tiger Lily, Green, 7 Piece 165.00

LETTER OPENERS have been used since the eighteenth century. Ivory and
silver were favored by the well-to-do. In the late nineteenth century, the letter
opener was popular as an advertising giveaway and many were made of metal
or celluloid. Brass openers with figural handles were also popular.

Acorn, Silver, Georg Jensen 118.00
Black Tribal Chieftain, Headdress, Ebony, 12 In. 6.00
Brass, Blumer Products, Ice Cream 25.00
Brass, Chicago Sun Times 15.00
Bronze, Hailand, Bronze, Box 20.00
Carew Tower, Cincinnati On Shield 22.00
Demon Buckle Handle, Sterling Silver & Jade, 10 In. 600.00
Folding Knife, R.J. Prentiss & Co, Ruler, Brass, 8 3/4 In. 18.00
Francis I, Reed & Barton, Silver 19.00
Fuller Brush, Salesman Figure 4.00
Horsehead Handle, Wide Curved Blade, Bronze, France, 8 1/4 In. 22.00
Marquette Prison, Carved Wood, Painted 55.00
Marshall Best Flour, Girl On Handle, Brass 45.00
Mason & Risch, Tin, 6 In. 90.00
Mother-Of-Pearl, Sterling Silver Band 6.00
Nabisco Boy, Metal 75.00
San Francisco Exposition, 1939 .... 26.50
Sonny Jim, Black Man's Head Top, Cast Iron, 11 In. 88.00
Spear, Openwork Austrian Silver Handle, Wiener Werkstatte, 9 3/8 In. 2420.00

LIBBEY Glass Company has made many types of glass since 1888, including
the cut glass and tablewares that are collected today. The stemwares of the
1930s and 1940s are once again in style. The Toledo, Ohio, firm was
purchased by Owens-Illinois in 1935 and is still working under the name
Libbey as a division of that company. Additional pieces may be listed under
Amberina, Cut Glass, and Maize.

Banana Boat, Cut Glass, Eulalia Pattern, 1906, 11 3/4 x 8 x 4 1/2 In. 875.00
Bottle, Whiskey, Senora, Signed, 13 1/4 In. 785.00
Bowl, Amberina, Rectangular, 5 1/2 In. 295.00
Bowl, Brilliant Cut, Intaglio, 2 Handles, 8 In. 195.00
Bowl, Cetus, 10 1/2 In. 2600.00
Bowl, Christmas, Ruffled, Holly Leaves & Berries, Icicles On Rim, Signed, 7 In. 225.00
Bowl, Cut Glass, Faceted, Fruits, Leafy Stems, Sabre Mark, 10 1/2 In. 880.00
Bowl, Cut Lovebirds, Signed, 8 Sides 825.00
Bowl, Ellsmere, Cut Glass, 9 In. 550.00
Bowl, Engraved Allover Floral, Footed, 8 In. 120.00
Bowl, Flower, Amberina, Optic Panels, Ruffled Flared Rim, Signed, 4 3/4 In. 595.00
Bowl, Lovebirds & Wisteria Blossoms, Diamond-Cut Band Rim, Signed, 8 In. 325.00

Bowl, Moonstone Elephant Stem, Crystal Bowl, 11 In. 385.00
Bowl, Scalloped, Hobstar Chain, Strawberry Diamonds, Star Center, 1919, 8 In. 190.00
Carafe, Star & Feather, Cut Glass, Signed 320.00
Chalice, Allover Deer & Foliage, Teardrop Stem, Green, Signed, 5 1/2 In. 295.00
Champagne, Jewel Pattern, Leaded, c.1904, 6 Piece 750.00
Champagne, Sharpe Cut Stem, Horizontal Ribbed Bowl, 6 In. 8.00
Champagne, Squirrel 125.00
Claret, Bear 165.00
Compote, Amberina, 1917, 10 In. 2310.00
Compote, Lovebirds, 4 1/2 x 7 In. 975.00
Cordial, Greyhound 175.00
Cordial, Sherry, Monkey 145.00
Decanter, Spillane, Scalloped Hobstar Foot, Signed, 14 In. 650.00
Dish, Cheese, Strawberry Diamond & Fan, Dome Cover, Signed, 1906, 9 In. 525.00
Dish, Prism, Cut Glass, 7 In. 185.00
Fernery, Diamond Shape Panels Of Nail Heads, Hobstar Base, 6 7/8 In. 275.00
Goblet, Princess, Cut Glass, 6 1/4 In. 85.00
Jar, Candy, Brilliant Cut, Barrel Shape, Signed, 8 In. 1200.00
Match Safe, Daisy & Button, Amber 225.00
Pitcher, Aztec, Cut Glass, 9 In. 3100.00
Pitcher, Comet, Cylindrical Shape, Signed, 10 In. 775.00
Pitcher, Flower Cutting, Notched Cut Loop Handle, Marked, 13 1/2 In. 305.00
Pitcher, Harvard Pattern, Cut Glass, Cut Handle, 9 x 6 1/2 In. .... 325.00 to 375.00
Pitcher, Kingston, Signed, 9 In. 395.00
Pitcher, Prism, 10 In. 325.00
Pitcher, Puritania, Cut Glass, Squat, Signed, 7 1/2 In. 800.00
Plate, Allover Holly & Snowflake, Cut Glass, Signed, 7 In. 295.00
Plate, Wedgemere, 7 In. 625.00
Punch Bowl, Kimberly, Cut Glass, 6 x 12 In. 850.00
Punch Cup, Double Lozenge, Pedestal, 3 In. 85.00
Relish, Glenda, Cut Glass, Divided, Signed, 8 x 5 In. 265.00
Salt & Pepper, Intaglio Flowers & Swags, Signed 250.00
Saltshaker, Saloon, Cut Hobstars, Cross Hatching & Fans, Rayed Base 165.00
Sherbet, Rabbit, Low 75.00
Sherbet, Sharp Cut Stem, Horizontal Ribbed Bowl 8.00
Sherbet, Squirrel, Black Silhouette, Signed 145.00
Sherry, Monkey Stem, Camphor 65.00
Sherry, Venetia 65.00
Toothpick, Diamond Quilted, Amberina, Square Mouth 235.00
Toothpick, Floppy Hat, Frosted, Columbian Exposition, 1939 .... 225.00
Toothpick, Little Lobe 95.00
Tray, Corinthian, Cut Glass, Signed, 12 In. 975.00
Tray, Flower Design, Signed, 11 3/4 In. 465.00
Tray, Ice Cream, Corena, Signed, 15 1/2 x 9 1/2 In. 1290.00
Tray, Ice Cream, Kimberly, Cut Glass, 18 x 10 1/2 In. 995.00
Tumbler, Brilliant, Cut Glass, 4 In., 4 Piece 132.00
Vase, Allover Diamond Hobstar & Fan, Flaring Sawtooth Rim, 17 1/2 In. 1430.00
Vase, Ellsmere, Signed, 16 In. .... 1600.00 to 2600.00
Water Set, Stars, Fans, Strawberry Diamond & Miters, Signed, 9 In., 7 Piece 1200.00

LIGHTERS for cigarettes and cigars are collectible. Cigarettes became
popular in the late nineteenth century, and with the cigarette came matches
and cigarette lighters. All types of lighters are collected, from solid gold to
the first of the recent disposable lighters. Most examples found were made
after 1940.

Baltimore Colts, Musical, Bluebird, Box 125.00
Baseball, Rests On 3 Crossed Bats, Occupied Japan, 1940s .... 40.00 to 95.00
Big Boy, Tan Plastic & Silvered Metal, 1960s, 2 1/2 In. 23.00
Bolser Flares 18.00
Bowling Ball 18.00
Bowling Ball & Pins, Metal, Table 24.00
Brass, 1914 .... 30.00
Camel Cigarettes Pack, Figural .... 5.50 to 10.00

*Lighter, Light Up A Kool, Willie
The Penguin, Cast Iron, 4 In.*

◆◆◆◆◆◆◆◆◆◆◆◆◆◆◆◆◆◆◆◆◆◆◆◆

Decorated glasses given as promotions at fast food restaurants
often fade in sunlight.

◆◆◆◆◆◆◆◆◆◆◆◆◆◆◆◆◆◆◆◆◆◆◆◆

Cannon, Bronze	75.00
Cigar, Cinco, Lamp Shape, Liberty, Reverse Glass Shade, 11 In.	495.00
Cigar, Elmer Fudd, Ceramic	125.00
Cigar, Figural, Indian, Chalkware, Milk Glass Glove, 23 In.	275.00
Cigar, Midland, Model L, Jump Spark, Oak, Brass Reservoir, Mechanism, 15 In.	330.00
Cigar, Tiered Oak Case, Nickel Plated Reservoir, 15 In.	121.00
Coin Form, John F. Kennedy 35th President, USA, 1 1/2 In.	35.00
Coors, Can Style	20.00
Craftsman, Raised Golfer	50.00
De-Light	10.00
Desk, Figural, Airplane, Negbaur	150.00
Dueling Pistol	75.00
Dunhill, 14K Gold Jacket, 1950s	275.00
Dunhill, Flip Top, 18K Gold Jacket, Metal Interior	345.00
Dunhill, Gold Monogram, Sterling Silver	30.00
Dunhill, Painted Aquarium Scene, Clear Plastic	125.00
Dunhill, Rollalite	40.00
Dunhill, Silent Flame, Sally Rand	50.00
Dunhill, Wick, Sterling Silver	110.00
Dunhill, World War II Service, Instruction, Box	15.00
Elgin, Large	18.00
Esso	20.00
Evans, Cowboy Boots	45.00
Evans, Grecian Style, Fluid, Table, 4 1/4 x 3 In.	25.00
Fox Hole, World War II	25.00
Frostie, 14K Gold Plated	48.00
Gold Poodle, Green Eyes	18.00
Golf Bag, Cast Metal, Copper Finish, 5 In.	45.00
Golf Bag, Table	20.00 to 32.00
Hotel Mapes, Reno, Nevada	50.00
Knight's Bust	40.00
L. & M. Cigarettes, Box	12.00
Light Up A Cool, Willie The Penguin, Cast Iron, 4 In. .... *Illus*	382.00
Lime Cola, Bottle Shape	23.00
Lizard Shape, Table, Germany	250.00
Mayflower Transit Company, Germany	75.00
Monkey, Bronze	150.00
Music Box	100.00
Musical, Advertising	65.00
Oasis Brand Cigarettes, Enameled	35.00
Oil Derrick, Table	30.00
Oil Filter Shape, Attached Ashtray, Auto	30.00
Orlando Magic	3.00
Penguin, Kools Cigarettes, Chrome	195.00
Philip Morris, Silvered Brass, Plastic Panels, 1960s, 2 In.	10.00
Pistol, Black, Chrome, Japan	25.00
Playboy	8.50 to 20.00

Red Fire Engine, Pumper, Cast Metal	65.00
Roly Poly, Crystal	20.00
Ronson, Black Barman, Touch Tip, Chrome, 1935	1500.00
Ronson, Crown, Silver, Table, 1964	7.00
Ronson, Fantasy, Ceramic, Fluid	40.00
Ronson, Lion Gasoline	25.00
Ronson, Melrose, Silver, Table	15.00
Ronson, Penciliter, Gold-Filled, 1936 .... 55.00 to 105.00	
Ronson, Queen Anne, Silver, England, Table	15.00
Ronson, Senator, Table, Box .... 18.00 to 30.00	
Ronson, Varaflame Premier, Hard Case, Box	35.00
Ronson, Vernon, Table	20.00
Royal Crown Cola, Bottle Shape, 3 In. .... 19.00 to 25.00	
Scripto Vu-Lighter, Clear Plastic, 1960s .... 15.00 to 24.00	
Sterling Silver, Monogram B.F.R.	19.00
Strikalite, Elephant	20.00
USS Porter	40.00
Vulcan, N.C.O. Club, Gunter Air Force Base, Doctor Insignia	15.00
White Rock, Painted Enamel, Idealine	40.00
Willie, Light Up A Kool, Head Lifts, Cast Iron, 4 In.	382.00
Woman's Head, Electric, Table	80.00
Zippo, 1935 Windy-Varga Girl, With Tin	22.00
Zippo, Advertising .... 12.00 to 22.00	
Zippo, Enameled Hammond Organ	35.00
Zippo, Engraved Oriental Scene, Sterling Silver	45.00
Zippo, Kleenex	38.00
Zippo, Masonic Emblem	25.00
Zippo, Mr. Camel	10.00
Zippo, Sterling Silver	40.00
Zippo, Travelodge Motels	40.00

LIGHTNING RODS and lightning rod balls are collected for their variety of shapes and colors. These glass balls were at the center of the rod that was attached to the roof of a house or barn to avoid lightning damage.

Arrow, Full Bodied Horse, Metal, Large	25.00
Arrow, Purple Stained Glass Tail, Brass, St. Louis	40.00
Ball, Blue Opaque .... 15.00 to 22.50	
Ball, Carnival Glass, Electra	50.00
Ball, Cobalt Blue, Julius F. Goetz Mfg., Co.	50.00
Ball, Milk Glass, Julius F. Goetz Mfg., Co.	35.00
Ball, Red Flashed, Wide Collar, SLR Co.	75.00
Ball, Staircase, Cobalt Blue	18.00
Ball, Sun Colored Amethyst, Diddie	35.00
Ball, True Red, Reyburn Hunter Foy Co.	675.00
Pendant, Plain, Metal, 4 Piece	60.00

LIMOGES porcelain has been made in Limoges, France, since the mid-nineteenth century. Fine porcelains were made by many factories, including Haviland, Ahrenfeldt, Guerin, Pouyat, Elite, and others. Modern porcelains are being made at Limoges and the word *Limoges* as part of the mark is not an indication of age. Haviland, Limoges is listed as a separate category in this book.

Biscuit Jar, Yellow Mums, Brushed Gold, Branch Handle	110.00
Bone Dish, Lavender Flower	12.00
Bowl, Bell Flowers, Gold Border, Flowers Into Bowl, Signed, 10 In.	160.00
Bowl, Flower, Ivory Ground, Gold Scrolls, Signed, 8 5/8 In.	35.00
Bowl, Leaves & Flowers, Raised Gold Buds, Gold Pierced Handle, Straus, 9 1/2 In. ..	130.00
Butter Chip, Forget-Me-Nots	35.00
Butter Chip, Ornate Holder	95.00
Celery, Roses, Rococo Gold Rim	88.00
Chocolate Pot, Flowers, Butterflies, Gold Ribbons In Twine Handle	145.00
Chocolate Set, Cobalt Blue, Gold & White, c.1910, 7 Piece	395.00
Cider Set, Berries, Leaves, Gold, 6 Piece	165.00

Coffee Set, Hand-Painted Flowers, Wedgwood Blue Borders, 19 Piece 295.00
Compote, Polychrome Floral, Shallow, Marked, 9 3/8 x 4 1/4 In., Pair 55.00
Dish, Blue Flowers, Gold Rim, Rectangular, Signed, 9 x 4 In. 18.00
Dresser Set, Violets, Purples, Greens, 3 Piece 225.00
Dresser Tray, Colonial Couple Courting, Pink Luster Grape Border, 8 x 13 In. 165.00
Fernery, Floral Design, Baroque Feet 225.00
Jardiniere, Bust, Young Woman, Roses, Hand Painted, 11 1/4 x 11 In. 275.00
Jardiniere, Yellow Roses, Bulbous 725.00
Lamp, Pink Rose, Gray & Tan Ground, Cylinder, 8 x 5 3/4 In. 235.00
Oyster Plate Set, 10 Piece 770.00
Pitcher, Hand Painted Apple 175.00
Plaque, 2 Facing Stags, 2 Facing Does, Signed, 13 1/4 In., Pair 845.00
Plaque, Dutch Scene, Gold Rococo Border, 12 1/2 In. 245.00
Plaque, Game Birds, Signed, 13 In. 325.00
Plaque, Portrait Of King Charles I & Danielle, Cadish, 3 3/4 x 5 In., Pair 535.00
Plaque, Portrait, Child, 4 3/4 In. 60.00
Plate, Cabbage Roses, Shaded Ground, Gold Rim, 8 1/2 In. 45.00
Plate, Cherries, Signed, 1902 .... 155.00
Plate, Desert Flowers, Pink & White Ground, Marked, 9 In., 6 Piece 195.00
Plate, Different Flowers, Pansies, Asters, 7 In., 6 Piece 165.00
Plate, Fish Design, 9 In., 6 Piece 275.00
Plate, Floral & Gilt Design, Multicolored, 9 5/8 In., 11 Piece 110.00
Plate, Fruit, Scalloped Gold Rim, Pierced For Hanging, Marked, 13 1/4 In. 265.00
Plate, Game Bird, Hanging, Pink Flowers, Beaded Rim, Marked, 13 3/4 In. 225.00
Plate, Gold Floral Rim, Polychrome Flowers, 11 1/4 In., 12 Piece 462.00
Plate, Hand Painted Pink & Gold Roses, Gold Rim, Coronet, Demitasse 30.00
Plate, Hanging, Deer & Dog, 10 In. 115.00
Plate, Lafayette At North Island, South Carolina, 8 1/2 In. 28.00
Plate, Portrait, Enameled, Union Ceramique, 1909 .... 225.00
Plate, Woman & Man On Horse, Rococo Gold Border, Signed, 12 3/4 In. 295.00
Platter, Fish, Painted, 22 In. 115.00
Platter, Magenta Flowers, Blank No. 118, Haviland, 14 In. 28.00
Platter, Roses In Almond, Gold, Olive, Yellow, 14 In. 75.00
Pot De Creme, Gold Bands, Handle, White, Gilded Rosebud Finial, 11 Piece 165.00
Powder Jar, Cover, Gold Leaf Fronds 30.00
Punch Bowl, Hand Painted Floral, 12 Piece 950.00
Punch Bowl, Violets Inside & Out, White With Gold Trim, 12 1/2 In. .... 395.00 to 495.00
Ramekin Set, Underplate, Stylized Pink Leaf & Scroll Border, Signed 10.00
Sugar & Creamer, Nut Finial, Acanthus Leaves 150.00
Teapot, Silver Overlay Floral & Scroll, 2 1/4 x 5 1/2 In. 110.00
Tile, Angel, Sitting On Garden Wall, Signed 225.00
Tray, Allover Grapes & Vines, Green & Red, 16 x 12 In. 145.00
Tray, Blue Flowers, Pink Buds, Beaded Scalloped Rim, 10 1/2 x 8 1/4 In. 60.00
Tray, Dresser, Baroque, Pink Blossoms, Gold Trim, 9 x 11 1/2 In. 55.00
Tray, Dresser, Floral & Insect Design, Multicolored, Gilt Handles, 17 In. 50.00
Tray, Lilacs, Autumn Foliage, Gold Rococo Trim, 12 1/2 x 9 1/4 In. 145.00
Tray, Violets, Green To Apricot Ground, Gold Split Center Handle, 11 x 6 In. 125.00
Trivet, Yellow Roses, Pastel Ground, 3 Button Footed, Artist E. Thau, 6 1/2 In. 48.00
Urn, Mantel, Figural Reserves, Gilt, Cover, Square Base, 1900s, 14 In., Pair 330.00
Vase, 2 Bird Panels, Gold Trim, Historical Design, Marked, 15 In. 375.00
Vase, Colonial Figures, Blue, Gold Trim, 8 In. 145.00
Vase, Pillow, Chrysanthemums 1 Side, Purple Flowers Other, Footed, 6 x 4 1/2 In. ... 60.00
Vase, Pillow, Orange Blossoms On Back, Violets On Front, Gold Trim, 9 x 6 In. 350.00
Vase, Woman, Long Brown Hair, Pink Gown, Turquoise Luster Ground, 13 In. 695.00
Water Set, Dragon Handle, Artist 985.00

LINDBERGH was a national hero. In 1927, Charles Lindbergh, the aviator, became the first man to make a nonstop solo flight across the Atlantic Ocean. In 1932, his son was kidnapped and murdered, and Lindbergh was again the center of public interest. He died in 1974. All types of Lindbergh memorabilia are collected.

Bank, Bust 235.00
Book, The Lone Eagle, 1929, 8 x 9 In. 20.00

Button, Lucky Lindbergh, Pinback, Ribbon, Metal Plane 75.00
Doorstop, Spirit Of St. Louis, 6 x 9 3/4 In. 550.00
Pencil Box, Picture & Plane, Blue Tin 50.00
Photograph, Charles Lindbergh, Formal, Paris, 1927 .... 85.00
Photograph, Homecoming, Reception, Pres. Coolidge, June 11, 1927, 36 x 12 In. 400.00
Plate, Commemorative, 1927 .... 40.00
Sheet Music, Lindbergh, Eagle Of The USA, Spirit Of St. Louis, 1927 .... 40.00
Trolley Broadside, Welcome To L.A., Picture, 6 x 16 In. 150.00
Watch, Statue Of Liberty & Eiffel Tower On Case 300.00

LITHOPHANES are porcelain pictures made by casting clay in layers of various thicknesses. When a piece is held to the light, a picture of light and shadow is seen through it. Most lithophanes date from the 1825–1875 period. A few are still being made. Many lithophanes sold today were originally panels for lampshades.

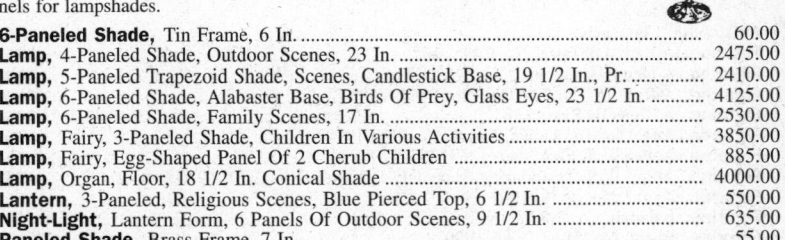

6-Paneled Shade, Tin Frame, 6 In. 60.00
Lamp, 4-Paneled Shade, Outdoor Scenes, 23 In. 2475.00
Lamp, 5-Paneled Trapezoid Shade, Scenes, Candlestick Base, 19 1/2 In., Pr. 2410.00
Lamp, 6-Paneled Shade, Alabaster Base, Birds Of Prey, Glass Eyes, 23 1/2 In. 4125.00
Lamp, 6-Paneled Shade, Family Scenes, 17 In. 2530.00
Lamp, Fairy, 3-Paneled Shade, Children In Various Activities 3850.00
Lamp, Fairy, Egg-Shaped Panel Of 2 Cherub Children 885.00
Lamp, Organ, Floor, 18 1/2 In. Conical Shade 4000.00
Lantern, 3-Paneled, Religious Scenes, Blue Pierced Top, 6 1/2 In. 550.00
Night-Light, Lantern Form, 6 Panels Of Outdoor Scenes, 9 1/2 In. 635.00
Paneled Shade, Brass Frame, 7 In. 55.00
Stein, Infanterie Rgt. II, Courting Couple, Pewter Lid, Lion Thumb Rest, 10 In. 192.00

LIVERPOOL, England, was the site of several pottery and porcelain factories from 1716 to 1785. Some earthenware was made with transfer decorations. Sadler and Green made print-decorated wares from 1756. Many of the pieces were made for the American market and feature patriotic emblems, such as eagles, flags, and other special-interest motifs.

Bowl, Motto, Columbia's Favorite Son, 9 3/4 In. 5225.00
Bowl, Waste, Chinese In Garden, Pearlware, c.1780, 6 1/2 In. 660.00
Creamer, Lafayette Crowned & Surrender Of Cornwallis, Copper Luster, 4 In. 375.00
Creamer, Lord Nelson In Shell, Neptune, Blue Ground, 4 In. 450.00
Cup & Saucer, Mt.Vernon, Seat Of The Late Gen. Washington, Black Transfer 125.00
Jug, Cooper's Arms 2000.00
Pitcher, 15 States Surround Liberty Poem, Jefferson Quote, Creamware, 20 In. 1870.00
Pitcher, 3-Masted American Ship, Rope-Makers Arms, Creamware, 10 1/4 In. 1980.00
Pitcher, 3-Masted Ship, American Flag On Back, Creamware, 6 3/4 In. 665.00
Pitcher, American Ship With Eagle & Banner 1200.00
Pitcher, Apotheosis, George Washington, Eagle Other Side, Transfer 1045.00
Pitcher, Commodore Preble, Attack On Tripoli, Creamware, 8 In. 2200.00
Pitcher, General Brown & Decatur, Squatty, 4 1/2 In. 895.00
Pitcher, Hibernia & English Ship 550.00
Pitcher, Map Of Ireland & Hibernia, 8 3/4 In. 900.00
Pitcher, Masonic Compass & Square Transfer, Ship Named Osiris 1100.00
Pitcher, Merry Andrew 1 Side, Landscape Other, Repaired Handle, 6 1/2 In. 190.00
Pitcher, Peace, Plenty & Independence, Apotheosis Of Washington, 8 1/2 In. 1150.00
Pitcher, Peace, Plenty & Independence, U.S. Ship, 7 1/2 In. 1650.00
Pitcher, Peace, Plenty & Independence, U.S. Ship, 10 1/2 In. 2400.00
Pitcher, Plan Of The City Of Washington, U.S. Ship Other, 8 3/4 In. 4800.00
Pitcher, Seal Of The U.S., Chain Of States Around, 6 1/4 In. 2200.00
Pitcher, Ship & Map Of Colonies, Alexander Thomas Of Maine 2200.00
Pitcher, Ship Building & Peace, Plenty & Independence, 1830s, 8 3/4 In. 1200.00
Pitcher, Transfer Of Washington & Map Of Colonies, 10 In. 4100.00
Pitcher, Washington & Map, Independence On Back, Creamware, 10 In. 935.00
Pitcher, Washington Bust, He In Glory, American In Tears 2475.00
Pitcher, Washington In Glory, Creamware, 6 3/4 In. 1320.00
Pitcher, Washington Memorial, 11 In. 1550.00
Plaque, George Washington, Black Transfer, Oval, 5 In. .... 1550.00 to 2400.00

Plate, British Ship, 1810, 9 3/4 In. 235.00
Plate, Flowering Branch, Blue Rock Work, Sprays On Rim, c.1760, 8 7/8 In. 935.00
Plate, Magenta Transfer, 2-Masted Sloop, Acorn Boarder, c.1800, 9 3/4 In. 275.00
Plate, Reddish Tan Rim, Blue Marking, "3", c.1760, 9 In. 325.00
Plate, Yellow & Blue Birds, Yellow Insects, c.1760, 9 In. 1650.00
Punch Bowl, 3-Masted American Figate, Neptune & Amphitrite, 13 1/4 In. 4950.00
Tankard, Black Transfer, Immortal Washington, Favorite Son, 3 7/8 In. 2750.00
Teapot, Cover, Ovoid, Oriental Floral Spray, Pennington's, c.1780, 6 1/2 In. 345.00

LLADRO is a Spanish porcelain. Juan, Jose, and Vicente Lladro opened a
ceramics workshop in Almacera in 1951. They soon began making figurines
in a distinctive, elongated style. In 1958 the factory moved to Tabernes
Blanques, Spain. The company makes stoneware and porcelain vases and
figurines in limited and unlimited editions. Dates given are first and last years
of production.

I.LLADRÓ®

Bell, 1988, Christmas 35.00
Figurine, A Lady Of Taste, No. 1495, 1986 .... 625.00
Figurine, A New Hat, 12 In. 400.00
Figurine, A Ride In The Country, No. 5354, 1986 .... 300.00
Figurine, A Time To Rest, 5 In. 225.00
Figurine, Angel Laying Down, No. 5728, 1990-1992 .... 70.00
Figurine, Angel With Flute, No. 1253, 1972-1988 .... 70.00
Figurine, Angel With Tambourine, Heavenly Dreamer, No. 1320, 1976-1985 .... 495.00
Figurine, Angel, No. 4539, 1969 .... 70.00
Figurine, Balancing Act, 3 1/2 In. 150.00
Figurine, Bison, No. 5312, 1985-1990 .... 3000.00
Figurine, Boy & Girl, No. 1039, 1969 .... 108.00
Figurine, Boy, With Yacht, No. 4810, 1972 .... 120.00
Figurine, Can I Play?, No. 7610, 1990-1992 .... 250.00 to 450.00
Figurine, Cat & Ball 70.00
Figurine, Centaur Boy, No. 1013, 1969-1989 .... 575.00
Figurine, Centaur Girl, No. 1012, 1969-1989 .... 600.00
Figurine, Charlie The Tramp, No. 5233, 1984-1993, 11 1/4 In. 1050.00
Figurine, Countryman, Matte, No. 4664, 1969-1979, 11 1/2 In. 375.00
Figurine, Couple From The Arctic, No. 2038, 1971-1982 .... 315.00
Figurine, Debutantes, No. 1431, 1982 .... 500.00
Figurine, Dentist, No. 4762, 1971-1978 .... 250.00 to 425.00
Figurine, Dog, Great Dane, No. 1068, 1969-1989 .... 750.00
Figurine, Dog, Pekinese, No. 4641, 1969-1985 .... 250.00
Figurine, Don Quixote & Sancho Panza, No. 1318, Limited Edition, 1976 .... 5000.00
Figurine, Donkey In Love, Picking Daisy, No. 4524, 1969-1985 .... 350.00
Figurine, Donkey, Manger, No. 4679, 1969 .... 75.00
Figurine, Dove, 7 1/2 In. 145.00
Figurine, Duck, White, No. 4551, 1969, 2 1/2 In. 35.00
Figurine, Faun Head, No. 1195, 1972 .... 600.00
Figurine, Flower Peddler, No. 5029, 1980-1985, 11 3/4 In. 375.00
Figurine, Full Moon, No. 1438, 1983-1988 .... 600.00
Figurine, Girl, Soccer Player, No. 5134, 1982-1983, 9 In. 700.00
Figurine, Girl, With Basket, No. 4665, 1969-1979, 11 1/2 In. 375.00
Figurine, Girl, With Flowers No. 1088, 1969-1989 .... 395.00
Figurine, Girl, With Kittens, Following Her Cats, No. 1309, 1974 .... 250.00
Figurine, Girl, With Lamb, No. 4835, 1972, 10 5/8 In. 130.00
Figurine, Girl, With Pig, No. 1011, 1969 .... 100.00
Figurine, Girl, With Wheelbarrow, No. 4816, 1972-1981 .... 375.00
Figurine, Heavenly Solo, Box, No. 2196, 1990 .... 95.00
Figurine, Hebrew Student, No. 4684, 1970-1985 .... 400.00
Figurine, Horned Owl, 5 3/4 In. 175.00
Figurine, I Love You Truly, No. 1528, 1987, 14 In. 425.00
Figurine, Just A Little Kiss, Girl & Boy With Flowers 265.00
Figurine, King Baltasar, No. 1425.3, 1983-1985 .... 70.00
Figurine, King Baltasar, No. 1425.3, 1983-1985, Box 275.00
Figurine, King Gaspar, No. 1424.3, 1983-1985 .... 70.00
Figurine, King Melchior, No. 1423.3, 1983-1985 .... 75.00

Figurine, Little Leaguer, Catcher, No. 5290, 1985-1990, 6 1/2 In. 350.00
Figurine, Little Leaguer, Exercising, No. 5289, 1985-1990, 12 1/4 In. 425.00
Figurine, Little Leaguer, On Bench, No. 5291, 1985-1990, 7 1/2 In. 375.00
Figurine, Little Pals, 1985 .... 1265.00
Figurine, Male Tennis Player, No. 1426, 1982-1988 .... 325.00
Figurine, Mary, No. 1387.3, 1983-1985 .... 50.00
Figurine, Mermaid, No. 1348, 1978-1983 .... 345.00
Figurine, Monk, Brown, No. 2060, 1977, 12 In. 100.00
Figurine, Mother & 2 Children, 15 In. 445.00
Figurine, My Buddy, No. 7609, 1989-1990 .... 400.00
Figurine, Nude, Matte, No. 4512, 1969-1985, 18 In. 295.00
Figurine, Obstetrician, No. 4763, 1971-1975 .... 200.00
Figurine, Old Folks, No. 1033, 1969-1985, 16 1/2 In. 1500.00
Figurine, Penguin, No. 5248, 1984-1988, 5 1/2 In. 200.00
Figurine, Peter Pan, No. 7529, Limited Edition, 1993 .... 1500.00 to 1600.00
Figurine, Petite Maiden, No. 5383, 1986-1990, 4 1/4 In. 350.00
Figurine, Petite Pair, No. 5384, 1986-1990, 4 1/4 In. 400.00
Figurine, Pharmacist, No. 4844, 1973-1985 .... 2000.00
Figurine, Pigs, Resting 175.00
Figurine, Pilar, 5 3/4 In. 400.00
Figurine, Serenade, No. 5381, 1986-1990 .... 825.00
Figurine, Shepherdess, Traditional Dress 400.00
Figurine, Spanish Dancer, 6 In. 250.00
Figurine, Storyhour, No. 5786, 1991 .... 700.00
Figurine, Teresa, 5 3/4 In. 475.00
Figurine, Tern, 5 In. 275.00
Figurine, The Family, No. 1201, 1971-1979 .... 1300.00
Figurine, Tinker Bell, No. 7529, Limited Edition, 1992 .... 1850.00
Figurine, Woman On Horse, No. 4516, 1969 .... 520.00

LOCKE ART is a trademark found on glass of the early twentieth century. Joseph Locke worked at many English and American firms. He designed and etched his own glass in Pittsburgh, Pennsylvania, starting in the 1880s. Some pieces were marked *Joe Locke*, but most were marked with the words *Locke Art*. The mark is hidden in the pattern on the glass.

Pitcher, 2 Hobstars, Stars & Fans, Engraved Poinsettias, 9 In. 295.00
Sherbet, Poppy, Saucer Base 160.00
Whiskey 95.00

LOETZ glass was made in many varieties. Johann Loetz bought a glassworks in Austria in 1840. He died in 1848 and his widow ran the company; then in 1879, his grandson took over. Most collectors recognize the iridescent gold glass similar to Tiffany, but many other types were made. The firm closed during World War II.

Ashtray, Applied Design, Iridescent, Attached Burner 175.00
Bowl, Celery Green, Fuchsia Iridescent Streaks, Footed, Globular, 9 1/2 In. 2587.00
Bowl, Green, Signed, 9 In. 150.00
Bowl, Papillon Design, Ruffled Rim, Iridized Red, 11 In. 350.00
Bowl, Ruffled Quatrefoil Rim, Basket Weave, Iridescent, 8 In. 715.00
Bowl, Scalloped Rim, Webbed, Plum Iridescent, 9 1/2 In. 585.00
Bowl, Thumbprint, Lobed Rim, 5 x 11 1/2 In. 625.00
Garniture Set, Box, Vases, Pink & Blue, Enameled Design, c.1916, 3 Piece 1725.00
Lamp, Bronze, 2 Arms, Amber Iridescent Shade, Red Marble Base, 1900, 27 In. 4888.00
Lamp, Bronze, Amber Pulled Feather Shade, Iridescent Glass, 1900, 21 1/2 In. 2875.00
Lamp, Desk, Adjustable Arm, Spherical Glass Shade, Green Pulled Feather, 15 In. 2640.00
Lamp, Desk, Bronze, Amber Shade With Oil Spots, 1900, 13 1/2 In. 1725.00
Lamp, Desk, Streaked Shade, Stepped Pyramidal Top, Pink Oil Spot, 13 In. 4180.00
Lamp, Silvered-Metal Tripod, Green & Blue Iridescent Shade, 1900, 19 1/2 In. 2588.00
Vase, 4 Protruding Branch-Like Necks, Amber, Rainbow Iridescent, 9 In. 2070.00
Vase, Amber, Random Threading, Gold Iridescent Fruits & Leaves, 4 In. 470.00
Vase, Amphora Shape, Blue-Gold Iridescent Oil Spots, 4 7/8 In. 770.00
Vase, Applied Snake & Coyote, Green & Blue, 5 In. 150.00
Vase, Applied Tadpoles, Oil Spots, Peacock Blue, 9 In. 1500.00

Vase, Art Deco Irises On Black, Blue Iridescent, 6 1/4 In. 975.00
Vase, Art Nouveau, Full-Length Nude Woman Each Side, Pewter Mount, 6 3/4 In. 330.00
Vase, Blue & Gold Flecked, Silver Styled Tree, Silver Overlay, 6 3/4 In. 720.00
Vase, Blue & Silver Wave Design, Red, 7 In. 3000.00
Vase, Blue Art Glass, Silver Floral Overlay, 4 1/4 In. 825.00
Vase, Blue Oil-Spot Design, Bell Shaped, Blue, 6 7/8 In. 368.00
Vase, Bottle Green, Arabesque & Stylized Leafage, Iridescent, Cameo, 9 7/8 In. 1725.00
Vase, Bulbous, Conical Neck, Violet Shaded To Apricot, Silver Iridescent, 6 1/4 In. .. 2760.00
Vase, Butterfly, Peacock Blue, 10 1/2 In. 2695.00
Vase, Cattail, Art Nouveau, Blue Iridescent, 10 In. 2500.00
Vase, Chalice Shape, Amber, Blue Oil Spots, Gilt Metal Frame, c.1900, 7 5/8 In. 1035.00
Vase, Cobalt Blue Iridescent, Applied Amber Rim, Double Reeded Handles, 11 In. ... 525.00
Vase, Cobalt Blue, Oil Spots, 9 1/2 In. 225.00
Vase, Conch Shell, Amber, Blue Oil Spots, Floriform Base, c.1900, 6 7/8 In. 920.00
Vase, Coral & White Marbleized Pull-Ups, Gold Ground, 7 In. 325.00
Vase, Dark Red & Gray, Silver Iridescent & Blue Pulled Feather, 15 1/4 In. 1380.00
Vase, Deep Rosaline, Oyster Iridescent, Floral Silver Overlay, 4 1/2 In. 467.00
Vase, Dimpled Sides, Silver Blue Drapery, 7 In. 1200.00
Vase, Double Handle, Green, Oil Spots, 4 1/4 x 3 1/2 In. 475.00
Vase, Elongated Curved Gooseneck Rim, Pulled Feather Design, 10 1/2 In. 1320.00
Vase, Free-Form, Pewter Mounts, 4 3/4 In. 1995.00
Vase, Gold Hearts & Vines, Opalescent, 11 1/2 In. 575.00
Vase, Gold Iridescent Wavy Pulls, Yellow Ground, Ovoid, Waisted Neck, 6 7/8 In. 1725.00
Vase, Gold Iridescent, Wild Rose Silver Overlay, Pinched, 3 1/2 In. 495.00
Vase, Gold Raindrop Iridescent, Carnations Silver Overlay, 4 1/2 x 2 1/2 In. 605.00
Vase, Gold Threading, Oil Spots, Pinched Sides, Ruffled Top, 10 1/2 In. 750.00
Vase, Gold Waves On Body, Burgundy Striped Spots, Marked, 9 In. 6325.00
Vase, Gourd, Papillon Pattern, Gold, Blue Luster, 11 x 5 In. 220.00
Vase, Green Iridescent, Amber Oil Spots, Swollen Cylindrical, 14 In. 315.00
Vase, Green Iridescent, Carnations & Leaves Silver Overlay, 3 x 3 1/2 In. 440.00
Vase, Green Iridescent, Free-Form, 10 In. 165.00
Vase, Green Snakeskin Scaling, Green, 7 3/4 In. 350.00
Vase, Green, Spotted Pale-Blue Iridescent, Compressed Globular, Neck, 18 In. 1725.00
Vase, Iridescent Raindrop Finish, Silver Overlay Iris, Gold Peppering, 8 3/4 In. 1100.00
Vase, Jack-In-The-Pulpit, Amber Pulled Feathers, Blue & Gold Iridescent, 13 In. 1450.00
Vase, Lemon Opalescent, Salmon & Cinnamon Wavy Lines, Oil Spots, 14 5/8 In. 3165.00
Vase, Lime Green Dripping Into Iridescent Blue, 8 7/8 In. 2090.00
Vase, Lime Green, Blue Ovals, Stringing, c.1900, 7 In. 1035.00
Vase, Octopus, Air Trap, Rich Brown Cased To Opal, No. 9159, 6 3/4 In. 2100.00
Vase, Oil Spots, Deep Cobalt Blue, 4 1/2 In. 240.00
Vase, Oil Spots, Gourd Shape, Blue, 5 In. 350.00

Loetz, Vase, Silver Overlay, Melon Ribs,
Iridescent Swirls & Raindrops, 7 1/4 In; Loetz,
Vase, Silver Overlay, Gold, Iridescent Raindrop
Finish, 8 3/4 In.

Loetz, Vase, Silver Overlay, Peacock Blue
Iridescent, 10 1/2 In.

Vase, Oil Spots, Green Drape, 7 In. 160.00
Vase, Ovoid, Cylindrical Neck, Purple Iridescent, Blue Pulled Feathers, c.1900, 6 In. 1265.00
Vase, Pale Amber Glass, Silver Oil Spots, 1900, 6 1/2 In. 402.00
Vase, Pale Bronze Iridescent, Bleeding Hearts Silver Overlay, 9 1/2 In. 2255.00
Vase, Pale Green, Melon Rib, Art Nouveau Silver Overlay, 7 x 5 In. 880.00
Vase, Peacock Blue Iridescent, Allover Papillon Design, Floral, 10 1/2 In. 2690.00
Vase, Peacock Iridescent Crackled Finish, 3 Handles, Squat, 8 5/8 In. 805.00
Vase, Pinched Bowl, Cased Yellow, Gold Iridescent Spots, 6 1/2 In. 1430.00
Vase, Pinched Sides, Gold Oil Spots, 4 In. 300.00
Vase, Pulled Cobalt Loops & Swags, Ground Lip, 12 In. 1050.00
Vase, Pulled Iridescent Rainbow Oil Spots, Everted Rim, 7 In. 2640.00
Vase, Raised Stylized Branch Design, Dimpled Rim, 5 In. 748.00
Vase, Red Oil Spot & Platinum Design, 10 In. 1400.00
Vase, Ribbed, Fan Shape, Green Shaded To Burgundy, 9 In. 395.00
Vase, Rose Iridescent, Silver-Blue Oil Spots, Geometric, 1900, 19 3/4 In. 3750.00
Vase, Silver & Gold Oil Spot Design, Gold Body, Trellis At Waist, 8 1/4 In. 1380.00
Vase, Silver Oil Spot Design, Dimpled At Waist, Everted Rim, 8 In. 390.00
Vase, Silver Oil Spots, Turned Rim, Green, Gold Trim, 5 1/2 x 7 In. 1700.00
Vase, Silver Overlay Design Of Bleeding Hearts, 9 1/2 In. 2255.00
Vase, Silver Overlay Trailings, Tangerine Ground, Paperweight, 1900, 7 5/8 In. 6325.00
Vase, Silver Overlay, Gold, Iridescent Raindrop Finish, 8 3/4 In. .... *Illus* 1100.00
Vase, Silver Overlay, Iridescent Brown, c.1890, 1 1/2 In. 600.00
Vase, Silver Overlay, Melon Ribs, Iridescent Swirls & Raindrops, 7 1/4 In. .... *Illus* 880.00
Vase, Silver Overlay, Peacock Blue Iridescent, 10 1/2 In. .... *Illus* 2695.00
Vase, Silver Spots At Waist, Iridescent Wavy Lines, Signed, 8 1/2 In. 7475.00
Vase, Silver Wave Design At Neck, Green Wavy Lines, Below, Signed, 6 In. 1955.00
Vase, Silver Waves At Top, Lime Green Cylinder, 11 3/8 In. 2450.00
Vase, Silvery-Blue & Amber Iridescent, c.1900, 11 1/2 In. 6900.00
Vase, Tree-Trunk Form, Holes On Side, Scalloped Rim, 10 In. 690.00
Vase, Trefoil Rim, Iridescent Blue & Green Waves, Pinched Cylinder, 9 1/2 In. 2100.00
Vase, Trefoil Rim, Iridescent Green & Blue Waves, Tear-Drop Form, 6 1/4 In. 1045.00
Vase, Trumpet Form, Blue, Silver & Green Waves, Floral Silver Overlay, 4 3/4 In. 3225.00
Vase, Trumpet Form, Gold Iridescent Streaks, Maroon Bottom, Signed, 7 In. 5525.00
Vase, Whiplash Tendrils, Lilies, Blue Glass, Green Iridescent Spot, Ovoid, 7 1/8 In. . . 980.00
Vase, Yellow Chartreuse, Silver Iridescent Feathered Overlay, 4 x 3 1/2 In. 1650.00
Vase, Yellow Iridescent, Art Nouveau Silver Overlay Design, 6 1/2 In. 1925.00

LONE RANGER, a fictional character, was introduced on the radio in 1932.
Over three thousand shows were produced before the series ended in 1954. In
1938, the first Lone Ranger movie was made. Television shows were started
in 1949 and are still seen on some stations. The Lone Ranger appears on
many products and was even the name of a restaurant chain for several years.

Badge, Chief Scout 90.00
Badge, Club, Horseshoe Shape, With Picture, Brass, 1930s .... 28.00 to 30.00
Badge, Deputy 40.00
Badge, Deputy, Secret Compartment 85.00
Badge, Safety Scout, Lone Ranger Riding Silver, 1 In. 28.00
Badge, Watch & Mask, Lone Ranger & Tonto, Package 38.00
Belt Hanger, Figural, Lone Ranger On Horse, 1938 .... 135.00
Book, Coloring, Whitman, 1950s 18.00
Book, Lone Ranger & The Black Shirt Highwayman, Whitman, 1939 .... 80.00
Book, Lone Ranger & The Mystery Ranch, Grossett & Dunlap, 1938 .... 22.00
Book, Lone Ranger Outlaw Stronghold, 1939 .... 19.00
Book, Lone Ranger Taps The Smugglers, 1941 .... 19.00
Book, Paint, Whitman, 1938, 11 x 14 In. 62.00
Booklet, His Mark & How He Met Tonto 40.00
Box, Pencil, Embossed Image Of Ranger On Silver, Top Opens To Tray 80.00
Card, Gum, No. 18, Barrier Of Fire, 1940 .... 20.00
Card, Trading, Silver Cup Bread Premium, 1938 .... 45.00
Card Set, Arcade, 16 Piece 15.00
Cereal Box, Cheerios, Deputy Kit 45.00
Coupon, Comic Book, 1940 .... 125.00
Dart Board, Tin 95.00

Dart Board, Tin, 1938	50.00
Doll, Linda Toys, 1966, 12 In., Box	100.00
Eggcup, Tonto, Raised Image, Keele Pottery, England, 1961, Pair	60.00
Figurine, Hartland	285.00
Flashlight, Signal Siren, With Silver Bullet Decoder, Box	150.00
Flashlight Gun, Victory Corps, Mailer	225.00
Game, Dart, Tin, 1938	125.00
Game, Parker Brothers, 1956	95.00
Game, Shooting, Lone Ranger & Tonto, Welsotoys, 1959	75.00
Guitar, Black & White Images, Tonto, 1947	115.00
Guitar, Lone Ranger & Tonto, Wooden	24.00
Gun, Click, Metal	45.00
Gun, Western Collection, American Cast Toy, 1940s	80.00
Hairbrush, Box, 1939	145.00
Hairbrush, Decal, 1939	75.00
Horseshoe Set, Ranger & Tonto, Rubber	65.00
Kit, Cheerios, Movie, 1980	35.00
Kit, First Aid, Graphics On Tin Lithographed Box	65.00
Kit, Tonto, Aurora, Box, 1974	70.00
Lunch Box, 1954	375.00
Mask, Wheaties Cutout, 1950s, 7 x 10 In.	65.00
Model Kit, Tonto, 1/10 Scale, Box, Aurora, 1967, 13 x 7 In.	249.00
Pedometer, Box, 1948	55.00
Pedometer, Mailing Box, 1943	95.00
Pedometer, Radio Premium	48.00
Pencil, Bullet	25.00
Pencil Box, Red Cardboard, American Lead Pencil Co.	45.00
Pencil Case, 1930s	65.00
Pencil Sharpener, Bullet Shape, Merita Bread	55.00
Photograph, On Plaque, Clayton Moore, Autographed	75.00
Pin, Celluloid	20.00
Plate, 1938	135.00
Play Set, Legend Of Lone Ranger, 1980	35.00
Postcard, 1939	6.00
Poster, Lone Ranger 6-Shooter Ring, Kix Cereal, c.1950	325.00
Puppet, Push	50.00
Puppet, Tonto, Vinyl, 1966	45.00
Puzzle, Clayton Moore Cover, 1947	75.00
Puzzle, Stagecoach Ambush, Jaymar, 1950, 8 1/2 x 14 In.	45.00
Record Player, Wooden	150.00
Rifle, Carbine, Plastic, Marx, c.1950, 26 In., Box	145.00
Ring, Atomic Bomb	65.00
Ring, Flasher, Caption Action Series, 1960s	20.00
Ring, Flashlight	45.00
Ring, Flashlight, Battery, Instructions	110.00
Ring, Six-Shooter, Gray Pistol, Silver Grips, Premium, 1947	125.00
Sign, Merita Bread, Tin, Embossed, 1950s, 24 x 36 In. .... 500.00 to 1100.00
Silver Bullet	5.00
Sleeping Bag, Lone Ranger & Tonto, 1978	65.00
Squirt Gun, Figural, On Card	45.00
Target Board, Box, 1939	150.00
Tattoo, Lone Ranger Fighting Indian, Philadelphia Gum Corp, 1966, 1 x 3 In.	32.00
Tent, Box, 1958 .... 125.00 to 300.00
Toothbrush Holder, 1938	45.00
Toy, Click Pistol, Decal	45.00
Toy, Figure, Moving Arm, Lasso, Marx	350.00
Toy, Lone Ranger, On Horse, Clockwork, Tin Lithographed, Marx	220.00
Toy, On Silver, Moving Arm, Holding Gun, Rotating Lasso, Windup .... 350.00 to 375.00
Toy, On Silver, Rotating Lasso, Windup, Marx	395.00
Wallet, 1940s	40.00
Watch, 1950	175.00
Watch, Lone Ranger, Pocket, Box	595.00
Watch, New Haven Clock, Pocket, Box, 1940	450.00

Wrapper, Weber's Bread, Red, White & Blue Radio Lone Ranger Ad 30.00

LONGWY Workshop of Longwy, France, first made ceramic wares in 1798. The workshop is still in business. Most of the ceramic pieces found today are glazed with many colors to resemble cloisonne or other enameled metal. The factory used a variety of marks.

Bowl, 12 Sides, Turquoise Crackle, Floral Border, Gilt Trim, c.1925, 13 3/8 In.	1495.00
Bowl, Black On Green, 13 1/2 In.	225.00
Charger, Crested Bird On Flowering Branch, Blue Ground, 14 In.	85.00
Pitcher, Persian Design, 5 In.	265.00
Plaque & Tray, Polychrome Floral, Black Enamel Ground, c.1925	385.00
Plate, Enamel Design, Textured Effect, 8 In.	195.00
Plate, Geometric Vertical Chain Links, Crackle Glaze Ground, 11 In.	695.00
Toothpick, Enamels On Crackle Glaze, 2 In.	95.00
Tray, Nude Black Woman, Signed, 6 1/4 x 4 7/8 In.	75.00
Trivet, Bird, Metal Mount, 6 In.	280.00
Vase, Elephant Head Handles, 10 In.	200.00
Vase, Multicolored Flowers, Chinese Blue Ground, Marked, 6 1/2 In., Pair	225.00

LONHUDA Pottery Company of Steubenville, Ohio, was organized in 1892 by William Long, W. H. Hunter, and Alfred Day. Brown underglaze slip-decorated pottery was made. The firm closed in 1896. The company used many marks; the earliest included the letters *LPCO*.

Pitcher, Fish Handle, Raised Waves, Orange & Yellow Glaze, 11 In.	159.00
Vase, Denver, Yellow & Orange Jonquils, Green Stems, L.F. In Shield, 9 1/2 In.	110.00
Vase, Orange Nasturtiums, Orange, Green & Brown Ground, 5 1/2 In.	550.00

LOTUS WARE was made by the Knowles, Taylor & Knowles Company of East Liverpool, Ohio, from 1890 to 1900. Lotus Ware, a thin porcelain which resembles Belleek, was sometimes decorated outside the factory. Other types of ceramics that were made by the Knowles, Taylor & Knowles Company are listed under KTK.

Creamer, Fish Net Around Body, 3 In.	625.00
Vase, Network Of Porcelain, Forming Cage Work, c.1890, 4 1/2 In.	1275.00

LOW art tiles were made by the J. and J. G. Low Art Tile Works of Chelsea, Massachusetts, from 1877 to 1902. A variety of art and other tiles were made. Some of the tiles were made by a process called *natural*, some were hand modeled, and some were made mechanically.

Tile, Blue & Buff Zigzag Design, Square, 4 1/2 In.	85.00
Tile, Franklin, Brown, 12 In.	250.00

LOY-NEL-ART, see McCoy category

LUNCH BOXES and lunch pails have been used to carry lunches to school or work since the nineteenth century. Today, most collectors want either early tobacco advertising boxes or children's lunch boxes made since the 1930s. Boxes listed here include the original Thermos bottle inside the box unless otherwise indicated. Movie, television, and cartoon characters may be found in their own categories.

LUNCH BOX, 3 Little Pigs, 1982	85.00
A-Team, Papers, Unused, 1983	25.00
Adam-12, 1972	65.00
Alice In Wonderland, Vinyl... 300.00 to 350.00
Alvin & The Chipmunks, Vinyl, King Seeley, 1963 .... 275.00 to 415.00
America On Parade	35.00
American Girl Barbie & Francie, Square Shape, 1965	55.00
Archie, 1969	75.00
Astronaut, Dome Top, 1960	80.00
Astronauts, 1969	80.00
Atom Ant, 1966	135.00
Barbie, Black Vinyl, 1962	45.00
Barbie, Vinyl, Pink	45.00

Barbie & Midge, Brunch Bag, Black Patent, 1963 .... 200.00
Barbie & Midge, Vinyl Dome, 1964 .... 400.00
Beany & Cecil, Vinyl, White, 1962 .... 250.00
Bednobs & Broomsticks, 1972 .... 35.00
Bee Gees, Maurice On Back, Metal, 1978 .... 48.00 to 50.00
Bee Gees, Robin On Back, Metal, 1978 .... 35.00
Beverly Hillbillies, 1967 .... 38.00
Beverly Hillbillies, Metal, Aladdin, 1963 .... 120.00 to 165.00
Bionic Woman, Metal, 1977-1978 .... 20.00 to 50.00
Black Hole, 1979 .... 150.00
Blondie, 1968 .... 65.00
Bonanza, Brown Rim, 1965 .... 75.00
Boston Red Sox, Vinyl, 1960s 75.00
Boston Red Sox, Vinyl, 1970s 95.00
Brave Eagle, 1957 .... 120.00
Brotherhood Tobacco .... 325.00 to 395.00
Bugaloos, 1971 .... 207.00
Burley Boy, Child Boxing, The White Man's Hope, Metal, 6 1/2 x 4 x 5 In. 2420.00
C.H.I.P.S., 1977 .... 50.00
Cable Car, Aladdin 195.00
Campbell Kids, Ohio Art, 1975 .... 230.00
Campus Queen, 1967 .... 35.00
Captain Power, Canada, 1987 .... 60.00
Casper The Friendly Ghost, Vinyl, King Seeley, 1966 .... 400.00
Central Union Cut Plug, Tin, Painted 45.00
Chuck Wagon, Domed Top, Aladdin .... 150.00 to 165.00
Circus Wagon, Domed Top, 1958 .... 275.00
Clash Of Titans 18.50
Close Encounters, 1977 .... 40.00 to 80.00
Daffy Diner, Vinyl Dome 600.00
Dallas Cowboys, Plastic, 1985 .... 15.00
Daniel Boone, Fess Parker, 1965 .... 70.00
Deputy Dawg, Vinyl, Beige 450.00
Dick Tracy, Aladdin, 1967 .... 90.00
Dixie Kid, White 195.00
Donny & Marie, Vinyl, Aladdin, 1978 .... 115.00
Dr. Doolittle, 1969 .... 80.00
Dr. Doolittle, Aladdin, 1967 .... 85.00
Dudley Do-Right, Metal, Universal, 1962 .... 775.00
Dudley Do-Right, Nell, Horse, Tin Lithographed, Ohio Art, 1962 .... 2200.00
Dukes Of Hazzard, Aladdin, 1980 .... 22.00 to 30.00
E.T., The Extra Terrestrial, Metal, Aladdin, 1982 .... 19.00 to 40.00
Emergency, Aladdin, 1973 .... 15.00
Emergency, Domed, 1973 .... 40.00 to 65.00
Empire Strikes Back, Spaceship Pictured, 1983 .... 20.00 to 25.00
Evil Knievel, Metal, Aladdin, 1974 .... 50.00
Family Affair, 1969-1970 .... 75.00
Fashion Tobacco 200.00
Fat Albert & The Cosby Kids, 1973 .... 20.00 to 60.00
Flintstones & Dino, Aladdin, 1962 .... 85.00
Flipper, 1967 .... 68.00 to 75.00
Flying Nun, 1968 .... 25.00 to 135.00
Flying Nun, Brunch Bag, Vinyl, 1960s 425.00
G.I. Joe, 1967 .... 70.00
G.I. Joe, 1982 .... 15.00
Gene Autry, 1954 .... 150.00
Gentle Ben, Aladdin, 1968 .... 29.00 to 65.00
Get Smart, King-Seeley, 1966 .... 95.00
Ginger Bread House, England, 1985 .... 207.00
Gomer Pyle, U.S.M.C., 1966 .... 50.00 to 95.00
Great Wild West, Universal, 1959 .... 75.00
Green Hornet, 1967 .... 200.00
Green Turtle 95.00

Grizzly Adams, Dome Top, 1977 .... 75.00 to 110.00
Gunsmoke, 1959 .... 45.00 to 690.00
Gunsmoke, Stagecoach On Back, 1973 .... 95.00
Hanna-Barbera, 1978 .... 55.00
Happy Days, Metal, 1977 .... 48.00
Hardy Boys, Mysteries, 1977 .... 75.00
Harlem Globetrotters, 1971 .... 75.00
Heathcliff, 1982 .... 22.00
Holly Hobbie, Metal, 1973-1981 .... 75.00
Holly Hobbie, Vinyl, 1972 .... 70.00
Hopalong Cassidy, 1950s 100.00
Horse Trailer Truck, Roy Rogers, Vinyl & Tin 275.00
Hot Wheels, 1969 .... 35.00
Huckleberry Hound & His Friends, 1963 .... 115.00
Incredible Hulk, 1978 .... 25.00 to 60.00
Indiana Jones, 1984 .... 42.00
James Bond 007, 1966 .... 150.00 to 690.00
Jetsons, 1962 .... 200.00
Joe Palooka, 1948 .... 95.00
Jonathan Livingston Seagull, Vinyl, Aladdin, 1974 .... 145.00
Julia, Diahann Carroll TV Show, 1969 .... 65.00
Jungle Book, 1960 .... 75.00
Jungle Book, 1966 .... 150.00
King Kong, 1977 .... 100.00
Kiss, 1977 .... 88.00
Knight Rider, 1981 .... 5.00
Knight Rider, Paper, Unused, 1983 .... 25.00
La Petite Cafe De Paris, Vinyl Dome 500.00
Land Of The Giants, 1968 .... 75.00 to 90.00
Land Of The Lost, 1975 .... 25.00 to 125.00
Laugh-In, Tricycle, 1970 .... 39.00
Lidsville, 1971 .... 207.00
Little Friends, Ohio Art, 1982 .... 1035.00
Little Red Riding Hood, Ohio Art, 1982 .... 35.00 to 45.00
Lolly's New Look, Merle Norman, Pink Plastic Box, 1980s 25.00
Lone Ranger, ADCO Liberty, 1954 .... 300.00
Lost In Space, Dome, 1967 .... 275.00
Lucky Curve Cut Plug, Baseball Player 395.00
Man From U.N.C.L.E., 1966 .... 95.00 to 110.00
Man On Moon 65.00
Mary Poppins, Aladdin, Vinyl, 1973 .... 22.00
Mary Poppins, Metal, 1965 .... 105.00
Mary Poppins, Vinyl, Brunch Bag, Blue, 1967 .... 135.00
Miner's, Lisk Sales, Nickel Over Brass, Sample 390.00
Miss America, 1972 .... 161.00
Monkees, Metal, King Seeley, 1967 .... 140.00
Monkees, Plastic, 1967 .... 107.00
Munsters, 1965 .... 175.00 to 225.00
Muppets, Metal, 1978-1979 .... 20.00
NFL, Stripes On Band, 1975 .... 22.00
NFL Quarterbacks, Bears, Packers, Browns, Giants, 1964 .... 253.00
Old Southern Coffee 85.00
Orbit, John Glenn 22.00
Osmonds, 1973 .... 18.00
Padlock Style, Yellow Brass, Bird Design, Original Folding Key, Large 20.00
Partridge Family, 1978 .... 50.00
Partridge Family, King Seeley, 1971 .... 45.00
Peanuts, Charlie Against Tree, 1973 .... 35.00
Peanuts, Charlie Pitching, Red Rim, 1976 .... 25.00
Peter Pan, 1969 .... 135.00
Peter Pan Peanut Butter, Sandwich Form 275.00
Pickle, Green, Pickle Shape, Plastic, 1972 .... 161.00
Pink Panther, Vinyl, Aladdin, 1980 .... 75.00

Planet Of The Apes, Aladdin, 1974 .... 85.00
Play Ball, 1969 .... 230.00
Pony Tail, Vinyl, 1960 .... 45.00
Ponytailed Girl, Walking 2 Poodles, Vinyl, American Thermos, 1960 .... 195.00
Popeye, S.S. Popeye, 1964 .... 60.00
Popeye, She's Mine, 1980 .... 55.00
Porky's Lunch Wagon, Dome, 1959 .... 190.00 to 552.00
Pro Sports, Variety Of Sports Represented, 1980 .... 104.00
Psychedelic, Dome, 1969 .... 275.00
Pussycats, Josie & Me, Vinyl, 1960s 85.00
Raggedy Ann & Andy, Brunch Bag, Vinyl, 1973 .... 60.00
Raggedy Ann & Andy, Metal, 1973 .... 30.00 to 35.00
Rat Patrol, 1967 .... 89.00
Red Barn, Dome, Closed Doors, 1957 .... 35.00
Redicut Tobacco 85.00
Rifleman, Metal, Aladdin, 1961 .... 150.00 to 250.00
Robin Hood, 1956 .... 90.00
Ronald McDonald, Red Plastic 18.00
S.W.A.T., 1975 .... 75.00
Saddle Bag, Roy Rogers, Vinyl 195.00
Scooby Doo, Plastic, Aladdin, 1984 .... 33.00
Secret Agent, 1968 .... 80.00
See America, Ohio Art, 1972 .... 138.00
Six Million Dollar Man, 1974 .... 25.00
Six Million Dollar Man, 1978 .... 20.00
Smoky The Bear, 1975 .... 175.00
Smurf, 1983 .... 175.00 to 184.00
Smurf, England, 1973 .... 50.00
Snow White & 7 Dwarfs, Aladdin, Plastic, 1974 .... 50.00
Snow White & 7 Dwarfs, Tin Lithograph, Double Handles, Belgium 395.00
Space 1999, 1974 .... 28.00 to 39.00
Sport Skwirts, Basketball, Ohio Art, 1972 .... 30.00
Star Wars, Canada, 1977 .... 125.00
Star Wars, Metal, 1977-1978 .... 30.00 to 52.00
Strawberry Shortcake, Vinyl, Unused, 1980 .... 35.00 to 40.00
Strawberry Shortcake, With Rainbow, Hang Tag, Unused, 1980 .... 15.00
Street Hawk, 1984 .... 288.00
Submarine, 1960 .... 80.00 to 110.00
Super Friends, 1976 .... 15.00
Tammy & Pepper, Vinyl, 1962 .... 110.00
Tarzan, 1966 .... 68.00
Thermos Only, Barbie, 1962 .... 40.00
Thermos Only, G.I. Joe, 1967 .... 30.00
Thermos Only, Get Smart, 1966 .... 35.00
Thermos Only, Gigi 18.00
Thermos Only, Guns Of Will Sonnett, 1968 .... 45.00
Thermos Only, James Bond 007, 1966 .... 65.00
Thermos Only, Junior Miss, Yellow, Steel, Glass, 1966 .... 20.00
Thermos Only, Partridge Family, Plastic, 1971 .... 20.00
Thermos Only, Peanuts, Steel, Glass, 1966 .... 16.00
Thermos Only, Shari Lewis & Her Friends, 1963 .... 60.00
Thermos Only, Smoky The Bear, 1965 .... 39.00
Thermos Only, Stars & Stripes 50.00
Thermos Only, Wild Bill Hickok, 1955 .... 35.00
Tiger Tobacco 32.50
Tom Corbett, Space Cadet, Red, 1952 .... 135.00 to 400.00
Transportation Images, Planes, Trains, Oval, Red & Blue, 1930s 85.00
UFO, 1973 .... 150.00
Union Leader, Tin, 7 x 4 x 4 In. 75.00
US Mail, Vinyl Dome 400.00
Virginia Dare Chewing Tobacco 120.00
Wagon Train, 1964 .... 60.00 to 120.00

Waltons, 1973 .... 75.00
Wayne Gretzky, Action Scene, Blue & Orange, Plastic 160.00
Wayne Gretzky, Plastic, Aladdin, 1980 .... 50.00
Weave Pattern, Ohio Art, 1971 .... 15.00
Welcome Back Kotter, 1977 .... 20.00 to 25.00
Western, Stagecoach Front, Cowboy Back, Red Rim, 1963 .... 40.00
Wild Bill Hickok & Jingles, 1955 .... 65.00 to 150.00
Wild Fruit Tobacco 200.00
Wonder Woman, Psychedelic, Blue Vinyl 65.00
Woody Woodpecker, Plastic, Aladdin, 1972 .... 90.00
World Of Barbie, Pink, Vinyl, 1973 .... 20.00 to 45.00
Yogi Bear And Friends, 1963 .... 60.00 to 165.00
Yogi's Treasure Hunt, 3-D 40.00
Zorro, Red Rim, Embossed, 1966 .... 322.00
LUNCH PAIL, Armour Star Lard, Lid, Tin, 4 Lb. 5.00
Armour's Peanut Butter, Nursery Rhyme Figures, Bail Handle, 4 In. 72.00
Capital Peanut Butter, Children Play, 14 Oz. 1200.00
Clark's Peanut Butter, Outdoor Scenes, Canada, 3 3/4 x 3 1/2 In. 605.00
Family Lard, Pigs 95.00
George Washington Tobacco 25.00
Hoody's Peanut Butter, 2 Girls On Teeter-Totter, 3 1/2 x 4 In. 137.00
Jackie Coogan Peanut Butter, Children In Classroom, 3 1/2 In. 125.00
Jackie Coogan Peanut Butter, Tin, 3 x 3 In. .... 250.00 to 350.00
Little Red Riding Hood, Candy, Lovell & Covel, Boston, 3 In. 255.00
Mayo's Tobacco 275.00
Miner's, Graniteware, No Cup 200.00
Monarch Teenie Weenie Popcorn, Elves Dodging Flying Popcorn 275.00
Montgomery Ward Peanut Butter, 5 Lb. 60.00
Mosemann's Peanut Butter 150.00
Old Partner 150.00
Ox-Heart Peanut Butter 100.00
Pedigree Peanut Butter, 3 x 3 1/2 In. 300.00
Peter Cottontail Scene, Lovell & Covel Candies, Tin, 3 x 3 In. 203.50
Peter Rabbit On Parade, Oval 1750.00
Rath's Pork Cutlets 15.00
Red Indian Tobacco, Black & Red, Feathered Indian Logo, 8 x 4 x 5 In. ... 715.00
Scudder's Brownie Brand Maple Spread 500.00
Squirrel Peanut Butter, Canada .... 175.00 to 200.00
Sultana Peanut Butter, Bail Handle, 4 In. 38.00
Sunny Boy Peanut Butter, Boy Eating Sandwich, 16 Oz. 100.00
Sweet Cuba Tobacco 25.00
Toyland Peanut Butter 200.00
Uncle Wiggly At The Seashore, Peanut Butter, 1 Lb. 715.00
Yankee Peanut Butter 220.00

LUNEVILLE, a French faience factory, was established about 1730 by Jacques
Chambrette. It is best known for its fine biscuit figures and groups and for
large faience dogs and lions. The early pieces were unmarked. The firm was
acquired by Keller and Guerin and is still working.

Plate, Man In Cape & Clogs, Keller & Guerin, 10 In. 75.00
Server, Asparagus, White & Green, Majolica 560.00
Vase, Art Nouveau, 14 1/4 In. 175.00
Vase, Lavender & Green, 13 In. 315.00

LUSTER glaze was meant to resemble copper, silver, or gold. It has been used
since the sixteenth century. Most of the luster found today was made during
the nineteenth century. The metallic glazes are applied on pottery. The
finished color depends on the combination of the clay color and the glaze. Tea
Leaf pieces have their own category.

Copper, Creamer, Albert & Victoria Portraits, Blue Band, 5 1/4 In. 33.00
Copper, Creamer, Canary Band, Brown Transfer, Woman & Children Scene, 4 3/4 In. 165.00
Copper, Creamer, Serpent Handle, Mask Spout, Basket Of Flowers, 4 3/4 In. 50.00

Copper, Creamer, Wide Yellow Band, Colored Adam Buck Transfer	150.00
Copper, Goblet, Black Transfer Oriental Band, 4 1/2 In.	38.50
Copper, Goblet, Blue & Green Band, Floral Design, 4 In., Pair	143.00
Copper, Jug, Magenta Transfer Clock Face, Charity, 6 3/4 In.	60.50
Copper, Pitcher, Applied Cherubs, Blue Band, 8 7/8 In.	220.00
Copper, Pitcher, Black Transfer On White, Lip Outlined In Copper, 7 In.	3465.00
Copper, Pitcher, Blue Floral Bands, 7 In.	150.00
Copper, Pitcher, Floral Design, Polychrome, 5 3/4 In.	72.00
Copper, Pitcher, Gaudy Floral, 6 7/8 In.	104.00
Copper, Pitcher, Leaf & Berry, England, 2 3/4 In.	22.00
Copper, Pitcher, Leaf & Berry, Harvest Ware, Wade, 4 1/4 In.	36.00
Copper, Pitcher, Pink Floral Designs, Painted, 19th Century, 5 1/2 In.	49.50
Copper, Pitcher, Polychrome Design, Blue Band, Mask Spout, 6 3/4 In.	33.00
Copper, Pot, Lid, Blue Bands, Pink Luster Floral, 6 1/2 In.	71.00
Copper, Sugar, Urn Shape, Ram's Head Handles, 5 1/4 In.	104.00
Copper, Tea Set, England, c.1820, 31 Piece	374.00
Copper, Teapot, Blue & Gold Medallion Trim, Rectangular, 6 Cup	225.00
Copper, Vase, Bud, Scalloped Rim, Pink Flowers, Blue Border, 6 1/2 In., Pair.	165.00
Copper, Wine, White Band, Purple Transfer, Faith & Hope	125.00
Fairyland luster is included in the Wedgwood category	
Gold, Pitcher, Ballerinas, Fancy Handle, England, 6 5/8 In.	40.00
Gold, Tea Set, Bavaria, 19 Piece	375.00
Green, Plate, Red Rose & Lily-Of-The-Valley, 6 1/4 In.	8.50
Jug, Hunt, Pink, Green, & Brown	200.00
Pink, Creamer, Black Transfer, Snipe Shooting, 6 In.	88.00
Pink, Pitcher, Floral Bird, 4 3/4 In.	165.00
Pink, Pitcher, Hunting Dogs Scenes, Raised, Green Enameled, 4 3/4 In.	105.00
Pink, Pitcher, Stylized Floral Band, Enameled, 6 5/8 In.	115.00
Pink, Plate, Fallow Deer, Wedgwood, Etruria, 10 In.	75.00
Pink, Plate, Green Enameled Dots, Scrolled, Scalloped, Square, 9 1/2 In.	17.00
Pink, Pot, Enameled Strawberries, Repaired, 11 In.	181.00
Pink, Sugar & Creamer, Roses, Spiral Ribs, Rope Handle, 4 x 3 In.	40.00
Pink, Sugar & Creamer, Tray	50.00
Pink, Tea Bowl, Luster Leaves & Rim	25.00
Pink, Tea Set, 25 Piece	900.00
Silver, Jug, Black Transfer, Marquis Wellington, Flower Under Spout, 6 5/8 In.	27.50
Silver, Jug, Cream, 1820s, 3 In.	95.00
Silver, Mug, Child's, Canary, Yellow Glazed	175.00
Silver, Mug, Floral	11.00
Silver, Mug, Yellow, Child's	60.50
Silver, Pitcher, English Country Scenes	104.50
Silver, Pitcher, Floral Design, Dalmatian & Bird, 5 5/8 In.	105.00
Silver, Pitcher, Molded Design, Red Enameled, 5 1/4 In.	60.00
Silver, Teapot, Queen Anne Pattern, 6 In.	195.00
Silver, Teapot, Rococo Revival, Staffordshire, 1850s	95.00
Silver, Teapot, Swan Finial, Oriental Scenes, Silver Luster Trim, 6 3/4 In.	155.00
Sunderland, luster pieces are in the Sunderland category	
Tea Leaf, luster pieces are listed in the Tea Leaf Ironstone category	

LUSTRES are mantel decorations or pedestal vases with many hanging glass prisms. The name really refers to the prisms, and it is proper to refer to a single glass prism as a lustre. Either spelling, luster or lustre, is correct.

Allover Enamel, Tulip Tops, 16 Cut Prisms, 14 In.	495.00
Blue Ground, White & Floral Painted Design, Bohemian, 9 In., Pair	165.00
Bristol, Hanging Crystal Prisms, Scalloped Tops, 12 1/4 In., Pair	595.00
Cobalt Blue Cut To Clear, Gilded & Cut Clear Prisms, 14 3/4 In., Pair	1100.00
Cranberry, Girls Facing, Floral Around, Prisms, Mary Gregory, 10 1/4 In.	2075.00
Cranberry Cut To Cream, 11 1/2 In.	750.00
Girandole Set, Jacob Bigelow Chapel, Prisms, W.F. Shaw, 3 Piece	550.00
Girandole Set, Marble Base, Gilded Brass, Prisms, 17 In., 3 Piece	275.00
Girandole Set, Paul & Virginia, 5-Light Center, Star, Snowflake Prisms, 3 Piece	1045.00
Mantle, Cut Prisms, Enameled Gold Bands, Florals, 12 In., Pair	450.00

Portrait & Floral Medallions, Spear Shape, Allover Gold Designs, 13 In., Pair 950.00
Ruby Glass, Gilt Decorated, Flowers, Spear Prisms, Domed Base, 13 1/4 In, Pr. 440.00

LUTZ glass was made by Nicolas Lutz working at the Boston and Sandwich
Glass Company from 1870 to 1888. He made delicate and intricate threaded
glass of several colors. Other similar wares made by other makers are now
known by the generic name *Lutz*.

Toothpick 210.00

MAASTRICHT, Holland, was the city where Petrus Regout established the
De Sphinx pottery in 1836. The firm was noted for its transfer-printed
earthenware. Many factories in Maastricht are still making ceramics.

Charger, Royal Sphinx, Blue, 16 In. 75.00
Plate, Castle, Floral Border, Blue & White, 8 3/8 In. 8.00
Plate, Gaudy Stick Spatter Blue, Green & Yellow, 9 In., Pair 120.00

MAIZE glass was made by W. L. Libbey & Son Company of Toledo, Ohio,
after 1889. The glass resembled an ear of corn. The leaves were usually
green, but some pieces were made with blue or red leaves. The kernels of
corn were light yellow, white, or light green.

Tumbler, Blue Leaves 195.00

MAJOLICA is a general term for any pottery glazed with an opaque tin
enamel that conceals the color of the clay body. It has been made since the
fourteenth century. Today's collector is most likely to find Victorian majolica.
The heavy, colorful ware is rarely marked. Some famous makers include
Wedgwood; Minton; Griffen, Smith and Hill (marked *Etruscan*); and
Chesapeake Pottery (marked *Avalon* or *Clifton*).

Basket, Duck, Ribbon & Wing Handle, Mottled, 6 1/2 x 9 1/2 In. 137.50
Basket, Handle, White Flowers, Green Leaves & Pink Bows, 8 x 8 1/2 In. 425.00
Basket, Server, Strawberry, 2 Spoons 1980.00
Basket, Yellow Basket Weave, Leaves, Pink Interior, 9 1/2 In. 325.00
Basket Server, Strawberry Center Handle, 2 Spoons 1980.00
Bowl, Dog & Deer, 8 In. 110.00
Bowl, Grape Leaf, Red Border, 10 In. 195.00
Bowl, Jester, Yellow & Green Leaves, Minton 8500.00
Bowl, Pond Lily, Footed, 10 1/4 In. 100.00
Bowl, Shell & Seaweed, 8 1/2 In. ....   275.00 to 990.00
Box, Flower Finial Handle, Mottled, 6 x 4 1/2 x 7 1/2 In. 65.00
Box, Sardine, Cobalt Blue, Etruscan 1100.00
Box, Sardine, Oriental, Wedgwood 415.00
Box, Sardine, Underplate, Etruscan 1100.00
Bread Tray, Classical Center Scene, Wheat Rim, 12 1/2 In. 330.00
Bread Tray, Eat Thy Bread, 13 In. 150.00
Bread Tray, Pineapple 155.00
Butter, Cover, Bamboo, Etruscan 495.00
Butter, Cover, Grid & Fan 165.00
Butter, Cover, Shell & Seaweed, Etruscan 1320.00
Butter, Cover, Stanley Pattern, Multicolored, Wedgwood, 3 1/4 x 6 1/4 In. 330.00
Butter, Cover, Swan & Water Lily, Pink Interior 415.00
Butter Chip, Cobalt & Yellow Pansy 60.00
Butter Chip, Green Leaf 15.00
Butter Chip, Leaf ....   20.00 to 44.00
Cachepot, Calla Lily 1045.00
Cachepot, Cobalt Blue, 1865, Pair 6900.00
Cake Plate, Green Grape Leaf On Cobalt, Footed, 2 1/4 x 9 1/4 In. 450.00
Cake Plate, Pedestal, Sepia, Etruscan 145.00
Cake Stand, Bird On Branch 195.00
Cake Stand, Floral, 9 In. 100.00
Cake Stand, Lavender Blossoms, Blue, Holdcraft 225.00
Candlestick, Gloomy Gus 85.00
Candlestick, Green, Brown, George Skey, Pair 480.00

Candlestick, Happy Hooligan 85.00
Celery Vase, Shell & Seaweed, Etruscan 880.00
Centerpiece, 2 Women Holding Basket 1760.00
Centerpiece, Bowl, Decorated Masks, Scrollwork, Oval Base, 12 1/2 x 16 In. 440.00
Charger, Rembrandt Portrait, Peacock Feather Design, 15 1/2 In. 176.00
Cheese Keeper, Apple Blossom, George Jones 1000.00
Cheese Keeper, Cobalt Lily, Etruscan 3300.00
Cheese Keeper, Cows & Trees, Cow-Form Finial, 8 x 10 1/2 In. 605.00
Cheese Keeper, Heron 3190.00
Cheese Keeper, Picket Fence, George Jones 1430.00
Cheese Keeper, Pink Swan, Etruscan 1980.00
Cheese Keeper, Stilton, Skep Shape 395.00
Cigar Caddy, Black Man Smoking Pipe, Wearing Crown, Striker Back, 6 In. 330.00
Coffeepot, Figural, Hound, 8 1/2 In. 175.00
Compote, Cauliflower & Leaf, Cobalt Center, Wedgwood, 11 In. .... 330.00 to 495.00
Compote, Fan & Floral, 9 In. 77.00
Compote, Sunflower, Etruscan 300.00
Creamer, Shell & Seaweed, Albino, Blue Seaweed, Gold Trim, Etruscan 165.00
Creamer, Shell & Seaweed, Albino, Blue Trim, Etruscan 55.00
Creamer, Shell & Seaweed, Etruscan, 4 In. 375.50
Creamer, Shell Molded, 3 1/2 x 4 1/2 In. 120.00
Creamer, Stork In Fan, 3 1/2 In. 185.00
Cup, Shell & Seaweed 150.00
Cup & Saucer, Bark & Blackberry, Brown Ground 140.00
Cup & Saucer, Shell & Seaweed 418.00
Cuspidor, Bird On Branch 385.00
Cuspidor, Fern & Basket Weave 165.00
Cuspidor, Floral 165.00
Cuspidor, Shell & Seaweed 220.00
Cuspidor, Sunflower, Cobalt Blue, Etruscan 2200.00
Decanter, Allover Floral, Rose Bud Stopper, Pair 285.00
Dish, Game, Hare & Duck, Minton 2310.00
Dish, Game, Pheasant, George Jones 2000.00
Dish, Grape Leaves, Pedestal, 5 1/2 In. 200.00
Dish, Green, White Flower, Layers Of Leaves, 8 In. 200.00
Dish, Leaf Shaped, Green Center, Pink Border, 9 In. 100.00
Dish, Nut, Brown, Minton 395.00
Dish, Pickle, Begonia, 8 1/4 x 6 In. 55.00
Dish, Sandwich, Cover, England, 1870 .... 450.00
Dish, Squirrel With Nut, Leaf Form, George Jones 1800.00
Ewer, Multicolored, Dark Green Ground, 13 In. 77.00
Figurine, Black Woman Holding Basket, 3 1/2 In. 88.00
Figurine, Cockatoo On Stump, 14 1/2 In. 275.00
Figurine, Dog, Googly-Eye, Blue Hat, Green Collar, 6 In. 135.00
Figurine, Man & Woman, Italy, 30 1/2 In., Pair 1100.00
Figurine, Man On Tree Stump, 9 1/2 In. 65.00
Figurine, Parrot, Blue, 10 In. 475.00

Majolica, Game Dish, Bird Finial Lid,
Rabbits & Ferns, 7 x 13 In.

◆◆◆◆◆◆◆◆◆◆◆◆◆◆◆◆◆◆◆◆◆◆

Most old majolica pieces have
a colored bottom. The newer
pieces have white bottoms.

◆◆◆◆◆◆◆◆◆◆◆◆◆◆◆◆◆◆◆◆◆◆

Figurine, Pheasant, 12 In. 45.00
Figurine, Rabbit, Pink Ears & Green Cabbage, 10 In. 325.00
Figurine, Young Black Girl, Lying On Stomach, Blue Bonnet, 3 1/4 x 5 1/4 In. 100.00
Game Dish, Bird Finial Lid, Rabbits & Ferns, 7 x 13 In. .... *Illus* 4000.00
Garden Seat, Cobalt Blue 1925.00
Garden Seat, Hexagonal, Pierced Floral, Minton, 1871, 19 In., Pair 3300.00
Goblet, Basket Weave, Green Glaze, 3 1/2 In., 6 Piece 110.00
Humidor, Black Boy On Melon 577.00
Humidor, Black Man With Pipe Handle, 10 1/2 In. 550.00
Humidor, Dog On Pillow 660.00
Humidor, Frog With Pipe Handle, 7 In. 305.00
Humidor, Hunting Scene, Dog On Pile Of Logs 175.00
Humidor, Man With Beanie Hat & Goggles 522.50
Humidor, Monkey 440.00
Humidor, Monkey With Pipe Handle, 8 1/2 In. 475.00
Humidor, Potbellied Man 495.00
Humidor, Pug Dog, Brown Glaze, 9 In. 895.00
Jam Jar, White Apple Blossom 305.00
Jardiniere, Bird On Branch, Turquoise Interior, 10 x 10 In. 275.00
Jardiniere, Foxglove, Minton 37040.00
Jardiniere, Pedestal, Reserved Of Putti & Griffins, Green Ground, 1880s, 48 In. 165.00
Jug, Baseball Player, Etruscan Monotone, Cobalt 295.00
Jug, Face, Sarreguemines 305.00
Jug, Gurgling Fish, 10 In. 295.00
Jug, Gurgling, Royal Winton 120.00
Jug, Tower, Minton 995.00
Lamp, Beaux Arts, Nacrous Glaze, Spider Cased Green Shade, 28 In. 795.00
Match Holder, Black Boy On Shell 550.00
Match Holder, Black Boy With Baskets 495.00
Match Holder, Black Man 305.00
Match Holder, Cat, 6 In. 60.00
Match Holder, Chicken 250.00
Match Holder, Monkey 467.00
Match Holder, On Leaf, Austria 78.00
Match Holder, Pug Dog 267.00
Match Holder, Town Crier 95.00
Mug, Leisey Brewing Co., Haynes 155.00
Oyster Plate, Pale Green & Gray, 1880, 9 1/2 In., 6 Piece 330.00
Pedestal, Dolphin, Cobalt Blue Ground, 38 x 15 1/4 In. 990.00
Pitcher, Allover Flowers, Pink Interior, Etruscan, 7 1/4 In. 245.00
Pitcher, Bird In Hand, 8 In. 325.00
Pitcher, Bird On Flowering Branch, Bark Handle, Lavender Interior, 8 In. 165.00
Pitcher, Blackberry, Red Interior, 8 In. 100.00
Pitcher, Corn, Cobalt Blue 155.00
Pitcher, Dogwood, 4 1/2 In. 70.00
Pitcher, Double Fish, Brownfield & Son, 1879, 11 In. 1100.00
Pitcher, Duck, Red Interior, Signed, 9 1/4 In. 195.00
Pitcher, Face, Sarreguemines, 8 1/2 In. 175.00
Pitcher, Fern & Floral, 6 Sides, 7 1/2 In. 110.00
Pitcher, Figural, Fish, Pink Interior, 10 In. 225.00
Pitcher, Figural, Fish, Pink Interior, 11 In. 265.00
Pitcher, Figural, Monkey In Brown, Black & Red, 9 3/4 In. 605.00
Pitcher, Figural, Owl, 8 1/2 In. 165.00
Pitcher, Figural, Parrot, 8 In. 220.00
Pitcher, Figural, Pig, Cream With Red, 8 1/4 In. 220.00
Pitcher, Figural, Ugly Woman, Pig Under Arm, Umbrella & Bag In Hand 290.00
Pitcher, Fish, Lavender Interior, 11 In. 175.00
Pitcher, Fish, Mottled Green & Brown 320.00
Pitcher, Floral & Drapery, 5 In. .... 60.00 To 195.00
Pitcher, Floral, 7 1/4 In. 135.00
Pitcher, Floral, Greenery, Twig Handle, Bamboo Ground, 4 1/4 In. 75.00
Pitcher, Flying Crane, Lavender Interior, 7 1/4 In. 77.00
Pitcher, Frog On Melon, 8 In. 525.00

Pitcher, Grape & Leaf On Bark, Pewter Lid 155.00
Pitcher, Green Leaves, Tan Faces & Interior, Griffin Spout, 11 1/2 In. 165.00
Pitcher, Gurgling Fish, 1880s, 13 In. 450.00
Pitcher, Hawthorne 250.00
Pitcher, Jack & Beanstalk 100.00
Pitcher, Knights, Spears, Cherubs, Shields, 9 1/2 In. 275.00
Pitcher, Leaf & Acorn Lid, Oak Leaves, Acorns, Twig Handle 165.00
Pitcher, Lily Pattern, Gold Ground, Orchid Interior, France 225.00
Pitcher, Lion, Red Interior, 4 1/4 In. 165.00
Pitcher, Maple Leaf & Basket Weave, 4 5/8 In. 195.00
Pitcher, Multicolor Leaves & Flowers, Basket Weave Ground, 4 3/4 In. 55.00
Pitcher, Owl & Fan, Triangular, 6 In. 88.00
Pitcher, Owl, Triangular 250.00
Pitcher, Pewter Hinged Top, Raised Circles, 12 1/2 In. 245.00
Pitcher, Pig Waiter 440.00
Pitcher, Pineapple, 6 In. 160.00
Pitcher, Pineapple, 8 1/2 In. 88.00
Pitcher, Ram, 8 In. 300.00
Pitcher, Red Lily, Cream Ground, Rope Medallion, Rope Braid Top, 5 In. 45.00
Pitcher, Rooster 385.00
Pitcher, Rose & Bud, Yellow Basket Weave Base, Greek Key Top, 7 In. 225.00
Pitcher, Running Elephant, 10 In. 550.00
Pitcher, Rustic, 8 1/2 In. 330.00
Pitcher, Sheaf Of Wheat, Cobalt Blue 355.00
Pitcher, Shell & Seaweed, Etruscan, 5 1/2 In. 825.00
Pitcher, Shell, Fielding 330.00
Pitcher, Stork In Rushes, Lavender Interior, 7 In. 120.00
Pitcher, Sunflower 250.00
Pitcher, Tree Trunk Base, Bird & Nest Of Eggs, 9 1/2 In. 155.00
Pitcher, U.S. Grant 550.00
Pitcher, Water Lily, 1890s, 9 In. 395.00
Planter, Gnome With Trojan Helmet, 13 In. 280.00
Plaque, Woman, Head To Side, Water Lilies, Setting Sun, 12 x 19 1/2 In. 475.00
Plate, Asparagus, Blue & Green, Luneville 225.00
Plate, Blackberry, 10 In. 115.00
Plate, Fan & Prunus, Green On White, c.1878, 6 1/2 In. 185.00
Plate, Fern & Picket, 6 In. 135.00
Plate, Floral, Basket Weave, 8 1/4 In. 50.00
Plate, Fruit, Turquoise, Wedgwood, 9 In. 95.00
Plate, Grape Leaf, Wedgwood 247.00
Plate, Green Leaf 125.00
Plate, Joan Of Arc, 8 1/2 In. 40.00
Plate, Leaf, Brown & Green, 9 1/2 x 2 In. 45.00
Plate, Leaf, Multicolored, 8 1/2 In., Pair 110.00
Plate, Maple Leaf, Etruscan, 9 In. 100.00
Plate, Mockingbird 45.00
Plate, Morning Glory, Red Ground 355.00
Plate, Palissy, Jose A. Cunha, 1880, 5 In. 275.00
Plate, Palissy, Jose A. Cunha, 1880, 6 In. .... 165.00 to 407.00
Plate, Pineapple, 8 Piece 2650.00
Plate, Rabbits, 9 In. 175.00
Plate, Shell & Seaweed, 7 In. 137.00
Plate, Shell & Seaweed, 8 In. 275.00
Plate, Shell & Seaweed, 9 1/4 In. 495.00
Plate, Shell, Carr, 7 1/2 In. 130.00
Plate, Swan & Water Lily, 6 1/2 In. 77.00
Plate, Tree Branch, Shell Border, Wedgwood 235.00
Plate, Water Lily, 7 1/2 In. .... 45.00 to 50.00
Plate, Yellow Dragons, Shield, Fruit, White Center, Brown Rim, 11 In. 75.00
Platter, Asparagus, Dipping Well, 16 1/2 x 10 3/4 In. 220.00
Platter, Banana, Leaf Design 295.00
Platter, Corn, 13 1/2 x 11 In. 85.00

Platter, Flying Crane, Turquoise Border, 10 1/4 x 7 In.	155.00
Platter, Grape Leaf, Gray & Yellow Rim, Twig Handles, Wedgwood, 11 x 9 In.	360.00
Platter, Greek Key Border, Lavender Ground, 10 1/2 x 8 In.	100.00
Platter, Prunus, Wedgwood	440.00
Platter, Strawberry & Bow, 13 1/2 x 11 In.	250.00
Platter, Wild Rose, Brown Border, Yellow Ground, 13 1/2 x 11 In.	210.00
Salt, Figural, Monkey, Holdcroft	412.00
Sardine Box, Cobalt Blue	1100.00
Saucer, Cauliflower	140.00
Saucer, Fern & Bamboo, Brown, Registry Mark, Pair	60.00
Sugar, Basket & Fern, Turquoise Ground, Colored Leaves	220.00
Sugar, Seashell, Handles	110.00
Sugar, Shell & Seaweed	632.00
Sugar & Creamer, Blackberry, White, Green & Gold Trim	110.00
Sugar & Creamer, Fish Shape	75.00
Syrup, Bamboo, Cobalt & Cream Ground	550.00
Syrup, Coral, Cobalt & Cream Ground	550.00
Syrup, Floral & Berry, Pewter Lid, Pink Interior	230.00
Syrup, Maple Leaf, Pewter Lid, 7 1/2 In.	137.50
Syrup, Moreley Pottery, 5 1/2 In.	360.00
Syrup, Sunflower, Cobalt Blue, Etruscan	275.00 to 425.00
Tea Set, Cauliflower, 3 Piece	495.00 to 715.00
Teapot, Albino, Turquoise, Gold & Lavender, Etruscan	525.00
Teapot, Blue, Wedgwood	595.00
Teapot, Cauliflower, Etruscan	380.00
Teapot, Cauliflower, Etruscan, 5 1/4 In.	375.00
Teapot, Chinaman, Minton	1925.00
Teapot, Fan & Bird	220.00
Teapot, Figural, Monkey, France, Criel	885.00
Teapot, Fish Swallowing Fish	715.00
Teapot, Flowers, Butterfly & Stork	120.00
Teapot, Man In The Moon	660.00
Teapot, Shell & Seaweed	495.00 to 1815.00
Teapot, Twig Handle, Mottled Green Wash, England	275.00
Teapot, Water Lily, Pink, White, Yellow & Green	155.00
Toothpick, Figural, Bird Stump, 4 1/ 2 In.	55.00
Tray, Applied Foliage, Longchaps Manner, 1900s, 8 In.	195.00
Tray, Flowers, Butterfly & Stork, Handles, Oval, 15 In.	115.00
Tray, Seaweed, Seals Handles, Wedgwood	1000.00
Tureen, Cover, Dove, Minton	8500.00
Tureen, Duck, Sarreguemine	330.00
Umbrella Stand, Figural Turkey On Base, 30 In.	2700.00
Umbrella Stand, Rushes	990.00
Umbrella Stand, Ships, Seagulls, Fish & Water Lilies, 22 In.	140.00
Umbrella Stand, Stork In Rushes At Brick Wall, Turquoise Ground, 18 1/2 In.	192.50
Umbrella Stand, Sunflower, Hexagonal, Wedgwood, 21 1/2 In.	275.00
Urn, Allover Frogs, Lizards, Bees & Beetles, Snake Handle, 14 In.	550.00
Urn, Coral Shell, Minton	6875.00
Vase, Albino, White Glazed, 7 In.	85.00
Vase, Applied Flowers & Leaves, 1870s, 10 In.	850.00
Vase, Applied Lizards, Frogs, Snake Handles, 14 In.	495.00
Vase, Black Man & Woman, 11 In., Pair	750.00
Vase, Dove, Minton	935.00
Vase, Enameled Design, Central Portrait, Italy, 19th Century, 11 In.	305.00
Vase, Heads At Handle, c.1890, 23 1/2 In.	950.00
Vase, Iris, 5 In.	265.00
Vase, Lion & Palm Tree, 10 In.	65.00
Vase, Polychrome Floral, Lizard Handles, 13 1/2 In.	165.00
Vase, Relief Roses, Hanging Plaster Base, 1880, Continental, 37 In.	330.00
Vase, Reserve Of Woman, Grotesques At Neck, 48 In.	5750.00
Vase, Thistles, Leaves, Art Nouveau, Cobalt Blue Shoulder Handles, 10 In.	85.00
Vase, Water Lily, 1880	185.00

Wall Pocket, Cabbage Leaf, 8 In. 172.00
Wall Pocket, Shoe, Longchamps Manner, Pair 710.00

MAPS of all types have been collected for centuries. The earliest known
printed maps were made in 1478. The first printed street map showed London
in 1559. The first road maps for use by drivers of automobiles were made in
1901. Collectors buy maps that were pages of old books, as well as the
multifolded road maps popular in this century.

Alaska Sportsman, Pub. 1950, Pocket, 17 x 24 In. 3.00
Anglesea, New Jersey, Streets & Building Lots, Fold-Out On Linen, 1900 .... 39.00
Aroostook War, Frame, February To May, 1843, 29 x 23 In. 995.00
Atlas, Road, Blue, 1916 .... 50.00
Atlas, Scott's Emulsion Cod Liver Oil, 1926, 40 Pages, Pocket 15.00
Auto & Cycling Route New England States, 1905 .... 55.00
Carte De La Virginie & Maryland, 1755, 20 1/2 x 27 In. 770.00
China, Japan & West Coast Of North America, A. Ortelius, c.1570, 14 x 18 In. 660.00
Devonshire & Hartfordshire, Hand Colored, Frame, 9 1/4 x 11 1/4 In. 44.00
England & Wales, Thomas Kitchen, Frame, 9 1/4 x 10 5/8 In. 50.00
Europe, Africa & Asia, World War II, Color, 1944, 20 x 26 In. 6.00
Europe, Hand Colored, Ashlet & Adams, 1870, 17 x 24 In. 25.00
European War, Sears, Roebuck & Co., Silvertone Radio, World War II 10.00
Flanders, Engraved, Black & White, 20 x 24 1/2 In. 50.00
Florida, Crown Gasoline, Standard Oil, 1924, 12 x 18 In. 18.00
France, Frame, Thomas Kitchen, 9 1/4 x 10 5/8 In. 50.00
Galveston, Texas, Lists Of Hotels, Public Buildings, Depots, 1915 .... 15.00
Globe, Celestial & Terrestrial, Boston, Joshua Loring, 18 In., Pair 5500.00
Globe, Celestial, Gilman Joslin, Boston, 1860s, 14 1/2 In. 2420.00
Globe, Celestial, Merriam Moore & Co., 1870s, 12 In. 1210.00
Globe, Celestial, W. Bardin, Fleet Street, London, 14 In. 990.00
Globe, Juvet & Co., Canajoharie, N.Y., Brass Stand 6000.00
Globe, Terrestrial & Celestial, C. Smith & Son, 1847, 34 In., Pair 5500.00
Globe, Terrestrial, Ginn & Heath, 19th Century, 9 1/2 In. 1210.00
Globe, Terrestrial, Metal Stand, C. S. Hammond Co., 31 1/2 In. 605.00
Globe, Terrestrial, Victorian, Walnut, W. & A.K. Johnston, Late 1800s, 65 x 36 In. 4315.00
Guide To Savannah, Georgia, Pocket, 1927 .... 15.00
Highways Of Texas, Rand McNally, Texas & Pacific Coal & Oil Co., 1930 .... 15.00
Holy Land, Hand Colored & Engraved, Frans Hogenberg 2420.00
Italy, Frame, Thomas Kitchen, 9 1/4 x 10 5/8 In. 28.00
Los Angeles, Bekins Van & Storage Co., Pre-1940s 10.00
Los Angeles, Union Oil, 1941, Large 5.00
Maine, Hand Colored, Coltons, Folds Into Leather Cover, 1870s 75.00
Maine, Railroads, Plantations, Town & Wild Land, 1900, 30 x 42 In. 25.00
Massachusetts, Copperplate, Hand Colored, 1838 .... 125.00
Minnesota Territory, Hand Colored, Thomas Cowperthwait, 1850, 13 x 16 In. 95.00
Moon, Black On White & White On Black, Goodacre, 1910 .... 110.00
Nashville Official City Map, Christian Endeavor Convention, Fold-Out, 1879 .... 18.00
New England & New York, Richfield Motor Routes, 1920 .... 10.00
New England Journeys, Ford Dealers, Pocket 5.00
New World, Hand Colored, Spanish Perspective, Matted, Frame, 27 x 31 In. 302.00
Niagara Falls, Illustrations, Wood Cuts, Steele's, 1838, 12 x 15 In. 40.00
Ohio, Hand Colored Engraved, Colton & Co., Frame, Mid-19th Century, 20 x 23 In. . 104.50
Ohio, Hand Colored Engraved, Thomas Cowperthwait, Frame, 23 x 20 1/2 In. 170.50
Olinville & Wakefield, New York, Color, 18 x 28 In. 22.50
Palm Beach, 1940s, 17 x 32 In. 13.50
Paraguay, DeCharlevoix, Printed In French, 1756 .... 45.00
Pennsylvania & New Jersey, In Latin, Nova Jersey Et Nova York, Frame, 1750 ...... 467.00
Plymouth County, Hand Drawn, Pen & Ink, Frame, 8 1/2 x 10 In. 150.00
Portland, Oregon, Columbia Driver Highway, 1926, 22 x 33 In. 15.00
Romania, Frame 27.50
Scotland, Revised By I. Senex, Hand Colored, 1721, 22 x 18 1/2 In. 385.00
St. Paul City, Thresher's, Doin G. Clay & Co., Fold-Out, 1888, 6 x 3 In. 25.00
Subway, New York City, Color Lithograph, 1903, 20 x 23 In. 25.00
Swampscott, Mass., Fold-Out, 1915 .... 15.00

*Clockwise from left: Marble, Clambroth,
Black Lines, 13/16 In.; Marble, Lutz, Green,
7/8 In.; Marble, Clambroth, Light & Dark
Blue Lines, 1 5/8 In.; Marble, Swirl,
Joseph's Coat, 11/16 In.*

Travel Missouri With Conoco, 1930	15.00
U.S., New York Central Line, 1930s	18.00
Vermont, c.1850, 5 x 7 In.	7.50
Vermont, Pen, Ink & Watercolor, Schoolgirl D.J. Houghton, 1833, 20 1/2 x 18 In.	425.00
War, AAF, Peking 1 Side, Area Around Yellow Sea Reverse, Silk, 12 x 12 In.	25.00
Western United States, Northern Pacific Railroad Co., c.1890	100.00
Wisconsin Fun Map, Conservation Dept., 1936, 24 x 28 In.	5.00
Worcester, Maine, Plan Of Building Lots, 1899, 13 x 17 In.	17.50
World War II, AAF Cloth Chart Of Kanazawa, Japan, 1943, 24 1/2 x 24 1/2 In.	45.00

MARBLE collectors pay highest prices for glass and sulphide marbles.
Marbles has been a popular game since the days of the ancient Romans.
American children were able to buy marbles by the mid-eighteenth century.
Dutch glazed clay marbles were least expensive. Glazed pottery marbles,
attributed to the Bennington potteries in Vermont, were of a better quality.
Marbles made of pink marble were also available by the 1830s. Glass
marbles seem to have been made later. By 1880, Samuel C. Dyke of South
Akron, Ohio, was making clay marbles and The National Onyx Marble
Company was making marbles of onyx. The Navarre Glass Marble company
of Navarre, Ohio, and M. B. Mishler of Ravenna, Ohio, made the glass
marbles. Ohio remained the center of the marble industry, and the Akron-
made Akro Agate brand became nationally known. Sulphides are glass
marbles with frosted white figures in the center.

Advertising, Cote's Master Loaf, 1930s	1000.00
Agate, Christensen Agate Co., 3/4 In.	10.00
Bumblebee, Wasp, Cub Scout, Marble King Inc., 1 In.	84.00
Clambroth, 1 5/8 In.	750.00
Clambroth, Black Lines, 13/16 In. *Illus*	210.00
Clambroth, Black, Opaque White Lines, 2 1/8 In.	1050.00
Clambroth, Cased Black, 13/1 6 In.	210.00
Clambroth, Light & Dark Blue Lines, 1 5/8 In. *Illus*	750.00
Clambroth, Opaque White, Pink Lines, Large	998.00
Clambroth, Purple Lines On White	255.00
Clambroth, White Lines On Opaque Black	400.00
Comb, Box, 1920s, 8 x 10 In.	115.00
Double Patch, 1 1/4 In.	5.00
End Of Day, Joseph's Coat, 1 3/8 In.	775.00
End Of Day, Onionskin, 1 3/4 In.	168.00
End Of Day, Onionskin, 2 In.	275.00
End Of Day, Onionskin, Handmade, 1 7/8 In.	40.00
Flame, Christensen Agate Co., 3/4 In.	20.00
Guinea, Christensen Agate Co., 5/8 In.	310.00
Guinea, Christensen Agate Co., 7/8 In.	2126.00
Indian Swirl, 11/16 In.	115.00
Joseph's Coat, Mark Matthews, 1 1/2 In.	105.00
Latticinio, Orange Core, Outer Bands, 1 1/16 In.	400.00

Latticinio, Orange, Swirls, 1 5/8 In. 600.00
Latticinio, Peewee 10.00
Latticinio Swirl, Blue 15.00
Latticinio Swirl, Large 75.00
Limeade, Fluorescent Opaque, 5/8 In. 15.00
Lutz, Black, 3/4 In. 700.00
Lutz, Blue Swirl, 7/8 In. 110.00
Lutz, Cased Indian, 5/8 In. 474.00
Lutz, Cased Indian, 11/16 In. 483.00
Lutz, Green Ribbon, 3/4 In. 405.00
Lutz, Green, 7/8 In. ....*Illus* 405.00
Lutz, Onionskin, 3/4 In. 560.00
Lutz, Onionskin, Polished, 1 5/8 In. 2100.00
Lutz, Onionskin, White 350.00
Lutz, Red Lines On Opaque Black, Clear Casing 250.00
Lutz, Ribbon, 5/8 In. 450.00
Malachite, 1 1/4 In. 55.00
Mica, Turquoise, Oxblood, 1 7/8 In. 3150.00
Onionskin, 4 Panels, Flecks Of Mica, 2 In. 450.00
Onionskin, With Mica, 1 15/16 In. 875.00
Onionskin, Yellow Base, Red & Green Spots, 2 5/16 In. 675.00
Oxblood, Cornelian, Akro Agate, 9/16 In. 95.00
Oxblood, Egg Yolk, Akro Agate, 3/4 In. 70.00
Oxblood, Green Base, 11/16 In. 280.00
Oxblood, Lemonade, Akro Agate Co., 9/16 In. 75.00
Peewee, 1/2 In., 3 Piece 6.00
Slag, Blue, 5/8 In. 5.00
Sparkler, Akro Agate, 2 3/4 In. 10.00
Sulphide, Bead, Standing, 2 1/8 In. 220.00
Sulphide, Clambroth, Green Lines, Milky Lime Base, 5/8 In. 150.00
Sulphide, Cow, Standing, 2 In. 115.00
Sulphide, Doe On Grass Mount, 1 5/8 In. 85.00
Sulphide, Dog On Cushion, 2 1/4 In. 60.00
Sulphide, Fish Center, Large 85.00
Sulphide, Flying Goose 460.00
Sulphide, Fox With Chicken 600.00
Sulphide, Frog, Green Tint, 1 3/4 In. 575.00
Sulphide, Girl, Standing, Blue Swirls Around Head, 1880-1915, 1 1/2 In. 220.00
Sulphide, Grizzly Bear 210.00
Sulphide, Hen, 4 Colors, Clear, 1 5/8 In. 4410.00
Sulphide, Indian Swirl, Red, Gray Lines, Black Opaque Base, 11/16 In. 95.00

◆◆◆◆◆◆◆◆◆◆◆◆◆◆◆◆◆◆◆◆◆◆◆◆◆

Small cracks in marble can be
concealed with a mixture of colored wax and chalk dust. The
same mixture can be used to
make a new nose or finger for a
damaged marble figure.

◆◆◆◆◆◆◆◆◆◆◆◆◆◆◆◆◆◆◆◆◆◆◆◆◆

Marble Carving, Boy, Fisher, Italy, c.1900

Sulphide, Lamb, 1880-1915, Germany, 1 3/4 In. 66.00
Sulphide, Lion, Lying Down, 2 1/16 In. 82.00
Sulphide, Lizard On Rock 550.00
Sulphide, Male Lion, Standing, 2 In. 270.00
Sulphide, Man Seated On Tree Stump, With Hat, Clear, 2 In. 245.00
Sulphide, No. 1, 3/34 In. 275.00
Sulphide, Onionskin, Pink, White & Dark Blue, 3/4 In. 50.00
Sulphide, Peasant Boy, Seated On Stump, Legs Crossed, 1 11/16 In. 283.00
Sulphide, Porcupine, 1 3/4 In. 105.00
Sulphide, Rabbit, 1 1/2 In. 50.00
Sulphide, Rearing Stallion, 2 In. 136.00
Sulphide, Rooster, 1 3/4 In. 130.00
Sulphide, Sheep, Clear, 1 3/4 In. 82.00
Sulphide, Sheep, Standing, Cobalt Blue, 1 1/4 In. 1418.00
Sulphide, Spread-Wing Eagle, 2 1/4 In. 1150.00
Sulphide, Squirrel, Eating Nut, 2 3/16 In. 205.00
Swirl, 1 3/8 In. 65.00
Swirl, Clear Center, 1 1/8 In. 34.00
Swirl, Divided Core, 1 1/2 In. 150.00
Swirl, Divided Core, 2 In. 145.00
Swirl, Double Ribbon Swirl, Red, White & Blue 400.00
Swirl, Joseph's Coat, 11/16 In. .... *Illus* 180.00
Swirl, Lattice Center, 1 3/4 In. 50.00
Swirl, Multicolored, 5/8 In. 5.00
Swirl, Yellow Core, Latticinio Co., 2 1/4 In. 260.00
Tricolor Flame, 15/16 In. 128.00

MARBLE CARVINGS, such as large or small figurines, groups of people or animals, and architectural decorations, have been a special art form since the time of the ancient Greeks. Reproductions, especially of large Victorian groups, are being made of a mixture using marble dust. These are very difficult to detect and collectors should be careful. Other carvings are listed under Alabaster.

Bowl, Egg & Dart Border, Tripartite Base, Italy, 6 1/2 x 14 In. 1495.00
Boy, Fisher, Italy, 1900 .... *Illus* 16100.00
Bust, Augustus Rex, Marble Plinth Base, 8 In., Pair 1210.00
Bust, Beatrix Violantes, Professor Petrilli, 24 In. 1320.00
Bust, Child, Unsmiling, Plinth Base, O.L. Warner, U.S., 1889, 16 1/2 In. 2860.00
Bust, Diana, 19th Century, 25 1/2 In. 2875.00
Bust, Girl, Clown Suit, White, A. Piazza, 1900, 16 1/4 In. 875.00
Bust, Man, Mutton-Chop Whiskers, P. Costas, Firenze, 1859, 18 3/4 In. 330.00
Bust, Woman, Gilt Accents, F. Saul, 1900, 23 In. 1320.00
Classical Maiden, Raised Arms, Carrara, A. Piazza, c.1900, 29 1/2 In. 2750.00
Column, Scagliola & White Marble, 43 In., Pair 8050.00
Girl, Holding Up Hem Of Dress, Signed Page, c.1900, 18 1/2 In. 715.00
Head, Kwan Lin, With Stand 400.00
Mask, White, Signed Caruso No. 49, 9 In. 20.00
Obelisk, Twisted Border, Quiver Of Arrows, 1870s, 24 In., Pair 9200.00
Pedestal, Marble Socle, Levanto Marble, 31 1/2 In., Pair 9775.00
Pedestal, Revolving Top, Turned Column, Octagonal Base, 34 1/2 In. 330.00
Pedestal, Sienna, Faux Marble Plinth, Molded Base, 41 1/2 In. 990.00
Reclining Nude, Flowing Tresses, Italian School, c.1880, 9 x 22 In. 1540.00
Shakespearean Couple, Signed Homanelli 1375.00
Slave Girl, Standing, In Chains, 19th Century 11000.00
Sphinx, Rose, Harriette Miller, 15 x 9 x 18 In. 5250.00
Statue, Angel, Standing, 1860 .... 3500.00
Urn, Berried Domed Cover, Foliate Scrolls, 28 In., Pair 6325.00
Woman, Holding Umbrella, Carrara, c.1870, 39 In. 6875.00
Young Woman, L. Pampaloni, Marble Pedestal, 30 In. 6613.00

MARBLEHEAD Pottery was founded in 1905 by Dr. J. Hall as a rehabilitative program for the patients of a Marblehead, Massachusetts, sanitarium. Two years later it was separated from the sanitarium and it continued operations until 1936. Many of the pieces were decorated with marine motifs.

Basket, Hanging, Gray Glaze, 3 x 3 3/4 In. 285.00
Bowl, Blue Matte Glaze, Light Blue Interior, 5 1/2 In. 220.00
Bowl, Closed-In-Mouth, Dark Matte Blue Glaze, Marked, 4 x 9 In. 220.00
Bowl, Dark Blue, Light Blue Interior, 8 In. 375.00
Bowl, Flared, Dark Blue Glaze, Lighter Blue Interior, Marked, 5 x 7 1/2 In. 275.00
Bowl, Flared, Matte Pink Glaze, 4 x 7 1/2 In. 247.00
Bowl, Incised Indian Scene, Matte Sand Ground, M.T., 3 3/4 x 7 1/4 In. 1870.00
Bowl, Inverted Rim, Olive Green, 2 3/4 x 6 In. 380.00
Candlestick, Saucer Base, Clay Ribbons Either Side, 3 1/4 In. 295.00
Candlestick, Speckled Green Glaze, Marked, 14 1/4 In., Pair 1700.00
Chamberstick, Dark Blue Matte Glaze, 6 x 4 3/4 In. 450.00
Chamberstick, Ring Handle, Green Glaze, 4 3/4 In. 750.00
Tile, Sailing Ship, Pink With Sky Blue Underglaze, 5 x 5 In. 165.00
Tile, Woodland Scene, Glazed Green Shades, Mark, Square, 6 1/8 In. 385.00
Vase, Allover Incised Lines, Dark Green Matte Glaze, 4 x 3 1/4 In. 357.00
Vase, Band Of Flowers On Shoulder, Allover Leaves, 1920, 8 1/2 In. 1210.00
Vase, Berries & Leaves, 5-Color Outlining, 5 1/2 In. 1300.00
Vase, Blue Incised Birds, 6 In. 1995.00
Vase, Blue Speckled Matte Ground, Stylized Florals, H. Tutt, c.1909, 4 1/2 In. 880.00
Vase, Brown & Gold Matte Glaze, 5 In. 286.00
Vase, Brown Speckled, Egg-Shape, Signed, 8 3/4 In. 550.00
Vase, Bud, Gray, 5 1/2 In. 185.00
Vase, Bulbous Shoulder, Feathered Matte Mustard Glaze, Marked, 8 In. 400.00
Vase, Closed-In Rim, Feathered Matte Blue Glaze, 8 1/2 In. 350.00
Vase, Corseted, Stylized Flying Cranes, Speckled Gray Glaze, 8 x 4 In. 2090.00
Vase, Dark Blue Matte, Egg-Shape, 8 1/2 In. 550.00
Vase, Elongated Peacock Feathers, Blue Glaze, Marked, 4 1/4 In. 650.00
Vase, Flared, Green, 3 In. .... 230.00 to 240.00
Vase, Flat Shoulder, Smooth Matte Green Glaze, Marked, 8 1/4 In. 850.00
Vase, Gray & Blue Leaf Border, 4 In. 1100.00
Vase, Gray, Blue Interior, 3 3/4 In. 250.00
Vase, Green & Brown Feathered Glaze, Signed, 7 In. 467.00
Vase, Green Speckled Glaze, Egg-Shape, 6 1/2 x 3 3/4 In. 550.00
Vase, Incised Pinecones, Long Stems, Egg-Shape, 5 1/4 In. 1000.00
Vase, Incised Stylized Flowers, Speckled Ground, Marked, 3 3/4 In. 750.00
Vase, Ivy & Berries At Shoulder, Teal Ground, Azure Blue Interior, 6 1/2 In. 1380.00
Vase, Lavender To Light Blue Matte Glaze, 2 1/2 In. 210.00
Vase, Matte Blue, 5 1/4 x 4 In. 215.00
Vase, Matte Speckled Ocher Glaze, Baluster Shape, Marked, 9 1/4 In. 650.00
Vase, Mottled Dark Mustard, Brown Shading To Green, Egg-Shape, 5 1/8 In. 230.00
Vase, Pear Shape, Lavender Matte Glaze, 8 1/4 x 6 1/2 In. 660.00
Vase, Smooth Blue Speckled Glaze, Signed, 4 1/2 x 4 1/2 In. 220.00
Vase, Speckled Matte Glaze, Black Rim, Stylized Flowers, c.1907, 3 1/4 In. 440.00
Vase, Stylized Design, Olive Green, Arthur Baggs, 5 1/4 In. 395.00
Vase, Stylized & Tooled Flower Buds, Hannah Tutt, 4 1/4 In. 2100.00
Vase, Trumpet, Blue, 4 1/2 In. .... 235.00 to 245.00
Vessel, Incised Floral, Matte Blue Ground, Marked, 3 3/4 x 4 1/2 In. 750.00

MARTIN BROTHERS of Middlesex, England, made martinware, a salt-
glazed stoneware, between 1873 and 1915. Many figural jugs and vases were
made by the three brothers. Of special interest are the fanciful birds, usually
made with removable heads.

Martin Bros.
London

Bird, Bird's-Head Cover, No. 71890, 15 In. 7475.00
Humidor, Grotesque Bird, Wooden Base, Marked, 1889, 9 In. 7600.00
Jug, Incised Foxgloves, Asters, Butterflies, Signed, 9 1/2 In. 750.00
Tobacco Jar, Grotesque Bird, Snake Around Leg, Signed, 13 1/4 In. 3000.00
Tobacco Jar, Grotesque Grinning Beast, Signed, 5 1/2 In. 4600.00
Vase, All-Over Incised Jellyfish, Copper Luster Glaze, 1894, 9 1/4 In. 900.00
Vase, Cream Glaze, Blue Wash, Grotesque Fish, Signed, 1889, 10 1/4 In. 1495.00
Vase, Incised Bluebirds On Branch, Beige Ground, Marked, 5 3/4 In. 600.00
Vase, Incised Insects, Blue Ground, Marked, 1904, 9 In. 2000.00
Vase, Vertical Ridges, Curdled Green & Brown Glaze, Marked, 5 1/2 In. 450.00

MARY GREGORY is the name used for a type of glass that is easily identified. White figures were painted on clear or colored glass as the decoration. The figures chosen were usually children at play. The first glass known as Mary Gregory was made about 1870. Similar glass is made even today. The traditional story has been that the glass was made at the Sandwich Glass works in Boston by a woman named Mary Gregory. Recent research suggests that it is possible that none was made at Sandwich. In general, all-white figures were used in the United States, tinted faces were probably used in Bohemia, France, Italy, Germany, Switzerland, and England. Children standing, not playing, were pictured after the 1950s.

Bottle, Barber, Girl & Flowers, Amethyst	175.00
Box, Girls With Rose Wreaths On Lid, Black Amethyst, 7 In.	1010.00
Box, Hinged, Heavy Enameled, Lime Green, 3 1/2 In.	150.00
Box, Jewelry, Sunday Dress, Bonnet, Brass Frame, 5 1/4 In.	550.00
Cruet, Green	145.00
Cruet, Inverted Thumbprint, Sapphire	225.00
Cruet, Vinegar, Little Boy, Bubble Stopper, Green, 8 1/4 In.	265.00
Decanter, 1 Man, Other Woman, Cranberry Flashed, Pinch, Pair	400.00
Decanter, Boy, Large	110.00
Decanter, Wine, Boy Sitting In Chair, Lime Green, 10 1/4 In.	245.00
Lamp, Hanging, Inverted Thumbprint, Brass Top, Green, 15 1/2 In.	1295.00
Lamp, Oil, Girl At Easel, 12 In.	650.00
Lamp, Urn Shape, Girl In Gown, Riding Butterfly, Black Amethyst, 18 In.	345.00
Mug, Girl Carrying Bouquet, Applied Handle, Optic Pattern Ground, 4 In.	55.00
Pickle Caster, Young Boy & Flowers, Cranberry, Metal Frame	245.00
Pitcher, Girl, Sapphire Blue, 2 In.	225.00
Pitcher, Little Girl With Flowers, Crystal	125.00
Pitcher, Tankard Shape, Girl, Emerald Green, 6 1/4 In.	195.00
Rose Bowl, 1 Boy, Other Girl, Cranberry, Miniature, Pair	215.00
Salt, White Enameled Girl, Bottle Green, 1 5/8 In.	95.00
Scent Bottle, Young Girl, Hinged Lid, Black	450.00
Scent Flask, Boy & Butterfly, Cranberry	425.00
Syrup, Child In Color, Holds Bird On Hand, Silver Lid	195.00
Tankard Set, Children At Play, Hinged Pewter Lid, 7 Piece	680.00
Tea Warmer, Boy, Girl & Woman, Pink	675.00
Toothpick, Little Girl Standing In Foliage, Watching Bird, Citron, c.1890	250.00
Tray, Dresser, Boy & Girl Feeding Deer, Cobalt Blue, 10 3/4 x 8 /12 In.	375.00
Tray, Dresser, Boy Fishing, Cranberry, 6 3/8 x 9 3/8 In.	375.00
Tumbler, Girl, Sapphire Blue, Barrel Shape, 4 1/4 In.	55.00
Tumbler, Little Boy, Trees & Flowers	25.00
Vase, Birds On Hoop Held By Woman, Green, 12 1/2 In.	330.00
Vase, Boy & Girl On Pear, Cobalt Blue, 3 1/2 In.	150.00
Vase, Boy & Girl, Blue, 12 In.	425.00
Vase, Boy & Girl, Cranberry, Gold Design, 10 In., Pair	295.00
Vase, Boy, Snail Handle, Amber, 7 1/4 In.	150.00
Vase, Bud, Boy Holding A Flower, Light Amethyst, 6 In.	110.00
Vase, Daisies & Lily-Of-The-Valley, 7 1/2 In., Pair	145.00
Vase, Girl & Boy, Butterfly Net, Cranberry, Frosted	550.00
Vase, Girl In Tree Branches, Green, Cylinder, Filigree Brass Base	325.00
Vase, Girl Picking Flowers, Emerald Green, Optic Ribbed, 10 1/2 In.	245.00
Vase, Girl Sitting On Bench, Royal Blue, 8 In.	195.00
Vase, Girl Wearing Hat, Black Amethyst, 9 3/4 In.	225.00
Vase, Girl With Umbrella, Reading A Book, Sapphire Blue, 5 1/4 In.	245.00
Vase, Girl, Brass Base Set With Jewels, Lime Green, 6 1/2 In.	235.00
Vase, Girl, Hands Near Chin, Flower Frame, Cobalt Blue, 8 1/2 In.	145.00
Vase, Leprechauns Under Toadstools, Pipes, Cranberry, 10 In., Pair	595.00
Vase, Young Boy Blowing Horn, Sapphire Blue, 8 1/4 In.	225.00
Vase, Young Girl, Floral Spray On Back, Brass Stork Shape Holder, 7 3/4 In.	750.00
Water Set, Clear, Boy Blowing Bubbles, Ribbed Handle, 6 Piece	495.00
Water Set, Young Girl, In Swing, Children On Tumblers, Gold Trim	620.00

MASONIC, see Fraternal

MASSIER, a French art pottery, was made by brothers Jerome, Delphin, and Clement Massier in Vallauris and Golfe-Juan, France, in the late nineteenth and early twentieth centuries. It has an iridescent metallic luster glaze that resembles the Weller Sicard pottery glaze. Most pieces are marked *J. Massier.*

Plaque, Flowers, Leaves & Birds, Multicolored Glaze, 18 In.	2250.00
Umbrella Stand, Carved Peacock Feathers, Green Glaze, 1900, 26 In.	1438.00
Vase, Applied Butterfly, Matte Brown Ground	350.00
Vase, Enamel Over Unglazed Buff Body, Black Lines, Signed	350.00
Vase, Iridescent Glaze, 4 In.	950.00
Vase, Landscape Of Marsh, Orange, Green & Brown, Signed, 4 3/4 In.	275.00
Vase, Japanesque, Gold Paste, Pyramid Neck, 14 In.	1875.00
Vase, Olive Iridescent Abstract Pattern, Glazed, Low Cylindrical, 1900, 9 In.	1380.00
Vase, Purple Iridescent Palm, Wrigglework, Square Mouth, 4 Handles, 7 1/2 In.	1610.00
Vase, Storks, Landscape, Copper Blue & Purple Luster, 9 1/2 In., Pair	3500.00
Vase, Thorny Branches, Fungi Cluster, Red Glaze, Gold, 1900, 31 5/8 In.	2300.00
Vessel, Double-Gourd Shape, Purple & Gold Glaze, Signed, 10 In.	700.00

MATCH HOLDERS were made to hold the large wooden matches that were used in the nineteenth and twentieth centuries for a variety of purposes. The kitchen stove and the fireplace or furnace had to be lit regularly. One type of match holder was made to hang on the wall, another was designed to be kept on a tabletop. Of special interest today are match holders that have advertisements as part of the design.

American Manure Spreader, Tin, Wall, Color, 5 In.	418.00
Ape, Crane & Breed Mfg.	45.00
Black Boy, Figural, Seated, With Baskets, Striker	495.00
Black Man, Stovepipe Hat, Emerging From Chimney, Bisque, 3 In.	95.00
Bliss Native Herbs, Tin Litho, Capitol Building, Wall, 6 1/2 In.	94.00
Brunswick Havana Cigar, Ceramic, Striker, 4 In.	242.00
C. Parker, Swing Lid, Pat. Sept.14, 1867, Cast Iron, Wall, 5 3/4 In.	99.00
Clothesline, Strike Plate	32.00
Clown, Beside Barrel, Wooden	20.00
Cover, Design, Cast Iron, 19th Century, Wilton, Wall	42.00
De Laval Cream Separator, Tin, 7 1/2 In. 110.00 to	250.00
De Laval Separator, 6 1/2 In.	85.00
Dog & Basket, Pottery, Occupied Japan	15.00
Dog On Cover, Creamware	250.00
E.O. Webber Lumber & Building Material, Stenciled Tin, Wall, 6 1/2 In.	50.00
Elephant, Figural, C.D. Kenny	28.00
F.H. Ohaus Grocer, Arrowhead Shape, Indian Chief, Tin, Wall, 5 1/2 In.	155.00
Gale Manufacturing Co., Agricultural Implements, Tin, Aerial View, Wall, 5 In.	330.00
Goebel Pure Food Beer, Metal Box, Double Shields	65.00
Graniteware, Gray Mottled, Wall	240.00
Happy Hooligan, Figural, Striker	93.00
J.H. Martin, Grocery Store Interior, Embossed Tin, Wall, 5 In.	155.00
Judd's, Cast Iron	50.00
Juicy Fruit, Front Striker Bin, Wall	115.00
Knights Of Columbus, 1919	24.00
Lithograph Of Mines Building, Columbian Exhibition, Tin	70.00
Man Juicy Fruit Made Famous, Portrait, Tin, Red Ground, Wall, 4 3/4 In.	247.00
Milwaukee Binders & Mowers, Tin	50.00
Moxie, Bottle & Box, Die-Cut Tin, Wall, 7 x 3/4 In.	275.00
Old Judson, J.C. Stevens, Tin, Wall	175.00
Old Judson Whiskey, Kansas City, Tin, Wall	135.00
Rochester American Brewing Co., Stoneware	125.00
Rolling Pin Form, Black, Chef Atop	95.00
Salem, Store, Wall	50.00
Section Of Tree, Transfer Of Black Man, Souvenir, Wooden, 6 In.	95.00
Sharples Tubular Cream Separators, Tin Litho, Wall, 6 3/4 In.	467.00
Skull, Movable Jaw, Striker, Bisque	30.00

Slipper, Brass, Wall .... 18.00 to 25.00
Solarine Metal Polish, Tin Litho, Match Holder, Slipper, Brass, Wall, 5 In. 88.00
Striker, Boy & Dog, Porcelain 45.00
Tall Boots, Orange Top, Gold Trim, Bootjack Striker 79.00
Universal Stoves & Ranges, Tin, Tan Ground, Wall, 4 3/4 In. 220.00

MATCH SAFES were designed to be carried in the pocket. Early matches
were made with phosphorus and could ignite unexpectedly. The matches
were safely stored in the tightly closed container. Match safes were made in
sterling silver, plated silver, or other metals. The English call these *vesta
boxes.*

Alligator, Nickel Plated Cast Iron 235.00
Anheuser-Busch, Brass 75.00
Anheuser-Busch, Eagle With Wings In A, Pat. Aug.14, '83 .... 198.00
Art Nouveau, Nude Woman, Sterling Silver 82.50
Blatz Brewing Co. 135.00
Bliss Herb 95.00
Book Shape, Combined With Coin Holder 55.00
Brass, Marble, Dated 1900 .... 35.00
Ceresota 195.00
Charles Parker, Self-Closing 125.00
Edward VII, Gutta-Percha, Embossed 48.00
Embossed Indians, World's Fair, St. Louis, Tin, 1904 .... 90.00
Enameled British Flag, Brass, 1900 .... 35.00
Frisco Line, Telephone Shape, Cast Iron 295.00
Gold, Faceted Stones, Europe 330.00
Harding Memorial 15.00
Hunting Scene, Embossed Metal 35.00
Jester's Head, Cast Iron 62.00
King Edward, Embossed Bust, Silver Plate, 1 1/2 x 2 In. 100.00
Knights Of Columbus, 1919 .... 15.00
Mouse, Figural, Leather Ears & Tail, 1 x 2 1/4 In. 175.00
National Cigar Stands 15.00
Parker Gun Co. 55.00
Pig, Figural, Striker On Base, Nickel Plate, 11/2 x 2 1/2 In. 135.00
Schlitz Beer 120.00
Silver, Chest Shape, Hoof Supports, Beresford, London, 1889, 2 3/4 In. 115.00
Silver, Enameled Tessellated Design, Russia, 1 7/8 In. 330.00
Silver Plate, Gold Wash Interior 45.00
Slipper, Figural, Cigar Cutter On Back Of Heel, Brass, 7/8 x 3 In. 195.00
St. George & Dragon Coin Each Side, Brass, 1 1/2 In. 175.00
St. Louis Fair, Leather, 1904 .... 25.00
Stein, Figural, Woman & Man By Tree, Front & Back, 1 x 1 5/8 In. 175.00
Sterling Silver, Cheese Grater Form, 3 In. 65.00
Tin, Tulips, Hanging 5.00
United Cigars, Embossed, 1904 .... 48.00
Victoria Jubilee, Embossed Head, Book Shape, Bakelite 110.00
Willow Springs Brewing Co., Engraved Eagle & Flag, 1 1/2 x 3 In. 93.50
Wise Wives Work Wonders, Solarine, 4 x 5 x 3 1/2 In. 150.00

MATSU-NO-KE was a type of applied decoration for glass patented by
Frederick Carder in 1922. There is clear evidence that pieces were made
before that date at the Steuben glassworks. Stevens & Williams of England
also made an applied decoration by the same name.

Rose Bowl, 12-Crimp Top, Thorny Base, Pink Cased, 3 1/4 x 3 In. 395.00

MATT MORGAN, an English artist, was making pottery in Cincinnati, Ohio,
by 1883. His pieces were decorated to resemble Moorish wares. Incised
designs and colors were applied to raised panels on the pottery. Shiny or
matte glazes were used. The company lasted less than two years.

Vase, Excised Design, Gilded Heraldic Patterns, Marked, 18 1/2 In., Pair. 550.00

MCCOY pottery was made in Roseville, Ohio. The J. W. McCoy Pottery was founded in 1899. It became the Brush McCoy Pottery Company in 1911. The name changed to the Brush Pottery in 1925. The word *Brush* was usually included in the mark on their pieces. The Nelson McCoy Sanitary and Stoneware Company, a different firm, was founded in Roseville, Ohio, in 1910. The firm made art pottery after 1926. In 1933 it became the Nelson McCoy Pottery. Pieces marked *McCoy* were made by the Nelson McCoy Company. Cookie jars were made from the 1930s until December 1990 when the McCoy factory closed. In 1990 the McCoy mark was put back on pottery by a firm unrelated to the original company.

McCoy

Bank, Dry Dock Savings, Gray	12.00
Bank, Eagle	25.00
Bank, Seaman's Bank, White Sailor	30.00
Bank, Woodsey Owl	68.00 to 75.00
Basket, Yellow, Basket Weave, Flowers At Base Of Handle	23.00
Bowl, Brown, Heinz Mark, Small	3.00
Bowl, Mixing, Ovenproof, 14 In.	43.00
Butter, Cover, Strawberries	5.00
Coffeepot, El Rancho	60.00 to 135.00
Cookie Jar, 2 Kittens	600.00
Cookie Jar, Apollo	550.00 to 875.00
Cookie Jar, Astronauts	650.00 to 1000.00
Cookie Jar, Astronauts On Globe	850.00
Cookie Jar, Bananas	90.00
Cookie Jar, Barnum's Animals	270.00 to 375.00
Cookie Jar, Bear & Beehive	50.00
Cookie Jar, Betsy Baker	195.00 to 375.00
Cookie Jar, Black Engine	125.00
Cookie Jar, Bobby The Baker	45.00
Cookie Jar, Boy On Baseball	100.00 to 350.00
Cookie Jar, Boy On Football	225.00 to 250.00
Cookie Jar, Bulldog	45.00
Cookie Jar, Caboose	125.00
Cookie Jar, Cat, On Black Coal Bucket	135.00 to 275.00
Cookie Jar, Cauliflower With Mammy	1250.00
Cookie Jar, Chef	125.00
Cookie Jar, Chipmunk	75.00
Cookie Jar, Christmas Tree	900.00 to 1250.00
Cookie Jar, Circus Horse, Black	125.00 to 150.00
Cookie Jar, Clown Bust	40.00
Cookie Jar, Clown In Barrel, Yellow	55.00
Cookie Jar, Clyde Dog	325.00
Cookie Jar, Coalby Cat	350.00 to 365.00
Cookie Jar, Coffee Grinder	25.00

  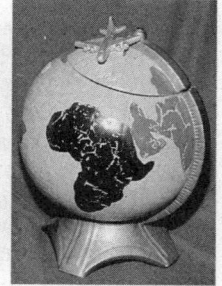

Left to Right: McCoy, Cookie Jar, Rocking Chair, Dalmatians; McCoy, Cookie Jar, Teepee; McCoy, Cookie Jar, Indian Head, Light Color; McCoy, Cookie Jar, World Globe, 1960

Cookie Jar, Cookie Cabin	35.00
Cookie Jar, Cookie House	95.00
Cookie Jar, Covered Wagon	95.00
Cookie Jar, Duck	110.00
Cookie Jar, Engine	175.00 to 190.00
Cookie Jar, Engine, Yellow	225.00
Cookie Jar, Friendship 7, 1962	110.00
Cookie Jar, Globe	210.00
Cookie Jar, Grandfather Clock	65.00 to 75.00
Cookie Jar, Grandma	75.00 to 105.00
Cookie Jar, Hamm's Bear	150.00 to 275.00
Cookie Jar, Happy Face	30.00
Cookie Jar, Honey Bear, Yellow	50.00
Cookie Jar, Hot Air Balloon	35.00
Cookie Jar, Indian Head, Light Color .... *Illus*	305.00
Cookie Jar, Jack-O'-Lantern	400.00
Cookie Jar, Kangaroo, Blue	425.00
Cookie Jar, Kangaroo, Tan	450.00 to 475.00
Cookie Jar, Keebler	45.00 to 57.00
Cookie Jar, Kittens, In Basket	400.00
Cookie Jar, Kola Bear	75.00
Cookie Jar, Liberty Bell, 1776-1976	25.00 to 35.00
Cookie Jar, Mammy	175.00
Cookie Jar, Mammy, Aqua	195.00
Cookie Jar, Mammy, Cookies On Base	175.00 to 255.00
Cookie Jar, Monk	25.00 to 35.00
Cookie Jar, Mushroom On Stump	65.00
Cookie Jar, Owl	18.00
Cookie Jar, Penguin	60.00
Cookie Jar, Picnic Basket	65.00
Cookie Jar, Pirate's Chest	135.00
Cookie Jar, Puppy With Sign	95.00
Cookie Jar, Rocking Chair, Dalmatians .... *Illus*	500.00
Cookie Jar, Snoopy On Doghouse	295.00
Cookie Jar, Snoopy, All White	60.00 to 65.00
Cookie Jar, Teddy Bear & Friend	40.00 to 45.00
Cookie Jar, Teepee .... *Illus*	305.00
Cookie Jar, Thinking Puppy	22.00
Cookie Jar, Touring Car	80.00 to 110.00
Cookie Jar, Tudor Cookie House	75.00
Cookie Jar, W.C. Fields	135.00 to 185.00
Cookie Jar, White Stagecoach	1000.00
Cookie Jar, Winking Pig	185.00 to 395.00
Cookie Jar, Woodsey Owl	175.00 to 295.00
Cookie Jar, World Globe, 1960 .... *Illus*	240.00
Cookie Jar, Wren House	110.00
Cookie Jar, Yosemite Sam.	140.00 to 150.00
Decanter, Apollo, Sims Distillery	190.00
Decanter Set, Jupiter	90.00
Dog Dish, Turquoise	15.00
Figurine, Frog, c.1950	480.00
Flowerpot, Basket Weave, Green, 4 1/4 In.	3.00
Flowerpot, Beetle Bands, Orange & Green, 5 In.	6.00
Jardiniere, Blossom Time, Square, 4 In.	10.00
Jardiniere, Floral, Brown & Green, Loy-Nel-Art, 5 In.	165.00
Jardiniere, Hanging Basket Shape, Ivy Relief, Yellow, Footed	12.00
Jardiniere, Rosewood, Pre-1900	175.00
Jardiniere, Vines Around Edge, Tufted, 9 In.	245.00
Lamp Base, Footed, Yellow & Orange Nasturtiums, Green Ground, Oil Font, 8 In. ...	330.00
Lamp Base, Orange Flowers, Dark Brown, Green, 14 In.	99.00
Mug, Barrel Shape, Green, 5 In.	4.00
Pie Bird, Mammy	95.00
Pitcher, Brown, 5 In.	10.00

Pitcher, Grape, Silver Deposit, 9 In.	40.00
Pitcher, Grapes & Leaves, 8 In.	15.00
Pitcher, Water Lily, Fish Handle, 9 In.	50.00
Planter, Banana Boat	35.00
Planter, Basket Weave, Orange, 7 1/2 x 4 In.	8.50
Planter, Bird Dog	75.00
Planter, Bowl, With Bird, Green, 10 1/4 In.	9.00
Planter, Carousel Horses, Yellow, Round	75.00
Planter, Chinese Man, Black, Red, Green Yellow	10.00
Planter, Cowboy Boots	35.00
Planter, Double Leaves, Blue, 6 1/2 x 2 In.	10.00
Planter, Down By The Old Mill Stream	10.00
Planter, Dutch Shoe, Yellow, Applied Pink Rose & Green Leaves, 8 x 4 In.	11.50
Planter, Fish	425.00
Planter, Frog	8.00
Planter, Hanging, Yellow Daisies, Olive Green Ground, 8 1/2 In.	120.00
Planter, Oval, 3-Footed, Dark Green, Glossy, 10 x 9 x 3 In.	10.00
Planter, Pine Cone Window Box, Rose, 7 1/2 x 4 In.	14.00
Planter, Quail	32.00
Planter, Raised Berries & Leaves, Marked, Oval	3.50
Planter, Rocking Chair, 8 1/2 In.	38.00
Planter, Triple Calla Lily	28.00 to 30.00
Planter, Under The Spreading Chestnut Tree	20.00
Planter, Wishing Well, Gray-Green	20.00
Salt & Pepper, Cabbage	40.00
Stein, German Street Scene Decal	30.00
Stein, Halften Bier, 8 1/4 In.	19.00
Sugar, Cover, Strawberries	5.00
Sugar, Pine Cone, Green & Brown	8.00
Tankard, Loy-Nel-Art, 12 In.	65.00
Tea Set, Daisy, Sugar, Creamer & Covered Pot, 3 Piece	47.00
Tea Set, Pine Cone, Sugar, Creamer & Covered Pot, 3 Piece	45.00
Teapot, Ivory, Relief Flowers	22.00
Teapot, Pine Cone	25.00
Tobacco Jar, Woodland, Brown	100.00
Tureen, Soup, El Rancho	165.00
Vase, Bird & Cherries, Urn Shape, Pink, Side Tab Handles, Footed, 8 1/4 In.	9.00
Vase, Bud, Olympia, 9 In.	95.00
Vase, Butterfly Line, Yellow, 9 In.	20.00
Vase, Floral, Loy-Nel-Art, 13 In.	250.00
Vase, Jewel, No. 042, 8 1/2 In.	395.00
Vase, Loy-Nel-Art, 13 In.	210.00 to 250.00
Vase, Olympia, 9 In.	165.00
Vase, Pleated Sides, Double Handles, White, 12 In.	100.00
Vase, Rosewood, 3 In.	50.00
Vase, Standard Glaze, Loy-Nel-Art, 10 1/2 In.	1500.00
Vase, Swan, Glossy Black, 9 3/8 In.	38.00
Vase, Tulips, Buds, Footed, Green, 8 In.	18.00
Vase, Uncle Sam	40.00
Vase, Yellow & Orange Pansies, Dark Brown Glaze, 3-Footed, 3 Handles, 9 1/2 In.	66.00
Vase, Yellow, No. 593, 10 In.	6.00
Wall Pocket, Banana	20.00
Wall Pocket, Clown	40.00
Wall Pocket, Fan	30.00
Wall Pocket, Grape	35.00
Wall Pocket, Woman, With Bonnet	38.00
Warmer, Food, Chuck Wagon	165.00

MCKEE is a name associated with various glass enterprises in the United States since 1836, including J. & F. McKee (1850), Bryce, McKee & Co. (1850 to 1854), McKee and Brothers (1865), and National Glass Co. (1899). In 1903, the McKee Glass Company was formed in Jeannette, Pennsylvania. It became McKee Division of the Thatcher Glass Co. in 1951 and was bought

PRESCUT

out by the Jeannette Corporation in 1961. Pressed glass, kitchenwares, and tablewares were produced. Jeannette Corporation closed in the early 1980s. Additional pieces may be included in the Custard Glass category.

Bonbon, Sunburst, High Footed, 6 1/2 x 8 In.	26.00
Bowl, Mixing, Red Ships, White, 6 In.	7.00
Bowl, Wiltec	45.00
Butter, Cover, Button & Star, Large	40.00
Cake Stand, Sunburst, Double Scalloped, 5 5/8 x 11 1/2 In.	30.00
Compote, Crowfoot, 8 In.	35.00
Compote, Frosted Moon & Star, 9 In.	45.00
Compote, Wiltec, 5 1/2 x 8 In.	20.00
Cruet, Orinda, 1910	12.00
Cup, Patrician Spoke	5.00
Dish, Moses In Bulrushes, Milk Glass	175.00
Dish, Swan Cover, Raised Wings, Lattice Base, Milk Glass	220.00
Dish, Uncle Sam On Battleship Cover, Milk Glass	175.00
Punch Set, Aztec, 14 Piece	120.00
Salt & Pepper, Roman Arch	55.00
Soup, Dish, Patrician Spoke, Amber	13.00
Tom & Jerry Set, Custard Glass, Gold Trim, 12 Piece	35.00
Toothpick, Colonial, Apple Green	40.00
Toothpick, Lone Star	30.00
Toothpick, Spearpoint Band, Clear, Gold Trim	40.00
Vase, Nudes, 3 Sides, 3 Footed, Black Amethyst, 8 In.	175.00

MEDICAL office furniture, operating tools, microscopes, thermometers, and other paraphernalia used by doctors are included in this category. Medicine bottles are listed in the Bottle category. There are related collectibles listed under Dental.

Almanac, Dr. Miles, Alka-Seltzer Advertising, 1931, 1936	9.50
Bag, Cowhide	85.00
Bag, Doctor's, Alligator	750.00
Bag, Doctor's, Black Leather	50.00
Bag, Doctor's, Brown Leather	5.00
Bedpan, Enamel Ware, Blue Speckled, Relax, Box, Unused	45.00
Bedpan, Porcelain Enamel Ware, White, Box, 1930s	25.00
Bleeder, 3 Blades, Horn Handle, Civil War	90.00
Bleeder, 3 Blades, Rosewood Handle	200.00
Bleeder, 12 Blades, Automatic Spring Loaded, Brass	275.00
Booklet, First Aid, Mutual Life Ins., Directions For Accidents, 1875	9.50
Bottle, Eye Dropper Top, Cobalt Blue, 3 1/2 In.	2.50
Box, Black, Painted, Wood Insert Tray, Leather Handle, 1930s	75.00
Box, Red Paint, Walker & Macara Wholesale & Retail Druggist, Bottles	250.00
Cabinet, Apothecary, 17 Drawers, 36 x 24 In..	325.00
Cabinet, Dr. Frost's, Homeopathic Remedies, Tin Litho Door, Wood, 19 In.	413.00
Cabinet, Dr. M.A. Simmons Liver Medicine, Stained Wood, Lettering, 30 1/2 In.	687.00
Chair, Physician, Koken	800.00
Chest, Apothecary, 16 Drawers, Pine, Cupboard Top	2400.00
Chest, Apothecary, 16 Drawers, Pine, Square Nail Construction, 33 x 36 In.	2310.00
Chest, Apothecary, 16 Nailed Drawers, Scrolled Apron, Pine	2100.00
Chest, Apothecary, 20 Drawers, Bracket Feet, Pine, England, c.1870, 33 x 63 In.	715.00
Chest, Apothecary, 20 Drawers, Parnall & Sons, Dished Knobs, Mahogany	2300.00
Chest, Apothecary, 24 Drawers, Spruce, England, 19th Century, 23 1/2 x 49 In.	1100.00
Chest, Apothecary, 39 Drawers, White Knobs	935.00
Chest, Hinged Lid, Original Bottles, Fitted	154.00
Crutch, Soldiers, Hand Carved Wood, Primitive, Civil War	35.00
Device, Orthopedic, Iron & Wood, Missing Leather Straps, 19th Century	55.00
Diabetes Test Kit, Graduated Cylinder, Hand Etched Graduations, 1800s	298.00
Diascope, No. 4, Glass Plate, September 1, 1908, I.A. Dubernet	110.00
Dose Glass, Dr. Henrich, Mascoutah, Ill., Pure Medicines Only	40.00
Dose Glass, Gavitt's Medical Co., Topeka, Ks.	16.00
Dose Glass, Lewis Medicine Co., Bolivar, Mo.	16.00

Dose Glass, Mercantile Co., New Orleans, Mobile & Cincinnati 40.00
Dr. Pollack Vagix, Feminine Hygiene, Bulb, Movable Parts, Metal, Box, 7 x 2 In. 65.00
Eyecup, Cobalt Blue, Paneled, Marked W.T. Co., Pedestal 30.00
Eyecup, Crystal, Fish Bowl Type, Squatty 14.00
Eyecup, Crystal, Tulip Bowl, Pedestal, 2 1/2 In. 30.00
Eyecup, Dark Green, Tulip Bowl, Pedestal 35.00
Eyecup, Green, Tulip Bowl, Pedestal 28.00
Eyecup, John Bull, Crystal, 1917 .... 22.50
Eyecup, John Bull, Green 22.00
Eyecup, Milk Glass, Paneled, Pedestal 15.00
Eyecup, Orange & Red Slag Glass, Stemmed 7.00
Eyecup, W. T. Co., Cobalt Blue, Pedestal 20.00
Eyecup, Wyeth, Cobalt Blue 15.00
Feeder, Invalid, Crowned x Mark, 5 In. 27.50
Feeder, Invalid, White, Gold Trim 20.00
Fleam, Bone Handle, G. Gregory, Pre-Civil War 120.00
Fleam Knife, 2 Blades 65.00
Homeopath Kit, Pharmacy, Nux Vom, Otis Clapp & Sons, Box, 3 3/4 x 6 3/8 In. 145.00
Hot Water Bottle, Baby's, ABC, 1930s, Box 40.00
Hot Water Bottle, Baby's, This Little Piggy, 1930s 35.00
Hot Water Bottle, Figural, Jane Mansfield, 22 In. 125.00
Inhaler, Roots Drug Store 35.00
Kit, Optical, American Optical Co., 111 Lenses, Leather Case 200.00
Kit, Optical, Eye Charts, Lenses, Eye Measuring Instrument, Frames, Case 300.00
Kit, Surgeon's, Gutta-percha Handled Instruments, Case, 19th Century 550.00
Lamp, Vapo Cresoline, Medication, Box 80.00
Lamp, Vaporizer, Simplex, 7 1/2 In. 50.00
Machine, Arthritis, Electrical, Box 70.00
Mold, Pill, Walnut & Brass, Civil War, 7 x 13 x 16 In. 290.00
Mortar & Pestle, Burlwood, 7 In. 77.00
Mortar & Pestle, Cast Iron, Civil War Era 135.00
Mortar & Pestle, Drug Store, Stoneware, 6 1/2 In. 65.00
Mortar & Pestle, Hand Painted Rose Buds, Cranberry & Gold, France, 3 3/4 x 2 In. .. 48.00
Mortar & Pestle, Lignum Vitae & Maple, 7 In. 105.00
Mortar & Pestle, Unpainted Wood, 19th Century, 3 1/2 x 7 In. 45.00
Mortar & Pestle, Wooden, c.1870 .... 225.00
Nasal Douche, Glass, Box 20.00
Sign, Dr. A.C. Livingston, Chiropractor, Metal, 12 x 24 In. 42.00
Speculum, Vaginal, 4 Blades, Mathieu, France, c.1870s, 9 1/2 In. 560.00
Table, Examination, Pediatric, With Scale, Walnut, Late 1800s 1375.00
Urinal, Clear Glass, Applied Handle, Calibrated, 11 1/2 In. 10.00
Urinal, Enamel Ware, Blue Speckled 25.00
Vaporizer, Electric, 1938 .... 12.50
Wheelchair, Late-1800s 150.00

MEERSCHAUM pipes and other pieces of carved meerschaum, a soft
mineral, date from the nineteenth century to the present.

Pipe, Bacchanalian Scene, Amber Stem, Fitted Case, 8 5/8 In. 660.00
Pipe, Black Man's Head, Wearing Hat, 4 1/4 In. 300.00
Pipe, Cottage & Horse, 1810 .... 125.00
Pipe, Deer, Buck, Doe, Fawn, Bellflower Bowl, Amber Stem, Case, 11 5/8 In. 467.50

MEISSEN is a town in Germany where porcelain has been made since 1710.
Any china made in the town can be called Meissen, although the famous
Meissen factory made the finest porcelains of the area. The crossed swords
mark of the great Meissen factory has been copied by many other firms in
Germany and other parts of the world. Pieces of Meissen dinnerware in the
Onion pattern are listed in their own category in this book.

Basket, Floral, Gilt, Twisted Handles, Openwork, 19th Century, 9 3/4 In. 605.00
Basket, Oval, Double Rope-Twist Handles, Pierced Sides, 2 x 10 x 7 In. 220.00
Bowl, Cover, Birds On Flowering Branches, Insect, Marked, c.1740, 5 11/16 In. 2013.00
Bowl, Floral Enameled, Gilt, Shallow, Marked, 14 In. 330.00
Bowl, Waste, Animal Vignettes, Black Bear, Horse, Marked, 6 7/16 In. 1725.00

Meissen, Figurine, Cherubs, Holding Fish,
8 3/4 In.; Meissen, Figurine, Cupid,
Holding 2 Hearts, 7 1/4 In.

◆◆◆◆◆◆◆◆◆◆◆◆◆◆◆◆◆◆◆◆◆◆◆

Don't use rubber gloves when
washing figurines with protruding arms and legs. The gloves
may snag and cause damage.

◆◆◆◆◆◆◆◆◆◆◆◆◆◆◆◆◆◆◆◆◆◆◆

Bowl, Yellow & White, Gilt Trim, Crossed Swords, 20 1/2 In.	181.00
Butter, Cover, Round, Flattened Lid Ivy Edges, Scroll Handles, 8 In.	275.00
Cake Stand, Scalloped Rim, Pedestal Base, 5 x 14 In.	385.00
Candelabra, 3-Light, Floral Encrustations, 11 1/2 In., Pair	715.00
Candelabra, 5-Light, 20 In., Pair	3500.00
Carafe, Undertray, Teardrop Form, Floral Sprays, Flat Stopper, 10 In.	467.00
Charger, Raised Flowers & Leaves, Allover Gold Relief, 11 In.	275.00
Clock, Brass Dial, Enameled Numerals, Floral & Figures, 1890s, 24 In.	7762.00
Clock, Figures On Top & Around Base, Late 19th Century	7762.00
Compote, Enameled Floral Design, Gilt, Crossed Swords, 8 3/4 x 9 In., Pair	990.00
Compote, Indian Purple Design, Reticulated Border, Marked, 8 3/4 In.	550.00
Cup, Watteau-Style, Painted Green	7300.00
Cup & Saucer, Birds & Insects, Gilt, Crossed Swords	71.00
Cup & Saucer, Blue Underglaze, White, Gilt, Crossed Swords	88.00
Cup & Saucer, Figures Around Tables, Insects, Marked, 5 3/16 In.	2300.00
Cup & Saucer, Rows Of Petals, Gilt Rim, Stem Handle, Marked, 5 1/2 In.	1035.00
Cup & Saucer, Tea, Landscape & Figures, Insects On Cup, Marked	2875.00
Dish, Bird & Floral Design, Multicolored, Gilt, 12 1/4 In.	100.00
Dish, Birds Surrounded By Floral Swags, Square, 10 1/2 In., Pair	690.00
Dish, Gilt Bird & Floral, 12 1/4 In.	100.00
Dish, Leaf-Form, Branch Handle, 10 1/2 x 8 1/2 In.	220.00
Eggcup, Underplate, Marked	155.00
Figurine, 2 Cherubs, Monkey & Cow In Cradle	575.00
Figurine, 2 Lovers, 18th-Century Dress, Cupid Above, 9 In.	1265.00
Figurine, 2 Putti Frolicking, 7 In.	1347.00
Figurine, Bird On Stump, 15 1/2 In., Pair	2875.00
Figurine, Bird, Molded & Incised Feathers, On Tree Stump, 3 11/16 In.	175.00
Figurine, Boy With A Crutch, 8 1/2 In.	400.00
Figurine, Butler, With Tray, Marked, 6 In.	695.00
Figurine, Cherub Holding Wheat & Scythe, Marked, 5 In.	575.00
Figurine, Cherub Placing Heart In Cage, Signed, 1890, 4 1/2 In.	650.00
Figurine, Cherub, Crossed Swords, 6 In., Pair	869.00
Figurine, Cherubs, Holding Fish, 8 3/4 In. *Illus*	660.00
Figurine, Count Bruhl's Tailor, Astride Shaggy Goat, 17 1/4 In.	8050.00
Figurine, Cupid, Holding 2 Hearts, 7 1/4 In. *Illus*	825.00
Figurine, Grape Seller, Black Tricorn, Yellow Slippers, Marked, 5 9/16 In.	4600.00
Figurine, Malabar Musicians, Man & Woman, Marked, 6 3/4 & 6 7/8 In., Pair	3450.00
Figurine, Monkey Band, 1870s, 5 In., 5 Piece	4312.00
Figurine, Monkey, Marked, 5 3/4 In.	995.00
Figurine, Parrot, Perched On Tree Trunk Base, Marked, 8 1/2 In.	770.00
Figurine, Putto, Seated On Rookery, Holding Ribbons, Tes Les Accouple, 5 1/8 In.	385.00
Figurine, Woman Card Player, Crossed Swords, 6 1/2 In.	605.00
Figurine, Woman Sculptress, Marked, 5 1/8 In.	192.00
Figurine, Woman, With Fan, Gold, Brown, Pink, Black, Scheurich, 1929, 18 1/4 In.	7475.00
Figurines, Man & Woman, 18th-Century Clothes, 19th Century, 7 3/8 In., Pair	1210.00
Fruit Bowl, Cherubs Supporting Bowl, Signed, 16 x 9 In.	1200.00

◆◆◆◆◆◆◆◆◆◆◆◆◆◆◆◆◆◆◆◆◆◆

If you have a lightweight
vase that tips easily, fill it
with sand.

◆◆◆◆◆◆◆◆◆◆◆◆◆◆◆◆◆◆◆◆◆◆

Meissen, Tureen, Soup, Cover,
Stand, Multicolored, 1740, 12 3/4 x 14 In.

Group, Departure Scene	495.00
Group, Europa & Bull, Crossed Swords, 8 1/4 In.	1430.00
Group, Female Seated On Reclining Lion, Cherubs & Garlands, Marked, 10 In.	3300.00
Group, Good Mother, Crossed Swords, 8 3/4 In.	1650.00
Group, Happy Family, Crossed Swords, 8 1/2 In.	1870.00
Group, Venus & Mercury, Crossed Swords, 16 1/2 x 11 In.	3025.00
Group, Young Man & Protesting Maiden, Marked, 5 1/4 In.	203.00
Inkwell, Floral, Insect Reserves, 19th Century, 2 1/2 In.	235.00
Paperweight, Recumbent Pug, Gilt-Edged Collar, Marked, 7 13/16 In.	1725.00
Plate, Bird Center, 3 Birds On Rim, Gold Trim, Marked, 9 1/2 In., 12 Piece	1495.00
Plate, Floral Center, Butterflies & Flower Border, Marked, 9 In.	225.00
Plate, Floral Spray, 12 In., Pair	575.00
Plate, Scalloped Rim, Floral Design, 8 1/4 In., 12 Piece	412.50
Plate, Scene, Floral Rim, Reticulated Rim, Gilt, Crossed Swords, 9 In.	137.00
Plate, Shell, Blue & White	245.00
Plate, Songbird In Flight, Bamboo Between Pines, Marked, 5 11/16 In., Pair	5175.00
Platter, Cranes & Swans, Oval, c.1900, 19 In.	880.00
Platter, Floral Sprays & Insects, Elongated Oval, 23 In.	920.00
Platter, Upturned Ends, Shell Tips, 4 x 19 x 13 In.	495.00
Pot, Bough, Alternating Figural & Floral Panels, Yellow Ground, 7 1/2 In.	990.00
Potpourri, Figural Panel, Bouquet Of Flowers On Reverse, 30 1/2 In.	6325.00
Sauce Boat, Attached Saucer, Birds & Insects, Marked, 10 1/4 In.	104.00
Snuffbox, Basket Of Flowers Interior, Scrollwork, Silver Mount, 2 11/16 In.	2645.00
Snuffbox, Palace Garden Scene Under Lid, Allover Trellis Work, 3 In.	7475.00
Snuffbox, Portrait Of Friedrich Christian, Gilded Interior, 3 3/16 In.	3450.00
Tea Set, White, Gilt Trim, Crossed Swords, 19-In. Tray, 9 Piece	797.00
Teapot, Figural Landscape, Gilt Highlights, 11 1/2 In.	180.00
Teapot, Quatrefoil Panels, Figures, Puce Sprigs, Yellow, Marked, c.1735	1265.00
Tray, Cartouche Shape, Leafy Ends, Gilt Rim, 12 x 17 In.	385.00
Tray, Center Floral, Embossed & Gilt Border, Square, 16 In.	895.00
Tray, Central Reserve Of Birds, Green Basket Weave Cartouche, Oval	1210.00
Tray, Enameled Floral, Gilded Scrolled Rim, Corner Shells, Crossed Swords, 16 In.	687.00
Tray, Serving, Floral Center & Edges, Shell Corners, Square, Handles, 16 In.	660.00
Tureen, Soup, Cover, Floral Pattern, Gilt Edge, Underplate, Ladle, 19th Century	600.00
Tureen, Soup, Cover, Stand, Multicolored, 1740, 12 3/4 x 14 In. .... *Illus*	5460.00
Urn, Applied Flowers & White Banding, 19 In.	2300.00
Urn, Gold Drapery, Mask Terminals, Snake Handles, 17 In., Pair	1540.00
Vase, Cobalt Blue Glaze, Serpent Handles, Shield Shape, 19 In.	747.00
Vase, Scene, Yellow, Pink, White & Gilt, Handles, Crossed Swords, 15 1/2 In.	495.00
Wall Brackets, Cherubs, 10 In., Pair	3575.00

MERCURY GLASS, or silvered glass, was first made in the 1850s. It lost
favor for a while but became popular again about 1910. It looks like a piece
of silver.

Lamp, Table, 22 In., Pair	125.00

Tieback, Pair	55.00
Vase, Enameled Flowers, 9 In., Pair	38.50
Vase, Painted Flowers At Middle, 12 1/2 In.	65.00
Vase, Silver, 5 3/8 In.	22.00
Wig Stand, 9 1/2 In.	220.00

MERRIMAC POTTERY Company was founded by Thomas Nickerson in Newburyport, Massachusetts, in 1902. The company made art pottery, garden pottery, and reproductions of Roman pottery. The pottery burned to the ground in 1908.

Vase, Curdled Green Matte Glaze, Paper Label, 8 x 5 1/2 In.	900.00
Vase, Green & Black Thick Glaze, 5 1/2 In.	345.00
Vase, Matte Blue Glaze, Impressed Mark, 3 3/4 In.	137.50
Vase, Matte Green Glaze, Squared Rim, Over Dimpled Shoulder, 1904, 4 1/4 In.	110.00
Vase, Narrow Neck, Green Mottled Glaze, 4 x 3 3/4 In.	285.00
Vase, Wide Mouth, Matte Green Glaze, Marked, 6 1/2 In.	450.00

METTLACH, Germany, is a city where the Villeroy and Boch factories worked. Steins from the firm are known as Mettlach steins. They date from about 1842. *PUG* means painted under glaze. The steins can be dated from the marks on the bottom, which include a date-number code. Other pieces may be listed in the Villeroy & Boch category.

Beaker, No. 2327-1290, 1/4 Liter, German Eagle, PUG	176.00
Charger, No. 1044/352, Geishas Tossing Flowers From Balcony, 17 1/2 In. .. 390.00 to 500.00
Clock, No. 2487, Etruscan, 15 1/2 In.	2310.00
Creamer, No. 3321, 4 1/2 In.	135.00
Ewer, No. 7012, White On Green, 12 In., Pair	1800.00
Flagon, No. 2270, 18 In.	600.00
Mug, Beer, Atlantic Garden, May 8, 1908	235.00
Mug, Hires Root Beer, 1905, 5 In.	165.00
Mug, Hires Root Beer, Toasting Boy, With Bib, 4 1/4 In.	195.00
Pitcher, Applied Green Leaves, Birch Handle, 8 1/2 In.	265.00
Planter, No. 2417, Art Nouveau, 8 x 16 In.	1100.00
Plaque, Mythological Scene, 18 In.	800.00
Plaque, No. 1044-3056, Birds, 17 In.	600.00
Plaque, No. 1044-9028, Dachshund, PUG, 13 3/4 In.	600.00
Plaque, No. 1108, Castle On The Rhine, Gold Rim, 17 In.	1250.00
Plaque, No. 1385, Man With Shield, Fighting Club, 1910, 14 3/4 In.	1200.00
Plaque, No. 1488, Woman Holding Flowers, Leather Frame	1750.00
Plaque, No. 1489, Woman Picking Grapes	1750.00
Plaque, No. 2274-104, Man Smoking Pipe, 18 x 25 In.	3900.00
Plaque, No. 2322, Cavalier & Bar Maid, 1909, 14 1/2 In.	1200.00
Plaque, No. 2443, Woman With Attendants, Green Ground, 18 1/4 In.	1250.00
Plaque, No. 2507, Mermaid	1200.00
Plaque, No. 2593, Hawk Sitting In Branches, 17 In.	1050.00
Plaque, No. 2597, Girl With Cherries, 15 In.	1265.00
Plaque, No. 2621, Cavalier Pouring Wine, 7 5/8 In.	325.00
Plaque, No. 2641, Lovers With Cupid, 9 In.	400.00
Plaque, No. 5174, Woman At Docks, Oak Frame, 26 1/2 x 18 1/2 In.	550.00
Plaque, Woman, Cameo Oval, Green Ground, 7 1/2 x 8 3/4 In.	475.00
Plate, Cheese, No. 2961, Art Nouveau, Cover, 4 1/2 In.	525.00
Plate, Christmas, 12 In.	95.00
Punch Bowl, No. 2814, Art Nouveau Maidens, 2 Handles, 1905, 11 In.	1265.00
Stein, 1/2 Liter, Art Nouveau, Brass Lid	155.00
Stein, 5 Liter, Elks, Art Nouveau Style, Inlaid Lid, c.1900	125.00
Stein, No. 1403, 1/2 Liter, Inlaid Lid	455.00
Stein, No. 1536, 1/2 Liter, Tapestry, Pewter Lid	350.00
Stein, No. 1968, 3 Liter, Inlaid Lid Of A & Eagle, Anheuser-Busch	1787.50
Stein, No. 1987, 1/4 Liter, Flowers	225.00
Stein, No. 1998, 1/2 Liter, Cavalier, Inlaid Lid Of Castle	525.00
Stein, No. 2002, 1/2 Liter, City Of Munich, Munich Maid Thumb Lift	450.00

Stein, No. 2025, 3 Liter, Cherubs 300.00
Stein, No. 2036, 1/2 Liter, Owl .... 850.00 to 1050.00
Stein, No. 2069, 1/2 Liter, Monkey & Fish 1650.00
Stein, No. 2092, Dwarf Setting Time On Clock, Inlaid Lid 1100.00
Stein, No. 2123, 3/10 Liter, Knight With A Beer 1320.00
Stein, No. 2126, 5 1/2 Liter, Symphony Composers Around Rim, Pewter Lid 6875.00
Stein, No. 2192, 1/2 Liter, Etruscan Scene, Inlaid Lid 910.00
Stein, No. 2193, 3 Liter, Pewter Cover, Tavern Figures, Shield Thumb Piece, 16 In. .. 580.00
Stein, No. 2206, 3 Liter, Tavern Scene, Many Cavaliers, Inlaid Lid 1350.00
Stein, No. 2231, 5/10 Liter, Cavaliers Having Good Time, Inlaid Lid 690.50
Stein, No. 2248, 3/10 Liter, Peasants Dancing.................................. 190.00 to 210.00
Stein, No. 2270-994, 5/10 Liter, 2 Soldiers With Bar Maid, PUG, Pewter Lid 825.00
Stein, No. 2520, 1 Liter, Schlitt 775.00
Stein, No. 2721, 1/2 Liter, Cabinet Maker, Tools Etched In Lid, 8 1/2 In. 1500.00
Stein, No. 2833F, 5/10 Liter, Students, Inlaid Lid 440.00
Stein, No. 2882, Castle Scene 695.00
Stein, No. 2951, 1 Liter, Prussian Eagle Cameo, 10 1/4 In. 795.00
Tobacco Jar, No. 436, Boy By Tree Stump, 7 In. 385.00
Vase, Classical Maidens, Tulip-Form Mouth, Scroll Handle, 13 1/2 In., Pair 800.00
Vase, No. 1573, Floral Design, Jewel-Like Colors, Teal Ground, 6 3/4 In., Pair 330.00
Vase, No. 1681, Geometric Floral, Browns, Blue, 8 3/4 In. 357.00
Vase, No. 1709, Strawberries On Vine, Bird On Reverse, 12 1/2 In. 385.00
Vase, No. 1728, Geometric Floral, Browns & Blues, 7 1/4 In. 300.00
Vase, No. 1870, Elephant Handles, 13 1/2 In. 615.00
Vase, No. 2017, Floral, Serpent Forms Base & Neck, 12 In. 357.50
Vase, No. 2414, Foliage Design, Blue Ground, Open Handles, 13 1/2 In. 385.00
Vase, No. 2457, Tropical Birds, Blue & Beige Shades, 18 7/8 In. 522.00
Vase, No. 2913, Incised Flower Pods, White Ground, 13 3/4 In. 400.00
Vase, Woman, Reading By Candlelight, Brown Ground, Green Stamp, 11 1/2 In. 415.00

MILK GLASS was named for its milky white color. It was first made in
England during the 1700s. The height of its popularity in the United States
was from 1870 to 1880. It is now correct to refer to some colored glass as
blue milk glass, black milk glass, etc. Reproductions of milk glass are being
made and sold in many stores. Related pieces may be listed in the Cosmos,
Vallerysthal, and Westmoreland categories.

Banana Stand, Openwork Rim & Base, Triple Split Stem, 11 x 8 In. 28.00
Bell, Smoke 7.00
Bottle, Grotesque, Lion Heads, Scrolls, Enameled, Stopper, 9 In., Pair 53.00
Bottle, Mushroom Stopper, Pinch, Opaque Green 375.00
Bowl, H Pattern, Atterbury, 7 In. 55.00
Bowl, Serving, Horizontal Lacy Rim, Atterbury, Oval 40.00
Bowl, Wicket, Atterbury, 8 x 2 1/2 In. 65.00
Box, Glove, Shell On Beach 160.00
Butter, Cover, Lacy Dewdrop 40.00
Cake Plate, H Pattern, Atterbury, 8 In. 45.00
Cake Stand, 1-In. Openwork Rim, 14 x 5 In. 18.00
Candleholder, Crucifix, Pair 60.00
Candlestick, Dolphin, 9 In. 45.00
Candlewick, Ashtray, Eagle 50.00
Centerpiece, Dolphin, Shell Compote, Candlesticks, 3 Piece 85.00
Cigarette Holder, Top Hat, Decal Flowers 105.00
Compote, Basket Weave, Pedestal, Atterbury 140.00
Compote, Fleur-De-Lis Border, Low Pedestal 75.00
Compote, Hobnail, Blue, Crimped, Ruffled, 8 x 5 In. 14.00
Compote, Hobnail, White, Crimped, Ruffled, Fluted Stem, 8 x 5 In. 14.00
Compote, Lattice Rim, Atterbury, 10 1/2 In. 50.00
Creamer, Cane & Scroll, Blue 30.00
Creamer, Cover, Oval 40.00
Creamer, Cover, Rectangular 40.00
Cruet, Alba, Lavender Floral 110.00
Cruet, Nesting Swan & Heron, Ribbed Body 130.00

Dish, Cat On Drum Cover 65.00
Dish, Chicken On Egg Nest Cover 125.00
Dish, Cover, Dolphin Footed, Shell Garlands, Shell Finial, 6 1/2 In. 35.00
Dish, Deer On Fallen Tree Base Cover 275.00
Dish, Dove In Hand Cover, Atterbury 125.00
Dish, Duck Cover, Blue, Wavy Base, Large 55.00
Dish, Flaccus Deer, Fallen Tree 250.00
Dish, Hen On Nest Cover, Chicks Around Nest, Flaccus 45.00
Dish, Hen On Nest Cover, Red Comb 65.00
Dish, Mallard On Nest Cover, Gold, Large 65.00
Dish, Pig On Drum Cover 42.00
Dish, Rabbit Cover, McKee Mark 165.00
Dish, Ram With Curved Horns Cover, Scalloped Base, 3 3/4 In. 165.00
Dish, Rooster Head Cover, Blue 65.00
Dish, Rooster, Lattice Edged Basket, Imperial 45.00
Dish, Swan, Raised Wings, Arched Neck 185.00
Figurine, Duck, Glass Eyes, Painted Beak 125.00
Figurine, Polar Bear, 4 In. 220.00
Goblet, Beaded Jewel 55.00
Goblet, Buttons & Arches 25.00
Goblet, Ivy In Snow 65.00
Hat, Ruffled Brim, 4 x 5 1/2 In. 14.00
Humidor, Floral, Art Nouveau Brass Lid 90.00
Jar, Cover, Eagle, Old Abe 120.00
Knife, Candlewick 250.00
Lamp, Aqua, Ornate, Large 375.00
Lamp, Hanging, Painted With Roses, Brass Frame, 14 In. 220.00
Perfume Bottle, Design, 9 In. 150.00
Pitcher Set, Spanish Lace, 5 Piece 425.00
Plate, 3 Owls, Pat. 1901, 7 1/4 In. 20.00
Plate, Anchor & Sailing Ship, 7 1/2 In. 45.00
Plate, Flag & Alternating Gilt Eagles, Fleur-Di-Lis, Dated 1903, 7 1/4 In. 65.00
Plate, Forget-Me-Not, 7 In. 40.00
Plate, Wicket, Atterbury, 8 In. 35.00
Powder Box, Court Jester, Black 78.00
Punch Bowl, Child's, Nursery Rhyme, Blue 400.00
Punch Set, Buzz Star, Complete, Ladle 700.00
Punch Set, Feather, Pink, 25 Piece 200.00
Salt & Pepper, Raised Grape & Leaf Design, Tin Tops 45.00
Server, Swan, 5 1/4 x 2 3/8 In. 18.50
Snack Tray, Cup, Feather, Pink 12.00
Spooner, Wild Rose 45.00
Sugar, Cover, Hexagonal 40.00
Sugar, Cover, Maple Leaf, Blue 110.00
Sugar & Creamer, Lace Dewdrop 55.00
Sugar Shaker 175.00
Syrup, Banded Shells, 5 1/2 In. 65.00
Syrup, Chain & Bead, Atterbury 85.00
Syrup, Tree Of Life, Challinor-Taylor 70.00
Table Set, Child's, Wild Rose, 4 Piece 275.00
Table Set, Versailles, 4 Piece 110.00
Toothpick, Frog & Shell 35.00
Towel Bar, Iron Brackets, Wall Mount, Round 7.50
Tray, Pin, Figural, Rabbit, 4 x 6 In. 45.00
Tureen, Cover, Mustard, Miniature 75.00
Vase, Everglades, 5 In. 40.00

MILLEFIORI means, literally, a thousand flowers. Many small pieces of glass resembling flowers are grouped together to form a design. It is a type of glasswork popular in paperweights and some are listed in that category.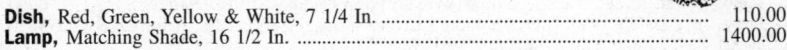

Dish, Red, Green, Yellow & White, 7 1/4 In. 110.00
Lamp, Matching Shade, 16 1/2 In. 1400.00

Mocha, Waste Bowl, Cat's Eyes Band, Pearlware, London Shape, 1820, 6 5/8 In.; Mocha, Bowl, Wavy Brown Line, Pearlware, 1810-1820, 7 3/8 In.; Mocha, Waste Bowl, Cat's Eyes Cluster, Pearlware, London Shape, 1810, 6 9/16 In.

Mocha, Pitcher, Double Worm, 7 1/2 In.

MINTON china has been made in the Staffordshire region of England from 1793 to the present. The firm became part of the Royal Doulton Tableware Group in 1968, but the wares continued to be marked *Minton*. Many marks have been used. The one shown dates from about 1873 to 1891, when the word *England* was added.

Cachepot, Underplate	1155.00
Cake Stand, Blue & Rust, White Ground, 19th Century, 2 5/8 x 12 In.	50.00
Charger, Willoware, Square, Large	195.00
Charger, Secessionist Ware, White Flowers, Green Outlined, Marked, 15 In.	850.00
Chocolate Pot, Gold Butterfly & Trees, Gold Finial, Apple Green, 1873-1879 Mark	95.00
Dish, Condiment, 4 Sections, Turquoise Interior, 11 x 9 1/2 In.	192.50
Dish, Game, Hare & Duck	2310.00
Dish, Squirrel	1595.00
Figurine, Grecian Dancer, Bronze Detail	650.00
Figurine, Parrot, Blue	467.50
Figurine, Sea Breezes, Porcelain, Bronze, 9 1/2 In.	80.00
Flask, Dragon Mask, Polychrome Enamel & Gilt Cloisonne, 10 1/4 In.	1955.00
Foot Tub, Egg-Shape, Handle, Mosaics, Mid-19th Century, 8 x 19 1/2 x 13 3/4 In.	1320.00
Garden Seat, Yellow Glazed, Chinese Style, Barrel Shape, 1880, 21 In.	357.00
Inkstand, Trefoil Shape, Painted Fruits, Yellow Ground, c.1810, 7 In., 4 Piece	1035.00
Jam Jar, Flowers	65.00
Jardiniere, Oyster Shell In Relief, Yellow, 9 x 9 In.	660.00
Jardiniere, Yellow Flower, Turquoise Panels, Brown Ground, 10 x 13 In.	1000.00
Match Pot, Rectangular, Gilt Scrollwork, Floral Sprays, Dresden, c.1830, 4 1/2 In.	575.00
Pie Dish, Hare & Duck, 13 1/2 In.	2310.00
Pitcher, Holly Berries & Leaves, Molded, Twisted Twig Handle, Parian, 5 1/2 In.	110.00
Plate, Dessert, Ducks, Oriental Shrubs, Rococo Rim, c.1830, 8 3/4 In., 10 Piece	1725.00
Plate, Dinner, Turquoise & Gold Border, Crest, Monogram, c.1880, 10 In., 6 Piece	143.00
Plate, Floral Bouquets, J. Colclough, 1883, 9 1/4 In., 24 Piece	5750.00
Plate, Floral Design, Burgundy & White Ground, Gilt Swag, 10 3/4 In., 12 Piece	1700.00
Plate, Medallion Floral Design, Cobalt Blue, Ivory Ground, 10 1/2 In., 12 Piece	375.00
Plate, Stylized Foliate Design, Gold Rim, 10 1/2 In., 12 Piece	460.00
Platter, Palissy-Style, Oval, 15 x 12 1/2 In.	440.00
Platter, Well & Tree, c.1820, 20 1/2 In.	695.00
Teapot, Figural, Chinaman	1925.00
Tile, Hawthorne Branches & Flowers Show Through Black Glaze, 6 In.	75.00
Vase, Bud, Secessionist Ware, Squeeze-Bag Flowers, Marked, 7 1/2 In.	450.00
Vase, Cover, Allegorical Medallions, Wreath Form Handles, 16 In., Pair	6900.00
Vase, Lily-Of-The-Valley, Overlapping Leaves, Sprigs, c.1860, 5 In., Pair	3450.00
Wash Set, Lotus, Pink & Green, Dated 1865, 5 Piece	600.00

MOCHA pottery is an English-made product that was sold in America during the early 1800s. It is a heavy pottery with pale coffee-and-cream coloring. Designs of blue, brown, green, orange, black, or white were added to the pottery and given fanciful names, such as *Tree, Snail Trail,* or *Moss.*

Bowl, Blue Band, Black Stripes, Dark Earthworm Design, 6 1/4 In.	275.00
Bowl, Cover, Blue & White Stripes, Rope Twist Handles, 6 x 7 In.	385.00
Bowl, Cover, Wide Seaweed Band, 8 x 9 In.	395.00
Bowl, Exterior Wavy Double Line, Green Glazed Border, 1810, 7 3/8 In.	518.00
Bowl, Geometric Band, Leaf Handle, 2 3/4 x 4 1/4 In.	110.00
Bowl, Wavy Brown Line, Pearlware, 1810-1820, 7 3/8 In. .... *Illus*	520.00
Creamer, Blue-Green Striped, 4 In.	150.00
Creamer, Brown, Blue & White Stripes, Embossed White, 6 3/4 In.	140.00
Cup, Child's, Yellow	1095.00
Flower Pot, Earthworm, Blue, White & Ocher, 4 1/4 In., Pair	3190.00
Jug, Cat's-Eye, Earthworm & Dendrite	3800.00
Measure, Tankard, Blue Band, Teal Stripes, Leaf Handle, 6 1/4 In.	195.00
Mug, Banded Seaweed	450.00
Mug, Blue & Teal Bands, Black Seaweed, Stripes, 5 In.	357.00
Mug, Blue Earthworm	305.00
Mug, Brown Checkered Design, Dark Lines, Herringbone Border, c.1790, 6 In.	690.00
Mug, Brown Seaweed, Pumpkin Ground, 19th Century, 6 In.	467.00
Mug, England, 1820s, 5 1/2 In.	1320.00
Mug, Fan-Type Designs	2200.00
Mug, Molded Reeding, Stripes, Blue, Dark Brown & Mustard, 5 5/8 In.	115.00
Mug, Seaweed Design, England, 19th Century	468.00
Mug, Tan Bands, Black Stripes, Seaweed, Green Rim, Molded Leaf Handle, 6 In.	412.00
Mustard Pot, Blue & White Bands, Gold & Black Stripes, 4 In.	605.00
Mustard Pot, Green Glaze, Brown Vertical & Horizontal Stripes, Handle, 3 In.	95.00
Pitcher, Banded, 5 In.	160.00
Pitcher, Banded, 7 In.	440.00
Pitcher, Brown Greenish Gray & White Stripes, Earthworm Design, 6 3/4 In.	600.00
Pitcher, Double Worm, 7 1/2 In. .... *Illus*	440.00
Shaker, Blue Band, Black Stripes, Blue Ground, 4 7/8 In.	635.00
Shaker, Earthworm Design, Brown & Blue Stripes, 5 In.	632.50
Waste Bowl, Cat's Eyes Band, Pearlware, London Shape, 1820, 6 5/8 In. ...... *Illus*	575.00
Waste Bowl, Cat's Eyes Cluster, Pearlware, London Shape, 1810, 6 9/16 In. .... *Illus*	575.00

MONMOUTH Pottery Company started working in Monmouth, Illinois, in 1892. The pottery made a variety of utilitarian wares. It became part of Western Stoneware Company in 1906. The maple leaf mark was used until 1930. If *Co.* appears as part of the mark, the piece was made before 1906.

Jardiniere, Signed, 7 x 10 In.	60.00
Pitcher, Tan, Horizontal Ribbed, 5 1/2 In.	8.00
Vase, Aztec, Brown, 9 In.	95.00

MONT JOYE, see Mt. Joye

MOORCROFT pottery was first made in Burslem, England, in 1913. William Moorcroft had managed the art pottery department for James MacIntyre & Company of England from 1898 to 1913. The Moorcroft pottery continues today although William Moorcroft died in 1945. The earlier wares are similar to the modern ones, but color and marking will help indicate the age.

Basket, Pomegranates, Multicolor On Blue, Silver Plated Handle, 4 In. .... 375.00 to	425.00
Bowl, African Lily Pattern, Green To Blue Ground, Signed, 12 In.	220.00
Bowl, Cover, Pink & Purple Floral, Signed, 6 1/2 In.	300.00
Bowl, Eventide, 9 In.	2450.00
Bowl, Pomegranate, Sterling Silver Band, 5 1/2 x 6 In.	750.00
Cup, Cloisonne Medallion, 2 Handles, Signed, 5 1/4 x 7 In.	165.00
Ginger Jar, Anemone Pattern, Cobalt Blue Ground, Signed, 6 In.	220.00
Ginger Jar, Cover, Landscape, Teal, Green, Cobalt Blue, Cobridge Ware, 11 In.	4600.00
Jar, Condiment, Cloisonne With Poppies & Forget-Me-Nots, Plated Lid, 4 1/2 In.	550.00

Jar, Cover, African Lily Pattern, Red Blossoms, Signed, 3 3/4 x 3 1/2 In. 193.00
Jar, Cover, Queen Mary, Hibiscus-Like Flower, Paper Labels, 4 3/4 In. 275.00
Jar, Cover, Stylized Trees, Red Flambe, Egg-Shape, 10 1/2 In. 6325.00
Lamp, Baluster Form, Fruit Design, 23 In. 165.00
Lamp, Eventide, Landscape, Brass Fittings, c.1930, 14 1/4 In. 2420.00
Lamp, Orchid On Flambe, Paper Label, 10 1/2 In. 1500.00
Lamp, Orchid, 10 x 6 In., Pair 1350.00
Lamp, Pomegranate Pattern, Cobalt Blue Centers, Brown Foliage, 7 1/2 In. 220.00
Lamp Vase, Fuchsia Pattern, Cloisonne Blossoms, Silver Plated Mount, 11 In. 1000.00
Mug, Landscape & Sailboats 225.00
Urn, Berries, Large Leaves, Teal Shading To Green, Signed, 3 1/2 In. 185.00
Urn, Red & Purple Berries, Yellow Leaves, Green Ground, Signed, 3 1/2 In. 225.00
Vase, Anemone, 3 1/2 In. 95.00
Vase, Baluster Shape, Incised Iris, Green, Blue, Early 1900s, 16 1/4 In. 1955.00
Vase, Blue Flowers, Green Leaves, 4 In. 95.00
Vase, Eagle, Owl, 1988, 12 In. 495.00
Vase, Embossed Floral, Florian Ware, Initialed W.M., 5 5/8 In. 412.00
Vase, Fan-Shaped Trees, Blue-Green, 16 In. 4250.00
Vase, Florian Ware, Cloisonne Cornflowers, Sprays, c.1902, 5 1/4 In. 800.00
Vase, Florian Ware, Iris Blossoms, England, c.1900, 11 3/4 In. 1150.00
Vase, Iris, Cloisonne Blossoms, 3 3/4 In. 175.00
Vase, Magnolia Design, Cobalt Blue Ground, Marked, 4 1/8 In. 220.00
Vase, Multicolored Leaves, Grapes, Signed, 5 In. 245.00
Vase, Orchid Design, Blue Ground, Marked, 8 1/2 In. 425.00
Vase, Pink, White & Blue Floral, Green Ground, Marked, 5 In. 350.00
Vase, Pomegranate, Orange & Blue Fruit, Mottled Ground, 7 In. 440.00
Vase, Pomegranate, Signed, c.1915, 13 1/2 In. 495.00
Vase, Pomegranate, Sterling Silver Band & Rim, 12 In. 1100.00
Vase, Poppy, Cloisonne Blossoms, Paper Label, 6 In. 150.00
Vase, Rose, Ochre, Purple & Blue, Cobridge Ware, 12 5/8 In. 1725.00
Vase, Shaped Trees, Cloud-Like Foliage, 7 In. 4250.00
Vase, Trumpet, Wisteria, Dark Blue, Pewter Base, Tudric Ware, 7 1/4 In. 495.00
Vase, Tulip Design, Green & Gold, MacIntyre, 7 1/4 In. 1005.00
Vase, Wisteria, c.1920, 12 In. 850.00
Vase, Wisteria, Sterling Silver Rim, 4 1/2 In. 265.00

MORIAGE is a special type of raised decoration used on some Japanese
pottery. Sometimes pieces of clay were shaped by hand and applied to the
item; sometimes the clay was squeezed from a tube in the way we apply cake
frosting. One type of moriage is called *Dragonware* and is listed under that
name.

Butter, Holes In Bowl, Floral Band, 2 Piece 40.00
Cup & Saucer, Floral Medallions On Green, Footed 95.00
Humidor, Sailing Ships, Palm Trees 45.00
Plaque, Boat, Mountain, Trees, Marked, 7 1/2 In. 65.00
Sugar & Creamer, Medallions, Vines, Flowers, Marbleized 175.00
Vase, Enameled Flowers, Medallion Center, Flattened Oval, 4 1/2 In. 65.00
Vase, Poppy & Butterfly, 9 1/2 In. 375.00

MOSAIC TILE Company of Zanesville, Ohio, was started by Karl
Langerbeck and Herman Mueller in 1894. Many types of plain and
ornamental tiles were made until 1959. The company closed in 1967. The
company also made some ashtrays, bookends, and related giftwares. Most
pieces are marked with the entwined *MTC* monogram.

Box, Cover, Brown Metallic Glaze, Dog Resting On Cover, 8 x 4 In. 154.00
Figurine, Bear, 10 In. 295.00
Figurine, Buffalo, White, 13 1/4 In. 395.00
Figurine, German Shepherd, Lying, Tan, 10 1/2 x 6 In. 95.00
Hot Plate, Nantucket Island, Map, Brown On Ivory, 6 x 6 In. 25.00
Paperweight, General Pershing 40.00
Paperweight, Lincoln 35.00
Paperweight, World Globe, Light Green, 4 In. 35.00
Plaque, Franklin D. Roosevelt, 12 In. 295.00

Moser, Perfume Bottle, Cobalt Blue, Enamel Design, Atomizer, 1920, 5 1/2 x 4 In.

◆◆◆◆◆◆◆◆◆◆◆◆◆◆◆◆◆◆◆◆◆◆

Graniteware pieces made in the 1950s were lighter in weight, brighter in color than early 19th century wares. The finish is smoother on old pieces. Most 1930s and after teapots and coffeepots had hinged lids and the handles were attached very close to the top of the pots.

◆◆◆◆◆◆◆◆◆◆◆◆◆◆◆◆◆◆◆◆◆◆

Tile, Betsy Ross, 6 x 9 In.		35.00
Tile, General Pershing, Blue Basalt, White Bust, Oval		65.00
Tile, Pilgrims, Miniature		25.00

MOSER glass is made by Ludwig Moser und Sohne, a Bohemian glasshouse founded in 1857. Art Nouveau-type glassware and iridescent glassware were made. The most famous Moser glass is decorated with heavy enameling in gold and bright colors. The firm is still working in Czechoslovakia. Few pieces of Moser glass are marked.

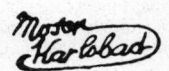

Box, Dresser, Brass Mount, Enameled Desire, 1900-1915		450.00
Box, Jewelry, Hinged Cover, Green, Gold Trim, 3 Footed		250.00
Centerpiece, Intaglio Cut Flowers, Green, 5 x 9 In.		425.00
Cologne Bottle, Cut Glass, Pink, Clear Faceted Stopper, Signed		695.00
Cordial Set, Decanter, Tray, Applied Acorns, Enameled Leaves, 6 Piece		1320.00
Cup & Saucer, Gold Scrolls, Multicolored Flowers, Amber		295.00
Decanter, Enameled Flowers, White Overlay, White, Pair		300.00
Decanter, Oval Panel, Gold Outlining, Scrolls & Branches, 11 In.		225.00
Decanter Set, Molded With Nude Women, Frosted, Smoky Topaz, 5 Piece		250.00
Decanter Set, Stemmed Liqueur Goblets, 7 Piece		895.00
Dish, Trinket, Polar Bears, Clear & Frosted, Signed		85.00
Ewer, Clear Opalescent, Blue Pedestal, Enameled, Signed		130.00
Finger Bowl, Leaf Scrolls & Lattice Design, Signed, 4 1/2 In.		160.00
Glass, Juice, Allover Multicolor Florals & Gold, Amber		85.00
Lamp, Enameled Flowers, Hanging Crystals, White Overlay, Green, 19 In.		450.00
Paperweight, Kissing Doves, Signed		125.00
Perfume Bottle, Amethyst, Angular Facets, Cut Crystal Stopper, 3 3/4 In.		165.00
Perfume Bottle, Cobalt Blue, Enamel Design, Atomizer, 1920, 5 1/2 x 4 In. .... *Illus*		275.00
Pitcher, Bladder Form, Apricot Handle, Allover Enameled, 7 In.		505.00
Pitcher, Enameled Flowers & Scrolls, Gilded, Red, 4 3/4 In.		700.00
Pitcher, Inverted Thumbprint, Bunches Of Grapes, Pinched Spout, 6 3/4 In.		3025.00
Pitcher, Oriental, With 2 Goblets, Pedestal, 3 Piece		1295.00
Pokal, Cover, Gold Enamel & Gilding, Leaf Design, 17 1/2 In.		1400.00
Rose Bowl, Gold Traced Branches & Leaves, Pedestal, Footed, 11 In.		175.00
Rose Bowl, Rainbow Mother-Of-Pearl		700.00
Scent Bottle, Enameled		495.00
Sherbet, Green, Pedestal, Gilded, Small Flowers, Underplate, 3 1/4 x 4 1/2 In.		475.00
Tankard, Apple Green To Clear, Intaglio Cut Poppy, Crystal Handle, 12 1/4 In.		765.00
Toothpick, Allover Gold Scrolled Leaves, Cranberry, 2 1/2 In.		225.00
Toothpick, Malachite, Cherubs		225.00
Vase, Applied Blue Glass Fish, Enameled Flowers, Signed, 6 1/2 In.		500.00
Vase, Applied Hawk, Glass, Victorian, Tall		4800.00
Vase, Blue & Gold Enameled Panels, 6 In.		195.00
Vase, Cranberry Glass, Bird, Acorns & Leaves, Gilded Feet, 4 In.		760.00
Vase, Diamond Point, Gold Angelfish, Seaweed, Signed, 8 1/2 In.		275.00
Vase, Elephants & Palm Trees, Cobalt Blue, Double Marked, 8 1/4 In.		3995.00
Vase, Enameled Flowers & Berries, Cranberry, 4 1/2 In.		625.00

Vase, Enameled Flowers, Hanging Crystals, White Overlay, Cranberry, 12 In. 450.00
Vase, Enameled Mums, Green Shaded To Clear, Ribbed, 12 In. 395.00
Vase, Flowers & Leaves, Green Tinged, Signed, c.1900, 6 3/4 In. 805.00
Vase, Flowers Enameled, Gold Trim, Cranberry, 2 1/4 In. 225.00
Vase, Gold Angelfish, c.1950, 8 In. 235.00
Vase, Gold Butterfly & Grape Florals, Thorn Handle 375.00
Vase, Gold Filigree Enameled, Green To Clear, 9 In. 175.00
Vase, Gold Medallions, Raised Enameled Beading, Cranberry, 9 In. 450.00
Vase, Greek Warriors, Signed, 8 In. 675.00
Vase, Pendant Leaves, Egg-Shape, Signed, 2 3/4 In. 150.00
Vase, Trumpet Shape, Bronze Ormolu Base, Signed, 30 In. 910.00
Vase, Tulip & Leaves Both Sides, Gold Trim, 12 1/2 In. 225.00
Vase, Violet, White Enameled Figure, 6 In. 195.00
Water Set, Gold Design, Crystal, 9-1/4 In. Pitcher, 7 Piece 965.00
Water Set, Wisteria Blossoms, Petals, 24K Gold Enameled, Presentation, 5 Piece 5500.00
Whiskey, Cranberry Cut To Clear 50.00
Whiskey, Flowers In Paperweight Bottom, Gilded Cocks 195.00
Wine, Intaglio Florals, Gold Enameled, Cranberry, 6 Piece 1200.00
Wine, Purple To Clear, Pair 500.00

MOSS ROSE china was made by many firms from 1808 to 1900. It has a
typical moss rose pictured as the design. The plant is not as popular now as it
was in Victorian gardens, so the fuzz-covered bud is unfamiliar to most
collectors. The dishes were usually decorated with pink and green flowers.

Bowl, Pedestal, Gold Rim, 9 3/4 x 5 In. 20.00
Cake Plate, Gold Trim, Pierced Handle 65.00
Cigarette Set, Rosenthal, 4-In. Underplate 24.00
Cup & Saucer 22.00
Dinner Set, Rosenthal, Germany, 47 Piece 625.00
Plate, Luncheon 15.00
Sugar, Cover, Ironstone 45.00
Sugar, Domed Lid, Rope Handle 65.00
Tea Set, Child's, Service For 6 .... 200.00
Tea Set, Fancy Handles & Footed, Demitasse, 15 Piece 75.00
Teapot, Blank, Scrolled Shoulder 15.00

MOTHER-OF-PEARL GLASS, or pearl satin glass, was first made in the
1850s in England and in Massachusetts. It was a special type of mold-blown
satin glass with air bubbles in the glass, giving it a pearlized color. It has been
reproduced. Mother-of-pearl shell objects are listed under Pearl.

Bowl, Tricorn, Looped Feet, Frosted Rim, Blue, 4 1/4 In. 335.00
Box, Heart Shape, Iridescent, Hand Wrought, 1950s 25.00
Brides Basket, Ruffled Ormolu Base, 14 In. 595.00
Card Tray, Diamond-Quilted, Pie-Crust Edge, Gilt Stand, Blue, 10 In. 665.00
Creamer, Raindrop, Frosted Blue Handle, White Interior, 4 1/2 In. 225.00
Cup & Saucer, Shell Shaped Cup, Swirl Pattern Saucer, Pink To Amber 250.00
Dish, Sweetmeat, Ribbon, Green 595.00
Ewer, Frilly Spout, Thorn Handle, Pink, 8 1/2 In. 385.00
Ewer, Herringbone, Pink, Ruffled Spout, Thorn Handles, 8 1/2 In. 385.00
Fairy Lamp, Herringbone, Canary To White, Ball Shade, Birds, 5 1/4 In. 1750.00
Pitcher, Diamond-Quilted, Camphor Handle, Oval Shape, 6 In. 385.00
Pitcher, Rain Spot Pattern, Frosted Handle, Ruffled, Blue, 6 3/4 In. 275.00
Rose Bowl, 3-Crimp Top, Frosted Foot, 3 x 2 3/4 In. 225.00
Rose Bowl, Herringbone, 4-Crimp Top, White Interior, 3 1/4 In. 165.00
Scent Bottle, White, Dora On Sterling Cap, 4 In. Diam. 535.00
Sugar Shaker, Herringbone, Blue, Brass Fittings, 6 1/4 In. 650.00
Sugar Shaker, Raindrop Pattern, Silver Plated Top, Blue, 6 1/4 In. 415.00
Tumbler, Herringbone, Rose On Upper Portion, White Base, 2 7/8 In. 185.00
Tumbler, Raindrop, Blue 135.00
Vase, Blue, Coralene Design, 6 1/4 In. 350.00
Vase, Coin Spot, Pink To Pristine White, Bulbous Base, 3 1/2 x 2 In. 325.00
Vase, Diamond Pattern, Yellow, Ruffled 95.00
Vase, Diamond-Quilted Pattern, Rose Pink, 7 1/4 x 4 1/2 In. 175.00

◆◆◆◆◆◆◆◆◆◆◆◆◆◆◆◆◆◆◆◆◆◆◆

If you have a small-neck decanter or bottle that doesn't seem to dry after it is washed, try putting a small amount of rubbing alcohol in the bottle. Shake, pour out, and wait for the remaining drops to evaporate.

◆◆◆◆◆◆◆◆◆◆◆◆◆◆◆◆◆◆◆◆◆◆◆

Mt. Washington, Pitcher, Mother-Of-Pearl, Ribbed, Blue to White, 8 3/4 In.

Vase, Diamond-Quilted, Blush Pink, Slender, 10 In.	275.00
Vase, Diamond-Quilted, Deep Apricot, 7 In.	225.00
Vase, Diamond-Quilted, Ruffled Rim, 5 1/2 In.	175.00
Vase, Herringbone, Flared Ruffled Rim, Blue, 6 3/4 In.	100.00
Vase, Herringbone, Gourd Shape, Clear Threading, 8 In.	450.00
Vase, Hobnail, Folded-In Sides, 5 3/4 In.	500.00
Vase, Pinched Sides, Rolled Rim, Rose Pink, 5 In.	425.00
Vase, Raindrop, Ruffled, White Interior, Green, 4 1/2 x 3 1/8 In.	195.00
Vase, Ruffled Top, Ormolu Feet, Satin Finish, 6 3/4 In.	450.00
Vase, Stick, Herringbone, Gourd Shape, 8 x 2 1/2 x 5 In.	450.00
Vase, Swirl Design, Square Folded Rim, Pink, 8 1/4 In.	175.00
Vase, Tiers Of Air Traps, 7 1/2 In.	285.00

MOUNT WASHINGTON, see Mt. Washington

MT. JOYE is an enameled cameo glass made in the late nineteenth and the twentieth centuries by Saint-Hilaire Touvier de Varraux and Co. of Pantin, France. This same company made De Vez glass. Pieces were usually decorated with enameling. Most pieces are not marked.

Bowl, Turned-In Rim, Enamel Iris, Glass Footed, 7 In.	435.00
Vase, Cameo Cut Flowers, Gold & Green, Hammered Amber Ground, 6 1/2 In.	595.00
Vase, Enameled Peony, Cameo, Signed, 8 1/2 In.	220.00
Vase, Pigeon Blood, Enameled, Signed, 11 In.	275.00
Vase, Stem & Blossoms, Green Cased, White, Enameled Gilt, Globular, 20 In.	690.00

MT. WASHINGTON Glass Works started in 1837 in South Boston, Massachusetts. In 1870 the company moved to New Bedford, Massachusetts. Many types of art glass were made there until 1894, when the company merged with Pairpoint Manufacturing Co. Amberina, Burmese, Crown Milano, Cut Glass, Peachblow, and Royal Flemish are each listed in their own category.

Biscuit Jar, Melon Ribbed, Butterfly, Blossoms, Clear, 6 1/4 x 6 1/2 In.	650.00
Biscuit Jar, Pink Floral, White Ground	350.00
Biscuit Jar, Silver Plated Lid & Bail, Butterfly, Branches, 6 x 6 1/2 In.	650.00
Bottle, Bitters, Cut Glass, Blank, Sterling Silver Top, 5 1/2 In.	195.00
Bowl, Peppermint Stick, 9 In.	120.00
Box, Blown-Out Flower On Lid, 8 1/4 In.	1495.00
Cologne Bottle, Blown Stopper, Lusterless White, 10 In.	150.00
Flower Bowl, Pillow Shape, Diamond-Quilted, Yellow Rim, 4 1/2 In.	275.00
Flower Bowl, Raised Diamond-Quilted, Pillow, 4 1/2 x 4 In.	295.00
Ice Tub, Russian With Single Star, Tab Handles, c.1870	425.00
Jar, Cover, Rose, Lusterless Glass, 6 In.	55.00
Lemonade Set, Egyptian Style Pitcher, Square Handles, 7 Piece	2250.00
Mustard, Flowers, Ribbed, Metal Lid	300.00
Perfume Bottle, Bell Shape, Birds & Florals, Steeple Stopper, 6 In.	295.00
Perfume Bottle, Daisy Design, Silver Stopper	525.00
Pickle Castor, Albertine, Pink To White, Star, Pairpoint Frame, 8 1/2 In.	1125.00
Pitcher, Hobnail, Glossy Finish, Loop Handle, Burmese, 6 In.	1450.00

Pitcher, Mother-Of-Pearl, Ribbed, Blue to White, 8 3/4 In. .... *Illus*   495.00
Powder Box, Pairpoint Lid, 3 x 5 1/2 In. .... 225.00 to 275.00
Rose Bowl, 12 Protruding Fingers, Pansies, White Ground, 4 In. 285.00
Rose Bowl, Verona, Pond Lilies, Brown & Gold 300.00
Saltshaker, Brownie, Beaded Corners, Square 195.00
Saltshaker, Egg In Blossom 110.00
Saltshaker, Egg In Cup, Band Of Red Berries, Leaves Around Body 110.00
Saltshaker, Lobe, Yellow 175.00
Saltshaker, Pillar, Tapered, Cranberry 125.00
Sugar Caster, Flowers, Blue & Pink, Satin Glass, Ostrich Egg Shape 250.00
Sugar Caster, Violets, Egg Shape 450.00
Sugar Shaker, Spider Mums, Yellow & White 295.00
Toothpick, Melon Sectioned, Blue Flowers, Yellow Centers, 2 1/4 In. 110.00
Vase, Black, Lava Glass, Bulbous, Handles, Colorful Interior, 5 3/4 In. 2250.00
Vase, Cherubs At Knee Of Half Naked Woman, Gold Tracery, 9 /12 In. 850.00
Vase, Lily, Burmese, Forget-Me-Nots, 8 In. 975.00
Vase, Pinched Scalloped Rim, 6 Feet, Ostrich-Egg Shape, 7 In. 395.00
Vase, Verona, Raised Parrot Tulips, Raised Gold & Green Leaves, 9 In. 350.00

MUD FIGURES are small Chinese pottery figures made in the twentieth century.
The figures usually represent workers, scholars, farmers, or merchants. Other
pieces are trees, houses, and similar parts of the landscape. The figures have
unglazed faces and hands but glazed clothing. They were originally made for
fish tanks or planters. Mud figures were of little interest and brought low prices
until the 1980s. When the prices rose, reproductions appeared.

Chinaman, Seated, 9 In. 165.00
Fish In Basket 40.00
Lady, Carrying Water & Basket, China, 6 1/2 In. 125.00
Man, 3 1/2 In. 35.00
Man, 5 In. 45.00
Man, Dish In Hand, Large Hat 60.00
Man, Emerald Green Glazed Robe, 10 In. 35.00
Old Man, With Fishing Pole, Hat On Back, Signed, 6 In. 85.00
Woman, Copper Glaze Dress, 12 In. 40.00

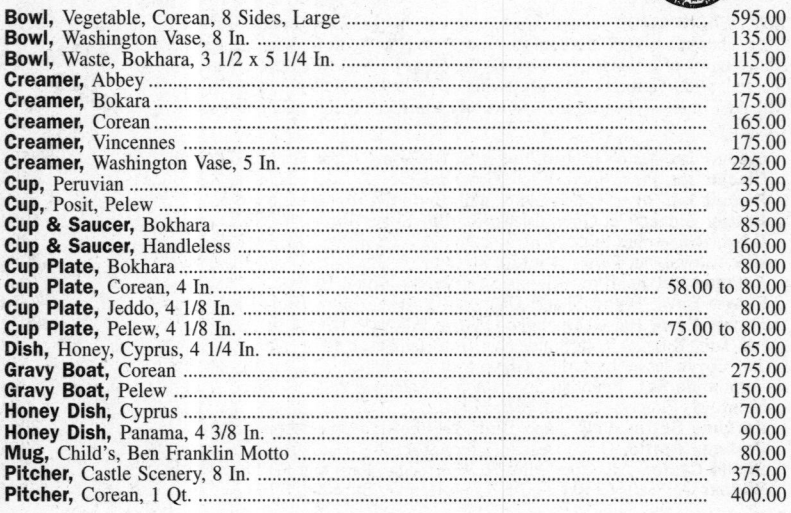

MULBERRY ware was made in the Staffordshire district of England from
about 1850 to 1860. The dishes were decorated with a reddish brown transfer
design, now called *mulberry.* Many of the patterns are similar to those used
for flow blue and other Staffordshire transfer wares.

Bowl, Vegetable, Corean, 8 Sides, Large 595.00
Bowl, Washington Vase, 8 In. 135.00
Bowl, Waste, Bokhara, 3 1/2 x 5 1/4 In. 115.00
Creamer, Abbey 175.00
Creamer, Bokara 175.00
Creamer, Corean 165.00
Creamer, Vincennes 175.00
Creamer, Washington Vase, 5 In. 225.00
Cup, Peruvian 35.00
Cup, Posit, Pelew 95.00
Cup & Saucer, Bokhara 85.00
Cup & Saucer, Handleless 160.00
Cup Plate, Bokhara 80.00
Cup Plate, Corean, 4 In. .... 58.00 to 80.00
Cup Plate, Jeddo, 4 1/8 In. 80.00
Cup Plate, Pelew, 4 1/8 In. .... 75.00 to 80.00
Dish, Honey, Cyprus, 4 1/4 In. 65.00
Gravy Boat, Corean 275.00
Gravy Boat, Pelew 150.00
Honey Dish, Cyprus 70.00
Honey Dish, Panama, 4 3/8 In. 90.00
Mug, Child's, Ben Franklin Motto 80.00
Pitcher, Castle Scenery, 8 In. 375.00
Pitcher, Corean, 1 Qt. 400.00

MULBERRY, Pi

Pitcher, Corean, 7 1/2 In. .... 375.00 to 435.00
Pitcher, Cyprus, 8 1/8 In. 325.00
Pitcher, Jeddo, 12 In. 395.00
Pitcher, Nan, 8 In. 315.00
Pitcher, Nan, 8 1/2 In. 365.00
Pitcher, I, Corean, Paneled, 12 3/8-In. Bowl 650.00
Platter, 4 1/4 In. 55.00
Plate, 8 In. 38.00
Plate, 9 In. 45.00
Platter, 10 3/4 In. 85.00
Platter, 9 In. 32.00
Platter, 10 1/2 In. 85.00
Platter, 1/4 In. 55.00
Platter, 1/4 In. 70.00
Platter, Scenery, 4 1/4 In. 55.00
Platter, 1/2 In. 60.00
Platter, Podmore Walker, 9 In. 45.00
Platter, ton Vase, 7 3/4 In. 55.00
Platter, ton Vase, 10 In. 55.00
Platter, ton Vase, 16 x 12 3/8 In. 250.00
Platter, swick, Polychrome, 17 In. 350.00
Platter, asan, Adams, 15 1/4 x 11 3/4 In. 300.00
Platter, Corean, 13 x 17 In. .... 245.00 to 350.00
Platter, Corean, 18 1/4 x 14 1/4 In. 395.00
Platter, Incennes, 15 1/2 x 11 3/4 In. 265.00
Platter, Jeddo, 15 1/2 x 12 In. 225.00
Platter, Pelew, 10 x 7 1/2 In. 125.00
Platter, Peru, 13 1/8 x 10 1/8 In. 155.00
Platter, Temple, 10 7/8 x 8 1/4 In. 125.00
Platter, Tonquin, 10 3/4 In. 100.00
Platter, Udina, Ironstone, 14 1/4 x 18 In. 195.00
Platter, Vincennes, 15 1/2 x 11 3/4 In. .... 250.00 to 265.00
Platter, Vincennes, 17 1/2 x 13 7/8 In. 350.00
Platter, Washington Vase, 16 x 12 1/4 In. 150.00
Relish, Bokhara 250.00
Sauceboat, Fish, Handle, Walker, Pair 325.00
Soup, Dish, Cyprus, 10 1/2 In. 90.00
Soup Dish, Jenny Lind, Staffordshire, 7 7/8 In. 6.00
Sugar, Bokara 300.00
Sugar, Castle Scenery, Furnival 275.00
Sugar, Corean, Cover 300.00
Sugar, Cyprus, Cover 195.00
Sugar, Hyson, Clementson 275.00
Sugar, Jeddo, Cover 225.00
Sugar, Washington Vase, Cover, Lion's Handle 275.00
Sugar & Creamer, Abbey, Cover 325.00
Teapot, Bokara 425.00
Teapot, Corean .... 425.00 to 650.00
Teapot, Jeddo .... 450.00 to 650.00
Teapot, Rhone Scenery 650.00
Teapot, Temple 425.00
Teapot, Washington Vase 525.00
Waste Bowl, Bokhara, 5 1/4 In. 115.00

MULLER FRERES, French for Muller Brothers, made cameo and other glass from the early 1900s to the late 1930s. Their factory was first located in Luneville, then in nearby Croismaire, France. Pieces were usually marked with the company name.

Bowl, Light, Half-Round, Mottled Yellow, Orange Blue, 3 Chains, 12 In. 415.00
Bowl, Light, Half-Round, Orange, Blue, Red, Hanging Ring Mount, 15 1/2 In. 825.00
Bowl, River Scene, Gray, Green, Raspberry, Purple, Cameo, 1920, 10 In. 2875.00
Box, Orange & Purple, Etched Red Currants, Oval, Cover, Signed, 7 In. 1610.00
Chandelier, Center Shade, 6 Cylinder Shades, Wrought Iron, 1925, 40 In. 2300.00

Chandelier, Floriform Mount, 3 Shades, Signed, Iron & Glass, 1925, 16 In.
Ewer, Shepherdess, Enameled Frieze, Clear, Cameo, 8 In. ....
Lamp, 3-Light, Poppy Blossoms & Leaves, Metal, Signed, 1925, 13 In. ....
Lamp, Boudoir, Art Glass Shade, Orange & Green, Gilt Metal Base, 23 In. ......
Lamp, Egg-Shaped Dome, Rural Scene, Mountains, Pearl Sky & Lake, 12 In. ...
Lamp, Hanging, Conical Shade, Frosted, Ribbed, 3 Peach Cords, 1930, 14 In. ....
Vase, Blossoms, Trumpet Vines, Sea Green, Gray Ground, Cameo, 11 1/2 In. ....
Vase, Concentric Arches, Internal Silver Foil, Signed, 8 In. ....
Vase, Cream Sheep, Pumpkin Ground, Cameo, 1920, 6 1/4 In. ....
Vase, Cylindrical, Eggplant Cased, Etched Flutes, Silver Foil Interior, 9 In. ....
Vase, Enamel Crocus Blossoms, Buds, Leaves, Signed, c.1915, 6 In. ....
Vase, Etched & Enameled Berries, Signed, 8 1/2 In. ....
Vase, Etched Butterflies, Foil Inclusion Interior, Signed, 13 3/4 In. ....
Vase, Mottled Brown & Orange, Bulbous Tapering Body, Marked ....
Vase, Mottled Mustard, Tangerine Streaks, Tortoiseshell Border, 1925, 9 In. ....
Vase, Mottled Orange & Blue, 6 In. 3
Vase, Mountain Lake Scene, Frosted Ground, Spherical, Signed, 10 In. 299
Vase, Olive Marguerite Blossoms, Clear, Cameo, 1910, 6 3/8 In. 1438
Vase, Shades Of Orange, Gold Ground, 13 1/2 In. 4500
Vase, Thorny Roses, Gray, Peach, Yellow, Red, Cameo, 1920, 19 1/2 In. 4025.0
Vase, White Peony Blossoms, Gray, Turquoise Ground, Cameo, 5 3/4 In. 2013.0
Vase, Wooded River Scene, Etched, Mottled Ground, Signed, 8 In. 1012.00
Vase, Yellow, Mottled Blue, 6 1/2 x 6 In. 600.00

MUNCIE Clay Products Company was established by Charles Benham in
Muncie, Indiana, in 1922. The company made pottery for the florist and
giftshop trade. The company closed by 1939. Pieces are marked with the
name *Muncie* or just with a system of numbers and letters, like *1A*.

Figurine, Canoe, Green To Lavender, 11 1/2 In. 90.00
Lamp, Lovebirds, 8 In. 115.00
Vase, Glossy White, Signed, 5 In. 65.00
Vase, Handles, Pink, 10 In. 30.00

MURANO, see Glass-Venetian

MUSIC boxes and musical instruments are listed here. Phonograph records,
jukeboxes, phonographs, and sheet music are listed in other categories in this
book.

Accordion, Brut-Piccolo, Box, Early 1900s 95.00
Accordion, Tanzbar, Player 850.00
Accordion, Tanzbar, Roll Operated, 7 Rolls 950.00
Autoharp, Zimmermann 110.00
Band Box, Model W/7, 7 Monkeys, Germany 2500.00
Banjo, Concertone, 4 Strings, Case 180.00
Banjo, Kay, 5 Strings 125.00
Banjo, North Carolina, 1890 .... 225.00
Banjo Ukulele, Bruno, Bird's-Eye Maple 130.00
Baton, Conductor's, Telescoping, 19th Century 65.00
Box, Bird, Boy & Girl With Dog, Gilt Metal, c.1890, 4 In. 1840.00
Box, Bird, Cityscapes On Sides & Cover, Green Ground, 19th Century, 4 1/8 In. 2300.00
Box, Bird, Watch, Green, Scroll Supports, Silver Gilt & Enamel, 4 1/4 In. 3450.00
Box, Dancing Maiden, Countryside Scene, Windmill Blades Rotate, Handmade 650.00
Box, Empress, Parlor Grand, Lion Paw Feet, Tin Disc, 41 x 26 In. 3360.00
Box, Harmonia, 10 Metal Discs, 16 x 12 x 6 In. 5000.00
Box, Hinged Cover, 11-In. Brass Roll 1650.00
Box, Imperial Symphonion, Double Comb, 12 Discs 3900.00
Box, Komet, Coin-Operated, Painted Front Glass, 16 Discs 3500.00
Box, Langdorf & Fils, Burl Walnut & Inlaid 5750.00
Box, Mira, Matching Storage Cabinet, 18 1/2-In. Disc 7500.00
Box, Organ Grinder, Oak, Uniflute Caviou & Cie., S.C.D.G., Paris 4125.00
Box, Orphenion, Storage Drawer, Tabletop 3200.00
Box, Polyphone, 1 1/2 Comb, Tabletop, 15 1/2 In. 3895.00

MUSIC, Box

2185.00
7475.00
2875.00
385.00
...0.00
...?

MUNCIE

Music, Box, Symphonion, Mahogany, 30 x 39 x 24 In.

Music, Gong, Gamewell Excelsior, Wooden Case, Windup Key, 6-In. Diam.

Box, Regina, Citerior, Carved Mahogany Case, 66 Discs, 10 1/2 x 21 In. 5720.00
Box, Regina, Coin-Operated, Double Comb, Oak, 5 Cents, 22 In. 4290.00
Box, Regina, Dual Comb, Mahogany, Tabletop, 15 1/2 In. 3995.00
Box, Regina, Duplex Combs, Coin-Operated, 1 Cent, 10 Discs, c.1900 .... 4290.00
Box, Regina, Oak, 12 Discs, 1895, 14 x 13 In. 1650.00
Box, Regina, Oak, Double Comb, Plays 15 1/2-In. Disc, 1896, 22 In. 3740.00
Box, Reginaphone, Mahogany, 15-Tune Disks 4400.00
Box, Rococo, Lacquer, Ivory, 150th Anniversary Mozart's Death, 11 1/2 In. 880.00
Box, Singing Bird, Alpine Scene On Cover, Continental Silver & Enamel, 3 3/4 In. ... 5750.00
Box, Singing Bird, Bird Cage, Brass Cage 3500.00
Box, Singing Bird, In Cage, Windup, Germany, 11 x 8 In. 225.00
Box, Snoopy & Woodstock, Plays Release Me, Ceramic, 1980s 45.00
Box, Snoopy, Astronaut, On Doghouse 65.00
Box, Snoopy, Plays Over There, Schmid, 1963 .... 85.00
Box, Sonora, 4 Keys Play Bells, Oak, 1908 .... 225.00
Box, Stella, Mahogany Veneer, Upright, 35 Discs, 25 1/2-In. Discs 6050.00
Box, Swiss, 6 Tunes, Cylinder & Single Comb, Tune Card, 4 x 11 In. 715.00
Box, Swiss, 10 Tunes, Card, Rosewood, Round, 9 5/8 In. 247.00
Box, Swiss, 10 Tunes, Inlaid Satinwood, Single Comb, 9 x 22 In. 880.00
Box, Swiss, 12 Tunes, Inlaid, Cylinder & Single Comb, Tune Card, 7 x 26 In. 1760.00
Box, Swiss, 12 Tunes, Instrument Inlaid On Lid, 1896, 6 1/2 x 21 In. 1050.00
Box, Swiss, Cylinder, Enameled Bell Striker, 17 x 10 x 8 In. 1450.00
Box, Symphonion, Clock In Top, Double Comb, Coin-Operated, Table Model 7500.00
Box, Symphonion, Mahogany, 30 x 39 x 24 In. .... *Illus* 6500.00
Box, Tournaphone, 10 Tunes, Enameled Butterflies, Bells 2250.00
Box, Vienna, Cabinet, With Pipe Organs, Enameled Drawers, Scenic Panels, Gilt 2850.00
Concert Harp, Hohner, Box, 9 In. 65.00
Concertina, Mother-Of-Pearl Keys, Brass Fret Work, Czechoslovakia 125.00
Drum, Field, 19th Century 250.00
Dulcimer, North Carolina, 1890 .... 850.00
Gong, Gamewell Excelsior, Wooden Case, Windup Key, 6-In. Diam. .... *Illus* 715.00
Guitar, Concert, Spanish, Rosewood, Mosaic Edge, Enrique Sanfelui, 1930, 25 In. 1495.00
Guitar, Electric, Zephyr, Maple Body, Celluloid Binding, Epiphone Inc., 1956 .... 680.00
Guitar, Gibson, Arch-Top, Model L-7, 1937 .... 2000.00
Guitar, Gibson, Model L-75, 1935 .... 1500.00
Guitar, Kent, Mother-Of-Pearl Inlay, Case 125.00
Harmonica, Blue & Silver Box, Prewar Germany 45.00
Harmonica, Blue Ribbon, Germany, Box 21.00

Harmonica, Hohner Chromatic 69.00
Harmonica, Hohner Marine Band .... 9.00 to 12.50
Harmonica, Hohner Orchestra, Inner Wrapper 20.00
Harmonica, Hohner, 64 Chromonica, Brown Plastic Case 45.00
Harmonica, Hohner, Hoosier Boy, Herb Shriner 75.00
Harmonica, Opera, Germany, c.1950, 6 1/2 In. 18.00
Harmonica, Tremolo Concert Harp, 4 Keys, 192 Reeds 145.00
Harp, Sebastian Erand, 1820s 4500.00
Hurdy-Gurdy, Child's, Painted, Cart, 6 Tunes, Faventia 240.00
Mandolin Harp, 32 Strings, Eagle & Gold Leaf, Yendrice & Co., c.1921 .... 250.00
Mandolin, Inlay Abalone, Ivory & Tortoiseshell, 1897, 24 In. 165.00
Mandolin, St. Louis, 1904 .... 125.00
Mandolin, W.A. Cole, Various Woods, Ivory & Mother-of-Pearl Inlay, Case, 1893 ..... 235.00
Melodeon, Folding Legs, Rosewood 500.00
Melodeon, Philot & Camp, 4 Stops, 72 Keys, 1875 .... 1200.00
Metronome, Mahogany, Paquet, France 75.00
Metronome, Seth Thomas, Box 75.00
Nickelodeon, Engelhardt, Piano, With Xylophone, Stained Glass, Oak 5500.00
Nickelodeon, Seeburg, Dog Sled 7495.00
Nickelodeon, Wurlitzer, Model IXB 2000.00
Nickelodeon, Wurlitzer, Original Art Glass, 1912 .... 7500.00
Orchestration, Piano, Triangle, Cymbals & Drum, 2 Discs, Coin-Operated 5600.00
Organ, Aeolian Duo Art, Orchestrelle Player, Mahogany, Folds, 200 Rolls, 1900 .... 4400.00
Organ, Beckwith, Oak 650.00
Organ, Kimball, Pump 1000.00
Organ, Mason & Hamlin, Pump 210.00
Organ, Moller, Art Deco Console, 2 Built-In Cabinets, 145 Rolls 6500.00
Organ, Monkey, Harmonipan Style 4500.00
Organ, Pipe, Seeburg, 120 Wood & Metal Pipes, 2 Keyboards, Rolls, Blower 3500.00
Organ, Player, Moller, Art Deco Console, 2 Roll Cabinets, 145 Boxed Rolls 6500.00
Organ, Player, Orchestrelle 6900.00
Organ, Player, Wangerin, Plays 88 Note Rolls, 47 Rolls 700.00
Organ, Pump, 36-Note Keyboard, Couplers, Mirror, Ferrand & Votey, 79 In. 800.00
Organ, Pump, Hamilton, Beveled Mirrors, Walnut Case, Claw Footed Stool, 1900 ..... 5000.00
Organ, Pump, Packard, 72 Keys, 11 Stops, Oak Case 750.00
Organ, Reed, Aeolian, Orchestrelle, Player, Mahogany, Folding Keyboard, 1900s 4400.00
Organ, Roller, Little Gem 800.00
Organ, Seybold, Church, Reed Pipe, Oak 995.00
Organ, Street, Gasparini, 52 Keys, Holland 8500.00
Orthophonic, Victor, Spring Driven, Gold Plated Accessories, Walnut 1000.00
Piano, Ainsley, Dynatone, Built-In Phonograph & Radio, Art Deco Case 200.00
Piano, Apollo, Push-Up, 58 Note, Player 2000.00
Piano, Arlington Piano, Grand, Cherry Wood, Boston, 1840-1860 .... 4500.00
Piano, Chickering, No. 180364, Baby Grand, Mahogany Case, Bench, 5 Ft. 1320.00
Piano, Chickering & Sons, Baby Grand, 1941 .... 1430.00
Piano, Cohler & Cambell, Upright, 1930s 300.00
Piano, Coinola, Player, Upright, Oak Case, Stained Glass Panels, 63 1/2 In. 4125.00
Piano, Exceltone, Chase-Hackley, Player .... 800.00 to 1000.00
Piano, Franklin Ampico, Player, Baby Grand 1800.00
Piano, Gulbronsen, Player, Electric, Walnut Finish, Roll Cabinet, Rolls 2000.00
Piano, John Broadwood & Sons, Oyster Walnut Veneer, 1870, 37 x 57 x 103 In. 3750.00
Piano, Joseph Brodmann, Forte, Vienna, c.1810 .... 6900.00
Piano, Karnish & Bach, Player, Manual Or Electric, 1915 .... 2295.00
Piano, Kurtzmann, Grand, 1885 .... 6000.00
Piano, Lindeman & Sons, Rosewood, 82 Keys, Square, 1861 .... 7000.00
Piano, M.H. Baillie Scott, Upright, c.1898 .... 7150.00
Piano, Marshall & Wendell, Ampico, Upright 3500.00
Piano, Mason & Hamlin, Baby Grand, 38 x 74 In. 5280.00
Piano, Mason & Hamlin, Baby Grand, Bench, Ebonized 5520.00
Piano, Melville Clark, Art-Apollo, Player, Mirror, 400 Rolls, Walnut 2500.00
Piano, Milton, Player, Electrified, Octaves & Climate Control, Burl Walnut 4000.00
Piano, Milton, Player, Mandolin Attachment, Octave Changer, Burl Walnut 4000.00
Piano, Poole, Upright, 1930s 250.00

Piano, Steger, Baby Grand, 1915, 6 Ft. 5000.00
Piano, Steinway, Baby Grand, 1920s 6600.00
Piano, Steinway, Baby Grand, Bench, Ebonized 9487.00
Piano, Steinway, Baby Grand, Stool, Ebonized 5980.00
Piano, Steinway, Duo Art, Upright 9500.00
Piano, Steinway, Grand, Ebonized Finish, 1896 .... 9500.00
Piano, Steinway, Model A, Grand, Walnut 4000.00
Piano, Steinway, Model L, Baby Grand, Alligatored Brown Finish, 1926, 70 In. 7150.00
Piano, Steinway, Model XR, Grand, Bench, 1921, 6 Ft. 2 In. 5750.00
Piano, Steinway, No. S311847, Baby Grand, Mahogany, 38 x 62 In. 3740.00
Piano, Stella, Oscar Schmidt, Mandolette, 2-Octave Keyboard, 1880, 15 x 21 In. 1250.00
Piano, Stroud, Duo-Art, Baby Grand, 1933, 5 Ft. 3 In. .... 7300.00 to 8500.00
Piano, Waterfall, Player, Walnut, Electric, Matching Bench 1995.00
Piano, Wm. Knabe, Spinet, Mahogany, Faux Ivory & Ebony Board, 60 x 40 In. 85.00
Piano, Wurlitzer Recordo, Player, Grand, 4 Ft. 8 In. 1500.00
Piano, Wurlitzer, Model 1XB, Roll Changer, Bells, Mandolin, Coin-Operated 7959.00
Piano, Wurlitzer, Player, Art Glass, Oak Finish, 26 Rolls 6500.00
Piano, Wurlitzer, Style A, Player, Upright, Oak Case, Glass Panels, 65 Key, Electric . 7500.00
Polyphone, Bells, 22 1/2 In. 5700.00
Rack, Sheet Music, Gustav Stickley, No. 670, c.1912 .... 1980.00
Rolmonica, 10 Rolls, Bakelite, Box 175.00
Rolmonica, 6 Rolls, Box 125.00
Solovox, Hammond, Organ Attachment For Piano, With Book, 1930-1940 .... 500.00
Stand, Lyre, Victorian 95.00
Stand, Sheet Music, Metal 35.00
Tubephone, Brass Tubes, Wooden Case, Lock, c.1870, 29 1/4 x 13 3/4 In. 290.00
Ukulele, Martin 85.00
Ukulele, Martin, Case, 1940s 550.00
Ukulele, Martin, Ivory Trim 250.00
Viola, Thomas Hardie, Double Case, 1828 .... 8625.00
Violin, Carlo Carletti, 1906 .... 8050.00
Violin, Child's, Shell Inlays In Violin, Ivory On Bow, Violin-18 3/4 In. 190.00
Violin, Gustave Bazin, c.1910 .... 2070.00
Violin, Hans Poulsen, 1928 .... 1150.00
Violin, Honore Derazey, Case, c.1870 .... 4140.00
Violin, Jean Louvet, Case, Outer Canvas Cover, 1750 .... 3680.00
Violin, Joseph Kloz, c.1778 .... 6900.00
Violin, Matthew Hardie, With Bow, 1830s 2070.00
Violin, Matthias Hofmans, Antwerp, 1670s 2760.00
Xylophone, Coinola, Model CX, Walnut Case 7000.00
Xylophone, Deagan, 1917 .... 875.00
Zither, Silver, Ivory & Nacar Shell Neck, Case, c.1910 .... 3000.00

MUSTACHE CUPS were popular from 1850 to 1900 when the large, flowing
mustache was in style. A ledge of china or silver held the hair out of the liquid
in the cup. This kept the mustache tidy and also kept the mustache wax from
melting. Left-handed mustache cups are rare but are being reproduced.

Large Floral Spray, Scalloped 35.00
Lily-Of-The-Valley, Pierced Soap Shelf, Pink Luster 36.00
Multicolored Floral Spray, Scrolled Base Lip & Handle, Left Handed 37.00

MZ AUSTRIA is the wording on a mark used by Moritz Zdekauer on
porcelains made at his works from about 1900. The firm was established in
the town of Alt-Rohlau, Austria, in 1884 and was nationalized in 1945. The
pieces were decorated with lavish floral patterns and overglaze gold
decoration. Full sets of dishes were made as well as vases, toilet sets, and
other wares.

MZ Austria

Chocolate Set, Green & Gold Bands, Pink Roses, Gold, 13 Piece 245.00
Vase, Portrait, Blue, Gold, 10 In. 150.00

NAILSEA glass was made in the Bristol district in England from 1788 to
1873. It was made by many different factories, not just the Nailsea Glass
House. Many pieces were made with loopings of either white or colored glass
as decoration.

Cracker Jar, Silver Top	695.00
Darner, Blue Swirled Design, 5 1/2 In.	35.00
Flask, Cranberry Looping, Opaque White, 7 In.	120.00
Flask, Red Looping, Flattened Shape, 7 In.	165.00
Lamp, Fairy, Camphor Glass Ruffled Base, Clarke Insert, 3 1/2 In.	450.00
Lamp, Fairy, Camphor Glass Ruffled Base, 5 1/2 In.	450.00
Lamp, Fairy, Satin Moire, Clarke Base	195.00
Lamp, White, Pink, Crystal Footed, Berry On Pontil, Ruffled Shade	2475.00
Rolling Pin, Red, White & Blue Spatter	25.00

NAKARA is a trade name for a white glassware made about 1900 by the C.F. Monroe Company of Meriden, Connecticut. It was decorated in pastel colors. The glass was very similar to another glass made by the company called *Wave Crest.* The company closed in 1916. Boxes for use on a dressing table are the most commonly found Nakara pieces. The mark is not found on every piece.

NAKARA

Bonbon, Pink Flowers, Blue	385.00
Box, Cover, Rose Blossoms, 5 x 8 In.	1350.00
Box, Hinged Lid, Florals, Green Leaves, Dotting, Octagonal, Signed, 6 In.	485.00
Box, Jewelry, Mums On Cream To Rose Ground, Lined	1950.00
Box, Petal Flowers, Pink Centers, Octagonal, 4 1/2 x 6 1/4 In.	960.00
Box, Pink & White Flowers, Raised Beading, Gold Lining, 6 In.	795.00
Box, White Dots Line Rim, Gilt Finish Of Metal Fittings, Cream Lining, 3 3/4 x 4 In. .	375.00
Humidor, Cigars In Gold, Hand Painted Pink Flowers, Blue Mottled Ground, 5 In.	795.00
Humidor, Owl, In Tree Design, C.F. Monroe	1220.00
Saltshaker, Transfer Of Niagara Falls, Concave Bulb	145.00
Vase, Orchid Center & Back, Orange Ground, 13 1/2 In.	1095.00
Wave Crest, Box, Rose Blossoms, 5 x 8 In.	1350.00

NANKING is a type of blue-and-white porcelain made in Canton, China, since the late eighteenth century. It is very similar to Canton, which is listed under its own name in this book. Both Nanking and Canton are part of a larger group now called *Chinese Export* porcelain. Nanking has a spear-and-post border and may have gold decoration.

Bowl, Salad, 19th Century, 9 In.	825.00
Coffeepot, Lighthouse Shape, Blue & White, 19th Century	1100.00
Dish, Blue & White, Leaf Shape, 7 1/2 In.	110.00
Dish, Hot Water, Cover, Inclined Pines, Oval, 1810, 18 13/16 In.	1495.00
Dish, Serving, 19th Century, 12 1/4 In.	330.00
Jug, Cider, Masonic, 19th Century, 11 In.	2200.00
Plate, Octagonal, 19th Century, 9 1/4 In., 6 Piece	660.00
Platter, Figural Landscape Design, Oval, 1800, 14 1/2 In.	412.00
Platter, Inclined Pines, Oval, 21 3/8 In.	1035.00
Platter, Oval, 19th Century, 16 In.	412.00
Sauce Boat, Strap Handle, Pair	825.00
Tray, Blue & White, 7 1/4 In.	220.00
Tureen, Sauce, Cover, Crossed Strap Handles, Oval, 8 x 10 In.	1000.00
Tureen, Soup, Cover, 9th Century, 8 1/4 x 12 1/2 In.	1100.00
Water Bottle, Cover, Ship Scene	2090.00

NAPKIN RINGS were in fashion from 1869 to about 1900. They were made of silver, porcelain, wood, and other materials. They are still being made today. The most popular rings with collectors are the silver-plated figural examples. Small, realistic figures were made to hold the ring. Good and poor reproductions of the more expensive rings are now being made and collectors must be very careful.

Bakelite, Bunny	28.00
Bakelite, Elephant	28.00
Figural, Cat On Hind Legs Pushing Ring, Silver Plate	120.00
Figural, Chick On Wishbone, Best Wishes, Silver Plate	25.00
Figural, Chicken, Reed & Barton	240.00
Figural, Cupid, Silver Plate	75.00
Figural, Cupid, Silver Plate, Chain Fragments On Hands, Pair	350.00

Figural, Hummingbird, Sitting On Ornament Next To Ring, Silver Plate, Derby 295.00
Figural, Indian Boy With Headdress, Pottery 35.00
Figural, Rabbit, Pairpoint 650.00
Figural, Rip Van Winkle, On Mountain, Silver Plated, New England 950.00
Figural, Squirrel, After Bird On Ring, Silver Plate 225.00
Figural, Water Lily, Meridan 75.00
Figural, Wheelbarrow, Glass Insert, Silver Plate 45.00
Horseshoe Base, Triangular Ring, Flying Bird, Pairpoint 235.00
Pewter, Old Point Comfort, Virginia, Scenes, Scrolled Border 10.00
Ring On Leaf, Flowers, Silver Plate 70.00

NASH glass was made in Corona, New York, from about 1928 to 1931. A.
Douglas Nash bought the Corona glassworks from Louis C. Tiffany in 1928
and founded the A. Douglas Nash Corporation with support from his father,
Arthur J. Nash. Arthur had worked at the Webb factory in England and for the
Tiffany Glassworks in Corona.

NASH

Bowl, Red Pulled-Up Striping, Silver Mottling, Blue, 4 1/2 In. 145.00
Bowl, Veined Design, Gold Iridescent, Signed, 2 3/8 x 3 In. 350.00
Compote, Chintz, Green Zig-Zag Line Around, Blue, Scalloped, Pedestal, 5 x 4 In. .. 95.00

NAUTICAL antiques are listed in this category. Any of the many objects that
were made or used by the seafaring trade, including ship parts, models, and
tools, are included. Other pieces may be found listed under Scrimshaw.

Ashtray, USS Cone, DD866, Flagship Destroyer Squadron Six, Oval, 7 In. 15.00
Barometer, Gimbal, Rope Carved, Spiral Reeding, Gadrooned Pediment 3850.00
Bell, California, Mounting Bracket, Brass, Sunk 1887, 10 In. 895.00
Bell, USS Cimarron, Pacific Fleet Oiler, World War II, 1939 .... 2100.00
Bellows, Diving, Morse, 2 Man, Hand Crank, Hard Hat 6800.00
Binnacle, Wooden Base, Japanese Compass, 42 In. 550.00
Binnacle, Yacht, Brass, Gimbal Compass, Charles Hutchinson, Boston, 23 In. 1430.00
Binnacle, Yacht, 32 In. 2100.00
Binnacle, Yacht, Original Compass, Baker, Boston, Established 1873 .... 5500.00
Bomb Lance Gun, Whaling, H.W. Chapman 2575.00
Box, Document, Captain's, Copper Lid, Steel Wire Bale, 7 1/2 x 4 1/2 In. 302.50
Candleholder, Wall Mount, Brass, 7 1/2 In. 290.00
Cannon, Boarding, Sea Serpent Sights, Swivel Mount, Spain, Bronze, 47 In. 660.00
Cap, Steward's, Steamship, Polar Bear Logo 5.00
Cards, Playing, Holland American Line, Red Box, 2 Decks 6.00
Cards, Playing, US Lines, Night & Day Ship Pictures, 2 Decks, Box 15.00
Case, Needle, Sail Maker's 192.50
Case, Sewing, Sail Maker's, Black Paint, Oak, 7 1/2 In. 120.00
Chest, Apothecary, Captain's, Hand-Blown Stoppered Bottles, Mahogany 715.00
Chest, 6-Board Construction, Wrought Iron Lock, Strap Hinges, 43 In. 195.00
Chest, Domed, Marked Perley Pollar, Captain Of Schooner, 1725, Small 137.50
Chest, Lift Top, Painted Landscape Scene, 19 x 40 x 17 In. 660.00
Chest, Paneled, Maple Trim, 21 x 44 In. 373.00
Chest, Sea, 6 Board, Canted Side, Rope Handles 295.00
Chest, Sea, Camphor Wood 495.00
Chest, Sea, Dark Blue Paint, 1830 .... 350.00
Chest, Seaman's, Painted Design On Front & Sides, Poplar & Pine, 38 In. 925.00
Chronometer, Bailey & Co., Mahogany Case 3025.00
Chronometer, 2-Day, 55 Hour, Mahogany Box, Brass, Peter De Mory, N.Y., 1890 ..... 1650.00
Chronometer, Hamilton, Gold Hands, Silvered Dial, U.S. Navy, 1869 .... 2200.00
Chronometer, Heath & Co., Late 19th Century 1155.00
Clock, Chelsea, Ship's, Bell Shape, 1940s 545.00
Clock, Sestral, Olympic Laurel On Face, Brass, 8 In. 220.00
Clock, Seth Thomas 325.00
Clock, Ship's Bell, Walnut Plaque, Brass Case, Bezel Marked Elske, 1910, 5 x 10 In. 400.00
Clock, U.S. Life Savings Service 2464.00
Compass, Binnacle, Wooden Base, 1800s 2400.00
Compass, Brass, Signed, Wooden Case, 7 In. 220.00
Compass, Lifeboat, Palmer, Box 275.00

Compass, Surveyor's, HM Poole Easton, Mass., Brass, Case, 14 1/2 In. 660.00
Compass, Whaleboat, Mahogany Box, Oil Lamp, c.1830, 7 1/2 x 6 1/4 x 6 1/4 In. ... 110.00
Compass, Wood & Brass, Large 150.00
Crutch, Wooden Shaft, Whalebone Arm Rest, 51 In. 1275.00
Deck Plan, Furness Lines, Queen Of Bermuda, Fold-Out, 1934, 33 x 40 In. 29.50
Desk, Davenport, Leather Top, Side Drawers, 1860-1870 .... 2900.00
Dish, Cobalt Blue, France, Ship Picture, 4 1/2 In. 6.00
Dresser, Captain's, Faded Mahogany, 5 Drawers, Adjustable Mirror, England, 40 In. . 302.00
Engine, Outboard, Johnson, Sea Horse, 1930 .... 130.00
Figure, Eagle, Pilot House, Upraised Wings, Open Beak, Wooden, Gilded, 21 In. 2530.00
Figure, Sperm Whale, Wooden, Ben Holmes, 27 In. 5225.00
Figure, Whale Man, Throwing Harpoon, Metal, 25 In. 660.00
Figurehead, Female, Hand Across Waist, c.1840, 29 In. 6875.00
Figurehead, Woman, Bare Breasted, Ponytail 4675.00
Finger Bowl, Southern Pacific Steamship 60.00
Gun, Flare, Steel Barrel, World War II, International Flare Signal Co., 10 3/4 In. 295.00
Handkerchief, Remember The Maine, Ship Surrounded By Bunting, Framed 250.00
Harpoon, Toggle Head, 19th Century 385.00
Harpoon, Toggle, Sheath, Macy 935.00
Helmet, Diving, 3 Lights, Boston Signature 3570.00
Horn, River Boat Barge, Brass, 19th Century, 20 1/2 In. 65.00
Inclinometer, Ship's Engine Room 125.00
Key, Cabin, Eastern SS Lines, Evangeline, Brass, 4 In. 55.00
Knife, Sailor's, Bone Handle, Folding, Large 155.00
Lamp, Anchor, Civil War Period, 2 Ft. 1430.00
Lamp, Oil, Cast Iron, c.1830, 4 3/4 In. 295.00
Lamp, Signal, Battery Operated, Brass, Canada 225.00
Lamp, Starboard, Brass, Russell & Watson, c.1870 .... 425.00
Lamp, Whale Oil, Hanging, Brass, From Clipper Ship 110.00
Lantern, Inspection, Officer's, Brass, New York, 19th Century 175.00
Lantern, Kerosene, Perkins Marine Lamp Corp. 440.00
Ledger, Sea Captain's, Schooner Melinda, 1885-1893 .... 95.00
Log, Whaling, Ship Magnet, From 1829-1831 & 1831-1834, Sperm Whale Oil 4400.00
Map, Cape Cod To Sandy Hook, U.S. Coast Pilot, Fold-Out, 326 Pages 8.50
Menu, USS Lurline, 1964 .... 10.00
Menu, USS Neville, Crews Mess, Christmas, 1941 .... 7.00
Menu, USS United States, Sept. 18, 1959 .... 15.00
Model, 2-Masted Brig, Mary, Walnut, Glass Case, 13 5/8 x 19 In. 550.00
Model, 3 Masts, Female Figurehead, Copper Hull, 28 x 43 In. 1265.00
Model, 3-Masted Ship, Benmore Of Liverpool, 32 In. 517.00
Model, 3-Masted Ship, D. & E. Heddinger, 31 In. 550.00
Model, Beetle Whale Boat, Oars, Harpoon, Whalebone, Case, 22 In. 2310.00
Model, Brigantine Satan, Flag Of Worley, Tallow Bottom, 19 1/2 x 22 In. 1320.00
Model, British 10 Gun Naval Cutter, Case, 11 1/2 In. 1980.00
Model, British Barque, Revenges Of 1577, 22 x 22 In. 880.00
Model, Catamaran, Lead Keel, America, 20th Century, 65 x 26 In. 880.00
Model, Chris-Craft, Inboard Motor, Working, 1949, 3 Ft. 850.00
Model, Dixie II, Speedboat, 6 Ft. 3300.00
Model, Elco PT, R.J. Sprague, World War II 66.00
Model, French Prisoner-Of-War, 78 Gun, Case, 14 1/2 In. 9900.00
Model, Glouchester Fishing Schooner, 20 In. 412.00
Model, Half, 3-Masted Merchant Vessel, H.E. Boucher Mfg. Co., 48 In. 3375.00
Model, Half, Whale Ship, Antarctic, 7 Lifts, Red, Black Topside, 37 1/4 In. 3250.00
Model, Half, Yacht, Pine & Mahogany, 40 1/2 In. 1985.00
Model, HMS Bounty, Wooden, Glass Case, 20 1/2 x 23 1/2 In. 1150.00
Model, Lap Strake Row Boat, Carved & Painted, 1/2 Model, 22 1/2 x 37 In. 880.00
Model, Mayflower, 1/3rd Scale, 40 Ft. 5500.00
Model, Motor Yacht Gustave W. Arnhold, Metal Fittings, Wooden, 38 3/4 In. 495.00
Model, Mt. Washington, 45 In. 1650.00
Model, Pond Boat, Birkenhead Star, 1930 .... 200.00
Model, Pond Boat, Brane Gear, All Original, 40 x 56 In. 2500.00
Model, Pond Boat, Original Paint, Replaced Sails, 1920s 1200.00

Model, Sailboat, Raccoon, Framed, 25 x 19 In. 467.00
Model, Sailing Ship, Rigged, Guns, Power Kegs, Display Case, 32 x 37 In. 770.00
Model, Sloop, Shadow Box, 40 x 40 In. 3960.00
Model, Steamer, American, Wooden, Cradle, 20th Century, 19 1/2 x 27 In. 770.00
Model, Submarine, Kittery-Portsmouth Built 2310.00
Oar, Double Side, 1900 .... 140.00
Obelisk, Sailor's Memorial, Shell Covered, Dates Of Crooker Family, 19th Century .. 385.00
Octant, Label, S.N. Parkman, Boston, Case, 14 In. 605.00
Octant, Swing-Away Magnifier, 2 Lenses, French, Brass, c.1870, 9 1/2 In. 525.00
Peg Leg, Wooden 975.00
Pitcher, Whale Oil, Lighthouse, 19th Century, SGD 65.00
Plate, Great Republic, Hamilton 45.00
Plate, USS Constitution, Hamilton 85.00
Print, 2 Ships At Sea, Seamen's Bank For Savings, Frame, 1962, 23 x 29 1/2 In. 18.00
Quadrant, Davis, Rosewood Limbs, Boxwood Arcs, c.1740 .... 3575.00
Quadrant, Hadley, Diagonally Divided Boxwood Scale, London, 20 In. 3300.00
Rifle, Whaling, Muzzle Loading, Iron Barrel, c.1850, 17 3/4 In. 3900.00
Rope Winder, Whalebone Gears, Large 8250.00
Sailor's Valentine, Compass Rose, Heart, Octagonal Case, Shellwork, 13 3/4 In. 2860.00
Sailor's Valentine, Heart, Shellwork, Hinged Case, 8 1/2 In. 1430.00
Sconce, Electrific, Mercer's Ship, 1920, Pair 700.00
Scope, Tri-Pod, Leather-Covered Brass Barrel, Case, c.1890 .... 2750.00
Sextant, B.K. Hagger & Son, Limbs Of Ebony, Engraved Ivory Scales 660.00
Sextant, B.K. Hagger, Wooden Frame, Baltimore, c.1830 .... 660.00
Sextant, Parnell, London, Brass Arm, Pivoting Sight, 3 Lenses, c.1860 .... 2250.00
Ship Model, see nautical, model
Spyglass, 5 Pulls, Brass, 36 In. .... 395.00 to 495.00
Stove, Ship's, Iron, Brass, Grape Tiles, 1840 .... 1500.00
Telephone, Captain's, Pilothouse, Mitchell, 1892 .... 295.00
Telescope, Adjustable, Brass, 6 Ft. 1540.00
Telescope, Single Draw, Sliding Cover, Brass Lens Cap, England, c.1800, 20 3/4 In. ... 375.00
Tin, Norwegian-American Line, Christmas, Bail Handle, 9 1/4 In. 10.00
Trumpet, Speaking, Captain's, Silver-Plated, 1875 .... 1045.00
Trunk, Sea Captain's, Late 1700s 1800.00
Vent, Tugboat, Mushroom 250.00
Watch Tower, Inlaid, Daguerreotype Of Captain's Daughter, Pocket, 13 1/2 In. 3575.00
Wheel, Ship's, Tugboat, 1900, 48 In. 450.00
Whiskey Glass, Queen Mary 8.00
Whiskey Glass, Spruce Goose 8.00
Whistle, Boatswain, Brass & Copper, Chain 9.50
Whistle, Bosun's, Copper & Brass, Chain, 1800s 110.00
Whistle, Buckeye, Brass, 11 In. 295.00
Whistle, Lunkenheimer, Brass, 10 In. 275.00

NETSUKES are small ivory, wood, metal, or porcelain pieces used as toggles
on the end of the cord that held a Japanese money pouch. The earliest date
from the sixteenth century. Many are miniature, carved works of art.

Boxwood, Endo Morita Holding Head Of Kesa, Meikei, Box 2875.00
Boxwood, Happy Water Carrier, 2 In. 185.00
Boxwood, Shinzan Wood Urchin, 1 1/2 In. 1035.00
Boxwood, Two Blind Men On Raft, Sosui, 2 In. 1495.00
Coral, Elder's Profile, 19th Century, 2 In. 520.00
Iron, Man, With Cane, Holding Temple Figure, 2 1/2 In. 90.00
Ivory, Baku, Mythical Devourer Of Dreams, 19th Century 11500.00
Ivory, Beak & Fanged Face, Holding Cucumber, 19th Century, Signed Jugyoko 900.00
Ivory, Boy With Hatchet, Morning Glory, Metal Himotoshi, 19th Century 165.00
Ivory, Chestnut Group, With Branch, Japan, 19th Century 440.00
Ivory, Dancer With Drum, Signed Seisho, 19th Century, 1 3/4 In. 330.00
Ivory, Daruma, Recumbent, Base, Japan, 19th Century 275.00
Ivory, Fighting Heron On Cobra, 2 In. 170.00
Ivory, Hotei, Jolly Immortal, 19th Century 488.00
Ivory, Hotei With Tongue Out, Bulging Eyes, Meiji Period 110.00

Ivory, Kappa On Lotus Leaf, Inlaid Eyes, Signed Tomokazu 495.00
Ivory, Laughing Elongated Figure, 4 1/2 In. 450.00
Ivory, Man On A Bench, Fan, Gourd, 19th Century, 1 3/4 In. 300.00
Ivory, Man With Hoe Digging Bamboo Shoots, Signed Mitsumasa, 1 1/2 In. 525.00
Ivory, Manju, Plant Spirit, 19th Century, Signed Gyokuzan 880.00
Ivory, Manju, Sword, Fan, Meiji Period 165.00
Ivory, Mask Of Comic Demon Bukaku, 1 1/2 In. 430.00
Ivory, Monkey Group, Hear No Evil, See No Evil, 19th Century 220.00
Ivory, Octopus With 3 Monkeys, 1 1/4 In. 1725.00
Ivory, Oni Carrying A Drum On Back 220.00
Ivory, Ono-No-Komachi, Walking Stick, Signed Hidemasa, Early 1800s, 1 1/2 In. 1045.00
Ivory, Rat On A Mokugyo, Box, Hogan Rantei, 1 1/2 In. 1050.00
Ivory, Shishi, Hind Leg Raised To Scratch Chin, 19th Century 690.00
Ivory, Shishi, Large Ball, 19th Century 250.00
Ivory, Skull Topped By Black Raven, Meigyokusai, 1 1/2 In. 4850.00
Ivory, Wrestling Group, 18th Century, Signed Tomotada 1100.00
Pottery, Fox Mask, 2 In. 185.00
Wood, Seated Boy Holding Fan, Signed Toshinaga, 19th Century, 1 1/4 In. 445.00
Wood, Seated Man, Holding Mask 195.00

NEW MARTINSVILLE Glass Manufacturing Company was established in
1901 in New Martinsville, West Virginia. It was bought and renamed the
Viking Glass Company in 1944 and is still producing fine glasswares.

Bonbon, Meadow Wreath Etched, 2 Handles, 6 In. 15.00
Bookends, Nautilus Shell 120.00
Bookends, Seal 85.00
Bowl, Epic, Orange, Clear Rim, Scalloped, 9 1/4 x 3 3/4 In. 28.00
Bowl, Janice, Basket Shape, Red, 7 x 12 In. 40.00
Cake Plate, Prelude 40.00
Candlestick, 2-Arms, Clear, Pair 35.00
Candlestick, Swan, Green, 6 In. 28.00
Card Holder, Wheelbarrow 20.00
Compote, Leaf & Flower, Silver Deposit, Lyre Stem, 7 In. 28.00
Compote, Prelude 12.00
Figurine, Bear, Baby 45.00
Figurine, Bear, Mama 17.50
Figurine, Horse, Rearing, Head Up, 6 1/2 x 8 In. 48.00
Figurine, Seal, Balancing Ball, 7 In. 55.00
Figurine, Swan, Amber, 6 In. 17.00
Figurine, Tiger, Head Down, 8 1/2 x 5 1/4 In. 165.00
Figurine, Tiger, Head Up, Pair 280.00
Figurine, Wolfhound, 9 1/4 x 7 In. 46.00
Goblet, Georgian, Ruby, 5 5/8 In. 15.00
Mustard, Cover, Janice, Blue 50.00
Plate, Prelude, Salad 5.00
Punch Bowl, Carnation, Pedestal 135.00
Sherbet, Georgian, Ruby, Flared, Footed, 2 3/4 In. 10.00
Sherbet, Janice, Blue 22.00
Sugar & Creamer, Holder, Call Of The Wild Silver Overlay, Triangular 90.00
Tumbler, Hostmaster, Ruby, 4 1/4 In. 12.00

NEWCOMB Pottery was founded by Ellsworth and William Woodward at
Sophie Newcomb College, New Orleans, Louisiana, in 1895. The work
continued through the 1940s. Pieces of this art pottery are marked with the
printed letters *NC* and often have the incised initials of the artist as well. Most
pieces have a matte glaze and incised decoration.

Bowl, Beige Bands, Mauve Field, Sadie Irvine, 4 x 8 3/8 In. 275.00
Bowl, Green Abstract Foliage Band, Sadie Irvine, 1933, 4 In. 600.00
Bowl, Incised Flowers, Buds, Leona Nicholson, 1908, 5 3/4 In. 3250.00
Bowl, Rice, Gulf Stream Glaze, Pair 450.00
Bowl, Wavy Band, Pink & Blue, 1921, 2 1/2 x 6 1/2 In. 605.00
Chamberstick, Geometric Design, Pink & Purple, Sadie Irvine, 1925, 3 x 4 In. 990.00

Chamberstick, Spouted, Blue Blossoms, Green Ground, 1912, A.F. Mason, 5 In. 935.00
Match Holder, Spanish Moss Oak Trees, White Ground, S. Irvine, 2 1/4 In. 743.00
Plaque, Palms Scene, Matte Glaze, Frame, A.F. Connor Simpson, 1915, 9 3/4 In. 4400.00
Tea Tile, Floral Band, Carved, Light Green, Alma Mason, 1911, 3 1/2 In. 440.00
Tile, Band Of Nasturtium & Green Vines, Desiree Roman, 1904, 5 3/4 In. 2200.00
Tile, Sailing Ship, Ivory & Clear Overglaze, Henrietta Bailey, 1902, 5 3/4 In. 600.00
Vase, Bayou Scene, 14 In. 7700.00
Vase, Blossoms, Yellow Hearts, Sadie Irvine, 1918, 8 In. 2090.00
Vase, Blue Flowers, Tall Stems, Blue Ground, Henrietta Bailey, 1915, 7 /14 In. 2800.00
Vase, Blue, White & Yellow Flowers, Matte Glaze, M. Morel, 10 1/2 In. 1650.00
Vase, Bud, Bulbous, Pink Flowers, Blue Ground, Sadie Irvine, 1914, 5 1/4 In. 880.00
Vase, Bulbous, Green & Yellow, Floral Band, Blue Ground, 1931, 6 1/2 In. 990.00
Vase, Bulbous, White Flowers, Gray-Green Glaze, Blue Ground, 6 x 5 1/2 In. 1980.00
Vase, Carved Flowers, Blue Ground, A. Bailey, 1924, 3 3/4 In. 700.00
Vase, Corseted, Dripping Glossy Glaze, Marked, 11 1/4 In. 800.00
Vase, Crackled Sant-De-Boeuf Glaze, 8 In. 400.00
Vase, Floral Design, Pink Flowers, Purple Ground, No. SV72, 5 1/2 In. 700.00
Vase, Flowers & Foliage, 2 Handles, M.W. Summery, 1909, 4 x 4 1/2 In. 1540.00
Vase, Incised Blue Berries On Ivory Band, E.A. Horner, 1913, 3 3/4 In. 750.00
Vase, Incised Green Leaves, Blue Ground, S. Irvine, 6 x 6 In. 1100.00
Vase, Incised White Flowers, Blue Ground, A.f. Simpson, 1910, 4 3/4 In. 1540.00
Vase, Landscape, Oak Trees, Spanish Moss, Ivory Glaze, Marked, 8 3/4 In. 2500.00
Vase, Luster Red Glaze, Stove-Pipe Neck, Marked, 5 1/2 In. 650.00
Vase, Matte Blue-Green Glaze, Poppy Blossoms, C. Littlejohn, c.1912, 5 1/2 In. 1870.00
Vase, Moon & Moss, Joseph Meyer, 8 3/4 In. 2750.00
Vase, Moon & Moss, Joseph Meyer, 12 1/2 In. 5225.00
Vase, Moonlit Landscape, Blue & Green Glaze, Sadie Irvine, 1918, 7 1/2 In. 2900.00
Vase, Moss Hanging From Oaks, Moonlit Sky, Sadie Irvine, c.1925, 6 1/2 In. 1955.00
Vase, Night Scene Of Spanish Moss, Full Moon, A.F. Simpson, 1930, 5 1/4 In. 1500.00
Vase, Pine Tree, Scenic, A.F. Simpson 9000.00
Vase, Spherical, Yellow Blossoms, Green Foliage, Ivory Ground, 1904, 6 x 6 In. 7150.00
Vase, Stylized Floral Design, Esther Huger Elliot, 1902, 3 3/4 In. 4180.00
Vase, Trees Extending To Base, Sadie Irvine, 14 In. 4750.00
Vase, White Blossoms, Blue Leaves, H. Bailey, 1926, 2 1/2 x 3 In. 665.00
Vase, White Carved Lilies, Blue & Green Bands, Bailey, 1905, 5 x 7 In. 5500.00
Vase, White Jonquils, Stems, Blue Ground, Anna F. Simpson, 1924, 10 In. 3800.00
Vase, Yellow Buds, Green & Blue Leaves, Marie Benson, 1908, 13 In. 9900.00

NILOAK Pottery (Kaolin spelled backward) was made at the Hyten Brothers
Pottery in Benton, Arkansas, between 1909 and 1946. Although the factory
did make cast and molded wares, collectors are most interested in the
Marbleized art pottery line made of colored swirls of clay. It was called
Mission Ware.

Candlestick, Marbleized, Brown, Blue & Ivory, Bisque, 20 x 5 1/4 In., Pair 257.00
Candlestick, Marbleized, Flares To Base, 10 In. 275.00
Cornucopia, Pale Blue, Feathered Rim, Fluted Tail, 7 x 8 In. 20.00
Figurine, Camel, Green 40.00
Figurine, Rabbit, Green 25.00
Pitcher, Ozark Dawn, 6 In. 45.00
Planter, Circus Elephant, 6 In. 48.00
Planter, Deer, 6 In. 32.00
Planter, Kangaroo, White Matte 30.00
Planter, Marbleized, Cream & Strawberry, 7 In. 12.50
Planter, Ozark Dawn, 6 In. 48.00
Planter, Squirrel, 6 In. 28.00
Planter, Wishing Well 28.00
Tumbler, Marbleized 60.00
Vase, Blue, 7 In., Pair 95.00
Vase, Blue, 7 Tulips Form Openings, 7 In. 36.00
Vase, Bulbous, Melon Rib, Flared, Wing Side Handles, Blue, 6 x 5 In. 10.00
Vase, Dark Brown To Blue Swirls, 2 In. 66.00
Vase, Marbleized Blue, 5 In. 95.00

Vase, Marbleized Brown, 5 In. 95.00
Vase, Marbleized, 5 In. 65.00
Vase, Marbleized, 6 3/4 In. 90.00
Vase, Marbleized, 12 In. 550.00
Vase, Marbleized, Clay, Tapering To Bulbous Top, 10 In. 200.00
Vase, Marbleized, Cylindrical, Blue, Brown, Cream, 8 In. 121.00
Vase, Marbleized, Hourglass Shape, 8 In. 185.00
Vase, Marbleized, Orange, Blue, Cream, 8 In. 143.00
Vase, Marbleized Polychrome, Bisque, Marked, 8 3/4 In. 165.00
Vase, Melon Ribbed, Pea Green, Wing Side Handles, Bulbous, Gold Label, 6 1/2 In.   10.00
Vase, Stick, Cylindrical, Round Base, Browns, Blue, Rust, Cream, 6 1/2 In. 99.00

NIPPON porcelain was made in Japan from 1891 to 1921. *Nippon* is the
Japanese word for *Japan.* A few firms continued to use the word *Nippon* on
ceramics after 1921 as a part of the company name more than as an
identification of the country of origin. More pieces marked Nippon will be
found in the Dragonware, Moriage, and Noritake categories.

Basket, Hand Painted Roses, Pastel, Gold Trim, 5 In. 85.00
Basket, Jasperware, Cherry Blossoms 375.00
Berry Set, Mocha Roses & Foliage, Cobalt Blue Rim, Torii Mark, 7 Piece 175.00
Biscuit Jar, Pink Roses, Gold Moriage 595.00
Blotter Holder, Red Poinsettia 110.00
Bowl, Autumn Lakeside Scene, Gold Rim & Handles, 9 In. 110.00
Bowl, Cover, Multicolor Flowers, Gold, Handle, Rising Sun, 6 1/2 In. 56.00
Bowl, Flowers, Geometric Medallion, Open Loop Handles, Green Wreath, 8 3/4 In. ..   65.00
Bowl, Fruit, Pedestal, Red Roses, Gold Side Handles, Green M Wreath, 8 x 5 In. 125.00
Bowl, House & Tree, Lake, Pastel Ground, Open Gold Handles, Rising Sun, 9 1/2 In.   58.00
Bowl, Interior Pearl Design, Gold Edge, 8 In. 100.00
Bowl, Nuts & Leaves, Marked, 7 1/2 In. 35.00
Bowl, Pink Roses, Garlands, Gold Beading & Scrolls, 10 In. 75.00
Box, Cover, Flowers, Gold Banding, Square, 3 3/4 In. 42.00
Box, Trinket, Raised Beaded Gold Roses, Cylindrical, Blue M Wreath 48.00
Cake Plate Set, Rose Swags, Gold Bands & Chain, Open Handles, 7 Piece 48.00
Candlestick, Jasperware, 1911, Pair 575.00
Celery Set, Geometric Border, Plums On Branch, Oval Tray, Marked, 7 Piece 170.00
Celery Set, Plums On Branch, Geometric Border, Handled Tray, Green Wreath 150.00
Celery Set, Tray & 4 Salts, Gold Designs, 5 Piece 65.00
Celery Tray, Dogwood, Oval, Handles, 14 In. 65.00
Centerpiece, Coralene, Tulips & Geometric, Handles, Pedestal 125.00
Cheese & Cracker, Plate, Apple Blossoms, Gold Trim, Blue Rising Sun, 8 1/2 In. ...   44.00
Chocolate Set, Royal Kinran 350.00
Cider Set, House In Meadow, Bisque, Green M Wreath, 6 Piece 240.00
Coffee Set, Blue-White-Gold, 12 Piece 110.00
Cracker Jar, Cover, Roses, Raised Gold, Cobalt Blue Ground, Large 280.00
Creamer, Child's Face, Marked 50.00
Cup & Saucer, Yellow Roses, Black Ground, Gold Handle & Rim, Green M Wreath   20.00
Dish, Red & Orange Flowers, Gold Trim, Scallops, 3-Footed, Triangular, 7 In. 80.00
Ewer, Marbleized Medallions, Raised Green & White Slip Work, Jeweled, 7 3/4 In. ... 245.00
Ewer, Moriage, Man & Woman On Side, Blue Mark, Squatty 60.00
Ewer, Pink Roses, Gold Triangular Medallions, Reticulated Rim, Art Nouveau Style .. 125.00
Humidor, Camel & Rider, Blown Out 395.00
Humidor, Deer & Doe Under Orange Tree, Signed, 6 In. 265.00
Humidor, Incised Greek Warrior On Side, Floral On Other, 7 In. 350.00
Humidor, Owl, Blown Out 550.00
Lemonade Set, Floral, Gold Trim, 7 Piece 135.00
Mayonnaise, Azalea, 3 Piece 35.00
Mug, Sailboat, Pines 135.00
Mustard, Attached Saucer, Lakeside Sunset, Raised Gold Beading 75.00
Nut Set, American Indian Hunter, Canoe, Gold Trim, Green M Wreath, 7 Piece 190.00
Nut Set, Enameled, White Ground, Octagonal, Footed, 5 Piece 80.00
Plaque, Bison, Blown Out, Green, 10 1/2 In. 795.00
Plaque, Sheep & Shepherd, 10 In. 225.00
Plaque, Wall, Head Of Dog, Blue Moriage Border, 8 1/2 In. 425.00

Plaque, Wild Roses, Pierced, 9 In. 65.00
Plaque, Windmill Scene, Narrow Brown Border, Green M Wreath, 10 In. 250.00
Plate, Azalea, 7 3/4 In., 6 Piece 45.00
Plate, Hunt Scene, Handles, Marked, 10 1/2 In. 120.00
Plate, Jeweled Floral Panels, Turquoise Ground, Footed, Gold Footed, 5 3/8 x 2 In. .. 50.00
Plate, Stag & Trees, Blown Out, 10 1/2 In. 395.00
Relish, Indian Handles 150.00
Relish, Matte Scene, Slit Handles, Gold Rim, Green Wreath, 8 1/2 x 4 1/2 In. 55.00
Relish, Roses, Green, Embossed Gold Trim 35.00
Sugar Shaker, Red Flowers, Fluted Body, Raised Beading, Blue Mark 175.00
Sugar & Creamer, Floral Design On Upper Half & Lid, Signed 65.00
Syrup, Cover, Underplate, Gold Flowers & Outlining, Spokes In Circle, 4 1/4 In. 90.00
Tea Set, Boat & Lake Scene, Gold Trim, Blue Rising Sun, 11 Piece 220.00
Tea Set, Jasperware, 3 Piece 475.00
Tea Set, Orange Luster, Service For 4 .... 45.00
Tea Strainer, Holder, Floral, Marked 60.00
Teapot, Peter Rabbit, Child's 75.00
Toothpick, Loving Cup Shape 25.00
Vase, Allover Iris & Foliage, Signed, 10 In. 325.00
Vase, Blown Out Leaves & Strawberries, Green Mark, 10 In. 365.00
Vase, Blown Out Strawberries, Marked, 10 In. 465.00
Vase, Blue & White Flowers, 13 In. 165.00
Vase, Camel & Rider, Palm Trees, 2 Handles, 10 1/2 In. 375.00
Vase, Coralene, Poppies, Yellow Ground, Gilding, 6 3/4 In. 250.00
Vase, Desert Village, River Scene, Jeweled Borders, Handles, Green M Wreath, 8 In. 175.00
Vase, Dragons, Gold, Raised, Footed, 6 In. 65.00
Vase, Dutch Fishing Scene, Ribbon Handles, 16 In., Pair 895.00
Vase, Flowers, Gilt Outlining, Smoky Pastel Ground, Royal Nishiki, 12 In., Pair 295.00
Vase, Jasperware, 7 1/2 In. 450.00
Vase, Lake Scene, Allover Jeweled, Olive Borders, Green M Wreath, 4 3/4 In. 58.00
Vase, Lavender Flowers, Gold Outlining, Shoulder Handles, Green M Wreath, 3 In. .. 110.00
Vase, Scenic, Taupe Trim, Green Wreath Mark, 11 In. 365.00
Vase, Tree & Lake Scene, Olive Handles, Squared, Green M Wreath, 5 3/4 In., Pair .. 135.00

NODDERS, also called nodding figures or pagods, are porcelain figures with
heads and hands that are attached to wires. Any slight movement causes the
parts to move up and down. They were made in many countries during the
eighteenth, nineteenth, and twentieth centuries. A few Art Deco designs are
also known. Copies are being made. A more recent type of nodder is made of
papier-mache or plastic. These often represent sports figures or comic
characters.

Andy Gump 95.00
Bank, Black Boy With Fruit, Chalkware 58.00
Bank, China Man 45.00
Bank, Fisherman, Comical Figure, Reeling In Mermaid, 1950s, 5 x 7 In. 40.00
Bellhop Monkey, Celluloid Head 60.00
Ben Casey, Ceramic, Lego, 1962, 7 In. 98.00
Black Cat, Ashtray 55.00
Black Woman, With Watermelon Slice 175.00
Cat, Colored Paint, Papier-Mache, 5 1/4 In. 30.25
Chester Gump 80.00
Chicago Bear, Composition, Green Base 50.00
Chicken, Wooden, Papier-Mache, Metal Legs, Yellow 42.00
Chinese Dragon, Floating Parade, Papier-Mache & Chalk, Red 20.00
Cleopatra, Lego, Japan, 7 In. 95.00
Clown, Pincushion & Tape Measure, Box, Japan, 5 1/2 In. 225.00
Colonel Sanders 135.00
Daddy Warbucks 95.00
Dallas Cowboy, Gold Base 85.00
Detroit Tigers, Mascot, Square Base 225.00
Dodger, Baseball Player 95.00
Donald Duck, Windup 575.00
Donkey, Celluloid, 3 3/4 x 5 In. 20.00

Dr. Kildare, Ceramic, Lego, 1962, 7 In. 98.00
Dutch Boy & Girl, Pair 20.00
Elf, On Log Ashtray 20.00
Falls City Beer .... 150.00 to 300.00
Fat Boy, Red Top Hat, Red Outfit, 2 1/2 In. 75.00
Fireman, Bisque, 3 1/2 In. 85.00
Girl, Green Shawl, Germany, 3 In. 75.00
Girl, Kneeling, Holding Basket, Pink Dress, Bisque 155.00
Golfer, Golf Ball Head, 1900, 6 In. 195.00
Goose, Celluloid, Germany 20.00
Green Bay Packer, Football Player, Composition 45.00
Henry Aaron, Plastic 22.00
Jiggs, Wooden, 1930s, 6 In. 235.00
John F. Kennedy & Jackie, Composition, Pair 235.00
Lord Plush Bottom 95.00
Man, Porcelain 65.00
Man & Woman, c.1880 .... 295.00
Minnesota Twins, Composition, Hand Painted, 1960s, 2 1/2 x 6 In. 45.00
Minnie Gump 80.00
Oriental, Seated, Holding Dagger, Sheath 145.00
Oriental Boy & Girl, Kissing, Papier-Mache, Pair 50.00
Oriental Man & Woman, Fans Behind Heads, Arms Uplifted, Pair 580.00
Phillies, Baseball Player, Plastic 18.00
Pig Pen, Composition, Painted, Lego, 1960s, 2 x 5 In. 22.00
Pigs, Bride & Groom 95.00
Planter, Duck Head 25.00
Pluto, 7 In. 175.00
Rabbit, Chalkware, 19th Century, 3 1/4 In. 1100.00
Rabbit, Composition, White & Pink Flocked, Glass Eyes, 8 In. 22.00
Rainier Beermaster, 18 In. 165.00
Salt & Pepper, Fish 38.00
Salt & Pepper, Skeleton 38.00
Santa Claus, Germany 110.00
Santa Claus, Head Rocks, Elastic Windup, Celluloid, 1930s 325.00
Santa Claus, Stand, Wicker Basket In Arm 675.00
Smokey Bear, Composition 85.00
Snoopy, Composition, 1970s, 4 In. 25.00
Topo Gigio, Bobbing Head 65.00
Woman, On Couch 45.00

NORITAKE porcelain was made in Japan after 1904 by Nippon Toki Kaisha.
The best-known Noritake pieces are marked with the M in a wreath for the
Morimura Brothers, a New York City distributing company. This mark was
used until 1941. Another famous Noritake china was made for the Larkin
Soap Company from 1916 through the 1930s. This dinnerware, decorated
with azaleas, was sold or given away as a premium. There may be some
helpful price information in the Nippon category, since prices are
comparable.

Ashtray, Dancing Couple, Tan Luster, Art Deco, Signed, 3 1/2 x 3 In. 125.00
Bowl, Azalea, 5 3/4 In. 22.00
Bowl, Azalea, 10 In. 20.00
Bowl, Baroda, 8 1/2 In. 22.00
Bowl, Bouillon, White & Gold 25.00
Bowl, Flowers, Shaded Brown, Blown Out Peanuts, Green M Wreath, 7 In. 50.00
Bowl, Nut, Orange Dog, Blue 35.00
Bowl, Vegetable, White & Gold, Oval, 9 In. 32.00
Bowl, White & Gold, 5 1/4 In. 18.00
Bowl, Woodland Stream, Stylized Cloverleaf Shape, Green M Wreath 58.00
Box, Sardine, White & Blue, Gold Trim 150.00
Butter Chip, Azalea, 3 1/4 In. .... 70.00 to 75.00
Butter Tub, Insert, Azalea, 5 1/8 In. 40.00
Cake Plate, Azalea, 9 3/4 In. .... 38.00 to 45.00

Cake Plate, Boat, Purple Sage & Mountain Scene, Handle, 8 In. 45.00
Cake Plate, Hand Painted Flowers & Garlands, Ivory Wreath, Red M, 6 Piece 22.00
Cake Plate, Scenic Landscape, Oval, 9 1/2 In. 50.00
Candlestick, Gold Flowers, Bird, Blue Luster, Pair 125.00
Candy Dish, Cover, Stylized Floral, Turquoise Ground, 6 1/2 In. 90.00
Casserole, Azalea, 10 3/4 In. 350.00
Cheese Dish, Slanted Cover, Swan 75.00
Chocolate Set, Floral 139.00
Condiment Set, White & Gold, 5 Piece 95.00
Cracker Jar, Cover, Tree In Meadow, 6 1/2 x 6 In. 105.00
Cruet, Azalea, Stopper .... 125.00 to 170.00
Cup, Azalea 15.00
Cup, Pink & Blue Flowers, Wreaths, Marked 6.00
Cup & Saucer, Azalea .... 9.00 to 18.00
Cup & Saucer, Azalea, After Dinner 38.00
Cup & Saucer, Desert Flowers 9.00
Cup & Saucer, White & Gold 24.00
Cup & Saucer, White & Gold, After Dinner 25.00
Cup & Saucer, Windmill Scene 10.00
Dinner Set, Azalea, 60 Piece 1095.00
Dresser Tray, Art Deco Woman, Blue-Green Luster, Gold Handle 275.00
Easter Egg, 1975, Mallard Ducks 18.00
Easter Egg, 1982 .... 18.00
Eggcup, Azalea, 3 1/8 In. .... 38.00 to 120.00
Figurine, Woman, Art Deco, White Dress, Orange Luster Ground 165.00
Gravy Boat, Lilybell 24.50
Gravy Boat, Milford, Attached Liner 10.00
Grill Plate, Azalea, 10 1/4 In. 110.00
Hair Receiver, Geometric, Allover Gold Luster Ground, Art Deco, 3 1/4 x 3 1/2 In. ... 50.00
Humidor, Floral Striped, 5 1/2 In. 85.00
Humidor, Tree In Meadow .... 200.00 to 300.00
Jam Jar, Raised Gold Design, 5 In. 30.00
Loving Cup, Scene In Medallion, Enamel & Moriage Trim 95.00
Luncheon Set, Art Deco Woman In Cups, Blue, 4 Piece 400.00
Luncheon Set, Rosemary, Box 125.00
Mug, Purple Irises Border 60.00
Mustard, Cover, Azalea, Handle, Ladle, 1 7/8 x 2 3/4 In. 40.00
Mustard, Cover, Tree In Meadow 15.00
Napkin Ring, Man & Woman, Art Deco, Box 60.00
Nappy, Woman Medallion, Art Deco, Tan Luster, Scalloped Black Trim, 5 1/4 In. 160.00
Plaque, Swans On Lake, 8 3/4 In. 85.00
Plate, 3 Floral Medallions, Gold Rim, 6 3/8 In. 2.50
Plate, Amerita, Dinner, 8 Piece 120.00
Plate, Ansonia, 6 1/4 In. 3.75
Plate, Ansonia, 9 1/2 In. 7.00
Plate, Azalea, 8 1/2 In. 15.00
Plate, Azalea, 10 In. 15.00
Plate, Googly-Eyed Girl Inside Base, Blue, Gold Handle, Marked 450.00
Plate, Multicolored Flowers, Brown Rim, 6 In., 4 Piece 10.00
Plate, Serving, Cover, Orange & Black Floral, Luster, 9 In. 40.00
Plate, White & Gold, 6 In. 15.00
Plate, White & Gold, 9 In. 22.00
Plate, White & Gold, 10 In. 24.00
Platter, Beaded Floral Medallions, Gold Encrusted, Ivory Band, 16 In. 22.00
Platter, Desert Flowers, 14 In. 30.00
Platter, Lorna, 14 In. 18.00
Platter, White & Gold, 14 In. 85.00
Relish, 2 Sections, Loop Handle, Green, Pink Flowers 300.00
Relish, Azalea, 4 Sections, Handle .... 130.00 to 135.00
Relish, Orange Bird Center 95.00
Salt & Pepper, Azalea 39.00
Salt Dip, Swan, Figural, White, Orange, 3 In., Pair 25.00

Saucer, Azalea 2.00
Saucer, Pink & Blue Flowers, Wreaths 6.00
Spooner, Scenic, Matte 65.00
Sugar, Cover, Azalea, Gold Finial .... 30.00 to 70.00
Sugar & Creamer, Ansonia 25.00
Sugar & Creamer, Azalea 32.00
Sugar & Creamer, Cover, Flowering Trees, Ivory Band, Red M Wreath 15.00
Sugar & Creamer, Japanese Lanterns, Basket Handle, Art Deco, Cobalt Ground 40.00
Sugar & Creamer, Pheasants, Hand Painted 55.00
Sugar Shaker, Azalea, 6 1/2 In. 85.00
Syrup, Azalea 65.00
Syrup, Azalea, Underplate 130.00
Syrup, Cover, Blue & Gold Florals, 4 1/2 In. 40.00
Table Set, Tree In Meadow, 4 Piece 325.00
Tea Set, Child's, Teapot, Sugar & Creamer, 3 Piece 850.00
Tea Set, Pink Peonies, Black Band, Pearl Luster, 21 Piece 90.00
Tile, Tea, Azalea 35.00
Toothpick, Azalea, 2 1/2 In. .... 85.00 to 130.00
Tray, Beaded Medallions, Green & Blue, White Ground, Green Wreath, 11 x 8 In. 65.00
Tray, Black Medallions, Orange Luster Band, Mother-Of-Pearl Center, 12 In. 18.00
Vase, Iridescent Copper Luster Over Browns, Bulbous, 5 5/8 In. 32.00
Vase, White House, Black Tree, Blue Luster, Art Deco 80.00
Wall Pocket, Flowers, Art Deco Vase, Blue Luster 65.00
Wall Pocket, Swan 55.00

NORTH DAKOTA SCHOOL OF MINES was established in 1892 at the University of North Dakota. A ceramic course was included and pieces were made from the clays found in the region. Students at the university made pieces from 1909 to 1949. Although very early pieces were marked *U.N.D.*, most pieces were stamped with the full name of the university.

Bookends, Planter, Ivy, Flat Bowl 750.00
Bowl, Carved Band Of Flowers, C.A. Sorbo, 6 3/4 In. 247.00
Bowl, Green Matte, M. Cable, 3 1/4 x 5 1/2 In. 425.00
Bowl, Green, Incised Geometric, 2 x 4 In. 95.00
Bowl, Multicolored Fruit, Leaves, Berries, Rust Ground, 9 In. 214.50
Cookie Jar, Farm Animal 1200.00
Creamer, Blue, M. Cable, 2 1/2 In. 125.00
Curtain Pull, Indian Head 80.00
Decanter, Bands Of Indian Designs, Mattson, Marked, 9 In. 465.00
Ewer, Floral, M. Cable, 6 In. 275.00
Figurine, Coyote 250.00
Flower Frog, Bird Shape, Blue & Tan, JIT, 5 1/2 In. 137.50
Flower Pot, Kissing Cardinals 2250.00
Ginger Jar, Cover, Chinese Sgraffito Design, 6 x 7 In. 1600.00
Lamp Base, Tapered, Blue, Green & Rust Matte Glaze, 10 In. 330.00
Lamp, Carved Palm Trees, Green Glaze, 1951, 9 In. 300.00
Mustard, Cover 175.00
Sugar, Cover, Cream, Cobalt Trim, 3 1/2 In. 480.00
Sugar & Creamer, Blue 150.00
Vase, Band Of Ducks, Brown & Ochre, Julia Mattson, 4 In. 715.00
Vase, Band Of Stylized Flowers, Signed, 7 x 6 In. 275.00
Vase, Black & Blue Bands, Glossy Glaze, Marked, 7 3/4 In. 410.00
Vase, Brown Tones, Havelson, 11 In. 190.00
Vase, Bud, Incised Leaf Design, Ivory Glaze, 6 In. 250.00
Vase, Carved Floral Band, Prairie Rose Glaze, M. Cable, 9 In. 467.00
Vase, Carved Roses & Leaves Band, Marked, 4 3/4 In. 550.00
Vase, Cobalt Blue & Taupe, Tan Ground, Signed, 5 In. 185.00
Vase, F.L.H., 4 In. 150.00
Vase, Holly Leaves & Berries, Green Ground, 1947, 6 In. 880.00
Vase, Incised Ivy, M. Peterson, 6 x 6 In. 440.00
Vase, Incised Wheat Stalks, Celadon Ground, Marked, 7 3/4 In. 700.00
Vase, Incised Wheat, F.C. Huckfield, Marked, 6 1/4 In. 620.00
Vase, Inscribed Why Not Minor, Cowboy, Marked, 5 3/4 In. 275.00

Vase, Interior Flowers, Lavender Glaze, 1929, 5 3/4 In. 275.00
Vase, Iris Blossoms & Leaves, L.M. Barlow, 9 In. 425.00
Vase, Lilac Glaze, Julia Mattson, 1927, 4 1/2 In. 135.00
Vase, Painted Black Buffalo, Rust Ground, Marked, 4 1/2 In. 600.00
Vase, Prairie Rose, Signed, 3 In. 250.00
Vase, Ring Of Girls, Brown, M. Kutson, 1946, 3 x 6 In. 275.00
Vase, Sgraffito Blossoms, Leaves, Incised, 1950, 9 In. 425.00
Vase, Shaded Blue, Huck, 4 In. 215.00
Vase, Squatty, Blue, 3 In. 100.00
Vase, Yellow, Gold Indian Designs, Red Ground, 1939, 4 In. 247.00

NORTHWOOD Glass Company was founded by Harry Northwood, a glassmaker who worked for Hobbs, Brockunier and Company, La Belle Glass Company, and Buckeye Glass Company before founding his own firm. He opened one factory in Indiana, Pennsylvania, in 1896, and another in Wheeling, West Virginia, in 1902. Northwood closed when Mr. Northwood died in 1923. Many types of glass were made, including carnival, custard, goofus, and pressed. The underlined N mark was used on some pieces.

Berry Bowl, Memphis, Green, Gold Trim 20.00
Berry Set, Atlas, Clear, 5 Piece 60.00
Berry Set, Cherry & Cable, 1908, 7 Piece 155.00
Berry Set, Cherry Thumbprint, Ruby & Gold Trim, 5 Piece 125.00
Berry Set, Intaglio, Ivory, 7 Piece 425.00
Berry Set, Plum & Cherry, 4 Piece 220.00
Bowl, Grape & Cable, Pie Crust Edge, Basket Weave, Marigold 130.00
Bowl, Pansy, Ruffled, 8 In. 250.00
Bowl, Regent, Amethyst, Gold Trim, 9 1/2 In. 50.00
Butter, Cover, Argonaut Shell 190.00
Butter, Cover, Cable, Ruby & Gold Trim 125.00
Butter, Cover, Cherry Thumbprint, Clear, Ruby & Gold Trim 100.00
Butter, Cover, Gold Rose, Green, Gold Trim 125.00
Butter, Cover, Intaglio, Green, Gold Trim 100.00
Butter, Cover, Strawberry & Cable, Clear, Ruby & Gold Trim 100.00
Chrysanthemum Sprig, Creamer, Milk Glass, 4 3/4 In. 192.00
Cologne Bottle, Grape & Cable, Stopper, Light Marigold, Carnival Glass 175.00
Creamer, Atlas, Clear, Gold Trim 30.00
Creamer, Hobnail, Canary Opalescent 45.00
Creamer, Pagoda, Milk Glass, Blue, 4 3/4 In. 192.00
Cruet, Paneled Sprig, Rubina 125.00
Hatpin Holder, Grape & Cable, Amethyst, Carnival Glass 140.00
Lemonade Set, Enameled Floral, Gold Trim, Paneled Tumblers, 9 Piece 475.00
Mug, Singing Bird, Blue, Carnival Glass 150.00
Mug, Singing Bird, Marigold, Carnival Glass 120.00
Pin Tray, Grape & Cable, Amethyst, Carnival Glass 200.00
Pitcher, Apple Blossom, Blue 235.00
Pitcher, Cherry & Cable, Green Opalescent, 1/2 Gal. 125.00
Pitcher, Cherry & Plum, Ruby & Gold Trim 125.00
Pitcher, Leaf Umbrella, Cranberry, c.1905, 9 In. 395.00
Pitcher, Pagoda, Milk Glass, Blue, 8 In. 660.00
Pitcher, Plums & Cherries, Clear, Ruby & Gold Trim 125.00
Plate, Grape & Cable, Basketweave, Amethyst, Carnival Glass, 9 In. 150.00
Plate, Strawberry, Amethyst, Carnival Glass, 9 In. 165.00
Rose Bowl, Inverted Fan & Feather, Vaseline 40.00
Salt & Pepper, Quilted Phlox, Blue Opaque 65.00
Spooner, Beaded Circle, Ivory, Enameled Flowers 150.00
Spooner, Cherry Thumbprint, Ruby & Gold Trim 60.00
Spooner, Singing Birds, Clear 35.00
Sugar, Cover, Cherry Thumbprint, Ruby & Gold Trim 75.00
Sugar, Cover, Hobnail, Opalescent 135.00
Sugar, Cover, Memphis, Green, Gold Trim 80.00
Sugar, Creamer & Spooner, Argonaut Shell, 3 Piece 225.00
Sugar Shaker, Aurora, Rubina 150.00
Syrup, Poinsettia, Blue Opalescent 700.00

Table Set, Cherry & Cable, 1908, 4 Piece 250.00
Toothpick, Leaf Mold, Cranberry, Vaseline Spatter Stain 225.00
Toothpick, Rubina Optic 110.00
Tumbler, Grape & Cable, Amethyst, Carnival Glass 32.50
Tumbler, Grape & Cable, Green, Carnival Glass 55.00
Tumbler, Oriental Poppy, Amethyst, Carnival Glass 80.00
Tumbler, Oriental Poppy, Green, Carnival Glass 67.50
Tumbler, Pagoda, Milk Glass, Blue, Gilt Trim, 3 3/4 In. 77.00
Vase, Pull-Up Overlay, Pink Loopings, 3 3/4 In. 325.00
Water Set, Gothic Arches, Green, Gold Trim, 5 Piece 225.00
Water Set, Memphis, Carnival Glass, Gold Trim, 7 Piece 295.00
Water Set, Memphis, Gold Trim, 7 Piece 225.00
Water Set, Regent, Blue, 7 Piece 475.00
Water Set, Springtime, Marigold, Carnival Glass, 7 Piece 1000.00

NU-ART was a trademark registered by the Imperial Glass Company of
Bellaire, Ohio, about 1920.

Bookends, Dogs, Scotties, Bronze, Art Deco 68.00
Bookends, Lincoln's Bust 65.00
Figurine, Nude, Holds Ashtray, Cigarette Box On Base 95.00
Plate, Homestead, 10 1/2 In. 700.00
Sugar & Creamer 50.00

NUTCRACKERS of many types have been used through the centuries. At
first the nutcracker was probably strong teeth or a hammer. But by the
nineteenth century, many elaborate and ingenious types were made. Levers,
screws, and hammer adaptations were the most popular. Because nutcrackers
are still useful, they are still being made, some in the old styles.

Black Man's Face, Bronze, 5 1/2 In. 135.00
Dog, Black Paint, Cast Iron, Harper Supply Co., 13 In. 94.00
Dog, Mastiff 125.00
Dog, Mechanical, Cast Iron, Table Top 17.50
Elephant, 4 5/8 x 9 1/2 In. 176.00
Parrot 125.00
Perfection, Mechanical, Iron 12.00
Rocket, Reeds 20.00
Topless Black Woman, Wooden 35.00
Wall Mount, Freeport, Illinois, Arcade 95.00

NYMPHENBURG, see Royal Nymphenburg

OCCUPIED JAPAN was printed on pottery, porcelain, toys, and other goods
made during the American occupation of Japan after World War II, from 1945
to 1952. Collectors now search for these pieces. The items were made for
export.

Ashtray, Classical Maidens, Bisque, Jasperware, Scalloped, Square, 2 3/4 In. 6.00
Ashtray, Dog, Boston Bulldog, At Hydrant 25.00
Ashtray, Elephant, Figural, Brown, 3 In. 3.50
Ashtray, Floral Spray, Scalloped, Square, 3 1/4 In. 2.50
Ashtray, Gold Bamboo & Leaves, Matte Gray, Rectangular, Ucagco, 4 In. 2.50
Ashtray, Map Of North Carolina, Figural, Bear, Dogwood, Indian, 6 1/4 In. 8.00
Ashtray, Strawberry, Figural, Gold Seeds, Stem & Rim, 4 In. 3.00
Box, Cover, Capo-Di-Monte Type, Andrea, 7 1/4 x 6 x 5 In. 98.00
Butter Chip, Country Scene, Man, Flute, Woman, Fan, Gold Rim, 3 1/4 In. 4.00
Cigarette Holder, Tray, Flowers, Caterpillars, Hokutosha 16.00
Climber, Fishbowl, Frog, Bisque, 4 In. 18.50
Condiment Set, Cobalt Blue Glass, Chrome, Musical, Wooden Box 100.00
Creamer, Corn 18.00
Cup & Saucer, Cherry Blossoms, Fruit 9.00
Cup & Saucer, Flowers, Blue Luster Rim, After Dinner 9.00
Cup & Saucer, Gold Tracery Design, Brick Red, After Dinner 8.50
Cup & Saucer, Roses, Gold Trim, After Dinner 9.50

Dinner Set, Lavonia, 75 Piece 700.00
Dish, Cheese, Cover, Cottage 70.00
Dish, Lemon, Lovers, In Garden, Loop Handle, Square, Elephant Mark, 5 3/4 In. 10.00
Ewer, Classical Maidens, Blue, Bisque, Jasperware, 4 1/4 In. 10.00
Figurine, Accordion Player, 3 1/4 In. 10.00
Figurine, Armchair, Porcelain, Hand Painted, Pair 45.00
Figurine, Bacchante Cherubs, Grapes, Basket, 3 1/4 In. 18.00
Figurine, Boy, Duck & Basket Of Apples, 4 In. 12.00
Figurine, Boy, Fence, Holds Horn & Bird, Hummel Type, 3 1/2 In. 8.00
Figurine, Boy, Holding Book, Bisque, Shorts, Suspenders, 4 3/4 In. 18.00
Figurine, Boy, Knapsack, Red Umbrella, Hummel Type, 4 1/4 In. 18.00
Figurine, Boy, Musician, Violin, On Wall, Tyrolean Hat, 4 In. 10.00
Figurine, Bride & Groom, Bisque, 1930s Clothes, 4 3/4 In. 6.00
Figurine, Colonial People, Cornucopia, Paulux, 8 x 8 In. 145.00
Figurine, Dog, Cocker Spaniel, Ozarks, 7 x 4 1/2 In. 15.00
Figurine, Dutch Children, Blue, Delft Type, 5 In., Pair 36.00
Figurine, Dutch Girl, Basket, Blue Delft Type, 4 7/8 In. 20.00
Figurine, Elf, Rides Snail, Red Cap, Pink Clothes, 4 In. 18.00
Figurine, Gentleman, Musician, Pink Jacket, Striped Breeches, 10 In. 60.00
Figurine, Girl, Singing, Music Book, 3 3/4 In. 11.00
Figurine, Man & Woman, Brown Coat, Flowered Skirt, 6 1/2 In. 22.00
Figurine, Man & Woman, Courting, Striped Breeches, 4 In. 20.00
Figurine, Man & Woman, Dancing, Pink Coat, Flowered Skirt, 6 In. 34.00
Figurine, Man, Musician, Lute, Blue & Yellow Cape, Bisque, 10 In. 60.00
Figurine, Shoe, Floral, Medium Heel, 4 In. 6.00
Figurine, Songbird, 7 In., Pair 58.00
Figurine, Victorian Lady, Porcelain, Gold Trim, Moruyama, 7 In. 105.00
Figurine, Woman & Man, Musicians, 4 5/8 In. 18.00
Figurine, Woman, Feathered Hat, Umbrella, Blue, Delft Type, 5 In. 20.00
Figurine, Woman, Flower Basket, Green Hat, Hadson, 6 1/2 In. 24.00
Lamp, Lacquered, Metal, Elongated Bell Shape, Silver Ferns, Maruni, 14 In. 120.00
Lamp, Man & Woman, Figural, Pastoral, 10 1/2 In. 28.50
Lamp, Shepherd Boy, With Horn, Tree Trunk, Pastel, Andrea, 11 3/8 In., Pair 70.00
Nappy, Floral Border, Pale Green, Yameka, 5 1/2 In. 2.50
Nappy, Flowers, Kent China, 5 3/8 In. 3.50
Pitcher, Scotty, Mottled Black, Brown 22.00
Planter, Donkey, Cart, Brown, Cream, Blue Trim, 4 3/4 In. 6.00
Planter, Duck, Turned Head, Horseshoe Mark, 4 x 5 1/2 In. 12.00
Planter, Woman, Bisque, 6 In. 80.00
Plaque, Woman, Headdress, Man, Hat, Bisque, Frame, 4 1/2 In., Pair 45.00
Plate, Floral Scrolled Border, Ivory Band, Mira, 7 1/2 In. 3.50
Plate, Floral, Geometric Rim, Octagonal, W In Wreath, 4 In. 10.00
Plate, Gold Flowers, Plums, Leaves, Reticulated, Ucagco, 8 1/4 In. 20.00
Plate, Leaf, Floral Spray, Open Handle, Gold Trim, Artist, 5 In. 8.00
Plate, Leaf, Floral Spray, Stem Hole, Berkshire, 4 3/4 In. 7.00
Plate, Maple Leaf, Lilies, Gold Rim, Hand Painted, 4 In. 5.00
Plate, Portrait, Renaissance Woman, Black Ground, Andrea, 4 In. 18.00
Plate, Renaissance Man & Woman, Pierced, Gold Rim, SGK, 4 In., Pair 18.00
Rice Bowl, Flower, Leaf Branch, Celadon, 4 1/2 x 2 3/8 In. 6.50
Server, Raised Gold Scrolls & Flowers, 2 Tiers, Loop Handle, Andrea, 10 In. 30.00
Shelf Sitter, Boy & Girl, Fishing, Bisque, 4 1/4 In., Pair 20.00
Soup, Dish, Multicolored Wildflowers Rim, Kent, 8 1/2 In. 5.00
Sugar, Tomato, Figural 12.00
Sugar & Creamer, Cottage, Figural 50.00
Sugar & Creamer, Cover, Floral Sprays, Yamaka 12.00
Sugar & Creamer, Swan Handle & Finial, Pastel 40.00
Teapot, Cottage, Figural 60.00
Vase, Flowers, Relief, High Handles, Matted, 4 x 2 1/2 In. 10.00
Vase, Jasperware, Bisque, Shoulder Handles, Pink Flower, 2 3/4 In. 9.00
Vase, Metal, Gold Dust Chrysanthemums, Lacquered, Classic Shape, 6 x 3 In. 40.00
Vase, Pillow, Pink Tulip, Brick Ground, Ruffled, Shoulder Handles, 4 1/4 In. 8.00
Vase, Woman & Man, Large, Pair 150.00

Wall Pocket, Bird, Apple Tree Branch, Figural, 5 x 4 1/2 In. 28.00

OHR pottery was made in Biloxi, Mississippi, from 1883 to 1918 by George
E. Ohr, a true eccentric. The pottery was made of very thin clay that was
twisted, folded, and dented into odd, graceful shapes. Some pieces were
lifelike models of hats, animal heads, or even a potato. Others were decorated
with folded clay *snakes*. Reproductions and reworked pieces are appearing on
the market. These have been reglazed, or snakes and other embellishments
have been added.

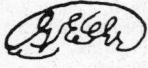

Bell, Indian, 12 In.	3500.00
Bell, Indian, 14 In.	2500.00
Bowl, Black & Brown Luster Glaze, Paper Thin, Signed, 2 x 3 In.	850.00
Bowl, Closed-In Rim, Mottled Glaze, Marked, 4 x 6 In.	950.00
Bowl, Spherical, Folded Rim, Black Sponged Design, Marked, 4 3/4 In.	700.00
Chalice, Ruffled Cup, Gray Glaze, Green Blistered Flaring Base, Signed	990.00
Inkwell, Geometric Buildings, Gray Glaze, Square Base, 2 3/4 x 6 In.	475.00
Inkwell, House Form, American Flag Speckled Base, Signed, 3 1/2 x 9 In.	1700.00
Jug, Owl, 7 In.	1500.00
Jug, Water, Ring Handle, Buff, Marked, 9 x 6 1/4 In.	357.00
Mug, 3 Strap Handles, In-Body Twist, Buff Bisque Clay, Signed, 7 In.	850.00
Mug, Ear-Form Handle, Spotted Glaze, Signed, 1901, 6 3/4 x 6 In.	2750.00
Mug, Puzzle, Brown Speckled, Gun-Metal Glaze, Signed, 4 x 5 In.	550.00 to 600.00
Mug, Puzzle, Green & Brown	600.00
Mug, Puzzle, Green Glaze	1000.00
Mug, Puzzle, Green Mottled Glaze	1200.00
Pitcher, Free-Form Spout, Scoddled Bisque Clay, Pinched Handle, Signed, 4 3/4 In.	715.00
Pitcher, Gunmetal Gray Glazed Handle, Signed, 5 1/2 In.	885.00
Pitcher, Pinched & Folded-In Rim, Cutout Handle, Signed, 7 In.	1880.00
Pitcher, Pinched & Dimpled, Cut-Out Handle, Caramel Glaze, Marked, 4 1/4 In.	1400.00
Pitcher, Puzzle, Gulf Shore Scene, Caramel Glaze, Marked, 1899, 8 1/4 In.	2700.00
Pitcher, Ruffled Rim, Blue & Green Glaze, Signed, 6 1/4 In.	2100.00
Pitcher, Twist & Folded Handle, Green & Black Glaze, Marked, 3 1/4 x 3 1/2 In.	1900.00
Plaque, Crab In Dark Green Glaze, Signed, 1899, 8 x 8 1/2 In.	4500.00
Plate, Tortured Ruffles, Flat Center, Bisque Clay, Signed, 7 1/2 In.	1100.00
Teapot, Banded Body, D Handle, Sponged Green On Red, Marked, 5 x 8 In.	8800.00
Teapot, Banded Body, Orange & Brown Glossy Glaze, Signed, 7 1/4 In.	2175.00
Teapot, Serpent Spout, Clear Green & Caramel Glaze, Marked, 8 3/4 In.	400.00
Vase, Dimpled Body, White Bisque Glaze, Signed, 5 In.	550.00
Vase, Dimpled, Floriform Folded Rim, Speckled Glaze, Marked, 7 x 5 1/2 In.	1300.00
Vase, Dimpled, Ruffled Neck, Green Glaze Over Dark Blue Glaze, Signed, 5 3/4 In.	1800.00
Vase, Folded & Rumpled, Black Mirror Glaze, Marked, 4 x 4 3/4 In.	1500.00
Vase, Folded Rim, Bulbous Base, Ochre, Rust & Green Glaze, 4 x 3 In.	825.00
Vase, Folded Rim, Dimples & Flat Folds At Rim, Black Glaze, Marked, 4 1/2 In.	1100.00
Vase, Folded Rim, In-Body Twist, Terra-Cotta Clay, Signed, 1905	1000.00
Vase, Folded Rim, Incised Band, Swollen Mid-Section, Mottled Glaze, Marked, 5 In.	900.00
Vase, In-Body Twist At Neck, Khaki Green Glaze, Signed, 9 1/4 In.	3400.00
Vase, Marbleized Glaze, Ripped & Folded Rim, Marked, 4 1/4 In.	1000.00
Vase, Mottled Red, Green, Blue & White Glaze, Baluster Shape, Marked, 5 1/2 In.	1600.00
Vase, Open Folded Rim, Orange & Buff Bisque Clay, Signed, 4 1/2 x 3 3/4 In.	1100.00
Vase, Pigeon-Feathered Glaze, Caramel Ground, Marked, 8 In.	850.00
Vase, Pink & Blue Blistered Glaze, Signed, 4 3/4 In.	715.00
Vase, Pink & Brown Leopard Skin, Grand Feu, 10 In.	4125.00
Vase, Protruding Mouth, Gunmetal Black Glaze, Signed, 4 1/2 In.	1100.00
Vase, Red & Tan, Tortured, Bisque, Unglazed, 5 In.	4125.00
Vase, Ruffled Rim, Pear Shape, Red Glossy Glaze, Signed, 4 1/2 x 4 In.	5250.00
Vase, Twisted Top, Speckled Glaze, Marked, 5 1/2 x 3 3/4 In.	1900.00
Vase, Twisted, Bisque, Brown Clay, Marked, 3 1/4 x 3 In.	750.00
Vessel, Dimples, Pinched Face, Green & Gunmetal Glaze, Signed, 4 3/4 In.	1300.00
Vessel, Folded Rim, Gunmetal Black Bisque Clay, Signed, 6 1/4 In.	600.00
Vessel, Free Form, Folded & Pinched, Burnt Orange, Signed, 5 1/2 x 7 In.	1700.00
Vessel, Iridescent Brick Red Glaze, Signed, 3 1/2 x 3 1/2 In.	665.00
Vessel, Leathery Blue Undulating Waist, Yellow & Green Neck, Signed, 2 3/4 In.	500.00

Vessel, Pinched Body, Terra-Cotta Bisque Clay, Signed, 1906 .... 3100.00
Vessel, Ruffled Rim, Footed 2860.00

OLD IVORY china was made by Hermann Ohme in Silesia, Germany, at the
end of the nineteenth century. The ivory-colored dishes have flowers, fruit, or
acorns as decoration and are often marked with a crown and the word *Silesia*.
Some pieces are also marked with the words *Old Ivory*. The pattern numbers
appear on the base of each piece.

OLD IVORY
84

Berry Bowl, Holly, 10 In. 195.00
Biscuit Jar, No. 16 .... 375.00
Bowl, Cupped Sides, Poppies, No. 112, Double Handles, 8 x 12 1/2 In. 150.00
Bowl, No. 75, 9 1/2 In. 70.00
Bowl, No. 84, 9 1/2 In. .... 95.00 to 125.00
Cake Plate, 10 In. 75.00
Cake Plate, Clarion, Pink & Yellow Roses, Silesia 125.00
Cake Plate, No. 16, Marked, 10 1/2 In. 120.00
Cake Plate, No. 84, 11 In. 125.00
Cake Stand, Hexagonal Shape, Pedestal, Fancy Foot, Silesia, 9 x 9 x 4 In. 550.00
Celery Tray, No. 16 .... 145.00
Celery Tray, No. 112, Rose Design, Marked, 11 1/2 In. 70.00
Chocolate Pot, Silesia, No. 16 .... 350.00
Chocolate Pot, Silesia, Pear Shaped, Yellow Roses, Gold Trim, 10 1/2 In. 275.00
Chocolate Pot, Thistle 235.00
Chocolate Set, No. 11, 12 Piece 975.00
Chop Plate, No. 11, 13 In. 135.00
Cold Meat Platter, No. 90, 8 Matching Plates, Platter-11 1/2 x 8 1/4 In. 350.00
Cookie Plate, No. 82, Scalloped Rim, 7 1/2 In. 75.00
Hatpin Holder, La Touraine, Scalloped Base, Gold Trim, 5 In. 195.00
Mustard, No. 16, Silesia 225.00
Mustard, No. 28, Silesia 240.00
Plate, No. 84, 7 1/2 In. 50.00
Plate, Silesia, No. 16, 7 1/2 In. 55.00
Relish, No. 84 .... 65.00
Spooner, No. 200, Flat, Cut-Out To Hang 95.00
Sugar & Creamer, Cover, No. 16 .... 100.00
Sugar & Creamer, No. 84 .... 100.00
Toothpick, No. 16, Silesia 185.00
Toothpick, No. 75, Silesia .... 175.00 to 185.00
Toothpick, No. 84 .... 275.00
Tray, Dresser, Touraine, Lily-Of-The-Valley, Gold Accents, 11 1/2 x 6 In. 165.00

OLD PARIS, see Paris

OLD SLEEPY EYE, see Sleepy Eye

ONION PATTERN, originally named *bulb pattern*, is a white ware decorated
with cobalt blue or pink. Although it is commonly associated with Meissen,
other companies made the pattern in the late nineteenth and the twentieth
centuries. A rare type is called *red bud* because there are added red accents on
the blue-and-white dishes.

Bowl, Reclining Male Figure Support, Meissen, 11 1/2 In. 385.00
Bowl, Reticulated Basketweave, Floral Medallions, Meissen, 11 x 3 1/2 In. 140.00
Box, Cover, Meissen, 3 3/4 In. 140.00
Butter Chip, Meissen, 3 Piece 55.00
Compote, Pierced Rim, Spiral Painted Stem, Meissen, 8 In. 165.00
Cup & Saucer, Germany 30.00
Feeder, Infant, 6 1/4 In. 60.00
Funnel, Loop Handle 75.00
Pitcher, Tettau, 4 1/2 In. 45.00
Plate, B.W.M. & Co., 10 In. 90.00
Plate, Flowering Chrysanthemum, Fruit Sprigs, Meissen, 8 13/16 In. 2070.00
Plate, Germany, 8 1/4 In. 2.00
Plate, Meissen, Crossed Swords, 9 1/2 In. 55.00

Plate, Open Edge, Meissen, 8 1/4 In.		110.00
Platter, Fish, Crossed Swords, 11 x 23 In.		375.00
Platter, Germany, 10 x 7 1/4 In.		23.00
Relish, 4 Sections, Meissen		150.00
Rolling Pin, Meissen		245.00
Soup, Dish, Oval, Meissen, 8 In.		30.00
Sugar, Cover, Villeroy & Boch		85.00
Trivet, Fireplace, Metal & Porcelain, Wooden Handle		350.00
Tureen, Underglazed, Crossed Swords, Oval, Meissen, 10 x 14 x 9 1/2 In.		550.00

OPALESCENT GLASS is translucent glass that has the tones of the opal gemstone. It originated in England in the 1870s and is often found in pressed glassware made in Victorian times. Opalescent glass was first made in America in 1897 at the Northwood glassworks in Indiana, Pennsylvania. Some dealers use the terms *opaline* and *opalescent* for any of these translucent wares. More opalescent pieces may be listed in Hobnail, Northwood, Pressed Glass, Spanish Lace, and other glass categories.

Basket, Green, Applied Clear Glass Handle, 3 3/4 In.		60.00
Berry Set, Iris With Meander, Blue, Jefferson Glass, 6 Piece		150.00
Bottle, Barber, Arabian Nights, Beaumont Glass, Cranberry, 1899		495.00
Bottle, Wine, Rib Optic, Cranberry, 1953, 13 1/2 In.		125.00
Bowl, Barbells, Aqua, 8 x 2 1/2 In.		30.00
Bowl, Beaded Fan, Green, Footed, Crimped, 6 3/4 In.		28.00
Bowl, Drapery, White, 9 In.		70.00
Bowl, Laura, White, Ruffled		22.00
Bowl, Polka Dot, Cranberry, 6 In.		135.00
Bowl, Reverse Drapery, Green, 8 1/4 x 2 1/4 In.		35.00
Bowl, Ruffles & Rings, Green		50.00
Butter, Cover, Diamond Spearhead, Green		260.00
Butter, Cover, Frosted Leaf & Basket Weave, White		110.00
Butter, Cover, Hobnail, Blue		65.00
Butter, Cover, Jewel & Flower, Blue, Gold Trim		450.00
Butter, Cover, Swag With Brackets, Green		160.00
Butter, Cover, Wreath & Shell, Blue		295.00
Candleholder, Green, 1959		30.00
Celery, Chrysanthemum Base Swirl, White		135.00
Compote, Argonaut Shell, Blue, Footed, 7 1/2 x 4 In.		52.00
Compote, Jelly, Rayed Heart, Blue		85.00
Compote, Popsicle Sticks, Green, 8 x 4 In.		44.00
Creamer, Flora, White		50.00
Creamer, Fluted Scrolls, Blue		65.00
Creamer, Fluted Scrolls, White		38.00
Creamer, Jewel & Flower		75.00
Creamer, Stars & Stripes, Cranberry, 4 In.		60.00
Creamer, Swag & Bracket, Blue		45.00
Creamer, Tokyo, Blue		85.00
Cruet, Argonaut Shell		115.00
Cruet, Chrysanthemum, Cut Stopper, Cranberry		395.00
Cruet, Daisy & Fern, Blue	110.00 to	125.00
Cruet, Everglades, Blue		450.00
Cruet, Inverted Thumbprint, Tapered, Blue		135.00
Cruet, Iris With Meander, Vaseline		485.00
Cruet, Paneled Grape		55.00
Cruet, Paneled Sprig, White		165.00
Cruet, Ribbed Opal Lattice, Blue		125.00
Cruet, Tokyo, Blue		175.00
Cruet, Windows, Swirled, White		90.00
Cuspidor, Diamond Spearhead, Vaseline		125.00
Cuspidor, Plum Opalescent, Souvenir, 1984		60.00
Cuspidor, Woman's, Wreath & Shell		65.00
Dish, Berry Patch, Green, Pedestal, 2 x 5 1/2 In.		27.00
Dish, Blooms & Blossoms, Green, Handle, Square, 5 7/8 In.		30.00

Dish, Hobnail, White, 5 1/2 In.	7.50
Dish, Honey, Roman Rosette	52.00
Dish, Spokes & Wheels, 8 In.	45.00
Finger Bowl, Beatty Rib, Blue	28.00
Finger Bowl, Diamond Quilted, Flared Ruffled Rim, Blue	50.00
Hat, Lime Green, Swirl, Fenton, 3 x 4 1/2 In.	55.00
Hat, Top, Dot Optic, Blue, 1931, 4 1/2 x 5 1/2 In.	90.00
Hat, Top, French Spiral, Cranberry, 1939, 6 x 9 In.	95.00
Lamp, Daisy & Fern, Cranberry Satin, 10 In.	395.00
Mug, Diamond Spearhead, Vaseline	68.00
Nappy, Sea Spray, Green	27.00
Pitcher, Alaska, Blue	495.00
Pitcher, Beaumont, Green Swirl	385.00
Pitcher, Buttons & Birds, Blue	225.00
Pitcher, Christmas Snowflake, Blue, 8 3/4 In.	175.00
Pitcher, Dot Optic, Green, 1931, 9 In.	175.00
Pitcher, Fluted Scrolls, Blue	250.00
Pitcher, Honeycomb & Clover, Gold Trim, Green	400.00
Pitcher, Jeweled Heart, Green	650.00
Pitcher, Leaf Medallion, Amethyst, Gold Trim	350.00
Pitcher, Poinsettia, Blue	275.00
Pitcher, Polka Dot, Cranberry	995.00
Pitcher, Regal, Green	625.00
Pitcher, Ribbed Lattice, Blue	500.00
Pitcher, Swag With Brackets, Green	575.00
Pitcher, Swirl, Cranberry	695.00
Pitcher Set, Water, Seaweed Pattern, Blue, 4 Piece	375.00
Plate, Cashews, White	27.50
Plate, Iris With Meander, 7 In.	35.00
Rose Bowl, Expanded Flutes, Blue	50.00
Rose Bowl, Fancy Fantails, Vaseline	45.00
Rose Bowl, Keyhole, White	28.00
Rose Bowl, Spiral Optic, Blue, 1939	45.00
Rose Bowl, Spiral Optic, Cranberry, 1939	45.00
Rose Bowl, Swirl, Pink Petal Feet, Pink Handles, Amber, 4 3/4 In.	75.00
Salt, Cotton Bale, Pink	55.00
Salt, Sawtooth, Footed, 3 5/8 In.	50.00
Salt, Wreath & Shell, Blue	95.00
Salt, Wreath & Shell, Green	75.00
Saltshaker, Jewel & Flower, White, Original Top	95.00
Spooner, Alaska, Blue	55.00
Spooner, Argonaut Shell, Blue	95.00
Spooner, Everglades, Blue	55.00
Spooner, Fern, Blue	140.00
Spooner, Flora, Blue	175.00
Spooner, Hobnail, Footed, Ruffled Top, Lavender	95.00
Spooner, Jewel & Flower	75.00
Spooner, Regal, Blue	95.00
Spooner, Ribbed Spiral, White	65.00
Spooner, Swag & Bracket, Blue	45.00
Spooner, Wreath & Shell, Vaseline	80.00
Sugar, Cover, Flora, Blue	175.00
Sugar, Cover, Fluted Scrolls, Blue	110.00
Sugar, Cover, Hobnail	45.00
Sugar, Cover, Swag & Bracket, Green	125.00
Sugar, Peacock Feather	25.00
Sugar, Sunburst-On-Shield, Blue	45.00
Sugar, Wreath & Shell, Blue	60.00
Sugar & Creamer, Argonaut Shell, Blue	225.00
Sugar & Creamer, Beaded Block, Vaseline	55.00 to 75.00
Sugar Shaker, Bubble Lattice, Vaseline	295.00
Sugar Shaker, Coin Spot, Wide Waist, Blue	165.00

Sugar Shaker, Cranberry	85.00
Sugar Shaker, Daisy & Fern, 9 Panel Mold, Cranberry	235.00
Sugar Shaker, Red & White Swirl	150.00
Sugar Shaker, Reverse Swirl, Vaseline	325.00
Sugar Shaker, Ribbed Lattice, Blue	295.00
Sugar Shaker, Spanish Lace, Vaseline	265.00
Sugar Shaker, Stripe, Vaseline	275.00
Sugar Shaker, Swirl, Green	25.00
Sugar Shaker, Windows, Blue	350.00
Sugar Sifter, Vaseline & White	165.00
Syrup, Beatty Swirl, White	365.00
Syrup, Bubble Lattice	225.00
Syrup, Coin Dot, 9-Panel	175.00
Syrup, Coin Spot, Blue	195.00
Syrup, Cranberry, Applied Handle	130.00
Syrup, Daisy & Fern, Blue	165.00
Syrup, Daisy & Fern, Cranberry	275.00
Syrup, Reverse Swirl, Blue	235.00
Syrup, Seaweed, Blue	425.00
Syrup, Windows, Blue	395.00
Table Set, Jewel & Flower, Blue, 4 Piece	650.00
Table Set, Tokyo, Green, 4 Piece	450.00
Tankard, Blown Twist, Green, Twisted Handle	225.00
Toothpicks are listed in the Toothpick category.	
Tumble-Up, Swirl, Cranberry, 8 1/4 In.	390.00
Tumbler, Buttons & Braids, Cranberry	125.00
Tumbler, Cranberry, Seaweed, Pair	100.00
Tumbler, Diamond Spearhead, Vaseline	55.00
Tumbler, Diamonds, Cranberry	95.00
Tumbler, Everglades, Vaseline	50.00
Tumbler, Hobnail, Blue	55.00
Tumbler, Hobnail, White, 5 Piece	100.00
Tumbler, Iris With Meander, Blue	85.00
Tumbler, Polka Dot, Cranberry	75.00
Tumbler, Spanish Lace, Vaseline	48.00
Tumbler, Swirl, Cranberry	30.00
Tumbler, Water Lily & Cattails, Blue	38.00 to 45.00
Vase, Clubs & Spades, 10 In.	40.00
Vase, Fluted Bars & Beads, Vaseline, Cranberry Trimp, Cupped, Ruffled	46.00
Vase, Green Feather, Signed Northwood, 9 In.	45.00
Vase, Hobnail, Triangular Top, Blue, 5 In.	65.00
Vase, Lined Heart, Blue, Ribbed, Flared, Crimped, 7 x 5 3/4 In.	28.00
Vase, Spiral Twist Stem, Vaseline Petal Feet, Green, 8 In.	70.00
Vase, Tokyo, Green	35.00
Vase, Windows, Ruffled Top, Urn Shape, Cranberry, 8 In.	95.00
Wall Pocket, Tree Trunk & Shell, Blue, 6 3/4 x 4 3/8 In.	110.00
Water Set, Buttons & Braids, Blue, 7 Piece	625.00
Water Set, Daisy & Fern, Cranberry, 5 Piece	375.00
Water Set, Daisy & Fern, Cranberry, 7 Piece	275.00
Water Set, Drapery, Blue, 6 Piece	450.00
Water Set, Palm Beach, Vaseline, 6 Piece	650.00
Water Set, Regal, Blue, 7 Piece	595.00
Water Set, Swag With Brackets, Blue, 7 Piece	595.00
Water Set, Tokyo, Green, 7 Piece	695.00

OPALINE, or opal glass, was made in white, green, and other colors. The glass had a matte surface and a lack of transparency. It was often gilded or painted. It was a popular mid-nineteenth-century European glassware.

Bottle, Cologne, Floral Enamel Motifs, Finial, 6 In.	99.00
Cruet, Lavender	95.00
Dresser Jar, Floral Enamel Motifs, Bowl Shaped Finial, Cover, 8 In.	66.00
Lamp, Oil, Green, Foliate Form, Fluted Support, Electric, 35 In.	410.00

Vase, Birds & Leaves, Gilded Banding, Hand Painted, 8 1/4 In., Pair 450.00
Vase, Straight Optic, Corset Shape, 13 x 4 1/2 In. 39.00

OPERA GLASSES are needed because the stage is a long way from some of
the seats at a play or an opera. Mother-of-pearl was a popular decoration.

Cabordion Sapphire Slide, 14K Yellow Gold 2760.00
Chevaliar, Paris, Brass, Leather Case, Hunting Scene 50.00
Chevalier, Paris, Embossed Leather Over Brass, Hunting Scene 47.50
Flower, Red Enamel, Mother-Of-Pearl 155.00
Iris, Paris 15.00
Leather Case, Occupied Japan 45.00
Lorgnette, Foliate Decoration, Suspended From Grosgrain Ribbon, Gold 1100.00
Mother-Of-Pearl, Brass, Collapsible Handle, Iris, Paris, c.1880 .... 110.00
Mother-Of-Pearl, Brass, France 110.00
Mother-Of-Pearl, Case 75.00
Mother-Of-Pearl, Collapsible Handle, Chevalier, Paris, c.1880, Pair 99.00
Mother-Of-Pearl, Lemaire, Lacquered Brass, Velvet Interior Case 190.00
Mother-Of-Pearl, Negretti & Zumbra 137.00
Mother-Of-Pearl, Smoky, Brass, Audeaiare, Paris 42.00
Porcelain, Enamel, Mother-Of-Pearl, Leather Case, France, 19th Century 400.00
Sportiere, Brass, Nickel Plate, Paris 15.00

ORPHAN ANNIE first appeared in the comics in 1924. The redheaded girl
and her friends have been on the radio and are still on the comic pages. A
Broadway musical show and a movie in the 1980s made Annie popular again
and many toys, dishes, and other memorabilia are being made.

Badge, Decoder, Mysto-Magic, 1939 .... 50.00
Bank, Gumball, Box, 1982 .... 40.00
Big Little Book, Little Orphan Annie & Mysterious Shoemaker, 1938 .... 14.00
Big Little Book, Orphan Annie Big Train Robbery 35.00
Book, Annie & The Gila Master Gang, Illustrations, 1934 .... 25.00
Book, Big Little Book, Little Orphan Annie & The Ancient Treasure Of Am, 1939 .... 39.00
Book, Little Orphan Annie And Daddy Warbucks, Whitman, 1934, 3 x 4 In. 12.00
Coloring Book, Little Orphan Annie, No.107 .... 16.00
Comic Book, Puffed Wheat Premium, 1938 .... 15.00
Decoder Badge, Ovaltine Premium, Secret Compartment, 1936 .... 65.00
Decoder Badge, Sunburst, Radio Premium, 1937 .... 55.00
Doll, Cloth, Box 550.00
Doll, Oilcloth, Yellow, Red & Black, With Sandy, 10 In. 175.00
Doll & Sandy Walker, Wood Jointed, Tin Plate Sandy, Marx, 5 In., Pair 475.00
Figure, Wood, Jointed, Harold Gray, 6 In. 185.00
Figurine, Sandy, Bisque, Germany, 1930s 50.00
Light Bulb, Christmas, Figural, 1935 .... 45.00
Map, Simmons Corners, Framed, 18 x 24 In. 125.00
Mug, Beetleware, Domed Top 43.00
Mug, Ovaltine, Beetleware 48.00
Mug, Ovaltine, Ceramic, 1930s, 3 In. 52.00
Mug, Ovaltine, Orphan Annie & Sandy 95.00
Mug, Shake-Up, Ovaltine, 1940 .... 70.00
PEZ, Container 55.00
Pin, Membership, 1937 .... 25.00
Pin, Sunburst Decoder, 1937 .... 45.00
Ring, 2 Initials 165.00
Scarf Set, 1930s, Box 75.00
Sewing Kit, For Cloth Doll, Patterns, Loop Needle, Wool, Silks, Box 215.00
Stove, Little Orphan Annie, 1930s 75.00
Tea Set, Box, 13 Piece 395.00
Toy, Bubble Set, Box, 1930s 80.00
Toy, Jacks Set, Ball, 1933, On Card 95.00
Wristwatch, 1935, Box 395.00
Wristwatch, 1948, Box 315.00
Wristwatch, Character, Box 395.00

Wristwatch, Character, Leather Strap, 1940 .... 349.00

ORREFORS Glassworks, located in the Swedish province of Smaaland, was established in 1898. The company is still making glass for use on the table or as decorations. There is renewed interest in the glass made in the modern *Orrefors* styles of the 1940s and 1950s. Most vases and decorative pieces are signed with the etched name.

Bowl, Asymmetrical, Tapering 3-Lobed Base, 13 x 4 In. 121.00
Bowl, Domed Cover, Foliate Finial, Death Of Cleopatra, Signed, 13 In. 2640.00
Bowl, Floral Medallions, Liner, Under Dish, Trapezoidal Windows, c.1929, 5 In. 2800.00
Bowl, Internal Abstract Design, Dark Amethyst, Signed, 9 1/4 In. 1725.00
Bowl, Male Nudes, Footed, Signed, 5 In. 285.00
Bowl, Red & Blue Overlapping Designs, Sven Palmquist, 1953, 7 3/4 In. 2300.00
Bowl, Sailor's Dream, Enameled, Expo. 682-68, Gunnar Cyren, 9 1/4 In. 1540.00
Bowl, Underplate, Mythological Scene, Couples In Garden, 1920, 14 3/4 In. 2875.00
Bowl, Underplate, Nude Women, Flowing Hair, No. 107.28, 7 3/4 In. 1840.00
Candleholder, Signed, 2 x 2 In., Pair 80.00
Decanter, Engraved Cancan Dancer, Simon Gate, 1922, 7 5/8 In. 288.00
Liqueur, Silvia 40.00
Pitcher, Cow, Green & Ivory, 8 In. 450.00
Vase, Abstract Design, Opaque Base, Vicke Lindstrand, 1935, 7 5/8 In. 115.00
Vase, Ariel, Blue, Inlaid Bubble Stripes, Ingeborg Lundin, No. 351K, 5 1/4 In. 440.00
Vase, Ariel, Profile Of Woman & Dove Of Peace, Blue, 6 In. 4500.00
Vase, Bubble, Sphere, Engraving, Naked Child Blowing Bubbles, V. Lindstrand 550.00
Vase, Crystal Optical Ribs, Black Base, Model HU 97, 1932, 7 In. 460.00
Vase, Elongated Teardrop Form, Dot Optical Pattern, 12 1/2 In. 575.00
Vase, Engraved Girl In Flower Field, 5 In. 185.00
Vase, Fish & Seaweed, Clear Ground, Paperweight, Edward Hald, 5 1/2 In. 522.00
Vase, Inclusions Of Fish & Underwater Plants, Signed, 6 In. 368.00
Vase, Interior Tropical Fish, Aquatic Plants, Edward Hald, 1947, 6 In. 518.00
Vase, Internal Black & Green Fish Amidst Seaweed, 5 1/4 In. 690.00
Vase, Jellyfish Amid Aquatic Plants, Edward Hald, c.1941, 6 3/4 In. 1380.00
Vase, Naked Male Diver, Seen Through Rippled Waves, Marked, 11 1/4 In. 935.00
Vase, Nude Diver Swimming To Pearl Clam, Signed, 10 1/2 In. 350.00
Vase, Topaz, Medallions, Bubbles, Expo. Dec. 30, 1953, 14 1/2 In. 550.00
Vase, Trumpet Form Neck & Foot, Edward Hald, c.1930, 12 3/8 In. 345.00

OTT & BREWER Company operated the Etruria Pottery at Trenton, New Jersey, from 1863 to 1893. They started making belleek in 1882. The firm used a variety of marks that incorporated the initials *O & B*.

Bowl, Gold Paste Florals, 3 In. 95.00
Creamer, Gold Florals, Gold Handle, Cylindrical, 4 1/2 In. 75.00
Cup & Saucer, Tridacna, Twig Handle, Gilded Trim 155.00
Pitcher, Gilt-Tipped Twig Stumps, Forked Twig Handles, 1883, 8 7/16 In. 1035.00
Sugar & Creamer, Gold Paste Florals, Matte Finish 250.00
Vase, Hand Painted Over Glaze, Etruria, 11 In. 350.00
Wash Set, Belleek Type, 1860-1880, 5 Piece 500.00

OVERBECK pottery was made by four sisters named Overbeck at a pottery in Cambridge City, Indiana. They started in 1911. They made all types of vases, each one-of-a-kind. Small, hand-modeled figurines are the most popular pieces with today's collectors. The factory continued until 1955 when the last of the four sisters died.

Compote, Fruit, Turquoise Exterior Glaze, Yellow Interior Glaze, Marked, 9 3/4 In. .. 165.00
Figurine, Basket Of Flowers 300.00
Figurine, Blue Jay, 7 x 4 In. 313.50
Figurine, Boy In Snowsuit, Green, Pink, Lavender Glaze, 3 In. 230.00
Figurine, Cockatoo 210.00
Figurine, Collie 145.00
Figurine, Dachshund, Pink, Blue & Black Glaze, 11 In. 275.00
Figurine, Dog, Standing, 5 In. 200.00

Figurine, Girl Placing Vase On Table 375.00
Figurine, Girl With Goose, Miniature 270.00
Figurine, Man, Playing Cymbals 325.00
Figurine, Man, With Book Of Music 300.00
Figurine, Robin 110.00
Figurine, Skunk 185.00
Figurine, Woman In Full Skirt, Hat, Purse, Blue & Pink Glaze, 4 In. 253.00
Figurine, Woman Singing, Blue Bows, Brown Matte Glaze, 3 In. 242.00
Figurine, Woman, Signed EF 450.00
Figurine, Woman, Wearing Shawl 275.00
Vase, Children & Cats, 11 In. 5500.00
Vase, Cut-Out Panels, Fish Swimming Through Water Plants, 3 1/2 In. 1550.00

OWENS Pottery was made in Zanesville, Ohio, from 1891 to 1928. The first
art pottery was made after 1896. Utopian Ware, Cyrano, Navarre, Feroza, and
Henri Deux were made. Pieces were usually marked with a form of the name
Owens. About 1907, the firm began to make tile and discontinued the art
pottery wares.

Ashtray, Feroza, 4 7/8 In. 195.00
Jardiniere, Lotus, Butterflies Circle Rim, Slip Painted, 10 1/2 x 7 1/2 In. 200.00
Jardiniere, Molded Design 85.00
Jug, Floral Design, Brown Shading To Green, 7 In. 99.00
Jug, Surano 250.00
Loving Cup, Utopian, Cherries, 6 3/4 In. 395.00
Loving Cup, Utopian, Strawberries, Brown Matte, 6 3/4 In. 495.00
Mug, Charles Chilcote, 6 In. 150.00
Mug, Eutopia, 4 In. 115.00
Mug, Orange Berries, Green Leaves, T.S., 5 In. 159.50
Mug, Utopian 145.00
Mug, Utopian, Blackberries, T.S., 5 In. 82.50
Pin Box, Bleeding Heart, Lid 185.00
Pitcher, Utopian, Matte, Peach & Brown Grapes, A. Haubrich, 1901, 12 In. 385.00
Plaque, Path Into Mountain, Green & Pink Glaze, Frame, Marked, 13 x 13 In. 1100.00
Poppy Florals, Standard Glaze, 6 In. 175.00
Powder Jar, Aborigine 275.00
Tile, Goose In Flight, Faience, Rectangular, 1923, 11 1/2 x 17 1/2 In. 373.00
Vase, Aborigine, Tan Ground, Rust & Black, 5 1/2 In. 170.50
Vase, Art Nouveau Woman, Henri Deux, 8 1/2 In. 465.00
Vase, Bust Of A Woman, Art Nouveau, 2-Handles, Henri Deux, 10 In. 660.00
Vase, Dark Brown Glaze, Woman's Face, Molded Leaves, Henri Deux, 7 In. 99.00
Vase, Feroza, Gold Luster, 11 1/2 In. 795.00
Vase, Floral, Profile Of Indian On Back, 12 In. 400.00
Vase, Hand Painted In Underglaze Slip Colors, 14 1/2 In. 375.00
Vase, Matte, 1900s, 4 x 4 In. 95.00
Vase, Mirror Black Glaze, Handles, 11 In. 175.00
Vase, Olympian, Brushed Ground, 5 1/2 In. 225.00
Vase, Orange Flowers, Green & Gold Coralene Surface, Marked, 11 In. 650.00
Vase, Profile Of Indian On Reverse, Floral, Standard Glaze, 12 In. 400.00
Vase, Stylized Roses Covered In Green Matte Glaze, 2 Handles, Signed, 9 3/4 In. 385.00
Vase, Utopian, Bottle Shape, Daisy, 6 In. 125.00
Vase, Utopian, 3 In. 135.00
Vase, Utopian, Footed, Yellow & Orange Nasturtiums, T.S., 4 In. 99.00
Vase, Utopian, Grapes & Vines Around Body, Signed, 7 In. 205.00
Vase, Utopian, Matte, Peach & Gray Flowers, Green Ground, C.E., 7 1/2 In. 230.00
Vase, Utopian, Pillow, Orange Roses, 4-Footed, S.T., 8 In. 187.00
Vase, Utopian, Pillow, Painted Shepherd & Dog With Flock, Leffler, 13 In. 1650.00
Vase, Utopian, Shepherd With His Dog Herding A Flock 1500.00
Vase, Utopian, Signed S.T., 10 In. 195.00
Vase, Utopian, Thistle In Underglaze Slip, 11 3/4 In. 230.00
Vase, Utopian, Yellow & Brown Roses, S.T., 4 In. 230.00
Vase, Utopian, Yellow & Orange Roses, Green & Brown Ground, 10 In. 88.00
Vase, Woman's Head With Flowing Hair, Brown Matte Glaze, Henri Deux, 9 In. 258.50

Top row: Oyster Plate, 1 Green & 1 Pink Shell Design, 9 & 9 1/2 In., Pair; Oyster Plate, Dark Green, France, 9 3/4 In.; Bottom row: Oyster Plate, White Basket Weave, France, 9 1/2 In.; Oyster Plate, Light Green Basket Weave, Rope Border, 9 1/2 In.; Oyster Plate, Pink & White, Cresent Shape, 9 In.

OYSTER PLATES were popular from the 1880s. Each course at dinner was served in a special dish. The oyster plate had indentations shaped like oysters. Usually six oysters were held on a plate. There is no greater value to a plate with more oysters although that myth continues to haunt antiques dealers. There are other plates for shellfish, including cockle plates and whelk plates. The appropriately shaped indentations are part of the design of these dishes.

1 Green & 1 Pink Shell Design, 9 & 9 1/2 In., Pair .... *Illus*	260.00
5 Sections, Center Saucer Dip, 2 Small Dips, Pink & Green	90.00
Brown Oysters, 2 Mussel &1 Scalloped Shell, White, Gold Trim, 9 In., 7 Piece	40.00
Dark Green, France, 9 3/4 In., 6 Piece .... *Illus*	320.00
Garlands Of Pink Roses, Gold Trim, Limoges, 5 Piece	495.00
Gold Rim, Union Porcelain, Pair	325.00
Gray & Coral, Sarreguemines, 9 3/4 In.	145.00
Half Moon, Copeland	660.00
Hand Painted Flowers, Logs Of Gold, Haviland, 6 Piece	395.00
Holdcroft	650.00
Light Green Basket Weave, Rope Border, 9 1/2 In., 4 Piece .... *Illus*	240.00
Marine Shell Design, Hand Painted, Square	165.00
Mottled Outside Wells, Turquoise Centers, 9 1/4 x 7 1/2 In.	550.00
Ocean, Wedgwood	412.50
Pink & White, Crescent Shape, 9 In., Pair .... *Illus*	190.00
Porcelain, 9 7 10 In., Pair	132.00
Raised Center Shell, George Jones, Majolica, Turquoise, 120 In.	1100.00
Sarreguemines, 9 1/2 In.	192.50
White, Gold Border	25.00
White Basket Weave, France, 9 1/2 In., 6 Piece .... *Illus*	275.00
Yellow Roses, Brown Leaves & Stems, 4 Wells, Haviland, c.1885, 8 Piece	595.00

PADEN CITY Glass Manufacturing Company was established in 1916 at Paden City, West Virginia. It is best known for glasswares but also produced a pottery line. The firm closed in 1951.

Basket, Forest Green, Handle, 7 1/2 In.	22.00
Bookends, Pouter Pigeon, Clear, 6 In.	85.00
Bowl, Art Deco, World's Fair, 1939, 10 In.	95.00
Candy Dish, Cover, Crow's Foot, Frosted, Silver Deposit, 3 Lobes	38.00
Cheese & Cracker, Underplate, Largo, Frosted, Silver Deposit, 10 1/2 In.	45.00
Compote, Cover, Ruby, Floral Etch, Ball Stem & Finial, 9 1/2 x 6 3/4 In.	70.00

Creamer, Green	3.50
Dispenser, Cotton, Rabbit, Pink	60.00
Figurine, Asian Pheasant, Crystal, 12 In.	60.00
Figurine, Chanticleer, 7 1/4 x 9 1/2 In.	82.00
Figurine, Pony, Standing, 11 1/2 In.	95.00
Figurine, Pouter Pigeon	42.00
Figurine, Rooster, Blue, 9 1/2 In.	200.00
Flower Frog, Dish, Pigtailed Girl	65.00
Ice Tub, Cupid	175.00
Mayonnaise, Underplate, Topaz	119.00
Pitcher, Buckskin Joe, Green, 5 In.	40.00
Pitcher, Penney Line, Ruby	65.00
Plate, Mrs. Bee, Amber, 8 1/4 In.	2.00
Platter, Nasturtiums, Oval, Shenandoah Ware, 13 1/2 In.	20.00
Saucer, Mrs. Bee, Topaz	1.50
Server, Mrs. Bee, Amber, Center Handle	16.00
Shaker, Party Line, Amber	9.00
Sherbet, Aristocrat, Ruby, Ball Stem, 3 7/8 In.	15.00
Sugar, Colonial, Green	14.00
Vase, Crow's Foot, Ruby Red, 8 1/4 In.	45.00
Wine, Futura, Ruby, 3 Oz.	12.00

PAINTINGS listed in this book are not works by major artists but rather decorative paintings on ivory, board, or glass that would be of interest to the average collector. To learn the value of an oil painting by a listed artist you must contact an expert in that area.

Oil On Board, Indian Camp, 12 x 24 In.	495.00
Oil On Board, Portrait, Old Collective Farmer, 16 x 12 In.	154.00
Oil On Board, Primitive 2 Story House, Trees, Pine Frame, 22 x 27 In.	275.00
Oil On Board, Primitive People Scene, Frame, 21 3/4 x 27 1/2 In.	82.00
Oil On Board, Primitive Still Life, Gilt Frame, 21 1/2 x 26 In.	82.00
Oil On Board, Sailing Ships Near Port, Frame, 19th Century, 8 x 12 In.	2090.00
Oil On Board, Toy Elephant & Red Trunk, Frame, 1900s, 17 x 21 In.	165.00
Oil On Canvas, 4 Puppies, Frame, 14 1/4 x 22 1/4 In.	192.00
Oil On Canvas, At The Old Swimming Hold, Frame, 22 x 26 1/2 In.	990.00
Oil On Canvas, Basket Of Peaches, Gilt Frame, 19 3/4 x 25 1/2 In.	104.00
Oil On Canvas, Blacksmith, 25 x 30 In.	71.00
Oil On Canvas, Bouquet Of Flowers, Gray Ground, Frame, 18 x 14 In.	105.00
Oil On Canvas, Connecticut Townscape, 1905, Frame, 25 x 46 In.	1650.00
Oil On Canvas, Cow's Head, Revarnished, Gold Frame, 15 1/4 x 13 1/4 In.	220.00
Oil On Canvas, Duck Hunting, American, 19th Century, Frame, 14 x 21 1/2 In.	385.00
Oil On Canvas, European City Scene, 1952, 18 x 25 In.	40.00
Oil On Canvas, European Landscape, Gilt Frame, 19 1/4 x 27 1/4 In.	220.00
Oil On Canvas, Farmyard, Horses & Riders, Gilt Frame, 30 x 39 In.	110.00
Oil On Canvas, Fish & Oyster Shell, Gilt Frame, Velvet Mat, 7 x 9 In.	55.00
Oil On Canvas, Fisherman's Farewell, Unstretched, Glass, Frame, 18 1/2 x 24 In.	110.00
Oil On Canvas, Floral Still Life, 25 x 21 In.	40.00
Oil On Canvas, Floral Still Life, Continental, 1860, Frame	2900.00
Oil On Canvas, Gentleman Portrait, Red Book, Restored, Gilt Frame, 30 x 25 In.	880.00
Oil On Canvas, Gentleman, Black Stock Hat, Oval, 1840, 30 In.	440.00
Oil On Canvas, Girl Portrait, Lace Collar, Oval In Gilt Frame, 17 3/4 x 16 1/4 In.	110.00
Oil On Canvas, Girl With Pitcher, Gilt Frame, 14 x 11 In.	165.00
Oil On Canvas, Girl, Red Dress, Heart-Shaped Locket, Oval, Frame, 37 In.	1200.00
Oil On Canvas, Girl, White Dress, 1852, Marked AB, Frame, 26 x 32 In.	3740.00
Oil On Canvas, Hispanic Girl At Water Fountain, Frame, 20 x 16 In.	110.00
Oil On Canvas, Horse, Frame, 15 x 23 In.	1100.00
Oil On Canvas, House Portrait, Figures, 20 x 24 In.	220.00
Oil On Canvas, Hunters & Bears, 36 x 19 In.	198.00
Oil On Canvas, Lafitte's Blacksmith Shop, Mariam, Signed, 11 3/4 x 16 In.	99.00
Oil On Canvas, Lake Scene, Frame, 30 x 36 In.	225.00
Oil On Canvas, Landing Party, Harbor View, Frame, 24 x 18 In.	715.00
Oil On Canvas, Landscape With Trees, Frame, 18 x 28 In.	137.00
Oil On Canvas, Landscape, Cows, Gilt Frame, 25 x 16 3/4 In.	115.00

Oil On Canvas, Landscape, Mountains, Lake, Gilt Frame, 29 1/2 x 34 1/4 In. 495.00
Oil On Canvas, Man & Woman Portrait, 30 x 25 In., Pair 1100.00
Oil On Canvas, Man & Woman, Well, Cows, Folk Art, 1896, 37 x 48 In. 700.00
Oil On Canvas, Man, Bust, Relined On Masonite, Frame, 19th Century, 27 x 22 In. .. 220.00
Oil On Canvas, Man, Portrait, Mid-19th Century, Frame, 30 x 25 In. 440.00
Oil On Canvas, Mountainous Landscape, 1899, 18 x 24 In. 50.00
Oil On Canvas, Old Couple With Book, Gilt Frame, 20 1/2 x 26 In. 247.00
Oil On Canvas, Pastoral Scene, Cows At Sunset, 17 x 28 In. 192.50
Oil On Canvas, Portly Gentleman, Chin Whiskers, Frame, 11 1/2 x 26 In. 247.00
Oil On Canvas, Portrait Of A Man, Frame, 36 x 30 In. 192.00
Oil On Canvas, Portrait Of A Yellow Farmhouse, Frame, 14 x 18 In. 467.00
Oil On Canvas, Prairie Scene, House & Barn, 20 x 26 In. 27.00
Oil On Canvas, Primitive Landscape, Classical Ruins, Frame, 15 1/4 x 19 1/4 In. 115.00
Oil On Canvas, Rocky Mountain Landscape, 18 x 24 In. 115.00
Oil On Canvas, Rocky Mountain Landscape, Frame, 36 x 47 In. 93.00
Oil On Canvas, Scene In Venetian Lagoon, Gilt Frame, Signed, 18 x 26 1/4 In. 575.00
Oil On Canvas, Sea, Boat In Rough Water, Frame, 48 1/4 x 38 1/4 In. 137.00
Oil On Canvas, Ships In A Harbor, White & Blue, Frame, 17 x 20 In. 880.00
Oil On Canvas, Still Life With Fruit, Unsigned, Frame, 16 1/8 x 23 1/8 In. 192.00
Oil On Canvas, Still Life, Flowers, Vase, Frame, 25 x 29 In. 357.00
Oil On Canvas, Sunflowers, Signed, 25 x 30 In. 100.00
Oil On Canvas, The Hay Stacks, Twilight, 14 x 20 In. 247.00
Oil On Canvas, Village Scene & Worker, 22 x 15 In. 30.00
Oil On Canvas, Winter Landscape, J.W.S., 1890, 12 1/4 x 17 1/4 In. 220.00
Oil On Canvas, Woman's Hand With Peach, Gilt Frame, 8 3/8 x 10 1/2 In. 137.00
Oil On Canvas, Woman, Portrait, Red Dress, Gold Frame, Oval, 14 1/4 x 12 1/2 In. . 385.00
Oil On Canvas, Young Woman In Blue Dress, Gilt Frame, 24 x 20 In. 275.00
Oil On Panel, Gentleman, Portrait, Open Book, Ogee Frame, 37 x 31 In. 1540.00
Oil On Panel, Girl & Dog In Forest, Frame, 14 x 17 In. 440.00
Oil On Panel, Girl Spinning, Gilt Frame, 15 x 11 3/4 In. 135.00
Oil On Panel, Portrait, Young Gentleman, Signed, Dated, Frame, 26 x 21 In. 467.00
Oil On Panel, The Brick Farmhouse, Frame, 13 x 21 In. 880.00
Oil On Tin, Bavarian Village Scene, 1878, 16 1/2 x 12 In. 440.00
Oil On Tin, English Landscape, Cows In Stream, Gilt Frame, 18 x 24 In. 220.00
On Canvas, Flower Garden, Two Figures, Gilt Frame, 32 x 38 In. 247.50
On Canvas, Scene Of 2 Cats On Branch, Bird's-Eye Frame, 14 1/2 x 18 1/2 In. 55.00
On Ivory, 2 Young Girls, Open Book, Pastel, Gilded Brass Frame, 2 3/4 x 2 1/4 In. ... 275.00
On Ivory, Alexander I, Uniform, Gilt Rim, c.1810, 1 7/8 In. 2415.00
On Ivory, George Bowles, Gilt Metal Frame, Oval, 1810, 5 In. 633.00
On Ivory, Girl, Red Dress, Lock Of Hair In Back, 3 In. 137.00
On Ivory, Madonna & Child, Oval, Brass Frame, Signed Silver, 4 1/8 In. 60.00
On Ivory, Man In Uniform, Signed, Gilt Brass Frame, 5 1/2 x 4 1/4 In. 187.00
On Ivory, Man, Frock Coat, Blue Ground, Oval, Brass Frame, 2 1/2 In. 165.00
On Ivory, Man, Sideburns, Gold-Filled Oval Case, 2 1/2 In. 580.00
On Ivory, Military Man, Bearded, Gilt & Velvet Frame, 7 1/4 x 5 3/4 In. 1045.00
On Ivory, Mother & Child, Arms Around Mother's Waist, c.1815, 3 1/2 In. 1955.00
On Ivory, Mother & Child, Frame, 1807, 3 In. 300.00
On Ivory, Napoleon, Signed Duval, Black Lacquered Frame, 5 1/2 In. 275.00
On Ivory, Naval Officer, Child, 2 Sides, 19th Century, Continental, 2 1/4 x 2 In. 522.00
On Ivory, Nobleman, Waist Length, Suit Of Armor, Locket Frame, c.1725, 2 3/8 In. .. 805.00
On Ivory, Officer Peter Pailou, Powdered Hair, Gilt Oval Frame, 1808, 3 1/8 In. 635.00
On Ivory, Officer, Louis Napoleon, White Uniform, c.1810, 2 1/4 In. 1955.00
On Ivory, Queen, English, Early 19th Century, 4 In. 375.00
On Ivory, Regal Woman, Blue & Brown Costume, Frame, 6 3/4 x 5 3/4 In. 137.50
On Ivory, Sir Joshua Reynolds, Gilt Gesso Frame, 5 1/2 In. 1150.00
On Ivory, Soldier, Continental, Rope-Twist Gilt Frame, 5 1/2 In. 715.00
On Ivory, Thomas Richmond, 3/4 Figure, Gold & Enamel Frame, c.1795, 2 1/4 In. 1050.00
On Ivory, Watercolor, Woman, Green Dress, Coral Beads, Gold Jewelry.4 x 3 1/2 In. . 330.00
On Ivory, Woman, Ivory Frame, Signed, 3 3/4 x 3 1/4 In. 192.00
On Ivory, Young Man, Gilt Frame, 5 x 4 1/2 In. 247.00
On Ivory, Young Man, Rose Gold-Filled Case, 2 3/8 In. 110.00
On Ivory, Young Woman, Cameo & Ribbon, Gold Filled Oval Case, 2 1/2 In. 715.00

On Ivory, Young Woman, Lace Cap, Holding Roses, Locket Frame, c.1815 .... 1380.00
On Ivory, Young Woman, Oval Molded Wooden Frame, 4 3/4 x 4 1/8 In. 247.00
On Porcelain, A Morning Meal, 6 1/2 x 4 1/4 In. 350.00
On Porcelain, Gentleman, Black Jacket, Waistcoat & Cravat, 1839, 2 1/4 In. 345.00
On Porcelain, James Peale, Gray Jacket, White Waistcoat, 1796, 2 3/4 In. 1725.00
On Porcelain, Madonna & Child, Cloisonne Frame, 7 3/8 x 4 3/4 In. 250.00
On Porcelain, Officer, Curly Hair, Blue Uniform, Hair In Locket, 1829, 2 3/4 In. 5175.00
On Porcelain, Woman, Large Hat, Frame, 6 x 4 1/4 In. 395.00
On Porcelain, Woman, Period Dress, Shawl, Frame, 4 x 6 In. 550.00
On Porcelain, Women Picking Flowers, Frame, 4 1/2 x 6 1/2 In. 850.00
On Silk, Eagle With Olive Branch, American Flag, Frame 110.00
On Silk, Hanging Scroll, Bamboo & Grasses, 58 x 19 In. 412.00
On Silk, Hanging Scroll, Tiger, Korea, 19th Century, 33 x 21 In. 1045.00
On Silk, Hanging Scroll, Two Puppies, Bamboo, c.1840, 41 1/2 x 14 In. 165.00
On Silk, Ladies In A Garden, Frame, China, 19th Century, 65 1/2 x 32 1/2 In. 302.00
On Velvet, Primitive Scene Of English Church, Gilt Frame, 26 1/4 x 33 1/2 In. 330.00
Reverse On Glass, George Washington, Frame 220.00
Reverse On Glass, House, Snowy Winter Landscape, 19th Century, 14 x 24 In. 30.00
Reverse On Glass, Last Supper, Frame, Italy, 9 7/8 x 12 1/8 In. 165.00

PAIRPOINT Manufacturing Company started in 1880 in New Bedford,
Massachusetts. It soon joined with the glassworks nearby and made glass,
silver-plated pieces, and lamps. Reverse-painted glass shades and molded
shades known as *puffies* were part of the production until the 1930s. The
company reorganized and changed its name several times but is still working
today. Items listed here are glass or glass and metal. Silver-plated pieces are
listed under Silver Plate.

Bonbon, Baltic, Tall Pedestal, 6 1/2 In. 110.00
Bowl, Neoclassical Style, Gilt Metal Stand, 6 3/4 In. 143.00
Candelabra, 3-Light, Gilt Metal, Crystal Ball Finials, Onyx Base, 9 In., Pair 154.00
Candleholder, Cherub Supports, Gilt Metal, 7 1/2 In., Pair 50.00
Candleholder, Tapered Bowl, Gilt Metal, Garland, Cherubs, 9 3/4 In., Pair 187.00
Candlestick, Engraved, Line-Cutting, 12 In., Pair 640.00
Candlestick, Overall Cut Floral, Balluster Stem, 14 1/2 In., Pair 165.00
Candlestick, Pewter, 4 Scrolling Feet, Cylindrical, 1900, 11 1/2 In., Pair 747.00
Candy Dish, Cover, Vintage, Chartreuse 200.00
Candy Dish, Cover, Vintage, Dark Yellow 150.00
Carafe, Water, Cambridge, Ovals & Miters, 7 1/2 In. 200.00
Cheese Dish, Butterfly & Daisy 385.00
Cigar Holder, Ashtray, Full-Figure Palmer Cox Brownie 335.00
Compote, Wexford, Cobalt Blue Trim, 7 In. 165.00
Console Set, Cut Glass, Amber, 3 Piece 575.00
Cracker Jar, Embossed Borders, Delft Design, Silver Mount, 5 3/4 In. 595.00
Decanter, Double Octagon, Double Gooseneck, Teardrop Stopper, 12 1/2 In. 495.00
Dish, Baked Apple, Carved Apples, Cherries & Leaves, 12 In. 375.00
Lamp, Autumn Scene, River, Castle, Mountains, Drum-Form Shade, c.1900, 20 In. 840.00
Lamp, Berkeley, Reverse Painted, Floral & Chipped Ice Shade, 16 In. 3800.00
Lamp, Boudoir, Puffy, Pink & Purple Dogwood Shade, Pineapple Base, 8 In. 3250.00
Lamp, Boudoir, Puffy, Reverse Painted, Roses & Butterflies, No. 3047, 16 x 9 In. 1495.00
Lamp, Boudoir, Reverse Painted, Scenic Shade, Sky, Sea & Trees, Signed, Pair 700.00
Lamp, Boudoir, Vassar, Reverse Painted Flowers, Onyx Cherub Base, 14 1/2 In. 885.00
Lamp, Copley Shade, Vase Shape With Handles 3575.00
Lamp, Floral Panel Shade, Directoire, Candelabra Base, Glass Sphere 2450.00
Lamp, Hummingbird & Roses Shade, 4-Arm Support, Signed, 1915, 22 In. 5750.00
Lamp, Leaded Glass, 1910, 23 x 18 In. 440.00
Lamp, Metal, Reverse Painted, Birds & Flowers Scene Domed Shade, 23 1/4 In. 2875.00
Lamp, Metal, Reverse Painted, Blossoming Orchard Shade, 21 1/2 In. 862.00
Lamp, Metal, Reverse Painted, Landscape Conical Shade, 20 3/4 In. 362.00
Lamp, Metal, Reverse Painted, Paneled Conical Shade, Octagonal Base, 22 In. 1725.00
Lamp, Metal, Reverse Painted, Rural Scene Domed Shade, H. Fisher, 20 In. 1380.00
Lamp, Metal, Reverse Painted, Spider Chrysanthemums Shade, 1915, 21 In. 2070.00
Lamp, Painted Seashore & Trees Domical Shade, Gilt Metal, 22 1/4 In. 1380.00

Lamp, Parrot, Floral Ground, Bronzed Metal Base, Signed, 18 In. 2640.00
Lamp, Puffy, Floral Painted Glass Shade 2850.00
Lamp, Puffy, Metal Butterflies & Roses, Signed, 1910, 15 1/2 In. 2875.00
Lamp, Puffy, Reverse Painted Shade, Metal Standard, Marked, 22 In. 9900.00
Lamp, Puffy, Reverse Painted Yellow Roses, Silvered Metal Base, 21 In. 7150.00
Lamp, Puffy, Shade & Base Signed, 1907, 14 In. 2800.00
Lamp, Red London Bridge Shade, 2-Handled Base, Signed, 20 In. 3875.00
Lamp, Reverse Painted, Butterflies & Roses Shade, Bronze Base, 1915, 24 In. 6900.00
Lamp, Reverse Painted, Desert Scene Shade, Gilt Metal, 25 In. 862.00
Lamp, Reverse Painted, Desert Scenes, Marble Base, 2 Candle Arms, c.1920, 16 In. ... 1725.00
Lamp, Reverse Painted, Etched, Mahogany Base, G. Morley, c.1915, 19 In. 1100.00
Lamp, Reverse Painted, Lake Scene, 12 In. 2530.00
Lamp, Reverse Painted, Leaf Shade, Antique Brass Finish Base, Signed, 10 In. 975.00
Lamp, Reverse Painted, Metal Delphinium, Signed, c.1915, 14 In. 4888.00
Lamp, Reverse Painted, Pansies & Poppies Shade, Bronze Base, 1915, 23 In. 7500.00
Lamp, Reverse Painted, Parrots & Exotic Flowers, Blue, Orange, Green, Brown 7425.00
Lamp, Reverse Painted, Peacocks In A Garden, Bronze Urn-Shaped Base, 22 In. 3300.00
Lamp, Reverse Painted, Puffy Rosebuds Shade, Silvered Metal, 15 1/2 In. 3737.00
Lamp, Reverse Painted, River Scene Shade, Silvered Metal, 21 3/4 In. 2300.00
Lamp, Reverse Painted, Scene, Birch Trees, 12 In. 2200.00
Lamp, Reverse Painted, Tulip Blossoms, 4-Armed Gilt-Metal Base, 19 In. 1760.00
Lamp, Rose Bonnet Shade 2800.00
Lamp, Rose Bouquet Puffy 7150.00
Pitcher, Irma Pattern, Hobstar Base, 8 1/2 x 9 1/4 In. 850.00
Ring Tree, Rabbit 128.00
Salt & Pepper, Dutch Scene, Ribbed 250.00
Vase, Cut Floral Design, Knob Stem, 9 1/2 In. 285.00
Vase, Shells, Flowers & Branches, 6 In. 45.00
Vase, Tavern, Sailing Galleon, 1900-1938, 6 In. 485.00
Vase, Trumpet, Clear Green Controlled Bubble, Green Foot, 12 In. 95.00

PALMER COX, BROWNIES, see Brownies

PAPER collectibles, including almanacs, catalogs, children's books, stock
certificates, and other paper ephemera, are listed here. Paper calendars are
listed separately in the Calendar category.

Almanac, Harrick's, 1888 .... 39.00
Almanac, Kate Greenaway, Geo. Ruthledge & Sons, 1886, 3 x 4 In. 125.00
Almanac, Lum & Abner's Family Almanac, Horlick's Malted, 1937, 32 Pages 10.00
Almanac, Public Ledger, Phila., 57 Pages, 1883 .... 15.00
Almanac, The American Almanac & Repository Of Useful Knowledge, 1838 .... 22.50
Almanac, The Illustrated Family Christian, 60 Pages, 1850 .... 15.00
Blotter, Borden's, Elmer, Santa Claus Clothes, War Bonds, 1940s, 3 x 6 In. 15.00
Blotter, General Electric, Mazda, Woman Holding Light Bulbs, Art Nouveau, 1912 ... 26.00
Blotter, Heinz Baby Foods, Unused, 1950s, 3 3/4 x 9 In. 18.00
Blotter, Kellogg's Rice Krispies, Vernon Grant, 1940s, 5 1/2 x 5 1/2 In. 12.00
Blotter, Morton Salt, Black & White Photo, White Ground, 1930s, 3 1/4 x 6 1/4 In. .. 13.00
Blotter, Red Goose Shoes, Every Day Is Circus Day, 1930s, 3 1/2 x 6 In. 10.00
Blotter, Reddy Kilowatt Says, 1930s, 3 1/2 x 5 In. 23.00
Blotter Pad, Bastian Brothers, 1930s, 6 Pages 19.00
Bond, Gold, Railroad, Chicago Rock Island Pacific, Coupons, 1902 .... 55.00
Book, Better Little Book, Terry & The Pirates 25.00
Book, Big Little Book, Beast Of Tarzan, Whitman, 1937 .... 57.00
Book, Big Little Book, Bell Boy Detective, Mickey Mouse 27.00
Book, Big Little Book, Blondie & Dagwood, Everybody's Happy 28.00
Book, Big Little Book, Buck Rogers & The Doom Comet, 1935 .... 50.00
Book, Big Little Book, Buck Rogers, Depth Men Of Jupiter 60.00
Book, Big Little Book, Charley Chan, 1938 .... 45.00
Book, Big Little Book, Flash Gordon & Ape Men Of Mor, 1942 .... 100.00
Book, Big Little Book, Flash Gordon, Water World & Witch Queen Of Mongo 65.00
Book, Big Little Book, G-Man 20.00
Book, Big Little Book, Laurel & Hardy 20.00

Book, Big Little Book, Magic Lantern, Mickey Mouse	20.00
Book, Big Little Book, Peck's Bad Boy, Jackie Cooper	25.00
Book, Big Little Book, Tim McCoy & The Sandy Gulch Stamped, 1939	25.00
Book, Big Little Book, Uncle Wiggly	50.00
Book, Coloring, Betty Grable, Uncolored, 1953	25.00
Book, Coloring, Buffalo Bill, 1950s	15.00
Book, Coloring, Eve Arden, 1953	15.00
Book, Coloring, Leave It To Beaver, Soft Bound, 120 Pages, Saalfield, 1963	55.00
Book, Coloring, Roy Rogers, Uncolored, 1948	35.00
Book, Coloring, Time Tunnel, 1966	50.00
Book, Little Golden Book, Bobby And His Airplanes, 1949	20.00
Book, Little Golden Book, Bozo The Clown, 1973	15.00
Book, Little Golden Book, Donald Duck On Parade	8.00
Book, Little Golden Book, Donald Duck's Sailboat	6.00
Book, Little Golden Book, Donald Duck's Toy Train	10.00
Book, Little Golden Book, Gun Smoke, 1958	12.00
Book, Little Golden Book, Johnny Appleseed	6.00
Book, Little Golden Book, Life & Legend Of Wyatt Earp, Hardbound, 1958	15.00
Book, Little Golden Book, Mickey Mouse & His Space Ship	14.00
Book, Little Golden Book, Tom And Jerry's Party, 1955	20.00
Book, Pop-Up, Bookano Zoo, 1930s	100.00
Book, Pop-Up, Goldilocks, 1934	125.00
Book, Pop-Up, Hopalong Cassidy, 1950	125.00
Book, Pop-Up, Huckleberry Hound	25.00
Book, Pop-Up, Jack & Beanstalk, Cloth Binding, 1962	45.00
Book, Pop-Up, Terry & The Pirates, Original Blue Ribbon, 1935, 3 Piece	65.00
Book, Puzzle, Uncle Wiggly, 1928	37.00
Book, Things To Do Book, Elsie The Cow, Paperback	40.00
Book Plate, Fraktur, Anna Cassel, Born March 15, 1804, Frame, 5 3/4 x 7 3/4 In.	258.00
Book Plate, Pierret's Serenade, Parrish	24.00
Book Plate, Pool Of The Villa D'Este, Parrish	22.50
Catalog, Aldens, 1959-60, Fall & Winter, 792 Pages	12.50
Catalog, American Steel & Wire Co., 1928, 40 Pages	16.00
Catalog, Bastian Brothers, 1901-1903, Pins, Rings, Medals, 40 Pages, 4 x 6 In.	29.00
Catalog, Bennett Brothers, 1953, Hardcover, 600 Pages	68.00
Catalog, Bonwit Teller, 1925, Gift Book, 22 Pages	45.00
Catalog, Catalogue Of Piano Rolls, Connorized Music Co., N.Y., 1910, 552 Pages	55.00
Catalog, Charles Atlas, New York, N.Y., 1937, 47 Pages, 6 x 8 In.	10.00
Catalog, Colburn Trolley Track Co., Holyoke, Mass., 1927, 56 Pages	18.00
Catalog, Diamond Match Co., New York, N.Y., 1928, 20 Pages, 6 1/2 x 9 1/2 In.	34.00
Catalog, Domestic Sewing Machine, New York, N.Y., 1882, 10 Pages, 6 x 10 In.	28.00
Catalog, Eureka Elastic Paint Co., 1900, 200 Pages, 7 1/4 x 5 In.	45.00
Catalog, FAO Schwarz, 1962, Christmas	100.00
Catalog, Firestone, 1950s, 67 Pages, Toys & Dolls	38.00
Catalog, Fisher-Price, 1957	50.00
Catalog, Fostoria Glass Co., 1950s, 450 Pages	75.00
Catalog, General Electric Co., Schenectady, N.Y., 1933, 5 1/2 x 8 In.	22.00
Catalog, H.W. Johns Mfg. Co., New York, N.Y., 1886, 12 Pages, 5 1/4 x 8 1/2 In.	68.00
Catalog, Hershey Metal Products, Derby, Conn., 1937, 52 Pages	19.00
Catalog, International Harvester, Chicago, 1921, Repair Parts, 260 Pages	21.00
Catalog, Ithaca Gun Co., Ithaca, N.Y., 1930, 22 Pages, 8 1/2 x 13 1/2 In.	29.00
Catalog, J.C. Penney, 1964, Christmas	85.00
Catalog, J.C. Penney, 1987, Christmas, 548 Pages, Wrapper	17.50
Catalog, John J. Frye Manufacturer, Portland, Me., 1870, 16 Pages	29.00
Catalog, John Wanamaker, New York, N.Y., 1920, 96 Pages, 8 x 11 In.	29.00
Catalog, Kendall & Whitney Seeds, 1931	55.00
Catalog, Lane Bryant, 1917, New York, Fall & Winter, 52 Pages	33.00
Catalog, Lane Bryant, 1926, Fall & Winter, Babies & Children, 43 Pages	45.00
Catalog, Lane Bryant, 1935, Spring & Summer, 76 Pages	38.00
Catalog, Lane Bryant, 1938	45.00
Catalog, Lauerman Bros. Co., Marinette, Wis., 1927, Fashion, 81 Pages	7.00
Catalog, Leece-Neville Co., Cleveland, Ohio, 1916, 24 Pages, 6 x 9 In.	28.00

Catalog, Leroy Plow Co., Leroy, N.Y., 1925, 12 Pages, 6 x 12 In. 15.00
Catalog, Loudon Farm Machinery & Equipment, 1929 .... 30.00
Catalog, Marlin Firearms, 1915, 136 Pages 175.00
Catalog, Miles Kimball Co., 1956, Christmas, 109 Pages 5.00
Catalog, Montgomery Ward, 1899, 28 Pages, 9 3/4 x 12 3/4 In. 17.00
Catalog, Montgomery Ward, 1924, February, 124 Pages 35.00
Catalog, Montgomery Ward, 1925, Monuments & Tombstones, Markers, 29 Pages 30.00
Catalog, Montgomery Ward, 1931, Fall & Winter 40.00
Catalog, Montgomery Ward, 1931, Spring & Summer 25.00
Catalog, Montgomery Ward, 1949, Christmas 40.00
Catalog, Montgomery Ward, 1950, Sample Wallpapers, 82 Pages 75.00
Catalog, Montgomery Ward, 1966, Christmas, 100 Pages 79.00
Catalog, National Bellas Hess Co., 1930s, Spring & Summer, 266 Pages 65.00
Catalog, National Cloak & Suit Co., 1910, New York Fashions, 177 Pages, 9 1/2 In. 83.00
Catalog, National Cloak & Suit Co., 1925, Spring & Summer, 345 Pages 50.00
Catalog, Old Town Canoes & Boats, 1955 .... 20.00
Catalog, Philipsborn, 1917, Fall & Winter, Ladies Fashions 30.00
Catalog, Portland Cement Association, 1927, 16 Pages 11.00
Catalog, Quaker City Rubber Co., Philadelphia, Pa., 1910, 164 Pages, 6 x 9 In. 17.00
Catalog, R.B. Anger & Co., Jewelers, Oshkosh, 1925, 16 Pages 6.00
Catalog, Remington Arms Union, Ilion, N.Y., 1918, 208 Pages, 5 3/4 x 8 3/4 In. 33.00
Catalog, Remington Typewriter Co., New York, N.Y., 1925, 16 Pages, 6 x 8 In. 16.00
Catalog, Rice Miller Wholesale Hardware, 1909, Hard Back, Bangor, Maine 28.00
Catalog, Richards-Wilcox, 1936, No. 90, Doorway Hardware, 424 Pages 35.00
Catalog, Sears, 1910, Hardware, 124 Pages 92.00
Catalog, Sears, 1922, Hard Cloth, Shoe Fashions, 8 x 11 In. 55.00
Catalog, Sears, 1927, Fall & Winter 58.00
Catalog, Sears, 1927, Fall Bargains, Philadelphia, 53 Pages 25.00
Catalog, Sears, 1934, Fall & Winter, 984 Pages 21.00
Catalog, Sears, 1942, Christmas 100.00
Catalog, Sears, 1961, Diamond Jubilee, 1460 Pages 80.00
Catalog, Sears, 1964, Christmas 75.00
Catalog, Sears, 1965, Summer 20.00
Catalog, Sears, 1966, Christmas 70.00
Catalog, Sears, 1971, Christmas Wish Book 35.00
Catalog, Shapleigh Keen Kutter, 1957, Leather Bound 525.00
Catalog, South Bend Fishing, 1937 .... 38.00
Catalog, Spiegel, 1930s, Christmas, 128 Pages 45.00
Catalog, Spiegel, 1941, Fall & Winter, 663 Pages, 10 x 14 In. 48.00
Catalog, Spiegel, 1942, Christmas, 148 Pages 24.00
Catalog, Spiegel, 1946, Christmas 75.00
Catalog, Spiegel, 1971, Christmas 25.00
Catalog, Stanley Tool, 1939, 240 Pages 20.00
Catalog, Starrett Tool, 545 Pages, 1965 .... 9.00
Catalog, The Hustler, 1933, 475 Pages 75.00
Catalog, Tilbert Toys, 122 Pages 15.00
Catalog, United States Heater Co., Detroit, Mich., 1931, 119 Pages, 5 x 7 1/2 In. 15.00
Catalog, White Co. Bus Chassis, Cleveland, Ohio, 1926, 78 Pages, 8 x 11 In. 43.00
Catalog, White Sewing Machine Co., Cleveland, Ohio, 1926, 16 Pages, 3 x 6 In. 9.00
Catalog, Woolworth's, 1955, Christmas 35.00
Circular, Wanted, Kansas Embezzler, Pinkerton, 1910 .... 115.00
Fraktur, Birth In Pennsylvania, Frame, 1828, Died 1880, 20 1/2 x 17 3/4 In. 93.00
Fraktur, Birth, Elizabeth Krimm, Floral Roundel, 12 3/4 x 16 In. 1150.00
Fraktur, Bookplate, Hanna Hunsberger, 1804, 6 3/4 x 4 In. 700.00
Fraktur, Bookplate, Johannes Biebighaus, November 18, 1812, 5 3/4 x 3 3/4 In. 4000.00
Fraktur, Certificate, Pen & Ink, Watercolor, Framed, P. Bergman 1776, 15 x 18 In. 225.00
Fraktur, Geburts Und Taufschein, 1795 Birth, John Ritter, Frame, 18 x 15 In. 247.00
Fraktur, Geburts Und Taufschein, Cathrina Boyer, Lebanon County, 9 1/2 x 7 1/2 In. 350.00
Fraktur, Geburts Und Taufschein, Knoxville, Ohio, Frame, 12 1/2 x 9 1/2 In. 120.00
Fraktur, Hex, Tulips, Judiah Andersin, 1804, 9 1/4 x 7 1/4 In. 4100.00
Fraktur, Jonathan Prescott Birth Notice, March 1, 1801, 8 1/2 x 10 1/2 In. 935.00
Fraktur, Mahlon B. Spang, May 30, 1840 Birth, Frame, 11 5/8 x 9 5/8 In. 1210.00

Fraktur, P. Bergman, 1776, Pen & Ink, Watercolor, Frame, 18 1/2 x 15 In. 220.00
Fraktur, P. Mockinghaupt Schoolmaster, Union Vorschrift, 1800, 10 1/2 x 14 1/2 In. . 300.00
Fraktur, P.W.J. Brown, 1792, Pen & Ink, Watercolor, Frame, 16 x 18 In 550.00
Fraktur, Taufschein, Birth In Daulphin County, Penn., Frame, 15 3/8 x 18 1/8 In. 305.00
Fraktur, Vorschrift, Floral Sides, 1811 .... 1200.00
Leaflet, Lufkin Precision Tools, No. 7, 128 Pages, 1920s 4.00
Magazine, 10th Anniversary Issue, 1962 .... 20.00
Magazine, Hustler, Vol. 1, No. 1, 1974 .... 500.00
Magazine, Journal Of National Dental Assoc., 1917, 1919, 1922, 1937, 1938 .... 40.00
Magazine, Life, Greta Garbo, November 8, 1937 .... 35.00
Magazine, Life, Ingrid Bergman, December 2, 1946 .... 25.00
Magazine, Life, Vivien Leigh, July 29, 1946 .... 30.00
Magazine, Playboy, 1970, 12 Piece 65.00
Magazine, Playboy, Barbi Benton, December 1973 .... 20.00
Magazine, Playboy, Elke Sommers, September 1964 .... 15.00
Magazine, TV Guide, Dinah Shore, 1953 .... 45.00
Magazine, TV Guide, Jimmy Durante, 1953 .... 65.00
Magazine, TV Guide, Red Buttons, 1954 .... 45.00
Menu, Gardner Field, Christmas, 1941 .... 12.00
Menu, Old Wagon Wheel, Restaurant 10.00
Menu, Ships, Dinner, HMS Queen Mary, 1936 .... 12.00
Program, American Legion National Commander's Dinner, Autographed, 1938 .... 110.00
Program, Broadway Show, Cinderella, Royal Lyceum Theatre, 1893 .... 15.00
Program, Broadway Show, Damn Yankees, Gwen Verdon, 1955 .... 10.00
Program, Broadway Show, Happy Hunting, Ethel Merman, 1956 .... 12.00
Program, Broadway Show, The King And I, Yul Brynner, Gertrude Lawrence, 1951 .. 10.00
Program, Circus, Ringling Brothers, 1945 .... 15.00
Program, Folies Bergere, Josephine Baker, 1937 .... 195.00
Program, Memorial Day, Arlington National Cemetery, 1915 .... 15.00
Program, Radio, Campbell's Soups, Christmas Carol, 4 Pages, 1933, 5 x 8 In. 25.00
Stock Certificate, California Railway Co., Train Avignette, 1891 .... 120.00
Stock Certificate, Camden-Philadelpha Steamboat, Train, Factory, Cattle, 1973 .... 45.00
Stock Certificate, Crackerjack King Mining Co., Death Valley, Calif., 1882 .... 115.00
Stock Certificate, Ishpeming Livery Co., Ishpeming, Mich., Unissued, 1905 .... 5.00
Stock Certificate, Moody & Place Mining Co., Arizona, Globe Vignette, 1881 .... 155.00
Stock Certificate, Narragansett Electric Co., 2 Shares, 1887 .... 20.00
Stock Certificate, National Mortgage Co., Boston, Mass., 1887 .... 10.00
Stock Certificate, Seven Devils Copper Co., Arizona Territory, 1910 .... 12.00

PAPER DOLLS were probably inspired by the pantins, or jumping jacks,
made in eighteenth-century Europe. By the 1880s, sheets of printed paper
dolls and clothes were being made. The first paper doll books were made in
the 1920s. Collectors prefer uncut sheets or books or boxed sets of paper
dolls. Prices are about half as much if the pages have been cut.

Airline Hostess & Pilot, Merrill, 1950s 23.00
American Toy Works, Original Signed Envelope 85.00
Amos 'n' Andy, Pepsodent, 1930s, Cut, 4 Piece 175.00
Ann Sothern, Clothes, Saalfield, 1943, Cut 39.50
Annette Funicello, 1961, Cut 30.00
Annie Oakley, 1956, Uncut 45.00
Annie Oakley, No. 2056, Whitman, 1960 .... 65.00
Aunt Jemima, Saalfield Publishing, 1910, 6 In. 315.00
Aunt Jemima & Uncle Mose, Uncut, 1949, Pair 195.00
Baby Sparkle Plenty, 1948, Uncut 65.00
Betty Bonnet, Ladies Home Journal, Mounted, Matted, 1918, 14 x 18 In., 9 Piece ... 66.00
Betty Bonnet, Wedding, 1918, Uncut 18.00
Betty Boop, 1984, Uncut 22.00
Betty Grable, 1940s, Cut 25.00
Beverly Hillbillies, Elly May, 1963, Uncut 50.00
Buffy, 1969, Uncut 35.00
Caroline Kennedy, Box, Uncut 15.00
Cheerful Tearful 15.00

Debbie Reynolds, Whitman, 1953, Uncut 95.00
Debbie Reynolds, Whitman, 1962, Uncut 16.00
Dolly Dingle & Friends, 1927, Uncut 75.00
Donny & Marie, Whitman, 1970s 25.00
Doris Day, 1955 .... 65.00
Dress Up For World's Fair, Outfits From Participating Countries, Uncut 20.00
Elizabeth Taylor, Whitman, 1950, Uncut 125.00
Elizabeth Taylor, Whitman, 1955, Uncut 115.00
Family Affair, Whitman, 1968 .... 35.00
Famous Flying Marvels, 3 Piece, Uncut 60.00
Faye Emerson, Saalfield, 1952, Uncut 115.00
First Ladies, Saalfield, 1937, Cut 45.00
First Ladies Of White House, 1937, Uncut 135.00
Flintstones, Jack & Jill Magazine, Uncut, March 1963 .... 22.00
Flintstones, Whitman, 1963, Uncut 60.00
Flying Nun, No. 5124, Artcraft, 1968, Uncut 75.00
Gilda Radner, Uncut 25.00
Gone With The Wind, 18 Doll Set, 53 Outfits, Cut & Uncut 100.00
Gone With The Wind, 1940, Uncut 275.00
Gone With The Wind, Merrill, Uncut 120.00
Greer Garson, 2 Dolls, 1940s, Cut 25.00
Hayley Mills, Cardboard Case, 1963, Cut 35.00
Heath & Milligan Mfg. Co., Sunshine Finish, 2 Girls, 1 Boy, 1905, Uncut 50.00
Jackie Kennedy, Magic Wand Corp., 1960s, 29 In. 45.00
Jane Powell, Whitman, 1952, Uncut 90.00
Jane Russell, 1943 .... 90.00
Jeanette MacDonald, 1940s 55.00
Jetsons, Uncut 95.00
John Wayne, Tom Tierney, 1981, Uncut 10.00
Judy Garland, Tom Tierney, 32 Pages, Uncut 25.00
Kewpies In Kewpieville, 1966, Uncut 80.00
Laugh-In, 1969 .... 25.00
Lennon Sisters, 1957, Cut 35.00
Lennon Sisters, Whitman, Uncut 40.00
Lettie Lane, Ladies Home Journal, 1911, Uncut 88.00
Lettie Lane's Around The World Party, 1918, Uncut 18.00
Liberty, Military Uniforms, World War II 55.00
Little Kiddie, Whitman, 1969, Uncut 25.00
Little Lulu, Valentines, 1951, 8 x 10 In. 11.00
Little Lulu & Tubby, 1974, Uncut 25.00
Lucy & Desi, Clothes, Cut 70.00
Marge's Little Lulu, Book, 1971, Uncut 25.00
Marilyn Monroe, 1979 .... 12.00
Mary Lou, Milton Bradley, 1955, Uncut 10.00
Mary Martin, 1952 .... 75.00
Mary Martin, Saalfield, 1942, Uncut 135.00
Mary Poppins, Disney, 1964 .... 35.00
Mary Poppins, Sands/Whitman, Australia, 1966, Uncut 35.00
Mary Poppins, Whitman, Uncut, 1964 .... 50.00
Mrs. Beasley, 1972, Uncut 30.00
Nancy & Sluggo, Whitman, Uncut 15.00
Nanny & The Professor, 1970, Uncut .... 18.00 to 25.00
Nurses Three, 1964 .... 15.00
Old Lady In Shoe, Whitman, 1940, Uncut 68.00
Partridge Family, Box, 1971, Uncut 95.00
Pat Boone, Whitman, 1959, Uncut 35.00
Patty Duke, 1964, Cut 30.00
Raggedy Ann, Marcela, 1944, Uncut 225.00
Raggedy Ann & Andy, Saalfield, 1954, Uncut 125.00
Reagan Family, Uncut 12.00
Rhonda Fleming, Saalfield, 1954 .... 45.00
Rock Hudson, 1957 .... 60.00

Teddy Bear, 5 Outfits, 1910, Cut .... 295.00 to 325.00
Twiggy, Uncut 75.00

PAPERWEIGHTS must have first appeared along with paper in ancient Egypt. Today's collectors search for every type, from the very expensive French weights of the nineteenth century to the modern artist weights or advertising pieces. The glass tops of the paperweights sometimes have been nicked or scratched and this type of damage can be removed by polishing. Some serious collectors think this type of repair is an alteration and will not buy a repolished weight; others think it is an acceptable technique of restoration that does not change the value. Baccarat paperweights are listed separately under Baccarat.

Advertising, Bear, Standing, Parker Vises, 3 3/8 x 1 3/4 In. 132.00
Advertising, Buick, Big News Is Buick, Cast Iron, c.1930 .... 65.00
Advertising, Connecticut Mutual Life Insurance 35.00
Advertising, Crescent Hotel, Eureka Springs, Ruby & Clear Glass, 3 In. 45.00
Advertising, Marvel Motor Car 30.00
Advertising, Maryland Casualty Insurance, 2 3/4 In. 25.00
Advertising, Metropolitan Museum Pop Art, Signed F. Stella, 1970 .... 75.00
Advertising, National Liberty Insurance, Glass, Silver Rim, Silver Coin, 1928 .... 40.00
Advertising, Penguin, Swanson Products, Metal 125.00
Advertising, Pig Shape, Iron, Kaiser Company, 1st Pig Iron, 1/1/43, 4 In. 95.00
Advertising, Pig, H.W. Adams & Co., 2 1/8 x 3 In. 132.00
Advertising, Prudential 50th Anniversary, 1925 .... 40.00
Advertising, Sherwin-Williams Co. Paint, Cast Iron, 8 1/2 In. 193.00
Advertising, South Western Bell Telephone, Bell Shape, Blue 175.00
Advertising, State Farm Insurance, Apple 45.00
Advertising, Traveller's Insurance, 1925 .... 40.00
Banford, Blue Flower & Ruby Flower, White Ground, 3 1/2 In. 600.00
Blenko, Controlled Bubble Spiral, Cylinder, Dome Top 45.00
Boy & Girl Kissing, Full Figured, 3 1/8 x 2 1/4 In. 82.50
Boy Kissing Girl, Fishing Pole & Hat At Bottom, Cast Iron 200.00
Bronze, Oval Frame, Mother-Of-Pearl In Base, France, 19th Century, 5 1/2 In. 660.00
Caithness, Christmas Star, Poinsettia, Purple Ground, Canes 350.00
Cape Cod, Rose Center, Purple & White Swirl 250.00
Christopher Columbus, Intaglio, 1892 Exposition 140.00
Clichy, Chain Of 13 Roses, Cinquefoil Garland 7150.00
Clichy, Millefiori Canes, Multi-Colored, Opaque White Ground, 3 In. 2860.00
Clichy, Millefiori, 15 Roses 9350.00
Clichy, Pansy, Purple & Yellow, Clear, 2 3/4 In. 1380.00
Clichy, Spaced Millefiori, 1 Rose 2450.00
Cristal D'Albret, Audubon 100.00
D'Albret, 4 Moon Astronauts, Signed 250.00
D'Albret, Jenny Lind, Sulphide, Double Overlay, 1970s 150.00
D'Albret, Sulphide, Prince Charles 175.00
Edinburgh, 6 Petal Purple Flower, Canes, Dark Violet Ground 110.00
Football, Frosted Glass 20.00
George Washington, Cast Iron 40.00
Gilded Classical Scene, Satyr, Cranberry Glass, 3 In. 71.50
Gordon Smith, Frog, Strawberry Dart Amid Foliage, Rocks, 3 5/8 In. 900.00
Gordon Smith, Moorish Idols Amid Coral On Reef, 3 1/2 In. 800.00
Kaziun, Triple Overlay Crimp Rose 6600.00
Kaziun III, Striped Flowers, 2 Buds, Red & White Jasper Ground, 2 1/4 In. 320.00
Lincoln, Piece Of Black Cloth, Funeral Car, 1865, 5 1/2 x 5 1/2 In. 275.00
Lion, Brown & Black Glaze, Red Clay, 3 3/4 In. 165.00
Lundberg, Daisy Cluster, White, Yellow & Mauve 350.00
Lundberg, Mixed Flowers Of Narcissus Family, Blue Ground 380.00
Lundberg, Shamrock Oxalis, Heart Shape Leaves, Blue Ground 290.00
Lundberg, Water Hyacinth & Bud, Over Floating Lily Pads, 3 1/4 In. 320.00
Marble, New York, New Haven & Hartford Railroad Co. 6.50
Maul, Blue & White Striped Petals, Mauve Ground 240.00
Maul, Red & White Striped Flower & Buds, Light Blue Ground 240.00

Millefiori, 7 Rings, 20 Canes, Gold Aventurine Bed 375.00
Millefiori, Bacchus, Silhouettes Of Women, Stars, 3 7/16 In. 2300.00
Millefiori, Concentric, Central Cane, Rows Of Cogwheel Canes, 3 7/16 In. 1150.00
Millefiori, Multicolor Canes, Spiral Cones, Gold Dust, 3 In. 50.00
Millefiori, Whale, Label, 6 In. 140.00
Millefiori, Whitefriars, Honeycomb, 1960s 350.00
New England Glass, Busts Of Queen Victoria & Consort, 1851 .... 195.00
New England Glass, Millefiori, Swirling White Latticinio 475.00
New England Glass, Nosegay, 3 Floret Canes, 4 Leaves On Stem 300.00
Orange & Blue Peacock Design, White Glass, Signed, Dated 1979 .... 55.00
Pelican, Cast Iron 48.00
Perthshire, 2 Rings Of Canes, Cobalt Ground, Marked P 1974, 3 In. 210.00
Perthshire, Garland, Ruby Overlay, 8 Point Star Base 565.00
Perthshire, Penguin & Bird Silhouette, Canes, 1972 .... 140.00
Perthshire, Pink & Green Floral, Cane Border, Signed, 1 3/4 In. 50.00
Rosenfeld, Fiesta, Corn & Peppers, 3 5/8 In. 400.00
Rosenfeld, Vegetable Garden, Radishes, Carrots, Asparagus, 3 1/2 In. 300.00
Salazar, American Dream, Red Rose, Blue Ground, 3 1/2 In. 600.00
Sandwich Glass, Double Poinsettia, Red 1100.00
Sikorsky-Todd, Blossoming Fruit Tree, Canes With Rocks, 3 1/2 In. 390.00
Sikorsky-Todd, White Birch, Vines, Flowers, In Grass, 3 1/2 In. 390.00
Snow Dome, Child On Sled 85.00
Snow Dome, Lighthouse 85.00
Snow Dome, MacArthur 85.00
Snow Dome, Mammy 235.00
Snow Dome, Nativity, Mary, Joseph, Jesus In Manger 25.00
Snow Dome, Yellowstone Park, Bear, Plastic 30.00
Snow Globe, Black Watermelon Eater 250.00
St. Clair, Apple, Caramel Flower 85.00
St. Clair, Apple, Red Controlled Bubble 125.00
St. Clair, Pink Flower, Dome Shape 58.00
St. Louis, Bouquet, Magnum Faceted, Clear, 3 15/16 In. 4600.00
St. Louis, Concentric Millefiori, Clear, 3 In. 920.00
St. Louis, Double Clematis, Lilac & Turquoise, Clear, Latticinio, 2 15/16 In. 1495.00
St. Louis, Fruit Basket 1430.00
St. Louis, Millefiori, Swirling White Latticinio, Star Canes 725.00
St. Louis, Nosegay, Strawberry Cut Base 795.00
St. Louis, Pansy, Latticinio Ground, Faceted Octagonal Form, 2 1/2 In. 825.00
St. Louis, Pink Double Clematis, Cane Center, 5 Green Petals 1275.00
St. Louis, Plum, Forked Branch, 3 Serrated Leaves, 2 3/4 In. 575.00
St. Louis, Red, White & Blue Canes, Millefiori 575.00
St. Louis, Strawberry, 1 Red & 1 Pink Strawberry, 3 Leaves, 2 1/2 In. 1100.00
St. Louis, Strawberry, White Ribbed, Clear, 2 11/16 In. 863.00
St. Louis, White Fish, Red & Black Face, Blue & White Sea Bed, 2 3/4 In. 1430.00
Stankard, Blackberry, Berries Under Leaves & Buds, Cane, 2 3/5 In. 1870.00
Stankard, Cattleya Orchid, Pink Petals About White Stamen, 3 In. 920.00
Stankard, Day Lily, Orange Leaves, Yellow Pistil, 3 Buds, 2 7/8 In. 633.00
Stankard, Lady Slipper, Pink Flower, Blue Ground, Cane, 1972, 2 1/4 In. 605.00
Stankard, Poinsettia, Floating Red Blossom, Cane, 1973, 2 1/4 In. 715.00
Stankard, Spiderwort, Variegated Green Petals, Signed, 2 13/16 In. 690.00
Star, Texas Centennial, Cobalt Blue, 5 x 5 In. 110.00
Sulphide, George Washington, Colored Particles, 1820s, 3 In. 500.00
Sulphide, Lee, Cobalt Blue Ground, Crystal, 3 In. 60.50
Swan, Cast Iron 35.00
Winchester, Glass, 1910 .... 60.00
Ysart, Butterfly, Multicolored, Green Ground, Garland, 2 15/16 In. 1210.00

PAPIER-MACHE is made from paper mixed with glue, chalk, and other
ingredients, then molded and baked. It becomes very hard and can be painted.
Boxes, trays, and furniture were made of papier-mache. Some of the
nineteenth-century pieces were decorated with mother-of-pearl. Furniture
made of papier-mache is listed in the Furniture category.

  Box, Jewelry, Mother-Of-Pearl Inlay, Painted Designs 800.00

Box, Sewing, Floral Design, Compartmentalized, 2 x 13 In. 145.00
Candy Container, Lobster, Separates In Middle, 1900 .... 125.00
Card Case, Mother-Of-Pearl Inlay, 1860s 250.00
Case, Cigar, Painted, Man Playing Lute, Pouch Inside, 2 3/4 x 5 1/2 In. 185.00
Mask, Tengu, Orange, Red & Gilt, Japanese, 11 3/4 In. 65.00
Tea Caddy, Birds & Flowers, Gold Enamel, Brown Lacquer Ground, 4 x 7 In. 425.00
Tray, Bird & Landscape, Mother-Of-Pearl Inlay, On Table Base, 21 In. 175.00
Tray, Center Floral Bouquet, Gilt Scrolled Design, Oval, 31 x 23 In. 1210.00
Tray, Faux Bamboo Stand, Mountain Lake Scene, Victorian 578.00
Tray, Handle, Victorian 88.00
Tray, Mahogany Stand, Marlborough Feet, Jennings & Beltridge 6500.00
Tray, Regency Style, Hunt Scene, Stand, 20 x 29 In. 1100.00
Tray, Victorian, Gilt Floral & Bird Design, Bamboo Base, 20 x 28 In. 935.00

PARASOL, see Umbrella

PARIAN is a fine-grained, hard-paste porcelain named for the marble it
resembles. It was first made in England in 1846 and gained in favor in the
United States about 1860. Figures, tea sets, vases, and other items were made
of Parian at many English and American factories.

Bust, Lord Byron, 8 1/8 In. 66.00
Bust, Man With Long Hair, Mutton Chops, 11 1/2 In. 230.00
Bust, Wistful Little Girl, Scarf Around Head, Winter, J & T B, 8 In. 95.00
Compote, Boy & Girl Feeding Swan, Pedestal, 9 1/2 In. 175.00
Creamer, Camping Scenes, 4 1/4 In. 19.00
Figurine, Child Kneeling On Cushion, 6 1/4 In. 100.00
Figurine, Havelock, Signed Macbride, 1868, 14 In. 357.00
Figurine, John Milton, 19th Century, 14 In. 290.00
Figurine, Medieval Warrior, Classical Ruins, 17 In. 345.00
Flower Bowl, Wheat Design, 7 In. 10.00
Pitcher, Cranes, Blue & White, 8 In. 135.00
Pitcher, Molded Bundled Reeds & Berries, 10 3/4 In. 193.00
Pitcher, Molded Foliage & Medallions, 9 In. 138.00
Planter, Relief Figure, Young Girl, 2 Turkeys & Chicks, 6 x 10 1/2 In. 200.00
Plaque, George Washington, Brass Hanger, 6 1/4 x 4 1/2 In. 120.00

PARIS, Vieux Paris, or Old Paris, is porcelain ware that is known to have
been made in Paris in the eighteenth or early nineteenth century. These
porcelains have no identifying mark but can be recognized by the whiteness
of the porcelain and the lines and decorations. Gold decoration is often
used.

Coffee & Tea Set, Gilt, Blue Highlights, Flowers, c.1820, 16 Piece 5225.00
Cologne Bottle, Lobed Stoppers, Multifaceted, Green, Lavender, Gold Base, Pair 1073.00
Cup & Saucer, Enamel Decorated, Portrait Of Woman, Flags, New Orleans, c.1862 .. 1760.00
Cup & Saucer, Flowers, Chinoiserie, Gilt Border, Black Ground, c.1820, 12 Piece 440.00
Cup & Saucer, Swan Form, Feathers Molded In Relief, Burnished Gilding, 4 1/2 In. 1650.00
Cuspidor, Gilt Masked-Head Handles, Floral Decorated, c.1825, 9 In. 248.00
Inkwell, Flowers, 2 Children On Top, Gold Trim 185.00
Jardiniere, Gilt Bordered, Vignettes, Chinese Nobles, Underplate, 8 3/4 In., Pair 5845.00
Night-Light, Floral Design 1450.00
Plate, Each Different Flower Or Fruit, Gilded Rim, 9 1/2 In., 12 Piece 1540.00
Plate, Topographical, Brown Transfer, Bay & Citadel Of Marseilles, 10 1/2 In. 880.00
Quill Holder, Figural, Hunter, Seated, 9 In. 193.00
Scent Bottle, Figural, 18th Century European Couple, c.1850, 13 1/2 In., Pair 550.00
Teapot, Inverted Pear, Gilded Scrollwork, c.1845, 9 In. 99.00
Urn, Campana Shape, Bisque Mask Handles, Painted Landscapes, c.1830, 12 In., Pair 1100.00
Urn, George Washington, Winged Horses Form Handle, Gilbert Stuart, 1798, 12 In. ... 3300.00
Urn, Gilt Designs, Floral Roundels, 19th Century, 10 1/4 In., Pair 605.00
Urn, Palace, Flocks Of Wild Fowl, 19th Century, 20 In. 935.00
Urn, Portrait, Blue Ground, Campana Form, Pair .... *Illus* 5175.00
Vase, Amphora Shape, Gilt Borders & Latticework, Flowers, c.1840, 10 In., Pair 1100.00
Vase, Baluster Shape, Greco-Roman Decoration, 24 In., Pair 880.00
Vase, Cobalt Blue, Gold Trim, Flared, Tall 750.00

*Paris, Urn, Portrait, Blue Ground,
Campana Form, Pair*

♦♦♦♦♦♦♦♦♦♦♦♦♦♦♦♦♦♦♦♦♦♦♦♦

When cleaning ceramics be
sure to remove your rings
so you don't scratch the
dishes. Wear tight sleeves
to avoid snagging any figurine's arms or legs. Hold
pieces with both hands.
Don't pick up teapots by
handles or spouts.

♦♦♦♦♦♦♦♦♦♦♦♦♦♦♦♦♦♦♦♦♦♦♦♦

Vase, Court Musician Scenes, Pair	825.00
Vase, Figural Panel, Cobalt Blue, Gilt Design, 22 1/4 In.	550.00
Vase, Floral Panel, Scrolling Gilt Border, Scrolled Handles, 17 In., Pair	2875.00
Vase, Floral, Rococo Gilt Borders, 11 5/8 In., Pair	880.00
Vase, Mantel, Gold Floral, Raised, Red Ground, Hand Painted, 15 In.	220.00
Vase, Ovoid, Gilt Stars, Purple Trelliswork, Gilt Handles, c.1800, 8 3/4 In., Pair	4025.00
Vase, Painted & Parcel Gilt, Campana Form, Courting Peasant, 10 In., Pair	1430.00
Vase, Pierced Metal Neck, Vine-Form Handles, 20 3/4 In., Pair	1430.00
Vase, Rococo, Leafy Gilded Rim, Flowers, Applied Blossoms, c.1850, 14 In., Pair	990.00
Veilleuse, Cherubs Standing Each 4 Corners	1485.00

PATE-DE-VERRE is an ancient technique in which glass is made by blending
and refining powdered glass of different colors into molds. The process was
revived by French glassmakers, especially Galle, around the end of the
nineteenth century.

Perfume Bottle, Atomizer, Deep Rose, Berries & Leaves Top, 3 3/4 In.	2500.00
Plaque, Cupid & Psyche, Henri Cros, c.1910, 9 3/4 x 7 5/8 In.	8050.00
Plaque, Nude Woman, 1/2 Length, Green Shawl, Henri Cros, 10 3/4 x 7 In.	1265.00
Vase, Blue, Green & Amber Swirls, Rectangular, A. Leperlier, 1982, 8 3/4 In.	546.00
Vase, Lime, V-Shaped Side Opening, Turquoise Streaks, A. Leperlier, 5 In.	345.00
Vase, Smoky, Grape, Aubergine Streaks, Handles, E. Leperlier, 5 5/8 In.	402.00

PATE-SUR-PATE means paste on paste. The design was made by painting
layers of slip on the ceramic piece until a relief decoration was formed. The
method was developed at the Sevres factory in France about 1850. It became
even more famous at the English Minton factory about 1870. It has since
been used by many potters to make both pottery and porcelain wares.

Plaque, Adam, Victoria Ware, Rust, White, Wedgwood, c.1880, 5 1/4 x 11 In.	2090.00
Plaque, Soldier, Victoria Ware, Blue, White, Wedgwood, c.1880, 5 1/4 x 11 In.	1540.00
Plaque, White, Blue Ground, Bronze Mounted, Small	1600.00
Vase, Gold Serpent Skin Handles, Gold Trim, 7 1/4 In.	995.00
Vase, Oriental Style, White Bird, Dark Green, 2 Handles, 14 3/8 In.	550.00
Vase, White Slip Buildup To Figure, Art Nouveau, 8 1/2 In.	730.00

PAUL REVERE POTTERY was made at several locations in and around
Boston, Massachusetts, between 1906 and 1942. The pottery was operated as
a settlement house program for teenage girls. Many pieces were signed
S.E.G. for Saturday Evening Girls. The artists concentrated on children's
dishes and tiles. Decorations were outlined in black and filled with color.

Bowl, Duck	7975.00

◆◆◆◆◆◆◆◆◆◆◆◆◆◆◆◆◆◆◆◆◆

American brilliant period cut glass will fluoresce a pale lime green under a black light. Newly cut glass will look purple-pink under the same light.

◆◆◆◆◆◆◆◆◆◆◆◆◆◆◆◆◆◆◆◆◆

Peachblow, Pitcher, Red-Fuchsia Shaded to Amber, Handle, Wheeling, 8 In.

Bowl, Goose Border, Yellow Glaze, SEG	250.00
Bowl, Tulip Band, SEG, 8 1/2 In.	850.00
Bowl Berry, Saucer, White Floral Band, Blue Ground, SEG, 5 x 6 1/2 In.	412.00
Canister, Cover, Hexagonal, Rabbit, Cream, Blue, SEG, 4 1/2 In.	550.00
Canister, Cream Rabbit, Blue, Medallion, Yellow & Green, SEG, 4 1/2 In.	550.00
Creamer, Matte Blue Glaze, SEG, 5 In.	325.00
Creamer, Yellow Ducks, SEG	300.00
Cup, Cone Tree In Circle, Multicolor, 3 1/2 In.	400.00
Dinner Set, Blossoms, Wavy Band, SEG, Service For 8	880.00
Dish, Cover, Multicolored Landscape Band, Ivory Ground, 5 x 10 In.	935.00
Dish, Hand Incised, SEG, 6 1/4 In.	340.00
Jar, Cover, Band Of Stylized Florals, SEG, 4 1/4 In.	625.00
Jar, Stylized Winged Insects, SEG, Ivory Ground, Cover, 4 1/2 In.	1700.00
Mug, Motto, Incised Tree Landscape, Sara Galner, 4 In.	1430.00
Mug, Rabbit, Cream Ground, Blue Band, Christmas, c.1914, SEG, 3 In.	385.00
Mug, Rabbit, Standing, Green Band	231.00
Paperweight, Stylized Swan, SEG, 5 x 2 1/2 In.	250.00
Paperweight, Stylized Tree, Blue Ground, SEG, 3/4 x 2 1/2 In.	250.00
Pitcher, Flowing Mottled Blue Glaze, SEG, 7 1/4 In.	525.00
Pitcher, Purple Flambe, 3 In.	85.00
Pitcher & Bowl, Child's, Chicks, Tan, 2 Piece	300.00
Pitcher & Bowl, Child's, Ducks, Tan, 2 Piece	325.00
Plate, Deep Blue Glaze, Black Band, 8 In.	28.00
Running Pigs Rim Monogram, Shapiro & Bikini, 3 1/2 In., Pair	3190.00
Sugar, Landscape Band, Blue Glaze, 4 In.	132.00
Tankard, Snow Capped Mountains Around Top, SEG, 5 In.	275.00 to 300.00
Toothpick, Rabbit Border, SEG	110.00
Trivet, Yellow & Black Design, SEG, Square, 5 1/4 In.	225.00
Vase, Band Of Trees, SEG, Dark Blue Matte Ground, 4 1/2 In.	500.00
Vase, Blue To Teal Drip Glaze, SEG, 10 1/2 In.	385.00
Vase, Cobalt Blue Drip Over White, 7 1/2 In.	125.00
Vase, Floral, SEG, 4 1/2 x 5 In.	500.00
Vase, Flying Geese Band, Light Blue Ground, Black Outlining, 8 3/8 In.	1320.00
Vase, Silver Crystals On Pale Green, SEG, 3 1/4 In.	130.00
Vase, Stylized Floral Band, Black Outlining, Yellow Glaze, SEG, 9 1/8 In.	522.00

PEACHBLOW glass originated about 1883 at Hobbs, Brockunier and Company of Wheeling, West Virginia. It shades from yellow to peach and is lined with white glass. New England peachblow is a one-layer glass shading from red to white. Mt. Washington peachblow shades from pink to blue. Reproductions of all types of peachblow have been made. Some are poor and easy to identify as copies, others are very accurate reproductions and could fool the unwary. Related pieces may be listed under Gunderson and Webb Peachblow.

Bowl, Frosted Squared Briar Handles, 9 1/4 In.	450.00

Bowl, Scalloped Rim, New England, 2 1/2 x 5 1/4 In. 300.00
Celery Vase, New England, Wild Rose, Crimped Top 545.00
Celery Vase, Raspberry To White, 6 1/4 In. 950.00
Celery Vase, Wild Rose Fades To Light Pink Base, Pie Crust Crimp, 6 3/4 In. 545.00
Creamer, Wheeling, 4 1/4 In. 785.00
Cruet, Wheeling, Teardrop Shape, 6 3/4 In. 1085.00
Fairy Lamp, Cranberry Glass Base 220.00
Flask, Wheeling, Dark Gold To Mahogany, Tooled Lip, 7 In. 750.00
Mustard, Gold Prunus, 2 1/2 In. 395.00
Pitcher, Mt. Washington, Crimped, Ruffled Lip, Amber Handle, 9 1/4 In. 550.00
Pitcher, Red-Fuchsia Shaded to Amber, Handle, Wheeling, 8 In. .... *Illus* 1760.00
Pitcher, Thorny Handle, Amber Lining, 9 In. 695.00
Pitcher, Wheeling, Quatrefoil Top, Amber Handle, c.1870, 7 1/4 In. 850.00
Rose Bowl, Footed, Diamond Quilted 225.00
Rose Bowl, New England, 7-Crimp Top, Raspberry To White, 2 5/8 In. 300.00
Saltshaker, Wheeling, Cherry Red To Yellow, 2 3/4 In. 485.00
Sugar & Creamer, 2 1/2 In. 850.00
Sugar & Creamer, World's Fair, 1893 On Sugar, 2 1/2 In. 850.00
Sugar Shaker, Wheeling, Screw-On Top, 5 1/2 In. 1250.00
Toothpick, Tri-Cornered, Raspberry To White 750.00
Tumbler, Mt. Washington 200.00
Tumbler, New England 295.00
Tumbler, Wheeling, 3 1/2 In. 500.00
Tumbler, Wheeling, Double Layers Of Glass, White Lining 485.00
Vase, Wheeling, Classic Shape, White Lining, 6 1/2 x 6 1/2 In. 850.00
Vase, Wheeling, Fuchsia At Top, Yellow Base, c.1885, 10 1/2 In. 1250.00

PEARL items listed here are made of the natural mother-of-pearl from shells. Such natural pearl has been used to decorate furniture and small utilitarian objects for centuries. The glassware known as mother-of-pearl is listed by that name. Opera glasses made with natural pearl shell are listed under Opera Glasses.

Card Case, Silver Plated Inset 88.00
Carving Set, Sterling Ferrules 30.00
Dressing Case, Inlaid Hongmu, China, 19th Century, 8 x 15 x 11 In. 275.00

PEARLWARE is an earthenware made by Josiah Wedgwood in 1779. It was copied by other potters in England. Pearlware is only slightly different in color from creamware and for many years collectors have confused the terms.

Pearl

Bowl, Waste, Blue & White Oriental Design, Repaired, 6 1/4 x 3 In. 165.00
Bowl, Waste, Gaudy Floral, 6 3/8 In. 33.00
Bust, George Washington, Ralph Wood, Jr., Color, c.1790, 10 In. 4950.00
Bust, Henry Wadsworth Longfellow, 13 1/2 In. 220.00
Can, Masks Design, Cylindrical, 5 In. 275.00
Charger, Blue & White Floral, Blue Feather Edge, 14 1/4 In. 412.50
Charger, Floral Design, Scalloped Border, Blue & White, 13 3/4 In. 165.00
Creamer, Black Transfer, Girl With Horse, Hounds, Pink Luster Trim, 4 3/4 In. 52.00
Creamer, Children In Hearts, Polychromed, 4 7/8 In. 434.50
Creamer, Helmet Shape, Floral Swags, Pink, Purple, Green, 4 1/2 In. 72.00
Cup, Mask Form Body, Mounted With Cross, 5 In., Pair 120.00
Cup & Saucer, Handleless, Blue Transfer Of Cows 77.00
Cup & Saucer, Handleless, Enameled Floral, Strawberries 110.00
Cup & Saucer, Handleless, Enameled Strawberry & Rose 72.00
Cup & Saucer, Handleless, Enameled Transfer Of Birds & Flowers 95.00
Cup & Saucer, Handleless, Floral Design, Blue & Pink Luster, Sewell 155.00
Cup & Saucer, Handleless, King's Rose Design, Pink Border 85.00
Cup & Saucer, Handleless, Polychrome Floral Design 72.00
Dish, Leaf Shape, Molded Ribs, Blue Oriental Transfer, 5 In. 115.00
Figurine, Lion, Curly Mane, Open Mouth, Paw On Ball, 11 In. .... 1380.00 To 2300.00
Figurine, Man And Woman, Strolling Arm-In-Arm, Yellow Gloves, c.1820, 8 3/8 In. .. 920.00
Figurine, Sailor Boy, Curly Hair, Striped Trousers, 1775-1785, 5 3/4 In. 2875.00

Figurine, Shepherdess, Blue Dress, Wood, 1785-1795, 10 1/4 In. 805.00
Figurine, Squirrel, Mocha & Brown Spots, 1790-1800, 6 13/16 In. 1955.00
Figurine, Vicar And Moses, Sleeping Vicar, Wood Family, c.1790, 9 5/8 In. 690.00
Invalid Feeder, Blue Oriental Transfer, 5 In. 93.00
Jug, Bacchus, Fruiting Grapevines, Monkey Handle, c.1780, 12 13/16 In. 1150.00
Jug, Puzzle, 3 Whistles Over Disc Body, Sunburst & Mask, 11 In. 488.00
Jug, Puzzle, Fluted Rim, Putti On Oval Foot, 9 1/2 In. 1150.00
Mug, Black Transfer, Cornwallis, Pink Luster Striping, 2 1/8 In. 470.00
Mug, Lattice Design, Polka Dots, Polychrome, 2 3/4 In. 104.50
Mug, Pink Luster, Black Transfer, Polychrome Enamel, God Save The King, 4 In. 55.00
Mug, Sand-Banded, Dated 1828, Initialed W.F. On Bottom, Painted Flowers 675.00
Pipe, Serpent Form, Green Glaze, Triple-Coiled Body, c.1810, 8 1/2 In. 920.00
Pitcher, Chinoiserie, Blue & White, England, c.1820, 6 In. 350.00
Pitcher, Floral Design, Polychrome, Brown Striping, 4 5/8 In. 72.00
Pitcher, Flower & Swag Design, Gamella Bingley, 1800, 7 In. 1150.00
Pitcher, Molded Hearts With Children, 8 1/8 In. 330.00
Pitcher, Purple Transfer, Faith Scenes, 4 1/8 In. 40.00
Pitcher, Silver Luster Floral, 6 In. 95.00
Plate, Blue Transfer, Scene, Stubbs, 8 1/2 In. 110.00
Plate, Embossed Daisy Rim, Polychrome Floral, 12 Sides, 7 1/4 In. 140.00
Plate, Hot Water, Sprig Design, Blue Rim, Crown Mark, 8 3/8 In. 95.00
Plate, Landscape Design, Blue & White 110.00
Platter, Blue Willow Transfer, 17 1/4 In. 215.00
Platter, Feather Rim, Gaudy Floral Design, 13 In. 1870.00
Punch Bowl, Another Bowl & Then, England, c.1790 .... 495.00
Punch Pot, Buffalo Pattern, Blue Transfer, Ribbed Spout, 10 1/2 In. 715.00
Saucer, Pink Luster House Design, Mayer & Co., 4 5/8 In. 55.00
Shaker, Molded Band, Blue & White, 4 3/8 In. 95.00
Sugar Bowl, Strawberries & Roses, Pink Enamel, Cover, 5 3/4 In. 300.00
Tea Set, Black Transfer, English Country Scenes, Blue Striping, 3 Piece 160.00
Tea Set, Swags & Floral Design, Crazed, 6 Piece 522.00
Tea Set, Swags, Polychrome Florals, New Hall Type, 6 Piece 475.00
Vase, 5-Finger, Pair 550.00

PEKING GLASS is a Chinese cameo glass first made popular in the eighteenth century. The Chinese have continued to make this layered glass in the old manner, and many new pieces are now available that could confuse the average buyer.

Bowl, Blue, Leafage Around Foot, 18th Century, 2 x 6 1/2 In. 2750.00
Bowl, Red Rooster & Flower Design, Cream Ground, 12 In. 715.00
Bowl, White Snowflake Ground, Green Overlay, 6 1/2 In. 95.00
Jar, Blue Overlay, Tripod, Clouds & Beast, Royal Blue Ground, 2 1/2 In. 3850.00
Jar, Yellow, Carved Flowers, Ovoid, 19th Century, 4 1/4 In. 550.00
Saucer, Ruby, Qianlong, 18th Century, 6 1/2 In. 1210.00
Snuff Bottle, Beast, Carved, Frosted, Round, Carnelian Stopper, 3 1/2 In. 247.00
Snuff Bottle, Birds In Landscape, Nephrite Stopper 230.00
Snuff Bottle, Blue Figures In A Garden, Frosted, Green Stopper, 2 3/8 In. 412.00
Snuff Bottle, Flowers, Butterflies, Blue, Red, Amber, Green, 1800s, 1 1/2 In. 715.00
Snuff Bottle, Green Jade Top, Blue & White With Red, 3 1/8 In. 165.00
Snuff Bottle, Multicolored Tendrils Of Leaves, Silver Topped 525.00
Snuff Bottle, Red, Snowflake, Foo Lion, Bat, Tiger, Late 19th Century 165.00
Snuff Bottle, Ring Loop Handles, Avian & Fu Lion Design, Yellow Ground 100.00
Snuff Bottle, Snowstorm Ground, Ruby Carving 220.00
Snuff Jar, Olive Cut To White, Pegasus, Crane & Turtle, 3 1/4 In. 60.50
Snuff Jar, Opaque White, Oriental Relief, 3 In. 308.00
Snuff Jar, White, Mottled Green & Tan, 2 3/4 In. 93.50
Vase, 3 Color Overlay, Foo Dogs, Lime Green Ground, Ring Handles, 6 In. 6600.00
Vase, Baluster, White, Landscape, 19th Century, 8 1/4 In., Pair 385.00
Vase, Bird & Flower Reserves, Red Overlay, Yellow, 18th Century, 9 3/4 In. 1045.00
Vase, Cobalt Blue, Inverted Rim, 5 In. 440.00
Vase, Opaque White, Pink Overlay, Cameo Lotus Flowers, Lily Pads, 7 3/4 In. 210.00
Vase, Prunus & Bamboo Design, Red Overlay, White, Bottle Shape, 8 3/4 In. 1320.00

PELOTON glass is a European glass with small threads of colored glass rolled onto the surface of clear or colored glass. It is sometimes called spaghetti, or shredded coconut, glass. Most pieces found today were made in the nineteenth century.

Plate, Ruffled, Colored Coconut Strings, 6 In.	95.00
Rose Bowl, Allover Coconut Strings, 4-Pointed Rim, Petal Feet, 3 3/4 In.	295.00
Vase, Coconut Strings Outside, Embossed Rib Effect, 3 1/2 In.	245.00
Vase, Colored Coconut Strings Outside, Ruffled Top, 3 1/2 In.	195.00
Vase, Colored Coconut Strings Outside, Pink Cased, Ruffled, 6 In.	245.00
Vase, Enameled Flowers, 6 3/4 In.	350.00
Vase, Folded Over Tricorner Shape Top, Coconut Strings Body, 4 x 5 In.	295.00
Vase, String, 5 x 5 In.	495.00

PENS replaced hand-cut quills as writing instruments in 1780 when the first steel pen point was made in England. But it was 100 years before the commercial pen was a common item. The fountain pen was invented in the 1830s but was not made in quantity until the 1880s. All types of old pens are collected.

PEN, Aiken Lambert Skywriter, Brown Marbleized	5.00
Ball-Point, Tooled Menorah & Hebraic Design, Sterling Silver, Israel, 4 1/2 In.	10.00
Baseball Bat Shape, Mickey Mantle, Louisville Slugger, Wooden	7.25
Conklin, All American, Marbleized, Price Sticker	50.00
Conklin, Black, Gold Filled Trim, 1927	65.00
Conklin, Fountain, Mottled Brown, Lever Filler	45.00
Conklin, No. 210, Crescent, Filler, 1921	175.00
Conklin, No. 25p, Crescent Filler, Gold Filled Engraved Trim, 1917	150.00
Conklin, Woman's, Wood Grain	45.00
Conklin PNL, Crescent Filler, Gold Filled Trim, 1922	249.00
Diamond, Green Marbleized, Gold Tip	6.00
Dunn-Pen, Eagle, 1899	150.00
Dunn-Pen, Eclipse, Gold Filled, 1924	15.00
Enameled Foliage, Black Ground, Swiss, Gold, 3 5/8 In.	1725.00
English, Spencerian Deluxe, Gold Filled	65.00
Eversharp, Doric, Marbleized Blue	275.00
Eversharp, Gold Seal Doric, Garnet Color, 5 1/2 In.	700.00
Eversharp, Skyline Presentation, Black, Gold Filled Metal Cap, 1943	99.00
Eversharp, Skyline Presentation, Blue, Gold Filled Cap	70.00
Eversharp, Skyline, Black, Gold Filled Trim, 1946	49.00
Eversharp, Skyline, Gold Filled Cap, Brown	45.00
Gold Bond, Stonite, Green Jade, Gold Filled Trim, 1928	69.00
Gorham, Golf, Riding Design, Sterling Silver, c.1915	230.00
Grieshaber, No. 8, Black & Gold Pattern, 1930s	403.00
Harold Orr, Green Marbleized	4.50
Kraker, Filigree Design, Gold Filled	200.00 to 632.50
Laymon, Green Marbleized, Black Cap, Gold Tip	4.50
Lord Baltimore, Black & Gold, Gold Tip	6.00
Mabie Todd & Co., Dip, Ebony, Gold Filled Metal, c.1877	125.00
Manager's, Hess Gas & Oil Co., Logo, 1960s	45.00
Moore, No. 96c, Jade Green, Lever Fill, 1926	400.00
Moore, Pearl, Black	225.00
Morrison, Gold Filled Metal, 1929	89.00
National, Cream & Brown Marbleized, Gold Tip	7.50
Parker, Blue Diamond Senior Maxima, Gold Pearl, Gold Filled Trim, 1939	725.00
Parker, Blue Diamond Vacumatic, Gold Pearl Stripes, 1946	75.00 to 82.00
Parker, Deluxe Challenger, Burgundy, 1938	99.00
Parker, Deluxe Standard Challenger, Black, Gold Filled Trim, 1936	89.00
Parker, DQ, Lucky Curve	75.00
Parker, Duofold Jr., Yellow	200.00
Parker, Duofold Sr., Black, Gold Filled Trim, 1931	365.00
Parker, Duofold Sr., Red, Gold Filled Trim, 1925	425.00
Parker, Duofold Sr., Streamline, Burgundy	225.00

Parker, Duofold, Black & Mother-Of-Pearl Stripe	50.00
Parker, Duofold, Woman's, Orange	125.00
Parker, Lady Duofold, Red, Gold Filled Trim, 1931	95.00 to 149.00
Parker, Lucky Curve, Gold Filled Trim, 1909	625.00
Parker, No. 15, Mother-Of-Pearl & Abalone, Gold Filled Filigree Cap	3500.00
Parker, No. 26, Black Hard Rubber,	242.00
Parker, No. 41, Aqua, Alloy Nib, 1958	55.00
Parker, Parkette Deluxe, Green Pearl Marble, 1937	89.00
Parker, Vacumatic Jr., Emerald Stripes, Gold Filled Trim, 1947	85.00
Parker, Vacumatic, Black, Gold Filled Trim, 1936	179.00
Parker, Vacumatic, Black, Gold Filled Trim, Canada, 1935, Oversize	599.00
Parker, Vacumatic, Emerald Pearl Stripes, Gold Filled Trim, 1945	69.00
Parker 51, Black, Gold Filled Cap	90.00
Parker 75, Sterling Silver, Box, 1960	115.00 to 139.00
Pilot, Dunhill, Hand Painted Maki-E-Lacquer, Red, 1927	2700.00
Reynolds, Roerig, Rocket Ball-Point	15.00
Salz Brothers, Peter Pan, Mottled Yellow, 3 1/4 In.	125.00
Scheaffer, Lifetime, Desk, 1945	125.00
Scheaffer, Lifetime, Green Marble, Gold Filled	150.00
Scheaffer, Lifetime, White Dot, Jade	90.00
Scheaffer, Valiant, 1950	55.00
Sheaffer, Cadet, 1945	110.00
Sheaffer, Fineline, Red, Gold Tip	7.50
Sheaffer, Green, 1940s	25.00
Sheaffer, Green, Gold Filled Trim, 1928	75.00
Sheaffer, Lifetime, Balance, Red, Lever Fill, 1935	3795.00
Sheaffer, Lifetime, Black, 14K Gold Trim & Tip, Marked	245.00
Sheaffer, Lifetime, Black, Gold Filled Trim, 1925	110.00
Sheaffer, Lifetime, Gold Pearl Stripes, Gold Filled Trim, 1937	89.00
Sheaffer, Lifetime, Green Marbleized, 1932	100.00
Sheaffer, Lifetime, Pearl & Black	250.00
Sheaffer, Lifetime, Pearl, Black Ends, 1920s	4830.00
Sheaffer, Lifetime, Triumph 1250, Black, Gold Filled Trim, 1947	69.00
Sheaffer, No. 2, Self Filling, 1918	99.00
Sheaffer, No. 2, Self-Filling, Sterling Silver, 1919	215.00
Sheaffer, No. 3-25, Silver, Speckled Pink, Gold Filled Trim, 1935	89.00
Sheaffer, No. 8, 14K Gold Band, Line Pattern	6555.00
Sheaffer, Silver, Pearl Stripes, White Gold Filled Trim, 1938	39.00
Sheaffer, Telephone Dialer, Jade, 1930	100.00
Sheaffer, Triumph Snorkel, Maroon, Paladium Silver Nib, 1953	39.00
Sheaffer, White Dot, Black & Pearl	100.00
Sheaffer, White Dot, Black Onyx Base, 2 Pens, 1920s, 7 x 7 1/2 In.	300.00
Sheaffer, White Dot, Lifetime, 14K Gold Tip	75.00
Stratford, Red Marbleized, 14K Gold Tip	7.00
Stratford, Regency, Black, Gold Tip	5.00
Swan, Gold Filled Trim, 1923	395.00
Swan, No. 48, E.T.N., Gold Filled Trim, 1927	449.00
Tillamook Cheese, Tillamook, Oregon, Black, Retractable, Ball-Point	1.00
Vulcan, Stylographic, 1906	149.00
Wahl, Fountain, Gold Filled, Lever Fill, 1928	150.00
Wahl, Line & Flower Design, 14K Gold, 1920s	632.50
Wahl, No. 2, Gold Filled Trim, 1921	395.00
Wahl, Woman's, 14K Gold Filled, Ribbon Ring	75.00
Wahl-Eversharp, Gold Seal, Personal Point, Black, 1931	595.00 to 795.00
Wahl-Eversharp, No. 3, Gold Filled Trim, 1920	175.00
Wahl-Eversharp, No. 5, Gold Filled Trim, 1920	395.00
Wahl-Eversharp, Skyline, Maroon, c.1940	385.00
Wahl-Oxford, Green Cross Hatched, Long	40.00
Waterman, 14K Gold Filigree Overlay, c.1923	1495.00
Waterman, Fountain, Gold Filled, Checkerboard	150.00
Waterman, Ideal, Match Stick, Gold Filled Trim, Box, 1902	8500.00
Waterman, Ideal, No. 7, Red Ripple, 1928	395.00

Waterman, Ideal, No. 12, Mottled Red, 1898 .... 199.00
Waterman, Ideal, No. 14, Sterling Filagree, 1919 .... 449.00
Waterman, Ideal, No. 48, Safety, Gold Filled Metal, 1924 .... 7995.00
Waterman, Ideal, No. 52, 1928 .... 99.00
Waterman, Ideal, No. 52, Gold Filled Filagree, 1927 .... 525.00
Waterman, Ideal, No. 452, Safety, 1924 .... 129.00
Waterman, Ideal, No. 452, Sterling Filigreed, 1924 .... 375.00
Waterman, No. 12, Sterling Silver Filigree, c.1908 .... 350.00
Waterman, No. 44, Fountain, Safety, Sterling Filigree 3575.00
Waterman, No. 52, Red Ripple, 1925 .... 95.00
Waterman, No. 58, Red Hard Rubber, c.1922 .... 3195.00
Waterman, No. 402, Sterling Chased Overlay, 1898-1915 .... 1300.00
Waterman, No. 514, Fountain, 14K Gold Filigree 660.00
Waterman, No. 552 1/2, Fountain, Pansy Panel, 14K Gold 715.00
Waterman, Supersize Hundred Year, Black, Gold Filled Trim, 1943 .... 599.00
Waterman, Wirt, Overfeed, 1904 .... 565.00
Waterman, Woman's, Ideal 65.00
Windsor, Black, Gold Cap 4.00
PEN & PENCIL, Dunn-Pen, Eclipse, Gold Filled 200.00
Eversharp, Ball-Point, Maroon, Box 8.00
Eversharp, Doric, Cathay, Silver Green Pearl, 1936 .... 399.00
Eversharp, No. 64, Black, Solid 14K Gold Caps & Trim, 1942 .... 349.00
Eversharp, Symphony Deluxe, Black, Chrome, Gold Banded Caps, 1950 ... 65.00
Grieshaber, Ambassador, 1931 .... 65.00
Onward, Brass Trim, Marbleized 8.00
Mont Blanc, Leather Case, 1920s 425.00
Parker, 41, Black, Lustraloy Caps, 1956 .... 79.00
Parker, 51, Wine, Silver, Green Jewel Top 110.00
Parker, Duofold, Green & Gold, Box 150.00
Parker, Vacumatic 70.00
Sheaffer, 14K Yellow Gold, 1922 .... 4505.00
Sheaffer, Balance, Pearl & Black, Box, Made 1 Year, 1929 .... 132.00
Wahl-Eversharp, Fifth Avenue, Beige, 1943 .... 125.00
Wahl-Eversharp, Gold Seal, Gold Filled Trim, 1928 .... 285.00
Wahl-Eversharp, Skyline, Maroon, 1945 .... 89.00
Wahl, Hand Engraved Floral Design, 14K Green Gold 1121.00
Waterman, Crusader, Taperite, Black, Lumaloy Caps, 1947 .... 49.00
Waterman, Ideal, No. 454, Gothic Sterling 895.00
Waterman, Italy 385.00
Waterman, No. 7, Ripple 242.00
Woman's, Penvelope, Hand Painted, Sterling, Celluloid Box, 1920s 1035.00

PENCILS were invented, so it is said, in 1565. The eraser was not added to
the pencil until 1858. The automatic pencil was invented in 1863. Collectors
today want advertising pencils or automatic pencils of unusual design. Boxes
and sharpeners for pencils are also collected.

PENCIL SHARPENER, Clock, Red, Bakelite 45.00
Donald Duck, Plastic Head 75.00
Elephant, Celluloid, Germany 20.00
Little Shaver, Mechanical, Decal 205.00
Nestle's, Battery Operated, 1940s 175.00
Scotty Dog, Green Bakelite 30.00
Wolfman, Bust, Green Plastic, U.P. Co., 1963, 3 In. 29.00
World Globe, Brass, Germany 15.00
PENCIL, AC Auto Parts, Gold Plated, Floating Oil Filter, 1940s 35.00
Bowling Pin, Mechanical 12.00
Box, Barbie, Black Patent, Ponytail, 1961 .... 66.00
Box, Jackie Coogan, ... 95.00
Box, Lucky Lindy, Spirit Of St. Louis, Original Contents, Tin, Wallace, 1920s 60.00
Box, Multiplication Tables, Lithographed Printed Surface, Tin, 9 In. 30.00
Cascade Dairy, Bellingham, Wash., Unused 1.25
Chevrolet Dealer, Christmas Premium 20.00
Chicago Fair, East View Of Administration Building, Brass & Celluloid, 1933 .... 10.00

Conklin, Black, Gold Filled Trim, 1930	69.00
Dance Card, Retractable, Gold Filled Metal, Glass Stone End, 1920s	65.00
Eversharp, Ventura Repeater, Green, Gold Tone Top, 1953	35.00
Holmes Ice Cream, Union Springs, Ala., Unused	1.25
Just For Fun, Eagle Pencil Co., Wooden, Large	20.00
Mechanical, Dr Pepper, Drink A Bite	30.00
Mechanical, Esso	12.00
Mechanical, Harley Davidson	110.00
Mechanical, Kennedy Supply Co., Kansas City, Silver, Engraved	4.50
Mechanical, Morrison, Woman's, Navy Insignia, 14K Gold Trim	28.00
Mechanical, Pepsi-Cola	35.00
Mechanical, Reddy Kilowatt	65.00
Mechanical, Tan & Black Checkered	2.50
Mechanical, U.S. Air Corps	10.00
Mechanical, U.S. Air Force Base	10.00
Mechanical, Wahl Eversharp, Tan, Box	5.00
Mechanical, Western Transport Co., Calendar, 1947	2.50
Mechanical, Woman's, Brass, Ribbon Ring, Chased Scrolls, 3 In.	6.00
Mechanical, Woman's, Gold Filled, Tooled, Ring, 2 3/4 In.	5.50
Mechanical, Woman's, Silver Color, Ring	4.50
Moore, Blue, Gold Filled Trim, 1925	69.00
Parker, Duofold Jr., Green Jade, Gold Filled Trim, 1927	115.00
Parker, Duofold Sr., Black & Pearl, 1931	249.00
Parker, Gold Filled Trim, 1920	175.00
Parker, No. 51, Gray, Gold Filled Trim, 1953	69.00
Parker, Parkette, Green Pearlized	9.50
Parker, Pastel, Magenta, Gold Filled Trim, 1927	69.00
Parker, Pastel, Naples Blue, Gold Filled Trim, 1928	79.00
Parker, Vacumatic, Emerald Stripes, Gold Filled Trim, 1947	69.00
Parker, Vacumatic, Red Pearl Stripes, Gold Filled Trim, 1940	79.00
Parker 51 Repeater, Blue, Lustraloy Top, 1950	69.00
Parker 51 Special, Burgundy, Chrome Cap, 1957	39.00
Pencil Box, Wonder Woman, Vinyl	12.00
Sealect Skim Milk Powder, Sheffield Condensed Milk Co., 1/2 In. Diam.	3.00
Sheaffer, Jade Green, Large, 1928	90.00
Sheaffer, Lifetime, Jade Green, Gold Filled Trim, 1926	49.00
Sheaffer, Lifetime, Lady's, Black, Gold Filled Trim, 1925	12.00
Sheaffer, No. 500, Red Pearl Stripes, Gold Filled Trim, 1946	29.00
Sheaffer, Pearl & Black Marble, Gold Filled Trim, 1930	149.00
Sheaffer, Vigilant, Emerald Stripes, Gold Filled Trim, 1942	110.00
Sheaffer, Woman's, Mechanical, Gold Filled, Pat. 1918, 3 1/2 In.	7.50
Shell Oil, Shell Figure On Clip, Mechanical, 1940s	35.00
Stratford, Brown & Tan Marbleized	8.00
Sunnybrook Whiskey, Bottle Shape, Chrome	60.00
Wahl-Eversharp, 1920	35.00
Wahl-Eversharp, 1928	129.00
Wahl-Eversharp, Rosewood, 1929	105.00
Wahl-Eversharp, Sterling, 1925	85.00
Waterman, Ideal, Gothic Sterling, 1925	325.00
Waterman, Ideal, Red Speckled Silver, 1936	79.00
Waterman, Red-Ochre Ripple, Gold Filled Trim, 1924	17.00

PENNSBURY Pottery worked in Morrisville, Pennsylvania, from 1950 to 1971. Full sets of dinnerware as well as many decorative items were made. Pieces are marked with the name of the factory.

Pennsbury Pottery

Ashtray, Amish Couple	14.00 to 35.00
Ashtray, It's Makin' Down	15.00
Ashtray, Man	30.00
Ashtray, Outen The Light	20.00
Ashtray, What Giffs	18.00
Bird, Nuthatch, No. 110	75.00
Bird, Red Start, No. 113	110.00
Candy Box, Eagle, Bellows	69.50

Candy Dish, Heart Shape	45.00
Cookie Jar, Amish Scene	125.00
Cookie Jar, Harvest	160.00
Creamer, Red Rooster, 3 1/2 In.	14.00
Cruet, Amish	100.00
Cruet, Man & Woman, Amish Head Stopper, Pair	90.00 to 125.00
Cruet, Man's Head Stopper	50.00
Cruet, Rooster	75.00
Cup, Red Rooster	15.00
Figurine, Blue Jar, 10 1/2 In.	650.00
Figurine, Bluebird, No. 103	140.00
Figurine, Goldfinch, No. 102	140.00
Figurine, Hen, Cream & Brown, 10 In.	250.00
Figurine, Magnolia Warbler, No. 112	140.00
Figurine, Nuthatch, No. 110	110.00
Figurine, Rooster, Cream, Brown Trim, 12 In.	295.00
Figurine, Wren, No. 109	75.00 to 85.00
Mug, Rooster	30.00
Mug, Sweet Adeline	25.00
Pitcher, Black Rooster, 1/2 Pt., 4 In.	22.00
Pitcher, Black Rooster, 2 Qt., 7 1/4 In.	75.00 to 95.00
Pitcher, Eagle	80.00
Pitcher, Eagle, 1 Qt.	55.00
Pitcher, Hex, 1/2 Pt., 4 In.	28.00 to 35.00
Plaque, Commemorative, U. S. Steel, 1958	25.00
Plaque, Eagle, 22 In.	300.00
Plaque, Fish, Round	125.00
Plate, Harvest, 11 In.	65.00
Salt & Pepper, Oil & Vinegar, Amish Heads	130.00
Salt & Pepper, Red Rooster	20.00
Stein, Here's Looking At You	25.00
Sugar, Cover, Red Rooster	20.00
Sugar & Creamer, Cover, Red Rooster	35.00
Tile, Basket Of Flowers, 6 In.	35.00
Trivet, Amish Man & Woman	45.00
Wall Pocket, Black Rooster	42.00

PEPSI-COLA, the drink and the name, was invented in 1898 but was not trademarked until 1903. The logo was changed from an elaborate script to the modern block letters on the 1970 Pepsi label. All types of advertising memorabilia are collected, and reproductions are being made.

Ashtray, LaFayette Beverages	55.00
Blackboard, Menu	20.00
Bottle, Amber, Straight Sides, 1907-1912	125.00
Bottle, Clear, Straight Sides	17.50
Bottle, Desert Storm, Long Neck, 1991, 12 Oz.	20.00
Bottle, Pinched, Italy, Green	35.00
Bottle Opener, With Knife, 5 Cent Pepsi	12.00
Calendar, 1950, Ice Skater	210.00
Can, Bank Top	25.00
Carrier, 6-Pack, Take Me Home The Safe Way, Red Letters, Silver Metal, 7 3/4 In.	132.00
Clip, Pencil, Metal, Celluloid Depicts Bottle Cap, Logo, 1940s	8.00
Clock, Bottle Cap, Square, 1940s	835.00
Clock, Double Glass	475.00
Clock, Reverse Painted Milk Glass Dial, Wood, 15 In.	357.00
Cooler, Aluminum	150.00
Crate, Wooden	2.00
Display, Santa Claus, Cutout, Stand-Up, Norman Rockwell, 1950s, 32 x 24 In.	65.00 to 75.00
Door Push, Enjoy Pepsi-Cola Iced, Porcelain	110.00
Door Push, Horizontal	50.00
Door Push, Porcelain	165.00
Fan, Hand, Pepsi & Pete, 1940	75.00

◆◆◆◆◆◆◆◆◆◆◆◆◆◆◆◆◆◆◆◆◆◆◆◆◆

Don't put a message on your
answering machine indicating
when you will return.

◆◆◆◆◆◆◆◆◆◆◆◆◆◆◆◆◆◆◆◆◆◆◆◆◆

*Pepsi-Cola, Tumbler, Joker, Batman Series;
Pepsi-Cola, Tumbler, Riddler, Batman Series;
Pepsi-Cola, Tumbler, Colonel Hathi,
Jungle Book*

Glass, Commemorative, Butte, Mont., 1963	44.00
Glass, Daisy, 1979	8.00
Glass, Stemmed, 50th Anniversary, Seattle, Wash., 1963	41.00
Glass, Tennessee Grocer's Assoc.	23.00
Lighter, Bottle Shape	28.00
Menu Board, 1940s	200.00
Menu Board, Hits The Spot, Tin Litho, 4 Nail Holes, 30 x 19 1/2 In.	110.00
Pencil, Bullet, c.1940s	18.00
Pencil, Wooden, Unused	1.00
Radio, Bottle Shape, Bakelite	440.00
Radio, Bottle Shape, Crack In Base, Large	295.00
Radio, Dispenser, 1960s, 12 In.	700.00
Radio, Indiana Jones, Transistor	25.00 to 35.00
Sign, Black Couple, Oval, Celluloid, 1960	120.00
Sign, Bottle Cap, 19 In.	150.00
Sign, Delicious Delightful, Embossed Tin, Strip Type, 1910-1915	303.00
Sign, Drink Pepsi-Cola, Metal, 30 x 10 In.	325.00
Sign, Enjoy Pepsi, Metal, 26 x 10 In.	250.00
Sign, Hanging, World War II Paper On Back, Cardboard, 16 x 16 In.	25.00
Sign, Neon, Metal Bracket, No Wiring & Transformer, 18 In.	220.00
Sign, Pepsi & Pete, Cops, 5 Cents, Embossed Tin Litho, Strip Type, 3 1/2 x 21 In.	357.00
Sign, Pepsi Bottle, Porcelain Enameled Steel, 1945, 6 x 21 In.	17.00
Sign, Pepsi-Cola, 5 Cents, 1940, 6 x 18 In.	13.00
Sign, Pepsi-Cola, Here's Health, Double Dot, Tin, 27 1/2 x 19 1/2 In.	330.00
Sign, Say Pepsi Please, Bottle Cap, 1950s, 30 x 11 In.	110.00
Sign, Trolley, Man & Woman, More Bounce To The Ounce, c.1940s	145.00
Sign, Where The Fun Begins, Bottle Cap, Paperboard, Wood Frame, 10 x 27 In.	198.00
Straw, Pepsi-Cola Printed On Entire Straw, 1950s	2.00
Straw Holder, Double Dot, Chrome	220.00
Tap Knob, Musical, 1940	250.00
Thermometer, Bottle, Stenciled Sheet Metal, 1940s, 27 In.	210.00
Thermometer, Long Straw, Woman, With Bottle, Sheet Metal, 27 In.	275.00
Thermometer, Red, White & Blue, 1942, 8 x 27 In.	125.00
Thermometer, Say Pepsi Please, Yellow Ground	42.00
Thermometer, Square, Metal, Glass Covered Thermometer, c.1960s	45.00
Tip Tray, Girl With Glass, 4 1/4 x 6 1/2 In.	750.00
Toy, Truck, Crates Of Bottles	495.00
Toy, Truck, Ny-Lint, 1958	95.00
Tray, Coney Island, 1955, 12 In.	35.00 to 55.00
Tray, Double Dash Logo, c.1940s	80.00
Tray, Pin, Black Boy, Straw Hat, Eating Watermelon, 1916	275.00
Tray, Red, White & Blue, 1940s, 14 x 11 In.	85.00
Tumbler, Collector Series, Porky Pig, 1973	8.00
Tumbler, Colonel Hathi, Jungle Book .... *Illus*	35.00
Tumbler, Cool Cat, Cartoon Character	35.00
Tumbler, Daffy Duck, In Pot	38.00

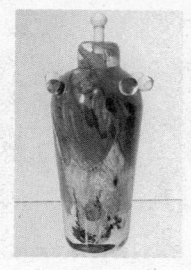

Perfume Bottle, Le Verre Schneider, Atomizer, Silver Floral Overlay, 1925, 9 In.

Perfume Bottle, Pink Opalescent, Floral Enameled, Atomizer, 19th Century, 6 In.

Perfume Bottle, Yellow & White, Blue Accents, Applied Knops, 7 3/4 In.

Tumbler, Joker, Batman Series	*Illus*	15.00
Tumbler, Riddler, Batman Series	*Illus*	15.00
Tumbler, Wonder Woman, 1976		12.00

PERFUME BOTTLES are made of cut glass, pressed glass, art glass, silver, metal, enamel, and even plastic or porcelain. Although the small bottle to hold perfume was first made before the time of ancient Egypt, it is the nineteenth- and twentieth-century examples that interest today's collector. DeVilbiss Company has made atomizers of all types since 1888 but no longer makes the perfume bottle tops so popular with collectors. These were made from 1920 to 1968. The glass bottle may be by any of many manufacturers even if the atomizer is marked *DeVilbiss*. Glass or porcelain examples may be found under the appropriate name such as Lalique, Czechoslovakia, etc.

Amber, Flowers & Bee, 4 1/4 In.	100.00
Amber, Gold Band, Stopper, Etched	65.00
Amber, Opalescent, Etched, Gold, Egypt	125.00
Amberina, Inverted Thumbprint, Amber Faceted Stopper, 5 In.	275.00
Arabic Sunburst Stopper, Brass Chased Leaf Flowers, Brass Chain, 3 In.	18.00
Azurite, Gold Laurel Band, Stopper	160.00
Black Amethyst, Urn Shape, Stork Circled In Florals, Lily Stopper, 7 1/4 In.	250.00
Blue Forget-Me-Nots, Gold Lattice & Scroll, Pair	65.00
Blue Hobnail, Sculptured Floral Finial, Atomizer	45.00
Bubble Stopper, Cut Ovals Allover Body, Vaseline Glass, 4 1/2 In.	70.00
Caron, Tabac Blond, 3 1/2 In.	25.00
Chanel, Cuir De Russie, Square, 8 1/4 x 3 1/2 In.	50.00
Colgate, Radiant Rose	25.00
Crystal, Ruby Inset, Crystal Stopper, Large	130.00
Cut Glass, Amber	55.00
Cut Glass, Atomizer, Miters, Oval Thumbprints, Stars, Bulbous, 4 1/4 In.	52.00
Cut Glass, Crystal, Tall	55.00
Cut Glass, Faceted Squares, Stopper, 4 7/8 In.	50.00
Cut Glass, Silver Lid, Birmingham Hallmark, 1906, 4 1/8 In.	192.00
D'Orsay, Intoxication, Teepee Shape	45.00
D'Orsay, Tojours Fidele	250.00
DeVilbiss, Atomizer, Gold Plate, Crackle Finish	60.00
DeVilbiss, Deco, Triangle Shape, Black, Atomizer, 3 1/4 In.	85.00
Dior, Frosted Top, Glass Stopper, 1950s	45.00
Dior, Ornate Filigree Atomizer, Original Box	125.00
Electrolytic, Trenton, N.J., Clear, Silver Overlay, Stopper, 2 1/2 In.	71.50
Emerald Green, Silver Overlay, Allover Scroll, Sterling Silver Deposit, 6 In.	660.00
Etched Glass, Silver Courting Scene, Germany, 7 1/2 In.	220.00
Evening In Paris, Box	46.00
Evening In Paris, Cologne, Navy, 15 Oz.	25.00

Evening In Paris, Lipstick Shape, Tassel, Purse Size 35.00
Evening In Paris, Purse Flask, Box 10.00
Feather Pattern, Stopper 12.00
Givenchy, Gold, Purse 16.00
Gold Crackle, Intaglio Birds, DeVilbiss Atomizer 325.00
Golliwog, Vigny, Box, 6 In. .... 395.00 to 425.00
Guerlain Shalimar, Rosebud Stopper, Box, 1/2 Oz. 100.00
Hobstars, Lapidary Stopper, 7 In. 250.00
Jean Patou, Black, With Red Stopper 95.00
Jean Patou, Moment Supreme 95.00
Le Verre Schneider, Atomizer, Silver Floral Overlay, 1925, 9 In. .... *Illus* 330.00
Lightner's Maid Of The Mist, Glass Stopper 33.00
Madame Pompadour 35.00
Marshall Field, Hand Painted Field's Clock, Florals 145.00
Melon Ribbed, Fan Stopper, 6 1/4 In., Pair 40.00
Melon Ribbed, Verre De Soie, Amber Stopper, Steuben, 7 In. 325.00
Melon Ribbed, Verre De Soie, Pink Stopper, Steuben, 4 1/2 In. 425.00
Milk Glass, Embossed Face, Goo Goo Eyes, Germany, 1920s, 3 In. 35.00
Miniature Perfume Bar, 4 Bottles 70.00
My Sin, Gold, Purse 16.00
Orloff, Eagle, Silk Box 65.00
Pantaloon Leaning On Tree Trunk, Diamond Eyes, Agate, 3 In. 5175.00
Pink Opalescent, Floral Enameled, Atomizer, 19th Century, 6 In. .... *Illus* 110.00
Prince Matchabelli, Green, Gold, Glass Stopper, 1950s 35.00
Purse, Enameled Floral, Dabber, 1 In. 75.00
Richard Hudnut, LeDebut, Glass, Blue, c.1927 .... 85.00
Roger & Gallet, Salesman's Sample, Label, 1900s 25.00
Satin Glass, Enameled Arabian Design, Atomizer 24.00
Schiaparelli, Candlestick, 6 1/2 In. 150.00
Schiaparelli, Dress Shape .... 75.00 to 125.00
Schiaparelli, Mini, Original Label 35.00
Schiaparelli, Shocking 40.00
Seguso, Twisted Form, Internal Design Of Red, Green & Amber 375.00
Star & Panel, Sandwich Glass 850.00
Sterling Silver Top, Birmingham, 1892, Pair 650.00
Stuart, Figural, Grandfather Clock 40.00
Theo Ricksecker's Sweet Clover Cologne, Urn Shape, Gold Lettering, 8 In. 143.00
Yellow & White, Blue Accents, Applied Knops, 7 3/4 In. .... *Illus* 130.00

PETERS & REED Pottery Company of Zanesville, Ohio, was founded by
John D. Peters and Adam Reed in 1897. Chromal, Landsun, Montene, Pereco,
and Persian are some of the art lines that were made. The company, which
became Zane Pottery in 1920 and Gonder Pottery in 1941, closed in 1957.
Peters & Reed pottery was unmarked.

Bowl, Berries, Leaves, Dark Blue, Pereco, 8 1/2 x 3 1/4 In. 45.00
Bowl, Pereco, 7 In. 38.00
Jardiniere, Green Lions Heads, Beige Ground, Fluted, 6 1/2 x 7 1/2 In. 62.00
Jug, Cavalier, 6 In. 75.00
Jug, Raised Design, 6 1/2 In. 150.00
Vase, 3 Applied Cavaliers, 3 Shoulder Handles, Brown, 3-Footed, 5 x 6 In. 40.00
Vase, Abstract Design, Globular Base, Tall Neck, 10 1/2 In. 175.00
Vase, Brownware, Floral & Cherries, 14 In. 35.00
Vase, Landsun, 6 In. 50.00
Vase, Landsun, 10 In. 350.00
Vase, Landsun, Brown & Purple Glaze, 6 1/2 In. 125.00
Vase, Molded Flower Medallions, 6 Sides, Brown, 4 x 6 In. 46.00
Vase, Moss Aztec, 12 In. 125.00
Vase, Olive Green Ivy Leaves, Trumpet Form, 7 1/2 In. 140.00
Vase, Scenic, 7 1/2 In. 100.00
Vase, Sheen Ware, 3 1/2 In. 50.00
Vase, Sky Blue Flambe Exposing Clay Body, Marked, 6 1/4 In. 600.00
Vase, Sprig Design Under Rim, Brown Glaze, 6 1/4 In. 130.00

Wall Pocket, Moss Aztec 75.00

PETRUS REGOUT, see Maastricht

PEWABIC POTTERY was founded by Mary Chase Perry Stratton in 1903 in
Detroit, Michigan. The company made many types of art pottery, including
pieces with matte green glaze and an iridescent crystalline glaze. The
company continued working until the death of Mary Stratton in 1961. It was
reactivated by Michigan State University in 1968.

Bookends, Bisque Court Jesters	550.00
Bookends, Incised Frontal View Of Rabbits, Blue Ground, 5 1/4 x 3 3/4 In.	550.00
Bowl, Iridescent Gray-Blue, c.1910, 3 1/8 In.	302.50
Bowl, Repeating Leaves, High Relief, Matte Green Glaze, Impressed Mark, 6 In.	1540.00
Bowl, Translucent Glaze Over Yellow-Brown, 3 Feet, 5 1/2 In.	275.00
Candlestick, Saucer Base, Orange Glaze, 8 3/4 In.	350.00
Jar, Wide Mouth, Squat, Yellow Glaze, Lavender Collar, 3 x 5 1/2 In.	330.00
Tile, Sea Horse, 2 Colors	75.00
Vase, Brown Specks, Turquoise High Glaze, Bulbous, 6 In.	375.00
Vase, Tapering Body, Ribbed Collar, Mottled Blue Glaze, 7 1/2 In.	1045.00
Vase, Volcanic Glaze, Iridescent Silver Over Translucent Blue, c.1910, 10 In.	2970.00
Vase, White & Black Drip Glaze, 4 In.	225.00
Vessel, Mottled Blue-Gray & Bold Glaze, Marked, 5 x 5 1/2 In.	650.00
Vessel, Red Luster Patches, Gray-Green Glaze, Marked, 3 3/4 x 4 1/2 In.	400.00

PEWTER is a metal alloy of tin and lead. Some of the pewter made after 1840
has a slightly different composition and is called *Britannia metal*. This later
type of pewter was worked by machine; the earlier pieces were made by
hand. In the 1920s pewter came back into fashion and pieces were often
marked *Genuine Pewter*. Eighteenth-, nineteenth-, and twentieth-century
examples are listed here.

Basin, Blakslee Barns, Philadelphia, 6 5/8 x 1 1/2 In.	176.00
Basin, Gersham Jones, Providence, R.I., Eagle Touch, 7 3/4 In.	275.00
Basin, I.M., England, 10 3/4 x 3 1/2 In.	110.00
Basin, John Skinner, 18th Century, 8 In.	550.00
Basin, Semper Eadem, Boston, 8 x 1 7/8 In.	440.00
Basin, Thomas Danforth, Eagle Touch, 10 x 2 3/4 In	357.00
Basin, Thomas Swanson, London, 1765-1783, 9 In.	265.00
Basin, Townsend & Compton, London, 11 x 2 3/4 In.	220.00
Beaker, Thomas Danforth Boardman, Connecticut, 1830s, Marked, 3 5/8 In.	220.00
Biscuit Jar, Liberty Tudric, Embossed Lily Pads At Rim, 5 1/2 In.	350.00
Box, Tobacco, James Dixon & Son, Sheffield, 3 x 4 3/4 In.	82.50
Bread Tray, Kayserzinn, No. 322, Raised Floral Design, 13 x 7 1/2 In.	350.00
Candlestick, 3-Light, Domical Base, Harold Buchrucher, 1930, 3 x 10 1/2 In.	173.00
Candlestick, Art Nouveau, Kayserzinn, 16 1/2 In., Pair	330.00
Candlestick, Henry Hopper, New York City, c.1840, 10 In., Pair	880.00
Candlestick, Push-Up, 10 In., Pair	192.50
Candlestick, Reed & Barton, 9 1/4 In., Pair	165.00
Candlestick, Roswell Gleason, Dorchester, Mass., 7 In.	330.00
Candy Dish, 4 Sections, Sculptured Bird Center Handle, England, 9 1/2 In.	25.00
Castor Set, Child's, 7 In.	95.00
Centerpiece, Art Nouveau, Nymph, Long Hair, Leaves Handle, 1900, 14 In.	230.00
Chalice, Communion, Sheldon & Feltman, Albany, 6 3/8 In.	247.50
Charger, Center Tulips, Gilbert Marks, 1899, 16 1/2 In.	322.00
Charger, Clothyer, R.C. & Rampant Lion, 16 1/2 In.	275.00
Charger, Continental, Angel Touch, Engraved Crown Rim, 15 3/4 In.	248.00
Charger, E.W., London Touch, 16 1/2 In.	247.00
Charger, May United States Of America Flourish, England, 16 3/4 In.	412.50
Charger, Samuel Ellis, Engraved Shell On Rim, 14 3/4 In.	220.00
Charger, Spread Eagle, Dated 1744, 15 In.	175.00
Chocolate Pot, Continental, Swirled Ribs, Hinged Lid, 8 In.	33.00
Clock, Stylized Honesty, Tudric, Liberty Co., 11 1/2 In.	1840.00
Coffeepot, Cast Flower Finial, H. Homan, 9 /34 In.	45.00
Coffeepot, Dunhan, 1816	925.00

Coffeepot, G. Richardson, Domed Lid, Double Bulbous, Repaired, 11 In. 357.50
Coffeepot, Hinged Dome Cover, Scroll Spout, Wooden Handle, Dutch, 11 1/2 In. 825.00
Coffeepot, J. Danforth, Wooden Finial, 10 In. 242.00
Coffeepot, Lighthouse, Ear Handle, Hinged Lid, Porter, Maine, 10 In. 150.00
Coffeepot, Peter Behrens, Art Deco, Germany, 1900s 1500.00
Coffeepot, Reed & Barton, c.1850, 11 In. 145.00
Coffeepot, Roswell Gleason, Massachusetts, Marked, 11 In. 275.00
Coffeepot, Rufus Dunham, Lighthouse, 11 In. 247.50
Coffeepot, Rufus Dunham, Westbrook, Maine, 19th Century, 12 In. 275.00
Coffeepot, Sellew & Co., Cincinnati, Ear Handle, 10 In. 412.00
Coffeepot, Ward, c.1820, 9 In. 300.00
Coffeepot, William Calder, Rhode Island, 1830s, Marked, 12 In. 302.50
Coffeepot, Wooden Handle & Finial, Sheldon & Feltman, Albany, 10 1/2 In. 280.00
Creamer, Reed & Barton, c.1850, 4 1/2 In. 50.00
Creamer, Sellew, 6 3/8 In. 110.00
Cup, Footed, Ear Handle, 4 3/4 In. 11.00
Cup, Nursery Rhyme 20.00
Dish, Bird Handles, Hammered, Denmark, 6 1/4 In. 16.50
Dish, Jugendstil, Central Flower, Tulip Stem Handle, c.1900, 12 In. 316.00
Dish, Samuel Ellis, Single Reed, London, 1721-1765, 14 1/2 In. 375.00
Flagon, Boardman & Jacob, Marked, 12 1/2 In. 1595.00
Flagon, Communion, Roswell Gleason, 10 In. .... 450.00 to 495.00
Flagon, Communion, Smith & Feltman, Albany, 10 1/2 In. .... 275.00 to 550.00
Flagon, Kayserzinn, Cubist Design 395.00
Flagon, L. Trask, 10 1/2 In. 770.00
Flask, Calder, Scroll Handle, 11 1/2 In. 715.00
Ink Sander, Cube, 1 3/4 In. 90.00
Jardiniere, Ruffled, Flared, Applied Foliage, Green Stone Berries, China, 6 In., Pair . 48.00
Jug, Osiris, Bunches Of Grapes, Domed Cover, Cylindrical, 13 3/4 In. 143.00
Ladle, Ebonized Wooden Handle, 14 1/2 In. 82.00
Lamp, Camphene, Morey & Ober, Bell Shape, Boston, 1852-1855, 5 In. 325.00
Lamp, Chamber, Whale Oil, 7 1/4 In. 357.50
Lamp, Figural, Woman, At Spinning Wheel, France, 1920, 12 In. 395.00
Lamp, Fluid, E. Smith, Brass & Pewter, Beverly, Mass., 8 In. 440.00
Lamp, Orivit, Ribbed Flower Head Shade, Glass Beads, 1900, 14 3/4 In. 2875.00
Lamp, Screw Ring, American, 6 In. 27.50
Measure, Bellied, 1/4 Gill To Quart, 6 3/8 In., 6 Piece 825.00
Measure, Bellied, Chambers, Birmingham, England, 1 Pt., 5 1/4 In. 44.00
Measure, Bellied, England, 5 1/2 In. 104.50
Measure, Double Volute, Fleur-De-Lis Hinge, Crown Thumbpiece, England, 1/2 Pt. . 71.50
Measure, England, 1 Pt., 5 In. 38.00
Measure, France, Early 1800s 110.00
Measure, G. Farmilor & Sons, London, 1 Pt., 4 7/8 In. 50.00
Measure, Imperial Medallion, Shell Thumbpiece, Glasgow, Pint To Gill, 5 Piece 1550.00
Measure, Marked Pint, G. Kent, 4 7/8 In. 27.50
Measure, Side Spout, England, Marked Quart, 6 In. 95.00
Measure, Tankard, Cover, English, 1/2 Pint 110.00
Measure, Tankard, James Birch Touch, Quart, 6 1/4 In. 165.00
Mold, Candle, 24 Tubes, Pine, c.1800 .... 2400.00
Mold, Ice Cream, Basket, Hinged 60.50
Mold, Ice Cream, Broken Heart 25.00
Mold, Ice Cream, Chick In Nest, Hinged 50.00
Mold, Ice Cream, Cupid .... 35.00 to 55.00
Mold, Ice Cream, Darky Choking Turkey, E & Co. 125.00
Mold, Ice Cream, Doves .... 35.00 to 55.00
Mold, Ice Cream, Egg, ML & F 25.00
Mold, Ice Cream, Heart With Cupid, E & Co., 3 3/4 In. 44.00
Mold, Ice Cream, Otter, E. & Co., N.Y., 5 1/4 In. 30.00
Mold, Ice Cream, Puss 'n Boots 750.00
Mold, Ice Cream, Rabbit, 2 Parts, 4 1/2 In. 115.50
Mold, Ice Cream, Racehorse & Jockey .... 75.00 to 125.00
Mold, Ice Cream, Rose, Cupid's Face In Center 40.00
Mold, Ice Cream, Rose, E & Co. 50.00

Mold, Ice Cream, Slipper, 3 Piece 35.00
Mold, Ice Cream, Tulip 47.00
Mold, Ice Cream, Turkey 45.00
Mold, Ice Cream, Wreath, 3 3/4 x 5 In. 72.00
Mug, England, Dated 1795 .... 125.00
Mug, Samuel Hamlin, Providence, Rhode Island, c.1800, Quart, 6 In. 1540.00
Mug, Thomas Danforth III, Connecticut & Philadelphia, 1 Qt. 1540.00
Pitcher, Ale, Domed Lid & Thumbpiece, Monogram, England, 8 In. 330.00
Pitcher, Eagle, Kayserzinn 475.00
Pitcher, Hinged Lid, Sellew & Co., Cincinnati 675.00
Pitcher, Rum, Naval, Marked HMS Eden, Richard Yates, 1890s, 8 1/4 In. 875.00
Pitcher, Steiff, Wooden Handle, 9 In. 35.00
Pitcher, Syrup, Ear Handle, Shell Thumb Piece, 8 1/8 In. 99.00
Pitcher, Water, Flagg & Homan, Ear Handle, 9 In. 248.00
Pitcher, Water, Hinged Lid, R. Gleason, 8 1/2 In. 302.00
Pitcher, Water, Sellew & Co., Cincinnati, Hinged Lid, 9 1/4 In. 743.00
Plate, Amos Treadway, 8 In. 220.00
Plate, Blakeslee Barns, 7 7/8 In. 155.00
Plate, Boardman & Co., 10 3/4 In. 465.00
Plate, Boardman Warranted, J No. 40, 9 3/8 In. 340.00
Plate, Brob Zinn, 8 In. 77.00
Plate, Compton, London, 8 In. .... 82.00 to 115.00
Plate, Edgar Curtis, 8 In. 93.00
Plate, Edward Danforth, Middletown, Connecticut, Lion Touch, 8 In. 176.00
Plate, Engraved Rim Initials, S.E., England, 8 1/4 In. 55.00
Plate, George Grenfell, London, 8 5/8 In. 66.00
Plate, Gershom Jones, Providence, R.I., Anchor Touch, 8 3/8 In. 121.00
Plate, John Skinner, Smooth Brim, 9 1/4 In. 357.50
Plate, John Townsend & Thomas Griffin, , Wavy Edge, c.1780, 9 1/2 In. 275.00
Plate, Joseph Danforth, 8 In. 350.00
Plate, P.W. On Brim, John Townsend, 1748, 9 In., 4 Piece 425.00
Plate, Rimmed, England, 18th Century, 8 1/4 In. 135.00
Plate, Roswell Gleason, 10 In. 138.00
Plate, Roswell Gleason, 10 7/8 In. 248.00
Plate, Sheldon & Feltman, Albany, 10 1/4 In. 182.00
Plate, T. Danforth, Philadelphia, Eagle Touch, 7 3/4 In. 412.00
Plate, Thomas Danforth Boardman, 7 3/4 In. 357.00
Plate, Thomas Danforth Boardman, No. 39, 8 1/2 In. 205.00
Plate, Thomas Danforth, Middleton Touch, 8 In. 275.00
Plate, Thomas Griffin, London, 13 1/2 In. 192.50
Plate, Thomas Griffin, London, 15 In. 302.50
Plate, Townsend & Compton Touch, 7 3/4 In. 50.00
Plate, William Kirby, New York, Hammered Booge, 8 7/8 In. 660.00
Platter, Compton, Hollow, London, 25 In. 190.00
Platter, John Duncomb, Birmingham, England, 1740s, 21 In. 467.50
Platter, John Townsend, England, Marked, 20 In. 770.00
Porringer, Cast Crown Handle, Marked G.S., 5 1/2 In. 330.00
Porringer, Cast English Handle, 5 1/2 In. 357.00
Porringer, Cast Heart & Crescent Handle, 4 1/2 In. 220.00
Porringer, Crown Handle, American, c.1800, 5 3/8 In. 250.00
Porringer, Crown Handle, 19th Century, 5 1/4 In. 275.00
Porringer, Eagle Touch, Hamlin Providence, Cast Handle, 4 1/4 In. 495.00
Porringer, Gero-Holland, Cover, Fan Handle, Bail Finial, 6 In. 45.00
Porringer, Gershom Jones, Cast Flower Handle, 6 In. 935.00
Porringer, Gershom Jones, Rhode Island, Marked, 5 1/2 In. 2090.00
Porringer, Handle, New York, 5 1/2 In. 412.00
Porringer, Handle, Pennsylvania, 5 1/2 In. 962.00
Porringer, Heart Handle, 4 1/2 In. 330.00
Porringer, T.D. & S.B., Cast Handle 550.00
Porringer, Thomas Danforth Boardman, Crown Handle With T.D. & S.B., 5 In. 412.00
Porringer, Thomas Danforth Boardman, English Handle, T.D. & S.B. Touch, 4 In. 605.00
Pot, Boardman & Hart, New York, 11 3/8 In. 330.00

Pot, R. Dunham, 11 3/4 In. 275.00
Pot, R. Gleason, Lighthouse, 10 5/8 In. 688.00
Silent Butler, Hank & Debler, Lucite Handle, 5 5/8 In. 35.00
Soup, Dish, Ashbill Griswold, J No. 152, 11 In. 355.00
Soup, Dish, M. Ernst, 8 1/2 In. 92.50
Soup, Dish, T. Danforth, J No. 120, 11 1/2 In. 275.00
Spoon, Scalloped Handles, RK In Shield, Buffed, 18th Century, 7 1/8 In., Pair 165.00
Syrup, Homan & Co., Flower Finial, Ear Handle, Cincinnati, 6 In. 55.00
Tankard, Alderson, Cover, Side Spout, Says Pint, 5 3/4 In. 160.00
Tankard, Boardman, T.D.B. Touch, 4 In. 495.00
Tankard, Cover, Fleur-De-Lis Thumbpiece, Ireland, 6 In. 165.00
Tankard, Domed Lid, England, 7 1/2 In. 357.00
Tankard, England, 1 Pt., 4 3/4 In. 159.00
Tankard, Frederick Bassett, New York & Hartford, Marked, 7 In. 9900.00
Tankard, Watts & Harton, London, 1 Pt., 5 1/4 In. 93.00
Tea Set, Royal Holland, Wooden Handle & Finial, Corset Shape, 3 Piece 110.00
Tea Set, Sellew & Co., Cincinnati, 3 Piece 495.00
Tea Set, Tudric, Hammered, 5 Piece 750.00
Teapot, Acorn Cover, T.D. & S.B., 8 In. 105.00
Teapot, Boadman, Eagle Hallmark, c.1836 .... 575.00
Teapot, Boardman & Hall, 7 In. 65.00
Teapot, Boardman & Hart, New York, 7 1/2 In. 330.00
Teapot, Figural Spout, Swivel Handle, Wooden Grip, 7 1/4 In. 120.00
Teapot, Freeman Porter, Westbrook, Maine 440.00
Teapot, G. Richardson, 7 5/8 In. 495.00
Teapot, G. Richardson, Warranted, 9 1/4 In. 605.00
Teapot, George Richardson, Rhode Island, 1830s, 8 1/4 In. 247.50
Teapot, Georgian, Empire Design, Paul Storr, 1816 .... 3250.00
Teapot, H.B. Ward & Co., 8 1/2 In. 105.00
Teapot, J. Danforth, No.14, 8 In. 385.00
Teapot, John Munson, Yalesville, Connecticut 247.50
Teapot, Plumly & Pelton, 1840, 7 In. 440.00
Teapot, Queen Anne Style, Rose Mark, 7 1/2 In. 55.00
Teapot, R. Gleason, Lighthouse 195.00
Teapot, R. Gleason, 7 1/4 In. 247.00
Teapot, R. Gleason, 8 5/8 In. 275.00
Teapot, Reed & Barton, c.1850, 9 1/2 In. 75.00
Teapot, Roswell Gleason 66.00
Teapot, Sellew & Co., Cincinnati, 7 1/2 In. 220.00
Teapot, Smith & Co., Boston, c.1847 .... 300.00 to 395.00
Teapot, Tudric 225.00
Teaspoon, C. Barter & Co., 5 3/8 In., Pair 125.00
Toddy, Engraved, R.H., England, 4 3/4 In. 38.00
Tray, Silberzinn, Flowers, Butterfly, Art Nouveau, Oval, 11 3/4 In. 68.00
Tumbler, Boardman, Eagle Touch, 2 3/4 In. 77.00
Tureen, Cover, Georgian, 10 In. 165.00
Tureen, Soup, Cover, Swirling Flutes, Shell & Scroll Handles, Germany, 14 3/4 In. .. 385.00
Vase, Kayserzinn, Art Nouveau, 3 Slender Handles, 4 3/4 In. 80.00
Warmer, Wooden Ball Feet & Handles, Marrior & Crowe, 14 1/4 x 18 In. 265.00

PHOENIX BIRD, or Flying Phoenix, is the name given to a blue-and-white kitchenware popular between 1900 and World War II. A variant is known as Flying Turkey. Most of this dinnerware was made in Japan for sale in the dime stores in America. It is still being made.

Bowl, Japan, 4 3/4 In. 7.00
Bowl, Oval, Japan, 7 3/4 x 6 In. 20.00
Creamer, Japan 12.00
Cup & Saucer, Demitasse 16.00
Plate, Japan, 7 1/4 In. 8.00
Platter, Japan, 10 In. 22.00
Salt & Pepper, Self Top, 3 In. 16.50
Sugar & Creamer, Cover, Squatty, Blue M Wreath 30.00

PHOENIX GLASS Company was founded in 1880 in Pennsylvania. The firm made commercial products, such as lampshades, bottles, and glassware. Collectors today are interested in the sculptured glassware made by the company from the 1930s until the mid-1950s. The company is still working.

Banana Server, Lace Dewdrop, 10 1/2 In.	200.00
Bowl, Lily, 14 1/4 In.	400.00
Candy Dish, Cover, Lavender, Crystal, Round	120.00
Candy Dish, Phlox, Gold Label, 6 3/4 In.	180.00
Compote, Moon & Star, 8 x 8 In.	150.00
Creamer, Lace Dewdrop, 5 In.	90.00
Dish, Cover, Violets, Lavender	95.00
Lamp, Island Scene Shade, Creams, Oranges, Browns, Bronze Base, 18 In.	1475.00
Plate, 5 Fruits, White, 12 In.	95.00
Platter, Jonquil, 14 In.	300.00
Tumbler, Lemonade, Pair	70.00
Vase, Bittersweet, 3 Colors, 10 In.	125.00
Vase, Design, Tan Shadow, Wavy Leaves, Wilson	95.00
Vase, Madonna, Gold Label, 10 In.	225.00
Vase, Mallards, Beige & White, Paper	125.00
Vase, Pillow, Blue Geese, Label, 9 1/2 In.	145.00 To 160.00
Vase, Thistle, Pearlized Blue, 18 In.	425.00
Vase, Umbrella Shape, 18 In.	425.00
Vase, Wavy Leaves, Tan Shadow, 5 In.	95.00
Vase, Yellow Daisies, Butterfly, Shaded Green Ground, L. Shively, 4 1/4 In.	125.00

PHONOGRAPHS, invented by Thomas Edison in the 1880s, have been made by many firms. This category also includes other items associated with the phonograph. Jukeboxes and records are listed in their own categories.

Columbia, Grafonola, Brass Parts	675.00
Columbia, Gramophone, Mahogany, Records, Floor Model	65.00
Columbia, Gramophone, Oak, Cylinder Disc, Metal Horn, 12 1/2 In.	413.00
Columbia, Gramophone, Oak, Cylinder Disc, Metal Horn, Stenciled, 15 In.	713.00
Columbia, Model AK, Brass Horn	1100.00
Decca, Bakelite, Radio, 1950s	65.00
Edison, Amberola, Bakelite Cylinders, Case, c.1905	675.00
Edison, Amberola, Model 30, Oak Case	500.00
Edison, Amberola, Oak, Cylinder, Floor Model	375.00
Edison, Cylinder, Oak	750.00
Edison, Diamond Disc, Plays 78 RPM	450.00

Phonograph, Edison, Reproducer Triumph Model H

Edison, External Horn, Oak Case, 1905 .... 2200.00
Edison, Home, Model E, Oak, Cygnet Horn 2000.00
Edison, Morning Glory Horn, Refinished Oak, Cylinder 750.00
Edison, Reproducer Triumph Model H .... *Illus* 1200.00
Edison, Spring Motor, Brass Horn, Floor Stand 3500.00
Edison, Standard, Oak, Cylinder Disc, Hanging Metal Horn, 13 In. 385.00
Edison, Triumph, 33-In. Horn 1300.00
Edison, Wax Cylinder, Oak Horn, c.1900 .... 1650.00
Oxford Jr., Cast Iron 55.00
Popeye's Dynamite Music Machine, Illustrations Inside & Out 50.00
RCA Victor, Model 2, Gold Leaf Horn, Nipper Logo, c.1906 .... 2400.00
RCA Victor, Victrola-Radio 125.00
Sonora, Nocturne 365.00
Sonora, Windup 245.00
Sonora, Windup, Mahogany 275.00
Standard, Model A, Oak, Red Metal Horn, Square, 11 In. 413.00
Talk-O-Phone, Brooke 600.00
Victor, Monarch Special, Oak, 1903 .... 2000.00
Victor, Style VIC III, Oak, Horn, Square, 14 In. 1980.00
Victor, Type O 1375.00
Victor VV-IV, Inside Horn, Oak 235.00

PHOTOGRAPHY items are listed here. The first photograph was a view from
a window in France taken in 1826. The commercially successful photograph
started with the daguerreotype, introduced in 1839. Today all sorts of
photographs and photographic equipment are collected. Albums were popular
in Victorian times. Cartes de visite, popular after 1854, were mounted on
2 1/2-by-4-inch cardboard. Cabinet cards were introduced in 1866. These were
mounted on 4 1/4-by-6 1/2-inch cards. Stereo views are listed under Stereo
Card. The cases for daguerreotypes are listed in the Gutta-Percha category.

Albumen, Cave Of The Winds, Niagara Falls, c.1880, 18 3/4 x 16 In. 100.00
Albumen, Waterfront View Of Oswego Harbor, 1869, 13 1/4 x 16 1/4 In. 185.00
Albumen, Workers Aboard Dry Docked Snag Boat, 8 3/4 x 12 1/2 In. 143.00
Ambrotype, Chief Maungwudas 3190.00
Ambrotype, Girl, With Dog, E.G. McElroy, Traveling Ambrotypist, Frame 110.00
Ambrotype, Man, Gutta-Percha Case 35.00
Ambrotype, Post Mortem Child, Bowl Of Fruit, Gutta-Percha, 4 x 5 In. 95.00
Ambrotype, Six-Man Boat Crew 1100.00
Cabinet, Fireman, Hoseman, Maltese Cross Badge, Haverhill Fire Dept., 1880 .... 30.00
Cabinet, Girl In Wicker Rocker, Boy Standing, Mildred & Edward Kurrie 20.00
Cabinet, Morning Star, Missionary Ship, J.C. Higgins, Bath, Maine 15.00
Cabinet Card, Bismark, Seated, In Uniform, April, 1875, 4 1/4 x 6 1/2 In. 32.50
Cabinet Card, Boy On Tricycle, 2 Little Girls At Side, 1890s, 4 x 6 In. 30.00
Cabinet Card, Camp Scene, 6 x 8 In. 165.00
Cabinet Card, Chicago Ferris Wheel, 1893 .... 75.00
Cabinet Card, Child, Lace Dress, Purse, Eastlake, Frame 48.00
Cabinet Card, General Fitzhugh Lee, Confederate 150.00
Cabinet Card, General George Washington Curtis Lee, Confederate 150.00
Cabinet Card, Man In Horse Driven Sleigh, Belvidere, Ill., c.1885 .... 15.00
Cabinet Card, Man Next To Singer Sewing Machine, 4 x 5 In. 75.00
Cabinet Card, Phineas T. Barnum, Signed, 1885 .... 605.00
Cabinet Card, Seated Woman & Girl, Mounted, 1900, 4 x 5 In. 5.00
Cabinet Card, Soldier In Uniform, Holding Sword 50.00
Cabinet Card, Victorian Black Ladies, 1882 .... 95.00
Cabinet Card, Young Woman, Born 1891, 4 x 5 In. 6.00
Camera, Aerial, Fairchild, World War II 70.00
Camera, Ansco No. 1, Ready Set Royal, 1926 .... 65.00
Camera, Ansco Viking Pronto, Bellows, U.S. Zone, Germany 25.00
Camera, Ansco, Folding, Vest Pocket 25.00
Camera, Ansco, No. 2-A 17.50
Camera, Asahi Pentax, Model K100, Flash 72.50
Camera, Brownie, Model 2A 35.00

Camera, Brownie, No. 620 .... 20.00
Camera, Charlie Tuna 75.00
Camera, Cine-Kodak, Model K, 16 mm 40.00
Camera, Conley, 5 x 7 In. Plate, Wallensack Lens, 1901 .... 95.00
Camera, Huckleberry Hound, Plastic 48.00
Camera, Kodak, Beau Brownie, Faux Leather Case, 5 1/4 In. 345.00
Camera, Kodak, Leather Covered, Folding, Colored Bellows, No. 6 Cartridge 120.00
Camera, Kodak, Model B, Folding Cartridge, Autograph, 1920s 110.00
Camera, Kodak, No. 2C, Autographic Brownie, Folding 25.00
Camera, Kodak, Retina Reflex, Telephoto Lens, Filters, Case, 1950s 250.00
Camera, Kodak, Target Hawkeye, Six-16 .... 18.00
Camera, Mamiya Sekor, 35 mm 37.50
Camera, Minolta, Rekker, Carrying Case 55.00
Camera, Rochester, Poco A, Rochester Camera Co., Pat.1897 .... 110.00
Camera, Speed Graphic, Top Handle, 1915 .... 150.00
Camera, Super Ricohflex, Twin Lens 47.50
Camera, Univex, Model A, Instructions, Box 30.00
Camera, Voightlander, Folding, Holder Pace, Case, 9 x 12 In. 120.00
Camera, Winchester Quicksnap, 1970s 35.00
Carte De Visite, Abraham Lincoln, Embracing Washington, Clouds, Angels 18.00
Carte De Visite, Bombardment Of Vera Cruz, Mexican War Lithograph, Sarony 200.00
Carte De Visite, Boy Trapeze Artist, Signed 32.00
Carte De Visite, Civil War Soldier, Rolled Pants 30.00
Carte De Visite, Collir's Zouaves, Mary Tippie, 114 Pennsylvania Reg. 220.00
Carte De Visite, Commodore Nutt & Minnie Warren, Circus Midgets 25.00
Carte De Visite, Confederate General Johnston 90.00
Carte De Visite, General Grant, In Uniform, Holding Small Child 12.00
Carte De Visite, General James Garfield, Uniform 20.00
Carte De Visite, General U.S. Grant & Family, Oval 15.00
Carte De Visite, John A. Dix, Major General, 7th Corps, Uniform 352.00
Carte De Visite, John Brown, Messotint, Sartain 150.00
Carte De Visite, John Wilkes Booth & The Devil 125.00
Carte De Visite, Lincoln & Tad, Looking At Album Of Brady Photos 352.00
Carte De Visite, Lincoln Mourning, 1865 .... 150.00
Carte De Visite, Lincoln Photograph, Profile Of Patriarch, Union Case 325.00
Carte De Visite, Lincoln, Seated Near Table With Inkwell 660.00
Carte De Visite, Little Boy With Rocking Horse, 1860s 40.00
Carte De Visite, Mary Whitcher, Shaker, Canterbury Sister 115.00
Carte De Visite, Mrs. Stephen Douglas 25.00
Carte De Visite, President Andrew Johnson 25.00
Carte De Visite, Quantrill's Raiders, Guerrilla Leader & Lieutenant, 1864 .... 4180.00
Carte De Visite, Stonewall Jackson 75.00
Carte De Visite, Thomas Edison 125.00
Carte De Visite, Thomas Nast, By Sarony 125.00
Carte De Visite, U.S. Grant, Virginia City, Nevada, 1879 .... 85.00
Daguerreotype, Bull, 1/2 Plate 4400.00
Daguerreotype, Carpenter, Elaborate Saw 450.00
Daguerreotype, Cigar Salesman, Full Box, 1/4 Plate 2750.00
Daguerreotype, Indian, Headdress, Gauntlets, Tomahawk, 1/6 Plate 2750.00
Daguerreotype, Odd Fellow, Gilt Vest & Apron, 1/4 Plate 495.00
Daguerreotype, Portrait Of A Child, 6th Plate, 19th Century 220.00
Daguerreotype, Rattlesnake, Rattle In Pointed Position, 1/6 Plate 1430.00
Exposure Meter, GM, Model B 20.00
Film, 3 Stooges, Box, 1940s 35.00
Film Tank, Kodak 12.50
Glass Negative, Cyclist, Riding Bike, 5 x 7 In. 24.00
Lantern, Darkroom, Amber Window, Large 25.00
Lens, Camera, Universal Rapid Aplionat, Series N. 12 .... 35.00
Magic Lantern, Bausch & Lomb Radioptician, 1922, 8 x 8 3/4 In. 265.00
Magic Lantern, Kerosene Burner, 2 Glass Sides, Tin 155.00
Photograph, 2 Girls & Dolls, Snow, Albumen, 1920, 5 x 3 1/2 In. 12.00
Photograph, 2 Seated Indians, Ornate Clothes, Jacob Cox, Frame, 18 x 15 In. 412.00

Photograph, Abraham Lincoln, Matthew Brady, 1864	150.00
Photograph, Abraham Lincoln, Oval, Frame, 1865	175.00
Photograph, Alaskan Panhandle, Taken From Boat, c.1900	130.00
Photograph, Animal Men, Ringling Bros., 1898, Frame, 11 1/4 x 13 In.	77.00
Photograph, Atlantic City Inner Cities Beauty Contest, Sepia, 1926, 3 Ft.(RiteJ)	18.00
Photograph, Bells Of Old Town, Ramone's Wedding, March 29, 1893, 4 x 5 In.	7.00
Photograph, Benito Mussolini, Signed, Framed, 1936, 11 x 24 In.	700.00
Photograph, Buffalo Bill Cody, Formal Clothes, Wooden Frame, 13 1/2 x 8 In.	185.00
Photograph, Captain Jack Crawford, Poet Scout, 1897	175.00
Photograph, Cowboys In Wyoming Territory, 1888, 7 x 10 In.	235.00
Photograph, Dining Room North Family, Mt. Lebanon, Shaker, 1890, 5 x 8 In.	250.00
Photograph, Doll, In Wicker Buggy, 3 Children, Albumen, 1900, 4 x 2 3/4 In.	12.00
Photograph, Eldress Anna Case, Watervliet, Shaker	100.00
Photograph, Harvard University, Scene, 1920-1930	9.00
Photograph, High Wheel Bicycle Group, Brooklyn Club	375.00
Photograph, Iowa Police Dept., Ottumwa, Frame, 1932, 8 x 10 In.	5.00
Photograph, Lamppost Lawn & Gardens, Mt. Lebanon, Shaker, 1890, 5 x 8 In.	250.00
Photograph, Late-President McKinley, 4 1/4 x 6 1/2 In.	10.00
Photograph, Leslie Howard, Signed, 8 x 10 In.	275.00
Photograph, McCormick Tractor Works, Club Congress, 1928, 10 x 34 In.	22.00
Photograph, Minstrel Show, Jenkins Shoe Store, Albumen, 1890, Mounted	20.00
Photograph, Sam Houston, 1850s	850.00
Photograph, School Building, American Flag, Mounted, 1900, 10 x 12 In.	10.00
Photograph, Shaker Attic, Mt. Lebanon, William Winter, 4 1/2 x 6 1/2 In.	175.00
Photograph, Sister Angelina Brown, Enfield, Shaker Chair, Lace Bonnet	110.00
Photograph, South Family, Watervliet Sisters, Shaker, Frame, 7 x 7 In.	75.00
Photograph, Trotters Racing, Miss Tilly, Hambletonian Winner, Frame, 1949	55.00
Photograph, Upton Sinclair, Hope For Social Progress, Signed, 8 x 10 In.	120.00
Photograph, View Of San Francisco Exposition, 1939, 1 1/4 In., 18 Pc.	15.00
Photograph, World War I Soldier, Color, Wooden Frame, 10 x 14 In.	15.00
Projector, Bell & Howell, 1926, 16 In.	40.00
Projector, Brownie 300 Movie, 8 mm, Original Box, 1950s	40.00
Projector, Magic Lantern, Kerosene, 4 Boxes Cartoon Slides, Germany, Box	230.00
Projector, Magic Lantern, Latema, 22 Slides, Box	350.00
Projector, Viewmaster Junior, Maroon	15.00
Scale, Eastman Studios, Weights	22.00
Slide Kit, Keystone, Lantern, Box	15.00
Speed Graphic, Top Handle, 1915	150.00
Tintype, 2 People With Bicycles, Full View	62.00
Tintype, 3 Standing Musicians, 2 1/4 x 3 1/2 In.	55.00
Tintype, 6 Baseball Players, Equipment, 1/6 Plate	198.00
Tintype, Abraham Lincoln, 1864, 2 3/4 x 3 1/4 In.	1455.00
Tintype, Baby, Carriage, Cross Leaf Frame, 1877, Large	110.00
Tintype, Civil War Private, With Colt Pistol	325.00
Tintype, Edward Hobart, Horse & Wagon, Randall Homestead, 6 x 8 In.	55.00
Tintype, Grandpa Brannock, Syracuse Family, Civil War	65.00
Tintype, Lincoln-Hamlin Campaign, 1860	450.00
Tintype, Soldiers, 3 Tough Guys Of Co. H, New York Artillery, 1/4 Plate	550.00
Tintype, Uniformed Baseball Player, Full-Length View, 1880s, 1/6 Plate	110.00
Tintype, Union Cavalry Soldier, Gutta-Percha Case, Lock Of Hair	200.00
Tintype, Woman, Seated At Table, Gutta-Percha Case, 2 3/8 x 2 7/8 In.	15.00
Tintype, Young Man, Gutta-Percha Case, 2 3/8 x 2 7/8 In.	11.00
Viewer, 3-D, Guild, Box	12.50

PIANO BABY is a collector's term. About 1880, the well-decorated home had a shawl on the piano. Bisque figures of babies were designed to help hold the shawl in place. They range in size from 6 to 18 inches. Most of the figures were made in Germany. Reproductions are being made. Other piano babies may be listed under manufacturers' names.

Crawling, Heubach, 7 In.	225.00
Dutch Boy & Girl, Seated, Heubach, 6 In., Pair	575.00
Girl, Seated, Curly Hair, Straw Hat, Green Dress, Gold Beaded Trim	95.00

Holding Ball, Heubach 85.00
Laying, Head On Pillow, Dog On Back, Pacifier In Mouth, 6 1/2 In. 175.00
Laying On Tummy, Holding Dog In Arm, Handwerck, 5 1/2 In. 125.00
Lying Down On Stomach, Playing With Toes, Gown & Bonnet, Heubach, 7 In. 375.00
Nightshirt, Raised Arms, Heubach 895.00
Seated, Playing With Toes, Pink Gown, 4 1/2 In. 85.00
Sitting, Boy & Girl, Floppy Hats, RPM Mark, 10 In., Pair 295.00
Sitting, Heubach, 9 x 8 In. 220.00
Sitting On Feet, Starburst Mark, Gebruder Heubach, 10 In. 595.00
Sitting Upright, Gebruder Heubach, Marked 450.00
Tying Bonnet, 2 In. 65.00

PICKARD China Company was started in 1898 by Wilder Pickard. Hand-painted designs were used on china purchased from other sources. In the 1930s, the company began to make its own chinawares in Chicago, Illinois. The company now makes many types of porcelains, including a successful line of limited edition collector plates.

Bowl, Modern Conventional, Hessler, Pedestal, 9 1/4 x 4 3/4 In. 300.00
Bowl, Raised Gold Floral Center, Fruit Border, Signed, 7 In. 150.00
Bowl, Side Handles, 3 Ball Feet, Lavender, Gold Trim, 7 1/2 In. 45.00
Bowl, Strawberries, Handles, Yeschek 98.00
Cake Plate, Gilded Outlined, Multicolored Leaves, Handles, Signed, 13 In. 95.00
Cake Plate, Yellow Trumpet Flowers, Handle, Gold Trim, 11 In. 175.00
Charger, Yellow Flowers, Leaves, Hand Painted, Signed, 12 1/2 In. 175.00
Chocolate Pot, Clusters Of Grapes & Leaves, Vokral 395.00
Ginger Jar, Cover, Floral Tracery Band, Mottled Gold Top & Base, 1915, 8 x 6 In. ... 80.00
Ginger Jar, Cover, Gilt Floral, Etched, 8 5/8 x 6 In. 80.00
Gravy Boat, Signed, c.1905, 8 In. 295.00
Pitcher, Modern Conventional, Hessler, 1905, 4 In. 185.00
Pitcher, Water Lilies, Gold Handle, Signed, 1898, 7 In. 395.00
Pitcher, Water Lily, Green, Gold Trim, 6 1/2 In. 395.00
Pitcher, Yellow Cherries, Gold-Outlined, Leaves, Marked, 5 3/4 x 7 1/2 In. 395.00
Plate, Currants & Foliage, 1910, 6 In. 75.00
Plate, Easter Lilies, Otto Goess, 8 1/4 In. 138.00
Plate, Italian Gardens, Signed, 6 In. 135.00
Plate, Scene Of Yosemite, Matte Finish, 8 1/2 In. 295.00
Plate, Stylized Design, Hessler, 8 1/4 In. 138.00
Plate, Walnuts, Almonds, Filberts, Brown Tone, Vokral, 8 In. 145.00
Punch Bowl, Grape Leaves, Bunches Of Grapes, Gold Claw Feet, 14 In. 1100.00
Stein, Garden Scene, Handles, 1898, 7 In. 345.00
Stein, Grapes, 1898 .... 385.00
Sugar, Cover, Stylized Art Deco Design, Efdon 65.00
Sugar & Creamer, Currants & Foliage, Gold Trim 165.00
Sugar & Creamer, Italian Gardens, Gold Trim 225.00
Sugar & Creamer, Turquoise & Gold, 1925 .... 85.00
Sugar & Creamer, Violets, Silesia, 1898, 4 1/4 In. 325.00
Sugar & Creamer, Wildwood Scene, James 295.00
Tankard, Stylized Trees, Grapes & Leaves, 11 In. 540.00
Tile, Dutch Merchant Ship, 1905-1910, Round, 6 3/4 In. 395.00
Tile, Tea, Apple Blossom & Gold Design, 6 3/4 In. 225.00
Tray, Allover Gold, Etched Florals, Marked, 12 In. .... 65.00 to 75.00
Tray, Autumn Leaves, Gold & Green, Gold Veining, Signed, 11 1/4 In. 295.00
Tray, Round, 3 Sections, Peacock Handle, Etched Flower Basket, Gold, 10 1/2 In. 70.00
Vase, Garden Scene, Handles, Marked, 7 In. 345.00
Vase, Hand Painted Fish, Aladdin Lamp Shape, Signed 395.00
Vase, Scenic, Matte Finish, E. Challinor, 7 1/2 In. 395.00

PICTURES, silhouettes, and other small decorative objects framed to hang on the wall are listed here. Some other types of pictures are listed in the Print and Painting categories.

Beadwork, Flower & Bud Forms, Natural Chintz Ground, Frame, 11 x 11 1/2 In. 395.00
Bust, Man's, Wax Profile, Georgian Rosewood Oval Frame, Stand 220.00
Calligraphy, Landscape, Ink & Watercolor On Paper, Frame, China, 32 x 16 In. 60.50

Calligraphy, Tree, Birds, Names, Merry Christmas, 1904, Frame, 22 In. 16.50
Collage, Ribbon & Paper, Pink Woman, Cutout Black, Silk Petal Dress, 8 x 10 In. 20.00
Collage, Ruined Abbey, Watercolor, Embossed Gray Frame, Matted, 20 x 16 In. 27.50
Crewel, Cottage Scene, Matted, Frame, 1920, 21 1/2 x 27 1/2 In. 55.00
Crewel, Exotic Bird, Black Sky, Matted, Frame, 28 1/2 x 19 1/2 In. 55.00
Crewel, Galleon, Wool On Linen, Frame, Glass, 19 x 21 In. 25.00
Diorama, 2 Ministers To Louis XVI, Wooden, France, 19th Century, 16 x 19 In. 660.00
Embroidered, The Lord Will Provide, Reds, Rectangular Frame 125.00
Embroidered, Water Lilies, Pink, Ecru Linen, Frame, 18 3/4 x 14 3/4 In. 13.00
Embroidered, Wool, Naval Ship, Flags Of Nations, Frame, 1860, Square, 29 In. 195.00
Engraving, Ex-Minister & Meteor, Colored, England, 1805, Frame, 16 x 12 In. 220.00
Engraving, Wooden, Ship, American Flag, Hand Colored, Frame, 6 x 7 In. 143.00
Feather, Exotic Birds, On Flowered Branch, Frame, 15 3/8 x 7 3/8 In., Pair 48.00
Ink On Paper, Napoleon At The Encampment, Frame, 10 x 14 1/2 In. 260.00
Micro-Mosaic, Plaque, Bouquet Of Flowers In Vase, 7 1/2 In. 5175.00
Micro-Mosaic, Plaque, Women In Field, Phini, Oval, 6 x 9 In. 3300.00
Mosaic, Wooden, Bay Scene, Trees, Building, Leaf Petit Point Border, 7 x 9 1/2 In. . 25.00
Needlepoint, Mosque Design, Shades Of Purple, 11 x 14 In. 70.00
Needlepoint, Salvadore Dali Pattern, Pink & Wine, 12 x 13 In. 70.00
Needlework, Eagle, Shield, Flags, E Pluribus Unum, Frame, 17 1/2 x 20 In. 80.00
Needlework, Memorial, Shaw Family, Essex, England, 1858, 23 x 22 In. 302.00
Needlework, Paint, Silk, Figures, Romantic Landscape, Frame, 20 x 27 In. 550.00
Needlework, Silk Panel, Woman, Large Hat, Watercolor Sky, Frame, 8 x 6 In. 160.00
Pinprick, Woman, Landscape Scene, Sc. L. Heyde, Frame, 14 x 34 In. 1500.00
Punched Paper, God Bless Our Home, Cottage, Trees, Walnut Cross Frame 145.00
Reverse On Glass, Morning Prayer, Children, Oak Frame, 12 1/4 x 15 1/4 In. 195.00
Sandpaper, Castle Scene, Blues, Greens & Browns, Frame, 15 1/2 x 19 1/2 In. 225.00
Sandpaper, Landscape, Great Elm Tree, Pa., 1827, Frame, 29 x 25 In. 852.00
Sandpaper, Mourning, Woman, Headstone, Frame, 1800s, 39 x 52 In. 3000.00
Sandpaper, Snow Owl, Mrs. H.B. Thompson, May 1887, Frame 110.00
Sandpaper, Springfield Maine Hotel, 1869 .... 125.00
Silhouette, 3 Men & 2 Women Busts, Hollow Cut, Gilt Frame, 3 3/4 x 4 1/2 In. 240.00
Silhouette, Alexander Hamilton, Hollow Cut, Frame, 6 3/4 x 5 1/2 In. 220.00
Silhouette, Brooding Gentleman, Gilt Frame, 5 1/2 x 4 3/8 In. 70.00
Silhouette, Colonial Man, Black Frame, 4 3/4 x 5 3/4 In. 78.00
Silhouette, Family Of Four & Cat, August Edouart, 11 x 14 In. 4070.00
Silhouette, General Henry Dearborn, Full-Length, 10 1/2 x 8 In. 165.00
Silhouette, Gentleman, Black Ink, Gilt Detail, Bird's-Eye Frame, 8 x 6 1/2 In. 220.00
Silhouette, Gentleman, Full-Length, Lithographed Scene, Frame, 10 x 14 In. 415.00
Silhouette, Gentlemen Of Boston, Full Figures, 1859, 14 3/4 x 10 In. 195.00
Silhouette, Girl, Flowers & Basket, Watercolor, 5 x 4 In. 250.00
Silhouette, John Quincy Adams, Wm. H. Brown, 1844, 17 x 12 In. 75.00
Silhouette, Landscape, Woman, Brass Frame, 5 1/2 In., Pair 920.00
Silhouette, Man, Seated, August Edouart, 11 x 14 In. 1430.00
Silhouette, Man, White Brushed, Frame, Gilded Liner, 15 3/4 x 13 3/4 In. 522.00
Silhouette, Man, With Sword, Lt. W.B. Knipe, Frame, June 1838, 13 3/4 x 10 In. 302.50
Silhouette, Martin Van Buren, Wm. H. Brown, Dated 1844, 17 x 12 In. 75.00
Silhouette, Old Man, Gilt Frame, 5 5/8 x 4 7/8 In. 135.00
Silhouette, Patriotic, Soldier With Flag, Soldier Saluting, Frame, 20 3/4 In. 365.00
Silhouette, Reading, Frame, 2 3/4 x 3 1/4 In. 120.00
Silhouette, Scotty, On Haunches, Begging For Handout 300.00
Silhouette, Sled, Can't You Go No Faster Tommy, Frame, 2 1/4 x 3 1/4 In. 135.00
Silhouette, William Kerr, Esq., 13 1/2 x 7 1/2 In. 275.00
Silhouette, Woman, Bouquet & Fan, Primitive, Frame 230.00
Silhouette, Young Man, Oval Embossed Brass Frame, 5 1/2 In. 100.00
Silhouette, Young Officer, Charcoal Gouache, Black Lacquer Frame, 5 3/8 x 4 1/2 In. 220.00
Theorem, Basket Of Fruit, 19th Century, Frame, 10 x 14 In. 1870.00
Theorem, Flower Basket, Silk, Frame, 19th Century, 10 x 12 In. 275.00
Theorem, Flowers & Butterfly, Mustard, Early 19th Century 365.00
Theorem, Fruit Flowers, Velvet, Gilt Frame, Eglomise Glass, 20 x 20 In. 495.00
Theorem, Fruit In Bowl, 1830s, 9 1/2 x 13 3/4 In. 715.00
Theorem, Oriental Bowl, Fruit & Vintage, Frame, 24 3/4 x 28 1/2 In. 660.00
Theorem, Parrot, Cluster Of Flowers, Gilt Frame, 16 3/4 x 21 1/2 In. 510.00

Theorem, Peaches, Pears, Plums & Squash, c.1830, 13 x 20 In. 805.00
Tinsel, 2 Birds, Frame, 6 3/4 x 8 3/4 In. 55.00
Tinsel, Reverse Painted Vase Of Flowers, Gilt Frame, 13 x 11 In. 105.00
Trapunto Pin-Pricked, Woman, Child, 19th Century, Frame, 11 x 9 In., Pair 2200.00
Wax, Admiral Adam Duncan, Mahogany Shadow Box Frame, 6 1/4 In. 395.00

PIERCE, see Howard Pierce

PIGEON FORGE Pottery was started in Pigeon Forge, Tennessee, in 1946. Red clay found near the pottery was used to make the pieces. Molded or thrown pottery with matte glaze and slip decoration was made. The pottery is still working.

Bowl, Volcanic Green Glaze, 13 In. 150.00
Cookie Jar, 3 In. 22.00
Figurine, Mama Bear & 2 Cubs, Gunmetal Black Glaze 65.00
Vase, Blue Splatter On Black, Signed, 3 1/2 In. 25.00

PILKINGTON Tile and Pottery Company was established in 1892 in England. The company made small pottery wares, like buttons and hatpins, but soon started decorating vases purchased from other potteries. By 1903, the company had discovered an opalescent glaze that became popular on the Lancastrian pottery line. The manufacture of pottery ended in 1937, but decorating continued until 1948.

Bowl, Vine & Grape Design Exterior, Floral Spray Interior, Griffin Center, 7 In. 3850.00
Vase, Fish & Seaweed, Luster Gold & Blue Glaze, Richard Joyce, 6 1/2 In. 1700.00
Vase, Green Matte, Squatty, 1908, 3 1/4 x 3 1/2 In. 40.00
Vase, Silver Luster Galleons, Maidens Rowing, W. Mycock, 11 In. 1380.00

PINCUSHION DOLLS are not really dolls and often were not even pincushions. Some collectors use the term *half-doll*. The top half of each doll was made of porcelain. The edge of the half-doll was made with several small holes for thread, and the doll was stitched to a fabric body with a voluminous skirt. The finished figure was used to cover a hot pot of tea, powder box, pincushion, whisk broom, or lamp. They were made in sizes from less than an inch to over 9 inches high. Most date from the early 1900s to the 1950s. Collectors often find just the porcelain doll without the fabric skirt.

Arms Away, Art Deco, Germany, No. 7111, 3 1/4 In. 150.00
Arms Extended, Lace Cushion, Germany 85.00
Art Deco, Fan, Eyeliner, 5 1/2 In. 250.00
Bathing Beauty, Germany 145.00
Bisque, Jointed Arms, Molded Hair, Germany, 5 In. 165.00
Bisque, Jointed Arms, Smile, Germany, 2 In. 250.00
Blue Painted Eyes, Germany, 5 In. 125.00
Blue Painted Eyes, Germany, 6 In. 95.00
Carmen, On Clothes Brush, 5 In. 125.00
Colonial Dame, Both Hands Away, 3 3/4 In. 125.00
Colonial Maid, Bisque, Jointed Arms, 4 In. 300.00
Curved Arms Extended, Porcelain, Marked, 6 In. 250.00
Dutch Girl, Jointed Arms, Germany, 3 3/4 In. 275.00
Flapper, Arms Away, Holding Fan, Applying Makeup, Germany, 2 1/2 In. 125.00
Flapper, Closed Arms 45.00
Flapper, Hand Away Holding Fan, Art Deco, 5 1/2 In. 225.00
Flapper, With Rose, 3 1/2 In. 45.00
Flapper Hairstyle, Head Facing Parrot On Shoulder 175.00
Frog, Seated, Pewter, Germany, 1 1/2 In. 45.00
Hand In Front & On Waist, Germany, 3 1/4 In. 45.00
Hand On Shoulder & Front, Germany, 3 3/4 In. 45.00
Holding Grapes, Blond Hair, 3 1/2 In. 45.00
Large Hat, Pink Off-The-Shoulder Dress, Pink Body 195.00
Porcelain Legs, Red Skirted Cushion 95.00
Queen Of The Nile Headdress, Arms Away, 3 In. 225.00
Toodles, Flirty Eyes 85.00

Woman, Flowers In Hair, Germany, 3 1/2 In. 55.00

PIPES have been popular since tobacco was introduced to Europe by Sir Walter Raleigh. Meerschaum pipes are listed under Meerschaum.

Box, Fan-Carved Small Drawer, Brass Pull, Birch, 19 1/4 x 5 1/4 In. 3163.00
Briar, Covered Bowl, Copper Deer, Amber Stem, BBK, Zurich 18.00
Hand Carved, Alligator 60.00
Meerschaum, Dark Amber Stem, Chieftain, Beard, Yellow Stem, 5 3/4 In. 28.00
Meerschaum, Face-Of-Man Bowl, Tall Hat, Long Nose, Beard 70.00
Meerschaum, Gibson Girl, Amber Stem, 4 1/2 In. 70.00
Meerschaum, Moorish, Ornamented Turban 58.00
Meerschaum, Turk's Head, Amber Stem 75.00
Opium, Brass Inlays, Pewter Bands, Chip Carving, Bone Mouthpiece, 1857 .... 357.50
Opium, Engraved Dragons, China 250.00
Opium Set, Metal Inserts, China, Wooden Box, 1850 .... 2450.00
Regimental, 15 Field Artillery, 1896, 45 In. 275.00
Regimental, Garde Du Corps, Potsdam, 1910, 7 Ft. 5 In. 825.00
Streamline, Aluminum, Disposable Corncob, 1950s 200.00

PIRKENHAMMER is a porcelain manufactory started in 1802 by Friedrich Holke and J. G. Lilst. It was located in Bohemia, now Brezova, Czechoslovakia. The company made tablewares usually decorated with views and flowers. Lithophanes were also made. The mark of the crossed hammers is easy to remember as the Pirkenhammer symbol.

Bowl, Fruits & Flowers, Gilt & Enamel, Marked, 6 1/2 In. 415.00

PISGAH FOREST pottery was made in North Carolina beginning in 1926. The pottery was started by Walter R. Stephen in 1914, and after his death in 1941 the pottery continued in operation. The most famous kinds of Pisgah Forest ware are the cameo type with designs made of raised glaze and the turquoise crackle glaze wares.

Bowl, Crystalline, Ivory-To-Green, Flambe Glaze, 4 x 5 1/2 In. 330.00
Creamer, White Wagon Trains, Matte Green Ground, Blue Body, 5 In. 200.00
Humidor, Streaked Green Glaze, 4 In. 75.00
Lamp Base, Cameo Ware, Pioneer Scene, Blue Ground, 10 3/4 In. 450.00
Mug, Fiddler & Dog .... 195.00 to 245.00
Pitcher, Forest, Signed Stephan 75.00
Pitcher, Simple Form, Streaked Glaze, 6 1/2 In. 95.00
Sugar & Creamer, 2-Tone, Date 68.00
Tea Set, Beige, Pink Interior Glaze, 3 Piece 485.00
Teapot, Green High Glaze, 6 x 8 1/2 In. 50.00
Vase, Aunt Nancy, Celadon Glossy Glaze, Marked, 7 1/2 In. 165.00
Vase, Blue To Lavender Glaze, Pink Interior, 1939, 4 1/2 In. 77.00
Vase, Cameo, Stephan Longpine, 5 In. 300.00
Vase, Crystalline Glaze, 5 In. .... 375.00 to 485.00
Vase, Turquoise & Yellow, 1930, 5 In. 55.00
Vase, Turquoise Glossy Glaze, Marked, 15 x 8 1/2 In. 1240.00
Vase, Yellow & White Crystalline Glaze, Bulbous, 5 1/2 In. 400.00
Vase, Yellow, Pink Interior, 1936, 3 1/2 In. 40.00

PLANTERS PEANUTS memorabilia is collected. Planters Nut and Chocolate Company was started in Wilkes-Barre, Pennsylvania, in 1906. The Mr. Peanut figure was adopted as a trademark in 1916. National advertising for Planters Peanuts started in 1918. The company was acquired by Standard Brands, Inc., in 1961. Standard Brands merged with Nabisco in 1981. Some of the Mr. Peanut jars and other memorabilia have been reproduced and, of course, new items are being made.

Alarm Clock, Yellow Face 85.00
Ashtray, Figural, Silvertone, 50th Anniversary, Die Casters, 1956 .... 36.00
Ashtray, Mr. Peanut, Bisque 95.00
Bag, Mr. Peanut Waving Red Pennant, Glassine, 1930s 8.00
Bank, Molded Plastic, Hat Turns To Open, 1950s, 8 1/2 In. 23.00

Top row (left to right): Planters Peanuts, Popgun, Paper, Fold Up, 1930s, 8 3/4 x 5 In.;
Planters Peanuts, Doll, Mr. Peanut, Wooden, Jointed, Blue Hat, 9 In.;
Planters Peanuts, Scale, Mr. Peanut, Iron, Platform, 20 x 45 x 22 In.;
Bottom row (left to right): Planters Peanuts, Costume, Mr. Peanut, Fiberglass, 50 In.;
Planters Peanuts, Car, Figural, Mr. Peanut Driving, Plastic, 5 x 2 1/2 In.

Bank, Mr. Peanut, Yellow, Box, 1938	530.00
Beach Ball, 1960s	10.00
Book, Around The World With Mr. Peanut, Canada, 1930	35.00
Book, Historical And Educational Paint Book, 1949	35.00
Book, Painting, Presidents Of The United States Of America, 1953	13.00
Book, Painting, Seeing The U.S.A. With Mr. Peanut, 1950, 7 3/4 x 10 1/2 In.	11.00
Bookmark, 1939	15.00
Bookmark, Mr. Peanut, Diecut Figure, World's Fair, New York, 7 In.	25.00
Bowl, Mr. Peanut, Ruffled, Metal, 6 In.	6.50
Bowl Set, Mr. Peanut, 5 Piece	15.00
Bowl Set, Mr. Peanut, World's Fair, Tin, Trylon & Perisphere, 6 Piece	50.00
Can, Peanut Oil	66.00
Candy Wrapper, Planter's, 5 Cents, Pencil Premium Picture	15.00
Car, Figural, Mr. Peanut Driving, Plastic, 5 x 2 1/2 In. *Illus*	550.00
Charm Bracelet, c.1950	40.00
Cookie Jar, Mr. Peanut	30.00 to 39.00
Costume, Mr. Peanut, Fiberglass, 50 In. *Illus*	523.00
Crate, Shipping, Wooden	350.00
Dish, Metal, World's Fair, 1939	20.00
Dish, Mr. Peanut In Center, Gold Metal, 1956	60.00
Dish, Mr. Peanut Nut Tray, Figural Handle, Blue Plastic, 3 Sections, 4 x 5 In.	10.00
Display, Mr. Peanut On Top Of Dispenser, On Blocks, Die Cut	1000.00
Doll, Mr. Peanut, Cloth, 19 In.	25.00
Doll, Mr. Peanut, Rubber Squeeze	2550.00
Doll, Mr. Peanut, Wooden, Jointed, Blue Hat, 9 In. *Illus*	171.00
Figurine, Man, Jointed, Wooden, 1940s, 8 1/2 In.	400.00
Figurine, Mr. Peanut, Metal, Heavy Base, 8 In.	250.00
Figurine, Mr. Peanut, With Peanut Tray, Bisque, 1930s, 4 In.	120.00
Figurine, Mr. Peanut, Wooden, 7 In., 1930s	195.00 to 285.00

Fry Pot, Planters Hi Hat Peanut Oil, Embossed 70.00
Glass, Champagne, Figural Plastic, Green 35.00
Glass, Champagne, Figural, Plastic, Red 35.00
Grinder, Figural, Mr. Peanut, Peanut Butter Maker, Between Ears, 12 In. 30.00
Jar, Barrel, Figural Peanut Handle, Clear Glass, 12 1/2 In. 170.00
Jar, Clear Glass, Mr. Peanut On Tin Lid, 10 In. 83.00
Jar, Fish Bowl, Frosted Base, Large 175.00
Jar, Planters Pennant Peanuts, Clear, Figural Peanut Handle, 12 In. 176.00
Jar, Running Peanut, Figural Finial Lid, Embossed, 8 x 12 In. 275.00
Jar Holder, Die Cut Tin 1650.00
Knife, Pocket 5.00
Magazine, Our Fighting Forces, Premium, 1943 .... 125.00
Mug, Tan Plastic, 3 3/4 In. 8.50
Nodder, Mr. Peanut 150.00
Nut Set, 1939, 5 Piece 25.00
Peanut Butter Maker, Mr. Peanut, Box, 1967 .... 35.00 to 55.00
Peanut Sack, Mr. Peanut, Burlap, 1950s 25.00
Pencil, Figural Top, Mechanical, Tin 20.00
Pencil, Figural, Retractable, Yellow & Blue, Metal 12.00
Popgun, Paper, Fold Up, 1930s, 8 3/4 x 5 In. .... *Illus* 220.00
Poster, Mr. Peanut, Presents Chazente, Radio Program, 11 x 17 In. 100.00
Radio, Figural, Box 125.00
Ring, 3-Dimensional Mr. Peanut, Plastic 95.00
Roaster, Royal No. 5, Planters Nut & Chocolate, Iron, Copper, 45 x 41 In 1320.00
Salt & Pepper, Blue, 3 In. 8.00
Salt & Pepper, Figural, Glass Eyes .... 20.00 to 95.00
Salt & Pepper, Mr. Peanut, Gloves, Spats, Beige & Black, 4 In. 9.50
Salt & Pepper, Mr. Peanut, Green Plastic, 3 In. 8.00
Salt & Pepper, Red 8.00
Scale, Mr. Peanut, Iron, Platform, 20 x 45 x 22 In. .... *Illus* 17875.00
Sign, Mr. Peanut In Canoe, With Girl, Parasol, Cardboard, 1920s 450.00
Sign, Nut Center, Plastic, 12 x 30 In. 60.00
Snack Set, Mr. Peanut, Tin 25.00
Spoon, Blue Plastic, Mr. Peanut Handle, Pierced, 5 1/2 In. 6.50
Spoon, Serving, Mr. Peanut, Full-Figure, Metal, 1950s, 5 In. 25.00
Straw, Mr. Peanut, Figural, Holder, 6 Piece 20.00
Tin, 10 Lb. 50.00
Tin, Nutola Peanuts, Paper Label, 10 Lb. 2000.00
Trade Card, Mr. Peanut, Spooky Magic Trick 1.00
Train Set, Battery-Operated, Box 125.00
Wristwatch, Mr. Peanut, Yellow Face 45.00
Wristwatch, Yellow Dial, Blue Leather Strap, Metal Hands, 1970s 55.00

PLASTIC objects of all types are being collected. Some pieces are listed in
other categories; gutta-percha cases are listed in photography, celluloid in its
own category.

Drink Mixer Set, Zulu-Lulu, Women, Figural, 1960s, Box, 6 Piece 10.00
Pitcher, Milk, With Tumbler, Aladdin 60.00

PLIQUE-A-JOUR is an enameling process. The enamel is laid between thin
raised metal lines and heated. The finished piece has transparent enamel held
between the thin metal wires. It is different from cloisonne because it is
transparent.

Boat, Dragon Head & Handles, 1900 .... 750.00
Bowl, Figural, Viking Ship, Dragon's Head, Silver, M. Hammer, 7 x 14 In. 9075.00
Bowl, Floral Design, 4 In. 165.00
Vase, Baluster Shape, Floral, Apple Green Ground, Japan, 4 5/8 In. 880.00

POLITICAL memorabilia of all types, from buttons to banners, is collected.
Items related to presidential candidates are the most popular, but collectors
also search for material related to state and local offices. Many reproductions
have been made. A jugate is a button with photographs of both the
presidential and vice presidential candidates.

Apron, Harrison, Log Cabin, Tippecanoe & Tyler Campaign, 1840, 21 1/2 In. 1870.00
Ashtray, Senator Thomas Eagleton 43.00
Badge, Abraham Lincoln & Andrew Jackson, Ferro-Type, 1864 .... 600.00
Badge, Lincoln, Union & Liberty For Lincoln, Paper, 7 1/4 x 3 1/4 In. 825.00
Balloon, Wallace For President, 1972 .... 5.00 to 8.00
Banner, Hubert Humphrey, 10 x 32 In. 25.00
Banner, Landon & Knox, Canvas 1050.00
Banner, Lyndon B. Johnson, 18 x 24 In. 25.00
Banner, Washington With Horse, Shields, Cotton, 24 1/2 x 17 In. 385.00
Bracelet, Charm, Peanut, Jimmy Carter 12.00
Bracelet, John F. Kennedy, PT 109 .... 78.00
Broadside, Daniel Webster Campaign, Silk 595.00
Bumper Sticker, Kennedy For President, Red, White, Blue, Photo, 18 In. 8.50
Button, 4 More Years, Re-Elect Bush In '92, Picture In Center, 3 In. 3.00
Button, Adlai Stevenson, Our Next President, Photograph, Large 2.50
Button, Aids Walk, '93, Square On End, 1 x 1 In. 2.00
Button, Al Smith, Derby 22.50
Button, Alaskans For Humphrey, 3 Letter Center 193.00
Button, America 1st, Vote Ford In '76, 1 1/2 In. 5.50
Button, America's Choice, President, Ann Richards, Picture Center, 1 /14 In. 1.50
Button, Barbara Jordan 1992, Democratic Nat'l Convention, Pictured, 1 3/4 In. 5.00
Button, Don't Let This Happen To You, Vote For Ike, Picture, Large 2.50
Button, Draft Rockefeller, Blue & White, 1960, 3 In. 17.50
Button, Dukakis In '88, Pictured, 6 In. 3.00
Button, Dwight D. Eisenhower, Picture 10.00
Button, Elect Hillary's Husband In '92, Picture Center, 1 1/4 In. 3.00
Button, Elephant, With Glasses, Goldwater 12.00
Button, For America In '92, Bentsen Of Texas, Picture Center, 1 In. 2.00
Button, Gen. Douglas MacArthur, Picture, Red, White, Blue, 2 1/2 In. 35.00
Button, Gen. MacArthur, Celluloid, Leather Strap, Washington & Lee '16 .... 40.00
Button, Goldwater & Miller, Photograph, 1964 .... 2.25
Button, Goldwater, Vote In '64, Red, White, Blue, 4 In. 9.00
Button, Goldwater, With Pearl 8.50
Button, Grits For Tom, Aug. 4, 1976, Blue, White, Gray, 1 1/2 In. 3.00
Button, H. Ross Perot, Jobs For America, President 1992, U.S. Flag, 1 In. 17.50
Button, Harding, Coolidge & Penrose, Republican Candidates, 1932 .... 6500.00
Button, I Am A Democrat For Eisenhower, 5/6 In. 24.00
Button, I Like Ike, Lithograph, Red, White & Blue, 1 In. 2.00
Button, I Saw ELVIS At The Republican National Convention, 1 1/4 In. 2.00
Button, I Was For Perot But Now I Don't Know, 1 1/2 In. 3.00
Button, I'm A Republican For Johnson, Blue & White, 1 1/4 In. 7.00
Button, Ike Sure To Click Dick, Red, White, Blue, 2 1/2 In. 35.00
Button, Ike, Rhinestone 18.00
Button, Inauguration, Clinton & Gore, A New Beginning, Full Color, 3 1/2 In. 4.00
Button, J.F. Kennedy, Swainson, Jugate Flasher 15.00
Button, JFK, PT Boat, Kennedy 60, Brass 45.00
Button, Joe Louis Wants Willkie, Center Of Louis 492.00
Button, John Kennedy, Inaugural Day January 20, 1961, The Man Of The 60s, 6 In. .. 32.00
Button, John P. Elkin Governor For Indiana, July 21, 1896, Colorful 20.00
Button, Johnson & Humphrey, 1964, Lithograph, Red, White, Blue, 1 In. 2.50
Button, Kennedy & Peace, Red, White & Blue, 1968, 3/4 In. 15.00
Button, Kennedy, Senator, Center Photograph, Red, White, Blue, 1 1/4 In. 10.00
Button, Kennedy, The Spirit Of '68, U.S. Map, Red, White, Blue, 2 In. 20.00
Button, Knows America's Needs, Picture Of Robert Kennedy, 3/4 In. 3.00
Button, Landon & Knox, Daisy 12.50
Button, LBJ All The Way, Cowboy Hat, 1964 .... 2.35
Button, Let's Back Ronald Reagan For Governor 48.00
Button, Long Live The President, Copper, Gold Wash 850.00
Button, Lyndon Johnson & Kennedy, 3 1/2 In. 27.50
Button, Maddox, Dyke 7.50
Button, McKinley & Roosevelt, Dinner Bucket Design, Pin Back, 1900, 1 1/4 In. 129.00
Button, Mitchell Day, Franklin D. Roosevelt & John L. Lewis, 1936 .... 450.00
Button, Mondale, Ferraro, West Virginia's Choice 7.00

Button, Nixon Now, Red, White & Blue 2.50
Button, Nixon With Honor, Peace Symbol In Center, 1 3/4 In. 10.00
Button, Nunn In 1992, Picture Center, 1 In. 1.00
Button, On Our Way, Elephant Dancing On U.S. Map, Red, White, Black, 2 1/2 In. .. 75.00
Button, Our President Harry S. Truman, Picture In Center, 1 1/2 In. 39.50
Button, Outline Of State Of Texas, 3/4 In. 2.00
Button, Perfumidor, Franklin D. Roosevelt, Celluloid, 1930s, 2 In. 625.00
Button, Perot For President, '92, 3/4 In 25.00
Button, President Ford '76, Photograph, Blue & White, 1 3/4 In. 5.00
Button, President William McKinley, Is This Imperialism, 1900 .... 1455.00
Button, Remember The Maine, 2 In. 20.00
Button, Robert LaFollette & B.K. Wheeler, Portraits, Bronze, 7/8 In. 125.00
Button, Ross For Boss '92, Stars At Outer Rim, 1 1/2 In. 2.00
Button, Ross Perot For President, Red, White & Blue Flag, 2 1/4 In. 2.00
Button, Scoop Jackson For Vice President, 2 In. 22.00
Button, Score A Touchdown With Willkie, Blue & White, 1 1/4 In. 12.00
Button, Senior Citizens For Kennedy, Lithograph, Red, Gold, 1 In. 4.50
Button, Stevenson & Kefauver, 1956 .... 2.25
Button, Taft, Chicago To Washington, On Elephant, Carrying Big Stick 2500.00
Button, Taft, Eagle, Navy Border, 3/4 In. 325.00
Button, Taft, With Running Mates 20.00
Button, Teddy Roosevelt & Johnson, Moose, With Ribbon, 1/4-In. Cartoon Image 6000.00
Button, Teddy Roosevelt, Fairbanks, Bear, Inaugural, C. Berryman, 1904 .... 6250.00
Button, The Nation Needs Richard M. Nixon, Photograph, Stars & Stripes, 4 In. 11.00
Button, Truman & Barkley Inauguration, Democratic Donkey, 1949 .... 650.00
Button, U.S. Grant, Brass, Framed, 1 x 3/4 In. 90.00
Button, Vote Perot U.S.A. 1992, The People's Choice, 1 In. 14.50
Button, Waiting For Perot, 1 1/4 In. 3.00
Button, Wallace For President, Large 10.00
Button, Warren Harding For President, Picture, 1920 .... 2.50
Button, Wendell Willkie, America's Hope, Photograph 2.50
Button, Wendell Willkie, Elephant Holding United States Flag, Metal 18.00
Button, Willkie For Millionaires, Roosevelt For Millions, Red, White, 1 1/4 In. 8.00
Button, Win With Goldwater, Stars & Bars On Rim, Picture Center, 1 In. 12.00
Button, Win With Wilson, Photograph, 1912 .... 3.00
Button, With Ribbons & Medallion, John Kennedy, Inaugural Day 45.00
Button, Women For Humphrey, Woman Figure In Center, 1 1/4 In. 17.50
Button, Year Of The Woman, U.S. Senate Nominees, All Pictured, 2 1/2 In. 10.00
Card, Birthday, Nixon, Velvet, 1972 .... 18.00
Card, Bridge, Hoover, 1928, 4 x 8 In. 15.00
Cards, Playing, Kennedy Kards, 1963, Complete 22.50
Cards, Trading, John F. Kennedy, Topps, 1963, 25 Piece 25.00
Chess Set, Watergate, All Different Pieces, Nixon, Mitchell 150.00
Cigar Case, Martin Van Buren, Image, Lacquered Papier-Mache 4620.00
Cigarette Pack, Stevenson For President, 1950s 6.00
Clicker, Click With Dick, Picture 22.50
Coin, Good Luck, Roosevelt & Garner, Embossed Portraits, 1/4 In. 40.00
Coloring Book, John F. Kennedy, 1962 .... 35.00
Comic Book, Eisenhower, Nixon, Congress & Senate Committees, 1956 .... 10.00
Comic Book, LBJ Great Society, Color 22.00
Doll, Barry Goldwater, Remco, 1964, 5 In., Box 75.00
Doll, Elephant, Republican Team, 1988 .... 9.00
Doorstop, Horace Greeley, Liberal Democrat Candidate, Figural, 1872 .... 2500.00
Fan, Portraits Of American Presidents, Washington To Polk, 1844, 20 x 11 In. 3300.00
Fan, Vandenburg For President, Convention Item 35.00
Ferrotype, Douglas, Johnson, 2-Sided, 1860 .... 150.00
Figurine, Donkey, Bryan Picture On Side Of Body 455.00
Figurine, Elephant, Sits On Donkey, Clay, 1948 .... 50.00
Figurine, Elephant, Taft, Sherman Picture On Side Of Body 1.50
Flag, Antennae, Nylon, Kennedy, Red, White, Blue, 7 1/2 In. 12.50
Football, Car Aerial, Nixon, Agnew, Styrofoam, 1968 .... 25.00
Glass, McKinley & Hobart White Transfer, 3 1/2 In. 65.00
Gum Cigars, Win With Dick, Photograph On Box, 1968 .... 25.00

Hat, Campaign, Kennedy	32.00
Hat, Vote Straight Democrat Kennedy-Johnson, Garrison Style, 1960	20.00
Invitation, Dinner, Millard Fillmore, December, 1852	300.00
Invitation, Reagan, Bush, Inaugural, Framed	12.50
Kerchief, Behold The Man, Washington's Farewell Address, 1800, 11 3/4 In.	465.00
Kerchief, Love Of Truth, Cherry Tree Incident, c.1800, 12 1/4 x 11 In.	520.00
Kerchief, Portrait, Bowling Green Washington, Frame, c.1819, 25 1/4 x 19 In.	1760.00
Key Chain, Spiro Agnew, Plastic, 1972, 3 In.	15.00
Letter, Barbara Bush Autographed	90.00
License Attachment, Donkey, Red Plastic Ears, Tail, Move When Car Driven	220.00
License Plate, America Needs Roosevelt	175.00
License Plate, Goldwater, 2 x 4 In.	13.00
License Plate, Hoover, Herbert Hoover Campaign, Red, White & Blue, 1928	28.00
License Plate, LBJ 464, California	14.00
License Plate, Win With Willkie	260.00
Lunch Pail, Dolph Briscoe, Texas	35.00
Match Cover, F.D. Roosevelt, Diamond Match, Biography, 1940s	2.50
Match Cover, George Washington, Diamond Match, Blue, Biography, 1940s	2.50
Match Cover, Wilson, Diamond Match, Biography, 1940s	2.50
Matchbook, Goldwater, Picture	6.50
Medal, Charles Evans Hughes For President, 1916	38.00
Medal, Inaugural, Taft & Sherman, 1909	175.00
Medal, Inaugural, Theodore Roosevelt, 1905	165.00
Medallion, Pres. Of United States, Franklin D. Roosevelt, Portrait, Bronze	30.00
Medallion, William Jennings Bryan, Silver Plate, Campaign Of 1896, 3 1/8 In.	90.00
Memorial Ribbon, John Kennedy, Woven Cloth, Photo, Poem, 9 In.	12.00
Menu, Democratic National Convention, 1924, Large	24.00
Mirror, F.D.R.-Times, Pocket	115.00
Mug, Archie Bunker For President	15.00
Mug, Bobby Kennedy For President, 1960s	27.00
Mug, Dwight Eisenhower, Yellow Flat Glaze, Porcelain, c.1952, 5 In.	89.00
Mug, Lyndon B. Johnson & Family	10.00
Necktie, Bob Taft, I Like Taft, 3 Pictures	35.00
Necktie, I Like Ike, Red	42.00
Pamphlet, Appeal To The Old Whigs Of Massachusetts, 20 Pages, 1806	1870.00
Paperweight, Hoover, Metal, 2 In.	45.00
Pencil, Bullet Shape, FDR & Landon	80.00
Pennant, Nixon, 1973, Large	20.00
Pin, Dewey For Students, 5/6 In.	47.50
Pincushion, Abraham Lincoln, Sterling Silver	1600.00
Ping-Pong Paddle, Nixon-Mao	25.00
Plaque, Bust, A. Lincoln, Copperplated Lead-Framed, 5 x 6 In.	85.00
Plate, James A. Garfield For President, Black & White, 8 In.	250.00
Plate, Portrait, James A. Garfield For President, Black & White, 8 In.	215.00
Plate, President Garfield, Memorial, Crystal, 10 In.	25.00
Plate, Republican National Convention, Signed By Governor, 1956, 14 In.	60.00
Postcard, Bryan, Kern, Picture Of Capitol Building	18.00
Postcard, Gephardt For President, Autographed By Gephardt, Oversized	20.00
Postcard, Harry Truman Campaign	25.00
Postcard, LBJ, USA, Picture, Unused	6.50
Postcard, Roosevelt Campaign, Wooden, 1904	1172.00
Poster, For President, Alfred E. Smith, Honest-Able-Fearless, 1928, 22 1/2 x 14 In.	50.00
Poster, Issue, 1900, Liberty, Justice, Humanity, W.J. Bryan, 28 1/2 x 18 1/2 In.	1210.00
Poster, Kennedy & Johnson, Vote Liberal Row C, License Tag	225.00
Poster, Kennedy For President, Leadership For The 60s, Photo, 1960, 13 x 21 In.	75.00
Poster, McGovern, President '72, Color Portrait, 21 x 28 In.	4.00
Program, Democratic National Convention, Philadelphia, 1936, Oversized	20.00
Program, Eisenhower, Nixon Inauguration, 1953	16.00
Program, Inauguration, JFK & Johnson, Envelope, 8 x 11 In.	65.00
Program, McKinley Inaugural Ball, Gold Leaf, Capitol, White House, 5 Pages	150.00
Program, Republican National Convention, Chicago, 1960	7.00
Program, Richard Nixon, Inauguration Ceremonies, Signed, 1973	440.00
Record, R.F. Kennedy, Sing Along For RFK, 33 1/3 RPM	45.00

Record, Voice Of President John F. Kennedy, Nomination Speech, 45 Rpm.	6.50
Ribbon, Lincoln, Hamlin, Free Homes For The People, Embossed Silk	1200.00
Ribbon, McKinley, Gold Color, May 8, 1901	80.00
Ribbon, Mourning, Andrew Jackson's Death, Silk, 1847, 8 1/8 x 3 In.	355.00
Ribbon, Mourning, Harrison's Unexpected Death, Silk, 7 x 3 1/4 In.	175.00
Ribbon, Philadelphia Mayor	105.00
Ribbon, Prohibitory Law Passed In New York, 1855, Myron Clark, Governor	25.00
Ribbon, Republican Party, Lincoln, Under The Oaks, Tree Shape, 1854-1904	400.00
Salt & Pepper, John F. Kennedy, Sitting In Rocking Chair, Ceramic, 1960s, 2 In.	25.00
Sewing Kit, We Want Rockefeller For President, 1960	22.00
Sheet Music, Jim Reed Of Missouri For President, 1928	45.00
Sheet Music, To You Roosevelt, 1933	22.00
Soap, Carter, 1980	18.00
Soap, Clean Up With Ike	20.00
Songbook, Coolidge & Dawes Rally, Jugate Photograph, 1924	38.00
Spoon, Measuring, Nixon, Plastic	25.00
Stickpin, Al Smith, Plastic Derby	30.00
Stickpin, Bear, Roosevelt, Figural	45.00
Stickpin, Theodore Roosevelt, Our Choice, Brass, 1904	65.00
Straw Hat, John F. Kennedy, Convention, 1960	45.00
Stud, F.D. Roosevelt, Picture	14.00
Stud, Hoover, Elephant	12.50
Stud, Taft, His Last Stop, Picture	80.00
Thimble, Reagan, Bush, Dated 1984	1.25
Ticket, Ball, Richard Nixon, 1973, 7 1/4 x 3 1/2 In.	6.00
Ticket, Republican National Convention, St. Louis, 1896, Ornate Engravings	35.00
Tie Bar, Goldwater	8.00
Tie Bar, Wallace	8.00
Tie Clip, Donkey, Democrat, Celluloid, Box	25.00
Tie Tack, Humphrey	7.50
Toby Jug, Teddy Roosevelt	1500.00
Toby Jug, Woodrow Wilson	1950.00
Toy, Jimmy Carter, Walking Peanut, Box	25.00
Trade Card, Hancock	18.00
Trade Card, Harrison	18.00
Tray, Teddy Roosevelt Rough Rider, Tin Litho, Oval	750.00
Umbrella, McKinley, Hobart, Campaign, Red, White & Blue	290.00
Watch, George Wallace, The Fighting Judge, Bill Dinken Time, 1970	125.00
Watch Fob, President Carter, Painted Flag Ground	10.00
Watch Fob, Taft & Sherman, Bust, Set Into Horseshoe, Brass, 1908	75.00
Watch Fob, Taft For President	75.00
Window Sticker, I Put Barry On T.V., Goldwater, 1964	18.00
Wristwatch, Woodrow Wilson, No Band	360.00

POMONA glass is a clear glass with a soft amber border decorated with pale blue or rose-colored flowers and leaves. The colors are very, very pale. The background of the glass is covered with a network of fine lines. It was made from 1885 to 1888 by the New England Glass Company. First grind was made from April 1885 to June 1886. It was made by cutting a wax surface on the glass, then dipping it in acid. Second grind was a less expensive method of acid etching that was developed later.

Berry Set, Amber Scalloped Rim, Frosted, 9 Piece	110.00
Berry Set, Inverted Thumbprint, Turned-In Scalloped Rim, 9 Piece	225.00
Bowl, 1st Grind, 4 1/2 In.	385.00
Bowl, Underplate, Ruffled, 2nd Grind, 3 & 4 1/2 In.	60.00
Castor, Pickle, Thumbprint, Enamel, Cranberry	325.00
Celery Vase, Amber Scalloped Rim, Frosted, Oval, 13 1/2 In.	28.00
Celery Vase, Blue-Stained Cornflower, 1st Grind, 6 1/2 In.	485.00
Celery Vase, Cornflower, Blue, 1st Grind, 6 1/2 x 4 1/2 In.	485.00
Dish, Handle, Gold Leaves, Blueberries, Ruffled, 4 x 3 In.	125.00
Finger Bowl, Cornflower, 1st Grind	100.00 to 125.00
Finger Bowl, Cornflower, Ruffled, 2nd Grind, 2 1/2 x 5 1/2 In.	155.00
Pitcher, Diamond Quilted, Twisted Rope Handle & Collar, 7 1/2 In.	110.00

Pitcher, Water, Diamond Quilted, 7 1/4 In. 40.00
Punch Cup, Cornflower, Amber Rim & Handle, 2 1/2 In. 195.00
Spooner, Flower & Pleat 50.00
Sugar, Flower & Pleat 70.00
Tumbler, Butterfly, Flower & Leaves 80.00
Tumbler, Inverted Thumbprint, Enameled Flowers & Ferns, Amber Rim .... 85.00 to 95.00
Vase, Amber, Rose & Silver Mineral Stained Flowers, Gold Rim, 1880s, 10 In. 275.00
Vase, Fan, Cornflower, Spray Of Violets, 1st Grind, 3 x 6 In. 237.50
Vase, Flowers & Butterflies, Amber, Rose & Silver, 2nd Grind, 1860s, 10 In. 350.00
Water Set, Flower & Pleat, c.1895, 6 Piece 140.00

PONTYPOOL, see Tole

POPEYE was introduced to the Thimble Theater comic strip in 1929. The character became a favorite of readers. In 1932, an animated cartoon featuring Popeye was made by Paramount Studios. The cartoon series continued and became even more popular when it was shown on television starting in the 1950s. The full-length movie with Robin Williams as Popeye was made in 1980.

Bank, Dime Register, 1929 .... 150.00
Bank, Figural, Plaster, 1950s 195.00
Bank, Knockout, Straits Mfg., Box, 1935 .... 2455.00
Bank, Olive Oyl 60.00
Bank, Pipe 450.00
Bank, Popeye Daily Dime, Tin Lithograph, 1956 .... 75.00
Bank, Popeye Knockout, Straits Mfg., Box, 1935 .... 2455.00
Bank, Socko, Mechanical 495.00
Book, Big Little Book, 1946 .... 30.00
Book, Big Little Book, Popeye In Poodleburg, Saalfield, 1934 .... 30.00
Book, How To Draw Cartoons, David McKay, 1939 .... 85.00
Book, Little Wonder, 1955 .... 14.00
Box, Popeye Express, Marx, No Toy, 1935 .... 650.00
Bubble Blower, Box 1350.00
Butler Set, Box, 1936 .... 65.00
Candy Container, PEZ, Olive Oyl 110.00
Candy Container, PEZ, Popeye With Removable Pipe, Package 60.00
Clock, Windup, Smiths 260.00
Coloring Set, 1950s 10.00
Cookie Jar, American Bisque .... 900.00 to 1000.00
Cookie Jar, No Pipe, ABC 575.00
Cookie Jar, Olive Oyl, American Bisque 2400.00
Cookie Jar, Pipe, AB Label 1100.00
Cookie Jar, Popeye In Spinach Can, Corl Collection 450.00
Cookie Jar, Vandor .... 400.00 to 550.00
Costume, Box, 1950s 50.00
Costume, Collegeville, 1950s 35.00
Costume, Mask, 2-Piece Body Suit, Collegeville, Box, 1960 .... 32.00
Costume, Mask, Collegeville, Box, 1950s 40.00
Decanter Set, Napco, Japan, 6 Piece 500.00
Dippy Dumper, Windup, Toy 1195.00
Doll, Stuffed, Oilcloth, 1930s, 16 In. 125.00
Doll, Wimpy, Rubber, 1930s 85.00
Doll, Wimpy, Stuffed, 1985, 11 In. 8.50
Doorstop, Popeye, Spinach Can, White Pants, Red Shirt, Stamped P1938, 6 1/2 In. ... 325.00
Eggcup 100.00
Figure, Folk Art, Wooden, 1930s, 2 1/2 In. 75.00
Figure, Popeye, Wooden, Jointed, Jaymar, 5 In. 70.00
Figurine, Celluloid, 5 1/4 In. 195.00
Figurine, Chalkware, 1933 .... 200.00
Figurine, Chalk, Original Paint, 10 In. 45.00
Game, Adventures Of Popeye, Transogram, Box, 1957 .... 135.00 to 140.00
Game, Ball Toss, Linemar, Box 1800.00
Game, Card, Popeye In Various Action Scenes, Ed-U-Cards, 1958, 3 x 4 In. 15.00

Popeye, Toy, Motorcycle, Popeye Patrol,
Movable Arms, Hubley, 5 x 9 In.

Popeye, Toy, Heavy Hitter, J. Chein; Popeye,
Toy, Overhead Puncher, J. Chein & Co.

Game, Juggler, 1929	80.00
Game, Pipe Toss, 1935	55.00
Game, Popeye's Menu Pinball, Durable Toy Co., 1935, 14 x 23 In.	425.00
Game, Ring Toss, 1933	65.00
Game, Ring Toss, Rosebud Art Co., 1937	100.00
Glass, 1920s	50.00
Harmonica, 1929	60.00
Harmonica, Red, Plastic, 3 Step By Step Songs, 1958	39.00
Key Ring, Vinyl, 1950s	10.00
Lamp, Desk, Lamppost, 1930, 16 In.	275.00
Lamp, Figural, Seated, Cross-Legged, Can Of Spinach Between Knees, Vinyl	85.00
Lamp, Popeye, Olive & Sweetpea, Leaded Glass Shade, 6 Sides, 20 1/2 x 13 In.	185.00
Lunch Box, Blue Plastic Dome, 1979	20.00
Lunch Box, Popeye Arm Wrestling With Bluto, 1980	184.00
Mold, Cookie, Tin	85.00
Music Box, Mattel, 1950s	200.00
Music Box, Olive Oyl, Schmid, c.1960	85.00
Music Box, Popeye & Olive Oyl, Japan, c.1960	95.00
Music Box, Popeye Pops Up, Crank, Mattel, 5 1/2 In.	225.00
Night-Light, Figural, Dell, 1950s	85.00
Paint Box, Unused, 1933	75.00
Paint Kit, 3 Numbered Canvas Panels, 6 Oil Paints, Brush, Hasbro, 1958, 7 x 10 In.	49.00
Paint Tin, American Crayon, 1949	20.00
Paperweight, Olive Oyl, Standing, Hubley, 1 1/4 x 1 In.	248.00
Paperweight, Wimpy, Hubley, 3 1/8 x 2 In.	220.00
Pencil, Giant, A Marvelusk Pencil, Box, 1929	80.00
Pencil, Mechanical, Box	50.00 to 55.00
Pencil Box, 1929	30.00
Pencil Box, 1934	50.00
Pencil Box, Eagle Pencil Co., 1929, 10 1/2 In.	120.00
Pin, Olive Oyl, Metal, 1 1/4 In.	15.00
Pin, Popeye, Metal	20.00
Pipe, Yazoo, 1934	75.00
Plate, Ceramic, I Yam So Strong 'cause I Eats My Spinach, TST Co., 7 1/4 In.	135.00
Popeye & Wimpy, Walker, Dated 1964, Box	90.00
Popeye Express, Wheelbarrow, Parrot, Windup, Marx, 1935	395.00
Poster, Popeye, With Robin Williams, 1980, 1 Sheet, 27 x 41 In.	5.00
Punching Bag, Overhead Puncher	4400.00
Puppet, Finger, Molded Rubber, King Features, 1968	65.00
Puzzle, No. 2764-29, Frame Tray, Jaymar, c.1950	25.00
Ring, Flasher, Olive Oyl	15.00
Salt & Pepper, Popeye & Olive Oyl	95.00
Sheet, Popeye & Friends, Famous Studios	200.00
Skater, Linemar	975.00
Soaky	65.00
Soap, Figural, 3 In.	45.00

Soap, Figural, 4 In., Early 1940s 16.00
Soap, Figural, Box, 1930s 65.00
Sparkler, Chein, Box, 1959 .... 375.00
Tank, Turnover, Windup, Linemar 550.00
Toy, Acrobat, Box 4400.00
Toy, Balancing Olive Oyl In Chair, Box, Linemar 4400.00
Toy, Basketball Player, Mechanical, Linemar, Box 4180.00
Toy, Bubble Blowing Set, Box, 1936 .... 150.00
Toy, Bubble Blowing, Battery-Operated, Linemar, Box, 12 In. 2255.00
Toy, Bubble Pipe, World Toy House, 1950s 40.00
Toy, Car, Paddle Wagon, Corgi, Box 395.00
Toy, Carrying Parrot Cages, Windup, 1930s, 8 In. 550.00
Toy, Colorforms, 1957 .... 60.00
Toy, Heavy Hitter, J. Chein .... *Illus* 5225.00
Toy, Marble Shooter, Bag & Box, Akro Agate Co., 1929, 7 x 3 In. 500.00
Toy, Motorcycle, Hubley 5000.00
Toy, Motorcycle, Popeye Patrol, Movable Arms, Hubley, 5 x 9 In. .... *Illus* 6300.00
Toy, Musical, I Turns Me Head As I Play, Box 400.00
Toy, Olive Oyl, Push-Button Puppet 20.00
Toy, On Tricycle, Linemar, Celluloid 875.00
Toy, Overhead Puncher, J. Chein & Co. .... *Illus* 4400.00
Toy, Popeye & Olive Oyl On Roof, Mechanical, Tin Plate, Marx, 1935, 9 1/4 In. 1035.00
Toy, Popeye & Olive Oyl, Juggling, Mechanical, Linemar 4400.00
Toy, Popeye Boxer, Clockwork, Lithographed, Chein 743.00
Toy, Popeye In Barrel, Windup, Tin, J. Chein, 1932, 6 1/2 In. .... 675.00 to 775.00
Toy, Popeye In Dippy Dumper, Windup, Tin 650.00
Toy, Popeye On The Roof, Tin, Jigger, Windup, 1930s 950.00
Toy, Popeye Pushing Wheelbarrow, Windup, Lithographed, Tin, Marx, 1930s, 8 In. 275.00
Toy, Popeye The Pilot, Marx Express Highway, Windup, Tin, Box 150.00
Toy, Popeye The Sailor, Pull Bell Toy, Paper On Wood, Fisher-Price, 12 In. 440.00
Toy, Popeye With Parrot Cages, Walker, Chad Valley 895.00
Toy, Popeye With Parrots, Marx, 1935 .... 225.00
Toy, Popeye With Punching Bag, Clockwork, Tin Plate, Chein, 7 1/4 In. 920.00
Toy, Popeye, Stretch Neck, Windup, Prewar Japan, Box 2250.00
Toy, Punching Bag, Windup 635.00
Toy, Ramp Walker, Marx, c.1960 .... 55.00
Toy, Roller Skating Popeye, Linemar, Box .... 975.00 to 1832.00
Toy, Roly Poly Popeye Target, Original Corks, Knickerbocker, Box, 1958 .... 275.00
Toy, Smoking Popeye, Battery Operated, Linemar, 1950s 1925.00
Toy, Spinach Can, Mechanical Popeye Face, Pipe Pop-Up 95.00
Toy, Spinach Eater, Fisher-Price 795.00
Toy, Surfboard, Pull, Wooden, American Preschool, 1950s 975.00
Toy, Tank, Mechanical, Line-Mar 395.00
Toy, Thumb Drummer, Tin, J. Chein 1045.00
Toy, Tumbling Popeye, Linemar, Box 1350.00
Toy, Turnover Tank, Linemar 1980.00
Truck, Transit Co., Friction 500.00
Viewmaster, 3 Reels, Booklet, Sawyer, 1962 .... 20.00
Watch, Pocket, 1930s 410.00
Wheelbarrow, Express, Windup, Marx 1045.00

PORCELAIN factories that are well known are listed in this book under the
factory name. This category lists pieces made by the less well-known
factories.

Bed Pan, Jonesware Of Ohio 9.00
Bowl, Blue & White, Flared Rim, Flowers, Fruits, China, Xangxi Period, 7 1/2 In. 600.00
Bowl, Floral Enameled, Gilt, Reticulated Rim, Ormolu Fittings, 10 In. 258.00
Bowl, Floral, Molded & Gilded Rim, Shallow, 11 In. 148.00
Bowl, Fukugawa, Polychrome Exterior, Dragon, Interior Carp, 1800s, 16 1/2 x 9 In. .. 825.00
Bowl, Molded Leaf Design, Gilded Leaves, Enameled Floral, Crossed Swords, 11 In. 247.00
Bowl, Open Basketwork Design, 5 In. 20.00
Bowl, Pink Roses, Pale Green Ground, Scalloped, Beaded Rim, Germany, 9 In. 32.00

◆◆◆◆◆◆◆◆◆◆◆◆◆◆◆◆◆◆◆◆◆◆

A hair dryer set for cool can be used to blow the dust off very ornate pieces of porcelain.

◆◆◆◆◆◆◆◆◆◆◆◆◆◆◆◆◆◆◆◆◆◆

Porcelain, Dish, Chicken & Egg Lid, 4 In.;
Porcelain, Dish, 3 Chicks & Eggs Lid,
Basket Weave, 6 1/2 In.

Bowl, Roses, Thuringia, 10 In.	25.00
Bowl, White Rims, Sang De Boeuf, Qianlong, 9 3/8 In., Pair	990.00
Box, Couple On Cover, Yellow Enameled, Ormolu Fittings, 2 3/4 In.	93.00
Box, Floral Enameled & Gilt, Ormolu Fittings, France, Round, 1 3/4 In.	105.00
Box, Trinket, Flowers & Cupid On Lid, 4 1/2 In.	80.00
Bread Plate, Roses, Gold Filigree Border, Give Us This Day, Germany, 10 1/2 In.	40.00
Cachepot, Landscape Scenes, Blue On White, Japan, 8 1/4 In.	110.00
Cake Plate, Flower Spray, Gold Trim, Scalloped, Handles, Austria, Urn, 9 1/2 In.	24.00
Cake Set, Pink Roses, Beaded, Scalloped Green Luster Rim, Silesia, 7 Piece	55.00
Celery, Blackberries, Flat, Silesia	18.00
Centerpiece, Figural, Shell, Calla Lilies, Wood Maidens, Austria, c.1900, 15 In.	800.00
Charger, Woman Portrait, 1840	325.00
Chest, 4 Movable Drawers, Polychrome Florals, Crossed Swords, 5 1/4 In.	412.50
Chocolate Pot, Bluebird, Victoria, Crown, Austria, 10 In.	125.00
Chocolate Set, Grapes & Roses, White Ground, Austria, 15 Piece	395.00
Coffee Set, Floral Sprays, 8 1/4-In. Coffee Pot, Gray's, 15 Piece	219.00
Cracker Jar, Cover, Classical Medallion, Blank, Blenheim, Signed Moreau	150.00
Cup & Saucer, Black Transfer, Woman, Classical Clothes, Gilt Trim, England	16.50
Cup & Saucer, Factory Reserve, Gilt Wreaths, Presentation, 1822-1872	115.00
Cup & Saucer, Flowers, Brown Transfer, Medway, Meakin, Demitasse	12.00
Cup & Saucer, Sunset Scene, Swan, Blue Luster Rim, Gold Bamboo Handle, Japan	6.00
Dessert Set, Roses, Gold Scalloped, Crown Mark, 5 Piece	65.00
Dish, 3 Chicks & Eggs Lid, Basket Weave, 6 1/2 In. .... *Illus*	625.00
Dish, Chicken & Egg Lid, 4 In. .... *Illus*	500.00
Dish, Dragon, Jiaqing Green, Pair	3850.00
Dish, Leaf Shape, Rose On Stem, Eaves, Sitzendorf, c.1890, 11 In.	375.00
Dish, Seated Figure Of Nude On Pumpkin, Black, Lenci, 18 In.	1725.00
Easter Egg, Monogram Of Alexandra Feodorovna, Russia, c.1900	750.00
Figure, Nude, Seated On Lotus Blossom, Arms, Head, Karl Ens, 1920, 12 1/2 In.	402.00
Figurine, Black Man Playing Tambourine, 3 7/8 In.	45.00
Figurine, Blackamoor, White Turban, Purple & Yellow Jacket, c.1760, 6 1/2 In.	2010.00
Figurine, Cockatoo, Will George, 13 In., Pair	350.00
Figurine, Dancing Boy, Gilt-Edged Hat, Tree-Stump Base, Bow, c.1765, 7 3/4 In.	920.00
Figurine, Girl, Sitting, Pigtails, Lace Skirt, Holding Flowers, Sitzendorf, 4 In.	150.00
Figurine, Golfer, Walking, White Knickers, 4 1/2 In.	28.00
Figurine, Man & Woman, Gold Anchor Mark, 13 In., Pair	1320.00
Figurine, Nude, With Water Lily, ENS, Germany, 1930	250.00
Figurine, Oriental Dancer, Seated, Shiny, Nancy China Co., 1942-1950, 13 In.	125.00
Figurine, Tailor, Riding A Goat, Theieme Saxonian, 10 In.	660.00
Fish Bowl, Blue & White, Dragons, Clouds, 19th Century, 14 x 18 In.	1760.00
Fish Bowl, Blue & White, River Scene, Flat Rim, 19th Century, 16 x 24 In.	2750.00
Fish Service, Fish Designs, Early 20th Century, 14 Piece	605.00
Flower Frog, Bashful Nude, September Morn Style, Ivory, Oval Base, 4 1/4 In.	17.50
Flower Frog, Bird, Cobalt, Majolica-Type Glaze, Brown Rock, Japan, 6 3/4 In.	24.00

Flower Frog, Birds, 1 Large, 1 Small, Majolica-Type Glaze, Japan, 6 4 5/8 In. 22.00
Flower Frog, Nude Standing In Flower, Corbett, England, 1800s 85.00
Flower Frog, Nude, Dancing, Art Deco, Scalloped Round Base, Germany, 5 1/2 In. .. 40.00
Flower Frog, Nude, Dancing, Art Deco, White, Oval Base, 6 1/2 x 8 3/4 In. 45.00
Flower Frog, Turtle, White, Pierced Shell, 7 x 2 3/4 In. 20.00
Flowerpot, 4 Cupids, Lion Pulling Cart, Gold Handles, France 245.00
Ginger Jar, Wood Cover, Blue & White, Prunus, Cracked Ice, Kangxi Period, 8 In. ... 825.00
Group, 3 Women & 1 Man, Around Table, 1920, A. Bloch & Co., 8 x 12 x 9 In. 950.00
Group, Nobleman & Cherub, L. Fabris, 17 3/8 In. 110.00
Holder, Denture, Transfer On Lid, Germany 50.00
Humidor, Black Man, Germany, 1910s 395.00
Humidor, Sheep Scene, Sunset Hour, Lewis, Empire Ware, 4 x 5 In. 45.00
Jar, Blue & White, Lopsided Shape, Sage Roundel, Korea, 9 1/2 In. 6325.00
Jar, Blue & White, Scrolling Lotus, Bronze Rim, China, Ming Dynasty, 11 In. 935.00
Jar, Cover, Eagle Finial, Reserves Of Courting Figures, c.1880, 15 In., Pair 1540.00
Jar, Cover, Famille Verte, Baluster, Animals, Flowers, Symbols, 18th Century, 17 In. .. 880.00
Luster, Candy Dish, Blue, Gold Swans, Raised Star, Japan 55.00
Mug, Black Transfer, Entrance To Blackburn Park, 3 In. 15.00
Mug, Harrods, London, Bobbie, 1970s 15.00
Panel, Enameled Oriental Figures, Wooden Frame, 8 1/8 x 5 3/8 In., Pair 143.00
Pitcher, Green & White, Raised Romans, Handle, S.F.A. 45.00
Pitcher, White Prunus Branches, Stippled Brown Ground, Twig Handle, 6 3/4 In. 46.00
Plaque, Blue & White, Dragons, Clouds, Frame, 19th Century, 9 1/4 x 8 In. 247.50
Plaque, The Bride In Prayer, Germany, c.1900, 9 x 7 In. 522.50
Plaques, Rectangular, Painted Flowers, Gilt Frame, c.1830, England, 7 In., Pr. 4485.00
Plate, Flowers, Painted Edge, Gilt Rim., J. Petit, c.1840, 9 1/4 In., 8 Piece 1100.00
Plate, Gilt Scrollwork, Green Border, Center Flowers, Feuillet, 9 1/4 In., 8 Piece 880.00
Plate, Luster Fruit, Gray's, 10 In. 185.00
Plate, Oyster, Floral Decoration, France, 10 In., 12 Piece 220.00
Plate, Scene, 4 Frolicking Nymphs In A Pond, 12 1/4 In. 88.00
Plate, Soft Past, Lee's Type, Floral, 1810, 9 3/4 In. 650.00
Plate, The Cage, Cobalt Blue, Gold Trim, Suhl, 7 1/2 In. 695.00
Plate, Violets, Raised Gilt Decoration, Hand Painted, Scalloped Edge, 10 In. 49.50
Platter, Florals, Scalloped, Gold Rim, Grindley, 14 In. 28.00
Platter, Peony, Blue & White, Booth, 16 In. 52.00
Portrait, Lady Wearing Hat, White Feather, Bronze Frame, 11 x 9 1/2 In. 100.00
Sauce, Cover, Blue Floral, Latticework Borders, Oval, Tournay, 5 1/4 In., Pair 385.00
Stirrup Cup, Hound's Head, Spotted Coat, Gilt Collar, England, c.1825, 5 1/2 In. 1380.00
Sugar & Creamer, Sheraton, Johnson Bros. 20.00
Teapot, Cover, Stand, Japan Pattern, Oblong, New Hall, c.1815, 5 3/4 In. 800.00
Teapot, Figural, Duck, Russia, c.1870 .... 950.00
Temple Jar, Cover, Blue & White, Baluster Shape, Prunus, China, c.1800, 19 In. 357.50
Temple Jars, Blue & White, Deer, Cranes, Pines, China, Kangxi Period, 16 In., Pair 5225.00
Toothpick, 14K Gold Design, China 45.00
Tray, Figural, Woman's Torso, Blossoms, E. Wahliss, Austria, c.1900, 11 1/4 In. 800.00
Tureen, Sauce, Cover, Floral, Gilt Trim, Hard Paste, Locre, 1780, 9 In. 275.00
Tureen, Transfer, Stubbs, 1825 .... 1095.00
Vase, Abstract Decoration, Green, Brown, Blue, Rozenburg, c.1894, 11 1/2 In. 1650.00
Vase, Art Deco, Yellow-Tan Flambe, Eljer, 1920s, 8 3/4 In. 600.00
Vase, Blue & White, Teardrop Shape, Dragons, Clouds, Qianlong, 19th C., 11 3/4 In. 247.50
Vase, Blue Crystalline Over Green Glaze, Adelaide Robineau, c.1905, 4 In. 2860.00
Vase, Bottle Form, Aqua Ground, England, 24 In., Pair 523.00
Vase, Cornucopia, Rococo Revival, Flowers, J. Petit, c.1840, 11 1/2 In., Pair 1760.00
Vase, Cover, Panels Of Foliage, Gilded, Leaf-Scrolled Feet, 13 3/4 In., Pair 8050.00
Vase, Cupid With Bow & Quill, Sitzendorf, c.1887, 12 1/2 In. 250.00
Vase, Deer Handles, Yongzberg, China, c.1723, 11 1/2 In. 660.00
Vase, Famille Verte, France, Late 19th Century, 14 In., Pair 605.00
Vase, Flambe, Teardrop Shape, China, 19th Century, 12 1/2 In. 168.00
Vase, Hand Painted Daisies, Black & White Transfer Portrait, Austria Crown 175.00
Vase, Kutani Decoration, Figures In Shaped Panels, Meiji Period, Japan, 18 In. 357.50
Vase, Pansy Flowers & Green Leaves, Gold Outline, 2 Handles, 8 In. 70.00
Vase, Pedestal, Painted Scrolled Foliage, 13 In., Pair 1210.00
Vase, Scene Of Maidens, Gilt Decoration, 3 Handles, 7 1/2 In. 71.50

Vase, Tulip, Open Blossom & Bud, Yellow, Purple, Puce, England, c.1820, 6 In. 3738.00
Vase, Tulip, Partially Open White Blossom, Striated Bud, England, c.1825, 6 1/4 In. 2300.00
Vase, Worship Of Hera Scene, Austria, Artist 350.00
Vase, Yellow Daffodils, Brown Ground, Silver Overlay, Gorham, 1890, 9 1/4 In. 715.00
Vase, Yellow Roses, Pale Aqua Ground, Gold Trim, Red Crown Mark, 9 In. 55.00
Washbowl & Pitcher Set, Doll's, Floral, Gilt, Box, 1885, 6-In. Pitcher, 5 Piece 425.00
Window Stop, Head Of Bearded Man, Foliage Plume Chapeau, 4 In. 225.00

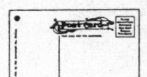

POSTCARDS were first legally permitted in Austria on October 1, 1869. The United States passed postal regulations allowing the card in 1872. Most of the picture postcards collected today date after 1910. The amount of postage can help to date a card. The rates are: 1872 (1 cent), 1917 (2 cents), 1919 (1 cent), 1925 (2 cents), 1928 (1 cent), 1952 (2 cents), 1959 (3 cents), 1963 (4 cents), 1968 (5 cents), 1973 (8 cents), 1975 (7 cents), 1976 (9 cents), 1978 (10 cents), 1981 (12 cents), 1981 (13 cents), 1985 (14 cents), 1988 (15 cents), 1991 (19 cents).

Alabama, Blacks Picking Cotton, Eagle, U.S. Shield 17.50
Albert I Of Belgium Set, 8 Piece .... *Illus* 302.50
Bambi, Paper Holder, Disney, France, 10 Piece 150.00
Barney Oldfield, Racer Lightning Penz 522.50
Baseball, Autographed, Babe Ruth, Swing Bat, Photograph 660.00
Baseball, Autographed, Cy Young 440.00
Baseball, Comiskey Park 11.00
Bernie, Missouri, Baseball Team With Equipment, Unused, c.1910 .... 20.00
Betty Grable, Pinup, El Rancho Vegas 25.00
Beverly Hillbillies Fan Club, Facsimile Signatures Of Cast, 1963, 3 x 5 In. 15.00
Black Boy, Sitting On Chair, By Shanty, Unused, 1940s 6.50
Black Gentleman, Dog, Holds Cigar, Photograph 12.00
Book, Close Encounters, 48 Piece 15.00
Buffalo Bill, Gravesite, Inset Photograph, 1937 .... 4.00
Buffalo Bill, Young, With Rifle, White Border 20.00
Cartoon, WAC Hitting Hitler Over Head With Rolling Pin 12.00
Children, Schoolhouse, Mt. Lebanon, Shaker, Photograph, 1890 .... 85.00
Class With Teacher, Girls, Button Shoes, Photograph, 1910 .... 2.00
Cognac-Bisquit, Alphonse Mucha, 1909 .... *Illus* 4100.00
Columbian Exposition, 1893, 8 Piece 65.00
Elsie & Beauregard, Borden's Family, Traveling Exhibit, 1950s 5.00
Enrico Caruso, 1921 .... 15.00
Everett, Oregon, Waterfront View, E.H. Mitchell 2.00
Fall River, Maine, No. Main Street, Street Cars, Wagons, People, 1920s 7.00
Farmer At R.R. Station, Wonder If I Can Spend That, Boston, Unused, 1908 .... 8.00
Father Christmas Caught In Snow, Louis Wain 330.00
Fenway Park, Yankee Stadium 12.00
Flag Girl, Holding Horn Of Plenty, Flag, U.S. Seal, Used, 1907 .... 15.00

Postcard, Albert I Of Belgium Set, 8 Piece

Postcard, Cognac-Bisquit, Alphonse Mucha, 1909

Postcard, Ship, Titanic, Photograph

Postcard, Socialist Caravan, Horse & Wagon,
Photograph, 1916 Election

Postcard, Women's Suffrage League,
Photograph, 1914

Flood & Ice Gorge, Cincinnati, 1918, 4 Piece	20.00
Florida, Peninsula State, Flag, Flowers, Indian Center, In God We Trust	17.50
Fred Harvey, Map Of Western States Locating Hotel, Dining & Lunch Room	8.00
G.H. Curtis, 8-Cylinder, 40-Horsepower Motorcycle, 1907	495.00
G.H. Curtis, Atop Wind Wagon, Silver Tone	330.00
Golliwog, Courtship, Marriage English, Full Color, c.1910, 6 Piece	300.00
Great Northern Steam Locomotive, Wooden Bridge, Unused, Large	2.00
Grenfell Scene, Tuck, 3 Piece	45.00
Halloween, Peters' Weatherbird Shoes, Advertising	100.00
Inaugural Day, Clinton & Gore, Die Cut, Shape Of America	2.50
Jack Dempsey's Restaurant, Broadway, Unused	10.00
Jersey Cream Coffee, Dollar Coupon, 1910	3.50
Joyful Easter, Baby Chicks, Wicker Basket, 1910	1.50
Kellogg's, Tony The Tiger, Fishing In Lake, Whale, 1966, 3 1/2 x 5 1/2 In.	13.00
Kellogg's Factory, Tony, Yogi Bear, Huckleberry Hound, Crackle, 1960s, 5 1/2 In. ..	50.00
Kokomo, Indiana, Flood, Postmarked 1908	7.00
La Danza Macabra Europea, World War I, 54 Piece	1320.00
Little Black Boy, Outcault, 1903	25.00
Louisiana, Pelican State, 2 Pelicans, Eagle Center	17.50
Louisiana Purchase Exposition, St. Louis, Woven Silk, 1904	495.00
Miller Beer, 1911	20.00
Monday's Child Is Fair Of Face, Swift's Pride Soap, Wiedersheim	65.00
Musical Turn, One-Legged Organ Grinder, Small Monkey, Unused, c.1909	5.00
National Cash Register, 1912	75.00
New Lexington, Ohio, Court House, Leather	6.00
Photograph, Buffalo Bill, Buckskins, Rifle	15.00
Photograph, Eugene Victor Debs, Presidential Campaign	825.00
Rose Bowl, Aerial View, Postmarked 1936	8.00
Roycroft Scenes, 4 Piece	50.00
Santa Claus In Plane, Throwing Toys, Winsch	10.00
Ship, Titanic, Different Times During Sinking, 6 Piece	880.00
Ship, Titanic, Photograph .... *Illus*	650.00

Socialist Caravan, Horse & Wagon, Photograph, 1916 Election .... *Illus*   3600.00
South Family, Photograph, Watervliet, Shaker, 1912 ....   195.00
Springfield Telescope Makers, To Burton Fitzgerald, Meeting Date, 1934 ....   60.00
St. Louis, City Hall, Hold-To-Light, 1905 ....   15.00
St. Louis World's Fair, Buxton & Skinner, 1904, 6 Piece 50.00
State Capitals, c.1910, 18 Piece 25.00
Stockton, California, Harvesting Scene, San Joaquin City, Pacific Novelty Co. 4.00
Sunbonnet Babies, Bliss, 1-Cent Stamp 10.00
Teddy Roosevelt & Hoxsey Seated In Bi-Plane, 1910 ....   192.00
Tournament Of Roses Parade, Pasadena, Ohio President Float, Leather, 1908 ....   15.00
Tri-Plane, Photograph 324.50
U.S. Battleship Alabama, Color Photograph, Unused 20.00
U.S. Grant, 1893 Expo Souvenir, 8 Different Scenes 65.00
Union Station Railroad, Kansas City, 1944 ....   1.50
United Citizens For Nixon, Agnew, Nixon At Piano, 1968 ....   5.00
Votes For Our Mothers, Rose O'Neill, Unused 715.00
War Effort 1915, Embroidered Lace 15.00
Will Rogers Memorial Museum, 1946 ....   1.00
Winseh Halloween Greetings 45.00
Woman's Rights, Woman, Taking $2 From Husband's Pants, 1910 ....   35.00
Women's Suffrage League, Photograph, 1914 .... *Illus*   490.00
World's Fair, Buildings & Scenes, 1939, 12 Piece 24.00

POSTERS have informed the public about news and entertainment events since ancient times. Nineteenth-century advertising or theatrical posters and twentieth-century movie and war posters are of special interest today. The price is determined by the artist, the condition, and the rarity. Other posters may be listed under Political and World War I and II.

A Day At The Races, Marx Brothers, 1937, 27 x 41 In. 5500.00
A Farewell To Arms, Rock Hudson, Jennifer Jones, 1963, 27 x 41 In. 40.00
A Gentleman From Mississippi, President Taft Laughed, Color, 39 x 26 In. 176.00
A Space Odyssey, Movie, 1971, 27 x 41 In. 15.00
Aliena, c.1986, 41 x 27 In. 10.00
American Red Cross, Colorful, 1929, 12 x 17 In. 18.00
American Tobacco Co., Uncle Sam, Cowboy, John Bull, 1899, 15 x 23 In., 4 Pc. 1800.00
Artillery Heroes At Front Say Get Into A Man's Uniform, 27 x 42 In. 50.00
Beech-Nut Gum, Billboard Size, Color, 1951, 8 Ft. 6 In. x 19 Ft. 6 In. 55.00
Black Gold, Kathryn Boyd, Norman Film Mfg. Co., 1928, 27 x 41 In. 1000.00
Black Patti's Troubadours, Lloyd G. Gibbs, Wooden Frame, 1954, 29 x 20 In. 187.00
Buffalo Bill, Chief Of Scouts & Guide For U.S. Army, c.1888, 25 1/2 x 20 In. 7700.00
Bugs Bunny In Space, Batman, Robin & Wonder Woman, Vivid Colors 150.00
Bull-Dogger, Bill Pickett, Norman Film Mfg. Co., 1923, 27 x 41 In. 2000.00
Catlin's Patent Pouch Smoking Tobacco, Kitty, 1890s, 12 x 16 In. 750.00
Champion Tennis Shoes, Woman, With Racket, 1903, 22 1/2 x 16 In. 880.00
Chase & Sanborn's Teas, Metal Border Top & Bottom, 27 x 21 In. 44.00
Chicago Flexible Shaft Co., Get More & Better Wool, Frame, 32 x 39 In. 50.00
Cistani Bros., Greatest Riding Troupe of All Time, c.1960, 21 x 28 In. 80.00
Cleveland Bicycle, Couple, Niagara Lithograph Co., 17 x 24 In. 110.00
Cole Bros. Circus, Something New, Boxing Horses, 28 x 20 1/2 In. 60.00
Colgate & Co.'s Harness & Stable Soaps, Gilt & Plaster Frame, 28 x 33 1/2 In. ..   600.00
Colgate Talc Powder, Lady With Baby, Frame, c.1910 ....   595.00
Compliments Of New York Life Insurance Co., Origin Of Stars & Stripes, Frame .   20.00
Continental Rouge Ferre Tires, Muscled Worker, 1930s, 63 x 46 1/4 In. 325.00
Dorothy Lamour, Sarong, Royal Crown Cola, Cardboard, 1940s, 19 x 36 In. 25.00
East Lynne, Chromolithograph, 28 x 41 In. 93.50
Eureka Mower, Painted Wooden Frame, 23 1/4 x 33 1/4 In. 150.00
F.S. Wolcott, Rabbit Foot Minstrel, Black Man With Cigar, c.1935 ....   195.00
Favor Cycles, Celomoteurs & Motos, 63 x 47 In. 350.00
Ferry Seeds, Children, Flowers 100.00
Foster Hose Supporters, Celluloid Over Cardboard, Frame, 16 1/2 x 8 1/2 In. 303.00
Foster Hose Supporters, Name On Buckles, Woman, Corset, Celluloid, 8 x 17 In. ..   1750.00
Four Freedoms, Norman Rockwell, 1943, 20 x 28 In. 375.00
General Custer, Reunion Of 7th Cavalry 600.00

Greta Garbo, On Linen, 112 x 50 In. 4675.00
Happy The Clown, Brenner Litho Open House, 1954, 18 x 25 In. 4.00
Houdini, 8 x 6 Ft. 8500.00
I Want You, James Montgomery Flagg, Frame, 30 x 42 In. 950.00
International Poultry Food, Makes Hens Lay More Eggs, Frame, 27 x 20 In. 231.00
International Stock Food, Cattle Yard, Wooden Frame, 27 x 21 In. 154.00
Joe Louis, King Levinsky, Norman Film Mfg. Co., 1935 .... 2500.00
John Dillinger, Wanted, FBI, 1934 .... 525.00
John Dillinger, Wanted, Ohio, 1933 .... 200.00
Jungle River Cruise, Disneyland Adventureland, Silk Screen, 54 x 36 In. 497.00
Kar-Mi Swallows A Loaded Gun Barrel, Magician, Color, 28 x 33 In. 375.00
King Bros. & Crisiani, 3 Laughing Clowns With Pig, c.1945, 28 x 41 In. 165.00
King Kong, France, 1 Sheet, 1933 .... 7700.00
King Solomon's Mines, Paul Robeson, Sweden, 1937, 27 x 41 In. 1250.00
Kool, Willy Doing Guard Duty, World War II, 12 x 18 In. 90.00
L' Automobile, Black & Orange Car, 47 1/4 x 31 1/2 In. 550.00
Laroute Des Vosges, Countryside View, 39 1/4 x 24 1/4 In. 250.00
Magniscope & Phonograph, c.1905, 50 x 38 In. 400.00
Michelin, Bibendau, Cigar In Mouth, Pedaling Bicycle, 47 1/4 x 32 In. 800.00
Minstrel Show, 1912, 77 x 41 In. 500.00
Monroe County Fair, Woman With Horse, Frame, 19 x 24 In. 175.00
Montana Frank Shows, Western, 27 x 20 In. 385.00
Never Say Good-Bye, Errol Flynn, Eleanor Parker, 1946, 27 x 41 In. 75.00
Newton Beers In Lost London, Chromolithograph, 40 x 27 1/2 In. 126.50
Oliver Chilled Plow Works, Carved Giltwood Frame, 34 1/2 x 41 1/2 In. 450.00
OM, Open Cockpit Race Car, Grille Of Car, 1924, 6 x 4 1/2 Ft. 2600.00
Order Coal Now, U.S. Fuel Administration, Leyendecker, World War I 517.00
Parker & Watts Circus, Kit Carson, c.1930, 28 x 40 In. 175.00
Pet Evaporated Milk, Colorful, Dated 1927, 10 x 21 In. 39.00
Putman Fire Insurance Co., Putman Leaving Plough, Frame, 28 1/2 x 35 1/2 In. 2400.00
Red Gate Coffee, Color, 1900, 10 x 5 In. 22.00
Remember Belgium, 4th Liberty Loan, World War I, 30 x 20 In. 55.00
Riders In The Sky, Gene Autry & Pat Buttram Signatures, 28 x 22 In. 125.00
Ringling Bros. & Barnum & Bailey, Prairie Bill Rough Riders, 1930, 20 x 28 In. ... 200.00
Sarah Bernhardt, La Dame Aux Camelias, Paper On Canvas, 82 x 29 1/2 In. 1700.00
Star Wars, 10th Anniversary, 24 x 36 In. 25.00
The Enforcer, Clint Eastwood, 1976, 27 x 41 In. 7.00
The Home Run King, Roger Maris, Icicle, Yankee Uniform, 17 x 11 In. 125.00
Tuberculosis Christmas Seals, Color, 1942, 11 x 15 In. 2.25
Tucker Car, Man & His Dream, LucasFilms 18.00
Twinkle Toes, Movie, Colleen Moore, First National Picture, 1926, 41 x 27 In. 485.00
USA Bonds, Boys Scouts Of America, Frame, 23 1/2 x 33 1/2 In. 75.00
Waterfront, John Carradine, J.C. Nash, Fold, 1944, Half Sheet 60.00
Wizard Of Oz, 1939, 24 x 18 In. 20.00
Wizard Of Oz, Judy Garland, Full Cast, 28 x 20 In. 115.00
Wood Taber & Morse's Steam Engine Works, Lithographed, Frame, 30 x 39 In. ... 1500.00
Zaza, Claudette Colbert, Paramount, Tooker Litho, 1938 .... 1200.00

POTLIDS are just that, lids for pots. Transfer-printed potlids had their heyday from the 1840s to the early 1900s. The English Staffordshire potteries made ceramic containers with decorative lids for bear's grease, shrimp or meat paste, cold cream, and toothpaste. Printed advertising and pictures of historical events, portraits of famous people, or scenic views were designed in black and white or color. Reproductions have been made.

Bazin Genuine Beef Marrow, Blue, Staffordshire 450.00
Dr. Johnson, Pratt, Square, Frame 125.00

POTTERY and porcelain are different. Pottery is opaque; you can't see through it. Porcelain is translucent. If you hold a porcelain dish in front of a strong light, you will see the light through the dish. Porcelain is colder to the touch. Pottery is softer and easier to break and will stain more easily because it is porous. Porcelain is thinner, lighter, and more durable. Majolica, faience, and stoneware are all pottery. Additional pieces of pottery are listed in this book in the Art Pottery category and under the factory name.

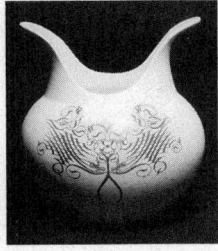

Left to Right: Pottery, Bowl, Ivory, Black, Eva Zeisel, 5 3/4 In.; Pottery, Bowl, Reptiles, Blue-Green, Mexico, Los Castillos, 1980s, 14 In.; Pottery, Figurine, Girl, Mindy, Teddy Bear, Josef, 4 3/4 In.

Ashtray, Streamlined, Green, William J. Gordy, 1 1/5 In.	45.00
Bean Pot, Open Apple, Shows Seeds	65.00
Biscuit Jar, Floral Design, Swan Finial, Silver Fittings, W. Wood & Co., 8 In.	175.00
Bottle, Incised Fish-People, Glossy Ground, Scheier, 8 In.	440.00
Bottle, Pinch, Amber Glaze, Galena, 7 3/4 In.	192.00
Bowl, 3 Figures Over Rim, Green & Blue, Japan, c.1900, 9 In.	247.00
Bowl, Band Of Incised Figures & Fish, Scheier, 5 3/4 x 6 In.	660.00
Bowl, Black, Brown & Gray Branch Type Drips, American Studio, 13 x 3 In.	130.00
Bowl, Blue Glaze, Rowantrees Kilns, Small	90.00
Bowl, Boat Shape, Irregular Matte Stripes, Glidden, 18 1/4 In.	200.00
Bowl, Brown, Dark Brown Speckles, Scatchard, American Studio, 13 x 4 1/2 In.	90.00
Bowl, Combed Design, Mottled Yellow, Green & Brown, Winchcombe, 10 1/2 In.	322.00
Bowl, Edwin Scheier, 11 In.	350.00
Bowl, Green Flambe Glaze, Red Clay Body, W.J. Walley, Marked, 3 x 6 In.	200.00
Bowl, Green, Terra-Cotta, Dandelion Relief, 8 1/4 x 2 3/4 In.	23.00
Bowl, Ivory, Black, Eva Zeisel, 5 3/4 In. .... *Illus*	30.00
Bowl, Leopard Drip Glaze, Earthenware, Maija Grotell, Cranbrook, 6 1/2 In.	935.00
Bowl, Modeled Fish, People, Black, Sgraffito, E. & M. Scheier, 1960, 7 3/4 In.	1320.00
Bowl, Mottled White, Oxblood Craquel Glaze, Earthenware, Maija Grotell, 5 7/8 In.	220.00
Bowl, Reptiles, Blue-Green, Mexico, Los Castillos, 1980s, 14 In. .... *Illus*	500.00
Bowl, Sea-Green Glaze, Lobed, California Faience, 2 3/4 x 6 3/4 In.	287.00
Bowl, Swirl Pattern, Mottled Blue Glossy Interior, E. & M. Scheier, 1950, 15 In.	302.00
Bowl, Woman & Tree, Pillin, 3 3/4 x 5 In.	325.00
Butter, Cover, Cow, Regal	240.00
Candlestick, Ruffled Flower Pot Form, Speckled, William J. Gordy, 5 In., Pair	80.00
Carafe, Coffee, Orange, Pacific Pottery, 1930s, 8 In.	125.00
Carpet Ball, Black & White Stripes, 3 1/8 In.	165.00
Carpet Ball, Stick Spatter, Black & White, 3 In.	225.00
Casserole, Cover, Feathered Brown Satin Glaze, Scheier, 7 x 13 In.	100.00
Cat, Hanging, Dark Yellow, Blue & White Hearts & Dots, Wemysware, 19 In.	632.00
Centerpiece, 3 Stylized Maiden Standards, White Glaze, M. Powolny, 10 In.	2875.00
Chalice, Art Nouveau Designs, Macintyre	1700.00
Chalice, Flared Cup, Feathered High Glaze Clay, Harding Black, 1956, 11 In.	150.00
Chamber Pot, Rose & Fish Scale	360.00
Charger, 3 Panels, 3 Women Embracing Boy & Girl, Scheier, 19 In.	3000.00
Coffeepot, Lid, Peacock, Blue & White	2722.00
Coffeepot, Tin Base & Insert	1000.00
Cooler, Ice Water, Blue & White, Floral Spray Center, 4 Gal.	1350.00
Creamer, Mask Spout, Black Transfer, Richard Reynolds, Philanthropist, Gilt, 5 In.	27.00
Cup, Quatrefoil, Floral Bas Relief, White Glaze, China, Qing Dynasty, 1 1/2 In., Pair	330.00
Cup, Tulips, Verse, Mercer, 5 In.	1100.00
Cuspidor, Blue & Gold, White Ground, 3 Handles, Spain	65.00

Cuspidor, Rectangular Cartouche, Clipped Corners, Remmey Pottery Co. 315.00
Decanter, Hillbilly In Outhouse, Woodpecker, Blue Ridge 75.00
Dish, Abstract Design, White Matte Ground, Brown Rim, Peter Voulkos, 5 In. 250.00
Dish, Feeding, Child's, Blue, Water Reservoir 12.50
Dish, Lobster, 3 Sections, Brad Keller 125.00
Ewer, Painted Design, American Pottery Co., 10 1/2 In. 250.00
Figurine, Bambi, American Pottery, 8 1/2 In. 100.00
Figurine, Dog, Cocker Spaniel, Morten Studios 55.00
Figurine, Dog, Dachshund, Keramos 75.00
Figurine, Girl, Mindy, Teddy Bear, Josef, 4 3/4 In. .... *Illus* 22.00
Figurine, Hedi Schoop, Ballet Dancer, 9 In., Pair 100.00
Figurine, Horse, Art Deco, Tan, 3 1/4 x 3 In. 10.00
Figurine, Jon, Brayton Laguna, 8 In. 65.00
Figurine, Lion, Reclining, Modeled Mane, Curled Tail, Yellow Glaze, 11 In. 575.00
Figurine, Lion, Rectangular Base, White, Blue & Brown, B.F.W. 1911, 9 3/4 In. 385.00
Figurine, Miranda, Brayton Laguna, 7 In. 55.00
Figurine, Nip The Cat, Josef, 1952 .... 15.00
Figurine, Oriental Boy & Girl, Coolie Hats, Vilas, 1950s, 8 In., Pair 45.00
Figurine, Panther, Stalking, Black, 9 1/4 x 1 3/4 In. 12.00
Figurine, Pig, Thistles, Wemyss, 12 1/2 In. 1725.00
Figurine, Setter, Curly White Coat, Dark Gray Spots, R. Wood, 5 /14 In. 1438.00
Figurine, Siamese Cat, Mama, Lying, Josef, 6 In. 22.00
Figurine, Woman, Hedi Schoop, 1990, 12 1/2 In., Pair 80.00
Figurine, Young Woman, Blackamoor, Art Nouveau, Michael Powolny, 1907, 16 In. . 895.00
Flower Frog, Nude, Figural, On Rock, Hands On Head, Maroon, 7 x 5 In. 18.00
Flower Frog, Sphere, Turquoise Over Tan Clay, Glazed Scrolls, Italy, 2 x 3 In. 8.00
Flower Pot, Attached Underplate, Brown, Egg Shape, Dalton 55.00
Flower Pot, Charcoal, Twist Rope Handles, Side Waterers, Baird, 1885, Large 850.00
Flower Pot, Green, Dalton 40.00
Jar, Butter, Indian With Deer, Bail Handle 600.00
Jar, Cosmetic, Crimson Glaze, Gardenias On Cover, Bradshaw, 5 In. 65.00
Jar, Preserving, Peoria Pottery, Brown Glaze 22.00
Jar, Ribbed Handles, Tooled Band, Brown Glaze, Boscowin, 6 In. 38.50
Jar, Tobacco, Basket Weave 900.00
Jardiniere, Lime Green To Dark Green, H. Guimard, France, c.1900, 16 1/2 In. 2300.00
Jardiniere, Sunburst & Circle Relief, Brown Over Green, U.S.A., 7 x 8 In. 26.00
Jug, Blistered Yellow & Brown Glaze, Pillin, Cover, 7 3/4 In. 275.00
Jug, Pinched Spout, Looped Handle, Green Glaze, 16th Century, 5 3/16 In. 690.00
Jug, Pinched Spout, Truncated Body, Tudor Green, 16th Century, 6 3/4 In. 1035.00
Mug, Horse, Prancing, Blues, Hadley, 4 5/8 In. 25.00
Mug, Puzzle, With Frog 195.00
Nappy, Brown Design, Yellow Glossy, Poillion, 4 1/2 x 3 3/4 In. 45.00
Paperweight, Mottled Ocher & Yellow, Relief Scarab, 5 7/8 In. 2875.00
Pie Plate, Amber Spotted Glaze, Galena, 9 1/2 In. 82.50
Pie Plate, Lettuce Ware, Wannopee, 6 1/4 In. 60.00
Pie Plate, Star Pottery 110.00
Pitcher, Brown, Margaret Mears Gabriel, 1940s, 9 In. 65.00
Pitcher, Figural, Floral, Scroll Design, Raised, Victorian, 11 3/4 In. 50.00
Pitcher, Flambe, Wannopee, 10 In. 450.00
Pitcher, Green Glaze, William J. Gordy, 2 In. 20.00
Pitcher, Shakespeare Festival, Ford's Theater In 1892, Haynes & Bennet, 7 In. 150.00
Pitcher, Spiral Pansy, Blue Ridge 60.00
Pitcher, Stag, Blue Top & Base 925.00
Pitcher & Bowl, Rose & Fish Scale, Blue & White 210.00
Planter, Blue Ridge Mountain Boys, Tree Stump, Jug & Snake 75.00
Planter, Native Girl, By Hut, Hollywood Ceramics 30.00
Planter, Wolfhound, Girl, Figural, Pink Dress, Brayton Laguna, 10 5/8 In. 60.00
Plate, Feather Design, Gray, Square, Glidden, 7 In. 15.00
Plate, Historical Buildings, Black Transfer, France, 8 5/8 In., Pair 495.00
Plate, Horse, Blues, Hadley, 6 In. 11.00
Plate, Lettuce Ware, Wannopee, 7 3/4 In. 40.00
Plate, Thames River Scenes, Pallisy Pottery, Blue & White, 9 In. 40.00

Poultry Fount, Albany Slip, Dalton Pottery 30.00
Relish, Lettuce Ware, Wannopee, 7 3/4 In. 125.00
Relish, Lobster, Brad Keller 48.00
Rolling Pin, Swirl, Blue & White 1125.00
Rolling Pin, Wildflower, Cash Store, Frank C. Burch, Coshocton, Ohio 650.00
Soap Dish, Wildflower, Rectangular 170.00
Sugar, Cover, Hen, Regal 135.00
Sugar & Creamer, Pink Glaze, William J. Gordy, 3 In. 55.00
Sugar & Creamer, Semi-Matte Black Glaze, William J. Gordy, 4 In. 75.00
Syrup, Enamel Over Glaze, Avalon Faience, David Francis Haynes, 5 1/2 In. 125.00
Syrup, Majolica, Edwin Bennett, 1846 .... 155.00
Teapot, Chicken, Chick Finial, Black Glaze 22.00
Teapot, Light Orange, Pacific Pottery Co., 1930s, 7 In. 85.00
Teapot, Rebecca At The Well, Brown Glaze, 6 In. .... 45.00 to 95.00
Teapot, Sailing Ships, Della Robbia 1100.00
Teapot, Strawberry, Hand-Enameled, England 585.00
Teapot, Swirl, Blue & White, Bail Handle 775.00
Umbrella Stand, Abstract Relief Pattern, Sargon, c.1955, 20 In. 258.00
Umbrella Stand, Stags, Deer, Oak Trees & Pheasant, Blue, Large 1600.00
Urn, Vase Shape, Oxblood, Catalina, 5 In. 195.00
Vase, Abstract Figure All Sides, Sponged Ground, Pillin, 1 1/2 In. 2600.00
Vase, Band Of Stylized Doves, California Faience Pottery, c.1924, 6 1/2 In. 357.00
Vase, Blue, Brown, Over Mottled Olive, Williams, American Studio, 13 x 7 In. 450.00
Vase, Blue, Green, Brown, Sand, Desert Sands, 5 In. 20.00
Vase, Blue-Green, R. Carlson, 1923 .... 65.00
Vase, Bottle Shape, 2 Women In Blue, Mottled Ground, Pillin, 15 In. 450.00
Vase, Bowl Shape, Green & Cobalt Blue Bubbled, North State Pottery, 3 1/2 In. 48.00
Vase, Broken & Jagged Glaze, Bauche, 1920s, 9 3/4 In. 450.00
Vase, Brown, Green & Gold Crystalline Glaze, Pierrefonds, 9 In. 300.00
Vase, Bulbous, Matte Green, Yellow & Brown, Fantoni, 9 x 8 In. 365.00
Vase, Bulbous Body, Purple & Ivory Flambe Glaze, Christopher Dresser 500.00
Vase, Carnelian Red, Silver Overlay Tulips, B. Moore, 1900, 7 In. 690.00
Vase, Catalin, Yellow, Burgundy, Fluted, 5 In. 38.00
Vase, Crystalline Drip Glaze, William Jervis, 4 In. 850.00
Vase, Curved Buttress Handles, Frey 250.00
Vase, Dark Brown Matte Glaze, Vertical Stripes, E. & M. Scheier, 1950, 33 In. 1100.00
Vase, Dark Cobalt Blue, 3 Small Shoulder Handles, Bybee, 11 1/4 x 6 In. 200.00
Vase, Design Outline In Brown, Green Ground, Austria, 11 1/2 In. 900.00
Vase, Dutch Sunset Scene, Multicolored, Haynes Ware, 5 x 6 In. 28.00
Vase, Everted Rim, Stylized Tulip Field, C.M. Beryen, Signed, 10 /4 In. 115.00
Vase, Figure Resting On Rock In Relief, Green, Japan, c.1900, 7 In. 165.00
Vase, Flared & Rolled Silver Mouth, Harrach, 6 In. 365.00
Vase, Flaring Rim, Canary Yellow Glaze, Natzler, 6 3/4 In. 1300.00
Vase, Floor, Ribs, Cream, U.S.A., 9 x 18 In. 22.00
Vase, Floral Spray, Flared, Pedestal, Ivory Ground, Trenton Potteries Co., 8 In. 45.00
Vase, Gray-Purple, Shell & Metal Mounted, Continental, 7 1/2 In. 143.00
Vase, Green Feathered Matte, 2 Handles, Bybee, 7 In. 150.00
Vase, Green Flambe, Red, Yellow & Green, Bretby, 5 1/2 In. 145.00
Vase, Green Luster Leaves, Swastika Keramos Ware, 10 1/2 In. 1250.00
Vase, Horizontal Stripes, White Glaze, Robert Arneson, 1954, 6 1/4 In. 303.00
Vase, Horses, Pillin, 7 In. 395.00
Vase, Incised Figures Of Pregnant Women, Animals, Scheier, 18 1/2 In. 1320.00
Vase, Japanesque Vignettes On White, Mary P., 9 1/4 In. 575.00
Vase, Mottled Green, Gray Interior, Cube, Glidden, 4 In. 22.00
Vase, Multicolor Roundel Design, Herman Kahler, c.1925, 12 In. 185.00
Vase, Nicodemus, Carved, 4 In. 160.00
Vase, Painted Woman & Horse, Periwinkle Blue, Pillin, 6 3/4 In. 380.00
Vase, Paneled Neck, Della Robbia, 9 In. 700.00
Vase, Pink Filigree, Cream Ground, 3 Gold Footed, Bulbous, Collins, 6 1/2 x 6 In. ... 95.00
Vase, Polychrome Enamel Figure In Landscape, Japanese Export, 24 1/2 In. 95.00
Vase, Polychrome Floral, Cream Ground, Carter, Stabler & Adams, c.1925, 11 In. 165.00
Vase, Raised Spikes Of Clay, Brown Matte Glaze, 8 x 7 In. 500.00

Vase, Rim Hand Pinched Into Ruffles, Marco Pottery, 4 1/2 In. 125.00
Vase, Rose & Purple Luster, Fraunfelter China Co., 6 In. 270.00
Vase, Sang De Boeuf, Bybee, 5 3/4 x 4 In. 50.00
Vase, Silver Mounted, Lucien Gaillard 1760.00
Vase, Spherical, Narrow Mouth, Brown, Abstract Slip, P. Voulkos, c.1950, 15 In. 4830.00
Vase, Stylized Maidens, Amid Trees, Gold Ground, Edouard Cazaux, 12 In. 2070.00
Vase, Tan Luster Glaze, Islamic Arabesques Scrolls, 15 In. 325.00
Vase, Tulip, 1930, Dalton, Small 275.00
Vase, Turquoise Glaze, Royal Crown Pottery, 1909, 7 1/2 In. 65.00
Vase, Turquoise, Glidden, 3 1/2 x 4 In. 22.00
Vase, Violet, Pink, Broadmoor, 4 In., Pair 70.00
Vase, Woman With Birds, Pillin, 6 In. 425.00
Vase, Woman With Flower & Bird, Pillin, 6 In. 350.00
Vase, Yellow Crackle Glaze, Oriental Shape, Hazel Bray 325.00
Vase, Young Girl, Yellow Outfit, Green, Austria, 8 In. 900.00
Vessel, Closed-In Rim, Incised Fish-People, Scheier, 5 x 4 In. 440.00
Wall Pocket, Face With Hands Holding Browneric Gronberg, 9 x 6 In. 350.00
Wall Pocket, Green Pepper, Green Leaves, White Flower, 4 3/4 In. 12.00

POWDER FLASKS AND POWDER HORNS were made to hold the
gunpowder used in antique firearms. The early examples were made of horn
or wood; later ones were of copper or brass.

POWDER FLASK, Brass Cap, Tin, Civil War, 4 1/2 In. 45.00
Copper, Embossed Dog & Pheasants 69.00
Flat, Brass Fittings, Revolutionary War, 9 3/4 In. 170.00
Musketeer's, Horn Body, Belt Hook, Germany, c.1650, 9 In. 850.00
Pewter Cap, Hazard Powder Co., Paper Label, Painted Green, 7 In. 85.00
POWDER HORN, Bullet Compartment, Floral Carved, Pivoted, European, c.1700 ...... 350.00
Carved Spout, Wire Wrap, Zulu Wars Period, 1870s 475.00
Engraved, Fish, Dogs, Indians, Eagle, 11 In. 2860.00
Etched Scroll Design, Center Initials, America, 18th Century, 13 1/2 In. 137.00
Fighting Soldiers, Levi Gaschet, November 30, 1775, 15 In. 9200.00
Gunner's, Priming, Revolutionary War 450.00
Incised Compass Design, Buckshot Highlighted, No Plug, 7 1/2 In. 115.00
Pewter Mounted, Scotland, 16 In., Pair 165.00
Red & Black, Painted, Cloth Strap, Cowry Shells 55.00
Relief Carved Animal, Horsehead, Lion Body, Inscription, 10 1/2 In. 55.00
Revolutionary War, Germantown, Monmouth, Valley Forge, 1777 .... 2200.00
Scratch Carved Design, 18th Century, 17 In. 110.00
Ships, Buildings & Geometric Devices, Joseph Hollifler, Feb. 21, 1776, 13 In. 4950.00

PRATT ware means two different things. It was an early Staffordshire pottery,
cream-colored with colored decorations, made by Felix Pratt during the late
eighteenth century. There was also Pratt ware made with transfer designs   PRATT
during the mid-nineteenth century in Fenton, England. Reproductions of the   FENTON
transfer-printed Pratt are being made.

Figurine, Dog, Seated, Spotted Brown Dimpled Coat, c.1805, 2 2/3 In. 690.00
Figurine, Eagle, Spotted Plumage, Brown Crest, c.1810, 9 5/8 In. 2875.00
Figurine, Hawk, Ochre Sponged Neck And Breast, c.1805, 6 5/8 In. 2300.00
Figurine, Squirrel, Pricked Ears, Nut In Paw, 1800-1810, 6 3/4 In. 1150.00
Jar, Cavalier Lid, Transfer Design 245.00
Jar, Lady, Boy & Mandolin Transfer Lid, Seaweed Ground 495.00
Jar, Polychrome Scene, Middle Eastern City, Transfer Design, 3 1/4 In. 155.00
Jar, Seashells Lid, Transfer Design, Large 245.00
Jug, Cider, Barnyard Fowl In Reserve, c.1800, 7 3/4 In. 1430.00
Lid, Pegwell Bay, Transfer Design, 4 In. 77.00
Perfume Pot, Washington Crossing The Delaware On Lid, Transfer Design 522.50
Pitcher, Lord Jarvis Both Sides 950.00
Tea Caddy, Mandarin Figures, Pearlware, 5 3/4 In. 126.00
Teapot, Woman, Bonnet, Arm Forms Handle, Other Arm Spout, 7 13/16 In. 460.00
Toby Mug, Hearty Good Fellow, 11 In. 975.00

PRESSED GLASS was first made in the United States in the 1820s, after the invention of glass pressing machines. Hundreds of patterns of pressed glass were made in complete table settings. Although the Boston and Sandwich Works was the most famous of the pressed glass factories, there were about sixteen other factories making pressed glass from 1830 to 1850, and still more from 1850 to 1900, when pressed glass reached its greatest popularity. It is now being widely reproduced. The pattern names used in this listing are based on the information in the book *Pressed Glass in America* by John and Elizabeth Welker. There may be pieces of pressed glass listed in this book in other categories, such as Lamp, Ruby, Sandwich, and Souvenir.

1000-Eye pattern is listed here as Thousand Eye	
Acanthus pattern is listed here as Ribbed Palm	
Acorn Band, Spooner, Flint	45.00
Acorn Medallion pattern with beading is listed here as Beaded Acorn Medallion	
Actress, Bowl, Footed, 4 1/2 In.	30.00
Actress, Bread Tray, Miss Nielson	85.00
Actress, Cake Stand, Annie & Maud, Frosted Base	125.00
Actress, Compote, 10 In.	350.00
Actress, Creamer, 5 1/2 In.	95.00
Actress, Goblet	85.00
Actress, Jam Jar	115.00
Actress, Pitcher	350.00
Actress, Platter, Bread	95.00
Actress, Sauce, Footed	15.00
Actress, Spooner, 6 In.	95.00
Actress, Sugar & Creamer	138.00
Admiral Dewey pattern is listed here as Spanish American	
Adonis, Compote	20.00
Alabama, Mustard, Green	35.00
Alabama, Toothpick	70.00
Alaska, Banana Boat, Enameled Elephant Ears, Green	165.00
Alaska, Berry, Master, Green	75.00
Alaska, Creamer	45.00
Alaska, Spooner	45.00
Alaska, Sugar & Creamer, Yellow	170.00
Alaska Variant, Sugar & Creamer, Yellow	110.00
Alhambra, Goblet	425.00
Almond Thumbprint, Pomade	95.00
Almond Thumbprint, Sugar, 5 1/2 In.	95.00
Amazon, Creamer, Child's	25.00 to 35.00
Amazon, Spooner, Child's	30.00 to 35.00
Amberette, Bowl, Oval, 9 x 5 1/2 In.	135.00
Amberette, Bowl, Scalloped, Amber Crosses, 7 In.	195.00
Amberette, Klondike, Creamer, Square	285.00
Amberette, Pitcher	245.00

Pressed Glass, American Shield

Pressed Glass,
Arched Grape

Pressed Glass,
Beaded Grape

Pressed Glass,
Bethlehem Star

Pressed Glass,
Bellflower

Amberette, Relish, Oval, 6 x 9 1/4 In.	175.00
Amberette, Salt & Pepper	150.00
Amberette, Spooner, Square	225.00
Amberette, Tumbler	85.00
Amberette, Vase, 8 In.	18.00
Amberette, Vase, Trumpet	275.00
American Shield, Goblet	50.00
Anthemion, Sugar, Cover	25.00
Apollo, Goblet, Frosted	36.00 to 38.00
Apollo, Pitcher, Water, Frosted, Applied Reeded Handle	79.00
Apollo, Syrup, Engraved Tulip Design	95.00
Arch & Forget-Me-Not, Jar, Cover	50.00
Arched Grape, Goblet	15.00 to 28.00
Arched Leaf, Plate, 10 In.	15.00
Arched Leaf, Plate, Bread	20.00
Argent, Wine	20.00
Argus, Celery Vase, Flint	85.00
Argus, Eggcup, Flint	15.00
Argus, Goblet	75.00
Argus, Mustard Pot, Pewter Lid, Hinged, Bail Handle	300.00
Argus, Tumbler, Flint, 3 5/8 In.	5.00
Art, Sugar, Cover	23.00
Art, Tumbler	30.00
Ashburton, Bottle, Barber, Pewter Lip & Screw-Off Cap, 7 3/4 In.	11.00
Ashburton, Eggcup, Flint, 8 Piece	150.00
Ashburton, Goblet	45.00
Ashburton, Sugar, Cover, 7 3/8 In.	16.50
Ashburton, Vase, Scalloped Rim, Applied Baluster Stem, 10 1/2 In.	22.00
Ashburton, Whiskey, Handled, Flint	125.00
Ashman, Cake Stand, 9 In.	70.00
Atlanta, Cake Stand, Square	95.00
Atlanta, Compote, 8 3/8 x 8 1/2 In.	35.00
Atlanta, Sugar, Cover, Etched	70.00
Atlanta, Syrup, Lion Heads, Frosted, Square	225.00
Atlas, Butter, Cover	60.00
Atlas, Creamer, Gold Trim, Footed	18.00 to 30.00
Atlas, Goblet	22.00
Austrian, Nappy, Cover, Handles	20.00
Aztec, Punch Cup	5.00
Baby Face, Pitcher	275.00
Baby Thumbprint pattern is listed here as Dakota	
Bakewell Block, Butter, Cover	125.00
Balder pattern is listed here as Pennsylvania	
Balky Mule pattern is listed here as Currier & Ives	
Ball & Bar, Tumbler, 4 In.	14.00

Baltimore Pear, Butter, Cover 60.00
Banded Barrel, Toothpick 20.00
Banded Buckle, Goblet, Miniature 25.00
Bar & Block, Nickel Plate Glass Co., Clear 33.00
Bar & Diamond pattern is listed here as Kokomo
Barberry, Bowl, Cover, Oval Berries, 8 In. 40.00
Barberry, Celery 40.00
Barberry, Compote, 8 In. 120.00
Barberry, Eggcup 26.00
Barley, Bowl, Oval, 6 x 8 1/2 In. 18.50
Barley, Cake Stand 57.00
Barley, Relish, Handles, 9 3/4 In. 15.00
Barley & Oats pattern is listed here as Wheat & Barley
Barley & Wheat pattern is listed here as Wheat & Barley
Barrel Honeycomb, see also the related pattern Honeycomb
Barreled Block pattern is listed here as Red Block
Basket Weave, Basket, Amber Spun Rope Handle, Blue, 6 1/4 In. 118.00
Basket Weave, Goblet, Amber 28.00
Basket Weave, Tray, Water, Scenic Center 30.00
Bead & Scroll, Pitcher 55.00
Bead & Scroll, Tumbler, 6 In. 40.00
Bead & Swirl, Breakfast Set, Blue, 4 Piece 325.00
Beaded Acorn Medallion, Goblet 45.00
Beaded Bull's-Eye & Drape pattern is listed here as Alabama
Beaded Dewdrop pattern is listed here as Wisconsin
Beaded Frog's Eye, Goblet 36.00
Beaded Grape, Bowl, Square, Green, 6 1/2 In. 20.00
Beaded Grape, Cake Stand, Square 70.00
Beaded Grape, Compote, Green 55.00
Beaded Grape, Creamer 30.00
Beaded Grape, Creamer, Green .... 35.00 to 50.00
Beaded Grape, Cruet, Green 95.00
Beaded Grape, Saltshaker, Green 47.50
Beaded Grape, Toothpick, Emerald, Gold Trim .... 50.00 to 75.00
Beaded Grape Medallion, Banded, Goblet 32.00
Beaded Grape Medallion, Banded, Goblet, Buttermilk 45.00
Beaded Grape Medallion, Pitcher, Water, Handle 155.00
Beaded Grape Medallion, Spooner 30.00
Beaded Loop, Pitcher, Milk 15.00
Beaded Ovals In Sand, Table Set, 4 Piece 325.00
Beaded Scroll, Creamer 40.00
Beaded Star pattern is listed here as Shimmering Star
Beaded Swirl, Sugar, Cover, Emerald Green, 3 Footed, 7 1/2 In. 45.00
Beaded Swirl & Disc, Berry Set, 7 Piece 150.00
Beaded Tulip, Pitcher 55.00
Bearded Head pattern is listed here as Viking
Bearded Man pattern is listed here as Queen Anne
Beehive, Bread Plate, Frosted 65.00
Belladonna, Butter, Cover, Green 25.00
Bellflower, Bowl, Scalloped Rim, 8 3/8 In. 60.50
Bellflower, Creamer, 7 In. 49.50
Bellflower, Eggcup .... 30.00 to 45.00
Bellflower, Goblet .... 45.00 to 70.00
Bellflower, Lamp, Brass Stem, Marble Base, 9 In. 33.00
Bellflower, Plate, 6 In. 125.00
Bellflower, Salt, Footed, Master 55.00
Bellflower, Sauce 14.00
Bellflower, Syrup, 6 1/2 In. 575.00
Bellflower, Tumbler, Flint, 7 Piece 490.00
Bellflower, Wine, Flared, Hexagonal Stem, 3 7/8 In. 38.00
Bellflower Double Vine, Plate, 10 1/2 In. 12.00
Bellflower Double Vine, Plate, Bread 20.00
Bent Buckle pattern is listed here as New Hampshire

Bethlehem Star, Cruet, Indian Glass 20.00
Bethlehem Star, Goblet 25.00
Bethlehem Star, Tumbler 30.00
Bird & Strawberry, Bowl, 10 In. 45.00
Bird & Strawberry, Bowl, Cover, Vegetable 85.00
Bird & Strawberry, Butter, Cover .... 60.00 to 100.00
Bird & Strawberry, Compote, Cover, 10 In. 145.00
Bird & Strawberry, Creamer, Red & Blue Trim, 5 In. 95.00
Bird & Strawberry, Pitcher, Reds & Blues, 5 In. 95.00
Bird & Strawberry, Punch Cup 18.00
Bird & Strawberry, Sugar & Creamer 110.00
Bird & Strawberry, Wine 70.00
Birds At Fountain, Goblet .... 45.00 to 55.00
Bleeding Heart, Wine 130.00
Block, Sugar Shaker, Red Flashed, c.1890 .... 175.00
Block & Bar, Creamer, Flint, 1850s 125.00
Block & Fan pattern is listed here as Romeo
Block & Fine Cut pattern is listed here as Fine Cut & Block
Block & Prism, Celery Vase 18.00
Block & Star pattern is listed here as Valencia Waffle
Block With Thumbprint, Celery Vase, Flint 100.00
Block With Thumbprint, Goblet 100.00
Bluebird pattern is listed here as Bird & Strawberry
Bohemian Grape, Tumbler, Red 40.00
Bowtie, Goblet 62.50
Box-In-Box, Toothpick 30.00
Branched Tree, Pitcher 65.00
Brazen Shield, Goblet 60.00
Britannic, Dish, Honey 65.00
Britannic, Toothpick, Red Flashed 110.00
Broken Column, Compote, Cover, Square, 5 In. 40.00
Broken Column, Jam Jar, Glass Cover 110.00
Broughton pattern is listed here as Pattee Cross
Bryce pattern is listed here as Ribbon Candy
Bucket pattern is listed here as Oaken Bucket
Buckle, Goblet 18.00
Buckle & Star, Sugar 18.50
Bulging Loops, Saltshaker, Yellow Cased 85.00
Bull's-Eye, Tumbler 70.00
Bull's-Eye & Daisy, Decanter, 2 Wines, Green, Gold Trim, 3 Piece 95.00
Bull's-Eye & Daisy, Goblet, Clear, Green Eyes 17.00
Bull's-Eye & Diamond Point, Celery 185.00
Bull's-Eye & Fan, Bowl, Green, 5 x 3 1/2 In. 18.00
Bull's-Eye & Fan, Celery Dish, 12 x 7 In. 45.00
Bull's-Eye & Spearhead, Butter, Cover 65.00
Bull's-Eye & Spearhead, Cruet 45.00

Pressed Glass, Bull's Eye With Diamond Point

Pressed Glass, Croesus

Pressed Glass, Cube

Bull's-Eye With Diamond Point, Goblet, Flint 65.00
Bull's-Eye With Diamond Point, Pitcher 110.00
Bullet Emblem, Sugar Bowl 350.00
Button Arches, Condiment Set, 5 Piece 100.00
Button Arches, Creamer, Ruby Stained, Etched 35.00
Button Arches, Syrup, Souvenir, Ruby Stained 170.00
Button Panel, Spooner, Child's, Gold Trim 50.00
Button Panel, Sugar, Cover, Child's 125.00
Buttressed Sunburst, Wine 15.00
Cabbage Rose, Goblet 44.00
Cabbage Rose, Relish, Oval 15.00
Cabbage Rose, Wine .... 36.00 to 42.50
Cable, Bowl, 9 In. 45.00
Cable, Eggcup .... 50.00 to 55.00
Cable, Goblet, Flint 110.00
Cactus, Tumbler 28.00
Cadmus, Cake Stand, 9 1/4 In. 38.00
California pattern is listed here as Beaded Grape
Camel Caravan, Pitcher, Etched 65.00
Camel Caravan, Tumbler, Etched 25.00
Cameo pattern is listed here as Profile & Sprig
Canadian, Celery Vase 75.00
Candlewick as a pressed glass pattern is properly named *Banded Raindrop*. There is
also a pattern called *Candlewick*, which has been made by Imperial Glass Corporation
since 1936. It is listed in this book in the Imperial category.
Candy Ribbon pattern is listed here as Ribbon Candy
Cane, Goblet, Amber 32.00
Cane, Goblet, Vaseline 45.00
Cane, Goblet, Yellow 27.50
Cane, Water Set, 6 Piece 150.00
Cape Cod, Goblet 55.00
Cape Cod, Jam Jar 65.00
Cardinal pattern is listed here as Cardinal Bird
Cardinal Bird, Goblet 45.00
Carolina, Sugar, Cover, Frosted, Enamel Floral 32.50
Cat On Pillow, Toothpick, Amber 65.00
Cathedral, Cruet, Amber 135.00
Celtic Cross, Compote, Cover, Footed, Square, 6 1/2 In. 83.00
Centennial, Goblet, 1876 .... 20.00
Ceres pattern is listed here as Profile & Sprig
Chain & Shield, Plate, Bread 15.00
Chain & Star Band, Goblet 30.00
Chandelier, Celery 30.00
Checkerboard, Wine 17.50
Chestnut Band, Butter, Cover 13.00
Chrysanthemum Leaf, Bowl, Gold Trim, 6 In. 20.00
Chrysanthemum Leaf, Tumbler 35.00
Church Windows pattern is listed here as Tulip Petals
Classic Medallion, Creamer 30.00
Classic Medallion, Spooner 35.00
Clear Block, Goblet, Ruby Stain 25.00
Coin Spot pattern is listed in this book in its own category
Colonial Panel, Bowl, Flared, Star Base, 9 x 2 3/4 In. 8.00
Colorado, Bowl, Violet, Blue, Gold Trim 45.00
Colorado, Cake Stand, Green, Gold Trim, 9 1/4 In. 125.00
Colorado, Creamer, Green, Large 45.00
Colorado, Spooner, Green 25.00
Colorado, Sugar, Cover, Green, Etched 50.00
Colorado, Sugar, Green, Gold Trim 110.00
Colorado, Violet Bowl, Cobalt Blue 65.00
Columbian Coin, Goblet, Frosted 100.00
Columbian Coin, Toothpick, Frosted 100.00
Comet, Goblet .... 95.00 to 125.00

Compact pattern is listed here as Snail
Constitution, Bread Plate, Liberty & Freedom 65.00
Continental Hall, Bread Plate 75.00
Corcoran, Goblet 30.00
Cord & Tassel, Cake Stand, 10 1/4 In. 65.00
Cord Drapery, Wine 37.50
Cornell, Wine, Green, Gold Trim 45.00
Cornucopia, Platter, Blue, 12 In. 70.00
Cornucopia, Sugar & Creamer, Cover, Blue 55.00
Cosmos pattern is listed in this book as its own category
Cottage, Cake Stand, Blue 86.00
Cottage, Goblet 28.00
Cottage, Pitcher 95.00
Croesus, Berry Bowl, Green 235.00
Croesus, Berry Bowl, Purple 260.00
Croesus, Berry Set, Green, Gold Trim, 6 Piece 165.00
Croesus, Butter, Cover, Green .... 150.00 to 265.00
Croesus, Celery Vase, Green, Gold Trim 130.00
Croesus, Compote, Jelly, Stem, Green 255.00
Croesus, Creamer, Green 235.00
Croesus, Cruet, Amethyst, Gold Trim 375.00
Croesus, Salt & Pepper, Green 160.00
Croesus, Sauce, Footed, Green 65.00
Croesus, Spooner, Amethyst 55.00
Croesus, Sugar & Creamer, Green 250.00
Croesus, Sugar, Cover, Purple 185.00
Croesus, Table Set, Green, 4 Piece 395.00
Croesus, Toothpick, Purple 235.00
Croesus, Water Set, Green, Gold Trim, 7 Piece 480.00
Crowfoot, Cake Stand 40.00
Crowfoot, Goblet 34.00
Crown Jewels is a name used for two different patterns listed here as Chandelier or
Queen's Necklace
Crystal Wedding, Banana Stand 90.00
Crystal Wedding, Compote, Cover, Pair 60.00
Crystal Wedding, Pitcher, 12 In. 85.00
Crystal Wedding, Relish, 7 1/2 x 4 In. 24.00
Crystal Wedding, Tankard 165.00
Cube, Butter, Cover .... 35.00 to 40.00
Cube with Fan pattern is listed here as Pineapple & Fan
Cupid & Psyche pattern is listed here as Psyche & Cupid
Cupid & Venus, Bread Tray 45.00
Cupid & Venus, Cordial 85.00
Cupid & Venus, Creamer 65.00
Cupid's Hunt, Berry Set, 5 Piece 135.00
Currier & Ives, Bread Plate 85.00
Currier & Ives, Goblet 20.00
Currier & Ives, Pitcher, Milk 65.00
Curtain, Bowl, Cover, 7 In. 125.00
Curtain Tieback, Goblet 18.00
Curtain Tieback, Sugar 20.00
Cut Log, Cruet, Original Stopper 50.00
Cut Log, Goblet 55.00
Cut Log, Sugar, Cover 55.00
Cyclone, Creamer, Fern Etch 30.00
Dahlia With Petal, Toothpick, Green, Gold Trim 150.00
Dahlia With Petal, Tumbler, Emerald Green, Gold 30.00
Daisies, Toothpick, Frosted 20.00
Daisies, Vase, Pedestal, 14 In. 85.00
Daisies in Oval Panels pattern is listed here as Bull's-Eye & Fan
Daisy & Button, Ashtray, 3 Footed, 3 3/4 In. 4.50
Daisy & Button, Ashtray, Black Amethyst, Kettle Type, 3 3/4 In. 8.00

Daisy & Button, Berry Set, Amberette, 11 Piece 225.00
Daisy & Button, Bowl, Amber, 6 Sides, 8 3/4 In. 30.00
Daisy & Button, Butter, Cover, Triangular, Blue 65.00
Daisy & Button, Compote, Scalloped, 8 3/8 x 9 5/8 In. 38.00
Daisy & Button, Goblet, Blue 22.50
Daisy & Button, Hat, Amber, 2 3/8 In. .... 14.00 to 20.00
Daisy & Button, Saltshaker, Pewter Cap, Yellow, Pair 50.00
Daisy & Button, Table Set, Prisms, 4 Piece 150.00
Daisy & Button, Toothpick, Brim Top Hat Shape, Blue 55.00
Daisy & Button With Crossbar, Compote, Blue, Square, 13 In. 175.00
Daisy & Button With Crossbar, Sugar, Cover, Blue 75.00
Daisy & Button With Crossbar, Tray, Amber 45.00
Daisy & Button With Crossbar, Tray, Dinner, Amber, 8 Piece 150.00
Daisy & Button With Narcissus, Punch Cup 10.00
Daisy & Button With Narcissus, Wine, 4 1/2 In. 18.50
Daisy & Button With Thumbprint, Celery, Square 25.00
Daisy & Button With V-Ornament, Castor, Pickle 40.00
Daisy & Plume, Candy Dish, Green 48.00
Dakota, Butter, Cover 45.00
Dakota, Celery, Etched 40.00
Dakota, Compote, 7 In. 30.00
Dakota, Compote, Golf Ball Standard, 8 x 8 In. 34.00
Dakota, Goblet 100.00
Dakota, Goblet, Etched 30.00
Dakota, Goblet, Flint 100.00
Dakota, Sugar, Cover 25.00
Dakota, Tumbler 80.00
Dakota, Tumbler, Ruby Stained, From Atlantic City 45.00
Dakota, Wine 65.00
Deer & Dog, Spooner, Etched 95.00
Deer & Oak Tree, Pitcher 225.00
Deer & Pine Tree, Bread Plate, Blue 85.00
Deer & Pine Tree, Cake Stand 85.00
Deer & Pine Tree, Compote, Cover, 8 x 6 In. 225.00
Deer & Pine Tree, Pitcher, Water .... 105.00 to 135.00
Deer & Pine Tree, Platter, Green, 8 x 13 In. 85.00
Deer Alert, Pitcher 250.00
Delaware, Banana Boat 75.00
Delaware, Banana Boat, Pink 210.00
Delaware, Pitcher, Claret 95.00
Delaware, Pitcher, Green, Gold Trim 150.00
Delaware, Pitcher, Rose To Clear 245.00
Delaware, Powder Jar, Rose, Gold Trim 35.00
Delaware, Punch Cup, Green, Gold Trim 35.00
Delaware, Spooner, Gold Trim 75.00
Delaware, Sugar & Creamer, Gold Covers 250.00
Delaware, Sugar, Cover, Green, Gold Trim 50.00
Delaware, Tankard, Green, Gold Trim, 9 1/4 In. 100.00
Delaware, Toothpick, Clear 40.00
Delaware, Toothpick, Green, Gold Trim 135.00
Delaware, Tray, Dresser, Green, Gold 50.00
Delaware, Tray, Pin, 5 x 10 In. 40.00
Delaware, Tumbler, Rose 65.00
Dewdrop, Goblet 25.00
Dewdrop In Points, Bread Plate 15.00
Dewdrop In Points, Compote, Open 20.00
Dewdrop In Points, Plate, Closed Handle, Clear 18.00
Dewdrop With Sheaf Of Wheat, Platter, 11 In. 45.00
Dewdrop With Star, Sugar, Cover 47.50
Dewey, see also the related pattern Spanish American
Dewey, Butter, Cover, Vaseline, 4 In. 75.00
Diagonal Band, Goblet 15.00

  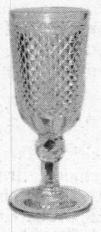 

Pressed Glass, Dewdrop With Star	*Pressed Glass, Diamond Cut With Leaf*	*Pressed Glass, Diamond Point*	*Pressed Glass, Excelsior*

Diamond & Button, Plate, Ice Cream, Fuchsia, Amberina 95.00
Diamond & Button, Spooner, Amber 15.00
Diamond & Fan, Spooner, 6 1/4 In. 30.00
Diamond Cut With Leaf, Sugar, Cover 30.00
Diamond Medallion pattern is listed here as Grand
Diamond Point, Cordial, Vaseline 35.00
Diamond Point, Tumbler, 3 5/8 In. 22.00
Diamond Point With Panels, Whiskey, Handle, Flint 135.00
Diamond Quilted, Goblet, Amber 40.00
Diamond Spearhead, Toothpick, Green 50.00
Diamond Splendor, Goblet 25.00
Diamond Sunburst, Cake Stand 15.00
Diamond Thumbprint, Bowl, 8 In. 85.00
Diamond Thumbprint, Compote, Flint, 11 1/2 In. 300.00
Diamond Thumbprint, Goblet, Flint 450.00
Dickinson, Sugar, Cover, Flint 40.00
Dog With Rabbit In Mouth, Plate 90.00
Dogwood, Berry, Master, Gold Trim 30.00
Doric pattern is listed here as Feather
Double Arch, Toothpick, Ruby Stain 295.00
Double Beetle Band, Goblet 15.00
Double Dahlia With Lens pattern is listed here as Dahlia with Petal
Double Daisy pattern is listed here as Rosette Band
Double Disced Prisms, Goblet 60.00
Double Loop pattern is listed here as Ribbon Candy
Double Ribbon, Butter, Cover 18.00
Double Spear, Goblet 28.00
Double Vine pattern is listed here as Bellflower Double Vine
Double Wedding Ring pattern is listed here as Wedding Ring
Doyle's Doyle, Goblet 22.00
Drapery, Creamer .... 18.00 to 35.00
Drapery, Goblet, Buttermilk 60.00
Drapery Band with Stars pattern is listed here as Doyle's Doyle
Drum, Creamer, Child's 65.00
Duchess, Berry Set, Green, Gold Trim, 7 Piece 280.00
E Pluribus Unum pattern is listed here as Emblem
Eagle, Toothpick, Green 20.00
Earl pattern is listed here as Spirea Band
Early Moon & Star, Tumbler 85.00
Early Thistle, Goblet 50.00
Egg In Sand, Bread Tray 25.00
Egg In Sand, Spooner, Amber 45.00
Egyptian, Compote, Sphinx Base, 8 In. .... 200.00 to 225.00
Egyptian, Creamer 50.00
Egyptian, Goblet 50.00
Egyptian, Plate, Pyramid & Camel, 10 In. 42.00
Elephant Toes, Toothpick, Green, Gold Trim 95.00

Elephant Toes, Tumbler	10.00
Elongated Thumbprint, Tumbler, Flint, 4 1/8 In.	22.00
Emblem, see also the related patterns American Shield	
Emerald Green Herringbone, Pitcher, Green	95.00
Empress, Compote, Jelly, Emerald Green, Gold	125.00
Empress, Spoon, Emerald Green	75.00
Empress, Table Set, Green, Gold Trim, 4 Piece	385.00
Empress, Toothpick, Green, Gold Trim	115.00
English Hobnail Cross pattern is listed here as Amberette	
Esther, Berry Set, 9 Piece	265.00
Esther, Berry Set, Green, Gold, 6 Piece	215.00
Esther, Butter, Cover	75.00
Esther, Celery Dish, Green, Gold Trim	40.00
Esther, Compote, Green, Gold Trim	40.00
Esther, Compote, Jelly	45.00
Esther, Cruet, Ball-Shaped Stopper	110.00
Esther, Salt & Pepper	6500.00
Esther, Sauce, Green, Gold Trim, 4 In.	25.00
Esther, Toothpick, Green, Gold Trim	95.00
Etched Dakota pattern is listed here as Dakota	
Eureka, Bread Plate, 11 3/4 In.	28.00
Eureka, Goblet, Flint	34.00
Eureka, Spooner	35.00
Eureka, Toothpick, Ruby Stained	110.00
Excelsior, Candlestick, Scalloped Base, Flint, 8 In.	27.50
Excelsior, Candlestick, Scalloped Base, Flint, 9 1/4 In.	72.00
Excelsior, Lamp, Finger	195.00
Eyewinker, Compote, Cover, Clear, 7 In.	45.00
Eyewinker, Compote, Turned-Up Rim, 8 1/2 In.	75.00
Eyewinker, Goblet	27.50

Top row: Pressed Glass, Fine Cut & Block; Pressed Glass, Fine Rib With Cut Ovals;
Pressed Glass, Horn of Plenty;
Bottom row: Pressed Glass, Hidalgo; Pressed Glass, Grape and Festoon; Pressed Glass, Horseshoe.

Eyewinker, Pitcher, Water, Clear, 1/2 Gal. 75.00
Fan with Diamond pattern is listed here as Shell
Fancy Cut, Toothpick 30.00
Feather, Celery Vase 45.00
Feather, Compote, Jelly 35.00
Feather, Goblet 65.00
Feather, Spooner 35.00
Feather Duster, Pitcher 95.00
Fern & Berry, Pitcher, Etched 145.00
Fernland, Creamer, Child's 15.00
Festoon, Cake Stand, 9 In. 14.00
Festoon, Tumbler 23.00
Festoon & Grape pattern is listed here as Grape & Festoon
Findlay, Dog Plate 70.00
Fine Cut & Block, Compote, Cover, Blue Sawtooth Edge, 10 x 9 In. 110.00
Fine Cut & Block, Creamer, Amber Trim 75.00
Fine Cut & Block, Dish, Handle, Blue, 9 1/2 In. 44.00
Fine Cut & Block, Goblet, Water, Blue, 8 Piece 302.00
Fine Cut & Block, Pitcher, Blue Trim 65.00
Fine Cut & Block, Soap Dish, Hanging 44.00
Fine Cut & Block, Sugar & Creamer, Cover, Yellow 88.00
Fine Cut & Feather pattern is listed here as Feather
Fine Cut & Panel, Creamer 42.50
Fine Cut & Panel, Goblet 6.00
Fine Cut With Block, Creamer, Amber 45.00
Fine Rib, Wine 44.00
Fish, Pitcher, Water 20.00
Fish, Plate, 8 In. 32.50
Flamingo Habitat, Celery Vase 45.00
Flattened Diamond & Sunburst, Punch Bowl, Child's 24.00
Flattened Finecut, Compote 20.00
Fleur-De-Lis & Drape, Plate, Green, 8 In. 12.00
Flora, Cruet, Green, Gold Trim 180.00
Flora, Pitcher, Amber, 1898 .... 75.00
Flora, Sugar, Creamer & Spooner, Crystal, Gold Trim 75.00
Flora, Tumbler, Green, Gold 30.00
Florette, Toothpick, Blue, 2 1/8 In. 65.00
Florida pattern pieces are listed here as Sunken Primrose if made of clear class and as
Emerald Green Herringbone if made of green glass
Florida Palm, Compote 25.00
Flower & Pleat, Pitcher, Pastel Flowers, Frosted 145.00
Flower & Pleat, Sugar Shaker 115.00
Flower & Pleat, Syrup, Frosted 165.00
Flower Flange pattern is listed here as Dewey
Flower Medallion, Tumbler 10.00
Flute, Goblet, Flint 25.00
Flying Birds, Goblet, Butterfly Each Side 47.50
Flying Robin pattern is listed here as Hummingbird
Four Petal, Sugar, Cover 140.00
Frosted patterns may also be listed under name of main pattern
Frosted Circle, Compote, 7 x 7 1/2 In. 22.00
Frosted Eagle, Compote, 7 In. 265.00
Frosted Eagle, Spooner 55.00
Frosted Eagle, Sugar, Cover 195.00
Frosted Leaf, Goblet 80.00
Frosted Leaf, Tumbler 35.00
Frosted Stork, Goblet 145.00
Frosted Stork, Waste Bowl 175.00
Frosted Waffle pattern is listed here as Hidalgo
Fuchsia, Goblet 65.00
Galloway, Butter, Cover .... 21.00 to 55.00
Galloway, Carafe, Water 45.00

Galloway, Castor, Pickle, Frame 75.00
Galloway, Finger Bowl 25.00
Garden Fruits, Goblet 15.00
Garden Of Eden, Butter 68.00
Garden Of Eden, Pitcher 140.00
Garfield Drape, Plate 45.00
Garfield Memorial, Bread Plate .... 20.00 to 35.00
Garland Drape, Goblet 25.00
Giant Bull's-Eye, Toothpick 35.00
Giant Prisms With Thumbprint Band, Goblet, Flint 245.00
Girl With Fan, Goblet 75.00
Gladiator, Tumbler, Blue 32.50
Golden Rule, Plate 110.00
Gonterman Swirl, Toothpick, Amber, Frosted 165.00
Good Luck pattern is listed here as Horseshoe
Gooseberry, Creamer 35.00
Gothic, Celery Vase, Flint 245.00
Gothic, Dish, Oblong, 6 x 8 In. 38.50
Gothic, Eggcup 50.00
Gothic, Goblet, Flint 90.00
Gothic Arch, Spooner 40.00
Gothic Arch, Spooner, Green, Gold Trim 30.00
Graduated Diamonds, Goblet 20.00
Grand, Pitcher 35.00
Grant, U.S., Bowl, Patriot & Soldier 25.00
Grape, see also the related patterns Beaded Grape, Beaded Grape Medallion, and
Magnet & Grape
Grape & Festoon, Punch Cup 430.00
Grape With Thumbprint, Goblet 45.00
Grape With Vine, Bowl, Footed, 10 In. 40.00
Grapevine With Ovals, Butter, Cover, Child's 75.00
Grasshopper, Spooner 43.00
Halley's Comet, Spooner 55.00
Hamilton, Eggcup 30.00
Hamilton With Clear Leaf pattern is listed here as Hamilton With Leaf
Hamilton With Leaf, Goblet 90.00
Hand, Compote, Electric Blue 95.00
Heart Band, Toothpick, Souvenir, Ruby Stained 20.00
Heart Plume, Relish, Heart Shape, Gold Trim 10.00
Heart With Thumbprint, Creamer, Individual 30.00
Heart With Thumbprint, Cruet, Stopper, Pair 135.00
Heart With Thumbprint, Goblet, Green 125.00
Heart With Thumbprint, Mustard, Silver Plate Cover 95.00
Heart With Thumbprint, Wine, Pair 165.00
Heavy Drape, Toothpick 30.00
Heavy Paneled Fine Cut pattern is listed here as Paneled Diamond Cross
Hercules Pillar, Goblet, Flint 38.00
Hero, Tumbler, Etched Florals, Ruby Flashed 20.00
Heron, Pitcher 90.00
Herringbone, Creamer 10.00
Hidalgo, Goblet, Enamel Design 15.00
Hinoto pattern is listed here as Diamond Point with Panels
Hobnail pattern is in this book as its own category
Honeycomb, Compote, Flint, 6 x 7 In. 75.00
Honeycomb, Goblet, Large 20.00
Honeycomb, Water Set, Ruffled Rim Pitcher, Amber, Frosted, 5 Piece 335.00
Horizontal Threads, Spooner, Child's, Ruby Stained 40.00
Horn Of Plenty, Compote, 8 x 5 In. .... 120.00 to 130.00
Horn Of Plenty, Eggcup 60.00
Horn Of Plenty, Goblet 70.00
Horn Of Plenty, Sugar, Flint 125.00
Horn Of Plenty, Tumbler, Flint 85.00

Pressed Glass, Inverted Fern   *Pressed Glass, Liberty Bell*   *Pressed Glass, Jefferson*

Horseshoe, Bowl, Cover, 5 x 8 In. 295.00
Horseshoe, Cake Stand, 10 In. .... 75.00 to 95.00
Horseshoe, Cake Stand, 11 In. 145.00
Horseshoe, Celery 125.00
Horseshoe, Goblet 35.00
Horseshoe, Plate, 10 In. 95.00
Horseshoe, Tray, Water, Double-Handled 95.00
Huber, Goblet 40.00
Huckle pattern is listed here as Feather Duster
Hummingbird, Pitcher, Amber 175.00
Hummingbird, Wine 55.00
Humpty-Dumpty, Breakfast Set, Child's, 3 Piece 70.00
Ida pattern is listed here as Sheraton
Idaho, Spooner 38.00
Indiana Swirl pattern is listed here as Feather
Interlocking Crescents, Sugar, Cover 16.00
Inverted Fan, Spooner 40.00
Inverted Fan & Feather, Tumbler, Green, Gold Trim, 6 Piece 495.00
Inverted Fern, Goblet, Flint 50.00
Inverted Fern, Sugar, Cover 60.00
Inverted Strawberry, Punch Set, Child's, 7 Piece 215.00
Inverted Strawberry, Table Set, Child's, 3 Piece 75.00
Inverted Thumbprint, Bottle, Knobbed Stopper, Blown, Amber, 8 In. 30.00
Inverted Thumbprint, Goblet, Amber 40.00
Inverted Thumbprint & Star, Goblet 15.00
Iowa, Jelly, Open 17.00
Iris With Meander, Berry Set, Green, 6 Piece 55.00
Iris With Meander, Salt & Pepper, Amethyst 145.00
Ivy In Snow, Tumbler, Gold Leaves & Rim 38.00
Jacob's Ladder, Butter, Cover .... 35.00 to 60.00
Jacob's Ladder, Compote, Scalloped, 8 1/2 In. 30.00
Jacob's Ladder, Saltshaker, Footed, 1 7/8 In. 24.00
Jacob's Ladder, Spooner, 6 In. 32.00
Jacob's Ladder, Sugar & Creamer 58.00
Jefferson's Optic, Berry Set, Amethyst, 7 Piece 85.00
Jewel & Dewdrop, Compote, Pointed Rim, 6 In. 35.00
Jewel & Dewdrop, Toothpick 55.00
Jewel Band, Wine 13.00
Jeweled Heart, Pitcher, Blue Opalescent 175.00
Jeweled Heart, Tumbler, Blue Opalescent 40.00
Jeweled Moon & Star pattern is listed here as Moon & Star Variant or Moon & Star
Job's Tears pattern is listed here as Art
Jumbo, Goblet 1200.00
Jumbo, Pitcher, Amber 395.00
Jumbo, Spoon Rack .... 600.00 to 750.00
Kamoni pattern is listed here as Pennsylvania
Kansas pattern is listed here as Jewel & Dewdrop

Pressed Glass,
Lily-Of-The-Valley

Pressed Glass,
New England Flute

Pressed Glass,
Open Rose

Pressed Glass, Ostrich
Looking at the Moon

Kayak, Plate, Bread 15.00
Kentucky, Toothpick, Green 115.00
Keystone Grape, Goblet 40.00
King's Crown, see also the related pattern Ruby Thumbprint
King's Crown, Bowl, Oval, 6 1/2 x 10 In. 67.50
King's Crown, Butter, Cover 65.00
King's Crown, Creamer, Green .... 30.00 to 35.00
King's Crown, Goblet, Ruby 45.00
Klondike pattern is listed here as Amberette
Knights Of Labor, Bread Plate, Amber 145.00
Knights Of Labor, Mug 70.00
Knobby Bull's-Eye, Wine 14.00
Kokomo, Wine 15.00
Lacy Medallion, see also the related pattern Princess Feather
Lacy Valance, Sugar, Cover 25.00
Lamb, Creamer, Child's 100.00
Lamb, Sugar, Cover, Child's .... 150.00 to 175.00
Large Drop, Salt, Master 50.00
Last Supper, Plate, Bread 20.00
Leaf & Dart, Goblet, Buttermilk 30.00
Leaf Medallion, Sugar, Cover, Amethyst 210.00
Leaf Medallion, Tumbler, Green, Gold Trim 35.00
Leaf Umbrella, Sugar Shaker 435.00
Leverne pattern is listed here as Star in Honeycomb
Liberty Bell, Bread Plate 75.00
Liberty Bell, Creamer .... 85.00 to 145.00
Liberty Bell, Goblet .... 20.00 to 30.00
Liberty Bell, Mug, Snake Handle, 1876 Centennial 300.00
Liberty Bell, Plate, Signers Border, 6 1/4 In. 125.00
Lily-Of-The-Valley, Creamer 65.00
Lily-Of-The-Valley, Goblet 95.00
Lily-Of-The-Valley, Salt, 3-Footed 85.00
Lincoln Drape, Eggcup 75.00
Lincoln Drape, Goblet, Flint .... 135.00 to 160.00
Lincoln Drape, Syrup, Pewter Shell Top 75.00
Lion, Bread Plate, Rope Edge, Closed Handles, Frosted 50.00
Lion, Cheese Dish, Cover, Frosted .... 300.00 to 425.00
Lion, Compote, Cover, Oval, Frosted, 8 3/4 In. 185.00
Lion, Compote, Frosted, 13 In. 240.00
Lion, Compote, Frosted, 8 x 7 1/2 In. 70.00
Lion, Creamer, Frosted 75.00
Lion, Creamer, Miniature 35.00
Lion, Creamer, Square, Frosted .... 65.00 to 85.00
Lion, Goblet, Frosted 85.00
Lion, Spooner 85.00
Lion, Sugar, Cover, Frosted 75.00
Lion, Syrup, Frosted 295.00

Lion's Head, Compote, 8 In. 85.00
Lion's Leg pattern is listed here as Alaska
Little Bopeep, Bowl, 7 1/2 In. 95.00
Little Bopeep, Tumbler 95.00
Little Gem, Sugar, Cover, Green, Gold Trim 45.00
Log Cabin, Compote 350.00
Log Cabin, Pitcher, Blue, 4 1/2 In. 125.00
Log Cabin, Spooner 65.00
Loganberry & Grape, Pitcher 110.00
Loop, see also the related pattern Seneca Loop
Loop, Celery Vase, Flint, 10 In., Pair 150.00
Loop, Compote, Flint, 6 x 8 1/2 In. 27.50
Loop, Sugar, Cover, Flint, 10 In. 33.00
Loop & Dart, Celery 30.00
Loop & Dart, Creamer 35.00
Loop & Dart With Round Ornaments, Goblet 30.00
Loop & Moose Eye, Creamer, Flint 85.00
Loop & Pyramid, Goblet 25.00
Loops & Drops pattern is listed here as New Jersey
Louis XV, Creamer, Green, Gold 45.00
Magnet & Grape, Goblet, Frosted Leaf .... 70.00 to 90.00
Maine, Cake Stand, Green 30.00
Man's Head, Spooner 90.00
Manhattan, Nappy, Scalloped, 5 In. 6.50
Manhattan, Punch Set, 15 Piece 290.00
Manhattan, Toothpick, Yellow Eyes 35.00
Maple Leaf, Pitcher 45.00
Mardi Gras, Spooner, Child's, Gold Trim 40.00
Mardi Gras, Toothpick 40.00
Marquisette, Goblet 30.00
Marsh Fern, Cake Stand 47.50
Maryland, Compote 20.00
Mascotte, Pitcher, Etched 110.00
Massachusetts, Tumbler, Juice 17.00
Massachusetts, Whiskey Glass 10.00
McKinley Memorial, Bread Plate, It Is God's Way, Oval, 10 3/8 In. 50.00
Medallion, Cake Stand, 9 In. 35.00
Medallion, Goblet, Amber 35.00
Medallion Sunburst, Punch Cup 8.00
Medallion Sunburst, Toothpick 42.50
Memphis, Punch Bowl, Base, Crystal 125.00
Memphis, Punch Cup 5.00
Memphis, Water Set, Gold Trim, 7 Piece 175.00
Menagerie, Punch Set, Child's, 7 Piece 75.00
Menagerie, Sugar, Cover, Child's, Bear, Amber 185.00
Menagerie, Table Set, Child's, 4 Piece 45.00
Mephistopheles, Tumbler, Ale 85.00
Michigan, Butter, Cover, Child's, Gold Rim 125.00
Michigan, Celery Vase 30.00
Michigan, Goblet, Gold 36.00
Michigan, Spooner, Child's 40.00
Michigan, Sugar, Cover, Child's 85.00
Michigan, Toothpick, Art Deco, Blue & Yellow 80.00
Minerva, Compote, 8 In. 165.00
Minerva, Creamer 40.00
Minerva, Goblet 120.00
Minnesota, Jug 60.00
Minnesota, Syrup 65.00
Missouri, Cake Stand 40.00
Monkey, Stein, Child's, Milk Glass, Gold Trim, Big 70.00
Monkey, Stein, Child's, Milk Glass, Small 25.00
Monkey, Sugar, Cover 210.00

Pressed Glass, Oval Miter

Pressed Glass,
Paneled Forget-Me-Nots

Pressed Glass,
Paneled Nightshade

Moon & Star, Bowl, Cover	50.00
Moon & Star, Bread Tray, 6 1/2 x 11 In.	65.00
Moon & Star, Cake Stand	45.00
Moon & Star, Celery Vase, Clear & Frosted	45.00
Moon & Star, Compote, 8 x 6 3/4 In.	52.00
Moon & Star, Goblet, Frosted	50.00 to 55.00
Moon & Star, Spill Holder, 4 7/8 In.	11.00
Moon & Star, Syrup, Tin Lid, 7 1/2 In.	49.50
Moon & Stork pattern is listed here as Ostrich Looking At The Moon	
Nail, Wine, Souvenir, Ruby	30.00
Nailhead, Wine	25.00
Narcissus Spray, Table Set, 4 Piece	95.00
Narrow Swirl, Creamer	20.00
Nestlings, Celery, Etched	65.00
Nestor, Berry Set, Green, 7 Piece	125.00
Nestor, Cruet, Green	85.00
Nestor, Sauce, Blue, Gold Trim, Enamel Design, 4 In.	35.00
New England Pineapple, Champagne	195.00
New England Pineapple, Decanter, Flint, 1 Qt.	280.00
New England Pineapple, Eggcup	60.00
New England Pineapple, Goblet, Flint	65.00 to 75.00
New Hampshire, Creamer, Gold Trim, Individual	25.00
New Hampshire, Goblet	22.00
New Hampshire, Mug	12.00
New Hampshire, Toothpick, Clear	45.00
New Jersey, Butter, Cover	60.00
New Jersey, Creamer	35.00
New Jersey, Tumbler	18.00
New Jersey, Water Set, Gold Flashed, 4 Piece	75.00
Niagara, Goblet	15.00
Nursery Tales, Berry Set, Child's, 6 Piece	170.00
Nursery Tales, Punch Cup, Child's	15.00
Nursery Tales, Tumbler, Child's	95.00
Oaken Bucket, Creamer, Blue	45.00 to 65.00
Oaken Bucket, Tumbler, Amber	85.00
Oasis, Creamer	65.00
Ohio Star, Toothpick	60.00
Old Abe pattern is listed here as Frosted Eagle	
One Hundred-One, Toothpick, Pink	55.00
One-O-One pattern is listed here as One-Hundred-One	
One-Thousand Eye pattern is listed here as Thousand Eye	
Open Rose, Eggcup	12.00 to 20.00
Open Rose, Goblet, 6 In.	32.00
Oregon, see also the related pattern Beaded Loop	
Orion pattern is listed here as Cathedral	
Ostrich Looking At The Moon, Goblet	125.00 to 150.00

Pressed Glass, Pillar

Pressed Glass, Primrose

Oval Miter, Bowl, 7 1/2 In.	40.00
Oval Panels, Goblet, Flint	40.00
Oval Star, Pitcher, Child's	57.50
Oval Star, Tumbler	18.00
Overshot, Pitcher, Braided Handle, Flint	150.00
Overshot, Pitcher, Champagne	125.00
Overshot, Tankard, Orange To Clear	295.00
Owl pattern is listed here as Bull's-Eye with Diamond Point	
Owl & Possum, Goblet	90.00 to 105.00
Owl in Fan pattern is listed here as Parrot	
Paddlewheel, Toothpick, Clear, Gold Trim	30.00
Palmette, Dish, Honey	10.00
Panama, Cake Stand	28.00
Paneled Dewdrop, Bread Plate, 1878	35.00
Paneled Dewdrop, Sugar & Creamer, Cover	45.00
Paneled Dewdrops, Plate, Bread	20.00
Paneled Diamond Cross, Goblet	25.00
Paneled Dogwood, Banana Boat, Green, 12 x 7 1/4 In.	36.00
Paneled Forget-Me-Nots, Celery	45.00
Paneled Forty-Four, Creamer, Gold Trim	45.00
Paneled Forty-Four, Pitcher, Platinum Stain	145.00
Paneled Heather, Celery Vase	20.00
Paneled Herringbone, Goblet	20.00
Paneled Holly, Tumbler, Green, Gold Trim	45.00
Paneled Honeycomb, Creamer, Pewter Lid	85.00
Paneled Jewel, Wine, Blue, 4 In.	10.00
Paneled Nightshade, Goblet, Amber	25.00 to 35.00
Paneled Palm, Berry Set, 7 Piece	65.00
Paneled Stippled Scroll, Goblet	15.00
Paneled Sunflower, Goblet	12.00
Paneled Thistle, Honey Dish, Higbee	120.00
Paneled Zipper, Cake Stand, Clear, 6 x 3 3/4 In.	68.00
Parrot, Goblet	37.00 to 42.00
Pattee Cross, Goblet, Green	30.00
Pattee Cross, Pitcher, Child's	50.00
Pavonia, Bowl, Waste, Underplate, 6 1/2 In.	45.00
Pavonia, Butter, Cover, Oak Leaf, Etched	80.00
Pavonia, Compote, Cover, 6 1/2 In.	55.00
Pavonia, Goblet, Etched	28.00 to 45.00
Pavonia, Sauce	12.00
Pavonia, Spooner, Etched	42.50
Pavonia, Tumbler, Ruby Stained, Etched	35.00
Peach, Butter, Green, Gold	145.00
Peacock Feathers, Cake Plate, Child's	65.00
Peacock Feathers, Compote, 6 3/4 In.	19.00
Peacock Feathers, Lamp, Finger, 7 1/2 In.	85.00
Peacock's Eye pattern is listed here as Peacock Feathers	

Pressed Glass, Princess Feather   *Pressed Glass, Rose in Snow*   *Pressed Glass, Royal*

Peas In Pods, Wine	18.00
Peerless, Toothpick, Green, Gold Trim	195.00
Pennsylvania, see also the related pattern Hand	
Pennsylvania, Goblet, Gold Trim	30.00
Pennsylvania, Punch Cup	8.00
Pennsylvania, Vase, 6 1/2 In.	40.00
Petal & Loop, Bowl, Flat, Flint, 8 In.	85.00
Petal & Loop, Compote, Cover, 9 3/4 In.	148.50
Pheasant, Compote, Cover	165.00
Philadelphia Centennial, Goblet	42.50 to 55.00
Picket, Compote, 7 x 7 1/4 In.	36.00
Pigs In Corn, Goblet	595.00 to 875.00
Pillar, Bowl, 9 1/2 In.	17.00
Pillar, Spooner, Pink Spatter	70.00
Pillar, Sugar, Flint	205.00
Pillar & Bull's-Eye pattern is listed here as Thistle	
Pillow Encircled, Celery Vase	11.00
Pinafore pattern is listed here as Actress	
Pineapple & Fan, Butter, Cover, Round	12.00
Pioneer, Sugar, Cover, Green	21.00
Pittsburg, Cake Stand, 8 In.	38.00
Plain Smocking pattern is listed here as Smocking	
Pleating, Wine	25.00
Pointed Thumbprint pattern is listed here as Almond Thumbprint	
Polar Bear, Bread Tray	165.00
Polar Bear, Goblet, Flared Rim, Frosted	115.50 to 175.00
Polar Bear, Tray, Water, Frosted, Signed	245.00
Portland, Jug, Molasses, Hinged Pewter Lid	28.00
Portland, Sugar, Cover	40.00
Portland, Syrup, Pewter Lid	95.00
Portland, Toothpick, Gold Trim	35.00
Post, Celery, Etched	48.50
Powder & Shot, Creamer	80.00
Powder & Shot, Creamer, Bulbous, Flint	95.00
Powder & Shot, Goblet, Flint	65.00 to 70.00
Prayer Rug pattern is listed here as Horseshoe	
Pressed Diamond, Butter, Cover, Blue	55.00
Pressed Diamond, Goblet, Amber	20.00
Pressed Leaf, Spooner	25.00 to 28.00
Primrose, Creamer, Lime Green	38.00
Primrose, Pitcher	45.00
Primrose, Tray, Water, 11 In.	40.00
Princess Feather, Spooner	15.00
Priscilla, Spooner	45.00
Prism & Daisy Bar, Goblet, Vaseline	40.00
Prize, Toothpick, Clear, Gold Trim	35.00
Profile & Sprig, Butter, Cover, Helmeted Head Finial	125.00

Psyche & Cupid, Creamer 42.50
Psyche & Cupid, Pitcher 90.00
Queen, Butter, Domed Cover, Blue .... 70.00 to 80.00
Queen, Goblet, Amber 35.00
Queen Anne, Creamer 65.00
Queen's Necklace, Compote, 10 In. 100.00
Queen's Necklace, Toothpick 55.00
Quilted Phlox, Sugar Shaker 270.00
Quintec, Compote, 6 1/2 In. 26.00
Radiant Daisy, Punch Set, 12 Piece 90.00
Red Block, Goblet, 8 Piece 300.00
Red Block, Goblet, Yellow Stain 40.00
Red Block, Spoon Holder 35.00
Red Block, Table Set, 4 Piece .... 220.00 to 500.00
Regent pattern is listed here as Leaf Medallion
Reverse Forty-Four, Butter, Cover, Ruby, Gold Trim 75.00
Reverse Forty-Four, Table Set, Red Stained, Gold Trim, 3 Piece 295.00
Reverse Forty-Four, Toothpick 65.00
Reverse Torpedo, Cake Stand, 10 In. .... 60.00 to 65.00
Reverse Torpedo, Compote, Fruit, High Standard, 8 In. 101.00
Rex, Pitcher, Child's 50.00
Rexford, Wine 12.50
Ribbed Grape, Goblet 55.00
Ribbed Palm, Champagne 195.00
Ribbed Palm, Eggcup .... 30.00 to 45.00
Ribbed Palm, Goblet, Flint .... 20.00 to 45.00
Ribbed Palm, Tumbler 125.00
Ribbed Pillar, Toothpick, Pink Frosted 75.00
Ribbon, Celery 35.00
Ribbon, Compote, Cover, 7 3/4 x 10 7/8 In. 72.00
Ribbon, Compote, Cover, 8 1/2 In. 130.00
Ribbon Candy, Cake Stand, 3 1/2 x 6 In. 65.00
Ringed Framed Ovals, Lamp, Whale Oil 140.00
Rising Sun, Goblet, Ruby, Gold Trim 25.00
Riverside's Victoria, Tumbler, Vaseline, Gold 50.00
Rochelle pattern is listed here as Princess Feather
Rock Of Ages, Bread Tray, Milk Glass Center 165.00
Roman Medallion, Compote, ... 18.00
Roman Rosette, Creamer 40.00
Romeo, Bowl, Square, 7 1/4 In. 35.00
Roosevelt Teddy Bears, Bread Plate, Frosted Portrait, Eagle, Flag 175.00
Roosevelt Teddy Bears, Bread Tray 150.00
Rooster, Creamer, Child's 120.00
Rope Bands pattern is listed here as Argent
Rose, Sugar & Creamer 27.00
Rose In Snow, Creamer 11.00
Rose In Snow, Goblet, Amber .... 45.00 to 55.00
Rose In Snow, Goblet, Vaseline .... 65.00 to 75.00
Rose In Snow, Plate, 9 1/2 In. 45.00
Rose Sprig, Bowl, Pedestal, Oval, Canary, 10 In. 85.00
Rose Sprig, Bowl, Vaseline 85.00
Rose Sprig, Cake Stand, 10 In. 67.50
Rose Sprig, Salt, Master 145.00
Rosette, Cake Stand, 8 1/2 In. 20.00
Rosette, Pitcher, Water, 9 1/2 In. 54.00
Rosette & Palms, Compote, Scalloped, 6 3/4 x 8 In. 23.00
Rosette Band, Goblet, Etched 27.00
Rosette Medallion pattern is listed here as Feather Duster
Royal, Bread Tray 65.00
Royal Ivy, Berry Set, Craquelle, 4 Piece 175.00
Royal Ivy, Spooner, Crackle 325.00
Royal Ivy, Sugar Shaker .... 100.00 to 285.00
Royal Oak, Butter, Cover, Acorn Finial, Frosted 180.00

Pressed Glass, Ruby Thumbprint

Royal Oak, Toothpick	110.00
Ruby Rosette pattern is listed here as Hero	
Ruby Thumbprint, see also the related pattern King's Crown	
Ruby Thumbprint, Butter, Cover	65.00
Ruby Thumbprint, Claret, Etched	65.00
Ruby Thumbprint, Pitcher, Etched Leaf & Berry	265.00
Ruby Thumbprint, Pitcher, Squatty	250.00
Ruby Thumbprint, Spooner, Etched	65.00
S Repeat, Pitcher, Green	85.00
Sandwich Loop, Tumbler, Flint	35.00
Sandwich Star & Buckle, Syrup, Lid	350.00
Sawtooth, Bowl, Scalloped, 7 1/2 x 3 3/4 In.	15.00
Sawtooth, Butter, Cover	65.00
Sawtooth, Celery	45.00
Sawtooth, Compote, 10 x 6 3/4 In.	42.00
Sawtooth, Compote, Wafer Foot, Amber, 8 In.	30.00
Sawtooth, Creamer, Molded Handle, 6 1/4 In.	29.00
Sawtooth, Dish, Footed, 7 x 4 3/4 In.	14.00
Sawtooth, Goblet, 5 5/8 In.	34.00
Sawtooth, Salt, Cover, Flint	75.00
Sawtooth, Spooner, 5 1/2 In.	28.00
Sawtooth, Toothpick, Barrel Shape, Green	15.00
Sawtooth Band pattern is listed here as Amazon	
Scarab, Goblet, Flint	170.00
Scroll, Pitcher, Flowers	85.00
Scroll With Cane Band, Celery, Amber Stained	25.00
Scroll With Cane Band, Compote, 8 1/2 x 8 1/4 In.	220.00
Scroll With Cane Band, Tumbler, Amber	45.00
Scroll With Flowers, Cake Plate	40.00
Scroll With Flowers, Compote, Cover, Small Handles	75.00
Scroll With Flowers, Goblet	27.50
Seashell, Spooner, Etched	45.00
Seneca Loop, Pitcher, Flint	110.00
Sequoia, Compote, Cover	35.00
Sheaf of Wheat pattern is listed here as Wheat Sheaf	
Sheaf Of Wheat With Star & Fan, Bowl, Ruffled, Star Base, 8 In.	10.00
Shell, Goblet	28.00
Shell & Tassel, Bowl, Oval, 12 In.	65.00
Shell & Tassel, Butter, Cover, Dog Finial	275.00
Shell & Tassel, Cake Stand, 10 In.	85.00
Shell & Tassel, Compote, Duncan	130.00
Shell & Tassel, Tray, Ice Cream, 14 x 8 In.	125.00

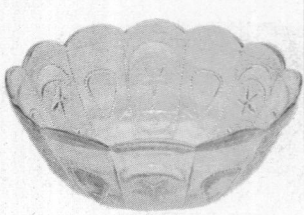

Pressed Glass,
Scroll with Flowers

Pressed Glass, Shrine

Pressed Glass,
Shell and Tassel

Sheraton, Creamer, Amber	21.00
Sheraton, Goblet	17.50 to 22.00
Sheraton, Sugar, Cover, Amber	40.00
Shields, Butter, Cover, Blue	175.00
Shimmering Star, Tumbler	45.00
Short Teasel pattern is listed here as Teasel	
Shoshone pattern is listed here as Victor	
Shrine, Pitcher, Water, 8 1/2 In.	47.00
Shrine, Tumbler, 6 Piece	175.00
Simplicity Scroll, Toothpick	20.00
Smocking, Goblet, Flint, 2 Row, 6 1/2 In.	85.00
Snail, Butter, Cover	95.00
Snail, Tumbler, Ruby Stained, 6 Piece	1200.00
Snake Drape, Goblet	18.00
Spanish American, Pitcher	45.00
Spanish American, Tumbler	60.00
Spanish Coin pattern is listed here as Columbian Coin	
Spirea Band, Sugar, Cover, Etched	25.00
Sprig, Butter, Cover	65.00
Sprig, Goblet	40.00
Sprig, Spooner	30.00
Sprig, Sugar	25.00
Square Fuchsia, Goblet	38.00
Square Fuchsia, Mug, Amber	37.00
Squirrel, Pitcher, 9 In.	75.00
Squirrel In Bower, Saucer	12.00
Star & File, Cake Stand, 8 1/4 x 4 1/2 In.	22.00
Star & Punty pattern is listed here as Moon & Star	
Star In Bull's Eye, Creamer, Gold Trim, Individual	20.00
Star In Bull's Eye, Toothpick	75.00
Star In Honeycomb, Wine	15.00
Star Medallion, Bowl, 5 x 2 1/2 In.	9.00
Starglow, Goblet	15.00
Stars & Bars, Creamer, Child's, Blue	30.00
Stars & Bars, Goblet	25.00
States pattern is listed here as The States	
Stippled Chain, Spooner	22.00
Stippled Chain, Sugar, Cover	19.00
Stippled Dahlia pattern is listed here as Square Fuchsia	
Stippled Double Loop, Creamer	35.00
Stippled Flower Band, Goblet	15.00
Stippled Forget-Me-Not, Plate, Baby In Tub Reaching For Ball, 7 In.	65.00
Stippled Forget-Me-Not, Wine	30.00
Stippled Fuchsia, Goblet	15.00
Stippled Medallion, Goblet	36.00
Stippled Paneled Flower pattern is listed here as Maine	
Stippled Peppers, Goblet	45.00

Stippled Scroll pattern is listed here as Scroll
Stippled Star, Creamer .... 45.00 to 65.00
Stippled Vine & Beads pattern is listed here as Vine & Beads
Stork Looking at the Moon pattern is listed here as Ostrich Looking At The Moon
Strawberry, Goblet, Buttermilk 30.00
Sunbeam, Toothpick, Blue 100.00
Sunburst, Syrup, Tin Lip & Spout, 6 7/8 In. 49.50
Sunk Diamond & Lattice, Pitcher, Water, 1885 .... 50.00
Sunken Button, Goblet, Amber 32.00
Sunken Primrose, Water Set, Clear, Red Trim, 7 Piece 475.00
Sunrise pattern is listed here as Rising Sun
Swag With Brackets, Butter, Green Opalescent 135.00
Swan, Cake Stand 110.00
Swan, Dish, Cheese, Cover 250.00
Swan, Sugar, Silver Plate Lid 65.00
Swan With Tree, Pitcher 95.00
Sweetheart, Table Set, Child's, 4 Piece 110.00
Tandem Bicycle, Goblet 20.00
Tape Measure pattern is listed here as Shields
Teardrop pattern is listed here as Teardrop & Thumbprint
Teardrop & Tassel, Sugar & Creamer, Opaque 175.00
Teardrop & Thumbprint, Pitcher 60.00
Teardrop & Thumbprint, Spooner, Blue 45.00
Teardrop & Thumbprint, Spooner, Clear 20.00
Teasel, Goblet 25.00
Tennessee, Cake Stand, 9 In. 38.00
Tennessee, Dish, Jelly, Open 40.00
Tennessee, Relish 20.00
Tennessee, Wine 125.00
Texas, Compote, Cover, Scalloped Lid, 6 In. 165.00
Texas, Creamer, Gold Trim 20.00
Texas, Sherbet, Footed, Gold Trim 12.00
Texas, Toothpick 35.00
Texas Star, Toothpick 70.00
The States, Goblet, Emerald Green 20.00
The States, Plate, Gold Trim, 5 3/8 In. 20.00
Thistle, Bowl, Crown Finial On Cover, Round, 5 1/2 x 7 In. 605.00
Thistle, Wine 75.00
Thistleblow, Wine, 4 1/2 In. 9.00
Thousand Eye, Cake Stand 135.00
Thousand Eye, Cruet, Amber 95.00
Thousand Eye, Goblet, Blue 45.00
Thousand Eye, Pitcher, Riverside 18.00
Thousand Eye, Tumbler, Blue, 3 3/4 In. 25.00
Thousand Eye, Water Set, Child's, 6 Piece 65.00
Thousand Eye, Wine, Amber, 4 In. 24.00
Three Birds, Pitcher 140.00

Pressed Glass, Star Medallion   *Pressed Glass, Frosted Stork*   *Pressed Glass, Strawberry*

Two Left: Pressed Glass, U.S. Coin;
Right: Pressed Glass, Westward Ho

Three Face, Cake Plate, 8 3/4 In.	125.00
Three Face, Compote, Cover, 6 In.	65.00
Three Face, Creamer, Face Under Lip	125.00
Three Face, Goblet	60.00
Three Face, Pitcher	550.00
Three Fruits, Goblet, Buttermilk	30.00
Three Graces, see also the related pattern Three Face	
Three Graces, Bread Tray	55.00
Three Panel, Bowl, Amber	25.00
Three Panel, Creamer, Amber	25.00 to 28.00
Three Panel, Spooner	10.00
Three Panel, Sugar, Cover	28.00
Three Presidents, Bread Plate	65.00 to 85.00
Three Sisters pattern is listed here as Three Face	
Three Stories, Sugar, Cover	25.00
Thumbprint, Compote, Scalloped Rim, Low Standard, 9 1/4 In.	125.00
Thumbprint, Goblet, Peacock Blue, Flint, 5 7/8 In.	280.00
Thumbprint, Spooner, Flint	35.00
Thumbprint, Wine, Knob Stem	75.00
Thumbprint, Wine, Reeded Stem	55.00
Tiny Lion, Celery	60.00
Tiny Lion, Pitcher	90.00
Tokyo, Toothpick, Green Opalescent	135.00
Tom Thumb pattern is listed here as Humpty-Dumpty	
Torpedo, Pitcher, Milk	95.00
Torpedo, Spooner	17.00
Torpedo, Sugar, Cover	95.00
Torpedo, Syrup	75.00
Torpedo, Wine, Ruby Stained	95.00
Tree Of Life, Cake Stand	275.00
Tree Of Life, Celery	75.00
Tree Of Life, Jam Jar, Holder	85.00
Tree Of Life With Hand, Compote, 10 In.	50.00
Tree Of Life With Hand, Spooner	42.00
Trilby, Goblet	225.00
Trophy, Toothpick, Ruby Stained, Souvenir	25.00
Truncated Cube, Water Set, 7 Piece	400.00
Tulip & Honeycomb, Punch Bowl, Child's	28.00
Tulip & Honeycomb, Sugar & Creamer, Child's	50.00
Tulip & Honeycomb, Table Set, 4 Piece	125.00
Tulip Petals, Butter, Cover, Gold Trim	60.00
Tulip Petals, Creamer, Gold Trim	30.00
Tulip Petals, Sugar, Cover	30.00
Tulip With Sawtooth, Decanter, Handle	100.00
Tulip With Sawtooth, Goblet, Flint, 6 5/8 In.	60.00
Tulip With Sawtooth, Salt	35.00

Tulip With Sawtooth, Wine 45.00
Twist, Celery, Vaseline, Opalescent, Pink Edge 48.00
Two Panel, Compote, Cover, Amber 60.00
Two Panel, Goblet 18.00
Two Panel, Goblet, Green 35.00
Two Panel, Goblet, Vaseline 45.00
Two Panel, Wine 29.00
U.S. Coin, Bowl, Quarters, Ruby Flashed, 6 1/2 In. 3300.00
U.S. Coin, Butter, Cover, 1892 .... 390.00
U.S. Coin, Butter, Cover, Frosted 450.00
U.S. Coin, Cake Stand, Dollars 385.00
U.S. Coin, Compote, Cover, 20 Cents, 6 In. 495.00
U.S. Coin, Compote, Quarters, 7 In. 465.00
U.S. Coin, Goblet, Half Dollars .... 690.00 to 715.00
U.S. Coin, Sauce, Scalloped, Quarters 660.00
U.S. Coin, Toothpick, Dollars, Ruby Flashed 335.00
U.S. Coin, Tumbler, Frosted 125.00
U.S. Coin, Wine, Half Dimes 800.50
Valencia Waffle, Goblet 30.00
Valentine pattern is listed here as Trilby
Victor, Bowl, Ruffled, Green, 8 In. 30.00
Victor, Butter, Cover, Gold Trim 55.00
Victor, Cake Stand, Emerald Green 50.00
Victor, Compote, Jelly, Green 22.00
Victor, Plate, Green, 7 In. 20.00
Victor, Toothpick, Gold Trim 45.00
Viking, Butter, Cover 75.00
Viking, Celery 20.00
Viking, Spooner 25.00
Vine & Beads, Creamer, Child's 70.00
Vine & Beads, Spooner, Child's 75.00
Vine & Beads, Sugar, Cover, Child's 125.00
Vine & Beads, Table Set, 4 Piece, Child's 202.00
Wading Heron, Compote, 8 x 8 In. 70.00
Waffle & Thumbprint, Goblet 100.00
Waffle & Thumbprint, Sugar, Flint 100.00
Waffle & Thumbprint, Wine, Flint 55.00
Washboard, Compote 20.00
Washington, Decanter, Flint, 1 Qt. 245.00
Washington, Sugar, Cover 135.00
Waterford, Candy Dish, Cover, Stacking, 5 In. 28.00
Wedding Bells, Spooner, Pink Stained 25.00
Wedding Ring, Syrup, Applied Handles 150.00
Wee Branches, Spooner, Child's .... 70.00 to 85.00
Wee Branches, Sugar, Cover, Child's 175.00
Westward Ho, Compote, Oval 150.00
Westward Ho, Goblet .... 60.00 to 85.00
Westward Ho, Pitcher, Milk 375.00
Westward Ho, Wine, 6 Piece 350.00
Wheat & Barley, Creamer, Enamel Dotted Florals .... 27.50 to 35.00
Wheat & Barley, Goblet, Amber 22.00
Wheat & Barley, Pitcher 30.00
Wheat & Barley, Tumbler, Amber 28.00
Wheat & Barley, Water Set, Amber, 7 Piece 175.00
Wheat Sheaf, Punch Cup, Child's 9.00
Whirling Star, Spooner, Child's 18.00
Whirling Star, Sugar, Cover, Child's 22.50
Wildflower, Creamer, Blue 45.00
Wildflower, Goblet, Amber 35.00
Willow Oak, Cake Stand, Amber 45.00
Willow Oak, Goblet .... 30.00 to 35.00
Willow Oak, Pitcher, Amber .... 55.00 to 70.00
Winged Scrolls, Box, Trinket, Green, Gold Trim, 3 In. 65.00

Wisconsin, Pitcher 95.00
Wooden Pail pattern is listed here as Oaken Bucket
X-Ray, Amethyst, Riverside 130.00
X-Ray, Berry Set, Green, 7 Piece 95.00
X-Ray, Creamer, Green, Gold Trim 65.00
X-Ray, Table Set, Green, 4 Piece 135.00
Yale pattern is listed here as Crowfoot
Zipper, Goblet .... 20.00 to 24.00
Zipper Slash, Toothpick, Ruby Stained 35.00

PRINT, in this listing, means any of many printed images produced on paper by one of the more common methods, such as lithography. The prints listed here are of interest primarily to the antiques collector, not the fine arts collector. Many of these prints were originally part of books. Other prints will be found in the Advertising, Currier & Ives, and Poster categories.

Audubon bird prints were originally issued as part of books printed from 1826 to 1854. They were issued in two sizes, 26 1/2 inches by 39 1/2 inches and 11 inches by 7 inches. The quadrupeds were issued in 28-by-22-inch prints. Later editions of the Audubon books were done in many sizes, and reprints of the books in the original size were also made. The bird pictures have been so popular they have been copied in myriad sizes by both old and new printing methods. This list includes originals and later copies because Audubon prints of all ages are sold in antiques shops.

Audubon, American Redstart, 19 1/2 x 12 1/4 In. 1725.00
Audubon, Black Billed Cuckoo, Frame, c.1834, 24 3/8 x 30 1/8 In. 3450.00
Audubon, Blue Grosbeak, 25 7/8 x 20 7/8 In. 2400.00
Audubon, Boat-Tailed Grackle, 25 7/8 x 20 3/4 In. 2300.00
Audubon, Brant Goose, Double Matted, Frame 300.00
Audubon, Canada Jay, 25 1/8 x 20 3/4 In. 800.00
Audubon, Fish Crow, 39 1/8 x 26 1/8 In. 2875.00
Audubon, Labrador Flacon, 39 x 26 1/8 In. 2875.00
Audubon, Least Bittern & Common Gallinule, Matted, 6 1/2 x 10 1/2 In., Pair 110.00
Audubon, Loggerhead Shrike & Swamp Sparrow, Matted, 10 1/2 x 6 1/2 In., Pair 187.00
Audubon, Mississippi Kite, 26 x 20 7/8 In. 2185.00
Audubon, Pigeon Falcon & Acadian Owl, Matted, 10 1/2 x 6 1/2 In., Pair 143.00
Audubon, Pine-Creeping Warbler, 19 1/4 x 12 1/4 In. 1265.00
Audubon, Purple Gallinule, 12 1/2 x 19 3/4 In. 2875.00
Audubon, Rathbone Warbler, 19 1/2 x 12 1/4 In. 1150.00
Audubon, Rice Bunting, 19 1/2 x 12 1/4 In. 1265.00
Audubon, Snow Geese, Double Matted, Frame 350.00
Audubon, Stellers Jay & Canada Jay, Matted, 10 1/2 x 6 1/2 In., Pair 99.00
Audubon, Swallowtail Hawk, Plate 18, J. Bien, N.Y., 1860, 21 x 29 In. 500.00
Audubon, Trumpeter Swan, Double Matted, Frame 400.00
Audubon, Turkey Buzzard, 39 x 26 1/4 In. 1850.00
Audubon, White-Fronted Goose, Double Matted, Frame 350.00
Audubon, White-Headed Eagle, 39 1/8 x 26 In. 3450.00
Audubon, White-Headed Eagle, Whatman Watermark, 1837, 25 x 38 In. 4500.00
Audubon, Wood Pewee & Ferruginous Thrush, 39 1/2 x 26 1/8 In. 3450.00
Baillie, Washington's Reception By The Ladies On The Bridge, Frame, 1848 .... 85.00
Bien, Rose-Breasted Grosbeak, Chromolith, 35 x 24 In. 2100.00
Bowen, American Flamingo, Frame, 9 1/4 x 6 In. 380.00
Courcelles, In Repose, Russian Wolfhound, Girl On Couch, Frame, 12 x 16 In. 120.00
Daumier, Social Satire, Child, Hanging On Door, Party, 12 1/2 x 14 In. 40.00
Fisher, 6 Greatest Moments In Woman's Life, Oak Frame 75.00
Fisher, Her Man, 1918 .... 135.00
Fox, June Mom, Original Frame 215.00
Fox, Sweet Dreams, 10 x 16 In. 70.00
Frances Brundage, The Mother, Daughter, Matted, Frame, 16 x 20 In. 55.00
Gutmann, Awakening, Frame, 18 1/2 x 13 1/2 In. .... 85.00 to 125.00
Gutmann, Bit Of Heaven 125.00
Gutmann, Friendly Enemies, 14 x 11 In. 50.00
Gutmann, Happy Dreams 275.00

Gutmann, Message Of Rose 250.00
Gutmann, On The Up & Up, Boy & Dog, Going Upstairs 30.00
Harris, Harbor Scene, Sepia Etch, 1891, Small Folio 250.00
Havell, Pigeon Hawk, No. 19, 1837, 34 x 24 7/8 In. 4100.00
Havell, Swamp Sparrow, Male, 1929, 26 x 18 In. 795.00
Icart, Carmen, 1927, Frame, 20 1/4 x 13 78 In. 862.00
Icart, Conchita, Signed, 1929, 20 1/4 x 13 7/16 In. 1150.00
Icart, Hydrangeas, 1927, Frame, 16 7/8 x 21 In. 1150.00
Icart, Joan Of Arc, Signed, 1929, 19 x 14 5/8 In. 920.00
Icart, In The Nest, Frame, 19 1/2 x 11 1/4 In. 865.00
Icart, Laziness, Frame, Signed, 1925, 15 x 19 In. 1495.00
Icart, Leda & Swan, Frame, 11 3/4 x 9 3/4 In. 4100.00
Icart, Madame Butterfly, 1927, 21 1/8 x 14 1/8 In. 977.00
Icart, Miss California, 1927, Frame, 21 x 16 3/4 In. 1725.00
Icart, Nude Woman, c.1930, 19 x 15 1/8 In. 575.00
Icart, Perfect Harmony, Frame, Signed, 1932, 13 1/8 x 17 3/8 In. 2875.00
Icart, Repose, 1934, Frame, 19 3/4 x 46 1/2 In. 1840.00
Icart, Salome, Etched, Windmill Stamp, 13 1/4 x 19 3/4 In. 1210.00
Icart, Sleeping Beauty, Frame, Signed, 1927, 14 3/4 x 18 1/2 In. 1495.00
Icart, Speed, 1927, Frame, 15 1/2 x 25 1/2 In. 2300.00
Icart, Spilled Milk, Frame, 17 x 21 1/2 In. 862.00
Icart, Symphonie En Bleur, Etched, Windmill Stamp, 18 3/4 x 22 1/4 In. 1760.00
Icart, Young Girl With Parrot, Oval Frame, Signed 715.00
Kellogg, Washington's Reception By Ladies At Trenton, April 1789, 12 3/4 x 16 3/4 In. .. 72.00

Japanese woodblock prints are listed as follows: Print, Japanese, name of artist, title or description, type, and size. Dealers use the following terms: Tate-e is a vertical composition. Yoko-e is a horizontal composition. The words Aiban (13 by 9 inches), Chuban (10 by 7 1/2 inches), Hosoban (12 by 6 inches), Oban (15 by 10 inches), and Koban (7 by 4 inches) denote size. Modern versions of some of these prints have been made.

Japanese, Cat, T. Inoue, Frame, Glazed 192.00
Japanese, Eisen, Bust-Length Portrait Of Courtesans, Kiwame Seal, Oban Tate-e 522.00
Japanese, Eisen, Courtesans, Kiwame Seal, Oban Diptych 715.00
Japanese, Hasui, Temple Steps In Snow, Oban Tate-e, 1926, 3 Piece 275.00
Japanese, Hirosada, Actors As Samurai, Ship, Chuban Triptych 302.00
Japanese, Hokusai, Reflected Moon Bridge, Yamashiro, Oban Yoko-e 385.00
Japanese, Hokusai, Shuitsu Mu-Tamagawa, Chuban Tate-e 192.00
Japanese, Jacoulet, Coucher De Soleil A Menado/Celebes, Dai Oban Tate-e 220.00
Japanese, Jacoulet, Joaquina Et Sa Mere Au Sermon Du Pere Pons, Dai Oban 385.00
Japanese, Jacoulet, Le Betel Yap, Dai Oban Tate-e, 15 1/2 x 11 3/4 In. 302.00
Japanese, Jacoulet, Retour De La Jungle/Tondano: Celebes, Dai Oban 467.00
Japanese, Kuniyoshi, Samurai Fighting Men Under Bridge, Oban Triptych .. 247.00
Japanese, Landscape, Canal, Koho, Frame, 14 x 11 In. 27.00
Japanese, Scene From Genji Monogatari, Triptych, Toyokuni III 605.00
Japanese, Shunsen, Young Man, Courtesan, Hashira-e 302.00
Japanese, Utamaro, Courtesan & Korean Soldier, Kiwame Seal, Oban Tate-e 220.00
Japanese, Utamaro, Courtesan And Young Man With Tea Bowl, Kakemono-e 165.00
Japanese, Utamaro, Courtesan Of The Matsuba-Ya Teahouse, Oban Tate-e .. 357.00
Japanese, Woman With Umbrella, Frame, 17 1/2 x 12 1/2 In. 55.00
Japanese, Yoshida, El Capitan, United States Series, Oban Tate-e, 1925 ...... 880.00
Japanese, Yoshida, Moraine Lake, Oban Tate-e, 1925 .... 522.00
Japanese, Young Woman, Choki, Frame, 10 3/4 x 8 3/4 In. 27.00
Kellogg, Happy Mother, Small Folio 79.00
Kellogg, Presidents Of United States, Frame, 8 3/4 x 14 3/4 In. 27.00
Kellogg, Red, White & Blue, Children & Roses, Frame, 16 x 13 In. 27.00
Kelly & Sons, Summer Scene In The Country, Frame, 26 1/2 x 32 1/2 In. ... 165.00
McKenny & Hall, Ca Ta He, Black Hoof, Shawnee 225.00
McKenny & Hall, Encampment Of Piekam Indians Near Fort McKenzie 750.00
McKenny & Hall, Wa Kaun Ha Ka, Winnebago 325.00
McKenny & Hall, Wanata, The Charger 395.00
Moran, In The Newark Meadows, Black & White, Small Folio 195.00

Nutting prints are now popular with collectors. Wallace Nutting is known for his pictures, furniture, and books. Nutting *prints* are actually hand colored photographs issued from 1900 to 1941. There are over 10,000 different titles.

Wallace Nutting

Nutting, A Tap At The Squire's Door, 1904	265.00
Nutting, Early June Brides, Frame, 9 1/2 x 4 In.	130.00
Nutting, Slack Water, 13 x 16 In.	80.00
Nutting, Thatched Cottage, Frame, 3 x 4 In.	110.00

Parrish prints are wanted by collectors. Maxfield Frederick Parrish was an illustrator who lived from 1870 to 1966. He is best known as a designer of magazine covers, posters, calendars, and advertisements.

Maxfield Parrish

Parrish, Air Castles, 1906, 24 x 19 In.	200.00
Parrish, Cleopatra, Medium	695.00
Parrish, Daybreak, Medium	150.00
Parrish, Dinkey Bird, 11 x 15 In.	150.00
Parrish, Dream Garden, Frame, 1915, 14 x 24 1/2 In.	325.00 to 450.00
Parrish, Garden Of Allah, 1918	350.00
Parrish, Giant, Frame	100.00
Parrish, Italian Villas	250.00
Parrish, Knave Of Hearts	1200.00
Parrish, Knave Of Hearts, Frame, 1924, 11 1/2 x 9 1/2 In.	350.00
Parrish, Reveries	185.00
Parrish, Thy Rocks & Rills, Frame, 1944, 15 x 12 1/2 In.	250.00
Parrish, Waterfall, 7 x 10 In.	125.00
Parrish, When Day Is Dawning, Winter Scene	225.00
Parrish, Wild Geese, Frame	200.00 to 225.00
Powers, World War I Soldier, Embracing Girl, Frame, 8 x 15 In.	25.00
Prang, Battle Of Kenesaw Mountain, 15 x 21 1/2 In.	80.00
Prang, Sheridan's Final Charge At Winchester, 15 x 21 1/2 In.	170.00
Prang, Spring Song, 14 x 18 In.	85.00
Yard Long, Fruit, Oak Frame	100.00
Yard Long, R.H. Parker Whiskey, Churchill Downs, Oak Frame, 1912	150.00

PURSES have been recognizable since the eighteenth century, when leather and needlework purses were preferred. Beaded purses became popular in the nineteenth century, went out of style, but are again in use. Mesh purses date from the 1880s and are still being made. How to carry a handkerchief and lipstick is a problem today for every woman, including the Queen of England.

Alligator, Brown, 1940-1950	35.00
Alligator, Child's, Brown, No Chain, 1890, Small	45.00
Alligator, Head Flap, Head On Back, Shoulder Strap, Glass Eyes, Child's	8.50
Alummesh, Whiting & Davis, 1940s	35.00
Art Deco, Large Lucite Clasp	18.50
Beaded, Black To Blue, Leaf Motif, France	55.00
Beaded, Black, Cocktail Clutch, Sequins	38.00
Beaded, Blue & Black, Metal Handles, Clasp	65.00
Beaded, Child's	10.00
Beaded, Coin, Black Metallic, Flying Horses On Metal Top	75.00
Beaded, Draped Panels, Drawstring, 4 3/4 x 5 In.	75.00
Beaded, Evening, Scarlet, Silver & Gold, Beaded Strap, Moralito Of Pair	110.00
Beaded, Flapper Era, Peacock Motif, Beaded Fringe, 10 In.	115.00
Beaded, Flapper, Red & Silver Squares, Beaded Fringe, Sterling Silver Frame	125.00
Beaded, Gathered At Neck, Chain, Cut Steel, Fringe Top & Bottom, 9 x 6 In.	75.00
Beaded, Glass Pearl, Clutch, 1920s	15.00
Beaded, Heavy Upholstery, Side Pockets, 2 Handles, Bright Colors	28.00
Beaded, Iridescent Crystal	40.00
Beaded, Jewel Encrusted, Brass Filigree Frame, France, 19th Century	165.00
Beaded, Mother-Of-Pearl Sequins, Seed Pearl Clusters, Strap Handle, 7 x 6 In.	18.00
Beaded, Poodle, Matching Baby Poodle Key Chain, Belgium, 1950s	3450.00
Beaded, Raised Beadwork, Flowers, 1940s, 11 x 7 In.	85.00
Beaded, Seed Pearl, White On White, Floral Design, Spring Clasp, 8 1/2 x 6 In.	7.00
Beaded, Silver, Pouch Bag, Diamond Design, Fringes Top & Bottom	75.00

Beaded, Steel, Fringe, Fancy Frame, France, 6 x 8 In. 95.00
Beaded, Swan, Ivorine Handle 165.00
Black Suede, Calf Piping, Faux Amber Frame, Gucci, 1930s 285.00
Brocade, Evening, Fitted With Compact & Lipstick, Satin Lining, 1940s 105.00
Brown Alligator, Carteras De Calidad, Large 258.00
Drawstring, Wide Ribbon Of Chine Taffeta Woven In Pattern Of Roses, 1910s 105.00
Evening, Woven Brocade, Woven Sprays Of Prunus, Tiffany, 1950s 115.00
Faille, Black, Snap Closure, Narrow Faille Handle, 9 x 8 In. 6.50
Faille, Rhinestone Clasp 18.00
Flame Stitch, Pink Silk Lining, 1780s, 5 3/4 x 4 1/2 In. 625.00
Fur, Leather & Seal, Kilt, Child's, Sporran 65.00
Gilt Metal, Evening, Oriental Design, Strap, Hand Made .... *Illus* 50.00
Gold Metal, Clutch, Rhinestone Closure 20.00
Gold Plated, Evening, Embossed Basket Weave, Snake Chain, 1950s 95.00
Leather, Art Nouveau Embossed Front, Small 22.00
Leather, Basket Weave, Tan & Ivory, Strap, Judith Leiber 247.00
Leather, Brown, Silver Frame & Locks, Child's, 1880s 65.00
Leather, Marcasite Trim 30.00
Leather, Silver, Evening, Judith Leiber .... *Illus* 325.00
Leather, Silver, Rhinestone Buckle, Judith Leiber 82.00
Leather, Tooled Acorns, Leaves, Light Brown, Shoulder Bag 65.00
Leather, Tooled Floral Design, Black, 1950s 45.00
Leather, Tooled, In The Defense Of American Liberties, 1777 .... 2970.00
Leather, White, Evening, Kenneth Lane For Rosenfield .... *Illus* 150.00
Leather, Woven, Judith Leiber .... *Illus* 225.00
Lizard, Red Leather Interior, Lizard Handle, 9 x 6 In. 16.00
Lucite, Lunch Box Style, Gunmetal Gray 50.00
Lucite, Red Clear, Gold Strings Inserts, Dorset, 9 x 3 3/4 x 4 In. 55.00
Lucite, Rialto, Marbled White 75.00
Lucite, Woven Brass, Basket Form 35.00
Mesh, 14K Gold, Change, Zigzag Pattern, Diamond Frame, Sapphire Handle 2860.00
Mesh, Beadlite, Enameled, Whiting & Davis 125.00
Mesh, Coin, Sterling, Signed 85.00
Mesh, Enameled & Silver, 3 x 6 In. 80.00
Mesh, Enameled, Art Deco Frame, Black & Red, Whiting & Davis, 6 x 5 In. 250.00
Mesh, Gold, Whiting & Davis, 1940 .... 45.00
Mesh, Jeweled Top, Change 550.00
Mesh, Mandolin, Floral Design, Mesh Fringes, Inset Onyx In Frame Corners 175.00
Mesh, Piccadilly, Whiting & Davis, Compact In Frame 125.00
Mesh, Pierced Frame, Sapphire Closure, Chain, Seed Pearl Tassell 660.00
Mesh, Shield Shape Top, Change, Sapphires & Seed Pearls, 14K Gold 550.00
Mesh, Silver, Black & Rose Beads, Germany, 1920s 55.00
Mesh, Silver, Chain, Embossed Frame, Germany 37.50
Mesh, White Enamel, Whiting & Davis, Brown .... 100.00 to 125.00

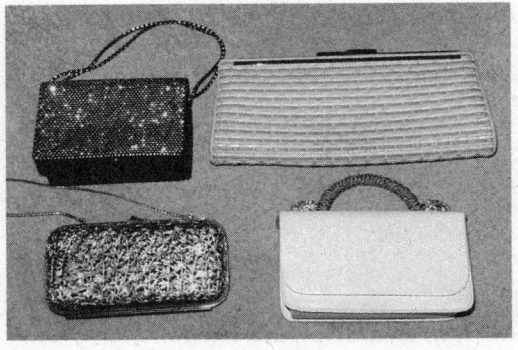

*Top row: Purse, Gilt Metal,
Evening, Oriental Design, Strap,
Hand Made; Purse, Leather,
Woven, Judith Leiber;
Bottom row: Purse, Leather, Silver,
Evening, Judith Leiber; Purse,
Leather, White, Evening, Kenneth
Lane for Rosenfield*

Mesh, Zigzag, Open Filigree Frame, Whiting & Davis 125.00
Mother-Of-Pearl, Change, Chain 70.00
Nantucket Basket, Faux Ivory Whale, 6 3/4 In. 95.00
Needlepoint, Floral, Original Change Purse, Mirror 48.00
Needlework On Canvas, Beadwork, Lucite Handle 28.00
Orange Tree Bark Textured, Synthetic Silk, Envelope Flap, Jean Patou, 1930s 145.00
Patent, Black, Clutch, Judith Leiber 247.00
Petit Point, Evening, Flowering Urn, Multicolored, France 82.00
Petit Point, Silver Plate Frame, Cherubs, Flowers & Foliage, 19th Century 176.00
Pocketbook, Nantucket, Carved Ivory Plaque Of Dolphin On Lid, 8 In. 1100.00
Pouch, Beaded, Black & Silver Checkerboard Design, Beaded Tassel Bottom 30.00
Rhinestone, Chain Handle, France, 1910s 35.00
Rhinestone, Evening, Strap, David's Of Palm Beach 88.00
Rhinestone, Gold Poodle Front, Gold Metal Leash 75.00
Satin, Black, Evening, Rhinestone Leopard Clasp, Kenneth Lane 137.00
Seed Pearl, Cocktail, Pearl Bugle Beaded 45.00
Silk, Pleated, Black, Embossed & Engraved Frame, Early 1900s, 4 x 6 In. 45.00
Silver, Coin, Art Nouveau, Pocket Watch Shape 125.00
Silver, Mounted, Engraved Thistle, Black & White Horsehair, Sporran 150.00
Snakesin, Clutch 60.00
Snakeskin, Brass Ring, Bass, 1940s 100.00
Tapestry, Evening, Red Beaded Roses, Red Satin Lining, Silver Frame 150.00
Tapestry Weave Cloth, Gilded Brass Fitting, White Enameled, 6 In. 55.00
Tortoiseshell, Gilt Metal, Victorian, Rectangular 110.00
Tortoiseshell, Plastic, Llewellyn, Honeycomb With Bees 85.00
Velvet, Black, Children & Cherub Frame, Marked 800 Italy 150.00
Velvet, Cut, Red, Yellow & Rust Flowers, 2-Tone Black, Strap Handle, 16 x 6 In. 5.00
Velvet, Openwork Pattern, People, Children, Medallion Chain, Silver Top 175.00
Wooden, Collins Of Texas 20.00
Woven Cigarette Packs, 11 x 7 In. 95.00

QUEZAL glass was made from 1901 to 1920 by Martin Bach, Sr., in Brooklyn, New York. Other glassware by other firms, such as Loetz, Steuben, and Tiffany, resembles this gold-colored iridescent glass. After Martin Bach's death in 1920, his son continued the manufacture of a similar glass under the name *Lustre Art Glass*.

Quezal

Bowl, Tree Form, Gold & Purple Crackle, Calcite Body, 11 In. 355.00
Compote, Gold Aurene, Footed, Signed, 4 1/2 x 6 In. 325.00
Decanter, Stopper, Green & Gold Double-Hooked Feathers, M. Bach, 11 1/2 In. 3850.00
Lamp, Bronze, Green Iridescent Mushroom Shade, 4 Acanthus Leaves, 26 In. 1610.00
Lamp, Desk, Art Nouveau Style, Ivory, Gold, Bronze Base, c.1920, 14 In. 220.00
Lamp, Desk, Gooseneck, Gold, Green & White Double-Hook Feather Shade, 12 In. .. 305.00
Shade, Gas, Snakeskin, White 295.00
Shade, Gold Hook Feathers, Gold Lining, 7 In. 345.00
Shade, Hearts & Vines, Gold Webbing 265.00
Shade, Iridescent Gold, Bell Form, 6 In. 225.00
Shade, Pulled Feather 85.00
Vase, Auto, Metal Holder, Gold, Signed 600.00
Vase, Blue & Green, Iridescent, 6 x 3 1/2 In. 300.00
Vase, Blue, White Lines, 11 In. 950.00
Vase, Double Bulbed, Flared Rim, Blue, Signed, 8 In. 550.00
Vase, Floriform, Amber, Green Feathering, Footed, c.1910, 11 7/8 In. 2415.00
Vase, Green & Gold Pulled Feathers, Band Of Gold Hearts, 9 3/4 In. 1265.00
Vase, Jack-In-The-Pulpit, Green & Gold Feather Pulls, Signed, 15 In. 1725.00
Vase, Jack-In-The-Pulpit, Pulled Feathers, Amber Interior, 1920, 13 1/8 In. 4600.00
Vase, Limousine, Gold Trim, Marked 550.00
Vase, Silver Frame, Cast With Berried Leaves, Signed, 11 3/4 In. 2070.00
Vase, White & Green, Gold Lining, 6 In. 1225.00

QUILTS have been made since the seventeenth century. Early textiles were very precious and every scrap was saved to be reused. A quilt is a combination of fabrics joined to a filler and a backing by small stitched designs known as quilting. An appliqued quilt has pieces stitched to the top of a large piece of background fabric. A patchwork, or pieced, quilt is made of many small pieces stitched together. Embroidery can be added to either type.

Amish, Patchwork, 15 Center Quilted Flowers, 41 x 58 In. 60.00
Amish, Patchwork, 16 Patch Variation, 76 x 73 In. 475.00
Amish, Patchwork Applique, Nine Patch & Irish Chain, Red & Cream, 102 x 83 In. .. 2070.00
Amish, Patchwork, Basket Pattern, Blue & Black, 68 x 78 In. 247.00
Amish, Patchwork, Basket Pattern, Multicolored, Cotton, 1930s, 90 x 63 In. 2645.00
Amish, Patchwork, Black & Green Sateen, 75 x 80 In. 770.00
Amish, Patchwork, Cables, Diamonds, Ferns, Heart, Black Cotton, 1940s, 79 x 67 In. 1375.00
Amish, Patchwork, Double Four-In-Nine, Cable Stitching, 88 x 68 In. 3450.00
Amish, Patchwork, Double Wedding Ring, Flowerhead Quilting, c.1890, 80 x 80 In. . 2185.00
Amish, Patchwork, Flower Garden, Lancaster County, c.1930, Crib 450.00
Amish, Patchwork, Geometric Pattern, Shades Of Green, 39 1/2 x 39 In. 65.00
Amish, Patchwork, Gray, Red & Orange, Faded, 75 x 88 In. 225.00
Amish, Patchwork, Lone Star, Blue Background, Lancaster County, 81 x 80 .... 1950.00
Amish, Patchwork, Nine Patch, Multicolored, Deep Green Border, 83 x 73 In. 3220.00
Amish, Patchwork, Star Design, Dark Solid Colors, 73 x 80 In. 137.50
Amish, Patchwork, Sunshine & Shadow, 20th Century, 36 x 54 In. 148.00
Amish, Patchwork, Sunshine & Shadow, Flannel Back, 85 x 85 In. 275.00
Amish, Patchwork, Sunshine & Shadow, Wool, Cotton & Synthetic, 84 x 80 In. 3450.00
Amish, Patchwork, Tumbling Blocks, Solid Colors, 45 x 52 In. 195.00
Amish, Patchwork, Variation Of Nine Patch, Cotton & Flannel, 76 x 72 In. 5463.00
Appliqued, 3 Rose Medallions, Border Swags & Tassels, Summer Weight, 83 x 97 In. . 715.00
Appliqued, 9 Oak Leaf Medallions, Vining Floral Border, 82 x 83 In. 225.00
Appliqued, 9 Stylized Baskets, Flowers & Puffed Berries, 75 x 100 In. 880.00
Appliqued, Album, Calico & Solids, Signed Names, 109 x 110 In. 8030.00
Appliqued, Baltimore Album, Hand-And-Heart & Eagle, c.1845 .... 20000.00
Appliqued, Basket, In White Blocks, Red Ground, 1880s, 89 x 78 In. 395.00
Appliqued, Bear's Paw, Dark Blue Borders, Dated 1884, 69 x 85 In. 275.00
Appliqued, Bowtie, Red, White & Light Blue, 3 Borders, 1920s, 79 x 71 In. 350.00
Appliqued, Calico, Fleur-De-Lis, Quilted Feather Wreaths, c.1850, 88 x 88 In. 1840.00
Appliqued, Chimney Sweep, Pastels, Dated 1927 & 1935, 70 x 80 In. 350.00
Appliqued, Dogwood Blossoms & Branches, Spider Web Quilting, 77 x 94 In. 303.00
Appliqued, Double Wedding Ring, Red & White, Scalloped Sides, 1920s, 86 x 82 In. ... 350.00
Appliqued, Drunkard's Path, Red & White, 1 In. Squares Quilted, 1920s, 81 x 64 In. 315.00
Appliqued, Floral Design, Red & Green, White Ground, 83 x 88 1/2 In. 880.00
Appliqued, Flower Basket, Fine Border, Shelbyville, Ind., 1848, 65 x 72 In. 950.00
Appliqued, Grandmother's Garden, Twin Size, Pair 550.00
Appliqued, Irish Chain, White, Blue Ground, Embroidered Names, 1930, 65 x 72 In. 850.00
Appliqued, Log Cabin Variation, 25 Printed & Solid Block, 58 1/4 x 58 In. 1725.00
Appliqued, Lone Star, Multicolored, 3 Row Border, 1920s, 82 x 85 In. 600.00

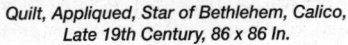

Quilt, Appliqued, Star of Bethlehem, Calico,
Late 19th Century, 86 x 86 In.

Quilt, Patchwork, Glazed Chintz,
Anna M. Stoeffer, 1852, 83 x 85 In.

Appliqued, Morning Glory Vines, Pastel Pink, Blue & Orchid, 88 x 88 In. 465.00
Appliqued, Nine Patch, Irish Chain Quilted Border, 66 x 74 1/2 In. 1550.00
Appliqued, Presidential Wreath, 1870s, 72 x 82 In. 1500.00
Appliqued, Red & Olive On White Ground, Feather Quilting, 82 x 84 In. 440.00
Appliqued, Rolling Stone, Calico, Brown With Green Border, 1870s, 77 x 68 In. 175.00
Appliqued, Roses & Buds, Feather Wreaths, 85 x 86 In. 990.00
Appliqued, Spools, Red, Blue, Calif. Street Methodist Church, 1904, 65 x 78 In. 250.00
Appliqued, Star of Bethlehem, Calico, Late 19th Century, 86 x 86 In. .... *Illus* 1150.00
Appliqued, Stylized Floral, Feather Quilted Medallions, 86 x 86 In. 550.00
Appliqued, Trees, Red, White & Green, Pennsylvania, Late 1800s, 70 x 64 In. 775.00
Appliqued, Whig Rose, 70 x 64 In. 250.00
Appliqued, Yo-Yo, Bright, 1920s, 60 x 72 In. 225.00
Crazy, Patchwork, 130 Felt Pieces From Packages Of Tobacco, 1930s 140.00
Crazy, Patchwork, American Pictorial, c.1875 .... 5500.00
Crazy, Patchwork, Cotton, Biblical Quotations, 1870s, Crib 1200.00
Crazy, Patchwork, Embroidered, Satin & Velvet, c.1880, 66 x 54 In. 445.00
Crazy, Patchwork, Embroidered, Satin & Velvet, Signed E.Y. 1883, 60 x 72 In. 445.00
Crazy, Patchwork, Silk, Velvet, Embroidered, 1900, 64 x 50 In. 425.00
Crazy, Spider Web Pattern, Silk & Velvet, 56 x 68 In. 2760.00
Linsey-Woolsey, Early 19th Century, 78 x 69 In. 325.00
Linsey-Woolsey, Floral, Cutout For Posts, Salmon 1 Side, Gold Other, 86 x 101 In. .. 275.00
Linsey-Woolsey, Geometric & Floral, Caliman Co., Cutout For Posts, 84 x 90 In. 935.00
Mennonite, Patchwork, Friendship, Wool, Embroidered, 1916, 69 x 81 In. 340.00
Mennonite, Patchwork, Lavender, Blue & White, Mrs. Orlin Byrer, 73 x 73 In. 275.00
Mennonite, Patchwork, Log Cabin, Green & Red Calico, 1870-1880s, 86 x 84 In. 475.00
Mennonite, Patchwork, Roman Stripes, 64 x72 In. 105.00
Mennonite, Patchwork, Weather Vane, Green & Blue Print, 78 x 82 In. 1215.00
Mennonite, Rolling Stone, Green & Red Strip, Jasper, Ind., Dated 1868, 90 x 90 In. 725.00
Patchwork, 13 Diamonds, Red Centers, Blue Grid, Sawtooth Edges, 77 x 79 In. 385.00
Patchwork, 16 Pinwheel Squares, Calico Ground, 75 x 76 In. 495.00
Patchwork, 16 Stars, 83 x 81 In. 525.00
Patchwork, 20 Squares, Red Star Pattern, Navy Ground, Cotton, 87 x 70 In. 1265.00
Patchwork, 25 Stars, Pinwheel Centers, Blue Print, 78 x 78 In. 220.00
Patchwork, Album, 20 Star Medallions, Embroidered Names, 1876, 69 x 84 In. 605.00
Patchwork, American Eagle, Red, Green & Yellow On White, 1930, 90 x 80 In. 675.00
Patchwork, Basket, Green & Magenta, White Ground, 80 x 96 In. 440.00
Patchwork, Basket, Orange & White, Machine-Sewn Binding, 82 x 82 In. 104.00
Patchwork, Basket Pattern, Red Border, 62 x 80 In. 137.50
Patchwork, Baskets Of Lilies, Blue, Beige & White, 68 x 84 In. 360.00
Patchwork, Baskets Of Pansies, Butterflies, Embroidered, 60 x 86 In. 150.00
Patchwork, Bear's Paw, Navy & Wine, 64 x 74 In. 350.00
Patchwork, Block, Late 19th Century, 74 x 68 In. 132.00
Patchwork, Blocks Of Butternut & Blue Patches, Chintz, c.1830, 91 1/2 x 90 In. 385.00
Patchwork, Calico, Prints, Solids, Pink Ground, 66 x 82 In. 110.00
Patchwork, Checkerboard Design, Multicolored Prints, 74 x 84 In. 71.50
Patchwork, Courthouse Steps, Wool Patches, 1910s, 74 x 82 In. 2013.00
Patchwork, Crazy Patch, Bible Quotes, Crib 1200.00
Patchwork, Crazy, Multicolor, Handstitched, c.1910 .... 195.00
Patchwork, Double Irish Chain Variation, 93 x 91 In. 900.00
Patchwork, Double Irish Chain, Green & White Calico, 104 x 104 In. 575.00
Patchwork, Double Wedding, 70 x 76 In. 240.00
Patchwork, Dresden Plate, White Ground, Blue Edge, 100 x 84 In. 115.00
Patchwork, Drunkard's Path, Vining Borders, 76 x 88 In. 358.00
Patchwork, Fan, Repeating Lattice, 68 x 68 In. 225.00
Patchwork, Fan, Turkey Tracks, Black & Plaid Wool, Dated 1876, 64 x 80 In. 2875.00
Patchwork, Floral, c.1870, 72 x 84 In. 1100.00
Patchwork, Flower Garden, Pink & White, c.1940, 75 x 60 In. 250.00
Patchwork, Friendship, Blue & White, Red Names, 1916, 69 x 82 In. 125.00
Patchwork, Friendship, Calico, Prints, Red, Blue, Gray, Yellow Grid, 90 x 92 In. 335.00
Patchwork, Geometric, Rose, Brown & Magenta, 85 x 88 In. 110.00
Patchwork, Glazed Chintz, Anna M. Stoeffer, 1852, 83 x 85 In. .... *Illus* 1265.00
Patchwork, Hired Man's, Calico, Brown, Yellow & Lavender, 1880s, 75 x 35 In. 245.00
Patchwork, Irish Chain, Feather Quilted Medallions, 82 x 92 In. 440.00

Patchwork, Irish Chain, Lavender, Pink & Green, 84 x 88 In.	85.00
Patchwork, Irish Chain, Quilted Floral Circle In Each Square, 82 x 90 In.	220.00
Patchwork, Irish Chain, Navy Blue Print, 72 x 84 In.	385.00
Patchwork, Lob Cabin Variant, 78 x 80 In.	99.00
Patchwork, Log Cabin, Brown & Blue Silk, 53 x 58 In.	192.50
Patchwork, Log Cabin, Multicolored Prints, Red Center, 80 x 80 In.	770.00
Patchwork, Log Cabin, Square, Lancaster County, c.1840, 80 In.	275.00
Patchwork, Lone Star, 1922, 78 x 88 In.	605.00
Patchwork, Lone Star, Calico Prints, Navy Blue, 79 x 81 In.	450.00
Patchwork, Lone Star, Goldenrod Binding, White Ground, 7 x 76 In.	82.50
Patchwork, Lone Star, Red Ground, 64 x 72 In.	300.00
Patchwork, Lone Star, Red & White Borders, 33 1/2 x 43 In.	110.00
Patchwork, Mickey Mouse, Crib, 1939	750.00
Patchwork, Monkey Wrench, Blue, Yellow Calico, 67 x 83 In.	192.50
Patchwork, Monkey Wrench, Green Calico, 88 x 88 In.	55.00
Patchwork, Moon & Stars, Swag Borders, c.1860, 60 x 76 In.	1380.00
Patchwork, Multiple Stars, Bars Back, 79 1/2 x 79 1/2 In.	375.00
Patchwork, Nine Patch, 1890, Crib	175.00
Patchwork, Nine Patch, Floral, Geometric & Bird Patterns, 1840, 49 x 68 In.	110.00
Patchwork, Nine Patch, Pink, Green, Dark Orange Ground, Square, 74 In.	300.00
Patchwork, Plume Pinwheels, 80 x 83 In.	605.00
Patchwork, Presentation, Strip, Red & Black, Providence, Ind., 1901, 68 x 71 In.	250.00
Patchwork, Princess Feather, Silk, Chenille, Cotton, Vine Border, 120 x 120 In.	1725.00
Patchwork, Sawtooth Design, Calico, Lancaster Co., Pa., 87 x 87 In.	957.00
Patchwork, Schoolhouse, Multicolored, 30 Squares, Cotton, 71 x 60 In.	3680.00
Patchwork, Schoolhouse, Navy & Salmon, 75 x 60 In.	425.00
Patchwork, Schoolhouse, Red & White, 77 x 69 In.	475.00
Patchwork, Schoolhouse, Red, Black, Gray, White, Penn., Early 1900s, 78 x 74 In.	1000.00
Patchwork, Snowflakes, Diamond Border, 66 x 80 In.	325.00
Patchwork, Souvenir Tobacco Silks, Baseball Players, National Flags, c.1910	55.00
Patchwork, Star Design, Pink On White, Feather Quilted Border, 95 x 96 In.	825.00
Patchwork, Star Of Bethlehem, Printed Fabrics, Field Of Tulips, Stars, 116 x 114 In.	1840.00
Patchwork, Star Of Bethlehem, White Ground, 98 x 75 In.	385.00
Patchwork, Star, 4 Shades Of Goldenrod & Orange, White Ground, 77 x 90 In.	192.00
Patchwork, Star, Green & Yellow Calico, 88 x 88 In.	165.00
Patchwork, Sunburst, America, 6 Ft.6 In. x 7 Ft.2 In.	40.00
Patchwork, Teal & White, Pinwheel Pattern, Feather Quilting Border, 80 x 80 In.	660.00
Patchwork, Triple Irish Chain, Mary Elizabeth McCauley, c.1870, 80 x 80 In.	1495.00
Patchwork, Tulips, 16 Sets Of 4, Yellow, Red & Green On White, 82 x 82 In.	725.00
Patchwork, Worsted Wool & Silk, 19th Century, 100 x 98 In.	715.00
Patchwork, Yo-Yo, Points On Edges, 82 x 85 In.	115.00
Trapunto, Cornucopia Center, Blossoms, Feathered Wreath, Child's, 36 x 36 In.	1380.00
Trapunto, Diamond Quilting, Rectangular Reserve, Child's, 52 x 60 In.	1380.00

QUIMPER pottery has a long history. Tin-glazed, hand-painted pottery has been made in Quimper, France, since the late seventeenth century. The earliest firm, founded in 1685 by Jean Baptiste Bousquet, was known as HB Quimper. Another firm, founded in 1772 by Francois Eloury, was known as Porquier. The third firm, founded by Guillaume Dumaine in 1778, was known as HR or Henriot Quimper. All three firms made similar pottery decorated with designs of Breton peasants and sea and flower motifs. The Eloury (Porquier) and Dumaine (Henriot) firms merged in 1913. Bousquet (HB) merged with the others in 1968. The group was sold to a United States family in 1984. The American holding company is Quimper Faience Inc., located in Stonington, Connecticut. The French firm has been called Societe Nouvelle des Faienceries de Quimper HB Henriot since March 1984.

Bowl, Peasant Woman, Handles, 5 In.	45.00
Creamer, Signed	35.00
Eggcup, Pair	75.00
Figurine, Baby Girl, B. Sevigny	225.00
Figurine, Dancing Peasants, Signed, c.1920, 10 In.	335.00
Figurine, Swan, 8 x 11 1/2 In.	850.00
Inkwell, Figural, Hat, Man Design	195.00

Mug, Chowder, Breton Woman & Man, Pair 95.00
Oyster Plate, Musicians & Dancers, Black & Yellow Trim, 9 1/2 In. 125.00
Pipe Rack, Man's Head, Black Hat, Hand Carved 900.00
Pitcher, Breton Peasant Man & Woman, Signed, Matched Pair 300.00
Planter, Centerpiece, 7 x 15 3/8 x 5 3/4 In. 1000.00
Plate, Faience, 9 3/4 In. 165.00
Plate, Peasant Girl, Cobalt Blue & Yellow Border, 10 1/2 In. 75.00
Plate, Shrimp Dip, Faience, Henriot 210.00
Plate, St. Michel, Slaying The Devil, 1850s 435.00
Soupier, Man, Handle, 1920s, Petite 185.00
Soupier, Woman, Handle, 1920s, Petite 185.00
Sugar, Breton Woman 48.00
Sugar, Cover, Cloverleaf Pattern, 1940 .... 95.00
Sweetmeat, Trefoil Shape 225.00
Wall Pocket, Bagpipe, 2 Musicians, 15 In. 2750.00

RADFORD pottery was made by Alfred Radford in Broadway, Virginia, Tiffin
and Zanesville, Ohio, and Clarksburg, West Virginia, from 1891 until 1912.
Jasperware, Ruko, Thera, Radura, and Velvety Art Ware were made. The $\qquad$ *RADURA.*
jasperware resembles the famous Wedgwood ware of the same name.

Ewer, Applied Grapes & Raspberries, Old Man Winter Handle, 9 In. 350.00
Jardiniere, Green & Brown, Drip Glaze, 10 In. 295.00
Mug, Applied Grapes 275.00
Vase, Radura, Mottled Green, Brown Matte Glaze, 4 Looped Handles, 10 In. 165.00

RADIO broadcast receiving sets were first sold in New York City in 1910.
They were used to pick up the experimental broadcasts of the day. The first
commercial radios were made by Westinghouse Company for listeners of the
experimental shows on KDKA Pittsburgh in 1920. Collectors today are
interested in all early radios, especially those made of Bakelite plastic or
decorated with blue mirrors. Figural advertising radios and transistor radios
are also collected.

Abbotwares, Metal Horse On Top, 13 3/4 In. 305.00
Addison, Catalin, Model 5F, Butterscotch & Red 1300.00
Addison, Peanut Butter Swirl 550.00
Admiral, AC Fire Ring Spark Plugs .... 200.00 to 250.00
Admiral, Model 6C22AN, Art Deco Grill 50.00
Air King, Black, Egyptian Design 3850.00
Arco Supreme Motor Oil Can, Transistor 45.00
Arvin, Check Mark, Red, Transistor 55.00
Atwater Kent, Cathedral, Model 84-V 200.00
Atwater Kent, Model 10A Breadboard, Horn, Battery, 1923 .... 1500.00
Auto, Tucker, Box 795.00
Bendix, Catalin, Model 526C, Marbleized Green & Black .... 675.00 to 750.00
Blue Max, No. 519, Transistor 45.00

Radio, California Raisin, Plastic,
Rubber Arms & Legs, 7 1/2 In.

◆◆◆◆◆◆◆◆◆◆◆◆◆◆◆◆◆◆◆◆◆◆◆◆◆

In half of all burglaries, the thief
came in through an unlocked
window or door.

◆◆◆◆◆◆◆◆◆◆◆◆◆◆◆◆◆◆◆◆◆◆◆◆◆

Bottle, Lone Star Beer, Box 850.00
Bulova, Transistor, Leather Case 68.00
California Raisin, Plastic, Rubber Arms & Legs, 1988, 7 1/2 In. .... *Illus* 48.00
Camcorder, Box, Transistor 75.00
Channelmaster, Model 6506, Red, Transistor 10.00
Coin-Operated, 1 Hour For 10 Cents, Box 150.00
Coronado, Table Model, Battery Operated, Wooden 40.00
Cosmopolitan, USA, Transistor 85.00
Country Bell, Guild, Wall Phone Type 125.00
Crosley, Metallic Blue 375.00
Crosley, Model 51, Wooden, Small 50.00
Crosley, Model 5TWE, Musical Chef 30.00
Crosley, Model D25MN, Coloradio, Maroon 125.00
Crosley, Select-A-Matic, Table, 1950s Jukebox Shape 40.00
DeWald, K-544, Transistor 100.00
Donny & Marie Osmond, Red, 1977 .... 30.00
Dr Pepper, Cooler Shape, Wooden Case, 12 x 8 1/2 x 8 In. 1320.00
Elgin, R-1400, Case, Transistor 15.00
Emerson, Eldorado, No. 911, Butterscotch, Transistor 35.00
Emerson, Model 569, Power Supply Plug, Portable, Ivory Bakelite Case 115.00
Emerson, Model 652, White Bakelite 45.00
Emerson, Rambler, Black, Transistor 75.00
Emerson, Vanguard 888, Turquoise, Transistor 50.00
Fada, Bright Green 485.00
Fada, Bullet, Model 1000, Blue, With Butterscotch Trim, 1946 .... 3500.00
Fada, Bullet, Model 1000, Catalin, Butterscotch, Red .... 1000.00 to 1760.00
Fada, Bullet, Model 115, Butterscotch, Red Trim, 1946 .... 4500.00
Fada, Catalin, 1941 .... 2000.00
Fada, Model 1000, Bullet, Maroon & Caramel .... 750.00 to 900.00
Fada, Model 652, Catalin, Caramel 850.00
Fada, Model 790, Wooden, 2 Band, Large 150.00
Film Pack 600, AM/FM, Box 25.00
Freed Eisemann, Neutrodyne, Model NR5, 1920s 80.00
Garod, Butterscotch, 1941 .... 2500.00
General Electric, AM/FM, Transistor 25.00
General Electric, Ivory & Gold, 1959 .... 35.00
General Electric, Model 202, Brown Bakelite 35.00
General Electric, Model 620-622, CD, Red, 1950 .... 45.00
General Electric, Model P797A, Beige Leather Case, Transistor, 1958 .... 35.00
General Electric, No. 50, Brown 36.00
General Electric, P766A, Plaid Grill, Transistor 35.00
General Electric, P850D, Black & Chrome, Transistor 30.00
Ghost Buster, Marshmallow Man, Transistor, Box 40.00
Ghost Buster, Slimer, Transistor, Box 50.00
Golf Cart, Transistor 75.00
Goodyear Wings, Short Wave, Wooden 195.00
Grand Piano, Bakelite, Lid Opens To Reveal Speaker & Dial, c.1940, 8 1/2 In. 690.00
Gridiron, Football 875.00
Guild, Country Belle, Wooden, Hanging, Crank, 1956 .... 125.00
Guild, Town Crier, Wooden, Metal, Glass Lantern, Transistor, 1958 .... 150.00
Gumby, Box, 1985, 10 In. 40.00
Hallicrafters, Model S-38 .... 65.00
Head Set, Holtzer Cabot 6.50
Heinz Ketchup, Bottle Shape 47.00
Jukebox, Windsor, AM/FM, Box 45.00
Ladybug, With Phonograph, Portable, 1970s 30.00
Lloyd's, Cylinder, Black, Japan 15.00
Magnavox, Model AM-20, With Clock, Black & Silver, Solid State 25.00
Magnavox, Transistor, Earphones, Leather Case, 1950s 5.00
Majestic, Model 59, Art Deco 250.00
Majestic, Model 921, Sailing Ship, Wooden Hull 325.00
Matsushita, T-7, Blue, Transistor 30.00
Michael Jackson, AM/FM, Transistor 20.00

Mork & Mindy, Eggship, AM, Concept 2000, Box, 1979 .... 30.00
Mork In Egg, Transistor, Box 45.00
Motorola, Catalin, Red, 1940 .... 5000.00
Oscar The Grouch, Trash Can 20.00
Owl, Ivory Plastic, Brass, Jeweled Eyes 85.00
Pee Wee, Crystal 180.00
Philco, Bakelite, Table Model, 1940s 38.00
Philco, Beehive, c.1930 .... 185.00
Philco, Model 19, Cathedral, Wooden, 1933 .... 150.00
Philco, Model 37-610B, Art Deco, 22 x 20 In. 85.00
Philco, Model T-7-126, Transistor, Leather Case, 1956 .... 85.00
Philco, Pocket, USA 60.00
Philco, Roll Top 75.00
Philco, With Clock, Grandfather, 1930s 995.00
Pillsbury, Doughboy, Quartz Clock, AM/FM Radio, Plastic, 1986, 4 1/2 In. 60.00
Plastic, Table Model, FM, 1940s, Police Emergency Dial 35.00
Pocket, Boy's Radio, Red, Transistor 45.00
Poppin' Fresh, Advertising 45.00
Pound Puppy, Transistor 25.00
Racing Car, John Player, No. 22, Transistor 35.00
Radio Shack, Battery Shape, 4 1/2 In. 60.00
Radio Shack, Red 25.00
Radio USA, AM/FM, Transistor 30.00
Railroad Crossing Signal, Box, Transistor 60.00
RCA, 1939 World's Fair 1100.00
RCA, Catalin, Model 66 x 8, Marbleized Black & Yellow 685.00
RCA, Model 8-R-71, Brown Marbleized Bakelite, 1949 .... 50.00
RCA, Radiola, External Speaker, c.1900 .... 200.00
RCA Victor, Levermatic, A.M. Clock, Beige, 1950s 55.00
RCA Victor, Model-X 71, Brown Bakelite, AM/FM, 1949 .... 80.00
Silvertone, Console, Cat's Eye Tuning, 5 Band, 1941 .... 389.00
Sinclair, Gas Pump, Dino 40.00
Sinclair Gasoline Pump Form, Transistor .... 35.00 to 50.00
Snoopy, Apollo, 1970 .... 50.00
Snoopy, On Doghouse, Transistor 40.00
Snoopy, Transistor, Earplugs, Box 24.00
Spartan, Fort Knobs, Model 558, Blue Glass 1850.00
Spartan, Model 409, 7 Sides, Blue Glass 2000.00
Spartan, Model 506, Bluebird, Blue Glass .... 2300.00 to 2750.00
Sparton, Blue Mirror, 4 Knobs, 1937 .... 3500.00
Sparton, Model 557, Blue Mirror Glass, Chrome Fins, Black Base, 3 Knobs, Table, 1936 2000.00
Sports, AM/FM, Yellow, Transistor 15.00
Stewart Warner, No. A72T3, AM/FM, Table, 1948 .... 35.00
Stewart Warner, Tan & Maroon, Celluloid, Table Model 10.00
Strawberry Shortcake, Transistor 20.00
Stromberg Carlson, Kitchen, Red & White, 1940s 65.00
Stromberg Carlson, Tombstone, No. 60, Wooden, c.1930 .... 250.00
Sylvania, Model 510B, Beige Painted Bakelite, 1950 .... 60.00
Teacup & Saucer, Transistor, Box 35.00
Tester, Tube, National Radio Institute, Metal Carrying Case 62.50
Thunderbird, 1963, Transistor 75.00
Tom Thumb, Bakelite, Box 95.00
Tony The Tiger, Transistor, Box .... 30.00 to 45.00
Touring Car, 1917 Model, Metal, Japan 55.00
Trophy, Baseball, Tube Type, Transistor 850.00
Tropicana Orange, AM/FM 25.00
Western Auto Supply, Model 557, Pearl Formica, Table, 1950s 26.00
Westinghouse, Aeriola, Wooden Case, Globe Crystal Set, Pat. June 1921 .... 165.00
Wuzzle Butter Bear, Transistor 25.00
Zenith, Clock, Model 520R 35.00
Zenith, Console, Model 8-S-463 .... 150.00
Zenith, No. 3000-1, Leather, Telescope Antenna .... 65.00 to 125.00

Zenith, R40, Transistor	40.00
Zenith, Royal 800, Black, Transistor	150.00

RAILROAD enthusiasts collect any train memorabilia. Everything is wanted, from oilcans to whole train cars. The Chessie system has a store that sells many reproductions of their old dinnerware and uniforms.

Ashtray, Canadian Pacific, Ceramic, Brown & White	55.00
Ashtray, Chessie Cat	55.00
Ashtray, Clinchfield RR, Blue Ridge	50.00
Ashtray, New York Central, Rooster Logo	45.00
Ashtray, Pullman Co.	35.00
Baggage Cart, 2 Wheels, 1870-1880	525.00
Baggage Tag, Indiana Funeral Directors, Golden Gate Special, San Francisco, 1940	10.00
Bowl, Cereal, Portland Rose	345.00
Bread Plate, Winged Union Pacific	18.00
Button, Uniform, CV	3.50
Button, Uniform, Rock Island	3.50
Cart, Baggage, Ames RR. Co.	125.00
Chisel, Santa Fe Railroad, Iron	4.50
Condiment Set, Santa Fe, 3 Piece	15.00
Creamer, Seaboard Line, International Silver	70.00
Crossing Light, Pair	20.00
Cup, Folding, Kansas & Oklahoma, Tin, 1897	50.00
Cup & Saucer, Baltimore & Ohio, Blue & White, Lamberton Mark	105.00
Flag, Centennial, ICRR, 6 x 4 Ft.	1000.00
Hat, Lapel Badge, Chicago Elevated Railroads, Enameled Brass, 3 Piece	40.00
Lamp, Desk, Kerosene, Railroad Depot, Tin, Fancy Cast Iron Base	60.00
Lamp, Inspector's, Ham	2001.00
Lamp, Oil, Coach, With Bracket	60.00
Lantern, Anaconda & Pacific RR, Bell Bottom	95.00
Lantern, Battery, Baltimore & Ohio RR	7.50
Lantern, C & O RR, Red Globe, Weighted Base	135.00
Lantern, City Of New York, Dietz, Red Cast Globe	75.00
Lantern, Colorado & Southern, Bell Bottom, Etched	350.00
Lantern, Conductor's, Brass, Blake's Patent 1852, Etched Globe A. Carter, 14 In.	990.00
Lantern, Dietz, BRT, Bell Bottom, Blue-Green, 5 3/8 In.	125.00
Lantern, Dietz, New York Central, Protection Track Walker	150.00
Lantern, Embossed Globe, Bell Bottom, NYNH & RR, 5 3/8 In.	125.00
Lantern, Great Northern, Clear	200.00
Lantern, Inspector's, Pennsylvania RR	85.00
Lantern, Milwaukee Road, Brass Top, Bell Bottom	275.00
Lantern, New York Central, Clear Globe, Pat. 1911	35.00
Lantern, New York Central, Red Globe	65.00
Lantern, Northern Pacific, Red Globe	200.00
Lantern, Pennsylvania RR, Blue Globe	65.00
Lantern, Presentation, Clear Globe	100.00
Lantern, Rock Island	55.00
Lantern, Tall Globe, Frisco Logo, Extended Base	125.00
Lantern, Westlake, LLU RR, Embossed Red Globe	120.00
Lantern, Wizard	15.00
Lantern Frame, Wabash Railroad, Bell Bottom	125.00
Lock, Alabama Southern, With Key, Cast Iron	35.00
Lock, C & NW	15.00
Lock, Frisco Railroad, Original Key	400.00
Lunch Box, Canadian	75.00
Mirror, With Comb Case & Towel Bar, Railroad Hotel, Tin, Framed	12.50
Mug, New York Central Railroad, Pottery, Large	5.50
Mug, Rock Island Railroad, Pottery, Large	5.50
Nail, Copper, 1934	1.00
Padlock, DL & WRR, Large Lock, Hasp, 1940	25.00
Padlock, Wabash Railroad, Yellow Brass, Heart Shape	25.00
Pamphlet, New England, Timetables Of Railroads & Steamboats, 1886	30.00

Paperweight, Rock Island, Glass, 1880s 85.00
Photograph, Southern Pacific Train Scene, Black & White, 11 x 14 In. 12.00
Pin, Collar, Rock Island Railroad, Enameled Gold 3.50
Pin, Lapel, Kerosene Lantern, Railroad Switchman's, Enameled Silver 2.50
Plate, Missouri Pacific Lines, State Flower, 10 1/2 In. 250.00
Plate, Missouri Pacific Steam & Diesel Locomotive, China, Pair 575.00
Plate, New York Central RR, DeWitt Clinton, 9 In. 52.00
Plate, New York Central, Wedgwood 55.00
Plate, The B & O, Staffordshire, 9 In. 660.00
Platter, Atchison, Topeka & Santa Fe, Adobe, 9 In. 85.00
Platter, CB & QRR, Violets, Daisies, 12 1/2 x 8 1/2 In. 375.00
Platter, CM & PS, Puget, 9 1/4 x 13 1/2 In. 195.00
Postcard, Florida E. Coast RR Co., Lure To Settlers, Postmark, Fold-Out 12.00
Shovel, Santa Fe 20.00
Sign, Boston & Main Railroad, Reverse Paint On Glass, 12 x 47 In. 5500.00
Sign, Crossing, Porcelain, Reflector, Yellow, Black, Round, 24 In. 65.00
Sign, Grand Texas Excursion, Steamer Telegraph & Railroad, 1870s, 13 x 6 1/2 In. ... 38.00
Sign, Railroad Crossing, Embossed Steel, Black, Yellow Ground, Round, 30 In. 28.00
Sign, Western Railroad, St. Louis, Iron Mount & Southern Railway, 1870s, 21 x 7 In. 44.00
Signal Flags, Case, 1961 Museum Label 185.00
Telephone Earpiece, Black Bakelite, Southern Pacific, Attached Cord & Plug 32.00
Timetable, Atchison, Topeka & Santa Fe, 64 Pages, 1944 .... 12.50
Timetable, Burlington Route, California Zephyr, Ticket Stubs, 1955 .... 5.00
Timetable, Direct Route To World's Fair, Pennsylvania, 4/30/39 .... 13.00
Timetable, Dunard, Anchor Line, Napoli, New York, 1923 .... 10.00
Timetable, Santa Fe, 1934 .... 10.00
Torch, LVRR RR, Johnson Urgana 35.00
Towel, Hand, Linen, White, Blue Stripes, 25 x 16 In., 1923 .... 25.00
Towel, Hand, Linen, White, Blue Stripes, 25 x 16 In., 1915 .... 25.00
Towel, Santa Fe Railroad, Cloth 3.50
Uniform, Conductor's, New York Central, Cap, Jacket, Vest 125.00

RAZORS were used in ancient Egypt and subsequently wherever shaving
was in fashion. The metal razor used in America until about 1870 was made
in Sheffield, England. After 1870, machine-made hollow-ground razors were
made in Germany or America. Plastic or bone handles were popular. The
razor was often sold in a set of seven, one for each day of the week. The set
was often kept by the barber who shaved the well-to-do man each day in the
shop.

Atlantic Cutlery Co., Straight, Bone Handle, 1900 .... 12.00
Baker, Straight, Carved Ivory Handle, Box, Germany 25.00
Bank, For Razor Blades, Mug Shape 30.00
Black Boy, McKeever Bros., Straight, Mingo, Iowa, Green Celluloid Case 25.00
Blade, Asco, Single, Blue Wrapper, Unused 1.00
Blade, Continental, 5-Pack, 1920s, Unused 5.00
Blade, Curvfit, Single, Unused 1.25
Blade, Don Juan, Single, Unused .... .50
Blade, Enders, Envelope .... .50
Blade, Eureka, Oxford, Ohio, Pack, 1907 .... 15.00
Blade, Gillette Blue, Single, Dark Blue Wrapper, Unused 1.00
Blade, Gillette Techmatic, Single, Unused 1.00
Blade, Marlin, Pack, Unused 1.50
Blade, Sani-Steel, Double Edge, Pack, Unused 2.50
Blade Bank, Frog, Figural, Listerine Shaving Cream 25.00
Blade Dispenser, Brass Wall Plaque, With Slot, For Used Razor Blades, Hotel 12.50
Blade Dispenser, Ever Ready Razor, Domed Trunk, Tin, Tan & Gold 15.00
Box, Auto Strop Razor Co., Brass, Hinged Lid 2.25
Box, Gillette, Man's Picture 1.00
Box, Twenty Grand Razor Blades, Race Horse Wrappers, 4 Piece 3.00
Christy, Directions, Box 9.00
Christy Safety, Box 20.00

Crater Guarded, Folding, Ivory Celluloid Handles, Metal Case 95.00
Curvfit, Woman's, Safety, Gold Plated, 1920s 8.00
Daisy, Safety, Lipstick, Woman's, In Tube 50.00
Durham Duplex, Straight, Ivoroid Handle 5.00
Durham Duplex, Straight, Ivory Celluloid Travel Case .... 10.00 to 18.00
Edw. Saville Eclipse, Straight, Horn Handles 12.00
Emir, Woman's, Safety, Boudoir Type, 1920s 15.00
Fred Dolle, Straight, Black Steel, Bone Handle, Knight Riding Frog 14.00
Gem, Brass 2.50
Gem, Micromatic, Brown Plastic, 2 Blade Case, 1930s 10.00
Gem, Safety, Basket Weave Metal Case, Gold Plated, 1912 .... 10.00
Gem, Tuckaway Style Case, 1912 .... 18.00
Gem Micromatic, NRA Emblem, Unused, Box 15.00
Genco, Folding, Riveted Blade Guard, Ivory Celluloid Handles 100.00
Geneva Cutlery Co., Straight, Ivory Celluloid Handles, Case 15.00
Gillette, Safety, Blades, Box 10.00
Gillette, Yellow Brass 3.50
Gillette Big Boy, Nickel Plated, Case 25.00
Gillette Goodwill, Variant No. 162 Cap & Guard, Box 75.00
Gillette Milady, Case, 1920s 10.00
Gillette Super-Speed, Red & Clear Plastic Case 7.00
Griffon Angle Corn, Germany 50.00
Hone, Dixon 5.00
Hone, Keen Kutter, K20, Tin Box 25.00
Hone, Novell Shapleigh Diamond Edge, Box 10.00
Hone, Primble, Leather Strop 40.00
Hone, Toncarial Gem, Stone 2.25
Kampfe, Safety, Star Safety, Patented 1901 .... 92.00
Keen Kutter, Safety 11.00
Keen Kutter, Straight Edge, Red Handle, Box 50.00
Kewtie, Lady's Personal Hygenic, Midget, Pink Case 25.00
Kit, Autostrop, Green Canvas 17.50
Kit, Valet Autostrop, Metal Box 20.00
Laurel, Woman's, Boudoir, Tin Litho Case, Unused 40.00
Neillite 400, Safety, Black Bakelite 4.00
Norelco, Electric, Triple Head, Cased, 1970s, Directions 8.00
Nude Handle, Straight 35.00
Nude Handle, Woman Picking Grapes, Celluloid, Straight, Germany 20.00
Pathfinder, Big Chief, Indian On Blade, Straight, Box 34.00
Pearl Cutlery Co., Straight, Ivory Celluloid Handles, Case 15.00
Pearl Handle, Straight 125.00
Remington, Electric, Illustration Of Electrical Building, World's Fair, 1939 .... 165.00
Remington, Electric, New York World's Fair, Box, 1939 .... 225.00
Remington De Luxe, Electric, Hard Case 5.00
Reynolds, Straight, Our Own Etched On Blade, Black Handle 10.00
Rolls, Self Contained Strop & Sharpening Stone 15.00
Rolls, Stropping Machine, Hard Case 25.00
Safety, Dime, Tin Litho Can, Directions, 1915 .... 80.00
Schick, Repeater, Barber, Brass 20.00
Schick Injector, 4 Speed Stick 5.00
Shapleigh, Straight, Marbleized Celluloid Handles, Sterling Case 20.00
Simmons, Straight, Box 45.00
Slant Stroke, Brown Bakelite 8.00
Straight, 7 Days, Missing Tuesday, Box, 6 Piece 175.00
Straight, Tortoiseshell Celluloid Handle, Box 50.00
Strop, Valet Auto, Dome Top Iron Case 5.25
Wade & Butcher, Large Blade 25.00
Wade & Butcher Original Arrow, Straight, Black Horn Handle, Gold Wash 12.00
Wallet, Straight Razor, 7 Individual Slots In Stitched Lining 10.00
Weller, Folding, Imitation Ivory Handle 45.00
Wilkinson, Safety, 4, Wedge Blades 50.00
Women's, Round Shape, Woman Illustrated On Silver Box, 1930s 45.00

REAMERS, or juice squeezers, have been known since 1767, although most of those collected today date from the twentieth century. Figural reamers are among the most prized.

Arcade No. 2, Ironstone Insert	85.00
Black Glass	10.00
Clown	45.00
Cobalt Blue Glass, Handle, Large	14.00
Criss-Cross, Hazel Atlas	5.00
Delphite	95.00
Green, Fry	30.00
Green, Loop Handle, Anchor Hocking	12.00
Horizontal Fine Rib, Clear, Ribbed Handle	3.00
Lemon, Clear, Vertical Rib, Seed Guard, Tab Handle, Federal	3.00
Lemon, Clear, Vertical Rib, Tab Handle, Anchor Hocking	3.00
Lemon, Green	11.00
Orange Juice Extractor, Green, Tab Handle	48.00
Ribbed Body, Loop Handle, Hocking Glass	12.50
Shelley, Green & White	145.00
Sunkist, 100th Anniversary, Blue	75.00
Sunkist, Milk Glass	12.00
Sunkist, Yellow	20.00
Yellow Glass, 2 Cups	300.00

RECORDS have changed size and shape through the years. The cylinder-shaped phonograph record for use with the early Edison models was made about 1889. Disc records were first made by 1894, the double-sided disc by 1904. High-fidelity records were first issued in 1944, the first vinyl disc in 1946, the first stereo record in 1958. The 78 RPM became the standard in 1926 but was discontinued in 1957. In 1932, the first 33 1/3 RPM was made but was not sold commercially until 1948. In 1949, the 45 RPM was introduced. Compact discs became available in the U.S. in 1982 and many companies began phasing out the production of phonograph records.

A Frog He Would A-Wooing Go., Book, Harper Bros. & Columbia, 5 1/2-In. Records	125.00
Al Jolson, Album, Souvenir, 78 RPM, 4 Piece	35.00
Album, A Star Is Born, Barbra Streisand & Kris Kristofferson, Columbia	10.00
Album, Bugs Bunny In Storyland, Picture Book, 78 RPM, 1949	14.00
Album, Bugs Bunny, Daffy Duck, Elmer Fudd, Capitol, 45 RPM, 1950s, Pair	30.00
Album, Cowboy Songs, Bing Crosby, Decca, 1948, 4 Piece	27.50
Album, Judy Garland Concert, Trophy Record, 1974	15.00
Album, Little Black Sambo's Jungle Band, Victor, 1939	70.00
Album, Marjorie Morningstar, Natalie Wood & Gene Kelly, RCA	10.00
Album, Rumba Lesson, Vogue, 2 Piece	175.00
Album, Showtime, Best Of Broadway, Streisand, Lansbury, Judy Holliday	6.00
Album, Wondrous World Of Sonny & Cher, Atco	5.00
Album, ZZ Top, American Blues	35.00
Around The World In 80 Days	25.00
Arthur Murray, Square Dances, 45 RPM	5.00
Brave Little Sambo, 78 RPM, 1959	45.00
Captain Kangaroo & His Friends Sing Songs Of The Treasure House, 1960s	8.00
Children's, Heckle & Jeckle, 45 RPM, Little Golden, 1958	24.00
Christmas Hymns & Carols, Mario Lanza, Album, RCA	5.00
Christmas With Julie Andrews, Album, RCA, 1969	5.00
Great Songs Of Christmas, Album, Nelson Eddy, Others, Columbia, For Goodyear	10.00
Holder, Dick Clark's Face As Music Note, Signed	75.00
I Can Hear It Now, E.R. Murror, Album	40.00
I Love Lucy, Lyrics, Desi Arnaz, 78 RPM, 1950s	52.00
James Bond, Dr. No Original Motion Picture Sound Track, United Artists, 1963	49.00
John Kennedy, Musical Narration Tribute To JFK, Jim Ameche, RCA, 45 RPM	15.00
Mike Hammer, Mickey Spillane's, Original Sound Track, RCA, 1959	32.00
Nursery Rhyme, Decca, 1946	2.00
Oh Susanna, Black Boy & Girl Pictured, Plastic, 1948	23.00
Roamin' In The Gloamin', Annie Laurie & Guy Lombardo	8.00

Roy Orbison, Sings Don Gibson, MGM, 33 1/3 RPM	400.00
Six Presidents Speak, Album, 78 RPM	25.00
Songs I Sing On The Jackie Gleason Show, Frank Fontaine, 1950s	10.00
Spiderman, 1974, 33 1/3 RPM	12.50
Sweet Georgia Brown, Harlem Globetrotters	15.00
War Of The Worlds, Album, Orson Welles	15.00

RED WING Pottery of Red Wing, Minnesota, was a firm started in 1878. The company first made utilitarian pottery. In the 1920s art pottery was made. Many dinner sets and vases were made before the company closed in 1967. Rumrill pottery was made for George Rumrill by the Red Wing Pottery and other firms. It was sold in the 1930s. For more information, see *Kovels' Depression Glass & American Dinnerware Price List.*

Ashtray, Land Of 1,000 Lakes, Full Figure Fish	40.00
Bean Pot, 1/2 Gal.	120.00
Bean Pot, Large	30.00
Bean Pot, Village Green	28.00
Beater Jar, 1925	140.00
Beater Jar, Advertising, Baker-Johnson Co., Ridgeway, Iowa	135.00
Beater Jar, Gray Line	180.00
Berry Bowl, Blossom Time, Concord Shape	3.00
Bowl, Blossom Time, Concord Shape, 8 1/2 In.	9.00
Bowl, Bob White, 2 Sections, 15 In.	22.00
Bowl, Floral Relief Design, Oval, Gunmetal Brown, 13 1/2 x 8 In.	25.00
Bowl, Magnolia, Square, 5 1/4 In.	4.00
Bowl, Red & Blue Band, 9 1/2 In.	50.00
Bowl, Reverse Picket Fence, Blue, 11 1/4 In.	55.00
Bowl, Sponged Panels, 11 In.	125.00
Bowl, Tampico, 5 1/4 In.	6.00
Bowl, Vegetable, Crazy Rhythm	15.00
Butter, Cover, Smart Set	200.00
Butter Pail, Lid, No. 5, Gray Line	300.00
Casserole, Cover, Advertising, It Pays To Mix With Peter Bootzin, Saffronware	250.00
Casserole, Cover, Gray Line, Signed Made In Red Wing, Largest	270.00
Chicken Waterer, Button Top	10.00
Churn, Butter, Large Wing, 10 Gal.	2150.00
Churn, Elephant Ear, Minnesota Oval, 5 Gal.	1225.00
Console, Feathery Leaves, Tan Patina, Cream Ground, 15 1/2 x 10 In.	24.00
Cookie Jar, Bob White	110.00 to 165.00
Cookie Jar, Carousel	145.00
Cookie Jar, Chef, Beige	110.00
Cookie Jar, Chef, Yellow	60.00 to 90.00
Cookie Jar, Jack Frost	500.00
Cookie Jar, King Of Tarts	460.00
Cookie Jar, King Of Tarts, Multicolored	695.00
Cookie Jar, Monk, Green	275.00
Crock, Blue Leaf, Minnesota Co., Salt Glaze, 15 Gal.	575.00
Crock, Boysenberry, MSCo., 20 Gal.	4300.00
Crock, Butter, 20 Lb.	190.00
Crock, Butter, Crescent Milk Co., No. 3	220.00
Crock, Butterfly, MSCo., 20 Gal.	1175.00
Crock, Cheese, Bail Handle, Liberty Brand Creamed Cottage Cheese, No. 10	325.00
Crock, Cobalt Blue Quill Design, Leaves & 20, 22 1/2 In.	165.00
Crock, Dart Pattern, 3 Gal.	95.00
Crock, Grape Leaf Design, MSCo., 25 Gal.	1275.00
Crock, Large Wing, Red Wing, 2 Gal.	80.00
Crock, Marked, Wing-5 In., 50 Gal.	700.00
Crock, Wing, 20 Lbs.	200.00
Crock, Wing-4 In., 1 Gal.	375.00
Cruet Set, Round-Up, With Stand	200.00
Cup & Saucer, Blossom Time, Green, Concord	4.50
Cup & Saucer, Bob White	14.00
Cup & Saucer, Lotus, Chartreuse	4.25

Cup & Saucer, Tampico 9.50
Dinner Set, Tampico, 43 Piece 120.00
Feeder, Ko-Roc, Signed, 1 Gal. 100.00
Figurine, Boy Holding A 10-Gallon Crock 2100.00
Figurine, Gopher, Football, Brown, Signed 85.00
Figurine, Lady With Tambourine, No. B1416 .... 125.00
Figurine, Man With Accordion, No. B1417 .... 125.00
Fruit Jar, 1/2 Gal. 190.00
Gravy Boat, Attached Liner, Magnolia, Chartreuse, Ivory Interior 10.00
Jam Jar, Village Green 12.00
Jar, Beater, Blue Bands, Marked Eggs, Cream & Salad Dressing 120.00
Jar, Butter, Small Wing, 20 Lb. 425.00
Jar, Pantry, 3 Lb. 625.00
Jar, Pantry, 10 Lb. 750.00
Jar, Pantry, Blue Band, 1930s, 6 In. 375.00
Jar, Preserving, Blue Logo, Patent Jan. 24, 1899, 1 Gal. 500.00
Jar, Refrigerator, Lid, Bail Handle, Word Butter On Front, Blue & White 250.00
Jug, Union Stoneware Co., 3 Gal. 70.00
Jug, White, 1 Gal. 75.00
Jug, Wing, Shoulder, 1 Gal. 95.00
Mug, Bratwurst Haus .... 45.00 to 60.00
Mug, Hamm's Krug Klub 28.00
Mustard, Bob White 25.00
Nappy, Tampico, 8 x 9 In. 12.00
Pitcher, Barrel Shape, Brown, Marked 75.00
Pitcher, Blue Cherry Band, Advertising 400.00
Pitcher, Bob White, 62 Oz. 25.00
Pitcher, Bottom Wing, Yellow & Green, 4 1/2 In. 1000.00
Pitcher, Cherry Band, 6 In. 175.00
Pitcher, Cherry Band, 8 In. 260.00
Pitcher, Gray Line, Large 200.00
Pitcher, Lunch Hour 950.00
Pitcher, Water, Bob White, Large 28.00
Planter, Art Deco, Square, 5 In. 38.00
Planter, Speckled Pink, 12 1/2 x 6 /2 In. 12.00
Planter, Violin 20.00
Plate, Capistrano, 6 1/2 In. 3.00
Plate, Crabapple, Red Border, Colonial Blank, 9 In. 5.00
Plate, Dinner, Lute Song 8.00
Plate, Hors D'oeuvre, Bird Shape 30.00
Plate, Lotus, 10 1/2 In. 5.50
Plate, Random Harvest, 10 1/2 In. 5.00
Plate, Round-Up, 9 1/2 In. 60.00
Platter, Blossom Time, Concord, 13 1/4 In. 10.00
Platter, Bob White, 20 In. 45.00
Platter, Crazy Rhythm, 15 In. 38.00
Platter, Town & Country, Orange Teardrop, 10 3/4 In. 25.00
Relish, 3 Sections, Turquoise, 9 In. 7.00
Salt & Pepper, Bob White, Bird Shape 18.00
Salt & Pepper, Brittany 10.00
Salt & Pepper, Tampico 20.00
Salt & Pepper, Village Green 20.00
Saltshaker, Gray Line 725.00
Saucer, Capistrano 2.00
Server, Beverage, Smart Set 90.00
Sugar, Cover, Lotus, Brown 6.50
Sugar, Cover, Morning Glory, Pink Flowers 3.50
Sugar, Cover, Rodeo 65.00
Syrup, Bob White, Stand 45.00
Teapot, Bob White 48.00
Tidbit, Normandy, 2 Tiers 11.00
Tray, French Bread, Bob White 85.00

Trivet, Minnesota Centennial, 1958 .... 20.00 to 75.00
Tumbler, Bob White, 4 Piece 700.00
Urn, Burgundy Handle, Marked Red Wing Art Pottery, 8 In. 75.00
Vase, Corset Shape, Gray Top, Maroon Base, Gold Label, 1878-1953, 10 In. 28.00
Vase, Cream Ground, Green Interior, Classic, 10 x 6 1/2 In. 24.00
Vase, Fan, 2 Leaf Shape, Cream Ground, Green Interior, 7 1/2 In. 18.00
Vase, Fan, Cornucopia-Style Swirl, Ivory Ground, Peach Interior, 7 3/4 In. 27.00
Vase, Geometric Style, Terra-Cotta, 13 In. 45.00
Vase, Green Ground, Pink Interior, Base Handles, 7 1/2 In. 14.00
Vase, High-Top Shoe Shape 85.00
Vase, Leopard Skin Glaze 195.00
Vase, Lion, Tan & Gray, Marked, 10 In. 80.00
Vase, Salt Glaze, Marked, 10 In. 75.00
Vase, Stylized People, 15 In. 350.00
Vase, With Perch, 12 In. 2500.00
Wall Pocket, Magnolia, White, 7 1/2 In. 52.00
Water Cooler, 5 Gal. 400.00
Water Cooler, Lid, Small Wing, Union Oval 500.00
Water Cooler, Small Wing, 6 Gal. 425.00

REDWARE is a hard, red stoneware that originated in the late 1600s and
continues to be made. The term is also used to describe any common clay
pottery that is reddish in color.

Bank, Save All You Can Is A Very Good Plan, March 14th, 1883 .... 137.00
Bowl, Brown Sponge Glaze, Applied Ribbed Handles, 8 x 5 In. 104.00
Bowl, Brown Spots, Clear Glaze, 9 1/4 In. 125.00
Bowl, Cup Shape, Brown Splotches, Strap Handle, 5 1/4 x 3 1/2 In. 110.00
Bowl, Divided, White Slip Design, Oval, England, 12 1/2 x 16 1/2 In. 16.50
Bowl, Floral Design, Colorful Glaze, 8 1/4 In. 286.00
Bowl, Freeform, Black, Yellow & Cream Glaze, A.R. Cole Pottery, Oval, 11 1/2 In. .. 94.00
Bowl, Milk, Clear Greenish Glaze, 17 1/4 In. 132.00
Bowl, Milk, Dark Brown Interior Glaze, 15 In. 192.40
Bowl, Yellow Slip, Brown Wavy & Straight Lines, 10 In. 280.00
Candleholder, Figural, Indian Girl, Pot On Head 3.50
Charger, 2 Line Yellow Slip, Coggeled Rim, 11 1/4 In. 220.00
Charger, 3 Line Design, Coggled Rim, 11 3/4 In. 693.00
Charger, Coggled Rim, 4 Line, Yellow Slip, 12 In. 385.00
Charger, Decorated, Pennsylvania, 19th Century, 11 x 16 1/4 In. 1950.00
Charger, Yellow Slip, Orange & Brown, 11 1/2 In. 632.00
Coffeepot, England, 1800, 11 In. 650.00
Creamer, Brown Splotches, Greenish Clear Glaze, 3 5/8 In. 93.00
Crock, Yellow Line Around Top, 8 1/4 In. 55.00
Cruet, Yellow Glaze Upper Half, Unglazed Bottom, c.1730 .... 650.00
Dish, Baking, Fluted Edges, Handles, Brown Glaze, 13 In. 60.00
Dish, Slip, Beaded, Trim, 1880, 10 1/4 In. 450.00
Figurine, Chicken, Cole Slaw Base, Amber Glaze, 12 1/2 In. 467.00
Figurine, Dog, 4 In. 450.00
Figurine, Roaster, Roof Ornament 685.00
Flask, 2-Tone Dark Brown Glaze, 6 3/8 In. 110.00
Flask, Book, Deep Brown, 3 5/8 x 4 5/8 x 1 7/8 In. 255.00
Flask, Dark Brown Splotches, Clear Glaze, 7 1/4 In. 170.00
Flowerpot, Attached Saucer, Crimped Rims, Foliage, Green Glaze, 5 1/2 In. 137.00
Flowerpot, Attached Saucer, Tooled Rim, Brown Splotches, 4 In. 22.00
Flowerpot, Brown Glazed, 5 1/4 In. 80.00
Flowerpot, Crimped Rim, Amber Glaze, Incised Love Haralson, Biloxi, 1898, 5 In. .. 357.00
Flowerpot, Greenish Amber Glaze 137.00
Hat, Yellow Slipware, Scroddleware, 1881, England 175.00
Inkwell, Molded Floral, Dark Paint, 4 5/8 In. 71.00
Inkwell, Quill Holder, 2 In. 60.00
Jar, 2 Stripes Of Yellow Slip At Shoulder, Egg Shape, Cover, 8 In. 55.00
Jar, Amber Glaze, Brown Splotches, Egg Shape, Strap Handle, 5 7/8 In. 93.00
Jar, Apple Butter, Mottled Greenish Amber & Brown Glaze, Strap Handle, 5 In. 125.00

Jar, Apple Butter, Tan Fleck Glaze, 7 In. 27.50
Jar, Brown Glaze, Impressed Label, John Bell, Waynesboro, 7 1/4 In. 82.00
Jar, Cover, Amber Speckled Glaze, Egg Shape, 7 3/4 In. 165.00
Jar, Cover, Splotched Manganese Design, 10 7/8 In. 1100.00
Jar, Fish Body Handles, Oriental 195.00
Jar, Green Glaze, 19th Century, 10 1/4 In. 165.00
Jar, Greenish Brown, Egg Shape, 12 In. 22.00
Jar, Mottled, Green Glaze, 2 Handles 165.00
Jar, Preserving, Brown Flecks, Greenish Beige Glaze, 6 12/4 In. 50.00
Jar, Storage, 2-Eared, Olive Green Glaze, Black Spots 250.00
Jar, Tan Fleck, Impressed, W. Smith Womelsdorf, Egg Shape, 5 1/2 In. 192.00
Jar, Tooled Line Rim, Shoulder Handles, Brown Splotches, Egg Shape, 9 1/4 In. 160.00
Jug, Dark Brown Glaze, Ribbed Strap Handle, Egg Shape, 13 1/4 In. 275.00
Jug, Glazed, New Hampshire, 11 1/2 In. 1095.00
Jug, Green Glaze, Amber Spots, Strap Handle, 8 In. 247.50
Jug, Green Glazed, Continental 275.00
Jug, Harvest, Applied Flowers, E.F.J.H., 19th Century, 10 1/2 In. 55.00
Jug, Manganese Splotches, 8 In. 137.00
Loaf Pan, Yellow Slip Glaze 440.00
Mold, Food, Scalloped, Brown Flecks, Clear Glaze, John Bell, 5 3/4 In. 335.00
Mug, Brown Sponge Glaze, 4 In. 22.00
Mug, Strap Handle, Brown Splotches, Elmer Webster, 6 In. 247.50
Pan, Milk, Brown & Yellow Slip Design, 11 3/4 In. 137.00
Pan, Milk, Dark Mustard Glaze Interior, Mid-19th Century, 15 In. 135.00
Pie Plate, Coggled Rim, 3 Line Yellow Slip Decoration, 10 3/8 In. 220.00
Pie Plate, Coggled Rim, Greenish Amber Glaze, 9 In. 72.00
Pie Plate, Coggled Rim, Yellow Slip Crow's Foot Designs, 7 1/2 In. 187.00
Pie Plate, Yellow Slip, Straight & Wavy Lines, 8 1/4 In. 302.00
Pitcher, Amber Glaze, Brown Splotches, White Slip, 7 In. 93.00
Pitcher, Applied Handle, Impressed Leaf, Amber Glaze, Brown Swirl, 7 3/4 In. 83.00
Pitcher, Bulbous, Sponge Decorated, 9 In. 250.00
Pitcher, Manganese Splotches, 19th Century, 10 1/2 In. 357.00
Pitcher, Ribbed Strap Handle, 4 1/4 In. 38.00
Pitcher, Slip Design, 18th Century 165.00
Pitcher, Vertical Stripes Of Brown Sponging, Cover, 6 3/4 In. 115.00
Plate, Coggled Rim, 9 3/4 In. 55.00
Plate, Comb Design 907.00
Plate, Green Over Yellow, 8 3/4 In. 650.00
Plate, Notched Rim, Wavy Lines, Stylized Leaf Design, 10 5/8 In. 805.00
Plate, Slip Sgraffito Design Center 125.00
Plate, Stylized Yellow Slip, 13 In. 2090.00
Pot, Flared Rim, Dark Brown Streaks On Yellow Ground, 1830s, 9 In. 1150.00
Preserve Jar, Cover, Handle, 19th Century, 7 1/2 In. 220.00
Salt & Pepper, Chef & Mammy 100.00
Sugar, Cover, Tooled Bands 82.50
Sugar, Dome Lid, Marbleized White & Black Slip, 12 In. 4600.00
Teapot, Yellow Glaze, 6 In. 125.00
Vase, Deep Green Glaze, 3 3/4 In. 115.00
Whistle, Child's, Rabbit, Germany 90.00
Whistle, Yellow, 4 In. 90.00

REGOUT, see Maastricht

RICHARD was the mark used on acid-etched cameo glass vases, bowls,
night-lights, and lamps made in Lorraine, France, during the 1920s. The
pieces were very similar to the other French cameo glasswares made by
Daum, Galle, and others.

Toothpick, Purple On Frosted Ground, Metal Base, 3 In. 275.00
Vase, Amethyst Etched Flowers, Low, Bulbed Shape, 4 1/4 In. 550.00
Vase, Cylindrical, Landscape, Gray, Amber Interior, Cameo, c.1925, 21 3/4 In. 1380.00
Vase, Dragonfly & Butterfly, Blue Flowers, 5 In. 625.00
Vase, Teardrop Shape, Landscape, Gray, Orange, Green, Cameo, 1925, 13 3/4 In. 1150.00
Vase, Twin Peaks, Brown Flowers, Lime, 3 x 4 In. 675.00

◆◆◆◆◆◆◆◆◆◆◆◆◆◆◆◆◆◆◆◆◆◆◆

To remove old gummed labels
use Bestine solvent found at artist supply stores.

◆◆◆◆◆◆◆◆◆◆◆◆◆◆◆◆◆◆◆◆◆◆◆

*Ridgway, Platter, Capitol Building,
Washington, D.C. , Dark Blue, 21 In.*

RIDGWAY pottery has been made in the Staffordshire district in England since 1808 by a series of companies with the name Ridgway. The transfer-design dinner sets are the most widely known product. They are still being made. Other pieces of Ridgway are listed under Flow Blue.

Cake Stand, Oriental Floral Design, Butterflies, Gilt, Marked, 9 1/2 In., Pair	121.00
Creamer, Pewter Lid, Brown & Orange Transfer, Birds, Fruits	95.00
Cup, Handleless, State House, Boston	93.50
Custard, Boston State House, Dark Blue	375.00
Dish, Vegetable, View From Ruggles House, Black Transfer, Cover, 6 1/2 x 9 3/4 In.	255.00
Dish, Soup, Octagon Church, Boston, Dark Blue, 9 3/4 In.	395.00
Ice Cream Set, Pomona, 5 Piece	155.00
Mug, Boating Days, Brown, Copper Luster Handle & Rim, 4 In.	35.00
Mug, Coaching Days, Amber Glaze, Silver Luster Trim, Black Transfer, 4 3/8 In.	11.00
Mug, Walking Up The Hill	28.00
Pitcher, Blueware, Tavern Scene, Man On Horse, 2 Witches, 1835, 11 In.	99.00
Pitcher, Congressional Library, Caramel, Silver Luster	60.00
Plate, Blackpool Transfer, Caramel, 9 In.	16.00
Plate, Blacksmith Shop, 10 In.	65.00
Plate, Caldwell, Lake George, Black, 7 3/4 In.	30.00
Plate, City Hall, New York, Beauties Of America Series, Blue, 9 In.	210.00
Plate, Columbian Star, Green, 10 1/4 In.	245.00
Plate, Insane Hospital, Boston, Blue Transfer, 7 1/4 In.	248.00
Plate, Kosciuszko's Tomb, West Point, 1844	150.00
Plate, Library, Philadelphia, Blue Transfer, 8 In.	170.50
Plate, Oriental Scene, Blue & White, 1790s, 9 1/2 In.	70.00
Plate, Park Theatre, New York, Blue Transfer, 10 In.	275.00
Plate, View From Ruggles House, Newburgh Hudson River, Light Blue, 10 1/4 In.	110.00
Platter, Capitol Building, Washington, D.C., Dark Blue, 21 In. .... *Illus*	2200.00
Platter, Floral, Lavender, John Ridgway, 1830-1855	425.00
Platter, Hartford Deaf & Dumb Asylum, Dark Blue, 15 In.	1100.00
Platter, St. Paul's Church, Boston, Dark Blue, 9 1/2 In.	1150.00
Platter, View From Port Putnam, Light Blue, Lace Border, 15 1/8 In.	295.00
Tankard Set, Coaching Days, Black Transfer, Silver Luster Handles, 4 Piece	300.00

RIFLE is a firearm that has a rifled bore and that is intended to be fired from the shoulder. Other firearms are listed under Gun.

Air, Airsporter	195.00
Air, Beeman, R-1, Power Scope	300.00
Air, Beeman, R-I, Tyrolean Stock, 66-R Scope, 22 Caliber	500.00
Air, Beeman, Scope, 20 Caliber,	375.00
Air, Benjamin, Model 342, Pump-Up, 22 Caliber	75.00
Air, Benjamin, No. 132, Wood Grips, 1950s	40.00
Air, Benjamin, No. 310, Tootsie Roll Pump	43.00
Air, Crosman, 140, Early Sights & Trigger	50.00
Air, Crosman, 150, Slab Grips	50.00
Air, Crosman, CG, Straight Tank	300.00

Air, Crosman, Model 1100, Shotgun, Trap, Plastic Targets, New 200.00
Air, Crosman, No. 120, Pump-Up, 22 Caliber 85.00
Air, Crosman, No. 140, X-Bolt Safety, Complete 27.00
Air, Crosman, No. 760, New Seals 14.00
Air, Daisy 300, BB 45.00
Air, Daisy, Air, Model 1894, Buffalo Bill 110.00
Air, Daisy, No. 50, Golden Eagle 125.00
Air, Daisy, No. 118, Targeteer, Nickel 35.00
Air, Daisy, No. 889, Pump Action Repeater, Box 90.00
Air, Daisy, No. 953, Single Stroke Pneumatic, Box 85.00
Air, Daisy, No. 1160, Plastic Stock 22.00
Air, Diana 27, Walnut Stock, Huntress Tamp On Receiver 90.00
Air, Haenel, Model II, Slab-Sided Receiver, 1928 .... 300.00
Air, Haenel, Model II, Smoothbore, Dated 1929 .... 77.00
Air, Hammerli, CO2, Bolt Action, Lead Ball 500.00
Air, Hy-Score, Model 806 .... 35.00
Air, Logo Of Diana Discarding Bow & Arrow 115.00
Air, Mars, No. 115, 4.4 mm Trainer, World War II 94.00
Air, Red Ryder, Copper Bands 280.00
Air, Red Ryder, Iron Lever 140.00
Air, S & W, 77A, 22 Caliber 75.00
Air, Sheridan BS, 20 Caliber, CO2 .... 73.00
Air, Sheridan CB, Blue Streak, Hold-Down Thumb Safety, Walnut 100.00
Air, Walther, LP3 .... 325.00
Air, Webley, No. S13XXX, Pre-World War II 117.00
Air, Winchester, No. 333, Recoilless Match, Barrel Latch Lever 298.00
Blunderbuss, Percussion Converted From Flint, Flat Lock, France, 15-In. Barrel 425.00
Browning .22, Semi-Automatic, 11 Shot, Adjustable Rear Side, 36 3/4 In. 305.00
Carbine, U.S. M-1, 3 Magazines, 30 Caliber 325.00
D.R. Hilliar, Walnut, Brass Fitted, 36 Caliber, 30 1/4 In. Octagonal Barrel 1100.00
Field Target, Theoban Imperator, No. 177, Thumbhole Stock Adjustable 1250.00
Kentucky, Curly Maple Full Stock, Brass Patch Box, 59 In. 825.00
Kentucky, Curly Maple Full Stock, Percussion Lock, Brass Patch Box, 56 In. 1320.00
Kentucky, Curly Maple Full Stock, Percussion Lock, H.E. Leman, 41-In. Barrel 550.00
Kentucky, Curly Maple Stock R.W. Booth, Cincinnati, 52 In. 687.00
Kentucky, Curly Maple Stock, Percussion, Brass, c.1835 .... 1750.00
Kentucky, Flintlock, New England 220.00
Kentucky, Mahogany, Half Stock, Percussion, Patchbox, R.M. Wilder 550.00
Kentucky, Walnut Half Stock, Percussion Lock, Henry Parker Warranted, 48 1/2 In. . 935.00
Kentucky, Walnut, Half Stock, Percussion, Pewter Nose Cap, O. Perine 440.00
Kentucky, Woman's, Full Stock 470.00
Kentucky, Woman's, Tiger Maple, Silver Inlaid, Eagle, Wildcat, Signed H. Elwell 1430.00
Musket, Johnathan Goodwin, Connecticut, 1775 .... 4500.00
Musket, Springfield, Underslung Bayonet, 1851 .... 1045.00
Musket, Springfield, US M1863, 1864 .... 875.00
Musketoon, Indian Trade, Dog Lock, John Whately, 21-In. Barrel, 1740 .... 1800.00
Percussion, Bayonet, 1861 .... 1045.00
Percussion, Carved Inlay, Pennsylvania 4000.00
Percussion, Muzzle Loading, 1 Barrel, Marked JMC 145.00
Percussion, Walnut Stock, Octagonal Barrel, Maple Ramrod, James Miller 660.00
Percussion, Walnut, Half Stock, Kentucky, Patchbox, Rawson Armstrong 385.00
Practice, Wooden, Old Paint, 19th Century, 58 In. 55.00
Remington, 700, Scope & Sling, .30-06 .... 330.00
Remington, Carbine, 43 Caliber, c.1870 .... 125.00
Remington, U.S. Springfield, 50-70 Caliber, c.1874 .... 135.00
Remington, Zouave 1210.00
Rim-Fire, Switzerland, c.1870 .... 100.00
Southern, Iron-Mounted Half Stock, 36 Caliber 235.00
Springfield, 1862 .... 2420.00
Stephenson, Peep Sight, Extra Barrel, 1915 .... 160.00
Target, Boy's, Underhammer, Walnut Stick, Brass Fittings, 1840s, 30 3/8 In. 380.00
Trapdoor, US M1873, Blue Traces 410.00
U.S. Springfield, Model 1884, Trap Door Loader, c.1890, 49 In. 165.00

Winchester, .30-06 Caliber, 1903	190.00
Winchester, 38 Caliber, Lever Action, c.1886	550.00
Winchester, Automatic Pump, 351 Caliber, c.1907	195.00
Winchester, Lever Action, 38 Caliber, c.1892	440.00
Winchester, Model 12, Ducks Unlimited, Dinner Gun, 1974	1100.00
Winchester, Model 61, Pump, 22 Caliber	350.00
Winchester, Model 70, Featherweight, 308 Caliber, Box, Unused	350.00
Winchester, Model 94, 32 Caliber	450.00
Winchester, Model 1873, Lever Action	467.00
Winchester, Pump Action, 22 Caliber, c.1890	385.00

RIVIERA dinnerware was made by the Homer Laughlin Co. of Newell, West Virginia, from 1938 to 1950. The pattern was similar in coloring and in mood to Fiesta and Harlequin. The Riviera plates and cup handles were square. For more information, see *Kovels' Depression Glass & American Dinnerware Price List*.

Butter, Cobalt Blue, 1/2 Lb.	150.00
Creamer, Ivory	8.00
Cup & Saucer, Ivory, After Dinner	100.00
Plate, Fruit, Ivory, 5 1/2 In.	9.00

ROCKINGHAM, in the United States, is a pottery with a brown glaze that resembles tortoiseshell. It was made from 1840 to 1900 by many American potteries. Mottled brown Rockingham wares were first made in England at the Rockingham factory. Other types of ceramics were also made by the English firm. Related pieces may be listed in the Bennington category.

Bank, Anna L. Curtis, Pittsfield, Mass., 6 1/2 In.	275.00
Bottle, Mermaid, 7 1/4 In.	72.00
Bowl, 3 1/2 x 8 1/2 In.	60.00
Bowl, Embossed Sides, 6 1/2 In.	48.00
Bowl, Straight Fluted Sides, 9 1/4 In.	60.00
Bowl, Straight Sides, Applied Handles, 6 1/2 x 9 In.	71.00
Creamer, Cow, Lid, 5 1/2 In.	105.00
Creamer, Toby, 6 In.	50.00
Cuspidor, Glazed, 8 In.	27.50
Cuspidor, Octagonal, 8 1/2 In.	27.00
Dessert Set, Center Flowers, Salmon Border, c.1860, 14 Piece	660.00
Dish, Octagonal, 12 1/2 In.	95.00
Dish, Soap, 3 3/4 x 6 3/8 In.	27.50
Dish, Soap, 7 1/4 In.	44.00
Dish, Soap, Molded Leaf Design, 4 x 6 1/4 In.	27.50
Figurine, Lion, Large, Pair	650.00
Figurine, Lion, Reclining	500.00
Figurine, Poodle, Empty Basket In Mouth, Coleslaw Mane, 9 1/4 In.	920.00
Figurine, Spaniel, Seated, 1850s, 10 3/8 In.	302.00
Inkwell, Boy Asleep, 5 3/4 In.	71.00
Jar, Cover, Leaf Design, Molded Panel, 7 1/4 x 7 1/2 In.	33.00
Mustard Pot, Molded Edge Designs, 3 In.	27.50
Pie Plate, 10 In.	71.00
Pie Plate, Glazed, 9 In.	155.00
Pipkin, Mid-19th Century, 5 1/2 In.	165.00
Pitcher, Deer & Hanging Game, 9 In.	165.00
Pitcher, Horsehead Handle, Marked, 8 In.	125.00
Pitcher, Hound Handle, Hanging Game, 7 3/4 In.	71.50
Pitcher, Hunter With Hound, 8 1/2 In.	175.00
Pitcher, Jenny Lind, 9 In.	325.00
Pitcher, Man's Head On Handle, Medallions Of Profiles, 8 In.	65.00
Pitcher, Molded Hunt Scenes, 6 3/8 In.	38.50
Pitcher, Toby, Tricorner Hat, 9 1/4 In.	110.00
Teapot, Circular, Lobed Shell Rim, Scroll Spout, 9 1/4 In.	460.00
Teapot, Enamel Floral Design, A Present To A Friend, 1874, 14 In.	330.00
Teapot, Rebecca At The Well, 8 1/2 In.	125.00

Urn, Hot Water, Baluster-Form, Brown & Gold, Enamel, Handles, 21 In. 9200.00

ROGERS, see John Rogers

ROOKWOOD pottery was made in Cincinnati, Ohio, from 1880 to 1960. All of this art pottery is marked, most with the famous flame mark. The R is reversed and placed back to back with the letter P. Flames surround the letters. After 1900, a Roman numeral was added to the mark to indicate the year. The name and some of the molds were purchased in 1984. A few new pieces were made, but these were glazed in colors not used by the original company.

Ashtray, Advertising Boss Stoves	85.00
Ashtray, Boss Kerosene Ranges, Blue, 1947	35.00
Ashtray, Cirrus Glaze, 1955, K.S.	265.00
Ashtray, Frog	50.00
Basket, Mustard, Glossy, 1887, 5 x 4 1/2 x 4 In.	165.00
Bookends, Donkey, McDonald	225.00
Bookends, Elephants, Matte Blue Glaze, Flame Mark, 5 x 5 3/4 In.	300.00
Bookends, Lady	195.00
Bookends, Lotus Blossom, Pink, 1926	195.00
Bookends, Oriental Woman, Lotus Position, Blue & Purple, 7 3/4 x 5 In. ..... 220.00 to	385.00
Bookends, Owl, Ivory	250.00
Bookends, Owl, Wm. Purcell McDonald, 1929	715.00
Bookends, Polar Bear, Ivory Semi-matte Glaze, Marked, 4 3/4 x 6 3/4 In.	485.00
Bookends, Rook, Dark Blue	260.00
Bookends, Rook, Inside Open Book, 6 1/2 x 6 In.	220.00
Bookends, Rook, Light Blue Matte, 7 In.	475.00
Bookends, Seated Woman, Reading, 1921, 6 3/4 x 7 In.	125.00
Bookends, Shape 2275, William P. McDonald, 1943, 5 1/2 In.	247.00
Bowl, Dragonfly, Charles McDonald, 9 1/4 In.	850.00
Bowl, Green Speckling Glaze, Geometric Band, 1910, 7 In.	220.00
Bowl, Hammered Glaze, Pink Blossoms, Laura A. Fry, 1882, 3 1/2 x 7 3/4 In.	770.00
Bowl, Tourmaline, Blue, 8 In.	70.00
Bowl, White Glaze, Turquoise Interior, Maiden Form Handles, 1927, 7 x 12 In.	495.00
Candleholder, Blue, 1947, Pair	145.00
Candlestick, Semi-Glaze, Blue, 1923, Pair	250.00
Cigarette Holder, Frog Finial, Light Green	185.00
Coffeepot, Domed Cover, Silver Overlay, Baluster, 1893, 9 In.	1150.00
Creamer, 3-Leaf Clovers, Brown Glaze, 1883, 4 In.	595.00
Creamer, Clover Design, Bookprinter, 1885, 4 1/2 In.	250.00
Decanter, Whiskey, Grapes & Leaves, Stopper, 1900, 10 In.	995.00
Ewer, Floral Design, Standard Glaze, 1899, 8 1/2 In.	645.00
Ewer, Holly Design, 1896, 7 In.	675.00
Ewer, School Of Swimming Fish, Albert R. Valentien, 1894, 13 1/8 In.	978.00
Ewer, Silver Overlay, Brown & Green Carnations, Schor, 1898, 6 In.	1150.00
Ewer, Standard Glaze, Floral Design, Hurley, Showroom Sticker, 1901	350.00
Ewer, White Wild Roses, Yellow-Green Glaze, Grace Young, 1889, 6 1/2 In.	330.00
Ewer, Yellow Daffodils, Standard Glaze, Josephine E. Zettel, 1897, 7 In.	330.00
Ewer, Yellow Fruit Blossoms, William P. McDonald, 1893, 12 In.	550.00
Ewer, Yellow Hibiscus, 1887, 19 In.	2700.00
Figurine, Cat, Sleeping, White	225.00
Figurine, Colonial Girl, Light Green, 8 In.	225.00
Figurine, Elephant, Green Glazed	140.00
Figurine, Pheasant, Pink, 1946, Pair	295.00
Flower Frog, Blue, Logo, 1911, 2 x 3 3/4 In.	65.00
Flower Frog, Half Boy, Half Goat, Blue Matte, 1920	275.00
Flower Frog, Pan Playing Pipes, Cream Glaze, 6 In.	195.00
Ginger Jar, Standard Glaze, Albert Valentien	295.00
Humidor, Copper Dust Glaze	495.00
Humidor, Salmon Pansies, 1889, 6 In.	467.00
Inkwell, Arts & Crafts, 1905	595.00
Jar, Cover, Design On Shoulders, 4 1/2 In.	1200.00
Jar, Cover, Leaves & Berries, K. Van Horne, 1916, 7 In.	750.00

Jar, Lid, Dimpled, Snails & Insects, Rust Ground, Maria Nichols, 1882, 6 In. 1500.00
Jug, 2 Ears Of Corn, Husks, Brown Ground, Sprague, 1902, 5 3/4 In. 315.00
Jug, Perfume, Kiln Mark, Harriet Wenderoth, Green, 1883 .... 350.00
Jug, Stopper, Standard Glaze, Swing, 7 In. 475.00
Jug, Whiskey, Cherries, Sara Sax, 1899 .... 350.00
Loving Cup, 3 Handles, Green Vellum Glaze 695.00
Mug, Owl, Green & Rust Matter, Sharp Mold, 1905, 5 1/2 In. 250.00
Mug, Stalk Of Corn, Lenore Asbury, Flame Mark, 1898, 4 3/4 x 5 In. 275.00
Paperweight, 2 Schooner, 1928 .... 100.00
Paperweight, Brown Glaze, 1925 .... 200.00
Paperweight, Dog, Brown Glaze, 1946 .... 110.00
Paperweight, Dog, High Glaze, Tan, 1947 .... 180.00
Paperweight, Duck .... 150.00 to 200.00
Paperweight, Elephant, 1943 .... 185.00
Paperweight, Elephant, Light Green, 1946 .... 165.00
Paperweight, Potter At Wheel, Matte Green, 1940 .... 195.00
Pitcher, Cherries & Green Foliage, Lenore Asbury, 1902, 10 1/2 In. 950.00
Pitcher, Green & Brown Holly, Red Berries, Shape 18, Abel, 1890, 6 3/8 In. 605.00
Pitcher, Hand Painted Berries, Martin Rettig, 1882, 6 1/2 In. 350.00
Pitcher, Limoges Style, Grasses, Butterflies, Shape 36, Valentien, 1883, 7 In. 495.00
Pitcher, Maple Leaves, Dark-Green To Burnt-Orange Field, 1982, 6 1/2 In. 660.00
Plaque, Bayou At Twilight, Trees, Arts & Crafts Frame, Asbury, 15 x 17 In. 1980.00
Plaque, Faience, Tree Scene, Blue Lake, Mountains, 13 In. 2750.00
Plaque, Forest Stream, Waterfall, Vellum Glaze, E.T. Hurley, 10 x 8 In. 5170.00
Plaque, Landscape, Glazed, Carl Schmidt, Frame, 1916, 11 x 8 1/2 In. 4600.00
Plaque, River Landscape, Blue, Green, Peach, Frame, Hurley, 1946, 9 x 12 In. 4025.00
Plaque, Tree Landscape, Reflecting Pool, Carl Schmidt, 1916, 12 1/2 In. 8800.00
Plaque, Vellum, Evening Mist, Lenore Asbury, 1923 .... 2900.00
Plaque, Venetian Harbor Scene, Carl Schmidt, 9 1/2 In. 7425.00
Sign, Dealer, Brown, 1936 .... 1100.00
Stein, Cincinnati Cooperage Co. Banner 190.00
Stein, Cincinnati Cooperage Co., Cherubs Toasting 125.00
Sugar & Creamer, Silver Overlay, H. Pabodie Stuntz, 1894, 2 7/8 In. 1150.00
Tankard, Beer, Cincinnati Cooperage Co. 215.00
Tea Set, Sailing Pirate Ships, Marked, 1886, 9 Piece 850.00
Tile, Alternating Pink Flower & Green Leaves, Flower Center, 6 1/2 In. 215.00
Tile, Dutch Scene, Multicolor, Junior Decorator, 1946 .... 260.00
Tile, Grapes, Matte Glaze, 1927 .... 350.00
Tray, Central Trust Co., Cincinnati, 4 x 6 In. 45.00
Tray, Pin, Rook, Brown, 1946 .... 595.00
Trivet, Tulips, 6 In. 140.00
Vase, 2 Birds, Bowl Of Fruit, 6-Sided, 6 Feet, Arthur Conant, 1920, 4 3/4 In. 165.00
Vase, 3 Chrysanthemums, Wisteria & Green, White, Wareham, 15 In. 5175.00
Vase, 3 Floral & Foliate Reserves, Ivory Ground, 6 In. 110.00
Vase, 3 Swimming Fish, E.T. Hurley, 1905 .... 2500.00
Vase, 3 Tortoises, Water Landscape, Gilt, Valentien, 1895, Ovoid 2587.00
Vase, 5 Poppies, Blue To Pink Ground, E.N. Lincoln, 1927, 14 7/8 In. 3450.00
Vase, Apple Blossoms, Iris Glaze, Lincoln, 1906, 7 x 4 In. 825.00
Vase, Applied Prunus Flowers & Leaves, 10 1/2 In. 1800.00
Vase, Art Deco Leaves, Blue, 1945, 5 1/2 In. 135.00
Vase, Band Of Incised Design, Dusty Rose Matte, 1927, 5 1/4 In. 135.00
Vase, Black Iris Glaze, Peacock Feathers, Carl Schmidt, 6 In. 5500.00
Vase, Blackberries, Yellow Blossoms, Elizabeth Lincoln, 1903, 8 In. 457.00
Vase, Blue Violets, Khaki Field, E.R. Felten, 1899, 4 1/2 In. 165.00
Vase, Blue, Green, Daisies, Vellum, Shape 950E, Edith Noonan, 1908, 7 1/4 In. 825.00
Vase, Blue, National Conference Catholic Charities, Cincinnati, 1934 .... 90.00
Vase, Blue, Yellow Interior, 1922, 15 1/2 In. 425.00
Vase, Blue-Ribbed Body, Yellow Interior, 1922, 15 1/2 In. 395.00
Vase, Blueberry Branches, Bulbous Top, Lorinda Epply, 1907, 7 x 3 In. 880.00
Vase, Bottle Shape, Pansies, Green Foliage, Lenore Asbury, 1907, 8 1/2 In. 900.00
Vase, Broad Band Of Stylized Grapes, Brown Leaves, S. Sax, 1915, 9 3/4 In. 850.00
Vase, Brown, Gray Streaked, 7 1/4 In. 60.00
Vase, Bud, Arches & Flowers, Pink & Blue On Ivory, Conant, 1919, 6 x 2 In. 605.00

Rookwood, Vase, Limoges Style, Maria Longworth Nichols, 1882, 16 3/8 In.

♦♦♦♦♦♦♦♦♦♦♦♦♦♦♦♦♦♦♦♦♦♦

Some tea and coffee stains on dishes can be removed by rubbing them with damp baking soda.

♦♦♦♦♦♦♦♦♦♦♦♦♦♦♦♦♦♦♦♦♦♦

Vase, Bud, Celadon Glaze, 1944, 7 In. 50.00
Vase, Bud, Jasmine Blossoms, Burgundy To Green Field, 1901, 5 1/4 In. 330.00
Vase, Celadon, 1944, 10 In. 165.00
Vase, Corseted, Blue & Lavender Trees, Rothenbusch, 1910, 7 x 3 In. 1100.00
Vase, Crocuses, Lavender To Blue Ground, H.E. Wilcox, 1926, 7 1/4 In. 1320.00
Vase, Daffodils, Butterfat Glaze, Sallie E. Coyne, 1928, 11 3/4 In. 1400.00
Vase, Dogwood Blossoms, Gray To Blue Ground, Sara Sax, 1907, 9 In. 1500.00
Vase, Dogwood Vellum, E.T. Hurley, 1910, 8 3/4 In. 775.00
Vase, Fish & Flowers, Bubbled Overglaze, Jens Jensen, 1946, 7 1/4 In. 900.00
Vase, Floral Thistle, Brown & Green Ground, Signed, 1896, 6 In. 800.00
Vase, Floral, Velum, Joseph Bailey, 1919, 7 In. 825.00
Vase, Flowers & Leaves, Handles, Bisque, Grace Young, 3 3/4 In. 750.00
Vase, Flowers Around Top, Green Shaded To Pink, 6 1/4 In. 165.00
Vase, Flowers, Lorinda Epply, Incised No. 9010, 1915, 8 In. 545.00
Vase, Foliate & Berry Design At Neck, Baluster Form, No. 2139, 4 3/4 In. 315.00
Vase, Forget-Me-Nots, Brown To Green Ground, Olga Reed, 1895, 7 In. 330.00
Vase, Glazed Landscape, Teal, Pink, Green Lavender, Sallie E. Coyne, 15 In. 3450.00
Vase, Golden Pine Cones, Green Needles, C. Duell, 1903, 8 1/4 In. 375.00
Vase, Grape Vines, Blue To Pink Field, L. Asbury, 1907, 7 3/4 In. 880.00
Vase, Green & Rose Clematis & Vines, Blue To Ecru Ground, 8 In. 660.00
Vase, Green Glaze, Gray Flecks, 1918 .... 125.00
Vase, Hand Painted Trumpet Vine, Shirayamadani, 1889 .... 2500.00
Vase, Incised Geometric Design, Matte Green Glaze, 1910s, 4 In. 175.00
Vase, Incised Sea Horse, Mottled Brown Glaze, 6 In. 207.00
Vase, Incised, Painted, Shirayamadani, 1902, 6 5/8 In. 5500.00
Vase, Indian, Yellow Matte, 5 1/2 In. 175.00
Vase, Iris Glaze, Ribbon Handles, Poppies, Rothenbusch, 1903, 7 In. 1320.00
Vase, Iris Glaze, S.E. Coyne, 1906, 9 3/4 In. 1210.00
Vase, Iris, Colored Blossoms & Buds, Carl Schmidt, 1904, 10 1/2 In. 5100.00
Vase, Iris, Poppy Blossom & Buds, Crazed, Clara C. Lindeman, 1904, 6 3/4 In. 880.00
Vase, Iris, Violets, Fred Rothenbusch, 1903, 6 3/8 In. 660.00
Vase, Jack-In-The-Pulpit, Black To Green Ground, S. Sax, 1902, 10 In. 3400.00
Vase, Jewel Porcelain, 2 Birds In Landscape, Arthur Conant, 1929, 6 3/4 In. 750.00
Vase, Jeweled, Carved Poppies, Harriet Wilcox, 1929, 8 In. 1325.00
Vase, Landscape, Frederick Rothenbusch, 1921, 8 1/8 In. 1495.00
Vase, Leaves & Berries, Brown-Green, Ivory, McDonald, 1939, 11 1/2 In. 775.00
Vase, Lenore Asbury, 1916, 10 1/2 In. 1600.00
Vase, Lily Blossoms, Royal Blue, Teal & Red, Hentschel, 1912, 25 1/4 In. 3450.00
Vase, Lily-Of-The-Valley, Burgundy To Burnt Orange Ground, 1901, 8 In. 440.00
Vase, Limoges Style, Maria Longworth Nichols, 1882, 16 3/8 In. .... *Illus* 13750.00
Vase, Matte Glaze, Margaret McDonald, 1930, 5 3/4 In. 550.00
Vase, Matte Glazed Multicolored Design, Jens Jensen, No. 2831, 1930, 5 1/2 In. 575.00
Vase, Molded Design, Matte Green Glaze, 8 1/2 In. 275.00
Vase, Multicolor On Metallic Blue, 1915, 8 In. 650.00

Vase, Musical Design, High Glaze, 1941, 5 1/2 In.	168.00
Vase, Mustard Glaze, c.1921, 7 3/4 In.	192.00
Vase, Ocher & Green Flowers, K. Shirayamadani, 1890, 13 In.	743.00
Vase, Ovoid, Black Bamboo, Butterflies, Valentien, 1883, 8 3/4 In.	920.00
Vase, Painted Design, Shirayamadani, 1938, 8 In.	4620.00
Vase, Painted Palm Leaves, Black Ground, F. Rothenbusch, 1900, 5 1/2 In.	2530.00
Vase, Pansies, Shaded Ground, Edward Hurley, 1945, 4 1/2 In.	975.00
Vase, Pea Pods, Teal Blue, 1932, 6 1/2 x 6 In.	185.00
Vase, Pillow, Floral, Brown, 4 In.	400.00
Vase, Pine Cone, 1925, 6 1/2 In.	160.00
Vase, Pink Dogwood, Vellum Glaze, 5 1/2 In.	575.00
Vase, Pink Roses, Thorny Stems, Frederick Rothenbusch, 1927, 11 In.	2750.00
Vase, Pocket, Standard Glaze, 1900, 4 In.	575.00
Vase, Purple Flowers, Pink Ground, J. Swing, c.1930, 7 1/2 In.	385.00
Vase, Red Flowers, Brown Stems, E. Lincoln, 1925, 14 1/2 In.	1400.00
Vase, Roses, Brown, Orange & Olive Ground, Flared Neck, 1897, 8 In.	495.00
Vase, Roses, Sage & Ginger, Handles, Cylindrical, McDonald, 1891, 10 In.	546.00
Vase, Scenic Vellum, Landscape, Body Of Water, E.T. Hurley, 1930, 10 1/2 In.	2600.00
Vase, Shell, Nautilus Shell Handles, Celadon, 1947, 8 1/2 x 7 In.	285.00
Vase, Silver Maple Leaf Design, Tan & Green, c.1896	1400.00
Vase, Silver Overlay Florals, Waisted Shape, Bulbous Bottom, Dibowski, 8 In.	1925.00
Vase, Sky, Meadows, Trees, Vellum, Shape 1660D, E. Diers, 1920, 9 1/4 In.	1320.00
Vase, Sprigs Of Maple Leaves, Matt A. Daly, 1901, 10 1/2 In.	385.00
Vase, Stylized Butterfly, 1928, Teal Blue, Dark Blue, 1928, 4 1/2 x 7 In.	235.00
Vase, Stylized Incised Iris, Vellum, K. Van Horne, 1910, 7 1/2 In.	600.00
Vase, Stylized Leaves & Berries, W.E. Hentschel, 1930, 9 x 5 In.	440.00
Vase, Sunflowers, Yellow Matte, 5 1/2 In.	175.00
Vase, Sweet Peas, Trumpet Shape, Ed Diers, 1925	1400.00
Vase, Tall Daffodils, Pink To Green Ground, E.N. Lincoln, 1910, 6 1/2 In.	1210.00
Vase, Tiger Eye, Asters, Amelia B. Sprague, 1894, 6 3/4 In.	825.00
Vase, Trees Beside Lake, c.1916, 7 In.	522.00
Vase, Trumpet, Blue & Brown, Dogwood Flowers, Jens Jensen, 1946, 10 x 4 In.	440.00
Vase, Tulip, Brown Ground, 9 In.	220.00
Vase, Vellum Glaze, Sara Sax, 1908, 11 In.	1500.00
Vase, Water Lilies, Green Round, Constance A. Baker, 1904, 7 1/4 In.	2200.00
Vase, White & Yellow Flowers, Gray Ground, I. Bishop, 1908, 5 1/2 In.	550.00
Vase, White Poppies, Thin Stems, L. Asbury, 1908, 10 3/4 In.	2300.00
Vase, White Shrub Roses, Iris Glaze, Irene Bishop, 5 1/2 In.	575.00
Vase, Wide Mouth, Magnolia, Black, Ivory & Yellow Ground, 1905, 7 In.	550.00
Vase, Wild Roses, Buds, Peach & Green, Brown To Cream Shaded, Diers, 7 In.	977.00
Vase, Winter Landscape, Vellum, Fred Rothenbusch, 1917, 7 1/2 In.	1375.00
Vase, Yellow Gloss Glaze, Molded Relief Iris, Shape 6171, Wilcox, 1931, 16 In.	770.00
Wall Pocket, Embossed Panels, Designs At Top, 9 1/2 In.	125.00

ROSALINE, see Steuben category

ROSE BOWLS were popular during the 1880s. Rose petals were kept in the open bowl to add fragrance to a room, a popular idea in a time of limited personal hygiene. The glass bowls were made with crimped tops, which kept the petals inside. Many types of Victorian art glass were made into rose bowls.

Coin Dot, Topaz, 1960, 4 In.	60.00
Emerald Green, Silver Overlay, Floral Design, Alvin, 4 1/2 x 5 In.	798.00
Frosted White, Pedestal, Fenton	32.00
Pink-Cased Satin Glass, Blown-Out Shell Design, Victorian	125.00
Purple, Double, 8 x 3 1/2 In.	65.00
Satin Glass, Flowers, Gold	95.00
Satin Glass, Hand Painted Flowers, Gold Tracery, Cream, Pleated Top, 6 In.	78.00
Satin Glass, Lavender Flowers	75.00
Vaseline Opalescent, Alhambra Pattern, 5 1/2 In.	150.00
White Opalescent, Cobalt Blue, 6 1/2 x 4 1/4 In.	55.00

ROSE CANTON china is similar to Rose Medallion, except no people are pictured in the decoration. It was made in China during the nineteenth and twentieth centuries in greens, pinks, and other colors.

Plate, Bird & Butterfly Border, 8 1/2 In.	150.00
Seat, Garden, Barrel-Shaped, 18 In.	1320.00

ROSE MEDALLION china was made in China during the nineteenth and twentieth centuries. It is a distinctive design picturing people, flowers, birds, and butterflies. Pieces are colored in greens, pinks, and other colors. It is similar to Rose Canton.

Bowl, 3 Figures, 7 1/2 In.	65.00
Bowl, 5 1/2 x 13 1/2 In.	1045.00
Bowl, Polychrome Design, 9 1/4 In.	264.00
Brush Pot, 4 1/2 In., Pair	220.00
Charger, 14 3/4 In.	105.00
Chocolate Pot, 8 1/4 In.	105.00
Cup & Saucer, Birds & People	38.00
Dish, Hot Water, Domed Cover, 1835, 10 1/2 In.	825.00
Dish, Kidney Shape, 1850, 11 In.	330.00
Dish, Shrimp, 19th Century, 10 In.	685.00
Flowerpot, Hexagonal, 4 3/4 In.	220.00
Plate, Birds & Figures, 6 In.	20.00
Plate, Figures, Birds, 9 1/2 In.	40.00
Platter, Orange Peel Glaze, 15 In.	412.50
Platter, Oval, 13 1/2 In.	214.50
Platter, Oval, 19th Century, 17 3/4 In.	715.00
Platter, Strainer, 19th Century, 16 1/2 In.	880.00
Punch Bowl, 1830s, 15 In.	862.00
Punch Bowl, 19th Century, 16 In.	935.00
Punch Bowl, Famille Rose Exterior & Interior, Fretwork, 12 7/16 In.	345.00
Salt & Pepper	9.00
Sugar, 2 Handles, 4 1/4 In.	38.00
Sugar, Cover, Birds & People, Handles, Bulbous, 4 x 6 In.	98.00
Sugar & Creamer, 4 1/2 In.	143.00
Sugar & Creamer, Cover, People On Porch, Bulbous, 5 1/2 In.	145.00
Sugar & Creamer, Terrace & Butterfly, 5 1/2 In.	145.00
Tea Set, Figural Reserves, Foliate Ground, 19 Piece	1650.00
Teapot, 9 In.	275.00
Teapot, Drum Form, 1830, 5 In.	165.00
Tureen, Sauce, Cover, Undertray, 8 In.	522.00
Umbrella Stand, 23 1/2 In.	825.00
Urn, Umbrella, 15 1/2 In.	1100.00
Vase, 19th Century, 17 In.	495.00
Vase, 9 x 8 1/2 In., Pair	825.00
Vase, Baluster, 18th Century	1100.00
Vase, Cylindrical, 9 1/2 x 4 In.	247.00
Vase, Polychrome Design, 19th Century, 14 In., Pair	467.00

ROSE O'NEILL, see Kewpie category

ROSE TAPESTRY porcelain was made by the Royal Bayreuth factory of Tettau, Germany, during the late nineteenth century. The surface of the porcelain was pressed against a coarse fabric while it was still damp, and the impressions remained on the finished porcelain. It looks and feels like a textured cloth. Very skillful reproductions are being made that even include a variation of the Royal Bayreuth mark, so be careful when buying.

Basket, 4 x 4 1/4 In.	285.00
Basket, 6 1/2 x 7 1/4 In.	685.00
Box, Jewelry, Blue Mark, 3 x 5 1/2 In.	375.00
Box, Trinket, Pink & White Roses, Ferns, Blue Mark, 4 1/2 In.	225.00
Cake Plate, Pierced Hold Handies, Blue Mark, 10 1/2 In.	450.00

Creamer, Pink Roses, 2 1/2 In. 215.00
Creamer, Pink Roses, Pinched Spout, 3 1/2 In. .... 165.00 to 245.00
Creamer, Scenic, Goat, Pinched Spout, 4 In. 210.00
Dish, Leaf Shape, Pink Roses 225.00
Hair Receiver, Scenic, Goat, Blue Mark 225.00
Hairpin Box, Pink And White 235.00
Hatpin Holder, Scroll Base 450.00
Humidor, Woman, Leaning On Horse, 6 1/2 In. 1675.00
Jug, Miniature 150.00
Pitcher, Pinched Spout, Blue Mark, 4 1/2 In. 240.00
Rose Bowl, 3-Color, Blue Mark 325.00
Toothpick 510.00
Toothpick, 3 Handles, Blue Mark 495.00
Tray, Dresser, Roses, Gold Trim, Blue Mark 200.00
Tumbler, Scenic, Castle By The Lake, 3 3/4 In. 200.00
Tumbler, Scenic, Castle On Mountain, Blue Mark, 4 In. 195.00
Tumbler, Scenic, Gazebo, Deer In Stream, Blue Mark, 4 In. 195.00
Vase, Pink & Yellow Roses, 4 1/4 In. 330.00
Vase, Scenic, Bathing Beauties Beneath Castle, 8 1/4 In. 435.00
Vase, Scenic, Train On Bridge, River, Pinched Spout, 8 1/4 In. 480.00
Vase, Woman, Flowers In Hair, Footed, Handles, 3 In. 260.00

ROSEMEADE Pottery of Wahpeton, North Dakota, worked from 1940 to
1961. The pottery was operated by Laura A. Taylor and her husband, R.I.
Hughes. The company was also known as the Wahpeton Pottery Company.
Art pottery and commercial wares were made.

Rosemeade

Ashtray, Equitable Life Assurance Society, Embossed Mother, Child 35.00
Bank, Black Grizzly Bear 450.00
Bank, Rhinoceros, Gold 500.00
Bookends, Wolfhound, Wine 250.00
Can, Watering, Rabbit 50.00
Console Set, Blue, Square Candleholder, 3 Piece 30.00
Egg Timer, Double, Friar Tuck 69.00
Egg Timer, Praying Lady 30.00
Ewer, Minnesota Centennial, 1958 .... 115.00 to 120.00
Figurine, Buffalo, Miniature 65.00
Figurine, Duck, Blue Bill, Brown Body 85.00
Figurine, Mouse, 2 In., Pair 25.00
Figurine, Pheasant, 10 In. .... 100.00 to 150.00
Figurine, Pheasant, 12 In. 190.00
Figurine, Robin, Perching 150.00
Flower Frog, Jumping Fawn, Label 65.00
Jam Jar, Barrel Shape, White 110.00
Lamp, Television, Palomino 400.00
Planter, Bird On Log 45.00
Salt & Pepper, Bears 30.00
Salt & Pepper, Bluegill 250.00
Salt & Pepper, Cactus 38.00
Salt & Pepper, Chickens, Black, Label 45.00
Salt & Pepper, Chow Chow 22.00
Salt & Pepper, Coyote Pup 225.00
Salt & Pepper, Ducks 18.50
Salt & Pepper, English Setters 25.00
Salt & Pepper, Grouse 30.00
Salt & Pepper, Kangaroo, Rose On Feet, White 140.00
Salt & Pepper, Mallards 55.00
Salt & Pepper, Mountain Goat 125.00
Salt & Pepper, Palomino 45.00
Salt & Pepper, Pheasants, Tails Up 35.00
Salt & Pepper, Prairie Rose 25.00
Salt & Pepper, Quail 25.00
Salt & Pepper, Swordfish 175.00
Salt & Pepper, Turkey, 5 1/2 In. 95.00

Sugar & Creamer, Blue, Individual, 2 1/4 In. 6.00
Vase, Floral, Marked AK, 5 In. 500.00
Vase, Wheat Design, Cylindrical, Light Blue, 5 In. 55.00

ROSENTHAL porcelain was made at the factory established in Selb, Bavaria, in 1880. The factory is still making fine-quality tablewares and figurines. A series of Christmas plates was made from 1910. Other limited edition plates have been made since 1971.

MARKE
Rosenthal

Bowl, Portrait, Marked, 9 1/2 In. 85.00
Coffeepot, Donatello, 7 In. 65.00
Dinner Set, Raised Gilded Scrolls, Floral Medallions, Cream Ground, 44 Piece 522.50
Figurine, Angelfish, 16 In. 750.00
Figurine, Ballerina, Arms Outstretched, 13 In. 225.00
Figurine, Bird On Branch, No. 1648, 6 In. 128.00
Figurine, Boy, Holding Bowl, Parrot On Head, Lieberman, 1908, 10 1/4 In. 450.00
Figurine, Cocker Spaniel, Seated, Kuspert, 3 3/4 In. 135.00
Figurine, Dachshund, Begging, No. 243 .... 150.00
Figurine, Dachshund, Sitting, 6 In. 190.00
Figurine, Dog, Boxer 400.00
Figurine, Kneeling Nude, Hands Cupped Toward Face, Signed 325.00
Figurine, Poodle, White 475.00
Figurine, Princess & Frog, 11 1/2 In. 495.00
Figurine, Puppy, Signed, 3 1/2 x 5 In. 98.00
Figurine, Seagulls, H. Meisel, 18 1/2 In. 1450.00
Figurine, Stylized, Narrow Face, Robe, White Glazed, Schliepstein, 18 1/2 In. 920.00
Figurine, Woman, Seated, Talking To Parrot, 6 1/2 In. 325.00
Mug, Hand Painted Fruit 45.00
Plate, Christmas, Winter Peace 370.00
Plate, Ivory, 11 In., 12 Piece 200.00
Plate, Portrait, Woman, Marked, 8 1/2 In. 65.00
Plate, Rheinstein Castle, 10 1/2 In. 100.00
Plate, Scrolled & Floral Border, Center Gilt Rosette, 11 In., 10 Piece 175.00
Soup, Dish, Springtime 9.00
Vase, Blue Floral, White Ground, 17 In. 143.00

ROSEVILLE Pottery Company was organized in Roseville, Ohio, in 1890. Another plant was opened in Zanesville, Ohio, in 1898. Many types of pottery were made until 1954. Early wares include Sgraffito, Olympic, and Rozane. Later lines were often made with molded decorations, especially flowers and fruit. Pieces are marked *Roseville*.

Roseville
U.S.A.

Ashtray, Capri, Green, 7 In. 50.00
Ashtray, Hyde Park .... 20.00 to 40.00
Ashtray, Ming Tree 70.00
Ashtray, Peony, Green .... 85.00 to 95.00
Ashtray, Pine Cone, Blue, 4 1/2 In. 95.00
Ashtray, Silhouette, Red 55.00
Ashtray, Snowberry, Blue 45.00
Ashtray, Snowberry, Green, 5 1/2 In. .... 44.00 to 90.00
Basket, Apple Blossom, Green, 10 In. .... 115.00 to 195.00
Basket, Bittersweet, Gray, 10 In. 140.00
Basket, Bleeding Heart, Handle, Blue, 10 In. .... 250.00 to 295.00
Basket, Bushberry, Blue, 8 In. 135.00
Basket, Capri, Green 95.00
Basket, Clematis, Blue, 7 In. 135.00
Basket, Columbine, Blue, 10 In. 198.00
Basket, Columbine, Pink, 8 In. 145.00
Basket, Dogwood II, 10 In. 165.00
Basket, Donatello, Small 275.00
Basket, Florentine, Brown, 9 In. 154.00
Basket, Foxglove, Blue, 8 In. 160.00
Basket, Freesia, Blue, 8 In. .... 65.00 to 145.00
Basket, Freesia, Blue, 10 In. 160.00

Basket, Fuchsia, Attached Flower Frog, Brown 295.00
Basket, Fuchsia, Blue, 10 In. 350.00
Basket, Gardenia, Brown 135.00
Basket, Hanging, Apple Blossom, Pink, 5 In. 140.00
Basket, Hanging, Blackberry 650.00
Basket, Hanging, Bushberry, Brown, 5 In. 160.00
Basket, Hanging, Clematis, Brown 150.00
Basket, Hanging, Columbine, Pink 185.00
Basket, Hanging, Dogwood II, 6 In. 242.00
Basket, Hanging, Foxglove, Blue, 5 1/2 In. 220.00
Basket, Hanging, Fuchsia, Green 285.00
Basket, Hanging, Imperial I, 4 In. 176.00
Basket, Hanging, LaRose, 6 In. 253.00
Basket, Hanging, Mostique, Large 145.00
Basket, Hanging, Zephyr Lily, Blue 165.00
Basket, Magnolia, Black 120.00
Basket, Mock Orange, Pink, 10 In. 325.00
Basket, Monticello, Blue 450.00
Basket, Morning Glory, White 375.00
Basket, Peony, Gold, 8 In. 75.00
Basket, Peony, Green, 10 In. 145.00
Basket, Pine Cone, Brown, 11 In. 330.00
Basket, Silhouette, Red 135.00
Basket, Snowberry, Rose, 12 In. 195.00
Basket, Teasel, Tan, Cream 250.00
Basket, Vista, 6 1/2 In. 198.00
Basket, Water Lily, Blue, 8 In. 125.00
Basket, White Rose, Blue, 10 In. 175.00
Basket, White Rose, Pink, 8 In. 95.00
Basket, Wincraft, Tan, 15 x 8 In. 90.00
Basket, Zephyr Lily, Blue, 10 In. 185.00
Basket, Zephyr Lily, Green .... 95.00 to 125.00
Bookends, Apple Blossom, Green 175.00
Bookends, Bleeding Heart, Green, 5 In. 210.00
Bookends, Burmese, Turquoise, Gold Trim, 6 In. 165.00
Bookends, Columbine, Pink 185.00
Bookends, Freesia, Green 60.00
Bookends, Ming Tree, White 145.00
Bookends, Pine Cone, 4 In. .... 135.00 to 270.00
Bookends, Snowberry, Blue 150.00
Bookends, Water Lily, Brown 135.00
Bookends, Zephyr Lily, Blue, 5 In. 77.00
Bookends, Zephyr Lily, Green .... 115.00 to 125.00
Bowl, Apple Blossom, Pink, 4 In. 300.00
Bowl, Baneda, Green, 3 x 8 In. 225.00
Bowl, Bittersweet, 6 In. 75.00
Bowl, Bleeding Heart, Blue, 4 In. 150.00
Bowl, Columbine, Blue, 6 In. 75.00
Bowl, Cosmos, Brown, 6 In. 89.00
Bowl, Earlam, 4 In. 140.00
Bowl, Ferella, Pedestal, Green & Yellow Molded Design, Brown Glaze, 5 In. 357.50
Bowl, Florane, 5 x 8 In. 110.00
Bowl, Florane, Brown, 6 In. 35.00
Bowl, Freesia, Blue, 14 In. .... 125.00 to 145.00
Bowl, Freesia, Oblong, 12 In. 1335.00
Bowl, Fuchsia, Blue, 4 In. 110.00
Bowl, Imperial I, 10 In. 38.00
Bowl, Imperial, Handle, 10 1/2 In. 62.00
Bowl, Iris, Brown, 8 In. 125.00
Bowl, Iris, Tan, 9 In. 95.00
Bowl, Ixia, Pink, 7 In. 65.00
Bowl, Jonquil, Oval, 12 In. 99.00
Bowl, Laurel, Oval, Yellow, 9 In. 132.00

Bowl, Luffa, Rust, 4 1/2 In.	154.00
Bowl, Magnolia, Conch Shell, 6 In.	77.00
Bowl, Magnolia, Green, Conch Shell, 6 1/2 x 9 In.	125.00
Bowl, Ming Tree, 9 In.	195.00
Bowl, Moderne, Aqua, 6 In.	85.00
Bowl, Moss, Oval, Blue, 10 In.	99.00
Bowl, Moss, Oval, Blue, 14 In.	125.00
Bowl, Moss, Pink, 6 In.	75.00
Bowl, Peony, Aqua, Conch Shell,	225.00
Bowl, Peony, Gold, Conch Shell, 9 1/2 By 6 1/2 In.	105.00
Bowl, Pine Cone, Banana Shape, Blue, 10 In.	143.00
Bowl, Pine Cone, Green, Oval, Twig End Handles, 9 1/2 x 6 In.	125.00
Bowl, Pine Cone, Leaf Shape, Brown, 8 In.	66.00
Bowl, Pine Cone, Oval, Green, 14 In.	225.00
Bowl, Poppy, Gray, 5 In.	75.00
Bowl, Silhouette, Brown, 1 Handle, 12 In.	60.00
Bowl, Thorn Apple, Blue, 7 In.	88.00 to 95.00
Bowl, Topeo, Blue, 13 In.	275.00 to 285.00
Bowl, Velmoss Scroll	98.00
Bowl, Velmoss, Pink, 6 In.	225.00
Bowl, Water Lily, Pink, Conch Shell, 8 In.	99.00
Bowl, White Rose, Green, 6 In.	95.00
Bowl, White Rose, Pink, 4 In.	50.00
Bowl, Wisteria, Brown-Green, 8 In.	250.00
Bowl, Zephyr Lily, Brown, Green, 9 x 2 1/2 In.	68.00
Bowl, Zephyr Lily, Green, 8 In.	98.00
Candlestick, Apple Blossom, Blue, Pair	85.00
Candlestick, Apple Blossom, Green, 2 In., Pair	85.00
Candlestick, Apple Blossom, Green, 4 In., Pair	100.00
Candlestick, Baneda, Red, Pair	475.00
Candlestick, Bittersweet, Gray	110.00
Candlestick, Bittersweet, Yellow, 3 In., Pair	66.00
Candlestick, Carnelian I, Blue, 3 In., Pair	55.00
Candlestick, Carnelian I, Turquoise, 3 In., Pair	99.00
Candlestick, Carnelian I, Dark Green Drip Glaze, Light Green Ground, 2 In., Pair ...	190.00
Candlestick, Columbine, Blue, 4 1/2 In., Pair	85.00 to 89.00
Candlestick, Freesia, 4 1/2 In., Pair	75.00
Candlestick, Freesia, Blue, 2 In., Pair	85.00
Candlestick, Freesia, Brown, Pair	110.00
Candlestick, Jonquil	90.00
Candlestick, Luffa, Brown, 5 In., Pair	176.00
Candlestick, Mock Orange, Green, 2 In.	20.00
Candlestick, Morning Glory, White, 5 In.	125.00
Candlestick, Peony, Green, 2 In., Pair	65.00
Candlestick, Pine Cone, Blue	225.00
Candlestick, Primrose, Tan, 4 1/2 In.	35.00
Candlestick, Rozane, Ivory, Cone Shape, 1917, 7 3/4 In.	70.00
Candlestick, Snowberry, Blue, Pair	75.00
Candlestick, Sunflower, Label, 4 In.	250.00
Candlestick, Thorn Apple, Green, Pair	55.00
Candlestick, Tuscany, Gray, 3 1/2 In., Pair	48.00
Candlestick, Tuscany, Pink, 5 In., Pair	75.00
Candlestick, Futura, Orange Matte, Tiered Design, Triangles, 10 1/2 In., Pair	1100.00
Cider Set, Peony, Pitcher, 8 Mugs	400.00
Coffee & Tea Set, Mock Orange, Green, 4 Piece	695.00
Coffeepot, Wincraft, Cover, Orange-To-Brown Glaze, 10 In.	198.00
Compote, Donatello, 12 x 6 In.	210.00
Compote, Egypto, Green Matte With Branches	550.00
Compote, Moderne, Pink, 6 In.	125.00
Compote, Rosecraft, Black, 11 In.	110.00
Console, Baneda, Green, 3 x 9 In.	295.00
Console, Blackberry, 13 In.	325.00
Console, Bushberry, Blue, Footed	120.00

Console, Ferella, With Frog, 8 In.	550.00
Console, Foxglove, Pink	125.00
Console, Fuchsia, Brown, 12 In.	185.00
Console, Monticello, Blue, 13 x 3 In.	230.00
Console, Monticello, Brown, 2 Handles, 14 In.	395.00
Console, Moss, Pink, 13 In.	195.00
Console, Pine Cone, Blue, 11 In.	310.00
Console, Rozane, Blue, 1940s, 14 In.	65.00
Console, Topeo, Red	185.00
Console, Velmoss Scroll	98.00
Console, Wisteria, Brown	375.00
Console, Zephyr Lily, Blue, Footed, 8 In.	110.00
Console Set, Apple Blossom, Pink, 3 Piece	220.00
Console Set, Bleeding Heart, Pink, 17 In.	265.00
Console Set, Clematis, 3 Piece	65.00
Console Set, Snowberry, Pink, 12-In. Bowl, 2-In. Candlesticks, 3 Piece	185.00
Cookie Jar, Clematis, Teal Blue	325.00
Cookie Jar, Freesia, 1945	300.00
Cookie Jar, Water Lily	295.00
Cookie Jar, Water Lily, Cover, Brown, 8 In.	198.00
Cookie Jar, Zephyr Lily, Brown	395.00 to 425.00
Cornucopia, Apple Blossom, Pink, 6 In.	75.00
Cornucopia, Bushberry, Green, 8 In.	135.00
Cornucopia, Clematis, Brown, 8 In.	70.00
Cornucopia, Foxglove, Green, 6 In.	70.00 to 75.00
Cornucopia, Ivory, 7 In.	40.00
Cornucopia, Ivory, Russco Shape, 9 In.	75.00
Cornucopia, Magnolia, Green	100.00
Cornucopia, Primrose, Pink, 6 In.	95.00
Cornucopia, Snowberry, Green, 7 In.	75.00
Creamer, Medallion	25.00
Cuspidor, Donatello	125.00
Dish, Feeding, Juvenile, Bunny, Rolled Edge, Large	125.00
Dish, Feeding, Juvenile, Little Jack Horner	125.00
Dish, Feeding, Juvenile, Rabbits, Rolled Edge, 6 In.	135.00
Dish, Feeding, Juvenile, Sunbonnet Girl, Rolled Edge, 8 In.	88.00
Dish, Feeding, Juvenile, Tom He Was A Piper's Son, Rolled Edge, Green, 8 In.	88.00
Ewer, Apple Blossom, Green, 8 In.	70.00
Ewer, Apple Blossom, Pink, 15 In.	280.00 to 375.00
Ewer, Bleeding Heart, Pink, 6 In.	165.00
Ewer, Clematis, Brown, 10 In.	120.00
Ewer, Clematis, Brown, 15 In.	230.00
Ewer, Clematis, Green, Red Flower, 10 In.	95.00
Ewer, Columbine, Brown	110.00
Ewer, Cosmos, Blue, 15 In.	357.50
Ewer, Foxglove, Blue, 15 In.	335.00
Ewer, Foxglove, Rose, 6 1/2 In.	120.00
Ewer, Freesia, Blue, 15 In.	350.00
Ewer, Gardenia, Brown, 15 In.	250.00
Ewer, Magnolia, Blue, 10 In.	190.00
Ewer, Ming Tree, Green, 10 In.	135.00
Ewer, Mock Orange, Green	95.00
Ewer, Pine Cone, Blue, 18 In.	1495.00
Ewer, Pine Cone, Candlesticks, Blue, 3 Piece	300.00
Ewer, Poppy, Gray, 10 In.	135.00
Ewer, Rozane, Brown, 16 In.	220.00
Ewer, Snowberry, 15 In.	325.00
Ewer, Snowberry, Blue, 10 5/8 In.	160.00
Ewer, Snowberry, Green, 15 In.	225.00
Ewer, Water Lily, Blue, 15 In.	295.00 to 350.00
Ewer, White Rose, 15 In.	365.00
Ewer, White Rose, Green, 6 In.	75.00 to 95.00
Ewer, Wincraft, Rust Glaze, 8 In.	88.00

Ewer, Zephyr Lily, Blue, 10 In. 135.00
Flower Frog, Clematis, 4 1/2 In. 35.00
Flower Frog, Columbine, Brown 95.00
Flower Frog, Donatello, 2 1/2 In. 15.00
Flower Frog, Iris, Pink 85.00
Flower Frog, Ixia, Green 55.00
Flower Frog, Pine Cone, Brown 150.00
Flower Frog, Poppy, Brown 100.00
Flower Frog, Primrose, Yellow, 5 In. 132.00
Flower Frog, Teasel, 3 x 4 In. 65.00
Flower Frog, Tourmaline, Blue, Sticker, 11 In. 225.00
Flower Frog, Tuscany, Pink, 6 In. .... 20.00 to 30.00
Flower Frog, Water Lily, Pink 95.00
Flowerpot, Donatello, Ivory, 5 In. 65.00
Flowerpot, Donatello, Saucer, 4 In. 95.00
Flowerpot, Flower Frog, Jonquil 295.00
Flowerpot, Foxglove, Saucer, Green, 5 In. 165.00
Flowerpot, Mayfair, Saucer, Brown, 5 In. 82.00
Ginger Jar, Tourmaline, 10 In. 275.00
Humidor, Dutch, Creamware 395.00
Jar, Band Of Holly, Cover, Ocher Field, 8 1/2 In. 330.00
Jardiniere, Apple Blossom, Green, 6 In. 82.00
Jardiniere, Apple Blossom, Pedestal, Pink, 8 In. 975.00
Jardiniere, Autumn, 7 In. 400.00
Jardiniere, Baneda, Pink, 5 In. 285.00
Jardiniere, Bleeding Heart, 4 In. 60.00
Jardiniere, Bushberry, Green, 4 In. 75.00
Jardiniere, Cherry Blossom, Pink, Blue, 7 In. 565.00
Jardiniere, Columbine, 3 In. 45.00
Jardiniere, Columbine, Blue, 8 In. 350.00
Jardiniere, Columbine, Blue, 10 In. 230.00
Jardiniere, Corinthian, 9 In. 176.00
Jardiniere, Dahlrose, 8 In. 175.00
Jardiniere, Dogwood I, 6 In. 130.00
Jardiniere, Dogwood II, Pedestal, 10 In. 825.00
Jardiniere, Donatello, 6 x 7 In. 75.00
Jardiniere, Donatello, 7 1/2 x 10 In. 110.00
Jardiniere, Florentine, 7 In. 50.00
Jardiniere, Foxglove, Blue, 4 In. 75.00
Jardiniere, Foxglove, Pink, 3 In. 45.00
Jardiniere, Fuchsia, 2 Handles, No. 346, 4 x 7 1/4 In. 40.00
Jardiniere, Fuchsia, Brown, 10 In. 650.00
Jardiniere, Futura, 8 In. 275.00
Jardiniere, Futura, Pedestal, Geometric Design, 28 In. 950.00
Jardiniere, Green, Pedestal, 10 In. 1250.00
Jardiniere, Imperial II, Pedestal, 28 In. 330.00
Jardiniere, Iris, Brown, 3 In. 60.00
Jardiniere, Iris, Tan 55.00
Jardiniere, Jonquil, Pedestal, 27 In. 1045.00
Jardiniere, Luffa, Brown, 4 In. 100.00
Jardiniere, Magnolia, Pedestal, Green, 8 In. 625.00
Jardiniere, Mock Orange, Pedestal, Yellow 725.00
Jardiniere, Mostique, Pedestal, Gray, Flower Design, 28 1/2 In. 825.00
Jardiniere, Mostique, Tan Flowers, 8 1/2 In. 77.00
Jardiniere, Normandy, 7 In. .... 99.00 to 230.00
Jardiniere, Peony, Pedestal, Gold, 10 In. 1250.00
Jardiniere, Pine Cone, Blue, 8 In. 525.00
Jardiniere, Poppy, Pink, Green 150.00
Jardiniere, Primrose, Pink, 4 In. 75.00
Jardiniere, Primrose, Rust, 9 In. 275.00
Jardiniere, Rosecraft, Grapevines On Brown Ground, 9 x 12 In. 247.00
Jardiniere, Rozane, Leaves, 6 1/2 In. 150.00
Jardiniere, Snowberry, Pedestal, Green, 8 In. 825.00

Jardiniere, Sunflower, 9 In. 1300.00
Jardiniere, Vista, 6 1/2 In. 295.00
Jardiniere, Water Lily, Pink And Green, 8 In. 275.00
Jardiniere, Wisteria, Brown, 12 In. 1100.00
Lamp, Tuscany, Brown & Gray, Metal Base & Fittings, 20 In. 302.00
Match Holder, Pine Cone, Blue, 2 1/2 In. 145.00
Mug, Bushberry, Blue, 3 1/2 In. .... 85.00 to 115.00
Mug, Dutch 65.00
Mug, Elk 95.00
Mug, Peony, Yellow, 3 1/2 In. 80.00
Mug, Pine Cone, Brown .... 145.00 to 190.00
Mug, Pine Cone, Green, 4 In. 55.00
Mug, Rozane, Brown, 1900s, 4 1/4 In. 55.00
Pedestal, Bushberry, Blue 225.00
Pedestal, Foxglove, Blue, 16 1/2 In. 176.00
Pedestal, Moss, Pink And Green, 17 In. 297.00
Pedestal, Wisteria, Brown, 16 1/2 In. 330.00
Pitcher, Apple Blossom, Green 150.00
Pitcher, Cider, Bushberry, Brown, 8 1/2 In. 320.00
Pitcher, Cider, Magnolia, 7 In. 225.00
Pitcher, Cider, Pine Cone, Green, 9 In. 330.00
Pitcher, Cow, 7 1/2 In. 185.00
Pitcher, Donatello, 6 3/8 In. 185.00
Pitcher, Dutch, 2 Dutchmen Smoking Cigars, Decal, 11 1/2 In. 115.50
Pitcher, Freesia, Blue 115.00
Pitcher, Magnolia, Green, 7 In. 295.00
Pitcher, Mayfair, Brown, 10 In. 75.00
Pitcher, Ming Tree, Green Foliage, Brown Branches, White Glaze, 10 In. .... 95.00 to 135.00
Pitcher, Peony, 6 In. 225.00
Pitcher, Peony, Yellow, 7 1/2 In. 295.00
Pitcher, Pine Cone, Brown, 9 In. 320.00
Pitcher, Pine Cone, Brown, Ice Lip 400.00
Pitcher, Primrose, Blue, 6 In. 100.00
Pitcher, Raymor, White 100.00
Pitcher, Rozane Woodland, Blue 850.00
Planter, Apple Blossom, Red 80.00
Planter, Artwood, 8 In. 65.00
Planter, Columbine, Brown 95.00
Planter, Donatello, Hanging 210.00
Planter, Earlam, 5 1/2 x 10 1/2 In. .... 125.00 to 150.00
Planter, Freesia 125.00
Planter, Lotus, Brown, Tan, 4 1/2 In. 75.00
Planter, Medallion, Footed 40.00
Planter, Ming Tree, 10 In. 55.00
Planter, Ming Tree, Turquoise, 9 In. 75.00
Planter, Nova, Blue Matte Glaze, Orange Interior, 6 x 4 In. 44.00
Planter, Nova, Green, 4 In. 45.00
Planter, Peony, 8 In. 85.00
Planter, Pine Cone, Blue, 8 In. 175.00
Planter, Thorn Apple, Blue, 5 In. 89.00
Planter, Water Lily, 9 x 4 In. 95.00
Sign, Rose Color, 6 1/2 x 2 1/2 In. 1100.00
Sign, Self-Standing, Ivory Letters On Blue Ground, 4 1/2 x 8 In. 1100.00
Stein, Dutch, Boy And Girl With Geese, 6 In. 27.50
Sugar & Creamer, Peony 80.00
Tankard, Mayfair, Green 135.00
Tankard Set, Creamware, Knights Of Pythias, 12-In. High Tankard, 7 Piece 440.00
Tankard Set, F. O. E., Eagle & Shield, Different Shapes, 7 Piece 655.00
Tea Set, Apple Blossom, Pink, 3 Piece .... 390.00 to 425.00
Tea Set, Bushberry, 3 Piece 200.00
Tea Set, Forget-Me-Not, Blue 450.00
Tea Set, Peony, 3 Piece 295.00
Tea Set, Peony, Gold 260.00

Tea Set, Snowberry, Green, 3 Piece 350.00
Tea Set, Wincraft, Blue 185.00
Tea Set, Zephyr Lily, Green, 3 Piece 285.00
Teakettle, Raymor, Swinging, 3 Piece 425.00
Teapot, Magnolia, Blue, Lid 15.00
Teapot, Peony, Cover, Gold, 8 In. 134.00
Teapot, Snowberry, Green 195.00
Toiletry Set, Autumn, Landscape, Rust & Yellow, 8 Piece 440.00
Tray, Foxglove, Green, 8 x 10 1/2 In. 60.00
Tray, Pine Cone, Green, 12 In. .... 100.00 to 295.00
Trivet, Raymor, 3-Footed, Light Gray 35.00
Tumbler, Green, 5 In., 8 Piece 300.00
Umbrella Stand, Chloron, Floral, Matte Green Glaze, Octagonal, 1907, 23 1/4 In. 275.00
Umbrella Stand, Florentine, Cream & Brown, 18 1/2 In. 357.00
Umbrella Stand, Imperial I 625.00
Umbrella Stand, Magnolia, 18 In. 650.00
Umbrella Stand, Matte Green 1100.00
Umbrella Stand, Mostique, 20 In. 350.00
Umbrella Stand, Normandy, 20 In. 795.00
Umbrella Stand, Vista, 20 In. 1600.00
Urn, Baneda, 6 x 6 In. 395.00
Urn, Freesia, Blue 185.00
Urn, Laurel, Green, 6 1/2 In. 200.00
Urn, Magnolia, Brown, 6 In. 60.00
Urn, Monticello, Blue, 5 In. 135.00
Urn, Monticello, Brown, 9 In. 550.00
Urn, Moss, Pink 175.00
Urn, Russco, Yellow & Green 140.00
Urn, Silhouette, 8 In. 225.00
Urn, Silhouette, Nude, Rust, 6 In. 225.00
Urn, Sunflower, 5 x 7 In. 470.00
Urn, Sunflower, 6 1/2 In. 650.00
Urn, Wisteria, Blue, 5 In. .... 325.00 to 345.00
Vase, Apple Blossom, Blue 210.00
Vase, Apple Blossom, Blue, Base Handles, 10 In. 125.00
Vase, Apple Blossom, Green, 7 In. .... 95.00 to 98.00
Vase, Apple Blossom, Pink, 9 In. 140.00
Vase, Artwood, Double Bud, 8 In. 65.00
Vase, Aztec, Art Nouveau-Style Decoration, White, Blue, Yellow, Rust, 10 In. 495.00
Vase, Aztec, Blue, 10 In. 125.00
Vase, Aztec, Cylindrical, Applied Decoration, Green, Cream, Orange, 10 In. 357.00
Vase, Baneda, Green, 6 In. .... 318.00 to 350.00
Vase, Baneda, Pink, 4 1/2 In. 265.00
Vase, Baneda, Pink, 7 In. 80.00
Vase, Bittersweet, 14 In. 395.00
Vase, Bittersweet, Double Bud, Green 155.00
Vase, Bittersweet, Floor, Yellow, 16 In. 355.00
Vase, Bittersweet, Gray & Tan, Floor 395.00
Vase, Bittersweet, Green, 8 In. 140.00
Vase, Blackberry, 2 Piece 420.00
Vase, Blackberry, 5 In. 285.00
Vase, Bleeding Heart, Pink 225.00
Vase, Bushberry, Blue, 18 In. 450.00
Vase, Carnelian II, 9 In. 175.00
Vase, Carnelian, Double Bud, Tan Over Green 75.00
Vase, Carnelian, Green, Blue, 8 In. 150.00
Vase, Cherry Blossom, 7 In. 250.00
Vase, Cherry Blossom, Brown, 5 In. 210.00
Vase, Cherry Blossom, Jug Shape, 4 In. 215.00
Vase, Cherry Blossom, Pink & Blue, 12 In. 600.00
Vase, Chloron, 5 Designs, 9 1/2 In. 350.00
Vase, Clematis, Brown, 6 1/2 x 5 1/2 In. .... 45.00 to 65.00
Vase, Clematis, Green, 6 In. 70.00

Vase, Columbine, Brown, 6 In. 60.00
Vase, Columbine, Brown, 7 In. 120.00
Vase, Cornelian, Raspberry, Green, 9 In. 175.00
Vase, Cosmos, Brown, 18 In. 650.00
Vase, Cosmos, Handles, Green, 10 In. 125.00
Vase, Cosmos, Wide Flared Top, 2 Looped Handles, Molded Design, 9 In. 198.00
Vase, Cremona, Pink, 5 In. 95.00
Vase, Cremona, Pink, 8 In. 75.00
Vase, Cremona, Pink, 12 In. 195.00
Vase, Dahlrose, Bud, 8 In. 135.00
Vase, Dahlrose, Triple Bud, 8 In. 125.00
Vase, Dawn, Green, 4 In. .... 55.00 to 75.00
Vase, Della Robbia, Drilled Base, 10 3/4 x 4 1/4 In. 1800.00
Vase, Della Robbia, Excised Grape Clusters, Marked, 11 1/2 In. 800.00
Vase, Donatello, 6 3/8 In. 45.00
Vase, Donatello, Double Bud 75.00
Vase, Donatello, Torch Shape, 8 1/4 In. 130.00
Vase, Earlam, 6 In. 125.00
Vase, Earlam, Orange & Gray-Blue Glaze, White Overglaze, 7 In. 176.00
Vase, Egypto, Flared Top, Arts & Crafts Banded Design, Green Glaze, 16 In. 330.00
Vase, Falline, Brown, 6 In. 270.00
Vase, Falline, Green Crescents, Pumpkin Field, 6 1/2 In. 303.00
Vase, Ferella, Brown, 10 In. .... 550.00 to 600.00
Vase, Ferella, Red, 4 In. 275.00
Vase, Florane, Rust & Brown, 12 1/2 In. 300.00
Vase, Florentine, 2 Handles, 12 In. 110.00
Vase, Florentine, Tan, Footed, 10 x 6 In. 98.00
Vase, Foxglove, Blue, 8 In. 150.00
Vase, Foxglove, Blue, 15 In. 450.00
Vase, Foxglove, Pale Green & Pink, 7 In. 55.00
Vase, Freesia, Blue, 7 In. 80.00
Vase, Freesia, Blue, 8 In. .... 80.00 to 135.00
Vase, Freesia, Blue, 15 In. 330.00
Vase, Freesia, Brown, 10 In. .... 66.00 to 175.00
Vase, Freesia, Green, 7 In. 120.00
Vase, Freesia, Tan, 10 In. 120.00
Vase, Fuchsia, Blue, 6 In. .... 135.00 to 154.00
Vase, Fuchsia, Tan, 15 In. 500.00
Vase, Futura, Ball Shape, Angular Base, Blue & Green Leaves, Gray, 7 1/2 In. 600.00
Vase, Futura, Ball Shape, Circular Neck, Square Handles, Green, 9 In. 467.00
Vase, Futura, Cylindrical, Flared Top, Graduated Handles, Yellow Tulip, 13 In. 1210.00
Vase, Futura, Cylindrical, Four Buttresses, Brown, Yellow Spots, 10 In. 825.00
Vase, Futura, Flat Center, Flaring Body, Diamond Designs, 9 In. 660.00
Vase, Futura, Graduated Neck, Orange & Green Glaze, 10 x 8 1/2 In. 300.00
Vase, Futura, Light And Dark Blue, Matte Glaze, 5 In. 187.00
Vase, Futura, Olive, Tan, 7 In. 310.00
Vase, Futura, Pedestal Base, Flaring Bottom, 2 Handles, Geometric Flowers, 10 In. .. 770.00
Vase, Futura, Pillow, Blue Rays On Gray Ground, Paper Label, 5 1/4 In., Pair 350.00
Vase, Futura, Pink & Gray, 8 In. 325.00
Vase, Futura, Square Base, Ball-Shaped Body, Green & White Spots, 8 In. 250.00
Vase, Gardenia, Brown, 8 In. 120.00
Vase, Gardenia, Double Bud, Gray, 8 In. 60.00
Vase, Gardenia, Gray, 8 In. .... 95.00 to 115.00
Vase, Gardenia, Green, 6 In., Pair 80.00
Vase, Imperial I, 8 In. 95.00
Vase, Imperial I, 10 In. 130.00
Vase, Imperial, 12 In. 225.00
Vase, Iris, Blue-Green, 9 1/2 In., Pair 250.00
Vase, Iris, Pink, 6 In. 135.00
Vase, Iris, Tan, 9 In. 250.00
Vase, Jonquil, 5 In. 140.00
Vase, Jonquil, 7 In. .... 150.00 to 165.00
Vase, Jonquil, 8 In. .... 165.00 to 275.00

Vase, Jonquil, Flower Frog, 5 1/2 In. 132.00
Vase, Jonquil, Flower Frog, 6 In. 195.00
Vase, Jonquil, Round, 4 In. 105.00
Vase, Landscape, Raised, Cylindrical Form, 5 1/2 x 4 3/4 In. 90.00
Vase, Laurel, Green, 7 In. 140.00
Vase, Laurel, Mottled Orange & Yellow, Mistletoe, 8 In. 176.00
Vase, Laurel, Persimmon, 6 In. 175.00
Vase, Laurel, Red, 6 In. 175.00
Vase, Laurel, Yellow, 9 In. .... 175.00 to 200.00
Vase, Lotus, 10 In. 155.00
Vase, Luffa, Brown, 6 In. 115.00
Vase, Luffa, Green, 6 In. 135.00
Vase, Luffa, Green, 8 In. .... 165.00 to 185.00
Vase, Luffa, Pastel Colors, 5 In. 120.00
Vase, Magnolia, Green, 8 In. 200.00
Vase, Mayfair, Brown, 12 1/2 x 5 1/4 In. 60.00
Vase, Ming Tree, Green, Pitcher Type, 10 In. 125.00
Vase, Ming Tree, Orange Matte, Green Leaves On Trees, 8 In. 357.00
Vase, Ming Tree, Vase, Brown Branches As Handles, Turquoise, 8 1/4 In. 300.00
Vase, Ming Tree, White, Handle, 10 In. 145.00
Vase, Mock Orange, 10 In. 125.00
Vase, Mock Orange, Trial Glaze, 7 In. 195.00
Vase, Modern, Green, 10 In. 95.00
Vase, Mongol, Dark Red, Cylindrical, Flared Bottom, 3-Footed, 3 Handles, 8 1/2 In. 600.00
Vase, Monticello, Blue, 6 In. 350.00
Vase, Monticello, Tan, 7 In. 265.00
Vase, Morning Glory, 10 In. 495.00
Vase, Morning Glory, White, 6 1/2 In. 275.00
Vase, Mostique, 12 In. 185.00
Vase, Mostique, Gray, Incised Yellow Flowers, Green Glazed Interior, 12 In. 242.00
Vase, Orian, Blue, 10 1/2 In. 130.00
Vase, Orian, Red Glaze, Light Green, 7 1/2 In. 150.00
Vase, Orian, Turquoise, 9 In. 187.00
Vase, Orian, Yellow, 10 1/2 In. 135.00
Vase, Panel, Brown, 12 1/2 In. 286.00
Vase, Panel, Brown, 6 In. 88.00
Vase, Panel, Double Bud, Green 95.00
Vase, Panel, Green, 4 In. 95.00
Vase, Pauleo, 17 In. 1500.00
Vase, Pauleo, 19 In. .... 750.00 to 850.00
Vase, Pauleo, Painted Landscape, c.1914, 16 1/2 In. 1600.00
Vase, Peony, 9 In. 90.00
Vase, Peony, Aqua, 10 In. 300.00
Vase, Peony, Gold, 9 In. 77.00
Vase, Peony, Gold, Shoulder Handles, 6 x 5 In. 70.00
Vase, Peony, Green, 9 In. 190.00
Vase, Peony, Yellow, 15 In. 300.00
Vase, Pillow, Pine Cone, Brown, 10 x 9 In. 295.00
Vase, Pillow, Rozane, Hunting Dog & Pheasant, Ruffled Edge, 2 Handles, I.S., 9 In. 935.00
Vase, Pine Cone, Blue, 7 In. .... 210.00 to 285.00
Vase, Pine Cone, Blue, 13 In. 350.00
Vase, Pine Cone, Brown, 10 In. .... 225.00 to 265.00
Vase, Pine Cone, Green, 6 In. 60.00
Vase, Pine Cone, Triple Bud, Brown, 8 1/2 In. 187.00
Vase, Poppy, Pink, 9 In. 130.00
Vase, Primrose, 2 Handles, Brown, 6 In. 55.00
Vase, Primrose, Pink, 9 In. 99.00
Vase, Rosecraft, Black, 6 In. 65.00
Vase, Rozane Royal, Green Ground, Peach Roses, 15 In. 605.00
Vase, Rozane, Della Robbia, 3 Handles, Oak Trees, Acorns, 9 1/4 In. 8500.00
Vase, Rozane, Della Robbia, Pedestal, Curled Handles, Classical Figures, 12 In. 3850.00
Vase, Rozane, Egypto, Embossed Flowers, Swirling Stems, 6 In. 357.00
Vase, Rozane, Indian Brave, Green, Orange & Brown Ground, 14 In. 1870.00

Vase, Rozane, Medium Green, 8 1/8 In. 488.00
Vase, Rozane, Mongol, Bulbous, Footed, Deep Red To Red-Brown Glaze, 7 1/2 In. .. 770.00
Vase, Rozane, Olympic, Juno Commanding The Sun To Set, 20 In. 5225.00
Vase, Rozane, Pillow, 2 Handles, Hunting Dog With Pheasant, Dunlavy, 9 In. 1100.00
Vase, Rozane, Portrait Of Dog, Orange, Brown, M. Timberlake, 13 1/2 In. 1540.00
Vase, Rozane, Woodland, Twisted Shape, Bisque Ground, Incised Flowers, 10 1/2 In.   55.00
Vase, Rozane, Woodland, Yellow & Brown Flowers, 11 In. 1430.00
Vase, Rozane, Yellow Flowers, Gray-Green Ground, 11 In. 2070.00
Vase, Russco, Ball Shape, Green & Yellow Crystals, 6 In. 88.00
Vase, Russco, Double Bud, 9 In. 65.00
Vase, Russco, Turquoise, 12 1/2 In. 115.00
Vase, Savona, Orange & Yellow, Handles, 6 In. 145.00
Vase, Silhouette, 12 In. .... 150.00 to 170.00
Vase, Silhouette, Fan Shape, Nude, Turquoise, 7 In. 198.00
Vase, Silhouette, Fan, Nude, White 210.00
Vase, Silhouette, Nude, Turquoise, 8 In. 165.00
Vase, Snowberry, Blue, 8 In. 125.00
Vase, Snowberry, Bud, Green 78.00
Vase, Snowberry, Pink, 12 In. 165.00
Vase, Sunflower, 10 In. 1200.00
Vase, Sunflower, 2 Handles, 9 1/2 In. 665.00
Vase, Sunflower, 5 1/2 In. 308.00
Vase, Sunflower, 6 In. .... 165.00 to 245.00
Vase, Sunflower, 8 In. .... 200.00 to 800.00
Vase, Thorn Apple, 6 1/2 In. 75.00
Vase, Thorn Apple, Blue, 12 In. 225.00
Vase, Thorn Apple, Blue, Cylinder, 7 In. 98.00
Vase, Thorn Apple, Brown, 4 In. 65.00
Vase, Thorn Apple, Bud, Pink, 7 In. 55.00
Vase, Thorn Apple, Pink, 6 In. 75.00
Vase, Topeo, 12 In. 475.00
Vase, Topeo, Egg Shape, 9 In. 350.00
Vase, Topeo, Red, 10 In. 300.00
Vase, Topeo, Red, 6 1/2 In. 150.00
Vase, Tourmaline, 8 In. 125.00
Vase, Tourmaline, Blue, 7 1/2 In. 210.00
Vase, Tourmaline, Blue, 10 In. 295.00
Vase, Tourmaline, Green Glaze, Pale Green Drip, 9 In. 143.00
Vase, Tourmaline, Orange & Yellow Glaze, Molded Design On Neck, 4 1/2 In. 72.00
Vase, Tourmaline, Turquoise, 4 1/2 In. 50.00
Vase, Tuscany, Pink, 5 In. 120.00
Vase, Tuscany, Pink, 8 In. 165.00
Vase, Velmoss II, Green, 6 In. 120.00
Vase, Vista, 2 Handles, 10 In. 253.00
Vase, Volpato, 12 1/2 In. 200.00
Vase, Water Lily, 14 In. 220.00
Vase, Water Lily, 16 In. 500.00
Vase, Water Lily, Brown, 10 In. 77.00
Vase, White Rose, Blue & Green, Open Handles, 8 1/2 In. 88.00
Vase, White Rose, Blue, 9 In. 125.00
Vase, White Rose, Blue, 15 In. 140.00
Vase, White Rose, Brown To Green, Loop Handles, 18 In. 485.00
Vase, White Rose, Brown, Floor 485.00
Vase, White Rose, Pink, 15 In. 375.00
Vase, Wincraft, Branch Handles, Step Base, 14 In. 155.00
Vase, Wincraft, Green, 6 In. 65.00
Vase, Wincraft, Green, Brown Glaze, 12 In. 55.00
Vase, Windsor, Brown, 8 1/2 In. 285.00
Vase, Windsor, Green Leaves, Rose Ground, 7 3/4 In. 275.00
Vase, Windsor, Yellow Rectangles, Green Squares, Blue Glaze, 6 In. 176.00
Vase, Wisteria, Brown, 6 In. .... 250.00 to 295.00
Vase, Wisteria, Brown, 8 In. 395.00
Vase, Wisteria, Embossed Vines, Ocher & Brown Ground, Signed, 6 3/4 In. 375.00

Vase, Wisteria, Handles, 6 In. 275.00
Vase, Wisteria, Handles, 8 In. 325.00
Vase, Zephyr Lily, Blue, 9 In. 150.00
Vase, Zephyr Lily, Brown, 2 Piece 170.00
Vase, Zephyr Lily, Floor, Rust, 15 In. 275.00
Vase, Zephyr Lily, Handle, 18 In. 375.00
Vase, Zephyr Lily, Rust, 8 In. 55.00
Wall Pocket, Apple Blossom, 8 In. 140.00
Wall Pocket, Blackberry 665.00
Wall Pocket, Bleeding Heart, 8 In. 250.00
Wall Pocket, Bleeding Heart, Blue 450.00
Wall Pocket, Cherry Blossom, Brown, 8 In. 495.00
Wall Pocket, Columbine, 9 In. 195.00
Wall Pocket, Corinthian, 12 In. 150.00
Wall Pocket, Cosmos, Blue, 6 In. 300.00
Wall Pocket, Dahlrose, 10 In. 245.00
Wall Pocket, Dogwood II, Green 125.00
Wall Pocket, Donatello, 12 In. 160.00
Wall Pocket, Foxglove, Blue .... 195.00 to 275.00
Wall Pocket, Freesia, Brown 140.00
Wall Pocket, Fuchsia, Blue, 8 1/2 In. 395.00
Wall Pocket, Gardenia, 8 In. 150.00
Wall Pocket, Imperial II, Orange, Green Drip, 6 1/2 In. 308.00
Wall Pocket, Imperial II, Triple 295.00
Wall Pocket, La Rose 175.00
Wall Pocket, Lombardy, Blue-Green Glaze, 8 In. 187.00
Wall Pocket, Lotus 185.00
Wall Pocket, Ming Tree, 8 3/4 x 8 3/4 In. 110.00
Wall Pocket, Mostique, 10 1/2 In. 145.00
Wall Pocket, Panel, Nude, Green .... 375.00 to 525.00
Wall Pocket, Rosecraft, Blue, 10 In. 185.00
Wall Pocket, Rosecraft, Yellow, Ink Stamp 135.00
Wall Pocket, Silhouette, Nude, Brown, 10 In. 295.00
Wall Pocket, Snowberry 90.00
Wall Pocket, Thorn Apple, Pink 500.00
Wall Pocket, White Rose, Pink & Green, 8 In. 275.00
Wall Pocket, Zephyr Lily, Brown 175.00
Window Box, Bushberry, Rust, 8 In. 49.50
Window Box, Clematis, Blue, Handle To Handle, 11 In. 75.00
Window Box, Cosmos, Brown 165.00
Window Box, Cosmos, Tan & Green 250.00
Window Box, Dahlrose, 11 1/2 In. 195.00
Window Box, Donatello, Ivory, 14 In. 175.00
Window Box, Ming Tree, Blue 120.00
Window Box, Pine Cone, Brown, 8 In. .... 110.00 to 260.00
Window Box, Snowberry, Blue 98.00
Window Box, Water Lily, Brown, 18 In. 390.00

ROWLAND & MARSELLUS Company is part of a mark that appears on
historical Staffordshire dating from the late nineteenth and early twentieth
centuries. Rowland & Marsellus is believed to be the mark used by the
British Anchor Pottery Co. of Longton, England, for some pieces made for
export to a New York firm. Many American views were made. Of special
interest to collectors are the blue and white plates with rolled edges.

Plate, Alaska-Yukon-Pacific Exposition, Seattle, Oriental Women, 1909 .... 125.00
Plate, Jefferson Center, Scenes Of Fair Rim, St. Louis, 1904, 10 In. 85.00
Plate, New Bedford, 6 1/2 In. 25.00

ROY ROGERS was born in 1911 in Cincinnati, Ohio. In the 1930s, he made
a living as a singer; in 1935, his group started work at a Los Angeles radio
station. He appeared in his first movie in 1937. From 1952 to 1957, he made
101 television shows. Roy Rogers memorabilia is collected, including items
from the Roy Rogers restaurants.

Badge, Deputy, 5-Pointed Star, 1950s .... 10.00 to 28.00
Badge, Nellybelle, Tin, Post Raisin Bran Premium .... 35.00 to 38.00
Bandanna, Roy On Horse, Blue, Green & White Trim, 1950s 40.00
Bank, Figural, Boot, Bronze Finish, Die Cast Metal, 1950s, 6 In. .... 55.00 to 125.00
Book, My Favorite Christmas Story, 1960 .... 15.00
Book, Raiders Of Sawtooth Ridge, Whitman, 1946 .... 14.00 to 25.00
Book, Roy Rogers And Cowboy Toby, Little Golden Book, 1954 .... 27.00
Book, Roy Rogers And The Desert Treasure, Cozy Corner Book, Whitman, 1950s 20.00
Book, Roy Rogers At The Lane Ranch, Tell-A-Tale, Whitman, 1950 .... 19.00
Book, Surprise For Donnie, Whitman, 1954 .... 15.00
Box, Crayon Set, Only Box .... · 8.00
Button, Pinback, Celluloid, 1 1/2 In., c.1950 .... 23.00
Camera, Flash, Box 245.00
Cap Pistol, Kilgore, 9 In. 85.00
Cards, Playing, King Of Cowboys, 2 Decks, Plastic Box 20.00
Chaps, Roy On Trigger 295.00
Clock, Alarm, Animated, Roy On Horse Rocks With Each Tick 175.00
Clock, Alarm, Roy Rogers & Trigger 110.00
Coloring Book, 1955 .... 35.00
Dishes, Western Dinner Set, Ideal, Box 225.00
Figurine, Dale Evans, On Horse, Hartland .... 95.00 to 120.00
Fix It Stagecoach, Box 60.00
Flip Book, Classy Holsters, 1958 .... 75.00
Gloves, Leather, Roy Rogers & Trigger, Felt Lining, Jeweled, Size 7 .... 145.00
Guitar, Wooden, 1954 .... 275.00
Harmonica 20.00
Harmonica, Riders 42.00
Hat, Cowboy 185.00
Hat, Roy Rogers & Trigger 15.00
Holster, Double, Leather, Merit, c.1950, Box 150.00
Horseshoe, Roy & Trigger, Good Luck 25.00
Horseshoe Set, Tin Lithograph, Ohio Art .... 195.00 to 200.00
Key Chain, Pocket Knife, Triangle Shape, Picture Of Roy In Horseshoe 12.00
Lamp, Roy On Rearing Trigger, Composition 195.00
Lamp, Roy On Trigger, Signed Many Happy Trails, Composition 275.00
Lantern, Ohio Art, c.1950 .... 145.00 to 150.00
Lunch Box, Dale Evans & Roy, 1954 .... 299.00
Lunch Box, Metal, Cowhide Red Band 110.00
Lunch Box, Roy & Dale Evans, Double Bar Ranch 50.00
Lunch Box, Saddlebag, Vinyl 250.00
Mug, Official, Plastic, F & F .... 20.00 to 39.00
Neckerchief, Square, 26 In. 95.00
Paper Doll, Roy & Dale Evans, Original Folder, 1956, Uncut 45.00
Paper Doll, Roy & Dale Evans, Whitman, 1950, Uncut 75.00
Paper Doll, Roy & Dale Evans, Whitman, 1953, Uncut 125.00
Paper Doll, Roy Rogers Corral, Uncut 95.00
Pencil, Republic Pictures, Wooden, Dated 1942, Unused 1.25
Pencil Box, Double R Bar Ranch, Contents 125.00
Play Set, Mineral City, Jail Side, Marx 465.00
Play Set, Mineral City, Saloon Side, Marx, Box 625.00
Play Set, Rodeo Ranch, No. 3985, Marx 235.00
Play Set, Rodeo Ranch, No. 3987, Series 750, Marx 125.00
Poster, Advertising Ranch Set, Post Cereal 75.00
Puzzle, Roy Holding 2 Puppies, Whitman, 1952, 11 x 15 In. 18.00
Record Set, Pecos Bill, 3 Piece 25.00
Rifle, Carbine, Plastic, Marx, c.1950, 26 In., Box 135.99
Ring, Fold-Up Microscope, Quaker Oats Premium, 1949 .... 80.00
Ring, Microscope 75.00
Ring, Saddle, Tin, Post Raisin Bran Premium, Package .... 38.00 to 45.00
Scarf, Hat Slide, Silk, 1945, Large 130.00
Sheet Music, Bible Tells Me So, Dale Evans & Roy Rogers Photograph, 1955 .... 5.00
Songbook, Cowboy, 1943 .... 10.00
Sticker Album, Rodeo, 2 x 1 In. 15.00

Suit, Cowboy, 1948, 3 Piece	190.00
Tent, Canvas	200.00
Thermos, Pictures Dale Evans And Roy	55.00
Thermos, Roy Rogers Ranch	30.00
Toy, Wagon Train, Marx, Box, 1950s	250.00
Viewmaster Reel, Roy & Trigger, 1950	10.00
Watch, Dale Evans, Time Teacher, Germany, On Card, 1956	200.00 to 225.00
Wood-Burning Set	60.00
Wristwatch, Dale Evans, Box, 1950	315.00 to 350.00
Wristwatch, Flasher Dial	225.00
Wristwatch, Roy & Dale, 3-D Box, Pair	650.00
Wristwatch, Roy & Rearing Trigger, Ingraham, c.1954	82.50
Wristwatch, Roy Rogers, Box	375.00
Yo-Yo, Picture, 1950s	12.00
Yo-Yo, Round Top King, Western Plastics	25.00
Yo-Yo, With Trigger	125.00

ROYAL BAYREUTH is the name of a factory that was founded in Tettau, Bavaria, in 1794. It has continued to modern times. The marks have changed through the years. A stylized crest, the name *Royal Bayreuth*, and the word *Bavaria* appear in slightly different forms from 1870 to about 1919. Later dishes may include the words *U.S. Zone*, the year of the issue, or the word *Germany* instead of *Bavaria*. Related pieces may be found listed in the Rose Tapestry, Sand Babies, Snow Babies, and Sunbonnet Babies categories.

Ashtray, Elk, 6 In.	235.00
Ashtray, Flying Goose, Frog In Mouth, Blues & Oranges	475.00
Ashtray, Gray Eagle, Claws Extending Upward, Blue Mark	525.00
Ashtray, Hunt Scene, Woman On Horse, Dogs, Marked, 4 5/8 In.	55.00
Ashtray, Red Devil	395.00
Ashtray, Turkey, Blue Mark	390.00
Bell, Ocean Liner Scene, Wooden Clapper	150.00
Bowl, Corinthian, 8 In.	95.00
Bowl, Cover, Tomato, 4 In.	60.00
Bowl, Musicians Scene, Scalloped Rim, 3 Scroll Feet, Marked, 6 7/8 In.	101.00
Box, Stamp, Devil & Cards, Blue Mark	800.00
Box, Tomato, Cover, Blue Mark, 4 In.	45.00
Box, Trinket, Jack & Jill On Cover, 2 1/2 x 3 1/2 In.	75.00
Butter Chip, Violets	20.00
Candleholder, Basset Hound, Blue Mark	500.00
Candleholder, Clown, Seated Position, Blue Mark	425.00
Candleholder, Elk	675.00
Candleholder, Elk, Low	385.00
Candleholder, Monk, Gray Robes, Holding Jug & Candle	1200.00
Candleholder, Pelican, Yellow, Handle, Pair	195.00
Candleholder, Under Tray, Owl, Blue Mark	1000.00
Candleholder, Woman Clown, Blue Mark	1900.00
Candy Dish, Clown, Pearlized, White	425.00
Chamberstick, Center Grip Handle, Orange Roses	195.00
Chamberstick, Green, Transfer Of Woman Climbing Stairs, 7 In.	275.00
Chamberstick, Ring Around The Rosy, Blue Mark	225.00
Cracker Jar, Tomato	375.00
Creamer, 3 Cows In Pasture, Blue Mark, 3 1/2 In.	73.00
Creamer, Bell Ringer	235.00
Creamer, Bird Of Paradise, Blue Mark	230.00
Creamer, Black Crow	60.00
Creamer, Butterfly	295.00 to 350.00
Creamer, Card	185.00
Creamer, Cat Handle, Green, White, Blue Mark	250.00
Creamer, Cat Handle, Marked	445.00
Creamer, Chimpanzee, Blue Mark	500.00
Creamer, Clown, Blue Mark	185.00
Creamer, Cow, Brown	250.00
Creamer, Cow's Head, Yellow Horns, Black & Gray, 4 x 5 In.	135.00

Creamer, Crow, Black, Gold Beak & Eyes, Blue Mark, 2 1/2 x 4 3/4 In. .... 125.00 to 135.00
Creamer, Dachshund 195.00
Creamer, Eagle .... 195.00 to 275.00
Creamer, Elk 125.00
Creamer, Frog, Green 110.00
Creamer, Girl With Basket 600.00
Creamer, Girl With Basket, Blue Mark 600.00
Creamer, Girl With Geese 75.00
Creamer, Gray Striped Cat 275.00
Creamer, Jack & Jill 155.00
Creamer, Lemon 165.00
Creamer, Lobster 95.00
Creamer, Maple Leaf, Blue Mark 350.00
Creamer, Milk Maid .... 625.00 to 695.00
Creamer, Miss Muffet 85.00
Creamer, Monk 700.00
Creamer, Monkey, Green .... 395.00 to 495.00
Creamer, Mountain Goat, Blue Mark 275.00
Creamer, Orange 235.00
Creamer, Owl, Gray, Pink Eyes .... 325.00 to 375.00
Creamer, Pansy, Dark Pink 250.00
Creamer, Pelican, Pink, Blue Mark .... 225.00 to 350.00
Creamer, Pig 525.00
Creamer, Pig, Gray 650.00
Creamer, Pinched Spout, 3 Color 225.00
Creamer, Poodle, Black, Blue Mark 145.00
Creamer, Poodle, Blue Mark .... 180.00 to 200.00
Creamer, Purple Grape, Blue Mark 95.00
Creamer, Rooster 345.00
Creamer, Rose, Blue Mark, 3 1/2 In. 395.00
Creamer, Seal .... 295.00 to 350.00
Creamer, Strawberry, Blue Mark .... 165.00 to 275.00
Creamer, Woman, With Basket 45.00
Dish, Leaf Shape, Tapestry, Courting Couple, Gold Handle, 5 x 5 In. 235.00
Ewer, Pink Flowers, Multicolor Leaves, Handle 155.00
Hair Receiver, Man In Horse-Drawn Wagon, 3 1/4 x 3 1/4 In. 110.00
Hatpin Holder, Coachman, Blue Mark 265.00
Hatpin Holder, Dachshund, 4 3/4 In. 800.00
Hatpin Holder, Musicians 325.00
Hatpin Holder, Owl 795.00
Hatpin Holder, Pink Roses 350.00
Humidor, Chimpanzee, Blue Mark, 6 1/2 In. 700.00
Humidor, Jester, More Than Enough Is Too Much, Blue Mark 650.00
Humidor, Man In Canoe, Tapestry, Blue Mark 1000.00
Inkwell, Children Playing 345.00
Jug, Tavern Scene, 4 x 4 In. 95.00
Match Holder, Devil & Cards, Hanging, Blue Mark 400.00
Match Holder, Red Clown 450.00
Match Holder, Snow Babies 275.00
Match Holder, Tavern Scene 200.00
Match Holder, Wall, Devil & Cards 350.00
Mug, Beer, Devil & Cards, 5 In. 425.00
Mug, Musketeers At Table, Drinking, 4 x 4 In. 75.00
Mustard, Lobster 95.00
Mustard, Red Poppy 195.00
Mustard, Spiky Mother-Of-Pearl 80.00
Mustard, Tomato .... 160.00 to 275.00
Mustard, Tomato, Cover, With Spoon 100.00
Pipe Rest, Basset, Blue Mark 450.00
Pitcher, Alligator, 5 1/4 In. 550.00
Pitcher, Classical Figures, Orange Interior, Marked, 7 1/8 In. 135.00
Pitcher, Clown, Red, 4 1/2 In. 335.00
Pitcher, Clown, Yellow, 4 1/2 In. 650.00

Pitcher, Coachman, Blue Mark .... 450.00 to 750.00
Pitcher, Corset, Pink Roses, 4 1/2 In. 325.00
Pitcher, Devil & Cards, 5 In. 325.00
Pitcher, Duck 198.00
Pitcher, Elk 295.00
Pitcher, Elk, 5 In. 95.00
Pitcher, Fish Head, 6 In. 85.00
Pitcher, Goose Girl, 5 In. 85.00
Pitcher, Jester, Never Say Die, Up Man & Try, Blue Mark 375.00
Pitcher, Lemonade, Lemon Shape, 1920, 7 3/4 In. 695.00
Pitcher, Melon, 4 1/2 In. 325.00
Pitcher, Owl, 5 In. 575.00
Pitcher, Poppy 650.00
Pitcher, Red Parrot Handle, Signed, 5 In. 250.00
Pitcher, Red Parrot Handle, White, Blue Mark, 6 1/2 In. 550.00
Pitcher, Santa Claus, Blue Mark, 5 1/4 In. 3500.00
Pitcher, St. Bernard, 4 In. 250.00
Plaque, Arab, 2 Maidens, Desert Background, 9 In. 185.00
Plate, Devil & Clock, Full-Bodied Red Devil, 4 1/2 In. 575.00
Plate, Lettuce, Handle, 4 x 4 In. 67.00
Plate, Lettuce, Yellow Flowers, Ring Handle, Blue Mark, 7 In. 33.00
Relish, Courtship Scene, Blue Mark, 4 x 8 1/4 In. 200.00
Relish, Poinsettia 295.00
Salt & Pepper, Grapes, Leaves, White 135.00
Salt & Pepper, Grapes, Purple .... 100.00 to 110.00
Salt & Pepper, Shell 75.00
Saltshaker, Grape, White, 2 In. 135.00
Saltshaker, Woman Feeding Chickens 65.00
Shaving Mug, Elk, Blue Mark 625.00
Shaving Mug, Woman's, Daisy & Pansy 148.00
Stein, Floral, Cow In Pasture Scene, Blue Mark, 8 In. 195.00
Stein, Tankard, Sailing Ship Design, Jewel Trim, Blue Mark, 8 In. 195.00
String Holder, Rooster 350.00
String Holder, Rooster, Wall Mount .... 170.00 to 235.00
Sugar, Boy & Donkey, Blue Mark 120.00
Sugar, Cover, Turtle, Blue Mark, 5 In. 475.00
Sugar, Cover, Turtle, Blue Mark, 6 In. 325.00
Sugar, Devil & Cards, Cover, Blue Mark 350.00
Sugar, Grape 30.00
Sugar, Purple Grape, Cover, Black Mark, 3 3/4 In. 155.00
Sugar, Tomato 68.00
Sugar & Creamer, Cover, Brittany Girls, Blue Mark 85.00
Sugar & Creamer, Lobster 125.00
Sugar & Creamer, Tomato, 4 In. 190.00
Tea Set, Child's, Children Running, 3 Piece 195.00
Tea Set, Murex Shell, 3 Piece 425.00
Tea Strainer, Poppy 300.00
Tea Strainer, Purple 395.00
Teapot, Girl & Geese 85.00
Toothpick, Badminton Scenes, Dice Shape, Blue Mark, 2 1/2 In. 600.00
Toothpick, Bell Ringer, Blue Mark, 3 In. 425.00
Toothpick, Black Corinthian, Footed, Signed 110.00
Toothpick, Dutch Boy & Girl In Sailboat, Overhead Handle, Blue Mark 135.00
Toothpick, Floral Ring, Handle 150.00
Toothpick, Hunt Scene, Man & Woman On Horse, Gold Handle, 3 3/4 In. ... 125.00
Toothpick, Lobsters, Green 65.00
Toothpick, Orange Exterior, Yellow Interior, Blue Mark 75.00
Toothpick, Red Clown, Blue Mark 450.00
Toothpick, Stork 80.00
Toothpick, Table Tennis Scene, Dice Shape, Blue Mark, 2 1/2 In. 950.00
Toothpick, Triangular, Penguin On Each Side, Blue Mark 235.00
Toothpick, Woman Holding Candle, Silver Rim, Blue Mark, 3 In. 75.00
Tray, Dresser, Girl With Goose, Blue Mark 425.00

Tray, Fox Hunt, Blue Mark, Square, 4 1/4 In. 45.00
Tray, Pearlized Grapes & Leaves, 5 x 7 In. 135.00
Vase, 3 Cows, 5 In. 100.00
Vase, Gold Flowers, Multicolor Floral, Gold Band, Footed, Red Crown, 20 In. 350.00
Vase, Little Miss Muffet, Ring Handles, Ruffled Rim, 3 1/2 x 4 1/4 In. 165.00
Vase, Man With Dog, Hunting Ducks, 4 1/4 In. 225.00
Wall Pocket, Penny In Pocket, Jester, Blue Mark 550.00

ROYAL BONN is the nineteenth- and twentieth-century trade name for the
Bonn China Manufactory. It was established in 1755 in Bonn, Germany. A
general line of porcelain was made. Many marks were used, most including
the name *Bonn*, the initials *FM*, and a crown.

Cheese Dish, Cover, Flowers, Twisted Handle, Triangular 55.00
Ewer, Floral, Raised Gold Design, Signed, 15 1/2 In. 200.00
Ewer, Multicolored Flowers, Front & Back, Raised Gold Design, 2 x 4 In. 155.00
Figurine, Romeo & Juliet, Clothed & Draped, 12 In., Pair 500.00
Ginger Jar, Hand Painted, Dogwood, Embossed Designs, 13 1/2 In. 150.00
Pitcher, Pink & Gold Flowers, Leaves, 6 1/2 In. 65.00
Umbrella Stand, Red Iris, Green To Yellow-Orange 375.00
Vase, Blue Floral, 5 1/2 In. 70.00
Vase, Floral, 13 In. 140.00
Vase, Floral, Hand Painted, Gold Outline & Handles, Dated 1825 .... 95.00
Vase, Flowers, Gold Beading, 15 In. 230.00
Vase, Rooster, Signed, 10 In. 495.00
Vase, Spider Mums, Art Nouveau Handles, 8 1/2 In. 95.00

ROYAL COPENHAGEN porcelain and pottery have been made in Denmark
since 1772. The Christmas plate series started in 1908. The figurines with
pale blue and gray glazes have remained popular in this century and are still
being made. Many other old and new style porcelains are made today.

Bowl, Open Work Rim, Ribbed, Blue & White, 11 In. 195.00
Bread Plate, Lace, Blue Fluted, 1960s, 6 In., 12 Piece 621.00
Cake Dish, Lace, Blue Fluted, 1960s 189.00
Candleholder, Lace, Blue Fluted, 1960s, 3 3/4 In., Pair 158.00
Coffeepot, Lace, Blue Fluted, 1960s 272.00
Compote, Blue Onion Pattern, Pierced Rim & Foot, 5 In. 200.00
Compote, Seagull 68.00
Compote, Triangular Low Bowl, Trumpet Foot, 5 In. 920.00
Decanter, Egeskov Castle 115.00
Decanter, Stopper, Rosenburg Castle, Blue & White, 9 3/4 In. 45.00
Dish, Flora Danica, Center Rose Branch, Square, Marked, 9 1/2 In. 345.00
Dish, Vegetable, Cover, Flora Danica, Twig Handle, Marked, 9 3/16 In. 2415.00
Eggcup, Stand, Blue Lace 40.00
Figurine, Apple Basket Boy, No. 4532, 6 3/4 In. 130.00
Figurine, Boy With Calf, No. 772 .... 290.00
Figurine, Boy With Gourd, No. 4539 .... 225.00
Figurine, Boy With Horn, No. 3689 .... 95.00
Figurine, Faun, On Pedestal, No. 433 .... 275.00
Figurine, Faun, Playing Pipes, No. 1736 .... 235.00
Figurine, Faun, Riding Bear, No. 1804 .... 585.00
Figurine, Fox, No. 1475 .... 150.00
Figurine, Girl With Calf, No. 779 .... 290.00
Figurine, Goose Girl, No. 528 .... 150.00 to 175.00
Figurine, Icelandic Flacon, No. 263 .... 300.00
Figurine, Koala Bear, No. 5402 .... 275.00
Figurine, Little Girl With Doll, No. 3539, 5 3/4 In. 40.00
Figurine, Mermaid, No. 4431, 7 In. 395.00
Figurine, Mermaid, No. 4431, Signed, 10 In. 385.00
Figurine, Milkmaid, No. 899 .... 425.00
Figurine, Nude, No. 4431 .... 245.00
Figurine, October, No. 4532 .... 275.00
Figurine, Owl, No. 2999 .... 150.00
Figurine, Pan, With Goat, No. 1012/498, 5 In. 260.00

Figurine, Polar Bear, No. 320 .... 50.00
Figurine, Rabbit, No. 4676 .... 245.00
Figurine, Seal, No. 1441, 5 In. 100.00
Figurine, Seated Girl, Braids, 5 3/4 In. 115.00
Figurine, Terrier, No. 1452 .... 130.00
Figurine, Two Children, No. 1761 .... 625.00
Pickle, Leaf Shape, Lace, Blue Fluted, 1960s, 9 In. 79.00
Plaque, Allegorical Day & Night Figures, White Parian, 11 In., Pair 295.00
Plaque, Angel, Sleeping Babies, Owl, White Parian, Pierced, 6 In. 25.00
Plate, 5 Fishermen, With Net, Shore, Rectangular, 6 5/8 x 4 1/4 In. 26.00
Plate, Christmas, 1924, Christmas Star Over Sea, 7 In. 55.00
Plate, Christmas, 1926, View Of Christianshavn Canal, Copenhagen, 7 In. 38.00
Plate, Christmas, 1930, Fishing Boats On Way To Harbor, 7 In. 44.00
Plate, Christmas, 1936, Roskilde Cathedral, 7 In. 66.00
Plate, Christmas, 1942, Bell Tower Of Old Church In Jutland, 7 In. 45.00
Plate, Christmas, 1943, Flight Of Holy Family To Egypt, 7 In. 210.00
Plate, Christmas, 1948, Nodebo Church At Christmas Time, 7 In. 83.00
Plate, Christmas, 1955, Fano Girl, 7 In. 88.00
Plate, Christmas, 1971, Hare In Winter, 7 In. 10.00
Plate, Christmas, 1981, Admiring Christmas Tree, 7 In. .... 8.00 to 30.00
Plate, Christmas, Winter Sleigh Ride, 1964 .... 65.00
Plate, Christmas, Winter Windmill, 1963 .... 65.00
Plate, Factory Bicentennial, 1975 .... 6.00
Plate, Lace, Blue Fluted, 1960s, 10 In., 12 Piece 918.00
Platter, Blue, Fluted, Oval, 14 1/2 In. .... 195.00 to 215.00
Platter, Blue, Oval, 10 1/2 In. 185.00
Platter, Flora Danica, Berries & Blossom Center, Marked, 9 3/4 In. 805.00
Platter, Flora Danica, Oval, Marked, 18 3/16 In. 2875.00
Platter, Flora Danica, Serrated Rim, Marked, 18 1/8 In. 2588.00
Relish, Leaf, 10 1/2 In. 115.00
Teapot, Open Face Trim, Face On Spout & Handle, 8 1/2 In. 350.00
Teapot, Seagull 125.00
Vase, Langelinie, Signed 250.00
Vase, Mother & Child, Blue, Brown, 6 1/2 In. 225.00
Vase, Seagull 168.00
Vase, Taaske, 1927, 7 In. 75.00

ROYAL COPLEY china was made by the Spaulding China Company of
Sebring, Ohio, from 1939 to 1960. The figural planters and the small
figurines, especially those with Art Deco designs, are of great collector
interest.

Creamer, Chick 15.00
Figurine, Angel, Blue 20.00
Figurine, Angel, Pink 25.00
Figurine, Blackamoor Prince, 8 In. 30.00
Figurine, Cockatoo, 8 1/4 In. 36.00
Figurine, Deer On Stump 20.00
Figurine, Dog With Picnic Basket, Large 52.50
Figurine, Dog, 6 1/2 In. 15.00
Figurine, Dutch Girl With Bucket 15.00
Figurine, Lamb On Sled 49.50
Figurine, Pan, Riding Turtle 175.00
Figurine, Puppy, In Basket 38.50
Figurine, Rooster, Black & White .... 45.00 to 58.00
Figurine, Spaniel 15.00
Lamp, Bird On Tree Stump 35.00
Planter, Angel, 6 1/2 In. 28.00
Planter, Deer & Fawn 24.00
Planter, Dog, Spaniel 18.00
Planter, Duck & Wheelbarrow 12.00
Planter, Elf On Log, Gold Trim 25.00
Planter, Leaf, Gold Trim 12.00
Planter, Panda, 8 In. 35.00

Planter, Pirate Head, 8 In.		40.00 to 48.00
Planter, Pony, 5 1/4 In.		24.00
Planter, Puppy & Mailbox		18.00
Planter, Rooster & Wheelbarrow		45.00
Planter, Rooster, High Tail, 7 3/4 In.		25.00
Planter, Teddy Bear		20.00
Planter, Wall, Oriental Girl, Pink		26.00
Plaque, Fruit Plate		14.00
Vase, Deer & Fawn, 9 1/4 In.		12.00
Vase, Mare & Foal, Pair		60.00
Wall Pocket, Bamboo, 7 In.		35.00
Wall Pocket, Hat		25.00
Wall Pocket, Rooster, White		38.00

ROYAL CROWN DERBY Company, Ltd., was established in England in 1890. There is a complex family tree that includes the Derby, Crown Derby, and Royal Crown Derby porcelains. The Royal Crown Derby mark includes the name and a crown. The words *Made in England* were used after 1921. The company is now a part of Royal Doulton Tableware Ltd.

Bowl, Tea Strainer		65.00
Cake Plate, Mikado, 2 Handled, 11 In.		110.00
Chop Plate, Roses, Shaded Dark Green Ground		95.00
Creamer, Blue Oriental Figures, Landscape, Gold Trim, 3 1/8 In.		22.00
Cup, Lump Sugar, Mikado, Blue, White Ground		18.50
Cup & Saucer, Mikado		30.00
Cup & Saucer, Pink Floral, Pair		22.00
Dish, Imari, Oval, 11 3/4 In.		187.00
Dish, Vegetable, Rectangular, Cover, 1800s		495.00
Plate, Green Derby Panel, 8 1/2 In., 10 Piece		260.00
Plate, Imari, 9 In., 8 Piece		495.00
Plate, Imari, 9 In., 12 Piece		75.00 to 475.00
Plate, Imari, Shaped Rim, c.1923, 8 1/2 In., 12 Piece		330.00
Plate, Mikado, 6 In.		11.50
Plate, Mikado, 8 In.		27.00
Plate, Mikado, Blue, White, 10 1/2 In.		30.00
Plate, Queen Victoria & 7 Canadian Province Shields, 6 In.		68.00
Platter, Foliage, Gilt Cobalt Border, Circular, 12 In.		72.00
Platter, Mikado, Oval, 11 1/2 x 9 In.		135.00
Sugar & Creamer, Mikado		75.00
Tea Set, Japan Pattern, 3 Piece		325.00
Tea Strainer, With Bowl		65.00
Teapot, Imari, 3 1/2 x 2 In.		450.00

ROYAL DOULTON is the name used on Doulton and Company pottery made from 1902 to the present. Doulton and Company of England was founded in 1853. Pieces made before 1902 are listed in this book under Doulton. Royal Doulton collectors search for the out-of-production figurines, character jugs, and series wares.

Animal, Cat, Seated, Flambe, 5 In.		80.00
Animal, Dog, Airedale, HN 1023		225.00
Animal, Dog, Alsatian, HN 1115		695.00
Animal, Dog, Boxer, Tan Coat, HN 2643		125.00
Animal, Dog, Bull Pup, K2		125.00
Animal, Dog, Bulldog, HN 1047		100.00 to 135.00
Animal, Dog, Bulldog, K1		65.00
Animal, Dog, Bulldog, Union Jack, HN 6407		250.00
Animal, Dog, Bulldog, White, HN 1074		225.00
Animal, Dog, Cairn, HN 1035		115.00
Animal, Dog, Cairn, HN 2589		60.00
Animal, Dog, Cairn, K11		50.00
Animal, Dog, Cocker Spaniel, Black, HN 1020		145.00
Animal, Dog, Cocker Spaniel, HN 1002		350.00
Animal, Dog, Cocker Spaniel, In Basket, HN 2585		70.00

Animal, Dog, Cocker Spaniel, Pheasant, HN 1028 .... 155.00 to 200.00
Animal, Dog, Cocker Spaniels, Sleeping, HN 2590 .... 80.00
Animal, Dog, Cocker, HN 1036 .... 150.00
Animal, Dog, Collie, HN 1057 .... 575.00
Animal, Dog, Dachshund, HN 1128 .... 95.00
Animal, Dog, Doberman, HN 2645 .... 150.00
Animal, Dog, English Setter, HN 1050 .... 100.00 to 150.00
Animal, Dog, English Setters, HN 1051 .... 120.00
Animal, Dog, Foxhound, K7 .... 45.00
Animal, Dog, Head Turned, HN 2508 .... 90.00
Animal, Dog, Irish Setter, 6 In. 90.00
Animal, Dog, Irish Setter, HN 1056 .... 135.00
Animal, Dog, Pekinese, HN 1012 .... 115.00
Animal, Duck, Floating, Flambe, 10 In. 350.00
Animal, Fox, D 6449 .... 185.00
Animal, Fox, Flambe, 13 In. 350.00
Animal, Fox, Lying, Flambe, 5 In. 275.00
Animal, Hare, Flambe 75.00
Animal, Horse, Merely A Minor, Dappled Gray, 12 In. 850.00
Animal, Horse, Palomino 90.00
Animal, Kitten Sleeping, HN 2581 .... 70.00
Animal, Kittens, HN 2580 .... 45.00
Animal, Lucky The Cat, K12 .... 100.00 to 125.00
Animal, Panda, Portrait Of Inn, Martha Carey 90.00
Animal, Persian Cat, HN 999 .... 300.00
Animal, Rhinoceros, Flambe Glaze, 9 3/4 In. 550.00
Animal, River Hog, Chatcull Range, HN 2663 .... 350.00
Animal, Salmon, Flambe Glaze, Marked, 12 1/4 In. 220.00
Animal, Tiger, Stalking, Flambe, 17 In. 800.00
Ash Pot, Auld Mac 125.00
Ash Pot, Farmer John 125.00
Ash Pot, Old Charley 115.00
Ash Pot, Paddy .... 120.00 to 145.00
Ash Pot, Sairey Gamp .... 85.00 to 135.00
Ashtray, Dick Turpin 115.00
Ashtray, John Barleycorn 115.00
Ashtray, Parson Brown .... 75.00 to 115.00
Bank, Book, Bunnykins 18.00
Bottle, Sherry, Sandeman, Black Cloak & Hat 50.00
Bottle, Whiskey, John Bull 70.00
Bottle, Whiskey, Old Mr.Turveytop, 5 In. 75.00
Bowl, Canterbury Pilgrims, 9 1/2 In. 110.00
Bowl, Child's, See Saw Margery Daw 65.00
Bowl, Child's, The House That Jack Built 115.00
Candlestick, Bobbie Burns, Pair 165.00
Candlestick, Golfer, Promise Little Do Much, Square, c.1920, 7 In. 165.00

Royal Doulton character jugs depict the head and shoulders of the subject.
They are made in four sizes: large, 5 1/4 to 7 inches; small, 3 1/4 to 4 inches;
miniature, 2 1/4 to 2 1/2 inches; and tiny, 1 1/4 inches. Toby jugs portray a
seated, full figure.

Character Jug, 'ard Of 'earing, Miniature 865.00
Character Jug, 'arriet, Large 225.00
Character Jug, 'arriet, Miniature 75.00
Character Jug, 'arriet, Small 90.00
Character Jug, 'arriet, Tiny 200.00
Character Jug, 'arry, Tiny 200.00
Character Jug, Ann Of Cleaves, Large 250.00
Character Jug, Anne Boleyn, Large .... 100.00 to 115.00
Character Jug, Annie Oakley 80.00
Character Jug, Apothecary, Miniature 60.00
Character Jug, Athos, Large 100.00
Character Jug, Auld Mac, Large 100.00

Character Jug, Auld Mac, Small 45.00
Character Jug, Beefeater, Miniature 45.00
Character Jug, Blacksmith, Large 110.00
Character Jug, Bootmaker, Small 70.00
Character Jug, Busker, Large 85.00
Character Jug, Buz Fuz, Small 85.00
Character Jug, Cap'n Cuttle 115.00
Character Jug, Cap'n Cuttle, Miniature .... 80.00 to 115.00
Character Jug, Captain Henry Morgan, Small 60.00
Character Jug, Captain Hook, Large 525.00
Character Jug, Cardinal, A Mark, Miniature 55.00
Character Jug, Cardinal, Miniature 50.00
Character Jug, Cardinal, Tiny 50.00
Character Jug, Cavalier, A Mark, Large .... 65.00 to 135.00
Character Jug, Cavalier, Large 155.00
Character Jug, Chelsea Pensioner, Large .... 90.00 to 110.00
Character Jug, Cliff Cornell, Blue, Large 325.00
Character Jug, Cliff Cornell, Brown, Large 350.00
Character Jug, Clown, Red, Large 3500.00
Character Jug, Clown, White, Large 850.00
Character Jug, Cook & Cheshire Cat, Large 130.00
Character Jug, Dick Turpin, Small 70.00
Character Jug, Dick Turpin, Tiny 50.00
Character Jug, Drake, Small 175.00
Character Jug, Fat Boy, Miniature 75.00
Character Jug, Fat Boy, Tiny 100.00
Character Jug, Fortune Teller, Large 350.00
Character Jug, Gardener, Miniature 70.00
Character Jug, George Washington, Miniature 50.00
Character Jug, Golfer, Large 95.00
Character Jug, Gondolier, Large 575.00
Character Jug, Gondolier, Miniature 340.00
Character Jug, Granny, A Mark, Large 100.00
Character Jug, Granny, Small 50.00
Character Jug, Guardsman, Williamsburg, Miniature 60.00
Character Jug, Hamlet, Large 105.00
Character Jug, Henry V 250.00
Character Jug, Henry VIII, Large 95.00
Character Jug, Jockey, Large 400.00
Character Jug, John Barleycorn, Large 150.00
Character Jug, John Peel, Tiny 200.00
Character Jug, Johnny Appleseed, Large 275.00
Character Jug, Lawyer, Large 90.00
Character Jug, Lobster Man, Large 50.00
Character Jug, Long John Silver, Large 75.00
Character Jug, Macbeth, Large 115.00
Character Jug, Mikado, Miniature 425.00
Character Jug, Mr. Bumble, Tiny 45.00
Character Jug, Mr. Micawber, 4 In. 185.00
Character Jug, Mr. Micawber, Tiny 105.00
Character Jug, Mr. Pickwick, Miniature 50.00
Character Jug, Neptune, Large 100.00
Character Jug, North American Indian, Canadian Centennial 350.00
Character Jug, Old Charley, Miniature 55.00
Character Jug, Old Charley, Small 200.00
Character Jug, Old Salt, Large 100.00
Character Jug, Othello, Large 105.00
Character Jug, Paddy, Large 88.00
Character Jug, Paddy, Miniature 45.00
Character Jug, Paddy, Tiny 105.00
Character Jug, Parson Brown, Small .... 55.00 to 65.00
Character Jug, Pearly Boy, Large 2000.00
Character Jug, Pearly Boy, Miniature 900.00

Character Jug, Pied Piper, Large	105.00
Character Jug, Pied Piper, Miniature	50.00
Character Jug, Punch & Judy Man, Miniature	400.00
Character Jug, Queen Victoria, Large	100.00
Character Jug, Robinson Crusoe, Large	120.00
Character Jug, Ronald Reagan, Large	450.00
Character Jug, Sairey Gamp, Large	165.00
Character Jug, Sairey Gamp, Tiny	75.00 to 100.00
Character Jug, Sam Weller, Miniature	55.00
Character Jug, Sam Weller, Tiny	100.00
Character Jug, Santa Claus, Large	95.00 to 100.00
Character Jug, Scaramouche, Large	650.00
Character Jug, Scaramouche, Miniature	500.00
Character Jug, Simon The Cellarer, Large	150.00
Character Jug, Simple Simon, Large	470.00
Character Jug, Sleuth, Red, Small	85.00
Character Jug, Tam O'Shanter, Large	135.00
Character Jug, Toby Jug, Cuttle, 4 1/2 In.	150.00
Character Jug, Toby Jug, Sam Weller, 4 1/2 In.	150.00
Character Jug, Toby Philpots, Large	165.00
Character Jug, Tony Philpots, Small	65.00
Character Jug, Tony Weller, A Mark, Large	225.00
Character Jug, Tony Weller, Miniature	45.00 to 50.00
Character Jug, Town Crier, Small	95.00
Character Jug, Trapper, Small	55.00
Character Jug, Ugly Duchess, Large	500.00
Character Jug, Uriah Heep, Tiny	45.00
Character Jug, Vicar Of Bray, Large	175.00
Character Jug, Viking, Large	165.00
Character Jug, Viking, Miniature	95.00
Character Jug, Viking, Small	100.00
Character Jug, Winston Churchill, Small	60.00
Character Jug, Witch, Large	250.00
Character Jug, Yeoman Of The Guard, Large	95.00
Charger, Long John Silver, 15 1/2 In.	250.00
Charger, Mums Between Branched Leaves, 16 In.	175.00
Creamer, Pickwick, Dickensware	65.00
Cup & Saucer, Coaching Scene	50.00
Cup & Saucer, Granthan, Demitasse	15.00
Cup & Saucer, Topographical, Pair	55.00
Decanter, Liqueur, Falstaff	105.00
Decanter, Liqueur, Poacher	105.00
Decanter, Liqueur, Rip Van Winkle	115.00
Ewer, Gold Design Of Lovebirds, Chinese Red	315.00
Ewer, Stopper, Flambe, Silver Overlay	550.00
Figurine, A Courting, HN 2004	475.00
Figurine, A Stitch In Time, HN 2352	175.00
Figurine, Abdullah, HN 2104	550.00
Figurine, Afternoon Tea, HN 1747	220.00 to 247.00
Figurine, Alexandra, HN 2398	125.00
Figurine, Alice, HN 2158	90.00
Figurine, Amy, HN 2958	100.00
Figurine, Annabella, HN 1875	535.00
Figurine, Antoinette, HN 2326	160.00
Figurine, Ashley, HN 3420	110.00
Figurine, At Ease, HN 2473	195.00
Figurine, Auctioneer, HN 2988	180.00
Figurine, Autumn Breezes, HN 1911	160.00
Figurine, Autumn Breezes, HN 1913	255.00
Figurine, Autumn Breezes, HN 1934	143.00
Figurine, Autumn Glory, HN 2766	125.00
Figurine, Autumn, HN 2087	500.00
Figurine, Babie, HN 1679	90.00

Figurine, Bachelor, HN 2319 .... 300.00
Figurine, Ballerina, HN 2116 .... 300.00 to 375.00
Figurine, Balloon Man, HN 1954 .... 150.00 to 225.00
Figurine, Beachcomber, HN 2487 .... 200.00
Figurine, Bedtime Story, HN 2059 .... 150.00
Figurine, Bedtime, HN 1978 .... 75.00
Figurine, Bess, HN 2003 .... 150.00
Figurine, Biddy Penny Farthing, HN 1843 .... 180.00
Figurine, Blacksmith Of Williamsburg, HN 2240 .... 190.00
Figurine, Bluebeard, HN 2105 .... 350.00
Figurine, Boatman, HN 2417 .... 160.00
Figurine, Bopeep, HN 1328 .... 1750.00
Figurine, Bride, HN 2166 .... 185.00
Figurine, Broken Lance, HN 2041 .... 350.00 to 400.00
Figurine, Bumble, M 76 .... 50.00
Figurine, Captain Cook, HN 2889 .... 325.00
Figurine, Carolyn, HN 2112 .... 225.00
Figurine, Carolyn, HN 2974 .... 165.00
Figurine, Carpet Seller, Flambe, HN 2776 .... 150.00
Figurine, Carpet Seller, HN 1464 .... 245.00
Figurine, Cellist, HN 2226 .... 395.00
Figurine, Cherie, HN 2341 .... 60.00 to 120.00
Figurine, Cheryl, HN 3253 .... 200.00
Figurine, Chinese Dancer, HN 2840 .... 925.00
Figurine, Christine, HN 1840 .... 650.00
Figurine, Christine, HN 2792 .... 300.00
Figurine, Christmas Morn, HN 1992 .... 120.00 to 140.00
Figurine, Christmas Parcels, HN 2851 .... 240.00
Figurine, Cissie, HN 1809 .... 130.00
Figurine, Claribel, HN 1951 .... 550.00
Figurine, Clarissa, HN 2345 .... 105.00
Figurine, Clockmaker, HN 2279 .... 225.00
Figurine, Clown, HN 2890 .... 210.00
Figurine, Coachman, HN 2282 .... 400.00
Figurine, Collinette, HN 1999 .... 450.00
Figurine, Columbine, HN 2738 .... 700.00
Figurine, Curly Locks, HN 2049 .... 380.00
Figurine, Daphne, HN 2268 .... 60.00
Figurine, Darling, HN 1319 .... 10.00 to 125.00
Figurine, Darling, HN 1985 .... 75.00
Figurine, Daydreams, HN 1731 .... 130.00
Figurine, Debbie, HN 2385 .... 110.00
Figurine, Denise, HN 2273 .... 310.00
Figurine, Dinky Do, HN 1678 .... 60.00 to 90.00
Figurine, Discovery, HN 3428 .... 160.00
Figurine, Doctor, HN 2858 .... 175.00
Figurine, Duchess Of York, HN 3086 .... 400.00
Figurine, Duke Of Edinburgh, HN 2386 .... 180.00
Figurine, Elegance, HN 2264 .... 105.00 to 150.00
Figurine, Enchantment, HN 2178 .... 135.00
Figurine, Ermine Coat, HN 1981 .... 140.00
Figurine, Eventide, HN 2814 .... 175.00 to 180.00
Figurine, Fair Lady, HN 2193 .... 90.00 to 195.00
Figurine, Fair Lady, HN 2835 .... 145.00
Figurine, Fair Maiden, HN 2211 .... 60.00
Figurine, Family Album, HN 2321 .... 300.00
Figurine, Fighter Elephant, HN 2640 .... 1500.00
Figurine, Fiona, HN 2694 .... 95.00
Figurine, Fleur, HN 2368 .... 185.00 to 210.00
Figurine, Flora, HN 2349 .... 210.00
Figurine, Florence, HN 2745 .... 199.00
Figurine, Flower Seller's Children, HN 1342 .... 375.00
Figurine, Fortune Teller, HN 2159 .... 375.00

Figurine, Fragrance, HN 2334 .... 210.00
Figurine, French Peasant, HN 2075 .... 500.00
Figurine, Friar Tuck, HN 2143 .... 425.00
Figurine, Gardening Time, HN 3401 .... 180.00
Figurine, Gay Morning, HN 2135 .... 375.00
Figurine, Gentleman From Williamsburg, HN 2227 .... 200.00
Figurine, Geraldine, HN 2348 .... 150.00
Figurine, Giselle, HN 2139 .... 298.00 to 400.00
Figurine, Good Catch, HN 2258 .... 140.00
Figurine, Good Morning, HN 2671 .... 235.00
Figurine, Gossips, HN 2025 .... 425.00
Figurine, Grand Manner, HN 2723 .... 225.00
Figurine, He Loves Me, HN 2046 .... 275.00
Figurine, Honey, HN 1909 .... 350.00
Figurine, Indian Temple Dancer, HN 2830 .... 975.00 to 1500.00
Figurine, Ink Holder, Flambe, Desert Scene, Palms 150.00
Figurine, Innocence, HN 2842 .... 150.00
Figurine, Ivy, HN 1768 .... 75.00
Figurine, Jack Point, HN 2080 .... 1800.00
Figurine, Jack, HN 2060 .... 195.00
Figurine, Jacqueline, HN 2000 .... 600.00
Figurine, Jane, HN 2806 .... 200.00
Figurine, Janice, HN 2022 .... 350.00 to 395.00
Figurine, Janice, HN 2165 .... 400.00
Figurine, Janine, HN 2461 .... 110.00
Figurine, Jennifer, HN 2392 .... 210.00
Figurine, Jester, HN 2016 .... 170.00
Figurine, Joan, HN 1422 .... 300.00
Figurine, Judith, HN 2089 .... 350.00
Figurine, Kate, HN 2789 .... 140.00 to 175.00
Figurine, Katrina, HN 2327 .... 250.00
Figurine, King Charles, HN 2084 .... 2200.00
Figurine, Kurdish Dancer, HN 2867 .... 1000.00
Figurine, L'Ambitieuse, HN 3359 .... 295.00
Figurine, Lady Anne Nevill, HN 2006 .... 550.00
Figurine, Lady From Williamsburg, HN 2228 .... 200.00
Figurine, Lambing Time, HN 1890 .... 160.00 to 190.00
Figurine, Last Waltz, HN 2315 .... 125.00
Figurine, Lavinia, HN 1955 .... 90.00
Figurine, Leading Lady, HN 2269 .... 125.00
Figurine, Leda & The Swan, HN 2826 .... 1900.00
Figurine, Legolas, Tolkien Series, HN 2917 .... 110.00
Figurine, Leisure Hour, HN 2055 .... 450.00
Figurine, Lights Out, HN 2262 .... 250.00
Figurine, Little Bridesmaid, HN 1433 .... 175.00
Figurine, Lobster Man, HN 2317 .... 275.00
Figurine, Lorna, HN 2311 .... 80.00 to 150.00
Figurine, Lucy Ann, HN 1502 .... 150.00
Figurine, Lucy Lockett, HN 524 .... 425.00
Figurine, Lunch Time, HN 2485 .... 220.00
Figurine, Lynne, HN 2329 .... 175.00 to 200.00
Figurine, Madonna Of Square, HN 2034 .... 650.00
Figurine, Marguerite, HN 1928 .... 220.00 to 350.00
Figurine, Market Day, HN 1991 .... 275.00
Figurine, Mary Had A Little Lamb, HN 2048 .... 90.00 to 175.00
Figurine, Mask Seller, HN 2103 .... 200.00 to 215.00
Figurine, Maureen, HN 1770 .... 110.00
Figurine, Maxine, HN 3199 .... 150.00
Figurine, Memories, HN 2030 .... 460.00
Figurine, Mexican Dancer, HN 2866 .... 850.00
Figurine, Michelle, HN 2234 .... 140.00
Figurine, Minuet, HN 2019 .... 310.00

Figurine, Miss Demure, HN 1402 .... 135.00 to 165.00
Figurine, Moor, HN 2082 .... 1100.00
Figurine, Mr. Micawber, M 42 .... 75.00
Figurine, Mr. Pickwick, M 41 .... 75.00
Figurine, Mrs. Fitzherbert, HN 2007 .... 575.00
Figurine, Nadine, HN 1886 .... 900.00
Figurine, Ninette, HN 2379 .... 130.00
Figurine, Noelle, HN 2179 .... 325.00
Figurine, Old Balloon Seller, HN 1315 .... 160.00 to 200.00
Figurine, Old King, HN 2134 .... 475.00
Figurine, One That Got Away, HN 2153 .... 400.00
Figurine, Orange Lady, HN 1759 .... 180.00
Figurine, Orange Vendor, HN 1966 .... 750.00
Figurine, Paisley Shawl, HN 1987 .... 325.00
Figurine, Patricia, HN 3365 .... 160.00
Figurine, Pecksniff, HN 2098 .... 350.00
Figurine, Peggy, HN 2038 .... 95.00
Figurine, Penny, HN 2338 .... 78.00
Figurine, Polish Dancer, HN 2836 .... 650.00
Figurine, Pope John Paul II, HN 2888 .... 180.00
Figurine, Queen Elizabeth I, HN 3099 .... 475.00
Figurine, Rebecca, HN 2805 .... 475.00
Figurine, Regal Lady, HN 2709 .... 125.00
Figurine, Rosabelle, HN 1620 .... 1450.00
Figurine, Roseanna, HN 1926 .... 240.00 to 250.00
Figurine, Samurai Warrior, Flambe 450.00
Figurine, Santa Claus, HN 2725 .... 245.00
Figurine, Sara, HN 2265 .... 165.00
Figurine, Scottish Highland Dancer, HN 2436 .... 1100.00
Figurine, Sea Harvest, HN 2257 .... 125.00
Figurine, Seafarer, HN 2455 .... 50.00
Figurine, Shepherd, HN 1975 .... 140.00 to 225.00
Figurine, Silks & Ribbons, HN 2017 .... 115.00
Figurine, Silversmith Of Williamsburg, HN 2208 .... 130.00
Figurine, Skater, HN 3439 .... 200.00
Figurine, Sophie, HN 3257 .... 225.00
Figurine, Southern Bell, HN 2229 .... 190.00
Figurine, Spring Flowers, HN 1807 .... 350.00
Figurine, Stephanie, HN 2811 .... 210.00
Figurine, Sweet & Twenty, HN 1298 .... 225.00
Figurine, Sweet Seventeen, HN 2734 .... 215.00
Figurine, Taking Things Easy, HN 2267 .... 195.00
Figurine, Tea Time, HN 2255 .... 180.00
Figurine, Tess, HN 2865 .... 165.00
Figurine, Thanksgiving, HN 2446 .... 200.00
Figurine, To Bed, HN 1805 .... 200.00
Figurine, Toby Philpots, D5737 .... 60.00
Figurine, Tom Bombadil, HN 2924 .... 400.00
Figurine, Top O' The Hill, HN 1834 .... 200.00
Figurine, Top O' The Hill, HN 1849 .... 160.00 to 195.00
Figurine, Town Crier, HN 2119 .... 250.00
Figurine, Ulysses S. Grant, HN 3403 .... 775.00
Figurine, Vase, Flambe, Mottled, Pear Shape, No. 1665 .... 175.00
Figurine, Veneta, HN 2722 .... 60.00
Figurine, Vera, HN 1730 .... 825.00
Figurine, Votes For Women, HN 2816 .... 245.00
Figurine, Wigmaker Of Williamsburg, HN 2239 .... 180.00
Figurine, Winter, HN 2088 .... 450.00
Figurine, Wintertime, HN 3060 .... 250.00
Ink Holder, Desert Scene, Flambe 150.00
Jam Jar, Coaching Scene 200.00
Jardiniere, Country Landscape, Cottage & Waterwheel, 3 3/4 x 5 In. 40.00

Jug, Whiskey, Mr. Pickwick, Jim Beam Handle 70.00
Lighter, Bacchus 350.00
Lighter, Beefeater 150.00
Lighter, Falstaff 150.00
Lighter, Lawyer, Small 225.00
Lighter, Long John Silver 150.00
Lighter, Poacher 150.00
Music Box, Auld Mac, D 5823 .... 850.00
Music Box, Paddy 900.00
Music Box, Tony Weller 800.00
Napkin Ring, Sairey Gamp 550.00
Pitcher, Kingware, Pilgrim Golfer, c.1925, 9 3/8 In. 765.00
Pitcher, Madras, Early 1900s, 6 In. 425.00
Pitcher, Proverbs, 8 1/2 In. 195.00
Pitcher, Robin Hood, King Of The Archers, 9 In. 395.00
Planter, Standing Pig, Flambe, Silver Trim 595.00
Plaque, Gleaners, 2 Women & 2 Boys, 15 1/2 In. 245.00
Plate, Admiral 95.00
Plate, Balloon Man, No. 18 .... 110.00
Plate, Biddy Penny Farthing, No. 24 .... 110.00
Plate, Blue Banding, Ivory Ground, 8 1/2 In., 9 Piece 90.00
Plate, Bunnykins, 5 1/2 In. .... 50.00 to 55.00
Plate, Bunnykins, 8 1/2 In. 80.00
Plate, Dickens Ware, Mr. Micawber, 7 1/2 In. 100.00
Plate, Falconer, No. 6279, 10 1/4 In. 80.00
Plate, Falconer, Rack, 10 1/4 In. 80.00
Plate, Hunting Man 135.00
Plate, Jackdaw Of Rheims, 10 In. 100.00
Plate, Jackdaw Of Rheims, 14 In. 195.00
Plate, Jester 160.00
Plate, King Arthur's Court, Blue & White 50.00
Plate, Mayor, 10 1/2 In. 42.50
Plate, Owl, Burslem 195.00
Plate, Parson, No. 6280, 10 1/4 In. 80.00
Plate, Pomeroy Pattern, 8 3/4 In., 11 Piece 145.00
Plate, Running Free, 1977 .... 115.00
Plate, Squire, No. 6284, 10 1/4 In. 80.00
Plate, Under The Greenwood Tree, 13 3/8 In. 165.00
Plate, Valentine, 1980, Box 5.00
Plate, Watchman With Lantern, Gray Buildings, Marked, 10 3/8 In. 95.00
Plate, Wildflower, Crazing, 10 3/8 In., 9 Piece 1425.00
Plate, Woodcut, Flambe, 6 In. 95.00
Potty, Phoenix Bird, Rose Garland, Lion & Crown Mark, 1927, 9 1/2 In. 285.00
Punch Bowl, White, Blue, 1890 .... 650.00
Spittoon, Woman's, Gold & Green Accents, 7 x 7 In. 195.00
Sugar, Old Charlie, 1939 .... 900.00 to 1200.00
Sugar & Creamer, Coaching Days 200.00
Sugar & Creamer, Old Charlie, No. 787515 .... 220.00
Tea Set, Green & Cream Design, 13 Piece 77.00
Teapot, Coaching Days, 4 3/4 In. 150.00
Teapot, Dutch Harbor Scene, Windmill Finial, 9 1/2 In. 210.00
Toby Jug, Father Christmas, D.6940, Small 82.00
Toby Jug, Len Lifebelt The Lifeboatman, D.6811, Doultonville 50.00
Toby Jug, Miss Nostrum The Nurse, D.6700, Doultonville 50.00
Toby Jug, Monsieur Chasseur The Chef, D.6769, Doultonville 50.00
Toby Jug, Mr. Tonsil The Towncrier, D.6713, Doultonville 120.00
Toby Jug, Sairey Gamp, A Mark, D.6263, Small 135.00
Toby Jug, Sam Weller, A Mark, D.6265, Small 25.00
Vase, Chang Ware, Red Flambe Glaze, Charles John Noke, 1925, 13 1/2 In. ... 2600.00
Vase, Chang Ware, White Crackle Glaze, Charles John Noke, 1925, 6 In. 2588.00
Vase, Country House, Flambe 300.00
Vase, Desert Scene, Flambe, Marked, 8 7/8 In. 220.00
Vase, Mottled Celadon, Flowers, Beige Tapestry Ground, Marked 175.00

Vase, Panel Of 4 Nudes, Handles, 11 1/2 In.	750.00
Vase, Pear Shape, Mottled, Flambe	175.00
Vase, Ship Scene, Flambe, 8 1/4 In.	195.00
Vase, Silicon, No. 6419	95.00
Vase, Tan Textured Top, Green & Blue Glaze Base, 10 In.	40.00

ROYAL DUX is the more common name for the Duxer Porzellanmanufaktur, which was founded by E. Eichler in Dux, Bohemia, in 1860. By the turn of the century, the firm specialized in porcelain statuary and busts of Art Nouveau–style maidens, large porcelain figures, and ornate vases with three-dimensional figures climbing on the sides. The firm is still in business.

Bowl, Boy On Branch, Hanging Over Shell Pool, Marked, 9 1/2 In.	495.00
Bowl, Tree Trunk Base, Calla Lilies, Art Nouveau Maidens, Marked, 17 7/8 In.	632.00
Bust, Girl, c.1880, 21 In.	2750.00
Bust, Victorian Woman, Hat, Parian Finish, 16 In.	550.00
Centerpiece, Figural, Woman Seated On Shell, Tritons, Green, c.1900, 23 1/4 In.	1725.00
Dish, Figural, Harem Woman, Mustard, Pink, Gray, Ivory, Gilt, c.1900, 10 7/8 In.	690.00
Ewer, Florals, Maroon, Cream Ground, Marked, 21 1/2 In.	600.00
Figurine, 2 Dogs, White & Gold, 11 In.	325.00
Figurine, 3 Elephants, Large	500.00
Figurine, Beetle, Large	350.00 to 450.00
Figurine, Bird On Stand, 6 In.	90.00
Figurine, Bird, 4 1/2 In.	85.00
Figurine, Boy Kissing Girl, 7 1/4 In.	80.00
Figurine, Buck & Doe, Paper Label, 5 1/2 In., Pair	150.00
Figurine, Camel Driver Astride Camel, White, Cobalt, Gold Trim, 23 x 19 In.	750.00
Figurine, Cat, Black	85.00
Figurine, Cinderella, Rocino	150.00
Figurine, Cockatoo, Marked, 8 In.	165.00
Figurine, Cockatoo, On Limb, White & Pink Head, Marked, 15 In.	175.00 to 210.00
Figurine, Colonial Girl, Fan, Blue Dress, Marked	225.00
Figurine, Courting Couple On Settee	375.00
Figurine, Dachshund	60.00
Figurine, Dancers, 13 In.	200.00
Figurine, Deer, Reclining, Pink Triangle	135.00
Figurine, Dog, With Pheasant, 12 In.	350.00
Figurine, Elephant, 2 1/2 In.	70.00
Figurine, Elephant, 4 In.	100.00
Figurine, Elephant, 6 In.	175.00
Figurine, Fish	150.00
Figurine, German Shepherd	55.00
Figurine, Girl At Waterfall, Green Tin, Pink Triangle, 12 3/4 In.	995.00
Figurine, Harlequin, Male Dancer Enfolding Female, 20 x 15 In.	850.00 to 900.00
Figurine, Horse, Rearing, Marked, 11 1/2 In.	250.00 to 425.00
Figurine, Hunting Dog, Pair	140.00
Figurine, King & Queen, Katri, No. 15588 & 15589, Pair	95.00
Figurine, Lion, 4 In.	65.00
Figurine, Lion, Marked, 4 3/4 x 9 In.	60.00
Figurine, Male & Female Field Workers, 21 1/2 In., Pair	205.00
Figurine, Man & Woman Reaping, Triangle Mark	495.00
Figurine, Michele, Pink, Red, Green, Beige, Green Base, Mark, 1900s, 18 In.	895.00
Figurine, Nude, Butterfly On Knee, Marked, 8 1/2 In.	165.00
Figurine, Owl, White, 10 In.	125.00
Figurine, Parrot, Blue Macaw, 16 In.	400.00
Figurine, Parrot, Pink, White, 7 1/2 In.	95.00
Figurine, Peacock, 12 In.	125.00
Figurine, Pig	40.00
Figurine, Ram	90.00
Figurine, Sheepherder, Pink Triangle, 16 3/4 In.	895.00
Figurine, Woman & Child, Pink Triangle, 16 In.	695.00
Figurine, Woman, Sitting Atop Seashell, 17 1/2 In.	500.00
Figurine, Zebra	85.00
Group, Bavarian Couple, Dancing	255.00

*Royal Flemish, Pitcher, Water, Fish Design,
Mt. Washington*

◆◆◆◆◆◆◆◆◆◆◆◆◆◆◆◆◆◆◆◆◆◆◆◆◆

Wipe glass dry with newspapers
for a special shine.

◆◆◆◆◆◆◆◆◆◆◆◆◆◆◆◆◆◆◆◆◆◆◆◆◆

Group, Boy, Leading Harnessed Oxen, Matte Green, Pink & Cream, 1905, 15 In. 795.00
Group, Camel & Driver, Grassy Base, Pink Triangle, 20 1/4 In. 690.00
Jardiniere, Molded Girl Reclining Against Poppies, White Ground, c.1900, 12 In. 575.00
Vase, Art Nouveau, Handles, Amphora, 9 1/2 In. 200.00
Vase, Art Nouveau, Olive Tree, Swirling Branches, Marked, 15 1/2 In. 435.00
Vase, Black & Gold Highlights, White Ground, c.1900, 12 In., Pair 770.00
Vase, Figural, Nude Woman Sitting On Pink Conch Shell, c.1900, 14 3/8 In. 920.00
Vase, Gold Highlights, Green On Cream Ground, c.1900, 19 In. 415.00
Vase, Oriental Woman Gathering Flowers, Ivory, 12 In. 395.00
Vase, Peacock, Marked, Pair 365.00

ROYAL FLEMISH glass was made during the late 1880s in New Bedford,
Massachusetts, by the Mt. Washington Glass Works. It is a colored satin glass
decorated with dark colors and raised gold designs. The glass was patented in
1894. It was supposed to resemble stained glass windows.

Pitcher, Water, Fish Design, Mt. Washington .... *Illus* 7480.00
Vase, Gold Enamel Griffin, Scrolling, Amber Ground, 4 In. 1210.00
Vase, Pansies, Gold Enamel, Double Bulbed Frosted Body, 6 In. 1210.00

ROYAL HAEGER, see Haeger category

ROYAL NYMPHENBURG is the modern name for the Nymphenburg
porcelain factory, which was established at Neudeck-ob-der-Au, Germany, in
1753 and moved to Nymphenburg in 1761. The company is still in existence.
Marks include a checkered shield topped by a crown, a crowned *CT* with the
year, and a contemporary shield mark on reproductions of eighteenth-century
porcelain.

Bowl, Cherub, White 275.00
Butter, Gray Dome Lid, Berry Finial, 12 Sides, Crown & Shield, 5 1/2 In. 23.00
Cane Handle, Bust Of Lady, Curling Tresses, White, c.1780, 3 In. 1380.00
Figurine, German Shepherd, Reclining, No. 398, 10 In. 137.00
Group, 3 Putti Surrounding Tree, Bird In Cage, 9 1/4 In. 550.00
Plate, Judgment Of Paris, Gilded Rim, Marked, c.1810, 12 3/8 In. 1265.00

ROYAL RUDOLSTADT, see Rudolstadt

ROYAL VIENNA, see Beehive category

ROYAL WORCESTER is a name used by collectors. Worcester porcelains
were made in Worcester, England, from about 1751. The firm went through
many different periods and name changes. It became the Worcester Royal
Porcelain Company, Ltd., in 1862. Today collectors call the porcelains made
after 1862 *Royal Worcester*. In 1976, the firm merged with W. T. Copeland to
become Royal Worcester Spode. Some early products of the factory are listed
under Worcester.

Biscuit Jar, Flowers, Green Leaves, Silver Plated Rim, Lid & Handle 245.00
Bowl, Ribbing Radiating From Finial To Edges, Matte Beige, 6 In. 475.00

Cake Stand, Pink Border, Center Floral Bouquet, c.1876, 9 1/4 In. 220.00
Candle Snuffer, Monk 135.00
Candle Snuffer, Nun 195.00
Candlestick, Flowers & Leaves, 6 In. 80.00
Coddler, Egg, King Size, Box 48.00
Cup & Saucer, English Garden, Fluted Blank, Demitasse 16.00
Dish, 3 Sections, Gold Trim, Flowers, Leaves, Marked, 1904, 10 3/4 In. 235.00
Dish, Large Dahlias, Gold Rim, 4 In. 5.00
Dish, Shell Shape, Signed, c.1890, 9 In. 125.00
Ewer, Artist's Monogram, 7 1/2 In. 220.00
Ewer, Chameleon Handle, 9 In. 400.00
Ewer, Coiled Lizard Handle, Glass Eyes, c.1890, 11 1/2 In. 750.00
Ewer, Gold Leaves, Spout & Handle, Purple Mark, 7 In. 435.00
Figurine, Bird, Indigo, Bunting, Doughty 2400.00
Figurine, Bullfinch, No. 3238, 1938 .... 85.00
Figurine, December, No. 3458, 1949 .... 275.00
Figurine, Exmoor Pony 1250.00
Figurine, First Dance, No. 3629, 1957 .... 150.00
Figurine, Grandmother's Dress, No. 3081, 1935 .... 140.00
Figurine, Horse, Appaloosa, No. 3869, Lindner .... 795.00 to 1250.00
Figurine, Horse, Clydesdale 1395.00
Figurine, Horse, Palomino, No. 3882, Lindner 1250.00
Figurine, Kingfisher On Stump, No. 2666, F. Gertner, 1917 .... 125.00
Figurine, Nijinsky The Racehorse, No. 3893, Lindner, 1969 .... 1695.00
Figurine, November 145.00
Figurine, Prince Charles, On Pan's Folly, Horse, Lindner 1495.00
Figurine, Queen Elizabeth I 3250.00
Figurine, Queen Elizabeth II .... 990.00 to 2700.00
Figurine, Queen Mary, No. 3090, 1935 .... 3495.00
Figurine, Raimondo D'inzeo, Lindner 1395.00
Figurine, Royal Horse Guard 1395.00
Figurine, Santa Gertrudis Bull, No. 3702, Lindner, 1960 .... 850.00
Figurine, September, No. 3457, Doughty, 1949 .... 100.00
Figurine, Sir Walter Raleigh, Green Mark, 1885, 6 1/2 In. 190.00
Figurine, Tea Party, Ruth Van Ruyckevelt, 1960 .... 2500.00
Figurine, The Curtsey, No. 3360, 1941 .... 275.00
Figurine, The Dandelion, Girl With 2 Rabbits, 4 1/4 In. 100.00
Figurine, Thief 275.00
Figurine, Welsh Mountain Pony, Model No. 80, Lindner, Certificate 4000.00
Fish Set, Platter, Gravy Boat, Stand, 12 Plates, Platter, 23 In. 1035.00
Jug, Owl On Branch, Moonlit Sky, Serpent Handle, 1885, 11 1/4 In. 935.00
Lamp, Inverted Funnel Shape, Gold & Colored Flowers, Handles, 27 In. 175.00
Loving Cup, Florals, Interior Gold Garland 225.00
Match Holder, Boy Holding Twigs 295.00
Pitcher, Bicentenary, Signed, 4 3/4 In. 75.00
Pitcher, Floral Design, Embossed & Gilt Leaves, Marked, 8 In. 495.00
Pitcher, Mask, 7 1/2 In. 365.00
Pitcher, Shell, 1892 .... 375.00
Plate, Black Transfer Rim, Blue, Gilt, 1881 Mark, 9 In. 11.00
Plate, Cordova, 1928, 9 In. 185.00
Plate, Different English Cathedral, 10 3/4 In., 4 Piece 165.00
Plate, Dinner, Melba, White, Cream & Blue Band, Pink Roses, 11 Piece 220.00
Plate, Ivory, Scrollwork Borders, Flowers, c.1925, 10 1/2 In., 12 Piece 275.00
Plate, Lavender Border, Gilt Scrollwork, c.1925, 10 3/4 In., 12 Piece 412.50
Plate, Oriental Flowers, Blue Rim, Early 20th Century, 9 In., 12 Piece 330.00
Plate, Pink & Blue Flowers, Gold Tracery, c.1889, 8 In. 95.00
Plate, Silver Chantilly, 6 In. 12.50
Tea Set, Neoclassical Form, Yellow, Silver Mounted, 1892, 11 Piece 1210.00
Teapot, Pumpkin Shape, Applied Leaves, Purple Mark, 6 1/2 In. 395.00
Toothpick, Hand Painted Flowers, 1 1/2 In. 85.00
Tray, Floral Reserves, Bouquet, Gilt, Oval, 1770s, 10 In., Pair 770.00
Urn, Flower Sprays, Gold Design, c.1903, 6 1/2 x 4 1/2 In. 180.00
Vase, 2 Pheasants At Center, Reticulated Collar, Stinton 795.00

Vase, Bird, Hand Painted, Gilded Border, Signed, c.1880, 9 1/8 In. 75.00
Vase, Gourd Shaped, Pierced Neck, Gold Flowers, c.1888, 17 In. 650.00
Vase, Hand Painted Roses, Yellow On Green Ground, 4 In. 70.00
Vase, Sack Shape, Applied Twisted Rope & Bow, 1886, 6 x 5 1/2 In. 185.00

ROYCROFT products were made by the Roycrofter community of East
Aurora, New York, in the late nineteenth and early twentieth centuries. The
community was founded by Elbert Hubbard, famous philosopher, writer, and
artist. The workshops owned by the community made furniture, metalware,
leatherwork, embroidery, and jewelry. A printshop produced many signs,
books, and the magazines that promoted the sayings of Elbert Hubbard.
Furniture by the Roycroft community is listed in the furniture category.

Bookends, 1 Embossed Blossom Each, Hammered Copper, 5 1/2 x 5 1/2 In. 400.00
Bookends, Pulls Attached With Rivets, Hammered Copper, 5 1/4 In. 275.00
Box, Mahogany, Hinged Lid, Impressed Logo, Iron Hardware, 1910, 9 x 23 x 12 In. .. 385.00
Candlestick, Bobeches, 4-Sided Shaft, Ball Rivets, Hammered Copper, 12 In., Pr. 1200.00
Candlestick, Brass Wash, 12 In., Pair 425.00
Candlestick, Hammered Copper, Straight Stem, Lily-Pad Base, 8 In., Pair 385.00
Candlestick, Princess, Square Stem, Riveted To Base, 8 In., Pair 400.00
Lamp, Copper, Riveted Strapwork Over Mica Band, Domed Shade, 15 In. 1430.00
Letter Rack, Repousse Large Poppy, Brown Patina, Copper, 6 1/2 x 7 1/4 In. 330.00
Nut Set, Hammered Copper, Cylindrical Center Bowl, Nutcracker & 4 Picks 300.00
Tray, 2 Riveted Handles, Incised Border, Signed, 16 In. 300.00
Vase, 4 Full-Length Buttresses, Silver Squares At Rim, Marked, 8 In. 2200.00
Vase, Band Of Stylized Roses At Rim, Signed, 6 In. 550.00
Vase, Geometric Silver Overlay, Hammered Copper, Marked, 6 In. 1800.00
Vase, Glossy Dark Patina, Squat, Marked, 4 1/2 x 6 1/4 In. 550.00
Vase, Hammered Copper & Silver, Stylized Band, Marked, 6 1/2 In. 750.00
Vase, Hammered Copper, Footed, Long Neck, Brass Wash, 12 x 6 In. 495.00
Vase, Hammered Copper, Nickel Silver Band, Stylized Pattern, 8 x 4 In. 467.00

ROZANE, see Roseville category

ROZENBURG worked at The Hague, Holland, from 1890 to 1914. The most
important pieces were earthenware made in the early twentieth century with
pale-colored Art Nouveau designs.

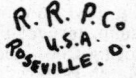

Plate, Birds, Flowers, Glazed, 10 7/8 In. 488.00
Tile Picture, Village Street Scene, Signed, Framed, 18 x 22 In. 1760.00
Vase, Polychrome Eggshell Porcelain, Orchids & Foliage, Marked, 10 In. 3220.00

RRP is the mark used by the firm of Robinson-Ransbottom. It is not a mark
of the more famous Roseville Pottery. The Ransbottom brothers started a
pottery in 1900 in Ironspot, Ohio. In 1920, they merged with the Robinson
Clay Product Company of Akron, Ohio, to become Robinson-Ransbottom.
The factory is still working.

Cookie Jar, Frosty The Snowman 650.00

RRP, Cookie Jar, Jocko the Monkey

RRP, Cookie Jar, Wise Bird

Cookie Jar, Hootie Owl, Gold	225.00
Cookie Jar, Jocko The Monkey .... *Illus*	200.00
Cookie Jar, Sheriff Pig	100.00
Cookie Jar, Wise Bird .... *Illus*	325.00
Vase, Yellow, Handle, Tall	15.00

RS GERMANY is part of the wording in marks used by the Tillowitz, Germany, factory of Reinhold Schlegelmilch from about 1869 until about 1956. The porcelain was sold decorated and undecorated. The Schlegelmilch families made porcelains marked in many ways. See also ES Germany, RS Poland, RS Prussia, and RS Tillowitz.

Berry Set, Chestnut Design, 5 Piece	270.00
Biscuit Jar, Green, Straight Sides	100.00
Biscuit Jar, Painted Lilies	85.00
Biscuit Jar, Satin Finish	85.00
Biscuit Jar, Yellow Roses, Greenery, Side Handles	115.00
Bowl, Shaded Roses, 9 In.	75.00
Cake Plate, Cotton Plant, 10 1/2 In.	45.00
Celery, Bird Of Paradise, 10 1/2 In.	195.00
Chocolate Pot, White & Apricot Floral, Shaded Ground, 10 1/2 In.	175.00
Dish, Hydrangeas, Leaves, Beige Ground, Gold Trim, Blue Wreath, Oval, 6 1/4 In. ...	28.00
Dish, Olive, Rose Spray, Floral Rim, Loop Handles, Green Wreath, 9 1/2 In.	30.00
Pitcher, Poppy, 12 In.	145.00
Plate, Portrait, Woman	85.00
Plate, White Orange Blossoms, Muted Green & Rose, 8 1/2 In.	20.00
Sugar & Creamer, Blue Florals, Gold Outlining, Oblong	75.00
Sugar & Creamer, Shaded Roses	65.00
Toothpick, Flowers, Blue & Cream, Signed	65.00

RS POLAND (German) is a mark used by the Reinhold Schlegelmilch factory at Tillowitz from about 1946 to 1949, although the factory continued production until 1956. This is one of many of the RS marks used. See also ES Germany, RS Germany, RS Prussia, RS Suhl, and RS Tillowitz.

Ewer, Golden Pheasants, Left-Handed, 6 1/4 In.	640.00
Server, Center Handle, Lavender & Orange Roses, 11 x 8 In.	515.00
Vase, Cavaliers, 4 In.	315.00
Vase, Cottage, Woman With Sheep, Gold Rim, 10 In.	640.00

RS PRUSSIA appears in several marks used on porcelain before 1915. Reinhold Schlegelmilch started his porcelain works in Tillowitz, Germany, in 1869. See also ES Germany, RS Germany, RS Poland, RS Suhl, and RS Tillowitz.

Berry Set, Reflecting Lilies, Red Mark, 7 Piece	450.00
Berry Set, White Flowers, Green Luster, 7 Piece	295.00
Bowl, 6 Lebrun Medallions, 11 In. .... *Illus*	1950.00
Bowl, Acorn, Poppies, 10 In.	275.00
Bowl, Autumn Season, 10 In.	1250.00
Bowl, Blown-Out Flowers, Center Roses, Green & Cobalt, 10 1/2 In.	775.00
Bowl, Cabbage Mold, Yellow & Green, 10 1/4 In.	195.00
Bowl, Castle Scene, 11 In.	495.00
Bowl, Floral, Crimped, Red Mark, 15 In.	850.00
Bowl, Lilies, Green Foliage, Fishscale Mold, Red Mark, 1830, 11 x 3 In.	395.00
Bowl, Lily-Of-The-Valley, Star Shape, Red Mark	475.00
Bowl, Masted Schooner, Red Mark, 8 1/2 x 13 In.	695.00
Bowl, Melon Eaters, Red Mark, 10 In.	800.00
Bowl, Old Mill Scene, Open Handles, Red Mark, 8 In.	435.00
Bowl, Peach, Ornate, Red Star, 10 1/2 x 3 1/2 In.	380.00
Bowl, Roses & Hydrangeas, Gold Trim, Handles, Oblong, 12 1/2 x 8 1/2 In.	235.00
Bowl, Sailing Ship, 10 1/2 In.	850.00
Bowl, Scalloped, Gold Rim Lines, Downward Arrows, Red Mark, 10 In.	265.00
Bowl, Schooner, Masted, Jeweling, Luster Finish, 10 1/2 x 3 In.	695.00
Bowl, Snowball, 10 In.	425.00

Bowl, Swan, Urn On Portico, Red Mark 450.00
Bowl, Swans, Evergreens In Relief, Lavender Shading, 11 In. 395.00
Bowl, Tea Rose Spray, Pale Green-Yellow, 10 1/4 x 3 In. 250.00
Bowl, Victorian Woman With Fan, 10 1/2 In. 1200.00
Bowl, Water Lilies, Red Mark 275.00
Bowl, Wild Roses & Wisteria, Pierced Rim, Shallow, Red Mark 245.00
Bowl, Winter Season, Iris Mold, 10 In. 2800.00
Box, Dresser, Heart Shape, Floral, Multicolored, 4 3/4 x 4 In. 150.00
Bread Tray, Carnations, Lily-Of-The-Valley Mold, Leaf Shape, 12 1/2 In. 145.00
Cake Plate, Barnyard, Swallows, Chickens & Duck, 9 3/4 In. 1005.00
Cake Plate, Blown-Out Pearlized Sunflowers, Handles, 11 In. 350.00
Cake Plate, Blue Boy Center, Gold Trim, Red Mark 700.00
Cake Plate, Castle Scene, Gold & Brown, Red Mark, 10 In. 635.00
Cake Plate, Clusters Of Shaded Roses, Shadow Leaves, Red Mark, 10 3/4 In. 215.00
Cake Plate, Diana The Huntress, Open Handles, Cupid In Relief, 10 1/2 In. 500.00
Cake Plate, Dice Players, Ribbon & Jewel Keyhole, 8 1/8 In. 675.00
Cake Plate, Dice Throwers, Point & Clover Mold, Red Mark, 11 In. 1100.00
Cake Plate, Poppies With Gold 95.00
Cake Plate, Sawtooth Rim, Cottage Scene, Red Mark, 10 1/4 In. 750.00
Cake Plate, Scalloped Gold Rim, Gold Leaves, Center Flowers, 10 1/2 In. 165.00
Cake Plate, Sunflower Mold, Red Mark 250.00
Cake Plate, Woman In Relief, Green Hair, Hidden Image, 11 In. 450.00
Candleholder, Pink Roses, Blue Ground, Handles, Red Mark 145.00
Celery, Daffodils, Beaded, Gold Trim, Handle, 12 1/4 x 6 In. 110.00
Celery, Dice Throwers, Point & Clover Mold, Red Mark 950.00
Celery, Hidden Image 375.00
Celery, Man In Mountain, Medallion Mold 650.00
Celery, Medallions Of Snow Birds, Sheepherders, Red Mark 2450.00
Celery, Reflecting Poppies, Red Mark, 14 In. 225.00

RS Prussia, Vase,
Melon Eaters, Jeweled

RS Prussia, Bowl, 6 Lebrun
Medallions, 11 In.

RS Prussia, Plate, Summer Season,
Keyhole, White, Gold, 9 1/2 In.

Celery, Roses, Crimped Rim, Open Handles, 12 In. 185.00
Celery, Water Lilies 175.00
Chocolate Pot, Floral 400.00
Chocolate Pot, Green Roses, Yellow, Red Mark 295.00
Chocolate Pot, Pearlized Swans, Red Mark, 9 1/2 In. 700.00
Chocolate Set, Gold Trim, Red Mark, 13 Piece 700.00
Cracker Jar, Red Roses 200.00
Cracker Jar, Reflecting Water Lilies, Icicle Mold 300.00
Cracker Jar, Roses & Snowballs 400.00
Cracker Jar, Sitting Basket 500.00
Cracker Jar, Sunflower Mold, 6 Petal Feet, Red Mark, 6 1/ 2 In. 275.00
Cracker Jar, Sunflower, Green Flower Centers, White Pearl Luster 150.00
Creamer, Barnyard Birds, Ribbon & Jewel Mold, Signed, 3 3/4 In. 300.00
Creamer, Small Roses, Gold Trim, Red Mark 40.00
Cup, Pedestal, Red Mark 42.50
Cup & Saucer, Dogwood, Footed, Green 100.00
Cup & Saucer, Pheasant & Swallow, Building, Shadow Trees, Red Mark 197.00
Cup & Saucer, Quiet Cove, Icicle Mold 130.00
Dish, Floral, Lily Mold, Pierced Handle 350.00
Hair Receiver, 4-Petal Shape, Pink Roses, Marked 150.00
Hair Receiver, Swan, Chinese Pheasant, Bluebird & Chicken 700.00
Mustard, Morning Glory, Floral, Blue & Lavender Trim 145.00
Nut Set, Peach Roses, Footed, 5 3/4 In. Bowl 550.00
Pitcher, Morning Glory Mold, Pink Carnations, 5 In. 165.00
Plate, Castle Scene, 8 1/2 In. 475.00
Plate, Cottage Scene, Blown-Out Lily Mold, 8 In. 295.00
Plate, Magnolias, Mold 56, Rose & Yellow, 7 1/2 In. 150.00
Plate, Melon Boys Eating & Playing Craps, Red Mark, 8 1/2 In. 800.00
Plate, Reflecting Poppies, Red Mark, 8 In. 95.00
Plate, Roses, Cobalt Blue, Red & Orange, 8 7/8 In. 150.00
Plate, Roses, Red Mark, 8 1/2 In. 150.00
Plate, Roses, Yellow, 6 3/8 In. 25.00
Plate, Sheepherder, With Swallows, 7 1/2 In. 125.00
Plate, Summer Season, Keyhole, White, Gold, 9 1/2 In. ...... *Illus* 1700.00
Plate, Surreal Dogwoods, Red Mark, 8 In. 85.00
Plate, Swan, Lavender & Blue Design, 8 1/2 In. 195.00
Plate, Swan, Satin, 9 In., 4 Piece 500.00
Plate, Swans, Blue, 7 3/4 In. 275.00
Plate, White Dogwood, Raised Gold Branches, 8 1/4 In. 95.00
Relish, Divided, Acorns & Leaves, Gold Trim 270.00
Relish, Swan & Trellis 495.00
Shaving Mug, Pink Roses, Green & Ivory, Red Mark 175.00
Shaving Mug, Scuttle, Mirror, Iris Mold 425.00
Sugar, Quiet Cove, Red Mark 145.00
Sugar & Creamer, Castle & Cottage Scenes, Corduroy Mold, Marked 495.00
Sugar & Creamer, Castle, Green 575.00
Sugar & Creamer, Cupids Playing Horns, Pink Roses, Gold Trim, Marked 490.00
Sugar & Creamer, Pheasants, Pedestal, Red Mark 725.00
Sugar & Creamer, Scalloped, Yellow & Pink Roses, Beaded Handles 385.00
Syrup, Roses, Green Ground, Red Mark 125.00
Syrup, Roses, Shaded Green Ground 125.00
Syrup, Underplate, Roses & Dogwood, Pearlized Luster 295.00
Tankard, Blown-Out Carnation Mold, Cerise 975.00
Tankard, Carnation Mold, Pink Roses, 11 1/2 In. 895.00
Tankard, Carnation Mold, Summer Season 6500.00
Tankard, Pink, Yellow Roses, Poppy Mold 595.00
Tankard, Plume Mold, Magnolia Design 500.00
Tankard, Roses, Stippled Floral 700.00
Tankard, Summer Season, Mill Scene 3600.00
Tea Set, California Poppy, 3 Piece 575.00
Tea Set, Child's Portrait, 11 Piece 1000.00
Tea Set, Child's, White Flowers, Aqua Trim, 17 Piece 1750.00
Toothpick, Carnation Mold 275.00

Toothpick, Icicle Mold	250.00
Tray, Bun, Castle Scene	675.00
Tray, Dresser, Icicle Mold, Hanging Basket	360.00
Tray, Swans In Lake, Icicle Mold, Red Mark, 11 1/2 x 7 In.	475.00
Vase, Boy & Girl, Handles, Red Mark, 4 1/2 In.	450.00
Vase, Crosshatch, Gold Thorns, Cobalt, 4 3/8 In.	195.00
Vase, Lebrun Portrait, 9 In.	675.00
Vase, Melon Eaters, Jeweled .... *Illus*	2350.00
Vase, Melon Eaters, Mountain Background, 4 1/2 In.	495.00
Vase, Mill Scene, Jeweled, Low Handles, 10 In.	725.00
Vase, Ostrich, Brown Tones, 9 1/2 In.	550.00
Vase, Pillow, Castle Scene, Red Mark, 7 In.	800.00
Vase, Pillow, Swans, Red Mark, 7 In.	800.00
Vase, Portrait Medallions, Pink Roses Background, Red Mark, 7 /12 In.	650.00
Vase, Rembrandt's Night Watchman, Gold Trim, Marked, 9 In.	495.00
Vase, Swan & Pines, 9 1/2 In.	550.00
Vase, Swans, Evergreens, Handles, 11 1/2 In.	495.00
Vase, Woman Feeding Chickens, Red Mark, 7 1/2 In.	395.00
Vase, Woman Watering Flowers, Cylindrical, Cobalt Blue, 8 3/4 In.	895.00
Vase, Woman With Dog, Handles, Art Nouveau Shape, 6 1/4 In.	895.00
Vase, Yellow Daisies, Multicolored Ground, Handles, Marked, 8 In.	365.00
Water Set, Child's, Oval Star, Gold Edge, 4 Piece	100.00

RS SUHL is a mark used by the Erdmann Schlegelmilch factory in Suhl, Germany, before 1917. The Schlegelmilch families made porcelains in many places. See also ES Germany, RS Germany, RS Poland, RS Prussia, and RS Tillowitz.

Chocolate Set, Floral, 1868	1495.00
Coffee Set, Coffeepot, Creamer, Sugar, 6 Cup & Saucers, 9-In Pot.	1675.00
Dish, Powder, Night Watch, Green Shading	410.00
Plate, The Cage, Cobalt Blue, Gold Trim, 7 1/2 In.	695.00

RS TILLOWITZ was marked on porcelain by the Reinhold Schlegelmilch factory at Tillowitz in the 1930s and 1940s. Table services and ornamental pieces were made. See also ES Germany, RS Germany, RS Poland, RS Prussia, and RS Suhl.

Vase, Golden Pheasants, 6 In.	260.00
Vase, White Pheasants, 6 In.	260.00

RUBENA is a glassware that shades from red to clear. It was first made by George Duncan and Sons of Pittsburgh, Pennsylvania, about 1885. This coloring was used on many types of glassware. The pressed glass patterns of Royal Ivy and Royal Oak are listed under Pressed Glass.

Perfume Bottle, Gold Band Trim, Faceted Stopper, Frosted, 5 1/4 In.	75.00
Pitcher, Inverted Thumbprint, Cranberry To Clear, 4 In.	185.00
Pitcher, Inverted Thumbprint, Crystal, Applied Handle, 4 In.	185.00
Pitcher, Square Mouth, Handle, Frosted, c.1898, Circumference 23 In.	275.00
Spooner, Opalescent, Inverted Thumbprint, Scalloped Top	135.00
Spooner, Venecia, Cranberry	110.00
Syrup, Coin Spot, Opalescent	245.00
Syrup, Medallion Sprig .... 265.00 to	275.00
Vase, Applied Leaves, Egg Shape, 9 In.	350.00
Vase, Enameled Lilies Of Valley, 10 1/2 In.	115.00

RUBENA VERDE is a Victorian glassware that was shaded from red to green. It was first made by Hobbs, Brockunier and Company of Wheeling, West Virginia, about 1890.

Castor, Pickle, Hobb's Hobnail, Frame, Tongs	495.00
Celery, Hand Painted Cherry Blossoms, Butterflies, c.1880, 6 x 12 In.	265.00
Cruet, Inverted Thumbprint, Trefoil Spout, Faceted Stopper, 7 In.	485.00
Cup, Enameled Flowers & Branches, 2 3/4 In.	90.00
Vase, Rigaree Around Body, Cranberry To Green, 8 1/4 In.	95.00
Vase, Spiral Trim Around Body, Ribbed, 8 In.	95.00

RUBY GLASS is the dark red color of the precious gemstone known as a *ruby*. It was a popular Victorian color that never went completely out of style. The glass was shaped by many different processes to make many different types of ruby glass. There was a revival of interest in the 1940s, when modern-shaped ruby table glassware became fashionable. Sometimes the red color is added to clear glass by a process called flashing or staining. Flashed glass is clear glass dipped in a colored glass, then pressed or cut. Stained glass has color painted on a clear glass. Then it is refired so the stain fuses with the glass. Pieces of glass colored in this way are indicated by the word *stained* in the description. Related items may be found in other categories, such as Cranberry Glass, Pressed Glass, and Souvenir.

Bowl, Vertical Ribbed, Scalloped, 10 3/4 x 4 7/8 In.	32.00
Cocktail Shaker, Silver Deposit Bands	65.00
Saltshaker, Glossy Flower Band	110.00
Saltshaker, Pansy Six	125.00
Table Set, Triple Triangle, 4 Piece	160.00

RUDOLSTADT was a faience factory in the Thuringia region of Germany from 1720 to about 1791. In 1854, Ernst Bohne began working in the area. From about 1887 to 1918, the New York and Rudolstadt Pottery made decorated porcelain marked with the RW and crown familiar to collectors. This porcelain was imported by Lewis Straus and Sons of New York, which later became Nathan Straus and Sons. The word *Royal* was included in their import mark. Collectors often call it *Royal Rudolstadt*. Most pieces found today were made in the late nineteenth or early twentieth century. Additional pieces may be listed in the Kewpie category.

Bottle, Cover, Flowers, Ernst Bohne Sohne, Gourd Shape, 9 1/4 In., Pair	302.00
Chocolate Set, Gold Handle & Pot Handle, Curved Stems, Poppies, 6 Piece	425.00
Cup & Saucer, Flowers	35.00
Dish, 2 Pierced Handles, 10 In.	30.00
Dish, Leaf, Multicolored Mother-Of-Pearl, Gold, 6 In.	14.00
Ewer, Floral Sprays, Gold Trim, Dragon Handle	140.00
Figurine, Young Girl In Rocker, Marked, 7 1/2 In.	135.00
Figurine, Young Woman, Hands Behind Back, Blue Dress	1295.00
Plate, Leaf Shape, Gold & White, 8 1/2 In.	50.00
Plate, Rose Sprays, Scalloped, Gold Border, Blue Mark, 13 In.	135.00
Plate, Satin Roses, 8 1/2 In.	55.00
Salt & Pepper, Jam Jar, Toothpick & Tray, 4 Piece	75.00
Sugar & Creamer, Roses	65.00
Tea Set, Child's, Happifats, Service For 6	275.00
Vase, Art Nouveau, Lily Pad, Pale Green	195.00
Vase, Footed, Venetian Ladies, Pair	495.00
Vase, Medallion Scene Of Castle, Handles, 5 In.	50.00
Vase, Reticulated Front, Gold Center Design, Gold Handles, c.1887, 9 1/2 In.	195.00

RUGS have been used in the American home since the seventeenth century. The oriental rug of that time was often used on a table, not on the floor. Rag rugs, hooked rugs, and braided rugs were made by housewives from scraps of material.

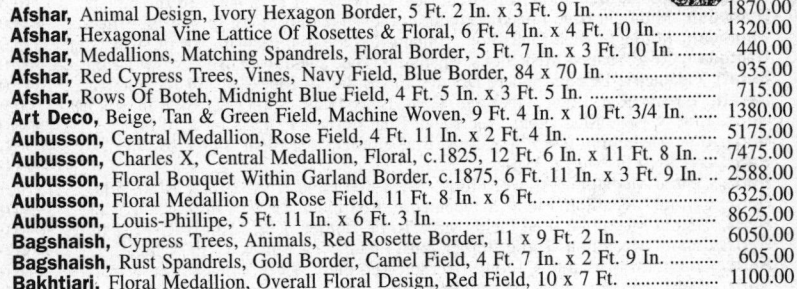

Afshar, Animal Design, Ivory Hexagon Border, 5 Ft. 2 In. x 3 Ft. 9 In.	1870.00
Afshar, Hexagonal Vine Lattice Of Rosettes & Floral, 6 Ft. 4 In. x 4 Ft. 10 In.	1320.00
Afshar, Medallions, Matching Spandrels, Floral Border, 5 Ft. 7 In. x 3 Ft. 10 In.	440.00
Afshar, Red Cypress Trees, Vines, Navy Field, Blue Border, 84 x 70 In.	935.00
Afshar, Rows Of Boteh, Midnight Blue Field, 4 Ft. 5 In. x 3 Ft. 5 In.	715.00
Art Deco, Beige, Tan & Green Field, Machine Woven, 9 Ft. 4 In. x 10 Ft. 3/4 In.	1380.00
Aubusson, Central Medallion, Rose Field, 4 Ft. 11 In. x 2 Ft. 4 In.	5175.00
Aubusson, Charles X, Central Medallion, Floral, c.1825, 12 Ft. 6 In. x 11 Ft. 8 In.	7475.00
Aubusson, Floral Bouquet Within Garland Border, c.1875, 6 Ft. 11 In. x 3 Ft. 9 In.	2588.00
Aubusson, Floral Medallion On Rose Field, 11 Ft. 8 In. x 6 Ft.	6325.00
Aubusson, Louis-Phillipe, 5 Ft. 11 In. x 6 Ft. 3 In.	8625.00
Bagshaish, Cypress Trees, Animals, Red Rosette Border, 11 x 9 Ft. 2 In.	6050.00
Bagshaish, Rust Spandrels, Gold Border, Camel Field, 4 Ft. 7 In. x 2 Ft. 9 In.	605.00
Bakhtiari, Floral Medallion, Overall Floral Design, Red Field, 10 x 7 Ft.	1100.00

Bakhtiari, Geometric & Floral Motifs, Blue Field, Ivory Border, 70 x 48 In. 852.00
Bakhtiari, Hexagon, Floral & Geometric, Red & Ivory, 6 Ft. 10 In. x 10 Ft.1 In. 1100.00
Bakhtiari, Medallion & Flowering Vines, Palmette Border, 18 Ft. 4 In. x 12 Ft. 6050.00
Bakhtiari, Stepped Diamond Lattice, Floral, Ivory Border, 6 Ft. 6 In. x 5 Ft. 385.00
Baluchi, Aubergine Palmettes, Blue Field, 5 Ft. 5 In. x 3 Ft. 4 In. 330.00
Baluchi, Aubergine Tree Of Life, Red Border, 5 Ft. 4 In. x 2 Ft. 9 In. 330.00
Baluchi, Blue, Red & Brown Stripes, Multicolored Border, 5 Ft. x 2 Ft. 10 In. 495.00
Baluchi, Hexagonal Lattice, Rust Border, Brown Field, 5 Ft. 6 In. x 2 Ft. 9 In. 605.00
Baluchi, Red Rectangles, Red Border, Midnight Blue Field, 9 Ft. 2 In. x 6 Ft. 660.00
Baluchi, Rust, Red & Blue, Tree Of Life, Camel Field, Ivory Border, 42 x 27 In. 275.00
Baluchistan, Wool, Dark Blues, Reds & Green, 3 Ft. 9 In. x 6 Ft. 10 In. 440.00
Bergamo, Prayer, Floral Motifs, Multicolored Border, Red Field, 4 Ft. 6 In. x 3 Ft. .. 550.00
Bidjar, Mina Khani Design, Geometric Border, 19th Century, 7 Ft. 6 In. x 4 Ft. 550.00
Bidjar, Navy & Green Rosette Medallion, Red Field, Blue Spandrels, 52 x 58 In. 495.00
Bidjar, Navy & Rose Rosette Medallion, Red Field, Rose Border, 4 Ft. x 2 Ft. 6 In. .. 440.00
Bidjar, Quatrefoil Medallion, Spandrels, Red Field, Rose Border, 4 Ft. x 2 Ft. 8 In. ... 357.00
Bidjar, Red Hexagonal Medallion, Ivory Border, Blue Field, 4 Ft. 7 In. x 3 Ft. 2 In. .. 770.00
Bokhara, Geometric Design, Red & Blue Border, Ivory Ground, 2 x 5 Ft. 8 In. 125.00
Bokhara, Red Center, Geometric, Multiple Borders, Navy & Red, 5 x 9 Ft. 770.00
Bokhara, Runner, Wool, Oriental, 2 Ft. 9 In. x 9 Ft. 192.00
Bokhara, Silk, Pakistan, 6 Ft. 2 In. x 8 Ft. 10 In. 412.00
Cabistan, 3 Ft. 4 In. x 6 Ft. 4 In. 250.00
Caucasian, 3 Diamond Medallions, Navy Field, Red Border, 3 Ft. 7 In. x 6 Ft. 9 In. 467.00
Caucasian, Hexagonal Medallions, Red Field, Stripe Border, 172 x 42 In. 220.00
Chinese, Amber Ground, Poppy Blossoms, Grapevines, Wool, 1925, 137 x 108 In. ... 4025.00
Chinese, Blue Medallion, Urns Of Flowers, Beige Field, 10 Ft. 6 In. x 7 Ft. 3 In. 110.00
Chinese, Ducks & Water Plants, Navy Field, Tan Border, 13 Ft. 2 In. x 10 Ft. 4 In. .. 1100.00
Chinese, Empty Field, Floral Corners, 13 Ft. x 10 Ft. 6 In. 550.00
Chinese, Floral Motif, Rose Field, Blue Border, Wool, 7 Ft. 8 In. x 5 Ft. 165.00
Chinese, Nine Blue Dragons, Gold Field, Multicolored Border, 96 x 60 In. 1045.00
Chinese, Tan Medallion, Overall Floral Border, 9 Ft. 10 In. x 13 Ft. 6 In. 1870.00
Chinese, Wool, Floral Design, Sand Field, 11 Ft. 3 In. x 14 Ft. 6 In. 467.00
Dagestan, Rows Of Palmette, Multicolored Border, Ivory Field, 54 x 38 In. 550.00
Donegal, Stylized Tulips, Budding Roses, Blue Ground, 189 x 192 In. 9775.00
Ersari, 19th Century, 9 Ft. 6 In. x 7 Ft. 825.00
Ersari, Curled Leaf Inner Border, 5 Ft. 2 In. x 3 Ft. 8 In. 1100.00
French, Art Deco, Geometric Devices, c.1930, 9 Ft. 6 In. x 6 Ft. 2 1/2 In. 2300.00
Gendje, 3 Stepped Diamond Medallions, Ivory Border, 7 Ft. 2 In. x 4 Ft. 1540.00
Gendje, 4 Stepped Red Hexagons, Ivory Border, Navy Field, 77 x 50 In. 880.00
Green & White, Colored Stripes Of String Warp, 36 x 54 In. 440.00
Grenfell, 2 Dogs, 7 3/4 x 9 1/4 In. 300.00
Grenfell, Figures, Label-History Of The Eskimo, Mat 2000.00
Grenfell, Flying Geese Over Pine Trees, Crescent Moon, Blue Ground, 26 x 39 In. ... 1200.00
Grenfell, Husky Dog's Head, 11 x 13 1/2 In. 300.00
Grenfell, Sled Dogs, Snow Scene, 17 x 25 In. 975.00
Hamadan, Boteh Medallion, Rust Field, Blue Border, 6 Ft. 7 In. x 4 Ft. 4 In. 1045.00
Hamadan, Central Pole Medallion, Orange Ground, 4 Ft. 2 In.x 7 Ft. 2 In. 2530.00
Hamadan, Herati Design, Rust, Blue & Gold, Turtle Border, 13 Ft. x 9 Ft. 10 In. 3080.00
Hamadan, Lobed Medallion, Rust-Red Field & Border, 7 Ft. x 4 Ft. 10 In. 1210.00
Hamadan, Midnight Blue Lobed Medallion, Ivory Field, 6 Ft. 10 In. x 4 Ft. 8 In. 440.00
Hamadan, Midnight Blue Medallion, Tomato Red Field, 6 Ft. 4 In. x 4 Ft. 4 In. 275.00
Hamadan, Rose Shaped Medallions, Spandrels, Blue Field, 6 Ft. 4 In. x 3 Ft. 4 In. ... 302.00
Herati, Geometric Design, Square Divided Field, Red & Blue, 46 x 74 In. 247.00
Herati, Variant, Red, Blue, Aubergine, Gold, Ivory Field, Border, 21 Ft. 6 In. x 8 Ft. 1100.00
Heriz, Blue & Rose Medallions, Red Field, Blue Border, 12 Ft. 8 In. x 10 Ft. 2860.00
Heriz, Blue Medallion, Ivory Spandrels, Blue Border, Red Field, 140 x 102 In. 1650.00
Heriz, c.1950, 9 Ft. x 6 Ft. 11 In. 575.00
Heriz, Central Medallion, Allover Floral, Brick Red Field, 7 Ft. 2 In. x 10 Ft. 5 In. 1210.00
Heriz, Central Medallion, Floral & Geometric, Red Field, 12 x 20 In. 3960.00
Heriz, Central Medallion, Red Field, Navy Turtle Border, 7 Ft. 11 In. x 11 Ft. 1 In. ... 2090.00
Heriz, Central Medallion, Turtle Border, Rust Field, 7 Ft. 9 In. x 11 Ft. 4 In. 3850.00
Heriz, Cruciform Medallions, Flower Border, Red Field, 15 Ft. 6 In. x 3 Ft. 5 In. 770.00
Heriz, Medallion, Palmette Pendants, Terra-Cotta Field, Spandrels, 149 x 112 In. 1430.00

Heriz, Overall Geometric Design, 38 Ft. 6 In. x 13 Ft. 6 In. 1540.00
Heriz, Red & Blue Medallion, Ivory Spandrels, Blue Field, 140 x 100 In. 2475.00
Heriz, Rose & Gold Medallion On Red Field, 12 Ft. x 6 Ft. 8 In. 2420.00
Heriz, Rosette Medallion On Terra-Cotta Field, 11 Ft. 4 In. x 8 Ft. 6 In. 2530.00
Hooked, 2 Deer, Standing, Polychrome Yarn, 1934, 30 1/2 x 51 In. 165.00
Hooked, 2 Pigs, 18 3/4 x 36 In. 385.00
Hooked, 2 Scottish Terriers, 26 x 46 In. 275.00
Hooked, 3-Masted Ship Blue Nose, 34 x 45 In. 247.00
Hooked, 40 Squares, Various Symbols, 22 x 3 Ft. 2 In. 2100.00
Hooked, Abstract Pattern, Multicolored, Cotton & Wool, 90 x 117 In. 805.00
Hooked, Black & Green Scrolls, Multicolored Ground, 53 x 34 In. 575.00
Hooked, Blue Oval Center, Cream Dots, Angled Stripe Border, Cotton, 27 x 39 In. ... 575.00
Hooked, Bopeep & 3 Sheep, Rag, 18 1/2 x 37 In. 220.00
Hooked, Brick Pattern, Braided Circles Border, 78 x 44 1/2 In. 935.00
Hooked, Center Dog, Surrounded By Florals, 5 Ft. 1980.00
Hooked, Center Galloping Horse, Sawtooth Border, Dated 1880, 36 1/2 x 53 In. 6900.00
Hooked, Central Oval Medallion, Winter Snow Scene, Wool & Cotton, 26 x39 In. 3105.00
Hooked, Commemorating William Jennings Bryan, Cross Of Gold, 48 x 29 In. 595.00
Hooked, Country Scene, 1930s, 8 x 2 Ft. 250.00
Hooked, Crowing Rooster, Light Blue Ground, Black Border, 20 x 24 1/2 In. 522.00
Hooked, Figure Of Cat, Floral Border, 39 x 46 In. 3850.00
Hooked, Floral Design, Brown With Gray & Pink, 26 1/2 x 33 In. 55.00
Hooked, Floral Design, On Stretcher, 28 x 39 1/2 In. 467.00
Hooked, Floral, 36 x 60 In. 99.00
Hooked, Folky Cat On Platform, Foliage, Green, White & Red, Rag, 20 x 38 In. 275.00
Hooked, Fort With U.S. Flag, One Star, Round, 29 In. 190.00
Hooked, Geometric, Log Cabin, Red, Green & Brown, 39 x 29 In. 95.00
Hooked, Geometric, Squares, Diagonal Pattern, Variegated Reds, Blue, 56 x 32 In. ... 220.00
Hooked, Geometric, Variegated Brown Yarn, Green, Red, Light Blue, 47 1/2 x 24 1/2 In. 195.00
Hooked, Harbor Scene, Earth Colors, 27 1/2 x 15 In. 192.50
Hooked, House In Landscape, 31 x 52 In. 330.00
Hooked, Interior Scene With Cat, Fireplace, 23 x 42 In. 275.00
Hooked, Landscape With 2 Houses, 24 x 41 In. 522.00
Hooked, Leaping Deer, 20th Century, 26 1/4 x 45 3/4 In. 247.00
Hooked, Lion, King Of The Beasts, 30 x 56 In. 1400.00
Hooked, Man Smoking Pipe, Riding Horse, Animal Corners, 42 x 40 In. 1840.00
Hooked, Morning Glories, Ivory Ground, Purple Border, Rag, 26 x 38 In. 27.50
Hooked, Navy Bear, Gray Ground, Deep Pink Border, 22 x 32 1/2 In. 577.00
Hooked, Polychrome Yarns On Burlap Ground, 14 Ft. 8 In. x 12 Ft. 2090.00
Hooked, Rag, 2 Black Cats, Green Vines, Gray Ground, 24 x 30 In. 330.00
Hooked, Recumbent Lion, 25 x 52 In. 330.00
Hooked, Roses, Buds, Bluebells, 64 x 36 1/2 In. 240.00
Hooked, Rows Of Medallions, Polychrome Roses, Beige Ground, 46 x 88 In. 357.00
Hooked, Scene Of Rooster Crowing At Sunrise, Yarn, 18 1/2 x 31 In. 30.00
Hooked, Scroll Design, On Multicolored Purple Ground, 24 x 46 In. 247.00
Hooked, Star Burst, Black, Salmon, Navy, Gray, Maroon, Early 1900s, Round, 37 In. 225.00
Hooked, Swan, Cattails, Water Lilies, Braided Border, 20 x 36 In. 65.00
Hooked, Swan, On Blue Oval Pond, Gray Ground, Stretcher-Mounted, 25 x 36 In. 385.00
Hooked, Tiger Design, Linen-Backed, 1870s, 45 x 83 In. 1760.00
Hooked, Tree Of Life, Butterfly & Squirrel, Vine Border, 1940s, 61 x 88 In. 1935.00
Hooked, Trees, Animals, Mustard Ground, 1900, 32 x 65 In. 4200.00
Hooked, Winter Landscape, House & Trees, Rag & Yarn, 16 1/2 x 26 In. 72.00
Hooked, Winter Townscape, Gray & Black Border, 18 1/4 x 34 1/2 In. 860.00
Hooked, Wool, Floral Medallion, 9 x 12 In. 1800.00
Hooked, Yarn, Floral Medallions, Gray Field, Ribbons & Bows, 34 x 54 In. 93.00
Joshogan, Snowflake Design, Brick Red Field, 7 Ft. x 10 Ft. 5 In. 880.00
Karabagh, Blue Stepped Polygons, Red Field & Border, 7 Ft. 6 In. x 5 Ft. 330.00
Karabagh, Central Geometric Design, Red Field, 20th Century, 4 Ft. x 5 Ft. 6 In. 605.00
Karabagh, Concentric Hooked Diamonds, Brown Field, 7 x 4 Ft. 660.00
Karabagh, Hexagonal Medallions, Flower Heads, Red Field, 8 Ft. 2 In. x 5 Ft. 2 In. . 1540.00
Karabagh, Medallions & Spandrels, Flower Head Border, 7 Ft. 4 In. x 4 Ft. 6 In. 880.00
Karabagh, Medallions, Navy Blue, Red Field, Navy Border, 8 Ft. x 5 Ft. 3 In. 522.00
Karabagh, Red Gabled Squares, Blue Field, Ivory Border, 19th Century, 103 x 62 In. 550.00

Karabagh, Rows Of Diamonds, Wineglass & Leaf Border, 51 x 36 In. 385.00
Karabagh, Stylized Roses Overall, 19 Ft. 7 In. x 3 Ft. 7 In. 3450.00
Karadja, Open Field, Blue & Rust, c.1900, 8 Ft. 1 In. x 11 Ft. 6 In. 6500.00
Karadja, Red, Apricot & Blue Medallion, Blue Field, Red Border, 50 x 38 In. 412.00
Karadja, Wool, 1880, Persia, 6 Ft. 2 In. x 9 Ft. 10 In. 5400.00
Kashan, Scalloped Diamond Medallion, Burgundy Field, 12 Ft. 4 In. x 8 Ft. 8 In. 1540.00
Kashan, Silk, 51 1/2 x 86 In. 3245.00
Kasvin, Central Medallion, Navy Field, Floral & Arabesque, 8 Ft. 1 In. x 10 Ft. 5 In. 2420.00
Kasvin, Oval Medallion, Red Palmette, Flowering Vine Border, 12 x 9 Ft. 3410.00
Kazak, Blue & Gray Stars, Burgundy Field, 98 x 155 In. 800.00
Kazak, Central Medallions, Blue Ground, 11 Ft. 7 In. x 6 Ft. 3300.00
Kazak, Diamond Medallions, Navy Field, Serrated Leaf Border, 103 x 42 In. 330.00
Kazak, Floral Border, Center Medallions, Blue & Red, 83 x 44 In. 1300.00
Kazak, Octagonal Medallion, Diamonds, Red Border, Navy Field, 110 x 68 In. 2640.00
Kermanshah, Central Lozenge, Geometric Design, 3 Borders, 4 Ft. 3 In. x 6 Ft. 6 In. 550.00
Khotan, Blue & Blue-Green, Floral Sprays, Red Field & Border, 108 x 55 In. 330.00
Khotan, Oval Rosettes, Vines, Flower Head Border, Silk, 7 x 4 Ft. 1100.00
Kilim, Bakhtiari, Wool, Stripes, Blues, Gold, Reds, 1900, 4 Ft. 9 In. x 6 Ft. 10 In. 3700.00
Kilim, Geometric Design, Multicolored, Brown Ground, 50 x 112 In. 400.00
Kilim, Geometric Design, Multicolored, 8 Ft. 8 In. x 14 Ft. 2 In. 600.00
Kilim, Geometric Motif, Squares, Red Ground, Black Border, 58 x 96 In. 357.00
Kilim, Persian Village, Faded, 4 Ft. x 7 Ft. 9 In. 302.00
Kirman, Allover Floral Sprays, Ivory Field, Border, 10 Ft. 8 In. x 8 Ft. 1100.00
Kirman, Allover Palmettes, Blossoms & Vines, Ivory Field, Cochineal, 14 x 10 Ft. ... 2640.00
Kirman, Central Medallion, Red Field, Stylized Floral Borders, 12 x 9 Ft. 770.00
Kirman, Diamond Medallion, Cochineal Field, Fringe, 11 Ft. 8 In. x 8 Ft. 8 In. 1540.00
Kirman, Floral On Blue & Pink Ground, 11 Ft. 8 In.x 18 Ft. 5 In. 2090.00
Kirman, Floral Spray, Ivory Ground, Apricot Border, 12 Ft. x 8 Ft. 6 In. 4950.00
Kirman, Pale Blue Field, Bird, Willow Tree, Urn Reserves, 4 Ft. 3 In.x 6 Ft. 2475.00
Konya, Serapi Design, Copper Field, 8 Ft. 6 In. x 11 Ft. 6 In. 1540.00
Konya, Serapi Design, Traditional Colors, 6 Ft. 2 In. x 9 Ft. 6 In. 935.00
Kuba, 4 Lesghi Stars, Blue Field, 5 Ft. 8 In. x 3 Ft. 8 In. 440.00
Kum, Scrolling Floral, Avian & Deer, Red Ground, 4 Ft. 4 In. x 7 Ft. 7 In. 450.00
Kurd, Gabled Rectangular Medallions, Blue Field, 6 Ft. 10 In. x 5 Ft. 2 In. 522.50
Kurd, Oriental, Medallion, Midnight Blue Field, Red Border, 1901, 105 x 53 In. 885.00
Kurd, Rows Of Boteh, Human Figures, Ivory Border, Navy Field, 79 x 45 In. 495.00
Kurd, Rows Of Geometric Motifs, Ivory Border, 20th Century, 6 Ft. 4 In. x 3 Ft. .. 220.00
Kurd, Vases Of Vines, Peacocks, Ivory Border, Rust Field, 74 x 44 In. 358.00
Lilihan, Detached Floral Sprays, Midnight Blue Field, Red Border, 11 x 8 Ft. 4 In. 4400.00
Lilihan, Floral Spray, Serrated Leaves, 5 Ft. x 3 Ft. 6 In. 385.00
Lilihan, Floral Sprays, Floral Meander Border, 6 Ft. 8 In. x 5 Ft. 1650.00
Lilihan, Overall Floral & Foliate Design, Black Ground, 6 Ft. 6 In. x 5 Ft. 415.00
Lilihan, Rose & Blue Herati Design, Dark Blue Field & Border, 56 x 40 In. 330.00
Lilihan, Rows Of Flowering Plants, Red Border, Navy Field, 12 Ft. x 8 Ft. 10 In. 3080.00
Luri, 3 Palmette Designs, Flower Head Border, 7 Ft. 4 In. x 4 Ft. 4 In. 2750.00
Luri, Blue & Green, Rows Of Boteh, Rust Field, Ivory Border, 70 x 50 In. 1045.00
Mahal, Allover Floral, Red Field, Turtle Border, 10 Ft. 7 In. x 13 Ft. 4 In. 990.00
Mahal, Allover Flower & Vine, Red Field, Navy Border, 8 Ft. 10 In. x 11 Ft. 8 In. 825.00
Mahal, Empty Green Field, 1910s, 11 Ft. 4 In. x 10 Ft. 4 In. 4125.00
Mahal, Overall Herati Design, Blue Border, 7 Ft. x 5 Ft. 3 In. 522.00
Malayer, Staggered Rows Of Boteh, Blue Border, Red Field, 74 x 50 In. 1100.00
Marasali, Rows, Hooked Diamonds, Black Field, Ivory Boteh Border, 55 x 44 In. 1430.00
Mimosa, Henri Matisse, 58 x 36 In. 4250.00
Moroccan, Center 6-Petaled Floral Medallion, 6 Ft. 5 In. x 8 Ft. 330.00
Mudjur, Prayer, Red Mihrab Field, Rosette Border, 6 Ft. x 4 Ft. 8 In. 3300.00
Nain, Central Medallion, Navy Ground, Wool & Silk, 10 x 14 Ft. 8140.00
Needlepoint, Overall Tile Design, 1930s, 9 Ft. 6 In. x 6 Ft. 4 In. 1438.00
Needlepoint, Rows Of Rosettes, Green Field, Portugal, 13 Ft. 6 In. x 10 Ft. 1980.00
Oushak, Overall Palmettes & Vines, Cream, Mandarin Field, 12 Ft. 9 In. x 10 Ft. . 2875.00
Oushak, Salmon Medallion, Steel Blue Field, Border, 14 Ft. 8 In. x 11 Ft. 11 In. 3163.00
Penny, Multicolored 3 Graduated Circles, Short Pile Fringe, 1920s, 39 x 21 In. .. 465.00
Persian, Allover Medallion Design, Red Field, 13 Ft. 3 In. x 10 Ft. 4 In. 8525.00
Persian, Hooked, Diamonds On Blue Field, 1900, 66 x 48 In. 1760.00

Persian, Red, Blue & Sand Medallions, Cobalt Field, 16 Ft. 8 In. x 3 Ft. 2 In. 1210.00
Persian, Rows Of Diamonds, Leaf Borders, 15 Ft. 6 In. x 3 Ft. 6 In. 660.00
Persian, Star Medallion, Blossoming Vines, Red Border, 4 Ft. x 2 Ft. 2 In. 715.00
Persian, Vases Of Flowers & Sprays, Palmette Border, 9 Ft. 6 In. x 6 Ft. 2 In. 3575.00
Qashqai, 3 Diamond Medallions, Rosette Border, 7 Ft. 2 In. x 5 Ft. 10 In. 2860.00
Qashqai, Diamond Medallions, Ivory Field & Border, 55 x 33 In. 1320.00
Qashqai, Diamond Medallions, Spandrels, Blue Field, Brown Border, 84 x 41 In. 550.00
Rag, Burlap, Appliqued Floral, Crocheted Border, 26 1/2 x 36 In. 82.50
Sarouk, Blue Vases Of Flowers & Border, Camel Tan, Green, Red Field, 11 x 9 Ft. .. 1100.00
Sarouk, Burgundy & Tan, 1920, 4 x 6 1/2 Ft. 650.00
Sarouk, Floral Design, Burgundy Field, Navy Border, 11 Ft. 10 In. x 8 Ft. 8 In. 1320.00
Sarouk, Floral Medallion, Spandrels, Red Border, Blue Field, 82 x 52 In. 1210.00
Sarouk, Floral Motif, Red Field, Blue Floral Border, 5 Ft. x 3 Ft. 4 In. 302.00
Sarouk, Floral Sprays, Blue Border, Burgundy Field, 4 Ft. 10 In. x 3 Ft. 4 In. 1045.00
Sarouk, Floral Sprays, Burgundy Field, Midnight Blue Border, 140 x 104 In. 3520.00
Sarouk, Midnight Blue Leaves & Floral Sprays, Wine Field, 11 Ft. 9 In. x 9 Ft. 4125.00
Senneh, Shub Design, Floral, Beige, Herati Border, 1900, 6 Ft. 5 In. x 4 Ft. 4 In. 3850.00
Serapi, Gabled Square Medallions, Red Field, 15 Ft. x 12 Ft. 6 In. 7700.00
Serapi, Stylized Floral & Vine, Red, Turtle Main Border, 9 Ft. 2 In. x 18 Ft. 3 In. 4620.00
Shiraz, Hexagon Medallions, Organic & Geometric Design, 63 x 45 In. 660.00
Shirvan, Floral & Geometric, Navy Field, Dragon's Tooth Border, 11 Ft. x 3 Ft. 2 In. 880.00
Shirvan, Octagonal Medallions, Dragon's Tooth Border, 7 Ft. 6 In. x 3 Ft. 6 In. 385.00
Shirvan, Octagonal Medallions, Ivory Border, Blue Field, 5 Ft. 2 In. x 3 Ft. 3 In. 880.00
Shirvan, Peacock Design, Blue, Barber Pole Border, 1900, 3 Ft. 10 In. x 5 Ft. 9 In. .. 1320.00
Shirvan, Prayer, 5 Stripes, Floral, Red, White, Blue & Yellow, 3 Ft. 1 In. x 5 Ft. 1155.00
Shirvan, Red & Blue Hooked Medallion, Ivory Field & Border, 5 Ft. 4 In. x 4 Ft. 2200.00
Shirvan, Tan & Gold Lesghi Stars, 4 Ft. 9 In. x 3 Ft. 10 In. 385.00
Sivas, Violet Medallion, Matching Spandrels, 5 Ft. 7 In. x 4 Ft. 2 In. 110.00
Soumak, Blue Indented Diamond Medallions, Rust Field, 6 Ft. 6 In. x 5 Ft. 880.00
Soumak, Indented Diamond Medallions, Red Field, 10 Ft. 2 In. x 7 Ft. 8 In. 2310.00
Soumak, Staggered Diamond Medallions, Star Border, 11 Ft. 8 In. x 8 Ft. 1870.00
Sultanabad, Red Herati Design, Ivory Border, 9 Ft. 7 In. x 5 Ft. 660.00
Tabriz, Ardebil Design, Medallion, Spandrels, Red, Blue Border, 12 Ft. x 8 Ft. 8 In. .. 2750.00
Tabriz, Herati Design, Turtle Border, 14 Ft. 10 In. x 9 Ft. 3080.00
Tabriz, Hunt Scenes, 11 Ft. 11 In. x 18 Ft. 9 In. 4950.00
Tabriz, Ivory Ground, Tan Border, 76 x 106 In. 400.00
Tabriz, Stylized Floral Design, Olive Field, 3 Ft. 5 In. x 6 Ft. 5 In. 132.00
Tekke, 6 Blue, Ivory And Magenta Octagonal Guls, Rust Field, 43 x 27 In. 385.00
Tekke, Columns Of Guls, Octagon Border, 19th Century, 10 Ft. 9 In. x 7 Ft. 6 In. 2200.00
Tekke, Columns, Rust Field, Octagon Border, Floral Motif, 140 x 78 In. 880.00
Tekke, Torba, Guls, Rust-Red Field, Gotshak Border, 3 Ft. 9 In. x 1 Ft. 6 In. 1100.00
Turkoman, Turkoman Door, Latch Hook Design, 41 In. Opening, 61 In. 55.00
Ushak, Blue Octagonal Medallion On Red Field, 14 Ft. 2 In. x 9 Ft. 2 In. 660.00
Yomud, Lattice Of Ashik Guls, Blue-Green Border, 4 Ft. x 2 Ft. 7 In. 1540.00
Yomud, Staggered Rows Of Kepse Guls, 9 Ft. 4 In. x 7 Ft. 2200.00
Yomud Chuval, 9 Chuval Guls, Rust Field, 3 Ft. 10 In. x 2 Ft. 7 In. 385.00

RUMRILL Pottery was designed by George Rumrill of Little Rock, Arkansas. From 1933 to 1938, it was produced by the Red Wing Pottery of Red Wing, Minnesota. In 1938, production was transferred to the Shawnee Pottery in Zanesville, Ohio. Production ceased in the 1940s.

RumRill

Pitcher, No. 304, Turquoise 20.00
Vase, 2-Tone Green, 8 In. 17.50
Vase, 6 In. 17.50
Vase, Cattail Handles, Green, 4 In. 5.00
Vase, Nude Holding Bowl, White 165.00
Vase, Nudes 65.00
Vase, Off-White, 7 1/2 In. 10.00

RUSKIN is a British art pottery of the twentieth century. The Ruskin Pottery was started by William Howson Taylor, and his name was used as the mark until about 1899. The factory, at West Smethwick, Birmingham, England, stopped making new pieces in 1933 but continued to glaze and sell the remaining wares until 1935. The art pottery is noted for its exceptional glazes.

Jar, Cover, Oriental Shape, Blue Flambe Glaze, 1908, 4 1/2 In.	275.00
Vase, Art Nouveau Whiplash Handles, Leathery Brown Glaze, 13 1/2 In.	700.00
Vase, Flat Shoulder, Pigeon Feather Gray & Red, 1910, 4 1/4 In.	350.00
Vase, Ivy Vines, Lemon Ground, Squat Baluster, Glazed, 1910, 7 1/8 In.	250.00
Vessel, Stovepipe Neck, Pigeon Feather Glaze, 9 x 8 1/2 In.	750.00

RUSSEL WRIGHT designed dinnerwares in modern shapes for many companies. Iroquois China Company, Harker China Company, Steubenville Pottery, and Justin Tharaud and Sons made dishes marked *Russel Wright*. The Steubenville wares, first made in 1938, are the most common today. Wright was a designer of domestic and industrial wares, including furniture, aluminum, radios, interiors, and glassware. Dinnerwares and other pieces by Wright are listed here. For more information, see *Kovels' Depression Glass & American Dinnerware Price List.*

Ashtray, Sterling, Ivory	65.00
Berry Bowl, American Modern	7.50
Bowl, American Modern, Gray, 11 In.	55.00
Bowl, American Modern, Gray, Lug Handle	11.00
Bowl, Iroquois, Divided, Avocado	14.00
Bowl, Iroquois, Pink, 5 1/4 In.	6.00
Bowl, Oceania Wave, Salad	250.00
Bowl, Rice, Cover, Individual, 3 x 4 1/2 In.	795.00
Bowl, Salad, American Modern, Chartreuse	40.00
Bowl, Vegetable, American Modern, Coral, 10 In.	15.00
Bread Plate, American Modern, Coral, 6 In.	4.00
Bread Plate, American Modern, Granite, 6 In.	4.00
Butter, Black, Chutney	250.00
Carafe, American Modern, Chartreuse	65.00
Carafe, American Modern, Gray	125.00
Carafe, Iroquois, Blue	110.00 to 125.00
Carafe, Iroquois, White	150.00 to 165.00
Casserole, American Modern, Cover, Gray	40.00
Chop Plate, American Modern, Bean Brown	45.00
Chop Plate, American Modern, Granite, Square, 13 In.	25.00
Creamer, American Modern, Coral	8.00
Creamer, American Modern, Gray	9.00
Cup, American Modern, Chartreuse	3.00
Cup & Saucer, American Modern	9.00
Cup & Saucer, Chartreuse, After Dinner	16.00
Cup & Saucer, Iroquois, Dark Gray	9.00
Cup & Saucer, Iroquois, Pink	9.00
Cup & Saucer, Seafoam	16.00
Cup & Saucer, Seafoam, After Dinner	20.00
Dinner Set, Doll's, American Modern, Plastic, Ideal, 30 Piece	140.00
Goblet, American Modern, Smoke	14.00
Pitcher, American Modern, Bean Brown	150.00
Pitcher, American Modern, Black Chutney, Cover	195.00
Pitcher, Iroquois, Apricot	85.00
Pitcher, Seafoam, 10 1/2 In.	70.00 to 95.00
Plate, American Modern, 6 In.	8.00
Plate, American Modern, Chartreuse, 10 In.	13.50
Plate, American Modern, Gray, 8 In.	9.00
Plate, Iroquois, Pink, 10 In.	6.00
Platter, American Modern, Chartreuse, 13 x 9 In.	10.00
Platter, Iroquois, Brown, 12 1/2 In.	15.00
Salt & Pepper, American Modern, Gray	12.50
Saucer, American Modern, Coral, After Dinner	6.00
Sugar & Creamer, Iroquois, Stacking, Pink	25.00
Sugar & Creamer, Nutmeg, Stacking	25.00
Teapot, Iroquois, Brown	150.00
Teapot, Knowles, Solar	125.00
Teapot, Sterling, Cedar Brown	40.00
Vase, Flaring Cylinder, Chromed Metal, c.1935, 10 1/8 In.	1150.00

SABINO glass was made in the 1920s and 1930s in Paris, France. Founded by Marius-Ernest Sabino (1878–1961), the firm was noted for Art Deco lamps, vases, figurines, and animals in clear, colored, and opalescent glass. Production stopped during World War II but resumed in the 1960s with the manufacture of nude figurines and small opalescent glass animals. The new pieces are a slightly different color and can be recognized.

SABINO FRANCE

Clock, Lovebirds In Flowering Branches, Gilt Metal, 1925, 10 1/4 In.	1438.00
Figurine, Dove, 5 x 7 In.	145.00
Figurine, Dove, Large	265.00
Figurine, Isadora Duncan, 1930s	800.00
Figurine, Lady & The Lamb, 1935	1000.00
Figurine, Rooster, Large	375.00
Plaque, Cherubic Head, Opalescent, Oval, Wooden Stand, Signed, 17 1/2 In.	2640.00
Scotty Dog	95.00
Vase, Gaiete, Art Deco Style Nudes, Late 1920s, 14 1/8 In.	1650.00

SALOPIAN ware was made by the Caughley factory of England during the eighteenth century. The early pieces were blue and white with some colored decorations. Another ware referred to as *Salopian* is a late nineteenth-century tableware decorated with color transfers.

Salopian

Bowl, Blue & Gilt Floral Design, Fluted Form, Round, 6 x 3 In.	120.00
Cup & Saucer	175.00
Plate, Blue & Gilt Landscape Design, Ivory Ground, 8 1/8 In., 10 Piece	1500.00
Sugar & Creamer	500.00
Tea Set, Oriental Stoneware, U.S. Hotel, Philadelphia, 1830, 17 Piece	700.00

SALT AND PEPPER SHAKERS in matched sets were first used in the nineteenth century. Collectors are primarily interested in figural examples made after World War I. *Huggers* are pairs of shakers which appear to embrace each other. Many salt and pepper shakers are listed in other categories and can be located through the index at the back of this book.

101 Dalmatians	25.00
Aladdin & Genie	24.00
Aladdin Genie & Lamp	30.00
Alarm Clock, Pottery	4.50
Apple Head People	15.00
Apples, With Leaves, Mawhon Ware, Large	10.00
Aunt Jemima & Uncle Mose, F & F, Large	67.00
Aunt Jemima & Uncle Mose, F & F, Small	30.00 to 60.00
Bakelite, Bakelite Box	17.00
Barney Google & Snuffy Smith	55.00
Bear, Gold Trim, American Bisque	35.00
Bears, Hugger, Van Tellingen	22.00
Bears, With Coats	20.00
Bert & Harry, With Blue Suits	165.00
Bette Farms Dairy, Dairy Bottles	45.00
Birthday Cake & Present	3.50
Black Boy & Dog, Van Telligen	45.00
Black Cat Chef, Wooden	25.00
Black Waiter, With Mustard	45.00
Bob's Big Boy	350.00
Borden's, Dairy Bottles	35.00
Boy Holding Melon	75.00
Brown Bear Huggers, Van Tellingen	45.00
Budman, Bud Bear	250.00
Budweiser, Bud Man, Box	30.00 to 50.00
Bunnies, Huggers	22.00
Butler & Mammy	95.00
Cabbage Rose, Amber	30.00
Cactus	59.00
Carnival Glass, Miters & File, Footed, Chrome Top, 5 In.	25.00
Cat, Black, Occupied Japan, 10 In.	27.00

Cat & Fiddle 22.00
Catskill Mountains, 1947 .... 5.00
Charlie Brown & Lucy 55.00
Chef, Holding Rabbit, Cook Holding Spoon, 2 1/2 In. 45.00
Chef, Man & Woman, Wooden 3.00
Cobalt Blue, Ribbed, Glass, 6 In. .... 25.00 to 32.00
Coffeepot On Cafe Hot Plate, Glass Pots 6.00
Colonel Sanders, Plastic 95.00
Coors Beer, Bottle Shape, Golden Export Lager, Ceramic, 1930s, 3 3/4 In. 35.00
Corn Head & Radish Head Ladies, Dressed Up 25.00
Cow & Calf, Japan 30.00
Cow & Moon 32.00
Cranberry, Swirl, Opalescent 80.00
Dairy Queen Cones 30.00
Desert Rose, Large 40.00
Dick Tracy & Junior, Chalkware 45.00
Dobbin 65.00
Donald Duck, Sitting 35.00
Donkey, Sitting, Chalkware 3.00
Droids, Sigma 495.00
Dumbo, Large & Small 40.00
Dutch Boy & Girl, Van Tellingen 20.00
Dutch Woman Holding Baskets 18.00
Elephants, Circus, Standing 25.00
Elsie, Ice Cream 45.00
Elsie & Elmer Busts, Borden Co., 1940s 125.00
Elsie The Cow, Stackable 125.00
Eskimos 12.00
Fat Mammy 35.00
Ferdinand The Bull, Japan 50.00
Fish & Fishing Basket 20.00
Gas Pump, Shell, Premium Label, TCP, 1950s 80.00
Gas Pumps, Phillips 66, Square Top .... 30.00 to 32.00
Gas Pumps, Texaco, Silver & Red .... 17.50 to 35.00
Geometrics, Green, Red Flowers, Gold Tops, Japan 4.00
Glass, Hexagonal, Silver Lid 2.50
Glass, Tapered Octagonal, Silver Lid, Anchor Hocking 3.00
Golden Guernsey Dairy, Dairy Bottles 40.00
Goose & Golden Egg 15.00
Green Glass, Floral Design, Metal Lids 6.50
Greyhound Bus 55.00
Hamm's Bears, Black & White 110.00
Heinz Ketchup, Plastic 12.00
Hershey's Kisses 15.00
House Beside Tree, Self Tops, 3 In. 10.00
Huggers, Van Tellingen 40.00
Humpty Dumpty, Enesco, 15 In. 110.00
Humpty Dumpty, Yellow, Plastic 8.00
Humpty Dumpty & Little Miss Muffet 20.00
Ice Cream Cones, Glass, Steel Rack, 4 1/2 In. 19.00
Indian, Nodder 25.00
Indians, In Drum, Nodder 35.00
Ken-L-Ration, Dog & Cat, F & F Plastics 20.00
Kettle, Red, Porcelain 4.50
Kittens, Nodder 35.00
Lambchop 10.00
Lambs, Range Top, Twin Winton 20.00
Laurel & Hardy, Beswick China, England 45.00
Liquor Bottle, 1 Brown, 1 Green, Iron Wire Holder, 5 1/4 x 6 3/8 In. 10.00
Little Sprout 12.00
Log Cabin, Chalkware 3.50
Love Bug, Huggers, Bendel, 4 1/2 In. 60.00

Luzianne Mammy, Green Skirt	225.00
Maggie & Jiggs	95.00
Magic Chef, Plastic	50.00
Mammy, Butler	85.00 to 138.00
Mammy, Range Size, Pearl China	150.00
Mammy, Yellow Dot, Metlox, Box	450.00
Mammy & Chef, Black Glaze, With Gold, 6 In.	35.00
Mammy & Chef, Brayton, Yellow	85.00
Mammy & Chef, Gold Trim	85.00
Mammy & Chef, Hand Painted, Gold, 5 1/2 In.	65.00
Mammy & Chef, New Orleans	36.00
Mammy & Chef, New Orleans, Porcelain, 4 In.	40.00
Mammy & Chef, With Cookie Jar, Japan, 3 Piece	225.00
Mary & Her Little Lamb, Huggers, Van Tellingen	25.00
Mermaid & Sailor, Huggers, Van Tellingen	110.00 to 125.00
Mice, Dressed, Bisque, Hand Painted, Japan	18.00
Milk Bottle Shape, Gold Medal Dairy Co., Dakota, Decals	30.00
Model T Ford, USA, Large	10.00
Moon Mullins & Kayo, Chalkware	45.00
Mother-Of-Pearl, Gold Tops, 1 Piece, 2 3/4 In.	4.50
Mushrooms, 2 1/2 In.	8.00
New York World's Fair, Orange, Blue Base, Plastic, 1939	15.00
Nipper	45.00
Oil & Vinegar	65.00
Old MacDonald, Churn	48.00
Old Woman & Shoe	30.00
Onion Cart, Soft Plastic	24.00
Orange Flower, Black Trim, Japan, 5 In.	8.00
Oriental, Nodder	25.00
Peek-A-Boo, Van Tellingen, Large	170.00
Peek-A-Boo, Van Tellingen, Small	190.00 to 200.00
Penguins, Kool Cigarettes, Willie & Millie,	193325.00
Persian Cats, Twin Winton	40.00
Pink Poodle, Lounge Chair	35.00
Pinocchio, Japan	95.00
Plaid Mammy & Butler	95.00
Popeye & Olive Oyl, Vandor, 9 In.	37.00
Poppin' Fresh & Poppie Fresh, Plastic	35.00
Poppin Fresh, Pillsbury, Ceramic	20.00
Pumpkin, With Leaves, Yellow, Porcelain	3.00
Pumpkins, Germany	12.00
Raggedy Ann & Andy	14.50
RCA, Box	35.00
RCA Victor Dog, Nipper, 2 In.	30.00 to 45.00
Refrigerator, Milk Glass, General Electric	20.00
Robin Hood & Fox	32.00
Sad Sack, Ceramic, 1 Carries Heavy Gear, Other Takes Army Pledge, 4 In.	38.00
Sailor & Mermaid, Huggers	145.00
Salty & Peppy, Pearl China, Large	185.00
Scottish Girl & Boy, Occupied Japan	12.50
Seagram's Gin	18.00
Shell & Tassel	225.00
Ship, Red & White	5.00
Silent Sam, Adamson	65.00
Smiley Pig, 5 In.	85.00
Sneezy & Sleepy	35.00
Snowman & Wife	10.00
Snuffy Smith & Brother	60.00
Snuggle Bear, Huggies	25.00
Squirt, Bottles	5.00 to 12.00
Tomato, With Leaves, Red, Porcelain	3.50
Tony The Tiger	15.00

Toonerville Folks, Hand Painted, Ceramic, 1 x 4 In. 65.00
Tumbling Clowns, Box 29.00
U.S. Mail Box, With Birds 10.00
Wizard Of Oz 16.00
Yellow, Half Round, Catalin 40.00
Ziggy & Fuz, Ceramic 15.00

SALT GLAZE has a grayish white surface with a texture like an orange peel.
It is a method of decoration that has been used since the eighteenth century.
Salt-glazed pieces are still being made.

Bowl, Mixing, Butterine, Handle, Advertising, Blue Letters 175.00
Creamer, Molded Designs On Blue Trim, 4 3/8 In. 72.00
Crock, Blue Design, 10 Gal. 32.50
Crock, Butterfly Design, 15 Gal. 650.00
Crock, Cobalt Blue Bird On Stump, Brady & Ryan, c.1870, 10 In. 230.00
Crock, Cobalt Blue Squatting Quail, N. Clark Jr., c.1860, 2 Gal. 690.00
Figurine, Cat, Seated, Blue Eyes, Staffordshire, c.1760, 5 7/8 In. 9350.00
Jar, M. Worther, Philadelphia, Ill., Freehand Incised, 1 Qt. 300.00
Jug, Cover, Pear Shape, Crab Stock Handle & Finial, Staffordshire, c.1755, 6 In. 3520.00
Jug, Handle, Cobalt Blue Incised Name, Design, 1862, 4 1/2 In. 310.00
Jug, Molded Portrait Medallion, Foliage, c.1765, 6 In. 385.00
Jug, White, Silver Plated Lid, Molded Heraldry, Albion, Cobridge, 7 1/2 In. 56.00
Mortar, Wooden Pestle, 8 In. 145.00
Mug, Hunting, Vauxhall, Bust Of Queen Anne, Beefeaters, 1727, 8 3/16 In. 2875.00
Mug, Medallions, Bust Of William III, Queen Anne, Charles I, 1726, 7 1/2 In. 2875.00
Mug, Strap Handle, Allover Brown Glaze, Fulham, c.1720 .... 1650.00
Pedestal, Blue Foliate & Figural Design, Gray Ground, 41 1/4 In., Pair 715.00
Pitcher, 2 Cherries, Leaves, 8 In. 125.00
Pitcher, Albany Slip, 8 In. 150.00
Pitcher, Milk, Tree Bark Texture, Farm Scene, Blue Roses, 9 In. 275.00
Pitcher, Pennsylvania Bavarian Man 350.00
Pitcher, Pewter Lid, White Classical Figures, Lid Marked J. Deakins, 8 1/4 In. 110.00
Syrup, Gothic Design, Apostles, Pewter Lid, 1842, 7 5/8 In. 137.50
Teapot, Bamboo Branches, Bamboo Handle, White, 5 Cup 175.00
Teapot, Gothic Design, Apostles, 6 1/4 In. 44.00
Tile, Stylized Rosette Within Circle, Nottingham, 1770s, 5 1/4 In., Pair 1980.00
Tureen, Soup, Fritz Helmut Ehmeke, 1908 .... 650.00
Umbrella Stand, Overall Fruited Vines, Wreath Form Handles, 24 In. 4313.00

SAMPLERS were made in America from the early 1700s. The best examples
were made from 1790 to 1840. Long, narrow samplers are usually older than
square ones. Early samplers just had stitching or alphabets. The later
examples had numerals, borders, and pictorial decorations. Those with
mottoes are mid-Victorian. A revival of interest in the 1930s produced
simpler samplers, usually with mottoes.

ABCDE

Alphabet, Crosses, Elizabeth Manher, 1786, 9 3/4 In. x 7 3/4 In. 600.00
Alphabet, Deborah Longachre, Montgomery County, Penn., 1835, 17 1/2 x 13 In. 400.00
Alphabet, Elizabeth Buntin, Age 12, 10 1/2 x 8 In. 1430.00
Alphabet, Fannie Cary's, Richfield, 7 Years, March 22, 1858, Frame, 8 x 14 In. 205.00
Alphabet, Flowers, Homespun, Cornelia McGear, Born 1776, Frame, 17 x 15 In. 770.00
Alphabet, House, Silk & Linen, Anne Isbister, Age 12, 1809, Frame, 18 x 11 In. 605.00
Alphabet, Linen Homespun, June Potter, 1802, Frame, 15 1/2 x 13 1/4 In. 440.00
Alphabet, Linen Homespun, Mary Spencer, 1826, Frame, 14 x 11 In. 1210.00
Alphabet, Linen, Silk Thread, Sally Whitney, Age 11, Frame, 1797, 15 x 12 In. 1760.00
Alphabet, Log Cabin, Sarah Buckman, Bucks County, Penn., 8 x 17 1/2 In. 850.00
Alphabet, Margaret Buckman, 9th Month, 1816, 17 1/2 x 8 In. 375.00
Alphabet, Memorial, Mary Ann Wood, Age 9, 1838, Frame, 15 x 13 In. 660.00
Alphabet, Numbers, Sarah Baker, March 6, 1822, Frame, 18 x 14 In. 550.00
Alphabet, Numerals, Blue Fringe Edging, Silk On Linen, Framed, 18 x 18 In. 165.00
Alphabet, Quotes, M. Boyd, 1812, 13 x 17 1/4 In. 1000.00
Alphabet, Silk On Linen, Green Floss, Mary Bell, 1831, 3 1/4 x 3 1/2 In. 660.00
Alphabet, Verse, 1809, Maria Noyes, Age 7, Frame, 16 x 16 In. 1760.00

Alphabet, Verse, Birds, Eleanor Dyer, Bucks County, Penn., 1842, 17 1/4 In. 1100.00
Alphabet, Verse, Elizabeth Lanyon, Age 8, March 1820, Frame, 16 x 9 In. 742.50
Alphabet, Verse, Linen, Cecilia Peterson's Work 1839, Frame, 17 x 10 3/4 In. 495.00
Alphabet, Verse, Silk On Linen, Homespun, 1775, Frame, 23 x 14 In. 550.00
Alphabets, 3 Letter Series, Diamond Border, Frame, 1825, 13 x 9 In. 295.00
Alphabets, 3 Letter Series, Flower Basket, Eliza Howlett, Age 9, 1838, 12 x 10 In. .. 355.00
Alphabets, 3 Letter Series, Landscape Panels, Continental, Frame, 1804, 19 x 28 In. 412.00
Alphabets, Adam & Eve Figures, Flowers, Birds, Dated 1740s, 42 x 9 3/4 In. 1100.00
Alphabets, Floral Border, Silk On Linen Homespun, Frame, 10 1/2 x 19 1/2 In. 3300.00
Alphabets, Flowers, Birds, Initials, Silk On Homespun, 1836, Frame, 11 x 14 In. 275.00
Alphabets, Flowers, Chain Border, Anstice Wilson, Born 1811, Frame, 16 x 11 In. ... 275.00
Alphabets, Gingerbread, Christmas, Emma Vincent, 1872, Frame, Square, 11 In. 300.00
Alphabets, Hannah Currier, Born January 2, 1799, Age 11, 8 1/2 x 7 1/2 In. 1980.00
Alphabets, House, Dog, American Flag, Anna Waller, 12 Years, Frame, 18 In. 1550.00
Alphabets, House, Willows, Eliza Ann Hammond, Age 11, Frame, 21 x 17 In. 1815.00
Alphabets, Numbers, Floral Design, Dated 1671, Frame, 16 x 9 In. 1320.00
Alphabets, Verse, Vining Border, Trees, Sarah Frend 1789, Frame, 17 x 12 In. 247.50
Barnyard Scene, Dated 1720, 12 x 15 In. 1500.00
Berlin Work, 8 Wool-Stitched Squares, 10 x 7 1/2 In. 175.00
Berlin Work, House, Cat, Wreath, People, Taste Not, Touch Not, 1850, 10 1/2 In. 295.00
Black Alphabets, Mary Carver, Silk On Homespun, Frame, 12 x 11 In. 467.00
Brick Building, Center Spray Of Flowers, Hannah E. Nye, 1838, 19 x 16 3/4 In. 920.00
Brick House, Linen, Silk Stitches, Emma C. Potter, Frame, 1830, 17 3/4 x 15 In. 2645.00
Buildings, Verse, Wool On Canvas, Frame, Eva Aged 10, 1885, 21 1/2 x 15 1/4 In. ... 72.00
Cornucopia Border, Lois Newhall, 12 Years, Framed, 1808, 15 1/2 x 16 In. 605.00
Eliza P.W. McClung, Wool On Punched Paper, 1853, 25 1/2 x 21 In. 550.00
Family Record, Collins Family, Gilt Frame, 1784, 17 3/4 x 17 3/4 In. 175.00
Family Record, Floral Border, Homespun, Hannah Ball 1798, Frame, 21 x 17 In. 495.00
Family Record, Genealogical, Mary E. Adams, Age 10 Yrs., 1825, 17 1/2 x 18 In. ... 1210.00
Floral & Vine Border, Olive Hardley, 11 Years, Frame, 1820, 16 1/4 x 17 In. 1100.00
Floral Border, Phebe M. Hayward, Age 12, August 6, 1828, 19 x 18 In. 632.00
Floral Border, Rebekah Parker, Age 14, 1820, Frame, 15 3/4 x 15 3/4 In. 715.00
Flowers, Birds, Cherubs, Ana Hall, 1836, Frame, 18 1/4 x 14 In. 880.00
Flowers & Baskets, Sara Waldner, Dated 1900, Frame, 29 In. 975.00
Hearse, Buds, Crown, Silk On Linen Homespun, Frame, 16 1/2 x 25 1/2 In. 1485.00
Group Of Images, Shield With Lions, Frame, Rec.e.g. Arno, 1774, 19 1/4 x 16 1/4 In. 770.00
Margaret E. Earnest, Petit Point, Flowers In Garlands, Frame, 15 1/2 x 14 1/2 In. .. 375.00
Motto, Garland, Leaves, Beaded, Blue, Natural Punched Ground, Germany, Frame ... 135.00
Needlework, Elizabeth Stockman, Born Feb. 3 1816, Age 12, 9 3/4 x 7 In. 880.00
Needlework, Priscilla Stearns Born May 14, 1806 In Bethel, 11 x 13 In. 1210.00
Pots Of Flowers, Landscape, Thomazine Everhart, Age 9, 1834, 17 1/2 x 17 In. 1375.00
Silk On Homespun Linen, Adam & Eve, Catherine Carpenter, Age 9 Yrs., Frame 2100.00
Silk Threads, Linen, Ashvah E. Potter, Frame, 13 3/4 x 13 1/2 In. 302.50
Strawberry Border, Alphabets, Verse, Mary Kates, 1814, Age 9, 23 x 22 In. 660.00
Symbols, Witch, Horse, Elephant, Crucifix, All Wool, Frame, 22 x 23 In. 302.50
Verse, Flower Border, Linen Homespun, Thomasin Lenn, Frame, 30 1/2 x 25 In. 220.00
Verse, Garden, Willows, Vine Border, Lydia Kephart, 1829, 21 In. Square 5000.00
Verse, Homespun, Floral Border, Hannah Ware, Sept. 29, 1760s, 29 x 24 In. 302.50
Verse, Martha Wood, Aged 12 Years, Sept. 28, 1855, Frame, 19 x 15 1/2 In. 325.00
Verse, On The Last Day, Frame, Sophia Fisher's Work, 1807, 14 1/4 x 14 1/4 In. 450.00
Verse, Stylized Animals, Elizabeth Yost, 1836, 21 1/2 x 17 1/2 In. 2760.00
Verse, Vine Border, Catherine Carpenter, Age 9, 1787, Frame, 17 x 18 In. 2310.00
Wool & Silk, Death Of A Sister, July 6, 1836, Frame, 18 1/4 x 18 1/2 In. 660.00

SAMSON and Company, a French firm specializing in the reproduction of collectible wares of many countries and periods, was founded in Paris in the early nineteenth century. Chelsea, Meissen, Famille Verte, and Chinese Export porcelain are some of the wares that have been reproduced by the company. The firm uses a variety of marks on the reproductions. It is still in operation.

Box, Pin, Courting Couple On Lid, Floral Still Life On Body, 4 In. 132.00
Bulb Pot, Dome Cover, Polychrome Applied Flower Holders, c.1880, 11 1/2 In., Pr. . 660.00

Candelabra, Young Man & Woman, Gilt Bronze Mounted, 10 3/4 In., Pair 345.00
Dish, Worcester Scale, Peacocks, Incised Mark, 19th Century, Oval 357.00
Figurine, Monkey Conductor, Salopian Mark, 1850, 5 In. 210.00
Ginger Jar, Panels Of Birds & Flowers, Gilt Bronze Rim, 17 In., Pair 4025.00
Group, Europa & Bull, 19th Century 690.00
Plate, Armorial Style, Polychrome & Gold, 9 In. 210.00
Plate, Colored Cocks, Leaves, Green Washed Ground, 1890s, 9 3/16 In., 12 Piece 460.00
Vase, Beaker, Chinese Style, Enameled Figural Scene, Ormolu Base, 9 In., Pair 1430.00

SANDWICH GLASS is any of the myriad types of glass made by the Boston
and Sandwich Glass Works in Sandwich, Massachusetts, between 1825 and
1888. It is often very difficult to be sure whether a piece was really made at
the Sandwich factory because so many types were made there and similar
pieces were made at other glass factories. Additional pieces may be listed
under Pressed Glass and in related categories.

Bowl, Squared Frosted Briar Handles, 9 1/4 In. 450.00
Candlestick, Crucifix, Opalescent 250.00
Candlestick, Opaque Starch Blue Hexagonal Socket, Opaque Base, 8 In. 467.50
Compote, Horn Of Plenty, Flint, 9 x 10 1/2 In. 350.00
Dish, Lace, Oval, 2 7/8 In. 539.00
Epergne, Snake Coils Pedestal & Bowl, 17 In. 395.00
Lamp, Base, Cranberry To Clear, 9 1/2 In. 825.00
Lamp, Camphene, Rose Overlaid, Triple Cut 330.00
Lamp, Kerosene, Blue Pedestal, Lavender Font 4070.00
Lamp, Whale Oil, Pewter Double Wick Burner, Sawtooth, Pair 575.00
Perfume Bottle, Hexagonal, 6 In. 825.00
Plate, Blue, Lace, 2 5/8 In. 115.00
Punch Bowl, 3-Mold, Geometric, 1820-1830, 9 In. 880.00
Salt Boat, Lafayette, B & S Glass Co., Blue 860.00
Salt Boat, Opalescent Purple, Mottled 605.00
Syrup, Star & Buckle 110.00
Tieback, Opalescent, 2 1/4 In., Pair 75.00
Toothpick, 3-Mold, Blown 125.00
Toothpick, Moss Rose, Milk Glass 40.00
Tureen, Cover, Underplate, Lace, 3 In. 126.00
Vase, Thumbprint, Canary Yellow, Flint, 11 1/2 In., Pair 770.00

SARREGUEMINES is the name of a French town that is used as part of a
china mark. Utzschneider and Company, a porcelain factory, made ceramics
in Sarreguemines, Lorraine, France, from about 1775. Transfer-printed wares
and majolica were made in the nineteenth century. The nineteenth-century
pieces, most often found today, usually have colorful transfer-printed
decorations showing peasants in local costumes.

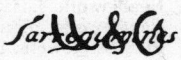

Basket, Quilted, Leopard Skin Crystallization, 9 In. 250.00
Bowl, Raised Fruits, Square, 9 1/4 In. 98.00
Bowl, Strawberries & Leaves Exterior, Yellow Interior, Marked, 14 In. 190.00
Bust, Madonna & Child, Pink Bisque 25.00

Sarreguemines, Oyster Plate,
Dark Green, 9 3/4 In., Pair

◆◆◆◆◆◆◆◆◆◆◆◆◆◆◆◆◆◆◆◆◆◆

Remove the handles from jalou-
sie or casement windows to
make them more burglar proof.

◆◆◆◆◆◆◆◆◆◆◆◆◆◆◆◆◆◆◆◆◆◆

Candlestick, Glazed Yellow Ware, Silver Luster, 8 In., Pair 300.00
Figurine, Praying Madonna, Standing, 15 In. 90.00
Fishbowl, Dark Green, 8 In. 27.50
Humidor, French Peasants, Unglazed, 1870s, 7 In. 285.00
Oyster Plate, Dark Green, 9 3/4 In., Pair .... *Illus* 200.00
Pitcher, Etna, Arts & Crafts Design, Brown Crystalline, 7 In. 195.00
Pitcher, Face, 8 1/2 In. 220.00
Pitcher, Frog On Melon, 8 1/2 In. 522.50
Pitcher, Rooster, 8 1/2 In. 385.00
Tureen, Cover, Duck, 8 1/2 x 11 In. 330.00
Vase, Clear Amber Brown Glaze, Blue Interior, Signed, 6 1/2 In. 33.00
Vase, Fisheye Pattern, Green Ground, Marked, 11 1/2 In., Pair 550.00
Vase, Folded Over Rim, Crystalline Glaze On 3/4ths Of Body, 6 3/4 In. 750.00
Wreath, Grave, Neoclassical Form, 12 In. 975.00

SASCHA BRASTOFF made decorative accessories, ceramics, enamels on copper, and plastics of his own design. He headed a factory, Sascha Brastoff of California, Inc., in West Los Angeles, from 1953 until about 1973. He died in 1993.

Sascha Brastoff

Ashtray, 2 Igloos, Ceramic, 9 1/2 In. 25.00
Ashtray, Blue & Gold Ray Design, White Ground, Ceramic, 5 In. 26.00
Ashtray, Clamshell Shape, Glass, Gold & Black 30.00
Ashtray, Dove Design, Oval, Ceramic, 8 1/4 In. 43.00
Ashtray, Houses, Ceramic, Signed 60.00
Ashtray, Leaf Design, Hooded, Green Ground, Ceramic 30.00
Ashtray, Mosaic, Ceramic 14.00
Bowl, 3 Pagodas, 3 Feet, Ceramic, 7 In. 30.00
Bowl, Alaska, Igloo, Ceramic 45.00
Bowl, Leaf, Hand Painted, Large, Ceramic 75.00
Bowl, Western Design, Gold, Glass, 3 x 8 In. 60.00
Cigarette Holder, Pipe Shape, Matching Tray, Stylized Design 55.00
Cup & Saucer, Gold Trim, Ceramic 35.00
Dish, Flowers, Brick Glaze, Ceramic, 6 In. 28.00
Dish, Horse, Square, Green Ground, Ceramic, 6 1/2 In. 52.00
Figurine, Owl, Amber, Signed, 14 3/4 In. 200.00
Head Vase, Abstract, Ceramic, 10 In. 160.00
Lamp, Rooster, Gold, 18 In. 250.00
Place Setting For 8, Yellow & Gold, Extra Serving Pieces, 50 Piece 400.00
Plate, Grape Cluster, Green, Ceramic, 11 In. 75.00
Plate, Roses & Leaves, Gold Painted, Glass 30.00
Service For 6, Dinner Set, Black, With Serving Pieces 850.00
Table Lighter & Cigarette Holder, Turquoise, Abstract Design, Ceramic 35.00
Toothpick, Enameled 45.00
Tray, Silver & Gold Floral, Glass, 8 In. 22.00
Vase, Alaska, Walrus, 6 In. 50.00
Vase, Blue Resin, 9 In., Pair 125.00
Vase, Gold On Gold 48.00

SATIN GLASS is a late nineteenth-century art glass. It has a dull finish that is caused by hydrofluoric acid vapor treatment. Satin glass was made in many colors and sometimes has applied decorations. Satin glass is also listed by factory name, such as Webb, or in the Mother-of-Pearl category in this book.

Basket, Lavender & White Cased, Blue & White Flowers, Ruffled Rim, 6 In. 225.00
Basket, Pink & White, Gold Decoration, Applied Handle, 7 x 8 In. 100.00
Biscuit Jar, Pink Cased, Diamond-Quilted Pattern 85.00
Bobeche, Citron, Fluted Rim, 3 1/2 In., 25 Piece 375.00
Bowl, Diamond-Quilted, Rainbow, Mother-Of-Pearl, Marked, 2 1/2 x 4 1/4 In. 700.00
Bowl, Ruffled Rim, Pink, 3 3/4 x 6 1/2 In. 20.00
Cruet, Diamond Pattern, Loop Handle, Mother-Of-Pearl, 1920, 8 In. 77.00
Dresser Jar, Rose Pink, Hinged, 5 x 5 In. 150.00
Pitcher, Guttate Pink, Clear Handle 185.00
Pitcher, Mother-Of-Pearl, Rainbow, 5 In. 60.00
Pitcher, Water, Quilt Design, Applied Handle, Frosted, Pink, 9 1/4 In. 100.00

Powder Box, Nude, Kneeling, Holding Garland	45.00
Rose Bowl, Deep Rose To Pale Pink, 2 1/4 x 2 1/2 In.	70.00
Rose Bowl, Deep Rose To Pink, 3 1/4 x 3 1/2 In.	130.00
Rose Bowl, Jack-In-The-Pulpit Rim, Citron To White, 5 1/2 x 5 3/4 In.	55.00
Rose Bowl, Leaf & Flower Design, Molded, Dark To Light Green, 3 x 4 In.	70.00
Rose Bowl, Petal Design, Molded, Blue To White, 4 x 4 In.	70.00
Vase, Bud, Enameled Orange Meadow Grass, Flowers, Flared, 6 In.	50.00
Vase, Bulbous Body, Slender Neck, Yellow With White Interior, 7 1/2 In.	145.00
Vase, Diamond-Quilted, Pinched Rim, Blue, Cut Velvet, 4 In.	60.00
Vase, Stick Neck, Peach To Rust, White Ground, c.1880, 10 In.	35.00
Vase, Twining Floral	185.00
Water Set, Diamond-Quilted, Mother-Of-Pearl, Apricot To White, 7 Piece	1300.00

SATSUMA is a Japanese pottery with a distinctive creamy beige crackled glaze. Most of the pieces were decorated with blue, red, green, orange, or gold. Almost all Satsuma found today was made after 1860. During World War I, Americans could not buy undecorated European porcelains. Women who liked to make hand painted porcelains at home began to decorate plain Satsuma. These pieces are known today as *American Satsuma*.

Bowl, Arhats, Gilt Decoration, Scalloped Rim, 19th Century, 7 In.	357.50
Bowl, Cobalt Ground, 19th Century, 5 1/2 In.	220.00
Bowl, Interior Legendary Scene, 19th Century, 5 In.	715.00
Bowl, Samurai In Battle, Greek Key Border, 19th Century, 6 In.	192.50
Box, Egg Shape, Cover, Dragons Inside And Outside, 19th Century, 3 In.	1540.00
Box, Scene & 14 Figures On Lid, Gold Halos, 3 1/8 In.	412.50
Dinner Set, For 11, 5 Arhats, Brocaded Robes, Brown Ground, Serving Pieces	875.00
Dish, Floral, Early 19th Century, 7 In.	550.00
Dish, Leaf- & Blossom-Shaped, Kozan, 6 In.	1100.00
Dish, Leaf Shape, Kinkozen, c.1900	145.00
Ewer, Cover, Floral Design, 15 In.	220.00
Figurine, Goddess, Standing, Polychromed & Gold Enamel, 9 1/2 In.	60.00
Figurine, Man, Pipe, Seated, Late Edo Period, 8 1/2 In.	1685.00
Incense Burner, Enamel Floral, Gold Slip, Foo Dog Handles & Finial, 10 In.	145.00
Jar, 14 Figures, 3 In.	247.00
Jar, Globular, Figures On Silver Ground, 19th Century, 4 In.	220.00
Jardiniere, Stand, Figural & Floral Design, 30 In.	165.00
Koro, Gold Dragons On Blue Waves, Wirework Cover, Shuzan, 3 In.	1650.00
Koro, Seated Sages, Wirework Cover, Hatori Sei Zo, 19th Century, 3 1/2 In.	550.00
Plate, 3 Arhats, Brown Ground, Kutani Style, 7 1/4 In.	8.00
Plate, Flying Cranes, Green & Red Floral, Scalloped, Edo Period, 1840, 7 In.	125.00
Punch Bowl, Cockerels In Center Roundel, Cranes, Scalloped Rim, 16 3/4 In.	1650.00
Sake Pot, Lappets, Early 19th Century, 2 1/2 In.	675.00
Salt, Blue & Orange Flower, Gold Exterior	16.00
Tea Set, Iris Decoration, 21 Piece	660.00
Teapot, Gilt, Jewel Blue Enameling, 4 1/4 In.	16.50
Toothpick, Owl, c.1900	225.00
Urn, Cover, Bird In Flight, 11 1/2 In.	160.00
Urn, Cover, Samurai Warriors, c.1910, 17 1/2 In.	250.00
Urn, Warriors Front, Landscape Reverse, Dragon Handles, 24 In.	1200.00
Vase, Animal Paneled, 12 In.	4125.00
Vase, Bijin Decoration, Gilt, Cobalt Background, Meiji Period, 6 1/4 In.	302.50
Vase, Cone Shape, Patterned Vertical Bands, Late 19th Century, 12 In.	220.00
Vase, Cover, Nobles, Metal Mounting, Handles & Finial, 19th Century, 25 In.	770.00
Vase, Egg Shape, Birds In Flight, Flowers, Grasses, Late 19th Century, 12 In.	440.00
Vase, Egg Shape, Flowering Branches, Brick Work, 19th Century, 13 In.	5225.00
Vase, Enamel & Gilded Design, 4 Scenes, 24 In.	2640.00
Vase, Flying Birds, Flora, 12 In..	610.00
Vase, Maidens, Flowering Trees, 7 1/2 In.	99.00
Vase, Monkey, Vine, Floral & Fruit Design, Bulbous, 19th Century, 21 In.	8250.00
Vase, Mountain & Lake Scene, Figures, 15 In.	180.00
Vase, Samurai Design, Floor, Large, 26 In.	5500.00
Vase, Samurai, Pheasant & Floral Design, Cylinder Form, 18 In., Pair	1540.00

Vase, Urn Shape, Raised Figures Of Elephants & Humans, Beaded, c.1900, 15 In. 605.00
Vase, Warrior On Side, Flowers Other Side, Scrolled Top, Fish Handles 200.00
Vase, Wirework Cover, Octagonal, Floral Reserves, 19th Century, 8 1/2 In. 3575.00
Vase, Woman In Flower Garden Scene, Polychrome Enamel, Wood Base, 10 In. 65.00

SATURDAY EVENING GIRLS, see Paul Revere Pottery

SCALES have been made to weigh everything from babies to gold. Collectors
search for all types. Most popular are small gold dust scales and special
grocery scales.

Baby, Angile Dile, Headlight Type 800.00
Baby, Matching Wicker Basket, Greenware, Hanson 150.00
Balance, 2 Circular Trays, Weights Box, Drawer, Jones & McDonald, Brass 1265.00
Balance, Brass & Iron, England, 21 In. 55.00
Balance, Brass, Cherry, Weights 105.00
Balance, Gillard, Brass & Mahogany, 19th Century 460.00
Balance, Hanging, Tin Pans, Wrought Iron, 18 In. 214.50
Balance, Laboratory, Glass Mahogany Case, Voland & Sons 315.00
Balance, Mahogany, Weights 250.00
Balance, Store, Stube, White Metal, Germany 45.00
Balance, Wrought Iron, Stamped A.N.O.D. 1868, 10 In. 83.00
Bathroom, Charlie The Tuna 45.00
Buffalo Hide, c.1880 .... 55.00
Candy, Cast Iron & Brass, Painted, Stars & Stripes, Tin Scoop, 2 Lb., 11 In. 467.00
Candy, International Business Machine, Canada 200.00
Candy, Iron, 2 Brass Scoops 195.00
Candy, National Store Specialty Co., Nickel Plated Cast Iron, 4 Lb., 14 In. 275.00
Candy, National, Store Specialty Co. 975.00
Candy, Sliding Bell Shaped, Red, Original Pan, 7 Lb. Capacity 65.00
Candy, Toledo No. 2 .... 125.00
Candy, Toledo, Countertop, 1930s 295.00
Candy, Wrigley's Spearmint Pepsin Gum, Red Repainted Tin, 4 Lb., 8 In. 660.00
Candy, Wrigley's Spearmint Pepsin Gum Embossed On Brass, Restored, Small 300.00
Chatillon, Brass 20.00
Chatillon, Painted Cast Iron, Stenciled Dial, 66 In. 205.00
Counter, National, Black, Iron, Chicopee Falls, Massachusetts 165.00
Eagle, Spring, Brass Face, Cast Iron, Hanging 9.50
Egg, Jiffy-Way, Box 20.00
Egg, Purina 35.00
Fairbanks, Brass Pan, 2 Sets Of Extra Weights, Cast Iron 137.50
Fairbanks, No. 3 .... 150.00
Glass Shelf, Sliding Door, Base Drawer, Balance, Chemical, Becker, 1938, 19 In. 220.00
Gold, Electronic, Portable, Battery-Operated, Up To 150 Grams, Hand-Held 140.00
Gold, Pocket, 1790 .... 120.00
Gold, Steel & Brass, Various Weights, Box, 6 In. 11.00
Grain, Winchester, Brass, With Bucket 235.00
Hanging, Buffalo Hide, Iron, Brass 70.00
Hanging, Round Brass Dial, Blue Pan 95.00
Henry Troemner, 30 Weights, Pans, Glass Case 300.00
Howe Scale Co., Brass Scoop, 1800s 155.00
Meat, Brass, England, 19th Century, 58 In. 2495.00
Mercury Athletic 800.00
Micrometer, Brass Plated, 10 Lb. 575.00
National, Automatic, Painted Cast Iron, Porcelain Sign & Dial, 68 In. 990.00
Oak Box, Weights, Small 69.00
Peerless Junior, 1 Cent, Porcelain Steel, Tile Platform, 63 In. 330.00
Penny, Floor Model 66.00
Pharmacy, Brass, Wood & Glass Case 225.00
Pharmacy, Cast Iron, Fancy 35.00
Pharmacy, Henry Troemner, Glass-Covered Marble Top 125.00
Pharmacy, Marble Top, Wooden Block, Brass Weights 115.00
Postal, Cast Iron, Brass Tray, Balance Beam 40.00

Postal, Liberty 15.00
Postal, Pelouze, 2 Cent Letters, 24 Oz., 1897 .... 20.00
Projecting Arms, 2 Dished Trays, Brass, Henry Troemner, 1840s, 25 1/2 In. 1380.00
Silver, 1 Troy Ounce Increments To 200 Troy, Brass Case 69.95
Steelyard, Brass 38.00
Store, U.S. Slicing Machine Co., White Enameled, Vertical Indicator 175.00
Texas, Wooden 25.00
Universal, Mechanical, Patent 1865, 8 x 8 x 5 1/2 In. 65.00
Weights, E.H. Sargent Co., Germany, 1920s, Case 95.00

SCHAFER & VATER, makers of small ceramic items, are best known for
their amusing figurals. The factory was located in Volkstedt-Rudolstadt,
Germany, from 1890 to 1962. Some pieces are marked with the crown and R
mark, but many are unmarked.

Ashtray, Googly-Eye Little Boy, Hugging Girl, 3 1/4 In. 150.00
Bottle, Boot Shape, Mustachioed Man 150.00
Bottle, Monk Pouring Drink, 5 In. 110.00
Box, Cover, Woman Holding Rose, Wreaths & Bows Base, 3 1/4 In. 95.00
Creamer, Maid With Keys, Blue & White, 3 1/2 In. 100.00
Creamer, Witch With Fan, Blue 95.00
Cup & Saucer, Pink Cartouches On Woman's Head Matte 150.00
Decanter, Full Figure Skeleton, Tray, Shot Glass, Brown Glaze 275.00
Figurine, Mr. Tenor, Black Tuxedo & Shoes, Red Stockings, Bug Eyes, 8 In. 125.00
Hair Receiver, Cameo Heads, Jasper, 3 Colors 75.00
Hair Receiver, Cupids On Cover, Faces Around Bottom 125.00
Hair Receiver, Lavender & Light Green, Jewels, Signed 35.00
Hair Receiver, Tricolor Jasperware 65.00
Hatpin Holder, Pink Egyptian Heads, 4 1/2 In. 170.00
Hatpin Holder, Woman's Face Both Sides 248.00
Humidor, Woman Cameo Ovals 125.00
Match Holder, Blind Man Holding Kettle 140.00
Match Holder & Ashtray, Couple, Heads Under Hat, 3 3/4 In. 175.00
Mug, Stag's Head, Embossed, Beige, Brown & Rust, 3 1/4 x 3 In. 75.00
Pin Tray, Skeleton & Coffin, Brockton Fair, If You Please, 1912, 4 x 5 In. 135.00
Pitcher, Dressed Cow, Signed, Small 25.00
Pitcher, Dutch Girl Holding Jug, Basket On Back, 5 In. 100.00
Pitcher, Maid With Jug & Keys, Multicolor, 3 1/2 In. 98.00
Pitcher, Milk, Cow Dressed As Woman, 6 1/2 In. 195.00
Toothpick, Egg Shape, Jasper, Jewels 65.00
Tray, Pin, Black Skeleton Holds Open Coffin, 1912, 5 In. 135.00
Tray, Pin, Egyptian 135.00
Vase, Grecian Woman & Child, 6 In. 145.00
Vase, Man, Woman & 2 Cupids, Blue Jasperware, 6 1/2 In. 150.00

SCHNEIDER Glassworks was founded in 1903 at Epinay-sur-Seine, France,
by Charles and Ernest Schneider. Art glass was made between 1903 and
1930. The company still produces clear crystal glass.

Bowl, Air-Bubble Design, Etched Cover Of Rectangles, Signed, 6 1/2 In. 745.00
Compote, Double-Knob Amethyst Pedestal, Lime Green, 8 1/2 In. 595.00
Compote, Red & Purple Frosted, 15 In. Diam. 950.00
Flower Frog, Woman, Germany 90.00
Pitcher, Art Deco, Spherical, Blue, Orange, Amethyst Handle, 6 In. 300.00
Shade, Lamp, Inverted On Base, Held By Cherub, Orange To Frosted, 18 In. 275.00
Sherbet Set, Tray, Purple, Pink & White, Signed, 7 Piece 450.00
Vase, Cameo, Egg Shape, Pastel Orange Layers, Etched Berries, Mottled, 24 In. 1320.00
Vase, Cut Geometric Design, Chevron Border, Flared, Signed, 8 1/4 In. 865.00
Vase, Geometric Design, Candy Cane Mark, 4 In. 495.00
Vase, Orange To Dark Blue, Signed, 10 In. 375.00
Vase, Striated Base, Slender Neck, Cushion Foot, Signed, 17 3/4 In. 5175.00
Vase, Swirled Amethyst & Bubbles, Signed, 8 1/2 x 8 1/2 In. 550.50
Vase, Yellow Mum, Green Foliage, Black Trellis, Acid Etched, Red, 12 1/2 In. 295.00
Vase, Yellow, Orange, 12 In. 750.00

SCIENTIFIC INSTRUMENTS of all kinds are included in this category. Other categories such as Barometer, Binoculars, Dental, Nautical, Medical, and Thermometer may also price scientific apparatus.

Armillary Sphere, Hand Forged, Lead, 19th Century, 2 Ft. Diam.	5800.00
Astro Chronometer, Ackermann, c.1820	1450.00
Compass, Hinged Lid, W. & L.E. Gurley, Troy, New York, 3 x 3 In.	110.00
Compass, Map Measure, Mind Matter Corp., Germany, Leather Case	55.00
Compass, Marine, Pelorus, Brass, Carrying Handle, 10 x 10 In.	320.00
Compass, Surveyor's, Brass, T. Greenough, 1735, 4 1/2 In.	2900.00
Compass, Surveyor's, Signed Hagger & Brother, Brass	1045.00
Compass, Surveyor's, Thomas Greenough, Wooden, 1850s, 13 In.	1210.00
Compass, Surveyor's, With Level, Brass, Signed & Cased, 7 1/2 In.	770.00
Dividers, Brass, Steel Tips, Benjamin Martin, Case, 6 1/2 In.	795.00
Drawing Set, Architect's, K & E, Velvet Case, 11 Piece	35.00
Field Glass, 50 mm, U.S. Naval Gun Factory, Sunshades, LeMaire	45.00
Geiger Counter, RCA, 1954	90.00
Heliometer, Multiple Dial, Wood & Brass Fittings, Risch, 1868	3250.00
Hydrometer, Sikes, British Navy	295.00
Inclinometer, Rufus Porter, Paper Face	1540.00
Magnifier, Machinist's, Swivel Stand, Desk, Brass, 4 In.	80.00
Micrometer, Crystal & Split Lens Eyepiece, Dollond, c.1825	1650.00
Micrometer, Inspection, Brass, Focus Thread, 1960s, 5 In.	195.00
Microscope, 4 Eyepieces, Leaflet In German, Carl Zeiss Jena	260.00
Microscope, Bausch & Lomb, Double Pillar, No. 11, Brass, c.1880	525.00
Microscope, Bausch.& Lomb, No. 26690, Wooden Case, Chart, 1880s	525.00
Microscope, Binocular, Brass & Cast Iron, Carl Zeiss Jena, 1870s	180.00
Microscope, Cased Brass, Slides, Tweezer, Lens, 19th Century, Case	395.00
Microscope, Student, 10X Eyepiece, Bausch & Lomb, 20th Century	70.00
Microscope, Student, Brass, Bausch & Lomb, 1876	390.00
Octant, Ivory Scale, Ebony & Rosewood, W. Kin, Dublin, 1771	4850.00
Octant, Spencer, Browning & Rust, London, Green Painted Case	935.00
Ophthalmoscope, 19 Position Wheel, Paxton, C.1880	295.00
Periscope, M16G, World War I, Erfle Eyepiece	45.00
Planetarium, Literature, Laing, c.1900, 12 x 19 In.	6050.00
Quadrant, Brass, Ebony, Thos. Jones, Liverpool, Stenciled Case	575.00
Quadrant, Navigational Backstaff, C. Elliot, Walnut, Cherry	8250.00
Refractor, Alvan Clark Type, Erecting Eyepiece, Case	4400.00
Refractor, Brass Barrel Assembly, Bardou, 3 In.	300.00
Refractor, Brass Cell, Lens Cap, Clark, 3 In.	1900.00
Refractor, Jaegers, Aluminum Tube	600.00
Ruler, Folding, Brass, Millimeters, Lenoir, Open-10 In.	595.00
Sextant, C. Plath, Case, 9 x 12 In.	675.00
Sextant, Ivory Veneer, Accessories, Case, Hutchison, c.1870	825.00
Signal Set, Western Union Telegraph, Box	75.00
Telescope, 1 Drawer, Gilt Leaves, Painted, Stenciled Wood, 43 In.	575.00
Telescope, 3 Draw, English, Wood & Brass, 1850s	247.00
Telescope, 45 mm Aperture, 4 Draw, Brass, 1870s, 36 In.	85.00
Telescope, Bardou & Son, Tripod, Mahogany, France, 63 In.	1430.00
Telescope, Big Bertha, Bulova Watch Co., Model 326, 1943	190.00
Telescope, Black Leather Covering, Brass, 16 In.	27.50
Telescope, Dolland, London, Day Or Night, Brass, 1830s, 35 In.	130.00
Telescope, Gundlach Optical Co., Tripod, Brass, 19th Century	1375.00
Telescope, Lawrence May Co., Brass, Leather Case	99.00
Telescope, Pancractic presentation, leather bound, c. 1860, 31 in	950.00
Telescope, Single-Drawer, Cased Brass, 19th Century, 26 In.	357.00
Telescope, Spenser, Browning & Rust, Draw Tube, Sliding Covers	210.00
Telescope, Tripod, Brass, G.D. King, Boston, Case	1430.00
Theodolite, Buff & Buff Co., Patent 1900, Brass, Case, 13 1/2 In.	1250.00
Transit, Surveyor's, W. & L.E. Gurley, Leather Case	120.00
Transit, Wissler, St. Louis, Box	110.00
Transit Level, Bostrom-Brady Mfg., Atlanta, Ga., Brass, 1913	195.00
Transit Level, K & E, Germany, Fitted Case	225.00

Transit With Compass, K & E, Brass-Bound Box, 1940 .... 395.00
Vibrating Gong, Polarized, Faraday, 11 In. Diam. 65.00

SCRIMSHAW is bone or ivory or whale's teeth carved by sailors and others for entertainment during the sailing-ship days. Some scrimshaw was carved as early as 1800. There are modern scrimshanders making pieces today on bone, ivory, or plastic. Other pieces may be found in the Ivory and Nautical categories.

Basket, Sewing, 6 In. Diam. 2550.00
Billiken, Whale Tooth, Brass Penholder Centerpiece, Alaska 325.00
Block, Whalebone, Double Sheaves, c.1840, 13 3/4 In. 450.00
Block, Whalebone, Iron Thimble, c.1830, 3 3/4 x 2 1/2 In. 1590.00
Blubber Hook, Whalebone, Iron, 19th Century, 12 In. 1100.00
Blubber Mincer, Whalebone 550.00
Bodkin, Carved Fist, Round And Square Sections, 19th Century, 4 In. 192.00
Bodkin, Fist, Left & Right Hands, Ivory, 19th Century, 3 1/2 In., Pair 330.00
Bodkin, Whale, Crosshatched Top, 4 Openwork Columns, 4 3/4 In. 385.00
Bone, Tool, Engraved Scene Of Ship, 5 3/8 In. 93.50
Box, Ditty, Inlaid Geometric Shapes Lid, Whalebone, c.1850, 4 x 8 1/2 In. 3985.00
Box, Ditty, Open-Carved Whalebone, Oval, c.1840, 4 3/4 x 10 1/4 In. 5600.00
Box, Equestrian, Fox Hunt Scene, Cheltenham Races, Ivory, 4 x 3 In. 495.00
Box, Polar Bear Finial Cover, Baleen & Walrus, 4 1/2 In. 715.00
Busk, 3 Whaling Ships, Leaf Vines Border, 19th Century, 14 In. 550.00
Busk, Columns Of Soldiers, Marching, Red Jackets, 19th Century 4400.00
Busk, Engraved Full-Length Woman, Ship, Lighthouse, 12 15/16 .... 885.00
Busk, Figure Of Columbia, Flowers, Lighthouse & Lady Slipper, 12 1/2 In. 440.00
Busk, Houses, Trees, Plants, 19th Century, 13 In. 2000.00
Busk, Inlaid Sealing Wax, Geometric & Fish Design, Wooden, 13 3/4 In. 825.00
Busk, Mourning Scene, Bird & Primrose, Engraved, 19th Century, 14 In. 470.00
Busk, Verse, Architectural Views, Geometric & Floral Design, 15 In. 1650.00
Busk, Whalebone, Decorated With Lady & Gentleman, Inscribed, 12 In. 165.00
Busk, Whalebone, Memorial, Flowers, Clipper Ship, 19th Century, 13 1/2 In. 1100.00
Candlestick, Pickwick, Whale, Red & Green Lines, Ivory Candles, 3 1/4 In., Pair 880.00
Candlestick, Whale, Walnut & Abalone Base, 19th Century, 8 1/4 In. 1870.00
Chest, Storage, Mahogany 6600.00
Clothespin, Whalebone, 19th Century, 4 3/4 In., 3 Piece 495.00
Clothespin, Whalebone, 7 Piece 302.50
Clothespin, Whalebone, Man In Top Hat Form, 5 1/4 In. 495.00
Cribbage Board, Carved Walrus Ivory Tusk, Animals, 1890s 7500.00
Crochet Hook, Ball Top, Reeded Carvings, Whale Ivory, 19th Century, 4 In. 137.00
Dipper, Coconut Shell, Ivory & Wooden Handle 467.50
Gong, Dinner, Hippopotamus Tusk 220.00
Jagging Wheel, Whale's Fluke Handle, Hand Held Fork, Whale, 6 1/2 In. 1925.00
Jagging Wheel, Whalebone, Hollow Handle, Pierced Scroll Carving, 9 In. 3300.00
Knitting Needles, Baleen & Wood-Turned Sections, 19th Century, 14 In., Pair 357.00
Ladle, Whalebone & Coconut Shell, 19th Century, 15 3/4 In. 330.00
Orange Peeler, Whalebone, Catalina Island, Patent No. 2260, 1897, 5 1/2 In. 695.00
Pickwick, Candlestick Form, Pair 5225.00
Pie Crimper, Baleen Banded Handle 412.50
Pie Crimper, Whale Ivory, Cutout Hearts, c.1840, 5 In. 1200.00
Pie Crimper, Whale Ivory, Lady's Leg Shape, Iron Stand, 1850, 5 In. 2400.00
Pipe, Whale, 6 In. 440.00
Plaque, Engraved Clipper Ship, 19th Century, 6 1/2 x 10 1/2 In. 2000.00
Rolling Pin, Exotic Wood, Ivory & Tortoiseshell 715.00
Rolling Pin, Whalebone Handles, Tropical Wood, c.1840, 16 In. 675.00
Shaker, Whale, Graduated Octagon, Dome Cover, c.1773 .... 935.00
Swift, Double, Whalebone, Round Turned Clamp, 19th Century, 16 In. 2200.00
Swift, Whalebone Clamp, Tortoise & Mother-Of-Pearl Inlay, 1840, 22 1/2 In. 3950.00
Tooth, Basket Of Flowers, Red & Green, Ivory, 4 1/2 In. 192.00
Tooth, Walrus, Vicksburg Paddleboat, Confederate Designs, 1880 .... 60.00
Tooth, Whale's, Battle Of Lake Erie Scenes, 1801, 6 In. 6325.00
Tooth, Whale's, Captain Howe Portrait, c.1860, 6 In. 6050.00
Tooth, Whale's, Clipper John Adams, Square-Rigged Ship, c.1870, 4 1/2 In. 4510.00

Tooth, Whale's, Clipper Ship Under Sail, 5 In. 330.00
Tooth, Whale's, Death Of Sir J. Moor, Military Symbols, American Ship, 7 In. 210.00
Tooth, Whale's, Engraved, Two-Masted Ship, Fashionable Lady, 4 1/2 In. 715.00
Tooth, Whale's, Essay On Man, c.1845, 6 3/4 In. 3300.00
Tooth, Whale's, Fashionable Lady, 19th Century, 5 1/2 In. 495.00
Tooth, Whale's, Full-Length Portraits On 4 Sides 2420.00
Tooth, Whale's, Girls Holding Balloons & Flowers, 7 1/2 In., Pair 1705.00
Tooth, Whale's, Naval Battle, War Of 1812, Rosewood Stand, c.1840, 6 1/2 In. 3300.00
Tooth, Whale's, Polychrome, 4 Warships, Wooden Mount, c.1845, 6 3/4 In. 4400.00
Tooth, Whale's, Polychrome, Sawtooth Band, Constitution Liberty, 5 1/2 In. 2750.00
Tooth, Whale's, Portrait Of Sailor, Black Iron Base, c.1850, 5 In. 690.00
Tooth, Whale's, Rescue Scene, Fort Background, c.1830, 7 1/4 x 3 In. 4450.00
Tooth, Whale's, Rigged Ship, For Grog Is Our Larbord, c.1840, 5 1/2 In. 3575.00
Tooth, Whale's, Ship & 4 Longboats, Sperm Whale At Bottom, 6 1/2 In. 3300.00
Tooth, Whale's, Whaleman's Woe, 3 Anchors, Stand, 19th Century, 4 3/4 In. 1870.00
Tooth, Whale's, Woman Acrobat, 1920 .... 2035.00
Tooth, Whaling Ship & Longboats, Capturing Sperm Whales, 8 1/4 In. 3975.00
Tusk, Indian Woman, Minnehaha, 19 In. 302.00
Tusk, Walrus, American Flag, Ship, 2 Female Portraits Other Side, 13 1/2 In. 2800.00
Tusk, Walrus, Animals & Ship, 19th Century 1750.00
Tusk, Walrus, Slave & His Master, Polychrome Paint, Pair 6600.00
Tusk, Walrus, Woman, Seated, Primitive, Scandinavian Style, 6 3/4 In. 160.00
Walrus, Cribbage Board, Animals, Late 1890s 7500.00
Walrus Tusk, Giraffe, Elephant & Leopard, Native Huts, 17 In. 1760.00
Watch Hutch, Whale Bone & Whale Ivory, Tall Clock Form, 35 1/4 In. 7475.00
Whale, Cup & Ball, Toy, William H. Chappell, 1855 .... 4400.00
Whistle & Rattle, Ivory, 4 In. 22.00
Winder, Thread, 10 1/2 In. 1155.00

SEBASTIAN MINIATURES were first made by Prescott W. Baston in 1938 in
Marblehead, Massachusetts. More than 400 different designs have been
made, and collectors search for the out-of-production models. The mark may
say *Copr. P. W. Baston U.S.A.,* or *P. W. Baston, U.S.A.,* or *Prescott W. Baston.*
Sometimes a paper label was used.

Candy Store 95.00
David Copperfield & Wife .... 5.00 to 40.00
Doctor .... 65.00 to 125.00
Gibson Girl 65.00
Lancaster Bible College 35.00
Little Girl, Lamppost, Signed 87.00
Mr. Obocel 75.00
Pioneer Couple 20.00
Plymouth Plantation 125.00
Scrooge .... 25.00 to 30.00
Shoemaker, Penholder 45.00
Swan Boat .... 37.50 to 175.00

SEG, see Paul Revere Pottery category

SEVRES porcelain has been made in Sevres, France, since 1769. Many
copies of the famous ware have been made. The name originally referred to
the works of the Royal Porcelain factory. The name now includes any of the
wares made in the town of Sevres, France. The entwined lines with a center
letter used as the mark is one of the most forged marks in antiques. Be very
careful to identify Sevres by quality, not just by mark.

Bowl, Blue & Cream Mother-Of-Pearl, Crystal Foot, 6 1/2 x 8 In. 650.00
Box, Jewel, Courting Scene In Wreath Of Gold, Marked, 3 x 5 1/2 In. 500.00
Box, Jewel, Stagecoach On Lid, Landscapes On Sides, 12 In. 1380.00
Bread Basket, Reticulated, Center Foliate Reserve, Painted & Parcel Gilt, 10 In. 115.00
Centerpiece, Figural Oval Panels, Scrolled Handles, Pierced Rim 18 In. 5195.00
Clock, Ormolu, Porcelain, 2 Vases, 1880, 7 1/4 In., 3 Piece 850.00
Coffee Can & Saucer, Central Vitruvian Scroll, c.1780, 5 1/2 In. 1150.00
Compote, Floral & Figural Reserved, Acanthus-Form Handles, 10 In. 685.00

Sevres, Urn, 5 Dancing Maidens,
Cupid, 32 1/2 In.

◆◆◆◆◆◆◆◆◆◆◆◆◆◆◆◆◆◆◆◆◆◆◆

Fill an old pair of panty hose with
cedar shavings from the pet
store and put it in your closet to
discourage moths.

◆◆◆◆◆◆◆◆◆◆◆◆◆◆◆◆◆◆◆◆◆◆◆

Cooler, Fruit, Multicolored Foliage, Gilded Foliate Borders, c.1810, 12 1/2 In., Pr. 2860.00
Decanter, Iris Blossoms & Leaves, Silver-Mounted Neck, Signed, 10 1/2 In. 575.00
Garniture Set, Urn Form Clock, Courting Scene Reserves, Masks, 3 Piece 2420.00
Group, Allegorical, Barian, 18th Century 3500.00
Lamp, Electric, Cobalt Blue, Hand Painted Design, 20 In. 300.00
Lamp, Painted Scenes Of Lovers, Landscape Panels, Gilt Bronze, 31 In., Pair 925.00
Plaque, Cameo, Napoleon, Blue Ground, Circular Frame, 1810, 10 In. 825.00
Plate, 2 Men Seated In Front Of House, 1837, 8 1/2 In. 70.00
Urn, 5 Dancing Maidens, Cupid, 32 1/2 In. .... *Illus* 2500.00
Urn, Amphora Shape, Ormolu Mounted, Cupid, Maiden, Scene, c.1880, 26 1/2 In. 3025.00
Urn, Cover, Continuo's, Painted, Figural, Scrolled Handles, 1890s, 38 In. 4000.00
Urn, Cover, Courtyard Scene Panels, Bronze Mounted, 18 1/4 In., Pair 1980.00
Urn, Cover, Figural Oval Panel, Landscape On Reverse, Gilt Bronze, 29 In., Pr. 6900.00
Urn, Cover, Figural Oval Panel, Landscape Panel, Gilt Bronze, 35 In. 5500.00
Urn, Figural Panels, Cream Ground, Fitted As Lamp, 31 In. 4300.00
Urn, Finial Cover, Ormolu Mounted, Scenes, 20 In., Pair 2900.00
Urn, Palace, Shades Of Pink & Turquoise On Ivory, S. Bellanger, 34 In. 4657.00
Vase, Cover, Allegorical Figures, Bronze Mounted, 13 In. 862.00
Vase, Cover, Flowers, Dark Green Ground, Shield-Shaped Body, 26 In. 6900.00
Vase, Cover, Portrait Of Woman & Cupid In Garden, Blue & Gold, Signed, 15 In. 350.00
Vase, Gilt Band Of Leaves At Shoulder, Gilt Leaves & Blossoms, 1914, 17 In. 1380.00
Vase, Lamp Mounted, Porcelain, Ormolu, Bleu Celeste Ground, 19 In. 350.00
Vase, Mantel, Porcelain, Gilt Bronze Mounted, Royal Blue, 10 In., Pair 3525.00
Vase, Turquoise Banded Figural Reserves, Mounted As Lamp, 23 In. 1385.00

SEWER TILE figures were made by workers at the sewer tile and pipe
factories in the Ohio area during the late nineteenth and early twentieth
centuries. Figurines, small vases, and cemetery vases were favored. Often the
finished vase was a piece of the original pipe with added decorations and
markings. All types of sewer tile work are now considered folk art by
collectors.

Bank, Pig, Seated, Green-Brown Salt Glaze, 9 1/4 In. 423.00
Bank, Rabbit, Incised, 10 1/2 In. 412.00
Bookends, Indian, Headdress, 5 1/2 In. 45.00
Bookends, Tooled, 4 1/2 In. 71.50
Bowl, 4-Footed, Incised Elwood Oct. 6, 1949, Oblong, 17 1/2 In. 82.50
Brick, Bust Of Lincoln, 4 x 8 1/4 In. 181.00
Brick, Newell's Patent Foot Warmer, Rounded Top, 9 In. 11.00
Cat, Unglazed, Traces Of Yellow Paint, 7 1/4 In. 137.50
Desk Set, Outdoor Fireplace Shape, Louis Staley, 1946, 8 1/4 In. 71.50

Desk Set, Pig, Tan Glaze, 5 1/2 In. 27.50
Dog, Seated, 7 In. 44.00
Dog, Seated, Dark Glaze, 10 1/2 In. 330.00
Dog, Seated, Flat Back, 11 3/4 In. 110.00
Dog, Seated, Hand Tooling, 10 1/4 In. .... 220.00 to 275.00
Dog, Seated, Olive Brown Glaze, 7 In. 50.00
Dog, Seated, Orange Tan Glaze, 10 In. 55.00
Dog, Seated, Tooled Eyes, Mounted As Lamp, 10 In. 95.00
Duck, Incised Initials, E.J.E., 6 3/4 In. 335.00
Frog, 7 In. 247.00
Frog, 7 1/4 In. 159.50
Frog, Incised T, 8 In. 192.50
Horse Head, 7 In. 236.00
Lamp Base, Stump, 13 In. 93.50
Marker, Boundary, Inscribed N.U.W., 45 In., Pair 550.00
Mother & Baby Gorilla, Granite Base 395.00
Paperweight, Eagle On Log, F.O.E. On Eagle's Breast, 1944, 8 In. 38.50
Pig, Full-Bodied, National Sewer Pipe Co., Akron, 14 In. 1320.00
Pig, Incised E.R., 9 In. 165.00
Pig, Olive Brown Glaze, National Sewer Pipe Co., Akron, Ohio, 13 1/2 In. 3630.00
Planter, Hanging, Log Shape, Tooled Bark, 15 1/2 In. 33.00
Planter, Incised Design Of Trees At Bottom, 2 Flags, B 1901, 6 3/4 In. 50.00
Planter, Stump, 4 Open Branches, 25 3/4 In. 110.00
Planter, Tree Trunk, 4 Branches, 2 Ft., Pair 850.00
Planter, Tree Trunk, Hurtford, c.1890, 42 In. 850.00
Salt & Pepper, Tooled Bark Surface 82.50
Siamese Cat, Red, 11 5/8 In. 50.00
Squirrel, Hand Tooled, 8 3/8 In. 66.00
Squirrel, With Nut, Green Eyes, 11 In. 302.00

SEWING equipment of all types is collected, from sewing birds that held the
cloth to old wooden spools.

Bird, 2 Pincushions, Brass, 5 In. 115.50
Bird, 2 Pincushions, Silver Plate, Patent Feb. 15, 1853 .... 210.00
Block, Fabric Printing, Wooden, Border-Type Repeat Design, 6 x 2 1/2 In. 35.00
Book, Holds Embroidery Silk, Art Novelty Co., 8 Pages, 9 1/2 x 12 In. 66.00
Box, Anglo-Indian, Ivory-Mounted, Octagonal, Sandalwood, 1870s, 13 In. 2300.00
Box, Bakelite 40.00
Box, Child's, Mirror, Needles, Thread, Thimble, Buttons, Illustrated Box 135.00
Box, Chinese Export, Lacquered, Bone Implements, c.1810 .... 675.00
Box, Floral Wallpaper-Covered, Cardboard, Scalloped Rim, 2 1/2 In. 27.50
Box, Hanging, Wooden 22.00
Box, Ivory, Anglo-Indian, Ball-Footed, 1850 .... 275.00
Box, Lacquer, Chinese Export Ivory Toys & Tools, 19th Century, 11 x 17 In. 285.00
Box, Lacquer, Inlaid, Fitted, Ivory Tools, Octagonal 1050.00
Box, Leather Cover, Blue Paper Lining, Red Heart Pincushion, 10 x 6 3/4 x 5 In. ... 225.00
Box, Mother-Of-Pearl Inlay, Lid, Round 145.00
Box, Needle, Queen Victoria & Prince Albert On Lid, c.1850 .... 300.00
Box, Paint Design, Scalloped Sides, Pennsylvania 750.00
Box, Poplar, Red Traces, Dovetailed, Painted Finials, Refinished, 11 In. 60.50
Box, Sewing, Regency, Mahogany, Sarcophagus, Fitted, 12 In. 242.00
Box, Stand, Hinged Domed Top, 3 Drawers, Satinwood, 36 1/2 In. 1045.00
Box, Stenciled Floral Designs, Yellow Paint, Poplar 1200.00
Box, Work, Rosewood Veneer, Octagonal, Fitted Interior, 10 1/4 In. 60.00
Cabinet, Spool, see Advertising category under Cabinet, Spool
Caddy, Spool, Carved Detail, Red Paint, White Trim, 12 1/2 In. 77.00
Caddy, Spool, Laminated Bentwood, Numbers For Gauge, 1878, 4 3/8 In. 49.50
Chest, Child's, Paper Cover Wood, Lift-Up Top, Fitted, France, 14 x 11 x 7 In. ... 605.00
Crochet Color Card, Geo. A. Clark & Bros., N.Y., 58 Samples, 8 1/4 x 43 In. 290.00
Darner, Sock, Wooden, Black, 6 In. 4.50
Darning Egg, Amethyst Stone, Sterling Silver Handle 45.00
Dispenser, Thread, Tartanware, McLean, Clark Logo, 3 3/4 Diam. 450.00
Distaff, Weaving, Wooden, Pewter Inlaid, Chip Carved, Freestanding 165.00

Frame, Quilting, Sawhorse Construction, 32 x 48 x 100 In. 27.50
Holder, Needle & Thread, Egg Shape, Tartanware, McBeth, 1 1/8 x 2 1/8 In. 295.00
Holder, Needle, Ivory, Umbrella Shape 57.00
Holder, Thimble, Knife Box Shape, Tartanware, Prince Charlie, 7/8 x 1 1/2 In. 600.00
Holder, Thimble, Machine, Barrel Shape 50.00
Kit, Hamm's, Case 10.00
Kit, Knights Life Insurance Co., Pittsburgh, 1940s 4.00
Kit, Lydia Pinkham, Metal Tube 25.00
Kit, Metal, Red Velvet Mirrored Top, Occupied Japan 20.00
Kit, National Bank, Brooklyn, Iowa, Metal, Cylinder, Round, Pocket 5.00
Machine, Book, Singer, Instructions, 1949 .... 12.50
Machine, Florence, Stenciled, Attachments, Instructions, Pat. 1861 .... 595.00
Machine, New Home, Books, Accessories 60.00
Machine, Oak Cabinet, Pedal Power 175.00
Machine, Singer, Black Cast Iron, Ornate Treadle 40.00
Machine, Singer, Child's, Hand Crank, Carrying Case 75.00
Machine, Singer, Featherweight, Model 221, 1952 .... 125.00 to 325.00
Machine, Treadle, Walnut, Elias Howe 475.00
Machine, Wilcox & Gibbs, 1871 .... 95.00
Machine, Wrought Iron Pedestal, Oak, 4 Drawers, 1920s 200.00
Mannequin, Dress, Muslin Cover, Wooden Trim, 1903, 25 In. 550.00
Needle, Knitting, Wooden, Help Uncle Sam Win The War, Puritan Flour, 1940s 8.00
Needle, Tatting, Brass, Retractable, 2.5 Oz. 24.00
Needle, Yarn, Mechanical, Wooden Handle, Brass 2.50
Needle Case, Broadway Needle Card, Lithograph Picture, Envelope, Early 1900s 10.00
Needle Case, Girl, Coca-Cola, 1924, 2 x 3 In. 55.00
Needle Case, Glove Darner, Sterling Silver 85.00
Needle Case, Home, Enclosed Needles, 2 3/4 x 4 1/2 In. 15.00
Needle Case, Paper, Fulton Trouser Co., 1904 .... 10.00
Needle Case, Tetley Tea 20.00
Needle Holder, Prudential Life Advertisement, Round Case With Picture 8.00
Needles & Threader, Advertising Top Sweet Snuff, Folder, 1930s 10.00
Pattern, Dress, Package, 1887 .... 45.00
Pattern, Rag Doll, Standard Fashion Co., 1 Painted Linen Head, Envelope, 1890 ...... 95.00
Pattern, Simplicity, Black Rag Dolls, 1947 .... 30.00
Pincushion, Amish Star, Black, Green & Purple Wool Yarn, Crocheted Edge 45.00
Pincushion, Barbell Shape, Silk 38.00
Pincushion, Blackamoor, Umbrella Overhead Is Cushion, Cast Iron 650.00
Pincushion, Boot, Silver Plated 20.00
Pincushion, Cat, Persian, Metal Pot, Victorian 52.00
Pincushion, Cradle Form, Sterling Silver, 2 3/4 x 3 In. 145.00
Pincushion, Daisy Duck, Beaded 98.00
Pincushion, Dog, Red Trim, Germany, 3 1/2 In. 16.50
Pincushion, Elephant Shape, Sterling Silver 125.00
Pincushion, Figural, Swan & Cygnet, Green Waves, Occupied Japan, 3 x 2 3/8 In. ... 12.00
Pincushion, Nodder, Turtle, Florenza 50.00
Pincushion, Poodle, Fur 15.00
Pincushion, Shoe Shape, Sterling Silver 110.00
Pincushion, Snow Bear, White, 5 In. 32.00
Pincushion, Success Manure Spreaders, Tin 95.00
Pincushion & Spool Stand, 2-Tier, Exotic Woods, Carved Ivory Fittings, 10 In. 715.00
Pincushion dolls are listed in their own category
Ruler, Dressmaker's, Advertising, 1870 .... 25.00
Scissors, Wurlitzer Musical Instruments, Early 1900s 85.00
Scissors Rest, Quilter's, Padded Fabric, Amish, Oblong 32.00
Sewing Bird, 2 Cushions 285.00
Sewing Kit, Bone, Thimble, Fitted, Green Velvet Case, 5 Piece 48.00
Shuttle, Bone 30.00
Shuttle, Tatting, Lydia E. Pinkham, Celluloid, Portrait On Front, C.1910, 3 In. 16.00
Shuttle, Tatting, Silver Sterling 65.00
Shuttle, Tortoiseshell 35.00
Spool cabinets are in the Advertising category under Cabinet, Spool

Spool Holder, Brass, 2 Tiers, Lift-out Rod, Holds 24 Spools, 16 In. 235.00
Spool Rack, Folding, Ruler On Bottom, 9 In. 40.00
Stand, Bottom Shelf, Wicker Basket Top, Handle, Natural, Victorian 145.00
Stand, Regency, Japanned, Fitted Interior, Tripod Ball & Claw Feet, 33 x 13 In. 880.00
Stand & Swift, 4 Drawers, 32 1/2 In. 4500.00
Swift, Table Clamp, Wooden, 22 In. 60.50
Tape Measure, Abbotts Ice Cream, Celluloid, Waitress Serving Sundae 40.00
Tape Measure, Alarm Clock, Metal, Germany 145.00
Tape Measure, Atlantic City Million Dollar Pier 45.00
Tape Measure, Black Mammy 55.00
Tape Measure, Black Man's Head, Wearing Fez, Pincushion Top, 1 3/4 In. 188.00
Tape Measure, Bon's Knoll Bourbon, Woman, Flowing Hair 95.00
Tape Measure, Brass Turtle, Tail Winds 95.00
Tape Measure, Burger King, Blue Plastic, Paper Tape, Side Crank, 1980, 1/2 x 1/2 In. . 4.00
Tape Measure, Clock Face, Metal, Square, Germany 125.00
Tape Measure, Clock, Figural, Germany 50.00
Tape Measure, Clock, Mantel, Bakelite, Hands Rotate As Tape Is Pulled 175.00
Tape Measure, Cloth, Spring Wound, Advertising 16.00
Tape Measure, Coffeepot Shape, Brass, Agate Handle, Pull From Spout 175.00
Tape Measure, Darning Egg, Insect Pull, 2 1/2 In. 85.00
Tape Measure, Dog Head, Celluloid 60.00
Tape Measure, Elvis Presley, Heart Shape 20.00
Tape Measure, Fab Detergent 25.00
Tape Measure, Fisher Floor Coverings 6.00
Tape Measure, General Electric Refrigerators, Blue Rim, Fabric, 1930s 25.00
Tape Measure, Green Parrot, Celluloid 135.00
Tape Measure, Hill Brand Coffee, Deland, Potter & Co., 1920s, 1 1/2 In. 90.00
Tape Measure, John Deere, Celluloid, 1918 .... 60.00
Tape Measure, Lewis Lye, Quaker Logo, Celluloid, 1918 .... 95.00
Tape Measure, Lux, Clock, Black 35.00
Tape Measure, Man's Head, Celluloid, 1920s, 1 1/2 In. 185.00
Tape Measure, Marston Coal Co. 48.00
Tape Measure, Otis Elevator 25.00
Tape Measure, Pecking Chick, Rewound By Worm In Beak, Metal, Germany 165.00
Tape Measure, Pig, Copper 85.00
Tape Measure, Pink Flowers, Celluloid 75.00
Tape Measure, Rozien Metal Co., Soodward, OK 12.00
Tape Measure, Sailing Ship, Celluloid 65.00
Tape Measure, Skookum, 3 1/4 In. 30.00
Tape Measure, Smokey Bear 35.00
Tape Measure, Stanley Tools, Marbelized Plastic Case 15.00
Tape Measure, White Pig In Red Boot, Celluloid 40.00
Thimble, Brass, Thread Cutter Top, Duke, Pat. May 15, 1900, Size 10 .... 5.00
Thimble, Engraved, Brass Purse 35.00
Thimble, Hoover, Home & Happiness Emblem, Metal 6.50
Thimble, Perma Cote Co., Davenport, Iowa, Advertising 1.00
Thimble, Silver Sterling, Simons, Size 6 .... 28.50
Thimble, Singer Sewing Machines, Silvered Aluminum, Red Band, 1950s 4.00
Thimble, Sterling Silver, 10 Cathedral Window Fleur-De-Lis 42.00
Thimble Case, Egg Shape, On Chain, Chatelaine Brass, Victorian 100.00
Thread, Aunt Lydia's, 12 Spoons, Box, 1918 .... 75.00
Tool, Scissors-Type, Stork-Form, Beak Opens, Sterling Silver, Tiffany, 5 In. 385.00
Winder, Yarn, Metal, Wooden Handles 39.00
Winder, Yarn, Red Paint, New England, 32 1/2 In. 175.00
Winder, Yarn, Table, Apple Green Paint, 30 In. 875.00

SHAKER items are characterized by simplicity, functionalism, and order-
liness. There were many Shaker communities in America from the eighteenth
century to the present day. The religious order made furniture, small wooden
pieces, and packaged medicines, herbs, and jellies to sell to *outsiders*. Other
useful objects were made for use by members of the community. Shaker
furniture is listed in this book in the Furniture category.

Basket, 4 Handles, 19 1/2 In. 660.00
Basket, Canterbury, 2 Handles 2860.00
Basket, Domed Lid, 10 x 12 3/4 In. 412.50
Basket, Sewing, Base Stamped Sabbathday Lake Shakers Maine, 9 In. 275.00
Blanket, Linsey-Woolsey, Embroidered Trim, Blue & Gray, 72 x 79 In. 150.00
Bottle, Medicine, Shaker Anodyne, Aqua, Enfield, N.J., 3 1/2 In. 35.00
Box, 2-Finger, Unpainted, Oval, 2 1/2 x 6 1/2 x 5 In. 225.00
Box, 3-Finger, Bentwood, Copper Tacks, Blue Repaint, Yellow Interior, 11 1/4 In. 195.00
Box, 3-Finger, Round, Red Paint, 9 In. 335.00
Box, 4-Finger, Oval, New England, 3 1/4 x 8 3/4 In. 250.00
Box, 4-Finger, Yellow Wash Exterior, Salmon-Colored Interior, 11 1/2 In. 1430.00
Box, 5-Finger, Maple, Oval, 13 1/2 In. 660.00
Box, 6-Finger, Graduated, Set Of 6 .... 1650.00
Box, 6 Compartments, Red, Yellow Interior, 17 x 29 x 11 In. 1540.00
Box, Blanket, Child's, Drawer, Red Stain, Pine, 24 3/4 x 33 1/4 In. 8250.00
Box, Canterbury, Leather Handles, Utensils For Making Wool Dusters, C.1830 .... 1250.00
Box, Copper Tacks, Finger Construction, Oval, Bentwood, 10 1/2 In. 225.00
Box, Copper Tacks, Hardwood & Pine, Brown Patina, Oval, 6 1/8 In. 302.50
Box, Harvard Type, Copper Tacks, Oval, Manufactured By Sam'l Hersey, 6 1/8 In. 275.00
Box, Lid Inscribed 1852 K.E. Myers, Oval, 6 1/2 In. 5225.00
Box, Salmon Pink Over White, Copper Tacks, Oval, Bentwood, 11 3/4 In. 550.00
Box, Stenciled From John Meane & Son, Augusta Me, Oval, 11 1/2 In. 715.00
Box, Tool, Fitted Interior Tray, Walnut & Bird's-Eye Maple, c.1850, 24 5/8 In. 1210.00
Box, Utility, Swallowtail Finger Fasteners, Red Sponging, Oval, 2 x 5 In. 5175.00
Box, Wooden, Label Says Handles Of Knives For Cutting Straw 775.00
Box, Wooden, Natural Finish, Oval, 8 3/4 In. 885.00
Box, Wooden, Oval, Label Says Bee's Wax, Ochre, 13 1/2 In. 5500.00
Box, Work, Compartmented, Red Stain Exterior, Yellow Interior, 29 1/2 In. 1540.00
Carrier, Fixed Handle, Red Stain 4675.00
Carrier, Oval, Painted Red, 11 In. 4675.00
Carrier, Sewing, Accessories, 20th Century, 7 5/8 x 5 1/2 In. 250.00
Chocolate Pot, Tin, 1850-1875 .... 200.00
Cloak, Rose Colored 1250.00
Cup, Measuring, Tin, 1850-1875 .... 25.00
Dipper, Painted Ochre, 5 1/2 In. 220.00
Dustpan, Scoop, Tinware, 2 Piece 38.00
Herb Crusher 68.00
Label, Coltsfoot, Tussilago Farfara, D.M. & Co., Watervliet, 7/8 x 1 3/4 In. 20.00
Label, Extract Of Sarsaparilla, Watervliet, N.Y., 2 1/4 x 3 1/2 In. 95.00
Label, Lily, White, Root, Nymphae Adorata, Watervliet, Yellow, 1 x 1 3/4 In. 20.00
Label, Liverwort, Hepatica, Triloba, Watervliet, N.Y., 1 1/8 x 2 In. 20.00
Label, Rosewater, Prepared By Society, Mt. Lebanon, 2 3/8 x 2 3/8 In. 55.00
Label, Shakers' Currant Wine, D.C. Brainard, Mt. Lebanon, Blue, 2 x 2 1/2 In. 85.00
Ladder, Canterbury, Painted, 109 In. 1650.00
Lap Robe, Multicolored Fabrics, Lined With Patterned Cotton, 53 1/2 x 69 In. 900.00
Latch & Strap Hinge, Door 125.00
Pail, Cover, Bail Handle, Wooden, Yellow, Oval, 6 In. 1540.00
Pail, New England, Painted Green, 4 In. 220.00
Photograph, North Family, Mount Lebanon, 5 1/4 x 8 1/4 In. 210.00
Pincushion, Screw Stand, Large 770.00
Pincushion, Stuffed Green Velvet On Maple Screw Stand, 10 1/2 In. 770.00
Postcard, Schoolchildren, Mount Lebanon, c.1890 .... 85.00
Postcard, View Of South Family, Watervliet, 20 Members, c.1912 .... 195.00
Rack, Drying, Cherry, 3 Bars, Trestle Feet, New England, 36 1/2 x 30 In. 302.00
Rug Whip, Label 145.00
Seed Packet, Beans, Early White Mountain, New Lebanon, N.Y., 10 x 5 1/2 In. 75.00
Seed Packet, Winter Crookneck Squash, F.W., Canterbury, 2 3/4 x 2 1/2 In. 85.00
Steps, Yellow Paint 2090.00
Trade Card, Quaker & Shaker New Tariff Ranges, Taunton Iron Works Co. 30.00
Tub, Interlocking Stave Construction, Mustard Paint 357.50
Wrapper, Herb, Borage, Watervliet, Light Blue Ground, 6 x 4 1/2 In. 125.00

SHAVING MUGS were popular from 1860 to 1900. Many types were made, including occupational mugs featuring pictures of men's jobs. There were scuttle mugs, silver-plated mugs, glass-lined mugs, and others.

Dr. Coklin, T & V	65.00
F.C. Peterson, Pink Luster, Gold Trim	75.00
Fraternal, I.O.O.F., Chain	75.00
Fraternal, Knight Templar, Gold Name & Design	110.00
Fraternal, Odd Fellows, Acme Lodge 469, 1923	150.00
Girl, Man Playing Stringed Instrument, Allenburg	48.00
Gold Fringed Curtain Backdrop, Cecil Bell	165.00
Limoges, Pennant, Initials WJ, 1901	360.00
Maryland Casualty Insurance, c.1905	125.00
Milk Glass Insert, Lid, Handles, Brush, Silver Plate, Van Bergh, 5 In.	100.00
Occupational, 5 People In Scene	450.00
Occupational, Autoist	1500.00
Occupational, Bartender	145.00
Occupational, Butcher	350.00 to 400.00
Occupational, Compass & Ruler, Wm. Dateman, Gold Band	77.00
Occupational, Delivery Wagon Driver	650.00
Occupational, Dentist, Set Of Teeth, Gold Trim	500.00
Occupational, Farmer, Man Pushing Plow, Name In Gold	345.00
Occupational, Furniture Maker, Man Working On Piece	475.00
Occupational, Hunter, Dogs & Birds In Flight, W. Eaton, Worn	100.00
Occupational, Koken Barber's Supply, Knight's Helmet, J.G. Leach	66.00
Occupational, Locomotive	290.00
Occupational, Oyster & Ice Cream Bar, People At Tables	250.00
Occupational, Passenger Train	290.00
Occupational, Photographer, Camera On Tripod	1100.00
Occupational, Policeman	195.00
Occupational, Railroad	90.00
Occupational, Telegraph Operator, Worn Gilt Band, Germany	395.00
Roses, Gray Luster Rim, Melon Ribbed, Castle Mark, Germany	48.00
Scuttle, Bull Elk, Germany	40.00
Scuttle, Pink Poppies, RS Poland, 3 1/2 In.	100.00
Scuttle, Welsh Ladies, Tea Party, White, Gold Trim, 4 In.	88.00
Shell, Multicolored, Lavender Interior, Majolica	192.50
Shield, Red, White & Blue Stars, Flower Design, Man's Name, Gold Rim	175.00
Silver Plate, Milk Glass Insert, Open Design, Brush Rest On Handle	50.00
Swallows Over Mountain Lake, ES Germany	85.00
Tea Leaf Ironstone, 12 Panels, Berries Around Handles, Shaw	95.00

SHAWNEE POTTERY was started in Zanesville, Ohio, in 1937. The company made vases, novelty ware, flowerpots, planters, lamps, and cookie jars. Three dinnerware lines were made: Corn, Lobster Ware, and Valencia (a solid color line). White Corn pattern utility pieces were made in 1945. Corn King was made from 1946 to 1954; Corn Queen, with darker green leaves and lighter colored corn, from 1954 to 1961. Shawnee produced pottery for George Rumrill during the late 1930s. The company closed in 1961.

Ashtray, Three Geese	45.00
Bank, Howdy Doody	375.00
Bank, Smiley Pig, Chocolate Base	250.00
Bank, Winnie Pig, Marked	250.00
Bowl, Corn Queen, No. 8	35.00
Bowl, Fruit, Corn Queen	33.00
Bowl, Kenwood, Embossed Silverware	25.00
Bowl, Mixing, Corn King, No. 5	45.00
Butter, Corn King, Cover	60.00
Canister, Fernware, Blue	55.00
Casserole, Corn King, Cover	75.00
Casserole, Corn King, Large	60.00
Casserole, Cover, Lobster	40.00

Casserole, Sundial, Medium 22.00
Cookie Bank, Smiley, Chocolate Base 650.00
Cookie Bank, Winnie, Chocolate Base 550.00
Cookie Jar, Cooky, Gold 250.00
Cookie Jar, Corn King .... 140.00 to 195.00
Cookie Jar, Corn Queen 195.00
Cookie Jar, Drummer Boy .... 300.00 to 550.00
Cookie Jar, Dutch Boy .... 120.00 to 185.00
Cookie Jar, Dutch Boy, Gold Trim, Decals, Original Label 450.00
Cookie Jar, Dutch Boy, Striped Pants .... 95.00 to 150.00
Cookie Jar, Dutch Girl, Gold Tulip 150.00
Cookie Jar, Dutch Girl, Yellow Dress 150.00
Cookie Jar, Dutch Jug, Pennsylvania 150.00
Cookie Jar, Great Northern Dutch Boy 325.00
Cookie Jar, JoJo Clown .... 290.00 to 375.00
Cookie Jar, Muggsy .... 250.00 to 525.00
Cookie Jar, Muggsy, Gold 795.00
Cookie Jar, Muggsy, Green Scarf 1900.00
Cookie Jar, Owl .... 90.00 to 175.00
Cookie Jar, Pig, Flowers, Gold Trim, Flower On Scarf 585.00
Cookie Jar, Puss 'n Boots .... 150.00 to 225.00
Cookie Jar, Puss 'n Boots, Gold Flowers, Maroon Bow 485.00
Cookie Jar, Puss 'n Boots, Gold Trim 595.00
Cookie Jar, Puss 'n Boots, Gold Trim, Decals 550.00
Cookie Jar, Puss 'n Boots, Gold Trim, Long Tail 495.00
Cookie Jar, Puss 'n Boots, Tail Over Foot, Gold, Decals 250.00
Cookie Jar, Sailor Boy, Gold 450.00
Cookie Jar, Sailor, Commemorative 425.00
Cookie Jar, Smiley & Winnie The Pig, Pair .... *Illus* 450.00
Cookie Jar, Smiley, Black Hair, Gold, Flowers 750.00
Cookie Jar, Smiley, Blue Collar, Brown Hooves 425.00
Cookie Jar, Smiley, Chrysanthemums .... 375.00 to 425.00
Cookie Jar, Smiley, Clover Bud 350.00
Cookie Jar, Smiley, Gold Trim, Black Buttons 285.00
Cookie Jar, Smiley, Shamrocks .... 175.00 to 250.00
Cookie Jar, Smiley, Tulip 375.00
Cookie Jar, Smiley, Yellow Bib, Gold Trim, Decals 595.00
Cookie Jar, Winnie Bank Head 325.00
Cookie Jar, Winnie, Blue Collar .... 265.00 to 325.00
Cookie Jar, Winnie, Clover Bud 389.00
Cookie Jar, Winnie, Peach Collar .... 188.00 to 345.00
Cookie Jar, Winnie, Red Collar, Gold .... 300.00 to 425.00
Cookie Jar, Winnie, Shamrocks 275.00
Cottage House Set, Cookie Jar, Teapot, Salt & Pepper, Covered Sugar 3900.00
Creamer, Corn King 30.00
Creamer, Corn Queen 25.00

◆◆◆◆◆◆◆◆◆◆◆◆◆◆◆◆◆◆◆◆◆◆

Don't sticky tape a top on a teapot. The decoration may come off with the tape. Secure a top with special wax.

◆◆◆◆◆◆◆◆◆◆◆◆◆◆◆◆◆◆◆◆◆◆

Shawnee, Cookie Jar, Smiley & Winnie The Pig,
Pair; Shawnee, Salt & Pepper, Winnie & Smiley,
4 Piece

Creamer, Elephant .... 15.00 to 34.00
Creamer, Pig 48.00
Creamer, Puss 'n Boots .... 28.00 to 45.00
Creamer, Puss 'n Boots, Gold Trim .... 175.00 to 225.00
Creamer, Smiley, Blue & Yellow 125.00
Creamer, Smiley, Blue Scarf, Yellow Ground 60.00
Creamer, Smiley, Peach Flower, Gold Trim 140.00
Creamer, Smiley, Yellow 85.00
Creamer, Snowflake, Green 15.00
Creamer, Sunflower 30.00
Cup & Saucer, Corn King 48.00
Jar, Great Northern Girl 145.00
Jug, Corn King, No. 71 .... 75.00
Pie Bird, Pink 40.00
Pitcher, Batter, Snowflake, Green 45.00
Pitcher, Bo Peep .... 95.00 to 125.00
Pitcher, Bo Peep, Large 75.00
Pitcher, Bo Peep, No. 47 .... 100.00
Pitcher, Chanticleer 60.00
Pitcher, Charlie Chicken .... 65.00 to 75.00
Pitcher, Milk, Dutch Boy 45.00
Pitcher, Milk, Pig 45.00
Pitcher, Milk, Smiley, Clover Bud 145.00
Pitcher, Smiley, Gold Trim, Peach Flowers 525.00
Pitcher, Smiley, Small 105.00
Pitcher, Water, Chanticleer 35.00
Pitcher, Water, Corn King 55.00
Planter, Deer 30.00
Planter, Dutch Children At Wishing Well, Blue, Green .... 17.50 To 20.00
Planter, Gazelle With Baby, 10 3/4 In. 45.00
Planter, Gazelle, Black 42.00
Planter, Globe 22.00
Planter, Open Car, Gold Trim 24.00
Planter, Pig 15.00
Planter, Red Pony 20.00
Platter, Corn King, 12 In. 60.00
Relish, Corn Queen 10.00
Salt & Pepper, Bo Peep & Boy Blue, Small 140.00
Salt & Pepper, Bo Peep & Sailor Boy .... 18.00 to 20.00
Salt & Pepper, Cat 18.00
Salt & Pepper, Chanticleer, Large 55.00
Salt & Pepper, Charlie Chicken, 3 In. 30.00
Salt & Pepper, Charlie Chicken, 5 In. 48.00
Salt & Pepper, Corn King, 3 1/4 In. 24.00
Salt & Pepper, Corn King, 5 1/4 In. 30.00
Salt & Pepper, Daisy, Large 35.00
Salt & Pepper, Duck, 8 1/4 In. .... 19.00 to 35.00
Salt & Pepper, Dutch Boy & Girl .... 40.00 to 55.00
Salt & Pepper, Flower Pots .... 15.00 to 25.00
Salt & Pepper, Milk Can .... 16.00 to 20.00
Salt & Pepper, Muggsy, Large .... 115.00 to 165.00
Salt & Pepper, Muggsy, Small 90.00
Salt & Pepper, Owl 20.00
Salt & Pepper, Owl, Green Eyes 35.00
Salt & Pepper, Pigs .... 90.00 to 100.00
Salt & Pepper, Puss 'n Boots 30.00
Salt & Pepper, Smiley, Green Scarf 90.00
Salt & Pepper, Starflower, Barrel Shape 150.00
Salt & Pepper, Sunflower .... 48.00 to 55.00
Salt & Pepper, Swiss Boy & Girl 45.00
Salt & Pepper, Watering Can 18.00
Salt & Pepper, Winnie & Smiley, 4 Piece .... *Illus* 160.00
Salt & Pepper, Winnie & Smiley, Green, Large 95.00

Salt & Pepper, Winnie & Smiley, Small 30.00
Sugar, Cover, Clover Bud 65.00
Sugar, Cover, Corn King 45.00
Sugar, Cover, Snowflake, Blue 20.00
Sugar Shaker, Lobster, 2 Piece 35.00
Teapot, Blue Flower .... 44.00 to 45.00
Teapot, Blue Flower, Gold Trim 45.00
Teapot, Blue Leaves 39.00
Teapot, Corn King, Large .... 80.00 to 90.00
Teapot, Corn Queen 58.00
Teapot, Fernware 49.50
Teapot, Flower & Fern 32.00
Teapot, Granny Anne, Lavender Apron .... 75.00 to 90.00
Teapot, Granny Anne, Peach Apron 75.00
Teapot, Granny Anne, Peach Apron, Label 90.00
Teapot, Granny Anne, Purple Apron 110.00
Teapot, Pennsylvania Dutch 80.00
Teapot, Pink Flower, Embossed 48.00
Teapot, Rose, Embossed .... 39.00 to 48.00
Teapot, Sunflower .... 28.00 to 55.00
Teapot, Tom Tom The Piper's Son, Multicolor 140.00
Teapot, Tom Tom The Piper's Son, White .... 65.00 to 75.00
Vase, Ruffled, Gray 25.00
Wall Pocket, Birds At Birdhouse 28.00
Wall Pocket, Grandfather Clock 20.00

SHEARWATER pottery is a family business started by Mr. and Mrs. G. W.
Anderson, Sr., and their three sons. The local Ocean Springs, Mississippi,
clays were used to make the wares in the 1930s. The company is still in
business.

Bowl, Floral Shoulder, Semi-Matte Glaze, Marked, 4 x 6 1/2 In. 400.00
Figurine, Pirate, Large 45.00
Figurine, Pirate, Small 35.00
Figurine, Sea Gull, Aqua 225.00
Pitcher, Bulbous, 8 1/4 In. 85.00
Pitcher, Dark Green, Blue Drip, 5 1/2 In. 49.50
Vase, Bulbous, Matte Green, 6 In. 68.00
Vase, Flowing Stylized Curtain, Metallic Glaze, M. Anderson, 1946, 9 1/2 In. 700.00
Vase, Stylized Animals & Figures, Gold Dust & Crystals, 11 1/2 In. 550.00
Vase, Top Hat Turned Over Shape, Metallic Green Glaze, 2 1/2 In. 150.00
Vessel, Ridged, Matte Green & Metallic Glaze, Marked, 6 In. 150.00

SHEET MUSIC from the past centuries is now collected. The favorites are
examples with covers featuring artistic or historic pictures. Early sheet music
covers were lithographed, but by the 1900s photographic reproductions were
used. The early music was larger than more recent sheets and you must watch
out for examples that were trimmed to fit in a twentieth-century piano bench.

101 Best Songs Book, Advertising, 1915 .... 2.00
A Lovely Way To Spend An Evening, Frank Sinatra, 1943 .... 5.00
A Marshmallow World, Vaughn Monroe, 1949 .... 5.00
Adventures Of Ichabod & Mr. Toad, Ichabod & Others 15.00
Ain't Got A Dime To My Name, Bob Hope, Crosby, Lamour, 1942 .... 5.00
Ain't Misbehavin', Connie's Hot Chocolates, Black Sax Player, 1929 ...... 13.00
All Shook Up, Elvis Presley Photograph 65.00
Allegheny Moon, Patti Page, 1956 .... 15.00
Alone, Marx Brothers, 1935 .... 8.00
Always Leave Them Laughing, Milton Berle, Virginia Mayo, 1949 .... 7.00
Anna In Indiana, Eddie Cantor In Black Face, 1921 .... 12.00
Annie Get Your Gun, Ethel Merman 15.00
Are You Sorry, Sophie Tucker Photograph, Barbelle Cover, 1925 .... 10.00
As Time Goes By, Hupfeld & Harms, Bogart, Bergman & Henreid 8.00
Baby It's Cold Outside, Esther Williams In Swimsuit, c.1948 .... 5.00
Barney Google, 1923 .... 22.00

Bebe, Ziegfield Follies, Eddie Cantor Photograph, 1923	9.00
Bonanza, TV Series	20.00
Bromo-Seltzer, Contains No Cocaine Or Morphine, 13 1/2 In.	38.00
Bromo-Seltzer, Starlight Polka	5.00
Burning Of Rome, Paul	12.00
Buttons & Bows, Movie, Bob Hope & Jane Russell, 1948	12.00
By The Watermelon Vine, 1904	15.00
Cake Walk, Frame, c.1895	125.00
Campin' On De Ole Suwanee, Blacks Cakewalking, 1899	20.00
China Seas, Freed, Brown, Robbins, Gable & Harlow Cover	14.00
Christmas Alphabet, McGuire Sisters Cover, 1954	5.00
Circus Parade, E.T. Paul	45.00
Come Josephine In My Flying Machine, 1910	10.00 to 12.00
Dan Patch	55.00
Dancing In The Dark, Band Wagon, Fred & Adele Astaire Photograph, 1931	10.00
Days Of Wine & Roses, Lee Remick & Jack Lemmon, 1962	5.00
Does She Love Me? Positively Absolutely, Sophie Tucker, 1927	20.00
Down Where The Swanee River Flows, Al Jolson, 1916	5.00
Driftwood, Bix Beiderbecke Illustration, 1924	60.50
Edgewood Yacht Club March, 1909	55.00
Ev'rybody Calls Me Honey	15.00
Five O'Clock Whistle, Woody Herman Photograph, 1940	6.00
Free Again, Barbra Streisand, 1965	5.00
Full Moon & Empty Arms, Frank Sinatra, 1946	6.00
Girl Of The Old West, 1922	8.00
Glad Rag Doll, Dolores Costello	20.00
Gold Diggers Of 1937, Vic Pall	15.00
Gold Mine In The Sky, Pat Boone, 1950s	12.00
Gold Rush, Chaplin, Lyman & Arnheim	10.00
Good Bye Teddy Roosevelt	25.00
Good Morning, Babes In Arms, Judy Garland, Mickey Rooney, 1941	15.00
Good Morning Carrie, Black Banjo Player, Serenading His Lady, 1901	12.80
Harbor Lights, Lighthouse, 1937	2.00
Heart O'Mine, Noah's Ark, Dolores Costello, 1913	5.00
Heaven Help A Sailor	10.00
Hello, Frisco, Hello, Tilzer & Murphy, Alice Faye On Cover	5.00
Hidden, Movie Phantom Rider, Buck Jones Portrait By Randall, 1936	25.00
High Noon, Gary Cooper, Grace Kelly, 1952	5.00
Hold Me In Your Loving Arms, Ziegfeld Follies, DeTakacs Cover, 1915	18.00
Home Is Where The Heart Is, Under Many Flags, DeTakacs Cover, 1912	11.00
Horse Feathers, Kalmar & Ruby, 4 Marx Bros.	6.00
I Didn't Raise My Dog To Be A Sausage, 1915	25.00
I'll Be Home For Christmas, Bing Crosby, 1943	5.00
I'll Give The World For You, Woman Cover, 1924	2.50
I'll Never Smile Again, Frank Sinatra, 1939	25.00
I'll See You In C-U-B-A, Berlin, 1920	13.00
I'm Feelin' Like A Million, Judy Garland, Eleanor Powell, Robert Taylor, 1937	10.00
I'm Wearing My Heart Away For You, 1902	1.50
In Society, Abbott & Costello, 1944	20.00
Is It True What They Say About Dixie, 1936	15.00
Just You & I & The Moon, Ziegfeld Follies, Couple Dancing, 1913	25.00
Kissing Bandit, Frank Sinatra & Kathryn Grayson, 1948	6.00
Liberty Bell March, Sousa, 1894	10.00
Little Black Me, 1899	15.00
Little Ford Rambled Right Along	5.00
Little French Mother, Good-Bye, Norman Rockwell Picture, 1919	15.00
Little Pal, Al Jolson, 1929	8.00
Lorraine, 1917	12.00
Louise, Maurice Chevalier	20.00
Louisville Lou	15.00
Love In Bloom, Bing Crosby, 16 Other Songs, 1930-1940	11.00
Love Me Tender, Elvis Presley	40.00
Lovely To Look At, Ginger Rogers, Fred Astaire	15.00

Lucky In Love, Flapper, Holding Newspaper, Good News Musical Comedy	10.00
Lullaby Of The Rain, Glenn Miller, 10 Other Songs, 1930-1940	9.00
Mairzy Doats, 1943	4.00
Make Believe Island, Glen Miller, 1940	7.00
Mary You Must Marry Me, Haskell Coffin, 1919	7.00
May I, Carole Lombard & Bing Crosby, 1934	5.00
Meet Me In St. Louis, Judy Garland, 1944	25.00
Melody Of Love, Engelmann, 1903	22.00
Michelle, Beatles, 1965	14.00
Moon River, Breakfast At Tiffany's, Audrey Hepburn Cover	20.00
Moxie, Rolls Royce Moxiemobile Pictured, Frank Archer On Reverse Side	65.00
My Blue Heaven, Arlen, Blane, Ed Morris, Grable & Dailey	5.00
My Buddy, Al Jolson, 1922	8.00
My Foolish Heart, Dana Andrews, Susan Hayward, 1949	7.00
Napoleon's Last Charge, Lithographed Battle Scene, E.T. Paul, 1910	30.00
Naughty Nineties, Brooks, Fairchild & Saunders, Abbott & Costello	8.00
Night At The Opera, Marx Brothers, 1935	35.00
Oh Boy Gum, Goudey Gum, 1925	20.00
Oh Johnny! Oh, Johnny! Oh!, Nora Bayes Photograph, 1918	9.00
Oh! How I Hate To Get Up In The Morning, Eddie Cantor, 1917	32.00
Old Black Joe & Medley Waltz, Empire Music Co., Starmer Cover	35.00
On Parade, Jeanette MacDonald & Nelson Eddy, 1938	7.00
Over There, Rockwell Cover	65.00
Over Yonder Where The Lilies Grow, Norman Rockwell Picture, 1918	15.00
Paul Revere's Ride, Lithographed Cover, E.T. Paul, 1905	45.00
Perfect Song, Pepsodent Hour Theme, Amos 'n' Andy, 1929 .... 14.00 to 60.00
Princess Pocahontas March & Two Step, 1903	35.00
Pullman Porter Blues, Ulrich & Hamilton............................. 15.00 to 20.00
Radio Favorites Song Book, 1940s	1.50
Reaching For The Moon, Berlin, Douglas Fairbanks, Bebe Daniels	15.00
Right Somebody To Love, Shirley Temple On Cover, 1936	15.00
River Of No Return, Darby, Newnab & Simon House	20.00
Rose Of Washington Square	55.00
Sailin' On The Robert E. Lee, Baby Rose Marie, 1931	15.00
Sam The Old Accordion Man, Walter Donaldson	20.00
Samson & Delilah, Livingston & Yound, Lamarr & Mature	20.00
Santa Claus Is Coming To Town, 1934	15.00
September Of My Years, Frank Sinatra, 1965	6.00
Seven Year Itch, Cahn, Newman, Robbins, Monroe & Ewell On Cover	7.00
Sleigh Ride In July, Randolph Scott, Dinah Shore, Gypsy Rose Lee, 1944	7.00
Smiles, 1917	4.00
Snow White, Walt Disney, 9 Songs, 1937	50.00
So Long Mother, Al Jolson, Mother's Song, W.W. I Soldier Saying Good-Bye	30.00
Sonny Boy, The Singing Fool, Al Jolson, 1928 .... 4.00 to 20.00
South Of Pago Pago, Wright, Pollack & Mills, John Hall & Farmer	20.00
South Pacific, Mary Martin	15.00
Southern Soldier Boy, 1880	34.00
Strike Up The Band, Freed, Edens & Feist, Judy Garland	8.00
Suppose I Had Never Met You, Weber Presents Little Jesse James, 1923	10.00
Thanks For The Memories, W.C. Fields & Bob Hope, 1938	20.00
That International Rag, Irving Berlin, Artist Phiffer	5.00
The Continental, Gay Divorcee, Fred Astaire & Ginger Rogers, 1934	10.00
Theme From Untouchables, Robert Stack, 1959	5.00
They Gave Him A Gun, Kahn & Romberg, Tracy & George Brent	15.00
Thinking Of You, Three Little Words, Fred Astaire, Red Skelton, Vera Ellen	6.00
Three Little Words, Fred Astaire, Red Skelton, 1953	20.00
Tico-Tico, Red Skelton, Esther Williams, 1943	5.00
To My Mammy, Al Jolson, 1929	25.00
To You Roosevelt, Ed Bamber, Cityscape Cover, 1935	27.00
Too Late, Bing Crosby, 1931	25.00
Top Hat, Berlin, Astaire & Rogers	6.00
True Love, Grace Kelly, Sinatra & Crosby, 1955	6.00
Wee, Wee, Marie, Will You Do Zis For Me, Doughboy & French Girl, 1918	10.00

When It's Nighttime Down In Dixieland	15.00
When It's Springtime, Rudy Vallee	8.00
When The Boys Come Home, Doughboys Cover, Schirmer, 1917	22.00 to 25.00
When The Lusitania Went Down, 1915	10.00
Whistle While You Work, Walt Disney Enterprise, 1937	100.00
Yo-Ho-Hurrah, Wonder Bakers Advertising Theme, Radio, 1929	11.00
You Belong To My Heart, 3 Caballeros, Disney, 1943	6.00
You Gave Me Your Heart, Rudolph Valentino, 1922	5.00
You Keep Coming Back Like A Song, Blue Skies, Berlin, 1940	4.00
You'll Always Be The One I Love, Frank Sinatra On Cover, 1946	18.00
You'll Never Know, Alice Faye, John Payne, 1943	7.00
Ziegfeld Follies, 1912	5.00
Ziegfeld Follies, 1924, Albert Vargas	40.00

SHELLEY first appeared on English ceramics about 1912. The Foley China Works started in England in 1860. Joseph Ball Shelley joined the company in 1862 and became a partner in 1872. Percy Shelley joined the firm in 1881. The company went through a series of name changes, and in 1910 the then Foley China Company became Shelley China. In 1929 it became Shelley Potteries. The company was acquired in 1966 by Allied English Potteries, then merged with the Doulton group in 1971. The name *Shelley* was put into use again in 1980.

Breakfast Set, Child's, Mabel Lucie Attwell Design, 3 Piece	225.00
Butter, Cover, Harebell, Square	325.00
Cup, Begonia, 6 Flute, Demitasse	30.00
Cup, Saucer & Plate, Rosebud	88.00
Cup & Saucer, 6 Flutes, Demitasse	38.00
Cup & Saucer, Blue Rock	55.00
Cup & Saucer, Crochet	65.00
Cup & Saucer, Daffodil Time, 8-Notch Shape	32.50
Cup & Saucer, Dainty Blue	65.00
Cup & Saucer, Demitasse	115.00
Cup & Saucer, Flowers, Gold Trim	52.00
Cup & Saucer, Fluted	34.00
Cup & Saucer, Forget-Me-Not, Demitasse	95.00
Cup & Saucer, Harebell	40.00
Cup & Saucer, Lilac	46.50
Cup & Saucer, Lily-Of-The-Valley	35.00
Cup & Saucer, Pagoda & Fountain Scene	55.00
Cup & Saucer, Pansy, Demitasse	95.00
Cup & Saucer, Primrose	40.00
Cup & Saucer, Regency	50.00
Cup & Saucer, Rose, Demitasse	95.00
Cup & Saucer, Rosebud	35.00 to 55.00
Cup & Saucer, Violets	20.00
Dinner Set, Dainty Blue, 80 Piece	1870.00
Dish, Mint, Bridge Scene	35.00
Eggcup, Double, Harebell	60.00
Eggcup, Rosebud	42.50
Jam Jar, Rosebud, Cover, Scalloped	70.00
Mug, Child's, Begonia, 2 In.	75.00
Mug, Elizabeth & Philip, Visit To Canada, 1959	75.00
Mustard, Begonia	85.00
Plate, Begonia, Pedestal	100.00
Plate, Bridal Rose, 8 In., 6 Piece	200.00
Plate, Heavenly Blue, 10 1/2 In.	75.00
Plate, Rambler Rose, 6 Flutes, 8 In.	35.00
Sugar, Dainty Blue, Handleless	22.50
Sugar & Creamer, Blue Rock	55.00
Sugar & Creamer, Glamis	28.00
Sugar & Creamer, Rosebud	55.00
Sugar & Creamer, Rosebud, Miniature	30.00
Tankard, Grapes, Gold Trim, 12 In.	150.00

Toast Rack, Campanula 220.00
Vase, Bird, Orange, 10 In. 150.00
Vase, Egrets, 8 In. 100.00

SHIRLEY TEMPLE, the famous movie star, was born in 1928. She made her
first movie in 1932. Thousands of items picturing Shirley have been and still
are being made. Shirley Temple dolls were first made in 1934 by Ideal Toy
Company. Millions of Shirley Temple cobalt blue glass dishes were made by
Hazel Atlas Glass Company and U.S. Glass Company from 1934 to 1942.
They were given away as premiums for Wheaties and Bisquick. A bowl, mug,
and pitcher were made as a breakfast set. Some pieces were decorated with
the picture of a very young Shirley, others used a picture of Shirley in her
1936 *Captain January* costume. Although collectors refer to a cobalt creamer,
it is actually the 4 1/2-inch-high milk pitcher from the breakfast set. Many of
these items are being reproduced today.

Book, Susannah Of The Mounties, Random, 1936 .... 25.00
Bowl, Cobalt Blue .... 30.00 to 45.00
Box, Cereal, Quaker Puffed Wheat, This Is My Cereal, 1930s, 9 x 6 In. 179.00
Card, Window, Adventure In Baltimore, 2 Poses 35.00
Cards, Bridge Set, U.S. Playing Card, 1930s 55.00
Carriage 95.00
Charm, Silver 50.00
Clock, Alarm 100.00
Coloring Book, Curly Top Front & Back, 13 x 14 In. 55.00
Cutouts, Wheaties, 1940s, 12 Piece 650.00
Doll, Composition, Hazel Sleep Eyes, Lashes, Mohair Wig, Panties, 13 In. 150.00
Doll, Flirty-Eye, Pink Party Dress, Mohair Wig, Box, 27 In. 1195.00
Doll, Ideal, 1950s, 15 In. 325.00
Doll, Ideal, 1950s, 17 In. 365.00
Doll, Ideal, Composition, Blond, 5 Piece Body, Red Dress, 1935, 13 In. 800.00
Doll, Ideal, Composition, Original Wig & Underwear, 1930s, 15 In. 220.00
Doll, Ideal, Composition, Sleep Eyes, 5 Piece Body, Sailor Suit, 18 In. 1000.00
Doll, Ideal, Nylon Flocked Dressed, 1972, 16 In. .... 45.00 to 70.00
Doll, Ideal, Vinyl Head, Hazel Sleep Eyes, 6 Upper Teeth, 35 In. 850.00
Doll, Ideal, Vinyl, Stand Up & Cheer, 1980s, 16 In. 60.00
Doll, White, Red Polka Dot Dress, 1973, 15 In. 125.00
Mirror, Wee Willie Winkle, Pocket, 1935 .... 30.00 to 40.00
Mug, Cobalt Blue 40.00
Night-Light 20.00
Paper Doll, 17 Costumes, 1938, Pair, Cut 95.00
Paper Doll, 1959, Uncut, 20 In. 100.00
Paper Doll, 1976, Uncut 25.00
Paper Doll, Accessories, 7 Dolls, Cut 95.00
Paper Doll, Advertising, 8 1/2 In. 17.00
Paper Dolls, Masquerade Costumes, Saalfield, 1940, Uncut 150.00
Pitcher, Cobalt Blue, 4 In. .... 23.00 to 40.00
Plate, Baby Take A Bow 85.00
Plate, Cobalt Blue 40.00
Sheet Music, Goodnight My Love, 1936 .... 12.00
Sugar, Cobalt Blue 35.00

SHRINER, see Fraternal category

SILVER DEPOSIT glass was made during the late nineteenth and early
twentieth centuries. Solid sterling silver was applied to the glass by a
chemical method so that a cutout design of silver metal appeared against a
clear or colored glass. It is sometimes called silver overlay.

Cheese & Cracker, Underplate, Flower Border, 10 1/4 In. 32.00
Coffee & Cake Set, Germany, 1900, Setting For 12 .... 1500.00
Decanter, Rose & Scroll, Cranberry Cut To Clear, Alvin, 12 1/2 In. .... *Illus* 2035.00
Teapot, Brown, Floral, Gibson, 8 Cup 35.00
Vase, Allover Floral & Scroll, Emerald Green, Alvin Mark, 7 In. .... *Illus* 550.00
Vase, Black Satin Glass, Cattail Flower & Bud Overlay, 5 1/2 In. 330.00
Vase, Bud, Green, Floral Design, 7 In., Pair 220.00

Silver Deposit, Vase, Spider Mum Overlay, Cranberry, 12 1/2 In.; Silver Deposit, Decanter, Rose & Scroll, Cranberry Cut To Clear, Alvin, 12 1/2 In.

Silver Deposit, Vase, Flared, Carnation & Arch, Emerald Green, 8 1/4 In.; Silver Deposit, Vase, Allover Floral & Scroll, Emerald Green, Alvin Mark, 7 In.

Vase, Clear, Silver Art Deco Roses & Buds, 12 1/4 x 7 In. 638.00
Vase, Cranberry, Pedestal, Daisy Design Silver Overlay, 10 In. 1485.00
Vase, Cranberry, Wild Rose Silver Overlay, Monogram, 1899, Alvin, 4 1/2 In. 165.00
Vase, Emerald Green, Allover Carnations, Buds, Monogram, 3 1/2 x 5 1/2 In. 798.00
Vase, Emerald Green, Allover Floral & Scroll, Shield, Alvin, 7 In. 550.00
Vase, Flared, Carnation & Arch, Emerald Green, 8 1/4 In. .... *Illus* 660.00
Vase, Pale Blue, Art Deco Pond Lilies & Leaves Overlay, 8 In. 137.00
Vase, Spider Mum Overlay, Cranberry, 12 1/2 In. .... *Illus* 330.00
Vase, Turquoise, Silver Floral & Scroll Design, 2 3/4 x 2 1/2 In. 550.00

SILVER FLATWARE includes many of the current and out-of-production silver and silver-plated flatware patterns made in the past eighty years. Other silver is listed under Silver-American, Silver-English, etc. Most silver flatware sets that are missing a few pieces can be completed through the help of one of the many silver matching services listed in *Kovels' Guide to Selling Your Antiques & Collectibles.*

SILVER FLATWARE PLATED, Alhambra, Ladle, 10 3/4 In. 65.00
  Ambassador, Cream Soup Spoon 4.00
  Ambassador, Iced Tea Spoon 7.00
  Arbutus, Salad Fork, 1908 .... 12.50
  Avalon, Luncheon Fork, 1901 .... 6.00
  Avon, Fruit Spoon, 1901 .... 7.00
  Berkshire, Bonbon Spoon, Gold Wash Bowl, Rogers 75.00
  Berkshire, Jelly Trowel, Rogers 48.00
  Bird Of Paradise, Poultry Set, Rogers 48.00
  Cardinal, Dinner Fork, Wallace 8.00
  Cardinal, Salad Fork, Wallace 8.00
  Charter Oak, Salad Fork 32.00
  Floral, Pickle Fork, Long Handle, Rogers 45.00
  Floral, Salad Fork, Rogers 48.00
  Floral, Seafood Fork, Wallace 14.00
  La Vigne, Tea Strainer, Rogers 175.00
  Meadowbrook, Service For 8, Wm. Rogers, Case, 73 Piece 200.00
  Nenuphar, Soup Ladle, 10 In. 60.00
  Old Colony, Gravy Ladle 25.00
  Old Colony, Gumbo Spoon 12.00
  Romanesque, Gravy Ladle, 1847 Rogers 29.00
  Sheraton, Seafood Fork 6.00
  Wildwood, Seafood Fork 7.00
SILVER FLATWARE STERLING, 14th Century, Dinner Set, Shreve & Co., 123 Piece . 8000.00
  Acanthus, Pickle, Fork, Georg Jensen 45.00
  Adams, Service For 12, Frank Whiting & Co., 104 Piece 550.00
  Afterglow, Service For 12, Oneida, Serving Pieces 875.00
  American Beauty, Cold Meat Fork, Shiebler 80.00
  American Beauty, Lettuce Fork, Shiebler 55.00

American Beauty, Teaspoon, Shiebler 20.00
Angelo, Berry Spoon, Wood & Hughes 125.00
Antique Lily, Teaspoon, Frank Whiting, 1890, 12 Piece 350.00
Arabesque, 8 Settings, Pearl Handled Knives, 1890, 48 Piece 2400.00
Avalon, Asparagus Server, International 225.00
Avalon, Meat Fork, International 125.00
Avalon, Soup Ladle, International 400.00
Baronial, Sandwich Tongs, Gorham 400.00
Baronial, Seafood Fork, Gorham 22.00
Baronial, Service For 12, 138 Piece 1650.00
Baronial, Stuffing Spoon, Gorham 275.00
Bead, Fish Slice, Durgin, 9 1/2 In. 95.00
Berain, Citrus Spoon, Wallace, c.1907, 8 Piece 195.00
Blossom, Dinner Fork, Dominick & Haff 38.00
Blossom, Pancake Server, Dominick & Haff 250.00
Blossom, Teaspoon, Dominick & Haff 15.00
Bridal Rose, Berry Spoon, Alvin .... 275.00 to 295.00
Bridal Rose, Chocolate Spoon, Alvin 55.00
Bridal Rose, Cream Soup Spoon, Alvin, 6 3/4 In. 75.00
Bridal Rose, Dinner Knife, Alvin 55.00
Bridal Rose, Gravy Ladle, Alvin 175.00
Bridal Rose, Meat Fork, Alvin 195.00
Bridal Rose, Pie Server, Alvin 495.00
Bridal Rose, Salad Set, Alvin, 2 Piece 295.00
Bridal Rose, Sugar Shell, Alvin 55.00
Bridal Rose, Sugar Sifter, Alvin 175.00
Bridal Rose, Sugar Spoon, Alvin 65.00
Bridal Rose, Teaspoon, Alvin 18.00
Bridal Veil, Salad Fork, Rogers 15.00
Buckingham, Dinner Set, Monogram H, Shreve & Co., 119 Piece 2185.00
Buckingham, Ice Cream Fork, Gorham 28.00
Buckingham, Iced Tea Spoon, Gorham 25.00
Buttercup, Dinner Service, Gorham, 191 Piece 2185.00
Buttercup, Olive Fork, Gorham 75.00
Buttercup, Sardine Fork, Gorham 150.00
Buttercup, Sauce Ladle, Gorham 75.00
Buttercup, Sugar Spoon, Gorham 35.00
Buttercup, Tomato Server, Gorham 95.00
Buttercup, Vegetable Serving Fork, Gorham 395.00
Cactus, Baby Fork, Jensen 45.00
Cambridge, Chocolate Spoon, Gorham 26.00
Cambridge, Punch Ladle, Gorham 220.00
Cambridge, Strawberry Fork, Gorham 25.00
Cambridge, Tomato Server, Gorham, 1899 .... 50.00 to 150.00
Camellia, Gorham, Service For 6, 44 Piece 495.00
Candlelight, Cocktail Fork, Towle 12.00
Cattails, Coffee Spoon, Durgin 35.00
Chantilly, Bouillon Spoon, Gorham, 12 Piece 300.00
Chantilly, Butter Fork, 2 Tines, Gorham 45.00
Chantilly, Cigar Cutter, Gorham 195.00
Chantilly, Dinner Service, Gorham, Fitted Case, 81 Piece 920.00
Chantilly, Mustard Ladle, Gorham 125.00
Chantilly, Nut Spoon, Gorham 495.00
Chantilly, Oyster Ladle, Gorham 325.00
Chantilly, Pea Spoon, Gorham 595.00
Chantilly, Pie Server, Gorham 275.00
Chantilly, Punch Ladle, Twisted Stem, Gorham 150.00
Chantilly, Service For 12, Gorham, Fitted Case, 87 Piece 1495.00
Charles II, Cheese Scoop, Dominick & Haff 150.00
Charles II, Dinner Set, Monogram, Lunt, 75 Piece 1265.00
Charles II, Fish Server, Dominick & Haff 250.00
Charles II, Ice Cream Spoon, Dominick & Haff 35.00
Charles II, Lettuce Fork, Dominick & Haff 75.00

Chateau, Service For 8, Lunt, Box, 50 Piece 450.00
Chateau Rose, Cream Soup Spoon, Alvin 20.00
Chateau Rose, Salad Fork, Alvin 17.00
Chateau Rose, Tablespoon, Alvin 40.00
Chrysanthemum, Berry Spoon, Durgin 250.00
Chrysanthemum, Cheese Scoop, Durgin 250.00
Chrysanthemum, Gravy Ladle, Durgin 225.00
Chrysanthemum, Meat Fork, Durgin 110.00
Chrysanthemum, Pie Server, Durgin 395.00
Chrysanthemum, Salad Set, Durgin 450.00
Chrysanthemum, Sardine Fork, Durgin 125.00
Colfax, Salad Fork, Durgin 14.00
Coligni, Cheese Knife, Gorham 175.00
Coligni, Cheese Scoop, Gorham 250.00
Colonial, Soup Ladle, Gorham .... 160.00 to 175.00
Continental, Dinner Set, International, 88 Piece 2587.50
Corinthian, Cake Knife, Serrated Blade, Shiebler 225.00
Corinthian, Nut Pick, Shiebler, 6 Piece 180.00
Corinthian, Teaspoon, Shiebler 25.00
Custis, 9 Piece Place Setting, Wallace, c.1912, 72 Piece 1600.00
Damask Rose, Teaspoon, Oneida 13.00
Dorchester, Mustard Ladle, Watrou 25.00
Douvaine, Cream Ladle, Unger 85.00
Douvaine, Pickle Fork, Unger, 6 1/4 In. 65.00
Dresden, Berry Spoon, Whiting 95.00
Dresden, Cucumber Server, Whiting 120.00
Dresden, Fish Set, Whiting 300.00
Empire, Meat Fork, Whiting 100.00
English Shell, Dinner Set, Monogram, Lunt, 67 Piece 575.00
Essex, Pie Knife, Durgin 98.00
Essex, Sugar Shell, Durgin 65.00
Etruscan, Dinner Set, Gorham, 97 Piece 920.00
Etruscan, Grapefruit Spoon, Gorham 22.00
Etruscan, Sugar Spoon, Gorham 35.00
Evangeline, Stuffing Spoon, Alvin 175.00
Fairfax, Bouillon Spoon, Durgin 20.00
Fairfax, Gumbo Spoon, Durgin 32.00
Fairfax, Olive Spoon, Durgin 45.00
Fairfax, Pickle Fork, Durgin 30.00
Fairfax, Service For 8, Gorham, 55 Piece 1595.00
Fairfax, Sugar Tongs, Durgin 30.00
Fairfax, Teapot, Durgin 285.00
Fiorito, Cold Meat Fork, Shiebler 165.00
Fiorito, Sugar Shell, Shiebler 45.00
Five Flowers, Bonbon Tongs, Reed & Barton 200.00
Five Flowers, Oyster Server, Reed & Barton 275.00
Florentine, Cold Meat Fork, Gorham, 8 1/2 In. 175.00
Fork, Pickle, Madrigal, Lunt 16.00
Francis I, Service For 12, Reed & Barton, 129 Piece 3850.00
Francis I, Service For 20, Chest, Reed & Barton, 145 Piece 3300.00
French Provincial, Dinner Set, Towle, Fitted Case, 83 Piece 1150.00
French Renaissance, Serving Spoon, Reed & Barton 52.00
Frontenac, Cheese Knife, International 225.00
Frontenac, Five O'Clock Spoon, International 75.00
Frontenac, Gumbo Soup Spoon, International 55.00
Frontenac, Lettuce Fork, International 195.00
Frontenac, Sardine Fork, International 150.00
Georgian, Soup Ladle, Towle 600.00
Georgian, Tomato Server, Towle 150.00
Gothic, Olive Fork, Shiebler 75.00
Grande Baroque, Dinner Knife, Wallace 45.00
Grande Baroque, Dinner Set, Wallace, Fitted Case, 114 Piece 3450.00
Grande Baroque, Gravy Ladle, Wallace 85.00

Grapevine, Ladle, Claret, Dominick & Haff 110.00
Grecian, Gravy Ladle, Gorham 110.00
Grecian, Ice Cream Set, 12 Spoons & Server, Gorham 600.00
Heiress, Fork, Cocktail, Oneida 14.00
Heiress, Fork, Cold Meat, Oneida 32.00
Heiress, Spoon, Cream Soup, Oneida 18.00
Heraldic, Dessert Spoon, Whiting 22.00
Heraldic, Serving Spoon, Long Handle, Whiting, c.1880 .... 192.50
Imperial Chrysanthemum, Cheese Knife, Gorham 195.00
Imperial Chrysanthemum, Ice Cream Knife, Gorham, 10 5/8 In. 250.00
Imperial Chrysanthemum, Oyster Fork, Gorham, Pair 40.00
Imperial Chrysanthemum, Spoon, 7 1/2 In. 35.00
Imperial Queen, Berry Spoon, Whiting 150.00
Imperial Queen, Ice Cream Slice, Whiting 225.00
Imperial Queen, Meat Fork, Whiting 100.00
Intermezzo, Place Setting, National, 5 Piece 85.00
Irian, Cocktail Fork, Wallace 20.00
Irian, Cream Ladle, Wallace 120.00
Irian, Master Butter Knife, Wallace 125.00
Iris, Butter Fork, Durgin 110.00
Iris, Fish Slice, Durgin 400.00
Iris, Salt Spoon, Master, Durgin, Pair 70.00
Joan Of Arc, Service For 8, International, Box 1195.00
John Alden, Dinner Set, Watson Co., Fitted Case, 147 Piece 1380.00
King, Dinner Fork, Dominick & Haff 48.00
King Edward, Dinner Set, 199 Piece 2300.00
King Edward, Lunch Knife, Silver Plated Blade, Whiting 40.00
King Edward, Tablespoon, Whiting 60.00
King Richard, Dinner Set, Towle, 119 Piece 1610.00
Kings III, Ice Cream Knife, Gorham, Gold Washed, 1900 .... 400.00
La Parisienne, Punch Ladle, Twist Handle, Reed & Barton 350.00
La Parisienne, Teaspoon, Reed & Barton 18.00
La Reine, Teaspoon, Reed & Barton 16.00
La Scala, Teaspoon, Gorham 21.00
Lace Point, Dinner Set, Lunt, 21 Piece 258.75
Lady Mary, Teaspoon, Towle 10.00
Lady Mary, Towle, Case, Service For 12 .... 450.00
Lancaster, Claret Ladle, Gorham 295.00
Lancaster, Dessert Spoon, Gorham 28.00
Lancaster, Jelly Knife, Gorham 150.00
Lancaster, Pie Server, Ruffled Edge, Gorham 495.00
Lancaster, Relish, Oval, Gorham 150.00
Lancaster, Salad Fork, Gorham, 12 Piece 341.00
Lancaster, Teaspoon, Gorham 12.00
Lansdowne, Service For 12, Gorham, Fitted Case, 211 Piece 2300.00
Laurate, Dessert Spoon, Whiting 18.00
Les Cinq Fleurs, Soup Spoon, Gumbo, Reed & Barton 38.00
Les Cinq Fleurs, Sugar Tongs, Reed & Barton 35.00
Lily, Bouillon Spoon, Monogram, Whiting, 12 Piece 330.00
Lily, Dessert Spoon, Whiting 75.00
Lily, Knife, Wedding Cake, Gorham, 1902 .... 75.00
Lily, Olive Fork, Whiting 95.00
Lily, Oyster Fork, Monogram, Whiting, 12 Piece 385.00
Lily, Pea Spoon, Whiting 795.00
Lily, Preserve Spoon, Whiting 195.00
Lily Of The Valley, Grapefruit Spoon, Whiting 55.00
Lily Of The Valley, Sugar Shell, Whiting 95.00
Lily Of The Valley, Sugar Tongs, Whiting 150.00
Lily Of The Valley, Teaspoon, Whiting, 12 Piece 350.00
Louis Silver Flatware Sterling, Asparagus Server, Whiting 325.00
Louis XV, Cocktail Fork, Durgin 22.00
Louis XV, Fish Knife, Whiting 165.00
Louis XV, Mustard Ladle, Whiting 65.00

Louis XV, Olive Spoon, Whiting 30.00
Louis XV, Service For 6, Whiting, 36 Piece 1800.00
Louis XV, Soup Ladle, Whiting 180.00
Louis XV, Tablespoon, Whiting, 6 Piece 132.00
Louise, Stuffing Spoon, Whiting 395.00
Love Disarmed, Fish Set, Reed & Barton, 2 Piece 935.00
Love Disarmed, Place Setting, Reed & Barton, c.1910, 84 Piece 9500.00
Love Disarmed, Salad Set, Gold Wash, Reed & Barton 875.00
Lucerne, Fish Server, Wallace 150.00
Lucerne, Sugar Spoon, Wallace 50.00
Lyric, Teaspoon, Gorham 11.00
Madame Royale, Cracker Scoop, Durgin 195.00
Madrigal, Sugar Spoon, Lunt 18.00
Majestic, Bouillon Spoon, Alvin 30.00
Majestic, Butter Pick, Alvin 75.00
Majestic, Fish Fork, Alvin 50.00
Majestic, Olive Spoon, Alvin 85.00
Majestic, Seafood Fork, Alvin 20.00
Marechal Niel, Asparagus Fork, Durgin 325.00
Marguerite, Cocktail Fork, Gorham 10.00
Marie Antoinette, Salad Set, Gorham, 8 3/4 In. 200.00
Marlborough, Teaspoon, Reed & Barton 11.00
Mary II, 8-Piece Place Setting, Servers, Lunt, 1920s, 96 Piece 2100.00
Mazarin, Ice Cream Knife, Dominick & Haff 335.00
Medallion, Knife & Fork, Juvenile, Schulz & Fischer 125.00
Medici, Fork, Luncheon, Gorham 26.00
Medici, Knife, Luncheon, Gorham 23.00
Medici, Teaspoon, Gorham 20.00
Melrose, Gravy Ladle, Gorham 55.00
Melrose, Tablespoon, Gorham 65.00
Melrose, Teaspoon, Gorham 20.00
Memory Lane, Teaspoon, Lunt 12.00
Michelangelo, Dinner Set, Oneida, 30 Piece 345.00
Milan, Ice Cream Knife, Gorham, 9 5/8 In. 100.00
Modern Classic, Dinner Set, Lunt, Fitted Case, 46 Piece 517.50
Modern Victorian, Service For 8, Monogram, Lunt, 50 Piece 467.00
Monarque, Sardine Fork, Howard 45.00
Mythologique, Pie Fork, Gorham, 12 Piece 1320.00
Mythologique, Salad Fork & Spoon, Gorham 357.50
National, Berry Fork, Durgin, Pair 45.00
New Art, Berry Spoon, Durgin .... 150.00 to 300.00
New Art, Gravy Ladle, Durgin 175.00
New Art, Sardine Fork, Durgin 125.00
New King, Dinner Fork, Dominick & Haff 45.00
New King, Orange Knife, Dominick & Haff 20.00
New Vintage, Berry Spoon, Durgin 95.00
Newberry, Dessert Spoon, Towle 18.00
Newcastle, Almond Server, Gorham, c.1895 .... 38.00
Nuremburg, Dinner Knife, Alvin 75.00
Old Baronial, Fish Fork, Gorham, 7 1/4 In. 55.00
Old Baronial, Tablespoon, Gorham 60.00
Old Colonial, Beef Fork, Towle 125.00
Old Colonial, Lettuce Fork, Towle 195.00
Old Colonial, Salad Fork, Towle, 8 Piece 55.00
Old Colony, Butter Knife, Lunt, 1895 .... 15.00
Old English, Soup Ladle, Towle 145.00
Old Lace, Service For 8, Monogram, Towle, 52 Piece 412.00
Old Lace, Teaspoon, Towle 15.00
Old Newberry, Sardine Fork, Towle 95.00
Old Newberry, Toast Fork, Towle 295.00
Olive, Spoon, Branch Of Coral Form, Seashells, Gorham, c.1890 ...... 690.00
Olympian, Soup Ladle, Applied Monogram Shield, Tiffany & Co. 546.25
Orange Blossom, Berry Spoon, Alvin 275.00

Orange Blossom, Bouillon Spoon, Alvin	35.00
Orange Blossom, Butter Knife, Master, Durgin	65.00
Orange Blossom, Cream Ladle, Alvin	100.00
Orange Blossom, Cucumber Server, Durgin	75.00
Orange Blossom, Ice Cream Fork, Alvin	75.00
Orange Blossom, Ice Cream Spoon, Alvin	55.00
Orange Blossom, Meat Fork, Alvin	150.00
Orange Blossom, Sardine Fork, Alvin	150.00
Orange Blossom, Soup Ladle, Monogram, Alvin, 12 In.	522.00
Orange Blossom, Sugar Shell, Alvin	55.00
Page Turner, Gorham, 11 x 2 1/2 In.	105.00
Paul Revere, Horseradish Spoon, Towle	85.00
Phoebe, Almond Scoop, Watson Newel	90.00
Piper, Teaspoon, Gorham	28.00
Plymouth, Butter Knife, Master, Gorham	30.00
Prelude, Luncheon Fork, International	24.00
Prince Eugene, Teaspoon, Alvin	16.00
Puritan, Cocktail Fork, Amston	11.00
Puritan, Dessert Spoon, Amston	20.00
Puritan, Salad Fork, Amston	18.00
Pusher, Puritan, Stieff	42.00
Queens, Service For 12, Gorham, 88 Piece	1210.00
Radiant, Soup Ladle, Gold Washed Bowl, Whiting, 14 In.	425.00
Raleigh, Lettuce Fork, Alvin	48.00
Raphael, Tomato Server, Alvin	275.00
Regent, Fish Slice, Gold Wash, Gorham	135.00
Renaissance, Meat Fork, Dominick & Haff	150.00
Repousse, Bacon Fork, Kirk	85.00
Repousse, Gravy Ladle, Kirk	90.00
Repousse, Iced Tea Spoon, Kirk	28.00
Repousse, Kirk, 97 Piece	3080.00
Repousse, Punch Ladle, Kirk	350.00
Repousse, Service For 12, Kirk, 109 Piece	3080.00
Roanoke, Teaspoon, Gorham	12.00
Rococo, Berry Spoon, Dominick & Haff	85.00
Rococo, Ice Cream Spoon, Dominick & Haff	35.00
Rococo, Seafood Fork, Dominick & Haff	22.00
Rococo, Sugar Sifter, Dominick & Haff	75.00
Rondo, Gravy Ladle, Gorham	55.00
Rose, Waffle Server, Stieff	395.00
Salem Witch, Berry Fork, Durgin, Pair	85.00
Salem Witch, Bonbon, Durgin	175.00
Salem Witch, Coffee Spoon, Durgin	160.00
Sir Christopher, Service For 12, Wallace, Fitted Case, 60 Piece	1100.00
Six Fleurs, Salad Set, Reed & Barton	650.00
Six Flowers, Berry Spoon, International	395.00
Sonja, Cold Meat Fork, International	75.00
Southern Charm, Place Setting, Alvin, 30 Piece	30.00
St. Cloud, Asparagus Fork, Gorham	695.00
St. Cloud, Soup Ladle, Gold Washed Bowl, Gorham	500.00
Strasbourg, Mustard Ladle, Gorham	125.00
Strasbourg, Sauce Ladle, Gorham	35.00
Strasbourg, Sugar Shell, Gorham	32.50
Stratford, Sugar Shell, International	28.00
Stratford, Sugar Tongs, International	45.00
Stratford, Teaspoon, International	18.00
Suffolk, Strawberry Fork, Alvin	25.00
Swan Lake, Fork, International, 7 1/4 In.	27.00
Symphony, Dinner Set, Monogram B, Towle, 121 Piece	980.00
Symphony, Service For 8, Towle, Fitted Case, 86 Piece	690.00
Tablespoon, Old Kings, Whiting, c.1890, 6 Piece	225.00
Tara, Dinner Set, Reed & Barton, 42 Piece	1000.00
Tatteau, Cold Meat Fork, Durgin, 1895	78.00

Tea Infuser, Dominick & Haff 65.00
Teaspoon, Arabesque, Whiting, 12 Piece 350.00
Theseum, Gumbo Soup Spoon, International 22.00
Theseum, Salad Fork, International 21.00
Theseum, Soup Spoon, Oval, International 19.00
Theseum, Teaspoon, International .... 12.00 to 15.00
Thistle, Hors D'Oeuvre Fork, Birmingham 27.00
Threaded, Tablespoon, S. Kirk & Son, c.1860 .... 65.00
Tomato Server, Francis I, Reed & Barton 135.00
Tomato Vine, Soup Ladle, Tiffany & Co. 805.00
Tranquility, Butter Knife, Fine Arts 17.50
Tranquility, Cold Meat Fork, Fine Arts 55.00
Tranquility, Gravy Ladle, Fine Arts 32.00
Tranquility, Sugar Spoon, Fine Arts 17.00
Trianon, Gumbo Soup Spoon, International 22.00
Trianon, Sugar Spoon, International 20.00
Tuileries, Dessert Fork, Gorham, Gold Washed, 12 Piece 450.00
Valencia, Butter Knife, International 16.00
Valencia, Knife, International 15.00
Valencia, Pickle Fork, International 19.00
Valencia, Teaspoon, International 14.00
Versailles, Asparagus Server, Gorham 535.00
Versailles, Cake Knife, Serrated, Gorham 300.00
Versailles, Cocktail Fork, Gorham 32.00
Versailles, Service For 12, Monogram, Gorham, 125 Piece 3740.00
Vespera, Salad Fork, Towle 18.00
Vespera, Soup Spoon, Oval, Towle 22.00
Vintage, Chocolate Spoon, Durgin 18.00
Violet, Tomato Server, Whiting 250.00
Virginian, Bread Knife, Oneida 26.00
Virginian, Cake Breaker, Oneida 30.00
Virginian, Cream Soup Spoon, Oneida 13.00
Virginian, Letter Opener, Oneida 26.00
Vision, Fork, International, 7 1/4 In. 29.00
Vision, Iced Tea Spoon, International 17.00
Vision, Sugar Spoon, International 21.00
Vision, Teaspoon, International 11.00
Vivant, Baked Potato Server, Oneida 25.00
Vivant, Citrus Spoon, Oneida 15.00
Vivant, Ice Cream Spoon, Oneida 15.00
Vivant, Lemon Fork, Oneida 7.00
Vivant, Olive Fork, Oneida 10.00
Wadefield, Fork, Kirk, 7 1/4 In. 18.00
Wadefield, Salad Fork, Kirk 17.00
Wallace, Butter Knife, Wallace 8.00
Wallace, Ice Cream Fork, Wallace 14.00
Wallace, Sugar Spoon, Wallace 10.00
Warwick, Citrus Spoon, International 14.00
Warwick, Potato Server, International 25.00
Warwick, Serving Spoon, Pierced, International 25.00
Warwick, Teaspoon, International, 5 3/4 In. 9.00
Watteau, Bread Serving Fork, Durgin 150.00
Watteau, Pastry Fork, Durgin 30.00
Waverly, Gumbo Soup Spoon, Wallace 26.00
Waverly, Sardine Fork, Wallace 45.00
Wedding Bells, Baked Potato Server, Rogers 25.00
Wedding Bells, Butter Fork, Rogers 6.80
Wedding Bells, Serving Spoon, Rogers 25.00
Wedding Bells, Soup Spoon, Rogers 10.20
Wedgwood, Gravy Ladle, Gorham 58.00
Wedgwood, Gumbo Spoon, Gorham 26.00
Wedgwood, Salad Fork, International 35.00
Wedgwood, Soup Spoon, Oval, Gorham 30.00

Wentworth, Bouillon Spoon, Watson	8.00
Wentworth, Knife, Watson, 9 3/4 In.	12.00
Wild Flower, Bread Knife, Royal Crest	28.00
Wild Flower, Butter Fork, Royal Crest	12.00
Wild Flower, Cake Breaker, Royal Crest	29.00
Wild Flower, Gravy Ladle, Royal Crest	30.00
Wild Rose, Bread Knife, International	29.00
Wild Rose, English Server, International	28.00
Wild Rose, Fork, International, 7 3/8 In.	23.00
Wild Rose, Letter Opener, International	26.00
Wild Rose, Steak Knife, International	29.00
Wild Rose, Youth Fork, International, 6 1/4 In.	18.00
Will O'Wisp, Dessert Spoon, Oneida	12.00
Will O'Wisp, Teaspoon, Oneida	12.00
William & Mary, Butter Fork, Lunt	7.00
William & Mary, Butter Spreader, Lunt	10.00
William & Mary, Cake Breaker, Lunt	29.00
William & Mary, Coffee Spoon, Lunt, 5 3/8 In.	7.00
William & Mary, Soup Spoon, Lunt	15.00
Willow, Berry Spoon, Gorham, 9 In.	50.00
Willow, Gravy Ladle, Gorham	29.00
Willow, Lemon Fork, Gorham	12.00
Willow, Olive Fork, Gorham	14.00
Winchester, Bouillon Spoon, Alvin	13.00
Woodlily, Teaspoon, F. Smith	18.00
Wreath, Salt, 1870	125.00

SILVER PLATE is not solid silver. It is a ware made of a metal, such as nickel or copper, that is covered with a thin coating of silver. The letters *EPNS* are often found on American and English silver-plated wares. Sheffield is a term with two meanings. In this section, Sheffield refers to a type of silver plate, usually English.

Ⓔ Ⓟ ⓝ Ⓝ Ⓢ

Basket, Bride's, Floral, Bird & Fruit Design, Raised, C-Scroll, Handle, 18 In.	625.00
Basket, Cake, Chased Hummingbirds, Florals, Bees, Meriden	55.00
Basket, Cake, Embossed Roses, Fruit, Scalloped Rim, 12 In.	85.00
Basket, Floral, Reticulated, Engraved Shell, 12 In.	160.00
Basket, Raised Art Nouveau Flowers, 8 x 10 1/2 In.	60.00
Biscuit Box, Victorian, Domed Top, Beaded Border, Chased Foliage, 8 1/2 In.	220.00
Bowl, Flower & Leaf Scroll Rim, Shell Shape, English Silver Mfg., 16 In. Diam.	65.00
Bowl, Open Wire Sides, Oval Base, Diamond Shape, Germany, 5 x 3 In.	13.00
Bun Warmer, Victorian, 3 Sections, 19th Century, 9 In.	550.00
Butter, Cooler, Scalloped, Wreath Finial Is Handle, Oneida	70.00
Butter, Cow, Resting Lid, Insert & Knife Rests, 1880s	125.00
Butter, Telescoping Domed Lid	66.00
Candelabra, 3-Light, Reeded Arms, M. Boulton, c.1820, 22 1/2 In., Pair	3450.00
Candelabra, 5-Light, George III Style, Square Foot, 19 In., Pair	1100.00
Candlestick, Art Nouveau, Pairpoint, 10 In., Pair	800.00
Candlestick, Baluster Stem, M. Boulton, Sheffield, c.1810, 12 1/4 In., Pair	805.00
Candlestick, Classical Column, Sheffield, 6 1/4 In., Pair	99.00
Card Tray, Art Nouveau Woman, No. 290, Wurttembergische, c.1906, 12 In.	800.00
Castor, Egg, 4 Each Cups, Spoon, Holder, Scotch	120.00
Centerpiece, Woman, Flowing Gown Forms Trays, WMF, c.1900, 8 5/8 In.	700.00
Chafing Dish, Cover, Stand, Lion Head & Paw Legs, Alcohol Burner, 11 In.	65.00
Charger, Classical Woman, Attendants, Elkington, Morel, 1876, 20 1/4 In.	445.00
Cider Pot, Cover, Globular, Tusk Handles, Cut Glass Bowl, 14 In.	445.00
Coaster, Wine, Barbour Silver Co., 1890s, Pair	1400.00
Cocktail Set, Bakelite Knobs, Barbour, c.1930, 11 Piece	690.00
Cocktail Shaker, Lid, Striped, Hawkes	156.00
Cocktail Shaker, Milk Pale, Reed & Barton, c.1920	160.00
Coddler, Egg, Bird Feet, Swan Finial, 9 In.	148.50
Coffee Server, Ornate, Swing Stand, Pairpoint	310.00
Coffee Set, Coronation, Community, 6 Piece	1195.00
Coffee Set, Heritage, 21-In. Tray, Rogers, 4 Piece	175.00

Coffee Set, Kentshire, Sheffield, 4 Piece	80.00
Coffee Set, Tray, Oneida, 4 Piece	45.00
Coffeepot, Fairmont Hotel, Reed & Barton	38.00
Coffeepot, Treen Handle, Sheffield, c.1810, 9 In.	155.00
Coffin Plate, Father	10.00
Coffin Plate, Our Darling	15.00
Condiment Dish, Cobalt Inserts, Spoon, Scrolled Collar, Pair	285.00
Cruet, Victorian, 6 Cut Glass Bottles, Stand, England, c.1880, 12 1/2 In.	225.00
Cup, Baby's, Playing Children	14.00
Dish, Bacon, Hinged Lid, Inner Tray, Lion & Crown Medallion, London, 1774	450.00
Egg Cruet, 6 Cups & Spoons, Stand, Scrolled Feet, Victorian, England, 12 In.	245.00
Egg Warmer, Victorian	120.00
Entree Dish, Cover, Hot Water Base, Sheffield, c.1820, 14 In., Pair	1035.00
Epergne, 3 Arms, Domed Base, Pierced Acanthus Leaves, Glass Bowls, 26 In.	1725.00
Epergne, Regency, Scroll Arms, Paw Feet, Gadrooned Neck, c.1815, 11 3/4 In.	1725.00
Fish Service, Celluloid, Cased, England, 14 Piece	100.00
Flask, Cap Opens To Jigger, 6 In.	95.00
Flower Frog, Flower Finial, 7 1/4 x 6 In.	20.00
Frame, Meiji Period, Floral Sprays, Basketry Ground, Japan, 13 In.	245.00
Frame, Picture, Chased, Embossed, 17 x 13 In.	285.00
Goblet, Wine, 4 Panels, Baluster Stem, Reed & Barton, 4 1/2 In., 8 Piece	50.00
Ice Bucket, Swing Hinge, Glass Vacuum Liner, Poole	225.00
Inkstand, George III, Matthew Boulton, Sheffield	1100.00
Jardiniere, Boat Riding Waves Form, Eagle At Prow, W.M.F., 15 In.	1955.00
Jardiniere, Oval Form, Bow Knots, Acanthus, French, 16 In.	302.00
Kettle, On Stand, Sheffield, England, 19th Century, 10 3/4 In.	330.00
Knife Rest, Sailor Having Tug Of War, 2 1/4 x 3 1/2 In.	95.00
Knife Rest Set, Animal Kingdom, Gallia, Box, 1925, 12 Piece	3450.00
Ladle, Punch, Kings, Victorian, 12 1/2 In., Pair	175.00
Mirror, Shaving, Victorian, 19th Century, 20 x 17 In.	660.00
Napkin rings are listed in their own category	
Nut Bowl, Squirrel Seated On Edge, Twigs, Leaves, Victorian	195.00
Pill Box, Georgian, Shagreen Veneer, Round, 3 In.	88.00
Pitcher, Ancestral, Rogers	135.00
Pitcher, Coronation, Community	325.00
Pitcher, Eternally Yours, Rogers	135.00
Pitcher, Tilting, Victorian, Mask Spout, Pairpoint, c.1890, 22 In.	412.50
Punch Set, Hand Chased, Thomas Turner & Co., England, 19-In. Tray, 15 Piece	850.00
Roast Tray, Cover, Engraved Arms, Sheffield, 28 In.	935.00
Saltshaker, Black Bear, Meriden, 1880s	55.00
Server, 2 Tiers, Scalloped, Twist Stem, Center Loop Handle, FB Rogers, 8 & 6 In.	32.00
Server, Squash Finial, Lobed Lid, Alcohol Burner, England, 12 In.	330.00
Shield, Allegorical Figural Scenes, Elkington & Co., 1866, 34 1/2 In.	1725.00
Spoon, Souvenir, see Souvenirs category	
Syrup, Engraved Columbia, Hinged Lid, Reed & Barton, 1900	38.00
Syrup, Roman Finial & Handle, Meriden, c.1868	100.00
Tankard, Eastlake Design, Derby	185.00
Tea & Coffee Set, Bud Finials, Gadrooned, Ellis Barker, 5 Piece	247.00
Tea & Coffee Set, Tray, Melon Pattern, Community, 1940s, 6 Piece	1000.00
Teapot, Floral Design, Repousse, Ebony Handle, Sheffield, 19th Century	935.00
Teapot, Floral Engraved, Cast Footed & Finial, 6 1/4 In.	50.00
Teapot, Stand, Gadrooned Banding, Loop Handle, 1 Burner, c.1910	247.00
Toothpick, Dog & Basket, Tuft	40.00
Tray, 2 Covered Sections On Sides, Gadrooned, Well, 18 x 14 In.	34.00
Tray, Gallery, Oval, Pierced Gallery, Engraved, England, c.1890, 19 3/4 In.	1760.00
Tray, Octagon, Gadroon Edges, Foliage Handles, Ellis-Barker, c.1900, 26 In.	495.00
Tray, Oval, Gadroon Noble Crest, Mappin & Webb, London, 24 x 17 In.	225.00
Tray, Oval, Gadrooned Border, England, 20 In.	60.50
Tray, Oval, Raised Gadroon Rim, Embossed Palmettos, 21 1/2 x 17 In.	225.00
Tray, Well, Scalloped, Flower Scroll Rim, Footed, International Silver, 17 In.	55.00
Tray, Winthrop, Reed & Barton, 26 x 21 In.	286.00
Trophy, Hunting Dog, Rifles, Resilvered, Simpson, Hall, Miller	350.00
Tureen, Cover, 3 Splayed Legs, Wood Handles, Ebony Finial, 1880	3200.00

Silver Plate, Tureen, Soup, Cover, Liner,
Sheffield, England, 1820

◆◆◆◆◆◆◆◆◆◆◆◆◆◆◆◆◆◆◆◆◆◆

Don't clean the impressed hallmarks or names on the bottom
of a piece of silver. You may
eventually rub them off.

◆◆◆◆◆◆◆◆◆◆◆◆◆◆◆◆◆◆◆◆◆◆

Tureen, Ram's Head Handles, Gorham	330.00
Tureen, Repousse Flowers, Scrolls, Glass Liner, Handles, 14 1/2 In.	1100.00
Tureen, Sauce, Cover, Regency, Crested, Rectangular, Claw Supports, 9 In., Pair	575.00
Tureen, Soup, Bombe, Applied Shell, Gadroon Rim, Paw Feet, c.1820, 14 In.	431.25
Tureen, Soup, Cover, Liner, Sheffield, England, 1820 *Illus*	3163.00
Urn, Hot Water, Scrolling Acanthus, Shell Rims, Sheffield, 50 3/4 In.	440.00
Urn, Hot Water, William IV, Curved Handles, Urn Finial, Sheffield, 18 In.	550.00
Urn, Tea, George III, Ring Handles, Spherical, Ball Footed, Sheffield, 13 1/2 In.	460.00
Urn, Tea, William IV, Foliate Finial, Lion Paw Feet, Sheffield, 17 In.	550.00
Vase, Cylinders Joined By Square Bracket, Christofle, France, c.1940, 12 7/8 In.	925.00
Vase, Victorian, Bacchic Masks, Square Base, Swirling Gadroons, 17 1/2 In.	484.00
Vase Holder, Squirrel, Seated On Mound, Green Bud Vase, Meriden	275.00
Vase Holder, Victorian Butterfly, Green Bud Vase, Meriden	275.00
Water Set, Bird Design, Meriden, 8 1/2-In. Pitcher, 2 Piece	137.00
Wine Cooler, Bell-Shaped, Stepped Foot, Early 19th Century, 9 1/4 In., Pair	1380.00
Wine Cooler, Engraved Crest, Campana Form, Leaf Borders, c.1820, 10 1/2 In.	632.50
Wine Cooler, Neoclassical, Campana, Grapevine Rim, England, 17 1/2 In.	2420.00
Wine Cooler, Ribbed, Satyr Head Handles, A. Goodman, 10 1/4 In.	230.00

SILVER, SHEFFIELD, see Silver Plate; Silver-English

SILVER-AMERICAN. American silver is listed here. Most of the sterling
silver listed in this book is subdivided by country. There are also other pieces
of silver and silver plate listed under special categories, such as Napkin Ring,
Silver Flatware, Silver Plate, Silver-Sterling, and Tiffany Silver.

SILVER-AMERICAN, Asparagus Fork, Wellington, Durgin	165.00
Basin, Designs, Fluted Form, Durgin-Gorham, 1928, 14 3/8 In.	2015.00
Basket, Beaded Bail Handle, Jones, Ball & Poor, c.1839, 6 1/2 In.	315.00
Basket, Fenestrated, Applied Border, Monogram, Roger Williams, 9 x 7 In.	280.00
Basket, Openwork, Monogram, J.E. Caldwell & Co., 10 1/2 In.	225.00
Basket, Scrolled Foliage, Monogram, Coin, N. Harding, 19th Century, 12 In.	474.00
Bouillon Cup & Saucer, Maintenon, Lenox Liner, Gorham, 24 Piece	1540.00
Bowl, Applied Floral Border, Gorham, 2 1/2 x 8 3/4 In.	143.00
Bowl, Basket Form, Oblong, Frank Whiting Co., 7 x 12 x 8 In.	220.00
Bowl, Centerpiece, Foliate Handles, Beaded Rim, Gorham, 8 In.	1870.00
Bowl, Chased, Engraved T, Reticulated, Gorham, 1906, Round, 10 3/4 In.	330.00
Bowl, Circular, Pentafoil Shape, Handwrought, Kalo Shop, 9 1/4 In.	520.00
Bowl, Collet Base, Handwrought, Handicraft Shop, Boston, 1906, 5 In.	375.00
Bowl, Curled-Over Sides, Monogram, Jenkins & Jenkins, c.1910, 12 In.	1380.00
Bowl, Double, Triangular Wells, Handwrought, Kalo Shop, c.1920, 13 In.	1495.00
Bowl, Engraved, Gorham, c.1932	82.00
Bowl, Everted Pierced Flora Rim, Gorham, 17 1/2 In.	605.00
Bowl, Flower, Princess Anne, Reticulated Lid, Wallace, 13 In.	357.00
Bowl, Francis I, Reed & Barton, 8 In., Pair	575.00
Bowl, Hexagonal Lobed Sides, Everted Lip, Art Nouveau, Whiting, 12 In.	575.00
Bowl, Leaf-Flanked Lobes, Flowers On Rim, Gorham, c.1905, 10 3/4 In.	2415.00
Bowl, Louis XIV, Footed, Towle, 5 x 10 In.	195.00

Bowl, Modern Pattern, Stepped Circular Foot, Gorham, 9 1/4 In. 2300.00
Bowl, Molded Rim, Scrolling Monogram, Joseph Loring, c.1790, 3 1/4 In. 1850.00
Bowl, Monogram, Applied Border, Wallace, 2 1/4 x 9 In. 250.00
Bowl, Monogram, Ornate Border, Gorham, 10 3/4 In. 275.00
Bowl, Paneled Neoclassical, Everted Rim, Durgin, 1927, 13 In. 330.00
Bowl, Paul Revere, Watson, 6 In. 77.00
Bowl, Quatrefoil, Openwork Foliage Footed, Cellini Craft, Oval, 5 1/2 In. 105.00
Bowl, Repousse Swirl, Floral Garlands, Footed, Duhme, 3 In. 126.00
Bowl, Reticulated, Hexagonal Form, C-Scroll Border, Gorham, 1898, 12 In. 360.00
Bowl, Reticulated, Monogram, Watson, 10 In. 250.00
Bowl, Ring Foot, Scroll Design, Joseph Loring, c.1790, 5 3/4 In. 1850.00
Bowl & Creamer, Bright Cut Design, Ephraim Brasher, 4 3/4 In. 1550.00
Buckle, Figures Of Moses & Aaron, Shreve & Lowe, 1870s, 6 1/2 In. 715.00
Butter, Cover, Embossed Floral, Sheep Finial, Mitchell & Tyler 495.00
Butter, Domed Cover, Beaded Rim, Flower Heads, Vanderslice, 1865 .... 2300.00
Cake Lifter, Empire, Durgin 275.00
Candlestick, Monogram, Baluster, W. Gale & Sons, 1852, 11 In., Pair 2875.00
Candlestick, Monogram, Watson, Weighted, 10 In., 4 Piece 300.00
Candlestick, Urn Shaped Nozzle, Hexagonal, S. Kirk, c.1840, 12 In., Pair 6900.00
Candlestick, Weighted, Arthur Stone, c.1918, 11 In., Pair.. 2200.00
Carving Set, Maryland, Fitted Case, Alvin, 3 Piece 40.00
Centerpiece, Applied Floral Border, Graff, Washbourne & Duhn, 12 1/2 In. 300.00
Centerpiece, Ribbed Petal Form Bowl, Handle, Gorham, 1869, 11 In. 1650.00
Centerpiece, Stand, Monogram, Signed, 1930-1940, Cloth Bags, 15 3/4 In. 1610.00
Cheese Scoop, Bright Cut, Ball, Black & Co. 150.00
Cigarette Case, Engraved Scrollwork, William Kerr, c.1910 .... 70.00
Cocktail Shaker, Tray, Arts & Crafts, No. 1457, Randahl Shop, c.1928 .... 1265.00
Coffee Set, Floral, Monogram, Baluster, Coin, J. & I. Cox, 1840, 3 Piece 2200.00
Coffee Set, Monogram, Watson Silver Co., Demitasse, 3 Piece 275.00
Coffee Set, Swan Neck Spout, J.E. Caldwell, 3 Piece 4500.00
Coffee Urn, Greek Key, Beaded, Coin, Bigelow Bros., 1845, 17 In. 2100.00
Coffeepot, Chased Vintage, Baluster, Coin, Ball, Black & Co., 1851, 10 In. 525.00
Coffeepot, Foliate Design, Scroll Spout, Handle, Gorham, 1899, 11 1/2 In. 7475.00
Coffeepot, Grapevines, Crest, Coin, Ball, Tomkins & Black, 11 In. 770.00
Coffeepot, Princess Mary, Wallace, 10 1/2 In. 250.00
Coffeepot, Repousse Neck, Bifurcated Scroll Handle, Durgin, 1890 .... 1495.00
Compote, Flowers & Leaves Rim, Hamilton, 6 x 6 1/2 In. 55.00
Compote, Footed, Chased Design, Gorham, 4 1/2 x 10 In. 165.00
Compote, Green Glass, Twisted Stem, Overlay, Rockwell Silver Co., 1920 .... 75.00
Compote, Presentation Inscription, Whiting, 1879, 7 x 11 In. 330.00
Compote, Putto Holding Swag Of Flowers, Crests & Arms, Gorham, Pair 2875.00
Compote, Winchester, No. 8411, Shreve & Co., 7 In., Pair 345.00
Creamer, Bands Of Pearls & Greek Key, Galt & Bros., c.1850, 8 1/4 In. 345.00
Creamer, Double Scroll Handle, Jonathan Otis, c.1770, 5 3/4 In. 2300.00
Creamer, Repousse Floral, Initials, Lincoln & Reed, Coin Silver, 4 3/4 In. 550.00
Creamer, Repousse Floral, Reed & Barton 40.00
Creamer, Sugar, Cover, Lady Diana, Towle 220.00
Creamer, Union Square, Children In Band At Top, Gorham 320.00
Cup, Chased Calyx Of Acanthus, Thomas Whartenby, 1810, Pair 3738.00
Cup, Chased Design, Engraved Symbols, Coin 98.00
Cup, Child's, Etched Scene, Bell Shape, C Shaped Handle, Gorham, 1885 .... 373.50
Cup, Child's, Graham, c.1913 .... 325.00
Cup, Flowers & Leaves, W.H. Talbot & Co. 235.00
Cup, Julep, Engraved J.A. Cox, W.R. Evans, 3 7/8 In. 522.50
Cup, Julep, Monogram, 3 3/8 In. 83.00
Cup Holder, J.E. Caldwell & Co., 1 1/2 In., 12 Piece 90.00
Demitasse Set, Colonial Revival, Graff, Washburn & Dunn, 3 Piece 330.00
Demitasse Set, Maintenon, Tray, Gorham, 4 Piece 2750.00
Desk Set, Pen, Inkwell, Stamp Box, Blotter, Dominique & Haff 305.00
Dessert Stand, Monogram, Presentation, Howard & Co., 1905, 1 1/2 In. 747.50
Dish, Alms, Sacred Monogram In Star Burst, G. Aiken, 1798, 10 In., Pair 3163.00
Dish, Cover, Bead Molding, Stylized Leaves & Grapes, Petersen 1840.00
Dish, Embossed Shells, Gorham, 1873, 2 1/2 In. 40.00

Dish, Nut, Interior Relief Flowers, Arthur Stone, c.1918, 3 5/8 In., 6 Piece	770.00
Dish, Repousse Fruit & Flowers, Ball Footed, Kirk, 5 3/4 In.	80.00
Dish, Serving, Applied Border, Arts & Crafts, L.S. & Co., c.1920, 12 In.	400.00
Dish, Serving, Chased Border, Monogram, Dominick & Haff, 12 In.	330.00
Dish, Serving, Chased, Engraved, Monogram, Dominick & Haff, 14 x 8 In.	825.00
Dish, Serving, Footed, 3 Sections, Shreve, Crump & Lowe, 13 In.	632.00
Dish, Vegetable, 2 Sections, Gadroon Border, Fisher, 11 1/4 In.	385.00
Dish, Vegetable, Cover, International Silver, 11 1/2 In.	195.00
Dish, Vegetable, Cover, Maintenon, Scroll Handle, Gorham, 12 3/4 In.	990.00
Dresser Set, Repousse, Colony Pattern, Fitted Case, Gorham, 3 Piece	137.00
Ewer, Embossed Flower & Grape Design, Harris & Hoit, 9 3/4 In.	1950.00
Ewer, Presentation, Ohio State Board Of Agriculture Premium, 10 In.	1200.00
Flagon, Cover, Ornate Border, Inscription, International Silver, 14 1/2 In.	1430.00
Flagon, Stepped Cover, Scroll Handle, Elias Pelletreau, 1726-1810	2640.00
Food Pusher, Duvaine, Helen On Blade, Unger	50.00
Fork, Fiddle-Tipped Handles, H. Cogswell, 7 1/4 In., 6 Piece	235.00
Fork, Olive Pattern, F. & H., c.1850, 6 Piece	245.00
Fruit Bowl, Stylized Flowers Set In Rim, International, 13 1/2 In.	375.00
Goblet, Garland Swags, Presentation, Vandyck Der Beitenne, 5 1/8 In.	203.50
Goblet, Wallace, 6 3/4 In., 8 Piece	360.00
Goblet, Water, Chased, Monogram, Heer-Schofield, 6 5/8 In., 12 Piece	3450.00
Gravy Boat, Underplate, Chrysanthemum, Gorham Martele .... *Illus*	2475.00
Gravy Ladle, Madrigal, Lunt	34.00
Ice Tongs, Mary Chilton Pattern, Towle, 1912	110.00
Inkwell, Figural, Seated Camels, Theodore B. Starr, c.1905, Pair	4000.00
Jug, Cream, Wavy Rim, 3 Scroll Feet, Philip Hulbeart, c.1764, 3 3/4 In.	575.00
Kettle, Stand, William Gale & Son, 1852, 16 3/4 In.	935.00
Knife, Butter, Memory Lane, Lunt, Individual	13.00
Ladle, Bright Cut Handle, Geo. W. Webb & Co., 13 In.	357.50
Ladle, Coffin End, Joel Sayer, 1880s.15 In.	750.00
Ladle, Cream, Fiddle-Tipped Handle, J.S.Porter, c.1845	48.00
Ladle, Gravy, Fiddle-Tipped Handle, Baldwin & Jones, c.1815	85.00
Ladle, Mustard, A.C. Benedict, c.1830	32.00
Ladle, Mustard, Basket Of Flowers, T. Stebbins, c.1830	58.00
Ladle, Sauce, D. Miller, c.1830	35.00
Ladle, Sauce, Pouring Spout, Shell Handle, Olsen, 1867, 7 3/8 In.	22.00
Ladle, Sauce, Rococo Handle, Reed & Barton, 6 In.	66.00
Ladle, Soup, Bead, Ball, Black & Co., 13 1/2 In.	225.00
Ladle, Soup, Bright Cut, C. Wiltberger, c.1790	975.00
Ladle, Soup, Curved Handle, Monogram, W.A. Williams, 1810, 12 1/2 In.	1495.00
Ladle, Soup, Paul Revere, c.1770, 13 7/8 In.	8625.00
Ladle, Soup, Pointed Oval Handle, John Vernon, c.1800, 13 5/8 In.	403.00
Ladle, Soup, Spiral Twist Shank, Flat Ovoid Handle, Schultz & Fisher	365.00
Loving Cup, Bird, Palm Fronds, Spider, Dragon, Glass Bottom, Gorham, 1883	4375.00
Marrow Scoop, Rattail Handle, Vautrot, 5 In.	60.00
Match Safe, Jester, Gorham, 1890	300.00
Mirror, Daffodil, Beveled Mirror, Easel, George Scheibler, 1890, 9 x 7 In.	357.00

*Silver-American, Gravy Boat, Underplate,
Chrysanthemum, Gorham Martele*

◆◆◆◆◆◆◆◆◆◆◆◆◆◆◆◆◆◆◆◆◆◆◆◆◆

Be careful how you handle clean
silver. Fingerprints will show and
eventually tarnish.

◆◆◆◆◆◆◆◆◆◆◆◆◆◆◆◆◆◆◆◆◆◆◆◆◆

Mug, Engraved Design, Coin, 3 1/2 In.	155.00
Mug, Inscription, 1866, Coin, Shreve, Stanwood & Co., 4 1/2 In.	220.00
Napkin Clip, Apollo, 4 Piece	50.00
Paperweight, Crab, S. Kirk & Son	165.00
Pitcher, Baluster Form, Bigelow, Kennard, 8 In.	522.50
Pitcher, Bulbous Form, Open Handle, Dominick & Haff, 10 1/2 In.	250.00
Pitcher, Chased Flowers & Foliage, Jacobi & Jenkins, 16 In.	2300.00
Pitcher, Cover, Design, Crest, Acanthus, Beaded, Gorham, 1863, 7 1/2 In.	440.00
Pitcher, Embossed Grapevine Spreading From Handle, J. Conning, c.1860	3163.00
Pitcher, Engraved, Octagonal Base, Waisted, W.B. Durgin Co., 8 1/4 In.	635.00
Pitcher, Flowers & Foliage, Shield Shaped Body, International, 12 In.	747.00
Pitcher, Gnarled Tree Trunk Form, Branch Handle, R. & W. Wilson, c.1845	6038.00
Pitcher, Hammered Finish, Kalo Shops, 1911, 22 Oz.	1540.00
Pitcher, Navarre Pattern, Whiting, 8 In.	415.00
Pitcher, Overall Chased Flowers & Leaves, Bigelow, Kennard, 8 1/2 In.	1870.00
Pitcher, Pierced Foliate Handle, Globular Form, Gorham, 9 In.	747.00
Pitcher, Pyriform Design, Chased Lily Pads, John Cox, 12 In.	2530.00
Pitcher, Underplate, Flowers, Vine Wrapped Handle, W. Wilson, 14 In.	4315.00
Pitcher, Water, Chased, Repousse, Monogram, S. Kirk, c.1915, 7 1/4 In.	1610.00
Pitcher, Water, Chased, Vine Monogram, Shreve & Co., c.1910, 13 1/2 In.	1610.00
Pitcher, Water, Gorham, 10 1/2 In.	522.00
Pitcher, Water, Joseph Lownes, 1800	6000.00
Pitcher, Water, Louis XIV, Chased, Monogram, Towle, 9 1/4 In.	495.00
Pitcher, Water, Octagonal, C-Scroll Handle, Howard, 9 1/2 In.	660.00
Pitcher, Water, Plain, Fred Hirsch Co., 1930s, 24 Oz., 9 1/2 In.	575.00
Pitcher, Water, Repousse Design, Monogram, Kirk, 9 In.	1870.00
Pitcher, Water, Repousse, Spherical, Cylindrical Neck, S. Kirk, 1905, 8 In.	1610.00
Pitcher, Water, William Heyer, c.1815	1210.00
Plate, Butter, Monogram, Gorham, 6 1/2 In., 12 Piece	225.00
Plate, Communion, Engraved, Whiting, 5 1/4 In.	44.00
Plate, Monogram, J.E. Caldwell & Co., 9 3/4 In., 12 Piece	5100.00
Plate, Pierced Rim, Lattice, Flowers, J.E. Caldwell, c.1900, 12 In., 12 Piece	9775.00
Plate, Presentation, Handwrought, Kalo Shop, 1915, 11 In., 12 Piece	5750.00
Plate, Serving, Louis XIV Pattern, Monogram, Towle, 12 In.	187.00
Plate, Shell & Foliate Scroll Rim, Dominick & Haff, 11 1/4 In., 12 Piece	8050.00
Platter, Well & Tree, Molded Rim, Foliate Feet, Baldwin, Miller, 19 In.	287.50
Platter, Well & Tree, Presentation, Shreve & Co., c.1911, 23 1/4 In.	690.00
Porringer, Edward Lownes, c.1820	2090.00
Porringer, Engraved Mary Perry, Benjamin Bunker, 1790s, 6 In.	2300.00
Porringer, George Hanners, Boston, c.1720, 4 3/4 In.	2640.00
Porringer, Pierced Keyhole Handle, John Andrew, 1784, 5 1/2 In.	1380.00
Powder Jar, Repousse, S. Kirk & Son	385.00
Punch Boat, Arts & Crafts, Scirotta, Ladle, 6 1/4 x 11 In.	825.00
Punch Bowl, Grapevine & Clusters, Gilt Interior, Howard, 1893, 14 1/2 In.	5175.00
Punch Bowl, Presentation, Lion Head & Ring Handles, Tuttle, c.1960	1210.00
Punch Ladle, R.E. Smith, 1820-1830, 12 1/2 In.	385.00
Ramekin Set, Underplate, Shreve & Co., 24 Piece	660.00
Salad Fork & Spoon, Onslow, Tuttle	395.00
Salad Server, Scroll Design, Monogram, Knowles, Pair	192.00
Salad Set, Arts & Crafts, Hammered, Shield Shape, Marshall Field, 2 Piece	132.00
Salt, Shell Shape, Foliate Handle, Rouyer, New Orleans, c.1860, 2 3/4 In.	275.00
Salver, Bright-Cut Designs, George W. Riggs, Baltimore, 10 1/2 In.	660.00
Server, Fish, Sea Horses, Seaweed Ground, Whiting, c.1885, Pair	4025.00
Shovel, Salt, Lows, Ball & Co., c.1850	20.00
Shovel, Salt, W. Beebe, c.1830	18.00
Spoon, Dessert, John Campbell, 6 Piece	850.00
Spoon, Dessert, Palmer & Ramsay	195.00
Spoon, Dessert, Shell & Scroll, Monogram, Coin, J.B. Jones & Co., 12 Piece	247.00
Spoon, Fiddle Thread, J. Titus, c.1840	55.00
Spoon, J.G. Joseph, 9 In., 4 Piece	375.00
Spoon, Marrow, Spiral Twist Shank, Geo. Sharp, c.1850	345.00
Spoon, Serving, Bright Cut Handle, Wm. Brown, 1810, 7 1/4 In., Pair	100.00
Spoon, Serving, Scalloped Bowl, T.B. Humphries	195.00

Silver-American, Tea & Coffee Set, Chased, Gorham, 1895-1902, 6 Piece

Wash silverware immediately after dinner. If this isn't possible, a quick rinse will help to remove food residues.

Spoon & Fork, Wood Scroll Handle, Silver Dragon, Whiting, 11 1/2 In. 3450.00
Spur, Heart Inlaid, G.S. Garcia, Elko, Nev., 1910, Pair 6600.00
Sugar, Cover, Oak Leaf, Monogram, Coin, Curry & Preston, 8 1/2 In. 302.00
Sugar, Repousse, Bigelow Kennard & Co. 40.00
Sugar & Creamer, Allover Hammered Pond Flowers, Dominick & Haff 850.00
Sugar & Creamer, Arts & Crafts, Carmel, Monogram 305.00
Sugar & Creamer, Greek Revival, Monogram, Gorham, 1874 .... 412.00
Sugar & Creamer, Joseph Richardson, Jr., Helmet Shape, Weighted 3250.00
Sugar Bowl, Acanthus Leaf Design, William Thomson, c.1830, 8 1/8 In. 825.00
Sugar Bowl, Grape Leaves & Vines, Edward Rockwell, c.1825, 7 In. 287.00
Sugar Nips, Engraved Flowerhead Each Side, c.1750, 5 In. 675.00
Sugar Urn, Cover, Basket Weave Border, William Seal, c.1825, 8 1/2 In. 632.00
Sugar Urn, Cover, Trailing Grape Vines, Peter Chitry, c.1825, 9 1/2 In. 315.00
Tablespoon, Bright Cut Wriggle Work Rim, Paul Revere, c.1780, Pair 2875.00
Tablespoon, Fiddle Thread, Ball, Tompkins & Black, c.1850, Pair 85.00
Tablespoon, Gregg Hayden Co. 75.00
Tablespoon, Newel Harding, 8 7/8 In., Pair 44.00
Tablespoon, Rattail Handle, Burritt & Son, 8 3/4 In. 33.00
Tablespoon, Rattail Handle, John Stevenson, 8 1/4 In. 8.50
Tankard, Cover, Corkscrew Thumbpiece, Samuel Gray, c.1742, 7 3/4 In. 8050.00
Tazza, Maintenon, Gorham, 9 1/8 In., Pair 1430.00
Tazza, Pierced, Footed, Monogram, Watson, 10 3/4 In., Pair 275.00
Tea & Coffee Set, Acanthus, C-Scroll, Gorham, 1875, 6 Piece 2310.00
Tea & Coffee Set, Banded & Floral, Ivory, Arthur Stone, c.1918, 8 Piece 9350.00
Tea & Coffee Set, Chased, Gorham, 1895-1902, 6 Piece .... *Illus* 14950.00
Tea & Coffee Set, Engraved Monogram, Gorham, c.1910, 6 Piece 977.50
Tea & Coffee Set, Flower Heads, Scrolls, George B. Sharp, 1850, 6 Piece 8050.00
Tea & Coffee Set, Georgian, Reed & Barton, 6 Piece 3737.50
Tea & Coffee Set, Granulated Ground, Eoff & Shepherd, c.1855, 4 Piece 2415.00
Tea & Coffee Set, Jones, Ball & Co., Grape & Vine, 1840, 4 Piece 3650.00
Tea & Coffee Set, Maintnon, Gorham, 7 Piece 7700.00
Tea & Coffee Set, Octagonal, Floral, Monogram, Durgin, 7 Piece 2090.00
Tea & Coffee Set, Ovoid, Engraved Design, Plated Tray, Durgin, 5 Piece 1650.00
Tea & Coffee Set, Princess Anne, Wallace, 5 Piece 1000.00
Tea & Coffee Set, Repousse Vine, Monogram, C. Bard & Son, 6 Piece 5225.00
Tea & Coffee Set, Strapwork Edge, Shreve & Co., 1900, 5 Piece 1760.00
Tea & Coffee Set, Tray, Engraved Foliage, Gorham, 1918, 6 Piece 5463.00
Tea & Coffee Set, Twig Handles, Eoff & Shepherd, c.1855, 8 Piece 5175.00
Tea & Coffee Set, William & Mary, Lunt, 4 Piece 1265.00
Tea & Coffee Set, Winchester, No. 5879, Shreve & Co., 5 Piece 1380.00
Tea Caddy, Repousse, Jacobi Jenkins 868.00
Tea Service, Rectangular, Paw Feet, J. Lownes, Phila., c.1816, 6 Piece 4675.00
Tea Set, Basket Weave, Charters, Dunn & Dunn, c.1850, 5 Piece 5500.00
Tea Set, Beaded Borders, Urn Finials, Hugh Wishart, c.1790, 3 Piece 4600.00
Tea Set, Chased Grape Vines, Hyde & Goodrich, 1850, 5 Piece 9200.00
Tea Set, Coral & Foliage Design, William Thompson, c.1815, 4 Piece 1495.00
Tea Set, Empire Period, William Thompson, 1831, 4 Piece 2640.00

Silver-American, Tea Set, Engraved, John Sayre, 1810, 3 Piece

Tea Set, Engraved, John Sayre, 1810, 3 Piece .... *Illus*	3850.00
Tea Set, Hyde & Goodrich, 1850, 5 Piece	9200.00
Tea Set, Plymouth, Chased, Gorham, c.1920, 5 Piece	1092.50
Tea Set, Urn Form, Ram's Head, Shreve, Standwood & Co., 1860, 5 Piece	3300.00
Tea Set & Waiter, Melon Form, Monogram, Goodnow & Jenks, 6 Piece	2750.00
Tea Strainer, Gorham, 2 Piece	50.00
Tea Strainer, Umbrella Shape, Webster Co.	40.00
Teapot, Armorial Cartouche, Philip Syng, Jr., c.1760, 6 1/2 In.	3850.00
Teapot, Chased Flowers & Scrolls, Scroll Feet, N. Harding, 8 1/2 In.	606.00
Teaspoon, Ruby Pattern, Shiebler, 6 Piece	120.00
Toby, Man, Military Uniform, Atop Tricorn, E. Leverich, c.1865, 7 In.	6325.00
Tray, Asparagus, Art Nouveau, Reed & Barton	3000.00
Tray, Cake, Art Nouveau, Alvin	150.00
Tray, Cake, Watson, 10 1/2 In.	55.00
Tray, Cocktail, Monogram, Black, Starr & Frost, Square, 10 In.	346.00
Tray, Egg & Dart Border, Oval, International, 15 In.	220.00
Tray, Lady Mary, Towle, c.1918, 26 5/8 In.	2950.00
Tray, Minuet, International Silver, 11 In.	121.00
Tray, Monogram, Applied Border, Frank Whiting, 12 In.	220.00
Tray, Monogram, Rectangular, Rounded Corners, Fisher, N.Y., 25 In.	1150.00
Tray, Monogram, Reed & Barton, Oval, 18 In.	440.00
Tray, Octagonal, Black Starr & Frost, 24 In.	1430.00
Tray, Oval, Handwrought, Rolled Rim, Kalo Shop, 1922, 9 1/4 In.	316.25
Tray, Oval, Louis XIV, Towle, c.1924, 22 1/2 x 16 In.	1540.00
Tray, Regency, Gadroon Rim, Acanthus Handles, Elkington, 1946, 29 In.	3220.00
Tray, Repousse, Monogram, Oval, Kirk, 15 In.	522.00
Tray, Tea, Everted Rim, Floral Swags, Gorham, 31 In.	2875.00
Trophy, Golf, Raised Foliate, Oakhurst Tournament, 1909, Gorham, 3 In.	88.00
Tumbler, Presentation, Pilletreau, Bennett & Cooke, 4 1/8 In.	249.50
Tureen, Soup, Cover, Floral Chased, Bombe, Round, Whiting, 1880, 11 In.	2587.50
Urn, Tea, Pear Form, Water Mill & Buildings, Taylor & Lawrie, c.1850	2588.00
Vase, Chased Cattails & Leaves, John C. Moore, Tiffany, c.1853, 9 3/4 In.	7475.00
Vase, Chased Grapevines, T.B. Starr, 10 1/2 In.	1210.00
Vase, French Border, Chased, Graff, Washburn & Dunn, 1909, 9 1/2 In.	805.00
Vase, Plants, Dragonflies, Turtle, Frog & Crayfish Feet, Gorham, 11 In.	3220.00
Vase, Trophy, Band Of Flowers, Pendant Fruit & Birds, Black, Starr & Frost	1100.00
Vase, Trumpet, Reed & Barton, Large	412.50
Vase Holder, Embossed Putti Musicians & Wreaths, Watson Co.	65.00
Vessel, Minerva Head Handle, Anthony Rasch, 6 1/2 In.	687.50
Waiter, Octagonal, Handles, Reed & Barton, 28 In.	1980.00
Waste Bowl, Coin, Monogram, Chased Foot & Rim, 19th Century, 6 In.	110.00
Wine Cooler, Pinched Body, 3 Scrolling Handles, Gorham, 1899, 9 x 7 In.	1430.00

SILVER-ARABIAN, Belt, Dancing Girls, Bells 1900.00
SILVER-AUSTRIAN, Candlestick, Chased Flowers, Baluster, 12 In., Pair 440.00
  Candlestick, Columnar, Round Base, Sphinx Head, 11 1/2 In., Pair 2185.00
  Dresser Set, Glass, 6 Piece 605.00
  Mirror, Table, Oval, Beaded Molding, 21 x 15 In. 412.00
  Tea & Coffee Set, Tapering Oval Form, Schwarz & Steiner, 5 Piece 715.00
  Tea & Coffee Set, Tray, 2 Handles, Schwartz & Steiner, c.1910, 8 Piece 5750.00
  Tea & Coffee Set, Tray, Ivory Handles, Bruder Frank, 1925, 6 Piece 8050.00
  Tray, Undulating Lobed Rim, 1910-1920, Otto Prutscher, Square, 10 1/2 In. 1150.00
SILVER-BALTIC, Vase, Rising from Dolphin, Seaweed & Shell Base, c.1900, 13 5/8 In. 2300.00
SILVER-BELGIAN, Candlestick, Paneled Vase Form, Marked fd, 1820, 11 In., Pair 3025.00
  Coffee Pot, Vase Shape, Flower Festoons, Medallion, c.1810 .... 5175.00
SILVER-CANADIAN, Coffee Set, Collet Base, Bright Cut Scroll, Birks, 1943, 3 Pc. 488.75
SILVER-CHINESE, Container, Opium, 19th Century, 1 1/2 In. 485.00
  Mug, Tapered Cylinder, Engraved Grapes, Khecheong, c.1850 .... 330.00
  Punch Bowl, Repose Writhing Dragon, Late 19th Century 1870.00
  Snuffbox, Scenes, Figures, Landscapes, Gilt Interior, Cutsing, c.1838, 3 In. 1093.00
SILVER-CONTINENTAL, Bowl, Oval, Marked Holm, 19th Century, 14 In. 302.50
  Bowl, Sabbath, Beaded Rim, Hebrew Inscription, 19th Century, 8 In. 200.00
  Box, Animal & Landscape Repousse, Hinged Top, 2 5/8 In. 100.00
  Box, Tortoiseshell, 19th Century, 3 In. 440.00
  Candelabra, 3-Light, Figural, Man In 17th-Century Clothes, 16 In., Pair 1725.00
  Chalice, Leaf Banding, 19th Century, 8 1/2 In. 520.00
  Plate, Applied Scrolls & Leaves, Shaped Rim, 11 In. 165.00
  Salt, Shell Shape, Child On Dolphin On Standard, 6 In., 4 Piece 977.00
  Spoon, Stuffing, Monogram, Fiddle Handle, 16 In. 247.00
  Tea Caddy, Repousse Panels, Scenes Of Village, Swing Handle, 4 5/8 In. 250.00
  Tea Set, Egg Shape, Chased Panels, Finials, 4 Piece 1045.00
  Tea Urn, Swan Finial, Dolphin Form Legs, 16 1/2 In. 4950.00
  Teapot, Stand, Blossom Finial, Swing Handle, Houret 79, 1870s, 10 In. 1210.00
  Tray, Octagonal, Ebonized Handles & Finials, 1937, 5 Piece 2588.00
SILVER-DANISH, Bowl, 3 Sections, Bud Finials, No. 323B, Georg Jensen, c.1925, 9 In. 2587.50
  Bowl, Footed, Decagonal Base, Silver Beads, Georg Jensen, c.1925, 5 1/8 In. 862.50
  Bowl, Free-Form, Asymmetric Tripod Foot, Georg Jensen, 15 3/4 In. 8625.00
  Bowl, Hammered Exterior, Beaded Foot, Georg Jensen, 7 3/8 In. 1100.00
  Bowl, Leaf Form, Flared, Hammered Surface, 9 Sides, Georg Jensen, 5 x 4 In. 600.00
  Bowl, Stylized Berries & Leaves On Foot, Georg Jensen, 1945, 6 1/8 In. 3600.00
  Box, Bead Feet, Chased Lobes, Scalloped Rim, Georg Jensen, 4 1/2 In. 2420.00
  Box, Dolphin Finial, Georg Jensen, 2 x 3 1/2 In. 375.00
  Box, Hammered Body, Beaded Rim, Amber Set Finial, G. Jensen, 4 3/4 In. 6900.00
  Box, Jewel, Swan Finial, Stepped Base, Georg Jensen, 1919, 9 7/8 In. 6325.00
  Cactus, Salt & Pepper, Jensen, 2 1/4 In. 250.00
  Candelabrum, 3-Light, Spot Hammered, Georg Jensen, 15 1/2 In. 7150.00

Silver-Danish, Tray, Georg Jensen,
Oval, 26 In.

Silver-French, Cruet Stand,
Pierre Denis DeLaRonde

Candlestick, Pendant Grapes, Twist Stem, Georg Jensen, 5 7/8 In., Pair 4000.00
Canister, Cover, Scalloped Rim With Pearls, Georg Jensen, 7 1/4 In. 3520.00
Carving Set, Knife, Fork, Poultry Shears, Georg Jensen, 17-In. Case 1650.00
Centerpiece, Hammered, Fluted Sides, AD, Copenhagen, 1922, 13 In. 1265.00
Cocktail Shaker, Leaf & Berry Cluster Finial, Georg Jensen, 1930, 12 In. 1725.00
Coffee & Tea Set, Blossom, Georg Jensen, 4 Piece 7475.00
Coffee Set, Hammered Surface, Hans Hansen, 1936, 3 Piece 1150.00
Compote, Blossom, Leaf Stem, Georg Jensen, 1940s, 7 In. 6325.00
Compote, Grapevine, Lobed Stem, Shallow, Georg Jensen, 1935, 6 In. 4025.00
Compote, Lily-Form Support, C.C. Hermann, 9 1/4 In. 550.00
Crumber & Tray, Openwork Foliate Design, Georg Jensen, 11 1/4 In. 2860.00
Cup, Cover, Stem Of Leaves & Beads, Georg Jensen, 5 1/2 In., Pair 3680.00
Dinner Set, Acorn, Georg Jensen, Fitted Case, 52 Piece 5450.00
Dish, Blossom, Openwork Edge, Marked, Georg Jensen, 6 In. 770.00
Dish, Cover, Openwork Blossoms, Blossom & Bead Finial, G. Jensen 6670.00
Ewer, Basin, Fluted Sides, S. Bernadotte, Jensen, c.1950, 6-In. Ewer 2587.50
Flatware, Service For 12, Evald Nielsen, Fitted Case, 91 Piece 2070.00
Fork & Spoon, Salad, Cactus Blossom Terminal, Georg Jensen, 7 1/2 In. 632.50
Kettle, Hot Water, Lampstand, Ebony Swing Handle, H. Hansen, 11 1/2 In. 1265.00
Pitcher, Beaded & Rope Twist Borders, Georg Jensen, 1945, 9 In. 3220.00
Pitcher, Scalloped Foot, Ebony Handle, Georg Jensen, 8 3/4 In. 4025.00
Pitcher, Water, Ebony Handle, Vase Form, Georg Jensen, 1920, 9 In. 1725.00
Plate, Shallow Well, Georg Jensen, 10 1/4 In., 12 Piece 6325.00
Salt, Owl, Hard Stone Eyes, Georg Jensen, 2 1/2 In., Pair 440.00
Sauceboat, Blossom Handle, Openwork, Georg Jensen, 8 1/4 In. 6325.00
Service For 12, Parallel Pattern, Georg Jensen, Wooden Box, 84 Piece 8625.00
Service For 8, Acorn Pattern, Monogram, Georg Jensen, Box, 109 Piece 5750.00
Spoon, Serving, Blossom, Georg Jensen, Pair 302.00
Strainer, Stand, Pierced Flowerhead, Ebony Handle, G. Jensen, 7 3/16 In. 1610.00
Sugar Caster, Grape, Leaf & Berry Finial, Georg Jensen, 7 1/4 In. 2185.00
Tazza, Grapevine Pattern, Georg Jensen, 1918, 7 5/8 In., Pair 3738.00
Tea & Coffee Set, Tray, Ebony Handles, Georg Jensen, 1915, 4 Piece 4025.00
Tray, Georg Jensen, Oval, 26 In. .... *Illus* 12000.00
Tray, Nordic Bands Engraved, A. Michelsen, 1916, Oval, 23 1/2 In. 1725.00
SILVER-DUTCH, Bowl, Brandy, Incised Lines, Leeuwarden, 1733, 9 1/2 In. 1760.00
Brandy Bowl, 2 Handles, Oval, Panels, S. Zshammer, Amsterdam, 1684, 9 In. 3738.00
Brandy Bowl, Boat Shape, Embossed Deer, J.A. Karsten, 1770, 9 1/2 In. 920.00
Coffee Urn, Pear Shape, Fluted, Fruit Finial, Amsterdam, 1778, 14 1/2 In. 6900.00
Perfume, Figural, Lute, Chased Landscape Scenes, c.1900, 7 1/4 In. 920.00
Tea Set, Reeded Form, 4 Piece 440.00
Teakettle, Stand, Neoclassical Style, 12 In. 3575.00

SILVER-ENGLISH. English silver is marked with a series of four or five small
hallmarks. The standing lion mark is the most commonly seen sterling quality
mark. The other marks indicate the city of origin, the maker, and the year of
manufacture. These dates can be verified in many good books on silver.

SILVER-ENGLISH, Basket, Circular, R. Eames & E. Barnard, 1828, 13 3/4 In. 2875.00
Basket, George III, Floral Handles, Reticulated Body, 1759, 5 In. 600.00
Basket, Incised Swag & Bellflower, Ovoid, Hester Bateman, 1795 .... 495.00
Basket, Oval, Birds, Flowers, Edwin Charles Purdie, 1897, 11 3/4 In. 2300.00
Beaker, Embossed & Chased Scrolling Flowers, J. Duck, 1679, 3 5/8 In. 4300.00
Beaker, Flared Rim, Engraved Initials, FS Mark, 1693, 3 5/8 In. 4025.00
Bowl, Bleeding, Openwork Trefoil Handle, 1653, 5 1/2 In. 9200.00
Bowl, Reticulated, Strapwork, 4 Scroll Feet, T. Bradbury, 1899, 9 In. 2600.00
Box, Heart Shape, Sheffield Hallmarks, c.1894, 1 1/2 In. 445.00
Box, Toilet, Hinged Lid, Shell Feet, Joseph Ward, 1697, 10 x 7 1/2 In. 8800.00
Cake Basket, Boat Shape, Beaded Border, Hester Bateman, 1786, 13 1/2 In. 6900.00
Cake Basket, Chinoiserie, Fretwork, S. Herbert & Co., 1758, 13 1/2 In. 4150.00
Cake Basket, Circular, Openwork Swing Handle, R. Gainsford, 1824, 13 In. 2000.00
Cake Basket, Oval, Trellis Sides, E. Aldridge & J. Stamper, 1754, 13 1/2 In. 2875.00
Cake Basket, Wirework, Raffia-Like Rim, Wakelin & Garrard, 1795 .... 7475.00
Candelabrum, 2-Light, George II Style, Caryatid Branches, 14 In., 1928, Pair 4025.00
Candlestick, Enameled Medallions, Fluted, Liberty & Co., 6 3/4 In., Pair 1610.00

Candlestick, Square Base, Ionic Stem, J. Carter, 1775, 11 In., 4 Piece 8625.00
Candlestick, Stepped Base, Ebenezer Coker, London, 1766, 10 1/2 In. 4900.00
Caster, George II, Vase Form, Engraved, Pierced, Samuel Wood, 6 In., Pair 2070.00
Caster, George III, Baluster Form, 1804, 6 1/8 In. 495.00
Chalice, Interlocked Stems, Onyx Mounted, Archibald Knox, 9 1/2 In. 9200.00
Chamberstick, Gadroon Rim, Shells, Storey & Elliott, 1912, 6 In., Pair 7200.00
Chamberstick, George II, Flying Scroll Handle, John White, 5 1/4 In. 2300.00
Chamberstick & Snuffer, Isaac Cookson, 1772 .... 825.00
Coffee Urn, Vasiform Body, Lion Head & Ring Handles, 19 1/2 In. 495.00
Coffeepot, George I, Swan Neck Spout, Daniel Sleamaker, 6 1/2 In. 4600.00
Coffeepot, George II, Leaf Capped Swan Neck Spout, T. Whipham, 8 In. 1725.00
Coffeepot, George II, Tapered Cylindrical Form, Gabriel Sleath, 5 7/8 In. 4600.00
Coffeepot, George III, Baluster Shape, Stepped Base, T.W., 1782, 12 In. 925.00
Coffeepot, George III, John Sheehan, c.1790 .... 6200.00
Coffeepot, John Emes, c.1802, 10 1/2 In. 1800.00
Coffeepot, Reeded Borders, Peter & Ann Bateman, 1799, 13 In. 2550.00
Coffeepot, Squat Body, 4 Scrolling Feet, Ivy, Barnard & Sons, 1872, 9 1/4 In. 690.00
Coffeepot, Tapered Cylinder, Cover, Urn Finial, J. Swift, 1738, 9 7/8 In. 4400.00
Compote, Art Nouveau, Mappin & Webb, c.1923, 7 x 9 1/2 In. 890.00
Cream Jug, George II, c.1741, 3 3/4 In. 695.00
Creamer, Floral Chased Design, Monogram, 1907 Hallmark, 4 1/4 In. 82.50
Creamer, George II, Helmet Form, Peter Archambo, 1735, 4 3/4 In. 5175.00
Creamer, Repousse Floral Design, Birmingham, 1868, 4 1/2 In. 55.00
Creamer, S-Curved Handle, Ovoid Form, Hester Bateman, 1777, 5 1/2 In. 495.00
Cruet, 2-Bottle, George II, Diaper Pattern, John Edwards II, 1739, 6 1/2 In. 7475.00
Cup, 2 Handles, Chased Leaves, Aldwinckle & Slater, London, 1883, 8 In. 1380.00
Cup, Cover, 2 Handles, Fluted Vase Shape, Hester Bateman, 1784, 14 3/4 In. 3750.00
Cup, Figural, Skull And Crossbones, Alexander Macrae, 1862, 7 5/8 In. 5750.00
Cup, George III, Campana Shape, Bands, Vines, Story & Elliott, 1810, 9 In. 1265.00
Cup, Standing, Panels Of Stylized Flowers, EW Mark, 1664, 3 7/8 In. 6325.00
Cup, Wine, Beaker Shape Bowl, Flared Rim, 1655, 7 In. 7475.00
Cup, Wine, Incised Line Border, TI Mark, 1638, 7 5/8 In. 8625.00
Desk Stand, Regency, Shield, Paw Feet, S. Hougham, 1813, 13 3/4 In. 2600.50
Dessert Service, Grapevine Pattern, Gilt, Crichton Bros., 1916, 72 Piece 2875.00
Dish, Shell, George III, Shell, Edward Aldridge, Jr. & Sr., 5 3/4 In., 4 Piece 7475.00
Dish, Sweetmeat, Boat Form, Corn Cobs Under Scrolls, IG Mark, 7 In. 8050.00
Dish, Sweetmeat, Floral Pendants, Corn Cobs, W. Maddox, 1634, 8 In. 6325.00
Dish, Vegetable, On Copper, Liner & Lid, Sheffield, 14 In. 300.00
Dish, William IV, Butterfly Finial, Cabbage Form, Undertray, 5 3/4 In. 4850.00
Dresser Set, Traveling, London, 1926, Fitted Leather Case, 7 Piece 550.00
Epergne, George III, Fleur-De-Lis, Roberts & Cadman, 1818, 14 In. 4600.00
Ewer, George II, Elongated Helmet Spout, Chased, P. Gardner, 1756, 14 In. 4025.00
Fish Set, Victorian, Engraved Fittings, Dolphin Blade, G. Unite, 2 Piece 375.00
Flatware Set, Fiddle Pattern, c.1810, 84 Piece 7475.00
Fruit Set, Bone Handles, Fitted Oak Case, Sheffield, 1895, 25 Piece 242.00
Fruit Set, Cased, Engraved Scrolls, T.W., Birmingham, 1899, 24 Piece 632.50
Grape Shears, Shell Thread, Charles Rawlings & William Summers 275.00
Holder, Place Card, Figural, Bacchante, Set Of 12 .... 770.00
Inkstand, Floral Scroll Feet, John & Edward Barnard, c.1838, 13 In. 550.00
Inkstand, Rectangular, Molded Rim, Peter Taylor, c.1752, 9 1/4 In. 4025.00
Inkstand, Scrolled Strapwork, Edward Barnard & Sons, 1852, 11 3/4 In. 1495.00
Jug, Beer, George III, Applied Reeded Bands, W. Grundy, 1774 .... 1725.00
Jug, Hot Water, George III, London, 1769 .... 5800.00
Kettle, Hot Water, On Stand, Ribbed, Wooden Handle, London Marks 495.00
Kettle, Lampstand, Inverted Pear Shape, John Pero, London, 1742, 14 3/4 In. 3750.00
Kettle Stand, George II, Triangular, Robert Abercromby, 9 1/2 In. 4600.00
Knife & Fork Set, Pistol Handle, England, 1750-1780, 12 Piece 3800.00
Ladle, George III, Onslow Pattern, John Mackhoule, 14 In. 500.00
Ladle, George IV, Fiddle Pattern, J. Barber & Wm. Whitwell, 1820, 7 In. 165.00
Ladle, Georgian, King Pattern, Mary Chawner, 1837, 13 In. 160.00
Ladle, Old Baronial, Alvin 125.00
Ladle, Sauce, Curved Stem, Circular Bowl, Paul De Lamerie, 1750, 7 1/2 In. 6050.00
Ladle, Soup, Waved Fluted Bowl, Elizabeth Oldfield, London, 1754, 14 In. 1725.00

Ladle, William III, Egg-Shaped Bowl, Seth Lofthouse, 1701, 16 1/4 In. 4300.00
Lemon Fork, King, Kirk 29.00
Lettuce Fork & Spoon, Old Colonial, Towle 250.00
Marrow Scoop, Thomas Watson, 2 Grooved Channels, 9 1/2 In. 110.00
Meat Fork, Ann & Peter Bateman, London, 1817, 11 1/2 In. 335.00
Muffin Dish, Cover, Beaded Rim, A. Fogelberg & S. Gilbert, 1784, 7 1/4 In. 2600.00
Mug, Baluster Shape, Molded Foot, Monogram, P. De Lamerie, 1733, 5 In. 6600.00
Mug, Beaker Form, Scrolled Strap Handle, John Ruslen, 1706, 2 In. 1495.00
Mug, Christening, Foliage & Beading, George Angell, 1867, 4 1/4 In. 175.00
Mug, George III, Baluster Shape, Chased, B. Brewood, 1763, 6 1/4 In. 750.00
Mug, Queen Anne, Harp-Shaped Handle, Samuel Wastell, 1706, 2 1/8 In. 3740.00
Pepper, George I, Octagonal, Scroll Strap Handle, G. Johnson, 3 1/2 In. 5175.00
Pepper, Strap Handle, Central Flowerhead, Charles Adam, 1708, 3 1/4 In. 3740.00
Place Card Holders, Recumbent Putti, Scrollwork, England, c.1890, 6 Piece 308.00
Place Marker, Tortoise Centers, W. Comyns & Sons, 1909, 6 Piece 660.00
Plate, Gadroon Rim, Acanthus Leaves, Paul Storr, 1813, 10 3/8 In., Pair 2000.00
Plate, Queen Anne, Engraved Initials, Samuel Lee, 9 3/4 In. 2200.00
Platter, George V, Oval, Molded Edge, Crichton & Co., 1927, 18 1/2 In. 800.00
Platter, Meat, George III, Gadroon Rim, Border, Paul Storr, 1805, 18 7/8 In. 4025.00
Platter, Octagonal, Cartouches, R. Garard & Bros., 1833, 18 5/8 In., Pair 8050.00
Platter, Oval, Gadroon Rim, Leaves, Paul Storr, 1819, 18 1/4 In., Pair 9200.00
Platter, Oval, Gadroon Rim, Paul Storr, London, 1801, 23 1/4 In. 8625.00
Platter, Ovolo Rim, Engraved Border, Paul Storr, London, 1810, 22 In. 5450.00
Punch Bowl, George V, Montieth Style, Crichton Bros., 1914, 10 In. 1035.00
Punch Bowl, Lion Mask, Handles, Wakely & Wheeler, 1931, 11 1/2 In. 2300.00
Punch Bowl, Monteith, Chased, Repousse Flowers, W.B.T., 1883, 13 1/4 In. 2860.00
Rose Bowl, George V, Hawksworth, Eyre & Co., 1912, 6 1/4 In. 1090.00
Salt, 3 Paw Feet, Floral Sprays, Cobalt Liner, R.Harper, 1867, 2 3/4 In., 4 Piece 635.00
Salt, Bombe Rectangular Shape, Everted Rim, R. Sibley, 1818, 4 In., 6 Piece 1265.00
Salt, Cutout At Rim, Peter & Ann Bateman, Glass Liner, 1792, Pair 500.00
Salt, Floral Design, Spoon, Cobalt Insert, Hoof Feet, 1750, Pair 210.00
Salt, Gadroon Rims, Paw Feet, T. Holland, 1808, 3 1/4 In., 4 Piece 2300.00
Salt, George II, D. Hennel, London, 1758, Pair 165.00
Salt, Spreading Sides, Engraved Arms, Thomas Ash, 1701, 3 3/8 In., 4 Piece 5175.00
Salver, Circular, Applied Rim, Profile Medallions, R. Rugg, 1776, 15 1/4 In. 2300.00
Salver, Gadroon Rim, Leaves & Shells, R. Rugg, London, 1769, 14 3/8 In. 3450.00
Salver, George I, Footed, Monogram, Thomas Bradbury, 1940, 17 In. 1150.00
Salver, George II, Chinoiserie, Fretwork Border, Richard Rugg, 11 1/8 In. 5750.00
Salver, George II, Gadrooned, Engraved Crest, Richard Rugg, 11 In. 605.00
Salver, George II, Shaped Square, Scroll Support, John Tuite, 8 5/8 In., Pair 5750.00
Salver, George III, 3 Ball & Claw Footed, 1785, Thomas Chawner, 10 In. 920.00
Salver, George III, Beaded Border, Hannam & Crouch, 1783, 8 1/4 In. 690.00
Salver, Molded Rim, Incurved Angles, W. Partis, Newcastle, 1738, 13 In. 5463.00
Salver, Queen Anne, Gadroon Rim, Arms Center, B. Pyne, 1702, 9 In. 8625.00
Salver, Shaped Acanthus Shell, David Bell, 1760, 12 In. 2860.00
Salver, Shell & Scroll Rim, Engraved Vignettes, J. & J. Angell, 1839, 16 In. 2013.00
Sauce, Strainer In Bowl, Smith & Fearn, 1795, 11 3/8 In. 275.00
Snuff Bottle, Engraved Monogram, London, 2 1/2 In. 180.00
Soup, Dish, Gadroon Rims, Acanthus Leaves, P. Storr, 1808, 10 1/4 In., Pair 2300.00
Spoon, Berry, George III, Fruit Repousse Bowl, Thomas Dealtry, 8 3/4 In. 60.00
Spoon, Serving, Apostle, Fitted Case 200.00
Spoon, Stuffing, Eley & Fern, 1822, 12 In. 165.00
Spoon, Stuffing, Old English Pattern, Peter & William Bateman, 1789-1790 .... 187.00
Spoon & Fork, Winged Putti, Birds, c.1690, 8 & 7 5/8 In. 6325.00
Strainer, Lemon, George I, Flowerhead, Handles, John Albright, 6 In. 3900.00
Strainer, Punch, Bracket Handles, Pierced Bowl, 1726, 4 1/2 In. 715.00
Sugar, Domed Cover, George I, Matthew Lofthouse, 4 3/8 In. 2300.00
Sugar, Domed Cover, Queen Anne, William Fleming, 4 1/2 In. 4600.00
Sugar, George III, Knob Finial , Gadrooned Collar, Upturned Handles, 8 In. 825.00
Sugar Basket, George III, Pierced Vase Form, Robert Hennell, 1776, 5 In. 1495.00
Sugar Basket, George III, Swing Handle, Edward Fernell, 1788, 7 1/8 In. 495.00
Sugar Sifter, Pierced Bowl, Curved Handle, W. Eley & W. Fearn, 1804 .... 165.00
Sugar Tongs, 18th-Century Style Chasing, Newcastle, 1878 .... 65.00

Tankard, Baluster Shape, Pastoral Scene, C. Hougham, 1790, 8 3/8 In. 1725.00
Tankard, Cover, Baluster Shape, Battle Scene, Francis Crump, 1743, 8 In. 2013.00
Tankard, Queen Anne, Timothy Ley, 1708, 5 1/4 In. 5000.00
Tankard, Regency, Flaring Base, Applied Band, W. Bateman, 1815, 6 1/2 In. 2600.50
Tankard, Scrolled Handle, Engraved, John Langlands, 5 1/2 In. 415.00
Tankard, Scrolled Handle, Engraved, T. Whipham & C. Wright, 5 In. 465.00
Tankard, Tapered Cylinder, Chased, Langlands & Robertson, 1782, 8 1/4 In. 2875.00
Tea & Coffee Set, Compressed Baluster Shape, Tray, Marked E.B., 5 Piece 3165.00
Tea & Coffee Set, Engraved, Victorian, E. & J. Barnard, 1857, 4 Piece 1540.00
Tea & Coffee Set, Ivory Finials & Handles, Sheffield, 1937, 4 Piece 2015.00
Tea & Coffee Set, Octagonal Pear Shape, Crichton Bros., London, c.1910 .... 1495.00
Tea Caddy, Cover, Octagonal, Bright Cut, Henry Chawner, 1791, 5 3/4 In. 4600.00
Tea Caddy, George III, Motto, Hinged Cover, E. Darvill, 1768, 3 3/4 In., Pair 2600.00
Tea Caddy, Hester Bateman, 1790 .... 4500.00
Tea Caddy, Queen Anne, Vase Form, Baluster, John Elston, 5 3/8 In. 4600.00
Tea Caddy Spoon, Poet Wadsworth Handle 195.00
Tea Kettle, Stand, Scroll & Dolphin Mounts, Bail Handle, London, 1790 .... 2530.00
Tea Service, Regency, Oblong, Gadrooned, Ball Feet, Exeter, c.1814, 3 Piece 1320.00
Tea Set, Fluted Form, Chased Ribbon & Floral Band, Barnard, 4 Piece 885.00
Tea Set, Pear-Shaped, Fluted Sides, Peaked Cover, Mayer, 1850, 5 Piece 4400.00
Tea Urn, Bright-Cut Borders, Heating Rod, H. Chawner, 1791, 21 In. 2875.00
Tea Urn, Vase Shape, Beaded Borders, James Young, London, 1775, 21 In. 2875.00
Teakettle, George III, Stand, Bail Handle, Scroll & Dolphin Mounts, 12 In. 2530.00
Teapot, Engraved Floral Design, William & John Deane, 6 In. 1000.00
Teapot, George II, Carved Wooden Handle, Aldridge, 1755, 8 3/4 In. 1100.00
Teapot, George III, Armorial, Motto, D. Smith & R. Sharp, 1782, 4 5/8 In. 1610.00
Teapot, George III, Drum, Side Handle, John Carter, 1776, 4 1/8 In. 2300.00
Teapot, George III, Pineapple Finial, G. Smith & T. Hayter, 1801-1802 .... 990.00
Teapot, George III, Straight Sides & Spout, Cover, W. Sutton, 1791, 6 In. 1035.00
Teapot, George V, Oval Form, Crichton Bros., 1915 .... 600.00
Teapot, Stand, George III, Engraved Armorial, H. Bateman, 1787, 6 1/4 In. 3737.50
Teaspoon, Acorn Shaped Bowls, London, c.1750, 12 Piece 1600.00
Teaspoon, George III, Hester Bateman, 1786, 8 Piece 275.00
Teaspoon, William & Mary, Trifid, Scrolled, Jean Harache, 1695, 6 Piece 1955.00
Toast Rack, 8 Naturalistic Bars, Bulrush Sprays, J.S. Hunt, 1848, 7 1/4 In. 3165.00
Toast Rack, Wirework Frame, Bead Feet, Beaded Corners, 1881 .... 1430.00
Tray, C-Scroll Rim, Lion & Rose Monogram, Benjamin Smith, 11 3/4 x 17 In. 880.00
Tray, Foliate Decoration, Oval, 27 In. 220.00
Tray, Snuffer, George II, Thumb Ring, Exeter, 1732, 5 3/4 In. 935.00
Tray, Snuffer, George III, C-Scroll Thumb Ring, Edward Cooke, 6 1/2 In. 665.00
Tray, Tea, George III, John Crouch & Thomas Hannan, 1791 .... 6200.00
Tumbler, Engraved Initials, John East, 1702, 2 3/4 In. 6900.00
Tumbler Cup, Queen Anne, Gilt Interior, Matthew Lofthouse, 2 In. 1850.00
Tureen, Soup, George III Style, Foliate Form Handles, 15 In. 1450.00
Urn, Cover, Handles, Square Base, Crichton Bros., 1910, 8 In. 525.00
Vegetable Dish, Gadroon Shell & Foliate Rim, Paul Storr, 1813, 12 In., Pair 8050.00
Waiter, Elizabeth II, Scroll Handles, Oval, 1967, 25 In. 1650.00
Whistle, Bosun's, Stamped Shells, Joseph Steward II, London, 1762, 5 In. 1265.00
Wine Coasters, Shell & Scrollwork, Pierced, Paul Storr, 1832, 6 In., Pair 6325.00
SILVER-FRENCH, Bowl, Cover, Rounded Rosewood Block Handles, Puiforcat, 11 In. .. 9200.00
Bowl, Scrolls & Stylized Leaves Border, Keller, 1940s, 13 In. 1150.00
Box, Cigarette, Hinged Lid, Center Cut Sapphire, Cartier, 1930, 8 5/8 In. 5750.00
Centerpiece Set, 4 Fan Sloped Dishes, Vase, Tetard Freres, 1935, 16 1/4 In. 3450.00
Chocolate Pot, Foliate Finial, Duck Bill Form Spout, Ivory Handle 1100.00
Condiment Set, Regency Style, Boin-Taburet, Paris, 20th Century, 9 Piece 1840.00
Container, Baby Form, Gift Presentation, Cutlery 1400.00
Cruet Stand, Pierre Denis DeLaRonde .... *Illus* 2530.00
Dessert Dish, Pierced Arches, Festoons, Gilt, Boin-Taburet, 8 1/2 In., Pair 1380.00
Ecuelle, Cover, Stand, Rococo Style, Bud Finial, 12 1/4 In., c.1900, Pair 3450.00
Ewer, Seashell Finial, Man With Fish Body Handle, Puiforcat, 12 1/2 In. 3500.00
Mirror, Hand, Black Panel With Monogram, Jean E. Puiforcat, 7 7/8 In. 1150.00
Pitcher, Water, Barrel Shape, Boucheron, 10 1/4 In. 2970.00

Roast Cart, 4 Wheels, Cover Engraved Francia Hotel, Ercuis, 40 1/2 In. 9200.00
Sauceboat, 2 Scroll Handles, Shell Terminals, Foliate Spout, c.1780, 9 In. 1200.00
Sugar, Cover, Louis XVI, Pierced Satyrs, Marc-Etienne Janety, Paris, 1782 .... 690.00
Tea & Coffee Set, Rococo Style, Maison La Vallee, F. Nicoud Sucr., c.1880 .... 2875.00
Tea & Coffee Set, Tray, Empire Style, Mask Handles, E-Mullet-V, 5 Piece 5750.00
Toothpick Holder, Porcupine Shape, Hyacinthe-Prosper Bourg, c.1850, Pair 4900.00
Tray, Scrolling Poppies, Monogram CC, Handles, Cardeilhac, 26 3/4 In. 6325.00
Vase, Crystal, Sterling Mount, Chinese Archaistic Form, Cartier, 12 In., Pair 5400.00
Wine Cooler, Regency Style, Dolphins, Grapevine, Cardeilhac, 1800s, 10 In. 8625.00
SILVER-GERMAN, Basket, Louis XVI Style, Floral Garlands, Pierced Ground, Courting Scene   805.00
Basket, Louis XVI Style, Reticulated, Garlands, Bucolic Scenes, 15 In. 2185.00
Basket, Scrolling Pierced Sides, Swing Handle, Glass Liner, 8 In. 977.00
Beaker, Granulated Band, Molded Rim, M.Messner, Augsburg, c.1670, 4 In. 1955.00
Beaker, Trumpet Shape, Foliage, Gilt, Jeremias Zobel, c.1700, 6 In. 4025.00
Bowl, Reticulated, Rococo Style, Footed, Monogram, c.1900, 11 In. 330.00
Candelabrum, 4-Light, Lion Passant, Balhsen, c.1825, 22 5/8 In., Pair 5463.00
Candlestick, Ram's-Head Pilasters, Hanselman, c.1825, 7 3/4 In., Pair 2300.00
Case, Calling Card & Coin Purse, 1903 .... 150.00
Centerpiece, Cover, Cut Glass, 4 Column Supports, 1900-1910, 16 1/4 In. 2588.00
Centerpiece, Hammered, Shell Handles, M.H. Wilkens & Sohne, 15 In. 2070.00
Centerpiece, Lion & Dragon Figures, Hexagonal, F. Gleichen, 1897, 16 In. 8050.00
Cornucopia, Chased Waves, Dolphin Stem, Crowned R & Heart, 8 1/4 In. 1840.00
Cup, 2 Tusk Handles, Roundels, Baluster, WHS, 1910-1920, 10 3/4 In. 2300.00
Dish, Panel Of Amorous Couple, Pierced Sides, 1890s, 10 x 15 3/8 In. 440.00
Figurine, Frederick William III, On Monument Base, 10 1/2 In. 1150.00
Goblet, Renaissance Design, Inscribed, 1880, 9 In. 275.00
Gravy Boat, Louis XVI Style, Squat Stem, Domed Foot, Oval Body, 7 In. 805.00
Jardiniere, Maiden, String Instrument, Girl, Pipes Other End, 22 In. 9200.00
Jug, Claret, Pinecone Finial, Cardinal's Face Spout, Ulm, 11 1/2 In. ....:........... 1035.00
Nef, 3-Masted Galleon, Detachable Hull, 4 Wheels, 16 1/2 In., c.1900 .... 3738.00
Punch Cup, Star Of David, Fluted Scrolled Panels, c.1890, 12 Piece 605.00
Sugar Box, Cover, Rectangular, Leaf Border, Marked SS, 7 3/8 In., c.1800 .... 2588.00
Tea & Coffee Set, Oriental, Ebony Handles, Bruckmann & Sohne, 4 Piece 2300.00
Tea & Coffee Set, Reeded Neoclassical, Marked Posen, 6 Piece 3100.00
Tea Caddy, Figural Design, Marked 930, 5 In. 445.00
SILVER-HUNGARIAN, Candlesticks, Campana Sconce, Koszeghy, 1830, 7 1/4 In, Pair . 1035.00
Coffeepot & Hot Water Jug, Fluted, Hammered, 1940, 8 3/4 In., 2 Piece 1380.00
SILVER-INDIAN, Box, Dome Hinged Lid, Hammered Pattern, 3 1/4 x 2 1/4 In. 500.00
Casket, Hinged Cover, Embossed Man Smoking Hookah, 15 In. 2075.00
Goblet, Cover, Repousse Arabesques & Medallions, Ceremonial, 18 In. 2300.00
Salver, Relief Dancing Girls, Gilt, 13 1/2 In. 315.00
Teapot, Elephant Finial, Overall Scrolled Design, Bracket Handle 275.00
SILVER-IRISH, Coffee Pot, Pear Shape, Engraved Neck, Strapwork, Dublin, 1738, 9 3/4 In. .. 3450.00
Dish Ring, George III, Reel Shape, Pierced, John Lloyd, 1780, 7 1/2 In. 8050.00
Hot Water Jug, Vase Shape, Beaded Borders, John Lloyd, c.1785, 12 In. 1850.00
Salver, Shaped Gadroon Rim, 3-Footed, William Homer, Dublin, 1771, 13 In. 1725.00
Sauce Boat, George III, Bombe Shape, Footed, M. West, c.1770, 6 1/2 In., Pair 2588.00
Sauce Boat, George III, Lion Head & Paw Footed, Dublin, 18th Century 715.00
Spoon, Marrow, Engraved P.M. & Dolphin, 9 1/4 In. 148.50
Tablespoon, J. Locker, Dublin, c.1866 .... 275.00
Tea & Coffee Set, Foliate Repousse, 1970, 4 Piece 675.00
Teapot, George IV, Engraved Crest, Compressed Sphere, W.N., 1824, 5 1/4 In. 975.00
Tray, Shaped & Molded Rim, Engraved, R. Calderwood, c.1750, 6 In., Pair 7200.00
Tureen, George III, Compressed Oval, Domed Cover, Jas.LeBass, c.1810, 9 In. 6600.00
SILVER-ISLAMIC, Belt Buckle, Applied & Filigree Designs, Silver Gilt, 11 In. 247.50
SILVER-ITALIAN, Biscuit Box, Shell-Shaped Containers, Tripod Frame, 9 1/4 In. 1725.00
Bowl, Oval, Lobed, Fluted, Brackets For Spoons, Engraved GA, c.1770, 5 In. 690.00
Kettle, Lampstand, Bombe Oval, Fluted Sides, Lid, Floral Finial, 16 1/2 In. 2070.00
Tea & Coffee Set, 2-Handled Tray, Baroque Style, 20th Century, 4 Piece 3738.00
Tureen, Soup, Cover, Bombe Oval, Paneled Sides, Pear Finial, 20th Century 1725.00
Vase, Repousse Panels, Scrolls, Venice, 17th Century, 7 1/2 In. 1100.00
SILVER-JAPANESE, Bowl, Iris On Hammered Ground, Arthur & Bond, 13 3/4 In. 4600.00

Mirror, Hand, Repousse Dragon, Arthur & Bond, 1900, 11 In. 165.00
Salt & Pepper, Rickshaws, 3 In. 145.00
Tea & Coffee Set, Knob Finials, Oversized Spouts, 20th Century, 3 Piece 575.00
SILVER-MEXICAN, Bookmark, Poulat 135.00
Bowl, Footed, Sanborns, 5 3/4 x 3 In. 110.00
Bracelet, Turquoise, Miguel 95.00
Button, Spratling, Pair 350.00
Cake Server, Geometric Design, Wood Handle, William Spratling, 9 In. 675.00
Coffee Set, Treen Handles, Sanborns, 4 Piece 660.00
Crucifix, Jade, Bernice Goodspeed 195.00
Dish, Native Design, God Figures Feet, Sanborn 195.00
Ladle, La Paglia, 1950s 695.00
Pin, Aztec Face, Black Enamel, Margot 175.00
Plate, Bread & Butter, Flowering Vine Border, Sanborns, 6 In., 12 Piece 575.00
Punch Set, Rosewood Handles, Post-1950, 27 Piece 4900.00
Salt & Pepper Castors, William Spratling 290.00
Sauce Ladle, Art Deco Floral Handle, Sanborns, 1948, 7 In. 71.00
Sugar & Creamer, Foliate Rims, Pedestal 395.00
Tea & Coffee Set, Chippendale Border, Maciel, 6 Piece 2875.00
Tea Set, Melon Form, Foliate Feet, 4 Piece 485.00
Teapot, Tapered Quadrangle, Embossed Montezuma, 7 3/4 In. 1035.00
Wine Cooler, Urn Shape, Leafy Handles, Gadrooned Foot, 12 1/2 In. 1760.00
SILVER-MONGOLIAN, Lamp, Crane, Turtle, Jadeite Cups, Coral & Turquoise Inlay, 15 In. .. 467.50
SILVER-PORTUGUESE, Coffee Pot, Vase Shape, Reeded, Marked, Oporto, c.1800, 12 3/4 In. .. 2013.00
Cup, Coconut, Rococo Ornaments, Square Base, 1700s, 7 5/8 In., Pair 3738.00
Dish, Chased Flowerhead, Sea Monsters In Waves, 1780s, 10 5/8 In. 920.00
Tray, 2 Handles, Pierced Grapevine, Marked, Oporto, c.1880, 31 In. 3738.00

SILVER-RUSSIAN. Russian silver is marked with the Cyrillic, or Russian,
alphabet. The numbers 84, 88, or 91 indicate the silver content. Russian silver
may be higher or lower than sterling standard. Other marks indicate maker,
assayer, or city of manufacture. Many pieces of silver made in Russia are
decorated with enamel. Faberge pieces are listed in their own category.

SILVER-RUSSIAN, Bowl, Pierced Handles, 10 x 16 In. 550.00
Box, Cigar, Cyrillic Makers Mark, V.R., c.1900, 6 5/8 In. 2588.00
Chalice, Engraved Savior, Holy Virgin & St. John, c.1890, 11 1/4 In. 2530.00
Cigar Case, St. Petersburg Scene, Moscow, 1878, 4 1/8 In. 230.00
Cigarette Case, Enamel Oyster, Diamond-Set Thumbpiece, c.1910. .... 5060.00
Cigarette Case, Simulated Wood Grain, Paper Stamps, Moscow, 1885, 4 In. 1840.00
Creamer, Ivory Handle, H.A. & B.C., Dated 1835 .... 185.00
Inkwell, Traveling, Cube Form, Inscribed Habana Flor, c.1890, 3 In. 3220.00
Kovshi, Enameled, Boat Form, Scroll Handles, 19th Century, 3 1/8 In., Pair 1610.00
Match Box, Striker Inside Cover, Village Hut Form, 1892, 3 3/4 In. 1380.00
Mirror, Dressing, Foliate Scrolling, Fiodor Ruckert, 20 x 14 In. 1035.00
Mug, Niello Entrelocs, Vacant Cartouches, c.1890, 3 1/4 In. 1265.00
Plate, Hammered, Enameled Rim, 6 In. 145.00
Pot, Hot Water, Hinged Cover, Foliage & Wheel Work, 1757, 9 3/4 In. 3450.00
Samovar, Presentation Inscription, Dated March, 1892, 19 1/2 In. 6325.00
Snuff Box, Figural Dog, Gilt-Copper Color, Marked AP, Moscow, 2 3/4 In. 2013.00
Snuff Box, St. Petersburg Scenes, Moscow, 1847, 2 1/8 In. 143.75
Spice Tower, 4 Bells, Central Bell, Flag Finial, M. Kharlap, 1887, 9 1/2 In. 1035.00
Spoons, Coffee, Twisted Handle, Vase Shaped Finial, c.1874, 12 Piece 143.00
Tankard, Hinged Cover, Bifurcated Thumbpiece, 1888, 5 1/4 In. 1150.00
Tea Caddy, Cut Glass Body, Silver Slip-On Cover, c.1900, 7 1/2 In. 920.00
Teapot, Ceramic Pot Wrapped In Basket Frame, A.N. Sokolov, 1880 .... 1150.00
Tray, Gadroon Border, Corner Shells, Raised Handles, 1826, 17 1/2 In. 2760.00
SILVER-SCOTTISH, Candlestick, Weighted, 10 1/4 In. 550.00
Salver, George II, Shaped Molded Rim, Footed, James Weems, 10 In., Pair 5175.00
Spoon, Basting, Hanoverian, Ratail Bowl, R. Innes, Edinburgh, c.1720 .... 5520.00
Sugar, George II, Hemispherical, Footed, Edinburgh, 1750, 5 1/4 In. 3220.00
Tablespoon, J. Sawyer, 1795 .... 150.00
Tablespoon, Ker Dempster, 1747 .... 375.00
Tea Urn, Monogram, Cartouche, Inverted Egg Shape, W. Mortimer, 1841, 19 In. 6325.00

Teapot, Apple Shape, C-Scroll Handle, Johan Gotlieff-Bilsinds, 5 In. 2760.00
Teapot, Engraved Band & Crest, W. Robertson, 1793. .... 440.00
Teapot, George II, Silver Bullet, Spherical, Thomas Mitchell, 6 In. 3738.00
SILVER-SPANISH, Inkstand, Rectangular, 4 Scroll Supports, Puiol, Madrid, 1804, 8 3/4 In. .. 4600.00
Soup Tureen, Cover, Mirror Plateau, Boat Shape, J.J. Girod, 20th Century 5175.00

SILVER-STERLING. Sterling silver is made with 925 parts silver out of 1,000
parts of metal. The word *sterling* is a quality guarantee used in the United
States after about 1860. The word was used much earlier in England and
Ireland. Pieces listed here are not identified by country. Other pieces of
sterling quality silver are listed under Silver-American, Silver-English, etc.

SILVER-STERLING, Bowl, Child's, Nursery Rhyme Design, Lebuecher & Co, 2 x 4 1/2 In.   25.00
Bowl, Urn Form, Footed, 4 In. 33.00
Box, Lift Top, Speckled Trout, Rising To Fly, Engraved Uinta, 1953, 8 In. 99.00
Cake Server, Serrated Stainless Blade, Danish Style Handle, Marked, 9 1/4 In. 25.00
Carving Set, Art Deco Handles, Case, Flint Hollow Ground Cutlery, 3 Piece 120.00
Case, Cigarette, Turquoise Stones, 1920s 125.00
Cheese Scoop, Ball Form Handle, Hart Bros., Late 19th Century, Box 300.00
Cigar Box, Hinged Cover, Gilt Interior, Fluted, Early 20th Century, 11 In. 4025.00
Coffee Set, Neoclassical Style, 3 Piece 198.00
Compote, Applied Leaves, Scrolled Handles, c.1870, 7 3/4 In. 300.00
Compote, Candy, Concentric Circles, Weighted, 6 x 2 3/4 In. 32.00
Compote, Repousse Scrollwork Rim, Footed, 3 x 6 In. 44.00
Creamer, Hinged Top, Wicker Wrapped Handle, 5 In. 50.00
Cup, Child's, Rabbit Handle, Saart, 2 1/2 In. 150.00
Cup, Julep, Engraved Ida 1899-1949, 3 5/8 In. 50.00
Cup Holders, 1 1/8 In., 12 Piece 110.00
Demitasse Set, Classical Style, Scroll Design, Sweetser, 3 Piece 465.00
Dish, Embossed Flower & Bead Design Rim, 9 1/2 In. 60.00
Dish, Scalloped, P.S. Co., Square, 7 In. 45.00
Dresser Set, 7 Assorted Brushes, 2 Jars, Hand Mirror 500.00
Dresser Set, Brush & Comb, 2 Piece 70.00
Dresser Set, Floral, Monogram In Shield, 4 Piece 192.00
Dresser Tray, Shaped, Weidlich, 11 In. 38.50
Flask, Etched, Pocket 195.00
Frame, Art Nouveau Floral, Oval, Marked B.B., 6 5/8 In. 83.00
Frame, Floral & Butterfly Design, Fish Scale Ground, Scrolling, 10 In. 2000.00
Fruit Bowl, Londonderry Pattern, Pedestal 250.00
Grater, Nutmeg, Bands Of Stylized Foliage, Cylindrical, 2 1/8 In. 1725.00
Holder, Place Card, Figural, Hunting Horse & Rider, Set Of 6 .... 715.00
Humidor, Chased Scrolling Leaves, Horse & Rider, Ball Footed, 9 1/2 In. 660.00
Kettle, Hot Water & Teapot, On Stand, Lexington Pattern, R. Denes, 13 In. 577.00
Knife, Fish, Danish Style Handle, Stainless Blade, Marked, 9 5/8 In. 25.00
Ladle, Sauce, Whiting, Ivory Handle, 5 1/2 In. 275.00
Ladle, Soup, Neptune Face, Gold Washed Fluted Bowl, 1984, 14 In. 295.00
Note Pad Holder, Repousse Art Nouveau Decoration 82.50
Pill Box, Repousse Scrolled Decoration, Circular 40.00
Pincushion, Elephant, Figural 95.00
Pitcher, Water, Undertray, Hammered, Monogram, 8 1/2 In. 825.00
Pitcher, Water, Vasiform, Chased Scrolling & Handle, Ellmore, 10 1/4 In. 990.00
Plate, Floral & Foliate Repousse, Gadrooned Border, 7 1/2 In., 12 Piece 950.00
Punch Bowl, Presentation, Flared Foot, Inscription, 10 In. 1980.00
Salt, Cupid, On Venetian Boat, 1 1/2 In. 135.00
Salt, Open, Cobalt Blue Liner, Spoon, Box, 4 Piece 120.00
Salt & Pepper, Open Salt, Lion Heads, Cobalt Blue Liner 225.00
Salver, Monogram, Impressed Border, Dated 1917-1942, 16 1/4 In. 357.00
Server-Mirror, Turned Wooden Handle, 15 In. 66.00
Spoon, Souvenir, see Souvenir category
Spoon, Tea Caddy, Figural Handle 28.00
Stretcher, Glove, Amethyst Color Stones On Handle 200.00
Sugar Shovel, Whiting, Ivory Handle, 6 1/4 In. 220.00
Tea & Coffee Set, Shield Shaped Body, Engraved Foliage, 5 Piece 1265.00
Tea Service, Poole, Ivory Resists, Raised Floral, Paneled Body, 5 Piece 1540.00

Teapot, Baltimore Floral, Hand Chased, 12 3/4 In. 2000.00
Teapot, Ebony Handle & Finial 2250.00
Teapot, George II, Cylindrical Form, Carved Wood Handle, 8 3/4 In. 1100.00
Teaspoon, Head Of Black Man, Paye & Baker, March 2, 1904 .... 195.00
Tray, Corset Shape, Ornate Rim, 9 In. 90.00
Urn, Cigarette, Glass, Lion Heads Sides, Gadroon Footed, Pair 28.00
SILVER-SWEDISH, Beaker, Wave Border, Parcel Gilt, O. Fernlof, 1739, 4 In. 920.00
Jewelry Box, Wriggle Work Borders, Bail Handles, C.G. Hallberg, 11 In. 2875.00
Salt, Figural, Stylized Lizard, M. Molleer, 8 1/8 In., Pair 935.00
Tea Caddy, Oval, Scrolling Flowers, Adolf Zethelius, 1833, 6 7/8 In. 1955.00
Tea Set, Flying Scroll Ivory Handles, Frantz Hingelberg, c.1930, 3 Piece 3520.00
SILVER-SWISS, Dish, Serving, Molded Rim, Gely Freres, Lausanne, c.1815, 13 1/4 In. 1150.00
SILVER-THAI, Punch Bowl, Repousse Scenes, Daily Life, 3 Ball Feet, 19th Century 660.00
SILVER-VIENNESE, Bowl, Shell Shape, Mother-Of-Pearl, 2 Satyr Supports, 9 1/4 In. ... 4025.00

SINCLAIRE cut glass was made by H. P. Sinclaire and Company of Corning,
New York, between 1905 and 1929. He cut glass made at other factories until
1920. Pieces were made of crystal as well as amber, blue, green, or ruby glass.
Only a small percentage of Sinclaire glass is marked with the S in a wreath.

Bowl, Canoe Shape, Engraved Flowers, Fine Rib Top, 11 x 7 1/2 In. 175.00
Bowl, Serving, Diamond & Silver Threads Pattern, 8 Sides, 3 1/2 x 9 In. 445.00
Bread Tray, Intaglio Dahlias, Dotted Border, Signed, 13 1/2 x 6 In. 350.00
Candlestick, Gooseberries & Leaves, 9 1/4 In. 275.00
Candlestick, Honey Amber, Tulip Cup, Bobeche, Cut Glass Prisms, Signed, 9 In. 295.00
Candlestick, Intaglio & Blown Blank, Petticoat Base, 8 In., Pair 475.00
Compote, Dotting, Green To Clear, Folded Rim, Pair 395.00
Dish, Relish, 2 Sections, Engraved Ivy Leaves & Vines, Signed, 14 In. 120.00
Plate, Diamonds & Silver Threads, Octagonal, Signed, 9 3/4 In. 950.00
Plate, Holly & Snowflake, 7 In. 1000.00
Plate, Stars & Pillar, Signed, 7 In. 425.00
Plate & Wine Set, Luncheon, Celeste Blue, Signed, 12 Piece 180.00
Tankard, Bengal, Triple Notched Handle, 10 In. 950.00
Tray, 5 Sections, Engraved Leaf Design, 10 x 14 In. 160.00
Tray, Chain Of Hobstars, Diamonds Of Crosshatching, Signed, 11 1/2 In. 110.00
Tray, Holly & Snowflake Pattern, Brilliant Cut, Signed, 10 1/2 x 8 1/4 In. 1750.00
Tray, Persian, Engraved Band, Signed, 10 In. 980.00
Urn, Celeste Blue, 8 In. .... 150.00 to 160.00
Vase, Elongated Stem, Engraved Flared Bowl, S In Wreath Mark, 12 In. 467.50
Vase, Ribbed, Blue, Signed, 11 In. 125.00
Wine, Adam, Signed 125.00

SKIING, see Sports category

SLAG GLASS resembles a marble cake. It can be streaked with different
colors. There were many types made from about 1880. Pink slag was an
American Victorian product of unknown origin. Purple and blue slag were
made in American and English factories. Red slag is a very late Victorian and
twentieth-century glass. Other colors are known but are of less importance to
the collector. New versions of chocolate glass and colored slag glass are
being made.

Blue, Candy Dish, Hen On Nest, Wright 145.00
Caramel slag is listed in the Chocolate Glass category
Green, Compote, Pedestal, 8 x 8 In. 60.00
Orange, Candlestick, Northwood, 9 In., Pair 35.00
Pink, Berry Bowl, Inverted Fan & Feather, Northwood, Small 265.00
Pink, Butter, Cover, Inverted Fan & Feather, 4 In. 185.00
Pink, Compote, Jelly, Inverted Fan & Feather, Scalloped Rim, 5 In. 350.00
Pink, Punch Cup, Fan & Feather 225.00
Pink, Sauce Dish, Inverted Fan & Feather 115.00
Pink, Sauce, Inverted Fan & Feather, Ball Feet, 4 1/2 In. 210.00
Pink, Spooner, Flaring Rim, 4 1/2 In. 675.00
Pink, Toothpick, Inverted Fan & Feather 800.00

Pink, Toothpick, Inverted Feather & Fan, St. Claire 80.00
Pink, Tumbler, Inverted Fan & Feather, 4 In. 375.00
Purple, Bread Tray, 13 In. 55.00
Purple, Candlestick, Light Blue, Cable & Jewel, Shell Design, Pair 175.00
Purple, Celery Vase, Flute 95.00
Purple, Dish, Hen On Nest Cover 125.00
Purple, Figurine, Alley Cat 55.00
Purple, Mustard, Bull's Head 35.00
Purple, Toothpick, Scroll With Acanthus 140.00
Red, Pitcher, Milk, Windmill 45.00

SLEEPY EYE collectors look for anything bearing the image of the nineteenth-century Indian chief with the drooping eyelid. The Sleepy Eye Milling Co., Sleepy Eye, Minnesota, used his portrait in advertising from 1883 to 1921. It offered many premiums, including stoneware and pottery steins, crocks, bowls, mugs, and pitchers, all decorated with the famous profile of the Indian. The popular pottery was made by Western Stoneware and other companies long after the flour mill went out of business in 1921. Reproductions of the pitchers are being made today. The original pitchers came in only five sizes: 4 inches, 5 1/4 inches, 6 1/2 inches, 8 inches, and 9 inches. The Sleepy Eye image was also used by companies unrelated to the flour mill.

Butter Crock .... 650.00 to 800.00
Cookbook, Loaf Of Bread 220.00
Creamer, 4 In. 180.00
Flour Sack, Paper 120.00
Label, Egg Crate 30.00
Mug, Blue & White, Double Blue Band, 4 1/2 In. .... 220.00 to 425.00
Mug, Blue, Yellow, Signed, 4 1/4 In. 370.00
Mug, With Verse, Minnesota Stoneware Co. 1200.00
Paperweight, Glass, Marked 325.00
Pillow Cover, President Monroe 250.00
Pitcher, Brown On Green, 1 Qt. .... 400.00 to 700.00
Pitcher, No. 1, Blue & White, 4 In. 185.00
Pitcher, No. 2, Blue On White 225.00
Pitcher, No. 3, Blue On Buff, 6 1/2 In. 275.00
Pitcher, No. 3, Blue On Gray 425.00
Pitcher, No. 3, Blue On White .... 280.00 to 325.00
Pitcher, No. 4, Blue On White, Blue Rim .... 235.00 to 450.00
Pitcher, No. 4, Blue On White, National Wine & Cordial, Peoria 900.00
Pitcher, No. 5, Blue On White, Blue Rim 210.00
Pitcher, No. 5, Brown On White 1975.00
Salt Bowl, 6 1/2 In. 500.00
Sign, Sleepy Eye Flour & Cereals, Die Cut Tin, 13 1/2 In. 1650.00
Stein, Blue On Gray, 7 3/4 In. .... 400.00 to 650.00
Stein, Blue On White, Koehler & Henrichs, St. Paul 925.00
Stein, Brown On Yellow 1300.00
Stein, Brown, 1952 .... 300.00
Sugar, Blue On White 675.00
Sugar, Cover 600.00
Vase, Blue On White 220.00
Vase, Cattail, Light Brown 1500.00
Vase, Cattail, Solid Green 4100.00
Vase, Indian, Cattails, Blue On Gray, 7 In. 450.00

SLIPWARE is named for *slip,* a thin mixture of clay and water, about the consistency of sour cream, which is applied to pottery for decoration. It is a very old method of making pottery and is still in use.

Cup, Strap Handle, Band Of Brown Dots Between Brown Lines, c.1700 .... 1650.00
Dish, Baking, Cream Interior, Spirals & Squiggles, Wales, 13 In. 920.00
Dish, Baking, Parallel Lines Interior, North Wales, 18th Century, 11 1/4 In. 1380.00
Dish, Strainer, Pierced Interior, Brown Glaze, Wales, 1880s, 11 In. .... 1035.00 to 2013.00

SMITH BROTHERS glass was made after 1878. Alfred and Harry Smith had worked for the Mt. Washington Glass Company in New Bedford, Massachusetts, for seven years before going into their own shop. They made many pieces with enamel decoration.

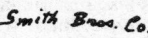

Dish, Sweetmeat, Blossoms, Queen Victoria Bust, Signed, 5 In.	385.00
Dish, Sweetmeat, Cover, Embossed Foliage, Queen Victoria Bust	385.00
Loving Cup, 2 Handles, Black Amethyst, 8 In.	35.00
Rose Bowl, Daisies	110.00
Rose Bowl, Pansies, Burmese Ground, Raised Gold, 5 In.	450.00
Syrup, Floral Design, 4 3/4 In.	685.00
Syrup, Melon-Ribbed, Floral, Lid, 4 3/4 In.	685.00
Vase, Birds Perched On Limb, Apple Blossoms, Lake Scene, 6 In.	385.00
Vase, Dancing Nymphs, Black Amethyst, Handles, 7 In.	30.00
Vase, Greenaway Style Figure, Dog, Signed, 8 In.	395.00
Vase, Rampant Lion, Balustrade Shape, Embossed Rope At Rim, 6 1/4 In.	150.00

SNOW BABIES, made from bisque and spattered with glitter sand, were first manufactured in 1864 by Hertwig and Company of Thuringia. Other German and Japanese companies copied the Hertwig designs. Originally, Snow Babies were made of candy and used as Christmas decorations. There are also Snow Babies tablewares made by Royal Bayreuth. Copies of the small Snow Babies figurines are being made today and can easily confuse the collector.

Box, Cover, Playing In Snow, Sledding, 3 1/2 x 3 3/4 In.	195.00
Chamberstick, Funnel Shape	295.00
Creamer, Royal Bayreuth	135.00
Doll, Cloth Body, Bisque Hands & Feet, 4 In.	725.00
Figurine, Baby, Sitting, 2 In.	195.00
Figurine, Bear, On All Fours	95.00
Figurine, Bear, Standing, 2 1/2 In.	115.00
Figurine, Boy & Girl Skating, Germany, 2 In.	105.00
Figurine, Hugging, Twin, Germany	220.00
Figurine, Kneeling, Arms Up, 1 1/4 In.	38.00
Figurine, On Red Sled, Germany, 1 1/2 In.	55.00
Figurine, Riding Polar Bear, Holds Banjo, Germany, 2 1/8 In.	75.00
Figurine, Seated, Arms & Legs Outstretched, 1 1/4 In.	40.00
Figurine, Standing & Waving, 2 In.	28.00
Ornament, On Sled	125.00
Santa Claus, Skating	55.00

SNUFF BOTTLES are listed in the Bottle category.

SNUFFBOXES held snuff. Taking snuff was popular long before cigarettes became available. The gentleman or lady would take a small pinch of the ground tobacco or snuff in the fingers, then sniff it and sneeze. Snuffboxes were made of many materials, including gold, silver, enameled metal, and wood. Most snuffboxes date from the late eighteenth or early nineteenth centuries.

Amber, Engraved Figure & Horn Top, Oriental, 3 1/2 In.	126.00
Birch, Hinged Lid, Engraved Designs, German Inscriptions, Oval, 4 In.	93.50
Black, Portrait On Ivory, Papier-Mache, 18th Century Clothes, 3 1/2 In.	137.00
Black Tortoiseshell, Silver Inlaid, Family Shield, Gold	295.00
Brass, Cut Corners, Oblong, Handmade, 2 1/2 In.	27.50
Brass, Engraved Lid, Oval, 3 3/8 In.	71.00
Brass, Naval Officer Commodore Decatur, c.1816, 1 x 2 1/8 In.	990.00
Burled Maple, Dated 1741	290.00
Charles II, Walnut, Brass Mounted, Carved Top, Dated 1679, 3 1/4 In.	522.00
Copper & Abalone Inlay, Victorian, Mother-Of-Pearl, 3 In.	175.00
Declaration Of Independence, Double-Sided, Papier-Mache, c.1820, 3 5/8 In.	440.00
Enamel, Field Of Geometric Designs, Diamond Thumbpiece, Cartier	1035.00
Enamel, Floral Motif, Green Ground, Oval, Oriental, 2 1/2 In.	22.00
General Jackson, N. Edmond Inside Cover, Pewter, Federal Period, 3 5/8 x 2 In.	425.00

General Lafayette, Transfer, Papier-Mache, c.1824, 3 1/2 In. 440.00
George III, Hinged Rectangular Form, London, Sterling Silver, 1804 .... 402.50
Gold, Young Girl On Cover, Swiss, c.1820, 3 1/2 In. 3910.00
Gold & Enamel, Cupid With Young Lady On Lid, Swiss, 2 3/4 In. 5483.00
Gold & Enamel, Lady With Putti On Lid, Swiss, 2 3/4 In. 3738.00
Gold & Enamel, Riverside Scenes On Lid, Vases Of Flowers, Swiss, 2 3/4 In. 7475.00
Gold Mounted & Rock Crystal, Scrolls & Flower Heads On Domed Cover 5750.00
Gold Seekers' Arrival In California, 7 Figures, Mining Tools 880.00
Hardstone, Oval Micro-Mosaic Of 2 Birds On Lid, c.1820, 3 1/4 In. 7475.00
Horn, France 75.00
Ivory, Glass Enclosed Portrait Of General Washington, 3 In. 330.00
Micro-Mosaic, Hound On Hinged Cover, Leather Case, 3 1/2 In 6325.00
Nickel-Plated Brass, Containing Corkscrew & Knife, Eriksson 800.00
Ogdens Snuff 35.00
Papier-Mache, Allegorical Scene, John Bettridge, English, 1830, 3 3/8 In. 2000.00
Papier-Mache, Elegant Woman, 3 In. 110.00
Papier-Mache, Elizabethan Woman, Black Over Gold, 2 7/8 In. 75.00
Papier-Mache, Fox Hunters, 3 1/2 In. 130.00
Papier-Mache, Gentleman's Club Scene, Cylindrical, England, 4 3/16 In. 660.00
Papier-Mache, Girl With Bonnet, 3 In. 140.00
Papier-Mache, Hand Design, 2 1/2 In. 75.00
Papier-Mache, Seated Girl, 2 1/2 In. 125.00
Papier-Mache, Sterling Inlay, 2 1/2 x 1 x 1 In. 85.00
Pewter, Shoe Shape, 3 5/8 In. 160.00
Pontipool, Castle Illustration, Yellow Sky, 18th Century 395.00
Railroad, Early Engine & Cars, Floral Border, c.1840, 3 In. 308.00
Scenes Of Childbirth, Double Opening, Germany, 1850s, 2 3/4 In. 2530.00
Shepherd & Flock On Lid, Pastoral Scenes On Sides, English, c.1765, 2 3/4 In. 863.00
Silver, Enamel, 4-Part, Hinged, Calligraphy, Late 19th Century 302.50
Silver, Niello, Russian, 3 In. 285.00
Silver, Regency, Hinged, Reeded Cover, S. Pemberton, England, 1816, 2 3/8 In. 230.00
Silver, Vase Of Flowers, Matted Ground, Foliage Borders, Swiss, c.1820, 3 In. 6325.00
Silver Plate, Figures, Oval, 2 1/4 In. 33.00
Tinned Steel, Engraved Brass Name Plate, Oval, 2 5/8 In. 50.00
Wood, Hand Painted Castle, German, c.1890, 2 1/4 x 4 In. 95.00

SOAPSTONE is a mineral that was used for foot warmers or griddles because of its heat-retaining properties. Soapstone was carved into figurines and bowls in many countries in the nineteenth and twentieth centuries. Most of the soapstone seen today is from China or Japan. It is still being carved in the old styles.

Ashtray, Goldfish, Gray 80.00
Box, Stylized Horse 64.00
Figurine, Bearded Sage Holding Staff & Fruit, Tan, Greenish, 5 5/8 In. 26.00
Figurine, Buildings, Trees & Mountains, Oriental 38.00
Figurine, Elephant, Gray 60.00
Figurine, Fu Lion, Nativewood Base, 7 In., Pair 155.00
Figurine, Geisha, Gray, Brown 100.00
Figurine, Monkey, 2 Babies & Bird, Brown, 6 1/4 In. 48.00
Figurine, River Hog, 6 In. 40.00
Figurine, Tiger On Rock, 3 x 5 In. 30.00
Figurine, Trees, Lions, & Mountain Peaks, Green, Stand, 6 1/4 In. 49.50
Figurine, Woman, Jade Green, Red Base, 9 3/4 In. 27.00
Foot Warmer, Buggy, Iron Bail Handle 12.00
Jar, Dragon, Elephant Head Handles, Foo Dog Finial, 7 3/4 In. 71.00
Jar, Translucent 130.00
Plaque, Birds, Trees, Flowers, Tan, Oval, 9 1/2 In. 120.00
Vase, 4 Entwined Vases, Birds, Floral Array, 12 x 8 In. 440.00
Vase, Birds, Monkeys, Urns & Bat, Gray-Green, 5 1/4 x 11 In. 50.00
Vase, Flowers, Tan, 9 1/2 x 6 In. 75.00
Vase, Multi-Paneled Glass Shade, Mounted As Lamp, 21 1/4 In. 55.00

SOFT PASTE is a name for a type of pottery. Although it looks very much like porcelain, it is a chemically different material. Most of the soft-paste wares were made in the early nineteenth century. Other pieces may be listed under Gaudy Dutch or Leeds.

Creamer, King's Rose, Striping, Vine Border, Staffordshire, 4 3/4 In.	187.00
Creamer, Polychrome Design, Late 18th Century	235.00
Dish, Sardine, Brown Transfer, Sardine Finial	35.00
Teapot, King's Rose, Striping, Vine Border, Staffordshire, 6 In.	300.00
Vase, Pear Shape, Scholar Unwrapping Scroll, Marked, 7 3/8 In.	85.00

SOUVENIRS of a trip—what could be more fun? Our ancestors enjoyed the same thing and souvenirs were made for almost every location. Most of the souvenir pottery and porcelain pieces of the nineteenth century were made in England or Germany, even if the picture showed a North American scene. In the twentieth century, the souvenir china business seems to have gone to the manufacturers in Japan, Taiwan, Hong Kong, England, and America. Another popular souvenir item is the souvenir spoon, made of sterling or silver plate. These are usually made in the country pictured on the spoon. Related pieces may be found in the Coronation and World's Fair categories.

Ashtray, Boulder Dam, Figural, Pot Metal	22.00
Buckle, Belt, Flag, Red, White, Blue, Enamel, Revolutionary Figures, 1976	8.00
Bust, Mayor Daley, Chicago, Plaster, 16 In.	150.00
Button, National Farmers Association, Pinback	.25
Canoe, Ruby Stained, Little Rock, Dated 1911	25.00
Coat Rack & Mirror, Wall, Remember The Maine, 1893	250.00
Cuff Links & Tie Tack, Marilyn Monroe, Nude Pose	26.00
Cup, Pressed Glass, Monroe City, Handle, 3 In.	25.00
Cup & Saucer, Empire State Building, Demitasse	12.00
Cup & Saucer, Will Rogers Portrait, Memorial, Claremore, Okla., Demitasse	20.00
Dance Card, West Point, Brass, 1912	15.00
Dish, Bone China, Niagara Falls, Gold Trim, Paragon, 4 1/2 In.	5.00
Handkerchief, Declaration Of Independence, 19th Century, 19 x 21 In.	88.00
Handkerchief, Silk, Lewis & Clark Portland Centennial, 1905	95.00
Handkerchief, Silk, Spanish American War	60.00
Hat, Stovepipe, Wales, Long Welsh Name Around Brim	22.00
Ice Bucket, Ice Follies	95.00
Lamp, Oil, Admiral Dewey, Brass	340.00
Medal, Alaska-Yukon-Pacific Expo, Seattle, Heart Shape, 1909	35.00
Mug, Beer, Prohibition, Good-Bye Forever, Hanged In Effigy, 11 In.	225.00
Mug, Old Wentworth Mansion Brown Transfer, JHT & Co., 1875	15.00
Mug, St. Francis De Sales Ossian, Handles, 3 1/2 In.	15.00
Pendant, Embossed Gold, Freedom 7 Space Launch, 1961	5.00
Pennant, Felt, Chillicothe, Mo. High School Seniors, 1917	5.00
Pennant, Felt, Illinois State, Eagle & Shield, 3 Ft.	7.00
Pennant, Felt, Yale University, Bulldog Picture, Large	7.50
Pin, Lapel, Maple Leaf, Canada	4.00
Pitcher Set, Stoneware, San Francisco, Windy City, 5 Piece	800.00
Plate, Grand Hotel, Colfax Wheelock, 8 In.	27.50
Plate, Lexington, Ma., Adams, 8 In.	12.00
Plate, Lookout Mountain, Tenn., Jonroth, 10 In.	25.00
Plate, Pan American Expo, 3 Kittens, 1901	40.00
Plate, Rainbow Falls, Watkins Glen, Ivory, Gold Trim, Square, Adams, 9 3/4 In.	9.00
Plate, Valley Forge, Pa., Washington's Headquarters, Jonroth, 10 In.	18.50
Plate, Washington D.C., Landmarks Border, Silver Trim, Box	25.00
Ribbon, Silk, Oklahoma Territory, For Free Homes & Dennis Flynn, 1 1/2 x 8 In.	25.00
Spoon, Admiral Dewey Handle, Ship Olympix On Spoon, 1898	10.00
Spoon, Delft Windmill Handle, Man On Horse In Bowl, Holland, Box	20.00
Spoon, Silver Plate, Coney Island	8.00
Spoon, Silver Plate, George Washington Bicentennial, Wm. Rogers	10.00
Spoon, Silver Plate, Harlem Opera House	125.00
Spoon, Silver Plate, James Monroe, Rogers	10.00
Spoon, Silver Plate, New Orleans, Palm Tree & Swan Handle	35.00

Spoon, Silver Plate, Toronto, Figural Indian Handle	35.00
Spoon, Sterling Silver, Bergen, Enameled Castle Crest, Demitasse	12.00
Spoon, Sterling Silver, Black Hills, S.D.	22.00
Spoon, Sterling Silver, California, City Hall, Oakland In Bowl	29.00
Spoon, Sterling Silver, California, Mt. Tamalpais In Bowl	29.00
Spoon, Sterling Silver, California, State Capitol Building	20.00
Spoon, Sterling Silver, Camp Sheridan, Alabama, Soldier In Bowl	30.00
Spoon, Sterling Silver, Catalina Island, Demitasse	18.00
Spoon, Sterling Silver, Chicago Skyline, Masonic Temple	65.00
Spoon, Sterling Silver, Cliff House, Ornate	29.00
Spoon, Sterling Silver, Colorado, Miners On Handle	45.00
Spoon, Sterling Silver, Columbian Exposition, Liberty Figures, 1893	70.00
Spoon, Sterling Silver, Court House, Corning N.Y., Pictures On Handle	32.00
Spoon, Sterling Silver, Crawford, Nebraska, Figural, Indian	85.00
Spoon, Sterling Silver, Crouse College, Syracuse, Girl Graduate, 1905	22.00
Spoon, Sterling Silver, Cutout Woolworth Building Handle, New York	20.00
Spoon, Sterling Silver, DAR, Betsy Ross At Spinning Wheel	85.00
Spoon, Sterling Silver, Detroit, Scene On Front	29.00
Spoon, Sterling Silver, Enameled French Crest, Paris In Bowl, Demitasse	16.00
Spoon, Sterling Silver, Enameled Race Dog Handle, London, 1893	20.00
Spoon, Sterling Silver, Golden Gate, San Francisco, Figural, Bear Top	55.00
Spoon, Sterling Silver, Head Of Black Man, Daytona, Florida, 4 In.	165.00
Spoon, Sterling Silver, Homestead In Hot Springs, Black Man, 5 3/4 In.	220.00
Spoon, Sterling Silver, Indian Chief, Full Figured	75.00
Spoon, Sterling Silver, Indian Maiden, Full Figured	75.00
Spoon, Sterling Silver, Indian, Canoe, Detroit, Pontiac	50.00
Spoon, Sterling Silver, Jacksonville, Florida, Figural, Alligator	55.00
Spoon, Sterling Silver, Knox College, Galesburg, Illinois	20.00
Spoon, Sterling Silver, Los Angeles, Enameled Handle, Eureka	45.00
Spoon, Sterling Silver, Louisiana Purchase, St. Louis Expo, Transportation Building	65.00
Spoon, Sterling Silver, Maine, Plain Bowl	29.00
Spoon, Sterling Silver, Mission San Gabriel, Los Angeles	49.00
Spoon, Sterling Silver, Nebraska, Post Office, Omaha In Bowl	29.00
Spoon, Sterling Silver, Pan American Exposition Tower, 1901	22.00
Spoon, Sterling Silver, State Capitol, Albany	45.00
Spoon, Sterling Silver, Vermont	29.00
Spoon, Sterling Silver, Washington, D.C., Teddy Roosevelt & Rough Rider Top	95.00
Spoon, Sugar, Sterling Silver, LaGrange, Texas, Fancy	38.00
Trivet, George Washington, Cast Iron, 9 1/4 In.	104.00
Tumbler, Dewey, Flags On Side, 3 1/2 In.	55.00
Tumbler, Indiana State Fair, Ruby Stained, 1955	8.00
Vase, Grand Canyon National Park, Ariz., Cream, Jamroth Royal Winton, 4 5/8 In.	7.00

SPANGLE GLASS is multicolored glass made from odds and ends of colored glass rods. It includes metallic flakes of mica covered with gold, silver, nickel, or copper. Spangle glass is usually cased with a thin layer of clear glass over the multicolored layer. Similar glass is listed in the Vasa Murrhina category.

Dresser Bottle, Blue, Square, Cut Glass Stopper, 7 3/4 In.	60.00
Ewer, Apricot, Curved Clear Handle & Spout, 7 1/4 In.	165.00

Pitcher, Amberina, Gold Flecks,
Diamond-Quilted, 7 1/4 In.

Pitcher, Blue Nugget, Silver Mica, Hobbs,
Brockunier, 8 1/2 In.

Ewer, Pink To White, C. Hobbs Brockunier, 19th Century, 11 In. 193.00
Pitcher, Amberina, Gold Flecks, Diamond-Quilted, 7 1/4 In. .... *Illus* 220.00
Pitcher, Blue Nugget, Silver Mica, Hobbs, Brockunier, 8 1/2 In. .... *Illus* 3000.00
Pitcher, Flowers & Leaves, 6-Rib Blowouts, Silver Mica, 8 In. 650.00
Rose Bowl, Gold Flecks, Crimped Rim, 4 x 5 In. 95.00
Vase, Swirl Pattern, 10 In. 325.00

SPANISH LACE is a type of Victorian glass that has a white lace design.
Blue, yellow, cranberry, or clear glass was made with this distinctive white
pattern. It was made in England and the United States after 1885. Copies are
being made.

Bride's Bowl, Ruffled Rim, Cranberry, 10 In. 250.00
Butter, Cover, White 150.00
Cruet, Northwood, White 100.00
Pitcher, Cranberry 975.00
Pitcher, Ruffled Top, Ice Blue Opalescent 185.00
Pitcher, Ruffled, Blown, Applied Handle 220.00
Pitcher, Water, Opalescent To Clear 145.00
Sugar Shaker, Canary 100.00
Sugar Shaker, Opalescent, Cranberry 495.00
Sugar Shaker, Vaseline 195.00
Syrup, Cranberry 300.00
Water Set, White Opalescent, 5 Piece 350.00

SPATTER GLASS is a multicolored glass made from many small pieces of
different colored glass. It is sometimes called *End-of-Day* glass. It is still
being made.

Lamp, Fairy, Green, Clear Rigaree & Base, 4 1/4 In. 400.00
Pitcher, Ruffled Rim, Cranberry Into Pink, 8 In. 295.00
Rolling Pin, Bristol, Case 412.50
Sugar & Creamer, Applied Clear Feet & Handle, 6 1/4 x 4 1/4 In. 120.00
Vase, Yellow, Orange, Polished Base & Pontil, 8 1/2 6 3/4 In. 110.00

SPATTERWARE is the creamware or soft paste dinnerware decorated with
colored spatter designs. The earliest pieces were made in the late eighteenth
century, but most of the spatterware found today was made from about 1800
to 1850, or it is a form of kitchen crockery with added spatter designs, made
in the late nineteenth and twentieth centuries. The early spatterware was
made in the Staffordshire district of England for sale in America. The later
kitchen type is an American product.

Bowl, Peafowl, Blue, 5 In. 40.00
Bowl & Pitcher, Adam's Rose, Blue, 12 In. 880.00
Creamer, Paneled, Rainbow, 6 In. 165.00
Creamer, Red, Green & Black Rose, Blue, 5 1/4 In. 247.50
Creamer, Rose Design, Brown & Black, 4 In. 247.00
Creamer, Tulip, Red & Green, Paneled 357.50
Cup, Handleless, Peafowl, Green, Red, Blue & Black 66.00
Cup & Saucer, Blue & White Sponge, Oversize 60.00
Cup & Saucer, Handleless, 4-Part Flower, Red 60.50
Cup & Saucer, Handleless, Black Deer On Saucer, Red 358.00
Cup & Saucer, Handleless, Bull's-Eye Saucer, Flower On Cup 275.00
Cup & Saucer, Handleless, Fort Pattern, Black, Green & Red 302.50
Cup & Saucer, Handleless, House, Blue 159.50
Cup & Saucer, Handleless, Purple 60.50
Cup & Saucer, Handleless, Rainbow, Blue & Red 192.50
Cup & Saucer, Handleless, Rooster, Blue, Red, Black, Yellow Ochre, Marked 440.00
Cup & Saucer, Peafowl, Green, Handleless, 6 In. .... 467.00 to 480.00
Cup & Saucer, Stick Flowers, Red 205.00
Custard, Blue & White Sponged, 2 3/4 In. 50.00
Lamp, Fairy, Ivy Leaves, Pottery Base, 4 1/4 In. 50.00
Pitcher, Blue, Flower, Black Stripes, 7 5/8 In. 330.00
Pitcher, Light Blue & Navy Sponge, Cream Ground, 10 In. 143.00
Pitcher, Peafowl, Blue, Yellow, Green & Black, Red Ground, 5 3/8 In. 345.00

Plate,	Adams Rose, 8 In.	320.00
Plate,	Center Tulip, Multicolor Rim, 9 1/2 In.	137.50
Plate,	Eagle & Shield, Blue Transfer, 9 1/8 In.	467.50
Plate,	Floral, 5 In.	25.00
Plate,	Peafowl, 9 1/2 In.	400.00
Plate,	Peafowl, Red, 8 3/8 In.	467.50
Plate,	Purple & White Stick, George Jones, Stoke On Trent	27.50
Plate,	Rabbit, Yellow, Red, Blue & Green, 9 In.	450.00
Platter,	Red Transfer, Cowboys & Wild Horses, Blue, 12 3/8 In.	193.00
Sauce,	Peafowl, Red, Blue, Green & Black, 5 In.	170.50
Saucer,	Columbine, Rosebud & Thistle Center, Purple Design Border, 6 In.	93.00
Saucer,	Peafowl, Red, 4 1/8 In.	60.00
Saucer,	Peafowl, Red, Green, Blue & Black, 5 3/8 In.	160.00
Sugar,	Peafowl, Blue	75.00
Sugar,	Tulip, Blue Sponge	350.00
Toddy Plate,	Red & Green Thistle, Yellow, 6 1/4 In.	1595.00
Vase,	Jack-In-The-Pulpit, Diamond Quilted, Green, White & Pink, 6 3/4 In.	95.00
Waste Bowl,	Cows, Stick, Yellow Geometric Border In & Out	225.00

SPELTER is a synonym for a zinc alloy. Figurines, candlesticks, and other pieces were made of spelter and given a bronze or painted finish. The metal has been used since about the 1860s to make statues, tablewares, and lamps that resemble bronze. Spelter is soft and breaks easily. To test for spelter, scratch the base of the piece. Bronze is solid; spelter will show a silvery scratch.

Candleholder,	Winged Figure, Arms Raised, 15 In.	110.00
Clock,	Rosee De Printemps, Art Nouveau, Francois Moureau, 28 1/4 In.	600.00
Figurine,	African Woman, c.1935, 20 In.	400.00
Figurine,	Don Juan, 17th Century Dress, Sword, Patinated Base, 21 1/2 In.	175.00
Figurine,	Nude Woman, Standing On Sphere, Gold Paint, 23 In.	100.00
Frame,	Mirror, Mask Of Lady At Base, Floral Crest, Easel Back, c.1910, 11 x 8 In.	110.00
Lamp,	Art Nouveau, Young Woman, Raised Arms, Jeweled Metal Shade, 33 In.	200.00
Lamp,	Base, Gargoyle Relief, Mushroom Style Globe, Green Glass, 18 In.	330.00
Lamp,	Figural, Woman, With 3 Lights, Art Nouveau, 32 In.	445.00
Match Holder,	2 Black Boys, Cotton Bale, Cotton Exposition, 1884, 2 5/8 In.	137.00
Match Holder,	2 Black Boys, Cotton Bale, Holding Watermelon, 1884, 2 5/8 In.	55.00
Trophy,	Tennis, Painted Gold, 1920s, 11 In.	550.00

SPINNING WHEELS in the corner have been symbols of earlier times for the past 100 years. Although spinning wheels date back to medieval days, the ones found today are rarely more than 200 years old. Because the style of the spinning wheel changed very little, it is often impossible to place an exact date on a wheel.

Chip Carved & Turned Detail,	Oak, 35 1/2 In.	247.50
Hardwood,	Red Paint, 41 1/2 In.	170.00
Mixed Hardwood,	17 In.	275.00
Mustard Paint,	Small	245.00
Pukin Paint		425.00
Punched Carved Designs,	Black Striping, J.H.W., 1847, 37 1/2 In.	165.00

SPODE pottery, porcelain, and bone china were made by the Stoke-on-Trent factory of England founded by Josiah Spode about 1770. The firm became Copeland and Garrett from 1833 to 1847, then W. T. Copeland or W. T. Copeland and Sons until 1976. It then became Royal Worcester Spode Ltd. The word *Spode* appears on many pieces made by the factories. Most collectors include all the wares under the more familiar name of Spode. Porcelains are listed in this book by the name that appears on the piece. Related pieces are listed under Copeland and Copeland Spode.

Chop Plate,	Tower, Blue, 12 In.	150.00
Chop Plate,	Tower, Blue, 15 In.	165.00
Creamer,	Tower, Pink	60.00
Cup & Saucer,	Imari, Cobalt Ground, 4 1/2 In.	220.00
Cup & Saucer,	Tower, Pink, Auld Lang Syne	170.00

Dish, Divided, Blue & White Oriental Design, 6 In. 148.00
Garniture Set, Landscape Medallions, Gilt Borders, 3 Piece 300.00
Gravy Boat, Attached Underplate, Tower, Blue 75.00
Planter, Ring, Ivory, Floral Panels, Scalloped, Velamour, 9 x 2 In. 110.00
Plate, Hawthorne, Medium Blue, White, c.1810, 10 In. 25.00
Plate, Square, Flowers In Yellow Urn, Baskets & Eagles On Rim, c.1825, 8 1/4 In. .. 1495.00
Platter, Tower, Pink, 14 In. 110.00
Platter, Tower, Scenic, Blue & White, 16 x 13 In. 275.00
Service For 8, Buttercup Pattern 120.00
Service For 20, Rose Briar, 88 Piece 385.00
Spill Vase, Cylindrical, Birds At Fountain, Footed, c.1820, 3 In. 690.00
Sugar, Cover, Tower, Pink 65.00
Tumbler, R.A.F. British War Relief Society 95.00

SPONGEWARE is very similar to spatterware in appearance. The designs
were applied to the ceramics by daubing the color on with a sponge or cloth.
Many collectors do not differentiate between spongeware and spatterware
and use the names interchangeably. Modern pottery is being made to
resemble the old spongeware, but careful examination will show it is new.

Bowl, Green & Yellow, 7 1/2 In. 70.00
Bowl, New Richland Advertising 210.00
Bowl Set, Brown & Blue, Nested, 5 Piece 550.00
Creamer, Grape & Leaf Panels, Scalloped, Blue, Cream Ground, Octagonal, 3 In. 54.00
Cuspidor, Blue & White 85.00
Dish, Scalloped Rim, Blue & White, 9 In. 70.00
Jug, Blue & Gray, Handle, Cork 8.50
Jug, Merry Christmas, Weeks, 1 Qt. 1100.00
Mug, Flying Bird, Blue & White 110.00
Pitcher, Embossed Lattice, Vines, Roses, Cream, Tan, Blue, 9 1/2 In. 400.00
Syrup, Green, Rust 395.00

SPORTS equipment, sporting goods, brochures, and related items are listed
here. Other categories of interest are Bicycle, Card, Fishing, Gun, Rifle,
Sword, and Toy.

Auto Racing, Program, Indianapolis 500, 1936 .... 150.00
Baseball, Ad, Bob Feller, Tip-Top Bread, 1940 .... 8.00
Baseball, Ad, Bob Feller, Wheaties Strikeout, 1939 .... 6.00
Baseball, Ad, Stan Musial, Red Hart Baseball Cap, 1955 .... 6.00
Baseball, Ad, Ted Williams, Nabisco, Ring, 1948 .... 6.00
Baseball, Ashtray, Baseball Player Standing On Edge, China 154.00
Baseball, Ball, Autographed, All-Star Teams, 1953 .... 325.00
Baseball, Ball, Autographed, Babe Ruth, 1938 .... 1995.00
Baseball, Ball, Autographed, Babe Ruth, Idol Of American Boy, May 4, 1931 .... 660.00
Baseball, Ball, Autographed, Babe Ruth, On Sweet Spot, 1920s 2500.00
Baseball, Ball, Autographed, Bob Feller 35.00
Baseball, Ball, Autographed, Chicago, Team, 1954 .... 175.00
Baseball, Ball, Autographed, Cincinnati Reds, Bench & Rose, 1980 .... 150.00
Baseball, Ball, Autographed, Cleveland Indians, 26 Signatures, 1957 .... 1150.00
Baseball, Ball, Autographed, Cy Young 1650.00
Baseball, Ball, Autographed, Henry Aaron & Others, 1962 .... 75.00
Baseball, Ball, Autographed, Joe DiMaggio 225.00
Baseball, Ball, Autographed, Orioles, Team, 1955 .... 175.00
Baseball, Ball, Autographed, Sinclair Babe Ruth Contest 302.00
Baseball, Ball, Autographed, Steve Carlton 30.00
Baseball, Ball, Autographed, Ty Cobb, 3/26/48 .... 240.00
Baseball, Ball, Autographed, Yankees, Team, 1943 .... 275.00
Baseball, Ball, Autographed, Yankees, Ruth & Gehrig, 1928 .... 4950.00
Baseball, Ball, Autographed, World Series, Boston Braves Vs Cleveland, 1948 .... 192.00
Baseball, Ball, Kellogg's, Tony The Tiger, Rawlings Major League 10.00
Baseball, Ball, Major League, 1968 .... 35.00
Baseball, Bank, Cleveland Indians, Figural, Ceramic, 1940s 175.00
Baseball, Bat Rack, Stan Musial, 1964 .... 65.00
Baseball, Bat Rack, Stan Musial, Sealed, 1954 .... 65.00

Baseball, Bat, Autographed, Bob Meusel, Yankees, Hillerich & Bradsby, 1927	1100.00
Baseball, Bat, Autographed, Mickey Mantle	995.00
Baseball, Bat, Autographed, Roy Campanella, Letter Of Authenticity	375.00
Baseball, Bat, Bill Dickey, Game-Used	3025.00
Baseball, Bat, Lee Mazzilli, Maz On Knob, Lot Of Tape & Pine Tar, Uncracked	90.00
Baseball, Bat, Louisville Slugger	27.50
Baseball, Bat, Louisville Slugger, Babe Ruth	175.00
Baseball, Bat, Paul Waner Signature, World Series, 1927	90.00
Baseball, Bat, R.C.F.C. Stars Of Boston, Against Howards Of Brockton, 1874	3025.00
Baseball, Bat, Spalding	12.50
Baseball, Bat, Ted Williams, Sears, 1950s	85.00 to 90.00
Baseball, Bat, Winchester	225.00
Baseball, Booklet, Mickey Mantle Great Hitters, Carvel Premium	45.00
Baseball, Bottle, Coca-Cola, Rod Carew, Minnesota Twins, 1987	50.00
Baseball, Bust, Bill Dickey, Sports Hall Of Fame, 1963	65.00
Baseball, Button, Babe Ruth, Brass	90.00
Baseball, Button, Briggs Stadium, Detroit Tigers, Flasher, 3 In.	35.00
Baseball, Button, Dave Kingman, Oakland A's, Large	1.25
Baseball, Button, Detroit Tigers, Large	1.25
Baseball, Button, Hank Aaron, Atlanta Braves, 1969	1.25
Baseball, Button, Jackie Robinson, Dated 1947	250.00
Baseball, Button, Keith Hernandez, New York Mets, Large	1.50
Baseball, Button, Larry Doby, Long White & Red Ribbon, 1947	100.00
Baseball, Button, New York Yankees, World Series, 1923	1000.00
Baseball, Button, Ozzie Smith, St. Louis Cardinals, Large	1.50
Baseball, Button, Willie Mays, San Francisco Giants, 1969	1.25
Baseball, Button, Yogi Berra, Yankees, 1969	1.25
Baseball, Cap, MacDonald's Restaurants, Red & Yellow Cloth, Unused	2.50
Baseball, Catcher's Mitt, Builtwell No. 211	20.00
Baseball, Clock, Alarm, Ted Williams	175.00
Baseball, Condiment Set, Baseball Bat Salt & Pepper, Tray, Porcelain, 1940s	120.00
Baseball, Fan, Milwaukee Braves, Mascot, Silk, c.1950	15.00
Baseball, Figurine, Autographed, Bust, Ted Williams	125.00
Baseball, Figurine, Babe Ruth, With Bat, Wooden Base, Hartland	165.00
Baseball, Figurine, Baseball Player, Rubber, 1930s, 4 In.	20.00
Baseball, Figurine, Rittgers, 1941	50.00
Baseball, Glove, Al Kaline	22.50
Baseball, Glove, Andy Palfko	20.00
Baseball, Glove, Batting, Mike Schmidt, 1989	125.00
Baseball, Glove, Batting, Rod Carew, 1980	80.00
Baseball, Glove, Claw Trapper, Dick Sisler Model, Rawlings, c.1920	125.00
Baseball, Glove, Johnny Temple, Fielder's, Model G111, Box, c.1960	290.00
Baseball, Glove, Luis Aparicio, Wilson	100.00
Baseball, Glove, Nellie Fox	30.00
Baseball, Glove, Robin Roberts	48.00
Baseball, Glove, Tom Seaver's, Spalding	*Illus* 4400.00
Baseball, Glove, Triple Play, Spalding, c.1930	65.00

Sports, Baseball, Glove, Tom Seaver's, Spalding

◆◆◆◆◆◆◆◆◆◆◆◆◆◆◆◆◆◆◆

Trim shrubs near the house so
they don't hide burglars trying to
break in basement or first-floor
windows.

◆◆◆◆◆◆◆◆◆◆◆◆◆◆◆◆◆◆◆

Baseball, Guard, Catcher's, Spaulding 90.00
Baseball, Jersey, Autographed, Darryl Strawberry, Mets 90.00
Baseball, Jersey, Autographed, Mickey Mantle, 1951 .... 300.00
Baseball, Jersey, Autographed, Ted Williams 300.00
Baseball, Key Ring, Frankie Robinson, Cincinnati Reds 35.00
Baseball, Lapel Pin, World Series, New York Mets, 1969 .... 20.00
Baseball, Mask & Chest Protector, Catcher's 65.00
Baseball, Mask, Catcher's, 1950-1960 .... 45.00
Baseball, Mask, Catcher's, Rawling's 20.00
Baseball, Mitt, Catcher's, J.C. Kiggins & J. Walker 95.00
Baseball, Nodder, Mickey Mantle 300.00
Baseball, Pencil Clip, Babe Ruth 6.00
Baseball, Pencil, Mickey Mantle Portrait, Display Card, 9 x 3 1/2 In., Pair 75.00
Baseball, Pennant, Cleveland Indians, 1950s 75.00
Baseball, Pennant, Milwaukee Braves, 1950s 35.00
Baseball, Pennant, Washington Senators, 1950s 45.00
Baseball, Pennant, World Series, Dodgers Vs. Yankees, 1963 .... 75.00
Baseball, Photograph, Autographed, Joe DiMaggio 95.00
Baseball, Photograph, Ernie Lombardi, Most Valuable Player, 1938 .... 27.50
Baseball, Photograph, Jimmie Foxx, Tour Of Japan, 1934 .... 170.00
Baseball, Picture, Mickey Mantle In Yankee Uniform, Autographed 200.00
Baseball, Pillow, Cincinnati Red Stockings, Players Pictured 3250.00
Baseball, Poster, Welcome Home Dinner, N.Y. Yankees, April 18, 1958, 14 x 22 In. . 60.00
Baseball, Press Pin, World Series, Fenway Park, 1967 .... 275.00
Baseball, Program & Scorecard, Giants Vs.Yankees, 1936 .... 200.00
Baseball, Program, World Series, Cardinals Vs. Red Sox, 1946 .... 100.00 to 175.00
Baseball, Program, World Series, Dodgers Vs. Yankees, 1950 .... 225.00
Baseball, Program, World Series, Giants Vs. Yankees, 1962 .... 65.00
Baseball, Program, World Series, Yankees Vs. Cubs, 1938........................ 275.00
Baseball, Radio, Roger Maris & Mickey Mantle Signatures, Stellar, 1959 .... 500.00
Baseball, Record, Greatest Moments In Sports, Ruth, Gehrig, Actual Voices 125.00
Baseball, Ring, Andy Pafko, Records Balls, Strikes & Outs, Quaker Oats 200.00
Baseball, Schedule, National & American League Home Games, 1941 .... 8.00
Baseball, Score Book, N.Y. Yankees, c.1942 .... 48.00
Baseball, Shirt, Game, Red Sox 25.00
Baseball, Sign, Boston Garter Co., Fred Clarke, F.L. Chance Picture, Paper, Frame ... 4400.00
Baseball, Sign, Chesterfield, Baseball Man's Cigarette, 6 Autographs .... *Illus* 990.00
Baseball, Sign, Chesterfield, New York Champions, 26 x 26 In. .... *Illus* 990.00
Baseball, Sign, White Sox Park Today, Comiskey Park, 18 x 25 In. .... *Illus* 1925.00
Baseball, Stock Certificate, Brooklyn Ball Club, Charles Ebbets To Himself, 1907 .... 1760.00
Baseball, Ticket Stub, World Series, St. Louis Cardinals Vs. Detroit Tigers, 1934 ..... 310.00
Baseball, Uniform, Batavia, New York 125.00

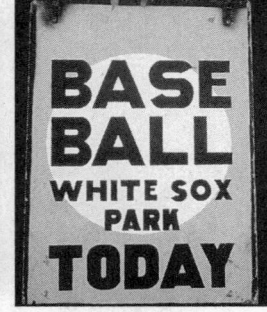

Sports, Baseball, Sign, Chesterfield, Baseball Man's Cigarette, 6 Autographs

Sports, Baseball, Sign, Chesterfield, New York Champions, 26 x 26 In.

Sports, Baseball, Sign, White Sox Park Today, Comiskey Park, 18 x 25 In.

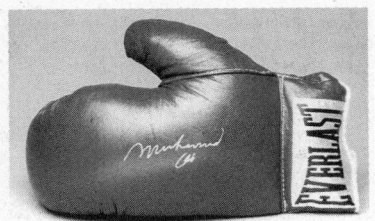

Sports, Boxing, Glove,
Muhammad Ali Autograph, Everlast

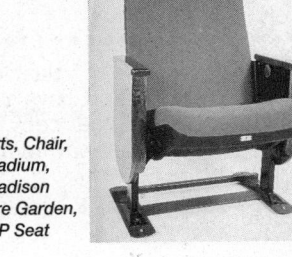

Sports, Chair,
Stadium,
Madison
Square Garden,
VIP Seat

Baseball, Uniform, Maynard Athletic Goods, 1920s		120.00
Baseball, Wrapper, Candy Bar, Pete Rose		10.00
Baseball, Wrapper, Candy Bar, Reggie! Bar		12.00
Baseball, Yearbook, Cleveland Indians, 1949		100.00
Baseball, Yearbook, Flag Form, St. Louis, American League Champions, 1944		120.00
Baseball, Yearbook, Los Angeles Dodgers, 1958		125.00
Baseball, Yearbook, Milwaukee Braves, 1957		125.00
Baseball, Yearbook, Photos Of Roy Campanella, Satchel Paige, Etc., 1944	225.00 to	450.00
Baseball, Yearbook, Pittsburgh Pirates, 1973		8.00
Basketball, Bank, Bobbin' Head, N.Y. Knicks, Ceramic, 1969, 9 In.		70.00
Basketball, Figurine, Lil' Dribbler, Ceramic, N.Y. Knicks, 1969		40.00
Basketball, Jersey Warm-Up, Autographed, Michael Jordan		3000.00
Basketball, Jersey, Bobby Jones, Denver Nuggets, No. 24, Powder, 1977-1978		465.00
Basketball, Jersey, Wilt Chamberlain, Game-Used, 1961-1962		1600.00
Basketball, Model Kit, Jerry West & Opponent, 1/12 Scale, Aurora, 1965, 12 x 9 In.		198.00
Basketball, Photograph, ABA, Kentucky Colonels Advertising, 1974, 10 x 12 In.		17.00
Basketball, Record, 45 Rpm, Harlem Globetrotters, Original Jacket, 1950s		22.00
Basketball, Record, Sweet Georgia Brown, Harlem Globetrotters, 45 RPM, 1950s		15.00
Basketball, Sneakers, Michael Jordan, Autographed, Nike Airs, 1986-1987		1320.00
Billiards, Ball, Autographed, Willie Mosconi		100.00
Billiards, Table, Brunswick, Balke, Collender Co., Rosewood, c.1860		6750.00
Booklet, How To Play, Brunswick-Balke Collender Co., 56 Pages		13.50
Bowling, Ashtray, Man, Bowling, Silver On Glass		8.00
Boxing, Can, Shoe Polish, Muhammad Ali, Unused		32.00
Boxing, Candy Bar Wrapper, Crunch Bar, Muhammad Ali, 1978		48.00
Boxing, Glove, Autographed, Muhammad Ali		85.00
Boxing, Glove, Muhammad Ali Autograph, Everlast	*Illus*	98.00
Boxing, Gloves, Autographed By Ali, Chuck, Wepner Vs. Ali, 3-24-75		1540.00
Boxing, Gloves, Everlast, Leather		75.00
Boxing, Gloves, Leather, 2 Pair		60.00
Boxing, Medal, Commemorative, Joe Louis		35.00
Boxing, Movie, Dempsey-Tunney Fight, 16 mm., Box		15.00
Boxing, Paperweight, Jimmy Weeden, Pittsburgh, PA		250.00
Boxing, Plate, 12 Rounds, France, Signed, 9 In., 12 Piece		800.00
Boxing, Poster, Sammy Harris, 1930		40.00
Boxing, Program & Magazine, Madison Square Garden, 1946-1947		48.00
Boxing, Score Card, Tommy Collins Vs. Glen Flanagan, 1950s		20.00
Boxing, Ticket, Ali Vs. Patterson, $50 Ringside Seat, November 22, 1965		450.00
Boxing, Ticket, Fritzie Zivic Vs. Al Davis, June 25, 1941		55.00
Boxing, Ticket, Joe Louis Vs. Ezzard Charles, Sept.27, 1950		69.00
Boxing, Ticket, Rocky Marciano Vs. Joe Walcott, Picture, May 15, 1953		285.00
Chair, Stadium, Madison Square Garden, VIP Seat	*Illus*	358.00
Curling, Plate, Curling Cup, 3 Men, Signed, 8 In.		22.50
Equestrian, Riding Crop, Brass Tip & Bezel, Bone Handle, 24 In.		65.00
Equestrian, Spurs, Buffalo Bill Cody's, With Autographed Photograph, 1907		4950.00
Equestrian, Spurs, Heart Buttons, North & Judd		150.00

◆◆◆◆◆◆◆◆◆◆◆◆◆◆◆◆◆◆◆◆◆◆◆◆◆

If you have an old, valuable tin-type or photograph, have a copy made. Display the copy, and keep the original away from sunlight and dirt.

◆◆◆◆◆◆◆◆◆◆◆◆◆◆◆◆◆◆◆◆◆◆◆◆◆

Sports, Horse Racing, Glass, Pimlico, 100th Preakness, 1975; Sports, Horse Racing, Glass, Pimlico, Daisies, Preakness, 1978

Fishing, Trophy, 2nd Place Sail Fish Prize, Miami, Fla., Silver Plate, 8 1/4 In.	45.00
Football, Ball, Autographed, Joe Namath	85.00
Football, Ball, Autographed, Marino, Elway, Montana	215.00
Football, Ball, Autographed, Walter Payton, Silver Sharpie, Wilson	105.00
Football, Charm, Cleveland Browns, Champions, 1948	330.00
Football, Glass, Super Bowl XXI	7.50
Football, Helmet, Bo Jackson, Los Angeles Raiders, Desert Storm Flag	1495.00
Football, Helmet, Leather, 1930s	225.00
Football, Holder, License Plate, Green Bay Packers	285.00
Football, Jersey, Ron Johnson, New York Giants, No. 30, Sand-Knit, 1970s	495.00
Football, Kerchief, Cleveland Browns, 1988	10.00
Football, Mirror, Missouri College Football Team, Celluloid, 1928, Oval, Pocket	8.00
Football, Program, Army-Navy, 1964	22.00
Football, Program, Army-Pennsylvania University, Nov. 17, 1945	25.00
Football, Program, Chicago Bears Vs. Redskins, Sept.15, 1968	5.00
Football, Program, Chicago Bears, 1962	12.00
Football, Program, LSU Vs. Ole Miss., College, Nov. 4, 1961	20.00
Football, Program, Minn.Vs. Ohio State, Oct.15, 1949	23.00
Football, Program, Northwestern Vs. Purdue, College, Oct.1, 1948	16.00
Football, Program, Notre Dame Vs. Army, Autographed, Notre Dame Team, 1946	450.00
Football, Program, Notre Dame Vs. Drake University, 56 Pages, 1932	163.00
Football, Sheet Music, Maybe It's Love, All America Team, Joe E. Brown, 1930	75.00
Football, Shoes, Athletic, O.J. Simpson, Papers, Box, 1975	45.00
Football, Shoes, Leather	5.00
Football, Thermos, NFL, Quarterback, 1964	40.00
Football, Tumbler, Pittsburgh Steelers, Mel Blount, 1976	6.00
Football, Tumbler, St. Louis Cardinals, NFL	5.00
Golf, Ad, Ben Hogan, Camel Cigarettes, 1941	3.00
Golf, Ball Marker, Falstaff Beer	5.00
Golf, Ball, Autographed, Sam Snead	303.00
Golf, Calendar, Desk, Lead Lady Golfer Figure, Perpetual, Unfinished, 4 3/4 In.	72.00
Golf, Charm, Golf Bag, Sterling Silver, 9/16 In.	25.00
Golf, Club, Driver, Bryon Nelson, 563	145.00
Golf, Club, Driver, Tony Lema Westerner	145.00
Golf, Club, Iron, Hickory Shaft	16.00
Golf, Club, MacGregor, Wood Shaft, Bag, Gloves, 1930s, 9 Clubs	450.00
Golf, Club, Mashie, Mac, JN 271, No.11	30.00
Golf, Club, Putter, George Low Bristol 600	150.00
Golf, Club, Putter, Hickory Shaft	22.00
Golf, Club, Putter, Ping Kushin, Wide Black Band	40.00
Golf, Club, Putter, Ping Zing-5, Becu, Engraved, All Original	59.00
Golf, Club, Putter, Spalding Touring Pro III	35.00
Golf, Club, Putter, Tourney Classic TCP2, 8802	60.00
Golf, Club, Putter, Wooden Shaft, Brass Head, Otye Cirsma	150.00
Golf, Club, Wood, Hickory Shaft	35.00
Golf, Figurine, Golfer's Dilemma, Bisque	35.00

Golf, Figurine, Old Duffer, Teeing Off, Plaster	205.00
Golf, Glove, Autographed, Trevino	85.00
Golf, Money Clip, Detroit Golf Assoc.	5800.00
Golf, Plate, Wendell August Forge, Aluminum, Golfer In Action, 8 In.	65.00
Golf, Trophy, Mauser USA, Horn Handle, Sterling Silver & Hammered Copper	132.00
Golf, Vase, Florida Seniors Golf Association, Etched Glass, Trophy	25.00
Hockey, Book, U.S. Field Hockey Assoc. Official 1932 Guide, Spalding	12.00
Hockey, Doll, Bobbin' Head, Papier-Mache, Detroit Red Wings, 1962, 3 1/2 In.	50.00
Hockey, Doll, Bobbin' Head, Papier-Mache, Montreal Canadiens, 1962, 3 1/2 In.	50.00
Hockey, Doll, Bobbin' Head, Papier-Mache, Toronto Maple Leafs, 1962, 3 1/2 In.	50.00
Hockey, Ice Skates, Red Doran	385.00
Hockey, Program, Chicago Black Hawks Vs. Montreal, 1947	26.00
Hockey, Program, NHL All-Star, Detroit, 4th Annual Game, Dec. 8, 1950	297.00
Hockey, Program, Stanley Cup, Chicago Black Hawks, 1970-1971	12.00
Hockey, Skate, Barney & Berry, WRA Co.	25.00
Hockey, Stick, Boston Bruins, 17 Signatures, 1935-1936	100.00
Hockey, Stick, Marcel Dionne, Game Used, CCM, 1970s	345.00
Hockey, Uniform, Red Wings, Red Doran	550.00
Horse Racing, Ad, Eddie Arcaro, Gillette, 1949	3.00
Horse Racing, Blazer, Roosevelt Raceway, Blue	50.00
Horse Racing, Glass, Belmont Park, Complimentary, 7 Piece	70.00
Horse Racing, Glass, Kentucky Derby, 1948, Churchill Downs	118.00
Horse Racing, Glass, Kentucky Derby, 1949, Portrait	119.00
Horse Racing, Glass, Kentucky Derby, 1950, Horse Racing Scene	232.00
Horse Racing, Glass, Kentucky Derby, 1952	110.00 to 160.00
Horse Racing, Glass, Kentucky Derby, 1954	90.00
Horse Racing, Glass, Kentucky Derby, 1955	125.00
Horse Racing, Glass, Kentucky Derby, 1955, 5 Fastest Runners	90.00
Horse Racing, Glass, Kentucky Derby, 1956	65.00
Horse Racing, Glass, Kentucky Derby, 1958	16.00 to 45.00
Horse Racing, Glass, Kentucky Derby, 1968	40.00
Horse Racing, Glass, Kentucky Derby, 1969	20.00
Horse Racing, Glass, Kentucky Derby, 1971	32.00
Horse Racing, Glass, Kentucky Derby, 1979	7.50
Horse Racing, Glass, Pimlico, 100th Preakness, 1975 *Illus*	53.00
Horse Racing, Glass, Pimlico, Daisies, Preakness, 1978 *Illus*	45.00
Horse Racing, Glass, Preakness, 1983	42.00
Horse Racing, Glass, Preakness, 1986	27.00
Horse Racing, Glass, Preakness, 1990	6.00
Horse Racing, Tray, Kentucky Derby, 1974	25.00
Horse Racing, Tumbler, Belmont Park, Triple Crown Winner, 1978	8.00
Horse Racing, Tumbler, Kentucky Derby, 100th Anniversary, 1974	8.00
Hunting, Crow Call, Mallardtone, Wooden	85.00
Hunting, Duck Call, 2 Bands, Cedar, Charles Perdew	625.00
Hunting, Duck Call, Carved Duck Head, Flapping Bill	800.00

Sports, Pool, Table, Brunswick, c. 1880

◆◆◆◆◆◆◆◆◆◆◆◆◆◆◆◆◆◆◆◆◆◆

When cleaning dolls or furniture or other wooden pieces use the foam from a mixture of 1 tablespoon of soap to 1 quart of water. Whip the mixture with a beater and clean with the foam.

◆◆◆◆◆◆◆◆◆◆◆◆◆◆◆◆◆◆◆◆◆◆

◆◆◆◆◆◆◆◆◆◆◆◆◆◆◆◆◆◆◆◆◆◆

Don't store wooden bowls and other pieces on their sides. This can cause them to warp.

◆◆◆◆◆◆◆◆◆◆◆◆◆◆◆◆◆◆◆◆◆◆

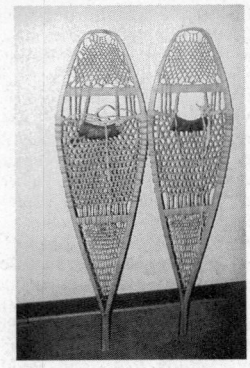

Sports, Snowshoes, Hand Made, Ontario, Canada, 48 In.

Hunting, Duck Call, Cerratta, Head	110.00
Hunting, Duck Call, Cherrywood, Pair	30.00
Hunting, Duck Call, Kankakee Crow	40.00
Hunting, Duck Call, Louisiana Brass Belle, Johnny Bill Weiss	65.00
Hunting, Duck Call, Metal Reed Design, Mangrum	325.00
Hunting, Duck Call, Octagonal Barrel, Label, Oscar Quam	75.00
Hunting, Goose Call, Fuller	275.00
Hunting, Hand Trap, Winchester-Western	50.00
Hunting, License, California, 1920	25.00
Hunting, License, Hunter & Trapper, State Of Ohio, Migratory Bird Stamp, 1936	90.00
Hunting, License, Tennessee, 1937	45.00
Hunting, Peep Sight, Lyman 48m, Box	50.00
Hunting, Print, Quail Shooting, A. Lasalle Ripley, 14 1/2 x 9 1/2 In.	225.00
Hunting, Print, Roland Clark, Duck Stamp Etched, Frame	1100.00
Hunting, Rifle Shell, Winchester Avon Red Shot	10.00
Hunting, Shotgun Shell, Berdan No. 1, 10 Gauge, Yellow Brass	3.35
Hunting, Shotgun Shell, W.R.A. Rival, 12 Gauge, Yellow Brass	3.50
Hunting, Turkey Call, 1958	25.00
Motorcycle Racing, Program, Dayton 200, 1969	10.00
Pool, Cue Rack, Brunswick Bolke Collendar, Gilt Trim	925.00
Pool, Table, Brunswick, c.1880 .... *Illus*	2860.00
Pool, Table, Burroughs, Folding, Equipment	150.00
Racing, Glass, Indianapolis 500 Speedway, 1951	48.00
Racing, Glass, Indianapolis 500, 1971	25.00
Racing, Poster, Indy 500, 1967	45.00
Racing, Program, Indy 500, 1947	70.00
Racing, Program, Indy 500, 1949	75.00
Rowing Scull, 8-Man, Princeton, Mahogany, Accessories, 1940-1950, 60 Ft.	3500.00
Skating, Skates, Inchester, Clamp On, Iron	35.00
Skiing, Chair, Ski Lift, Oak Seat, 1950s	250.00
Skiing, Skis, Oak, With Poles, 1940s	50.00
Skiing, Skis, Strand, Handmade, Leather Straps, Cedar, 96 In.	85.00
Snowshoes, Handmade, Ontario, Canada, 48 In. .... *Illus*	121.00
Softball, Postcard, Softball Club, St. Petersburg, Fla., 1944	30.00
Tennis, Press Ticket, Bobby Riggs Vs. Billie Jean King, Sept. 20, 1973, 8 In.	138.00
Tennis, Program, Bobby Riggs, World Championship Tour, 1940s	25.00
Tennis, Racquet, 1890s	120.00
Tennis, Racquet, Dayton	25.00
Tennis, Racquet, Dayton Steel, Wooden Handle, Wire Strings	20.00
Tennis, Racquet, Don Budge, Wilson, Allstar Model	40.00
Tennis, Shirt, Match Used, Jimmy Connors, U.S. Open, Slazenger, 1988	935.00

Wrestling, Sign, All Star Wrestling, Women, Cardboard, 1940s, 14 x 22 In. 15.00

STAFFORDSHIRE, England, has been a district making pottery and porcelain since the 1700s. Hundreds of kilns are still working in the area. Thousands of types of pottery and porcelain have been made in the many factories that worked and still work in the area. Some of the most famous factories have been listed separately, such as Adams, Davenport, Ridgway, Rowland & Marsellus, Royal Doulton, Royal Worcester, Spode, Wedgwood, and others. Some Staffordshire pieces are listed under categories like Fairing, Flow Blue, Mulberry, Shaving Mug, etc.

Bank, Black Man	160.00
Bank, Cottage, Polychrome, 4 1/2 In.	148.00
Bookends, Dog & Cat, Pottery, 6 In.	242.00
Bowl, Commodore MacDonnough's Victory, Beaded Rim, Wood, 11 1/2 In.	1320.00
Bowl, Old Foley, Blue & White, James Kent, 4 3/4 x 5 1/2 In.	100.00
Bowl, Vegetable, Cover, Ship Of The Line In The Downs, Enoch Wood	2250.00
Bowl, Underplate, Dark Brown Transfer, Olympic Games, 10 3/4 In.	330.00
Bowl & Undertray, Reticulated, Blue Transfer, Roman Ruins, Rogers, 10 In.	852.50
Box, Pin, Baby In Bed, Polychrome Enamel, 6 5/8 In.	192.50
Box, Trinket, Boy Paddling Boat, Mirror Frame	110.00
Box, Trinket, Little Red Riding Hood & Wolf On Lid, 2 1/2 x 3 In.	35.00
Bust, Washington, 8 In.	192.00
Bust, Washington, Born 1732, Died 1799, Cherub Riding Eagle, 8 1/2 In.	2100.00
Butter, Cover, Silver Luster Leaf Sprays	25.00
Butter Tub, Cover, Stand, White Salt Glaze, 1760, Oval, 6 1/2 In.	1495.00
Cask, Beer, Barrel Shape, Allover Brown Glaze, Slipware, Dated 1774, 9 In.	990.00
Chimney Piece, Scotsman On Horseback, Slain Deer, 14 1/4 In.	247.50
Coffeepot, California, Podmore & Walker, c.1850	325.00
Coffeepot, Commodore MacDonnough's Victory, Blue, Wood, 10 1/2 In.	2400.00
Coffeepot, Lafayette At Franklin's Tomb, Domed Lid, Blue, 11 1/2 In.	1450.00
Cracker Jar, Cottage, Bail Handle	65.00
Cream Boat, Helmet Shape, Marbled, c.1750, 4 1/16 In.	2300.00
Creamer, California, Podmore & Walker, c.1850	165.00
Creamer, Child's, Sailboats, Fans, Calico Print, 4 In.	65.00
Creamer, Christmas Eve, Dark Blue, 5 1/2 In.	246.50
Creamer, Cow, Cover, Tail Handle, Open Mouth Forms Spout, c.1900, 6 In.	1440.00
Creamer, Cow, Gray, Black Spot, Gilt Horns, Oval Base, Grass, 4 1/2 x 7 In.	300.00
Creamer, Cow, Lusterware, 6 In.	71.50
Creamer, Cow, On Base, 5 x 5 In.	350.00
Creamer, Houses, Ruins In Landscape, Salt Glaze, c.1760	1320.00
Creamer, Toby, Polychrome & Luster, 5 1/4 In.	192.50
Cup, Stirrup, Hound Form, 19th Century	1650.00
Cup, University Of Maryland, Dark Blue	475.00
Cup, Washington With Scroll In Hand, Dark Blue	175.00
Cup & Saucer, Almshouse, N.Y., Staughnton's Church, Phila., Black	300.00
Cup & Saucer, Boston Coffee Exchange & State House, Medium Blue	1400.00
Cup & Saucer, Handleless, Bust Of Maj. Gen. Wm. H. Harrison	385.00
Cup & Saucer, Handleless, Lafayette At Franklin Tomb	275.00
Cup & Saucer, MacDonnough's Victory, Dark Blue	575.00
Cup & Saucer, Plate, Child's, Brown Transfer, Child & Dog, Ironstone, 3 Piece	38.50
Cup & Saucer, Swan, Medium Dark Blue	150.00
Cup & Saucer, Washington Standing At His Tomb, Scroll In Hand	385.00
Cup Plate, Lafayette, Washington, Line Border, Enoch Wood, 3 3/4 In.	770.00
Cup Plate, Medium Blue Transfer, Italian Scenery, Santa Croce, 4 5/8 In.	65.00
Dinner Set, London View, Blue & White	4620.00
Dish, Cover, Morning Glories, Small	45.00
Dish, Hen On Basketweave Cover, Oval, Brown, 6 x 6 3/4 In.	245.00
Dish, Hen On Nest Cover, Polychrome, 7 1/2 In.	330.00
Dish, Soup, Lakes Of Killarney, Dark Blue, 10 In.	110.00
Dish, Soup, Table Rock Niagara, Dark Blue, Wood, 10 In.	395.00
Dish, Sweetmeat, White Salt Glaze, Leaf Shape, 1760, 5 7/16 In.	925.00
Dish, Vegetable, Cover, Spoletto, Dark Blue Transfer, 13 In.	137.50
Drinking Cup, Satyr's Head, Smiling, Tortoiseshell Glaze, 1780, 3 3/8 In.	345.00

Figurine, A Night Watchman & Vicar 375.00
Figurine, Bagpiper, Front Of Column, Beaded Base, Creamware, 5 3/4 In. 7700.00
Figurine, Bagpiper, Seated On Stump, 1770, 5 3/8 In. 1850.00
Figurine, Bird, Parrot, 7 1/4 In. 205.00
Figurine, Bonaparte, Standing, 8 In. 142.00
Figurine, Boy & Cow, 8 In. 750.00
Figurine, Boy, Holding Flowerpot, Bisque, 6 In. 145.00
Figurine, Cat, Black & Tan Sponging, Glass Eyes, 5 1/4 In. 275.00
Figurine, Cat, Blue-White, Lavender Pillow, Shorter & Son, 6 In. 125.00
Figurine, Cat, Curled Tail, c.1880, 10 9/16 In. 300.00
Figurine, Cat, Seated, Glass Eyes, 12 1/2 In., Pair 600.00
Figurine, Cat, Seated, Salt Glaze, Agate, Marbelized, 1745-1755, 4 1/8 In. 1495.00
Figurine, Cobbler & Wife, 7 1/2 In., Pair 250.00
Figurine, Costumed Farm Couple, Vegetables, Wheat, Double, 6 In. 525.00
Figurine, Couple, Seated Under Arbor, 14 In. 121.00
Figurine, Cow, Recumbent, White, Gilt Ears, Oval Base, c.1835, 5 1/2 In., Pair 1035.00
Figurine, Cow, Tortoiseshell Glaze, Cream Body, c.1765, 8 In. 2875.00
Figurine, Doe, Tan & Green Enamel, Pearlware, 5 3/8 x 6 1/4 In. 525.00
Figurine, Dog, 13 1/2 In. 210.00
Figurine, Dog, Brown Mottled, 8 In., Pair 193.00
Figurine, Dog, Copper Luster Spots, Chain, 9 1/2 In. 225.00
Figurine, Dog, Greyhound, 11 1/2 x 9 In., Pair 600.00
Figurine, Dog, Greyhound, Rabbit In Mouth, Glazed, 10 In., Pair 415.00
Figurine, Dog, Pekingese, Orange & White, 9 x 9 In., Pair 835.00
Figurine, Dog, Poodle, Birds In Mouth, Raised Base, 4 In. 192.50
Figurine, Dog, Poodle, c.1880, 5 In., Pair 260.00
Figurine, Dog, Poodle, Sanded Coat, Yellow Stripe On Base, 3 In., Pair 165.00
Figurine, Dog, Pug, Creamware, 1770-1780, 3 In. 1265.00
Figurine, Dog, Pug, Tortoiseshell Glaze, Punch Work Collar, c.1770, 3 1/8 In. 920.00
Figurine, Dog, Spaniel, 10 In. 135.00
Figurine, Dog, Spaniel, 12 1/2 In., Pair 517.00
Figurine, Dog, Spaniel, Brown & White, Late 19th Century, 9 In., Pair 396.00
Figurine, Dog, Spaniel, Green Mottled Luster, 11 In., Pair 240.00
Figurine, Dog, Spaniel, Rust Spots, 10 In., Pair 325.00
Figurine, Dog, Spaniel, Rust Spots, Gold Chain, 8 1/4 In., Pair 295.00
Figurine, Dog, Spaniel, White, 10 In., Pair 495.00
Figurine, Dog, Spaniel, Wood, England, 11 1/2 In., Pair 175.00
Figurine, Dog, St. Bernard, Brown Glaze, 13 In., Pair 358.00
Figurine, Dog, St. Bernard, Standing, 10 In., Pair 305.00
Figurine, Dog, White, Black & Gilt, Glass Eyes, 13 3/4 In., Pair 440.00
Figurine, Fisherman & Fisher Girl, 13 1/2 In., Pair 275.00
Figurine, General Gordon, 18 In. 220.00
Figurine, Girl And Goat, Polychrome Enamel, Cole Slaw Trim, 4 7/8 In. 180.00
Figurine, Girl Riding Animal, 4 x 5 In. 145.00
Figurine, Goat, 2 3/4 In. 140.00
Figurine, Hawk, Tortoiseshell Glaze, Incised Plumage, c.1765, 7 7/8 In. 920.00
Figurine, Highland Lord & Lass, 11 1/2 In., Pair 950.00
Figurine, Highland Lord, 10 In. 625.00
Figurine, Highlander, Late 19th Century, 15 In. 875.00
Figurine, Horn Player, Before Tree Stump, Creamware, c.1745, 6 In. 8250.00
Figurine, Horn Player, French Horn, 1850s, 5 5/16 In. 1265.00
Figurine, Horse & Rider, 12 In., Pair 275.00
Figurine, Hurdy-Gurdy Man, 15 In. 287.00
Figurine, Il Spinario, Naked Youth, Salt Glaze, c.1755, 5 1/4 In. 1045.00
Figurine, King & Queen Of Sardinia, 13 1/2 In. 110.00
Figurine, King Charles Spaniel, 11 In., Pair 330.00
Figurine, Lad & Lassie, Lambs At Feet, 7 1/2 In., Pair 265.00
Figurine, Lady Macbeth & Macbeth, c.1852, 8 In., Pair 325.00
Figurine, Lamb, Reclining, Pebble Finish, 3 x 6 In. 125.00
Figurine, Lion Slayer, 12 In. .... 350.00 to 358.00
Figurine, Lion, Reclining, Glass Eyes, Brown Glaze, 12 In. .... 210.00 to 325.00
Figurine, Lion, Salt Glazed, 1830, Pair 4900.00
Figurine, Lion, Standing, Brown Glaze, 11 In. 990.00

Staffordshire, Pitcher, Boston State House,
Dark Blue, Rogers, 11 In.

Staffordshire, Punch Bowl, Arms Of Maryland,
Footed, 5 x 11 3/4 In.

Staffordshire, Platter, Bridge Over River
Schuylkill, Dark Blue, Stubbs, 18 3/4 In.

Staffordshire, Platter, Castle Garden, New York,
Dark Blue, Wood, 18 5/8 In.

Figurine, Lion, Tortoiseshell Glaze, Shaggy Mane, Teeth, c.1765, 3 1/2 In. 2000.00
Figurine, Lost Sheep, Shepherd Carrying Lamb On Shoulder, c.1780, 8 5/8 In. 990.00
Figurine, Man & Woman, Poole & Unwin, 1871-1876, 6 In. 275.00
Figurine, Man Patting Plump Maid, If You Please Sir, Polychrome, 4 In. 25.00
Figurine, Mythical, Sheaf Of Wheat, 15 In. 135.00
Figurine, Old Woman, Jug & Glass, Pink Luster, 6 3/8 In. 225.00
Figurine, Prince Albert, 15 In. 275.00
Figurine, Prince Louis & Marquis Of Lorne, 10 In., Pair 385.00
Figurine, Prince Of Wales, 17 In. 440.00
Figurine, Princess On Goat, 5 1/2 In. 275.00
Figurine, Princess Royal On Goat, c.1845, 5 1/2 In. 295.00
Figurine, Queen Victoria, 11 In. 250.00
Figurine, Queen Victoria, 17 In. 385.00
Figurine, Rabbit, Black & White, Green Cole Slaw Grass, 3 1/2 In. 250.00
Figurine, Ram, Green Enamel With Black, Pearlware, 4 3/4 In. 193.00
Figurine, Returning Home, Polychrome, 8 3/4 In. 192.50
Figurine, Robin Hood, 15 In. 195.00
Figurine, Scotsman With Deer & Dog, White, 14 In. 220.00
Figurine, Scotsman, Mounted, Bagged Deer Across Saddle, 12 In. 195.00
Figurine, Scottish Couple, Man, Bagpipes, Mounted, 19th Century, 14 In., Pair 385.00
Figurine, Scottish Couple, With Clock, 14 In. 110.00
Figurine, Scottish Shepherd, 16 In. 248.00
Figurine, Shakespeare, 10 In. 522.00
Figurine, Sheep, 3 In. 160.00
Figurine, Shepherdess, Lamb At Feet, Creamware, c.1780, 8 5/8 In. 880.00
Figurine, Shoemaker & His Wife, 6 3/4 In., Pair 195.00
Figurine, Squirrel, Tortoiseshell Glaze, Eating, Oval Base, c.1780, 4 1/2 In. 1495.00
Figurine, St. George & Dragon, Creamware, c.1780, 11 In. 2000.00
Figurine, St. John With Goose, White, 11 1/4 In. 215.00
Figurine, Turkish Couple, Drawing Water, 9 In. 358.00

Figurine, Uncle Tom, 8 1/4 In. 195.00
Figurine, Vicar & Moses, 8 In. 250.00
Figurine, War, Man On Horse, 11 1/2 In. 500.00
Figurine, Water Buffalo, Tortoiseshell Glaze, Brown Glaze, c.1760, 10 In. 7475.00
Figurine, White Cottage, Gray Thatched Roof, Shrubbery, 5 1/2 In. 55.00
Group, 2 Men & Deer, 8 In. 155.00
Group, Boy, Holding Dove, Dog At Side, 9 In. 100.00
Group, Courting Couple, Grapevine Arbor, 1810, 14 In. 525.00
Group, Death Of Munrow, Obadiah Sherratt Type, 1830, 13 1/2 In. 1600.00
Group, Ewe & Lamb, Recumbent Ewe, Lamb At Side, c.1775, 6 In. 885.00
Group, Man & Woman, Lamb, Tenderness Inscribed, Walton, 6 1/2 In. 385.00
Group, Man, With Dog, 9 1/2 In. 275.00
Group, Mother & Child, 6 In. 121.00
Group, Tenderness, Walton, c.1815, 7 In. 1100.00
Group, Youth & Maiden, White, 12 1/2 In. 220.00
Incense Burner, Cottage, Polychrome, 6 3/4 In. 220.00
Incense Burner, Gazebo Shape, England, 18th Century, 4 1/4 In. 192.00
Jug, Cider, World In Planisphere, Tythe Pig, Creamware, 1790, 11 In. 2640.00
Jug, Milk, Cover, White Salt Glaze, Pear Shape, 1745-1750, 5 3/4 In. 1265.00
Jug, Nelson Form, 11 In. 248.00
Ladle, Flora Transfer, Polychrome Enamel, 12 1/2 In. 27.50
Mug, Black Transfer, Hunting Dog, 2 1/4 In. 71.50
Mug, Child's, Inscribed, A Present For My Dear Boy, 19th Century, 2 In. 330.00
Mug, Children On Early Cycles, Brown Transfer, 2 7/8 In. 115.00
Mug, Scratch-Blue, Initials JG, Cylindrical, 1750-1755, 4 5/8 In. 2013.00
Pap Boat, Scallop Shell, Marbelized Cream, Blue, Brown, Agate, c.1750, 5 In. 1440.00
Pen Stand, Swan, 4 In. 110.00
Pepper Pot, Blue On Cream Floral 70.00
Pickle, Creamware, Tortoiseshell Glaze, Leaf Shape, 1765, 5 1/8 In. 1725.00
Pitcher, 3-Masted American Ship, George Clotts, Mask Spout, 7 In. 1760.00
Pitcher, Barrel, Erie Canal Views, Dark Blue, 6 1/2 In. 1600.00
Pitcher, Boston State House, Dark Blue, Rogers, 11 In. .... *Illus* 1045.00
Pitcher, Boston State House, New York City Hall, Blue, Stubbs, 6 1/2 In. 1200.00
Pitcher, Figural, Dog, Tall 17.50
Pitcher, New York City Hall & Insane Asylum, Dark Blue, 7 1/2 In. 1275.00
Pitcher, Pearlware, 3-Masted British Ship, Seal Of United States, 7 1/2 In. 825.00
Pitcher, Tradesman's Arms, 7 In. 175.00
Pitcher, Wash, Franklin's Tomb, Dark Blue, 8 1/2 In. 1100.00
Pitcher & Bowl, Light Blue Transfer, Byzantium, 10 x 13 In. 275.00
Pitcher & Bowl, View Of Deaf & Dumb Asylum, c.1825, Bowl-14 In. 2760.00
Plate, A.B.C., Black Transfer, Stilt Walking, Meakin, 5 1/4 In. 94.00
Plate, Arms Of New York, Dark Blue, Mayer, 9 7/8 In. 660.00
Plate, Arms Of South Carolina, Dark Blue, Mayer, 7 1/2 In. 220.00
Plate, B & O, Dark Blue, Wood, 10 In. 895.00
Plate, Bakers Falls, Black, 9 In. 65.00
Plate, Bank Of The United States, Philadelphia, Blue Transfer, 10 1/4 In. 302.00
Plate, Battle Monument, Baltimore, Red Transfer, 9 In. 110.00
Plate, Black Transfer, Gen. Jackson, Hero Of New Orleans, 8 3/4 In. 1155.00
Plate, Blue Transfer, America & Independence, States Border, 10 1/2 In. 330.00
Plate, Blue Transfer, Barrington Hall, Stevenson, 8 7/8 In. 192.00
Plate, Blue Transfer, Dunraven, Gladmorgan, Enoch Wood & Son, 6 1/2 In. 60.00
Plate, Blue Transfer, Fruit & Flowers, Stubbs & Kent, 10 In. 93.00
Plate, Blue Transfer, Italian Scene, Fisherman's Island, Wood & Sons, 8 3/8 In. 82.00
Plate, Blue Transfer, Llanarth Court, Monmouthshire, 10 In. 192.00
Plate, Blue Transfer, Marine Hospital, Louisville, Ky., Wood, 9 1/8 In. 440.00
Plate, Blue Transfer, Molded Foliage, 8 3/4 In. 632.00
Plate, Captain John Smith, 1906, 10 In. 100.00
Plate, Catskill House, Hudson, Dark Blue, Enoch Wood, 6 1/2 In. 675.00
Plate, Catskill Mountain House, U.S., Red Transfer, 10 3/8 In. 170.00
Plate, Chinese River Scene, Medium Blue, 8 1/4 In. 95.00
Plate, Christ Church Oxford, Blue Transfer, 10 In. 100.00
Plate, City Hotel, New York, Medium Blue Transfer, 9 In. 300.00
Plate, City Of Albany, Impressed Wood, Blue Transfer, 10 In. 415.00

Plate, City Of Benares, Blue & White, R. Hall, 1820, 6 In. 88.00
Plate, Commodore MacDonnough's Victory, 10 In. 137.50
Plate, Commodore MacDonnough's Victory, Dark Blue, Wood, 6 1/2 In. ...... 330.00 to 375.00
Plate, Dark Blue Oriental Transfer, Wood, 9 1/4 In. 165.00
Plate, Dark Blue Transfer, Fairmount Near Philadelphia, 10 1/4 In. 205.00
Plate, Dark Blue Transfer, Fonthill Abbey, Wilstshire, 10 In. 40.00
Plate, Dark Blue Transfer, Nahant Hotel Near Boston, 8 5/8 In. 325.00
Plate, Dark Blue Transfer, Union Line, Wood, 10 1/4 In. 300.00
Plate, Dr. Syntax, Drawing After Nature, 10 1/2 In. 315.00
Plate, Dr. Syntax Reading His Tour, Dark Blue, 8 7/8 In. 175.00
Plate, Dr. Syntax, Returned From Tour, 8 1/4 In. 255.00
Plate, Erie Inscription, Dark Blue, High Glaze, 6 1/2 In. 650.00
Plate, Fairmount New Philadelphia, Blue Transfer, 10 1/4 In. 165.00
Plate, Falls Of Montmorenci, Near Quebec, Dark Blue, Wood, 8 1/2 In. 250.00
Plate, Fort Gansevoort, New York, Dark Blue, Stevenson, 5 1/4 In. 1250.00
Plate, Franklin's Birthplace, Dark Blue, 10 In. 195.00
Plate, Fruit & Flowers, Stubbs & Kent, 10 In. 175.00
Plate, Fulham Church, Middlesex, Dark Blue, Hall, 8 1/2 In. 75.00
Plate, General W.H. Harrison, Hero Of The Thames, 1813 .... 1800.00
Plate, Gilpin's Mills On The Brandywine Creek, Dark Blue, Wood, 9 In. 650.00
Plate, Hadley's Falls, Sepia, 6 5/8 In. 85.00
Plate, Hartford, Black, Jackson, 10 In. 145.00
Plate, Harvard College, Acorn Border, 8 1/4 In. 170.00
Plate, Harvard Hall, Mass., Pink, Jackson, 7 In. 165.00
Plate, Landing Of The Pilgrims, Medium Blue, Enoch Wood, 10 In. 225.00
Plate, Llanarth Court, Monmouthshire, Dark Blue, Hall, 10 In. 165.00
Plate, Louise, New Wharf Pottery, 9 3/4 In., 8 Piece 150.00
Plate, Marine Hospital, Louisville, Ky., Impressed Wood, 9 1/4 In. 160.00
Plate, Medium Blue Transfer, Boston State House, 10 In. 220.00
Plate, Meeting Of Sancho & Dapple, Don Quixote Series, Dark Blue, 8 7/8 In. 195.00
Plate, Moulin Sur La Marne A Charenton, Dark Blue, Wood, 9 1/4 In. 175.00
Plate, Nahant Hotel Near Boston, Blue Transfer, 9 In. 330.00
Plate, New York Battery, Vine Leaf Border, Blue, Ralph Stevenson, 6 7/8 In. 850.00
Plate, New York From Brooklyn Heights, Dark Blue, Stevenson, 10 In. 1200.00
Plate, Oriental Pagoda, Dark Blue, 5 5/8 In. 58.00
Plate, Park Theater, Spread Wing Eagle Border, Dark Blue, Stubbs, 6 In. 550.00
Plate, Philadelphia Waterworks & Dam, Dark Blue, Henshall, 10 In. 650.00
Plate, Philadelphia Waterworks, Dark Blue, R.S. & W., 10 In. 650.00
Plate, Southampton, Hampshire, Impressed Wood, 7 5/8 In. 220.00
Plate, States, Sheep On Lawn, Dark Blue, 8 3/4 In. 325.00
Plate, Staughton's Church, Philadelphia, Blue Transfer, 8 1/4 In. 115.00
Plate, Table Rock Niagara, Hudson River, Dark Blue Beaded, 11 1/2 In. 1700.00
Plate, Texan Campaign Scene, Purple Transfer, 8 1/2 In. 200.00
Plate, Thornton Castle, Medium Dark Blue, Wood, 10 In. 135.00
Plate, Toddy, America & Independence, Dark Blue Transfer, 5 5/8 In. 165.00
Plate, Toddy, Court House Boston, Dark Blue, R.S. & W., 5 1/4 In. 1400.00
Plate, Tortoiseshell Glaze, Basket Rim, Cream Ground, c.1765, 11 1/4 In. 460.00
Plate, Tortoiseshell Glaze, Octagonal, Milled Rim, c.1765, 8 1/4 In., Pair 290.00
Plate, Tortoiseshell Glaze, Reticulated, Fruit, c.1765, 9 3/4 In. 1440.00
Plate, Union Forever On Rim, Centennial, 1776-1876, 6 In. 145.00
Plate, Upper Ferry Bridge Over The River Schuylkill, Blue Transfer, 9 In. 93.50
Plate, Vevay, Indiana, Dark Blue, Henshall, 6 5/8 In. 1650.00
Plate, View Of Trenton Falls, Dark Blue, Wood, 7 1/2 In. 350.00
Plate, Washington Vase, 10 In. 60.00
Plate, Washington, Canova's Statute, Red Border, Brown Transfer, Wood, 7 In. 135.00
Plate, Waterworks, Philadelphia, Dark Brown, Jackson, 9 In. 175.00
Plate, Woman's Portrait, Cobalt Blue Border, 14 1/2 In. 225.00
Platter, America & Independence, States Border, Dark Blue, 16 5/8 In. 1045.00
Platter, Ancient Ruins, Green Transfer, 15 1/4 In. 115.00
Platter, Arms Of Georgia, Dark Blue, Mayer, 12 3/4 In. 4125.00
Platter, Arms Of North Carolina, Dark Blue, Mayer, 14 3/4 In. 2420.00
Platter, Blue Transfer, Landing Of General Lafayette, 17 In. 920.00
Platter, Boston & Bunker's Hill, Brown & White, T. Godwin, 8 Sides, 16 In. 209.00

Platter, Boston State House, Dark Blue Transfer, 16 In. 880.00
Platter, Boston State House, Medium Dark Blue, Rogers, 16 5/8 In. 1100.00
Platter, Bridge Over River Schuylkill, Dark Blue, Stubbs, 18 3/4 In. .... *Illus* 1210.00
Platter, Canova, Light Blue Transfer, 15 3/4 In. 192.50
Platter, Castle Garden, New York, Dark Blue, Wood, 18 5/8 In. .... *Illus* 2090.00
Platter, Center Concentric Ovals, Stripes On Rim, 1835, 18 In. 690.00
Platter, Christianburg, Danish Settlement On Gold Coast Africa, Blue, 21 In. 275.00
Platter, Columbus, Ohio, Dark Blue, 14 1/2 In. 880.00
Platter, Fairmount Near Philadelphia, Dark Blue, 20 1/2 In. 2420.00
Platter, Louisville, Kentucky, Cities Series, Medium Dark Blue, 12 1/2 In. 3200.00
Platter, Lucerne, Light Blue, 20 In. 187.00
Platter, Niagara Falls, Blue 1850.00
Platter, Panoramic Scenery, Dark Blue, Stevenson, 16 In. 695.00
Platter, Residence Of Late Richard Jordan, Purple Transfer, 19 1/2 In. 962.50
Platter, Richard Jordan, Pink, 13 1/2 In. 125.00
Platter, Standard Willow Pattern, c.1809, 16 1/2 x 21 In. 850.00
Platter, Well & Tree, Deer & Temple, Blue & White 450.00
Punch Bowl, Arms Of Maryland, Footed, 5 x 11 3/4 In. .... *Illus* 9350.00
Quill Stand, Nesting Birds Form, 2 In. 121.00
Sauceboat, Fox, Swan, Pearlware, 1790, 7 1/8 In., Pair 690.00
Sauceboat, Woman Playing Harpsichord, Salt Glaze, c.1760, 7 7/8 In. 3850.00
Saucer, MacDonnough's Victory, Wood 235.00
Scent Bottle, Book Shape, Salt Glaze, 1725, 2 1/16 In. 1438.00
Soup, Dish, Blue, White, C. Harvey & Son 175.00
Soup, Dish, Dark Blue, Mambrino's Helmet, 9 3/4 In. 27.50
Soup, Dish, Doctor Syntax Mistakes House For Inn, Blue, 9 7/8 In. 138.00
Soup, Dish, Fisherman, Wife & Child, Medium Blue Transfer, 10 In. 82.00
Spill Vase, Boy & Girl, Lamb 325.00
Spill Vase, Couple, Dog & Lamb, Tree, 10 1/2 In 300.00
Spill Vase, Group, Children, Dog & Goat Over Clock, 9 1/2 In. 550.00
Stand, Teapot, Pierced Bracket Feet, Salt Glaze, c.1760, 6 In. 4400.00
Stirrup Cup, Fox Head, Pearlware, 1785, 5 5/8 In. 700.00
Stirrup Cup, Hound Head, Brown Spotted, Pearlware, 1825, 5 1/16 In. 575.00
Stirrup Cup, Hound Head, Spotted Coat, Pink Luster Collar, c.1830, 5 In. 1035.00
Stirrup Cup, Stag Form, 5 In. 1430.00
Sugar, Cover, California, Podmore & Walker, c.1850 .... 245.00
Sugar, Cover, Hunter & 2 Dogs, Medium Blue Transfer, Lid, 5 In. 150.00
Sugar, Cover, Lafayette At Franklin's Tomb, Dark Blue, Wood 1750.00
Sugar, Cover, Swans, Blue & White, Marked, 5 1/2 x 7 In. 80.00
Sugar Bowl, Oriental Scene, Dark Blue, 7 In. 71.50
Sugar Bowl, Zebra & Horse, Dark Blue Transfer, 5 3/4 In. 165.00
Tea Caddy, Chinese Figures, Mottled Brown Glaze, c.1775, 4 1/2 In. 2200.00
Tea Canister, Cauliflower, Green Glaze, Shoulder Florets, 1765, 3 3/4 In. 575.00
Tea Set, Child's, Punch & Judy, Blue & White, 20 Piece 450.00
Tea Set, Embossed Leaves & Florals, Seal Of United States, Pearlware, 3 Piece 990.00
Tea Set, Swan Design, J. Stubbs, 1820, 19 Piece 4175.00
Tea Set, Washington, Scroll In Hand, Enoch Wood, 12 Piece 2000.00
Teapot, Cover, Spherical, Scallop Shell, Paw Feet, Agateware, c.1750, 4 In. 4900.00
Teapot, Crabstock Handle & Finial, Hexagonal, Creamware, c.1755, 4 In. 5500.00
Teapot, Dolphin Handle, Serpent Spout, Redware, c.1745, 4 1/4 In. 3520.00
Teapot, Flowerhead Finial, Rococo, Scroll Handle, c.1850 .... 345.00
Teapot, Italianate Ruins, Trees, Floral Sprig, c.1770, 4 5/8 In. 7475.00
Teapot, John Bull, Tricornered Hat, Large 110.00
Teapot, Lafayette At Franklin Tomb, Dark Blue, 8 1/4 In. 1045.00
Toby Jugs are listed in their own category
Tray, Gravy, Estate View, Dark Blue, Acorn Border, Stevenson 225.00
Tray, Gravy, William Penn's Treaty With The Indians, Brown, Round 175.00
Tray, Medium Blue Transfer, Chillicothe, 9 5/8 In. 4345.00
Tureen, Blue & White, Grecian Scenery, Flower Knop, E.W. & S., 9 5/8 In. 250.00
Tureen, Cover, Swans, Blue & White Transfer, Mid-19th Century, 9 x 13 In. 895.00
Tureen, Medium Blue Transfer, Country Scenes, 15 1/2 In. 165.00
Tureen, Soup, Cover, White Salt Glaze, Lozenge Shape, 1750, 11 1/2 In. 1840.00
Tureen, Underplate, Unfinished Cathedral Of Batalha, Portugal View 2250.00

Undertray, Gravy, Arms Of Connecticut, Dark Blue, Nayer 3800.00
Undertray, Light Blue Transfer, Priory, 6 1/2 In. 100.00
Urn, Garniture, Botanical Design, 1840, Pair 300.00
Vase, Bud, Snake Around Tree, Dog Protecting Sleeping Maiden 305.00
Vase, Cow & Milkmaid, 8 1/2 In. 577.00
Vase, Figural, Gardener, Holding Spade, Blue Hat, c.1790, 7 3/4 In. 345.00
Vase, Figural, Girl In Orange Shawl, Dog, 10 In. 99.00
Vase, Figural, Girl, Pink Dress, Fox & Swan, 9 In. 187.00
Vase, Pedestal, Stone Bridge, House, 5 Sheep, c.1880, 9 In. 95.00
Vase, Spill, Scotsman On Side 715.00
Vase, Tulip, Blossom, Purple & Puce Striations, Pink Interior, c.1825, 4 In. 1495.00
Wall Pocket, Flowers, Green Leaves, Creamware, c.1765, 9 1/2 In., Pair 7700.00
Wash Bowl, Boston State House, Medium Dark Blue, Rogers, 12 In. 1200.00
Wash Bowl, Seashell & Flower Transfer, Dark Blue, Stubbs & Kent, 11 3/4 In. 55.00
Watch Holder, Clock Tower, 11 7/8 In. 105.00
Window Stop, Polychrome, England, 19th Century, 4 1/2 In. 440.00

STANGL Pottery traces its history back to the Fulper Pottery of New Jersey.
In 1910, Johann Martin Stangl started working at Fulper. He bought into the
firm in 1913, became president in 1926, and in 1929 changed the company
name to Stangl Pottery. The pottery made dinnerwares and a line of limited-
edition bird figurines. The company went out of business in 1978.

Ashtray, Big Top, Seal, Clown & Giraffe 60.00
Ashtray, Fantasy 25.00
Ashtray, Fish, Round, 8 1/4 In. 35.00
Ashtray, Hunting Dog, 8 1/4 In. 75.00
Ashtray, Mallard, No. 3915, 9 In. .... 45.00 to 50.00
Ashtray, Mallard, No. 3926, 10 5/8 In. 38.00
Ashtray, Partridge, No. 3926, Oval, 10 5/8 In. 45.00
Ashtray, Pheasant, No. 3926, 10 1/2 In. 80.00
Basket, Pastel Yellow, 1930s, 9 In. 30.00
Bird, Bird Of Paradise, No. 3408, 5 1/2 In. .... 70.00 to 150.00
Bird, Blue-Headed Vireo, No. 3448 .... 70.00 to 83.00
Bird, Bluebird, No. 3276 .... 28.00 to 80.00
Bird, Brewers Blackbird, No. 3591 .... 125.00
Bird, Broadbill Hummingbird, No. 3629 .... 125.00
Bird, Cardinal, Gray, No. 3596 .... 62.00
Bird, Cardinal, No. 3444 .... 72.00
Bird, Chat, No. 3590 .... 101.00
Bird, Chickadee, No. 3581 .... 175.00
Bird, Cockatoo, Medium, No. 3580 .... 75.00 to 99.00
Bird, Cockatoo, No. 3405S 72.00
Bird, Cockatoo, No. 3584 .... 235.00
Bird, Cockatoos, No. 3405D .... 85.00 to 195.00
Bird, Evening Grosbeak, No. 3813 .... 120.00
Bird, Flying Duck, No. 3443, 14-In. Wingspan .... 167.00 to 225.00
Bird, Golden-Crowned Kinglet, No. 3848 .... 85.00 to 95.00
Bird, Goldfinch, Group, No. 3635, 12 In. 135.00
Bird, Gray Cardinal, No. 3596 .... 80.00
Bird, Gray Hen, No. 3446 .... 128.00
Bird, Gray Rooster, No. 3445 .... 150.00
Bird, Hen Pheasant, No. 3491 .... 200.00
Bird, Hummingbirds, Double, No. 3599D 225.00
Bird, Indigo Bunting, No. 3589 .... 60.00
Bird, Kentucky Warbler, No. 3598 .... 45.00 to 55.00
Bird, Key West Quail Dove, No. 3454 .... 145.00 to 176.00
Bird, Kingfisher, Double, No. 3406D 105.00
Bird, Kingfisher, No. 3406S 90.00
Bird, Nuthatch, No. 3593 .... 32.00 to 50.00
Bird, Oriole, No. 3402S 55.00
Bird, Painted Bunting, No. 3452 .... 70.00 to 105.00
Bird, Parula Warbler, No. 3583 .... 39.00 to 65.00
Bird, Redstarts, No. 3448D 175.00

Bird, Redstarts, No. 3490, Pair 210.00
Bird, Rieffers Hummingbird, No. 3628 .... 115.00
Bird, Rivoli Hummingbird, No. 3627 .... 130.00
Bird, Rufous Hummingbird, No. 3585 .... 55.00 to 75.00
Bird, Scarlet Tanagers, Double, No. 3750 .... 395.00
Bird, Shoveler Duck, No. 5455 .... 500.00
Bird, Titmouse, No. 3592 .... 45.00 to 60.00
Bird, Wilson Warbler, No. 3597 .... 25.00 to 40.00
Bird, Wren, No. 3401S 72.00
Bird, Wrens, No. 3401D 150.00
Bird, Yellow Warbler, No. 3447 .... 60.00 to 95.00
Bowl, Country Garden, 8 In. 30.00
Bowl, Orchard Song, 5 1/2 In. 6.00
Bowl, Rainbow Ware, 6 In. 55.00
Bowl, Thistle, 8 In. 26.00
Bowl, Vegetable, Thistle, Divided, 10 1/2 x 7 1/4 In. 16.00
Box, Cigarette, Garden Flower, Square 40.00
Box, Cigarette, Gladiola 30.00
Box, Cigarette, Ivy, Rectangular 30.00
Candleholder, Double 10.00
Candy Dish, Cover, Terra Rose 22.00
Chop Plate, Colonial, Blue, 12 1/2 In. 12.00
Coffee Server, Amber Glo .... 40.00 to 45.00
Coffee Warmer, Golden Harvest 12.00
Coffeepot, Amber Glo 35.00
Coffeepot, Carnival 45.00
Creamer, Jeweled Christmas Tree, 1/2 Pt. 50.00
Creamer, Magnolia 10.00
Creamer, Thistle 4.50
Creamer, Wild Rose 10.00
Cup, Bittersweet 8.00
Cup, Country Garden 8.00
Cup, Dahlia 3.50
Cup, Dogwood .... 7.00 to 10.00
Cup & Saucer, Blueberry 15.00
Cup & Saucer, Country Garden .... 5.00 to 10.00
Cup & Saucer, Fruit .... 9.00 to 12.00
Cup & Saucer, Thistle 11.00
Dinner Set, Blue Bell, Hand Painted, 57 Piece 495.00
Eggcup, Golden Blossom .... 8.00 to 10.00
Figurine, Giraffe 500.00
Flowerpot, Red Rose, 5 x 5 1/2 In. 14.00
Flowerpot, Yellow Tulip, 5 x 5 3/4 In. 14.00
Gravy Boat, Fruit 18.00
Grill Plate, Thistle 10.00
Holder, Cotton, Bunny, All Light Green 185.00
Mug, Apple Delight 14.00
Pitcher, Amber Glo, 1 Qt. 25.00
Pitcher, Terra Rose 15.00
Plate, Apple Delight, 8 In. 9.00
Plate, Country Garden, 8 In. 3.00
Plate, Country Life, Farmhouse, 12 In. 225.00
Plate, Country Life, Rooster, 6 In. 9.00
Plate, Daisy, 8 In. 4.00
Plate, Dinner, Blueberry, 10 In. 16.50
Plate, Fruit & Flowers, 10 In. 18.00
Plate, Fruit, 10 In. 8.00
Plate, Golden Harvest, 10 In. 7.50
Plate, Star Flower, 6 In. 2.00
Plate, Thistle, 6 In. 5.00
Platter, Terra Rose, Yellow, 12 In. 35.00
Salt & Pepper, Magnolia 12.00
Server, Antique Gold, Center Handle, Green Ground, 10 In. 15.00

Server, Bella Rosa, Center Handle 10.00
Server, Country Garden, 3 Tiers 38.00
Server, Fairlawn, Center Handle 10.00
Sign, Dealer, Della Ware, Easel Back 295.00
Soup, Americana, Cream, Orange 4.00
Soup, Dish, Thistle, Lug 7.00
Sugar, Cover, Bittersweet .... 10.00 to 12.00
Sugar, Cover, Fruit 13.00
Sugar, Fruit, Frosted 18.00
Sugar, Golden Harvest 10.00
Sugar, Tiger Lily, Individual 10.00
Teapot, Amber Glo 30.00
Teapot, Blueberry 35.00
Teapot, Thistle 50.00
Vase, Horse Head, Blue & White, Terra Rose .... 325.00 to 595.00
Vase, Terra Rose, Green, 7 In. 45.00
Wig Stand .... 225.00 to 295.00

STEINS have been used by beer and ale drinkers for over 500 years. They
have been made of ivory, porcelain, stoneware, faience, silver, pewter, wood,
or glass in sizes up to nine gallons. Although some were made by Mettlach,
Meissen, Capo-di-Monte, and other famous factories, most were made by
less important German potteries. The words *Geschutz* or *Musterschutz* on a
stein are the German words for *patented* or *registered design*, not company
names. Steins are still being made in the old styles. Lithophane steins may be
found in the Lithophane category.

2 Horses, Floral Design, Pewter Lid, 1 Liter, Dated 1777 .... 825.00
Alpine Lodges, Wildlife, Man & Women, Pewter Lid, Germany, 11 1/2 In. 75.00
American Brewing Co., St. Louis, Pewter Lid, 3 Liter 2420.00
Artist, Enamel, Pewter Lid 440.00
Bacchanalian Scenes, God Of Vineyard, Pewter Lid, Salt Glaze 105.00
Baker, Porcelain, Pewter Lid, ... 660.00
Boot, Falstaff, Ceramic, Black & Gray, 8 In. 50.00
Bowl Set, 2 Handles Bowl, Cover, 1920s, 7 Piece 225.00
Budweiser, Ceramarte, Clydesdales & Wagon 335.00
Budweiser, Katakombe .... *Illus* 185.00
Budweiser, Red Wagon, Black, St. Louis, Hammered Lid 187.00
Budweiser, Sports Legends, Jim Thorpe, Box 35.00
Budweiser, St. Louis Cardinals 19.00
Budweiser, Summer Olympics, 1988, Lid 19.00
Busch Gardens, Tampa, Thewalt, Sticker 50.00
Bustle Woman, Pewter Lid Of Upper Torso 1815.00
Ceramarte, Opumph, Woman's Body Handle, 1971 .... 95.00
Children's Wooden Toys, Porcelain, Pewter Lid 308.00
Cobalt Blue Entwined Vines, Gray Salt Glaze, Remmy Fils, 4 1/4 x 3 3/4 In. 22.00
Couple, Drinking, Blue, Orange Luster Rim, Motto, Pewter Lid, Germany, 1/4 Liter . 35.00
Crossed Rifles, Hammered, Copper, New York Jewelry Co., 1875, 13 1/4 In. 225.00

Stein, Budweiser, Katakombe

Devil, Porcelain, Inlaid Lid	852.00
Ducks Unlimited, Wood Duck, Wooden Box, Ceramarte, 1987	95.00
Falstaff, Lid, Music, Original Tag	100.00
Figure, Long Robe & Hood, Carries Beer Mugs, Germany, 9 In.	40.00
Floral Enameled, Clear Glass, Pewter Top, 9 1/2 In.	75.00
German Cities, Tall	420.00
Gothic, Coat Of Arms, Cut Panels, Porcelain Lid, Pewter Rim, Blue To Clear, 6 In. ..	1100.00
John Bull Type Portrait, Quote, Hinged Pewter Lid, Germany, 1/2 Liter	88.00
Mettlach steins are listed in the Mettlach category.	
Michelob Dry, Pewter, Box	75.00
Military, Infantry, Porcelain, Germany, 11 In.	330.00
Military Man, Stoneware	200.00
Miller, Pewter Lid	286.00
Miller High Life Lite, 3 Colors	36.00
Monkey, Glazed Ceramic, Germany, c.1875, 8 1/2 In.	175.00
Mushroom, Dwarfs On Handle & Finial	1045.00
Peptomalt, King Of Tonics, White Ceramic, Pewter Lid, Glass Base, 4 In.	83.00
Regimental, 117 Infantry, 4 Side Scenes, Lion Thumb Lift, Porcelain, 13 In.	495.00
Regimental, 14 Dragoon, Scene Of Germania, Eagle Thumb Lift, Pottery	715.00
Regimental, Christmas, 130 Infantry, 4 Side Scenes, Eagle Thumb Lift, Porcelain	440.00
Schlitz, 125 Anniversary, No. 23263	40.00
Schlitz Buffet Of Germany, Compliments Of E. Vierke, A.H. Tebber	125.00
Soccer Player, Porcelain, O'Hara Dial Co.	195.00
Statue Of Liberty Head, SCI 1974 Convention, Ceramarte	235.00
Stroh's, National Audubon Wildlife, Grizzly Bear, Box	100.00
Visit To Technical School, Organization Logo, 1/2 Liter	143.00

STEREO CARDS that were made for stereoscope viewers became popular after 1840. Two almost identical pictures were mounted on a stiff cardboard backing so that, when viewed through a stereoscope, a three-dimensional picture could be seen. Value is determined by maker and by subject. These cards were made in quantity through the 1930s.

Brewster, 20 Cards, 1885	225.00
Burial Vault, Funeral Of President McKinley, 1901	12.50
Columbian Exposition, 11 Piece	125.00
Egypt, Box	90.00
H. Greely 1872 Campaign, Phantom Leaves, I.L. Rogers	25.00
Niagara Falls, New Suspension Bridge, C. Bierstadt, c.1890	7.50
Palestine, Box	65.00
President's Wedding, Excelsior	5.00
Professor Lowe's Balloon Ascension, Civil War	250.00
Public Sale Dinner, Man & Women, Long Table, Western Stereoscopic Co., 1904	11.00
San Francisco Earthquake, 25 Piece Set	75.00
Scenes Of New York, 8 Piece	95.00
Ship Builders, Albumen, 6 Children, Toy Boats, 1880, Mounted	18.00
Washington, Box	65.00

STEREOSCOPES were used for viewing stereo cards. The hand viewer was invented by Oliver Wendell Holmes, although more complicated table models were used before his was produced in 1859. Do not confuse the stereoscope with the stereopticon, a magic lantern that used glass slides.

Metal, Folding, With Cards, Tiny	100.00
Pierced Metal, Wooden	60.00
Realist, Box	22.50
View Master, 24 Reels, 1946	75.00

STERLING SILVER, see Silver-Sterling category

STEUBEN glass was made at the Steuben Glass Works of Corning, New York. The factory, founded by Frederick Carder and T. C. Hawkes, Sr., was purchased by the Corning Glass Company. They continued to make glass called *Steuben.* Many types of art glass were made at Steuben. The firm is still making exceptional quality glass but it is clear, modern-style glass. Additional pieces may be found in the Aurene and Cluthra categories.

Atomizer, Fired Gold, Engraved, Hawkes, 10 In. 660.00
Bowl, Calcite Body, Gold Iridescent Interior, Flaring, 11 7/8 In. 520.00
Bowl, Calcite, Iridescent White, Broad Everted Rim, Gold Interior, 12-In. Diam. 172.00
Bowl, Celeste Blue, 5 x 12 In. 295.00
Bowl, Footed, Amethyst, 10 In. 150.00
Bowl, Grotesque, 12-Ribbed, Ivorene, 6 3/4 x 14 In. 550.00
Bowl, Grotesque, Blue, 13 In. 800.00
Bowl, Grotesque, Clear To Green, 4 1/4 In. 325.00
Bowl, Grotesque, Ruby, 12 1/2 In. 320.00
Bowl, Grotesque, Signed, 6 3/4 x 11 1/2 In. 325.00
Bowl, Ivrene, Blue Iridescent Interior 5 3/4 In. 325.00
Bowl, Line Drawing, Flemish Blue, 12 In. 335.00
Bowl, Millefiori, Ivory, Gray, Green, Yellow, Frederick Carder, 3 x 5 1/2 In. 3450.00
Bowl, Plum Jade, 16 In. 3000.00
Bowl, Rosaline, Folded & Pinched, 8 x 7 x 3 In. 335.00
Bowl, Steuben Gold Thread & Glass, 18 In. 375.00
Bowl, Sunflower, 15 1/2 In. 495.00
Bowl, Underplate, Rosaline, 5 In. 245.00
Box, Cigarette, Millefiori Glass, Silver Mount At Rim, c.1915, 6 1/4 In. 2600.00
Candlestick, Clear, Spiral Ribbed, Baluster, 1930, 10 3/8 In. 201.00
Candlestick, Green Twist, 12 In., Pair 450.00
Candlestick, Jade Green, Intaglio Carved, c.1930, 14 5/8 In., Pair 1600.00
Candlestick, Ribbed, Crystal Wafer Foot, Celeste Blue, 12 In. 150.00
Candlestick, Twisted Rosa Stem, Green Ribbed Top & Bottom, 12 In., Pair 675.00
Candy Dish, Cover, Ram's Head, Signed, c.1943, 6 In. 220.00
Centerpiece, 6 Triangular Sections, Circular Base, c.1925, 15 1/4 In. 1035.00
Champagne, 2-Color Threading, Signed 350.00
Cintra Interior, Controlled Bubbles, Frederick Carder, 9 In. 4600.00
Cocktail, Teardrop In Base, Signed, 3 3/4 In. 25.00
Compote, Art Glass, Oriental Jade, 7 x 7 In. 275.00
Compote, Engraved Floral, Hollow Stem, Light Green & Crystal, 7 In., Pair 300.00
Console Set, Thorn Handles, Prunts, Amber, 3 Piece 400.00
Cordial, Tall Stem, Signed, 10 Piece 250.00
Cordial, Wheel Cut Spanish Sailing Ship, Selenium Red, 5 3/4 In., Pair 220.00
Cornucopia, Ivrene, Signed, 6 In. 425.00
Cup & Saucer, Rosaline 175.00
Dish, Mint, Figural Leaf At Base Of Clear Handle, Signed, 5 1/2 In. 175.00
Dish, Nut, Black Threading, Bristol Yellow, Signed, 3 x 5 In. 195.00
Figurine, Owl, 2 1/2 In. 75.00
Figurine, Owl, 5 In. 200.00
Figurine, Owl, Clear, 1955, Marked, 5 1/4 In. .... 250.00 to 325.00
Figurine, Pheasant, Stylized Feathers, Frederick Carder, 1932, 6 x 11 In., Pair 2588.00
Figurine, Rabbit, Clear, Marked, 3 1/2 In. 302.00
Figurine, Salmon, 8 In., Pair 862.50
Figurine, Teddy Bear, Clear, Marked, 5 5/8 In. 605.00
Finger Bowl, Underplate, Calcite, Ribbed, Gold Lining 250.00
Fixture, 3-Light, Ceiling, Pulled Feather Design, Marked 575.00
Fixture, Ceiling, Gold Feather & Calcite, 8 x 4 In. 695.00
Flatware Set, Glass Handles, 1920-1930, 25 Piece 2750.00
Flower Frog, Green Ribbon Edge, Signed 110.00
Goblet, 2-Color Threading, Signed 350.00
Goblet, Topaz, Celeste Blue Reeding 85.00
Goblet, Van Dyke, Engraved, Signed, 8 In. 295.00
Goblet, Water, Van Dyke Pattern, Amber Stem 90.00
Goblet, Wheel Cut, Pomona Green Turned Stems, 6 1/2 In., 12 Piece 1210.00
Jar, Dresser, Pomona Green, Swirl Ribbed, Threaded Stopper, 6 In. 165.00
Lamp, Cluthra, Brass Harp Base, 7 In. 1500.00
Lamp, Mantle, Art Nouveau, Gold Lily Shade, Stylized Brass Base, 10 1/2 In., Pair .. 975.00
Lamp Base, Vasiform, Vine Handles & Leaves, Acanthus Base, c.1925, 27 In. 1265.00
Paperweight, Nautilus Form, Signed, c.1940, 3 1/2 In. 185.00
Perfume Bottle, Rosaline to Alabaster, Art Glass, Stopper, 1925, 8 In. .... *Illus* 440.00
Pitcher, Bristol Yellow, Quilted Body, Black Reeding At Top, Signed, 9 In. 325.00
Pitcher, Double Loop Handles, Signed, 1955, 10 In. 305.00

*Steuben, Perfume
Bottle, Rosaline to
Alabaster, Art Glass,
Stopper, 1925, 8 In.*

◆ ◆

Rub Bakelite hard for 30 seconds, then sniff it. You will soon learn to recognize its distinctive smell.

◆ ◆

Pitcher, Ivory, Black Handle, 9 3/8 In. 795.00
Pitcher, Jade Green & Alabaster 400.00
Pitcher, Teardrop 150.00
Plate, Calcite, Gold Color, 8 1/4 In. 185.00
Plate, Cluthra, Large Bubbles, 6 1/2 In. 85.00
Plate, Luncheon, Gold Ruby, White Rim 85.00
Plate, Luncheon, Ruby 55.00
Plate, Teardrop, 8 1/2 In. 125.00
Sculpture, Excalibur, Crystal Rock, Inset Sterling Sword, Leather Case, 8 1/2 In. 1380.00
Shade, Moss Agate, Gold, Amber, Red & Green, 7 1/4 In. 850.00
Sherbet, Celeste Blue, Signed, 6 Piece 695.00
Sherbet, Teardrop 125.00
Sherbet, Underplate, Van Dyke Pattern, Amber Stem, 16 Piece 950.00
Sherry Set, Pattern 6401, Carder, 6 3/4 In., 8 Piece 187.00
Sherry Set, With Teardrop, Box, 8 Piece 385.00
Smoke Set, 2 Ashtrays, Box, Cover, 4 1/2 In. 140.00
Syrup, Coreopsis 300.00
Vase, 2 Scrolling Supports, c.1942, 8 3/4 In. 440.00
Vase, Applied Swirls At Base, 11 In. 440.00
Vase, Bell Form, Geometric Devices, Teague, c.1932, 10 1/8 In. 1035.00
Vase, Bud, Ivrene, White, Trumpet Shape, 8 In. 302.50
Vase, Celeste Blue, Signed, 3 1/2 x 6 In. 90.00
Vase, Chang, Plum Jade, 10 In. 4900.00
Vase, Cluthra, 4 1/2 In. 500.00
Vase, Cut Repeating Floral Design, Green Cintra, Alabaster, 15 In. 715.00
Vase, Cylindrical, Geometric Lines & Dots, Teague, 1930, 10 In. 1265.00
Vase, Green & Silver Pulled Feathers, Cream Ground, Signed, 11 5/8 In. 4400.00
Vase, Grotesque, Green To Clear, 4 In. 425.00
Vase, Grotesque, Intarsia, 8 In. 1500.00
Vase, Grotesque, Ivory Shade, Footed Form, Undulating Rim, 8 1/4 In. 635.00
Vase, Grotesque, Rosaline Shaded To Alabaster, 4 1/2 In. 350.00
Vase, Grotesque, Undulating Rim, 8 1/4 In. 635.00
Vase, Internal Mica Flecks & Diamond Design, Signed, 10 In. 325.00
Vase, Ivrene, Iridescent White, 12-Pillar Flared Shape, No. 7565, 10 In. 550.00
Vase, Ivrene, Mushroom Shape Base, Flared Top, 5 In. 110.00
Vase, Maplewood Pattern, Alabaster, Green, White, Oviform, Footed, 12 1/4 In. 1100.00
Vase, Matzu, Rose Over Alabaster, 7 In. 4000.00
Vase, Paneled Teardrop Shape, Red Glass, Signed, 1920s, 12 In. 1725.00
Vase, Reeded Top, Spinach Green, Bubbly, Signed, 8 x 7 In. 150.00
Vase, Ribbed, Folded Rim, Flared Top & Bottom, 10 1/4 In. 140.00
Vase, Rose Over Alabaster, Carved Matzu, 7 In. 4000.00
Vase, Ruffled, Blue Baluster, 8 In. 600.00
Vase, Ruffled Lip, Green Threaded Design, Controlled Bubbles, 8 In 110.00
Vase, Selenium Ruby, 7 In. 450.00
Vase, Verre De Soie, Aquamarine, 6 In. 135.00

Wine, Tear Drop Stem, Signed, 4 In., 7 Piece 385.00
Wine, Twisted Stem, Selenium Red, Signed, 4 1/2 In. 75.00

STEVENGRAPHS are woven pictures made like fancy ribbons. They were manufactured by Thomas Stevens of Coventry, England, and became popular in 1862. Most are marked *Woven in silk by Thomas Stevens* or were mounted on a cardboard that tells the story of the Stevengraph. Other similar ribbon pictures have been made in England and Germany.

Bookmark, Father Of Our Country 55.00
Bookmark, Last Roses Of Summer, Frame 95.00
Children At Play, Gilt Frame, 6 x 7 1/2 In. 38.50
Good Old Days, Framed, Signed, Label On Back 135.00
H.M.S. Hannibal, Framed, 5 1/4 x 7 3/4 In. 210.00
The Start, Framed, 1 3/4 x 6 In. 185.00
Wellington & Blugher At Waterloo 185.00

STEVENS & WILLIAMS of Stourbridge, England, made many types of glass, including layered, etched, cameo, and art glass, between the 1830s and 1930s. Some pieces are signed *S & W*. Many pieces are decorated with flowers, leaves, and other designs based on nature.

Basket, Gold Mica Flakes, Amber Rim, Twisted Handle, 7 1/2 In. 275.00
Basket, Red Flower, White Stripes, Vaseline Handles, c.1850, Pair 350.00
Basket, Strawberries, Thorn Handles & Feet, Amber, 7 1/2 x 6 3/4 In. 1250.00
Biscuit Jar, White Outside, Ruffled Leaves, Pink Interior, 7 1/2 In. 395.00
Bowl, 1 Large Flower, Branch Handles, 6 1/2 x 9 3/4 In. 650.00
Bowl, Clear Applied Acorn, 3 Thorn Handles, Footed, 7 x 8 1/2 In. 400.00
Creamer, Scissor-Cut Top, Blue Flower, Amber Handle, 2 7/8 In. 245.00
Cruet, Arboresque, Amber Foot & Handle, White Spatter, 9 1/2 In. 145.00
Cruet, Arboresque, Blue, Bubble Stopper, 8 In. 145.00
Jardiniere, Leaves & Stems, Thorn Feet, 1 Sunflower, 10 In. 350.00
Pitcher, Silver Rim, Matching Tumbler, 9 1/4 In. 495.00
Plate, Strawberries, Rolled Rim, Amber Handle & Feet, 10 In. 760.00
Rose Bowl, Box-Pleated Top, Stripes, 4 1/2 In. 145.00
Rose Bowl, Diamond Quilted, Box Pleated Top, Blue, 4 In. 225.00
Vase, 4 Opalescent Ruffled Leaves, Cream Lining, 11 1/2 In. 395.00
Vase, 8-Crimp Top, Amber Ruffled Leaf, Pink Lining, 6 3/4 In. 165.00
Vase, Amber Fluted Rim, Amber Leaves, White, 5 1/2 In. 125.00
Vase, Amber Rim, Ruffled Foot, Bell-Shaped Flowers, 7 1/8 In. 135.00
Vase, Amber, Plums & Leaves, Amber Handle, 8 In. 125.00
Vase, Appliqued Flowers & Leaves, Pink Lining, 10 3/4 In. 225.00
Vase, Jack-In-The-Pulpit, White, White To Rose Interior, 7 1/2 In. 37.50
Vase, Mother-Of-Pearl, Green To Rose, White Lining, 5 3/8 In. 850.00
Vase, Mother-Of-Pearl, Swirl Pattern, 12 1/4 In. 1000.00
Vase, Opalescent Scroll Feet, White Lining, Intaglio Flowers, 4 In. 165.00
Vase, Orange Swirl, Mother-Of-Pearl, White Lining, 11 In. 245.00
Vase, Rainbow Colored Flowers, White Ground, c.1900, 5 3/8 In. 2500.00
Vase, Red Cherries, Blue Overlay Top, 4 3/4 In. 165.00
Vase, Red Cherries, Pink Overlay Top, 4 1/4 In. 145.00
Vase, Trapped Swirl Design, Pink Cased, 11 1/4 In. 715.00

STOCKTON Terra Cotta Company was started in Stockton, California, in 1891. The art pottery called *Rekston* was made there after 1897. The factory burned in 1902 and never reopened.

Vase, Grapes, Scroll Handles, 13 In. 750.00
Vase, Green & Yellow Flowers, Ruffled Neck, Bulbous Base, 9 x 4 3/4 In. 302.00

STONEWARE is a coarse, glazed, and fired potter's ceramic that is used to make crocks, jugs, bowls, etc. It is often decorated with cobalt blue decorations. Stoneware is still being made.

Batter Jar, Blue Decorated, Cowden & Wilcox, Harrisburg 575.00
Batter Jar, Full-Bellied Teakettle Shape, Grady L. Ryan 275.00
Bean Pot, Friends Beans, 1 Pt. 35.00
Beater Jar, Wesson Oil, Blue Stripe, 14 In. 85.00

Bottle, D.W. Defreest, Cobalt Blue LL On Opposite Side 100.00
Bottle, Display, Ginger Beer, Gurds 875.00
Bottle, Hot Water, Flat Side, White Glaze, Chas. E. Brauer, 10 3/4 In. 115.00
Bottle, J.R. Cronks Sarsaparilla Beer, Ribbed Neck 100.00
Bottle, Kamp Distilling Co., Paper Label 28.00
Bowl, Gray Drip Design, Peter Voulkos, 12 In. 990.00
Bowl, Milk, Brushed Design, Applied Handles & Spout, H. Smith & Co., 11 In. 1100.00
Bowl, Raised Design, Green Glaze, 9 1/2 In. 45.00
Butter, Blue & White, Bail Handle, 5 x 5 In. 60.00
Butter, Cover, Cherries, Bail, Blue & Gray 225.00
Churn, 6-Pointed Star, Flower In Middle, H.M. Whitman, 5 Gal. 4290.00
Churn, 8-Point Starface Design, Eared, 6 Gal. 4620.00
Churn, Cobalt Blue Design, Edmands & Co., 13 In. 154.00
Churn, Cobalt Blue Foliage & Flower, White's Utica, 5 Gal. 525.00
Churn, Cobalt Tulip, Green Leaves, c.1870, 5 Gal. 357.50
Churn, Cornucopia Of Flowers, John Burger, Rochester, c.1855, 6 Gal. 8525.00
Churn, Dotted & Ribbed Flower & Leaves, C.W. Braun, 4 Gal. 3080.00
Churn, E. Norton & Co., Bennington, Vt., Stylized Floral, No. 4, 17 1/2 In. 165.00
Churn, McDonald & Benjamin, Cincinnati, Ohio, 3 Gal. 330.00
Churn, Small Blue Floral, 4 Gal. 200.00
Churn, Standard Pottery Co., Brazil, Ind., 4 Gal. 60.00
Churn, Stenciled Birch Leaves, Minnesota Stoneware Co., 5 Gal. 3000.00
Churn, Swan Design, Harts, c.1860, 4 Gal. 1980.00
Churn, W.H. Farrar, Geddes, N.Y., Bird, Ears, 5 Gal. 3575.00
Churn, Welch & Atcheson, Annapolis, Ind. 250.00
Churn, White & Wood, Binghamton, N.Y., Paddletail Bird, 6 Gal. 4950.00
Churn, Whites Utica, 5 Gal. 550.00
Colander, Miss Mary Mansfield, Lyons, N.Y., Albany Slip, Footed, 2 Gal. 1100.00
Colander, Straight Sides, July 1895 .... 1300.00
Cooler, 5 With Flourish, Blue Quill Work, Wooden Spigot, Barrel Shape, 14 1/4 In. .. 55.00
Cooler, Alderman & Scott, No. 16 In Wreath, Double Ear Handles, 23 1/2 In. 825.00
Cooler, Barrel, Blue Bands, 3 Gal. 143.00
Cooler, Ithaca, N.Y. 1879 In Cobalt Script, 6 Gal. 3190.00
Cooler, Molded Floral Relief, Words Ice Water, Brass Spigot, Cover, 16 3/4 In. 137.50
Cooler, Niagara Falls, 3 Colors, Whites Utica Factory 5500.00
Cooler, Parrot On Branch, Burger 8525.00
Cooler, Spigot, Whiteways Devon Cyder, 5 Gal. 125.00
Cooler, Stenciled Label, Alderman & Scott, 16-In. Wreath, Ovoid 750.00
Cooler, Water, Gold Medal Products, Mauve Glaze 75.00
Cooler, Water, White, Brass Spigot, Counter Top 35.00
Cooler, Whites, Utica, Salt Glaze, 3 Colors, Niagara Falls, 1900 .... 5500.00
Cream Pot, Basket Of Flowers, Ovoid, 1 Gal. 1815.00
Cream Pot, T. Harrington, Lyons, Bird, 3 Gal. 1210.00
Cream Pot, Whites, Utica, Basket Of Flowers, 1 Gal. 1800.00
Crock, Anchor, Rope & Water, West Troy Pottery, 4 Gal. 2200.00
Crock, Bird In Brush, F.A. Plaaisted & Co., 2 Gal. 325.00
Crock, Bird On Branch, Haxstun & Co., Fort Edward, N.Y., 2 Gal. 330.00
Crock, Blue Decorations, Handles, 15 1/2 In., 5 Gal. 115.00
Crock, Blue Foliage, Incised Lines Around Rim, Handles, Ovoid, 6 3/4 In. 350.00
Crock, Brushed Floral Design, Impressed 4, 10 In. 330.00
Crock, Butter, Cobalt Blue Design, Cover, 19th Century, 13 In. 220.00
Crock, Butter, Cobalt Blue Floral Design, Impressed 1 1/2, 12 In. 412.00
Crock, Butter, Stenciled Cobalt Blue Label, A. Conrad, 6 x 9 In. 180.00
Crock, Clarke & Bros., Cannelton, Ind., Eagle, 3 Gal. 1600.00
Crock, Cobalt Blue 1832 1 Side, Leaf Reverse, Ovoid, 12 In. 357.00
Crock, Cobalt Blue Design, 3 Gal., 14 In. 275.00
Crock, Cobalt Blue Design, BC Millburn Under Handle, 4 Gal., 14 In. 415.00
Crock, Cobalt Blue Design, John Burger Rochester, 2 Gal., 12 In. 357.00
Crock, Cobalt Blue Floral, 19th Century, 11 3/4 In. 132.00
Crock, Cobalt Blue Stenciled & Free Hand Label, Williams & Reppert, 8 1/2 In. 325.00
Crock, Cobalt Blue Stenciled Label, Donaghho, 9 1/2 In. 45.00
Crock, Cobalt Blue Tree Hand Label, Hamilton & Jones, Pa 2, 8 1/4 In. 60.00
Crock, Cobalt Blue, Flower 4, Quill Work, 12 3/4 In. 302.00

Crock, Cobalt Design, Flying Bird, 19th Century, 3 Gal. 467.00
Crock, Cobalt Design, Lyons, 3 Gal. 247.00
Crock, Cobalt Vines, Tapered Sides, Ballard & Brothers, 3 Gal. 165.00
Crock, Cornflower, G. Hart, Sherburne, Vt., 2 Gal. 125.00
Crock, Crossed Birds On Branch, J.A. & C.W. Underwood, 4 Gal. 1017.00
Crock, Daisy & Blue 4, John Burger, 4 Gal. 330.00
Crock, Dotted Fish In Water, 2 Gal. 1650.00
Crock, Eberly, Rhyme, 2 Gal. 7000.00
Crock, Elephant Ear Leaves, 30 Gal. 550.00
Crock, Factory Building, New York Stoneware Co., 4 Gal. 6400.00
Crock, Floral Design, Ears, 5 Gal. 70.00
Crock, Floral Design, Impressed 2, Ovoid, 10 3/4 In. 250.00
Crock, Floral Design, John Burger, 6 Gal. 775.00
Crock, Folk Art Man, 1 Qt. 5000.00
Crock, Geo. Husher, Brazil, Ind., 1/2 Gal. 175.00
Crock, Guinea On Ground, Haxstun, Ottman & Co., 2 Gal. 2420.00
Crock, Hudson Pottery, Chicken Pecking Corn, 5 Gal. 2750.00
Crock, Ideal Salt Feeder Co., Writing Inside 350.00
Crock, J. & E. Norton, Bennington, Vt., Floral, 5 Gal. 1375.00
Crock, J.P. Convers & Co., Gray Glaze, Design 400.00
Crock, Jas. Hamilton, Stenciled & Freehand, 4 Gal. 410.00
Crock, Mammy Design 6500.00
Crock, Milk Cooling, Sawtooth, White Hall, Blue 75.00
Crock, Milk, Blue, Gal. 50.00
Crock, N. Clark & Co., Double-Floral Design, 4 Gal. 2530.00
Crock, New York Stoneware, Bird On Branch, 4 Gal. 550.00
Crock, Orchid Design, N.A. White & Son, 12 Gal. 4290.00
Crock, Oyster, Brown & White, Albany Slip, E. Swasey & Co., 1 Qt. 88.00
Crock, Oyster, Brown Glaze, Label, A.E. Jones & Sons, 1 Qt. 330.00
Crock, Oyster, Salt Glaze, Stenciled, Albany Slip, E.A. Gowan, 1 Qt. 525.00
Crock, Oyster, Stencil, Blue & White Striping, Ackers, 1 Qt. 412.00
Crock, Oyster, Stenciled, Salt Glaze, Cork Lid, Walker Brothers, 1 Qt. 143.00
Crock, Paste, Diamond Ink Co., 1 Gal. 35.00
Crock, Peanut Butter, Store, Holds 32 Lbs. 325.00
Crock, Pecking Chicken & Chick, 4 Gal. 440.00
Crock, S. Hart Fulton, Dog, Carrying Basket, 5 Gal. 3850.00
Crock, Salt Glazed, G.A. McCarthy & Bro., Maysville, Ky., Blue, 1 Qt. 175.00
Crock, Squirrel Brand Peanut Butter, 21 Lb. .... '15.00
Crock, Stenciled 8, E.S. & B. Newbrighton, 16 In. 126.00
Crock, Stenciled Shield, Jas. Hamilton & Co. 175.00
Crock, Stylized Floral, O. Whittemore, 10 In. 203.50
Crock, T. Harrington, Deer Standing By Tree, 4 Gal. 3630.00
Crock, Toloma Creamery, 6 x 3 In. 15.00
Crock, Upton Stuckey, Freehand Cobalt Squiggle 200.00
Crock, West Troy, 5 Gal. 275.00
Crock, West Troy New York, Pottery 3, Handles, 10 3/4 In. 247.50
Crock, Whites Utica, New York, Floral, 3 Gal. 660.00
Cuspidor, Blue Freehand Design 190.00
Cuspidor, Gray Salt Glaze, Brown Highlights, 8 1/2 In. 55.00
Cuspidor, Peacock At Fountain, Blue & White 390.00
Figurine, Cocker Spaniel, Incised Collar & Leash, 7 1/8 In., Pair 403.00
Figurine, Dove, Gray, Han Dynasty, 3 x 10 In. 350.00
Flask, Boot Shape, 1 Pt., 6 1/2 x 8 In., Pair 185.00
Flask, Marked ST, WT, 1829, Sailing Ship, Albany Slip 3850.00
Flask, Tavern Scenes, J. Saimders Wine & Spirit Merchant, 5 1/2 In. 93.50
Flowerpot, Blue Decoration, 5 1/4 x 6 In. 125.00
Foot Warmer, Sgraffito Design, Round 425.00
Jar, A.P. Donagho, Parkersburg, West Virginia, Gal. 75.00
Jar, Blue Floral, C. Wilber, Double-Handled, c.1850, 6 Gal. 1600.00
Jar, Blue Stenciled Label, 3 Shields, L.B. Milliner, Pa. 6, Ovoid, 16 1/2 In. .. 715.00
Jar, Blue Stenciled Label, Fine Maccoboy, 9 1/4 In. 143.00
Jar, Brushed Cobalt Blue At Shoulder Handles, I.M. Mead & Co., 13 3/4 In. .. 71.50
Jar, Brushed Tulip, Shoulder Handles, T. Reed, 3, Ovoid, 13 1/4 In. 550.00

Jar, Canning, 3 Cobalt Blue Stripes, Gray, 1 Qt. 105.00
Jar, Canning, 4 Blue Stripes, 8 1/2 In. 160.00
Jar, Canning, 6 Light Blue Stripes, 8 1/2 In. 145.00
Jar, Canning, A. Conrad, New Geneva, Pa., 8 1/2 In. 220.00
Jar, Canning, A.P. Donagho, Parkersburg, W.Va., Cobalt Blue Stencil, 8 1/2 In. 93.00
Jar, Canning, Blue Decorated 200.00
Jar, Canning, Blue Stenciled Label, A.P. Donagho, 8 In. 60.00
Jar, Canning, Blue Stenciled Label, E.B. Taylor, 8 In. 132.00
Jar, Canning, Cobalt Blue Label, Hamilton & Jones, Greensboro, 9 3/4 In. 60.00
Jar, Canning, Cobalt Blue Label, Jas. Hamilton & Co., Greensboro, 9 1/2 In. 192.00
Jar, Canning, G. Hiser & Sons, 9 3/4 In. 155.00
Jar, Canning, Harrington & Burger, Double Flower, 3 Gal. 520.00
Jar, Canning, Peoria Pottery, Brown 325.00
Jar, Canning, S. Hart, Fulton, N.Y., Striped Dog, Carrying Basket, Ears, 2 Gal. 4950.00
Jar, Canning, Stenciled Design, Hamilton & Jones, Greensboro, 8 1/2 In. ...... 325.00 to 350.00
Jar, Canning, Strap Handle, Cobalt Blue Brushed Design & 1, 10 1/4 In. 45.00
Jar, Canning, T.F. Reppert, Greensboro, Pa., 9 1/2 In. 50.00
Jar, Canning, Wilkinson & Fleming, Shinnston, W. Va., Blue Label, Rose, 10 In. 275.00
Jar, Cobalt Blue Brush Work, Tulips, Hamilton & Pershing, No. 3, 13 In. 715.00
Jar, Cobalt Blue Brushed Tulip & 4, 14 3/4 In. 55.00
Jar, Cobalt Blue Floral Design, Circled Mark, 11 1/4 In. 395.00
Jar, Cobalt Blue Floral Design, I.M. Mead, Portage Co., Ohio, Handles, 15 In. 275.00
Jar, Cobalt Blue Floral, Foliage Band, Impressed 3, 14 1/2 In. 467.50
Jar, Cobalt Blue Floral, Ovoid, 12 1/2 In. 357.00
Jar, Cobalt Blue Free Hand & Stenciled Label, Hamilton & Jones, 13 3/4 In. 330.00
Jar, Cobalt Blue Quill Design, Bird, Stylized Wings, No. 4, Ovoid, 14 1/2 In. 140.00
Jar, Cobalt Blue Quill Work, 2 With Flourishes, 11 In. 95.00
Jar, Cobalt Blue Stenciled Label, Donagho Co., 12 In. 55.00
Jar, Cobalt Blue Stenciled Label, Endix & Frankenbert, Shoulder Handles, 15 In. 230.00
Jar, Cobalt Blue Stenciled Label, McIntire & Brand, Pa. 2, 10 In. 165.00
Jar, Cobalt Brush Work, Hamilton, Greensboro, Pa. 8, Shoulder Handles 500.00
Jar, Cobalt Flower, Dated 1798, Double Handles, Ovoid, 1798 .... 1705.00
Jar, Cover, Cobalt Blue Floral, I.M. Mead, 15 1/2 In. 275.00
Jar, Cover, Pen Yan, Cobalt Blue Floral Design, 9 In. 95.00
Jar, Cover, Serpent Lid Handle, Tobacco 200.00
Jar, Farrar, Geddes, N.Y., Rooster, Ovoid, 3 Gal. 3300.00
Jar, Floral Design, Blue Quill Work, J. Norton & Co., 10 1/2 In. 220.00
Jar, Floral, Shoulder Handles, A.O. Whittemore, Havana, N.Y., No. 2, 9 3/4 In. 66.00
Jar, Flower In Cobalt Blue Quill Work, A.O. Whittemore, Havana, N.Y., 11 3/4 In. 60.00
Jar, Freehand Tiger's Head, 1 Gal. 45.00
Jar, Gray Salt Glaze, Lewis 4, 15 In. 50.00
Jar, Green Ash Glaze, Southern, 5 In. 27.50
Jar, Hartford City Slat Co., Hartford City, W.Va. 275.00
Jar, Hummingbird, On Vine, Incised Flower, Handles, 3 1/2 Gal. 1550.00
Jar, Incised Blue Profile Of Colonial Man's Head, Remmey, 1 Gal. 6875.00
Jar, Incised Cobalt Bird, 2 Flowers, I. Seymour, Double Handle 1100.00
Jar, Incised Seed Pod Front, Freehand 1823 Reverse, J.H. Remmey, 3 Gal. 1265.00
Jar, J. Burger Jr., Rochester, N.Y., Stylized Flower, 1881, 4 Gal. 852.50
Jar, J. Dillon, Burlington, Ovoid, 10 1/4 In. 60.00
Jar, Lye, McCormick-Deering, 2 Gal. 60.00
Jar, M. Dustin, Jeffersonville, Iowa, 6 Gal. 650.00
Jar, M. Worther, Philadelphia, Ill., Freehand, 1 Qt. 300.00
Jar, Man In The Moon & Stylized Rain Clouds, c.1820, 2 Gal. 1100.00
Jar, Miss Sadie Rogerson, Moundsville, W.Va., 6 Gal. 400.00
Jar, New York Stoneware Co., NY., Stylized Foliage, 5 Gal., 14 1/2 In. 300.00
Jar, Olive Ash Glaze, Incised LM/ Jan. 29, 1859/ Dave, 5 Gal. 7425.00
Jar, Preserving, Cobalt Blue Stenciled Label, Hamilton & Jones, 9 3/4 In. 88.00
Jar, Sipe & Sons, W'msport, Pa., 4, Cobalt Flowers, 12 3/4 In. 242.00
Jar, Stenciled Label, Eagle & A.P. Donagho, 9 3/4 In. 962.00
Jar, Stylized Floral, Brushed Cobalt Blue, Shoulder Handles, 16 1/4 In. 330.00
Jar, T. Reed, Cobalt Brush Tulip, Handles 550.00
Jar, Tooled Shoulder Lines, Stenciled & Free Hand Label, C.L. Williams, 20 3/4 In. .. 1100.00
Jar, W.H. Farrar & Co., Geddes, N.Y., Rooster, 3 Gal. 3300.00

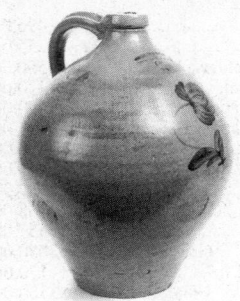

*Stoneware, Jug, Blue Flowers &
Leaf Design, I. Seymour, 2 Gal.*

Jug, 2 Handles, Marked RA & GB Weaver, Roseville	225.00
Jug, 2-Tone Gray Salt Glaze, Brown Top, Ohio Stoneware Co., Akron, 11 In.	82.00
Jug, 3 In Center Of Stylized Flower, Trapp-Chandler, Brown Slip, c.1850	4125.00
Jug, A.K. Ballard, Cobalt Design, Spout, 2 Gal.	121.00
Jug, Beehive, Cobalt Leaves, 5 Gal.	1400.00
Jug, Beehive, Imperial, Canada, 5 Gal.	425.00
Jug, Bellarmine, Germany	770.00
Jug, Bergan & Foy 3, Impressed Label, Blue Quill Work, 15 In.	1072.00
Jug, Bleeding Bull's-Eye, 5 Gal.	50.00
Jug, Blue Flowers & Leaf Design, I. Seymour, 2 Gal. *Illus*	500.00
Jug, Brown & White, Buckeye Pottery, 2 3/4 In.	120.00
Jug, Brown Over White, Bee-Sting Design, 2 Gal.	27.00
Jug, Burger & Land, Rochester, N.Y., Flower & 2, Ovoid, 14 7/8 In.	165.00
Jug, C. Schrack's Varnish Mfg., Ovoid, 16 In.	120.00
Jug, Chas S. Gove Co. Liquor Merchants, Blue Stencil, Miniature	70.00
Jug, Chemical, Eastman Kodak, 5 Gal.	45.00
Jug, Cobalt Bird On Branch, J. & E. Norton, c.1850, 1 1/2 Gal.	4125.00
Jug, Cobalt Blue Codfish, Ovoid, 1800-1810, 17 In.	1870.00
Jug, Cobalt Blue Decoration, John Young & Co., Harrisburg Pa., 3 Gal., 17 In.	935.00
Jug, Cobalt Blue Design, Boston, Massachusetts, 15 In.	1540.00
Jug, Cobalt Blue Design, Inscribed Geo. Washington, 13 In.	990.00
Jug, Cobalt Blue Design, Man's Head, Wm. E. Warner, 2 Gal.	7425.00
Jug, Cobalt Blue Design, Medallion, Gray Glaze	550.00
Jug, Cobalt Blue Design, New York Stoneware Co., 1876, 5 Gal.	1540.00
Jug, Cobalt Blue Design, Ottoman Bros., For Edward N.Y., 2 Gal., 14 1/2 In.	137.00
Jug, Cobalt Blue Design, T. & J. Ducey, 1850s, 14 In.	1320.00
Jug, Cobalt Blue Floral Design, 19th Century, 16 In.	357.00
Jug, Cobalt Blue Floral, Number 3, Ovoid, Gray Salt Glaze, 16 1/2 In.	330.00
Jug, Cobalt Blue Freehand Jumping Deer, Norton & Fenton, 1845-1847	550.00
Jug, Cobalt Blue Label, J.F. Weller, Allentown, Pa., 9 In.	275.00
Jug, Cobalt Blue Stenciled Label, C.B. Somerville & Co., 11 In.	275.00
Jug, Cobalt Blue, Louis J. Miller & Co., Boston, Mass., 1 Gal.	90.00
Jug, Commeraws, Blue Incised Swag & Tassel, c.1800, 3 Gal.	4125.00
Jug, Dean Foster & Co., 2 Birds, 5 Gal.	600.00
Jug, Devil, Painted Red, Black & White, Robert Brown, Cork	385.00
Jug, Double Flower, I. Seymour & Son, 2 Gal.	154.00
Jug, E.W. Farrington & Co., Elmira, N.Y., Profile, 1 Gal.	2860.00
Jug, F. Stetzenmeyer & Co., Rochester, N.Y., Tree Design, Male Profile, 2 Gal.	1650.00
Jug, F. Stetzenmeyer & Goetzman, Floral Design, 2 Gal.	715.00
Jug, Farmmato, Down On The Farm, Shadyside, Ohio	50.00
Jug, Farrington, Elmira, Male Profile, 1 Gal.	2860.00
Jug, Floral Design, Cobalt Blue Quill Work, Impressed Label, 12 In.	192.00
Jug, Floral Design, Impressed Label, Brushed Cobalt Blue, 15 In.	165.00
Jug, Floral Design, Mead, Mogadore, Ohio, Double Ear Handles, No. 5, 18 1/2 In.	385.00
Jug, Floral Design, Norton, 2 Gal.	225.00
Jug, Floral Design, Stezenmeyer-Goetzman, Rochester, N.Y., Ovoid, 2 Gal.	715.00

Jug, Floral Spray, J. & E. Norton, Bennington, Vt., 3 Gal. 495.00
Jug, Gray, Dripping Green Ash Glaze, Southern, 6 1/4 In. 55.00
Jug, Hamilton, Greensboro, Pa., Blue Floral, No. 8, Shoulder Handles, 18 In. 550.00
Jug, Harrington & Burger, Rochester, Double Floral Design, 2 Gal. 1430.00
Jug, Hoffman House Blended Whiskey, H.F. Carein & Co., Miniature 90.00
Jug, I. Seymour, Troy Factory, Ovoid, 12 In. 45.00
Jug, Impressed 1809 Paul Cushman's Stoneware, 1/2 Gal. 3300.00
Jug, Impressed M.C. Webster & Co., Mottled Surface, 15 1/2 In. 165.00
Jug, Incised Bird & Branch, J. Matheis, 5 1/4 In. 3327.50
Jug, Incised Design, Continental 468.00
Jug, J. & E. Norton, Bennington, Stylized Floral, 10 12 In. 357.00
Jug, J. & E. Norton, Bennington, Vt., Dotted Peacock On Stump, 2 Gal. 3080.00
Jug, J. Hayes & Co., Manchester, N.H., Cobalt Blue Label, 9 1/2 In. 170.00
Jug, J.F. Cartouche In Oval, Roped Border, Jonathan Fenton, 1793, 1 Gal. 3300.00
Jug, John Burger, Daisy Design, 3 Gal. 935.00
Jug, N. Clark & Co., Blue Double Flower Design, 2 Gal. 2145.00
Jug, N. Clark & Co., Cobalt Sheep, Foliage, 2 Gal. 7000.00
Jug, N. Clark, Athens, N.Y., 2 Gal. 3850.00
Jug, N.A. Qhite & Son, Brushed Cobalt Blue Flower, 14 In. 300.00
Jug, P.M. Dannell, Incised 2, 13 In. 72.00
Jug, S. Routson, Wooster, Ohio, Gal. 250.00
Jug, S.S. Perry & Co., W. Troy, Cobalt Blue Floral, Strap Handle, 15 1/2 In. 247.00
Jug, S.T. Brewer, Havana, Floral, Spigot Hole, 2 Gal. 205.00
Jug, Salt Glaze, Raised Label, Ohio Stoneware Co., Akron, Ohio 75.00
Jug, Sgraffito Label, Kauffman Latimer Co., Albany Slip, 13 1/2 In. 88.00
Jug, Sgraffito Label, Louis Zable & Co., Louisville, Ky., Albany Slip, 13 1/2 In. 45.00
Jug, Stacker, Incised Man, Smoking Cigarette, Otto Brown, Handle, 1925 .... 2200.00
Jug, Stenciled Design, Blue Bands, Greensboro, Pa., 1 Gal. 247.00
Jug, Stenciled Getty & Co., Ovoid 130.00
Jug, Stenciled Label, A.P. Donagho, Parkersburg, W.Va., 9 3/8 In. 104.00
Jug, Stenciled Label, T.F. Reppert, 11 3/4 In. 71.00
Jug, Stylized Tree, Stetzenmeyer 2200.00
Jug, Triple Hearts, Geddes, 2 Gal. 412.50
Jug, W. Lunn, Cobalt Blue Labels, 10 & 1882, Double Ear Handles, 19 1/2 In. 187.00
Jug, W.H. Ferrar & Co., Geddes, N.Y., Cobalt Blue Bird, 2 Gal. 1210.00
Jug, Whiskey, Fink Family Liquor, St. Paul, 1 Gal. 600.00
Jug, Whiskey, Hidden Door 575.00
Match Holder, Stump With Mouse, Bluish Glaze On White, 3 1/4 In. 132.00
Mold, Food, Turk's Head 330.00
Mug, Flying Bird 195.00
Mug, Golfer Scene, Portabello Ware, Scotland, c.1949 .... 195.00
Mug, Windy City, Blue & White, Advertising 250.00
Mug, Zigzag Dot Design, Strap Handle, 4 3/8 In. 275.00
Pie Pan, Brown, 9 In. 8.00
Pitcher, Auburn, N.Y., Albany Slip, Ovoid, 11 1/4 In. 38.50
Pitcher, Blue & White Sponging, Brown Albany Slip Interior, 11 1/4 In. 192.00
Pitcher, Brown & White Jasperware, Paxton, 7 In. 165.00
Pitcher, Brown Tree Bark Texture, Cut-Off Limbs, Minnesota Stoneware 950.00
Pitcher, Brown-Gray Salt Glaze, Strap Handle, Pinched Spout, 10 3/4 In. 165.00
Pitcher, Brushed Cobalt Blue Tulip, Sawyer & Smith, Akron, O., 2, 12 1/4 In. 1265.00
Pitcher, Castle & Fishscale, Blue & White, 8 In. .... 240.00 to 250.00
Pitcher, Cattail, Blue & White, 8 In. .... 150.00 to 195.00
Pitcher, Cherryband, Small 220.00
Pitcher, Cobalt Blue Floral, Ribbed Strap Handle, 14 1/2 In. 1760.00
Pitcher, Daisies, John Meeks, Blue & White Sponge Design, 10 In. 475.00
Pitcher, Dutch Children, Windmill, Blue & White, 7 In. 100.00
Pitcher, Eagle & Shield, Blue & White 475.00
Pitcher, Edelweiss, Prosit, Blue & White, 8 In. 275.00
Pitcher, Embossed Tulip, Brown, 6 In. 65.00
Pitcher, Fishscale & Wild Rose, Blue & White, 12 1/2 In. 275.00
Pitcher, Harrington & Burger, Blue Slip Cabbage Flower, 1 Gal. 2200.00
Pitcher, Indian Head, Blue, 8 In. 350.00
Pitcher, Indian Head, Brown, 6 In. 87.00

Pitcher, Indian In War Bonnet, Blue & White 400.00
Pitcher, Keg Shape, Strap Handle, Blue Bands, 7 1/4 In. 27.00
Pitcher, Keister, Blue Design, Lip, 18 In. 5600.00
Pitcher, North Star Grape, Brown, 6 In. 65.00
Pitcher, Tan Glaze, Applied Lions, Rose & Thistle, Coat Of Arms, Burslem, 10 In. ... 38.00
Pitcher, Yellow & Blue Sponging, 8 In. 125.00
Pot, Stenciled, Freehand Wave, A. Conrad & Co., New Geneva, Penna., 8 1/2 In. 350.00
Rolling Pin, White 125.00
Salt Box, Hanging, Daisy On Snowflake 120.00
Soap Dish, Cat's Face In Relief, Blue & White 85.00
Sugar & Creamer, Brown & White Jasperware, Paxton, 3 3/4 In. 150.00
Syrup, Herons In Reeds, January 23, 1873 .... 145.00
Teakettle, Flower Design, South Carolina, Large 350.00
Teapot, Brown & White Jasperware, Paxton, 6 1/2 In. 125.00
Umbrella Stand, Whites Of Utica, c.1900, 20 In. 1150.00
Urn, J.B. Cairie & Co., Poughkeepsie, 2 Gal. 450.00
Vase, Fuchsia & Pink Flowers, Rust Ground, Griffin Handles, 18 x 10 In. 160.00
Vase, Overlapping Circles, White Slip, Claude Conover, 1960, 19 In. 1265.00
Vase, Textured, Green & White Glaze, Marguerite Wildenhane, 1950, 6 1/2 In. 920.00

STORE fixtures, cases, cutters, and other items that have no advertising as
part of the decoration are listed here. Most items found in an old store are
listed in the Advertising category in this book.

Back Bar, Carved Oak, Walnut Top, Bird's-Eye Maple Panels, 13 x 9 1/2 Ft. 7500.00
Bar, With Backbar, Mirrors, Oak, 22 Ft. 4500.00
Bin, Grain, Pine, Refinished, 5 Ft.2 In. x 30 x 20 In. 595.00
Bin, Japan Tea, Tin, 20 In. 185.00
Butcher Block, Maple 795.00
Cabinet, Display, Excelsior Showcase Works, Mahogany, Mirror Doors, 96 x 39 In. . 4950.00
Cabinet, Display, Mahogany, Rear Door, 60 In. 577.00
Cabinet, Dye Makers, Soft Pine, Birth To Death Insignia 950.00
Cabinet, Hardware, Revolving, 120 Drawers, With Base 1650.00
Cabinet, Hardware, Wooden, Revolving Octagonal Top, 9 Base Drawers, 62 x 30 In. 880.00
Cabinet, Jeweler's, Walnut, 4 Drawers, Pullout Work Desk, 1800 .... 565.00
Cabinet, Printing, Oak, 20 Drawers, American Type Founders Co., Refinished, 1860s 845.00
Cabinet, Seed & Feed, Pine, 30 Drawers, 2 Bins, 1840 .... 1600.00
Cabinet, Seed Rack, Stained Oak, 18 Glass Front Drawers, 90 In. 935.00
Cabinet, Thread, Oak, 10 Beveled Glass Front Drawers 475.00
Candy Jar, Clear Glass, 4 Sides, Pedestal, 26 In. 440.00
Candy Jar, Clear Glass, Fish Bowl, Pedestal, 24 In. 550.00
Cart, Peanut, Bartholomew, Factory Decal 3800.00
Case, Display, Beveled Glass Sides & Top, Oak, 12 Ft. x 20 In. 315.00
Case, Salesman's, Oak, Pine, 10 Drawers, Handle, Lock, 9 3/4 x 16 x 14 In. 290.00
Cash Drawer, Saloon, Oak, 3 Top & 2 Bottom Keys, 19th Century, 13 x 18 x 5 In. .. 300.00
Chest, Hardware, Wooden, 36 Drawers 150.00
Counter Top, Soda Fountain, Long Dome Lid For Pastries 35.00
Dispenser, Chocolate, Inset Clock, Schilling, Stollwereck, Clockwork, 5 Cent, 50 In. 4500.00
Mirror, 3 Adjustable Oval Mirrors, Footed Cast Iron Stand, Counter Top, 38 In. 330.00
Rack, Seed, Wire, 2 1/2 x 17 3/4 In. 10.00
Seed Rack & Cabinet, 18 Illuminated Glass Fronts, Oak, 19 Rear Drawers, 12 In. .. 990.00
Stool, Shoe Store, Twisted Iron Legs 80.00
Table, Swing-Out Stools, Ice Cream, Display Case Top 3500.00
Tobacco Cutter, Griswold, Red & Gold Pin Striping, Marked 195.00

STOVES have been used in America for heating since the eighteenth century
and for cooking since the nineteenth century. Most types of wood, coal, gas,
kerosene, and even some electric stoves are collected.

Blue & White Tile, European Style 38.00
Brookline Somerset, Cast Iron, Restored, 1910-1925 .... 1250.00
Cook, French Canadian, Beveled Mirror, Pink Roses On White Tile 4000.00
Cook, Gold Carion, Water Tank 2500.00
Cook, Home Clarion, Water Tank 1600.00
Cook, Ideal Clarion, No. 21 .... 550.00

*Stove, Corona,
Figural, Iron,
Painted, Late 19th
Century, 69 In.*

◆◆◆◆◆◆◆◆◆◆◆◆◆◆◆◆◆◆◆◆◆◆

Remove the rust from iron by
soaking the piece in kerosene
for twenty-four hours or use any
one of several commercial
preparations made for the re-
moval of rust. Wash, dry, and
coat the piece with a light oil to
protect it.

◆◆◆◆◆◆◆◆◆◆◆◆◆◆◆◆◆◆◆◆◆◆

Cook, Ideal Clarion, No. 25	650.00
Cook, Kineo Franklin, Size 18	600.00
Cook, King Kinwo Kitchen	1400.00
Cook, Mayflower	320.00
Cook, Modern Glenwood, No. 223	600.00
Cook, Modern Glenwood, No. 225	650.00
Cook, Our Clarion, Side Shelf	2000.00
Cook, Our Clarion, Water Tank	2200.00
Cook, Queen Atlantic, Imperial, Overhead Oven, 4 Wood & 4 Gas Burners	2800.00
Cook, Queen Atlantic, Overhead Gas Ovens, 2 Wood & 4 Gas Burners	2500.00
Cook, Quick-Meal, 2 Burners, Kerosene, Towel Bar 1 Side, Flip-Up Shelf Other	195.00
Cook, Water Tank	1400.00
Corona, Figural, Iron, Painted, Late 19th Century, 69 In. *Illus*	4950.00
Crescent, Wood, With Pots & Pans, Salesman's Sample	485.00
Delft Type Tiles On 3 Sides, France	1000.00
Empire, Iron, Marble Top & Shelf, Urn-Shaped Brass Finials, c.1820, 58 x 31 In.	990.00
Florence Stove Co., White Porcelain, Legs, Gas, Late 1920s	1350.00
Franklin, Corner Style, Cast Iron Grates, Open, 1890s	80.00
General Electric, 1950s	300.00
Graniteware, Blue, Silver, Black Skirts, Black Pierced Lid, Oil, 27 1/2 In.	750.00
Heating, Magic Chef, Kerosene, Tin, Legged	20.00
Heating, Oak-Gnarled, Chrome Trim	2000.00
Heating, Perfection, Kerosene, Blue Enameled, Portable, Legged	28.00
New Method, Model 660, Mansfield, Ohio, Gas, 2 Colors	105.00
Parcel Gilt Design, On Cream Ground, French, Pottery, 20th Century, 79 In.	1380.00
Parlor, Brass Finials, Sheet Iron Heat Exchanger Top, Cast Iron	450.00 to 495.00
Parlor, Coal Base, With Vent Oven, Estate Stove Co., Refurbished, 1860, 6 Ft.	5500.00
Parlor, Franklin-Type, Paw Feet, Foliage & Eagle In Relief, Iron, 39 1/2 In.	220.00
Parlor, Glenwood, Tauton, Nickel Plate & Cast Iron, 59 x 27 In.	1200.00
Parlor, Second Empire	8250.00
Peterborough, New Hampshire, 4 Tall Legs, Cast Iron	400.00
Table Top, Oil, 1 Burner, Gray & White Mottled Enameled, With 2 Qt. Pan	275.00

STRETCH GLASS is named for the strange stretch marks in the glass. It was
made by many glass companies in the United States from about 1900 to the
1920s. It is iridescent. Most American stretch glass is molded; most European
pieces are blown and may have a pontil mark.

Basket, White, 10 1/4 In.	90.00
Bowl, Amber Iridescent, Flared, 12 In.	28.00
Bowl, Amber Rainbow Iridescent, 10 x 3 In.	28.00
Bowl, Blue Opaque, Ribbed, Flared, 9 1/2 x 3 1/4 In.	40.00
Bowl, Hand Painted Flowers, White, 9 3/4 x 3 In.	28.00

Bowl, Vaseline, 12 x 5 1/2 In. 42.00
Candlestick, Colonial Style, Olive, 8 1/2 In., Pair 50.00
Candlestick, Green, Hollow, 9 3/4 In., Pair 40.00
Candy Dish, Cover, Blue, Art Glass 55.00
Sherbet, Amberina, Ribbed, Footed, 3 3/8 x 4 In. 38.00
Tumble Up, Blue 28.00
Vase, Car, Green 22.00

SUMIDA, or Sumida Gawa, is a Japanese pottery. The pieces collected by that name today were made about 1895 to 1970. There has been much confusion about the name of this ware, and it is often called *Korean Pottery.* Most pieces have a very heavy orange-red, blue, or green glaze, with raised three-dimensional figures as decorations.

Jar, Cover, Tortoise Glaze, 18th Century, 8 x 7 In. 425.00
Jug, Frog Design, Signed, 9 In. 450.00
Mug, Bull, Boy On Rim 60.00
Vase, Children Playing With Ball, 11 1/2 In. 210.00
Vase, Dragon Design, 26 In. 2100.00
Vase, Monkeys 225.00

SUNBONNET BABIES were first introduced in 1902 in the *Sunbonnet Babies Primer.* The stories were by Eulalie Osgood Grover, illustrated by Bertha Corbett. The children's faces were completely hidden by the sunbonnets. The children had been pictured in black and white before this time, but the color pictures in the book were immediately successful. The Royal Bayreuth China Company made a full line of children's dishes decorated with the Sunbonnet Babies. Some Sunbonnet Babies plates have been reproduced, but are clearly marked.

Candlestick, Fishing, Blue Mark, 4 1/4 In. 185.00
Creamer, Fishing, Royal Bayreuth 345.00
Cup & Saucer, Cleaning, Royal Bayreuth 250.00
Cup & Saucer, Getting Acquainted 50.00
Dish, Cover, Fishing 225.00
Dish Set, Child's, Victorian Children Scenes, 30 Piece 150.00
Hair Receiver, Blue Mark 250.00
Pitcher, Washing, Blue Mark, 4 In. 295.00
Plate, Cleaning, Royal Bayreuth, 6 In. 110.00
Postcard, 7 Piece 70.00
Saucer, Fishing, Blue Mark 55.00
Tile, Fishing, Blue Mark 195.00

SUNDERLAND luster is a name given to a special type of pink luster made by Leeds, Newcastle, and other English firms during the nineteenth century. The luster glaze is metallic and glossy and appears to have bubbles in it. Other pieces of luster are listed in the Luster category.

Butter Pot, Lid, 8 Lines Of Doggerel On 1 Side, Nautical 935.00
Creamer, Brown Transfer, Red & Green Enameling, Verse, 3 In. 71.00
Cup & Saucer 65.00
Jar, Cover, Black Transfer, Sailor's Farewell, 4 1/2 In. 148.00
Mug, 2 1/2 In. 60.00
Mug, Frog Interior 500.00
Pitcher, Black Transfer, Ship Caroline & The Shipwright Arms, 12 In. 137.00
Pitcher, Black Transfers, Polychrome Enamel, 6 1/4 In. 115.50
Pitcher, Historical, 1810 .... 425.00
Pitcher, Milk, House 85.00
Pitcher, Polychrome Transfer, Reverse Ship, 2 Seamen, 2 Flags, 19th Century 770.00
Plaque, Black Transfer, Prepare To Meet Thy God, 6 5/8 x 7 3/4 In. 230.00
Plaque, Black Transfer, Rejoice In The Lord, 8 5/8 x 9 5/8 In. 330.00
Plaque, Black Transfer, The Best Of All God Is With Us, 5 1/4 x 6 3/4 In. 220.00
Plate, Fluted Rim, 6 3/4 In. 68.00
Shaving Mug, Saucer 200.00
Vase, 8 In. 18.00
Waste Bowl 95.00

SUPERMAN was created by two seventeen-year-olds in 1938. The first issue of *Action* comics had the strip. Superman remains popular and became the hero of a radio show in 1940, cartoons in the 1940s, a television series, and several major movies.

Bank, Dime Register, Lithograph, Sliding Trapdoor, 1940s, 2 1/2 In.	110.00
Bank, Figural, 1974	35.00
Belt, Brown Leather, Embossed, Metal Buckle, 1940s	165.00
Box, Pep, 1940s	400.00
Brush, Avon, 1978	16.00
Cake Decoration Set, Superman With Buildings, DC Comics, 6 Piece	1.50
Card, 6 Different, 1940	79.00
Cereal Box, Kellogg's Pep, Superman Vs. The Solar Firebugs, 1947	150.00
Colorforms, 1964, Box	60.00
Comic Book, 3-D, 1953	65.00
Container, Orange Drink & Fruit Punch, 1/2 Gal.	12.50
Cookie Jar, Brown, California Originals	325.00 to 550.00
Cookie Jar, Silver, California Originals	950.00
Display, 12 Wallets, With Header, 1966	180.00
Doll, Kenner, Package, 5 In.	5.50
Figure, Energized, Remco, 9 In.	50.00
Figure, Mego, 1979, 3 3/4 In.	40.00
Figure, Super Powers, Card, Large	15.00
Flashlight, Flip, Bantamlite, 1966, On Card	31.00
Flippers, Membership Card, Box	145.00
Game, Calling Superman, Board, 1954	95.00
Game, Card, Whitman, 1966	35.00
Game, Quoit, 1950s, Box	28.00
Game, Superman III, Parker Bros., 1982	28.00
Glass, Superman Finds The Spaceship, 1964	70.00
Kiddie Paddlers, Card, Box, 1950s	115.00
Lobby Card, Columbia Serial Chapter 5, 1950s, 11 x 14 In.	85.00
Model Kit, Superboy, With Dog Krypto At Cave, Aurora, 1965, Box, 13 x 5 In.	325.00
Nutcracker, Wooden, DC Comics, 1979	30.00
Paint Set, Superman Sparkle, Kenner, Original Shrink Wrap, 1966	40.00
Pinback, Action Comics, 1940s	85.00
Pinback, Kellogg's Pep	12.00
Planter, Superman Super Plants, 1976	20.00
Play Money	10.00
Poster, Superman & The Mole Men, George Reeves, 1951, 3 Sheets	4400.00
Puppet, Hand, Ideal, 1965, Box	125.00
Puzzle, Superman Battling Aliens, Space Cycles, Whitman, 1966, 14 x 18 In.	15.00
Radio, Transistor, Box, 1973	50.00 to 60.00
Ray Gun, Daisy, Krypto, With Film	485.00
Ray Gun, Krypto, Instructions & Film, Box	595.00
Record Player	100.00
Ring, Airplane, Pep Cereal Premium, 1948	245.00
Soaky	45.00
Suspenders, 1978	5.00
Tin, Superman Curad Bandages, Colgate-Palmolive	20.00
Tumbler, Superman In Action, Red, 1964	10.00
Valentine, 1940	20.00 to 30.00
Watch, 1938	150.00
Wristwatch, DC Comics Inc., Dabs, Swiss, 1977	90.00
Wristwatch, Death Of Superman, Timex, Box	195.00

SUSIE COOPER began as a designer in 1925 working for the English firm A.E. Gray & Company. In 1932 she formed Susie Cooper Pottery, Ltd. In 1950 it became Susie Cooper China, Ltd., and the company made china and earthenware. In 1966 it was acquired by Josiah Wedgwood & Sons, Ltd. The name Susie Cooper appears with the company names on many pieces of ceramics.

Dish, Black Fruit	15.00

SWANKYSWIGS are small drinking glasses. In 1933, the Kraft Food Company began to market cheese spreads in these decorated, reusable glass tumblers. They were discontinued from 1941 to 1946, then made again from 1947 to 1958. Then plain glasses were used for most of the cheese, although a few special decorated Swankyswigs have been made since that time. A complete list of prices can be found in *Kovels' Price Guide to Depression Glass & American Dinnerware*.

Band No. 2, Red & Black	3.00
Bustling Betsy, Brown	3.50
Bustling Betsy, Red	3.00
Carnival, Red	3.50
Cornflower, No. 2, Light Blue	3.00
Forget-Me-Not, Blue	2.75
Kiddie Cup, Red	3.50
Posy, Cornflower	3.00
Posy, Tulip	3.00
Posy, Violet	4.00
Tulip, No.1, Red	3.00

SWORDS of all types that are of interest to collectors are listed here. The military dress sword with elaborate handle is probably the most wanted. Be sure to display swords in a safe way, out of reach of children.

Ames Saber, U.S., 1850	330.00
Artillery Officer's, British, 1850	220.00
Bayonet, Enfield, Scabbard, Civil War	95.00
Bayonet, Ger Mauzer	65.00
Bayonet, Officer's, Triangular Blade, Revolutionary War, 12 In.	145.00
Bayonet, World War II Mauser, Scabbard & Frog	35.00
Brass Hilt, England, 28 In.	82.00
Brass Hilt, Walnut Grip, Revolutionary War, 24 3/4 In.	245.00
Cadet's, West Point, Standard Pattern Hilt	190.00
Cutlass, Ames, Naval	525.00
Cutlass, Naval, Spear Point, Brass Hilt, Ribbed Leather Grip, England, 25 In.	210.00
Dagger, Brass Mounted Hilt, Tortoiseshell Covered Grip, China, 9 1/2 In.	85.00
Dagger, Challenge Cutlery, Stag Handle, Leather Sheath, 1800s	45.00
Dagger, Hand Forged, 800-1000 A.D., 14 1/2 In.	200.00
Dagger, Nazi Railway Leader	500.00
Dagger, Nubby Crocodile Skin Grip, Sudanese, 5 In.	85.00
Dagger, Pacific Islanders, Carved Wooden Handle, Leather Sheath, Large	42.50
Dagger, Silver, Sheath, Arabian, Large	45.00
Dirk, Naval Officer's, Brass Hilt, Napoleonic, 17 1/4 In.	275.00
Executioner's, Chiseled & Pierced Design, Pewter Hilt, 15 In.	325.00
Executioner's, Field Of 4 Pierced Eyes, Wooden Grip, 23 1/2 In.	675.00
Infantry Officer's, Brass Hilt, Walnut Grip, U.S., 1840s	750.00
Infantry Officer's, Wire Wrap Sharkskin Grip, British, 32 3/4 In.	255.00
Machete, Red Chinese Army, Wooden Handle, Canvas Sheath	12.00
Molly McGuire, Labor Riots, Plated F Scabbard.1870s, 30 In.	350.00
Naval Officer's, Ivory Hilt, Gilt Lion Pommel, 1810, England	250.00
Naval Officer's, Non-Regulation, Blade Stamped P.D.L., c.1850s	357.00
Naval Officer's, Sharkskin Grip, Civil War Period, 28 3/4 In.	275.00
Nickel Plate Hilt, Continental, 37 In.	77.00
Officer's, Artillery, With Scabbard, Mounted, S & K, 1820s, 34 In.	275.00
Officer's, Brass Hilt, Shell Guard, Knights Head Pommel, France, 32 3/4 In.	625.00
Officer's, Coast Guard, Dress, Brass Bound Sheath, 1800s	127.00
Officer's, Double Fullered Blade, Spiral Grip, Italy, c.1850, 31 In.	250.00
Officer's, Plated Hilt, Imperial German, 32 3/4 In.	150.00
Officer's, World War II, Scabbard, Paper Label, Japanese Characters, 39 In.	495.00
Pirate's, Iron, Brass Mounted Hilt, Bone Grip, Floral, Malay, 1800, 20 In.	145.00
Police, World War II, Germany	325.00
Presentation, General Arthur Brealler, c.1872	715.00
Saber, Eagle Pommel, French, c.1805, 35 In.	525.00
Saber, Hungarian Hussar, Curved Blade, Etched Man In The Moon, c.1650, 31 In.	1150.00

Saber, Iron Hilt, Bronze Monster Head Pommel, Swiss, 1650, 28 1/2 In. 1350.00
Saber, Short, Brass Hilt & Wire Grip, Turk's Head Finials, England, 1720, 31 In. 475.00
Saber, Tooled Steel, Ornate Brass Mounts, Bone Grip, Leather Sheath, 29 In. 160.00
Saber, U.S. Cavalry Trooper's, German Made 375.00
Samurai, Carved Ivory Scabbard & Hilt 44.00
Samurai, Shinto Blade, Japan, 18th Century 1522.00
Scimitar, Carved Bone & Brass Hilt Guard, Leather, Wood 580.00
Scimitar, Turkish, Steel, Iron Hilt 330.00
Staff & Field Officer's, Civil War, Shell Guard, Eagle-Form Pommel, 28 3/4 In. 275.00
West Point Cadet, Marked Challenger, Etched Scenes Of West Point 265.00
Wooden Hilt & Scabbard, Pyramidal Design, Sinew Binding, Shona, 25 In. 425.00

SYRACUSE is a trademark used by the Onondaga Pottery of Syracuse, New York. The company was established in 1871. It is still working. The name became the Syracuse China Company in 1966. It is known for fine dinnerware and restaurant china.

Cup & Saucer, Bracelet 28.00
Pitcher, Herbert Hoover, Cream, First Limited Edition, No. 1390, 6 x 7 In. 80.00
Plate, Bombay, 10 In. 15.00
Plate, Corabell, 6 1/4 In. 5.00
Plate, Corabell, 8 1/2 In. 5.00
Plate, Corabell, 9 3/4 In. 7.00
Soup, Dish, Corabell 10.00

TAPESTRY, PORCELAIN, see Rose Tapestry category

TEA CADDY is the name for a small box made to hold tea leaves. In the eighteenth century, tea was very expensive and it was stored under lock and key. The first tea caddies were made with locks. By the nineteenth century, tea was more plentiful and the tea caddy was larger. Often there were two sections, one for green tea, one for black tea.

Abalone, Georgian, Fitted Interior, c.1800, 5 1/2 x 8 x 5 In. 550.00
Alternating Floral & Cobalt Panels, Russia, 5 1/2 In., Pair 250.00
Birds In Sunburst Medallion, Blue, Red & Gilt, 5 1/2 In. 385.00
Bronze, Louis Phillippe, Overall Florals, 3 Compartments, 5 x 8 In. 440.00
Brown Stoneware, 19th Century 165.00
Burl Walnut, Banded Kingwood, 8 1/4 In. 193.00
Burl Walnut, Regency, Ivory Inlaid Escutcheon, 6 x 12 1/2 In. 385.00
Burl Walnut, Satinwood, 2 Sections, Ivory Escutcheon, Bun Feet, 6 x 12 In. 550.00
Copper, Ginger Jar Form, Silver Leaves & Flowers, Gorham, 1882, 4 1/8 In. 6325.00
Creamware, Black Transfer, Amorous Couple In Garden, 4 1/8 In. 71.50
Delft, Flower Heads, Single Leaves, Initialed, 1737, 4 3/4 In. 6900.00
Double Compartment, Present To Miss Eliza Johnson, 1843, 7 1/2 In. 88.00
Faux Bois, Oval Painted Medallions, 4 3/4 x 8 In. 1150.00
Fruitwood, Apple Shape, Inset Stem, 19th Century, 5 In. 3750.00
Fruitwood, George III, Feather & Leaf Decoupage, Hexagonal, 4 3/4 x 7 In. 805.00
Fruitwood, George III, Pear Shape, Wooden Stem, 6 3/4 In. 8625.00
Fruitwood, George III, Shell & Patera Inlay, 1830s, 4 1/2 x 7 In. 465.00
Fruitwood, Pear Shape, Inlaid Ivory Escutcheon, 19th Century, 7 1/2 In. 2590.00
George III, Apple Shape, Red Stain Traces, Wooden Stem, 4 In. 7475.00
George III, Ivory, Tortoiseshell Mounts, 10 Sides, 1800s, 5 x 6 In. 3450.00
Grain Painted, Floral & Putti Painted Design, Ring Handles, 7 3/4 In. 300.00
Inlay Work Tea On Lid, Cut Glass Jars, Mixing Bowl, Rosewood Veneer, 13 In. 220.00
Iron, Silver Dragon & Fan, Silver Crab Finial, 1883, 6 1/4 In. 6900.00
Lacquered, Divided, 8 1/2 In. 116.00
Lignum Vitae, Apple-Four, 4 In. 825.00
Mahogany, Chippendale, Handle, 1788, 9 In. 193.00
Mahogany, Edge Line Inlay, Brass Bale, England, 8 1/2 In. 93.00
Mahogany, Fitted Interior, Rectangular, Hinged, 6 1/2 x 13 x 6 1/2 In. 110.00
Mahogany, George III, Hinged Lid, Rectangular, 12 x 7 1/2 x 7 In. 330.00
Mahogany, George III, Inlaid, Gilt, Painted Paper Scroll, 1780, 4 3/4 x 5 1/2 In. 1265.00
Mahogany, Inlaid Knight Lid, 13 In. 247.00
Mahogany, Ivory Inlay, Fitted Interior, England, Mid-19th Century, 10 1/4 In. 660.00

Mahogany, Marquetry Musical Instruments, 8 In. 412.50
Mahogany, Oval, 18th Century 475.00
Mahogany, Regency, Parquetry Lid, Early 19th Century, 5 x 8 1/2 In. 275.00
Mahogany, William IV, Sideboard Shape, Hinged Top, c.1840, 9 x 13 x 6 1/2 In. 2590.00
Mahogany, With Glass Mixing Bowl, Faded, 13 1/2 In. 440.00
Mahogany Veneer, Figural, Brass Inlaid Escutcheon, 11 In. 192.50
Mahogany Veneer, Hepplewhite, Inlaid Ivory Escutcheon, 13 3/4 In. 313.00
Mahogany Veneer, Hepplewhite, Shell Inlay, 2 Compartments, 12 In. 247.50
Maple, Inlaid Conch, Hinged Lid, Single Compartment, 1780-1800, 5 x 7 In. 345.00
Oriental, Fuji, Bird & Floral Design, Lacquered, 8 x 11 In. 15.00
Polychrome, French Faience, Rouen, 4 1/4 In. 115.00
Porcelain, Coral & Gilt Flowers, Key Border, Silver Neck, China, 18th Century 550.00
Rosewood, Regency, 9 1/2 x 12 1/2 In. 577.00
Rosewood, Regency, Inlaid, Brass, 12 In. 247.00
Rosewood, Sarcophagus Form, Abalone Floral Inlay, 2 Compartments 330.00
Silver, George II, Pear Form, Ayme Videau, 1744, 4 1/2 In. 660.00
Silver, Monogram, Square, American, 3 1/2 In. 110.00
Sterling Silver, Repousse Floral Festoons, Medallions, Floral Feet 395.00
Tin, English Breakfast Tea, Cylinder Lid, 14 1/2 x 14 x 14 In. 77.00
Tin, Faux Tortoiseshell, 19th Century, 4 1/2 x 4 7/8 In. 220.00
Tin, Gold Bird, Flowers, Black Ground, Japan, 5 1/2 In. 25.00
Tole, Dark Brown Japanning, Floral Design, 5 3/4 In. 165.00
Tole, Red Paint 285.00
Tole, White Band, Floral Design, 5 1/ 2 In. 440.00
Tortoiseshell, 10 Sides, Brass Footed, 4 In. 990.00
Tortoiseshell, 2 Compartments, Ball Feet, 5 1/2 x 7 In. 770.00
Tortoiseshell, Name Plate, Silver Plated Feet, Divided, 5 1/4 In. 742.50
Tortoiseshell, Rectangular, 6 3/4 In. 650.00
Tortoiseshell, Regency, 2 Compartments, c.1820, 5 1/2 x 7 1/2 In. 1430.00
Tortoiseshell, Regency, 2 Lidded Compartments, 1820s, 6 x 6 In. 1840.00
Tortoiseshell, Regency, Bombe, 2 Caddies, Glass Bowl, Loop Handles, 13 In. 5750.00
Tortoiseshell, Regency, Brass Mounted, Ivory Bun Footed, 7 x 12 In. 4888.00
Tortoiseshell, Regency, Corner Columns, 6 1/2 x 7 In. 605.00
Tortoiseshell, Silver Plated Fittings, 2 Compartments, 6 3/4 In. 880.00
Tortoiseshell, Victorian, 19th Century, 6 x 6 1/2 In. 880.00
Tunbridge Ware, Regency, Cube Design, Rectangular, 5 1/2 x 10 In. 1150.00
Vermeil, Pineapple, Green Tinted Leaves, Portugal, 1938, 8 In. 475.00
Victorian, Oxbow Form, Mother-Of-Pearl, Abalone & Tortoiseshell, 5 1/4 In. 2070.00
Walnut, Egyptian King, Brass Mounting, 9 In. 303.00
Walnut, Victorian, 15 In. 500.00
Walnut Inlay, Bracket Footed, 9 In. 154.00

TEA LEAF IRONSTONE dishes are named for their decorations. There was a
superstition that it was lucky if a whole tea leaf unfolded at the bottom of
your cup. This idea was translated into the pattern of dishes known as *tea
leaf.* By 1850, at least twelve English factories were making this pattern, and
by the 1870s, it was a popular pattern in many countries. The tea leaf was
always a luster glaze on early wares, although now some pieces are made
with a brown tea leaf.

Bowl, Apple, Meakin 450.00
Brush Box, Lily-Of-The-Valley, A. Shaw 725.00
Butter Chip 9.00
Butter Chip, Square 40.00
Coffeepot, Luster, Square, Meakin, Marked, 9 1/2 In. 150.00
Cup & Saucer, Handleless, Lily-Of-The-Valley, Tea Leaf In Cup Bottom 135.00
Cup & Saucer, Paneled Teaberry 85.00
Gravy Boat, Handled Tray, Meakin 165.00
Pitcher, East End Pottery, 6 In. 90.00
Pitcher, Hot Water, Meakin 525.00
Plate, Meakin, 9 In. 8.00
Platter, Meakin, 12 In. 40.00
Platter, Meakin, 14 In. 50.00
Platter, Vegetable, Individual, Meakin, 6 x 4 In. 65.00

Punch Bowl, Meakin 600.00
Punch Bowl, Teaberry, Clementson 1700.00
Saucer, Meakin 2.75
Teapot, Chinese Pattern, A. Shaw 425.00
Toothbrush Holder, Interior Holes For Draining, Shaw 200.00
Tureen, Vegetable, Cover, Square 85.00

TECO is the mark used on the art pottery line made by the American Terra Cotta and Ceramic Company of Terra Cotta and Chicago, Illinois. The company was an offshoot of the firm founded by William D. Gates in 1881. The Teco line was first made in 1885 but was not sold commercially until 1902. It continued in production until 1922. Over 500 designs were made in a variety of colors, shapes, and glazes. The company closed in 1930.

$$\mathsf{T}\!\!\begin{array}{c}\mathsf{e}\\\mathsf{c}\\\mathsf{o}\end{array}$$

Bowl, Berry & Swirl Design, No. 196, Signed, 9 1/2 In. 288.50
Bowl, For Cut Flowers, Nested Flower Frog, Leaves At Shoulder, 3 x 9 In. 895.00
Bowl, Gray Matte, Fritz Albert, Impressed Mark, 2 1/2 x 8 In. 350.00
Bowl, Matte Green Glaze, Cross Style Pedestal, 10 1/2 In. 400.00
Bowl, Rolled Rim, Smooth Matte Green Glaze, Stamped, 2 1/2 x 7 In. 400.00
Bowl, Saucer Shape, Cross-Shaped Foot, Green Glaze, 10 1/2 In. 1400.00
Bowl, Scalloped Rim, Smooth Matte Green & Black Glaze, Signed, 8 In. 467.00
Coaster, Cubs, Team Insignia, Oatmeal Ground, Impressed Mark, 4 1/4 In. 137.50
Pitcher, Split Handle, 9 In. 450.00
Vase, 2 Buttressed Handles, Gourd Shape, W.D. Gates, Marked, 5 1/2 In. 680.00
Vase, 2 Full-Length Buttressed Handles, Matte Brown Glaze, 6 1/2 In. 495.00
Vase, 2 Full-Length Buttressed Handles, Gray Glaze, 5 1/2 In. 770.00
Vase, 4 Buttressed Handles, Wide Mouth, Bulbous, J. K. Cady, 10 x 7 1/4 In. 3300.00
Vase, 4 Buttresses Attached At Base & Rim, W.J. Todd, Marked, 12 In. 950.00
Vase, 4 Full-Length Buttresses, Green Glaze, W.D. Gates, Marked, 7 In. 1100.00
Vase, 4 Long Square Buttresses, Green Glaze, Signed, 7 /14 In. 950.00
Vase, 4 Round Handles, Orchid Shape, Green Glaze, 4 1/2 x 3 In. 990.00
Vase, 4-Sided Neck Extending To Bulbous Base, Green, Signed, 16 3/4 In. 1760.00
Vase, Allover Green Veined Glaze, Signed, 3 1/2 x 4 In. 385.00
Vase, Brown Matte Glaze, 3 1/2 In. 385.00
Vase, Bulbous, Undulating Rim, Matte Green Glaze, Stamped, 5 x 4 1/2 In. 325.00
Vase, Dimpled Sides, Squat Globular, 4 1/4 In. 740.00
Vase, Fanned Crystals, Celadon, Rust & Rose, c.1905, 6 In. 750.00
Vase, Gourd-Shaped, Flared Neck, Buttressed Handles, Mossy Green, 7 x 4 In. 715.00
Vase, Light & Soft Green, 5 In. 795.00
Vase, No. 12, Matte Green Glaze 605.00
Vase, No. 61, Gourd Shaped, Matte Yellow Glaze 467.50
Vase, Pompeian Style, 9 1/2 In. 1450.00
Vase, Pompeian, Green, 8 In. 500.00
Vase, Raised & Shaped Neck, Dimpled Body, Marked, 4 1/2 In. 247.50
Vase, Rolled Rim, Gourd Shape, Green Glaze, Marked, 5 1/2 In. 475.00
Vase, Smooth Green Glaze, Egg Shape, F. Albert, Marked, 9 1/2 In. 750.00
Vase, Spherical, No. 52, Matte Green Glaze, Protruding Mouth, 4 1/2 x 4 1/4 In. 412.00
Vase, Square Buttressed Handles On Rim, Green Glaze, Marked, 6 3/4 In. 1400.00
Vase, Squat Base, Long Thin Neck, Matte Green Glaze, Stamped, 5 1/2 In. 400.00
Vase, Stick, Tiger Eye Glaze, 5 1/2 In. 780.00

TEDDY BEARS were named for a President of the United States. The first teddy bear was a cuddly toy said to be inspired by a hunting trip made by Teddy Roosevelt in 1902. Morris and Rose Michtom started selling their stuffed bears as *teddy bears* and the name stayed. The Michtoms founded the Ideal Novelty and Toy Company. The German version of the teddy bear was made about the same time by the Steiff Company. There are many types of teddy bears and all are collected. The old ones are being reproduced. Other bears are listed in the Toy section.

C.L. Marland, Brown Wool, 12 In. 250.00
Gumar, Mohair, Size 10 .... 345.00
Ideal, Mohair, Shoebutton Eyes, Embroidered Nose & Claws, Jointed, 24 In. 1210.00
Ideal, Sam, Hump Back, Gold, Shoebutton Eyes, Straw Stuffed, c.1915, 14 In. 345.00

TEDDY BEAR, Knickerbocker

Knickerbocker, Cinnamon Color, c.1930, 21 In. 265.00
Knickerbocker, Hump, Jointed Mohair, Glass Eyes, 1920s, 27 In. 250.00
Kramer, Mechanical, 1920s, 12 In. 1250.00
Mohair, Gold, Stitched Eyes, 21 In. 302.00
Mohair, Tan, Shoebutton Eyes, 17 In. 1045.00
Mohair, Yellow, Embroidered Nose & Claws, Fully Jointed, 1920s, 19 In. 165.00
Schoenhut, Ball-Jointed Neck, Glass Eyes, Brown 650.00
Sitting, Long Wool, Kidskin Body, Solid, 9 In. 495.00
Steiff, Baby, Gold, Chest Tag, U.S. Zone Tag, Jointed, 3 1/2 In. 900.00
Steiff, Blue Velvet Suit, c.1910 .... 520.00
Steiff, Clown 295.00
Steiff, Curly Mohair, Blond, Shoebutton Eyes, Excelsior Stuffing, 1905, 23 In. 2200.00
Steiff, Gold Plush, Button, 1915, 23 1/2 In. 4025.00
Steiff, Mohair, Blond, Shoebutton Eyes, Embroidered Nose, 1906, 14 In. 1650.00
Steiff, Mohair, Tan, Shoebutton Eyes, Jointed, 12 In. 2055.00
Steiff, Mohair, Yellow, Jointed, Steel Eyes, c.1906, 9 3/4 In. 960.00
Steiff, Mohair, Yellow, Mr. Bear, Shoebutton Eyes, Jointed, 1910, 24 In. 715.00
Steiff, Ophelia, Box, 1980s, 18 In. 175.00
Steiff, Silver Plush, Button, Black Boot Button Eyes, 1910, 9 1/2 In. 805.00
Steiff, Silver, Black Button Eyes, Stitched Nose & Snout, Straw Filled, 12 In. 1430.00
Steiff, Wool, Light Brown, Blue Jacket, Short Pants, c.1910, 13 1/2 In. 518.00
Straw Stuffing, Jointed, Glass Eyes, FAO Schwartz, c.1910, 16 In. 385.00
Wool, Jointed, Pointed Nose, Felt Pads, 17 In. 395.00
Wool, Light Brown, Jointed, Suede Pads, 17 In. 395.00
Wool, Yellow, White Trim, 22 In. 195.00

TELEPHONES are wanted by collectors if the phones are old enough or unusual enough. The first telephone may have been made in Havana, Cuba, in 1849, but it was not patented. The first publicly demonstrated phone was used in Frankfurt, Germany, in 1860. The phone made by Alexander Graham Bell was shown at the Centennial Exhibition in Philadelphia in 1876, but it was not until 1877 that the first private phones were installed. Collectors today want all types of old phones, phone parts, and advertising. Even recent figural phones are popular.

Advertising, 7-Up Spot, Box 55.00
Airplane, Canada 175.00
Alvin Chipmunk 30.00
Booth, Maple, With Phone 1495.00
Booth, Oak, With Phone & Fan 2395.00
Candlestick, Stromberg-Carlson, Rochester, N.Y., Lamp Mounted, 1930s 127.50
Candlestick, Western Electric, Pay Phone, Gray, 1898-1910 .... 720.00
Chicago Telephone Supply, Wall, Beveled Glass Window, 32 x 14 In. 550.00
Crest Gel-Man .... 35.00 to 45.00
Elliot Ness Pay Station, Black Metal, Bakelite Receiver, 1920 .... 600.00
Hand Crank, German, 1930s 90.00
Keebler Elf 96.00
Kellogg, Grade A, 1919 .... 595.00
Kellogg, Oak 155.00
Kellogg, Walnut 235.00
Li'l Sprout, Advertising .... 35.00 to 50.00
Monophone, Phillips Telephone Co., Black & Chrome 75.00
North Electric, Wooden Tool, Fluter, Genivieve, Ripple Pattern, 2 Piece 40.00
Paperweight, Bell Shape, Missouri Kansas Telephone Company, Blue Glass 78.00
Paperweight, Pioneers Of America, Bell Shape, Blue 45.00
Pizza Inn 85.00
Public, Porcelainized Steel Flange, Blue & White, Square, 12 In. 44.00
Sign, Bell System Public Telephone, Porcelain, Round, 7 In. Diam. 200.00
Sign, Bell System, Lollipop, Enameled, 2 Sides 695.00
Sign, Bell Telephone Of Canada, Porcelain, 12 x 17 In. 175.00
Switchboard, Western Electric, Oak Console, 30 Connections 350.00
Wall, Chicago Telephone Supply, Beveled Glass Window, 32 In. Long 500.00
Wall, Kellogg, U.S. Navy, World War II, Oak Case 85.00

Wall, Slanted Writing Surface, Oak 120.00
Westinghouse, Crank, Wall, 20 1/2 In. 250.00

TELEVISION sets are twentieth-century collectibles. Although the first
television transmission took place in England in 1925, collectors find few
sets which pre-date 1946. The first sets had only five channels, but by 1949
the additional VHF channels were included. The first color television set
became available in 1951.

Changer, 1950 .... 20.00
Philco, Floor Model 11.00
Philco, Predicta .... 600.00 to 750.00
Predicta, Danish Modern Console, 1961 .... 2450.00

TEPLITZ refers to art pottery manufactured by a number of companies in the
Teplitz-Turn area of Bohemia during the late nineteenth and early twentieth
centuries. The Amphora Porcelain Works and the Alexandra Works were two
of these companies.

Basket, Cherubs Entangled In Garlands Of Rosettes, Amphora, 11 x 15 In. 795.00
Basket, Embossed Flowers, Oval, Amphora, 5 x 9 1/2 In. 250.00
Bowl, White Blossoms, Hummingbird, Lavender Interior, Signed, 4 1/2 x 7 1/2 In. 250.00
Bust, Female, Pedestal Base, 9 In. 220.00
Charger, Warrior On Horseback, Jeweled Border, Amphora, 12 In. 475.00
Ewer, Bluish Flowers, Salamander Handle, 8 In. 195.00
Ewer, Molded Orchids, Gilt Outlining, Green Spout & Handle, Amphora 225.00
Figurine, Bird Of Prey, Marked, Amphora, 15 In. 825.00
Figurine, Girl, With Dog, Shell Type Ground, Ernst Wahlis, Crown Mark, 1900 .... 750.00
Figurine, Woman, Flowing Hair, Draped, Amphora, Marked, c.1904, 28 In. 2310.00
Humidor, Yellow Flowers, Green, Signed 350.00
Jardiniere, Man, Wagon & Horses, Brown & Beige, Amphora, 10 x 13 In. 975.00
Mug, Warrior Profile 195.00
Pitcher, Gold & Floral, Reticulated Handles 285.00
Planter, Tan, Glazed Interior, 4 Footed 145.00
Vase, Bleeding Hearts, Gold Outline, Fold Handles, Purple & Pink, 13 x 6 In. 350.00
Vase, Bulbous, Looped Handle, Wisteria Blossoms, c.1900, 19 3/8 In. 460.00
Vase, Carved Polychrome Birds, Dead Matte Ground, Marked, 21 1/4 In. 550.00
Vase, Egyptian, Art Deco, 10 In. 420.00
Vase, Figure Of Rooster Attached To Side, Amphora 900.00
Vase, Floral Motif, Raised, Green Matte Ground, Signed, 10 In. 660.00
Vase, Floral, Gold Outlines, 5 1/2 In. 135.00
Vase, Floral, Salamander Handles, Amphora, 16 In. 350.00
Vase, Footed, 3-Dimensional Sitting Woman, Amphora, 24 1/2 In. 3800.00
Vase, Genre Scene, Amphora, 14 In. 400.00
Vase, Gold Spider Web, Reticulated Top & Handle, 20 In. 750.00
Vase, Green Neck, Pink Leaves At Base, 4 Gold Handles, Amphora, Marked, 8 In. ... 225.00
Vase, Incised Birds & Flowers, Blue & Gray, Mottled Ground, Amphora, 13 1/2 In. .. 335.00
Vase, Incised Designs, Condor In Band Of Vines, Amphora, Signed, 1925, 20 In. 1725.00
Vase, Man's Profile, Multicolored, Amphora, 15 In., Pair 900.00
Vase, Pink Leaves & Blueberries, Double Handle, Amphora, Marked, 8 3/4 In. 275.00
Vase, Salamander Handles, Amphora, 16 In. 350.00
Vase, Stylized Tree Form, Gold Ground, Marked, 10 1/4 In. 280.00
Vase, Symbolist, Woman Rising Out Of Water, Blue, Green, Cream, c.1900, 12 In. ... 800.00
Vase, Waist Of Mother, Holding Nude Baby, White Scarf, 7 In. 225.00
Vase, White Enameled Flowers & Butterflies, Cobalt Blue, Wahliss, 15 In. 585.00
Vase, Woman's Head, Long Hair, Holding Enameled Flowers, Marked, 6 3/4 In. 375.00
Vase, Woman's Profile, Background Of Trees & Foliage, Amphora 900.00
Vessel, 2 Spouts, Stylized Floral, Cream Ground, Amphora, 7 1/2 In. 540.00

TERRA-COTTA is a special type of pottery. It ranges from pale orange to dark
reddish-brown in color. The color comes from the clay, which is fired but not
always glazed in the finished piece.

Bust, Abraham Lincoln, Black Velvet Field, Pine Frame, 12 x 9 1/2 In. 70.00
Bust, Caesar Augustus, Allegorical Scenes On Mantle, 23 In. 3450.00
Bust, Medusa, A. Blashe, c.1900 .... 9500.00

Bust, Young Girl, Turned Walnut Socle, 20 In. 690.00
Figurine, Cherub, Reclining, With Flower Basket, Giltwood Base, France, 12 In. 2090.00
Figurine, Chinese Maiden, Holding Dove, France, 19th Century, 14 3/4 In., Pair 1495.00
Figurine, Polo Player, Polychrome Glaze, Wiener Werkstatte, 7 1/4 In. 745.00
Fruit Bowl, Polychrome Glaze, 2 Curved Handles, Wiener Werkstatte, 8 3/4 In. 1400.00
Humidor, Cover, Greek Black Figure Design, England, 4 3/4 In. 55.00
Lamp, Base, Abstract Design, Wiener Werkstatte, 1928, 14 1/4 In. 1955.00
Lion's Head, 1860, 10 In. 2800.00
Plaque, Benjamin Franklin, Marked Date 1777, 4 1/2 In. 410.00
Plaque, Musterschutz, Hand Painted, Adolph Schreyer, 19th Century, 12 In. 375.00
Teapot, Imari Decoration, England, 6 In. 45.00
Umbrella Stand, Gilded Raised Dragons, 24 In. 12.00
Urn, Rim Loop Handles, Baluster Form, Brown Glaze, 30 In., Pair 495.00
Vase, Pleated Corners, Polychrome Glaze, Wiener Werkstatte, 6 5/8 In. 1400.00

TEXTILES listed here include many types of printed fabrics and table and
household linens. Some other textiles will be found under Clothing, Coverlet,
Rug, Quilt, etc.

Altar Cloth, Figures Of Saints, Gilt Braid & Trim, Embroidered, Velvet, 31 x 25 In. . 410.00
Banner, American, 18 Stars, Printed & Sewn, 13 x 90 In. 85.00
Banner, American, 92 Stars, Printed, 29 1/2 x 136 In. 140.00
Banner, Band, Military, Painted, Sienna & Gilt, Silk, Frame, 29 x 23 In. 275.00
Banner, Harvard University, Red Felt, 1910, 22 x 43 In. 125.00
Bed Tick, Blue & White Cotton Check, 2 Sides, Buttons, Pennsylvania, 68 x 45 In. .. 175.00
Bed Tick, Cotton, Blue & White Plaid, Tie Closure, Pennsylvania, 31 x 30 In. 75.00
Bedspread, Chenille, Peacock, Twin Size 175.00
Bedspread, Chenille, Twin Peacocks, Full Size 175.00
Bedspread, Crewel Work, Floral & Urn Design, Multicolored, 92 x 87 In. 60.00
Bedspread, Crocheted, Snow Flake Design, Popcorn, Knotted Fringe, 90 x 100 In. ... 185.00
Bedspread, Crocheted, Star & Popcorn, Twin Size 295.00
Bedspread, Crocheted, White, Dark Green, 3 In. Fringe, 80 x 100 In. 200.00
Bedspread, Embroidered Bird & Flowers, Red, 1920, Double 95.00
Bedspread, Homespun, White Woven Design, 69 x 99 In. 215.00
Blanket, Crocheted, Pastel Petal Strips, Acrylic, 42 x 42 In. 9.00
Blanket, Hudson Bay, Red, Yellow, Green, Navy, 4 Points, 68 x 86 In. .... 110.00 to 185.00
Blanket, Red & Blue, TWA 60.00
Blanket, Wool, Blue & White, Hand Sewn Hems, 62 x 80 In., 1 Piece 115.00
Blanket, Wool, Striped Homespun, Red, Blue, Brown, 19th Century, 91 x 68 In. 325.00
Cover, Mattress, Homespun Linen, Linen Back, 51 x 64 In. 220.00
Curtain, Gold Metallic Greek Key Border, Velvet, 96 x 118 In. 1725.00
Doily, Battenburg Lace, 17 x 17 In. 35.00
Doormat, 260 Hearts 295.00
Drapes, Sienna Italian Renaissance, Gray, Cotton, Fortuny, 100 x 137 In., Pair 1870.00
Flag, American, 12 Stars, 13 Stripes, Bon Homme Richard, 36 x 60 In. 352.00
Flag, American, 14 Stars, Linen, Wool, Homemade, 33 1/2 x 44 In. 1870.00
Flag, American, 37 Stars, 19th Century, 15 x 9 In. 264.00
Flag, American, 38 Stars, Hand & Machine Stitching, 41 x 70 In. 385.00
Flag, American, 44 Stars, 71 x 105 In. 120.00
Flag, American, 45 Stars, 1896-1907, 60 x 96 In. 65.00
Flag, American, 45 Stars, 5 Uncut, Printed Muslin, 2 x 3 Ft. 200.00
Flag, American, 46 Stars, 60 x 96 In. 85.00
Flag, American, 46 Stars, 98 x 128 In. 100.00
Flag, American, 48 Stars, 1940s, 3 3/4 x 5 In. 15.00
Flag, American, 48 Stars, Silk, 57 x 34 In. 25.00
Flag, American, 49 Stars, Cotton, 24 x 36 In. 35.00
Flag, Texas, Dura-Lite, 5 x 8 Ft. 20.00
Handkerchief, Imperial Monogram Of Empress Marie Feodorovna, Frame 920.00
Hanging, Peacock & Dragon, Blue, Teal, Cream, William Morris, 96 x 60 In. 1438.00
Hanging, Tent, Caucasian, Geometric & Figural Border, c.1860, 71 In. x 52 In. 5500.00
Mat, Braided, Green & Black, Crocheted Border, Round, 13 In. 60.00
Mat, Braided, Pink, Brown & Rust, Round, 16 In. 60.00
Napkin, Cocktail, Linen, Blue Embroidered Rooster In Corner, 7 In., 5 Piece 5.00
Obi, Dragon Designs, Silk Brocade 85.00

Panel, Apotheosis Of Franklin, Roller Print, Brown On White, Frame, 58 x 27 In. 126.00
Panel, Death Of Gen.Washington, Printed Scene, Cotton, Gilt Frame, 27 x 31 In. 275.00
Panel, Oriental Equestrian Soldiers, In Battle, Matted, Frame, 17 x 13 In., Pair 198.00
Panel, Print, E. Pluribus Unum, Les Presidents Des Etats-Unis, Frame, 26 x 28 In. ... 467.00
Panel, Roller Print, Portraits Of Franklin Pierce, Eagles, Framed, 10 1/2 In. 412.50
Panel, Roller Print, William Henry Harrison, Framed, 26 1/2 x 28 1/4 In. 660.00
Panel, Silk, Equestrian Figure, Hunting Lion, Oriental, Frame, 40 x 16 In. 38.50
Panel, Washington Medallion, Eagle, Ship Border, Frame, 25 x 29 In. 4510.00
Picture, Liberty & Unity Forever, Golden Eagle, 42-Star Flag, Needlework 82.50
Pillow, Aubusson Tapestry Cover, Urn & Bouquets, Square, 22 In., Pair 5750.00
Pillowcase, Calico, Button Closure, Penna. German, 19th Century, Pair 220.00
Ribbon, Mourning, Silk, Andrew Jackson's Death In 1847, 8 1/8 x 3 In. 325.00
Runner, Crochet, Ecru Fine Thread, 4-In. Rosettes, 20 x 40 In. 15.00
Scarf, Dresser, Raised Needlework, Victorian 30.00
Tablecloth, Battenburg, Vine & Grape, Round, 49 In. 145.00
Tablecloth, Blue & White Cotton Homespun, 78 x 58 In. 214.50
Tablecloth, Cotton Brocade, Stylized Flowers, 49 x 68 In. 150.00
Tablecloth, Crochet, White, Large Roses, Windowpane, Scalloped, 54 x 50 In. 40.00
Tablecloth, Cutout & Embroidered, Florals, Ivory & Brown, 18 Napkins, 76 In. 135.00
Tablecloth, Damask, Ireland, 96 x 144 In. 150.00
Tablecloth, Light & Dark Blue Cross Stitched, Pineapple Border, 56 x 80 In. 65.00
Tablecloth, Linen, Ecru, Pulled Thread Hem, Cutwork, Napkins, 80 x 60 In. 65.00
Tablecloth, Luncheon, Embroidered Butterflies, 4 Napkins 18.00
Tablecloth, Palm Trees, Cacti, Sombreros, Square, 34 In. 14.00
Tablecloth, Pointe Venice, 12 Napkins, 66 x 144 In. 450.00
Tablecloth, Quaker Lace, 54 x 72 In. 80.00
Tablecloth, Wool, Embroidered, Folk Art Scenes, England, 1831, 90 x 64 In. 2750.00
Tapestry, Country Scene, 18th Century Figures, Chateau, 25 x 76 In. 45.00
Tapestry, Forest Scene, Verdure, Flemish, 18th Century, 102 x 150 In. 7150.00
Tea Cozy, Flower Design, Battenburg Lace, 16 x 12 In. 72.00
Tea Cozy, Linen, White Satin Stitch Emblem, Florals, Scalloped, Kapok Insert 45.00
Throw, Paisley, Wool, Fringed, Square, 68 In. 375.00
Towel, Show, Cross-Stitch Embroidery, Stars, Chairs, Lea Sartman, 1834, 51 In. 100.00
Towel, Show, Embroidered Floral, Homespun Linen, 18 x 27 1/2 In. 50.00
Towel, Show, Peacocks & Flowers, Red & Blue, Dated 1833 .... 375.00
Towel, Show, Tree Of Life Openwork, Dated 1838 .... 200.00
Towel, Tea, Raggedy Ann, Calendar, 1975 .... 5.00
Wall Hanging, Stylized Foliate, Machine-Woven, Continental, 108 x 60 In. 517.00

THERMOMETER is a name that comes from the Greek word for heat. The thermometer was invented in 1731 to measure the temperature of either water or air. All kinds of thermometers are collected, but those with advertising messages are the most popular.

1st Prize Meat Products, Round, 12 In. 95.00
7-Up, Porcelain, 1950s 75.00
7-Up, Round, 1960, 12 In. .... 100.00 to 120.00
Allis Chalmers, Tractors, Tin 45.00
Anthracite, Coal, Porcelain, 1930s 115.00
Arbuckles' Coffee, Summer & Winter, Tin Lithographed, 19 In. 132.00
Baby's Bath, Glass, Hand Painted Flowers, Lithographed Box, 1919 .... 33.00
Battery, Red Seal, 1915 .... 135.00
Bireley's, Tin 95.00
Borden, Elsie, Round, 12 In. 100.00
California Milk Advisory Board, Storage, Plastic, 0 To 80 Degrees 15.00
Camel, Picture Of Pack Of Cigarettes 60.00
Carey Salt, Tin, 20 In. 26.50
Cigar, 1950s, 30 In. 135.00
Clinchfield Railroad, Tin, Large 10.00
Clown Cigarettes, Lithographed Paper Dial, Black & Yellow, White, 9 In. 60.00
Columbus Dispatch, Ohio's Greatest Home Daily, Porcelain, 7 x 27 In. 220.00
Country Kitchen White Bread, Round, 12 In. 110.00
Dairy, Glass, Paper Insert, 1893 Patent, Freezing To 150 Degrees 8.00
Desk, Christmas Club, New York, Egyptian Revival, Cast Metal, 6 3/8 In. 50.00

Doan's Pills, Wooden Figure, Is Your Back Bad Today?, 20 In. 185.00
Dr Pepper, 1930s 140.00
Dr Pepper, 1960s, Small 95.00
Dr Pepper, Drink A Bite To Eat, Tin Litho, 1936, 13 In. 825.00
Dr Pepper, Hot Or Cold, Tin, 16 In. .... 75.00 to 100.00
Dr Pepper, Tin Lithograph, White & Black, Yellow Ground, 1939, 17 1/4 In. 440.00
Dr Well 20.00
Dr. Scholl's, Metal, 1960s, 37 In. 38.95
Ex-Lax, Chocolate Laxative, Porcelainized Steel, Black Letters, 36 In. 132.00
Five Roses Flour, Porcelain, 39 In. 200.00
Fleur-De-Lis Flour, Porcelain, 1930s 115.00
Folger's Coffee, Painted Tin Dial, Red & Black, White Ground, 9 In. 220.00
Frostie, Small 50.00
Gibson Appliance, Round, 12 In. 95.00
Gilbey's Gin, Brass Bound, Die Cut Bottle, Round, 9 In. 55.00
Have You Seen The New Studebaker, Stenciled Wood, Checkered, 11 3/4 In. 220.00
Hires Root Beer, Bottle Shape, 1960s, 29 In. .... 125.00 to 135.00
Indiana Furniture Co. & Funeral Service, Outdoor Scene, 1920s 26.00
Joan Of Arc, Red Kidney Beans, Painted Stenciled Wood, 15 In. 38.00
Keen Kutter, Round 180.00
Keep Regular With Ex-Lax, Porcelain, 8 x 36 x 1 1/4 In. 100.00
Ken-L-Ration, Can Shape, Dog, 4 Colors 100.00
Kist, Bottle & Girls Face, 5 x 16 In. 20.00
Land O' Lakes Butter, Steel, 27 In. 65.00
Lowey's Chocolates, Porcelain 450.00
Mail Pouch, Porcelain, 39 In. 85.00
Mail Pouch Chewing Tobacco, Cobalt Blue, 6 Ft. 695.00
Mail Pouch Tobacco, 36 In. 170.00
Mail Pouch Tobacco, Porcelain, 40 In. 250.00
Mason's Root Beer, Bottle Picture 125.00
Mission Orange 5.00
Mobil Oil 660.00
Nesbitts, Little Professor, Don't Say Orange, Say Nesbitts, 27 In. 125.00
Nesbitts Orange, 1939 Bottle, 27 In. 85.00
Noll's Ice Cream & Bakery, Wooden, 12 In. 65.00
Northrup, King & Co., Clover & Alfalfa Seed, Porcelainized Steel, 27 In. 88.00
Oakhurst Milk, Square, 12 In. 40.00
Obelisk Form, Malachite & Floral Design, Pietra Dura, 15 In. 805.00
Old Crow, Tin 40.00
Oliva Olive Oil, Pictures Can, 19 x 9 1/2 In. 65.00
Orange Crush, 19 x 6 In. 75.00
Orange Crush, Bottle Shape 110.00
Orange Crush, Orange, White & Turquoise, 6 x 16 In. 40.00
Orange Crush, Round 100.00
Orange Crush, Tin, 19 x 6 In. 80.00
Oxo, Porcelain 225.00
Peter Schuyler, Cigar Shape 125.00
Prestone Anti-Freeze, Porcelain, 1940s .... 75.00 to 100.00
Ramon's Pills, Real Laxative For Adults, Wood, Stenciled, 21 In. 143.00
Red Crown Gasoline 400.00
Red Seal, Guarantee Protects You, Porcelainized Steel, 27 In. 66.00
Royal Crown Cola, 1947, 26 x 10 In. 85.00
Royal Crown Cola, Red & White, 1961, 24 In. 38.00
Salem Cigarettes 20.00
Sauer's, Wooden, c.1920, 4 x 8 In. 575.00
Squirt, Tin 40.00
Sunoco Oil 32.00
Texaco, Plastic, 1950s, 7 In. 45.00
Tile, Bambi, Walt Disney Productions 24.00
Waterman's Pen, Die Cut Tin, 19 1/2 x 3 3/4 In. .... 700.00 to 750.00
Wells Fargo & Co. Express, Tin, Wall, Large 12.00
Winston Cigarettes Pack, Embossed 55.00
Yellow Cab, Buick & Chrysler Sedans, Painted Stenciled Wood, 15 In. 264.00

TIFFANY is a name that appears on items made by Louis Comfort Tiffany, the American glass designer who worked from about 1879 to 1933. His work included iridescent glass, Art Nouveau styles of design, and original contemporary styles. He was also noted for stained glass windows, unusual lamps, bronze work, pottery, and silver. Other types of Tiffany are listed under Tiffany Glass, Tiffany Pottery, or Tiffany Silver. The famous Tiffany lamps are listed in this section. Tiffany jewelry is listed in the jewelry and wristwatch categories. Reproductions of some types of Tiffany are being made.

Louis C. Tiffany

Ashtray, Bronze, Gold Dore, Raised Line Design, 2 Cigarette Rests, 4 x 3 In.	135.00
Ashtray, Bronze, Griffin With Canister, Liner, Brown & Green Patina, 31 In.	2990.00
Ashtray, Bronze, Oval, Raised Ribs, 4 x 2 1/2 In.	95.00
Ashtray, Bronze, Slender Stand, Circular Dish, Liner, 28 1/4 In.	1265.00
Ashtray-Match Safe, Zodiac, Octagonal Tray, 4 1/2 x 4 In.	250.00
Basket, Bronze, Enameled, Shaped Handle, Pedestal, 8 x 3 1/2 In.	1500.00
Bill File, Zodiac, Bronze, Octagon Shaped Base, 7 3/4 In.	500.00
Blotter, Hand, Abalone, Bronze, Gold Dore, Knob Handle, Signed, 6 x 2 3/4 In.	300.00
Blotter, Hand, Adam, 5 x 3 In.	150.00
Blotter, Hand, Chinese, Knob Handle, 3 x 5 3/4 In.	200.00
Blotter, Hand, Ninth Century, Bronze, Jeweled, Knob Handle, 5 3/4 x 3 In.	350.00
Blotter, Rocker, Adam, Bronze	195.00
Blotter Ends, Grapevine, Bronze, 19 x 2 In., Pair	350.00
Blotter Ends, Grapevine, Green Patina, Signed, 4 Piece	150.00
Blotter Ends, Pine Needle, 19 x 2 In., Pair	350.00
Blotter Ends, Pine Needle, 5 1/2 x 5 1/2 x 8 In., 4 Piece	350.00
Blotter Ends, Zodiac, 3 3/4 x 3 3/4 In., 4 Piece	200.00
Blotter Ends, Zodiac, Bronze, 3 3/4 x 3 3/4 x 5 In., 4 Piece	200.00
Book Rack, Grapevine, Beaded Border, 2 Sections, Bronze & Glass, Signed, 9 1/2 In .	1800.00
Bookends, Arch Form, 5 1/4 In.	176.00
Bookends, Bookmark, Bronze, Gold Dore, 4 3/4 x 6 In.	750.00
Bookends, Bookmark, Bronze, Trees In 14K Gold Plate, Signed, 6 In.	750.00
Bookends, Bookmark, Gilt Bronze, No. 1056, 6 In.	550.00
Bookends, Buddha, Gilt Bronze, Coppery Patina, No. 1025, 6 In.	360.00
Bookends, Line Design, Curved Scroll Pattern, Bronze, Signed, 4 1/2 In.	450.00
Bookends, Ninth Century, Bronze, Jeweled, 14K Gold Plate, 4 1/2 x 6 In.	900.00
Bookends, Zodiac, Bronze	395.00
Bowl, Centerpiece, Marine Design, Sailboat, Bronze, Signed	225.00
Bowl, Flower, Glass Design Of Lily Pads, 2 Tiers, Favrile, Signed	3500.00
Box, Card, Pine Needle, Green Slag Glass, 2 Compartments, Hinged Lid, 3 x 5 In.	800.00
Box, Enameled Star, Hinged Cover, Ball Footed, Bronze, 6 x 3 3/4 x 2 In.	650.00
Box, Favrile, Hexagonal, Blue, Low Relief Crackle, Gilt Bronze Edges, 5 7/8 In.	920.00
Box, Glove, Grapevine, Green Slag Glass, Cover, Bronze, 13 x 4 x 3 In.	2700.00
Box, Glove, Hinged Cover, Beaded Border, Bronze Openwork, Signed	2530.00
Box, Grapevine, Amber Slag Glass, Ball Footed, Bronze, 5 1/2 x 3 1/2 x 2 In.	500.00
Box, Grapevine, Green Slag Glass, Etched Metal, 3 1/4 x 6 3/4 x 4 In.	440.00
Box, Hinged Cover, Green Enameled Geometric, Orange Accents, 2 3/4 x 1 3/4 In.	450.00
Box, Jewel, Abalone, Key	1100.00
Box, Jewel, Grapevine, Amber Slag Glass, Hinged Lid, Bronze, 6 1/2 x 4 x 3 In.	1200.00
Box, Pine Needle, Amber Slag Glass, Gold Dore, Bronze, 4 x 3 x 1 1/2 In.	400.00
Box, Pine Needle, Gold Dore, Bronze, Square, 8 x 2 1/2 In.	1200.00
Box, Pine Needle, Paneled, 6 In.	350.00
Box, Stamp, Graduate, Bronze, 4 x 2 x 1 1/4 In.	125.00
Box, Stamp, Pine Needle, Gold Dore, Amber Slag, 3-Section Tray, Bronze, 4 x 2 In. .	550.00
Box, Stamp, Venetian, Gold Dore, Bronze, 4 x 2 x 1 3/4 In.	400.00
Box, Stamp, Zodiac, 3-Section Tray, Bronze, 3 3/4 x 2 1/4 x 1 In.	300.00
Box, Twine, Grapevine, Green Slag Glass, Bronze, 4 x 3 1/4 In.	1500.00
Buckle, Enamel On Bronze, Foliate Design, Impressed Ovals, EL 265, 3 1/4 In.	1870.00
Candelabrum, Bronze, 2-Light, Green Glass, Center Candle Snuff, Signed, 15 In.	8625.00
Candelabrum, Bronze, 3-Light, Brown-Green, Bobeches, Snuffer, 14 1/4 In.	4600.00
Candelabrum, Bronze, 4-Light, 2 Candle Cups Each Side, Stick Body, 15 x 14 In.	2200.00
Candelabrum, Bronze, 4-Light, Favrile Green Glass, Lotus, 13 In.	2587.00
Candelabrum, Bronze, 6-Light, Quezal Shades, Pulled Feathers, 15 7/8 In.	4600.00

Candelabrum, Bronze, 6-Light, Snuffer In Stem, 21 In. 9775.00
Candelabrum, Bronze, 14-Light, 2 Adjustable Arms, Signed, 19 1/2 In. 330.00
Candle Lamp, Ruffled Quilted Shade, Swirl Rib Base, Gorham Riser, 13 1/2 In. 1400.00
Candleholder, Bronz, Hook For Snuffer, Fleur-De-Lis Base, 8 7/8 In. 1380.00
Candlestick, 2-Light, Art Nouveau, Green Glass Into Bronze, Signed, 13 In. 1540.00
Candlestick, 2-Light, Gold Dore, Oval Base, Bronze, 6 x 9 1/2 In., Pair 2000.00
Candlestick, 4 Reeded Legs, Paw Feet, Bronze, 11 1/4 In., Pair 3738.00
Candlestick, Bronze Standard & Foot, Green Favrile, No. D383, 17 1/2 In., Pair 1600.00
Candlestick, Bronze, C-Scroll Handle, Ring Base, Gimbal, 6 1/2 In. 1312.00
Candlestick, Bronze, Double Stem, Detachable Bobeches, Signed, 9 1/2 In. 920.00
Candlestick, Bronze, Favrile, Green Glass, Reticulated, 19 3/4 In., Pair 3163.00
Candlestick, Bronze, Favrile, Reticulated, Green Glass, Queen Anne's Lace, 20 In. .. 5750.00
Candlestick, Bronze, Gold Does, Stick, 17 In., Pair 2100.00
Candlestick, Bronze, Gold Dore, Stick Body, 6 Leaf Arms, Bobeche, 10 In., Pair 2500.00
Candlestick, Bronze, Green Patina, Signed, 12 1/4 In., Pair 1265.00
Candlestick, Bronze, Griffin & Turtle, 7 1/2 In., Pair.. 1665.00
Candlestick, Bronze, Round Platform, Stick Body, 17 x 5 3/4 In. 2100.00
Candlestick, Bronze, Stick, 4-Footed, Blown Green Glass, 13 In. 2200.00
Candlestick, Bronze, Tripod Base, Twisted Vine, Green Glass, Bobeche, 13 1/4 In. .. 4140.00
Candlestick, Bronze, Urn Shape Socket, Paw Feet, No. 1301, 11 3/8 In., Pr. 1095.00
Candlestick, Bronze, Wild Carrot, Champagne, Favrile, Amber Glass, 19 3/4 In. 7188.00
Candlestick, Striated Feather, Bronze Base, Signed, 8 1/2 In. 1320.00
Candlestick, Wisteria, Pastel, Signed, 3 1/2 In., Pair 1250.00
Centerpiece, Bronze, Enameled, Gold Dore, Floral Handles, 10 In. 2000.00
Chamberstick, Bronze, Blown Green Glass, Fleur-De-Lis, 2 Arms, 9 In. 2000.00
Chamberstick, Bronze, Purple Enameled, Loop Handle, 4 x 3 1/2 In., Pair 1500.00
Chandelier, Bronze, 7 Sockets, Shade Supports, Chain Connectors, 29 x 22 In. 1100.00
Chandelier, Bronze, Inverted Domical Geometric Shade, Favrile, 16 3/8 In. 2587.00
Chandelier, Gold Design, Glass Finial, Bronze Mount, 3 Swan Arms, 16 1/4 In. 5520.00
Chandelier, Moorish Style, 4 Arms, Hanging Beads, Iridescent Prisms, 22 In. 5520.00
Clock, Art Deco, Repeating, Inlay At Base 1210.00
Clock, Desk, Bronze, Gold Dore, Platform Base, Large 2250.00
Clock, Grapevine, Carriage, Favrile, Bronze, Green, Opalescent, 1899-1918, 6 1/8 In. 2185.00
Clock, Venetian, Gilt Bronze, No. 1679, 4 /14 x 3 3/4 x 3 In. 715.00
Clock, Venetian, Gold Dore, Sculptured Minds Around, 4 1/2 x 2 1/4 x 5 1/2 In. 1500.00
Clock, Zodiac, Bronze, Gold Dore, 4 x 4 1/2 In. 1500.00
Coaster, Openwork Floral, Cut Glass Hobstar, 7 1/2 In. 550.00
Desk Set, Abalone, Gilt Bronze, 9 Piece 1090.00
Desk Set, American Indian, Gilt Bronze, Signed, 1909-1918, 8 Piece 1725.00
Desk Set, Bookmark, Bronze, 5 Piece 1095.00
Desk Set, Bookmark, Gilt Bronze, Signed, 13 Piece 5280.00
Desk Set, Enameled, Blue-Green, 7 Piece 3080.00
Desk Set, Grapevine, Green & White Striated Glass, 3 Piece 1725.00
Desk Set, Heraldic, Enameled Bronze, Silvered, 11 Piece 2300.00
Desk Set, Pine Needle, Bronze & Glass, 4 Piece 2200.00
Desk Set, Venetian, Gilt Bronze, Signed, 18 Piece 3850.00
Desk Set, Zodiac, Bronze, 7 Piece 1150.00
Figurine, Indian, Action Pose, Tomahawk & Knife In Hand, Bronze, 7 In. 750.00
Figurine, Lion, Brown Patina, Bronze, Signed, 4 3/4 In. 775.00
Frame, Abalone Discs Set In Floral Design, Bronze, Signed, 10 1/4 x 7 1/2 In. 2000.00
Frame, Adam, Bronze, Wreath & Sunburst Design, Beading, 9 1/2 x 6 1/2 In. 950.00
Frame, Calendar, Abalone Discs, Bronze, 6 x 3 1/4 In. 675.00
Frame, Calendar, Abalone, Bronze, Gold Dore, 6 1/2 x 6 In. 650.00
Frame, Chinese, Bronze, Brown Patina, Signed, 8 3/4 In. 1150.00
Frame, Chinese, Easel Style, Bronze, 6 3/4 x 8 3/4 In. 950.00
Frame, Gilt Bronze, Floral Border, No. 1611, 11 7/8 x 9 3/4 In. 690.00
Frame, Gilt Bronze, Meandering Flowers, Flower In Urn, 11 3/4 In. 3163.00
Frame, Grapevine, Beaded Border, Silvered Openwork, Signed, 10 In. 2200.00
Frame, Grapevine, Bronze, Glass, Easel, 9 3/4 x 11 1/2 In. 2800.00
Frame, Grapevine, Bronze, Green Slag Glass, 2-In. Border, 12 x 14 In. 3200.00
Frame, Grapevine, Etched Metal, Amber Slag Glass, 10 x 8 In. 770.00
Frame, Grapevine, Favrile, Bronze Openwork, 9 1/2 In. 1840.00
Frame, Grapevine, No. 9, 7 1/4 x 8 1/4 In. 770.00

Frame, Ninth Century, Bronze, Jeweled, Gold Dore, 8 x 6 1/2 In. 1800.00
Frame, Pine Needle, 18 1/2 x 15 1/4 In. 2310.00
Frame, Pine Needle, Beaded Border, Amber Glass, Bronze, Signed, 14 1/4 In. 2420.00
Frame, Pine Needle, Beaded Border, Bronze Openwork, Signed, 12 In. 3910.00
Frame, Pine Needle, Bronze, Amber Slag Glass, Easel Type, 9 3/4 x 12 In. 2500.00
Frame, Pine Needle, Favrile, Bronze Openwork, 10 In. 1380.00
Frame, Reticulated Bronze, Vintage Design, Verdigris Finish, Folding, 8 x 9 1/2 In. .. 1265.00
Frame, Spanish, Seahorse Each Side, Bronze, Gold Dore, 8 1/2 x 11 3/4 In. 1800.00
Frame, Spring Flower, Etched Metal, Glass, 12 1/2 x 14 1/2 In. 2310.00
Frame, Venetian, Gilt Bronze, Signed, 11 3/4 x 9 In. 1035.00
Frame, Venetian, Rectangular, Gilt Bronze, Signed, 11 3/4 In. 1540.00
Frame, Zodiac, Bronze, 8 x 7 In. 850.00
Globe, Hanging, Gold Iridescent Feather & Swirl, 3 Chains, 13 In. 2800.00
Globe, Hanging, Gold Iridescent, Diamond Quilted, Chain, 12 In. 1800.00
Handle, Parasol, Art Nouveau, Tortoise Shell & Enamel, Signed 8050.00
Holder, Note Pad, Pine Needle, Bronze, Green Slag Glass, 7 1/2 x 5 In. 450.00
Humidor, Pine Needle, Removable Liner, Cover, Bronze, Signed 2000.00
Inkwell, Abalone, Curve & Leaf Around, Hinged Cover, Bronze, Octagonal, 3 1/2 In. ... 650.00
Inkwell, Adam, Bronze, Gold Dore, Hinged Cover, Oval, 4 x 3 x 2 1/2 In. 350.00
Inkwell, Art Nouveau, Bronze, Gold Dore, Raised Swirls, 2 1/2 x 8 x 6 In. 1200.00
Inkwell, Bronze, Glass Blown In Rectangular Opening, Signed, 3 1/2 In. 2000.00
Inkwell, Bronze, Green Glass, Hinged Top, Signed, 4 In. 1093.00
Inkwell, Butterflies In Flight, Bronze, Orange Iridescent Well, 3 x 5 In. 4887.00
Inkwell, Chinese, Bronze, Octagon Shape, Tapered Sides, Hinged Lid, 5 x 4 In. 550.00
Inkwell, Chinese, Geometric Scrolls, Bronze, 4 x 5 1/2 In. 275.00
Inkwell, Chinese, Gold Roe, Line & Curved Design, Insert, Signed, 5-In.Base 550.00
Inkwell, Dog Chained To Post, Figural, Bronze, c.1875, 5 1/4 In. 920.00
Inkwell, Grapevine, Double, Green Slag Glass, Bronze, Ball Footed, 5 1/2 x 3 x 3 In. 2000.00
Inkwell, Green, Rectangular Openings, Bronze Hinged Cover, Signed, 7 In. 2000.00
Inkwell, Nautical, Hinged Seashell Cover, Bronze, 5 1/4 x 3 1/2 In. 1200.00
Inkwell, Ninth Century, Bronze, Jeweled, Dome Hinged Cover, 14K Gold Plate, 4 In. 750.00
Inkwell, Nude Men Pulling Chest, Gilt Bronze, Signed, 11 In. .... 4200.00 to 4600.00
Inkwell, Pine Needle, Bronze, Green Slag Glass, Round, 7 In. 1500.00
Inkwell, Pine Needle, Green Slag Glass, Bronze, Ball Feet, Signed, 4 x 3 In. 400.00
Inkwell, Spanish, Gold Dore, Brass Knob Cover, 4 1/2 x 6 In. 1200.00
Inkwell, Spanish, Hinged Knob Cover, Gold Dore, 4 1/2 x 6 In. 1200.00
Inkwell, Turtleback Medallion, Gold Favrile, Gilt Bronze, 3 Legs, Gold Jewels, 4 In. 1870.00
Inkwell, Venetian, Bronze, Gold Dore, Octagonal, Glass Insert, 3 x 2 1/2 In. 550.00
Inkwell, Venetian, Octagon, Sculptured Minks, Glass Insert, Hinged Lid, 3 In. 550.00
Inkwell, Zodiac, Hinged Cover, Bronze, Hexagonal, 6 1/2 x 4 In. 550.00
Inkwell, Zodiac, Hinged Cover, With 10-Section Tray, Bronze, Gold Dore, 7 x 8 In. .. 1800.00
Inkwell & Letter Rack, Grapevine, Bronze 1500.00
Jar, Chinese Gold Iridescent, Sterling Silver Lid & Handle, 4 x 6 1/2 In. 750.00
Jar, Cover, Intaglio Cut Top Knob, Favrile, 8 In. 1500.00
Jar, Lid, Gold Iridescent, Floral Festoons, Silver Ring, Swing Handle, 5 1/2 In. 546.00
Lamp, 3-Light, Bronze, Favrile, Iridescent Green & Gold Pulled Feather, 16 In. 5463.00
Lamp, 3-Light, Bronze, Lily Form Shade, Favrile, 13 3/4 In. 2375.00
Lamp, 3-Light, Gilt Bronze, Favrile, Amber Lily Form Shade, 13 In. .... 2300.00 to 4300.00
Lamp, 3-Light, Wintergreen Feathering, Bronze, 15 3/4 In. 3738.00
Lamp, 4-Light, Leaves On Base, Green Jewels On 5 Ball Feet, 1918, 13 In. 1380.00
Lamp, 7-Light, Lily, Bronze, Favrile, Lime Green Feathered Shade, 21 1/4 In. 6325.00
Lamp, Abalone, Panel Shade, Favrile Fabrique Glass, 8-Sided Platform, 12 In. 8500.00
Lamp, Acorn, Art Nouveau Bronze Base, Bronze Collar Shade, 16 In. 6995.00
Lamp, Acorn, Bronze, Favrile, Butterscotch & White Opalescent Shade, 23 In. 6325.00
Lamp, Acorn, Domed Shade, Band Of Acorns, Bronze, Signed, 22 In. 7475.00
Lamp, Acorn, Gilt Bronze, Favrile, Opalescent Yellow Glass, 22 1/2 In. 8050.00
Lamp, Acorn, Leaded Green Glass Shade, Yellow Acorns Band, Bronze, 58 1/2 In. 7700.00
Lamp, Acorn, Yellow & White, Leaded Glass, Bronze Tortoiseshell Base, 23 In. 6670.00
Lamp, Adam, Green Octagon Shaped Shade, Gold Dore, 17 In. 5000.00
Lamp, Aladdin, Conical Shade, Rows Of Dots, Signed, 14 1/2 In. 2200.00
Lamp, Arabian, Caramel Favrile Shade, 3 Applied Amber Punts, Bronze, 15 In. 4500.00
Lamp, Bamboo Stick, Bronze, Favrile Green & Gold Shade, 14 1/2 In. 2200.00

◆ ◆ ◆ ◆ ◆ ◆ ◆ ◆ ◆ ◆ ◆ ◆ ◆ ◆ ◆ ◆ ◆ ◆ ◆ ◆

Fishing line is strong and almost invisible and can be used to tie fragile items to a base or wall. This will prevent damage from earthquake, two-year-olds, and dogs with wagging tails.

◆ ◆ ◆ ◆ ◆ ◆ ◆ ◆ ◆ ◆ ◆ ◆ ◆ ◆ ◆ ◆ ◆ ◆ ◆ ◆

Tiffany, Lamp, Poppy, Favrile
Shade, Bronze, 1899-1920

Lamp, Brass, Favrile, Amber Iridescent Glass Shade, 15 In. 5750.00
Lamp, Bridge, Bronze, Domed Shape, Adjustable Arm, No. 676, 52 In. 2415.00
Lamp, Bridge, Bronze, Favrile, Green Damascene Shade, 4 Ft. 7 In. .... 4888.00 to 6900.00
Lamp, Bridge, Steuben Shade, Adjustable Harp, Bronze, c.1915, 4 Ft. 10 In. 3163.00
Lamp, Bronze, Damascene, Cased Pearl Opal, Favrile, Base No. 418, 13 1/2 In. 3080.00
Lamp, Bronze, Favrile Glass, Rainbow Iridescent, Tripod, 25 1/2 In. 4025.00
Lamp, Bronze, Favrile, Amber Iridescent Shade, 20 In. 5175.00
Lamp, Bronze, Green Glass Cased Over White Shade, 13 In. .... 3738.00 to 4025.00
Lamp, Bronze, Harp Shape, Ash Receiver, Petal Circular Base, 1890-1920, 56 In. 1840.00
Lamp, Bronze, Harp Shape, Bell Shaped Green Shade, Favrile, 13 In. 2500.00
Lamp, Bronze, Harp Shape, Domed Silver Wave Shade, Green Ground, 18 3/4 In. 2300.00
Lamp, Bronze, Harp Shape, Yellow Steuben Domed Shade, Marked, 13 1/4 In. 670.00
Lamp, Bronze, Mottled Yellow Adam Octagonal Shade, 17 In. 5000.00
Lamp, Bronze, Tree Trunk Base, Stick Body, Bamboo Ribs, 14 1/2 In. 2200.00
Lamp, Bronze, Weight-Balance, Metal Hemispherical Shade, 51 In. 1265.00
Lamp, Bronze, Whirling Leaf Shade, Emerald Green Ground, 26 x 18 In. 14000.00
Lamp, Candlestick, 3 Foliate Supports, Bronze, Signed, 1920, 16 In. 1610.00
Lamp, Candlestick, Blue Favrile, Gilt Metal, Quilted Shade, 1899-1928, 14 1/4 In. 2300.00
Lamp, Candlestick, Bronze, Favrile, Bulbous Candle Cup, Triform Base, 16 In. 1610.00
Lamp, Candlestick, Bronze, Favrile, Glass, 3 Foliate Supports, 1920, 16 In. 1610.00
Lamp, Candlestick, Ribbed Base, Ruffled Shade, Favrile, Signed, 15 In., Pair 4620.00
Lamp, Chinese, Bronze, Amber Slag Glass Octagonal Shade, 17 In. 6000.00
Lamp, Circular Base, Gooseneck Arm, Weighted Ball, Favrile, No. 415, 16 1/2 In. 6900.00
Lamp, Colonial, Bronze, Mottled Green-Yellow Glass Tiles, 22 1/2 In. 7475.00
Lamp, Colonial, Geometric, Yellow-Amber Glass, Bronze Base, 21 In. 2310.00
Lamp, Daffodil, Bronze, Yellow & Gold Daffodils Shade, Ball Footed, 23 In. 9200.00
Lamp, Damascene, Opal Favrile Shade, Bronze Base, 21 1/2 In. 4400.00
Lamp, Double Harp, Green Damascene Wave Shade, 5 Padded Floor Base 8995.00
Lamp, Floor, Weight-Balance, Favrile Glass, Bronze, Blue Iridescent Shade, 53 In. 9775.00
Lamp, Floor, Weight-Balance, Gold Dore, 5-Footed, Ball Lever Socket, 54 In. 825.00
Lamp, Geometric Pomegranate Shade, Bronze Base & Cap, 20 1/2 In. 9000.00
Lamp, Geometric Shade, Mottled Green Glass, Bronze, Footed, Signed, 26 In. 7000.00
Lamp, Geometric, Bronze, Favrile, Conical Brickwork Tiles Shade, 21 1/2 In. 4600.00
Lamp, Gilt Bronze, Tree Trunk, 6 Light Sockets, Alligator Finish, 30 1/4 In. 9775.00
Lamp, Gilt Bronze, Wave Domical Shade, 16 1/2 In. 3162.00
Lamp, Globe, Hanging, Gold Iridescent Diamond-Quilted, Dore Bronze, 12 x 5 In. 1500.00
Lamp, Globe, Hanging, Gold Iridescent Feather & Swirl, Bulbous, 6 x 13 In. 2500.00
Lamp, Grapevine, Etched Bronze, Green Favrile Bent Panels, 16 x 14 In. 5225.00
Lamp, Grapevine, Green Slag Glass, Bronze, Curved Panels, 17 In. 7500.00

Lamp, Grapevine, Green Slag Glass, Bronze, 17 In. 7500.00
Lamp, Greek Key, Leaded Glass, Bronze Stem & Base, Signed, 22 In. 9900.00
Lamp, Greek Key, Mottled Amber Leaded Glass, 15th-Century Base, 25 In. 9350.00
Lamp, Linen Fold, 10 Panels, Gilt Bronze Frame, Signed, 21 1/2 In. 4888.00
Lamp, Linen Fold, Leaded Glass, 12 Panels, Bronze, Signed, 55 In. 6325.00
Lamp, Linen Press, Weight-Balance Arms, Bronze, 15 In. 2860.00
Lamp, Lyre-Shaped Shade, Horizontal Panels, Leaded Glass, Bronze, 18 1/2 In. 4600.00
Lamp, Moorish Luminor, Octagonal Shade, Pulled Feather, Wooden Base, 8 In. 1980.00
Lamp, Mosque, Deep Olive Green Feather, Gold Iridescent, 8 1/2 In. 2800.00
Lamp, Nautilus, Green & White Shade, Wishbone Standard, Bronze, 13 1/4 In. 6325.00
Lamp, Nautilus, Pivoting Bronze Base, Signed, 14 In. 2530.00
Lamp, Oil, Foliate Base, Green Shade, Patinated Bronze, 1928, 21 In. 2875.00
Lamp, Piano, 3-Light, Lily, Gold Favrile Shades, Bronze Base No. 320, 9 In. 1100.00
Lamp, Piano, Bronze Turtleback Tile, Blue-Green Iridescent Glass, 15 In. 5750.00
Lamp, Pine Needle, Student, 1 Arm, Adjustable, Bronze, 19 3/4 In. 2875.00
Lamp, Pomegranate, Emerald Green, Bronze Cap, 20 1/2 In. 9000.00
Lamp, Pomegranate, Green Favrile, Yellow Border, Base No. 168, 18 x 16 In. 4400.00
Lamp, Poppy, Favrile Shade, Bronze, 1899-1920 .... *Illus* 40250.00
Lamp, Spanish, Gold Dore, Bronze Sculptured Wings Base, 14 In. 2800.00
Lamp, Swirling Leaf Border, Bronze, Favrile, Emerald Green Tiles, 22 In. 9775.00
Lamp, Swirling Leaf, Domed Shade, Band Of Leaves, Bronze Base, 22 1/2 In. 6900.00
Lamp, Teal Green Geometric Colonial Type Shade, Art Nouveau Base, 16 In. 8960.00
Lamp, Turtleback Favrile, Wishbone Standard, Green Jewels On Base, 14 In. 7475.00
Lamp, Turtleback Tile Shield, Bronze, 15 In. 4025.00
Lamp, Turtleback Tile Shield, Bronze, Favrile, 13 1/2 In. 3450.00
Lamp, Undulating Bronze Foot, Dark Verdigris Patina, Signed, 64 In. 1200.00
Lamp, Weight-Balance, Bronze Shade, Pivoting Gooseneck Arm, 14 In. 5520.00
Lamp, Weight-Balance, Bronze, Gold Domical Shake, 7 1/8 In. 2300.00
Lamp, Weight-Balance, Bronze, Green Glass Damascene Shade, 14 1/2 In. 4888.00
Lamp, Weight-Balance, Gilt Bronze, Gold Iridescent Shade, 15 3/4 In. 2875.00
Lamp, Weight-Balance, Green Favrile Shade, 5 x 7 In. 6000.00
Lamp, Wire Mesh, Enameled & Jeweled, Floral, Gold Dore Bronze, 12 In., Pair 1800.00
Lamp, Zodiac, Bronze, Stick Body, Leaded Mica Shade, Hexagon, Finial, 18 In. 2500.00
Lamp Base, Adjustable Arm, Weight-Balance, Bronze, 54 1/4 In. 1900.00
Lamp Base, Bronze, Applied Stringing, 22 1/2 In. 3163.00
Lamp Base, Bronze, Paneled, 1899-1928, 24 1/2 In. 2875.00
Lamp Base, Gilt Bronze, Hexagonal Paneled Standard, No. 638, 21 3/4 In. 1495.00
Lamp Base, Gilt Bronze, Hexagonal Standard, Acid Etched, No. 581, 29 5/8 In. 1610.00
Lantern, Turtleback, Blue-Gold Iridescent Sides, 13 x 6 1/2 In. 5500.00
Letter Holder, Graduate, Bronze, Gold Dore, 4 1/2 x 6 1/4 x 2 3/4 In. 350.00
Letter Opener, Bookmark, Gold Dore, Symbol Both Sides Handle, 10 1/2 In. 200.00
Letter Opener, Entwined Design, Gold Dore, Signed, 9 In. 225.00
Letter Opener, Ninth Century, Gold Dore, 10 1/4 In. 250.00
Letter Opener, Pine Needle, Gold Dore, Amber Glass In Handle, 9 In. 275.00
Letter Opener, Venetian, Gold Dore, Pattern Both Sides Handle, 10 1/2 In. 250.00
Letter Opener, Zodiac, Gold Dore, Amber Slag Glass In Handle, 10 1/2 In. 225.00
Letter Rack, Abalone, Bronze, Gold Dore, 2 Sections, Signed 900.00
Letter Rack, Adam, Bronze, 2 Sections, 9 1/4 x 2 1/4 x 6 In. 450.00
Letter Rack, American Indian, Bronze, Tall Divider, 6 1/2 x 3 x 4 1/2 In. 550.00
Letter Rack, Chinese, Bronze, 2 Sections, 9 1/2 x 6 In. 550.00
Letter Rack, Chinese, Symbols, Bronze, Signed, 6 x 9 1/2 In. 550.00
Letter Rack, Graduate, 2 Sections, Gold Dore Finish, 9 In. 375.00
Letter Rack, Grapevine, Bronze, Green Slag Glass, 10 x 6 1/2 x 2 1/2 In. 950.00
Letter Rack, Ninth Century, Bronze, Jeweled, 14K Gold Plate, 10 x 6 x 2 1/2 In. 900.00
Letter Rack, Pine Needle, Green Slag Glass, 2 Sections, 10 x 6 1/2 In. 950.00
Letter Rack, Spanish, Bronze, 2 Sections, Gold Dore, 10 In. 950.00
Letter Rack, Spanish, Bronze, 2 Sections, Signed, 10 In. 950.00
Letter Rack, Venetian, Bottom Border, Signed, 4 1/2 x 6 In. 600.00
Letter Rack, Venetian, Bronze, 2 Sections, Gold Dore, 10 x 3 x 6 In. 650.00
Magnifying Glass, Bookmark, Bronze, Gold Dore, 8 3/4 In. 500.00
Magnifying Glass, Bookmark, Gilt Bronze, 8 3/4 In. 825.00
Magnifying Glass, Indian, Bronze, Gold Dore, 8 3/4 In. 500.00
Magnifying Glass, Pine Needle, Gold Dore, Amber Slag Glass In Handle, 8 1/4 In. 750.00

Magnifying Glass, Zodiac, Bronze, Gold Dore, 8 3/4 In. 500.00
Mirror, Mother-Of-Pearl & Favrile Glass Mosaic, Wood Frame, 24 x 21 1/2 In. 8050.00
Mirror, Turtleback Border, Bronze, 14 x 18 In. 2800.00
Night-Light, Scarab 1800.00
Note Pad, Chinese, Knob Handle, Signed, 3 x 5 3/4 In. 200.00
Pad Holder, Sea Horses, Sailboat & Wave Design, Gold Dore Finish, 7 1/4 In. 550.00
Paper Clip, Abalone, Bronze, Gold Dore, 2 x 2 3/4 In. 350.00
Paper Clip, Adam, Bronze, Gold Dore, 2 1/2 x 4 In. 250.00
Paper Clip, Indian, Bronze 225.00
Paper Clip, Venetian, Bronze, Gold Dore, Signed, 2 1/4 x 3 1/4 In. 350.00
Paper Clip, Zodiac, Bronze, Gold Dore, 2 1/4 x 3 3/4 In. 250.00
Paperweight, Art Nouveau Green Glass Swirl, Bronze, 3 1/2 x 2 3/4 In. 2800.00
Paperweight, Bulldog, Sitting, Bronze, 2 1/4 x 1 1/2 In. 475.00
Paperweight, Commemorative, Bronze, Fancy Letters, Knob Handle, 3 1/2 In. 250.00
Paperweight, Letter Forms, Top Knob Handle, Dinner March 1905, 3 1/2 In. 250.00
Paperweight, Lioness, Bronze, Gold Dore, 5 x 1 1/2 x 1 1/2 In. 700.00
Paperweight, Pointer, Shando, Bronze, 3 1/4 x 2 x 2 1/2 In. 850.00
Pen Brush, Grapevine, Bronze, 2 x 2 1/4 In. 250.00
Pen Brush, Ninth Century, Bronze, Jeweled, 2 3/4 x 2 In. 350.00
Pen Brush, Venetian, Gold Dore, Signed, Square, 3 x 2 1/4 In. 400.00
Pen Tray, Nautical, Shell Shape, Bronze, 9 1/2 x 2 3/4 In. 550.00
Pen Tray, Ninth Century, Bronze, Jeweled, Signed, 8 3/4 x 3 1/2 In. 300.00
Pen Tray, Spanish, Bronze, 9 3/4 x 3 3/4 In. 350.00
Pen Tray, Spanish, Bronze, Signed, 9 3/4 x 3 3/4 In. 350.00
Perfume Bottle, Green Leaves, White Centers, Tendrils, Signed, 4 In. 2500.00
Planter, Bronze, Jeweled, Round, 6 1/2 In. 2800.00
Planter, Pine Needle, Bronze, Green Slag Glass, 10 1/2 x 8 1/2 In. 1800.00
Plate, Lily-Of-The-Valley Center & Rim, 9 In., 12 Piece 565.00
Punch Cup, Opalescent & Green Design, Scroll Handle, Signed, 3 In. 350.00
Salt, Ruffled Edge, Gold Iridescent, Rainbow Colors, Signed 200.00
Scale, Postage, Abalone Discs, Bronze, Gold Dore, 1 1/2 x 3 x 3 3/4 In. 750.00
Scale, Postage, Grapevine, Gold Dore Finish, Amber Slag Glass, Signed 650.00
Scale, Postage, Pine Needle, Gold Dore Finish, Amber Slag Glass, Signed 650.00
Scissors, Line Design In Bronze Handle, Signed, 9 1/2 In. 175.00
Sconce, Bronze, 6-Sided Gold Iridescent Shades, 10 In., Pair 660.00
Sconce, Bronze, Blue Favrile Tiles, Oriental Style, 16 In. 4125.00
Sconce, Favrile, Bronze, Urn Shape Mount, 2 Upturned Arms, 10 1/4 In., Pair 9200.00
Sconce, Favrile, Turtle-Back Tile, Bronze, 3-Panel Shade, Brown/Green, 14 In., Pr. .. 9775.00
Seal, Letter, 3 Scarabs, Gold Iridescent, 1 3/4 In. 385.00
Smoking Stand, Berries Ending With 3 Balls Base, Wrought Iron, 28 1/2 In. 1840.00
Smoking Stand, Bronze, Round Reeded Ring, Onion-Form Base, 1906, 31 1/2 In. ... 3162.00
Smoking Stand, Griffin At Top Holding Canister, Bronze, 34 1/4 In. 1955.00
Smoking Stand, Leaf, Stick Body, Match Holder, Bronze, 26 In. 750.00
Thermometer, Bronze, Green Slag Glass, Grapevine, Easel Type, 8 1/2 x 3 3/4 In. ... 850.00
Thermometer, Foliate & Shell Collar, Curved To Follow Elephant Tusk, 10 In. 1150.00
Tray, Bronze, Enameled Floral & Leaf, Gold Dore, Handles, 8 1/4 In. 400.00
Tray, Bronze, Geometric Design Edge, Gold Dore Finish, Signed, 9 3/4 In. 225.00
Tray, Bronze, Round, Raised Rim, No. 1722, Early 20th Century, 14 In. 121.00
Tray, Nautical, Bronze, Gold Dore, 12 x 15 In. 650.00
Tray, Pen, Grapevine, Green Glass Under Bronze, Signed, 2 3/4 x 9 1/2 In. 250.00
Tray, Red Enameled, Monogram Center, 8 In. 175.00
Tray, Serving, Bronze & Abalone, Round, Leaf & Vine Border, Signed, 12 In. 350.00
Tray, Serving, Bronze, Gold Dore, 12 x 15 In. 650.00
Tray, Venetian, Bronze, 2 Sections, 8 1/2 x 2 3/4 In. 250.00
Umbrella, Handle, Tortoiseshell & Enamel, Foliage, Fitted Box 8050.00
Vase, Bronze, Alternating Ribs & Panels, No. 28215B, 15 In. 990.00
Vase, Bronze, Raised Pods, Raised Vines, Golden Green Iridescent, 2 1/8 x 3 In. 950.00
Vase, Favrile, Blue, Shaded Green Leaves & Vines, Bronze Flower Frog, 4 x 6 In. 2500.00
Vase, Heart & Vine, Drilled For Lamp 300.00
Vase, Peacock Zipper Design, Black Ground, Favrile, 3 In. 1800.00
Vase, Poppy Pod Design, Bronze, Silver Clad, 9 In. 4675.00
Vase, Raised Pods, Silver Finish, Gold-Green Iridescent, 2 1/2 x 3 In. 950.00
Vase, Tel Al Amarna, Black, Blue & Silver Design, Handles, Signed, 10 1/4 In. 7500.00

Vase, White Leaves Pulled From Foot, Onion Shape, Signed, 10 In. 2750.00
TIFFANY GLASS, Bonbon, Blue Favrile, Leaf Decorations, 4 3/4 In. 660.00
Bonbon, Gold Iridescent, Favrile, Short Pedestal, 2 x 4 3/4 In. 275.00
Bowl, Cobalt Blue Favrile, 10 Ribs & Scallops, 7 In. 715.00
Bowl, Cobalt Blue, Scalloped, 8 Ribs, 5 3/4 In. 440.00
Bowl, Favrile Gold Iridescent, Purple Highlights, Flared, 4 1/2 In. 600.00
Bowl, Favrile, Amber, Green Leaves, No. 2220L, c.1917, 14 In. 920.00
Bowl, Favrile, Gold Iridescent, Ruffled Edge, Ribbed, 7 1/4-In. Diam. 650.00
Bowl, Favrile, Vertical Bands, Dark Pink Ground, No. 1891, c.1925, 12 In. 575.00
Bowl, Gold Bowl, Scalloped Leaf Shape, Favrile, Signed, 10 1/4 In. 705.00
Bowl, Gold Favrile, 12 Ribs & Scallops, 1925, 10 In. 410.00
Bowl, Gold Favrile, Crimped, Pink Iridescent, Round, 4 3/8 In. 230.00
Bowl, Gold Iridescent, Double-Tiered Flower Frog, 1 1/2 x 7 In. 1100.00
Bowl, Gold Iridescent, Favrile, Flared, Center Well, 2 1/2 x 4 1/2 In. 600.00
Bowl, Pastel Aqua Favrile, Flared, Flowers, Diamond-Quilted, 12 1/4 In. 990.00
Bowl, Petalled Outline, Flattened Foot, Favrile, Signed, 1937, 4 1/2 In. 863.00
Bowl, Raised Trailings, Amber Ground, Favrile, c.1902, 2 3/4 In. 2070.00
Bowl, Ruffled Flare, Gold Iridescent, Favrile, 2 1/2 x 8 1/4 In. 600.00
Bowl, Scalloped, Gold Iridescent, Paperweight Base, 10 Ribs, 5 x 2 1/2 In. 395.00
Bowl, Underplate, Blue Iridescent, Flared, Opalescent Gold Center, 5 In. 700.00
Bowl, Underplate, Electric Blue Pastel, Gold Iridescent, 5 In. 700.00
Candlestick, Blown Green Glass, Bronze Tripod Base, Signed, 9 3/4 In. 3300.00
Candlestick, Favrile Swirl, Pair 1350.00
Candlestick, Gold Iridescent, Favrile, Oval Top, Saucer Base, 3 3/4 In., Pair 2100.00
Candlestick, Green Feather, Iridescent, 8 1/2 In., Pair 1200.00
Centerpiece, Pink, Footed, Wide Optic Stripes, Oval Shape, 12 x 9 1/2 x 4 In. 850.00
Charger, Favrile, Radiating Rays, Pulled Feather Center, 17 3/4 In. .... 4600.00 to 5980.00
Compote, Center Quilted Pattern, Gilt Bronze Base, Signed, 12 In. 1760.00
Compote, Cover, Blue Favrile, Goblet Shape, 9202M, 9 1/2 In. 465.00
Compote, Favrile, Cobalt Blue, Purple Iridescence, Footed, No. 1838, 6 3/8 In. 880.00
Compote, Favrile, Gold Iridescent, Flared, Footed, No. 1848, 8 In. 770.00
Compote, Floriform, Flared Ruffled Lip, Amber, No. 8853B, 1907, 4 5/8 In. 520.00
Compote, Gold Iridescent, Favrile, Intaglio Leaf & Vine, Pedestal, 4 1/2 In. 1200.00
Compote, Gold Iridescent, Favrile, Raised Ruffled, Pedestal, 4 x 2 1/2 In. 450.00
Compote, Oval, Green Favrile, Clear Bowl, Stem & Foot, No. 1919C, 8 In. 385.00
Compote, Ribbed, Morning Glory Blossoms Interior, 1921, 7 3/8 In. 4025.00
Compote, Ruffled, Leaves & Vines, Teardrop Stem, Signed, 6 In. 695.00
Compote, Ruffled Rim, Iridescent Gold, Favrile, Signed, 6 In. 150.00
Compote, Stepped Circular Bowl, Cylindrical Stem, Footed, 4 1/4 x 7 1/4 In. 632.00
Cordial, Gold Aurene, Signed, 4 In. 295.00
Cordial Set, Applied Lily Pad Pulls, Favrile, Signed, 5 Piece 805.00
Cordial Set, Intaglio Grapevine Band, Favrile, Signed, 5 Piece 5290.00
Dish, Blue Favrile, Everted Rim, 2 Scroll Handles, Gold & Violet Iridescent 546.00
Dish, Blue Favrile, Leaf Shape, Oval, Pinched Ring Handle, 4 3/4 In. 575.00
Figurine, Scarab, Blue Iridescent, 3/4 In. 125.00
Finger Bowl, Underplate, Earl Pattern, Amber, Signed, 1928, 3 Sets 1150.00
Finger Bowl, Underplate, Ruffled, Signed, 2 1/4 In. 550.00
Flower Bowl, Favrile Blue, 5 Green Lily Pads & Leaves, 2-Tier Holder, 12 In. 3500.00
Flower Frog, Frog, 16 Holes, Favrile, Blue 450.00
Flower Holder, Rolled Rim, Olive Green Flowers, No. 1131, 1918, 11 In. 2070.00
Jar, Chinese Gold Iridescent, Sterling Silver Lid & Handle, 4 x 6 1/2 In. 750.00
Liquor Set, Gold Iridescent, Diagonal Ribs, Star Stopper, 4-In. Goblet, 9 Pc. 4500.00
Ornament, Moth, Outspread Wings, Green & Amber, 11 1/4 In. 2300.00
Pitcher, 3 Large Leaves, Vines On Gold Iridescence, 4 In. 1275.00
Pitcher, Favrile, Amber, C-Scroll Handle, No. 1192, 1892-1928, 6 1/2 In. 515.00
Plate, Egyptian Chain, Experimental, Favrile, Opalescent, 8 1/4 In. 1610.00
Plate, Pastel Pink, Signed, 10 1/2 In. 450.00
Platter, Chintz, Flashed Stripes, Gold Iridescent, 8 1/2 In. 95.00
Salt, 8 Protruding Rattails, 2 1/4 x 3 1/2 In. 875.00
Salt, Gold Favrile, Open, 2 In. 165.00
Salt, Gold Iridescent, Favrile, Blue & Red Highlights, Round, Pedestal, 1 1/2 In. 275.00
Salt, Gold Iridescent, Favrile, Flared, Footed, 1 1/2 x 2 In. 250.00

Salt, Gold Iridescent, Favrile, Flared Top, 4 Footed, 1 1/2 In. 250.00
Salt, Gold Iridescent, Favrile, Raised Twists, 1 x 2 In. 375.00
Salt, Gold Iridescent, Favrile, Ribs, Pedestal Base, Stand-Up Collar, 2 In. 275.00
Salt, Gold Iridescent, Favrile, Ruffled, Signed 200.00
Salt, Gold Iridescent, Favrile, Silver-Blue Tones, Flared, 4-Footed, 1 1/2 In. 250.00
Salt, Gold Iridescent, Favrile, Silver-Blue Tones, 2 In. Diam. 375.00
Salt, Gold Iridescent, Ruffled, 2 3/4 In., 5 Piece 550.00
Salt, Peacock Blue Iridescent, Favrile, Ruffled, Flat Base 650.00
Scarab, Favrile, Blue Iridescent, 3/4 In. 125.00
Shade, Dome Shape, Amber Swirls, 1899-1920, 7 In. 2645.00
Shade, Lamp, Boudoir, Gold Favrile, Peacock Feather, 5 x 5 In. 275.00
Shade, Linen Fold, Gilt Bronze Frame, Mother-Of-Pearl Discs, Signed, 10 In. 700.00
Sherbet, Blue & Violet Tone, Signed, 3 1/2 In. 225.00
Sherbet, Gold Iridescent, Blue & Violet Highlights, Signed, 3 1/2 In. 275.00
Sprinkler, Rose Water, Gooseneck Lip, Amber, c.1901, 13 7/8 In. 5750.00
Sprinkler, Rose Water, Gooseneck Lip, Turquoise, c.1902, 12 3/4 In. 4600.00
Tazza, Venetian Optic, 6 1/2 In. 800.00
Tile, Surface Of Cypriote Glass, Square, 4 In. 450.00
Toothpick, 8 Twisted Prunts, Gold Iridescent, 1 3/4 In. 250.00
Toothpick, Dimpled Sides, Gold Iridescent, 2 In. 210.00
Toothpick, Dimpled, Gold, Signed 290.00
Toothpick, Favrile, Iridescent Gold, 4 Pinched Sides, Signed, 1 3/4 In. 225.00
Toothpick, Favrile, Light Blue, 2 5/8 In. 495.00
Toothpick, Lily Pads, Signed 220.00
Tumbler, Juice, Applied Pulled Lily Pads, No. M1853, 1899-1928, 3 3/4 In. 345.00
Vase, Agate, Bulbous, Cylindrical Neck, No. 1995K, c.1916, 2 5/8 In. 1955.00
Vase, Amber Opalescent, Leafage, Gold Iridescent, c.1896, 16 1/2 In. 5483.00
Vase, Baluster, Cylindrical Neck, Handles, Bright Blue, No. 28H, 6 3/8 In. 1265.00
Vase, Bud, Favrile, Trumpet Shape, Amber Feathering, No. 7150, c.1915, 8 In. 460.00
Vase, Bud, Peacock Feather, Signed, 12 In. 250.00
Vase, Cypriote, Favrile, Iridescent Green, Textured, Gold Swags, 5 3/4 In. 5175.00
Vase, Cypriote, Mottled Cream, Bronze, Copper, Bulging Ovoid, 1895, 9 1/2 In. 4600.00
Vase, Egg Shape, Elongated Neck, Blue, Vertical Rows, No. 03000, 4 3/4 In. 2070.00
Vase, Egg Shape, Everted Rim, Green, Blue Feathering, No. H1462, 1897, 3 5/8 In. 1265.00
Vase, Egg Shape, Melon Green, Millefiori, Silver, Gold & Violet Vines, 5 In. 2875.00
Vase, Engraved Bumble Bee, Green & Ochre Agate, c.1904, 3 1/8 In. 2070.00
Vase, Favrile, Agate, Green-Brown Stripes, Pale Green Ground, 2 1/2 In. 2500.00
Vase, Favrile, Alabaster, Gold Iridescent Leaf Design, Barber Shape, 8 In. 650.00
Vase, Favrile, Amber Iridescent, Pulled Damascene Feathering, 18 3/4 In. 8050.00
Vase, Favrile, Amber Trailing Pulled Feathers, Blossoms, 8 3/8 In. 4025.00
Vase, Favrile, Band Of Metallic Gold Plumage, Peacock Eyes, 22 In. 9900.00
Vase, Favrile, Black Amethyst, Oval, Egyptian Designs, c.1890, 7 5/8 In. 1980.00
Vase, Favrile, Blue Iridescent, Ribbed Body, Pedestal Base, 2 x 2 1/2 In. 1800.00
Vase, Favrile, Blue, 8 Pillars, No. 6263, 2 1/2 In. 715.00
Vase, Favrile, Blue, Classic Form, Signed, 5 1/2 In. 1795.00
Vase, Favrile, Blue, Cylindrical Neck, Everted Rim, c.1918, 12 In. 4600.00
Vase, Favrile, Blue, Ribbed Ovoid, Scalloped Everted Rim, 1919, 15 In. 1955.00
Vase, Favrile, Blue, Urn Shape, Shell Handles, Silver Tones, 6 1/2 x 5 In. 1800.00
Vase, Favrile, Blue-Gold, Free Form Style, Bulbous, 4 1/2 In. 950.00
Vase, Favrile, Bottle Shape, Amber, No. M779, c.1900, 2 1/8 In. 690.00
Vase, Favrile, Cased Over Amber, Red, c.1916, 8 1/4 In. 4600.00
Vase, Favrile, Cased, Cylindrical, Green, White, No. 7718D, c.1909, 5 3/8 In. 920.00
Vase, Favrile, Cobalt Blue, 10 Herringbone Ribs, 6 1/2 In. 880.00
Vase, Favrile, Cobalt Blue, Double Bulb Shape, Swirls, No. A581E, 8 In. 600.00
Vase, Favrile, Cypriote, Elongated Baluster, Gold, No. 8922, 12 1/2 In. 4400.00
Vase, Favrile, Double Cone Shape, Rolled Foot, No. G1859, c.1897, 4 3/8 In. 1265.00
Vase, Favrile, Flared, Amber, Heart-Shaped Leaves, No. 6644L, c.1917, 12 In. 980.00
Vase, Favrile, Floriform, Lime Feathering, Amber, No. 5281C, c.1908, 5 In. 700.00
Vase, Favrile, Gold Iridescent, Deep Green Feathering, 7 3/4 In. 875.00
Vase, Favrile, Gold Iridescent, Trifold Shape, Straight Neck, 2 x 1 1/2 In. 500.00
Vase, Favrile, Gold Iridescent, Trifold Shape, Straight Neck, 2 1/4 x 1 1/2 In. 500.00
Vase, Favrile, Gold, Baluster, Engraved Grape Leaf Border, No. 1824, 9 In. 550.00

Vase, Favrile, Gold, Favrile, Bean Pot Shape, Handles, 1 3/4 x 2 In. 500.00
Vase, Favrile, Gourd Shape, Amber, Ribbed, No. 6246H, c.1913, 3 1/2 In. 460.00
Vase, Favrile, Green Iridescent, Gold Thread, Narrow Neck, 2 1/2 In. 1300.00
Vase, Favrile, Green Vine Leaves & Stems, Signed, 9 In. 2070.00
Vase, Favrile, Heart-Shaped Leaves, Random Trailings, c.1910, 9 In. 2300.00
Vase, Favrile, Iridescent Green, All Around Ribbed, 5 In. 1300.00
Vase, Favrile, Irregular Ovoid, Amber, Lozenges, No. 908D, c.1909, 5 3/8 In. 575.00
Vase, Favrile, Millefiori Design, Amber, Green, No. K1144, c.1916, 2 3/4 In. 1495.00
Vase, Favrile, Opal, Green & Gold Pulled Feather, No. 7804E, 8 1/2 In. 1430.00
Vase, Favrile, Ovoid, Amber Loopings, 2 5/8 In. 690.00
Vase, Favrile, Ovoid, Amber Ribs, White Stripes, Caramel Banding, 3 3/4 In. 1265.00
Vase, Favrile, Paperweight, Brown Leaves, Green Walls, 1892-1928, 4 1/4 In. 1840.00
Vase, Favrile, Pastel Opalescent, Pink, Bulbous, No. 958, c.1921, 5 1/4 In. 920.00
Vase, Favrile, Peacock Blue, 2 Applied Shell Handles, 6 1/2 In. 1800.00
Vase, Favrile, Peacock Blue, Rolled Neck, Collar, 1 1/2 In. 1200.00
Vase, Favrile, Red Iridescent, Trailing Gold Lines, Squat Waisted, 1 3/8 In. 1840.00
Vase, Favrile, Ribbed, Bell Shape, Domed Foot, c.1909, 10 3/4 In. 474.00
Vase, Floriform, Favrile, Opalescent, Pulled Green Feather, c.1903, 11 1/4 In. 6325.00
Vase, Floriform, Favrile, Pulled Green Feathering, Signed, 17 3/8 In. 5175.00
Vase, Floriform, Gold Blossom, Ruffled, Saucer Foot, Marked, 12 1/2 In. 1045.00
Vase, Floriform, Gold Iridescent, Violet & Red Highlights, 4 1/2 In. 850.00
Vase, Floriform, Ribbed, Silvery-Blue To Purple, c.1916, 16 In. 1380.00
Vase, Floriform, Ruffled Rim, Amber Base, Favrile, c.1902, 7 3/4 In. 2300.00
Vase, Gold Iridescent, Leaf Molding, Flared, Signed, c.1919 .... 3400.00
Vase, Gold With Violet Iridescence, Ribbed, Waisted, c.1917, 8 1/2 In. 805.00
Vase, Iridescent, Gold, Pedestal, Signed, 5 1/2 In. 375.00
Vase, Jack-In-The-Pulpit, Favrile, Rainbow Iridescence, Signed, 18 In. 7475.00
Vase, Jack-In-The-Pulpit, Undulated Mouth, Crackled Rim, Favrile, 12 1/2 In. 3850.00
Vase, Lava, Egg Shape, Surface Bubble Design, Vines & Leaves, 7 3/4 In. 550.00
Vase, Mottled Tortoiseshell Design Interior, Red, Signed, 6 1/4 In. 3000.00
Vase, Paperweight, Millefiori Design, c.1900, 2 3/8 In. 1725.00
Vase, Peacock Blue Iridescent, Blue-Purple Base, Signed, 6 1/4 In. 1200.00
Vase, Peacock Blue Iridescent, Flower Form, Leaves, 9 1/4 In. 2800.00
Vase, Red & Yellow Seed Pods, Leaves, Urn Shape, Signed, 7 1/4 In. 8800.00
Vase, Rib Optic, Opalescent, Yellow Stretch Rim, Signed, Label, 4 1/2 In. 425.00
Vase, Trumpet, Favrile, Gilt Bronze, Amber, Pulled Feathering, No. 160, 14 In. 1265.00
Vase, Trumpet, Favrile, Gold, Pink Iridescent, Ivy, Knopped Base, 12 In. 2070.00
Vase, Trumpet, Favrile, Signed, 12 In. 1650.00
Vase, Wheel-Carved Woodbine Leaves, Vines, Gourd Shape, Signed, 7 In. 6050.00
Vase, White, Gold Iridescent, Folded Foot, Trumpet Flower, No. 1669, 11 In. 1320.00
Whiskey, Gold Favrile Glass, D Initial 375.00
Wine, Favrile, 4 In., 4 Piece 425.00
TIFFANY POTTERY, Pitcher, Cat-O'-Nine Tails, Unglazed, Green Interior, 12 In. 1800.00
Pitcher, Embossed Fruit, Clear Green Glaze, Signed, 10 1/2 In. 475.00
Vase, Boughs Of Trumpet Vines, Mottled, Signed, c.1910, 12 5/8 In. 3750.00
Vase, Bud, Yellow-Green & Blue, Vines & Hanging Pods, 5 In. 2200.00
Vase, Classical Figures, Grecian Dress, Irregular Shape, Signed, 4 In. 750.00
Vase, Classical Figures, Unglazed, Top Border Design, Signed, 4 In. 750.00
Vase, Cylindrical, Molded Foliage, Green, Brown, c.1910, 5 1/4 In. 575.00
Vase, Egg Shape, Lobed Sides, Green & Brown Glaze, Signed, 16 In. 2645.00
Vase, Eggplant Shape, Raised Overlay Leaves, Chocolate, Yellow, 4 In. 2800.00
Vase, Green Glaze, Narrow Neck, Deep Green Horizontal Line, 6 x 4 In. 950.00
Vase, Green Shades, Raised Branches, Green Leaves, Ribbed, 8 x 6 In. 2500.00
Vase, Hanging Pods, Leaves Around Top, Blue-Green Speckled, 6 x 4 In. 2200.00
Vase, Leafing Vines, Mottled, Squat Base, 6 In. 518.00
Vase, Overlapping Iris Leaves, Apple Green Glaze, Signed, 8 In. 2500.00
Vase, Yellow, Queen's Lace Border, Allover Design, Tapered Top, 8 x 5 In. 3500.00
TIFFANY SILVER, 4 Piece Setting, Beekman, c.1902, 12 Sets 4000.00
Berry Shovel, Persian 495.00
Blotter, Hobnail Edge & Handle, Heraldic, Green Enameled, 5 x 3 In. 300.00
Bonbon, Cupid & Psyche Handles, 1902, 13 1/4 In., Pair 3450.00
Bowl, Applied Arts & Crafts Floral Stripes, Round, 1938-1947 .... 880.00

Bowl, Applied Scrolling Border, Leaves, Berries, No. 14619, c.1900, 9 1/2 In. 1035.00
Bowl, Bombe Shape, Hammered, c.1915, 10 1/4 In. 3500.00
Bowl, Child's, Scenes From Sing A Song Of Sixpence, c.1905, 5 1/8 In. 1495.00
Bowl, Chrysanthemum, c.1895, 11 1/4 In. 2990.00
Bowl, Monogram, Scalloped Edge, Reeded Molding, No. 4115B, 8 1/2 In. 690.00
Bowl, Pierced Clover Design, Late 19th Century, 10 1/4 In. 70.00
Bowl, Revere, Monogram, 8 1/2 x 4 1/4 In. 495.00
Bowl, Twig Form, Openwork, Van Day Truex 1100.00
Bowl, Vine Shaped Handles & Base, Oval, 11 In. 747.00
Box, Scrolled Design On Top, Monogram, Oval, 6 1/4 In. 660.00
Bread Tray, Pierced & Repousse Border, Oval, Marked, 14 In. 880.00
Buckle, Belt, Barnum & Bailey Circus, 1908 .... 550.00
Cake Basket, Regence Design, Swing Handle, 10 1/2 In. 770.00
Candlestick, 2-Light, Fleur-De-Lis Base, Pair 900.00
Candlestick, Ribbed, Swag Waist, Monogram, J. Parson, c.1784, 11 In., Pair 2365.00
Cane, Presentation, Bear-Shaped Handle 880.00
Case, Cigarette, 3/8 x 3 x 5 In. 154.00
Centerpiece, Hammered, Stepped Borders, Monogram, c.1920, 16 1/2 In. 8050.00
Cocktail Set, Art Deco, Sterling, c.1925, 9 Piece 2600.00
Coffee Set, Kettle, On Stand, Monogram, Sterling, 3 Piece 1980.00
Coffee Set, Sugar, Creamer & Demitasse Pot, 3 Piece 675.00
Coffeepot, Allover Repousse & Chased Flowers & Leaves, 8 5/8 In. 4370.00
Cologne Flask, Floral Chased, Teardrop Shape, c.1880, 4 1/8 In. 373.50
Compote, Chrysanthemum, 1902, 9 In., Pair 4600.00
Compote, Flowers & Ferns, Frosted Gilt Center, c.1881, 9 1/2 In., Pair 2875.00
Compote, Monogram, Reticulated, Sterling, 2 x 6 1/2 In., Pair 550.00
Compote, Repousse, Inscription, 1890-1900, 5 1/2 x 9 In. 1045.00
Compote, Wavy Rim, Foliate Scrolls, Monogram, 1856 & 1902, 3 In., Pair 2990.00
Creamer, Rope Twist Border, Basket Weave Design, c.1860, 5 3/4 In. 1955.00
Crumber, Bright Cut, Bamboo Branches, Spider Web, 1880s, 12 3/4 In. 1380.00
Dish, Asparagus, Liner, Pierced Ends, Trellis Surround, c.1895, 14 1/4 In. 4315.00
Dish, Cover, Serpentine Oval, Gadroon Border, Monogram, 11 In. 165.00
Dish, Serving, Cover, Chrysanthemum, Monogram, 11 1/2 In. 7150.00
Flask, Engraved, Rectangular, Screw-Off Gilt Lined Cup, No. 1882, 6 1/8 In. 2880.00
Flask, Hammered Design, Monogram, 10 Oz. 357.00
Flask, Presentation, To Porto Rico, Victory Wreaths Sides, c.1898 .... 3738.00
Flask, Tennis Scene, c.1893 .... 1430.00
Flatware Set, Antique Ivy, No. 20, Hand Chased, E.C. Moore, 156 Piece 9600.00
Fork, Dessert, Queen Anne, 12 Piece 900.00
Fork, Fruit, Windham 45.00
Fork, Ice Cream, Beekman, 12 Piece 550.00
Fork, Lettuce, Chrysanthemum, Sterling 300.00
Fork, Luncheon, Chrysanthemum 70.00
Fork, Olive, Olympian 125.00
Fork, Sardine, Holly, 5 5/8 In. 235.00
Fork, Winthrop, 6 5/8 In. 25.00
Frame, Rococo Style, Late 19th Century, 9 In. 1320.00
Ice Bucket, Scalloped Edge, Rope Swing Handle, 5 3/4 In. 805.00
Ice Bucket, Tub Shape, Barrel Staves & Hoops, Marked, 1860s, 10 1/2 In. 5175.00
Ice Cream Ax, Chrysanthemum 695.00
Ice Cream Server, Grapes, 11 In. 400.00
Ice Cream Server, Olympian 795.00
Kettle, Hot Water, On Stand, Pear Shape, Chased Leaf Design, 13 1/4 In. 2310.00
Kettle, On Lampstand, Chrysanthemum, Engraved Arms, 13 1/2 In. 5750.00
Knife, King William, Pistol Handle 60.00
Ladle, Gravy, Chrysanthemum 395.00
Ladle, Oyster, Oysters & Seaweed, Lapover Ledge 1800.00
Ladle, Soup, Chrysanthemum, Shell-Form Bowl, 1880, 12 1/2 In. 715.00
Ladle, Tomato Soup, Vine, Oval, Scalloped Rim, 1870s, 12 1/4 In. 1265.00
Mug, Chased Flowers, Leaves & Vines, Marked, 1880s, 3 1/2 In. 1495.00
Mug, Spot Hammered Handle, Gilt Interior, 1880s, 3 1/2 In. 1610.00
Pie Server, San Lorenzo Pattern, Monogram, 11 1/2 In. 165.00

Pie Server, Serrated, Holly 725.00
Pie Server, Serrated, Renaissance 795.00
Pitcher, Band Of Spear Tips, Interlace Circles, c.1869, 13 3/4 In. 3450.00
Pitcher, Japanese Style, Spot-Hammered Surface, Band Of Leaves, c.1885 .... 9200.00
Pitcher, Water, Chased Wind Band, Goddesses, 1890-1900, 8 1/2 In. 3300.00
Place Setting, Ivy, Hand Chased, c.1872, 156 Piece 9600.00
Plate, Twisted Ribbon & Flowerhead Border, Monogram, 10 In., 16 Piece 9775.00
Platter, Meat, Chrysanthemum, Monogram, 22 In. 5225.00
Platter, Serving, Chrysanthemum, Oval, 18 In. 3190.00
Pot, Jelly, Apple Form, Spoon, 4 1/2 x 4 In. 300.00
Punch Bowl, Borders, Pendant Ring Handles, Monogram, 1944, 13 In. 4025.00
Rose Bowl, Regence, Plated Liner, 12 1/2 In. 935.00
Salad Set, English King .... 750.00 to 895.00
Salt, Urn Form, Buck's Head Handle, 2 1/2 In., Pair 467.00
Salt Cellar & Spoon, Gilt Interior, Corners Form Undulating Rim, 1 In., 4 Sets 575.00
Sauceboat, Stand, Greek Key Border, Leaf Handle, Marked, 1860s, 6 5/8 In. 1150.00
Service For 6, Winthrop, 36 Piece 2700.00
Service For 12, Beekman, c.1902, 48 Piece 4000.00
Spoon, Berry, 9 1/8 In. 325.00
Spoon, Berry, Grapevine, Silver-Gilt Bowl, 1870s, 9 1/2 In. 1095.00
Spoon, Fruit, Chrysanthemum 85.00
Spoon, Iced Tea, Chrysanthemum 45.00
Spoon, Oak Leaf, 1860s, 12 3/4 In. 650.00
Spoon, Persian, Monogram, 4 Piece 75.00
Spoon, Serving, Vine, Square Bowl, Ruffles 395.00
Spoon, Statue Of Liberty 50.00
Spoon, Stuffing, Gramercy 275.00
Spoon, Vegetable, Wave Edge, c.1884 .... 300.00
Strawberry Fork, Shell & Thread 75.00
Sugar Sifter, Gold Gilded, Dated 1916 .... 150.00
Tablespoon, Persian 100.00
Tazza, Scalloped Garland & Ribbon Border, Foliate Foot, 9 In. 605.00
Tea Caddy, 5 In. 385.00
Tea Caddy, Floral Repousse, Floral Knob Finial, c.1885, 4 3/8 In. 805.00
Tea Caddy, Scrolling Flowers & Greyhounds, Oval, 5 In. 770.00
Tea Set, Kettle On Lampstand, Islamic & Oriental Designs, c.1870, 5 Piece. 4313.00
Teaspoon, St. Dunstan 20.00
Tongs, Richelieu, Monogram, 5 1/2 In. 385.00
Tongs, Sandwich, Olympian, 7 1/2 In. 660.00
Tool, Sewing, Stork, Scissors Type Handles, Beak Opens, 5 In. 385.00
Tray, Bread, Reeded Edge, Pierced Border, No. 18197, c.1925, 10 5/8 In. 460.00
Tray, Chippendale Style, M Mark, 12 1/4 In. 935.00
Tray, Raised Rim, Etched Running Foliage, Flower Heads, c.1915, 28 3/4 In. 4888.00
Tray, Tea, Floral Panels, Plated, Handles, c.1870, 32 In. 990.00
Vase, Art Nouveau, Monogram, 1891-1902, 17 3/4 In. 3190.00
Vase, Bud, Chased, Love Knots Handles, Engraved 1874, Monogram, 10 In. 880.00
Vase, Bud, Trumpet, 6 1/2 In. 220.00
Vase, Etched Band Of Running Leaves Under Rim, c.1915, 14 In. 1380.00
Vase, Multiple Baluster Form, Etched Butterflies, Marked, 1902, 10 In. 2300.00
Vase, Presentation, Acanthus, Entwined Monogram, c.1950, 11 In. 1092.50
Vase, Trumpet, Fluted, 1891-1902, 9 1/8 In. 495.00
Vase, Trumpet, Monogram, No. 11094, c.1900, 13 1/4 In. 977.50
Waiter, Chrysanthemum, Monogram, Round, 13 In. 2860.00
Wine Coaster, Gadrooned Border, Plated, c.1895, 5 3/4 In. 165.00
Wine Cooler, Cylindrical Bottle Holder, 11 1/2 In. 8250.00

TIFFIN Glass Company of Tiffin, Ohio, was a subsidiary of the United States
Glass Co. of Pittsburgh, Pennsylvania, in 1892. The U.S. Glass Co. went
bankrupt in 1963, and the Tiffin plant employees purchased the building and
the inventory. They continued running it from 1963 to 1966, when it was sold
to Continental Can Company. In 1969, it was sold to Interpace, and in 1980,
it was closed. The black satin glass, made from 1923 to 1926, and the
stemware of the last twenty years are the best-known products.

Ashtray, Ruby, Crystal, 9 In.	125.00
Candlestick, Black Satin, 8 1/2 In., Pair	45.00
Candy Dish, King's Crown, Cover, Ruby Stained, Pedestal	22.00
Centerpiece, Sand Carved Flowers, Square, 4 1/2 x 10 In.	55.00
Champagne, Cascade	22.00
Champagne, June Night	10.00
Cocktail, Apollo, Diana, Gold, Vaseline Stem	25.00
Cocktail, Florence, 6 3/8 In.	12.00
Cocktail, June Night	15.00
Compote, Twist Stem, Vaseline, 7 1/2 In.	55.00
Cordial, Florence, 4 1/4 In.	12.00
Goblet, Byzantine	35.00
Goblet, Flanders, Pink, 8 1/4 In.	35.00 to 48.00
Goblet, Raindrops, Rose	21.00
Goblet, Shawl Dancer	38.00
Goblet, Water, Florence, 8 1/4 In.	12.00
Pilsner, Shawl Dancer	55.00
Pitcher, Lemonade, Arcadian, Green Handle & Base	375.00
Punch Set, Williamsburg, 13 Piece	140.00
Sherbet, Corona, 4 1/2 In.	18.00
Sherbet, June Night, Reeded Stem	20.00
Sherry, Shawl Dancer	55.00
Sugar & Creamer, Beaded Handles, Fuchsia	50.00
Vase, Black Satin, Floral, 10 In.	125.00
Vase, Bud, Swedish Modern, 11 In.	40.00
Vase, Diamond Pattern, Orange-Topaz, Footed Stem, Large	35.00
Vase, Poppy, Amethyst, c.1920, 5 1/2 In.	95.00
Vase, Poppy, Black Amethyst, 5 In.	85.00
Vase, Royal, Flared, Twilight & Green	400.00

TILES have been used in most countries of the world as a sturdy building material for floors, roofs, fireplace surrounds, and surface toppings. Many of the American tiles are listed in this book under the factory name.

Adam & Eve, Under The Apple Tree, Majolica, 11 x 8 In.	357.00
Animals, Empire, Square, 3 In.	28.00
Arthur's Knights.	80.00
Calendar, 1908, Harvard Medical School Building	55.00
Calendar, 1912, Cunard Line	70.00
Calendar, 1925, Flying Cloud	70.00
Calendar, 1928, Coolidge Homestead	70.00
China & Dolls, Painted Flowers, Louis Wolfe & Co	75.00
Cinderella Scenes, Minton Blank, Frame, 4 Piece	400.00
Dog & Doghouse, Majolica	88.00
Dr. Syntax Taking Possession Of His Living, Clews	175.00
Eve Offering Adam Fruit Of Tree Of Knowledge, Moravian Pottery, Square, 4 In.	50.00
Floral Design, White Ground, Frame, William DeMorgan & Co., 6 x 6 In.	385.00
Floral Sprays, Green & Purple, William DeMorgan & Co., 9 x 9 In.	440.00
Flowing Glaze, Hamilton Art Tile Co., Square, 6 In.	95.00
Frieze, Stylized Scroll, Pale Brown & Blue, 3 3/4 x 7 1/2 In., 14 Piece	172.00
Garden With Fountain, Brown & Blue Glaze, Square, 4 1/4 In.	165.00
Geometrics, Empire, Square, 3 In.	28.00
Grueby Type Floral, Green Shades, VBP Co., 6 1/8 In.	225.00
Hunting, 3-Tile Scene, Aetco	375.00
Lady In The Lake, Minton Blank, John Moyr Smith	95.00
Lily, Cross, Mercer, Moravian, 7 x 6 In.	100.00
Lion's Head, Hamilton, 6 x 6 In.	125.00
Nursery Rhyme, Old Lady In A Shoe, Square, 5 1/2 In.	65.00
Oak Tree, Yellow & Brown, Walrich Tile Co.	265.00
Owl, Fired Paint, Square, 6 In.	55.00
Pisces, Cutout, Brown, 4 In.	30.00
Roof, Ming Dynasty, Woman Seated On Animal, Foo Lions On Base	605.00
Roof, Phoenix, China	235.00
Sea Shells, S. Alcock, Mounted In Wood & Cloth Frame, c.1875, 7 x 14 1/2 In.	1210.00

Spanish Girl, Roses & Lace, Signed, 5 x 7 In.	145.00
Stylized Berries, Ochre, White, Blue, Umber, Terra-Cotta, 1915, 21 x 10 In.	332.00
Table, Black, Orange & Peach, Taylor Tile Co., 1930s, 17 In.	125.00
Woman & Bearded Man Portrait, Brown Glazed, 6 x 6 In., Pair	93.00
Woman Portrait, Pale Yellow Craquelle Glaze, Ceramic, 6 x 6 In., 3 Sections	71.00

TINWARE containers for household use have been made in America since the seventeenth century. The first tin utensils were brought from Europe, but by 1798, tin plate was imported and local tinsmiths made the wares. Painted tin is called *tole* and is listed separately. Some tin kitchen items may be found listed under Kitchen. The lithographed tin containers used to hold food and tobacco are listed in the Advertising category under Tin.

Baker, Bread, Tubular, Snap Closures, 2 Part	35.00
Boiler, Coffee, Side Spout, 13 1/4 In.	150.00
Bonnet, Anniversary, Bouquet Of 8 Tin Flowers, 16 In.	550.00
Bonnet, Anniversary, Cloth Trim, Tin Flowers & Feathers, 8 In.	770.00
Bottle, Fire Hydrant Liquor	12.50
Box, Bank Note Cigar	35.00
Box, Tinder, Candle Socket, Flint, Steel, Flax Tinder & Damper, 3 1/4 In.	275.00
Box, Tinder, With Candle Holder, Damper & Flints, 3 x 4 3/8 In.	215.00
Canister, Wig, Black Paint, A.A. Scanlon, Esq. London, Rack, 9 x 9 1/2 x 9 In.	190.00
Chamberstick, Push-Up, Conical Snuffer, Oblong Base, 6 In.	148.50
Chamberstick, Push-Up, Embossed Lion & Unicorn In Base, 5 In.	165.00
Coffee Urn, Brass Fittings, Eclipse Copper Co., 23 1/2 In.	115.00
Coffeepot, Hand-Punched Top, 7 In.	120.00
Coffeepot, Punched, Lovebirds & Tulips	7500.00
Cooler, Lemonade, Spigot, Domed Top	65.00
Foot Warmer, Punch, Walnut Frame, Turned Posts, Heart & Circle Design, 7 x 9 In.	330.00
Foot Warmer, Punched Heart, Circle Design, Mortised Walnut Frame, 7 1/4 In.	335.00
Ink Sander, 3 3/4 In.	65.00
Invitation, Anniversary, Mr. & Mrs. Charles Cook, Envelope, 3 x 5 In.	27.50
Mold, Candle, 12 Tube	495.00
Mold, Candle, 12 Tube, 11 1/2 In.	82.50
Mold, Candle, 24 Tube, Ear Handles, 8 1/2 In.	352.00
Mold, Candle, 36 Tube, 9 In.	308.00
Mold, Candle, 36 Tube, Wooden, Signed Walker	1475.00
Mold, Candle, Hanging Chain, 52 In.	357.50
Mold, Chocolate, Rabbit, 11 1/4 In.	47.00
Mold, Chocolate, Santa Claus, 7 1/2 In.	95.00
Recipe Box, Blue, Borrowman Label, With Recipes	15.00
Sconce, Candle, Diamond Shaped Reflector, Crimped Edge Pan, 16 1/2 In.	137.50
Sconce, Handle, Fluted Hood, 13 In.	135.00
Sconce, Hooded Semi-Circular Crest, Crimped, 16 In.	1155.00
Sconce, Red Flowers, Cream, Green Border, 12 In.	200.00
Sieve, Cheese, Cylindrical Punched, Footed, Handles, 4 In.	99.00
Teakettle, Stand, Chinoiserie Painted Design, England, 19th Century	1400.00
Umbrella Stand, Painted, 21 In.	200.00

TOBACCO JAR collectors search for those made in odd shapes and colors. Because tobacco needs special conditions of humidity and air, it has been stored in special containers since the eighteenth century.

Alligator, Majolica	275.00
Arabian, Majolica, 6 In.	155.00
Barrel Shape, Tan & Brown, Dolton Lambeth, 6 In.	95.00
Black Bearded Man, Gray Hat, Ceramic, 7 1/8 In.	1045.00
Black Child, Standing, Ceramic, 7 1/4 In.	165.00
Black Head, Detailed Hair, Eyes & Teeth, 9 In.	140.00
Black Man, Wearing Cap, Smoking Cigarette, Majolica, 7 In.	330.00
Black Woman's Head, Feather Crown, Ceramic, 7 1/2 In.	330.00
Black Man's Face, Form Of Watermelon, Austrian, Ceramic, 6 In.	1265.00
Black Man's Head, Green Cap, Majolica, Austrian, 4 1/4 In.	185.00
Figural, Bulldog	295.00
Grape & Cable, Purple Slag, Fenton	125.00

Mask Of Disraeli, Pagoda Shape, Majolica	165.00
Pouty Man, Cigar Butt In Mouth, Majolica	65.00
Urn Finial, America As Feather Headdressed Native, Cobalt Blue, 14 1/2 In.	2300.00
Winking Scotsman, Cover, Blue Beret, Plaid Band, 6 In.	135.00

TOBY JUG is the name of a very special form of pitcher. It is shaped like the full figure of a man or woman. A pitcher that shows just the top half of a person is not correctly called a toby. More examples of toby jugs can be found under Royal Doulton and other factory names.

Admiral Lord Howe, Brown Tricorner, Pearlware, 1785-1795, 10 In.	3738.00
Balding Man, Beard, Mustache, Occupied Japan, 2 1/4 In.	18.00
Blue & Polychrome Enamel, Staffordshire, 8 1/2 In.	440.00
Brown Sponging, Black, Yellow & Tan, Creamware, Staffordshire, 10 In.	440.00
Brown Tricorn, Brown Hair, Teal Blue Coat, Pratt, c.1795, 7 1/2 In.	460.00
Brown Tricorn, Yellow Edge, Blue Coat, Holding Jug, Pratt, c.1825, 7 1/2 In.	345.00
Chef, Tin	75.00
Creamware, Brown Tricorn, Brown Coat, Holding Jug, c.1795, 6 1/4 In.	460.00
Creamware, Brown Tricorn, Gray Hair, Blue Coat, Staffordshire, c.1780, 6 1/2 In.	575.00
Creamware, Dark Brown Tricorn, Amber Coat, Staffordshire, c.1820, 9 1/2 In.	345.00
Earthenware, Brown Tricorn, Gray Hair, Green Coat, Staffordshire, c.1830, 10 In.	460.00
French Officer, Full Figure, Occupied Japan	15.00
Gentleman, Gray Hair, Lancaster's Ltd., 2 1/2 In.	30.00
Gentleman, Seated, Tricorner Hat Spout, H & K Tunstall, 5 1/2 In.	30.00
Henry VIII, Wood & Sons, 5 1/2 In.	50.00
Hobo, Winking, White Beard, Porkpie Hat, Occupied Japan, 2 3/8 In.	22.00
Lord Nelson, Wood & Sons, 5 1/2 In.	50.00
Man, Seated, Holds Beer Stein, Back Of Chair Spout, Souter Johnny, 9 1/4 In.	72.00
Monkey, Polychrome, Crown Mark, 1980, 6 In.	19.00
Napoleon, Wood & Sons, 5 1/2 In.	50.00
Old Lady, Black Straw Bonnet, Umbrella Handle, Occupied Japan, 2 3/8 In.	22.00
Pearlware, Gray Tricorn, Gray Hair, Sponged Coat, Staffordshire, c.1785, 10 In.	345.00
Pearlware, Squire, Brown Tricorn, Long Brown Hair, Blue Coat, c.1795, 11 In.	800.00
Rodney's Sailor, Brown Hat, Yellow Neckerchief, Pearlware, c.1780, 11 3/4 In.	3738.00
Woman, Full Figure, Brown Hair, Flowered Skirt, Occupied Japan, 3 In.	20.00

TOLE is painted tin. It is sometimes called *japanned ware*, *pontypool*, or *toleware*. Most nineteenth-century tole is painted with an orange-red or black background and multicolored decorations. Many recent versions of toleware are made and sold. Related items may be listed in the Tin category.

Bank, House, Red, Stenciled Gold Trim, Blue Japanned Roof, 4 In.	93.50
Birdcage, Gilt Scrolling Design, Yellow Ground, 29 1/2 In.	75.00
Bowl, Apple, Hand Stenciled & Painted, 11 In.	95.00
Box, Black Transfer, Dark Green Paint, Oval, 4 3/4 In.	60.00
Box, Brown Graining, Yellow Border, German Inscription On Lid, Oval, 16 In.	50.00
Box, Deed, Colored Floral Design, Black Ground, 8 In.	110.00
Box, Deed, Dark Brown Japanning, Fruit, Bird & Floral, 10 1/2 In.	66.00
Box, Deed, Dome Top, Brown Japanning, Design, 9 In.	330.00
Box, Deed, Dome Top, Dark Brown Japanning, Floral, White Band, 8 In.	302.00
Box, Deed, Red, Green & Mustard, 1820-1830, 9 1/4 x 5 3/4 x 6 1/2 In.	345.00
Box, Deed, Red Paint, Gold Stenciling, 4 In.	82.50
Box, Deed, Stenciled Basket Of Flowers, Wire Bale Handle, 9 1/2 In.	82.00
Box, Document, Painted, New England, c.1830, 5 1/8 x 9 In.	715.00
Box, Hat, Red Stripe On Hinged Lid, Yellow Graining, 15 In.	27.50
Box, Red Thistle Type Design, 1820-1830, 8 x 4 x 4 1/2 In.	345.00
Box, Silver Stenciled Design On Lid, Yellow Striping, 5 In.	27.50
Box, Spice, Black Stenciled Labels, Mustard Paint, 14 In.	93.50
Box, Spice, Red Striping, 6 Square Canisters, Stenciled Labels On Lids	105.00
Box, Tobacco, Girl & Flowers Cover, Pornographic Nude Woman Interior, 3 x 4 In.	220.00
Bucket, Red Paint, Gold Stenciled Floral, Wire Bale, 3 1/2 In.	275.00
Cache Pot, Reserves Of Chinamen In Landscape, 6 3/4 In., Pair	690.00
Canister, Ginger, Gold & Blue Stenciled Label, Phil Becker & Co., 10 In.	110.00
Canister, Red Cherries, Mustard Design, 1820-1830, 8 x 8 In.	275.00
Coal Scuttle, Bail Handle, Painted Mask Heads, Floral Garland, 21 In.	132.00

Coffeepot, Gooseneck, Brown Ground 4400.00
Cup, Red, 1850-1860, 2 x 1 1/2 In. 38.00
Jardiniere, Figural, Moorish Male & Female, Period Costumes, 14 In., Pair 4888.00
Jardiniere, Flared, Neoclassical Design, Red Ground, Claw Feet, 14 3/4 In., Pair 4025.00
Lamp, Circular Tapering Stem, Faux Bois 690.00
Lamp, Pierced Conical Shade, 1 Candlearm, Electrified, France, 19 1/4 In. 575.00
Mirror, Fora Frame, Italy, 24 x 16 In. 275.00
Mug, Polychrome Fruit & Flowers, Black Ground, 4 3/4 In. 38.50
Needle Case, Brown Japanning. Yellow Design, 9 In. 16.50
Sugar, Red Paint, Comma Foliage, 3 1/2 In. 165.00
Tea Caddy, Brown Japanning, Stylized Floral, Red & Yellow, 4 In. 148.50
Tea Caddy, Red, Yellow, Pink & Black 770.00
Tea Caddy, Red & Yellow Design, Black, 6 1/4 In. 30.50
Tray, 2 Tiers, Vintage & Landscape Scene, Black Ground, 16 1/2 x 16 1/2 In. 275.00
Tray, Apple, Scalloped Sides 5500.00
Tray, Bread, Dark Brown Japanning, Stylized Floral Center, 12 3/4 In. 192.00
Tray, Chippendale, Allover Hand Painted Flowers, Gold Trim, 12 In. 70.00
Tray, Empire, Perspective City View Center, Foliate Border, Bamboo Stand, 24 In. 5400.00
Tray, European Landscape Reserve, Ribbon & Wreath Design, Oval, 27 In. 1650.00
Tray, Fruit Design, Blue Border, Round, 14 In. 100.00
Tray, Hudson River Style Oil With Ruins, c.1880, 20 x 27 1/2 In. 285.00
Tray, Hunting Dog, With Pheasant, 19th Century, England, 28 x 20 1/2 In. 385.00
Tray, Regency, Cartouche Shape, Gilt Flowers, Landscape, England, 32 x 24 In. 825.00
Tray, Regency, Gilt Decorated, Red, Eagles & Wreaths, Pierced Handles, 28 In. 4600.00
Tray, Reticulated, Rectangle, Gilt Decorated Center, Handles, 14 1/2 x 9 3/8 In. 165.00
Tray, Stenciled Floral Design, Yellow Striping, 8 3/4 x 11 3/4 In. 71.50
Tray, Victorian, Overall Floral Design, Stand, 27 In. 410.00
Tumbler, Comma Design On Rim, Dark Brown Japanning, 4 In. 120.00
Urn, Landscape Reserve, Fruit Finial, Lion Head Handles, France, 15 3/8 In., Pair 605.00

TOM MIX was born in 1880 and died in 1940. He was the hero of over 100
silent movies from 1910 to 1929, and 25 sound films from 1929 to 1935.
There was a Ralston Tom Mix radio show from 1933 to 1950, but the original
Tom Mix was not in the show. Tom Mix comics were published from 1942 to
1953.

Belt, Championship, Red & Black 125.00
Book, Big Little Book, Rider Of Death Valley, Universal Pictures 25.00
Book, Big, Big Book, Tom Mix & The Scourge Of Paradise Valley, Whitman, 1937 .. 75.00
Booklet, No. 39, National Chicle Co., 1934 .... 35.00
Bracelet, ID, Straight Shooters, Ralston 95.00
Brochure, Contest, Autographed Stetson Hat 50.00
Button, Straight Shooters, Ralston Premium, 1949, Card & Mailer, 5 Piece 125.00
Card Game, Wild Cat, Box, 1935 .... 48.00 to 55.00
Catalog, Straight Shooters Premium, 1933 .... 30.00
Chaps, Leather, Brown, Black Trim, Ralston Premium, 1930s 295.00
Compass, Magnifier, Glow-In-The-Dark, Ralston Premium, 1947 .... 45.00 to 72.00
Flashlight, Bird Call 75.00
Game, Card, Wild Cat, 1935 .... 48.00 to 65.00
Parachute, Mailer, Instruction Book 100.00
Periscope, Official Tom Mix, Ralston .... 30.00 to 90.00
Pin, Lithograph .... 30.00 to 90.00
Pitcher, Water, Little Joe, Teal Decal 15.00
Postcard, Captains Medal Order, 1940 .... 1.00
Poster, Tom Mix In Daredevil, Romance Of Hard-Boiled Tenderfoot, 80 x 41 In. 132.00
Ring, Look-Around, 1946 .... 90.00
Ring, Mystery Picture 365.00
Ring, Signet, With Embossed Six-Shooters, 1936 .... 175.00 to 325.00
Ring, Sliding Whistle .... 50.00 to 95.00
Ring, Straight Shooter, 1935 .... 65.00
Ring, Tiger Eye, Glow-In-The-Dark, 1950 .... 200.00 to 250.00
Safety Poster, 1947, 17 x 22 In. .... 15.00 to 35.00
Secret Manual, 1944 .... 50.00

Shirt, 1920s 660.00
TV Set, Model RCA Victor, Film Discs 55.00
Watch Fob, Straight Shooters, Gold Ore 85.00
Water Set, Child's, Cobalt Blue, 5 Piece 35.00
Wristwatch, Anniversary, Ralston, 1983 .... 350.00

TOOLS of all sorts are listed here, but most are related to industry. Other tools may be found listed under Iron, Kitchen, Tinware, and Wooden.

Adding Machine, Victor, Black Bakelite 32.00
Adding Machine, Victor, Black, Green Keys 75.00
Adze, Connecticut-Style, 9 In. Head, 4 In. Bit 210.00
Anvil, Jeweler's 15.00
Anvil, Shoemaker's, Iron, 9 1/2 x 3 1/2 x 10 In. 15.00
Auger, Bung Hole, Barrel, Wooden, Tee Handle 12.00
Auger, Hand, Keen Kutter 25.00
Auger Bit, Winchester, No.6, 8 1/2 In. 20.00
Ax, Broad, Winchester, Single Bevel 25.00
Ax, Goosewing, Multiple Touch Marks, 9 In. 205.00
Ax, Red Goose On Blade & Handle 1500.00
Ax, Shapleigh 25.00
Ax, Splitting, Goosewing, Billansbruk 155.00
Beater, Bed, Wicker 30.00
Bee Smoker 25.00
Bench, Carpenter's, Wooden Vises, Shelves 575.00
Bit Brace, Stanley, Bell System, 1950s 40.00
Book Press, Cast Iron, Black & Gold Paint, 10 3/4 x 20 In. .. 440.00
Bootjack, American Bulldog, Iron, Embossed, Folding 20.00
Box, Clock Maker's, Stenciled Clock Face Interior, Poplar, 20 3/4 In. .. 165.00
Box, Keen Kutter, Oak, 2 Doors 400.00
Box, Machinist's, Oak, 8 Compartments, Complete 145.00
Box, Shoe Shine, Esquire, Mahogany, Brass Lion Handles .. 125.00
Brace, Brass Frame, Ebony, William Marples Patent 400.00
Brace, Carpenter's, Wooden, Brass Bound, Iron Bit 125.00
Bucksaw, Wagon Maker's, Carved, Nameplate, T. H. Edgerly, Rochester, N.H. .. 1500.00
Butt Plate, Black Hard Plastic, WRA Co. 20.00
Calipers, Log, Wm. Greenlief, 55 In. 770.00
Carder, Flax 35.00
Caulking Mallet, Shipwright's, With Caulking Wedge 82.50
Chainsaw, Fairbanks & Morse 275.00
Change Sorter, Oak, Separated Fitted Drawers, Hand Crank .. 575.00
Cheese Press, Pine & Hardwood, Primitive, 45 3/4 In. 82.50
Cheese Press, Wooden, Strainers, Drain Boards, Primitive .. 25.00
Chest, Cabinet Maker's, Blue Sides, Ends & Back, Sliding Compartments, 35 In. 385.00
Chest, Machinist's, Oak Drawers, Metal Covered 145.00
Cigarette Roller, Tin, Brown, Williamson 12.00
Clamp, Bliss Co., Barn Size, Pair 65.00
Clamp, Quilt, Handmade, 4 Piece 45.00
Clamp, To Remove Articles From High Shelves 20.00
Clippers, Hair, Keen Kutter, No. 4, Cover 30.00
Comb, Cast Iron, Curry, 6 Rows Of Teeth, Horse Center, 5 x 8 In. .. 85.00
Comb, Curry, Horse, Iron, Wooden Handle, Round 2.00
Compass, Barometer, 14K Gold, Pocket, 1 1/4 In. 605.00
Compass, Surveyor's, Brass, W.I. Young, Philadelphia 357.00
Cork Puller, Bronze, Industrial Strength, Large 150.00
Corn Planter, Iron, John Deere, Moline, Ill., Raised Deer Design .. 12.00
Cow Kicker, Farmer's, Iron Chain 2.35
Cutter, Cottage Cheese Curd 48.00
Cutter, Sugar, Hand Forged Iron, Wooden Base, 12 1/2 In. .. 140.00
Damper, Stove Pipe, Cast Iron, Griswold 6.50
Doweling Jig, No. 60, 9 Guides, c.1920s 85.00
Drill Press, W.F. & J. Barnes 150.00
Flashlight, Eveready, Pat. 1912, Box, Miniature 40.00

Flashlight, Winchester 35.00
Fleam, Brass Frame, Livestock Or Horse, England 50.00
Fly Chaser, Clockwork, Nickel Plated, Cloth Covered Wire Wands, 50 In. 165.00
Gauge, Milk Can, Stanley 310.00
Gauge, Mortise, 1920s 45.00
Glove Stretcher, Ivory 45.00
Glue Pot, Copper, Double Boiler-Style, 2 Piece 135.00
Gum Chipper, Wooden Handle, Net 145.00
Hair Dryer, Oster, Chrome, Box 50.00
Hammer, Coal, Iron, Wooden Handle, Sunshine Coal Co., Centerville, Iowa 18.00
Hammer, Farrier's, Horseshoe, Wooden Handle 5.00
Hammer, Log Marker 65.00
Hammer Head, Log Marking, Double-Ended, Star With Center Dot 275.00
Hand Beader, 6 Cutters 325.00
Handcuffs, Policeman's, Peerless, Key 30.00
Handcuffs, Policeman's, Smith & Wesson, Key 28.00
Hatchet, Camp, Wooden Handle, Winchester 65.00
Hatchet, Rig Builders Pattern, New Handle, Winchester, 13 In. 40.00
Hatchet, Sheath 25.00
Honey Press, Iron 30.00
Ice Chipper, Pick, For Horse's Hooves, Cast Iron, c.1890, 9 1/2 In. 65.00
Jointer, Iron, Diamond-Patterned Bottom & Floral Design, Morris Patent, 21 5/8 In. .. 850.00
Knitter, Home Profit, Instruction Book 185.00
Labeling Machine, Monarch Marking System, Print Box 95.00
Lamp Lighter, Gas, Brass Head, Walnut Turned Handle, 28 In. 145.00
Lathe, Metal, W.F.& J. Barnes, Foot Powered, Dated 1876 .... 400.00
Lathe, South Bend, Westinghouse Motor, 4 Foot Bed, 1934 .... 1850.00
Level, Brass, Cast Iron, The Davis Level & Tool Co., Springfield, 1883, 24 In. 165.00
Level, Davis, Patent September 17, 1867, 7 In. 350.00
Level, Machinist's, 1950s, 24 In. 65.00
Level, Sighting, Brass, Stackpole & Brother, New York, Tripod Base 467.00
Level, Spirit, Cast Iron, Adjustable, L. L. Davis, 24 In. 240.00
Level, Spirit, Mahogany, Brass Trim, D. Miyon, 30 In. 49.50
Lice Killing Machine, Schild's Lightning Poultry, Canvas, Wooden, Primitive, 1897 ...... 40.00
Lock, Brass, Yale, Ordinance Dept. 65.00
Loom, Tape, Walnut, Dovetailed Case 295.00
Loupe, Bausch & Lomb, 3 Matched Lenses, Zinc Plated Slip-Out Case 47.95
Meal Bin, Poplar, Dark Stain, 3 Sections, Lift Top, Hinges, 7 Ft. 485.00
Measure, Grain, Wooden, Signed 32.00
Miter Box, Instruction Sheet, Box, 1950s 120.00
Miter Jack, Wooden Screws, Walnut & Maple, 28 In. 205.00
Model, Man, Artist's, Wooden, Articulated, 19th Century, 33 1/2 In. 1705.00
Mold, Bullet, Winchester, 44WCF, Wooden Handles 30.00
Mold, For Pewter Spoons, Bronze, 2 Piece, 9 In. .... 325.00 to 330.00
Multiplane, No. 405, Dovetailed Box 285.00
Niddy-Noddy, Birch, Carved, Mortised & Pinned, 18 In. 75.00
Niddy-Noddy, Chip Carved, Old Varnish Finish, 18 In. 205.00
Niddy-Noddy, Hardwood, Dark Red Finish, Chip Carved Detail, 20 In. 220.00
Night Stick, Policeman's, Wooden, Long 3.50
Padlock, Winchester, Brass 165.00
Peel, Baker's, Wrought Iron, Scroll Handle, 45 1/2 In. 66.00
Pick, Miner's 3.50
Pitchfork, True Temper, Wooden, Cast Iron, Salesman's Sample, 30 In. 385.00
Plane, Carpenter's, W. Butcher, 21 In. 40.00
Plane, Dado, Japanned Finish, Box, 1920s 200.00
Plane, Jointer, Holy's Patent, Iron, 20 In. 325.00
Plane, Molding, Gate, Brass Trim, 11 1/2 In. 49.50
Plane, Molding, Yellow Birch, Fuller & Field, 10 In. 525.00
Plane, Plow, Miller, No. 141, Fillister Bed, Nose Piece, 6 Cutters 510.00
Plane, Rabbet, E. Smith, Handle, 14 1/2 In. 115.00
Plane, Rabbet, Weatherstrip, Box, 1940s 175.00
Plane, Rabbet, Wedged Slide Arms, Yellow Birch, Nicholson Stamp 2100.00
Plane, Stanley, Block, Edge Rimming 150.00

Plane, Stanley, No. 4 .... 27.00
Plane, Stanley, No. 10, Rabbet, Carriage Maker's 125.00
Plane, Stanley, No. 13, Circular, Side Wheel Adjustment 70.00
Plane, Stanley, No. 20, Circular, Victor, Bailey Patent 200.00
Plane, Stanley, No. 113, Circular 75.00
Plane, Stanley, No. A78, Duplex Fillister 400.00
Plane, T Rabbet, Carriage Maker's, Brass 150.00
Plane, Tongue & Groove, B Casting, No. 49 .... 100.00
Plane, Tongue, John Sleeper, 9 3/4 In. 100.00
Plane, Tongue, Veerploeg, 13-In. Fence, 10 1/4 In. 100.00
Plane, Winchester, No. 3026, Corrugated Bottom 60.00
Plane, Wood, Stothert Bath 20.00
Planter, Plow, Miller, No. 42, Adjustable, Gunmetal, Filllister Bed & Cutter 2200.00
Pliers, Pistol Grip, Keen Kutter 110.00
Pole, Measuring, Equestrian, Brass, Presentation Plaque, 19th Century, 75 In. 165.00
Pounce Sander, Maple, Tooled Bands Top & Base, 2 x 2 3/4 In. 45.00
Press, Book, Wood Screws, Walnut, W.O. Hickok, Harrisburg, 1830s, 25 x 3 In. 265.00
Press, Cigar, With 12 Cigar Molds, 1850 .... 750.00
Press, Printing, C. & P., Foot Pedal, 8 x 12 In. 800.00
Press, Tie, Man's, Horne 20.00
Press, Tie, Wooden, England 15.00
Press, Wine, Oak, Stenciled, 3 Ft. 90.00
Press & Grinder, Apple Cider, Original Paint 450.00
Pump, Bilge, Brass, Nantucket, 1897 .... 65.00
Pump, Pitcher, Cast Iron, Brass Cylinder, T. I. Savey 35.00
Pump, Pitcher, Hartley, Cast Iron, Brass, Cylinder, Wall Mount 30.00
Pump, Well, Wooden, Orange Paint Traces, Cast Iron Spigot, Stearns Mfg. Co. 42.50
Punch, Poultry, J.C. Petty, Iron 1.50
Rake, Cranberry, Pine & Maple, Wire Tines, No. S. Jos. Breck & Sons, 45 In. 165.00
Ruler, Architect's, 4 Fold, 2 Ft. 45.00
Ruler, Caliper, 2 Fold, Type 6, 1 Ft. 35.00
Ruler, Folding, Ivory, No. 29 .... 255.00
Ruler, Folding, Keen Kutter, No. 620, 24 In. 15.00
Ruler, Folding, Wooden, 72 In. 10.00
Ruler, Zig-Zag, Stanley Bell System, Patent 1913, 72 In. 45.00
Saw, 2-Man, Double Handles, Wooden Sheath, Steel, 50 In. 38.50
Saw, Crosscut, 1 Man 10.00
Saw, Dehorning, Keen Kutter 80.00
Saw, Ice, 7 Ft. 37.50
Saw, Ice, Horse Drawn, Blade Guard, Gifford Wood Co., 84 In. 825.00
Scaler, Lumber, William Greenleaf 660.00
Scissors, Keen Kutter, 8 In. 20.00
Scoop, Black Powder, Bronze, Hand Hammered, 3 1/2 x 5 3/4 In. 115.00
Scoop, Cranberry, Wood, Carved E.D., 11 x 16 In. 297.00
Screwdriver, 3 Bits, Box, 1950s 95.00
Scribe, Carpenter's, Wooden, Adjustable 2.50
Scythe, Farmer's, Wooden Handle 10.00
Shears, Grape, Fox & Grape Design, Silver Plate 75.00
Shears, Sheep 10.00
Shell Crimper, For 12 Gauge Shotgun, Cast Iron, Wooden Handle 20.00
Shovel, Snow, Wooden 10.00
Slate Remover, Roof, Bangor Slate Co., Easton Penna., c.1850, 32 In. 75.00
Sled, Hauling Freight, Iron Fittings, Pine, 36 x 64 In. 137.50
Sorter, Bean, Treadle, Primitive, Stenciled, 1880 .... 85.00
Sorter, Cranberry, Gray Slates, 6 Ft. 4 In. 95.00
Spokeshave, Rabbet, Japanned Finish, 1920s 85.00
Spokeshave, Razor Edge, Hanging Holes, Rosewood, No.82 .... 110.00
Spokeshave, Stanley, No. 51 .... 15.00
Sprayer, Insect, Spra-Well, Tin 28.00
Stapler, Hotchkiss, No. 1 .... 95.00
Stencil Kit, Sign Painter's, Brass Alphabet, Paint Pots, 12 3/4 In. 110.00
Stone, Sharpening, Dietz Milk 17.50
Straight Edge, Draftman's, Adie London, Brass, Wooden Case, 19 1/2 In. 73.50

◆ ◆ ◆ ◆ ◆ ◆ ◆ ◆ ◆ ◆ ◆ ◆ ◆ ◆ ◆ ◆ ◆ ◆ ◆ ◆

New security idea: Have one of
the neighbors park a second car
in your driveway. Your house will
look occupied and the car will
be seen coming and going.

◆ ◆ ◆ ◆ ◆ ◆ ◆ ◆ ◆ ◆ ◆ ◆ ◆ ◆ ◆ ◆ ◆ ◆ ◆ ◆

Tool, Wrench, Bed Rope, Painted Design,
19th Century

Ticker Tape Machine, Glass Dome	7000.00
Time Lock, Bank Vault, 4 Movement, 1892	240.00
Tooth Setter, Mill Saw, Aikens Saw	5.00
Torch, Hand, Jeweler's, Jim Dandy, Alcohol, Brass, Small	6.50
Trammel, Sawtooth, Wrought Iron, 48 In.	220.00
Vacuum Cleaner, Fairfax, Art Deco, Chrome, With Attachments	145.00
Vise, Box Lid Bench, Wooden Foot Activates Spring Clamp, 33 x 13 1/2 In.	214.50
Vise, Harness Maker's, 43 In.	55.00
Vise, Saw, Brass Thumbscrew, Rosewood, 14 x 15 1/4 In.	155.00
Washing Machine, Double, Wooden, Jonas L. Noll, Lebanon, Pa., 1889	375.00
Water Pump, Cast Iron, Green, Salesman's Sample, 8 x 4 1/4 In.	140.00
Wheelbarrow, Red, Stencil, Iron Wheel	165.00
Wheelbarrow, Wooden, Black Paint	110.00
Wheelbarrow, Yellow, Detachable Sides, Bittersweet Wheel, 1920s	350.00
Whistle, Steam, Buckey Brass Works, Pigtail, 3 x 14 In.	265.00
Windmill, Aero Mfg. Co., Model 12B, Aluminum, Salesman's Sample, 16 3/4 In.	143.00
Wrench, Adjustable, Gordon Automatic	45.00
Wrench, Adjustable, Keen Kutter, 4 In.	155.00
Wrench, Bed Rope, Painted Design, 19th Century .... *Illus*	4000.00
Wrench, Crescent, Keen Cutter	19.00
Wrench, Ford, Adjustable, 8 In.	10.00
Wrench, Hex, Walco, No. 0	25.00
Wrench, Pipe, Keen Kutter, No. 14, Simmons	25.00
Wrench, Pipe, Winchester, No. 1022, Wooden Handle	50.00
Wrench, Reed, Cast Iron, Adjustable	3.50
Wrench, Spark Plug, Model T, Marked	5.00
Wrench, Winchester, No. 1837, Curved Double Open End	30.00
Wringer, Bench, Universal Ball Bearing, Folding	88.00
Wringer, Bicycle, Anchor Brand, Advertising, Patent 1899, 7 x 7 1/2 In.	495.00

TOOTHPICK HOLDERS are sometimes called *toothpicks* by collectors. The
variously shaped containers used to hold small wooden toothpicks are made
of glass, china, or metal. Most of the toothpick holders are Victorian.
Additional items may be found in other categories, such as Bisque, Silver
Plate, Slag Glass, etc.

Acorn	75.00
Amberette, Clear	95.00
Arched Ovals, Donnelson, Iowa	30.00
Art Novo, White Flowers, Green Leaves	73.00
Atlas, Milk Glass	55.00
Beatty's Honeycomb, Blue	50.00
Beatty's Honeycomb, White	40.00
Beatty's Rib, Blue	40.00
Bees In Basket, Ivory, Blue & Gold Bees	45.00
Boy, Sitting On Fence, Tree Trunk, Bisque, Occupied Japan, 2 1/2 In.	7.00

Boy, In Wheat, Metal 40.00
Bulldog, Pot Metal 18.00
Bundle Of Cigars, Milk Glass 18.00
Button Arches, Syracuse, N.Y., Ruby 12.00
Buxx Star, Light Gold 15.00
Cactus, Milk Glass, Green 45.00
Can Pattern, Iridescent, Robert Hanson 50.00
Child, In Clown Suit, Beside Vase, 2 1/2 In. 3.00
Chrysanthemum Base, Blue Speckled 239.00
Colorado, Cobalt Blue, Gold Trim 35.00
Colorado, Green, Gold Trim 20.00
Criss-Cross, White Opalescent 165.00
Daisy & Button, Celeste Blue, Footed 15.00
Diamond & Button, Coal Hod, Vaseline 22.00
Diamond Quilted, Reverse Amberina, Corset Shape 225.00
Dicken's Days, Porcelain 35.00
Dog, At Side Of Blue Hat, Cat On Rim, Occupied Japan 8.00
Forget-Me-Not, Blue 60.00
Galloway, Clear 15.00
Hobnail, White Opalescent 20.00
Indian Head, Chocolate Glass 195.00
Indian Head, Milk Glass, Light Lilac 45.00
Intaglio Sunflower 35.00
Inverted Fan & Feather, Custard 695.00
Iris With Meander, Amethyst 45.00
Iris With Meander, Blue Opalescent 75.00
Jefferson Colonial, Gold Between Scallops & Top 45.00
Lace, Carnival Glass, Amber, Imperial 25.00
Ladder With Diamond, Ruby Stain 145.00
Little Lobe, Pink Violets, Yellow Between Lobes 75.00
Man & Woman, Figural, In Front Of Blue Vases, Occupied Japan, Pair 12.00
Monkeys, Amber 22.00
Moon & Stars, Amberina 75.00
National's Eureka, Ruby Stain 45.00
Paneled, Amberina 55.00
Phlox, Blue, Translucent 475.00
Pony Pulling 2-Wheel Glass Cart 50.00
Red & Blue Floral, Cloisonne, Scrolled Yellow Ground, Porcelain, 1 1/2 In. 26.00
Reverse Swirl, Cranberry Opalescent 235.00
Ribbed Spiral, Vaseline Opalescent 115.00
Ribbed Spirals, Blue Opalescent 85.00
Ribbed Thumbprint, Custard 90.00
Ring Band, Custard, Heisey 70.00
Royal Ivy, Multicolored, Cased 145.00
Royal Ivy, Rainbow Craquelle 325.00
Ruby Thumbprint, Etched 25.00
Scotty, Large Cylinder, Blue Bow, Occupied Japan 4.50
Scroll With Cane Band 70.00
Shamrock, Ruby Stain, Detroit, Michigan 40.00
St. Clair, Bicentennial, Cobalt Blue, Gold 25.00
Sunset Pattern, Pink Cased, 2 1/4 In. 80.00
Swag & Baskets, Vaseline Opalescent, 2 1/2 In. 165.00
Swirl, Opalescent Reverse 90.00
Tan & Gray Slag, Marked Joe St. Clair In Script 45.00
Thousand Eye, Vaseline 40.00
Urn, Square Base, Ice Blue Carnival Glass, Imperial 35.00
Urn, Sterling Silver, Gadroon Rim, 2 3/4 x 2 5/8 In. 38.00
Venetian Diamond, Amberina 235.00
Wild Bouquet, Blue Opalescent 695.00
Woodpecker, Mechanical, Head Picks Up Toothpick 3.25
Wreath & Shell, White Opalescent 150.00
Wreath & Wheel, Vaseline Opalescent 225.00

TORQUAY is the name given to ceramics by several potteries working near Torquay, England, from 1870 until 1962. Until about 1900, the potteries used local red clay to make classical-style art pottery vases and figurines. Then they turned to making souvenir wares. Items were dipped in colored slip and decorated with painted slip and sgraffito designs. They often had mottoes or proverbs, and scenes of cottages, ships, birds, or flowers. The *Scandy* design was a symmetrical arrangement of brushstrokes and spots done in colored slips. Potteries included Watcombe Pottery (1870–1962); Torquay Terra-Cotta Company (1875–1905); Aller Vale (1881–1924); Torquay Pottery (1908–1940); and Longpark (1883–1957).

TORQUAY

Bean Pot, Pixie, Footed, Embossed Figure, 2 1/2 In.	65.00
Biscuit Jar, Kingfisher	260.00
Bottle, Devon Violets	30.00 to 35.00
Bowl, Silver Plated Rim, 9 In.	195.00
Candlestick, Cockerel, Black, Motto Ware, Longpark, 4 In.	128.00
Chamberstick, Crocus, Longpark, 3 1/2 In.	58.00
Coffeepot, Motto Ware, 5 In.	100.00
Compote, Daunee Be Afraid Of Now, Motto Ware, Devon	42.00
Creamer, Cottage Motto Ware, Square, 2 3/4 In.	65.00
Creamer, Watcombe Cottage, 4 In.	45.00
Cup, A Stitch In Time, Motto Ware, Devon	48.00
Cup & Saucer, Motto Ware, Scandy, Allervale	55.00
Eggcup, Cottage, Just Laid, Watcombe, 1 3/4 In.	28.00
Eggcup, Lighthouse, Pedestal, Watcombe, 3 In.	40.00
Hatpin Holder, Cockerel	140.00
Hatpin Holder, Longpark Ship	125.00
Hatpin Holder, Scandy, I'll Take Care Of Hat Pins, Allervale, 5 In.	95.00
Jam Jar, Cottage, Isle Of Wight, Go Aisy Wi' It Now, Cover, 4 1/4 In.	55.00
Jam Jar, Cottage, Take A Little Marmalade, Cover, 4 1/2 In.	55.00
Jam Jar, Cottage, Time Ripens All Things, Cover, 4 1/4 x 3 In.	45.00
Jug, Hot Water, Cottage	145.00
Jug, Puzzle, Scandy	180.00
Pitcher, Cover, 6 3/4 In.	135.00
Pitcher, Ruby	375.00
Pitcher, Sailboat Scene, Be Canny With Cream, Exeter, Miniature	48.00
Pitcher, Scandy, Motto Ware, Allervale, 3 In.	38.00
Plate, Scandy, Motto Ware, Watcombe, 4 In.	52.00
Puzzle Jug	95.00
Salt & Pepper, Cottage, Snowdon On Back, Egg Shape	60.00 to 65.00
Teapot, Child's, Cottage, 2 1/2 In.	85.00
Teapot, Cockerel	145.00
Teapot, Cottage, Motto Ware, Longpark, 5 In.	170.00
Tile, Tea, 5 1/2 In.	70.00
Tobacco Jar, Scandy, Motto Ware, Longpark, 5 In.	175.00
Vase, Kerswell, Motto Ware, Allervale, 4 In.	115.00
Vase, Moonlight Sailing Boat, 7 In., Pair	175.00
Vase, Peacock, Blue Ground, c.1917, 6 In.	165.00
Vase, Sailboat, Ship On Front, Be Not Weary In Well Doing, 4 In.	55.00

TORTOISESHELL is the shell of the tortoise. It has been used as inlay and to make small decorative objects since the seventeenth century. Some species of tortoise are now on the endangered species list, and objects made from these shells cannot be sold legally.

Box, Allegorie Sur La Bataille D'jena Scene Lid, 3 1/8 In.	192.00
Box, Ivory Bun Feet, Victorian, England, 1 1/4 x 3 1/2 x 2 1/4 In.	302.50
Box, Oriental Carved, Oval, 4 In.	121.00
Box, Patch, 2 1/4 In.	99.00
Box, Pill, 2 1/8 In.	77.00
Box, Pill, Horn, 4 In.	94.00
Box, Silver Plated Brass, Lift Out Tray, Scissors, Thimble, 3 1/4 In.	434.00
Box, Trinket, 4 3/4 In.	357.00
Box, Trinket, Ivory, 7 In.	193.00

Toy, Airplane, Ford Trimotor, Tin, Schieble, 29 1/2 x 26 1/2 In.

Top to Bottom: Toy, Airplane, America, Cast Iron, 13 1/2-In. Wingspan; Toy, Airplane, Lindy, Cast Iron, Hubley, 10-In. Wingspan

Brush, Child's, 6 In.	33.00
Clock, Carriage, Victorian, Silver-Mounted, JB, London, French Movement	4310.00
Comb, Enameled Dancing Scenes, Goldtone Case, England	80.00
Compact, Silver Mounted, Rectangular	286.00
Glove Box, Ivory Edge, Large	990.00
Mirror, Hand	154.00
Pill Box, Domed Lid, Rectangular	99.00
Shoe Horn, Child's, Velvet Box	25.00
Snuff Bottle, Semi-Precious Stones	77.00
Tea Caddy, England, 1800-1820	1800.00
Tea Caddy, Regency, Bombe, Silver Plaque, Early 1800s, 6 1/2 x 7 3/4 In.	1840.00
Tea Caddy, Silver Mount, Inlaid Ivory, Ten Sides, c.1810, 5 3/4 x 6 In.	4600.00

TORTOISESHELL GLASS was made during the 1800s and after by the Sandwich Glass Works of Massachusetts and some firms in Germany. Tortoiseshell glass is, of course, named for its resemblance to real shell from a tortoise. It has been reproduced.

Bowl, 8 1/2 In.	90.00
Dresser Jar, 2 With Amber Finial & Footed, 1 With Clear Finial, 3 Piece	165.00
Pitcher, Amber Handle, 8 1/2 In.	125.00

TOY collectors have special clubs, magazines, and shows. Toys are designed to entice children, and today they have attracted new interest among adults who are still children at heart. All types of toys are collected. Tin toys, iron toys, battery operated toys, and many others are collected by specialists. Dolls, Games, Teddy Bears, and Bicycles are listed in their own categories. Other toys may be found under company or celebrity names.

10 Pin Bowling, Wooden, 1950s, Package, Unused	10.00
Accordion, Carrying Case, 1950s	35.00
Accordion, Emenee, Box	50.00
Acrobat, Pinocchio, Windup, 1939	450.00
Adama, Battlestar Galactica, On Card, 1978	12.00
Adding Machine, Wolverine	12.00
Air-E-Go-Round, Reeves, Box, 11 In.	295.00
Airplane, Air Ford, Cast Iron, Prop Turns, 1928, 3 1/2 x 4 In.	198.00
Airplane, Airmail, Cast Iron, Kenton	895.00
Airplane, America, Cast Iron, 13 1/2-In.Wingspan *Illus*	495.00
Airplane, America, Tri-Motor, Hubley, c.1931	2760.00
Airplane, American DC-7, Friction, Linemar, Box	375.00
Airplane, American Eagle, Metal, Hubley, Box, 11-In. Wingspan	165.00
Airplane, American Flyer, Pressed Steel, Lithographed, Rubber Tires, 20 In.	385.00

Airplane, Army, Olive, Wooden Wheels, Marx, c.1941, 7 1/2 In. 95.00
Airplane, Bi-Plane, Cast Iron Pilot, Pressed Steel, Kingsbury, c.1925, 16 In. 425.00
Airplane, Boeing 707, Linemar, TWA, Marx, Lighted 4 Engines, Stop & Go Action .. 195.00
Airplane, Boeing 747, Swissair, Blinking Wing Lights, Stop & Go Action 125.00
Airplane, Carvelle, Dinky, Box, 7 In. 50.00
Airplane, Catapult Aeroplane, No. 111, Katz, 9 x 5 1/2 In. 475.00
Airplane, China Clipper, Pressed Steel, Wyandotte, 13-In. Wingspan. 225.00
Airplane, Circling Hanger, Globe Center, Tin, Cardini, c.1925, 23 In. 1840.00
Airplane, Circus Jet, Battery Operated, Box 185.00
Airplane, Douglas DC-3, Display Stand, IKO, Box 40.00
Airplane, Flying Circus, Metal, Hubley, Box 195.00
Airplane, Fokker, Windup, Japan, 13-In. Wingspan 1850.00
Airplane, Ford Trimotor, Tin, Schieble, 29 1/2 x 26 1/2 In. .... *Illus* 1000.00
Airplane, Globemaster, Troop Carrier, Bandai, 17-In. Wingspan, 13 1/2 In., Box 785.00
Airplane, Helio Jet, Dad's Root Beer, Tin 12.00
Airplane, Jabula Toys, Pressed Steel, Jabula Toys, 22-In. Wingspan 310.00
Airplane, Lindy Embossed On Wing, Cast Iron, Hubley, c.1929, 13 1/4 In. 1955.00
Airplane, Lindy, Cast Iron, Hubley, 10-In. Wingspan .... *Illus* 550.00
Airplane, Martin Bomber, Tri-Motor, Nomura, 1930s, Box 3950.00
Airplane, Monocoupe, Buddy L 395.00
Airplane, Monoplane, Black & Orange, Buddy L, 10-In. Wingspan 595.00
Airplane, Pan Am Jet, Battery Operated, Linemar, Box 85.00
Airplane, Pennzoil, Vega, Yellow, Red Z, 1927 .... 34.00
Airplane, Sea Patrol, Windup, Tin, Ohio Art, 10-In.Wingspan 110.00
Airplane, Seaplane, Battery Operated, Chein 66.00
Airplane, Silver Eagle, Pressed Aluminum, Automatic Toy Co., Box 300.00
Airplane, Spirit Of St. Louis, Metalcraft, Box 375.00
Airplane, Spirit Of St. Louis, Metalcraft, Pressed Steel, 11-In. Wingspan, 1928 .... 300.00
Airplane, Spitfire, Windup, Tin, England, 1950s, 10 In. Wingspan .... 195.00 to 295.00
Airplane, Take-Off & Land, Battery Operated, Box 375.00
Airplane, Tin, Windup, Chein, 7-In.Wingspan 240.00
Airplane, Turbo Jet, Box Back, Aluminum Wings Inside Box, Kellogg's Pep Flakes .. 60.00
Airplane, TWA, Boeing 707, Stop & Go Lighted Engines, Linemar 145.00
Airplane, Twin Engine, Cast Iron, Steel, No. 3630, Arcade, 7 In. 145.00
Airplane, U.S. Mail, 3-Motor, Steelcraft, 27-In. Wingspan .... 800.00 to 1195.00
Airplane, U.S. Marine Air-Sea Rescue, Ideal, Box 50.00
Airplane, Windup, Tin, Marx 250.00
Airplane Set, Tootsietoy, Box 1400.00
Airport And Flying Planes, Liberty, Box 365.00
Airport Tower, Sky Hawk, Windup, Marx, 8 1/2 In. 335.00
Alabama Coon Jigger, Clockwork, Lithographed, Ferdinand Strauss, 10 In. 550.00
Aladdin & Lamp, Hard Rubber, 1920s, 14 x 20 In. 950.00
Ambulance, Graham, Camouflage, Tootsietoy, 1940 ....: 165.00
Ambulance, Tin, Lupor, 1950s, 7 In. 135.00
Ambulance Unit, British Motor, Britain 1210.00
Amos 'n' Andy, Walker, Shuffle Action, Tinplate, Windup, c.1932, 11 1/2 In. 1265.00
Andy Gump, Driving 348 Roadster, Cast Iron, c.1932, 7 In. 1495.00
Apollo, Astronaut, Tin, Japan, 1970s, Box, 9 In. 80.00
Aquaman, Mego, 1979, 3 3/4 In. 90.00
Army Set, Matchbox, Box 675.00
Arnold Ice Cream Vendor, Windup 350.00
Arty The Trapeze Artist, Gymnast, Overhead Bar, Windup, Celluloid, 7 1/2 In. 325.00
Astronaut, Battery Operated, Swing Door Open, Shooting Gun, Noise, Box 109.00
Astronaut, Rotate-O-Matic, Silver, Battery Operated, Box .... 275.00 to 375.00
Astronaut Space Explorer, Inflatable Ball, In Bag, Japan, 1950s 10.00
Atomic Reactor, Steam, Tin, Windup, Linemar, 1950s 200.00
Autobus, Lehman, 8 In. 1795.00
Baby, Crawling, Windup, Plastic, Cloth, TN Japan, 1950s, Box 75.00
Backdrop Panel, Humpty Dumpty Circus, 2 Sides, Colorful, Pair 2125.00
Badge, Deputy Sheriff, Gold, 1930s, On Card 10.00
Bake-A-Cake Cooking Set, Wolverine 100.00
Balky Pony & Cart, Windup, Marx, Box 275.00
Ballerina, Spinning, Tin Lithograph, Marx, c.1930 .... 275.00

Band, Royal Marines, Box 880.00
Band, Salvation Army & Colors 1540.00
Barn, Lazy Day, Tin, 22 Accessories 75.00
Barn, Silo, No. 915, Fisher-Price 50.00
Barn, With Horses, Ohio Art 48.00
Barney Google, On Scooter, Lithographed Tinplate, Fischer, c.1924, 9 In. 2990.00
Barney Google, Pull Toy, Racing, c.1924 .... 6270.00
Barrel Wagon, Wilkins 1850.00
Bartender, Charlie Weaver, Battery Operated, Box .... 65.00 to 95.00
Bashful Suitor, Windup, Tin, Germany, 1920s 500.00
Basket, Easter, Tin, Chein, 9 In. 29.00
Bathroom Set, Tootsietoy, 5 Piece 55.00
Bathtub, Doll's, Tin, Black Bottom, Mustard Paint 35.00
Batman, Pix-A-Go-Go, Ideal, 1966, Box 65.00
Batmobile, Batman & Robin, Battery Operated, Lights & Gun, 11 1/2 In. 400.00
Batmobile, Corgi, 1st Issue 75.00
Battery Maker, Build Your Own Flashlight Batteries, 1930s, Box 50.00
Battle Action, Road Block, Ideal, 1965 .... 125.00
Battleship, Conqueror, Cannons, 2 Life Boats, Paper On Wood, Bliss, c.1890 .... 1725.00
Battleship, Exploding, Bazooka Gum, Mailer 35.00
Battleship, New Jersey, 3 Stacks, Key Wind, Tin & Wood, Orkin, c.1920, 35 In. 1265.00
Beach, Water Pumper, Tin Lithograph, Ohio Art, 1939, 9 In. 135.00
Beany & Cecil, Leapin' Lena, Pull Toy, Pressman 125.00
Bears are also listed in the Teddy Bear category
Bear, Baby Bear Cries, Momma Feeds Hungry Baby, Battery Operated, Box, 10 In. .. 195.00
Bear, Ball Playing Bear, Battery Operated, Box .... 700.00 to 725.00
Bear, Barney, Drumming, Battery Operated, Box 275.00
Bear, Beauty Parlor, Battery Operated, Box 1250.00
Bear, Bruno The Spectacle Bear, Windup, Japan, Box 165.00
Bear, Busy Housekeeper, Battery Operated, 1950s 195.00
Bear, Dentist, Battery Operated, Box 795.00
Bear, Drinking Maxwell Coffee, Battery Operated, Box, Japan 225.00
Bear, Drumming, Mechanical, Alps Toys, Box 300.00
Bear, Fishing, Battery Operated, Box 325.00
Bear, Hungry Cub, Pours Milk & Drinks, Windup, Box, 6 In. 150.00
Bear, Knitting, Windup, Tin 125.00
Bear, Maxwell, Battery Operated, Box 175.00
Bear, Mechanical, Ives, c.1890 .... 550.00 to 650.00
Bear, Mighty Mike, Barbell Lifter, Battery Operated, Box 450.00
Bear, Mother Polar & Baby, Mechanical, Head Moves, Walks, 1930-1940, Box, 5 In. .. 475.00
Bear, News-Cub, Windup 275.00
Bear, Polar, Fishing, Battery Operated, Alps, 1950s, Box 195.00
Bear, Pull Toy, Tin, 3 1/4 In. 347.00
Bear, Roller-Skating, Plastic, Battery Operated, Musical, Eidelweiss, 14 In. 38.50
Bear, Sleeping, Battery Operated, Box 325.00
Bear, Teddy Zilo, Fisher-Price 75.00
Bear, Telephone, Battery Operated, Box 300.00
Bear, Traveler, Battery Operated, Remote Control, Box 350.00
Bear, Walking Lovely, Modern Toys, Early 1950s, Box 95.00
Bear, Walking, Windup, Occupied Japan, Box, 3 x 5 In. .... 80.00 to 125.00
Bear, Windup, Metal, Chein 45.00
Bear, With Celluloid Fish, Walks, Stops, Growls, Windup, Box, 4 x 5 In. 160.00
Bed, Doll's, Empire, Curly Maple 675.00
Bed, Doll's, Rope, Crazy Quilt, 1880-1890 .... 185.00
Bed, Doll's, Sleigh, Paneled, Original Stain, 1850, 22 x 15 In. 225.00
Bed, Doll's, Wooden, Painted, Folding, Springs, Early 1900s, 9 1/2 x 17 In. 89.00
Bed & Wardrobe, Doll's, Ruffled Canopy, Furnishings, 1940s, 14 In. 57.50
Bed Set, Doll's, Hollywood, Amsco, Box, Large 125.00
Beetle, Windup, Lehmann, 1886 .... 225.00 to 250.00
Bell, Buster Brown & Friend, On Seesaw, Cast Iron 770.00
Bell, Camel, Painted Tinplate, Althof Bergmann, c.1874, 8 1/4 x 9 In. 2530.00
Betty Jane Glasbake Set, McKee, Box 15.00
Bicycles are listed in their own category

Toy, Bonzo, Brown, Steiff, 13 In.

••••••••••••••••••••••••••

Take batteries with you to the
toy sales if you plan to buy a
battery operated toy. Check to
see if the toy really works.

••••••••••••••••••••••••••

Bicycle Siren, Fire Chief, Metal, 1930s, Box ....:..	35.00
Big Joe Chef, Action, Box	75.00
Binoculars, Kit Carson	45.00
Bird, Flying, Paper Wings, Mechanical, Lehmann, c.1890	1400.00
Birdcage, Chirpee, Windup, Mid 1950s, Box	160.00
Birdcage, Scarlet Tanager, Box Back, Kellogg's Raisin Bran	14.95
Bisque Head Doll, Pull, Arms Move, Head Turns, Donkey's Head Moves, 13 In.	5500.00
Black Boy, Jungle, Native Rocks Back & Forth, Beats Drum, Windup, Marx, 7 In. ...	225.00
Black Boy, Stealing Watermelon, Dog, Celluloid, Windup, Japan, 1930s	595.00
Black Boy On Tricycle, Repainted, Stevens & Brown	1650.00
Black Boy On Velocipede, Clockwork, Tin, Iron, Stevens & Brown, Pat. 1870	6820.00
Black Man, Jigger With Accordion, Crank	2100.00
Black Man, On Animal, Ramp Walker, Marx, Package	55.00
Black Man, Walking, Lindstrom, 1920s, 7 In.	575.00
Black Zulu, Large Earrings, Pull String Eyes Roll, Germany, 1910, 3 x 3 In.	65.00
Blackboard & Desk, Flip-Over, Falcon Toy, 1930s	295.00
Blacksmith, Steam, Germany, Early 1900s	1300.00
Blocks, American Skyline Building, 1950s	25.00
Blocks, Anchor, Anker-Baukasten, Box	200.00
Blocks, Blondie & Dagwood, Interchangeable, King Features, 1950s, Box	175.00
Blocks, Changeable, No. 1501, Gaston, Paper Lithograph, Wood, 1953	45.00
Blocks, Children At Play, With Seasons, Box, 1 5/8 In.	375.00
Blocks, Hills Alphabet Blocks, Wooden, Box, 27 Piece	132.00
Blocks, Kiddie Blox Set, Castles Of Imagination, 1930s, Box	45.00
Blocks, Little Tots, Pictorial, Schoenhut, Wooden Box	110.00
Blocks, Mother Goose Living Picture, Lithographed Paper On Wood, c.1890	575.00
Blocks, Nested, Lithographed Paper On Wood, Milton Bradley, c.1910, 6 x 6 In.	460.00
Blocks, Sifo's Mailbag Of Blocks, Land Of Hiawatha, No. 142, Cloth Bag	55.00
Blocks, Stacking, Children At Play Scenes, Ges Geschutz, Box, 3 To 6 In., 8 Piece ...	1050.00
Blocks, Windows, Special Shape, Illustrated Box, 1940s, 6 x 6 In.	25.00
Blushing Willie, Battery Operated	45.00
Boat, Air, Windup, Arnold	435.00
Boat, Atomic Submarine, Sea Wolf, Friction, Tin, Box	150.00
Boat, Battery Operated, Wooden, 1950s, Box	85.00
Boat, Battleship New York, Cast Iron, Dent, c.1910, 20 In.	3450.00
Boat, Cabin Cruiser, Key Wind, Tin Plate, Chein, 1950s, Box, 15 In.	95.00
Boat, Cabin Cruiser, Outboard, Battery Operated, Linemar, 13 1/2 In., Box	395.00
Boat, Clockwork, Composition Figures, Lionel, Key Wind, 1930s	550.00
Boat, Coast Guard Patrol, Tin Lithograph, Windup Propeller, Japan, 13 In.	165.00
Boat, Ferry, Windup, Lindstrom	275.00
Boat, Harbor Patrol, Tin, Japan, 1950s, 13 In.	95.00
Boat, Harbor Queen, Battery Operated, Box	295.00
Boat, Hudson Ferry, Windup, Japan	450.00
Boat, Merchant Marine, Key Wind, Ives, Box	2500.00
Boat, Miss America, Mahogany & Brass, Stand	950.00
Boat, Mystery, Tin Lithograph, Alcohol Propelled, Gobar Products, Box, 9 1/2 In.	93.50
Boat, Oarsman, Clockwork, Hand Painted, Cloth Dressed, Nathan S. Warner, 13 In. ..	3850.00

Boat, Ocean Liner New York, Lifeboats, Key Wind, Tin, Ives, c.1915, 13 In. 805.00
Boat, Ocean Liner United States, Battery Operated, Japan, Box, c.1965, 18 In. 345.00
Boat, Ocean Liner, Clockwork, 6 Lifeboats, Propeller, Bing, Tin, c.1912, 40 In. 5775.00
Boat, Ocean Liner, Tin, Windup, German 700.00
Boat, Outboard, Mermaid, Battery Operated, Japan, Box 125.00
Boat, Paddle, City Of New York, Wilkins, 1910, 15 In. 1785.00
Boat, Pirate Gunboat, Paper On Wood 1100.00
Boat, Ride, Kiddie, Electric, 1950s 495.00
Boat, Sea Queen, Siren, Battery Operated, Box 235.00
Boat, Side-Wheeler, Live Steam, Tin Plate, Bramwell-Smith, 1872, Box 6050.00
Boat, Speed Launch, Carette 1250.00
Boat, Speed, Clockwork, Orkin, Box 2090.00
Boat, Speed, Inflatable, Vinyl, Battery Operated Outboard Motor, Cragstan, Box 185.00
Boat, Speed, Key Wind, Lionel, 1930s 625.00
Boat, Steam Fired, Repainted White & Gray, Bing, 1910, 19 1/4 In. 546.00
Boat, Tanker, Windup, Tin, Fleischman, 21 In. 1450.00
Boat, Torpedo, Rover, Paper On Wood, Bliss, c.1896, 20 In. 1495.00
Boat, Warship, Uncle Sam Lithograph, Bliss 1595.00
Boat, Water Pumping, Siren, Battery Operated, Ideal, Box, 15 In. 145.00
Boat Set, Wooden, International Navy, Tied In Box, 3 Piece 175.00
Bonzo, Steiff, Brown, 13 In. .... *Illus* 1350.00
Bop-A-Loop, Wooden, 1930s, Box 25.00
Bow & Arrow Set, Wooden, Feathers, Rubber Suction Tips, Eastel, Late 1930s 22.00
Bowl, Waste, Child's, Buster Brown & Tige, 4 1/2 In. 35.00
Boxers, Celluloid Figures, Windup, Lithographed Tin, Box .... 210.00 to 225.00
Boxing Game, Knockout, Electronic, Tin Lithograph, Northwester Products, Box 250.00
Boy, Drinking From Stoneware Beer Mug, Windup, Germany 400.00
Boy, On Sled, Celluloid Figure, Windup, Occupied Japan, 5 In. 95.00
Boy & Girl, Dance, Pull Toy, Jointed, Wooden, Box, 4 x 6 In. 65.00
Brownie Artillery, 20 Lithographed People, Cannon & Balls, McLoughlin, c.1895 .... 1380.00
Bubble Blower, Tin, Windup, Marusan, Japan 195.00
Bubble Machine, Soapy Solution, Large Bubbles, 1940s, Box 35.00
Buckboard, Child's, Wooden Spokes, Metal Wheel Rims 1300.00
Bucket Loader, Barber-Green High Capacity, Doepke, Late 1940s 275.00
Buckle, Star Trek, 1976 .... 20.00
Bucky Beaver, Steiff 770.00
Buddy Bullfrog, Fisher-Price, Box, 1959 .... 125.00
Buffalo Bill Cody, Rifle, Pistol, Hat, Box, Mego, 8 In. 85.00
Bugs Bunny, Dakin, 1970s, 9 In. 8.00

♦ ♦

Restoration of an old dollhouse should be restrained. Wash it, repair the structural problems, repaint as little as possible, and redecorate with appropriate old wallpaper fabrics and paint colors.

♦ ♦

Toy, Bus, Cast Iron, Nickel Plated Driver, Arcade, 13 In.

Toy, Cement Mixer, Jaeger, Green, Cast Iron, Revolving, Kenton, 9 x 4 In.; Toy, Car, Chevrolet, 1928 Sedan, Cast Iron, Arcade

Building Set, Astrolite, Future Cities, Clear Plastic, Hasbro, 1969, Box 45.00
Building Set, Built E-Z, A-1924, Metal, Instructions, Box 85.00
Building Set, Falcon Lumber, Dovetailed Box 125.00
Building Set, No. 820, Complete, American Logs, 1950s, 22 x 6 In. 42.00
Bulldozer, Caterpillar, Marx, Box 495.00
Bulldozer, Handy Hank, Battery Operated, On-Off Switch At Top 70.00
Bulldozer, Robotrac, Battery Operated, Linemar, Box, 10 In. 695.00
Bunny Basket Cart, No. 301, Pull, Fisher-Price 70.00
Bunny Belltoy, Robot, Television Spaceman, Battery Operated, Alps 575.00
Bus, Bico Bus To Joyville, Tin Lithograph, Key Wind, Distler, 9 In. 3025.00
Bus, Buddy L, No. 955, Steel, 1939, Box 795.00
Bus, Cast Iron, Nickel Plated Driver, Arcade, 13 In. .... *Illus* 1925.00
Bus, Coast To Coast Bus Line, Wyandotte, White, Blue 375.00
Bus, Deluxe, Tin Lithograph, Windup, Curtained Windows, Strauss, c.1925, 13 In. 633.00
Bus, Double Decker, Gunthermann, 20 In. 3200.00
Bus, Double Decker, Kenton, 10 1/2 In. 695.00
Bus, Double Decker, Mobilgas, Friction, 1950s 125.00
Bus, Double Decker, Open Top, Cast Iron, Kenton, c.1925, 10 In. 1093.00
Bus, Double Decker, Pressed Steel, Triang 450.00
Bus, Double Decker, Tin Lithograph, Penny Toy, c.1915, 3 1/2 In. 322.00
Bus, Great Eastern Bus System, Cast Iron, Arcade, 1930s 1700.00
Bus, Greyhound, Buddy L 75.00
Bus, Greyhound, Century Of Progress, Cast Iron, Arcade, 1933, 10 In. .... 165.00 to 260.00
Bus, Greyhound, Century Of Progress, Chicago 260.00
Bus, Greyhound, Great Lakes Exposition, 1937 .... 1210.00
Bus, Greyhound, Scenic Cruiser, Friction, Box 125.00
Bus, Greyhound, Scenic Cruiser, Tin, 10 x 13 In. 45.00
Bus, Greyhound, Tin Plate, S.A.N., Japan 550.00
Bus, Jackie Gleason Honeymooners Special, Mechanical, Tin Litho, Wolverine, 1955 ... 425.00
Bus, Overland Bus, Red, Tootsietoy 95.00
Bus, Side Mounts, Cor Cor 445.00
Bus, Touring Coach, Buddy L, 28 In. 2400.00
Bus, Trailways, Nickel-Plated Grill, Rubber Tires, Arcade, Cast Iron, c.1939, 9 In. 748.00
Bus, United Bus Line, Highway Traveler, Tin, Japan, 14 In. 110.00
Bus, Volkswagen, KLM, Battery Operated 120.00
Bus Terminal, Keystone, 1940s, Box 155.00
Bus Terminal, Marx, 1938 .... 50.00
Butcher With Pig, Cast Iron, Key Wind, Stock 1200.00
Butterfly, Friction, Tin, Wings Move Up & Down, Japan 65.00
Cab, Hansom, Kenton 750.00
Cab, Landau, Horse Drawn, Driver, All White Horses, Hubley, c.1900, 17 In. 4370.00
Cabriolet, Horse Drawn, Cast Iron, 15 1/2 In. 1850.00
Calypso Joe, Windup, TPS 265.00
Camel, Dromedary, Mohair, Glass Eyes, Straw, Steiff 90.00
Camel, With Rider, Tin, Windup, German U. S. Zone, 6 In. 82.50
Camera, Kiddle Kamera, 12 Filmstrips, 1930s, Box 275.00
Camp Play Set, Boy's, Marx 500.00
Cane, Shooting, Secret Sam, Lion's Head Top, Plastic, Topper, 1965 .... 89.00
Cannon, Electric, Wood & Metal, ElecToy 75.00
Cannon, Fire Cracker, Cast Iron 70.00
Cannon, Napoleonic, Britains, 1960s 45.00
Cap Gun, American, Unused, Box 685.00
Cap Gun, Apache, Lone Star 100.00
Cap Gun, Atomic Disintegrator, Hubley .... 325.00 to 525.00
Cap Gun, Big Bill, Kenton 50.00
Cap Gun, Big Horn, 7 1/2 In. 65.00
Cap Gun, Big Scout, Cast Iron 50.00
Cap Gun, Border Patrol, Kilgore 50.00
Cap Gun, Buck 'n Bronc, Box, c.1950 .... 125.00
Cap Gun, Buck, Kilgore, Box 50.00
Cap Gun, Buffalo Bill, Cast Iron, 8 In. .... 40.00 to 60.00
Cap Gun, Captain Cutlass 150.00
Cap Gun, Champion, Smoker, Box 325.00

Toy, Car, Amphibious, Tin, Windup,
Lehman, 9 1/2 In.

◆◆◆◆◆◆◆◆◆◆◆◆◆◆◆◆◆◆◆◆◆◆◆

Remove the batteries from
a stored toy.

◆◆◆◆◆◆◆◆◆◆◆◆◆◆◆◆◆◆◆◆◆◆◆

Cap Gun, China Man's Head, Bomb, Cast Iron	245.00
Cap Gun, Cowboy King, Steven, Cast Iron	225.00
Cap Gun, Cowboy, No. 275, Die Cast, Hubley, 1950s, 12 In., Box	195.00 to 225.00
Cap Gun, Derringer Type, Ejectable Cap Firing Bullet, Dyna-Mite, 3 1/4 In.	13.00
Cap Gun, Dragnet, Box, 1950s	65.00
Cap Gun, Dyna-Mite Derringer, Nichols, Presentation Box	20.00 to 25.00
Cap Gun, Fanner 50, Smoking, Mattel, Box	50.00 to 175.00
Cap Gun, Flintlock Jr., Hubley, 1955, Box, 7 1/2 In., Pair	40.00 to 50.00
Cap Gun, G-Man, Cast Iron, 6 In.	50.00
Cap Gun, Galaxy, Cast Iron & Plastic, Box, 3 1/2 In.	27.00
Cap Gun, Hawkeye, No. 4, Kilgore	50.00 to 65.00
Cap Gun, Kilgore Pal	35.00
Cap Gun, Kit Carson, Kilgore	65.00 to 75.00
Cap Gun, Lasso 'em Bill	110.00
Cap Gun, Mountie, Hubley, Box	45.00
Cap Gun, National, Automatic, Brown Grips, Mason	40.00
Cap Gun, Nichols Mustang No. 500, Box	250.00
Cap Gun, Nicklus, No. 38, Holster, Pair	175.00
Cap Gun, Pioneer, Hubley	60.00
Cap Gun, Pirate, Single Barrel, 3 1/2 In.	65.00
Cap Gun, Pluck, Cast Iron	35.00
Cap Gun, Pony Boy, Jr. Marshall, Black Leather Holster, White Fringe	65.00
Cap Gun, Red Ranger Jr., Box	95.00
Cap Gun, Red Ranger, Wyandotte, Gold Finish, 8 1/2 In.	165.00
Cap Gun, Remington, 44 Caliber, 1965, Miniature, Box	40.00
Cap Gun, Repeating, Benton Harbor Novelty Co., 1950s	75.00
Cap Gun, Rodeo, Repeating, Hubley, Box	75.00
Cap Gun, Rodeo, White Grips, Hubley, Tin Box	50.00
Cap Gun, Silver Pony, Nichols	45.00
Cap Gun, Six-Shooter, Kilgore	50.00
Cap Gun, Smokey Joe, With Cowboy	8.00
Cap Gun, Snake, Fourth Of July, 1809, Bomb, Iron & Wood	600.00
Cap Gun, Space Police Neutron Blaster, Stevens, 1950	225.00
Cap Gun, Stevens, Peace Maker, Cast Iron	75.00
Cap Gun, Texan, Revolving Cylinder, Hubley, 9 In., Box	175.00
Cap Gun, Trooper, Die Cast, Hubley, 1950, Box	65.00
Cap Gun, Victor, Stevens, 1880	275.00
Cap Gun, Wild Bill Hickok, Pop-Up Top Load	130.00
Cap Gun, With Holster, Hubley Cowpoke	25.00
Cap Gun, Wyatt Earp, 9 In.	60.00
Cap Gun Set, Historic Guns, Marx, 1974, Miniature, Box, 8 Piece	120.00
Cappy The Caterpillar, Pull Toy, Wooden, On Wheels, Jointed, 1940s, Box	35.00
Captain America, Mego, 1979, 3 3/4 In.	90.00
Captain America, With Shield Launcher, 5 In.	10.00
Captain Kangaroo's TV Eras-O-Board, Hasbro, 1956, Box	50.00
Car, Amphibious, Tin, Windup, Lehman, 9 1/2 In.	*Illus* 1100.00
Car, Andy Gump, Cast Iron, Arcade, 1923, 7 1/2 In.	4250.00

Top row: Toy, Car, Lincoln, Sedan, Pressed Steel, Turner, 27 In.;
Toy, Truck, Coal, Pressed Steel, Sturdy Toy, 27 1/2 In.;
Bottom row: Toy, Car, Fire Chief, Packard Roadster, Pressed Steel, American
National, 29 In.; Toy, Truck, Delivery, Pressed Steel, Kingsbury, Keene, N. H. , 25 In.

Car, Antique, Shaking, Battery Operated, Box	125.00
Car, Aston-Martin, James Bond, Ejecting Figure, Battery Operated	170.00 to 345.00
Car, Bluto Dippy Dump, Marx	795.00
Car, Buick, Remote Control, Cragston, Box	660.00
Car, Buick, Renwal, 1950s	65.00
Car, Buick, Tin, Friction, Marx, 1950s, 20 In.	150.00
Car, Bump, Pop-Up Clown, Windup, Japan	95.00
Car, Bump-And-Go, Japan, 7 In.	45.00
Car, Cadillac, Battery Operated, 1952, 7 1/2 In., Box	275.00
Car, Cadillac, Convertible, Bandai, 1959	285.00
Car, Cadillac, Convertible, Battery Operated, Bandai, 1964, 11 1/2 In., Box	225.00
Car, Cadillac, Friction, 2-Tone Red & Black, Tin Litho, Japan, 1952, 14 In.	425.00
Car, Cadillac, U-Turn, Battery Operated, Box	225.00
Car, Carabo, Green, Hot Wheels	182.00
Car, Carrier, Blue Cab, Orange Trailer, 2 Cars, Ramp, Structo, 1940s	175.00
Car, Champion Racer, Helmeted Driver, Friction, Tin, Japan	3410.00
Car, Champion, Friction, Box	395.00
Car, Checker Cab, Windup, Courtland	135.00 to 175.00
Car, Chevrolet Station Wagon, 1956 Bandai, 10 In.	325.00
Car, Chevrolet, 1928 Sedan, Cast Iron, Arcade	*Illus* 1100.00
Car, Chevrolet, 2-Tone Green, Tin, Friction, Ichiko, 1955, 10 1/2 In., Box	450.00
Car, Chevrolet, Bel Air, ATC, 1960, Box	595.00
Car, Chevy Coupe, Arcade, 1929	1950.00
Car, Chitty Chitty Bang Bang, Mattel, Box, 1968	75.00
Car, Chrysler Airflow, Royal Blue, Hubley, 4 1/2 In.	210.00
Car, Chrysler, 1958, 2-Tone Green, Japan, 11 1/2 In.	650.00
Car, Chrysler, Airflow, Windup, Kingsbury, 1934	995.00
Car, Citroen Convertible, 1930s, Canvas Top, Michelin Tires, Tinplate	990.00
Car, Convertible, Blue, No. 458, Hubley Kiddie Toy, 1940s	40.00 to 45.00
Car, Convertible, Sportsman, Wyandotte, Box, 12 In.	335.00
Car, Corvette Stingray, 1968 Model, Eldon, Box	50.00
Car, Corvette, Yellow, Split Window, Ertl	25.00
Car, Coupe, Chevy, 1929 Model, Arcade	1950.00
Car, Couple, Kingsbury, Windup, Pressed Steel, 9 In.	500.00
Car, Crazy Kar, Open Air, Canvas Top, Mr. Magoo Driving, Hubley	275.00
Car, Dagwood The Driver, Windup, Tin Lithographed	990.00
Car, Delivery, Pressed Steel, Buddy L, 1924	850.00
Car, Doepke, Unassembled, Box	700.00
Car, Edsel Sedan, Blue, Friction, Japan, Box, 9 In.	750.00
Car, Evil Knievel, Funny Car, Die Cast, Ideal, Box, 1976	25.00

Car, Fire Chief, Battery Operated, Friction, Japan, c.1950 .... 165.00
Car, Fire Chief, Packard Roadster, Pressed Steel, American National, 29 In. .... *Illus* 4125.00
Car, Fire Chief, Tin Lithograph, Pull Toy, Bell, T. Cohn Inc., 1940s, Box 90.00
Car, Fix-It Convertible, Plastic, Ideal, 12 In., Box 225.00
Car, Flivver, Fred Flintstone, Linemar 375.00
Car, Ford Convertible, 1950, Renwal, Box 50.00
Car, Ford Fairlane, Ranch Wagon, Friction, Tailgate & Window Open, 1952, 14 In. ... 765.00
Car, Ford Model B, Renwal, Box 50.00
Car, Ford Mustang, 1967, Driver Arm Goes Up & Down, Y Japan, Box, 13 1/2 In. 295.00
Car, Ford Station Wagon, Friction, 9 In. 395.00
Car, Ford T-Bird, 2-Door Hardtop, Bandai, 1965 .... 100.00
Car, Ford Type, Driver, Pull String Action, 1930s, 9 In. 315.00
Car, Ford, Convertible, Tin, Friction, Japan 75.00
Car, Ford, Fairlane, Friction, Toymaster, Early 1950s, 7 In. 90.00
Car, Green Hornet, Black Beauty, Corgi 225.00
Car, Highway Patrol, Oldsmobile, Tin, Friction, Battery Operated, 1958 .... 295.00
Car, Hot Rod Racer, Sparking, Friction, Early 1950s, 5 1/4 In., Box 95.00
Car, Hot Rod, Friction, Tin Litho, Red, 7 1/2 In. 125.00
Car, Hot Wheels, Redline, Hot Heap, Orange, Mattel, 1968 .... 55.00
Car, Hot Wheels, Redline, Lotus Turbine, Aqua, Mattel, 1969 .... 45.00
Car, Humphreymobile, Mechanical, Wyandotte, Box 975.00
Car, Indian Traffic, Red & Blue Cast Iron, White Rubber Tires, Hubley, 1938, 9 In. ... 3250.00
Car, Jaguar, XK-150, Tin, Red, Black, Bandai, Japan, 1960s, 9 1/2 In. 375.00
Car, Jetmobile, Captain America, No. 263, Corgi, Box 45.00
Car, Johnny Speed, Topper, 1966 .... 200.00
Car, Jolly Jalopy, Fisher-Price 18.00
Car, Jolly Joe, Krazy Kar, Tin Machine Guns, Marx 275.00
Car, Krazy Kar, Windup, Original Driver, Strauss 695.00
Car, Landaulet, Tin, Fischer, 7 1/2 In. 2500.00
Car, LaSalle, Green, 3 In., Tootsietoy 85.00
Car, Limousine, Carette, 8 1/2 In. 3630.00
Car, Limousine, Carette, Beveled Windows 6820.00
Car, Limousine, Closed Rear Quarters, Cast Iron, Kenton, c.1915, 7 1/4 In. 575.00
Car, Lincoln Continental, No. 170, Die Cast, Dinky Toy 40.00
Car, Lincoln Mark III, Convertible, Bandai, 1959 .... 250.00
Car, Lincoln, Sedan, Pressed Steel, Turner, 27 In. .... *Illus* 4675.00
Car, Matchbox, Crosley, 1918 .... 18.00
Car, Matchbox, Ford A, 1930 .... 18.00
Car, Matchbox, Models Of Yesteryear, No. 12, Lipton's Tea Wagon, Die Cast, 1950s . 72.00
Car, Matchbox, Models Of Yesteryear, No. 15, 1907 Rolls Royce Silver Ghost, 1960s 68.00
Car, Matchbox, No. 851, Auburn, 1935 .... 18.00
Car, Matchbox, Rolls Royce, Silver Ghost, 1906 .... 35.00
Car, Maxwell, Trigger Mechanism, Box 100.00
Car, Mercedes 360 SL, No. 6, Matchbox 20.00
Car, Mercury, Rear Drive, Brown, Made For Ralston Purina 3195.00
Car, Milton Berle, Chein 375.00
Car, Model A Ford, 1929, Tootsietoy 45.00
Car, Model A Ford, Sedan, Red, Arcade 700.00
Car, Model T Ford, Black Paint, Replacement Driver, Arcade, 6 1/2 In. 240.00
Car, Model T, Cast Iron, Arcade 195.00

Toy, Car, Nash, Sedan, Cast Iron,
Blue, Kenton

Toy, Car, Packard, Cast Iron, 2 Colors
Hubley, 11 x 4 In.

Car, Model T, Woman Driver, Windup, Bing, Germany, 6 1/4 In. 192.00
Car, Monkeemobile, Corgi 50.00
Car, Moon Mullins Patrol, Cast Iron, 8 1/2 In. 450.00
Car, Mountain Wagon, Tin Lithograph, Friction, Cragston, 1950s, 7 1/2 In. 150.00
Car, Mr. Magoo, Battery Operated, Hubley, 1961 .... 235.00
Car, Nash, Sedan, Cast Iron, Blue, Kenton .... *Illus* 5720.00
Car, Old Jalopy, Marx, Box 475.00
Car, Oldsmobile '88, Convertible, Tootsietoy, 1959, 6 In. 45.00
Car, Oldsmobile Super 88, Lithograph, Friction, Cragstan, 1950s, 7 In. 100.00
Car, Oldsmobile, Rubber, Auburn, 6 In. 55.00
Car, Packard, Cast Iron, 2 Colors, Hubley, 11 x 4 In. .... *Illus* 27500.00
Car, Packard, Clockwork, Lithographed, Automatic Steering, Schuco, Box, 11 In. 660.00
Car, Penny, Driver, Kellerman, 3 1/2 In. 175.00
Car, Phaeton, Woman's, Horse Drawn, Cast Iron, Wilkins, c.1900, 17 In. 3450.00
Car, Plymouth, Woody Station Wagon, Die Cast, Dinky Toy, Box 135.00
Car, Police, Battery Operated, 1960s 125.00
Car, Police, Buick Riviera, Bandai, 11 In. 80.00
Car, Police, Bump-And-Go, Man Holding Mounted Machine Gun, Battery Operated .. 185.00
Car, Police, Tin, Battery Operated, Linemar, Japan 125.00
Car, Pontiac Firebird III, Battery Operated, Flashing Lights, Cragston, Japan, Box 650.00
Car, Pontiac, Blue-Gray Paint, Nickeled Grill, Original Tires, Arcade, 1935, 4 1/4 In. 275.00
Car, Pontiac, Red Paint, Nickeled Grill, Replaced Tires, Arcade, 1935, 6 In. 495.00
Car, Racer Set, Whee-Whiz, Marx, 13 1/2 In., Box 895.00
Car, Racing Horses, National Derby, Tin Lithograph, Convex Sign Co., 1925, Box 250.00
Car, Racing Set, A-Team 85.00
Car, Racing, American Flyer, Stock Car Race, A.C. Gilbert, 1960 .... 375.00
Car, Racing, Arcade, Cast Iron, White Tires, 1935, 5 1/2 In. 200.00
Car, Racing, Battery Operated, Yonezawa, 17 In. 625.00
Car, Racing, Capitol Hill, Windup, Unique Art, Box 275.00
Car, Racing, Cast Iron, Kenton, 9 In. 1900.00
Car, Racing, Clockwork, Structo, Painted Tin, 1930s, 15 In. 275.00
Car, Racing, Electro, Yonezawa, Box 5995.00
Car, Racing, Firebird, Indianapolis 500, Waving Driver, Battery Operated, 15 In., Box . 1250.00
Car, Racing, Indy 500, Aluminum, Wilber Shaw 170.00
Car, Racing, Kiddie Toy Racer, No. 457, Hubley, 7 In., Box 175.00
Car, Racing, Midget, Yonezawa, 8 In. 2195.00
Car, Racing, Red Streak, Buffalo Toy Co., 3 x 20 In. 925.00
Car, Racing, Schuco, 6 1/2 In. 195.00
Car, Racing, Set, American Flyer, Box 65.00
Car, Racing, Silver Bullet, 1930s, 26 In. 295.00
Car, Racing, Special Racer No. 98, Tin, Yonezawa, 1950s, 18 In. 4250.00
Car, Racing, Speedway, 2 Windup Racers, Track, Tin, Box, 1930s 225.00
Car, Racing, Thunderbolt, Key Wind, Tin, Kingsbury, c.1938, 18 In. 403.00
Car, Racing, Tin Plate, Red Paint, Driver, Hercules, 1920s, 19 In. 1035.00
Car, Racing, Windup, Plastic, Rite Spot Plastic, 9 In. 85.00
Car, Racing, Windup, Tin, Marx, 5 In. 95.00
Car, Racing, World's Fair Track, Figure 8, 2 Cars, Key, Marx 425.00
Car, Renault, 2-Seater, Matchbox, Box 20.00
Car, Roadster, Mr. Magoo, Hubley 295.00
Car, Roadster, With Driver, Friction, Tin Plate, Turner, 1922, 8 In. 225.00
Car, Rocket Racer, Windup, Marx 485.00
Car, Rodeo Joe Krazy Kar, Windup, Unique Art, 1930-1940 .... 275.00
Car, Rollback Auto, Gunthermann 3250.00
Car, Rolls-Royce, Bumper Car From Amusement Park 3000.00
Car, Rolls-Royce, Orange 50.00
Car, Speedway, 2 Cars, Wolverine, Partial Box 400.00
Car, Spider Man, Friction, Tin Lithograph, Marx, 1967, 4 In. 100.00
Car, Squad, G-Men, Tin, Multi-Action, Battery Operated, Box, 1953 .... 350.00
Car, Station Wagon, Dinky Toy, 1948 .... 95.00
Car, Take-Apart, Hubley 265.00
Car, Thunderbird, Tootsietoy, 1955, 4 In. 35.00
Car, Tom & Jerry, Comic, Vinyl Characters, Battery Operated, Bouncing, Spinning 395.00
Car, Touring, 1915 Model, Green Metal, Lever Action, Japan, 1950s, 6 In. 42.00

Car, Touring, 3 Figures, A.C. Williams, 9 1/2 In. 900.00
Car, Touring, 4 Passengers, Carette 5170.00
Car, Touring, Hill Climber, Gray, Red, Schieble, c.1910, 14 In. 475.00
Car, Touring, Mercedes, Fuhremobile, Tippco 2420.00
Car, Touring, Model T, White Wheels, Orbor, 6 In. 525.00
Car, Touring, Open, Steam Powered, Doll & Co., Instructions, c.1920, 19 In. 5500.00
Car, Transport, 2 Plastic Cadillacs, Wyandotte, 1950s 185.00
Car, Transport, 4 Cars, Cast Iron, Arcade, 11 1/4 In. 895.00
Car, Transport, 4 Cars, Hubley, 10 In. 595.00
Car, Transport, Structo, 1953 .... 130.00
Car, Transport, Tin Lithograph, Marx, 1940s 125.00
Car, Tricky Taxi, Marx, 1940s 300.00
Car, Uncle Wiggly, Clockwork, Lithographed, Marx, 7 1/2 In. 550.00
Car, Volkswagen Dune Buggy, Powered, Cox, Box 25.00
Car, Volkswagen, Convertible, Battery Operated, Maroon 395.00
Car, What's Wrong, Tin Plate, Key Wind, Distler, c.1930 .... 770.00
Car, Whoopee, Milton Berle, Marx 350.00
Car, Woody, Convertible Top, Tin, Wyandotte 85.00
Car & Truck Set, Tootsietoy, Die Cast, 1970s, Package, Miniature, 7 Piece 25.00
Car Wash, Car, Ideal, Box... 85.00
Carousel, Gnome, Windup, Metal, West Germany, Box 145.00
Carousel, Swan, Animals, Tin, Lever, Wyandotte, 5 1/2 In. 295.00
Carousel, Tin Cars, Germany, 1910s 9500.00
Carpet Ball, Brown Dotted, Victorian 165.00
Carpet Ball, Striped Maroon, Victorian 165.00
Carriage, Doll's, 3 Wheels, 3 x 2 Ft. 450.00
Carriage, Doll's, Iron Spoked Wheels, Leather Hood, Wooden Handle 125.00
Carriage, Doll's, Metal, 1940s 98.00
Carriage, Doll's, Pressed Metal, Wicker Pattern, Maerklin, 1910, 5 In. 800.00
Carriage, Doll's, Raggedy Ann, Ohio Art 48.00
Carriage, Doll's, Tin, Painted, Hood 125.00
Carriage, Doll's, White Rubber Tires, France, 10 x 14 In. 375.00
Carriage, Doll's, Wicker, 1930s, 30 x 30 In. 99.00
Carriage, Doll's, Wicker, Green, Mary-Lu, No. 4805/4, J.C. Penney, c.1930 .... 440.00
Carriage, Doll's, Wicker, Hood, Turned Wood Handlebar, Natural 225.00
Carriage, Doll's, Wood & Metal, Oil Cloth Hood, 20th Century, 26 1/2 In. 82.00
Carriage, Doll's, Wooden Body, Wire Spoke Wheels 90.00
Carriage, Doll's, Wooden Sides, Vinyl Hood, Rubber Tires, Whitney, c.1950 .... 137.00
Carriage, Doll's, Wooden, 3 Wheels, Green, Oilcloth Hood, Joel Ellis, c.1870 .... 440.00
Carriage, Doll's, Wooden, Collapsible Hood, Leather Interior, English Style, c.1900 . 550.00
Carriage, Doll's, Wooden, Mattress & Pillow, 1905, 16 In. 175.00
Carriage, George Washington Inauguration, Wooden, Horses, Schoenhut, 8 x 23 In. .. 400.00
Carrier, Airplane, Wolverine, Box 225.00
Carrier, Car, 3 Buicks Molded Into Chassis, Kenton, 10 In. 2050.00
Cart, Coal Dump, Mule, Kenton, 14 1/2 In. 545.00
Cart, Dog, Girl Driver, John Harris, Cast Iron, c.1895, 7 In. 437.00
Cart, Doll's, Wicker, Open Weave, Painted Base, c.1895, 25 x 10 In. 165.00
Cart, Doll's, Wooden, Black, Stenciling, Collapsible Hood, c.1860 .... 550.00
Cart, Pony Drawn, Paper Lithograph, Wooden, c.1900, 6 In. 195.00
Cartoon Charm Set, Felix, Popeye, Katzenjammer, Phantom, 1950s, Box, 21 Piece . 135.00
Case, Barbie, Cream, Ponytail, Vinyl, 1959 .... 15.00
Case, Bubble Cut Barbie, Red Patent, Dated 1963 .... 8.00
Case, Ken, Campus Hero, Dark Mustard Color, 1963 .... 7.00
Cash Register, American Flyer 95.00
Cash Register, Benjamin Franklin 110.00
Cash Register, Tom Thumb, Metal, Box .... 25.00 to 32.00
Cash Register, Tom Thumb, No. 248, Green, Yellow, Western Stamping Co., Box 65.00
Cash Register, Uncle Sam, Green 15.00
Castle, Crusade, Ideal 500.00
Cat, Drinking Licking, Battery Operated, 1950s, Box 325.00
Cat, Jumping Rope, Tin, Key Wind, Germany 95.00
Cat, Lever Action, Tin Lithograph, Marx, 1930s, 8 In. 95.00
Cat, Long Plush, Glass Eyes, Germany, 1915, 3 In. 250.00

Cat, Tabby, Steiff, 6 In.	125.00
Cat, Tailspin Tabby, Fisher-Price, No. 600	185.00
Cat, With Ball, Friction, Tin, Japan, 5 In.	27.50
Cat, With Ball, Windup, Tin, Marx, 1930s	90.00
Cavalry, Milton Bradley, Box, 5 Piece	325.00
Cement Mixer, Cast Iron	250.00
Cement Mixer, Jaeger, Green, Cast Iron, Revolving, Kenton, 9 x 4 In. .... *Illus*	1100.00
Cement Mixer, Jaeger, Kenton	550.00
Cement Mixer, Linemar, 1950s	230.00
Chair, Doll's, Painted Red, Pennsylvania, Late 19th Century	300.00
Chair, Doll's, Wooden, Mustard Milk Paint, Stenciled, Woven Seat, 1880, 14 In.	275.00
Chair, Doll's, Wooden, Spindles, Arms, Gold Leaf, France, 1890, 11 In.	650.00
Chalkboard, Stand-Up, Spaceman, Lithograph Cardboard, 1950s, 16 x 32 In.	55.00
Charleston Trio, Tin, Windup, Marx .... *Illus*	900.00
Charlie Chimp Hula Expert, Box, Japan, 1950s	95.00
Chemical Wagon, Pratt & Litchworth	7500.00
Chemistry Set, Gilbert, No. 5	85.00
Chemistry Set, Microscope, Slides, Test Tubes, 50 Piece, 1930s, Wooden Box	235.00
Chest, Doll's, Circassian Walnut, 3 Small Over 3 Lower Drawers, 15 x 16 In.	1600.00
Chest, Doll's, Empire, Mahogany, 1850, 9 x 9 1/2 In.	375.00
Chest, Doll's, Mahogany, Pine, Porcelain Knobs, New England, 1850, 8 1/2 In.	200.00
Chick, Checkered Vest, Chein, Windup	35.00
Chief Robotman, Battery Operated, Japan, Box	900.00
Child On Tricycle, Windup, Tin, 8 In.	275.00
Chuck Wagon, Cowboy Joe, Musical, Tin Lithograph, Mattel, 13 In., Box	75.00
Church, No. 3601, HO Scale, White, Gray Roof, Plasticville, Early 1960s	17.50
Cinderella & Prince, Dancing, Windup, Box	195.00
Circus, Amusement Park, Wolverine, Jet Roller Coaster, 1930s, Box	375.00
Circus, City Dairy, Wood, Tin, Milk Bottles, Rich Toys, 18 In.	412.00
Circus, Humpty-Dumpty, No. 2036, Schoenhut, Box, c.1925	3680.00
Circus, Humpty-Dumpty, Painted Wood, Windup, Schoenhut, Box, c.1915, 7 In.	2185.00
Circus, Magnet, On Card, American, 1930s, 4 Piece	25.00
Circus, Mammoth, Britains, No. 1359, Box	1800.00
Circus, Mammoth, Figures, Kangaroo, Horses, Britains, No. 1054, 1955, Box	450.00
Circus, Overland, Band Wagon, Cast Iron, Hand Painted, Kenton, 15 In.	630.00
Circus, Overland, Bear Wagon, 3 Drivers, Kenton, Pre-1940	475.00
Circus, Royal, Horse Drawn, Cast Iron, Hubley, 1920s	5950.00
Circus, Seesaw Circus, Tin, Windup, Lewco Products, Box	200.00
Circus, Sticker Kit, Raggedy Ann And Andy, No. 1042, Kits Inc., 1941, Box	120.00
Circus Overland, Band Wagon, Cast Iron, Hand Painted, Kenton, 15 In.	525.00
Circus Set, Wooden, Schoenhut, 1930s, 7 Piece	160.00
Circus Wagon, Overland Horses, Kenton	550.00
Circus Wagon, Toby Tyler Circus, Wooden, 11 In.	175.00
Clock, Crazy Cuckoo, Plastic, Remco, 1954	55.00
Clock, Hickory Dickory, Nursery Rhyme, Ideal	30.00
Clown, Artie, Tin, Windup, Unique Art	295.00
Clown, Ball Blowing, Battery Operated, 1950s	150.00
Clown, Bill Ding, Wooden, Strombecker, 20 Piece, Box	100.00
Clown, Bimbo, Windup, Circles, Jumping Up & Down, Tin Lithograph, France	225.00
Clown, Bouncing, Clockwork, Tin Lithographed, Unique Art Mfg. Co., 7 In.	130.00
Clown, Boxing, Celluloid, Tin Lithograph, Chein, 1940s	695.00
Clown, Charlie The Drumming Clown, Battery Operated, Box	300.00
Clown, Climbing, Zippo, Tin, Battery Operated	125.00
Clown, Happy Fiddler, Battery Operated, Box	595.00
Clown, Herman, Unicycle, Wooden, Directions, Card, 1940-1950, 18 1/2 In.	36.00
Clown, Horse Trainer, Mechanical, Tokyo Shei	797.00
Clown, In Chariot, Drawn By Burro, Schoenhut	3740.00
Clown, Magic Man, Puffs Smoke, Battery Operated, Maruson, Box	425.00
Clown, Mobile, Action, Mattel, 1952, Box	200.00
Clown, On Animal, Ramp Walker, Marx, Package	45.00
Clown, On Electric Trapeze, Plastic Head & Feet, 1940s, 25 In.	125.00
Clown, On Roller Skates, Windup, Box	400.00
Clown, Pinky The Juggling Clown, Battery Operated, Illfelder, Box .... 495.00 to 525.00	

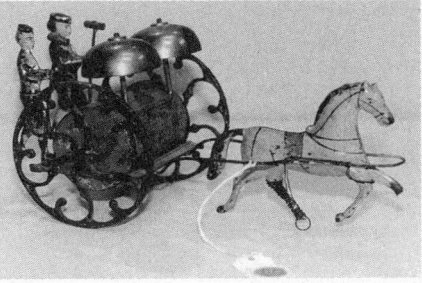

Toy, Fire Alarm Cart, Horse, 2 Men, Mechanical, Tin, c. 1900, 10 In.

Toy, Charleston Trio, Windup, Tin, Marx

Clown, Playing Violin, Battery Operated, 1950s	150.00
Clown, Plays Drum, Windup, Papier-Mache, 1930s, Box	125.00
Clown, Riding Mule, Clockwork, Tin Lithograph, Germany	412.00
Clown, Rollover, Windup, Japan, 1950s	65.00
Clown, Smiling Sam, Tin, Cloth Clothes, Up & Down Movement, Twirling Cane, Alps	325.00
Clown, Squeaky, Fisher-Price, Box	295.00
Clown, Stationary Head, Spins From Weighted Inside Mechanism, 4 In.	100.00
Clown, Suitcase, Windup, Schuco	65.00
Clown, Tambourine, Hand Crank, Original Clothes, 17 In.	850.00
Clown, Triky Trike, On Motor Scooter, Windup, 1950s	65.00
Clown, Tumbles, Mechanical, Papier-Mache Head, Germany, 1925, 8 In.	175.00
Clown, Tumbling Peter, Celluloid, Windup, Japan, 7 In., Box	195.00
Clown, Vibrates While Playing Fiddle, Schuco, 4 1/2 In.	250.00
Coach, Cinderella, Twin Horse Drawn, Paper On Wood, c.1900, 26 In.	2760.00
Coffee Set, Aluminum, 1940s	75.00
Colorforms, 3 Stooges, 1959, Box	165.00
Colorforms, Addams Family, Box, 1965	88.00
Compass, Space, On Card, 1940s	22.00
Construction Set, Tin, Windup, Daiya, Japan, 1950s, Box	60.00
Covered Wagon, Horses Go Up & Down When Moving, Battery Operated	180.00
Cow, Elsie Jumps Over The Moon, Pull Toy, Box	150.00
Cowboy, On Horse, Pull Toy, Wooden Wheels, 1950s	40.00
Cowboy, Rodeo, Rope Spinner, Tin Lithograph, Battery Operated, Alps, Japan, Box	275.00
Cowboy & Indian, Barclay No. 716/14, Box	445.00
Cowboy Range Rider, Moving Arm, Lasso, Rocker, Marx	295.00
Cowboy Rider, Key Wind, Tin Plate Horse Jumps, Marx, Box, 8 1/4 In.	285.00
Cradle, Doll's, Hardwood, 15 1/2 x 24 1/2 In.	143.00
Cradle, Doll's, Hooded, Pine, Red Flame Graining, Wire Nail Construction, 25 In.	105.00
Cradle, Doll's, Hooded, Poplar, 25 In.	440.00
Cradle, Doll's, Poplar, Green & Yellow Paint, 17 3/4 In.	165.00
Cradle, Doll's, Red Bentwood	25.00
Cradle, Doll's, Stenciled Flowers & Ostrich, Scrolled Ends, Poplar, 13 In.	85.00
Cradle, Doll's, Yellow Grained, 19 1/2 x 9 In.	75.00
Crapshooter, Cragston, Battery Operated, Box	200.00 to 275.00
Crawling Baby, Battery Operated, Box, 1950s	155.00
Crib, Doll's, Amsco, Box, Large	125.00
Curious George, Yes/No, Jointed, Schuco, 1930, 9 In.	195.00
Cutter Sleigh, Painted & Stenciled Wood, Velvet Seat, c.1880, 33 In.	173.00
Cycle, Rider, Windup, U.S. Zone Germany	395.00
Cycling Daddy, Battery Operated, Box	225.00
Dancing Couple, Celluloid, Windup, Occupied Japan, Box	150.00

Dancing Couple, Clockwork, Dressed, Hand Painted, Ferdinand Martin, 7 1/2 In. 990.00
Dancing Dan, Bell Products, 1950s, Box 145.00
Dancing Sam, With Cane, Windup, Tin Plate, Box 350.00
Dennis The Menace, Plays The Xylophone, Battery Operated, Box 385.00
Depot, Bus, Keystone 125.00
Derrick, Clamshell, Structo 265.00
Dining Set, Doll's, Tubular Metal, Gray, Pink Floral, 6 Piece 15.00
Dinner Set, Cobalt Blue Floral, Pottery, 1840, 29 Piece 650.00
Dinner Set, Doll's, Faience, Decanter, Tumblers, C.G.B.Paris, 1890, Box 700.00
Dinner Set, Doll's, Porcelain, Pink Rose Pattern, Partial Cutlery, France, 1920, Box . 500.00
Dish Set, Doll's, Plastic, Ideal Toy, 1946, Box 75.00
Dishwasher, Tin, Battery Operated, Cragstan, 10 In. 125.00
Ditch Digger, Cast Iron, Kenton 1155.00
Doctor's Kit, Dr. Kildare, With Bag, Box 50.00
Doctor's Kit, Ken, Fitted, Pressman, Box, 1963 .... 225.00
Dog, Begging, Heubach, 7 1/2 In. 595.00
Dog, Dachshund, Bee On Tail, Stung Him, Windup, Fur Type, Occupied Japan, 5 In. 65.00
Dog, Drinking, Battery Operated, Yone Toys, Japan, Box 350.00
Dog, Long Plush, Glass Eyes, Germany, Label, 1915, 4 In. 295.00
Dog, Piano Playing, Tin & Plastic, Battery Operated, Japan, 9 x 5 In. 77.00
Dog, Poodle, Glass Eyes, Schoenhut 350.00
Dog, Poodle, Riding, White Rubber Wheels 225.00
Dog, Running Spaniel, Marx, 1940, Box 285.00
Dog, Salon, Poodle, Brown Mohair, Papier-Mache, France, 1900, 19 In. 650.00
Dog, Salon, Reclining, White Fur, Papier-Mache, France, 1900, 18 In. 550.00
Dog, Scotty, Wags Tail, Pull Toy, Lithograph Tin, Marx, 1940s, 12 In. 135.00
Dog, Sitting, Long Plush, Glass Eyes, 1915, 3 1/2 In. 150.00
Dog, Sniffing, Wind Up, TN, Japan, 1950s 150.00
Dog, Spin, Fisher-Price 100.00
Dog, Wee Scotty, Tin, Windup, Marx 175.00
Dog, Wooden, Jointed, Press Bottom, Wiggle, Sit, Jump, 1940s, Box, 6 1/2 In. 35.00
Dolls are listed in their own category
Doll-E-Detector Scales, Amsco, Box 100.00
Dollhouse, 3 Story, Green, Elevator, Crank Handle, Germany, c.1925, 14 In. 690.00
Dollhouse, Barbie's New Dream House, 1963 .... 350.00
Dollhouse, Bliss, 2 Story, Paper On Wood, Keyhole, Early 20th Century, 16 In. 805.00
Dollhouse, Bliss, Front Porch, Hinged Front, Paper On Wood, 19th Century, 16 In. ... 460.00
Dollhouse, Coffee Serving Set, Flowered, Porcelain 85.00
Dollhouse, Colonial, Half-Style, 6 Rooms, Hand-Crafted, 20th Century, 33 x 37 In. .. 110.00
Dollhouse, Furniture, Baby Carriage, Cast Iron, Kilgore 65.00
Dollhouse, Furniture, Bed, Spindle, With Linens 40.00
Dollhouse, Furniture, Bliss, ABC, Box, 10 Piece 1100.00
Dollhouse, Furniture, Bureau, Walnut, 4 Drawer, Victorian, 18 x 20 In. 248.00
Dollhouse, Furniture, Chair, Mary Had A Little Lamb Theme, Chein, Tin, 5 Piece 125.00
Dollhouse, Furniture, Chiffonier, Double Door, Shelves, Trays, Hangers, 22 In. 295.00
Dollhouse, Furniture, Crib, Cast Iron, Kilgore 65.00
Dollhouse, Furniture, Cupboard, Green 24.00
Dollhouse, Furniture, Dining Room Set, 4 High Back Chairs, Table, Marx, 1964 .... 45.00
Dollhouse, Furniture, Dining Room Set, Stromberger 45.00
Dollhouse, Furniture, Dresser, Converse, 1905, 28 x 19 In. 345.00
Dollhouse, Furniture, Fainting Couch 95.00
Dollhouse, Furniture, Go-Cart, Cast Iron, Kilgore 65.00
Dollhouse, Furniture, Ice Cream Table, 4 Chairs, 5 Piece 375.00
Dollhouse, Furniture, Kitchen Set, Wooden, Green, Schoenhut, 1930, 7 Piece 65.00
Dollhouse, Furniture, Parlor Set, Porcelain, Piano, Fainting Couch, 3 Chairs, 5 Piece 225.00
Dollhouse, Furniture, Potty Chair, Cast Iron, Kilgore 55.00
Dollhouse, Furniture, Rocker, Cast Iron, Kilgore 45.00
Dollhouse, Furniture, Sink, Cast Iron, Arcade 110.00
Dollhouse, Furniture, Stove, Cast Iron, Royal 20.00
Dollhouse, Furniture, Table, Bamboo, 2 Chairs, 1910, 5 1/2 In. 32.00
Dollhouse, Furniture, Table, Drop Leaf, 4 Chairs, 1930s, 7 In. 45.00
Dollhouse, Marx, Colonial, With Furniture, Box 55.00
Dollhouse, No. 952, Blue & Brown Trim, Fisher-Price 45.00

Dollhouse, Play Time, Cardboard, Box 45.00
Dollhouse, Schoenhut, Cottage, 2 Story, c.1920 .... 1045.00
Dollhouse, Schoenhut, Mansion, 2 Story, 8 Rooms, 1923 .... 1500.00
Dollhouse, Tin, With Furniture 69.00
Dollhouse, Tootsietoy, Half House, Slanted Roof, Other Furniture, 26 x 23 In. 825.00
Dollhouse, Town, 2 Story, Early 20th Century, Electric, England, 22 1/2 In. 403.00
Dollhouse, Victorian, Blue Roof, Germany, 1850-1860, Large 8500.00
Dollhouse, Victorian, Front Open, 4 Rooms, Staircase, 35 x 36 x 21 In. 605.00
Dollhouse, Wacker, 3 Story, Early 1900s, 27 In. 8500.00
Dollhouse, Warren Paper Products, Brick, 1920s, 6 x 10 x 8 In. 55.00
Dolly Seamstress, Battery Operated, Box 425.00
Donkey, Boxing, Boxing Gloves, Windup, Schuco, c.1935, 8 In. 920.00
Donkey, Stubborn, Key Wind, Clown, Cart, Lehmann, Box 875.00
Dragonfly, Friction, Japan 55.00
Dresser, Doll's, 3 Drawers, Cream & Green, Mirror, 1930s, 13 x 11 x 4 In. 120.00
Drinking Captain, Eyes Roll, Drinks & Face Reddens, Smoke From Belly 175.00
Drum, Cowboys & Indians, Tin Lithograph 85.00
Drum, Felix The Cat, Tin Lithograph 375.00
Drum, Noah's Ark Animals Pictured, Tin 110.00
Drummer, Bunny Bell, Fisher-Price 115.00
Drummer, Pink Panther, Battery Operated 45.00
Drummer Boy, Battery Operated, Chein 125.00
Drummer Boy, Windup, Celluloid, Pre-War Japan 145.00
Duck, Daffy Wooden Jointed, Label On Foot, 1930s, 6 1/2 In. 125.00
Duck, Daffy, Pull Toy, Paper Lithograph, Brice, 1940s, Sealed Bag 135.00
Duck, Granny Duck, Fisher-Price, 1940 .... 45.00
Duck, Pulling A Wagon Of Ducklings, Windup, Lehmann, 1920s 490.00
Duck, Ramp Walker 20.00
Duck, Waddling, Windup, Chein, 1940s 55.00
Duck, Windup, Wings Flap, Germany 465.00
Easy Bake Oven, Kenner 19.50
Elephant, Boxing, Gray Felt, Windup, Schuco, c.1935, 8 In. 748.00
Elephant, Bubble Blowing, Battery Operated, Box .... 95.00 to 195.00
Elephant, Circus, Ball, Umbrella, Windup 125.00
Elephant, Jumbo, Bubble Blowing, Tin & Plastic, Battery Operated, 8 x 9 In. 82.50
Erector Set, A.C. Gilbert, No. 10057, Electric, c.1956, Box 175.00
Erector Set, Builds Parachute Jump & Merry-Go-Round, Gilbert, No. 10 1/2 .... 350.00
Erector Set, Gilbert, No. 2, Junior, 1949 .... 250.00
Erector Set, Gilbert, No. 7, Wooden Box 100.00
Erector Set, Gilbert, Tin Box, Instructions 100.00
Erector Set, Motorized, Gilbert, Blue Steel Case, 1935 .... 225.00
Erector Set, Rocket Launcher, Gilbert, No. 10053, c.1958 .... 140.00
Eric The Bat, Steiff, Tag & Button 600.00
Farm, Hammer & Nail Set, Wooden, Playschool, Box 45.00
Farm, Manure Spreader, 2 Horses, McCormick Deering, Arcade 750.00
Farm Set, Auburn Rubber, Plastic Box 85.00
Farm Wagon, Cast Metal, Stanley, 1940s 95.00
Farmer, Massey Ferguson 390.00
Felix The Cat, Figural, Squeak, 1962, 7 In. 78.00
Felix The Cat, Movable Feet & Arms, Smiling, Schoenhut, c.1924, 7 1/4 In. 230.00
Felix The Cat, On Orange Scooter, Green Wheels, Windup, Tin, 1930s .... 695.00 to 975.00
Felix The Cat, Schoenhut, Dated 1924, 4 In. 265.00
Felix The Cat, Walker, Windup, German 200.00
Felix The Cat, Wooden Jointed, Schoenhut, Dated 1924, 8 In. 375.00
Ferdinand, Windup, Tin, Marx, 1938 .... 195.00
Ferris Wheel, Chein, 1930s .... 350.00 to 375.00
Ferris Wheel, Chein, 1940s 375.00
Ferris Wheel, Giant Ride, Ohio Art 275.00
Ferris Wheel, Hercule, Windup, Chein, 1930s 275.00
Ferris Wheel, Windup, Fisher-Price, 1960s 12.00
Figure, Ice Skating, Metal, Victorian Clothes, Flatback, Germany, 30 Piece 176.00
Fire Alarm Cart, Horse, 2 Men, Mechanical, Tin, c.1900, 10 In. .... *Illus* 7000.00
Fire House, Iron Front, Twin Horse-Drawn Cast Iron Pumper, Ives, c.1890 .... 4600.00

Fire Patrol Wagon, Cast Iron, Ives, 1890 .... 1995.00
Fire Pumper, Bing 6500.00
Fire Pumper, Bing, Tin, 16 In. 2200.00
Fire Pumper, Horse Drawn, Dent, 1905 .... 1045.00
Fire Truck, 1957 Model Ford, 17 In. 295.00
Fire Truck, Aerial Ladder, Buddy L, Steel, 1935, 37 In. .... 1100.00 to 1200.00
Fire Truck, Buddy L, 1920s, 29 In. 895.00
Fire Truck, Cast Ladders, Doepke 395.00
Fire Truck, Fisher-Price, No. 720 .... 55.00
Fire Truck, Hook & Ladder, Blue, Tootsietoy 95.00
Fire Truck, Hook & Ladder, Buddy L, No. 205 .... 3190.00
Fire Truck, Hook & Ladder, Marx, Box, 33 In. 300.00
Fire Truck, Hook & Ladder, Rossmoyne, Doepke 80.00
Fire Truck, Hook & Ladder, Structo, No. 902, 1950, 26 In. Box 195.00
Fire Truck, Hook & Ladder, Triple-Team, Chrome Body, Cast Iron, 1890s, 30 In. 1320.00
Fire Truck, Ladder Trailer, Arcade, 1934, 15 1/2 In. 1475.00
Fire Truck, Ladder, Dent Hardware Co., Cast Iron 2595.00
Fire Truck, Ladder, Horse, Bell & Driver, Arcade, 18 In. 650.00
Fire Truck, Ladders, Doepke 25.00
Fire Truck, Pumper, Buddy L 1605.00
Fire Truck, Pumper, Kenton, Cast Iron, 6 1/2 In. 320.00
Fire Truck, Pumper, Kenton, Cast Iron, 8 In. 425.00
Fire Truck, Pumper, LaFrance, Doepke 335.00
Fire Truck, Pumper, Lincoln, Red, Turner, 29 In. 1250.00
Fire Truck, Renwal, No. 105, Plastic, 1950s .... 85.00 to 125.00
Fire Truck, Suburban Pumper, Tonka 395.00
Fire Truck, Super Fire Truck, Plastic, Friction, Saunders, Box, 12 In. 145.00
Fire Truck, The Big Alarm, Battery Operated, Plastic, Marx, 1961, Box 75.00
Fire Truck, Yellow, Cast Iron, Dayton 495.00
Fire Truck & Station, Sheet Metal, Clockwork Doors, Kingsbury, 19 1/2 In. 403.00
Fire Truck & Station, Wilkins Horse Drawn Pumper, Ives, 17 In. 2750.00
Fire Wagon, Horse Drawn, Carved Nozzle, Cast Iron, Dent, c.1910, 31 In. 1955.00
Fire Wagon, Horse Drawn, Cast Iron, 26 In. 800.00
Fire Wagon, Ladder, 3 Horses, Cast Iron, 18 In. 115.50
Firefly, Battery Operated, Japan, Box 75.00
Fireman, Climbing, Remote Control & Battery Operated, France, 7 1/2 In. 165.00
Fireman, Climbing, Windup, Marx 140.00
Fish, Terror Fish, Friction, Tin 225.00
Fish, Walking, Balance, Paper, 1940s 18.00
Flash Space Patrol, Battery Operated, Whirling Rotor Blade, Flashing Lights, Box . 225.00
Flashlight, Captain Ray-O-Vac, Rocket Ship Form, Box 35.00
Flashlight, Planet Patrol Atomic Pistol, Marx, Box 125.00
Flashlight, Secret Detective, Lithographed, 1940s 65.00
Flashlight, Space Ranger, Tin Lithograph, 1950s, 6 In. 65.00
Flying Saucer, Space Patrol 3, Battery Operated, K.O., Japan, c.1950, Box 395.00
Flying Saucer, Space Pilot, Battery Operated, Cragstan, Box 275.00
Football, Foto Electric, Cadaco, c.1962, Box 50.00
Fort, Turrets, Flag & Soldiers, Paper On Wood, Bliss, c.1880, 14 1/2 x 13 1/2 In. 1265.00
Fort Apache Stockade, Marx, Box 50.00
Fox, Mr. Fox The Magician, Tin, Windup, Yone, Japan 275.00
Foxy, Standing, Steiff Chest Tag, 7 In. 145.00
Foxy Grandpa, Sticks Out Tongue, Papier-Mache, Tape Measure, 13 In. 175.00
Foxy Grandpa In Donkey Cart, Nodder, Hubley, Cast Iron, c.1905, 6 In. 322.00
Frankenstein, Battery Operated, Rosko, 1960s, Box 275.00
Frankenstein, Monster, Battery Operated, Box 175.00
Fred Flintstone & Pal, On Dino, Tin Lithograph, Windup, Linemar, 1962, 8 In. 225.00
Frisbee, Wham-O, 1959, Box 250.00
Frogs, Fighting, Pull Toy, Cast Iron, Sheet Metal, Fallows 825.00
Frontier Scouting Kit, Daisy, 1950, Box 375.00
Frontier Town Kit, Celluloid, Blackman, Box, 1960s 75.00
Fun Fair, Sunny Andy, Tin Plate, Colorful Ground, 1920s, Wolverine, Box, 14 In. 575.00
Funny Jungleland, Moving Pictures, Panels Flip To Change Outfits, Kellogg's 79.95
G.I. Joe, Action Pilot, Orange Jumpsuit, Boots, Painted Hair, Hasbro, 1964, 11 In. 75.00

G.I. Joe, Action Soldiers Of The World, British Commando, No. 8304, 1960s, Box ...   300.00
G.I. Joe, Action Soldiers Of The World, Russian Infantry Man, No. 8302, 1960s, Box   250.00
G.I. Joe, Adventure Team, Wind Boat, No. 7353, Hasbro, c.1972, Box 40.00
G.I. Joe, Air Cadet, Accessories 350.00
G.I. Joe, Army Jet Helicopter 275.00
G.I. Joe, Astronaut, Silver Jumpsuit, Painted Hair, Hasbro, 1964, 11 In. 60.00
G.I. Joe, Black Commander, Talking 225.00
G.I. Joe, British Commando, Accessories 320.00
G.I. Joe, Combat Helmet Set, Card 50.00
G.I. Joe, Deep Diving Gear, Complete 135.00
G.I. Joe, Doll, Mouth Of Doom, Painted Hair 275.00
G.I. Joe, Eisenhower Uniform 85.00
G.I. Joe, Frogman, No. 7602 ....   375.00
G.I. Joe, Imperial Soldier, Japan 675.00
G.I. Joe, Japanese Soldier 585.00
G.I. Joe, Jeep & Trailer 95.00
G.I. Joe, Krazy War, Unique Art 225.00
G.I. Joe, Land Adventurer, Box 130.00
G.I. Joe, Military Police Set, Accessories 175.00
G.I. Joe, Motorcycle & Sidecar, Camouflage, Japanese Stickers, Irwin 90.00
G.I. Joe, Mountain Troop Ski-Patrol, Accessories 225.00
G.I. Joe, Navy Jet, Irwin 450.00
G.I. Joe, Revenge Of The Spy Shark, Box 225.00
G.I. Joe, Sea Adventurer 110.00
G.I. Joe, Talking, Box 375.00
G.I. Joe, Training Center, Box 235.00
G.I. Joe, White Tiger Hunt, Adventure Team 150.00
G.I. Joe & Jeep, Metal, 1940s 200.00
G.I. Joe & K-9 Pups, Tin Lithograph, Windup, Unique Art .... 154.00 to 225.00
G.I. Joe Jouncing Jeep, Windup, Tin, c.1950, 7 In. 475.00
G.I. Joe Krazy Kar, Windup, Unique Art, 1930-1940 ....   250.00
Gallant Men, No. 4634, Marx 175.00
Games are listed in their own category
Garage, Automatic Opener, Marx, Tin Lithograph, 1950s .... 75.00 to 85.00
Garage, Double, Tin Lithograph, Lehmann 250.00
Garage, Limousine, Race Car, Bing 775.00
Gardener, Sam, Several Tools, Windup, Marx 175.00
Gas Station, Keystone 125.00
Gertie The Galloping Goose, Windup, Unique Art, 1930s 250.00
Getta-1 Robot, Metal, Windup, Colorful Headpiece, 7 1/ 2 In. 175.00
Giraffe, Button, Steiff, 27 In. 300.00
Giraffe, Mohair, Steiff, 8 Ft. 253.00
Giraffe, Open Mouth, Button, Steiff, 31 In. 325.00
Giraffe, Painted Eyes, Schoenhut 450.00
Girl, On Potty, Jumps Up, Mouse Pops To Bite Her, Tin, Germany 225.00
Girl In Swan, Shell Seat, Pull Toy, Cast Iron, 1885, 10 1/2 In. 6900.00
Glider Gun, Metal, Balsa, American, 1940s, Box 65.00
Globe, On Stand, Ohio Art, Tin 6.50
Go Kart, Tom & Jerry, Friction, Marx, 1973 ....   90.00
Goat, Navy Mascot, Glass Eyes, Plush, 6 1/2 In. 495.00
Golliwog, Holds Dolls & Soldier, Rocker, Raphael Tuck, Cardboard 225.00
Gong Bell, Mower Chime, Box 100.00
Good Time Charlie, Battery Operated, Japan, Box .... 135.00 to 200.00
Gorilla, Growls, Prowls, Battery Operated, Box 295.00
Gramophone-Cinema, Kinephone, 5 Discs, Charlie Chaplin & Felix The Cat, Box ...   275.00
Grasshopper, Cast Iron, Hubley 1000.00
Green Checkered Cab, Cast Iron, Painted Wheels, 8 In. 2750.00
Greyhound Bus, Friction, Tin, Japan, Box, 12 In. 42.00
Guitar, Beany & Cecil, Mattel, 1962 ....   60.00
Gun, Atomic Disintegrator, Hubley 295.00
Gun, Atomic, Sparking Ray, Tin Lithograph, Plastic Muzzle, Haji, Japan, 1969, 9 In. .   45.00
Gun, Cheyenne Shooter, Hamilton 54.00
Gun, Click, Red Ranger, Wyandotte 15.00

◆◆◆◆◆◆◆◆◆◆◆◆◆◆◆◆◆◆◆◆◆◆

Wooden items should be
kept off the sunny window
sill. Direct sunlight will harm
wood finishes.

◆◆◆◆◆◆◆◆◆◆◆◆◆◆◆◆◆◆◆◆◆

Toy, Hen On Nest Skittles, Composition,
Germany, 9 x 11 In. , 9 Piece

Gun, Click, Tom Corbett	195.00 to 225.00
Gun, Cork, Red Ryder, Daisy, Training Rifle	85.00
Gun, Cosmic Ray, Metal, Lithograph, Sparks, Siren, 1940s, Box, 13 In.	48.00
Gun, Dart, Astro Ray Laser Lite Beam, No. 563, Ohio Art, 1960s, 10 In., Box	175.00
Gun, Defender, Cap & Cork	275.00
Gun, Fanner 50	52.00
Gun, Guided Missile, Box	95.00
Gun, Pompom, US Navy, Remco, Box	50.00
Gun, Ray, Atom-Buster, Plastic, Target, Box, 1950s	175.00
Gun, Ray, Atomic Flash, Chein, Box, 1950s	70.00
Gun, Secret Agent Hideaway, Pewter Type, Smokes, I.D. Card, Box, 1930-1940	53.00
Gun, Shootin' Shell 38, Mattel	72.00
Gun, Space Rocket, Battery Operated, Sparking, Box	110.00
Gun, Space, Guided Missile, 2 Missiles, Box	95.00
Gun, Stallion 32 Six-Shooter, Nichols, 1955, Box, 8 In.	165.00
Gun, Texas Star, Bakelite Horsehead Handle	62.00
Gypsy Wagon, 1 Horse, Gibbs, c.1910	425.00
Gyroscope, 1930s	65.00
Gyroscope, Chandler, Instructions, Box	38.00
Ham & Sam, Clockwork, Tin Lithographed, Ferdinand Strauss, 7 1/2 In.	577.00
Ham & Sam, Windup, Strauss, Box	1850.00
Ham & Sam Minstrel Team, Windup, Strauss	595.00 to 605.00
Hammock, Baby, Frame	325.00
Handcar, 2 Figures Moving Handles, Rubber Track, Windup, Japan, Box	145.00
Handcar, Peter Rabbit, Floor Model, Lionel, Box	1795.00
Handcar, Railroad, Tom & Dick, Moving Handles, Rubber Track, Unique Art	175.00
Handcar, Windup, Tin, K.P.C. Japan, 6 In.	125.00
Handcuff Set, Junior Police, Whistle, On Card, 1940s	48.00
Hansom Cab, Cast Iron, Kenton, Box	797.00
Hansom Cab, Horse Drawn, Cast Iron, Pratt & Letchworth, c.1895	978.00
Hansom Cab, Windup, Lehmann	440.00
Happy Hooligan, Jigger	1275.00
Happy Jack & Happy Jane, Steam, Walter Kraus, Jigger	1400.00
Happy Violinist, Battery Operated, TPS, 1950, Box	375.00 to 775.00
Harold Lloyd, Action, Glasses, Eyes Blink, Bell Rings, Smile, Frown, 1930s, 8 In.	425.00
Harold Lloyd, Bell Toy, Rolls Eyes, Mouth Moves, Tin Plate, 6 In.	375.00
Harold Lloyd, Shuffles, Swings Cane, Expressions Change, Tinplate, Walker, c.1930	1725.00
Harold Lloyd, Squeeze, Eyes & Mouth Go Up & Down, Bell Rings	225.00
He-Man, Masters Of The Universe, No. 5040, Mattel, 1981	10.00
Helicopter, 2 Blade, Die Cast, Hubley, 1940s, 9 In.	110.00
Helicopter, Moon Scout, Battery Operated, Marx, Box	150.00
Helicopter, Tin, Plastic, Japan, Box	140.00
Helmet, Crash, Dennis The Menace, Ideal, Box	50.00
Helmet, Jet, Steve Canyon, Box	100.00
Helmet, Lost In Space, Plastic, 1966	1294.00
Helmet & Grenade, Camouflage, On Card, Maco Toys, 1964	12.00
Hen, Cackling, Fisher-Price	50.00
Hen On Nest Skittles, Composition, Germany, 9 x 11 In., 9 Piece ... *Illus*	2530.00

High Chair, Doll's, Metal, 1940s	12.50
High Chair, Doll's, Red & Black Graining, Gold Trim, 28 3/4 In.	132.00
Highway Set, Tonka, 1956	675.00
Hike-O-Meter, Wheaties	27.00
Hip Hop Dancers, Windup	800.00
Hobbyhorse, Carved Wood, Kid Covering, Leather Harness, France, 1885	1100.00
Hobbyhorse, Glider, Horsehair Mane & Tail, Glass Eyes, Wood, Carved, 58 x 54 In.	935.00
Hobbyhorse, Papier-Mache, Hide Cover, Leather Harness, France, 1885, 16 In.	600.00
Hobbyhorse, Papier-Mache, Original Gray Paint, Large Dark Eye	375.00
Hobo Train, Windup, Unique Art, 8 1/2 In.	750.00
Holster, Cap Gun, Leather, 1950s	20.00
Honeymoon Express, Key Wind, Marx, 1930s	295.00
Honeymoon Express, Tin Plate, With Christmas Card, Marx, Box	495.00
Honeymoon Express, Windup, Marx, Square, Box, c.1950, 7 In. .... 150.00 to	225.00
Horse, Pull, Hair Cloth, Straw Stuffed, Replaced Pewter Wheels, 27 In.	385.00
Horse, Pull, Oversize Chair Cart, Tin, 5 In.	165.00
Horse, Pull, Tan Felt Coat, Glass Eyes, On Wheels, c.1900, 18 x 18 In.	220.00
Horse, Rocking, Bent Wire, Wooden Head & Seat	28.00
Horse, Rocking, Carved & Painted, Maple, 23 x 42 In.	1210.00
Horse, Rocking, Carved Wood, Red Paint, Whitney Reed Corp, 34 x 46 In.	440.00
Horse, Rocking, Dappled Gray, England, 1920s, 48 In.	2100.00
Horse, Rocking, Hopalong Cassidy, Windup, Tin	450.00
Horse, Rocking, Horse Hair Mane & Tail, Brass Stirrups, 19th Century	520.00
Horse, Rocking, Pull Voice Box, Steiff, No. 9860, 29 x 51 In.	750.00
Horse, Rocking, Straw Filled, Detachable Wheels, Red Paint	650.00
Horse, Rocking, Wonder Horsesprings	155.00
Horse, Rocking, Wood & Leather, Ellis, Britton & Eaton	800.00
Horse, Walking, Traces Of Old Paint, Ives, Cast Iron, c.1880	2795.00
Horse & Jockey, Wheeled Platform, Fallows, Tin, c.1875, 7 In.	920.00
Horse & Wagon, Black, Red & Yellow Paint, Cast Iron, 13 In.	100.00
Horse & Wagon, Pull Toy, Wooden, 2 Wheels, Gibbs	145.00
Horse Drawn Wagon, Calliope, Driver, Hubley, c.1915, 13 1/2 In.	1955.00
Hose & Reel Wagon, Single Horse & Driver, Cast Iron, Wilkins, 1895	825.00
Hose Reel, Wilkins, 16 In.	2800.00
Hose Wagon, 3-Horse Team, Cast Iron, Kenton, 1911, 13 In. .... *Illus*	440.00
Hyster, Druge Bros.	500.00
Ice Skates, Keen Kutter, c.1890	20.00
Ice Skates, Klipper Klub, Clamp-On, Box, 1921	55.00
Ice Skates, Winchester, Figure, Lake Placid	145.00
Ice Skates, Wrought Steel Blades, Wooden	60.00
Ice Wagon, No. 12, Canvas Cover, Removable Rider, Buddy L, 1933, 27 In.	990.00
Iron, No. 24A, Wolverine, Box	30.00
Iron, Raggedy Ann, Tin	10.00
Iron, Red, Electric, Wolverine, 6 1/4 In.	55.00
Iron, Sensible, No. 6, Trivet	150.00
Iron, Sunnie Miss, Yellow, Plastic Handle, Tin	8.00
Iron, Wolverine, Box	10.00

Rusted toys have very low value.

Toy, Hose Wagon, 3-Horse Team, Cast Iron, Kenton, c. 1911, 13 In.

Toy, London General Omnibus Ltd. , Raphael Tuck & Sons, c. 1890, 22 x 18 In.

Ironing Board, Sunnie Miss	20.00
Jack-'o-Panda, Riding Donkey, Box	75.00
Jack-In-The-Box, Dr. Seuss Cat In The Hat, Tin Lithograph, 1970	45.00 to 125.00
Jack-In-The-Box, Foxy Grandpa, Papier-Mache	125.00
Jack-In-The-Box, Music Man, Mattel, 1952, Box	110.00
Jack-In-The-Box, Pop Goes The Weasel, Tin & Plastic, Mattel, 6 x 5 1/2 In.	22.00
Jackie The Hornpipe Dancer, Windup, Tin Lithograph, Strauss	700.00
Jazzbo Jim, Strauss, 1921	400.00
Jazzbo Jim Roof Dancer, Marx, Box	675.00
Jeep, Gumby's, Yellow & Red, Plastic, Lakeside Toys, 1966, 10 x 5 x 4 In.	100.00
Jeep, Jouncing, College Kids, Tin, Windup	275.00
Jeep, Jouncing, Unique Art	275.00
Jeep, Jumping, Clockwork, Tin Lithograph, Marx, Box, 6 In.	230.00 to 350.00
Jigger, Dancing Dan, Bell Products, 9 In.	295.00
Jimmy The Acrobat, Arnold, Box	140.00
Joe Penner, Tin Plate, Walker, Marx	495.00
Jolly Pianist, Battery Operated, Box	245.00
Julia Hospital Set, Nurse's Kit, Candy Dispensing Syringe, Microscope, Box	52.50
Jungle Trio, Battery Operated, Animals Play Instruments, Box	975.00
Junior Police Kit, Metal Badge, Whistle, Night Stick, Box, 1930s	65.00
Kaleidoscope, C.G. Bershe, Ct., 1874	1800.00
Kaleidoscope, Turned Walnut Base, Rhode Island, C.C. Bush, 1870s, 14 In.	935.00
Kazoo, Bronze Tin, 1930s, 7 In.	12.00
Keystone Fire Department, Building, 3 Tin Doors, 17 In.	145.00
Kidd-E-Simonize Kit, Amsco, Box, 1955	200.00
Kiddy Cyclist, On Tricycle, Ringing Bell, Windup, Unique Art, 1930-1940	275.00 to 350.00
King Kong, Battery Operated, Marx, Box, 12 In.	225.00
Kitchen, Doll's, Wooden, Donna Lee, Box	45.00
Kitchen, Tin, 19th Century	225.00
Kitchen Set, Aluminum, 19 Piece	45.00
Kitchen Set, Porcelain, Teapot, Molds, Rolling, Pin, Strainer, Masher, 6 Piece	300.00
Kitchen Set, Tootsietoy, 8 Piece	120.00
Kite, Casper The Ghost, Saalfield, Uncut	25.00
Kite, Cosmic, With Spaceship, 1923	15.00
Kite, Inflatable, Captain Carvel, Unused	12.00
Kite, Jell-O, 1940s	15.00
Kittens, Turn Knob & Moves, Madame Alexander, 1950s, 16 In.	145.00
Ladder Wagon, Cast Iron, Arcade	925.00
Lamb, On Wheels, Riding, Original Paint, 1920s	145.00
Laundry Set, Bench, Wringer, Tin Washtub, Washboard, Pins, Ironing Board, Wood	175.00
Lawnmower, Victorian	90.00
Lazy Day Farm Set, Marx, Box	50.00

Leopard, Green Glass Eyes, Steiff Label In Ear, 15 In. 195.00
Li'l Abner Dogpatch Band, Unique Art .... 450.00 to 875.00
Lincoln Logs, Double Set, Design Book, c.1924 .... 80.00
Lincoln Tunnel, Lithographed Tin, Key Wind, Unique Art, 24 In., c.1935 ..... 230.00 to 490.00
Lion, Bubble Blowing, Battery Operated, Box 225.00
Lion, On Wheels, Plush, Embroidered Nose, Amber Glass Eyes, Steiff, 1915, 12 In. .. 1150.00
Lioness, Steiff, 11 In. 225.00
Little Henry, Black Boy & Elephant, Windup, Celluloid 1425.00
Little Henry, Wheeled Platform, Pulling Little Brother, Celluloid, Windup 1000.00
Little Lulu, 1944, 15 In. 275.00
Lobster, Painted Tin, Windup, Goes Backwards, Germany 575.00
London General Omnibus Ltd., Raphael Tuck & Sons, c.1890, 22 x 18 In. ...... *Illus* 3000.00
Loom, Bead Craft, 1935 .... 55.00
Luggage Set, Charlie's Angels, Box, 3 Piece 125.00
Magic Garage, Windup Car, Tin Lithograph, Marx, 12 x 8 In. 325.00
Magic Slate, Hector Heathcote, Lowe, 1963 .... 69.00
Magician, Mr. Fox, Disappearing Rabbit 275.00
Makeup Kit, Little Miss Movie, 1937, Box 40.00
Mammy, Wilson Walkie, Wooden, 1930 .... 35.00
Mangle, Hand Crank 60.00
Mary Had A Little Lamb, Windup, Animated, Schuco, 1930 .... 475.00
Mask, Zorro Secret Sight 30.00
Mattel-A-Tune, Jingle Train, Animated Musical Story Book, 1958 .... 25.00
Merry-Go-Round, 4 Cars, Musical, Tin Lithograph, 1945, 10 In. 550.00
Merry-Go-Round, Musical, 5 Children On Horses, Brass, Tin, Wood, Windup, 1920s 550.00
Merry-Go-Round, Musical, Wooden Finial, Stop & Go Switch, Germany, 1920s 590.00
Merry-Go-Round, Plays Music, Wolverine, 1930s 525.00
Merry-Go-Round, Pull Toy, Ringing Bell, Rubber Wheels, Wooden 145.00
Merrymakers, Tin Lithograph, Clockwork, Marx, 5 1/2 In. .... 250.00 to 880.00
Microscope, Lab Set, Gilbert 65.00
Microscope, Slides, Tools, Oak Box 45.00
Microscope Set, Aristo Craft, Slides, 1950s, Box 45.00
Microscope Set, Meccano, Box 24.00
Milk Cart, Horse-Drawn, Windup, Marx Toyland 95.00
Milk Wagon, Borden's, Horse, Pull Toy, Wooden, 32 In. .... *Illus* 1155.00
Milk Wagon, Horse-Drawn, American Milk Co., Wooden, c.1900, 25 In. 330.00
Milk Wagon, Original Bottles, Marx, 1930s 450.00
Miss Friday At Desk, Typewriter, Telephone, Battery Operated, Tin .... 150.00 to 275.00
Mixer, Battery Operated, Marx, 1950s 22.00
Model Kit, Airplane, Fokker D-VIII, Aurora, 1959, Box 60.00
Model Kit, Alfred E. Newman, Aurora, 1965, Unbuilt, Box 185.00
Model Kit, American Firefighters, Revell 20.00
Model Kit, Astronaut, Aurora, 1967 .... 35.00
Model Kit, Aurora Sea View, Black Plastic, Box, 1966 .... 300.00
Model Kit, Beverly Hillbillies, MPC, Box, Sealed 240.00
Model Kit, BJ & Bear, AMT 50.00

Toy, Milk Wagon, Borden's, Horse, Pull Toy, Wooden, 32 In.

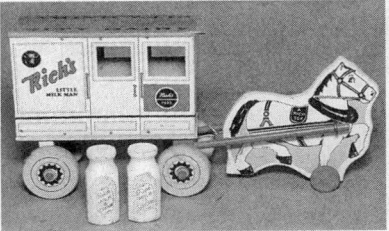

Toy, Rich's Wagon, Little Milk Man, Horse, Pull Toy, Wooden, Tin, 18 In.

◆◆◆◆◆◆◆◆◆◆◆◆◆◆◆◆◆◆◆◆◆◆◆◆◆

Use opaque window shades or drapes so the contents of your rooms can't be seen from outside.

◆◆◆◆◆◆◆◆◆◆◆◆◆◆◆◆◆◆◆◆◆◆◆◆◆

Motorcycle, Harley Davidson, Swivel Head Driver, Hubley, 7 In.

Model Kit, Build A Road, Matchbox	85.00
Model Kit, Car, Li'l Coffin, Monogram, 1964, Box	150.00
Model Kit, Car, Pontiac, Club-De-Mer, Revell, 1956, Box	175.00
Model Kit, Dr. Seuss, Tingo Revell	25.00
Model Kit, Dracula, Glow-In-The-Dark, Remco	25.00
Model Kit, Drag-U-La, Munsters, AMT, 1964	175.00
Model Kit, Engine, Visible V-8, Renwal, 1960	100.00
Model Kit, Falcon Building Lumber, Interior Lithographed Dovetailed Box	125.00
Model Kit, Frankenstein, 1/8 Scale, Plastic, Aurora, 1961	429.00
Model Kit, Frankenstein, Frightening Lightning, Aurora, Box	450.00
Model Kit, Jalopy, Motorized, Ungai, 1950s	75.00
Model Kit, Kit, Dr. Seuss's Gowdy, The Dowdy Gragle, Revell, 1960, Window Box	210.00
Model Kit, LaSalle Hearse, Aurora, 1939	37.00
Model Kit, MG Sports Car, Dopke, Box, Unused	995.00
Model Kit, Mod Squad, Station Wagon, 1/25 Scale, Includes Figures, Aurora, 1970	169.00
Model Kit, Moonship S, Revell	245.00
Model Kit, Mummy's Chariot, Aurora	450.00
Model Kit, Phantom & Witch Doctor, Revell, 1965	225.00
Model Kit, Phantom Of The Opera, 1/12 Scale, Plastic, Aurora, 1963, 13 x 4 In.	449.00
Model Kit, Prehistoric Scenes, Cave Bear, Aurora, Box	60.00
Model Kit, PT 109, Lindbert, Unbuilt, Box	65.00
Model Kit, Rat Patrol, Play Set, HO, Aurora, 1967, Box, 10 x 15 In.	229.00
Model Kit, Restless Gun, Pyro, 1958	40.00
Model Kit, Tarzan, Standing On Slain Lion, 1/11 Scale, Box, Sealed, 13 x 5 In.	169.00
Model Kit, Thing, Mego, 8 In., Box	125.00
Model Kit, UFO, Invaders, Aurora, Box	215.00
Model Kit, Zorro, Aurora	245.00
Monkey, Banjo Player Minstrel, Celluloid, Windup, Occupied Japan	125.00
Monkey, Bartender, Windup, Box	495.00
Monkey, Bartender, Windup, Japan	100.00
Monkey, Bellhop, Tumbling, Schuco	200.00
Monkey, Bongo Monkey, Battery Operated, Box	250.00
Monkey, Clancy, Roller Skating, Battery Operated, Ideal	90.00
Monkey, Frankie, Roller Skating, Battery Operated, Box	165.00
Monkey, Grinning, On Go-Cart, Rubber Wheels, Steiff	325.00
Monkey, Happy, Drummer, Windup, Tin, Plastic Head, Japan	90.00
Monkey, Hy Que The Amazing Monkey, Battery Operated, Box	395.00
Monkey, Jocko, Tumbling, Windup, Celluloid, Japan	95.00
Monkey, Juggling, Tin, Windup, Alps, Japan, Box	95.00
Monkey, Kazoo, Penny Toy, Germany	395.00
Monkey, Mechanical, Glass Eyes, Jointed Head & Arms, 1930s, 8 In.	395.00
Monkey, Metal Acrobat, Pull String, Runs Up & Down On String, 1930s, 8 In.	225.00
Monkey, Minstrel, Banjo Playing, Windup, Celluloid, Occupied Japan	125.00 to 145.00
Monkey, Mischievous, Battery Operated, Box	400.00
Monkey, On All 4 Legs, Windup, Painted, Guntermann, 1910	685.00
Monkey, Playing Trumpet, Battery Operated, Box	250.00
Monkey, Sheriff, Clockwork	675.00

Monkey, Sitting, Ringing Bells, Clockwork, Cloth Dressed, Ives, 1872, Box 5500.00
Monkey, Tumbling, On Trapeze, Marx, 1932 .... 140.00
Monkey, Yes-No, Green & Black Bellhop Clothes, Schuco .... 250.00 to 550.00
Monkey, Zippo, Climbing, Tin Lithograph, Marx 90.00
Monorail Car, Friction, Tin, Japan, 24 In. 150.00
Moon Ranger, Space Vehicle, 2 Astronauts, Tin, Box 795.00
Motorbike, Friction, Tin, 1950s, 4 In. 100.00
Motorcycle, Friction, Japan, 9 In. 195.00
Motorcycle, Halloh, Hand Painted Tin Lithographed, Lehmann, 1909, 9 In. 3450.00
Motorcycle, Harley Davidson, Swivel Head Driver, Hubley, 7 In. .... *Illus* 1000.00
Motorcycle, Harley Davidson, Tin Lithograph, Japan 650.00
Motorcycle, Hill Climber, Driver, Hubley, 6 3/4 In. 435.00
Motorcycle, Patrol, Cast Iron, Green, Hubley, 6 1/2 In. 485.00
Motorcycle, Police, Hubley, Box, 8 1/2 In. 250.00
Motorcycle, Policeman Driver, Harley Davidson, Cast Iron, Hubley, 5 1/2 In. 450.00
Motorcycle, Policeman Rider, Iron 225.00
Motorcycle, Policeman, Battery Operated, Modern Toys, Japan 300.00
Motorcycle, Policeman, Cast Iron, White Rubber Tires, Side Wheel, 1930s, 7 In. 300.00
Motorcycle, Policeman, Sidecar, Sparking Siren, Marx 350.00
Motorcycle, Rider, Harley-Davidson, Cast Iron, Swivel Head 300.00
Motorcycle, Rumbler, Hot Wheels 450.00
Motorcycle, Sidecar, Cast Iron, Yellow, 4 In. 210.00
Motorcycle, Sidecar, Police Squad, Mechanical, Marx, c.1930, Box 650.00
Mr. & Mrs. Potato Head, Box, Pair 395.00
Mr. Dan, Hot Dog Man, Tin, Windup, Box 110.00
Music Box, Casper The Friendly Ghost, Mattel, Box 150.00
Music Box, Easter Egg, Windup, Mattel 75.00
Music Box, Farmer In The Dell, Mechanical 195.00
Music Box, Lithographed Angels, Elaine Ends Hileman, Ohio Art Box 50.00
Musical Man On The Flying Trapeze, Mattel, Box 225.00
Musician, Bubble Blowing, Soap Package, Instructions, 1960s, 10 In. 285.00
Navy Set, 6 Ships, Tootsietoy, 1930, Box 595.00
Negro, Pull Toy, Tin, Spinning Bug Eyes, 1930s 50.00
Noah's Ark, Bliss-Type, Paper Covered Base, 13 Animals, c.1880 .... 299.00
Noah's Ark, Hand Painted, Hinged Roof, Wooden, c.1895, 15 In. 978.00
Organ, Church, Crank, Tin, Chein 95.00
Organ Grinder, Mattel, 1952 .... 175.00
Oven, Easy Bake, Kenner, 1964, Box 50.00
Oven, Electric, Turquoise, Wolverine, c.1950s 50.00
Oven, Pizza Hut, Electric, Coleco, Box, 1975 .... 25.00
Paddy & Pig, Key Wind, Tin, Lehmann 880.00
Pail, Circus Animals, Ohio Art 12.50
Pail, Circus Animals, Tin, Bail Handle, Chein, 4 1/4 In. 8.00
Pail, Embossed Seaside, Lithographed Tin, Germany 215.00
Pail, Fairy Tale Characters, Chein, Tin 30.00
Pail, Happynak, English, 6 In. 100.00
Pail, Little Red Riding Hood, 1940s 20.00
Pail, Little Red Riding Hood, 7 1/2 In. 25.00
Pail, Oriental Children, Carousel, Wolverine, 8 In. 30.00
Pail Play Set, On Display Card, Ohio Art 425.00
Paint Box, Blondie & Dagwood Family, Tin, 1932 .... 36.00
Paint Set, Li'l Abner, Box, 1940s 75.00
Pan Gee The Funny Dancer, Windup, Carter Toy Co. 475.00
Parrot, Pretty Peggy, Wings Flap, Eyes Light, Battery Operated, Box .... 300.00 to 325.00
Pastry Set, Mirro, Box, 11 Piece 45.00
Patrol Car-Tricycle, Police Box 450.00
Patrol Wagon, Wagon & Fire Men, Nickel Plated, Cast Iron, Shimer, 21 In. 1760.00
Pedal Car, Airplane, Red, Chrome Trim, Murray Steel Craft, 1940s 2200.00
Pedal Car, Airplane, Single Engine, Falcon, Toledo Mfg. Co., 63 In. 3245.00
Pedal Car, Airplane, Spirit Of St. Louis 3500.00
Pedal Car, Army Pursuit Plane, Steel Body, Disk Wheels, 46 1/2 In. 1100.00
Pedal Car, Barbie, Pink, Murray, 1962 .... 595.00
Pedal Car, Bi-Wing Plane, Steel Body, Rubber Tires, Toledo, 41 In. 2200.00

Pedal Car, Buick Torpedo, Red, Portholes 900.00
Pedal Car, Cadillac, Blue Streak 5000.00
Pedal Car, Casey Jones 400.00
Pedal Car, Caterpillar Tractor 2500.00
Pedal Car, Champion, 1958 .... 750.00
Pedal Car, Chrysler, Steelcraft, Ivory, 2-Tone Brown, Restored, 1932, 51 In. 8050.00
Pedal Car, Cord, Black, Red Interior, Restored, 1935, 57 1/2 In. 6900.00
Pedal Car, Dump Truck 4450.00
Pedal Car, Earth Mover, Yellow, Murray, 1959 .... 550.00 to 695.00
Pedal Car, Fire Chief, AMF, 1950s 5500.00
Pedal Car, Fire Chief, Murray, 1963 .... 395.00 to 600.00
Pedal Car, Fire Engine, American National, Hose, Fireman Hood Ornament 3850.00
Pedal Car, Fire Engine, Murray, 1959 .... 395.00
Pedal Car, Fire Truck, American National, Restored 3850.00
Pedal Car, Fire Truck, Garton, 1949 .... 525.00
Pedal Car, Fire Truck, Steel Body, Disk Wheels, Pneumatic Tires, c.1927, 55 In. 2310.00
Pedal Car, Garton, Fenders, Running Boards, Hood Ornament, Headlights 1250.00
Pedal Car, Lasalle, Silver, Maroon Wheel Arches & Lining, Restored, 1938, 52 In. ... 2415.00
Pedal Car, On Go-Cart Frame, Fiberglass 295.00
Pedal Car, Packard, Electric, Rumble Seat, 1920s, 72 In. 20000.00
Pedal Car, Phaeton, Double Cowl, Auburn, Maroon, 1932, 62 In. .... 2300.00 to 5500.00
Pedal Car, Pioneer Lines, Red, Gendron, 36 In. 4950.00
Pedal Car, Racer, Powell, Red & Orange, 1950s 400.00
Pedal Car, Rocket, 1950s 425.00
Pedal Car, Studebaker, Steelcraft, Restored, 1930 .... 5000.00
Pedal Car, Sunbeam Racer, Genfron, 1928 .... 4495.00
Pedal Car, Tank Truck, Mack Gasoline, Red 2325.00
Pedal Car, Toledo Racer, Black, Red Wheels, American National, 1927 .... 3200.00
Pedal Car, Tow Truck, Gulf, 24 Hr. Service 1155.00
Pedal Car, Tractor, John Deere .... 75.00 to 225.00
Pedal Car, U.S. Mail Truck, 1955 .... 1500.00
Pedal Car, Western Flying, Blue Paint, 1950s 300.00
Pedal Plane, Olive Green, Restored, 1927, 30-In. Wingspan, 45 In. 2900.00
Penguin, Action, Papa Pulls Baby, Sled, Walks Down, Plastic, 1940, 2 3/4 In. 4.50
Penguin, Big Bill, Fisher-Price 85.00
Penguin, Eyes Roll, Windup, Tin, Japan, 1960s 45.00
Penguin, Steiff, 8 1/2 In. 300.00
Penguin, Windup, Tin, Fur, 4 Actions, MT Japan, 5 1/2 In. 145.00
Penny, Beetle, Tin, Germany, 1 7/8 In. 100.00
Percolator, Red Handle, Aluminum 14.00
Periscope, Skippy Peanut Butter, Skiparoo 15.00
Pet Rock, Carrying Case, Rock Bottom Productions, California, 1975 .... 35.00
Pete Hustler, Driver, Movable Arms & Legs, Pull 100.00
Peter Rabbit Chick-Mobile, Box 1275.00
Phonograph, Barbie, Composition, Sing Along Microphone 87.00
Phonograph, Winnie The Pooh, Sears, 1971 .... 28.00
Piano, Charlie Brown 25.00
Piano, Futurland Grand, Mattel, 1948, 12 x 9 In. 125.00
Piano, No. 108, Schoenhut, 10 1/2 x 8 x 6 In. 75.00
Piano, Play-A-Way, Song Book, Marx, Box 250.00
Piano, Upright, Ebony, Gilt Pencil Striping, 8 Keys, France, c.1885, 13 In. 550.00
Piano, Upright, Tin Lithographed, Bliss, 8 x 6 1/2 In. 85.00
Piano, Wooden, 10 Keys, Olympia, 8 In. 125.00
Pig, Blue Glass Eyes, Pink Felt Ears & Nose, Steiff, Box, 11 In. 95.00
Pig, Checkered Pants, Windup, Chein 35.00
Pig, Walking, Windup, Chein 68.00
Piggy Cook, Flipping Omelet, Battery Operated 175.00
Pinball Machine, Flintstones 12.00
Pip-Squeak, Bird On Box, Papier-Mache, Spring Legs, 3 1/2 In. 71.50
Pip-Squeak, Boy, On Pig, Mechanical, 3 x 6 1/2 In. 3000.00
Pip-Squeak, Cat & Kittens, Bellows Base, Composition, c.1880, 4 1/2 x 2 In. 230.00
Pip-Squeak, Exotic Bird, Spring Legs, c.1884, 7 1/2 x 2 1/2 In. 173.00
Pip-Squeak, Froggy Gremlin, 5 In. 115.00

Pip-Squeak, Goose, Papier-Mache, Leather Covered Bellows, Spring Legs, 6 In. 49.50
Pip-Squeak, Pecking Bird, On Bellows Base, c.1882, 7 x 2 1/2 In. 173.00
Pip-Squeak, Rabbit, Felt Coat, 8 In. 22.50
Pip-Squeak, Sheep, Papier-Mache, Leather Covered Wooden Bellows, 4 1/4 In. 170.50
Pirate, Metal & Plastic, Wood Base, 1940s, 7 In. 29.00
Pistol, Mystery, Target Master, Ohio Art, Box 45.00
Play Set, Battle Of The Blue & Gray, 1965 .... 225.00
Play Set, Cape Canaveral, Marx, Box 250.00
Play Set, Captain Blood & The Buccaneers, Marx 50.00
Play Set, Captain Space Solar Port, No. 7018, Marx, 1950s, Box 255.00
Play Set, Castle Fort, Marx, 1950s 145.00
Play Set, Flintstones, 30th Anniversary, Marx 55.00
Play Set, Fort Apache, No. 3647, Marx 95.00
Play Set, Fort Apache, No. 4202, Marx 225.00
Play Set, International Airport, Late 1950s, Box 225.00
Play Set, Lunar Exploration, 4 Scenes, Marx, 1960s 350.00
Play Set, Operation Moon Base, No. 4654, 1962, Box 400.00
Play Set, Prince Valiant Castle Fort, No. 4706, Marx, 1950s, Box 200.00
Play Set, Star Trek, Mission To Gamma VI, Mego 650.00
Play Set, Ten Commandments, Marx, 1960s, Miniature, Box 435.00
Play Set, Tracy Island, Electronic, Matchbox 150.00
Play Set, Western Town, HO Scale, Marx, 1960s, Box 250.00
Play Set, Zorro, No. 3758, Marx, Box 795.00
Playhouse, Play Time, Cardboard, Box 45.00
Police Set, Gun, Holster, Handcuffs, Whistle, Badge, Night Stick, Tin Plate, 1940s, Box 110.00
Police Station, Howetown, Motorcycle Cop, Convict, Desk Sergeant, Marx 225.00
Policeman, Officer Clancy, Walking, Marx 550.00
Polly The Talking Parrot, Battery Operated 250.00
Pool Player, Standing, Table, Penny Toy, Germany, 1916 .... 165.00
Popcorn Vendor, Duck Pushing Popcorn Machine, Battery Operated, Box 575.00
Popgun, U.N.C.L.E., Luger-Style, 1965 .... 15.00
Praxinoscope, Metal, Paper Strip Scenes, Candle Center, France, Box, 9 In. Diam. .. 2500.00
Pretty Boy Singing Canary, With Mirror, Off & On Switch, HHI, Box 115.00
Printing Set, Favorite Funnies, Stampkraft, c.1935, Box 75.00
Printing Set, Ringling Brothers & Barnum & Bailey, 1940s, Box 65.00
Projector, Give-A-Show, Kenner, 1963, Box 35.00
Projector, Lantern, With Burner, Victorian, 6 Color Slides 85.00
Projector, Lindstrom, Box 125.00
Projector, Slide, Dr. Dolittle Ugly Mugly, Remco, Box, 1968 .... 30.00
Puppet, String, Sam The Scary Skeleton, Box Back, Side Panel, Kix Cereal, 1952 .... 34.95
Push, 2 Horses Between Cast Wheels, Cast Iron & Tinplate, c.1895, 30 In. 2185.00
Pushcart, Doll's, Bentwood, Stick & Ball Design, Rattan Back, c.1910 .... 275.00
Rabbit, Bunny Bell, No. 508, Fisher-Price 45.00
Rabbit, Oswald, Squeeze, Sun Rubber, Early 1950s 55.00
Rabbit, Peter Cottontail, Easter Basket, Easter, Mattel, 1952 .... 95.00
Rabbit, Pulling 3 Carts, Lithographed Tin, Chein 35.00
Rabbit, Rock-A-Bye Bunny Cart, Fisher-Price 475.00
Rabbit Trade Stimulator, Composition, Cloth Dressed, Germany, 22 In. 8250.00
Radar Station, Early Warning, Battery Operated, Box 375.00
Railroad, Gondola, Marx, Box 35.00
Railway, Elevated, Lithographed Paper On Wood, Shepard Hardware, 1890, 27 In. 2300.00
Ramp Walker, Wooden, Black, Original Clothes, 1930s, 4 1/2 In. 105.00
Rastus Shimandy, Toy Dances On Windup Record Player, Dated 1915, Box 700.00
Rattle, Humpty Dumpty's Head, Victorian Style 154.00
Reel, For Viewmaster, San Francisco, Calif., 1962, 1 Pack 15.00
Rich's Wagon, Little Milk Man, Horse, Pull Toy, Wooden, Tin, 18 In. .... *Illus* 413.00
Ride A Rocket, Spins Around, Bell Rings, Tin, Chein, 1930s 760.00
Riding Car, Plywood & Pine, Fading Paint, 1940s 175.00
Rifle, Cork, Wyandotte, Wooden Stock 5.00
Rifle, Indian Scout, Mattel, Box 11.00
Rifle, Johnny Seven, OMA, Topper, Box, 1964 .... 275.00
Rifle, Lasermatic, Battlestar Gallactica, Box, 1979 .... 65.00
Rifle, Space, Sparking, Tom Corbett 325.00

Rifle, Spitfire, Nichols, 1950s, Miniature, Box 65.00
Ring, Flicker, 3 Stooges, Curly, Gold Plastic, 1950s 18.00
Ring, Rat Fink, Detachable Membership Card, Macman Ent., 1963, 1 1/4 In. 29.00
Ring, Siren Whistle, Metal, 1950s, Package 3.00
Ring, Sky King, Teleblinker, Instructions, Box 475.00
Ring, Sky King, With Magnifier Pen 100.00
Ring, Tom Corbett, Metal, Silver, 1950s 230.00
Road Construction Set, Truck, 2 Road Scrapers, Trailer, Signs, Tootsietoy, Box 450.00
Road Grader, Metal, Marx, 1950s, Box, 16 In. 125.00
Roadrunner, Dakin, 1970s, 8 In. 15.00
Robot, Airplanet, Windup, KO, Box 150.00
Robot, Astronaut, Blue, Daiya, 14 In. 1895.00
Robot, Astronaut, Blue, Rosco 1100.00
Robot, Astronaut, Rotatomatic, Battery Operated, Box 165.00
Robot, Astrosound, Hasbro, Box 155.00
Robot, Atomic Man, Windup, 5 In. 495.00
Robot, Biotron, Battery Operated, Mego, Box 150.00
Robot, Blink-O-Gear, 1960s 795.00
Robot, Chief Robotman, Battery Operated, 1950s, Box 800.00
Robot, Commando, Ball, Rocket & Instructions, Box, Ideal .... 325.00 to 425.00
Robot, Dalek, Silver, Marx, 1964, Box 275.00
Robot, Dino, Battery Operated, Box 975.00
Robot, Driving Bulldozer, Marvelous Mike, Battery Operated .... 225.00 to 375.00
Robot, Fighting, Gray, Tin, Japan, 1960s, Box 600.00
Robot, Giant Commander, Remote Control, Voltron, Box, 26 In. 200.00
Robot, Lilliput, Red Highlights, Orange Tinplate, Key Wind, Japan, 1930s, 6 In. 1100.00
Robot, Linemar, Windup, Tin, 6 In. 410.00
Robot, Lost In Space, Stop & Go Action, Blinking Lights, China, Box, 1977 160.00 to 175.00
Robot, Lunar, Windup, Box 685.00
Robot, Magic Mike, Battery Operated, 9 In. 45.00
Robot, Mighty, Windup, Chest Sparks, Metal, Box, 5 1/2 In. 135.00
Robot, Monster, Opening Helmet, Lighted Red Growling Dragon, Battery Operated .. 75.00
Robot, Mr. Flash, Walking, Battery Operated, Plastic, Cragstan, Box 165.00
Robot, Mr. Robot, Battery Operated, Red, Cragston, 1950s, Box 1500.00
Robot, R-35, Windup, Japan, Box, 1984 .... 15.00
Robot, Radar Scope Space Scout, S-H Co., 1960s 150.00
Robot, Radar, Battery Operated, Remote Control, Eyes Light Up 900.00
Robot, Radar, Remote Control, Battery Operated, Box 2600.00
Robot, Robby, Windup, 8 In. 1100.00
Robot, Robert The Robot, Ideal, 1950s, Box .... 225.00 to 375.00
Robot, Robotank 550.00
Robot, Rock 'em, Sock 'em, Marx, c.1964, Box 150.00
Robot, Roto-Robot, Cragstan, c.1960 .... 225.00
Robot, Rudy, Remco, 1960 .... 155.00
Robot, Rudy, Remco, 1968 .... 300.00
Robot, Scorpio, Mattel, 1966 .... 750.00
Robot, See-Through Sparking Chest, Windup 145.00
Robot, Space Commander, 1960 .... 300.00
Robot, Sparky, Walker, Silver Finish, Key Wind, Tin Plate, Box 395.00
Robot, Sparky, Windup, Box 325.00
Robot, Steel & Plastic, Painted, Battery Operated, Japan, 11 1/4 In. 33.00
Robot, Strenco, Key Wind, Tin Plate, Silver Finish, Red Accents, 1950s, 7 1/2 In. 375.00
Robot, Super Astronaut, Mechanical, Blinking & Shooting Guns, Sounds, 1 1/4 In. .. 225.00
Robot, Super Space Commander, TV Space Scenes, Box 95.00
Robot, Television Spaceman, Battery Operated, Alps, 1950 .... 525.00 to 575.00
Robot, Verbot, Tomy 85.00
Robot, Walking, Windup, Green, Red Ear Muffs, Tin, 1950s 65.00
Robot, Winkie, Early 1950s 975.00
Robot, Zoomer The Robot, Battery Operated, Blue, TN, Japan, Box .... 950.00 to 1200.00
Robot Clock, Wooden, Black Metallic Finish, Battery Operated, 14 In. 175.00
Rocker, Shoofly, Black & White Paint 150.00
Rocket, Friendship 7, Battery Operated, Box 375.00
Rocket Launcher, Friction, Linemar, Box 60.00

Rocket Light, Space Patrol, c.1950, Box 350.00
Rocket Ship, Space Frontier, Battery Operated, Box 235.00
Roller Coaster, 1 Car, Chein, Box, 1950s 290.00
Roller Coaster, Coney Island, 2 Cars, Windup, Ohio Art, Box 250.00
Roller Coaster, Windup, Chein, 1950, Box 195.00
Roly Poly, Dutch Girl, Celluloid, Hand Painted, Germany, 1930s, 4 In. 8.00
Roly Poly, Irish Boy, Celluloid, Hand Painted, Germany, 1930s, 4 In. 8.00
Roly Poly, Monkey, Dressed As Porter, Suitcases, Celluloid, Germany, 1930s, 4 In. ... 20.00
Roly Poly, Mr. Pip, Smoking Pipe, Celluloid, Hand Painted, Germany, 1930s, 4 In. ... 15.00
Roly Poly, Rabbit, Celluloid 95.00
Roly Poly, Rooster, Carrying Purse, Horn, Celluloid, Germany, 1930s, 4 In. 12.00
Roly Poly, Santa Claus, Schoenhut, 12 In. 1900.00
Rookie Cop, On Motorcycle, Marx, Box, 1930 .... 795.00
Rooster & Hen, Plush, Stitched Felt Tail Feathers, Steiff, 1960, 11 In., Pair 400.00
Roulette Wheel, Instructions, Marx, Box, 6 1/2 In. 35.00
Round-Up Carnival Ride, 4 Celluloid Passengers, Mechanical, Japan, 1930s 825.00
Rudolph The Red Nose Reindeer, Steiff, Sold By Montgomery Ward, 1939 .... 150.00
Sailor, Rowing Boat, Friction, Mystery Action, Celluloid Figure, Tin, Japan, 1950s ... 125.00
Sam The City Gardner, Marx, Box 330.00
Samson The Strong Man, Tin, Windup, Box 1100.00
Sand, Dancing Fireman, Holding Horn Dances By Moving Box, c.1850, 7 1/2 In. 288.00
Sand, Seesaw, Busy Mike, Chein 100.00
Sand, Tools, Ohio Art, 1940s, On Card, 7 x 10 In., 4 Piece 45.00
Sand Crawler, Jawa, Star Wars, Radio Control 250.00
Sand Screener, Buddy L 1500.00
Sand Set, Felix The Cat, Box 130.00
Sand Toy, Black Dancer, Jointed 675.00
Sandy Andy Automatic Sand Toy, Wolverine .... 120.00 to 160.00
Scar, Convertible, Thunderbird, Cragstan, Retractable Top, Battery Operated 42.50
Scooter, Cushman Eagle, Red, White Stripe, 1959 .... 3000.00
Scooter, Metal, Red Paint, Wooden Handles, J.G. Rideout, c.1930, 43 x 32 In. 375.00
Scooter, Pee Wee, Box 250.00
Scooter, Push, Allstate, Original Paint, Pneumatic Tires 45.00
Scooter, Radio Flyer, c.1950 .... 145.00
Scooter, Skeeter, Aluminum, 4 Wheels 125.00
Seal, Spinning Ball, Celluloid, Windup, Japan 95.00
Search Light, Tom Thumb, Battery Operated, 1951, Miniature 4.50
Service Station, #866, Superior 175.00
Service Station, With Cars, Marx 200.00
Sewing Machine, All Metal, 1930s, Box 35.00
Sewing Machine, Casige 45.00
Sewing Machine, Germany, 1920s 125.00
Sewing Machine, Kayanee Sewmaster 50.00
Sewing Machine, Kramer, Wooden Box, Opens Into Cabinet, 1950s 25.00
Sewing Machine, Little Beauty, Germany 85.00
Sewing Machine, Little Red Riding Hood 185.00
Sewing Machine, Singer, Hand Operated, 7 In. 95.00
Sewing Machine, Singer, Sewhandy, Model 20, 1953 .... 100.00
Sewing Machine, Straco Sewomatic 47.00
Shell Tanker, Ford, Tootsietoy, 1950 .... 65.00
Sheriff, 2 Guns, Tin, Windup, Cragston 180.00
Shoe Shine Joe, Battery Operated 150.00
Shooting Gallery, Arcade, Circus Clown Ground, Tin Litho, Plastic, Marx, Box 115.00
Shooting Gallery, Windup, Ohio Art, 17 In. 90.00
Shovel Dozer, Battery Operated, Bandai, Box, 10 In. 75.00
Showboat, Whistle, Smoke, Battery Operated, Box 220.00
Shutter-Bug, Boy Takes Picture, Battery Operated, Box 775.00
Sink, Plastic, White, Red Hardware, Renwal, 3 x 2 1/2 In. 25.00
Six Million Dollar Man, Action, 12 In. 65.00
Six Million Dollar Man, Bionic Man, Engine Block, Kenner, 1975, 13 In. 40.00
Skating Hobo, Key Wind, Comic Face, Hands Flail In Air, Tin Plate, 7 In. 325.00
Skeleton, Dragon Blaster, Masters Of The Universe, Mattel, 1986, 6 In. 10.00
Ski Boy, Tin, Windup, 1940s 160.00

Ski Jumper, Flips Over On Bottom Of Slope, Key Wind, Wolverine 225.00
Ski Lift, Battery Operated, Early 1950s, Box 165.00
Sled, Belle Of Rochester New York, Brown Paint, Gold Lettering, 27 In. 1700.00
Sled, Cutter Sleigh, Velvet Seat, c.1880 .... 172.50
Sled, Dark Wood, Radio, 1930s 225.00
Sled, Flexible Flyer, Original Paint, Foot Braces, Decal, 65 In. 180.00
Sled, Fly Away 37.50
Sled, Goose Head, Iron 200.00
Sled, Hand Painted Wood, Steel Runners, American, 39 In. 368.00
Sled, Log Pulling, Miniature 250.00
Sled, Paint & Gilt Design, Word Friendship On Side, Dated 1874, 42 In. 1100.00
Sled, Push, Red Paint 50.00
Sled, Push, Victorian, Brown Paint 165.00
Sled, Red Putty Inlaid Reindeer, Wooden, Long & Narrow, 73 In. 82.50
Sled, Red, Chamfered Handle & Seat, Elegant Back Support, Nova Scotia, 1880 .... 585.00
Slinky, Frog, #440, c.1960, Box 65.00
Slinky, Worm, 1955, Box 80.00
Smitty Scooter, Tin Plate, Clockwork, Marx, 8 In. 1093.00
Smokey The Bear, Tag, Dakin, 1970s, 8 In. 25.00
Smoking Grandpa, Battery Operated 150.00
Smoky Sam The Wild Fireman, Tin, Plastic, Windup, Marx, Box 275.00
Snow Plow, Treads On Wheels, Tonka, 7 In. 25.00
Soldier, 6th Inniskilling Dragoons, Whisstock Box, 1935 .... 1100.00
Soldier, 7th Bengal Infantry, Armies Of The World Box, c.1935 .... 1045.00
Soldier, American Dime Store, 10 Piece 200.00
Soldier, American Infantry, German, c.1920, Box 650.00
Soldier, British Infantry, Britains, No.1614 .... 300.00
Soldier, Cavalry, McLaughlin Bros., Box, 14 Piece 550.00
Soldier, Coldstream Guard Band, Pre-1938, Britains, No.37 .... 600.00
Soldier, Combat, Windup, Metal, Hard Plastic, Turns, Fires Gun, Box 125.00
Soldier, Composition, Red Coat, Gold Buttons, Rifle, 4 1/2 In. 95.00
Soldier, Finn, With Skis, Manoil 80.00
Soldier, Indian Army Cavalry, Britains, 1948, 12 Piece 3520.00
Soldier, Infantry, Hard Board, Milton Bradley, 1900, Box, 21 Piece 425.00
Soldier, Japanese Infantry, Britains, No. 134 .... 1100.00
Soldier, Kaiser Wilhelm I, Bismarck & 8 Others, Heyde, Wooden Box, c.1890 .... 2860.00
Soldier, Kneeling Riflemen, Red Coats, Black Headdress, Britains, 11 Piece 195.00
Soldier, Knight With Mace, Britains 88.00
Soldier, Knight With Sword, Britains 88.00
Soldier, Life Guards, Mounted Band, Britains 870.00
Soldier, Lord Strathcona's Horse & Royal Canadian Regiment, 13 Piece. 2860.00
Soldier, Lying Prone Riflemen, Black Headdress, Britains, 5 Piece 110.00
Soldier, Mess Hall, American Dime Store, 15 Piece 275.00
Soldier, Mexican Infantry, Britain, Whisstock Box, c.1935 .... 1045.00
Soldier, Mounted, Blue Uniforms, Flag Bearers, Britains, 4 Piece 155.00
Soldier, Papier-Mache, Blue Coat & Hat, Black Boots, 1899-1925, 4 In. 125.00
Soldier, Pod Feet, American Dime Store, 7 Piece 150.00
Soldier, Queen's Own Cameron Highlanders, Britains, No. 2025, Box 1000.00
Soldier, Royal Air Force, Asbestos Suits & Gauntlets, Britain, Box, 8 Piece 2970.00
Soldier, Royal Horse Artillery At The Halt, Britain, c.1935 .... 990.00
Soldier, Royal Marines, Tropical Dress, Box, Britain, 1938, 8 Piece 1650.00
Soldier, Royal Suffix Regiment, Britains, No. 1323 .... 950.00
Soldier, Salvation Army Band, Britains 1540.00
Soldier, Seaforth At The Charge, Britains, No. 88, Pre-1938 .... 640.00
Soldier, Sharp Shooter, Key Wind, Clicks, Celluloid, Occupied Japan, Box, 9 In. 110.00
Soldier, Standing Guard, Red Coats, White Helmets, Britains, 5 Piece 100.00
Soldier, Starlux, 50 Pieces 165.00
Soldier, Wilson Walkie, Wood, Cardboard, 1940s 75.00
Son Of Garloo, Windup, Tin, Marx, 1960 .... 135.00
Space Explorer, Metal, Key Wind, Under Plastic Bubble, Guns, Christmas Box 175.00
Space Explorer, No. 103C, Battery Operated, Moran, Box 1200.00
Space Man, Captain Hap Hazard, Box 1100.00
Space Men, Ramp Walker, Package, 1960s 25.00

Space Patrol, Cardboard, Center Spinner, 1930s, Round, 3 In. 9.00
Space Ride, Chein, Box 485.00
Space Scientist Drafting Set, Precision Instruments, Unused, 1965 .... 15.00
Space Shuttle, James Bond Moonraker, Corgi, Box, 1979 .... 55.00
Space Sled, Land Of The Giants, Battery Operated, Remco, Box 595.00
Space Trip, Rocket Cars, Battery Operated, Box 725.00
Spaceship, Enterprise, From Star Trek, Dinky, On Card, 3 In. 15.00
Sparky, Doghouse, Battery Operated, Box 105.00
Speaker, Darth Vader, Star Wars 85.00
Speedway, Auto, 2 Race Cars, Windup, Tin 250.00
Spelling Board, Cress, 1916 .... 40.00
Spider-Man, Die Cast, Mego, 1979, 5 1/2 In. 90.00
Stagecoach, Fix-It, Ideal, Box, 1950s 75.00
Star Trek, Captain Kirk, Figure, 8 In. 40.00
Star Trek, McCoy, Mego, 1974, 8 In. 80.00
Star Trek, Talos, Mego, 1974, 8 In. 400.00
Star Wars, B-Wing Pilot, On Card 15.00
Star Wars, Imperial Dignitary, On Card 40.00
Station, Cities Service, Car, Battery Operated, Linemar, 10 x 6 In. 275.00
Station, Railroad, Brick, Green Doors, Ticket Taker Window, Tin 65.00
Station, Railroad, Schoenhut, c.1917, 17 In. 650.00
Steam Engine, Wilesco, Operates On Heat Tablets, Wilesco, Small 135.00
Steam Engine Plant, Falk, 17 In. 825.00
Steam Roller, Hubley, 10 In. 125.00
Steam Roller, Keystone 350.00
Steam Roller, Red Paint, Wood Roller, Nickeled Wheels, Hubley, 3 1/2 In. 95.00
Steam Roller, With Trailer, Light, Smoke & Chugging Sound, Japan, 1950s 250.00
Steam Shovel, Buddy L, Black Paint, Label 209.00
Steam Shovel, Metal, Tonka 150.00
Steam Shovel, Power, Steel, No. 220, Decal, Painted, Buddy L, 1920s, 19 In. 165.00
Steam Shovel, Sheet Metal, Structo, 10 1/4 In. 60.50
Steamship, 4 Stacks, Twin Props, 17 In. 2800.00
Store, Corner Grocer, Wolverine, 30 In. 275.00
Stove, Black, Nickled Top & Legs, 5 Utensils, Western Electric 140.00
Stove, Cast Iron, Eagle, 12 x 13 In. 695.00
Stove, Cook, Charm, Nickel Finish, Cast Iron, 4 3/4 In. 38.50
Stove, Cook, Green & Cream Enamel, 1930s 20.00
Stove, Crescent, Cast Iron 60.00
Stove, Eagle, Cast Iron 180.00
Stove, Electric, Tin, Little Chef, 12 x 14 In., Box 95.00
Stove, Empire, Metal, 2 Burners, White Enameled, Black, Oven Door, 17 x 9 In. 75.00
Stove, Gas, Royal, Cast Iron 45.00
Stove, Hughes Electric, Tin 20.00
Stove, Karr Range Co., Blue Enamel, Warming Oven, c.1900, 13 x 20 In. 1300.00
Stove, Lady Junior, Blue & Black, Metro Electric Co. 100.00
Stove, Little Chef 30.00
Stove, Little Orphan Annie .... 48.00 to 75.00
Stove, Marklin, Electric 125.00
Stove, Royal, Cast Iron, 1920s, 4 1/2 In. .... 50.00 to 85.00
Stove, Sunny Suzy, Tin Lithograph 30.00
Stove, Wolverine, Tin, Electric, 11 1/2 In. 20.00
Street Car, Gunthermann, 18 In. 1600.00
Street Sweeper, Nylint, 1948, Box 495.00
Strutting My Fair Dancer, Battery Operated, Box 175.00
Strutting Sam, Battery Operated, Box 550.00
Submarine, Atomic Sea Wolf, Dives & Surfaces, Windup, Sutcliffe, Box ...... 150.00 to 195.00
Submarine, Baking Soda, 4 1/2 In. 50.00
Submarine, Bing, Tin, Windup, c.1910, 8 In. 295.00
Submarine, Diving, Key Wind, Wolverine 150.00
Submarine, Diving, Unda-Wunda, Tin, Clockwork, Box 175.00
Submarine, U-Boat, German, Shark Type, Painted Wood & Metal, 1940, 36 In. 275.00
Submarine, Wolverine, Windup, Tin, 13 In. 350.00
Sun Picture Camera, Develops Pictures, 1930s, Package 8.00

Superior Service Station, Frank Studios, 1949 .... 45.00
Surrey, 2 Horses, Driver, Woman Passenger, Hubley, c.1900, 12 1/2 In. 748.00
Sweeper, Little Helper, Bissel, Ohio Art 10.00
Sweeper, Musical, Suzie Goose 18.00
Swing, Racing Bronco, Wood Cutout, Yellow, Black & Blue Paint, Metal Rods 65.00
Swing Set, Boy, Girl & Monkey, Moving Swings, Windup, Celluloid 195.00
Swing Set, Playground, Celluloid Boy, Girl & Monkey On Swing, Windup, Tin 225.00
Switchboard Operator, Battery Operated, Box 950.00
Sword, Celluloid, 13 In. 10.00
Table, Child's, Nursery Rhymes, Alphabet, Numbers, Graniteware 175.00
Table, Doll's, Folding, 1900s, Top Measures 16 x 10 In. 65.00
Table, Sewing, Folding 45.00
Tank, Army, Renault, Tootsietoy, c.1930 .... 60.00
Tank, Army, Sparking, Gunner Pops Up While Tank Rolls, Marx, Box 525.00
Tank, Centurion, Dinky, Box 85.00
Tank, Climbing, Army No. 12, Khaki, Mechanical, Marx, Box 275.00
Tank, Climbing/Fighting, Marx, 1950s, Box 150.00
Tank, Doughboy, Marx 275.00
Tank, Robotank, TR2, Battery Operated, Box 325.00
Tank, Rollover, Marx 150.00
Tank, Space Explorer, Bump-And-Go, Tin Lithograph, Japan 95.00
Tank, Space, Robot, Friction, Box 875.00
Tank, Sparking Space, Tin Plate, Key Wind, Sounds, Marx, Box 850.00
Tank, Sparking, Clockwork, Tin Lithograph, Louis Marx, Box 302.00
Tank, Tin Lithograph, Marx, 1930s, 9 In. 150.00
Tank, Turn-Over, Casper The Ghost, Tin Lithograph, Lineman, 1960s 350.00
Tank, Turn-Over, No. 3, Marx 235.00
Tank, Turn-Over, No. 5, Blue, Orange, Marx, 4 In. 120.00
Tank, U.S. Army Battery Operated, Tin, Japan, 1950s 250.00
Tank, Windup, Marx, 10 In. 285.00
Tanker, Esso, Painted Tin, Key Wind, Fleischmann, c.1938, 20 In. 805.00
Tanker, Gasoline, Mobil, No. MP8A1, Matchbox, 1960 .... 80.00
Tanker, Texaco, Buddy L, Metal, 23 In. 95.00
Tap Dancer, Circus, Tappin' Tom, Paper, Post's Cereal, 6 x 7 3/4 In. 24.95
Target, Dragnet, Tin Lithograph, Plastic, 1955, Box 150.00
Target, Red Ryder, 1939 .... 50.00
Target Set, Cap 'N Crow, Knickerbocker, 1958, Box 75.00
Target Set, Launch A Rocket, Knickerbocker, 1950s, Box 95.00
Target Set, Rabbit Hunt, Double Barrel Shotgun, Marx, Box 95.00
Taxi, Arcade, 9 In. 3000.00
Taxi, Black Driver, Cast Iron, Freidag, 1925 .... 1320.00
Taxi, Yellow Cab, Cast Iron, Arcade 975.00
Taxi, Yellow Cab, Skyview, Tin, Windup, Marx, 1950s, 7 In. 285.00
Taxi, Yellow Checker, 5 Cents Per Mile, Die Cast, Ledo, Box, 4 In. 25.00
Taxi, Yellow, Stop & Go On Back, Tin, Friction 120.00
Tea Set, Alice In Wonderland, Plastic, Box, 1930s 50.00
Tea Set, Bird Scene, Tin, Ohio Art, 13 Piece 145.00
Tea Set, Birds, Hand Painted, English, 5 Piece 300.00
Tea Set, Black Prints Of Children, Animals, England, 1835, 13 Piece 525.00
Tea Set, Clown, Palfair, Teapot, Sugar & Creamer 30.00
Tea Set, Cobalt Glass, Art Deco Design, 1930s, 21 Piece 154.00
Tea Set, Doll's, Admiral Perry At North Pole, 21 Piece 2500.00
Tea Set, Floral, Blue & Green, RS Prussia 395.00
Tea Set, Forget-Me-Not Pattern, Tin Litho, With Tray, Ohio Art 135.00
Tea Set, Kittens, Duck, Goldfish, 4 Spoons & Napkins, French 395.00
Tea Set, Little Miss Muffet, Polyethylene, Gotham, Ind., Box, 33 Piece 30.00
Tea Set, Mother Goose, Tin, Ohio Art, 19 Piece 44.00
Tea Set, Multicolor Flowers, Orange & Blue Luster, Japan, 13 Piece 72.00
Tea Set, Parseley China, 1840, England, 14 Piece 575.00
Tea Set, Peter Pan, 6 Punch-Out Stand Up Figures, Marx, Box, 23 Piece 675.00
Tea Set, Pink Transfer, Scenes Of Girls In Garden, English, 3 Piece 190.00
Tea Set, Queen Of Hearts, Tin 25.00
Tea Set, Rose, Wolverine, Metal 160.00

Tea Set, Sailboats, Umbrellas, Playing Horsey, Germany, 11 Piece 100.00
Tea Set, Staffordshire, c.1889, 17 Piece 410.00
Teddy Bears are also listed in the Teddy Bear category
Teeter-Totter, Boy, Girl, Hand Painted, Tin, Gibbs, c.1890 .... 650.00
Telegraph Radio De Luxe Set, 1950s, Box 55.00
Telephone, Stick, Tin, Wood, Bell, c.1920 .... 95.00
Telescope, 40 Power, Gilbert, Box 50.00
Ten Pin, Brownie, Box 1200.00
Ten Pins, Baseball Team Portraits On Each Pin, 1880 .... 4000.00
Theater, Child Life Puppet, Rand McNally Promotion, Box 250.00
Thresher, McCormick Deering, Yellow & Red Paint, Nickeled Wheels, Arcade, 9 In. 450.00
Tiger, Bengal, Open Mouth, Wooden Teeth, Steiff, 1959 .... 110.00
Tiger, Cub, Steiff, c.1980, 3 Ft. 85.00
Toaster, Pop-Up, Cloth Cord 25.00
Toilet, Doll's, Enameled Gray Cast Iron, Hinged Lid, 1 3/4 x 1 In. 10.00
Tom & Jerry, Bendable, Amscan, Inc., 1968, Pair, 7 In. Tom, 2 1/2 In. Jerry 42.00
Tool Set, Greycraft, 1940, 9 Piece 65.00
Tool Set & Box, Die Cast, Ideal, 1960s, Box, 5 Tools 15.00
Top, Metal, Gyro Top, c.1920, Box 75.00
Top, Nursery Rhyme, Tin, Ohio Art 5.00
Top, Red & White, Advertising, Frigidair Is Tops 3.50
Top, Spinning, 10 Little Indians, Ohio Art 12.00
Top, Tulip Petals Open As Spinning, Ballerina Inside, Tin 145.00
Toyland Farm Products, Tin Horse & Wagon, Windup, Marx 145.00
Tractor, Allis-Chalmers WD45, In D21 Box 18.00
Tractor, Battery Operated, Japan, 1950s, Box 145.00
Tractor, Buddy L 2750.00
Tractor, Caterpillar, Tootsietoy, No. 410, Box 50.00
Tractor, Climbing, Windup, Marx, Orange, Box, 8 1/2 In. 185.00
Tractor, Disstler, Windup, 7 In. 420.00
Tractor, Dozer Blade & Driver, Ideal 70.00
Tractor, Fordson, Nickel Wheels, Cast Iron, 4 In. 130.00
Tractor, Grader, Orange, Marx, 1940s 325.00
Tractor, International Harvester No. 1086, Radio Controlled, Ertl, Box 35.00
Tractor, International Harvester, Hard Rubber 13.00
Tractor, John Deere, No. 6, Pull Combine, Handmade 275.00
Tractor, Marvelous Mike, Electronic, Saunders-Swader Toy Co., Box, 9 In. 231.00
Tractor, Minneapolis Moline, Cast Metal 13.00
Tractor, Red, Yellow Cast Iron Wheels, Hubley, 3 1/2 In. 75.00
Tractor, Scoop, Shovel Wagon, No. 290, Tootsietoy, 1953, Box 250.00
Tractor, Show, Massey Ferguson 145.00
Tractor, Sparking, Climbing, Driver, Marx, Windup, Ox 195.00
Tractor, Sparking, Driver, Marx, Box 125.00
Tractor, Steam Shovel, Wooden, Noma, 1930s, Box 225.00
Tractor, With Driver, Auburn Rubber, 4 In. 15.00
Tractor, Wooden, XL Products, Des Moines, 21 In. 100.00
Tractor & Manure Spreader, Allis Chalmers, Cast Iron, Arcade, 1950s, 8 In. 365.00
Tractor Trailer, Coca-Cola, Buddy L 25.00
Tractor Trailer, Parkay, Ertl 45.00
Train, American Flyer, Diesel, 4 Cars, Box 850.00
Train, American Flyer, Tank Car, No. 4010, Two-Tone Blue 550.00
Train, American Flyer, Tunnel, No. 4267, Telegraph Poles, Box 605.00
Train, Amtrak, Battery Operated 45.00
Train, Auburn, Army, Rubber, Box, 10 Piece 225.00
Train, Baker's Chocolate, Tank Car 200.00
Train, Bassett Lowke, Locomotive, Spirit Fired, Steam, Maroon, Black, 21 1/4 In. 1093.00
Train, Beggs, Locomotive & Tender, Spirit Fired, Steam, Wooden Box, 21 In. 1955.00
Train, Boxcar, Central Of Georgia, No. 6464-375, Maroon, Red & White 85.00
Train, Boxcar, New Haven, No. 984 .... 80.00
Train, Boxcar, Rock Island, No. 6464-75, Dark Green & Gold 110.00
Train, Boxcar, Western Pacific, No. 6464-250, Orange & White, Box 225.00
Train, Buddy L, Caboose, No. 1001 .... 935.00
Train, Buddy L, Coal Car, No. 1005 .... 880.00

Train, Buddy L, Stock Car, No. 1004, Red 770.00
Train, Bump 'n Go Choo Choo, Windup, Tin Lithograph, Japan, Box 70.00
Train, Burro, Crane Car, No. 33/60, Yellow 200.00
Train, Burro, Maintenance Car, No. 69, Yellow 250.00
Train, Caboose, U.S. Marine Corps, No. 6017-50 .... 60.00
Train, Car, Railway Express Baggage, No. 1530, Presidential 260.00
Train, Carette, Gauge I, Mail Van, Double Bogie, Olive, Hinged Gray Roof, 11 In. 259.00
Train, Choo-Choo, Smurf, Durham, Box, 1981 .... 12.00
Train, Circus, Driver, Steiff 1600.00
Train, Ding Dong Train, Ohio Art, 1950s, 11 In. 125.00
Train, Dinky, Battery Operated, Plastic, Andy Gard, Box, 1950s 35.00
Train, Earlham Hall, Locomotive & Tender, Steam, Brass Display Track, 47 In. 1495.00
Train, Fisher-Price, Huffy, Puffy, No. 999 .... 75.00
Train, Fisher-Price, Toot Toot Engine, No. 643, 1964 .... 12.00
Train, Freight, Hiawatha, No. 757W 2310.00
Train, Gebruder Bing, Locomotive, Tender, Spirit Fired, Gauge III .... 2100.00 to 2645.00
Train, Gilbert Chemical, Tank Car, No. 910 .... 300.00
Train, Gunthermann, Engine & Tender, Tin Litho, Painted, Clockwork 143.00
Train, Ives, Hero, Engine & Tender, Passenger, Gondola, Cast Iron, 14 In. 357.00
Train, Ives, No. 3238, Locomotive, Electric 775.00
Train, Ives, No. 50 Baggage Car, Loop Couplers, Red, 4 1/2 In. 475.00
Train, Jefferson, Transformer, Model 535, 125 Watts 65.00
Train, Lady Cicely, Locomotive & Tender, Coal Fired, Steam, 30 1/2 In. 748.00
Train, Lionel Standard Gauge No. 4, Engine, Rapid Transit, 1908-1913, 14 In. 7475.00
Train, Lionel, Bild-O-Co, No. 381, Standard Gauge 495.00
Train, Lionel, Boat Loader, No. 6416 .... 200.00
Train, Lionel, Bridge, No. 105, Hand Painted Cardboard, Papier-Mache, Box 1155.00
Train, Lionel, Caboose, Smoking, No. 6557, Tuscan & White 200.00
Train, Lionel, Coal Elevator, Sante Fe, Tin 125.00
Train, Lionel, Crane, No. 2660 .... 99.00
Train, Lionel, Fire Car, No. 3512, Silver Ladders 154.00
Train, Lionel, Floodlight Tower, No. 92 .... 440.00
Train, Lionel, Freight Flyer, Locomotive, Track, 4 Cars 140.00
Train, Lionel, Gondola, No. 212, 205 Canisters, Wine 522.50
Train, Lionel, Gondola, No. 512, Brass, Peacock, Box .... 176.00 to 270.00
Train, Lionel, Hiawatha Passenger, 5 Piece 400.00
Train, Lionel, Locomotive, 1912 .... 2970.00
Train, Lionel, No. 5, Engine, 1918 .... 1485.00
Train, Lionel, No. 17, Caboose 440.00
Train, Lionel, No. 50, Engine, Standard Gauge, Illinois Central 185.00
Train, Lionel, No. 217, Caboose, Red, Peacock 137.00
Train, Lionel, No. 630, Observation Car 50.00
Train, Lionel, No. 736, Steam Engine 308.00
Train, Lionel, No. 6827, Bulldozer Flat 176.00
Train, Lionel, Pullman Car, No. 2630 .... 75.00
Train, Lionel, Signal Tower, No. 438 .... 1045.00
Train, Lionel, Station, No. 115, Box 935.00
Train, Lionel, Switch Tower, No. 437 .... 506.00
Train, Lionel, Tank, Shell, No. 2815, 1938-Style Couplers 230.00
Train, Lionel, Tank, Sunoco, No. 215, Brass 550.00
Train, Lionel, Transformer, Model T, 100 Watts 75.00
Train, Lionel, Trestle Bridge, No. 280, Green, Box 55.00
Train, Lionel, Trolley, No. 60, O Gauge, 7 1/2 In. 125.00
Train, Lionel, Tunnel, Illuminated, Brass, Tin, O Gauge, c.1930 .... 125.00
Train, Lionel, Tunnel, No. 104, Hand Painted Felt & Composition, Box 176.00
Train, Locomotive & Tender, Lionel, No. 736, O Gauge 320.00
Train, Locomotive, 3 Passenger Cars, Ives, No. 3243, Standard Gauge 990.00
Train, Locomotive, Clockwork, 2 Passenger Cars, Hubley, c.1906, 24 In. 1150.00
Train, Locomotive, Lionel, No. 2332, Electric 605.00
Train, Locomotive, Tender, 2 Cars, Cast Iron 375.00
Train, Log Loader, American Flyer, No. 787, c.1956 .... 275.00
Train, Marklin, Derrick, No. 10000K 577.00
Train, Marklin, Gauge I, Dining Car, Brown, 6 Tables, Chairs, Kitchen, 12 1/2 In. 748.00

Train, Marklin, Gauge I, Locomotive & Tender, Electric, Gray & Black 2185.00
Train, Marklin, Locomotive & Tender, Spirit Fired, Steam, Black, Red, Gold, Silver .. 633.00
Train, Marklin, Tank Locomotive, Black, Control Levers Cab 978.00
Train, Marx, Flintstones Choo-Choo, Tin, Windup, 1960s 495.00
Train, Marx, Honeymoon Express Cottage, Windup, Box .... 225.00 to 250.00
Train, Marx, Union Pacific, No. 10000, Box 495.00
Train, Mother Goose, Paper On Wood, Reed, c.1895, 38 In. 2100.00
Train, Ohio Art, Switch & Dump, Windup, Tin, Box 100.00
Train, Pratt & Letchworth, Engine & Tender, N.Y. Central, Cast Iron, c.1895, 25 In. .. 978.00
Train, Pratt & Letchworth, New York Central & Hudson, c.1900, 60 In. 4830.00
Train, Schoenner, Clockwork, c.1905, 18 In., 2 Piece 2100.00
Train, Stevens, Dreadnought, Locomotive, Spirit Fired, Steam, 1890, 14 1/2 In. 978.00
Train, Tinker, Pull Toy, Metal, Wooden, 13 In. 45.00
Train, Wilkins, Locomotive, Cast Iron, People In Cab 193.00
Train Set, American Flyer Frontiersman, Box .... 325.00 to 350.00
Train Set, American Flyer, 0 Gauge 137.00
Train Set, American Flyer, Klondike, No. 20764, 7 Piece, Boxes 550.00
Train Set, American Flyer, No. 3, Clockwork Locomotive, Tender, Baggage, Coach .. 605.00
Train Set, American Flyer, No. 5, Locomotive, Tender, Baggage, Coach, Boxes 577.50
Train Set, American Flyer, No. 282 .... 350.00
Train Set, American Flyer, No. 1101, Locomotive, 2 Pullmans, Boxes 385.00
Train Set, American Flyer, No. 4687, President Special Passenger, Track, Box, 1927 3400.00
Train Set, American Flyer, No. 21140, Northern, Locomotive, Tender 1595.00
Train Set, American Flyer, Pocahontas, Standard Gauge, 5 Piece 1045.00
Train Set, American Flyer, Silver Flash Freight, 5 Piece 429.00
Train Set, American Flyer, Silver Streak, Locomotive, Combine, Coach, Vistadome .. 143.00
Train Set, American Flyer, Union Pacific, No. 20535, Boxes, 6 Piece 1870.00
Train Set, Big Boy, No. 40445, Brass Engine & Tender, 4 Cars, 1932 .... 950.00
Train Set, Carette, Live Steam, 0 Gauge, Baggage, 2 Coaches 660.00
Train Set, Fisher-Price No. 215, Engine & 4 Cars 140.00
Train Set, Flintstones, Battery Operated, Marx, Box 185.00
Train Set, Hafner, Century Of Progress, Locomotive, Tender, Baggage, Pullman 302.50
Train Set, Hafner, No. 802, Clockwork Locomotive, Tender, 2 Coaches 825.00
Train Set, Hornby, Track, Clockwork Windup, Green & Black, 4 Piece 375.00
Train Set, Ives, 0 Gauge, Engine, 2 Cars, Track 1650.00
Train Set, Ives, 0 Gauge, Limited Vestibule Express 1870.00
Train Set, Ives, Gray Ghost, Locomotive, Combine, Pullman, Observation 605.00
Train Set, Ives, No. 690, Locomotive, Combine, Observation, Boxes 522.50
Train Set, Ives, No. 692, Locomotive, Buffet, Parlor, Observation, Boxes 352.00
Train Set, Ives, No. 3243 R, Banker's Special, Electric Engine 2750.00
Train Set, Katz, 515 LTD, Track 230.00
Train Set, Lionel, Alaska RR, Switcher, Flat, Quadhopper, Gondola, Caboose 275.00
Train Set, Lionel, American, Electric, 1955 .... 920.00
Train Set, Lionel, Blue Comet, 5 Piece 5720.00
Train Set, Lionel, Blue Comet, Locomotive, Tender, Faye, Westphal, Tempel 7480.00
Train Set, Lionel, Chessie Systems, Box 275.00
Train Set, Lionel, Coal Train, Locomotive, 3 Hoppers, Caboose 1430.00
Train Set, Lionel, Freedom, HO, Box 125.00
Train Set, Lionel, Girl's, Locomotive, 2 Box Cars, Gondola, Hopper, Caboose 2640.00
Train Set, Lionel, Inspection Car, No. 68, Red, Cream 440.00
Train Set, Lionel, Laser Train, No. 1150, Box 110.00
Train Set, Lionel, Lines Hudson, Passenger, Aluminum, Red, 1954 .... 550.00
Train Set, Lionel, Navy, Locomotive, Carrier, Missile Launcher 2 Flats, Caboose 742.50
Train Set, Lionel, No. 221, 2 Pullmans, Observation Car, Boxes 231.00
Train Set, Lionel, No. 254E, Searchlight Car, Hopper, Gondola, Caboose 282.00
Train Set, Lionel, No. 342, Locomotive, Baggage, 2 Pullmans, Observation Car 1045.00
Train Set, Lionel, No. 358, Work Engine, Tender & Rolling Stock, Box 4950.00
Train Set, Lionel, No. 773, NYC Hudson, Boxes 1000.00
Train Set, Lionel, No. 1615, Steam Switcher Work Train, 1958 .... 395.00
Train Set, Lionel, No. 1666, Steam Freight, Whistle Tender, 1947 .... 295.00
Train Set, Lionel, No. 1800, General Frontier Pack, Box, 4 Piece 400.00
Train Set, Lionel, No. 2023, Union Pacific AA Diesel Freight, Yellow & Gray, 1950 395.00
Train Set, Lionel, No. 2055, Steam Freight, Smoke, Whistle, 1956 .... 395.00

Toy, Trolley Car, Horses, Bowery & Central Park, c. 1900, 27 x 9 In.

◆◆◆◆◆◆◆◆◆◆◆◆◆◆◆◆◆◆◆◆◆◆

Remove mildew and mold stains from dolls with a commercial bathroom shower cleaning product that is chlorine-free.

◆◆◆◆◆◆◆◆◆◆◆◆◆◆◆◆◆◆◆◆◆◆

Train Set, Lionel, O Gauge, Engine, 1930-1940, 7 Piece	600.00
Train Set, Lionel, Royal Limited, 1980, Box	499.00
Train Set, Marx, Army, No. 5925, Locomotive, Tender, 4 Flats, Radio Car	880.00
Train Set, Marx, Mercury, New York Central Lines, Brass Color, 5 Piece	135.00
Train Set, Marx, No. 897, Locomotive, Tender, Hopper, 2 Gondolas, Cattle, Caboose	247.50
Train Set, Marx, Passenger, Joy Line	175.00
Train Set, Marx, Passenger, Windup	95.00
Train Set, Marx, Santa Fe Diesel, Box	310.00
Train Set, Marx, Union Pacific, Track, 4 Piece	45.00
Train Set, New York Central, Tin Plate, Tracks, Complete, Box	125.00
Train Set, Presidential Set, No. 12088, Silver, Red Trim, 1962, Box, 7 Piece	1350.00
Train Set, Pride Lines Hiawatha, Locomotive, Tender, Coach, Diner, Observation	770.00
Train Set, Tyco, Iron Horse, HO Scale, 1967, Box	130.00
Train Set, Varney, Olympian, Locomotive, Combine, 2 Parlors, Observation	1870.00
Train Set, Wooden, On Card, 1940s, Box, 5 Piece	85.00
Train Station, American Flyer, Metal	20.00
Train Station, Lionel, No. 134, Box	467.00
Train Tower Floodlight, Lionel, No. 92, Red & Silver, Box	253.00
Tram, Double-Decker, Electric Motor, Tinplate, Bing, c.1912, 10 In.	1495.00
Transformer, Bombshell, Insecticon, 1984	15.00
Transformer, Mixmaster, Construction, 1984	10.00
Transformer, Scavenger, Construction, 1984	10.00
Transformer, Shrapnel, Insecticon, 1984	15.00
Transformer, Twin Twist, 1984	15.00
Transformer, Ultra Magnus, 1985	25.00
Trapeze, Windup, Celluloid, Box	180.00
Tricycle, Wooden, Painted, Upholstered Seat, Iron-Bound Wheels, 35 x 51 In.	1650.00
Tricycle Rider, Bell, Celluloid, Windup, Suzubel, 5 In.	95.00
Trolley, Clockwork, Kingsbury	275.00
Trolley, Open, Horse Drawn, Bowery & Central Park, Paper On Wood, Reed, 1895	2990.00
Trolley, Toonerville, Tin, Windup, 1922, 6 3/4 In.	665.00 to 1210.00
Trolley, Twin Horse Drawn, Wilkins, Cast Iron, c.1895, 18 1/2 In.	2760.00
Trolley, Windup, Strauss, 1920s, 7 1/2 In.	295.00
Trolley Car, Horses, Bowery & Central Park, 1900, 27 x 9 In. .... *Illus*	2000.00
Truck, Aerial Hook & Ladder, Structo No. 902, Box	200.00
Truck, Air Compressor, Hubley, Box	175.00
Truck, Air Mail, Painted, Enclosed Body, Decal Plate 68502, Buddy L, 1930s, 22 In.	660.00
Truck, Animal Circus, Animals On Side, Bonnett Style	1200.00
Truck, Armored Fargo, Pressed Steel, Sturditoy, c.1927, 24 In.	2300.00
Truck, Army Lorry, With Driver, Black, 6 Wheels, Britain, No. 1335, Box, 6 In.	295.00
Truck, Auto Transport, Wyandotte	85.00
Truck, Baby Dump, Red Paint, Replacement Driver, Arcade, 10 3/4 In.	450.00
Truck, Bell Telephone, Cast Iron, Original Paint, Hubley, 3 3/4 In.	185.00
Truck, Bell Telephone, Plastic, Battery Operated, Remote, G.M.P., 1950s	195.00
Truck, Bell Telephone, Red Paint, Replacement Tools, Hubley, 10 In.	795.00
Truck, Black Diamond Coal, Cortland	110.00
Truck, Borden's Milk, Cast Iron, Rubber Tires, Hubley, 6 In.	880.00
Truck, Camper Pickup, Turquoise, Plastic, Buddy L, 1961, 14 1/2 In.	85.00
Truck, Car Carrier, 3 Austins, Cast Iron, A.C. Williams, 1920s	895.00

Truck, Cement Mixer, Ideal, Original Sleeve, 1950s 50.00
Truck, Cement Mixer, Linemar, 1950s 240.00
Truck, Cement, Friction, Japan, 7 In. 70.00
Truck, Cement, Red & Yellow, Structo, 20 In. 100.00
Truck, Circus, Lion & Tiger Heads Moving In & Out 145.00
Truck, Coal, Black Diamond, Courtland, 10 In. 85.00
Truck, Coal, Courtland, Box 110.00
Truck, Coal, Kenton, 1910 .... 685.00
Truck, Coal, Noisemaker Crank, Giant 990.00
Truck, Coal, Pressed Steel, Sturdy Toy, 27 1/2 In. .... *Illus* 2970.00
Truck, Coca-Cola, General Motors, Orange, Buddy L 300.00
Truck, Concrete Mixer, Tonka 225.00
Truck, Concrete Mixer, Wel-Don, Tin Lithograph, Japan, 8 In. 95.00
Truck, Curtiss Candy, Buddy L, Crank Operated Rear Gate, 29 In. 1100.00
Truck, Dairy, Insert With Milk Bottles, Marx, 13 3/4 In. 3850.00
Truck, Delivery Van, White Rubber Tires, Grill, Cast Iron, 1930s 100.00
Truck, Delivery, Flavor Ice Cream, 7 1/2 In., Box 375.00
Truck, Delivery, Junior Supply Co., Cast Iron, Dent, c.1925, 15 1/2 In. 9775.00
Truck, Delivery, Plastic Ice Blocks, Tongs, Canvas Cover, Steel, Buddy L, 1930 .... 1495.00
Truck, Delivery, Pressed Steel, Kingsbury, Keene, N.H., 25 In. .... *Illus* 4675.00
Truck, Delux Deliveries, Marx, Pressed Steel, 1930s, 15 In. 65.00
Truck, Dump, Arcade Mack, Red, 1925 .... 2495.00
Truck, Dump, Black Diamond Coal, Windup, Courtland, Box 175.00
Truck, Dump, Buddy L, Pressed Steel, Chain Driven .... 400.00 to 495.00
Truck, Dump, Cast Iron, Wyandotte 295.00
Truck, Dump, Coal, Battery Operated, Marx, 1930s 425.00
Truck, Dump, Friction Flywheel, Pressed Steel, Turner 1210.00
Truck, Dump, GMC, National Products, 1950 .... 275.00
Truck, Dump, Green & Red Paint, Rubber Tires, Hubley, 3 3/4 In. 175.00
Truck, Dump, Green Cab, Red Bed, 6 Wheels, Silver Grill, Hubley, 9 1/2 In. 150.00
Truck, Dump, Heavy Hauling, Buddy L 75.00
Truck, Dump, Hydraulic, Green & Orange, Structo, c.1940 .... 125.00
Truck, Dump, Hydraulic, No. 4600, Nylint, Box 395.00
Truck, Dump, Lumar Contractors, Marx, 17 1/2 In., c.1940 .... 190.00
Truck, Dump, Marx, 20 In. 275.00
Truck, Dump, Metal Scoop, Plastic Cab, Wyandotte, 6 1/2 x 19 1/2 In. 225.00
Truck, Dump, Scotty Boy, Pressed Steel, Turner 425.00
Truck, Dump, Steel, Yellow, Day Fran, 1960s 10.00
Truck, Dump, Tonka, 1956 .... 110.00
Truck, Dump, Trailer, Buddy L, 1950s 39.00
Truck, Dump, Turner, Pressed Steel 350.00
Truck, Dump, Windup, Cortland, Box 195.00
Truck, Dumper, Trojan, Pressed Steel, Sutcliffe, Box, 7 In. 60.00
Truck, Elsie's Dairy, No. 745, Paper Lithograph, Wood, Fisher-Price 625.00
Truck, Excavating, Windup, Crank, 1940s, 15 In. 55.00
Truck, Express, Steel, Painted, Spoked Wheels, Buddy L, 1930, 26 In. 990.00
Truck, Fanny Farmer, Marx, Box 75.00
Truck, Farm, Light Green, Tonka, 1960s 120.00
Truck, Farm, Stakes, Tonka, 1961 .... 150.00
Truck, Ferris Wheel, Friction, Chein, Tin 195.00
Truck, Firestone Service, Buddy L 595.00
Truck, Firestone Tire Service, Buddy L 900.00
Truck, Fix-All Wrecker, Tools, Marx, Box 220.00
Truck, Flatbed, Advertising, Dinky, 1950s 50.00
Truck, Flatbed, International, Ertl 175.00
Truck, Ford, Ford Sales & Service Sign, Die Cast, Ledo, Box, 4 In. 25.00
Truck, Gasoline, Cast Iron, Tin, Arcade, 1932, 13 In. 5500.00
Truck, Goodrich Tires, Open Hutch, Die Cast, Ledo, Box, 4 In. 25.00
Truck, Grain Hauler, No. 550, Red, Silver, Wooden Bed Trailer, Tonka, 6 x 22 In. 485.00
Truck, Gravel, Front End Scoop, Marx, 1950 .... 50.00
Truck, Grocery, Tin Plate, Miniature Boxes, Marx, Box, 1950s, 14 1/2 In. 265.00
Truck, Hathaway's Bread & Cake, Arcade, 9 1/2 In. 2090.00
Truck, Heinz 57, Battery Operated Lights, Metal Craft 575.00

Toy, Truck, Mack, Gasoline,
Cast Iron, c. 1900, 13 In

◆◆◆◆◆◆◆◆◆◆◆◆◆◆◆◆◆◆◆◆◆◆◆◆

Never try to play a disc on
your music box that was not
made for that box. The machine will be damaged and
the disc ruined.

◆◆◆◆◆◆◆◆◆◆◆◆◆◆◆◆◆◆◆◆◆◆◆◆

Truck, Heinz Pickles, Battery Headlights, Metal Craft	450.00
Truck, Heinz, Cream Of Tomato Soup, Die Cast, Ledo, Box, 4 In.	25.00
Truck, Highway Maintenance, Orange, Green, Structo, 1950s, 12 In.	80.00
Truck, Hydraulic, Blue, Tonka, 1960s	130.00
Truck, Ice, Pressed Steel, Buddy L, c.1930, 26 In.	1495.00
Truck, Ice, Yellow & Green Paint, Buddy L, 22 In.	30.00
Truck, Inner City Delivery Service, Tin, Marx, 18 In.	165.00
Truck, Kodak, Illustrated Film, Die Cast, Ledo, Box, 4 In.	25.00
Truck, Livestock Trailer, Gold Lettering, Landing Gear, Pressed Steel, Tonka, 1954	155.00
Truck, Log Carrier, Buckeye, Box	500.00
Truck, Log, Friction, Tin, Japan, 12 In., Box	180.00
Truck, Mack Wrecker, Mack In Raised Script On Cab, Cast Iron, 13 In.	4750.00
Truck, Mack, Gasoline, Cast Iron, c.1900, 13 In. .... *Illus*	1300.00
Truck, Meadow Gold Butter, Metal Craft	695.00
Truck, Merry-Go-Round, Buddy L, Friction .... 175.00 to	195.00
Truck, Military Police, Tin Plate, 5 Soldiers, Driver, Movable Windshield, 6 1/2 In.	185.00
Truck, Morrell Meats, Tonka	345.00
Truck, Moving And Storage, Plastic, Renwal, 1950s	95.00
Truck, Oil Delivery, Tin Plate, Windup, Courtland, 1930s, Box	300.00
Truck, Okie Oil Co., Phillips 66, Arcade, 13 In.	2200.00
Truck, Overland Transport Express, Battery Operated, Japan, 16 1/2 In.	275.00
Truck, Pickup, Marx, Tin Lithographed, Pressed Steel, Electric Lights, 11 In.	110.00
Truck, Pickup, Steel, Red, 1960s, Box	10.00
Truck, Polar Ice, Insert With Ice & Tongs, Marx, 13 3/4 In.	495.00
Truck, Police Patrol, Siren, Electric Lights, Marx, 15 In.	325.00
Truck, Pull Toy, Wooden Horse Pulling Merry-Go-Round, Kids On Horses, N.N. Hill	350.00
Truck, Railway Express, Keystone, Cast Iron	715.00
Truck, Ramp Hoist Flat Bed, Tonka, 1963	125.00
Truck, Ramp, Chain Crank Hoist, Orange, Structo, c.1940	125.00
Truck, Reads Drug Store, 1940s, 13 In.	75.00
Truck, Ready-Mix Concrete, No. K-13, Matchbox, 1960s, King Size, Box	55.00
Truck, Red Star Express, Buckeye, Box	750.00
Truck, Rescue, Convoy, No. 384, Dinky	22.00
Truck, Ride 'm, White & Red, Structo, 1930s	250.00
Truck, Rocket Launcher, Ideal, 1950s, Box	100.00
Truck, Sand Loader, Automatic, Wolverine	125.00
Truck, Sand Loader, Red, No. 994, Tonka, 1950s	80.00
Truck, Sanitation, Off-White, Marx, c.1950	125.00
Truck, Searchlight, Doepke	800.00
Truck, Searchlight, Pressed Steel, Battery Operated Light, Wyandotte, 10 In.	275.00
Truck, Semi, Circus, Buddy L	95.00
Truck, Semi, Grain Hauler, Dunwell	125.00
Truck, Semi, Grain Hauler, Tonka	290.00
Truck, Semi, Moving Van, Allied, Tonka, 24 In.	135.00
Truck, Semi, Western Auto, Structo	275.00
Truck, Service, Firestone, Buddy L	750.00
Truck, Service, White, Black Trim, Structo, c.1960	85.00
Truck, Shell, Buddy L	75.00

Truck, Sohio Oil, Drums, Pressed Steel 350.00
Truck, Stake, Heinz 57, Smith Miller 385.00
Truck, Steel, Cargo Co., Blue Cab, Red Trailer, Structo, 1940s 150.00
Truck, Sun Rubber, 5 In. 45.00
Truck, Tank, Keystone 3520.00
Truck, Tanker, Texaco, GMC-550, Buddy L, 1959, 25 In. .... 159.00 to 225.00
Truck, Tanker, Texaco, Oil, Republic, 23 In. 26.00
Truck, Telephone, Nickel Wheels, Hubley 450.00
Truck, Tipper, Bedford, No. 3, Gray, Red Dump, Black Tires, Matchbox, 1960s, Box 19.00
Truck, Tow, Esso Decal, Matchbox King Size, No. K-2, 1960s, Box 50.00
Truck, Tow, Wooden, Tick Tock Toys, 1940, 15 In. 100.00
Truck, Tow, Wrecker, Revver Series, Mattel, Box 100.00
Truck, Trailer, Century Of Progress, Arcade, 10 1/2 In. 200.00
Truck, Trailer, Colonial Brand Ham, Japan, Box 350.00
Truck, U.S. Army Signal Corps, Marx, Box 165.00
Truck, U.S. Mail, Buddy L, 6 Wheel, Buy U.S.War Bonds 550.00
Truck, Winnebago, White, Tonka, 1970s 100.00
Truck, Wooden, Tick Tock Toys, 1940, 17 In. 100.00
Truck, Wrecker, Die Cast, 1940s, Hubley 55.00
Truck, Wrecker, No. 171, Tootsietoy 75.00
Truck, Wrecker, Steel, Orange, Day Fran, Box, 1960s 10.00
Truck, Wrigley's Spearmint Gum, Buddy L, 1955 .... 150.00
Trunk, Barbie, Francie & Skipper, Black Patent, SPP, 1966 .... 83.00
Trunk, Doll's, Camel Back, Lithographs, Tray 350.00
Trunk, Doll's, Camel Back, Paper Over Wood, Tray 65.00
Trunk, Doll's, Dome Lid, Linen Cover, Wood, Brass Studs, Tray, 17 1/2 x 11 In. 303.00
Trunk, Doll's, Leather Cover, Wooden Slat Design, Brass Studs, Key, 13 1/2 x 9 In. .. 660.00
Trunk, Doll's, Victorian Children, Original Paper Lining, Restored, 20 x 10 x 10 In. . 115.00
Turtle, Tip Toe, No. 773, Fisher-Price 30.00
Twirly Whirly Rocket Ride, Box 1195.00
Typewriter, Delux Dial 62.00
Typewriter, Deluxe, Tin, Marx 125.00
Typewriter, Simplex, Lithographed, Box 45.00
Typewriter, Tin Lithograph, Letters On Metal & Rubber Wheel, 1940s, Box 35.00
Typewriter, Tom Thumb, Metal, Green, Gold Lettering, Cover, Booklet .... 55.00 to 65.00
Typewriter, Wolverine 30.00
Ukulele, Islander Baritone, French American Reeds Mfg., 1955, Box 100.00
Uncle Sam, Jigger, Wooden, Hand Painted, 15 1/2 In. 33.00
Uncle Sam's Big Show, Acrobatic Tricks, Instructions, Box 295.00
Vac-U-Form, Mattel, 1962, Box 65.00
Van, Delivery, Clockwork, Lithographed, G & K, Germany, 5 3/4 In. 465.00
Van, Hess, Box, 1980 .... 250.00
Van, Moving, Buddy L, 1920s 995.00
Van, Postal, Bing 1500.00
Van, Superman, Corgi, 1978 .... 22.00
Van, Transport, Steel Plate, Toy Illustrations, Rubber Wheels, England, 1950s, 18 In. 575.00
Viewmaster, Adventures Of Tarzan, Tarzan Rescues Cheetah, 1950 .... 10.00
Viewmaster, Captain Kangaroo, Sealed, 1970 .... 18.00
Viewmaster, Cisco Kid & Pancho, 1950 .... 10.00
Viewmaster, Lassie & Timmy, The Runaway Mummy, Sawyer, 1956 .... 7.00
Viewmaster, M*A*S*H, Sealed, 1978 .... 10.00
Viewmaster, Mighty Mouse, 3 Reels, Booklet, Sawyer, 1951 .... 42.00
Viewmaster, Monster Gift Pack, GAF, 1978 .... 35.00
Viewmaster, Rin Tin Tin, 3 Reel Set, Photograph Cover 30.00
Viewmaster, Road Runner, Warner, 1967 .... 12.00
Viewmaster, Star Trek, Mr. Spock's Time Trek, 3 Reels, 16 Page Booklet, 1974 .... 12.00
Viewmaster, Tom Corbet, Space Cadet, 3 Reels, Storybook, 1954 .... 25.00
Viewmaster, Welcome Back Kotter, Sealed, 1977 .... 10.00
Viewmaster, Wizard Of Oz, Sealed, 1970s 10.00
Viewmaster Reel, Dennis The Menace, 1967 .... 18.00
Wagon, Artillery, A2 Horses, Ives, 1880s 1750.00
Wagon, Circus, Cage, 2 Dappled Horses, Schoenhut 5445.00

Wagon, Circus, Horse & Driver, Wooden, Polychrome, 22 In. 55.00
Wagon, Eagle Coaster, Coil Springs 385.00
Wagon, Good-Will Soap, Large Wheels 1950.00
Wagon, Milk, Fisher-Price, 1965 .... 65.00
Wagon, Radio Flyer, Chicago Fair, 1933 .... 45.00 to 125.00
Wagon, Radio Flyer, Decals, 4 Ft. 165.00
Wagon, Radio Flyer, Green, Rubber Tires, Steel, Chicago World's Fair, 1933 .... 275.00
Wagon, Radio Flyer, Miniature 150.00
Wagon, Radio Flyer, White Rubber Ties, Red, Decal 225.00
Wagon, Red Metal, Compliments Of Radio Steel & Mfg. Co., Radio Flyer, 1950s 125.00
Wagon, Simmons Hi-Speed, Hand Brake 75.00
Wagon, Wooden, Dark Green & Yellow, Large Back Wheels, 1840 .... 985.00
Wagon, Wooden, Handmade, Accessories 625.00
Walkie Talkie, 2-Way, Box, Remco, 1953 .... 45.00
Walkie Talkie, Space, QX-2, Remco, 1950s, Box 80.00
Walkie Talkie, Space, Remco, 1950s, Box .... 35.00 to 80.00
Walkie Talkie, Spaceman, Magnet Powered, Remco, 1953, 12 x 9 x 3 In. 45.00
Washboard, Midget Washer, Glass, 8 1/2 x 6 In. 18.50
Washer, Glass Washboard, Midget 50.00
Washer-Dryer, Marx, Box 175.00
Washing Machine, Doll's, Marx 95.00
Watercolor Set, Artist's, Hand Carved Wooden Box, Porcelain Containers, 1890 ...... 95.00
Whale, Billy, Ball Blowing, Windup, Box 75.00
Whale, Monstro, Dives & Spouts Water, Windup, Tin, Disney 150.00
Wheelbarrow, Apple Green, Yellow Striping, Berlin Bilt 165.00
Wheelbarrow, Tin, Wooden Handles 32.50
Whistle, Guitar Shape, Celluloid .... .50
Window Box, Plastic, Sunbonnet Child, Yellow, Bernard Edward Co., 1940, 9 In. 12.00
Woman, Old, Walking, With Umbrella, Windup, Gunthermann 875.00
Woman With Watering Can & Hoe, Windup, Tin, 7 1/4 In. 368.50
Wonder Woman, Action, Box, 1976, 13 In. 46.00
Woody Woodpecker, Squeeze, 1960, 8 1/2 In. 65.00
Xylophone, Aristokratt, Book, Box 25.00
Xylophone, Brass Tubes, 2 Mallets, Musical Charts, 10 x 5 In., Box 125.00
Xylophone, Decal, Schoenhut 250.00
Xylophone, Lithographed Metal, Schoenhut 250.00
Xylophone, Metal, Wooden Mallets, 1950s, Box 45.00
Xylophone Player, Windup, Occupied Japan 135.00
Yeti, Abominable Snowman, Remote Control, Battery Operated, Box 900.00
Yo-Yo, Duncan, Butterfly, 1960 .... 45.00
Yo-Yo, Space Orbit, 1959, On Card 15.00
Yosemite Sam, Hat, Dakin, 1970s, 8 In. 25.00
Zeppelin, Construction Set, Metalcraft, Box 650.00
Zeppelin, Graf, Metal Wheels, Silver Finish, Boycraft, 25 In. 275.00
Zeppelin, Pull Toy, Cast Iron, 1920s 175.00
Zippo, Human Cannon Ball, Paper, Post's Cereal, 1947, 6 x 7 3/4 In. 24.95

TRAMP ART is a form of folk art made since the Civil War. It is usually
made from chip-carved cigar boxes. Examples range from small boxes and
picture frames to full-sized pieces of furniture.

Box, 3 Levels, Each With Drawer 750.00
Box, All Sides Carved, Center Drawer, Mirrors 3 Sides, 7 1/2 x 14 1/4 In. 345.00
Box, Anchor, Heart & Crosses On Cover, German Wording Front, 19th Century 302.50
Box, Dresser, Lift Top 150.00
Box, Heart Pattern, Carved, 4 Legs, Small 100.00
Box, Jewelry, Geometric & Heart Design, 10 1/2 x 9 x 6 In. 330.00
Box, Jewelry, Geometric Inlay 130.00
Box, Match Stick, 6 In. 195.00
Box, Mirrored Lid, Paper Lining, Footed 285.00
Chair, 5 In. 20.00
Clock, Tall Case, Snail Shells, Green & Maroon Paint, 1920s 5200.00
Cottage, Wood Roof Shingles, Copper Trim, c.1880 .... 195.00

Cupboard, Glass Door, 4 Shelves, Chip Carved	6000.00
Cupboard, Lower Doors, Top Shelves, Glass Doors, 71 x 42 In.	4950.00
Dresser, 2 Drawers, Mirror, Made Of Cigar Boxes, Labels Intact, 1920s, 11 In.	275.00
Frame, 11 3/4 x 14 In.	55.00
Plant Stand, Pedestal, Hourglass Shape, Layered Wooden Pyramids	125.00
Stand, Covered With Cigar Bands, 1910-1920	650.00
Summer Cottage, Hand Cut Wood Shingles, Copper Trim, c.1880	195.00
Vase, Tin, Within Cube, 10-Sided Pyramids, 17 Layers Of Wood, 14 In.	175.00

TRAPS for animals may be handmade. One of the most unusual is the mousetrap made so that when the mouse entered the trap, it was hit on the head with a mallet. Other traps were commercially manufactured and often are marked with the name of the manufacturer. Many traps were designed to be as humane as possible, and they would trap the live animal so it could be released in the woods.

Animal, Hand Forged Iron, 17 In.	50.00
Bear, Herters Kodiak Model, 52 Lbs., 44 In.	850.00
Bear, Oneida Newhouse, No. 5, Iron	150.00
Fly, Table Top, Wooden, Wire, Round	18.00
Lobster, Buoy, Maine	90.00
Mouse, Maple & Pine	40.00
Mouse, Sur Catch, Wooden	1.50
Mouse, Wire Mesh	20.00
Mouse, Wire, 9 In.	35.00
Rat, McGill 4 Way, Large	2.00
Rat, Vidtor Hold Fast, Wooden, Large	2.00

TREEN, see Wooden category

TRENCH ART is a form of folk art made by soldiers. Metal casings from bullets and mortar shells were cut and decorated to form useful objects, such as vases.

Key Ring, Bullet, 22 Caliber, Brass, From Military M-16 Rifle	3.50
Lamp, Art Nouveau, Large	85.00
Lighter, Brass, World War I	35.00
Paperweight, Shell Casing, Brass, Oval, 1919	3.00
Shell, Lighter, World War II	20.00

TRIVETS are now used to hold hot dishes. Most trivets of the late nineteenth and early twentieth centuries were made to hold hot irons. Iron or brass reproductions are being made of many of the old styles.

Brass, 1 Cutout Heart, Shoe Shape Feet, 9 In.	38.00
Brass, 3-Legged, Wooden Handle, 1884, 10 1/2 In.	175.00
Brass, Hearts & Diamonds, 9 In.	33.00
Brass, Horseshoe, 1888 In Center, Handle, 3 Footed	74.00 to 82.00
Brass, Lyre Shape, Iron Legs, Wooden Handle, 11 1/2 In.	6050.00
Brass, Odd Fellows, 3 Circles In Center, Hand With Heart Handle	115.00
Brass, Reticulated Heart Shape, 3 Stamped Flowers, 1849, 11 1/4 In.	82.00
Iron, Adjustable Fork Rest, Twisted Shank, 23 In.	50.00
Iron, Floral, Star Handle, 9 In.	70.00
Iron, Fork Rest	93.00
Iron, Girl, House, Tree, Paddle Shape, 4 Footed, 11 1/4 In.	38.00
Iron, Girl's Face, 8 In.	93.50
Iron, Grapes & Scrolls, 8 In.	38.50
Iron, Hearts, 9 1/2 In.	105.00
Iron, Horseshoe, Footed	12.50
Iron, Maple Handle, Scrolled Feet, 11 1/4 In.	22.00
Iron, Pineapple & Scroll, Wilton	30.00
Iron, Star & Sunburst	35.00
Iron, Tulip, S.B. Miller, 8 In.	49.50
Penny Footed, 1 Foot Forms Large Handle, New England	95.00
Pierced Design, Wooden Handle, England, Brass & Steel, 10 In.	475.00
Strauss Gas, I Want You	38.00

Typewriter, Tin, Panama, Manifold Supplies Co.

If you have a smelly tin, try filling it with fragrant peppermint tea for a few weeks. When you empty it the tin will still smell, but like peppermint.

Wedgwood, Stanley Pattern, 7 In. 192.00

TRUNKS of many types were made. The nineteenth-century sea chest was often handmade of unpainted wood. Brass-fitted camphorwood chests were brought back from the Orient. Leather-covered trunks were popular from the late eighteenth to mid-nineteenth centuries. By 1895, trunks were covered with canvas or decorated sheet metal. Embossed metal coverings were used from 1870 to 1910. By 1925, trunks were covered with vulcanized fiber or undecorated metal.

Camphorwood, Brass Bail Handles, 23 x 44 x 23 In. 495.00
Coach, Leather, Wooden Base, Rectangle, U.S., Mid-19th Century 385.00
Dome Top, Hide Covered, Leather, Iron Lock, 1818 Newspaper Lined, 10 1/4 In. 110.00
Dome Top, Hide Covered, Leather Trim, Brass Studs, Iron Lock, 18 1/2 In. 93.50
Dome Top, Putty Design, Green & Salmon, New England, 1830s, 13 3/4 x 32 In. 522.50
Dome Top, Red & Green Painted, G.M.C. Initials On Top, 30 1/2 In. 600.00
Dome Top, Tendrils, Flowers & Swags, Floral Wallpaper Lined, c.1830, 24 In. 2300.00
Hide Bound, Leather Trim, Brass Studs, Iron Lock & Hasp, Cylindrical, 24 In. 205.00
Hide Covered, Brass Stud Trim, Initials I.V.V.B., Iron Lock & Handles, 24 In. 66.00
Humpback, Original Paper Lining, Victorian Picture In Lid 225.00
Immigrant's, Marked Marte Olds, 1854, Scandinavia 645.00
Leather Covered, Oval Brass Tacks On Lid, Camphor Lined, Handles, 41 3/4 In. 2645.00
Louis Vuitton, Brass Bound, Leather Trim, 18 x 12 x 5 3/4 In. 495.00
Louis Vuitton, Cube Shape, Logo Tapestry, Wooden, Metal Trim 5500.00
Louis Vuitton, Fitted, 4 Divided Shelves, 20 x 35 x 15 In. 1210.00
Louis Vuitton, Overnight 770.00
Louis Vuitton, Shoe Case, Fitted, 8 1/4 x 24 x 21 In. 935.00
Louis Vuitton, Steamer, 16 x 44 x 21 3/4 In. 935.00
Louis Vuitton, Steamer, Fitted, Dated 1910, 2 x 3 x 2 Ft. 2500.00
Louis Vuitton, Suitcase, 8 x 29 x 18 In. 880.00
Louis Vuitton, Suitcase, Lift Top, Removable Compartment, 10 x 28 x 15 In. 715.00
Pine, Dome Top, Cotter Pin Hinged, Swag & Tassel Drapery, 9 1/2 x 20 In. 805.00
Stagecoach, Iron Straps, Pine, 1800s 155.00
Steamer, Vuitton, Leather 2860.00
Storage, 2 Drawers, Brass Clad, 18 1/2 x 34 1/4 In. 135.00
Tacked, Spanish, c.1950, 17 x 9 In. 135.00
Wardrobe, Oshkosh, 42 x 22 x 20 In. 100.00
Wooden, Leather, Hand Painted Oriental Scene, Small 100.00

TUTHILL Cut Glass Company of Middletown, New York, worked from 1902 to 1923. Of special interest are the finely cut pieces of stemware and tableware.

Bottle, Cologne, Wild Rose, Engraved Sterling Silver Stopper, 4 3/4 x 5 In. 375.00
Bowl, Allover Brilliant Cut, 8-Sided, 9 1/4 x 6 1/2 In. 390.00
Bowl, Roses Within Diamond & Star Cut Miters, Signed, 9 In. 350.00
Bowl, Vintage, Rolled Rim, 3 1/4 x 12 In. 665.00
Compote, Cherry, Intaglio, Signed, 7 In. 225.00

Compote, Rolled Rim, 4 x 8 In. 450.00
Compote, Rosaceae Pattern, Flowering Raspberry Swirl, Signed 375.00
Cruet, Primrose, Teardrop Stopper, Signed 265.00
Cruet, Wild Roses, Leaves & Thorns, Signed, 8 1/2 In. 225.00
Dish, Cheese, Intaglio Pumpkin Pattern 275.00
Mayonnaise Set, 6-Sided, Signed, 2 Piece 750.00
Plate, Primrose Pattern On Rim, Hobstars & Crosshatching Bottom, 9 In. 625.00
Sugar & Creamer, Cut Florals, Oval, Signed 195.00
Tray, Dresser, Vintage, Intaglio, 7 1/2 x 5 1/2 In. 425.00
Tray, Intaglio Vintage Center, Hobstar Border, Oval, Signed, 7 1/2 x 5 In. 425.00
Tray, Primrose & Geometric, Center Handle, 10 In. 885.00
Tray, Rosemere, Geometric, Oval, 7 1/2 In. 225.00
Tray, Woodlily, Serrated Teeth, Round, 12 In. 475.00
Vase, Alternating Hobstar & Floral Panels, Flaring Form, 8 In. 165.00

TYPEWRITER collectors divide typewriters into two main classifications: the index machine, which has a pointer and a dial for letter selection, and the keyboard machine, most commonly seen today. The first successful typewriter was made by Sholes and Glidden in 1874.

Blickensderfer, No. 5, Oak Case, 1 Extra Head, c.1885 .... 125.00 to 175.00
Corona, 1910 .... 45.00
Corona, Pre-1930s 35.00
Crandall Machine Co., Extra Long Carriage 4250.00
Gunka, No. 5 .... 205.00 to 250.00
Hammond Multiplex, Folding Keyboard, Cover 100.00
Hammond Varityper, Case 175.00
Oliver No. 9, Visible, Oil Bottle, Box, Booklet, Contract .... 58.00 to 75.00
Royal, No. 5 .... 75.00
Smith-Corona, Commemorative, Gorham Mfg. Co., Original Case, 11 x 12 In. 4600.00
Tom Thumb, Green, Original Cover, Instructions 75.00

TYPEWRITER RIBBON TINS are now being collected. The lithographed tin containers have been used since the 1870s.

Tin, Battleship 8.00
Tin, Beaver Old Reliable 11.00
Tin, Carter's Cabalier 6.00
Tin, Chicago Super 13.00
Tin, Lith-O-Rote 6.00
Tin, Panama, Manifold Supplies Co. .... *Illus* 7.50
Tin, Roytype Ribbon, Typewriter 15.00
Tin, Secretarial De Luxe 4.00
Tin, Star Brand 6.00
Tin, Vetex Roytype 5.00
Tin, Vogue Roytype 5.00

UHL pottery was made in Evansville, Indiana, in 1854. The pottery moved to Huntingburg, Indiana, in 1908. Stoneware and glazed pottery were made until the mid-1940s.

Bean Pot, Blue 190.00
Bean Pot, Brown & White 40.00
Casserole, Cover, Blue 40.00
Figurine, Frog, Brown, Green, 6 In. 500.00
Figurine, Frog, Natural, Hand Painted, 9 In. 900.00
Jar, Strawberry, Hanging 30.00
Jug, Army Tank Shape, Marked 225.00
Jug, Creme-De-Mint, Blue, 26 Oz. 10.00
Jug, Elephant Shape, Blue, Miniature .... 40.00 to 50.00
Jug, Evansville, Ind., 5 Gal. 250.00
Jug, Handle, Christmas Cheer, 1930, Small 850.00
Jug, Shoulder, Kentucky State Fair, Cream, Brown Top 140.00
Mug, Blue & White, Dillsboro Sanitarium, Dillsboro, Ind. 450.00
Pitcher, Barrel, Blue 35.00
Pitcher, Barrel, Brown 30.00

◆◆◆◆◆◆◆◆◆◆◆◆◆◆◆◆◆◆◆◆◆

Rinse food off plates as soon after use as possible to avoid
stains.

◆◆◆◆◆◆◆◆◆◆◆◆◆◆◆◆◆◆◆◆◆

Union Porcelain Works, Pitcher,
United States Hotel, c. 1880, 9 9/16 In.

Pitcher, Barrel, Pink, Rustic, 1 Qt. 35.00
Pitcher, Barrel, Rustic, 1 Qt. 50.00
Pitcher, Batter, Blue 60.00
Pitcher, Blue & White, 1 Gal. 430.00
Pitcher, Cover, Grape, Blue, Squat 80.00
Pitcher, Grape, Bulbous 90.00
Pitcher, Lincoln, Blue & White, 1 Gal. 2100.00
Pitcher, Spongeware, Bellied, 1/2 Gal. 975.00
Planter, Cow Shape, Yellow 160.00
Roaster, Cover, Blue, Marked 650.00
Teapot, Blue, 8 Cup 80.00
Vase, Black, 2 x 8 In. 20.00
Vase, Cut Flower, Blue, 5 In. 170.00

UMBRELLA collectors like rain or shine. The first known umbrella was
owned by King Louis XIII of France in 1637. The earliest umbrellas were
sunshades, not designed to be used in the rain. The umbrella was embellished
and redesigned many times. In 1852, the fluted steel rib style was developed
and it has remained the most useful style.

Parasol, Black Lacquer, Red Parchment, Wooden Handle & Spokes, 1940s 25.00
Parasol, Black Taffeta, Silk Lines, Maroon Fringe, Bone Handle, Folding, 19th C. 200.00
Parasol, Facial, Ivory Handle, Seashell Finial, Tassels, 19th Century 185.00

UNION PORCELAIN WORKS was established at Greenpoint, New York, in
1848 by Charles Cartlidge. The company went through a series of ownership
changes and finally closed in the early 1900s. The company made a fine
quality white porcelain that was often decorated in clear, bright colors.

UNION
PORCELAIN
WORKS
GREENPOINT
N.Y.

Oyster Plate, Seaweed, Coral & Crabs, White, Gold Trim 325.00
Pitcher, Milk, Shells 425.00
Pitcher, Molded Foliate Edged Cartouche, c.1880, 9 9/16 In. 805.00
Pitcher, United States Hotel, c.1880, 9 9/16 In. .... *Illus* 805.00
Vase, Century, Karl Mueller, White, 12 1/2 In., Restored 6500.00
Vase, Enamel, Gilt Flowers, Monkey Handles, c.1880, 12 In. 2420.00
Water Filter, Floral & Foliate Border, Spigot, 1889, 14 1/8 In. 575.00

UNIVERSITY OF NORTH DAKOTA, see North Dakota School of Mines

VAL ST. LAMBERT Cristalleries of Belgium was founded by Messieurs
Kemlin and Lelievre in 1825. The company is still in operation. All types of
table glassware and decorative glassware were made. Pieces were often
decorated with cut designs.

Val St Lambert

Ashtray, Triangular, 4 1/2 In. 20.00
Bone Dish, 12 Piece.. 192.50
Candlestick, Crystal, 23 In., Pair 170.00
Candlestick, Lluxval, 11 In., Pair 600.00
Charger, Signs Of Zodiac, 1970, 11 1/2 In. 305.00
Compote, Amberina, Ruby Rim, Mottled, Applied Foot & Handles, 3 1/2 In. 165.00

Decanter & Tumbler, Amber, Crystal 95.00
Ewer, Cameo, Acid-Etched, Red Overlay, Cut Flowers, c.1900, 14 In. 920.00
Figurine, Madonna & Child, 10 1/2 In. 190.00
Paperweight, Millefiori, White & Red Canes, 2 5/8 In. 175.00
Vase, Crystal, 9 1/2 In. 20.00
Vase, Gilt Central Medallion, Flattened Oval, Emerald To Clear, 8 In. 120.00
Vase, Handkerchief, 9 In. 65.00
Vase, Textured Frosted Ground, Sea-Holly Overlay, Signed, 21 3/4 In. 2990.00

VALLERYSTHAL Glassworks was founded in 1836 in Lorraine, France. In
1854, the firm became Klenglin et Cie. It made table and decorative glass,
opaline, cameo, and art glass. A line of covered, pressed glass animal dishes
was made in the nineteenth century. The firm is still working.

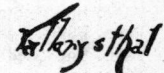

Box, Cover, Irish Setter, Frosted 95.00
Dish, Hen On Nest Cover, Milk Glass, 2 In. 35.00
Dish, Hen On Nest Cover, Milk Glass, 9 In. 125.00
Plate, Ice Blue, 5 Petal Shape, Floral Design 7.50
Vase, Berried Leafy Branches, Signed, c.1920, 7 3/4 In. 345.00

VAN BRIGGLE pottery was made by Artus Van Briggle in Colorado Springs,
Colorado, after 1901. Van Briggle had been a decorator at Rookwood Pottery
of Cincinnati, Ohio. He died in 1904. His wares usually had modeled relief
decorations and a soft, dull glaze. The pottery is still working and still making
some of the original designs.

Ashtray, Turquoise, 9 1/2 In. 25.00
Bookends, Dogs, Green 150.00
Boot, Cowboy, Black & White Froth, Glossy, 6 1/4 In. 35.00
Boot, Persian Rose, Santa Claus Style, 2 1/2 x 2 1/4 In. 35.00
Bowl, 3-Frog Flower, Dragonfly Bowl, Turquoise, 8 x 2 1/2 In. 165.00
Bowl, 5 Stylized Petals, Turquoise, 6 x 3 In. 45.00
Bowl, Art Deco, Stepped Open Handles, Blue Flambe On Cafe Au Lait, 9 In. 250.00
Bowl, Embossed Leaves, Mottled Brown Glaze, 1914, 6 1/4 In. 450.00
Bowl, Frog, Persian Rose, Tulips, Scalloped Oval, 8 1/4 In. 95.00
Bowl, Leaves & Acorns, Mountain Craig Brown, 5 1/2 x 3 In. 80.00
Bowl, Leaves, Shape No. 776, Turquoise, 6 3/8 In. 135.00
Bowl, Persian Rose, Stylized Leaves, 6 1/2 In. 50.00
Bowl, Stylized Leaves At Rim, Curdled Green Glaze, 2 x 5 In. .... 200.00 to 400.00
Bowl, Yucca Leaves, Turquoise, 4 1/2 x 5 1/2 In. 30.00
Candlestick, Double, Tulip, Turquoise 30.00
Card Holder, Pike's Peak 125.00
Chalice, Persian Rose, Hollow Foot, Buff Bottom, 4 x 3 In. 45.00
Console, Flower Frog, Swan, Turquoise, 3 Piece 125.00
Creamer & Sugar, Turquoise Bowl, Ridges 35.00
Ewer, Persian Rose, Bowling Pin Shape, 7 x 3 1/4 In. 48.00
Figurine, Elephant, White, 7 3/4 x 4 1/2 In. 60.00
Figurine, Elephant, Turquoise 125.00
Figurine, Lady Of The Lakes, Persian Rose Glaze, Marked, 10 1/2 x 16 In. 302.00
Flower Bowl, Dragonfly, Blue, 9 In. 55.00
Flower Bowl & Frog, Oval, Burgundy, Blue Tulips, 8 1/4 x 3 1/4 In. 75.00
Flower Frog, Turquoise, 11 Holes, Ribs, 1 3/8 x 3 1/2 In. 18.00
Lamp, Damsel Of Damascus, Original Shade, 1940s 275.00
Lamp, Indian Heads Base, Plastic Shade With Pressed Grass, 11 1/2-In. Base 253.00
Lamp, Kneeling Indian Woman, Urn On Shoulder, Lavender, 19 In. 275.00
Lamp, Maiden At The Well, White, Pair 650.00
Lamp, Peacock In Tree, Aqua To Blue, Tail Feathers Design 225.00
Lamp, Tree Trunk With Parrot On Branch, 2-Tone Matte Blue, 14 In. 120.00
Lamp, Turquoise, Butterfly 75.00
Pen Holder, Maroon 110.00
Pitcher, Dark Brown, 3 1/2 In. 195.00
Pitcher, Sweetheart, Heart Shaped Mouth, Turquoise, 3 1/2 x 4 In. 35.00
Plaque, Indian Squaw, Persian Rose, So Ya Zhe, Little Star, Oval, 5 x 4 In. 140.00

Vase, 2 Women, Flowing Gowns, Plum Glaze, c.1915, 7 1/2 In. 1300.00
Vase, 3 Indian Heads, Green, Blue Over Spray, 11 1/2 In. 550.00
Vase, 3 Moths, Panels, Green, Logo, Initial, 3 In. 40.00
Vase, 4 Buttressed Handles, Peacock Feathers, 1915, 13 3/4 In. 1000.00
Vase, Acorns & Oak Leaves, Turquoise, 6 In. 50.00
Vase, Allover Robin's-Egg Blue Glaze, 1906, 5 3/4 In. 330.00
Vase, Arrow Root Leaves, Stems, Ochre Glaze, 1904, 11 x 5 In. 1100.00
Vase, Blue Matte Glaze, Molded Poppies, 1917, 11 In. 495.00
Vase, Brown Matte Glaze, Leaf Design, 1914, 7 In. 385.00
Vase, Bud, Turquoise, 8 3/4 In. 50.00
Vase, Elongated Leaves, Curdled Apple Green Glaze, Marked, 9 In. 550.00
Vase, Embossed Crocuses, Frog-Skin Matte Glaze, 1904, 3 1/2 In. 1200.00
Vase, Embossed Peacock Feathers, Matte Glaze, 1903, 5 1/2 x 6 In. 2000.00
Vase, Embossed Poppy Pods, Blue Matte Glaze, Marked, 1908, 7 1/2 In. ...... 550.00 to 700.00
Vase, Flower Buds, Mustard Matte Glaze, Marked, 1906, 9 1/2 In. 1100.00
Vase, Flowers & Leaves, Jug Shape, White Frosting, 9 In. 35.00
Vase, Flowers & Leaves, Pattern No. 645, Turquoise, 4 5/8 In. 38.00
Vase, Green Shading To Brown, Dated 1916, 8 In. 900.00
Vase, Indian Head, Green With Blue Spray, 1920 .... 425.00
Vase, Irises, 2 Small Base Handles, Marked, 1920s, 13 1/4 In. 225.00
Vase, Lady Of The Lily, Ming Blue, 1930s 485.00
Vase, Lady Of The Lily, Reclining Nude, Marked, 1920s, 11 In. 900.00
Vase, Lorelei, Matte Turquoise Glaze, Incised Mark, 1902, 11 In. 550.00
Vase, Luna Moth, Dark Blue, 1912 .... 295.00
Vase, Male Figure Curled Around Rim, Blue To Red Glaze, 13 1/4 In. 357.00
Vase, Matte Green, Shape No. 29, Artus Van Briggle, 1902, 7 1/2 In. 990.00
Vase, Matte Turquoise Glaze, No. 754, Anne Gregory Van Briggle, 9 1/2 In. 385.00
Vase, Mistletoe, 7 Berries, Barrel Shape, Turquoise, c.1903 .... 290.00
Vase, Mistletoe, Mottled Turquoise, Buff Ground, 1907, 4 1/2 In. 525.00
Vase, Mulberry Leaves, 1920, 5 In. 250.00
Vase, Mustard Glaze, Rystals, 1907, 8 In. 995.00
Vase, Oak Leaves With Acorns, Green, 1916, 5 1/2 In. 395.00
Vase, Persian Rose, Dragonflies, 6 1/2 In. 390.00
Vase, Persian Rose, Floral Band, Shoulder Handles, 10 1/2 x 8 In. 175.00
Vase, Persian Rose, Water Lilies, 5 In. 165.00
Vase, Persian Rose Glaze, No. 890, 7 1/2 In. 330.00
Vase, Persian, Rose & Blue, Flowers, Squatty Base, Flared Neck, 4 x 3 In. 50.00
Vase, Ribbed, Robin's-Egg Blue, Handles, Dark Blue Glaze, 13 1/2 In. 137.00
Vase, Spider Wort, Green Glaze, 1912 .... 585.00
Vase, Stylized Flowers, Dark Maroon, Blue Matte Glaze, 3 1/2 In. 77.00
Vase, Stylized Peacock Feathers, Dark Green Glaze, 1904, 4 x 4 1/2 In. 1210.00
Vase, Stylized Poppy Seed Pods At Rim, Matte Blue Glaze, 1916, 7 1/4 In. 400.00
Vase, Tulip Design, Turquoise Blue Glaze, Marked, c.1907, 13 3/4 In. 880.00
Vase, Turquoise Blue, 1920s, 8 1/2 In. 200.00
Vase, Turquoise, 1905, 3 3/4 In. 350.00

VASA MURRHINA is the name of a glassware made by the Vasa Murrhina
Art Glass Company of Sandwich, Massachusetts, about 1884. The glassware
was transparent and was embedded with small pieces of colored glass and
metallic flakes. The mica flakes were coated with silver, gold, copper, or
nickel. Some of the pieces were cased. The same type of glass was made in
England. Collectors often confuse Vasa Murrhina glass with aventurine,
spatter, or spangle glass. There is uncertainty about what actually was made
by the Vasa Murrhina factory. Related pieces may be listed under Spangle
Glass.

Basket, Green, Blue, 11 In. 125.00
Biscuit Jar, Blue, Gold Mica Spatter, Silver Plated Lid & Handle 135.00
Bowl, Clear Edging On Ruffled Rim, Shaded Gold, 8 In. 95.00
Candlestick, Spangled Black Amethyst, Hollow Stem, 18 In. 220.00
Rose Bowl, 8-Crimp Top, Mica Flakes, White Lining, 3 1/2 In. .... 85.00 to 105.00
Rose Bowl, Thorny Handle, White Lining, Mica Flakes, 7 1/4 x 4 1/8 In. 195.00
Scent Bottle, Screw-On Silver Cap, Butterfly Design, 5 In. 395.00
Vase, 3-Petal Top, Mica Flakes, Clear Rim, 9 1/4 In. 145.00

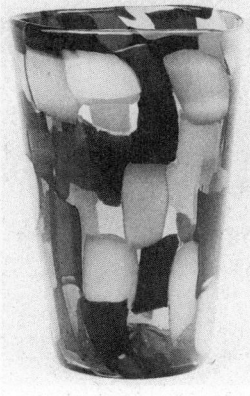

◆◆◆◆◆◆◆◆◆◆◆◆◆◆◆◆◆◆◆◆◆◆◆

Antique glass should be handled as if it has been repaired and might fall apart. Hold a pitcher by the body, not the handle. Pick up stemware by holding both the stem and the bowl. Hold plates in two hands, not by the rim.

◆◆◆◆◆◆◆◆◆◆◆◆◆◆◆◆◆◆◆◆◆◆◆

Venini, Vase, Clear & Black Patches, Murano, Bianconi, c. 1955, 9 In.

Vase, 3-Petal Top, Orange To Pink, White Interior, 8 1/2 In. 135.00
Vase, Ruffled Top, Mica Flakes, White Lining, 9 In. 100.00

VASELINE GLASS is a greenish-yellow glassware resembling petroleum jelly. Some vaseline glass is still being made in old and new styles. Pressed glass of the 1870s was often made of vaseline-colored glass. Additional pieces of vaseline glass may also be listed under Pressed Glass in this book.

Aquarium, Art Deco, Metal Stand, Round 350.00
Berry Set, Frosted, Vertical Panels, Star Base, 5 Piece 28.00
Bread Tray, Finecut & Panel 40.00
Butter, Cover, Ranson 90.00
Coaster, 3 1/4 In., 6 Piece 12.00
Dish, Finial Cover, Vertical Panels, Footed, 3 1/2 x 3 3/4 In. 35.00
Sugar, Cover, Bagware 80.00
Sugar, Ranson 90.00
Sugar Shaker, Reverse Swirl, Opalescent 145.00
Toothpick, Diamond Spearhead, Opalescent 90.00
Toothpick, Hobnail 30.00
Tray, Argonaut Shell, Opalescent 90.00
Vase, Car, Bracket, Mosswell 75.00

VENETIAN GLASS, see Glass-Venetian

VENINI glass was first designed by Paolo Venini, who established his factory in Murano, Italy, in 1925. He is best known for pieces of modern design, including the famous *handkerchief* vase. The company is still working. Other pieces of Italian glass may be found in the Glass-Contemporary, Glass-Midcentury, and Glass-Venetian categories of this book.

venini mmTano ITALIA

Bottle, Inciso, Mushroom Shaped Stopper, Red Cased, 5 1/4 In. 575.00
Bottle, Occhi, Opaque Black & White Squared Murrines 4000.00
Bowl, Amber Stripes Alternating With Latticinio Ribbons, Marked, 5 3/4 In. 220.00
Bowl, Black, Radiating Green & Red Stripes On Yellow Interior, 11 1/4 In. 460.00
Bowl, Pulegoso, Walled Green, Oval, Iridescent Surface, Murano, 16 1/2 In. 357.50
Bowl, Red, Black, Gray & Clear, 1940, 8 3/8 In. 3450.00
Charger, Clear Reserve, Orange Center, Green Rim, c.1970, 19 1/4 In. 460.00
Decanter, Hammered Finish, Oviform, Topaz, Signed, 7 1/4 In. 748.00
Figurine, Chicken, Fulvio Bianconi, 1950, Pair 6500.00
Figurine, Rooster & Hen, Latticinio & Swirled Hollow Cone Body, 7 In., Pair 5775.00
Fish Tank, Giant Fish Form, c.1950, 10 In. 900.00
Frame, Picture, Twisted Clear Glass Rope, 10 x 12 In. 350.00
Hourglass, Pear Shaped Containers, 1 Cobalt Blue, Turquoise, 7 1/4 In. 230.00
Mirror, Clear Molded Frame, Glass & Bronze, c.1930, 22 1/4 x 20 In. 1380.00

Obelisk, Internal Spiral Threading, Green Base, Signed, 10 3/8 In., Pair 460.00
Perfume Bottle, Clear Ribbed Body, Enclosed Layers Of Gold Dust 425.00
Perfume Bottle, Inciso, Amber, 8 In. 700.00
Pitcher, Pulled Spout, Green, Lavender Stripe, Bianconi & Venini, c.1951, 9 In. 750.00
Shade, Multicolored, Signed, 15 In. 700.00
Vase, Blue & Green Vertical Canes, Signed, 1955, 15 In. 2588.00
Vase, Clear & Black Patches, Murano, Bianconi, 1955, 9 In. .... *Illus* 8250.00
Vase, Corroso, Applied Globules, Signed, 1936, 8 1/4 In. 1150.00
Vase, Fazzoletto, Slumped Handkerchief Form, Marked, 6 1/4 In. 247.50
Vase, Flattened Cylinder, Disk Stopper, White & Pink Spirals, c.1960, 21 1/2 In. 1380.00
Vase, Handkerchief, Alternating Zanfirico Canes, Marked, 6 3/4 In. 690.00
Vase, Handkerchief, Rose-Cased, White, Venini & Bianconi, c.1950, 9 1/4 In. 800.00
Vase, Mosaico-Zanfirico, White Net Design, 10 3/4 In. 4370.00
Vase, Patchwork Squares, Paper Label, Signed, 1955, 8 5/8 In. 6325.00
Vase, Rippled Tiers, Blue Ribbed, Signed, c.1930, 11 3/4 In. 230.00
Vase, Spherical, Off-Center Internal Green Wall, c.1970, 7 In. 460.00
Vase, Spiral Threading, Gunmetal & Violet, Cylindrical, 1962, 9 1/2 In. 2875.00
Vase, Tooled Handle, Conical, Clear, Signed, 1930, 8 7/8 In. 575.00
Vase, Wavy Indentations Around Body, Egg Shape, c.1930, Signed, 8 In. 95.00
Vase, White Cane Slices, Amber Centers, Wide Mouth, Egg Shape, 1988, 7 In. 747.00

VERLYS glass was made in France after 1931. It was made in the United
States from 1935 to 1951. The glass is either blown or molded. The American
glass is signed with a diamond-point-scratched name, but the French pieces
are marked with a molded signature. The designs resemble those used by
Lalique.

Bowl, Birds & Bees, Signed, 11 In. 200.00
Bowl, Kingfisher, Frosted, V-1038, 13 1/2 In., Pair 220.00
Bowl, Pinecone, Frosted, 7 In. 50.00
Bowl, Tassels, Signed, 11 In. 100.00
Bowl, Thistle, Signed, 8 1/2 In. 68.00
Vase, Alpine Thistle, Topaz On Clear, 9 1/2 In. 500.00
Vase, Frosted Dogwood Blossoms, 8 In. 125.00
Vase, Lovebirds, 5 In. 150.00
Vase, Thistle, Topaz, 9 3/4 In. .... 750.00 to 795.00

VERNON KILNS was the name used after 1958 by Vernon Potteries, Ltd. The
company, which started in Vernon, California, in 1931, made dinnerware and
figurines until it closed in 1958. Collectors search for the brightly colored
dinnerware and the pieces designed by Rockwell Kent, Walt Disney, and Don
Blanding. For more information, see *Kovels' Depression Glass & American
Dinnerware Price List.*

Ashtray, Santa Fe, Red 18.00
Bowl, Divided, Heavenly Days 18.00
Bowl, Flower, Pekingese Marked, 12 In. 135.00
Bowl, Gingham, 9 In. 12.00
Carafe, Cover, Raffia-Wrapped Handle 30.00
Carafe, Tam O'Shanter 48.00
Casserole, Sherwood 35.00
Charger, Our America, 13 In. 195.00
Charger, Salamina, Polychrome Transfer, c.1939, 16 1/2 In. 220.00
Chop Plate, Gingham, 12 In. 12.00
Chop Plate, Homespun, 12 In. 12.00
Chop Plate, Moby Dick, Pink, 13 In. 195.00
Coaster-Ashtray, Organdie, Signed Gale Turnbull, 4 In. 10.00
Coffeepot, Coral Reef, 6 Cup 150.00
Coffeepot, Lei Lani, After Dinner 200.00
Cup, Organdie 6.50
Cup & Saucer, Tickled Pink 7.00
Eggcup, Homespun 12.00
Gravy Boat, Homespun 18.00
Gravy Boat, Mayflower .... 40.00 to 65.00
Mug, Organdie 12.00

Pitcher, Barkwood, 2 Qt.	15.00
Pitcher, Homespun, 11 1/2 In.	25.00
Pitcher, Raffia	18.00
Pitcher, Rose-A-Day	30.00
Planter, Bird	30.00
Plate, California, Blue, 10 1/2 In.	15.00
Plate, Colonial Annapolis, Brown, 10 1/2 In.	15.00
Plate, Commemorative, Will Rogers	18.00
Plate, Down On The Levee, Bits Of Old South, 14 In.	29.00
Plate, Eisenhower, Red, 10 1/2 In.	18.00
Plate, Frontier Days, Winchester Rifle, 14 In.	60.00
Plate, Hawaiian Flowers, Maroon, 9 In.	25.00
Plate, Lei Lani, 9 In.	40.00
Plate, Massachusetts, Red, 10 1/2 In.	12.00
Plate, Moby Dick, Brown, 9 In.	55.00
Plate, North American Aviation, Red, 10 In.	38.00
Plate, Organdie, 7 In.	8.00
Plate, Salamina, 9 In.	120.00
Plate, Statue Of Liberty, 10 In.	25.00
Plate, Tickled Pink, 10 In.	5.00
Plate, Vermont, Red, 10 1/2 In.	12.00
Platter, Organdie, 10 In.	12.00
Platter, Organdie, 12 1/2 In.	15.00
Salt & Pepper, Chintz	18.00
Salt & Pepper, Homespun	12.00
Salt & Pepper, Mayflower	30.00
Salt & Pepper, Mushroom	265.00
Salt & Pepper, Organdie	12.00
Saltshaker, Fantasia Mushroom People, 3 In.	125.00
Server, Homespun, 14 In.	15.50
Sugar, Cover, Organdie	10.00
Sugar & Creamer, Barkwood	10.00
Sugar & Creamer, Chintz	45.00
Sugar & Creamer, Cover, Homespun	15.00
Sugar & Creamer, Mayflower	40.00 to 65.00
Sugar & Creamer, Salamina	40.00
Teapot, Arcadia	65.00
Teapot, Chintz	110.00
Teapot, Mayflower	75.00 to 90.00
Teapot, Sherwood	40.00
Tumbler, Rose-A-Day	22.00

VERRE DE SOIE glass was first made by Frederick Carder at the Steuben Glass Works from about 1905 to 1930. It is an iridescent glass of soft white or very, very pale green. The name means *glass of silk*, and it does resemble silk. Other factories have made verre de soie, and some of the English examples were made of different colors. Verre de soie is an art glass and is not related to the iridescent, pressed, white carnival glass mistakenly called by its name. Related pieces may be found in the Steuben category.

Bowl, Engraved Florals, Frosted Interior, Amber Rim, 10 In.	150.00
Bowl, Flower, Optic Panels, 4 1/4 x 6 1/2 In.	110.00
Powder Box, Enameled Tiger Lilies, White Satin	145.00

VIENNA ART plates are round metal serving trays produced at the turn of the century. The designs, copied from Royal Vienna porcelain plates, usually featured a portrait of a woman encircled by a wide, ornate border. Many were used as advertising or promotional items and were produced in Coshocton, Ohio, by J. F. Meeks Tuscarora Advertising Co. and H. D. Beach's Standard Advertising Co.

Plate, Coca-Cola, Western, Framed, 1905	500.00
Tray, The Landing Of The Fathers, Plymouth, Dec. 22, 1620, 15 1/2 In.	110.00

VIENNA, see Beehive category

VILLEROY & BOCH Pottery of Mettlach was founded in 1841. The firm made many types of wares, including the famous Mettlach steins. Collectors can be confused because although Villeroy & Boch made most of its pieces in the city of Mettlach, Germany, they also had factories in other locations. The dating code impressed on the bottom of most pieces makes it possible to determine the age of the piece. Additional items may be found in the Mettlach category.

Bowl, Gaudy Stick Spatter Design, 9 In.	137.00
Charger, Castle On Rhine, Pierced For Hanging, 12 In.	250.00
Ewer, Figural, Cupid	115.00
Mug, Hires Root Beer, Pair	305.00
Pitcher, Cover, Red Poppy, Green Leaves, White, 7 1/2 In.	110.00
Pitcher, Purple Plums, Green Leaves, 7 In.	145.00
Plaque, Maiden Sniffing Yellow Rose, Leaf Border, c.1900, 20 In.	805.00
Plate, Baby's, Little Miss Muffet	125.00
Plate, Enameled Tulips, Yorkshire Ware, 9 1/2 In., 10 Piece	110.00
Plate, Konigin Louise, 10 1/4 In.	29.00
Vase, Stylized Polar Bear, Cream Ground, c.1925, 9 In.	275.00

VOLKMAR pottery was made by Charles Volkmar of New York from 1879 to about 1911. He was associated with several firms, including the Volkmar Ceramic Company, Volkmar and Cory, and Charles Volkmar and Son. Volkmar had been a painter, and his designs often look like oil paintings drawn on pottery.

VOLKMAR
Corona N.y

Bowl, Scalloped Leaf, Matte Green Glaze, 9 1/2 In.	275.00
Candlestick, Green Matte Glaze, Flower Shaped Top, 14 1/2 In., Pair	522.50
Lamp, Yellow Chrysanthemums, Brown Ground, Stamped, 11 x 6 1/4 In.	465.00
Mug, Matte Green, Marked, 4 In.	275.00
Plaque, Scenic, c.1882	4675.00
Plaque, Underglaze Pastoral Scene, Haviland Style, c.1882, 15 5/8 x 9 1/4 In.	4675.00
Vase, Incised Geometric Design, Mottled, Gray-Green, 6 In.	485.00
Vase, Matte Brown, Oriental Blue Glaze, Durant, Volkmar, 1920, 11 1/2 In., Pr.	357.50
Vase, Mottled Green Glaze On Brown Ground, 10 1/4 In.	303.00

VOLKSTEDT was a soft-paste porcelain factory started in 1760 by Georg Heinrich Macheleid at Volkstedt, Thuringia. Volkstedt-Rudolstadt was a porcelain factory started at Volkstedt-Rudolstadt by Beyer and Bock in 1890. Most pieces seen in shops today are from the later factory.

Bowl, Whiplash Tendrils, Art Nouveau Maiden, Marked, 1900, 10 1/4 In.	460.00
Figurine, Boy Playing Flute, Dog At Side, Karl Ens, 5 In.	125.00
Figurine, Young Woman, Holding Bouquet, Lace Skirt, c.1930, 9 1/2 In.	295.00
Snuffbox, Gilt Scrollwork, Animals, Leaping Stag On Lid Interior, 2 3/4 In.	4025.00

WAHPETON POTTERY, see Rosemeade category

WALLACE NUTTING photographs are listed under Print, Nutting. His reproduction furniture is listed under Furniture.

WALRATH was a potter who worked in New York City, Rochester, New York, and at the Newcomb Pottery in New Orleans, Louisiana. Frederick Walrath died in 1920. Pieces listed here are from his Rochester period.

Walrath
Pottery

Bowl, 3 Frogs On Leaf, 10 In.	1200.00
Bowl, Attached Flower Frog Of Seated Nude, Green Matte Glaze, 9 In.	357.50
Bowl, Mustard-Brown Matte Glaze, Tapered, 2 1/2 x 4 1/2 In.	192.00
Figurine, Lion & Leopard Battling, Green & Brown, Circular Base, 7 x 7 In.	357.00
Vase, Yellow Flowers, Brown Leaves, Marked, 4 1/2 In.	1200.00

WALT DISNEY, see Disneyana

WALTER, see A. Walter

WARWICK china was made in Wheeling, West Virginia, in a pottery working from 1887 to 1951. Many pieces were made with hand painted or decal decorations. The most familiar Warwick has a shaded brown background. The

name *Warwick* is part of the mark and sometimes the mysterious word *IOGA*
is also included.

Bowl, Cover, White & Pink Roses, Green, Handles, IOGA, 6 In. 85.00
Chocolate Set, Wild Roses & Daisies, 12 Piece 245.00
Cuspidor, Bouquets Of Flowers, Brown & Yellow, IOGA, 8 In. 150.00
Ewer, Hibiscus, 8 In. 125.00
Mug, Indian Portrait, Brown Glaze 90.00
Pitcher, Poppies, Leaves, Scrolled, Brown To Beige, 9 1/2 In. 105.00
Pitcher, Tankard Shape, Brown Mums, IOGA 70.00
Syrup, Orange Poppies, Spring Lid, Signed 85.00
Vase, Duchess, Brown & Rust, 7 1/4 In. 225.00
Vase, Twig, Woman Holding White Rose, 10 1/2 In. 200.00
Water Set, Monks, Various Scenes, 9 Piece 395.00

WATCH pockets held the pocket watch that was important in Victorian times
because it was not until World War I that the wristwatch was used. All types
of watches are collected: silver, gold, or plated. Watches are arranged by
company name or by style. Pocket watches are listed here; wristwatches are a
separate category.

Accutron, Asymmetric, Square, Black Dial, 14K Yellow Gold 575.00
Agassiz, 17 Jewel, Open Face, Silvered Dial, Arabic Numbers, 14K Gold 220.00
American Watch Co., Key Wind, Enamel, 18K Gold, No. 189574 .... 825.00
Ansonia, Sundial, Brass, 1880, 3 x 2 In. 95.00
Appleton Tracey, Nickel Damascened Movement, 17 Jewel, 1889, Size 18 .... 137.50
Art Deco, Back Wind, 18K Gold, Rock Crystal, France 935.00
Audemars Piguet, Micrometer Regulator, Open Face, Monogram, c.1923 .... 5463.00
Audemars Piguet, Open Face, Quarter Hour Repeating, Gun Metal, No. 45552 .... 907.50
Beyer, Chronograph, Steel 300.00
C.H. Meylan, Repeater, 31 Jewel, White Porcelain Dial, Signed 2970.00
Ch. H. Grosclaude, Wolf Tooth Wind, 19 Jewel, Varicolored Gold Flowers, 1880 ..... 2300.00
D. Brown, Silver & Tortoiseshell Case, Brass Movement, Key Wind, 3 In. 1155.00
Dueber, Hunting Case, Jeweled Nickel Movement, Scenic Outer Case, 14K Gold 220.00
E. Howard, 14K Gold, 15 Jewel, Size 18 .... 1155.00
E. Howard, Open Face, Key Wind, Silveroid, With Chain, 1861, Size N 440.00
Elgin, 14K Gold Case, Dated 1883 .... 300.00
Elgin, Buffalo On Prairie, 1907 .... 365.00
Elgin, Buffalo Under Tree 325.00
Elgin, Hunting Case, 17 Jewel, White Porcelain Dial, 14K Gold 495.00
Elgin, Hunting Case, Key Wind, Coin Silver 100.00
Elgin, Longhorn, 1897 .... 295.00
Elgin, Open Face, Key Wind, Coin Silver, 1874 .... 95.00
Elgin, Open Face, White Dial, Second Hand 198.00
Elgin, Raymond, 21 Jewel 350.00
Elgin, Woman's, 14K Gold Hunter Case, 22 In. 14K Gold Chain 395.00
Ettenheimer & Co., Jeweled Nickel Movement, 14K Tricolor Gold, No. 81412 .... 1265.00
Exacta, Babe Ruth, 1949 .... 1000.00
Fres. Wiss & Menu, Open Face, Key Wind, Enameled 1540.00
Geneva, Woman's, Florentine Finish, 14K Yellow Gold 137.50
Gouvernoa, Pocket, Key Wind, No Key, Silveroid 48.00
Gruen, Veri-Thin, Pentagonal Shape, Chain 38.50
Gucci, Rosewood & Silver Links Band, Signed, c.1960 .... 1725.00
Hamilton, 18K Gold Pear Case, Matching Handmade Chain 5000.00
Hamilton, Chronometer, Model 21 .... 450.00
Hamilton, Hunting Case, Porcelain Enameled Dial, Gold Plated, No. 53204 .... 110.00
Hamilton, Model 940, Open Face, 21 Jewel, 5 Position, Size 18 .... 250.00
Hamilton, Railroad, 10K Gold Rolled Case, Nickel Movement 88.00
Hamilton, Railroad, Ball Gold Filled Case, 23 Jewel, Size 16 .... 995.00
Hamilton, Railroad, Model 992B, 21 Jewel, 10K White Gold Filled, Size 16 .... 250.00
Hamilton, U.S. Navy, Deck, Sterling Silver, 24 Hour, World War II 350.00
Hamilton, Woman's, Lapel Watch, Silver Filigree, Butterfly, Flip Up Wings 125.00
Hampden, Swingout, 17 Jewel, Gold 225.00

Hampton, Hunting Case, Key Wind, Porcelain Dial, 18K Gold, No. 315733 .... 605.00
Henry Moser & Co., Hunting Case, Porcelain Enamel Dial, Repeating, No. 132423 . 660.00
Howard, Flip-Out Case, 19 Jewel, 14K Gold 350.00
Hunting Case, White Porcelain Dial, Key Wind, 15 Jewel, 18K Gold, Woman's 247.50
Illinois, Autocrat, 17 Jewel, 14K Gold Filled, 1924 .... 85.00
Illinois, Lincoln, 21 Jewel, 10K Solid Hunting Case, Porcelain Dial 495.00
Illinois, Mexican Eagle, 1900 .... 395.00
Illinois, Silver Open Face, Gold Hunting Case 75.00
Ingersoll, Jumbo Model, Nickel Plated, Clockwork, 10 1/4 In. 247.00
Junghans, Open Face, Gun Metal, c.1940 .... 55.00
Lapel, Framed By Pearls, Gold Bar, Amethyst Bead Chain, 14K Yellow Gold 747.00
Lapel, Half Pearl & Diamond, Turtle Slide, Enamel Dial, Rope Chain, 14K Gold 2530.00
Lapel, Key Wind, Wreath Of Pink Roses & Bluebells, 18K Gold 402.00
Longines, Chronograph, 17 Jewel, Stainless Steel 700.00
Longines, Hunting Case, Silver, Scenic 105.00
Minerva, Chronograph, Stainless Steel 275.00
Movado, Hermetic, Tricolor Gold Striped Case, Easel Back, c.1935 .... 4888.00
Movado, Open Face, White Dial, Seconds Dial, 17 Jewel, 14K Gold 467.50
New York Standard, Railroad, Locomotive Engraved 77.00
Patek Philippe, Porcelain Dial, Scrolled Hands, Gold & Enamel, 18K Gold 2970.00
Patek Philippe, Wolf Tooth Wind, Regulator, Gold Foliate Hands, c.1890 .... 1955.00
Pendant, Woman's, 14K Gold Repousse, Blue Enameled, Fleur De Lis, Chain 445.00
Pin, 4-Leaf Clover, Green Enamel Leaves, Diamond Center 145.00
Pocket, Hunter Case, White Dial, Roman Numerals, 14K Gold 247.50
Reddy Kilowatt 75.00
Rockford, Key Wind, Hunting Case, Coin Silver, 1885 .... 95.00
Roskopf, House & Shield, Lion Back, Silver Chain, With 1912 Coin Fob, 1880 .... 220.00
Sears, Roebuck, Pendant, Piecrust Hunting Case, Woman's, 17 Jewel, Size 6 .... 165.00
Seth Thomas, 14K Gold, 1890 .... 250.00
Smokey The Bear, With Smokey's Face Watch Fob 110.00
Stop, Richard Petty, Box 48.00
Swiss, Woman's, Bouquet Spring, Rubies, Enamel Face, Beetle Hands 165.00
Swiss, Woman's, Diamond Set Monogram, Gold & Enamel, c.1880, 1 3/8 In. 1725.00
The Nassau, Enameled Face, Scene Of Side-Wheeler On Back, Yellow Gold 192.50
Thos. Russel, Convertible, Enamel Dial, 18K Gold, Liverpool, c.1860 .... 1380.00
Trinity, A. Calame Fils, 7 Jewel, Swiss 75.00
Turkish Trade, Coin Silver Hunting Case, Key Wind, Gold Beetle Hands 225.00
Vacheron, Girod, Jeweled Key Wind, Engraved Silver Dial, 18K Gold, No. 39123 .... 357.50
Vacheron & Constantin, 2-Tone Dial, Stainless Steel Strap 990.00
Waltham, 14K Gold, 15 Jewel, Size 16 .... 440.00
Waltham, 7 Jewel, Coin Silver Case 95.00
Waltham, Bicycle Rider, 1891 .... 387.50
Waltham, Hunting Case, 7 Jewel, Gold Filled, Size 0 .... 175.00
Waltham, Hunting Case, 17 Jewel, White Porcelain Dial, Engraved Case, 14K Gold . 302.50
Waltham, Hunting Case, 23 Jewel, 14K Gold, ... 1450.00
Waltham, Hunting Case, Enamel Dial, Curb Link Chain, 14K Yellow Gold 375.00
Waltham, Railroad, 21 Jewel, 5 Adjustable Positions, Box, Size 18 .... 165.00
Waltham, Texas Centennial, 1836-1936 .... 465.00
Waltham, Vanguard, 23 Jewel, 6 Positions, Up & Down Indicator .... 250.00 to 375.00
Waltham, Vanguard, Lossier Inner Terminal Hair Spring, 23 Jewel 525.00
Waltham, Veterans Of Mexican War, 1872 .... 465.00
Woman's, Ring Watch, 14K White Gold, 1920s 400.00
Zenith, Art Deco, Blue & Black Enamel Highlights, 18K Gold, c.1920 .... 2070.00

WATCH FOBS were worn on watch chains. They were popular during
Victorian times and after. Many styles, especially advertising designs, are still
made today.

1863 Dime, With 6 Linked Drop Garnet Set In Coin 65.00
A.C., Caterpillar Tractor, Strap 45.00
Adams Grader 30.00
Adams Road Machinery 15.00
Alaska Yukon Exposition, 1909 .... 85.00

Allis Chalmers, Cat	65.00
Allis Chalmers Farm Tractor, Brass	7.25
Allis Chalmers Grader	15.00
Alumina Soapalite	65.00
Anheuser-Busch, Horseshoe, Enameled Red A & Blue Shield, Silver	116.00
Arrowhead, Saddle, Texas	35.00
Art Nouveau Women, Seattle Expo, 1909	95.00
Bardner Denver Drill	15.00
BPOE, West Virginia, Clock & Deer Head	35.00
Bulldog Cylinder, Litcheifle Mfg., Waterloo, Iowa	85.00
Case	60.00
Chicago Central Business Men's Assn.	12.00
Colt	75.00
Columbia Exposition	35.00
Delegate Pos Of A, Blue Enameled, Gold Ground, Harrisburg, Pa., 1946	6.50
Doctor's Bag, Sterling	25.00
Economy 1 Cylinder Gas Farm Engine, Brass	6.50
Elks, Advertising	40.00
Euclid Dozer	25.00
Fairbanks Morse Z Farm Engines, Enameled Brass	7.75
Galion Iron Works, Machinery	15.00
Galion Roller	25.00
Grand Lodge, State Of New York, Annual Session, Eagle, Shield, Skyline	10.00
Green River Whiskey	85.00
Hair Work, Victorian, Watch Chain	324.00
Hamley Saddle	150.00
Hat Shape, Ship Picture, 1915 Expo, Brass	45.00
Heinz, White Cap Girl	60.00
Heinz Pickle, Figural, 57 Varieties, Brass	50.00
Heraldry On Bloodstone Seal, 18K Gold	200.00
Hopto Digger, Winona, Minnesota	20.00
IATSE, 45th Convention, Chicago, Red, White & Blue, 1960	8.00
Imperial Council Atlanta 1914, Enamel & Compass	60.00
International Harvester, Centennial Coin, 1831-1931	35.00
John Deere, Mother-Of-Pearl, Shield Shape, Missing Strap	85.00
John Deere Bulldozer	15.00
Kellogg's Corn Flakes, Box Shape, Brass, Red & Black Enameled, 1920	95.00
Kentucky	45.00
Keystone Co.	45.00
Leroy Plow Co., Miller Bean Harvester, Spinner, Celluloid & Brass	125.00
Lima Shovels, Move Earth	15.00
Lincoln, Illinois Watch Co.	25.00
Linkbelt Crane	28.00
Lipton Tea Bags, Tin	17.00
Luther League Of Penna., 36th Annual Con. Allentown, 1929, Pewter	6.50
Lynch & McKee Co., Bear, Steer & Ear Of Corn On Strap	80.00
Mack Highway Truck, Bulldog, Copper	30.00
Mack Tractor Truck, Model B, Enameled Brass	12.50
Mack Truck, Enamel, On Silver, Parkersburg	10.00
Marion Steam Shovel Co.	20.00
Mayflower, Calf Skin, German	15.00
McCormick-Deering Farm Machines, Enamel	45.00
Miami, Palm Trees, Leaping Fish, 1934	6.00
Nash, White & Blue, Porcelain	125.00
New York Commercial Tercentenary, 1914	18.00
Old Dutch Cleanser	35.00
Our Freedom Must Live, Black, On Gold, Rectangular, 1960	6.00
Oval Citrine, Chased Foliate Mounting	825.00
Packard Automobile, Enameled Brass, Oval	8.50
Playboy Bunny, White, Silver, Black	6.00
Port Of New York, Indian, Pilgrim On Map, Bayonne Bridge, Bronze Color, 1931	6.50
Railway Express Agency, Enameled Brass	9.50

Red Intaglio Cut Stone Charm, Striped Agate Obverse, Gold Mesh	65.00
Relieve Fatigue, 1907	95.00
Rochester, N.Y., Niagara Falls	18.00
Rock Island Railroad, Enameled Brass	14.00
Rumely Oil Pull Farm Tractor, Enameled Brass	7.00
Salvation Army, Red, White & Blue Enameled Shield, Blood & Fire	8.00
Samuel Rosenthal & Bros., Boy Holding Up Trousers, c.1890	32.00
Schrock's Buggy Works, Millerburg, Ohio	35.00
Shell Oil, Yellow Enamel, Metal	60.00
Swift & Co., Red Steer, Celluloid	55.00
Union Pacific Railroad, Locomotive, Enameled Brass	8.00
Wabco Heavy Equipment	20.00
Walters & Dunbar Stockyards, Chicago	35.00
Washburn Crosby Foods, Gold Medal	75.00
West Cast Steel Truck Wheels	55.00
Western Association	40.00

WATERFORD type glass resembles the famous glass made from 1783 to 1851 in the Waterford Glass Works in Ireland. It is a clear glass that was often decorated by cutting. Modern glass is being made again in Waterford, Ireland, and is marketed under the name *Waterford*.

Bowl, Diamond & Notched Cutting, 7 1/4 In.	85.00
Chandelier, 12 Candlearms, Alternating Lengths, Prisms, Chains, 28 In.	3850.00
Cocktail, Colleen, 4 1/2 In.	40.00
Condiment Set, 4 Clear Cut Bottles, Silver Plated Frame, 6 In.	170.00
Cordial Set, Colleen, Decanter & 6 Short Stems	450.00
Cruet, Stopper, Leaf Pattern, Diamond Cut Facets, Stopper, 8 In.	40.00
Decanter, Crisscross Miters, Center Crosses, Fluted, Stopper, 10 1/2 In.	150.00
Decanter, Inverted Arches, Thumbprint Centers, Honeycomb Stopper, 10 In.	150.00
Jelly Jar, Cover, Diamond Cut Facets & Fans, 4 1/8 In.	45.00
Lamp, Cut Crystal Shade & Base, 14 In., Pair	1825.00
Punch Bowl, 25 Cups, 9 x 12 In.	2090.00
Salt, Cut Glass, Sheffield Silver Plate Top, Pair	88.00
Salt & Pepper	55.00
Tumbler, Colleen, 5 1/2 In.	45.00
Tumbler, Lismore, 10 Piece	350.00
Vase, Posy, Signed, 2 1/2 In.	50.00
Wine, Colleen, 3 7/8 In.	40.00

WATT family members bought the Globe pottery of Crooksville, Ohio, in 1922. They made pottery mixing bowls and dishes of the type made by Globe. In 1935 they changed the production and made the pieces with the freehand decorations that are popular with collectors today. Apple, Starflower, Rooster, Red & Blue Tulip, and Autumn Foliage are the best-known patterns. Apple, the most popular pattern, can be dated from the leaves. Originally, the apples had three leaves; after 1958 two leaves were used. The plant closed in 1965. For more information, see *Kovels' Depression Glass & American Dinnerware Price List.*

Bean Pot, Apple	165.00 to 210.00
Bean Pot, Apple, No. 502, Advertising, Oversized	900.00
Bean Pot, Cover, Tulip, No. 76	240.00
Bean Pot, Double Apple, No. 76	775.00
Bean Pot, Teardrop	245.00
Bowl, Apple, No. 8	65.00
Bowl, Apple, No. 9	80.00
Bowl, Apple, No. 04	65.00
Bowl, Apple, No. 63	15.00
Bowl, Apple, No. 64	20.00
Bowl, Apple, No. 131, Yellow & Brown	50.00
Bowl, Apple, Spaghetti	75.00
Bowl, Apple, Spaghetti, No. 62	175.00
Bowl, Apple, Spaghetti, No. 73	95.00

Bowl, Autumn Foliage, 8 In. 35.00
Bowl, Decagon, Pink, Oval, 10 1/2 In. 12.00
Bowl, Double Apple, No. 5 .... 200.00
Bowl, Double Apple, No. 63 .... 240.00
Bowl, Mexican, No. 64 .... 28.00
Bowl, Mixing, No. 12, Brown Banded 80.00
Bowl, Mixing, Pansy, No. 6 .... 35.00
Bowl, Moon & Star, No. 7 .... 60.00
Bowl, Moon & Star, No. 10 .... 95.00
Bowl, Rooster, No. 5 .... 85.00
Bowl, Rooster, No. 8 .... 150.00
Bowl, Serving, 11 In. 275.00
Bowl, Spaghetti, Pansy .... 40.00 to 120.00
Bowl, Stacking, Blue & Rose, 14 In. 75.00
Bowl, Starflower, Green On Brown, No.15 .... 195.00
Bowl, Starflower, No. 8 .... 47.00 to 65.00
Bowl, Starflower, No. 55 .... 48.00 to 85.00
Bowl, Teardrop, 6 In. 20.00
Bowl, Teardrop, 7 In. 49.00
Bowl, Teardrop, No. 5 .... 40.00
Bowl, Tulip, No. 65 .... 115.00
Bowl Set, Corn Row, Nested, Nos. 5-9, 5 Piece 150.00
Bowl Set, Teardrop, Nested, Nos. 5-7, 3 Piece 130.00
Bowl Set, Tulip, Nested, Nos. 63-65, 3 Piece 285.00
Canister, Cover, Apple, No. 91 .... 2300.00
Canister, Cover, Eagle, No. 72 .... 500.00
Canister, Esmond, Bulbous, No. 62 .... 60.00 to 90.00
Canister, Starflower, Flour 230.00
Canister Set, Starflower, 4 Piece 1500.00
Carafe, Electric Warmer, Orchard Ware, No. 132, Brown Glaze 390.00
Casserole, Cover, Apple, No. 15 .... 105.00
Casserole, Cover, Apple, No. 60 .... 60.00
Casserole, Cover, Apple, No. 601 .... 175.00 to 300.00
Casserole, Cover, Cherries 95.00
Casserole, Cover, Dutch Tulip, Large 250.00
Casserole, Cover, Moon & Star 65.00
Casserole, Cover, Peedeeco 20.00
Casserole, Cover, Rooster, No. 67 .... 250.00
Casserole, Cover, Rooster, Oval, No. 86 .... 1400.00
Casserole, Cover, Starflower, No. 67 .... 120.00
Casserole, Cover, Tulip, No. 600 .... 235.00
Casserole, Cover, Tulip, No. 601 .... 225.00
Casserole, Dutch Tulip, Handled, No.18 .... 230.00
Casserole, French, Handle, Raised Pansy 135.00
Casserole, Peedeeco, Individual 42.00
Casserole, Raised Pansy, Stick Handle 165.00
Casserole, Starflower .... 75.00 to 110.00
Casserole, Teardrop, No. 66 .... 300.00
Cheese Crock, Cover, Dutch Tulip 775.00
Cookie Jar, Apple 475.00
Cookie Jar, Blue & White Banded 175.00
Cookie Jar, Cover, Tulip, Large, No. 503 .... 345.00 to 395.00
Cookie Jar, Cross Hatch Pansy 265.00
Cookie Jar, Happy-Sad Face 950.00
Cookie Jar, Starflower, Green & Brown .... 180.00 to 200.00
Cookie Jar, Starflower, No. 21 .... 160.00 to 190.00
Cookie Jar, Tulip, No. 503 .... 595.00
Creamer, 4-Petal Starflower, No. 62 .... 500.00
Creamer, 5-Petal Starflower, No. 8 .... 200.00
Creamer, Apple, No. 62 .... 35.00 to 95.00
Creamer, Cut Leaf Pansy 130.00
Creamer, Morning Glory, No. 97 .... 500.00 to 650.00

Creamer, Quilted Morning Glory, Yellow, No. 97 .... 1500.00
Creamer, Raised Pansy 100.00
Creamer, Rooster, Advertising 225.00
Creamer, Rooster, No. 62 .... 135.00 to 150.00
Creamer, Starflower, Advertising 45.00
Creamer, Starflower, No. 62 .... 165.00
Creamer, Teardrop 300.00
Creamer, Tulip, No. 62 .... 75.00 to 125.00
Custard, Teardrop & Apple, Pair 50.00
Dispenser, Ice Tea 280.00
Ice Bucket, Apple 250.00
Ice Bucket, Cover, Apple, 2 Leaves 150.00
Ice Bucket, Rooster .... 345.00 to 375.00
Ice Bucket, Splatter, Pink 450.00
Ice Bucket, Starflower 500.00
Ice Bucket, Teardrop 200.00
Jar, Esmond, Happy/Sad Face 225.00
Jar, Grease, Apple, No. 01 .... 500.00
Mug, Apple, No. 121 .... 195.00 to 325.00
Mug, Esmond, No. 31 .... 375.00
Mug, Starflower, No. 501 .... 75.00 to 95.00
Pepper Shaker, Rooster, Hourglass Shape, Advertising 280.00
Pepper Shaker, Starflower 48.00
Pie Plate, Apple 160.00
Pie Plate, Apple, No. 33, Watkins Bake Shop 195.00
Pie Plate, Pilger, Nebraska 110.00
Pie Plate, Starflower 125.00
Pitcher, Apple, No. 15 .... 75.00 to 95.00
Pitcher, Apple, No. 16 .... 115.00
Pitcher, Apple, No. 17, Advertising 260.00
Pitcher, Apple, No. 17, Ice Lip .... 150.00 to 350.00
Pitcher, Apple, No. 62 .... 75.00
Pitcher, Autumn Foliage, Advertising, No. 15 .... 90.00
Pitcher, Autumn Foliage, No. 15 .... 55.00
Pitcher, Bank Advertising, No. 15 .... 70.00
Pitcher, Bleeding Heart, No. 15 .... 70.00
Pitcher, Blue & White Bands 55.00
Pitcher, Double Apple, No. 15 .... 425.00
Pitcher, Dutch Tulip, No. 15 .... 125.00 to 150.00
Pitcher, Iced Tea, Gold Prize Iced Tea 195.00
Pitcher, Refrigerator, Dutch Tulip, No. 69 .... 625.00
Pitcher, Rooster, No. 15 .... 79.00 to 95.00
Pitcher, Rooster, No. 16 .... 100.00 to 190.00
Pitcher, Silhouette, No. 16 .... 10.50
Pitcher, Starflower, No. 15 .... 45.00 to 65.00
Pitcher, Starflower, No. 15, 4 Petal 95.00
Pitcher, Starflower, No. 16 .... 80.00 to 165.00
Pitcher, Starflower, No. 16, Green On Brown 125.00
Pitcher, Starflower, No. 17 .... 240.00
Pitcher, Teardrop & Apple 65.00
Pitcher, Teardrop, No. 5 .... 45.00
Pitcher, Teardrop, No. 15 .... 65.00
Pitcher, Tulip, No. 16 .... 145.00 to 225.00
Pitcher, Tulip, No. 16, Advertising 185.00
Pitcher, Tulip, No. 17, Ice Lip 185.00
Pitcher, Tulip, No. 62 .... 56.00
Plate, White Daisy, 8 1/2 In. 75.00
Platter, Apple, No. 49 .... 250.00
Platter, Esmond, Apple/Pear, 15 In. 225.00
Platter, Pizza, Starflower 190.00
Salt & Pepper, Apple, Hourglass .... 215.00 to 250.00
Salt & Pepper, Autumn Foliage, Advertising 120.00
Salt & Pepper, Hourglass .... 275.00 to 300.00

Salt & Pepper, Starflower, No. 2, Barrel Shape .... 190.00 to 200.00
Saltshaker, Apple, Hourglass 140.00
Saltshaker, Starflower, Barrel Shape 95.00
Sugar, Autumn Foliage 125.00
Sugar, Cover, Morning Glory, No. 98 .... 325.00 to 350.00
Sugar, Rooster, No. 15 .... 95.00
Sugar, Starflower, No. 16 .... 110.00
Sugar, Tulip, No. 62 .... 225.00
Teapot, Autumn Leaf, No. 505 .... 2150.00
Tumbler, Starflower, Slant Sides, No. 56 .... 400.00
Underplate, Starflower, 12 In. 85.00
Underplate, Starflower, 18 In. 155.00

WAVE CREST glass is a white glassware manufactured by the Pairpoint
Manufacturing Company of New Bedford, Massachusetts, and some French   **WAVE CREST**
factories. It was decorated by the C. F. Monroe Company of Meriden,
Connecticut. The glass was painted in pastel colors and decorated with   **WARE**
flowers. The name *Wave Crest* was used after 1898.

Biscuit Jar, Egg Crate Mold 395.00
Biscuit Jar, Floral Panels, Scroll Edges, Silver Lid, Beaded Handle, 11 In. 440.00
Biscuit Jar, Hand Painted Ferns, Pale Yellow To White 280.00
Biscuit Jar, Lavender Lilacs & Foliage 265.00
Box, 2 Cherubs On Lid, Footed, Pink, Rectangular, Large 1850.00
Box, Black Stripe Across Swirls On Lid, Pink Blossoms, Gold Outlined 885.00
Box, Blown Out Rococo Lid, Hand Painted Pink Flowers, Signed, 7 1/2 In. 550.00
Box, Collar & Cuff, Egg Crate Mold 485.00
Box, Collar & Cuff, Puffy Mold, Brass Collar, Daisies, 6 1/2 x 6 1/2 In. 1075.00
Box, Cover, Pink & White Flowers, Rococo Trim, Marked, 5 1/2 x 7 1/4 In. 695.00
Box, Dresser, Flowers, Hinged Cover, 5 x 6 In. 440.00
Box, Egg Crate Mold, Gold Outlined Enamel Dots, Square, 7 In. 650.00
Box, Footed, Blue, 9 x 6 In. 1450.00
Box, Helmschmied Swirls, Blue Forget-Me-Nots, 7 In. Diam. 885.00
Box, Hinged, Cover, Pale Pink, 4 1/2 In. 300.00
Box, Jewelry, Hinged Lid, Baroque Shell, Satin Lining, 4 x 7 In. 750.00
Box, Ring, Florals, Square, Signed 550.00
Box, Swivel Mirror Inside Lid, Sterling Silver Fittings, Signed, 8 In. 1500.00
Card Holder, Pink Flowers, Blue Border 310.00
Dish, Dresser, Coral Flowers, Brass Throat, 3 1/8 x 4 In. 149.00
Dish, Trinket, Blue & Red Flowers, 5 In. 175.00
Fernery, Florals, Shaded Pink Ground 250.00
Flower Frog, Nude, 6 1/4 In. 54.00
Humidor, Brass Top, Three Guardsmen, Heads Of Bulldogs, 6 1/2 In. 525.00
Humidor, Cigar, 7 x 5 In. .... 700.00 to 975.00
Lamp, Molded Floral Design Shade & Base, Brass Mounts, 22 In. 825.00
Perfume Bottle, Lavender & Blue Pansies, Gold Stems, Square 325.00
Salt & Pepper, Erie Twist, Forget-me-nots, Daisies 145.00
Salt & Pepper, Tulip Pattern .... 65.00 to 100.00
Salt Dip, Tulip Mold, Florals 165.00
Saltshaker, Draped Column, Cat Design 85.00
Sugar Shaker, Helmschmied Swirl, Blue Scrolls & Flower Panels 480.00
Syrup Jug, Hinged Cover, Pink Florals 165.00
Toothpick, Blue Floral 140.00
Vase, Burgundy Mums, Enameled Swags, Doted Rim, 9 In. 595.00
Wall Pocket, Whisk Broom, Daisies, Scrolled Medallion, Marked 250.00

WEAPONS listed here include instruments of combat other than guns, knives,
rifles, or swords. These are listed in their own sections.

Bayonet, Remington Zouave 330.00
Club, Throwing, Carved Head, Fiji 225.00
Club, Throwing, Ula, Ivory Stars & Crescent Moon Inlay 1650.00
Club, War, Tapered, Diamond Section Striking Gace, Solomon Island, 97 In. 500.00
Parrying, Iron Haft, Chinese, 17th Century 365.00
Spear, Trench, Crude, Iron, 17 3/8 In. 185.00

Spear Head, Scabbard, Leaf Form, Wooden Scabbard, 18 1/2 In. 175.00

WEATHER VANES were used in seventeenth-century Boston. The direction
of the wind was an indication of coming weather, important to the seafaring
and farming communities. By the mid-nineteenth century, commercial
weather vanes were made of metal. Today's collectors often consider weather
vanes to be examples of folk art, even though they may not have been
handmade.

Airplane, Copper Over Wood, 62-In. Wingspan 2500.00
American Eagle, Full-Bodied, Outstretched Wings, Copper, 30 1/4 In. 2990.00
Arrow Directional, Gilt, 37 In. 105.00
Automobile, 1910 .... 4950.00
Banner, Flowers, Green, Victorian, Late 19th Century 1650.00
Blacksmith, Sheet Metal, Painted, 30 x 28 In. 1955.00
Butterfly, Sheet Metal, 1880s, 16 1/2 x 23 In. 1550.00
Centaur Archer, Copper 900.00
Codfish, Carved, New England, 19th Century, 37 In. 8250.00
Codfish, Swell-Bodied, Repousse Eyes & Scales, Copper, 57 In. 2000.00
Copper Top & Ball, Iron Directions & Shaft, 72 In. 900.00
Cow, Copper & Zinc, Cushing & White, Massachusetts, 27 In. .... 2090.00 to 4350.00
Cow, Silhouette, Sheet Iron, 22 1/2 x 22 1/2 In. 515.00
Duck, Cast Iron 450.00
Eagle, Spread Wings, Perched On A Ball, Molded Copper, 24 x 37 In. 1840.00
Eagle, Standing On Orb, Gilt Metal, 50-In. Wingspan 5175.00
Eagle, Wooden Ball, Metal Feet, Gold Repaint, 18-In. Wingspan, 18 In. 75.00
Fish, Carved & Gilt Painted 165.00
Fisherman, Holding Fish, Sheet Iron, Painted, 24 x 18 In. 2530.00
Gabriel, Blowing Horn, Copper 550.00
Gabriel, Silhouette, Painted Sheet Iron, 33 x 59 In. 2990.00
Goddess Of Liberty, Copper 1980.00
Grasshopper, Copper, Mounted On Rod, Ball Finial, 31 In. 500.00
Halley's Comet, Mustard Paint, Late 18th Century, 59 In. 3800.00
Horse, Copper 3295.00
Horse, Prancing, Raised Foreleg, Zinc Head, Copper, 15 1/2 In. 4600.00
Horse, Running & Jockey 3575.00
Horse, Running, Cast Iron 5060.00
Horse, Running, Directionals, Bullet Holes 935.00
Horse, Running, Flowing Mane, Molded Copper, 19 x 26 In. 2300.00
Horse, Running, Gilt Copper, 19th Century, 38 In. 1045.00
Horse, Running, Hollow Copper, Zinc Head, 31 In. 660.00
Horse, Running, Hollow Sheet Copper, Cast Iron Head, 17 x 24 In. 577.50
Horse, Running, Lightning Rod, Brass Arrow 395.00
Horse, Running, Molded Copper, 29 x 48 In. 9775.00
Horse, Running, Silhouette, Riveted Sheet Iron, 28 In. 715.00
Horse, Running, Zinc Head, Traces Of Gilt, Copper, 31 In. 1430.00
Horse, Trotting, Cast Iron, Directions, Red & Gold Paint 1795.00
Horse & Jockey, Full Gallop, Copper, Cast Bronze, 30 In. 1540.00
Horse & Jockey, Parcel Gilt, Painted Metal 4400.00
Horse & Rider, Sheet Copper, 26 x 27 1/2 In. 4830.00
Horse & Sulky, Molded Copper, 33 x 18 In. 6900.00
Horse & Sulky, Molded Copper, Full-Bodied, 32 1/2 In. 690.00
Indian, Bow & Arrow, Yellow Paint, Sheet Copper, 54 x 43 In. 4025.00
Indian, Silhouette, Drawn Bow & Arrow, Sheet Metal 550.00
Indian, Wooden, Strap Hinges, c.1820, 72 In. 800.00
Indian With Tomahawk, 19th Century, 24 In. 300.00
Locomotive, Steam, Sheet Metal, 19th Century, 64 In. 2310.00
Marsh Bird, Standing 5775.00
Men In Boat, Sperm Whale, Carved, Metal Base, 1925, 46 In. 2350.00
Moose, Silhouette, Zinc & Copper, 20th Century, 28 1/2 x 39 In. 330.00
Rooster, Cast Zinc, 14 1/4 x 11 1/2 In. 2990.00
Rooster, Copper, Fisk 3995.00
Rooster, Copper, Painted, Early 20th Century, 31 In. 6600.00
Rooster, Crowing, Yellow Paint, Sheet Metal, 38 1/2 x 34 In. 2300.00

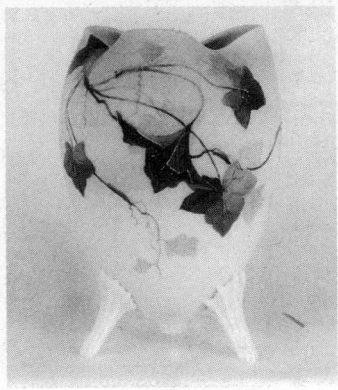

*Webb Burmese, Vase, Ivy Design,
Applied Feet, Signed, 7 In.*

Rooster, Gilded, 19th Century, 26 5/8 In.	770.00
Rooster, Gilt Cast & Sheet Iron, 37 In.	1540.00
Rooster, Sheet Copper, Black Paint	125.00
Rooster, Standing, 1870	3200.00
Sailboat, Iron, 1930s	425.00
Sailboat, Maine, Early 20th Century	950.00
Shore Bird, Gilt Metal, 18 1/2 x 24 In.	1210.00
Stag, Leaping, Brass, Fiske & Co., 28 x 26 In.	4730.00
Touring Car, Copper, c.1910, 13 x 31 In.	1430.00
Writing Quill, Gilded	3850.00

WEBB glass is made by Thomas Webb & Sons of Stourbridge, England.
Many types of art and cameo glass were made by them during the Victorian
era. The factory is still producing glass. Webb Burmese and Webb Peachblow
are special colored glasswares of the Victorian era. They are listed at the end
of this section. Glassware which is not Burmese or Peachblow is included
here.

Webb

Biscuit Jar, Geometric Designs, Sterling Silver Rim, Bale & Cover, 7 1/4 In.	935.00
Bowl, 8-Crimp Top, 3 Feet With Clear Leaf Up Onto Body, 4 1/4 In.	145.00
Bowl, Foxglove, Branch Of Blossoms On Rim, 6 In.	875.00
Decanter, Diamond Design Lower Band, 3 Oval Reserves, c.1900, 11 In.	1150.00
Jar, Sweetmeat, Gold Leaves & Flowers, Bamboo Each Corner, 3 1/4 In.	195.00
Lamp, Cameo, Blue Base, White Blossoms, Morning Glory Shade, 8 3/4 In.	3300.00
Lamp, Chartreuse Shade, Off-White Lined, Green, 7 3/8 In.	850.00
Perfume Bottle, Opaque White, Cameo Blossoms & Leaves, Silver Top, 5 In.	475.00
Punch Cup, Alexandrite, Barrel Shape, Citrine Handle, 2 3/4 In.	550.00
Shade, Pink Floral Swags, Cameo, Cream Ground, 4 x 6 In., Pair	1500.00
Vase, 8-Crimp Top, Cranberry Threading, Opaque, Clear Rigaree, 4 1/2 In.	95.00
Vase, Cameo, Tri-Color, Red & White Cameo Cut Blossoms, Yellow Ground, 8 In.	2860.00
Vase, Crystal Garlands & Berries, Crystal Teardrops On Sides, Cranberry, 5 In.	265.00
Vase, Gold & Silver Enamel, Dragonfly, Flowering Branches, c.1880, 12 In.	215.00
Vase, Gold Prunus & Butterfly, White Lining, Facing Pair, 6 5/8 In.	265.00
Vase, Gold Prunus & Pine Needles, Cream Lining, Brown Ground, 5 In.	595.00
Vase, Opaque Yellow Overlaid With White & Red, Cameo Roses, 4 In.	255.00
Vase, Pink Cased Floral, Enamel, Signed, 5 1/2 In.	140.00
Vase, Poppy Blossoms, Lemon, Crimson, White, Cameo, 1890, 9 In.	2875.00
Vase, Shaded Orange, Gold Maiden Hair Fern, Gold Butterfly, 7 1/4 In., Pair	495.00
Vase, White Geraniums, Lime Green, Baluster Type Neck, Ovoid, 1900, 5 1/8 In.	920.00
Vase, Wild Geranium Leaves & Blossoms, Butterfly At Reverse, 9 1/4 In.	3300.00

WEBB BURMESE is a colored Victorian glass made by Thomas Webb &
Sons of Stourbridge, England, from 1886.

Bowl, Blue Butterfly, Flying To Blossoms, Leafed Branches, 4 In.	585.00

Bowl, Floral Design, Crystal Rim, Marked, 3 3/4 x 6 1/4 In. 1120.00
Fairy Lamp, Bowl Base, Clear Candle Cup Holder, 5 1/2 In. 950.00
Fairy Lamp, Cream Pottery, Clarke Base, Marked, 4 1/4 In. 225.00
Fairy Lamp, Pyramid, Clear Candle Cup, Dome Shape Shade, 3 7/8 In. 1050.00
Petal Top, Internal Ribbing, 6 1/2 In. 1250.00
Rose Bowl, 8-Crimp Top, 3 x 3 1/8 In. 200.00
Rose Bowl, Pink To Yellow, 6-Crimp Top, Enamel Flowers, 2 1/4 In. 300.00
Toothpick, Unfired 100.00
Vase, Enamel Flowers, Leaves & Foliage, Ruffled, 4 In. 295.00
Vase, Flower Form, Optic Ribs, 7 3/4 In. 750.00
Vase, Ivy Design, Applied Feet, Signed, 7 In. .... *Illus* 950.00
Vase, Ivy Leaves, Bottle Shape, 10 In. 995.00
Vase, Orange Berries, Leaves, 8 1/2 In. 750.00
Vase, Queen's, Painted, 21 Pine Cones & Branches, 3 1/2 In. 365.00
Vase, Reverse Teardrop Shape, Butter Base, Blossom Top, 7 3/4 In. 750.00
Vase, Ruffled Top, Lavender 5-Petal Flowers, Leaves, 3 3/4 In. 300.00
Vase, Star Shaped Top, Ball Shape, 3 x 2 1/2 In. 200.00

WEBB PEACHBLOW is a colored Victorian glass made by Thomas Webb &
Sons of Stourbridge, England, from 1885.

Bowl, Branch Of Foxglove, Butterfly On Side, Marked, 6 In. 875.00
Bowl, Ruffled Rim, Shell Shape, Gold Flowers, Pine Needles, 8 In. 295.00
Rose Bowl, Gold Flowers & Butterfly, Satin, 2 1/2 In. 385.00
Vase, Gold Branches & Prunus Flowers, Butterfly, 6 3/4 In. 375.00
Vase, Gold Branches, Flowers, Off-White Lining, 7 3/4 In. 325.00
Vase, Gold Prunus Blossoms & Leaves, Butterfly, 3 1/2 In. 350.00
Vase, Raised Flowers & Pears, Gold & Silver, 10 In., Pair .... 850.00 to 950.00
Vase, Ruffled, White Enamel Flowers, Leaves, Gold Trim, 5 3/8 In. 225.00
Vase, Stick, Allover Gold & Silver Design, Butterfly, 10 In. 450.00

WEDGWOOD, one of the world's most successful potteries, was founded by
Josiah Wedgwood, who was considered a cripple by his brother and was
forbidden to work at the family business. The pottery was established in
England in 1759. A large variety of wares has been made, including the well-
known jasperware, basalt, creamware, and even a limited amount of
porcelain. There are two kinds of jasperware. One is made from two colors of
clay, the other is made from one color of clay with a color dip to create the
contrast in design. The firm is still in business. Other Wedgwood pieces may
be listed under Flow Blue or in other porcelain categories.

WEDGWOOD

Ashtray, Jasperware, Pegasus & Maidens, Blue-Gray, 3 5/8 In. 12.00
Atomizer, Jasperware, Cherubs, Ribbed Neck, Chrome Top, Blue 30.00
Basket, Orange, Cover, Stoneware, Strap Handle, c.1860, 7 1/4 In. 935.00
Biscuit Barrel, Blue Basalt, Neoclassic, 19th Century 110.00
Bookends, Pan, Green Glaze, E.B. Olsen, c.1932, 6 1/2 In. 247.50
Bookends, Rosewood & Brass, 2 x 2 1/2 In. Oval Blue Medallions, Pair ...... 550.00 to 605.00
Bottle, Barber, Cover, Salmon Glaze, Raised Leaf Festoons, 10 1/4 In. 330.00
Bouquetiere, Biscuit, Matte Black Glazed Strapwork, 1790, 7 In. 3300.00
Bowl, Boat Shape, Ironstone, Bently 45.00
Bowl, Boat Shape, Ironstone, Clarke 45.00
Bowl, Butterfly Luster, Butterflies Exterior, Orange Interior, c.1920, 8 In. 550.00
Bowl, Butterfly Luster, Gold Butterflies, Purple Band, 3 1/2 In. 250.00
Bowl, Butterfly Luster, Gold Ground, Rainbow Interior, Signed, 4 x 2 1/2 In. 250.00
Bowl, Dancing Hours, Black Basalt, 11 In. 875.00
Bowl, Dragon Luster, Mottled Exterior, Green Interior, 2 x 3 3/4 In. 250.00
Bowl, Earthenware, Shell Shape, Lobster Base, Servers, c.1889, 7 In., 3 Piece 880.00
Bowl, Fairyland Luster, Snake Coiled Around Animal Interior, 2 1/4 In. 160.00
Bowl, Gilt Dragon In Clouds, Famille Rose Exterior, M. Tatton, c.1910, 8 In. 165.00
Bowl, Ram's Head Handles, Footed, Marked, 8 1/4 x 5 1/2 In. 50.00
Box, Heart, Pink, 4 1/2 In. 100.00
Box, Sardine, Cover, Basket Weave, Attached Tray, c.1878, 7 1/2 In. 165.00
Bridge Set, Jasperware, Oak Leaf Border, Classical Figures, Blue, 4 Piece 45.00
Brush Pot, Blue & White, Classical, 4 1/4 In., Pair 88.00
Bust, Bacchus, Jasperware, White, Early 19th Century, 3 3/8 In. 220.00

Bust, Black Basalt, Early 19th Century, 8 In. 715.00
Bust, Byron, Black Basalt, Wyon, Mid-19th Century, 14 1/2 In. 440.00
Bust, Ceres, Black Basalt, Silver Banded Stem, 19th Century, 2 1/2 In. 305.00
Bust, Mercury, Black Basalt, Wings On Helmet, Early 19th Century, 9 1/2 In. 935.00
Bust, Napoleon, Black Basalt, Early 19th Century, 8 3/4 In. 550.00
Bust, Shakespeare, Black Basalt, c.1880, 12 1/2 In. 825.00
Bust, Shakespeare, Black Basalt, c.1880, 17 In. 770.00
Bust, Stephenson, Parian, Circular Base, c.1858, 14 3/4 In. 467.50
Bust, Voltaire, Black Basalt, 19th Century, 5 3/4 In. 357.50
Butter Dish, Cover, Caneware, Applied Drabware Ferns, c.1800, 8 1/2 In. 330.00
Cake Plate, Cover, Medium Blue, Large 275.00
Candlestick, Black Basalt, Bronzed, Classical Relief, c.1880, 5 1/4 In., Pair 1210.00
Candlestick, Figural, Jasperware, Classical Woman, 10 1/4 In., Pair 1980.00
Candlestick, Gothic Style, Ivory, c.1896, 11 In., Pair 225.00
Candlestick, Jasper Dip, Pale Lilac, Medallions, Garlands, c.1850, 5 1/2 In. 302.50
Candy Box, Cover, Jasperware, Light Blue, Square, 4 In. 20.00
Candy Box, Cover, Jasperware, Vine, Green, Round, 5 In. 20.00
Charger, Creamware, Brown Transfer Printed Hound, c.1878, 12 In. 165.00
Cheese Keeper, Jasperware, Medium Green 345.00
Chimney Ornament, Enameled Medallion Of Children, c.1875, 6 7/8 In. 220.00
Coffeepot, Cover, Queensware, Red Transfer Printed Landscape, 9 1/4 In. 523.00
Coffeepot, Cover, Rosso Antico, Enamel, c.1850, 7 1/4 In. 413.00
Compote, Creamware, Greek Key Border, 5 1/2 In. 165.00
Creamer, Fallow Deer, Blue & Silver Luster 95.00
Creamer, Jasperware, Mother & Child, Crimson, 3 1/4 In. 395.00
Crocus Pot, Underplate, Hedgehog Shape, Celadon Body, c.1868, 6 In. 1210.00
Cup, Jasperware, Yellow, White Applied Latticework, 2 1/2 In. 1320.00
Cup, Luster, Butterflies, Blue Interior, Orange Exterior, 3 Handles 200.00
Cup & Saucer, Countryside, Blue & White 6.00
Cup & Saucer, Harvest Fruit Cluster, Gold Trim, Tunstall Lts., Unicorn 10.00
Cup & Saucer, Terra-Cotta, After Dinner 40.00
Cuspidor, Majolica, Blue, Yellow & Brown, c.1885, 7 1/4 In. 110.00
Custard Cup, Cover, Jasperware, Blue, White Rope Handle, 2 1/2 In. 880.00
Dinner Set, Queensware, Lavender, Cream Ground, Service For 8 .... 1100.00
Dish, Flowers & Foliage, Footed, Pearlware, 8 1/2 x 11 In. 192.00
Dish, Jasperware, Grape & Vine Border, Chariot, 2 Horses, Black, 4 In. 14.00
Dish, Pin, Luster, Gold Bull In Center, Gold Rim, 3 3/4 In. 165.00
Door Knob, Jasperware, Blue, Classical Relief, Brass Knob, 2 3/8 In., Pair 275.00
Ewer, Water, Seated Triton Holding Monster's Horns, Blue, 16 1/4 In. 440.00
Figurine, Apollo, Pearlware, Enamel Decorated, Early 1800s, 7 3/8 In. 550.00
Figurine, Bull, Plain, Machin, 1930s 400.00
Figurine, Bull, Zodiac Design, Machin, 1930s 750.00
Figurine, Eagle, Pearlware, Enamel Decorated, Early 1800s, 7 1/2 In. 990.00
Figurine, Fisherman, Earthenware, c.1870, 10 1/4 In. 990.00
Figurine, Shakespeare, At Podium, Basalt, 1850, 16 In. 1200.00
Flowerpot, Jasperware, Blue, White Applied Quatrefoils, c.1790, 3 1/2 In. 522.50
Flowerpot, Jasperware, Classical Women Under Lion's Head, 3 5/8 In. 175.00
Game Dish, Cover, Caneware, Latticework, Twig Finial, c.1800, 8 1/4 In. 440.00
Game Pie Dish, Cover, Caneware, Molded Rabbit Finial, Grapevine, c.1874, 9 1/2 In. 357.50
Game Pie Dish, Cover, Applied Vine, Pastry Design, Early 19th Century, 4 In. 715.00
Garniture, Porphyry Style, Gilt Acanthus Leaves, Late 18th Century, 3 Piece 1320.00
Ginger Jar, Cover, Stoneware, Turquoise Enamel Decorations, c.1871, 9 1/4 In. 605.00
Hat Pin, Jasperware & Cut Steel, Star Form, Steel Beads, Blue Button, 4 1/2 In. 440.00
Incense Urn, Lattice Cover, Jasper Dip, Classical Relief, c.1870, 7 1/4 In. 1540.00
Jar, Jasperware, White Vintage, Green, 5 In. 93.00
Jardiniere, Dark Blue & White, Marked, 7 1/2 In. 150.00
Jardiniere, Stand, Stoneware, Mask Handles, Enameled Florals, Brown, 6 In. 605.00
Jug, Britannia Lid, c.1840, 6 3/4 In. 195.00
Jug, Cover, Creamware, Strainer, Polychrome Stripes, c.1800, 11 In. 950.00
Lamp, Desk, Green Ceramic Shade, Brass Arm, Copper Base, c.1933, 15 In. 275.00
Lamp, Oil, Black Basalt, Woman Holding Book, Gilded, Bronzed, 8 1/2 In. 1320.00
Lamp, Oil, Jasper Dip, Classical Medallion, Zodiac Symbols, 5 1/4 In. 385.00
Mold, Jelly, Creamware, Wedge Shape, Floral Enamel, c.1800, 6 1/2 In. 2310.00

Mortar & Pestle, Vitreous Ware, c.1785, 4 1/4-In. Mortar, 5 3/4-In. Pestle 385.00

Perfume Bottle, Jasperware, Lilac Medallions, White Relief, 3 In. 715.00

Pill Box, Blue Basalt, Royal Profile Plaque 44.00

Pin, Circle, 6 Dancing Girls, Discs, Light Blue 30.00

Pitcher, Cream, Black Basalt, Lady Templetown's Poor Maria, c.1785, 3 5/8 In. 468.00

Pitcher, Hunting Scene, Hound Handle, 8 In. 345.00

Pitcher, Jasperware, Barrel Shape, Bust Of Washington & Franklin, 4 7/8 In. 120.00

Pitcher, Jasperware, Raised Green Figures Of Ladies, 4 1/2 In. 165.00

Pitcher, Light Blue, Metal Lid, Marked, 6 1/2 In. 70.00

Pitcher, Neoclassical Maidens, Grape Vine Border, 8 In. 88.00

Pitcher, Presentation, Old Hall, Birth & Death, c.1870 .... 375.00

Pitcher, Shell & Seaweed, Cobalt Blue 495.00

Pitcher, Water, Longfellow, 10 In. 145.00

Pitcher, White Classical Figures, Salmon, 5 3/4 In. 193.00

Plaque, Black Relief, Hercules, Wood Mounted, 5 1/4 x 7 1/4 In., Pair 440.00

Plaque, Blue & White, Basalt, 2 1/2 x 7 1/4 In., 4 Piece 94.00

Plaque, Fairyland Luster, Picnic By River, Z5280, c.1922, 5 x 10 1/2 In. 4400.00

Plaque, Jasper Dip, Tri-Color, Hercules In Garden, 7 1/4 x 20 In. 1045.00

Plaque, Jasperware, Blue, White Cupid On Lion, 4 x 4 1/2 In. 385.00

Plaque, Jasperware, Blue, White, Children, Rectangular, 4 1/8 x 5 1/2 In. 330.00

Plaque, Jasperware, Light Blue, Relief Of Coriolanus, Round, 10 1/2 In. 1100.00

Plaque, Judgment Of Hercules, Black Basalt, Late 18th Century, 11 1/2 In. 825.00

Plaque, Lafayette, White On Green Jasperware, Silver Rim, Hanger, 3 1/8 In. 185.00

Plaque, Medusa, Jasperware, Blue, White Applied Portrait, 5 1/4 In. 110.00

Plate, Baltimore From Federal Hill, Black Transfer, 1830 .... 35.00

Plate, Basket, Majolica 247.00

Plate, Bennington Battle Monument, c.1900, 9 1/2 In. 35.00

Plate, Blue Floral, White Ground, Spiral Relief, Ironstone, Platinum, 10 In. 32.00

Plate, Boston Tea Party, Blue Transfer, 10 1/2 In. 65.00

Plate, Christmas, 1969, Windsor Castle, Jasperware .... 100.00 to 200.00

Plate, Christmas, 1972, St. Paul's Cathedral 25.00

Plate, Countryside, Blue & White, 10 In. 5.00

Plate, Dominion Of Canada, Province Crest 88.00

Plate, Duke University, Etruria, 1937 .... 22.00

Plate, Floral, Silver Sterling Rim, 11 1/2 In. 77.00

Plate, Grape Leaf, Majolica 247.00

Plate, Green & Black Shells, Green Feather Edge, Pearlware, 9 1/8 In. 95.00

Plate, Ivanhoe, Flow Blue, 10 In. 100.00

Plate, Jasper Dip, Light Blue, Leaf And Berry Border, Floral Festoons, 9 3/4 In. 165.00

Plate, Jasperware, Putti Cameo Banding, Signed, c.1805, 8 In. 130.00

Plate, Mother's Day, 1971, Sportive Love 15.00

Plate, Nigpo Pattern, 1860, 10 In., 5 Piece 176.00

Plate, Old Meeting House, Blue & White, Bingham, Mass., 9 In. 40.00

Plate, Patrician, 10 In. 40.00

Plate, Railroad Limited Edition, New York Central 55.00

Plate, Shakespeare Theater 45.00

Plate, Silver Jubilee, Jasperware, 5 Colors, Queen Elizabeth, 109/750, 9 In. 440.00

Plate, Williamsburg, Virginia, 1956 .... 25.00

Platter, California, Flow Blue, c.1849, 16 In. 250.00

Platter, Chapoo, Flow Blue, 15 1/2 x 20 In. 950.00

Platter, Cow, Blue, 17 In. 200.00

Platter, Cows, Flow Blue, 17 x 13 1/2 In. 400.00

Posy Pot, Jasperware, Seasons, Light Blue, 3 3/8 In. 20.00

Punch Bowl, Fairyland Luster, Firbolgs, Thumbelina Interior, 11 In. 3575.00

Scale Set, Jasper Mounted, Parkins & Gotto, Late 1800s, 2 1/2 In. 440.00

Server, Dessert, Rose & Jasmine, Pedestal, 1875-1900 .... 365.00

Sugar & Creamer, Jasperware, White Classical Scenes, c.1900 .... 65.00

Sugar Bowl, Cover, Jasperware, Pale Blue, Domestic Scene, c.1790, 4 In. 880.00

Sugar Bowl, Cover, Rosso Antico, Black Basalt, Classical, c.1820, 4 1/2 In. 440.00

Sugar Box, Caneware, Signed, c.1800 .... 135.00

Tea Bowl & Saucer, Caneware, Blue Enamel Bands, c.1800, 3 1/4 In. 413.00

Tea Set, Jasperware, Terra-Cotta, Primrose, 3 Piece 125.00

Teapot, Black Basalt, Classical Relief Medallions, c.1865, 5 1/4 In. 358.00

Teapot, Busts Of Franklin & Washington, White On Green, Drum Shape, 3 1/2 In.	145.00
Teapot, Caneware, Bacchanalian Boys, Blue Enamel Trim, c.1790, 4 3/4 In.	220.00
Teapot, Chintz, Creamware, Ovoid, c.1770, 5 5/16 In.	4025.00
Teapot, Depicting Benjamin West's Painting, Death Of Wolfe, 1770	5800.00
Teapot, Grape Pattern, Blue, 2 Cup	45.00
Teapot, Jasperware, Blue & White, Classical Ladies On Sides, 6 1/4 In.	295.00
Teapot, Jasperware, Lilac, Applied Leaves & Flowers, 5 1/2 In.	605.00
Teapot, Jasperware, White Classical Figures, Salmon, 5 In.	247.00
Teapot, Stoneware, Leaf Molded Oval Body, White Applied Stems, 7 3/4 In.	495.00
Thimble, Blue & White, Jasper, 1988	25.00
Tile, Spring, Earthenware, Polychrome Decorations, 6 1/2 x 8 3/4 In.	303.00
Tobacco Jar, Fox Hunt, Fox Finial, D'ye Ken John Peel, Marked, 7 In.	250.00
Tobacco Jar, Jasper Dip, Dark Blue, White Classical Relief, 6 1/2 In.	330.00
Toothpick, Butterfly Luster, 3 Handles	295.00
Tray, Fairyland Luster, Lily, Garden Of Paradise Scene, 1920, 11 In.	2300.00
Tureen, Soup, Corea, Cover, Flow Blue	695.00
Tureen, Soup, Indian Festoon, Cover, Underplate & Ladle, Flow Blue	1950.00
Vase, Basalt, Raised Neoclassical & Vintage Design, 6 In.	192.00
Vase, Black Basalt, Classical Female Figure, Early 19th Century, 8 In.	1000.00
Vase, Bud, Pear Shape, Cupids & Leaves, Blue, 5 x 3 In.	25.00
Vase, Celadon, White Handles & Base, K.Murray, c.1940, 8 In.	330.00
Vase, Classical Ladies & Cupid, Dark Blue, Marked, 4 7/8 In.	125.00
Vase, Classical Scene, Blue Ground, Portland, 8 In.	517.00
Vase, Column, Creamware, Brown Enamel, Black Basalt Base, 12 In., Pair	1980.00
Vase, Cover, Creamware, Blue Landscapes, Satyr Handles, c.1876, 13 In., Pair	1760.00
Vase, Cover, Creamware, Satyr-Head Handles, c.1770, 8 1/2 In.	2310.00
Vase, Cover, Jasper Dip, Yellow & Black Ground, White Muses, 10 1/4 In.	220.00
Vase, Cover, Variegated Agate, Creamware, c.1770, 7 1/4 In., Pair	2860.00
Vase, Fairyland Luster, Argus Pheasant, Shape 3451, c.1920, 11 3/4 In.	3025.00
Vase, Fairyland Luster, Imps On Bridge, Shape 3451, c.1925, 11 3/4 In.	6600.00
Vase, Ivory Glaze, Enamel & Gilt Bird & Flowers, 1800s, 14 1/2 In., Pair	990.00
Vase, Jasper Dip, Black, Apollo Finial, Latin Verse, c.1930, 9 1/4 In.	1320.00
Vase, Jasper Dip, Dark Blue, Classical Relief, Trophies To Neck, 6 In., Pair	468.00
Vase, Jasper Dip, Green, Canopic, Hieroglyphic Relief, c.1800, 9 1/2 In.	3300.00
Vase, Jasperware, 3-Color, White Body, Lilac Pilasters, c.1780, 5 1/4 In., Pair	1380.00
Vase, Jasperware, 3-Color, White Relief Of Flaming Torches, 7 In.	1100.00
Vase, Jasperware, 4-Color, White Pilasters, Lion Rings, 1882, 6 1/2 In.	2015.00
Vase, Jasperware, Classical Ladies, Child, Cherub, Light Blue, 3 7/8 In.	22.00
Vase, Jasperware, Column Shape, White Columns, Blue Ground, 6 In.	248.00
Vase, Portland, Jasper Dip, Dark Blue, White Classical Figures, 10 In.	2310.00
Vase, Spill, Jasper Dip, Green, Dancing Hour Figures, Fluting, 5 3/8 In.	330.00
Vase, Stoneware, White, Bronzed & Gilt, Applied Floral Festoons, 6 1/2 In.	303.00
Vase, Stoneware, White, Gilded Leafy Festoons, Lion Mask Columns, 5 1/4 In.	275.00
Vase, Trumpet, Fairyland Luster, Butterfly Woman, c.1920, 7 3/4 In.	2420.00
Vase, Vellum, Ivory, Gilded Dragon-Head Handles, Late 1800s, 9 1/2 In.	358.00
Vase, Victoria Ware, Columns With Lions Masks & Paws, c.1875, 6 3/4 In.	715.00
Vase, Victoria Ware, Deep Blue Ground, Classical Relief, c.1875, 4 1/4 In.	220.00
Wine Cooler, Caneware, Mask Handles, Early 19th Century, 10 1/2 In., Pair	935.00

WELLER pottery was first made in 1873 in Fultonham, Ohio. The firm moved to Zanesville, Ohio, in 1882. Art wares were introduced in 1893. Hundreds of lines of pottery were produced, including Louwelsa, Eocean, Dickens Ware, and Sicardo, before the pottery closed in 1948.

LOUWELSA
WELLER

Ashtray, Figural, Black Seal .... 55.00 to 60.00
Ashtray, Patricia, Swan, White	65.00
Basket, Cameo, Brown, White Flowers	35.00
Basket, Copra, 12 1/2 In.	350.00
Basket, Hanging, Claywood	20.00
Basket, Hanging, Owl, 5 1/2 x 10 In.	325.00
Basket, Ivoris, Paper Label	35.00
Basket, Tivoli, 8 1/2 In.	125.00
Bowl, Ardsley, 12 In.	175.00
Bowl, Classic, Green, 14 1/2 In.	125.00

Weller, Charger, Aurelian, Dog, Brown Glaze   Weller, Charger, Aurelian, Chicks, Brown Glaze

Bowl, Claywood, 2 In.	50.00
Bowl, Gloria, 6 In.	65.00
Bowl, Louwelsa, Gold Floral, Brown, 7 1/4 In.	95.00
Bowl, Lustre, Cinnamon, 7 x 3 In.	50.00
Bowl, Mixing, Pierre, Green, 10 1/2 x 5 1/2 In.	35.00
Bowl, Muskota, Black, Red Medallions	85.00
Bowl, Paragon, Blue, 5 x 7 1/2 In.	280.00
Bowl, Pumila, Flower Form, Pink, Green Leaves, 3 1/2 In.	35.00
Bowl, Rosemont, Blue Jays, Ivory & Green Branches, 9 1/2 In.	220.00
Bowl, Squirrel, Matte Glaze, Mark	95.00
Bowl, Woodcraft, Full Squirrel, 5 1/2 x 8 In.	60.00
Bowl, Woodcraft, Squirrels, 6 In.	125.00
Box, Sicardo, Gold Fleur-De-Lis, Crimson & Blue Ground, c.1905, 2 3/4 In.	550.00
Candleholder, Classic, Tan, Pair	65.00
Candleholder, Lavonia, Lavender, Ribbed, Pair	50.00
Candleholder, Marvo, Double	100.00
Candleholder, Woodcraft, Owl & Tree, Pair	660.00
Candlestick, Clarmont, 8 In., Pair	195.00
Charger, Aurelian, 3 Baby Chicks, Brown, Yellow, Haubrich, 13 In.	4000.00 to 4400.00
Charger, Aurelian, Chicks, Brown Glaze	*Illus* 4400.00
Charger, Aurelian, Dog, Brown Glaze	*Illus* 1760.00
Clock, Louwelsa, Pansies, Star Shaped, Footed, Yellow, Orange & Brown, 11 In.	880.00
Compote, Flemish, Fruit Garlands, 6 In.	77.00
Compote, Roma	100.00
Console, Glendale, Seagull, Nest Flower Frog	575.00
Console, Lavonia, Bowl, Frog, Candlesticks	255.00
Console, Sabrinian	225.00
Console Set, Orange & Brown Glaze, 10-In. Bowl, 2-In. Candlesticks, 3 Pc.	93.50
Console Set, Silvertone, 3 Piece	250.00
Console Set, Warwick, 3 Piece	200.00
Cookie Jar, Mammy	3480.00
Cookie Jar, Teapot	1500.00
Cookie Jar, Watermelon Mammy	2500.00
Cornucopia, Wild Rose, Green, 6 In.	32.00
Creamer, Mammy	495.00 to 950.00
Ewer, Aurelian, Yellow & Orange Flowers, A.H., 7 1/2 In.	270.00
Ewer, Oak Leaf	40.00
Ewer, Pine Cones, 4 1/2 In.	1200.00
Figurine, Cat, Reclining, White Matte Glaze, Black & Orange Eyes, 14 In.	1760.00
Figurine, Dachshund, Brown	75.00
Figurine, Dog, Pop-Eyed, Black & White Matte Glaze, Blue Eyes, 4 In.	440.00

Figurine, Garden, Gnome, Long Nose 7900.00
Figurine, Garden, Owl On Apple Stump 1995.00
Figurine, Goose, Evergreen, Black Eyes, 6 In. 75.00
Figurine, Kingfisher, Brighton 245.00
Figurine, Scotty Dog, Seated, Black & White 3500.00
Figurine, Woodpecker, Brighton .... 175.00 to 225.00
Flower Frog, Brighton Kingfisher, 9 In. 264.00
Flower Frog, Brighton Pheasant, 12 x 8 In. 286.00
Flower Frog, Crab, Muskota 35.00
Flower Frog, Hobart, Fisher Boy 250.00
Flower Frog, Lorbeek, Art Deco 75.00
Flower Frog, Low Bowl, Matte Green Glaze, 2 1/4 x 8 1/4 In. 137.00
Flower Frog, Muskota, Hunting Dogs 350.00
Flower Frog, Muskota, Lobster .... 115.00 to 135.00
Flower Frog, Muskota, Lotus .... 115.00 to 135.00
Flower Frog, Muskota, Poppy, 1 3/4 In. 30.00
Flower Frog, Muskota, Swan 60.00
Flower Frog, Muskota, Water Lilly 110.00
Flower Frog, Woodcraft, 3 1/2 x 6 In. 85.00
Garden, Figure, Pan, 16 1/2 In. 2310.00
Ginger Jar, Chase 400.00
Humidor, Dickens Ware, Indian Chief, Clay Outlined, Painted Face & Feathers 750.00
Jar, Turada, Lid 375.00
Jar, Velvetone 575.00
Jardiniere, Bells Of San Juan, 9 In. 425.00
Jardiniere, Burntwood, Faces Of Men, Women, Children & Angels, 9 1/2 In. 247.50
Jardiniere, Dickens Ware I, Oriental Lady, Olive Green Ground, 7 In. 330.00
Jardiniere, Etna, Roses, 8 x 10 In. 250.00
Jardiniere, Flemish, Lion Heads With Garlands, 11 In. 375.00
Jardiniere, Forest, Marked, 5 1/2 In. 150.00
Jardiniere, Leaf Design, Matte Green, 11 In. 695.00
Jardiniere, Lorber, Satyr, 10 In. 575.00
Jardiniere, Louwelsa, Woodland Colors, Leaves, Berries 95.00
Jardiniere, Pedestal, Art Nouveau Ivory, Molded Women, Floral Border, 36 In. 2090.00
Jardiniere, Pedestal, Forest Pattern, Marked, 29 x 12 1/2 In. 705.00
Jardiniere, Pedestal, Forest, 30 In. 990.00
Jardiniere, Pedestal, Ivory, 31 1/2 In. 385.00
Jardiniere, Raised Roses, 10 x 9 In. 125.00
Jardiniere, Woodcraft 135.00
Jardiniere, Woodcraft, Woodpecker & Squirrel, 9 1/2 In. 350.00
Jug, Dickens Ware, Looped Handle, Dark Green & Brown Ground, 10 3/4 In. 172.00
Kitchen Set, Mother's Little Helper, Tools, Beater Jar, Mixing Bowl 250.00
Lamp, Louwelsa, Integral Handle, Ruffled, Scalloped Base 595.00
Lamp, Woodcraft, Owl, Cherry Boughs, Electric, 15 In. 585.00
Lamp Base, Camelot, Green Background, Incised Greek Key Design, 11 1/2 In. 275.00
Lamp Base, Louwelsa, Yellow Wild Roses, Brown Ground, 9 1/2 In. 200.00

Weller, Planter, 2-Faced Dog

♦♦♦♦♦♦♦♦♦♦♦♦♦♦♦♦♦♦♦♦♦♦♦♦♦

Smoke stains can be removed from a stone fireplace with an artgum eraser. Soot on the carpet in front of the fireplace can be removed with salt. Sprinkle dry salt on the soot, wait 30 minutes, then vacuum.

♦♦♦♦♦♦♦♦♦♦♦♦♦♦♦♦♦♦♦♦♦♦♦♦♦

Lamp Base, Turada, Brown Ground, Oil Lamp Canister Insert, c.1898, 9 3/4 In. 440.00
Lamp Base, Yellow & Orange Daffodil, Brown Ground, 10 In. 181.50
Mug, Dickens Ware, Dark Green Glaze, Raised Orange Flowers, Horseshoe, 7 In. 170.00
Mug, Dickens Ware, Light Blue, 4 In. 395.00
Mug, Dickens Ware, Monk, Drinking Beer, Green 395.00
Mug, Etna, 5 1/2 In. 75.00
Mug, Floretta, Tulips, Gray Glaze 80.00
Pitcher, Cream, Louwelsa, Yellow Lilies 120.00
Pitcher, Eocean, Light Cream To Lavender Ground, Yellow Corn, 8 1/2 In. 165.00
Pitcher, Etna, Raised Pink Flowers, Green Leaves, Gray To Pink Ground, 10 1/2 In. . . 165.00
Pitcher, Grape Cluster On Brown Ground, Cylindrical, 11 In. 65.00
Pitcher, Kingfisher, 8 1/2 In. 210.00
Pitcher, Louwelsa, Pouring Lip, Blackberries & Leaves, 6 In. 300.00
Pitcher, Marvo 95.00
Planter, 2-Faced Dog .... *Illus* 35.00
Planter, Lido, Turquoise, 9 1/2 x 3 1/2 In. 25.00
Planter, Roma, Mythological Design, Square, 6 In. 65.00
Planter, Woodcraft, Log, 10 In. .... 40.00 to 55.00
Plaque, Abraham Lincoln, World's Fair .... 95.00 to 135.00
Plate, McKinnley, 4 1/2 In. 75.00
Potpourri Jar, 3-Footed, Matte Green Glaze, 3 1/2 x 4 1/4 In. 192.00
Sand Jar, Forest, 14 In. 695.00
Syrup, Mammy Form, 6 3/8 In. 550.00
Tankard, Art Nouveau, Green Bisque, Applied Grapes & Leaves, 12 In. 330.00
Tankard, Eocean, Red Berries, Green Leaves, Gray To Cream Ground, 10 1/2 In. 357.50
Teapot, Forest 225.00
Teapot, Pumpkin, Green, Bisque 100.00
Umbrella Stand, Ardsley, Cattails, c.1928 .... 695.00
Umbrella Stand, Denton, Cream Ground, 22 1/2 In. 1100.00
Umbrella Stand, Ivory, Floral Panels, 22 In. 385.00
Umbrella Stand, Louwelsa, Yellow & Brown Daffodils, Footed, 20 In. 605.00
Umbrella Stand, Raised Purple Apple In Tree, Brown Ground, 21 3/4 In. 853.00
Umbrella Stand, Zona 2750.00
Urn, Cloudburst, Orange, 5 In. 120.00
Vase, Ardsley, 10 1/2 In. 55.00
Vase, Ardsley, Double, 9 1/2 In. 85.00
Vase, Aurelian, Leaf Design, 8 7/8 In. 275.00
Vase, Aurelian, Yellow Lily, Footed, 6 In. 330.00
Vase, Baldin, 7 In. 95.00
Vase, Baldin, Blue, 13 In. 325.00
Vase, Barcelona, 6 In. .... 150.00 to 160.00
Vase, Barcelona, 7 In. 450.00
Vase, Barcelona, Handles 150.00
Vase, Besline, Narrow Cylindrical Neck, Etched Blue Florals, 12 In. 358.00
Vase, Bonito, 9 1/4 In. 145.00
Vase, Bonito, Roses, Daisies, Fuchsias, 12 x 9 In. 295.00
Vase, Boy In A Tree, Modeled, Hugging The Side, Green Glaze, 15 3/4 x 9 In. 3575.00
Vase, Burnt Wood, Wise Men, 9 In. .... 345.00 to 385.00
Vase, Camelot, 6 In. 140.00
Vase, Chase, Fox Hunt Scene, White Raised Slip, 8 In. 595.00
Vase, Chengtu, 12 In. 125.00
Vase, Chengtu, Bright Orange Glaze, 7 In. 49.50
Vase, Claywood, 13 In. 125.00
Vase, Claywood, 4 1/2 In. 60.00
Vase, Cloudburst, Stick, White, Maroon, 6 1/2 In. 100.00
Vase, Copra, Red & Blue Berries, Green Leaves, Applied Handles, 11 In. 275.00
Vase, Cornish, Orange & Green Leaves, Green & Blue Berries, 8 In. 66.00
Vase, Dancing Girls, Blueware, 10 In. 200.00
Vase, Dickens Ware II, Bleak House Scene, Grandfather Smallwood, 10 1/2 In. 495.00
Vase, Dickens Ware II, Golfer In Landscape, Marked, 8 3/4 In. 1600.00
Vase, Dickens Ware, Captain Cuttle Gives Lovely Peg, 9 1/2 In. 1850.00
Vase, Dickens Ware, Colorful Peacock On Branch, Bisque, 14 1/2 In. 468.00

Vase, Dickens Ware, Football Players 1000.00
Vase, Dickens Ware, Incised Figure Of Golfer, Tree Lined Ground, 9 In. 1000.00
Vase, Dickens Ware, Indian, 2 Feathers, Incised "White Man," Daughtery, 10 In. 1100.00
Vase, Dickens Ware, Mr. Micawber, 13 In. 1400.00
Vase, Dickens Ware, Street Scene, David Copperfield, Bisque, 13 1/2 In. 385.00
Vase, Eocean, Dog Portrait, Blake, 7 1/2 x 7 In. 1000.00
Vase, Eocean, Floral, 6 1/2 In. 225.00
Vase, Eocean, Morning Glories, 7 In. 150.00
Vase, Eocean, Rectangular Top, Squared Handles, 2-Footed, Raspberries, 7 1/2 In. 413.00
Vase, Eocean, Signed McL, 6 1/2 In. 300.00
Vase, Eocean, Stemmed Pink Flowers, Gray, 13 In. 475.00
Vase, Etna, 5 1/2 In. 95.00
Vase, Etna, Blue & Gray Raised Grape Design, Art Nouveau, 2 Handles, 7 1/2 In. 308.00
Vase, Etna, Pink Flowers, Gray & Pink Ground, 6 1/2 In. 176.00
Vase, Fan, Marvo, Green, 5 Holes 24.00
Vase, Flemish, Red Rose, Blue Ribbon, Cylinder 110.00
Vase, Fleron, 6 1/2 In. 65.00
Vase, Fleron, Green, Ruffled, 6 In. 60.00
Vase, Floretta, Brown Glaze, 7 In. 110.00
Vase, Floretta, Light And Dark Brown Glaze, Molded Grapes, 7 1/2 In. 60.00
Vase, Flowers In Relief, Bracket Handles, 6 In. 90.00
Vase, Flowers, Light To Medium Blue Ground, Signed, 6 1/4 In. 193.00
Vase, Forest Scene, Signed, 8 In. 95.00
Vase, Fruitone, 5 In. 110.00
Vase, Fruitone, Green, Brown, Shoulder Handles, 4 1/2 In. 22.00
Vase, Fudzi, Incised Flowers, 1905, 7 In. 1200.00
Vase, Glendale, Lovebirds 685.00
Vase, Glendale, Orange Lustre, Molded Birds, Nest, Leaves, 9 In. 522.50
Vase, Gourd Bottle Shape, Stemmed Cover 60.00
Vase, Greenbriar, Boat, 5 In. 60.00
Vase, Hudson, Bird, 9 In. 585.00
Vase, Hudson, Blue, 7 1/2 In. 175.00
Vase, Hudson, Blue, Cream Flowers, Green Leaves, 9 In. 297.00
Vase, Hudson, Cherry Blossoms, Lavender Ground, Signed, 6 In. 275.00
Vase, Hudson, Cherry Blossoms, Narrow Neck, 7 In. 250.00
Vase, Hudson, Floral, 8 In. .... 275.00 to 325.00
Vase, Hudson, Glazed White, Apple Blossoms, 7 In. 325.00
Vase, Hudson, Handles, Timberlake, 7 In. 700.00
Vase, Hudson, Iris, 15 In. 2200.00
Vase, Hudson, Iris, Timberlake, Gray-Green, 8 1/2 In. 450.00
Vase, Hudson, Light To Dark Gray-Tea, Hester Pillsbury, 12 1/2 In. 220.00
Vase, Hudson, Lilacs & Foliage, Dark Blue, 8 1/2 In. 220.00
Vase, Hudson, Multicolored Irises, Lavender Ground, Marked, 15 1/4 In. 1100.00
Vase, Hudson, Parrot, Handles, Mae Timberlake, 24 In. 6875.00
Vase, Hudson, Raspberries, Yellow Flowers, 4 1/2 In. 140.00
Vase, Hudson, White Flowers & Leaves, Cream To Gray, 11 In. 225.00
Vase, Hudson-Perfecto, Ball Shape, Orange Florals & Circles, F. Dedonatis, 8 In. 467.50
Vase, Hudson-Perfecto, Blue Flowers, Dorothy Laughead, 13 In. 1100.00
Vase, Hudson-Perfecto, Woman, Iris, 11 In. 175.00
Vase, Hunter, Navy, Leaping Dog 225.00
Vase, Incised Woman's Bust In Profile, Green Ground, E.L. Pickens, 20 In. 880.00
Vase, Kenova, Embossed Frog Climbing Up Side, Egg Shape, 6 3/4 In. 475.00
Vase, Knifewood, Owls & Moon, 8 In. 425.00
Vase, Knifewood, Peacock, 9 In. 415.00
Vase, L'Art Nouveau, Cameo Of Woman's Face, 12 In. 375.00
Vase, LaSa, 11 1/2 In. 950.00
Vase, LaSa, 2 Pine Trees, Clouds, Iridescent Gold, 7 1/2 In. 275.00
Vase, LaSa, 3 1/2 In. 150.00
Vase, LaSa, 3 Pine Trees, 4 In. 365.00
Vase, LaSa, 9 In. 485.00
Vase, LaSa, Desert Landscape, Palm Trees, Gold & Magenta Glaze, 12 In. 385.00
Vase, LaSa, Landscape Scene, Mountains, Water, Clouds, Sunset, 6 1/2 In. 264.00

Vase, LaSa, Single Pine Tree, Mountains, Clouds, Rose, 5 1/2 In. 250.00
Vase, LaSa, Stick, Palm Tree, Mountains, 6 1/2 In. 195.00
Vase, Lebanon, 10 1/2 In. 400.00
Vase, Lido, 6 In. 25.00
Vase, Louwelsa, Blue, 10 1/4 In. 995.00
Vase, Louwelsa, Blue, 11 In. 1200.00
Vase, Louwelsa, Burnt Orange Roses, Swirling Stems, Brown Ground, 14 In. 825.00
Vase, Louwelsa, Chrysanthemums, Pillsbury, 11 In. 575.00
Vase, Louwelsa, Jug Shape, 2 5/8 In. 185.00
Vase, Louwelsa, Orange, Yellow & Green Flowers, 2 Handles, Mitchell, 12 In. 357.50
Vase, Louwelsa, Pocket Shape, Footed, Brown & Orange Dog, Blake, 7 1/2 In. 880.00
Vase, Louwelsa, Portrait Of Indian Chief, Marked, 10 1/2 x 7 In. 1600.00
Vase, Louwelsa, Portrait, Cavalier, Pillow Shape, 7 In. 357.00
Vase, Louwelsa, Portrait, L.J. Burgess, 12 1/4 In. 1400.00
Vase, Louwelsa, Roses, Shaded Brown, Green & Yellow Ground, 29 In. 1265.00
Vase, Louwelsa, Silver Overlay Leaf Design, Orange Rose, 10 In. 1320.00
Vase, Lustre, Orange Glaze, 5 In. 99.00
Vase, Malvern, Reticulated Top, Strap Design, Green, Brown & Orange, 10 In. 165.00
Vase, Marengo, Luster Ground, White Outlines 400.00
Vase, Marvo, Blue, 8 In. 100.00
Vase, Marvo, Rust, 9 In. 44.00
Vase, Muskota Figural, Cat Perched, Matte Yellow, Red & Green, 11 In. 770.00
Vase, Patricia, Gooseneck Handle, 8 1/2 In. 100.00
Vase, Patricia, Green Drips, Molded Design, Tan To Brown, 4 In. 50.00
Vase, Patricia, Swan, Handle, Green 85.00
Vase, Perfecto, Underglaze Slip Design, 8 In. 425.00
Vase, Pillow, Ansonia, 9 In. 225.00
Vase, Pillow, Dickens Ware II, Monk & Beer Mug 425.00
Vase, Pillow, Dickens Ware, Ducks In Marsh Setting, 5 In. 350.00
Vase, Pillow, Florals, 7 In. 290.00
Vase, Portrait Of Indian Chief, K. Kappes, 10 1/2 In. 1760.00
Vase, Protruding Shoulder, Embossed Butterflies, Elephant-Skin Glaze, 7 In. 350.00
Vase, Purple Violets, Marked, 8 1/2 In. 150.00
Vase, Raceme, Round, 6 In. 70.00
Vase, Roma, Bands Of Leaves & Flowers, Cylinder, 7 5/8 x 3 1/4 In. 46.00
Vase, Roma, Double, 8 1/2 In. 55.00
Vase, Roma, Triple, 7 1/2 In. 75.00
Vase, Scandia, Yellow Design, Black Glaze, 9 In. 110.00
Vase, Scrolled Tendrils, Floral, Blue Over Violet, Cylindrical, 4 1/2 In. 373.00
Vase, Selma, 4 White Swans 195.00
Vase, Sicard, Blue & Green Irises, Rose Ground, 8 1/2 In. 550.00
Vase, Sicard, Bulbous Top, Purple Wild Flowers, Textured Ground, 9 1/4 In. 935.00
Vase, Sicard, Floral Design, Bulbous Body 825.00
Vase, Sicard, Green Peacock Feathers, Magenta & Gold Ground, 10 x 3 In. 1045.00
Vase, Sicard, Mums On Curving Stems, Green & Rose Iridescence, 13 1/2 In. 2420.00
Vase, Sicard, Purple Ground, Iridescent Green Flowers & Leaves, 6 1/2 In. 550.00
Vase, Sicard, Tapering Cylinder, Gold & Silver Iris, Rose Ground, 10 In. 1320.00
Vase, Sicard, Twisted Form, Blue, Green & Blue Iridescence, 5 In. 660.00
Vase, Sicardo, Daisies, 5 In. 500.00
Vase, Sicardo, Landscape, 7 5/8 In. 287.00
Vase, Sicardo, Scrolling Stems, Floral, Fuchsia Ground, 4 3/4 In. 345.00
Vase, Sicardo, Swirling Mistletoe, Gold & Lavender Glaze, Signed, 7 In. 550.00
Vase, Stellar, Black Matte Glaze, White Stars, 5 1/2 In. 605.00
Vase, Sydonia, Blue & Cream, 7 In. 55.00
Vase, Sydonia, Double, Blue, 10 In. 95.00
Vase, Tree Trunk Shape, Small 75.00
Vase, Utopian, 4 In. 145.00
Vase, Utopian, 6 In. 185.00
Vase, Velvetone, Yellow, 8 In. 55.00
Vase, Warwick, 12 1/2 In. 125.00
Vase, White Rose, 9 1/2 In. 45.00
Vase, Woodcraft, 9 In. 120.00

Vase, Woodcraft, 10 1/2 In.	65.00
Vase, Woodcraft, Owl, Tree, 16 In.	925.00
Vase, Woodrose, 7 In.	50.00
Vase, Yellow Daisies, Light Green, 10 In.	50.00
Wall Pocket, Flowers & Columns, Ivory	70.00
Wall Pocket, Glendale, Mother Bird & 4 Chicks On Branch, 8 In.	450.00
Wall Pocket, Lavonia Lady	325.00
Wall Pocket, Oak Leaf With Acorn	85.00
Wall Pocket, Roma, 11 In.	110.00 to 150.00
Wall Pocket, Roma, Dupont Design, 12 In.	125.00
Wall Pocket, Woodcraft, Squirrel On Front, 9 1/2 In.	160.00
Wall Pocket, Woodrose, White With Yellow Roses, 5 1/2 x 6 1/2 In.	65.00
Wall Vase, Double, Glendale	225.00

WESTMORELAND GLASS was made by the Westmoreland Glass Company of Grapeville, Pennsylvania, from 1890 to 1984. They made clear and colored glass of many varieties, such as milk glass, pressed glass, and slag glass.

Appetizer Set, Paneled Grape, 3 Piece	55.00
Ashtray, Beaded Grape, Gold Paint, 4 In.	18.00
Banana Boat, Doric, 11 In.	40.00
Banana Boat, Ring & Petal, Footed	38.00
Basket, Pansy, Split Handle, Dogwood	20.00
Bowl, Maple Leaf, 10 In.	45.00
Bowl, Paneled Grape, Bell Shape, 9 In.	55.00
Bowl, Waterford, Lipped, Ruby, 11 1/2 In.	45.00
Butter, Cover, English Hobnail, Ruby	75.00
Cake Plate, Moonstone, Blue, 11 In.	55.00
Cake Plate, Ring & Petal, Square, 11 In.	55.00
Cake Plate, Skirted, 11 In.	75.00
Candy, Cover, Ashburton	50.00
Candy, Cover, Ball & Swirl, Marigold	15.00
Candy, Cover, Della Robbia, Mother-Of-Pearl	30.00
Compote, Cover, Sawtooth, 14 In.	50.00
Compote, Green & White	25.00
Compote, Paneled Grape, Ruffled Rim, 6 In.	50.00
Cookie Jar, Plantation	95.00
Decanter, Thousand Eye, Crystal & Ruby	85.00
Decanter Set, Paneled Grape, 9 Piece	165.00
Dish, Sweetmeat, Doric	55.00
Gravy Boat, Paneled Grape	52.00
Honey Jar, Old Quilt	45.00
Ivy Bowl, Paneled Grape	45.00
Jam Jar, Strawberry Design	20.00
Nappy, Heart, 5 In.	35.00
Nappy, Heart, 8 In.	45.00
Plate, Paneled Grape, 10 1/2 In.	35.00
Plate, Thousand Eye, 8 In.	20.00
Punch Cup, Three Fruits	4.00
Punch Set, Three Fruits, 15 Piece	225.00
Rose Bowl, English Hobnail, 5 In.	25.00
Salt & Pepper, Forget-Me-Not Design	44.00
Sugar & Creamer, Paneled Grape	35.00
Table Set, Child's, Flattened Diamond, 3 Piece	37.50
Tumbler, Ice Tea, Paneled Grape, Flat	22.00
Water Set, Old Quilt, 7 Piece	120.00

WHEATLEY Pottery was established in 1880. Thomas J. Wheatley had worked in Cincinnati, Ohio, with the founders of the art pottery movement, including M. Louise McLaughlin of the Rookwood Pottery. Wheatley Pottery was purchased by the Cambridge Tile Manufacturing Company in 1927.

Bowl, Water Plant Design, Green Glaze, 2 1/2 x 8 In.	795.00
Ewer, Kezonta Ware, 11 In.	2500.00

Lamp, Oil, Green, Wicker & Silk Shade, Four-Footed, Electrified, 18 1/2 In. 1540.00
Vase, Purple & White Flowers, Green Leaves, 1880s, 13 In. .... 950.00 to 2200.00

WHIELDON was an English potter who worked alone and with Josiah
Wedgwood in eighteenth-century England. Whieldon made many pieces in
natural shapes, like cauliflowers or cabbages.

Basket, Tortoiseshell Glaze, Reticulated, Circular, c.1760, 11 1/8 In. 2875.00
Box, Hinged Cover, Green, Brown, Ochre & Gray, c.1770, 2 1/2 In. 990.00
Creamer, Skating 90.00
Plate, Combed Edge, Tortoise Pattern, Label, 18th Century, 8 In. 375.00
Sauceboat, Double Strap Handles, Solid Agate, Staffordshire, c.1760, 5 3/4 In. 8250.00
Teapot, Brown & White, Mottled Green, c.1770, 4 3/4 In. 575.00
Teapot, Cover, Tortoiseshell Glaze, Floral Vines, Staffordshire, c.1760, 4 1/2 In. 1150.00
Teapot, Cover, Tortoiseshell Glaze, Pear Shape, Staffordshire, c.1765, 5 In. 3150.00
Teapot, Pineapple Shape, Floral Finial, Green & Yellow, c.1765, 4 7/8 In. 5500.00
Teapot, Tortoiseshell Glaze, Cover, 18th Century, 5 1/4 In. 385.00
Teapot, Tortoiseshell Glaze, Hexagonal, Chinoiserie, c.1765, 4 1/2 In. 1265.00
Whistle, Birds On Branches, Pair 950.00

WILLETS Manufacturing Company of Trenton, New Jersey, began work in
1879. The company made belleek in the late 1880s and 1890s in shapes
similar to those used by the Irish Belleek factory. They stopped working
about 1912. A variety of marks were used, all including the name Willets.

Bowl, Rose Design, Double Handle, Hand Painted, Belleek, 7 1/4 x 4 In. 44.00
Mug, Dragon Handles, Enamel Dog Portraits, G.Y. Houghton, 1904, 5 3/4 In., Pair ... 825.00
Pitcher, Roses, 1885, 5 1/2 In. 600.00
Salt, Heart Shape, Gold Trim, Crimped 55.00

WILLOW, see Blue Willow category

WINDOW glass that was stained and beveled was popular for houses during
the late nineteenth and early twentieth centuries. The old windows became
popular with collectors in the 1970s; today, old and new examples are seen.

Beveled, Textures, Jeweled, 35 x 43 In. 1100.00
Casement, Leaded, Textured, Frank Lloyd Wright, c.1900, 41 x 21 In. ..... 4830.00 to 5520.00
Casement, Yellow Squares In Clear Glass, Wright, 1908, 32 x 20 In., Pr. 7475.00
Figural Roundels, Pointed Arch, 102 x 14 In., Pair 230.00
Leaded, Stylized Lozenge Pattern, Frank Lloyd Wright, 1900, 25 3/8 x 22 In. 2070.00
Leaded Clear Glass, Frank Lloyd Wright, 35 5/8 x 26 1/2 In. 3680.00
Rounded Top, White Paint, 18 Panes 295.00
Segments Arranged As Wisteria Landscape, 58 x 48 1/4 In. 2530.00
Stained Glass, Pink, Green, Amber, With Jewels, 1880-1890, 39 x 44 In. 2000.00
Victorian, Mosaic Form, Demilune, c.1885, 24 x 50 In. 2200.00

WOOD CARVINGS and wooden pieces are listed separately in this book.
There are also wooden pieces found in other categories, such as Kitchen.

Antelope, Bronze Horns, Hagenauer, c.1930, 13 1/2 In. 1150.00
Black Bears, Playing Doctor, White, Black, Red Paint, 9 x 9 3/4 In. 126.50
Bust, Man, Cartoon-Like, Protruding Eyes, Sticking Out Tongue, 20 In. 1725.00
Chicken, Red & Yellow Detail, Himmelreicht, 6 1/2 In. 1815.00
Creche Figure, Cloth & Ivory Arms, Kneeling, 18th Century, 6 In. 450.00
Decanter, Chef, Open To Hold Bottle 65.00
Decanter, Football Player, Open To Hold Bottle 65.00
Eagle, Banner In Mouth, Over Shield, J.H. Bellemy, 1890, 24 1/2 In. 13500.00
Eagle, E Pluribus Unum Banner, Polychrome Paint, 48-In. Wingspan 3500.00
Eagle, Federal, Gilded, Oak, c.1800, 7 1/2 x 14 1/4 In. 365.00
Eagle, Feeding Young, Polychrome & Gilt, 7 1/2 In. 132.00
Eagle, Gesso & Gold 550.00
Eagle, On Rock, Gilded, Israel Sack, 40-In. Wingspan, 29 In. 6325.00
Eagle, Pine, Old Finish, 20th Century, 9 x 18 1/2-In. Wingspan 440.00
Goblet, Fruitwood, 4 Seasons, 19th Century, Austria, 12 1/2 In. 385.00
Goose, In Flight, Hand Painted, On Driftwood, Wing Spread-12 1/2 In. 175.00

Hawk, Perched On Log, Carved, Shinnecock Indian 1100.00
Horse, Rearing, 10 1/2 In. 60.00
Lectern, Eagle, Flat Back With Ledge To Hold Book, 1880s 1875.00
Lectern, Eagle, Stained Pine, c.1850 .... 2500.00
Man, Ivory Signed Cartouche In Base, Oriental, 7 1/8 In. 236.00
Man, Profile, Polychrome Paint, John W. Saur, Newark, Ohio, Aug., 7 x 6 In. 55.00
Mice, Resting On A Bed Of Pine Nuts, Japan, 7 In. 990.00
Ornament, Circus Wagon, Man With Mustache, Painted, 33 x 49 In. 522.00
Ornament, Heart Finial, Chip Carved Edge, Initials E. R., 1 3/4 x 5 1/2 In. 198.00
Plaque, Indian Head, Mahogany, 19th Century, 20 In., Pair 1760.00
Plate, Walnut, Floral & Leaf Trim, Victorian Style, 10 3/4 In. 23.00
Santos, Aged Patina, Painted Dress, No Legs, 18th Century, 10 1/2 In. 325.00
Smiling Lion, Glass Eyes, Carved Pine, Gesso & Wood, 32 x 41 In. 4255.00
Soldier, Style Of Ohio Militia Man, Polychrome Paint, 67 1/2 In. 605.00
St. Joseph & Baby Jesus, Estofado Technique, Mexican 5500.00
Statue, Wellington Victor At Waterloo, Polychrome Repaint, 74 In. 1980.00
Swallow, Black Paint, 2 Large, 3 Small, 5 1/2 In., 5 Pieces 165.00
Virgin Mary, Estofado Technique, Mexican 3000.00
Watch Hutch, Polychrome Paint, 9 1/2 x 5 1/4 In. 220.00
Whale, Full Bodied, Ben Holmes, Stratford, Conn., 1890, 27 1/2 In. 5225.00
Youth, Renaissance Costume, 3 Socket Candle Arm, 36 In. 1750.00

WOODEN wares were used in all parts of the home. Wood was used for many containers and tools. Small wooden pieces are called *treenware* in England, but the term *woodenware* is more common in the United States. Additional pieces may be found in the Advertising, Kitchen, and Tool categories.

Blotter, Rocker, Tartanware, Hay & Leith, 5 1/2 In. 385.00
Book Rack, Folding, Carved, Large 485.00
Bowl, Ash Burl, Deep, 10 x 4 3/4 In. 385.00
Bowl, Ash Burl, Scrubbed, Notched, 13 x 4 1/4 In. 495.00
Bowl, Bird Shape, Polychrome, Gilt, Russia, 9 1/2 In., Pair 55.00
Bowl, Black & Red Stripes, Poplar, 20 In. 115.00
Bowl, Chopping, American, 19th Century, 24 1/2 In. 357.50
Bowl, Chopping, Round, Late 19th Century, 19 In. 192.50
Bowl, Dough, Oblong, 21 In. 175.00
Bowl, Orange & Red, 23 1/2 In. 2310.00
Bowl, Salad, Carved, 19th Century, 27 1/2 x 17 x 6 In. 264.00
Box, Blue-Green Paint, 19th Century, 9 x 11 x 5 In. 160.00
Box, Carved, White Carved Stone Insert In Lid, Oriental, 1 7/8 In. 66.00
Box, Inscribed North Visitors Room Box, 2 Handles 3025.00
Box, Land & Sailing Ship Scene, Mustard, Green, Rufus Porter Style, Coin Clasp 3520.00
Box, Lehnware, Saffron, Poplar, Painted Design, Decoupage, 5 In. 467.00
Box, Slant Lid, Eagle Painted, Pine, Varnish Finish, Primitive, 16 x 16 x 33 In. 286.00
Bucket, Cover, Stave Construction, Forged Iron Bands, Painted 335.00
Bucket, Cover, Sugar, Wooden Stave, Bands, Orange Stain, 7 1/4 In. 192.00
Bucket, Flower & Leaf Engraved, Tooled, Wire Handle, 1900s, 3 1/2 x 4 1/2 In. 45.00
Bucket, Grain, Red Paint, Iron Bands, 19th Century, 10 x 11 1/2 In. 95.00
Bucket, Hollowed Log, Iron Bands & Bail, 7 1/2 x 7 1/4 In. 155.00
Bucket, Lid, Sugar, Yellow Paint, Red Bands, Sweet Pickles Stencil, 13 In. 192.00
Bucket, Sugar, Stave Constructed, Green Paint, Cover, 14 In. 210.00
Bucket, Sugar, Stave Constructed, Wire Bale Handle, Dark Finish, 6 3/4 In. 148.00
Cabinet, Spice, Stained Pine, 2 Small Over 2 Large Drawers, Treenware 290.00
Canteen, Field, Iron & Splint Bands, 1750s, 11 In. 145.00
Casket, Wooden, White, Fancy, 40 In. 35.00
Comb Case, Hanging, Applied Hearts On Front, 1900s, 7 3/4 x 4 3/4 In. 35.00
Container, 3 Iron Bands, Blue Paint, Staved, 1850-1860, 19 x 17 In. 320.00
Container, Storage, Swing Handle, 12 x 14 In. 1800.00
Cup & Saucer, Floral Design, Pink Ground 60.50
Dipper, c.1760, 14 1/2 In. 45.00
Dipper, Large Bowl, Hook Handle, 20 In. 50.00
Dish, Leaf Shape, Mahogany, 8 In. 5.00
Dressing Set, Oyster Walnut, Silver Plated Cups, Crystal Bottles, Tray, Victorian 413.00
Eggcup, Tartanware, MacDuff, Mauchline Base, 1900, 3 1/4 In. 160.00

Finial, Painted, From Hearse 297.00
Firkin, Cover, Wooden Handle 85.00
Frame, Tartanware, Prince Charlie, 3 x 4 3/4 In. 600.00
Frame, Walnut, Raised Leaves, Milk Glass Jewels 22.00
Funnel, Ear, Hollowed Log, 5 3/4 In. 55.00
Gameboard, 6 Wrought Iron Hooks For Wild Game, Scalloped Edge, 34 In. 125.00
Hammer, Sugar, Incised Design, 10 5/8 In. 55.00
Hanger, Stag Shape, Germany 595.00
Hatbox, Oval, Flower And Leaf Decorations, Mustard Paint, c.1830 .... 2400.00
Hatchel, Hardwood, Worn White Paint, Floral Design, 25 In. 38.50
Jar, Cover, Laminated Layers, Treenware, 5 3/4 In. 50.00
Jardiniere, Regency, Beechwood, Slatted Sides, Stand, Brass Liner, 1800s, Pr. 3735.00
Keg, Walnut Bung, Pewter Spout, Iron Bands, Oak, 11 3/4 x 8 1/2 In. 120.00
Measure, Stave Constructed, Steel Bands, Old Red Paint, 11 1/2 x 9 In. 137.00
Mirror, Shaving, Sheraton, Inlaid Mahogany, 1780 .... 165.00
Napkin Holder, Doll, Marble Type Base, 1930s, 11 1/2 In. 38.00
Scoop, Cranberry, Maple, W.T. Makepeace, 15 x 17 In. 132.00
Scoop, Cranberry, Pine, Maple, D & G Co., 22 x 19 1/2 In. 302.00
Scoop, Hand Carved, Handle, 4 1/2 x 8 1/2 In. 86.00
Shovel, Grain, Branded E. J. S., Poplar, 40 1/2 In. 71.50
Shovel, Grain, Walnut, Treenware, 36 In. 137.00
Stand, Tartanware, Caledonia, Footed, 5 In. 525.00
Stand, Umbrella, Oak, Carved Panels, Brass Pan, 28 In. 137.00
Tankard, Hollowed Log, Pegged Band, 6 5/8 In. 165.00
Tray, Carved Boxwood, Lotus Leaf Shape, Late 19th Century, 27 x 17 In. 2200.00
Tray, Cutlery, Dovetailed, 9 x 16 In. 85.00
Tray, Regency, Painted Bouquet In Basket, Gilt Border, 19th Century 1800.00
Tub, Hollowed Log, Carved Ears, Oval, c.1740, 9 x 15 3/8 In. 185.00
Vase, Bud, Satinwood, Inlaid Mahogany, George III Style, 4 1/2 In., Pr. 800.00
Wall Pocket, Eagle Design 285.00

WORCESTER porcelains were made in Worcester, England, from 1751. The
firm went through many name changes and eventually, in 1862, became The
Royal Worcester Porcelain Company Ltd. Collectors often refer to *Dr. Wall*,
Barr, *Flight*, and other names that indicate time periods or artists at the
factory. It became part of Royal Worcester Spode Ltd. in 1976. Related pieces
may be found in the Royal Worcester category.

Basket, Blue & White, Reticulated, Oval, Pine Cone, c.1775, 11 In. 920.00
Bough Pot, Blue & White, Bombe, Globe Flower Sprays, c.1770, 8 3/4 In. 1150.00
Bowl, Blue & Gilt Floral Design, Ivory Ground, Barr, Flight & Barr, 7 x 4 In. 90.00
Bowl, Blue & White, Oriental Village Scene, Late 18th Century, 8 1/4 In. 440.00
Bowl, Blue, Oriental Landscape, c.1780, 6 In. 303.00
Bowl, Fruit, Scalloped Rim, Blue Flowers, c.1775, 10 1/4 In. 302.00
Caudle Cup, Cover, Stand, Transfer Printed, Couple, Blackamoor, c.1765, Pair 2875.00
Coffeepot, Cover, Pear Shape, Mandarin Holding Tea Bowl, c.1770, 8 7/8 In. 920.00
Cup & Saucer, Chrysanthemum, Handles, c.1775, Pair 330.00
Cup & Saucer, Floral, 1770-1785 .... 375.00
Dish, Kidney Shape, Bengal Tiger, c.1770, 10 1/4 In., Pair 2875.00
Dish, Shell Shape, Blind Earl, Rose Branch, Barr & Barr, c.1825, 8 1/4 In. 1725.00
Dish, Square, Scalloped, Blue Ground, Bird, Barr, Flight & Barr, c.1810, 9 In. 575.00
Fruit Cooler, Cover, Dragon In Compartments, Chamberlain's, 9 1/4 In., Pair 9775.00
Jug, Cabbage Leaf, Leaf-Molded Body & Neck, S-Scroll Handle, c.1765, 9 In. 690.00
Junket Dish, Blue & White, Flower, Scallop Shells, c.1770, 9 3/4 In. 800.00
Mug, Beckoning Chinese Man, Oriental Flowering Branch, c.1758, 5 3/4 In. 1955.00
Pitcher, Gargoyle Handle, Cobalt Blue, 13 In. 308.00
Plate, Dessert, Full-Blown Pink Rose, Barr, Flight & Barr, c.1810, 8 1/8 In. 575.00
Plate, Dinner, Regent China, Japan Pattern, c.1820, 10 In., 24 Piece 3160.00
Platter, Oval, Armorial, Arms & Crest Of Oliveira, Chamberlain's, c.1840, 12 In. 748.00
Platter, Rectangular, Chamfered, Phoenix, Kakiemon Palette, c.1770, 13 In. 1725.00
Platter, Rectangular, Chamfered, Phoenix, Kakiemon Palette, c.1770, 15 In. 2015.00
Sauce Tureen, Cover, Hundred Antiques, Shell Handles, c.1775, 6 1/2 In. 630.00
Sauce Tureen, Cover, Quatrefoil, Blue & White, Floral Spray, c.1770, 7 In. 345.00
Spill Vase, Turquoise, Gilt Edge, Cylindrical, Barr & Barr, c.1820, 4 1/4 In. 2010.00

Sugar Bowl, Cover, Blue Scale, Bucket Shape, Exotic Birds, c.1770, 4 In., Pair 8050.00
Teacup & Saucer, Fluted, Jabberwocky Pattern, Kakiemon Palette, c.1770 .... 575.00
Teacup & Saucer, Transfer Printed, Figures, Classical Ruins, c.1770 .... 400.00
Urn, Cylindrical, Suffolk Abbey, Flight, Barr & Barr, c.1820, 3 1/2 In. 1035.00
Vase, Animal Scenes, 1810, Pair 1995.00
Vase, Cone Shape, 3 Cows, Distant Landscape, Flight & Barr, c.1795, 6 In. 920.00
Vase, Cover, Shield Shape, Mask Handles, Chamberlain's, c.1810, 11 In. 4025.00
Waste Bowl, Japan, Flight & Barr, c.1800, 6 1/2 In. 460.00

WORLD WAR I and World War II souvenirs are collected today. Be careful
not to store anything that includes live ammunition. Your local police will tell
you how to dispose of the explosives. See also Gun, Sword, and Trench Art.

WORLD WAR I, Banner, Heroes, Painted, Cotton, J.S. Miller & Co., 11 x 15 3/4 In. 140.00
Canteen, Marked 319 Machine Gun Co. 35.00
Cloth, German P.O.W., Iron Cross, Oak Leaves, Embroidered Military Flags 50.00
Figurine, American Doughboy, Metal, Dated 1918, 8 In. 17.50
Hand Grenade, U.S. Army, Pineapple, Cast Iron 6.50
Helmet, Doughboy 40.00
Medal, He Died For Freedom & Honor, Arthur Jakeman, Cast Brass, 5 In. 100.00
Oil Can, U.S. Army Machine Gunner, Brass Spout, Chained Cap, Tin, Oval 4.00
Periscope, Trench, R & J Beck Ltd., Adjustable, 1917, 17 x 23 In. 265.00
Poster, And They Thought We Couldn't Fight, Clyde Forthe, 41 x 30 1/2 In. 55.00
Poster, Be Patriotic, Woman, Flag Dress, Faithhorn Co., 28 x 20 In. 88.00
Poster, Beat Back The Hun, Fred Strothmann, 1918, 28 1/2 x 20 1/2 In. 49.50
Poster, Blood Or Bread, Raleigh, 29 x 21 In. 55.00
Poster, Buy More Liberty Bonds, Walter Whitehead, 1918, 29 x 20 In. 110.00
Poster, Halt The Hun!, Raleigh, 1918, 29 1/2 x 20 In. 77.00
Poster, Keep Him Free, Buy War Saving Stamps 198.00
Poster, Keep Your War Savings Pledge, C. Emerson, Jr., 1918, 30 x 20 In. 66.00
Poster, Red Cross Christmas Roll Call, Blashfield, 1918, 29 x 18 In. 143.00
Poster, The Navy Is Calling, Enlist Now, L.N. Britton, 41 x 28 In. 187.00
Poster, Uncle Sam, I Am Telling You, June 28th Enlistment, New Frame 60.00
Poster, YMCA Lend Your Strength To The Red Triangle, Spear, 27 x 20 In. 77.00
Print, U.S. Soldier, Rifle, Color, Hardboard, 8 x 10 In. 2.00
Ring, Black Enameled Maltese Cross, 1914-1917 .... 12.00
Trench Dagger, Knuckle Duster Type, 1917 .... 125.00
U.S. Army Canteen, Cover, With Cup, Dated 1918 .... 8.00
Uniform, Battle Star, Complete, With History 150.00
War Map, Europe, Lists War Strengths Each Country, 1914, 20 x 28 In. 6.00
WORLD WAR II, Armband, U.S. Army Air Force Observer, Cloth 6.50
Badge, Flak, German Army 135.00
Badge, Golden Wound, Germany 99.00
Badge, Nazi, Reichparteitag, 1936 .... 26.00
Badge, Wound, Nazi 35.00
Banner, 5 x 16 Ft. 150.00
Banner, Nazi, Black Swastika Center, Red, Large 100.00
Belt Buckle, Nazi, Army, Metal, With Eagle & Swastika 14.00
Camera, MP, Aircraft Firing, GSAP, Original Lenses 75.00
Cap, Officer's, Nazi 225.00
Cap, Officer's, Waffen-SS Infantry 1653.00
Card, Window, Keep Japs Out Of California, Cardboard, 5 1/2 x 8 1/2 In. 75.00
Clock, Fighter Plane, 24 Hour 85.00
Cross, Mothers, Gold, Germany 59.00
Cuff Links, Nazi Officer's, Silver 10.00
Dagger, German, Officer's Dress 250.00
Dagger, Nazi, NSKK 2000.00
Door Push, Nazi, Brass, Embossed Eagle & Swastika 15.00
Hatchet, Military Aircraft Survival, Britain 20.00
Head, Adolph Hitler, Carved, Painted 165.00
Helmet, Anti-Artillery, Luftschutz Decal, Wings With Swastika, 55 In 220.00
Helmet, French Army, Liner, Badge On Front 45.00
Helmet, French Army, Steel 6.00
Helmet, German Navy 250.00

Helmet, German, Steel, Leather Liner 43.00
Helmet, Luftwaffe, Paratrooper, Camouflaged .... 1700.00 to 1870.00
Helmet, SS, Nazi 900.00
Housewife Kit, Soldier's, Oil Cloth, Cylindrical 12.50
Insignia, Collar, U.S. Military, Brass, Round 2.25
Jacket, Aviator's, U.S. Air Force, Leather 250.00
Jacket, Aviator's, U.S. Navy, Cooper Goatskin 295.00
Jacket, Flight, Leather 250.00
Jacket, U.S. Army Air Force, High Altitude 595.00
Lapel Pin, Hitler Youth, H.J. Arbeiter, Enameled, Round 25.00
Lapel Pin, Hitler Youth, H.J. Membership, Cloisonne Diamond Shape 27.00
Lead Flat, SS, Swastika Flag, Hitler Marked Card, 6 Piece 175.00
Medal, Mother's Cross, Gold, Ribbon, Germany 65.00
Medal, Nazi, Blue Max 12.00
Pants, Flight 90.00
Patch, Nazi Walfen SS Foreign Volunteer, Sleeve Shield, Italy 20.00
Pendant, Nazi, Cloisonne, For Necklace, 3 Colors 5.00
Periscope, Trench, Japan 195.00
Photograph, Mussolini & Mistress, Shot & Hanging By Heels 20.00
Pilot Wing, USAAF, Sterling, 3 In. 89.00
Pin, Edelweiss, German 12.00
Pin, Lapel, Nazi, Zeppelin Corps 40.00
Plate, Bundles For Britain, Dieu Et Mon Droit, Steubenville 10.00
Poster, Buy War Bonds, Wyeth, 14 x 22 In. 150.00
Poster, Save For Security-Buy Defense Savings Stamps, GPO, 1941, 21 x 28 In. 4.00
Poster, Your War Bonds Are A Stake In The Future, Saalberg, 10 x 14 In. 12.00
Propeller, Drone, Wooden, Walthem Clock Factory, 32 In. 250.00
Raft, Navy 500.00
Ration Book, Box Of Tokens 17.50
Rifle, Training 37.50
Sheet, Gasoline Ration Stamps, 30 Coupons, Unused 7.50
Sign, 2nd Liberty Loan Of 1917, Boy & Girl, Flag, Dewey, Frame, 30 x 20 In. 143.00
Sign, U.S. Army Mine Field, Steel 2.50
Suit, Sailor, Woolen, Blue 40.00
Sword Guard, Japan 20.00
Telephone, Battle, U.S. Navy, Sound Powered 30.00
Telephone, Field, U.S. Army 30.00
Telescope, Japan, Original Wooden Box, 31 In. 200.00
Tunic, General's, Nazi 1075.00
Tunic, Luftwaffe Flight Lieutenant 550.00
Tunic, SS-Oberstaturmbannfuhrer Hermann Pister 9030.00
Uniform, Red Cross 75.00
Uniform, U.S. Coast Guard 25.00
Watch Fob, Fighter Airplane, Enameled Brass 8.00

WORLD'S FAIR souvenirs from all of the fairs are collected. The first fair
was the Great Exhibition of 1851 in London. Other important exhibitions and
fairs include Philadelphia, 1876 (Centennial); Chicago, 1893 (World's
Columbian); Buffalo, 1901 (Pan-American); St. Louis, 1904 (Louisiana
Purchase); San Francisco, 1915 (Panama-Pacific); Philadelphia, 1926
(Sesquicentennial); Chicago, 1933 (Century of Progress); Cleveland, 1936
(Great Lakes); San Francisco, 1939 (Golden Gate International); New York,
1939 (World of Tomorrow); Seattle, 1962; New York, 1964; Montreal, 1967;
New Orleans, 1984; Tsukuba, Japan, 1985; Vancouver, B.C., 1986; Brisbane,
Australia, 1988; Seville, Spain, 1992; and Genoa, Italy, 1992. Memorabilia of
fairs include directories, pictures, fabrics, ceramics, etc.

Ashtray, 1893, Chicago, Manufacturers & Liberal Arts Bldg., Copper 20.00
Ashtray, 1904, St. Louis, Seashell, 3 x 2 1/2 In. 22.00
Ashtray, 1939, New York, Maple Leaf Shape, Syroco Wood, 6 In. 35.00
Ashtray, 1939, New York, Vanity Fair Transfer, Japan, 3 1/2 In. 32.50
Ashtray, 1964, New York, 4 Different Scenes, Gold Rim, Ceramic, 4 Piece 14.00
Badge, 1933, Chicago, American Legion Convention, Ft. Dearborn, Ribbon 22.00
Banner, 1876, Philadelphia, Flags Of The Nations, Cotton, 15 x 25 In. 30.00

Blotter, 1933, Chicago, Hall Of Photography Photograph 15.00
Book, 1893, Chicago Tribune Souvenir, 192 Photos, 6 1/2 x 5 In. 16.00
Book, 1893, Columbian Exposition In Pictures, H.S. Smith 125.00
Book, 1939, New York, Souvenir, Large 15.00
Book, 1939, New York, Story Of Lucky Strike, 94 Pages, 5 x 7 1/2 In. 16.00
Bookends, 1939, Trylon & Perisphere, Marble 95.00
Booklet, 1893, Chicago, Aultman Machine Co., Color Lithos 145.00
Booklet, 1904, St. Louis, Louisana Expo, Singer Sewing Machine 75.00
Booklet, 1939, New York, GM Highways & Horizons, Foldout, 10 x 14 In. 6.00
Booklet, 1964, New York, Guide To GM Futurama 3.00
Booklet, Sears, Roebuck, At The Century Of Progress, 1933, 16 Pages 16.50
Bottle, Vinegar, 1939, San Francisco, Figural Image, Milk Glass, 5 x 8 1/2 In. 40.00
Bottle Globe, 1939, New York, 9 In. 40.00
Bowl, 1964, New York, Lacquerware, Unisphere, Black, 8 1/2 In. 4.00
Box, 1876, Philadelphia, Clark's Spool Cotton, 2 12 x 3 3/4 In. 50.00
Box, 1893, Chicago, Beveled Glass, Brass Footed, Original Lining, 2 1/2 In. 65.00
Box, 1933, Chicago, Button & Stretch Penny, Century Of Progress 12.00
Bracelet, 1939, San Francisco 20.00
Bread Tray, 1964, New York, Silver Plastic, Unisphere Center, 11 x 7 In. 8.00
Brush, Dog Bead, 1933, Chicago 85.00
Bust, Shakespeare, 1876, Philadelphia, Frosted, Gillander, 5 In. 30.00
Button, 1893, Chicago, Bust Of Columbus, White Ceramic 17.00
Button, 1904, St. Louis, Festival Hall & Cascades, Celluloid 55.00
Candy Container, 1904, St. Louis, Celluloid, Cigar Shape, Flag Band, 4 In. 65.00
Card, Playing, 1893, Chicago, 52 Multicolor 66.00
Card, Playing, 1933, Chicago 32.00
Change Purse, 1893, Chicago, Leather, 2 Compartments, Columbus 83.00
Clock, Alarm, World's Fair, Century Of Progress 225.00
Coaster, 1964, New York, Unisphere Center, Black Rim, Metal 4.00
Coaster, 1967, Montreal, Expo Symbol, Metal, Red, Gold, Round, 4 In. 3.00
Coaster Set, 1964, New York, Unisphere, US Steel, Chrome, 3 In., 4 Piece 10.00
Compact, 1939, New York 52.00
Compact, 1939, New York, Trylon & Perisphere, Mother-Of-Pearl, Rhinestones 85.00
Compact & Cigarette Case, Mirror, 1933, Chicago, Century Of Progress 55.00
Cookbook, 1964, New York, Good Housekeeping 20.00
Cufflinks, 1876, Philadelphia, Scrimshaw Liberty Bell 165.00
Cufflinks, 1964, New York, Festival Of Gas, Box 7.00
Cufflinks & Tie Bar, 1964, New York, Swank 17.50
Cup, 1904, St. Louis, Norvell-Shapleigh Hardware Co., 2 1/2 In. 39.00
Fan, 1893, Chicago, Agriculture, Machinery & Manufacturing, 25 In. 73.00
Fan, 1893, Chicago, Bird's Eye View Of Grounds, J.W. Green, Paper, 24 In. 80.00
Fan, 1904, St. Louis, Panoramic View, Multicolor, Wooden Trim 42.00
Fan, Hand, Ladies, 1904, St. Louis, Lithograph Paper Of Fair Building 42.00
Flip Book, 1939, New York, Hawaiian Girl Dancing, Bromide Seltzer Character 16.00
Folder, 1933, Chicago, Heinz Century Of Progress 3.00
Game, 1964, New York World's Fair, Milton Bradley 20.00
Globe, Bobbing, 1964, New York 40.00
Harmonica, 1876, Philadelphia, Wilhelm Thie, Original Box 200.00
Hatchet, 1893, Chicago, George Washington, Libbey Glass 100.00
Holder, Thimble, 1893, Chicago, Sailboat Shape, Mother-Of-Pearl Sails, 4 In. 8.00
Ice Pick, 1939, San Francisco, Iron, Wooden Handle 2.50
Kerchief, 1893, Chicago, Columbian Exposition 75.00
Key, 1939, New York, Box 48.00
Knife, 1933, Chicago, Mickey Mouse, Pocket 75.00
Knife, 1939, New York, Pocket, 2 1/2 In. 20.00
Knife, Pocket, 1893, Chicago, Bronze Handle, Leather Case 300.00
Knife, Pocket, 1939, New York 25.00
Letter Opener, 1904, St. Louis, Embossed Building On Handle 28.00
Letter Opener, 1904, St. Louis, Indian Figure 45.00
Letter Opener, 1933, Chicago, Carillon Tower, Brass 15.00
Letter Opener, 1933, Chicago, Century Of Progress, Ornate, 7 In. 9.00
Letter Opener, 1933, Chicago, Lincoln 20.00
Lighter, 1962, Seattle, Space Needle, Figural, 10 1/2 In. 45.00

Map, 1933, Chicago, Pictorial Map Of 1934 World's Fair, Pure Oil Co. 8.50
Map, 1933, Chicago, Street Car Map & Brochure, 10 Pages 10.00
Map, 1962, Seattle, World's Fair Streets & Vicinity, Chevron Dealers 4.00
Map, 1964, New York, World's Fair Edition, AAA's 5.00
Marbles, 1933, Chicago, Bag 17.50
Match Cover, 1939, San Francisco, Golden Gate, Anacin, 20 Stick, Unused 2.00
Match Safe, 1893, Chicago, Profile Of Columbus, 2 1/2 In. 130.00
Matchbox, 1967, Montreal, USSR Building, Photograph, Unused 2.00
Mirror, 1933, San Francisco, Checking Bureau, Inc., 3 1/2 In. Diam. 95.00
Napkin Ring, 1893, Chicago 18.00
Official Guide Book, 1939, New York, 1st Edition, 256 Pages 12.50
Paper Doll, 1964, New York, Uncut 35.00
Paperweight, 1876, Philadelphia, Memorial Hall, Oval 125.00
Paperweight, 1893, Chicago 25.00
Paperweight, 1967, Montreal, Plastic, Snow Dome, Monorail 3.00
Paperweight-Mirror, 1876, Philadelphia, 2 1/2 x 4 In. 137.00
Pencil, 1939, New York, Westinghouse, 3 1/2 In. 2.50
Photograph, 1904, St. Louis, T. Roosevelt Family, Tin Frame, 6 In. Diam. 695.00
Pin, 1939, New York, Heinz Pickle 10.00
Pin, 1939, New York, Lapel, Hand Holding Medallion Trylon & Perisphere, Enameled   40.00
Pin, Locket, 1940, New York, Trylon & Perisphere 30.00
Pipe Rest, 1933, Chicago, Century Of Progress, Dog Figural, Bronze 35.00
Pitcher, 1893, Chicago, Ruby Stained, 4 In. 45.00
Plate, 1893, Chicago, Electrical Building, China 50.00
Plate, 1904, St. Louis, Glass, Festival Hall, Floral, Open Edge, Gilt, 7 3/8 In. 37.00
Plate, 1933, Chicago, Century Of Progress, Ft. Dearborn, Johnson Bros., 9 In. 39.00
Plate, 1964, New York, 7 Scenes 32.00
Plate, 1964, New York, Molded Fair Views, U.S. Steel 12.00
Plate, 1967, Montreal, Plastic, Photographs, Triangular, 5 In. 4.00
Pocket Clip, 1964, New York, Ford Logo, Pennsylvania, Plastic, 1 1/2 x 2 In. 4.50
Postcard, 1893, Chicago, Woman's Building, Multicolored, Unused 15.00
Postcard, 1904, St. Louis, Mechanical 150.00
Postcard, 1933, Chicago, Central Tower, Ford Expo. Building, Unused 4.00
Postcard, 1939, New York, Firestone Building, Unused .... 4.00 to 5.00
Postcard, 1962, Seattle, China Pavilion, Unused 3.00
Postcard, 1964, New York, Plaza Of Astronauts, Rocket Thrower 2.50
Poster, 1940, New York, International Stamp Exhibit, British Pavilion, Frame 175.00
Poster, 1984, New Orleans, Coca-Cola 20.00
Punch Cup, 1904, St. Louis 35.00
Razor, Straight, 1893, Chicago, Black Celluloid Handle, Germany 66.00
Ribbon, 1893, Chicago, Ohio Day, Seal, Silk, 6 In. 20.00
Ribbon, 1901, Buffalo, Pan Am Expo, Electric Tower, Hot Air Balloon 125.00
Ring, 1939, New York, Spirit Of The Fair, Gold, Semi-Draped Figure 12.00
Salt & Pepper, 1933, Chicago 52.00
Salt & Pepper, 1939, New York .... 18.00 to 45.00
Salt & Pepper, 1964, New York, Ceramic 28.00
Salt & Pepper, Tray, 1964, New York, Coffeepot Shape, Unisphere Paper Label 6.00
Scarf, 1893, Chicago, Machinery Hall, Black & Silver Silk, 20 1/2 In. 56.00
Sign, 1878, Paris, Gale Plow, Philadelphia & Paris 325.00
Sponge, 1934, Chicago, Old Dutch Cleanser, Figural, Cleaning Woman 100.00
Spoon, 1893, Chicago, Ship In Bowl, 4 In. 10.00
Spoon, 1893, Chicago, Umbrella, Wooden Box, 24 In. 50.00
Spoon, 1904, St. Louis, Palace Of Varied Industries, Sterling Silver 50.00
Spoon, 1904, St. Louis, Transportation Building, Leonard Mfg. Co. 8.00
Spoon, 1939, New York, Textile Building, Silver Plate 10.00
Stein, 1904, St. Louis, 1/4 Liter, Machinery Building 75.00
Stereo Card, 1893, Chicago, Views Of Fair, 11 Piece 125.00
Stickpin, 1876, Philadelphia, 1 Dollar, Open Wreath 35.00
Stud, 1893, Chicago, Eagle Center 17.00
Sugar & Creamer, 1893, Chicago, Frosted Pink Satin Glass 340.00
Swizzle Stick, 1939, New York, Ruby Foo's Sundial Restaurant 12.50
Teapot, 1939, New York, Cobalt Blue, Gold Trylon & Perisphere, Hall 75.00
Teaspoon, 1939, New York, Exchange Building In Bowl, Silver Plate, Rogers 12.00

Textile, 1893, Chicago, Columbian Exposition, Chicago, Frame, 3 Piece 412.50
Thermometer, 1933, Chicago, Sky Ride Picture, 7 x 5 In. 25.00
Thermometer, 1964, New York, Unisphere, Wooden Wall Plaque, 4 x 6 In. 6.00
Tie Bar, 1939, New York 12.00
Tip Tray, 1964, New York, Unisphere, 7 1/4 x 5 In. 3.00
Toothpick, 1876, Philadelphia, Baby Eagle Next To Egg, Just Out 65.00
Toothpick, 1893, Chicago, Wooden, E.B. Estes & Sons, 3 1/2 In. 121.00
Toy, 1933, Chicago, Bus, Arcade 310.00
Toy, 1939, San Francisco, Tram, Cast Iron, 8 1/2 In. 500.00
Tray, 1904, St. Louis, Administration Building, Floral, 5 x 4 In. 32.00
Tray, 1933, Chicago, Ford Building, Century Of Progress 32.00
Tray, 1964, New York, Unisphere Center, Black Rim, Metal, Round, 12 In. 18.00
Tray, 1967, Montreal, Smoky Glass, Gold & White Scenes, 4 x 4 3/4 In. 5.00
Tumbler, 1893, Chicago, Administration, 3 1/2 In. 25.00
Tumbler, 1893, Chicago, Machinery Hall, 3 1/2 In. 35.00
Tumbler, 1901, Buffalo, Pan Am, Temple Of Music, 3 1/2 In. 25.00
Tumbler, 1901, Buffalo, Pan American, Horticultural Building 20.00
Tumbler, 1904, St. Louis, Cairo Street Transfer, 3 1/2 In. 75.00
Tumbler, 1939, New York, Amusement Rides Transfer, 6 In. 17.50
Tumbler, 1939, New York, Marine Trans. Building, Blue, Yellow, 5 1/4 In. 12.00
Tumbler, 1964, New York, Circus 3.50
Tumbler, 1964, New York, Kids With Balloons 15.00
Tumbler, Iced Tea, 1964, New York, Federal Pavilion, Maroon, Orange, 6 1/2 In. 8.00
Tumbler, Iced Tea, 1964, New York, Hall Of Science, Red, Blue, 6 1/2 In. 8.00
Tumbler Set, 1962, Seattle, 5 Piece 40.00
Watch Fob, 1893, Chicago, Keystone Watch Case Co. 35.00
Watch Fob, 1933, Chicago, Bronze, Research, Industry, 1833-1933 .... 10.00
Window Box, 1933, Chicago, Ford Exhibit 20.00

WRISTWATCHES came into use during World War I. Wristwatches are listed here by manufacturer or as advertising or character watches. Pocket watches are listed in the Watch category.

Advertising, Bunny, Energizer 48.00
Advertising, Denim Jeans, Timex, Box 40.00
Advertising, Kraft, Macaroni & Cheese 10.00
Advertising, Real Dairy Products, Plastic Strap, Digital Display, China 10.00
Advertising, Ritz Cracker, Box 695.00
Advertising, Ritz Crackers, Crackers Indicate Hour, Steel, 1960s 825.00
Advertising, Ronald McDonald, Center Image Of Ronald, Black Band, 1970s 50.00
Andersen, Chronograph, Sun & Moon Indicators, 18K Gold 4025.00
Audemars Piguet, Calendar, Chronograph, Self-Winding, Stainless Steel 4313.00
Audemars Piguet, Raised Gold Markers, Leather Strap, 18K Gold, 1949 .... 3200.00
Audemars Piguet, Royal Oak, Gray Dial, Stainless Steel & 18K Gold 5650.00
Bailey Banks & Biddle, Woman's, Single Cut Diamonds, 14K Gold 345.00
Barbie, Vinyl Band, Mattel, Bradley, 1973 .... 60.00
Baume & Mercier, 18K Gold Face & Band 2900.00
Baume & Mercier, Oval Lapis Dial, Lapis Bead Bracelet, 14K Gold 165.00
Braille, Flip Top 100.00
Breitling, Chronomat, 3 Registers, Stainless Case, c.1990 .... 1650.00
Breitling, Navitimer, Chronograph, c.1950 .... 950.00
Bucher, Woman's, Silver, 1 In., Floral Filigree Band 190.00
Bulova, Gold-Filled Speidel Band, 21 Jewels, 14K Gold, c.1940 .... 165.00
Bulova, Woman's, 14K White Gold, Diamonds Around Face & Band, 1950s 500.00
Bulova, Woman's, Numerals Outside Case, 1950 .... 75.00
Carrol, 17 Jewel, Chronograph, 18K Pink Gold, c.1940 .... 522.50
Cartier, Santos, Black Roman Numbers, 18K Gold Case & Bracelet 7700.00
Cartier, White Oval Dial, Roman Numerals, 18K Gold, No. 50674, France 3410.00
Character, 3 Stooges, 1970s 75.00
Character, Abbott & Costello, Bradley, 1986, Large 75.00
Character, Alice In The Teacup, Box 345.00
Character, Bozo, Tin, Plastic, 1960s 15.00
Character, Bullwinkle, Buren, Original Box 800.00
Character, Captain Marvel, Box 600.00

Character, Charlie Chaplin, Goes Backwards, Bradley 145.00
Character, Clint Eastwood, Any Which Way You Can 75.00
Character, Dudley Do-Right, 1971 .... 500.00
Character, Fonz, Happy Days 50.00
Character, Fred Flintstone, 1972 .... 150.00
Character, G.I. Joe, Combat Watch, Gilbert, 1964, Box 360.00
Character, Hazel, Wide Vinyl Band, 1971 .... 250.00
Character, Holly Hobbie, Full Dress 16.00
Character, Holly Hobbie, Windup, Bradley, Box 30.00
Character, Jolly Green Giant Sprout 85.00
Character, Laurel & Hardy, 1985, Small 70.00
Character, Pink Panther, 1979 .... 129.00
Character, Porky Pig, Box 395.00
Character, Snoopy & Red Baron, Timex, Box 50.00
Character, Snoopy, Playing Tennis, Timex, Box 55.00
Character, Snoopy, Timex, Date 1958 .... 35.00
Character, Spiderman, Dabs, 1977 .... 75.00
Character, Spiro Agnew, Face Front, Stars 17.00
Character, Spiro Agnew, Red, White & Blue Shorts, Dirty Time, c.1968 .... 135.00 to 140.00
Character, Star Wars, Bradley, 1979 .... 90.00
Character, Tom Corbett, Rocket Ship, Box 825.00
Character, Tom Corbett, Space Cadet 450.00
Character, Viking, Robin Hood, Box 650.00
Character, Woody Woodpecker, Rotating Disc, 1970 .... 130.00
Character, Yogi Bear, 1968 .... 125.00
Character, Zorro, U.S. Time, 1960s 200.00
Charles Nicolet, Chronograph, 2 Registers, Stainless Case, 1949 .... 245.00
Cortina, Woman's, Cover, 17 Jewel, Opals & Diamonds, Gold Band 385.00
Daumier, Flexible Bracelet, Envelope Conceals Watch, 14K Gold, c.1950 ...... 880.00
Duoplan, Black Dial, Leather Strap, 9K Yellow Gold 660.00
Ebel, Chronograph, Gold Buckle On Leather Strap, 18K Yellow Gold .... 5850.00 to 6550.00
Elgin, 7 Jewel, Gold Filled, Lever Set, Size 16 .... 185.00
Gallet, Button Chronograph, Hours At Top, Minutes At Bottom, Stainless ... 1275.00
Genault, Woman's, Platinum, 18K Gold, 17 Jewel, Diamond &Sapphire Band 650.00
Geneva, By Orloff, Woman's, Rhinestone, 17 Jewel 85.00
Geneve, Woman's, 14K Gold 225.00
Gruen, 3 Diamond Markers, Faceted Crystal, 14K Gold Mesh Band 715.00
Gruen, Curvex, Driver's 375.00
Gruen, Curvex, Gold Numbers, 14K Gold Case, c.1938 .... 850.00
Gruen, Doctor's Watch, Duo Dials, 14K White Gold Case, c.1932 .... 1275.00
Gruen, Quadron Silvered Dial, Second Hand, 14K White Gold 275.00
Gubelin, Ipso/Day, Stainless Steel 150.00
Hamilton, 22 Jewel, 10 Full-Cut Diamonds, Stretch Band, 14K White Gold 650.00
Hamilton, Chronograph, Gold Ring Bezel, Black Dial, Stainless Steel, 1970s 650.00
Hamilton, Day, Date Calendar, Automatic, 14K Gold 200.00
Hamilton, Driver's Watch, Raised Arabic Numbers, Sub Seconds, 1952 .... 475.00
Hamilton, Perry, Bowed Sides, Sub Seconds, 14K Gold Filled, 1932 .... 325.00
Hamilton, Piping Rock, 19 Jewel, Gold Numerals, 14K Gold Bracelet, 1945 ..... 1725.00
Hamilton, Piping Rock, Enamel Bezel & Numbers, 14K Gold, 1930s 1600.00
Hamilton, Second Hand, 19 Jewel, 1940s, 14K Yellow Gold 275.00
Hamilton, Silver Dial, Black Bezel, Speidel Band, Gold Filled 770.00
Hamilton, Silver Dial, Diamond Markers, 19 Jewel, White Gold 660.00
Hamilton, Woman's, 48 Single-Cut Diamonds, Link Band, 14K White Gold 230.00
Hamilton Electric Spectra, 14K Gold, Box 600.00
Hampden, 14K Pink Gold, Square 150.00
Harwood, 1st Automatic, Rotating Setting Bezel, 14K Gold Filled 950.00
Harwood, Fluted Bezel, 14K Yellow Gold, Leather Strap 550.00
Heuer, Chronograph, Triple Date Calendar, 14K Yellow Gold, 1949 .... 1800.00
Hunter Case, Repeating, Blacksmiths Hammering On Anvil, Gold, c.1890 .... 4888.00
Illinois, Ritz, 14K Yellow & White Gold, c.1938 .... 950.00
Ingersoll, Big Bad Wolf, 1934 .... 1150.00
IRA WC, Gold Band, 30 Diamond Ends, 17 Jewel, 18K White Gold 345.00
Jaeger LeCoultre, 17 Jewel, Auto Alarm, Date Window, Gold Filled 220.00

Jaeger LeCoultre, Raised Gold Markers, 18K Yellow Gold, 1952 .... 1800.00
Jaeger LeCoultre, Rose Gold Dial, Raised Gold Markers & Hands, 1940s 475.00
Juvenia, Abstract & Arabic Numerals, Leather Strap, 18K Pink Gold 247.50
Lady's, Platinum, 17 Jewel, Rope Band, Diamonds, Sapphires, Genault, 18K 650.00
Lady's, Tortoiseshell Bracelet, Gold Hinge Clip, 18K Gold, c.1935 .... 5075.00
LeCoultre, Alarm, 2-Tone Dial, 18K Gold 990.00
LeCoultre, Rear Wind, Woven Brickwork Band, 14K Yellow Gold 690.00
Longines, Rectangular, 14K Gold, c.1940 .... 295.00
Longines, Woman's, 15 Jewels, Silver Link Band, 18K Gold 90.00
Morabito, Quartz Movement, Oval Twin Gold Dial, Leather Strap 66.00
Movado, 2 Bands Of Sapphires & Diamonds, Woven Bracelet, 14K Gold 1092.00
Movado, Black & White Dial, Day & Date Window, 18K Rose Gold 797.50
Movado, Calendar, Moon Phases, 15 Jewel, 18K Pink Gold, c.1940 .... 2415.00
Movado, Chronograph, Register & Pulsemeter, Black Dial, c.1935 .... 5750.00
Nardin, Single Button Chronograph, 18K Gold, c.1940 .... 3163.00
National, 17 Jewel, Cobra Link Bracelet, Ruby Edges, 14K White Gold 440.00
Nobil, 17 Jewel, Crescent Shaped Gold Band, 14K, Woman's 192.50
Omega, Second Hand, White Dial, Leather Strap, 18K Pink Gold 440.00
Patek Philippe, 18 Jewel, Silvered Dial, 18K Pink Gold, c.1950 .... 2760.00
Patek Philippe, 18 Jewel, Silvered Dial, Curved Case, 18K Gold, c.1950 .... 9775.00
Patek Philippe, 18 Jewel, Silvered Dial, Diamond Numerals, c.1930 .... 8050.00
Patek Philippe, 18 Jewel, Silvered Dial, Hinged Curved Case, c.1925 .... 8625.00
Patek Philippe, Man's, 18 Jewel, Curved Case, Platinum, Signed 5750.00
Patek Philippe, Metal Dial, Second Hand, 18K Yellow Gold 1980.00
Patek Philippe, Micrometer Regulator, Silvered Dial, c.1960 .... 2588.00
Patek Philippe, Silver Tone Dial, 18K White Gold 1092.00
Patek Philippe, Silvered Dial, Second Hand, Leather Strap, 18K Gold 2860.00
Patek Philippe, Woman's, Gold & Diamond, 18 Jewel, c.1960 .... 2875.00
Paul Ditisheim, Silvered Dial, Faceted Crystal, 17 Jewel, Platinum 1045.00
Perfecta, Diamond Dial, Rectangular, 14K Gold 325.00
Pery, 17 Jewel, Goose-Neck Bracelet, 14K Gold, Tiffany & Co. 440.00
Piguet, Gold Ribbed Dial, Swiss Movement, 18K Gold, 1960s 1210.00
Piguet, Jump Hour, 17 Jewel, Rectangular Case, 18K White Gold, c.1930 .... 12075.00
Rolex, 17 Jewel, 18K Gold, Leather Strap, Gold-Plated Clasp, Woman's 495.00
Rolex, Daytona, Stainless Steel Case, Oyster Bracelet 5200.00
Rolex, Explorer, Stainless Steel, 24 Hour-Bezal, 2nd Hour Hand 1900.00
Rolex, Jeweled Movement, Bubble-Back, Stainless Steel, c.1940 .... 1100.00
Rolex, Military, Stainless Steel, Black Dial, c.1940 .... 3450.00
Rolex, Oyster Air King, Manual Wind 435.00
Rolex, Oyster, Datejust, Calendar, Self-Winding, Pink Gold 4313.00
Rolex, Oyster, Self-Winding, Gold & Stainless Steel, Case, 1945 .... 2300.00
Rolex, Oyster, Woman's, Calendar, 26 Jewel, Bracelet, c.1970 .... 4313.00
Rolex, Oyster, Woman's, Self-Winding, Datejust, 18K Pink Gold, c.1970 .... 3680.00
Rolex, President, Woman's, 18K Gold Case 4800.00
Rolex, Submariner, Stainless Steel, Sapphire Crystal 1850.00
Schwab & Brandt, Masonic, Mother-Of-Pearl, Triangular, 15 Jewel, c.1900 .... 1840.00
Seiko, 10K Gold Band, Gold Ore Bezel, Quartz 450.00
Seth Thomas, Man's, 17 Jewel, 14K Rose Gold 275.00
Swatch, Black Friday 200.00
Swatch, Day & Date, 1983 .... 315.00
Swatch, Mickey Mouse, Marx, Animated Feet 35.00
Swiss, 14K Yellow Gold Bracelet, Spring Loaded Cover, 7 In. 440.00
Tissot, Automatic, Sub Seconds, 18K Gold Case, 1945 .... 850.00
Universal, 17 Jewel, Moon Phase, Stainless Steel, c.1940 .... 880.00
Universal, Fancy Lugs, 18K Pink Gold, c.1940 .... 357.50
Universal Compax, 17 Jewel, Stainless Steel 302.50
Universal Geneve, Dato-Compax, 17 Jewel, Chronograph, 14K Gold, 1950s 2100.00
Universal Geneve, Tri-Compax Moonphase, Calendar, Chronograph, Steel 770.00
Vacheron & Constantin, 15 Jewel, 2-Tone Gold, c.1935 .... 2875.00
Vacheron & Constantin, 18 Jewel, 18K Gold, c.1970 .... 2875.00
Vacheron & Constantin, 18 Jewel, Platinum, c.1969 .... 4313.00
Vacheron & Constantin, Chronograph, 3 Register, 18K Gold Case 8800.00
Vacheron & Constantin, Tonneau Case, 18K White Gold, c.1927 .... 2800.00

Waltham, Lady's Hunter Cased, 7 Jewel, 14K Gold Case, Signed, c.1914 .... 250.00
Whitnauer, Woman's, Gold Band, White Gold 105.00
Zenith, Gold & Enamel, Black Scroll Design, Art Deco, 18K, 1920s 2070.00
Zenith, Square, 18K Gold, c.1940 .... 400.00

YELLOWWARE is a heavy earthenware made of a yellowish clay. It varies in color from light yellow to orange-yellow. Many nineteenth- and twentieth-century kitchen bowls and jugs were made of yellowware. It was made in England and in the United States. Another form of pottery that is sometimes classed as yellowware is listed in this book in the Mocha catetgory.

Bank, Dog Head, Running Green & Brown Glaze, 4 In. 126.50
Bank, Piggy, 4 In. 60.00
Bank, Purse Shape 85.00
Bowl, 3 White Bands, 6 In. 35.00
Bowl, 4 Blue Bands, 7 1/4 In. 50.00
Bowl, 4 Blue Bands, 8 3/4 In. 44.00
Bowl, 5 1/4 In. 38.00
Bowl, Brown Bands, 2 1/4 x 3 3/16 In. 200.00
Bowl, Embossed Sides, 9 1/2 In. 58.00
Bowl, Green Mocha Seaweed, White Band, Brown Stripes, Ohio, 9 1/4 In. 192.00
Bowl, Light Blue & White Bands, 5 In. 50.00
Bowl, Mixing, Blue & White Stripes, Ovenware USA, 9 In. .... 22.00 to 25.00
Bowl, Mixing, Blue Seaweed, Mocha Design, Ohio, 12 In. 247.00
Bowl, Mixing, Brown & White Stripes, 4 3/4 In. .... , 10.00
Bowl, Mixing, Cottage, Girl Watering Flowers 70.00
Bowl, Mixing, Seaweed, Mocha Design, Blue Stripes, 6 1/4 x 13 1/2 In. 110.00
Bowl, White Band, Black Stripes, Blue Seaweed, East Liverpool, 5 3/4 In. 410.00
Butter Tub, Banded 174.00
Chamber Pot, Handle, White Band, Red Seaweed Design, Brown Stripes, 6 In. 192.00
Creamer, Blue Sponged, 4 In. 71.00
Crock, Red & Blue Sponge Band, Early 20th Century, 6 1/4 x 8 1/2 In. 115.00
Cup, Brown Slip Decoration 1210.00
Cup, Custard, Brown Bands 124.00
Figurine, Lion, 19th Century, Pair 450.00
Figurine, Lion, Olive-Amber Glaze, Oval Base, 14 1/2 In. 275.00
Figurine, Lion, Rectangular Base, Brown, 10 In. 440.00
Jar, Beater, 3 Brown Bands, 5 1/2 x 5 In. 75.00
Jar, Canning, Lid, 7 In. 66.00
Jar, Cover, Grease, Cobalt Blue 250.00
Jar, Mocha, Blue Seaweed, Dark Brown Stripes, White Band, 7 In. 105.00
Keg, Mahogany Bung, 6 x 6 1/4 In. 145.00
Mold, Food, Bunch Of Grapes In Center, 8 In. 33.00
Mold, Food, Ear Of Corn, Oval, 7 1/2 x 9 In. .... 65.00 to 72.00
Mold, Food, Pineapple 185.00
Mug, Child's, Yellow & Black Checkered Design 38.00
Mug, White & Brown Banding, 4 In. 145.00
Mustard, Blue & White Stripes, 2 1/8 In. 165.00
Pitcher, Brown Seaweed Design, White Band, Brown Stripes, 9 1/4 In. 1210.00
Pitcher, Milk, Blue Seaweed Design, White Band, Brown Stripes, 4 3/4 In. 577.50
Pitcher, Milk, Sponged 125.00
Pitcher, Seaweed Design, Black Stripe, Second Handle Under Spout 1320.00
Pitcher, White Band, Brown Stripes, Blue Mocha Seaweed, 6 5/8 In. 550.00
Salt, Green Seaweed Design, White Band, Footed, 2 1/8 x 2 3/4 In. 357.50
Tenderizer, Meat 175.00

ZSOLNAY pottery was made in Hungary after 1862 and was characterized by Persian, Art Nouveau, or Hungarian motifs. A series of new Zsolnay figurines with green-gold luster finish is available in many shops today. Early Zsolnay was not marked, but by 1878, the tower trademark was used.

Bowl, 3-Cornered, Reticulated, 15 In. 525.00
Ewer, Baluster Form, Woman & Satyr On Rim, Purple Luster, 17 3/4 In. 4025.00

Figurine, Little Boy, Cat On Shoulder, Peacock Iridescent Glaze, Marked, 6 In. 403.00
Figurine, Rooster, Iridescent Glaze, 8 In. 143.00
Group, Picasso Style Figures, Iridescent Green 595.00
Plaque, Man, Horse & Cart, Iridescent, Glazed, Frame, 10 1/4 x 15 1/8 In. 862.00
Tumbler, 4 Maidens In Vineyard, Green, Blue, Gold Iridescent, 6 In. 225.00
Urn, Persian Floral Designs, Braided Handles, Marked, 12 1/4 In. 250.00
Vase, 4 Mice, Gourd Shape, 4 Handles, Red & Ochre Glaze, Marked, 6 7/8 In. 748.00
Vase, Art Nouveau Maiden On Shoulder, Ovoid Base, Neck, Glazed, 9 1/4 In. 172.00
Vase, Flowering Peony, Butterflies, Spotted Ground, Marked, 14 3/4 In. 1725.00
Vase, Iridescent Glaze, High Relief Decoration, c.1903, 17 In. 2640.00
Vase, Iridescent Gold & Blue Swirl, c.1903, 5 7/8 In. 302.50
Vase, Lemon-Lime Iridescent, Emerald Streaks, Bulbous Base, 12 In. 172.00
Vase, Stylized Foliage In Geometric Patterns, Signed, c.1900, 10 1/2 In. 2300.00

INDEX

This index is computer-generated, making it as complete as possible. References in upper-case type are category listings. Those in lower-case letters refer to additional pages of the book where the piece can be found. There is also an internal indexing system used in the main part of the book, so if you look for a Kewpie doll in the doll section, you will be told it is in the Kewpie section. There is additional information about where to find prices of pieces similar to yours at the end of many paragraphs.

THE KOVELS' LIBRARY

KOVELS' AMERICAN ART POTTERY
The Collector's Guide to Makers, Marks, and Factory Histories

At last! *Kovels' American Art Pottery,* the book you have been waiting for. Here is information on 104 potteries and 95 tile factories. Fabulous color and black-and-white photographs show details of design, lists of makers with the identifying marks, factory marks with dating information, and hundreds of clues to help the collector identify all types of art pottery. More than 700 pictures of art pottery, from the $198,000 green Rookwood "fish" vase to the ordinary Weller bowl worth $50 are included. This is the book for the beginner or serious collector, with extensive history and production information written to aid you in identification of art pottery. Listed here from A to Z are the major potteries, such as Rookwood, Weller, Ohr, Roseville, Newcomb, Van Briggle, and Dedham, as well as the less well-known works of the North Dakota School of Mines, Arequipa, Avon, Ouachita, Roblin, or Walrath. Also included are tile companies, with marks, pictures, and histories. *Kovels' American Art Pottery* is a beautiful coffee-table color picture book that belongs in every collector's research library.

580128 336 pages / $60.00 hardcover

DICTIONARY
OF MARKS
Pottery and Porcelain
(1580–1880)

A classic in the field, the *Dictionary of Marks* is a comprehensive guide to more than 5,000 American and European pottery and porcelain marks. It shows at a glance the geographical location of the factory, family name or manufacturer's name, type of ware, color of mark, and the date the mark was used.

001411 288 pages / $16.00 hardcover

KOVELS' NEW DICTIONARY OF MARKS
Pottery and Porcelain
(1850–Present)

Kovels' New Dictionary of Marks provides the quickest and easiest way to identify more than 3,500 American, European, and Oriental marks. The perfect companion to the Kovels' original best-seller *Dictionary of Marks—Pottery and Porcelain*, this is the most comprehensive reference manual for nineteenth- and twentieth-century marks. Together, the two volumes are an indispensable guide to the porcelain and pottery marks of the last four centuries.

559145 304 pages / $19.00 hardcover

Ninth Edition

Kovels' Bottles Price List is the complete guide to collecting bottles of all types. More than 10,000 current pieces are included in this, the most complete bottle book available. More than 200 illustrations in full color and black and white aid in identification of bottles. Included are old and new bottles, bitters, perfumes, figurals, flasks, Avons, Beams, and a host of others. Notes on styles of manufacturers, lists of bottles magazines and clubs, recommended reading, and a bibliography for the serious collector make *Kovels' Bottles Price List* the best listing of current bottle prices available.

589443 240 pages / $14.00 paperback

KOVELS' DEPRESSION GLASS & AMERICAN DINNERWARE PRICE LIST

Fourth Edition

The inexpensive pastel-colored glassware that became popular from 1925 on and the ceramic dinnerware produced during the same period are now attracting collectors in great numbers. Here are the latest and most accurate prices, based on a comprehensive survey of actual sales, shows, catalogs, auctions, and other reliable sources. The more than 6,000 pieces are listed by pattern, along with dates, descriptions, marks and illustrations. Also included are charts of factories with all the known patterns and their name variations, and a 16-page, full-color quick-reference guide.

584441 256 pages / $13.00 paperback

KOVELS' KNOW YOUR ANTIQUES
Revised & Updated Edition

The best guide in print today for beginning collectors. Learn how to recognize, evaluate, and purchase virtually any type of antique—large or small—like an expert. There is detailed advice about caring for your antiques, identifying fakes, and finding bargains. This best-seller is used by collectors and college classes alike.

578069 368 pages / $15.00 paperback

KOVELS' KNOW YOUR COLLECTIBLES
Updated Edition

The up-to-date illustrated guide to today's most fascinating collecting trends: pottery, porcelain, silver, glass, furniture, toys, and other collectibles made since 1890. These items are not old enough to be officially called "antiques" but are rapidly increasing in value. Included here are more than 1,000 photographs and illustrations, information about marks, value, origin, availability, storage, and buying and selling, plus extensive bibliographies.

588404 416 pages / $16.00 paperback

KOVELS' GUIDE TO SELLING, BUYING, AND FIXING YOUR ANTIQUES AND COLLECTIBLES

Publication March 1995

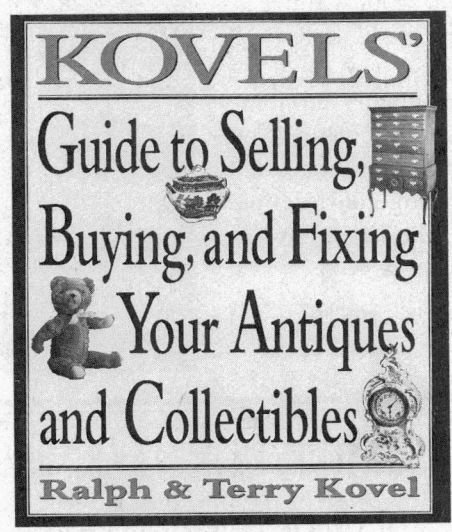

Looking for the parts and services needed to fix your antiques? Selling your antiques and collectibles? Thinking of having your treasures appraised? Renting table space at a flea market? Want to have a house sale? These are just some of the questions that the Kovels address in this comprehensive source book. Here in one place is almost everything the collector needs to know about repairing, buying, selling, and caring for antiques and collectibles. There is advice on how to sell more than one-hundred categories of collectibles—in all price ranges— from autographs, baseball cards, beer cans, carousel figures, decoys, furniture, and glass to movie memorabilia, musical instruments, paintings, toys, and Western art. Want a tail for your carousel horse or a belly button for your toy robot? The Kovels list names, addresses, and phone numbers of those who sell the parts and know how to repair antiques and collectibles. The Kovels also list clubs, publications, auctions and auction houses, professional appraisers, books and much more. This is a book for easy and frequent reference. A must for dealers, dedicated collectors, and those who love their antiques.

883139 352 pages / $18.00 paperback

K O V E L S

SEND ORDERS & INQUIRIES TO: **Crown Publishers, Inc.,**
c/o Random House, 400 Hahn Road,
Westminster, MD 21157

SALES & TITLE INFORMATION
1-800-733-3000

ATT: ORDER DEPT._____

NAME _____

ADDRESS _____

CITY & STATE _____ZIP _____

*PLEASE SEND ME THE FOLLOWING BOOKS:*_____

ITEM NO. QTY.	TITLE		PRICE	TOTAL
882590 _____	Kovels' Antiques & Collectibles Price List 27th Edition	PAPER	$14.00	_____
580128 _____	Kovels' American Art Pottery: The Collector's Guide to Makers, Marks, and Factory Histories	HARDCOVER	$60.00	_____
54668X_____	American Country Furniture 1780–1875	PAPER	$14.95	_____
001411 _____	Dictionary of Marks—Pottery and Porcelain	HARDCOVER	$16.00	_____
559145 _____	Kovels' New Dictionary of Marks	HARDCOVER	$19.00	_____
568829 _____	Kovels' American Silver Marks	HARDCOVER	$40.00	_____
589443 _____	Kovels' Bottles Price List 9th Edition	PAPER	$14.00	_____
584441 _____	Kovels' Depression Glass & American Dinnerware Price List 4th Edition	PAPER	$13.00	_____
578069 _____	Kovels' Know Your Antiques Revised and Updated	PAPER	$15.00	_____
588404 _____	Kovels' Know Your Collectibles Updated	PAPER	$16.00	_____
883139 _____	Kovels' Guide to Selling, Buying, and Fixing Your Antiques and Collectibles (available March 1995)	PAPER	$18.00	_____

_____TOTAL ITEMS   TOTAL RETAIL VALUE _____

CHECK OR MONEY ORDER ENCLOSED MADE PAYABLE
TO CROWN PUBLISHERS, INC.
or telephone 1-800-733-3000
(No cash or stamps, please)

Shipping & Handling
Charge $2.00 for one book;
50¢ for each additional book.
Please add applicable
sales tax.   _____

Charge: ☐ Master Card ☐ Visa ☐ American Express
Account Number (include all digits) Expires MO.   YR.

TOTAL AMOUNT DUE _____

_____

_____

PRICES SUBJECT TO CHANGE
WITHOUT NOTICE. If a more
recent edition of a price list has been
published at the same price, it
will be sent instead of the old edition.

Signature _____

Thank you for your order.

We Want to
Send You a Gift.

Because you love antiques, we know you will be interested in our monthly newsletter, *Kovels on Antiques and Collectibles*, a nationally distributed, fully illustrated publication now in its 21st year.

We report current prices, collecting trends, landmark auction results for all types of antiques and collectibles, and tax, estate, security, and other pertinent news for collectors. We alert you to the fakes and foibles of the marketplace, all in 12 information-packed pages each month.

For additional information and a **FREE** sample copy of the newsletter, just fill in your name and address on this postcard and drop it in the nearest mailbox. We already paid the postage.

[ ] **YES!** Please send me a FREE sample of *Kovels On Antiques and Collectibles.*

Name _____

Address _____
                                                    64KKPL

City _____ State _____ Zip _____

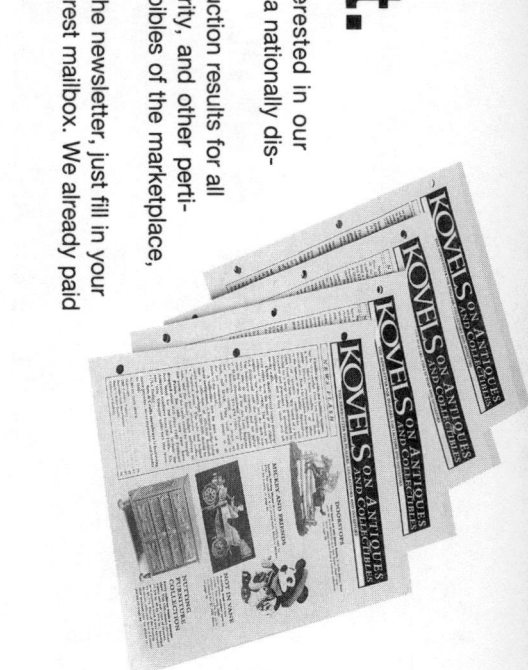

BUSINESS REPLY MAIL

FIRST CLASS PERMIT NO. 191 FLAGLER BEACH, FL

POSTAGE WILL BE PAID BY ADDRESSEE

KOVELS ON ANTIQUES AND COLLECTIBLES

P.O. BOX 420349

PALM COAST, FL 32142-9655

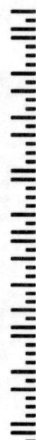